# THE ROUGH GUIDE TO
# FRANCE

This fifteenth edition updated by
**Samantha Cook, Emma Gibbs, Norm Longley,
Keith Munro, Victoria Trott and Greg Ward**

ROUGH
GUIDES

# Contents

## INTRODUCTION                                                          4

| | | | |
|---|---|---|---|
| Where to go | 8 | Things not to miss | 14 |
| When to go | 12 | Tailor-made trips | 26 |
| Author picks | 13 | | |

## BASICS                                                               28

| | | | |
|---|---|---|---|
| Getting there | 29 | Festivals | 46 |
| Getting around | 33 | Sports and outdoor activities | 47 |
| Accommodation | 39 | Shopping | 50 |
| Food and drink | 41 | Travelling with children | 51 |
| The media | 45 | Travel essentials | 51 |

## THE GUIDE                                                            60

| | | | |
|---|---|---|---|
| 1 Paris | 61 | 10 The Limousin, Dordogne and the Lot | 529 |
| 2 The North | 157 | 11 The Pyrenees | 585 |
| 3 Champagne and the Ardennes | 203 | 12 Languedoc | 639 |
| 4 Alsace and Lorraine | 223 | 13 The Massif Central | 683 |
| 5 Normandy | 259 | 14 The Alps and Franche-Comté | 725 |
| 6 Brittany | 307 | 15 The Rhône valley | 777 |
| 7 The Loire | 363 | 16 Provence | 809 |
| 8 Burgundy | 431 | 17 The Côte d'Azur | 865 |
| 9 Poitou-Charentes and the Atlantic coast | 475 | 18 Corsica | 935 |

## CONTEXTS                                                             992

| | | | |
|---|---|---|---|
| History | 993 | Books | 1035 |
| Art | 1012 | French | 1038 |
| Architecture | 1022 | Glossary of architectural terms | 1047 |
| Cinema | 1028 | | |

## SMALL PRINT & INDEX                                                  1048

THE FAMED PROMENADE DES ANGLAIS IN NICE

# Introduction to
# France

You could spend a lifetime of holidays in France and still not come close to exhausting its riches. Landscapes range from the fretted coasts of Brittany and the limestone hills of Provence to the canyons of the Pyrenees and the half-moon bays of Corsica, and from the lushly wooded valleys of the Dordogne and the gentle meadows of the Loire valley to the glaciated peaks of the Alps. Each region looks and feels different, has its own style of architecture, its own characteristic food and often its own dialect. Though the French word *pays* is the term for a whole country, people frequently refer to their own region as *mon pays* – my country – and this strong sense of regional identity has persisted despite centuries of centralizing governments, from Louis XIV to de Gaulle.

Industrialization came relatively late to France, and for all the millions of French people that live in its many vibrant cities, the idea persists that theirs is a **rural country**. The importance of the land reverberates throughout French culture, manifesting itself in areas as diverse as regional pride in local cuisine and the state's fierce defence of Europe's agricultural subsidies. Perhaps the most striking feature of the French countryside is the sense of space. There are huge tracts of woodland and undeveloped land without a house in sight, and, away from the main urban centres, hundreds of towns and villages have changed only slowly and organically over the years, their old houses and streets intact, seeming to belong to the natural landscape as much as the rivers, hills and fields.

Despite this image of pastoral tranquillity, France's **history** is notable for its extraordinary vigour. For more than a thousand years the country has been in the vanguard of European development, and the accumulation of wealth and experience is evident everywhere in the astonishing variety of things to see, from the Dordogne's prehistoric cave paintings and the Roman monuments of the south, to the Gothic cathedrals of the north, the châteaux of the Loire, and the cutting-edge architecture of the *grands projets* in Paris. This legacy of history and culture – *le patrimoine* – is so widely dispersed across the land that even the briefest of stays will leave you with a powerful sense of France's past.

The importance of these traditions is felt deeply by the French state, which fights to preserve and develop its **culture** perhaps harder than any other country in the world, and by private companies, which also strive to maintain French traditions in arenas as diverse as haute couture, pottery and, of course, food. The fruits of these efforts are evident in the **subsidized arts**, notably the film industry, and in the lavishly endowed and innovative museums and galleries. From colonial history to fishing techniques, aeroplane design to textiles, and migrant shepherds to manicure, an array of impressive collections can be found across the nation. Inevitably, however, first place must go to the fabulous displays of fine art in Paris, a city which has nurtured more than its fair share of the finest creative artists of the last century and a half, both French – Monet and Matisse for example – and foreign, such as Picasso and Van Gogh.

There are all kinds of pegs on which to hang a **holiday** in France: a city, a region, a river, a mountain range, gastronomy, cathedrals, châteaux. All that open space means there's endless scope for outdoor activities, from walking, canoeing and cycling to skiing and sailing, but if you need more urban stimuli – clubs, shops, fashion, movies, music – then the great cities provide them in abundance.

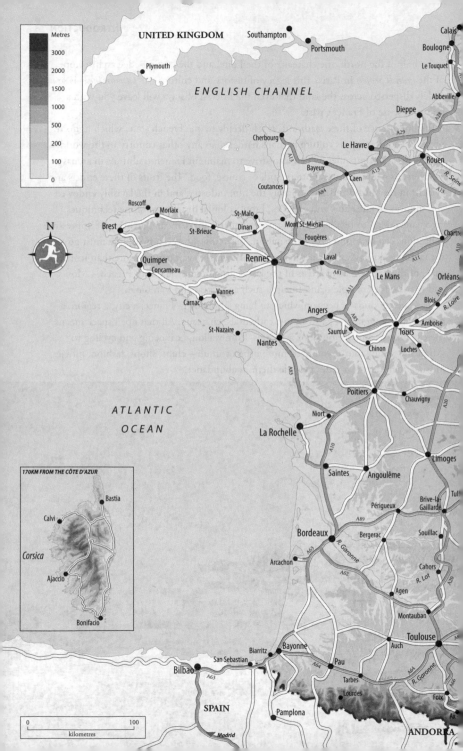

## FACT FILE

- With a land area of 547,000 square kilometres, France is the **largest country in the EU**; its population of 67.2 million is second only to that of Germany.
- France has a long secular republican tradition dating back to the revolution of 1789. Yet the majority of its population is **Roman Catholic** – nominally, at least – and there's a substantial Muslim minority of around 8 to 10 percent.
- Annual GDP per capita is around $44,000, making France **one of the world's richest countries**, but unemployment is a persistent problem, at around 9 percent. Taxes are high, at around 43 percent, but so is social spending, at almost 30 percent.
- France remains by far **the world's most popular tourist destination**, with some 86 million visitors annually.
- The French **film industry** is the world's third most prolific, after the US and India, with around 215 million tickets sold annually.
- Contrary to its self-image as a bastion of gastronomy, the country is also the second largest consumer of **McDonalds' burgers** after the US, flipping more than a million Big Macs daily.
- A great source of confusion when meeting and greeting French people is the **double kiss**, or *bise*. When it is appropriate, and how many times to do it, which cheek to start with, whether to touch or air kiss, what to do with your hands, or whether it's better to shake hands instead, are all matters that vex the French just as much as foreign visitors – not least because norms vary between regions, social situations and age groups. When in doubt, hang back, copy what everyone else does, and go left for the first one.
- In 1910, a **law** was passed in France forbidding couples from kissing on train platforms to avoid delayed departures. The law is still in place, though no longer enforced.

# Where to go

Travelling around **France** is easy. Restaurants and hotels proliferate, many of them relatively inexpensive when compared with other developed Western European countries. Train services are admirably efficient, as is the road network – especially the (toll-paying) *autoroutes* – and cyclists are much admired and encouraged. Information is highly organized and available from tourist offices across the country, as well as from specialist organizations for walkers, cyclists, campers and so on.

As for specific destinations, **Paris**, of course, is the outstanding cultural centre, with its impressive buildings – not least Frank Gehry's stunning Fondation Louis Vuitton – and unparalleled art, nightlife and ethnic diversity, though the great **provincial cities** – Lyon, Bordeaux, Toulouse, Marseille – all now vie with the capital and each other for prestige in the arts, ascendancy in sport and innovation in attracting visitors.

For most people, however, it's the unique characters of the **regions** that will define a trip. Few holiday-makers stay long in the largely flat, industrial **north**, but there are some fine cathedrals and energetic cities to leaven the mix. The picture is similar in **Alsace-Lorraine** where Germanic influences are strong, notably in the food. On the northern Atlantic coast, **Normandy** has a rich heritage of cathedrals, castles, battlefields and beaches – and, with its cream-based sauces, an equally rich cuisine. To the west, **Brittany** is renowned for its Celtic links, beautiful coastline, prehistoric sites and seafood, while the **Loire** valley, extending inland towards Paris, is famed for soft, fertile countryside and a marvellous parade of châteaux. Further east, the green valleys of **Burgundy**

## PÉTANQUE

For your average Frenchman, any recipe for a relaxing summer's evening would have to include the three Ps: plane trees (or palms at a pinch); *pastis*; and that most quintessentially French of games, **pétanque**. You'll see this Gallic version of **bowls** played on countless squares across the country, where groups of mostly middle-aged men in baggy shorts congregate around gravel-and-dirt boulodromes to lob heavy metal *boules* at diminutive wooden ones called *cochonnets* (literally "piglets"). *Pétanque* matches played after work and on weekends are part and parcel of the daily rhythm of life, especially in the south.

The game was invented in 1907 in the town of La Ciotat on the Côte d'Azur by an enthusiastic bowler whose rheumatism prevented him from making the usual extended run up. Instead, he devised a version of his favourite sport in which the bowler's feet stayed planted firmly on the ground (*pieds tanqués*). The pitch was shortened accordingly, and after the local bar owner firmed up a set of rules, the new game quickly caught on. A whole **lexicon** has evolved around *pétanque* to describe different throws and scenarios. Each team, for example, has a mix of "pointeurs" (pointers), players who place the ball as closely as possible to the jack, and "tireurs" (shooters), whose job it is to displace the opposition's balls with spectacular lobs. If the throw falls short, it's a "palouf". If it nudges one of the other team's balls, it's made a "biberon", or "baby's bottle". "Faire la Micheline" means to turn up for a game without your own set of boules. "Faire la chanson" refers to attempts to distract the opposition by chatting between points. And, most insulting of all for wannabe *pétanque* players from the UK, "faire de l'anglais" describes a totally hopeless throw.

Finally, if you're lucky enough to spectate at a complete whitewash, you'll experience the most ribald of all *pétanque* traditions, "Kissing the Fanny". When a team or individual player loses by 13 points to zero they have to kiss the bare buttocks of a statue or framed picture of a lady named "Fanny", usually kept in the nearest bar expressly for the purpose.

shelter a wealth of Romanesque churches, and their wines and food are among the finest in France. More Romanesque churches follow the pilgrim routes through rural **Poitou-Charentes** and down the Atlantic coast to **Bordeaux**, where the wines rival those of Burgundy. Inland from Bordeaux, visitors flock to the gorges, prehistoric sites and picturesque fortified villages of the **Dordogne** and neighbouring **Limousin**, drawn too by the truffles and duck and goose dishes of Périgord cuisine. To the south, the great mountain chain of the **Pyrenees** rears up along the Spanish border, running from the Basque country on the Atlantic to the Catalan lands of **Roussillon** on the Mediterranean; there's fine walking and skiing, as well as beaches at either end. Further along the Mediterranean coast, **Languedoc** offers dramatic landscapes, medieval towns and Cathar castles, as well as more beaches, while the **Massif Central**, in the centre of the country, is undeveloped and little visited, but beautiful nonetheless, with its rivers, forests and the wild volcanic uplands of the **Auvergne**. The **Alps**, of course, are prime skiing territory, but a network of signposted paths makes for great walking too; to the north, the wooded mountains of the **Jura** provide further scope for outdoor adventures. Stretching down from the Alps to the Mediterranean is **Provence**, which, as generations of travellers have discovered, seems to have everything: Roman ruins, charming villages, vineyards and lavender fields – and legions of visitors. Its cuisine is similarly diverse, encompassing fruit, olives, herbs, seafood and lamb. Along the Provençal coast, the beaches, towns and chic resorts of the **Côte d'Azur** form a giant smile extending from the vibrant city of **Marseille** to the super-rich Riviera hotspots of Nice and Monaco.

HIGH-PERCHED NONZA IN THE CAP CORSE REGION OF CORSICA

## "LA GRANDE BOUCLE"

Each year, in the sweltering heat of July, millions of people take up positions on roadsides around France to cheer, shout and bellow cries of encouragement to a peloton of nearly 200 cyclists as they speed past in a stream of day-glo lycra. Millions more watch on television – though few of them are cycling aficionados. Because the Tour de France is far more than a mere bike race. For the French, it's a national institution; a symbol of unity; a chance, as the riders pit themselves against the toughest terrain the mighty *héxagone* can throw at them, to admire the scenic splendour of the country in all its summer glory, with the fields of the Garonne's sunflowers in full bloom, the Côte d'Azur at its most sleek, and the craggy Alps basking under boundless blue skies.

Started in 1903, the Tour was born out of the **rivalry** between two sporting papers, *L'Auto* and *Le Vélo*, as a ruse to boost sales. The passion it incited nearly scuppered the event in its second year, when riders were beaten up by rival fans and cheating was rife (racers were spotted jumping into cars and taking trains). These days, in the wake of a series of high-profile doping scandals, performance-enhancing drugs pose the main threat to the survival of the 3600-km (2200-mile) race, though **La Grande Boucle** (the "Great Loop"), as it's known, still casts a powerful spell over the nation. And it's not just an obsession for the French. In 2012, Bradley Wiggins clinched the title – the Tour's first British winner – since which time Brits have dominated: Chris Froome won in 2013 and then in three consecutive years between 2015 and 2017, before Welsh wonder Geraint Thomas took the title in 2018.

For truly fabulous beaches, however, head for the rugged island of **Corsica**, birthplace of Napoleon and home to an Italian-leaning culture and cuisine, and some fascinating Neolithic sculptures.

# When to go

The most important factor in deciding when to visit France is tourism itself. As most French people holiday in their own country, consider avoiding the main **French holiday** periods – mid-July to the end of August. At this time almost the entire country closes down, except for the tourist industry itself. Easter, too, is a bad time for Paris: half of Europe's schoolchildren seem to descend on the city. For the same reasons, ski buffs should keep in mind the February school ski break. And don't be caught on the roads during the last weekend of July or August, and least of all on the weekend of August 15.

Generally speaking, **climate** (see page 52) needn't be a major consideration in planning when to go. Northern France, like nearby Britain, is wet and unpredictable. Paris has a marginally better climate than New York, rarely reaching the extremes of heat and cold of that city, but only south of the Loire does the weather become significantly warmer. West coast weather, even in the south, is tempered by the proximity of the Atlantic, and is subject to violent storms and close thundery days even in summer. The centre and east, as you leave the coasts behind, have a more continental climate, with colder winters and hotter summers. The most reliable weather is along and behind the Mediterranean coastline and on Corsica, where winter is short and summer long and hot.

# Author picks

Our authors have travelled the length and breadth of France, exploring pretty villages and busy markets, sipping heady red wines in Bordeaux and tackling myriad walking trails. Here are their (off-the-beaten-track) highlights:

**Multicultural adventures** Le Comptoir Général in Paris (see page 138), hidden away off the Canal St-Martin, is an irresistible and almost indefinable find – equal parts museum, thrift store, club and bar, with a freewheeling and inspiring emphasis on the African diaspora.

**Fine fizz** Where better to sample champagne than in the village of Dom Pérignon? At the laidback *Au 36* (see page 213), tastings come with expert advice and delicious, paired food.

**Wild swimming** The Pont d'Arc (see page 721), a natural limestone arch spanning the River Ardèche, forms a superb backdrop for a river swim.

**Must-see masterpiece** The Romanesque carving of Isaiah in Souillac's twelfth-century Church of Sainte-Marie (see page 564) captures a moment of pure ecstasy.

**Awesome castle** With its turreted towers soaring from a wooded hilltop in Alsace, Haut Koenigsbourg (see page 236) is like a vision from a medieval fairy tale.

**Mountain road** Panoramic views to the distant Alps extend from the spectacular Route des Crêtes (see page 242) in the Vosges – one of France's most scenic drives.

**Easy riding** The antithesis of the Tour de France, the tow path lining the Canal de Bourgogne (see page 442) between Migennes and Dijon offers a gentle ride through classic French scenery.

**Small-town festival** Scores of hot-air balloons and thousands of spectators converge on the northern French town of Chalon-sur-Saône (see page 468) over the weekend of Pentecost for this lively balloon fest.

**Into the blue** The turquoise shallows surrounding the Îles Lavezzi in Corsica (see page 981), are among the most transparent waters in all the Mediterranean – perfect for snorkelling and diving.

> Our author recommendations don't end here. We've flagged up our favourite places – a perfectly sited hotel, an atmospheric café, a special restaurant – throughout the Guide, highlighted with the ★ symbol.

HAUT KOENIGSBOURG, ALSACE

CYCLING ALONG THE CANAL DE BOURGOGNE

# 30
## things not to miss

It's not possible to see everything that France has to offer in one trip – and we don't suggest you try. What follows, in no particular order, is a selective taste of the country's highlights, including wonderful architecture, breathtaking landscapes and delectable food and wine. All entries have a page reference to take you straight into the Guide, where you can find out more. Coloured numbers refer to chapters in the Guide section.

### 1 CORSICAN BEACHES

See page 936

Some of France's best beaches are found on Corsica, with its white-shell sand and turquoise water.

### 2 ABBAYE DE FONTENAY

See page 444

This complex Burgundian monastery has a serene setting in a stream-filled valley.

### 3 CYCLING

See page 38

Cycling is an ideal way to explore France's scenic back roads, and there are some great long-distance cycle routes, too, such as those that lace the Alps.

### 4 CHAMPAGNE TASTING AT ÉPERNAY

See page 207

Dom Pérignon is the most famous, but there are plenty of other bubblies to try in the cellars of Épernay's *maisons*.

### 5 AIX-EN-PROVENCE

See page 847

Aix is Provence's regional capital, and with its wonderful market, top-class restaurants and lively bars, it makes a very satisfying stop.

### 6 WINTER SPORTS IN THE ALPS

See page 736

The French Alps are home to some of the world's most prestigious ski resorts, offering a wide range of winter sports.

### 7 BAYEUX TAPESTRY

See page 284

This 70-metre-long tapestry is an astonishingly detailed depiction of the 1066 Norman invasion of England.

### 8 THE LOUVRE

See page 73

The palace of the Louvre cuts a grand classical swathe through the centre of Paris and houses what is nothing less than the gold standard of France's artistic tradition.

### 9 LES GORGES DU VERDON

See page 854

The mighty gorges are Europe's answer to the Grand Canyon, and offer stunning views, a range of hikes, and colours and scents that are uniquely, gorgeously Provençal.

### 10 CHÂTEAUX OF THE LOIRE

See page 404

The River Loire is lined with gracious châteaux, of which Chenonceau is one of the most elegant.

### 11 LES CALANQUES
See page 881

The cliffs between Marseille and Cassis offer excellent hiking and isolated coves that are perfect for swimming.

### 12 MEDIEVAL PROVENÇAL VILLAGES
See page 845

Provence's hilltop villages attract visitors by the score. Gordes is one of the most famous.

### 13 MONT ST-MICHEL
See page 296

One of France's best-loved landmarks, Mont St-Michel is a splendid union of nature and architecture.

### 14 ST-OUEN FLEA MARKET
See page 113

It's easy to lose track of an entire weekend morning browsing the covetable curios at St-Ouen, the mother of Paris's flea markets.

### 15 WAR MEMORIALS
See pages 190, 187 and 188

World Wars I and II left permanent scars on the French countryside. The dead are remembered in solemn, overwhelming cemeteries.

11

12

### 16 BASTILLE DAY
See page 1000
July 14 sees national celebrations commemorating the beginning of the French Revolution, with fireworks and parties.

### 17 CARCASSONNE
See page 664
So atmospheric is this medieval fortress town that it manages to resist relentless commercialization and summer's visitors.

### 18 PREHISTORIC CAVE ART
See page 558
The most impressive prehistoric art in France is found at Lascaux, Dordogne.

### 19 CARNAC
See page 352
Archeologically, Brittany is one of the richest regions in the world and the alignments at Carnac rival Stonehenge.

### 20 DINING OUT IN A LYON BOUCHON
See page 792
Famed for its gastronomy, Lyon offers no end of wonderful eating places, not least the old-fashioned bouchons.

17

18

19

20

24

### 21 BORDEAUX
See page 509
Bordeaux was the principal English stronghold in France for years, and is still known for its refined red wines.

### 22 ANNECY
See page 750
One of the prettiest towns in the Alps, Annecy has a picture-postcard quality which even the crowds can't mar.

### 23 GORGES DE L'ARDÈCHE
See page 721
The fantastic gorges begin at the Pont d'Arc and cut their way through limestone cliffs before emptying into the Rhône valley.

### 24 CATHAR CASTLES
See page 622
These gaunt fortresses are relics of the brutal crusade launched by the Catholic church and northern French nobility against the heretic Cathars.

### 25 AMIENS CATHEDRAL
See page 192
The largest Gothic building in France, this lofty cathedral has a clever son et lumière show.

25

26

27

28

### 26 CANAL DU MIDI
See page 666
Cycling, walking or drifting along the Canal du Midi is the most atmospheric way of savouring France's southwest.

### 27 THE GR20
See page 958
Arguably France's most dramatic – and most demanding – long-distance footpath climbs through and over Corsica's precipitous mountains.

### 28 JARDIN DU LUXEMBOURG
See page 100
Paris's most beautiful park, in the heart of the laidback Left Bank, is the ideal spot for relaxing.

### 29 THE ISSENHEIM ALTARPIECE, COLMAR
See page 238
Grünewald's amazing altarpiece is one of the most extraordinary works of art in the country.

### 30 BASTIDE TOWNS
See page 550
Monpazier is the best preserved of Dordogne's medieval fortified towns – *bastides* – built when there was fierce conflict between the French and English.

# Tailor-made trips

The following itineraries are designed to lead you up, down and round about *la belle France* – picking out the crème de la crème of the country's cities, valleys and mountains, vineyards and coastline. The trips below give a flavour of what the country has to offer and what we can plan and book for you at www.roughguides.com/trips.

## LE GRAND TOUR

**❶ Paris** Crossing off the iconic sights takes up most visitors' first few days, but leave time for soaking up that legendary Parisian chic. See page 62

**❷ Normandy** The pretty port of Honfleur makes the obvious base for day-trips to the Bayeux tapestry (see page 284), D-Day Beaches (see page 288) and Mont St-Michel (see page 296).

**❸ Loire Valley** Use Amboise as your pied-à-terre in the beautiful Loire valley, famed for its fairy-tale castles. See page 401

**❹ Dordogne** Medieval clifftop castles, prehistoric cave art and sublime local cuisine account for its enduring popularity. See page 542

**❺ Carcassonne** Take in some of the southern Lot's *bastide* towns and Cathar castles en route to the Cité of Carcassonne. See page 664

**❻ Arles, West Provence** The elegant Pont du Gard (see page 647) and beautifully preserved theatre at Orange (see page 813) are just two of the many Roman vestiges within reach of Arles.

**❼ Gorges du Verdon, East Provence** String together as many *villages perchés* as you can on the high road across the Var to the awesome Gorges du Verdon. See page 854

**❽ The Alps** A jaw-dropping journey north through Europe's highest mountains culminates with the snowfields of Mont Blanc. See page 755

**❾ Nancy, Lorraine** A serene and refined city, Nancy has one of the most elegant *places* in Europe – Place Stanislas. See page 245

**❿ Verdun** Travel back to the capital via the sobering monument to World War I's fallen at Verdun. See page 254

## VITICULTURAL ODYSSEY

**❶ Saumur, Loire** Known for its cool-climate-style whites, the Loire's wines are best sampled from the pretty town of Saumur. See page 409

**❷ St-Émilion, Bordeaux** St-Émilion is an ideal springboard for visiting the famous châteaux around Bordeaux. See page 520

**❸ St-Jean-Pied-de-Port, Pays Basque** In the Pyrenean foothills, St-Jean is a picturesque medieval town where you can taste the luscious sweet wines of nearby Jurançon. See page 598

**❹ Béziers, Languedoc** This sun-drenched land is the world's largest wine-producing region, and its capital Béziers is perfectly placed for tasting forays to Collioure, Banyuls and Faugères. See page 657

**You can book these trips with Rough Guides, or we can help you create your own**. Whether you're after adventure or a family-friendly holiday, we have a trip for you, with all the activities you enjoy doing and the sights you want to see. All our trips are devised by local experts who get the most out of the destination. Visit **www.roughguides.com/trips** to chat with one of our travel agents.

**❺ Bandol, Côte d'Azur** Low rainfall and oodles of sunshine are the hallmarks of the region to the east of Marseille, where the fishing village of Bandol is home to the flagship wine; reds and rosés rule the roost here. See page 883

**❻ Châteauneuf-du-Pape, Provence** The wines produced around this ancient village in the southern Rhône are legendary. See page 815

**❼ Beaune, Bourgogne** Burgundy boasts more AOP designation wine than anywhere else, and the medieval town of Beaune is the recommended base. See page 465

**❽ Colmar, Alsace** The Fecht valley, just west of Colmar, is striped with steeply shelving vines – source of Alsace's finest Rieslings and Gewürztraminers. See page 238

**❾ Épernay, Champagne** France's champagne capital, Épernay, is the place to sample the country's best bubbly. See page 207

## ICONIC LANDSCAPES

**❶ Les Falaises d'Étretat, Normandy** The chalk cliffs, needles and arches of Étretat inspired Monet, Courbet, Flaubert and Maupassant in their day, and now offer a superb, if dizzying, coastal walk. See page 266

**❷ Les Volcans d'Auvergne** With their grassy slopes, cratered summits and ridgetops, the extinct volcanoes running across the Massif Central create a mountain environment unlike any other. See page 687

**❸ Grande Cascade de Gavarnie, Pyrenees** France's tallest waterfall crashes 423 metres from the awesome Cirque de Gavarnie in the Pyrenees. See page 613

**❹ Gorges de l'Ardèche** Kayak down the magnificent Gorges de l'Ardèche, lined by 300-metre-tall limestone cliffs. See page 721

**❺ Lavender fields, Provence** Immortalized in the paintings of Van Gogh and Cézanne, the lavender fields of the southeast are at their most fragrant in early summer. See page 844

**❻ Golfe de Porto, Corsica** The red porphyry cliffs of Corsica's wild northwest coast rise from a bay of exquisite cobalt blue to a wall of snow-streaked granite mountains. See page 958

**❼ Gorges du Verdon, Vaucluse** France's own Grand Canyon forms a spectacular trench in the Provençal limestone. See page 854

**❽ Mer de Glace, French Alps** Hop on the rack railway from Chamonix for a stupendous view of Europe's largest glacier. See page 760

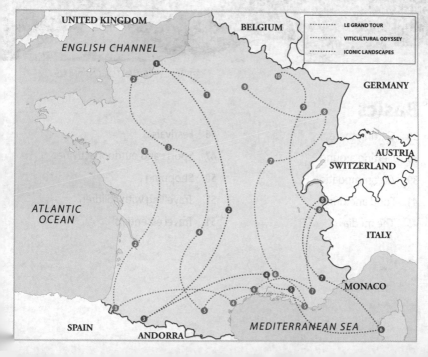

FRESH LOAVES ON A MARKET STALL IN PROVENCE

# Basics

29 Getting there

33 Getting around

39 Accommodation

41 Food and drink

45 The media

46 Festivals

47 Sports and outdoor activities

50 Shopping

51 Travelling with children

51 Travel essentials

# Getting there

**The quickest way to reach France from most parts of the United Kingdom and Ireland is by air. From southern England, however, the Eurostar provides a viable alternative, making the journey from London to Paris in as little as two and a quarter hours. The Channel Tunnel is the most flexible option if you want to take your car to France, though cross-Channel ferries are usually cheaper. From the US and Canada a number of airlines fly direct to Paris, from where you can pick up onward connections. You can also fly direct to Paris from South Africa, while the best fares from Australia and New Zealand are generally via Asia.**

Whether you are travelling by air, sea or rail, prices increasingly depend on how far in advance you book, but will also depend on the **season**. Fares are at their highest from around early June to the end of August, when the weather is best, drop during the "shoulder" seasons – roughly September to October and April to May – and are at their cheapest during the low season, November to March (excluding Christmas and New Year when prices are hiked up and seats are at a premium). Note also that flying at weekends can be more expensive; price ranges quoted below assume midweek travel, and include all taxes and surcharges.

## Flights from the UK and Ireland

Flights between the UK, Ireland and France are plentiful, even from regional airports, though industry consolidation and higher departure taxes mean that the bargain-basement fares of the budget airlines' heyday are much rarer than they were – so look out for special offers advertised on the airline websites or in the media. The main budget airlines are easyJet, Flybe, Jet2 and Ryanair, which between them cover forty or so airports across France, including Bergerac, Carcassonne, Chambéry, La Rochelle, Montpellier,

Nantes, Perpignan, Toulon and Tours, as well as more established hubs such as Paris, Lyon and Nice. Routes change frequently and many destinations are not served all year round, so again keep an eye on the airlines' websites. It's also worth double-checking exactly where the airport is in relation to your destination; Ryanair claims to fly to Paris, for example, but in reality flies to Beauvais, a 1hr 15min coach journey from Porte Maillot, west of the city. **Tickets** work on a quota system, and it's wise to book ahead for the cheapest fares. In theory it's still possible to travel for as little as £50/€58 return including taxes, if you're prepared to be flexible about routes and to go out of season – but surcharges for things like checked-in baggage and priority boarding can all bump up the price considerably, so the price you actually pay will probably be higher than these figures.

It's worth checking out the **traditional carriers**, such as Air France, British Airways and Aer Lingus, which have streamlined their schedules and lowered prices in response to the budget airline challenge, and can sometimes be just as cheap. Low-season return fares to Paris start at around £80 from London, £100 from Edinburgh and €115 from Dublin.

**Air France** flies direct to Paris Charles-de-Gaulle (CDG) several times daily from London Heathrow, Dublin and regional airports such as Birmingham and Manchester. Flights to most other French destinations involve a change at Paris. **British Airways** has several flights a day to Paris CDG from London Heathrow but its flights from provincial airports to Paris involve a change at London. BA also operates flights from London to Bordeaux, Lyon, Marseille, Nice and Toulouse. In Ireland, **Aer Lingus** offers nonstop flights from Dublin and Cork to Paris CDG; from Dublin to Bordeaux, Lyon, Marseille, Nantes, Nice, Perpignan, Rennes and Toulouse; and from Cork to Rennes; note, though, that some of these routes are seasonal.

## Flights from the US and Canada

Most major airlines operate scheduled flights to Paris from the US and Canada. Air France has the

## A BETTER KIND OF TRAVEL

At Rough Guides we are passionately committed to travel. We believe it helps us understand the world we live in and the people we share it with – and of course tourism is vital to many developing economies. But the scale of modern tourism has also damaged some places irreparably, and climate change is accelerated by most forms of transport, especially flying. We encourage our authors to consider the carbon footprint of the journeys they make in the course of researching our guides.

most frequent service, with good onward regional connections and competitive fares that sometimes undercut US carriers; it also operates a codeshare with Delta. One possible disadvantage, if your destination is not Paris, is that while Air France transatlantic flights often terminate at Charles-de-Gaulle, domestic connections frequently depart from Orly, entailing an inconvenient transfer between the two airports. Other airlines offering **nonstop** services to Paris from a variety of US cities include: American Airlines from New York, Charlotte, Chicago, Dallas, Philadelphia and Miami; Delta from Boston, Washington, Los Angeles, Seattle, San Francisco and Cincinnati; and United from Chicago, New York, San Francisco and Washington DC. Air Canada offers nonstop services to Paris from Montréal and Toronto, while Air Transat offers good-value scheduled and **charter flights** to Paris from a number of bases and to other destinations from Montréal, Québec or Toronto. Another option is to fly with a European carrier – such as British Airways, Iberia or Lufthansa – to its European hub and then continue on to Paris or a regional French airport.

Transatlantic **fares** to France have risen sharply in recent years, reflecting green taxes and variable fuel costs. An off-season midweek direct return flight to Paris can be US$1145 including taxes from New York, US$1335 from Los Angeles and US$1255 from Houston. From Canada, prices to Paris start at around CAN$800 from Montréal or Toronto.

## Flights from Australia, New Zealand and South Africa

Most travellers from **Australia** and **New Zealand** choose to fly to France via London, although the majority of airlines can add a Paris leg (or a flight to any other major French city) to an Australia/New Zealand–Europe ticket. Flights via Asia or the Gulf States, with a transfer or overnight stop at the airline's home port, are generally the cheapest option; those routed through the US tend to be slightly pricier. Return **fares** start at around AUS$1520 from Sydney, AUS$1420 from Perth, AUS$1500 from Melbourne and NZ$2830 from Auckland.

From **South Africa**, Johannesburg is the best place to start, with Air France flying direct to Paris from around R7150 return; from Cape Town, they fly via Johannesburg or Doha and are more expensive, starting at around R8300.

## By train

**Eurostar** operates high-speed passenger trains daily from London's St Pancras International to France through the **Channel Tunnel**; many but not all services stop at either Ebbsfleet or Ashford in Kent (15min and 30min from London, respectively). There are 1–2 services an hour from around 5.40am to 8pm for Paris Gare du Nord; fast trains take 2hr 15min; Brussels-bound trains stop at Lille (1hr 20), where you can connect with TGV trains heading south to Bordeaux, Lyon and Marseille; some also stop at Calais (1hr). In addition, Eurostar runs direct trains from London to Disneyland Paris (daily during UK school holidays; otherwise Mon, Wed, Fri & Sun; 2hr 40min) and to the south: Lyon (4hr 40min), Avignon TGV (5hr 50min) and Marseille (6hr 30min), with 1–5 trains running weekly. There is also a special direct twice-weekly ski service to Moutiers, Aime-la-Plagne and Bourg-St-Maurice in the French Alps (mid-Dec to mid-April; 8hr 15min–9hr 35min).

Standard **fares** from London to Paris or Lille start at £58 (£98 to Avignon) for a non-refundable, non-exchangeable return; availability is limited so it's best to book as early as possible. Fares are non-refundable but can be changed to another date and train for a fee of £30, plus the difference in fare. Return fares to Disneyland Paris start at £92 for adults. Child fares apply for 4–11-year-olds while under-4s travel for free provided they travel on the lap of a fare-paying passenger.

**Tickets** can be bought online or by phone from Eurostar, as well as through travel agents and websites like ⓦlastminute.com. InterRail and Eurail **passes** (see page 31) entitle you to discounts on Eurostar trains. Under certain circumstances, you can also take your bike on Eurostar (see above).

### By car via the Channel Tunnel

The simplest way to take your car to France from the UK is on one of the drive-on drive-off shuttle trains operated by **Eurotunnel**. The service runs continuously between Folkestone and Coquelles, near Calais, with up to four departures per hour (one every 1hr 30min from midnight–6am) and takes 35 minutes. It is possible to turn up and buy your ticket at the check-in booths, though you'll pay a premium and at busy times booking is strongly recommended; if you have a booking, you must arrive at least thirty minutes before departure. Note that Eurotunnel does not transport cars fitted with LPG or CNG tanks.

Standard **fares** start at £72 one-way if you book far enough ahead and/or travel off peak, rising to around £90. Fully refundable and changeable FlexiPlus fares cost £169 each way for a short stay (up to 5 days) and £219 for longer periods. There room for only six **bicycles** on any departure, so book ahead in high season – a standard return costs £30 for a bike plus rider.

## Rail passes

There is a variety of rail passes useful for travel within France, some of which need to be bought in your home country (for details of railcards that you can buy in France, see below). **Rail Europe** (see page 32), the umbrella company for all national and international rail purchases, is the most useful source of information on availability and cost.

### InterRail Pass

**InterRail Passes** are only available to European residents, or those who have lived in a European country for at least six months, and you will be asked to provide proof of residency (and long-stay visa if applicable) before being allowed to buy one. They come in first or second-class senior (over 60), first- or second-class over-27 or second-class under-27 versions, and cover thirty European countries. Children from 4–11 years can travel free as part of a family pass; those under 4 travel free, though they may not get a seat.

There are two types of passes: **global** and **one-country**. The global pass covers all thirty countries with various options: five days travel in a fifteen-day period (under-27 £192/over-27 £322); ten days travel within a month (£281/£351); 15 days (£311/£388), 22 days (£363/£454); and one month (£470/£587) continuous travel. The family pass is the same price as the over-27 pass per adult. Similarly, the one-country pass allows you to opt for various periods, ranging from three days to eight days travel in one month with prices varying between countries (see Ⓦ winterrail.eu). In each case, first-class passes are also available.

InterRail Passes do not include travel within your country of residence, though pass-holders are eligible for discounts on Eurostar and on ferries from Rosslare.

### Eurail Pass

**Eurail Passes** are not available to European residents but once ordered can be delivered to a European address (see Ⓦ eurail.com). Again, there are various options; the most useful are likely to be the **regional passes**, covering France with Benelux, Germany, Italy, Spain or Switzerland. The France-Italy pass offers four days of unlimited train travel within two months for €211 under-27/€257 adult travelling second class, or up to ten days within two months for €341 under-27/€418 adult. The Saverpass offers 15 percent discount on Eurail passes for between two and five

---

### TRAVELLING WITH PETS FROM THE UK

If you wish to take your dog or cat to France, the **Pet Travel Scheme (PETS)** enables you to avoid putting it in quarantine when re-entering the UK as long as certain conditions are met. Current regulations are available on the Department for Environment, Food and Rural Affairs (DEFRA) website Ⓦ gov.uk/take-pet-abroad or through the PETS Helpline (Ⓣ 0370 241 1710).

---

people travelling together, and children named on the pass go free.

## Ferries

Though slower than travelling by plane or via the Channel Tunnel, the ferries plying between Dover and Calais offer the cheapest means of travelling to France **from the UK** and are particularly convenient if you live in southeast England. If you're coming from the north of England or Scotland, you could consider the overnight crossing from Hull (13hr) to Zeebrugge (Belgium) operated by P&O Ferries. It's also worth bearing in mind that if you live west of London, the ferry services to Roscoff, St-Malo, Cherbourg, Caen, Dieppe and Le Havre can save a lot of driving time. **From Ireland**, putting the car on the ferry from Cork (14hr) or Rosslare (17hr 30min) to Roscoff in Brittany, or Rosslare to Cherbourg (19hr) in Normandy cuts out the drive across Britain to the Channel.

Ferry **prices** are seasonal and, for motorists, depend on the type of vehicle. In general, the further you book ahead, the cheaper the fare and it's well worth playing around with dates and times to find the best deals: midweek and very early or late sailings are usually cheapest. At the time of writing, one-way fares for a car and up to four passengers are available for £39 with DFDS on the Dover–Dunkerque and Dover–Calais routes. One-way fares from Ireland kick off at around €123 for a car and two adults.

Some ferry companies also offer fares for **foot passengers**, typically from around £40 return on cross-Channel routes; accompanying **bicycles** can usually be carried free.

## Buses

**Eurolines** runs regular services from London Victoria to forty French cities (fewer in winter), with between six and eight a day to Paris, crossing the Channel by ferry or Eurotunnel. Prices are lower than for the same journey by train, with adult return "Advance" fares (must be booked at least ten days in advance) starting at around £40 to Paris or Lille. If you're travelling frequently, a Eurolines Discount Card (three months €29/six months €39) will give you 25 percent off fares, subject to certain restrictions. There's also a Eurolines Pass which offers Europe-wide travel between 50 European cities for fifteen or thirty days. Prices range from €195 for a fifteen-day youth pass in low season (€315 in high season) to €340 for a low-season thirty-day adult pass (€490 in high season).

## Airlines, agents and operators

There are a vast number of travel agents and tour operators offering holidays in France, with options varying from luxury, château-based breaks to adventure trips involving skiing and hiking. The following is a list of the most useful contacts.

### AIRLINES

**Aer Lingus** ⓦ aerlingus.com.
**Air Canada** ⓦ aircanada.com.
**Air France** ⓦ airfrance.com.
**Air Transat** ⓦ airtransat.com.
**American Airlines** ⓦ aa.com.
**British Airways** ⓦ britishairways.com.
**Cathay Pacific** ⓦ cathaypacific.com.
**Delta** ⓦ delta.com.
**easyJet** ⓦ easyjet.com.
**Emirates** ⓦ emirates.com.
**Flybe** ⓦ flybe.com.
**Jet2** ⓦ jet2.com.
**KLM** ⓦ klm.com.
**Lufthansa** ⓦ lufthansa.com.
**Qantas** ⓦ qantas.com.
**Ryanair** ⓦ ryanair.com.
**Singapore Airlines** ⓦ singaporeair.com.
**South African Airways** ⓦ flysaa.com.
**United Airlines** ⓦ united.com.

### AGENTS AND OPERATORS

**Allez France** ⓦ allezfrance.com. UK tour operator offering accommodation only as well as short breaks and other holiday packages throughout France.
**Arblaster & Clarke** UK ☎ 01730 263 111, ⓦ winetours.co.uk. Wine-themed tours to all the great wine regions, from Champagne to Bordeaux.
**Austin-Lehman Adventures** US ☎ 1 800 575 1540, ⓦ austinadventures.com. Good range of bike and walking tours all over France for family groups or solo travellers.

**Belle France** UK ☎ 01580 214 010, ⓦ bellefrance.com. Walking and cycling holidays throughout France.
**Canvas Holidays** UK ☎ 0345 268 0827, ⓦ canvasholidays.co.uk. Tailor-made caravan and camping holidays.
**Chez Nous** UK ☎ 0845 268 1102, ⓦ cheznous.com. Thousands of self-catering and B&B properties online, including ski rentals.
**Corsican Places** UK ☎ 01489 866 931, ⓦ corsica.co.uk. Corsica specialists.
**Cycling for Softies** UK ☎ 020 3918 7866, ⓦ cycling-for-softies. co.uk. Easy-going cycle holiday operator to rural France.
**Discover France** US ☎ 1-800-929-0152, ⓦ discoverfrance.com. Self-guided cycling and walking holidays throughout France.
**Eurocamp** UK ☎ 01606 787 125, ⓦ eurocamp.co.uk. Camping holidays with kids' activities and single-parent deals.
**European Waterways** ☎ 0808 168 1458, ⓦ ewaterways.co.uk. Wide range of river cruise options, from hotel barge cruises through Burgundy to boat hire or trips on the Loire.
**Fields Fairway** France ☎ 01376 327 636, ⓦ fieldsfairway.co.uk. British-run company offering all-inclusive golfing holidays in France and Belgium.
**France Afloat** UK ☎ +33 (0)3 86 81 54 55 , ⓦ franceafloat.com. France-based UK operator offering canal and river cruises across France.
**Headwater** UK ☎ 01606 369 588, ⓦ headwater.com. UK-based operator offering walking, cycling, and canoeing tours throughout France, and cross-country skiing.
**Holiday France Direct** ☎ 0330 159 6868, ⓦ holidayfrancedirect. co.uk. Website offering thousands of properties throughout the country, from cottages and villas to châteaux and mobile homes.
**HouseTrip** UK ⓦ housetrip.com. Holiday home rental website offering a wide range of affordable family accommodation with thousands of properties across rural France.
**Inntravel** UK ☎ 01653 617 001, ⓦ inntravel.co.uk. Broad range of activity holidays, including riding, skiing, walking and cycling, as well as property rental.
**Le Boat** US ☎ 1-800 734 5491, UK ☎ 023 9222 2177, ⓦ leboat. com. Self-drive canal holidays all over France.
**Locaboat** ☎ +33 (0)3 86 91 72 72, ⓦ locaboat.com. French company specializing in holidays on *pénichettes* (scaled-down replicas of commercial barges).
**North South Travel** UK ☎ 01245 608 291, ⓦ northsouthtravel. co.uk. Friendly, competitive travel agency, offering discounted fares worldwide. Profits are used to support projects in the developing world, especially the promotion of sustainable tourism.

### RAIL, CHANNEL TUNNEL AND BUS CONTACTS

**Eurail** ⓦ eurail.com.
**Eurolines** UK ☎ 08717 818181, ⓦ nationalexpress.com.
**Eurostar** UK ☎ 03432 186 186, ⓦ eurostar.com.
**Eurotunnel** UK ☎ 08443 35 35 35, ⓦ eurotunnel.com.
**International Rail** UK ☎ 0871 231 0790, ⓦ internationalrail.com.
**Rail Europe** US ☎ 1-800 622 8600, Canada ☎ 1-800 361 7245, ⓦ raileurope.com.

**Rail Plus** Australia ☎ 1300 555 003, New Zealand ☎ 09 377 5415; ⓦ railplus.com.au.

**SNCF** ☎ +33 892 35 35 35, ⓦ sncf.com. For regional train tickets and timetables.

**Trainseurope** UK ☎ 0871 700 7722, ⓦ trainseurope.co.uk.

### FERRY CONTACTS

**Brittany Ferries** UK ☎ 0330 159 7000, ⓦ brittany-ferries.co.uk; Republic of Ireland ☎ 021 427 7801, ⓦ brittanyferries.ie.

**Condor Ferries** UK ☎ 01202 207 216, ⓦ condorferries.co.uk.

**Corsica Ferries** UK ☎ 0825 095 095, ⓦ corsica-ferries.fr.

**DFDS** UK ☎ 0871 574 7735 (Dover-Calais, Dover-Dunkerque), ⓦ dfdsseaways.co.uk.

**Direct Ferries** UK ☎ 03333 000 128, ⓦ directferries.co.uk.

**Ferry Savers** UK ☎ 0844 371 8021, ⓦ ferrysavers.com.

**Irish Ferries** Republic of Ireland ☎ 0818 300 400, ⓦ irishferries.com.

**MyFerryLink** UK ☎ 0844 248 2100, ⓦ myferrylink.com.

**P&O Ferries** UK ☎ 0800 130 0030, ⓦ poferries.com.

# Getting around

**With the most extensive train network in Western Europe, France is a great country in which to travel by rail. The national rail company, SNCF (Société Nationale des Chemins de Fer), runs fast, efficient trains between the main towns. Buses cover rural areas, but services can be sporadic, with awkward departure times. If you want to get off the beaten track the best option is to have your own transport.**

## By train

**SNCF** (☎ 0844 848 5848, ⓦ oui.sncf) operates one of the most efficient, comfortable and user-friendly railway systems in the world. Staff are generally courteous and helpful, and its trains – for the most part, fast, clean and reliable – continue, in spite of the closure of some rural lines, to serve most of the country.

### Trains

Pride and joy of the French rail system is the high-speed **TGV** (*train à grande vitesse*), capable of speeds of up to 300kph, and its offspring Eurostar. The continually expanding TGV network has its main hub in Paris, from where main lines head north to Lille, east to Strasbourg and two head south: one to Marseille and the Mediterranean, the other west to Bordeaux and the Spanish frontier. Spur lines service Brittany and Normandy, the Alps, Pyrenees and Jura.

A subsidiary of SNCF, **Ouigo** (ⓦ ouigo.com) works on the budget airlines no-frills premise, whereby tickets are only bookable online, there is only one class (ie no first class), there are no on-board buffet facilities, and a fee (€5) is payable for each extra piece of baggage (hand baggage is free). Moreover, passengers must check-in at least thirty minutes before departure. There are seven main routes, which operate out of Paris (typically from Paris Gare Montparnasse or Marne-la-Vallée outside the city): Strasbourg, Nantes, Bordeaux, Lyon, Marseille, Montpellier and Rennes, and fares are extremely cheap, starting at a rock bottom €10, even for a train from Paris to Marseille. **Intercité** is the catch-all brand name for trains providing intercity services on routes not yet upgraded to TGV. Though not as fast, they have decent facilities including restaurant cars. Intercité sleeper services, of which there are now less than a handful, link Paris, Toulouse, the Alps and the south. Local services are covered by **TER** regional express trains.

Aside from the regular lines there are a number of special **tourist trains**, usually not part of the SNCF system or covered by normal rail passes, though some offer a discount to rail-pass holders. One of the most popular is the spectacular Petit Train Jaune, which winds its way up through the Pyrenees (see page 635).

### Tickets and fares

**Tickets** can be bought online (see above) or at train stations (*gare SNCF*). If you have language problems or there are long queues at the counter, note that touch-screen vending machines with instructions in English sell tickets for express services in most stations; separate vending machines for regional (TER) services have basic English labelling. All tickets – but not passes or computerized tickets printed out at home – must be validated in the orange machines located beside the entrance to the platforms, and it's an offence not to follow the instruction *Compostez votre billet* ("validate your ticket").

**Timetables** covering particular destinations are available free at stations. The word *Autocar* (often abbreviated to *car*) on the timetable signifies that the service is covered by an SNCF bus, on which rail tickets and passes are valid.

**Fares** are cheaper if you travel off-peak (*période bleue* or blue period) rather than during peak hours (*période blanche* or white period); peak period generally means Monday mornings and Friday and Sunday evenings. Tickets are sold a maximum of three months in advance on national trains and four months in advance on TER. You can choose your

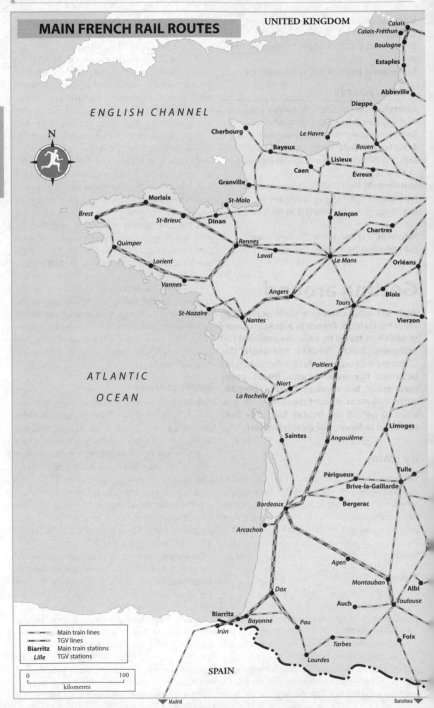

## MAIN FRENCH RAIL ROUTES

UNITED KINGDOM

ENGLISH CHANNEL

N

ATLANTIC OCEAN

SPAIN

Calais
Calais-Fréthun
Boulogne
Estaples
Abbeville
Dieppe
Le Havre
Rouen
Cherbourg
Bayeux
Lisieux
Évreux
Caen
Granville
Alençon
Chartres
Morlaix
St-Malo
Brest
St-Brieuc
Dinan
Quimper
Rennes
Le Mans
Orléans
Laval
Lorient
Blois
Vannes
Angers
Vierzon
St-Nazaire
Tours
Nantes
Poitiers
Niort
La Rochelle
Limoges
Saintes
Angoulême
Tulle
Périgueux
Brive-la-Gaillarde
Bordeaux
Bergerac
Arcachon
Agen
Montauban
Albi
Dax
Toulouse
Auch
Biarritz
Bayonne
Pau
Foix
Irún
Tarbes
Lourdes
Madrid
Barcelona

Main train lines
TGV lines
**Biarritz** Main train stations
*Lille* TGV stations

0        100
kilometres

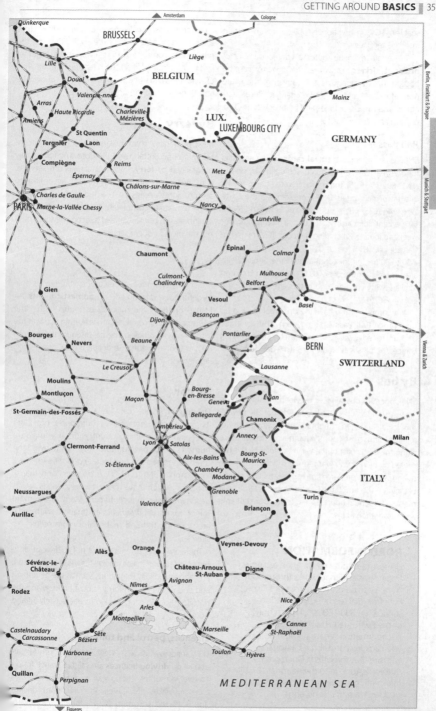

seat on TGV; reservation is obligatory on certain Intercité services.

On certain mainline routes a limited number of **discount tickets**, known as *tarifs Prem's* can be bought up to ninety days in advance; these are non-refundable and cannot be changed. Prices start at €25. You can check times and book tickets at ⓦ en. oui.sncf and ⓦ trainline.eu.

### Rail passes

SNCF offers a range of **travel cards**, which are valid for one year, and can be purchased online, by phone (❶ 33 892 35 35 35), through accredited travel agents and from main *gares SNCF*. For example, the Carte Weekend (€75) offers a discount of between 25 and 50 percent for cardholders and a companion for weekend journeys including travel on TGV trains. The Carte Jeune (€50) for 12- to 27-year-olds implements a 30 to 50 percent discount at any time. Similar deals are available for the over-60s (Carte Senior; €60) and families with children under the age of 12 (Carte Enfant +; €75).

Non-Europeans also have the option of picking up the **France Rail Pass** (starting from $192 for three days unlimited travel in one month) before arriving in France. The pass is available for 3- to 9-day periods.

## By bus

SNCF operates bus services between train stations in areas no longer accessible by rail. Additionally, private, municipal and departmental buses can be useful for local and cross-country journeys – for instance along the long coast of the Var, much of which is not served by train. If you want to see much outside the main towns be prepared for early starts and careful planning – the timetable is often constructed to suit market and school hours. As a rule, buses are cheaper and slower than trains.

---

### ROAD INFORMATION

Up-to-the-minute information regarding traffic jams and road works throughout France can be obtained from the Bison Futé free-dial recorded information service (❶ 0800 100 200; French only) or their website ⓦ bison-fute.gouv.fr. For information regarding *autoroutes*, you can also consult the bilingual website ⓦ autoroutes.fr. Once on the *autoroute*, tune in to the national 107.7FM information station for 24-hour music and updates on traffic conditions.

---

Larger towns usually have a *gare routière* (bus station), often next to the *gare SNCF*. However, the private bus companies don't always work together and you'll frequently find them leaving from an array of different points (the local tourist office should be able to help locate the stop you need).

## By ferry

Most of France's coastal islands, which are concentrated around Brittany and the Côte d'Azur, can only be reached by **ferry**. Local companies run services, with timetables and prices varying according to season. Some routes have a reduced schedule or cease to operate completely in winter months, while in high season booking ahead is recommended on all but the most frequent services.

## By air

Arriving by air from outside Europe, you may be able to get a good deal on add-on **domestic flights**. Air France operates the majority of routes within the country, although competition is hotting up, with the likes of easyJet running internal discount flights from Paris or Lyon to Biarritz, Bordeaux, Brest, Corsica, Nice, Rennes and Toulouse.

## By car

**Driving** in France can be a real pleasure, with its magnificent network of *autoroutes* providing sweeping views of the countryside. If you're in a hurry, it's worth paying motorway tolls to avoid the often congested toll-free *routes nationales* (marked, for example, RN116 or N116 on signs and maps), many of which have been reclassified as *routes départementales* in recent years. Many of the more minor *routes départementales* (marked with a D) are uncongested and make for a more scenic – if slow – drive.

There are times when it's wiser not to drive at all: in big cities; around major seaside resorts in high season; and at peak holiday migrations such as the beginning and end of the month-long August holiday, and the notoriously congested weekends nearest July 14 and August 15.

### Licences, petrol and tolls

US, Canadian, Australian, New Zealand, South African and all EU **driving licences** are valid in France for up to twelve months, though an International Driver's Licence makes life easier. The minimum driving age is 18 and you must hold a full licence. Drive are required to carry their licence with them when driving, and you should also have the insurance and registration documents with you in the car.

All the major car manufacturers have garages and service stations in France, which can help if you run into mechanical difficulties. You'll find them listed in the Yellow Pages of the phone book under *"Garages automobiles"*; for breakdowns, look under *"Dépannages"*. If you have an accident or theft, contact the local police – and keep a copy of their report in order to file an insurance claim. Within Europe, most car **insurance policies** cover taking your car to France; check with your insurer. However, you're advised to take out extra cover for motoring assistance in case your car breaks down.

Note that **petrol stations** in rural areas tend to be few and far between, and those that do exist usually open only during normal shop hours – don't count on being able to buy petrol at night and on Sunday. Thankfully, some stations are equipped with automated 24-hour pumps. Most sell unleaded (*sans plomb*), and diesel (*gazole* or *gasoil*); some also sell LPG and an increasing number are selling SP95-E10, a form of unleaded which includes 10 percent ethanol. Not all cars can run on this, so check with the manufacturer before using it.

Most *autoroutes* have **tolls**: rates vary, but to give you an idea, travelling by motorway from Calais to Montpellier costs around €70; pay in cash or by credit card (get in a lane marked CB at the toll-gates). You can work out routes and costs of both petrol and tolls online at the useful Ⓦ viamichelin.com. UK motorists can use the Liber-T automatic tolling lanes if their cars are fitted with the relevant transponder; to register in advance for a transponder and for more information see Ⓦ emovis-tag.co.uk.

### Rules of the road

Since the French **drive on the right**, drivers of right-hand-drive cars must adjust their **headlights** to dip to the right. This is most easily done by sticking on glare deflectors, which can be bought at most motor accessory shops, at the Channel ferry ports or the Eurostar terminal and on the ferries. It's more complicated if your car is fitted with High-Intensity Discharge (HID) or halogen-type lights; check with your dealer about how to adjust these well in advance. Dipped headlights must be used in poor daytime visibility.

All non-French vehicles must display their **national identification letters** (GB, etc) either on the number plate or by means of a sticker, and all vehicles must carry a red warning triangle, a reflective safety jacket and a single-use breathalyser. You are also strongly advised to carry a spare set of bulbs, a fire extinguisher and a first-aid kit. **Seat belts** are compulsory and children under 10 years must travel in an approved child seat, harness or booster appropriate to their age and size.

In built-up areas the law of *priorité à droite* – **giving way** to traffic coming from your right, even when it is coming from a minor road – still sometimes applies, including at some roundabouts. A sign showing a yellow diamond on a white background indicates that you have right of way, while the same sign with a diagonal black slash across it warns you that vehicles emerging from the right have priority. *Cédez le passage* means "Give way"; *vous n'avez pas la priorité* means "You do not have right of way".

If you have an **accident** while driving, you must fill in and sign a *constat d'accident* (declaration form) or, if another car is also involved, a *constat à l'amiable* (jointly agreed declaration); in the case of a hire car, these forms should be provided with the car's insurance documents.

Unless otherwise indicated **speed limits** are: 130kph (80mph) on *autoroutes*; 110kph (68mph) on dual carriageways; 80kph (50mph) on other roads; and 50kph (31mph) in towns. In wet weather, and for drivers with less than two years' experience, these limits are 110kph (68mph), 100kph (62mph) and 80kph (50mph) respectively, while the town limit

---

### CANAL AND RIVER TRIPS

With over 7000km of navigable rivers and canals, **boating** is one of the most relaxed ways of exploring France. Expect to pay between around €800 and €2500 per week, depending on the season and level of comfort, for a four- to six-person boat. There are many companies (see page 32) offering boating holidays or you could contact the Fédération des Industries Nautiques (Ⓞ01 44 37 04 00, Ⓦfin.fr). If you want to bring your own boat, contact Voies Navigables de France (VNF) (Ⓞ0800 863 000, Ⓦvnf.fr), which has information in English on maximum dimensions, documentation, regulations and so forth. The **principal areas** for boating are Brittany, Burgundy, Picardy-Flanders, Alsace and Champagne. The eighteenth-century Canal de Bourgogne and 300-year-old Canal du Midi in particular are fascinating examples of early canal engineering, the latter being a UNESCO World Heritage Site.

## BUY-BACK LEASING SCHEMES

If you are not resident in an EU country and will be touring France for between 17 days (21 in the case of Peugeot and Renault) and six months, it's worth investigating the special **buy-back leasing schemes** operated by Peugeot ("Peugeot Open Europe"), Citroën ("Citroën DriveEurope") and Renault ("Renault Eurodrive"). Under these deals, you purchase a new car tax-free and the manufacturer guarantees to buy it back from you for an agreed price at the end of the period. In general, the difference between the purchase and re-purchase price works out considerably less per day than the equivalent cost of car hire. Further details are available from Peugeot, Citroën and Renault dealers and online at Ⓦ peugeot-openeurope. com, Ⓦ citroeneuropass.com.au and Ⓦ renault-eurodrive.com.

remains constant. Many towns and villages have introduced traffic-calming measures and 30kph limits particularly in town centres where there are lots of pedestrians. Fixed and mobile radars are now widely used. The **alcohol limit** is 0.05 percent (0.5 grams per litre of blood), and random breath tests and saliva tests for drugs are common. There are stiff **penalties** for driving violations, ranging from on-the-spot **fines** for minor infringements to the immediate confiscation of your licence and/or your car for more serious offences. Note that radar detectors and SatNav systems that identify the location of speed traps are illegal in France.

### Car rental

To rent a car in France you must be over 21 (25 with some agencies) and have driven for at least a year. The paper counterpart of UK driving licences is now obsolete and therefore for UK licence-holders to prove to any car rental agency that they have not exceeded the maximum twelve penalty points, it is essential to go to the "Share Driving Licence Service" with the DVLA website (Ⓦ gov.uk/dvla) prior to your rental, where you can attain the necessary evidence.

Car rental costs upwards of €60 a day and €100–250 for a week for the smallest car; reserve online well in advance to get the best price. You'll find the big-name international firms – Avis, Hertz and so on – represented at airports and in most major towns and cities. Local firms can be cheaper but they won't have the agency network for one-way rentals and you should check the small print. Unless you specify otherwise, you'll get a car with manual (stick shift) transmission.

### CAR RENTAL AGENCIES

**Avis** Ⓦ avis.com.
**Argus Car Hire** Ⓦ arguscarhire.com.
**Auto Europe** Ⓦ autoeurope.com.
**Europcar** Ⓦ europcar.com.
**Hertz** Ⓦ hertz.com.
**Holiday Autos** Ⓦ holidayautos.com.

## By scooter and motorbike

**Scooters** are ideal for pottering around locally. They're easy to rent – places offering bicycles often also rent out scooters. Expect to pay in the region of €35 a day for a 50cc machine. If you are over 24 years old, you don't need a licence for a 50cc moped – just passport/ID – but otherwise you'll need a driving licence. For anything 50cc–125cc you'll need to have held a driving licence for at least two years regardless of your age, and for anything over 125cc you need a full **motorbike** licence. Rental prices are around €60–70 a day for a 125cc bike and expect to leave a hefty deposit by cash or credit card – over €1000 is the norm – which you may lose in the event of damage or theft. Crash helmets are compulsory on all bikes, and the headlight must be switched on at all times. For bikes over 125cc it is compulsory to wear reflective clothing. It is recommended to carry a first-aid kit and a set of spare bulbs.

## By bicycle

**Bicycles** (*vélos*) have high status in France, where cyclists are given respect both on the roads and as customers at restaurants and hotels. In addition, local authorities are actively promoting cycling, not only with urban cycle lanes, but also with comprehensive networks in rural areas (often on disused railways). Most towns have well-stocked repair shops, but if you're using a foreign-made bike with non-standard wheels, it's a good idea to carry spare tyres.

You can take your bike free of charge without reservation on many TER and Intercité trains; look out for trains marked on the timetable with a bicycle symbol. Folding bikes travel free on TGV and Intercité trains if they're packed into a bag no more than 90cm x 120cm; for non-folding bikes you'll have to pay a €10 fee and it may be necessary to book a space in advance. On Ouigo trains a €5 fee is levied to take your bike ("additional baggage"), but if you haven't booked this before the day of departure it will cost you €40. Another option is to have your bicycle delivered to your destination for a fee of €80. Eurostar has similar arrangements. On ferries, bikes count as your "vehicle" and attract much lower charges than taking a car across. Some airlines, such as British Airways, will not charge an additional fee for a bicycle if it's within your free baggage allowance; others now charge – check when making your booking.

Bikes – usually mountain bikes (*vélos tout-terrain* or VTT) or hybrid bikes (*vélos tout-chemin* or VTC) – are often available to **rent** from campsites and hostels, as well as from specialist cycle shops and some tourist offices for around €15 per day. Many cities, including Lyon, Marseille, Nice and Paris, have public self-service bike hire schemes with hire points scattered widely throughout the city.

# Accommodation

**At most times of the year, you can turn up in any French town and find a room or a place in a campsite. Booking a couple of nights in advance can be reassuring, however, as it saves you the effort of trudging round and ensures that you know what you'll be paying; many hoteliers, campsite managers and hostel managers speak at least a little English. In most places, you'll be able to get a simple double for €35–40, though expect to pay at least €50 for a reasonable level of comfort. Paris and the Côte d'Azur are more expensive, however, with equivalent rates of roughly €60 and €100. We've detailed a selection of hotels throughout this book, and given a price for each (see box); as a general rule the areas around train stations have the highest density of cheap hotels.**

**Problems** may arise between mid-July and the end of August, when the French take their own vacations en masse. During this period, hotel and hostel accommodation can be hard to come by, particularly in the coastal resorts, and you may find yourself falling back on local tourist offices for help.

All **tourist offices** can provide lists of hotels, hostels, campsites and bed-and-breakfast possibilities, and some offer a booking service, though they can't guarantee rooms at a particular price. With campsites, you can be more relaxed about finding an empty pitch, though it may be more difficult with a caravan or camper van or if you're looking for a place on the Côte d'Azur.

## Hotels

French hotels are graded in five bands, from one up to five, in addition to which there is a further designation called a palace hotel – truly regal establishments (and with correspondingly regal prices), and there are currently around twenty-five of these in France. The price more or less corresponds to the number of stars, though the system is a little haphazard, having more to do with ratios of bathrooms per guest and so forth than genuine quality; some unclassified and single-star hotels can be very good. Single rooms – if the hotel has any – are only marginally cheaper than doubles, so sharing slashes costs, especially since many hotels willingly provide rooms with extra beds for three or more people.

Big cities tend to have a good variety of cheap establishments; in small towns and rural areas, you may not be so lucky, particularly as the cheaper, family-run hotels find it increasingly hard to survive. Swanky resorts, particularly those on the Côte d'Azur, have very high **prices** in July and August, but even these are still cheaper than Paris, which is far more expensive than the rest of the country. If you're staying for more than three nights in a hotel it's sometimes possible to negotiate a lower price, particularly out of season.

**Breakfast** will often add anything between €6 and €30 per person to a bill – though there is no obligation to take it.

Note that many **family-run hotels** close for two or three weeks a year in low season. In smaller towns and villages they may also close for one or two nights a week, usually Sunday or Monday. Details are given where relevant in the text, but dates change from year to year; the best precaution is to phone ahead to be sure.

---

## ACCOMMODATION PRICES

Throughout this book we give a headline price for every accommodation reviewed. This indicates the **lowest rack rate price for a double/twin room during high season** (usually July & August). Single rooms, where available, usually cost between 60 and 80 percent of a double or twin; in many budget chain hotels in particular there is no discount for single occupancy of a double or triple-bed room. At **hostels**, where relevant, we have given the price of a double room and of a dormitory bed – and at **campsites**, the cost of two people, a pitch and a vehicle, unless otherwise stated.

A very useful option, especially if you're driving and are looking for somewhere late at night, are the **chain hotels** located at motorway exits and on the outskirts of major towns. They may be soulless, but you can usually count on a decent and reliable standard. Among the cheapest (from around €24 for a three-person room with communal toilet and shower) is the one-star *Formule 1* chain (☎0825 88 00 00 or 0871 663 0624, ⓦhotelf1.accorhotels.com). Other budget chains include *B&B* (☎0298 337 529, ⓦhotel-bb.com), the slightly more comfortable *Première Classe* (☎0892 234 814, ⓦpremiereclasse. com) and *Ibis* (part of the Accor group), which incorporates three brands: *Ibis Budget*, *Ibis*, and the more design-oriented *Ibis Styles* hotels (☎0825 88 22 22 or 0871 662 0628, ⓦibis.accorhotels.com). Slightly more upmarket is *Campanile* (☎0892 234 812, ⓦcampanile.com), where en-suite rooms with satellite TV and often broadband internet access cost from around €60–120.

There are a number of well-respected **hotel federations** in France. The biggest and most useful of these is *Logis de France* (☎01 45 84 83 84, ⓦlogishotels.com), an association of over 2800 hotels nationwide. They produce a free annual guide, available in French tourist offices, from *Logis de France* itself and from member hotels. Two other, more upmarket federations worth mentioning are *Châteaux & Hôtels de France* (☎0892 230 075, ⓦchateauxhotels.com) and the *Relais du Silence* (☎0826 103 909, ⓦrelaisdusilence.com), both of which offer high-class accommodation in beautiful older properties, often in rural locations.

## Bed and breakfast and self-catering

In country areas, in addition to standard hotels, you will come across *chambres d'hôtes* (ⓦchambres-hotes. fr) – bed-and-breakfast accommodation in someone's house, château or farm. Though the quality varies widely, on the whole standards are pretty high, and the best can offer more character and greater value for money than an equivalently priced hotel. If you're lucky, the owners may also provide traditional home cooking and a great insight into French life. Prices generally range between €50 and €120 for two people including breakfast; payment is almost always expected in cash. Some offer meals on request (*tables d'hôtes*), usually evenings only.

If you're planning to stay a week or more in any one place it's worth considering renting self-catering accommodation. This will generally consist of self-contained country cottages known as *gîtes*. Many

*gîtes* are in converted barns or farm outbuildings, though some can be quite grand. "Gîtes Panda" are *gîtes* located in a national park or other protected area and are run on environmentally friendly lines. The government-funded agency Gîtes de France has a list of *gîtes* (☎0871 277 0399, ⓦgites-de-france.com), which are available by location or theme (for example, *gîtes* near fishing or riding opportunities). In addition, every year the organization publishes a number of national guides, such as *Nouveaux Gîtes* (listing new addresses); these guides are available to buy online or from departmental offices of Gîtes de France, as well as from bookstores and tourist offices. Tourist offices will also have lists of places in their area which are not affiliated to Gîtes de France.

## Hostels

At around €12–26 per night for a **dormitory bed**, sometimes with breakfast thrown in, youth hostels – *auberges de jeunesse* – are invaluable for single travellers of any age on a budget. Many now offer rooms, occasionally en suite, but they don't necessarily work out cheaper than hotels – particularly if you've had to pay a taxi fare to reach them. However, many allow you to cut costs by eating in the hostels' cheap canteens, while in a few you can prepare your own meals in the communal kitchens. In the text we give the cost of a dormitory bed.

In addition to those belonging to the two French hostelling associations listed below, there are now also several independent hostels, particularly in Paris (for example, MIJE: ⓦmije.com). At these, dorm beds cost €30–40, with breakfast sometimes extra.

### Youth hostel associations

Slightly confusingly, there are two rival **French hostelling associations** – the *Fédération Unie des Auberges de Jeunesse* (FUAJ: ☎01 44 89 87 27, ⓦfuaj. org) and the much smaller *Ligue Française* (LFAJ: ☎01 44 16 78 78, ⓦauberges-de-jeunesse.com). In either case, you normally have to show a current Hostelling International (HI) **membership card**. It's usually cheaper and easier to join before you leave home, provided your national youth hostel association is a full member of HI. Alternatively, you can purchase an HI card in certain French hostels (€7 HI Welcome tariff for foreign visitors at FUAJ hostels, €11 under 26/€16 over 26 at LFAJ hostels).

### Gîtes d'étape and refuges

In the countryside, another hostel-style option exists in the form of **gîtes d'étape** (ⓦgites-refuges.

com). Aimed primarily at hikers and long-distance bikers, *gîtes d'étape* are often run by the local village or municipality and are less formal than hostels, providing bunk beds and primitive kitchen and washing facilities for around €15–25 per person. They are marked on the large-scale IGN walkers' maps and listed in the individual Topo guides. In addition, mountain areas are well supplied with **refuge huts**, mostly run by the Fédération Française des Clubs Alpins et de Montagne (FFCAM: ☎01 53 72 87 00, ⓦffcam.fr). These huts, generally staffed only in summer, offer dorm accommodation and meals, and are the only available shelter once you are above the villages. Costs are around €17–26 for the night, or half of this if you're a member of a climbing organization affiliated to FFCAM, plus around €20–25 for breakfast and dinner, which is good value when you consider that in some cases supplies have to be brought up by mule or helicopter. Outside the summer season, some *refuges* offer very limited, basic shelter at reduced cost.

## Camping

Practically every village and town in France has at least one **campsite** to cater for the thousands of people who spend their holiday under canvas. Most sites open from around Easter to September or October. Most are graded – from one to four stars – by the local authority. One-star sites are basic, with toilets and showers (not necessarily with hot water) but little else, and standards of cleanliness are not always brilliant. Facilities improve with more stars: at the top end of the scale, four-star sites are far more spacious, have hot-water showers and electrical hook-ups; most will also have a swimming pool (sometimes heated), washing machines, a shop and sports facilities, and will provide refreshments or meals in high season. A further designation, **Camping Qualité** (ⓦcampingqualite.com), indicates campsites with particularly high standards of hygiene, service and privacy, while the **Clef Verte** (ⓦlaclefverte.org) label is awarded to sites (and also hostels and hotels) run along environmentally friendly lines. For those who really like to get away from it all, **camping à la ferme** – on somebody's farm – is a good, simple option. Lists of sites are available at local tourist offices or from Gîtes de France (see page 40).

The Fédération Française de Camping et de Caravaning (☎0890 214 300, ⓦffcc.fr) has some 1200 affiliated sites and publishes an annual **guide** (€12.50), details of which can also be found online on the excellent Camping France website (ⓦcamp-ingfrance.com), which lists thousands of sites, with themed categories (campsite with beach access, with water parks, and so on). If you'd rather have everything organized for you, note that there are a number of companies that specialize in camping holidays (see page 32).

Most campsites charge per emplacement and per person, usually including a car, with extra charges for electricity. As a rough guide, two people with a tent and car might pay as little as €10 per day at an out-of-the-way rural one-star site, or as much as €45 at a four-star on the Côte d'Azur in July or August. In peak season it's wise to book ahead, and note that at many of the big sites the emphasis is more on letting caravans or chalet bungalows.

Lastly, a word of caution: always ask permission before **camping rough** (*camping sauvage*) on anyone's land. If the dogs don't get you, the guns might – farmers have been known to shoot first, and ask later. Camping on public land is not officially permitted and is often strongly discouraged, particularly in the south where in summer the risk of forest fires is high.

# Food and drink

**France is famous for producing some of the most sublime food in the world, whether it's the rarefied delicacies of haute cuisine or the robust, no-nonsense fare served up at country inns. Nevertheless, French cuisine has taken a bit of a knocking in recent years. The wonderful ingredients are still there, as every town and village market testifies, but those little family restaurants serving classic dishes that celebrate the region's produce – and where the bill is less than €25 – are increasingly hard to find. Don't be afraid to ask locals for their recommendations; this will usually elicit strong views and sound advice.**

In the complex world of **haute cuisine**, where the top chefs are national celebrities, a battle has long been raging between traditionalists, determined to preserve the purity of French cuisine, and those who experiment with different flavours from around the world. At this level, French food is still brilliant – in both camps – but can be astronomically expensive: at a three-star Michelin restaurant, even the set lunch menu is likely to cost €90, though you might get away with less than half that at a – still very impressive – one-star restaurant.

## CHEESE

Charles de Gaulle famously commented "How can you govern a country that has 246 kinds of cheese?" For serious **cheese**-lovers, France is the ultimate paradise. Other countries may produce individual cheeses which are as good as, or even better than, the best of the French, but no country offers a range that comes anywhere near them in terms of sheer inventiveness. In fact, there are officially over 350 types of French cheese, and the methods used to make them are jealously guarded secrets. Many cheese-makers have successfully protected their products by gaining the right to label their produce **AOP** (*appellation d'origine protégée*), covered by laws similar to those for wines, which – among other things – controls the amount of cheese that a particular area can produce. As a result, the subtle differences between French local cheeses have not been overwhelmed by the industrialized uniformity that has plagued other countries.

The best, or most traditional, restaurants offer a well-stocked *plateau de fromages* (cheeseboard), served at room temperature with bread, but not butter. Apart from the ubiquitous Brie, Camembert and numerous varieties of goat's cheese (*chèvre*), there will usually be one or two local cheeses on offer – these are the ones to go for. If you want to buy cheese, local markets are always the best bet, while in larger towns you'll generally find a *fromagerie*, a shop with dozens of varieties to choose from. We've indicated the best regional cheeses throughout the book.

As for **foreign cuisines**, North African is perhaps the best bet, but you'll also find Caribbean (known as *Antillais*), Vietnamese, Chinese and Indian, though French versions of spicy favourites tend to be more bland than you may be used to.

## Breakfast and lunch

A croissant or *pain au chocolat* (a light, chocolate-filled pastry) in a café or bar, with tea, hot chocolate or coffee, is generally the most economical way to eat breakfast, costing from €4. If there are no croissants left, it's perfectly acceptable to go and buy your own at the nearest bakery or patisserie. The standard hotel breakfast comprises bread and/or pastries, jam and a jug of coffee or tea, and orange juice if you're lucky, from around €6. More expensive places are likely to offer a breakfast buffet or even hot dishes cooked to order, though you could be paying anywhere up to €25.

The main meal of the day is traditionally eaten at **lunchtime**, usually between noon and 2pm. Midday, and sometimes in the evening, you'll find places offering a *plat du jour* (daily special) for €8.50–13, or *formules* (or simply *menus*), limited menus typically offering a main dish and either a starter or a dessert for a set price. **Crêpes**, or pancakes with fillings, served at ubiquitous crêperies, are popular lunchtime food. The savoury buckwheat variety (*galettes*) provide the main course; sweet, white-flour crêpes are dessert. **Pizzerias**, usually *au feu de bois* (baked in wood-fired ovens), are also very common. They are somewhat better value than crêperies, but quality and quantity vary greatly.

For **picnics**, the local outdoor market or supermarket will provide you with almost everything you need, from tomatoes and avocados to cheese and pâté. Cooked meat, prepared snacks, ready-made dishes and assorted salads can be bought at charcuteries (delicatessens), which you'll find even in most small villages, and at supermarket cold-food counters. You purchase by weight, or you can ask for *une tranche* (a slice), *une barquette* (a carton) or *une part* (a portion) as appropriate.

## Snacks

Outside tourist areas the opportunities for snacking on the run are not always as plentiful or obvious in France as in Britain or North America; the local boulangerie is often the best bet. Popular snacks include *croques monsieur* or *croques madame* (variations on the toasted cheese-and-ham sandwich) – on sale at cafés, brasseries and many street stands – along with *frites* (fries), crêpes, *galettes*, *gaufres* (waffles), *glaces* (ice creams) and all kinds of fresh-filled baguettes (which usually cost between €3 and €7 to take away). For variety, in bigger towns you can find Tunisian snacks like *brick à l'œuf* (a fried pastry with an egg inside), *merguez* (spicy North African sausage) and Middle Eastern falafel (deep-fried chickpea balls served in flat bread with salad). Wine bars are good for regional sausages and cheese, usually served with brown bread (*pain de campagne*).

## Regional dishes

French cooking is as varied as its landscape, and differs vastly from region to region. In **Provence**, in close proximity to Italy, local dishes make heavy use of olive oils, garlic and tomatoes, as well as Mediterranean vegetables such as aubergines (eggplant) and peppers. In keeping with its close distance to the sea, the region's most famous dish is bouillabaisse, a delicious fish stew from Marseille. To the southwest, in **Languedoc** and **Pays Basque**, hearty cassoulet stews and heavier meals are in order, with certain similarities to Spanish cuisine. **Alsace**, in the northeast, shows Germanic influences in dishes such as *choucroute* (sauerkraut), and a hearty array of sausages. **Burgundy**, famous for its wines, is the home of what many people consider classic French dishes such as *coq au vin* and *boeuf bourguignon*. In the northwest, **Normandy** and **Brittany** are about the best places you could head for seafood, as well as for sweet and savoury crêpes and *galettes*. Finally, if you're in the **Dordogne**, be sure to sample its famous foie gras or pricey truffles (*truffes*).

For more on which regional dishes to try, see the boxes at the start of each chapter.

## Vegetarian food

On the whole, **vegetarians** can expect a somewhat lean time in France. Most cities now have at least one specifically vegetarian restaurant, but elsewhere your best bet may be a crêperie, pizzeria or North African restaurant. Otherwise you may have to fall back on an omelette, salad or crudités (raw vegetables) in an ordinary restaurant. Sometimes restaurants are willing to replace a meat dish on the fixed-price menu (*menu fixe*); at other times you'll have to pick your way through the *carte*. Remember the phrase *Je suis végétarien(ne); est-ce qu'il y a quelques plats sans viande?* ("I'm a vegetarian; are there any non-meat dishes?"). **Vegans**, however, should probably stick to self-catering. That said Paris hasn't been immune to the recent vegan craze and does have an emerging vegan scene.

## Drink

In France, drinking is done at a leisurely pace, whether it's a prelude to food (*apéritif*) or a sequel (*digestif*), and **café-bars** are the standard places to do it. By law the full price list, including service charges, must be clearly displayed. You normally pay when you leave, and it's perfectly acceptable to sit for hours over just one cup of coffee, though in this case a small tip will be appreciated.

### Wine

French wines, drunk at just about every meal and social occasion, are unrivalled in the world for their range, sophistication, diversity and status. With the exception of the northwest of the country and the mountains, wine is produced almost everywhere. Champagne, Burgundy and Bordeaux are the most famous wine-producing regions, closely followed by the Loire, Rhône valleys and Languedoc region.

**Choosing wine** is an extremely complex business and it's hard not to feel intimidated by the seemingly innate expertise of all French people. Many *appellations* are mentioned in the text, but trusting your own taste is the best way to go. The more interest you show, the more helpful advice you're likely to receive.

The best way of **buying wine** is directly from the producers (*vignerons*) at their vineyards or at Maisons or Syndicats du Vin (representing a group of wine producers), or Coopératives Vinicoles (producers' co-ops). At all these places you can usually sample the wines first. It's best to make clear at the start how much you want to buy (particularly if it's only one or two bottles) and you'll not be popular if you drink several glasses and then fail to make a purchase. The most economical option is to buy *en vrac*, which you can do at some wine shops (*caves*), filling an easily obtainable plastic five- or ten-litre container (usually sold on the premises) straight from the barrel. Supermarkets often have good bargains, too.

The basic wine terms are: *brut*, very dry; *sec*, dry; *demi-sec*, sweet; *doux*, very sweet; *mousseux*, sparkling; *méthode champenoise*, mature and sparkling.

### Beer and spirits

Familiar light Belgian and German brands, plus French brands from Alsace, account for most of the **beer** you'll find. Draught beer (*pression*) – very often Kronenbourg – is the cheapest drink you can have next to coffee and wine; *une pression* or *un demi* (0.33 litre) will cost around €3. For a wider choice of draught and bottled beer you need to go to the special beer-drinking establishments such as the English- and Irish-style pubs found in larger towns and cities. A small bottle at one of these places can set you back double what you'd pay in an ordinary café-bar. Buying bottled or canned bear in supermarkets is, of course, much cheaper.

**Spirits**, such as cognac and armagnac, and liqueurs are consumed at any time of day, though in far smaller quantities these days thanks to the clampdown on drink-driving. *Pastis* – the generic name of aniseed drinks such as Pernod and Ricard – is served diluted with water and ice (*glace* or *glaçons*). It's very refreshing and not expensive. Among less familiar names, try Poire Williams (a pear-flavoured eau de vie)

## FINE FRENCH WINES

The most obvious guide to the quality of a wine is its **classification**, and in 2012 the system used to classify French wines changed. At the lowest level is now **vin de France**, suitable for everyday drinking, replacing the old **vin de table** but now allowing growers to provide information on vintage and grape variety. Then there's **Indication Géographique Protégée** (IGP), a new intermediate category indicating quaffable fare. IGP replaces the old Vin de Pays category. AOP – **appellation d'origine protégée** – is the highest category, taking the place of the old AOC classification. Within this category a number of exceptional wines qualify for the superior labels of **Premier Cru** or **Grand Cru**.

### WINE REGIONS

Within each wine region there's enormous diversity, with differences generated by the type of grape grown (there are over sixty varieties), the individual skill of the *vigneron* (producer) and something the French refer to as *terroir*, an almost untranslatable term meaning the combination of soil, lie of the land and climate.

**Burgundy's** luscious reds and crisp white wines can be truly sublime. The best wines come from the Côte de Nuits, which produces Burgundy's headiest reds made from the richly fruity Pinot Noir grape, and the Côte de Beaune, which yields the region's great white burgundy, made from the buttery Chardonnay grape. To the south, the Côte Chalonnaise and the Mâconnais also produce good-quality whites, while further south still the Beaujolais region is famous for its light, fruity reds. Out on its own, further north, is the Chablis region, known for its wonderfully fresh, flinty whites.

**The Bordeaux** wine-producing region, three times the size of Burgundy, produces a huge quantity of very fine, medium-bodied reds, delicious sweet whites, notably Sauternes, and dry whites of varying quality. The best-known area is the Médoc, known for its long-lived, rich reds, including such legendary names as Margaux and Lafitte, which are made from a blend of wines, chiefly the blackcurranty Cabernet Sauvignon. Graves produces the best of the area's dry white wines, while St-Émilion, where the Merlot grape thrives, yields warmer, fruitier wines.

**Champagne's** status as *the* luxury celebration drink goes back to a time when it was used to anoint French kings, and at its best is an extraordinarily complex and rich sparkling wine. This far north – Champagne is just an hour from Paris – where good weather cannot be relied on year in year out, the only way to achieve consistent quality is by blending the produce of different vineyards and vintages. The leading Champagne houses, known as *maisons*, such as Bollinger and Moët et Chandon, blend up to sixty different wines and allow them to age for some years before selling. Needless to say, they produce the best and most expensive champagnes; those of smaller growers are more variable in quality.

**The Loire's** wines tend to be rather overlooked, probably because their hallmark is subtlety and elegance rather than intensity and punch. Sauvignon Blanc is the dominant white grape variety, as manifested in the dry, fragrant Sancerre and the smoky Pouilly-Fumé, arguably the region's finest whites. Steely Muscadet, made from the hardy Melon de Bourgogne grape, is not to everyone's taste, but the best (try Sèvre-et-Maine) make a great accompaniment to seafood. The region's top reds include the light, aromatic Chinon and Bourgueil.

**The Rhône** is best known for its warm, flavoursome reds such as the blackberry-scented Hermitages, the peppery Gigondas and most famously of all the rich, spicy Châteauneuf-du-Pape.

**The Languedoc** is one of the largest vine-growing regions in the world, although the emphasis in recent years has been moving towards quality over quantity. There are so many different grape varieties grown here that the vineyards are often described as a "patchwork", and consequently many producers here make creative blends rather than single variety wines. Look out for the heady, full-bodied reds from Faugères, Fitou and Collioure, or pick up a bottle of Blanquette de Limoux, the region's economical answer to Champagne.

---

or Marc (a spirit distilled from grape pulp). Measures are generous, but they don't come cheap; the same applies for imported spirits like whisky (*Scotch*). The drinks designed to stimulate the appetite – *un apéritif* – are *pineau* (cognac and grape juice) and kir (white wine with a dash of Cassis – blackcurrant liqueur – or with champagne instead of wine for a Kir Royal). Cognac, armagnac and Chartreuse are among the many aids to digestion – *un digestif* – to relax over after a meal. Cocktails are served at most late-night bars, discos and clubs, as well as upmarket hotel bars and at every seaside promenade café; they usually cost upwards of €8.

## Soft drinks, tea and coffee

You can buy cartons of unsweetened **fruit juice** in supermarkets, although in cafés the bottled (sweetened) nectars such as apricot (*jus d'abricot*) and blackcurrant (*cassis*) still hold sway. Fresh orange (*jus d'orange pressé*) or lemon juice (*citron pressé*) is much more refreshing – for the latter, the juice is served in the bottom of a long ice-filled glass, with a jug of water and a sugar bowl to sweeten it to your taste. Other soft drinks to try are syrups (*sirops*) – mint or grenadine, for example, mixed with water. The standard fizzy drinks of lemonade (*limonade*), Coke (*coca*) and so forth are all available, and there's also no shortage of bottled mineral **water** (*eau minérale*) or spring water (*eau de source*) – whether sparkling (*gazeuse*) or still (*plate*) – from the big brand names to the most obscure spa product. But there's not much wrong with the tap water (*l'eau du robinet*), which will usually be brought free to your table if you ask for it. The only time you shouldn't drink the tap water is if the tap is labelled *eau non potable*.

**Coffee** is invariably espresso – small, black and very strong. *Un café* or *un express* is the regular; *un crème* is with milk; *un grand café* or *un grand crème* are large versions. *Un déca* is decaffeinated, now widely available. Ordinary **tea** (*thé*) – Lipton's, nine times out of ten – is normally served black (*nature*) or with a slice of lemon (*limon*); to have milk with it, ask for *un peu de lait frais* (some fresh milk). *Chocolat chaud* – **hot chocolate** – unlike tea, lives up to the high standards of French food and drink and is very common in cafés and bars. After meals, herb teas (*infusions* or *tisanes*), offered by most restaurants, can be soothing. The more common ones are *verveine* (verbena), *tilleul* (lime blossom), *menthe* (mint) and *camomille* (chamomile).

# The media

**French newspapers and magazines are available from newsagents (*maisons de la presse*) or any of the ubiquitous street-side kiosks, while TV, satellite and otherwise, is easy to track down in most forms of accommodation. A limited range of British and US newspapers and magazines is widely available in cities and occasionally in even quite small towns.**

## Newspapers and magazines

Of the **French daily papers**, *Le Monde* (W lemonde. fr) is the most intellectual; it's widely respected, and somewhat austere, though it does now carry such frivolities as colour photos. Conservative, and at times controversial, *Le Figaro* (W lefigaro.fr) – France's oldest newspaper – is the most highly regarded of the more right-wing dailies. *Libération* (W liberation. fr), founded by Jean-Paul Sartre in the 1960s, is moderately left-wing, pro-European, independent and more colloquial, while rigorous left-wing criticism of the government comes from *L'Humanité* (W humanite.fr), the Communist Party paper, though it is struggling to survive. The top-selling **tabloid**, predictably more readable and a good source of news, is *Aujourd'hui* (W aujourdhui-en-france. fr, published in Paris as *Le Parisien*), while *L'Équipe* (W lequipe.fr) is dedicated to sports coverage. The widest circulations are enjoyed by the **regional dailies**, of which the most important is the Rennes-based *Ouest-France* (W ouest-france.fr). For visitors, these are mainly of interest for their listings.

Weekly **magazines** of the *Newsweek/Time* model include the wide-ranging and left-leaning *Le Nouvel Observateur* (W nouvelobs.com), its right-wing counterpoint *L'Express* (W lexpress.fr) and the centrist with bite, *Marianne* (W marianne. net). The best investigative journalism is found in the weekly satirical paper *Le Canard Enchaîné* (W lecanardenchaine.fr), while *Charlie Hebdo* (W charliehebdo.fr) became a national bastion for free speech after two Islamic extremists entered its offices in 2015 and opened fire, killing twelve people, in revenge for the paper having published depictions of the Prophet. In the aftermath, millions of people all around the world marched in solidarity under the banner, "Je suis Charlie".

For gossip about stars and royalty there's *Paris Match* (W parismatch.com), and, of course, the French versions of *Vogue*, *Elle* and *Marie-Claire*, and the relentlessly urban *Biba*, for women's fashion and lifestyle.

**English-language** newspapers which are printed locally, such as the *International Herald Tribune*, are available on the day of publication. Others usually arrive the following day, and the prices are all heavily marked up.

## Television and radio

French **terrestrial TV** has six channels: three public (France 2, France 3 and Arte/France 5); one subscription (Canal Plus – with some unencrypted programmes); and two commercial (TF1 and M6). Of these, TF1 (W tf1.fr) and France 2 (W france2.fr) are the most popular channels, showing a broad mix of programmes.

In addition there are any number of **cable and satellite channels**, including CNN, BBC World, Euronews, Eurosport, Planète (which specializes in documentaries) and Jimmy (*Friends* and the like in French). The main French-run music channel is MCM.

**Radio France** (Ⓦ radiofrance.fr) operates seven stations. These include France Culture for arts, France Info for news and France Musique for classical music. Other major stations include Europe 1 (Ⓦ europe1. fr) for news, debate and sport. Radio France International (RFI, Ⓦ rfi.fr) broadcasts in French and various foreign languages, including English; programmes are broadcast on FM to Africa or you can listen on the website or through your mobile phone.

# Festivals

**It's hard to beat the experience of arriving in a small French village, expecting no more than a bed for the night, to discover the streets decked out with flags and streamers, a band playing in the square and the entire population out celebrating the feast of their patron saint. As well as nationwide celebrations such as the Fête de la Musique (June 21; Ⓦ fetedelamusique.culture.gouv.fr), Bastille Day (July 14) and the Assumption of the Virgin Mary (Aug 15), there are any number of festivals – both traditional and of more recent origin – held in towns and villages throughout France. For more information see Ⓦ culture.gouv.fr and Ⓦ viafrance.com.**

## Festival calendar

### JANUARY AND FEBRUARY

**Nantes** La Folle Journée (late Jan to early Feb; Ⓦ follejournee.fr); classical music.

### FEBRUARY TO APRIL

**Menton** Fête du Citron (two weeks following Mardi Gras, forty days before Easter; Ⓦ fete-du-citron.com); citrus-themed parades.
**Nice Carnival** (Feb–March; Ⓦ nicecarnaval.com).

### MAY

**Cannes** Festival de Cannes (Ⓦ festival-cannes.com); international film festival.
**Chalon-sur-Saône** Montgolfiades (mid-May; Ⓦ montgolfiades71. com); hot-air balloon racing.

**Les Saintes-Maries-de-la-Mer** Fête de Ste Sarah (May 24–25); Romany festival.
**Nîmes** La Féria de Nîmes (Pentecost, seven weeks after Easter); bullfights.

### JUNE

**Annecy** Festival International du Film d'Animation (early to mid-June; Ⓦ annecy.org); animated films.
**Bordeaux** Bordeaux Fête le Vin (late June in even-numbered years; Ⓦ bordeaux-fete-le-vin.com).
**Châlons-en-Campagne** Furies (early June; Ⓦ furies.fr); festival with circus and street theatre.
**Lyon** Les Nuits de Fourvière (June and July; Ⓦ nuitsdefourviere. com); performance arts.
**Montpellier** Montpellier Danse (mid-June to mid-July; Ⓦ montpellierdanse.com).
**Paris** La Marche des Fiertés Lesbiennes, Gaies, Bi & Trans, also known as Gay Pride (late June; Ⓦ inter-lgbt.org).
**Paris** Festival de St-Denis (May–June; Ⓦ festival-saint-denis.com); classical and world music festival.
**Reims** Flâneries Musicales d'Été (mid-June to mid-July; Ⓦ flaneriesreims.com); open-air concerts.
**Uzès** Uzès Danse (mid-June; Ⓦ lamaison-cdcn.fr); contemporary dance.
**Vienne** Jazz à Vienne (late June to early July; Ⓦ jazzavienne.com).

### JULY

**Aix-en-Provence** Festival International d'Art Lyrique (Ⓦ festival-aix.com); classical music and opera.
**Alès** Cratère/Surfaces (early July; Ⓦ cratere-surfaces.com); street theatre.
**Arles** Les Suds à Arles (mid-July; Ⓦ suds-arles.com); world music.
**Avignon** Festival d'Avignon (Ⓦ festival-avignon.com); contemporary dance and theatre.
**Beaune** Festival International d'Opéra Baroque (Ⓦ festivalbeaune. com).
**Belfort** Eurockéennes (early July; Ⓦ eurockeennes.fr); rock and indie music.
**Carhaix** Festival des Vieilles Charrues (mid-July; Ⓦ vieillescharrues. asso.fr); rock music festival.
**Colmar** Festival International de Colmar (early July; Ⓦ festival-colmar.com); classical music.
**Gannat** (near Vichy) Les Cultures du Monde (late July; Ⓦ cultures-traditions.org).
**Grenoble** Rencontres du Jeune Théâtre Européen (early July; Ⓦ crearc.fr); contemporary theatre.
**Juan-les-Pins** Jazz à Juan (mid-July; Ⓦ jazzjuan.com).
**La Rochelle** Festival International du Film (late June to early July; Ⓦ festival-larochelle.org); Francofolies (mid-July; Ⓦ francofolies. fr); contemporary French music.
**La Roque d'Anthéron** Festival International de Piano (mid-July to mid-Aug; Ⓦ festival-piano.com).
**Nice** Jazz Festival (mid-July; Ⓦ nicejazzfestival.fr).
**Orange** Chorégies d'Orange (July; Ⓦ choregies.fr); opera.

**Périgueux** Mimos (late July; Ⓦ mimos.fr); international mime festival.
**Prades** Festival Pablo Casals (late July to mid-Aug; Ⓦ prades-festival-casals.com); chamber music.
**Rennes** Les Tombées de la Nuit (early July; Ⓦ lestombeesdelanuit.com); concerts, cinema and performance arts.
**Saintes** Festival de Saintes (mid-July; Ⓦ abbayeauxdames.org); classical music.
**Samois-sur-Seine** Festival Django Reinhardt (early July; Ⓦ festivaldjangoreinhardt.com); jazz.
**Vaison-la-Romaine** Vaison Danse (July; Ⓦ vaison-danses.com); contemporary dance.

### AUGUST

**Aurillac** Festival International de Théâtre de Rue (late Aug; Ⓦ aurillac.net); street theatre.
**Lorient** Festival Interceltique (early Aug; Ⓦ festival-interceltique.bzh); Celtic folk festival.
**Menton** Festival de Musique (late July to early Aug: Ⓦ festival-musique-menton.fr); chamber music.
**Mulhouse** Festival Météo (late Aug; Ⓦ festival-meteo.fr); jazz.
**Paris** Rock en Seine (late Aug; Ⓦ rockenseine.com).
**Quimper** Semaines Musicales (mid-Aug; Ⓦ semaines-musicales.bzh); Baroque, classical and contemporary music.
**St-Malo** La Route du Rock (mid-Aug; Ⓦ laroutedurock.com).

### SEPTEMBER

**Limoges** Les Francophonies en Limousin (late Sept to early Oct; Ⓦ lesfrancophonies.fr); contemporary francophone theatre, dance and music.
**Lyon** Biennale de la Dance (every even-numbered year from mid-Sept; Ⓦ biennaledeladanse.com).
**Paris** La Biennale Paris (every even-numbered year in mid-Sept; Ⓦ lebiannaleparis.com) antiques fair; Jazz à la Villette (late Aug to early Sept; Ⓦ jazzalavillette.com); Festival d'Automne (mid-Sept to mid-Dec; Ⓦ festival-automne.com); theatre, concerts, dance, films and exhibitions.
**Perpignan** Visa pour l'Image (early to mid-Sept; Ⓦ visapourlimage.com); international photojournalism.
**Puy-en-Velay** Fêtes Renaissance du Roi de l'Oiseau (mid-Sept; Ⓦ roideloiseau.com); historical pageants, fireworks and re-creations.
**Strasbourg** Musica (late Sept to early Oct; Ⓦ festival-musica.org); contemporary music.

### OCTOBER

**Nancy** Jazz Pulsations (mid Oct; Ⓦ nancyjazzpulsations.com).
**Paris** Foire Internationale d'Art Contemporain, FIAC (mid Oct; Ⓦ fiac.com).

### NOVEMBER AND DECEMBER

**Bastia** Les Musicales (late Nov; Ⓦ musicales-de-bastia.com); chanson and world music.
**Rennes** Rencontres Transmusicales (early Dec; Ⓦ lestrans.com); contemporary music.
**Strasbourg** Jazz d'Or (mid Nov; Ⓦ www.jazzdor.com).

# Sports and outdoor activities

**France has much to offer sports fans, whether spectator or participant. It's not difficult to get tickets for football and rugby matches, while the biggest event of all, the Tour de France, is free. And if you prefer to participate, there's a host of activities and adventure sports available.**

## Spectator sports

More than any cultural jamboree, it's **sporting events** that excite the French – particularly cycling, football, rugby and tennis. In the south, bullfighting and the Basque game of pelota are also popular. At the local, everyday level, the rather less gripping but ubiquitous game of *boules* is the sport of choice.

### Cycling

The sport the French are truly mad about is **cycling**. It was, after all, in Paris's Palais Royal gardens in 1791 that the precursor of the modern bicycle, the *célérifère*, was presented; the French can also legitimately claim the sport of cycle racing as their own, with the first event, a 1200-metre sprint, held in Paris in 1868 – won by an Englishman.

The world's premier cycling race is the **Tour de France**, held over three weeks in July and covering around 3500 kilometres. The course changes each year, but always includes some truly arduous mountain stages and time trials, and ends on the Champs-Élysées. An aggregate of each rider's times is made daily, the overall leader wearing the coveted yellow jersey (*maillot jaune*). Huge crowds turn out to cheer on the cyclists and the French president himself presents the jersey to the overall winner. The last French cyclist to win the Tour was Bernard Hinault in 1985, while Bradley Wiggins, the 2012 champion, was the first Brit to clinch the title since 1903, followed a year later by team mate Chris Froome, and then in three consecutive years between 2015 and 2017. British domination continued in 2018 when it was won by Welshman Geraint Thomas.

Other classic long-distance bike races include the **Paris–Roubaix** (Ⓦ paris-roubaix.fr), instigated in 1896 and held in April, which is reputed to be the most exacting one-day race in the world, and the rugged seven-day **Paris–Nice** event (March; Ⓦ letour.fr).

## SPORTING CALENDAR

**January** Monte Carlo Car Rally (W acm.mc).
**February–March** Six Nations rugby tournament (Paris; W sixnationsrugby.com).
**April** Paris Marathon (W parismarathon.com); Le Mans 24-hour motorcycle rally (W lemans.org).
**May** Roland-Garros International Tennis Championship (Paris; W rolandgarros.com); Monaco Formula 1 Grand Prix (W acm.mc).
**June** Le Mans 24-hour car rally (W lemans.org).
**July** Tour de France (W letour.fr).
**October** Qatar Prix de l'Arc de Triomphe (Paris; W parislongchamp.com).

## Football

**Football** (soccer) is France's number-one team sport. After its legendary 3–0 win against Brazil on home soil at the 1998 World Cup, the national team's fortunes plummeted, to the extent that, at the 2010 World Cup, players refused to train after Nicolas Anelka was expelled from the squad for verbally abusing coach Raymond Domenech and the team crashed out at the group stage. In both the 2012 Euros and the 2014 World Cup they surpassed the group stages but were knocked out by eventual victors Spain (2012) and Germany (2014). There then followed a painful home final defeat against Portugal in the 2016 Euros in Paris. However, the glory days of 1998 were relived twenty years later at the 2018 World Cup in Russia, when France – comfortably the strongest team in the tournament – beat Croatia 4–2 in a pulsating final in Moscow.

The **domestic game** has been on the up in recent years, and average attendances have improved. The leading club side in *Ligue 1* (W ligue1.com) by far is Paris Saint-Germain, with its glittering array of stars, followed by AS Monaco, Olympique Lyonnais and Olympique de Marseille.

**Tickets** to see domestic clubs are available either from specific club websites, or in the towns where they are playing; ask at local tourist offices. To watch the national team, you can get tickets online at W fff.fr (Fédération Française de Football), or try W france-billet.com. Prices tend to start at around €10–15.

## Rugby

Although most popular in the southwest, **rugby** enjoys a passionate following throughout France. Although they have never won it, they have reached the final of the World Cup three times, losing to New Zealand in 1987 and 2011, and to Australia in 1999.

More international competition is provided by the **Six Nations** tournament – the other five nations being England, Ireland, Italy, Scotland and Wales. France has won the competition sixteen times (and shared it a further eight times), though it hasn't won the championship since 2010, when it also gained the Grand Slam (winning all its matches).

The **main French league** is *Top 14* and **domestic clubs** to watch out for include Toulouse (joint record-breaking four-time winners of the European Rugby Champions Cup), Toulon, Montpellier and Paris's Racing 92, and the Basque teams of Bayonne and Biarritz, which still retain their reputation as keepers of the game's soul, though both these clubs now languish in the second tier.

**Tickets** for local games can be bought through the clubs themselves, with prices starting at around €10. For bigger domestic and international games, they are available online at W francebillet.com. Information can be found on the Fédération Française de Rugby's website (W ffr.fr).

## Pelota

In the Basque country (and also in the nearby Landes), the main draw for crowds is **pelota**, a lethally (sometimes literally) fast variety of team handball or racquetball played in a walled court with a ball of solid wood. The most popular form today is played with bare hands in a two-walled court called a *fronton*. In other varieties wooden bats are used or wicker slings strapped to the players' arms. Ask at local tourist offices for details of where to see the game played.

## Bullfighting

In and around the Camargue, the number-one sport is **bullfighting**. Different from the Spanish version, the *course camarguaise* (W ffcc.info) involves variations on the theme of removing cockades from the base of the bull's horns, and it's generally the fighters, rather than the bulls, who get hurt. Further west, particularly in the Landes *département*, you'll come across the similar *courses landaises* (W www.courselandaise.org), where men perform acrobatics with the by no means docile local cows.

Spanish bullfights, known as *corridas*, do take place – and draw capacity crowds – in southern France. The major events of the year are the Féria de Nîmes (see page 645) at Pentecost (Whitsun) and the Easter *féria* at Arles (see page 836).

## Boules

In every town or village square, particularly in the south, you'll see beret-clad men playing *boules* or its variant, *pétanque* (in which contestants must keep both feet on the ground when throwing). Although more women are taking up *boules*, at competition level it remains very male-dominated: there are café or village teams and endless championships.

## Outdoor activities

France provides a fantastically wide range of outdoor activities. Most have a national federation (listed in the text where relevant), which can provide information on local clubs.

### Walking and climbing

France is covered by a network of some 180,000km of long-distance footpaths, known as *sentiers de grande randonnée* or **GRs**. They're signposted and equipped with campsites, *refuges* and hostels (*gîtes d'étape*) along the way. Some are real marathons, like the GR5 from the coast of Holland to Nice, the trans-Pyrenean GR10 and the magnificent GR20 in Corsica (see page 958). There are also thousands of shorter *sentiers de promenade et de randonnée*, the **PRs**, as well as nature walks and many other local footpaths. Note that in the south, many routes are subject to closure in summer at times of high forest fire risk.

Each GR and many PRs are described in the **Topo-guide series** (available outside France in good travel bookshops), which give a detailed account of each route, including maps, campsites, refuges, sources of provisions, and so on. In France, the guides are available from bookshops and some tourist offices, or direct from the principal French walkers' association, the Fédération Française de la Randonnée Pédestre (☎01 44 89 93 90, ⓦffrandonnee.fr). In addition, many tourist offices have guides to local footpaths.

**Mountain climbing** is possible all year round, although bear in mind that some higher routes will be snowbound until quite late in the year, and require special equipment such as crampons and ice axes; these shouldn't be attempted without experience or at least a local guide. Accommodation when mountain climbing comes in the form of *refuges* (see page 40).

No matter where you are walking, make sure you have your own water supplies, or find out locally if you'll be able to fill up your water bottles on the way. You'll also need decent footwear, waterproofs and a map, compass and possibly GPS system. Finally, don't forget sunblock, sunglasses and a hat.

In mountain areas associations of professional **mountain guides**, often located in the tourist office, organize walking expeditions for all levels of experience. In these and more lowland areas, particularly the limestone cliffs of the south and west, you'll also find possibilities for **rock climbing** (*escalade*). For more information contact the Fédération Française de la Montagne et de l'Escalade (ⓦffme.fr).

**Walking holidays** are popular in France, and there are many tour operators (see page 32) offering enticing packages.

### Cycling

There are around 60,000km of marked cycle paths (*pistes cyclables*) in France. Many towns and cities have established cycle lanes, while in the countryside there are an increasing number of specially designated **long-distance cycle routes** (*véloroutes* and *voies vertes*). Burgundy is particularly well served, with an 800km circuit, while the Loire à Vélo cycle route runs the length of the Loire valley from Nevers to St Nazaire. The Fédération Française de Cyclisme website (ⓦffc. fr) has useful information on mountain-biking sites and tourist offices can provide details of local cycle ways; the Fédération Française de Cyclotourisme website (ⓦffvelo.fr) provides links to local cycling clubs, and lists local trips by region. IGN sells various cycling guides through its website; their France-wide 1:100,000 maps are the best option for cyclists (see page 55).

A large number of tour operators (see page 32) specialize in French cycle holidays.

### Skiing and snowboarding

Millions of visitors come to France to go **skiing** and **snowboarding**, whether its downhill, cross-country or ski-mountaineering. It can be an expensive sport to arrange independently, however, and the best deals are often from package operators (see page 32). These can be arranged in France or before you leave (most travel agents sell all-in packages). Though it's possible to ski from early November through to the end of April at high altitudes, peak season is February and March.

The best skiing and boarding is generally in the **Alps** (see page 736). The higher the resort the longer the season, and the fewer the anxieties you'll have about there being enough snow. The foothills of the Alps in **Provence** offer skiing on a smaller scale; snow may not be as reliable. The **Pyrenees** are a friendlier range of mountains, less developed (though that can be a drawback if you want to get in as many different runs as possible per day) and warmer, which means a shorter season and – again – less reliable snow.

**Cross-country skiing** (*ski de fond*) is being vigorously promoted, especially in the smaller ranges of the Jura and Massif Central. It's easier on the joints, but don't be fooled into thinking it's any less athletic. For the really experienced and fit, though, it's a good way of getting about, using snowbound GR routes to discover villages still relatively uncommercialized. Several independent operators organize **ski-moun-taineering courses** in the French mountains (see page 32).

Lift **passes** start at around €35 a day, but can reach €55 in the pricier spots; six-day passes cost from €180 to around €270. **Equipment** hire is available at most resorts, and comes in at around €25 per day for skis and boots, while a week's hire will generally set you back anything from €80–150, but can climb to €200 for the most high-tech or stylish gear.

The Fédération Française de Ski (☎ 04 50 51 40 34, ⓦ ffs.fr) provides links to local clubs, while ⓦ france-montagnes.com is a good overall source of **information** in English, with links to all the country's ski resorts.

### Adventure sports

**Hang-gliding** and **paragliding** are popular in the Hautes-Alpes of Provence, the Pyrenees and Corsica. Prices are around €160 for a day; contact local tourist offices for more information.

**Caving** is practised in the limestone caverns of southwest France and in the gorges and ravines of the Pyrenees, the Alps and the Massif Central. You'll need to make an arrangement through a local club; they usually organize beginner courses as well as half- or full-day outings. For more information, contact the Fédération Française de Spéléologie (☎ 04 72 56 09 63, ⓦ ffspeleo.fr).

As for all adventure sports, it is important to make sure that your **insurance** (see page 54) covers you for these rather more risky activities.

### Horseriding

**Horseriding** is an excellent way to explore the French countryside. The most famous and romantic region for riding is the flat and windswept Camargue at the Rhône Delta, but practically every town has an equestrian centre (*centre équestre*) where you can ride with a guide or unaccompanied. **Mule-** and **donkey-trekking** are also popular, particularly along the trails of the Pyrenees and Alps. An hour on horseback costs from around €25; a day's horse- or donkey-trekking will cost €50 or more. Lists of **riding centres** and events are available from the Comité National de Tourisme Équestre (ⓦ ffe.com/tourisme), or from local tourist offices.

### Watersports and activities

France's extensive coastline has been well developed for recreational activities, especially in the south. In the towns and resorts of the Mediterranean coast, you'll find every conceivable sort of beachside activity, including boating, sea-fishing and diving, and if you don't mind high prices and crowds, the clear-blue waters and sandy coves are unbeatable. The wind-licked western Mediterranean is where **windsurfers** head to enjoy the calm saltwater inlets (*étangs*) that typify the area. The Atlantic coast is good for **sailing**, particularly around Brittany, while the best **surfing** (Fédération Française de Surf; ⓦ surfingfrance.com) is in Biarritz; further north, Anglet, Hossegor and Lacanau regularly host international competitions. Corsica and the Côte d'Azur – which has a number of World War II-era wrecks – are popular for **diving**; contact the Fédération Française d'Études et de Sports Sous-Marins (☎ 04 91 33 99 31, ⓦ ffessm. fr) for more information.

Most towns have a **swimming pool** (*piscine*), though outdoor pools tend to open only in the height of summer. You may be requested to wear a bathing cap and men to wear trunks (not shorts), so come prepared. You can also swim at many river beaches (usually signposted) and in the real and artificial lakes that pepper France. Many lakes have leisure centres (*bases de plein air* or *centres de loisirs*) at which you can rent pedaloes, windsurfers and dinghies, as well as larger boats and, on the bigger reservoirs, jet-skis.

**Canoeing** (Fédération Française de Canoë-Kayak: ⓦ ffck.org) is very popular in France, and in summer practically every navigable stretch of river has outfits renting out boats and organizing excursions. The rivers of the southwest (the Dordogne, Vézère, Lot and Tarn) in particular offer tremendous variety. **Canal-boating**, particularly in the Loire and Burgundy, is also a favourite water-based activity.

# Shopping

**France in general is a paradise for shoppers. Even outside Paris, most main towns have excellent department stores – usually a Galeries Lafayette – as well as a host of independent shops which make superb targets for window-shopping (known as lèche-vitrines, or literally "window-licking" in French).**

**Food** is a particular joy to shop for; well-stocked supermarkets are easy to find, while on the outskirts of most towns of any size you'll come across at least one *hypermarché*, enormous supermarkets selling everything from food to clothes and garden furniture. The most well-known chains include Auchan, Carrefour, Leclerc and Casino

Every French town worth its salt holds at least one **market** (marché) a week. These tend to be vibrant, mostly morning affairs when local producers gather to sell speciality goods such as honey, cheese and alcohol, alongside excellent quality vegetable, meat and fish stalls. Boulangeries are the best places to buy bread, while patisseries offer a broader range of pastries, cakes and sometimes also sandwiches and other snacks.

**Regional specialities** are mostly of the edible kind. If you're travelling in Brittany, be sure to pick up some of the local cider (cidre), while Normandy is famous for its calvados, and the south for its pastis. Provence is well known for its superb olive oil (huile d'olive) and pricey truffles (truffes), as is the Dordogne. No matter where you go, each region will produce at least one local cheese, and wine of course also varies from region to region. Cognac and the Champagne region are also obvious destinations if you're looking to stock up.

Other items to look out for include **lace** (dentelle) in the north, **pottery** in Brittany and **ceramics** in Limoges. The northeast, especially Lorraine, is renowned for its **crystal** production, while Provence, particularly the town of Grasse on the Côte d'Azur, is the place in France to buy **perfume**.

Non-EU residents are able to claim back **VAT** (TVA) on purchases that come to over €175. To do this, make sure the shop you're buying from fills out the correct paperwork, and present this to customs before you check in at the airport for your return flight.

# Travelling with children

France is a relatively easy country in which to travel with children. They're generally welcome everywhere and young children and babies in particular will be fussed over. There are masses of family-oriented theme parks and no end of leisure activities geared towards kids, while most public parks contain children's play areas.

Local **tourist offices** will have details of specific activities for children, which might include anything from farm visits, nature walks or treasure hunts to paintball and forest ropeways for older children. In summer most seaside resorts organize clubs for children on the beach, while bigger campsites put on extensive programmes of activities and entertainments. Children under 4 years travel free on public transport, while those between 4 and 11 pay half-fare. Museums and the like are generally free to under-12s

and half-price or free up to the age of 18; in some cases, citizens of the European Union aged under 26 get in free too.

**Hotels** charge by the room, with a small supplement for an additional bed or cot, and family-run places will sometimes babysit or offer a listening service while you eat or go out. Some youth hostels also now offer family rooms. Nearly all **restaurants** offer children's menus. Disposable **nappies/diapers** (couches jetables) are available at most pharmacies and supermarkets, alongside a vast range of **baby foods**, though many have added sugar and salt. **Milk powders** also tend to be sweet, so bring your own if this is likely to be a concern. You can **breastfeed** in public.

# Travel essentials

## Costs

France can be one of the more expensive European countries to visit, but how much a visit will cost depends on where in the country you go and when. Much of France is little or no more expensive than its Eurozone neighbours, with reasonably priced accommodation and restaurant food. But in prime tourist spots hotel prices can go up by a third during July and August, and places like Paris and the Côte d'Azur are always more expensive than other regions. If you're visiting a chic tourist hotspot like St Tropez, be prepared for a wallet-bashing.

For a reasonably comfortable existence – staying in hotels, eating lunch and dinner in restaurants, plus moving around, café stops and museum visits – you need to allow a **budget** of around €120 (£105/$140) a day per person, assuming two people sharing a mid-range room. By counting the pennies – staying at youth hostels or camping and being strong-willed about extra cups of coffee and doses of culture – you could probably manage on €60 (£50/$70) a day.

**Admission charges** to museums and monuments can also eat into your budget, though many state-owned museums have one day of the month when they're free or half-price. Reductions are often available for those under 18 (for which you'll need your passport as proof of age) and for students under 26, while many are free for children under 12, and almost always for kids under 4. Several towns and regions offer multi-entry tickets covering a number of sights (detailed within the text).

### Discount cards

Once obtained, various official and quasi-official youth/student ID cards soon pay for themselves in savings. Full-time students are eligible for the **International Student ID Card** (ISIC, Ⓦisic.org or Ⓦstatravel.co.uk in the UK) which entitles you to special air, rail and bus fares and discounts at museums and for certain services. You have to be 25 or younger to qualify for the **International Youth Travel Card (IYTC)**, while teachers are eligible for the **International Teacher Card (ITIC)**. A **university photo ID** might open some doors, but is not always as easily recognizable as the above cards.

Some cities issue their own discount cards, offering free or reduced price entry to museums or on public transport. These are mentioned in the relevant sections of the book.

# Crime and personal safety

### Theft and assault

While violent crime involving tourists is rare in France, **petty theft** is not uncommon in all the big cities, on beaches and at major tourist sights. In Paris, be especially wary of pickpockets at train stations and on the métro and RER lines; RER line B, serving Charles de Gaulle airport and Gare du Nord, and RER line D, serving Stade de France, have recently been the scene of several serious assaults. You'd do well to be wary when approaching the Channel ports, where migrants may seek to slow down traffic in order to break into the back of vehicles; in such instances, keep moving where possible and keep doors locked at all times; ensure, too, that it's secure if left unattended at any stage. Another recent trend, particularly in the south, is the targeting at night of foreign drivers on unlit sections of *autoroute* by fake police equipped with uniforms and flashing blue lights. Having stopped the drivers for some "offence", they make off with their documentation and a considerable "fine". Violence has sometimes been involved.

It obviously makes sense to take the normal **precautions**: don't flash wads of notes around; carry your bag or wallet securely and be especially careful in crowds; never leave valuables lying in view; and park your car overnight in a monitored parking garage or, at the very least, on a busy and well-lit street. Be wary of unmanned *aires* (rest areas) on the *autoroute* at night. It's also wise to keep a separate record of cheque and credit card numbers and the phone numbers for cancelling them. Finally, make sure you have a good insurance policy (see page 54).

To **report a theft**, go to the local gendarmerie or Commissariat de Police (addresses are given in

## AVERAGE DAILY TEMPERATURES AND RAINFALL

| | Jan | Feb | Mar | Apr | May | Jun | Jul | Aug | Sep | Oct | Nov | Dec |
|---|---|---|---|---|---|---|---|---|---|---|---|---|
| **PARIS** | | | | | | | | | | | | |
| Max/min (°C) | 6/2 | 7/2 | 11/4 | 14/6 | 18/9 | 21/12 | 24/14 | 23/14 | 20/12 | 16/9 | 10/5 | 7/2 |
| Max/min (°F) | 43/35 | 45/35 | 52/39 | 57/43 | 64/48 | 70/53 | 75/57 | 73/57 | 68/53 | 61/48 | 50/41 | 45/35 |
| Rainfall (mm) | 54 | 46 | 52 | 45 | 62 | 57 | 54 | 51 | 57 | 59 | 59 | 55 |
| **ST-MALO** | | | | | | | | | | | | |
| Max/min (°C) | 8/3 | 9/3 | 11/4 | 13/6 | 17/9 | 20/11 | 22/13 | 22/13 | 20/12 | 16/10 | 12/6 | 9/4 |
| Max/min (°F) | 46/37 | 48/37 | 52/39 | 55/43 | 62/48 | 68/52 | 71/55 | 71/55 | 68/53 | 61/50 | 53/43 | 48/39 |
| Rainfall (mm) | 82 | 68 | 63 | 50 | 57 | 48 | 41 | 48 | 62 | 75 | 95 | 89 |
| **LYON** | | | | | | | | | | | | |
| Max/min (°C) | 6/0 | 8/1 | 12/3 | 15/6 | 19/9 | 23/13 | 27/15 | 26/14 | 23/12 | 17/8 | 10/4 | 6/1 |
| Max/min (°F) | 43/32 | 46/33 | 53/37 | 59/43 | 66/48 | 73/55 | 80/59 | 78/57 | 73/53 | 62/46 | 50/39 | 43/33 |
| Rainfall (mm) | 58 | 58 | 66 | 69 | 89 | 78 | 61 | 77 | 78 | 79 | 73 | 64 |
| **TOULOUSE** | | | | | | | | | | | | |
| Max/min (°C) | 9/2 | 11/3 | 14/4 | 16/7 | 20/10 | 24/13 | 28/15 | 27/15 | 24/13 | 19/10 | 13/5 | 10/3 |
| Max/min (°F) | 48/35 | 52/37 | 57/39 | 61/45 | 68/50 | 75/55 | 82/59 | 80/59 | 75/55 | 66/50 | 55/41 | 50/37 |
| Rainfall (mm) | 59 | 59 | 57 | 67 | 77 | 71 | 44 | 57 | 67 | 58 | 63 | 69 |
| **NICE** | | | | | | | | | | | | |
| Max/min (°C) | 11/3 | 11/4 | 13/6 | 15/8 | 19/12 | 22/15 | 26/18 | 26/18 | 23/16 | 19/12 | 14/7 | 12/5 |
| Max/min (°F) | 52/37 | 52/39 | 55/43 | 59/46 | 66/53 | 71/59 | 78/64 | 78/64 | 73/61 | 66/53 | 57/45 | 53/41 |
| Rainfall (mm) | 77 | 79 | 74 | 66 | 61 | 46 | 22 | 43 | 65 | 104 | 101 | 78 |

accounts for major cities). Remember to take your passport, and vehicle documents if relevant. The duty officer will usually find someone who speaks English if they don't themselves.

### Drugs

**Drug use** is just as prevalent in France as anywhere else in Europe – and penalties for use remain harsh by European standards, despite public agitation for a softening of the law. The authorities make no distinction between soft and hard drugs. People caught smuggling or possessing drugs, even just a few grams of marijuana, are liable to find themselves in jail. Should you be arrested on any charge, you have the right to contact your consulate, though don't expect much sympathy.

### Racism

Though the self-proclaimed home of "liberté, égalité, fraternité", France has its share of **racist-related** issues. The majority of racist incidents are focused against the Arab community, although black and Asian visitors may also encounter an unwelcome degree of curiosity or suspicion from shopkeepers, hoteliers and the like. Anti-Semitic violence has had a high profile in France since the torture and murder of a young Jewish man, Ilan Halimi, in a Paris *banlieue* in 1996. In 2018, the anti-Semitic murder of 85-year-old Mireille Knoll shook the whole of France to the core. If you suffer a **racial assault**, contact the police, your consulate or one of the local anti-racism organizations (though they may not have English-speakers); SOS Racisme (ⓦsos-racisme.org) and Mouvement contre le Racisme et pour l'Amitié entre les Peuples (MRAP; ⓦmrap.fr) have offices in most regions of France. Alternatively, you could contact the **English-speaking helpline** SOS Help (ⓣ01 46 21 46 46, daily 3–11pm; ⓦsoshelpline.org). The service is staffed by trained volunteers who not only provide a confidential listening service, but also offer practical information for foreigners facing problems in France.

### Road safety

**Pedestrians** should take great care when crossing roads. Although the authorities are trying to improve matters, many French drivers pay little heed to pedestrian/zebra crossings. Never step out onto a crossing assuming that drivers will stop. Also be wary at traffic lights: check that cars are not still speeding towards you even when the green man is showing.

## Electricity

**Voltage** is officially 230V, using **plugs** with two round ïns. If you need an adapter, it's best to buy one

---

### EMERGENCY NUMBERS

**Police** ⓣ17
**Medical emergencies/ambulance (SAMU)** ⓣ15
**Fire brigade/paramedics** ⓣ18
**Emergency calls from a mobile phone** ⓣ112
**Rape crisis** (Viols Femmes Informations) ⓣ0800 05 95 95
All emergency numbers are toll-free.

---

before leaving home, though you can find them in big department stores in France.

## Entry requirements

Citizens of **EU countries** can enter France freely on a valid passport or national identity card, while those from many **non-EU countries**, including Australia, Canada, New Zealand and the United States, among others, do not need a visa for a stay of **up to ninety days**. South African citizens require a short-stay visa for up to ninety days, which should be applied for in advance and costs €60. At the time of writing the situation remains unclear with regards to citizens of the UK once the UK leaves the EU.

All non-EU citizens who wish to remain **longer than ninety days** must apply for a long-stay visa (€99), for which you'll have to show proof of – among other things – a regular income or sufficient funds to support yourself and medical insurance. Be aware, however, that the situation can change and it's advisable to check with your nearest French embassy or consulate before departure. For further information about visa regulations consult the Ministry of Foreign Affairs website: ⓦdiplomatie.gouv.fr.

### FRENCH EMBASSIES AND CONSULATES

**Australia** Canberra ⓣ02 6216 0100, ⓦau.ambafrance.org.
**Britain** London ⓣ020 7073 1000; ⓦuk.ambafrance.org.
**Canada** Montréal ⓣ514 878 4385, ⓦmontreal.consulfrance.org; Toronto ⓣ416 847 1900, ⓦtoronto.consulfrance.org.
**Ireland** Dublin ⓣ01 277 5000, ⓦie.ambafrance.org.
**New Zealand** Wellington ⓣ04 384 2555, ⓦnz.ambafrance.org.
**South Africa** Johannesburg ⓣ011 77 85 600, ⓦjohannesburg.consulfrance.org.
**USA** Washington ⓣ202 944 6000, ⓦfranceintheus.org.

## Health

Visitors to France have little to worry about as far as health is concerned. No vaccinations are required, there are no nasty diseases, and tap water is safe to drink. The worst that's likely to happen to you is a case of sunburn or an upset stomach from eating too much rich food. If you do need treatment, however, you should be in good hands: the French healthcare system is rated one of the best in the world.

Under the French health system, all services, including doctors' consultations, prescribed medicines, hospital stays and ambulance call-outs, incur a charge which you have to pay upfront. **EU citizens** are entitled to a refund (usually 70 percent) of medical and dental expenses, providing the doctor is government-registered (*un médecin conventionné*) and provided you have a European Health Insurance Card (EHIC; *Carte Européenne d'Assurance Maladie*). Present your EHIC card to avoid upfront charges if you're admitted to hospital; you'll generally only have to pay a 20 percent co-payment for treatment you receive there. Note that everyone in the family, including children, must have their own EHIC card, which is free. In the UK, you can apply for them online (☏ehic.org.uk) by phone (☎0300 330 1350) or by post – forms are available at post offices. Note that EHIC regulations are subject to change when/if Brexit comes into effect. Even with the EHIC card, however, you might want to take out some additional insurance to cover the shortfall. All **non-EU visitors** should ensure that they have adequate medical insurance cover. For minor complaints go to a **pharmacie**, signalled by an illuminated green cross. You'll find at least one in every small town and even in some villages. They keep normal shop hours (roughly 9am–noon & 3–6pm), though some stay open late and in larger towns at least one (known as the *pharmacie de garde*) is open 24 hours according to a rota; details are displayed in all pharmacy windows, or the local police will have information.

**Condoms** (*préservatifs*) are widely available in pharmacies, supermarkets and coin-operated street dispensers. The pill (*la pilule*) is available only on prescription but emergency contraception (*la pilule du lendemain*) can be obtained at pharmacies.

For anything more serious you can get the name of a **doctor** from a pharmacy, local police station, tourist office or your hotel. Alternatively, look under "Médecins" in the Yellow Pages of the phone directory. The consultation fee is in the region of €23 to €25; note that some practitioners charge an additional fee on top of the official rate. You'll be given a *Feuille de Soins* (Statement of Treatment) for later insurance claims. Any prescriptions will be fulfilled by the pharmacy and must be paid for; little price stickers (*vignettes*) from each medicine will be stuck on the *Feuille de Soins*.

In serious **emergencies** you will always be admitted to the nearest general hospital (*centre hospitalier*). Phone numbers and addresses of hospitals in all the main cities are given in the text.

## Insurance

Even though EU citizens are entitled to healthcare privileges in France, they would do well to take out an **insurance policy** before travelling in order to cover against theft, loss, illness or injury. Before paying for a new policy, however, it's worth checking whether you are already covered: some all-risks home insurance policies may cover your possessions when overseas, and many private medical schemes include cover when abroad.

After investigating these possibilities, you might want to contact a **specialist travel insurance** company. A typical travel insurance policy usually provides cover for the loss of baggage, tickets and – up to a certain limit – cash or cheques, as well as cancellation or curtailment of your journey. Most exclude so-called **dangerous sports** unless an extra premium is paid.

Rough Guides has teamed up with World Nomads to offer you **travel insurance** that can be tailored to suit the length of your stay. There are also annual **multi-trip** policies for those who travel regularly. You can get a quote on our website (☏roughguides.com/travel-insurance).

## Internet

Wireless internet (wi-fi) is pretty much the norm in even the cheapest French hotels and is often – though not invariably – free. Many hotels will also have a computer terminal in a public area for those who do not have laptops or smartphones. Internet cafés are less common than they were but can still be found in big cities, sometimes also offering cheap international calls or other services such as photo-copying. Unless specified otherwise, all accommodation establishments listed in this guide have wi-fi.

## Laundry

Self-service **laundries** are common in French towns – just ask in your hotel or the tourist office, or look in the phone book under "*Laveries automatiques*" or "*Laveries en libre-service*".

Most **hotels** forbid doing laundry in your room, though you should get away with just one or two items.

## LGBT+ France

In general, France is as liberal as other western European countries. The age of consent is 15, and same-sex couples have been able to get married since 2013.

Gay male communities thrive, especially in Paris and southern towns such as Montpellier and Nice. Nevertheless, gay men tend to keep a low profile outside gay communities and specific gay venues, parades, and the prime gay areas of Paris and the coastal resorts. Lesbian life is rather less upfront, although Toulouse has a particularly lively lesbian community. The biggest annual event is the Gay Pride march in Paris (ⓦ gaypride.fr), which takes place every June. Other cities with Pride celebrations in early summer include Lille, Lyon, Marseille, Montpellier, Strasbourg and Toulouse.

### USEFUL CONTACTS

**Spartacus** Published by Bruno Gmünder Verlag, the English-language *Spartacus International Gay Guide* has an extensive section on France and contains some information for lesbian travellers.

**Têtu** ⓦ tetu.com. France's best-selling LGBT+ magazine with events listings and contact addresses; you can buy it in bookshops or through their website, which is also an excellent source of information.

## Mail

French **post offices**, known as La Poste and identified by bright yellow-and-blue signs, are generally open from around 9am to 6pm Monday to Friday, and 9am to noon on Saturday. However, these hours aren't set in stone: smaller branches and those in rural areas are likely to close for lunch (generally noon to 2pm) and finish at 5pm, while big city centre branches may be open longer.

You can **receive letters** using the poste restante system available at the central post office in every town. They should be addressed (preferably with the surname first and in capitals) "Poste Restante, Poste Centrale, Town x, post code". You'll need your passport to collect your mail and there'll be a charge of €0.76 per item. Items are kept for 15 days.

For **sending mail**, standard letters (20g or less) and postcards within France cost €0.80 or €1.20 to other European Union countries. To the rest of the world it's €1.30. You can also buy stamps from *tabacs* and newsagents. To post your letter on the street, look for the bright yellow postboxes.

For **further information** on postal rates, among other things, log on to the post office website ⓦ laposte.fr.

## Maps

In addition to the maps in this guide and the various free town plans and regional maps you'll be offered along the way, the one extra map you might want is a good, up-to-date **road map** of France. The best are those produced by Michelin (1:200,000; ⓦ viam-ichelin.fr) and the Institut Géographique National (IGN; 1:250,000; ⓦ ign.fr), either as individual sheets or in one large spiral-bound *atlas routier*.

## Money

France's **currency** is the euro, which is divided into 100 cents (often still referred to as *centimes*). There are seven notes – in denominations of 5, 10, 20, 50, 100, 200 and 500 euros – and eight different coins – 1, 2, 5, 10, 20 and 50 cents, and 1 and 2 euros. At the time of writing, the **exchange rate** for the euro was around €1.15 to the pound sterling (or £0.85 to €1) and €0.95 to the dollar (or $1.15 to €1). See ⓦ xe.com for current rates.

You can change cash at **banks** and main **post offices**, and travellers' cheques at post offices and some BNP Paribas branches. Rates and commission vary, so it's worth shopping around. There are **money-exchange counters** (*bureaux de change*) at French airports, major train stations and usually one or two in city centres as well, though they don't always offer the best exchange rates.

By far the easiest way to access money in France is to use your credit or debit card to withdraw cash from an **ATM** (known as a *distributeur* or *point argent*); most machines give instructions in several European languages. Note that there is a transaction fee, so it's more efficient to take out a sizeable sum each time rather than making lots of small withdrawals.

**Credit and debit cards** are also widely accepted, although some smaller establishments don't accept cards, or only for sums above a certain threshold. Visa – called Carte Bleue in France – is widely recognized, followed by MasterCard (also known as EuroCard). American Express is accepted less often.

## Opening hours and public holidays

Basic **hours of business** are Monday to Saturday 9am to noon and 2 to 6pm. In big cities, **shops** and other businesses stay open throughout the day, as do most **tourist offices** and museums in July and August. In rural areas and throughout southern France places tend to close for at least a couple of hours at lunchtime. Small food shops may not reopen till halfway through the afternoon, closing around 7.30

## PUBLIC HOLIDAYS

**January 1** New Year's Day
**Easter Monday**
**Ascension Day** (forty days after Easter)
**Whit Monday** (seventh Monday after Easter)
**May 1** Labour Day
**May 8** Victory in Europe (VE) Day 1945
**July 14** Bastille Day
**August 15** Assumption of the Virgin Mary
**November 1** All Saints' Day
**November 11** Armistice Day
**December 25** Christmas Day

or 8pm, just before the evening meal. The standard **closing day** is Sunday, even in larger towns and cities, though some food shops and newsagents are open in the morning. Some shops and businesses, particularly in rural areas, also close on Mondays.

**Banking hours** are typically Monday to Friday 8.30am to 12.30pm and 1.30/2pm to 5 or 6pm. Some branches, especially those in rural areas, close on Monday, while those in big cities may remain open at midday and may also open on Saturday morning. All are closed on Sunday and public holidays.

**Museums** tend to open from 9 or 10am to noon and from 2 or 3pm to 5 or 6pm, though in the big cities some stay open all day and opening hours tend to be longer in summer. Museum closing days are usually Monday or Tuesday, sometimes both. **Churches** are generally open from around 8am to dusk, but may close at lunchtime and are reserved for worshippers during services (times of which will be posted on the door).

France celebrates eleven **public holidays** (*jours fériés*), when most shops and businesses (though not necessarily restaurants), and some museums, are closed.

## Phones

Payphones (*cabines*) are increasingly rare due to the proliferation of mobile phones/cellphones. You can make and receive calls – look for the number in the top right-hand corner of the information panel. The vast majority of public phones require a prepaid phonecard (*télécarte*) available from *tabacs* and newsagents; they come in units of 50 and 120 units (€10 and €17 respectively). Alternatively, a more flexible option is one of the many prepaid phonecards which operate with a unique code (*cartes téléphoniques*) on sale at Orange outlets, post offices, *tabacs*, newsagents and many super-markets, which

can be used from both private and public phones. Orange's Carte France Europe, for example, for domestic and European calls is available in €5 and €10 denominations, while the prices for the Carte Internationale are €7.50 and €15. The €15 card buys up to 588 minutes to the US and Canada. You can also use credit cards in many call boxes.

### Calling within France

For calls within France – local or long distance – simply dial all ten digits of the number. Numbers beginning ☎0800 and ☎0805 are free-dial numbers; those beginning ☎081 are charged as a local call; numbers beginning ☎086 cost €0.1 for the first minute and €0.02 per minute thereafter. Note that some of these ☎08 numbers cannot be accessed from abroad. Numbers starting ☎06 and 07 are mobile numbers and are therefore more expensive to call.

### Mobile phones

If you want to use your **mobile/cellphone**, contact your phone provider to check whether it will work in France and what the call charges are – they could potentially be pretty exorbitant, and remember that you may be charged for receiving calls. That said, roaming charges in the EU were abolished in 2017, meaning that UK and Irish travellers can use their home mobile data and call allowance while in France at no extra cost. However, monthly data allowances when abroad may vary so check with your provider. It's not yet known whether free roaming will still be in place if and when the UK leaves the EU. French mobile phones operate on the GSM standard; if you're travelling from the US your cellphone may not work if it is not tri-band or from a supplier that has switched to GSM. If your mobile does not work in France, or if roaming is prohibitively expensive, it may be worth buying a pay-as-you-go **French SIM card** from any of the big mobile providers (Orange, SFR, Bouygues Telecom and Free), all of which have high-street outlets and offer low cost SIM cards, typically around €5; you can then decide how much prepaid time to buy. Remember you'll need either a plug adapter for your phone charger or a charger compatible with French power sockets – phone shops stock the most popular models. One other option, of course – if you can find a wi-fi zone – is to make calls through a video-calling account like Skype or Face Time.

## Smoking

**Smoking** is banned in all indoor public places, including public transport, museums, cafés, restaurants and nightclubs.

# Time

France is in the Central European Time Zone (GMT+1). Daylight Saving Time (GMT+2) in France lasts from the last Sunday in March to the last Sunday in October.

# Tipping

At restaurants you only need to leave an additional cash **tip** if you feel you have received service out of the ordinary, since restaurant prices always include a service charge. It's customary to tip porters, tour guides, taxi drivers and hairdressers a couple of euros.

# Tourist information

The **French Government Tourist Office** (Maison de la France; Ⓦ rendezvousenfrance.com) generally refers you to their website for information, though they still produce a free magazine, *Traveller in France*, and dispense the *Logis de France* book (see page 40). For more detailed information, such as hotels, campsites, activities and festivals in a specific location, it's best to contact the relevant regional or departmental tourist offices.

In France itself you'll find a tourist office – usually an **Office du Tourisme** (OT) but sometimes a **Syndicat d'Initiative** (SI, run by local businesses) – in practically every town and many villages. Addresses, contact details and opening hours are detailed throughout the book, or try Ⓦ tourisme.fr. All local tourist offices provide specific information on the area, including hotel and restaurant listings, leisure activities, car and bike rental, bus times, laundries and countless other things; many can also book accommodation for you. If asked, most offices will provide a town plan (for which you may be charged a nominal fee), and will have maps and local walking guides on sale. In mountain regions they display daily meteorological information and often share premises with the local hiking and climbing organizations. In the big cities you can usually pick up free *What's On* guides.

## TOURIST OFFICES AND GOVERNMENT SITES

**Australia and New Zealand** Ⓦ au.france.fr.
**Canada** Ⓦ ca.france.fr.
**UK & Ireland** Ⓦ uk.france.fr.
**USA** Ⓦ us.france.fr.

# Travellers with disabilities

The French authorities have been making a concerted effort to improve facilities for **disabled travellers**. Though haphazard parking habits and stepped village streets remain serious obstacles for anyone with mobility problems, ramps or other forms of access are gradually being added to hotels, museums and other public buildings. All hotels are required to adapt at least one room to be wheelchair accessible and a growing number of *chambres d'hôtes* are doing likewise. Hotels, sights and other facilities are inspected under the nationwide "Tourisme & Handicap" scheme and, if they fulfil certain criteria, issued with a certificate and logo. A supplementary scheme, "Destination pour tous" was rolled out in 2011 to recognize communities that promote disabled access to tourism.

For **getting to France**, Eurotunnel (see page 30) offers the simplest option for travellers from the UK, since you can remain in your car. Alternatively, Eurostar trains have dedicated wheelchair spaces in Standard Premier and Business Premier carriages, but you only pay for a standard class ticket. A companion can also travel at a discounted rate. It's wise to reserve well in advance, when you might also like to enquire about the special assistance that Eurostar offers. If you're flying, it's worth noting that, while airlines are required to offer access to travellers with mobility problems, the level of service provided by some discount airlines may be fairly basic. All cross-Channel ferries have lifts for getting to and from the car deck, but moving between the different passenger decks may be more difficult.

**Within France**, most train stations now make provision for travellers with reduced mobility. SNCF produces a free booklet outlining its services, which is available from main stations or to download from SNCF's dedicated website for travellers with disabilities: Ⓦ accessibilite.sncf.com, where you can also find information on accessible stations. Note that you need to give 48 hours advance warning to gain assistance from the beginning to the end of your trip.

Specially adapted **taxi** services (such as Taxis G7's Horizon in Paris) are available in some towns: contact the local tourist office for further information or one of the organizations listed below. All the big **car hire** agencies can provide automatic cars if you reserve sufficiently far in advance, while Hertz offers cars with hand controls – again, make sure you give them plenty of notice.

As for finding suitable **accommodation**, guides produced by *Logis de France* (see page 40) and *Gîtes de France* (see page 40) indicate places with specially adapted rooms, though it's essential to double-check when booking that the facilities meet your needs.

Up-to-date **information** about accessibility, special programmes and discounts is best obtained before you leave home from the organizations listed below. French readers might want to get hold of the *Handi-tourisme* guide, published by Petit Futé (W petitfute.com), available online or from major bookstores.

## USEFUL CONTACTS

**Access in Paris** W accessinparis.org. Comprehensive (if slightly dated) information on accessible Paris in book form or online.
**Association des Paralysés de France (APF)** W apf-francehandicap.org. National association that can answer general enquiries and put you in touch with their departmental offices.
**Fédération Française Handisport** France W handisport.org. Among other things, this federation provides information on sports and leisure facilities for people with disabilities.
**Irish Wheelchair Association** Ireland W iwa.ie. Useful information about travelling abroad with a wheelchair, and good links.
**Mobile en Ville** France W mobileenville.org. Information on getting around, mainly in Paris
**Mobility International USA** US W miusa.org. Provides information and referral services and international exchange programmes.
**Tourism for All** UK W tourismforall.org.uk. Masses of useful information.

# Women travellers

Despite a relatively strong feminist movement, France can still feel like a very male-dominated country, with many men still holding rather strong chauvinist ideas. While change is in the air, with female politicians starting to take a higher profile and giving the male ruling class a run for their money, for the moment many women still suffer the double burden of being housewife and earner.

**French men** on rare occasions can be a little predatory, but are usually easily brushed off if you don't want the attention. It's not unusual, however, to be chatted up regularly, or have men (more often boys) call at you from cars in the street, and make comments as they pass you. The best way to deal with this is simply to avoid making eye contact and fail to react, and they'll soon get the message. On the beaches, especially on the Riviera, women young and old occasionally go **topless**. Be sensitive though; if on the rare occasion you find you're the only one baring all on the beach, do cover up.

# Work and study in France

**EU citizens** are able to work in France on the same basis as a French citizen. This means that you don't have to apply for a residence or work permit except in very rare cases – contact your nearest French consulate for further information (see page 53). You will, however, need to apply for a **Carte de Séjour** from a police station within three months of your arrival – consular websites have details. Non-EU citizens are not allowed to work in France unless their prospective employer has obtained an "autorisation de travail" from the Ministry of Labour before they arrive in France. Under the "Compétences et Talents" scheme, a three-year renewable work permit may be issued to individuals with specific skills. Students who have completed one academic year in France can work on renewable three-month work permits under strict conditions, subject to obtaining prior permission from the Ministry of Labour. Au pair visas must also be obtained before travelling to France. Contact your nearest French consulate for more information on what rules apply in your particular situation.

When **looking for a job**, a good starting point is to read one of the books on working abroad published by Crimson Publishing (W crimsonpublishing.co.uk). You might also want to search the online recruitment resource Monster (W monster.fr) and Job Étudiant (W jobetudiant.net), which focuses on jobs for students. In France, try the youth information agency CIDJ (W cidj.com), or CIJ (Centre d'Information Jeunesse) offices in main cities, which have information about temporary jobs and about working in France.

A degree and a TEFL (Teaching English as a Foreign Language) or similar qualification are normally required for **English-language teaching** posts. The online *EL Gazette* newsletter (W elgazette.com) is a useful source of information; so too is the annual *Teaching English Abroad* published by Vacation Work and the TEFL website (W tefl.com), with its database of English-teaching vacancies.

Foreign **students** pay the same as French nationals to enrol for a course, and you'll be eligible for subsidized accommodation. French universities are relatively informal, but there are strict entry requirements, including an exam in French for undergraduate courses if you don't already have a degree in French. If you're not a citizen of the EU or European Economic Area you'll also need a one-year extended-stay visa and residency permit. For 31 countries including the United States, enrolment is through a compulsory online process. See the Campus France website (W campusfrance.org) for more information.

Should you wish to study French in France, you can search online for language courses meeting recognized quality criteria at W qualitefle.fr.

## Further contacts

**AFS Intercultural Programs** Ⓦ afs.org. Opportunities for high-school students to study in France for a term or full academic year, living with host families.

**American Institute for Foreign Study** US Ⓦ aifs.com. Language study and cultural immersion for the summer or school year.

**Council on International Educational Exchange (CIEE)** US Ⓦ ciee.org. A non-profit organization with summer, semester and academic-year programmes in France.

**Erasmus** UK Ⓦ erasmusplus.org. EU-run student exchange programme enabling students at participating EU universities to study in another European member country.

**Experiment in International Living** US Ⓦ experiment.org. Summer programmes for high-school students.

**World Wide Opportunities on Organic Farms (WWOOF)** Ⓦ wwoof.fr. Volunteer to work on an organic farm in return for board and lodging.

# Paris

65 The islands

69 The Champs-Élysées and around

74 The Louvre

77 The Opéra district

78 Beaubourg and around

81 The Marais

87 Bastille

88 The 12<sup>e</sup> arrondissement

90 Quartier Latin

95 St-Germain

100 The Eiffel Tower quarter

106 Southern Paris

109 The Beaux Quartiers

111 Montmartre and around

114 La Villette and around

115 The eastern districts

147 Around Paris

THE LOUVRE

# 1 Paris

Long considered the paragon of style, Paris is perhaps the most glamorous city in Europe. It is at once deeply traditional – a village-like metropolis whose inhabitants continue to have a reputation for hauteur – and famously cosmopolitan. The city's reputation as a magnet for writers, artists and dissidents lives on, and it remains at the forefront of Western intellectual, artistic and literary life. The most tangible and immediate pleasures of Paris are found in its street life and along the banks and bridges of the River Seine. Cafés, bars and restaurants line every street and boulevard, and the city's compactness makes it easy to experience the individual feel of the different *quartiers*.

You can move easily, even on foot, from the calm, almost small-town atmosphere of **Montmartre** and parts of the **Quartier Latin** to the busy commercial centres of the **Grands Boulevards** and **Opéra-Garnier** or the aristocratic mansions of the **Marais**. The city's overall lack of open space is redeemed by unexpected havens like the **Mosquée de Paris** and the **place des Vosges**, and courtyards and gardens of grand houses like the **Hôtel de Soubise**. The gravelled paths and formal beauty of the **Tuileries** create the backdrop for the ultimate Parisian Sunday promenade, while the islands and quaysides of the Left and Right banks of the **River Seine** and the Quartier Latin's two splendid parks, the **Luxembourg** and the **Jardin des Plantes**, make for a wonderful wander.

Paris's architectural spirit resides in the elegant streets and boulevards begun in the nineteenth century under Baron Haussmann. The mansion blocks that line them are at once grand and human in scale, a triumph in city planning proved by the fact that so many remain residential to this day. Rising above these harmonious buildings are the more arrogant monuments that define the French capital. For centuries, an imposing classical style prevailed with great set pieces such as the **Louvre**, **Panthéon** and **Arc de Triomphe**, but the late nineteenth century onwards has also seen the architectural mould repeatedly broken in a succession of ambitious structures, the industrial chic of the **Eiffel Tower** and **Pompidou Centre** contrasting with the almost spiritual glasswork of the **Louvre Pyramide** and the audacious **Institut du Monde Arabe**. Paris is remarkable, too, for its **museums** – ranging from giants of the art world such as the Louvre, **Musée d'Orsay** and Pompidou Centre to lesser-known gems such as the Picasso, Rodin and Jewish museums – and the diversity of **entertainment**, from cinema to jazz music, on offer.

Brief history

Paris's **history** has conspired to create a sense of being apart from, and even superior to, the rest of the country. To this day, everything beyond the capital is known quite ordinarily as *province* – the provinces. Appropriately, the city's first inhabitants, the **Parisii**, a Celtic tribe that arrived in around the third century BC, had their settlement on an island: Lutetia, probably today's Île de la Cité. The **Romans** conquered the city two centuries later, and preferred the more familiar hilly ground of the Left Bank. Their city, also called Lutetia, grew up around the hill where the Panthéon stands today.

This hill, now known as the Montagne Ste-Geneviève, gets its name from Paris's first patron saint, who, as legend has it, saved the town from the marauding army of Attila in 451 through her exemplary holiness. Fifty years later **Geneviève** converted another invader to Christianity: Clovis the Frank, the leader of a group of Germanic tribes, went on to make the city the capital of his kingdom. His newly founded Merovingian dynasty promptly fell apart under his son Childéric II.

THE JARDIN DU LUXEMBOURG

# Highlights

**❶ Sainte-Chapelle** The stunning stained-glass windows of Sainte-Chapelle rank among the finest achievements of French High Gothic. See page 68

**❷ The Louvre** Quite simply, one of the world's greatest art museums. See page 73

**❸ Musée Picasso** An unrivalled collection of Picasso paintings, sculpture, drawings and ceramics housed in a handsome seventeenth-century *hôtel particulier*. See page 84

**❹ Musée d'Orsay** The Musée d'Orsay's fabulous collection of Impressionist paintings is a must-see. See page 95

**❺ Jardin du Luxembourg** These lovely gardens capture Paris at its most elegantly sociable. See page 100

**❻ Palais de Tokyo** Two exciting art spaces in a cool 1930s structure. See page 104

**❼ Musée Rodin** Rodin's intense and revolutionary sculptures are displayed to powerful effect in his elegant eighteenth-century townhouse. See page 106

**❽ Puces de St-Ouen** Even if it's less of a flea market now, and more of a mega-emporium for bric-a-brac and antiques, the St-Ouen market is a wonderful place for relaxed weekend browsing. See page 113

**HIGHLIGHTS ARE MARKED ON THE MAP ON PAGE 66**

**1**

Power only returned to Paris under **Hugues Capet**, the Count of Paris. He was elected king of France in 987, although at the time his territory amounted to little more than the Île de France, the region immediately surrounding Paris. From this shaky start French monarchs gradually extended their control over their feudal rivals, centralizing administrative, legal, financial and political power as they did so, until anyone seeking influence, publicity or credibility, in whatever field, had to be in Paris – which is still the case today. The city's cultural influence grew alongside its **university**, which was formally established in 1215 and swiftly became the great European centre for scholastic learning.

The wars and plagues of the fourteenth and fifteenth centuries left Paris half in ruins and more than half abandoned, but with royal encouragement, the city steadily recovered. During the **Wars of Religion** the capital remained staunchly Catholic, but Parisians' loyalty to the throne was tested during the mid-seventeenth-century rebellions known as the Frondes, in which the young Louis XIV was forced to flee the city. Perhaps this traumatic experience lay behind the king's decision, in 1670, to move the court to his vast new palace at **Versailles**. Paris suffered in the court's absence, even as grand Baroque buildings were being thrown up in the capital.

Parisians, both as deputies to the Assembly and mobs of *sans-culottes*, were at the forefront of the **Revolution**, but many of the new citizens welcomed the return to order under Napoleon I. The emperor adorned the city with many of its signature monuments, Neoclassical almost-follies designed to amplify his majesty: the Arc de Triomphe, Arc du Carrousel and the Madeleine. He also instituted the Grandes Écoles, super-universities for the nation's elite administrators, engineers and teachers. At the fall of the Empire, in 1814, Paris was saved from destruction by the arch-diplomat Talleyrand, who delivered the city to the Russians with hardly a shot fired. Nationalists grumbled that the occupation continued well into the Restoration regime, as the city once again became the playground of the rich of Europe, the ultimate tourist destination.

The greatest shocks to the fabric of the city came under Napoléon III. He finally completed the Louvre, rebuilding much of the facade in the process, but it was his Prefect of the Seine, **Baron Haussmann**, who truly transformed the city, smashing through the slums to create wide boulevards that could be easily controlled by rifle-toting troops – not that it succeeded in preventing the **1871 Commune**, the most determined insurrection since 1789. It was down these large boulevards, lined with grey bourgeois residences, that **Nazi troops** paraded in June 1940, followed by the Allies, led by General Leclerc, in August 1944.

Although riotous street protests have been a feature of modern Parisian life – most famously in **May 1968**, when students burst onto the streets of the Quartier Latin – the traditional barricade-builders have long since been booted into the satellite towns, known as *la banlieue*, alongside the under-served populations of immigrants and their descendants. Integrating these communities, riven with poverty, unemployment and discontent, has long been one of the greatest challenges facing the city. Meanwhile, the city's Socialist and first woman mayor, **Anne Hidalgo**, is continuing and expanding upon the green policies of her popular predecessor, **Bertrand Delanoë**, creating a more cycle-friendly environment and reclaiming for pedestrians more of the riverbank, as well as the city's famous squares, place de la Bastille and place de la Nation. In the wake of the horrific events of 2015, when Paris experienced two major terrorist massacres – the *Charlie Hebdo* shootings in January and the widespread attacks of November – the city experienced a renewed sense of unity and solidarity. This partly fuelled the bid to stage the **Olympic Games** in 2024, the success of which was a massive boost to the city and to Hidalgo. Consistent with her green policies, she has committed to foregrounding eco issues and sensible spending by repurposing existing sports venues rather than embarking upon a building frenzy, and has guaranteed that some events will be held in the poorer *banlieue*, in a bid to encourage development.

# The islands

There's nowhere better to start a tour of Paris than the two islands at its centre. The **Île de la Cité** is where Paris began, and boasts a number of important sights. The smaller **Île St-Louis**, linked to the Île de la Cité by a footbridge, is often considered the most romantic part of Paris. There are no particular sights on this little island, just austerely handsome seventeenth-century houses on single-lane streets, tree-lined *quais*, a church, restaurants, cafés and interesting little shops. It is particularly atmospheric in the evening, when an arm-in-arm wander along the *quais* is a romantic must.

## Île de la Cité

The earliest settlements were built here, followed by the small Gallic town of Lutetia, which was overrun by Julius Caesar's troops in 52 BC. A natural defensive site commanding a major east–west river trade route, it was an obvious candidate for a bright future. In 508 it became the stronghold of the Merovingian kings, then of the counts of Paris, who in 987 became kings of France.

The Frankish kings built themselves a splendid palace at the western tip of the island, of which the **Sainte-Chapelle** and **Conciergerie** survive today. At the other end of the island, they erected the great cathedral of **Notre-Dame**. By the early thirteenth century this tiny island had become the bustling heart of the capital, though it's hard to imagine this today: virtually the whole medieval city was erased by Baron Haussmann in the nineteenth-century and replaced by four imposing Neoclassical edifices, including the Palais de Justice.

# PARIS

N

La Grande Arche

Ile de la Jatte

CLICHY

ST-OUEN

BOULEVARD PERIPHERIQUE

PTE DE
ST-OUEN

PTE DE
CLICHY

BOULEVARD D'AUBRES

BOULEVARD BERTHIER

AVENUE DE CLICHY

RUE VICTOR-HUGO

LEVALLOIS-
PERRET

BOULEVARD BINEAU

PTE
D'ASNÈRES

BATIGNOLLES

LA
DÉFENSE

PONT DE
NEUILLY

NEUILLY

PTE DE
CHAMPERRET

AVENUE DE VILLIERS

17e

BOULEVARD DE BATIGNOLLES

Gare
St-Lazare

Ile de Puteaux

AVENUE CHARLES DE GAULLE

BOULEVARD DU CDT. CHARCOT

Jardin
d'Acclimatation

Fondation
Louis Vuitton

PORTE
MAILLOT

AV. DE LA GRANDE-ARMÉE

AVENUE DE WAGRAM

BOULEVARD DE COURCELLES

Parc
Monceau

BOULEVARD MALESHERBES

BOULEVARD

PLACE CHARLES
DE GAULLE

Arc de
Triomphe

AVENUE FOCH

8e

Église de la
Madeleine

BOIS DE
BOULOGNE

BOULEVARD PERIPHERIQUE

BOULEVARD LANNES

PTE
DAUPHINE

AVENUE DES CHAMPS-ELYSÉES

Petit Palais

Grand
Palais

PLACE DE LA
CONCORDE

Jardin
des
Tuileries

AVENUE VICTOR-HUGO

AVENUE KLEBER

Musée
Guimet

Palais
de Tokyo

ALBERT 1ER COURS LA REINE

PTE DE
LA MUETTE

Palais de
Chaillot Cité de
l'Architecture

6

QUAI D'ORSAY

Musée du
Quai Branly

Musée
d'Orsay

16e

AVENUE P. DOUMER

AVENUE DE NEW YORK

QUAI BRANLY

7e

BOULEVARD RASPAIL

PTE DE
PASSY

PASSY

Eiffel Tower

Hôtel des
Invalides

ST-GERMAIN

Longchamp

AVENUE DE ST-CLOUD

Auteuil

AVENUE MOZART

BOULEVARD SUCHET

Maison de
Radio France

AVENUE DU PRÉSIDENT KENNEDY

AVENUE BOSQUET

Musée
Rodin

7

Roland
Garros

PTE
D'AUTEUIL

PTE
MOLITOR

AUTEUIL

AVENUE DE VERSAILLES

BOULEVARD MURAT

QUAI LOUIS BLÉRIOT

École
Militaire

AVENUE DE LOWENDAL

BOULEVARD DES INVALIDES

Parc des
Princes

PTE DE
ST-CLOUD

AVENUE EMILE ZOLA

RUE DE LA CONVENTION

Parc
André-
Citroën

15e

RUE DE VAUGIRARD

BOULEVARD DU

Tour
Montparnasse

Gare Montparnasse

AVENUE E. VAILLANT

River Seine

BOULEVARD VICTOR

Palais
des Sports

PTE DE
VERSAILLES

RUE DE VAUGIRARD

Jardin
Atlantique

Montparnasse
Cemetery

AVENUE DU MAINE

BOULEVARD PERIPHERIQUE

PTE DE
SÈVRES

Parc
Georges-
Brassens

BOULEVARD LEFEBVRE

PERNETY

RUE D'ALESIA

ISSY-LES-
MOULINEAUX

PTE DE
LA PLAINE

PTE
BRANCION

PTE DE
VANVES

BOULEVARD BRUNE

ALESIA

PTE DE
CHATILLON

AVENUE P. BROSSOLETTE

MONTROUGE

PORTE
D'ORLEANS

## HIGHLIGHTS

1 Sainte-Chapelle
2 The Louvre
3 Musée Picasso
4 Musée d'Orsay
5 Jardin du Luxembourg
6 Palais de Tokyo
7 Musée Rodin
8 Puces de St-Ouen

1

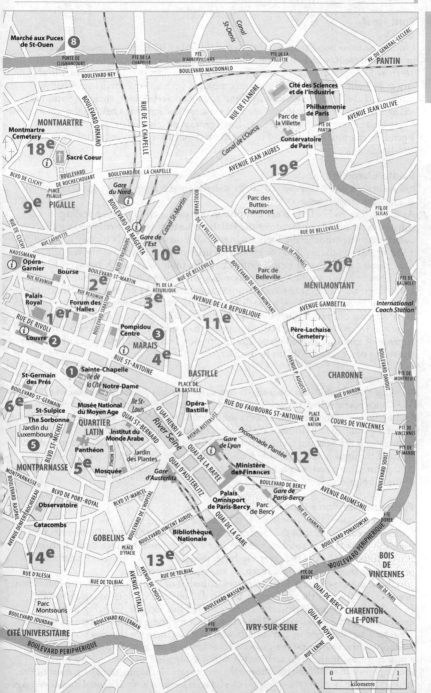

Marché aux Puces de St-Ouen 8

PORTE DE CLIGNANCOURT

PTE DE LA CHAPELLE

PTE D'AUBERVILLIERS

PTE DE LA VILLETTE

AV. DU GENERAL-LECLERC

**PANTIN**

BOULEVARD NEY

BOULEVARD MACDONALD

Canal St-Denis

RUE DE FLANDRE

Cité des Sciences et de l'Industrie

Philharmonie de Paris

AVENUE JEAN LOLIVE

Parc de la Villette

PTE DE PANTIN

BOULEVARD ORNANO

RUE DE LA CHAPELLE

RUE DE L'OURCQ

Canal de l'Ourcq

Conservatoire de Paris

**MONTMARTRE**

Montmartre Cemetery

18e

Sacré Coeur

AVENUE JEAN JAURES

**19e**

BLVD DE CLICHY

BOULEVARD DE ROCHECHOUART

BOULEVARD DE LA CHAPELLE

Gare du Nord

Parc des Buttes-Chaumont

PTE DE SLILAS

RUE DE CLICHY

PLACE PIGALLE

9e **PIGALLE**

BOULEVARD DE MAGENTA

Canal St-Martin

RUE DE BELLEVILLE

RUE LAFAYETTE

Gare de l'Est

BOULEVARD DE LA VILLETTE

**BELLEVILLE**

HAUSSMANN

10e

RUE DE PRENES

Opéra-Garnier

Bourse

BLVD ST-MARTIN

BOULEVARD ST-MARTIN

Parc de Belleville

**MÉNILMONTANT**

20e

PTE DE BAGNOLET

RUE REAUMUR

2e

RUE DE BELLEVILLE

BOULEVARD DE MENILMONTANT

Palais Royal

RUE REAUMUR

PL DE LA RÉPUBLIQUE

3e

AVENUE DE LA REPUBLIQUE

AVENUE GAMBETTA

International Coach Station

1er

Forum des Halles

BOULEVARD DE SEBASTOPOL

**11e**

Louvre 2

Pompidou Centre 3

Père-Lachaise Cemetery

RUE DE RIVOLI

**MARAIS**

RUE ST-ANTOINE

4e

**CHARONNE**

PTE DE MONTREUIL

St-Germain des Prés

Sainte-Chapelle 1 Île de la Cité Notre-Dame

AVENUE P. AUGUSTE

RUE D'AVRON

BOULEVARD DAVOUT

BOULEVARD ST-GERMAIN

Île St-Louis

**BASTILLE**

PLACE DE LA BASTILLE

RUE DU FAUBOURG ST-ANTOINE

PLACE DE LA NATION

COURS DE VINCENNES

PTE DE VINCENNES

6e

St-Sulpice

Musée National du Moyen Age

QUAI ST-BERNARD

Opéra-Bastille

The Sorbonne

Jardin du Luxembourg

5

**QUARTIER LATIN**

QUAI HENRI IV

River Seine

AVENUE AUSTERLITZ

Promenade Plantée

PTE DE ST-MANDE

BOULEVARD INOULT

BLVD ST-MICHEL

Institut du Monde Arabe

Gare de Lyon

**12e**

Panthéon

RUE MONGE

Jardin des Plantes

QUAI DE LA RAPEE

**MONTPARNASSE**

5e

Mosquée

Gare d'Austerlitz

Ministère des Finances

MONTPARNASSE

BLVD DE PORT-ROYAL

QUAI D'AUSTERLITZ

BOULEVARD DE BERCY

Gare de Paris-Bercy

AVENUE DAUMESNIL

BOULEVARD RASPAIL

BLVD ST-MARCEL

Palais Omnisport de Paris-Bercy

Parc de Bercy

RUE DE CHARENTON

Observatoire

AVENUE DENFERT-ROCHEREAU

BOULEVARD DE L'HOPITAL

QUAI DE LA GARE

PTE DOREE

Catacombs

BOULEVARD VINCENT AURIOL

Bibliothèque Nationale

BOULEVARD PONIATOWSKI

**GOBELINS**

PLACE D'ITALIE

BOULEVARD PERIPHERIQUE

PTE DE BERCY

**BOIS DE VINCENNES**

14e

13e

QUAI DE BERCY

RUE DE PARIS

RUE D'ALESIA

RUE DE TOLBIAC

RUE DE TOLBIAC

AVENUE D'ITALIE

AVENUE DE CHOISY

PTE DE BERCY

QUAI M. BOYER

**CHARENTON LE-PONT**

Parc Montsouris

BOULEVARD KELLERMAN

BOULEVARD MASSENA

RUE LENINE

BOULEVARD JOURDAN

PTE D'IVRY

**IVRY-SUR-SEINE**

**CITÉ UNIVERSITAIRE**

BOULEVARD PERIPHERIQUE

0          1

kilometre

1

## Pont-Neuf

Ⓜ Pont-Neuf

One of the most popular approaches to the Île de la Cité is via the graceful, twelve-arched **Pont-Neuf**, which despite its name is Paris's oldest surviving bridge, built in 1607 by Henri IV. It takes its name ("new") from the fact that it was the first in the city to be built of stone. Henri is commemorated with an equestrian statue halfway across, and also lends his nickname to the **square du Vert-Galant**, enclosed within the triangular stern of the island and reached via steps leading down behind the statue. "Vert-Galant", meaning a "green" or "lusty gentleman", is a reference to Henri's legendary amorous exploits, and he would no doubt have approved of this romantic, tree-lined garden.

## Sainte-Chapelle

Palais de Justice, bd du Palais, 1ᵉʳ • April–Sept 9am–7pm; Oct–March 9am–5pm • €10, combined admission with the Conciergerie €15 • ☎ 01 53 40 60 80, Ⓦ sainte-chapelle.fr • Ⓜ Cité

At the further end of leafy **place Dauphine**, one of the city's most appealing squares, looms the huge facade of the **Palais de Justice**, which swallowed up the palace that was home to the French kings until Étienne Marcel's bloody revolt in 1358 frightened them off to the greater security of the Louvre. A survivor of the old complex is the magnificent **Sainte-Chapelle**, built by Louis IX between 1242 and 1248 to house a collection of holy relics, including Christ's crown of thorns and a fragment of the True Cross, bought at extortionate rates from the bankrupt empire of Byzantium. Though much restored, the chapel remains one of the finest achievements of French High Gothic. Its most radical feature is its seeming fragility – created by reducing the structural masonry to a minimum to make way for a huge expanse of exquisite stained glass. The impression inside is of being enclosed within the wings of a myriad brilliant butterflies.

## Conciergerie

Palais de Justice, 2 bd du Palais, 1ᵉʳ • Daily 9.30am–6pm • €9, combined ticket with Sainte-Chapelle €15 • Ⓦ paris-conciergerie.fr • Ⓜ Cité

The **Conciergerie** is Paris's oldest prison, where Marie Antoinette and, in their turn, the leading figures of the Revolution were incarcerated before execution. Inside are several splendidly vaulted late Gothic halls, vestiges of the old Capetian kings' palace. Most impressive is the Salle des Gens d'armes (1315), originally the canteen and recreation room of the royal household staff. A number of rooms and cells, including Marie Antoinette's, have been reconstructed to show how they might have looked at the time of the Revolution.

## Cathédrale de Notre-Dame

Place du Parvis Notre-Dame, 4ᵉ • Ⓦ notredamedeparis.fr • Ⓜ St-Michel/Cité

One of the masterpieces of the Gothic age, the **Cathédrale de Notre-Dame** rears up from the Île de la Cité's southeast corner like a ship moored by huge flying buttresses. It was among the first of the great Gothic cathedrals built in northern France and one of the most ambitious, its nave reaching an unprecedented 33m.

Built on the site of the old Merovingian cathedral of Saint-Étienne, Notre-Dame was begun in 1160 under the auspices of Bishop de Sully and completed around 1345. In the seventeenth and eighteenth centuries it fell into decline, suffering its worst depredations during the **French Revolution** when the frieze of Old Testament kings on the facade was damaged by enthusiasts who mistook them for the kings of France. It was only in the 1820s that the cathedral was at last given a much-needed restoration, a task entrusted to the great architect-restorer, Viollet-le-Duc, who carried out a thorough (some would say too thorough) renovation, including remaking most of the statuary on the facade – the originals can be seen in the Musée National du Moyen Âge (see page 91) – and adding the steeple and baleful-looking gargoyles.

**1**

**April 15 fire**

While undergoing restoration, on the early evening of April 15 2019 a huge fire tore through Notre-Dame, destroying the 13th-century wooden frame fondly nicknamed "la forêt" (the forest), which in turn caused the roof and its steeple to collapse on the marble floor of the cathedral. Parisians – and the world – watched on in horror as some 400 firefighters fought to tame the devastating fire by pumping water directly from the Seine. The fire was extinguished in time to save the stone structure, including the two emblematic **towers**. The cathedral's most prized relics, including the supposed Crown of Thorns worn by Jesus prior to his crucifixion and a piece of the cross on which he was crucified, were taken away as the fire raged on and paintings and other priceless artworks saved from fire were sent to the Louvre for safekeeping and restoring. The altar, the 13th-century organ and the exquisite stained-glass rose windows were essentially intact. Thankfully, the fire claimed no victims and the interior was mostly spared bar some water and smoke damage.

Almost immediately, pledges from France's wealthiest families and donations from all over the world came pouring in – reaching almost €800m at the time of writing. Immortalized by Victor Hugo in his masterpiece *Notre-Dame de Paris* (*The Hunchback of Notre-Dame*), her fame far exceeds her status as head church of the Catholics of France; it was also here that Napoleon crowned himself emperor. Some experts have claimed that this sum will most probably surpass the actual cost of repairs and opinion in France and abroad has been divided as to whether this amount is justified in the current climate of austerity highlighted by the ongoing "gilets jaunes" protests.

Only days after the tragedy French president Emmanuel Macron promised that Notre-Dame would take only five years to rebuild – an ambitious claim indeed. But it is in everyone's interest that the most visited monument in Europe reopens as soon as possible. Until then, both the cathedral and the **Crypte Archéologique** – a large, well-presented excavated area revealing the remains of the original cathedral, as well as remnants of the streets and houses that once clustered around Notre-Dame – are closed indefinitely.

### Mémorial des Martyrs de la Déportation

Square de l'Île de France, 4ᵉ • Tues–Sun: April–Sept 10am–7pm; Oct–March 10am–5pm • Free • ⓂSt-Paul/Maubert Mutualité

At the eastern tip of Île de la Cité is the symbolic tomb of the 200,000 French who died in Nazi concentration camps during World War II – Resistance fighters, Jews and forced labourers among them. The stark and moving **Mémorial des Martyrs de la Déportation** is scarcely visible above ground; stairs hardly shoulder-wide descend into a space like a prison yard off which is a stifling, narrow crypt, its walls lined with thousands of illuminated quartz pebbles representing the dead. The monument ends in a raw aperture, with a single naked bulb hanging in the middle. Above the exit are the words "Pardonne, n'oublie pas" ("Forgive, do not forget").

# The Champs-Élysées and around

The **Champs-Élysées** sweeps through one of the city's most exclusive districts, studded with luxury hotels and high-end fashion boutiques. The famed avenue forms part of a grand 9km-long axis that extends from the Louvre, at the heart of the city, to the Grande Arche de la Défense, in the west. Referred to as the Voie Triomphale, or Triumphal Way, it offers impressive vistas all along its length and incorporates some of the city's most famous landmarks – not only the avenue itself but also the **Tuileries** gardens, **place de la Concorde**, and the **Arc de Triomphe**. The whole ensemble is so harmonious it looks as though it was laid out by a single town planner rather than by successive kings, emperors and presidents, all keen to add their stamp and promote French power and prestige.

**1**

## Arc de Triomphe

Place Charles-de-Gaulle, 8ᵉ; access is via underground stairs from the north corner of the Champs-Élysées • Daily: April–Sept 10am–11pm; Oct–March 10am–10.30pm • €12 • ⓦ paris-arc-de-triomphe.fr • Ⓜ Charles-de-Gaulle-Étoile

The **Arc de Triomphe** towers above the traffic in the middle of **place Charles-de-Gaulle**, also known as l'Étoile ("star") on account of the twelve avenues radiating out from it. The arch was started by Napoleon as a homage to the armies of France and himself, but it wasn't actually finished until 1836 by Louis-Philippe, who dedicated it to the French army in general. The names of 660 generals and numerous French battles are engraved on the inside of the arch, and reliefs adorn the exterior: the best is François Rude's extraordinarily dramatic *Marseillaise*, in which an Amazon-type figure personifying the Revolution charges forward with a sword, her face contorted in a fierce rallying cry. A quiet reminder of the less glorious side of war is the **tomb of the unknown soldier** beneath the arch, marked by an eternal flame that is stoked up every evening at 6.30pm by war veterans. Climbing the twisty, narrow 280 steps to the top (there is a lift you can ask to use) will be amply rewarded by the panoramic views; the best time to come is towards dusk on a sunny day, when the marble of the Grande Arche de la Défense sparkles in the setting sun and the Louvre is bathed in warm light.

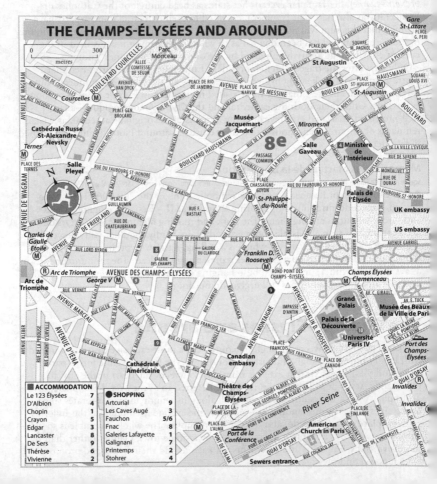

THE CHAMPS-ÉLYSÉES AND AROUND

| ■ ACCOMMODATION | |
| --- | --- |
| Le 123 Élysées | 7 |
| D'Albion | 4 |
| Chopin | 1 |
| Crayon | 5 |
| Edgar | 3 |
| Lancaster | 8 |
| De Sers | 9 |
| Thérèse | 6 |
| Vivienne | 2 |

| ● SHOPPING | |
| --- | --- |
| Artcurial | 9 |
| Les Caves Augé | 3 |
| Fauchon | 5/6 |
| Fnac | 8 |
| Galeries Lafayette | 1 |
| Galignani | 7 |
| Printemps | 2 |
| Stohrer | 4 |

# The Champs-Élysées

The celebrated **avenue des Champs-Élysées**, a popular rallying point at times of national crisis and the scene of big military parades on Bastille Day, sweeps down from the Arc de Triomphe towards the place de la Concorde. A number of major fashion brands have their flagship stores on the avenue, particularly on the southern side, where Louis Vuitton, Lanvin and the like flaunt their wares. On account of its high concentration of luxury hotels and flagship designer stores, the area bounded by the Champs-Élysées and, to the south, avenue Montaigne and rue François-1$^{er}$, is nicknamed the **Triangle d'Or** (Golden Triangle).

The Champs-Élysées began life as a leafy promenade, an extension of the Tuileries gardens. It was transformed into a fashionable thoroughfare during the Second Empire when members of the *haute bourgeoisie* built themselves splendid mansions along its length and high society would come to stroll and frequent the cafés and theatres. Most of the mansions subsequently gave way to office blocks and the beau monde moved elsewhere, but remnants of the avenue's glitzy heyday live on at the *Lido* cabaret, *Fouquet's* café-restaurant and the perfumier Guerlain's shop.

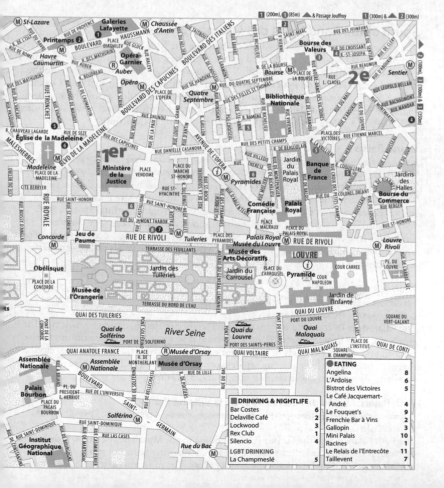

1

Every first Sunday of the month, the avenue closes to traffic. Also note that the Champs-Élysées is a favourite meeting place of the "gilets jaunes" (yellow vests) protesters and as such is best avoided on a Saturday.

## Musée Jacquemart-André

158 bd Haussmann, 8ᵉ • Daily 10am–6pm (Mon until 8.30pm during temporary exhibitions) • €13.50, or more including temporary exhibitions • ☎ 01 45 62 11 59, ⓦ musee-jacquemart-andre.com • ⓜ Miromesnil/St-Philippe-du-Roule

The **Musée Jacquemart-André**, just one of the select museums north of the Champs-Élysées, is a splendid mansion laden with the outstanding works of art that its owners, banker Édouard André and his wife, society portraitist Nélie Jacquemart, collected on their extensive trips abroad. Informative audioguides take you through sumptuous *salons*, mainly decorated in Louis XV and Louis XVI style. The pride of the couple's collection was their early Italian Renaissance paintings, on the upper floor, including Uccello's *St George and the Dragon*, a haunting *Virgin and Child* by Mantegna, and another by Botticelli. An excellent way to finish off a visit is with a reviving halt at the museum's **salon de thé**, with its lavish interior and ceiling frescoes by Tiepolo.

## South of the Rond-Point des Champs-Élysées

The lower stretch of the Champs-Élysées, between the Rond-Point des Champs-Élysées and place de la Concorde, is bordered by chestnut trees and flowerbeds and is the most pleasant part of the avenue for a stroll. Rising above the greenery to the south are the splendid **Grand Palais** and **Petit Palais**, both built for the World Fair in 1900. On the other side of the avenue, to the north of place Clemenceau, police guard the high walls round the presidential **Palais de l'Élysée** and the line of ministries and embassies ending with the US in prime position on the corner of place de la Concorde.

### Grand Palais

Av Winston Churchill; Galeries nationales entry at 3 av du Général Eisenhower, 8ᵉ • Opening times vary, but usually Mon & Thurs–Sun 10am–8pm, Wed 10am–10pm • Prices vary; usually €14–15 • ☎ 01 40 13 48 00, ⓦ grandpalais.fr • ⓜ Champs-Élysées-Clemenceau

The **Grand Palais** is a grandiose Neoclassical edifice topped with a huge glass cupola. The cupola forms the centrepiece of the *nef* (nave), an impressive events space for music festivals and art exhibitions – including the prestigious annual art fair, **FIAC** (ⓦ fiac.com), in October – as well as fashion shows and trade fairs. The **Galeries nationales** (the city's prime venue for blockbuster art exhibitions) occupy the eastern side of the Grand Palais, while its northern wing houses the **Palais de la Découverte** science museum.

### Palais de la Découverte

Tues–Sat 9.30am–6pm, Sun 10am–7pm • €9, combined ticket with planetarium €12 • ☎ 01 56 43 20 20, ⓦ palais-decouverte.fr • ⓜ Champs-Élysées-Clemenceau/Franklin D. Roosevelt

The **Palais de la Découverte** is Paris's original science museum, dating from 1937. The emphasis, as its name suggests, is very much on discovery and experiment; interactive exhibits and working models help you, for example, discover the properties of electro-magnets, or find out how ants and spiders communicate. In addition, there is an excellent planetarium and engaging temporary exhibitions.

### Petit Palais: Musée des Beaux-Arts de la Ville de Paris

Av Winston Chuchill, 8ᵉ • Tues–Sun 10am–6pm • Free; charges for temporary exhibitions • ☎ 01 53 43 40 00, ⓦ petitpalais.paris.fr • ⓜ Champs-Élysées-Clemenceau

The **Petit Palais,** facing the Grand Palais, is home to the **Musée des Beaux-Arts de la Ville de Paris**. It is hardly "petit" but certainly palatial, boasting beautiful spiral wrought-iron staircases, ceiling frescoes and a grand gallery. The museum's extensive holdings of

1

paintings, sculpture and decorative art range from the ancient Greek and Roman period up to the early twentieth century. At first sight it looks like it's mopped up the leftovers discarded by the city's other galleries, but there are some real gems here, such as Monet's *Soleil couchant sur la Seine à Lavacourt* and Courbet's provocative *Demoiselles des bords de la Seine*. Changing exhibitions allow the museum to display works from its vast reserves.

## Place de la Concorde

At the lower end of the Champs is the vast **place de la Concorde**, where crazed traffic makes crossing over to the middle a death-defying task. As it happens, some 1300 people did die here between 1793 and 1795, beneath the Revolutionary guillotine – Louis XVI, Marie Antoinette, Danton and Robespierre among them. The centrepiece of the square is a stunning gold-tipped **obelisk** from the temple of Luxor. From here there are sweeping vistas in all directions; the Champs-Élysées looks particularly impressive, and you can admire the alignment of the Assemblée Nationale in the south with the church of the Madeleine to the north.

## Jardin des Tuileries

East of place de la Concorde lies the **Jardin des Tuileries**, the formal French garden *par excellence*. It dates back to the 1570s, when Catherine de Médicis had the site cleared of the medieval warren of tilemakers (*tuileries*) to make way for a palace and grounds. One hundred years later, Louis XIV commissioned renowned landscape artist Le Nôtre to redesign them and the results are largely what you see today: straight avenues, formal flowerbeds and splendid vistas. Shady tree-lined paths flank the grand central alley, and ornamental ponds frame both ends. The much-sought-after chairs strewn around the ponds are a good spot from which to admire the landscaped surroundings and contemplate the superb statues executed by the likes of Coustou and Coysevox, many of them now replaced by copies, the originals transferred to the Louvre.

### Jeu de Paume

1 place de la Concorde, 8ᵉ • Tues 11am–9pm, Wed–Sun 11am–7pm • €10 • ☎ 01 47 03 12 50, ⓦ jeudepaume.org • Ⓜ Concorde

At the Concorde end of the Jardin des Tuileries is the **Jeu de Paume**, once a royal tennis court and now a venue for major exhibitions of photography and video art. There's also a small Japanese café and good bookshop.

### Musée de l'Orangerie

Jardin des Tuileries, 1ᵉʳ • Mon & Wed–Sun 9am–6pm • €9; book in advance as queues can be long • ☎ 01 44 77 80 07, ⓦ musee-orangerie.fr • Ⓜ Concorde

Originally designed to protect the Tuileries' orange trees, the **Musée de l'Orangerie**, an elegant Neoclassical-style building, now houses a private art collection including eight of Monet's giant water-lily paintings, vast, mesmerizing canvases executed in the last years of the artist's life. On the lower floor is a fine collection of paintings by his contemporaries. Highlights include a number of Cézanne still lifes, sensuous nudes by Renoir and vibrant landscapes by Derain.

# The Louvre

The palace of the **Louvre** cuts a magnificent classical swathe right through the centre of the city – a fitting setting for one of the world's grandest art galleries. Originally little more than a feudal fortress, the castle was rebuilt in the new Renaissance style from 1546, under François Iᵉʳ. Over the next century and a half, France's rulers steadily aggrandized their palace without significantly altering its style, and the result

**1**

is an amazingly harmonious building. Admittedly, Napoleon's pink marble Arc du Carrousel, standing at the western end of the main courtyard, looks a bit out of place, but it wasn't until the building of IM Pei's controversial Pyramid in 1989, followed by a new Islamic arts department in 2012, with its sinuous glass and gold roof, that the museum saw any significant architectural departure.

The origins of the art gallery, the **Musée du Louvre**, lie in the French kings' personal art collections. The royal academy mounted exhibitions, known as salons, in the palace as early as 1725, but the Louvre was only opened as a public **art gallery** in 1793, in the midst of the Revolution. Within a decade, Napoleon's wagonloads of war booty transformed the Louvre's art collection into the world's largest.

## Musée du Louvre

See "Information" (see page 76) for practicalities

It's easy to be put off by tales of long queues outside the Pyramid, endless foot-wearying corridors and multilingual selfie-stick forests in front of the *Mona Lisa*, but ultimately, the draw of the mighty collections of the **Musée du Louvre** is irresistible.

A **floor plan**, available free from the information booth in the Hall Napoléon, will help you find your way around. It's wise not to attempt to see too much – even if you spent the entire day here you'd only see a fraction of the collection. The museum's size does at least make it easy to get away from the crowds – beyond the Denon wing you can mostly explore in peace and you can always step outside for a break.

From the Hall Napoléon under the **Pyramid**, stairs lead into each of the three wings: Denon (south), Richelieu (north) and Sully (east, around the giant quadrangle of the Cour Carré). Few visitors will be able to resist the allure of the *Mona Lisa*, in the **Denon** wing, housed along with the rest of the Louvre's Italian paintings and sculptures and its large-scale French nineteenth-century canvases. A relatively peaceful alternative would be to focus on the grand chronologies of French painting and sculpture, in the **Richelieu** wing. For a complete change of scene, descend to the **Medieval Louvre** section on the lower ground floor of Sully where you'll find the dramatic stump of Philippe-Auguste's keep and vestiges of Charles V's medieval palace walls.

### Painting

The largest section by far is **Painting**. A good place to start a tour of **French painting** is in the Sully wing with the master of French classicism, Poussin, whose profound, mythological themes influenced artists such as Lorrain, Le Brun and Rigaud. After this grandly classical suite of rooms, the more intimate paintings of Watteau come as a relief, followed by Chardin's intense still lifes and the inspired Rococo sketches by Fragonard known as the *Figures of Fantasy*. From the southern wing of Sully to the end of this section, the chilly wind of Neoclassicism blows through the paintings of Gros, Gérard, Prud'hon, David and Ingres, contrasting with the more sentimental style that begins with Greuze and continues into the Romanticism of Géricault and Delacroix. The final set of rooms takes in Millet, Corot and the Barbizon school of painting, prefiguring the Impressionists.

The nineteenth century is most dramatically represented in the second area of the Louvre devoted to painting, on the first floor of the Denon wing. A pair of giant rooms is dedicated to Nationalism and Romanticism, respectively, featuring some of France's best-known works including such gigantic, epic canvases as David's *Coronation of Napoleon in Notre Dame*, Géricault's *The Raft of the Medusa*, and Delacroix's *Liberty Leading the People*, the icon of nineteenth-century revolution.

Denon also houses the frankly staggering **Italian collection**. The high-ceilinged Salon Carré – which has been used to exhibit paintings since the first "salon" of the Royal Academy in 1725 – displays the so-called Primitives, with works by Uccello, Giotto, Cimabue and Fra Angelico. To the west of the Salon, the famous Grande Galerie stretches into the distance, parading all the great names of the Italian Renaissance – Mantegna, Filippo Lippi, Leonardo da Vinci, Raphael, Correggio, Titian. The playfully troubled Mannerists kick in about halfway along, but the second half of the Galerie dwindles in quality and representativeness as it moves towards the eighteenth century. Leonardo's *Mona Lisa*, along with Paolo Veronese's huge *Marriage at Cana*, hangs in the Salle des États, a room halfway along the Galerie. If you want to catch *La Joconde* – as she's known to the French – without a swarm of admirers, go first or last thing in the day. At the far end of Denon, the relatively small but worthwhile **Spanish** collection has some notable Goya portraits.

The western end of Richelieu's second floor is given over to a more selective collection of **German**, **Flemish** and **Dutch** paintings, with a brilliant set of works by Rubens and no fewer than twelve Rembrandts, including some powerful self-portraits. Interspersed throughout the painting section are rooms dedicated to the Louvre's impressive collection of **prints and drawings**, exhibited in rotation.

## Antiquities

The **Antiquities** galleries cover the sculptures, stone-carved writings, pottery and other relics of the ancient Near East, including the Mesopotamian, Sumerian, Babylonian, Assyrian and Phoenician civilizations, plus the art of ancient Persia. The highlight of this section is the boldly sculpted stonework, much of it in relief. Watch out for the statues and busts depicting the young Sumerian prince Gudea, and the black, 2m-high Code of Hammurabi, a hugely important find from the Mesopotamian civilization, dating from around 1800 BC.

**Egyptian Antiquities** contains jewellery, domestic objects, sandals, sarcophagi and dozens of examples of the delicate naturalism of Egyptian decorative technique, such as the wall tiles depicting a piebald calf galloping through fields of papyrus, and a duck taking off from a marsh. Among the major exhibits are the Great Sphinx, carved from a single block of pink granite, the polychrome Seated Scribe statue, the striking, life-size wooden statue of Chancellor Nakhti, a bust of Amenophis IV and a low-relief sculpture of Sethi I and the goddess Hathor.

The collection of **Greek and Roman Antiquities**, mostly statues, is one of the finest in the world. The biggest crowd-pullers in the museum, after the *Mona Lisa*, are here: the *Winged Victory of Samothrace* and the *Venus de Milo*. Venus is surrounded by hordes of antecedent Aphrodites, from the graceful marble head known as the "Kaufmann Head" and the delightful *Venus of Arles* to the strange *Dame d'Auxerre*. In the Roman section a sterner style takes over, but there are some very attractive mosaics from Asia Minor and vivid frescoes from Pompeii and Herculaneum.

## Islamic arts

The **Islamic arts** department, in the Cour Visconti, displays more than 2500 objects from the Louvre's own collections and the Musée des Arts Décoratifs. Under a stunning, rippling glass-and-gold roof, evoking a silk headscarf or undulating sand dunes, you can admire early Islamic inscriptions, intricate Moorish ivories, ninth-century Iraqi moulded glass and exquisite miniature paintings from the court of Mughal India.

## French sculpture

The **French sculpture** section is arranged on the lowest two levels of the Richelieu wing, with the more monumental pieces housed in two grand, glass-roofed courtyards: the four triumphal *Marly Horses* grace the Cour Marly, while Cour Puget has Puget's dynamic *Milon de Crotone* as its centrepiece. The surrounding rooms trace the development of sculpture in France from painful Romanesque Crucifixions to the lofty public works of David d'Angers. The startlingly realistic Gothic pieces – notably the Burgundian *Tomb of Philippe Pot*, complete with hooded mourners – and the experimental Mannerist works are particularly rewarding, but towards the end of the course you may find yourself crying out for an end to all those gracefully perfect nudes

**1**

and grandiose busts. You'll have to leave the Louvre for Rodin, but an alternative antidote lies in the intense **Italian and northern European** sections, on the lower two floors of Denon, where you'll find such bold masterpieces as two of Michelangelo's writhing *Slaves*, Duccio's virtuoso *Virgin and Child Surrounded by Angels*, and some severely Gothic Virgins from Flanders and Germany.

### Objets d'art

The vast **Objets d'art** section, on the first floor of the Richelieu wing, presents the finest tapestries, ceramics, jewellery and furniture commissioned by France's wealthiest and most influential patrons. Walking through the entire 81-room chronology affords a powerful sense of the evolution of aesthetic taste at its most refined and opulent. The exception is the **Middle Ages** section, which is of a decidedly pious nature, while the apotheosis of the whole experience comes towards the end, as the circuit passes through the breathtakingly plush **apartments** of Napoléon III's Minister of State.

| INFORMATION | MUSÉE DU LOUVRE |
|---|---|

**Website** ⓦ www.louvre.fr.

**Opening hours** Mon, Thurs, Sat & Sun 9am–6pm, Wed & Fri 9am–9.45pm. The Wed and Fri "nocturnes" are an excellent time to visit, when the museum is often quieter. Note that almost a quarter of the museum's rooms are closed one day a week on a rotating basis, though the most popular rooms are always open.

**Admission** The entry fee is €15, free to all under-18s and EU residents aged 18–26; free to under-26s from any country on Fri after 6pm; free to all on the first Sun of each month Oct–March, as well as July 14.

**Tickets** Tickets can be bought at the museum or online

in advance through the website (€17); for temporary exhibitions you usually have to book online. Tickets bought in advance are time-stamped and you're expected to arrive within 30min of your allotted starting time.

**Access** The nearest métro station is ⓜ Palais Royal Musée du Louvre. The Pyramide is the main entrance, although the often lengthy queues can be avoided by using one of the alternative entrances: Porte des Lions, just east of the Pont Royal (though this is sometimes closed); Arc du Carrousel, 99 rue de Rivoli; or directly from the métro station Palais Royal-Musée du Louvre (line 1 platform). If you've already got a ticket or a museum pass you can join a fast-track queue at the Pyramide.

## Musée des Arts Décoratifs

Entrance at 107 rue de Rivoli, 1ᵉʳ • Tues, Wed & Fri–Sun 11am–6pm, Thurs 11am–9pm (late opening for temporary exhibitions only) • €11; free to all under-18s and EU residents aged 18–26 • ☏ 01 44 55 57 50, ⓦ madparis.fr

The westernmost wing of the Louvre palace houses **Musée des Arts Décoratifs**, an eclectic collection of art objects and superbly crafted furnishings. The works in the "historical" rooms (from the medieval period through to Art Nouveau) may seem humble in comparison with those in the Louvre's Objets d'art section, but these objects were made to be used, and feel more accessible as a result. There are curious and beautiful chairs, dressers and tables, religious paintings, Venetian glass and some wonderful tapestries. A number of "period rooms" have been reconstituted top-to-toe in the style of different eras; there's even an entire 1903 bedroom by Hector Guimard, the Art Nouveau designer behind Paris's métro stations. The topmost floors show off designer furnishings from the 1940s through to the present day, with some great examples from the prince of French contemporary design, Philippe Starck. Separate galleries focus on jewellery and toys, while the eastern half of the museum, to the left of the main entrance, puts on exhibitions dedicated to **fashion** and **advertising**. These can be among the city's most innovative, curated by industry professionals rather than state museum administrators.

# The Opéra district

Between the Louvre and **boulevard Haussmann**, **Montmartre**, **Poissonnière** and **Bonne-Nouvelle** to the north lies the city's main commercial and financial district. Right at its heart stand the solid institutions of the Banque de France and the Bourse, while just to the north, beyond the glittering **Opéra-Garnier**, are the large department stores **Galeries Lafayette** and **Printemps**. More well-heeled shopping is concentrated on the rue **St-Honoré** in the west and the streets around aristocratic place Vendôme, lined with top couturiers, jewellers and art dealers. Scattered around the whole area are the delightful, secretive **passages** (see box) – nineteenth-century arcades that hark back to shopping from a different era.

## Opéra-Garnier

Cnr rues Scribe & Auber, 9ᵉ • **Interior** Generally open for visits daily 10am–4.30pm; closes earlier if there are matinee performances • €11 • **Performances** See page 141 • Ⓦ operadeparis.fr • Ⓜ Opéra

Set back from the boulevard des Capucines and crowning the avenue de l'Opéra is the dazzling **Opéra-Garnier**, which was constructed from 1860 to 1875 as part of Napoléon III's new vision of Paris. The architect, Charles Garnier, whose golden bust by Carpeaux can be seen on the rue Auber side of his edifice, pulled out all the stops to provide a suitably grand space in which Second Empire high society could parade and be seen. The facade is a fabulous extravaganza of white, pink and green marble, colonnades, rearing horses, winged angels and niches holding gleaming gold busts of composers. You can look round the equally sumptuous **interior**, including the plush auditorium – rehearsals permitting – the colourful ceiling of which is the work of Chagall, and which depicts scenes from well-known operas and ballets. The visit includes the small **Bibliothèque-Musée de l'Opéra**, dedicated to the artists connected with the Opéra throughout its history, and containing model sets, paintings and temporary exhibitions on operatic themes.

## Église de la Madeleine

Place de la Madeleine, 8ᵉ • Daily 9.30am–7pm • Free • Ⓦ eglise-lamadeleine.com • Ⓜ Madeleine

Dominating place de la Madeleine, the imperious-looking **Église de la Madeleine** is the parish church of the cream of Parisian high society. Modelled on a Greek classical temple, it's surrounded by 52 Corinthian columns and fronted by a huge pediment depicting the Last Judgement. Originally intended as a monument to Napoleon's army, it narrowly escaped being turned into a railway station before finally being consecrated to Mary Magdalene in 1845. Inside, a wonderfully theatrical sculpture, *Mary Magdalene Ascending to Heaven*, draws your eye to the high altar; its organ, once regularly played by Gabriel Fauré, is one of the best in Paris.

---

### THE PASSAGES

Among the most attractive of the Opéra's **passages** is the **Galerie Vivienne**, between rue Vivienne and rue des Petits-Champs, its decor of Grecian and marine motifs providing a suitably flamboyant backdrop for its smart shops, including a branch of Jean-Paul Gaultier. But the most stylish examples are the three-storey **passage du Grand-Cerf**, between rue St-Denis and rue Dussoubs, and **Galerie Véro-Dodat**, between rue Croix-des-Petits-Champs and rue Jean-Jacques-Rousseau, named after the two butchers who set it up in 1824. This last is the most homogeneous and aristocratic *passage*, with painted ceilings and faux marble columns. North of rue St-Marc, the several arcades making up the **passage des Panoramas** are more workaday, though still full of character: there's *Caffè Stern* at no. 47, a former printshop with its original 1867 fittings (now home to an upmarket Italian restaurant), as well as bric-a-brac shops, stamp and secondhand postcard dealers. It's also become a foodie destination, with a number of popular wine *bistrots*, such as *Racines* (see page 128), setting up home here. **Passage Jouffroy**, across boulevard Montmartre, harbours a number of quirky shops, including one selling antique walking sticks and another stocking exquisite dolls' house furniture. The Marks and Spencer food shop feels somewhat out of place.

**1**

## Place Vendôme

A short walk east of the Madeleine along ancient rue St-Honoré, a preserve of top fashion designers and art galleries, lies **place Vendôme**, one of the city's most impressive set pieces. Built by Versailles' architect Hardouin-Mansart, it's a pleasingly symmetrical, eight-sided *place*, enclosed by a harmonious ensemble of elegant mansions, graced with Corinthian pilasters, *mascarons* and steeply pitched roofs. Once the grand residences of tax collectors and financiers, they now house such luxury establishments as the *Ritz* hotel, Cartier, Bulgari and other top-flight jewellers, lending the square a decidedly exclusive air. No. 12, now occupied by Chaumet jewellers, is where Chopin died in 1849.

Somewhat out of proportion with the rest of the square, the centrepiece is a towering triumphal **column**, surmounted by a statue of Napoleon dressed as Caesar, raised in 1806 to celebrate the Battle of Austerlitz – bronze reliefs of scenes of the battle, cast from 1200 recycled Austro-Russian cannons, spiral their way up the column.

## Palais-Royal

Place du Palais-Royal, 1ᵉʳ • Ⓜ Palais-Royal-Musée-du-Louvre

At the eastern end of rue St-Honoré stands the handsome, colonnaded **Palais-Royal**, built for Cardinal Richelieu in 1624, though much modified and renovated since. The current building houses various governmental bodies and the **Comédie Française**, a long-standing venue for the classics of French theatre.

To its rear lie gardens lined with stately three-storey houses built over arcades housing quirky antique and designer shops. It's an attractive and peaceful oasis, with avenues of limes, fountains and flowerbeds. You'd hardly guess that this was a site of gambling dens, brothels and funfair attractions until the Grands Boulevards took up the baton in the 1830s. Folly, some might say, has returned in the form of Daniel Buren's **art installation**, which consists of black-and-white striped pillars, all of varying heights, dotted about the palace's main courtyard.

## Bibliothèque Nationale

58 rue de Richelieu, 2ᵉ • Mon–Sat 9am–8pm, but times vary for temporary exhibitions • Admission prices vary, depending on the exhibition • ☎ 01 53 79 59 59, Ⓦ bnf.fr • Ⓜ Bourse

Across from the Palais-Royal, on the other side of rue des Petits-Champs, looms the huge **Bibliothèque Nationale**, the French National Library, dating back to the 1660s. At the time of writing, it was undergoing major renovation work, due for completion in 2020, to improve the conditions in which the library's remaining twenty million documents are kept, and to open up more of the building to the public. Included in the renovation work (and thus also closed until 2020) is the **Cabinet des Monnaies, Médailles et Antiques**, a collection of coins, Etruscan bronzes, ancient Greek jewellery and other ancient treasures built up by successive kings from Philippe-Auguste onwards. Parts of the library may remain open during this period for exhibitions; check the website for the latest updates.

# Beaubourg and around

The **Beaubourg** *quartier* centres on the **Centre Pompidou**, one of the city's most popular and recognizable landmarks and one of the twentieth century's most radical buildings. The area around the Centre Pompidou is home to more contemporary art. Jean Tinguely and Niki de Saint Phalle created the colourful moving sculptures and fountains in the pool in front of Église St-Merri on **place Igor Stravinsky**. This squirting waterworks pays homage to Stravinsky – each fountain corresponds to one of his compositions (*The Firebird, The Rite of Spring* and so on) – and shows scant respect for passers-by. To the north are numerous commercial **art galleries**, occupying the attractive old *hôtels particuliers* on pedestrianized **rue Quincampoix**, while to the west is the **Les Halles** underground shopping and leisure complex.

## Centre Pompidou

Rue St-Martin, 4ᵉ • Mon & Wed–Sun 11am–9pm (occasional late opening on Thurs) • ☎ 01 44 78 12 33, Ⓦ centrepompidou.fr • Ⓜ Rambuteau/Hôtel-de-Ville

The opening of the **Centre Pompidou** in 1977 gave rise to some violent reactions; since then, however, it has won over critics and public alike. Architects Renzo Piano and Richard Rogers freed up maximum space inside by placing all infrastructure outside: utility pipes and escalator tubes, all brightly colour-coded according to their function, climb around the exterior in crazy snakes-and-ladders fashion. The transparent escalator on the front of the building, giving access to the **Musée National d'Art Moderne**, affords superb views over the city. Aside from the hugely popular museum there are galleries, cinemas, a performance space, a café and a restaurant, bookshops,

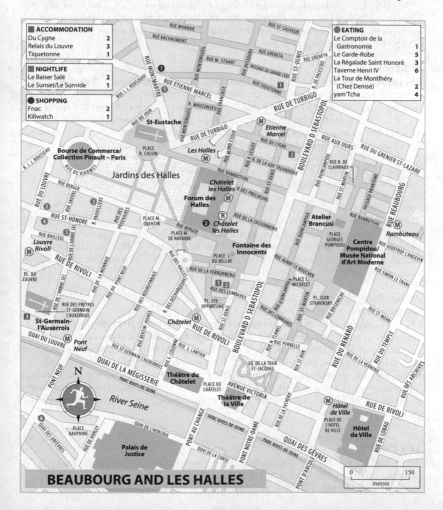

1

a design store and public reference library. The excellent **Galerie des enfants** stages regular exhibitions and workshops for children between 3 and 10 years old (Mon & Wed–Sun 11am–7pm; children must be accompanied by an adult; children's admission is free, adults need a museum ticket); also worth checking out is the free **Galerie de Photographies**, which organizes regular exhibitions drawn from the centre's fascinating archive of photographs.

To mark its fortieth anniversary in 2017, the Pompidou announced a major renovation programme, slated to finish in 2020, including repairs to the escalators on the outside of the building. The centre is set to remain open throughout the work, but it is worth checking in advance.

## Musée National d'Art Moderne
€14 (includes all exhibitions at the Pompidou); under-18s free; free to all first Sun of the month

The superb **Musée National d'Art Moderne** presides over the fourth and fifth floors of the Centre Pompidou, with the fifth floor covering 1905 to roughly the years 1970–80, while the fourth floor concentrates on contemporary art. Thanks to an astute acquisitions policy and some generous gifts, the collection is a near-complete visual essay on the history of twentieth-century art and is so large that only a fraction of the 50,000 works are on display at any one time.

### Fifth floor

On the **fifth floor**, Fauvism, Cubism, Dada, abstract art, Surrealism and abstract expressionism are all well represented. There's a particularly rich collection of Matisses, ranging from early Fauvist works to his late masterpieces – a standout is his *Tristesse du roi*, a moving meditation on old age and memory. Other highlights include a number of Picasso's and Braque's early Cubist paintings and a substantial collection of Kandinskys, including his pioneering abstract works *Avec l'arc noir* and *Composition à la tache rouge*. The characteristically colourful paintings of Robert and Sonia Delaunay contrast vividly with the darker mood of more unsettling works on display by Surrealists Magritte, Dalí and Ernst.

### Fourth floor

The **fourth floor** is given over to **contemporary art**, featuring installations, photography and video art, as well as displays of architectural models and contemporary design. Established French artists such as Annette Messager, Sophie Calle, Christian Boltanski, Daniel Buren and Dominique Gonzalez-Foerster often feature, alongside newer arrivals such as Anri Sala.

## Atelier Brancusi
Pompidou Centre piazza • Mon & Wed–Sun 2–6pm • Free

On the northern edge of the Pompidou Centre, down some steps off the sloping piazza, in a small separate building, is the **Atelier Brancusi**, the reconstructed home and studio of Constantin Brancusi. The sculptor bequeathed the contents of his workshop to the state on condition that the rooms be arranged exactly as he left them, and they provide a fascinating insight into how he lived and worked. Studios one and two are crowded with Brancusi's trademark abstract bird and column shapes in highly polished brass and marble, while studios three and four comprise the artist's private quarters.

# Les Halles

At the heart of the city is the sprawling underground shopping and leisure complex, gardens and métro interchange of **Les Halles**, which has recently been given a much-needed revamp. The most striking feature is the **Canopée** ("canopy") – a vast, undulating, metal-and-glass roof, suspended over the entrance to the complex, which allows light to flood into the underground **Forum des Halles** shopping mall. The roof itself, though, feels anything but light – its sheer size and weight feel oppressive as you walk under – a far cry from the original, elegant glass structures created by Victor Baltard in response to Napoléon III's request for "a covering as light as an umbrella".

The redevelopment includes landscaped gardens (Jardin Nelson-Mandela), a library, a music and arts conservatoire and, perhaps most significantly, a **hip-hop** performance and workshop space, **La Place** (Ⓦ laplace.paris), the first of its kind in the capital and in part an acknowledgement of the popularity of Les Halles with the *jeunes de banlieue* – the young people who come in from the housing estates in the suburbs.

## Forum des Halles

Mon–Sat 10am–8.30pm, Sun 11am–7pm • Ⓦ forumdeshalles.com • Ⓜ Les Halles/Châtelet/RER Châtelet-Les Halles

The **Forum des Halles** centre is spread over four levels. On the bottom level is the métro/RER station, where five métro lines and three suburban lines intersect, used by some 750,000 commuters a day. The other levels accommodate numerous shops, mostly international high-street fashion chains; there's also a decent Fnac bookshop, a swimming pool and a number of cinemas, including the **Forum des Images** (see page 141).

## St-Eustache

2 Impasse St-Eustache, 1er • Mon–Fri 9.30am–7pm, Sat 10am–7.15pm, Sun 9am–7.15pm • Ⓦ saint-eustache.org • Ⓜ Les Halles

At the foot of rue Montorgueil stands the beautiful, gracefully buttressed church of **St-Eustache**. Built between 1532 and 1637, it's a glorious fusion of Gothic and Renaissance styles, with soaring vaults, Corinthian pilasters and arcades. It was the scene of Molière's baptism, and Rameau and Marivaux are buried here.

## Bourse de Commerce/Collection Pinault – Paris

2 rue de Viarmes, 1er • Ⓦ collectionpinaultparis.com • Ⓜ Louvre Rivoli

Facing the Canopée at the western end of Les Halles gardens stands the striking **Bourse de Commerce**, the city's former corn market, an eighteenth-century circular building under a glass cupola, which is being converted into a museum of contemporary art, the **Collection Pinault – Paris**, due to open in 2019. The artworks, including pieces by Damien Hirst and Mark Rothko, will come from the huge collection built up by the luxury goods billionaire François Pinault, who already owns two galleries in Venice.

# The Marais

The **Marais** is one of the most seductive districts of central Paris, sophisticated and arty, and a neighbourhood of choice for LGBT+ Parisians. Largely untouched by Baron Haussmann and unscarred by modern development, the *quartier* is full of handsome Renaissance *hôtels particuliers*, narrow lanes and inviting cafés and restaurants. There's a significant, if dwindling, Jewish community here, established in the twelfth century and centred on **rue des Rosiers**.

Prime streets for wandering are **rue des Francs-Bourgeois**, lined with fashion and interior design boutiques, **rue Vieille-du-Temple** and **rue des Archives**, with their buzzy bars and cafés, and the streets of the so-called Haut Marais, home to sleek art galleries and chic young designers. The Marais' animated streets and atmospheric old buildings would be reason enough to visit, but the *quartier* also boasts a high concentration of excellent museums, not least the **Musée Picasso**, the **Carnavalet** history museum and the **Musée d'Art et d'Histoire du Judaïsme**, all set in fine mansions.

1

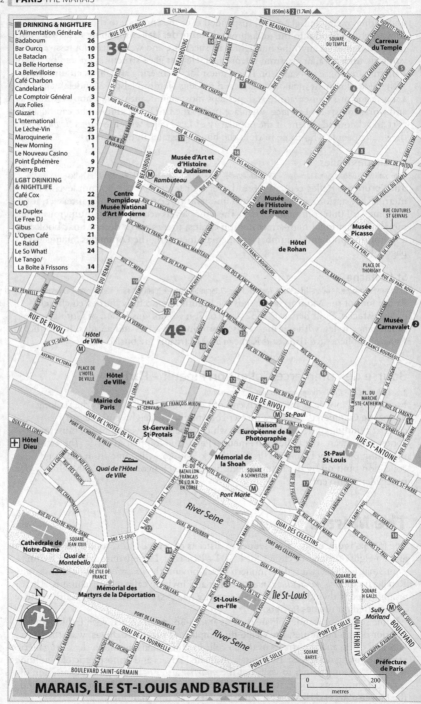

**■ DRINKING & NIGHTLIFE**

| | |
|---|---|
| L'Alimentation Générale | 6 |
| Badaboum | 26 |
| Bar Ourcq | 10 |
| Le Bataclan | 15 |
| La Belle Hortense | 23 |
| La Bellevilloise | 12 |
| Café Charbon | 5 |
| Candelaria | 16 |
| Le Comptoir Général | 3 |
| Aux Folies | 8 |
| Glazart | 11 |
| L'International | 7 |
| Le Lèche-Vin | 25 |
| Maroquinerie | 13 |
| New Morning | 1 |
| Le Nouveau Casino | 4 |
| Point Éphémère | 9 |
| Sherry Butt | 27 |

**LGBT DRINKING & NIGHTLIFE**

| | |
|---|---|
| Café Cox | 22 |
| CUD | 18 |
| Le Duplex | 17 |
| Le Free DJ | 20 |
| Gibus | 2 |
| L'Open Café | 21 |
| Le Raidd | 19 |
| Le So What! | 24 |
| Le Tango/ La Boîte à Frissons | 14 |

**MARAIS, ÎLE ST-LOUIS AND BASTILLE**

0        200
metres

1

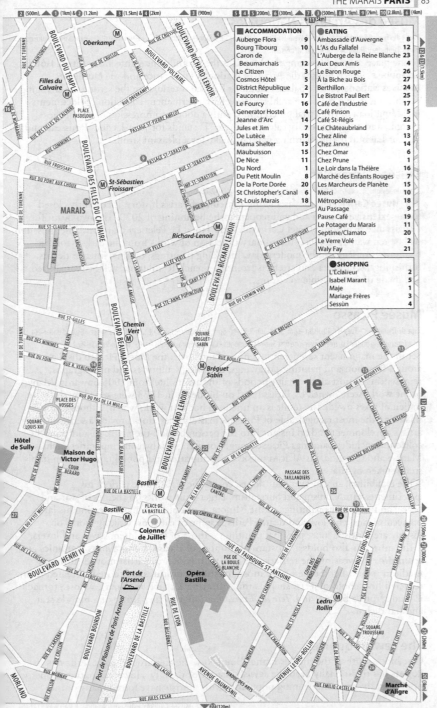

**■ ACCOMMODATION**

| | |
|---|---|
| Auberge Flora | 9 |
| Bourg Tibourg | 10 |
| Caron de Beaumarchais | 12 |
| Le Citizen | 3 |
| Cosmos Hôtel | 5 |
| District République | 2 |
| Fauconnier | 17 |
| Le Fourcy | 16 |
| Generator Hostel | 4 |
| Jeanne d'Arc | 14 |
| Jules et Jim | 7 |
| De Lutèce | 19 |
| Mama Shelter | 13 |
| Maubuisson | 15 |
| De Nice | 11 |
| Du Nord | 1 |
| Du Petit Moulin | 8 |
| De la Porte Dorée | 20 |
| St Christopher's Canal | 6 |
| St-Louis Marais | 18 |

**● EATING**

| | |
|---|---|
| Ambassade d'Auvergne | 8 |
| L'As du Fallafel | 12 |
| L'Auberge de la Reine Blanche | 23 |
| Aux Deux Amis | 4 |
| Le Baron Rouge | 26 |
| À la Biche au Bois | 27 |
| Berthillon | 24 |
| Le Bistrot Paul Bert | 25 |
| Café de l'Industrie | 17 |
| Café Pinson | 5 |
| Café St-Régis | 22 |
| Le Châteaubriand | 3 |
| Chez Aline | 13 |
| Chez Janou | 14 |
| Chez Omar | 6 |
| Chez Prune | 1 |
| Le Loir dans la Théière | 16 |
| Marché des Enfants Rouges | 7 |
| Les Marcheurs de Planète | 15 |
| Merci | 10 |
| Métropolitain | 18 |
| Au Passage | 9 |
| Pause Café | 19 |
| Le Potager du Marais | 11 |
| Septime/Clamato | 20 |
| Le Verre Volé | 2 |
| Waly Fay | 21 |

**● SHOPPING**

| | |
|---|---|
| L'Eclaireur | 2 |
| Isabel Marant | 5 |
| Maje | 1 |
| Mariage Frères | 3 |
| Sessùn | 4 |

**1**

## Musée des Archives Nationales

60 rue des Francs-Bourgeois, 3ᵉ • Mon & Wed–Fri 10am–5.30pm, Sat & Sun 2–5.30pm • €5–8 • ⓦ www.archives-nationales.culture.gouv.
fr • Ⓜ Rambuteau/Hôtel de Ville/Arts et Métiers

A fine place to start exploring the Marais is the magnificent eighteenth-century **Hôtel
de Soubise**, which houses the Archives Nationales de France and the **Musée des
Archives Nationales**. The palace's fabulous Rococo interiors are the setting for changing
exhibitions drawn from the archives, as well as a permanent collection of documents
including Joan of Arc's trial proceedings, with a doodled impression of her in the
margin, and a Revolutionary calendar where "J" stands for Jean-Jacques Rousseau and
"L" for Labourer. The charming gardens make for a pleasant stroll.

## Musée Carnavalet

23 rue de Sévigné, 4ᵉ • ☎ 01 44 59 58 58, ⓦ carnavalet.paris.fr • Ⓜ St-Paul

The **Musée Carnavalet**, the fascinating museum of Paris's history, is currently closed
for an extensive revamp and will reopen at the beginning of 2020. The two beautiful
Renaissance mansions (Hôtel Carnavalet and Hôtel Le Peletier) that house the museum
will be renovated, and its extraordinary collection of works from the early Neolithic
beginnings of Paris to the modern day, including paintings, original interior decors,
furnishings, sculptures and artefacts from the French Revolution, will be reorganized
and made more accessible to visitors.

## Musée Picasso

5 rue de Thorigny, 3ᵉ • Tues–Fri 10.30am–6pm, Sat & Sun 9.30am–6pm, last entry 5.15pm • €12.50; free to under-18s, and under-26s
from (or studying in) the EU; free to everyone first Sun of the month • ⓦ museepicassoparis.fr • Ⓜ Chemin-Vert/St-Paul

Set in the magnificent seventeenth-century Hôtel Salé, the **Musée Picasso** displays
around five thousand paintings, drawings, ceramics, sculptures and photographs,
representing almost all the major periods of the artist's life from 1905 onwards. Many
of the works were owned by Picasso and on his death in 1973 were seized by the state
in lieu of taxes owed. The result is an unedited body of work, which, although not
including the most recognizable of Picasso's masterpieces, does provide a sense of the
artist's development and an insight into the person behind the myth. In addition, the
collection includes paintings Picasso bought or was given by contemporaries such as
Matisse and Cézanne, his African masks and sculptures and photographs of him in his
studio taken by Brassaï.

The **exhibition**, spread over four floors, covers the artist's blue period; his
experiments with Cubism and Surrealism; larger-scale works on themes of war and
peace; and numerous paintings of the Minotaur and bullfighting, reflecting his later
preoccupations with love and death. Perhaps some of the most striking works on
display are Picasso's more personal paintings – those of his children, wives and lovers.

The museum also holds a substantial number of Picasso's **engravings**, **ceramics** and
**sculpture**, showcasing the remarkable ease with which the artist moved from one
medium to another. Some of the most arresting sculptures are those he created from
recycled household objects, such as the endearing *La Chèvre* (Goat), whose stomach
is made from a basket, and *Tête de Taureau*, an ingenious pairing of a bicycle seat
and handlebars.

## The Jewish quarter

One block south of the rue des Francs-Bourgeois, the area around narrow **rue des
Rosiers** has traditionally been the **Jewish quarter** of the city. However, soaring property
prices and the area's burgeoning popularity with tourists have forced many of the

MUSÉE D'ORSAY, HOUSED IN A FORMER RAILWAY STATION

**1**

traditional grocers, bakers, bookshops and cafés to close, and the area is in real danger of losing its identity. Some Jewish shops survive, however, such as the odd kosher food shop and a Hebrew bookstore, with the falafel takeaways testimony to the influence of the North African Sephardim, who replenished Paris's Jewish population, depleted when its Ashkenazim were rounded up by the Nazis and the French police and transported to the concentration camps.

### Musée d'Art et d'Histoire du Judaïsme

71 rue du Temple, 3ᵉ • Tues–Fri 11am–6pm, Sat & Sun 10am–6pm, (open Wed till 9pm during temporary exhibitions) • €10 • ☎ 01 53 01 86 60, ⓦ mahj.org • Ⓜ Rambuteau

The attractively restored Hôtel de St-Aignan, just northeast of the Centre Pompidou, is home to the **Musée d'Art et d'Histoire du Judaïsme**, which traces the culture, history and artistic endeavours of the Jewish people from the Middle Ages to the present day. The focus is on the history of Jews in France, but there are also many artefacts from the rest of Europe and North Africa. Some of the most notable exhibits are a Gothic-style Hanukkah lamp, one of the very few French Jewish artefacts to survive from the period before the expulsion of the Jews from France in 1394; an Italian gilded circumcision chair from the seventeenth century; and a completely intact late nineteenth-century Austrian *sukkah*, a brightly painted wooden hut built as a temporary dwelling for the celebration of the harvest. One room is devoted to the **Dreyfus affair**, documented with letters, postcards and press clippings. There's also a significant collection of paintings and sculpture by Jewish artists, such as Soutine and Chagall, who came to live in Paris at the beginning of the twentieth century. The Holocaust is only briefly touched on, since it's dealt with in depth at the Mémorial de la Shoah's museum (see opposite).

## Place des Vosges

A grand square of symmetrical pink brick and stone mansions built over arcades, the **place des Vosges**, at the eastern end of rue des Francs-Bourgeois, is a masterpiece of aristocratic elegance and the first example of planned development in the history of Paris. It was built by Henri IV and inaugurated in 1612 for the wedding of Louis XIII and Anne of Austria; Louis's statue – or, rather, a replica of it – stands hidden by chestnut trees in the middle of the grass and gravel gardens at the square's centre. The gardens are popular with families on weekends – children can run around on the grass (unusually for Paris the "pelouse" is not "interdite") and mess about in sandpits. Buskers often play under the arcades, serenading diners at the outside tables of restaurants and cafés, while well-heeled shoppers browse in the upmarket art, antique and fashion boutiques.

### Maison de Victor Hugo

6 place des Vosges, 4ᵉ • Tues–Sun 10am–6pm • Free; temporary exhibitions €6–8 • ☎ 01 42 72 10 16, ⓦ maisonsvictorhugo.paris.fr • Ⓜ Chemin-Vert/Bastille

Among the many celebrities who made their homes in the place des Vosges was Victor Hugo. His house, at no. 6, where he wrote much of *Les Misérables*, is now a museum, the **Maison de Victor Hugo**, where the author's life is evoked through a somewhat sparse collection of memorabilia, portraits, photographs and first editions of his works. As well as writing, Hugo drew – many of his ink drawings are exhibited – and designed his own furniture; he even put together the extraordinary Chinese-style dining room on display here.

### Hôtel de Sully

62 rue St-Antoine, 4ᵉ • Centre des monuments nationaux closed to the public; bookshop Tues–Sun 1–7pm • ⓦ hotel-de-sully.fr • Ⓜ St-Paul/Bastille

From the southwest corner of the place des Vosges, a door leads through to the formal château garden and exquisite Renaissance facade of the **Hôtel de Sully**, the headquarters of the Centre des monuments nationaux, which manages more than a hundred national monuments and publishes numerous books and guides, many of which are on sale in the excellent ground-floor bookshop.

## South of rue de Rivoli

The southern section of the Marais, below rues de Rivoli and St-Antoine, is quieter than the northern part and has some atmospheric streets, such as cobbled rue des Barres, perfumed with the scent of roses from nearby gardens and the occasional waft of incense from the church of **St-Gervais-St-Protais**, a late Gothic construction that looks somewhat battered on the outside owing to a direct hit from a Big Bertha howitzer in 1918. The church's interior contains some lovely stained glass, carved misericords and a seventeenth-century organ – one of Paris's oldest.

### Mémorial de la Shoah

17 rue Geoffroy-l'Asnier, 4ᵉ • Mon–Fri & Sun 10am–6pm, Thurs 10am–10pm • Free • ☏01 42 77 44 72, ⓦwww.memorialdelashoah.org • Ⓜ St-Paul/Pont-Marie

Since 1956 the **Mémorial de la Shoah** has been the site of the Mémorial du Martyr Juif Inconnu (Memorial to an Unknown Jewish Martyr), a sombre crypt containing a large black marble star of David, with a candle at its centre. In 2005 President Chirac opened a new **museum** here and unveiled a Wall of Names: four giant slabs of marble engraved with the names of the 76,000 French Jews sent to death camps from 1942 to 1944. In 2006, the **Mur des Justes** was added, a wall listing the names of French people who aided Jews at this time.

The museum gives a moving account of the history of Jews in France, especially Paris, leading up to and during World War II, but there is also background on the history of Jews in Europe as a whole. There are last letters from deportees to their families, videotaped testimony from survivors, numerous ID cards and photos. The museum ends with the Mémorial des Enfants, a collection of photos, almost unbearable to look at, of 2500 French children, each with the date of their birth and the date of their deportation.

# Bastille

A symbol of revolution since the toppling of the Bastille prison in the 1789, the **Bastille** quarter was a largely working-class district up until the construction of the new opera house in the 1980s. Since then, it has attracted artists, fashion folk and young people, who have brought with them stylish shops and an energetic nightlife, concentrated around rues Amelot, de Charonne and de Lappe.

## Place de la Bastille and around

The notorious Bastille prison once stood on **Place de la Bastille**, a large, traffic-choked square. The only visible remains of the prison have been transported to square Henri-Galli at the end of boulevard Henri-IV. The square is the scene of partying on the evening of July 13 to celebrate Bastille Day, and at other times of the year it's often used as a rallying point for left-wing demonstrations. In the centre towers a column topped with the gilded "Spirit of Liberty", erected not to commemorate the surrender of the prison, but the July Revolution of 1830 that replaced the autocratic Charles X with the "Citizen King" Louis-Philippe. On the eastern side of the square looms the **Opéra-Bastille**, built in 1989 to mark the 200th anniversary of the French Revolution.

1

Likened by one critic to "a hippopotamus in a bathtub", the sprawling building with its semicircular glass facade is difficult to warm to, but its high-calibre performances are nearly always a sell-out. The hurly-burly of the traffic around the place de la Bastille hardly invites you to linger and ponder its historical significance, though work is under way to reduce the volume of cars and make it more pedestrian-friendly, with the addition of benches, trees and plants.

# The 12ᵉ arrondissement

South of Bastille, the relatively unsung **12ᵉ arrondissement** offers an authentic slice of Paris, with its neighbourhood shops and bars and traditional markets, such as the lively **Marché d'Aligre**. Among the area's attractions are the **Promenade Plantée**, an ex-railway line turned into an elevated walkway running from Bastille to the green expanse of the **Bois de Vincennes**, and **Bercy**, once the largest wine market in the world, its handsome old warehouses converted into cafés and shops.

## Bercy

The riverside **Bercy** *quartier*, which extends southeast from the Gare de Lyon, was where the capital's wine supplies used to be unloaded from river barges. With many of the handsome old wine warehouses converted into shops, restaurants and, appropriately enough, wine bars, the district also boasts a welcome green space, the extensive **Parc de Bercy**.

### Parc de Bercy

**Parc** Daily 8am/9am–7pm/7.30pm/8.30pm/9pm • Free • **Maison du Jardinage** March & Oct Tues–Sun 1.30–5.30pm, April–Sept Tues–Fri 1.30–5.30pm, Sat & Sun 1.30–6.30pm; Nov–Feb 1.30–5pm • Free • ⓜ Bercy

The contemporary **Parc de Bercy** incorporates elements of the old warehouse site, such as disused railway tracks and cobbled lanes. The western section of the park is a fairly unexciting expanse of grass with a huge stepped fountain (popular with children) set into one of the grassy banks, but the area to the east has arbours, rose gardens, lily ponds and an orangerie.

### Cinémathèque

51 rue de Bercy, 12ᵉ • **Museum** Mon & Wed–Sun noon–7pm • €5 • ☎ 01 71 19 33 33, ⓦ cinematheque.fr • ⓜ Bercy

Overlooking the Parc de Bercy, the **Cinémathèque**, a striking glass, zinc and stone building designed by Guggenheim architect Frank Gehry, houses a huge archive of films dating back to the earliest days of cinema. Along with cinema screens it also has an engaging museum, with lots of early cinematic equipment and silent-film clips.

# Promenade Plantée

Ⓜ Bastille/Ledru-Rollin

The **Promenade Plantée** is a stretch of disused railway line, much of it along a viaduct, which has been converted into an elevated walkway and planted with a profusion of trees and flowers. The walkway starts near the beginning of avenue Daumesnil, just south of the Bastille opera house, and is reached via a flight of stone steps – or lifts (frequently out of order) – with a number of similar access points all the way along. It takes you to the Parc de Reuilly, then descends to ground level and continues nearly as far as the *périphérique*, from where you can follow signs to the Bois de Vincennes. The whole walk is around 4.5km long, but if you don't feel like doing it all you could just take a twenty-minute stroll along the first section – along the viaduct. This also happens to be the most attractive stretch, running past venerable old mansion blocks and giving a bird's-eye view of the area below and of architectural details not seen from street level. The arches of the viaduct itself have been converted into spaces for artisans' ateliers and craft shops (Ⓦleviaducdesarts.com).

# Bois de Vincennes

Main entrance on av de Paris, Vincennes • **Bois de Vincennes** Ⓜ Porte Dorée/Porte de Charenton/Château de Vincennes; buses #46 and #86 • Ⓦ parcfloraldeparis.com • Ⓜ Château de Vincennes, then bus #112 or a short walk

The **Bois de Vincennes** is a favourite family Sunday retreat and the largest green space in the city, aside from the Bois de Boulogne in the west. It's rather crisscrossed with roads, but there are some very pleasant corners, including the picturesque Lac Daumesnil, where you can hire boats, and the **Parc Floral**, perhaps Paris's best gardens, with an adventure playground attached. Flowers are always in bloom in the Jardin des Quatre Saisons; you can picnic amid pines and rhododendrons, then wander through concentrations of camellias, cacti, ferns, irises and bonsai trees.

## Parc Zoologique de Paris

Junction of av Daumesnil and route de la Ceinture du Lac, 12ᵉ • April, Sept & Oct Mon–Fri 9.30am–6pm, Sat & Sun 9.30am–7.30pm; May & Aug daily 10am–8.30pm; June & July Mon–Wed & Fri–Sun 10am–8.30pm, Thurs 10am–10.30pm; Nov–March Mon & Wed–Sun 10am–5pm • €20, 3–12-year-olds €15 • ☎ 08 11 22 41 22, Ⓦ parczoologiquedeparis.fr • Ⓜ Porte Dorée

North of the Lac Daumesnil lies the **Parc Zoologique de Paris**, the city's main **zoo**. Its landmark Grand Rocher, an extraordinary 65m-high fake boulder, built in 1934 when the zoo first opened, is still here, but just about everything else has been completely rebuilt, with the aim of recreating as far as possible the animals' natural habitats. Highlights include the giant tropical hothouse harbouring tortoises, iguanas, caimans and other reptiles; and the giraffe house, where you get a great view of the leggy beasts from the glass viewing balcony.

## Château de Vincennes

1 av de Paris, Vincennes • Daily: mid-May to mid-Sept 10am–6pm; mid-Sept to mid-May 10am–5pm • €9 • ☎ 01 48 08 31 20, Ⓦ chateau-vincennes.fr • Ⓜ Château-de-Vincennes

On the northern edge of the Bois de Vincennes lies the **Château de Vincennes**, the country's only surviving medieval royal residence, built by Charles V and subsequently turned into a state prison, then porcelain factory, weapons dump and military training school. Enclosed by a high defensive wall and still preserving the feel of a military barracks, it presents a rather austere aspect on first sight, but it's worth visiting for its Gothic **Chapelle Royale**, decorated with superb Renaissance stained-glass windows; and the restored fourteenth-century **donjon** (keep), where you can see some fine vaulted ceilings, Charles V's bedchamber, and graffiti left by prisoners, whose number included one Marquis de Sade.

**1**

# Quartier Latin

South of the river, the **Rive Gauche** (Left Bank) has long maintained an "alternative" identity, opposed to the formal ambience of the Right Bank. Generally understood to describe the 5ᵉ and 6ᵉ arrondissements, the Left Bank was at the heart of *les évènements*, the revolutionary political "events" of May 1968. Since that infamous summer, however, gentrification has transformed the artists' garrets and beatnik cafés into designer pads and top-end restaurants, and the legend is only really kept alive by the student population of the **Quartier Latin** – so-called for the learned Latin of the medieval scholars who first settled here, or possibly for the abundant Roman ruins. It is in fact one of the city's more palpably ancient districts.

The pivotal point is **place St-Michel**, where the tree-lined **boulevard St-Michel** begins. It's a busy commercial thoroughfare these days, but the universities on all sides still give an intellectual air to the place, and the cafés and shops are still jammed with young people. Meanwhile, on the riverbank you'll find old books, postcards and prints on sale from the **bouquinistes**, whose green boxes line the parapets of the **riverside quais**. It's a pleasant walk upstream to **Pont de Sully**, which leads across to the Île St-Louis and offers a dramatic view of Notre-Dame.

## Around St-Séverin

The Quartier Latin's touristy scrum is at its most intense around **rue de la Huchette**, just east of place St-Michel. Hemmed in by cheap bars and kebab shops, the tiny Théâtre de la Huchette (see page 142) is the last bastion of the area's postwar beatnik heyday, and it still shows Ionesco's absurdist plays more than sixty years on. Connecting rue de la Huchette to the riverside is **rue du Chat-qui-Pêche**, a narrow slice of medieval Paris as it was before Haussmann got to work. At the end of rue de la Huchette, **rue St-Jacques** follows the line of the main street of Roman Paris, and was the road up which millions of medieval pilgrims trudged at the start of their long march to Santiago de Compostela (Saint Jacques de Compostelle, in French) in Spain. Across rue Lagrange from the square Viviani, rue de la Bûcherie is the home of the celebrated English-language bookshop **Shakespeare and Company** (see page 144), a huge tourist attraction in its own right.

### St-Séverin

1 rue des Prêtres St-Séverin, 5ᵉ • Mon–Sat 11am–7.30pm, Sun 9am–8pm • Free • Ⓜ St-Michel/Cluny–La Sorbonne

One block south of rue de la Huchette, just west of rue St-Jacques, is the mainly fifteenth-century church of **St-Séverin**. It's one of the city's more intense churches, its Flamboyant (distinguished by *flamboyant*, or flame-like, carving) choir resting on a virtuoso spiralling central pillar and its windows filled with edgy stained glass by the modern French painter Jean Bazaine.

## Institut du Monde Arabe

1 rue des Fossés-St-Bernard, 5ᵉ • **Institute** Tues–Fri 10am–7pm (last entry to exhibitions 5.15pm), Sat & Sun 10am–8pm (last entry to exhibitions 6.15pm) • Free • **Museum** Tues–Fri 10am–7pm (last entry 5.15pm), Sat & Sun 10am–8pm (last entry 6.15pm) • €8 • ☎ 01 40 51 38 38, Ⓦ imarabe.org • Ⓜ Jussieu/Cardinal-Lemoine

Opposite Pont de Sully, you can't miss the bold glass and aluminium mass of the **Institut du Monde Arabe**, a cultural centre built to further understanding of the Arab world. Designed by Paris's favourite modern architect, Jean Nouvel, its broad southern facade, which mimics a *moucharabiyah*, or traditional Arab latticework, is made up of thousands of tiny, photo-sensitive metallic shutters. Inside, its **museum** aims to present a broad history of the Arab world, going back as far as prehistoric times (the oldest exhibit, a statuette of an earth goddess from Jordan, dates from the seventh century

BC). If the collection feels sparse in places and slightly confusingly arranged (by theme, rather than chronologically), you do at least get a sense of the cultural diversity and richness of the Arab peoples. The institute also puts on temporary exhibitions and concerts of Arab music, and there's a library and specialist bookshop.

Up on the ninth floor, the **terrace** (Tues–Sun 10am–6pm) offers fabulous views of the city, especially downriver towards the apse of Notre-Dame.

## Musée National du Moyen Âge

28 rue du Sommerard, 5ᵉ • Mon & Wed–Sun 9.15am–5.45pm • €5, €9 with temporary exhibitions, free to all first Sun of the month • ☎ 01 53 73 78 16, ⓦ musee-moyenage.fr • ⓜ Cluny-La Sorbonne

The area around the slopes of the **Montagne Ste-Geneviève**, the hill on which the Panthéon stands, is good for a stroll. The best approach is from **place Maubert** or from the St-Michel/St-Germain crossroads, where the walls of the third-century **Roman baths** are visible in the garden of the **Hôtel de Cluny**, a sixteenth-century mansion built by the abbots of the powerful Cluny monastery as their Paris pied-à-terre. With a smart new reception building off boulevard St-Michel, the complex houses the richly rewarding **Musée National du Moyen Âge**, a treasure house of medieval sculpture, stained glass, books, oddities and *objets d'art*. The real beauties here are the **tapestries**, and supreme among them is *La dame à la licorne* ("The Lady with the Unicorn"), a fifteenth-century masterpiece depicting the five senses along with an ambiguous and distinctly erotic image that may represent the "moral sense" in controlling them.

The museum is currently undergoing an extensive **restoration** programme, slated to continue until 2020. Some spaces may be closed when you visit, if only for an hour or so at a time. Depending on what's on show, look out for some wonderful backlit panels of **stained glass** from the Sainte-Chapelle; the vaults of the former Roman cold room, or *frigidarium*, which shelter the beautifully carved Gallo-Roman *Pillar of St-Landry*; the thermal baths; and the light-bathed, Flamboyant **chapel**.

The museum puts on high-quality **concerts** of medieval music throughout the week.

## The Sorbonne

ⓜ Cluny-La Sorbonne/RER Luxembourg

The elite educational institutions of the **Sorbonne**, **Collège de France** and the prestigious **Lycée Louis-le-Grand** number Molière, Robespierre, Sartre and Victor Hugo among its pupils. The hub of the quarter is **place de la Sorbonne**, overlooked by the dramatic Counter-Reformation facade of the Sorbonne's chapel, which was built in the 1640s by the great Cardinal Richelieu, whose tomb it houses. With its lime trees, fountains and cafés, the square is a lovely place to sit.

## The Panthéon

Place du Panthéon, 5ᵉ • Daily: April–Sept 10am–6.30pm; Oct–March 10am–6pm • €9 • ☎ 01 44 32 18 00, ⓦ paris-pantheon.fr • RER Luxembourg/ⓜ Cardinal-Lemoine

The Montagne Ste-Geneviève is topped by the grandly domed and porticoed **Panthéon**, Louis XV's grateful response to Ste-Geneviève, patron saint of Paris, for curing him of illness. After the Revolution it was transformed into a mausoleum, and the remains of giants of French culture such as Voltaire, Rousseau, Hugo and Zola are entombed in the vast, barrel-vaulted crypt below, along with Marie Curie (one of only five women), and Alexandre Dumas, of *Musketeers* fame, who was "panthéonized" in 2002. The interior is overwhelmingly monumental, bombastically classical in design. The **dome**, however, is pretty impressive – it was from here, in 1851, that French physicist Léon Foucault suspended a pendulum to demonstrate vividly the rotation of the earth: while the pendulum appeared to rotate over a 24-hour period, it was in fact the earth beneath

1

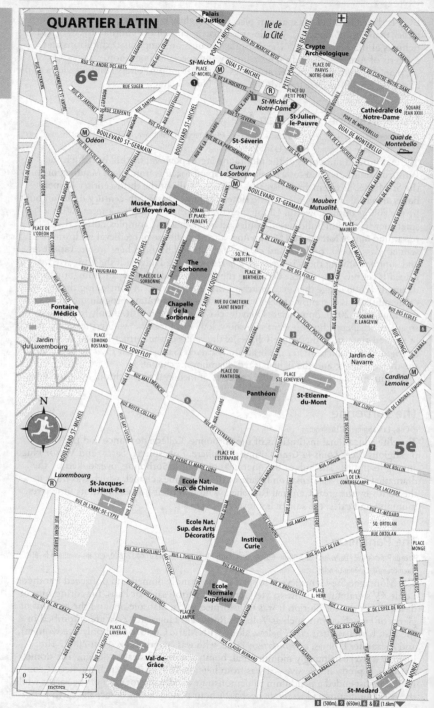

# QUARTIER LATIN

Palais de Justice

Ile de la Cité

Crypte Archéologique

6e

St-Michel

PLACE DU PARVIS NOTRE-DAME

St-Michel Notre-Dame

St-Julien-le-Pauvre

Cathédrale de Notre-Dame

SQUARE JEAN XXIII

Quai de Montebello

St-Séverin

Odéon

Cluny La Sorbonne

Maubert Mutualité

Musée National du Moyen Age

SQUARE ET PLACE P. PAINLEVE

The Sorbonne

SQ. F. A. MARIETTE

Fontaine Médicis

PLACE DE LA SORBONNE

PLACE M. BERTHELOT

SQUARE P. LANGEVIN

Jardin du Luxembourg

Chapelle de la Sorbonne

RUE DU CIMETIERE SAINT BENOIT

Jardin de Navarre

Cardinal Lemoine

PLACE EDMOND ROSTAND

PLACE DU PANTHEON

PLACE STE GENEVIEVE

Panthéon

St-Etienne-du-Mont

PLACE DE L'ESTRAPADE

5e

Luxembourg

St-Jacques-du-Haut-Pas

PLACE PIERRE ET MARIE CURIE

PLACE DE L'ESTRAPADE

PLACE DE LA CONTRESCARPE

Ecole Nat. Sup. de Chimie

Ecole Nat. Sup. des Arts Décoratifs

Institut Curie

SQ. ORTOLAN

PLACE MONGE

Ecole Normale Supérieure

PLACE P. LAMPUE

PLACE L. HERR

PLACE A. LAVERAN

Val-de-Grâce

St-Médard

N

0    150
metres

8 (500m), 9 (650m), 6 & 7 (1.6km) ▼

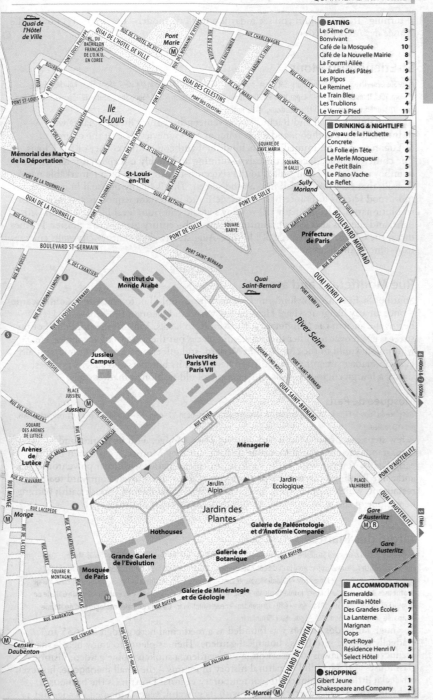

**● EATING**

| | |
|---|---|
| Le 5ème Cru | 3 |
| Bonvivant | 5 |
| Café de la Mosquée | 10 |
| Café de la Nouvelle Mairie | 8 |
| La Fourmi Ailée | 1 |
| Le Jardin des Pâtes | 9 |
| Les Pipos | 6 |
| Le Reminet | 2 |
| Le Train Bleu | 7 |
| Les Trublions | 4 |
| Le Verre à Pied | 11 |

**■ DRINKING & NIGHTLIFE**

| | |
|---|---|
| Caveau de la Huchette | 1 |
| Concrete | 4 |
| La Folie ejn Tête | 6 |
| Le Merle Moqueur | 7 |
| Le Petit Bain | 5 |
| Le Piano Vache | 3 |
| Le Reflet | 2 |

**■ ACCOMMODATION**

| | |
|---|---|
| Esmeralda | 1 |
| Familia Hôtel | 6 |
| Des Grandes Écoles | 7 |
| La Lanterne | 3 |
| Marignan | 2 |
| Oops | 9 |
| Port-Royal | 8 |
| Résidence Henri IV | 5 |
| Select Hôtel | 4 |

**● SHOPPING**

| | |
|---|---|
| Gibert Jeune | 1 |
| Shakespeare and Company | 2 |

**1**

it turning. The pendulum you see today is a working model – the original is now in the Musée des Arts et Métiers.

## St-Étienne-du-Mont

Place Ste-Geneviève, 5ᵉ • July & Aug Thurs–Sat 10am–noon & 4–7.45pm, Sun 10am–noon & 4.30–7.45pm; Sept–June Mon 6.30–7.30pm, Tues, Thurs & Fri 8.45am–7.45pm, Wed 8.45am–10pm, Sat 8.45am–noon & 2–7.45pm, Sun 8.45am–12.15pm & 2.30–7.45pm • Free • ⓦ saintetiennedumont.fr • RER Luxembourg/ⓜ Cardinal-Lemoine

The remains of Pascal and Racine, two seventeenth-century literary giants who didn't make the Panthéon, and a few relics of Ste-Geneviève, lie in the church of **St-Étienne-du-Mont**, immediately behind the Panthéon on the corner of rue Clovis. The church's garbled facade conceals a stunning and highly unexpected interior, its Flamboyant Gothic choir linked to the sixteenth-century nave by a remarkable narrow catwalk that transforms itself into a rood screen. This is highly unusual in itself, as most rood screens in France have fallen victim to Protestant iconoclasts, reformers or revolutionaries. Exceptionally tall windows at the triforium level fill the church with light, and there is also some beautiful seventeenth-century glass in the cloister. Further down rue Clovis, a huge piece of Philippe-Auguste's twelfth-century **city walls** emerges from among the houses.

## Rue Mouffetard and around

South of St-Étienne-du-Mont, rue Descartes heads uphill onto **place de la Contrescarpe** – once an arty hangout where Hemingway wrote and Georges Brassens sang. Here begins the ancient **rue Mouffetard** – rue Mouff' to locals. Most of the upper half of the street is given over to rather touristy eating places but the lower half, a cobbled lane winding downhill to the church of **St-Médard**, still offers a taste of the quintessentially Parisian market street that once thrived here, with its butchers and speciality cheese shops, a few greengrocers' stalls and a couple of old-fashioned market cafés.

### Mosquée de Paris

2bis place du Puits de l'Ermite, 5ᵉ • Daily except Fri & Muslim holidays 9am–noon & 2–6pm • €3 • ☎ 01 45 35 97 33, ⓦ mosqueedeparis.net • ⓜ Jussieu

A few steps east of rue Mouffetard, beyond place Monge, with its market and métro stop, stands the crenellated **Mosquée de Paris**, built by Moroccan craftsmen in the early 1920s. You can walk in the sunken garden and patios with their polychrome tiles and carved ceilings, but not the prayer room. There's also a lovely courtyard **tearoom/restaurant**, which is open to all, and an atmospheric **hammam** (Turkish bath); bathing here is one of the most enjoyable things to do in this part of the city.

## Jardin des Plantes

Rues Cuvier, Buffon & Geoffroy St-Hilaire, 5ᵉ • **Jardin** Daily: Feb & mid-Oct to late Oct 8am–6.30pm; early to mid-March 7.30am–7pm; mid- to end March 7.30am–7.30pm; April to mid-Sept 7.30am–8pm; mid-Sept to end Sept 8am–7.30pm; early Oct to mid-Oct 8am–7pm; Nov–Jan 8am–5.30pm • Free • ⓦ jardindesplantes.net • ⓜ Gare d'Austerlitz/Jussieu/Censier–Daubenton/Place Monge • **Hothouses** Daily except Tues: March to mid-Oct 10am–6pm; mid-Oct to Feb 10am–5pm • €7 • ⓦ mnhn.fr • **Grande Galerie de l'Évolution** Mon & Wed–Sun 10am–6pm • €10 • ⓦ grandegaleriedelevolution.fr • **Galerie de Paléontologie et d'Anatomie Comparée** Mon & Wed–Sun 10am–6pm • €9 • ⓦ mnhn.fr

The huge **Jardin des Plantes** was founded as a medicinal herb garden in 1635 and gradually evolved into Paris's botanical gardens. There is plenty to enjoy here – shady avenues of trees, lawns to sprawl on, a rose garden, a sunken alpine garden, historic glasshouses and a handful of natural history museums – the small **ménagerie**, however, can feel a little old-fashioned for contemporary visitors. Don't miss the **hothouses**, including the Art Deco *serre tropicale*, with its graceful, vegetal-themed facade, and a

1

pair of elegant hothouses that were revolutionary structures when built in the 1830s. Of the museums, the **Grande Galerie de l'Évolution**, housed in a dramatic nineteenth-century glass-domed building (the entrance is at the southwest corner of the gardens), tells the story of evolution with a huge cast of stuffed animals, some of them striding dramatically across the central space. Further into the gardens, and little changed since it was laid out in 1900 for the Universal Exhibition, the **Galerie de Paléontologie et d'Anatomie Comparée** has a real old-fashioned charm, full of the skeletons of strange beasts and ancient creatures that need no touch-screens or interactive gizmos to thrill.

# St-Germain

The northern half of the 6ᵉ arrondissement, centred on **place St-Germain-des-Prés**, is one of the most attractive, lively and wealthy square kilometres in the city – and one of the best places to shop for upmarket clothes. The most dramatic approach is to cross the river from the Louvre by the footbridge, the **Pont des Arts**, from where there's a classic upstream view of the Île de la Cité, with barges moored at the quai de Conti, the Tour St-Jacques and Hôtel de Ville breaking the skyline of the Right Bank. The dome and pediment at the end of the bridge belong to the **Institut de France**, seat of the Académie Française, an august body of writers and scholars whose mission is to safeguard the purity of the French language. This is the most grandiose part of the Left Bank riverfront: to the left is the **Monnaie de Paris**, redesigned as the Mint in the late eighteenth century; to the right is the **Beaux-Arts**, the School of Fine Art, whose students throng the *quais* on sunny days, sketchpads on knees. Inspiration for budding artists is in plentiful supply at the stunning **Musée d'Orsay**, just a little further west along the river. The perfect place to unwind after a little sightseeing is the lovely **Jardin du Luxembourg**, which borders the Quartier Latin towards the southern end of the *sixième*.

## Musée d'Orsay

1 rue de la Légion d'Honneur, 7ᵉ • Tues–Sun 9.30am–6pm, Thurs till 9.45pm • €14; free to under-18s and EU residents aged 18–25; free to everyone on the first Sun of the month; combined ticket with Musée Rodin (page 106) €18 • ☎ 01 40 49 48 14, Ⓦ musee-orsay.fr • Ⓜ Solférino/RER Musée-d'Orsay

Behind the handsome 1900 facade of a former railway station, the **Musée d'Orsay** is one of Paris's top attractions. While famed for its electrifying collection of **Impressionist** and **Post-Impressionist** works, in fact the Orsay highlights a broad range of French painting and sculpture dating between 1848 and 1914, an artistically revolutionary period that bridges the gap between the "classical" Louvre and the "modern" art of the Pompidou. You could spend almost a day meandering through the whole place, but it's easy enough – and maybe advisable – to confine your visit to a specific section or two. Note that the museum occasionally **rearranges rooms** and swaps paintings to make space for new acquisitions. While you can be pretty sure of seeing the big hitters, you should treat our account here as a loose guide.

There are three places to **eat**: the resplendent restaurant on the second floor, gilded in stunning period style; the postmodern Café Campana on level five (don't miss the wonderful view of Montmartre through the giant railway clock) and, for cheaper drinks and snacks, the tiny Café de l'Ours on the ground floor.

### The ground level

The **ground level**, under the great glass arch, is devoted mostly to pre-1870 works, with a double row of sculptures running down the aisle like railway tracks, and paintings in the little rooms on either side. Here you'll find pieces by Ingres, Delacroix and other serious-minded painters and sculptors acceptable to the mid-nineteenth century salons, as well as some relatively unusual Symbolist works by Gustave Moreau, Odilon Redon

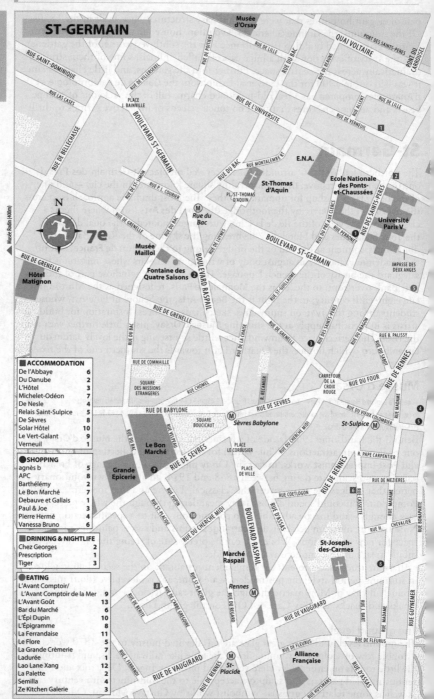

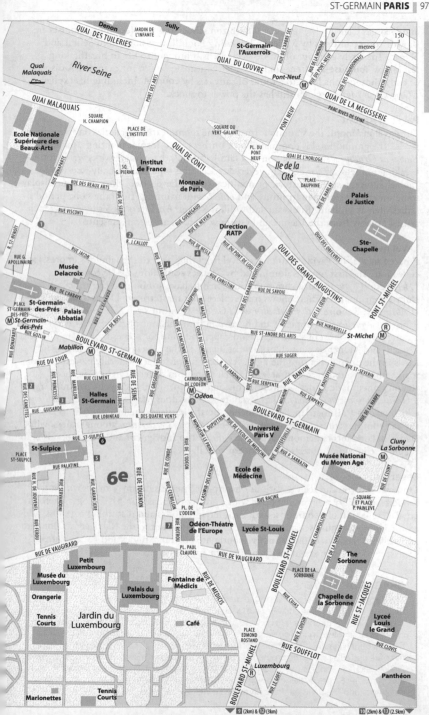

**1**

and Georges Clairin. The influential **Barbizon school** and the **Neo-Impressionists** are showcased in paintings by Millet and dazzling Pointilliste visions from Seurat and Signac. The seedy glamour of fin-de-siècle Paris is brought to life in breathtaking fashion by **Toulouse-Lautrec** – in his tenderly intimate *Le Lit*, for example. A display of **early photographs** leads to a room of canvases by **Courbet**, including his explicit *L'Origine du Monde*, which still has the power to shock.

## Pavillon Amont

The **Pavillon Amont**, the station's former engine room, features galleries on five different levels. The ground level is dominated by Courbet's large-format paintings, including *A Burial at Ornans*, a stark depiction of a family funeral; these huge works were groundbreaking in their day for depicting everyday scenarios on a scale usually reserved for "noble" subjects, such as historic or mythical scenes. Levels two, three and four display some superb **Art Nouveau** furniture and *objets*, with paintings from the same period by artists such as Vuillard, Rousseau and Odilon Redon. Art Deco pieces by non-French artists, notably from the Vienna and Glasgow schools, are also represented.

## Level five

Proceeding via the Pavillon Amont to level five brings you to the fabulous **Impressionist** collection. The first room is dominated by Manet's scandalous *Le Déjeuner sur l'Herbe* and *Olympia*, both commonly accepted to have announced the arrival of Impressionism. Thereafter follows masterpiece after masterpiece: Degas' *Dans un Café* (*L'Absinthe*); Renoir's *Bal du Moulin de la Galette*; Cézanne's *Les Joueurs de Cartes*; Monet's *Coquelicots* ("Poppies") and his two radiant versions of *Femme à l'Ombrelle*, among others. A host of small-scale landscapes and outdoor scenes by Renoir, Sisley, Pissarro and Monet owe much of their brilliance to the novel practice of setting up easels in the open to capture the light. A selection of Monet's waterlily paintings and works from his **Rouen cathedral series**, each painted in different light conditions, face Renoir's pneumatic nudes – a wonderful counterpoint. Renoir's joyous pairing *Danse à la Ville/Danse à la Campagne* has a wall to itself, as does Manet's smaller *Sur la Plage*, which reveals a distinct Japanese influence. **Berthe Morisot**, the first woman to join the early Impressionists, is represented by her famous *Le Berceau*, among others, while **Degas' ballet dancers** demonstrate his key interest in movement and line as opposed to the more common Impressionist concern with light.

## Level two

On **level two** you can see the various offspring of Impressionism – an edgier, more modern sensibility is emerging here, with a greater emphasis on psychology. There's a crucial collection of **Van Goghs**, with their fervid colours and disturbing rhythms, and an intriguing **Gauguin** selection. A suite of rooms devoted to the **Nabis** artists **Bonnard** and **Vuillard** includes their distinctively intimate portraits, nudes and Parisian street scenes, rendered with spontaneity, naturalism and emotion.

---

### BERGES DE SEINE

The **Berges de Seine**, a pedestrianized promenade running for 2.3km along the river between the pont d'Alma and Musée d'Orsay, is particularly lively on weekends in the warmer months, where you can listen to concerts, take part in a sporting event, play chess over a cup of coffee or simply relax in a deckchair and enjoy the river views. Near the Pont de l'Alma are five small floating gardens, each on a different theme, with plenty of space for picnics. Places to sit are dotted all along the promenade, while restaurant-bars such as *Faust, Bistrot Alexandre III, Flow* and *Rosa Bonheur* (see page 132) – the last three on huge floating barges – offer food and drink. The Berges de Seine was joined in 2017 to a similar promenade on the Right Bank, creating a loop known as the **Parc Rives de Seine** (see page 88).

On the **sculpture terraces**, amid works by Maillol, Bourdelle and others, it is pieces by **Rodin** that stand out, not least his exceptionally grim *Ugolin*. The painful imagery of *L'Age Mûr*, a heartbreaking appeal to Rodin from his pupil and lover **Camille Claudel**, shows the exceptional skill of this lesser-known artist.

## The St-Germain riverside

The riverside chunk of the 6e arrondissement is cut lengthwise by **rue St-André-des-Arts** and **rue Jacob**. It's an area full of bookshops, commercial art galleries, antique shops, cafés and restaurants, and if you poke your nose into the courtyards and side streets, you'll find foliage, fountains and peaceful enclaves removed from the bustle of the city. The houses are four to six storeys high, seventeenth- and eighteenth-century, some noble, some bulging and skew, all painted in infinite gradations of grey, pearl and off-white. Broadly speaking, the further west you go the posher the houses get.

**Historical associations** are legion: Picasso painted *Guernica* in rue des Grands-Augustins; Molière started his career in rue Mazarine; Robespierre et al split ideological hairs at the *Café Procope* in rue de l'Ancienne-Comédie. In rue Visconti, Racine died, Delacroix painted and Balzac's printing business went bust. In the parallel rue des Beaux-Arts, Oscar Wilde died, Corot and Ampère (father of amps) lived, and the poet Gérard de Nerval went walking with a lobster on a lead.

### Rue de Buci

You'll find numerous places to eat on **place** and **rue St-André-des-Arts** and along **rue de Buci**, up towards boulevard St-Germain. Rue de Buci preserves a flavour of its origins as a market street, with food shops, delis, cafés and brasseries galore. Before you get to rue de Buci, there is an intriguing little covered passage on the left, **Cour du Commerce St-André**, where Marat had a printing press and Dr Guillotin perfected his notorious machine by lopping off sheep's heads.

## St-Germain-des-Prés and around

**Place St-Germain-des-Prés**, the hub of the *quartier*, has the famous *Deux Magots* café on its corner, *Flore* adjacent and *Lipp* across the boulevard St-Germain. All three brasseries are renowned for the number of philosophical and literary backsides that have shined their banquettes, along with plenty of celebrity-hunters. Today they're touristy, and pricey, but still retain an undeniable historic charm. Picasso's chunky bust of a woman, dedicated to the poet Apollinaire, recalls the district's creative heyday.

### St-Germain-des-Prés

Place St-Germain-des-Pres, 6ᵉ • Mon 9am–8pm, Tues–Sun 8.30am–8pm • ⓦ eglise-saintgermaindespres.fr • Free • Ⓜ St-Germain-des-Prés

The tower dominating Place St-Germain-des-Prés belongs to the church of **St-Germain-des-Prés**, all that remains of an enormous Benedictine monastery. Inside, the transformation from Romanesque to early Gothic is just about visible under the heavy green-and-gold nineteenth-century paintwork.

### Musée National Eugène Delacroix

6 rue de Furstemberg, 6ᵉ • Mon & Wed–Sun 9.30am–5.30pm • €7 • ☎ 01 44 41 86 50, ⓦ musee-delacroix.fr • Ⓜ Mabillon/St-Germain-des-Prés

Halfway down rue de Furstemberg, opposite the tiny square of the same name, is Delacroix's old apartment and studio, now the **Musée National Eugène Delacroix**. Here you can see a small collection of the artist's personal belongings and minor exhibitions of his work; visitors are also welcome to sit a while in the peaceful walled garden.

**1**

## St-Sulpice

Place St-Sulpice, 6ᵉ • Daily 7.30am–7.30pm • Free • Ⓦ pss75.fr/saint-sulpice-paris • Ⓜ St-Sulpice

South of boulevard St-Germain, the streets round **place St-Sulpice** are calm and classy. The enormous, early eighteenth-century church of **St-Sulpice** is an austerely classical building with Doric and Ionic colonnades and Corinthian pilasters in the towers. On the south tower centuries-old uncut masonry blocks protrude from the top, still awaiting the sculptor's chisel. The church is famed for its three **Delacroix** murals, in the first chapel on the right; for its colossal organ, still used in recitals; and for its **gnomon**, a kind of astronomical clock whose origins and purpose were so compellingly garbled by *The Da Vinci Code*.

## Jardin du Luxembourg

Entrances on place Edmond Rostand, rue Guynemer and rue de Vaugirard, 6ᵉ • **Gardens** Daily dawn to dusk • Ⓦ senat.fr/visite/jardin • **Puppet shows** €6.40 • Ⓦ marionnettesduluxembourg.fr • **Musée du Luxembourg** 19 rue de Vaugirard, 6ᵉ • Hours vary depending on the exhibtion, but generally daily 10.30am–7pm; some late openings, check website for details • Prices vary • ☎ 01 40 13 62 00, Ⓦ museeduluxembourg.fr • Ⓜ St-Sulpice/Mabillon/RER Luxembourg

Belonging to the Palais du Luxembourg, seat of the French Senate, the **Jardin du Luxembourg** offers a lovely ensemble of formal lawns, broad gravel paths, more than one hundred sculptures and resplendent floral parterres, with citrus and olive trees in giant pots (taken inside in winter). Most people enjoy the view from the many elegant sage-green chairs dotted throughout the gardens; sprawling on the lawns is strictly forbidden, except on the southernmost strip, which gets fantastically crowded on sunny days. The shady **Fontaine Médicis**, in the northeast corner, is another pleasant spot to relax, and there are a couple of sit-down places to eat. The western side of the park is more active, with tennis courts and a historic **puppet theatre** that still puts on enthralling shows. The quieter, wooded southwest corner ends in a miniature orchard of heritage apple and pear trees.

With its entrance on rue de Vaugirard, the **Musée du Luxembourg** hosts some of the city's largest and most exciting temporary art exhibitions. Recent highlights have included an exhibition on the Tudors and another devoted to Alphonse Mucha.

# The Eiffel Tower quarter

The stretch of Paris in the shadow of the **Eiffel Tower** is home chiefly to diplomats, government officials and aristocrats, both old-school and new. The sheer monumental pomp can feel overwhelming: most visitors drop in by métro (or sail in by Batobus) to climb the **tower** and perhaps call in at one of the quarter's fine museums in the **Trocadéro**, a hop away on the north bank. The area at the tower's feet, to the east, is the **septième** (7ᵉ) arrondissement, home to the imposing **Hôtel des Invalides** and the French army's vast **war museum**. The splendid **Musée Rodin**, nearby, makes an interesting contrast, displaying the revolutionary sculptor's works in the intimate surroundings of a private mansion.

## The Eiffel Tower

Daily: mid-June to Aug 9am–12.45pm; Sept to mid-June 9.30am–11.45pm • €25 (for the top, by lift), €16 (second level, by lift); you can climb the stairs as far as the second level for €10 and buy a "supplément ascenseur" ticket to the top for a further €9; save queueing time by buying tickets online (well in advance), or turn up on the day around 1–2hr before the tower opens for the lift, around 20min in advance for the stairs • ☎ 0892 701 239, Ⓦ toureiffel.paris • Ⓜ Trocadéro/Bir-Hakeim/École Militaire/RER Champs de Mars-Tour Eiffel

It's hard to believe that the **Eiffel Tower**, the quintessential symbol both of Paris and a brilliant feat of industrial engineering, was designed to be a temporary structure for a fair. Late nineteenth-century Europe had a decadent taste for such giant-scale, colonialist-capitalist extravaganzas, but Paris's 1889 Exposition Universelle was particularly ambitious, and when completed the tower, at 300m, was the tallest building in the world. Outraged critics protested "in the name of menaced French art and history" against this "useless and monstrous" tower. "Is Paris", they asked, "going to be associated with the grotesque, mercantile imaginings of a constructor of machines?" Curiously, Paris's most famous landmark was only saved from demolition by the sudden need for "wireless telegraphy" aerials in the first decade of the twentieth century and nowadays the original crown is masked by an efflorescence of antennae. It's particularly spectacular after dark, an urban lighthouse illuminated by a double searchlight and, for the first five minutes of every hour until 1am, by thousands of effervescent lights that fizz across its grid lines.

Though you may have to wait a while for the lifts, it's arguable that you simply haven't seen Paris until you've seen it from the **top**. While the views are almost better from the second level, especially on hazier days, there's something irresistible about going all the way to the top, and looking down over the surreally microscopic city below. On the **first level**, meanwhile, a glass floor affords dizzying views of the ground (and queues) below. This is also the location of the tower's less formal restaurant – *Le 58 Tour Eiffel* – a more affordable option than the gastronomic *Jules Verne* on level two. Note that **security** is tight at the tower, which means queues can be slow; schedule plenty of time for a visit.

## Trocadéro

On the **Trocadéro** heights of the north bank of the river, facing the Eiffel Tower, stand the resplendent **Palais de Tokyo** and **Palais de Chaillot**. Between them they host some of the city's best art museums, including the **Palais de Tokyo art gallery**, the **Musée d'Art Moderne de la Ville de Paris** and the **Cité de l'Architecture et du Patrimoine**, with another scattering of good museums in the surrounding area.

### Cité de l'Architecture et du Patrimoine

Palais de Chaillot, 1 place du Trocadéro et du 11 novembre, 16ᵉ • Mon, Wed & Fri–Sun 11am–7pm, Thurs 11am–9pm • €8, €12 with temporary exhibitions • ☎ 01 58 51 52 00, Ⓦ citedelarchitecture.fr • Ⓜ Trocadéro

The eastern wing of the **Palais de Chaillot** is occupied by the superb **Cité de l'Architecture et du Patrimoine**, a stunningly put-together museum of architecture. On the loftily vaulted ground floor, the **Galerie des Moulages** displays giant plaster casts taken from the greatest French buildings (chiefly churches) at the end of the nineteenth century, before pollution and erosion dulled their detail. The **Galerie des Peintures Murales et des Vitraux**, with its radiant, full-scale copies of French frescoes and stained glass, is equally impressive. The **Galerie d'Architecture Moderne et Contemporaine** showcases the nineteenth and twentieth centuries, with models, photographs and a reconstruction of an entire apartment from **Le Corbusier**'s Cité Radieuse in Marseille.

### Musée de l'Homme

Palais de Chaillot, 17 place du Trocadéro, 16ᵉ • Mon & Wed–Sun 10am–6pm • €10, €12 with temporary exhibitions • ☎ 01 44 05 72 72, Ⓦ museedelhomme.fr • Ⓜ Trocadéro

Unlike the city's other ethnographical museum, Musée du Quai Branly (see page 104), which presents its objects as works of art, the **Musée de l'Homme** focuses on science. Intriguing thematic connections are made between the exhibits, which range from stuffed animals and skeletons to digital touchscreens. Look out for the history of waxworking, particularly the bizarre eighteenth-century model of a newborn as seen only by its arteries, veins and organs.

### Musée d'Art Moderne de la Ville de Paris

Palais de Tokyo, av du Président-Wilson, 16ᵉ • Tues–Sun 10am–6pm • Free; admission charges (€5–12) for temporary exhibitions • ☎ 01 53 67 40 00, Ⓦ mam.paris.fr • Ⓜ léna/Alma-Marceau

1

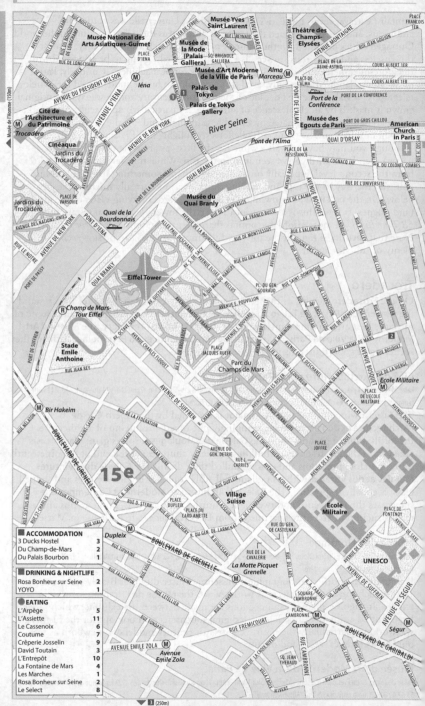

Musée de l'Homme (150m)

**Eiffel Tower**

River Seine

Parc du Champs de Mars

15e

| ◼ ACCOMMODATION | |
|---|---|
| 3 Ducks Hostel | 3 |
| Du Champ-de-Mars | 2 |
| Du Palais Bourbon | 1 |

| ◼ DRINKING & NIGHTLIFE | |
|---|---|
| Rosa Bonheur sur Seine | 2 |
| YOYO | 1 |

| ◼ EATING | |
|---|---|
| L'Arpège | 5 |
| L'Assiette | 11 |
| Le Cassenoix | 6 |
| Coutume | 7 |
| Crêperie Josselin | 9 |
| David Toutain | 3 |
| L'Entrepôt | 10 |
| La Fontaine de Mars | 4 |
| Les Marches | 1 |
| Rosa Bonheur sur Seine | 2 |
| Le Select | 8 |

▼ 3 (250m)

# TROCADÉRO, EIFFEL TOWER AND THE SEPTIÈME

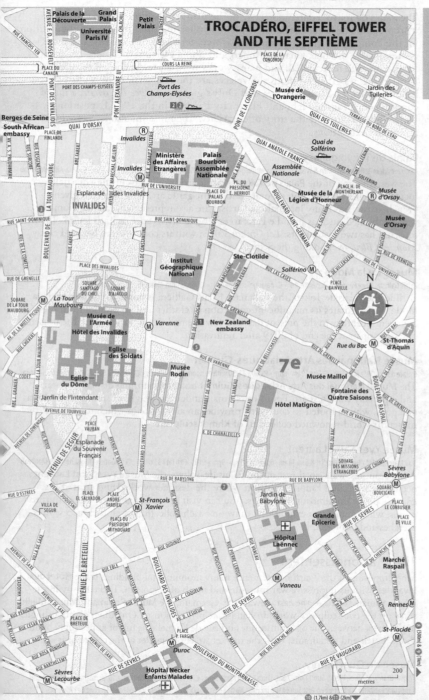

**1**

The **Palais de Tokyo**, contemporary with the nearby Chaillot, houses the **Musée d'Art Moderne de la Ville de Paris**. While the collection itself may be no competition for the Pompidou Centre, the museum is free, relatively uncrowded, and more contemplative. Braque, Chagall, Robert and Sonia Delaunay, Derain, Léger and Picasso are well represented, and many works were expressly chosen for their Parisian themes. The enormous showpieces are the two versions of Matisse's balletic mural, *La Danse de Paris*, and Dufy's gigantic *La Fée Électricité*, a mural commissioned for the Light and Electricity Pavilion in the 1937 Exposition Universelle to illustrate the story of electricity. The museum also hosts frequent temporary exhibitions.

### Palais de Tokyo gallery

Av du Président-Wilson, 16ᵉ • Mon & Wed–Sun noon–midnight • €12 • ☎ 01 81 97 35 88, ⓦ palaisdetokyo.com • Ⓜ léna/Alma-Marceau

The western wing of the **Palais de Tokyo** is occupied by a huge cutting-edge **gallery** focusing exclusively on contemporary and avant-garde art. Prominence is given to French artists, but many international artists are also represented, ranging from the well-established, such as Julio Le Parc, to emerging artists such as Taru Izumi. The museum has two **restaurants**: *Les Grands Verres*, with its cool cocktail bar, and classy *Monsieur Bleu*, overlooking the Seine.

### Musée de la Mode

Palais Galliera, 10 av Pierre 1er de Serbie, 16ᵉ • ⓦ palaisgalliera.paris.fr • Ⓜ léna/Alma-Marceau

Behind the Palais de Tokyo, the Italianate Palais Galliera is home to the **Musée de la Mode**, which rotates its magnificent collection of clothes and accessories from the eighteenth century to the present day in a few themed exhibitions a year. The museum due to re-open at the end of 2019 after renovation.

### Musée National des Arts Asiatiques-Guimet

6 place d'Iéna, 16ᵉ • Mon & Wed–Sun 10am–6pm • €8.50 €11.50 with temporary exhibitions • ☎ 01 56 52 53 00, ⓦ guimet.fr • Ⓜ léna

The **Musée National des Arts Asiatiques-Guimet** boasts a stunning display of Asian and especially Buddhist art. Four floors groan under the weight of statues of Buddhas and gods, while a roofed-in courtyard provides an airy space in which to show off the museum's world-renowned collection of **Khmer sculpture**.

### Musée Yves Saint Laurent

5 av Marceau, 16ᵉ • Tues–Thurs, Sat & Sun 11am–6pm, Fri 11am–9pm • €10 • ☎ 01 44 31 64 00, ⓦ fondation-pb-ysl.net • Ⓜ Monceau

A few minutes' walk northeast of the Palais de Tokyo, the **Musée Yves Saint Laurent** occupies the Second Empire mansion where the designer worked and created his couture pieces for almost thirty years. You can visit his atelier and the haute couture salons, while temporary exhibitions draw on a rich collection of clothes, accessories, sketches and photographs.

## The 7ᵉ arrondissement

Most imposing of the 7ᵉ arrondissement's many monumental buildings is the **Hôtel des Invalides**, with its impressive war museum and tomb of Napoleon. Tucked away in the more intimate streets to the east, towards St-Germain, the **Musée Rodin** and **Musée Maillol** show off the two sculptors' works in handsome private houses. One tiny neighbourhood in this area, between rue St-Dominique and rue de Grenelle, is full of appealingly bijou shops, hotels and restaurants, with the market street of **rue Cler** at the centre of it all.

### Musée du Quai Branly

37 quai Branly, 7ᵉ • Tues, Wed & Sun 11am–7pm, Thurs–Sat 11am–9pm • €10; temporary exhibitions €10; permanent collection and temporary exhibitions €12; free on first Sun of the month • ☎ 01 56 61 70 00, ⓦ quaibranly.fr • Ⓜ léna/RER Pont de l'Alma

A short distance upstream of the Eiffel Tower stands the intriguing **Musée du Quai Branly**, which gathers together hundreds of thousands of non-European objects bought or purloined by France over the centuries. The museum was the pet project of President Chirac, whose passion for non-Western art helped secure funding. Designed by Jean Nouvel, the Postmodern building unfurls in a sleek curve through the middle of an intriguing **garden** that is cut off from the riverbank by a high glass wall. Inside, areas devoted to Asia, Africa, the Americas and the Pacific ("Oceania") snake through semi-dark rooms lined by curving "mud" walls in brown leather. The **folk artefacts** on display at any one time are as fascinating as they are beautiful, with an especially amazing collection of textiles and masks that reveal incredible artistry.

## Musée des Egouts de Paris

Quai d'Orsay, 7ᵉ, entrance on northeast side of place de la Résistance • Mon–Wed & Sat: May–Sept 11am–6pm; Oct–April 11am–5pm • €4.40 • ☎ 01 53 68 27 81 • Ⓜ Alma-Marceau/RER Pont de l'Alma

The chief attraction of the **Musée des Egouts de Paris**, or **Sewers Museum**, is that it is actually in the sewers. Once you're underground it's dark, damp and noisy from the gushing water; the exhibition, which runs along a gantry walk poised above a main sewer, renders the history of the city's water supply and waste management surprisingly fascinating. The museum is currently closed for restoration and is due to reopen early in 2020; opening times and admission may well change.

## Hôtel des Invalides and around

The noble **Esplanade des Invalides** strikes south from **Pont Alexandre III** towards the proud dome of the **Hôtel des Invalides**, which was built as a home for wounded soldiers on the orders of Louis XIV. The surrounding complex, which still belongs to the army, is home to the **Musée de l'Armée**, a national war museum founded in 1905, and two **churches** – one of which contains **Napoleon's tomb**.

### Musée de l'Armée

Hôtel des Invalides, 51 bd de la Tour-Maubourg, 7ᵉ • Daily: April–Oct 10am–6pm; Nov–March 10am–5pm • €12 ticket also valid for Église du Dôme and Napoleon's tomb • Ⓦ musee-armee.fr • Ⓜ La Tour-Maubourg/Varenne

The vast **Musée de l'Armée** plots a course through French military history from the Middle Ages to the end of the Cold War. Perhaps the most affecting galleries cover the **world wars** and their aftermath, beginning with Prussia's annexation of Alsace-Lorraine in 1871 and ending with the fall of the Berlin Wall. Memorabilia is combined with stirring contemporary newsreels, most of which have an English-language option. The simplest artefacts – a rag doll found on a battlefield, an overcoat caked in mud from the trenches – tell a stirring human story. The **Extraordinary Cabinets** in the **east wing** display historical figurines, artillery models and **military musical instruments**, while the floor above, covering the years from 1643 to 1870, has a number of intriguing **Napoleon** exhibits – including, somewhat surprisingly, his horse Vizir (now stuffed).

On the top floor, the **Musée des Plans-Reliefs**, a collection of around 25 super-scale models of French ports, fortified cities and islands, is surprisingly engaging; the hagiographic **Charles de Gaulle Historial** (closed Mon), in the basement, less so.

### Église du Dôme and Église des Soldats

**Église du Dôme** April–Sept Mon & Wed–Sun 10am–7pm, Tues 10am–9pm; Oct daily 10am–6pm; Nov–March daily 10am–5pm • €12 including Musée de l'Armée • Ⓦ musee-armee.fr • Ⓜ La Tour-Maubourg/Varenne

The **Église du Dôme**, on the south side of the complex, was formerly the Église Royale, intended for the private worship of Louis XIV and the royal family. The big draw here is **Napoleon's tomb**, a mighty sarcophagus of deep red porphyry, without any name or inscription, entombed in a circular pit and overlooked by statues that represent his military victories. Napoleon was finally laid to rest in Paris on December 14, 1840, when his remains, freshly returned from St Helena – where he had died nineteen years

**1**

earlier – were carried through the streets from the newly completed Arc de Triomphe to Invalides. Half a million Bonapartists came out to watch the emperor's last journey.

The relatively spartan **Église des Soldats** (or **Soldiers' Church**) was – and remains – separated from the Église du Dôme by a glass wall, which avoided the risk of worshippers on either side coming into social contact. A commemorative Mass is still said here on May 5, the anniversary of the emperor's death.

### Musée Rodin

79 rue de Varenne, 7ᵉ • Tues–Sun 10am–5.45pm • €10, combined ticket with Musée d'Orsay €18 • ☎ 01 44 18 61 10, ⓦ musee-rodin.fr • Ⓜ Varenne/Invalides

The **Musée Rodin**, arguably Paris's loveliest museum, occupies a beautiful eighteenth-century mansion that the sculptor leased from the state in return for the gift of all his work at his death. Today, major projects like *The Burghers of Calais*, *The Thinker*, *The Gates of Hell* and *Ugolini and his Sons* are exhibited in the gardens – the last forming the centrepiece of an ornamental pond. Indoors, the mould-breaking, stormy vigour of the sculptures sits beautifully with the time-worn elegance of the wooden panelling and the age-tarnished mirrors. Well-loved works like the touchingly erotic *The Kiss* get most of the attention, but you can explore rooms full of tortured clay and plaster figures that still bear the imprint of the artist's hands. Don't miss the section dedicated to the sculptor Camille Claudel, Rodin's talented pupil, muse and lover. Finally, take in Rodin's collection of personal **artworks**, from quirky walls of ancient (sculpted) hands and feet to the Van Gogh masterpiece *Le Père Tanguy*.

# Southern Paris

The neighbourhood of **Montparnasse**, with its evocative literary and artistic associations, divides the well-heeled opinion-formers and powerbrokers of St-Germain and the 7ᵉ from the relatively anonymous populations to the south. The three arrondissements to the south of Montparnasse have suffered from large-scale housing developments, most notably along the riverfronts to both east and west, but villagey areas such as **rue du Commerce** in the 15ᵉ, **Pernety** in the 14ᵉ and the **Buttes-aux-Cailles** in the 13ᵉ are worth a foray. On the fringes of the city proper, hard up against the *périphérique* ring road, are three worthwhile **parks**: André-Citroën, Georges-Brassens and Montsouris.

## Montparnasse

Like other Left Bank *quartiers*, Montparnasse trades on its association with the wild characters of the interwar artistic and literary boom. Many were habitués of the cafés on **boulevard du Montparnasse** – the most famous of which are still going strong – and many of them are interred in the nearby **Montparnasse cemetery**. The quarter's artistic traditions are recalled in a couple of fascinating art museums, while elsewhere you can ascend the **Tour Montparnasse**, Paris's first and ugliest skyscraper, and descend into the bone-lined **catacombs**.

### Tour Montparnasse

Rue de l'Arrivée, 15ᵉ • Observation deck/viewing terrace: April–Sept daily 9.30am–11.30pm; Oct–March Mon–Thurs & Sun 9.30am–10.30pm, Fri & Sat 9.30am–11pm • €18 • ⓦ tourmontparnasse56.com • Ⓜ Montparnasse-Bienvenüe

At the station end of boulevard du Montparnasse, the colossal **Tour Montparnasse** has become one of the city's principal and most despised landmarks. Although central Paris is more distant, the view from the top is better than the one from the Eiffel Tower in that it includes the Eiffel Tower – and excludes the Tour Montparnasse. Alternatively, you could sit down for an expensive drink in the 56th-storey café, from where you get a tremendous view westwards.

**1**

## Musée Bourdelle

18 rue Antoine Bourdelle, 15ᵉ • Tues–Sun 10am–6pm • Free; charge for temporary exhibitions • ☎ 01 49 54 73 73, ⓦ bourdelle.paris.fr • Ⓜ Montparnasse Bienvenüe/Falguière

Northwest of the Montparnasse tower, the fascinating **Musée Bourdelle** has been built around the sculptor's atmospheric old studio. Bourdelle, Rodin's pupil and Giacometti's teacher, moved sculpture on from naturalism towards a more geometric, modernist style. Bronze versions of some of his better-known, monumental sculptures are dotted around the garden, while huge plaster models of mythological subjects such as *The Dying Centaur* take pride of place in the skylit Modernist **Great Hall**. You can also see a sequence of rooms displaying Bourdelle's works – including paintings – in **chronological order**, from 1883 to his death in 1929; the highlight here is a wonderful series of tumultuous **Beethoven** busts and masks.

## Jardin Atlantique

Place des Cinq Martyrs du Lycée Buffon, behind Montparnasse train station, 15ᵉ access from bd Pasteur or by the stairs alongside platform #3 • Mon–Fri 8am–7pm/9.30pm, Sat & Sun 9am–7pm/9.30pm (depending on season) • Free • Ⓜ Montparnasse-Bienvenüe

Montparnasse station was once the great arrival and departure point for travellers heading across the Atlantic, a connection commemorated in the unexpected **Jardin Atlantique** on the station roof. Hemmed in by high-rise apartment blocks, lawns – some planted with coastal grasses – rise and fall in symbolic waves, while a double line of trees (those on the eastern side are of American origin, those on the West, European) runs to the central **Île des Hespérides** water-jet fountain. Ventilation shafts dotted around the grass mean you can clearly hear the trains rumbling below, and at the southern end of the park, huge canopied ventilation holes reveal glimpses – if you crane your neck – of TGV roofs and rail sleepers.

## Montparnasse cemetery

Bd Edgar Quinet, 14ᵉ • Mid-March to Nov 5 Mon–Fri 8am–6pm, Sat 8.30am–6pm, Sun 9am–6pm; Nov 6 to mid-March closes 5.30pm • Free • Ⓜ Raspail/Gaîté/Edgar Quinet

Just south of boulevard Edgar-Quinet (which has a food market on Wed and Sat mornings) is the main entrance to the **Montparnasse cemetery**. Ranks of miniature temples pay homage to illustrious names from Baudelaire and Beckett to Gainsbourg and Zadkine; pick up a map at the entrance gates to track down your favourites. The simple joint grave of Jean-Paul Sartre and Simone de Beauvoir lies immediately right of the main entrance, while in Division 1, the tomb of singer **Serge Gainsbourg** is regularly festooned with métro tickets – the "lilacs" of his song *Le Poinçonneur des Lilas* – along with flowers, wine bottles and cigarettes. Look out, too, for a couple of poignant monuments marked by artist Niki de Saint Phalle's distinctive mosaic sculptures. In the southwest corner is an old sail-less windmill, remains of one of the seventeenth-century taverns frequented by the carousing students.

## The catacombs

Place Denfert-Rochereau, 14ᵉ • Tues–Sun 10am–8.30pm, last entry 7.30pm • €13 • ☎ 01 43 22 47 63, ⓦ catacombes.paris.fr • Ⓜ Denfert-Rochereau

For a surreal, somewhat chilling experience, head down into the **catacombs**. Abandoned quarries stacked with millions of bones, which were cleared from overstocked charnel houses and cemeteries between 1785 and 1871, the catacombs are said to hold the remains of around six million Parisians. Lining the gloomy passageways, long thigh bones are stacked end-on, forming a wall to keep in the smaller bones and shards, which can just be seen in dusty, higgledy-piggledy heaps behind. These high femoral walls are further inset with gaping, hollow-eyed skulls and plaques carrying macabre quotations. It's undeniably fascinating, but note that there are a good couple of kilometres to walk – it's 500m through dark, damp, narrow passageways before you even get to the ossuary – and it can quickly become claustrophobic.

**1**

## Fondation Cartier pour l'Art Contemporain

261 bd Raspail, 14ᵉ • Tues 11am–10pm, Wed–Sun 11am–8pm • €10.50 • ☎ 01 42 18 56 50, ⓦ fondation.cartier.com • Ⓜ Raspail

Rue Schoelcher and boulevard Raspail, on the east side of Montparnasse cemetery, have some interesting examples of twentieth-century architecture, from Art Nouveau to the modern glass-and-steel façade of the **Fondation Cartier pour l'Art Contemporain**. Built in 1994 by Jean Nouvel, this presents contemporary installations, videos and multimedia in high-quality temporary exhibitions.

## Observatoire de Paris

Av de l'Observatoire, 14ᵉ • ⓦ obspm.fr • Ⓜ Denfert-Rochereau/RER Port Royal

The classical **Observatoire de Paris** sat on France's zero meridian line from the 1660s, when it was built, until 1914, when France agreed to recognize the Greenwich Meridian as the standard. A couple of commemorative bronze medallions are set in the pavement on either side of the front gate; similar discs run through the city, marking the old meridian, now named the **Arago line**.

## The 15ᵉ arrondissement

Though it's the largest and most populous of them all, the **15ᵉ arrondissement** falls off the agenda for most visitors as it lacks a single important building or monument. It does have a pleasant villagey heart, however, in the **rue du Commerce**, and an appealing offbeat riverside walk on the narrow midstream island, the **Allée des Cygnes**, which you can reach in a short stroll south of the Eiffel Tower, via the Pont de Bir-Hakeim. The chief landmarks of the 15ᵉ, however, are its **parks**.

### Parc André-Citroën

2 rue Cauchy, 15ᵉ • **Park** Daily 8am/9am–dusk • **Balloon** Fine days only: 9am to 30min before the park closes • €12 • ☎ 01 44 26 20 00, ⓦ ballondeparis.com • RER Javel/Boulevard Victor

In the southwest corner of the 15ᵉ lies the hyper-designed, contemporary **Parc André-Citroën**, built on the old Citroën motor works site. Its best features are the glasshouses, the dancing fountains – which bolder park-goers run through on hot days – the themed serial gardens and the tethered hot-air **balloon**, which offers spectacular views.

### Parc Georges-Brassens and around

Rue des Morillons, 15ᵉ • Daily dawn to dusk • Ⓜ Convention/Porte-de-Vanves

**Parc Georges-Brassens**, in the southeast corner of the 15ᵉ, is a delight, with a garden of scented herbs and shrubs (best in late spring), a climbing wall, puppets and merry-go-rounds for kids, a stream lined with pine and birch trees, a tiny vineyard and a scented garden. To the west, in a secluded, semi-wild garden off rue Dantzig, stands an unusual polygonal studio space known as **La Ruche**. Home to Fernand Léger, Modigliani, Chagall, Soutine and many other artists at the start of the twentieth century, it's still used as studios. A **book market** is held every Saturday and Sunday morning in the sheds of the old horse market between the park and rue Brancion.

## The 13ᵉ arrondissement

The 13ᵉ is one of the most disparate areas of the city. **Place d'Italie**, with the ornate *mairie* and Kenzo Tange's huge **Grand Écran Italie** building, is the hub, with each of the major roads radiating out into very different *quartiers*. To the north, the genteel neighbourhood around the ancient **Gobelins** tapestry works has more in common with the adjacent Quartier Latin. Between boulevard Auguste-Blanqui and rue Bobillot, meanwhile, is the lively hilltop quarter of the **Butte-aux-Cailles**. If you're looking for unpretentious, youthful and vaguely lefty restaurants and nightlife, this area is worth the short métro ride from the centre.

1

Over to the east, in the middle of a swathe of high-rise social housing, is the **Chinese quarter** of Paris. Avenues de Choisy and d'Ivry are full of Vietnamese, Chinese, Thai, Cambodian and Laotian restaurants and food shops, as is **Les Olympiades**, a strange semi-derelict pedestrian area seemingly suspended between giant tower blocks. Along the riverside from the Gare d'Austerlitz down to the *boulevard périphérique* the old quays, mills and warehouses form an intriguing *quartier* called **Paris Rive Gauche**, centred on the flagship **Bibliothèque Nationale**. Between the **Passerelle Simone de Beauvoir** – a modern double-ribbon footbridge – and the pont de Bercy, a clutch of tethered **barges** have repurposed themselves as nightlife venues or, in the case of **Piscine Josephine Baker** (ⓦwww.piscine-baker.fr), as a swimming pool.

## Bibliothèque Nationale de France

Quai François-Mauriac, 13ᵉ • **Exhibitions** Tues–Sat 10am–7pm, Sun 1–7pm • €9 • **Public reading rooms** Tues–Sat 10am–8pm, Sun 1–7pm • €5 for a day pass; bring ID • ☏ 01 53 79 59 59, ⓦbnf.fr • Ⓜ Quai de la Gare/Bibliothèque-François Mitterrand

The impressive **Bibliothèque Nationale de France** has four enormous towers – L-shaped, and intended to look like open books – framing a sunken pine copse. Jaw-dropping as it is, architect Dominique Perrault's design attracted widespread derision after shutters had to be added to the towers to protect the books and manuscripts from sunlight. It's worth wandering around inside, and to pop into one of the occasional small-scale exhibitions; the garden level is reserved for accredited researchers only.

## Les Frigos

19 rue des Frigos, 13ᵉ • Open to the public during events only • ⓦ les-frigos.com • Ⓜ Quai de la Gare/Bibliothèque François Mitterrand

On the south side of rue de Tolbiac, the giant, decaying cold-storage warehouse of **Les Frigos** has been occupied by artists and musicians since the 1980s, when it was an infamous squat. It's now an officially sanctioned home to around two hundred artists' workshops, which hold open-door exhibitions in the spring; a couple of places also host individual shows throughout the year.

## Les Docks/Cité de la Mode et du Design

34 quai d'Austerlitz, 13ᵉ • Daily 10am–midnight • ☏ 01 76 77 25 30, ⓦ citemodedesign.fr • Ⓜ Gare d'Austerlitz/Quai de la Gare

Sitting on the quai d'Austerlitz upstream of the Pont de Bercy, a set of concrete warehouses have been rebuilt as **Les Docks/Cité de la Mode et du Design**, whose startling design of twisting, lime-green tubes, by Dominique Jakob and Brendan MacFarlane, is supposed to recall the sinuous shape of the river.

Hosting regular temporary exhibitions, the complex houses a fashion school – the **Institut Français de la Mode** (ⓦifm-paris.com) – and a number of places to eat, while a handful of bars and **clubs** draw the nightlife crowd.

# The Beaux Quartiers

Commonly referred to as the **Beaux Quartiers**, Paris's well-manicured western arrondissements, the 16ᵉ and 17ᵉ, are mainly residential and have few specific sights, the chief exceptions being the **Musée Marmottan**, with its collection of late Monets, and Frank Gehry's extraordinary building, the **Fondation Louis Vuitton** contemporary art centre, set in the **Bois de Boulogne**. Further west still bristle the gleaming skyscrapers of the purpose-built commercial district of **La Défense**, dominated by the enormous **Grande Arche**.

# Musée Marmottan

2 rue Louis-Boilly, 16ᵉ • Tues–Sun 10am–6pm, Thurs 10am–9pm • €12 • ☏ 01 44 96 50 33, ⓦ marmottan.fr • Ⓜ Muette

**1**

The **Musée Marmottan** showcases Impressionist works, the highlight of which is a dazzling collection of canvases from Monet's last years at Giverny, including several *Nymphéas* (Water Lilies). The collection also features some of his contemporaries – Manet, Renoir and Berthe Morisot.

## Bois de Boulogne

Ⓜ Porte-Maillot/Porte Dauphine • **Parc de Bagatelle** Daily: March & Oct 9.30am–6.30pm; April–Sept 9.30am–8pm; Nov–Feb 9.30am–5pm • Free, admission charged for special events • Ⓜ Porte Maillot, then bus #244, which takes you to the entrance on allée de Longchamp; there's also an entrance on rte de Sèvres in Neuilly

The **Bois de Boulogne** is an area of extensive parkland running down the west side of the 16ᵉ. The "bois" of the name is somewhat deceptive, though it does contain some remnants of the once great Forêt de Rouvray. Once the playground of the wealthy, it also established a reputation as the site of the sex trade and its associated crime. The same is true today and you should avoid it at night. By day, however, the park is an extremely pleasant spot for a stroll. Especially appealing is the **Parc de Bagatelle**, with its lovely rose garden and its beautiful displays of tulips, hyacinths and daffodils in the first half of April, irises in May, and water lilies and roses at the end of June.

### Jardin d'Acclimatation

Bois de Boulogne, by Porte des Sablons, 16ᵉ • Mon–Fri 10am–7pm, Sat & Sun 10am–8pm • €5; rides from €2.90 • Ⓦ jardindacclimatation.fr • Ⓜ Les Sablons/Porte-Maillot; the best way to get there is via the "petit train" from rue de la Porte des Sablons to Porte Maillot, near Ⓜ Porte Maillot (every 15min: Mon, Tues, Thurs & Fri noon–6pm, Wed, Sat & Sun and during hols from 10am)

The highlight of the Bois de Boulogne for children is the **Jardin d'Acclimatation**, a cross between a funfair, zoo and amusement park that dates back to 1860. Traditional temptations include bumper cars, merry-go-rounds, a mini canal ride, pony and camel rides, adventure playgrounds and a paddling pool, while newer attractions include roller coasters and ziplines.

## Fondation Louis Vuitton

8 av du Mahatma-Gandhi, Bois de Boulogne, 16ᵉ • Mon, Wed & Thurs 11am–8pm, Fri 11am–9pm, Sat & Sun 9am–9pm • €16, under-18s €5 (ticket includes entry to the adjoining Jardin d'Acclimatation) • ☎ 01 40 69 96 00, Ⓦ fondationlouisvuitton.fr • Ⓜ Les Sablons; rather than walk from the métro (10–15min) you could take the shuttle minibus (every 20min during museum opening hours; 5–10min; €2) from av de Friedland, just off place Charles-de-Gaulle (aka place de l'Étoile)

Rising amid the trees and greenery of the Bois de Boulogne is the dramatic, Frank Gehry-designed contemporary art centre, the **Fondation Louis Vuitton**, opened in 2014. It houses the collection of Bernard Arnault, head of the luxury goods empire LVMH. The huge, abstract structure, dubbed the "cloud of glass", consists of twelve glass "sails" and sits surrounded by a moat of water. Evoking a ship buffeted by the wind (or possibly a giant insect), the sails jut out at angles, occasionally revealing the dazzling-white inner walls.

Inside, escalators take you down to the moat level (or "grotto"), with its striking Olafur Eliasson installation of coloured glass, mirror and sound, while stairways spiral up to roof terraces revealing unexpected vistas of the Eiffel Tower and La Défense. The galleries display the fondation's **permanent collection**, including works by Rothko, Jeff Koons, Takashi Murakami and Jean-Michel Basquiat, and stage high-calibre temporary exhibitions of modern art.

## La Défense

An impressive complex of gleaming skyscrapers, **La Défense** is Paris's prestige business district and a monument to late twentieth-century capitalism. Its most popular attraction is the huge **Grande Arche** (Ⓜ RER Grande-Arche-de-la-Défense), an astounding 112m-high hollow cube clad in white marble, standing 6km out from the Arc de Triomphe at the far end of the Voie Triomphale. There are excellent **views** from the steps that lead up to the base of the arch; you can also take the glass elevator to the **roof** for more superb vistas.

# Montmartre and around

Perched on Paris's highest hill, towards the northern edge of the city, **Montmartre** was famously the home and playground of artists such as Renoir, Degas, Picasso and Toulouse-Lautrec. The crown of the Butte Montmartre, around place du Tertre, is a touristy scrum, but the cobbled streets around **Abbesses** métro preserve an attractively festive, village-like atmosphere with their tall, shuttered buildings and steep staircases – this *quartier* becomes more gentrified with each passing year. Edgier is **Pigalle**, the brassy sprawl at the southern foot of the Butte, where in the once gritty area now rebranded as **SoPi**, or "South of Pigalle", girly bars and seedy dives sit side by side with – or give way to – indie shops and boutique hotels. The **Goutte d'Or**, to the east, meanwhile, remains thoroughly multi-ethnic. Out at the northern city limits, the mammoth **St-Ouen market** hawks everything from extravagant antiques to the cheapest flea-market hand-me-downs.

## The Butte Montmartre

Despite being one of the city's chief tourist attractions, much of the **Butte Montmartre** manages to retain the peaceful air of its rural origins. The most popular access route is via the rue de Steinkerque and the steps below the Sacré-Coeur (the funicular railway from place Suzanne-Valadon is covered by normal métro tickets). For a quieter approach, wind your way up via **place des Abbesses**, the hub of a lively neighbourhood full of clothes shops, buzzing wine bars and convivial restaurants, or the winding rue Lepic.

One quiet and attractive way to get from place des Abbesses to the top of the Butte is to climb up rue de la Vieuville and the rue Drevet stairs to the minuscule **place du Calvaire**, a route with a lovely view back over the city; you could also head up rue Tholozé, turning right below the **Moulin de la Galette** – the last survivor of Montmartre's forty-odd windmills, immortalized by Renoir – into rue des Norvins. Artistic associations abound hereabouts: Zola, Berlioz, Turgenev, Seurat, Degas and Van Gogh lived in the area, while Picasso, Braque and Gris invented Cubism in an old piano factory in tiny place Émile-Goudeau.

### Musée de Montmartre

12 rue Cortot, 18ᵉ • Daily April–Sept 10am–7pm; Oct–March 10am–6pm • €9.50, occasionally more during temporary exhibitions; gardens only €4 • ☎ 01 49 25 89 39, ⓦ museedemontmartre.fr • Ⓜ Lamarck Caulaincourt

The intriguing **Musée de Montmartre**, occupying two fine old houses on one of Montmartre's loveliest streets, recaptures something of the feel of the quarter's bohemian days, with its old posters, paintings and photos and period rooms. One of the houses, the Maison du Bel Air, was rented at various times by Renoir, Dufy, Suzanne Valadon and her son Maurice Utrillo, and Valadon's spacious, light-filled studio-apartment has been convincingly re-created. The gardens (where you'll find a café) offer views over the terraces of the tiny **Montmartre vineyard** – which produces some 450 bottles a year – on the north side of the Butte. The historic cabaret *Au Lapin Agile* is nearby.

### Place du Tertre

The **place du Tertre**, the core of old Montmartre, is today best avoided. It's been sucked dry of all interest, clotted with tour groups, overpriced restaurants, tacky souvenir stalls and jaded artists knocking out garish paintings. Between place du Tertre and the Sacré-Coeur, the old church of **St-Pierre de Montmartre** (ⓦsaintpierredemontmartre.net) is all that remains of the Benedictine abbey that occupied the Butte Montmartre from the twelfth century on.

## Sacré-Coeur

Parvis du Sacré-Coeur, 18e · **Church** Daily 6am–10.30pm · Free · **Dome** Daily: May–Sept 8.30am–8pm; Oct–April 9am–5pm · €6 · ⓦ sacre-coeur-montmartre.com · ⓜ Abbesses/Anvers

Crowning the Butte is the **Sacré-Coeur** with its iconic ice-cream-scoop dome. Construction of this French–Byzantine confection was started in the 1870s on the

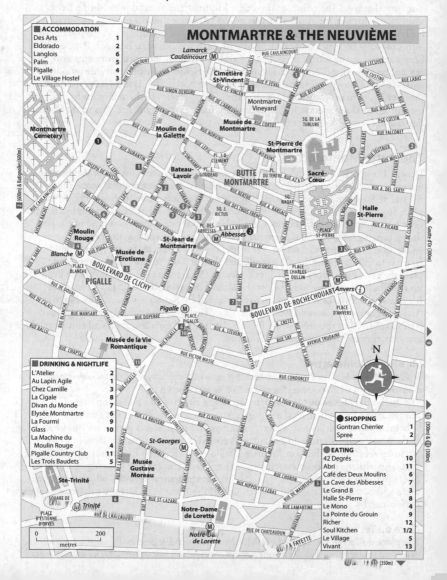

initiative of the Catholic Church to atone for the "crimes" of the Commune. **Square Willette**, at the foot of the monumental staircase, is named after the local artist who turned out on inauguration day to shout "Long live the devil!". Today the staircase acts as seating for visitors enjoying the views over Paris, munching on picnics and wielding selfie sticks; the crowds, and the guitar-strumming street entertainers, only increase as night falls. You also get stunning **views** from the top of the dome (a steep, claustrophobic climb of three hundred steps), which takes you almost as high as the Eiffel Tower.

## Montmartre cemetery

Entrance on av Rachel under the bridge section of rue Caulaincourt, 18ᵉ • Mid-March to Nov 5 Mon–Fri 8am–6pm, Sat 8.30am–6pm, Sun 9am–6pm; Nov 6 to mid-March closes 5.30pm • Free • ⓜ Blanche/Place-de-Clichy

West of the Butte lies the **Montmartre cemetery**. It's a melancholy place, tucked down below street level in the hollow of an old quarry, its steep tomb-dotted hills creating a sombre ravine of the dead. Consult the free map at the entrance to find the graves of Nijinsky, Stendhal, Berlioz, Degas and Truffaut, among others, as well as La Goulue, the *Moulin Rouge* dancer immortalized by Toulouse-Lautrec.

## St-Ouen flea market

Mon, Sat & Sun; different markets keep slightly different hours, but as a rule Mon 11am–5pm, Sat & Sun 10am–5.30pm • ⓦ marcheauxpuces-saintouen.com • ⓜ Porte de Clignancourt/Garibaldi

**Puces de St-Ouen** claims to be the largest flea market in the world, though nowadays it's predominantly a proper – and expensive – antiques market (mainly furniture, but including old café-bar counters, traffic lights, jukeboxes and the like), with many quirky treasures to be found. Of the fourteen or so individual markets, you could concentrate on Marché **Dauphine**, good for vintage movie posters, chanson and jazz records, comics and books, and Marché **Vernaison** for curios and bric-a-brac.

## Pigalle

From place Clichy in the west to Barbès-Rochechouart in the east, the hill of Montmartre is underlined by the sleazy **boulevards de Clichy and Rochechouart**. In the middle, between place Blanche and place **Pigalle**, sex shows, sex shops, girly bars and streetwalkers (both male and female) vie for custom. Toulouse-Lautrec's inspiration, the **Moulin Rouge**, survives here, albeit as a shadow of its former self, on the corner of place Blanche. A few steps south of Pigalle, the atmosphere shifts as you enter so-called SoPi, or "South of Pigalle"; it still has its seedy elements, but bohemian shops and bars have moved in, especially in the streets around **rue des Martyrs**, known for its upmarket food and flower shops.

## Goutte d'Or

Along the north side of the grimy boulevard de la Chapelle, between boulevard Barbès and the Gare du Nord rail lines, stretches the *quartier* of the **Goutte d'Or** ("Drop of Gold"), a name that derives from the medieval vineyard that once occupied this site. After World War I, and the arrival of large numbers of North Africans, the area gradually became an immigrant ghetto. Today, while the *quartier* remains poor, it is a vibrant place, home to a host of mini-communities, predominantly West African and Congolese, along with North African, South Asian, Haitian, Kurdish and other ethnicities. On rue Dejean, a few steps east of métro Château-Rouge, the **Marché Dejean** (closed Sun afternoon and Mon; roughly 9am–2pm) sells African groceries and has a couple of good, cheap eating places.

# 1 La Villette and around

The **Bassin de la Villette** and the **canals** at the northeastern gate of the city were for generations the centre of a densely populated working-class district, whose main source of employment were the La Villette abattoirs and meat market. These have long gone, replaced by the huge complex of La Villette, a postmodern park of science, art and music.

The Villette complex stands at the junction of the **Ourcq** and **St-Denis canals**. The first was built by Napoleon to bring fresh water into the city; the second is an extension of the Canal St-Martin built as a short cut to the great western loop of the Seine around Paris. The canals have undergone extensive renovation, and derelict sections of the *quais* have been made more appealing to cyclists, rollerbladers and pedestrians. A major arts centre, **Le 104**, has also helped to regenerate the area.

## Canal St-Martin

The **Canal St-Martin** runs underground at Bastille emerging after 2.5km near the **place de la République**, and continuing north up to the **place de la Bataille de Stalingrad**. The canal still has a slightly industrial feel, especially along its upper stretch. The lower part is more attractive, with plane trees, cobbled *quais* and elegant, high-arched footbridges, as well as lively bars and stylish boutiques. The area is particularly lively on Sunday afternoons, when the *quais* are closed to traffic, and pedestrians and cyclists take over the streets; on sunny days a young crowd hangs out along the canal's edge, nursing beers or strumming guitars.

### La Rotonde de la Villette

6–8 place de la Bataille de Stalingrad, 19e • ☎ 01 80 48 33 40, ⓦ larotonde.com • Ⓜ Stalingrad/Jaurès

On place de la Bataille de Stalingrad, where the Canal St Martin disappears underground, stands the beautifully restored Palladian-style **Rotonde de la Villette**, a former tollhouse, built by Ledoux in 1788. Cleaned and restored, the *rotonde* is used for occasional exhibitions and has a restaurant with a popular outdoor terrace. The outside tables on the square are a pleasant spot for a day-time or evening drink. The area has a dodgy reputation at night, however, as it's a known haunt of drug dealers.

### Bassin de la Villette

Ⓜ Stalingrad/Laumière/Riquet

Beyond the Rotonde de la Villette extends the **Bassin de la Villette** dock, once France's premier port. It's been recobbled and the dockside buildings have been converted into brasseries and a multiplex cinema (the MK2), which has screens on both banks, linked by a boat shuttle. In August, as part of the Paris Plages scheme (see page 143), there are canoes and pedaloes for rent. At rue de Crimée a unique hydraulic bridge marks the end of the dock and the beginning of the Canal de l'Ourcq. If you keep to the south bank on quai de la Marne, you can cross directly into the **Parc de la Villette**.

## Parc de la Villette

Between avs Corentin-Cariou and Jean-Jaurès, 19e • Information office daily 9.30am–6.30pm • ☎ 01 40 03 75 75, ⓦ villette.com • Ⓜ Porte-de-la-Villette/Porte-de-Pantin

The futuristic **Parc de la Villette**, a stimulating music, art and science complex, is so large in scope and size, it can feel a little overwhelming at first; pick up information at the office by the southern entrance and orientate yourself before you start. The park's main visitor attractions are the **Cité des Sciences et de l'Industrie** and the **Philharmonie de Paris**, comprising a new concert hall and the old Cité de la Musique with its superb

**museum of music**. The park also has twelve themed **gardens**, some aimed at children, including the Garden of Mirrors, of Shadows and of Dunes.

## Cité des Sciences et de l'Industrie

Parc de la Villette, 30 av Corentin-Cariou, 19ᵉ • **Cité des Sciences et de l'Industrie** • Tues–Sat 10am–6pm, Sun 10am–7pm • €12 • **Cité des Enfants** Tues–Sun 90min sessions (check online for times) • €12, €9 for under-25s; best to book in advance online • ☎ 01 40 05 80 00, ⓦ cite-sciences.fr • ⓜ Porte-de-la-Villette

The Parc de la Villette's dominant building is the **Cité des Sciences et de l'Industrie**, an enormous, glass-walled, high-tech science museum, four times the size of the Pompidou Centre, built into the concrete hulk of an abandoned abattoir. The main exhibition, called Explora, features temporary exhibits and covers subjects such as sound, aeronautics, energy, light, genes, maths, matter, automobiles and the universe, using interactive computers, videos, holograms, multi-media displays and games. You can have your head spun further in the **planetarium**.

The Cité des Sciences has a special section for children called the **Cité des Enfants**, with areas for 2- to 7-year-olds and 5- to 12-year-olds (all must be accompanied by an adult). It's hugely engaging; children can play about with water, construct buildings on a miniature construction site, manipulate robots and race their own shadows.

## Philharmonie de Paris

221 av Jean-Jaurès, 19ᵉ • ⓦ philharmoniedeparis.fr • **Musée de la Musique** Tues–Fri noon–6pm, Sat & Sun 10am–6pm • €8, under-26s free • ⓜ Porte-de-Pantin

Designed by Jean Nouvel, the **Philharmonie de Paris** concert hall opened in 2015, adding to La Villette's collection of futuristic architecture. It's a huge, angular, metal-clad structure, with a rather more relaxing interior of cream and ochre colours and rounded balconies. With its state-of the-art acoustics and modular seating and stage, it makes a wonderful venue for grand-scale symphonic concerts. Concerts are also held at the smaller hall in the nearby Cité de la Musique, **Philharmonie 2**. Here you'll also find the excellent **Musée de la Musique**, which presents the history of music from the end of the Renaissance to the present day, both visually – through a fabulous collection of instruments – and aurally, with headsets and interactive displays.

## Le Centquatre/Le 104

5 rue Curial, 19ᵉ • Tues–Sun 11am–7pm • ☎ 01 53 35 50 00, ⓦ 104.fr • ⓜ Riquet

Located in a former grand nineteenth-century funeral parlour, **Le 104** is a huge arts centre, with an impressive glass-roofed central hall (*nef curial*) and numerous artists' studios. It hosts exhibitions and installations, dance and theatre performances, with an emphasis on the experimental and cutting edge. The complex also houses a good bookshop, charity and fair-trade shops, a café and restaurant.

# The eastern districts

Traditionally working class, with a history of radical and revolutionary activity, the gritty **eastern districts** of Paris, particularly the old villages of **Belleville** and **Ménilmontant**, are nowadays among the most diverse and vibrant parts of the city, home to sizeable ethnic populations, as well as students and artists, attracted by the low rents. The main visitor attraction in the area is the **Père-Lachaise cemetery**, final resting place of many celebrated artists and writers. Visiting the modern **Parc de Belleville** will reveal the area's other main asset – wonderful views of the city below. Another park well worth seeing is the fairy-tale-like **Parc des Buttes-Chaumont**.

**1**

# Parc des Buttes-Chaumont

Ⓜ Buttes-Chaumont/Botzaris

At the northern end of the Belleville heights, a short walk from La Villette, the **parc des Buttes-Chaumont** was constructed by Haussmann in the 1860s to camouflage what until then had been a desolate warren of disused quarries and miserable shacks. Out of this rather unlikely setting a wonderfully romantic park was created – there's a grotto with a cascade and artificial stalactites, and a picturesque lake from which a huge rock rises up topped with a delicate Corinthian temple.

# Belleville and Ménilmontant

The route from Buttes-Chaumont to Père-Lachaise will take you through the one-time villages of **Belleville** and **Ménilmontant**. Absorbed into Paris in the 1860s and subsequently built up with high-rise blocks to house migrants from rural districts and the former colonies, this area might not be exactly "belle", but it's certainly vibrant and happening. The main street, rue de Belleville, abounds with Vietnamese, Thai and Chinese shops and restaurants, and numerous artists live and work in the area; the best time to view their work is during the **Journées portes ouvertes des ateliers d'artistes de Belleville** at the end of May (Ⓦateliers-artistes-belleville.fr).

You get fantastic views down onto the city centre from the higher reaches of Belleville and Ménilmontant: the best place to watch the sun set is the **Parc de Belleville** (ⓂCouronnes/Pyrénées), which descends in a series of terraces and waterfalls from rue Piat. And from **rue de Ménilmontant**, by rues de l'Ermitage and Boyer, you can look straight down to the Pompidou Centre. Rue de Ménilmontant's extension, **rue Oberkampf**, and parallel rue Jean-Pierre Timbaud are the hub of the city's nightlife, where you can hear anything from live rock to gypsy jazz.

## Père-Lachaise cemetery

Main entrance on bd de Ménilmontant, 20ᵉ • Mid-March to Oct Mon–Fri 8am–6pm, Sat 8.30am–6pm, Sun 9am–6pm; Nov to mid-March closes 5.30pm • Free • Ⓦ pere-lachaise.com • Ⓜ Gambetta/Père-Lachaise/Alexandre-Dumas/Philippe-Auguste

**Père-Lachaise cemetery**, final resting place of numerous notables, is an atmospheric, eerily beautiful haven, with little cobbled footpaths, terraced slopes and magnificent old trees that spread their branches over the tombs as though shading them from the outside world. The cemetery was opened in 1804, after an urgent stop had been put to further burials in the overflowing city cemeteries and churchyards. The civil authorities had Molière, La Fontaine, Abelard and Héloïse reburied here, and to be interred in Père-Lachaise quickly acquired cachet. A free **map** is available at all the entrances or you can buy a more detailed one from the shops on boulevard de Ménilmontant. Among the most visited graves is that of **Chopin** (Division 11), often attended by Poles bearing red-and-white wreaths and flowers. Fans also flock to the grave of **Jim Morrison** (Division 6), lead singer of The Doors, who died in Paris at the age of 27, and to **Oscar Wilde**'s tomb (Division 89), which is topped with a sculpture by Jacob Epstein of a mysterious Pharaonic winged messenger. You can also visit the graves of Edith Piaf, Marcel Proust, Corot, Balzac and Modigliani.

In Division 97 are the memorials to the victims of the Nazi **concentration camps** and executed **Resistance fighters**. Marking one of the bloodiest episodes in French history is the Mur des Fédérés (Division 76), the wall where the last troops of the Paris Commune were lined up and shot in the final days of the battle in 1871.

**ARRIVAL AND DEPARTURE**                                      **PARIS**

**BY PLANE**

The two main international airports are Roissy-Charles de Gaulle – usually referred to as Charles de Gaulle (CDG or Paris CDG) – 26km northeast of the city, and Orly 14km south. Both are well connected to the centre. The more distant Beauvais Airport, some 80km northwest of Paris, is used by some budget airlines, including Ryanair.

## ROISSY-CHARLES DE GAULLE AIRPORT

**Information** Detailed information at ⓦ parisaeroport.fr.

**Terminals** Charles de Gaulle has three main terminals: CDG 1, CDG 2 and CDG 3.

**TGV links** A TGV station links the airport (CDG 2) with a number of French cities and Brussels.

**RER into Paris** The quickest and easiest way to reach the centre of Paris is on the Roissy-Rail train link that runs on RER line B (daily 4.50am–11.50pm; every 10–20min; 25–50min; €11.40 one-way). The train stops at Gare du Nord, Châtelet-Les Halles, St-Michel and Denfert-Rochereau, all of which have métro stations for onward travel.

**Buses into Paris** Various bus companies provide services from the airport direct to city-centre locations, but they're slightly more expensive than Roissy-Rail and may take longer. The Roissybus connects all three terminals with the Opéra Garnier (corner of rues Auber and Scribe in the 9e; ⓦ Opéra/RER Auber; daily 6am–12.30am; every 15–20min; 1hr; €12.50). Le Bus Direct buses (daily; every 30min; €18 one-way, €31 return; ⓦ lebusdirect.com) run from CDG1 and 2; the green-coded line 2 runs to Av de Suffren, near the Eiffel Tower, stopping near the Champs-Élysées and at the Trocadéro on the way (5.45am–11pm; 1hr 10min to the Eiffel Tower), while the orange-coded line 4 stops at Gare de Lyon before terminating near Gare Montparnasse (6am–10.30pm; 1hr 15min to Montparnasse).

**Shuttles into Paris** The on-demand Paris Blue door-to-door minibus service costs from €50 for two people, with no extra charge for luggage; book at least 24 hours in advance (ⓦ paris-blue-airport-shuttle.fr).

**Taxis** Taxis into central Paris (50min–1hr) cost around €50–70 on the meter, more at night, plus a small luggage supplement (€1/item).

## ORLY AIRPORT

**Information** Detailed information at ⓦ parisaeroport.fr.

**Terminals** Orly Sud (South; international flights) and Orly Ouest (West; domestic flights) are linked by shuttle bus but are easily walkable.

**RER into Paris** The easiest way into the centre is via Orlyval, a fast train shuttle link to the suburban RER station Antony, where you can pick up RER line B trains to the central RER/métro stations Denfert-Rochereau, Gare du Nord and Châtelet-Les Halles (daily 6am–11.35pm; every 4–7min; €12.10 one-way; ⓦ orlyval.com).

**Shuttles into Paris** The useful Orlybus shuttle takes you direct to RER line B station Denfert-Rochereau, on the Left Bank, with good onward métro connections (6am–12.30am; every 10–20min; around 30min; €8.70 one-way).

**Trams into Paris** Tram T7 runs to métro Villejuif-Louis-Aragon, on métro line 7 (daily 5.30am–12.30am; every 8–15min; 45min; €1.90).

**Taxis** Taxis take about 35min to reach the centre of Paris (around €45).

## BEAUVAIS AIRPORT

**Information** ⓦ aeroportbeauvais.com.

**Coaches into Paris** Coaches shuttle between the airport and Porte Maillot in the 17e arrondissement, where you can pick up métro line 1 to the centre (1hr 15min; €17 one-way, €15.90 if reserved online on the airport website). The coach leaves around 20min after the flight has arrived and 3hr before the flight departs on the way back. Tickets can be bought online, at Arrivals, or at the Pershing bus station, near the Porte Maillot terminal.

## BY TRAIN

Paris has six mainline train stations and a motorail station, Paris-Bercy. All have cafés, restaurants, *tabacs*, ATMs and bureaux de change and are connected with the métro system; most also offer free wi-fi. All but St-Lazare and Paris Bercy have left luggage (*consigne*) facilities.

**Gare du Nord** Eurostar (ⓦ eurostar.com), along with trains from Calais and other north European countries, terminates at the busy Gare du Nord, on rue Dunkerque, in the northeast of the city. As you come off the train, turn left for the métro and the RER, and right for the taxi rank (around €10–15 to central Paris). Though the station isn't dangerous you should keep your wits about you, and watch out for scammers offering to "help" with tickets or taxis.

**Gare de l'Est** Near the Gare du Nord, on place du 11-Novembre-1918, 10e, Gare de l'Est serves eastern France and central and eastern Europe.

**Gare St-Lazare** Serving the Normandy coast and Dieppe, St-Lazare is the most central, at place du Havre, 8e, close to the Madeleine and the Opéra-Garnier.

**Gare de Lyon** On the southeast edge of the Right Bank, at place Louis-Armand, 12e, Lyon is the terminus for trains from Italy and Switzerland and TGV lines from southeast France.

**Gare Montparnasse** South of the river on bd de Vaugirard, 15e; the terminus for Chartres, Brittany, the Atlantic coast and TGV lines from southwest France.

**Gare d'Austerlitz** Bd de l'Hôpital, 13e; serves the Loire valley and the Dordogne.

**Gare de Paris-Bercy** The motorail station is down the tracks from the Gare de Lyon on bd de Bercy, 12e.

## BY BUS

Almost all the buses coming into Paris – whether international or domestic – use the main *gare routière* at 28 av du Général-de-Gaulle, Bagnolet, at the eastern edge of the city; métro Gallieni (line 3) links it to the centre.

## BY CAR

If you're driving in yourself, don't try to go straight across the city to your destination. Use the ring road – the *boulevard*

1

## TICKETS AND PASSES

Useful for a short stay in the city, **carnets** of ten tickets can be bought from any station or *tabac* (€14.90, as opposed to €1.90 for one ticket). The RATP is divided into **five zones**, and the métro system itself more or less fits into zones 1 and 2. The same tickets are valid for the buses (including the night bus), métro and, within the city limits and immediate suburbs (zones 1 and 2), the RER express rail lines, which also extend far out into the Île de France. Only one ticket is ever needed on the métro system, and within zones 1 and 2 for any RER or bus journey, but you can't switch between buses or between bus and métro/RER on the same ticket. For RER journeys beyond zones 1 and 2 you must buy an RER ticket. In order to get to La Défense on the RER rather than on the métro, for example, you need to buy a RER ticket, as La Défense is in zone 3. Children under 4 travel free and from ages 4 to 10 at half-price. Don't buy from the touts who hang round the main stations and be sure to keep your ticket until the end of the journey as you'll be fined on the spot if you can't produce it.

### PASSES

The **Mobilis day pass** (from €7.50 for zones 1 and 2 to €17.80 for zones 1 to 5) offers unlimited access to the métro, buses and, depending on which zones you choose, the RER. If you arrive early in the week and stay more than three days, consider a **Navigo weekly pass** (Ⓦnavigo.fr). A weekly pass costs €22.80 for zones 1 and 2, and is valid for an unlimited number of journeys on all modes of transport from Monday morning to Sunday evening. You can only buy a ticket for the current week until Thursday; from Friday you can buy a ticket to begin the following Monday. Monthly passes are also available (€75.20 for zones 1 and 2). Factor in the initial one-off purchase of the Navigo swipe card itself (€5, unrefundable); you'll also need a passport photo. **Paris Visites**, passes that cover one, two, three or five consecutive days, either in the central zones or extending as far as the suburbs and the airports (€12–65.80), are not as good value as the Navigo and Mobilis passes, but they do give reductions on certain tourist attractions.

*périphérique* – to get around to the nearest *porte*: it's much quicker, except at rush hour, and far easier to navigate, albeit pretty terrifying. For information on car parks in Paris, see Ⓦparkingsdeparis.com.

## GETTING AROUND

While walking is undoubtedly the best way to discover Paris, the city's integrated public transport system of bus, métro and trains – the RATP (Régie Autonome des Transports Parisiens; Ⓦratp.fr) – is cheap, fast and meticulously signposted. The métro, combined with the RER (Réseau Express Régional) suburban express lines, is the simplest way to get around. Free métro and bus maps of varying sizes and detail are available at most stations, bus terminals and tourist offices: the largest and most useful is the *Grand Plan de Paris avec rues numéro 2*, which overlays the métro, RER and bus routes on a city map so you can see exactly how transport lines and streets match up. If you just want a pocket-sized métro/bus map ask for the *Petit Plan des lignes*. There are downloadable maps at Ⓦratp.fr.

interchanges can involve a lot of legwork, including many stairs.

**The network** In addition to free maps (see above), every station has a big plan of the network outside the entrance and several inside, as well as a map of the local area. Lines are colour-coded and designated by numbers for the métro and by letters for the RER, although they are signposted within the system with the names of the terminus stations: for example, travelling from Montparnasse to Gare du Nord on métro line 4, follow the sign "Direction Porte de Clignancourt"; from Gare d'Austerlitz to Maubert Mutualité on line 10 follow "Direction Boulogne–Pont de St-Cloud". For RER journeys beyond the city, make sure the station you want is illuminated on the platform display board.

### THE MÉTRO AND RER

**Hours** The métro and the RER run from 5.30am to around 1.15am (the métro runs to 2.15 on Fri and Sat, with fewer services on Sun).

**Stations** Stations are evenly spaced and you'll rarely find yourself more than 500m from one in the centre, though the

### BUSES

**City buses** The city's buses (generally Mon–Sat 7am–8.30pm with some continuing to 12.30am and around half of them operating on Sun too; a restricted night bus service, Noctilien, takes over 12.30–5.30am, running roughly hourly) are straightforward to use. Every bus stop displays the numbers

1

of the services that stop there, a map showing all the stops on the route, and some form of timetable; you need to hail the driver if you want to get on. You can buy a single ticket (€1.90 from the driver), or use a pre-purchased carnet ticket or pass; validate your ticket by inserting it into one of the machines on board and press the red button to request a stop. All buses are accessible for wheelchairs and prams. You can download a map of the most useful tourist routes from ⓦ ratp.fr.

## TAXIS

**Fares** Taxi charges are fairly reasonable: between €8 and €17 for a central daytime journey, considerably more if you

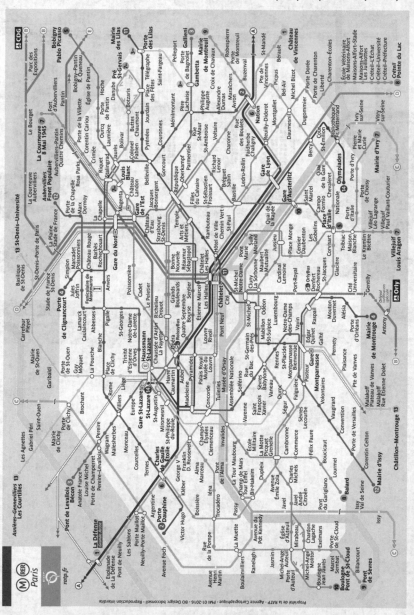

call one out. There's a minimum charge of €7, a pick-up charge of €2.60, and you'll pay €1 per item if you have more than one piece of (bulky) luggage. Taxis can take up to four passengers. A tip of ten percent will generally be expected.

**Taxi ranks** Waiting at a rank (*arrêt taxi*) is usually more effective than hailing a cab from the street. If the large green light on top of the vehicle is lit up the taxi is free; the red light means it's in use.

**Taxi firms** Booking a taxi will cost more than picking one up on the street; firms include Taxis G7 (☎01 41 27 66 99 for an English-speaking operator, ⬤g7.fr) and Alpha Taxis (☎01 45 85 85 85, ⬤www.alphataxis.fr).

**Uber** Despite angry protests from regular taxi drivers, use of the app-based taxi service Uber (⬤uber.com) has become very popular in Paris.

### VÉLIB' AND ELECTRONIC SCOOTERS

**Bikes** At the time of research, Paris's much-vaunted self-service bike scheme Vélib was in complete chaos, and thus impossible to recommend. Operated until 2018 under the Vélib' brand, it was then taken over as "Smoove" by the Smovengo group, whose promise to replace a third of the 20,000-strong bike fleet with up-to-the-minute electrically assisted e-bikes required them to dig up all the docking stations scattered throughout the city. That work remains drastically behind schedule, while software snarl-ups have caused local users to abandon the service, and prompted great political controversy. Watch this space!

### INFORMATION

**Tourist offices** At the city's tourist offices (⬤parisinfo. com) you can pick up maps and information, book accommodation and buy travel passes and the Paris

**Electronic scooters** Perhaps benefitting from the temporary demise of Vélib is the electronic scooter, which has gained immense popularity especially among young Parisians. The scheme is expanding at lightning speed but at the time of research there are six operators: Lime (⬤www.li.me/fr), Bird (⬤www.bird.co), Bolt (Txfy app), Wind (⬤www.wind.co/france), Voi (⬤www.voiscooters.com/fr) and Tier (⬤www.tier. app), all operating on a self-service basis via an app. This is a relatively new phenomenon and the Parisian authorities are still legislating rules of usage. In theory scooters should be allowed to circulate on pavements but in practise there have been a lot of incidents involving pedestrians as some scooters can go as fast as 25km/h. Therefore Paris road traffic agents can now fine you up to €135 for dangerous scooting. So it is highly recommended to use the cycle lanes. Some operators have a minimum age limit and others will require a valid driver's license.

### BATOBUS

One of the most enjoyable ways to get around Paris is on the Batobus (April–Aug every 10–25min 10am–9.30pm; Sept–March every 30–40min 10am–7pm; ⬤batobus. com), which stops at eight points along the Seine, including the Eiffel Tower and the Louvre. To do the entire trip in one go takes around 1hr 30min, but you can hop on and off as many times as you like – a day pass costs €17, two (consecutive) days €19; children are half-price.

Museum Pass. The main offices are in the Hôtel de Ville at 29 rue de Rivoli, 4ᵉ (Mon–Sat 10am–7pm; ⬤rendezvous. paris.fr; ⬤Hôtel de Ville), and at Gare du Nord (daily

---

## BOAT TRIPS

Most tourists are keen, rightly, to take a **boat trip** on the Seine. One good option is the Batobus (see above); otherwise **Bateaux-Mouches** is the best-known operator (daily every 20–45min: April–Sept daily 10am–10.30pm; Oct–March Mon–Fri 11am–9.20pm, Sat & Sun 10.15am–9.20pm; €14; ☎01 42 25 96 10, ⬤bateaux-mouches.fr). Leaving from the Embarcadère du Pont de l'Alma on the Right Bank in the 8ᵉ, boats take you past the major Seine-side sights, such as Notre-Dame and the Louvre, complete with commentary. Night-time cruises use dazzling lights to illuminate the streetscapes – much more fun for people on board than passing pedestrians. The pricey lunch and dinner trips are best avoided. Bateaux-Mouches has many **competitors**, all much of a muchness, including Bateaux Parisiens (⬤bateauxparisiens.com), Vedettes de Paris (⬤vedettesdeparis.fr) and Bateaux-Vedettes du Pont-Neuf (⬤vedettesdupontneuf.com).

Another option, which takes you past less-visited sights, is to take a **canal boat trip**. Canauxrama offers a number of narrated cruises on the St-Martin, Ourcq and St-Denis canals, along with the Seine and the River Marne (reservations essential; 9.45am & 2.30/2.45pm in summer, fewer at other times; €18; ☎01 42 39 15 00, ⬤canauxrama.com), while Paris Canal (☎01 42 40 29 00, ⬤pariscanal.com) offers catamaran tours of the Canal St-Martin between the Musée d'Orsay and the Parc de la Villette (Feb to mid-Nov; from Musée d'Orsay 9.45am & 2.25pm; from Parc de la Villette 10.30am & 2.30pm; 2hr 30min; €22).

**1**

8.30am–6.30pm). There's also a smaller information point in the Louvre (Mon & Wed–Sun 10am–8pm, Tues 11am–8pm).

**Reduced museum admissions** The permanent collections at all municipal museums are free year round, while the national museums (including the Louvre, Musée d'Orsay and Pompidou Centre) are free on the first Sun of the month and to under-18s. Elsewhere, the cut-off age for free admission varies between 18, 12 and 4. Reduced admission is usually available for 18- to 26-year-olds and for those over 60 or 65; you'll need to carry your passport or ID card around with you as proof of age. Some discounts are available for students with an ISIC Card (International Student Identity Card; ⓦ isic.org).

**Paris Museum Pass** If you're planning to visit many museums in a short time it might be worth buying the Paris Museum Pass (€48 two-day, €62 four-day, €74 six-day; ⓦ parismuseumpass.com). Available from the tourist

office, Fnac stores and participating museums, it's valid for more than thirty museums and monuments inside Paris, including the Louvre, Musée d'Orsay and the Pompidou (but not special exhibitions), and allows you to bypass ticket queues (though not the security checkpoints).

**Listings magazines** For detailed what's-on information, check Paris's weekly listings magazine *L'Officiel des Spectacles* (ⓦ offi.fr; €1), available from newsagents and kiosks. *Pariscope* (online only; ⓦ pariscope.fr) has details of concerts, dance performances, theatre and exhibitions, but no longer includes the cinema listings for which it was once famed. Look out too for the free weekly listings paper, *A nous Paris* (ⓦ anousparis.fr), which comes out on Mondays and is available from métro stations and online, and the English-language webzine *Paris Voice* (ⓦ parisvoice.com).

**Maps** For a comprehensive A–Z hard-copy map, your best bet is one of the pocket-sized "*L'indispensable*" series booklets, sold throughout the city.

## ACCOMMODATION

**Prices** Parisian hotels are among Europe's most expensive for what you get. Although it *is* possible to find a double room in a central location for around €70, these will usually be basic, with a sink (*lavabo*) in the room and a shared bathroom on the landing (*dans le palier*). As a rule, a double room in an old-fashioned two-star will cost between €90 and €150; for something with a bit more class you could easily spend as much as €200. Some bargains do exist, however, so it pays to shop around – we have listed many of the best-value options below. At the luxury end of the scale the sky's the limit, with prices above €400 not uncommon – though online and off-season deals can chop a dramatic amount off the official rack rates. The rates quoted in the following reviews are for the cheapest double room available on a weekend night in mid-June.

**Neighbourhoods** One of the best central areas for budget hotels is the 10ᵉ, especially around place de la République, and the 11ᵉ, especially along rue du Grand Prieuré. Quieter districts, further out, where you can get some good deals are the 13ᵉ and 14ᵉ, south of Montparnasse, and the 17ᵉ and 20ᵉ, on the western and eastern sides of the city respectively.

**Reservations** If you want to secure a good room it's worth booking a couple of months or more ahead, as even the nicer hotels often leave their pokiest rooms at the back for last-minute reservations, and the best places will sell out well in advance in all but the coldest months. If you find yourself stuck on arrival, the main tourist office can find you a room; this service is free of charge.

### THE ISLANDS

**De Lutèce** 65 rue St-Louis-en-l'Île, 4ᵉ ☎ 01 43 26 23 52, ⓦ hoteldelutece.com; ⓜ Pont-Marie; map p.82.

This narrow seventeenth-century townhouse has 23 tiny, pretty wood-beamed en-suites. All have been renovated in a contemporary style, and come with modern bathrooms. €243

### THE CHAMPS-ÉLYSÉES AND AROUND

**Le 123 Élysées** 123 rue du Faubourg-St-Honoré, 8ᵉ ☎ 01 53 89 01 23, ⓦ astotel.com; ⓜ St-Philippe-du-Roule; map p.70. Friendly, stylish hotel – one of the generally good *Astotel* chain – a 5min walk from the Champs-Élysées. Rooms are a good size with high ceilings, laminate floors and modern furnishings. Some have balconies. €245

**D'Albion** 15 rue de Penthièvre, 8ᵉ ☎ 01 42 65 84 15, ⓦ hotelalbion.net; ⓜ Miromesnil; map p.70. A small hotel in a nineteenth-century townhouse, set around a quiet courtyard garden. Just a 10min walk from the Champs-Élysées, it's not fancy, but it's clean, comfortable and excellent value for the area. Some rooms have a view over the garden. €135

**Lancaster** 7 rue de Berri, 8ᵉ ☎ 01 40 76 40 76, ⓦ hotel-lancaster.com; ⓜ George-V; map p.70. The rooms in this elegantly restored nineteenth-century townhouse retain original features and Louis XVI and Rococo antiques, with a touch of contemporary chic. A small interior garden and impeccable service make for a relaxing stay, and there's a swanky restaurant, too. €565

**De Sers** 41 av Pierre 1ᵉʳ de Serbie, 8ᵉ ☎ 01 53 23 75 75, ⓦ hoteldesers-paris.fr; ⓜ George-V; map p.70. This chic hotel, just off the Champs-Élysées, offers swish, sleek rooms with flashes of jewel colours. Some of the suites (from €1800) have panoramic terraces with views of the Eiffel Tower. Online deals can bring the rates right down. €470

## THE LOUVRE

**Crayon** 25 rue de Bouloi, 1er ☎01 42 36 54 19, ⓦhotelcrayon.com; ⓂLouvre-Rivoli; map p.70. Colourful, artist-owned hotel with a guesthouse feel. The funky rooms are all different, scattered with mismatched retro furniture. Check online for good deals. **€206**

★**Thérèse** 5–7 rue Thérèse, 1er ☎01 42 96 10 01, ⓦhoteltherese.com; ⓂPalais-Royal-Musée-du-Louvre; map p.70. Appealing, friendly boutique hotel on a quiet street within easy walking distance of the Louvre. Rooms are small and stylish, with luxury fabrics and cool furnishings; some overlook the leafy courtyard. Book early, as it's very popular, especially during the fashion shows. **€200**

## OPÉRA DISTRICT AND AROUND

**Chopin** 46 passage Jouffroy, 9e ☎01 47 70 58 10, ⓦhotelchopin-paris-opera.com; ⓂGrands-Boulevards; map p.70. Quiet, old-fashioned hotel in a period building at the end of a picturesque 1840s *passage*. The 36 rooms are clean, spruce and good value, though the cheaper ones are on the small side and a little dark. **€140**

★**Edgar** 31 rue d'Alexandrie, 2e ☎01 40 41 05 19, ⓦedgarparis.com; ⓂSentier; map p.70. Thirteen small rooms conceived by artists, stylists, film--makers and fashionistas and presented with wit and style – whether you want the soft greys of "Cocoon", the updated boudoir chic of "Ma Nuit" or the kooky kiddy kitsch of "Dream", you'll find a niche here. The street is quiet. **€205**

**Vivienne** 40 rue Vivienne, 2e ☎01 42 33 13 26, ⓦhotel-vivienne.com; ⓂGrands-Boulevards/Bourse; map p.70. A 10min walk from the Louvre, this family-run place has 44 clean, well-sized rooms with modern facilities; the cheapest are less impressive than the others, though OK for the price, with private showers and shared WC. En-suite rooms are £115. Good online deals available. **€90**

## BEAUBOURG AND AROUND

★**Du Cygne** 3–5 rue du Cygne, 1er ☎01 42 60 14 16, ⓦhotelducygne.fr; ⓂÉtienne-Marcel; map p.79. Friendly hotel in a four-storey seventeenth-century townhouse on a lively, pedestrianized Les Halles street. There's no lift, just a narrow staircase (staff will help with bags) – some of the twenty (small) rooms have beamed ceilings. Good online deals. **€125**

**Relais du Louvre** 19 rue des Prêtres St-Germain l'Auxerrois, 1er ☎01 40 41 96 42, ⓦrelaisdulouvre.com; ⓂPalais-Royal-Musée-du-Louvre; map p.79. The 21 rooms in this intimate hotel, on a quiet backstreet opposite the church of St-Germain l'Auxerrois, are rich fabrics, old prints and paintings. The relaxed atmosphere and charming service attract a repeat clientele. **€269**

★**Tiquetonne** 6 rue Tiquetonne, 2e ☎01 42 36 94 58, ⓦhoteltiquetonne.fr; ⓂÉtienne-Marcel; map p.79. On a pedestrianized street a block away from lively rue Montorgueil, this budget hotel in a 1920s building offers old-fashioned charm. Simple rooms are well maintained: some are quite spacious, with larger-than-average bathrooms, though walls are thin. It's worth spending €90 on an en-suite: other rooms have just a sink and bidet, with a shared shower on the landing. **€75**

## THE MARAIS

★**Bourg Tibourg** 19 rue du Bourg-Tibourg, 4e ☎01 42 78 47 39, ⓦbourgtibourg.com; ⓂHôtel-de-Ville; map p.82. Oriental meets medieval meets bordello, with a dash of Second Empire, at this stylishly designed little hotel. Rooms are small, but cosseted with rich velvets, silks and drapes; some have their own mini balconies. With well-chosen books and classic movies on offer, this is a hip little romantic hideaway. **€261**

**Caron de Beaumarchais** 12 rue Vieille-du-Temple, 4e ☎01 42 72 34 12, ⓦcarondebeaumarchais.com; ⓂHôtel-de-Ville; map p.82. Pretty hotel where all the furnishings – the original engravings and Louis XVI furniture, not to mention the piano in the foyer – evoke the refined tastes of high-society pre-Revolution Paris. Rooms overlooking the narrow courtyard are petite, while those on the street are more spacious, some with a small balcony, chandeliers and beams. **€185**

**Fauconnier** 11 rue du Fauconnier, 4e ☎01 42 74 23 45, ⓦmije.com; ⓂSt-Paul/Pont-Marie; map p.82. One of three hostels run by MIJE, all in the Marais. *Le Fauconnier* is in a superbly renovated seventeenth-century building with a courtyard. Dorms (single sex) sleep four to eight, and there are some single (€65) and en-suite doubles; breakfast included. Silence requested after 10pm. Dorms **€33.50**, doubles **€85**

**Le Fourcy** 6 rue de Fourcy, 4e ☎01 42 74 23 45, ⓦmije.com; ⓂSt-Paul; map p.82. Another good MIJE hostel, with the same rates as *Le Fauconnier*, including breakfast. Housed in a beautiful mansion, this has a small garden and an inexpensive restaurant. The same rules apply as at *Le Fauconnier*. Dorms **€33.50**, doubles **€85**

**Jeanne d'Arc** 3 rue de Jarente, 4e ☎01 48 87 62 11, ⓦhoteljeannedarc.com; ⓂSt-Paul; map p.82. This old Marais townhouse, just off place du Marché-Ste-Catherine, has small, elegant rooms, all different; some retain original features such as exposed brick walls. The triple at the top has views over the rooftops, and corner rooms have more light. **€159**

**Jules et Jim** 11 rue des Gravilliers, 3e ☎01 44 54 13 13, ⓦhoteljulesetjim.com; ⓂArts-et-Métiers; map p.82. Cool hotel with hip design features and quiet, swish rooms. There's a good bar opening onto the cobbled courtyard (it closes at 11pm, to avoid noise disturbing guests in courtyard rooms). **€240**

**Maubuisson** 12 rue des Barres, 4e ☎01 42 74 23 45, ⓦmije.com; ⓂPont Marie/Hôtel de Ville; map p.82. MIJE hostel in the same group as *Le Fauconnier* and *Le Fourcy*

1

in a magnificent medieval building on a quiet street. Shared use of the restaurant at Le Fourcy. Breakfast included. Dorms only. €33.50

★ De Nice 42bis rue de Rivoli, 4ᵉ ☎01 42 78 55 29, ⓦhoteldenice.com; ⓂHôtel de Ville; map p.82. A well-run, cosy little establishment, with old-world charm and lots of quirky style: the 23 colourful rooms have Indian-cotton bedspreads, carved wooden wardrobes, elaborate wallpaper and gilded mirrors. The rue de Rivoli is very busy, but double glazing helps to block out most of the traffic noise. €170

★ Du Petit Moulin 29–31 rue de Poitou, 3ᵉ ☎01 42 74 10 10, ⓦhoteldupetitmoulin.com; ⓂSt-Sébastien-Froissart/Filles-du-Calvaire; map p.82. Housed inside a former bakery, this luxurious Christian Lacroix-designed boutique hotel is infused with the designer's hallmark flamboyance. Rooms are a bold fusion of different styles, from elegant Baroque to Sixties kitsch. €270

St-Louis Marais 1 rue Charles-V, 4ᵉ ☎01 48 87 87 04, ⓦsaintlouismarais.com; ⓂSully-Morland; map p.82. Formerly part of the seventeenth-century Célestins Convent, this place retains some period feel, with stone walls, exposed beams and tiled floors. Some of the rooms are small, but the bathrooms are a good size and relatively luxurious. A major plus is the location, on a quiet road a short walk from the Marais action. Avoid at all costs the annexe rooms, which have little appeal. €175

## BASTILLE AND AROUND

★ Auberge Flora 44 bd Richard-Lenoir, 11ᵉ ☎01 47 00 52 77, ⓦaubergeflora.fr; ⓂBréguet-Sabin; map p.82. Cute boutique hotel with 21 rooms from singles to "gourmande" options and suites. The cheapest are tiny, but all are colourful and comfortable. Flora herself is also the chef at the restaurant below, which offers seasonal and tasty Mediterranean-influenced food. €121

★ De la Porte Dorée 273 av Daumesnil, 12ᵉ ☎01 43 07 56 97, ⓦhoteldelaportedoree.com; ⓂPorte-Dorée; map p.82. This welcoming, child-friendly hotel is not as central as some but it's close to the Bois de Vincennes, right next to the métro, and Bastille is just minutes away by métro or a pleasant 20min stroll along the Promenade Plantée. The contemporary en-suite rooms have traditional features including ceiling mouldings and fireplaces, and some antique furnishings. Regular online deals. €134

## QUARTIER LATIN

★ Esmeralda 4 rue St-Julien-le-Pauvre, 5ᵉ ☎01 43 54 19 20, ⓦhotel-esmeralda.fr; ⓂSt-Michel/Maubert-Mutualité; map p.92. Dozing in an ancient house on square Viviani, this rickety old hotel offers sixteen simple (and eccentrically decorated) en-suite rooms – a few with unrivalled views of Notre-Dame. There are plenty of worn corners and few mod cons but staff are friendly and the location is incomparable. €130

Familia Hôtel 11 rue des Écoles, 5ᵉ ☎01 43 54 55 27, ⓦfamiliahotel.com; ⓂCardinal-Lemoine/Maubert-Mutualité/Jussieu; map p.92. What this friendly, family-run hotel in the heart of the quartier lacks in luxury, it makes up for in charm – the small rooms may have beams or murals, views of Notre-Dame, or balconies. €134

★ Des Grandes Écoles 75 rue du Cardinal-Lemoine, 5ᵉ ☎01 43 26 79 23, ⓦhotel-grandes-ecoles.com; ⓂCardinal-Lemoine/Monge; map p.92. A cobbled private lane leads through to a large, peaceful garden – the feel of a country house, right in the heart of the Quartier Latin. Rooms are pretty in a chintzy way, with floral wallpaper and old-fashioned furnishings. €170

★ La Lanterne 12 rue de la Montagne Ste-Geneviève, 5ᵉ ☎01 53 19 88 39, ⓦhotel-la-lanterne.com; ⓂMaubert Mutualité; map p.92. Gorgeous boutique hotel in a classy location. The chic rooms are plush and welcoming; the real star, though, is the little spa – swimming pool, aromatherapy shower and steam room – hidden away in a vaulted stone cellar. Guests receive a smartphone for the length of their stay. €270

★ Marignan 13 rue du Sommerard, 5ᵉ ☎01 43 54 63 81, ⓦhotel-marignan.com; ⓂMaubert-Mutualité; map p.92. Great-value place, totally sympathetic to the needs of rucksack-toting foreigners, offering free laundry and ironing facilities plus a basic self-catering kitchen/diner. Rooms – some sleep up to five – are clean and comfortable; the cheapest have shared bathrooms. Simple, but one of the best value places in town – and breakfast is free. No elevator. €95

Port-Royal 8 bd Port-Royal, 5ᵉ ☎01 43 31 70 06, ⓦport-royal-hotel.fr; ⓂGobelins; map p.92. A good-value one-star that has been in the same family since the 1930s. The whole place, in a quiet area, is clean and comfy, but rooms do vary: some have shared facilities (€2.50/timed shower) while en-suite doubles (€97) are fairly large and attractive. €70

Résidence Henri IV 50 rue des Bernardins, 5ᵉ ☎01 44 41 31 81, ⓦresidencehenri4.com; ⓂMaubert-Mutualité; map p.92. Set back from busy rue des Écoles on a cul-de-sac, this hotel is discreet and elegant, with eight doubles and five larger suites with lounging areas. All are classically styled – some have original features such as fireplaces – and have small kitchenettes. €242

Select Hôtel 1 place de la Sorbonne, 5ᵉ ☎01 46 34 14 80, ⓦselecthotel.fr; ⓂCluny La Sorbonne; map p.92. This modern, 65-room four-star, right on the place, has a stylish feel, with exposed stone walls and contemporary furnishings. Standard rooms are comfortable, if tiny; larger rooms are available, some with views. €200

## ST-GERMAIN

De l'Abbaye 10 rue Cassette, 6ᵉ ☎01 45 44 38 11, ⓦhotelabbayeparis.com; ⓂSt-Sulpice; map p.96. An atmosphere of calm presides over this elegant four-star hotel. Rooms – all floral fabrics and brass fittings – are tasteful, but best of all is its courtyard garden and conservatory, where you can enjoy breakfast (often included in the rates, depending on season) or an *apéritif*. **€290**

**Du Danube** 58 rue Jacob, 6e 🅣01 42 60 34 70, 🅦hoteldanube.fr; 🅜St-Germain-des-Prés; map p.96. Tranquil, friendly hotel in the heart of St-Germain. The teeny standard rooms are fine, but the *supérieures* (€265) are the ones to go for, if you can: unusually spacious, each with a pair of handsome, tall windows. Book well in advance and look out for excellent deals. **€215**

★ **L'Hôtel** 13 rue des Beaux-Arts, 6e 🅣01 44 41 99 00, 🅦l-hotel.com; 🅜Mabillon/St-Germain-des-Prés; map p.96. Quirky boutique hotel with a dash of louche glamour and sumptuous rooms (the cheapest are tiny, however) accessed by a spiral staircase. There's a small steam room/pool, a good restaurant and cool bar. Oscar Wilde died here, "fighting a duel" with his wallpaper; he's honoured today in a themed room. **€351**

**Michelet-Odéon** 6 place de l'Odéon, 6e 🅣01 53 10 05 60, 🅦hotelmicheletodeon.com; 🅜Odéon; map p.96. A clean, comfortable and quiet choice – a bargain so close to the Jardin du Luxembourg. The best rooms face onto the *place*. A few triples, quads and apartments are available, making it a good deal for families. **€143**

★ **De Nesle** 7 rue de Nesle, 6e 🅣01 43 54 62 41, 🅦hoteldenesleparis.com; 🅜St-Michel; map p.96. Eccentric and sometimes chaotic hotel many of whose tiny rooms are decorated with cartoon historical murals that you'll either love or hate. The overgrown courtyard garden is a plus. Ideally, phone (it's best to have a little French) to reserve. **€150**

**Relais Saint-Sulpice** 3 rue Garancière, 6e 🅣01 46 33 99 00, 🅦relais-saint-sulpice.com; 🅜St-Sulpice/St-Germain-des-Prés; map p.96. Wonderfully located in a beautiful, aristocratic townhouse on a side street behind St-Sulpice's apse, this is a discreetly classy hotel – many rooms overlook the leafy patio or the church. The cosy lounge, with courtesy bar, is a nice place to relax. **€220**

★ **De Sèvres** 22 rue de l'Abbé Grégoire, 6e 🅣01 45 48 84 07, 🅦hoteldesevres.com; 🅜Rennes; map p.96. You get good value for this neighbourhood in this appealing contemporary hotel. The small rooms are comfortable and perfectly adequate, and service is great; extra touches incude a small spa and a little patio where you can drink a glass of wine or a coffee. **€155**

**Verneuil** 8 rue de Verneuil, 7e 🅣01 42 60 82 14, 🅦hotel-verneuil-saint-germain.com; 🅜St-Germain-des-Prés; map p.96. In a quiet street between St Germain, the Louvre and the Musée d'Orsay, this boutique hotel exudes understated style. The smallest doubles are tiny but cosy – many retain period features, including exposed beams. Guests are given use of a free smartphone throughout their stay. **€260**

### EIFFEL TOWER QUARTER

★ **Du Champ-de-Mars** 7 rue du Champ-de-Mars, 7e 🅣01 45 51 52 30, 🅦hotelduchampdemars.com; 🅜École-Militaire; map p.102. This good-value, quiet hotel in a handsome area just off rue Cler, has a comforting neighbourhood feel. Rooms are cosy, clean and colourful; a couple overlook pretty courtyards. **€165**

**Du Palais Bourbon** 49 rue de Bourgogne, 7e 🅣01 44 11 30 70, 🅦bourbon-paris-hotel.com; 🅜Varenne; p.102. This substantial old building in the hushed, posh district near the Musée Rodin, offers good doubles with plenty of old-fashioned charm. It's not luxurious, but has all the facilities you need in a good location. **€215**

### SOUTHERN PARIS

★ **3 Ducks Hostel** 6 place Etienne Pernet, 15e 🅣01 48 42 04 05, 🅦3ducks.fr; 🅜Commerce; map p.102. Lively, popular hostel in a historic building, offering four- to eight-bed en-suite dorms, both mixed and female-only. The terrace and streetside bar are good hangouts. Rates include breakfast and there's a kitchen. Dorms **€45**, doubles **€125**

**Oops** 50 av des Gobelins, 13e 🅣01 47 07 47 00, 🅦oops-paris.com; 🅜Gobelins; map p.92. This early "design hostel", opened in 2007, is decorated in the now almost obligatory hostel style of bright colours and funky patterns. They have two- and four-bed dorms, all en suite, plus en-suite doubles, and a guest kitchen. Cash only (although reservations must be made by card). Dorms **€32**, doubles **€102**

★ **Solar Hôtel** 22 rue Boulard, 14e 🅣01 43 21 08 20, 🅦solarhotel.fr; 🅜Denfert-Rochereau; map p.96. Budget hotel maintaining a determinedly ecological spirit, from its waste disposal to its cleaning products. Rooms are unfussy and comfortable, a little like an upmarket hostel, each with private bathroom. Rates include a simple organic breakfast, which you can eat in the small courtyard, and you also get access to a kitchen. Free bikes are available for guests; wi-fi only available in the breakfast room. **€89**

★ **Le Vert-Galant** 43 rue Croulebarbe, 13e 🅣01 44 08 83 50, 🅦vertgalant.com; 🅜Gobelins; map p.96. In a quiet spot overlooking the square René-le-Gall, this small hotel, with its pretty garden, seems to belong to a provincial French town rather than Paris – and in the evening you can eat at the attached *Auberge Etchegorry*. The plain rooms are clean and comfortable; some have French windows giving onto the garden. Rooms with kitchenettes available. **€140**

### MONTMARTRE AND AROUND

★ **Des Arts** 5 rue Tholozé, 18e 🅣01 46 06 30 52, 🅦arts-hotel-paris.com; 🅜Abbesses/Blanche; map p.112. Homely, welcoming and efficient, with lovely staff and good-value accommodation. Rooms, each named for an artist, vary in size but are all well maintained, quiet and comfortable, with attention to detail and style. There's a romantic room with a balcony, and some have Eiffel

**1**

Tower views. The location – in a side street in the heart of the Abbesses quarter, opposite a vintage arts cinema – is splendid. €165

★ **Eldorado** 18 rue des Dames, 17ᵉ ☎ 01 45 22 35 21, ⓦ eldoradohotel.fr; ⓜ Place-de-Clichy; map p.112. This idiosyncratic hotel in the bohemian Batignolles village, with its own restaurant and a sweet, flower-filled courtyard, is undertaking a major renovation, scheduled to end in November 2019. There may be changes, but historically this hotel has always been a favourite. Watch this space. Prices may change. €100

**Langlois** 63 rue St-Lazare, 9ᵉ ☎ 01 48 74 78 24, ⓦ hotel-langlois.com; ⓜ Trinité; map p.112. This genteel hotel feels as if it has scarcely changed in the last century, though it has all the facilities you'd expect of a three-star, plus excellent service. Each room is different, but they're all larger than average and handsome, with high ceilings, fireplaces, the odd antique and en-suite bathrooms, some of which are huge. Excellent online discounts. €160

★ **Palm** 30 rue de Maubeuge, 9ᵉ ☎ 01 42 85 07 61, ⓦ astotel.com/hotel/hotel-palm-opera; ⓜ Cadet; map p.112. Fresh, upbeat and family-friendly hotel typical of the excellent *Astotel* group – all poppy colours and retro styling – with nicely designed rooms and good bathrooms. Some have balconies and Eiffel Tower views. Free snacks and drinks, and in-room tea- and coffee-making facilities. €140

★ **Pigalle** 9 rue Frochot, 9ᵉ ☎ 01 48 78 37 14, ⓦ lepigalle.paris/en; ⓜ Pigalle; map p.112. In the heart of the hip SoPi nightlife district, this artsy hotel has plush, vintage-cool rooms, lovely staff and a good, late-opening restaurant/bar on the ground floor. Very cool. €216

**Le Village Hostel** 20 rue d'Orsel, 18ᵉ ☎ 01 42 64 22 02, ⓦ villagehostel.fr; ⓜ Anvers; map p.112. Reliable indie hostel in an attractively renovated nineteenth-century building with a view of Sacré-Coeur from the terrace. All dorms (some female only) and rooms (with phones) are en suite. There's a bar and a guest kitchen, and rates include breakfast. Dorms €45, doubles €99

## EASTERN PARIS

★ **Le Citizen** 96 quai de Jemmapes, 10ᵉ ☎ 01 83 62 55 50, ⓦ lecitizenhotel.com; ⓜ Jacques Bonsergent; map p.82. With a perfect setting on the banks of the Canal St-Martin, this is an eco-friendly, beautifully designed hotel with just twelve rooms, all of them airy and soothing, with iPads and great canal views. The cheaper options are compact; the more expensive are twice as big. Home-made buffet breakfast included. €199

**Cosmos Hôtel** 35 rue Jean-Pierre Timbaud, 11ᵉ ☎ 01 43 57 25 88, ⓦ cosmos-hotel-paris.com; ⓜ Parmentier; map p.82. Contemporary budget hotel, excellently located for the bars and cafés of Oberkampf, offering clean, minimalist en-suite rooms. The styling is a little bland, the fittings occasionally rough around the edges and the bathrooms are tiny – but it's a good base, a great price and the beds are super-comfortable. The larger doubles (€86) are worth the extra for a longer stay. €76

**District République** 4 rue Lucien Sampaix, 10ᵉ ☎ 01 42 08 20 09, ⓦ hoteldistrictrepublique.com; ⓜ Jacques Bonsergent; map p.82. A solid, reasonably priced option on the edge of the 10ᵉ, towards the canal. The 33 rooms are small but contemporary and well equipped, with coffee- and tea-making facilities, and the staff are super-helpful. €150

★ **Generator Hostel** 9–11 Place du Colonel Fabien, 10ᵉ ☎ 01 70 98 84 00, ⓦ generatorhostels.com; ⓜ Colonel Fabien; map p.82. Well-run party hostel by the métro, with spotless dorms (eight- to ten-bed; some women-only options), some with private bathrooms. As to be expected with the *Generator* group, facilities are generally good, with a handy café and a rooftop bar. Private rooms are en suite. Dorms €46, doubles €138

★ **Mama Shelter** 109 rue de Bagnolet, 20ᵉ ☎ 01 43 48 48 48, ⓦ mamashelter.com; ⓜ Alexandre-Dumas; map p.82. The relentless branding – "Mama says" this, "Mama says" that – can wear thin, but the buzzy *Mama Shelter*, designed by Philippe Starck, offers surprisingly good rates and can be fun. Free in-room movies and iMacs, plus a bar-restaurant and roof terrace. €149

★ **Du Nord** 47 rue Albert Thomas, 10ᵉ ☎ 01 42 01 66 00, ⓦ hoteldunord-leparivelo.com; ⓜ Jacques Bonsergent/République; map p.82. A pretty, ivy-strewn entrance leads into a cosy, charming hotel with 23 tasteful, simply decorated rooms. The cheaper ones look onto the courtyard and are smaller and darker. The friendly staff can loan out bikes. Wi-fi only in reception area. €86

**St Christopher's Canal** 159 rue de Crimée, 19ᵉ ☎ 01 40 34 34 40, ⓦ st-christophers.co.uk/paris-hostels/canal; ⓜ Crimée/Laumière; map p.82. Massive hostel in an eye-catching, renovated former boat hangar overlooking the Bassin de la Villette. The four- to twelve-bed dorms, some women-only, feature curtained-off pod beds, and there's a lively bar/restaurant, waterfront terrace, and dozens of activities on offer; prices fluctuate, but always include breakfast. Some of the doubles are en suite. Dorms €38, doubles €107

## EATING

**Cuisine** Even outside the Michelin-starred temples to high cuisine, of which the city has many, many Parisian restaurants remain defiantly traditional, offering classic *cuisine bourgeoise* based on well-sauced meat dishes, or regional French cuisines. You can find a tremendous variety of foods, from Senegalese to Vietnamese, however, while the so-called bistronomy movement sees accomplished chefs rejecting over-fussy concoctions in favour of more experimental cuisine, focusing on fresh flavours – and even, shockingly, giving a starring role to vegetables – usually served in less elaborate settings and at lower prices.

**Where to eat** Luxurious, hushed restaurants decked with crystal and white linen; noisy, elbow-to-elbow bench-and-trestle-table joints; intimate bistros with specials on the blackboard; grand seafood brasseries with splendid, historic interiors; artfully distressed boho cafés – Paris has them all. And today, many of the city's most talked about restaurants are the relatively relaxed so-called neo-bistros, where the focus is very much on creative food, not on traditional service or old-school decor, while a rash of hipster coffee houses, akin to those you'll find in cities around the world, serve the needs of caffeine heads not satisfied with the city's characteristically bitter brews. Our reviews are divided into restaurants – including brasseries, bistros and neo-bistros – and bars and cafés, encompassing any place you might go for a drink or a lighter meal, from wine bars and coffee houses to delis and *salons de thé*. For bars with less emphasis on eating, check "Nightlife".

**Prices** Eating out in restaurants tends to be expensive, with three-course evening meals rarely costing less than €45. You can cut costs by opting for the lunchtime set menus (known as *menus* or *formules*), typically priced at less than €25 even at quite classy restaurants, or as little as €15 for two courses at good inexpensive places. As a rule prices will usually vary for consuming at the bar (*au comptoir*; the cheapest option), sitting down (*la salle*), or on the terrace (*la terrasse*; generally most expensive). Addresses in the smarter or more touristy arrondissements set costs soaring and you'll generally pay more on main squares and boulevards than on backstreets.

**Reservations** For the more upmarket or fashionable places, and at weekends, it's wise to reserve. Generally you will only need to do this a day or so in advance, but the most renowned places may require booking up to several weeks (or in some cases, months) ahead.

**August** Note that many establishments close for at least a couple of weeks in August, and sometimes the whole month; it's always best to call to check.

## THE ISLANDS

### BARS AND CAFÉS

**Berthillon** 31 rue St-Louis-en-l'Île, Île St-Louis, 4ᵉ ☎01 43 54 31 61, ⓦberthillon.fr; ⓂPont-Marie; map p.82. *Berthillon* serves some of the best ice cream in Paris, in a range of tempting flavours – salted butter caramel is a highlight. Wed–Sun 10am–8pm.

★ **Café St-Régis** 6 rue Jean du Bellay, Île St-Louis, 4ᵉ ☎01 43 54 59 41, ⓦcafesaintregisparis.com; ⓂPont-Marie; map p.82. Lovely café-brasserie, designed to pay homage to traditional bistros – all gleaming white ceramic tiles, mirrored walls, dark wood, zinc bar and leather banquettes, with bustling waiters and a neighbourhood vibe. Daily 7am–2am.

**Taverne Henri IV** 13 place du Pont-Neuf, Île de la Cité, 1ᵉʳ ☎01 43 54 27 90; ⓂPont-Neuf; map p.79. Bustling with a comfortable atmosphere, this old-fashioned wine bar is buzziest at lunchtime, when it's full of quaffing lawyers and workers from the nearby Palais de Justice. Traditional *plats*, meat and cheese platters from €15. Mon–Sat noon–10.30pm.

### RESTAURANTS

**L'Auberge de la Reine Blanche** 30 rue St-Louis-en-l'Île, 4ᵉ ☎01 85 15 07 30, ⓦaubergedelareineblanche.fr/en; ⓂPont Marie; map p.82. Located on Île St-Louis's main street, this long-established little restaurant is a homey place with copper pans hanging from the wood-beamed ceiling. The menu focuses on classics such as soupe à l'oignon, *coq au vin* and *tarte tatin*. Mains from €16. Mon, Tues & Fri–Sun noon–2.30pm & 6.15–10pm, Thurs 6.30–9.30pm.

## MEAT-FREE EATING

Traditionally Paris's gastronomic reputation was largely lost on **vegetarians**, who had to subsist on salads, omelettes and cheese. Nowadays, however, most places will often offer at least one or two non-meaty dishes, and some of the new breed of chefs are turning their attention to the fresh flavours and possibilities of vegetables. In addition to the exclusively veggie restaurants, *salons de thé*, coffee houses and tapas bars offer lighter dishes; neo-bistros and hipper restaurants, along with the ethnic places, are also a good bet. Useful French phrases are *Je suis végétarien(ne)* ("I'm a vegetarian") and *Il y a quelques plats sans viande?* ("Are there any non-

meat dishes?"). The picture is increasingly good for **vegans**, too. Plant-based eating has caught on in a big way with the cool Parisian set, with a rash of exclusively vegan places popping up in some of the trendier neighbourhoods, from the Marais to the 10ᵉ and eastern Paris. "I'm a vegan" translates as *Je suis végétalien(ne)* but the English word vegan (pronounced "végane") is more frequently used. Top choices for meat-free eats include Michelin-starred **Arpège** (see page 132), **42 Degrés** (see page 134), **Café Pinson** (see page 129), **Le Potager du Marais** (see page 130) and **Soul Kitchen** (see page 134).

**1**

## THE CHAMPS-ÉLYSÉES AND AROUND

### BARS AND CAFÉS

**Le Café Jacquemart-André** 158 bd Haussmann, 8ᵉ ☎01 45 62 11 59, ⓦmusee-jacquemart-andre.com; ⓜSt-Philippe-du-Roule/Miromesnil; map p.70. Within the Musée Jacquemart-André, but with independent access, this is among the city's most opulent *salons de thé*. It's best to come for tea – you'll pay around €12 for tea and a pastry – or a Sunday brunch, as the lunch dishes are more uneven (from €16). Mon–Fri 11.45am–5.30pm, Sat 11am–5.30pm, Sun 11am–2.30pm.

**Le Fouquet's** 99 av des Champs-Élysées, 8ᵉ ☎01 40 69 60 50; ⓜGeorge V; map p.70. Dating from 1899, iconic *Le Fouquet's* (you pronounce the "t") is such a well-established celebs' watering hole that it's been classified a Monument Historique. You can sit out on the *terrasse*, a prime spot for people-watching, or sink into a red velvet banquette in the café-brasserie. Coffee from €8 (€10 on the *terrasse*), mains @18–85. Daily 7.30am–1am.

### RESTAURANTS

**Mini Palais** Av Winston-Churchill, 8ᵉ ☎01 42 56 42 42, ⓦminipalais.com; ⓜChamps-Élysées-Clemenceau; map p.70. A meal at the Grand Palais' lofty dining room or out on the colonnaded terrace is a real treat. Triple-Michelin-starred chef Eric Fréchon oversees the seasonal menu, a mix of French classics and modern dishes. You can also just come for a snack (cheese platters €13), or a drink at the bar. Mains €18–40. Daily 10am–2am.

**Le Relais de l'Entrecôte** 15 rue Marbeuf, 8ᵉ ☎01 49 52 07 17, ⓦrelaisentrecote.fr; ⓜFranklin-D.-Roosevelt; map p.70. No reservations are taken at this old-fashioned restaurant, so you may have to queue for the single main course on the menu: *steak-frites*. This is no ordinary steak though – the secret is in the delicious, buttery sauce. The set price of €26.50 includes a salad starter – and seconds. Mon–Fri noon–2.30pm & 7–11.30pm, Sat & Sun noon–2.45 & 7–11.30pm.

**Taillevent** 15 rue Lamennais, 8ᵉ ☎01 44 95 15 01, ⓦtaillevent.com; ⓜGeorge-V; map p.70. One of Paris's finest classic gourmet restaurants, with two Michelin stars. The Provençal-influenced cuisine and wine list are exceptional, the decor classy and refined. Eating à la carte, count on around €200; the tasting menus cost from €198, and there's a set lunch for €90. Mon–Fri 12.15–2pm & 7.15–10pm.

## THE LOUVRE

### BARS AND CAFÉS

**Angelina** 226 rue de Rivoli, 1ᵉʳ ☎01 42 60 82 00, ⓦangelina-paris.fr; ⓜTuileries; map p.70. This elegant *salon de thé* dates from 1903 and still has its murals,

gilded stucco and leather armchairs. It also does the best hot chocolate in town – a generous jugful with whipped cream on the side (€8.20) is enough for two. Mon–Thurs 7.30am–7pm, Fri 7.30am–7.30pm, Sat & Sun 8.30am–7.30pm.

### RESTAURANTS

**L'Ardoise** 28 rue du Mont Thabor, 1ᵉʳ ☎01 42 96 28 18, ⓦlardoise-paris.com; ⓜTuileries; map p.70. A tiny, good-value neo-bistro with a friendly atmosphere and a fresh take on the classics: think crab cakes with avocado purée or grilled lamb with celeriac *mousseline* and herb salad. Three-course *menu* €38. Mon–Sat noon–2.30pm & 6.30–11pm, Sun 6.30–11pm.

## THE OPERA DISTRICT AND AROUND

### BARS AND CAFÉS

**Frenchie Bar à Vins** 8 rue du Nil, 2ᵉ ☎01 40 39 96 19, ⓦfrenchie-bav.com ⓜSentier; map p.70. Join the crowds of anglophone foodies enjoying interesting wines and snacking on sharing platters (roasted artichoke with anchovy aioli, say, or pappardelle with octopus and chickpeas; €6–40) at Grégory Marchand's relaxed wine bar– it's best to arrive early (or much later, as the locals do). Daily 6.30–11pm.

**Racines** 8 passage des Panoramas, 2ᵉ ☎01 40 13 06 41, ⓦracinesparis.com; ⓜGrands Boulevards or Bourse; map p.70. A cosy, neighbourhood *bistrot à vins* in a lovely old tile-floored wine shop, with a short daily changing menu of home-cooked food that they will pair with natural wines from the store. This pretty old *passage* has become quite the foodie hotspot, in fact – *Le Coinstot Vino* is another good option along here. Mains from €25. Mon–Fri noon–2pm & 7.30–10pm.

### RESTAURANTS

★ **Bistrot des Victoires** 6 rue de la Vrillière, 1ᵉʳ ☎01 42 61 43 78; ⓜBourse; map p.70. Very reasonably priced for the area, this charming, old-fashioned *bistrot* with zinc bar, mustard-coloured walls, globe lamps and velvet banquettes serves good standbys such as *confit de canard* and *poulet rôti* for around €12, as well as huge salads and *tartines* (€9.50). Daily 9am–11pm.

**Gallopin** 40 rue Notre-Dame-des-Victoires, 2ᵉ ☎01 42 36 45 38, ⓦgallopin.com; ⓜBourse; map p.70. Endearing nineteenth-century brasserie, with original brass and mahogany fittings and beautiful painted glass. It's a popular choice for classic French dishes including *escargots*, beef *tartare* and foie gras *maison*. Menus €22 and €29 at lunch and dinner. Mon noon–2.30pm & 7–10.30pm, Tues–Fri noon–2.30pm & 7–11pm, Sat noon–3pm & 7–11.30pm, Sun noon–3pm & 7–10pm.

## BEAUBOURG AND AROUND

### BARS AND CAFÉS

★ **Le Comptoir de la Gastronomie** 34 rue Montmartre, 1ᵉʳ ☏ 01 42 33 31 32, ⓦ comptoirdelagastronomie.com; ⓜ Les Halles/Etienne-Marcel; map p.79. Gloriously old-fashioned deli serving fabulous takeaway baguettes (try the foie gras with fig chutney). Or sit down to a simple *plat* (roast duck, cassoulet, onion soup and the like, around €16) in the traditional dining room. A dream of a place. Deli Mon 9am–8pm, Tues–Sat 8am–8pm; restaurant Mon–Thurs noon–11pm, Fri & Sat noon–midnight.

★ **Le Garde-Robe** 41 rue de l'Arbre Sec, 1ᵉʳ ☏ 01 49 26 90 60, ⓦ facebook.com/pg/legarderobeparis; ⓜ Louvre-Rivoli; map p.79. Animated, cosy *bistrot à vins* with bare wood floors, retro wallpaper and globe lights. The wines, with many biodynamic and natural choices, are superb, as is the food: a couple of simple lunchtime *menus* (€15.50 and €19) focus on organic ingredients, with tasty veggie choices; in the evenings the likes of cheese and charcuterie plates, *croques* and foie gras take over. Mon–Fri noon–1am, Sat 4pm–1am.

### RESTAURANTS

**La Régalade Saint Honoré** 106 rue St-Honoré, 1ᵉʳ ☏ 01 42 21 92 40, ⓦ laregalade.paris; ⓜ Louvre-Rivoli/Les Halles; map p.79. Tourists and locals flock to taste Bruno Doucet's celebrated bistronomy at this cosy restaurant: the €41 three-course *menu* offers great value, with dishes such as cod poached in chicken broth with beets and curried crème fraiche followed by Mont Blanc with green apple. Booking essential. Daily 12.15–2.30pm & 7–11pm.

**La Tour de Montlhéry (Chez Denise)** 5 rue des Prouvaires, 1ᵉʳ ☏ 01 42 36 21 82; ⓜ Louvre-Rivoli/Châtelet; map p.79. An old-style, late-night and convivial market *bistrot*, chock-a-block with regulars tucking into rich, substantial French dishes, such as daube of beef, bone marrow, *tête de veau* or skate with *frites*, along with Loire wines from the barrel. Mains around €26. Mon–Fri noon–3pm & 7.30pm–5am.

★ **yam'Tcha** 121 rue St-Honoré, 1ᵉʳ ☏ 01 40 26 08 07, ⓦ yamtcha.com; ⓜ Louvre-Rivoli; map p.79. The delicate, Michelin-starred Chinese-French fusion food at this elegantly simple spot is outstanding – *menus découvertes* (€70/€150) might include red mullet with sweet and sour cucumber, followed by melting meringue with moscatel grapes and lychee with shiso (similar to mint) sorbet. Each course can be paired with either tea or wine. Reservations are like gold dust; book well in advance. Wed–Sat noon–1.30pm & 8–9.30pm.

## THE MARAIS

### BARS AND CAFÉS

**L'As du Fallafel** 34 rue des Rosiers, 4ᵉ ☏ 01 48 87 63 60; ⓜ St-Paul; map p.82. One of the best falafel shops in the Jewish quarter – and arguably the most famous. Falafels to take away start at €3.50 for ten, €6.50 in pitta with salad – or pay a bit more and sit in the buzzing little dining room. Mon–Thurs & Sun noon–11.30pm, Fri noon–3pm.

**Café Pinson** 6 rue du Forez, 3ᵉ ☏ 09 83 82 53 53, ⓦ cafepinson.fr; ⓜ Filles du Calvaire; map p.82. A gluten-free and vegan-friendly organic café turning out "cuisine haute vitalité" – for which read home-made dishes such as blanquette de légumes with quinoa or Chinese-style rice with tofu, ginger and tamari sauce. Eat in the airy dining area, with its potted plants and open kitchen, or sink into a sofa with a coffee or a fresh juice (€6). Reckon on spending around €20 for lunch, more at dinner. Mon–Fri 9am–10pm, Sat 10am–10pm, Sun 10am–6pm.

**Le Loir dans la Théière** 3 rue des Rosiers, 4ᵉ ☏ 01 42 72 90 61, ⓦ leloirdanslatheiere.com; ⓜ St-Paul; map p.82. A much-loved *salon de thé* decorated with arty posters and whimsical murals and a coupole of comfy leather armchairs for lounging. The enormous home-made cakes are a hit (around €11 for tea and cake), but you can also get light meals and brunch. Mon–Fri 9am–7.30pm.

**Marché des Enfants Rouges** 39 rue de Bretagne, 3ᵉ; ⓜ Filles-du-Calvaire; map p.82. A great picnic option: in addition to fresh produce, this venerable food market is a great spot for street food – rotisserie, Japanese, couscous, crêpes, Lebanese, Italian, Creole – which you can eat at communal picnic tables. Tues, Wed & Thurs 8.30am–1pm & 4–7.30pm, Fri & Sat 8.30am–1pm & 4–8pm, Sun 8.30am–2pm.

★ **Merci** 111 bd Beaumarchais, 3ᵉ ☏ 01 42 77 00 33, ⓦ merci-merci.com; ⓜ St-Sébastien-Froissart; map p.82. There are three eating options at this cool concept store: the *Used Book Café*, with books lining the walls and plump armchairs to sink into; family-friendly *La Cantine de Merci*, with its little garden; and the coolly retro *Cinéma Café*, offering simple charcuterie, salads and soup. Used Book Café Mon–Sat 10am–7pm; Cinéma Café Mon–Sat 10am–6.30pm; La Cantine de Merci Mon–Sat noon–6pm.

### RESTAURANTS

**Ambassade d'Auvergne** 22 rue de Grenier St-Lazare, 3ᵉ ☏ 01 42 72 31 22, ⓦ ambassade-auvergne.com; ⓜ Rambuteau; map p.82. Tourists love it, and for good reason: this is hearty Auvergne cuisine, served in a cosy dining room. For the ultimate in comfort food try the *saucisse* and *aligot* (creamy, cheesy potato; €18) – then try to resist the vast help-yourself bowl of chocolate mousse for dessert (€10). Mon–Thurs noon–2pm & 7.30–10pm, Fri–Sun noon–2pm & 7–10pm.

**Chez Janou** 2 rue Roger Verlomme, 3ᵉ ☏ 01 42 72 28 21, ⓦ chezjanou.com; ⓜ Chemin Vert; map p.82. Popular Provençal restaurant that serves generous portions of traditional southern food – rabbit, risotto, *daube* (mains

1

from €18) – and *pastis* in its warm, traditional dining room. Save room for dessert; the house chocolate mousse is served in a cavernous help-yourself bowl. Daily noon–3pm & 7pm–midnight.

**Chez Omar** 47 rue de Bretagne, 3ᵉ ☎ 01 42 72 36 26; ⓜ Arts-et-Métiers; map p.82. You can't reserve at this popular North African couscous restaurant, but it's no hardship to wait at the bar, taking in the handsome old brasserie decor and spirited atmosphere. It's not gourmet, but portions are copious and the couscous light and fluffy. The *merguez* (spicy sausage) variety costs €17, the *royale* (with three kinds of lamb) €29. No credit cards. Mon–Sat noon–2.30pm & 7–11.30pm, Sun 7–11.30pm.

★ **Métropolitain** 8 rue de Jouy, 4ᵉ ☎ 09 81 20 37 38, ⓦ www.metroresto.fr; ⓜ St-Paul; map p.82. This appealing contemporary *bistrot*, decorated with vintage métro posters, serves terrific, sophisticated food. The limited-choice menu lists such dishes as French asparagus, Corsican brocciu, lemon confit and wild sorrel; spicy stuffed squid with black rice; or steamed hake with nori, artichoke mousseline and satay sauce. Lunch *menu* from €20, dinner from €36. Mon–Sat noon–3pm & 7.30pm–midnight.

**Le Potager du Marais** 24 rue Rambuteau, 3ᵉ ☎ 01 57 40 98 57, ⓦ lepotagerdumarais.fr; ⓜ Rambuteau; map p.82. A small, welcoming vegan restaurant, rustically styled and with a menu featuring organic and gluten-free options. Dishes include pink lentils with smoked tofu, fresh seaweed and fennel or *seitan bourguignon*, and there are scrumptious vegan desserts (crème brûlée with apricot, for example). Mains €14–18. Wed–Sun noon–4pm & 7pm–midnight.

## BASTILLE

### BARS AND CAFÉS

★ **Le Baron Rouge** 1 rue Théophile-Roussel, 12ᵉ ☎ 01 43 43 14 32, ⓦ lebaronrouge.net;; ⓜ Ledru-Rollin; map p.82. Stallholders and shoppers from the nearby Marché Aligre gather at this glorious old spit-and-sawdust *bar à vins* for a light lunch or an *apéritif*. If it's crowded, join the locals around the barrels outside, lunching on simple platters of *saucisson*, cheese or fresh oysters (weekends only, in season). Unmissable. Mon 5–10pm, Tues–Fri 10am–2pm & 5–10pm, Sat 10am–10pm, Sun 10am–4pm.

★ **Café de l'Industrie** 16 rue St-Sabin, 11ᵉ ☎ 01 47 00 13 53, ⓦ cafedelindustrieparis.fr; ⓜ Bastille; map p.82. The relaxed atmosphere and shabby boho glamour – dark wood, huge potted plants, retro movie star photos and gypsy jazz soundtrack – attract a mixed crowd at this Bastille institution (actually two cafés, with another across the road). The menu ranges from pasta and salad bowls to traditional French *bistrot* dishes – not outstanding, but reasonably priced (*plats* from €12; lunchtime *formule* Mon–Fri €13). Daily 9am–2am.

**Chez Aline** 85 rue de la Roquette, 11ᵉ ☎ 01 43 71 90 75; ⓜ Voltaire; map p.82. Excellent gourmet deli serving inexpensive, creative picnic food – eat in at one of the few tables or take out baguettes (ham, artichoke and pesto; roast cod with tapenade), salads and daily specials, all from €7. Mon–Fri 11am–7pm.

**Pause Café** 41 rue de Charonne, corner of rue Keller, 11ᵉ ☎ 01 48 06 80 33; ⓜ Ledru-Rollin; map p.82. This café-*bistrot* is a long-established favourite with a lively, youthful crowd, who pack out the pavement tables at lunch and *apéritif* time. The food won't win any prizes, but the atmosphere is fun and the location enviable. *Plats du jour* including burgers and pasta are around €15. Mon–Sat 8am–2am, Sun 9am–8pm.

### RESTAURANTS

★ **Le Bistrot Paul Bert** 18 rue Paul Bert, 11ᵉ ☎ 01 43 72 24 01; ⓜ Faidherbe-Chaligny; map p.82. This Parisian bistro looks right, with its chalkboard menu, little wooden tables, tiled floor and marbled mirrors, and feels right, with a genuine neighbourhood buzz. The seasonal food, from fried eggs with truffles to steak *au poivre* with crispy *frites*, is delicious. Three-course dinner *menu* €40. Reservations advised. Tues–Sat noon–2pm & 7.30–11pm.

★ **Les Marcheurs de Planète** 73 rue de la Roquette, 11ᵉ ☎ 01 43 48 90 98, ⓦ lesmarcheursdeplanete.com; ⓜ Voltaire; map p.82. Great restaurant/bar with a good old-fashioned Parisian atmosphere: chess tables; books and graphic novels to read; musical instruments dotted about; posters covering the walls (and ceiling); and a friendly, wild-haired owner. More than 150 wines are on offer, plus cheeses, charcuterie and rustic French food at reasonable prices. Tues–Sun 5.30pm–2am; food served 7.30pm–midnight.

**Septime/Clamato** 80 rue de Charonne, 11ᵉ ☎ 01 43 67 38 29, ⓦ septime-charonne.fr; ⓜ Charonne; map p.82. Michelin-starred *Septime*, on the edge of the 11ᵉ, turns out inventive, delicate food – steamed cod with pickled turnips and yuzu sauce, say, or courgette with goat's cheese and rhubarb – on *menus dégustation* (four-course menu €42 for lunch, seven-course menu €80 for dinner). It gets booked quickly, but the adjoining tapas bar, *Clamato*, which serves fish and seafood small plates (€7–65), accepts walk-ins only. Septime Mon 7.30–10pm, Tues–Fri 12.15–2pm & 7.30–10pm; Clamato Wed–Fri 7–11pm, Sat & Sun noon–11pm.

**Waly Fay** 6 rue Godefroy-Cavaignac, 11ᵉ ☎ 01 40 24 17 79, ⓦ walyfay.fr; ⓜ Charonne/Faidherbe-Chaligny; map p.82. This West African restaurant on the eastern edge of the Bastille district has a stylish, intimate atmosphere, all dim lighting, white stone walls and dark wood beams. Smart young Parisians come to dine on fragrant spiced stews, plantain fritters, jumbo prawns and other delicacies (mains €14–26). Daily noon–3pm & 7pm–midnight.

## QUARTIER LATIN

### BARS AND CAFÉS

★ **Le 5ème Cru** 7 rue du Cardinal Lemoine, 5ᵉ ☎ 01 40 46 86 34, ☗ 5ecru-75.com; Ⓜ Cardinal-Lemoine; map p.92. The shelves at this welcoming *bistrot à vins* are piled high with bottles from French artisan winemakers; the perfect accompaniment to charcuterie, cheese and and pâté (around €7–10). Mon noon–3pm & 7pm–midnight, Sat 7pm–midnight.

**Bonvivant** 7 rue des Écoles, 5ᵉ ☎ 01 43 26 51 34, ☗ bonvivant.paris; Ⓜ Cardinal Lemoine; map p.92. This friendly wine bar, with biodynamic wines from €6 a glass, serves sharing platters (around €16) and pâtés, hummus or *rillettes* to nibble – and expands at the back into an elegant restaurant (mains from €15). Daily 9am–2am.

★ **Café de la Mosquée** 39 rue Geoffroy-St-Hilaire, 5ᵉ ☎ 01 43 31 38 20; Ⓜ Censier-Daubenton; map p.92. The *salon* at the Paris mosque has a lovely Arabic interior, and a courtyard where tajines and couscous are served (€12–18), while the tiled *terrasse* with its fig trees is a great spot to refuel with a glass of sweet mint tea and a honey-drenched cake. Daily 9am–midnight.

★ **Café de la Nouvelle Mairie** 19 rue des Fossés-St-Jacques, 5ᵉ; ☎ 01 44 07 04 41; Ⓜ Cluny-La Sorbonne/RER Luxembourg; map p.92. Set on a narrow, tree-shaded street near the Panthéon, this contemporary bistro-wine bar has a warm, convivial atmosphere. Small plates and sharing *assiettes* of cheese or charcuterie (€8–18) can be enjoyed all day, along with bigger mains and a really excellent selection of natural wines. Mon–Fri 8am –midnight.

**La Fourmi Ailée** 8 rue du Fouarre, 5ᵉ ☎ 01 43 29 40 99; Ⓜ Maubert-Mutualité; map p.92. This high-ceilinged *salon de thé,* with its colourful decor – mosaic facade, cloudy sky trompe l'oeil, yellow banquettes, book-lined walls – is a welcome stop. You'll pay around €14–19 for a home-made *plat* – including Provençal specialities and a handful of veggie options – €11 for a slab of quiche or €6.50 for home-made cake. Daily noon–midnight.

**Les Pipos** 2 rue de l'École Polytechnique, 5ᵉ ☎ 01 43 54 11 40; Ⓜ Maubert Mutualité/Cardinal Lemoine; map p.92. This charming old corner bar – named for the first-year students at the nearby *école* – is an unreconstructed Latin Quarter institution, full of *bon viveurs* and happy tourists enjoying natural wines by the glass and simple Auvergnat food. Two-course lunch *formule* (Mon–Fri) €15. Mon–Sat 9am–1am.

★ **Le Verre à Pied** 118bis rue Mouffetard, 5ᵉ ☎ 01 43 31 15 72, ☗ leverreapied.fr; Ⓜ Monge; map p.92. An old-fashioned, charming and authentic market bar where traders take their morning glass at the bar or sit down to eat a simple *plat du jour – steak haché, saucisson, entrecôte* – for around €12. Lunch *formule* €16. Tues–Sat 9am–9pm, Sun 9.30am–4pm.

### RESTAURANTS

**Le Jardin des Pâtes** 4 rue Lacépède, 5ᵉ ☎ 01 43 31 50 71, ☗ restaurant-lejardindespates.fr; Ⓜ Jussieu; map p.92. In this pretty plant-filled space you can dine on delicious pasta, home-made with freshly ground organic grains and served with gourmet sauces. Try the chestnut pasta with duck, nutmeg and mushrooms, or rice pasta with sautéed veg, soy sauce, ginger and tofu. Mains €12–15. Daily noon–2.30pm & 7–11pm.

**Le Reminet** 3 rue des Grands-Degrés, 5ᵉ ☎ 01 44 07 04 24, ☗ www.lereminet.fr; Ⓜ Maubert-Mutualité; map p.92. This postage-stamp sized *bistrot* is relaxed but classy: snowy-white tablecloths, mottled old mirrors and mini-chandeliers, with French windows opening out onto a leafy square. Dinner is very expensive, so come for lunch, when they offer a good-value, tasty three-course *menu* (€18.90) – split pea soup followed by wild guinea fowl and then cheese, for example. Daily noon–2.30pm & 7–10.30pm.

★ **Les Trublions** 34 rue de La Montagne Sainte-Geneviève, 5ᵉ ☎ 01 42 02 87 83, ☗ lestrublions.fr; Ⓜ Maubert Mutualité/Cluny La Sorbonne; map p.92. This smart bistro is a friendly local favourite, delivering bright, creative food made with market-fresh ingredients. It's particularly good for lunch, when the two-/three-course *menus* offer exceptional value at €14.90/€19 – goat's cheese wrapped in leek, say, or anchovy *rillettes* with ginger and lemongrass. Tues–7.30–11pm, Wed–Sat noon–3pm & 7.30–11pm.

## ST-GERMAIN

### BARS AND CAFÉS

★ **L'Avant Comptoir/L'Avant Comptoir de la Mer** 3 carrefour de l'Odéon, 6ᵉ ☎ 01 42 38 47 55, ☗ hotel-paris-relais-saint-germain.com; Ⓜ Odéon; map p.96. This hole-in-the-wall, standing room only, is home to a tremendous wlne/tapas bar where you can sample Yves Camdeborde's innovative cooking at affordable prices (tapas from €4). The food, from the duck confit hot dog to the ham and artichoke waffles, is outstanding, as are the natural wines; bread, butter and pickles are served communally. If you can't get in, console yourself with a takeout crêpe or sandwich from the stall at the front. *L'Avant Comptoir de la Mer,* next door, focuses on fish and seafood tapas (from €5) – Basque hake confit; squid with quinoa, lemon, mint and olives – with a takeout oyster bar at the front. No reservations at either. Both daily noon–11pm.

**Bar du Marché** 75 rue de Seine, 6ᵉ ☎ 01 43 26 55 15; Ⓜ Mabillon; map p.96. Perennially popular café with the rue de Buci market on its doorstep, and *serveurs* cutely kitted out in flat caps and market trader dungarees. The food – *plats* from €12, *tartines* from €8 – isn't bad, but really you're here for the colourful atmosphere. Mon & Fri 7.30am–2am, Tues–Thurs, Sat & Sun 8am–2am.

1

**Le Flore** 172 bd St-Germain, 6ᵉ ☎01 45 48 55 26, ⓦcafedeflore.fr; ⓜSt-Germain-des-Prés; map p.96. One of the city's iconic old literary brasseries, the great rival and neighbour of the even more touristy *Les Deux Magots*. Sartre, de Beauvoir, Camus et al used to hang out here – and there's still the odd reading and debate. It's fun, but expect to pay above the odds for all that history (espressos around €5). Daily 7.30am–1.30am.

**La Grande Crèmerie** 8 rue Grégoire de Tours, 6ᵉ ☎01 43 26 09 09, ⓦlagrandecremerie.fr; ⓜOdéon; map p.96. They keep it simple at this contemporary-rustic *bistrot à vins*, a godsend on such a touristy street, serving the best produce from France, Italy and Spain – Tuscan truffle sausage, Iberico Bellota chorizo, *moules* – alongside natural and organic wines. Tues–Sat 6pm–midnight.

**Ladurée** 21 rue Bonaparte, 6ᵉ ☎01 44 07 64 87, ⓦladuree.fr; ⓜSt-Germain-des-Prés; map p.96. Lovely Left Bank outpost of *Ladurée*'s mini-empire, with a pale-green muralled conservatory at the back of the shop and a Second Empire lounge upstairs. There's often a queue, particularly at weekends, but those famed *macarons* (€10.30 for four) and the beauty of the surroundings make it worth the wait. Mon–Fri 8.30am–7.30pm, Sat 8.30am–-8.30pm, Sun 10am–7.30pm.

**La Palette** 43 rue de Seine, 6ᵉ ☎01 43 26 68 15, ⓦcafelapaletteparis.com; ⓜOdéon; map p.96. This former Beaux Arts student bar is always buzzing. Inside decor features, of course, old oil paintings and paint-spattered palettes on the walls; the appealing *terrasse* is a big draw, too. There's a short menu of salads, *plats* and dishes to share. Mains €16–24; quiche €13. Daily 8am–2am.

**RESTAURANTS**

**L'Épi Dupin** 11 rue Dupin, 6ᵉ ☎01 42 22 64 56, ⓦwww.epidupin.com; ⓜSèvres-Babylone; map p.96. This friendly modern *bistrot* in an untouristy corner serves high-quality, seasonal food with imaginative touches and a focus on fresh veg: creamy leeks with citrus vinaigrette and buckwheat-crusted cod, for example. The decor is relaxed, and the dining room usually full with locals. *Menus* €30 and €42 at lunch, €42 and €56 at dinner. Tues–Fri noon–3pm & 7–11pm.

**L'Épigramme** 9 rue de l'Éperon, 6ᵉ ☎01 44 41 00 09, ⓦwww.lepigrammeparis.fr; ⓜOdéon; map p.96. The emphasis in this tiny restaurant – whitewashed stone walls, wood-beamed ceiling, contemporary decor – is on modern French cooking (try the guinea fowl with kumquats or "La texture chocolat"). When it's warm they throw the windows open to a peaceful courtyard. *Menus* €25 at lunch, €39 at dinner. Tues–Sat noon–2.30pm & 6–10.30pm.

**La Ferrandaise** 8 rue de Vaugirard, 6ᵉ ☎01 43 26 36 36, ⓦlaferrandaise.com; ⓜOdéon; map p.96. As the name suggests (Ferrandaise is a breed of cattle), meat is the

star at this largely Auvergnat *bistrot* – you might choose a hearty beef cheek *confit* with lentil and mustard – but the changing menu also lists such dishes as roasted scallops with broccoli purée and chorizo. *Menus* €16/€37 lunch, €37 dinner. Mon 7.30–10.30pm, Tues–Thurs noon–2pm & 7.30–10.30pm, Fri noon–2pm & 7.30pm–midnight, Sat 7.30pm–midnight.

★**Semilla** 54 rue de Seine, 6ᵉ ☎01 43 54 34 50; ⓜMabillon; map p.96. The food at this light, airy modern *bistrot* is fantastic, focusing as much on veg as on meat. Choose from such dishes as pumpkin fritters with roasted butternut squash cream and brocciu cheese or mullet with fennel purée, pak choi and hazelnut oil. Two-course lunch *menu* €29; otherwise mains €23–42, with a six-course tasting menu for €65. Mon–Sat 12.30–2.30pm & 7–11pm, Sun 12.30–2.30pm & 7–10pm.

**Ze Kitchen Galerie** 4 rue des Grands-Augustins, 6ᵉ ☎01 44 32 00 32, ⓦzekitchengalerie.fr; ⓜSt-Michel; map p.96. This contemporary Michelin-starred place mixes Asian influences with Mediterranean cuisine – pigeon with tamarind, perhaps. *Menus* from €41 (lunch); €85 (dinner, six courses). Their sister restaurant, *Kitchen Galerie Bis*, down the road at no. 25, is also excellent, slightly cheaper, and open on Sat. Mon–Fri noon–2.15pm & 7.15–10.30pm.

## EIFFEL TOWER QUARTER

### BARS AND CAFÉS

**Coutume** 47 rue Babylone, 7ᵉ ☎01 45 51 50 47, ⓦcoutumecafe.com; ⓜSaint-François-Xavier; map p.102. Quintessential coffee shop – all peeling walls and science lab chic – with an on-site roaster and a crowd of laptop-lugging caffeine heads enjoying superb brews and a short menu of simple food– Bircher muesli, salads, poached eggs, pâtisserie and the like (€5–16). Mon–Fri 8.30am–5.30pm, Sat & Sun 9am–6pm; kitchen Mon–Fri 9am–3.30pm, Sat & Sun 9am–3.45pm.

★**Rosa Bonheur sur Seine** Near Pont Alexandre III, 7ᵉ ☎01 47 53 66 92, ⓦrosabonheur.fr/rosa-seine; ⓜInvalides; map p.102. Lovely, informal Berges de Seine café/bar on a large floating barge, with huge windows, deck seating and cheery, colourful decor. There's a relaxed vibe, whether you're after a quick coffee or a cocktail, want to pick at tapas (from €4) or feast on oysters (€13 for six). Quai-side seating for landlubbers. Mon & Tues noon–10.30pm, Wed noon–12.30pm, Thurs–Sat noon–1.30am, Sun 11.30am–10.30pm; hours may change according to season and weather.

### RESTAURANTS

★**L'Arpège** 84 rue de Varenne, 7ᵉ ☎01 45 05 09 06, ⓦalain-passard.com; ⓜVarenne; map p.102. Alain Passard gives vegetables – all from his own *potager* (kitchen garden) – the spotlight in this three-Michelin-starred restaurant, which lacks the snootiness of many of its kind. Dishes such as asparagus sushi with green tea, cauliflower hummus with lovage pesto, or blue lobster poached in wine with smoked potato purée are astounding. *Menus* €175 (lunch) and €320/€390 (dinner; vegetarian/ non-vegetarian). Mon–Fri noon–2.30pm & 7–10.30pm.

★ **Le Cassenoix** 56 rue de la Fédération, 15ᵉ ☎01 45 66 09 01, ⓦle-cassenoix.fr; ⓜDupleix; map p.102. Cosy and convivial neighbourhood *bistrot*, conveniently near the Eiffel Tower, serving hearty portions of seasonal, hearty food – *gambas a la plancha* with basil risotto; quail with foie gras. It's prix fixe, with a three-course *menu* at €34 (lunch and dinner). Mon–Fri noon–2.30pm & 7–10.30pm.

★ **David Toutain** 29 rue Surcouf, 7ᵉ ☎01 45 50 11 10, ⓦdavidtoutain.com; ⓜInvalides; map p.102. This place has a Michelin star for its seasonal, perfectly judged flavours with lots of farm-fresh veg and delicate fish – typical offerings include beetroot rolls, scallops in Jerusalem artichoke *bouillon*, or smoked eel with black sesame sauce – in a light, modern-rustic space. Tasting menus only – €60/€80/€120/€160 (lunch) and €120/€160 (dinner). Booking essential. Mon 12.30–2.30pm & 8–10pm, Tues– Fri noon–2.30pm & 8–10pm.

**La Fontaine de Mars** 129 rue St-Dominique, 7ᵉ ☎01 47 05 46 44, ⓦfontainedemars.com; ⓜLa Tour-Maubourg; map p.102. Heavy, checked tablecloths, leather banquettes, attentive service: this restaurant, tucked under a colonnade with outdoor seating opposite an old stone fountain, feels quintessentially French. The food is meaty and southwestern: think snails, *magret de canard* and Basque *boudin*. Mains €18–46; *plats du jour* €23. Mon–Sat noon–3pm & 7.30–11pm, Sun 7.15–11pm.

★ **Les Marches** 5 rue de la Manutention, 16ᵉ ☎01 47 23 52 80, ⓦlesmarches-restaurant.com/en; ⓜléna; map p.102. This cheerfully traditional *bistrot* makes a handy lunch stop, with its sunny tables on the pavement opposite the side wall of the Palais de Tokyo. You might choose egg mayonnaise or lentil and sausage salad followed by steak *tartare* or (at the weekend) a delicious *poulet rôti* (*plats* €11–19). Daily noon–2.30pm & 7.30–10.30pm.

## SOUTHERN PARIS

### BARS AND CAFÉS

**L'Entrepôt** 7–9 rue Francis-de-Pressensé, 14ᵉ ☎01 45 40 60 70, ⓦlentrepot.fr; ⓜPernety; map p.102. Arts cinema with a relaxed café and a courtyard where you can enjoy *menus* of home-cooked food (lunch €17.80/€22.20, dinner €35.80), Sunday brunch (€24.50) and *plats du jour* – *magret de canard*, beef tartare and the like – for around €20. Mon–Sat noon– 2.30pm & 7–11pm, Sun 11.45am–2.45pm & 7–11pm.

**Le Select** 99 bd du Montparnasse, 6ᵉ ☎01 45 48 38 24, ⓦleselectmontparnasse.fr; ⓜVavin; map p.102. If you want to visit one of the great historic Montparnasse cafés –

as frequented by Picasso, Matisse, Henry Miller et al – make it this. Prices are high, so it's best for a coffee, but *Select* has kept a lot of traditional atmosphere, with little marble tables and an old tiled floor. The brasserie food isn't bad – the €23.20 weekday lunchtime *menu* gets you a main course, glass of wine and coffee. Mon–Thurs & Sun 7am–2am, Fri & Sat 7am–3am.

### RESTAURANTS

★ **L'Assiette** 181 rue du Château, 14ᵉ ☎01 43 22 64 86, ⓦrestaurant-lassiette.paris; ⓜPernety; map p.102. Bijou brasserie where David Rathgeber, previously head chef for Alain Ducasse, brings his gastronomic skills to a neighbourhood setting, serving impeccable country classics – the cassoulet is a house special – along with creative modern dishes. Mains from €25; two-course lunch *menu* (not Sun) €23. Reservations essential. Wed–Fri noon–2.30pm & 7–10.30pm, Sat & Sun 12.30–2.30pm & 7–10.30pm.

★ **L'Avant Goût** 26 rue Bobillot, 13ᵉ ☎01 53 80 24 00, ⓦlavantgout.com; ⓜPlace-d'Italie; map p.96. Unassuming Butte aux Cailles restaurant with a reputation for good French cuisine – try the rich, spicy signature *pot-au-feu* – and wines to match. *Menus* €16–44. Tues–Sat noon–2.30pm & 7.30–10pm.

**Crêperie Josselin** 67 rue du Montparnasse, 14ᵉ ☎01 43 20 93 50; ⓜEdgar Quinet/Montparnasse; map p.102. This crêperie – in Montparnasse, traditionally the Breton quarter of Paris – serves authentic, savoury and sweet crêpes (€6– 12), with jugs of cider, in a traditional setting of heavy wood furniture, lace and rustic porcelain. No reservations; no cards. Tues–Fri noon–3pm & 6–11pm, Sat & Sun noon–11pm.

**Lao Lane Xang** 102 av d'Ivry, 13ᵉ ☎01 58 89 00 00; ⓜTolbiac; map p.96. Reasonably priced Thai, Vietnamese and Lao cuisine. Try the popular toasted rice salad, served in a lettuce leaf, or the *panaché* of Laotian specialities (€26), including pork sausage. Mon, Tues & Thurs noon–3pm & 7–11pm, Fri noon–3pm & 7–11.30pm, Sat & Sun noon–4pm & 7–11.30pm.

## MONTMARTRE AND AROUND

### BARS AND CAFÉS

**Café des Deux Moulins** 15 rue Lepic, 18ᵉ ☎01 42 54 90 50, ⓦcafedesdeuxmoulins.fr; ⓜBlanche; map p.112. Though still sporting its *Amélie* poster (she waited tables here in the film), and welcoming a number of movie fans, this retro 1950s café remains a down-to-earth neighbourhood hangout. The French food is not bad but not outstanding – it's best for breakfast (*menus* €11.90/€15.90) or a drink and a plate of cheese (€22). Mon–Fri 7.30am– 2am, Sat & Sun 8am–2am.

★ **La Cave des Abbesses** 43 rue des Abbesses, 18ᵉ ☎01 42 52 81 54, ⓦcavesbourdin.fr/abbesses; ⓜAbbesses; map p.112. This humble neighbourhood

**1**

wine shop, with a couple of streetfront tables, hides a tiny secret dining room at the back. Squeeze in among the mixed neighbourhood crowd tucking into sharing platters of charcuterie and cheese – fresh oysters and foie gras are also on offer, along with fabulous wines. Try a *Grande Mixte* for a feast of cheeses, terrines, *rillettes* and ham, with endless supplies of fresh bread, for just €14. No reservations: arrive early. Tues–Fri 5–10.30pm, Sat & Sun noon–10.30pm; last entry 9.30pm.

★ **Halle St-Pierre** 2 rue Ronsard, 18ᵉ ☎ 01 42 58 72 89, ⓦ hallesaintpierre.org; ⓜ Anvers/Abbesses; map p.112. Relax surrounded by artworks in the light-filled *salon de thé* of this gallery of outsider art, housed in an old market building at the foot of Sacré-Coeur. Speciality teas, coffee and cakes (from €4) are on offer, along with a good selection of quiches (from €11). Mon–Fri 11am–6pm, Sat 11am–7pm, Sun noon–6pm.

**La Pointe du Grouin** 8 rue de Belzunce, 10ᵉ ⓦ 01 48 78 28 80, ⓦ lapointedugrouin.com; ⓜ Gare du Nord; map p.112. This high-spirited wine bar-tavern, on a small square near the Gare du Nord, has a strong Breton accent. There's a €10 minimum spend, you need to convert your euros into "grouin" tokens in a vending machine in order to pay, and you order at the bar. Once you've got the hang of it, you can enjoy tasty, inexpensive food, Breton cider and natural wines at the pub-like tables. Small plates (€4–12) – octopus with tapenade; Breton artichoke with vinaigrette; *moules*; *galettes* – are served all day, along with cheese and charcuterie platters (€8–14). Mon–Fri 11am–3pm & 6pm–midnight, Sat 6pm–midnight.

★ **Le Village** 36 rue des Abbesses, 18ᵉ ☎ 01 42 54 99 59, ⓦ bistrotlevillage.com; ⓜ Abbesses; map p.112. Retro little bar-café hidden among the larger pavement cafes on Abbesses. The *terrasse* is teeny, but the interior is a delight, with gleaming ceramic wall tiles, high stools, huge mirrors and a zinc bar held up by all manner of local *habitués*. Good for a morning coffee or a quick lunch (€8–18) – and most of all for people-watching. Daily 7am–2am.

### RESTAURANTS

**42 Degrés** 109 rue du Faubourg Poissonnière, 9ᵉ ☎ 09 73 65 77 88, ⓦ 42degres.com; ⓜ Cadet; map p.112. Elegant bistronomy restaurant on the fringes of the 10ᵉ, turning out organic, raw vegan food – sophisticated dishes like chia caviar with vegetable charcoal and buckwheat blinis, or cashew ricotta with aubergine chips. Mains €16–19. Weekday lunch *formules* €16 and €20; *menus* €34 and €42; Sun brunch *formule* €33. Mon–Sat noon–2.30pm & 7–10.30pm, Sun noon–4pm.

★ **Abri** 92 rue du Faubourg-Poissonnière, 10ᵉ ☎ 01 83 97 00 00; ⓜ Poissonnière; map p.112. The 10ᵉ is becoming quite the foodie destination, and this humble hole-in-the-wall is one of Paris's classiest places to eat,

turning out elegant French-Asian fusion from the tiny open kitchen. Reserve weeks in advance for the *menus dégustation* (€26 for four courses at lunch, €49 for six courses at dinner), or come (early) on Sat lunchtime for the gourmet toasted sandwiches (€13 including a drink). Tues–Fri 12.30–2pm & 7.30–10pm, Sat 12.30–3pm & 7.30–10pm.

★ **Le Grand 8** 8 rue Lamarck, 18ᵉ ☎ 01 42 55 04 55, ⓦ restaurant-legrandhuit.com; ⓜ Anvers; map p.112. It's hard to believe that you're just footsteps away from the Sacré-Coeur at this pared-down bistro, which serves simple, sophisticated French dishes using market-fresh produce. Prices are good for the area and the quality (mains €18–26) – book ahead for a table by the back window, and savour the view over the city. Wed–Fri 7–11.30pm, Sat & Sun noon–3pm & 7pm–2am.

**Le Mono** 40 rue Véron, 18ᵉ ☎ 01 46 06 99 20; ⓜ Abbesses; map p.112. Welcoming, casual Togolese restaurant with *soukous* on the playlist and African art on the walls. Mains (€13–18.50) focus on grilled fish or meat with sour, hot sauces and rice or cassava. Mon, Tues & Thurs–Sun 7pm–midnight.

★ **Richer** 2 rue Richer, 9ᵉ ☎ 01 48 24 44 80, ⓦ lericher. com; ⓜ Poissonier/Bonne Nouvelle; map p.112. Light, bright, modern brasserie. You could have a simple breakfast, coffee, a glass of wine or all-day tapas, but it's the short, seasonal menu that dazzles. Starters (€10–12) might include crispy ravioli of beef cheek with a salty broth of peanut and smoked eel, while typical mains (€17–28) include steamed hake with beetroot purée, horseradish and Thai basil. No reservations. Daily 8am–1am; full meals noon–2.30pm & 7.30–10.30pm.

★ **Soul Kitchen** 33 rue Lamarcq, 18ᵉ ☎ 01 71 37 99 95, ⓦ facebook.com/pg/soulkitchenparis; ⓜ Lamarck Caulaincourt; map p.112. Cosy, rustic veggie restaurant, offering good vegan options, in a pretty room filled with the aroma of baking. Along with fresh salads and savoury tarts, the daily changing €16.50 lunch *menu* lists such dishes as a mac'n'cheese *raclette* with butternut squash and roasted onion or a veg-packed "geisha bowl" in a miso/yuzu broth. It's perpetually full, so come early. Mon–Fri 8.45am–6pm.

★ **Vivant** 43 rue des Petites-Ecuries, 10ᵉ ☎ 01 42 46 43 55, ⓦ vivantparis.com/vivant; ⓜ Bonne Nouvelle/Château-d'Eau; map p.112. Pretty little *restaurant à vins* offering natural wines and a grazing menu of seasonal produce (€13–29) – oysters, white asparagus, foie gras and the like. Mon–Fri 7pm–1am.

### EASTERN PARIS

#### BARS AND CAFÉS

★ **À la Biche au Bois** 45 av Ledru-Rollin, 11ᵉ ☎ 01 43 43 34 38, ⓦ bit.ly/alabicheaubois; ⓜ Gare de Lyon; map

**1**

p.82. This terrific traditional restaurant mixes charming service with keenly priced, generous food. It's a carnivore's dream: don't miss the game dishes, the terrines, the wild duck and the huge, rich *coq au vin*. Four-course *menu* (including an array of cheeses) €33. Mon & Sat 7–10.45pm, Tues–Fri noon–2.30pm & 7–10.45pm.

**Aux Deux Amis** 45 rue Oberkampf, 11ᵉ ☎01 58 30 38 13; Ⓜ Oberkampf; map p.82. You'd never guess it from the outside, but this ordinary-looking neighbourhood café on the lower stretch of rue Oberkampf is a hot ticket – it fills quickly, so get there by 7pm. The fresh and inventive small plates (from around €10) and Spanish tapas can be paired with the fine selection of natural wines. Tues–Fri 4.30pm–1am, Sat noon–1.30am.

★ **Chez Prune** 36 rue Beaurepaire, 10ᵉ ☎01 42 41 30 47, Ⓜ Jacques-Bonsergent; map p.82. Named after the owner's grandmother (a bust of whom is inside), this laidback café-bar is the quintessential canalside haunt, gently buzzing with an artsy crowd enjoying everything from Sunday brunch to a charcuterie platter (€12) and glass of wine (full meals not served at night). Mon–Sat 8am–2am, Sun 10am–2am.

**RESTAURANTS**

★ **Au Passage** 1bis passage de Saint-Sebastien, 11ᵉ ☎01 43 55 07 52, Ⓦ restaurant-aupassage.fr; Ⓜ St-Sébastien-Froissart; map p.82. Quiet, subtle, market-fresh food served in a bright, noisy, bare-bones tapas/wine bar/restaurant. Small plates (€9–18) focus on seasonal ingredients in simple, contemporary dishes, with lots of fish

and veg; larger *plats* from €25. Tues–Sat 7pm–1.30am; food served until 11.30pm.

★ **Le Châteaubriand** 129 av Parmentier, 11ᵉ ☎01 43 57 45 95, Ⓦ lechateaubriand.net; Ⓜ Goncourt; map p.82. Helmed by famed Basque chef Inaki Aizpitarte, this innovative Michelin-starred *bistrot* offers a five-course *menu dégustation* (€75) featuring concoctions such as squid salad with sea asparagus, onions, redcurrants and wakame powder. Reservations are essential; if you don't bag a place, head to Aizpitarte's tapas bar, *Dauphin*, next door. Tues–Sat 7–11pm.

**Le Train Bleu** Gare de Lyon, 12ᵉ ☎01 43 43 09 06, Ⓦ le-train-bleu.com; Ⓜ Gare-de-Lyon; map p.82. The jaw-dropping decor at *Le Train Bleu* is from a bygone age – everything drips with gilt; chandeliers hang from lofty ceilings frescoed with scenes from the Paris–Lyon–Marseille train route; huge windows give onto the trains below. The traditional French cuisine, meanwhile, is acceptable, if pricey (two-course *menu* €49). You could simply have coffee and cake (€20) or breakfast, drinks and snacks in the bar. Daily 7.30am–10.30pm.

★ **Le Verre Volé** 67 rue de Lancry, 10ᵉ ☎01 48 03 17 34, Ⓦ leverrevole.fr; Ⓜ Jacques Bonsergent; map p.82. This wine shop doubles as a simple, cool venue for great food, with a handful of formica tables crammed into the small space. The short menu lists modern and traditional dishes (from €27) along with cheaper, simpler offerings such as sausage with lentils; there's a good-value three-course lunch *menu* for €22. The impeccable wine selection focuses on natural and biodynamic varieties – you pay the over-the-counter price plus €7 corkage fee. Daily 12.30–2pm & 7.30–10.30pm.

## DRINKING AND NIGHTLIFE

Paris's fame as the home of decadent, hedonistic nightlife has endured for centuries, and today the city has a vibrant bar and club scene and a world-class live music programme. World music and jazz are particularly strong, with gypsy jazz being very popular, but you'll find everything from house and electro-lounge to home-grown indie rock and *chanson*.

**Listings** To find out what's on, get hold of one of the city's listings magazines (see page 122). The online Ⓦ lylo.fr offers a pretty good run-down of gigs, searchable by genre. For more detail, try Ⓦ parisbouge.com and the arts and music magazine *Nova* (Ⓦ nova.fr). To find the latest club nights pick up flyers – or word-of-mouth tips – in the city's trendier shops, music stores, bars and cafés.

**Tickets** Concert tickets can be bought at the venues themselves, online, or through agents such as Fnac (Ⓦ fnac. com). It can also be worth checking Ⓦ billetreduc.com for cut-price tickets at the more mainstream venues.

## BARS

The following listings review the city's livelier venues for night-time drinking, places that stay open late and maybe have DJs or occasional live music. Also included are the more

vibrant, late-opening cafés, Alsatian/German-type beer cellars and cool cocktail bars. You'll find more relaxed cafés and *bars à vins*, geared more to eating than nightlife, listed in the "Eating" section.

**THE LOUVRE**

**Bar Costes** Hôtel Costes, 239 rue St-Honoré, 1ᵉʳ ☎01 42 44 50 00, Ⓦ hotelcostes.com; Ⓜ Concorde/Tuileries; map p.70. Though its star is waning a little, this hotel bar is still a decadent place for an *apéritif* or late-night drinks, all sexy red velvet, swags and columns, around an Italianate courtyard. Cocktails from €20; DJs from 9pm. Daily 5pm–2am.

**THE OPERA DISTRICT**

★ **Delaville Café** 34 bd de la Bonne Nouvelle, 10ᵉ ☎01 48 24 48 09, Ⓦ delavillecafe.com; Ⓜ Bonne-Nouvelle; map p.70. The grand staircase, gilded mosaics and marble columns hint at this bar's former incarnation as a bordello. It draws in crowds of pre-clubbers, who sling back a mojito or two before moving on. DJ nights Thurs–Sat. Daily 8.30am–2am.

**Lockwood** 73 rue d'Aboukir, 2ᵉ ⓦ lockwoodparis.com⊠ Ⓜ Sentier/Grands Boulevards; map p.70. Ticking all the hipster boxes, this artisan café/coffee house transforms into a cocktail bar after dark, its candlelit brick-walled cellar filled with cool young expats and locals quaffing creative whisky cocktails and chatting over the retro playlist. Mon–Sat 9am–2am.

### THE MARAIS

★ **La Belle Hortense** 31 rue Vieille du Temple, 4ᵉ ☎ 01 42 74 59 70, ⓦ cafeine.com/belle-hortense; Ⓜ St-Paul; map p.82. You can sip a glass while reading or chatting in this friendly little wine/champagne bar-cum-bookshop that has a zinc bar and book-lined walls. There's a snug room with sofas at the back, though you'll be lucky to get a seat there. Daily 5pm–2am.

**Candelaria** 52 rue de Saintonge, 3ᵉ ⓦ quixotic-projects. com; Ⓜ Filles du Calvaire; map p.82. An atmospheric, clandestine cocktail bar, set behind an unassuming-looking taqueria; just walk straight to the back and push open the door. You'll be lucky to snag one of the low tables, otherwise squeeze in around the bar and watch the staff mix up exotic concoctions (€12–14); try the classic La Guêpe Verte, made of pepper-infused tequila, lime, agave syrup and coriander. Daily 6pm–2am.

★ **Sherry Butt** 20 rue Beautreillis, 4ᵉ ☎ 09 83 38 47 80, ⓦ www.sherrybuttparis.com; Ⓜ St-Paul/Bastille; map p.82. This New York-style cocktail bar manages to feel both relaxed and a shrine to all things cool. The cocktails are great (€13) – try the Sassy Green (Scotch, pistachio and wasabi syrup, lime juice and sage leaves). Mon & Sun 8pm–2am, Tues–Sat 6pm–2am.

### BASTILLE

**Le Lèche-Vin** 13 rue Daval, 11ᵉ ☎ 01 43 55 06 70; Ⓜ Bastille; map p.82. Appealing, rough around the edges little bar, dotted with kitsch religious decor. The statue of Mary with a cross in the window sets the scene; the pics in the toilet, meanwhile, are far from pious. Daily 6pm–2am.

### QUARTIER LATIN

**Le Piano Vache** 8 rue Laplace, 5ᵉ ☎ 01 46 33 75 03; Ⓜ Cardinal-Lemoine; map p.92. Venerable, unpretentious *boîte* with poster-lined walls and dim lighting, crammed with students setting the world to rights. Live gypsy jazz, DJs, and occasional rock gigs. Mon–Sat 6pm–2am.

**Le Reflet** 6 rue Champollion, 5ᵉ ☎ 01 43 29 97 27; Ⓜ Cluny-La Sorbonne; map p.92. There's a nostalgic flavour of *la Nouvelle Vague* in this bar/café with its scruffy black decor, lights rigged up on a gantry, peeling movie posters, and Dylan, Coltrane and Cohen LP sleeves adorning the walls. Popular for a drink before or after a movie at one of the many arts cinemas on this street. Mon–Sat 11am–2am, Sun 3pm–midnight.

### ST-GERMAIN

★ **Chez Georges** 11 rue des Canettes, 6ᵉ ☎ 01 43 26 79 15, ⓦ facebook.com/barchezgeorges; Ⓜ Mabillon; map p.96. This spirited wine bar – all chipped walls and mosaic-tiled floor – is a neighbourhood institution in an area dominated by noisy theme pubs. The predominantly (but not entirely) young crowd keeps things lively, and it gets good-naturedly rowdy later on in its vaulted cellar bar, where you might hear anything from *chanson* to gypsy jazz.. Mon & Sun 6pm–1am, Tues–Fri 6pm–2am, Sat 3pm–2am.

**Prescription** 23 rue Mazarine, 6ᵉ ☎ 09 50 35 72 87; Ⓜ Odéon; map p.96. Tiny bar, a stalwart on the cocktail scene, with a swish interior and creative drinks (around €14). Frequent DJ nights. Mon–Thurs 7pm–2am, Fri & Sat 7pm–4am, Sun 8pm–2am.

★ **Tiger** 13 rue Princesse, 6ᵉ ☎ 01 84 05 81 74, ⓦ tiger-paris.com; Ⓜ Mabillon; map p.96. Paris's favourite gin bar – 130 gins and counting – decked out in Scandi wood, retro mosaics, bare bulbs and pot plants, pulls a laidback young crowd for G&Ts, martinis and other cocktails (from €13). DJs start up as the night proceeds. Tues–Sat 6.30pm–2am.

### THE EIFFEL TOWER QUARTER

★ **Rosa Bonheur sur Seine** Near Pont Alexandre III, 7ᵉ ⓦ rosabonheur.fr/rosa-seine; Ⓜ Invalides; map p.102. Few things beat having a relaxed beer, wine (from €4) or cocktail (from €8.50) at this laidback floating café-bar, enjoying river views with an *apéro*. Mon & Tues noon–10.30pm, Wed noon–12.30pm, Thurs–Sat noon–1.30am, Sun 11.30am–10.30pm; hours may change according to season and weather.

### SOUTHERN PARIS

★ **La Folie en Tête** 33 rue Butte-aux-Cailles, 13ᵉ ☎ 01 45 80 65 99, ⓦ facebook.com/Lafolieentete; Ⓜ Corvisart; map p.92. This vibrant, alternative Butte-aux-Cailles bar, littered with bric-a-brac, is a classic of the *quartier*. You can hear world music, laidback underground beats and *chanson*, both live and on the playlist. Mon–Sat 5pm–2am.

**Le Merle Moqueur** 11 rue Butte-aux-Cailles, 13ᵉ; Ⓜ Place-d'Italie/Corvisart; map p.92. Bohemian little Butte-aux-Cailles bar that saw the Paris debut of Manu Chao. Today it chiefly serves up a playlist French rock and home-made flavoured rums to a merry crowd of young Parisians. Daily 5pm–2am.

### MONTMARTRE AND AROUND

★ **L'Atelier** 6 rue Burq, 18ᵉ ☎ 01 42 51 32 27, ⓦ facebook.com/ateliermontmartre18; Ⓜ Abbesses; map p.112. Arty, welcoming and on the cool side of scruffy, this bar has the feel of an artist's garret – or a boho living room. Exhibitions and performances are staged in the tiny space, but above all it's a relaxed spot for an inexpensive drink (cocktails from €7). The bar food is good, too. Daily 4pm–2am.

★ **Chez Camille** 8 rue Ravignan, 18ᵉ ☎ 01 42 57 75 62, ⊚ facebook.com/Chez-Camille-112695022123953; Ⓜ Abbesses; map p.112. Cool little bar on the slopes of the Butte. With a simple list of drinks, and an effortlessly charming, retro decor – ceiling fans, a few old mirrors, mismatched school tables – it pulls a local crowd who could as easily be enjoying a quiet chat as spontaneously dancing to a playlist dominated by R&B and rockabilly. Mon–Sat 6pm–1.30am, Sun 6pm–midnight.

**La Fourmi** 74 rue des Martyrs, 18ᵉ ☎ 01 42 64 70 35; Ⓜ Pigalle/Abbesses; map p.112. The long bar and spacious, high-ceilinged room at this artfully distressed café-bar provide a home from home for a lively, trendy crowd; drinks are gratifyingly inexpensive (wine from €3.80) and the food isn't bad. DJs at the weekend. Mon–Thurs 8am–2am, Fri 8am–4am, Sat 9am–4am, Sun 10am–2am.

★ **Glass** 7 rue Frochot, 9ᵉ ☎ 09 80 72 98 83, ⊚ quixotic-projects.com/venue/glass; Ⓜ Pigalle; map p.112. This little bar, with its knowing take on hipster Americana, is a stalwart on the SoPi scene. The whisky-based cocktails (from €11), hot dogs and craft beers hit the spot with the young, up-for-it crowd – including lots of Americans and Brits. Daily 8pm–5am.

**EASTERN PARIS**

★ **Bar Ourcq** 68 quai de la Loire, 19ᵉ ☎ 01 42 40 12 26, ⊚ barourcq.free.fr; Ⓜ Laumière; map p.82. This canalside bar really comes into its own in the warmer months when you can sit out on the quay, or borrow the bar's *pétanque* set. DJs Thurs–Sun. Tues–Thurs 3pm–midnight, Fri & Sat 3pm–2am, Sun 3–10pm; closed Tues & Wed in winter.

**Café Charbon** 109 rue Oberkampf, 11ᵉ ☎ 01 43 57 55 13, ⊚ lecafecharbon.fr; Ⓜ St-Maur/Parmentier; map p.82. Established Oberkampf café-bar pulling in a young, fashionable crowd day and night for its attractively restored *belle époque* decor – all high ceilings, huge mirrors, comfy booths and dangling lights – and the long happy hour (daily 5–8pm). Good food, too. Mon–Wed 8am–2am, Thurs 8am–5am, Fri & Sat 8am–6am.

★ **Le Comptoir Général** 80 quai de Jemmapes, 10ᵉ ☎ 01 44 88 24 48, ⊚ facebook.com/pg/lecomptoirgeneral; Ⓜ République/Goncourt; map p.82. Tucked away behind the canal, this huge, rambling space, with a heavy emphasis on African creativity and retro vintage cool, is a shabby chic garage-style bar, with two bars, a mixed, friendly crowd and an impeccably cool playlist. Frequent live world music Mon–Thurs 6pm–2am, Fri 4pm–2am, Sat & Sun 2pm–2am.

**Aux Folies** 8 rue de Belleville, 20ᵉ ☎ 06 28 55 89 40, ⊚ aux-folies-belleville.fr; Ⓜ Belleville; map p.82. Once a café-théâtre hosting the likes of Édith Piaf and Maurice Chevalier, the charmingly tatty Aux Folies offers a slice of old

Belleville life; its terrasse and brass bar are packed with a mixed, cosmopolitan crowd enjoying cheap beer, cocktails and mint tea. Occasional live music. Daily 7am–2am.

**GIG VENUES**

Most of the venues listed here are primarily concert venues, though some double as clubs on certain nights, or after hours. The majority host bands on just a couple of nights a week. Note too that some clubs host gigs earlier on in the evening, and jazz venues often branch out into world music and folk.

**MONTMARTRE AND AROUND**

**La Cigale** 120 bd de Rochechouart, 18ᵉ ☎ 01 49 25 89 99, ⊚ lacigale.fr; Ⓜ Pigalle; map p.112. Opened in 1887 and formerly playing host to the likes of Mistinguett and Maurice Chevalier, this gorgeous 1400-seater Pigalle theatre is now a leading venue for world music, jazz and French and continental European bands. The adjoining *La Boule Noire* (⊚ laboule-noire.fr) is smaller, with a more indie vibe. Opening times vary.

**Divan du Monde** 76 rue des Martyrs, 18ᵉ ☎ 01 40 05 08 10, ⊚ divandumonde.com; Ⓜ Pigalle; map p.112. This venue, in one of Montmartre's many historic cabarets, offers a vibrant music programme of live music (largely Francophone) and cool club nights. Opening times vary.

★ **Élysée Montmartre** 72 bd de Rochechouart, 18ᵉ ☎ 01 44 92 78 00, ⊚ elysee-montmartre.com; Ⓜ Anvers; map p.112. Iconic concert hall – it's hosted everyone from Toulouse-Lautrec (in the audience) to David Bowie (on the stage) – presenting high-profile rock and indie acts from around the globe. Opening times vary.

**EASTERN PARIS**

★ **L'Alimentation Générale** 64 rue Jean-Pierre Timbaud, 11ᵉ ☎ 09 81 86 42 50, ⊚ alimentation-generale. net; Ⓜ Parmentier; map p.82. Great venue with a global line-up of live music ranging from Afro-rock to Balkan beats and trance. A DJ usually takes over later and there's some room for dancing. Wed 7pm–2am, Thurs–Sat 7pm–5am.

**Le Bataclan** 50 bd Voltaire, 11ᵉ ⊚ bataclan.fr; Ⓜ Oberkampf; map p.82. Historic pagoda-styled ex-theatre venue (the Velvet Underground played a legendary gig here, recorded on their *Le Bataclan '72* album) that hit the news again in November 2015 when ISL gunmen fired on the audience during a citywide terrorist attack that killed hundreds. The venue re-opened in 2016 and today it remains fiercely true to its heritage, putting on an eclectic line-up covering anything from international and local dance and rock to *chanson*, comedy and techno nights. Opening times vary.

★ **La Bellevilloise** 19–21 rue Boyer, 20ᵉ ☎ 01 46 36 07 07, ⊚ labellevilloise.com; Ⓜ Gambetta/Ménilmontant; map p.82. There's always something interesting going on at this former workers' cooperative, dating back to 1877, now a dynamic bar, restaurant and arts centre. The excellent basement club and live music venue might host anything from Afro jazz to alternative Arabic music, *chanson* to swing. Opening times vary, but generally: Wed & Thurs 7pm–1am, Fri & Sat 7pm–2am, Sun 11.30am–4pm.

★ **L'International** 5 rue Moret, 11e ☎ 09 50 57 60 50, ⓦ linternational.fr; Ⓜ Menilmontant; map p.82. With two stages and at least two gigs a night, this friendly *café-concerts* showcases the best new, indie and edgy acts – mostly French – in all genres. DJs take over later on. Tues–Thurs 7pm–1am, Fri & Sat 7pm–6am.

**Maroquinerie** 23 rue Boyer, 20e ☎ 01 40 33 35 05, ⓦ lamaroquinerie.fr; Ⓜ Gambetta; map p.82. Cool arts centre with a smallish concert venue downstairs. The line-up encompasses anything from folk and jazz to metal and hip-hop, with international names and a good selection of French musicians. Opening times vary.

★ **Point Éphémère** 200 quai de Valmy, 10e ☎ 01 40 34 02 48, ⓦ pointephemere.org; Ⓜ Jaurès/Louis Blanc; map p.82. Run by an arts collective in a disused boathouse, this superbly dilapidated cultural venue is a nexus for alternative and underground performers of all kinds. Gigs most nights. Mon–Sat 12.30pm–2am, Sun 12.30–10pm.

### JAZZ VENUES

**Le Baiser Salé** 58 rue des Lombards, 1er ☎ 01 42 33 37 71, ⓦ lebaisersale.com; Ⓜ Châtelet; map p.79. Small, crowded upstairs room with nightly live music – usually jazz, but also world music, funk, flamenco and soul (from around €12). There are free jazz jam sessions on Mon, and a chilled-out bar downstairs. Daily 5.30pm–6am; most sets start 7pm & 9.30pm.

**Caveau de la Huchette** 5 rue de la Huchette, 5e ☎ 01 43 26 65 05, ⓦ caveaudelahuchette.fr; Ⓜ St-Michel; map p.92. An atmospheric, historic cellar bar – self-styled "*temple du swing*", as seen in the movie *La La Land* – offering a slice of old Parisian life in this touristy area. The concerts, usually Dixieland, boogie woogie, blues or swing, inspire energetic dancing from the crowd. Mon–Thurs & Sun €13, Fri & Sat €15. Mon–Thurs & Sun 9pm–2.30am, Fri & Sat 9pm–4am.

★ **New Morning** 7–9 rue des Petites-Écuries, 10e ⓦ newmorning.com; Ⓜ Château-d'Eau; map p.82. This well-established, relatively understated place attracts big international jazz names and a knowledgeable crowd. Excellent blues, funk and world music, too. Admission varies. Days and concert times vary.

**Le Sunset/Le Sunside** 60 rue des Lombards, 1er ☎ 01 40 26 46 60, ⓦ sunset-sunside.com; Ⓜ Châtelet-Les Halles; map p.79. Two clubs in one: *Le Sunside* features mostly traditional, acoustic jazz, whereas the *Sunset* cellar tends towards electric and fusion. There are sometimes two shows per night. Performers have included Benny Golson

and Avishai Cohen. Admission €20–35, with some free gigs. Days and concert times vary.

### CHANSON VENUES

★ **Au Lapin Agile** 22 rue des Saules, 18e ☎ 01 46 06 85 87, ⓦ au-lapin-agile.com; Ⓜ Lamarck-Caulaincourt; map p.112. Legendary cabaret bar famously painted and patronized by Picasso, Utrillo and other leading lights of the early twentieth-century Montmartre scene, the "nimble rabbit" – in an adorable shuttered building with a pretty garden – is now an intimate *chanson* club much beloved by tourists. €28 including one drink, students €20 (except Sat). Tues–Sun 9pm–1am.

★ **Les Trois Baudets** 64 bd de Clichy, 18e ☎ 01 42 62 33 33, ⓦ lestroisbaudets.com; Ⓜ Blanche/Pigalle; map p.112. With a proud place on Pigalle's vibrant nightlife scene, this refitted 1940s theatre specializes in developing young, upcoming French singer-songwriters of all stripes. Concerts 7pm–midnight.

### CLUBS

While you could spend a night dancing to techno or deep house, the best of Paris's club scene is in the edgier, esoteric programmes put on at smaller venues – hip-hop, r'n'b, electro-lounge, rock, reggae, you name it. The clubs listed below are among the most popular, but the music and the general vibe really depend on who's running the "*soirée*" on a particular night. Note too that many bars bring in DJs, especially on weekend nights, while live music venues may well hold DJ sessions after hours. Venues rarely warm up before 1am or 2am, whatever their opening hours.

#### THE OPÉRA DISTRICT

★ **Rex Club** 5 bd Poissonnière, 2e ☎ 01 42 36 10 96, ⓦ rexclub.com; Ⓜ Bonne-Nouvelle; map p.70. The iconic *Rex* is serious about its music, which is strictly electronic, notably techno, played through a top-of-the-line sound system. Refreshingly unpretentious, with big-name DJs. Entry varies. Thurs–Sat 11.30pm–7am.

**Silencio** 142 rue Montmartre, 2e ☎ 01 40 13 12 33, ⓦ silencio-club.com; Ⓜ Bourse; map p.70. This club (with cinema, stage and library), set in a basement and reached via six flights of stairs, was conceived by director David Lynch, and everything – from the 1950s-style furniture to the striking gold-leaf walls – pays homage to the club in his film *Mulholland Drive*. Up until 11pm it's members only; after that, doors open to the public, and DJs play hip-hop, disco, rock and electro till the early hours. Occasional live music. Tues–Thurs 6pm–4am, Fri & Sat 6pm–6am.

#### BASTILLE

**Badaboum** 2bis rue des Taillandiers, 11e ☎ 01 48 06 50 70, ⓦ badaboum.paris; Ⓜ Bastille; map p.82. Relatively intimate club, concert venue and cocktail bar

1

rolled into one, in a converted warehouse. Music focuses on digital EDM, but can stray as far as zouk and hip-hop, with live bands earlier on. Entry €13–15. Cocktail bar Fri & Sat 7pm–6am; club nights Thurs–Sun 11pm–6am.

### EIFFEL TOWER QUARTER

**YOYO** Palais de Tokyo, 13 av du Président-Wilson, 16ᵉ ☎01 84 79 11 70, ⓦyoyo-paris.com; ⓜléna; map p.102. Housed in the huge basement of the super-cool Palais de Tokyo, this is one of the city's top dance clubs, serving up rap, techno, house anthems and electro to a cool crowd. Days and times vary.

### MONTMARTRE AND AROUND

★ **La Machine du Moulin Rouge** 90 bd de Clichy, 18ᵉ ☎01 53 41 88 89, ⓦlamachinedumoulinrouge. com; ⓜBlanche; map p.112. Next to the fabled *Moulin Rouge*, this club/bar/live music venue has a concert space hosting international names – from Moodymann to Fuck Buttons – plus a basement club/music venue known as "La Chaufferie", a tapas bar and a rooftop bar. EDM is the order of the day here, but a touch of hedonism lifts it above the usual monster club. Entry €10–22. Club nights generally Fri & Sat midnight–6am, often with gigs beforehand; days and times of live music and other events vary.

★ **Pigalle Country Club** 59 rue Jean-Baptiste Pigalle, 9ᵉ ⓦpigallecountryclub.com; ⓜPigalle; map p.112. A super-cool breath of fresh air on Paris's clubbing scene, with DJ sets spanning the range from Krautrock to glam rock plus open mics, movies, tarot readings and lots of quirky events. Entry varies, and is often free. Dates and times vary.

### SOUTHERN PARIS

★ **Le Petit Bain** 7 port de la Gare, 13ᵉ ☎01 80 48 49 81, ⓦpetitbain.org; ⓜQuai de la Gare; map p.92. One of a few intriguing floating venues along this stretch of the river, near the Bibiliothèque Nationale, this modernist bar/club/performance space ofers an eclectic schedule of club nights and live music, running the gamut from EDM to alt country. Mon–Thurs 6pm–midnight, Fri 6pm–2am, Sat noon–2am, Sun noon–midnight; club nights till 5am/6am.

### EASTERN PARIS

★ **Concrete** 69 port de la Rapée, 12ᵉ ⓦconcreteparis.fr; ⓜGare-de-Lyon; map p.92. Moored on the Seine, near the Gare de Lyon, this is one of the hottest spots on the clubbing scene, putting on all-night and all-day techno parties and featuring big-name DJs. €15; free before midnight. Fri & Sat 10pm–10am; sometimes nonstop Sat 10am–Mon 2am.

**Glazart** 7–15 av de la porte de la Villette, 19ᵉ ☎01 40 36 55 65, ⓦglazart.com; ⓜPorte de la Villette; map p.82. Artsy venue that's serious about its music, with an eclectic range of club nights and live acts covering everything from pagan metal to dub. It's spacious, and in summer there's an outdoor "beach". Entry around €10–20. Wed–Sun; club nights Thurs–Sat, times vary.

**Le Nouveau Casino** 109 rue Oberkampf, 11ᵉ ☎01 43 57 57 40, ⓦnouveaucasino.net; ⓜParmentier; map p.82. Next to *Café Charbon*, this venue puts on an interesting line-up of live gigs that makes way for a relaxed, dancey crowd later on, with music ranging from electro-pop or techno to funk. Entry €9–15, depending on whether you reserve online and when you arrive. Fri & Sat midnight–5am.

## ENTERTAINMENT

### CLASSICAL MUSIC AND OPERA

Paris is a stimulating environment for classical music, boasting the Orchestre de Paris, Orchestre National de France and, for Baroque music, Les Arts Florissants (ⓦarts-florissants.com), plus a number of impressive concert halls. Opéra National de Paris, meanwhile, produces a fine selection of opera and ballet, from core repertoire to new commissions, while the energetic electronic/contemporary scene has a major point of focus at IRCAM, near the Pompidou Centre. The following venues host regular concerts, but many other museums and churches – including Notre-Dame cathedral – stage occasional events; check *Pariscope* (ⓦpariscope.fr), *L'Officiel des Spectacles* (ⓦoffi.fr) or ⓦconcertclassic.com. Tickets can almost always be bought online; for big names you may find overnight queues at the actual box office.

### CONCERT HALLS

**Philharmonie de Paris** 221 av Jean-Jaurès, 19ᵉ ☎01 44 84 44 84, ⓦphilharmoniedeparis.fr; ⓜPorte de Pantin. Designed by celebrated architect Jean Nouvel,

this remarkable concert hall opened in 2015. The massive, aluminium-clad angular building, with a zigzagging ramp leading up to the roof, is intimate inside, with excellent acoustics; the resident Orchestre de Paris and the Ensemble Intercontemporain put on an exciting programme.

**Salle Gaveau** 45 rue la Boétie, 8ᵉ ☎01 49 53 05 07, ⓦsallegaveau.com; ⓜMiromesnil. This intimate concert hall, built in 1907, is a major venue for world-class piano recitals, and stages chamber music recitals and full-scale orchestral works.

**Théâtre des Champs-Élysées** 15 av Montaigne, 8ᵉ ☎01 49 52 50 50, ⓦtheatrechampselysees.fr; ⓜAlma-Marceau. Opened in 1913, this two-thousand-seater modernist theatre seeps history, with sculptures by Bourdelle and paintings by Vuillard. Now home to the Orchestre National de France and Orchestre de Chambre de Paris (ⓦorchestredechambredeparis. com), it also hosts international orchestras, superstar conductors and ballet troupes, and has a vigorous operatic programme. No-view tickets are a bargain, but you can pay up to €150 or so for star performers.

## OPERA HOUSES

**Opéra Bastille** Place de la Bastille, 12e ☎ 08 92 89 90 90, ⓦ operadeparis.fr; ⓜ Bastille. Opened in 1989, this opera house hasn't been entirely successful. The design is unlovable and opinions differ over the acoustics. The stage, at least, allows the auditorium uninterrupted views, prices are generally a little lower than at the Palais, and there's no doubting the high calibre of the Bastille orchestra.

**Opéra Comique** 5 rue Favart, 2e ☎ 08 25 01 01 23, ⓦ opera-comique.com; ⓜ Richelieu-Drouot. As well as lesser-known works in general, the venerable Opéra Comique offers something different – the rich, yet largely forgotten nineteenth-century French opera genre "opéra comique", reviving such obscure composers as Hérold and Auber with successful and surprising results.

**Opéra Garnier** Place de l'Opéra, 9e ☎ 08 92 89 90 90, ⓦ operadeparis.fr; ⓜ Opéra. An evening in this opulent nineteenth-century opera house, used for ballets and smaller-scale opera productions, is unforgettable. While views from some of the side seats can be poor, the acoustics are excellent.

## FILM

Paris is a city for cinema-lovers. The plethora of little arts cinemas screen unrivalled programmes of classic and contemporary films, and you can find mainstream movies at almost any time of the day or night.

**Venues** The city is littered with fine cinemas, from the megaplexes on the boulevards to the small venues in the Quartier Latin. In addition to those listed below, there is a cluster of venues around rue Champollion and rue des Écoles, 5e – check out in particular the mini-chain Les Écrans de Paris (ⓦ lesecransdeparis.fr). Many cultural institutions and embassies also offer screenings.

**Listings** The best source for current film listings is *L'Officiel des Spectacles* (ⓦ offi.fr). Note that foreign films shown in the original language are listed as *version originale* or *v.o.*; films dubbed into French are *v.f.*

**Tickets** The smaller, independent cinemas are the cheapest; tickets usually start at around €9. There are often discounts for off-peak *séances*, and almost all venues have reductions for students and the unemployed.

## CINEMAS

**Cinémathèque Française** 51 rue de Bercy, 12e ☎ 01 71 19 33 33, ⓦ cinematheque.fr; ⓜ Bercy. This Gehry-designed cinema screens around two dozen films and shorts every week (closed Tues), including retrospectives and silents.

**L'Entrepôt** 7–9 rue Francis-de-Pressensé, 14e ☎ 01 45 40 07 50, ⓦ lentrepot.fr; ⓜ Pernety. This Montparnasse classic has been keeping the city's cine-addicts happy for years with its three screens dedicated to the obscure and the subversive, plus regular events and themed seasons.

**Forum des Images** 2 rue du Cinéma, Porte St-Eustache, Forum des Halles, 1er ☎ 01 44 76 63 00, ⓦ forumdesimages.fr; ⓜ Châtelet-Les Halles/Châtelet. Classic movies, themed seasons, director-led events and festivals, with at least four films a day on its five screens. The Salle des Collections offers terminals with digital access to the (huge) archive and some obscure titles.

**Le Louxor** 170 bd de Magenta, 10e ☎ 01 44 63 96 98, ⓦ www.cinemalouxor.fr; ⓜ Barbès-Rochechouart. Legendary 1920s movie house with three screens showing arthouse and mainstream films; festivals and film courses, too.

**Max Linder Panorama** 24 bd Poissonnière, 9e ☎ 01 48 00 90 24, ⓦ maxlinder.com; ⓜ Grands Boulevards. This Art Deco cinema, with a big screen, always shows films – both arty and more mainstream – in the original language, and has state-of-the-art surround sound.

**Nouvel Odéon** 6 rue de l'École de Médicine, 6e ☎ 01 46 33 43 71, ⓦ nouvelodeon.com; ⓜ Odéon/Cluny la Sorbonne. A minimalist treat for anyone who loves old movies, with an enticing art-house programme that includes splendid little-known gems.

**Rex** 1 bd Poissonnière, 2e ☎ 01 45 08 93 89, ⓦ legrand rex.com; ⓜ Bonne-Nouvelle. A huge Art Deco cinema showing big-screen movies – dubbed, if the film is foreign.

**Studio 28** 10 rue Tholozé, 18e ☎ 01 46 06 36 07, ⓦ cinemastudio28.com; ⓜ Blanche/Abbesses. In its early days, after one of the first showings of Buñuel's *L'Âge d'Or*, this cinema was done over by extreme right-wing Catholics who destroyed the screen and the paintings by Dalí and Ernst in the foyer. It still hosts occasional avant-garde premieres, sometimes followed by Q&A sessions.

## THEATRE

Looking at the métro posters, you might think bourgeois farces starring gurning celebs form the backbone of French theatre. To an extent, that's true, though the classics – Molière, Corneille and Racine – are also regularly performed, and well worth a try if your French is up to it. You can get by with quite basic French at one of the plays by the postwar generation of Francophone dramatists, such as Anouilh, Genet, Camus, Ionesco and Samuel Beckett. For non-French-speakers, the most rewarding theatre in Paris is likely to be the genre-busting kind represented by the companies at the Cartoucherie, and at the Bouffes du Nord.

**Listings** Productions are detailed online at ⓦ pariscope.fr and ⓦ offi.fr; check too the monthly arts journal *La Terrasse* (ⓦ journal-laterrasse.fr).

**Prices** Prices are mostly around €20–40; inexpensive previews (*avant-première*) are advertised by listings websites and magazines, and there are discounts at some places for students.

**Tickets** Buy directly from theatres, Fnac shops (see page 144) or online at ⓦ fnac.com, ⓦ theatreonline.com or

**1**

ⓦbilletreduc.com (which offers discounts). For the more commercial plays you can buy same-day tickets, with a fifty percent discount (minus a small commission), from the kiosks on place de la Madeleine, 8ᵉ, and place Raoul Dutry, Montparnasse, 14ᵉ (both Tues–Sat 12.30–2.30pm & 3–7.30pm; Sept–June also Sun 12.30–3.45pm; ⓦkiosqueculture.com); and place des Ternes, 17ᵉ (Wed–Sat 12.30–2.30pm & 3–7.30pm). Be prepared to queue.

### VENUES

**Bouffes du Nord** 37bis bd de la Chapelle, 10ᵉ ☎01 46 07 34 50, ⓦwww.bouffesdunord.com; ⓜLa Chapelle/ Gare du Nord. Groundbreaking theatre director Peter Brook resurrected the derelict Bouffes du Nord in 1974 and was based here until 2010. The gorgeous old theatre's two current French directors, Olivier Mantei and Olivier Poubelle, continue Brook's innovative approach.

**Cartoucherie** Rte du Champ-de-Manœuvre, 12ᵉ; ⓜChâteau-de-Vincennes. This former army barracks is home to several cutting-edge theatre companies: workers' co-op Théâtre du Soleil (ⓦtheatre-du-soleil.fr); French-Spanish troupe Théâtre de l'Épée de Bois (ⓦepeedebois. com); Théâtre de la Tempête (ⓦla-tempete.fr); and Théâtre de l'Aquarium (ⓦtheatredelaquarium.net).

**Comédie Française** Place Colette, 1ᵉʳ ☎01 44 58 15 15, ⓦcomedie-francaise.fr; ⓜPalais-Royal. Venerable national theatre chiefly staging tragedies and comedies by Racine, Molière and Corneille, but also twentieth-century greats. There are three sites: the Théâtre du Vieux-Colombier, 21 rue du Vieux-Colombier, 6ᵉ; the mini Studio-Théâtre, under the Louvre, accessed via the Carrousel, 1ᵉʳ; and the headquarters – the Salle Richelieu or "Maison de Molière" – next to the Palais Royal on place Colette, 1ᵉʳ.

**Odéon Théâtre de l'Europe** Place de l' Odéon, 6ᵉ ☎01 44 85 40 40, ⓦtheatre-odeon.eu; ⓜOdéon. This Neoclassical, state-funded theatre puts on European plays and *version originale* productions by well-known foreign companies.

## LGBT PARIS

Paris is one of Europe's great centres for gay men, with the scene's focal point in the Marais, the "pink triangle" around rue Sainte-Croix-de-la-Bretonnerie. Lesbians have fewer dedicated addresses, but the community is energetic and visible. For information, check *Têtu* (ⓦtetu.com), the main French gay monthly magazine.

### BARS

**Café Cox** 15 rue des Archives, 3ᵉ ☎01 42 72 08 00, ⓦcox.fr; ⓜHôtel-de-Ville; map p.82. Muscular chaps, up for a seriously good time, pack out this loud bar – an essential fixture on the Marais circuit, with an extended happy hour (Mon–Sat 6–10pm, Sun 6pm–2am). Daily 5pm–2am.

**Théâtre de la Huchette** 23 rue de la Huchette, 5ᵉ ☎01 43 26 38 99, ⓦtheatre-huchette.com; ⓜSt-Michel. For more than sixty years now, this intimate theatre, seating ninety, has been showing Ionesco's *La Cantatrice Chauve* (*The Bald Prima Donna*; 7pm) and *La Leçon* (8pm), two classics of the Theatre of the Absurd, from Tues–Sat.

## DANCE

Paris is a key player in the nation's dance scene, and regularly hosts the best contemporary practitioners. Plenty of space and critical attention are also given to tap, tango, folk and jazz dancing, and to international traditional dance troupes. The free monthly arts journal *La Terrasse* (ⓦwww. journal-laterrasse.fr) is a good resource for news and events. Note, too, that some of the venues listed under "Theatre" host dance productions.

**Centre National de la Danse** 1 rue Victor Hugo, Pantin ☎01 41 83 98 98, ⓦcnd.fr; ⓜHoche/RER Pantin. Converted from a disused 1970s monolith in the suburb of Pantin into an airy, high-tech space, the national centre for dance is the base for hundreds of French dance companies. Performances, plus workshops, masterclasses and exhibitions.

**Opéra Garnier** Place de l'Opéra, 9ᵉ ☎08 92 89 90 90, ⓦoperadeparis.fr; ⓜOpéra. This extravagantly decorated opera house, the main home of the Ballet de l'Opéra National, still bears the influence of Rudolf Nureyev, its charismatic, controversial director from 1983 to 1989, and frequently revives his productions.

**Théâtre de la Ville** 2 place du Châtelet, 4ᵉ ☎01 42 74 22 77, ⓦtheatredelaville-paris.com; ⓜChâtelet. The biggest contemporary dance venue in Paris, specializing in mainstream and avant-garde productions by French companies as well as working with some of Europe's best choreographers.

**Théâtre National de Chaillot** Palais de Chaillot, place du Trocadéro, 16ᵉ ☎01 53 65 30 00, ⓦtheatre-chaillot. fr; ⓜTrocadéro. An exciting programme of contemporary dance from around the world.

**La Champmeslé** 4 rue Chabanais, 2ᵉ ☎01 42 96 85 20, ⓦlachampmesle.fr; ⓜPyramides; map p.70. Long-established, community-oriented lesbian address in a handsome old building. Popular among thirty-somethings, though it packs everyone in for the cabaret nights. Mon–Sat 4pm–4am.

★ **Le Duplex** 25 rue Michel-le-Comte, 3ᵉ ☎01 42 72 80 86; ⓜRambuteau; map p.82. Arty gay men's bar that's popular with intellectual and media types for its relaxed and chatty atmosphere. Friendly rather than cruisey. Mon–Thurs 8pm–2am, Fri & Sat 6pm–5am, Sun 6pm–2am.

**Le Free DJ** 35 rue Ste-Croix-de-la Bretonnerie, 4ᵉ ☎01 48 04 95 14, ⓦfreedj.fr; ⓜHôtel-de-Ville; map p.82. This stylish, welcoming DJ bar features big sounds (house,

## PARIS FESTIVALS

Paris has a vibrant festival schedule; just a few are listed here. For details of the following and more, check at tourist offices or Ⓦ parisinfo.com.

### MARCH–MAY

**Festival de Films de Femmes** Ⓦ filmsdefemmes.com. Held in mid- to late March in Créteil, just southeast of Paris (Ⓜ Créteil-Préfecture).

**Festival Jazz à St Germain** Ⓦ festivaljazzsaintgermainparis.com. Big names and new talent from around the world, performing in all manner of venues, in late May.

### JUNE/JULY

**Festival Chopin** Ⓦ frederic-chopin.com. Chopin recitals by candlelight or on weekend afternoons from mid-June to mid-July in the lovely setting of the Bois de Boulogne's Orangerie.

**Fête de la Musique** Ⓦ fetedelamusique.culture.fr. Free concerts and street performers all over Paris to coincide with the summer solstice (June 21).

**Gay Pride** Ⓦ marche.inter-lgbt.org. In late June, France's biggest LGBT march sees around 650,000 people hit the streets.

### JULY/AUG

**Bastille Day** Ⓦ parisinfo.com. The 1789 surrender of the Bastille is celebrated with parades of tanks down the Champs-Élysées, followed by fireworks, concerts and street dances.

**Paris l'Été** Ⓦ parislete.fr. Free music, theatre, circus and cinema around the city from mid-July to early Aug.

**Paris Plages** Ⓦ en.parisinfo.com. From early July to early Sept, the *quais* along the Seine between the Louvre and Pont de Sully are transformed into a sandy beach. There's another beach at the Bassin de la Villette.

**Tour de France** Ⓦ letour.fr. The race finishes along the Champs-Élysées on the third or fourth Sun of July.

**Festival du Cinéma en Plein Air** Ⓦ cinema.arbo.com. Free films in the Parc de la Villette from mid-July to late Aug.

**Rock en Seine** Ⓦ rockenseine.com. Three-day music festival in late Aug in a lovely Seine-side park on the western edge of the city.

### SEPT–DEC

**Festival d'Automne** Ⓦ festival-automne.com. Major festival of contemporary theatre, music, dance and avant-garde arts, held from mid-Sept to Dec in venues all over the city.

**Nuit Blanche** Ⓦ paris.fr. In early Oct, the "sleepless night" persuades Parisians to stay up all night for a stunning programme of arts events and parties.

**Paris Photo** Ⓦ parisphoto.com. This huge photography exhibition takes over the Grand Palais for four days in mid-Nov.

---

disco-funk) in the basement club at the weekends. Daily 5pm–4am.

**L'Open Café** 17 rue des Archives, 4ᵉ Ⓦ opencafe.fr; Ⓜ Hôtel-de-Ville; map p.82. *The* most famous gay bar in Paris is expensive and quite touristy, but still good fun, with not bad café food and lots of *terrasse* seating for observing the street scene. Mon–Thurs & Sun 11am–2am, Fri & Sat 11am–3am.

**Le Raidd** 23 rue du Temple, 4ᵉ ☎01 42 77 04 88, Ⓦ facebook.com/pg/raiddbarparis; Ⓜ Hôtel-de-Ville; map p.82. One of the city's biggest, glossiest bars, famous for its beautiful staff, topless waiters and go-go boys' shower shows. Mon–Thurs & Sun 6pm–4am, Fri & Sat 6pm–5am.

**Le So What!** 30 rue du Roi de Sicile, 4ᵉ ☎01 42 71 24 59, Ⓦ facebook.com/LeSoWhat; Ⓜ St-Paul; map

p.82. A lesbian bar aimed at a more mature crowd. Friendly ambience, with good DJ sets, and club nights at the weekend. Check the Facebook page for listings. Thurs 9pm–9am, Fri 11pm–5am, Sat 11.30pm–5am.

## CLUBS

A few classic club addresses are given here, and many mainstream clubs run gay *soirées*. Clubs are all pretty empty before at least 1am and keep going till at least dawn. Entry generally costs around €10–20 (usually including a *conso*, or "free" drink).

**CUD** 12 rue des Haudriettes, 3ᵉ ☎01 42 77 44 12, Ⓦ facebook.com/cudbar; Ⓜ Rambuteau; map p.82. The "Classic Up and Down" is just that: bar upstairs, club below. Low-key: no queues, door policies or overpriced drinks. More for bears than boys, though it's pretty mixed. Mon–Thurs & Sun midnight–6am, Fri & Sat midnight–7am.

**Gibus** 18 rue du Faubourg du Temple, 11e ☎01 47 00 78 88, ⓦgibusclub.fr; ⓂRépublique; map p.82. Hugely popular club/live music venue putting on some of the city's biggest gay nights, including Crazyvores and Menergy. The up-for-it crowd looks good and is generally friendly. Club nights (generally Fri–Sun) from 11pm.

**Le Tango/La Boîte à Frissons** 13 rue au Maire, 3e ☎01 48 87 25 71, ⓦboite-a-frissons.fr; ⓂArts-et-Métiers; map p.82. Unpretentious (and inexpensive) LGBT+ club in a retro 1930s dance hall, with a traditional Sunday-afternoon tea dance/*bal* from 6pm. Friday and Saturday nights also begin with couples of all sexual orientation dancing traditional *danse à deux*, until the legendary "Madison" line dance at 12.30am, after which it's pure fetish costume and disco. €6–9. Fri & Sat 10.30pm–5am, Sun 6–11pm.

## SHOPPING

Though chains both local and international have made advances in the city in recent years, the Parisian attachment to small local traders has kept alive a good variety of speciality shops. The nineteenth-century arcades, or *passages*, in the 2e and 9e arrondissements, offer intriguing opportunities, while the square kilometre around place St-Germain-des-Prés is hard to beat for anything from antiques to shoes – at a price. Other rewarding places for browsing include chic Marais, trendy Bastille, the quirky rues des Abbesses and Martyrs in Montmartre, the hip streets south of Pigalle and the broadly bohemian Oberkampf and Canal Saint-Martin areas of northeastern Paris. For haute couture the traditional bastions are avenue Montaigne, rue François-1er and the upper end of rue du Faubourg-St-Honoré in the 8e. The studenty *quartier Latin* is the home of most of the city's best independent bookshops; bibliophiles should also check out the Seine *quais*, with their rows of mostly secondhand bookstalls perched against the river parapet.

### BOOKS

★ **Artcurial** 7 Rond-Point des Champs-Élysées, 8e ☎01 42 99 16 19, ⓦlibrairie.artcurial.com; ⓂFranklin-D.-Roosevelt; map p.70. Based in an astonishingly grand townhouse that also houses an auctioneers, this is a swanky setting for excellent art books, including French and foreign editions. Mon–Fri 9am–7pm, Sat 10.30am–7pm.

**Fnac** Forum des Halles, Porte Pierre-Lescot, 1er; Ⓜ/RER Châtelet-Les Halles; map p.79; 74 av des Champs-Élysées, 8e; ⓂFranklin-D.-Roosevelt; map p.70; both ☎08 25 02 00 20, ⓦfnac.com. France's leading chain for books, CDs, games and electronics, and for concert and sports tickets. There are numerous branches in Paris, offering supermarket-style discounting, and the range of books and music is excellent. Forum des Halles Mon–Sat 10am–8pm, Sun 11am–7pm; Champs-Élysées Mon–Sat 10am–10.30pm, Sun 11am–8.45pm.

★ **Galignani** 224 rue de Rivoli, 1er ☎01 42 60 76 07, ⓦgalignani.com; ⓂConcorde; map p.70. Claims to be the first English bookshop established on the continent, opened (on a different site) way back in the early 1800s. The English-language selections are top-notch, including fiction, fine art and children's books. Mon–Sat 10am–7pm.

**Gibert Jeune** 6 place St-Michel, 5e ☎01 56 81 22 22, ⓦwww.gibert.com; ⓂSt-Michel; map p.92. There's a fair English-language and discounted selection at this branch of the classic Quartier Latin student bookshop. A vast selection of French titles can be found in the seven branches, which are dotted throughout and around the *place*, and easily spotted with their yellow awnings. Mon–Sat 9.30am–7.30pm.

**Shakespeare and Company** 37 rue de la Bûcherie, 5e ☎01 43 25 40 93, ⓦshakespeareandcompany.com; ⓂSt-Michel; map p.92. The original shop with the Shakespeare name – owned by Sylvia Beach, the first publisher of Joyce's *Ulysses* – was on rue de l'Odéon, but even the replacement has become a classic. A cosy, welcoming literary haunt run by Americans and staffed by earnest young Hemingway wannabes, it sells the best selection of secondhand English-language books in town, and lots of new stock, especially Paris-related. Regular readings and events, with a café in an adjacent building. Daily 10am–10pm.

### CLOTHES

**agnès b.** 6 (mostly women's; ☎01 44 39 02 60) & 10 (mostly men's; ☎01 45 49 02 05) rue du Vieux Colombier, 6e ⓦeurope.agnesb.com; ⓂSt-Sulpice; map p.96. Cool, simple staples from the queen of understatement – chic, timeless and relaxed. Numerous branches around town. Both Mon–Fri 10am–7.30pm, Sat 10am–8pm.

★ **Antoine et Lili** 95 quai de Valmy, 10e ☎01 40 37 41 55, ⓦantoineetlili.com; ⓂRépublique. The flagship of this quirky Parisian institution, with three neighbouring candy-coloured frontages (one for women's clothes, one for kids, and one for homeware) on the Canal St-Martin. There are several branches across the city, each as colourful. The clothes and accessories have a dose of kitsch and an emphasis on fun. Mon–Fri 10.30am–8pm, Sat 10am–8pm, Sun 11am–7pm.

**APC** 38 rue Madame, 6e ☎0142 22 12 77, ⓦapc.fr; ⓂSt-Sulpice; map p.96. This chain is perfect for young, urban basics – a kind of Parisian take on Gap. This is the main store; there are many other branches around town. Mon–Sat 11am–7.30pm.

**Le Centre Commercial** 2 rue de Marseille, 10e ☎01 42 02 26 08, ⓦcentrecommercial.cc; ⓂJacques-

## FOOD MARKETS

Many of Paris's most historic market streets, such as **rue Mouffetard** (5ᵉ) and **rue des Martyrs** (9ᵉ) are lined with food shops now, not stalls, but this is still one of the world's great cities for outdoor food shopping. A few of the best markets are recommended here.

**Marché d'Aligre** Place d'Aligre, 12ᵉ; Ⓜ Ledru-Rollin. Historic street and covered food market in the square; one of the cheapest and most popular in Paris. Tues–Sat 9am–1pm & 4–7.30pm, Sun 9am–1.30pm.

**Marché Bastille** Bd Richard Lenoir, 11ᵉ; Ⓜ Richard Lenoir. Huge, authentic street market, with lots of regional produce. Thurs & Sun 7am–2.30pm.

**Marché Belleville** Bd de Belleville, 11ᵉ; Ⓜ Belleville. Lively, noisy neighbourhood market selling a good range of fresh ethnic food. Tues & Fri 7am–2.30pm.

**Marché Edgar-Quinet** Bd Edgar-Quinet, 14ᵉ; Ⓜ Edgar-Quinet. Two separate markets: food and arts and crafts. The food market offers a vast range of fresh produce, from seafood and artisan cheese to fresh crêpes and home-made pizza. Food Wed & Sat 7am–2.30pm, art and crafts Sun roughly 10am–dusk.

**Marché des Enfants Rouges** 39 rue de Bretagne, 3ᵉ; Ⓜ Filles-du-Calvaire. Covered food market abounding in eating outlets and produce. Tues, Wed & Thurs 8.30am–1pm & 4–7.30pm, Fri & Sat 8.30am–1pm & 4–8pm, Sun 8.30am–2pm.

**Marché Monge** Place Monge, 5ᵉ; Ⓜ Place Monge. Fabulous (and quite pricey) produce set around the pretty Monge fountain; organic stalls on Sundays. Wed, Fri & Sun 7am–2.30pm.

**Marché Montorgueil** Rue Montorgueil 1ᵉʳ; Ⓜ Étienne-Marcel. Market stalls, artisan produce and gourmet food stores spread along this foodie street. Tues–Fri, plus Sat & Sun mornings.

**Marché Raspail/Marché Bio** Bd Raspail, 6ᵉ; Ⓜ Rennes. The city's main organic market, also selling herbal remedies and artisan produce. Sun 9am–3pm.

Bonsergent. The name may sound unpromising, but this is an interesting concept store dedicated to ecofriendly clothes for men, mostly, as well as accessories, travel and fashion books and furniture. There's a children's shop around the corner on rue Yves Toudic. Mon 1–7.30pm, Tues–Sat 11am–8pm, Sun 2–7pm.

**L'Éclaireur** 40 rue de Sévigné, 3ᵉ ☎ 01 48 87 10 22, Ⓦ leclaireur.com; Ⓜ Chemin Vert; map p.82. Paris's original concept store is still going strong and has three outlets; this one is particularly striking, styling itself as an experience rather than a shop, with clothes hidden behind screens and sliding panels. Well-known and offbeat designers, as well as perfumes, books and accessories for men and women. Mon–Sat 11am–7pm, Sun 2–7pm.

**Isabel Marant** 16 rue de Charonne, 11ᵉ ☎ 01 49 29 71 55, Ⓦ isabelmarant.com; Ⓜ Bastille/Ledru-Rollin; map p.82. Parisian Marant has an international reputation for her feminine and flattering clothes in quality fabrics; her Étoile line is less expensive. Four more Paris branches. Mon 11am–7pm, Tues–Sat 10.30am–7.30pm.

**Kiliwatch** 64 rue Tiquetonne, 2ᵉ ☎ 01 42 21 17 37, Ⓦ kiliwatch.paris; Ⓜ Étienne Marcel; map p.79. Vast concept store where vintage duds meet cheap'n'chic streetwear: match cool trainers/sneakers with army surplus, lumberjack shirts or 1970s boho gear. Also a great selection of jeans and vintage women's shoes. Mon 10.30am–7pm, Tues–Sat 10.30am–7.30pm.

★ **Maje** 49 rue Vieille du Temple, 4ᵉ ☎ 01 42 74 63 77, Ⓦ maje.com; Ⓜ St-Paul; map p.82. This Paris-based but now international brand offers relaxed, slightly bohemian, cool and elegant clothes. This is a sizeable store, offering a

good choice; there are many other branches around town. Mon–Sat 10.30am–7.30pm, Sun 10am–8pm.

★ **Paul & Joe** 64 rue des Sts-Pères, 7ᵉ ☎ 01 42 22 47 01, Ⓦ paulandjoe.com; Ⓜ Sèvres-Babylone; map p.96. Very French clothes, for men and women – quirky but not showy, playful but not radical. Several concessions in Paris, including Paul & Joe Sister, the slightly more youthful offshoot. Mon–Sat 10am–7pm.

**Sessùn** 34 rue de Charonne, 11ᵉ ☎ 01 48 06 55 66, Ⓦ sessun.com; Ⓜ Ledru-Rollin; map p.82. This bright and spacious boutique, on a trendy shopping street, sells all the womenswear you could want, from pretty prints and elegant winter coats to cosy knits and basic T-shirts. Prices can be good value, given the quality. Mon–Wed, Fri & Sat 11am–7pm, Thurs 11am–8pm.

★ **Spree** 16 rue de la Vieuville, 18ᵉ ☎ 01 42 23 41 40, Ⓦ spree.fr; Ⓜ Abbesses; map p.112. Funky, feminine clothing concept store/gallery with pieces by designers such as Isabel Marant and Christian Wijnants. Also vintage pieces, bigger-brand lines (Comme des Garçons, for instance), accessories, furniture and homeware. Tues–Sat 11am–7.30pm, Sun 3–7pm.

**Vanessa Bruno** 25 rue St-Sulpice, 6ᵉ ☎ 01 43 54 41 04, Ⓦ vanessabruno.com; Ⓜ Odéon; map p.96. Effortlessly beautiful women's fashions with a hint of floaty, hippy chic. There's another branch in the Marais. Mon–Sat 10am–7pm.

### DEPARTMENT STORES

★ **Le Bon Marché** 24 rue de Sèvres, 7ᵉ ☎ 01 44 39 80 00, Ⓦ 24sevres.com; Ⓜ Sèvres-Babylone; map p.96. The world's oldest department store, founded in 1852, and

**1**

now run by the luxury goods empire LVMH. It's a stunning building and a classy place to shop, with a legendary food hall. Mon–Wed, Fri & Sat 10am–8pm, Thurs 10am–9pm, Sun 11am–8pm.

**Galeries Lafayette** 40 bd Haussmann, 9ᵉ ☎01 42 82 34 56, ⓦhaussmann.galerieslafayette.com; Ⓜ Havre-Caumartin; map p.70. The store's forte is high fashion, with a huge parfumerie and a branch of *Angélina salon de thé*, all under a superb 1912 dome. Just down the road at no. 35 is Lafayette Maison/Gourmet, five floors of quality kitchen- and homewares, luxury food and wine. Galeries Mon–Sat 9.30am–8.30pm, Sun 11am–8pm; Maison/Gourmet Mon–Sat 8.30am–9.30pm, Sun 11am–8pm.

★ **Printemps** 64 bd Haussmann, 9ᵉ ☎01 42 82 50 00, ⓦdepartmentstoreparis.printemps.com; Ⓜ Havre-Caumartin; map p.70. The beautiful *belle époque* store on Haussmann is in a glorious building with a stunning stained-glass dome. There's another branch in the Carrousel du Louvre on rue de Rivoli, focusing more on accessories and make-up. Mon–Sat 9.35am–8pm, Thurs 9.35am–8.45pm, Sun 11am–7pm.

### FOOD AND DRINK

★ **Barthélémy** 51 rue de Grenelle, 7ᵉ ☎01 45 48 56 75; Ⓜ Rue-du-Bac; map p.96. Exquisite, traditional store packed to the rafters with carefully ripened and meticulously stored seasonal cheeses. Tues–Thurs 8.30am–1pm & 3.30–7.15pm, Fri & Sat 8.30am–1.30pm & 3–7.15pm.

**Les Caves Augé** 116 bd Haussmann, 8ᵉ ☎01 45 22 16 97, ⓦcavesauge.com; Ⓜ St-Augustin; map p.70. The oldest *cave* in Paris, dating back to 1850, and selling around six thousand French and foreign wines and champagne, many of them organic or natural. Mon–Sat 10am–7.30pm.

**Debauve et Gallais** 30 rue des Sts-Pères, 7ᵉ ☎01 45 48 54 67, ⓦdebauve-et-gallais.fr; Ⓜ St-Germain-des-Prés/Sèvres-Babylone; map p.96. This beautiful historic shop, specializing in chocolate and elaborate sweets, is designated a *monument historique*. Mon–Sat 9am–7pm.

**Fauchon** 30 place de la Madeleine, 8ᵉ ☎01 70 39 38 02, ⓦfauchon.fr; Ⓜ Madeleine; map p.70. Upmarket foodie gifts, including extravagantly beautiful groceries, patisserie, charcuterie, terrines and wines – at exorbitant prices. Mon–Sat 10am–8.30pm.

★ **Gontran Cherrier** 22 rue Caulaincourt, 18ᵉ ☎01 46 06 82 66, ⓦgontran-cherrier.com; Ⓜ Abbesses; map p.112. While the bread, croissants and sweet pastries at this contemporary *pâtissier* are amazing, the buns – try the squid-ink and nigella seed variety, filled with *jamón* – steal the show. Green (rocket and courgette) and red (paprika) buns are also available. Mon–Sat 7.30am–8pm.

**Mariage Frères** 30 rue du Bourg-Tibourg, 4ᵉ ☎01 42 72 28 11, ⓦwww.mariagefreres.com; Ⓜ Hôtel-de-Ville; map p.82. Hundreds of teas, prettily packed in tins, line the floor-to-ceiling shelves of this historic tea emporium that's been trading since 1854. There's also a classy *salon de thé* (serving from noon). Also at 32 and 35 rue du Bourg-Tibourg, with other branches throughout Paris. Daily 10.30am–7.30pm.

**Pierre Hermé** 72 rue Bonaparte, 6ᵉ ☎01 43 54 47 77, ⓦpierreherme.com; Ⓜ St-Sulpice; map p.96. The *macarons* made by this pastry demigod are widely considered to be the best in Paris, if not France. While the more unusual flavour pairings, such as foie gras and chocolate, may sound risky, Hermé hasn't earned his stellar reputation for nothing. Various branches around town. Mon–Fri & Sun 10am–7pm, Sat 10am–8pm.

★ **Stohrer** 51 rue Montorgueil, 2ᵉ ☎01 42 33 38 20, ⓦstohrer.fr; Ⓜ Sentier; map p.70. Patisserie, chocolate and deli delights have been produced in this lovely little shop since 1730. The window display is irresistible: from delectable chocolate eclairs to towering vol-au-vent and quail stuffed with foie gras. Daily 7.30am–8.30pm.

### FLEA MARKETS

**Puces de Vanves** Av Georges Lafenestre/av Marc Sangnier, 14ᵉ ⓦpucesdevanves.fr; Ⓜ Porte-de-Vanves. Bric-a-brac and Parisian knick-knacks, with professionals dealing alongside weekend enthusiasts. Sat & Sun 7am–1pm/3pm.

★ **Puces de St-Ouen** 18ᵉ ⓦmarcheauxpuces-saintouen.com; Ⓜ Porte-de-Clignancourt. By far the biggest and most visited of Paris's flea markets, just beyond the northern edge of the 18e arrondissement, with thousands of stalls selling new and used clothes, shoes, records, books and junk of all sorts, along with expensive antiques. Different markets keep slightly different hours, but as a rule Mon 11am–5pm, Sat & Sun 10am–5.30pm.

### DIRECTORY

**Banks and exchange** Cash machines (ATMs) are located at all airports and mainline train stations, and at most of the banks in town. Beware of money-exchange bureaux and automatic exchange machines, however, which may advertise the selling rather than buying rate and add on hefty commission fees.

**Embassies/Consulates** Australia, 4 rue Jean-Rey, 15ᵉ; Ⓜ Bir-Hakeim (☎01 40 59 33 00, ⓦfrance.embassy.gov.au); Canada, 35 av Montaigne, 8ᵉ; Ⓜ Franklin-D.-Roosevelt (☎01 44 43 29 00, ⓦcanadainternational.gc.ca); Ireland, 4 rue Rude, 16ᵉ; Ⓜ Charles-de-Gaulle-Étoile (☎01 44 17 67 00, ⓦdfa.ie/irish-embassy/france); New Zealand, 103 rue de Grenelle, 7ᵉ; Ⓜ Varenne (☎01 45 01 43 43, ⓦbit.ly/nzembassy); South Africa, 59 quai d'Orsay, 7ᵉ; Ⓜ Invalides (☎01 53 59 23 23, ⓦafriquesud.net); UK, 35 rue du Faubourg-St-Honoré, 8ᵉ; Ⓜ Concorde (☎01 44 51 31 00,

Ⓦ www.gov.uk/government/world/organisations/british-embassy-paris); US, 2 av Gabriel, 1ᵉʳ; Ⓜ Concorde (☎ 01 43 12 22 22, Ⓦ fr.usembassy.gov).

**Health** SOS Médecins (☎ 01 47 07 77 77) offers doctor call-out service. In emergencies, call the paramedics/fire brigade (*sapeurs-pompiers*) on ☎ 18; they are equipped to deal with medical emergencies and are the fastest and most reliable emergency service.

**Left luggage** Left luggage facilities (*consigne*) are available at all train stations except St-Lazare and Paris-Bercy.

**Lost property** The lost property office (Bureau des Objets Trouvés) is at the Préfecture de Police, 36 rue des Morillons, 15ᵉ; Ⓜ Convention (Mon–Thurs 8.30am–5pm, Fri 8.30am–4.30pm; ☎ 3430). If you have mislaid property on public transport within the last 48hrs, inform station staff. After 48hrs you will need to phone the RATP on ☎ 3246. If you lose your passport, report it to a police station and your embassy.

**Pharmacies** To find your nearest duty pharmacy call ☎ 32 37 or search on Ⓦ www.3237.fr (though note that not all of the city's pharmacies are listed). Many are closed on Sundays, though there are some in central areas that open from roughly 8am–8pm; at night, details of the nearest open pharmacy are posted in the windows. For a list of pharmacies that are open on particular nights, check Ⓦ pharmaciesdegarde.fr.

**Police** ☎ 17 for emergencies. To report a theft, go to the Commissariat de Police of the arrondissement in which the theft took place.

# Around Paris

The region around the capital – the **Île de France** – and the borders of the neighbouring provinces are studded with **châteaux**. Many were royal or noble hunting retreats, while some – like **Versailles** – were for more serious state show. **Vaux-le-Vicomte** has perhaps the most harmonious architecture, **Chantilly** the finest Classical art collection and **Fontainebleau** the most gorgeous interiors. Two of the world's greatest cathedrals also lie within easy reach of Paris: in the otherwise gritty suburb of **St-Denis** the Gothic style was born; at **Chartres**, it reached its exquisite pinnacle. The most popular attraction by far, however, is **Disneyland Paris**, out beyond the satellite town of **Marne-la-Vallée**.

## Basilique St-Denis

1 rue de la Légion d'Honneur, St-Denis, 10km north of the centre of Paris • April–Sept Mon–Sat 10am–6.15pm, Sun noon–6.15pm; Oct–March Mon–Sat 10am–5pm, Sun noon–5.15pm; closed for extra services on feast days • €9 • Ⓦ saint-denis.monuments-nationaux.fr • Ⓜ Basilique de St-Denis

The traditionally industrial *banlieue* (suburb) of **ST-DENIS** is perhaps a surprising place to find the most important cathedral in France. Begun in the first half of the twelfth century, the **Basilique St-Denis** is generally regarded as the birthplace of the Gothic style in European architecture. With its two towers (the northern one collapsed in 1837), three large sculpted portals and high rose window, the west front set the pattern of Gothic facades to come, but it's in the choir that you best see the emergence of the new style: the use of the pointed arch, the ribbed vault and the long shafts of half-column rising from pillar to roof. It's beautifully lit, thanks to the transept windows – so big that they occupy their entire end walls – and the clerestory, which is almost entirely made of glass (another first).

Legend holds that the first church here was founded by a mid-third-century Parisian bishop, later known as St-Denis. The story goes that after he was beheaded for his beliefs at Montmartre (Mount of the Martyr), he picked up his head and walked to St-Denis, thereby establishing the abbey. The site's **royal history** began with the coronation of Pepin the Short in 754, but it wasn't until the reign of Hugues Capet, in 996, that it became the customary burial place of the kings of France. Since then, all but three of France's kings have been interred here, and their fine tombs and effigies are distributed about the **necropolis** (closed during services) in the transepts and ambulatory.

Immediately on the left of the entrance, in the south transept, is one of the most bizarre sights: the bare feet of **François 1ᵉʳ** and his wife Claude de France peeking out of their enormous Renaissance memorial. Beside the steps to the ambulatory lies **Charles V**, the first king to have his funeral effigy carved from life, on the day of his coronation in 1364.

**1**

Alongside him is his wife Jeanne de Bourbon, who clutches the sack of her own entrails to her chest – royalty was traditionally eviscerated at death. Up the steps and round to the right, a florid Louis XVI and **Marie Antoinette** – often graced by bouquets of flowers – kneel in prayer. The pious scene was sculpted in 1830, long after their execution.

## Domaine de Chantilly

Rue du Connétable, Chantilly, 40km north of Paris • April–Oct daily 10am–6pm (grounds 8pm); Nov–March Mon & Wed–Sun 10.30am–5pm (grounds 6pm); French-language guided tours of the Duc and Duchesse d'Aumale's private apartments daily (45min; see website for schedule) • Château, grounds, horse museum & equestrian show €30; château, grounds & Musée du Cheval (including training session) €17; Musée du Cheval & equestrian show €21; tours of the Duc and Duchesse d'Aumale's private apartments €3; grounds only April–Oct €8, Nov–March €5; mini train through grounds €5 • ☎ 03 44 27 31 80, ⓦ domainedechantilly.com • Daily trains run from Gare du Nord to Chantilly Gouvieux station (every 30min–1hr; 25min) on the line to Creil: there is no taxi rank at Chantilly station but a list of phone numbers is displayed; you might otherwise pick up a free bus (get off by the Grandes Écuries and walk 500m to the château) but it's more pleasant to take a direct, 25min stroll along a signposted footpath – turn right outside the station, then almost immediately left at the roundabout along the av de l'Aigle (you'll pass the racetrack about a third of the way along)

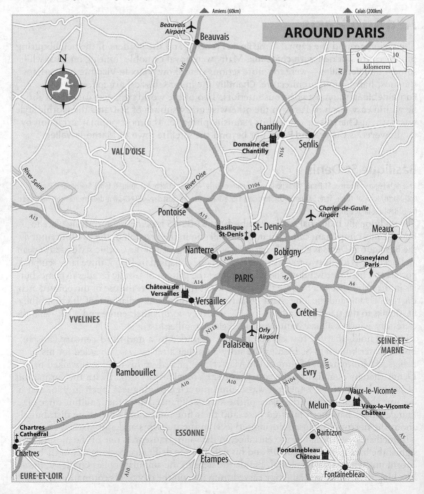

The small horse-racing town of Chantilly is also famous for the **Chantilly estate**, which has been the powerbase of two of the most powerful clans in France: the Montmorencys and then, through marriage, the Condés. It was the château's last private owners, the **Duc and Duchesse d'Aumale**, who, in 1886, donated it to the Institut de France, which owns the estate today. The Duc d'Aumale (Henri d'Orléans) had little reason to cling to it, in fact, as he was not actually a Condé at all, but the fifth son of King Louis-Philippe, France's last king. He inherited the château in 1830 – aged eight – from his godfather, Louis VI Henri de Bourbon-Condé, who had lost all six of his own children (the eldest son was murdered on the orders of Napoleon, in 1804). A great collector, the duke filled it with many of the precious works of art you see here today.

The present, mostly late nineteenth-century **château** replaced a palace, destroyed in the Revolution, which had been built for the Grand Condé (1621–86). It's a beautiful structure, surrounded by what's more a lake than a moat, looking out over a formal arrangement of pools and elegant **gardens** created by André Le Nôtre, Louis XIV's gardener.

### Cabinet des Livres and Petit Château

Just off an antechamber linking the sixteenth-century wing (the "Petit Château") and the nineteenth-century Grand Château, the Duc d'Aumale's **Cabinet des Livres** displays a perfect facsimile of the manuscript *Les Très Riches Heures du Duc de Berry*. The original, which is also held here, is the most celebrated of all the medieval Books of Hours, and the museum's single greatest treasure.

Beyond the Cabinet des Livres, the first floor of the **Petit Château** is filled with the opulent **apartments of the Princes de Condé**, decorated in the seventeenth and eighteenth centuries. Look out for the exquisite *boiseries* (wooden panelling) in the **Singerie**, or Monkey Gallery, painted with allegorical stories, all starring monkeys, in a pseudo-Chinese style. The nineteenth-century **apartments of the Duc and Duchesse d'Aumale**, on the ground floor – elegant but surprisingly intimate – are visitable on (French-language) guided tours only.

### Musée Condé

The **Musée Condé**, which occupies the nineteenth-century **Grand Château**, harbours the Duc d'Aumale's art collection, one of the greatest in France. Highlights can be found in the skylit **Painting Gallery** and its **Rotunda** – among them Poussin's *Massacre of the Innocents* and di Cosimo's *Simonetta Vespucci* – and in the Sanctuary, with its Italian Renaissance masterpieces: Raphael's *Three Graces* and the *Orleans Madonna*, as well as Filippino Lippi's *Esther and Assuerus*. Don't miss, either, the octagonal, red-walled Tribune, where Botticelli's resplendently fertile *Autumn* seems to rival Ingres' sexy *Venus Anadyomene*, and works by Delacroix, Poussin and van Dyck, among others, crowd in all around.

### Musée du Cheval

Five minutes' walk along the drive from the Château de Chantilly towards town stands the colossal stable block, the **Grandes Écuries**. The building was erected at the beginning of the eighteenth century by the incumbent Condé prince, who believed he would be reincarnated as a horse and wished to provide fitting accommodation for 240 of his future relatives. Equine exhibits at the **Musée du Cheval** cover everything from the history of domestication to the changing depiction of the animal in art. Spectacular **equestrian shows** are held in the central wing (check website for calendar).

## Disneyland Paris

Children will love **Disneyland Paris** – and most adults too, for all its rampant commercialism. The park marked its 25th anniversary in 2017 by revamping some of its most popular attractions and freshening up others. There are three areas: **Disneyland Park**, which has most of the really big rides; **Walt Disney Studios Park**, which offers

**1**

more technological rides based on animation – though there are plenty of thrill rides too; and the restaurant/entertainment/accommodation complex of **Disney Village**. Disneyland Paris is easy to visit in a day-trip from the capital, around 30km away.

## Disneyland Park

**Disneyland Park** has a variety of good thrill rides, though the majority of attractions remain relatively sedate. The Magic Kingdom is divided into four "lands" radiating out from **Main Street USA**. **Fantasyland** appeals to the tinies, with It's a Small World, Sleeping Beauty's Castle, Peter Pan's Flight and Dumbo the Flying Elephant among its attractions. **Adventureland** has the most outlandish sets and one of the best rides – Pirates of the Caribbean. **Frontierland**, loosely set in the Wild West, features the hair-raising roller coaster Big Thunder Mountain, modelled on a runaway mine train, and the gothic Phantom Manor. In **Discoveryland** there's the terrifyingly fast Star Wars Hyperspace Mountain ride. A grand **parade** of floats representing all your favourite characters sallies down Main Street USA every evening, and there are regular smaller events, special shows and firework displays.

## Walt Disney Studios Park

The **Walt Disney Studios Park** largely focuses on what Disney was and is still renowned for – animation. You can try your hand at drawing, be part of the audience in a mocked-up film or TV set, and enjoy special effects and stunt shows. This is where you'll find the wildly popular **Ratatouille** ride, where you're "shrunk" to the size of a rat and taken on a frantic 3D chase through a kitchen, plus three other thrilling rides: the corkscrew-looping, heavy metal-playing white-knuckler of the **Rock 'n' Roller Coaster Starring Aerosmith** – due to be updated on an Iron Man and the Avengers theme in 2020 – the plummeting elevator of the **Twilight Zone Tower of Terror** and the swirling, "undersea" exhilarations of **Crush's Coaster**.

### ARRIVAL AND DEPARTURE                                    DISNEYLAND PARIS

**By train** From Paris, take RER line A4 from Châtelet-Les Halles, Gare-de-Lyon or Nation to Marne-la-Vallée/Chessy station, which is opposite the main park gates (every 5–10min; 40min–1hr; €7.60 one-way). Marne-la-Vallée/Chessy also has its own TGV train station, linked to Lille and London (via Eurostar). Some Mobilis travel cards include Disneyland Paris.
**By plane** Shuttle buses from Charles de Gaulle and Orly

(every 15min–1hr from 9am; see ⓦ magicalshuttle.co.uk for timetables and pick-up points; 45min; €23 one-way, €10 for children aged 3 to 12).
**By car** Disneyland Paris is a 32km drive east of Paris along the A4: take the "Porte de Bercy" exit off the *périphérique*, then follow "direction Metz/Nancy", leaving at exit 14. From Calais follow the A26, changing to the A1, the A104 and finally the A4.

### INFORMATION

**Opening hours** Depending on the season and whether it's a weekend, the parks open from 10am to anywhere between 7pm and 11pm at Disneyland Park, or between 6pm and 7pm at Walt Disney Studios.
**Admission** One-day one-park costs €49–79 for

adults/€42–71 children aged 3–11; one-day two-park tickets cost €69–99/€62–91.
**Contact details** UK ☎ 0844 800 8898, France ☎ 0825 300 500, ⓦ disneylandparis.co.uk. ⓦ dlpguide.com is also useful.

### ACCOMMODATION

Disney's seven themed, heavily designed Disney Village hotels are a mixed bag, and only worth staying in as part of a multi-day package booked through an agent, or through Disneyland. Around 10km to the southwest, a new

venture, *Villages Nature Paris*, a somewhat incongruous collaboration between Disney and Center Parcs, adds eco-themed waterpark fun to the mix.

## Vaux-le-Vicomte

6km east of Melun, 50km southeast of Paris • Mid-March to early Nov daily 10am–7pm (last entry 5.15pm); Dec Wed–Fri 11am–7pm (last entry 6pm), Sat & Sun 11am–8pm (last entry 7pm); candlelight illumination of state rooms and gardens early May to early Oct Sat

1

7pm–midnight • €16.50, with candlelight illumination €19.50; gardens only €10, with candlelight illumination €15; dome €3 • ☎ 01 64 14 41 90, ⓦ vaux-le-vicomte.com • Driving, take the A4 or A6 then N104 and A5 (direction Troyes); by train take the Provins train (line P) from Gare de l'Est to Verneuil l'Étang (hourly; 35min) – from here a frequent "Châteaubus" service (€10 return) covers the 20min journey to the estate (check ⓦ vaux-le-vicomte.com timetables)

Of all the great mansions within reach of a day's outing from Paris, the classical **Château of Vaux-le-Vicomte** is the most architecturally harmonious and aesthetically pleasing – and the most human in scale. Louis XIV's finance minister, Nicolas Fouquet, had the château built between 1656 and 1661 at colossal expense, using the top designers of the day – architect Le Vau, painter Le Brun and landscape gardener Le Nôtre. The result was magnificence and precision in perfect proportion, and a bill that could only be paid by someone who occasionally confused the state's accounts with his own. In September 1661, weeks after his sumptuous and showy house-warming party, Fouquet was arrested – by d'Artagnan of **Musketeer** fame – and charged with embezzlement, of which he was certainly guilty, then clapped into jail for life. Thereupon, the design trio was carted off to build the king's own piece of one-upmanship, the palace of Versailles.

### The château and gardens

Seen from the entrance, the château is an austere grey pile surrounded by an artificial moat. It's only when you go through to the south side – where clipped box and yew, fountains and statuary stand in formal gardens – that you can look back and appreciate the very harmonious, very French combination of steep, tall roof and central dome with classical pediment and pilasters. Inside, the main artistic interest lies in the work of Le Brun. He was responsible for the two fine **tapestries** in the entrance, made in the local workshops set up by Fouquet specifically to adorn his house, as well as numerous **painted ceilings** including the one in the Salon des Muses, *Le sommeil* ("*Sleep*") in the Cabinet des Jeux, and the so-called King's Bedroom, whose decor is the first example of the style that became known as "Louis Quatorze". There is also a carriage museum, an audiovisual display on Le Nôtre and a dome to climb for panoramic views of the estate.

On Saturday evenings from May to October the state rooms and gardens are illuminated with two thousand **candles**, as they probably were on the occasion of Fouquet's fateful party, with classical music and fireworks in the gardens adding to the atmosphere. A fancy restaurant, and an alfresco champagne bar with deckchairs, are both open at this time, along with the standard self-service **restaurant** that's also open during the day. There are two designated **picnic** areas at either end of the gardens.

## Fontainebleau Château

60km south of Paris, 3km southwest of Fontainebleau-Avon train station • **Château** Daily except Tues: April–Sept 9.30am–6pm; Oct–March 9.30am–5pm • Grands Appartements and Musée Napoléon 1er €12; additional charges for various other apartments and museums • **Gardens** Daily: March, April & Oct 9am–6pm; May–Sept 9am–7pm; Nov–Feb 9am–5pm • Free • ☎ 01 60 71 50 70, ⓦ musee-chateau-fontainebleau.fr • Fontainebleau is 16km from the A6 autoroute (exit "Fontainebleau"); SNCF trains run from the Gare de Lyon to Fontainebleau-Avon station (40min), on the way to Montargis Sens, Montereau or Laroche-Migennes – line 1 bus "Les Lilas" (15min) takes you from the station to the château

The ramblingly magnificent **Fontainebleau Château** owes its existence to the surrounding forest, which made it the perfect base for royal hunting expeditions. A lodge was built here as early as the twelfth century, but it only began its transformation into a luxurious palace during the 1500s on the initiative of François Ier, who imported a colony of Italian artists – notably Rosso Fiorentino and Niccolò dell'Abate – to carry out the decoration. The palace's highlights are the sumptuous **interiors** worked by the Italians, chiefly the celebrated **Galerie François Ier**, which are resplendent in gilt, carved, inlaid and polished wood, and adorned by intricate stucco work and painted panels

**1**

covered in vibrant Mannerist brushwork. The paintings' classical themes all celebrate or advocate wise kingship, and had a seminal influence on the development of French aristocratic art and design.

Utterly contrasting in style to the rest of the château are the sober but elegant **Petits Appartements**, the private rooms of Napoleon, his wife and their intimate entourage. You have to buy a separate ticket to join the (obligatory) guided tour, but tours of the **Musée Napoléon** – which displays a wide variety of personal and official souvenirs – is included in the main château ticket.

The **gardens** are as splendid as the château, but if you want to escape to the relative wilds, note that the surrounding **forest** of Fontainebleau is full of walking and cycling trails, all marked on the Michelin map *Environs de Paris* (W travel.michelin.co.uk) and detailed on W fontainebleau-tourisme.com, which also has information on **rock climbing** in the forest – Fontainebleau's many rocks are a favourite training ground for Paris-based *grimpeurs* (climbers).

Note that there are no **restaurants** in the château complex.

## Chartres cathedral

Cloître Notre-Dame, Chartres • Jan–April & Sept–Dec Mon–Sat 9.30am–12.30pm & 2–5pm, Sun 2–5pm; May–Aug Mon–Sat 9.30am–12.30pm & 2–6pm, Sun 2–6pm • €6 • ☎ 02 37 21 22 07, W chartres-cathedrale.fr

The modest market town of **Chartres**, 91km from Paris, is almost entirely overshadowed by its extraordinary Gothic **cathedral**. Built between 1194 and 1260, the cathedral was one of the fastest ever to be constructed and, as a result, preserves a uniquely harmonious design. Its official name, Notre-Dame (Our Lady), and its staggering size and architectural richness are owed to its holiest relic, the **Sancta Camisia** – reputed to have been the robe Mary wore when she gave birth to Jesus – which was discovered here, miraculously unharmed, three days after an earlier Romanesque structure burnt down in 1194. Thereafter, hordes of **pilgrims** stopped here on their way south to the shrine of Santiago de Compostela in Spain, and the church needed to accommodate them with a sizeable crypt, for veneration of the relic, and a nave large enough to sleep hundreds.

A controversial ongoing **refurbishment** – slated for completion in 2020 – has largely cleaned up the once-gloomy interior, restoring it to how it is believed it would have originally appeared. Today's gilding and bright, whitewashed walls may appear startling – and inauthentic, some claim (incontrovertible when it comes to the new electric lighting, it has to be said) – but the new (or is it old?) look does help emphasize the rich jewel colours of the stained-glass windows. Sadly, chairs still cover up the **labyrinth** on the floor of the nave, whose diameter is the same size as that of the rose window above the main doors.

Whatever you make of the restoration, the geometry of the building is unique in being almost unaltered since its consecration, and virtually all the magnificent **stained glass** is original, and unsurpassed, thirteenth-century work. The **stonework** is captivating, particularly the **choir screen**, which curves around the ambulatory. Note, too, the mid-twelfth-century **Royal Portal**; like the south tower and spire that abuts it, it survives from the earlier Romanesque church.

### ARRIVAL AND INFORMATION                                          CHARTRES

**By train** Services run from Gare Montparnasse (hourly; roughly 1hr).

**By car** Chartres is 91km from Paris, around 1hr 15min by car. From the *périphérique*, take the A6B autoroute, then follow the signs just after Villejuif and L'Haÿ-les-Roses that lead you via the E50 onto the A10 near Massy. Follow the signs onto the A11 near Orsay, and follow this to Chartres, coming off at junction 2.

**Tourist office** 8 rue de la Poissonnerie, a 5min walk from the train station, by the cathedral (Jan & Feb daily 10am–1pm; March–Dec Mon–Sat 10am–6pm, Sun 10am–5pm; ☎ 02 37 18 26 26, W chartres-tourisme.com).

## EATING

**Café Bleu** Place de la Cathédrale ☎ 02 37 36 59 60, ⓦ cafebleu-chartres.com. This buzzy contemporary bistro, brilliantly situated opposite the cathedral, offers a creative range of dishes from *croque monsieur* to cod with chorizo and peppers. Mains €15–22; two-course lunchtime *formule* (Mon & Wed–Fri) €16.90. Daily except Tues 8am–midnight.

# Château de Versailles

Some 20km southwest of Paris lies Louis XIV's extraordinary **Château de Versailles** (ⓦ chateauversailles.fr). With 700 rooms, 67 staircases and 352 fireplaces alone, Versailles is, without doubt, the apotheosis of French regal indulgence. While it's possible to see the whole complex in one day, it's undeniably tiring, so you'd do best to plan ahead to avoid crowds and save time.

## The palace

Consumed with envy of his finance minister's château at Vaux-le-Vicomte (see page 150), the young Louis XIV recruited the same design team – architect Le Vau, painter Le Brun and gardener Le Nôtre – to create a **palace** a hundred times bigger. Construction began in 1664 and lasted virtually until Louis XIV's death in 1715. Second only to God, and the head of an immensely powerful state, Louis was an institution rather than a private individual. His risings and sittings, comings and goings, were minutely regulated and rigidly encased in ceremony, attendance at which was an honour much sought after by courtiers. Versailles was the headquarters of every arm of the state, and the entire court of around 3500 nobles lived in the palace (in a state of squalor, according to contemporaneous accounts).

Following the king's death, the château was abandoned for a few years before being reoccupied by Louis XV in 1722. It remained a residence of the royal family until the Revolution of 1789, when the furniture was sold and the pictures dispatched to the Louvre. Thereafter Versailles fell into ruin until Louis-Philippe established his giant museum of French Glory here – it still exists, though most is mothballed. In 1871, during the Paris Commune, the château became the seat of the nationalist government, and the French parliament continued to meet in Louis XV's opera building until 1879.

### Grands Appartements

Tues–Sun: April–Oct 9am–6.30pm; Nov–March 9am–5 30pm • €18, including audioguide, or included in the Passeport Versailles (see page 154); free for under-18s and EU residents under 26

The rooms you can visit without a guide are known as the **Grands Appartements**, used for the king's official business. A procession of gilded drawing rooms leads to the dazzling **Galerie des Glaces** (Hall of Mirrors), where the Treaty of Versailles was signed after World War I. More fabulously rich rooms, this time belonging to the **queen's apartments**, line the northern wing, beginning with the queen's bedchamber, which has been restored exactly as it was in its last refit, of 1787, with hardly a surface unadorned with gold leaf.

### The park and gardens

**Gardens** Daily: April–Oct 8am–8.30pm; Nov–March 8am–6pm • **Park** Daily: April–Oct 7am–8.30pm; Nov–March 8am–6pm • Free, or €8.50/€9.50/€26 during *spectacles* • A *petit train* shuttles between the terrace in front of the château and the Trianons

You could spend a whole day just exploring the **gardens** at Versailles. Beyond the great Water Parterres designed by André Le Nôtre, geometrically planned walks and gardens stretch out on all sides. The outer limits of the estate are known as the **park**, and are made up of woods and fields grazed by sheep; the northernmost area is part of the Domaine de Trianon (see page 154), visitable on a separate ticket.

**1**

## Domaine de Trianon

Château de Versailles park • Tues–Sun: April–Oct noon–6.30pm; Nov–March noon–5.30pm • €12 (buy tickets from Domaine entrance rather than at the palace entrance), or included in the Passeport Versailles, which has to be bought at palace entrance (see below); free for under-18s and EU residents under 26

Hidden in the northern reaches of the gardens is the **Domaine de Trianon**, young Marie Antoinette's country retreat, where she found relief from the stifling etiquette of the court. Here she commissioned some dozen or so buildings, sparing no expense and imposing her own style and tastes throughout (and gaining herself a reputation for extravagance that did her no favours). The centrepiece is the elegant Neoclassical **Petit Trianon** palace, built by Gabriel in the 1760s for Louis XV's mistress, Mme de Pompadour, and given to Marie Antoinette by her husband Louis XVI as a wedding gift. The interior boasts an intriguing *cabinet des glaces montantes*, a pale-blue salon fitted with sliding mirrors that could be moved to conceal the windows, creating a more intimate space.

You can also see the Italianate **Grand Trianon** palace, which was designed by Hardouin-Mansart in 1687 as a country retreat for Louis XIV and refurbished in Empire style by Napoleon, who stayed here intermittently between 1805 and 1813.

### The formal gardens and Hameau de la Reine

West of the Petit Trianon, in the formal **Jardins à la française**, is the **Petit Théâtre** where Marie Antoinette would regularly perform, often as a maid or shepherdess, before the king and members of her inner circle. To the east lies the bucolic **Jardin anglais**, impossibly picturesque with its little winding stream, grassy banks, classical temple and grotto, and the enchanting, if bizarre, **Hameau de la Reine**, a play village and farm where the queen indulged her fashionable Rousseau-inspired fantasy of returning to the "natural" life.

### ARRIVAL AND INFORMATION — CHÂTEAU DE VERSAILLES

**By train** Taking the train to Versailles is by far the best and quickest option; take the RER line C5 from a Left Bank station to Versailles–Château (20–40min; €7.50 return); turn right out of the station then take the first left onto av de Paris, which leads to the palace – an 8min walk.

**Opening times** The château is open all year, except on Mondays, public holidays and during occasional state events. We've given individual opening hours for each attraction within the account.

**Tickets and passes** There are several types of ticket available. If you've got limited time, buy separate tickets to the Grands Appartements and the Domaine de Trianon according to what you want to see (we've given individual prices in the account). Otherwise there's the Passeport Versailles, a one- or two-day pass for all the main sights (€20 one day/€25 two consecutive days; €27/€30 on *spectacle* days). All tickets and passes – except for the *spectacles* – are free to under-18s and EU residents under 26, year-round; head straight to Entrance A with proof of your status.

**Spectacles** In peak periods, the Versailles gardens host various "*spectacles*": in the Grandes Eaux Musicales (€9.50) fountains gush flamboyantly while piped classical music booms; the less exciting Jardins Musicaux (€8.50) feature the piped music without the fountains. Dates and times vary, so check online.

**Crowds, queues and saving time** Versailles can get extremely crowded and at peak times (10am–3pm, particularly Tues, Sat & Sun) queues can last several hours. There are things you can do to reduce queuing time, but some waiting is inevitable as security is strict. Buying tickets online at ⓦ chateauversailles.fr or ⓦ fnactickets.com is a good option; alternatively, pick them up from a Fnac (see page 144) or at the Versailles town tourist office, near the entrance to the palace at 2bis av de Paris (April–Oct Mon 9.30am–6pm, Tues–Sun 8.30am–7pm; Nov–March Mon 11am–5pm, Tues–Sat 8.30am–6pm; ☎ 01 39 24 88 88, ⓦ versailles-tourisme. com). You can then head straight to Entrance A for admission. It's best to avoid the Grands Appartements at the busiest times; the ideal route would be to head for the gardens and park between 9am and noon, following that with the Trianon palaces and Marie Antoinette's hamlet, and leaving the palace interior until last, ideally after 4.30pm or so.

**Getting around** Distances in the park are considerable. Shuttles ("le petit train") run a 5km loop between the château and the Trianons (every 15–20min; €7.50 hop-on hop-off ticket), while bikes can be rented (€6.50/half hr, €8.50/hr, €18/half day) by the Grand Canal, at the Grille de la Reine on bd de la Reine, and at Porte St-Antoine at the far end of the gardens.

**Guided tours** Tours (€10), including English-language options, are available, taking you to areas that can't otherwise be seen; some can be booked online, while more are bookable on the day at the information point – turn up early to be sure of a place – or via the Versailles town tourist office (see opposite).

# The North

**158** Dunkerque and around

**164** St-Omer

**165** Calais and around

**169** Boulogne-sur-Mer

**172** Le Touquet

**174** Montreuil-sur-Mer

**174** Crécy and Agincourt battlefields

**175** Parc Ornithologique du Marquenterre

**175** The Somme estuary

**176** Lille

**181** The Flemish Cities

**186** The Somme and its battlefields

**192** Picardy

THE CÔTE D'OPALE AT CAP BLANC-NEZ

# The north

When conjuring up exotic holiday locations, you're unlikely to light upon the north of France. Largely flat Artois and Flanders include some of the most heavily industrialized parts of the country. However, there are many good reasons to explore the area, not least its strong associations with the most devastating battles of World War I. Other big draws are the bustling port town of Calais, Dunkerque's university atmosphere, and the delightful village of Cassel, a rare example of a Flemish hill settlement. St-Omer, Le Touquet and Montreuil-sur-Mer are strong contenders in terms of charm and interest and the castle at Pierrefonds would make Walt Disney proud. Lille's rejuvenation is complete and its culture is thriving, and the architecture of the cathedrals in Laon and Beauvais isn't hard to admire.

Northern France has always been on the path of various invaders into the country, from northern mainland Europe as well as from Britain, and the events that have taken place in Flanders, Artois and Picardy have shaped both French and world history. The bloodiest battles were those of World War I, above all the five-month-long **Battle of the Somme**; at **Vimy Ridge**, near Arras, the trenches have been preserved in perpetuity. A visit to either of these is highly recommended for an understanding of the scale of sacrifice involved and the futility of the war.

 **Picardy**, meanwhile, boasts some of France's finest cathedrals, including those at **Amiens**, **Beauvais** and **Laon**. Other attractions include the bird sanctuary of **Marquenterre**; industrial archeology in the Lewarde coalfields around **Douai**, where Zola's *Germinal* was set; the great medieval castle of **Coucy-le-Château**; and the battle sites of the Middle Ages, **Agincourt** and **Crécy**, familiar names in the long history of Anglo–French rivalry. In **Lille**, you'll find your fill of food, culture and entertainment.

## GETTING THERE AND AROUND          THE NORTH

The Channel Tunnel emerges at Sangatte, 5km southwest of Calais. Crossing times under the "Chunnel" are just 30 minutes, with the efficient but pricey *autoroute* (the A16) waiting to whisk you away to your ultimate destination. **By train** Eurostar will get you to Calais or Lille from London, Brussels and Paris and a comprehensive local train network serves both large and small towns (🌐 ter-sncf.com).

**By bus** There is a good local bus network operating in and around the main towns, but long-distance bus routes only operate between large centres.

# Dunkerque and around

Less reliant than Boulogne-sur-Mer (see page 169) or Calais (see page 165) on the cross-channel ferry trade, **DUNKERQUE** is the liveliest of the three big Channel ports, a university town with an appealing, boat-filled inner harbour, the **Bassin du Commerce**. It was from the shores of **Malo-les-Bains**, an attractive beachfront suburb, that the evacuation of Allied troops took place in 1940. Dunkerque remains France's third-largest cargo port (following Marseille and Le Havre) and is a massive industrial centre, its oil refineries and steelworks producing a significant proportion of the total French output. Devastated during World War II, central Dunkerque is largely the brick-built product of postwar reconstruction, slightly more ambitious and stylish than the rebuild of Calais or Boulogne-sur-Mer. But among the 1950s

THE EXQUISITELY INTRICATE FACADE OF AMIENS CATHEDRAL

# Highlights

**❶ La Coupole** This vast complex, originally built to launch the V2 bombs on London, takes you from the 1930s through to the Cold War and the space race. See page 164

**❷ Cité Internationale de la Dentelle et de la Mode** Housed in a former factory, this entertaining museum tells the story of lacemaking in Calais through films, machines and fashions. See page 167

**❸ Parc Ornithologique du Marquenterre** From geese and godwits to storks and spoonbills, a huge variety of birds make their home amid briny meres and tamarisk-fringed dunes. See page 175

**❹ Lillois cuisine** Eat anything, from the ubiquitous *moules-frites*, washed down with micro-brewed beer, to fried *escargots* with onions roasted in lavender oil, in the historic centre of Lille, the cultural capital of northern France. See page 180

**❺ World War I monuments in the Somme** Moving memorials by Lutyens and others to the victims of the trenches still resonate today, over 100 years since the end of the conflict. See page 186

**❻ Son et lumière, Amiens cathedral** The biggest Gothic building in France, brought to life by sound and light shows on summer evenings. See page 192

**HIGHLIGHTS ARE MARKED ON THE MAP ON PAGE 160**

architecture, you come across some delightful Art Nouveau-style villas with curving forms and balconies.

Among the few buildings of any significance that survived World War II (or were rebuilt afterwards) are the tall medieval brick **belfry**, the town's chief landmark; the impressive, bullet-ridden fifteenth-century **church of St-Éloi** opposite, to which the belfry belonged; and, a few blocks north of the church on place Charles-Valentin, the early twentieth-century **hôtel de ville**, a giant Flemish fancy to rival that of Calais.

**HIGHLIGHTS**

1. La Coupole
2. Cité Internationale de la Dentelle et de la Mode
3. Parc Ornithologique du Marquenterre
4. Lillois cuisine
5. World War I monuments in the Somme
6. Son et lumière, Amiens cathedral

**THE NORTH**

**REGIONAL FOOD AND DRINK**

**French Flanders** has one of northern France's richest regional cuisines. Especially on the coast, the **seafood** – oysters, shrimps, scallops and **fish**, and above all, sole and turbot – are outstanding, while in Lille *moules-frites* (mussels and chips) are appreciated every bit as much as in neighbouring Belgium. Here, too, **beer** is the favourite drink, with pale and brown Pelforth the local brew. Traditional *estaminets* or brasseries also serve a range of dishes cooked in beer, most famously *carbonnade flamande*, a kind of beef stew; rabbit, chicken, game and fish may also be prepared *à la bière*. Other pot-cooked dishes include *hochepot* (a meaty broth), *waterzooi* (chicken in a creamy sauce) and *potjevlesch* (white meats in a rich sauce). In addition to *boulette d'Avesnes*, the **Flemish cheese** *par excellence* is the strong-flavoured *Maroilles*, used to make *flamiche*, a kind of open tart of cheese pastry also made with leeks (*aux poireaux*). For the sweet-toothed, *crêpes à la cassonade* (pancakes with muscovado sugar) are often on menus, but **waffles** (*gaufres*) are the local speciality and come in two basic varieties: the thick honeycomb type served with sugar or cream, or the wafer-like biscuit filled with jam or syrup. Game looms large on menus around the Ardennes, with *pâté d'Ardennes* being the most famous dish and juniper berries used to flavour food *à l'Ardennaise*.

## Musée Portuaire

9 quai de la Citadelle · **Museum** July & Aug daily 10am–12.30pm & 1.30–6pm; Sept–June Wed–Mon 10am–12.30pm & 1.30–6pm; **Ships** *Duchesse Anne* and *Sandettié* mid-March to mid-Nov daily 2–6pm; mid-Nov to mid-March guided tours only Sun 3pm & 4.30pm; *Guilde* mid-March to mid-Nov daily 10am–12pm· Museum €9 or €15 joint ticket with the ships; ships €9; lighthouse €5 · ☎ 03 28 63 33 39, ⓦ museeportuaire.com

The **Musée Portuaire**, or **Port Museum** has three parts to it: the museum itself, housed in a restored brick warehouse on the lively Bassin du Commerce; the three ships that make up the "floating" part of the museum; and a 60m lighthouse, 2km to the north, which can be climbed for fantastic views. In the child-friendly museum, engaging ship models, panoramas and period film footage lead you through the main events of Dunkerque's history, from its beginnings as a fishing hamlet. It's an easily digestible size and mounts good temporary exhibitions on related themes.

Opposite the museum are the three attractive preserved historic ships that make up the "floating" museum. You can visit the three-masted sailing ship *Duchesse Anne*, built in Germany in 1901, the *Sandettié* lightship, and the *Guilde* barge.

## Musée Dunkerque 1940

32 courtines du Bastion (off rue des Chantiers de France) · mid-March to mid-Sept daily 10am–6pm · €8 · ☎ 03 74 06 02 81, ⓦ dynamo-dunkerque.com

The **Musée Dunkerque 1940** is the place to learn all about the 1940 evacuations of Operation Dynamo that rescued over 340,000 Allied soldiers. It starts with a short film in English that sets the scene, then a wander through the vault – "Bastion 32", as per the address, was the Allied headquarters for the operation – which displays a rich collection of photographs, maps, uniforms and military equipment of the time.

## LAAC

Jardin de Sculptures, 302 av des Bordées · Tues–Sun 10am–12.15pm & 2–6pm · €3 · ☎ 03 28 29 56 00, ⓦ musees-dunkerque.eu

In a park of sculptures just south of the Musée Dunkerque 1940 in the Pont Lucien-Lefol area, the worthwhile **LAAC (Lieu d'Art et Action Contemporaine)** specializes in the period from 1950 to 1980 and features works by the likes of Andy Warhol, Pierre Soulages and César.

## Malo-les-Bains

**Malo-les-Bains** is a pleasant nineteenth-century seaside suburb on the east side of Dunkerque, from whose vast sandy beach the Allied troops embarked in 1940. Digue

**2**

## DUNKERQUE'S 1940 EVACUATION

The evacuation of nearly 350,000 Allied troops from the beaches of **Dunkerque** from May 27 to June 4, 1940, has become legendary, concealing the fact that the Allies, through their own incompetence, almost lost their entire armed forces in the first weeks of the war.

The German army had taken just ten days to reach the English Channel and could easily have cut off the Allied armies. Hitler, unable to believe the ease with which he had overcome a numerically superior enemy, ordered his generals to halt their advance, giving Allied forces trapped in the Pas-de-Calais time to organize **Operation Dynamo**, the largest wartime evacuation ever undertaken. Initially it was hoped that around 10,000 men would be saved, but thanks to low-lying cloud and more than 1750 vessels – including pleasure cruisers, fishing boats and river ferries – 140,000 French and more than 200,000 British soldiers were successfully shipped back to England. The heroism of the boatmen and the relief at saving so many British soldiers were the cause of national celebration.

In France, however, the ratio of British to French evacuees caused bitter resentment, since Churchill had promised that the two sides would go *bras dessus, bras dessous* ("arm in arm"). Meanwhile, the British media played up the "remarkable discipline" of the troops as they waited to embark, the "victory" of the RAF over the Luftwaffe and the "disintegration" of the French army all around. In fact, there was widespread indiscipline in the early stages as men fought for places on board; the battle for the skies was evenly matched; and the French fought long and hard to cover the whole operation, some 150,000 of them remaining behind to become prisoners of war. In addition, the Allies lost seven destroyers and 177 fighter planes and were forced to abandon more than 60,000 vehicles. After 1940, Dunkerque remained occupied by Germans until the bitter end of the war. It was the last French town to be liberated in 1945.

des Alliés is the urban end of an extensive beachfront promenade lined with cafés and restaurants, though things are rather nicer further east along Digue de Mer, away from Dunkerque's industrial side. Much of the promenade's attractive architecture survived wartime destruction; there's more *fin-de-siècle* charm a few blocks inland, along avenue Faidherbe and its continuation avenue Kléber, and around leafy place Turenne with its dainty old-fashioned bandstand.

To get to Malo from Dunkerque all year round, take buses #C3 or C4 from place de la République in the centre to Malo Plage, near the casino.

### ARRIVAL AND INFORMATION
### DUNKERQUE

**By train** Dunkerque's *gare SNCF* is on place de la Gare, a 10min walk from the town centre.
Destinations Calais-Ville (8–10 daily; 45min); Cassel (6–20 daily; 25min); Lille Europe (2 hourly; 35min); Paris (20 daily; 1hr 40min–2hr 20min).
**By bus** The *gare routière* is located next to the *gare SNCF* on rue Belle Vue. Information on the Boulogne-Calais-Dunkerque service is available at ⓦligne-bcd.com.
Destinations Boulogne (5 daily; 1hr 30min); Calais (12

daily; 45min), Cassel (Mon–Sat 3 daily; 1hr).
**Getting around** The extensive Dunkerque bus service is free throughout the city and its environs. For more information, see ⓦdkbus.com.
**Tourist office** Beffroi St-Eloi, rue de l'Amiral Ronarc'h (July & Aug Mon–Sat 10am–6.30pm, Sun 10am–noon & 2–4pm; Sept–June Mon–Fri 10am–12.30pm & 2–6.30pm, Sat 10am–-6.30pm, Sun & public hols 10am–noon & 2–4pm; ⓣ03 28 66 79 21, ⓦdunkirk-tourism.com).

### ACCOMMODATION

**Borel** 6 rue de l'Hermite ⓣ03 28 66 51 80, ⓦhotelborel. fr. Predominantly a business hotel, the *Borel* has good-sized rooms with conventional wooden furnishings and impressive bathrooms. It's a comfortable but rather anonymous four-star option, right on the Bassin du Commerce. Breakfast €13. **€105**
**Hirondelle** 46/48 av du Général Faidherbe, Malo-

les-Bains ⓣ03 28 63 17 65, ⓦhotelhirondelle.com. Located very near the beach, this bright hotel occupies two buildings with renovated, comfortable en-suite rooms, including three adapted for people with limited mobility. The restaurant offers regional fish and shellfish with *menus* from €14.50–€31, and a children's *menu* from €13.30. Breakfast €9.40. **€84**

**La Licorne** 1005 bd de l'Europe, Malo-les-Bains ☎ 03 28 69 26 68, ⓦ campingdelalicorne.com. On the eastern end of Digue de Mer, accessible by the #C3 bus, you can pitch your tent or take your campervan near the beach. You can also book comfortable and spacious eco-lodges, as well as static caravans, by the week (shorter stays available in low season). Closed Dec–March. Camping €19, lodges from €360/week

**Welcome** 37 rue Raymond Poincaré ☎ 03 28 59 20 70, ⓦ hotel-welcome.fr. A recent renovation has transformed the *Welcome*, in the centre of town, into a comfortable, modern hotel. The bright rooms are enlivened by splashes of colour and there's also a casual bar. Breakfast €10. €67

## EATING AND DRINKING

**Les 3 Brasseurs** rue des Fusiliers Marins ☎ 03 28 59 60 60, ⓦ les3brasseurs.com. Brass-and-wood decorated branch of the well-known artisanal microbrewery chain, overlooking the water. Beautifully simple choice of beers, classified by colour, plus burgers, grills and salads – or try the *flammeküche* for a regional twist on a pizza. Mains €10–22. Sun–Thurs 10am–11pm, Fri & Sat 10am–midnight.

**L'Auberge de Jules** 9 rue de la Poudrière ☎ 03 28 63 68 80. Funky modern restaurant just off the Bassin du Commerce, with plenty of fish and seafood, freshly caught by members of the family. *Menus* run from €24 to €38. Mon–Fri noon–2pm & 7–10pm.

**Le Country Grill** 54 place du Minck ☎ 03 28 66 66 25.

For a bit of change from seafood, visit this cheery place for an all-American diner experience with enormous burgers and generous portions of fries. Burgers start from €11, steaks and grills from €16. Mon & Wed–Fri noon–2pm & 7–10.30pm, Sat & Sun 7–10.30pm.

**Le Sweet** 2 bis Quai de la Citadelle ☎ 03 28 63 04 29, ⓦ lesweetrestaurant.fr. This small, unpretentious restaurant overlooking the water has a short but delicious menu. Expect the likes of prawns with Thai-style quinoa or steak stuffed with duck foie gras. Mains from €19, menus from €16 (lunctime) to €37. Mon, Wed & Fri noon–2pm & 7.30–10pm, Thurs & Sun noon–2pm, Sat 7.30–10pm.

# Cassel

The tiny hilltop town of **CASSEL** is just 30km southeast of Dunkerque. Hills are rare in Flanders, so Cassel was fought over from Roman times onwards. It was supposedly to the top of Cassel's hill that the "Grand Old Duke of York" marched his ten thousand men in 1793, though, as implied in the nursery rhyme, he failed to take the town. In more recent history, during World War I, Marshal Foch spent some of the "most distressing hours" of his life here.

The town was originally a Flemish-speaking community – until use of the language was suppressed by the authorities – and it still boasts a very Flemish **Grand'Place**, lined with some magnificent mansions, from which narrow cobbled streets fan out to the ramparts.

## Musée de Flandres

26 Grand'Place • Tues–Fri 10am–12.30pm & 2–6pm; Sat, Sun & school hols 10am–6pm • €6 • ☎ 03 59 73 45 59, ⓦ museedeflandre.fr

Housed in the splendid Flemish/Renaissance Hôtel de la Noble Cour, the **Musée de Flandres** mixes everyday *objets* and odd collectables from the Flemish past with contemporary art. Exhibits are beautifully displayed in wood-panelled rooms straight out of a Flemish Old Master painting. The museum stages interesting temporary shows; past exhibitions have included the *Splendours of Mannerism in Flanders*, which showed odd and exotic sixteenth-century Flemish paintings. Visit the museum's garden, which illustrates the principle of "atmospheric perspective", with its gradient of colours from green to blue, creating an illusion of depth by mimicking the natural effect of the atmosphere.

## ARRIVAL AND INFORMATION                                    CASSEL

**By train** Cassel's *gare SNCF* is 3km west of the town near Bavinchove (no taxis to town).
Destinations Dunkerque (7–24 daily; 27min); Lille Flandres (1–20 daily; 40min).
**By bus** Buses arrive in central Cassel on the Dunkerque to Hazebrouck route, bus #105.

Destinations Dunkerque (5 daily Mon–Sat, 1 daily Sun; 1hr).
**Tourist office** 20 Grand'Place (Tues–Sat 9.30am–noon & 2–6pm, Sun 2–6pm; ☎ 03 28 40 52 55, ⓦ coeurdefrlandre. fr).

## ACCOMMODATION AND EATING

**Châtellerie de Schoebeque** 32 rue du Maréchal Foch ☎ 03 28 42 42 67, ⓦ schoebeque.com. Set in an eighteenth-century château where Marshal Foch met Britain's George V in World War I, this delightful spa hotel has intriguing themed rooms: for a sense of the sea opt for "La Mer", or splash out on a suite for a little more space. Views from the dining room are wonderful. **€95**

**La Taverne Flamande** 34 Grand'Place ☎ 03 28 42 42 59, ⓦ taverne-flamande.fr. Try this cosy restaurant with its wooden panelling and red gingham-checked tablecloths for a typical Flemish experience. Hearty dishes like large plates of charcuterie or *carbonnade flamande* start at €10.50. The terrace has great views. Tues noon–2pm; Thurs–Mon noon–2pm & 7–9pm.

★ **Estaminet T'Kasteel Hof** 8 rue Saint-Nicolas ☎ 03 28 40 59 29. If it wasn't so well-executed, this might verge on the kitsch, but instead this lovely *estaminet* is a real find, with hops and pots hanging from the ceiling, board games to play, an open fire and small patio, and good Flemish dishes from €12. Wash them down with local beers. Thurs–Sun 11am–10pm.

# St-Omer

**ST-OMER**, a popular stop en route to or from the ports, is an attractive old Flemish town of yellow-brick houses, 44km southeast of Calais. The *hôtel de ville* on place Foch and the chapel of the former Jesuit college on rue du Lycée are genuine flights of architectural fancy, but for the most part the style is simple yet handsome. For a little greenery, head to the pleasant **public gardens** to the west of town or to the nearby **marais**, a network of Flemish waterways cut between plots of land on reclaimed marshes along the river.

## Cathédrale Notre-Dame

Enclos Notre-Dame • Daily: March–Sept 8.30am–6pm; Oct–Feb 8.30am–5pm • Free

It's hard to miss the Gothic **cathedral**, founded in the thirteenth century, and stuffed full of treasures such as an astronomical clock, an eighteenth-century Cavaillé-Coll organ and a rather odd shrine to St Erkembode – patron saint of children – that's covered with pairs of shoes, left by mothers whose children are struggling to start walking.

## Musée de l'Hôtel Sandelin

14 rue Carnot • Wed–Sun 10am–noon & 2–6pm • €5.50 • ☎ 03 21 38 00 94 ⓦ patrimoines-saint-omer.fr

The centrepiece of the delightful **Musée de l'Hôtel Sandelin**, housed in an eighteenth-century mansion, is the suite of panelled rooms on the ground floor. The museum displays focus on eleventh- to fifteenth-century Flemish art (including a Brueghel) and ceramics. Look out for the glorious piece of twelfth-century medieval goldsmithing known as the *Pied de Croix de St-Bertin*.

## The Blockhaus at Éperlecques

Rue de Sart, 12km north of St-Omer off the D300 • Daily: March 2.15–5pm; April–June & Sept 10am–6pm; July & Aug 10am–7pm; Oct 10am–5pm • €10 • ☎ 03 21 88 44 22, ⓦ leblockhaus.com

The Forêt d'Éperlecques feels remote, making it the perfect place for the largest-ever **Blockhaus**, a German concrete bunker, built in 1943–44 by six thousand half-starved prisoners of war. It was designed to launch V2 rockets against London, but the RAF and French Resistance attacked it so heavily – killing many Allied prisoners at the same time – that it was never ready for use. Walk around the massive bunker, originally named 5, which has multilingual commentaries on the story.

## La Coupole

Just off the D928 (A26 junctions 3 & 4) • Daily: July & Aug 10am–7pm; Sept–June 9am–6pm • €10 • ☎ 03 21 12 27 27, ⓦ lacoupole-france.com

Of all the World War II museums in northern France, **La Coupole**, 5km southwest of St-Omer, is the best. As you walk around the site of the intended V2 rocket launch pad, individual, multilingual infrared headphones tell you the story of the occupation of northern France by the Nazis, the use of prisoners as slave labour, and the technology and ethics of the first liquid-fuelled rocket – advanced by Hitler and later developed for the space race by the Soviets, the French and the Americans. Four excellent films cover all aspects.

## ARRIVAL AND INFORMATION ST-OMER

**By train** The ornate 1903 St-Omer railway station is on rue Saint-Martin, about a 15min walk south into the town centre.

Destinations Calais-Ville (18–26 daily; 32min); Lille Flandres (1–2 hourly; 45min).

**Tourist office** 7 place Victor Hugo (April–Sept Mon–Fri 10am––12.30pm & 2–6pm, Sat & Sun 10am–6pm;

Oct–March Mon 2–5.30pm, Tues–Sat 10am–12.30pm & 2–5pm; ☎ 03 21 98 08 51, ⓦ tourisme-saintomer.com).

**Boat trips** Société Isnor (3 rue du Marais, ☎ 03 21 39 15 15, ⓦ isnor.fr). Boat trips leave from the church in nearby Clairmarais. For information and details of kayak and canoe rental, contact the tourist office.

## ACCOMMODATION

**Le Bretagne** 2 place du Vainquai ☎ 03 21 38 25 78, ⓦ hotellebretagne.com. Located near the railway station, this hotel has 69 bright, if simple, rooms, and feels more business- than leisure-oriented. Comfortable and convenient for the town centre, and with a smart restaurant. Breakfast €10. **€72**

★ **Château Tilques** Rue du Château, Tilques ☎ 03 21 88 99 99, ⓦ tilques.najeti.fr. Originally a seventeenth-century manor house, this rebuilt red-brick château, set in a delightful park with peacocks, is the best hotel in the region. You can choose from rooms in the main château, some with four-poster beds and classic grand furniture, or more contemporary rooms in the Pavillon du Parc. The restaurant in the former stables offers good-value *menus* (€25–35). Leisure facilities include tennis and indoor

swimming pool. Free parking, breakfast €16. **€122**

**Le Clairmarais** Rue du Romelaëre ☎ 03 21 38 34 80, ⓦ camping-clairmarais.com. This countryside campsite, near the Forêt de Clairmarais, 4.5km east of St-Omer, has simple facilities in the picturesque centre of the Marais, including an indoor heated pool, and offers fishing and boating. Note that there's no transport between it and the town. Closed mid-Dec to Jan. **€12.50**

**St-Louis** 25 rue d'Arras ☎ 03 21 38 35 21, ⓦ hotel-saintlouis.com. Comfortable, simply decorated hotel in a quiet street near the cathedral, with pretty fabrics brightening up the rooms, some of which overlook the gardens, with more modern rooms in the annexe. Popular restaurant with regional-cuisine *menus* from €17. Breakfast €10, parking €9. **€79**

## EATING AND DRINKING

★ **Chez Tante Fauvette** 10 rue Ste Croix ☎ 03 21 11 26 08. A tiny restaurant with a wood floor, red-gingham tablecloths and quirky artefacts as decor. The Polish-heritage patron runs it single-handedly, producing a changing menu of good-value dishes. Expect the likes of home-made fish gratin (around €7), pork sautéed with curry powder and rice, or pollock with a creamy sauce (€13–16), plus great desserts. Booking is essential. Wed–Sat noon–1.30pm & 7.30–10.30pm.

**Le Cygne** 8 rue Caventou ☎ 03 21 98 20 52, ⓦ restaurantlecygne.fr. Elegantly decorated and offering

seasonal dishes, this is a favourite with Brits, who drop by for their good-value menu du marché (€18), which might include a lamb stew or prawn tartare. Tues–Sat 11.30am–2.30pm & 6.30–9.30pm, Sun 11.30am–2.30pm.

**De Drie Kalders** 18 place du Maréchal Foch ☎ 03 21 39 72 52, ⓦ restaurantles3caves.com. With a vaulted brick cellar for the winter, ground floor and terrace for summer months, this old-fashioned restaurant is a busy, atmospheric place with hearty Flemish specialities chalked up on a blackboard. *Menus* from €23.90. Tues–Sun noon–2pm & 7–10pm.

# Calais and around

**CALAIS** is less than 40km from Dover – the Channel's shortest crossing – and is by far the busiest French passenger port. In World War II, the British destroyed Calais to prevent it being used as a base for a German invasion, but the French still refer to it as "the most English town in France", an influence that began after the battle of Crécy in 1346, when Edward III seized it for use as a beachhead in the Hundred Years' War. It remained in English hands for over two hundred years until 1558, when its loss caused Mary Tudor to say: "When I am dead and opened, you shall find Calais lying in my heart." The association has continued over the centuries, and today Calais welcomes more than nine million British travellers and day-trippers per year.

## Calais-Nord

**Calais-Nord** (also the old town) was originally a fortified town on an island. It was rebuilt after World War II, with place d'Armes and rue Royale as its focus. The **Tour du Guet**, on place d'Armes, is the only medieval building on the square to have survived wartime bombardment. From here, rue de la Paix leads east to the **church of Notre-Dame**, where Charles de Gaulle married local girl Yvonne Vendroux in 1921. It's been carefully restored recently and is the only church in English Perpendicular style in Europe.

Walk north up rue Royale over the bridge to the city's **beaches**, where the chilly waters are swimmable, and from which on a fine day a white strip of English shore is visible; get a panoramic view from the top of the 59m **lighthouse** (Mon–Fri 2–5.30pm, Sat & Sun 10am–noon & 2–5.30pm; closes 6.30pm June–Sept; €4.50) at place Henri-Barbusse.

### Musée des Beaux-Arts

25 rue Richelieu • April–Oct Tues–Sat 1–6pm; Nov–March Tues–Sat 1–5pm, Sun 2–5pm • €2 • ☎ 03 21 46 48 40, ⓦ www.calais.fr.

The **Musée des Beaux-Arts** has an appealing collection of sixteenth- to twentieth-century art, including paintings by Picasso and Dubuffet, and a Rodin sculpture

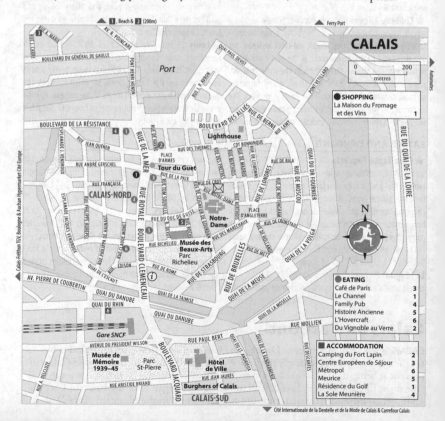

CALAIS

SHOPPING
La Maison du Fromage et des Vins ..... 1

EATING
Café de Paris ..... 3
Le Channel ..... 1
Family Pub ..... 4
Histoire Ancienne ..... 5
L'Hovercraft ..... 6
Du Vignoble au Verre ..... 2

ACCOMMODATION
Camping du Fort Lapin ..... 2
Centre Européen de Séjour ..... 3
Métropol ..... 6
Meurice ..... 5
Résidence du Golf ..... 1
La Sole Meunière ..... 4

> **AUTOROUTE DES ANGLAIS**
>
> Drivers keen to **avoid Calais** should take a left turn out of the ferry terminal – the appropriately named *Autoroute des Anglais* bypass begins almost immediately, leading to the A26 and the N1. Note however that this shortcut, particularly the N216 road, attracts, at the time of writing, a significant number of migrants and refugees seeking to stow away on lorries heading for the Channel.

exhibition. One of the permanent collections is inspired by the alternative realities of Lewis Carroll's *Alice in Wonderland*, and previous temporary exhibits include an underwater photographic study of artificial reefs.

# Calais-Sud

Just over the canal bridge is **Calais-Sud**, a nineteenth-century extension of the old town, and now the main **city centre**. Here the town's main landmark, the *hôtel de ville*, raises its belfry over 60m into the sky; this Flemish extravaganza was finished in 1926, and miraculously survived World War II. Nearby, Rodin's famous bronze, the *Burghers of Calais*, records for ever the self-sacrifice of local dignitaries, who offered their lives to assuage the blood lust of the victor at Crécy, Edward III – only to be spared at the last minute by the intervention of Queen Philippa, Edward's wife.

### Cité Internationale de la Dentelle et de la Mode de Calais

135 quai du Commerce • Wed–Mon: April–Oct 10am–6pm; Nov–March 10am–5pm • €4 temporary exhibition, €7 temporary exhibition and permanent collection • ☎ 03 21 00 42 30, ⓦ cite-dentelle.fr

Housed in a former lace factory, the extensive **Cité Internationale de la Dentelle et de la Mode** guides visitors from the early days of handmade lace – when it was worn only by the aristocracy – to the Industrial Revolution, when machines were smuggled in from England, and up to the present day. The working machines are particularly engrossing, as are the interactive exhibits and videos showing off the complex lace-making process itself. Models display early seventeenth-century costumes, the elegant clothes of the twentieth century and the futuristic inspirations of tomorrow's design names.

### Musée Mémoire 1939–1945

Parc Saint-Pierre • Feb–April, Oct & Nov Mon & Wed–Sat 11am–5pm; May–Sept daily 10am–6pm • €8 • ☎ 03 21 34 21 57, ⓦ musee-memoire-calais.com

For a record of Calais' wartime travails, don't miss the Musée Mémoire 1939–1945, dedicated to World War II, set in the ivy-covered former German blockhaus (bunker) in the Parc Saint-Pierre. It's quaintly old-fashioned, with its faded newspaper cuttings, stiff models in uniform and models, but it gives a good picture of Calais under occupation.

**ARRIVAL AND INFORMATION**                                                                          **CALAIS**

### BY TRAIN

**TGV** Eurostar trains from and to London, Lille and Paris arrive at the outlying Calais Fréthun *gare TGV*. Take the *navette*, usually a shuttle bus, occasionally a TER train, into Calais Ville station (€2.40).

Destinations Lille (8–10 daily; 30min); London (3 daily; 55min–1hr 15min); Paris (7 daily; 1hr 40min).

**SNCF** Calais-Ville, on av du Président Wilson, is the main station for regional services on the TER network and some TGV trains. A daytime bus (€2 one-way) runs from the ferry

terminal to place d'Armes and the central Calais-Ville *gare SNCF*, but needs to be booked at the ferry reception desk, either in Calais or in Dover.

Destinations Abbeville (4 daily; 2hr 5min); Boulogne-Ville (approx. hourly; 40min); Dunkerque (12 daily; from 35min); Étaples-Le Touquet (11 daily; 1hr); Lille (12 daily; 30min–1hr 20min); Paris (12 daily; from 1hr 40min).

### BY BUS

Buses to Boulogne, Wimereux and Wissant depart from in

front of the gare SNCF.

Destinations Boulogne (2–3 daily; 1hr 25min); Wimereux (2–3 daily; 1hr 10min); Wissant (2–3 daily; 30min).

## INFORMATION

**Tourist office** 12 bd Clemenceau (May–Aug Mon–Sat 10am–6pm Sun 10am–5pm; Sept–April Mon–Fri 10am–6pm Sat 10am–5pm; ☎03 21 96 62 40, ⊚ calais-cotedopale.com).

### BY CAR

From the Tunnel exit, road connections to Calais and the *autoroutes* are well signposted and easy to follow.

## ACCOMMODATION

**Camping du Fort Lapin** Route Nationale D940, Sangatte-Blériot ☎03 21 97 67 77, ⊚ www.camping dufortlapin.fr. A large site at the harbour end of Calais' adults' beach, with *pétanque* and playground. Closed Nov–March. €17.90

**Centre Européen de Séjour** Rue du Maréchal de Lattre-de-Tassigny ☎03 21 34 70 20, ⊚ auberge-jeunesse-calais.com. This modern, well-appointed hostel is just one block from the beach. One-, two- or three-bed rooms are available. Breakfast is included, while the good on-site restaurant offers meals from €14. Doubles from €25, singles €33

**Métropol** 45 quai du Rhin ☎03 21 97 54 00, ⊚ metropolhotel.com. Situated beside the canal close to the train station, and popular with the British, this feels like a classic "grand seaside hotel". The oldest hotel in Calais, it's comfortable, with unexciting rooms that are a little old fashioned, and a bar with an English pub feel. Breakfast €12.90. €91

**Meurice** 5–7 rue Edmond-Roche ☎03 21 34 57 03, ⊚ hotel-meurice.fr. With a rather *fin-de-siècle air*, this three-star hotel has spacious lounges and a club-like bar that gets crowded with British guests after dinner. A grand staircase (or lift) takes you up to rooms decorated with antique furniture, of which the most expensive have jacuzzis. It's in a quiet street behind the Musée des Beaux-Arts. Breakfast €14. €119

**Résidence du Golf** 745 Digue G. Berthe ☎03 21 96 88 99, ⊚ hoteldugolf-calais.com. The neat, bright motel-style rooms have kitchenettes and sea views. Rooms accommodating up to four people, and proximity to the beach, make this a good family choice. Breakfast €7.50. €87

**La Sole Meunière** 1 bd de la Résistance ☎03 21 34 43 01, ⊚ solemeuniere.com. Well situated near the ferry port, beach and the lighthouse, this friendly hotel has eighteen basic but comfortable rooms and a vibrant restaurant with a popular local reputation. Breakfast €9, garage parking €10. €75

## EATING AND DRINKING

**Café de Paris** 72 rue Royale ☎03 21 34 76 84, ⊚ cafedeparis-calais.com. This lively Calais-Nord brasserie swings along late into the night and is popular with locals and tourists for its inexpensive, straightforward dishes; *plats du jour* €10.50 and their various *menus* range from €21 to €29. Sun–Thurs 11am–12am, Fri & Sat 11am–2am.

**Le Channel** 3 bd de la Résistance ☎03 21 34 42 30, ⊚ restaurant-lechannel.com. A stylish gourmet restaurant overlooking the yacht basin, with wooden floors, a wall of wine bottles, plush red chairs and a classic menu that doesn't short-change on quality and flavour. The à la carte is expensive, but set meals (€18–61) are skilfully cooked. Closed two weeks in summer; reservations required. Wed–Sat & Mon noon–2.30pm & 6–10pm, Sun noon–2.30pm.

**Family Pub** 33 rue Royale ☎03 21 97 22 76, ⊚ familypub.fr. A late-night pub/brasserie with wooden booth seating, a good range of local and international beers, flatscreen TVs and food including pizza and burgers. It's laidback on non-party nights and a little rowdy on themed occasions. Daily 10am–2am.

★ **Histoire Ancienne** 20 rue Royale ☎03 21 34 11 20, ⊚ histoire-ancienne.com. A family-run brasserie with a charming, vaguely Art Deco interior, well-spaced tables and a warm welcome. On the menu, bistro dishes with a twist include veal kidneys with juniper (€19.50), while classics range from côte de boeuf (€48 for two people) to grilled king prawns (€24). Set options include the generous *menu bib gourmand* for €32. Tues–Sat noon–2pm & 6.45–9.30pm, Mon noon–2pm.

**L'Hovercraft** 11 place Foch ☎03 21 34 59 73, ⊚ hovercraft-calais.com. This popular bar and brasserie gets even busier when football matches are shown on a giant screen. It's a friendly spot – even British–French matches are watched in an entente cordiale spirit. Daily 10am–2am.

**Du Vignoble au Verre** 43 place d'Armes ☎03 21 34 83 29, ⊚ duvignoble-calais.com. The cosy interior matches the traditional French cooking – including pâté made on the premises alongside classics like steak with pepper sauce and scallops in white wine sauce. There's an emphasis on wine, including a selection of over four hundred cuvées. *Menus* at €15–24, bottles of wine from €13 to €1450. Sun & Tues noon–2pm, Wed & Thurs noon–2pm & 7–8.45pm, Fri & Sat noon–2pm & 7–9pm.

## SHOPPING

Street markets are around place d'Armes (Wed & Sat am) and place Crèvecoeur (Thurs & Sat am). For the *hypermarchés* and "booze cruise" stock-up sites, the main areas are around rue Gutenberg and rue de Judée.

**Auchan** Av Roger Salengro, west of town (bus #1) ☎ 03 21 46 92 92, ⓦ auchan.fr. Mainly food and drink, with weekly promotions on a large range of products. Mon–Thurs 8.30am–9pm, Fri & Sat 8.30am–9.30pm, Sun 8.30am–noon.

**Calais Vins** Rue Gutenberg, junction 44 of the A16 ☎ 03 21 36 40 40, ⓦ calais-vins.com. Over 2000 varieties of wines and 250 beer brands, plus tastings and expert advice. Mon–Sat 9am–7pm, Sun 10am–7pm.

**Carrefour** Av Georges-Guynemer, on the east side of town (bus #2 or #4) ☎ 03 21 46 75 55, ⓦ carrefour-calais.com. As to be expected from one of France's most popular chains, you'll find absolutely anything here – from washing powder to laptops, plus a staggering selection of

wine. Mon–Sat 8.30am–8.30pm, Sun 9am–12.30pm.

**Cité Europe** Bd du Kent, by the Channel Tunnel terminal (bus #1) ☎ 03 21 46 47 48, ⓦ citeeurope.com. Offers another Carrefour (Mon–Wed 9am–9pm, Thurs–Sat 9am–9.30pm), plus high-street clothing and food shops. Mon–Sat 10am–8pm.

**La Maison du Fromage et des Vins** 1 rue d'André-Gerschel. Has a good selection of cheeses and wine, which are served at the nearby *Le Channel* restaurant. Mon 3–7pm, Wed–Fri 8.30am–12.30pm & 3–7.30pm, Sat 8.30am–1pm & 2.30–7.30pm, Sun 10am–1pm.

**Majestic Wine** Rue de Judée, Zone Marcel Doret, on the eastern side of town (bus #7) ☎ 03 21 97 63 00, ⓦ majesticwinecalais.co.uk. For cheap wine, head for the French branch of this well-known British store. If you pre-order £250-worth of goods or more, Majestic will book a free return on the Eurotunnel for you. Mon–Sat 9am–7pm, Sun 9am–6pm.

# Wissant

**WISSANT**, some 20km from Calais south along the coast, is a small, attractive place, popular with windsurfers and weekending Britons drawn to its enormous beach. It's long been a preferred beach – indeed Julius Caesar launched his expedition to England from here in 55 BC. The drive from Wissant along the D940 towards Boulogne-sur-Mer is lined with beautiful and undeveloped dunes with frequent turn-offs for **walking paths** to the shore, each of which is tempting on a fine day.

## ARRIVAL AND INFORMATION                                          WISSANT

**By car** Follow the A16 southwest from Calais for the quicker journey or the D940 along the coast for the scenic route. Parking is available around place de la Mairie.

**Tourist office** Place de la Mairie (Mon–Sat 9.30am–noon & 2–6pm, Sun 10am–1pm & 3–6pm; ☎ 03 21 82 48 00, ⓦ terredes2capstourisme.fr).

## ACCOMMODATION

**Escale** 4 rue de la Mer, Escalles, 6km from Wissant ☎ 03 21 85 25 00, ⓦ hotel-lescale.com. In the little village of Escalles, this creeper-covered modern hotel has pretty rooms, many for three or four people. Facilities like tennis, a children's playground and a restaurant menu of tried and tested favourites make this a solid family choice. Breakfast €10.50. Closed mid-Dec to mid-Feb. **€77**

**De la Plage** 1 place Édouard-Houssin ☎ 03 21 35 91 87, ⓦ hotelplage-wissant.com. Old seaside hotel, very simply refurbished. Rooms are not well sound-proofed, but

it's friendly and family-oriented, and the restaurant serves excellent seafood. A good bet for a cheap and cheerful stay. Some rooms have a river view. Breakfast €8. Closed Jan to mid-Feb. **€70**

**La Source** 62179 Wissant ☎ 03 21 35 92 46. No reservations needed here; just turn up and pitch your tent in the municipal campsite just off the rue des Goérlans, a short walk from the sea. It has basic facilities but it's near the beach and Wissant's restaurants. Closed mid-Nov to mid-March. **€13.90**

# Boulogne-sur-Mer

**BOULOGNE-SUR-MER** is the smallest of the three main channel ports. The *ville basse* is pretty unprepossessing, but rising above the lower town is a diminutive, cobbled medieval quarter, the *ville haute*, contained within the old town walls and dominated by a grand, domed basilica. The main tourist street in the *ville haute* is **rue de Lille**, where you'll find the *hôtel de ville*, whose twelfth-century belfry is the most ancient monument in the old town (only accessible via guided tour arranged with the tourist office).

The most impressive sight in the *ville haute* is the **medieval walls** themselves, beautifully conserved and set out with rosebeds, gravel paths and benches, and providing panoramic views of the city below; it takes about 45 minutes to walk around them. Within the walls is the domed **Basilique Notre-Dame** (April–Aug daily 10am–noon & 2–6pm; Sept–March Tues–Sat 10am–noon & 2–5pm Sun 10am–noon), which is an odd building – raised in the nineteenth century by Father Haffreingue, the town's priest, without any architectural knowledge or advice – yet it seems to work. The vast medieval **crypt** (Tues–Sun: May–Sept 10am–6pm; Oct–April 10am–12.30pm & 2.30–5.30pm; €5) contains frescoed remains of the Romanesque building and various sacred objects.

## Musée de Boulogne-sur-Mer

Château Comtal, rue du Bernet • Mon & Wed–Sat: May–Sept 10am–6pm; Oct–April 10am–12.30pm & 2.30–5.30pm • €5 • ☎ 03 21 10 02 20

The **Musée de Boulogne-sur-Mer** is one of the more surprising discoveries in Boulogne, containing a beautiful collection of Greek and Etruscan vases. Created during the reign of King Louis XVIII, the permanent collections include Egyptian funerary objects such as a mummy, an unusual set of Eskimo masks and paintings including works by Corot and Fantin-Latour. The underground ramparts, part of the original 1825 building, are also worth a walk around.

## Nausicaá

Bd Ste-Beuve • Daily: July & Aug 9.30am–8pm; Sept–June 9.30am–6.30pm; closed for 3 weeks in Jan • €25, €24.20 if bought online • ☎ 03 21 30 99 99, ⓦ nausicaa.fr

Boulogne's number one attraction – and one of the most visited in northern France – is the Centre National de la Mer, or **Nausicaá**. You can wander from tank to tank while

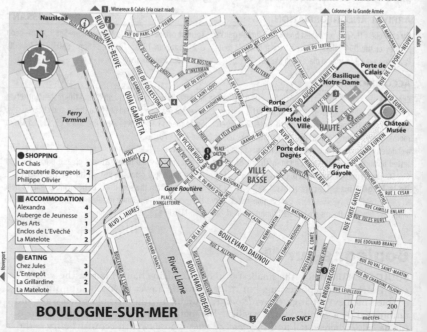

BOULOGNE-SUR-MER

hammerhead sharks, giant conger eels and jellyfish float and circle over your head. There are up-close-and-personal experiences with turbot and rays, and feeding sessions with the sea lions and exuberant penguins. Environmental issues are touched on in some of the display materials and, as you'd expect in France, there's an emphasis on the sea as a source of food; the restaurant offers appropriately caught fresh fish. In May and June the place is crawling with French and British school groups, and you may find it best to avoid – or at least get in early to beat the crowds.

## Around Boulogne

Three kilometres north of Boulogne on the A16/RD940 stands the **Colonne de la Grande Armée** where, in 1803, Napoleon is said to have changed his mind about invading Britain and turned his troops east towards Austria. The column was originally topped by a bronze figure of Napoleon, symbolically clad in Roman garb – though his head, equally symbolically, was shot off by the British navy during World War II; a replacement statue now tops the column.

For a pleasant excursion on a fine day, take bus #A 10min north to **Wimereux**, a charming seaside village with a broad promenade and a network of walking paths leading up into the windswept headlands.

### ARRIVAL AND INFORMATION           BOULOGNE-SUR-MER

**By train** The *gare SNCF* (Boulogne-Ville) is on bd Voltaire, a 10min walk to the centre.
Destinations Abbeville (5–11 daily; 50min–1hr 5min); Amiens (5–11 daily; 1hr 20min–1hr 30min); Calais-Ville (9–17 daily; 35min); Étaples-Le Touquet (9–24 daily; from 15min); Lille (6–8 daily; 1hr); Paris (10–13 daily; 2hr 25min).
**By bus** The bus station is on place de France; the centre is just a few minutes' walk. Services in the Boulogne area are run by Marineo (📞 03 21 83 51 51, 🖥 marineo.fr).

Destinations Calais (2–3 daily; 1hr 25min); Dunkerque (2–4 daily; 1hr 25min); Le Touquet (1–2 daily; 40min).
**Tourist office** Bd Sainte Beuve, Parvis de Nausicaá (April–June & Sept Mon–Sat 10am–12.30pm & 1.45–6pm, Sun 10am–1pm & 3–5pm; July & Aug Mon–Sat 10am–6.30pm, Sun 10am–1pm & 3–6pm; Oct–March Mon–Sat 10am–12.30pm & 2–5.30pm; 📞 03 21 10 88 10, 🖥 tourisme-boulognesurmer.com). Note that the office will be relocating in the near future; the address had not been confirmed at the time of writing, see website for up-to-date information.

### ACCOMMODATION

**Alexandra** 93 rue Adolphe Thiers 📞 03 21 30 52 22, 🖥 www.hotel-alexandra.fr. A small, unfussy hotel in the centre, with just eighteen bright rooms. Comfortable enough for a night or two. Breakfast €9. **€65**
**Auberge de Jeunesse** Place Rouget-de-Lisle 📞 03 21 99 15 30, 🖥 fuaj.org. Opposite the *gare SNCF* in the middle of a housing estate, this friendly modern HI hostel has en-suite rooms for 2–4 people. Breakfast included. Dorms **€22.50**, doubles **€54.80**
**Des Arts** 143 rue Carnot, Wimereux 📞 03 21 33 84 30. Set just a few streets back from the seafront, this appealing hotel has small but attractive rooms that combine old and new furnishings to very stylish effect. Some rooms have balconies, and there's also a bar. A great choice in lovely Wimereux. Breakfast €10. **€110**

★ **Enclos de L'Évêché** 6 rue de Pressy 📞 03 91 90 05 90, 🖥 enclosdeleveche.com. A classy *chambres d'hôtes* consisting of five individually and beautifully decorated large rooms and spacious bathrooms, set in a nineteenth-century townhouse in the heart of the medieval quarter. Around the corner from the cathedral and looking onto the ramparts, it's a peaceful place, with its own internal courtyard and terrace restaurant. **€75**
**La Matelote** 70 bd Ste-Beuve 📞 03 21 30 33 33, 🖥 la-matelote.com. Boulogne's most celebrated hotel has a swimming pool, jacuzzi, hamam and sauna. Smartly decorated and supremely comfortable, bedrooms come with minibar, a/c, and cable TV. Some have private balconies which look towards the sea and Nausicaá. **€130**

### EATING AND DRINKING

As a fishing port, Boulogne is a good spot to eat fish and seafood, with plenty of possibilities around place Dalton and a scattering on rue de Lille and around. There's a handful of bars in the *ville haute* and a rather livelier selection in place

Dalton, which surrounds the attractive Église Saint-Nicolas – a great backdrop for a drink.
**Chez Jules** 8 place Dalton 📞 03 21 31 54 12, 🖥 chez-jules.fr. On the main square of the *ville basse* this jolly

2

brasserie is perfect for families, with a pizza oven, fish tank, cheerful waiters and regional specialities including tripe. The terrace outside is perfect for people-watching. *Menus* €23.50–33. Mon–Sat 10am–10pm, Sun 10am–3pm.

**L'Entrepôt** 20–22 place Dalton ☎ 03 21 83 02 73, ⊛ restaurant-lentrepot.com. A cool, modern brasserie in the central and atmospheric place Dalton. Daily specials for food and a good selection of drinks, served in a softly lit bar with sofas or on the terrace. The menu includes "Welshes" (effectively Welsh rarebits in casserole dishes), pasta, fish and burgers from €12. Daily 10am–midnight.

**La Grillardine** 30 rue de Lille ☎ 03 21 80 32 94. Bright, small and cheerful restaurant in the *ville haute*. It has a

growing and glowing reputation for its focus on limited menus of bistro dishes, using locally sourced meat. At this standard of cooking, the €17 *menu* is particularly good value. Tues–Sat noon–2pm & 7–10pm.

**La Matelote** 80 bd Ste-Beuve ☎ 03 21 30 17 97, ⊛ la-matelote.com. In the eponymous hotel down by the sea, this restaurant, opened by Michelin-starred Tony Lestienne, is understandably high-end, if a little stuffy. Expect dishes like foie gras with stewed rhubarb or lobster fricassée, plus delectable desserts. *Menus*, priced at €35, €40, €68 or €82 are pretty reasonable for this level of quality. Daily 7.30–9.30pm, plus Fri–Wed noon–2pm.

## SHOPPING

On Wednesday and Saturday mornings, place Dalton hosts a general market with cheeses, meats and bric-a-brac. Boulogne also has some good artisan food shops in and around the Grande Rue. For the enormous Auchan hypermarket (☎ 03 21 10 11 12, ⊛ auchan.fr), catch bus #L along the N42 towards St-Omer.

**Le Chais** 49 rue des Deux Ponts ☎ 03 21 31 65 42, ⊛ lechais.com. Located in the Bréquerecque district by the *gare SNCF* and specializing in wines from Bordeaux and Bourgogne, this is the best place in the city to buy in bulk. Mon–Fri 9.30am–12.30pm & 2–7pm, Sat 9.30am–7pm.

**Charcuterie Bourgeois** 1 Grande Rue ☎ 03 21 31 53 57. One of the locals' favourite *traiteurs*, selling charcuterie and numerous cheeses. Tues–Fri 9am–noon & 2.30–7. pm, Sat 9am–12.30pm & 2.30–6.30pm.

★ **Philippe Olivier** 43 rue Adolphe-Thiers ☎ 03 21 31 94 74, ⊛ www.philippeolivier.com. With over a hundred years of family experience, this is quite simply the finest cheese shop in northern France, with over two hundred varieties in various states of maturation. Mon 3–7.15pm, Tues–Fri 9.30am–1pm & 3–7.15pm, Sat 8.30am–7.15pm.

# Le Touquet

Nestled among dunes and wind-flattened tamarisks and pines, leafy **LE TOUQUET** (officially called Le Touquet-Paris-Plage) resembles some of the snootier places on the English south coast. This is no real surprise, given its interwar popularity with the British smart set: Noel Coward spent weekends here, while the author P.G. Wodehouse lived in the town from 1934 to 1940. He was captured here by the rapidly advancing Germans, then interned, later making his notorious wartime broadcasts from Berlin. Though the town's seafront has been colonized by modern apartments, magnificent villas still hide behind the trees a few blocks inland.

## ARRIVAL AND INFORMATION

**By train and bus** Take the train from Boulogne to Étaples, then a local bus covers the last 4km. Alternatively, take the bus (Mon–Sat only; timetable from local tourist offices) directly from Boulogne down the coast through Le Touquet to Berck-sur-Mer.

**Tourist office** Palais des Congrès, place de l'Hermitage (Mon–Sat 9am–1pm & 2–6pm, Sun 10am–1pm & 2–6pm; ☎ 03 21 06 72 00, ⊛ letouquet.com).

## ACCOMMODATION

**Bristol** 17 rue Jean-Monnet ☎ 03 21 05 49 95, ⊛ hotel bristol.fr. Near the beach but very central, this 1920 villa-style hotel has renovated rooms decorated in pretty pastel colours with good bathrooms, a quiet inner courtyard, the comfortable *Ascot Bar* and a lounge with a fireplace for cosy winter evenings. Breakfast €12. **€125**

**Le Manoir** Av du Golf ☎ 03 21 06 28 00, ⊛ manoirhotel.

com. You don't get much more English than this manor-house-style hotel, loved by golfers for the course on its doorstep and the good-value golf breaks (see website for details). Bedrooms vary in size, with the largest having a huge window area, sofa and comfortable chairs. It's full of tasteful, old-fashioned furniture, and has something of the club feel about it. Breakfast €18. **€180**

## THE CÔTE D'OPALE

The **Côte d'Opale** is the stretch of Channel coast between Calais and the mouth of the River Somme, characterized by huge, windswept beaches. Along the northern stretch, as far as Boulogne, the beaches are fringed by white chalk cliffs, as on the English side of the Channel. Just here, between the prominent headlands of **Cap Blanc-Nez** and **Cap Gris-Nez**, the D940 coast road winds high above the sea, allowing you to appreciate the "opal" in the name – the sea and sky merging in an opalescent, oyster-grey continuum. The southern part of the coast is flatter, and the beach, uninterrupted for 40km, is backed by pine-anchored dunes and brackish tarns, punctuated by German pillboxes toppled over by the shifting sands. To help you appreciate the area even more, join a guided walk with Eden 62, an organization that protects natural areas, based at 2 rue Claude, Desvres (☏03 21 32 13 74, ⓦeden62.fr).

**Le Westminster** Av du Verger ☏03 21 05 48 48, ⓦwestminster.fr. The best hotel in the area is a grand old lady with impressive public spaces, traditional furnishings and rooms that seamlessly blend traditional furnishings with modern sensibilities. The list of past guests reads like a Who's Who, from Winston Churchill to Sean Connery. *Le Pavillon* restaurant is Michelin-starred. **€129**

### EATING AND DRINKING

**Le Café des Arts** 80 rue de Paris ☏03 21 05 21 55, ⓦrestaurant-lecafedesarts.com. Specializing in fish dishes, this is the place for sole, fresh tuna and crab. Classic meat dishes, like steak and roast lamb, are available, too. *Menus* at €23, €30 and €48. Mon & Thurs–Sun noon–2pm & 7.30–10pm.

**Côté Sud** 187 bd Docteur Jules-Pouget ☏03 21 05 41 24. Separate to, but part of, the Bristol, this is an elegant restaurant with a sea view. Oysters, foie gras, sole or smoked sea bass, as well as beef fillet with morels, are on offer on *menus* at €31–54 – head here for lunch when the set menus range from just €10 to €18.50. Tues–Sat 12.15–1.30pm & 7.15–9pm, Sun 12.15–1.30pm.

**Le Pavillon** Le Westminster, av du Verger ☏03 21 05 48 48, ⓦwestminster.fr. The best restaurant in the region, *Le*

*Pavillon* is smart, with an Art Deco interior and an outside terrace. Exciting, modern cooking ups the ante with the likes of red mullet with onions and chestnuts and langoustines with turnips and lemon caviar. The wine cellar features an impressive 25,000 bottles. *Menus* from €65 to €95, à la carte mains from €38. Daily except Wed 7.30–9pm, July & Aug daily.

**Les Sports** 22 rue St-Jean ☏03 21 05 05 22, ⓦbrasserielessports.fr. Both bar and brasserie have been serving classic French cuisine such as sole meunière since 1912; this down-to-earth place – but still good enough for Harrison Ford – has an extensive menu, with mains from around €17. Order the speciality, fish with "Ratte", Le Touquet's famous potato. Mon–Thurs & Sun 7am–2am, Fri & Sat 7am–4am.

# Étaples and around

Facing Le Touquet on the other side of the River Canche is the workaday **ÉTAPLES**, a fishing port whose charm lies in its relaxed air. To discover more about the local fishing industry, visit the engaging **Maréis La Coderie** (April–Sept daily 9.30am–1pm & 2–6pm; Oct–March Mon–Sat 10am–12.30pm & 2–5.30pm, Sun 2–5.30pm; €6.90; ☏03 21 09 04 00, ⓦmareis.fr), which shares the former rope factory with the tourist office. Apart from **Étaples**, the seaside towns in this area are only interesting in that they provide access to the beaches. Their quaint beauty is best experienced by walking the coastal GR path or any of the marked trails promoted by the local tourist offices. For drivers, the D119 between Boulogne and just north of Dannes provides turn-offs directly into the dunes.

### ARRIVAL AND INFORMATION                                ÉTAPLES

**By train** The station is on place de Huckeswagen, a few minutes' walk from the centre.

Destinations Boulogne (11–20 daily; 25min); Calais Ville (3–10 daily; 55min).

**Tourist office** La Corderie, bd Bigot Descelers (April–Sept daily 9.30am–1pm & 2–6pm; Oct–March Mon–Sat 10am–

12.30pm & 2–5.30pm, Sun 2–5.30pm; ☏03 21 09 56 94, ⓦetaples-tourisme.com).

**Boat trips** Depart from the port between April and September. A 45min sea jaunt costs €10.90, and a more rigorous twelve-hour fishing stint with experienced fishermen is €75. Book via the tourist office.

## EATING

**Aux Pêcheurs d'Étaples** Quai de la Canche ☎03 21 94 06 90, ⓦauxpecheursdetaples.fr. Set above the bustling fish market on the quayside, this restaurant is the perfect place for the freshest fish caught by the local fishing cooperative. From a long menu, the generous-sized bouillabaisse (€65 for two people) is outstanding; otherwise go for grilled sole, or a platter of langoustines. Daily noon–2pm & 7–9.30pm.

# 2 Montreuil-sur-Mer

Once a port, **MONTREUIL-SUR-MER** is now stranded 13km inland, after the River Canche silted up in the sixteenth century. Perched on a hilltop above the river and surrounded by ancient walls, it's compact and easily walkable, with fine views from its hilltop ramparts. Laurence Sterne spent a night here on his *Sentimental Journey*, and it is the scene of much of the action in Victor Hugo's *Les Misérables*, best evoked by the steep cobbled street of Cavée St-Firmin, first left after the Porte de Boulogne.

Two heavily damaged Gothic churches grace the main square: the **church of St-Saulve** and a tiny wood-panelled **chapelle** tucked into the side of the red-brick hospital. To the south, cobbled lanes are lined with little artisan houses. In the northwestern corner of the walls lies Vauban's **Citadelle** (daily except Tues: March–May & Nov 2–5pm; June–Sept 10.30am–5.30pm; Oct 10.30am–5.30pm; €5; ☎03 21 06 10 83 ⓦmusees-montreuilsurmer.fr), ruined and overgrown, with subterranean gun emplacements and a fourteenth-century tower that records the coats of arms of the French noblemen killed at Agincourt. Don't miss the World War I exhibition in the vaulted underground rooms of the tower.

## INFORMATION

**Tourist office** 11–13 rue Pierre Ledent (April–June, Sept & Oct Tues–Sat 10am–12.30pm & 2–6pm, Sun 10am–1pm; July & Aug Mon–Sat 9.30am–1pm & 2–7pm, Sun 10am–1pm & 3–5pm; Nov–March Tues–Sat 10.30am–12.30pm & 2–5pm; ☎03 21 06 04 27, ⓦtourisme-montreuillois.com). **Festivals** In mid-August, Montreuil stages a lively mini-festival of opera, theatre and dance, Les Malins Plaisirs (ⓦlesmalinsplaisirs.com).

## ACCOMMODATION AND EATING

**Château de Montreuil** 4 chaussée des Capucins ☎03 21 81 53 04, ⓦchateaudemontreuil.com. The best hotel in the region is a pretty *Relais & Châteaux* property with white walls and blue shutters, featuring a pool and surrounded by gardens. Individually themed rooms are beautifully done and have huge bathrooms. For a treat, book a room with a four-poster bed and old tapestries on the walls or traditional wooden panelling. The breakfast (€19–25) is one of the best in France, while its superb Michelin-starred restaurant serves dishes such as pigeon, scallops and show-stopping roast lamb. *Menu du Chef* €100. Restaurant: July & Aug Tues–Sun noon–1.45pm & 7–9.30pm; Sept–June Tues & Thurs 7–9.30pm, Wed & Fri–Sun noon–1.45pm & 7–9.30pm. €248

**Le Coq Hôtel** 2 place de la Poissonnerie ☎03 21 81 05 61, ⓦcoqhotel.fr. This red-brick hotel on a square has simple, comfortable rooms in the annexe and a courtyard garden. A convivial bar and good restaurant (mains from €18.50) complete a satisfying package. €95

**Le Darnétal** Place Darnétal ☎03 21 06 04 87, ⓦdarnetal-montreuil.com. A cosy restaurant full of odd objects, from plaster Buddhas to antique bags and rugby caps hanging from the ceiling, and offering a bistro menu of favourites. *Menus* from €22. Wed–Sun 9am–7pm.

**La Hulotte** Rue Carnot ☎03 21 06 10 83. A small, basic hostel in one of the citadelle's outbuildings. Closed Nov–Feb; reception 10am–6pm. Dorms from €14

# Crécy and Agincourt battlefields

Agincourt and Crécy, two of the bloodiest Anglo–French battles of the Middle Ages, took place near the attractive little town of **HESDIN**. Twenty kilometres southwest of Hesdin, at the **Battle of Crécy**, Edward III inflicted the first of his many defeats of the French in 1346. This was the first appearance on the continent of the new English weapon, the six-foot longbow, and reputedly the first use in European history of gunpowder. Today you just see the **Moulin Édouard III** (now an inconspicuous wooden watchtower), 1km northeast of **Crécy-en-Ponthieu** on the D111 to Wadicourt, site of the windmill from which Edward watched the hurly-burly of battle. Further south, on the D56 to Fontaine, the battered **croix de Bohème** marks the place where King John of Bohemia died fighting for the French, having insisted on leading his men into battle despite his blindness.

Ten thousand more died in the heaviest defeat ever of France's feudal knighthood at the **Battle of Agincourt** on 25 October 1415, the six hundredth anniversary of which was recently celebrated. Forced by muddy conditions to fight on foot in heavy armour, the French, though more than three times as numerous, were easy prey for the lighter, mobile English archers. The rout took place near present-day **AZINCOURT**, about 12km northeast of Hesdin off the D928. Agincourt Centre Historique Médiéval (closed at the time of research, but due to reopen in late 2019; ☎03 21 47 27 53, ⓦazincourt1415.fr) uses video and interactive facilities to bring the story to life and a map takes you for a circular drive around the English and French lines, including an orientation point by the crossroads of the D104 and the road to Maisoncelle.

# Parc Ornithologique du Marquenterre

30km south of Étaples off the D940 between the Canche and Somme estuaries • Feb, March & Oct to mid-Nov daily 10am–6pm; April–Sept daily 10am–7pm; mid-Nov to mid-Dec Sat & Sun 10am–5pm • €10.50 • ☎03 22 25 68 99, ⓦparcdumarquenterre.com

The landscape at the **Parc Ornithologique du Marquenterre** is beautiful and strange: all dunes, tamarisks and pine forest, full of salty meres and ponds, thick with water plants and birdlife. There's a choice of walking itineraries – two longer, more interesting walks (2–3hr) and a shorter one (roughly 1hr 30min). On both you can see dozens of species – ducks, geese, oyster-catchers, terns, egrets, redshanks, greenshanks, spoonbills, herons, storks, godwits – most taking a breather from their epic migratory flights. In April and May they head north, returning from the end of August to October; in early summer the young chicks can be spotted. You can rent binoculars or talk to the guides at some of the observation huts, who set up portable telescopes and will tell you about the nesting birds.

Keen natural historians might also want to drop into the **Maison de la Baie de Somme et de l'Oiseau** (daily: mid-Feb to March & Oct to mid-Nov 10am–5pm; April–Sept 10am–6.30pm; €6.90, ☎03 22 26 93 93, ⓦbaiedesomme.fr) on the other side of the bay, which has displays relating to birds and seals of the Somme bay and also organizes seal excursions.

# The Somme estuary

After Marquenterre, the D940 meanders through yet more silted-up fishing hamlets. Some, like **LE CROTOY**, have enough sea still to attract the yachties, and have enjoyed a boom in second homes. Le Crotoy's south-facing beach has attracted numerous writers and painters over the years: Jules Verne wrote *Twenty Thousand Leagues under the Sea* here.

## St-Valéry-Sur-Somme

**ST-VALÉRY-SUR-SOMME**, on the opposite side of the bay from Le Crotoy, is where William, Duke of Normandy, set sail to conquer England in 1066. With its intact medieval citadelle and brightly painted quays, St-Valéry is the jewel of the coast. The main sight is the **Musée Picarvie** (5 quai du Romerel; April–Sept Wed–Sat 10am–

12.30pm & 1.30–6pm, Sun 1.30–6pm; €5.90; ⓦbaiedesomme.fr), with its interesting collection of tools and artefacts relating to vanished trades and ways of life. Otherwise, **activities** include boat trips, cycling and guided walks, led by the Maison des Guides. Digging for shellfish is also popular, but be extremely careful about the tide: when it's high it reaches up to the quays, but withdraws 14km at low tide, creating a dangerous current; equally, it returns very suddenly, cutting off the unwary.

### ARRIVAL AND INFORMATION

**By train** St-Valéry-sur-Somme is accessible from April to Oct on the Chemin de Fer de la Baie de Somme steam train from Le Crotoy on its way to Cayeux-sur-Mer (see website for timetables; €14.50 return; ☎03 22 26 96 96, ⓦcfbs.eu).

### ST-VALÉRY-SUR-SOMME

**Tourist office** 2 place Guillaume le Conquérant (daily 9.30am–12.30pm & 2.30–6pm, closed Mon Sept–May; ☎03 22 60 93 50, ⓦsaint-valery-sur-somme.fr).

### ACCOMMODATION AND EATING

**Picardia** 41 quai du Romerel ☎03 22 60 32 30, ⓦpicardia.fr. This graceful, shuttered nineteenth-century building at the foot of the medieval quarter and a few steps from the water is a delightful, family-owned hotel. Pretty rooms follow the contours of the old house, many with beamed ceilings. Breakfast €14. **€115**

**Du Port et Restaurant des Bains** 1 quai Blavet ☎03 22 60 80 09, ⓦhotelhpb.com. Right on the estuary and offering simple but bright rooms and a friendly welcome, this long, low, fifteen-roomed hotel is particularly popular with families. Its bright, airy dining room, overlooking the water, buzzes with contented locals and visitors tucking into numerous seafood and shellfish specialities using the freshest local ingredients. *Menus* €19.90–49. Restaurant open daily noon–2pm & 7–10pm. **€90**

**Au Vélocipède** 1 Rue du Puits Salé ☎03 22 60 57 42, ⓦauvelocipede.fr. This charming B&B, with its smart, individually decorated rooms, some of which look onto the striking church of St-Martin, feels closer to a hotel than a traditional chambres d'hôtes. The owners are lovely and their restaurant serves up very good food, with a focus on local and seasonal ingredients. Daily noon–1.30pm & 7–10pm; closed Tues Sept–June. **€82**

# Lille

**LILLE** (Rijsel in Flemish), northern France's largest city, surprises many visitors with its impressive architecture, the winding streets of its tastefully restored **old quarter** (Vieux Lille), its plethora of excellent restaurants and its bustling nightlife. It boasts a large university, a modern métro system and a serious attitude to culture, with some great museums.

Historically the main stop on the rich trading route between Flanders and Paris, Lille was first and foremost a merchant city: instead of a soaring Gothic cathedral, taking pride of place are secular temples like the Flemish Renaissance gem, the **Ancienne Bourse**. The focal part of central Lille is the place du Général-de-Gaulle, always referred to as the **Grand'Place**, marking the southern boundary of Vieux Lille. South of this, the pedestrianized shopping area runs along rue de Béthune to the squares of place Béthune and place de la République. The city's **museums** are a short walk from the centre, though the top museums are outside the city limits: La Piscine in Roubaix and the Museum of Modern Art in Villeneuve d'Ascq. The city spreads far into the countryside in every direction, a jumble of suburbs and factories, and for the French it remains the symbol of the country's heavy industry and working-class politics.

## Ancienne Bourse

The east side of the Grand'Place is dominated by the lavishly ornate **Ancienne Bourse**. To the merchants of seventeenth-century Lille, all things Flemish were the epitome of wealth and taste and they lavished money on the Bourse and the imposing surrounding mansions. The courtyard holds a book **market** in the afternoons. A favourite Lillois pastime is lounging around the fountain at the centre of the Grand'Place, in the middle of which is a **column** commemorating the city's resistance to the Austrian siege of 1792, which is topped by *La Déesse* (the goddess), modelled on the wife of the mayor at the time.

2

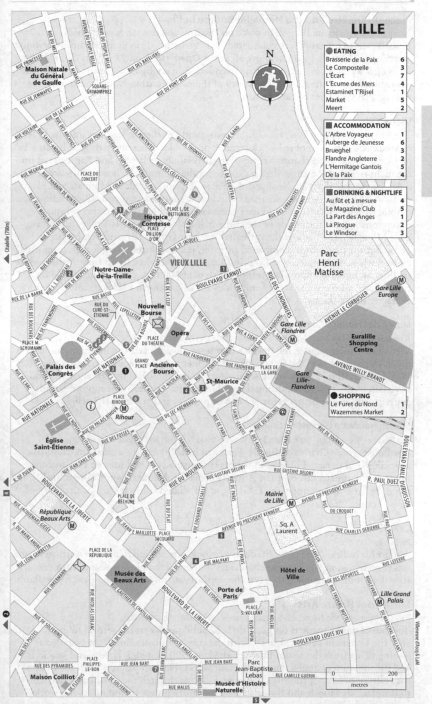

# LILLE

| ● EATING | |
|---|---|
| Brasserie de la Paix | 6 |
| Le Compostelle | 3 |
| L'Écart | 7 |
| L'Ecume des Mers | 4 |
| Estaminet T'Rijsel | 1 |
| Market | 5 |
| Meert | 2 |

| ■ ACCOMMODATION | |
|---|---|
| L'Arbre Voyageur | 1 |
| Auberge de Jeunesse | 6 |
| Brueghel | 3 |
| Flandre Angleterre | 2 |
| L'Hermitage Gantois | 5 |
| De la Paix | 4 |

| ■ DRINKING & NIGHTLIFE | |
|---|---|
| Au fût et à mesure | 4 |
| Le Magazine Club | 5 |
| La Part des Anges | 1 |
| La Pirogue | 2 |
| Le Windsor | 3 |

| ● SHOPPING | |
|---|---|
| Le Furet du Nord | 1 |
| Wazemmes Market | 2 |

### Place du Théâtre and the Nouvelle Bourse belfry

Next to the Ancienne Bourse, in **place du Théâtre**, you can see how Flemish Renaissance architecture was assimilated and "Frenchified" in grand flights of Baroque extravagance. This is apparent above all at the **Opéra** (☎03 62 21 21 21, ⊛opera-lille. fr), which was built at the turn of the twentieth century by Louis-Marie Cordonnier, who also designed the extravagant **belfry** of the neighbouring Nouvelle Bourse, now the regional Chamber of Commerce.

## 2 | Vieux Lille

The smart shopping streets, rues Esquermoise and Lepelletier, lead towards the heart of **Vieux Lille**, a warren of red-brick terraces on cobbled lanes and passages. It's an area of great character and charm, having been successfully reclaimed and reintegrated into the mainstream of the city's life. To experience the atmosphere, head up towards rue d'Angleterre, rue du Pont-Neuf and the Porte de Gand, rue de la Monnaie and place du Lion d'Or. Everywhere restaurants and bars are interspersed with chic boutiques.

Amid the city's secular pomp, Lille's ecclesiastical architecture is rather subdued. Exceptions include the facade of the cathedral, **Notre-Dame-de-la-Treille**, just off rue de la Monnaie. The body of the cathedral is a Neo-Gothic construction begun in 1854, but the new facade, completed in 1999, is a translucent marble skin supported by steel wires, best appreciated from inside, or at night when lit up from within. More traditional, but also impressive, is the **church of St-Maurice**, close to the station on rue de Paris, whose white stone front hides a classic Flemish Hallekerke, its five aisles characteristic of the style.

### Musée de l'Hospice Comtesse

32 rue de la Monnaie • Mon 2–6pm, Wed–Sun 10am–6pm • €3.70 • ☎ 03 28 36 84 00

Vieux Lille's main sight is the **Hospice Comtesse**. Twelfth century in origin, though much reconstructed in the eighteenth, the former hospital became an orphanage after World War I. The Hospice is the setting for a collection of paintings, tapestries and porcelain of the region, recreating the ambience of a seventeenth-century Flemish convent, and its medicinal garden, a riot of poppies and verbena, is a delight.

### Maison Natale du Général de Gaulle

9 rue Princesse • Wed–Sat 10am–1pm & 2–6pm, Sun 1.30–6pm • €6 • ☎ 03 59 73 00 30, ⊛maison-natale-de-gaulle.org

The house where **Charles de Gaulle** was born in 1890 is now a museum exhibiting keepsakes and personal objects in rooms that give a very real idea of a bourgeois home in the nineteenth century. A multimedia display takes you through his life and there are interesting temporary exhibitions on related subjects such as the story of Anne Frank.

### Citadelle

Rue de la Barre

A must for military buffs, the **citadelle** overlooks the old quarter to the northwest, and was constructed in familiar star-shaped fashion by Vauban in the seventeenth century. It's still in military hands today, but the outskirts are now a splendid park for walking.

### Musée des Beaux-Arts

Place de la République • Mon 2–6pm, Wed–Sun 10am–6pm • €7 • ☎ 03 20 06 78 00, ⊛pba-lille.fr

The **Musée des Beaux-Arts** on place de la République is France's second museum, after the Louvre in Paris, naturally, with the core of its collection from Napoleon's looting of art from the rest of Europe. The late 1990s redesign is sleek and spacious, and the museum contains some important works. Flemish painters form the bulk of the collection, from "primitives" like Dirck Bouts, through the northern Renaissance to Ruisdael, de Hooch and the seventeenth-century greats, including several works painted by Rubens for the Capuchin convent in Lille. French contributions include paintings by Delacroix, Courbet and Monet.

## Musée d'Histoire Naturelle

19 rue de Bruxelles • Mon & Wed–Fri 9.30am–5pm, Sat & Sun 10am–6pm • €3.70 • ☎ 03 28 55 30 80, ⓦ mhn.lille.fr

Located near the green avenue Jean-Baptiste Lebas, the charming **Musée d'Histoire Naturelle** is a manageable size for children, and has a lovely collection of dinosaur bones, fossils, as well as an impressive array of stuffed birds, including a dodo.

## Maison Coilliot and Hôtel de Ville

West of the Musée d'Histoire Naturelle, on rue de Fleurus, lies **Maison Coilliot**, one of the few houses built by Hector Guimard, who made his name designing the Art Nouveau entrances to the Paris métro – it's worth taking a look at the facade. East of the museum, near the triumphal arch of Porte de Paris, is the city's odd but serviceable *hôtel de ville*, which was executed in a Flemish-modernist style, not unlike German *jugendstil*, and has an extremely tall belfry.

## Euralille

100 Centre Commercial, off av Le Corbusier • Mon–Sat 9.30am–8pm • ☎ 03 20 14 52 20, ⓦ euralille.com

Thanks to Eurostar and the international extension of the TGV network, Lille has become the transport hub of northern Europe, a position it is trying to exploit by turning itself into an international business centre. Hence the creation of **Euralille**, the complex of shops and offices behind the old *gare SNCF*. Some of the structures are by big-name architects like Rem Koolhaas and Jean Nouvel, and the Jean-Marie Duthilleul-designed TGV station is bustling and audacious. The facility was expanded in 2000, in an unimaginatively named "Euralille 2" project.

## Lille Métropole Musée d'Art Moderne (LaM)

1 allée du Musée • Tues–Sun 10am–6pm, park open Tues–Sun 9am–6pm • €10 • ☎ 03 20 19 68 68, ⓦ musee-lam.fr

The suburb of **Villeneuve d'Ascq** is a mark of Lille's cultural ambition. Acres of parkland, an old windmill or two, and a whole series of mini-lakes form the setting for the renovated **Musée d'Art Moderne**. The ground floor holds exhibitions by contemporary French artists, while the permanent collection, on the first floor, contains canvases by Picasso, Braque, Modigliani and Rouault. The museum also has the largest collection of *art brut* ("raw art") in France, which includes graffiti and pieces by primitive artists working outside the fine art tradition.

## ARRIVAL AND DEPARTURE                                                                 LILLE

### BY AIR

Lille-Lesquin airport is located 7km southeast of Lille. A *navette*, or shuttle-bus (hourly on the hour; ⓦ lille.aeroport. fr; €8 one-way), can whisk you to Euralille, just by Gare Lille-Flandres, in 20min.

### BY TRAIN

**Gare Lille-Flandres** Situated in central Lille, a few minutes' walk from Grand'Place, this station serves regional trains plus a regular service to Paris. It was originally Paris's Gare du Nord, which was brought here brick by brick in 1865.

Destinations Arras (3 daily; from 20min); Boulogne (8 daily; 1hr); Brussels (TGV 7 daily; 40min); Calais-Ville (1–2 hourly; 1hr 25 min); Douai (10–18 daily; from 20min);

Dunkerque (approx. hourly; 1hr 10min); Lyon (TGV 8–11 daily; from 2hr 50min); Marseille (TGV 1–2 hourly; from 4hr 45min); Paris (TGV 23 daily; from 59 min).
**Lille-Europe** This station serves TGV and Eurostar trains from London, Brussels and further afield. Trains also connect with Lille-Flandres.
Destinations Amiens (hourly; 1hr 15min); Arras (hourly; 35min); Brussels (16 daily; from 34min); London (Eurostar 11 daily; from 1hr 22min); Paris (TGV 1–2 hourly; from 1hr).

### BY BUS

Eurolines buses from the UK and Europe pull into Lille-Europe.
Destinations London (3 daily; 5hr).

## GETTING AROUND

Lille's centre is small enough to walk around, and unless you choose to visit the modern art museum at Villeneuve-d'Ascq or La Piscine in Roubaix you won't even need to use the city's public transport system. Information on both the metro and bus routes can be found on ⓦ transpole.fr.

**By métro** Two VAL (Véhicule Automatique Léger, or automatic light vehicle) lines go from central Lille to the suburbs, including Villeneuve-d'Ascq and Roubaix.

**By bus** The Citadines route is a continuous loop running past the principal sights, from 5.30am to 9.30pm.

**Tickets** Public transport tickets are €1.65 for a single, €4.90 for a day pass and €2.25 for an evening pass (after 7pm).

## INFORMATION

**Tourist office** Place Rihour (Mon–Sat 9.30am–6pm, Sun & public hols 10am–4.30pm; ☎ 08 91 56 20 04, ⓦ lilletourism.com).

**Passes and tours** The tourist office runs regular city tours by bus and walking tours, plus a number of tours of the surrounding world war heritage sites from April to October (from €90). It can help book hotels, and sells a City Pass (one day €25, two days €35, three days €45), which offers free entry to various sites and attractions and free use of public transport. The passes are good value if you intend to hit the sightseeing trail hard.

**Festivals** The major festival of the year, the Grande Braderie, takes place over the first weekend of September, when a big street parade and vast flea market fill the streets of the old town by day, and the nights see a *moules-frites* frenzy in all the restaurants.

**Health** SOS Médecins, 3 av Louise Michel ☎ 08 26 46 91 91, ⓦ sosmedecins-lille.fr.

**Police** Commissariat Central, 5 bd du Maréchal-Vaillant ☎ 03 20 62 47 47.

## ACCOMMODATION

**L'Arbre Voyageur** 45 bd Carnot ☎ 03 20 20 62 62, ⓦ hotelarbrevoyageur.com. Though Boulevard Carnot itself is rather uninspiring, this smart contemporary hotel is just a stone's throw from Vieux Lille. The bright rooms are enlivened by colourful wallpaper that evokes the buildings 1970s heritage, and downstairs there's a chic restaurant and bar. **€109**

**Auberge de Jeunesse** 12 rue Malpart, off rue de Paris ☎ 03 20 57 08 94, ⓦ fuaj.org. Striking modern HI hostel in a fairly central position. Kitchen facilities and internet access available. Breakfast included. Closed Jan. Dorms **€26.10**, doubles **€40**

**Brueghel** 3–5 parvis St-Maurice ☎ 03 20 06 06 69, ⓦ hotel-brueghel.com. Tucked down a pedestrianized side street, this charming hotel with small but well-decorated rooms – no two are the same – is a real find. Prices are as attractive as the welcome. **€120**

**Flandre Angleterre** 13 place de la Gare ☎ 03 20 06 04 12, ⓦ hotel-flandre-angleterre.fr. Located near the train station, this two-star hotel has good-sized rooms with standard fittings and pretty fabrics. Double-glazed windows effectively keep out the noise outside. Breakfast from €4. **€58**

**L'Hermitage Gantois** 224 rue Pierre-Mauroy ☎ 03 20 85 30 30, ⓦ hotelhermitagegantois.com. This classy red-brick building is housed in a charity hospital dating back to 1462. Now a *Marriott* hotel, it successfully bridges the centuries, mixing medieval and modern. Large, luxurious bedrooms look out onto peaceful cobbled courtyards and you feel you're far from the city, though the location is central. Includes breakfast. **€146**

**De la Paix** 46bis rue de Paris ☎ 03 20 54 63 93, ⓦ hotel-la-paix.com. In a great central location just off the place du Théâtre, this hotel has standard rooms named after artists (Modigliani, Picasso and the like), each one livened up with classy posters and reproductions on the walls. Significant discounts are usually available on their website. **€130**

## EATING, DRINKING AND ENTERTAINMENT

A Flemish flavour and a taste for mussels characterize the city's traditional cuisine, with the main concentration of cafés, brasseries and restaurants around place Rihour and along rue de Béthune. Vieux Lille has a reputation for gastronomic excellence, particularly on the eastern side towards and along rue de Gand, where you'll find most of the worthwhile places. The student quarter along rue Solférino is good for ethnic eating – the former mostly Chinese or Japanese, the latter dominated by cheap kebab shops. The cafés around the Grand'Place and place Rihour buzz with life. Up near the cathedral in Vieux Lille, rue Royale, rue de la Barre, rue Basse and place Louise-de-Bettignies have trendier spots, with a few stretched out along rue de la Monnaie. West of the centre, Celtic-style pubs dominate in studenty rue Masséna, attracting a young crowd. Art and music events are always worth checking up on – there's a particularly lively jazz scene. Pick up a copy of the free weekly listings magazine, *Sortir* (ⓦ sortir.eu), from the tourist office, or look in the local paper, *La Voix du Nord* (ⓦ lavoixdunord.fr).

### CAFÉS AND RESTAURANTS

**Brasserie de la Paix** 25 place Rihour ☎ 03 20 54 70 41, ⓦ paix.restaurantsdelille.com. Red velvet banquettes, wooden tables, Art Deco stained glass and brass lamps decorate this bustling 1930s brasserie. The menu changes regularly, but expect classic dishes such as thyme-and-garlic lamb and platters of seafood, plus a good French wine list and Belgian beer. *Menus* €22–32. Mon–Sat noon–12.30pm & 7–11.30pm.

**Le Compostelle** 4 rue St-Étienne ☎ 03 28 38 08 30 ⓦ www.lecompostelle.fr. In a renovated Knights Templar Renaissance palace, this airy restaurant is the place for refined versions of traditional French specialities, including good vegetarian options. *Menus* from €29.80 to €36. Mon–Fri noon–2pm & 7.30–10.30pm, Sat noon–2pm & 7–10.30pm, Sun noon–2.30pm & 7–10.30pm.

**L'Écart** 26 rue Jeanne d'Arc ☎ 03 20 57 59 31, ⓦ cafelecart.free.fr. Cosy café-bar popular with students, but unpretentious and laid-back with it. Serves up the usual bistro dishes, but come to linger over a coffee during the day, or squeeze in for a beer come evening. Often hosts exhibitions or performances. Mon–Thurs 10am–midnight, Fri 10am–1am, Sat 2.30pm–2am.

**L'Écume des Mers** 10 rue de Pas ☎ 03 20 54 95 40, ⓦ ecume-des-mers.com. Large space with a pristine all-white decor sets the scene for top fish dishes from a daily changing menu. From tuna carpaccio with fresh leaf salad (€15) to rich bouillabaisse (€25), this is the place for seafood delicacies. Daily noon–2.30pm & 7–11pm.

**Estaminet T'Rijsel** 25 rue de Gand ☎ 03 20 15 01 59, ⓦ estaminetrijsel.fr. If you want the true Flemish *estaminet* experience, this is the place. Decorated with hops, old photos and candles on the tables, this crowded bistro serves the whole gamut of regional dishes, and over forty beers. *Plats* from €13.20, *menus* €26–39. Tues–Thurs & Sun noon–1.45pm & 7–10pm, Fri & Sat noon–2pm & 7–10.15pm.

**Market** 6 place Maurice-Schumann ☎ 03 20 54 98 02. Chic, red-brick-walled restaurant and bar with an up-to-date simple menu featuring dishes such as sea bass with oriental spices and New York strip steak, and a very good wine list. Mains from €25. Tues–Sat noon–2.30pm & 7–11pm.

★ **Meert** 27 rue Esquermoise ☎ 03 20 57 07 44 ⓦ meert.fr. Join Lille's high society in this old-fashioned *salon de thé* and shop, which has provided the locals (including General de Gaulle) with *gaufrettes* (crispy waffles) since 1761. The restaurant behind the shop now serves a more contemporary menu than previously, such

as veal tartare with a harissa cream. Main dishes from €19. Shop: Mon 2–7.30pm, Tues–Fri 9.30am–7.30pm, Sat 9am–7.30pm, Sun 9am–7m. Restaurant: Tues–Sun noon–2.30pm & 7.30–10pm, Sun 11am–2pm.

## BARS AND CLUBS

**Au fût et à mesure** 5 rue du Faisan ☎ 03 20 48 20 66, ⓦ aufutetamesure.com. The concept, imported from Spain, is simple: you pay in advance for a special card, and then have access to the beer tap on your table to fill up as you want. A good range of beers and big screens for sports events ensure its popularity. Sun–Wed 5pm–midnight, Thurs–Sat 5pm–2am.

**Le Magazine Club** 84 rue de Trévise ⓦ magazineclub. fr. Superstar DJs of world electro music plus great live acts in three comfortable bars make this one of Lille's most popular clubs. See website for hours.

**La Part des Anges** 50 rue de la Monnaie ☎ 03 20 06 44 01, ⓦ lapartdesangeslille.fr. A trendy wine bar with an enviable cellar (20,000 bottles), serving simple meals and oysters to accompany the wine. Mon–Thurs 9am–midnight, Fri 9am–1am, Sat 9am–2am.

**La Pirogue** 16 rue Jean-Jacques Rousseau ☎ 03 20 31 70 82. Antilles-themed bar with a suitably hot atmosphere and reasonably priced cocktails, especially popular with local students. Mon–Wed 5pm–1am, Thurs–Sat 5pm–3am.

**Le Windsor** 5 rue Jean-Roisin ☎ 03 20 57 45 64. Cool and atmospheric interior with dark lighting and a big-screen TV. Staggering range of enormous cocktails, which come served in vases, sweet jars and just about anything large and made of glass. Mon–Wed 6pm–1am, Thurs 6pm–2am, Fri & Sat 6pm–3am, Sun 7pm–1am.

## SHOPPING

**Le Furet du Nord** 15 place du Général-de-Gaulle ☎ 03 20 78 43 43, ⓦ furet.com. Spread over eight floors, this is one of Europe's largest bookshops, with a good number of books in English. Mon–Sat 9am–7.30pm.

**Wazemmes Market** Place de la Nouvelle Aventure/Rue Gambetta. A loud and colourful flea market in west central Lille; visitors can find a good-value snack or a clothing bargain in the market hall and the surrounding streets. Sunday is the main trading day. Tues, Thurs & Sun 7am–2pm; covered market Tues–Sat 8am–8pm, Sun 8am–3pm.

# The Flemish Cities

From the Middle Ages until the late twentieth century, great Flemish cities like **Roubaix**, **Douai** and **Cambrai** flourished, mainly thanks to their textile industries. The other dominating – but now virtually extinct – presence in this part of northern France was the **coalfields** and related industries, which, at their nineteenth-century peak stretched from Béthune in the west to Valenciennes in the east. At **Lewarde** you can visit one of the pits, while in the region's big industrial cities you can see what the masters built with their profits: noble townhouses, magnificent city halls, ornate churches and some of the country's finest art collections.

## Roubaix

Accessible by métro (line 2 to Gare Jean Lebas) and just 15km northeast of Lille, right up against the Belgian border, **ROUBAIX** is a once-great Flemish textile city that fell into decline and is still striving to rejuvenate itself – but it's worth a visit to see its showpiece museum, **La Piscine**.

### La Piscine – Musée d'Art et d'Industrie

23 rue de l'Espérance • Tues–Thurs 11am–6pm, Fri 11am–8pm, Sat & Sun 1–6pm; temporary and permanent collection €11; permanent collection only €9 • ☎ 03 20 69 23 60, ⓦ roubaix-lapiscine.com

Halfway between the *gare SNCF* and the Grand'Place is the magnificent **La Piscine – Musée d'Art et d'Industrie**, which was opened in 2001 and is in the improbable setting of one of France's most beautiful swimming pools and bath complexes, originally built in the early 1930s for the poor of the city. Architect Paul Philippon's contemporary conversion retains various aspects of the baths – part of the pool (it can't be swum in nowadays), the shower cubicles, the changing rooms and the bathhouses – and uses each part to display a splendid collection of mostly nineteenth- and early twentieth-century sculpture and painting, plus haute couture clothing, textiles and photographs of the pool in its heyday. A recent extension has added a further 2300m$^2$ of space, including more room for temporary exhibitions, and a new gallery dedicated to exploring modern sculpture.

## Douai

Right in the heart of mining country, 40km south of Lille, **DOUAI** is an unpretentious, surprisingly attractive town, despite being badly damaged in both world wars. Its handsome streets of eighteenth-century houses are cut through by the River Scarpe and a canal. Once a haven for English Catholics fleeing Protestant oppression in Tudor England, Douai later became the seat of Flemish local government under Louis XIV, an aristocratic past evoked in the novels of Balzac.

### Hôtel de Ville

83 rue de la Mairie • Guided tours (through the tourist office) Mon 3pm & 4.30pm, Tues–Sun: 10.30am, 11.30am, 3pm, 4.30pm; July & Aug 5.30pm • €6

Most of Douai's sights are west of the central place d'Armes, from which rue de la Mairie leads to the splendid fifteenth-century Gothic *hôtel de ville*, which is topped by a belfry of fairy-tale fabulousness, popularized by Victor Hugo and renowned for its carillon of 62 bells – the largest single collection in Europe. There are concerts every Saturday at 10.45am.

### Church of St-Pierre

Rue Bellegambe

Rising above the old town is the **church of St-Pierre**, its Baroque nave bracketed by a stone west tower, begun in 1513 but not finished until 1690, and by a dumpy round tower and dome at the opposite end. The church contains – among other treasures – a spectacular carved Baroque organ case.

### Musée de la Chartreuse

130 rue des Chartreux • Wed–Mon 10am–noon & 2–6pm • €4.70, free first Sun of the month • ☎ 03 27 71 38 80, ⓦ museedelachartreuse.fr

With the exception of the 1970s extension to the old Flemish Parliament, the riverfront west of the town hall is pleasant to wander along; across the river to the west are quiet streets of handsome two-storey houses. Here, the **Ancienne Chartreuse** has been converted into a wonderful **museum**, with a fine collection of paintings by Flemish, Dutch and French masters, including van Dyck, Jordaens, Rubens and Douai's own Jean Bellegambe. The adjacent chapel displays an array of sculptures including a poignant *Enfant prodige* by Rodin.

### Lewarde

A visit to the colliery at **LEWARDE**, 7km east of Douai, is a must for admirers of Zola's *Germinal*. It offers visitors a fascinating insight into the gruelling conditions of a nineteenth-century coal mine. Surrounded by flat, featureless beetroot fields, Lewarde's dour brick dwellings line streets named after Pablo Neruda, Jean-Jacques Rousseau, Georges Brassens and other luminaries of the Left. This is the traditional heart of France's coal-mining country, though you'll look in vain for winding towers or slag heaps hereabouts, demolition and landscaping having removed almost all visible traces.

#### Centre Historique Minier de Lewarde

Fosse Delloye, rue d'Erchin • March to mid-Nov daily 9am–7.30pm; mid-Nov to Feb Mon–Sat 1–7pm, Sun 10am–7pm; 1hr 30min • €12.50 • ☎ 03 27 95 82 82, ⊚ www.chm lewarde.com • From Douai's place de Gaulle, take tram A to Bougival then bus #1 one stop or 20min walk on the D132 towards Erchin.

The largest mining museum in France, the **Centre Historique Minier de Lewarde**, is in the former Delloye pithead where one thousand miners worked. You can tour the exhibition and surface installations with an English-language audioguide, but the tours of the mine itself (included in the admission fee) are led by retired miners. These pits were deep and hot, with steeply inclined narrow seams that forced the miners to work on slopes of 55 degrees and more, just as Étienne and the Maheu family do in Zola's story. After a simulated ride you see mining machinery, photographs, and the stables where the pit ponies were kept. There's a lot for children to see and do, and you should allow half a day to do it justice.

#### ARRIVAL AND INFORMATION
DOUAI

**By train** The *gare SNCF* is on bd de Liège, a 5min walk from the centre.
Destinations Amiens (5–11 daily; 1hr); Arras (1–3 hourly; from 12min); Cambrai (7–17 daily; 35min); Lille-Flandres

(10–18 daily; from 20min).
**Tourist office** 70 place d'Armes (Mon 2–6pm, Tues–Sun 10am–1pm & 2–6pm; ☎ 03 27 88 26 79, ⊚ douaitourisme. fr).

#### ACCOMMODATION AND EATING

**Le Prévert** 28 rue de la Comédie ☎ 03 27 98 59 51. Cosy bistro, with dishes chalked up on a blackboard and simple cooking in a friendly, unpretentious atmosphere. Main dishes from €12.50. Mon, Thurs & Fri noon–2pm & 7–10pm, Tues & Wed noon–2pm, Sat 7–10pm.

**La Terrasse** 36 terrasse St-Pierre ☎ 03 27 88 70 04, ⊚ laterrasse.fr. The food here is in the grand French tradition, with everything made in the on-site kitchens, from the breakfast croissants to the foie gras. Both Flemish (*potjevleich*) and classic French dishes (steak with pepper sauce) make an appearance. Old-fashioned maybe, but very reliable and well regarded. Accommodation and gastronomy tours also available. *Menus* €19.50–49.50. Daily noon–9.30pm. **€100**

## Cambrai

Despite the tank battle of November 1917 to the west of the town (see page 184), and the fact that the heavily defended Hindenburg Line ran through the town centre for most of World War I, **CAMBRAI** has kept enough of its character and cobbled streets to make a fleeting visit worthwhile, though it is less attractive than either Douai or Arras.

The large, cobbled, main **place Aristide-Briand** is dominated by the Neoclassical *hôtel de ville*. The imposing building hints at the town's former wealth, which was based

2

## CAMBRAI 1917

At dawn on November 20, 1917, the first full-scale **tank battle** in history began at Cambrai, when more than four hundred British tanks poured over the Hindenburg Line. In just 24 hours, the Royal Tank Corps and British Third Army made the biggest advance by either side since the trenches were dug in 1914. A fortnight later, however, casualties had reached 50,000, and the armies were back where they'd started.

Although the tanks were ahead of their time, they still relied on cavalry and plodding infantry as backup. The primitive tanks were operated by a crew of eight who endured almost intolerable conditions – with no ventilation, the temperature inside could reach 48°C. The steering alone required three men, each on separate gearboxes, communicating by hand signals through the mechanical din. Maximum speed (6kph) dropped to barely 1kph over rough terrain, and refuelling was necessary every 55km. Of the 179 tanks lost at Cambrai, few were destroyed by the enemy; most broke down and were abandoned by their crews.

on textiles and agriculture. Cambrai's chief ecclesiastical treasure is the **church of St-Géry**, off rue St-Aubert west of the main square, worth a visit for a celebrated *Mise au Tombeau* by Rubens.

### Musée des Beaux-Arts

15 rue de l'Épée • Wed–Sun 10am–noon & 2–6pm • €4, free entry first weekend of the month • ☎ 03 27 82 27 90, ⊛ musenor.com

The appealingly presented **Musée des Beaux-Arts** is worth a visit for its paintings by Velázquez, Utrillo and Ingres, alongside works by various Flemish old masters, plus great twentieth-century artists such as Zadkine and Van Dongen. Take the audio-tour and be sure to check out the archeological display in the atmospheric vaulted cellars, where you can see some fascinating exhibits, including elegant statues rescued from Cambrai's cathedral which was decimated after the French Revolution.

### ARRIVAL AND INFORMATION                                    CAMBRAI

**By train** The *gare SNCF* is located on rue Alsace Lorraine, a 5min walk from the *mairie*.
Destinations Amiens (4–14 daily; from 2hr); Douai (7–17 daily; 35min) Lille (5–12 daily; from 1hr 10min).

**Tourist office** Maison Espagnole, 48 rue de Noyon (mid-March to mid-Oct Mon–Sat 9.30am–12.30pm & 2.30–6pm, Sun 2.30–5.30pm; Dec–April Mon–Sat 9.30am–12.30pm & 2.30–5.30pm; ☎ 03 27 78 36 15, ⊛ tourisme-cambrai.fr).

### ACCOMMODATION AND EATING

**Château de la Motte Fénelon** Square du Val du Château ☎ 03 27 83 61 38, ⊛ cambrai-chateau-motte-fenelon.com. The château is oddly located within a suburban area of Cambrai, but its surrounding parkland shuts off the world nicely. Inside it's stately with large, well-decorated rooms and good bathrooms (ask for one in the château). The restaurant in the vaulted castle caves offers classic dishes and a good-value three-course *menu* (€30). Breakfast €11. €62

★ **Le Clos St-Jacques** 9 rue St Jacques ☎ 06 79 84 31 98, ⊛ leclosstjacques.com. A delightful bed and breakfast

with five individually themed rooms decorated with flair and imagination. All rooms can accommodate families. Breakfast €11. €101
**Mouton Blanc** 33 rue d'Alsace-Lorraine ☎ 03 27 81 30 16, ⊛ mouton-blanc.fr. Moderately priced and with smartly decorated rooms, this Flemish-style hotel is conveniently near the station. Its restaurant, *Le Carré*, features regional cooking and extensive use of local seasonal ingredients. *Menus* from €18. Restaurant open Tues–Thurs noon–2pm & 7.30–9.30pm, Fri noon–2pm & 7.30–10.30pm, Sat 7.30–10.30pm, Sun noon–2pm. €87

## Le Cateau-Cambrésis

Twenty-two kilometres east of Cambrai along an old Roman road, the small town of **LE CATEAU-CAMBRÉSIS** is the birthplace of Henri Matisse (1869–1954). As a gift to his home town, the artist bequeathed it a collection of his works, some of which are displayed in the remarkable **Musée Matisse** in the Palais Fénelon (Wed–Mon 10am–

6pm; €5, ☎03 59 73 38 03, ⓦmuseematisse.lenord.fr). Although it contains no major masterpieces, this is the third-largest Matisse collection in France, with many attractive and interesting paintings. The collection includes several studies for the Rosary Chapel in Vence (near Nice), plus a whole series of his characteristic simple pen-and-ink sketches. The work of local Cubist Auguste Herbin, particularly his psychedelic upright piano, and the magazines and books published by the editor-poet, Tériade, add depth to the collections.

**2**

# The Somme and its battlefields

Picardy, Artois and Flanders are littered with the monuments, battlefields and cemeteries of the two world wars, but they are nowhere as intensely concentrated as in the region northeast of Amiens, between **Albert** and the appealing market town of **Arras**. It was here, among the fields and villages of the Somme, that the main battle lines of World War I were drawn a hundred years ago.

You can get a real feel of trench warfare at **Vimy Ridge**, north of Arras, where the trenches have been left in situ. Lesser sites, often more atmospheric and thus more poignant, dot the countryside around Albert along the **Circuit du Souvenir**.

## Arras

**ARRAS** is one of the most architecturally striking towns in northern France, the cobblestoned squares of its old centre surrounded by ornate Baroque townhouses that hark back to its Flemish past. It was renowned for its tapestries in the Middle Ages, giving its name to the hangings behind which Shakespeare's Polonius was killed by Hamlet.

During World War I, British and New Zealand miners dug tunnels under the town to surprise the Germans to the northeast, while the Germans bombarded the town. Only a handful of the famous medieval Arras tapestries survived the conflict, including *The Annunciation*, now on display in the Metropolitan Museum of Art, New York.

Reconstruction after the war was meticulous, and the townhouses lining the grand arcaded Flemish squares in the central **Grand'Place** and the smaller **place des Héros** preserve the historic character. Inside the ornate *hôtel de ville* (daily during tourist office hours), on place des Héros, old photographs provide an interesting history of the town's wartime destruction and subsequent reconstruction.

For a panoramic view of the town and countryside, go up to the **belfry** viewing platform (€3.10), 150m above rue du 11 novembre. A lift then takes you the 43 steps to the top. Guided tours (ask for times in the tourist office, €4.50) take you round **Les Boves** – cold, dark passageways and spacious vaults beneath place des Héros and the rest of the city centre, tunnelled since the Middle Ages and developed by the British during World War I for a surprise attack on the Germans. The rooms – many of which have fine, tiled floors, pillars and stairways – were also used as a British barracks and hospital.

### La Carrière Wellington

Rue Arthur-Deletoille · Daily 10am–12.30pm & 1.30–6pm · €7 · ☎ 03 21 51 26 95, ⓦ carrierewellington.com

A few minutes' walk from the centre of town, **La Carrière Wellington** is a particularly moving and impressive exhibition involving a descent into the network of medieval chalk quarries adapted by British and New Zealand miners and engineers to create secret underground quarters for the 24,000 Allied troops awaiting the start of the Battle of Arras, a diversionary attack in preparation for the Chemin des Dames assaults. The troops emerged to mount their surprise attack on April 9, 1917. The visit is accompanied but there are also individual audioguides. Film footage on small screens, inscriptions on the walls and the words of poets such as Wilfred Owen bring the horrors of the battle to life. The visit finishes with a hauntingly effective film on the battle.

## Musée des Beaux-Arts

Abbaye St-Vaast, 22 rue Paul-Donnier • Mon & Wed–Fri 11am–6pm, Sat & Sun 10am–6.30pm • €7.50 • ☎ 03 21 71 26 43

Next to Arras' enormous cathedral is the eighteenth-century Benedictine Abbaye St-Vaast which houses the **Musée des Beaux–Arts**. The grey-stone classical building, still pockmarked by wartime shrapnel, contains an impressive collection, with works by seventeenth-century French and Dutch artists including Jordaens, Brueghels and Rubens – surprising to find outside Paris. Remnants of the history of Arras include sculpture, porcelain and one of the rare surviving Arras medieval tapestries. One room is filled with vivid seventeenth-century paintings by Philippe de Champaigne and his contemporaries, including his own *Présentation de la Vierge au Temple*.

## The war cemetery and Mémorial des Fusillés

Bd Général-de-Gaulle

On the southwestern edge of town is a **war cemetery** and memorial by the British architect Sir Edwin Lutyens. It's a movingly elegiac, classical colonnade of brick and stone, commemorating 35,928 missing soldiers, their names inscribed on the walls. Around the back of the barracks is the stark **Mémorial des Fusillés**, which commemorates two hundred Resistance fighters shot by firing squad during World War II – many of them of Polish descent, nearly all of them miners, and most of them Communists.

## Musée Lens-Louvre

99 rue Paul-Bert, Lens • Wed–Mon 10am–6pm • Free; temporary exhibitions €10 • ☎ 03 21 71 26 43, ⓦ louvrelens.fr

Just 16km from Arras and an easy day-trip is the **Musée Lens-Louvre** arts museum in **Lens**, part of the government's ongoing attempt to decentralize arts facilities from Paris. Collections on loan from the Paris Louvre include beautiful Greek, Etruscan and Roman antiquities, organized chronologically. The building, a futuristic glass pavilion, was designed by Japanese architectural firm SANAA after winning an international design competition.

## ARRIVAL AND INFORMATION ARRAS

**By train** Gare d'Arras, place du Maréchal-Foch, is a five-minute walk away from the centre.
Destinations Albert (5–11 daily; 23min); Boulogne (9–12 daily; from 1hr 50min); Calais (8–16 daily; from 1hr 20min); Étaples-Le Touquet (4–10 daily; 1hr 35min); Lille (9–15 daily; from 30min); Paris (17 daily; from 49min).
**Tourist office** Hôtel de Ville, place des Héros (Mon

10am–noon & 2–6pm, Tues–Sat 9am–noon & 2–6pm, Sun 10am–12.30pm & 2.30pm–6pm; ☎ 03 21 51 26 95, ⓦ explorearras.com).
**Festivals** On the last Sunday of August the town transforms itself into an open-air bistro for La Fête de l'Andouillette, with parades, colourful costumes and tasting of the sausage itself.

## ACCOMMODATION

**Les 3 Luppars** 49 Grand'Place ☎ 03 21 60 02 03, ⓦ hotel-les3luppars.com. Go for location in the Grand'Place. The ancient building has a superb Gothic facade on the front, though the small rooms are comfortable and a little old fashioned. Ask for a room at the back for peace and quiet. **€80**
**Moderne** 1 bd de Faidherbe ☎ 03 21 23 39 57, ⓦ hotel-moderne-arras.com. Opposite the station and just a short walk from the Grand'Place, this 1920 red-brick hotel has

reasonable-sized rooms, simply decorated but bright and comfortable. Breakfast included. **€70**
**De l'Univers** 3–5 place de la Croix Rouge ☎ 09 70 38 55 01, ⓦ univers.najeti.fr. The best hotel in town is set in a former seventeenth-century Jesuit monastery, built around a paved courtyard. Choose from a variety of rooms, all spacious and full of pretty fabrics and good furniture. **€86**

**2**

## EATING AND DRINKING

There's a good *fromagerie*, L'Alpage (Tues–Sat 9am–1pm & 2–7pm), just off the Grand'Place on rue de la Taillerie. Saturday is the best day for food and wine, when the squares are taken over by a morning market.

**La Faisanderie** 45 Grand'Place, ☎03 21 48 20 76, ⓦwww.restaurant-la-faisanderie.com. A gourmet restaurant in a knock-out Flemish baroque building; the adventurous cooking provides another revelation. Foie gras and *magret de canard* on the cheapest €30 *formule gastronomique* make this a really affordable treat. Tues 7–9.30pm, Wed–Sat noon–1.30pm & 7–9.30pm, Sun noon–1.30pm.

**La Rapière** 44 Grand'Place ☎03 21 55 09 92, ⓦlarapiere.com. Like many restaurants on the main square, the dining room is underground in a vaulted, red-brick seventeenth-century cellar, part of the old quarries under Arras. Typically, there are outside terrace tables for summer dining off an excellent regional menu. You can't get more local than a tart made with local Maroilles cheese followed by *andouillette*. Menus €16.60–36.60. Mon–Sat 9.30am–3pm & 6.30–10pm, Sun 9.30am–3pm.

## Vimy Ridge

Ten kilometres north of Arras off the D55 • April–Sept Mon noon–6pm, Tues–Sun 10am–6pm; Oct–March Mon 11am–5pm, Tues–Sun 9am–6pm; Tours daily every half hour before noon & after 1pm; book on arrival at the visitor's centre; 50min • Free • ☎03 21 50 68 68, ⓦveterans.gc.ca

**Vimy Ridge**, or Hill 145, was the scene of some of the fiercest trench warfare of World War I: almost two full years of battle, culminating in its capture by the Canadian Corps in April 1917. It's a vast site, given in perpetuity by the French to the Canadian people out of respect for their sacrifices, and the churned land has been preserved, in part, as it was during the conflict. Of all the battlefields, this is the best place to gain an impression of the lie of the land, and to imagine how it may have felt to be part of a World War I battle.

Near the visitor centre, long veins of neat, sanitized **trenches** wind through the earth, still heavily pitted by shells beneath the planted pines. Under the ground lie countless rounds of unexploded ammunition – visitors are warned not to stray from the paths. Free guided **tours** of the trenches are run by friendly, bilingual Canadian students, who supervise the visitor centre. An exhibition in the centre illustrates the well-planned Canadian attack and its importance for the Canadians: this was the first time they were recognized as fighting separately from the British, which hugely influenced their growing sense of nationhood.

On the brow of the ridge to the north, overlooking the slag-heap-dotted plain of Artois, a great white **monument** reaches for the heavens, inscribed with the names of 11,285 Canadians and Newfoundlanders whose bodies were never found. Back from the ridge lies a memorial to the **Moroccan Division** who also fought at Vimy, and in the woods behind, on the headstones of another exquisitely maintained **cemetery**, you can read the names of half the counties of rural England.

## La Targette and around

The **Musée de la Targette** (irregular hours: officially daily 9am–7pm; €4; ☎03 21 59 17 76) at La Targette, Neuville-Saint-Vaast, 8km north of Arras at the crossroads of D937/ D49, contains an interesting collection of World War I and II artefacts. It's the private collection of one David Bardiaux, inspired by his grandfather, a veteran of Verdun. Its appeal lies in the precision with which the mannequins of British, French, Canadian and German soldiers are dressed and equipped, down to their sweet and tobacco tins and such rarities as a 1915 British cap with earflaps – very comfortable for the troops but withdrawn because the top brass thought it made their men look like yokels. All the pieces exhibited have been under fire; some have stitched-up tears of old wounds.

North and south of La Targette along the D937 are several **cemeteries**, including a small British one, and south of the crossroads is the vast and moving German Neuville-Saint-Vaast cemetery, also known as "La Maison Blanche", containing the remains of 44,833 Germans, some four to a cross, others singly under a Star of David. To the north, a Polish memorial and a Czech cemetery face each other across the D937 between La Targette and Souchez.

## Notre-Dame de Lorette
Ablain-Saint-Nazaire, 5km north of La Targette • March 8am–5pm; April & May 8am–6pm; June–Sept 8am–7pm; Oct 8.30am–5pm; Nov–Feb 9am–5.30pm • Free

On a bleak hill a few kilometres further north of the cemeteries is the imposing church of **Notre-Dame de Lorette**, which stands on the site of a costly French offensive in May 1915. The Neo-Byzantine church was built in 1937, and is grey and dour outside but rich and bejewelled within. Around it stretches a vast graveyard with more than 20,000 crosses laid out in pairs, back to back. There are 20,000 more buried in the ossuary. Perhaps the most striking part of a visit here is the 'Ring of Remembrance', engraved as it is with the names of almost 600,000 soldiers and erected to commemorate the war's centenary. The **Lens' 1914–1918 War and Peace History Centre** (Tues–Sun 10am–1pm & 2–6pm; free; ☏03 21 74 83 15) at the foot of the church, covers the history of World War I in the region, through photographs, letters, maps and various other objects.

# Albert

The church at **ALBERT**, 40km south of Arras and 30km northeast of Amiens, was one of the minor landmarks of World War I. Its tall tower was hit by German bombing early on in the campaign, leaving the statue of the Madonna on top leaning at a precarious angle. The British, entrenched over three years in the region, called it the "Leaning Virgin". The superstition that when she fell the war would end inspired frequent pot shots by disgruntled troops. The town itself was completely rebuilt after the war in Art Deco style.

## Musée Somme 1916
Rue Anicet-Godin • Daily mid-Jan to mid-Dec 9am–6pm • €7 • ☏ 03 22 75 16 17, ⓦ musee-somme-1916.eu

This underground museum contains re-enactments of fifteen different scenes from life in the Somme trenches in 1916. The mannequins at the museum look slightly too jolly but it does go some way to bringing the war to life. The final section recreates the actual battle, complete with flashing lights and the sound of exploding shells.

---

### THE BATTLE OF THE SOMME

On July 1, 1916, the British and French launched the **Battle of the Somme** to relieve pressure on the French army defending Verdun. The front ran roughly northwest–southeast, 6km east of Albert across the valley of the Ancre and over the almost treeless high ground north of the Somme. The windy terrain had no intrinsic value, nor was there any long-term strategic objective; the region around Albert was the battle site simply because it was where the two Allied armies met.

There were 57,000 British casualties on the first day alone, approximately 20,000 of them fatal, making it the costliest defeat the British army has ever suffered. **Sir Douglas Haig** is the usual scapegoat, yet he was only following the military thinking of the day, which was where the real problem lay. As historian A.J.P. Taylor put it, "Defence was mechanized: attack was not." Machine guns were efficient, barbed wire effective, and, most important of all, the rail lines could move defensive reserves far faster than the attacking army could march. The often ineffective heavy bombardment before an advance only warned the enemy of an offensive and churned the trenches into a giant muddy quagmire.

Despite the bloody disaster of the first day, the battle wore on until bad weather in November made further attacks impossible. The cost of this futile struggle was roughly 415,000 British, 195,000 French and 600,000 German casualties.

**2**

**By train** The train station is on place du Général-de-Gaulle and is a few minutes' walk from the centre.
**Destinations** Amiens (22 daily; from 20min); Arras (5–11 daily; 25min).
**Tourist office** The appropriately named "Tourist Office of Poppy Country" is at 9 rue Gambetta (May–Aug Mon–Fri 9am–12.30pm & 1.30–6.30pm, Sat 9am–12.30pm & 2–6.30pm, Sun 9am–1pm; Sept–April Mon–Fri 9am–12.30pm & 1.30–5pm, Sat 9am–noon & 2–5pm; ☎ 03 22 75 16 42, ⓦ tourisme-paysducoquelicot.com).

**De la Paix** 43 rue Victor-Hugo ☎ 03 22 75 01 64, ⓦ hoteldelapaixalbert.com. The small rooms are simply decorated and have basic bathrooms, but you get a warm welcome here and it makes a good base. The old-fashioned, comfortable brasserie-style dining room offers locals specialities such as *ficelle picarde* (a savoury crêpe with cheese, mushrooms and ham), duck and snails, plus *menus* from €25. Breakfast €11. **€89**

# The Circuit du Souvenir

*Was it for this the clay grew tall?*
*O what made fatuous sunbeams toil*
*To break earth's sleep at all?*
                                                                    Wilfred Owen, Futility

The **Circuit du Souvenir** takes you from graveyard to mine crater, trench to memorial. There's little to show the scale of the destruction, nor do you get much sense of battle tactics. But you will find that, no matter what the level of your interest in the Great War, you have embarked on a sort of pilgrimage, as each successive step uncovers a more harrowing slice of history.

The **cemeteries** are deeply moving, with the grass perfectly mown and flowers by every gravestone. Tens of thousands of them stand in precise rows, all identical, with a man's name – if it is known, as nearly half the British dead have never been found – his rank and regiment and, often, a personal message chosen by the bereaved family. In the lanes between Albert and Bapaume you'll see cemeteries everywhere: at the angle of copses, halfway across a field, in the middle of a wood.

## Lochnagar and the Memorial to the Missing

The Circuit du Souvenir heads east from Albert to the giant mine crater of **Lochnagar** at La Boisselle before swinging north to **BEAUMONT-HAMEL**, where, pipes playing, the 51st Highland Division walked abreast to their deaths. On the hill where most of them died, a series of trenches, now grassed over and eroding, is preserved. You'll get a good sense of the battle at the **Newfoundland Memorial Park Visitor Centre** (Mon 11am–5pm, Tues–Sun 9am–5pm; ☎ 03 22 76 70 86, ⓦ veterans.gc.ca) on rue de l'Église/D73, a few minutes' walk south; of 800 Newfoundlanders who took part in the push, just 86 returned.

Across the river, near the village of **THIEPVAL**, the 5000 Ulstermen who died in the Battle of the Somme are commemorated by the **Ulster Memorial Tower** (March–Nov Tues–Sun 10am–5pm; free), a replica of Helen's Tower at Clandeboyne near Belfast.

Probably the most famous of Edwin Lutyens' many memorials is also at Thiepval: the colossal **Memorial to the Missing** (daily: March–Oct 9.30am–6pm; Nov–Feb 9.30am–

---

## GETTING AROUND THE CIRCUIT DU SOUVENIR

Perhaps not even the truly dedicated would try to see all four hundred Commonwealth cemeteries in the area. The easiest way to explore the circuit is by car, though the distances are short enough to do it by bicycle. Both Albert to the west and Péronne to the southeast make good starting points, their tourist offices and museums offering free **maps** of the circuit. The route is marked (somewhat intermittently) by arrows and poppy symbols, with Commonwealth graveyards also indicated in English.

5pm, closed mid-Dec to mid-Jan). Inscribed with the names of the approximately 72,000 British troops (the exact number varies depending on the source) whose bodies were never recovered at the Somme, the 43-metre-high memorial is visible for miles around. The interlocking-arch structure is dedicated to the men who were lost at the Somme between 1915 and 1918; staggeringly, according to the Commonwealth War Graves Commission, over ninety percent of these soldiers died in just a five-month period, during the first Battle of the Somme between 1 July and 18 November 1916. Here, an informative **visitor centre** (same opening hours as memorial; free) has a poignant photo wall of some of the missing, an exhibition on the Somme Offensive and short films in English on related themes.

## Devil's Wood

Delville Wood, known as "**Devil's Wood**", lies 10km east of Thiepval at **LONGUEVAL**. Here, where thousands of **South Africans** lost their lives, there's a memorial to the dead from both world wars and a **museum** (Tues–Sun: April–Oct 10am–6pm; Nov & March 10am–4pm; free). It describes not just the battle in France but also the longest march of the war, thousands of kilometres away, when South African troops walked 800km to drive the Germans out of East Africa (now Tanzania). The museum also touches upon South African involvement in other major conflicts, including the air force and navy in Korea and a section documenting the armed struggle against apartheid.

## Péronne: Historial de la Grande Guerre

Château de Péronne, Péronne • April–Oct daily 9.30am–6pm; Nov–March Thurs–Tues 9.30am–5pm; closed mid-Dec to mid-Jan • €9 • ☎ 03 22 83 14 18, ⓦ historial.org

The excellent **Historial de la Grande Guerre** museum in Péronne's château explains the political and cultural tensions before 1914, the conflict itself, and the consequences of World War I for civilians and the soldiers through an imaginative display of uniforms and accessories, posters, newsreel, film footage, Otto Dix drawings, artificial limbs and weaponry.

### ARRIVAL AND INFORMATION

**By train** Gare TGV Haute Picardie is near Berny-en-Santerre, 15km from Péronne and 100km from the Lille-Europe Eurostar stop. For a taxi to or from the station, use A2 Taxi (18 rue des Bouleaux, ☎ 03 22 84 40 00), based in Péronne, or ask at the tourist office.
**Tourist office** 16 place André-Audinot, Péronne (April–

### CIRCUIT DU SOUVENIR: PÉRONNE

July, Sept & Oct Mon–Wed 9.30am–noon & 2–6pm, Sat 9am–noon & 2–6pm; July & Aug Mon–Wed 9am–noon & 1.30–6pm, Sat 9.30am–12.30pm & 2–6pm; Nov–March Mon–Wed 9.30am–noon & 2–5.30pm, Sat 9am–noon & 2–5pm; ☎ 03 22 84 42 38, ⓦ hautesomme-tourisme.com).

### ACCOMMODATION AND EATING

**Le St-Claude** 42 place du Cdt-L-Daudré, Péronne ☎ 03 22 79 49 49, ⓦ hotelsaintclaude.com. Perfect for visiting the Historial directly opposite, this nineteenth-century former inn has spacious rooms including two that are especially suited for guests with reduced mobility. Rooms are a little garish, but it's a peaceful setting and there's a patio, plus a handy restaurant (closed Sat & Sun pm), with *menus* from €16. €92

## Villers-Bretonneux and The Australian Memorial

Near the village of **VILLERS-BRETONNEUX**, 18km from Albert near the River Somme, another Lutyens creation dominates. As at Vimy, the landscaping of the **Australian Memorial** is dramatic – for the full effect, climb up to the viewing platform of the stark white central tower. The monument was one of the last to be inaugurated, in July 1938, when the prospects for peace were again looking bleak, and it was damaged during World War II – bullet holes are still visible. There's a small **Franco–Australian Museum** (daily: April–Oct 9.30am–5.30pm; Nov–March 9.30am–4.30pm; €6; ☎ 03 22 96 80 79, ⓦ museeaustralien.com) on the first floor of the village school on rue de Victoria, just south of the memorial.

# Picardy

To the southeast of the Somme, away from the coast and the main Paris through-routes, the often rain-washed province of Picardy becomes considerably more inviting. **Amiens** is a friendly city whose life revolves around its canals, while both the Amiens and Beauvais cathedrals are highlights of the region. In the *départements* of **Aisne** and **Oise**, where Picardy merges with neighbouring Champagne (see Chapter 3), there are some real attractions amid the lush wooded hills. **Laon**, **Soissons** and **Noyon** all have handsome Gothic cathedrals, while at **Compiègne**, Napoleon Bonaparte and Napoléon III enjoyed the luxury of a magnificent château. The most rewarding overnight stop is off the beaten track in the tiny fortified town of **Coucy-le-Château-Auffrique**, which is perched on a hill between Soissons and Laon.

## Amiens

**AMIENS** was badly scarred during both world wars, but sensitively restored. Most people visit for the cathedral, but there's much more to the city: **Quartier St-Leu**, the renovated medieval artisans' quarter north of the cathedral with its network of canals, is charming, while the *hortillonnages* transport you into a peaceful rural landscape. A sizeable student population ensures enough evening entertainment to make an overnight stay worthwhile.

### Cathédrale Notre-Dame

April–June & Sept Mon & Wed–Fri 2.30pm–5.15pm, July–August Wed–Mon 2.30–5.15.pm; guided tours (book 48 hours in advance) April–June & Sept Mon & Wed–Fri 3 & 4.30pm; July & Aug Wed–Mon 11am; Oct–March Wed–Mon 3.45pm • €8 • ☎ 03 22 80 03 41, ⓦ cathedrale-amiens.monuments-nationaux.fr

The **Cathédrale Notre-Dame** dominates the city by sheer size – it's the biggest Gothic building in France – but its appeal lies mainly in its unusual style. Begun in 1220 under architect Robert de Luzarches, it was effectively finished by 1269. The west front shows traces of the original polychrome exterior, in stark contrast to its sombre modern appearance. A spectacular summer evening **sound and light show** shows how the west front would have looked, with an explanation of the various statues on the facade in French and then in English. The interior, on the other hand, is a light, calm and unaffected space. Later embellishments, like the sixteenth-century choir stalls, are works of breathtaking virtuosity, as are the sculpted panels depicting the life of St Firmin, Amiens' first bishop, on the choir screen. Visitors with strong legs can mount the cathedral's front **towers**. One of the most atmospheric ways of seeing the cathedral is to attend a Sunday morning Mass (9am and 10.30am), which is accompanied by sublime Gregorian chants.

### Quartier St-Leu

Just north of the cathedral, the **quartier St-Leu** is a Flemish-looking network of canals and cottages that was once the centre of Amiens' textile industry. The city still produces much of the country's velvet, but the factories moved out to the suburbs long ago, leaving St-Leu to rot in peace. Today the former slums have been transformed into neat brick cottages on cobbled streets, and the waterfront has been colonized by restaurants and bars.

### Hortillonnages

Boat trips: Association des Hortillonnages, 54 bd de Beauville • April–Oct daily 9am–noon & 1.30–6pm • €5.90 • ☎ 03 22 92 12 18 ⓦ hortillonnages-amiens.fr

On the edge of the city, the canals still serve as waterways for the **hortillonnages** – fertile market gardens cultivated since Roman times in the marshes of the Somme. Farmers travel between them in black, high-prowed punts and a few still take their produce into the city by boat for the Saturday morning **market** at place Parmentier. Each June farmers dress up in traditional garb and load their punts with produce for a festive *marché sur l'eau*. Taking a trip on one of these traditional boats is a particularly lovely way of experiencing the city.

## Musée de Picardie

48 rue de la République • ☎ 03 22 97 14 00, ⓦ amiens.fr

An opulent nineteenth-century mansion, originally modelled on Napoléon III's Louvre, houses the splendid **Musée de Picardie**, though it was closed at the time of writing for substantial refurbishment (due to reopen Autumn 2019 – check website for up-to-date information). The star exhibits in its previous incarnation were the Puvis de Chavannes paintings on the main stairwell, the room created by Sol LeWitt, and a collection of rare sixteenth-century paintings on wood donated to the cathedral by a local literary society.

## Maison de Jules Verne

2 rue Charles-Dubois • Mid-April to mid-Oct Wed–Mon 10am–12.30pm & 2–6.30pm, Tues 2–6.30pm; mid-Oct to mid-April Mon & Wed–Fri 10am–12.30pm & 2–6pm, Sat & Sun 2–6pm • €7.50 • ☎ 03 22 45 45 75, ⓦ amiens.fr

**Jules Verne** (1828–1905) spent most of his life in Amiens, and died here. His restored, four-storey house is a historic and attractive building, and a must for Jules Verne fans. It's laid out as a prosperous townhouse dating from the nineteenth century, with one room exactly as it was when the Verne family lived here. Large maps, posters,

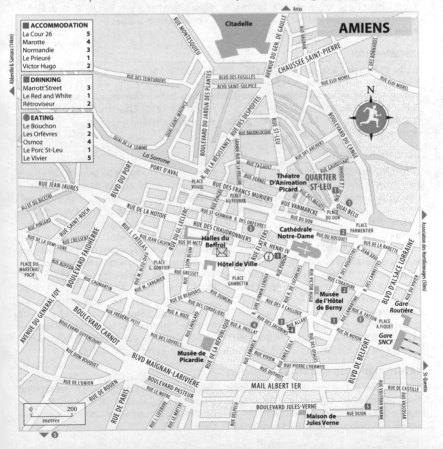

illustrations and models give an idea of the inspiration behind the writer and his science fiction works, *Twenty Thousand Leagues under the Sea* and *Around the World in Eighty Days*. They appear even more extraordinary when set against this evocation of life in a provincial French city.

## Samara

Rue d'Amiens, La Chaussée-Tirancourt, off the N1 to Abbeville • April–June & Sept to early Nov Mon–Fri 9.30am–5.30pm, Sat & Sun 10am–6pm; July & Aug daily 10am–6.30pm; closed early Nov to March • €10 • ☎ 03 22 71 83 83, ⓦ samara.fr

**Samara** (from "Samarobriva", the Roman name for Amiens), a large museum-cum-park, re-creates the life of prehistoric man in northern Europe. The open-air park is full of reconstructions of dwellings and displays illustrating the way of life – how people farmed, made oil lamps, cooked their dinners and coped with the weather. Live displays and recreations make it a worthwhile day-trip.

### ARRIVAL AND DEPARTURE                                    AMIENS

**By train** The *gare SNCF* (Amiens-Nord) is at place Alphonse Fiquet a five-minute walk west into the centre.
**Destinations** Abbeville (10–13 daily; 30min); Albert (22 daily; from 20min); Arras (13 daily; from 44min); Compiègne (9–18 daily; from 1hr); Laon (5–12 daily; 1hr 35min); Lille (hourly; from 1hr 15min); Paris (every 20min–1hr; from 1hr 30min); Reims (4 daily; from 2hr 45min).
**By bus** The *gare routière* is concealed beneath the Amiens 2 shopping complex next to the *gare SNCF*.
**Destinations** Beauvais (18 daily; from 1hr); Péronne (2–5 daily; 45min).
**By car** Much of central Amiens is traffic-free – the rest is full of cars circling in search of parking spaces. The most central car parks are on place Saint-Michel, rue du Général-Leclerc and rue Jules-Lardière.

### INFORMATION

**Tourist office** 23 place Notre-Dame (April–Sept Mon–Sat 9.30am–6.30pm, Sun 10am–noon & 2–5pm; Oct–March Mon–Sat 9.30am–6pm, Sun 10am–noon & 2–5pm; ☎ 03 22 71 60 50, ⓦ amiens-tourisme.com).
**City Pass** The Carte Pass Amiens (€17–21) provides reductions on up to four sites –including the cathedral and the Maison de Jules Verne – and is available at the tourist office.
**Festivals** On the third weekend in June, the local costumes come out for the Fête d'Amiens, which is the best time of year to visit the *hortillonnages*.

### ACCOMMODATION

**La Cour 26** 26 rue Dijon ☎ 06 26 30 73 89, ⓦ chambre-hote-amiens.fr. Set in a shuttered building close to the station, this charming B&B has just four bright rooms, one of which is a suite. An ample breakfast is served in the courtyard. €94
**Marotte** 3 rue Marotte ☎ 03 60 12 50 00, ⓦ hotel-marotte.com. A classic Flemish-style red-brick house originally built for an Amiens doctor has been converted into a graceful four-star property with surprisingly modern rooms. A new-build annexe (*the Cube*) was built on to high "green" standards and has three huge suites with private saunas. €165
**Normandie** 1bis rue Lamartine ☎ 03 22 91 74 99, ⓦ hotel-normandie-amiens.fr. This bright, comfortable two-star hotel in a little side street in an Art Deco building is close to the *gare SNCF*. It makes a good choice for a sightseeing base on a budget. Not all rooms have en-suite bathrooms; check when you book. Breakfast €8.50. €54
**Le Prieuré** 17 rue Porion ☎ 03 22 71 16 71, ⓦ hotel-prieure-amiens.com. You could be in Paris in this chic, beautifully renovated hotel very close to the cathedral. Each room of the former canon's house is different – with varying styles ranging from cosy antique to cool contemporary – so you can choose to match your mood and taste; there's even a chapel room with a truly beautiful ceiling. €92
**Victor Hugo** 2 rue de l'Oratoire ☎ 03 22 91 57 91, ⓦ hotel-a-amiens.com. This pretty hotel has just ten rooms, each differently decorated and with good bathrooms. It's near the cathedral and feels more like a rural bed and breakfast than a city hotel. Old photos and pictures give the place real character. Breakfast €8. €52

### EATING, DRINKING AND ENTERTAINMENT

If you're stocking up for a picnic or fancy some gourmet food shopping, La Halle au Frais in Les Halles du Beffroi at 22B rue du Général-Leclerc (Tues–Sat 9am–7pm, Sun 9am–12.30pm; ☎ 03 22 09 64 58, ⓦ leshalles-amiens.fr) is the place to head; it's a large covered market hall full of top producers and individual cheesemongers, like Julien Planchon who encourages local makers to produce new cheeses.

## RESTAURANTS

**Le Bouchon** 10 rue Alexandre-Faton ☎ 03 22 92 14 32, ⓦ lebouchon.fr. Simply elegant bistro menu of staples like roasted duck in blackcurrant jus, alongside more ambitious dishes, from a chicken and prawn ravioli in a spicy ginger broth to hot foie gras served with figs and Sichuan pepper, keep the locals happy at this popular restaurant. Mains start at €24 and there's a seriously good wine list. Tues & Thurs–Sat noon–2.30pm & 7.30–10.30pm, Wed & Sun noon–2.30pm.

**Les Orfèvres** 14 rue des Orfèvres ☎ 03 22 92 36 01, ⓦ lesorfevres.fr. Contemporary decor accompanies Jean-Michel Descloux's renowned cooking. Go for one of the *menus* (€45–83) and the chef will compose a "surprise" menu for the whole table. Tues–Sat noon–2pm & 6.45–10pm, Sun noon–1.30pm.

**Osmoz** 8 rue Lamarck ☎ 03 22 72 79 22, ⓦ restaurant-osmoz.fr. With bright yellow walls and a slightly industrial feel, Osmoz is a traditional restaurant with a stylish, contemporary feel. Expect the likes of salmon risotto and roast duck with goat's cheese. Mon 11.45am–2pm, Tues–Fri 11.45am–2pm & 7–10pm, Sat 7–10pm, Sun noon–2pm.

**Le Porc St-Leu** 45/47 quai Bélu ☎ 03 60 86 02 66, ⓦ porc-st-leu-amiens.fr. More traditional than its trendy neighbours, this brasserie-style restaurant has banquette seating, brass lamps and a tiled floor. It's the place for hearty meat dishes like *cochon de lait* (suckling pig) on *menus* running from €13 to €29. Sun–Thurs noon–2pm & 7–10pm, Fri & Sat noon–2pm & 7–11pm.

**Le Vivier** 593 route de Rouen ☎ 03 22 89 12 21, ⓦ restaurantlevivier-amiens.com. It's worth the slight trek to this pretty restaurant where you can eat in the glass conservatory. Dishes like blue lobster with mango and orange, groaning platters of seafood to share (from €29 to an eye-watering €160 for the *plateau prestige*), and pan-fried langoustines with sweetbreads and morels make this the best fish restaurant in Amiens. *Menus* from €35. Tues–Sat noon–2pm & 7–9.30pm.

## BARS

**Marott'Street** 1 rue Marotte ☎ 03 22 91 14 93. A chic champagne bar housed in a former insurance office, designed by Eiffel's architectural firm in 1892. It's an atmospheric spot next to the *Marotte*, with wood panelling, stained glass and funky tables and chairs. The wine list is excellent. Mon & Sat 2.30pm–1am, Tues–Fri noon–1pm.

**Le Red and White** 9 rue de la Dodane ☎ 03 22 72 34 00. The best gay bar in Amiens; it's busy and lively right into the small hours with live music. Tues–Sat 10pm–3am.

**Rétroviseur** 16 rue des Bondés ☎ 03 22 91 92 70, ⓦ leretroviseur.fr. One of a huddle of lively bars dotted around the waterfront, with busy decor and a student crowd. There's a solid choice of beers and wines and regular DJ slots, all beneath the colossal shadow of the cathedral. Mon 5pm–1am, Tues noon–2am, Wed–Fri noon–3am, Sat 5pm–3am.

## THEATRE

**Théâtre d'animation picard Chés Cabotans d'Amiens** 31 rue Edouard-David ☎ 03 22 22 30 90, ⓦ ches-cabotans-damiens.com. Traditional Picardy marionette (*cabotans*) performances are suitable for children as well as adults. Tickets from €8. You can buy the handmade marionettes at Jean-Pierre Facquier's workshop at 67 rue du Don (☎ 03 22 92 49 52).

# Beauvais

As you head south from Amiens towards Paris, the countryside becomes broad and flat; **BEAUVAIS**, 60km from Amiens, seems to fit into this landscape. Rebuilt in tasteful but unexciting fashion after World War II, it's not a town for aimless wandering – however, the cathedral is anything but boring.

## Cathédrale St-Pierre

Rue St-Pierre • Daily: April–Oct 10am–6.15pm; Nov–March 10am–12.15pm & 2–5.15pm • Free • ☎ 03 44 48 11 60, ⓦ cathedrale-beauvais.fr

The audacious, eccentric Gothic cathedral soars above the town and perfectly demonstrates the religious materialism of the Middle Ages – its main intention was to be taller and larger than its rivals. The choir, completed in 1272, briefly 5m higher than that of Amiens, collapsed in 1284. Its replacement also fell and, the authorities having overreached themselves financially, the church remained as it is today: unfinished, mutilated and rather odd. At over 155m high, the interior vaults are impressive, seemingly on a larger scale than at Amiens, though the props and brackets reinforcing the structure internally show its fragility. The building's real beauty lies in its glass, its sculpted doorways and the remnants of the so-called Basse-Oeuvre, a ninth-century Carolingian church incorporated into (and dwarfed by) the Gothic structure. It also contains a couple of remarkable **clocks**: a 12m-high astronomical clock built in 1865, with figures mimicking scenes from the Last Judgement on the hour; and a medieval clock that's been working for seven hundred years.

## Galerie Nationale de la Tapisserie
22 rue St-Pierre • Daily 10.30am–5.30pm • Free • ☎ 03 44 15 67 00

Beside the cathedral, the **Galerie Nationale de la Tapisserie** houses a collection of furniture and textiles from the fifteenth century to the present day. Louis XIV founded the royal tapestry works here in 1664; in 1939 they were transferred to Aubusson then brought back here in 1989. You can see the colourful products at the Manufacture Nationale de la Tapisserie on 24 rue Henri-Brisport (☎03 44 14 41 90).

## Musée Départemental de l'Oise
1 rue du Musée • Wed–Mon 11am–6pm • Free • ☎ 03 44 10 40 50, ⓦ mudo.oise.fr

The **Musée Départemental de l'Oise** is devoted to painting, local history and archeology, and is housed in the former episcopal palace. The magnificent Renaissance building houses French paintings from the sixteenth century, plus works by nineteenth-century artists like Corot. The Art Nouveau dining room is full of ceramics and there's a good representation of artists active between the two world wars.

### ARRIVAL AND INFORMATION · BEAUVAIS

**By air** The Paris-Beauvais Tillé airport – served by Ryanair from the UK and Ireland – is just outside the town (bus #6; every half hour).

**By train** The train station is on av de la République, and is a 10min walk from the centre.

Destinations Paris (at least hourly; from 1hr 15min).

**Tourist office** 1 rue Beauregard (Mon 2–6pm, Tues–Sat 9.30am–12.30pm & 1.30–6pm, Sun 10am–1pm & 2–5.30pm; ☎ 03 44 15 30 30, ⓦ visitbeauvais.fr).

### ACCOMMODATION AND EATING

★ **Al Karma** 21 rue de Calais ☎03 44 05 04 52. This Lebanese restaurant in a pretty yet inconspicuous building serves up huge platters of meze, hummus and various vegetarian delights from a family-run kitchen. A delicious assortment of hot and cold meze starts at €19.90. Mon–Sat noon–2.30pm & 7–10.30pm.

**Du Cygne** 24 rue Carnot ☎03 44 48 68 40, ⓦ hotel ducygne-beauvais-picardie.com. This serviceable small hotel in the centre of town makes a good base for sightseeing, with its simple rooms and a warm welcome. Breakfast €9. €58

**La Salamandre** 10 rue Marcelle-Geudelin ☎06 14 87 59 53, ⓦ lasalamandre-beauvais.fr. Set in extensive gardens, this sweet B&B has just five serene rooms that successfully blend traditional and modern styles. The "Plume" room has views of the cathedral. €105

# Laon

Looking out over the plains of Champagne and Picardy from the spine of a high narrow ridge, still protected by its gated medieval walls, **LAON** (pronounced "Lon") is one of the highlights of the region. Dominating the town, and visible for miles around, are the five great towers of one of the earliest and finest Gothic cathedrals in the country. Of all the cathedral towns in the Aisne, Laon is the one to head for.

## Cathédrale Notre-Dame
Place du Parvis Gautier-de-Mortagne • Daily 9am–6pm • Free

The magnificent **Cathédrale Notre-Dame**, built in the second half of the twelfth century, was a trendsetter in its day. Elements of its design, such as the gabled porches, the imposing towers and the gallery of arcades above the west front, were repeated at Chartres, Reims and – most famously – at Notre-Dame in Paris. The creatures craning from the uppermost ledges, looking like reckless mountain goats borrowed from a medieval bestiary, are reputed to have been carved in memory of the valiant horned steeds which lugged the cathedral's masonry up from the plains below. Inside, the effects are no less dramatic – the high white nave is lit by the dense ruby, sapphire and emerald tones of the medieval stained glass.

Crowded in the cathedral's surrounds is a quiet jumble of grey stone streets. South of the cathedral on rue Ermant is the crumbly little twelfth-century octagonal **Chapelle des Templiers** – the Knights Templar chapel – set in a secluded garden. The rest of the *ville haute*, which rambles along the ridge to the west of the cathedral, is enjoyable to wander around, with sweeping views from the **ramparts**.

### Musée d'Art et d'Archéologie

32 rue Georges-Ermant • Tues–Sun: June–Sept 11am–6pm; Oct–May 2–6pm • €4 • ☎ 03 23 22 87 01

The **Musée d'Art et d'Archéologie** contains a rather stuffy collection of classical antiquities, albeit with some fine Grecian ceramics among them, and a jumble of furniture and paintings, including an acclaimed seventeenth-century work, *Le Concert*, by local lad Mathieu Le Nain.

## ARRIVAL AND INFORMATION                                                    LAON

**By train** The train station is in the lower town (*ville basse*), in place des Droits de l'Homme. To get to the upper town – *ville haute* – without your own transport, you face either the stiff climb up the steps at the end of avenue Carnot, or the easier option of the cable railway.

Destinations Paris (8–15 daily; from 1hr 30); Soissons (7–17 daily; 30min).

**Cable Railway** The Poma 2000 (Mon–Sat 7am–8pm every 5min; same-day return ticket €1.20; tul-laon.fr) is a fully automated, rubber-tyred cable railway; you board next to the train station and alight by the town hall (Terminus "Hôtel de Ville") on place du Général-Leclerc; from there, a left turn down rue Sérurier brings you to the cathedral in the *ville haute*.

**Tourist office** Next to the cathedral, housed in the impressive Gothic Hôtel-Dieu in place du Parvis Gautier-de-Mortagne. (April–Sept daily 10am–12.30pm & 1.30–6pm; Oct–March Mon–Sat 10am–12.30pm & 1.30–5.30pm, Sun 1.30–5.30pm; ☎ 03 23 20 28 62, ⊛ tourisme-paysdelaon.com).

## ACCOMMODATION

**Bannière de France** 11 rue Franklin-Roosevelt ☎ 03 23 23 21 44, ⊛ hoteldelabannieredefrance.com. A comfortable hotel in the old town, very near the cathedral and in a building that dates back to the seventeenth century. There's eighteen pleasant, if unexciting, rooms and a restaurant serving authentic local food. *Menus* €18–62, Breakfast included. **€92**

**La Chênaie** Allée de la Chênaie ☎ 03 23 23 38 63, ⊛ camping-aisne.fr. Laon's well-established lakeside campsite is on the northwest side of town, just a few minutes from the centre. May–Sept. **€26.40**

**Les Chevaliers** 3–5 rue Sérurier ☎ 03 23 27 17 50, ⊕ hotelchevaliers@aol.com. Near the Poma stop in the old town, this is a charming wooden-floored hotel, though ask for a room at the back for a peaceful night. Breakfast €7. **€75**

**La Maison des 3 Rois** 17 rue Martin ☎ 03 23 20 74 24, ⊛ lamais3rois.com. Located in the middle of the old town, this boutique bed and breakfast is in a lovingly renovated fourteenth-century house. Spectacular views and rooms are smart and modern. **€110**

## EATING, DRINKING AND ENTERTAINMENT

**Crêperie Agora** 8 place du Marché aux Herbes ☎ 03 23 20 29 21, ⊛ creperieagora.fr. Just the place, after a visit to the cathedral opposite, for a cheap lunch or a full *menu* (€13.20–17.80). Good summer terrace. Mon–Wed 11.30am–2.30pm, Thurs–Sun 11.30am–2.30pm & 6.30–10.30pm.

**La Petite Auberge** 45 bd Brossolette ☎ 03 23 23 02 38, ⊛ zorn-lapetiteauberge.com. Located near the station, this Willy Marc Zorn Michelin-starred restaurant is far above average. Starters (€22) like scallops done three different ways, mains (€29) such as pan-seared veal with parsnip purée, and superb desserts (from €13) are served in a refreshingly contemporary space. The adjacent *Bistrot St-Amour*, under the same ownership, offers more casual eating. Mon noon–2pm, Tues–Sat noon–2pm & 7–9.30pm, Sat 7–9.30pm.

**Le Péché Mignon** 53 rue Châtelaine ☎ 03 23 29 35 19. This small, unpretentious restaurant gets rave reviews for its beautifully presented food and reasonably priced *formules* (from €9), which include the likes of tuna tartare and pork in mustard sauce. Mon & Thurs noon–2pm & 7–9.30pm, Tues & Sun noon–2pm, Fri & Sat noon–2pm & 7–10.30pm.

### THEATRE

**Maison des Arts de Laon** 2 place Aubry ☎ 03 23 22 86 86. MAL is based in a theatre to the north of the cathedral, and puts on concerts, dramas and other events, especially during Les Médiévales de Laon in May and the Laon Festival in October, sometimes in the cathedral itself (details from the tourist office).

## Soissons

Half an hour by train from Laon, or 30km down the N2, **SOISSONS** has a long and highly strategic history. Before the Romans arrived it was already a town, and in 486 AD the last Roman ruler, Syagrius, suffered a decisive defeat here at the hands of Clovis the Frank, making Soissons one of the first real centres of the Frankish kingdom. Napoleon, too, considered it a crucial military base, a judgement borne out in the twentieth century by extensive war damage.

### Cathédrale St Gervais-St Protais

23 rue des Déportés et Fusilliés • Daily 9.30am–noon & 2–4pm

Once one of the most beautiful Gothic cathedrals in northern France, the mainly thirteenth-century **Cathédrale St Gervais-St Protais** stands at the west end of the town square and dominates the countryside. Despite huge damage in World War I, its interior is still remarkable for the stone vaulting in the choir, majestic glasswork and the *Adoration of the Shepherds* by Rubens.

### Abbaye de St-Jean-des-Vignes

Rue St-Jean

More impressive than the cathedral is the ruined **Abbaye** to the south of place Marquigny. The gaping west front of the tremendous Gothic abbey rises sheer and grand, impervious to the empty space behind it – you get a superb view of the silhouette from the peaceful abbey precincts, but the ruin itself is in crumbly condition and fenced off. The rest of the complex, save for remnants of a **cloister** and **refectory** (free to visit), was dismantled in 1804.

### ARRIVAL AND INFORMATION SOISSONS

**By train** The train station is at place de la Gare from where it's a 20min walk into the centre.
**Destinations** Laon (7–17 daily; 25min); Paris (7–14 daily; from 1hr 5min).
**By bus** The bus station is on avenue de l'Aisne, a few minutes' walk from the centre.

Destinations Compiègne (9 daily; 1hr 15min); Coucy (5 daily; 25min).
**Tourist office** 16 place Fernand Marquigny (May–Sept Mon–Sat 10am–6pm, Sun 10am–12.15pm & 1.15–5pm; Oct–April Mon–Sat 10am–5pm; ☎03 23 53 17 37, ⓦ tourisme-soissons.fr).

### ACCOMMODATION AND EATING

**L'Arthé** 16 rue de la Bannière ☎03 23 76 29 64, ⓦ restaurant-larthe.fr. An informal *salon de thé* and restaurant on a side street between the cathedral and the river. On offer are simple *menus* from €12.30, or just coffee and desserts. Tues–Tues noon–2pm, Wed & Thurs noon–5.30pm, Fri & Sat noon–11pm.
**L'Assiette Gourmande** 16 av de Coucy ☎03 23 93 47 78, ⓦ agourmande.fr. This elegant restaurant does classy cooking, including a good-value €33 *menu gourmand* offering foie gras with fig and apricot compote, along with deliciously sweet lamb with *petits pois* and mushrooms. Mon–Fri noon–2pm & 7.30–9pm, Sat 7.30–9pm, Sun

noon–2pm.
**Francs** 62 bd Jeanne-d'Arc ☎03 60 71 40 00, ⓦ hotel desfrancs.fr. This Best Western hotel is strong on up-to-date facilities and eco-friendly practices. Good-sized rooms may lack period charm but the hotel is opposite the old abbey of St-Jean-des-Vignes, and has great views. There's also a pool and a chic brasserie with main meals starting at €17. **€109**
**Le Terminus** 56 av du Général-de-Gaulle ☎03 23 53 33 59. Above a bar and conveniently near the station, this hotel will entertain for an overnight stop – especially as it has table football and darts. **€63**

## Coucy-le-Château-Auffrique

About 30km west of Laon and 15km north of Soissons, in hilly countryside on the far side of the forest of St-Gobain, lie the straggling ruins of one of the greatest castles of the Middle Ages, **Château de Coucy** (daily: May–Aug 10am–1pm & 2–6.30pm; Sept–April 10am–1pm & 2–5.30pm; €6; ⓦ coucy.monuments-nationaux.fr).

The castle's walls still stand, encircling the attractive village of **COUCY-LE-CHÂTEAU-AUFFRIQUE**. In the past this was a seat of great power and the influence of its lords, the Sires de Coucy, rivalled and often even exceeded that of the king. The retreating Germans capped the destruction of World War I battles by blowing up the castle's keep as they left in 1917, but enough remains, crowning a wooded spur, to be extremely evocative.

Enter the village through one of three original gates, which are squeezed between powerful, round flanking towers – there's a footpath around the outside which is open even when the castle is not. A display of photographs, models and various historical objects in the museum (contact ☎03 23 52 44 55 for more information; free), at the Porte de Soissons, shows how the castle looked pre-1917. Go onto the roof to compare with today's postwar reconstruction. Also here are costumed characters and explanations of medieval life.

## ARRIVAL AND INFORMATION

**COUCY-LE-CHÂTEAU-AUFFRIQUE**

**By bus** Buses on the Soissons–St Quentin route (line 10) stop in Coucy-le-Chateau at the *Café des Sports* and the *Hôtel du Lion Rouge* at the bottom of the hill.
**Destinations** Soissons (6 daily; 25min).
**Tourist office** Pavillon Anne Morgan, place de l'Hôtel-

de-Ville (Tues–Sun 2–6pm; ☎03 23 52 44 55, ⓦcoucylec hateau.com).
**Festivals** Check out the many medieval spectacles (such as Coucy à la Merveille) on ⓦamvcc.com; note that you'll have to book in advance.

## ACCOMMODATION

**Belle Vue** 2 Porte de Laon ☎03 23 52 69 70, ⓦhotel-bellevue-coucy.com. A sense of faded grandeur in the bedrooms fits in perfectly with the romantic feel of being within the medieval walls; if possible opt for the superior

room, which has a sitting area and views of the ramparts. The restaurant specializes in Picardy cuisine (*menus* from €24.90), and serves special "medieval" meals to get you in the right frame of mind. Breakfast €8. **€56**

# Compiègne

Thirty-eight kilometres west of Soissons, **COMPIÈGNE** owes its reputation as a tourist centre to a vast royal palace, built at the edge of the Forêt de Compiègne so that generations of French kings could play at "being peasants", in Louis XIV's words. It's an attractive and lively town of pale stone houses, white shutters and dark slate roofs, and makes a good base for seeing the sites associated with the two world wars and for walks in the surrounding forest.

## Palais de Compiègne

Place du Général-de-Gaulle • mid-March to Oct Wed–Sat 10am–6pm, last admission 5.15pm; Nov to mid March Wed–Sat 10am–4pm • **Musée de la Voiture** mid-March to Oct Wed, Thurs, Sat & Sun 2–6pm; Nov to mid-March Mon & Fri 4.16–6pm, Wed, Thurs, Sat & Sun 2–6pm • €7.50 including **Musée de la Voiture**, €9.50 during temporary exhibitions • **Palace gardens** Daily: March to mid-April & mid-Sept to Oct 8am–6pm; mid-April to mid-Sept 8am–7pm; Nov–Feb 8am–5pm • Free • ☎03 44 38 47 00, ⓦpalaisdecompiegne.fr.

Compiègne's star attraction, the opulent **Palais de Compiègne**, is an eighteenth-century château, two blocks east of the Hôtel de Ville along rue des Minimes. Despite its pompous excess, it inspires a certain fascination. Napoleon commissioned a renovation of the former royal palace in 1807, and the work was completed in time for the emperor to welcome his second wife, Marie-Louise of Austria – a relative of Marie-Antoinette – here in 1810. The ostentatious post-revolutionary apartments stand in marked contrast to the more sober Neoclassicism of the few surviving late royal interiors, a monument to the unseemly haste with which Napoleon I moved in, scarcely a dozen years after the Revolution.

The **Théâtre Impérial** was first planned by Napoléon III in the historic apartments of the Second Empire. It was only completed with a restoration project in 1991 at a cost of some thirty million francs. Originally designed with just two seats for Napoleon and his wife, it now seats nine hundred and is used for concerts.

The **Musée de la Voiture**, in another part of the vast palace, contains a wonderful array of antique bicycles, tricycles and aristocratic carriages, as well as the world's first steam coach.

You can visit the extensive **palace gardens** separately, and they make excellent picnicking territory. Much of the original French-style garden was replanted on Napoleon's orders after 1811. The result is monumental; the great avenue that extends 4.5km into the Forêt de Compiègne was inspired by the Austrian imperial summer residence at Schönbrunn on the outskirts of Vienna.

## Place de l'Hôtel-de-Ville

The centre of town is more handsome than picturesque, though several half-timbered buildings remain on rue Napoléon and rue des Lombards, south of the main square, place de l'Hôtel-de-Ville. The *hôtel de ville* itself – Louis XII Gothic – features ebullient nineteenth-century statuary including the image of Joan of Arc, who was captured in this town before being handed to the English.

## Musée de la Figurine Historique

28 place de l'Hôtel-de-Ville • Tues–Sun 10am–1pm & 2–6pm • €4 • ☎ 03 44 20 26 04, ⓦ www.musee-figurine.fr

Beside the *hôtel de ville*, the **Musée de la Figurine Historique** reputedly holds the world's largest collection of toy soldiers in mock-up battles; the huge diorama of the Battle of Waterloo is the most impressive.

## Mémorial de l'Internement et de la Déportation

2bis av des Martyrs de la Liberté • Wed–Mon 10am–6pm • €5 • ☎ 03 44 96 37 00, ⓦ www.memorial-compiegne.fr

Southwest of the town centre is the sombre **Mémorial de l'Internement et de la Déportation**, which occupies the former barracks of Royallieu, transformed into a prisoner of war camp by the German army in 1940 and later used as a transit camp for political prisoners, Jews and others. It was from here in March 1942 that the first deportation from France to Auschwitz took place.

### ARRIVAL AND INFORMATION COMPIÈGNE

**By train** The station is a few minutes' walk from the centre of town on place de la Gare: cross the River Oise and go up rue Solférino to place de l'Hôtel-de-Ville.
Destinations Amiens (9–17 daily; from 55min); Paris (1–3 hourly; from 40min).
**By bus** The station is next to the train station, just off quai de la République.

Destinations Beauvais (4–10 daily; 1hr 5min); Soissons (3 daily; 50min).
**Tourist office** Place de l'Hôtel-de-Ville (April–Sept Mon–Sat 9.15am–12.15pm & 1.45–6.15pm; Oct–March Mon 1.45–5.15pm, Tues–Sat 9.15am–12.15pm & 1.45–5.15pm; also open Sun Easter–Oct 10am–12.15pm & 2.15–5pm; ☎ 03 44 40 01 00, ⓦ compiegne-tourisme.fr).

### ACCOMMODATION

**Les Beaux-Arts** 33 cours Guynemer ☎ 03 44 92 26 26, ⓦ hotellesbeauxarts.com. Some of the rooms at this Best Western hotel are looking a little dated, but it remains a reliable and comfortable choice. Breakfast €12. **€129**
**Flandre** 16 quai de la République ☎ 03 44 83 24 40, ⓦ hoteldeflandre.com. Between the station and the centre and overlooking the river, this cute hotel has some good-value, simple doubles with hall showers alongside its more expensive, plusher suites. Breakfast €8.50. **€75**

### EATING AND DRINKING

**Le Bistrot de Flandre** 2 rue d'Amiens ☎ 03 44 83 26 35, ⓦ bistrotdeflandre.fr. An authentic bistro with summer terrace and tasty dishes, from Burgundy snails (€6.90) to a thoroughly satisfying roast beef. *Menus* from €22–30. Mon–Sat noon–2.30pm & 7–11pm, Sun noon–2.30pm.
**Le Saint-Clair** 8 rue des Lombards ☎ 03 44 40 58 18, ⓦ lesaintclair.free.fr. You're guaranteed a good meal here (*menus* from €16.50), along with a big selection of Belgian beers and a warm welcome. There's live music and karaoke

on some nights and the bar becomes a gay meeting place after 1am. Sun–Wed 11am–1am, Thurs–Sat 11am–3am.
**La Table d'Élisa** 1 place de la Gare ☎ 03 44 83 22 30, ⓦ hoteldunordcompiegne.com. This restaurant, in Hôtel du Nord, serves well-presented traditional dishes in a classy, modern dining room with an open kitchen. *Menus* from €25.50. Tues–Fri noon–2pm & 7–9.30pm, Sat 7–9.30pm & Sun noon–2pm.

## The Forêt de Compiègne

Very ancient, and cut through by a succession of hills, streams and valleys, the **Forêt de Compiègne**, with the GR12 running through it, is ideal stomping ground for walkers and cyclists. East of Compiègne, some 6km into the forest and not far from the banks of the Aisne, is the sandy glade known as the **Clairière de l'Armistice**. Here, in what was a rail siding for rail-mounted artillery, World War I was brought to an end on November 11, 1918. A plaque commemorates the deed: "Here the criminal pride of the German empire was brought low, vanquished by the free peoples whom it had sought to enslave." To avenge this humiliation, Hitler had the French sign their capitulation on June 22, 1940, on the same spot, in the same rail carriage. The original car was taken to Berlin and destroyed by fire in the last days of the war. Its replacement, now housed in a small **museum** (March–Nov daily 10am–6pm; Dec daily 10am–5.30pm; €5, ☎03 44 85 14 18, ⓦmusee-armistice-14-18.fr), is similar, and the objects inside are the originals.

## Château de Pierrefonds

13km southeast of Compiègne • Daily: May–Sept 10am–6pm; Sept–April Tues–Sun 10am–5.30pm • €8 • ☎03 44 42 72 72, ⓦpierrefonds.monuments-nationaux.fr

**Pierrefonds** is home to an astonishing medieval **château** built in the twelfth century, dismantled in the seventeenth and restored by order of Napoléon III in the nineteenth to create a fantastic fairy-tale affair of turrets, towers and moat – one of the finest in the country. The nearby picturesque villages of **Vieux-Moulin** and **St-Jean-aux-Bois** are in the heart of the forest, the latter retaining part of its twelfth-century fortifications.

## Noyon

A possible day-trip from Compiègne, **NOYON** is another of Picardy's cathedral towns. Its quiet provinciality belies a long, illustrious history, first as a Roman prefecture, then as seat of a bishopric from 531. Here, in 768, Charlemagne was crowned king of Neustria, largest of the Frankish kingdoms; in 987, Hugues Capet was crowned king of France; and John Calvin was born here in 1509.

Rowing along the Oise on his *Inland Journey* of 1876, Robert Louis Stevenson stopped briefly at Noyon, which he described as "a stack of brown roofs at the best, where I believe people live very respectably in a quiet way". It's still like that, though the **cathedral**, to which Stevenson warmed, is impressive enough. Spacious and a little stark, it successfully blends Romanesque and Gothic, and is flanked by the ruins of thirteenth-century cloisters and an exquisitely shaped Renaissance library.

### Musée du Noyonnais

7 rue de l'Évêché • Tues–Sun: 10am–noon & 2–6pm; Nov–March closes 5pm • €4, includes Musée Calvin • ☎03 44 09 43 41

On the south side of the cathedral, the old episcopal palace houses the **Musée du Noyonnais**, a small, well-presented collection of local archeological finds and cathedral treasures. Close by, signs direct you to the **Musée Calvin** (same opening times as Musée du Noyonnais), ostensibly on the site of the reformer's birthplace. The respectable citizens of Noyon were never among their local boy's adherents and tore down the original building long before its tourist potential was appreciated.

| INFORMATION AND ACCOMMODATION | NOYON |
| --- | --- |
| **Tourist office** *Hôtel de Ville*, place Bertrand-Labarre (June–Sept Mon 2–6pm, Tues–Sat 10am–noon & 2–6pm; Oct–May Mon 2–5pm, Tues–Fri 10am–noon & 2–5pm; Sat 10–noon; ☎03 44 44 21 88, ⓦnoyon-tourisme.com). | **Le Cèdre** 8 rue de l'Évêché ☎03 44 44 23 24, ⓦhotel-lecedre.com. In a great, central position, directly opposite the cathedral, this is a comfortable and unfussy hotel offering simple rooms, enlivened by brightly coloured walls and fabrics. **€82** |

**2**

# Champagne and the Ardennes

**204** Reims

**210** Épernay

**213** Troyes

**216** The Plateau de Langres

**219** The Ardennes

THE VINEYARDS OF CHAMPAGNE-ARDENNE

# Champagne and the Ardennes

The bubbly stuff is the reason most people visit Champagne, drawn to the vineyards and cellars of the region's capital, the cathedral city of Reims. Some of the most extravagant champagne houses are here, the *caves* beneath them notable for their vaulted ceilings and kilometres of bottles. Épernay, a smaller town set in the scenic heart of the region, is dominated by an avenue of champagne *maisons*, where visitors can float from one to another like the bubbles they're drinking.

The cultivation of vines here was already well established in Roman times, when Reims was the capital of the Roman province of Belgae (Belgium), and by the seventeenth century still wines from the region had gained a considerable reputation. Contrary to popular myth, however, it was not Dom Pérignon, cellar master of the Abbaye de Hautvillers near Épernay, who "invented" champagne. He was probably responsible for the innovation of mixing grapes from different vineyards, but the wine's well-known tendency to re-ferment within the bottle was not controllable until eighteenth-century glass-moulding techniques produced vessels strong enough to contain the natural effervescence.

The region's other major attraction is **Troyes**, some way to the southwest, a town of cobbled streets, half-timbered houses and cut-price shopping. Further south still, the small, far-flung towns of **Chaumont, Essoyes** and **Langres** also merit a stop.

Many people miss out the **Ardennes** in the far north on the Belgian border, which is a mistake: it's a breathtakingly wild landscape offering nature lovers a tempting array of hiking, cycling and boating opportunities. The region's main town, **Charleville-Mézières**, is thrust into the limelight every two years by an international puppet festival but is worth a visit at other times for its lovely seventeenth-century main square.

## Reims

Laid flat by the shells of World War I, **REIMS** (pronounced like a nasal "Rance", and traditionally spelled Rheims in English) was rebuilt with taste and touches of Art Deco but lacks any great sense of antiquity. It makes up for this with a walkable centre, beneath which lies its real treasure – kilometre upon kilometre of bottles of fermenting champagne. The old centre of Reims clusters around one of the most impressive Gothic cathedrals in France – formerly the coronation church of dynasties of French monarchs going back to Clovis, the first king of the Franks. The northernmost section of the old town was protected by place de la République's triumphal Roman arch, the **Porte de Mars**, reached via the grand squares of place Royale, place du Forum and place de l'Hôtel-de-Ville. To the west, place Drouet d'Erlon is the main nightlife spot and an almost-complete example of the city's 1920s reconstruction. A fifteen-minute walk south from the cathedral is the other historical focus of the town, the **Abbaye St-Remi**, with the Jesuits' College nearby. Most of the champagne houses are to the east of here. These attractions, plus a handful of interesting museums and a big-city buzz unusual in this part of France, make it worth a day or two's stopover.

### Cathédrale Notre-Dame de Reims

Place du Cardinal-Luçon • Mon–Sat 7.30am–7.30pm, Sun 7.30am–7.15pm • **Towers** Guided tour only; March 15 to May 5 & Sept 9 to Oct Sat at 10am, 11am, 2pm, 3pm & 4pm, Sun 2pm, 3pm & 4pm; May 6 to Sept 8 Tues–Sat at 10am, 11am, 2pm, 3pm, 4pm & 5pm, Sun 2pm, 3pm, 4pm & 5pm • €8, or combined ticket with the Palais du Tau €11 • ⏲ cathedrale-reims.fr

# Highlights

**❶ Cathédrale Notre-Dame de Reims** Known as the Coronation Cathedral, Reims's Gothic masterpiece boasts a prime place in French history and stunning Chagall stained glass. See page 204

**❷ Champagne-tasting at Épernay or Reims** Taste vintage bubbly in the atmospheric cellars of world-famous sparkling wine emporia. See pages 210 and 204

**❸ Troyes** Delightful medieval town with historic churches and fascinating museums, from an old apothecary to a personal collection of modern art. See page 213

**❹ Essoyes** Visit the former summer home of Impressionist painter Pierre-Auguste Renoir in this lovely champagne-producing village. See page 218

**❺ Langres** Walk around the impressive fortified walls and towers of the town where the French philosopher Diderot was born. See page 218

**❻ The Ardennes** Explore the spectacular scenery and forested hills of the rugged Meuse river valley. See page 219

**HIGHLIGHTS ARE MARKED ON THE MAP ON PAGE 206**

The glorious Gothic thirteenth-century **Cathédrale Notre-Dame de Reims,** a UNESCO World Heritage Site, features prominently in French history: in 1429 Joan of Arc managed to get the Dauphin crowned here as Charles VII – an act of immense significance when France was more or less wiped off the map by the English and their allies. In all, 26 French kings were crowned here.

The chief draw inside the cathedral is the kaleidoscopic patterns in the stained glass, with fantastic **Marc Chagall** designs in the east chapel, and champagne processes glorified in the south transept. The exterior is also fabulous: an inexplicable joke runs around the restored but still badly mutilated statuary on the west front – the giggling

# CHAMPAGNE AND THE ARDENNES

## HIGHLIGHTS

1 Cathédrale Notre-Dame de Reims

2 Champagne-tasting at Épernay or Reims

3 Troyes

4 Colombey-les-Deux-Églises

5 Essoyes

6 Langres

7 The Ardennes

## CHAMPAGNE: THE FACTS

Nowhere else in the world are you allowed to make a drink called **champagne**, though many people do, calling it "champan", "shampanskoye" and all manner of variants. You can blend grape juice harvested from chalk-soil vineyards, double-ferment it, store the result for years at the requisite constant temperature and high humidity in sweating underground *caves*, turn and tilt the bottles little by little to clear the sediment, add some vintage liqueur, and finally produce a bubbling golden (or pink) liquid; but according to European law you may refer to it only as "*méthode traditionnelle*". The jealously guarded monopoly helps keep the region's sparkling wines in the luxury class, although the locals will tell you the difference comes from the squid fossils in the chalk, the lay of the land and its climate, the evolution of the grapes, the regulated pruning methods and the legally enforced quantity of juice pressed.

Three authorized **grape varieties** are used: chardonnay, the only white grape, grown best on the Côte des Blancs and contributing a light and elegant element; pinot noir, grown mainly on the Montagne de Reims slopes, giving body and long life; and pinot meunier, cultivated primarily in the Marne valley, adding flowery aromas.

The **vineyards** are owned either by *maisons*, who produce the *grandes marques* champagne, or by small cultivators called *vignerons*, who sell the grapes to the *maisons*. The *vignerons* also make their own champagne and will happily offer you a glass and sell you a bottle at two-thirds the price of a *grande marque* (ask at any tourist office in the Champagne region for a list of addresses). The difference between the two comes down to capital. The *maisons* can afford to blend grapes from up to sixty different vineyards and to tie up their investment while their champagne matures for several years longer than the legal minimum (one year for non-vintage, three years vintage). So the wine they produce is undoubtedly superior.

If you could visit the head offices of Cartier or Dior, you'd probably find the atmosphere similar to that of the champagne *maisons*, whose palaces are divided between Épernay and Reims. In 2015, the Hillsides, Houses and Cellars of Champagne, became a UNESCO World Heritage Site. Visits to the handful that organize regular **tours** are not free, and most require appointments, but don't be put off – their staff all speak English and a generous *dégustation* is thrown in. Their audiovisuals and (cold) cellar tours are on the whole very informative, and do more than merely plug brand names. Local tourist offices can provide full lists of addresses and times of visits or check out ⓦ maisons-champagne.com or ⓦ champagne.fr

If you want to work on the harvest, contact any of the *maisons* direct or Pôle Emploi Grand Est Vendanges (ⓦ pole-emploi.fr)

angels who seem to be responsible for a prank are a delight. Not all the figures on the cathedral's west front are originals – some have been removed to spare them further erosion and are now at the former bishop's palace, the Palais du Tau. The **towers** of the cathedral are open to the public; as well as a walk round the transepts and chevet, you get to see inside the framework of the cathedral roof; tickets available from the Palais du Tau. In December, the square in front of the cathedral hosts one of France's best Christmas markets.

## Palais du Tau

Tues–Sun early May to early Sept 9.30am–6.30pm; early Sept to early May 9.30am–12.30pm & 2–5.30pm • €8, or combined ticket with the towers €11 • ⓦ palais-du-tau.fr

At the **Palais du Tau**, next door to the cathedral, you can appreciate the expressiveness of the statuary from close up. Apart from the grinning angels, there is also a superb Eve, shiftily clutching the monster of sin, while embroidered tapestries of the Song of Songs line the walls. The palace also preserves the paraphernalia of Charles X's coronation in 1824, right down to the Dauphin's hat box and cathedral treasures. Stop off in the ground-floor tearoom for a delicious cake.

## Musée des Beaux-Arts

8 rue Chanzy • Daily except Tues & public hols 10am–noon & 2–6pm • €5 (includes entry to Chapelle Foujita) • ☏ 03 26 35 36 00, Ⓦ musees-reims.fr

West of the cathedral is the **Musée des Beaux-Arts**, the city's principal art museum, which, though ill-suited to its ancient building, effectively covers French art from the Renaissance to the present. Few of the works are among the artists' best but the collection includes one of David's replicas of his famous Marat death scene, a large selection of Corots, two great Gauguin still lifes, and some beautifully observed sixteenth-century portraits by the German artists Lucas Cranach the Elder and Younger. The highlight, however, is a collection of works by Franco-Japanese artist Léonard Foujita (1886–1968), who spent much of the latter part of his life in the city. The museum's ticket also gives entry to the Chapelle Foujita (33 rue du Champ-de-Mars; same hours as museum), his last major work.

## Musée de la Reddition

12 rue Franklin-Roosevelt • Daily except Tues & public hols 10am–6pm • €5 • ☏ 03 26 47 84 19, Ⓦ musees-reims.fr

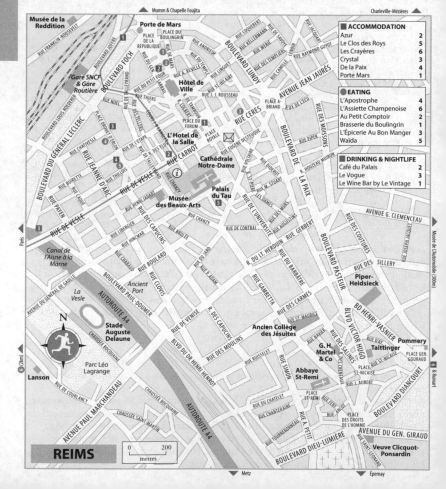

| ◼ ACCOMMODATION | |
|---|---|
| Azur | 2 |
| Le Clos des Roys | 5 |
| Les Crayères | 6 |
| Crystal | 3 |
| De la Paix | 4 |
| Porte Mars | 1 |

| ◼ EATING | |
|---|---|
| L'Apostrophe | 4 |
| L'Assiette Champenoise | 6 |
| Au Petit Comptoir | 2 |
| Brasserie du Boulingrin | 1 |
| L'Épicerie Au Bon Manger | 3 |
| Waïda | 5 |

| ◼ DRINKING & NIGHTLIFE | |
|---|---|
| Café du Palais | 2 |
| Le Vogue | 3 |
| Le Wine Bar by Le Vintage | 1 |

REIMS

West of the Porte behind the train station, the "Museum of the Surrender" is based around an old schoolroom that served as Eisenhower's HQ from February 1945. In the early hours of May 7, 1945, General Jodl agreed to the unconditional surrender of the German army here, thus ending World War II in Europe. The room has been left exactly as it was (minus the ashtrays and carpet), with the Allies' battle maps on the walls.

## The Abbaye St-Remi

Rue Simon • **Basilique St-Remi** Daily 8am–7pm, closed during service • Son et lumière show July–Sept Sat 9.30pm • Free • **Musée St-Remi** Tues–Sun 10am–noon & 2–6pm • €5 • ☎ 03 26 35 36 90, ⓦ musees-relms.fr

Most of the early French kings were buried in Reims's oldest building, the eleventh-century **Basilique St-Remi**, part of a former Benedictine abbey named after the 22-year-old bishop who baptized Clovis and three thousand of his warriors. An immensely spacious building, this UNESCO World Heritage Site preserves its Romanesque transept walls and ambulatory chapels, some of them with modern stained glass that fits in beautifully. Albert Nicart, the bell-ringer of St-Remi, was the inspiration for Victor Hugo's fictional Quasimodo in *The Hunchback of Notre Dame*; Hugo met Nicart and the gypsy girl Esméralda in 1825 while visiting Reims to attend Charles X's coronation.

The spectacular abbey buildings alongside the church house the **Musée St-Remi**, the city's rather dry archeological and historical museum that includes a fine collection of sixteenth-century Flemish tapestries depicting the life of Remi as well as some interesting Gallo-Roman finds.

## Musée de l'Automobile

84 av Georges-Clemenceau • Daily except Tues: April–Oct 10am–noon & 2–6pm; Nov–March 10am–noon & 2–5pm; also open Tues July & Aug • €9 • ☎ 03 26 82 83 84, ⓦ musee-automobile-reims-champagne.com

If you have even a passing interest in old cars don't miss the **Musée de l'Automobile**, fifteen minutes' walk southeast of the cathedral. The collection contains many prototypes and rarities; highlights include a string of sleek, powerful Delahaye coupés designed by Philippe Charbonneaux in the 1940s and 1950s, and a stunning Panhard et Levassor Dynamic 130 Coupé from 1936 – pure Art Deco on wheels.

### ARRIVAL AND INFORMATION                                    REIMS

**By train** Reims main station is on boulevard Joffre, about 10 minutes' walk north west of the centre.
Destinations Charleville-Mézières (almost hourly; 55min); Épernay (about 20 daily; from 30min); Paris (TGV 14 daily; 45min).
**By bus** The *gare routière* is on rue Pingat, beside the train station, with services to Troyes (6 daily; 2hr 20min; ⓦ courriersdelaube.fr).
**Tourist office** 6 rue Rockefeller, next to the cathedral (April–Sept Mon–Sat 9am–7pm, Sun & public hols

10am–6pm; Oct–March Mon–Sat 10am–6pm, Sun 10am–12.30pm & 1.30–5pm; ☎ 03 26 77 45 00, ⓦ reims-tourisme.com) and Parvis de la Gare outside the station (Mon–Sat 8.30am–12.30pm & 1.30–6pm ; April–Sept also Sun 10–11.30am & 12.30–4pm).
**Passes** The Reims City Pass (ⓦ reimscitypass.com) is valid for 1 day (€22), 2 days (€32) or 3 days (€42) and includes entry to the city's museums, a guided city tour, free use of public transport, and discounts at certain champagne cellars, shops and restaurants.

### ACCOMMODATION

**Azur** 9 rue des Écrevées ☎ 03 26 47 43 39, ⓦ hotel-azur-reims.com. This charming small hotel, 5min from the station, is friendly, has spotless simple rooms, and is in the up-and-coming Boulingrin area, with its restaurants, shops and renovated 1920s market. In summer, take breakfast in the little courtyard. **€79**
**Le Clos des Roys** 3 rue d'Anjou ☎ 06 75 28 34 85, ⓦ leclosdesroys.fr. This charming B&B a short walk south

of the cathedral has just two tastefully decorated rooms: Clovis and Charles VII. The friendly owners can arrange champagne tastings and tours. If you're arriving by car, there's secure parking in the interior courtyard. **€100**
★ **Les Crayères** 64 bd Henry-Vasnier ☎ 03 26 24 90 00, ⓦ lescrayeres.com. Ideal for a special occasion, this gorgeous five-star hotel in a restored eighteenth-century château built by Louise Pommery is surrounded by

beautiful parkland. As you'd expect it has luxurious rooms and impeccable service as well as one of the region's most sophisticated restaurants, Le Parc (lunch menu €70) . **€380**

**Crystal** 86 place Drouet d'Erlon ☎03 26 88 44 44, ⓦ hotel-crystal.fr. Most of the renovated rooms here are spacious and look out onto a charming, flower-filled courtyard garden where you can eat breakfast in the summer months. The garden also blocks out much of the noise from the local nightlife. **€91**

★ **De la Paix** 9 rue Buirette ☎03 26 40 04 08, ⓦ hotel-lapaix.fr. The smart, contemporary rooms, some in the old building, others in the modern extension, come with contemporary art on the walls and Philippe Starck furniture. An indoor pool and a good restaurant complete the package. **€180**

**Porte Mars** 2 place de la République ☎03 26 40 28 35, ⓦ hotel-portemars.com. Cosy rooms, well insulated against noise, a colourful bar, and a sitting room with a fire for chilly evenings make this an attractive option. There's also a good breakfast and staff are friendly. **€95**

## EATING AND DRINKING

Place Drouet d'Erlon, a wide pedestrianized boulevard lined with bars and restaurants, is the place for most of the city's nightlife, though it's more pavement café lounging than high-octane partying. There's a big market held in Les Halles du Boulingrin on Wednesday, Friday and Saturday mornings. The area around here, between the *hôtel de ville* and Porte de Mars, is one of the up-and-coming districts, good for restaurants, bars, cafés and boutiques. From mid-June to mid-July, dozens of classical and jazz concerts – many of them free – take place as part of Les Flâneries Musicales de Reims (ⓦ flaneriesreims.com).

### EATING

**L'Apostrophe** 59 place Drouet d'Erlon ☎03 26 79 19 89, ⓦ restaurant-lapostrophe.com. Smart, modern café, bar, brasserie and terrace in an old building with a menu that goes from French classics like *tartare de boeuf* (€16.50) to Asian dishes such as noodles with chicken and prawns (€16.50). Three-course *menus* from €26. Daily 10am–2am.

★ **L'Assiette Champenoise** 40 avenue Paul Vaillant-Couturier, 51430 Tinqueux ☎03 26 84 64 64, ⓦ assiettechampenoise.com. About 2km west of the cathedral, this three-Michelin-star restaurant headed by Arnaud Lallement regularly appears in international lists of the world's best eating places. Each dish is an experience, like Brittany blue lobster 'in homage to my father', made with the finest local and national produce. *Menus* €95–285. Five-star accommodation is also available in this half-timbered manor house. Mon & Thurs–Sun noon–2pm & 7.30–10pm.

**Au Petit Comptoir** 17 rue de Mars ☎03 26 40 58 58, ⓦ au-petit-comptoir.fr. Close to the Marché du Boulingrin, this smart restaurant and bistro serves inventive dishes such as cod with bacon and pumpkin risotto. Bistro *menu* €26, restaurant *menu* €41. Mon–Thurs noon–2pm & 7–10pm, Fri & Sat noon–2pm & 7–10.30pm.

**Brasserie du Boulingrin** 31 rue de Mars ☎03 26 40 96 22, ⓦ boulingrin.fr. Art Deco glamour from 1925 including a wall-length fresco depicting a bucolic vineyard scene and good-value classics make this brasserie a winner. Order its famous seafood platters and *moelleux au chocolat*. Three-course *menu* at €27. Mon–Sat noon–2.30pm & 7–11pm.

★ **L'Épicerie Au Bon Manger** 7 rue Courmeaux ☎03 26 03 45 29, ⓦ aubonmanger.fr. This small deli with a few tables is the place to go for top-quality cheese and charcuterie (platters €17–23) accompanied by wine and/ or champagne from small producers. Don't leave without trying the chocolate mousse. Tues–Wed & Sat 10am– 7pm, Thurs & Fri 10am–11pm.

**Waïda** 5 place Drouet d'Erlon ☎03 26 47 44 49. Beautiful *pâtissier-glacier* and *salon de thé*, with pastries and ice cream made on the premises, plus one of the best original Art Deco interiors in Reims. Tues–Fri 7.30am–7.30pm, Sat 7.30am–8pm, Sun 8am–2pm & 3.30–7.30pm.

### DRINKING AND NIGHTLIFE

★ **Café du Palais** 14 place Myron-Herrick ☎03 26 47 52 54, ⓦ cafedupalais.fr. Long-running, large brasserie and bar stuffed full of improbable artefacts in its grand Art Deco setting. Food is served at lunch, with dinner on Sat. Tues–Fri 8.30am–8.30pm, Sat 9am–9.30pm.

**Le Vogue** 93 bd du Général-Leclerc ⓦ levogue.fr. The place to go clubbing into the small hours and dance to excellent DJs. Minimum age 18. Thurs–Sat 11.30pm– 5am.

**Le Wine Bar by Le Vintage** 16 place du Forum ☎03 26 05 89 94, ⓦ winebar-reims.com. Popular wine bar with a superb selection of champagnes, wines and spirits. Connoisseurs won't be disappointed. Tues–Thurs 6pm– 12.30am, Fri & Sat 6pm–1.30am.

# Épernay

There's no question that **ÉPERNAY**, 26km south of Reims, is a single-industry town. But it's beautifully situated below rolling, vine-covered hills, and the industry in question – champagne production – is a compelling reason for a visit. The town contains some

## CHAMPAGNE-TASTING IN REIMS

**Tours** of the Reims champagne houses and *caves* generally need to be prebooked but in summer it may be worth showing up on the off chance. Those in the southern part of town near the Abbaye St-Remi tend to have the most impressive cellars – some have been carved in cathedral-esque formations from the Gallo-Roman quarries used to build the city, long before champagne was invented. This is not a comprehensive list of all the *maisons* in the city but includes the most visitor-friendly. Note that the cellars can be cold, so it's worth taking another layer of clothing. All tours are available in English and last about an hour, unless otherwise stated.

**Lanson** 66 rue de Courlancy ☎ 03 26 78 50 50, ⓦ lanson.com. Worth the trip across the river because the in-depth tours take you into the factory and demonstrate the mechanized process of champagne-making. Most days you'll see the machines degorging the bottles, as well as labelling and filling them in preparation for the second fermentation. Reservations required. Mon–Fri 8.30am–12.30 & 1.30–6pm; closed weekends; tours (1hr 30min) €20.

**G.H. Martel & Co** 17 rue des Créneaux, near the Basilique St-Remi ☎ 03 26 82 70 67, ⓦ champagnemartel.com. A good-value tour with a *dégustation* of three champagnes as well as a film show and guided visit taking in the old equipment. Daily 10am–1pm & 2–7pm, last tour at 5.30pm; €15.

**Mumm** 34 rue du Champ-de-Mars ☎ 03 26 49 59 70, ⓦ mumm.com. Known for its red-slashed Cordon Rouge label, Mumm's un-French-sounding name is the legacy of its founders, German winemakers from the Rhine valley who established the business in 1827. The guided tour includes a short film and ends with a tasting of either Cordon Rouge or Cuvée Prestige, or a glass each of the Blanc de Blanc and Blanc de Noir. March–Oct daily 9.30am–1.30pm & 2–6pm (last tours 2pm & 4.30pm); Nov–Feb Mon–Sat 9.30am–noon & 2–6pm; (last tours 10.50am & 4.15pm); €20–39.

**Pommery** 5 place du Général-Gouraud ☎ 03 26 61 62 56, ⓦ champagnepommery.com. The creator of the cute one-eighth size "Pop" bottles has excavated Roman quarries for its cellars. Two tours are offered, lasting about an hour, and include either one or two glasses of champagne and a visit to their cellars and contemporary art gallery. Daily 10am–6pm; €22–30.

**Ruinart** 4 rue des Crayères ☎ 03 26 77 51 51, ⓦ ruinart. com. Founded in 1729, the fanciest of the champagne producers offers the most exclusive tours. The *maison* recommends booking at least two weeks in advance and the comprehensive 2hr visits are limited to ten people. The price includes a glass of champagne. Tues–Sat morning or afternoon; closed Nov–March; €70.

**Taittinger** 9 place St-Niçaise ☎ 03 26 85 84 33, ⓦ taittinger.com. Starts with a film show before a guided stroll through the ancient cellars, some of which have doodles and carvings added by more recent workers; there are also the remains of the crypt of an ancient Gothic church and statues of St Vincent and St Jean, patron saints respectively of *vignerons* and cellar hands. April to mid-Nov daily 9.30–5.30pm (last tour at 4.30pm); mid-Nov to March Mon–Fri 9.30am–1pm & 1.45–5.30pm (last tour at 4.30pm); €19–55.

**Veuve Clicquot-Ponsardin** 1 place des Droits de l'Homme ☎ 03 26 89 53 90, ⓦ veuveclicquot.com. In 1805 the widowed Mme Clicquot not only took over her husband's business – *veuve* means "widow" in French – but also later bequeathed it to her business manager rather than to her children. The *maison* is one of the least pompous, and its *caves* some of the most spectacular, sited in ancient Gallo-Roman quarries. March–Dec Tues–Sat 9.30am–12.30pm & 1.30–5.30pm (last tour at 4pm); closed Jan & Feb; €26–53.

of the most famous champagne *maisons* as well as several smaller houses, so start at the appropriately named **avenue de Champagne**, running east from place de la République. Dubbed "the most drinkable street in the world" by Winston Churchill, and now a UNESCO World Heritage Site, it's worth strolling along for its imposing eighteenth- and nineteenth-century champagne *maisons*. You can tour some of them, and many others welcome visitors to taste and buy. The town makes a sensible base for exploring the surrounding villages and vineyards and is especially fun on the last weekend of June for the Champagne en Fête festival.

## Moët et Chandon

18 av de Champagne • Daily 9.30–11.30am & 2–4.30pm; closed Jan • €25–40, including *dégustation* • ⓦ moet.com

The largest, and probably the most famous *maison*, though neither the most beautiful nor necessarily the most interesting to tour, is **Moët et Chandon**, one of the keystones of the LVMH (Louis Vuitton, Moët and Hennessy) empire which owns Mercier, Veuve Clicquot, Dior perfumes and other luxury brands. The house is also the creator of the iconic **Dom Pérignon** label. All tours end with a tasting of their truly excellent champagne, with the €40 option including a glass of both the white and rosé *Grand Vintage*.

## Mercier

70 av de Champagne • Daily 9.30–11.30am & 2–4.30pm; closed Jan & Feb • €18–25 including *dégustation* • ☎ 03 26 51 22 22, ⓦ champagnemercier.com

**Mercier**, whose visitor experience was renovated in 2018, runs a fairly rewarding tour around its cellars in an electric train. Nowadays the wine producer is known for being at the lower end of the champagne market in terms of price, demonstrating that M. Mercier has achieved his ultimate goal: he founded the house, aged 20, in 1858 with a plan to make champagne more accessible to the French people. In 1889 he carted a giant barrel that held 200,000 bottles' worth to the Paris Exhibition – only to be upstaged by the Eiffel Tower. The barrel is on display in the lobby.

## De Castellane

57 rue de Verdun • 12 March to 23 Dec daily 10am–noon & 2–6pm • From €14 including *dégustation* • ☎ 03 26 51 19 19, ⓦ castellane.com

A fifteen-minute walk from the train station, **De Castellane** provides Épernay with its chief landmark: a pastel edifice resembling a kind of Neoclassical water tower. Along with the cellars, the visit shows off the working assembly lines that fill the champagne bottles, and the huge vats that hold the grape juice prior to fermentation. After the tour you can wander the little museum and climb the tower for a great view of the surrounding vineyards.

## Around Épernay

The villages in the appealing **vineyards** of the Montagne de Reims (a Regional Natural Park and UNESCO World Heritage Site), Côte des Blancs and Vallée de la Marne surrounding Épernay are home to a range of curiosities, including the world's largest champagne bottle and cork in **Mardeuil**, a traditional *vigneron*'s house at **Oeuilly** (ⓦ ecomusee-oeuilly.fr) and a champagne discovery centre in a lighthouse in Verzenay (ⓦ lepharedeverzenay.com). The Route Touristique du Champagne (ⓦ tourisme-en-champagne.co.uk/champagne-trail), which is well signposted throughout the vineyard area, takes you through many of the champagne villages, where a number of small producers welcome visitors. Look out for the "Accueil" (Welcome) sign outside their establishments or check with the tourist office in Épernay or Reims for details. Many of the villages have a sleepy, old-stone charm: **Vertus**, 16km south of Épernay, is particularly pretty, and so too is **Hautvillers**, 6km north of town, where the famous monk Dom Pérignon lived and worked. You can see the abbey (closed to the public) where he was responsible for the wine cellars and helped improve champagne production methods. His tomb can be visited in the nave of the church.

### ARRIVAL AND INFORMATION                                                      ÉPERNAY

**By train and bus** Épernay's *gare SNCF* and *gare routière* are in place de la Gare, a 5min walk from the centre.

**Tourist office** 7 av de Champagne (mid-April to mid-Oct Mon–Sat 9am–12.30pm & 1.30–7pm, Sun 10.30am–1pm & 2–4.30pm; mid-Oct to mid-April Mon–Sat 9.30am–– 12.30pm & 1.30–5.30pm; ☎ 03 26 53 33 00, ⓦ ot-epernay. fr). **Vineyard tours** Échappée Bulles (☎ 06 95 90 33 47; ⓦ lechappee-bulles.com; from €55 for two hours) organizes bike tours in English, with all prices including a tasting.

## ACCOMMODATION

**Jean Moët** 7 rue Jean-Moët ☎03 26 32 19 22, ⓦhoteljeanmoet.com. Set in a beautifully restored eighteenth-century mansion, the four-star *Jean Moët* has twelve smart a/c rooms named after the sizes of champagne bottles; each with wooden floors, pastel-coloured walls and luxury fabrics. A spa, chic champagne bar and a conservatory for drinks and snacks in the internal courtyard, makes this hotel an excellent option. **€170**

**Parva Domus** 27 av de Champagne ☎06 73 25 66 60, ⓦparvadomusrimaire.com. The champagne producers Rimaire offer five simple, spacious rooms in their charming ivy-clad home on the av de Champagne. The warm welcome includes a glass of the bubbly stuff and you'll enjoy a copious breakfast in the morning. **€140**

**Villa Eugène** 84 av de Champagne ☎03 26 32 44 76, ⓦvilla-eugene.com. Housed in the former home of Eugène Mercier, founder of the famous *maison*, this five-star establishment offers country-style calm and luxury just a short walk from the town centre. The decor of the fifteen a/c rooms varies from modern and cosy to grandiose with period-style furnishings. Breakfast is served in the conservatory, and there's a heated outdoor swimming pool. **€190**

**La Villa St-Pierre** 1 rue Jeanne-d'Arc ☎03 26 54 40 80, ⓦvillasaintpierre.fr. In a quiet street away from the centre but near the main champagne houses, this good-value, welcoming hotel has simply decorated rooms, some with very small bathrooms. There's also a bar and restaurant. **€86**

## EATING AND DRINKING

★ **Au 36** 36 rue Dom-Pérignon, Hautvillers ☎03 26 51 58 37, ⓦau36.net. Excellent champagne tasting bar in the village of Dom Pérignon, where you can sample or buy a good selection of champagnes at reasonable prices. The €19 taster plate of local specialities is the perfect way to soak up the bubbly. Daily 10.30am–6pm.

**Les Berceaux** 13 rue des Berceaux ☎03 26 55 28 84, ⓦlesberceaux.com. Concentrating on classic bourgeois cooking and using seasonal, local ingredients where possible, this wonderful restaurant is the place for dishes like roasted wild turbot with stuffed courgette flowers or fresh snails cooked in champagne. It's pricey, but always busy and the elegant dining room with fireplace, flowers and crisp linen adds to the sense of occasion. The hotel's second restaurant, the good-value *Bistrot le 7* has *menus* at €29–35. *Menus* in *Les Berceaux* €45–95. Wed–Sun noon–2pm & 7–9pm.

**La Table Kobus** 3 rue Dr Rousseau ☎03 26 51 53 53, ⓦla-table-kobus.fr. Delightful brasserie, with traditional marble-topped tables and banquette seating, that's popular for dishes like *tartare de saumon* with coconut milk and lime, and veal roasted with nougat. You can take your own wine to lunch Tues–Fri at no extra cost (though their wine list is good value). *Menus* €19.90–65. Tues–Wed & Fri–Sat noon–2pm & 7–10pm, Thurs & Sun noon–2pm.

# Troyes

It is easy to find charm in the leaning medieval half-timbered houses and churches of **TROYES**, the ancient capital of the Champagne region. The town also offers top-quality museums and shopping outlets and is a good place to try the regional speciality, *andouillette* (see page 216).

## The churches

The centre of Troyes between the station and cathedral is scattered with marvellous **churches**, four of which are open to the public. The first you come to is the sumptuous, high-naved **St-Pantaléon** (April–Oct Mon–Sat 9.30am–12.30pm & 2–6pm, Sun 2–6pm; Nov–March Mon–Sat 9.30am–12.30pm & 2–5pm, Sun 2–5pm) on rue de Vauluisant, which is filled with sixteenth-century sculpture, stored here away from the ravages of the Revolution. A short walk to the north is Troyes' oldest church, the twelfth-century **Ste-Madeleine** (May–Oct Mon–Sat 9.30am–12.30pm & 2–6pm, Sun 2–6pm; Nov–April Mon–Sat 9.30am–12.30pm & 2–5pm, Sun 2–5pm), on the road of the same name and remodelled in the sixteenth century, when the delicate stonework rood screen – used to keep the priest separate from the congregation – was added. A lovely garden provides a peaceful oasis in the summer. A short way to the southeast, between rues Émile-Zola and Champeaux, is **St-Jean-au-Marché** (mid-April to Sept Mon & Thurs–Sun 2–6pm), the church where Henry V of England married Catherine of France after being recognized as heir to the French throne in the 1420

Treaty of Troyes. Between it and the cathedral is the elegant Gothic **Basilique St-Urbain** (May–Oct Mon–Sat 9.30am–12.30pm & 2–6pm, Sun 2–6pm; Nov–April Mon–Sat 9.30am–12.30pm & 2–5pm, Sun 2–5pm), on place Vernier, its exterior dramatizing the Day of Judgement.

## Musée d'Art Moderne

Closed for renovation until 2020 ☎ 03 25 76 26 80, ⓦ musees-troyes.com

Across the Canal de la Haute Seine lies the city's most outstanding museum, the **Musée d'Art Moderne**, housed in the old bishops' palace next to the cathedral on place St-Pierre. The museum displays the private collection built up by industrialist Pierre Lévy (1907–2002) and his wife Denise. Lévy developed a strong friendship with the Fauvist André Derain, and it's Derain's work (including the famous paintings of Hyde Park and Big Ben) that forms the collection's core. For the rest, there are works by Degas, Courbet, Gauguin and Bonnard, but it's in no sense a "greatest hits of modern art" and therein lies its charm: entire rooms are devoted to a particular theme or to the works of lesser-known artists. Another room is given over to a beautiful collection of African carvings.

## Quartier de la Cité

The ancient **quartier de la Cité**, across the canal from the centre, is home to many of the city's oldest buildings. They all huddle around the **Cathédrale St-Pierre-et-St-Paul** (April–Oct Mon–Sat 9am–12.30pm & 2–6pm; Sun 11.30am–6pm; Nov–March Mon–Sat 9am–12.30pm & 2–5pm, Sun 11.30am–5pm), whose pale Gothic nave is mottled with reflections from the wonderful stained glass. It was here in 1128/29 that the Order of the Knights Templar was officially formed by St Bernard of Clairvaux. On the other side of the cathedral from the Musée d'Art Moderne (see above), the once glorious **Abbaye St-Loup** houses the **Musée Saint-Loup** (April–Oct Mon & Wed–Sun 10am–1pm & 2–6pm; Nov–March Mon & Wed–Sun 10am–1pm & 2–5pm; €5.50 or part of museum pass; free Nov–March ☎ 03 25 42 20 09), whose broad collection takes in mainly French paintings, including a couple by Watteau, an impressive collection of medieval sculptures and gargoyles, and a selection of meteorites from around the world.

## Apothicairerie

Closed for renovation until 2020 • ☎ 03 25 80 98 97, ⓦ musees-troyes.com

Down rue de la Cité (entrance on quai des Comtes de Champagne), the **Apothicairerie**, a richly decorated early eighteenth-century pharmacy, occupies a corner of the majestic **Hôtel-Dieu-le-Comte**. Rows of painted wooden "silène" boxes adorn its shelves, each illustrating the medicines once found inside.

---

### CLOTHES SHOPPING IN TROYES

Troyes made its name in the clothing trade, and today the industry still accounts for more than half of the town's employment. **Factory outlets** are one of the chief attractions here: designer-label clothes can be picked up at two-thirds or less of the normal shop price. The best array is at the giant **Marques Avenue**, 114 bd de Dijon, St-Julien-les-Villas, a couple of kilometres south of the city on the D671 to Dijon or on bus #2 (Mon–Fri 10am–7pm, Sat 9.30am–7pm; ⓦ marquesavenue.com); there's also a special "shed" for household goods at 230 faubourg Croncels, including luxury glass and chinaware. At Pont-Ste-Marie, a short way to the northeast of Troyes between the D677 to Reims and the D960 to Nancy, are **Marques City** (Mon–Fri 10am–7pm, Sat 9.30am–7pm; ⓦ marquescity.fr) and **McArthurGlen** (Mon–Fri 10am–7pm, Sat 10am–8pm; ⓦ mcarthurglen.fr). Buses for the outlets depart from the bus stops by Marché les Halles (ask at the tourist offices for details).

## Maison de l'Outil et de la Pensée Ouvrière

7 rue de la Trinité • Daily 10am–6pm; Oct–March closed Tues • €7 or part of museum pass (see below) • 📞 03 25 73 28 26, 🌐 mopo3.com

Despite being raked by numerous fires since the Middle Ages, Troyes' old town has retained many timber-framed buildings. The most infamous fire, in 1524, led to a massive rebuilding scheme giving Troyes a wealth of Renaissance palaces. An outstanding example, just east of the church of St-Pantaléon, is the sixteenth-century Hôtel de Mauroy, once an orphanage, then a textile factory, and now the **Maison de l'Outil et de la Pensée Ouvrière**. Troyes' most original museum, it exhibits traditional tools from a myriad of trades, ranging from chair-caning to glove-making. It's worth a visit just to see the building.

## Hôtel de Vauluisant

4 rue de Vauluisant • Both museums: April–Oct Tues–Sun 10am–1pm & 2–6pm; Nov–March Wed–Sun 10am–1pm & 2–5pm • €3 for both museums or part of museum pass (see below); free Nov–March except during temporary exhibitions

Hosiery ("bonneterie") and woollens have been Troyes' most important industry since the late Middle Ages. Some of the old machines and products used for creating garments can be seen in the sixteenth-century palace, the **Hôtel de Vauluisant**. The **Musée de la Bonneterie** displays an array of looms, sewing machines and the like, as well as historic photographs and a collection of socks and stockings from the nineteenth and twentieth centuries. The stone Renaissance palace is also home to the more compelling **Musée d'art Champenois**, which contains some gorgeous sixteenth-century sculptures of the Troyes school as well as some fine winged triptychs.

### ARRIVAL AND DEPARTURE                                            TROYES

**By train** The *gare SNCF* is off boulevard Carnot, a 5min walk into the centre. Destinations Chaumont (approx every 1–2hr; 50min); Langres (10 daily; 1hr 15min); Paris (frequent; 1hr 30min). **By bus** The *gare routière* is beside the train station, with around six daily services to Reims (2hr 20min).

### INFORMATION

**Tourist office** 16 rue Aristide Briand (May–Oct Mon–Sat 9.30am–6.30pm; Nov–April Mon–Sat 9.30am–12.30pm & 2–6pm; 📞 03 25 82 62 70, 🌐 tourisme-troyes.com.
**Passes** The Pass'Troyes (€12) museum pass, available at the tourist office, includes entry to all Troyes' museums, some *Prunelle* (the local liqueur), a chocolate tasting, an audioguided tour, two hours of bike rental, and discount vouchers for the factory outlets.
**Festivals and events** During the weekends from late June to mid-Aug, the city organizes free Ville en Musiques concerts in picturesque locations in the historic centre; the programme ranges from classical and jazz to rock and hip-hop – pick up a schedule at the tourist office.

### ACCOMMODATION

**Arlequin** 50 rue Turenne 📞 03 25 83 12 70. Tucked away in the rambling alleyways of the old town, this traditional two-star hotel has sunny, individually decorated rooms. Some are small, so check on booking. **€68**
**Camping municipal** 7 rue Roger-Salengro, Pont Ste-Marie 📞 03 25 81 02 64, 🌐 troyescamping.net. Set in a wooded area, 5km out on the N60 to Châlons, with good facilities including washing machines, children's play area and free wi-fi. Closed mid-Oct to March. **€15.40**
**Les Comtes de Champagne** 54 rue de la Monnaie 📞 03 25 73 11 70, 🌐 comtesdechampagne.com. Located in the middle of the old quarter, but down a quiet street, this charming two-star in a twelfth-century house has odd-shaped rooms, fireplaces, slanted floors and creaking staircases. Friendly proprietors and covered parking. **€79**

★ **La Maison de Rhodes** 18 rue Linard-Gonthier 📞 03 25 43 11 11, 🌐 maisonderhodes.com. This sumptuous five-star establishment has an inner courtyard surrounded by medieval half-timbered buildings with staircases that seem to belong more to a theatre set than a boutique hotel. With antique furniture, beamed rooms and an outdoor pool, the hotel lives up to its reputation as one of France's most romantic getaways. It was recently amalgamated with the neighbouring four-star *Le Champ des Oiseaux*, which shares the same excellent restaurant (dinner Tues–Sat). **€269**
**Le Relais St-Jean** 51 rue Paillot-de-Montabert 📞 03 25 73 89 90, 🌐 hotel-relais-saint-jean.com. Behind the facade of a half-timbered building in the centre of the old town, you'll find a smart hotel, elegantly decorated with contemporary furniture and fabrics. The bar is a local

---

**IT TAKES GUTS …**

Troyes is famed for its **andouillette**. Translated euphemistically into English as "chitterling sausage", *andouillette* is an intestine crammed full of more intestines, all chopped up. It's an acquired taste (and texture), but it's better than it sounds – look out for the notation AAAAA, a seal of approval awarded by the Amicable Association of Amateurs of the Authentic Andouillette. In the Ardennes, fans of game are in for a treat, with *pâté d'Ardennes* the most famous dish, and juniper berries used to flavour food *à l'ardennaise*.

---

meeting place and fills up in the evenings. **€98**

**Le Royal** 22 bd Carnot ☎ 03 25 73 19 99, ⓦ royal-hotel-troyes.com. Decent, pleasantly restored hotel in a rather drab building near the station. Don't be put off

– it's welcoming and good value; rooms have spacious bathrooms, there's a copious breakfast and also a good restaurant. **€79**

### EATING, DRINKING AND NIGHTLIFE

Self-caterers should head for the Marché les Halles, a daily covered market on the corner of rue du Général-de-Gaulle and place St-Rémy, close to the *hôtel de ville*. Most of the restaurants cluster in the narrow streets around St-Jean.

### EATING

**Aux Crieurs de Vin** 4 place Jean-Jaurès ☎ 03 25 40 01 01, ⓦ auxcrieursdevin.fr. Delightfully unpretentious wine bar and shop with *andouillettes* on the menu and a jumble of different furniture. A good selection of wines come by the glass, with emphasis on organic varieties; during the week, the lunchtime *plat du jour* comes with a glass of wine for just €11.80. Tues–Sat noon–2pm & 7–9.30pm.

**Chez Félix** 5 ruelle des Chats ☎ 03 10 94 03 03, ⓦ chez-felix.fr. Quirky retro restaurant with a young, fun vibe and a pleasant summer terrace. Traditional French cuisine made with local produce is on the menu; the sharing platters of charcuterie (€12–15) are popular. There's a small but perfectly formed wine list and the desserts are delicious – try a café gourmand (coffee with several small desserts, €8). *Menus* €16–18. Daily noon–1.30pm & 7–9.30pm.

**La Mignardise** 1 ruelle des Chats ☎ 09 70 35 75 09, ⓦ lamignardise.eu. One of Troyes' most celebrated restaurants, *La Mignardise* is set in a sixteenth-century building looking onto a quiet courtyard where you can eat on summer evenings. Come here for the classics: duck *ballottine* with dried apricots; fillet of beef with a shallot and local red wine sauce. *Menus* €25–65. Tues–Sat noon–

2pm & 7.30–9.30pm, Sun noon–2pm.

**Le Valentino** 35 rue Paillot-de-Montabert (entrance cours de la Rencontre) ☎ 03 25 73 14 14, ⓦ levalentino.com. This chic and intimate restaurant with a pretty paved courtyard makes for a romantic dinner. Reasonable prices, local ingredients and emphasis on fish has earned it a top local reputation. Reservations essential; *menus* €29–58. Tues–Sat noon–1.30pm & 7–9.30pm.

### DRINKING AND NIGHTLIFE

**Le Bougnat des Pouilles** 29 rue Paillot-de-Montabert ☎ 03 25 73 59 85. Quirky decor with contributions from local artists, always packed, good wine list, concerts and exhibitions. Tues–Sat 5pm–3am.

★ **Chez Philippe** 11 rue Champeaux ☎ 03 25 43 17 96, ⓦ bullesetdouceurs.com. Smart champagne bar specializing in bubbles from ten small producers in the commune of Celles-sur-Ource in the Côte des Bar. Tues–Sat 5.30pm–1am.

**Cotton Club** 8 rue Charbonnet ☎ 03 25 76 11 71. Popular and lively bar in the centre of town, with a disco and a good line-up of live music in the vaulted cellars. Wed 11.45pm–4am, Thurs until 5am, Fri & Sat until 5.30am.

**L'Illustré** 8 rue Champeaux ☎ 03 25 40 00 88, ⓦ lillustre.com. Restaurant, café, bar and club downstairs in an old half-timbered building. Café daily 2.30–7pm; restaurant Mon–Sat noon–2.30pm & 7–11pm; bar and club Fri–Sat 6.30pm–1am.

# The Plateau de Langres

The Seine, Marne, Aube and several other lesser rivers rise in the **Plateau de Langres** between Troyes and Dijon, with main routes between the two towns skirting this area. To the west, the champagne town of **Essoyes** in the Côte des Bar was once home to Impressionist painter Pierre-Auguste Renoir (1841–1919); the family villa opened to the public in 2017. To the east, the D619 (which the train follows) takes in **Chaumont** and **Langres**, two towns that could briefly slow your progress if you're in no hurry, and the home village of Charles de Gaulle, **Colombey-les-Deux-Églises**.

# Chaumont

Situated on a steep ridge between the Marne and Suize valleys, **CHAUMONT** (Chaumont-en-Bassigny, to give its full name), lies 95km southeast of Troyes. Approach by train to cross the town's stupendous mid-nineteenth-century viaduct, which took an average of 2500 labourers working night and day two years to construct. It's also possible to walk across the viaduct, which gives you fine views of the Suize valley.

The town's most interesting historic building is the **Basilique St-Jean-Baptiste**. Though built with the same dour, grey stone of most Champagne churches, it has a wonderful Renaissance addition to the Gothic transept of balconies and turreted stairway, and a superb church organ. The decoration includes an *Arbre de Jessé* of the early sixteenth-century Troyes school, in which all the characters are sitting in the tree, dressed in the style of the day.

You shouldn't leave without taking a look at **Le Signe**, 1 place Émile-Goguenheim, near the *gare SNCF* (Wed & Fri–Sun 2–6pm; Thurs until 9pm; free, ☎03 25 35 79 01, ⓦcentrenationaldugraphisme.fr), a purpose-built centre, opened in 2016, dedicated to graphic design. As well as hosting temporary exhibitions, it's the main venue for Chaumont's international **poster festival** (Biennale de design graphique), which is held every two years from mid-May to mid-June (2019, 2021, etc.). As for the rest of the old town, there's not much to do except admire the thirteenth-century castle keep of the Comtes de Champagne, the delightfully named **Tour d'Arse** at the foot of the *vieille ville*, and the strange, bulging stair towers of the houses.

## ARRIVAL AND INFORMATION CHAUMONT

**By train** The *gare SNCF* is just off place du Général-de-Gaulle, from where it's a 10min walk into the centre along place Émile-Goguenheim.
Destinations Paris (15 daily; from 2hr 20min); Reims (11 daily; from 2hr); Troyes (10 daily; from 50min).

**By bus** The *gare routière* is beside the train station.
**Tourist office** 7 av du Général-de-Gaulle (July & Aug Mon–Sat 9am–12.30pm & 1.30–6.30pm; Sept–June Mon–Sat 9.30am–12.30pm & 2.30–6pm; ☎03 25 03 80 80, ⓦtourisme-chaumont-champagne.com).

## ACCOMMODATION

**Les Remparts** 72 rue de Verdun ☎03 25 32 64 40, ⓦhotel-les-remparts.fr. Handily situated between the station and the centre, this former coaching inn has been tastefully renovated in contemporary style. There are two good restaurants: one gourmet, one brasserie. Be warned that there is no car park, but there is free public parking nearby. €118

# Colombey-les-Deux-Églises

Twenty-seven kilometres northwest of Chaumont, on the D619 to Troyes, is **COLOMBEY-LES-DEUX-ÉGLISES**, the village where Gaullist leaders come to pay their respects at the grave of **Général Charles de Gaulle**. The former president's family home, **La Boisserie**, opens its ground floor to the public (April–Sept daily 10am–1pm & 2–6.30pm; Oct–March Mon & Wed–Sun 10am–12.30pm & 2–5.30pm; closed mid-Dec–Jan; €5.50), but more impressive are the pink-granite **Cross of Lorraine**, symbol of the French Resistance movement, standing over 40m high on a hill just west of the village, and the **Mémorial Charles de Gaulle** (May–Sept daily 9.30am–7pm; Oct–April Mon & Wed–Sun 10am–5.30pm; €13.50, or €16.50 including La Boisserie and Cross of Lorraine; ⓦmemorial-charlesdegaulle.fr), an exhaustive chronicle of the man's life and times in an ultra-sleek museum beneath the cross.

## ACCOMMODATION AND EATING COLOMBEY-LES-DEUX-ÉGLISES

**La Grange du Relais** 26 route Nationale 19 ☎03 25 02 03 89, ⓦlagrangedurelais.fr. It may be on the D619 but the charming, simply decorated rooms face towards the fields or are around the outdoor swimming pool. A dining room crowded with artefacts, most for sale, offers honest, classic dishes. *Menus* €14.90–36.90. €76

**Hostellerie La Montagne** 10 rue de Pisseloup ☎03 25 01 51 69, ⓦhostellerielamontagne.com. Run by a father and son team, this rustic-chic mansion is really a restaurant with rooms – chef Jean-Baptiste Natali gained his experience working under some famous culinary names. Rooms are individually designed and top-notch, as is the Michelin-starred cooking, which uses local ingredients. *Menus* €28–100. €115

## Essoyes

About 60km south east of Troyes, the village of **ESSOYES** in the middle of the Côte des Bar champagne-producing area is best known for its links to Pierre-Auguste Renoir. The Impressionist painter spent summers here from 1888 to 1919, after being entranced by the village where his wife Aline was born. The family home, garden and studio opened to the public in 2017 and form part of the **Parcours Renoir** (Renoir Trail; see website for opening times; €14; ☎03 25 29 10 94, ⓦrenoir-essoyes.fr), which also includes a good permanent exhibition on the artist, **L'Espace Renoir** (Place de la Mairie; see details for Parcours Renoir). Renoir, Aline and their three sons are buried in the village cemetery.

### ARRIVAL AND INFORMATION                                                ESSOYES

**By car** Essoyes is about an hour's drive south east of Troyes via the A5 then D79.
**By train** The nearest *gare SNCF* is at Bar-sur-Seine, from where you'd need to get a taxi.
**Tourist office** L'Espace Renoir, Place de la Mairie (same opening times as the Parcours Renoir; ☎ 03 25 29 21 27, ⓦ essoyes.fr).

### EATING AND DRINKING

**La Guinguette des Arts** 4 quai de l'Ource ☎03 25 29 70 59, ⓦlaguinguettedesarts.fr. Charming restaurant next to the river with a terrace. Dishes are French and regional, featuring the likes of *andouillette*, meat skewers and steak. As you'd expect, there's a good selection of champagnes. *Menus* €11.50–28. Mon & Wed–Sun noon–2pm & 7–9pm.

## Langres

**LANGRES**, 35km south of Chaumont and just as spectacularly situated above the Marne, retains its near-complete encirclement of gateways, towers and ramparts. If you're just here for an hour or so, the best thing to do is to walk this circuit, with its great views east to the hills of Alsace and southwest across the Plateau de Langres (you can download a discovery map off the tourist office website). Don't miss the **St-Ferjeux tower** with its beautiful metal sculpture, *Air and Dreams*. Wandering inside the walls is also rewarding – Renaissance houses and narrow streets give the feel of a place time has left behind, swathed in the mists of southern Champagne. Langres was home to the eighteenth-century Enlightenment philosopher **Diderot** for the first sixteen years of his life, and people like to make the point that, were he to return to Langres today, he'd have no trouble finding his way around.

The town's **Cathédrale St-Mammès** (daily: May–Oct 8am–7pm; Nov–April 8am–5pm) is worth a visit for the sixteenth-century tiles from Rouen, on display in one of the nave chapels. You'll also find an amusing sixteenth-century relief of the *Raising of Lazarus*, in which the apostles watch, totally blasé, while other characters look like kids at a good horror movie.

### Maison des Lumières Denis Diderot

1 place Pierre-Burelle • Tues–Sun: April–Sept 9am–noon & 2–6.30pm; Oct–March 1.30–5.30pm; €7 including Musée d'Art et Histoire • ⓦ musees-langres.fr

This impressive sixteenth-century mansion houses a well-executed collection celebrating the life of the town's most famous son. Setting Diderot's work within the context of the Enlightenment, the museum exhibits handwritten letters, personal effects, artworks and original editions of all 35 volumes of his groundbreaking encyclopedia, which courted considerable controversy for its secular view of the world.

### Musée d'Art et d'Histoire

Place du Centenaire • Mon & Wed–Sun: April–Sept 9am–noon & 2–7pm; Oct–March 1.30–5.30pm • €7 including Maison des Lumières Denis Diderot • ⓦ musees-langres.fr

Roman mosaics, medieval sculptures, eighteenth-century engravings and early photographs make this an eclectic collection, but the real highlight is the superbly restored Romanesque chapel of St-Didier, which houses a fourteenth-century painted ivory *Annunciation*.

### ARRIVAL AND INFORMATION

LANGRES

**By train** The *gare SNCF* is on avenue de la gare, a 10min walk into town.

Destinations Dijon (4 direct daily; 1hr); Reims (3 direct daily; 2hr 30min); Troyes (11 daily; 1hr 10min).

**Tourist office** Square Olivier Lahalle (April–June & Sept Mon–Sat 9am–noon & 1.30–6pm, Sun 10am–12.15pm & 1.45–6pm; July & Aug Mon–Sat 9am–6.30pm, Sun 10am–6pm; Oct–March Mon–Sat 9am–noon & 1.30–5.30pm; ☎03 25 87 67 67, ⓦ tourisme-langres.com).

### ACCOMMODATION

**Cheval Blanc** 4 rue de l'Estres ☎03 25 87 07 00, ⓦ hotel-langres.com. Once part of an ancient abbey church, this mellow stone building has been an inn since the 1790s. Huge windows, wooden floors and exposed stone retain the ecclesiastical feel, but rest assured, bedrooms and bathrooms are firmly twenty-first century. Good restaurant (see below). Closed Nov. **€80**

**Grand Hôtel de l'Europe** 23–25 rue Diderot ☎03 25 87 10 88, ⓦ relais-sud-champagne.com. The large, high-ceilinged, modestly decorated rooms and an inner courtyard recall the days when this was an old coaching inn in the centre of town. Old-fashioned and welcoming. **€74**

### EATING AND DRINKING

Langres has its own highly flavourful, strong-smelling – and excellent – cheese, which you can buy at the Friday market on boulevard du Maréchal de Lattre de Tassigny.

**Restaurant Diderot** Cheval Blanc, 4 rue de l'Estres ☎03 25 87 07 00, ⓦ hotel-langres.com. The restaurant is as elegant as the hotel, with high-beamed ceilings and polished wood floors. Classic dishes with inventive twists are the order of the day: marinated salmon with avocado sushi and yuzu cream; millefeuille of strawberries and almonds with minted strawberry coulis. *Menus* €18–49. Mon–Tues & Thurs–Sun noon–1.15pm & 7–9.15pm, Wed 7–9.15pm; closed Nov.

# The Ardennes

To the northeast of Reims, the scenery of the **Ardennes** region along the Meuse valley knocks spots off any landscape in Champagne. Most of the hills lie over the border in Belgium, but there's enough of interest on the French side to make it well worth exploring.

In war after war, the people of the Ardennes have been engaged in protracted last-ditch battles down the valley of the Meuse, which, once lost, gave invading armies a clear path to Paris. The rugged, hilly terrain and deep forests (frightening even to Julius Caesar's legionnaires) helped World War II Resistance fighters, but during peacetime life here has never been easy. The land is unsuitable for crops, and the slate and ironworks, the main source of employment during the nineteenth century, closed in the 1980s. The only major investment in the region has been a nuclear power station, to which locals responded by etching "Nuke the Élysée!" high on a half-cut cliff of slate just downstream. This said, tourism, the main growth industry, is developing apace – there are walking and boating possibilities, plus good train connections – though the isolated atmosphere of this region still lingers.

## Charleville-Mézières

CHARLEVILLE-MÉZIÈRES – an agglomeration of former stand-alone towns Charleville and Mézières – provides a good base for exploring the northern part of the region, which spreads across the meandering Meuse before the valley closes in and the forests take over.

The splendid seventeenth-century **place Ducale**, in the centre of town, was the result of the local duke's envy of the contemporary place des Vosges in Paris, which it somewhat resembles. Despite the posh setting, the shops in the arcades remain down-to-earth and the cafés charge reasonable prices to sit outside.

## PUPPETS IN CHARLEVILLE

Charleville is a major international puppetry centre (its school is justly famous), and every two years it hosts one of the largest puppet festivals in the world, the **Festival Mondial des Théâtres de Marionnettes** (Ⓦfestival-marionnette.com). For ten days in September, up to 250 professional troupes – some from as far away as Mali and Burma – put on around fifty shows a day on the streets and in every available space in town. Tickets are cheap, and there are shows for adults as well as the usual stuff aimed at kids. If you miss the festival you may still be able to catch one of the occasional puppet performances at the **Institut de la Marionnette** on place Winston-Churchill (☎03 24 33 72 50, Ⓦmarionnette.com; tickets often free). If you're passing by here during the day, you can see one of the automated episodes of the *Four Sons of Aymon* enacted on the facade's clock every hour from 10am–9pm, or all twelve scenes on Saturday at 9.15pm.

### Musée de l'Ardenne

Accessed from 31 place Ducale • May–Sept Tues–Fri 9.30am–12.30pm & 1.30–6pm, Sat & Sun 11am–1pm & 2–6pm; Oct–April Tues–Fri 9am–noon & 1.30–5.30pm, Sat & Sun 2–5.30pm • €5, combined ticket with Musée Arthur Rimbaud (see below) • ☎03 24 32 44 60

A complex of old and new buildings houses the **Musée de l'Ardenne**, a typically eclectic local museum which includes archeological finds from a local Merovingian cemetery, fascinating historic models of Charleville and Mézières in the seventeenth century, and paintings on nineteenth-century industrial and political themes by Paul Gondrexon.

### Musée Arthur Rimbaud

May–Sept Tues–Fri 9.30am–12.30pm & 1.30–6pm, Sat & Sun 11am–1pm & 2–6pm; Oct–April Tues–Fri 9am–noon & 1.30–5.30pm, Sat & Sun 2–5.30pm• €5, combined ticket with Musée de l'Ardenne (see above)

Reopened in 2015 after more than eighteen months of renovation work, the **Musée Arthur Rimbaud** honours the most famous person to emerge from Charleville, the poet Arthur Rimbaud (1854–91), who ran away from the town four times before he was 17, so desperate was he to escape its provincialism. Housed in a very grand stone watermill – a contemporary of the place Ducale – on quai Arthur-Rimbaud, two blocks north of the main square, the museum contains original sonnets and letters handwritten by the poet, as well as photos, paintings and sketches of him and his contemporaries, including his lover Verlaine. Nearby, you can also visit the house where he lived with his family from the age of 15 to 21, La Maison des Ailleurs (7 quai Arthur-Rimbaud; same times and tickets as museums). A few steps down the quayside is the spot where he composed his most famous poem, *Le Bateau Ivre*. After penning poetry in Paris, journeying to the Far East and trading in Ethiopia and Yemen, Rimbaud died in a Marseille hospital. His body was brought back to his home town – probably the last place he would have wanted to be buried – and true Rimbaud admirers can visit his **tomb** in the cemetery west of the place Ducale at the end of avenue Charles-Boutet.

### ARRIVAL AND INFORMATION

CHARLEVILLE-MÉZIÈRES

**By train** The *gare SNCF* is in place de la Gare, a 10min walk south east of place Ducale, with an almost hourly service to Reims (55min) and 12 per day to Paris (1hr 46min).

**By bus** The *gare routière* is a couple of blocks west of the square, by the Marché Couvert. Bus routes cover the immediate area only.

**Tourist office** 4 place Ducale (Daily: May–Sept 10am–12.30pm & 1.30–6pm; Oct–April 10am–noon & 2–5.30pm; ☎03 24 55 69 90, Ⓦcharleville-sedan-tourisme.fr).

### ACCOMMODATION

**Camping du Mont Olympe** ☎03 24 33 23 60. On a bend in the river and just a few minutes' walk into town, this small campsite is open April–Sept and has a snack bar, wi-fi and laundry. **€13.60**

**Le Dormeur du Val** 32bis rue de la Gravière ☎03 24 42 04 30, Ⓦhotel-dormeur-du-val.com. Four-star, seventeen-room boutique hotel with large, colourful and stylish rooms. Adding to the lively atmosphere is a bar with industrial steel girders and more mix-and-match contemporary furniture. **€86**

## EATING AND DRINKING

★ **Bar à Vin Le Concept** 37 place Ducale ☎ 03 24 22 57 03. Excellent wine bar in the attractive main square, not only serving a good selection of vino but champagne, local beers and snacks too – like tapas and platters or cheese and charcuterie (from €8.90). Tues 6.30–midnight, Wed–Sat noon–2pm & 6.30–midnight.

**Sel et Poivre** 12 av Forest ☎ 03 24 55 71 16. Small, cosy restaurant offering excellent value for money. Chef Olivier Houzet dreams up a new menu every day with fresh ingredients bought from the morning's market, creating inventive dishes (€12.50–24) that are reliably tasty. Reservations recommended. Tues–Sat noon–2pm & 7–9.30pm.

# North of Charleville-Mézières

Writing about the stretch of the Meuse that winds through the Ardennes, George Sand said: "its high wooded cliffs, strangely solid and compact, are like some inexorable destiny that encloses, pushes and twists the river without permitting it a single whim or any escape". What all the tourist literature emphasizes, however, are the legends of medieval struggles between Good and Evil whose characters have given names to some of the curious rocks and crests. The grandest of these, where the schist formations have taken the most peculiar turns, is the **Roc de la Tour**, also known as the "Devil's Castle", up a path off the D31, 3.5km out of **Monthermé**.

The **GR12** is a good **walking route**, circling the **Lac des Vieilles Forges**, 17km northwest of Charleville-Mézières, then meeting the Meuse at Bogny and crossing over to Hautes-Rivières in the even more sinuous **Semoy valley**. There are plenty of other tracks, too, though beware of *chasse* (hunting) signs – French hunters tend to hack through the undergrowth with their safety catches off and are notoriously trigger-happy. They're mostly after the local wild boar, who are nowhere near as dangerous as their pursuers; the animals would seem to be more intelligent, too, rooting about near the crosses of the Resistance memorial near **Revin**, while hunters stalk the forest. The abundance of wild boar is partly explained when you rummage around on the forest floor yourself and discover, between the trees to either side of the river, an astonishing variety of mushrooms, and, in late summer, wild strawberries and bilberries. For a quaint insight into life in the forest, stop at the **Musée de la Forêt**, situated right on the edge of the Ardennes, 2km north of **Renwez** on the D40 (mid-April to mid-Nov Tues–Sun 10am–6pm; €6; ☎ 03 24 54 82 66, ⓦ renwez.fr). All manner of wood cutting, gathering and transporting is enacted by wooden dummies along with displays of utensils and flora and fauna of the forest; it's also a tranquil spot for a picnic or lunch at the museum café.

## GETTING AROUND                                NORTH OF CHARLEVILLE-MÉZIÈRES

Journeys in this neck of the woods are best tackled on foot, on skis, by bike or on a boat.

**By train** Trains follow the Meuse towards Belgium, while local buses run as far as Nouzonville.

**By boat** There are various different kinds of pleasure boats, some just for the day and some to rent by the week or weekend – not wildly expensive if you can split the cost four or six ways. South of Charleville-Mézières at Pont à Bar, Ardennes Nautisme (☎ 03 24 54 01 50, ⓦ ardennes-nautisme.com) provides boats for weekly and weekend

rent; while north of Charleville-Mézières at Monthermé Le Roc (☎ 03 24 35 79 47, ⓦ lerocbateausurlameuse.net; €12 for 1hr 30min) takes trips along the Meuse from April to Sept.

**By bicycle** The Trans-Ardennes Bike Path provides over 80km of off-road bike trails following the Meuse valley; the regional tourist office at Charleville-Mézières (see opposite) can provide free route maps, as well as information on hiking, canoeing or riding.

## ACCOMMODATION

**Ferme Auberge du Malgré-Tout** Rte Malgré-Tout ☎ 03 24 40 11 20, ⓦ aubergeferme-malgretout.com. Situated in the middle of a forest just a few kilometres outside Revin, this charming farm-style bed and breakfast offers simple

rooms in a converted barn. The cooking is classic *ardennaise*, with plenty of tasty game dishes. At €24, the four-course *menu* is particularly good value. **€65**

# Alsace and Lorraine

**228** Strasbourg

**235** The Route des Vins

**238** Colmar and around

**242** Mulhouse

**245** Nancy

**249** Metz

**253** Amnéville

**254** Verdun

TRADITIONAL ALSACIEN HOUSES, COLMAR

# Alsace and Lorraine

Disputed for centuries by French kings and the princes of the Holy Roman Empire, and subsequently embroiled in a bloody tug-of-war between France and Germany, France's easternmost provinces, Alsace and Lorraine, share a tumultuous history. It's no surprise then that almost everything, from the architecture to the cuisine and the language, is an enticing mixture of French and German – so much so that you might begin to wonder which country you're actually in.

Cute Hansel-and-Gretel-type houses – higgledy-piggledy creations with oriel windows, carved timberwork, toy-town gables and geranium-filled window boxes – are a common feature in **Alsace**, especially along the winding **Route des Vins** (ⓦalsace-wine-route.com), which traces the eastern margin of the forests of the Vosges mountains. This road also represents the region's chief tourist *raison d'être* – wine – best accompanied with a regional cuisine that's traditionally more Germanic than French, although you'll find plenty of creativity in modern Alsatian cooking. Ruined medieval castles are scattered about, while outstanding churches and museums are concentrated in the handsome regional capital of **Strasbourg** and in smaller, quirkier **Colmar**. Bustling **Mulhouse** stands out for its industrial heritage and entertaining nightlife. A noticeably wealthy province, Alsace has historically churned out cars and textiles, not to mention half the beer in France.

Alsace's less prosperous and less scenic neighbour, **Lorraine**, shares borders with Luxembourg, Germany and Belgium. The graceful former capital, **Nancy**, is one of the most important centres of Art Nouveau and is well worth a visit, as is leafy **Metz**, with its sparkling contemporary art gallery. The bloody World War I battlefields around **Verdun** attract a large number of visitors, as does the zoo in Amnéville, one of the largest in France. Gastronomically no less renowned than other French provinces,

---

## ALSATIAN FOOD

Alsatians are hearty eaters, with their local cuisine characterized by generous helpings of pork, potatoes and *spaetzle* (a type of pasta usually fried in butter). But the region also has an international reputation for gastronomy, with exciting, new and well-established Michelin-starred restaurants dotted across its towns and villages.

The classic Alsatian dish is *choucroute*, the aromatic pickled cabbage known in German as **sauerkraut**. The difference here is the inclusion of juniper berries in the pickling stage and the addition of goose grease or lard. Traditionally it's served with smoked pork, ham and sausages, but some restaurants offer a succulent fish variant (*choucroute aux poissons*). The qualification *à l'alsacienne* after the name of a dish means "with *choucroute*". **Baeckoffe**, a three-meat hotpot comprising layers of potato, pork, mutton and beef marinated in wine and baked for several hours, is a speciality. **Onions**, too, crop up frequently, often in the guise of soup or tart. The food of choice to accompany a beer is *flammeküche* (*tarte flambée*), a thin, pizza-like base usually topped with onions, cream and pork lardons, although you'll encounter endless variations.

Alsatians are particularly fond of their **pastries**. In almost every patisserie, you'll find a mouthwatering array of fruit tarts, with yellow *mirabelle* plums a speciality, as well as delicacies such as *torche aux marrons*, a meringue base topped with chestnut puree. Cake-lovers should try *kugelhopf*, a dome-shaped cake with a hollow in the middle made with raisins and almonds.

For the classic Alsatian eating experience, head to a **winstub**, loosely translated as a "wine bar", a cosy establishment with bare beams, wood wall panels, benches and a convivial atmosphere.

VINTAGE MOTORS AT THE CITÉ DE L'AUTOMOBILE IN MULHOUSE

# Highlights

**❶ Strasbourg cathedral** Climb up to the lofty spire of this magnificent Gothic cathedral for stunning views as far as the Black Forest. See page 228

**❷ The Route des Vins** Surrounded by a sea of vines, Alsace's picturesque wine villages are overlooked by a wealth of ruined castles, perched on pine-clad fringes of the Vosges. See page 235

**❸ The Issenheim Altarpiece, Colmar** Luridly expressive, this early Renaissance masterpiece alone makes quaint Colmar worth a visit. See page 238

**❹ Bugattis at Mulhouse's Cité de l'Automobile** A matchless collection of vintage motors in the city of many unique museums. See page 244

**❺ Place Stanislas, Nancy** Along with some outstanding Art Nouveau furniture and glassware, elegant Nancy is home to one of the most grandiose eighteenth-century squares in all France. See page 245

**❻ Centre Pompidou-Metz** Explore the new branch of the famous Parisian Centre Pompidou. See page 251

**HIGHLIGHTS ARE MARKED ON THE MAP ON PAGE 226**

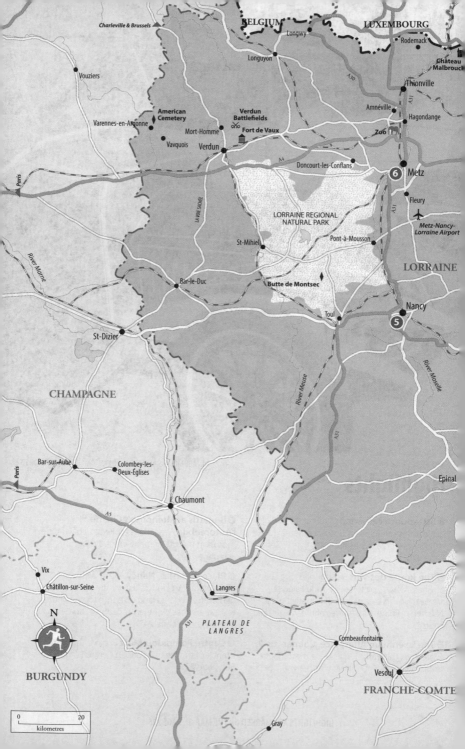

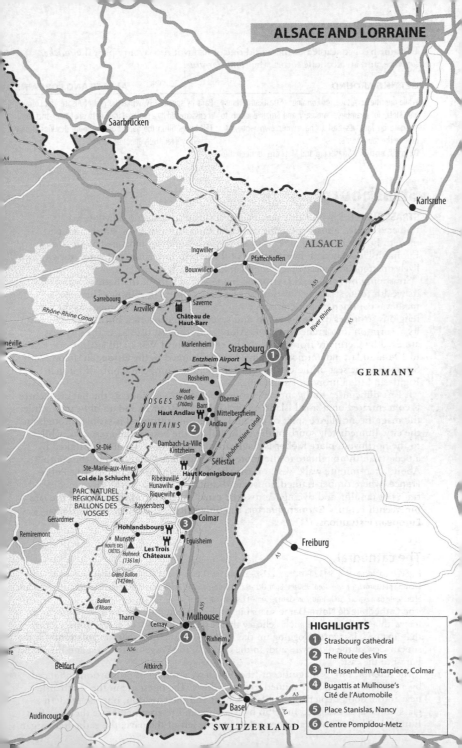

# ALSACE AND LORRAINE

Saarbrücken

Karlsruhe

Ingwiller

Pfaffenhoffen

ALSACE

Bouxwiller

Sarrebourg

Arzviller

Saverne

Château de
Haut-Barr

Rhône-Rhine Canal

Marlenheim

Strasbourg ①

Entzheim Airport

néville

River Rhine

GERMANY

Rosheim

VOSGES

Mont
Ste-Odile
(760m)

Obernai

Barr

Haut Andlau

Mittelbergheim

MOUNTAINS

Andlau

②

St-Dié

Dambach-La-Ville

Kintzheim

Sélestat

Ste-Marie-aux-Mines

Col de la Schlucht

Ribeauvillé

Haut Koenigsbourg

Hunawihr

Riquewihr

PARC NATUREL
RÉGIONAL DES
BALLONS DES
VOSGES

Kaysersberg

Gérardmer

Hohlandsbourg

Colmar ③

Remiremont

Munster

ROUTE DES
CRÊTES

Hohneck
(1361m)

Les Trois
Châteaux

Eguisheim

Freiburg

Grand Ballon
(1424m)

Ballon
d'Alsace

Thann

Cernay

Mulhouse

④

re

Rixheim

Belfort

Altkirch

Audincourt

Basel

SWITZERLAND

## HIGHLIGHTS

① Strasbourg cathedral

② The Route des Vins

③ The Issenheim Altarpiece, Colmar

④ Bugattis at Mulhouse's
Cité de l'Automobile

⑤ Place Stanislas, Nancy

⑥ Centre Pompidou-Metz

Lorraine has bequeathed to the world one of its favourite savoury pies, the *quiche lorraine*, and an alcoholic sorbet, the *coupe lorraine*.

## GETTING AROUND ALSACE AND LORRAINE

While the cities in Alsace and Lorraine – Strasbourg, Nancy and Metz, for example – are easy and small enough to navigate on foot, it's best to have your own wheels to explore the countryside.

**By train and bus** Strasbourg and Metz are connected to Paris by speedy TGV, while the rest of Alsace and Lorraine is crisscrossed by a regional train network (⑩ ter-sncf.com). TER buses fill in the gaps, but the Route des Vins is only served by a relatively sporadic service.

# Strasbourg

**STRASBOURG** is a hybrid city: part medieval village, characterized by lovely half-timbered houses, a soaring Gothic cathedral and narrow winding streets, and part modern European powerhouse, with sleek, glassy buildings inhabited by important European Union bodies. Boasting one of the largest universities in France, the city is a lively, metropolitan place that deserves at least three days' visit.

Strasbourg owes both its Germanic name – "the City of the Roads" – and its wealth to its strategic position on the west bank of the Rhine. The city's medieval commercial pre-eminence was damaged by its involvement in the religious struggles of the sixteenth and seventeenth centuries, but recovered with its absorption into France in 1681. Along with the rest of Alsace, the city was annexed by Germany from 1871 to the end of World War I and again from 1940 to 1944. Today, old animosities have been subsumed in the **European Union**, with Strasbourg the seat of the Council of Europe, the European Court of Human Rights and the European Parliament.

It isn't difficult to find your way around Strasbourg on foot, as the flat city centre is concentrated on a small island encircled by the River Ill and an old canal, while the magnificent filigree spire of the pink sandstone **cathedral** is visible throughout the city. Immediately south of the cathedral are the best of the museums, while to the northwest, **place Kléber** is the heart of the commercial district, linked by a pedestrian thoroughfare to the more attractive **place Gutenberg** to the south. About a ten-minute walk west, on the tip of the island, is picturesque **La Petite France**, where timber-framed houses and canals hark back to the city's medieval trades of tanning and dyeing. Across the canal to the east of the centre is the late nineteenth-century **German quarter**, the **University** and, further north, the city's **European institutions**.

## The cathedral

Place de la Cathédrale • Mon–Sat 8.30–11.15am & 12.45–5.45pm, Sun 11.15am–noon & 1.30–5.30pm; closed during services • Free
**Viewing platform** Daily: April–Sept 9.30am–8pm; Oct–March 10am–6pm • €5 **Astronomical clock** Tickets bought from the cash desk at the south door in place du Château Mon–Sat 11.30am–12.30pm • €3

The **Cathédrale de Notre-Dame** soars out of the close huddle of medieval houses at its feet with a single spire of such delicacy that it seems the work of confectioners rather than masons. It's worth slogging up the 332 steps to the spire's **viewing platform** for the superb view of the old town, and, in the distance, the Vosges to the west and the Black Forest to the east.

The **interior**, too, is magnificent, the high nave a model of proportion enhanced by a glorious sequence of stained-glass windows. The finest are in the south aisle next to the door, depicting the life of Christ and the Creation, but the modern glass in the apse designed in 1956 by Max Ingrand to commemorate the city's first European institutions is also beautiful. On the left of the nave, the cathedral's organ

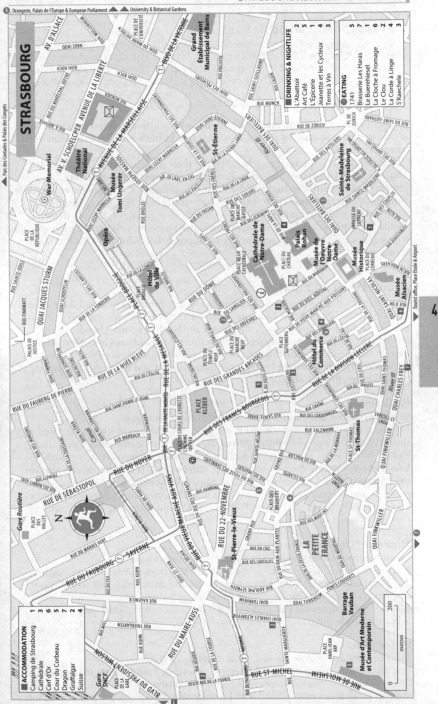

**STRASBOURG**

| DRINKING & NIGHTLIFE | |
|---|---|
| L'Abattoir | 2 |
| Art Café | 5 |
| L'Épicerie | 1 |
| Jeanette et les Cycleux | 4 |
| Terres à Vin | 3 |

| EATING | |
|---|---|
| 1741 | 5 |
| Brasserie Les Haras | 7 |
| Le Buerehiesel | 1 |
| La Cloche à Fromage | 6 |
| Le Clou | 2 |
| La Corde à Linge | 4 |
| S'Kaechele | 3 |

| ACCOMMODATION | |
|---|---|
| Camping de Strasbourg | 1 |
| Cathédrale | 3 |
| Cerf d'Or | 6 |
| Cour du Corbeau | 5 |
| Dragon | 7 |
| Graffalgar | 2 |
| Suisse | 4 |

4

perches precariously above one of the arches, while further down on the same side is the late fifteenth-century pulpit, a masterpiece of intricacy in stone by the aptly named Hans Hammer.

In the south transept are the cathedral's two most popular sights. The **Pilier des Anges** is a slender triple-tiered central column, decorated with some of the most graceful and expressive statuary of the thirteenth century. The huge and enormously complicated **astronomical clock** was built by Schwilgué of Strasbourg in 1842. It is a favourite with the tour-group operators, whose customers roll up in droves at midday to witness the clock's crowning daily performance, striking the hour of noon, which it does with unerring accuracy at 12.30pm – that being pre-GMT midday Strasbourg time.

## Around the cathedral

The old cobbled streets and colourful riverside quays around the cathedral are a great place to wander. Narrow rue Mercière, busy with cathedral-gazers, funnels west to **place Gutenberg**, with its steep-pitched roofs and brightly painted facades. It was named after the printer and pioneer of moveable type, Johannes Gutenberg, who lived in the city in the early fifteenth century and whose statue occupies the middle of the square. As well as being a hub for tourist restaurants and cafés, this area houses a number of worthwhile museums.

### Palais Rohan

Museums: Daily except Tues 10am–6pm • €6.50 each • ☏ 03 68 98 51 60, Ⓦ musees.strasbourg.eu

On the south side of the cathedral is the place du Château, which is enclosed to the south by the imposing **Palais Rohan**, designed for the immensely powerful Rohan family, who, for several generations, cornered the market in cardinals' hats. It now contains three museums: the **Musée des Arts Décoratifs**; the **Musée des Beaux-Arts**; and the rather specialist **Musée Archéologique**. Of the three, the Arts Décoratifs stands out; its collections include some fine eighteenth-century faïence tiles crafted in the city by Paul Hannong and some impressive trompe l'oeil crockery.

### Musée de l'Oeuvre Notre-Dame

3 place du Château • Tues–Sun 10am–6pm • €6.50 • ☏ 03 68 98 51 60, Ⓦ musees.strasbourg.eu

Next to the Palais Rohan, the excellent **Musée de l'Oeuvre Notre-Dame** houses the original sculptures from the cathedral exterior, damaged in the Revolution and replaced today by copies. Other treasures include mesmeric stained-glass windows and impressive still lifes by the sixteenth-century Strasbourg painter Sebastian Stoskopff.

### Musée Historique

2 rue du Vieux Marché aux Poissons • Tues–Sun 10am–6pm • €6.50 • ☏ 03 68 98 51 60, Ⓦ musees.strasbourg.eu

Past the picturesque place du Marché-aux-Cochons-de-Lait is the **Musée Historique**. Interactive exhibits, and an over-enthusiastic but worthwhile audioguide, steer you through Strasbourg's political and social history, as a prosperous free city of the Holy

Roman Empire, through the theological controversies of the Reformation to French annexation by Louis XIV and the revolutionary fervour of 1789. The prize exhibit is an enormous 3-D relief map of the city, commissioned in the 1720s to show the state of the city's fortifications.

### Musée Alsacien

23–25 quai Saint-Nicolas • Daily except Tues 10am–6pm • €6.50 • ☎ 03 68 98 51 60, ⓦ musees.strasbourg.eu

Across the river, in a rickety and typically Alsatian house on quai St-Nicolas, the delightful **Musée Alsacien** celebrates all things Alsatian: reconstructed rooms – a kitchen, nursery, bedroom, even a *winstub* and a farmyard – are packed with local artefacts, painting a vivid picture of Alsatian life in the eighteenth and nineteenth centuries. There's also a very pretty interior courtyard.

## La Petite France and the rest of the old city

The attractive Pont St-Martin marks the beginning of the district known as **La Petite France**, where the city's millers, tanners and fishermen used to live. At the far end of a series of canals are the so-called **Ponts Couverts** (they are in fact no longer covered), built as part of the fourteenth-century city fortifications. Just beyond, the **barrage Vauban** (daily 8am–7pm; free), a dam built by Vauban to protect the city from attack (making it possible to quickly flood the southern side of the city, thereby protecting the city from any attack by land), offers excellent views from its panoramic terrace. The whole area is picture-postcard pretty, with winding streets – most notably rue du Bain-aux-Plantes – bordered by colourful sixteenth- and seventeenth-century houses adorned with flowers and elaborate carvings.

### Musée d'Art Moderne et Contemporain

1 place Hans Jean Arp • Tues–Sun 10am–6pm • €7 • ☎ 03 68 98 51 60, ⓦ musees.strasbourg.eu

Housed in a purpose-built, glass-fronted building overlooking the river and Vauban's dam (see above), the light and airy **Musée d'Art Moderne et Contemporain** hosts temporary exhibitions, alongside its well-presented permanent collections. Most interesting is the ground floor, which includes a small group of Impressionist paintings by the likes of Pissarro and Renoir, Kandinsky's studies for the ceramic *salon de musique*, a couple of Picassos, and a good section on Surrealism, with plenty of folkloric, mystical paintings by Brauner. There's also a room devoted to the voluptuous, smooth curves sculpted by Strasbourg's own Jean Arp, who was influenced by Dada and Surrealism before turning to sculpture. The rooftop café is a popular brunch spot (see page 234).

### Place du Marché-Gayot and place Broglie

The area east of the cathedral, where rue des Frères leads to place St-Étienne, is good for a stroll. **Place du Marché-Gayot**, tucked away off rue des Frères behind the cathedral, is a lively cobbled square lined with café-bars and is one of the city's top nightspots. From the north side of the cathedral, rue du Dôme leads to the eighteenth-century **place Broglie**, where you'll find the *hôtel de ville*, the bijou **Opéra** and some imposing eighteenth-century mansions. It's here that the city's famous Christmas market is held (see page 235).

## The German quarter (Neustadt) and the European institutions

Across the canal from the cathedral, **place de la République** is surrounded by vast German Neo-Gothic edifices erected during the Prussian occupation, one example being the main **post office** on avenue de la Marseillaise. Along with the *Grande-Île* (city centre), this is a UNESCO World Heritage Site. At the other end of avenue de la Liberté, across the confluence of the Ill and Aar, is the city's **university**, where Goethe studied. From in front of the university, alleé de la Robertsau, flanked by handsome *fin-de-siècle* bourgeois residences, leads to the headquarters of three major European institutions: the bunker-like **Palais de l'Europe**, the 1970s-built home of the 47-member Council of Europe; the glass and steel curvilinear **European Parliament building**, opened in 1999; and the glass entrance and silver towers of Richard Rogers' **European Court of Human Rights**, completed in 1995. Individuals can arrange to visit the European Parliament during plenary sessions (free; Ⓦeuroparl.europa.eu); the European Court of Human Rights has public court hearings (free; Ⓦechr.coe.int). Booking is also required to visit the Council of Europe (free; Ⓦcoe.int). Opposite the Palais de l'Europe, the **Orangerie**, Strasbourg's best bit of greenery, hosts a variety of exhibitions and free concerts. There's also a small zoo with monkeys and exotic birds. Look out for the region's emblematic storks nesting in and around the park.

## Musée Tomi Ungerer

2 av de la Marseillaise • Daily except Tues 10am–6pm • €6.50 • ☎ 03 68 98 51 60, Ⓦ musees.strasbourg.eu

With a career spanning advertising, erotica, political satire and, most famously, children's books, award-winning Strasbourg illustrator Tomi Ungerer has enjoyed a rich and varied career. This hidden gem of a museum offers a fascinating insight into his life and works, with explanatory texts in English. Exhibitions change regularly, but the artist's imagination is always on show – especially in his often-startling erotic images.

## ARRIVAL AND DEPARTURE                                          STRASBOURG

**By plane** Entzheim International Airport (Ⓦstrasbourg. aeroport.fr) lies 15km outside the city and is connected with the *gare SNCF* via a shuttle that makes the journey in 8min around every 15min during the week, less often at weekends (€2.60).

**By train** The *gare SNCF* lies on the west side of the city centre, a 15min walk from the cathedral. It is a terminus for the TGV high-speed train.

Destinations Barr (1–2 hourly; 42min); Colmar (2–3 hourly; 30min); Lille (12 daily; 3hr 20min); Nantes (10 daily;

5hr 10min); Obernai (1–2 hourly; 30min); Metz/Nancy (9–13 daily; 1hr 20min); Mulhouse (1–2 hourly; 50min); Paris Gare de l'Est (1–2 hourly; 2hr 20min); Rennes (1 daily; 5hr 25min); Sélestat (1–4 hourly; 20min).

**By bus** Eurolines has an office at place de l'Étoile (☎0892 89 90 91). Ouibus (Ⓦouibus.com), which serves destinations in France and neighbouring countries, also stops here. Buses to destinations in Alsace leave from the place des Halles.

## GETTING AROUND

**By tram** While the compact centre can easily be explored on foot, the city boasts an efficient public transport system, which includes six tramlines (€4.50 unlimited 24hr pass; Ⓦcts-strasbourg.fr).

**By boat** Batorama (☎03 69 74 44 04, Ⓦbatorama. com) runs cruises on the Ill, which depart from in front of the Palais Rohan (daily: see website for times). The most popular itinerary takes in La Petite France, the Vauban dam, the European Parliament and the Palais de l'Europe. The trip lasts 1hr 15min and costs €13 (discounts for under-13s).

**By car and motorcycle** There are several car rental firms operating in the main station while Ⓦrhinocarhire.com can

pick the best price among all firms. Although much of the city centre is geared for pedestrian use, there are enough car parks available (Ⓦparcus.com).

**By bicycle** Strasbourg is a very bicycle-friendly city, and its 560km of cycle tracks and routes make bike rental a tempting option. Velhop is at the train station and at 3 rue d'Or (Mon–Fri 8am–7pm, Sat & Sun 9.30am–5.30pm; closed Sun mid-Nov to mid-March; ☎09 69 39 36 67, Ⓦvelhop.strasbourg.eu). The rental stations are open 24/7. All bikes cost €10/day, €150 deposit.

**By taxi** Taxi-13 (☎03 88 36 13 13; Ⓦtaxi13.fr) are available all through the day and night.

## INFORMATION

**Tourist office** The main tourist office is at 17 place de la Cathédrale (daily 9am–7pm; ☎03 88 52 28 28, Ⓦotstrasbourg.fr), and it can provide you with a map

(€1.50 for one with museums and sights marked on it; free otherwise).

**Tourist pass** Depending on your itinerary, it may be worth investing in a Strasbourg Pass (€21.50), which entitles you to one free museum entry, one half-price museum entry, a free boat tour, free access to the cathedral tower and clock and many more reductions; it's valid for three days.

**Markets** Place Broglie hosts a large market of produce and bric-a-brac every Wed and Fri (7am–6pm); there are fruit, vegetable and local produce markets every Tues and Sat am on bd de la Marne and on rue de la Douane on Sat. The flea market is on Wed and Sat (7am–4pm) on rue du Vieil-Hôpital (opposite the Musée Historique).

## ACCOMMODATION

When looking for a place to stay, bear in mind that once a month (except Aug, but twice in Oct) the European Parliament is in session for the best part of a week, bringing hundreds of MEPs and their entourages into town. To find out in advance when the parliament is sitting, check the calendar at ⓦ europarl.europa.eu.

**Camping de Strasbourg** Rue de l'Auberge de Jeunesse ⓣ 03 88 30 19 96, ⓦ camping-strasbourg.com. This smart campsite offers two-bedroom wooden chalets as well as simple pitches for tents. There's a pool on site, plus free wi-fi. Take bus #2 from the train station, direction "Elmerforst", to stop "Camping", or tram B or F from place Homme de Fer to "Montagne Verte" then bus #2 or L1 to "Camping". **€28.50**

**Cathédrale** 12–13 place de la Cathédrale ⓣ 03 88 22 12 12, ⓦ hotel-cathedrale.fr. Bang next to the cathedral, the location of this charming hotel can't be beaten. If you can, fork out for the pricier rooms, which have wonderful cathedral views. **€105**

**Cerf d'Or** 6 place de l'Hôpital ⓣ 03 88 36 20 05, ⓦ cerf-dor-strasbourg.fr. Attractive, family-run place in a sixteenth-century building, with a small swimming pool/sauna and its own restaurant (lunch *menu* €26) serving hearty Alsatian cuisine. Rooms are comfortably furnished, if a bit dark. Breakfast €11. **€98**

★ **Cour du Corbeau** 6–8 rue des Couples ⓣ 03 90 00 26 26, ⓦ cour-corbeau.com. Housed in an exquisite sixteenth-century building with an intricate wooden courtyard and 300-year-old cobbles in the dining room, *Cour du Corbeau* lays claim to being the oldest hotel in Europe, mentioned first in 1538 (although it was a factory between 1854 and 2007). The pale, whitewashed rooms, some with views of the cathedral, are luxurious and spacious and the service is suitably attentive. Breakfast €24. **€160**

**Dragon** 2 rue de l'Écarlate ⓣ 03 88 35 79 80, ⓦ dragon.fr. Painted in a pleasing shade of red ochre, this seventeenth-century house situated near the river has a little cobbled courtyard and comfortable rooms in soothing shades of grey. Buffet breakfast €15. **€92**

**Graffalgar** 17 rue Déserte ⓣ 03 88 24 98 40, ⓦ graffalgar-hotel-strasbourg.com. Each of the 38 rooms in this boutique hotel features a mural painting by a different artist, with additional works available for purchase. The decor is pleasingly minimalist, the staff friendly, and it's just a 3min walk from the train station. There's also a café serving brunch and lunch (Wed–Sat). Breakfast €10. **€100**

**Suisse** 2–4 rue de la Râpe ⓣ 03 88 35 22 11, ⓦ hotel-suisse.com. Friendly hotel in a labyrinthine old house just a stone's throw from the cathedral. It's a superb location, although the rooms (with the exception of the family rooms) are rather cramped. Buffet breakfast €11.90. **€105**

## EATING AND DRINKING

Traffic-free place du Marché-Gayot near the cathedral is one of the best spots for café-life, most of which stay open until 1.30am. In summer, when the sun comes out, the floating cafés and deckchairs along the quai des Pêcheurs make great hangouts. There's a good selection of less touristy restaurants, ranging from upmarket *winstubs* to simple neighbourhood brasseries, along the quai des Pêcheurs and on surrounding streets, such as rue de Zurich and rue de la Krutenau.

### EATING

**1741** 22 quai des Bateliers ⓣ 03 88 35 50 50, ⓦ 1741. fr. Named after the year of completion of the Palais Rohan, which sits opposite, this exquisite restaurant was awarded a Michelin star in 2014, just two years after opening. The interior design is suitably Baroque, with Hermès tableware and Baccarat chandeliers, except on the second floor, where a glass panel looks onto chef Guillaume Scheer's kitchen. Lunch *menus* start at €42, and the inventive cuisine is always exemplary. Mon & Thurs–Sun noon–3pm & 7–10pm.

**Brasserie Les Haras** 23 rue des Glacières ⓣ 03 88 24 00 00, ⓦ les-haras-brasserie.com. Set in the premises of Louis XV's former royal stud farm, this upmarket brasserie has won multiple awards for its stunning design, which includes a horseshoe-shaped open kitchen and a spectacular spiral stair-case leading to a dining area under the original eighteenth-century roof beams. The small, elegant menu was created by Marc Haeberlin of Bergheim's *Auberge de l'Ill* fame (see page 238) and includes an excellent spicy lamb burger (€22), as well as simpler tapas dishes from €8. Daily noon–2pm & 7–10pm.

**Le Buerehiesel** 4 parc de l'Orangerie ⓣ 03 88 45 56 65, ⓦ buerehiesel.fr. Run by Eric Westermann, son of the much-lauded, Michelin-starred chef Antoine Westermann, *Buerehiesel* is housed in a delightful, rustic farmhouse in the Parc de l'Orangerie. It's pricey – *menus* start at €37 for lunch, and à la carte mains hover around the €35–45 mark. Tues–Sat noon–1.30pm & 7.30–9.30pm.

4

## THE WINES OF ALSACE

Despite the long, tall bottles and Germanic names, Alsatian wines are unmistakably French in their ability to complement the region's traditional cuisine. This is white wine country – if you do spot a local red, it will invariably be a Pinot Noir. Winemakers take advantage of the long, dry autumns to pick extremely ripe grapes producing wines with a little more sweetness than elsewhere in France, but good wines will have a refreshing natural acidity, too. Each of the three main grape varieties listed below can be made with a sweetness level ranging from off-dry right through to "*Sélection de Grains Nobles*" for the most highly prized dessert wines (*vendanges tardives* being the label for the slightly less sweet late-harvested wines). Grand Cru labelled wines come from the best vineyard sites.

**Riesling** The ultimate thirst-quencher, limey, often peachy, excellent with fish dishes and *choucroute*.

**Gewurztraminer** Alsace's most aromatic grape, with roses, lychees, honey, spices and all manner of exotic flavours. Try with pungent Munster cheese or rich *pâté*.

**Pinot Gris** Rich, fruity, smoky and more understated than Gewurztraminer. A versatile food wine; try with white meat in creamy sauces and milder cheeses.

Other wines you're likely to come across include the grapey **Muscat**, straightforward **Sylvaner**, and delicate **Pinot Blanc/Auxerrois**, which also forms the base of the region's excellent sparkling **Crémant d'Alsace**. **Pinot Noir** is used for light, fruity reds and rosés.

**La Cloche à Fromage** 27 rue des Tonneliers ☎ 03 88 23 13 19, ⓦ fromagerie-tourrette.com. Don't come here if you don't like cheese: everything on the menu centres around it, from the delicious oven-baked goat's cheese platters (€21.30) to the *raclettes* (from €27.90) and fondues (from €25.90). They also have an excellent cheese shop across the road at no. 32. Tues–Sat noon–2pm & 7–11pm.

**Le Clou** 3 rue du Chaudron ☎ 03 88 32 11 67, ⓦ le-clou.com. Reliable, ever-popular *winstub* close to the cathedral, serving hearty meals such as *choucroute* (€19.90) and *pot-au-feu* (€21.90). Mon–Sat (and Sun in Dec) 11.45am–2pm & 5.30pm–midnight.

★ **La Corde à Linge** 2 place Benjamin-Zix ☎ 03 88 22 15 17, ⓦ lacordealinge.com. Popular brasserie with a prime location in La Petite France. The contemporary interior is decorated with washing lines (*cordes à linge*), while the canal-side terrace is perfect for people-watching. Simple, tasty food includes large salads (from €12), *spaetzle* pasta dishes (€11.50), burgers and meaty Alsatian classics. Daily 11.30am–11pm.

★ **S'Kaechele** 8 rue de l'Argile ☎ 03 88 22 62 36, ⓦ skaechele.com. Of all the city's *winstubs*, that of Alsatian couple Karine and Daniel has gained a reputation as *the* one to visit when in Strasbourg. *Jambonneau, choucroute* (€17.30), *escargots* and plenty of desserts are served in a cosy, half-timbered building where the house wine means wine from its own vineyard. Book in advance. Mon 7–9.30pm, Tues–Fri 11.45am–1.30pm & 7pm–-9.30pm.

### DRINKING AND NIGHTLIFE

**L'Abattoir** 1 quai Charles-Altorffer ☎ 03 88 32 28 12. With its funky lamps, painted black walls and wooden benches, L'Abattoir is a relaxed café-bar. A decent three-course menu (€12.50) is available each day as well as shisha

pipes. There's a lounging area with strange circular beds as well as two outside areas for a drink in the sunshine. Mon–Thurs & Sun 11–1.30am, Fri & Sat until 3.30am.

**Art Café** 1 place Hans-Jean-Arp (inside the Musée d'Art Moderne, see page 231) ☎ 03 88 22 18 88, ⓦ musees.strasbourg.eu. You don't have to get a ticket to the museum to come up to its superb café-restaurant which serves everything from teas and coffees to light snacks. There's a large terrace that looks out over the whole of Strasbourg, perfect for brunch (Sun only; €24). Mon noon–3pm, Tues–Sun 10am–6pm.

**L'Épicerie** 6 rue du Vieux Seigle ☎ 03 88 32 52 41, ⓦ lepicerie-strasbourg.com. This fun café-bar is a reconstructed grocers', with jolly tablecloths, ramshackle wooden furniture and vintage advertisements. It's always packed with people enjoying very reasonably priced *tartines* (open sandwiches), served daily until midnight. *Tartine* with prunes and *fourme d'Ambert* cheese €6.20. Daily 11.30am–1.30am; kitchen closes midnight.

★ **Jeanette et les Cycleux** 30 rue des Tonneliers ☎ 03 88 23 02 71. A biker theme dominates at this trendy little bar that serves a variety of coffees, cocktails, milkshakes and wines. Substantial snacks include local Frankfurter-like "knack" sausages and delicious *planchettes* of cold meat and cheese (from €7). Free alcotests and condoms offered for those who need them. Daily 11.30am–1am.

**Terres à Vin** 1 rue du Miroir ☎ 03 88 51 37 20, ⓦ terresavin.com. Excellent boutique wine shop/bar, brainchild of wine connoisseur Eric Demange, stocking 1600 different wines from high-quality producers around France, with an emphasis on biodynamic wines and *vins naturels*. There's a variety of snacks to accompany your tipple (glass from €3). Mon & Tues 3–10pm, Wed–Sat 10am–11pm, Sun 11am–10pm.

### ENTERTAINMENT

Strasbourg usually has lots going on, particularly when it comes to music. Pick up the free monthly magazine *Spectacles à Strasbourg et alentours* (ⓦspectacles-publications.com) for entertainment info and listings.

**Festivals** There are theatre, dance and musical festivals throughout the summer, with a particular emphasis on classical music in mid-June, jazz in July, and contemporary classical music at the Musica festival (ⓦfestivalmusica.org) from mid-Sept to early Oct. If you happen to be in town in July, August or September, don't miss the impressive illumination of the cathedral facade, accompanied by music (daily July 10.30pm–midnight; Aug 10.15–11.45pm; Sept 9.15–10.15pm).

**Christmas market** During the Marché de Noël (last weekend in Nov to Dec 30), an increasingly commercial event dating back over 400 years, central Strasbourg is taken over by wooden stalls selling mulled wine, crafts of varying quality and spicy Christmas cookies known as *bredele*.

# The Route des Vins

Flanked to the west by the rising forests of the southern Vosges, which stretch all the way down to Belfort, Alsace's picturesque **Route des Vins** ("Wine Route"; ⓦalsace-wine-route.com) follows the foot of the mountains along the western edge of the wide and flat Rhine valley. Beginning in Marlenheim, west of Strasbourg, the route, on or around the D35, snakes its way over 180km to Thann, near Mulhouse, through exquisitely preserved medieval towns and villages characterized by half-timbered houses, narrow cobbled streets and neighbouring ancient ruined castles – testimony to the province's turbulent past. The route is blanketed with neat terraces of vines, which produce the famous white wines (see page 234). Tasting opportunities are plentiful, particularly during the region's countless wine festivals that mainly coincide with the October harvest.

## Obernai

Picturesque little **OBERNAI** on the Strasbourg–Molsheim–Sélestat train line is the first place most people head for when travelling south from Strasbourg. Miraculously unscathed by the last two world wars, Obernai has retained almost its entire **rampart system**, including no fewer than fifteen towers, along with street after street of carefully maintained medieval houses, two Michelin-starred restaurants and three wine producers offering tastings a short stroll away from the centre. True, it gets more than its fair share of visitors, but with good reason.

## Barr and around

Every bit as charming as Obernai, **BARR**, only 6km south, is for some reason overlooked by mass tourism. Still, it is easy to while away a couple of hours wandering its twisting cobbled streets, at their busiest during the lively mid-July **wine festival**, when you can taste over two hundred local wines in the town hall. To break up the wine and the walking, you might like to drop into La Folie Marco (30 rue du Docteur-Sultzer; May–Sept daily except Tues 10am–noon & 2–6pm; Oct Sat & Sun 10am–noon & 2–6pm; €5; ☏ 03 88 08 94 72, ⓦmusee-foliemarco.com), an eighteenth-century mansion on the northern outskirts of town, which has interesting displays of furniture from the Renaissance to the late nineteenth century.

There are several delightful stops south of Barr, such as **Gertwiller** – virtually next door – the world capital of gingerbread-making, where the Palais du Pain d'Épices (114 rte de Strasbourg; mid-Feb to early Jan Mon–Sat 9am–noon & 2–6pm, Sun 10am–noon & 2–6pm; €4; ☏ 03 88 08 04 26, ⓦlepalaisdupaindepices.com) offers an interactive history of the art, plus a visit of the workshop and free tastings; **Mittelbergheim**, a peaches-and-cream cluster of houses lining narrow, undulating

**FOUR FABULOUS ALSACE FORTRESSES**

Alsace is dotted with medieval fortresses, heirlooms from a quarrelsome past. Here's a rundown of the very best castles in the region:

**Bernstein** Explore the marvellous ruins of this castle perched 562m up on a rock overlooking Dambach-la-Ville. It's a 45min walk from the village past the chapel of St-Sébastien or a drive up the D35, turning left at Blienschwiller towards Villé on the D203 and then following the sign to Bernstein on the GR5 until the Schulwaldplatz car park. From there it's a gentle 20min walk uphill through a spruce forest. Free access.

**Haut Koenigsbourg** A massive pile of honey-coloured sandstone that sits astride a 757m bluff, this castle dates from the twelfth century. It was heavily restored in the twentieth century under the tenacious management of Kaiser Wilhelm II and is today one of the most visited monuments in France – try to come midweek or out of season to avoid the crowds. It is a stunning spot with fantastic views on a clear day. Daily: March & Oct 9.30am–5pm; April, May & Sept 9.15am–5.15pm; June, July & Aug 9.15am–6pm; Nov–Feb 9.30am–noon & 1–4.30pm; audio tours available, plus guided tour in English daily June–Sept at 2pm. €9; ☎ 03 69 33 25 00, ⓦ haut-koenigsbourg.fr

**Château Hohlandsbourg** Six kilometres outside Eguisheim, this enormous castle surrounded by massive walls is the largest in the region. It was extensively damaged during the Thirty Years' War but there's still plenty to see, including beautiful gardens. The castle is also a venue for cultural activities, music concerts and children's workshops – check the website for events. July & Aug daily 10am–7pm; April–June Tues–Sat 10am–6pm; Sept Tues–Sat 1–6pm, Sun 10am–6pm; Oct Tues–Sat 1–5pm, Sun 10am–5pm; €7–9.50; ☎ 03 89 30 10 20, ⓦ chateau-hohlandsbourg.com/en.

**Château Kintzheim** Small but wonderful ruined castle built around a cylindrical refuge-tower and located just south of Haut Koenigsbourg (see above). Today Kintzheim is an aviary for birds of prey – the Volerie des Aigles – and puts on magnificent displays of aerial prowess by resident eagles and vultures. Daily: April–June 1.30–6pm; July & Aug 10am–6.30pm; Sept to mid-Nov 1.30–5.30pm. Demonstrations two to five times daily, depending on the period – consult website for times; €9.50 (under-14s €6.50); ☎ 03 88 92 84 33, ⓦ voleriedesaigles.com.

streets; **Andlau**, in the middle of a green ridge with a venerable abbey that dates back to 880 AD; the south-facing **Itterswiller**, which offers some of the best views on the Route des Vins; and the impossibly picturesque **Dambach-la-Ville** where the road enters from one village gate and leaves from the other. The focus in every village is wine, with plenty of opportunities for tastings.

## Bergheim

From Dambach you'll drive through a few medieval villages of varying attractiveness to reach the peaceful walled town of **BERGHEIM**, for many the most beautiful village on the Route des Vins. Just by the car park is one of the most easily accessible Grand Cru Alsatian cellars, that of **Gustave Lorentz**, established in 1836 and still in the same family.

## Hunawihr

**Reintroduction centre** Daily: April–May & Sept–Oct 10am–12.30pm & 1.30–5.30pm; June–July & late Aug 10am–6.30pm; early to late Aug 10am–7pm • Show times are always in the afternoons, check website for times • €10.50 • ☎ 03 89 73 72 62, ⓦ cigogne-loutre.com **Butterfly Garden** Daily: April–Sept 10am–6pm; Oct 10am–5pm • €8 • ☎ 03 89 73 33 33, ⓦ jardinsdespapillons.fr

Around 8km south of Bergheim lies the charming hamlet of **HUNAWIHR**, with its fourteenth-century walled church standing proud amid the green vines. Hunawihr is at the forefront of the Alsatian ecological movement aimed at protecting the stork – the *cigogne* – of the region, and there's a family-friendly **Reintroduction Centre** for them, along with otters, to the east of the village, as well as a Butterfly Garden (Jardins des Papillons). Along with Riquewihr (below), Hunawihr is one of Les Plus Beaux Villages de France (ⓦ france-beautiful-villages.org).

## Riquewihr

**La Tour des Voleurs and Maison de Vigneron** April–Oct 10.30am–1pm & 2–6pm; €5 combined ticket

An exceptionally well-preserved medieval town a couple of kilometres south of Hunawihr, **RIQUEWIHR** has its fair share of visitors but is still a lovely place to stay a night or two. To distract you from the tempting tastings at wine cellars that dot Riquewihr's cobbled streets, there are a few interesting sites including La Tour des Voleurs (Thieves' Tower), complete with torture chamber, and the sixteeenth-century Maison de Vigneron (Winegrower's House) next door.

## Kaysersburg

**Museum** 126 rue du Général-de-Gaulle • 9am–noon & 2–6pm: July & Aug daily; Jan–June & Sept–Nov daily except Wed; Dec Fri–Sun • €2.50 • ☎ 03 89 78 22 78, ⓦ kaysersberg.com

Considered one of the most striking villages on the Route des Vins, **KAYSERSBURG** suffers from a deluge of summertime visitors, thanks to its houses clustered in chocolate-box fashion around the River Weiss and its fortified bridge. Along with a wonderful sixteenth-century altarpiece in its Gothic church, the town's main claim to fame is as the birthplace of Nobel Peace Prize-winner Albert Schweitzer, who founded a leprosy hospital at Lambaréné in French Equatorial Africa. He is honoured with the **Musée du Docteur Schweitzer**. The neighbouring valley offers skiing in winter and a raft of outdoor activities in summer.

### ACCOMMODATION

THE ROUTE DES VINS

**ANDLAU**

**Zinck** 13 rue de la Marne ☎ 03 88 08 27 30, ⓦ zinckhotel. com. This quirky hotel occupies a former corn mill and each room has a different theme, from the 1930s browns and beiges in "Jazzy" to the more traditional "Vigneronne" and the colourful "Pop" suite. Breakfast €11. **€75**

**BARR**

**Le H** 19 rue Docteur-Sultzer ☎ 03 88 58 56 00, ⓦ hotel restauranth.com. Both charming and pleasant from the outside, set in the middle of a large park, *Le H* manages to have a cool, contemporary feel in its rooms inside. The swimming pool is a great draw in the summer months. "Bistronomie" is what it's all about in the restaurant. Breakfast €12. **€125**

**BERGHEIM**

**La Cour du Bailli** 57 Grand'Rue, Bergheim ☎ 03 89 73 73 46, ⓦ cour-bailli.com. A cheerful little place with studios and rooms housed in a charming lavender-coloured building – there's also a rather incongruous, but most welcome, spa. The restaurant, La Cave du Bailli, serves good Alsatian food. Breakfast €11. **€89**

**OBERNAI**

**À la Cour d'Alsace** 3 rue de Gail ☎ 03 88 95 07 00, ⓦ cour-alsace.com. This four-star grand hotel is tucked away next to the rampart walls; it has a pool, garden terrace, a sauna, a Turkish bath, two restaurants, closed parking and some excellent half-board deals. Breakfast €20. **€129**

**La Diligence** 23 place du Marché ☎ 03 88 95 55 69, ⓦ hotel-diligence.com. Slap bang in the centre of town with spotless, neat rooms and geranium-brimming balconies, above a pleasant *salon de thé* (Mon & Wed–Sun 1.30pm–-6.30pm). Buffet breakfast €9.50. **€65**

**Le Gouverneur** 13 rue de Sélestat ☎ 03 88 95 63 72, ⓦ hotellegouverneur.com. A wonderful sixteenth-century building named after Louis XIV's military governor who ensconced himself here when Alsace was conquered by France. It has 32 comfortable and peaceful rooms set around an old horse carriage entrance. Breakfast €9.80. **€65**

**RIQUEWIHR**

**Domaine Jean Sipp** 60 rue de la Fraternité ☎ 03 89 73 60 02, ⓦ jean-sipp.com. The wine-growing Sipp family offer two spacious and comfortable *chambres d'hôtes* in

4

a courtyard by their fifteenth-century home, just a few minutes' walk from the town centre. Breakfast is not provided, but both rooms have a kitchenette and fridge, and there is a private garage. Excellent value. **€80**

### EATING AND DRINKING

#### BERGHEIM

**Auberge de l'Ill** 📞 03 89 71 89 00, 🌐 auberge-de-l-ill. com. A Michelin three-starred restaurant since 1967, this gastronomic institution is the star of Illhaeusern, a small agglomeration of houses south of Bergheim. Behind a traditional, half-timbered facade, the restaurant's decor is a modern medley of camouflage carpet, crystal chandeliers and cream-coloured furniture, while the food and wines are spectacular. Expect a fair dent in your bank account, with dishes starting at €48 and rising to €160 – *menus* are €132 at lunch and €195 at dinner. Wed–Sun noon–2pm & 7–9.30pm.

★ **La Mosaïque** 28 Grand'Rue. Stop by for a bite to eat with the locals in this diminutive café where the *plat du jour* (€8) is excellent value and the house speciality, *matafan* – thick crêpes covered with a bechamel sauce and filled with onions, bacon and cheese – is particularly delicious. Daily 8am–8pm.

#### OBERNAI

**Le Bistrot des Saveurs** 35 rue de Sélestat 📞 03 88 49 90 41, 🌐 bistro-saveurs.fr. One-star Michelin restaurant by chef Thierry Schwartz, with few tables, a small menu with local produce and excellent service; it's notable also for making its own bread. It is generally not busy at lunch during weekdays so reservations might not be necessary. Three-course *menus* start at €59. Tues–Sat 12.15–2pm & 7.15–10pm.

**La Dîme** 5 rue des Pèlerins 📞 03 88 95 54 02, 🌐 ladime-obernai.fr. Busy, popular and very friendly restaurant. Try a Cynar aperitif (beer mixed with artichoke liqueur – full of iron, apparently) before moving onto one of the cheerful *menus*, starting from €19. Noon–2pm & 7–9.30pm; closed Wed.

**La Fourchette des Ducs** 6 rue de la Gare 📞 03 88 48 33 38, 🌐 lafourchettedesducs.com. One of the great restaurants in Alsace under chef Nicolas Stamm, situated very conveniently opposite the station and well worth travelling to from Strasbourg for a meal. Contemporary decor and dishes, but limited hours, so make reservations well in advance. Mains from €68, *menu dégustation* €135 and €170. Tues–Sat 7–9pm & Sun noon–1.30pm.

#### RIQUEWIHR

**La Table du Gourmet** 51 rue de la Première Armée 📞 03 89 49 09 09, 🌐 jlbrendel.com. Chef Jean-Luc Brendel has a monopoly on good food and accommodation in Riquewihr. As well as this Michelin-starred restaurant (three-course lunch €38), he also has a more reasonably priced *winstub*, Brendelstub (three-course menus from €20.50), along with five-star hotel rooms (B.Suites), a self-catering cottage (B.Cottage) and a hip vintage guesthouse (B.Vintage). Mon & Fri–Sun 12.15pm–1.30pm & 7.15–9. pm, Wed & Thurs 7.15–9pm.

# Colmar and around

The old centre of **COLMAR**, a thirty-minute train ride south of Strasbourg and lying east of the main Route des Vins villages, is *echt* Alsatian, with crooked half-timbered and painted houses. Its small canals and picturesque narrow streets are a flaneur's paradise. This is prime Elsässisch-speaking country, a German dialect known to philologists as Alemannic, which has waxed and waned during the province's chequered history. As the proud home of Mathias Grünewald's magnificent Issenheim altarpiece, the town is a magnet for tourists all year round.

## Musée d'Unterlinden

1 rue d'Unterlinden • Mon & Wed–Sun 9am–6pm • €13 • 🌐 musee-unterlinden.com

Colmar's foremost attraction, the **Musée d'Unterlinden** is an even richer experience after a lengthy period of renovation and extension. The core of the collection is housed in a former Dominican convent with a peaceful cloistered garden; it includes the museum's biggest draw, the **Issenheim altarpiece**, which is thought to have been made between 1512 and 1516 for the monastic order of St Anthony at Issenheim, whose members cared for those afflicted by ergotism and other nasty skin diseases. The extraordinary painted panels are the work of

Mathias Grünewald (1480–1528). The luridly expressive centre panel depicts the Crucifixion: a tortured Christ turns his outsize hands upwards, fingers splayed in pain, flanked by his pale, fainting mother and saints John and Mary Magdalene. The face of St Sebastian, on the right wing, is believed to have been modelled on Grünewald's own likeness. The reverse panels depict the annunciation, Christ's resurrection, the nativity and a flamboyant orchestra of angels, all splendidly bathed in transcendental light. On the rest of the panels, you'll find a truly disturbing representation of the temptation of St Anthony, who is engulfed by a pack of demons; note the figure afflicted with the alarming symptoms of ergotism. The renovated convent is now linked via an underground gallery of nineteenth- and early twentieth-century art to a brand-new wing, which houses modern and contemporary works, and to the town's former municipal baths, re-imagined as a venue for cultural events. Highlights include Impressionist paintings by Monet and Bonnard, plus a couple of Picassos. There's also a nice café-restaurant here.

## Dominican church and the Collégiale St-Martin

**Church** April–Nov daily 10am–1pm & 3–6pm • €1.50 **Collégiale St-Martin** Mon–Sat 8am–6.30pm, Sun 2–6.30pm • Free

The austere **Dominican church** on rue des Serruriers has some fine glass and a beautiful altarpiece known as *The Virgin in a Bower of Roses*, painted in 1473 by Schongauer. At the other end of the street you reach the **Collégiale St-Martin** on a busy café-lined square. It's known locally as "the cathedral" because for a short period it served as one; peek in to see its stonework and stained glass. The sixteenth-century **Maison Pfister**, with external painted panels, is on the south side of the church.

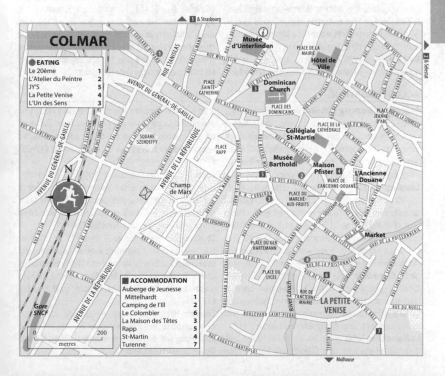

## Musée Bartholdi

30 rue des Marchands • March–Dec daily except Tues 10am–noon & 2–6pm; closed public hols • €6 • ⓦ musee-bartholdi.com

Frédéric Auguste Bartholdi, the sculptor of New York's Statue of Liberty, was born at 30 rue des Marchands, which now houses the **Musée Bartholdi**. It contains Bartholdi's personal effects and the original designs for the statue, along with 1870s memorabilia and scale models of his greatest works.

## Ancienne Douane and La Petite Venise

Rue des Marchands continues south to the **Ancienne Douane** or Koïfhus, its gaily painted roof tiles loudly proclaiming the town's medieval prosperity. This is the heart of Colmar's old town, a short step away from the canal quarter down the Grand'Rue known as **La Petite Venise** (Little Venice). The dolly-mixture colours of the old fishing cottages on quai de la Poissonnerie contrast with the much taller, black-and-white, half-timbered tanners' houses on **rue des Tanneurs**, which leads off from the Koïfhus.

### ARRIVAL AND INFORMATION COLMAR

**By train** The *gare SNCF* is a 10min walk south east from the centre of town, along avenue de la République.
Destinations Mulhouse (1–2 hourly; 20min); Munster (1 hourly; 30min); Sélestat (1–3 hourly; 10–12min);

Strasbourg (2–3 hourly; 30min).
**Tourist office** Place Unterlinden (Mon–Sat 9am–6pm; Sun 10am–1pm,during Christmas markets 10am–1pm & 2–5pm;ⓣ03 89 20 68 92, ⓦ tourisme-colmar.com).

### GETTING AROUND

**Boat trips** You can get up close to the charming half-timbered houses in La Petite Venise by taking a peaceful boat trip with Sweet Narcisse (March–Oct daily 10am–6.30pm;Jan, Feb & Nov contact for times; €6; ⓣ03 89 41 01 94, ⓦ sweetnarcisse.com), which has a 30min commentary, from 10 rue de la Herse; English is spoken.
**By bike** Colmar Vélo Vélodocteurs, 9 place de la Gare (April–Oct Mon–Fri 8am–noon & 2–7pm, Sat & Sun 9am–

7pm; Nov–March Mon–Fri 8am–noon & 2–6pm, Sat & Sun 9am–noon & 2–6pm; €6/half-day, €8/day, €15/2 days and €40/week; ⓣ03 89 41 37 90, ⓦ velodocteurs.com).
**By car** Colmar has a one-way system around the town which is not easy to manage. Hotels in the centre do not often offer parking and rates are high. There's free parking at the train station and, also, Manufacture in the north of the town and Montagne Verte to the east.

### ACCOMMODATION

**Auberge de Jeunesse Mittelhardt** 2 rue Pasteur ⓣ03 89 80 57 39, ⓦ colmar.fr/auberge-jeunesse. The town's only youth hostel is perfectly adequate but gets extremely busy in summer. It's 1km from town (15 min walk); take bus #2 to stop "Pont Rouge" or #6 to "Auberge de Jeunesse". Breakfast €6. Dorms (up to 9 beds), family and single rooms. **€12.50**
**Camping de l'Ill** 1 allée du Camping ⓣ03 89 41 15 94, ⓦ campingdelill.fr. Inexpensive but excellent campsite 2km east of Colmar by the river Ill. It offers a pool, wi-fi and bike rental. Take bus #1 from the station, direction "Horbourg-Wihr/Pommier", stop "Camping de l'Ill", or bus #20 direction "Fortschwihr" or bus #21 direction "Andolsheim Primevères". Closed Jan–March. **€21.20**
★ **Le Colombier** 7 rue Turenne ⓣ03 89 23 96 00, ⓦ hotel-le-colombier.fr. Colmar's best-known boutique hotel in the heart of the Petite Venise quarter. Modern rooms are swathed in cool lavender tones and back onto a calm internal courtyard. Large family suites available, too. **€126**
**La Maison des Têtes** 19 rue des Têtes ⓣ03 89 24 43 43, ⓦ la-maison-des-tetes.com. Colmar's only five-star hotel

is set in a well-appointed seventeenth-century house with a wonderful facade covered in grimacing faces. The rooms are clad in wood panelling, and there's a Michelin-starred restaurant downstairs (mains €42–68, breakfast €19–23). **€190**
**Rapp** 1–5 rue Weineimer ⓣ03 89 41 62 10, ⓦ rapp-hotel.com. Central three-star hotel with rooms rather on the small side but with a great swimming pool and sauna in the basement. Traditional restaurant on the ground floor with a good choice of wines. Breakfast €14. **€113**
**St-Martin** 38 Grand'Rue ⓣ03 89 24 11 51, ⓦ hotel-saint-martin.com. A riot of flowery wallpaper, flounces and painted headboards, for those who like the Renaissance style of decoration. In the shadow of the cathedral, the hotel couldn't be more central yet it's remarkably quiet. Breakfast €12. **€75**
**Turenne** 10 rte de Bâle ⓣ03 89 21 58 58, ⓦ turenne.com. Functional, multicoloured rooms in a jolly little hotel, overflowing with balcony geraniums in the heart of Petite Venise. Breakfast €10. **€65**

## EATING AND DRINKING

**Le 20ème** 2 rue Edouard-Richard ☎ 03 89 24 00 00, ⓦle20emecolmar.com. Top-quality, good-value French cuisine is on the menu at this stylish bistro with high ceilings and pale blue walls. There's also a decent wine list with plenty of local varieties to try. Lunch menu €16.50. Tues–Sat noon–1.30pm & 7–9.30pm.

**L'Atelier du Peintre** 1 rue Schongauer ☎ 03 89 29 51 57, ⓦatelier-peintre.fr. French contemporary cuisine that finally earned chef Lefèbvre a Michelin star in 2011. It is all served up in an attractive authentic ambience, all lime green and distressed wood, with some tables alfresco. Wide range of menus from €30 to €89, while à la carte dishes hover around €37. Tues 7–9.30pm, Wed–Sat noon–2pm & 7–9.30pm.

★ **JY'S** 17 rue de la Poissonnerie ☎ 03 89 21 53 60, ⓦjean-yves-schillinger.com. Sitting by the canal and with a lovely outdoor terrace, this is one of the top gastronomic restaurants in Colmar thanks to two Michelin stars. Inside, the decor is cool and contemporary, and the food simply sublime. *Menus* start at €49 (lunch) and €82 (dinner). Tues–Sat noon–1.45pm & 7–9.30pm.

**La Petite Venise** 4 rue de la Poissonnerie ☎ 03 89 41 72 59, ⓦrestaurantpetitevenise.com. It's like eating dinner in an old Alsatian house in this charming *winstub*: pots and pans, wooden benches and even an old oven adorn the interior. Alsatian classics prevail, with a three-course menu around €29. Mon–Tues & Fri–Sat noon 2pm & 7–9.30pm, Wed–Thurs & Sun 7–9.30pm; closed Wed off season.

**L'Un des Sens** 18 rue Berthe-Molly ☎ 03 89 24 04 37, ⓦcave-lun-des-sens.fr. Excellent *cave à vins*, where you can taste a wide range of wines and nibble on plates of cold meat and cheese (€7–24). Buy the wines you liked at the front from the boutique. Tues–Fri 5–10pm, Sat 11–3pm & 5–10pm.

# Sélestat

Less touristy and much larger than the pretty little villages that surround it, **SÉLESTAT** has nevertheless an interesting centre to amble around in. It's worth dropping into the town's two churches, the romanesque **Ste-Foy**, much restored since its construction by the monks of Conques and, close by, the attractive Gothic **St-Georges**, which sports spectacularly multicoloured roof tiles and some very beautiful stained glass. For a brief period in the late fifteenth and early sixteenth centuries, Sélestat was the intellectual centre of Alsace; its Latin School attracted a group of humanists led by Beatus Rhenanus, whose personal library was one of the most impressive collections of its time. Rhenanus' library is displayed in the **Bibliothèque Humaniste** (Humanist Library; 1 place Dr Maurice-Kubler; Tues–Sun May–Sept & Dec 10am–12.30pm & 1.30–6pm; Feb–April & Oct–Nov 1.30–5.30pm; €6; ☎ 03 88 58 07 20, ⓦbibliotheque-humaniste.fr), housed in the town's former corn exchange. Reopened in 2018 after three years of renovation and a redesign by Rudy Ricciotti, the modernized library displays Rhenanus' humanist texts alongside rare books and manuscripts dating back to the seventh century, including the 1507 *Cosmographiae Introductio*, the first document ever to use the word "America".

## EATING AND DRINKING                                                  SÉLESTAT

★ **L'Acoustic** 5 place du Marché Vert ☎ 03 88 92 29 40, ⓦrestobiolacoustic.com. A dinky organic café-bar just by the church of Ste-Foy, which serves tasty snacks and main meals – *plats* around €9, lunch *menu* €13; look out for the occasional amateur performances on weekends, ranging from jazz and classical concerts to comedy and drama (*menu* €22 for three courses, plus small fee for the show). Mon–Thurs noon–3pm, Fri & Sat noon–3pm & 7–10pm, Sun 10am–5pm.

# Munster

Some 19km west of Colmar, and accessible by train, the peaceful town of **MUNSTER** owes its existence and its name to a band of Irish monks who founded a successful monastery (monasterium = Munster) here in the seventh century. Today its name is associated with a rich, creamy and exceedingly smelly **cheese**, the crowning glory of many an Alsatian pretzel – or even meal. Overlooked by Le Petit Ballon (1272m) and

---

**THE ROUTE DES CRÊTES**

Above Munster, the main road west to the lakeside town of Gérardmer crosses the mountains by the principal pass, the Col de la Schlucht, where it intersects the "**Route des Crêtes**" (Crest Road), which was built for strategic purposes during World War I to facilitate the movement of munitions and supplies. It's a spectacular road traversing thick forest and open pasture, and in winter it becomes one long cross-country ski route. Starting in Cernay, 15km west of Mulhouse, it follows the main ridge of the Vosges, including the highest peak of the range, the **Grand Ballon** (1424m), north as far as Ste-Marie-aux-Mines, 20km west of Sélestat; a great experience especially if you are travelling on a motorbike. From Munster it's also accessible by a twisting minor road through Hohrodberg, which takes you past beautiful glacial lakes and the eerie World War I battlefield of Linge, where the French and German trenches, once separated by just a few metres, are still clearly visible; there is a small museum nearby (🌐linge1915.com).

---

Le Hohneck (1363m), among the highest peaks of the Vosges, the town itself is not as picturesque as the wine villages further east but nevertheless makes a pleasant day-trip from Colmar.

# Mulhouse

A large, sprawling, industrial city 35km south of Colmar, **MULHOUSE** was Swiss until 1798 when, at the peak of its prosperity (founded on printed textiles), it voted to become part of France. Today it bills itself as a "museum town", with at least four that might grab your interest. It's much cheaper to stay here than in neighbouring Colmar (or Basel), plus it offers the best nightlife in Alsace should you find yourself there over a weekend. Also, the thrice-weekly market (Tues, Thurs & Sat) is the largest in the north east. The *hôtel de ville* on the central place de la Réunion contains a beautifully presented history of the city in the **Musée Historique** (Mon & Thurs–Sun Jan–June & Sept–Dec 1–6.30pm; July & Aug 10am–noon & 1–6.30pm; free). The Neo-Gothic cathedral opposite the museum was built in 1866, replacing a twelfth-century church, yet its fourteenth-century stained glass is considered the most beautiful in the Upper Rhine; this is the only Protestant cathedral standing in a main square in France.

## Écomusée d'Alsace

Chemin Grosswald, Ungersheim • April–Oct Tues–Sun 10am–6pm; June–Aug daily 10am–6pm; Dec Tues–Sun 10.30am–6.30pm • €15; family with two children €46 • 🌐 ecomusee.alsace/en

Around 18km outside Mulhouse is the **Écomusée d'Alsace**, a successful reconstruction of a typical early twentieth-century Alsatian village – the seventy or so half-timbered huts were dismantled from elsewhere in the region and rebuilt in fields here, using Alsatian building methods. You could easily spend a couple of hours here, wandering at will around the farmyard and stables – complete with farm animals – pottery, school, bakery, ironmongers and buzzing apiary. There's even a barber, where brave souls can treat themselves to a shave and haircut *à l'alsacienne*. Enthusiastic staff dressed in traditional Alsatian garb – white aprons, ribboned headdresses and the like – are on site to help explain the ins and outs of the history. Throughout the year, usually at weekends, there are festivals and various workshops, ranging from pottery to stonemasonry. On weekends and

public holidays from May to August, it is possible to take a shuttle from Mulhouse train station (leaves 10.15am and returns 5.30pm; 30min) to the Écomusée (€1.50, €4.60 family ticket). Driving remains the simplest option, with the route well signposted.

## Cité de l'Automobile, Musée National-Collection Schlumpf

15 rue de l'Épée • Daily: April–Oct 10am–6pm; Nov–Dec & early Feb to March 10am–5pm; Jan to early Feb Mon–Fri 1–5pm, Sat & Sun 10am–5pm • €14 • Free audioguide in English and free app guide available for download in museum • Take tram #1 from *gare SNCF* to stop "Musée de l'Auto" • ⓦ citedelautomobile.com

A couple of tram stops north of Mulhouse's city centre, the **Cité de l'Automobile**, **Musée National-Collection Schlumpf**, houses an overwhelming collection of more than six hundred cars, originally belonging to local brothers Hans and Fritz Schlumpf, who made their fortunes running a nearby spinning mill. Lined up in endless rows, the impeccably preserved vehicles range from the industry's earliest attempts, such as the extraordinary wooden-wheeled Jacquot steam "car" of 1878, and the very first attempt at an environmentally friendly, solar-powered car made in 1942 to the 1968 Porsche racers. The highlights are the locally made Bugatti models: dozens of alluringly displayed, glorious racing cars, coupés and limousines, the pride of them being the two Bugatti Royales, out of only seven that were constructed. There's also a Veyron, one of the most expensive Bugattis in the world.

## Cité du Train

2 rue Alfred-de-Glehn • Daily: April–Oct 10am–6pm; Nov–March 10am–5pm • €12 • Free audioguide in English and free app guide on website • Take tram #3 from *gare SNCF* to stop "Musées" • ⓦ citedutrain.com

Several tram stops to the west of the town centre is the multicoloured, corrugated-iron building that houses the city's fantastic train museum; it's Europe's largest train museum, in fact. Slick and interactive, the Cité has impressive railway rolling stock on display, covering everything from the earliest 1840s locomotives to the latest TGV. A small train (what else?) transports you around a new outdoor part of the museum, where you can view modern-day engines in action.

## Musée de l'Impression sur Étoffes

14 rue Jean-Jacques-Henner • Tues–Sun 10am–noon & 2–6pm • €10 • ⓦ musee-impression.com

The wallpaper and textile museum, which is close to the *gare SNCF*, is rather more fun than the name would suggest. Mostly displayed in temporary exhibitions, the museum's vast collection of sumptuous fabrics includes the eighteenth-century Indian and Persian imports that revolutionized the European ready-to-wear market and made Mulhouse a prosperous manufacturing centre. It's worth trying to coincide with one of the daily demonstrations of fabric printing (consult the website).

### ARRIVAL AND DEPARTURE                                                     MULHOUSE

**By air** The international airport (ⓦ euroairport.com) Basel-Mulhouse-Freiburg is 30min by car outside Mulhouse (still in France, but near the Swiss/German border). Take the shuttle bus to the train station in St Louis and change onto a train there. It is a 15min nonstop ride to the *gare SNCF*.
**By train** The main square, place de la Réunion, is a 5min

walk north of the *gare SNCF*. It is a terminus for the TGV.
Destinations Colmar (4 hourly; 20min); Lyon (12 daily; 2hr 50min); Marseille (9 daily; 4hr 40min); Paris Gare de Lyon (10 daily; 2hr 40min); Sélestat (1–3 hourly; 30min); Strasbourg (1–2 hourly; 50min).

### INFORMATION

**Tourist office** 1 av Robert-Schuman (Jan–June & Sept–Dec Mon–Sat 10am–1pm & 2–6pm, Sun 10am–3pm;

July–Aug Mon–Sat 9.30am–6.30pm, Sun 10am–3pm; ☎ 03 89 35 48 48, ⓦ tourisme-mulhouse.com). The three-day ticket City Pass (€18) is valid for all public transport, a free visit to one museum and to others at a reduced rate, plus other reductions. Free city guide apps in English are available for download on the website.

## ACCOMMODATION

★ **Kyriad** 15 rue Lambert ☎ 03 89 66 44 77, ⍟ kyriad. com. Good-value hotel in the middle of the shopping area that's comfortable and modern, with little touches that make a big difference: own lift to (public) parking below, safe, fast wi-fi, Turkish bath and fitness room, varied buffet breakfast (€10). Worth checking out its occasional special offers (around €50 for a double). **€75**

## EATING

**Chez Auguste** 11 rue Poincaré ☎ 03 89 46 62 71, ⍟ chezauguste.com. Arguably the best restaurant in town, Chez Auguste is the place to go for refined cooking at a reasonable price. Chef Luc Chervy serves up traditional French dishes in a contemporary dining room, with steak at €15 and a selection of cheeses for €6. Tues–Sat noon–2pm & 7–9pm until late.

**Zum Saüwadala** 13 rue de l'Arsenal ☎ 03 89 45 18 19. This name of this popular *winstub* means "little pig's tail" so expect a good selection of hearty pork dishes on the menu (mains from €13). The traditional, cosy restaurant has its fair share of celebrity fans (including former French president François Hollande), who must have big appetites as the portions are huge. Mon–Sat noon–2pm & 7–9pm.

## DRINKING AND NIGHTLIFE

**Le Gambrinus** 5 rue des Franciscains ☎ 03 89 36 96 75, ⍟ legambrinus.com. Lively nocturnal hangout that hosts regular events and concerts, with works from local artists displayed on its red brick walls. Salads and *tarte flambée* are available until midnight on weekends, and there is a great choice of beers on tap. Mon–Sat 5pm–1am.

**La Quille** 10 rue de la Moselle ☎ 03 89 44 41 30. This stylish wine bar has more than 500 bottles on its list, including an excellent selection of Alsatian wines. If you want to make a make a night of it, they have platters of cheese and charcuterie to munch on for about €19. Mon–Sat 6pm until late.

# Nancy

The city of **NANCY**, on the River Meurthe, is renowned for the magnificent place Stanislas, cited as a paragon of eighteenth-century urban planning and one of the finest in France; it's a UNESCO World Heritage Site. For its spectacularly grand centre, Nancy has the last of the independent dukes of Lorraine to thank: the dethroned king of Poland and father-in-law of Louis XV, Stanislas Leszczynski. During the twenty-odd years of his office in the mid-eighteenth century, he ordered some of the most successful construction of the period in all France. The city is also home to some impressive examples of Art Nouveau furniture and glassware hailing from the days of the **École de Nancy**, founded at the end of the nineteenth century by glass-master and furniture-maker, Émile Gallé.

## Place Stanislas and around

From the *gare SNCF*, walk through **Porte Stanislas**, straight down rue Stanislas to reach the Rococo **place Stanislas**. Both this gate and Porte St-Catherine opposite are meticulously aligned with place Stanislas's solitary statue – that of the portly **Stanislas Leszczynski**, who commissioned architect Emmanuel Héré to design the square in the 1750s. On the south side of the square stands the imposing **hôtel de ville**, its roof topped by a balustrade ornamented with florid urns and winged cupids. Along its walls, lozenge-shaped lanterns dangle from the beaks of gilded cockerels; similar motifs adorn the other buildings on the square – look out for the fake, two-dimensional replacements. The square's entrances are enclosed by magnificent wrought-iron gates; the impressive railings on the northern corners frame fountains dominated by statues of Neptune and Amphitrite.

## Musée des Beaux-Arts

Place Stanislas · Daily except Tues 10am–6pm; closed public hols · €7, · ⓦ mban.nancy.fr

Set in the corner where rue Stanislas joins the square, the **Musée des Beaux-Arts** presents some excellent nineteenth- and twentieth-century French art, including a number of beautiful paintings by Émile Friant and Nancy's own Victor Prouvé. The layout of the basement – where works from Nancy's glass company, Daum, are beautifully lit – follows the shape of fortifications constructed from the fifteenth century through to Vauban's seventeenth-century alterations, discovered during the museum's 1990s renovation. For a glimpse of Daum's contemporary creations you can visit their shop on place Stanislas.

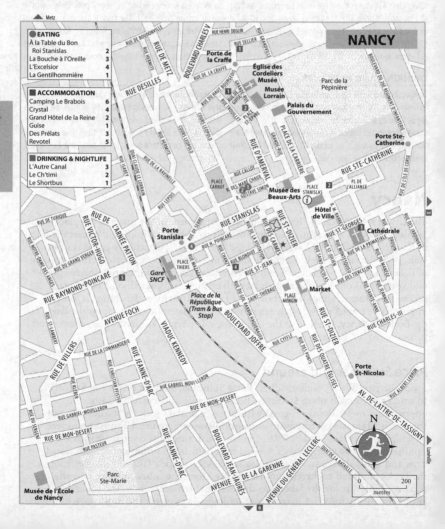

**NANCY**

**EATING**

| À la Table du Bon | |
| --- | --- |
| Roi Stanislas | 2 |
| La Bouche à l'Oreille | 3 |
| L'Excelsior | 4 |
| La Gentilhommière | 1 |

**ACCOMMODATION**

| Camping Le Brabois | 6 |
| --- | --- |
| Crystal | 4 |
| Grand Hôtel de la Reine | 2 |
| Guise | 1 |
| Des Prélats | 3 |
| Revotel | 5 |

**DRINKING & NIGHTLIFE**

| L'Autre Canal | 3 |
| --- | --- |
| Le Ch'timi | 2 |
| Le Shortbus | 1 |

4

---

### STANISLAS LESZCZYNSKI

**Stanislas Leszczynski**, born in the Polish–Ukrainian city of Lemberg (now Lviv) in 1677, lasted just five years as the king of Poland before being forced into exile by Tsar Peter the Great. For the next twenty-odd years he lived on a French pension in northern Alsace, but after fifteen years Stanislas's luck changed when he managed, against all odds, to get his daughter, Marie, betrothed to the 15-year-old king of France, **Louis XV**. Marie was not so fortunate: married by proxy in Strasbourg cathedral, having never set eyes on the groom, she went on to give birth to ten children, only to be rejected by Louis, who preferred the company of his mistresses, Madame de Pompadour and Madame du Barry. Bolstered by his daughter's marriage, Stanislas had another spell on the Polish throne from 1733 to 1736, but gave it up in favour of the comfortable dukedom of Barr and Lorraine. He lived out his final years in aristocratic style in the capital, Nancy, which he transformed into one of France's most beautiful towns.

## Musée Lorrain

64 Grande-Rue • Closed for renovation until 2023 • ⓦ musee-lorrain.nancy.fr

On its north side, place Stanislas opens into the long, tree-lined **place de la Carrière**. Its far end is enclosed by the classical colonnades of the **Palais du Gouvernement**, former residence of the governor of Lorraine. Behind it, housed in the fifteenth-century Palais Ducal, is the **Musée Lorrain**. It displays local treasures – pottery, sculptures, Renaissance painting – along with a worthwhile annexe showing off a collection of Gallo-Roman skeletons found in the Lorraine region. Back in the main building, don't miss the superb etchings by Nancy-born artist, Jacques Callot, whose concern with social issues, evident in series such as *The Miseries of War*, presaged much nineteenth- and twentieth-century art. Some of the highlights of the collection will be on show at the Musée des Beaux-Arts while the museum is being renovated.

## Musée des Cordeliers

64 Grande-Rue • Tues–Sun 10am–12.30pm & 2–6pm; closed public hols • Free • ⓦ musee-lorrain.nancy.fr

Next to the Musée Lorrain, in the Église des Cordeliers et Chapelle Ducale, is the **Musée des Cordeliers**, which illustrates the history of rural life in the region. You can access the church and adjacent octagonal chapel, which contain a few tombs belonging to various dukes of Lorraine. While the Musée Lorrain is undergoing renovation, an exhibition on the dukes is being held here. As a descendant of these nobles, Prince Otto von Habsburg (1912–2011) claimed the right to marry in the chapel in 1951 (and celebrate his golden jubilee in 2001). On the other side of the Palais du Gouvernement, the attractive **Parc de la Pépinière** contains a free zoo with resident macaque monkeys, ponies and a few sheep.

## Muséum Aquarium de Nancy

34 rue Ste-Catherine • Tues–Sun 9am–noon & 2–6pm • €5 • ⓦ museumaquariumdenancy.eu

Heading east towards the river from place Stanislas, you arrive at the **Muséum Aquarium de Nancy**, a great place to change register and while away an hour or so. Housed in a 1930s Art Deco building, the museum contains 57 aquariums inhabited by more than three hundred species of tropical and marine fish. Look out for the camouflaged Amazonian leaf fish, colourful frogfish and 2m-long electric eels. The usually informative temporary exhibitions are signed in English.

## Musée de l'École de Nancy

36–38 rue du Sergent-Blandan • Wed–Sun 10am–6pm • €6 • ⓦ ecole-de-nancy.com • Bus #7 or #8; stop "Nancy-Thermal"

A half-hour walk or a ten-minute bus ride southwest of the train station, the **Musée de l'École de Nancy** is housed in a 1909 villa built for the Corbin family, founders of the Magasins Réunis department stores. Even if you're not into Art Nouveau, this collection is exciting. The furniture is outstanding – all swirling curvilinear forms – and there's some extraordinary glassware by Émile Gallé, whose expressive naturalistic motifs and experimental techniques brought him international recognition. Some of Gallé's marquetry and furniture is also on display – look out for the stunning *Aube et Crépuscule* (*Dawn and Dusk*) bed, with its curvaceous headboard and exotic moths, inlaid with mother-of-pearl. While you're in town, you should also go and check out the newly restored facade of the **Villa Majorelle**, Nancy's Art Nouveau masterpiece (1 rue Louis-Majorelle). However, its interior is closed for renovation until the end of 2019.

## ARRIVAL AND INFORMATION                                    NANCY

**By train** The *gare SNCF* is near the town centre, a 15min walk west of place Stanislas.

Destinations Metz (2–4 hourly; 40min); Paris-Est (1 hourly; TGV; 1hr 30min); Strasbourg via Saverne (1 hourly; 1hr 25min).

**By bus** For bus and tram timetables and tickets, head to the STAN information centre, just around the corner from the *gare SNCF* at place de la République (Mon–Sat 7am–7pm;

w reseau-stan.com). The square is Nancy's main public transport hub.

**Tourist office** South side of place Stanislas in the *hôtel de ville* (April Mon–Sat 10am–6pm, Sun 10am–5pm; May–Oct Mon–Sat 9.30am–6.30pm, Sun 10am–5pm; Nov–March Mon–Wed & Fri–Sat 10am–6pm, Thurs 1–6pm, Sun 10am–1pm; ☎ 03 83 35 22 41, w nancy-tourisme.fr).

## ACCOMMODATION

**Camping Le Brabois** Av Paul-Muller ☎ 03 83 27 18 28, w campeole.com. Set in a large park near the hippodrome (racecourse), this campsite has a restaurant, sports facilities and free wi-fi. It's a basic site so ideal for a night or two. Bus #6 or #16 direction "Villers Clairlieu", stop "Camping". April to mid-Oct. Reception 8am–12.30pm & 2–9pm; July–Aug 7.30am–10pm. **€12.80**

**Crystal** 5 rue Chanzy ☎ 03 83 17 54 00, w bestwestern-hotel-crystal.com. Modern, no-nonsense three-star hotel with spotless large rooms decorated with brown and purple furnishings, comfortable beds, flat LSD TVs, private parking and easy-to-use wi-fi connection. Excellent weekend deals. The huge buffet breakfast is a steal at €14. **€68**

★ **Grand Hôtel de la Reine** 2 place Stanislas ☎ 03 83 35 03 01, w hoteldelareine.com. The grandest hotel in Nancy is surprisingly affordable. Marie Antoinette stayed here en route from Vienna to Paris and the service is as regal

as it was then. Breakfast €16. **€125**

★ **Guise** 18 rue de Guise, just off Grande-Rue ☎ 03 83 32 24 68, w hoteldeguise.com. An eighteenth-century seigneurial residence, atmospherically furnished with antiques and tucked away on a quiet side street off the lively, restaurant-lined Grande-Rue. Breakfast €10.50. **€80**

**Des Prélats** 56 place du Monseigneur-Ruch ☎ 03 83 30 20 20, w hoteldesprelats.com. Attractive, classic rooms in a light and airy seventeenth-century house. Breakfast (€12.90) is served in the elegant conservatory. **€97**

**Revotel** 43 rue Raymond-Poincaré ☎ 03 83 28 02 13, w revotel-hotel.com. Just a 5min walk from the train station, this is a smartly decorated two-star with budget prices. The rooms are small, but they all come with flat-screen TV and free wi-fi. The private car park is an additional €4 per night. Buffet breakfast €7.50. **€60**

## EATING AND DRINKING

There's a cluster of restaurants along and around the Grande-Rue, the rue des Maréchaux and the rue des Ponts, although some of those on the rue des Ports cater primarily to tourists. The cafés on place Stanislas are good for a drink and make great people-watching points. At night, head up the Grande-Rue towards place St-Epvre with its various lively bars.

### EATING

**À la Table du Bon Roi Stanislas** 7 rue Gustave-Simon ☎ 03 83 35 36 52. This unique restaurant allows

diners to try the Polish and Alsatian dishes that King Stanislas would have enjoyed, such as *pierogi* (dumplings) for starters and *Baba au Vin de Tokaji* for dessert. There's also a good selection of regional wine and beer. *Menus* from €20. Tues & Thurs–Sun 12.15–1.30pm, Mon–Sat 7.15–9.30pm.

**La Bouche à l'Oreille** 42 rue des Carmes ☎ 03 83 35 17 17. Hearty Alsatian and Savoyard food using lots of cheese is on offer in this adorable restaurant that's covered ceiling to floor in knick-knacks. *Tartiflette*, omelettes and fondue are on the large and varied menu (from €11.50). There's another slightly less festooned branch at 17 rue Stanislas (☎03 83 37 22 87). Both Mon 7–10pm, Tues–Thurs noon–1.30pm & 7–10pm, Fri noon–1.30pm & 7–10.30pm, Sat 7–10.30pm.

★ **L'Excelsior** 50 rue Henri-Poincaré ☎03 83 35 24 57, ⓦbrasserie-excelsior-nancy.fr. A lively 1911 Art Nouveau brasserie worth visiting for the grandeur of the interior alone; now part of the *Flo* brasserie chain but managing to retain its good classic food (mains from €17.90). Mon & Sun 8am–11pm, Tues–Sat 8am–12.30am.

**La Gentilhommière** 29 rue des Maréchaux ☎03 83 32 26 44, ⓦlagentilhommierenancy.fr. By far the trendiest establishment on this street of restaurants, with a busy terrace and generous portions, specializing in fish. Set *menus* at €26 and €40. Mon–Thurs noon–1.30pm & 7–9.30pm, Fri noon–1.30pm & 7–10pm, Sat 7–10pm.

**DRINKING AND NIGHTLIFE**

**L'Autre Canal** 45 bd d'Austrasie ☎03 83 38 44 88, ⓦlautrecanalnancy.fr. The main live venue for bands that are not quite stadium material, as well as an outlet for rap artists and electronica DJs from all over Europe. Prices and times vary.

**Le Ch'timi** 17 place St-Epvre ☎03 83 32 82 76. An institution in Nancy for thirty years under the stewardship of the formidable Natalie, offering sixteen beers on tap, 200 bottled ones and numerous beer cocktails. Mon 10am–1am, Tues–Fri 10am–2am, Sat 9.30am–2am, Sun 9.30am–9pm.

**Le Shortbus** 2 ter rue de la Citadelle (behind Porte de la Graffe) ☎03 83 39 04 49, ⓦshortbus.fr. Gay bar embraced by the mainstream student population. Packed to the rafters, loud and youthful, with a DJ spinning the decks after 10pm. Beers from €3. Wed–Sat 6pm–2am.

# Metz

**METZ** (pronounced "Mess"), the capital of Lorraine, lies on the east bank of the River Moselle, close to the autoroute de l'Est linking Paris and Strasbourg. Today the city has another connection to the capital in the much-lauded satellite branch of the Centre Pompidou. Along with its rather splendid cathedral, a strong dining scene (inspired by the Renaissance writer and famous gourmand, Rabelais, who lived here for two years), large and beautiful flower-lined public spaces and riverside setting, the honey-coloured city of Metz is worth a day or two of anyone's time.

The city's origins go back at least to Roman times, when, as now, it stood astride major trade routes. On the death of Charlemagne it became the capital of Lothar's portion of his empire. By the Middle Ages it had sufficient wealth and strength to proclaim itself an independent republic, which it remained until its absorption into France in 1552. Caught between warring influences, Metz has endured more than its share of historical hand-changing; reluctantly ceded to Germany in 1870, it recovered its liberty at the end of World War I, only to be re-annexed by Hitler until the Liberation.

Metz is, in effect, two towns: the original French quarters of the *vieille ville*, gathered round the cathedral and encompassing the **Île de la Comédie**, and the **Quartier Impérial**, undertaken as part of a once-and-for-all process of Germanification after the Prussian occupation in 1870. Developing with speed and panache is a third section: the **Quartier de l'Amphithéâtre**, south of the train station, heralded by the **Centre Pompidou** and the adjacent sports stadium – shops and offices are slowly following.

## Vieille Ville

From the north side of place de la République, **rue des Clercs** cuts through the attractive, bustling and largely pedestrianized heart of the *vieille ville*. Past the place St-Jacques, with its numerous outdoor cafés, you come to the eighteenth-century **place d'Armes**, where the lofty Gothic **Cathédrale Saint-Étienne** (daily: mid-April to mid-Sept 8am–7pm; mid-Sept to mid-April 8am–6pm) towers above the colonnaded classical facade of the **hôtel de ville**. Its nave is the third tallest in France – after Beauvais and Amiens cathedrals – but its best feature is without doubt the stained glass, both medieval and modern, including windows dating from the thirteenth century. Pride of place, however, goes to **Chagall's** 1963 masterpiece in the western wall of the north transept, representing the Garden of Eden, while his slightly earlier works in the ambulatory vividly depict Old Testament scenes – Moses and David, Abraham's Sacrifice and Jacob's Dream.

Some ten minutes' walk to the east of the cathedral along **En-Fournirue** is the popular drinking spot **place St-Louis**, with its Gothic arcades. On the way, wander up the Italianate streets climbing the hill of **Sainte-Croix** to your left, the legacy of the Lombard bankers who came to run the city's finances in the thirteenth century. It's also worth continuing east down the rue des Allemands to visit the splendidly renovated **Porte des Allemands** (Tues–Sun: May–Sept 2–7pm; Oct–April 2–5pm) – an imposing,

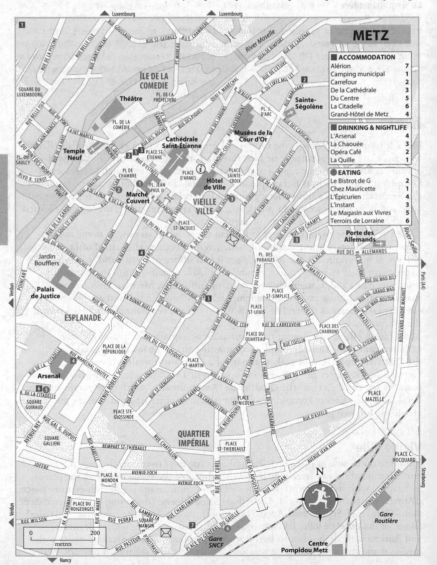

fortified double gate that once barred the eastern entrances to the medieval city. For the city's most compelling townscape, go down to the riverbank and cross over to the tiny **Île de la Comédie** which is dominated by its classical eighteenth-century square and theatre (the oldest in France) and a rather striking Protestant church erected under the German occupation.

## Musée de la Cour d'Or

2 rue du Haut-Poirier • Mon & Wed–Sun 9am–12.30pm & 1.45–5pm; closed public hols • €5 • ☎ 03 87 36 51 14, ⓦ musees. metzmetropole.fr

From the cathedral, a short walk up rue du Chanoine-Collin brings you to the city's main museum complex, the labyrinthine **Musée de la Cour d'Or**, a conglomeration of the town's old Roman baths, a Carmelite church and a medieval granary. It is a treasure trove of Gallo-Roman sculpture, with the original remains of the city's Roman baths, excavated during an extension in the 1930s. There are objects from the Middle Ages including a fantastic painted ceiling, as well as special sections showcasing local painters from the fifteenth century onwards and artefacts illustrating the city's Jewish community.

## Quartier Impérial

The **Quartier Impérial** makes up the southern section of the city, an elegant and stately collection of rose and yellow sandstone buildings, unmistakably Teutonic in style: the **gare SNCF** sets the tone, a vast and splendid granite structure of 1870 in Rhenish Romanesque, a bizarre cross between a Scottish laird's hunting lodge and a dungeon. Its gigantic dimensions reflect the Germans' long-term intention to use it as the hub of their military transport system. It's matched in style by the **post office** opposite and by some imposing bourgeois apartment buildings on the surrounding streets. The whole quarter was meant to serve as a model of superior town planning, in contrast to the squalid Latin hugger-mugger of the old French neighbourhoods further north.

To the northwest of the *gare SNCF*, the pedestrianized place de la République is bound on the east side by shops and cafés, with army barracks to the south and the formal gardens of the **Esplanade**, overlooking the Moselle, to the west. To the right, as you look down the esplanade from the square, is the handsome **Palais de Justice**. To the left, a gravel drive leads past the old arsenal, now converted into a prestigious concert hall, **L'Arsenal**.

## Centre Pompidou-Metz

1 parvis des Droits de L'Homme • April–Oct Mon & Wed–Thurs 10am–6pm, Fri–Sun 10am–7pm; Nov–March Mon & Wed–Sun 10am–6pm; €7–12, free for under-26 • ☎ 03 87 15 39 39, ⓦ centrepompidou-metz.fr

The **Centre Pompidou-Metz**, the first decentralized branch of the Georges Pompidou Centre in Paris, opened with much pomp and ceremony in Metz's Quartier de l'Amphithéâtre in May 2010. Designed by architects Shigeru Ban and Jean de Gastines, it's a curious, bright white building resembling a swimming stingray and, with its huge glass windows and wooden scaffolding, is extremely light and inviting. The same spirit reigns here as in Paris: showing off a varying percentage of the Parisian stock, the aim of the museum is to bring modern art to the masses, and judging by the queues it's working. Expect to spend around two hours here; there's a café, as well as workshops for children.

---

**ARRIVAL AND DEPARTURE**                                               **METZ**

**By train** The huge granite *gare SNCF* stands centre stage in the Quartier Impérial at the end of rue Gambetta.
Destinations Luxembourg (1–3 hourly; 40min–1hr); Nancy (2–4 hourly; 40min); Paris Est (10 daily; TGV 1hr

25min); Strasbourg (10–14 daily; 1hr 20min).
**By bus** The *gare routière*, where regional buses depart, is east of the train station on av de l'Amphithéâtre.

## INFORMATION

**Tourist office** By the side of the *hôtel de ville* at 2 place d'Armes in the old town (April–Sept Mon–Sat 9am–7pm, Sun 10am–4pm; Oct–March Mon–Sat 10am–6pm, Sun 11am–3pm; ☏ 03 87 39 00 00, ☎ tourisme-metz.fr).

**Car rental** There are rental offices at *gare SNCF*; book at ☎ rhinocarhire.com for all of them. Parking in Metz is relatively easy and it costs about €1.60 for an hour. .

## ACCOMMODATION

**Alérion** 20 rue Gambetta ☏ 03 87 66 74 03, ☎ alerion-hotel.com. Opposite the station and near the Centre Pompidou, this grandiose building, built when Metz was German, houses forty comfortable, clean rooms. Ask for a room with a view on the upper floors. Breakfast €9. **€65**

**Camping municipal** Allée de Metz-Plage ☏ 03 87 68 26 48. Quiet, very central and luxurious campsite, a 10min walk from the centre of town by the river and near where the city's sandy beach is put up every summer. Mid-April to Sept. **€4.90**

**Carrefour** 6 rue Marchant ☏ 03 87 75 07 26, ☎ carrefour-metz.asso.fr. Large HI hostel, a 5min walk north of the museums and cathedral; it's packed with teenagers in summer. Four-bed dorms €19; €21.40 for a double with shared bathroom. The en-suite private rooms are excellent value. **€25.40**

★ **De la Cathédrale** 25 place de Chambre ☏ 03 87 75 00 02, ☎ hotelcathedrale-metz.fr. Lovely, friendly hotel in a seventeenth-century townhouse, wonderfully located opposite the cathedral. Parquet floors, original beams and elegant furnishings give this place bags of character.

Breakfast €11. **€80**

**Du Centre** 14 rue Dupont des Loges ☏ 03 87 36 06 93, ☎ hotelducentremetz.fr. With a prime location in the pedestrianized centre, this two-star offers good value for money. The large rooms are tastefully furnished and the staff friendly. There's no garage, but the underground Parking de la République is just a 5min walk. Breakfast €9. **€69**

**La Citadelle** 5 av Ney ☏ 03 87 17 17 17, ☎ citadelle-metz.com. Extremely stylish four-star hotel housed in an impeccably converted fifteenth-century military building overlooking a peaceful little park. The rooms are chic, spacious and contemporary, with a touch of Japanese decor about them. Breakfast €24. **€130**

**Grand-Hôtel de Metz** 3 rue des Clercs ☏ 03 87 36 16 33, ☎ grandhotelmetz.com. Centrally located hotel on the main pedestrian shopping district with welcoming staff. Common areas look fussy but never overbearing – the paintings around reception are by local artist Denis Gaudinot – while the rooms are surprisingly business-like. Breakfast €11. **€74**

## EATING AND DRINKING

Metz celebrates Lorraine specialities with enthusiasm – you'll find quiche and *mirabelle* (yellow plum) tarts everywhere, as well as many a *menu rabelais*, involving such earthy delights as pigs' trotters, foie gras and snails. Place de Chambre, beside the cathedral, place St-Jacques and place St-Louis all have their fair share of restaurants and bars. For a picnic or snack, head to the covered market (Tues–Sat 7am–7pm).

### EATING

**Le Bistrot de G** 9 rue du Faisan ☏ 03 87 37 06 44, ☎ restaurant-bistrotdeg.com. Atmospheric Parisian-style bistro serving everything from *tartine fromagère* (€15.25) to duck breast with honey (€20.25). The three-course lunchtime *menu* is excellent value at €16.50. Tues–Sat noon–2pm & 7–10.30pm.

**Chez Mauricette** Marché couvert, place de la Cathédrale ☏ 03 87 36 37 69, ☎ chezmauricette.com. Serves vast sandwiches, made with the finest local cheese and charcuterie on crusty rustic bread; eat in or take away from €2. Tues–Sat 7am–6.30pm.

★ **L' Épicurien** 33 rue Vigne Saint-Avold ☏ 03 87 36 69 11. Jan from Yorkshire will serve you her French husband's creations with a beaming English smile. Their set *menu*

three-course lunch for €21.50 can't be beaten. Great choice of wines, too. Noon–1.30pm & 7–9pm; closed Wed evening, Sat lunch & Sun.

★ **L'instant** 27 rue Taison ☏ 03 54 62 17 35, ☎ l-instant.fr. Superb tearoom and restaurant with minimalist decor and a warm welcome. *Pâtissière* Julie and chef Maxime concoct a new menu every few weeks, with inventive, elegant mains and mouthwatering cakes and desserts. Meals (mains from €13) are served from noon until closing. Tues–Thurs 9am–5.30pm, Fri & Sat 9am–11pm, Sun 11am–3pm.

★ **Le Magasin aux Vivres** 5 av Ney ☏ 03 87 17 17 17. Metz's own Michelin-starred establishment under chef Christophe Dufossé. It belongs to *La Citadelle* hotel and offers cookery, patisserie or wine-tasting afternoons (usually Sat) starting from €52 per person. *Menu dégustation* four dishes for €85 or eight dishes for €125, and a lunch *menu* for €38. He also has a cheaper brasserie in the hotel with mains around €19. Tues–Fri noon–2pm & 7.30–10pm, Sat 7.30–10pm.

**Terroirs de Lorraine** Gare de Metz ☏ 03 87 66 64 03, ☎ terroirsdelorraine.com. Michelin-starred chef Michel Roth, a local boy, is now overseeing the buffet at the city's magnificent train station. His chefs are revisiting regional dishes, such as egg with snails and mushrooms in tarragon sauce (€12), with flair. The three-course lunch menu is well priced at €25.90. Daily 11.30am–9.30pm.

### DRINKING AND NIGHTLIFE

**L'Arsenal** 3 av Ney ☎ 03 87 74 16 16, ⊚ citemusicale-metz.fr. Metz's main cultural venue has superb acoustics and a great atmosphere for an eclectic programme of classical, jazz and dance. Most performances start at 8pm. It's associated with the city's two other big venues, BAM (for well-known music acts) and Trinitaires (rock, folk, electro etc), which you can find out about on the same website.

★ **La Chaouée** 1 rue du Champé ☎ 09 81 08 98 06. Hip and charming bar with a library and games corner. There's a good selection of beer, exhibitions and regular music concerts in the atmospheric cellar. Mon–Sat 6pm–1am.

**Opéra Café** 39 place de Chambre ☎ 03 87 36 80 26. One of the most popular drinking spots on this lively square – it stays open 'til late and attracts the barflies from all over town; the place to come if you want an impromptu chat with a stranger. Mon–Sat 10am–2am, Sun 5pm–2am.

**La Quille** 27 place de Chambre ☎ 03 87 66 76 57. This excellent wine bar offers a cool, contemporary atmosphere inside and a cathedral view from the terrace outside. Knowledgeable staff will guide you through the wine list, which includes plenty of local producers. The cheese and meat platters are recommended. Mon–Sat 6pm–2am.

# Amnéville

A thirty-minute drive north of Metz lies **Amnéville**, an easy-to-overlook town off the A31 motorway. But, just outside, in the Parc **Amnéville-Les-Thermes**, there is a gigantic tourist site with a conglomeration of attractions, cinemas, restaurants, spas and hotels you'd expect to see in North America rather than Europe. There are three large spas, Centre Thermal St Éloy (with a more therapeutic-medical orientation), Thermapolis (relaxation for all the family) and Villa Pompéi (offering massage and beauty treatments), which have been built over natural thermal springs; there are also sports arenas that include France's only indoor ski slope, an 18-hole golf and mini-golf course, a gym, an ice-skating rink and an Olympic-size swimming pool. But the main attraction is the **zoo** – one of the largest in France. You need a car to get there – and to move around the site.

## Amnéville zoo

1 rue du Tigre • Daily: April–Sept 9.30am–7.30pm (8pm Sun & holidays); Oct–March 10am–sunset • Adults and children over 12 €36; age 3–11 €30; under-3s free • ⊚ zoo-amneville.com

---

### CHÂTEAU DE MALBROUCK

Only 2km from France's border with Germany, the imposing and impregnable **Château de Malbrouck** (mid-April–June & Sept–Nov Tues–Fri 10am–5pm, Sat, Sun & public hols 10am–6pm; July & Aug Tues–Sun 10am–6pm; €5; ☎ 03 87 35 03 87, ⊚ chateau-malbrouck. com) is a restoration marvel. Every brick and turret has been placed in the medieval manner by masons re-schooled in bygone techniques.

The castle's history is pretty dramatic: it was built by the Sierck family between 1419–1436 and, then called Meinsberg Castle, it passed on through generations until the French Revolution. A change in fortune came during the War of Spanish Succession (1701–14) when, after the Battle of Blenheim, the **Duke of Marlborough** decided to invade France through the Moselle and reached the castle. On June 4 1705, it surrendered without resistance and the Duke set his headquarters there. His adversary, the **Duke of Villars**, one of Louis XIV's best generals, assembled a massive army and waited outside the castle. The one who blinked was the Duke of Marlborough; after long deliberation he withdrew from the castle during the night of June 16/17, thus abandoning his plans for the invasion of France. Even though he was there for only two weeks, the castle's name has remained in folk memory as **Malbrouck**, a Francification of Marlborough.

Amnéville zoo, rated one of the three largest in France, is alone worth travelling to Amnéville for because of the number of rare species on display. Many of them are photogenic mammals, such as snow leopards, Siberian tigers, dwarf hippos and a big number of monkey species. In 2015, a new arena was opened to host a choreographed tiger show (1–3 times daily). Feeding of animals takes place several times a day; the wolf-pack feed is the biggest draw.

### ACCOMMODATION AND EATING                                     AMNÉVILLE

★**La Forêt** Bois de Coulange ☎ 03 87 70 34 34, ⓦ restaurant-laforet.com. Nicely set apart in a forested turn, far from the rest of the rather touristy options, this is one of the best family restaurants in Lorraine, combining local produce in creative, yet familiar dishes (€20–32). The wine list is superb and the service impeccable. Reservation recommended. Tues–Sat noon–1.45pm & 7–9.30pm, Sun noon–1.45pm.

**Golden Tulip Amnéville** Parc de Coulange ☎ 03 87 71 82 86, ⓦ amneville.goldentulip.com. Modern and minimalist four-star hotel with pleasing curves and lines. As well as large rooms with plasma TV, which rises majestically with the press of a button, and superfast wi-fi, it also offers a gym, a pool and immaculate service. Breakfast €16.50. **€70**

# Verdun

**VERDUN** lies in a bend of the River Meuse, some 70km west of Metz. Of no great interest in itself, what makes this sleepy provincial town remarkable is its association with the horrific battle that took place on the bleak uplands to the north between 1916 and 1918. In 1916, aiming to break the stalemate of trench warfare, the German General Erich von Falkenhayn chose Verdun as the target for an offensive that ranked among the most devastating ever launched in the annals of war. His troops advanced to within 5km of Verdun, but never captured the town. Gradually the French clawed back the lost ground, but final victory came only in the last months of the war with the aid of US troops. The price was high: hundreds of thousands of men died on both sides. To this day, memorials in every village, hamlet and town of France are inscribed with the names of men slaughtered at Verdun. Not far from Verdun's railway station, the **Rodin memorial**, a disturbing statue of winged Victory, stands beside a handsome eighteenth-century gateway at the northern end of rue St-Paul where it joins avenue Garibaldi. Nearby, a simple engraving lists all the years between 450 and 1916 that Verdun has been involved in conflict. The fourteenth-century **Porte Chaussée** guards the river-crossing in the middle of town. Beyond it, further along rue Mazel, a flight of steps climbs up to the towering **Monument de la Victoire**, where a helmeted warrior leans on his sword in commemoration of the 1916 battle, while in the crypt below a roll is kept of all the soldiers, French and American, who took part.

## Cathédrale de Notre-Dame and around

The rue de la Belle Vierge leads round to the **Cathédrale de Notre-Dame** (daily: April–Sept 8.30am–7pm; Oct–March 9am–6pm; free), whose outward characteristics are Gothic; its earlier Romanesque origins were only uncovered by shell damage in 1916. The elegant **bishop's palace** behind it has been converted into the **Centre Mondial de la Paix, des Libertés et des Droits de l'Homme** (daily: mid-March–mid-Oct 10am–6pm, mid-Oct–mid-March 10am–12.30pm & 2–6pm; €9), which hosts exhibitions on themes such as peacekeeping and human rights.

## The citadelle

Av du 5ème R.A.P • Daily: Feb 9.30am–12.30pm & 1.30–5.30pm; March 9.30am––5.30pm; April–May & Sept–Oct 9am–6pm; June–Sept 9am–7pm; Nov 9.30am–5.30pm; Dec 10am–noon & 2–5pm • €9 • ☎ 03 29 84 84 42

Rue du Rû, the continuation of rue Mazel, takes you to the underground galleries of the **citadelle**, used as shelter for thousands of soldiers during the battle. The Unknown Soldier, whose remains now lie under the Arc de Triomphe in Paris, was chosen from among the dead who lie here. A small train takes visitors around the site that reconstitutes the lives of soldiers in World War I. You'll need to wrap up as it's 7°C underground, and also reserve in advance.

### ARRIVAL AND DEPARTURE                   VERDUN

**By car** It is best to reach Verdun and drive around the battlefields by car (1hr from Metz on the A4 motorway; exit 30). **By train** Verdun's *gare SNCF*, on av Garibaldi, is poorly served, although there are TER trains from Metz (3 daily; 1hr 30min); the TGV stops at Gare de Meuse about 30km from the city. You need to change there to reach Verdun by SNCF bus (30min).

### INFORMATION

**Tourist office** Place de la Nation (hours vary – call to check; ☎ 03 29 86 14 18, ⓦ tourisme-verdun.com).
**Champ de Bataille Pass** The tourist office sells a "Battlefield Pass" which gives entry to the Mémorial de Verdun, Fort de Douaumont, Ossuaire de Douaumont, Fort de Vaux and Citadelle Souterraine. It costs €25 for adults and €15 for ages 8 to 16.
**Guided tours** The tourist office runs a variety of guided minibus tours in French (Feb–Oct; booking advised if English is requested; €27 for half-day, including entry to sights) around some of the battlefields, memorials and forts.

### ACCOMMODATION AND EATING

★ **Château des Monthairons** Le Petit Monthairon, 26 rte de Verdun ☎ 03 29 87 78 55, ⓦ chateau desmonthairons.fr. Superb-value hostellerie with a spa in a plush nineteenth-century château, 18km south of Verdun, offering enormous apartment rooms overlooking its own forest and lake with its wading herons. The excellent restaurant (noon–1.30pm 7.30 9pm; closed Mon, Tues lunch & Sun eve, depending on season) open to non-residents has four-course *menus* from €48. Breakfast €17. Pay extra to have a view of the garden in front. **€110**
**Le Clapier** 34 rue des Gros Degrés ☎ 03 29 86 20 14. In the old town near the cathedral, this rabbit-themed restaurant with a small, contemporary dining room has an interesting menu featuring the likes of partridge stuffed with cabbage, venison flavoured with bay and, of course, rabbit terrine with hazelnuts. *Menus* from €14.50. Tues–Sat noon–2pm & 7–9.30pm.
**Montaublain** 4 rue de la Vieille Prison ☎ 06 13 56 47 08, ⓦ hoteldemontaulbain.fr. Modern rooms, decorated in brown, white and orange, provide no-nonsense comfort, while the location right in the centre of town is hard to beat. The friendly owners are a great source of tips about the local sights. Breakfast €11. **€89**

## The battlefields

The **Battle of Verdun** opened on the morning of February 21, 1916, with a German artillery barrage that lasted ten hours and expended two million shells. The battle concentrated on the forts of Vaux and Douaumont, built by the French after the 1870 Franco–Prussian War. By the time the main battle ended ten months later, nine villages had been pounded into oblivion.

The most visited part of the battlefield extends along the hills north of Verdun, but the fighting also spread to the west of the Meuse, to the hills of Mort-Homme and Hill 304, to Vauquois and the Argonne, and south along the Meuse to St-Mihiel, where the Germans held an important salient until dislodged by US forces in 1918. Unless you take an organized tour the only viable way to explore the area is with your own transport. The main sights are reached via two minor roads that snake through the battlefields: the D913 and D112.

## Mémorial de Verdun and Fort de Vaux

Fleury • Daily: Feb, March & Nov Mon–Fri 9am–5pm, Sat & Sun 9.30am–6pm; April–Aug daily 9.30am–7pm; Sept & Oct Mon–Fri 9.30am–6pm, Sat & Sun 9.30am–7pm; Nov Mon–Fri 9.30am–5pm, Sat & Sun 9.30am–6pm; Dec daily 9.30am–5pm • €11 • ☎ 03 29

> ## ST-MIHIEL AND THE VOIE SACRÉE
>
> As early as 1914, the Germans captured the town of **St-Mihiel** on the River Meuse to the south, which gave them control of the main supply route into Verdun. The only route left open to the French was the N35 (now downgraded to the D1916), winding north from Bar-le-Duc over the open hills and wheat fields. In memory of all those who kept the supplies going, the road is called **La Voie Sacrée** (The Sacred Way) and marked with milestones capped with the helmet of the *poilu* (the slang term for infantryman, literally "the hairy one" but used as a term of endearment in France).

88 19 16, ⓦ memorial-verdun.fr **Fort de Vaux** Daily: Feb–March & Oct–Nov 9.30am–5pm; April & Sept 9.30am–5.30pm; May–June 9.30am–6.30pm; July–Aug 9.30am–7pm; Dec 9.30am–4.30pm • €4

The full horror of the battle is graphically documented at **FLEURY**, in the **Mémorial de Verdun**, where, alongside contemporary newsreels and photos, a section of the shell-torn terrain that was once the village of Fleury has been reconstructed as the battle left it. Since undergoing renovation between 2013 and 2016, the memorial has been enlarged to include a state-of-the-art exhibition looking at the battle from a Franco-German viewpoint and offers an excellent view of the battlefield form the third-floor terrace.

Another major monument is the **Fort de Vaux**, 4km east of Fleury. After six days' hand-to-hand combat in the gas-filled tunnels, the French garrison were left with no alternative but to surrender. On the exterior wall, a plaque commemorates the last messenger pigeon sent to the command post in Verdun asking, in vain, for reinforcements. Having delivered its message, the pigeon expired, poisoned by the gas-filled air above the battlefield. It was posthumously awarded the Légion d'Honneur.

## Ossuaire de Douaumont

Douaumont • Hours vary wildly throughout the year: call for details • €6 • ☎ 03 29 84 54 81

The principal memorial to the carnage stands in the middle of the battlefield a short distance along the D913 beyond Fleury. The **Ossuaire de Douaumont** is a vast ossuary, with a central tower and two horizontal galleries shaped like a sword with its blade buried in the earth. Its vaults contain the bones of thousands upon thousands of unidentified soldiers, some of them visible through windows set in the base of the building. When the battle ended in 1918, the ground was covered in fragments of corpses; 120,000 French bodies were identified, perhaps a third of the total killed. Across the road, a separate memorial honours the 15,000 fallen Muslims of the French colonial regiments, while a nearby wall, beneath an eerily tree-less ridgetop, commemorates the Jewish dead.

## Fort de Douaumont

Douaumont • Daily: Feb–March & Nov–Dec 10am–5pm; April & Sept 10am–6pm; May–June 10am–6.30pm; July–Aug 10am–7pm; Oct 10am–5.30pm • €4 • ☎ 03 29 84 41 91

The **Fort de Douaumont** is 900m down the road from the cemetery. Completed in 1912, it was the strongest of the 38 forts built to defend Verdun. Inexplicably, however, the armament of these forts was greatly reduced in 1915, and when the Germans attacked in 1916, twenty men were enough to overrun the garrison. The fort is on three levels and its claustrophobic, dungeon-like galleries are hung with stalactites. The Germans held the fort for eight months while under continuous siege, housing 3000 men in these cramped, unventilated quarters, infested with fleas and lice and plagued by rats that attacked the sleeping and the dead indiscriminately.

## American Cemetery

Romagne-sous-Montfaucon • Daily: 9am–5pm, the American superintendent is available Mon–Fri during office hours • ☎ 03 29 85 14 18, ⓦ abmc.gov

The only other war site worth making a detour for is the **American cemetery** in Romagne-sous-Montfaucon, near Argonne – the biggest US graveyard in Europe, with 14,246 graves. Solemn, dignified and thought-provoking, it lies on ground leased to the US in perpetuity and is overseen by an American superintendent who lives in the house overlooking the chapel. There, on its Wall of the Disappeared, you can read the engraved names of 954 US soldiers whose bodies were never recovered. A visitor centre, renovated in 2016, tells the story of the Meuse-Argonne offensive.

4

# Normandy

**260** Seine Maritime

**278** Basse Normandie

**296** Mont St-Michel

**298** Inland Normandy

MONT ST-MICHEL

**5** # Normandy

Long since incorporated into the French mainstream, the seaboard province of Normandy has a history of prosperous and powerful independence. Colonized by Vikings from the ninth century onwards, it went on to conquer not only England but as far afield as Sicily and areas of the Near East. Later, as part of France, it was instrumental in the settlement of Canada.

Normandy's wealth has always depended on its ports: **Rouen**, on the Seine, is the nearest navigable point to Paris, while **Dieppe**, **Le Havre** and **Cherbourg** have important transatlantic trade. Inland, it is overwhelmingly agricultural – a fertile belt of tranquil pastureland, where the chief interest for many will be the groaning restaurant tables of regions such as the **Pays d'Auge**. While parts of the coast are overdeveloped, due either to industry, as with the huge sprawl of Le Havre, or tourism – as along the "Norman Riviera", around **Trouville** and **Deauville** – ancient harbours such as **Honfleur** and **Barfleur** remain irresistible, while numerous seaside villages lack both crowds and affectations. The banks of the Seine, too, hold several delightful little communities.

Although Normandy also boasts extraordinary Romanesque and Gothic **architectural treasures**, only its much-restored capital, Rouen, retains a complete medieval centre. Elsewhere, the attractions are more often single buildings than entire towns. Most famous of all is the spectacular *merveille* on the island of **Mont St-Michel**, but there are also the monasteries at **Jumièges** and **Caen**, the cathedrals of Bayeux and **Coutances**, and Richard the Lionheart's castle above the Seine at **Les Andelys**. Bayeux has its vivid and astonishing tapestry, while more recent creations include Monet's garden at **Giverny**. Furthermore, Normandy's vernacular architecture makes it well worth exploring inland – rural back roads are lined with splendid centuries-old half-timbered manor houses. It's remarkable how much has survived – or, less surprisingly, been restored – since the D-Day landings in 1944 and the subsequent **Battle of Normandy**, which has its own legacy in war museums, memorials and cemeteries.

**GETTING AROUND**                                                        **NORMANDY**

**By train** The main towns and cities are well served, though many routes in Haute Normandie require a change at Rouen, and services are less frequent at weekends.

**By bus** Services vary by *département*: the best served is Calvados, where Bus Verts (ⓦ busverts.fr), for example, link Caen to the D-Day beaches, and Honfleur to Le Havre.

Services to rural areas such as the Pays d'Auge are infrequent or non-existent.

**By car** To explore the countryside, you'll need a car. A vehicle is also useful for the coast, although guided tours head out from Bayeux and Caen to the D-Day beaches.

## Seine Maritime

The *département* of Seine Maritime comprises three distinct sections: Normandy's dramatic **northern coastline**, home to major ports like Dieppe and Le Havre and such delightful resorts as **Étretat**; the meandering course of the **River Seine**, where unchanged villages stand both up- and downstream of Rouen; and the flat, chalky **Caux plateau**, which makes for pleasant cycling country but holds little to detain visitors.

**Dieppe** in particular offers an appealing introduction to France, and with the impressive white cliffs of the **Côte d'Albâtre** (Alabaster Coast) stretching to either side, it makes a good base for a few days' stay. The most direct route to Rouen from here is simply to head south, but it's well worth tracing the shore west to **Le Havre**, then following the Seine inland.

MONET'S GARDEN AT GIVERNY

# Highlights

**❶ Rouen** This fine old medieval city would still seem familiar to Joan of Arc, whose trial and death here is commemorated by a high-tech museum. See page 270

**❷ Château Gaillard** The ruins of Richard the Lionheart's mighty fortress, at Les Andelys, command superb views along the River Seine. See page 276

**❸ Giverny** Claude Monet's house and garden remain just as he left them, with Japanese prints on the walls and, of course, water lilies in the pond. See page 277

**❹ The Bayeux Tapestry** One of the world's most extraordinary historical documents,

embroidering the saga of William the Conqueror in every colourful detail. See page 284

**❺ The war cemeteries** Memories of D-Day abound in Normandy, but nowhere more so than in the powerfully evocative American cemetery at Colleville-sur-Mer. See page 289

**❻ Mont St-Michel** Second only to the Eiffel Tower as France's best-loved landmark, the *merveille* makes a magnificent spectacle atop the sea-girt islet of Mont St-Michel. See page 296

**❼ The Pays d'Auge** With its luscious meadows and half-timbered farmhouses, the Pays d'Auge is a picture-perfect home for Camembert and other legendary cheeses. See page 298

**HIGHLIGHTS ARE MARKED ON THE MAP ON PAGE 262**

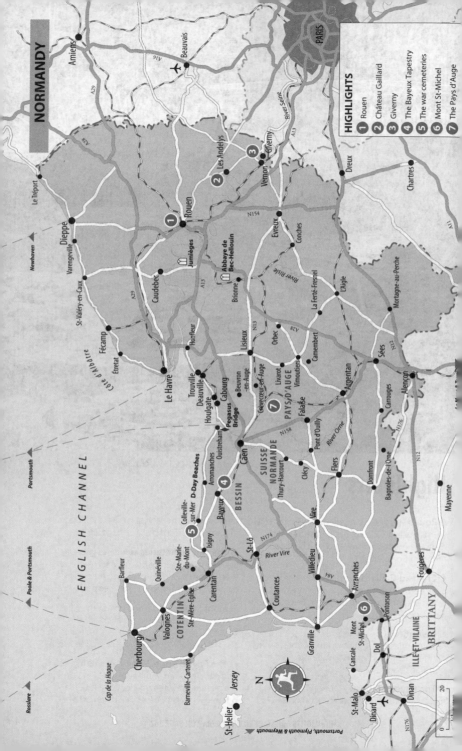

**5**

## THE FOOD OF NORMANDY

The **food of Normandy** owes its most distinctive characteristic – its gut-busting, heart-pounding richness – to the lush orchards and dairy herds of the region's agricultural heartland, and especially the Pays d'Auge, southeast of Caen. Menus abound in **meat** such as veal (*veau*) cooked in *vallée d'Auge* style, which consists largely of the profligate addition of **cream** and **butter**. Many dishes also feature orchard **fruit**, either in its natural state or in more alcoholic forms – either as apple or pear cider, or perhaps further distilled to produce brandies.

Normans relish blood and guts. In addition to gamier meat and fowl such as rabbit and duck (a speciality in Rouen, where the birds are strangled to ensure their blood gets into the sauce), they enjoy such intestinal preparations as *andouilles*, the sausages known in English as chitterlings, and *tripes*, stewed for hours *à la mode de Caen*. A full blowout at a country restaurant traditionally entails pauses between courses for the *trou normand*: a glass of the apple brandy Calvados to let you catch your breath.

Thanks to its long coastline, Normandy is also renowned for its **seafood**. Waterfront restaurants in its ports and resorts compete for attention, each with its *"copieuse" assiette de fruits de mer*. **Honfleur** is the most enjoyable, but **Dieppe**, **Étretat** and **Cherbourg** also offer endless eating opportunities. The menus tend to be similar to those in Brittany, if perhaps slightly more expensive.

The most famous products of Normandy's meadow-munching cows are, of course, their **cheeses**. Cheese-making in the Pays d'Auge started in the monasteries during the Dark Ages. By the eleventh century the local products were already well defined; in 1236, the *Roman de la Rose* referred to Angelot cheese, identified with a small coin depicting a young angel killing a dragon. The principal modern varieties began to emerge in the seventeenth century – **Pont l'Évêque**, which is square with a washed crust, soft but not runny, and **Livarot**, which is round, thick and firm, and has a stronger flavour. Although Marie Harel is generally credited with having invented **Camembert** in the 1790s, a smaller and stodgier version had already existed for some time. A priest fleeing the Revolution stayed in Madame Harel's farmhouse at Camembert, and suggested modifications in line with the techniques used to make Brie de Meaux – a slower process, gentler on the curd and with more thorough drainage. The rich, full cheese thus created was an instant success in the market at Vimoutiers, and the development of the railways (and the invention of the chipboard cheesebox in 1880) helped to give it a worldwide popularity.

Driving along the D982 on the northern bank of the Seine, you'll often find your course paralleled by mighty container ships on the water. Potential stops en route include the medieval abbey of **Jumièges**, but **Rouen** itself is the prime destination, with its role in the execution of Joan of Arc as the most compelling episode in its fascinating history. Further upstream, Monet's wonderful house and garden at **Giverny** and the English frontier stronghold of Château Gaillard at **Les Andelys** also justify taking the slow road to Paris.

## Dieppe

Squeezed between high cliff headlands, **DIEPPE** is an enjoyably small-scale port that used to be more of a resort. During the nineteenth century, Parisians came by train to take the sea air, promenading along the front while the English indulged in the peculiar pastime of swimming. Though ferry services have diminished, Dieppe remains a nice little place. If you have kids in tow, the aquariums of the **Cité de la Mer** and the strip of pebble **beach** are the obvious attractions; otherwise, you could settle for admiring the cliffs and the **castle** as you stroll the seafront lawns.

### The château

June–Sept Wed–Sun 10am–6pm, Oct–May Wed–Sat 10am–noon & 2–5pm Sun 10am–noon & 2–6pm • €4.50 • ☎ 02 35 06 61 99, ⓦ dieppe.fr

**5**

Perched on the clifftop above the western end of the seafront, Dieppe's medieval **château** is home of the **Musée de Dieppe**, whose collection includes carved ivories – virtuoso pieces of sawing, filing and chipping of the plundered riches of Africa, shipped back by early Dieppe explorers. It also holds paintings of local scenes by artists such as Pissarro, Renoir, Dufy, Sickert and Boudin, and works by Georges Braque, the co-founder of **Cubism**, who went to school in Le Havre, spent summers in Dieppe and is buried not far west at Varengeville-sur-Mer. The castle's separate newer wing stages temporary exhibitions.

### Boulevard de Verdun and around

Modern Dieppe is laid out along the three axes dictated by its eighteenth-century town planners. The **boulevard de Verdun** runs for more than 1km along the seafront, from just below the fifteenth-century **château** in the west, to the port entrance in the east. The **square du Canada**, at its western end, was originally named in commemoration of the role played by Dieppe sailors in the colonization of Canada. Now a small plaque is dedicated to the Canadian soldiers who died in the suicidal 1942 raid on Dieppe, a trial run for the 1944 Normandy landings. East from there, the boulevard de Verdun passes the Casino; "Les Bains", a large complex of indoor and outdoor **swimming pools**; and the town's grandest hotels.

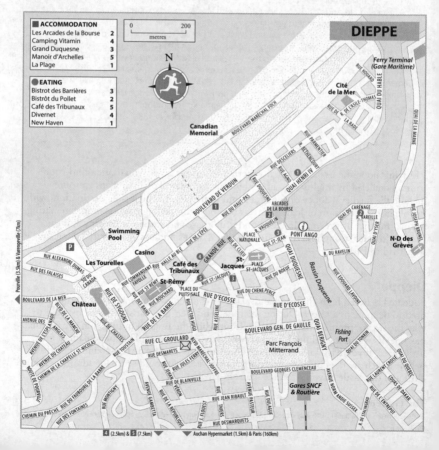

| ■ ACCOMMODATION | |
| --- | --- |
| Les Arcades de la Bourse | 2 |
| Camping Vitamin | 4 |
| Grand Duquesne | 3 |
| Manoir d'Archelles | 5 |
| La Plage | 1 |

| ● EATING | |
| --- | --- |
| Bistrot des Barrières | 3 |
| Bistrôt du Pollet | 2 |
| Café des Tribunaux | 5 |
| Divernet | 4 |
| New Haven | 1 |

**DIEPPE**

## Cité de la Mer

37 rue de l'Asile-Thomas • Mon–Fri 9.30am–6pm, Sat & Sun 9.30am–12.30pm & 1.30–6pm • €7.50 • ☎ 02 35 06 93 20, ☏ www.estrancitedelamer.fr

Tucked into the backstreets at the eastern end of town, just back from the harbour, Dieppe's **Cité de la Mer** is a museum and scientific research centre for all things sea-related. Unless you are a maritime history or marine biology enthusiast, little is likely to hold your attention for long: the small museum races through the history of seagoing vessels, including a Viking *drakkar* reconstructed using methods depicted in the Bayeux Tapestry, and an exhibition details Dieppe's relationship with the sea, with a pungent display of dried, salted fish. Visits culminate with the large **aquariums**, filled with the marine life of the Channel: flatfish with bulbous eyes and twisted faces, retiring octopuses, battling lobsters, and hermaphrodite scallops.

## Grande Rue and around

Dieppe's main shopping streets – the **rue de la Barre** and its pedestrianized continuation, the **Grande Rue**, scene of Saturday's all-day open-air **market** – run parallel to the seafront. The landmark *Café des Tribunaux* dominates place du Puits-Salé, at the centre of the old town, while along the harbour's edge, an extension of the Grande Rue, **quai Henri-IV**, has a colourful backdrop of cafés, brasseries and restaurants.

### ARRIVAL AND INFORMATION                                                    DIEPPE

**By train** The *gare SNCF*, with services from Paris-St-Lazare (19 daily; 2hr 10min) via Rouen (16 daily; 50min), is 500m south of the tourist office, on bd Clemenceau.

**By bus** The *gare routière*, on bd Clemenceau, alongside the train station, has services from Fécamp (4 daily; 2hr 20min).

**By ferry** DFDS (☏ dfdsseaways.co.uk) sail between Dieppe's *gare maritime*, 500m east of the centre, and Newhaven in England (2–3 daily; 4hr).

**Tourist office** Pont Ango (April Mon–Sat 9am–1pm & 2–6pm; May, June & Sept Mon–Sat 9am–1pm & 2–6pm, Sun 9am–1pm & 2–5pm; July & Aug Mon–Sat 9am–7pm, Sun 9am–1pm & 2–5pm; Oct–March Mon–Sat 9am–1pm & 2–5pm; ☎ 02 32 14 40 60, ☏ dieppetourisme.com).

### ACCOMMODATION

**Les Arcades de la Bourse** 1–3 arcades de la Bourse ☎ 02 35 84 14 12, ☏ lesarcades-dieppe.fr. Long-established central hotel under the arcades facing the port; you couldn't ask for a more convenient location. Cheaper rooms face the street. Restaurant with full, good-value *menus* from €23. **€85**

**Camping Vitamin** 865 rue des Vertus, St-Aubin-sur-Scie ☎ 02 35 82 11 11, ☏ camping-vitamin.com. Three-star site, well south of town in an unremarkable setting, with indoor and outdoor pools. It's really only convenient for motorists, though it is served by bus #2. Closed Oct–March. **€24.90**

**Grand Duquesne** 15 place St-Jacques ☎ 02 32 14 61 10. This small, central hotel is unusually plain for the *Logis de France*, offering eight old-fashioned en-suite rooms at bargain rates, plus two larger family suites, all accessible via steep stairs. Vegetarian and meat-rich menus in its restaurant start at under €20. **€73**

**Manoir d'Archelles** Rte de Neufchâtel, Arques-La-Bataille ☎ 02 32 83 40 51, ☏ manoir-darchelles.fr. Simple rooms, including some large family options, in an eccentric old château set in gorgeous gardens, 6km southeast of central Dieppe; restaurant next door. **€78**

**La Plage** 20 bd de Verdun ☎ 02 35 84 18 28, ☏ plage hotel-dieppe.com. Seafront hotel with rooms to suit all budgets, from the upmarket sea-view options to smaller but perfectly pleasant courtyard-facing doubles. No restaurant. **€77**

### EATING AND DRINKING

If you like to stroll and compare menus, the most promising area to look for restaurants in Dieppe is not the beach, but the quai Henri-IV, overlooking the port. For the very best food in town, though, it's worth heading a little further afield. The café-lined Place St-Jacques, dominated by the Gothic Église St-Jacques, is an ideal spot for a relaxed drink.

**Bistrot des Barrières** 5–7 arcades de la Poissonnerie ☎ 02 35 40 46 83. Welcoming little restaurant near the tourist office, where, apart from the great-value €17.50 lunch menu, everything is à la carte, with daily fish specials for around €20. Mon & Tues noon–1.45pm, Wed–Sat noon–1.45pm & 7–9.30pm.

**Bistrot du Pollet** 23 rue Tête de Boeuf ☎ 02 35 84 68 57. Little local restaurant just east of Pont Ango, especially cosy on a winter's evening, selling fresh seafood at low prices. Weekday lunch *menus* from €23, dinner from €30. Tues–Sat noon–2pm & 7.30–9.30pm; closed second fortnight in April and second fortnight in Aug.

**5**

**Café des Tribunaux** Place du Puits-Salé ☎ 02 32 14 44 65. The place du Puits-Salé is dominated by this cavernous café, built as an inn towards the end of the seventeenth century. Two hundred years later, it was favoured by painters and writers such as Renoir, Monet, Sickert, Whistler and Pissarro, but for English visitors, its most evocative association is with the exiled and unhappy Oscar Wilde, who drank here regularly. It's popular with students. Daily 8am–8pm.

**Divernet** 138 Grande Rue ☎ 02 35 84 13 87, ⓦ divernet. fr. Chic patisserie, brasserie and tearoom, with pavement seating on Dieppe's main shopping street. Delicious cakes and desserts, and simple lunch *formules* from €9. Daily 9am–7pm; closed Mon Sept to mid-July.

**New Haven** 53 quai Henri-IV ☎ 02 35 84 89 72, ⓦ restaurantdieppe.fr. Reliable seafood specialist, towards the quieter end of the quayside, with good *menus* from €21. Mon & Thurs–Sun noon–9.30pm, Tues noon–3pm.

## The Côte d'Albâtre

West of Dieppe, the shoreline of the **Côte d'Albâtre** ("Alabaster Coast") is eroding at such a ferocious rate that small resorts like **Fécamp** and **Étretat**, tucked among the cliffs at the ends of its successive valleys, may not last more than another century or so. For the moment, however, they are quietly prospering, with casinos, sports centres and yacht marinas ensuring a modest but steady summer trade.

### Varengeville

The lovely rural village of **VARENGEVILLE** stretches luxuriantly to either side of the D75 8km west of Dieppe, 1km or so inland from the steep coastal cliffs. Its main attractions are the **Bois des Moutiers** (mid-March to mid-Nov daily: house 10am–noon & 2–6pm; gardens 10am–8pm; €11; ☎ 02 35 85 10 02, ⓦ boisdesmoutiers.com), where a house built by English architect **Edwin Lutyens** features magnificent **gardens**, designed by owner Guillaume Mallet with Gertrude Jekyll, and the château-like **Manoir d'Ango** (April & Oct Sat & Sun 10am–12.30pm & 2–6pm; May–Sept daily 10am–12.30pm & 2–6pm; €5.50; ☎ 02 35 83 61 56, ⓦ manoirdango.fr), the splendid "summer palace" of sixteenth-century Dieppe shipbuilder Jean Ango.

Artist **Georges Braque** lies buried in Varengeville's clifftop church, where his marble **tomb** is topped by a sadly decaying mosaic of a white dove in flight. More impressive is his vivid blue *Tree of Jesse* stained-glass window inside the church, through which the sun rises in summer.

### St-Valéry-en-Caux

Open-air stalls beside the narrow harbour in the rebuilt but still attractive port of **ST-VALÉRY-EN-CAUX**, 30km west of Dieppe, sell fresh fish daily. Crumbling brown-stained cliffs soar to either side of its long shingle beach, busy with tourists in summer.

### Fécamp

Halfway between Dieppe and Le Havre, **FÉCAMP** is a serious fishing port with a pleasant seafront promenade. Its most distinctive attraction, the rambling **Benedictine Distillery**, is tucked away in the backstreets at 110 rue Alexandre-le-Grand (April to early July & early Sept to mid-Nov 10am–1pm & 2–6.30pm; early July to early Sept 10am–7pm; last admission always 1hr before closing; €12; fully guided tour at 3.30pm, €12; ☎ 02 35 10 26 10, ⓦ benedictinedom.com). Visits consist partly of self-guided wanderings through galleries of treasures, oddities and paintings, and partly of a guided tour through the production area, and culminate with a *dégustation* of the liqueur itself in their bar across the street.

### Étretat

Exquisite little **ÉTRETAT** has grown up simply as a pleasure resort. The alabaster cliffs are at their most spectacular here, complete with arches, tunnels and a solitary "needle" out to sea, and there isn't even a port of any kind: the seafront consists of a sweeping unbroken curve of concrete above a shingle beach. In the town itself, a lovely architectural ensemble surrounds the central **place Foch**. The ground floor of the old wooden market *halles* in the square now holds souvenir shops, but the beams of the balcony and roof are bare and ancient.

The cliffs

Footpaths climb the stunning **cliffs** to either side of town. The **Falaise d'Aval** to the south is a straightforward walk. Lush lawns and pastures stretch away inland, while German fortifications extend to the point where the turf abruptly stops. From the windswept top you can see further rock formations and even glimpse Le Havre. However, it's the views back to the town sheltered in the valley, and the **Falaise d'Amont** on its northern side – an idyllic green hillside, topped by the little chapel of Notre-Dame – that stick in the memory.

## INFORMATION                                   THE CÔTE D'ALBÂTRE

### ST-VALÉRY-EN-CAUX
**Tourist office** 1 quai d'Amont (April–Sept daily 9.30am–12.30pm & 2–6.30pm; Oct–March Mon–Sat 9.30am--12.30pm & 2–6pm; ☏02 35 97 00 63, ⓦwww.plateaudecauxmaritime.com).

### FÉCAMP
**Tourist office** Quai Sadi-Carnot (Sept–March Mon–Fri 9am–12.30pm & 2–5.30pm, Sat 10am–1pm & 3–5pm, Sun 9.30am–12.30pm in school hols only; April–June Mon–Fri 9am–6pm, Sat & Sun 10am–6.30pm; July & Aug

daily 9am–6.30pm; ☏02 35 28 51 01, ⓦfecamptourisme.com). Ask about each week's programme of sea cruises, typically priced at €25.

### ÉTRETAT
**Tourist office** Place Maurice-Guillard (Easter–June & Sept Mon–Sat 10am–12.30pm & 2–6pm, Sun 10am–12.30pm & 2–5.30pm; July & Aug Mon–Sat 9.30am–6.30pm, Sun 10am–6pm; Oct–Easter Mon–Sat 10am–12.30pm & 2–5.30pm, Sun 10am–12.30pm; ☏02 35 27 05 21, ⓦetretat.net).

## ACCOMMODATION

### VARENGEVILLE
★ **De la Terrasse** Rte de Vastérival ☏02 35 85 12 54, ⓦhotel-restaurant-la-terrasse.com. Slightly faded hotel in an irresistible setting, perched high above the cliffs at the end of a dead-end right turning just west of town. Fish *menus* in its panoramic dining room start at €23, and you can follow footpaths down through narrow cracks in the cliffs to reach the rocky beach below. Some large family rooms. Closed mid-Oct to mid-March. Look for good-value rates that include breakfast and dinner. €93

### ST-VALÉRY-EN-CAUX
**La Maison des Galets** 22 rue le Perrey ☏02 35 97 11 22, ⓦlamaisondesgalets.fr. Though housed in the unremarkable concrete block that lines St-Valery's beach, this hotel has a distinct pre-war, Art Deco flavour. All the simple tasteful rooms, of which half enjoy sea views, have good bathrooms. A panoramic ground-floor space operates as a bar and tearoom year-round, while the owners operate a separate restaurant nearby. €75

### FÉCAMP
**Angleterre** 91–93 rue de la Plage ☏02 35 28 01 60, ⓦfecamp-hotelangleterre.com. Just back from the sea above a crêperie, this hotel holds nicely refurbished sea-

view rooms, all en suite, as well as a lively "English pub" with a large outdoor terrace. The ambience is most suited to young budget travellers, and there's no lift. €88
**Camping de Renéville** Chemin de Nesmond ☏02 35 28 20 97, ⓦcampingdereneville.com. Lovely campsite, with beautiful views along the coast, just a short walk out of town on the western cliffs. Closed early Nov to March. €20
**De la Mer** 89 bd Albert-1er ☏02 35 28 24 64, ⓦhotel-dela-mer.com. The only sea-view accommodation in Fécamp offers eight very plain but unbeatably priced rooms above a bar; the cheapest has a toilet but no bath. €54

### ÉTRETAT
**Camping Municipal** 69 rue Maupassant ☏02 35 27 07 67. Spacious individual pitches in Étretat's campsite spread amid the trees east of the D39, 1km inland from the town centre. Closed mid-Oct to March. €12.20
**Détective** 6 av George-V ☏02 35 27 01 34, ⓦdetectivehotel.com. Quirky hotel with rooms themed according to fictional detectives, from Étretat's own Arsène Lupin to Sherlock Holmes and Inspector Clouseau. Set 200m back from the sea, it's among the cheapest options in town, but with its strong eco-friendly emphasis and all-round charm, it's great value. €69

**5**

**La Résidence** 4 bd René-Coty ☎02 35 27 02 87, ⓦhotels-etretat.com. Guest rooms in this dramatic half-timbered old mansion, also known as the Manoir de la Salamandre, vary enormously; the cheapest option has a toilet but no other en-suite facilities, while others are positively luxurious. €49

## EATING

### ST-VALÉRY-EN-CAUX

**Du Port** 18 quai Amont ☎02 35 97 08 93, ⓦrestaurant-du-port-76.fr. Stand-alone quayside restaurant that specializes in whisking deliciously fresh fish from boat to table with only the most minimal, subtle intervention. Dinner menus €27 and €46. Tues, Wed, Fri & Sat noon–2pm & 7.30–9.30pm; Thurs & Sun noon–2pm.

### FÉCAMP

**Chez Nounoute** 3 place Nicolas-Selle ☎02 35 29 38 08, ⓦcheznounoute.com. The blue chairs of this friendly, good-value bistro, housed in a former fishmonger's, spread across a nice little square by the port; fill up on moules frites for €12, or get the €15 lunch menu. Mon, Tues & Thurs–Sun noon–4pm & 7–11pm.

### ÉTRETAT

**Le Galion** Bd René-Coty ☎02 35 29 48 74, ⓦetretat-legalion.fr. Étretat's finest restaurant, adjoining the Résidence hotel just off the square, serves classic Norman dishes in a gloriously weathered medieval hall, on menus from €25. Daily noon–1.30pm & 7.30–9pm; closed Tues & Wed in winter.

# Le Havre

While **LE HAVRE** may hardly be picturesque or tranquil, it's not the soulless sprawl some travellers suggest. Its port, the second largest in France, takes up half the Seine estuary, but the town itself, home to almost 200,000 people, is a place of pilgrimage for fans of contemporary **architecture**.

Built in 1517 to replace the ancient ports of Harfleur and Honfleur, then silting up, Le Havre – "The Harbour" – swiftly became the principal trading post of northern France. Following its near-destruction during World War II, it was rebuilt by a single architect, **Auguste Perret**, between 1946 and 1964. The sheer sense of space can be exhilarating: the showpiece monuments have a winning self-confidence, and the few surviving relics of the old city have been sensitively integrated into the whole. While the endless mundane residential blocks can be dispiriting, even those visitors who fail to agree with Perret's famous dictum that "concrete is beautiful" may enjoy a stroll around his city.

It's easy to get to and from Le Havre without ever seeing its downtown area. If you do make the effort, the Perret-designed central **hôtel de ville** is a logical first port of call. A long, low, flat-roofed building topped by a seventeen-storey concrete tower, sitting in an attractive, lively square, surrounded by pergola walkways, flowerbeds and fountains, it hosts imaginative exhibitions.

## Church of St-Joseph

From the outside, Perret's major creation, the **church of St-Joseph**, is a mass of speckled concrete, the main doors thrown open to hint at dark interior spaces within. Once you get inside, it all makes sense: the altar is right in the centre, with the 100m bell tower rising directly above. Simple patterns of stained glass, extending right the way up the tower, create a bright interplay of coloured light, focusing on the altar.

## The Volcano

Le Havre's boldest specimen of modern architecture is a post-Perret creation – the cultural centre known as the **Volcano** (or, less reverentially, the "yoghurt pot"), dominating the Espace Oscar Niemeyer. Niemeyer, the Brazilian architect who oversaw the construction of Brasília, designed this slightly asymmetrical gleaming white cone in the 1970s, and remained hard at work until he died just short of his 105th birthday in 2012.

## Musée d'Art Moderne André Malraux – MuMa

2 bd Clemenceau • Tues–Fri 11am–6pm, Sat & Sun 11am–7pm • €7 • ☎ 02 35 19 62 62, 🌐 muma-lehavre.fr

The **Musée d'Art Moderne André Malraux**, overlooking the harbour entrance and widely known as **MuMa**, ranks among the best-designed art galleries in France, making full use of the natural light afforded by its seafront location to display an enjoyable array of nineteenth- and twentieth-century French paintings. Its highlights are more than two hundred canvases by Eugène Boudin, including greyish landscapes produced all along the Normandy coastline, as well as an entire wall of miniature cows. A lovely set of works by Raoul Dufy, born in Le Havre in 1877, make the city appear positively radiant, whatever the weather outside.

### ARRIVAL AND DEPARTURE
LE HAVRE

**By train** The *gare SNCF* is a 10min walk from the centre down bd de Strasbourg, not far from the ferry port.
Destinations Paris (11 daily; 2hr 30min); Rouen (15 daily; 50min).

**By bus** The *gare routière* stands alongside the *gare SNCF*.

Destinations Étretat (12 daily; 45min); Fécamp (11 daily; 1hr 20min); Honfleur (7 daily; 30min).

**By ferry** Brittany Ferries (🌐 brittanyferries.com) operate frequent sailings between Portsmouth and Le Havre. Shuttle buses connect the ferry terminal with the *gare SNCF*.

### INFORMATION

**Tourist office** 186 bd Clemenceau, on the main seafront drag (April–Oct daily 9.30am–1pm & 2–7pm; Nov–March Mon 2–6pm, Tues–Sat 10am–12.30pm & 2–6pm; ☎ 02 32 74 04 04, 🌐 lehavretourisme.com).

### ACCOMMODATION

**Best Western Art Hôtel** 147 rue Louis-Brindeau ☎ 02 35 22 69 44, 🌐 art-hotel.fr. Very smart hotel on the north side of the Espace Oscar Niemeyer, facing the Volcano cultural centre. Rooms do indeed have arty touches, and the largest have outdoor terraces. **€99**

★ **Carmin** 15 rue Georges-Braque ☎ 02 32 74 08 20, 🌐 hotelcarmin.com. Great-value hotel in a relatively quiet neighbourhood, not too far back from the sea; the large rooms may not be fancy, but they've got all the basic comforts. Buffet breakfasts €9. **€82**

**Richelieu** 132 rue de Paris ☎ 02 35 42 38 71, 🌐 hotel lerichelieu.fr. For a mid-priced hotel in a very central

| ACCOMMODATION | |
|---|---|
| Best Western Art Hôtel | 3 |
| Carmin | 1 |
| Richelieu | 4 |
| Vent d'Ouest | 2 |

| EATING | |
|---|---|
| Lyonnais | 4 |
| Nuage Dans La Tasse | 3 |
| Petite Auberge | 1 |
| Taverne Paillette | 2 |

**5**

location, where the cosy rooms have bright, colourful quilts and tapestries, and in some instances balconies, this friendly family-run place is hard to beat, though there's no lift and the wifi can be patchy. **€61**

★ **Vent d'Ouest** 4 rue de Caligny ☎ 02 35 42 50 69, ⓦ ventdouest.fr. Le Havre's smartest hotel is a stylishly designed boutique affair, with well-equipped rooms decorated on a nautical or mountain theme. Apartments that sleep four also available. **€100**

### EATING AND DRINKING

Head to the area around the *gare SNCF* for bars, cafés and brasseries. Otherwise, all sorts of restaurants, from traditional French to Japanese, fill the backstreets of the waterside St-François district.

**Lyonnais** 7–9 rue de Bretagne ☎ 02 35 22 07 31. Small, cosy restaurant with checked tablecloths and a welcoming atmosphere. The speciality is baked fish, though dishes from Lyon, such as *andouillettes*, are also available on *menus* that start at €15 at lunch, €20 at dinner. Tues–Fri 8am–10pm, Sat 7am–10pm.

**Nuage Dans La Tasse** 93 av Foch ☎ 02 35 21 64 94. Huge salads and simple, good-value bistro meals – or you can simply drop in for a cup of tea – near the town hall. Mon–Wed noon–2pm, Thurs–Sat noon–2pm & 7–10pm.

**Petite Auberge** 32 rue de Ste-Adresse ☎ 02 35 46 27 32, ⓦ lapetiteauberge-lehavre.fr. High-class traditional French cooking, aimed more at local businesspeople than at tourists, and offering few surprises but no disappointments. Lunch costs €25, dinner *menus* start at €35. Tues & Thurs–Sat noon–1.30pm & 7.30–9.30pm, Wed 7.30–9.30pm, Sun noon–2pm.

**Taverne Paillette** 22 rue Georges-Braque ☎ 02 35 41 31 50, ⓦ taverne-paillette.com. This venerable Bavarian brasserie can trace its roots – and its beer – back to the sixteenth century, even if its present incarnation is a postwar reconstruction. The twin specialities are *choucroute* and elaborate seafood platters; there's also a daily lunch *menu* for €15.50. Daily noon–midnight.

# Rouen

**ROUEN**, the capital of Upper Normandy, is one of France's most ancient cities. Standing on the site of Rotomagus, built by the Romans at the lowest point where they could bridge the Seine, it was laid out by Rollo, the first duke of Normandy, in 911. Captured by the English in 1419, it became the stage in 1431 for the trial and execution of **Joan of Arc**, before returning to French control in 1449.

Bombing during World War II destroyed all Rouen's bridges, the area between the cathedral and the *quais*, and much of the left bank's industrial quarter. When the city was rebuilt, its inner core of streets, north of the river, were turned into the closest approximation to a medieval city that modern imaginations could conceive. Rouen today can be very seductive, its lively and bustling centre well equipped with impressive churches and museums, and the effect is enhanced by the fact that they've finally, at long last, got round to restoring the riverfront.

While Rouen proper is home to a population of 110,000, its metropolitan area holds five times that number, and it remains the fourth-largest port in the country. The city spreads deep into the loop of the Seine, with its docks and industrial infrastructure stretching endlessly away to the south.

## Cathédrale de Notre-Dame

**Cathedral** Mon 2–6pm, Tues–Sat 9am–noon & 2–6pm, Sun 8am–6pm; crypt closed on Sun and during services **Cathédrale de Lumière** Daily: mid-June to end July 11pm; first half of Aug 10.30pm, second half of Aug 10pm; first 3 weeks of Sept 9.30pm • Free • ☎ 02 35 71 85 65, ⓦ cathedrale-rouen.net

Despite the addition of all sorts of towers, spires and vertical extensions, Rouen's **Cathédrale de Notre-Dame** remains at heart the Gothic masterpiece that was built in the twelfth and thirteenth centuries. Its intricately sculpted western facade was Monet's subject for multiple studies of changing light, several of which now hang in the Musée d'Orsay in Paris. Monet might not recognize it today, however – it's been scrubbed a gleaming white, free from the centuries of accreted dirt he so carefully recorded.

Inside, the **ambulatory** and **crypt** hold the assorted tombs of various recumbent royalty, such as Duke Rollo, who died "enfeebled by toil" in 933 AD, and the actual heart of Richard the Lionheart.

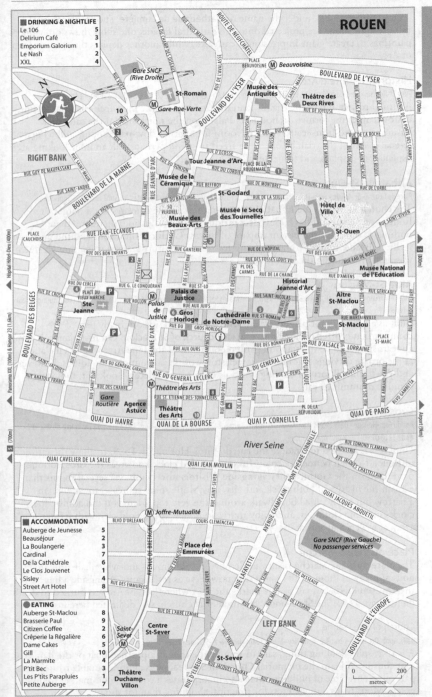

**ROUEN**

**DRINKING & NIGHTLIFE**
| | |
|---|---|
| Le 106 | 5 |
| Delirium Café | 3 |
| Emporium Galorium | 1 |
| Le Nash | 2 |
| XXL | 4 |

**ACCOMMODATION**
| | |
|---|---|
| Auberge de Jeunesse | 5 |
| Beauséjour | 2 |
| La Boulangerie | 3 |
| Cardinal | 7 |
| De la Cathédrale | 6 |
| Le Clos Jouvenet | 1 |
| Sisley | 4 |
| Street Art Hotel | 8 |

**EATING**
| | |
|---|---|
| Auberge St-Maclou | 8 |
| Brasserie Paul | 9 |
| Citizen Coffee | 2 |
| Crêperie la Régalière | 6 |
| Dame Cakes | 5 |
| Gill | 10 |
| La Marmite | 4 |
| P'tit Bec | 3 |
| Les P'tits Parapluies | 1 |
| Petite Auberge | 7 |

5

On summer nights, under the name of **Cathédrale de Lumière**, spectacular thirty-minute light shows are projected onto the cathedral facade; one show draws on Monet's paintings to create giant Impressionist canvases, while another depicts the story of Joan of Arc.

## Historial Jeanne d'Arc

7 rue St-Romain • Tues–Sun 10am–12.15pm & 12.45–7pm • €10.50 • ☎ 02 35 52 48 00, ⓦ www.historial-jeannedarc.fr

A virtual re-creation of the trial of Joan of Arc in 1431, the high-tech **Historial Jeanne d'Arc** occupies the former Archbishop's Palace, on the north side of the cathedral. Visitors proceed from sealed room to room for a rather slow-paced hour, following a re-enactment of the trial, before being freed to spend perhaps half an hour looking at explanatory displays and related exhibits.

## Abbatiale St-Ouen

Place du Général-de-Gaulle • Tues–Thurs, Sat & Sun: April–Oct 10am–noon & 2–6pm; Nov–March 10am–noon & 2–5pm • Free

The church known as the **Abbatiale St-Ouen**, next to the *hôtel de ville*, is larger than Rouen's cathedral and has far less decoration. From the outside, therefore, there's nothing to diminish the instant impact of its vast Gothic proportions and the purity of its lines. Inside, it holds some stunning fourteenth-century stained glass, though much was destroyed during the Revolution.

## Aître St-Maclou

188 rue Martainville • April–Oct Sat & Sun 9am–7pm; Nov–March Sat & Sun 9am–6pm; plus Mon–Fri 9am–6pm all year, during school hols only • Free

Built as a cemetery for plague victims, **Aître St-Maclou** was originally part of the complex that centred on the light, graceful **church of St-Maclou**. On first glance, it now appears simply to be the tranquil garden courtyard of the Fine Arts school; take a look at the ornate carvings that line the lower storey of the surrounding buildings, however, and you'll find all sorts of chilling symbols of death and decay. Look out, too, for a genuine mummified cat.

## Gros Horloge

Rue du Gros-Horloge • Daily except Mon: April–Oct 10am–1pm & 2–7pm; Nov–March 2–6pm; last admission 1hr before closing • €7 •
☎ 02 32 08 01 90, ⓦ rouen.fr/gros-horloge

Until it was lowered to straddle the rue du Gros-Horloge in 1529, to allow the citizens of Rouen to see it better, the colourful one-handed clock known as the **Gros Horloge** used to adorn the Gothic belfry alongside. Visitors now climb, via several rooms that explain the history of both clock and city, up a stone spiral staircase, to emerge on a narrow but safely railed boardwalk around the very top. Here you can admire the clock's intricate workings, and enjoy marvellous views of the old city, with its startling array of towers and spires.

## Place du Vieux-Marché

The **place du Vieux-Marché** is surrounded by fine old brown-and-white half-timbered houses; many of those on the south side now serve as restaurants. Alongside a huge cross (nearly 20m high), a small plaque marks the spot where Joan of Arc was burned to death on May 30, 1431; the **Ste-Jeanne**, her memorial church, was dedicated here in 1979.

### Church of Ste-Jeanne

Daily: April–Oct 10am–noon & 2–6pm; Nov–March 10am–noon & 2–5.30pm • Free

A wacky, spiky-looking thing, said to represent either an upturned boat or the flames that consumed Joan, the memorial **Church of Ste-Jeanne** is an indisputable triumph, part of an ensemble of buildings that also incorporates a covered food market (daily except Mon) that's designed less for practical shopping than for show.

## JOAN OF ARC

By the time the 17-year-old peasant girl known to history as **Joan of Arc** (Jeanne d'Arc in French) arrived at the French court early in 1429, the Hundred Years'War had already dragged on for more than ninety years. Most of northern France was in the grip of an Anglo–Burgundian alliance, but Joan, who had been hearing voices since 1425, was certain she could save the country, and came to present her case to the as-yet-uncrowned Dauphin. Partly through recognizing him despite a simple disguise he wore to fool her, she convinced him of her Divine guidance. After a remarkable three-week examination by a tribunal of the French *parlement*, she secured command of the armies of France. In a whirlwind **campaign**, which culminated in the raising of the siege of Orléans on May 8, 1429, she broke the English hold on the Loire Valley. She then escorted the Dauphin deep into enemy territory so that, in accordance with ancient tradition, he could be crowned King Charles VII of France in the cathedral at Reims, on July 17.

Within a year of her greatest triumph, Joan was **captured** by the Burgundian army at Compiègne in May 1430, and held to ransom. Chivalry dictated that any offer of payment from the vacillating Charles must be accepted, but in the absence of such an offer Joan was handed over to the English for 10,000 ducats. On Christmas Day, 1430, she was imprisoned in the château of Philippe-Auguste at Rouen.

### THE TRIAL

Charged with heresy, on account of her "false and diabolical" visions and refusal to give up wearing men's clothing, Joan was put on **trial** for her life on February 21, 1431. For three months, a changing panel of 131 assessors – only eight of them English-born – heard the evidence against her. Condemned, inevitably, to death, Joan recanted on the scaffold in St-Ouen cemetery on May 24, and her sentence was commuted to life imprisonment. The presiding judge, Bishop Pierre Cauchon of Beauvais, reassured disappointed English representatives "we will get her yet". The next Sunday, Joan was tricked into putting on male clothing, and taken to the archbishop's chapel in rue St-Romain to be condemned to death for the second time. On May 30, 1431, she was burned at the stake in the place du Vieux-Marché; her ashes, together with her unburned heart, were thrown into the Seine.

### BIRTH OF A LEGEND

Joan passed into legend, until the transcript of her trial was discovered in the 1840s. The forbearance and humility she displayed throughout her ordeal added to her status as France's greatest religious heroine. She was **canonized** in 1920, and soon afterwards became the country's patron saint.

The theme of the church's fish-shaped windows is continued in the scaly tiles that adorn its elongated roof, which forms a walkway across the square. The outline of its predecessor's foundations is visible on the adjacent lawns, which also mark the precise spot of Joan's martyrdom.

## Musée des Beaux-Arts

Esplanade Marcel-Duchamp • Daily except Tues 10am–6pm • free; temporary exhibitions may charge fees • ☎ 02 35 71 28 40, ⓦ mbarouen.fr

Rouen's imposing **Musée des Beaux-Arts** is home to an absorbing permanent collection, as well as regular temporary exhibitions. Unexpected highlights include dazzling Russian icons from the sixteenth century onwards, and an entertaining eighteenth-century crib from Naples. Many big names – Caravaggio (the centrepiece *Flagellation of Christ*), Velázquez, Rubens – tend to be represented by a single minor work, but there are several Modiglianis and a number of Monets, including *Rouen Cathedral* (1894), the *Vue Générale de Rouen* and *Brume sur la Seine* (1894). The central sculpture court, roofed but very light, holds a small tearoom.

## Musée da la Céramique

1 rue Faucon • Daily except Tues 2–6pm • free • ☎ 02 35 07 31 74, ⓦ museedelaceramique.fr

**5**

Rouen's history as a centre for *faïencerie*, or earthenware pottery, is recorded in the **Musée de la Céramique**, which is raised above the north side of the square Verdrel. A series of beautiful rooms, some of which incorporate sixteenth-century wood panelling rescued from a demolished nunnery of St-Amand, display specimens from the 1600s onwards. Assorted tiles and plates reflect the eighteenth-century craze for *chinoiserie*.

## Musée Le Secq des Tournelles

2 rue Jacques-Villon • Daily except Tues 2–6pm • free • ☎ 02 35 88 42 92, ⓦ museelesecqdestournelles.fr

Housed in the old, barely altered church of St-Laurent, behind the Beaux-Arts, the **Musée Le Secq des Tournelles** consists of a gloriously eccentric and uncategorizable collection of wrought-iron objects of all dates and descriptions. Prize exhibits include nutcrackers and door knockers, a huge double bed from sixteenth-century Italy, spiral staircases that lead nowhere and hideous implements of torture.

## Musée des Antiquités

198 rue Beauvoisine • Tues–Sat 1.30–5.30pm, Sun 2–6pm; also open Tues–Sat 10am–12.15pm during school hols • free • ☎ 02 76 30 39 50, ⓦ museedesantiquites.fr

The **Musée des Antiquités** provides a dry but comprehensive run-through of ancient artefacts found locally. Starting with an impressive Bronze Age helmet and various early iron tools, it continues with some remarkably complete and beautifully presented Roman mosaics. Then comes a long gallery filled with woodcarvings rescued from long-lost Rouen houses – including a lovely bas-relief of sheep that served as the sign for a medieval draper's shop – and also some fine fifteenth-century tapestries.

## Panorama XXL

Quai de Boisguilbert • Daily except Mon: May–Sept 10am–7pm, Oct–April 10am–6pm • €9.50 • ☎ 02 35 52 95 29, ⓦ panoramaxxl.com

Housed in a colossal metal cylinder, beside the right (northern) bank of the river Seine, Panorama XXL is a modern attraction with a strangely old-fashioned feel. Visitors climb a multi-level scaffolding tower in the centre of the building, to obtain changing, 360-degree views of a vast hyper-real panorama that's displayed on the surrounding walls. In summer, it depicts the city of Rouen as it looked at the time of the execution of Joan of Arc, in 1431. Each winter, a different image is presented, on themes such as the Great Barrier Reef.

### ARRIVAL AND INFORMATION ROUEN

**By train** The main *gare SNCF*, Gare Rive Droite, stands at the north end of rue Jeanne-d'Arc.

Destinations Dieppe (12 daily, 50min); Le Havre (13 daily, 1hr 10min); Paris-St-Lazare (25 daily; 1hr 20min); Vernon (12 daily; 30min).

**By bus** The *gare routière* is tucked away behind the riverfront on rue des Charrettes one block west of rue Jeanne-d'Arc.

Destinations Le Havre (hourly; 2hr 45min), via Jumièges

(30min); Lisieux (2 daily; 2hr 30min).

**By car** Rouen is a difficult and frequently congested city to drive into. With many of the central streets pedestrianized, it's best to park as soon as you can – there are plenty of central underground car parks, especially near the cathedral and the place du Vieux-Marché – and explore the city on foot.

**Tourist office** 25 place de la Cathédrale (Mon–Sat 9.30am–12.30pm & 1.30–6.30pm; ☎ 02 32 08 32 40, ⓦ rouentourisme.com).

### GETTING AROUND

**By métro** Rouen's métro system (ⓦ tcar.fr) follows the line of the rue Jeanne-d'Arc south from the *gare SNCF*, making two stops before resurfacing to cross the river by bridge. Individual journeys cost €1.60; a book of ten tickets is €14.30, or you can buy a 24hr pass for €5.

**By bus** Almost all local buses from the *gare SNCF* run down rue Jeanne-d'Arc to the centre, which takes 5min. Agence

Astuce, the headquarters of the bus network, is just north of the river.

**By bike** The city-sponsored Cy'clic network (ⓦ cyclic.rouen. fr) enables credit-card holders to unlock a simple bike from "stations" scattered along the streets, and leave it at any other station; journeys of less than 30min are free.

## ACCOMMODATION

**Auberge de Jeunesse** 3 rue du Tour, rte de Darnetal ☎02 35 08 18 50, ⓦfuaj.org. Housed in an eighteenth-century dyers' works, beside the little Robec river well east of the centre, Rouen's youth hostel offers dorm beds in rooms that sleep from two to eight, plus bright and friendly communal areas. **€19.70**

**Beauséjour** 9 rue Pouchet ☎02 35 71 93 47, ⓦbeausejour.rouentophotels.com. Good-value hotel near the station (turn right as you come out). Beyond the orange facade and nice garden courtyard, the rooms are nothing fancy, but they're crisply decorated and have large-screen TVs. The cheapest double room lacks its own shower, and they have even cheaper singles. **€58**

**La Boulangerie** 59 rue St-Nicaise ☎06 12 94 53 15, ⓦlaboulangerie.fr. Very welcoming three-room B&B, just north of St-Ouen and set above a half-timbered, red-painted boulangerie where the owners bake bread and serve breakfast. Bedrooms feature exposed beams, comfy beds, and in two instances bathtubs open to the room. **€92**

**Cardinal** 1 place de la Cathédrale ☎02 35 70 24 42, ⓦcardinal-hotel.fr. Very good-value hotel in a stunning – albeit potentially noisy – location, facing the cathedral. Rooms are spacious and clean, with good en-suite facilities and flatscreen TVs. Two family rooms available. All have views of the cathedral (the higher ones from balconies). Ample buffet breakfasts for €10. **€88**

**De la Cathédrale** 12 rue St-Romain ☎02 35 71 57 95, ⓦhotel-de-la-cathedrale.fr. Attractive hotel, in a pedestrian lane beside the cathedral, with a pleasant olde-worlde theme, nice breakfast room and flower-filled courtyard. The rooms are plainer than the public spaces might suggest, but it's still a peaceful haven. Discounts at public car park nearby. Buffet breakfasts €12. **€95**

★ **Le Clos Jouvenet** 42 rue Hyacinthe-Langlois ☎02 35 89 80 66, ⓦleclosjouvenet.com. Four beautifully decorated, comfortable rooms in an immaculate nineteenth-century house a 10min walk east of the train station. Breakfast is served in the conservatory, overlooking the enclosed garden. Rates drop for second night onwards. Closed mid-Nov to mid-Feb. **€130**

**Sisley** 51 rue Jean-Lecanuet ☎02 35 71 10 07, ⓦle-sisley.rouentophotels.com. Very central little budget hotel, an easy walk from the station, where each of the thirteen bright, comfortable double rooms is decorated in keeping with a different Impressionist painter, and has a shower rather than a bath. **€66**

**Street Art Hotel (was Arts et Seine)** 6 rue St-Étienne-des-Tonneliers ☎02 35 88 11 44, ⓦstreetarthotel.com. Inexpensive hotel, a block north of the river not far from the cathedral, redecorated in vaguely Asian style by friendly owners. Clean, well-equipped rooms of varying levels of comfort, accessible via stairs only, plus good buffet breakfasts. **€65**

## EATING AND DRINKING

Rouen's busiest bars and restaurants are especially concentrated around the streets that radiate out from the place du Vieux-Marché. Rue Martainville offers some excellent, often less touristy.

### RESTAURANTS

**Auberge St-Maclou** 224–226 rue Martainville ☎02 35 71 06 67. Half-timbered building in the shadow of St-Maclou church, with outdoor tables on a busy pedestrian street, and an old-style ambience. Well-priced traditional French *menus* – lunch is €14/€17, dinner €24/€30. Tues–Fri noon–2pm & 7–10pm, Sat 7–10.30pm, Sun noon–2.30pm.

**Brasserie Paul** 1 place de la Cathédrale ☎02 35 71 86 07, ⓦbrasserie-paul.com. Rouen's definitive bistro, an attractive *belle époque* place facing the cathedral. Daily lunch specials, with a €17.90 *formule* or Simone de Beauvoir's favourite goat's cheese and smoked duck salad for €15. Mon–Thurs & Sun 10am–11pm, Fri & Sat 10am–midnight.

**Citizen Coffee** 4 rue de l'Écureuil ☎02 35 71 49 42. Cool coffee house, with pavement tables on a pedestrianized central street, where along with fine coffee you can enjoy light food options including avocado toast for €11 and various salads, surrounded by local freelancers attempting to maintain their work/life balance. Mon–Fri 7.30am–7pm, Sat 9am–7pm.

**Crêperie la Régalière** 12 rue Massacre ☎02 35 15 33 33. Quaint, inexpensive but good-quality crêperie, in a quiet but very picturesque backstreet just north of the Gros Horloge, that's one of central Rouen's best bargains, with a lunch *menu* at €9.50 and good-value deals later on. They also serve a surprising array of fine teas. Tues–Sat 11.45am–11pm.

**Dame Cakes** 70 rue St-Romain ☎02 35 07 49 31, ⓦdamecakes.fr. Elegant tearoom, with a little garden, on a quiet street next to the cathedral, tempting the tastebuds with delicious desserts, savoury tarts and salads. Mon–Fri 10.30am–7pm, Sat 10am–7.30pm.

**Gill** 8–9 quai de la Bourse ☎02 35 71 16 14, ⓦgill.fr. A showcase for celebrated local chef Gilles Tournadre, this ultra-smart quayside restaurant boasts two Michelin stars. The Asian-influenced food is presented with all the fancy trimmings and extras that it might suggest; it can be hard to tell what you're eating, but it tastes sublime. There's a €40 weekday lunch *menu*, while set dinners cost €75 or €115. Tournadre's other Rouen restaurants include the cheaper and less formal *Le 37*, in the terrace behind at 37 rue St-Etienne-des-Tonneliers. Tues–Sat noon–1.45pm & 7.30–9.45pm; closed 2 weeks in April and 3 weeks in Aug.

★ **La Marmite** 3 rue de Florence ☎02 35 71 75 55, ⓦlamarmiterouen.com. Smart little place just north of

**5**

the place du Vieux-Marché, offering beautiful, elegantly presented gourmet dishes on well-priced *menus* at €34, €44 (featuring hot foie gras), and €65. Wed–Sat noon–2pm & 7–9.30pm, Sun noon–2pm.

**P'tit Bec** 182 rue Eau de Robec ☎02 35 07 63 33, ⓦleptitbec.com. Friendly brasserie that's especially popular at lunchtime. Simple *menus* at €14 and €17.50 include a fish or meat main course, plus vegetarian options, or you can get a salad for €12. There's seating indoors as well as out on the pedestrianized street. Mon–Wed noon–2.30pm, Thurs–Sat noon–2.30pm & 7–10.30pm.

**Les P'tits Parapluies** 46 rue Bourg-l'Abbé, place de la Rougemare ☎02 35 88 55 26, ⓦlesptits-parapluies.com. Elegant, secluded, half-timbered restaurant, on the edge of an attractive little square. Counting your calories (or your pennies) is not really an option; set *menus* start at €29 for lunch, €36 for dinner, and include oysters or duck carpaccio as a starter. Just €6 extra buys two glasses of wine per person. Tues–Fri noon–1.45pm & 7.45–10pm, Sat 7.45–10pm, Sun noon–1.45pm.

**Petite Auberge** 164 rue Martainville ☎02 35 70 80

18, ⓦrestaurant-petite-auberge.fr. Appealing, old-fashioned, indoor restaurant, serving delicious traditional Norman cuisine at reasonable prices; they're proud of their snails, but there are plenty of alternatives. Weekday lunch *formule* €14.30, dinner *menus* from €19 on weekdays, €24 at weekends. Tues noon–1.30pm, Wed–Sun noon–1.30pm & 7.15–10pm.

### BARS

**Delirium Café** 30 rue des Vergetiers ☎02 32 12 05 95, ⓦdeliriumcafe.be. In a splendid half-timbered house right under the big clock, this student-oriented pub, part of a Belgian chain, focuses entirely on beer, with a couple of dozen on draught – largely Belgian – and plenty more besides. Mon–Sat 5pm–2am.

**Le Nash** 97 rue Écuyère ☎02 35 98 25 24, ⓦnashcafe.com. Relaxed bar that's popular with locals. The interior has a lounge-like feel with its mood lighting and zebra stripes, while the outdoor terrace is much more akin to a classic French café, and serves light snacks. Music from ambient to Latin. Tues–Sat 6pm–2am.

### NIGHTLIFE AND ENTERTAINMENT

### CLUBS

**Emporium Galorium** 151 rue Beauvoisine ☎02 35 71 76 95, ⓦwww.facebook.com/EmpoGalorium. Busy, half-timbered student-dominated bar, a short walk north of the centre, hosting small-scale gigs and theatrical productions. Wed–Sat 8pm–2am.

**XXL** 25–27 rue de la Savonnerie ☎02 35 88 84 00. Gay (largely male) club near the river, just south of the cathedral, with theme nights and a small basement dancefloor. Tues–Sun 10pm–5am.

### LIVE MUSIC

**Le 106** 106 quai Jean-de-Béthancourt ☎02 32 10 88 60, ⓦle106.com. City-owned hangar-like venue with two halls, used for large gigs, as well as meetings and

exhibitions, on the southern side of the river a 15min walk from the centre, and served by night buses N2 and N3.

### THEATRE

**Hangar 23** Pied du Pont Flaubert ☎02 32 76 23 23, ⓦletincelle-rouen.fr. Major south-bank venue used by local and touring theatre companies, and also hosting dance, world music and jazz.

**Théâtre des Arts** 7 rue du Dr-Rambert ☎02 35 98 74 78, ⓦoperaderouen.com. This highbrow venue puts on a varied programme of opera, ballet and concerts.

**Théâtre des Deux Rives** ☎02 35 70 22 82, ⓦcdn-normandierouen.fr. Home to an adventurous repertory company, this small theatre, opposite the Antiquités museum at the top end of rue Louis-Ricard, also hosts touring productions.

## Along the Seine from Rouen

As well as idyllic pastoral scenery, the banks of the Seine hold some unmissable historical and cultural attractions. **Upstream** from Rouen, high cliffs on the north bank look down on green woodlands and scattered river islands. By the time you reach the splendid castle at **Les Andelys**, 25km southeast of Rouen, you're within 100km of Paris, while another 30km brings you to Monet's former home in the village of **Giverny**. **Downstream**, on the other hand, the highlight of the lovely riverside route is the intriguing ruins of **Jumièges abbey**.

### Château Gaillard

Les Andelys • Mid-March to mid-Nov daily except Tues 10am–1pm & 2–6pm • €3, grounds free all year • ⓦlesandelys.com/chateau-gaillard

The most dramatic sight along the Seine has to be Richard the Lionheart's **Château Gaillard**, perched high above **LES ANDELYS**. Constructed in a position of impregnable power, at the frontier of the English king's domains, it surveyed all movement on the river. Built within a single year (1196–97), the castle might have survived intact had Henri IV not ordered its destruction in 1603. As it is, the stout flint walls of its keep, roughly 4m thick, remain reasonably sound, and its overall outline is still clear, arranged over green and chalky knolls. To reach it on foot, climb the steep path that leads off rue Richard-Coeur-de-Lion in Petit Andely.

## Monet's house at Giverny

84 rue Claude-Monet, Giverny • late March to Oct daily 9.30am–6pm; last entry 5.30pm • €9.50, ages 7–12 €5.50; to avoid queues, book ahead online • ☎ 02 32 51 28 21, ⓦ fondation-monet.com

The house where **Claude Monet** lived from 1883 until his death in 1926 remains much as he left it – complete with lily pond – at **GIVERNY**, 20km south of Les Andelys near the Seine's north bank. While the **gardens** that Monet laid out are still lovingly tended, none of his original paintings are on display, so art-lovers who make the pilgrimage here tend to be outnumbered by garden enthusiasts.

Visits start in the huge **studio**, built in 1915, where Monet painted the last and largest of his many depictions of water lilies (*nymphéas*). It now serves as a well-stocked book- and giftshop. The **house** itself is a long two-storey structure, painted pastel pink with green shutters. Almost all the main rooms are crammed floor-to-ceiling with Monet's collection of Japanese woodblock prints. Most of the furnishings are gone, but you get a real sense of how the dining room used to be, with its walls and fittings a glorious bright yellow.

The flower-filled **gardens** stretch down towards the river, though the footpath that drops to the **water-lily pond** now burrows beneath the road. Once there, paths around the pond, as well as arching Japanese footbridges, offer differing views of the water lilies, cherished by gardeners in rowing boats. May and June, when the rhododendrons flower and the wisteria is in bloom, are the best times to visit.

## Abbaye de Jumièges

24 rue Guillaume le Conquérant, Jumièges • Daily: mid-April to mid-Sept 9.30am–6.30pm; mid-Sept to mid-April 9.30am–1pm & 2.30–5.30pm • €6.50 • ☎ 02 35 37 24 02, ⓦ www.abbayedejumieges.fr

Nestled into an especially delightful loop of the Seine, 23km west of Rouen, the majestic **abbey** of **JUMIÈGES** is said to have been founded by St Philibert in 654 AD. Now a haunting ruin, the abbey was burned by Vikings in 841, rebuilt a century later, then destroyed again during the Revolution. Its main surviving outline dates from the eleventh century – William the Conqueror himself attended its reconsecration in 1067. The twin towers, 52m high, are still standing, as is one arch of the roofless nave, while a one-sided yew tree stands amid what were once the cloisters.

| INFORMATION | ALONG THE SEINE FROM ROUEN |
|---|---|

**LES ANDELYS**
**Tourist office** 24 rue Reymond-Phélip, between Petit and Grand Andely (April–Oct Mon–Sat 10am–1pm & 2–5pm, Sun 10.30am–1.30pm & 2.30–4pm; Nov–March Tues–Sat 10am–12.30pm & 2–5pm; ☎ 02 32 54 41 93, ⓦ www.ville-andelys.fr).

## ACCOMMODATION AND EATING

**LES ANDELYS**
★ **Chaîne d'Or** 27 rue Grande ☎ 02 32 54 00 31, ⓦ hotel-lachainedor.com. Les Andelys' most upscale hotel, this luxurious old coaching inn is arrayed around a courtyard beside the river, opposite the thirteenth-century St-Sauveur church; Seine-view rooms cost from €20 extra. Its restaurant (closed Wed all year, plus Sun eve & Tues in winter) serves wonderful food on *menus* priced €52 and up. **€119**

**L'Île des Trois Rois** 1 rue Gilles-Nicole, Petit Andely ☎ 02 32 54 23 79, ⓦ camping-troisrois.com. Lovely – and lively – three-star campsite, stretching out beside the river far below the château, with a pool and snack bar. Closed mid-Nov to mid-March. **€27**

**5**

**GIVERNY**

**Jardin des Plumes** 1 rue du Milieu ☎02 32 54 26 35, ⓦ lejardindesplumes.fr. Opulent half-timbered country hotel, set in extensive gardens, 500m from Monet's house. Smart contemporary rooms with lots of polished wood and exposed brickwork; dinner *menus* start at €52. Hotel closed Mon & Tues Nov–March; restaurant closed Mon & Tues. **€184**

**Musardière** 123 rue Claude-Monet ☎02 32 21 03 18, ⓦ lamusardiere.fr. Ten comfortable en-suite rooms in a fine old rosy-hued townhouse, plus dinner *menus* from €26. Its well-shaded terrace makes a nice spot for lunch, and it also offers crêpes and snacks during the day. Closed Christmas–Jan. **€85**

**ABBAYE DE JUMIÈGES**

★ **Auberge des Ruines** 17 place de la Mairie ☎02 35 37 24 05, ⓦ auberge-des-ruines.fr. A relaxing and truly superb restaurant, with outdoor seating on a shaded terrace across from the abbey. *Menus* range from €33 up to €55. July & Aug daily noon–2pm & 7–9pm, Sept–Jun Mon, Tues & Thurs–Sat noon–2pm & 7–9pm, Sun noon–2pm.

# Basse Normandie

Setting off west along the coast of Basse Normandie from the mouth of the Seine, you come to a succession of exclusive resorts: **Honfleur** is a delightful medieval port, while **Trouville** and **Deauville** are the busiest centres. Continuing west brings you to the beaches where the Allied armies landed in 1944, and then to the wilder shore around the **Cotentin Peninsula**.

## Honfleur

**HONFLEUR** is Normandy's most beautiful seaside town, and its best-preserved historic port. All that holds it back from perfection is that it's now cut off from the Channel itself; as silt from the Seine has accumulated, the sea has steadily withdrawn, leaving the eighteenth-century waterfront houses of **boulevard Charles-V** stranded and a little surreal. The ancient port, however, still functions – the channel is kept open by regular dredging – and though only pleasure craft now use the harbour moorings, fishing boats tie up alongside the pier nearby.

Honfleur remains recognizable as the fishing village that so appealed to nineteenth-century artists. Its compact size, quaint waterside setting and abundant restaurants make it an ideal destination for a weekend break. Visitors inevitably gravitate towards the old centre, around the beautiful **Vieux Bassin**, where slate-fronted houses, each one or two storeys higher than seems possible, harmonize despite their tottering and ill-matched forms. They create a splendid backdrop for the **Lieutenance** at the harbour entrance, which has been the gateway to the inner town since at least 1608, when Samuel Champlain sailed from Honfleur to found Québec.

### Musée de la Marine

Quai St-Etienne • Mid-Feb to March, Oct & Nov Tues–Fri 2.30–5.30pm, Sat & Sun 10am–noon & 2.30–5.30pm; April–Sept Tues–Sun 10am–noon & 2–6.30pm • €4.20, €5.30 with Musée d'Ethnographie, €12 with Musée d'Ethnographie, Musée Eugène Boudin and Les Maisons Satie • ☎02 31 89 14 12, ⓦ musees-honfleur.fr

Honfleur's one-room **Musée de la Marine** somehow squeezes into the fourteenth-century church of **St-Étienne**, on the eastern side of the *bassin*. Exhibits tracing the town's intimate association with the sea include model sailing ships, displays on the local shipbuilding industry, and a cumbersome early diving suit.

### Musée d'Ethnographie

Rue de la Prison • Mid-Feb to March, Oct & Nov Tues–Fri 2.30–5.30pm, Sat & Sun 10am–noon & 2.30–5.30pm; April–Sept Tues–Sun 10am–noon & 2–6.30pm • 4.20, €5.30 with Musée de la Marine, €120 with Musée de la Marine, Musée Eugène Boudin and Maisons Satie • ☎02 31 89 14 12, ⓦ musees-honfleur.fr

Alongside the Musée de la Marine, a nice little ensemble that once held Honfleur's prison now serves as the **Musée d'Ethnographie**, filling ten rooms with a fascinating assortment of everyday artefacts from old Honfleur.

## Musée Eugène Boudin

Place Érik-Satie • April to early July & Sept daily except Tues 10am–noon & 2–6pm; early July to Aug daily except Tues 10am–6pm; Oct to mid-March Mon & Wed–Fri 2.30–5.30pm, Sat & Sun 10am–noon & 2.30–5.30pm • €8, €12 with Les Maisons Satie, Musée de la Marine and Musée d'Ethnographie • ☎ 02 31 89 54 00, ⓦ musees-honfleur.fr

Eugène Boudin, a forerunner of Impressionism, was born and worked in Honfleur, and was joined here at various times by Pissaro, Renoir, Cézanne and the 18-year-old Monet. He was also among the founders of what's now the **Musée Eugène Boudin**, west of the port, and left 53 works to it after his death in 1898. His pastel seascapes and sunsets hold a special resonance in this setting, where panoramic windows offer superb views of the Seine estuary.

## Église Ste-Catherine

**Church** Daily: summer 8.30am–7pm; winter 8.30am–6pm **Belfry** Mid-March to May & Sept Mon & Wed–Sun 10am–noon & 2–6pm; June–Aug Mon & Wed–Sun 10am–12.30pm & 2–6pm; Oct to mid-March Mon & Wed–Fri 2.30–5.30pm, Sat & Sun 10am–noon & 2.30–5.30pm • €2, or free with Musée Eugène Boudin

Honfleur's most remarkable building, the church of **Ste-Catherine**, is, like its distinctive detached **belfry**, built almost entirely of wood. The church itself has the added peculiarity of being divided into twin naves, with one balcony running around both. The belfry, a favourite subject for the young Monet, holds random ethnographic oddities; visitors are not permitted above ground level.

## Les Maisons Satie

67 bd Charles-V • daily except Tues: mid-Feb to April & Oct–Dec 11am–6pm; May–Sept 10am–7pm; last entry 1hr before closing • €8, €12 with Musée Eugène Boudin, Musée de la Marine and Musée d'Ethnographie • ☎ 02 31 89 11 11, ⓦ musees-honfleur.fr

From the outside, the red-timbered former home of **Érik Satie** – open to visitors as **Les Maisons Satie** – looks unchanged since the composer was born there in 1866. Step inside, however, and you'll find yourself in Normandy's most unusual and eccentric museum. As befits a close associate of the Surrealists, Satie is commemorated by all sorts of weird and wonderful interactive surprises. It would be a shame to give too many of them away here; suffice it to say that you're immediately confronted by a giant pear, bouncing into the air on huge wings to the strains of his best-known piano series, *Gymnopédies*.

### ARRIVAL AND INFORMATION    HONFLEUR

**By train** The nearest train station, 20km south at Pont-l'Évêque, is connected to Honfleur by the Lisieux bus #50 (20min).

**By bus** The *gare routière*, a 10min walk east of the Vieux Bassin, is served by frequent buses from Caen and Le Havre (☎ 09 70 83 00 14, ⓦ busverts.fr).

**Tourist office** Quai Le Paulmier (Easter–June & Sept Mon–Sat 9.30am–12.30pm & 2–6.30pm, Sun 10am–12.30pm & 2–5pm; July & Aug Mon–Sat 9.30am–7pm, Sun 10am–5pm; Oct–Easter Mon–Sat 9.30am–12.30pm & 2–6pm, Sun 10am–1pm in school hols only; ☎ 02 31 89 23 30, ⓦ ot-honfleur.fr).

**River cruises** In summer, several cruises sail upriver each day from well-signposted departure points either side of the Avant-Port, for a closer look at the Pont de Normandie (45min trip €8, 1hr 30min €11). Visit ⓦ ot-honfleur.fr for full listings.

### ACCOMMODATION

Honfleur is an expensive destination, especially in summer; budget travellers would do better simply to visit for the day. No hotels overlook the harbour itself, while motorists will find it hard to park anywhere near most central hotels.

★ **La Cour Sainte-Catherine** 74 rue du Puits ☎ 07 87 04 49 16, ⓦ coursaintecatherine.com. Beautiful B&B tucked down a quiet street beyond Ste-Catherine church. Comfortable, well-decorated rooms around a plant-filled courtyard, and some larger apartments; substantial buffet breakfasts served in the old cider press. **€120**

**Dauphin** 10 place Berthelot ☎ 02 31 89 15 53, ⓦ hotel dudauphin.com. Grey-slate townhouse around the corner from Ste-Catherine church, offering assorted rooms above a tearoom. All have been spruced up with contemporary decor; the cheapest are in an impersonal annex, and there are some larger family options. The creaky floorboards and thin walls are universal, however. **€89**

**L'Ex Voto** 8 place Albert-Sorel ☎ 02 31 89 19 69,

**5**

ⓦ hotel-honfleur-exvoto.com. Four clean, well-priced rooms, reached via a precarious spiral staircase above a friendly family-run café/bar, a short walk inland from the Vieux Bassin. Two are en suite, the others share a shower and toilet. Rates include breakfast; wifi in bar only. Closed Wed Sept–June. €67

**Le Fond de la Cour** 29 rue Eugène-Boudin ☎ 06 72 20 72 98, ⓦ lefonddelacour.com. Secluded little complex, run by a friendly Scottish couple and set around a courtyard a short walk from the centre, consisting of tastefully furnished rooms and suites in a former stables, plus a garden cottage sleeping up to four. Rates shown are cash only, and include excellent breakfasts; you can stay on a self-catering basis if you prefer. €99

★ **Les Maisons de Léa** Place Ste-Catherine ☎ 02 31 14 49 49, ⓦ lesmaisonsdelea.com. This magnificent hotel spreads through four seventeenth-century houses on Honfleur's central square. Rooms range from spacious doubles to family suites and a self-catering cottage; each has its own quirks and treasures, and all are luxurious. They also have a spa, while *menus* in the high-class on-site restaurant, with tables on the square itself, start at €26 for lunch. €180

★ **Monet** Rue Charrière du Puits ☎ 02 31 89 00 90, ⓦ hotel-monet-honfleur.com. Spruce, modern en-suite rooms in a quiet spot 10min walk uphill from the centre, with courtyard parking. Some are in the original old townhouse, the remainder in new extensions, and the management is exceptionally helpful. €90

## EATING

With its plentiful visitors, Honfleur supports a corresponding number of restaurants, many specializing in seafood. Few face onto the harbour itself, though; instead, most of the narrow buildings around its edge are home to cafés and ice-cream parlours.

**Le Bouillon Normand** 7 rue de la Ville ☎ 02 31 89 02 41. Old-fashioned bistro, with indoor and outdoor seating, in a spacious and quiet square just back from the *bassin* behind St-Étienne church. Fish, cider and cheese are prominent on simple, good-value *menus* at €22 and €30. Mon, Tues & Thurs–Sat noon–1.45pm & 7–9pm, Sun noon–1.45pm.

**Le Bréard** 7 rue du Puits ☎ 02 31 89 53 40, ⓦ restaurant-lebreard.com. Creative, contemporary take on classic French cuisine, in a remodelled old mansion just off the church square. Don't expect heavy sauces and huge portions; here things are very much lighter and more delicate, on dinner *menus* at €33–63. Mon–Thurs

7–9.30pm, Fri–Sun noon–2pm & 7–9.30pm; closed 3 weeks in Dec.

**La Cidrerie** 26 place Hamelin ☎ 02 31 89 59 85, ⓦ creperie-lacidrerie-honfleur.com. This lively and convivial old cider bar, set back just off the square, also serves crêpes and *galettes* for around €6, and has a €12 lunch *menu*. It might look like a tourist trap, but once you get deep inside it's pleasantly cosy. Daily noon–10pm; closed Tues & Wed in low season.

**Au P'tit Mareyeur** 4 rue Haute ☎ 02 31 98 84 23, ⓦ auptitmareyeur.fr. No distance from the centre, but all the seating is indoors and there are no views. Very good fish dishes, plus plenty of creamy *pays d'Auge* sauces and superb desserts. *Menus* from €29 for lunch, €36 for dinner, or you can get a sumptuous bouillabaisse for €35. Mon & Thurs–Sun noon–2pm & 7–10pm; closed Jan.

# Trouville and Deauville

As you head west along the corniche from Honfleur, green fields and fruit trees lull the land's edge, and cliffs rise from sandy beaches all the way to the sister towns of **Trouville**, 15km away, and **Deauville**, just beyond. Of the two, **TROUVILLE** is more of a real town, with a constant population and industries other than tourism. But it's still a resort, with a tangle of pedestrian streets, alive with restaurants and hotels, just back from a broad beach that's paralleled by a busy boardwalk.

**DEAUVILLE** is slightly larger than Trouville, and significantly smarter, its sleek streets lined with designer boutiques and chic cafés. In summer, life revolves around the beach and the *planches*, 650m of boardwalk, beyond which rows of primary-coloured parasols obscure the view of the sea. It's best known for its **American Film Festival** (ⓦ festival-deauville.com), held in the first week of September and offering public admission to a wide selection of previews.

## ARRIVAL AND DEPARTURE · TROUVILLE AND DEAUVILLE

**By train and bus** Trouville and Deauville share their *gare SNCF* and *gare routière*, located between the two just south of the marina.

Destinations (train) Lisieux (5 daily in winter, much more frequently in summer; 20min); Paris (5 daily in winter, much more frequently in summer; 2hr).

Destinations (bus) Caen (hourly; 1hr 15min); Honfleur (10 daily; 30min).

## INFORMATION

**Trouville tourist office** 32 quai Fernand-Moureaux (July & Aug Mon–Sat 10am–6pm, Sun 10am–4pm; Sept–June Mon–Sat 10am–6pm, Sun 10am–1.30pm; ☎02 31 14 60 70, ⓦtrouvillesurmer.org).

**Deauville tourist office** quai de l'Impératrice-Eugénie (July & Aug Mon–Sat 9am–7pm, Sun 10am–1pm & 2–6pm; Sept–June Mon–Sat 10am–6pm, Sun 10am–1pm & 2–5pm; ☎02 31 14 40 00, ⓦdeauville.org).

## ACCOMMODATION

★ **Flaubert** Rue Gustave-Flaubert, Trouville ☎02 31 88 37 23, ⓦflaubert.fr. If you fancy staying right on the seafront, it's hard to beat this great-value faux-timbered mansion at the start of Trouville's boardwalk, where the spacious, comfortable rooms have large bathrooms and in

many cases balconies. **€129**

**Des Sports** 27 rue Gambetta, Deauville ☎02 31 88 22 67. Nine well-priced en-suite rooms, two of which have balconies, above a popular local bar/restaurant behind Deauville's fish market. Closed March & Nov, plus Sun in winter. **€76**

## EATING

**Chez Miocque** 81 rue Eugène-Colas, Deauville ☎02 31 88 09 52. Everyone who's anyone in Deauville drops in at some point to this bustling, top-quality Parisian-style bistro, to snack on anything from hard-boiled eggs to steak and chips, or enjoy a full three-course meal for €44. Feb–Dec daily noon–11pm.

**La Petite Auberge** 7 rue Carnot, Trouville ☎02 31 88 11 07, ⓦlapetiteaubergesurmer.fr. Small, intimate restaurant just inland from the beach, where seafood is the speciality but the *menus*, from €42 in the evenings, include hearty meat dishes too. Mon & Thurs–Sun 12.15–1.45pm & 7.15–9.30pm; also open Wed in Aug.

# Caen

Few tourists go out of their way to visit **CAEN**, capital and largest city of Basse Normandie. It was devastated during the fighting of 1944, so busy roads now fill the wide spaces where pre-war houses stood, circling ramparts that no longer have a castle to protect. However, the former home to William the Conqueror remains impressive in parts, adorned with the scattered spires and buttresses of two abbeys and eight old churches, and makes a convenient base for the D-Day beaches.

Most of the centre is taken up with shopping streets and pedestrian precincts. On Friday, the main city **market** spreads along both sides of Fosse St-Julien. The **Bassin St-Pierre**, the pleasure port at the end of the canal that links Caen to the sea, is the liveliest area in summer.

## Château de Caen

Although almost nothing remains of the eleventh-century **Château de Caen**, its ancient **ramparts** are still in place. Walking the complete circuit gives a good overview of the city, with a particularly fine prospect of the reconstructed fourteenth-century facade of the nearby church of **St-Pierre**. Two modern structures within the castle precinct hold **museums**.

### Musée des Beaux-Arts

Mon–Fri 9.30am–12.30pm & 2–6pm, Sat & Sun 11am–6pm; closed Mon & Tues Nov–May • €3.50, special exhibitions extra; under-26s free • ☎02 31 30 47 70, ⓦmba.caen.fr

Upstairs galleries in the **Musée des Beaux-Arts** trace a potted history of European art from Renaissance Italy to eighteenth-century France. Downstairs brings things up to date with diverse twentieth-century and contemporary art as well as paintings by Monet, Bonnard and Gustave Doré.

### Musée de Normandie

Mon–Fri 9.30am–12.30pm & 2–6pm, Sat & Sun 11am–6pm; closed Mon & Tues Nov–May • €3.50, special exhibitions extra; under-26s free • ☎02 31 30 47 60, ⓦmusee-de-normandie.caen.fr

The **Musée de Normandie** provides a surprisingly cursory overview of Norman history, ranging from archeological finds from the megalithic period and glass jewellery from Gallo-Roman Rouen to artefacts from the Industrial Revolution.

**5**

## Abbaye aux Hommes

Rue St-Pierre • July & Aug Mon–Fri 8am–6.30pm, Sat & Sun 9.30am–6.30pm; Sept–June Mon–Thurs 8am–6pm, Fri 8am–5pm, Sat & Sun 9.30am–6.30pm; 1hr 15min guided tours leave adjacent *hôtel de ville*; tours in English July & Aug Mon–Fri 11am, 1.30pm & 4pm; tours in French all year, times vary • church free, cloisters €2, guided tours €4.50–7 • ☎ 02 31 30 42 81, ⓦ caenlamer-tourisme.fr

The spectacular Romanesque monument known as the **Abbaye aux Hommes** was founded by William the Conqueror and designed to hold his tomb within its huge, austere Romanesque church of St-Étienne. However, his burial here, in 1087, was hopelessly undignified. The funeral procession first caught fire and was then held to ransom, as factions squabbled over his rotting corpse for whatever spoils they could grab. During the Revolution the tomb was again ransacked, and now holds a solitary thigh bone rescued from the river.

## Abbaye aux Dames

Rue des Chanoines • Mon–Fri 8am–12.30pm & 1.30–6pm, Sat & Sun 2–6pm; guided tours, in French, daily 2.30pm & 4pm • Free • ☎ 02 31 06 98 45, ⓦ caenlamer-tourisme.fr

Corresponding to William the Conqueror's Abbaye aux Hommes, across town, the **Abbaye aux Dames** holds the tomb of William's queen, Mathilda, who commissioned the abbey church, La Trinité, well before the Conquest. It's starkly impressive, with a gloomy pillared crypt, superb stained glass behind the altar, and odd sculptural details like the fish curled up in the holy-water stoup.

## The Caen Memorial

Av Marshal-Montgomery • Late Jan to early Feb & Nov–Dec daily except Mon 9.30am–6pm; early Feb to Oct daily 9am–7pm; closed 3 weeks in Jan; last entry 1hr 15min before closing • €19.80, family pass €51 • ☎ 02 31 06 06 44, ⓦ normandy. memorial-caen.com • Bus #2 from stop "Tour le Roi" in central Caen

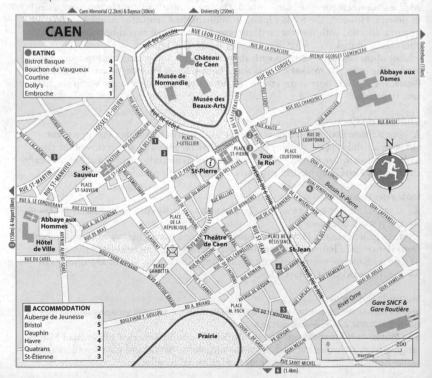

Just north of Caen, the excellent, high-tech **Caen Memorial** stands on a plateau named after General Eisenhower on a clifftop beneath which the Germans had their HQ in June and July 1944. Originally a "museum for peace", its brief has expanded to cover history since the Great War; allow two hours at the very least for a visit. Displays start with the rise of fascism in Germany, follow with resistance and collaboration in France, then chart all the major battles of World War II, with a special emphasis on D-Day and its aftermath. Further areas examine the Cold War. Most captions, though not always the written exhibits themselves, are translated into English. The memorial also hosts temporary exhibitions, and has a good-value self-service restaurant.

## ARRIVAL AND DEPARTURE                                                       CAEN

**By air** Caen's small airport (🖥 caen.aeroport.fr), served by British European flights from Southend (🖥 flybe.com), is 7km west on the D9, just outside Carpiquet.

**By train** Caen's *gare SNCF* is 1km south of the centre, across the River Orne.

Destinations Cherbourg (10 daily; 1hr 15min), via Bayeux (20min); Lisieux (21 daily; 30min); Le Mans (5 daily; 2hr), via Alençon (1hr 15min); Paris-St-Lazare (11 daily; 2hr 10min); Rennes (4 daily; 3hr), via St-Lô (50min), Coutances (1hr

15min) and Pontorson (2hr); Rouen (11 daily; 1hr 30min).

**By bus** The *gare routière* is alongside the *gare SNCF*, 1km south of the centre.

Destinations Arromanches (1 daily; 1hr 10min); Bayeux (3 daily; 50min); Clécy (4 daily; 50min); Falaise (10 daily; 1hr); Honfleur (9 daily; 2hr), via Deauville (1hr 15min), of which 5 continue to Le Havre (2hr 30min); Le Havre (3 daily express services; 1hr 20min), via Honfleur (1hr); Ouistreham (20 daily; 30min); Thury-Harcourt (5 daily; 40min).

## GETTING AROUND

**By bus and tram** Caen's buses and trams are run by TWISTO (☎ 02 31 15 55 55, 🖥 twisto.fr). Single journeys cost €1.50, and a 24-hour pass €4 per adult, €6.20 per family or group of 2–5 passengers. The main tram route

connects the southern and northern suburbs, running through the centre from the *gare SNCF* up av du 6-Juin to the university and beyond.

## INFORMATION

**Tourist office** Place St-Pierre (April–June & Sept Mon–Sat 9.30am–6.30pm, Sun 9.30am–1.30pm; July & Aug Mon–Sat 9am–7pm, Sun 10am–1pm & 2–5pm; Oct–March

Mon–Sat 9.30am–1pm & 2–6pm; ☎ 02 31 27 14 14, 🖥 caenlamer-tourisme.fr).

## ACCOMMODATION

**Auberge de Jeunesse** Résidence Robert-Remé, 68bis rue Eustache-Restout, Grâce-de-Dieu ☎ 02 31 52 19 96, 🖥 acahj-caen.fr. Lively and welcoming hostel in a sleepy area 2km southwest of the *gare SNCF*, on tramline B. Beds in four- or six-bed dorms. Reception 5–9pm. Closed Oct–May. Dorms **€17**

**Bristol** 31 rue du 11 Novembre ☎ 02 31 84 59 76, 🖥 hotelbristolcaen.com. Efficient, spruce and friendly hotel, in a quiet location an easy walk across the river from the train station. Rooms are small, but not bad for the price, and a substantial buffet breakfast is served in a pleasant dining room, for €9.50. **€85**

**Dauphin** 29 rue Gémare ☎ 02 31 86 22 26, 🖥 le-dauphin-normandie.com. Upmarket Best Western, where the public areas are impressive, and the rooms comfortable but relatively compact, at least at the lower end of the price scale. Spa and fitness facilities available, and a grand

restaurant serves dinner *menus* from €25 to €62. **€138**

★ **Havre** 11 rue du Havre ☎ 02 31 86 19 80, 🖥 caen-hotel.fr. Modern, cosy, and very good-value budget hotel, a block south of St-Jean church, close to the trams and with free parking. Rooms range from small singles to larger triples, and there are great discounts for advance bookings. **€70**

**Quatrans** 17 rue Gémare ☎ 02 31 86 25 57, 🖥 hotel-des-quatrans.com. Renovated hotel in an anonymous modern setting, near the tourist office and the château. The pastel theme of the facade continues inside; it's a bit cloying, but the service is friendly, and everything works well. **€85**

**St-Étienne** 2 rue de l'Académie ☎ 02 31 86 35 82, 🖥 hotelsaintetiennecaen.com. Hospitable budget hotel in a venerable stone house in the characterful St-Martin district, not far from the Abbaye aux Hommes. The rooms are far from fancy, but all are en-suite. **€61**

## EATING

Caen's town centre offers two major areas for eating, with cosmopolitan restaurants in the largely pedestrianized *quartier* Vaugueux and more traditional French options on

the streets off rue de Geôle, near the western ramparts.

**Bistrot Basque** 24 quai Vendeuvre ☎ 02 31 38 21 26, 🖥 le-bistrot-basque.com. Opposite the pleasure port,

**5**

an atmospheric restaurant with a bright interior, serving tasty Basque-influenced cooking, such as grilled cod with chorizo. There's a lunchtime *formule* at €21, while dinner is à la carte, with tasty tapas for €6–9 per portion, and larger servings for more like €14. Mon–Thurs noon–2pm & 7.30–10.30pm, Fri & Sat noon–2pm & 7.30–11pm.

★ **Bouchon du Vaugueux** 12 rue Graindorge ✆ 02 31 44 26 26, ⓦ bouchonduvaugueux.com. You'll need to reserve in advance for this intimate but hugely popular little brasserie in the Vaugueux quarter, which offers well-prepared French classics, such as duck with peaches, on just two *menus* (€23 and €35). Tues–Thurs noon–2pm & 7–10pm, Fri & Sat noon–2pm & 7–10.30pm.

**Courtine** 16 rue Caponière ✆ 02 31 79 19 16. Behind a simple side-street shopfront, a short walk west of the Abbaye aux Hommes, this friendly local restaurant serves up a different short menu daily; €25 buys a full meal of excellent local cuisine, with an emphasis on fresh salads as well as the expected meat and fish. Tues, Wed, Fri & Sat noon–2pm & 7.30–9.30pm, Thurs noon–2pm.

**Dolly's** 18 av de la Libération ✆ 02 31 94 03 29. Very popular, very central, English-style café and tearoom, serving not only tea and coffee but good salads, with lots of vegetarian options, and Anglophile snacks like fish'n'chips for €14. Tues 11am–11pm, Wed & Sun 11am–10pm, Thurs–Sat 10am–1am.

**Embroche** 17 rue de la Porte au Berger ✆ 02 31 93 71 31. Cosy place, where the open kitchen whips up simple regional specialities in full view of appreciative diners, with lunch from €20 and dinner from €27; there are also a few outdoor tables. Tues–Thurs noon–2pm & 7–10pm, Fri noon–2pm & 7–10.45pm, Sat 7–10.45pm.

## Bayeux

Home to a perfectly preserved medieval ensemble, magnificent **cathedral** and world-famous **tapestry**, BAYEUX is smaller and much more intimate than its near neighbour Caen, and a far more enjoyable place to visit. A mere 10km from the coast, Bayeux was the first French city to be liberated in 1944, the day after D-Day. Occupied so quickly that it escaped serious damage, it briefly became capital of Free France.

### Bayeux Tapestry (Centre Guillaume le Conquérant)

13bis rue de Nesmond • Daily: Feb, Nov & Dec 9.30am–12.30pm & 2–6pm; March, April, Sept & Oct 9am–6.30pm; May–Aug 9am–7pm; closed Jan; last admission 45min before closing • €9.50; €12 with either MAHB or Musée Mémorial de la Bataille de Normandie; €15 with both • ✆ 02 31 51 25 50, ⓦ bayeuxmuseum.com

A grand eighteenth-century seminary, remodelled as the **Centre Guillaume le Conquérant**, houses the extraordinary **Bayeux Tapestry**, known to the French as the *Tapisserie de la Reine Mathilde*. Unexpectedly, and unceremoniously, the first thing you see on entry is the tapestry itself, with an interesting audio-guided commentary to explain the events it so vividly depicts. Only afterwards comes an exhibition detailing the theories that surround the tapestry's creation, and explaining more about its turbulent history, followed by a film (shown in English at least once an hour in summer) that gives more of the historical background. As this book went to press, it was anticipated that the Bayeux Tapestry would travel on loan to Britain in 2022, and probably be displayed in London's British Museum.

### Cathédrale Notre-Dame

Daily: Jan–March 9am–5pm; April–June 8.30am–6pm; July–Sept 9am–7pm; Oct–Dec 9am–6pm • Free

The **Cathédrale Notre-Dame**, the first home of the Bayeux Tapestry, stands a short walk from the tapestry's current resting place. Although only the crypt and towers date from the original work of 1077, the building's Romanesque plan remains intact. The crypt is a beauty, its columns graced with frescoes of angels playing trumpets and bagpipes, looking exhausted by their performance for eternity.

### MAHB – Musée d'Art et d'Histoire Baron Gérard

37 rue du Bienvenu • Daily: Feb–April & Oct–Dec 10am–12.30pm & 2–6pm; May–Sept 9.30am–6.30pm; closed Jan; last admission 45min before closing • €7.50; €12 with either Tapestry or Musée Mémorial de la Bataille de Normandie; €15 with both • ✆ 02 31 92 14 21, ⓦ bayeuxmuseum.com

Beside the cathedral, the large **Musée d'Art et d'Histoire Baron Gérard**, or **MAHB**, covers local history from prehistoric axe-heads up to the present, and also includes the city's

5

fine-art collection. Although it's a slightly odd assortment, making no mention of the Tapestry, there's plenty to like, from the private chapel in the former bishops' palace, with its wood panelling and ceiling frescoes, to the very fancy displays of "bobbin" lace and drawers filled with butterflies in the newer building. Paintings include works by Eugène Boudin, and you'll even find a Sioux peace pipe and Inuit boots, brought home by a nineteenth-century explorer.

### Musée Mémorial de la Bataille de Normandie

Bd Fabian-Ware • Daily: Feb–April & Oct–Dec 10am–12.30pm & 2–6pm; May–Sept 9.30am–6.30pm; closed Jan; last admission 45min before closing • €7.50; €12 with either Tapestry or MAHB; €15 with both • ⓣ 02 31 51 46 90, ⓦ bayeuxmuseum.com

Set behind massive guns southwest of town, Bayeux's **Musée Mémorial de la Bataille de Normandie** provides an accessible, visceral and highly visual overview of the Battle of Normandy. Rather than endless military hardware, it's filled with colour photos, maps and display panels that trace the campaign, with good sections on German counter-attacks and the role of the press. The understated and touching **British War Cemetery** stands immediately across the road.

## ARRIVAL AND INFORMATION — BAYEUX

**By train** The *gare SNCF* is 15min walk southeast of the centre, just outside the ring road.

Destinations Caen (very frequent; 20min); Cherbourg (6 daily; 55min).

**By bus** Buses stop both at the *gare SNCF* and across town, on the north side of place St-Patrice.

## THE BAYEUX TAPESTRY

Created well over nine centuries ago, the 70m strip of linen known as the **Bayeux Tapestry** recounts the story of the Norman Conquest of England. Technically it's a piece of embroidery rather than a tapestry, with a palpable three-dimensional presence. The brilliance of its coloured wools has barely faded, and the tale is enlivened throughout with scenes of medieval life, popular fables and mythical beasts; its draughtsmanship, and the sheer vigour and detail, are stunning. Commissioned by Bishop Oddo, William's half-brother, for the inauguration of Bayeux Cathedral in 1077, the work is thought to have been carried out by nuns in England, most likely in Canterbury.

The tapestry looks, and reads, like a modern comic strip. While it's generally considered to be historically accurate, William's justification for his invasion – that Harold, during an enforced sojourn after he was rescued by William following a shipwreck on the coast of northern France, had sworn to accept him as King of England – remains in dispute.

In the tapestry itself, Harold is every inch the villain, with his dastardly little moustache and shifty eyes. At the point when he breaks his oath and seizes the throne, Harold looks extremely pleased with himself; however, his comeuppance swiftly follows, as William crosses the Channel and defeats the English armies at Hastings.

**Destinations** Arromanches (3–5 daily; 25min); Ouistreham (2–3 daily; 1hr 20min).

**Tourist office** On the arched pont St-Jean, in the centre (Jan–March & Nov–Dec Mon–Sat 9.30am–12.30pm & 2–5.30pm, Sun 10am–1pm & 2–5.30pm; April–June, Sept & Oct Mon–Sat 9.30am–12.30pm & 2–6pm, Sun 10am–1pm & 2–6pm; July & Aug Mon–Sat 9am–7pm, Sun 9am–1pm & 2–6pm; ☎ 02 31 51 28 28, ⓦ bayeux-bessin-tourisme.com).

## ACCOMMODATION

**Camping des Bords de l'Aure** Bd d'Eindhoven ☎ 02 31 92 08 43, ⓦ camping-bayeux.fr. Large three-star municipal campsite, near the river on the northern ring road (RN13). Well-shaded tent sites of varying sizes and prices, rental cabins, and free access to the local swimming pool alongside. Closed early Nov to March. **€13**

★ **Churchill** 14–16 rue St-Jean ☎ 02 31 21 31 80, ⓦ hotel-churchill.fr. Perfectly situated in the heart of town, with free parking, this beautifully furnished 32-room hotel has no restaurant, but offers personal and friendly service plus a €65 daily return shuttle to Mont-St-Michel. Closed Dec to mid-Feb. **€100**

**De la Gare** 26 place de la Gare ☎ 02 31 92 10 70, ⓦ hotel-delagare-bayeux.fr. Basic but perfectly adequate hotel, beside the station and a 15min walk from the cathedral, with fourteen en-suite rooms (showers not baths) and a simple brasserie. Normandy Tours (see page 289), based here, offer tours of D-Day beaches. **€49**

**Mogador** 20 rue Chartier ☎ 02 31 92 24 58, ⓦ hotel-mogador-bayeux.fr. Friendly little hotel facing Bayeux's main square, with free parking; the fourteen rooms are simple but very presentable, with quieter ones overlooking the inner courtyard. Some sleep three or four. **€65**

**Reine Mathilde** 23 rue Larcher ☎ 02 31 92 08 13, ⓦ hotel-bayeux-reinemathilde.fr. Well-equipped, well-priced en-suite rooms backing onto the canal, between the Tapestry and cathedral, with a nice open-air brasserie/crêperie downstairs. **€85**

## EATING

**L'Insolite** 16 rue des Cuisiniers ☎ 02 31 51 71 16. Cheap but chic crêperie serving an imaginative range of savoury *galettes*, with flavours such as salmon with crème fraiche (€9), followed by sweet crêpes. Set *menus* at €17 and €23. Tues–Sun noon–2pm & 6.30–9.15pm.

**Pommier** 38–40 rue des Cuisiniers ☎ 02 31 21 52 10, ⓦ restaurantlepommier.com. Traditional restaurant close to the cathedral, with terrace seating. Meat- and dairy-rich Norman cuisine on *menus* from €15 (weekday lunch only) up to €35.50, plus a wide range of vegetarian options including a soya steak served with local cheese. Daily noon–2.30pm & 7–9.30pm; closed Nov to mid-March.

**P'tit Resto** 2 rue du Bienvenu ☎ 02 31 51 85 40, ⓦ restaurantbayeux.com. Stylish contemporary restaurant all but across from the cathedral, where the "creative cuisine" extends to veal chop fried in wasabi, and rolled monkfish with tandoori stuffing. *Menus* from €18 at lunch, €25 at dinner. Mon 7–10pm, Tues–Sat noon–3pm & 7–10pm, closed Mon in low season.

★ **Rapière** 53 rue St-Jean ☎ 02 31 21 05 45, ⓦ larapiere.net. Hidden away just off the main pedestrianized street, this cosy little restaurant feels like it's been here forever. Its old-fashioned Norman cooking remains as dependable as ever, on copious €36 & €49 dinner *menus*. May–Oct Tues–Sat 6.30–9.15pm, Nov–April Tues & Thurs–Sat noon–1.30pm & 6.30–9.15pm, Wed 6.30–9.15pm.

**5**

## The D-Day beaches

At dawn on **D-Day**, June 6, 1944, Allied troops landed at points along the Normandy coast all the way from the mouth of the Orne to the eastern Cotentin peninsula. For the most part, the shore consists of innocuous beaches backed by gentle dunes, and yet this foothold in Europe was won at the cost of 100,000 lives. The ensuing **Battle of Normandy** killed thousands of civilians and reduced nearly six hundred towns and villages to rubble, but within a week of its eventual conclusion, Paris was liberated.

The various D-Day beaches are still widely referred to by their wartime code names. The British and Commonwealth forces landed on **Sword**, **Juno** and **Gold** beaches between Ouistreham and Arromanches; the Americans, further west on **Omaha** and **Utah** beaches. Substantial traces of the fighting are rare, the most remarkable being the remains of the astounding **Mulberry Harbour** at **Arromanches**, 10km northeast of Bayeux. Further west, at **Pointe du Hoc** on Omaha Beach, the cliff heights are deeply pitted with German bunkers and shell holes, while the church at **Ste-Mère-Église**, from whose steeple a US paratrooper dangled during heavy fighting throughout *The Longest Day*, still stands, and now has a model parachute permanently fastened to the roof.

World War II **cemeteries** dot the Normandy countryside. While most of the French dead were taken home for burial, the remains of fallen foreigners were gathered into cemeteries devoted to the separate warring nations. In total, over 140,000 young men were disinterred from their original battlefield graves; more than half of the 31,744 US casualties were repatriated. In addition, almost every coastal town has its own **war museum**, in which the wealth of incidental human detail can be overpowering.

### Ouistreham

**OUISTREHAM-RIVA BELLA**, on the coast 15km north of Caen, is that rare thing, a cross-Channel ferry port that remains a small seaside resort. From the harbour, at its eastern end, it's easy to head straight out, following the main road south towards Caen. Head west instead to reach the handful of charming streets at the heart of the old town. The sea itself lies a couple of hundred metres north, along the semi-pedestrianized **avenue de la Mer**. Strictly speaking, the waterfront, backing a long straight beach, is a separate community known as **Riva Bella**. Its large central **casino** has been remodelled to resemble a 1930s passenger liner, while gloriously old-fashioned bathing huts face onto the sands.

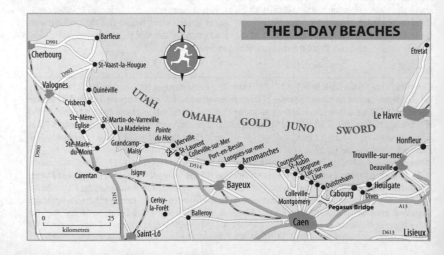

THE D-DAY BEACHES

### D-DAY TOURS

The Caen Memorial (see page 282) organizes bilingual **guided tours** of the beaches in summer (departs daily 1pm; €95, ages 3–17 €75; ☎02 31 06 06 45, ⓦmemorial-caen.fr); the price includes admission to the Memorial, which doesn't have to be on the same day.

Other operators offering D-Day tours, at typical prices from around €60/half-day and €100/day, include *Normandy Sightseeing Tours* (☎02 31 51 70 52, ⓦnormandy-sightseeing-tours.com), *Victory Tours* (☎02 31 51 98 14, ⓦvictorytours.com), and *Normandy Tours* (☎02 31 92 10 70, ⓦnormandy-landing-tour.com). Those three are based in Bayeux, while *D-Day Battle Tours* (☎02 33 01 26 12, ⓦddaybattletours.com) offer private group tours that start from Ste-Mère-Église.

## Grand Bunker – Musée du Mur de l'Atlantique

Av du 6-Juin • Daily: Feb, March & Oct–Dec 10am–6pm; April–Sept 9am–7pm • €7.50 • ☎02 31 97 28 69

This large and lofty bunker, known as both the **Grand Bunker** and the **Musée du Mur de l'Atlantique**, served as the headquarters to several German batteries defending the mouth of the River Orne, and fell to Allied forces on June 9, 1944. Inside, displays re-create the living quarters, with newspapers, cutlery and cigarette packets adding a welcome human touch to the moderately interesting explanations of the generators, gas filters and radio room.

## Pegasus Bridge

Av du Major-Howard, Ranville, 5km south of Ouistreham • **Mémorial Pegasus** Daily: Feb, March & Oct to mid-Dec 10am–5pm; April–Sept 9.30am–6.30pm • €8 • ☎02 31 78 19 44, ⓦmemorial-pegasus.org

South of Ouistreham, the main road towards Caen passes close by the site now known, in honour of its wartime code name, as **Pegasus Bridge**. On the night before D-Day, twin bridges across the Caen canal and the River Orne here were the target of a daring Allied glider assault. When replaced in 1994, the original bridge was moved to become the focus of the **Mémorial Pegasus** immediately east. This vaguely glider-shaped museum explains the attack in detail, accompanied by the expected array of helmets, goggles and medals, as well as photographs and models used to plan the attack.

## Arromanches

While basically a little seaside village, **ARROMANCHES**, cradled between high cliffs 31km west of Ouistreham, has the strongest identity of all the resorts hereabouts. Its huge beach looks directly out at the ruins of the artificial Mulberry Harbour used in the D-Day landings, while numerous war memorials are scattered throughout town.

## Musée du Débarquement

Place du 6-Juin • Daily: Feb, Nov & Dec 10am–12.30pm & 1.30–5pm; March & Oct 9.30am–12.30pm & 1.30–5.30pm; April 9am–12.30pm & 1.30–6pm; May–Aug 9am–7pm; Sept 9am–6pm • €8 • ☎02 31 22 34 31, ⓦmusee-arromanches.fr

The seafront **Musée du Débarquement**, in Arromanches' main square, recounts the story of the town's three-month spell as the busiest port in the world. A huge picture window faces the bulky remains of the **Mulberry Harbour**, "Port Winston", which facilitated the landings of two and a half million men and half a million vehicles. Two of these prefab concrete constructions were built in Britain, then towed across the Channel at 6kph as the invasion began; the other one, further west on Omaha Beach, was destroyed by a storm within a few weeks.

## Normandy American Cemetery and Memorial

Above Omaha Beach, 21km west of Arromanches, outside Colleville-sur-Mer • Daily: mid-April to mid-Sept 9am–6pm; mid-Sept to mid-April 9am–5pm • Free • ☎02 31 51 62 00, ⓦabmc.gov

In the vast **Normandy American Cemetery and Memorial**, near the Pointe du Hoc, neat rows of crosses cover the clifftop lawns. There are no individual epitaphs, just gold lettering for a few exceptional warriors. At one end, a muscular giant dominates

5

a huge array of battlefield plans and diagrams covered with surging arrows and pincer movements. Barack Obama is the most recent US president to have paid his respects here; another president's son, General Theodore Roosevelt Jr, is among those buried.

A high-tech visitor centre explains the events of 1944, while poignant displays focus on the personal angle, highlighting the stories of both casualties and survivors.

## Utah Beach

The westernmost of the Invasion Beaches, **Utah Beach** stretches up the eastern shore of the Cotentin Peninsula, running 30km north towards St-Vaast (see page 293). From 6.30am onwards on D-Day, 23,000 men and 1700 vehicles landed here. A minor coast road, the D421, traces the edge of the dunes and enables visitors to follow the course of the fighting, though there's precious little to see these days. Ships that were deliberately sunk to create artificial breakwaters are still visible at low tide, while markers commemorate fallen heroes.

In the comprehensive **Musée du Débarquement d'Utah-Beach** in **STE-MARIE-DU-MONT**, huge sea-view windows lend immediacy to the copious models, maps, films and diagrams (daily: June–Sept 9.30am–7pm; Oct–May 10am–6pm; last admission 45min before closing; €8; ☎02 33 71 53 35, ⓦutah-beach.com). The **Mémorial de la Liberté Retrouvée** in **QUINÉVILLE** focuses on everyday life for the people of Normandy under Nazi occupation (April to mid-Nov daily 10am–7pm; €7; ☎02 33 95 95 95, ⓦmemorial-quineville.com).

### ARRIVAL AND DEPARTURE
### THE D-DAY BEACHES

#### OUISTREHAM
**By boat** Brittany Ferries connect Ouistreham with Portsmouth (2–3 daily; 6–8hr; ☎02 31 36 36 36, ⓦbrittany-ferries.com). Buses timed to connect with each sailing run to Caen.

### GETTING AROUND

**By bus** Bus Verts (☎09 70 83 00 14, ⓦbusverts.fr) run all along this coast; for timetables, visit ⓦcommentjyvais.fr. From Bayeux, bus #74 goes to Arromanches, Courseulles and Ouistreham, and bus #70 to the Pointe du Hoc, the US cemetery at Colleville-sur-Mer and Port-en-Bessin. From Caen, bus #30 runs inland to Bayeux, and bus #3 to Courseulles.

### INFORMATION

#### OUISTREHAM
**Tourist office** Esplanade Lofi, alongside the casino (April–June & Sept daily 10am–1pm & 2–5.30pm; July & Aug daily 9.30am–6.30pm; Oct–March daily except Tues 10am–12.30pm & 2.30–5pm; ☎02 31 97 18 63, ⓦcaenlamer-tourisme.fr).

#### ARROMANCHES
**Tourist office** 2 rue Maréchal-Joffre (March daily 10am–1pm & 2–5pm; April–June, Sept & Oct daily 10am–1pm & 2–6pm; July & Aug Mon–Sat 9.30am–7pm, Sun 9.30am–1pm & 2–6.30pm; Nov–Jan Sat & Sun 10am–noon & 2–5pm; ☎02 31 22 36 45, ⓦbayeux-bessin-tourisme.com).

### ACCOMMODATION AND EATING

#### OUISTREHAM
**Normandie** 71 av Michel-Cabieu ☎02 31 97 19 57, ⓦlenormandie.com. Faded but convenient hotel, just off the square near the ferry port, where the rooms are comfortable but a little thin-walled, and the restaurant (closed Sun eve, plus Mon Nov–March) serves good three-course *menus* from €32. Closed Jan. €80
**Villa Andry** 51 av Andry ☎02 31 97 18 79, ⓦvilla-andry.fr. This place offers spacious, well-equipped rooms near the casino, many with great sea views, plus a garden – complete with chickens – and good food on *menus* from €32. Closed 3 weeks in Jan. €71

#### ARROMANCHES
★ **La Marine** 1 quai du Canada ☎02 31 22 34 19, ⓦhotel-de-la-marine.fr. At the centre of Arromanches' seafront, ideally placed for the D-Day sights and the beach, this restful hotel offers bright, sizeable, pastel-painted sea-view rooms and a high-class restaurant, sprawling through the entire ground floor, which serves fishy *menus* from €27. €96

# Cherbourg

Though its heyday as a transatlantic passenger port is now long gone, the sizeable town of **CHERBOURG**, at the northern tip of the Cotentin peninsula, makes an appealing point of arrival in France. Its **old town**, west of the quayside, is an intriguing maze of pedestrian alleys. The tempting cluster of small shops and boutiques around place Centrale offers the chance to buy the city's most famous product, the genuine **Cherbourg umbrella**, at 30 rue des Portes, while an excellent Thursday **market** is held on and off rue des Halles, near the majestic theatre with its *belle époque* facade. A pleasant stroll north leads to the Basilique de la Trinité and the former town beach, now grassed over to form the **Plage Verte**.

## Cité de la Mer

Daily: May, June & Sept 9.30am–6pm; July & Aug 9.30am–7pm; Oct–Dec & Feb–April 10am–6pm, with variations including longer hours in school hols, and Mon closures in March, Nov & Dec; last entry 1hr before closing • €18 • ☎ 02 33 20 26 69, ⓦ citedelamer.com

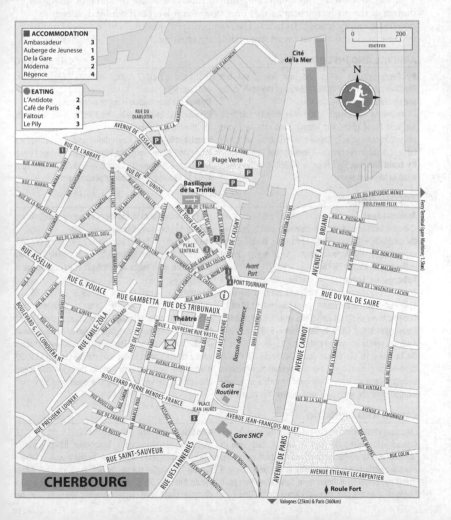

**5**

Just across the pleasure port from the town centre, the **Cité de la Mer** centres on Cherbourg's former Transatlantic ferry terminal. It's now divided into several sections, including a memorial to the *Titanic* that opened in 2012, a hundred years to the day since the ill-fated liner called here for two hours on her maiden voyage. Almost 300 passengers joined the *Titanic* at Cherbourg, including such famous names as John Jacob Astor IV, Benjamin Guggenheim, and the "unsinkable" Molly Brown. Rather than reconstruct the entire ship, superb mock-ups of her wireless room, mailroom, and a typical first-class cabin offer an "immersive experience" that, fortunately, stops short of a dunking in icy waters.

The complex also incorporates a museum that tells the story of underwater exploration in history and fiction, along with fish tanks holding jellyfish, seahorses and large squid, while descending walkways offer views at ever-greater depths into a vast cylindrical aquarium.

In a dry dock alongside is the *Redoutable*, France's first ballistic-missile **submarine**. Visitors can scramble through its labyrinth of tube-like walkways and control rooms, though as the nuclear generator that once powered it has been removed, there's a cavernous empty space at its heart. The cramped crew quarters will feel very familiar if you've just shared a cabin on an overnight ferry crossing.

## ARRIVAL AND INFORMATION                                    CHERBOURG

**By ferry** Brittany Ferries and Irish Ferries sail into Cherbourg's *gare maritime*, not far east of the town centre and served by regular shuttle buses.
Destinations Portsmouth (daily early May to mid-Sept; 3hr) and Poole (daily; 4hr 30min), with Brittany Ferries (ⓦ brittanyferries.com); Rosslare and Dublin, with Irish Ferries (ⓦ irishferries.com; 3–4 weekly; 18hr 30min).
**By train** The *gare SNCF* is on av J-F Millet, a short walk south of the town centre.

Destinations Paris (7 daily; 3–4hr); via Valognes (15min) and Caen (1hr 15min).
**By bus** The *gare routière* is opposite the *gare SNCF*.
Destinations St-Lô (3 daily; 1hr 30min); St-Vaast (3 daily; 1hr 10min), via Barfleur (1hr).
**Tourist office** 14 quai Alexandre-III (mid-June to mid-Sept Mon–Sat 9.30am–7pm, Sun 10am–5pm; mid-Sept to mid-June Mon–Sat 10am–12.30pm & 2–6pm, Sun 10am–1pm; ☎ 02 33 93 52 02, ⓦ cherbourgtourisme.com).

## ACCOMMODATION

**Ambassadeur** 22 quai de Caligny ☎ 02 33 43 10 00, ⓦ ambassadeurhotel.com. Inexpensive central hotel on the quayside, with four storeys of en-suite, double-glazed rooms, many with harbour views (there's a lift). Decent buffet breakfasts cost €9. **€64**
**Auberge de Jeunesse** 55 rue de l'Abbaye ☎ 02 33 78 15 15, ⓦ fuaj.org. Well-equipped red-brick hostel, a 15min walk west of the centre and on bus routes #3 and #5. Two rooms are designed for visitors with limited mobility. Breakfast included. Check-in 9am–1pm & 6–11pm. Closed 3 weeks over Christmas and early Jan. **€23.40**
**De la Gare** 10 place Jean-Jaurès ☎ 02 33 43 06 81, ⓦ hotel-gare-cherbourg.com. Conspicuous blue-trimmed budget hotel that's surprisingly quiet for such a convenient location, near the *gares SNCF* and *routière*. The rooms may

not be exactly stunning, but they do have en-suite facilities, and family-sized rooms are available. **€68**
**Moderna** 28 rue de la Marine ☎ 02 33 43 05 30, ⓦ hotel-moderna.com. Friendly, small hotel, set slightly back from the harbour, with reasonably well-priced en-suite rooms of all sizes. **€62**
**Régence** 42 quai de Caligny ☎ 02 33 43 05 16, ⓦ laregence.com. Slightly more upmarket than Cherbourg's other offerings, with antique-style British furnishings, this family-run *Logis de France* has neat rooms overlooking the harbour. The dining room downstairs starts with a reasonable €19.50 *menu*, and ranges up to €36.50; it's not the best restaurant along the *quai*, but there's something to be said for eating where you sleep. **€93**

## EATING AND DRINKING

Cherbourg's restaurants divide readily into the glass-fronted seafood places along the quai de Caligny, each with its "copious" *assiette de fruits de mer*, and the more varied, less expensive little places tucked away in the pedestrianized streets and alleyways of the old town. This is also where you'll find some animated bars, especially along rue de l'Union.

**L'Antidote** 41 rue au Blé ☎ 02 33 78 01 28, ⓦ restaurant-cherbourg.fr. Welcoming little restaurant whose multicoloured tables squeeze into a small courtyard just off the market square. As well as offering full dinner *menus* from €22.50, it's a good place to drop in for a quick daytime snack, and serves excellent desserts. The bar section stays open longer hours. Tues–Sat noon–3pm & 7–11pm.

**Café de Paris** 40 quai de Caligny ☎02 33 43 12 36, ⓦrestaurantcafedeparis.com. Diners seated inside this grand *belle époque* café, or out at its quayside tables, can savour fish-heavy *menus* (€23.50–42), or work their way up through the ranks of *assiettes de fruits de mer*, from the one-person *Matelot* up to the belly-straining *Amiral* at well over €100. Mon 7–9.30pm, Tues–Sat noon–1.45pm & 7–9.30pm; closed 3 wks in Nov.

★ **Faitout** 25 rue Tour-Carrée ☎02 33 04 25 04, ⓦrestaurant-le-faitout.com. Stylish, faux-rustic, fishing-themed restaurant that offers traditional French cuisine, centring on local specialities such as scallops, with good *menus* at €29 and €49. Reserve in summer. Mon 7.15–10pm, Tues–Sat noon–2pm & 7.15–10pm.

**Le Pily** 39 rue Grande Rue ☎02 33 10 19 29, ⓦrestaurant-le-pily.com. This tiny but smart little Michelin-starred restaurant, in the tangled heart of the old town, is a showcase for imaginative contemporary Norman cuisine, with a focus on fish and meat. Weekday lunch *menu* €29, dinner from €45. Mid-June to Aug Mon 7–9pm, Tues–Sat noon–1.45pm & 7–9pm; Sept to mid-June Tues–Sat noon–1.45pm & 7–9pm, Sun noon–1.45pm.

# The Cotentin peninsula

Hard against the frontier with Brittany, and cut off from the rest of Normandy by marshy terrain, the **Cotentin peninsula** has traditionally been seen as something of a backwater. By sea, on the other hand, it's very easily accessible. Beyond the peninsula's major port, **Cherbourg**, little ports such as **Barfleur** and **St-Vaast** on the indented northern headland presage the rocky Breton coast, while **La Hague** to the west offers a handsome array of heather-clad cliffs and stone-wall-divided patchwork fields.

The Cotentin's long western flank, with its flat beaches, serves primarily as a prelude to **Mont St-Michel**, with hill towns such as **Coutances** and **Avranches** cherishing architectural and historical relics associated with the abbey. Halfway down, the walled port of **Granville**, a popular destination for French holiday-makers, is a sort of small-scale mirror-image of Brittany's St-Malo.

## Barfleur

Seven centuries ago, the pleasant harbour village of **BARFLEUR**, 25km east of Cherbourg, was the biggest port in Normandy. Its population having dwindled along with its fortunes, it's now a low-key place, where the sweeping crescent of the picturesque grey-granite quayside sees little activity.

## St-Vaast

Pretty **ST-VAAST-LA-HOUGUE**, 11km south of Barfleur, is a relaxed resort that comes alive in summer. Countless tiny Channel-crossing yachts moor in the bay where Edward III landed on his way to Crécy, overlooked by a string of fortifications that date from Vauban's time.

## Barneville-Carteret

Backed by sand dunes that resemble miniature mountain ranges, the **beaches** along the Cotentin's northwestern coast rank among the finest in Normandy. The twinned villages known as **BARNEVILLE-CARTERET** make the best overnight halt. **Carteret** itself, sheltered by a rocky headland, is the nearest harbour to the English-speaking island of **Jersey**, just 25km away across seas made treacherous by the fast Alderney current.

Visitors who prefer to stay right beside a beach should head instead for **Barneville**, directly across the mouth of the bay. Here, an endless exposed stretch of clean, firm sand is backed by weather-beaten villas and the occasional hotel.

## Coutances

The hill town of **COUTANCES**, 65km south of Cherbourg, confined by its site to just one main street, is crested by the landmark **Cathédrale de Notre-Dame**. Essentially

**5**

Gothic, it remains very Norman in its unconventional blending of architectural traditions, and the octagonal lantern crowning the nave is nothing short of divinely inspired. The son et lumière that's staged on Sunday evenings and throughout the summer serves as a true complement to the light stone building. The fountained **public gardens** nearby are also illuminated on summer nights.

## Granville

The striking fortified coastal town of **GRANVILLE** is the Norman equivalent of Brittany's St-Malo, with a similar history of piracy and an imposing citadel – the **haute ville** – that guards the approaches to the bay of Mont St-Michel. Here, however, the fortress was originally built by the English, in the fifteenth century, as the springboard for an attack on Mont St-Michel that never materialized.

The great difference between Granville and St-Malo is that Granville's walled citadelle stands separate from the modern town, an intriguing enclave that remains resolutely uncommercialized. Sheltered behind a rocky outcrop that juts into the Channel, it's reached by steep stairs from alongside the beach, or circuitous climbing roads from the port. Once up there, you'll find three or four long narrow parallel streets of grey-granite eighteenth-century houses that lead to the church of Notre-Dame.

Granville today is a deservedly popular tourist destination. Thanks in part to the long beach that stretches away north, it's the Cotentin's busiest resort. Traffic in the maze-like new town, below the headland, can be nightmarish, but the beaches are excellent, with facilities for watersports of all kinds.

## Avranches

Perched high above the bay on an abrupt granite outcrop, **AVRANCHES** is the closest large town to Mont St-Michel, with which it has always had close connections. The Mont's original church was founded by a bishop of Avranches, spurred on by the Archangel Michael, who became so impatient with the lack of progress that he prodded a hole in the bishop's skull.

Robert of Torigny, a subsequent abbot of St-Michel, played host in Avranches on several occasions to Henry II of England, the most memorable being when Henry was obliged, barefoot and bareheaded, to do public penance for the murder of Thomas Becket, on May 22, 1172.

### Scriptorial d'Avranches

Place d'Estouteville • Feb–March & Oct–Dec Tues–Sat 2–6pm; April–June & Sept daily except Mon 10am–1pm & 2–6pm; July & Aug daily except Mon 10am–1pm & 2–7pm; closed Jan; last admission 1hr before closing • €8 • ☎ 02 33 79 57 00, ⓦ scriptorial.fr

For a vivid evocation of Normandy's medieval splendours, examine the illuminated manuscripts, mostly created on the Mont, displayed in the museum known as the **Scriptorial d'Avranches**. Exhibits trace the history of Avranches, and bring the story up to date by covering modern book-production techniques.

## ARRIVAL AND DEPARTURE                          THE COTENTIN PENINSULA

### COUTANCES
**By train** Coutances' *gare SNCF*, which greets trains from Caen (7 daily; 1hr 15min) and Rennes (7 daily; 1hr 45min), is 1.5km southeast of the centre, at the bottom of the steep hill.

### GRANVILLE
**By train and bus** Trains from Coutances (6 daily; 35min) arrive at the *gare SNCF*, well east of the centre on av du Maréchal-Leclerc; buses stop here, too.

### AVRANCHES
**By train** Avranches' *gare SNCF* is a long way below the town centre; the walk up discourages many rail travellers from stopping here at all.
Destinations Granville (2 daily; 55min); St-Malo (2 daily; 45min) via Pontorson (for Mont St-Michel; 15min).
**By bus** Buses to Mont St-Michel (1 daily; 45min) stop on the main town square, and also outside the *gare SNCF*.

## INFORMATION

### COUTANCES
**Tourist office** 6 rue Milon (July & Aug Mon–Sat 9.30am–6pm, Sun 9.30am–1.30pm; Sept–June Mon–Sat 9.30am–12.30pm & 2–6pm; ☎02 33 19 08 10, ⓦwww.tourisme-coutances.fr).

### GRANVILLE
**Tourist office** 4 cours Jonville, below the citadelle (Mon–Fri 8.30am–12.30pm & 1.30–5.30pm, Sat 9am–noon; ☎02 33 91 30 03, ⓦ ville-granville.fr).

### AVRANCHES
**Tourist office** 2 rue du Général-de-Gaulle (July & Aug Mon–Sat 9.30am–6.30pm, Sun 10am–5pm; Sept–June Mon–Sat 9.30am–12.30pm & 2–6pm; ☎02 33 58 00 22, ⓦ avranches.fr).

## ACCOMMODATION AND EATING

### BARFLEUR
★ **Comptoir de la Presqu'Île** 30 quai Henri-Chardon ☎02 33 20 37 51, ⓦlecomptoirdelapresquile.com. Relaxed, friendly waterfront brasserie, with lots of seating both indoors and out. Seafood enthusiasts can opt for seafood platters of varying sizes, or a substantial bowl of *moules barfleuraises* for €12; cheesy scallops stand out on the one set menu, at €29, and there's occasional live jazz. Mon–Wed, Fri & Sat 11.30am–2pm & 6.30–9pm, Sun 11.30am–2pm.

★ **Le Conquérant** 16–18 rue St-Thomas-à-Becket ☎02 33 54 00 82, ⓦhotel-leconquerant.com. Welcoming family-owned hotel, set in an elegant old stone-built townhouse on the main street, a few steps inland from the harbour. Ten relatively simple rooms, of which the six that overlook the garden are the largest and nicest, and have appealing Norman touches. No restaurant. Closed mid-Nov to mid-March. **€92**

**La Ferme du Bord de Mer** 43 rte du Val de Saire, Gatteville-le-Phare ☎02 33 54 01 77, ⓦcamping-gatteville.fr. This basic but appealing campsite, a couple of kilometres north of Barfleur, is exactly what its name suggests: a farm beside the sea, alongside a scruffy flat beach. As well as tent sites, it also has a few mobile homes for rent. **€13.90**

### ST-VAAST
**De France et des Fuchsias** 20 rue du Maréchal-Foch ☎02 33 54 40 41, ⓦfrance-fuchsias.com. Sprawling back from the main road a few blocks short of the sea, this popular hotel has splendid gardens and an excellent restaurant, and with rooms of all sizes and degrees of comfort it makes an ideal stopover for ferry passengers. Closed Jan–Feb, plus Mon in winter. **€80**

### BARNEVILLE-CARTERET
★ **Des Isles** 9 bd Maritime, Barneville ☎02 33 04 90 76, ⓦhoteldesisles.com. Very classy beachfront hotel, which resembles a bright and relaxing New England coastal inn. All the rooms have sea views, and there's a heated outdoor swimming pool plus a superb restaurant. **€145**

### COUTANCES
**Cositel** 29 rue de St-Malo ☎02 33 19 15 00, ⓦwww.cositel.fr. Large and exceptionally comfortable modern hotel, architecturally uninspiring but equipped with stylish rooms and spacious gardens, halfway up the hill towards Agon on the western outskirts of town. **€60**

**Taverne du Parvis** 18 place du Parvis ☎02 33 45 13 55, ⓦhotel-restaurant-taverne-du-parvis.com. Unexciting but adequate rooms, several of them family-sized, in an unbeatable location facing the cathedral on the main square, above a reasonable brasserie that serves lunch for €11 and a Norman dinner *menu* for €18. Hotel & restaurant closed Sun. **€55**

**Tanquerey de la Rochaisière** 13 rue St-Martin ☎06 50 57 22 55, ⓦbandb-hotel-coutances.fr. Very charming B&B, in a seventeenth-century townhouse in a quiet street close to the cathedral, offering two huge antique-furnished rooms, one with shower and one with bath, plus a courtyard garden and sumptuous breakfasts. **€125**

**Les Vignettes** 27 rue de St-Malo ☎02 33 45 43 13, ⓦville-coutances.fr. Excellent little year-round municipal campsite, offering lush pitches on a wooded hill just west of town. **€11.86**

### GRANVILLE
**Centre Régional de Nautisme** Bd des Amiraux ☎02 33 91 22 62, ⓦcrng.fr. This modern oceanfront building, 1km south of the station in the town centre, serves as Granville's hostel, with dorms and private rooms. Closed Sat & Sun Nov–Feb. Dorms **€20.10**, doubles **€50**

**Logis du Roc** 13 rue St-Michel ☎06 18 35 87 42, ⓦlelogisduroc.com. This nicely furnished townhouse B&B, run by a fluent English-speaker, is the only accommodation option in Granville's peaceful old citadelle, with three attractive and spacious en-suite rooms. **€62**

★ **Mer et Saveurs** 49 rue du Port ☎02 33 50 05 80, ⓦmeretsaveurs.fr. The cut of the fine crop of waterfront restaurants that line Granville's commercial port; its mouthwatering assortment of fishy *menus*, from €14.50 for lunch, €27 dinner, changes daily. Daily noon–2pm & 7–9.30pm; closed Sun eve in low season.

**5**

## AVRANCHES

★ **Croix d'Or** 83 rue de la Constitution ☎ 02 33 58 04 88, ⓦ hotel-restaurant-avranches-croix-dor.com. Gloriously old-fashioned hotel, consisting of a rambling former coaching inn plus a newer annexe hidden away in the beautiful hydrangea-filled gardens at the back. Good-value rooms, and the best restaurant in town, where dinner *menus* start at €35. Closed Jan, plus Sun eve in winter. **€79**

# Mont St-Michel

The stupendous abbey of **MONT ST-MICHEL** was first erected on an island at the very frontier of Normandy and Brittany more than a millennium ago. Until recently, however, that island was attached to the mainland by a long causeway, topped by a road. Now, thanks to a vast hydraulic and reconstruction project, it has become an island once more, connected to the shore by a futuristic curved bridge, surfaced with wooden decking. Crucially, that has enabled tidal waters to sweep all around, and thus flush away centuries of accumulated sand.

The real point of all this work was to control access for the millions of tourists who come here. It's therefore no longer possible to drive all the way to Mont-St-Michel in your own vehicle; instead you have to park on the mainland, roughly 2km away, and access the island either on foot, by bike, or riding in a shuttle bus or horse-drawn carriage.

### Brief history

The 80m-high rocky outcrop on which the abbey stands was once known as "the Mount in Peril from the Sea". Many a medieval pilgrim drowned while crossing the bay to reach it. The Archangel Michael was its vigorous protector, leaping from rock to rock in titanic struggles against Paganism and Evil.

The abbey itself dates back to the eighth century, after the archangel appeared to Aubert, bishop of Avranches. Since work on the sturdy church at the peak commenced in the eleventh century, new structures have been grafted to produce a fortified hotchpotch of Romanesque and Gothic buildings that clamber to the very pinnacle, forming arguably the most recognizable silhouette in France after the Eiffel Tower. Although the abbey was a fortress town, home to a large community, even at its twelfth-century peak it never housed more than sixty monks.

After the Revolution the monastery became a prison, but in 1966, exactly a thousand years after Duke Richard the First originally brought the order here, the Benedictines returned. They departed again in 2001, after finding that the present-day island does not exactly lend itself to a life of quiet contemplation. A dozen nuns and monks from the Monastic Fraternity of Jerusalem now maintain a presence.

## The island

The **island of Mont St-Michel** is almost entirely covered by medieval stone structures, encircled by defensive walls. Once through the heavily fortified **Porte du Roi**, you find yourself on the narrow **Grande Rue**, which spirals steadily upwards, passing top-heavy gabled houses amid the jumble of souvenir shops and restaurants. Amazingly enough, less than a third of all visitors climb up to the abbey itself at the summit.

Large crowds gather each day at the **North Tower** to watch the tide sweep in across the bay. Seagulls wheel away in alarm, and those foolish enough to be wandering too late on the sands have to sprint to safety.

### The abbey

**Abbey** Daily: May–Aug 9am–7pm; Sept–April 9.30am–6pm; last admission 1hr before closing; closed Jan 1, May 1 and Dec 25 • €10, EU citizens aged under 26 free, non-EU citizens aged 18–25 €8; fee includes optional 1hr 15min guided tour, available in English all year **Night visits** July & Aug Mon–Sat 7.30pm–midnight • €13, or €19 with daytime admission; ages 18–25 €10 • ☎ 02 33 89 80 00, ⓦ abbaye-mont-saint-michel.fr

Although visible from all around the bay, the **abbey**, an architectural ensemble that incorporates the high-spired, archangel-topped church and the magnificent Gothic buildings known since 1228 as the **Merveille** ("The Marvel") – which in turn includes the entire north face, with the cloister, Knights' Hall, Refectory, Guest Hall and cellars – becomes, if anything, more awe-inspiring the closer you get.

The Mont's rock comes to a sharp point just below what is now the transept of the **church**, where the transition from Romanesque to Gothic is only too evident in the vaulting of the nave. In order to lay out the church's ground plan in the traditional shape of the cross, supporting crypts had to be built up from the hillside, and the Chausey granite sculpted to match its exact contours. Space was always limited, and yet the building has grown through the centuries, with an ingenuity that constantly surprises – witness the shock of emerging into the light of the cloisters from the sombre Great Hall.

Not surprisingly, the building of the **monastery** was no smooth progression: the original church, choir, nave and tower all had to be replaced after collapsing. The style of decoration has varied, too. That you now walk through halls of plain grey stone is a reflection of modern taste. In the Middle Ages, public areas such as the refectory would have been festooned with tapestries and frescoes.

## ARRIVAL AND DEPARTURE

## MONT ST-MICHEL

**By car** All visitors have to park on the mainland (cars €12, motorbikes €4.40). Rates include the shuttle ride to the island; buses leave from beside the information centre, as do horse-drawn carriages, which operate to varying schedules and charge €6 per person. It's also possible to walk the 2km to Mont-St-Michel.

**By train** The nearest *gare SNCF* is at Pontorson, 6km south

(see below).

**By bus** Shuttle buses connect the *gare SNCF* in Pontorson with Mont-St-Michel itself (€3.30). In addition, Keolis Emeraude (☎02 99 26 04 80, ⓦ destination-montsaintmichel.com) run scheduled services to Mont-St-Michel from the *gares SNCF* in Dol (2 daily; 30min) and Rennes (4 daily; 1hr 15min).

## INFORMATION

**Information centre** Adjoining the parking areas and shuttle-bus stop on the mainland, with displays on the restoration project (daily 9am–7pm; ☎02 14 13 20 15, ⓦ bienvenueaumontsaintmichel.com). Note that they do not offer a left-luggage facility.

**Tourist office** The island's own tourist office is in the

lowest gateway (March & Oct Mon–Sat 9.30am–6pm, Sun 9am–12.30pm & 1.30–5.30pm; April–June & Sept Mon–Sat 9.30am–6.30pm, Sun 9am–12.30pm & 1.30–6pm; July & Aug daily 9.30am–7pm; Nov–Feb Mon–Sat 10am–5pm, Sun 10am–12.30pm & 1.30–5pm; ☎02 33 60 14 30, ⓦ ot-montsaintmichel.com).

## ACCOMMODATION AND EATING

Mont St-Michel holds a surprising number of hotels. Most are predictably expensive, and all charge extra for a view of the sea. Drivers have to leave their vehicles in the mainland car parks. Sadly, the restaurants on the island are consistently worse than almost anywhere in France; ideally, you should aim to eat elsewhere.

### MONT ST-MICHEL

**Croix Blanche** Grande Rue ☎02 33 60 14 04, ⓦ hotel-la-croix-blanche.com. This little hotel is the nicest on Mont St-Michel itself, with nine small but sprucely decorated rooms, reached via steep stairs. Expect to pay around €20 extra for a sea view, and €17 for breakfast. **€192**

**Du Guesclin** Grande Rue ☎02 33 60 14 10, ⓦ hotel duguesclin.com. The cheapest option on the island, a *Logis de France* with ten old-fashioned and mostly small en-suite rooms, of which five have sea views. Closed mid-Nov to March. **€100**

**Mouton Blanc** Grande Rue ☎02 33 60 14 08, ⓦ lemoutonblanc.fr. Wood-panelled fourteenth-century house, now a hotel with fifteen small and somewhat plain rooms, and a large old-fashioned restaurant. **€171**

### ON THE MAINLAND

**Camping du Mont St-Michel** Rte du Mont St-Michel ☎02 33 60 22 10, ⓦ www.camping-montsaintmichel. com. Three-star, 350-pitch campsite, on the mainland just short of the bridge, with well-shaded pitches separated by hedges. Closed early Oct to March. **€22**

**Gabriel** Rte du Mont St-Michel ☎02 33 60 14 13, ⓦ hotelgabriel-montsaintmichel.com. Modern hotel resembling an American motel, with a huge gleaming glass facade facing the Mont, and rooms sprucely decorated in a knowing Pop-art style. **€107**

# 5 **Inland Normandy**

Seeking out specific highlights is not really the point of travelling through **inland Normandy**. The pleasure lies not so much in show-stopping sights, or individual towns, as in the feel of the landscape, with its lush meadows, orchards and forests. On top of that, the major attraction in these rich dairy regions is the **food**. To the French, the **Pays d'Auge** and the **Suisse Normande** are synonymous with cheeses, cream, apple and pear brandies, and ciders.

This is also a place to be active. The Suisse Normande is canoeing and rock-climbing country, and there are countless good walks further south. Of the towns, **Falaise** is inextricably associated with the story of William the Conqueror, while **Lisieux** was home to France's best-loved modern saint.

## South of the Seine

Heading south from the Seine, you can follow the River Risle from the estuary just east of Honfleur, or the Eure and its tributaries from upstream of Rouen. The lowest major crossing point over the Risle is at **Pont-Audemer**, where medieval houses lean out at alarming angles over the crisscrossing roads, rivers and canals. From here, perfect cycling roads lined with timbered farmhouses follow the river south.

### Abbaye du Bec-Hellouin

Le Bec-Hellouin • Admission on guided tours only, Mon–Sat 10.30am, 3pm & 4pm, plus 5pm June–Sept only; Sun & hols noon, 3pm & 4pm • €6 • ☎ 02 32 43 72 60, ⓦ bec-hellouin.fr

The size and tranquil setting of the **Abbaye du Bec-Hellouin**, upstream from Pont-Audemer just before Brionne, lend a monastic feel to the whole Risle valley. Bells echo across the water and white-robed monks go soberly about their business. From the eleventh century onwards, the abbey was an important intellectual centre; the philosopher Anselm was abbot here before becoming Archbishop of Canterbury in 1093. Thanks to the Revolution, most of the monastery buildings are recent – the monks only returned in 1948 – but some have survived amid the appealing clusters of stone ruins, including the fifteenth-century **bell tower of St-Nicholas** and the cloister.

| ACCOMMODATION AND EATING | SOUTH OF THE SEINE |
| --- | --- |
| **Auberge de l'Abbaye** 12 place Guillaume-le-Conquérant, Bec-Hellouin ☎ 02 32 44 86 02, ⓦ hotel bechellouin.com. Pretty, half-timbered hotel-restaurant in the tiny and rather twee village adjacent to the Abbaye du | Bec-Hellouin, bedecked in flowers and offering ten rooms of varying degrees of luxury, plus a spa. Restaurant closed Mon & Tues; hotel closed Dec & Jan. **€79** |

## The Pays d'Auge

The rolling hills and green twisting valleys of the **Pays d'Auge**, stretching south of **Lisieux**, are scattered with magnificent manor houses. The lush pastures here are responsible for the world-famous **cheeses** of Camembert, Livarot and Pont L'Évêque. They are intermingled with orchards yielding the best of Norman **ciders**, both apple and pear (*poiré*), as well as Calvados apple brandy.

For really good, solid Norman cooking visit one of the many local *fermes auberges*, working farms that welcome paying visitors to share their meals. Tourist offices hereabouts can provide copious lists of these and of local producers from whom you can buy your cheese and booze.

### Lisieux

**LISIEUX**, the main town of the Pays d'Auge, is famous as the home of **Ste Thérèse**, the most popular French spiritual figure of the modern era, who was born here in

1873 and lived just 24 years. Passivity, self-effacement and a self-denial that verged on masochism were her trademarks, and she is honoured by the gaudy and gigantic **Basilique de Ste-Thérèse**, on a slope southwest of the centre. The huge modern mosaics that decorate the nave are undeniably impressive, but the overall impression is of a quasi-medieval hagiography. The faithful can ride on a white, flag-bedecked fairground train around the holiest sites, which include the infinitely restrained and sober **Cathédrale St-Pierre**.

Lisieux's large street **market**, on Wednesday and Saturday, is a great opportunity to get acquainted with its cheeses and ciders.

## Crèvecoeur-en-Auge
While it's fun to stumble across dilapidated old half-timbered farms in the Pays d'Auge, here and there you can visit prime specimens that have been beautifully restored and preserved. An especially fine assortment has been gathered just west of **CRÈVECOEUR-EN-AUGE**, 17km west of Lisieux on the N14, in the grounds of a small twelfth-century **château** (April–June & Sept daily 11am–6pm; July & Aug daily 11am–7pm; Oct Sun 2–6pm; €8; ☎02 31 63 02 45, ⓦwww.chateau-de-crevecoeur.com). Around a pristine village green, circled by a shallow moat, this photogenic group of golden adobe structures includes a manor house, a barn, an attractive little twelfth-century chapel, and a tall thin dovecote that dates from the fifteenth century. Displays in the manor house itself include a fascinating exhibition on the music and instruments of the Middle Ages.

## Beuvron-en-Auge
By far the prettiest Pays d'Auge village is **BEUVRON-EN-AUGE**, 7km north of the N13 halfway between Lisieux and Caen. It consists of an oval central *place*, ringed by a glorious ensemble of multicoloured half-timbered houses, including the yellow-and-brown sixteenth-century Vieux Manoir.

## Orbec
The town of **ORBEC**, 19km southeast of Lisieux, epitomizes the simple pleasures of the Pays d'Auge. Several houses along the rue Grande feature gaps between the timbers that are filled with intricate patterns of coloured tiles and bricks. Debussy composed *Jardin sous la pluie* in one, and the oldest and prettiest – a tanner's house dating back to 1568, known as the **Vieux Manoir** – holds a museum of local history. On the whole, though, it's more appealing just to walk down behind the church to the river, its watermill and paddocks.

## Livarot
In venerable **LIVAROT**, at the centre of cheese country, you can take a 1hr 30min tour of the **Fromagerie Graindorge**, 42 rue du Général-Leclerc (April–June, Sept & Oct Mon–Sat 9.30am–1pm & 2–5.30pm; July & Aug Mon–Sat 9.30am–5.30pm, Sun 10.30am–5.30pm; Nov–March Mon–Fri 10am–12.30pm & 2.30–5.30pm, Sat 10am–1pm; free; ☎02 31 48 20 10, ⓦgraindorge.fr), to get a closer look at how the town's eponymous cheese is made.

For superb views of the valley, climb up to the thirteenth-century church of **St-Michel de Livet**, just above town.

## Vimoutiers
The pretty little town of **VIMOUTIERS** is home to the **Musée du Camembert**, 10 av du Général-de-Gaulle (April–June, Sept & Oct daily 2–6pm; July & Aug daily 11am–6pm; €3; ☎02 33 39 30 29, ⓦvimoutiers.fr), a rather homespun affair which explains the production process of the famous cheese, with an optional €1 tasting at the end.

A statue in the main square honours **Marie Harel**, who, at the nearby village of Camembert, developed the original cheese early in the nineteenth century, promoting it with a skilful campaign that included sending free samples to Napoleon. Marie is

**5**

## WILLIAM THE BASTARD AND THE LAUNDRYWOMAN

William the Conqueror, or William the Bastard as he is more prosaically known in his homeland, was born in **Falaise**. William's mother, Arlette, a laundrywoman, was spotted by his father, Duke Robert of Normandy, at the washing place below the château. She was a shrewd woman, scorning secrecy in her eventual assignation by riding publicly through the main entrance to meet him. During her pregnancy, she is said to have dreamed of bearing a mighty tree that cast its shade over Normandy and England.

confronted across the main street by what might be called the statue of the Unknown Cow. Vimoutiers hosts a **market** on Monday afternoons.

### Camembert

The tiny, hilly, very rural and world-famous village of **CAMEMBERT**, 3km southeast of Vimoutiers, is home to far more cows than humans. The largest Camembert producers, **La Ferme Président**, run a museum in its little central square, aptly called **La Maison du Camembert** (March, April, Sept & Oct Wed–Sun 10–noon & 2–5pm; May daily 10am–noon & 2–5.15pm; June–Aug daily 10am–noon & 2–6.15pm; €4; ☎02 33 12 10 37; ⓦfermepresident.com), which whirls through the history of the cheese and the methods, both traditional and modern, used to make it. Afterwards comes a cheese tasting, in their café.

### Falaise

The historic town of **FALAISE**, 40km southwest of Lisieux, was almost entirely destroyed during the climax of the **Battle of Normandy** in August 1944. In the desperate struggle to close the so-called "Falaise Gap", the Allied armies sought to encircle the Germans and cut off their retreat. By the time the Canadians entered the town on August 17, they could no longer tell where the roads had been, and they had to bulldoze a new 4m strip straight through the middle. As a result, although its mighty **château**, the birthplace of William the Conqueror, still stands as a fascinating monument, Falaise itself has lost its former charm.

#### Château Guillaume-le-Conquérant

Daily: Feb–June & Sept–Dec 10am–6pm; July & Aug 10am–7pm; last admission 1hr before closing; closed Jan • €8 • ☎ 02 31 41 61 44, ⓦ chateau-guillaume-leconquerant.fr

Firmly planted on the massive rocks of the cliff (*falaise*) that gave Falaise its name, and towering over the **Fontaine d'Arlette** down by the river, the keep of the **Château Guillaume-le-Conquérant** is as evocative a historic sight as one could imagine. Nonetheless, it was so heavily damaged during the war that it took more than fifty years to reopen for regular visits.

Huge resources have been lavished on restoring the central **donjon**, reminiscent of the Tower of London with its cream-coloured Caen stone. Steel slabs, concrete blocks, glass floors and tent-like canvas awnings have been slapped down atop the bare ruins, and metal staircases squeezed into the wall cavities. The raw structure of the keep, down to its very foundations, lies exposed to view, while the newly created rooms are used for changing exhibitions that focus on the castle's fascinating past.

---

**INFORMATION**                                                    **THE PAYS D'AUGE**

**LISIEUX**
**Tourist office** 11 rue d'Alençon (mid-June to Sept Mon–Sat 8.30am–6.30pm, Sun 10am–12.30pm & 2–5pm; Oct to mid-June Mon–Sat 8.30am–noon & 1.30–6pm; ☎02 31 48 18 10, ⓦ www.lisieux-tourisme.com).

**FALAISE**
**Tourist office** 5 place Guillaume-le-Conquérant (May–Sept Mon–Sat 9.30am–12.30pm & 1.30–6.30pm, Sun 10am–1pm; Oct–April Tues–Sat 9.30am–12.30pm & 1.30–5.30pm; ☎02 31 90 17 26, ⓦfalaise-tourisme.com).

## ACCOMMODATION AND EATING

### LISIEUX

**St-Louis** 4 rue St-Jacques ☎ 02 31 62 06 50, ⓦ hotel saintlouis-lisieux.com. Friendly and ultra-enthusiastic management have transformed this former budget hotel, where the cheapest of the twelve individually decorated rooms lack en-suite facilities. Excellent organic breakfasts cost €9. **€75**

### BEUVRON-EN-AUGE

★ **Pavé d'Auge** ☎ 02 31 79 26 71, ⓦ pavedauge.com. Top-notch restaurant in Beuvron's timber-framed medieval market hall, in the central square, serving rich and opulent Norman cuisine on changing *menus* from €50; it also offers five comfortable B&B rooms, (**€118**), in the separate *Pavé d'Hôtes*. Mid-July to Aug daily except Mon noon–1.30pm & 7.30–9pm; Sept to mid-July Wed–Sun noon–1.30pm & 7.30–9pm.

### ORBEC

**Manoir de l'Engagiste** 15 rue de St-Rémy ☎ 06 84 75 67 33, ⓦ manoir-engagiste.fr. Gorgeous half-timbered B&B, dating back to the sixteenth century, offering two very comfortable rooms plus a larger suite, decorated to differing themes, and arrayed around a peaceful courtyard. **€125**

### VIMOUTIERS

**La Campière** Bd Docteur-Dentu ☎ 02 33 39 18 86, ⓦ vimoutiers.fr. Clean and very cheap two-star campsite, a short walk north of the centre. Closed Nov–March. **€10**

**L'Escale du Vitou** Rte d'Argentan ☎ 02 33 39 12 04, ⓦ domaineduvitou.com. Attractive half-timbered hotel, in a delightful rural setting not far south of Vimoutiers, where the Escale du Vitou lake offers windsurfing, swimming and horseriding. Seventeen rooms, half a dozen cottages, and a decent restaurant (closed Mon). **€75**

### FALAISE

**Camping Municipal** Rue du Val d'Ante ☎ 02 31 90 16 55, ⓦ camping-falaise.com. This well-equipped three-star municipal campsite is in a superb location, immediately below the castle, next to Arlette's fountain and a swimming pool to which guests get cut-price access. Closed Oct–April. **€15.20**

## The Suisse Normande

The area known as the **Suisse Normande** starts roughly 25km south of Caen, along the gorge of the River Orne, between Thury-Harcourt and Putanges. While the name may be a little far-fetched – there are certainly no mountains – the region is quite distinctive, with cliffs, crags and wooded hills at every turn. There are plenty of opportunities for **outdoor pursuits**: you can race along the Orne in canoes and kayaks, cruise more sedately on pedalos, or dangle on ropes from the sheer rock faces high above. For mere walkers the Orne can be frustrating: footpaths along the river are few and far between, and often entirely overgrown.

### Thury-Harcourt

**THURY-HARCOURT** is really two separate towns: a little village around a bridge across the Orne, and a larger market town on the hill that overlooks it. In summer, the grounds of the local manor house are open to visitors, providing access to the immediate riverside.

### Clécy

The small village of **CLÉCY**, 10km south of Thury-Harcourt, is perched on a hill about 1km up from the point where the D133A crosses the River Orne by means of the Pont du Vey. On the way up is the Parc de Loisirs, which holds a **Musée du Chemin de Fer Miniature**, featuring a gigantic model railway that's certain to appeal to children (mid-April to mid-May Mon & Fri 2–6pm, Tues–Thurs, Sat & Sun 10am–noon & 2–6pm; mid-May to early July Tues–Thurs, Sat & Sun 10am–noon & 2–6pm, Fri 2–6pm; early July to end Aug daily 10.30am–6.30pm; Sept daily except Mon 2–5pm; €8.50, ages 3–12 €6.50; ☎ 02 31 69 07 13, ⓦ chemin-fer-miniature-clecy.com).

Across from Clécy, the east bank of the Orne is dominated by the exposed rock face of the giant **Pain de Sucre**, or Sugarloaf, looming above the river. Small footpaths, and the tortuous Route des Crêtes, wind up to its flat top, making for some fabulously enjoyable walks. Picnic sites and parking places along the crest hold orientation maps

**5**

so weather-beaten as to be almost abstract, but the views down to the flat fields of the Orne Valley are stupendous.

## Pont d'Ouilly

For anyone planning to walk or cycle, the village of **PONT D'OUILLY**, a dozen kilometres upriver from Clécy, makes a good starting point. Upstream, a pleasant walk leads for 3.5km to the pretty little village of Le Mesnil Villement.

A short distance south of Pont d'Ouilly, the **Roche d'Oëtre** is a high rock with a tremendous view into the deep and totally wooded gorge of the Rouvre, a tributary of the Orne. The river widens soon afterwards into the **Lac de Rabodanges**, formed by the many-arched Rabodanges Dam.

---

**ARRIVAL AND INFORMATION**       **THE SUISSE NORMANDE**

**By bus** Bus Verts #34 stops in Thury-Harcourt and Clécy en route between Caen and Flers.

**Thury-Harcourt tourist office** 2 place St-Sauveur (May, June & Sept Tues–Sat 10am–12.30pm & 2–6pm, Sun 10am–12.30pm; July & Aug also open Mon; Oct–April Tues–Fri 10am–12.30pm & 2.30–5pm, Sat 10am–12.30pm; ☏ 02

31 79 70 45, ⓦ suisse-normande-tourisme.com).

**Clécy tourist office** Place du Tripot, behind the church (second half of April Tues–Sat 10am–12.30pm & 2.30–5pm; May, June & Sept Tues–Sat 10am–12.30pm & 2–6pm, Sun 10am–12.30pm; July & Aug also open Mon; ☏ 02 31 69 79 95, ⓦ suisse-normande-tourisme.com).

---

**ACCOMMODATION AND EATING**

**THURY-HARCOURT**

**Relais de la Poste** 7 rue de Caen ☏ 02 31 79 72 12, ⓦ hotel-relaisdelaposte.com. Elegant old country-house hotel, holding a dozen rooms of all shapes and sizes, plus an opulent restaurant (closed Sun eve and all Mon) that's perfect at the end of a long day. Dinner *menus* start at €32. **€65**

**CLÉCY**

★ **Au Site Normand** 2 rue des Châtelets ☏ 02 31 69 71 05, ⓦ hotel-clecy.com. Village hotel, facing the church, with pleasant, comfortable rooms in a modern annexe, and a stylish modern dining room in the main timber-framed building, serving good *menus* from €36 (restaurant closed Sun & Mon). The river is 1km away, down the hill. **€87**

# Southern Normandy

Drivers heading west from Paris towards Brittany can cut directly across southern Normandy by following the N12 through **Alençon**, and then continuing on the N176 and N976. Much of the terrain along Normandy's southern border is taken up by the dense woodlands of the **Forêt d'Écouves** and the **Forêt des Andaines**, so there's plenty of good walking, while the hill towns of **Carrouges** and **Domfront** make great stopovers.

## Alençon and around

**ALENÇON**, a medium-sized and lively town, is known for its traditional – and now largely defunct – lacemaking industry. Wandering around the town will take you to St Thérèse's birthplace on rue St-Blaise, just in front of the *gare routière*.

### Musée des Beaux-Arts et de la Dentelle

Cour Carrée de la Dentelle • July & Aug daily 10am–noon & 2–6pm; Sept–June closed Mon • €6.60 • ☏ 02 33 32 40 07, ⓦ paysdalencontourisme.fr

Housed in a former Jesuit school, the **Musée des Beaux-Arts et de la Dentelle** has all the best trappings of a modern museum. The highly informative history of lacemaking upstairs, can, however, be tedious for anyone not already riveted by the subject. It also contains an unexpected collection of gruesome Cambodian artefacts like spears and lances, tiger skulls and elephants' feet, gathered in the nineteenth century. The paintings in the adjoining Beaux-Arts section are nondescript, except for a few works by Courbet and Géricault.

## Forêt d'Écouves

Starting 10km north of Alençon, the **Forêt d'Écouves** is a dense mixture of spruce, pine, oak and beech. Unfortunately, though, it's a favoured spot of the military – and, in autumn, deer hunters, too. You can usually ramble along the cool paths, where you may happen upon wild mushrooms and even the odd wild boar.

## Mortagne-au-Perche

Famous for the Percheron horses who derive their name from this rural region, **Le Perche** is an ideal retreat for a few days' relaxation. An obvious base from which to explore southern Normandy's countryside is the pretty town of **MORTAGNE-AU-PERCHE**, 38km east of Alençon. Its historic centre includes the sixteenth-century **Église Notre-Dame**, as well as an impressive *hôtel de ville* set in some lovely formal gardens, from where there is an excellent view of the countryside beyond.

## Carrouges

The hill town of **CARROUGES**, perched along a high ridge at the western end of the Forêt d'Écouves, is noteworthy for its impressive moat-encircled **château**, set in spacious grounds at the foot of the hill.

### Château de Carrouges

Daily: May–Aug 10am–12.45pm & 2–6pm; Sept–April 10am–noon & 2–5pm • €6 • ☎ 02 33 27 20 32, ⓦ carrouges.monuments-nationaux.fr

The twin highlights of the **Château de Carrouges** are a superb restored brick staircase, and a room in which hang portraits of fourteen successive generations of the Le Veneur family, an extraordinary illustration of the permutations of heredity. Local craftsmen sell their work in the **Maison des Métiers**, the former castle chapel.

## Bagnoles-de-l'Orne

The quaint spa town of **BAGNOLES-DE-L'ORNE** is quite unlike anywhere else in this part of the world, attracting the moneyed sick and convalescent from all over France to its thermal baths, along with mainly elderly visitors keen to indulge themselves in the various spas. The layout is formal and spacious, centring on a lake surrounded by well-tended gardens. With so many visitors to keep entertained, there are also innumerable cultural events of a restrained and stress-free nature, such as tea dances and stage shows.

Anyone looking for more active pursuits has the choice of mini golf or a pedalo trip around the lake. The town as a whole operates to a **season** that lasts roughly from early April to the end of October; arrive in winter, and you may find everything shut.

## Domfront

**DOMFRONT** is a pretty hilltop town, dominated by the ruins of a redoubtable **castle**, perched at its very apex on an isolated rock. Eleanor of Aquitaine was born here in October 1162, and Thomas Becket came to stay for Christmas 1166, saying Mass in the **Notre-Dame-sur-l'Eau** church down by the river, which, sadly, has been ruined by vandals. The views from the flower-filled gardens that surround the castle's mangled keep are spectacular, including an impressive panorama of the ascent you've made to get up here. A slender footbridge connects the castle with the narrow little village itself, which holds an abundance of half-timbered houses.

## St-Lô

The city of **ST-LÔ**, 60km southeast of Cherbourg and 36km southwest of Bayeux, is still known as the "Capital of the Ruins". Memorial sites are everywhere, and what is new speaks as tellingly of the destruction as the ruins that have been preserved. In the main square, the gate of the old prison commemorates Resistance members executed by the Nazis, people deported east to the concentration camps and soldiers killed in action.

**5**

---

## THE BOCAGE

The region that centres on **St-Lô**, just south of the Cotentin, is known as the **Bocage**. That word describes a type of cultivated countryside common in western France, where fields are cut by tight hedgerows rooted into walls of earth standing well over 1m high. An effective form of smallhold farming in pre-industrial days, it also proved to be a perfect system of anti-tank barricades. When the Allied troops tried to advance through the region in 1944, it was almost impenetrable – certainly bearing no resemblance to the East Anglian plains where they had trained. The war here was hand-to-hand slaughter, and the destruction of villages was often wholesale.

---

When the bombardment of St-Lô was at its fiercest, the Germans refused to take measures to protect the prisoners; this gate was all that survived.

The newness of so much in St-Lô reveals the scale of fighting. It took sixty years for the canalized channel of the Vire, running between the *gare SNCF* and the castle rock, to be re-landscaped. Now known as **Port-St-Lô**, it's an attractive area to walk around, and pedalos are available for rent. But the most visible – and brilliant – reconstruction is the **Cathédrale de Notre-Dame**. The main body of this, with its strange southward-veering nave, has been conventionally repaired and rebuilt. Between the shattered west front and base of the collapsed north tower, however, a startling sheer wall of icy green stone makes no attempt to mask the destruction.

By way of contrast, a lighthouse-like 1950s folly spirals to nowhere on the main square. Should you feel the urge, you can climb its staircase and make your way into the even more pointless labyrinth of glass at its feet for a €1.50 admission fee.

### Villedieu-les-Poêles

Ever since the twelfth century, **VILLEDIEU-LES-POÊLES** – a lively place, 35km south of St-Lô – has been a centre for **metalworking**. To this day, copper souvenirs and kitchen utensils gleam from its rows of shops, and the tourist office can provide lists of dozens of local ateliers for more direct purchases. Much of the ancient town of retains significant elements of its medieval appearance. In its backstreets perfectly preserved old courtyards are tucked away behind unprepossessing wooden gateways.

---

**ARRIVAL AND DEPARTURE**                                    **SOUTHERN NORMANDY**

**ALENÇON**
**By train** The *gare SNCF* is northeast of the centre, on rue Denis-Papin.
Destinations Caen (8 daily; 1hr 10min); Le Mans (11 daily; 40min).
**By bus** The *gare routière* is a little short of the *gare SNCF*, northeast of the centre.
Destinations Bagnoles (3 daily; 1hr); Mortagne (2–3 daily;

1hr); Vimoutiers (1–3 daily; 1hr 55min).

**ST-LÔ**
**By train** The *gare SNCF* is on av Briovère, across the Vire river from the town centre.
Destinations Caen (12 daily; 50min), via Bayeux (25min); Rennes (4 daily; 2hr 10min), via Coutances (20min) and Pontorson (1hr 15min).

---

**INFORMATION**

---

**ALENÇON**
**Tourist office** Place de la Magdelaine (July & Aug Mon–Sat 9am–7pm, Sun 10am–1pm & 2–5pm; Sept–June Mon–Sat 9am–12.30pm & 2–6pm; ☎ 02 33 80 66 33, 🌐 visitalencon.com).

**MORTAGNE-AU-PERCHE**
**Tourist office** 36 place du Général-de-Gaulle (April–June Tues–Thurs 10am–noon & 2–5pm, Fri & Sat 10am–1pm &

2–6pm, Sun 10am–1pm; July & Aug Mon–Sat 9.30am–-6.30pm, Sun 10am–12.30pm & 2.30–6.30pm; Oct–March Tues–Thurs 10am–noon & 2–5pm, Fri & Sat 10am–1pm & 2–5pm; ☎ 02 33 83 34 37, 🌐 www.ot-mortagneauperche.fr).

**BAGNOLES-DE-L'ORNE**
**Tourist office** Place du Marché (mid-Feb to March & Nov Mon–Sat 9.30am–12.30pm & 2–6pm; April–Oct Mon–Sat

9.30am–1pm & 2–6.30pm, Sun 9.30am–1.30pm ; ☎ 02 33 37 85 66, ⓦ bagnolesdelorne.com).

### DOMFRONT
**Tourist office** 12 place de la Roirie (April–June & Sept Mon–Sat 10am–12.30pm & 2–6pm; July & Aug Mon & Sat 10am–12.30pm & 2–6pm, Tues–Fri 10am–6pm, Sun 10am–noon & 2.30–5.30pm; Oct–March Tues–Sat 10am–12.30pm & 2–6pm; ☎ 02 33 38 53 97, ⓦ ot-domfront.com). In summer, they offer guided tours of Domfront (mid-June to mid-Sept Wed 3pm).

### ST-LÔ
**Tourist office** 60 rue de la Poterne (April–June & Sept Mon–2–6pm, Tues–Fri 9.30am–12.30pm & 2–6pm, Sat 10am–12.30pm & 2–5pm; July & Aug Mon–Fri 9.30am–6.30pm, Sat 10am–12.30pm & 2.30–5.30pm, Sun 10am–1pm; Oct–March Tues–Fri 9.30am–12.30pm & 2–6pm, Sat 10am–1pm; ☎ 02 14 29 00 17, ⓦ ot-saintloagglo.fr).

### VILLEDIEU-LES-POÊLES
**Tourist office** 8 place des Costils (Feb–May Mon–Sat daily 10am–12.30pm & 2–5.30pm; June–Sept daily 9.30am–1pm & 2–6pm; Oct–Jan Mon 2–5.30pm, Tues, Wed, Fri & Sat 10am–12.30pm & 2–5.30pm, Thurs 10am–12.30pm; ☎ 02 33 61 05 69, ⓦ tourisme-villedieu.com).

## ACCOMMODATION AND EATING

### ALENÇON
**Château de Sarceaux** Valframbert ☎ 02 33 28 85 11, ⓦ chateau-de-sarceaux.com. Grand, yet comfortable and very welcoming eighteenth-century château, 3km north of central Alençon. Family-owned and run as an intimate B&B, it holds four luxurious antique-furnished rooms and copious breakfasts. Opulent dinners, served communally, are available for an additional €54 per person. €130
**De Paris** 26 rue Denis-Papin ☎ 02 33 29 01 64, ⓦ hotel deparis-alencon.com. Perfectly presentable rooms in a simple hotel above a bar facing the *gare SNCF*. All rooms have showers, but some don't have toilets. €40

### MORTAGNE-AU-PERCHE
★ **Ferme du Gros Chêne** Le Gros Chêne ☎ 02 33 25 02 72, ⓦ fermedugroschene.com. This working farm, just outside Mortagne on the D8, has five comfortable, colourful and imaginatively decorated guest rooms in a converted barn, plus three-course dinners for €24. €75
★ **Du Tribunal** 4 place du Palais ☎ 02 33 25 04 77, ⓦ hotel-tribunal.fr. Mortagne's nicest hotel, on a sleepy tree-lined square, consists of a few old stone buildings with exposed timbers. As well as tasteful if slightly old-fashioned rooms with updated bathrooms, it has a good restaurant, with outdoor seating and *menus* from €31. €80

### BAGNOLES-DE-L'ORNE
**Ô Gayot** 2 av de la Ferté-Macé ☎ 02 33 38 44 01, ⓦ ogayot.com. Bagnoles' nicest hotel, alongside the tourist office, offers a contemporary take on the spa experience with its minimalist rooms, and has a pleasant bistro/restaurant (closed Thurs eve) with outdoor garden seating. €60

### DOMFRONT
**France** 7 rue du Mont St-Michel ☎ 02 33 38 51 44, ⓦ hoteldefrance-domfront.fr. Old-fashioned but perfectly comfortable *Logis* on the main road below the old town, where it's somewhat exposed to traffic noise. Affordable rooms above a nice bar and good-value restaurant, with a garden at the back. €78

### ST-LÔ
**Mercure Saint-Lô** 1 av Briovère ☎ 02 33 05 10 84, ⓦ accorhotels.com. St-Lô's largest hotel, ranged atop a ridge beside the *gare SNCF*, just across the river. As well as 67 modern motel-style rooms, it's home to the *Tocqueville* restaurant, open for all meals on weekdays only, and serving *menus* from €21. €67

### VILLEDIEU-LES-POÊLES
**St-Pierre et St-Michel** 12 place de la République ☎ 02 33 61 00 11, ⓦ st-pierre-hotel.com. Very welcoming *Logis*, in the heart of the main street, housing a stylish restaurant that serves seriously gastronomic menus from €23. €56

# Brittany

**311** Eastern Brittany and the north coast

**330** Finistère

**348** The Nantes–Brest canal

**351** The southern coast

CÔTE DE GRANIT ROSE

# Brittany

Long before Brittany became subsumed into France, the inhabitants of this rugged Atlantic promontory were risking their lives fishing and trading on the violent seas, and struggling with the arid soil of the interior. Today that toughness and resilience continues to define the region, which is deeply infused with Celtic culture: mystical, musical, sometimes morbid and defeatist, sometimes vital and inspired. Archeologically, Brittany is among the richest sites in the world – the alignments at Carnac rival Stonehenge. It first appeared in history as the quasi-mythical "Little Britain" of Arthurian legend, and in the days when travel by sea was safer and easier than by land, it was intimately connected with "Great Britain" across the water. Settlements such as St-Malo, St-Pol and Quimper were founded by otherwise unrecorded Welsh and Irish missionary saints.

Brittany remained **independent** until the sixteenth century; after its last ruler, Duchess Anne, died in 1532, François Ier took her daughter and lands, and sealed the **union with France** with an act that supposedly enshrined certain privileges. Successive violations of this treaty by Paris, and subsequent revolts, form the core of Breton history since the Middle Ages.

Many Bretons continue to regard France as a separate country, even if few actively support Breton nationalism much beyond displaying Breizh (Breton for "Brittany") stickers on their cars. The Breton **language** remains very much alive, and the economic resurgence since the 1970s, helped partly by tourism, has largely been due to local initiatives, including the successful bid by Brittany Ferries to re-establish the old trading links with Britain and Ireland. At the same time a Celtic artistic identity has consciously been revived, and festivals – above all August's **Inter-Celtic Festival** at Lorient – celebrate Breton music, poetry and dance, with fellow Celts treated as comrades.

For most visitors, the Breton **coast** is the dominant feature. Apart from the Côte d'Azur, this is France's most popular resort area, for French and foreign tourists alike. Its attractions are obvious: warm white-sand beaches, towering cliffs, rock formations and offshore islands and islets, and everywhere the stone dolmens and menhirs of a prehistoric past. The busiest areas are the **Côte d'Émeraude** around **St-Malo**; the **Côte de Granit Rose** in the north; the **Crozon peninsula** in far western **Finistère**; the family resorts such as **Bénodet** that lie just to the south; and the **Morbihan coast** below **Vannes**. Hotels and campsites here are plentiful, if pushed to their limits from mid-June to the end of August.

Be sure not to leave Brittany without visiting at least one of its many **islands** – such as the **Île de Bréhat**, the **Île de Sein**, or **Belle-Île** – or taking in cities like **Quimper** or **Morlaix**, testimony to the riches of the medieval duchy. Allow time, too, to explore the much quieter interior, despite its sketchy transport and shortage of accommodation.

If you're looking for traditional Breton fun, and you can't make the large-scale summer events in Lorient or Quimper, look out for gatherings organized by **Celtic folklore groups** – Circles or Bagadou. You may also be interested by the **pardons**, pilgrimage festivals commemorating local saints. Bear in mind, though, that these are not phoney affairs kept alive for tourists, but deeply serious and rather gloomy religious occasions.

---

**GETTING AROUND**                                                        **BRITTANY**

Brittany is well served by public transport. Separate TGV train lines from Paris – one ending at Brest, the other at Quimper – serve the major cities along the north and south coasts respectively, and high-speed trains also connect Lille with Rennes. All are complemented by local buses and trains. Driving, too, is straightforward, and none of Brittany's *autoroutes* charges tolls.

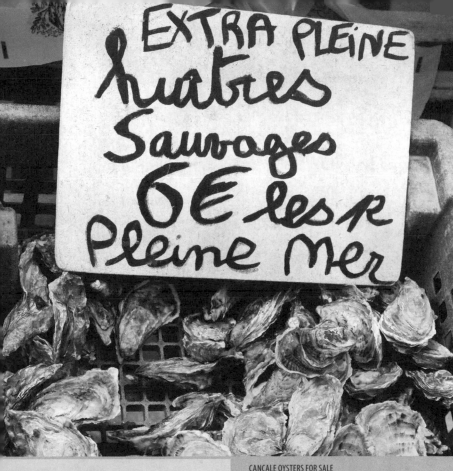

EXTRA PLEINE
huîtres
Sauvages
6€ les 12
Pleine Mer

CANCALE OYSTERS FOR SALE

# Highlights

**❶ Cancale** The stalls and restaurants in Cancale's little harbour will have oyster-lovers in raptures. See page 320

**❷ Dinan** Brittany's most complete walled medieval town, perched in a gorgeous setting above the Rance river. See page 321

**❸ The Côte de Granit Rose** With its bizarre pink rock formations and gem-like beaches, this memorable stretch of coastline is perfect for kids. See page 327

**❹ Île de Sein** Misty and mysterious island, barely rising from the Atlantic; a great day-trip from western Finistère. See page 341

**❺ The Inter-Celtic Festival** Celebrate the music and culture of the Celtic nations at Lorient's summer festival. See page 351

**❻ Carnac** France's most extraordinary megalithic monuments, predating even the Egyptian pyramids. See page 352

**❼ Belle-Île** The aptly named island offers a microcosm of Brittany, with wild coast in the south, beaches in the north, and beautiful countryside in between. See page 356

**HIGHLIGHTS ARE MARKED ON THE MAP ON PAGE 310**

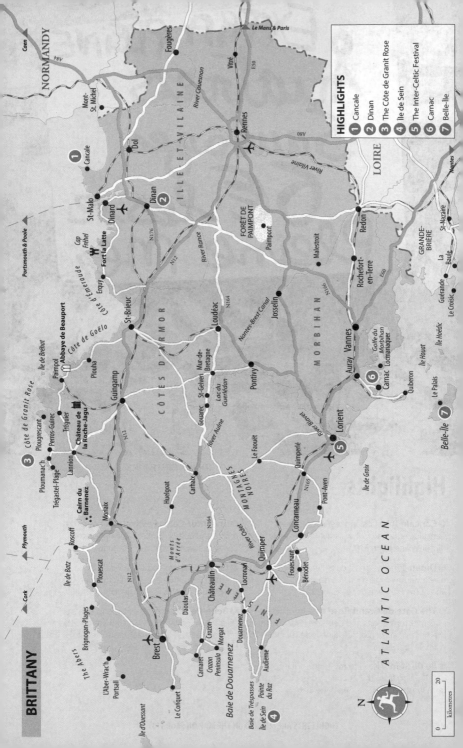

## A BRETON GLOSSARY

Although estimates of the number of **Breton-speakers** range from 400,000 to 800,000, you're unlikely to encounter Breton spoken as a day-to-day language. Learning Breton is not really a viable prospect for visitors who lack a grounding in Welsh, Gaelic or some other Celtic tongue. However, it's interesting to note the roots of Breton place names, many of which have a simple meaning. Below are some of the most common:

| | | | |
|---|---|---|---|
| aber | estuary | **lann** | heath |
| argoat | land | **lech** | flat stone |
| armor | sea | **mario** | dead |
| avel | wind | **men** | stone |
| bihan | little | **menez** | (rounded) mountain |
| bran | hill | **menhir** | long stone |
| braz | big | **meur** | big |
| coat | forest | **nevez** | new |
| cromlech | stone circle | **parc** | field |
| dol | table | **penn** | end, head |
| dolmen | stone table | **plou** | parish |
| du | black | **pors** | port, farmyard |
| enez | island | **roc'h** | ridge |
| goaz | stream | **ster** | river |
| gwenn | white | **stivel** | fountain, spring |
| hir | long | **traez henn** | beach |
| ker | village or house | **trou** | valley |
| kozh | old | **ty** | house |
| lan | holy place | **wrach** | witch |

# Eastern Brittany and the north coast

All roads in Brittany curl eventually inland to **Rennes**, the capital. East of Rennes, the fortified citadelle of **Vitré** protected the eastern approaches to medieval Brittany, which vigorously defended its independence against incursors. Along the north coast, west of Normandy's Mont St-Michel, stand some of Brittany's finest old towns. A spectacular introduction to the province greets ferry passengers: the **River Rance**, guarded by magnificently preserved **St-Malo** on its estuary, and beautiful medieval **Dinan** 20km upstream. Further west stretches a varied coastline that culminates in the seductive Île de Bréhat, and the colourful chaos of the **Côte de Granit Rose**.

## Rennes

The capital and power centre of Brittany ever since it united with France in 1532, **RENNES** is – outwardly at least – uncharacteristic of the region, with its Neoclassical layout and pompous major buildings. Any potential it had as a picturesque tourist spot was destroyed three centuries ago in 1720, when a drunken carpenter managed to set light to virtually the entire city. Only the area known as **Les Lices**, at the junction of the canalized Ille and the River Vilaine, survived undamaged.

Rennes' subsequent remodelling left the city, north of the river at any rate, as a muddle of grand eighteenth-century public squares interspersed with intimate little alleys of half-timbered houses. It's a lively enough place though, with around sixty thousand university **students** to stimulate its cultural life, and a couple of major annual **festivals**, the Tombées de la Nuit and the Transmusicales, to lure in visitors.

### The medieval quarter

Rennes' surviving **medieval quarter**, bordered by the canal to the west and the river to the south, radiates from the **Porte Mordelaise**, the old ceremonial entrance to the city.

Immediately northeast of the *porte*, the **place des Lices** is dominated by two usually empty market halls, but comes alive every Saturday for one of France's largest **street markets**. In a jousting tournament on this very spot in 1337, the hitherto unknown Bertrand du Guesclin, then aged 17, fought and defeated several older opponents. That set him on his career as a soldier, during which he was to save Rennes when it was under siege by the English. However, after the Bretons were defeated at Auray in 1364, he fought for the French, and twice invaded Brittany.

## Palais du Parlement

The one central building to escape Rennes' 1720 fire was the **Palais du Parlement** on rue Hoche, downtown. In 1994, however, the Palais was all but ruined by a mysterious conflagration, sparked by a flare during a demonstration by Breton fishermen. Rebuilt and restored, the entire structure is once more topped by an impressive array of gleaming gilded statues. Inside, its lobby stages temporary exhibitions.

## Musée des Beaux-Arts

20 quai Émile-Zola • Tues–Fri 10am–5pm, Sat & Sun 10am–6pm • €6 • ☎ 02 23 62 17 45, ⓦ mbar.org

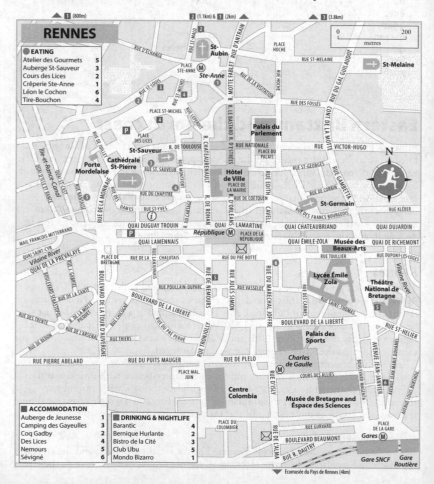

## FOOD IN BRITTANY

Brittany's proudest contribution to world cuisine has to be the **crêpe**, and its savoury equivalent the **galette**; crêperies throughout the region serve them with every imaginable filling. However, gourmets are more likely to be enticed by the magnificent array of **seafood**. Restaurants in resorts such as St-Malo and Quiberon jostle to attract fish connoisseurs, while some smaller towns – like Cancale, widely regarded as the best place in France for oysters (*huîtres*), and Erquy, with its scallops (*coquilles St-Jacques*) – depend on one specific mollusc for their livelihood.

Although they can't claim to be uniquely Breton, two appetizers feature on every self-respecting menu – **moules marinières**, giant bowls of succulent orange mussels steamed in white wine, shallots and parsley (and perhaps enriched with cream or crème fraîche to become *moules à la crème*), and **soupe de poissons** (fish soup), traditionally served with garlicky *rouille* mayonnaise (coloured with sweet red pepper), a mound of grated gruyère, and a bowl of croutons. Jars of fresh *soupe de poissons*, sold in seaside *poissonneries*, make an ideal way to take a taste of France home with you. Paying a bit more in a restaurant – typically on *menus* costing €30 or more – brings you into the realm of the **assiette de fruits de mer**, a mountainous heap of langoustines, crabs, oysters, mussels, clams, whelks and cockles, most raw and all delicious.

**Main courses** tend to be plainer than in neighbouring Normandy. Fresh fish is prepared with relatively simple sauces. Skate served with capers, or salmon baked with a mustard or cheese sauce, are typical, while even the **cotriade**, a stew containing sole, turbot or bass, as well as shellfish, is less rich than its Mediterranean equivalent, the bouillabaisse. Brittany is also better than much of France in its respect for fresh **vegetables**, thanks to local-grown peas, cauliflowers, artichokes and the like. Only with the **desserts** can things get a little heavy; **far Breton**, considered a great delicacy, is a baked concoction of sponge and custard dotted with chopped plums, while *îles flottantes* are soft meringue icebergs adrift in a sea of *crème anglaise*, a light egg custard.

Strictly speaking, no **wine** is produced in Brittany; although they're often regarded as Breton, the dry whites Muscadet and Gros-Plant are produced in the neighbouring *département* of Loire-Atlantique.

The south bank of the **River Vilaine**, which flows through the centre of Rennes, narrowly confined into a steep-sided channel, is home to the **Musée des Beaux-Arts**. Unfortunately, many of its finest artworks – which include drawings by Leonardo da Vinci, Botticelli, Fra Lippo Lippi and Dürer – are not usually on public display. Instead you'll find indifferent Impressionist views of Normandy by the likes of Boudin and Sisley, interspersed with the occasional treasure such as Veronese's depiction of a flying *Perseus Rescuing Andromeda*. Picasso makes a cameo appearance, with a nude from 1923, a simple *Baigneuse à Dinard* from 1928, and a very late and surprisingly Cubist canvas from 1970.

### Musée de Bretagne and Espace des Sciences

10 cours des Alliés • July & Aug Tues–Fri 1–7pm, Sat & Sun 2–7pm; Sept–June Tues–Fri noon–7pm, Sat & Sun 2–7pm • Musée de Bretagne €6, Espace des Sciences €6 • ☎ 02 23 40 66 00, ⓦ musee-bretagne.fr

The showpiece **Musée de Bretagne**, housed in the modern Champs Libres, 500m south of the river, provides a high-tech overview of Breton history and culture. It starts with a hearth used by humans in a Finistère sea cave half a million years ago that ranks among the oldest evidence of the deliberate exploitation of fire in the world. From here on, a quick, entertaining skate through regional history covers the dolmens and menhirs of the megalith builders, some magnificent jadeite axes and Bronze Age swords, and the arrival of first the Celts, next the Romans, and later still the spread of Christianity from the fifth century onwards. A separate section is devoted to the Dreyfus Affair (see Contexts), and there's also extensive coverage of World War II.

Under the same roof, the **Espace des Sciences** is a peculiar sort of scaly volcano that contains two floors of interactive scientific displays that change each year.

## ARRIVAL AND DEPARTURE

**By train** Rennes' *gare SNCF*, on the Paris–Brest TGV line, is 15min walk south of the Vilaine, and a little more from the medieval quarter.

Destinations Brest (11 daily; 2–2hr 30min); Caen (5 daily; 3–5hr); Lille (2 daily; 3hr 45min); Morlaix (10 daily; 1hr 45min); Nantes (10 daily; 1hr 25min); Paris-Montparnasse (12 daily; 2hr 10min); Pontorson (3 daily; 1hr); Quimper (9 daily; 2hr 15min); St-Malo (14 daily; 1hr); Vannes (6 daily; 1hr); Vitré (12 daily; 18–35min).

**By bus** The long-distance *gare routière* stands alongside the *gare SNCF* on bd Solférino; main operators include Illenoo (☎ 08 10 35 10 35, ⓦ www.illenoo-services.fr) and Keolis meraude (☎ 02 99 26 16 00, ⓦ destination-montsaintmichel.com).

Destinations Dinan (6 daily; 1hr 20min); Dinard (4 daily; 1hr 30min); Fougères (10 daily; 1hr); Mont St-Michel (4 daily; 1hr 15min); St-Malo (3 daily; 1hr 30min).

**By car** For drivers, it's best to park as soon as you reach the city centre; the most convenient car parks are beneath the place des Lices, and between the *quais* Duguay-Trouin and Lamennais.

## GETTING AROUND

**By métro and bus** An efficient métro system connects the *gare SNCF*, the place de la République in the heart of town, and the place Ste-Anne. Like the extensive local bus network, it's run by STAR (single journey, with transfers €1.50, all-day pass €4.10; ⓦ star.fr).

## INFORMATION

**Tourist office** Just north of the river at 11 rue St-Yves (July & Aug Mon–Sat 9am–7pm, Sun 10am–1pm & 2–5pm; Sept–June Mon 1–6pm, Tues–Sat 10am–6pm, Sun 10am–1pm & 2–5pm; ☎ 08 91 67 35 35, ⓦ tourisme-rennes.com).

## ACCOMMODATION

**Auberge de Jeunesse** 10–12 Canal St-Martin ☎ 02 99 33 22 33, ⓦ fuaj.org. Welcoming, attractively positioned HI hostel, by the canal 3km north of the centre (bus #8 from place Ste-Anne). It has a cafeteria and a laundry; hostelling association membership is compulsory. Closed Christmas to mid-Jan. **€23.55**

**Camping des Gayeulles** Rue du Prof-Maurice-Audin ☎ 02 99 36 91 22, ⓦ camping-rennes.com. An appealingly verdant municipal site, 1km east of central Rennes (bus #3, direction "St-Laurent"), in a park that offers good shade and a pool, with sporting facilities nearby. Open all year. **€16**

**Coq Gadby** 156 rue d'Antrain ☎ 02 99 38 05 55, ⓦ lecoq-gadby.com. Family-run for four generations, this self-styled "urban resort" is in a somewhat humdrum location, 1.5km north of the centre. Spread between the original seventeenth-century building and a modern annexe, it holds 24 comfortable rooms, an open-fire lounge, a pool and a spa. **€90**

**Des Lices** 7 place des Lices ☎ 02 99 79 14 81, ⓦ www. hotel-des-lices.com. Forty-eight smallish modern rooms, all with balcony, in a very comfortable and friendly hotel in the prettiest part of old Rennes, handy for the place des Lices car park. **€80**

★ **Nemours** 5 rue de Nemours ☎ 02 99 78 26 26, ⓦ hotelnemours.com. Cast as a boutique hotel, this central option has spotless, stylish, and well-lit rooms in white, green and earth tones, with comfortable beds. Warm, professional service, and you can take good breakfasts (€10) in bed. **€73**

**Sévigné** 47 av Jean-Janvier ☎ 02 99 67 27 55, ⓦ hotel lesevigne.fr. Smart, upmarket establishment 100m north of the *gare SNCF* en route to the centre, with buffet breakfasts, and a large brasserie next door. All rooms have good en-suite bathrooms, plus satellite TV; discounts at weekends. **€53**

## EATING AND DRINKING

Most of Rennes' more interesting bars and restaurants are just south of the place Ste-Anne, with the bar-lined rue St-Michel and rue Penhoët, each lined with ancient wooden buildings, forming the epicentre. Ethnic alternatives are

---

### RENNES FESTIVALS

Rennes is at its best in the first week of July, when the **Festival des Tombées de la Nuit** takes over the whole city to celebrate Breton culture with music, theatre, film, mime and poetry (ⓦ lestombeesdelanuit.com). A pocket version of the same festival is also held in the week between Christmas and New Year.

The city's busy calendar of rock festivals also includes **Youank**, in early November (ⓦ yaouank.bzh), which is geared towards young up-and-coming bands, and the **Transmusicales** in the first week of December (ⓦ lestrans.com).

concentrated along rue St-Malo to the north, and on rue St-Georges near the place du Palais.

**Atelier des Gourmets** 12 rue Nantaise ☎02 99 67 53 84, ⓦatelierdesgourmets-rennes.fr. Simple, old-fashioned bistro on the western edge of the centre, serving beautifully prepared French standards in a homely atmosphere; *menus* change daily, costing €13 for lunch and €31 for dinner. Tues–Thurs noon–1.30pm & 7.30–10pm, Fri & Sat noon–2pm & 7.30–10.30pm.

**Auberge St-Sauveur** 6 rue St-Sauveur ☎02 99 79 32 56, ⓦrestaurant-lesaintsauveur.fr. Classy, romantic restaurant, in an attractive medieval house near the cathedral, with light lunches for €15 and a richer, meaty dinner *menu* at €27. Mon noon–2pm, Tues–Sat noon–2pm & 7.30–10pm.

★ **Cours des Lices** 18 place des Lices ☎02 99 30 25 25, ⓦwww.lecoursdeslices.fr. Top-notch French restaurant, perfectly positioned to take advantage of the fresh produce in the adjoining market. Dinner *menus* at €35 and €46; the latter includes such dishes as roasted langoustines with crab, and de-boned pigeon. Tues–Thurs noon–2pm & 7.30–10pm, Fri & Sat noon–2pm & 7.30–11pm.

**Crêperie Ste-Anne** 5 place Ste-Anne ☎02 99 79 22 72. Appealing crêperie nicely situated on place Ste-Anne opposite the church, with plenty of outdoor seating and a good selection of *galettes* for €4–10. Mon–Sat 11.45am–10.30pm, Sun 11.45am–6pm.

**Léon le Cochon** 6 rue du Pré-Botté ☎02 99 79 37 54, ⓦleonlecochon.fr. Tasteful, contemporary but classically French restaurant; as the name suggests, there's a heavy emphasis on pigs, and their trotters in particular. The simple €14.40 lunch *menu* includes wine, while dinner *menus* cost €20.50 and €26.50. Daily noon–2pm & 7–10pm.

**Tire-Bouchon** 2 rue du Chapitre ☎02 99 79 43 43, ⓦtirebouchon.bzh. Part bistro, part wine bar, this friendly rendezvous chalks up a simple array of fresh-cooked dishes on its blackboard each day, from *tartines* to meat with pasta, and also offers plates of cheese or charcuterie. A full meal costs around €20. Mon–Fri noon–2pm & 7–11pm.

## NIGHTLIFE AND ENTERTAINMENT

### BARS

**Barantic** 4 rue St-Michel ☎02 99 79 29 24. One of the city's favourite bars, putting on occasional live music for a mixed crowd of Breton nationalists and boisterous students; if it's too full, you can head to half a dozen similar alternatives within spitting distance. Mon–Fri 9am–1am, Sat 7am–1am, Sun 2pm–midnight.

**Bernique Hurlante** 40 rue St-Malo ☎02 99 38 70 09, ⓦlaberniquehurlante.free.fr. This popular, yellow-painted haunt ranks among Rennes' most gay-friendly bars, and also serves as a rendezvous for artists and activists. Thurs–Sun 6pm–12.45am; also open Wed July & Aug.

★ **Bistro de la Cité** 7 rue St-Louis ☎02 99 79 24 34. This great little bar/bistro, with art on the walls and friendly staff and clientele, is the ideal place for a cider, a stronger house brew, or a quick meal. They host live music to suit a range of tastes on Saturday nights. Tues–Fri 4pm–1am, Sat noon–1am.

### LIVE MUSIC

**Club Ubu** 1 rue St-Helier ☎02 99 31 12 10, ⓦubu-rennes.com. The city's principal venue for big rock concerts, open year round, on the same site as the Théâtre National de Bretagne, but in a separate auditorium.

**Mondo Bizarro** 264 av Général-Patton ☎02 99 87 22 00, ⓦmondobizarro.free.fr. Rock, metal and especially punk club, 1km northeast of the centre (bus line #5), and kept busy most nights with local bands and punk stalwarts, plus tribute bands, ska, reggae and jazz. Tues–Sat 5pm–3am.

### THEATRE

**Théâtre National de Bretagne** 1 rue St-Helier ☎02 99 31 12 31, ⓦt-n-b.fr. A stimulating programme of varied events – with dance and music as well as theatre – throughout the year, except for July and most of August, when it's closed.

# Vitré

**VITRÉ**, 30km east of Rennes, rivals Dinan as the best-preserved medieval town in Brittany. While its walls are not quite complete, the thickets of medieval stone cottages that lie outside them have hardly changed. The towers of the **castle**, which dominates the western end of the ramparts, have pointed slate-grey roofs in perfect fairy-tale fashion, looking like freshly sharpened pencils, but sadly the municipal offices and **museum** of shells, birds, bugs and local history inside are not exactly thrilling (April–June & Sept daily 10am–12.30pm & 2–6pm; July & Aug daily 10am–6pm; Oct–March Mon & Wed–Fri 10.30am–12.30pm & 2–5pm, Sat & Sun 2–5pm; €4; ☎02 99 75 04 54).

Vitré's principal **market** is held on Mondays in the square in front of **Notre-Dame church**. The old city is full of twisting streets of half-timbered houses, a good proportion of which are bars – **rue Beaudrairie** in particular has a fine selection.

**By train** The *gare SNCF* is on the southern edge of the centre, where the ramparts disappear and the town blends into its newer sectors.

**Tourist office** Place du Général-de-Gaulle, left from the station (April–June & Sept Mon 2.30–6pm, Tues–Fri 9.30am–12.30pm & 2.30–6pm, Sat 10am-12.30pm

& 3–5pm; July & Aug Mon–Sat 9.30am–12.30pm & 2–6.30pm, Sun 2.30am–12.30pm & 3–6pm; Oct–March Mon & Tues 2.30–6pm, Wed–Fri 9.30am–12.30pm & 2.30–6pm, Sat 10am-12.30pm & 3–5pm; ☎02 99 75 04 46, ⓦ ot-vitre.fr).

**Du Château** 5 rue Rallon ☎02 99 74 58 59, ⓦ hotelduchateauvitre.com. Decent hotel, down below the castle, just outside the walls, and above a tearoom. All rooms are acceptable, but it's worth paying a little extra for those on the upper floors, which have views of the ramparts. €71

**Petit Billot** 5bis place du Général-Leclerc ☎02 99 75 02 10, ⓦ hotel-vitre.com. Very friendly, good-value hotel,

facing the station and offering clean, modest rooms of all shapes and sizes. €70

**La Soupe aux Choux** 32 rue Notre-Dame ☎02 99 75 10 86, ⓦ restaurant-vitre.fr. Fine old house, with exposed stone walls, converted into a smart restaurant with simple but classic French food,. The standard dinner *menu* costs €27. Mon–Wed & Fri noon–1.30pm & 7–9pm, Thurs noon–1.30pm, Sat 7–9pm.

# St-Malo

Walled with the same grey-granite stone as Mont St-Michel, the elegant, ancient, and beautifully positioned city of **ST-MALO** originally occupied a fortified island at the mouth of the Rance, controlling not only the estuary but also the open sea beyond. Now inseparably attached to the mainland, it's the most visited place in Brittany, thanks partly to its superb **old citadelle** and partly to its ferry service to England, and the lively streets that lie within the walls – the area known as *intra-muros* – are packed with restaurants, bars and shops. Yes, the summer crowds can be oppressive, but even then a stroll atop the walls should restore your equilibrium, while the vast, clean **beaches** beyond are a huge bonus, especially if you're travelling with children.

### The citadelle

The **citadelle** of St-Malo was long joined to the mainland only by a causeway; then the construction of the harbour basin concealed the original line of the coast forever. Although its streets of restored seventeenth- and eighteenth-century houses tend to be packed with visitors in high season, away from the more popular thoroughfares random exploration is fun, and you can always escape to the **ramparts** – first erected in the fourteenth century – to enjoy wonderful all-round views.

Venerable as they look, the **buildings** within the walls are almost entirely reconstructed; following the bombardment that forced the German surrender in 1944, eighty percent of the city was lovingly and precisely rebuilt, stone by stone. For a memorable account of St-Malo's experience in the war, read Anthony Duerr's Pulitzer-winning novel, *All The Light We Cannot See*.

#### Musée d'Histoire de la Ville

St-Malo Château • April–Sept daily 10am–12.30pm & 2–6pm; Oct–March Tues–Sun 10am–noon & 2–6pm • €6; free on first Fri of month • ☎02 99 40 71 57, ⓦ ville-saint-malo.fr

Inside St-Malo's **castle** – next to the main gate of the citadelle, the **Porte St-Vincent** – the **Musée d'Histoire de la Ville** commemorates the "prodigious prosperity" enjoyed by the city during its days of piracy, colonialism and slave trading. Climbing the 169 steps of the keep, you pass a fascinating mixture of maps, diagrams and exhibits – chilling handbills from the Nazi occupation, accounts of the "infernal machine" used by the English to blow up the port in 1693, and savage four-pronged *chausse-trapes* (a kind of early version of barbed wire), thrown by pirates onto the decks of ships being boarded to immobilize their crews. At the top a gull's-eye prospect takes in the whole citadelle.

## The beach

At several points, you can pass through St-Malo's ramparts to reach the open shore, where a huge **beach** stretches away east beyond the featureless resort-suburb of **Paramé**. When the tide is low, it's safe to walk out to the tiny island of **Grand-Bé** – the walk is so popular that sometimes you even need to queue to get onto the short causeway. Solemn warnings are posted of the dangers of attempting to return from the island once the tide has risen too far – if you're caught there, there you have to stay. The one "sight" is the tomb of the nineteenth-century writer-politician **Chateaubriand** (1768–1848).

6

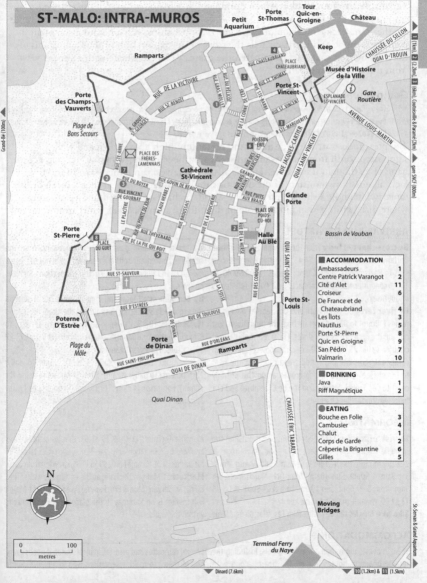

ST-MALO: INTRA-MUROS

**ACCOMMODATION**

| | |
|---|---|
| Ambassadeurs | 1 |
| Centre Patrick Varangot | 2 |
| Cité d'Alet | 11 |
| Croiseur | 6 |
| De France et de Chateaubriand | 4 |
| Les Ilots | 3 |
| Nautilus | 5 |
| Porte St-Pierre | 8 |
| Quic en Groigne | 9 |
| San Pédro | 7 |
| Valmarin | 10 |

**DRINKING**

| | |
|---|---|
| Java | 1 |
| Riff Magnétique | 2 |

**EATING**

| | |
|---|---|
| Bouche en Folie | 3 |
| Cambusier | 4 |
| Chalut | 1 |
| Corps de Garde | 2 |
| Crêperie la Brigantine | 6 |
| Gilles | 5 |

## St-Servan

The **St-Servan** district, within walking distance of the citadelle, south along the corniche, was the city's original settlement, converted to Christianity by St Malou (or Maclou) in the sixth century. Only later, in the twelfth century, did the townspeople move to the impregnable island now called St-Malo.

### Tour Solidor

April–Sept daily 10am–12.30pm & 2–6pm; Oct–March Tues–Sun 10am–noon & 2–6pm • €6; free on first Fri of month • ☎ 02 99 40 71 58, 𝕎 ville-saint-malo.fr

The distinctive **Tour Solidor**, which dominates St-Servan, consists of three linked towers. Built in 1382, it looks in cross-section just like the ace of clubs, and now holds a rather ramshackle **museum** of Cape Horn clipper ships. A haphazard assortment of paintings, models and artifacts tells the story of the exploration of the Pacific, and of the four-masters that once dominated the route. Visits culminate with a superb view from the topmost ramparts.

## Grand Aquarium

Av du Général-Patton • Daily: April–June & Sept 10am–7pm; first two weeks in July & second two weeks in Aug 9.30am–8pm; mid-July to mid-Aug 9.30am–9pm; Oct–March 10am–6pm as a rule, but closed for most of Jan & Nov; last admission 1hr before closing • €7, ages 4–12 €12 • ☎ 02 99 21 19 00, 𝕎 aquarium-st-malo.com • Bus #5 from *gare SNCF*

The postmodern structure of the **Grand Aquarium**, high above town and well signposted south from St-Servan, can seem a bit bewildering at first. Once you get the hang of it, though, it's an entertaining place, where you can either learn interesting facts about slimy monsters of the deep or simply pull faces back at them. Its eight fish tanks, which hold fish from all over the world, include one shaped like a Polo mint, where dizzy visitors stand in the hole in the middle as myriad fish whirl around them.

### ARRIVAL AND DEPARTURE ST-MALO

**By cross-channel ferry** From the Terminal Ferry du Naye, Brittany Ferries (☎ 02 99 40 64 41, 𝕎 brittany-ferries.com) sails to Portsmouth, while Condor Ferries (☎ 02 99 40 78 10, 𝕎 condorferries.co.uk) connects with Poole (via Jersey or Guernsey).

**By river ferry** Between April and Oct, regular passenger ferries (10min) to Dinard operate from the quai Dinan, just outside the ramparts (€5.70 single, €8.50 return; bikes cost double; ☎ 08 25 13 81 00, 𝕎 compagniecorsaire.com). Compagnie Corsaire also conduct excursions up the river to Dinan (see page 321), and cruises along the Brittany coast to Cap Fréhel, St-Cast and the Île Cézembre, and out to Jersey and the Îles Chausey.

**By train** St-Malo's *gare SNCF* is 2km inland from the citadelle, convenient neither for the old town nor the ferry. Destinations Rennes (14 daily; 1hr; connections for Paris on TGV).

**By bus** Almost all local and long-distance buses stop on the esplanade St-Vincent, just outside the citadelle. Illenoo (☎ 08 10 35 10 35, 𝕎 illenoo-services.fr) runs services to Dinard, Rennes and Mont-St-Michel; Tibus (☎ 08 10 22 22 22, 𝕎 tibus.fr) serves Dinan and Dinard. Destinations Cancale (6 daily; 45min); Dinan (6 daily; 1hr); Dinard (10 daily; 30min); Mont St-Michel (4 daily; 1hr 30min); Pontorson (4 daily; 1hr 15min); Rennes (3 daily; 1hr 30min).

### INFORMATION

**Tourist office** Esplanade St-Vincent, just outside the citadelle (April–June & Sept Mon–Sat 9am–1pm & 2–6.30pm, Sun 10am–1pm & 2–6pm; July & Aug Mon–Sat 9am–7.30pm, Sun 10am–7pm; Oct–March Mon–Sat 9am–1pm & 2–6pm, Sun 10am–1pm & 2–5pm; ☎ 08 25 13 52 00, 𝕎 saint-malo-tourisme.com).

**Bike hire** Bicycles can be rented from Les Vélos Bleus, 19 rue

Alphonse-Thébault (☎ 02 99 40 31 63, 𝕎 velos-bleus.fr; bikes available by reservation only Nov–March), or Cycles Nicole, 11 rue du Président, Paramé (☎ 02 99 56 11 06, 𝕎 cyclesnicole.com).

**Markets** St-Malo, in the Halle au Blé within the walls (Tues & Fri); St-Servan (Mon & Fri); Paramé (Wed & Sat). St-Malo's fish market is on Saturday in the place de la Poissonnerie, within the walls.

### ACCOMMODATION

St-Malo boasts more than a hundred hotels, including the seaside boarding houses just off the beach, along with several campsites and a hostel. In high season it needs every one of them, so make reservations well in advance. Some *intra-muros* hotels take advantage of summer demand by insisting you eat in their own restaurants. Cheaper rates can be found by the *gare SNCF*, or in suburban Paramé.

### IN THE CITADELLE

**Croiseur** 2 place de la Poissonnerie ☎ 02 99 40 80 40, ⓦ hotel-le-croiseur.com. Contemporary-style hotel with sleek and spotless rooms overlooking the old fish market, and a great bar and terrace. Friendly and good value. **€105**

**De France et de Chateaubriand** 12 place Chateaubriand ☎ 02 99 56 66 52, ⓦ hotel-chateaubriand-st-malo.com. While the standard *confort* rooms in this imposing old hotel, just off the main square, are rather ordinary, the *supérieures* – especially those with sea views – are well worth the extra €30–40, and the old-fashioned public spaces are ideal for lazy days. There's also a large, well-priced bistro downstairs and a fancier modern top-floor restaurant. Breakfast costs €12, parking €15. **€107**

★ **Nautilus** 9 rue de la Corne de Cerf ☎ 02 99 40 42 27, ⓦ www.hotel-lenautilus-saint-malo.com. Colourfully refitted hotel (with a lift) with small, bright, good-value rooms, all with shower and WC. Friendly staff ensure it's hugely popular with younger travellers, but it's welcoming to all. Bar but no restaurant. Closed Nov to late Dec. **€71**

**Porte St-Pierre** 2 place du Guet ☎ 02 99 40 91 27, ⓦ hotel-portestpierre.com. Comfortable *Logis de France*, peeping over the walls of the citadelle, near the small Porte St-Pierre and very handy for the beach; the modernized rooms have smart floors and in many cases sea views (€10 extra). One family room sleeps five. The owners also run a restaurant across the alley, recommended for seafood lovers. Closed mid-Nov to Feb. **€85**

★ **Quic en Groigne** 8 rue d'Estrées ☎ 02 99 20 22 20, ⓦ quic-en-groigne.com. Friendly little hotel run by accommodating owners, at the far end of the citadelle, with attractive en-suite rooms, refreshed with good bathroom fittings. Closed mid-Dec to late Jan. **€94**

**San Pédro** 1 rue Ste-Anne ☎ 02 99 40 88 57, ⓦ san pedro-hotel.com. Twelve compact but tastefully and stylishly furnished rooms in a nice quiet setting, just inside the walls. Great breakfasts and friendly advice. Higher rooms (reached via a minuscule lift) enjoy sea views, and

cost around €10 extra. Closed Dec to mid-March. **€79**

### OUTSIDE THE WALLS

**Ambassadeurs** 11 chaussée du Sillon, Coutoisville ☎ 02 99 40 26 26, ⓦ hotel-ambassadeurs-saintmalo. com. Twenty-room, four-floor hotel, right on the seafront, with free parking nearby. The rooms may be small, but they've been very tastefully refreshed, and those facing the sea (around €30 extra) come with balconies directly over the waves, and there's also a rooftop bar with a fabulous terrace. **€117**

**Valmarin** 7 rue Jean-XXIII, St-Servan ☎ 02 99 81 94 76, ⓦ levalmarin.com. Impressive eighteenth-century *malouinière* (sea captain's house) set in spacious flowery gardens 50m from the sea in St-Servan, that's now a hotel with a dozen very comfortable antique-furnished rooms. **€118**

### HOSTEL AND CAMPSITES

**Centre Patrick Varangot** 37 av du Père-Umbricht, Paramé ☎ 02 99 40 29 80, ⓦ centrevarangot.com. One of France's busiest hostels, near the beach 2km northeast of the *gare SNCF*, and usually dominated by energetic young travellers. Dorm beds are in shared en-suite rooms that can also be rented privately; hostelling association membership required. Rates include breakfast, and there's also a cut-price cafeteria where you can get a three-course meal for €8.70, plus kitchen facilities and tennis courts. No curfew, open all year. Dorms **€25.20**

★ **Cité d'Alet** Allée Gaston-Buy, St-Servan ☎ 02 99 81 60 91, ⓦ ville-saint-malo.fr/campings. The nicest local campsite is also by far the nearest to the citadelle, a municipally run gem in a dramatic location on the headland southwest of St-Malo, overlooking the city from within the wartime German fortified stronghold. Bus #1 from *gare SNCF* or Porte St-Vincent. Open July to early Sept, plus late March to late May. **€17.10**

**Les Îlots** Avenue de la Guimorais, Rothéneuf ☎ 02 99 56 98 72, ⓦ ville-saint-malo.fr/campings. Green little municipal site, reserved for caravans and mobile homes only, 5min walk inland from either of two crescent beaches, and roughly 5km east of the *citadelle*. Closed mid-Nov to late March. **€12**

## EATING AND DRINKING

*Intra-muros* St-Malo boasts even more restaurants and bars than hotels, but prices are probably higher than anywhere else in Brittany, especially on the open café terraces. Bear in mind that most crêperies also serve *moules* and similar snacks.

### RESTAURANTS

**Bouche en Folie** 14 rue du Boyer ☎ 06 72 49 08 89. This little place offers classic, seasonal French dishes, with a good lunch *menu* for €15, and an excellent €30 dinner

*menu*. Some outdoor seating. Mon & Thurs–Sun noon–2pm & 7–10pm.

**Cambusier** 6 rue des Cordiers ☎ 02 99 20 18 42, ⓦ cambusier.fr. Creative contemporary cuisine from one of Saint-Malo's top chefs, with plenty of seafood – oysters and lobsters are particular favourites – but also rich duck and other meat dishes. A two-course lunch costs €18, dinner costs €29 or €38. Mon–Sat noon–2pm & 7–9pm, Sun noon–2pm.

**Chalut** 8 rue de la Corne de Cerf ☎ 02 99 56 71 58. Blue-painted, fish-themed bistro a short way in from the Porte St-Vincent, where the €25 weekday lunch *menu* centres on the catch of the day. Otherwise you can pay €43 or €59 for a gourmet fish dinner, not quite as rich as the traditional norm, or €79 for a five-course *menu* of which three consist entirely of lobster. Reservations preferred. Wed–Sun noon–1.30pm & 7–10pm.

**Corps de Garde** 3 montée Notre-Dame ☏ 02 99 40 91 46, ⓦ le-corps-de-garde.com. The only restaurant that's right up on St-Malo's ramparts is a simple crêperie, serving delicious albeit far from unusual crêpes (€3–10). However, the views from its large open-air terrace (covered when necessary) are sensational, looking out over the beach to dozens of little islets. Daily: mid-Dec to mid-Nov noon–2pm & 7–9pm; July & Aug noon–9.30pm.

**Crêperie la Brigantine** 13 rue de Dinan ☏ 02 99 56 82 82, ⓦ la-brigantine.fr. Sweet and savoury pancakes at very reasonable prices, with a strong emphasis on organic ingredients – the seafood fillings are exceptional. An individual crêpe can cost just €2.40, and there's a full menu for €11, including a glass of cider. Daily noon–10pm; closed Tues & Wed in low season.

**Gilles** 2 rue de la Pie qui Boit ☏ 02 99 40 97 25, ⓦ restaurant-gilles-saint-malo.com. Bright, modern, good-value restaurant, just off the central pedestrian axis and lacking views or outdoor space. The €18 lunch *formule* is fine; for dinner, prices range €26 to €45 for two to four courses, potentially including lobster and scallops for a €10 supplement. Mon, Tues & Fri–Sun noon–1.30pm & 7–9pm, Thurs noon–1.30pm.

### BARS

**Java** 3 rue Ste-Barbe ☏ 02 99 56 41 90, ⓦ lajavacafe. com. Among its many eccentric features, this entertaining and unique cider bar – to give it its full official name, *Le Café du Coin d'en Bas de la Rue du Bout de la Ville d'en Face du Port ... La Java* – boasts a row of swings at the bar, old dolls on the wall, and an elevator door into the toilet. All is designed to keep the conversation flowing as smoothly as the drinks. Mon 8.12am–8.45pm, Tues 8.13am–8.45pm, Wed 8.14am–8.45pm, Thurs 8.15am–8.45pm, Fri 8.16am–8.45pm, Sat 8.18am–9.47pm, Sun 9.45am–8.45pm,.

**Riff Magnétique** 20 rue de la Herse ☏ 02 99 40 85 70. Busy, friendly bar, with a fine choice of wines plus regular café-concerts, and DJs at the weekend. Tues–Sun 7pm–3am.

## Cancale

The delightful harbour village of **CANCALE**, across the peninsula 15km east of St-Malo, is not so much a one-horse as a one-mollusc town – the whole place is obsessed with the **oyster**, and with "*ostréiculture*". It consists of two distinct halves: the old town up on the hill, and the very pretty and smart port area of **La Houle** down below. Glass-fronted hotels and restaurants stretch the length of the waterfront, always busy with visitors, while fishing boats bob in the harbour itself. At its northern end, demarcated by a stone jetty, local women sell fresh oysters by the dozen from stalls with bright striped canvas awnings.

In the old church of St-Méen at the top of the hill, the town's obsession is documented with meticulous precision by the small **Musée des Arts et Traditions Populaires** (daily: late June to early Oct 10am–12.30pm & 2.30–7pm; €4; ☏ 02 99 89 79 32, ⓦ museedecancale.fr).

Just north of town, the perilous and windy heights of the headland known as the **Pointe du Grouin** offer spectacular views of the pinnacle of Mont St-Michel, plus the bird sanctuary of the **Îles des Landes** to the east.

### ACCOMMODATION AND EATING

★ **Au Pied d'Cheval** 10 quai Gambetta ☏ 02 99 89 76 95, ⓦ restaurant-aupieddcheval.fr. A ramshackle, gloriously atmospheric little place to sample a few oysters, with baskets of bivalves spread across its wooden quayside tables. There's no set menu, but while seafood sharing platters for two start at €56, you can still get a dozen raw oysters on a bed of seaweed for €8.50, and cooked mussels for little more. July & Aug Mon–Fri 9am–10pm, Sat & Sun 9am–6pm; Sept, Oct & mid-April to June Mon, Tues, Thurs & Fri 9am–10pm, Sat & Sun 9am–6pm.

**Auberge de Jeunesse** Port Picain ☏ 02 99 89 62 62, ⓦ fuaj.org. Striking modern hostel 2km north of town and very close to the beach, where rates include breakfast; camping space and kitchen facilities are also available. Closed Nov–Feb. Dorms €25.25

**Chez Victor** 8 quai Thomas ☏ 02 99 89 55 84. Occupying a huge corner site, with indoor and outdoor tables beside the jetty and oyster stalls at the north end of the quayside, this all-day brasserie is a sure-fire option for good local seafood. There's a €15.50 *menu*, featuring oysters and mussels, and an excellent €27 one, along with a wide range of mixed platters and *moules frites* for €12.50. Daily noon–9pm.

**La Voilerie** 8 rue Ernest-Lamort ☎02 99 89 88 00, ⓦhotel-lavoilerie.com. Twelve simple but good-value, wood-panelled rooms, in a hotel that stands very slightly uphill from the point where the road reaches the southern end of Cancale's waterfront. **€70**

## Dinan

The wonderful citadelle of **DINAN**, sitting 30km south of St-Malo at the point just before the river Rance broadens towards the sea, has preserved almost intact its 3km encirclement of protective masonry, along with street upon colourful street of late medieval houses. However, despite its slightly unreal perfection, it's seldom overrun with tourists. There are no essential museums, the most memorable architecture is vernacular rather than monumental, and time is most easily spent wandering from crêperie to café and down to the pretty port.

During the third weekend of July, every even-numbered year, Dinan celebrates the **Fête des Remparts** with medieval-style jousting, banquets, fairs and processions, culminating in an immense fireworks display (ⓦfete-remparts-dinan.com).

### Port de Dinan

Like St-Malo, Dinan is ideally seen when arriving by boat, along the Rance. By the time the ferries reach the lovely **port de Dinan**, down below the thirteenth-century ramparts, the river has narrowed sufficiently to be spanned by a small but majestic old stone bridge. High above it towers a former railway viaduct. The steep, cobbled lane that

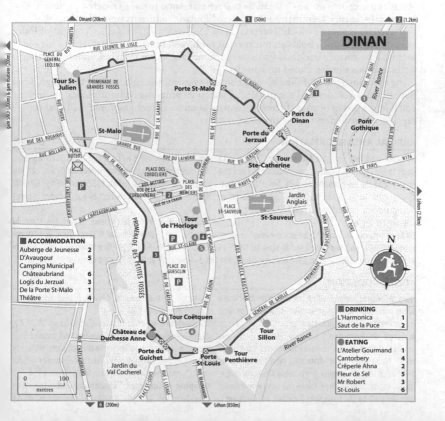

**DINAN**

**ACCOMMODATION**

| | |
|---|---|
| Auberge de Jeunesse | 2 |
| D'Avaugour | 5 |
| Camping Municipal Châteaubriand | 6 |
| Logis du Jerzual | 3 |
| De la Porte St-Malo | 1 |
| Théâtre | 4 |

**DRINKING**

| | |
|---|---|
| L'Harmonica | 1 |
| Saut de la Puce | 2 |

**EATING**

| | |
|---|---|
| L'Atelier Gourmand | 1 |
| Cantorbery | 4 |
| Crêperie Ahna | 2 |
| Fleur de Sel | 5 |
| Mr Robert | 3 |
| St-Louis | 6 |

twists up from the quayside makes a wonderful climb, passing ancient flower-festooned edifices of wood and stone, before it enters the city through the **Porte du Jerzual**.

## St-Sauveur church

Set on a little square not far above the imposing gateway of the Porte du Jerzual, **St-Sauveur church** sends the skyline of Dinan even higher. It's a real hotchpotch, with a Romanesque porch and an eighteenth-century steeple. Even its nine Gothic chapels feature five different patterns of vaulting in no symmetrical order; the most complex pair, in the centre, would make any spider proud.

The one small stretch of Dinan's medieval **ramparts** that's open to visitors leads from behind St-Sauveur church to just short of Tour Sillon, overlooking the river.

## Place du Guesclin and around

Dinan's large, central **place du Guesclin** hosts a large **market on Thursdays**, and serves as a car park for the rest of the week. In 1364, the Breton warrior **Bertrand du Guesclin** fought and defeated the English knight Thomas of Canterbury in single combat here.

The true heart of town these days consists of two much smaller squares nearby, the **place des Merciers** and the **place des Cordeliers**, which hold a magnificent assortment of medieval wood-framed houses.

## Château de la Duchesse Anne

Daily: Easter to end April 1.30–5.30pm; May–Sept 10.30am–7pm • €5 • ☎ 02 96 39 45 20, ⓦ dinan.fr

What's now known as the **Château de la Duchesse Anne** is not so much a castle as the fourteenth-century keep that once protected Dinan's southern approach, along with two separate towers to which it offers access. The keep itself, or *donjon*, consists of four storeys, each of which holds an unexpected mishmash of items, including two big old looms and assorted Greek and Etruscan perfume jars; at ground level, well below the walls, there's a slender, closed drawbridge.

The more intriguing of the two neighbouring towers, the ancient **Tour Coëtquen**, is all but empty. If you descend the spiral staircase to its waterlogged bottom floor, however, you'll find a group of stone fifteenth-century notables resembling some medieval time capsule, about to depetrify at any moment.

### ARRIVAL AND INFORMATION                                          DINAN

**By train and bus** Both the Art Deco *gare SNCF* – with trains to Dol (8 daily; 23min), for connections to Caen and Brest – and the *gare routière* (6 daily buses to St-Malo; 45min; ☎ 08 10 22 22 22, ⓦ tibus.fr) are in the rather gloomy modern quarter, on place du 11-Novembre, 10min walk west of the walls.

**By boat** Between May and Oct, boats sail along the Rance between Dinan's port and Dinard and St-Malo (☎ 08 25 13 81 00, ⓦ compagniecorsaire.com). The trip takes 2hr 45min,

and the schedule varies with the tides. Only on certain days, and only if you're starting from St-Malo or Dinard, can you do a day return by boat (adults €33.50, under-16s €20.10); otherwise, you have to come back by bus (included in price) or train.

**Tourist office** 9 rue du Château, just off the place du Guesclin (July & Aug Mon–Sat 9.30am–7pm, Sun 10am–12.30pm & 2.30–6pm; Sept–June Mon–Sat 9am–12.30pm & 2–6pm; ☎ 02 96 87 69 76, ⓦ dinan-capfrehel.com).

### ACCOMMODATION

Many of Dinan's hotels lie within the walled town or down by the port. Both locations are convenient if you're on foot, but parking can be difficult in summer.

**Auberge de Jeunesse** Moulin de Méen, 2 rue des Quatre-Moulins, Vallée de la Fontaine-des-Eaux ☎ 02 96 39 10 83, ⓦ fuaj.org. Attractive, rural former watermill, beside the river in green fields below the town centre. No bus access: to walk there, follow the quay downstream from the port on the town side. Breakfast €4. Camping is

permitted in the grounds. Closed Oct–March. Dorms **€15.90**, doubles **£31.80**

**D'Avaugour** 1 place du Champ-Clos ☎ 02 96 39 07 49, ⓦ avaugourhotel.com. Smart, elegant hotel, entered from the main square but backing onto the ramparts, with very tasteful rooms, lovely gardens, and exceptionally helpful staff. Closed Nov–Feb, plus Sun in low season. **€150**

**Camping Municipal Chateaubriand** 103 rue Chateaubriand ☎ 02 96 39 11 96. Verdant, minimally equipped little campsite, in a quiet spot just outside the western ramparts, offering just fifty pitches. Closed Oct–May. **€9.90**

**Logis du Jerzual** 25–27 rue du Petit-Fort ☎02 96 85 46 54, ⓦlogis-du-jerzual.com. Friendly B&B, with a lovely garden terrace, halfway up the exquisite lane that climbs from the port. The five assorted rooms have wonderful character, with four-poster beds, modern bathrooms and romantic views over the rooftops. **€85**

★ **De la Porte St-Malo** 35 rue St-Malo ☎02 96 39 19 76, ⓦhotelportemalo.com. Simple but spotless and very comfortable rooms in a hugely welcoming and tasteful small hotel just outside the walls, beyond the Porte St-Malo, away from the bustle of the centre. The €9.50 breakfasts are recommended. **€85**

**Théâtre** 2 rue Ste-Claire ☎02 96 39 06 91. Nine very basic rooms above a pleasant (and generally early-closing) bar, right by the Théâtre des Jacobins; the very cheapest comes with only a basin and its own bathroom on the landing, but the rest have en-suite bathrooms. Closed Mon Oct–May. **€53**

## EATING AND DRINKING

All sorts of restaurants are tucked away in the old streets of Dinan; stroll through town and down to the port, and you'll pass at least twenty places. For bars, explore the tiny alleyways between place des Merciers and rue du Marchix.

### RESTAURANTS

**L'Atelier Gourmand** 4 rue du Quai ☎02 96 85 14 18. Delightful riverside spot beside the bridge, with indoor and outdoor seating, and a well-priced menu of *tartines* (€12), *moules* (€12–15) and main courses (€15–18). July–Sept Mon 6.30–9.30pm, Tues–Sat noon–1.30pm & 6.30–9.30pm, Sun noon–1.30pm; Oct–June closed Mon.

**Cantorbery** 6 rue Ste-Claire ☎02 96 39 02 52. High-class food served in an old stone house with rafters, a spiral staircase and a real wood fire. Lunch from €16, while traditional dinner *menus* start with a good €33 option that includes fish soup and veal kidneys. June–Sept Mon–Sat noon–1.45pm & 7–9.30pm, Sun noon–1.45pm; Oct–May closed Wed & Sun.

**Crêperie Ahna** 7 rue de la Poissonnerie ☎02 96 39 09 13, ⓦcreperie-ahna.blogspirit.com. Smart central crêperie, with limited outdoor seating, that's hugely popular with lunching locals. Savoury pancakes cost €4–11, and they also serve potato blinis at similar prices, as well as grilled meats, including nice big sausages. Mon, Tues & Thurs–Sat noon–2pm & 7–10pm.

**Fleur de Sel** 7 rue Ste-Claire ☎02 96 85 15 14, ⓦwww.restaurantlafleurdesel.com. Central restaurant, just off the main square, that's a must for its quirky and inventive take on Breton cuisine. Highlights on its two set menus, at €30 and €42, range from raw oysters to guinea fowl roasted with honey and coriander, plus rich, creamy desserts. Wed–Sun noon–11pm.

**Mr Robert** 11 place des Cordeliers ☎02 96 85 20 37, ⓦwww.mrrobertrestaurant.fr. Named for its Irish chef-owner, this excellent central option offers a handful of tables on the square itself but plenty of room indoors. Classic French cuisine with subtle Asian-influenced flavourings, with a 3-course lunch at €16 and full dinner *menus* from €27.50. Tues–Sat noon–1.30pm & 7–9.30pm, Sun noon–1.30pm.

**St-Louis** 9–11 rue de Léhon ☎02 96 39 89 50. Good-value restaurant, just inside the Porte St-Louis, which specializes in buffets. *Menus* start at €21.50, and allow you to choose extensive buffets of hors d'oeuvres and desserts, with a conventional main course in between. Mon, Tues, Thurs & Fri noon–2pm & 7–9pm, Sat 7–9pm, Sun noon–2pm.

### BARS

★ **L'Harmonica** 34 rue du Petit-Fort ☎02 96 80 99 28. The terrace of this dynamic little bistro makes an ideal location for a sunset drink, and there's often live music too. Wed 10am–9pm, Thurs & Sun 10am–10pm, Fri & Sat 10am–1am.

**Saut de la Puce** 15 rue de la Cordonnerie ☎02 96 39 36 11. A long-standing stalwart of Dinan nightlife, one of several similar hangouts along the ever-lively rue de la Cordonnerie, this contemporary Breton dive continues to attract nightly crowds of drinkers. Tues–Sun 11.30am–1am, opens 5pm Oct–April.

# The north coast from Dinard to Lannion

The coast that stretches from the resort of **Dinard** to Finistère at the western end of Brittany is divided into two distinct regions, east and west of the bay of **St-Brieuc**. Between Dinard and St-Brieuc lie the exposed green headlands of the **Côte d'Émeraude**, while beyond St-Brieuc, along the **Côte de Goëlo**, the shore becomes more extravagantly indented, with countless secluded little bays and an increasing proliferation of huge pink-granite boulders, seen at their best on the **Côte de Granit Rose** near Tréguier.

**6**

## Dinard

Originally a fishing village, now a smart little resort blessed with several lovely beaches, **DINARD** sprawls around the western approaches to the Rance estuary, just across the water from St-Malo but a good twenty minutes' drive by road. With its casino, spacious shaded villas and social calendar of regattas and ballet, it might not feel out of place on the Côte d'Azur. Although Dinard is a hilly town, undulating over a succession of pretty coastal inlets, it attracts great numbers of older visitors; as a result, prices tend to be high, and pleasures sedate.

Central Dinard faces north to the open sea, across the curving bay that holds the attractive **plage de l'Écluse**. Hemmed in by venerable Victorian villas rather than hotels or shops, the beach itself has a low-key atmosphere, despite the casino and summer crowds. An unexpected statue of **Alfred Hitchcock** dominates its main access point. Standing on a giant egg, with a ferocious-looking bird perched on each shoulder, he was placed here to commemorate the town's annual festival of English-language films.

### Coastal footpaths

Enjoyable **coastal footpaths** lead off in either direction from the principal beach, enlivened by notice boards holding reproductions of paintings produced at points along the way. Surprisingly, Pablo Picasso's *Deux femmes courant sur la plage* and *Baigneuses sur la plage*, both of which look quintessentially Mediterranean with their blue skies and golden sands, were in fact painted here in Dinard during his annual summer visits throughout the 1920s.

---

**ARRIVAL AND INFORMATION**                           **DINARD**

**By plane** Dinard's small airport, off the D168 near Pleurtuit, 4km southeast of the centre, is served by Ryanair flights from London Stansted and East Midlands. Illenoo buses stop nearby en route between Dinard and Rennes.
**By boat** Companie Corsaire boats arrive from St-Malo.
**By bus** Local buses run regularly between Dinard and St-Malo, across the dam, while long-distance buses, run by Illenoo (☎ 08 10 35 10 35, ⊛ illenoo-services.fr) and Tibus (☎ 08 10 22 22 22, ⊛ tibus.fr), go from the former *gare SNCF*

and "Le Gallic" stop (near the tourist office).
**Destinations** Cancale (2 daily; 1hr 30min); Dinan (6 daily; 40min); Rennes (4 daily; 1hr 30min); St-Brieuc (8 daily; 25min).
**Tourist office** 2 bd Féart (April–June & Sept Mon–Sat 9.30am–12.30pm & 2–6pm, Sun 10am–12.30pm & 3–6pm; July & Aug daily 9.30am–6.45pm; Oct–March Tues–Sat 9.30am–12.30pm & 2–6pm; ☎ 02 99 46 94 12, ⊛ dinardtourisme.com).

---

**ACCOMMODATION AND EATING**

**Camping Le Port Blanc** Rue du Sergent-Boulanger ☎ 02 99 46 10 74, ⊛ camping-port-blanc.com. Dinard's finest campsite, run by the municipality, has the plage du Port-Blanc, west of the centre, almost to itself, with shady pitches right by the beach. Closed Oct–March. **€20.60**

★ **Didier Méril** 1 place du Général-de-Gaulle ☎ 02 99 46 95 74, ⊛ restaurant-didier-meril.com. High-quality gourmet restaurant, beside the main road on the edge of Dinard, just above a great beach. Open for lunch and dinner daily, it offers fancy menus from €31, and holds nine stylish designer bedrooms, of which the three sumptuous sea-

view suites, which sleep up to five, are much the largest and nicest. Room **€100**, suite **€280**
**La Plage** 3 bd Féart ☎ 02 99 46 14 87, ⊛ hoteldelaplage-dinard.com. Modern, good-value and very central hotel, just up from the main beach, and offering smart contemporary bedrooms with crisp white linens and spacious, well-equipped bathrooms. Expect to pay up to €40 extra for a full-on sea view, though guests can enjoy the buffet breakfast on an open-air, beach-facing terrace in summer. **€99**

---

## The Côte d'Émeraude

The splendidly attractive **Côte d'Émeraude**, west of Dinard, is one of Brittany's most traditional family resort areas, with old-fashioned holiday towns, and safe sandy beaches. It also offers wonderful camping, at its best around the heather-backed beaches near **Cap Fréhel**, a high, warm expanse of heath and cliffs where views can extend as far as Jersey and the Île de Bréhat.

### Fort la Latte

2km southeast of Cap Fréhel • Early July to late Aug daily 10.30am–7pm; April to early July & late Aug to Sept daily 10.30am–12.30pm & 2–6pm; Oct–March Sat, Sun & hols 1.30–5.30pm • €5.70 • ☏ 02 96 41 57 11, ⓦ castlelalatte.com

The fourteenth-century **Fort la Latte**, at the tip of a small headland 2km southeast of Cap Fréhel, is a gorgeous little gem. Visitors enter across two drawbridges; outbuildings scattered within include a cannonball factory, and there's also a medieval herb garden, but the highlight is the keep, which contains historical exhibits. Precarious walkways climb to its summit, for superb coastal views. Look out for the annual medieval festival, in early August.

**6**

### Erquy

In the delightful family resort of **ERQUY**, 20km west of Cap Fréhel, a perfect crescent beach nestles into a vast natural bay. At low tide, the sea disappears way beyond the harbour entrance, leaving gentle ripples of sand. You can walk right across its mouth, from the grassy wooded headland on the left side to the picturesque little lighthouse on the right.

| **INFORMATION** | **ERQUY** |
| --- | --- |

**Tourist office** 3 rue du 19 Mars (April–June & Sept Mon–Sat 9.30am–12.30pm & 2–6pm, Sun 10am–12.30pm; July & Aug Mon–Sat 9.30am–1pm & 2–7pm, Sun 10am–1pm & 4.30–6pm; Oct–March Mon–Sat 9.30am–12.30pm & 2–5pm; ☏ 02 96 72 30 12, ⓦ erquy-tourisme.com).

#### ACCOMMODATION AND EATING

★ **Beauséjour** 21 rue de la Corniche ☏ 02 96 72 30 39, ⓦ beausejour-erquy.com. Set in a seaside villa above the southern end of the beach, and festooned with eccentric art and artefacts, the *Beauséjour* represents Erquy at its quirkiest. There's no restaurant, but the breakfasts are good, and the rooms are nice. Closed mid-Nov to mid-April. **€85**

**Camping de la Plage de St-Pabu** Plage de St-Pabu ☏ 02 96 72 24 65, ⓦ saintpabu.com. The best local campsite, in a garden-like seafront location just beyond the second promontory southwest of town, with a kids' playground but no pool. Closed early Nov to March. **€22.60**

★ **Le Vivier** 64 rue du Port ☏ 02 96 72 34 24, ⓦ le-vivier-erquy.com. The best of a row of similar restaurants beside the fishing port, with weekday lunches for €17.90, and seafood-rich dinner *menus* from €23.50; the €32 option includes sumptuous grilled oysters and a stew made with the local speciality, scallops. Daily noon–2pm & 7–9pm; closed Jan.

## The Côte de Goëlo

As you move northwest from Erquy towards Paimpol along the **Côte de Goëlo**, the shoreline becomes wilder and harsher, while the seaside towns tend to be crammed into narrow rocky inlets or set well back in river estuaries.

### Abbaye de Beauport

2km south of Paimpol • Daily: April–June 10.30am–noon & 2–6pm; July–Sept 10.30am–7pm; Oct–March 2–6pm; closed first 3 wks of Dec • €6 • ☏ 02 96 55 18 58, ⓦ abbayebeauport.com

South of Paimpol, in a superbly romantic waterfront setting, the D786 passes the substantial ruins of the **Abbaye de Beauport**, established in 1202 by Count Alain de Goëlo. Its stone walls are covered with wild flowers and ivy, the central cloisters are engulfed by a huge tree, and there are birds flitting and flying everywhere. The Norman Gothic chapterhouse is the most noteworthy building to survive, and its roofless halls hold relics from all periods of its history. In late May, the abbey hosts a festival of choral music.

### Paimpol

At the northern end of the Côte de Goëlo, the attractive town of **PAIMPOL** consists of a tangle of cobbled alleyways and fine grey-granite houses. It centres on a port that has been stripped of much of its character in its transition from working fishing port to pleasure harbour. This was once the base for a cod and whaling fleet that sailed to Iceland each February. From then until September the town would be empty of its young men. Thanks to naval shipyards and the like, the open sea is not visible from Paimpol; a maze of waterways leads to its two separate **harbours**. Both are usually filled with the high masts of yachts, but are still also used by the fishing vessels that keep a fish market and a plethora of *poissonneries* busy.

## ARRIVAL AND INFORMATION                                                                    PAIMPOL

**By train and bus** The *gare SNCF* and *gare routière* are side by side on av du Général-de-Gaulle.
**Tourist office** Place de la République, 100m from the pleasure port (July & Aug Mon–Sat 9.30am–7.30pm, Sun

10am–12.30pm & 4.30–6.30pm; Sept–June Mon–Fri 9.30am–12.30pm & 2–6pm, Sat 9.30am–12.30pm & 2–6.30pm; closed Thurs Oct–March; ☎02 96 20 83 16, ⓦpaimpol-goelo.com).

## ACCOMMODATION AND EATING

**La Cabane sur les Quais** quai de Kernoa ☎02 96 55 58 52. Housed in what resembles a black quayside shed on the far side of the harbour, with terrace tables alongside, this inviting little restaurant serves small-plate sharing portions of each day's fresh catch, plus standards like fish'n'chips or *moules frites* for around €10. Daily except Mon 11am–3pm & 6pm–1am.

★ **K'Loys** 21 quai Morand ☎02 96 20 40 01, ⓦhotel-

kloys.com. This grand old mansion, overlooking the small boat harbour, houses an eccentric but extremely welcoming hotel, crammed with oddities. The comfortable rooms vary in price according to size and view; the wonderful top-floor Captain's suite, with its retractable ceiling, is highly recommended. A good bistro stretches from the front courtyard into the street. **€86**

## The Île de Bréhat

Hugely popular with French visitors in summer, the little **ÎLE DE BRÉHAT** – 2km offshore from Pointe de l'Arcouest, 6km northwest of Paimpol – is one of the most beautiful places in Brittany. Renowned as a sanctuary for rare species of wild flowers, including blue acanthus, it also abounds in birds of all kinds.

Consisting, in truth, of two islands, joined by a tiny bridge, Bréhat appears to span great latitudes. On its north side are windswept meadows of hemlock and yarrow, sloping down to chaotic erosions of rock; on the south, you find yourself amid palm trees, mimosa and eucalyptus. All around is a multitude of islets – some accessible at low tide, others *propriété privée*, most just pink-orange rocks.

### Port-Clos

Boats to Bréhat arrive at the small harbour of **PORT-CLOS**, though depending on the tide passengers may have to walk several hundred metres before setting foot on terra firma. **Cars** are banned, so many visitors rent **bikes** at the port, for around €15 per day. However, it's easy enough to explore on foot; walking from one end to the other takes less than an hour.

### Le Bourg

Each batch of new arrivals heads first to Bréhat's village, **LE BOURG**, 500m up from the port. Besides a handful of hotels, restaurants and bars, it also holds a limited array of shops, and hosts a small **market** most days. In high season, the attractive central square tends to be packed fit to burst, with exasperated holiday-home-owners trundling their little shopping carts through the throngs of day-trippers.

### The northern island

A short distance north of Le Bourg, the slender **Pont ar Prat** bridge leads across to the northern island, where the crowds thin out, and countless coves offer opportunities to sprawl on the tough grass or clamber across the rugged boulders. At the northernmost tip, the **Paon lighthouse** stands erect over the rock-scattered waters – girls of the island used to throw rocks into the wash, believing that if it landed in the water without hitting a rock they would marry their love, but if it hit a rock, it would be a cold bed for another year. Though the coastal footpath around this northern half offers the most attractive walking on the island, the best **beaches** line the southern shores, with the **Grève du Guerzido** at its southeastern corner being the pick of the crop.

## ARRIVAL AND INFORMATION                                                    ÎLE DE BRÉHAT

**By ferry** Bréhat is served by regular Vedettes de Bréhat ferries (☎ 02 96 55 79 50, ⊛ vedettesdebrehat.com) from Pointe de l'Arcouest, 6km northwest of Paimpol and served by summer buses from its *gare SNCF*. Parking for the day here costs €6. Broadly speaking, sailings are every 30min at peak times between April and Sept, and every 1hr 30min between Oct and March, with the first boat out to Bréhat at 8.15am year-round (9.30am on Sun in winter), and the last boat back at 7.45pm in summer, 6pm in winter. The direct crossing takes around 10min, and a return trip costs €10.30 for adults, €8.80 for ages 4–11 (bikes, €16 extra,

are only allowed outside peak crossing times). Roughly half the departures in summer, though, cruise for an hour around Bréhat before docking at the island; catching one, and then returning on a direct ferry, costs €16 for over-11s, €11 for ages 4–11. The same company also offers crossings in summer from Erquy, Binic and St-Quay-Portrieux.
**Tourist office** In Le Bourg's main square (July & Aug Mon–Sat 10am–1pm & 2–5pm, Sun 10am–1pm; March–-June & Sept Tues–Thurs & Sat 10am–1pm & 2–4pm, Fri 10am–1pm & 2–3.30pm; Oct–Feb Mon & Thurs–Sat 10am–1pm & 2–3.30pm; ☎ 02 96 20 04 15, ⊛ brehat-infos.fr).

## ACCOMMODATION

**Bellevue** Port-Clos ☎ 02 96 20 00 05, ⊛ hotel-bellevue-brehat.fr. This imposing white-with-blue-trim hotel, right by the *embarcadère*, has been nicely modernized; the best of its twenty rooms have sea-view balconies and whirlpool baths. Lunch downstairs costs €20, dinner €36. Compulsory *demi-pension* mid-July to Aug; closed mid-Nov to mid-Feb. **€95**, *demi-pension* **€183**
**Camping Municipal** Goaréva ☎ 02 96 20 02 46, ⊛ iledebrehat.fr. This wonderful municipal campsite is set

in the woods high above the sea at the southwest tip of the island. Camping wild elsewhere is strictly forbidden. Closed mid-Sept to mid-June. **€11.35**
**Men-Joliguet** Port-Clos ☎ 06 88 20 32 88, ⊛ locations-brehat.net. Bréhat's best value; this village house beside the *Bellevue* has been modernized to hold five bright, sleek B&B rooms, and has a lovely sea-view garden. Closed Nov–Easter. **€83**

## The Côte de Granit Rose

The northernmost stretch of the Breton coast, between Bréhat and Ploumanac'h, is loosely known as the **Côte de Granit Rose**. Great pink-granite boulders jut from the sea around the island of Bréhat, and are scattered along the headlands to the west. Perhaps the most memorable stretch of coast lies north of **Tréguier**, where the pink-granite rocks are eroded into fantastic shapes.

### Tréguier

West of Paimpol, the D786 passes over a green ria on the bridge outside Lézardrieux before arriving at **TRÉGUIER**, one of Brittany's very few hill towns. Its central feature is the **Cathédrale de St-Tugdual**, which contains the tomb of St Yves, a native of the town who died in 1303 and – for his incorruptibility – became the patron saint of lawyers. Attempts to bribe him continue to this day; his tomb is surrounded by marble plaques and an inferno of candles invoking his aid.

---

### LA PETITE MAISON DE PLOUGRESCANT

Perhaps the best-known photographic image of Brittany is of a small seafront cottage somehow squeezed between two mighty pink-granite boulders. Surprisingly few visitors, however, see the house in real life. It stands 10km north of Tréguier, and just 2km out from the village of **Plougrescant**, at a spot marked on maps as either **Le Gouffre** or Le Gouffre du Castel-Meuru. Although you can't visit the cottage itself – which actually faces inland, across a small sheltered bay, with its back to the open sea – the shoreline nearby offers superb short walks, and a summer-only café sells snacks.

**6**

## Château de la Roche-Jagu

D787, 10km southeast of Tréguier • Daily: early May to June & Sept 10am–noon & 2–6pm; July & Aug 10am–1pm & 2–7pm; Nov hols 2–5pm • park & ground floor free, special exhibitions €5 • ☎ 02 96 95 62 35, ⓦ www.larochejagu.fr

The fifteenth-century **Château de la Roche-Jagu** stands on a heavily wooded slope above the meanders of the Trieux river. A really gorgeous building, it hosts lavish **annual exhibitions**, usually on some sort of Celtic theme. Outside, the modern landscaped park, accessible free of charge, is traced through by several **hiking trails**.

## Ploumanac'h

For anyone in search of a beach holiday, the best base along the Granit Rose coast has to be the tiny resort of **PLOUMANAC'H**, a couple of kilometres west of the missable town of Perros-Guirec.

The small golden yellow beach fronting Ploumanac'h itself is a surreal treat, set in an alcove of soft-shaped and smooth pink-granite formations protected by numerous other outcrops in the bay, one of which barely separates a glorious private house from the waves.

A great walk along the **Sentier des Douaniers** pathway winds round the clifftops from Ploumanac'h to the plage Trestraou in Perros-Guirec, passing an astonishing succession of deformed and water-sculpted rocks. Birds wheel overhead towards the offshore bird sanctuary of **Sept-Îles**, and battered boats shelter in the narrow inlets or bob uncontrollably out on the waves. There are patches and brief causeways of grass, clumps of purple heather and yellow gorse.

## Trégastel-Plage

Three kilometres west of Ploumanac'h along a pretty coastal road, **TRÉGASTEL-PLAGE** boasts a delightful sheltered beach with a couple of huge lumps of pink granite slap in the middle. Sadly, however, the seafront in the village is an ugly stretch of concrete, centring on the **Forum**, a swimming pool and leisure complex.

## INFORMATION                                CÔTE DE GRANIT ROSE

**TRÉGUIER**
**Tourist office** rue Marcelin-Berthelot, down by the commercial port (early July to late Aug Mon–Sat 9.30am–6.30pm, Sun 10am–1pm; late Aug to early July Mon–Sat 10am–12.30pm & 2–5.30pm; ☎ 02 96 92 22 33, ⓦ bretagne-cotedegranitrose.com).

## ACCOMMODATION AND EATING

**TRÉGUIER**
**Aigue-Marine** 5 rue Marcelin-Berthelot, Port de Plaisance ☎ 02 96 92 97 00, ⓦ aiguemarine-hotel. com. Smart, welcoming hotel by the port in Tréguier, with swimming pool, private parking, whirlpool spa, good buffet breakfasts for €14.50, and a top-notch restaurant (closed Sat lunch & Mon) where dinner costs €49 and up. **€105**

★ **Manoir de Troezel Vras** Kerbors ☎ 06 63 41 43 71, ⓦ troezel-vras.com. Tranquil rural B&B, set in a sensitively converted old farmhouse 8km northeast of Tréguier. The five large guest rooms are splendidly furnished, and the friendly hosts serve an excellent nightly dinner for €25; there's no menu, you just eat what you're given. No credit cards. Closed late Sept to early May. **€90**

★ **Poissonnerie Moulinet** 2 rue Ernest-Renan ☎ 02 96 92 30 27. Tasting room above a fish shop just below the cathedral, where you can buy superb seafood platters for €18–50; you can also take them away and eat in the square. April–Sept daily noon–2.30pm & 6–9pm.

**PLOUMANAC'H**
**Castel Beau Site** Plage de Saint-Guirec ☎ 02 96 91 40 87, ⓦ castelbeausite.com. Lavish luxury hotel in prime beachfront position, modernized and enlarged to offer 33 ultra-chic sea-view rooms, plus a delicious restaurant that's open for dinner nightly, and lunch on Sundays only, with *menus* from €49. **€199**
**Le Ranolien** Bd du Sémaphore ☎ 02 96 91 65 65, ⓦ leranolien.fr. Four-star campsite in a superb position near a little beach halfway along the Sentier des Douaniers, boasting a great array of swimming pools, waterslides, a spa and a cinema. Rental cabins also available. Closed late Sept to early April. **€33**
**Des Rochers** 70 chemin de la Pointe ☎ 02 96 91 67 54, ⓦ hotel-desrochers-perros.com. Very stylish, very friendly modern hotel, beside the port rather than the beach, but

still enjoying a fabulous outlook across the harbour, and offering bright, well-equipped rooms. The restaurant downstairs (closed Mon) serves high-class *menus* from €20 for lunch, €28 for dinner. **€120**

**TRÉGASTEL-PLAGE**

★ **Beau Séjour** 5 plage du Coz-Pors ☎ 02 96 23 88 02,

ⓦ lebeausejourtregastel.fr. Exceptionally welcoming and hugely eccentric seafront hotel, with all kinds of nautical theming. The ten rooms vary enormously, but most have sea views, and one fabulous suite has boat-shaped beds and a large balcony. Best of all, the owners are bakers, so the €14 breakfast buffet spread is out of this world. Closed mid-Jan to mid-Feb & mid-Nov to mid-Dec. **€90**

## The Bay of Lannion

Despite being set significantly back from the sea on the estuary of the River Léguer, **Lannion** gives its name to a huge coastal bay – and it's the bay rather than the town that is most likely to impress. One enormous beach stretches from **St-Michel-en-Grève**, which is little more than a bend in the road, as far as **Locquirec**; at low tide you can walk hundreds of metres out on the sands.

### Lannion

Set amid plummeting hills and stairways, **LANNION** is a historic city with streets of medieval housing and a couple of interesting old churches. As a centre for high-tech telecommunications, this is one of modern Brittany's real success stories – hence its self-satisfied nickname, *ville heureuse* or "happy town". In addition to admiring the half-timbered houses around the **place du Général-Leclerc** and along **rue des Chapeliers**, it's worth climbing up the 142 granite steps to the twelfth-century Templar **Église de Brélévenez**, from where the views are stupendous.

### INFORMATION

BAY OF LANNION

**Tourist office** 2 quai d'Aiguillon (July & Aug Mon–Sat 9am–6.30pm, Sun 10am–1pm; Sept–June Mon– Sat 9.30am–12.30pm & 2–6pm; ☎ 02 96 05 60 70, ⓦ bretagne-cotedegranitrose.com).

### ACCOMMODATION AND EATING

**Grand Hôtel des Bains** 15bis rue de l'Église, Locquirec ☎ 02 98 67 41 02, ⓦ grand-hotel-des-bains.com. Grand indeed, this imposing seafront hotel stands in private gardens close to the heart of the little resort of Locquirec. Spacious rooms, many with terraces, plus a good restaurant and spa. **€139**

**Ibis** 30 av du Général-de-Gaulle, Lannion ☎ 02 96 37 03 67, ⓦ ibis.com. Lannion's only central hotel, facing the station, has seventy well-equipped modern rooms, but no restaurant. **€73**

**Tire-Bouchon** 8 rue de Keriavily ☎ 02 96 37 10 43. Good traditional restaurant in the heart of town, offering weekday lunches from €11.50, dinner menus from €22. Tues–Sat noon–1.45pm & 7.15–9pm.

### Cairn du Barnenez

13km northeast of Morlaix • Daily: May & June 10am–12.30pm & 2–6.30pm; July & Aug 10am–6.30pm; Sept–April 10am–12.30pm & 2–5.30pm • €6 • ☎ 02 98 67 24 73, ⓦ barnenez.fr

In a glorious position at the mouth of the Morlaix estuary, the prehistoric stone **Cairn du Barnenez** surveys the waters from the summit of a hill. As on Gavrinis in the Morbihan, its ancient masonry has been laid bare by excavations, and provides a stunning sense of the architectural prowess of the megalith builders. Dated to 4500 BC, this is one of the oldest large monuments in the world.

The site consists of two stepped **pyramids**, built of large flat stones chinked with pebbles, and encircled by terraces and ramps. The whole thing measures roughly 70m long by 15–25m wide and 6m high. Both pyramids were long buried under the same 80m-long earthen mound. While the actual cairns are exposed to view, most of the passages and chambers that lie within them are sealed off. Local tradition has it that one tunnel runs right through this "home of the fairies", and continues out deep under the sea.

**6**

# Finistère

It's hard to resist the appeal of the **Finistère coast**, with its ocean-fronting cliffs and headlands stretching all the way around the western tip of Brittany. Summer crowds may detract from the best parts of the **Crozon peninsula** and the **Pointe du Raz**, but elsewhere you can enjoy near solitude. Explore the semi-wilderness of the **northern stretches** west of the appealing little Channel port of **Roscoff**, where each successive estuary or **aber** shelters its own tiny harbour, or take a ferry to the misty islands of **Ouessant** and **Sein**. From the top of **Ménez-Hom** visitors can admire the anarchic limits of western France, while the cities of **Brest** and **Quimper** display modern Breton life as well as ancient splendours.

## Morlaix

**MORLAIX**, one of the great old Breton ports, thrived on trade with England during the "Golden Period" of the late Middle Ages. Its sober stone houses climbing the slopes of a steep valley, the town was originally protected by an eleventh-century castle and a circuit of walls. Little is left of either, but the centre remains in part medieval with its cobbled streets and half-timbered houses. The present grandeur comes from the pink-granite **viaduct**, carrying trains from Paris to Brest, which towers above the town centre.

### Maison à Pondalez

9 Grande Rue • July–Sept daily 10am–6pm; Sept–June Tues–Sat 10am–noon & 2–5pm • €4 • ☎ 02 98 88 68 88, ⓦ musee.ville.morlaix.fr

Morlaix's most impressive medieval relic, the **Maison à Pondalez**, is a fabulously restored sixteenth-century house that takes its name from the Breton word for the sculpted wooden internal gallery that dominates its ground floor. It's run in conjunction with the town museum, in the **Jacobin convent** on the nearby place des Jacobins, which was closed for restoration as this book went to press, but was expected to reopen shortly.

### ARRIVAL AND INFORMATION | MORLAIX

**By train** The *gare SNCF* is on rue Armand-Rousseau, high above the town at the western end of the viaduct.
Destinations Brest (20 daily; 40min); Roscoff (7 daily; 35min).
**By bus** All buses depart from place Cornic, right under the viaduct.
Destinations Lannion (4 daily; 1hr); Quimper (1 daily; 1hr

50min); Roscoff (5 daily; 1hr).
**Tourist office** 10 place Charles-de-Gaulle (June & Sept Mon–Sat 9am–12.30pm & 2–6.30pm; July & Aug Mon–Sat 9am–7pm, Sun 10.30am–12.30pm; Oct–May Mon–Sat 9am–12.30pm & 2–6pm; ☎ 02 98 62 14 94, ⓦ baiedemorlaix.bzh).

### ACCOMMODATION AND EATING

**Auberge de Jeunesse Éthic Étapes** 1 voie d'accès au Port, St-Martin-des-Champs ☎ 02 98 15 10 55, ⓦ aj-morlaix.org. Large, well-equipped, modern hostel, beside the pleasure port just over 1km downstream from the centre along the left (west) bank of river, with 35 rooms holding four dorm beds each, plus a communal kitchen.

Rates include breakfast. **€20**
**De l'Europe** 1 rue d'Aiguillon ☎ 02 98 62 11 99, ⓦ hotel europe-morlaix.com. Grand, if eccentric, old hotel in the centre of Morlaix, with a fabulous wooden staircase and nicely refurbished rooms – some plush and some plain, including some cut-rate singles – and €10 buffet breakfasts. **€94**

## Roscoff

The 1973 opening of the deep-water port at **ROSCOFF** played a crucial role in revitalizing the Breton economy. Its cross-Channel **ferry services** were designed not just to bring tourists, but also to revive the ancient trading links between the Celtic nations of Brittany, Ireland and southwest England. Roscoff had long been a significant port. Mary Queen of Scots landed here in 1548 on her way to Paris to be engaged

**THE JOHNNIES OF ROSCOFF**

In 1828, Henri Ollivier took **onions** to England from Roscoff, thereby founding a trade that flourished until the 1930s. The story of the "Johnnies" – that classic French image of men in black berets with strings of onions hanging over the handlebars of their bicycles – is told at **La Maison des Johnnies et de l'Oignon Rosé de Roscoff**, 48 rue Brizeux, near the *gare SNCF* (mid-June to mid-Sept daily 10am–noon & 2.30–6pm; mid-April to mid-June & mid-Sept to Oct daily 2.30–5pm; €4).

6

to François, the son of Henri II of France, as did Bonnie Prince Charlie, the Young Pretender, in 1746, after his defeat at Culloden.

Roscoff itself is still just a small resort, mixing an economy based on fishing with relatively low-key pleasure trips to the **Île de Batz**. Almost all activity is confined to **rue Gambetta** and to the lively old port. The sixteenth-century church, **Notre-Dame-de-Croas-Batz**, at the far end of rue Gambetta, is embellished with an ornate Renaissance belfry, complete with sculpted ships and a protruding stone cannon. Some way beyond is Roscoff's best **beach**, at Laber.

## ARRIVAL AND INFORMATION                                   ROSCOFF

**By boat** Brittany Ferries sailings from Plymouth and Cork (☎ 02 98 29 28 13, ⌨ brittany-ferries.com), some of which offer continuing service to Bilbao and Santander in Spain, dock not in Roscoff's original natural harbour, but at the Port de Bloscon, a couple of kilometres east of the town.

**By train** From the *gare SNCF*, a few hundred metres south of the town centre, a restricted rail service (often replaced by buses) runs to Morlaix (7 daily; 35min), with connections beyond.

**By bus** Local buses leave from the *gare SNCF* year-round, and also from the ferry terminal in summer (☎ 08 10 81 00 29, ⌨ viaoo29.fr).

**Tourist office** 46 rue Gambetta, just south of the old harbour (July & Aug Mon–Sat 9am–12.30pm & 1.30–7pm, Sun 10am–4pm; Sept–June Mon–Sat 9.15am–noon & 2–6pm; ☎ 02 98 61 12 13, ⌨ roscoff-tourisme.com).

## ACCOMMODATION

For a small town, Roscoff is well equipped with hotels, which are accustomed to late-night arrivals from the ferries. However, many close for some or all of the winter. There's also a hostel on the Île de Batz (see page 332).

**Des Arcades** 15 rue de l'Amiral-Réveillère ☎ 02 98 69 70 45, ⌨ hotel-les-arcades-roscoff.com. Very central sixteenth-century building where 14 of the 20 modernized en-suite rooms have superb sea views, and so, too, does the restaurant, which has dinner *menus* from €19.50, and an excellent €32.50 option. Closed mid-Nov to Jan. **€71**

**Du Centre** 8 rue Gambetta ☎ 02 98 61 24 25, ⌨ chezjanie.fr. Boutique hotel above the venerable *Chez Janie*, with modern, tastefully furnished bedrooms – sea

views €15 extra – and a decent bistro menu. Closed mid-Nov to mid-Feb. **€91**

**Chardons Bleus** 4 rue de l'Amiral-Réveillère ☎ 02 98 69 72 03, ⌨ roscoffhotel.com. Friendly hotel in the heart of the old town, with simple but comfortable rooms and a good restaurant (closed Thurs & Sun eve Sept–June) where dinner *menus* cost €26 or €39. Closed three weeks in Feb. **€77**

★ **Le Temps de Vivre** 19 place Lacaze-Duthiers ☎ 02 98 19 33 19, ⌨ letempsdevivre.net. Ultra-stylish contemporary hotel, in an old mansion near the Notre-Dame church. Luxuriously spacious rooms with designer bathrooms, some with wonderful close-up sea views, but no restaurant. Off-season rates are at least €60 lower. **€140**

## EATING

**Bonne Étoile** 36 rue de l'Amiral-Réveillère ☎ 02 98 69 71 58, ⌨ la-bonne-etoile-roscoff.fr. Jaunty little restaurant, in the centre near the port, with bright seaside decor and lots of baked goods – pies, tarts and sponges – as well as seafood on menus at €18 for lunch, and €22 for dinner. Tues & Sun noon–2pm, Wed–Sat noon–2pm & 7–9pm.

**Crêperie de la Poste** 12 rue Gambetta ☎ 02 98 69 72 81, ⌨ creperiedelaposte.fr. Cosy old stone house in the heart of town, offering inexpensive à la carte meals of

sweet and savoury pancakes; more exotic seafood crêpes cost up to €12. They also serve fish soup, mussels and other simple meals. Sept to mid-Nov & mid-Jan to June Thurs–Sun 11.30am until late; July & Aug Mon & Wed–Sun 11.30am until late.

**L'Écume des Jours** Quai d'Auxerre ☎ 02 98 61 22 83, ⌨ lecume-des-jours.pagesperso-orange.fr. Romantic restaurant in a grand house 500m south of town along the quayside, with outdoor seating in summer. Two-course lunch *formules* go for €23 on weekdays, while the *plat*

**6**

du jour with a coffee costs €16; dinner *menus*, from €35, feature such delights as braised oysters or scallops with

local pink onions. Jan to mid-Dec Mon & Thurs–Sun noon–1.30pm & 7–9pm.

## Île de Batz

Long, narrow, and very lovely, the **ÎLE DE BATZ** (pronounced "Ba") mirrors Roscoff across the water, separated from it by a sea channel that's barely 200m wide at low tide but perhaps five times that when the tide is high. Appearances from the mainland are deceptive: the island's old town fills much of its southern shoreline, but those areas not visible from Roscoff are much wilder and more windswept. With no cars permitted, and some great expanses of sandy beach, it makes a wonderfully quiet retreat, for families in particular.

Ferries from Roscoff arrive at the **quayside** of the old town. A nice small beach lines the edge of the harbour, but it turns into a morass of seaweed at low tide. All arriving passengers make the obvious 500m walk towards the town.

Turning left when you get to the **church** will bring you to the hostel (see below), and the 44m-high **lighthouse** on the island's peak, all of 23m above sea level (April–June & first half of Sept Sat & Sun 2–5pm; July & Aug daily 11am–5.30pm; €4). Turning right instead leads you towards the best beach, the white-sand **Grève Blanche** at the eastern end of the island.

### ARRIVAL AND INFORMATION                    ÎLE DE BATZ

**By ferry** Three rival ferry companies make the 10min crossing from Roscoff to Batz (frequent services daily: July & Aug 8am–8pm; Sept–June 8.30am–6.30pm; 10min; €9 return; bikes €9). Compagnie Maritime Armein (☎02 98 61 75 47, ⓦvedettesbatzroscoff.com), Compagnie Finistérienne or CFTM (☎02 98 61 78 87, ⓦvedettes-ile-de-batz.com), and Armor Excursions (☎02 98 61 79 66, ⓦvedettes.armor.ile.de.batz.fr) sell tickets at the landward end of Roscoff's pier; in summer, tickets are valid on any

ferry. At low tide, the boats sail from the far end of the pier, 5min walk further.

**Tourist office** At the ferry landing (April–June & Sept Tues, Thurs, Fri & Sat 9.15am–noon & 1.45–4.45pm, Wed 9.15am–noon; July & Aug Mon–Sat 9.15am–12.15pm & 1.30–5.30pm; Oct–Mar Mon, Tues, Thurs, Fri 9.15am–noon & 1.45–4.30pm, Wed 9.15am–noon; ☎02 98 61 75 70, ⓦwww.iledebatz.com).

### ACCOMMODATION AND EATING

**Auberge de Jeunesse Marine** Creach ar Bolloc'h ☎02 98 61 77 69, ⓦaj-iledebatz.org. The evocatively named Creach ar Bolloc'h makes a beautiful setting for this hostel, which faces south towards Roscoff from near the port. Two separate cottages hold dorm beds, with a lovely beach just a few steps away. Rates include breakfast, while dinner is available for €11. Closed Oct–March. **€17.50**

**Les Herbes Folles** Le Débarcadère ☎02 98 61 78 28, ⓦhotel-iledebatz.com. The island's one, simple hotel, on the ferry quay, is a rambling old place with an open-air

wooden deck, a garden, and abundant nooks and crannies. Seven of its ten en-suite rooms look out to sea. It also has a good restaurant, serving dinner from €22, and a very pleasant little bar, the *Bigorneau Langoureux* ("languorous periwinkle"). **€94**

**Terrain d'Hébergement** Porz Reter ☎02 98 61 77 76, ⓦwww.iledebatz.com. Batz's waterfront campsite, at the island's southeast corner, is as minimal as they come; you simply pick a spot, just back from the beach. It does however have a small shower block. Closed Sept to late June. **€8.16**

## The abers

The coastline west of Roscoff is among the most dramatic in Brittany, a jagged procession of **abers** – deep, narrow estuaries – that hold numerous small, isolated resorts. It's a little on the bracing side, especially if you're making use of the many **campsites**, but that just has to be counted as part of the appeal. In summer, at least, the temperatures are mild enough, and things grow more sheltered as you move around towards Le Conquet and Brest.

The first real resort west of Roscoff, **PLOUESCAT**, is not quite on the sea itself, but there are **campsites** nearby on each of three adjacent beaches. Roscoff to Brest

**buses** stop at Plouescat before turning inland. Pretty little **BRIGNOGAN-PLAGES**, on the first *aber* west of Plouescat, holds a small natural harbour, once the lair of wreckers, with beaches and weather-beaten rocks to either side, as well as its own menhir.

The *aber* between Plouguerneau and **L'ABER-WRAC'H** has a stepping-stone crossing just upstream from the bridge at Lannilis, built in Gallo-Roman times, where long cut stones still cross the three channels of water. L'Aber-Wrac'h itself, perched over the western side of the vast mouth of the Baie des Anges, is a small and attractive resort within reach of yet more sandy beaches.

**6**

## ACCOMMODATION AND EATING                                      THE ABERS

### PLOUESCAT

★ **Camping de Keremma** La Sablière, Tréflez ☎ 02 98 61 62 79, ⓦ campingdekeremma.fr. Lovely little village campsite, inland from the sea on the way between Plouescat and Brignogan, and set on a green avenue lined with meadows of purple-and-yellow flowers. Closed Dec–Feb. €13

**Roc'h-Ar-Mor** 18 rue Ar Mor, plage de Porsmeur ☎ 02 98 69 63 01, ⓦ rocharmor.com. Basic, long-standing and bargain-priced hotel, aimed especially at walkers. Only some rooms have showers, and all share toilets; and even though it's right on the beach at Porsmeur, none has a sea view. Four-person rooms are the best value. A bright, cheery dining room serves lunch from €16.50, dinner from €25. Closed Mon & Tues April–June & Sept–Nov, and only open Fri–Sun Dec–March. €36

### BRIGNOGAN-PLAGES

**Camping de la Côte des Légendes** Rue Douar ar Pont ☎ 02 98 83 41 65, ⓦ campingcotedeslegendes.com. Central three-star campsite, beside a good beach on the western side of the bay, north of the centre and 50m from the sailing school. Closed mid-Nov to Easter. €17.35

### L'ABER-WRAC'H

★ **Camping Municipal de Penn-Enez** 551 Penn-Enez, Landéda ☎ 02 98 04 99 82, ⓦ camping-penn-enez.com. Perched atop the dunes, enjoying superb views across the fine beach below and out to sea, this welcoming little campsite has a bakery and grocery that's open in July & Aug only. Closed Oct to mid-April. €11.29

## Le Conquet

**LE CONQUET**, at the far western tip of Brittany 24km beyond Brest, is a wonderful place, scarcely developed, with a long beach of clean white sand that's protected from the winds by the narrow spit of the Kermorvan peninsula. It's very much a working fishing village, with grey-stone houses leading down to the stone jetties of a cramped harbour. A good walk 5km south brings you to the lighthouse at **Pointe St-Mathieu**, with a much-photographed view out to the islands from its site amid the ruins of a Benedictine abbey.

### ACCOMMODATION                                               LE CONQUET

**Les Blancs Sablons** Kermorvan peninsula ☎ 02 98 36 07 91, ⓦ les-blancs-sablons.com. In July & Aug only, this well-equipped two-star campsite, in the splendid setting of the beach-lined Kermorvan peninsula, offers its own surf school, as well as wood-fired pizzas and a basic grocery. Closed Oct–March. €16.44

**Relais du Vieux Port** 1 quai Drellac'h ☎ 02 98 89 15 91, ⓦ lerelaisduvieuxport.com. A handful of inexpensive, attractive and nicely decorated rooms, right by the ferry jetty and mostly facing out to sea, plus a crêperie that also serves tasty seafood specials, with a full set dinner *menu* at €31. Closed Jan. €58

## Île d'Ouessant

The **Île d'Ouessant** (known to the English as "Ushant") lies 30km northwest of Le Conquet, and its lighthouse at **Creac'h** (said to be the strongest in the world) is regarded as the entrance to the English Channel. Ouessant is the farthest flung in a chain of smaller islands and half-submerged granite rocks. Most are uninhabited, or like Béniguet the preserve only of rabbits, though the **Île de Molène**, midway, has a village.

**6**

## Lampaul

Boats to **Ouessant** arrive at the modern **harbour** in the ominous-sounding Baie du Stiff. While there's a scattering of houses here, the only town is 4km distant at **LAMPAUL**, so that's where everyone heads, either by the bus that meets each arriving ferry, by bike, or in a long walking procession that straggles along the one road.

There's not a lot to Lampaul. The best beaches are sprawled around its bay, while the cemetery's **war memorial** lists all the ships in which townsfolk were lost, alongside graves of unknown sailors washed ashore and a chapel of wax "*proëlla* crosses" symbolizing the many islanders who never returned.

## Éco-Musée d'Ouessant

Niou • April–June & Sept daily 11.30am–6pm in school hols, 11.30am–5pm otherwise; July & Aug daily 10.30am–6pm; Oct–March Tues–Sun 1.30–5pm; €2.80 • ☎ 02 98 48 86 37, ⓦ pnr-armorique.fr

At **NIOU**, 1km northwest of Lampaul, two old houses have long served as the **Éco-Musée d'Ouessant**. Sadly, one of them, a reconstruction of a traditional island house, was destroyed in an arson attack in 2018. The other, however, remains open as a museum of local history and culture.

## Créac'h lighthouse

1km west of Niou **Musée des Phares et Balises** April–June daily 11.30am–6pm in school hols, 11.30am–5pm otherwise; July & Aug daily 10.30am–6pm, plus two varying nights each week 9–11pm; Sept daily 11.30am–5pm; Oct–March Tues–Sun 1.30–5.30pm • €4.30 • ☎ 02 98 48 80 70, ⓦ pnr-armorique.fr

The **Créac'h lighthouse**, 1km west of Niou, boasts a 500-million-candlepower beam capable of being seen from England's Lizard Point. You can't visit the lighthouse tower itself, but the complex at its base holds the **Musée des Phares et Balises**, a large museum devoted to lighthouses and buoys. None of the information is in English, however, and photography is not permitted.

The Créac'h lighthouse makes a good starting point from which to set out along the barren and exposed rocks of the north coast. Particularly in September and other times of migration, it's a remarkable spot for birdwatching, frequented as it is by puffins, storm petrels and cormorants.

**ARRIVAL AND DEPARTURE**         ÎLE D'OUESSANT

**By boat** Penn Ar Bed (☎ 02 98 80 80 80, ⓦ pennarbed.fr) offer one to six daily departures from Le Conquet to Ouessant all year. The timetables are extremely intricate, but broadly speaking the first sailing from Le Conquet is at 7.30am or 8.30am from mid-July to late Aug, and at 9.45am for the rest of the year. They also operate one or two daily services from Brest, with the first sailing always at either 8am or 8.20am, and between mid-July and late Aug they sail from Camaret to Ouessant at 8.45am daily except Sun, with some sailings to either side of that peak period. All round trips cost €34.90 June–Sept, €27.90 Oct–May, with bikes €15.50 extra. For similar prices, Finist'Mer (☎ 08 25 13 52 35, ⓦ www.finist-mer.fr) sail from Le Conquet to Ouessant three times daily, between mid-July and late Aug only, and once daily most days between mid-April and late Sept, and from Camaret on Wed only, at 9.10am, between late April and early July, and during Sept; and on Tues & Thurs at 9.30am between early July and late Aug.

**By plane** Finist'Air fly to Ouessant in just fifteen minutes from Brest's Guipavas airport all year – except, frustratingly, between mid-July and mid-Aug (Mon–Fri 8.30am & 4.30pm, Sat 8.30am; €47.70 each way; ☎ 02 98 84 64 87, ⓦ www.finistair.fr).

**GETTING AROUND**

**By bus** A bus meets the ferry to take passengers into Lampaul (€4 return, €15 for full island tour; ☎ 06 42 70 48 71, ⓦ ouessantevasion.bzh).

**By bike** Bike rental is available at the port (€10–15/day).

**INFORMATION**

**Tourist office** Lampaul (late July to late Aug Mon–Sat 9.30am–6.15pm, Sun 10.15am–12.15pm; late Aug to late July Mon–Sat 10am–noon & 2–5.45pm; ☎ 02 98 48 85 83, ⓦ ot-ouessant.fr).

PARADE IN TRADITIONAL BRETON COSTUME

## ACCOMMODATION AND EATING

**Auberge de Jeunesse** La Croix Rouge, Lampaul ☎ 02 98 48 84 53, ⓦ auberge-ouessant.com. Little hostel, north of the centre towards Niou, where rates for beds in the dorms (sleeping two to six) include breakfast. Closed Dec & Jan. **€22**

**Ti Jan Ar C'hafé** Lampaul ☎ 02 98 48 82 64, ⓦ tijan.fr. This attractively restored village house, in a peaceful setting with a pretty garden, offers eight tastefully decorated rooms but no restaurant. Breakfast is available for €10. Closed mid-Nov to mid-Feb. **€99**

# 6

# Brest

Set in a magnificent natural harbour known as the Rade de Brest, the city of **BREST** is sheltered from ocean storms by the Crozon peninsula to the south. Now home to France's Atlantic Fleet, Brest has been a naval town since the Middle Ages. During World War II, it was bombed to prevent the Germans from using it as a submarine base; when liberated in September 1944, after a six-week siege, it was devastated beyond recognition. The architecture of the postwar town is raw and bleak, and despite attempts to green the city, it has proved too windswept to respond. While it's reasonably lively, most visitors simply pass through.

## Château de Brest

Feb, March & Oct–Dec Mon & Wed–Sun 1.30–6.30pm; April–Sept daily 10am–6.30pm; closed Jan · €7, under-26s free · ☎ 02 98 22 12 39, ⓦ musee-marine.fr/brest

Perched on a headland where the Penfeld river meets the bay, Brest's fifteenth-century **château** offers a tremendous panorama of both the busy port and the roadstead. Not quite as much of the castle survives as its impressive facade might suggest, though new buildings in the grounds house the French naval headquarters. Three still-standing medieval towers, however, hold Brest's portion of the **Musée National de la Marine**. Collections include ornate carved figureheads and models, as well as a German "pocket submarine" based here during World War II, and visitors can also stroll the parapets to enjoy the views.

## Tour Tanguy

June–Sept daily 10am–noon & 2–6pm; Oct–May Wed & Thurs 2–5pm, Sat & Sun 2–6pm · Free · ☎ 02 98 00 80 803

Facing the château from the lower right bank of the Penfeld river, and topped by a conical slate roof, the **Tour Tanguy** was constructed in the fourteenth century. Thanks to a remarkable collection of large-scale dioramas – all the work of one man, Jim Sévellec, and peopled with intricately modelled ceramic figures – it now serves as a **history museum**-cum-memorial of Brest before 1939.

## Océanopolis

Port de Plaisance du Moulin-Blanc · Hours vary: first half of Feb, mid-March to mid-April, early Sept to mid-Oct & Nov to mid-Dec Tues–Sun 10am–5pm; mid-Feb to mid-March, mid-April to mid-July, late Aug to early Sept, second half of Oct & Christmas/New Year daily 9.30am–6pm; mid-July to late Aug daily 9.30am–7pm; closed most of Jan · €21, ages 3–13 €13.35 · ☎ 02 98 34 40 40, ⓦ oceanopolis.com · Bus #3

A futuristic complex of **aquariums** and related attractions, **Océanopolis** sprawls a couple of kilometres east of the city centre. Its original white dome, now known as the **Brittany Pavilion**, focuses on the Breton littoral and Finistère's fishing industry, and holds all kinds of fish, seals, molluscs, seaweed and sea anemones. To that has been added a **Tropical Pavilion**, with a tankful of ferocious-looking sharks plus a myriad of rainbow-hued smaller fish that populate a highly convincing coral reef; a **Polar Pavilion**, complete with polar bears and penguins; and a **3-D cinema**. Everything's very high-tech, and very earnest, and it's possible to spend a whole entertaining day here.

## ARRIVAL AND DEPARTURE

BREST

**By plane** Brest's airport, at Guipavas 9km northeast, is served by flights from Birmingham and Southampton with Flybe, and also offers local connections to Ouessant.

**By train** Brest's *gare SNCF* is on place du 19ème RI at the bottom of av Clemenceau.

Destinations Le Mans (2 daily; 3hr 50min); Morlaix (20

daily; 40min); Paris-Montparnasse (7 TGVs daily; 4hr 20min); Quimper (14 daily; 1hr 15min); Rennes (11 daily; 2hr–2hr 30min).

**By bus** The *gare routière* stands shoulder-to-shoulder with the train station.

Destinations Brignogan (8 daily; 1hr); Camaret (1–3 daily; 1hr 10min); Le Conquet (8 daily; 45min); Le Faou (2 daily;

1hr); Quimper (5 daily; 1hr 15min); Roscoff (5 daily; 1hr 45min).

**By boat** As well as the sailings to Ouessant, in summer boats make the 25min crossing from Brest's Port de Commerce to Le Fret on the Crozon peninsula (April–Sept daily 2 sailings each way; €9.50 one-way; ☎07 78 37 03 23).

## INFORMATION

**Tourist office** 8 Av Clemenceau, facing place de la Liberté (July & Aug Mon–Sat 9.30am–7pm, Sun 9.30am–1.30pm; Sept–June Mon–Sat 9.30am–6pm; ☎02 98 44 24 96, ⓦ brest-metropole-tourisme.fr).

## ACCOMMODATION

★ **Abalys** 7 av Clemenceau ☎02 98 44 21 86, ⓦ abalys. com. Small but good-value accommodation in a spruce little hotel above a bar near the stations. All rooms have en-suite facilities, though the bathrooms can be tiny. **€50**

**Citôtel Centre Gare** 4 bd Gambetta ☎02 98 44 47 01, ⓦ hotelgare.com. Convenient, well-priced option very near the stations. Pay a little extra to get a magnificent view of the Rade de Brest from the upper storeys. Cheaper weekend tariffs, and buffet breakfast for €9. **€55**

**Continental** 41 rue Émile-Zola, place de la Tour d'Auvergne ☎02 98 80 50 40, ⓦ oceaniahotels.com.

Despite its dull concrete facade, this grand hotel has some fine Art Deco features, and is very popular with business travellers. Spotless rooms; several on the fourth floor have large balconies. Look for discounted weekend rates. **€85**

**Hostel Ethic Étapes** 5 rue Kerbriant, Port de Plaisance du Moulin-Blanc ☎02 98 41 90 41, ⓦ aj-brest.org. Brest's year-round hostel, set in a wooded park, is modern and clean, with beds in four-person dorms and inexpensive meals. Price includes breakfast. It's 3km east of the *gare SNCF*, by the beach and Océanopolis – take bus #3. **€20**

## EATING

As well as several low-priced places near the stations, Brest offers a wide assortment of restaurants. Rue Jean-Jaurès, climbing east from place de la Liberté, holds plenty of bistros and bars, while place Guérin to the north is the centre of the student-dominated *quartier* St-Martin.

★ **La Maison de l'Océan** 2 quai de la Douane ☎02 98 80 44 84, ⓦ restaurant-fruit-mer-brest.com. Blue-hued fish restaurant down by the port, with a terrace facing across to the island ferries. It serves wonderful seafood

on *menus* from €20.20 – which features a mixed shellfish assortment – to €46.50. Daily noon–2pm & 7–11pm.

**Le Ruffé** 1bis rue Yves-Collet ☎02 98 46 07 70, ⓦ le-ruffe.com. Unpretentious, very reliable restaurant near the tourist office, entirely indoors, which prides itself on tasty, traditional French seafood dishes, and an affordable wine list. Weekday lunches from €19, dinner *menus* from €23.90. Tues–Sat noon–2pm & 6–10pm, Sun noon–2pm.

# The Crozon peninsula

A craggy outcrop of land shaped like a long-robed giant, arms outstretched, the **Crozon peninsula** is the central feature of Finistère's jagged western coastline. Much the easiest way for cyclists and travellers relying on public transport to reach the peninsula from Brest is via the **ferries** to Le Fret (see above).

As you approach the Crozon peninsula, it's well worth making a slight detour to climb the hill of **Ménez-Hom** ("at the giant's feet") for a fabulous preview of the alternating land and water across the southern side of the peninsula out to the ocean.

## Crozon

The main town on the peninsula, **CROZON**, has a nice little stone-built core that serves as the commercial hub for the surrounding communities, and plays host to a large-scale **market** on alternate Wednesdays. It's also, unfortunately, a traffic hub, its one-way traffic system distributing tourists among the various resorts – and in any case it's set back from the sea – so it's more of a place to pass through than to linger in.

**6**

## Morgat

**MORGAT**, 1km downhill from Crozon, makes a more enticing base. It has a long crescent beach that ends in a pine slope, and a sheltered harbour full of pleasure boats on the short haul from England and Ireland. The main attractions are **boat trips** around the various headlands, such as the **Cap de la Chèvre** (which is a good clifftop walk if you'd rather make your own way) and to the **Grottes**.

### The Grottes

April–Sept daily, departure times depend on tides • €14 • ☎ 06 60 93 97 05, ⓦ sirenes.bzh

The most popular boat trip from Morgat is the 45-minute tour out to the **Grottes**. From these multicoloured caves in the cliffs, accessible only by sea but with steep "chimneys" up to the clifftops, saints are said to have emerged in bygone days to rescue the shipwrecked.

## Camaret

One of the loveliest seaside towns in all Brittany, the sheltered port of **CAMARET** nestles at the western tip of the peninsula. Its most prominent building is the pink-orange **château de Vauban**, standing at the end of the long jetty that runs parallel to the main town waterfront. Walled, moated, and accessible via a little gatehouse reached by means of a drawbridge, it was built in 1689 to guard the approaches to Brest; these days it guards no more than a motley assortment of decaying half-submerged fishing boats, abandoned to rot beside the jetty. A short walk away, around the port towards the protective jetty, the quai du Styvel holds a row of excellent hotels.

There are two beaches nearby – a small one to the north and another, larger and more attractive, in the low-lying (and rather marshy) Anse de Dinan.

### ARRIVAL AND DEPARTURE                        THE CROZON PENINSULA

**By ferry** In summer, ferries run from Camaret to the islands of Ouessant and Sein. Ferries also run from Brest to the village of Le Fret on the north coast of the peninsula.

### INFORMATION

#### CROZON
**Tourist office** Bd de Pralognan-la Vanoise, west of the centre in the *gare routière* (July & Aug Mon–Sat 9.30am–1pm & 2–7pm, Sun 10am–1pm; Sept–June Mon–Sat 9.30am–noon & 2–6pm; ☎ 02 98 27 07 92, ⓦ crozon-tourisme.bzh).

#### CAMARET
**Tourist office** 15 quai Kléber (July & Aug Mon–Sat 9.15am–12.30pm & 2–7pm, Sun 10am–12.30pm; Sept–June Mon–Sat 9.30am–noon & 2–6pm; ☎ 02 98 27 93 60, ⓦ camaretsurmer-tourisme.fr).

### ACCOMMODATION

#### MORGAT
**Camping Plage de Goulien** Kernavéno ☎ 06 08 43 49 32, ⓦ camping-crozon-laplagedegoulien.com. Three-star campsite, just across the headland from Morgat and a few steps from a huge sandy beach. Pitches amid the trees, with an on-site grocery. Closed mid-Sept to mid-April. **€19.60**

**Julia** 43 rue de Tréflez ☎ 02 98 27 05 89, ⓦ hoteljulia.fr. Neat, quiet hotel in an impressive villa set 300m back from the beach, with comfortable single to family-sized rooms, some of which have sea views. Closed Jan & Feb. **€86**

**Kastell Dinn** Hameau de Kerlouantec ☎ 02 98 27 26 40, ⓦ sejour-insolitebretagne.com. One-of-a-kind B&B, in a gorgeous village atop the headland, 2km west of Morgat.

One "room" consists of a boat equipped with a thatched roof; one's a stone cottage with an upturned boat for a roof; and another is a wheeled wooden caravan. There are also a couple of conventional rooms in a converted granary. Rates do not include breakfast, at €6 per person. **€60**

#### CAMARET
**Camping Le Grand Large** Lambézen ☎ 02 98 27 91 41, ⓦ campinglegrandlarge.com. Four-star campsite, 2km east of the port and 500m up from the nearest beach, but offering nicely secluded grass pitches, plus a pool with waterslide and great views. Closed Oct–March. **€26.28**

**Du Styvel** 2 quai du Styvel ☎ 02 98 27 92 74, ⓦ hotel-du-styvel.com. Friendly seaside hotel, with a decent

restaurant. Ten of the thirteen small but comfortable en-suite rooms have harbour-view balconies. Closed Jan. **€65**
★ **Vauban** 4 quai du Styvel ☎ 02 98 27 91 36, ⊕ hotel-vauban-camaret.fr. Plain but exceptionally hospitable and more than adequate quayside hotel, with a simple brasserie (closed Sun eve, all Mon & Tues lunch). Rooms at the front look right out across the bay. Rates remain constant year-round; the one family room does not have a sea view. **€65**

## EATING AND DRINKING

### MORGAT

**Saveurs et Marée** 52 bd de la Plage ☎ 02 98 26 23 18, ⊕ saveurs-et-maree.com. The pick of Morgat's beachfront seafood restaurants, with the bonus of outdoor seating. Dinner *menus* €19.50–31. April–Sept daily noon–2pm & 7–10pm; Oct–March Wed–Sun noon–2pm & 7–10pm.

### CAMARET

**Les Frères de la Côte** 11 quai Toudouze ☎ 06 78 75 57 54, ⊕ breiz-ile.fr. Camaret's finest seafood restaurant, a funky little place that's open to the harbour and serves fresh fish accompanied by sauces and spices influenced by the owner's Guadalupe origins. The €15 weekday lunch is a real bargain, while the €30 Menu Caraïbes offers a memorable dinner. Mon & Wed–Sun 12.15–1.30pm & 7.15–9.30pm.

# Southwest Finistère

Moving south of the Crozon peninsula, you soon enter the ancient kingdom of **Cornouaille**. The most direct route to the principal city, **Quimper**, leaves the sea behind and heads due south, passing close to the unchanged medieval village of **Locronan**. However, it's worth following the supremely isolated coastline instead, around the Baie de Douarnenez to the **Pointe du Raz**, the western tip of Finistère. With a few exceptions – most notably its land's-end capes – this stretch of coast has kept out of the tourist mainstream. Nowhere does that hold more true than on the remote **Île de Sein**.

## Locronan

The beautifully preserved medieval town of **LOCRONAN** stands a short way from the sea on the minor road that leads down from the Crozon peninsula. From 1469 through to the seventeenth century, it thrived on trading in woven "lin" (linen), supplying sails to the French, English and Spanish navies, and thereby accumulating a glorious ensemble of fine mansions. It was first rivalled by Vitré and Rennes, before suffering the "agony and ruin" so graphically described in its small **museum** (mid-April to mid-Sept Mon–Sat 10am–12.30pm & 1.30–6pm, Sun 2–7pm; €5; ☎ 02 98 51 80 80). Film directors love the town's sense of time warp, even if Roman Polanski, filming *Tess*, deemed it necessary to change all the porches, put new windows on the Renaissance houses, and bury the main square in mud to make it all look a bit more English.

Today Locronan prospers on tourism, but this commercialization shouldn't put you off making at least a passing visit, as the town itself is genuinely remarkable, centred around the focal **Église St-Ronan**. Be sure to take the time to walk down the hill of the **rue Moal**, to the lovely little stone chapel of Notre-Dame de Bonne Nouvelle.

## INFORMATION
LOCRONAN

**Tourist office** Alongside the museum (April–June & Sept Mon–Sat 10am–6pm, Sun 2–6pm; July & Aug Mon–Sat 10am–6pm, Sun 11am–1pm & 3–6pm; school hols otherwise Mon–Fri 10am–12.30pm & 1.30–5pm; ☎ 02 98 91 70 14, ⊕ www.locronan-tourisme.com).

## ACCOMMODATION

**Camping Locronan** Rue du Troménie ☎ 02 98 91 87 76, ⊕ camping-locronan.fr. Municipal campsite, in a very pleasant wooded position a few hundred metres uphill, with rental cabins as well as tent sites and a heated pool. Closed Oct to mid-April. **€19.52**
**Du Prieuré** 11 rue du Prieuré ☎ 02 98 91 70 89, ⊕ hotel-le-prieure.com. Locronan's one hotel, on the main approach street, is not particularly attractive in itself, but it's lovely and quiet when the day-trippers have gone home, and offers well-equipped rooms, including some split-level family suites. Its restaurant serves lunch from €15.50, dinner from €19. **€80**

**6**

## Douarnenez

Though it's still home to the largest fish canneries in Europe, the sheltered, historic port of **DOUARNENEZ** has been transformed in its entirety into a superb living museum.

### Port-Musée

Place de l'Enfer • Early April to June & mid-Sept to early Nov daily except Mon 10am–12.30pm & 2–6pm, July & Aug daily 10am–6pm • €7.50 • ☎ 02 98 92 65 20, ⓦ port-musee.org

**Port-Rhû**, on the west side of Douarnenez, has been designated as the **Port-Musée**. The whole waterfront is taken up with fishing and other vessels gathered from throughout northern Europe, several of which are open for visitors to roam through. Its centrepiece, the **Musée du Bateau** (Boat Museum) in place de l'Enfer, houses slightly smaller vessels, such as Gallic coracles and a Portugese *moliceiro*, with a strong emphasis on fishing and exhaustive descriptions of construction techniques.

### ARRIVAL AND INFORMATION DOUARNENEZ

**By bus** Buses to Douarnenez stop outside the tourist office. Destinations Audierne (8 daily; 30min); Locronan (July & Aug 2 daily; 20min); Pointe du Raz (July & Aug 1 daily; 50min); Quimper (10–12 daily; 35min).
**Tourist office** 1 rue du Dr-Mével (April–June, Sept &

Oct Mon–Sat 10am–12.30pm & 2–6pm, Sun 10.30am–12.30pm; July & Aug daily 10am–6.30pm; Nov–March Mon–Sat 10am–12.30pm & 2–5.30pm; ☎ 02 98 92 13 35, ⓦ douarnenez-tourisme.com).

### ACCOMMODATION AND EATING

**Le Bretagne** 23 rue Duguay-Trouin ☎ 02 98 92 30 44, ⓦ le-bretagne.fr. Welcoming, good-value hotel in the heart of town, offering bright rooms plus a hot tub and sauna. €58

**Le Bigorneau Amoureux** 2 bd Richepin ☎ 02 98 92 35 55, ⓦ le-bigorneau-amoureux.lafourchette.rest. Artfully casual beachfront restaurant, serving good seafood *menus* from €29, and blessed with a terrace that enjoys a fabulous view over the plage des Dames. Tues–Thurs & Sun noon–2pm, Fri & Sat noon–2pm & 7–9pm.

**Camping Croas-Men** 27bis rue du Croas-Men, Tréboul ☎ 02 98 74 00 18, ⓦ croas-men.com. Two-star campsite,

a short walk west of town close to the lovely Sables Blancs beach, and offering shaded pitches plus rental cabins and fresh-baked bread in summer. Closed Oct–March. €12.20

★ **Ty Mad** 3 rue St-Jean, Tréboul ☎ 02 98 74 00 53, ⓦ hoteltymad.com. Charming and very stylish seaside hotel, just up from the delightful little St-Jean beach. The spacious rooms have stripped-wood floors and exposed stone walls – only the upper storeys have sea views, and there's no lift – while the modern dining room (closed Tues) serves creative and unusual French cuisine, with *menus* from €19 at lunch, €39 for dinner. Closed mid-Nov to early March. €105

## The Baie des Trépassés

The **Baie des Trépassés** ("Bay of the Dead"), 30km west of Douarnenez just north of the Pointe du Raz, gets its grim name from the shipwrecked bodies that once washed up here. However, it's actually a very attractive spot; green meadows, too exposed to support trees, end abruptly on the low cliffs to either side; there's a huge expanse of flat sand (in fact little else at low tide); and out in the crashing waves surfers and windsurfers get thrillingly thrashed to within an inch of their lives. Beyond them, you can usually make out the white-painted houses along the harbour on the Île de Sein, while the various uninhabited rocks in between hold a veritable forest of lighthouses.

In total, less than half a dozen scattered buildings intrude upon the emptiness, including the two parts of a hotel, both with tremendous views.

### ACCOMMODATION BAIE DES TRÉPASSÉS

**De la Baie des Trépassés** Baie des Trépassés ☎ 02 98 70 61 34, ⓦ baiedestrepasses.com. A spectacular hideaway, set on the grass just behind the magnificent fine-sand beach. Plain, simply decorated rooms in all sizes

and shapes – the cheapest option lacks en-suite facilities, while several sleep three or four – and the restaurant serves wonderfully fresh seafood *menus* (€28.50–65). Closed mid-Nov to mid-Feb. €65

## Pointe du Raz

Daily: April–June & Sept 10.30am–6pm; July & Aug 10.30am–7pm; Oct 10.30am–5.30pm • Parking €6.50 cars, €4 motorcycles • ☎ 02 98 70 67 18, ⓦ pointeduraz.com

Thirty kilometres west of Douarnenez, the **Pointe du Raz** – the Land's End of both Finistère and France – is designated a "Grand Site National", and makes a magnificent spectacle, buffeted by wind and waves and peppered with deep gurgling fissures. It's quite a wild experience to walk to the end and back, but don't expect to have the place to yourself; with three million visitors every year, they've had to build a huge car park 1km short of the actual headland, alongside an information complex which serves as the starting point for regular guided tours. To get to the *pointe*, take the €1 *navette*, then walk the most direct route, along an undulating, arrow-straight track, or take a longer stroll along the footpath that skirts the top of the cliffs.

## Île de Sein

Of all the Breton islands, the tiny **Île de Sein**, just 8km out to sea off the tip of the Pointe du Raz, has to be the most extraordinary. It's hard to believe anyone could survive here; nowhere does the island rise more than 6m above the surrounding ocean, and for much of its 2.5km length it's barely broader than the breakwater wall of bricks that serves as its central spine.

In fact, however, Sein has been inhabited since prehistoric times, and was reputed to have been the very last refuge of the druids in Brittany. It also became famous during World War II, when its entire male population answered General de Gaulle's call to join him in exile in England. Today, more than three hundred islanders make their living from the sea, gathering rainwater and seaweed, and fishing for scallops, lobster and crayfish.

Never mind cars, not even bicycles are permitted on Sein. Depending on the tide, boats pull in at one or other of the two adjoining harbours that constitute Sein's one tight-knit village, in front of which a little beach appears at low tide. There is a **museum** of local history here (daily: May, June & Sept 10.30am–noon & 2–4pm; July & Aug 9am–6pm; €4), packed with black-and-white photos and press clippings, and displaying a long list of shipwrecks from 1476 onwards.

The most popular activity for visitors, however, is to take a bracing walk, preferably to the far end of the island, from where you can see the **Phare Ar-men** lighthouse, peeking out of the waves 12km further west into the Atlantic.

### ARRIVAL AND DEPARTURE        ÎLE DE SEIN

**By boat** Boats to Sein depart from Ste-Evette beach, just outside Audierne; the crossing takes around 1hr. Services are operated by Penn Ar Bed (daily: mid-July to late Aug 3 daily, first usually at 8.45am; late Aug to mid-July 1–2 daily, first usually at 9.30am; ☎ 02 98 70 70 70, ⓦ pennarbed.fr).

On Sun from late June to early Sept, Penn Ar Bed also run trips to Sein from Brest (departs 8.40am; 1hr 30min) via Camaret (9.40am; 1hr), for the same round-trip fare: July–Sept €34.90, Oct–May €27.90.

### ACCOMMODATION AND EATING

★ **D'Armen** 32 rue Fernand-Crouton ☎ 02 98 70 90 77, ⓦ hotel-restaurant-d-armen-ile-de-sein.fr. The nicer of Sein's two good hotels is the very last building as you walk west out of town, which makes it the last restaurant in Europe. All of its simple but lovely rooms face the sea, and the excellent €25 dinner *menu* features mussels in cider,

skate, and delicious home-baked bread. Closed early Nov to mid-Feb. €58

**Trois Dauphins** 16 quai des Paimpolais ☎ 02 98 70 92 09. Seven cosy and attractive wood-panelled rooms, not all en suite or with sea views, above a bar in the middle of the port. €48

# Quimper

Capital of the ancient diocese, kingdom and later duchy of Cornouaille, **QUIMPER** is the oldest city in Brittany. Its first bishop, St Corentin, is said to have come with

**6**

the first Bretons across the English Channel at some point between the fourth and seventh centuries.

Still "the charming little place" known to Flaubert, Quimper takes at most half an hour to cross on foot. Though relaxed, it's active enough to have the bars and atmosphere to make it worth going out **café-crawling**. The word "kemper" denotes the junction of the two rivers, the Steir and the Odet, around which lie the cobbled streets (now mainly pedestrianized) of the **medieval quarter**. To the east of the Gothic **cathedral**, towering over place St-Corentin, ancient half-timbered buildings hold lively shops and cafés.

With no great pressure to rush around monuments or museums, the most enjoyable option may be to take a **boat** and drift down the Odet, "the prettiest river in France", to the open sea at Bénodet. Overlooking all is tree-covered **Mont Frugy**; climb to its 87m peak for good views over the city.

## Cathédrale St-Corentin

Quimper's focal point, the enormous **Cathédrale St-Corentin**, is the most complete Gothic cathedral in Brittany, though its Neo-Gothic spires date from 1856. When the nave was being added to the old chancel in the fifteenth century, the extension would either have hit existing buildings or the swampy edge of the then-unchannelled river. So the nave was placed at a slight angle – a peculiarity which, once noticed, makes it hard to concentrate on the other Gothic splendours within. The exterior, however, gives no hint of the deviation, with King Gradlon mounted in perfect symmetry between the spires.

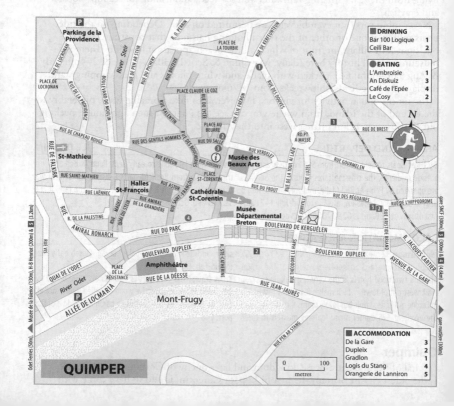

**QUIMPER**

DRINKING
Bar 100 Logique   1
Ceili Bar   2

EATING
L'Ambroisie   1
An Diskuiz   3
Café de l'Épée   4
Le Cosy   2

ACCOMMODATION
De la Gare   3
Dupleix   2
Gradlon   1
Logis du Stang   4
Orangerie de Lanniron   5

## Musée Départemental Breton

1 rue du roi Gradlon • Mid-June to mid-Sept daily 10am–7pm; mid-Sept to mid-June Tues–Fri 9.30am–5.30pm, Sat & Sun 2–5.30pm • €5
• ☎ 02 98 95 21 60, ⓦ musee-breton.finistere.fr

The quirky-looking Bishop's Palace, alongside Quimper's cathedral, holds the
beautifully laid-out **Musée Départemental Breton**. Collections start with Bronze Age
spear- and axe-heads and prehistoric golden jewellery, move rapidly through Roman
and medieval statues, and culminate with a fascinating assortment of Breton oddments
and *objets d'art*.

## Musée des Beaux-Arts

40 place St-Corentin • April–June, Sept & Oct daily except Tues 9.30am–noon & 2–6pm; July & Aug daily 10am–6pm; Nov–March Mon &
Wed–Sat 9.30am–noon & 2–5.30pm, Sun 2–5.30pm • €5 • ☎ 02 98 95 45 20, ⓦ mbaq.fr

Quimper's compelling **Musée des Beaux-Arts** stands across the main square
immediately north of the cathedral. Equipped by an impressive architectural
transformation with new floors and suspended walkways, it focuses on an amazing
assemblage of drawings by Max Jacob – who was born in Quimper – and his
contemporaries. Look out also for the museum's solitary work by Gauguin, a goose he
painted on the door of Marie Henry's inn in Pont-Aven itself (see page 348).

## Musée de la Faïence

14 rue Jean-Baptiste Bousquet • Mid-April to late Sept Mon–Sat 10am–6pm • €5, €7 with the H-B Henriot atelier • ☎ 02 98 90 12 72,
ⓦ musee-faience-quimper.com

Visiting Quimper, it is impossible to ignore the local ceramic tradition of **faïence**, or
tin-glazed earthenware. Its manufacture started here in the seventeenth century, and
boomed from around 1875, when the coming of the railways brought Brittany's first
influx of tourists, and some unknown artisan hit on the idea of painting ceramic ware
with naive "folk" designs. The **Musée de la Faïence**, beside the river in the southwest
corner of town, traces the history of the tradition.

## H-B Henriot

Rue Haute • Tours April Tues & Fri 2.30pm & 4pm; May & June Mon–Fri 11am, 2.30pm, 4pm & 5pm; July & Aug Mon–Sat 10.30am,
11.30am, 2pm, 3pm, 4pm & 5pm; Sept Mon–Fri 11am, 2.30pm, 4pm • €5, or €7 with the Musée de la Faïence • ☎ 02 98 90 09 36,
ⓦ henriot-quimper.com

Right next door to the Musée de la Faïence, the major atelier **H-B Henriot** continues to
produce hand-painted pottery, which it sells on site, and also offers half-hour tours that
explain the entire process, from design through firing to completion.

### ARRIVAL AND DEPARTURE

QUIMPER

**By train** Quimper's *gare SNCF* is on av de la Gare 1km east
of the centre, on bus route #6.

Destinations Brest (14 daily; 1hr 15min); Lorient (18 daily;
35min); Nantes (6 daily; 2hr 40min); Paris-Montparnasse (8
TGVs daily; 3hr 40min); Vannes (12 daily; 1hr 15min).

**By bus** To reach the coast on public transport, buses are
your only option (☎ 02 98 90 68 40, ⓦ cat29.fr). The *gare*

*routière* is beside the train station.

Destinations Audierne (10–12 daily; 1hr 15min); Bénodet
(12 daily; 50min); Brest (5 daily; 1hr 15min); Camaret (4–8
daily; 1hr 30min); Concarneau (8 daily; 40min); Douarnenez
(10–12 daily; 45min); Locronan (8–12 daily; 30min);
Morlaix (1 daily; 1hr 45min); Roscoff (1 daily; 2hr 20min).

### INFORMATION AND TOURS

**Tourist office** 8 rue Élie-Fréron (April & May Mon–Sat
9.30am–6.30pm; June & Sept Mon–Sat 9.30am–6.30pm,
Sun 2–5pm; July & Aug Mon–Sat 9am–7pm, Sun 10am–
1pm & 3–6pm; Oct–March Mon–Sat 9.30am–12.30pm &
1.30–6pm; ☎ 02 98 53 04 05, ⓦ quimper-tourisme.com).

**Tours** The tourist office arranges an intricate programme of
walking tours. In addition, between April and September,

Vedettes de l'Odet cruise down the Odet from Quimper to
Bénodet (1–3 daily departures, except Sun in July & Aug;
1hr 15min each way; €28 return, higher rates for gourmet
cruises including meals; ☎ 02 98 57 00 58, ⓦ vedettes-
odet.com). Schedules and precise departure points vary
with the tide and season; the tourist office sells tickets.

**6**

---

## THE FESTIVALS OF QUIMPER

Having originated in 1923, Quimper's **Festival de Cornouaille** is still going from strength to strength. This great jamboree of Breton music, costumes, theatre and dance is held in the week before the last Sunday in July, attracting guest performers from the other Celtic countries and a scattering of other, sometimes highly unusual, ethnic-cultural ensembles. The whole thing culminates in an incredible Sunday parade through town. The official programme appears in July; pick up provisional details in advance from the tourist office or at ⓦfestival-cornouaille.bzh.

Not so widely known are the **Semaines Musicales**, which stretch over two weekends in the middle of August (ⓦsemaines-musicales.bzh). Some events take place in the cathedral, others in the courtyard of the departmental museum. The music is predominantly classical, favouring French composers.

---

## ACCOMMODATION

**De la Gare** 17 av de la Gare ☎02 98 90 00 81, ⓦhoteldelagarequimper.com. Colourful and great-value en-suite rooms arranged around a floral patio and above a no-nonsense snack bar, across from the station. €69

**Dupleix** 34 bd Dupleix ☎02 98 90 53 35, ⓦhotel-dupleix.com. Modern concrete hotel, not very attractive from the outside but airy and bright within, in a good central location overlooking the Odet, with fine views across the river to the cathedral. Some rooms have balconies. The free private garage is a major advantage in this part of town. €92

**Gradlon** 30 rue de Brest ☎02 98 95 04 39, ⓦhotel-gradlon.fr. This quiet and exceptionally friendly hotel, a short walk north from the centre, makes an ideal base, and has a pleasant garden. Tastefully decorated rooms, plus a good bar, with an open fire in winter. €98

★ **Logis du Stang** 41 Allée du Stang-Youen ☎02 98 52 00 55, ⓦwww.logis-du-stang.com. Delightful B&B, 5km southeast in a nineteenth-century house, with four well-furnished en-suite rooms and a hortensia-filled garden. €92

**Orangerie de Lanniron** 87 Allée de Lanniron ☎98 90 62 02, ⓦcamping-lanniron.com. Five-star campsite, 4km south towards Bénodet in the grounds of a château, with its own aquapark, restaurant and tennis court, and also chalets and stone cottages for rent. Closed mid-Sept to mid-May. €18.55

---

## EATING AND DRINKING

### RESTAURANTS

**L'Ambroisie** 49 rue Élie-Fréron ☎02 98 95 00 02, ⓦambroisie-quimper.com. Upmarket French restaurant a short climb north from the cathedral, featuring fine seafood (including tuna) and meat dishes on *menus* from €25 for lunch on weekday, €48–65 for dinner. Tues & Thurs–Sat 12.15–1.30pm & 7.15–9pm, Wed 12.15–1.30pm.

**An Diskuiz** 12 rue Élie-Fréron ☎02 98 95 55 70. The pick of the crêperies in a city that's renowned for its pancakes, with outdoor seating, and located just up from the cathedral; the name means "place to rest". Crêpes and wholewheat *galettes* range €4–10. July & Aug Mon, Tues & Thurs–Sat 11.45am–2.15pm & 6.45–10pm, Wed 11.45am–2.15pm; Sept–March Mon & Thurs–Sun 11.45am–2.15pm & 6.45–10pm.

**Café de l'Épée** 14 rue du Parc ☎02 98 95 28 97, ⓦcafedelepee.fr. A glorious Art Nouveau brasserie when Max Jacob brought Picasso here, this Quimper institution, which has outdoor seating facing the river, has lost a certain charm since being modernized, but it still serves excellent food, with assorted fish and meat dishes for €15–25, a two-course lunch *formule* at €15.50, and dinner *menus* for €24–39 – and you can get a meal at 11pm, rare indeed for Brittany. Daily 10.30am–midnight.

**Le Cosy** 2 rue du Sallé ☎02 98 95 23 65. Pretty bistro just north of the cathedral, where the menu proudly insists they serve "pas de crêpes, pas de frites"; instead savoury *tartines* or daily *plats* cost €14–21, and set *menus* cost €17.50 for lunch, €33 for dinner. Tues–Sat noon–2pm & 7–9pm.

### BARS

**Bar 100 Logique** 9 rue des Réguaires ☎02 98 95 44 69, ⓦle100logiquequimper.skyrock.com. Classy little bar that's proud of its status as Quimper's number one gay and lesbian hangout. Tues–Sun 7pm–1am.

**Ceili Pub** 4 rue Aristide- Briand ☎02 98 95 17 61. This lively and convivial bar is the place to go for all things Breton: a great big ramshackle old place, it offers beer and opinionated conversation, plus live traditional Celtic bands and occasionally jazz. Mon–Sat 11am–1am, Sun 5pm–1am.

---

# South from Quimper

South of Quimper, no longer restrained into a narrow canalized channel, the Odet first broadens and then twists through successive tight corners to reach the sea.

The southern coast here, and especially the string of wonderful **beaches** between the family-friendly resort of **Bénodet** and **La Forêt-Fouesnant**, is the most popular tourist destination in Finistère. From Bénodet or Fouesnant, there's the opportunity to jump aboard a commercial boat and visit the lovely island of **St-Nicolas**, part of the Îles Glénan. A little further east, the walled, sea-circled old town of **Concarneau** makes a perfect day-trip destination, though a prettier place to spend a night or two would be the flowery village of **Pont-Aven**, immortalized by Paul Gauguin, slightly further east.

**6**

## Bénodet and around

**BÉNODET**, at the mouth of the Odet, is a much-developed resort that comes alive in summer, when its many hotels and campsites are filled with holidaying families. The long, sheltered beach on its ocean side, perfect for children, is packed day after day.

East of Bénodet, the coast is rocky and repeatedly cut by deep valleys. Each seems to hold another little village, and there are plenty of further seafront communities tucked into the nearby coastal coves. **Fouesnant** is the main commercial centre here, while **La Forêt-Fouesnant**, clustered along the waterfront 12km out from Bénodet, at the foot of a hill so steep that caravans are banned from even approaching, is known for its beaches and cider. For a quiet seaside stay, the sleepy beach town of **Cap-Coz**, languidly stretched along a sandspit facing Concarneau, is ideal.

| **ACCOMMODATION AND EATING** | **BÉNODET AND AROUND** |
| --- | --- |

**Armoric** 3 rue Penfoul, Bénodet ☎02 98 57 04 03, ⓦ www.armoric-benodet.com. Peaceful, family-run *Logis de France*, set in pleasant gardens near the tourist office and 800m up from the sea. Comfortable, if somewhat old-fashioned, carpeted rooms, plus a heated swimming pool, and a restaurant serving good-value dinner *menus* at €20 and €27. **€87**

**Belle Vue** 30 descente de Bellevue, Cap-Coz, Fouesnant ☎02 98 56 00 33, ⓦ hotel-belle-vue.com. Classic seaside hotel, poised at the west end of a lovely long beach. Owned by the same family for almost a century, but energetically maintained and modernised, it offers large and very pleasant sea-view bedrooms and a good-value restaurant. Closed Nov–Feb. **€96**

★ **Bot Conan Lodge** Hent Lantecost, Beg-Meil ☎06 11 05 19 43, ⓦ www.botconan.com. Brittany's premier glamping site, using African-style safari tents, permanently fixed on wooden decks. The setting is glorious, in rural meadows that roll down to an exquisite little beach, while the tents themselves hold double beds plus separate kitchens and outdoor seating areas. For the best rates, come in May, June or Sept. Seven-day minimum stay in high season. Closed late Sept to April. **€140**

**Camping du Letty** Chemin de Creisanguer ☎02 98 57 04 69, ⓦ campingduletty.com. Large, very well-equipped four-star campsite, southeast of the centre alongside the plage du Letty, with an aquapark, gym, squash and tennis courts, and supermarket/deli. Closed early Sept to mid-June. **€39**

**Du Port** 4 corniche de la Cale, la Forêt-Fouesnant ☎02 98 56 97 33, ⓦ hotelduport.fr. Peaceful, smart hotel a short walk from the port, with seven very reasonably priced and brightly furnished rooms and an attractive garden-view restaurant (closed Sun & Mon). **€75**

★ **Villa Tri Men** 16 rue du Phare, Ste-Marine ☎02 98 51 94 94, ⓦ www.trimen.fr. Gorgeous hotel, set on stately lawns above the jetty in Ste-Marine, reached by a 5min river ferry from Bénodet. With their wooden floors and light decor, the spacious rooms resemble a New England inn; the best have two balconies, and there are suites in separate cottages. The dining room (mid-April to Oct; dinner only in July & Aug, closed Mon & Sun in low season) is excellent, as it should be with *menus* costing from €50. **€172**

## Îles Glénan

The **Îles Glénan** are a cluster of tiny islands, set in a shallow lagoon that's renowned for its marvellous turquoise waters, 16km off the coast of Finistère. If you're lucky enough to own a yacht, or can borrow one, you'll find secluded coves all around the archipelago just waiting to be explored. Commercial day-trips, though, most of which leave from Bénodet or Forêt-Fouesnant, only go to the largest islet, **St-Nicolas**.

Once you're there, the big attraction is a luscious white-sand beach, which is technically a tombolo, in that it's a sandspit connecting St-Nicolas to another even tinier outcrop. You can walk around the entire island in under half an hour, along

6

boardwalks laid down to protect plants such as the endemic *narcisse de Glénan*, which carpets the central meadow with tiny white blossoms in April and May.

## ARRIVAL AND INFORMATION ÎLES GLÉNAN

### BY FERRY

Excursions to St-Nicolas are run by Vedettes de l'Odet (€45 return; ☎02 98 57 00 58, ⓦvedettes-odet.com). They set from Beg-Meil in April, July & Aug; from Bénodet between

April and mid-Sept; from Concarneau mid-April to mid-Sept; and from La Forêt-Fouesnant and Loctudy in July & Aug. Schedules change frequently; check the website for details.

## ACCOMMODATION AND EATING

**Sextant** St-Nicolas ☎02 98 50 68 88, ⓦsextant-glenan.org. Simple, modern bungalow that serves as a "gîte de mer", and has five dorms with six beds in each, available for a maximum stay of three nights per person. With no food or even drinking water available, guests have to bring all they plan to consume from the mainland. Closed Oct–March. **€16.60**

**Les Viviers** St-Nicolas ☎02 98 50 68 90, ⓦrestaurant lesviviers.wixsite.com. Advance reservations, made by 11am for lunch or 6pm for dinner, are compulsory if you want to eat at this family-run restaurant, at the ferry landing. Its €19 *menu* features fish soup followed by either crab or the day's fresh catch, but you can usually get lobster à la carte. Mid-April to mid-Sept daily, lunch 1pm, dinner 8pm.

## Concarneau

Although **CONCARNEAU**, 25km southeast of Quimper, is the third most important fishing port in France, it does a reasonable job of passing itself off as a holiday resort. Its greatest asset is its small and very well fortified **old city**, located just a few metres out in the rivermouth on an irregular rocky island.

### The ville close

Concarneau's walled core, the **ville close**, is a real delight. Its ramparts were completed by Vauban in the seventeenth century, but the island itself had been inhabited for at least a thousand years before that. The flowers that earn Concarneau its title of *ville fleurie* are most in evidence inside the walls, where climbing roses and clematis swarm all over the giftshops, restaurants and crêperies. Walk the central pedestrianized street to the far end, and you can pass through a gateway to the shoreline to watch the fishing boats go by. The best views of all come from the promenade on top of the **ramparts**; you can't make a complete circuit of the walls, but you can climb up for short stretches.

### Musée de la Pêche

3 rue Vauban • July & Aug daily 10am–7pm; April–June, Sept & Oct daily except Mon 10am–6pm; Feb, March, Nov & Dec daily except Mon 2–5.30pm • €5 • ☎02 98 97 10 20, ⓦmusee-peche.fr

By exploring the history of fishing all over the world, the **Musée de la Pêche**, in the *ville close*, provides an insight into the traditional life Concarneau shared with so many other Breton ports. Oddities include a three-thousand-year-old anchor from Crete, the swords of swordfish and the saws of sawfish, and a genuine trawler, moored behind the museum.

## ARRIVAL AND INFORMATION CONCARNEAU

**By bus** While there's no rail service to Concarneau, SNCF buses connect it with Quimper (8 daily; 40min), from the quai d'Aiguillon.

**Tourist office** Quai d'Aiguillon, just outside the *ville*

*close* (April–June & Sept Mon–Sat 9am–6.30pm, Sun 10am–1pm; July & Aug daily 9am–-7pm; Oct–March Mon–Sat 9am–12.30pm & 2–6pm; ☎02 98 97 01 44, ⓦtourismeconcarneau.fr).

## ACCOMMODATION

**Auberge de Jeunesse** Quai de la Croix ☎02 98 97 03 47, ⓦaj-concarneau.org. Budget travellers will love this very central hostel, which enjoys magnificent ocean views

just around the south tip of the headland from the town centre, and has a windsurfing shop nearby. Rates include breakfast; dinner available for €11. **€18**

**De France et d'Europe** 9 av de la Gare ☎ 02 98 97 00 64, ⓦ www.hotel-france-europe.com. Bright, modernized and very central hotel near the main bus stop, which, as well as well-furnished rooms, offers €12 buffet breakfasts, a garden terrace and a small gym. €95

**Des Halles** Rue Charles-Linement, place de l'Hôtel-de-Ville ☎ 02 98 97 11 41, ⓦ hoteldeshalles.com. Spruce, pastel-orange hotel near the fish market, across from the entrance to the *ville close*, offering light, recently refreshed rooms, with good showers, at reasonable rates. €77

★ **Ker Moor** 37 rue des Sables-Blancs ☎ 02 98 97 02 96, ⓦ hotel-kermor.com. Classic, beautifully restored seafront hotel, nautically themed throughout, on the beach 2km west of town. All rooms have sea views — some via portholes — but you can pay extra for a balcony. €114

★ **Prés Verts** ☎ 02 98 97 09 74, ⓦ presverts.com. This spacious, well-shaded campsite spreads through green fields at Kernous Plage at the far end of Sables-Blancs beach; facilities include pool and crazy golf. Closed Oct–April. €22.40

## EATING AND DRINKING

**Le Bélem** 15 av du Dr-Nicolas ☎ 02 30 97 03 42, ⓦ lebelemrestaurant.fr. Pretty little restaurant, near the south end of the quayside on the mainland, serving mussels from around €11 and good seafood *menus* from €29. Mon, Tues, Fri & Sat noon–1.30pm & 7–9.15pm; Thurs & Sun noon–1.30pm.

**La Coquille** 1 quai de Moros ☎ 02 98 97 08 52, ⓦ lacoquille-concarneau.com. Sophisticated French

cuisine served away from the crowds but with views of the *ville close* from a quayside terrace across the river, with a bar-bistro as well as more formal dining. The *plat du jour* costs €10, and a three-course lunch €20, while dinner *menus* range €32–€48. Tues & Thurs–Sat noon–2pm & 7–9.30pm, Wed & Sun noon–2pm.

**Crêperie des Remparts** 31 rue Théophile-Luarn ☎ 02 98 50 65 66. Slightly off the beaten track behind the main

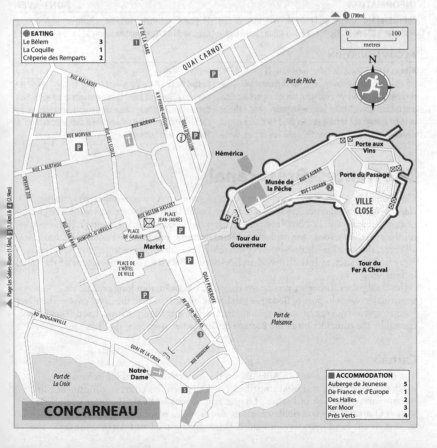

CONCARNEAU

**6**

street in the walled city, this place serves tasty, inexpensive crêpes, either indoors or on a nice terrace. There's also an appealing €16 lunch *menu*. Daily noon–2pm & 6–9.30pm; low season closed Wed.

## Pont-Aven

**PONT-AVEN**, 14km east of Concarneau, is a delightful little port that holds a prominent place in art history. **Paul Gauguin** came here to paint during the 1880s, before he left for Tahiti, and inspired the **Pont-Aven School** of artists, including Émile Bernard. Despite this, the town has no permanent collection of his work, though the spanking new, central **Musée de Pont-Aven** (Feb, March, Nov & Dec daily except Mon 2–5.30pm; April–June, Sept & Oct daily except Mon 10am–6pm; July & Aug daily 10am–7pm; €8; ☎02 98 06 13 43, ⓦmuseepontaven.fr) stages temporary exhibitions devoted to different aspects and influences of the school. Private galleries abound, though few show much connection with Pont-Aven's own traditions.

Gauguin aside, Pont-Aven is pleasant in its own right. Just upstream of the little granite bridge at the heart of town, the **promenade Xavier-Grall** crisscrosses the tiny river on landscaped walkways, offering glimpses of the backs of venerable mansions, dripping with ivy, and a little "chaos" of rocks in the stream itself. A longer walk – allow an hour – leads into the romantically named **Bois d'Amour**, wooded gardens that have long provided inspiration to painters, poets and musicians.

### INFORMATION                                                                 PONT-AVEN

**Tourist office** 5 place de l'Hôtel-de-Ville (July & Aug Mon–Sat 9.30am–12.45pm & 2.30–6.45pm, Sun 10am– 12.45pm; Sept–June Mon–Sat 9.30am–noon & 2–6pm; ☎02 98 06 04 70, ⓦpontaven.com).

### ACCOMMODATION

**Ajoncs d'Or** 1 place de l'Hôtel-de-Ville ☎02 98 06 02 06, ⓦajoncsdor-pontaven.com. The bedrooms inside this very central hotel are very ordinary, but it's a great location, and the restaurant (closed Sun eve) is pretty good, offering outdoor seating and serving *moules frites* for €12, a decent weekday lunch or dinner for €22, and full dinner *menus* from €33. **€70**

**Castel Braz** 12 rue du Bois d'Amour ☎02 98 06 07 81, ⓦwww.castelbraz.com. Lovely and very good-value B&B, in a charming old townhouse with peaceful gardens, where each room is decorated to a different theme from "Jazz" to "Asia". No credit cards. **€76**

# The Nantes–Brest canal

Completed in 1836, the meandering chain of waterways known collectively as the **Nantes–Brest canal** connects Finistère to the Loire. Interweaving rivers with stretches of canal, it was built at Napoleon's instigation to bypass the belligerent English fleets off the coast. As a focus for exploring **inland Brittany**, whether by barge, bike, foot, or all three, the canal is ideal. Not every stretch is accessible, but detours can be made away from it, such as into the wild and desolate **Monts d'Arrée** to the north of the canal in Finistère.

The canal passes through riverside towns, such as **Josselin**, that long predate its construction; the old port of **Redon**, a patchwork of water, where the canal crosses the River Vilaine; and a sequence of scenic splendours, including the long, narrow **Lac de Guerlédan**, created by the construction of the **Barrage de Guerlédan**, near Mur-de-Bretagne.

## Carhaix

The sizeable market town of **CARHAIX**, on the eastern frontier of Finistère 50km southeast of Morlaix and 60km northeast of Quimper, has come to prominence in recent years as the host of France's biggest annual **rock festival**. The massive four-day **Vieilles Charrues** (ⓦwww.vieillescharrues.asso.fr) takes place during the third weekend of July; recent headliners have included Bruce Springsteen and Arctic Monkeys. The most interesting building in town, meanwhile is the granite Renaissance **Maison du Sénéchal**, meanwhile, is on rue Brizeux, which houses the tourist office.

## Huelgoat and its forest

**HUELGOAT**, next to its own small **lake** halfway between Morlaix and Carhaix on the minor road D769, makes a pleasant overnight stop. Spreading north and east from the village, the **Forêt de Huelgoat** is a landscape of trees, giant boulders and waterfalls tangled together in primeval chaos. Various paths lead into the depths of the woods, allowing for long walks amid spectacularly wild scenery.

## Le Lac de Guerlédan

For the 15km between Gouarec, 30km east of Carhaix, and Mur-de-Bretagne, the N164 skirts the edge of **Quénécan Forest**, within which lies the artificial **Lac de Guerlédan** created when the dam of the same name was completed in 1928. It's a beautiful stretch of river, peaceful enough despite the summer influx of campers and caravans.

Just off the N164 near the village of **ST-GELVEN**, 5km east of Gouarec, the beautiful **Abbaye de Bon-Repos** nestles beside the water at the end of an avenue of ancient trees. This twelfth-century Cistercian abbey was largely destroyed during the French Revolution, but its ruins are open to visitors (April–June, Sept & Oct Mon–Fri 10am–noon & 2–6pm, Sun 2–6pm, closed Sat; July & Aug daily 10am–7pm; €5; ☎02 96 24 82 20; ⓦbon-repos.com), and play host to **son et lumière** spectacles on the first two weekends in August (€21).

From just west of **CAUREL**, 7km east of St-Gelven, the brief loop of the D111 leads to tiny sandy beaches. **MÛR-DE-BRETAGNE**, set back from the eastern end of the lake, is a lively town with a wide and colourful pedestrianized zone around its church.

## Josselin

The historic riverside town of **JOSSELIN** is full of medieval splendours. Its gargoyle-studded **basilica**, Notre-Dame-du-Roncier – the focus of an important *pardon* each September 8 – is ringed by twisted streets of half-timbered houses. The major attraction for visitors, however, is the **château**, looming high over the Oust.

### Château de Rohan

Early April to mid-July & Sept daily 2–6pm; mid-July to Aug daily 11am–6pm; Oct Sat, Sun & hols 2–5.30pm • Tours €9, musée €8; combined ticket €14.80 • ☎02 97 22 36 45, ⓦ chateaudejosselin.com

The three Rapunzel towers of the **Château de Rohan**, embedded in a vast sheet of stone above the water, are the most impressive sight along the Nantes–Brest canal. They now serve as a facade for the remnants of the much older castle behind, built by Olivier de Clisson in 1370, the original riverfront towers of which were demolished by Cardinal Richelieu in 1629 as punishment for Henri de Rohan's leadership of the Huguenots. It's still owned by the Rohan family, which used to own a third of Brittany. Although tours of the castle's oppressively formal apartments are not very compelling, the duchess's collection of ancient **dolls**, housed in the **Musée des Poupées** behind, is something special.

## Redon

Situated at the junction not only of the rivers Oust and Vilaine and the canal, but also of the train lines to Rennes, Vannes and Nantes, and of six major roads into the bargain, **REDON** is not easy to avoid. And you shouldn't try to, either. A wonderful mess of water and locks, it's a town with history, charm and life.

Until World War I, Redon was the seaport for Rennes. Its industrial docks – or what remains of them – are therefore on the Vilaine, while the canal remains almost totally rural. Shipowners' houses from the seventeenth and eighteenth centuries can be seen along quai Jean-Bart by the *bassin* and quai Duguay-Truin next to the river. A rusted wrought-iron workbridge still crosses the river, but the main users of the port now are cruise ships heading down to La Roche-Bernard.

## Église St-Sauveur

Redon's **Église St-Sauveur**, founded in 832 by St Conwoion, remains its most prominent church. Its unique four-storeyed Romanesque belfry is squat, almost obscured by later roofs and the high choir, and best seen from the adjacent cloisters; the Gothic tower was entirely separated from the main building by a fire. In the crypt, you'll find the tomb of the judge who tried the legendary Bluebeard – Joan of Arc's friend, Gilles de Rais.

| INFORMATION | THE NANTES–BREST CANAL |
| --- | --- |

### CARHAIX

**Tourist office** Rue Brizeux (June & Sept Mon–Sat 9.30am–12.30pm & 2–5.30pm; July & Aug Mon–Sat 9.30am–12.30pm & 2–6.30pm, Sun 10am–1pm; Oct–May Mon–Wed, Fri & Sat 10am–noon & 2–5.30pm, Thurs 2–5.30pm; ☎02 98 93 04 42, ⓦcarhaixpohertourisme.bzh).

### JOSSELIN

**Tourist office** 21 rue Olivier-de-Clisson (April–June & Sept Mon 1.30–5.30pm, Tues–Sat 10am–noon & 1.30–5.30pm; July & Aug daily 10am–6pm; Oct–March Mon 1.30–5.30pm, Tues, Wed & Fri 10am–noon & 1.30–5.30pm, Sat 10am–noon; ☎02 97 22 36 43, ⓦjosselin-tourisme.com).

### REDON

**Tourist office** Place de la République (July & Aug Mon–Sat 9.30am–1pm & 2–6.30pm, Sun 10am–12.30pm & 3.30–5.30pm; Sept–June Mon & Wed–Fri 9.30am–noon & 2–6pm, Tues 2–6pm, Sat 10am–12.30pm & 2–5pm; ☎02 99 71 06 04, ⓦtourisme-pays-redon.com).

## ACCOMMODATION AND EATING

### CARHAIX

**Noz Vad** 12 bd de la République ☎02 98 99 12 12, ⓦnozvad.bzh. This very central hotel, near the church, has en-suite rooms, ranging from tiny, plain "eco" rooms via plush "prestige" options to large family suites. There's a bar but no restaurant, and it also hosts live concerts in spring, plus exhibitions of art, sculpture and photography. Closed for 10 days in mid-Aug. **€51**

### HUELGOAT

**Camping du Lac** Le Fao ☎09 83 57 28 38, ⓦhuelgoat-camping.com. Two-star municipal campsite, in a gorgeous forested spot beside the lake, 800m from central Huelgoat towards Brest. Free tennis on the local courts. Closed Sept–June. **€13.80**
**Du Lac** 9 rue du Général-de-Gaulle ☎02 98 99 71 14, ⓦhoteldulac-huelgoat.com. Huelgoat's largest hotel faces the lake from across the road. While the rooms are nothing fancy, they're fine for the price, and there's both a bistro that serves hearty local food on a €29 *menu*, and a more casual pizzeria. **€75**
**Laura's Chambres d'Hôtes** 2 Impasse des Cendres ☎02 98 99 91 62. Very welcoming and good-value B&B, at the northern end of the village centre, offering six plain rooms with en-suite facilities, including some family-sized suites. **€60**

### JOSSELIN

**Camping Domaine de Kerelly** Bas de la Lande, Guégon ☎02 97 22 22 20, ⓦcamping-josselin.com. Very pleasant little three-star campsite, right beside the river, a 30min walk west from the castle, with a mini-golf course and simple rental chalets, as well as pitches. Closed Oct–March. **€18**
★ **Du Château** 1 rue du Général-de-Gaulle ☎02 97 22 20 11, ⓦhotel-chateau.com. Facing Josselin's fairy-tale castle from across the river, this lovely hotel is a perfect place to stay. Though the slightly more expensive rooms, with château views, are not particularly luxurious, they're worth it – the whole place looks fabulous lit up at night – while the dining room, serving lunch from €17.50 and dinner for €22.50–48.50, is first-rate. **€91**

### LAC DE GUERLÉDAN

**Beau Rivage** Site du Beau Rivage ☎02 96 28 52 15, ⓦwww.le-beau-rivage.info. This hotel/restaurant, 7km east of the Abbaye de Bon-Repos, may look that attractive from outside, and the four bedrooms, though modern and well equipped are carpeted all the way up the wall, but it commands magnificent views of the lake and serves great food, with dinner menus from €21.50 and even crêpes for breakfast. Restaurant closed Mon eve in July & Aug, all Wed June–Sept. **€59**

**REDON**

**Chandouineau** 1 rue Thiers ☏ 02 99 71 02 04, ⊛ hotel-restaurant-chandouineau.com. Smart hotel close to the station, with just seven comfortable bedrooms at great-value prices, and a gourmet restaurant (closed Sat) where dinner *menus* cost €28–59. **€94**

# The southern coast

6

Brittany's **southern coast** is best known for being home to mainland Europe's most famous prehistoric site, the megalithic alignments of **Carnac**, which are complemented by other ancient relics scattered around the beautiful, island-studded **Golfe du Morbihan**. Although the beaches hereabouts tend not to be as spectacular as in Finistère, there are more safe places to swim and the water is warmer. Of the cities, **Lorient** has Brittany's most compelling **festival** and **Vannes** is a dynamic medieval centre, while you can also escape to the islands of **Belle-Île**, **Hoëdic** and **Houat**.

## Lorient

Brittany's fourth-largest city, **LORIENT**, lies on an immense natural harbour, sheltered by the Île de Groix. A functional, rather depressing port today, it was founded in the mid-seventeenth century by the Compagnie des Indes, an equivalent of the Dutch and English East India Companies. Apart from the name, little else remains to suggest the plundered wealth that once arrived here from France's far-flung colonial possessions.

### Cité de la Voile Éric Tabarly

Base de Sous-Marins de Kéroman • Check website for the intricate calendar of opening hours, broadly summarized here: mid-Feb to mid-March, mid-April to mid-May daily 10am–6pm; mid-March to mid-April & first half of Oct daily except Mon 2–6pm; mid-May to early July Mon 2–6pm, Tues–Sun 10am–6pm; early July to Aug daily 10am–7pm; Sept Mon 2–6pm, Tues–Sun 10am–6pm; last admission 1hr 30min before closing • Adults €18.50, ages 7–17 €15 • ☏ 02 97 65 56 56, ⊛ citevoile-tabarly.com

The **Cité de la Voile Éric Tabarly**, a couple of kilometres south of central Lorient at the mouth of the Ter river, is a large, modern, interactive museum of **sailing**. M. Tabarly himself was a champion yachtsman and Breton hero who, sadly, drowned in 1998. Several of his yachts – all called *Pen Duick*, which roughly means "little black head" – are moored alongside, and can be visited.

### U-boat pens

Base de Sous-Marins de Kéroman • Feb–June & Sept–Dec daily 10am–6pm during school hols, daily except Mon 10am–12.30pm & 2–6pm outside school hols; first 3 weeks of July & last week of Aug daily 10am–7pm; late July to late Aug daily 10am–8pm • €9.50–18.03 depending on your chosen combination of visits and tours • ☏ 02 97 65 52 87, ⊛ la-flore.fr

---

**THE INTER-CELTIC FESTIVAL**

The world's largest Celtic event, Lorient's **Inter-Celtic Festival** takes place over ten days from the first Friday to the second Sunday in August. Representatives from all the Celtic nations of Europe – Brittany, Ireland, Scotland, Wales, Cornwall, the Isle of Man, Asturias and Galicia – come to celebrate cultural solidarity. Well over half a million people attend more than a hundred different shows, five languages mingle, and Scotch and Guinness flow with French and Spanish wines and ciders. There's a certain competitive element, with championships in various categories, but mutual enthusiasm and conviviality is paramount. Various activities – embracing music, dance and literature – take place all over the city, with mass celebrations around the central place Jules-Ferry and the fishing harbour, and the biggest concerts at the football stadium, the Parc du Moustoir. For full **schedules**, see ⊛ festival-interceltique.bzh. **Reserve tickets** for the major events well in advance.

During World War II, Lorient was a major target for the Allies; by the time the Germans surrendered, in May 1945, the city was almost completely destroyed. The only substantial traces to survive were the **U-boat pens**, which now stand alongside the Cité de la Voile in the port district of **Kéroman**. Subsequently expanded to hold French nuclear submarines, they're open these days for **guided tours**, of which the highlight is the chance to visit the decommissioned sub *La Flore*.

**6**

## Musée de la Compagnie des Indes

Port-Louis • Feb–April & Oct to mid-Dec daily except Tues 1.30–6pm; May–Aug daily 10am–6.30pm; Sept daily except Tues 10am–6pm; closed mid-Dec to Jan • €8 • ☎ 02 97 82 19 13, ⓦ musee.lorient.bzh

If you have the time, it's well worth catching a ferry across the bay from Lorient's Embarcadère des Rades to **Port-Louis**. In the citadelle here, the **Musée de la Compagnie des Indes** traces the history of French colonialism in Asia, with displays covering both the trading voyages and the goods they brought home.

### INFORMATION                                                                                   LORIENT

**Tourist office** Beside the pleasure port on the quai de Rohan (April to June & Sept Mon–Fri 10am–noon & 2–6pm, Sat 10am–noon & 2–5pm; July & Aug Mon–Sat 9.30am–1pm & 2–7pm, Sun 9.30am–1.30pm, except during the festival, when it's daily 9.30am–8pm; Oct–March Mon–Sat 10am–noon & 2–5pm; ☎ 02 97 84 78 00, ⓦ lorient-tourisme.fr).

### ACCOMMODATION

**Auberge de Jeunesse** 41 rue Victor-Schoelcher ☎ 02 97 37 11 65, ⓦ fuaj.org. Lorient's well-equipped, friendly hostel is in a plain, functional building beside the River Ter, 3km west of the centre (bus #21 from the *gare SNCF*). Five-person dorms, plus very minimal private doubles. Closed mid-Dec to mid-Jan. Dorm **€17.70**, double **€43**

**Les Océanes** 17 av de la Perrière ☎ 02 97 37 14 66, ⓦ www.hotel-lesoceanes.com. Very presentable modern hotel, slightly removed from the centre near the sailing museum, with simple but bright and attractive rooms and some good-value family suites. **€70**

**Pêcheurs** 7 rue Jean-Lagarde ☎ 02 97 21 19 24, ⓦ hotel-lespecheurs.com. Basic but decently renovated and perfectly acceptable hotel, close to the town centre, with a pub (closed Sun) and brasserie downstairs. The cheapest rooms lack en-suite facilities. **€39**

### EATING AND DRINKING

**Galway Inn** 18 rue de Belgique ☎ 02 97 64 50 77. Fine old stone pub, renowned for its fusion of Irish and Celtic traditions, with live music of all kinds at the weekend to go with its draught Guinness and cider. Daily 5pm–2am.

**Le Pic** 2 bd Franchet-d'Espèrey ☎ 02 97 21 18 29, ⓦ restaurant-lorient.com. Little restaurant, just south of the *gare SNCF*, with the look of a classy old-fashioned bistro and some outdoor seating. Lunch from under €15, inventive dinner *menus* of market-fresh produce from €28. Mon, Tues, Thurs & Fri noon–1.45pm & 7–9.30pm, Wed noon–1.45pm, Sat 7–9.30pm.

**Tavarn ar Roue Morvan** 17 rue Poissonnière ☎ 02 97 21 61 57. Infused with all things Breton, this lively tavern serves good, hearty meat and fish dishes, as well as offering home-made cider and live traditional music. Mon–Sat 11am–1am; also Sun 11am–1am in Aug only.

# Carnac

**CARNAC** is the most important prehistoric site in Europe – in fact this spot is thought to have been continuously inhabited longer than anywhere else in the world. Its **alignments** of two thousand or so menhirs stretch over 4km, with great burial tumuli dotted amid them. In use since at least 5700 BC, the site long predates Knossos, the Pyramids, Stonehenge and the great Egyptian temples of the same name at Karnak.

Divided between the original **Carnac-Ville** and the seaside resort of **Carnac-Plage**, modern Carnac has a special charm, especially in spring and autumn. For most visitors, the alignments are, if anything, a mere sideshow. The town and seafront remain well wooded, and the tree-lined avenues and gardens are a delight.

## The megaliths

Rte des Alignements, 1km north of Carnac-Ville • **Site** April–Sept tours only; occasional English-language tours, including Tues 11.30am & Fri 11.30am during July & Aug; Oct–March daily 10am–5pm • adults €9, ages 7–17 €5 **Maison des Mégalithes** Daily: April–June & Sept 9.30am–6pm; July & Aug 9.30am–7.30pm; Oct–March 10am–1pm & 2–5pm • ☎ 02 97 52 29 81, ⓦ menhirs-carnac.fr

Carnac's **megaliths** form three distinct major alignments, sited parallel to the sea alongside the **Route des Alignements**, north of Carnac-Ville. These are the **Alignements de Ménec**, "the place of stones" or "place of remembrance", with 1169 stones in eleven rows; the **Alignements de Kermario**, "the place of the dead", with 1029 stones in ten rows; and the **Alignements de Kerlescan**, "the place of burning", with 555 stones in thirteen lines. Each runs roughly in the same northeast–southwest direction, but has a slightly separate orientation.

Visitors can only walk freely around the best-preserved sites in winter. In summer, access is on guided tours – it's best to join one if this is your first exposure to the subject, or you may feel as though you're simply staring at rocks in a field. They start from the **Maison des Mégalithes**, across the road from the Alignements de Ménec, which also holds interesting displays, plus a model of the site.

## Musée de Préhistoire

10 place de la Chapelle, Carnac-Ville • March & Nov daily except Tues 2–5.30pm; April–June & Sept daily except Tues 10am–12.30pm & 2–6pm; July & Aug daily 10am–6.30pm; Oct daily except Tues 10am–12.30pm & 2–5.30pm; Dec–Feb school hols only, daily 2–5.30pm • €7 • ☎ 02 97 52 22 04, ⓦ museedecarnac.com

Carnac's rather dry **Musée de Préhistoire**, in the town centre, traces the history of the Morbihan from earliest times, starting with 450,000-year-old chipping tools and leading by way of the Neanderthals to the megalith builders and beyond. Captions are in French only. As well as authentic physical relics, it holds reproductions and casts of the carvings at Locmariaquer, a scale model of the Alignements de Ménec, and diagrams showing how the stones may have been moved into place.

---

### THE MEGALITHS OF BRITTANY

Along with Newgrange in Ireland, Stonehenge in England and the Ring of Brodgar in the Orkneys, the tumuli, alignments and single standing stones of Brittany are of pre-eminent status among the **megalithic sites** of Europe. Dated at 5700 BC, the tumulus of Kercado at Carnac is the earliest known stone construction in Europe. Little is known of the monuments' creators; the few skeletons unearthed indicate a short, dark, hairy race with a life expectancy of no more than the mid-30s. What is certain is that their civilization was long-lasting; the earliest and the latest constructions at Carnac are more than five thousand years apart.

Each megalithic centre had its own distinct styles and traditions. Brittany has relatively few stone circles, or **cromlechs**, and a greater proportion of free-standing stones, **menhirs**; fewer burial chambers, known as **dolmens**, and more evidence of ritual fires; and different styles of carving. Carnac's alignments are unique in their sheer complexity.

As for their actual **purpose**, the most fashionable theory sees them as part of a vast astronomical observatory centred on the fallen Grand Menhir of Locmariaquer. However, controversy rages as to whether the Grand Menhir ever stood at all, or, even if it did, whether it fell or was broken up before the surrounding sites came into being. Moreover, sceptics say, the measurements on which the theory depends ignore the fact that the sea level in southern Brittany 6600 years ago was 10m lower than it is today.

Alternative theories interpret the menhirs as a series of territorial or memorial markers. This annual or occasional setting-up of a new stone is easier to envisage than the vast effort required to erect them all at once – in which case the fact that they were arranged in lines, mounds and circles might have been of peripheral importance.

**6**

## The beaches

Carnac's five **beaches** extend for a total of nearly 3km. The two most attractive, usually counted together as one of the five, are **plages Men Dû** and **Beaumer**, which lie east towards La Trinité beyond Pointe Churchill. They're especially popular these days with **kite surfers**.

### ARRIVAL AND INFORMATION
CARNAC

**By train** In July and Aug, when the Tire-Bouchon ("corkscrew") rail link runs between Auray and Quiberon, trains call at Plouharnel, 4km northwest of Carnac.
**By bus** Buses from Auray (9 daily; 30min) and Vannes (7 daily; 1hr 20min) stop at the tourist office.

**Tourist office** 74 av des Druides, Carnac-Plage (April–June & Sept Mon–Sat 9.30am–12.30pm & 2–6pm, Sun 3–6pm; July & Aug Mon–Sat 9.30am–7pm, Sun 3–7pm; Oct–March Mon–Sat 9.30am–12.30pm & 2–5pm; ☎ 02 97 52 13 52, ⓦ ot-carnac.fr).

### ACCOMMODATION

Prices for hotels in Carnac are among the most expensive in all Brittany, and at a premium in July and August. As befits such a family-oriented place, Carnac features as many as twenty campsites.

**Rochers** 6 bd de la Base Nautique, Carnac-Plage ☎ 02 97 52 10 09, ⓦ www.les-rochers.com. Well-kept, family-friendly hotel offering the best value by the beach, especially if you are looking for sea-view balconies. Closed early Nov to early April. **€133**

#### HOTELS

★ **Plume au Vent** 4 venelle Notre-Dame, Carnac-Ville ☎ 06 16 98 34 79, ⓦ plume-au-vent.com. Central, welcoming and brilliantly decorated B&B, where the two suites ("low tide" and "high tide") draw tastefully on the nautical theme (for once), with pastel colours and some great found artefacts. **€130**

**Râtelier** 4 chemin de Douët, Carnac-Ville ☎ 02 97 52 05 04, ⓦ le-ratelier.com. Old, ivy-clad stone hotel with a handful of comfortable rooms, characterized by rustic colours and open wooden beams; the cheapest have showers but not toilets. Top-quality food on *menus* from €24. Closed 3 wks in Jan. **€74**

#### CAMPSITES

**Camping Le Dolmen** Chemin de Beaumer ☎ 02 97 52 12 35, ⓦ campingledolmen.com. Three-star campsite, just north of Carnac-Plage and an easy walk from the sea, with a grocery, snack bar, and seafood platters on demand, as well as a heated swimming pool. Closed late Sept to March. **€32**

**Men Dû** 22bis chemin de Beaumer ☎ 02 97 52 04 23, ⓦ camping-mendu.com. Two-star site near the sea, just inland from the plage du Men Dû, with a summer-only snack bar. Closed Oct–March. **€25**

### EATING AND DRINKING

**Chez Marie** 3 place de l'Église, Carnac-Ville ☎ 02 97 52 07 93. An old favourite in Carnac-Ville, this busy stone-clad crêperie offers good €15 *menus* with a *galette* as the main course. Mon & Wed–Sun noon–2pm & 7–9pm; closed Mon Sept–June.

**La Côte** 3 impasse Parc-er-Forn, Carnac-Ville ☎ 02 97 52 02 80, ⓦ restaurant-la-cote.com. Inside this venerable stone cottage, a very smart dining room serves inventive, modern gourmet cuisine, which you can sample at lunch for just €26, or from €39 in the evening. Ever more copious offerings stretch up to an €83 all-lobster menu. July & Aug Tues 7.15–9.15pm, Wed–Sun 12.15–2.15pm & 7.15–9.15pm; Sept–June Wed–Sat 12.15–2.15pm & 7.15–9.15pm, Sun 12.15–2.15pm.

## Locmariaquer

**LOCMARIAQUER** stands right at the narrow mouth of the Gulf of Morbihan. On the ocean side, there's a long sandy beach; on the Gulf side, a small tidal port. As with Carnac, however, the main reason to go out of your way to visit Locmariaquer is to see its fine crop of **megaliths**.

### Site des Mégalithes

Daily: May & June 10am–6pm; July & Aug 10am–7pm; Sept–April 10am–12.30pm & 2–5.15pm • €6, under-18s free • ☎ 02 97 57 37 59, ⓦ site-megalithique-locmariaquer.fr

Until 1991, Locmariaquer's principal **Site des Mégalithes** was thought to hold two monuments – the broken fragments of the **Grand Menhir Brisé**, which having originally stood 20m tall is the largest ever discovered, and a massive dolmen, the **Table des Marchands**. Then archeologists realized that the car park had inadvertently been created atop a third, even larger relic. Now known as *Er Grah*, it consists of a series of partially reconstructed stone terraces, the purpose of which remains unknown.

| ACCOMMODATION | LOCMARIAQUER |
|---|---|

**L'Escale** 2 place Dariorigum ☎ 02 97 57 32 51, ⓦ escale-hotel.com. Small, simple but great-value hotel, right on the waterfront. Its brasserie/restaurant is perched on the sea wall, so you get fabulous views as you feast on oysters, clams and mussels at €10–15 per *plat*, or €23 for a full *menu*. Closed Oct–March. **€55**

**Lann Brick** lieu-dit Lann-Brick ☎ 02 97 57 32 79, ⓦ camping-lannbrick.com. Three-star campsite, set in rich countryside 2.5km northwest of Locmariaquer and

300m from the beach, with a heated pool, grocery and snack bar. Closed late Oct to late March. **€23**

**Trois Fontaines** Rte d'Auray ☎ 02 97 57 42 70, ⓦ hotel-troisfontaines.com. Friendly and attractive modern hotel, looking out towards the bay from across the road into town, not far from the Table des Marchands. Several of the colourful, comfortable rooms have balconies. Closed mid-Nov to mid-Feb. **€94**

# Presqu'île de Quiberon

The **Presqu'île de Quiberon**, south of Carnac, is as close to being an island as any peninsula could conceivably be; the long causeway of sand that links it to the mainland narrows to as little as 50m in places. In summer, it attracts tourists in abundance, who come not so much for the towns, which, other than lively **Quiberon**, are generally featureless, but to use them as a base for trips out to **Belle-Île** or around the peninsula's contrasting coastline. Along the wild and highly unswimmable ocean-facing shore, known as the **Côte Sauvage**, the stormy seas look like snowy mountaintops. The sheltered eastern side has safe and calm sandy beaches, and plenty of campsites.

## Quiberon

Despite recent construction on its namesake peninsula, **QUIBERON**, at the southern tip, is still the only real town. Its most active area, **Port-Maria**, is home to the **gare maritime** for the islands of Belle-Île, Houat and Hoëdic, and also has a sardine-fishing harbour. At Quiberon's centre is a busy little park and miniature golf course, but few streets further back hold anything of great interest. The exception is the little hill that leads down to the port from the *gare SNCF*, where browsing is rewarded with some surprisingly good clothes and antique shops. Stretching away to the east of the harbour is a long curve of fine sandy **beach**, lined for several hundred metres with bars, cafés and restaurants.

| ARRIVAL AND INFORMATION | QUIBERON |
|---|---|

**By train** In summer, the Tire-Bouchon ("corkscrew") train links Quiberon's *gare SNCF* with Auray (second half of June & first half of Sept 4 trains on Sat & Sun only; July & Aug 8–10 daily; 45min).

**By bus** Bus #1 runs to the *gare maritime* from Auray via Carnac (8 daily; 1hr 15min; ⓦ breizhgo.bzh).

**Tourist office** 14 rue de Verdun (April–June & Sept Mon–Sat 9am–12.30pm & 2–6pm, Sun 9am–1pm; July & Aug Mon–Sat 9.30am–7pm, Sun 10am–1pm & 2–5pm; Oct–March Mon–Fri 10am–12.30pm & 2–5.30pm, Sat 10am–12.30pm; ☎ 02 97 50 07 84, ⓦ quiberon.com).

**ACCOMMODATION**

For most of the year, it's hard to get a room in Quiberon. In July and August, the whole peninsula is packed, while in winter it's so quiet that virtually all its facilities close down. The nicest area to stay is along the seafront in Port-Maria, where several good hotel-restaurants face the Belle-Île ferry terminal.

**Auberge des Dunes** av Surcouf, Penthièvre ☎ 02 97 52

34 00, ⓦ revesdemer.com. Secluded hostel complex, on the Côte Sauvage immediately north of the isthmus, with private double and dorms holding two to six beds each, plus a restaurant serving all meals, and a bar. Rates include breakfast. Dorms **€28**, double **€66**

**Au Bon Accueil** 6 quai de Houat, Quiberon ☎ 02 97 50 07 92, ⓦ aubonaccueil-quiberon.com. Spruced up seafront

**6**

6

hotel where the most basic rooms share bathrooms; pay €25 extra for an en-suite room with sea views. The restaurant downstairs has dinner *menus* from €25. €43

★ **Neptune** 4 quai de Houat, Quiberon ☎ 02 97 50 09 62, ⊛ hotel-le-neptune.quiberon.hotels-fr.net. Good-value hotel; twelve of the 21 bright, cheery rooms cost €15 extra and have sea-view balconies – though the bathrooms are drab – while larger family suites face inland. €72

### EATING AND DRINKING

**La Chaumine** 79 rue de Port Haliguen ☎ 02 97 50 17 67, ⊛ restaurant-lachaumine.com. This lovely little fish restaurant, away from the sea on the main road into Port Haliguen, serves *menus* from €24 at lunch, and from €27 for dinner. Mid-March to mid-Nov Tues 7–8.45pm, Wed–Sun noon–1.15pm & 7–8.45pm; also closed Sun eve except in July & Aug.

★ **De la Criée** 11 quai de l'Océan ☎ 02 97 30 53 09, ⊛ maisonlucas.com. Superb fish restaurant, serving whatever's freshest from the morning's catch; choose from over-flowing baskets of shellfish ranging up to the 79 plateau Gargantua; daily €20–25 specials; or good-value set *menus* starting at €20. Feb–Dec Tues–Sun 12.15–2pm & 7.15–10pm; closed Sun eve in low season.

# Belle-Île

Considerably larger than the other Breton islands, at 17km from east to west, gorgeous **BELLE-ÎLE**, 15km south of Quiberon, feels significantly less isolated than the rest. However, its towns – fortified **Le Palais**; **Sauzon**, arrayed along one side of a long estuary; and **Bangor**, inland – are consistently lovely, and it offers wonderful opportunities for walking and cycling. At different times in its turbulent history the island belonged to the monks of Redon, the English – who in 1761 swapped it for Menorca – and Lorient's Compagnie des Indes.

## Le Palais

When you dock at the port and main town of **LE PALAIS**, the abrupt star-shaped fortifications of the **citadelle** are the first thing you see. Built along stylish and ordered lines by the great fortress-builder, Vauban, it is startling in size, filled with doorways leading to mysterious cellars and underground passages and deserted cells. Much of it has been converted into an expensive hotel, but it still houses a **museum** (daily: April–June, Sept & Oct 9.30am–6pm; July & Aug 9am–7pm; Nov–March 9.30am–5pm; €8.50; ☎ 02 97 31 85 54, ⊛ citadellevauban.com), documenting the island's history in fiction as much as in fact.

## Côte Sauvage

Belle-Île is far too large to stroll round, but a coastal footpath runs on bare soil for the length of its exposed southern shore, the **Côte Sauvage**, where sparse heather-covered cliffs face out into the sea. To appreciate this and the rich and fertile landward side, some form of transport is advisable – **rental bikes** are widely available in Le Palais (see opposite).

## Grotte de l'Apothicairerie and around

Near the west end of the island, the **Grotte de l'Apothicairerie** is a cliff-face cave that earned its name because it was once full of cormorants' nests, arranged like the jars on a pharmacist's shelves. Inland, on the D25 back towards Le Palais, you pass the two **menhirs**, Jean and Jeanne, said to be lovers petrified as punishment for wanting to meet before their marriage. Another larger menhir used to lie near these two; it was broken up to help construct the road that separates them.

**ARRIVAL AND DEPARTURE**                                                **BELLE-ÎLE**

**FROM QUIBERON**
**Compagnie-Océane** All year, Compagnie-Océane (☎ 08 20 05 61 56 or ☎ 02 97 35 02 00, ⊛ compagnie-oceane.fr) sends 6–13 ferries daily from Quiberon to Le Palais. The first departure is generally around 8am, and the crossing takes 45min. Rates vary according to the season for adults, from

€15 to €17.50 each way – under-18s always cost €7.50 – and from €65 to €85 for the smallest size of car, with bikes always costing €7.50.

at 8.30am (adults €31 return, under-18s €26) and Port-Navalo at 9.45am (€30/€25), with a connecting service from Locmariaquer at 9.20am (€34.50/€31).

## FROM VANNES, PORT-NAVALO AND LOCMARIAQUER

**Navix** In summer, Navix (☎ 02 97 46 60 00, ⓦ navix.fr) sail to Le Palais from Vannes and Port-Navalo (March to mid-April Tues only; mid-April to June and almost all of Sept Tues–Thurs, Sat & Sun; July & Aug daily), leaving Vannes

## FROM LE CROISIC AND LA TURBALLE

**Navix** Between early July and late Aug, Navix (☎ 02 97 46 60 00, ⓦ navix.fr) offer daily excursions to Belle-Île that leave Le Croisic at 7.45am, and La Turballe, not far north of La Baule between Piriac and Guérande, at 8.35am (adults €42 return, under-18s €35).

## GETTING AROUND

**By bus** Belle-Île's bus system offers around six daily connections in summer from Le Palais to each of Sauzon, Bangor and Locmaria (☎ 02 97 31 81 88, ⓦ ccbi.fr).
**By car** Locatourisle (☎ 02 97 31 83 56, ⓦ locatourisle.com) rents cars from around €70/day in summer.

**By bike** Several waterfront outlets in Le Palais, including Loca Scoot, 4 quai Bonnelle (☎ 02 97 31 49 94, ⓦ velo-scooter-belle-ile-56.fr), rent bikes at around €12/day, as well as scooters from €45/day.

## INFORMATION

**Tourist office** Next to the *gare maritime* in Le Palais (July & Aug Mon–Sat 9am–7pm, Sun 9am–1pm; Sept–June

Mon–Sat 9am–12.30pm & 2–6pm; ☎ 02 97 31 81 93, ⓦ belle-ile.com).

## ACCOMMODATION AND EATING

**Atlantique** Quai de l'Acadie ☎ 02 97 31 80 11, ⓦ hotel-atlantique.com. Cheerful yellow-and-blue hotel in prime position on the quayside facing the ferries, offering good-value accommodation and a decent restaurant with a panoramic terrace, serving lunch from €18 and dinner from €26. The cheapest rooms are in a separate annexe, but even in summer a sea-view room in the main building costs less than €100. **€68**
**Auberge de Jeunesse** Haute-Boulogne, Le Palais ☎ 02 97 31 81 33, ⓦ fuaj.org. Hugely popular hostel on the heights above town, behind the citadelle, a 15min walk from the port. Small dorms, with cooking facilities and breakfast available. Advance bookings essential. Closed Oct–March. **€17**
**Camping de Port Andro** Locmaria ☎ 02 97 31 73 25, ⓦ locmaria-belle-ile.com/heb_campings. Belle-Île has plenty of fancier campsites, but if you like to camp close to

the beach, there's no beating this secluded little municipal site, beside its own perfect strand 3km from Locmaria, towards the southeast tip of the island. Closed late Sept to mid-May. **€12.50**
**Le Clos Fleuri** Rte de Sauzon, Le Palais ☎ 02 97 31 45 45, ⓦ hotel-leclosfleuri.com. This exceptionally welcoming and peaceful hotel, just outside Le Palais on the road towards Sauzon, offers spacious, comfortable and tastefully furnished rooms at reasonable prices, with private terraces. No restaurant. Closed Jan to mid-Feb. **€85**
**Villa Pen Prad** Rue du Chemin-Neuf, Sauzon ☎ 06 49 41 71 43, ⓦ villapenprad.com. Very pleasant B&B, in an unbeatable waterfront location beside the road into Sauzon – a tremendous vantage point for watching activity in the little port – with three charming rooms, a couple of luxurious suites and great breakfasts. **€180**

# Houat and Hoëdic

You can't take your car to Belle-Île's two smaller sisters, **HOUAT** and **HOËDIC**. Known as the *"îles du silence"*, both islands have a feeling of being left behind by the passing centuries. However, the younger fishermen of Houat have revived the island's fortunes by establishing a successful fishing cooperative, and it also has **beaches** – as ever on the sheltered (eastern) side – that fill up with campers in the summer (even though camping is not strictly legal). The more traditional and less developed Hoëdic, on the other hand, has a large municipal **campsite**, overlooking the port. The vast majority of visitors are day-trippers, but each island has at least one hotel.

## ARRIVAL AND DEPARTURE                    HOUAT AND HOËDIC

**By boat** Compagnie-Océane (☎ 02 97 35 02 00, ⓦ compagnie-oceane.fr) runs between one and six daily

ferries from Quiberon to Houat and Hoëdic all year, to widely varying schedules (40min to Houat, another 25min

**6**

to Hoëdic; one way fares €15–17.50). In July and Aug, to varying schedules, Navix (☎02 97 46 60 00, ⓦnavix. fr) sail to Houat and Hoëdic from Vannes, Port-Navalo, Locmariaquer and La Trinité (€32.60 return) and also from Le Croisic and La Turballe (€39.90 return).

## Golfe du Morbihan

The sheltered **Golfe du Morbihan** – *mor bihan* means "little sea" in Breton – is one of the loveliest stretches of Brittany's coast. While its only large town, medieval **Vannes**, is well worth visiting, its endlessly indented shoreline is the major attraction, with superb vistas at every turn, and countless secluded **beaches**.

It is said that the gulf used to hold an **island** for every day of the year, but rising seas have left fewer than one per week. A **boat tour** around them, or at least a trip out to **Gavrinis** near the mouth of the gulf, is a compelling experience, with megalithic ruins and stone circles dotted around the beguiling maze of channels, and solitary menhirs gazing down from small hillocks.

### Vannes

At the head of the Golfe du Morbihan, **VANNES**, southern Brittany's major tourist town, is such a large and thriving community that the size of the small walled town at its core, **Vieux Vannes**, may well come as a surprise. Its focal point, the old gateway of

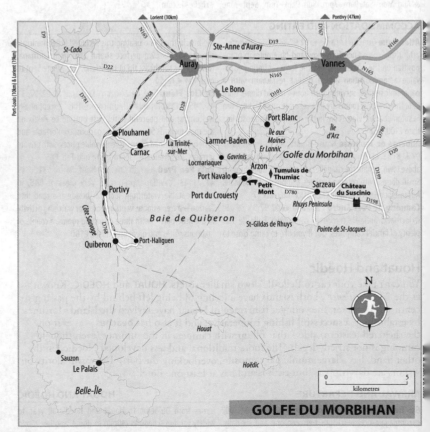

GOLFE DU MORBIHAN

---

### GULF TOURS

**Izenah Croisières** ☎ 02 97 57 23 24, ⓦ izenah-croisieres.com. Gulf tours from Port Blanc at Baden in summer (April–Sept; €21.50), and a year-round ferry service to the Île aux Moines (daily every 30min: July & Aug 7am–10pm, Sept–June 7am–7.30pm; €5.20 return).

**Navix** ☎ 02 97 46 60 00, ⓦ navix.fr. Between March and Dec, cruises from Vannes, Port-Navalo and Locmariaquer include half-day (€17) and full-day

(€28.50) trips around the gulf, and also lunch and dinner cruises, where the cost depends on your choice of *menu* (total €62.50–71). Between mid-July and late Aug, similar tours at similar prices also depart from Auray, Le Bono and La Trinité.

**Vedettes Angélus** ☎ 02 97 57 30 29, ⓦ vedettes-angelus.com. Up to five gulf tours of varying lengths daily from Locmariaquer and Port-Navalo (mid-April to Sept; €15–26).

---

**6**

the **Porte St-Vincent**, commands a busy little square at the northern end of a canalized port leading to the gulf itself. Inside the ramparts, the winding car-free streets – crammed around the cathedral, and enclosed by gardens and a tiny stream – make great strolling territory.

Modern Vannes centres on **place de la République**; the focus was shifted outside the medieval city during the nineteenth-century craze for urbanization. The grandest of the public buildings here, guarded by a pair of sleek bronze lions, is the **hôtel de ville** at the top of rue Thiers. By day, however, the streets of the old city, with their overhanging, witch-hatted houses and busy commercial life, are the chief source of pleasure.

### Musée des Beaux-Arts

9 place St-Pierre • June–Sept daily 1.30–6pm; Oct–May open to groups only, by appointment • €6.50 with Musée d'Histoire et d'Archéologie • ☎ 02 97 01 63 00

It was in the impressive medieval building known as **La Cohue** that the Breton *États* assembled in 1532 to ratify the Act of Union with France. It currently houses the **Musée des Beaux-Arts**, of interest primarily for its temporary exhibitions.

### Cathédrale St-Pierre

Place St-Pierre • Daily 8.30am–7pm • ☎ 02 97 47 10 88, ⓦ cathedrale-vannes.fr

Facing La Cohue, the **Cathédrale St-Pierre** is a rather forbidding place, with a stern main altar almost imprisoned by four solemn grey pillars. Light, tinted purple through the new stained glass, spears in to illuminate the desiccated finger of the Blessed Pierre Rogue, who was guillotined on the main square in 1796.

### Musée d'Histoire et d'Archéologie

2 rue Noé • June–Sept daily 1.30–6pm; Oct–May open to groups only, by appointment • €6.50 with Musée des Beaux-Arts; free Sun • ☎ 02 97 01 64 00

A sombre fifteenth-century mansion holds Vannes' summer-only **Musée d'Histoire et d'Archéologie**. Its collection of prehistoric artefacts is said to be one of the world's finest, but they're tediously arrayed in formal patterns in glass cases, and the Middle Ages exhibit on the upper floors is more entertaining.

### Parc du Golfe: L'Aquarium de Vannes and Jardin aux Papillons

21 rue Daniel-Gilard • Daily: April–June & Sept 10am–noon & 2–6pm; July & Aug 9.30am–7pm; Oct–March 2–6pm, except school hols 10am–noon & 2–6pm • Aquarium: adults €14, under-12s €10; combined ticket with Jardin aux Papillons €20/€14.50 • ☎ 02 97 40 67 40, ⓦ aquariumdevannes.fr

Vannes' major tourist attraction, its modern **aquarium**, 500m south of place Gambetta in the **Parc du Golfe**, claims to hold Europe's finest collection of tropical fish. Certainly it holds some pretty extraordinary specimens, including a type of fish from Venezuela with four sexes and four eyes; cave fish from Mexico that have no eyes at all; and *arowana* from Guyana, which jump 2m out of the water to catch birds.

**6**

Alongside, the separate **Jardin aux Papillons**, or Butterfly Garden, consists of a huge glass dome containing hundreds of beautiful, free-flying butterflies.

## ARRIVAL AND INFORMATION                                    VANNES

**By train** Vannes' *gare SNCF* is on av Favrel et Lincy, 25min walk north of the centre.

Destinations Lorient (16 daily; 30–50min), with connections to Quimper (12 daily; 1hr 40min); Nantes (4 daily; 1hr 20min).

**By bus** The *gare routière* faces the *gare SNCF* (☎ 02 97 01 22 01, ⓦ lactm.com).

**By car** Parking can be a problem, but there's plenty of space

on quai Tabarly on the port's west side.

**Tourist office** Quai Tabarly, on the west side of the port (July & Aug Mon–Sat 9.30am–7pm, Sun 10am–6pm; Sept–June Mon–Sat 9.30am–noon & 1.30–6pm; ☎ 02 97 47 24 34, ⓦ golfedumorbihan.bzh).

**Festivals** At the end of July, the Festival Jazz en Ville takes over clubs and spaces throughout Vannes (ⓦ www. festivaljazzenville.fr).

## ACCOMMODATION

**Bretagne** 36 rue du Méné ☎ 02 97 47 20 21, ⓦ hotel-lebretagne-vannes.com. Reasonably priced, friendly little hotel, backing onto the walls, around the corner from the Porte-Prison, with a dozen pleasantly decorated, triple-glazed en-suite rooms. **€66**

**Camping Conleau** 188 av du Maréchal-Juin ☎ 02 97 63 13 88, ⓦ vannes-camping.com. Very agreeable three-star municipal campsite, the closest to central Vannes, set right beside the gulf, 2km southwest of the centre, with a heated pool and snack bar. Closed Oct–March. **€28**

**Manche Océan** 31 rue du Colonel-Maury ☎ 02 97 47 26 46, ⓦ www.manche-ocean.com. Ordinary but perfectly acceptable modern rooms between the station and the walled town, used mainly by tour groups. Small-scale buffet breakfasts for €9.50; no restaurant. **€79**

**Maison de la Garenne** 2 rue Sébastien-de-Rosmadec ☎ 02 97 67 00 31, ⓦ maisondelagarenne.com. Very pleasant B&B, in a stately townhouse just outside the walls, with a welcoming owner, and offering four comfortable and tasteful rooms plus a suite, all decorated to different

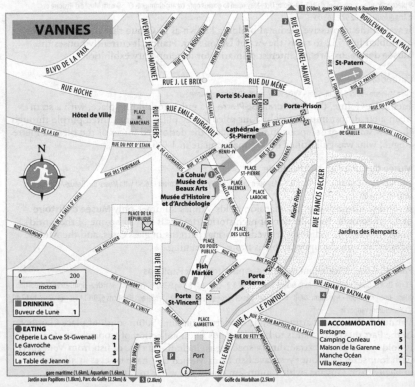

VANNES

themes, and its own spa. €145

**Villa Kerasy** 20 av Favrel et Lincy ☎02 97 68 36 83, ⓦvillakerasy.com. Luxurious little boutique hotel in an unlikely setting close to the station, with an Asian ambience throughout and its own spa. The finest rooms lead onto private Japanese gardens. No restaurant. €149

## EATING AND DRINKING

### RESTAURANTS

**Crêperie La Cave St-Gwenaël** 23 rue St-Gwenaël ☎02 97 47 47 94. Atmospheric, good-value crêperie in the cellar of a lovely old house, alongside the cathedral; a meal of one savoury and one sweet crêpe costs €11. July & Aug Mon–Sat noon–2.30pm & 6.30–9.30pm; Sept–Dec & Feb–June Tues–Sat noon–2.30pm & 6.30–9.30pm.

**Le Gavroche** 17 rue de la Fontaine ☎02 97 54 03 54, ⓦlegavroche-vannes.com. This cheerful, half-timbered, husband-and-wife restaurant is a godsend for meat-lovers. The steaks are cooked to perfection and original starters such as pig's trotters – along with the complimentary glass of home-made rum – will put hairs on your chest. *Menus* from €18.50 to €28.50. Tues–Sat noon–2pm & 7–10.30pm, Sun noon–2pm.

★ **Roscanvec** 17 rue des Halles ☎02 97 47 15 96, ⓦroscanvec.com. Superb formal restaurant, in a lovely half-timbered house, with some outdoor seating. Lunch at €26 is a bargain, while dinner *menus* (€55–92) feature unusual dishes such as *carbonara d'huîtres*. Tues–Sat 12.15–2pm & 7.15–9.30pm, Sun 12.15–2pm; closed Tues in low season.

**La Table de Jeanne** 13 place de la Poissonnerie ☎02 97 47 34 91, ⓦlatabledejeanne.com. Smart restaurant, entirely indoors, which faces the fish market and takes its inspiration from the changing daily catch. There's a good-value €18 lunch *menu*, while dinner is totally à la carte, with most main courses around €20. Tues, Wed & Sun noon–2pm, Thurs–Sat noon–2pm & 7–9.30pm.

### BAR

**Buveur de Lune** 8 rue Saint-Patern ☎02 97 54 32 32. A relaxed and good-natured spot for a fairly priced drink, with the night sky painted across the ceiling. Tues–Sun 6pm–2am.

## Gavrinis

The reason to visit the island of **GAVRINIS**, which can only be reached on guided boat tours from Larmor-Baden, the closest spot on the mainland immediately north, is its **megalithic site**. The most impressive and remarkable in Brittany, it stands comparison with Newgrange in Ireland and – in shape as well as size and age – with the earliest pyramids of Egypt.

The megalithic structure is essentially a **tumulus**, an earth mound covering a stone cairn and "passage grave". However, half of the mound has been peeled back and the side of the cairn that faces the water was reconstructed to make a facade resembling a step-pyramid. Inside, every stone of both passage and chamber is covered in carvings, with a restricted "alphabet" of fingerprint whorls, axe-heads and other conventional signs, including the spirals that, although familiar in Ireland, are seen only on this spot in Brittany.

### ARRIVAL AND DEPARTURE                                    GAVRINIS

**By ferry** Gavrinis can be reached April–Sept only. Tides permitting, ferries leave Larmor-Baden at half-hourly intervals, with the last boats of both morning and afternoon leaving 90min before the site closes. The cost includes a 45-minute guided tour (April & June–Sept daily 9.30am– 12.30pm & 1.30–6.30pm; May Mon–Fri 1.30–6.30pm, Sat & Sun 9.30am–12.30pm & 1.30–6.30pm; mid-Oct to early Nov daily except Tues 1.30–6pm; €18; ☎02 97 57 19 38, ⓦmorbihan.fr/gavrinis).

# The Loire

**364** Orléans and around

**379** Bourges

**382** The Cher and Indre

**390** Blois and around

**396** Tours and around

**406** Chinon and around

**409** Saumur and around

**413** Angers and around

**417** Nantes and around

**425** Le Mans

THE GARDENS AT VILLANDRY

# The Loire

The Loire has a justifiable reputation as one of the greatest, grandest and most scenic rivers anywhere in Europe. In its most characteristic stretch, from the hills of Sancerre to the city of Angers, it flows past an extraordinary parade of regal châteaux, majestic palaces and sweeping vineyards; unsurprisingly, when it came to choosing which should be awarded the title of World Heritage Site, UNESCO bestowed the label on the entire valley. The region's biggest draw might be the striking landscapes, but it's also famed for its rich gastronomy, laidback pace of life and hugely popular Loire à Vélo cycling trail.

The region's heartland, **Touraine**, long known as "the garden of France", has some of the best wines, the tastiest goat's cheese, and the most regal history in France, including one of the finest châteaux, in Chenonceau. Touraine also takes in three of the Loire's most pleasant tributaries: the **Cher**, **Indre** and **Vienne**. If you have just a week to spare for the region, then these are the parts to concentrate on. The attractive towns of **Blois** and **Amboise**, each with their own exceptional châteaux, make good bases for visiting the area upstream of Tours. Numerous grand **châteaux** dot the wooded country immediately south and east of Blois, including Chambord, the grandest of them all, while the wild and watery region of the Sologne stretches away further to the southeast. Downstream of Tours, around handsome Saumur, quirky troglodyte dwellings have been carved out of the rock faces.

Along with its many châteaux, the region has a few unexpected sights, most compelling of which are the gardens at **Villandry** and the abbey at **Fontevraud**. The major towns of **Angers**, **Tours**, **Nantes**, **Le Mans** and **Orléans** each have their own charms, from Orléans' astonishing cathedral, to Angers' lively nightlife.

The Loire itself is often called the last wild river in France, mostly because unpredictable currents and shallow water brought an end to commercial river traffic as soon as the railways arrived, and the many quays remain largely forgotten, except by the occasional tour boat. Such an untamed river also makes for dramatic floods, but for most of the year it meanders gently past its shifting sandbanks, shaded by reeds and willows, and punctuated by long, sandy islands beloved by birds.

**GETTING AROUND**                                                    **THE LOIRE**

Though most sites are accessible by public transport, buses and trains can be rather limiting. It's a good idea to rent some means of transport, at least for occasional forays away from the crowds. Renting a bike is perhaps the most enjoyable option of all, especially on the cycle routes that make up the Loire à Vélo network (see page 368).

# Orléans and around

ORLÉANS is the northernmost city on the Loire, sitting at the apex of a huge arc in the river as it switches direction and starts to flow southwest. Its proximity to Paris, just over 100km away, has always shaped this ancient city, and Orléans today is a vibrant cultural hub, with high-speed train and motorway links to the capital bringing in a steady influx of visitors. It's an attractive place, too: the ancient riverside quays have been redeveloped, and the pedestrianized old town buzzes with activity day and night.

Upstream from the city, the rambling Forêt d'Orléans spreads north. Along the river are plenty of lesser-known attractions, most notably the **abbey at St-Benoît**, the château at **Sully-sur-Loire**, the small town of **Gien**, the aqueduct at **Briare** and the hilltop town of **Sancerre**, where the famous dry white wines are produced.

# Highlights

❶ **Châteaux à vélo** The most scenic stretch of the Loire à Vélo cycle route, with 400km of bike paths that ramble past forests, fields and stunning châteaux. See page 368

❷ **Stained glass at Bourges cathedral** Some of France's finest stained-glass windows are preserved in Bourges's extravagant Gothic cathedral. See page 381

❸ **Château de Chambord** A fairy-tale castle set in 5440 hectares of parkland, where visitors can ride in a horse-drawn carriage, row a boat around the lake or cycle through the forest. See page 395

❹ **Amboise** Beautiful, archetypal Loire valley town, with a rich heritage, and a brilliant base for an exploration of the outlying regions. See page 401

❺ **The gardens at Villandry** Show-stopping Renaissance-style gardens complete with ornamental hedge-work, an intricate maze and expertly tended vegetable and flower gardens. See page 403

❻ **The Tapestry of the Apocalypse** Dramatically displayed in Angers' half-ruined fortress, this is an astonishingly well-preserved piece of medieval doom-mongering. See page 413

❼ **Les Machines de L'Île, Nantes** Thrilling steam-punk extravaganza, where visitors can ride on a 12m-tall mechanical elephant and operate fantastical sea creatures on an interactive carousel. See page 420

**HIGHLIGHTS ARE MARKED ON THE MAP ON PAGE 366**

## Cathédrale Sainte-Croix

Place du Martroi • Daily March–May & Oct 9.15am–6pm; June–Sept 9.15am–7pm (July & Aug Thurs, Fri & Sat until 11pm followed by son et lumière on the facade); Nov–March 9am–5pm

A short stroll from the mid-nineteenth-century Joan of Arc statue on **place du Martroi**, rue Jeanne-d'Arc marches arrow-straight up to the doors of the **Cathédrale Sainte-Croix**, where Joan celebrated her victory over the English. The uniformly Gothic structure actually dates from well after her death; Huguenot iconoclasts destroyed the transepts in 1568, and in 1601 Henri IV inaugurated a rebuilding programme that lasted until the nineteenth century. The lofty towers of the west front, which culminate in a delicate stone palisade, were only completed at the time of the Revolution. Inside, skeletal columns of stone extend in a single vertical sweep from the cathedral floor to the vault. Joan's canonization in 1920 is marked by a garish monumental altar next to the north transept, supported by two jagged golden leopards that represent the English. In the nave, the late nineteenth-century stained-glass windows tell the story of her life, starting from the north transept.

### HIGHLIGHTS

1. Châteaux à vélo
2. Stained glass at Bourges cathedral
3. Château de Chambord
4. Amboise
5. The gardens at Villandry
6. The Tapestry of the Apocalypse
7. Les Machines de l'Île, Nantes

## Musée des Beaux-Arts

1 rue Fernand-Rabier • Tues–Thurs & Sat 10am–6pm, Fri until 8pm, Sun 1–6pm • €6; same ticket for Hôtel Cabu and Maison de Jeanne d'Arc • ☎ 02 38 79 21 83, ⓦ orleans-metropole.fr

The **Musée des Beaux-Arts**, opposite the Hôtel Groslot, is probably the cultural high point of the city. The highlights of the main French collection on the first floor include Claude Deruet's *Four Elements*, the Le Nain brothers' dream-like and compelling *Bacchus Discovering Ariane on Naxos*, and an exquisite series of eighteenth-century pastel portraits. The suite of rooms on the mezzanine level leads from nineteenth-century Neoclassicism through Romanticism and on to a large chamber devoted to the early Realists, dominated by Antigna's taut, melodramatic *The Fire*. Foreign art, mainly Flemish and Italian sixteenth- and seventeenth-century works, is on the second floor – look out for Correggio's renowned *Holy Family* (1522) and Velázquez's *St Thomas*. Twentieth-century art lurks in the basement, where the big names include Picasso and Gauguin; a small inner chamber has a number of African-influenced sculptures by Henri Gaudier-Brzeska (1891–1915), who was born just outside Orléans.

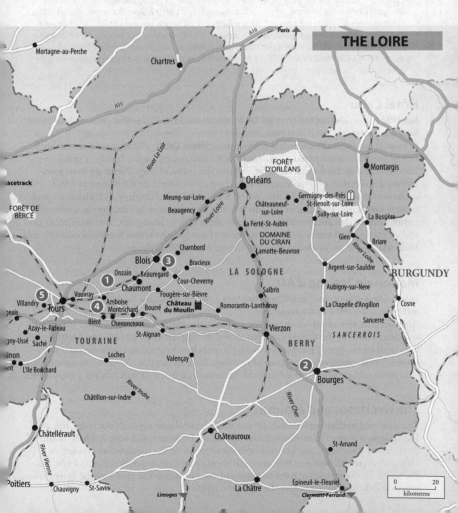

**7**

### THE LOIRE BY BIKE

Thanks to the **Loire à Vélo** scheme, the Loire valley is now one of the most charming places in the world to have a cycling holiday or take a day out on a rented bike. A mix of dedicated cycle paths and meticulously signposted routes along minor roads now run all the way along the Loire from Cuffy to St-Nazaire – a distance of more than 800km, that forms part of the EuroVelo 6 route (Ⓦ en.eurovelo6-france.com). The region around Blois is another popular choice for cyclists, with 400km of routes making up the **Châteaux à vélo** (Ⓦ chateauxavelo. com) network and taking in highlights such as Chambord, Chaumont and Cheverny.

Tourist offices provide detailed maps and information, but you can download maps, plan your route and book your trip on the **Loire à Vélo** website (Ⓦ loire-a-velo.fr). Almost all routes are easy and largely flat, making it simple for first-timers, and French villages and car drivers are well accustomed to cyclists.

### BIKE RENTAL

All larger towns have at least one rental agency and bikes can be rented at many hotels, campsites, tourist offices, train stations and even restaurants along the way. Look out for the green "Accueil Vélo" signs, which indicate accredited **Loire à Vélo** accommodation and services – here, cyclists are ensured secure bike parking, repair equipment and an energy-boosting breakfast. The cooperative bike scheme also means you can pick up a bike in one place and drop it off in another, and many offer baggage transfer services too. Expect to pay around €20 a day for bike rental and €20–50 for baggage transfer, but many companies offer special deals for groups or longer trips.

## Hôtel Cabu

Square Abbé-Desnoyers • Tues–Sun April–Sept 10am–1pm & 2–6pm; Oct–March 1–6pm • Same ticket as Musée des Beaux-Arts and Maison de Jeanne d'Arc ☎ 02 38 79 25 60, Ⓦ orleans-metropole.fr

A short stroll from the cathedral is the ornate **Hôtel Cabu**, whose three tiers faithfully follow the three main classical orders in strict Renaissance style. Inside, a small historical and archeological museum houses the extraordinary **Trésor de Neuvy-en-Sullias**, a collection of bronze animals and figurines found near Orléans in 1861. The cache was probably buried in the second half of the third century AD, either to protect it from Germanic invaders or to stop it being melted down for coinage at a time of rampant inflation, and possibly represents the last flourishing of Celtic religion at the end of the Gallo-Roman period. The floors above house various medieval oddities and Joan-related pieces, as well as exhibits on the history of Orléans.

## Maison de Jeanne d'Arc

3 place du Général-de-Gaulle • Tues–Sun: April–Sept 10am–1pm & 2–6pm; Oct–March 2–6pm • Same ticket as Musée des Beaux-Arts and Hôtel Cabu • ☎ 02 38 68 32 63, Ⓦ jeannedarc.com

An entertaining enough diversion for an hour, the **Maison de Jeanne d'Arc** is a 1960s reconstruction on the site where Joan stayed during the siege of Orléans. Despite the hundreds of images of Joan, many with the pageboy haircut and demure little face, there is no contemporary portrait of her, save for a clerk's doodle in the margin of her trial proceedings, kept in the National Archives in Paris, and you can see a copy here.

## The riverfront and around

The scattered vestiges of the old city are to the east, down towards the river. Rue de Bourgogne was the Gallo-Roman main street and is now lined with lively bars and restaurants. The Salles des Thèses is all that remains of the medieval university of Orléans where the hardline Reformation theologian Calvin studied Roman law. To the south lie the attractive narrow streets of the old industrial area and the busy hub of place de la Loire, which slopes down to the river.

## St-Aignan and St-Pierre-le-Puellier

Two of Orléans' historic churches are on the list of precious monuments: the remains of **St-Aignan** and its well-preserved eleventh-century crypt; and the Romanesque **St-Pierre-le-Puellier**, a former university church now used for concerts and exhibitions. St-Aignan was destroyed during the English siege, rebuilt by the Dauphin, then grew to become one of the greatest churches in France under Louis XII. More sieges of the city during the Wars of Religion took their toll, leaving just the choir and transepts standing. Tours of the crypt, which was built in the early eleventh century to house the relics of St-Aignan, can be arranged by the tourist office.

### ARRIVAL AND INFORMATION                                 ORLÉANS

**By train** The *gare SNCF* leads straight into the huge shopping centre on place d'Arc, at the top of the city's main shopping boulevard; the old town lies to the south. Destinations Beaugency (frequent; 20min); Blois (frequent; 40min); La Ferté-St-Aubin (frequent; 15–25min); Meung-sur-Loire (frequent; 15min); Paris (at least hourly; 1hr); Tours (frequent; 1hr–1hr 30min).

**By bus** The *gare routière*, on rue Marcel-Proust, is just north of place d'Arc.

Destinations Beaugency (10 daily; 1hr); Chartres (9 daily;

**7**

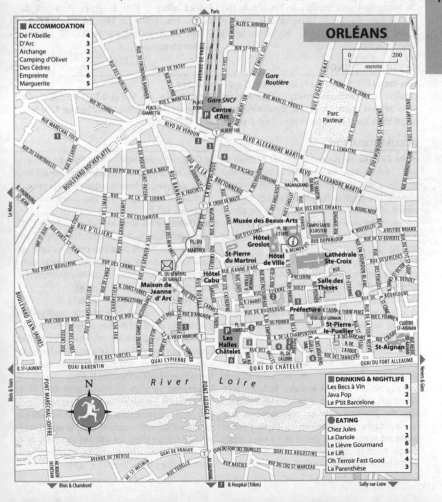

**7**

## JOAN OF ARC

Orléans is most famous for its heroine, **Joan of Arc**, and her deliverance of the city in May 1429. This was the turning point in the Hundred Years' War (1337–1453), when Paris had been captured by the English and Orléans, as the key city in central France, was under siege. The legend says that Joan, a 17-year-old peasant girl in men's clothing, had talked her way into meeting Charles, the heir to the French throne, and persuaded him to reconquer his kingdom. The reality may be a little different, as it seems that Joan was in fact born of nobility. The myth may have coloured her actual achievements, but she was undeniably an important symbolic figure. Less than three years later she was captured in battle, tried as a heretic, and burnt at the stake. Today, the Maid of Orléans is an omnipresent feature, whether in museums, hotels or in the stained glass of the vast Neo-Gothic cathedral. One of the best times to visit is on May 7 and 8 (Les Fêtes Johanniques/Joan of Arc Festival), when the city hosts parades, fireworks and a medieval fair.

1hr 10min–1hr 45min); Germigny-des-Prés (3 daily; 1hr); Gien (8 daily; 1hr 50min); Meung-sur-Loire (10 daily; 35min); St-Benoît-sur-Loire (3 daily; 1hr); Sully-sur-Loire (8 daily; 1hr 20min).

**Tourist office** 2 place de l'Étape (April–Sept daily 9.30am–7pm; Oct–March Mon–Sat 10am–12.30pm & 2–6pm, Sun 10am–1pm ☎02 38 24 05 05, ⓦtourisme-orleansmetropole.com).

## GETTING AROUND

**Bike rental** Orléans has a shared bike scheme (ⓦaggло-veloplus.fr) with stands across the city. It's €1 for a day and €3 for the week, and free for rides of 30min or less. Many central hotels have bikes to lend free of charge if you call in advance.

**Car rental** Avis, *gare SNCF* ☎02 38 71 31 95; Rent-a-Car, 3 rue Sansonnières ☎02 38 62 22 44; Europcar, 17 av de Paris ☎02 38 73 00 40.

## ACCOMMODATION

★ **De l'Abeille** 64 rue Alsace-Lorraine ☎02 38 53 54 87, ⓦhoteldelabeille.com. With its luxurious fabric wallpapers, glittering chandeliers and striking colour schemes, this gorgeous little hotel has just the right amount of glitz and bags of charm. Just off the buzz of the main shopping street, there's also a spacious terrace and an organic breakfast to look forward to in the morning (€12.50). **€84**

**D'Arc** 37 rue de la République ☎02 38 53 10 94, ⓦbestwestern.com. This long-established Art Nouveau hotel has touches of grandeur, though it's now a Best Western, with all the mod cons. For a change from the classical decor, book one of the two super-modern designer rooms on the fourth floor. No on-site parking. Breakfast €16.50. **€75**

★ **Archange** 1 Bd de Verdun ☎02 38 54 42 42, ⓦhotelarchange.com. It's impossible not to smile on entering *Archange*, which is crammed with quirky artefacts, bold artworks and bohemian keepsakes. Each room has a distinct personality: the Joan of Arc room has a medieval vibe; the Gutenberg room has newspaper-print bed-spreads; and the comparatively demure yin-yang room is decked out in monochrome. Best of all is a room entirely devoted to Tintin, complete with posters, figurines and printed bedspreads. Breakfast is €7.80. **€69**

**Camping d'Olivet** Rue du Pont Bouchet, Olivet ☎02 38 63 53 94, ⓦcamping-olivet.org. This is the closest site to town, 5km away by the river. There's free bike and canoe rental, ping pong, badminton and wet-weather games. To get there take Tram A, "Lorette" stop. Closed mid-Oct to end March. **€21.80**

**Des Cèdres** 17 rue Maréchal-Foch ☎02 38 62 22 92, ⓦhotelcedresorleans.com. Smart and well-serviced, with a good location close to the station and still walkable from the *centre ville*. Rooms are comfortable and clean, with a courtyard out back where you can have breakfast (€10) under the trees. Cheaper week rates. **€66**

**Empreinte** 80 quai du Châtelet ☎02 38 75 10 52, ⓦempreinte-hotel.com. This four-star boutique hotel and spa in a grand old building on the riverbank is the smartest accommodation in town. Rooms are stylish and contemporary; pay a bit more for a river view. The spa has a sauna, steamroom, whirlpool and beauty treatments. There's an excellent breakfast for €19. **€130**

**Marguerite** 14 place du Vieux-Marché ☎02 38 53 74 32, ⓦhotel-orleans.fr. Right in the centre of the old town, close to the river, *Marguerite*'s position is unbeatable, especially if you want to explore the city by night. Friendly and well-run, the rooms are light and airy with a subtle but cheery colour scheme, and are surprisingly quiet considering the location. Breakfast €7. **€60**

## EATING AND DRINKING

Rue de Bourgogne is the main street for restaurants and nightlife, where you'll find an incredible range of world cuisine, all at very reasonable prices. To buy your own provisions, head to the covered market halls on place du Châtelet.

### EATING

★ **Chez Jules** 136 rue de Bourgogne ☎ 02 38 54 30 80, ⓦ chezjulesorleans.fr. Stone-brick interiors, mood lighting and choice ornaments make this a cosy, romantic choice. There's a small but quality menu (in French only) of regional specialities and scrumptious desserts. *Menus* from €29. Tues–Sat noon–1.45pm & 7–9.45pm.

**La Dariole** 25 rue Étienne-Dolet ☎ 02 38 77 26 67. Tearoom-cum-restaurant in a picture-postcard half-

timbered building, serving fresh, wholesome food at inexpensive prices (*menus* from €23). It's fairly small so reserve if you want to be sure of grabbing a table. Mon–Fri 12.30–2pm, Tues & Fri also 7.30–9.30pm.

**Le Lièvre Gourmand** 20 quai du Châtelet ☎ 02 38 53 66 14, ⓦ lelievregourmand.com. Michelin-star cuisine is on the menu in this old townhouse with a contemporary interior on the banks of the Loire. Dishes are inspired by chef Tristan Robreau's travels in Asia. Menus start at €41 and there's an excellent cheese board. Wed–Mon noon–12.30pm & 8–8.30pm.

**Le Lift** Place de la Loire ☎ 02 38 53 63 48, ⓦ restaurant-le-lift.com. Spectacularly situated atop the huge Pathé cinema on place de la Loire, this funky modern restaurant is reached by glass elevators located at the side of the cinema.

7

## FOOD AND DRINK OF THE LOIRE

The Loire is renowned for its mild climate and rich soils, qualities that help produce some of the best **fruit** and **vegetables** you'll find anywhere. From Anjou's orchards come greengages, named Reine Claude after François I<sup>er</sup>'s queen, and the succulent Anjou pear, Doyenné du Comice. Tours is famous for its French beans and Saumur for its potatoes and shallots. Asparagus, particularly the fleshy white variety, appears in soufflés, omelettes and other egg dishes as well as on its own, accompanied by vinaigrette made (if you're lucky) with local walnut oil. Finally, from Berry, comes the humble green lentil, which often accompanies salmon or trout.

Given the number of rivers that flow through the region, it's hardly surprising that **fish** features on most restaurant menus, though this doesn't guarantee that it's from the Loire itself. Favourites are *sandre* (pikeperch, a fish native to Central Europe), usually served in the classic Loire *beurre blanc* sauce; stuffed bream; *matelote* (a kind of stew) of local eels softened in red wine; and little smelt-like fishes served deep-fried (*la friture*).

The favoured **meat** of the Loire is game, and pheasant, guinea fowl, pigeon, duck, quails, young rabbit, venison and even wild boar are all hunted in the Sologne. They are served in rich sauces made from the wild mushrooms of the region's forests or the common *champignon de Paris*, cultivated on a huge scale in caves cut out of the limestone rock near Saumur (see page 409). Both Tours and Le Mans specialize in *rillettes*, or potted pork (*rillauds* in Anjou); in Touraine charcuteries you'll also find *pâté au biquion*, made from pork, veal and young goat's meat.

Touraine makes something of a cult of its **goat's cheese**, and a local *chèvre fermier* (farm-produced goat's cheese) can be a revelation. Four named goat's cheeses are found on most boards: Ste-Maure is a long cylinder with a piece of straw running through the middle; Pouligny-St-Pierre and Valençay are pyramid-shaped; and Selles-sur-Cher is flat and round.

### WINE

Though not as famous as the produce of Bordeaux and Burgundy, the Loire valley has some of the finest **wines** in France, including 27 AOC classified wines (ⓦ vinsvaldeloire.fr). Sancerre, the easternmost Loire *appellation*, produces the best white wines in the region from the Sauvignon grape, and the whites of Muscadet around Nantes are a great accompaniment to the local shellfish. Touraine's finest reds – Chinon, Bourgueil and St-Nicolas de Bourgueil – get their ruby colour from the Cabernet Franc grape, while many of its white wines are made from the Chenin Blanc, including the highly fashionable Jasnières. At the other end of the spectrum is the honeyed complexity of Côteaux du Layon's dessert wines – best with blue cheese or foie gras rather than pudding. Saumur and Vouvray both have excellent sparkling varieties, a fraction of the price of champagne, while the orangey liqueur **Cointreau** is made in a distillery close to Angers.

Head here for brunch (€42 *menu* every Sun) and enjoy the creations of renowned chef, Philippe Bardau, with a serene view of the Loire. Reservations required. Mon–Sat noon–2.30pm & 7.30–11pm, Sun noon–2.30pm.

**Oh Terroir Fast Good** 3 rue des Halles ☎02 38 75 71 26, ℗ ohterroir-orleans.fr. Delicious burgers with fries (menu €13.90 including drink), pasta dishes and salads (both €8.90 including drink), made with (mostly) organic produce from the surrounding area. Mon–Fri 11.30am–3pm & 6.30–10pm, Sat & Sun 11.30am–10pm.

★ **La Parenthèse** 26 place du Châtelet ☎02 38 62 07 50, ℗ restaurant-la-parenthese.com. A leafy terrace and timber-fronted facade add character to this small but incredibly popular restaurant, and reservations are a must. *Menus* start from €19 for lunch and there's a wide range of expertly crafted traditional dishes, followed by show-stopping desserts. Tues–Sat: noon–1pm & 7.30–9pm.

**DRINKING AND NIGHTLIFE**
**Les Becs à Vin** 8 pl du Châtelet ☎09 65 16 64 09, ℗ becsavin.com. Cosy, traditional wine bar specializing in organic, biodynamic wine. There are around 200 labels on the menu, which you can accompany with a plat du jour (€9.50) made with local produce. Mon–Sat noon–2pm & 6pm–1am.

**Java Pop** 45 rue de la Charpenterie ☎06 75 45 35 42 ℗ javapop.fr. Hip, youthful bar with affordable prices, outdoor seating and DJs. There's also an ample cocktail list – just €5 during Happy Hour (6–8pm). Daily 5pm–1am.

**Le P'tit Barcelone** 218 rue de Bourgogne ☎09 53 53 55 05. A laidback student haunt, this budget bar has cheapish drinks (€3–4 for a beer or glass of wine) and a range of tapas (from €5) to accompany them. Daily 3pm–1am.

**DIRECTORY**

**Festivals** Les Fêtes Johanniques is a series of period-costume parades held at the end of April and in May to celebrate Joan of Arc. The Jazz or Jazz festival (℗ jazzorjazz. fr) is held in April, with concerts in the Théâtre d'Orléans. Every September in odd years, the Loire Festival (℗ festivaldeloire.com) takes place, with five days of boats, concerts and shows beside the Châtelet quay.

**Health Centre** Hospitalier Régional La Source, 14 av de l'Hôpital ☎02 38 51 44 44; emergencies ☎15.

**Police** 63 rue du Faubourg St-Jean ☎02 38 24 30 00; emergencies ☎17 or 112.

# Meung-sur-Loire

The village of **MEUNG-SUR-LOIRE**, 14km southwest of Orléans, is an agreeable place to spend an afternoon – little streams known as *les mauves* flow between the houses here, and the sound of gurgling water is omnipresent. Meung has accumulated a number of literary associations over the centuries, taking its name from Jean de Meun, or de Meung, whose iconic adaptation of Guillaume de Lorris's poem *Roman de la Rose* in the late thirteenth century inspired generations of European writers. Most recently, the town featured in the works of Georges Simenon – his fictional hero, Maigret, takes his holidays here.

## Château de Meung
16 pl du Martroi • See website for opening times • €9 • ☎02 38 44 36 47, ℗ chateau-de-meung.com

Looming at the western edge of Meung-sur-Loire is the **Château de Meung**, which remained in the hands of the bishops of Orléans from its construction in the twelfth century right up to the Revolution, though since then it has passed through seven or eight private owners. The exterior of the château on the side facing the old drawbridge looks grimly defensive with its thirteenth-century pepper-pot towers, while the park side presents a much warmer facade, its eighteenth-century windows framed by salmon-pink stucco. You can explore the older part on your own, even poking around under the roof, but bear in mind that most of this pleasantly shambolic section of the building was remodelled in the nineteenth century, and little sense of its history remains. More impressive is the eighteenth-century wing, where the bishops entertained their guests in relative comfort. Below here are the cellars where criminals condemned by the Episcopal courts were imprisoned. The most famous of the detainees was the poet François Villon, who was kept under lock and key between May and October 1461.

### MUST-SEE CHÂTEAUX

First things first; though it is tempting to try and pack in as many châteaux as you can in a short period of time, this is counter-productive and frustrating. It's far better to aim to visit three or four of the best in the area in which you're staying, possibly with a one-day trip to one of the most spectacular set-piece châteaux.

### ADMISSIONS

Entry prices are undeniably steep, particularly for the châteaux that have remained in private hands – and there are a surprising number of French aristocrats still living in their family homes. This means that picking and choosing the best really will help you. There is no consistency in concessions offered, and children rarely go free. If you're over 65, under 25, a student or still at school, check for any reductions and make sure you've got proof of age or a student card with you. Here's a rundown of the very best châteaux to aim for:

**Chenonceau** (see page 382). Renaissance-period château in a glorious setting by the river.

**Azay-le-Rideau** (see page 405). A marvellous encapsulation of a long-gone period of grandeur and power, in a serene setting, surrounded by a moat.

**Blois** (see page 391). An impressive stronghold, with its four wings representing four distinct eras.

**Chambord** (see page 395). The triumph of François I's Renaissance, this monstrously huge château features a dual-spiral staircase allegedly designed by Leonardo da Vinci.

**Cheverny** (see page 394). A prime example of seventeenth-century magnificence.

**Amboise** (see page 401). One of the most compelling and striking Loire châteaux, rearing above the Loire like a cliff.

**Loches** (see page 388). For an evocation of medieval times, the citadelle of Loches is hard to beat.

**Langeais** (see page 404). Impressive interiors are the main attraction here, especially the tapestries and intricate tile work.

**Villandry** (see page 403). The simple elegance of this sixteenth-century château is overshadowed by its series of resplendent Renaissance gardens.

Other châteaux are more compelling for their contents than for their architecture:

**Valençay** (see page 386). The interior of this Renaissance château is Napoleonic – and it's a great spot for children.

**Beauregard** (see page 394). Most famous for its wonderful portrait gallery.

**La Bussière** (see page 377). Witness the obsessive nineteenth-century decoration, entirely dedicated to freshwater fishing.

**Angers** (see page 413). This stark, largely ruined medieval castle houses the *Tapestry of the Apocalypse*, the greatest work of art in the Loire valley.

---

**INFORMATION** **MEUNG-SUR-LOIRE**

**Tourist office** 1 rue Emmanuel-Troulet, Moulin de la Poterne (see website or call for opening times; ☎ 02 38 44 32 28, ⓦ entre-orleans-et-chambord.com). You can hire bikes here for €10 per day.

## Beaugency

**BEAUGENCY**, 6km southwest of Meung along the Loire, is a pretty little town, which, in contrast to its innocuous appearance today, played its part in the conniving games of early medieval politics. In 1152 the marriage of Louis VII of France and Eleanor of Aquitaine was annulled by the Council of Beaugency in the church of Notre-Dame, allowing Eleanor to marry Henry Plantagenet, the future Henry II of England. Her huge land holdings in southwest France thus passed to the English crown – which already controlled Normandy, Maine, Anjou and Touraine – and the struggles between the French and English kings over their claims to these territories, and to the French throne itself, lasted for centuries.

Liberated by the indefatigable Joan of Arc on her way to Orléans in 1429, Beaugency was a constant battleground during the Hundred Years' War due to its strategic significance as the only bridge crossing point of the Loire between Orléans and Blois. Remarkably, the 26-arch bridge still stands, and the once heavily fortified medieval town now clusters tightly around a handful of central squares. Place St-Firmin, with its statue of Joan, is overlooked by the only remaining tower of a church destroyed during the Revolution, while place Dunois is bordered by the massive eleventh-century **Tour de César**, formerly part of the rather plain, fifteenth-century **Château de Beaugency** (July & Aug daily 10am–7pm; May–June & Sept–Oct Tues–Sun 1–6pm; mid-Feb–April Sat–Sun 1–6pm; €9; ☎02 38 44 36 47, ⓦchateau-de-beaugency. com). The square is completed by the Romanesque abbey church of Notre-Dame, the venue for the council's fateful matrimonial decision in 1152. Shady place du Docteur-Hyvernaud, two blocks north of place Dunois, is dominated by the elaborate sixteenth-century facade of the *hôtel de ville*. Inside, the main council chamber is graced by eight fine embroidered wall hangings from the era of Louis XIII, but you'll have to ask at the tourist office (see below) to be allowed inside.

## INFORMATION BEAUGENCY

**Tourist office** Place du Docteur-Hyvernaud (Mon–Sat 10am–12.30pm & 2–6.30pm; ☎02 38 44 54 42, ⓦentre- orleans-et-chambord.com).

## ACCOMMODATION

**De l'Abbaye** 2 quai de l'Abbaye ☎02 38 45 10 10, ⓦgrandhoteldelabbaye.com. Set in a beautiful seventeenth-century abbey with painted ceilings and huge fireplaces, this charming place offers traditional luxury with prime Loire river views. Breakfast €16. **€69**

**Relais des Templiers** 68 rue du Pont ☎02 38 44 53 78, ⓦhotelrelaistempliers.com. This simple, homely hotel is a good budget option, with original wooden beams and walls adorned with old photos and knick-knacks. It's run by a delightful couple who take pride in their work, and

the newly refurbished rooms each have a unique touch, while the older rooms are a bit faded, though clean and functional. Breakfast €9.50. **€64**

**De la Sologne** 6 place St-Firmin ☎02 38 44 50 27, ⓦhotel-de-la-sologne.fr. A small, basic hotel with some original stone-brick walls and timbered ceilings. Rooms vary, with the upstairs rooms bright and airy, while those downstairs look a little tired. The flower-filled garden terrace is an idyllic spot for breakfast (€10.50). **€74**

## EATING AND DRINKING

**Chez Henri** 43 rue du Pont ☎02 38 44 16 65. Good-value classic French cuisine served by cheerful staff. There's a shaded terrace area just off the narrow street and a tasty selection of burgers and meat dishes (from €11.50). Tues–Sat noon–2pm & 7–9.45pm.

**La Crep'zeria** 32 rue du Pont ☎02 38 46 47 30. Perched on one of the little waterways that dot the streets in Beaugency, this is the place for decent and inexpensive pizzas and crêpes on the sunny terrace; with mains from €10.50. Wed–Sat noon–1.30pm & 7–9.30pm, Sun 7–10pm.

**L'Idée** 3 place du Petit-Marché ☎02 45 48 24 78. You'll

find seasonal *terroir* cooking with a modern twist in this stone and timber restaurant that has elegant decor and overlooks the market square. Lunch *menus* from €13.80. Daily noon–2pm & 7–9.30pm.

**Le P'tit Bateau** 54–56 rue du Pont ☎02 38 44 56 38, ⓦrestaurant-lepetitbateau.fr. With ambitious cuisine served up in traditional surroundings, and a team of young, motivated staff, it's easy to see why this place is so popular. Opt for the *menu gourmand* (€42) and tuck into dishes like lobster or wild asparagus and truffle risotto. Wed–Sun noon–2.30pm & 7–9.30pm.

# Château de la Ferté-St-Aubin

Daily: Feb 2–6pm; March–May 10am–6pm; June–Aug 10am–7pm; Sept to mid-Nov 10am–6pm • €9 • ☎02 38 76 52 72, ⓦchateau-ferte-st-aubin.com

The **Château de la Ferté-St-Aubin** lies 20km south of Orléans, at the north end of the village of **LA FERTÉ-ST-AUBIN**. The late sixteenth- and early seventeenth-century building presents an enticing combination of salmon-coloured brick, creamy limestone and dark slate roofs, while the interior is a real nineteenth-century home – and you are invited to treat it as such, which makes a real change from the stuffier attitudes of most grand homes. You can wander freely into almost every room, playing billiards or the piano, picking up the old telephone, sitting on the worn armchairs or washing your hands in a porcelain sink; only the rather fancier grand salon is cordoned off. There are demonstrations down in the kitchens of how to make Madeleines (Sat & Sun; daily July & Aug) – the sweet sponge cake that so inspired Proust. At the rear of the château, there's a play fort with sponge balls supplied for storming it, little cabins with dummies acting out fairy tales, and a toy farm.

| **ARRIVAL AND DEPARTURE** | **CHÂTEAU DE LA FERTÉ-ST-AUBIN** |
| --- | --- |
| **By train** The *gare SNCF* is roughly 200m southwest of the village square. | Destinations Bourges (hourly; 1hr); Orléans (frequent; 15min); Vierzon (frequent; 30min). |

## Germigny-des-Prés

Heading east of Orléans on the D960, you pass through Châteauneuf-sur-Loire – whose château has very pleasant gardens of rhododendrons and magnolias and a museum of traditional Loire shipping (☎02 38 46 84 46, ⓦmusee-marinedeloire.fr) – en route to **GERMIGNY-DES-PRÉS**, 30km from the city.

The small **church** (daily: April–Sept 9.30am–6.30pm; Oct–March 10am–5pm) incorporates at its east end one of the few surviving buildings from the Carolingian Renaissance – a tiny, perfectly formed church in the shape of a Greek cross. The oratory's antiquity has been slightly spoiled by too-perfect restoration work, but the unique gold and silver mosaic on the dome of the eastern chapel preserves all its rare beauty.

| **INFORMATION** | **GERMIGNY-DES-PRÉS** |
| --- | --- |
| **Tourist office** Next to the church (Jan & Dec Tues–Sun 1.30–5pm; Feb–March & Oct–Nov Tues 1.30–5pm, Wed–Sun 10am–12.30 & 1.30–5pm; April–June & Sept daily 9am–12.30pm & 1.30–6.30pm; July & Aug daily | 9am–6.30pm; ☎02 38 58 27 97, ⓦtourisme-loire-foret. com). It has a gallery of local artists' work, a shop selling specialities such as saffron and pralines, plus free wi-fi and a computer to use. |

## St-Benoît-sur-Loire

**ST-BENOÎT-SUR-LOIRE**, 5km further upstream from Germigny-des-Prés, along the D60, is dominated by the striking edifice of the Romanesque **Abbaye de Fleury** (daily 6.30am–10pm; Mass daily noon, Sun 11am; ⓦabbaye-fleury.com), which is populated by around thirty Benedictine monks who still observe the original Rule – poverty, chastity and obedience – and whose Gregorian chants can be heard at Mass. Built between 1020 and 1218, the church dates from the abbey's greatest epoch. The oldest part, the porch tower, illustrates St John's vision of the New Jerusalem in Revelation, while the fantastically sculpted capitals of the heavy pillars are alive with acanthus leaves, birds and exotic animals. Three of them depict scenes from the Apocalypse, while another shows Mary's flight into Egypt. Inside, the choir has two levels: above, a marble mosaic of Roman origin covers the chancel floor; below, the ancient crypt houses the relics of St Benoît.

## Sully-sur-Loire

**SULLY-SUR-LOIRE** lies on the south bank of the Loire, 7km east of St-Benoît. The village of Sully itself holds little appeal, but its grand château (Feb–April & Oct–Dec Tues–Sun Mon–Fri 1.30–5.30pm, Sat & Sun 10am–noon & 1.30–5.30pm; May–June & Sept Tues–Sun 10am–6pm; July & Aug daily 10am–7pm; €8; ☎02 38 36 36 86,ⓦchateausully.fr) is pure fantasy, despite savage wartime bombing that destroyed the nearby bridge. From the outside, rising out of its gigantic moat, it has all the picture-book requirements of pointed towers, machicolations and drawbridge.

## ARRIVAL AND INFORMATION SULLY-SUR-LOIRE

**By train** The *gare SNCF*, on the Bourges–Étampes line, is 10min from the village.

**By bus** The #7 route from Orléans drops you off by the château.

**Tourist office** Place de Gaulle (May–June & Sept Mon–Sat 9.30am–12.30pm & 2–6.30pm, Sun 10am–12.30pm; July & Aug Mon–Sat 9.30am–6.30pm, Sun 10am–12.30pm; Oct–April Mon–Wed & Fri–Sat 9.30amam–noon & 2–6pm,

Thurs 2–6pm; ☎02 38 36 23 70, ⊛sully-loire-sologne.co.uk).

**Bike rental** Passion Deux-Roues, 10 rue des Épinettes ☎02 38 35 13 13.

**Festivals** Sully's international Music Festival (⊛festivalsully.com) runs from mid-May to mid-June, featuring classical concerts held in a huge marquee in the château grounds.

## ACCOMMODATION AND EATING

**Aux P'tits Oignons** 1 rue du Port-au-Bois ☎02 38 67 64 16. This cosy restaurant in the old fisherman's district serves good value traditional French dishes. The three-course lunch menu is a steal at €15.50 (Tues–Fri): try pork terrine to start, then steak with fries, followed by chocolate mousse. Friendly service. Tues–Sat noon–2pm & 7–9pm.

**Burgevin** 11 rue du Fbg-St-Germain ☎02 38 38 13 12, ⊛hotelburgevin.com. Minutes from the château, this stylish and modern three-star hotel has spacious rooms with original wooden ceiling beam features, and the owners are helpful and friendly. Breakfast €14. **€115**

**Camping Le Jardin de Sully** ☎02 38 67 10 84, ⊛camping-bord-de-loire.com. On the banks of the Loire; there's a swimming pool and paddling pool for little ones

and café-bar-style restaurant. **€22**

**La Closeraie** 14 rue Porte Berry ☎02 38 05 10 90, ⊛hotel-la-closeraie.fr. Eleven spacious, individually decorated rooms, with dark wood floors, fireplaces and crisp white duvets. There's also a pretty terrace garden, a jacuzzi and sauna. Breakfast €10. **€85**

**Hostellerie du Grand Sully** 10 bd du Champ-de-Foire ☎02 38 36 27 56, ⊛grandsully.com. Lovely three-star hotel and restaurant on the south side of town, which is part of the Logis de France group. Chef Yves Dessaint uses seasonal, local produce to create refined dishes served in the smart dining room. Three-course lunch from €18. Tues–Fri noon–2pm & 7–9pm, Sat 7–9pm, Sun noon–2pm.

# Gien

The pretty town of **GIEN** has been restored to its late fifteenth-century quaintness after extensive wartime bombing, and the sixteenth-century stone bridge spanning the river gives excellent views as you approach from the south.

## Musée International de la Chasse et de la Nature

1 pl du Château • May–Sept daily 10am–6pm; Oct–April Mon–Fri 1.30–5.30pm, Sat & Sun 10am–noon & 1.30–5.30pm • €8 • ☎02 38 67 69 69, ⊛chateaumuseegien.fr

The fifteenth-century château above the town centre – where the young Louis XIV and his mother, Anne of Austria, hid during the revolts against taxation known as the Frondes (see Contexts) – has been turned over to the **Musée International de la Chasse et de la Nature**, with the emphasis more on *la chasse* – hunting horns, tapestries, exquisite watercolours of horseback hunts, guns and falconers' gear – than *la nature*. One of the significant consequences of the French Revolution for rural people was the right to hunt, a right still vehemently guarded today. The château itself is modest, but unusual in its brick construction, a pattern of dark red interrupted by geometric inlays of grey.

## Musée de la Faïencerie

78 place de la Victoire • Mon–Sat 10am–7pm, Sun 10am–5pm (closed Sun Oct–March) • €5 • ☎02 38 05 21 06

Gien is famous for its fine china, and it's worth paying a visit to the **Musée de la Faïencerie**, adjacent to the factory shop (where you can buy beautiful china at vastly discounted prices), which displays the more extravagant ceramic knick-knacks produced over the centuries.

## ARRIVAL AND INFORMATION GIEN

**By bus** Bus #3, which runs between Briare and Orléans seven times daily, stops at place Leclerc, at the north end

of the bridge.

**Tourist office** Place Jean-Jaurès (May, June & Sept Mon–

Sat 9.30am–12.30pm & 1.30–6pm; July & Aug Mon–Sat 9.30am–6.30pm, Sun 9am–1pm; Oct–April Mon 1.30– 5pm; Tues–Sat 10am–12.30pm & 1.30–5pm; ☎02 38 67 25 28, ⓦgien-tourisme.fr).

## ACCOMMODATION AND EATING

**La Bodega** 17 rue Bernard-Palissy ☎02 38 67 29 01, ⓦhotel-restaurant-labodega.fr. Simple, functional rooms available above a very decent pizza and tapas restaurant. It's no-frills, but friendly and good value. Breakfast €6. **€45**

**Camping Touristique de Gien** ☎02 38 67 12 50, ⓦcamping-gien.com. Right on the riverbank, with a swimming pool and outdoor activities, including bike rental and canoe trips. Closed mid-Nov to Feb. **€20**

**L'Olivier** 22 quai Lenoir ☎02 38 38 13 45. Delicious Mediterranean cuisine with generous portions and decadent desserts are on offer at this chic waterfront restaurant and service comes with a smile. Lunch menus

from €18. Mon–Tues & Fri–Sat noon–2pm & 7.30–9.30pm, Sun noon–2pm.

**Le P'tit Bouchon** 66 rue Bernard-Palissy ☎02 38 67 84 40. Classic French cuisine served with minimal fuss and competitive prices (three-course *menus* from €27), makes *Le P'tit Bouchon* worth venturing away from the riverfront. It's a popular haunt for locals, so book ahead to be sure. Tues–Sat noon–1.30pm & 7.15–8.45pm.

**Du Rivage** 1 quai de Nice ☎02 38 37 79 00. Just a minute's walk out of town, across from the river, this hotel has spacious, classic-style rooms and friendly staff. Decide whether you want a room with a bath or a room with a Loire view, as those at the front only have showers. Breakfast €11. **€82**

# La Bussière

Twelve kilometres northeast of Gien is a surprising château dedicated to fishing: the so-called **Château des Pêcheurs** (April & Oct Mon & Wed–Sun 2–6pm; May–June & Sept daily except Tues 10am–noon 2–6pm; July & Aug daily 10am–6pm; Dec Sat & Sun 2–6pm; €9; ☎02 38 35 93 35, ⓦchateau-de-la-bussiere.fr) at **LA BUSSIÈRE**. Initially a fortress, the château was turned into a luxurious residence at the end of the sixteenth century, but only the gateway and one pepper-pot tower are recognizably medieval. Guided tours are available, but you're free to wander around, soaking up the genteel atmosphere evoked by the handsome, largely nineteenth-century furnishings and the eccentrically huge collection of freshwater fishing memorabilia bequeathed by Count Henri de Chasseval. The eighteenth-century walled vegetable garden is classed as one of France's "remarkable gardens".

# Briare

The small town of **BRIARE**, 10km southeast of Gien on the Orléans–Nevers road and the Paris–Nevers rail line, is known for its *belle époque* iron aqueduct, the **Pont Canal**. Linking the Canal de Briare to the north with the Canal Latéral à la Loire, it's the longest bridge canal in Europe. The design of the Pont Canal came from the workshops of Gustave Eiffel (of Tower fame), but parts of the canal date back to the early seventeenth century.

On the opposite side of town from the canal, at the northern end, is the tiny **Maison des Deux Marines** on 58 bd Buyser (daily: March–May & Oct–Nov 2–6pm; June–Sept 10am–12.30pm & 2–6.30pm; €5.50; ☎02 38 31 28 27, ⓦmusee-2-marines.com) which is dedicated to the rival boatmen who plied the Loire and the Canal Latéral; its basement houses a modest aquarium of Loire species.

## INFORMATION AND TOURS                                                    BRIARE

**Tourist office** 1 place Charles-de-Gaulle (April to mid-Aug Mon–Sat 10am–noon & 2–6pm; mid-Aug to Sept Mon–Sat 10am–noon & 2–6pm, Sun 10am–noon; Oct–March Mon 2–5pm, Tues–Sat 10am–noon & 2–5pm; ☎02 38 31 24 51, ⓦtourisme-briare.com). Provides details of boat rental.

**Boat tours** Les Bateaux Touristiques (Quai de la Trezee, ☎02 38 37 12 75, ⓦles-bateaux-touristiques-briare.com) run boat tours from April–Oct, starting from €8.50 for a 1hr 30min cruise.

## ACCOMMODATION AND EATING

**Le Cerf** 22 bd Buyser ☎02 38 37 00 80, ⓦhotelducerf. com. Basic and clean, offering bike garages and private

## THE VINEYARDS OF SANCERRE

If you're going to be staying in Sancerre, your first priority is probably going to be the wine, so it makes sense to have an idea of which are the best vineyards in the area. There are numerous quirks of wine production here; for instance, wines aren't allowed to carry an individual vineyard's name, instead being sold under the name of the producer or, very occasionally, the cuvée.

First port of call for wine enthusiasts should be the Maison des Sancerre on 3 rue du Méridien (April–Oct daily 10am–6.30pm; €8; ☏ 02 48 54 11 35, ⚅ maison-des-sancerre.com), a fourteenth-century townhouse with a great view over the vine-clad hills around. With its entertaining film shows and interactive exhibits, you'll get a comprehensive picture of winemaking in Sancerre and a tasting is included. The Maison also organizes bespoke tours of wine and cheese makers in the region combined with cycling or canoeing activities.

To accompany your wines, try the local *crottin de Chavignol*, a goat's cheese named after the neighbouring village, just 4km away, in which it's made; Dubois-Boulay (☏ 02 48 54 08 23, ⚅ dubois-boulay.fr) offers the best selection. Henri Bourgeois (☏ 02 48 78 53 20, ⚅ henribourgeois.com), up the hill, has been making wine for ten generations. Call ahead to book a 45-minute tour with a *dégustation* (from €40).

**7**

parking, a garden with clothes-drying space and BBQ. The rooms are reasonably well-sized but expect no frills. Breakfast €9. **€64**

**Chocolat et Chimères** Quai Mayzoyer ☏ 02 38 37 10 58. Follow the footpath at the right side of the bridge from quai Mayzoyer and you'll find Briare's most idyllic café, poised right on the banks of the Pont Canal. Artisan chocolatier Hervé Roussel whips up a decadent array of chocolates,

*macarons*, cakes and ice creams (from €2), plus there's a range of teas and cold drinks. Tues–Sun 10.30am–7pm.

**Le Petit St-Trop** 5 rue Tissier ☏ 02 38 37 00 31. Excellent-quality traditional cuisine with *menus* from €20 and a special children's menu, this popular haunt has ample outdoor seating with a view over the canal. Tues–Sat noon–2pm & 7.30–8.45pm, Sun noon–2pm.

# Sancerre

Huddled at the top of a steep, round hill with vineyards below, **SANCERRE** could almost be in Tuscany. The village trades heavily on its famous wines – there are endless *caves* offering tastings – rather than any particular sights or attractions, but it's certainly picturesque and the rolling hills of the Sancerrois, to the northwest, make an attractive venue for walks and cycle rides.

## ARRIVAL AND INFORMATION

SANCERRE

**By bus** The town is difficult to access by public transport, save for an infrequent bus service (#110) to and from Bourges, which leaves no more than twice a day.

**Tourist office** Esplanade Porte César (daily: April–June & Sept 10am–12.30pm & 1.30–6pm; July & Aug

10am–6.30pm; Oct–Dec & March 2–5pm; ☏ 02 48 54 08 21, ⚅ tourisme-sancerre.com). The tourist office offers a map with a walking tour of the village, including several panoramic viewpoints.

## ACCOMMODATION

★ **Le Cep en Sancerrois** 2 rue du Maréchal-Macdonald ☏ 06 85 71 72 20, ⚅ lecepensancerrois.com. The personal touches of Dutch-Belgian owners make this *chambre d'hôte* a home away from home, complete with creaky wooden staircases and bookshelves groaning with books. Rooms are spacious and modern with plenty of character, while the attic is a quirky space with partition walls and striking wooden beams. There's even a hammam. Breakfast is included and dinner available on request (€30). **€95**

**Le Clos Saint-Martin** 10 rue Saint-Martin ☏ 02 48 54 21 11, ⚅ leclos-saintmartin.com. Well located near the

main square, Le *Clos* is excellent value for money, with a range of rooms and suites. The windowless patio rooms are surprisingly bright and airy, while the rattan flooring adds a unique edge. Breakfast €11.50. **€65**

**La Côte des Monts-Damnés** Place de l'Orme, Chavignol ☏ 02 48 54 01 72, ⚅ montsdamnes.com. In the heart of goat's cheese country and nestled in a quiet village – which looks like the last place you'd find this modern, well-designed hotel – is the boutique-style *La Côte*. It's a fun mix of traditional on the outside and funky on the inside, plus there's a fine bistro on-site. Breakfast €14. **€115**

**EATING AND DRINKING**

**Auberge L'Écurie** Rue de la Tour du Chancelier ☎ 02 48 72 17 03, ⊕ auberge-ecurie.fr. Around the corner from the main square, Nouvelle Place, with plenty of outdoor seating, the no-frills *Auberge L'Écurie* is one of the town's longest running restaurants. The wide range of pizzas (around €14), grills, crêpes and salads (around €11) are both tasty and affordable. Service can be brusque. Daily noon–2pm & 7–10pm.

**La Tour** 31 Nouvelle Place, ☎ 02 48 54 00 81, ⊕ latoursancerre.fr. Transforming locally sourced meat and veg into gourmet creations that look almost too good to eat, *La Tour* is one of the best restaurants in the Loire, with a phonebook-length wine list. Splash out on the *menu dégustation* with wine for €110. If that's beyond your budget, then book in for lunch as the *menus* start at €25. Tues–Sun noon–2pm & 7.30–9.30pm.

# Bourges

**BOURGES**, the chief town of the region of Berry, is some way from the Loire valley proper but linked historically. It has one of the finest Gothic cathedrals in France, rising gloriously out of the well-preserved medieval quarter, which provides enough reason for making a detour.

7

## Musée des Arts Décoratifs and Musée Estève

Bourges's museums may be modest, but they are housed in some beautiful medieval buildings. Rue Bourbonnoux is worth a wander for the early Renaissance Hôtel Lallemant, richly decorated in an Italianate style. It contains the **Musée des Arts Décoratifs** (Tues–Sat 10am–noon & 2–6pm, Sun 2–6pm; €4; ☎ 02 48 70 23 57), a diverting enough museum of paintings, tapestries, furniture and *objets d'art*, including works by the Berrichon artist Jean Boucher (1575–1633).

Nearby, the fifteenth-century Hôtel des Échevins houses the **Musée Estève** (13 rue Édouard-Branly; Mon & Wed–Sat 10am–noon & 2–6pm, Sun 2–6pm; €4; ☎ 02 48 24 75 38), dedicated to the highly coloured, mostly abstract paintings and tapestries of local artist Maurice Estève, who died in 2001.

## Palais de Jacques-Coeur

Daily: April & Sept 10am–12.15pm & 2–6pm; May & June 9.30am–12.15 & 2–6.15pm; July & Aug 10am–12.45pm & 2–6.15pm; Oct–March 9.30am–12.30pm & 2–5.15pm • €8 • Guided tours every 30min–1hr, depending on the season

**Rue Jacques-Coeur** was the site of the head office, stock exchange, dealing rooms, bank safes and home of Charles VII's finance minister, Jacques Coeur (1400–56). A medieval shipping magnate, moneylender and arms dealer, Coeur dominates Bourges as Joan of Arc does Orléans. The **Palais de Jacques-Coeur** is one of the most remarkable examples of fifteenth-century domestic architecture in France. There are hardly any furnishings, but the house's stonework recalls the man who had it built, including a pair of bas-reliefs on the courtyard tower that may represent Jacques and his wife, and numerous hearts and scallop shells inside that playfully allude to his name.

## Musée du Berry

4 rue des Arènes • Mon & Wed–Sat 10am–noon & 2–6pm, Sun 2–6pm • €4 • ☎ 02 48 70 41 92

Housed in the sixteenth-century Hôtel Cujas, the **Musée du Berry** is made up of local artefacts, most notably ten of the forty *pleurants* (mourners) that survived the breaking up of Jean de Berry (John the Magnificent)'s tomb. Rodin considered these weeping statues so beautiful that he paid six thousand francs for one shortly before his death.

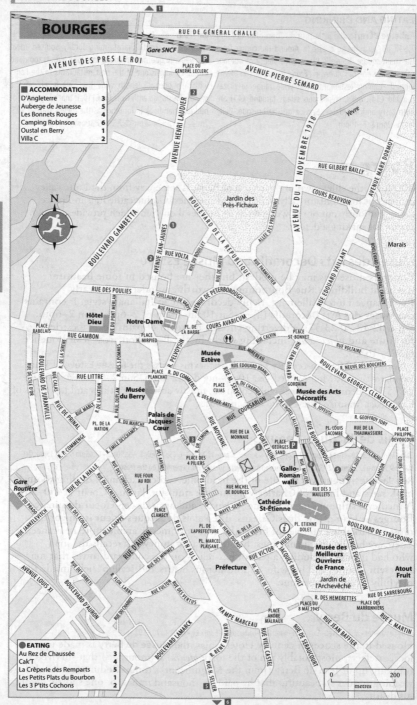

# BOURGES

Gare SNCF

PLACE DU
GENERAL LECLERC

AVENUE DES PRES LE ROI

AVENUE PIERRE SEMARD

**ACCOMMODATION**

| | |
|---|---|
| D'Angleterre | 3 |
| Auberge de Jeunesse | 5 |
| Les Bonnets Rouges | 4 |
| Camping Robinson | 6 |
| Oustal en Berry | 1 |
| Villa C | 2 |

Yèvre

RUE GILBERT BAILLY

AVENUE MARX DORMOY

Jardin des
Près-Fichaux

COURS BEAUVOIR

Marais

N

BOULEVARD GAMBETTA

AVENUE JEAN-JAURÈS

RUE VOLTA

BOULEVARD DE LA RÉPUBLIQUE

AVENUE DU 11 NOVEMBRE 1918

BOULEVARD DU GENERAL CHANZY

RUE EDOUARD VAILLANT

RUE DES POULIES

R. GUILLAUME DE VARYE

AVENUE DE PETERBOROUGH

RUE PARMENTIER

Hôtel
Dieu

RUE PARERIE

RUE DU PONT MERLIAN

Notre-Dame

PLACE
H. MIRPIED

PLACE DE
LA BARRE

COURS AVARICUM

RUE CALVIN

PLACE
ST-BONNET

RUE VOLTAIRE

PLACE
RABELAIS

RUE GAMBON

R. DE LA SIRÈNE

R. DES 3 POMMES

R. P'EVOYSIN

Musée
Estève

RUE MIREBEAU

RUE EDOUARD BRANLY

RUE JEAN GIRARD

BOULEVARD GEORGES CLEMENCEAU

BOULEVARD DE JURANVILLE

RUE DE L'ILE D'OR

RUE CALAIS

RUE MABLY

R. DE LA NATION

RUE LITTRE

PLACE
PLANCHAT

R. DU COMMERCE

R. DU CHARRIER

PL.
GORDAINE

Musée des Arts
Décoratifs

R. JOYEUSE

R. GEOFFROY IORY

PLACE
PHILIPPE
DÉVOUCOUX

BOULEVARD DE PRIMAL

R. PAUL DUPLAN

Musée
du Berry

PLACE
CUJAS

R. DES BEAUX-ARTS

RUE COURSARLON

R. DE L'HOTEL LALLEMAND

PL.-LOUIS
LACOMBE

RUE DE LA
THAUMASSIERE

PL. DE LA
NATION

R. DU MARCHE

Palais de
Jacques-
Cœur

RUE JACQUES CŒUR

R. DR. TEMOIN

RUE MOYENNE

RUE DE LA
MONNAIE

RUE PORTE JAUNE

RUE BOURBONNOUX

R. P. COMMENGE

R. ÉMILE DESCHAMPS

RUE DES ARÈNES

PLACE DES
4 PILIERS

PLACE-
GEORGES
SAND

Gare
Routière

RUE DE LA HALLE

RUE DU SECRETAIN

RUE FOUR
AU ROI

RUE MICHEL
DE BOURGES

Gallo-
Roman
walls

RUE DES 3
MAILLETS

R. MICHELET

BOULEVARD DE STRASBOURG

RUE DU PRADO

RUE JANKELEVITCH

RUE DES ÉCOLES

RUE DE LA CHAPPE

RUE DES CORDELIERS

PLACE
CLAMECY

RUE FERNAULT

RUE MAYET-GENETRY

PL. DE
LAPREFECTURE

RUE HENRI DUCROT

RUE DE LA
CAGE VERTE

Cathédrale
St-Étienne

PL. ETIENNE
DOLET

RUE HUGO

BOULEVARD AVENUE EUGENE BRISSON

AVENUE LOUIS XI

BOULEVARD D'AURON

RUE D'AURON

RUE DES MINIMES

PL. MARCEL
PLAISANT

Préfecture

RUE VICTOR

R. JACQUES RIMBAULT

Musée des
Meilleurs
Ouvriers
de France

Atout
Fruit

Jardin de
l'Archevêché

RUE FLOR LABRE

RUE DES VERTUS

RUE FULTON

AV. DU PISE DE LIGNE

PLACE DU
8 MAI 1945

R. DES HEMERETTES

PLACE DES
MARRONNIERS

RUE DE SARREBOURG

RUE E. MARTIN

RUE DU CHAMBOT

RAMPE MARCEAU

BOULEVARD LAMARCK

RUE RENE MENARD

RUE VIEIL CASTEL

PLACE ANDRE
MALRAUX

RUE DE SERAUCOURT

RUE JEAN BAFFIER

RUE R. SELLIER

**EATING**

| | |
|---|---|
| Au Rez de Chaussée | 3 |
| Cak'T | 4 |
| La Crêperie des Remparts | 5 |
| Les Petits Plats du Bourbon | 1 |
| Les 3 P'tits Cochons | 2 |

| 0 | | 200 |
|---|---|---|
| | metres | |

# The cathedral

Place Étienne-Dolet • Tower and crypt: daily except Sun morning: April &Sept 0—11.45am & 2—5.30pm; May—Aug 9.30—11.30am & 2—5.45 pm; Oct—March 9.30—11.30am & 2—4.45pm • Last entry 45min before closing • €6 for tower or €8 with the crypt • ☎ 02 48 65 49 44, ⓦ bourges-cathedrale.fr

The exterior of the twelfth-century **Cathédrale St-Étienne**, a UNESCO World Heritage Site, is characterized by the delicate, almost skeletal appearance of its flying buttresses and it's a captivating sight. A much-vaunted example of Gothic architecture, it's modelled on Notre-Dame in Paris but incorporates improvements on the latter's design, such as the astonishing height of the inner aisles.

The interior's top feature is the twelfth- to thirteenth-century **stained glass**. The most dazzling windows surround the choir and were all created between 1215 and 1225. You can follow various stories – the Prodigal Son, the Good Samaritan, Christ's Crucifixion and the Apocalypse; binoculars come in handy for picking up the exquisite detail. The painted decoration of France's oldest astronomical clock in the nave celebrates the wedding of Charles VII, who married Marie d'Anjou here on April 22, 1422. On the northwest side of the nave aisle is the door to the **Tour de Beurre**, which you can climb for fantastic views over the old city (396 steps). There are guided tours of the **crypt** (reservations required), which shelters the alabaster statue of a puggish Jean de Berry; a bear, the symbol of strength, lies asleep at his feet. It's also possible to climb unsupervised to the top of the north tower, rebuilt in Flamboyant style after the original collapsed in 1506.

## ARRIVAL AND DEPARTURE                                    BOURGES

**By train** The *gare SNCF* lies 1km north of the centre; it's a straightforward walk along avenues Henri-Laudier and Jean-Jaurès to place Planchat, from where rue du Commerce connects with the main street, rue Moyenne. Destinations Nevers (frequent; 45min); Orléans (frequent; 1hr 15min); Paris (frequent; 2hr 43min); Tours (frequent; 1hr 40min).

**By bus** The *gare routière* is on rue du Prado, west of bd Juranville, with one or two daily services to Sancerre (1hr 15min).

## INFORMATION

**Tourist office** Just off the top end of rue Moyenne, at 21 rue Victor-Hugo (April—Sept Mon—Sat 9am—7pm, Sun 10am—6pm; Oct—March Mon 2—6pm, Tues—Sat 10am—6pm) ☎ 02 48 23 02 60, ⓦ bourgesberrytourisme.com.

**Festivals** Un Eté à Bourges (ⓦ ville-bourges.fr) lasts from the end of June until late September and involves free concerts every night in unusual settings, from bandstands to boats. Le Printemps de Bourges (ⓦ printemps-bourges. com) features hundreds of contemporary music acts over a week in April; there's a medieval festival in June and atmospheric lighting transforms the old town every evening from June to September.

## ACCOMMODATION

**D'Angleterre** Place des Quatre-Piliers ☎ 02 48 24 68 51, ⓦ bestwestern-angleterre-bourges.com. This four-star hotel has classic rooms with red accents, all the mod cons, and an excellent location right next to the Palais de Jacques-Coeur. Breakfast €14. **€140**

**Auberge de Jeunesse** 22 rue Henri-Sellier ☎ 02 48 24 58 09, ⓦ fuaj.org. Decent hostel located a short way southwest of the centre, with a garden on the River Auron. Take bus #1 from the station or it's a 10min walk from the cathedral or *gare routière*. Reception hours mid-Jan to mid-Dec Mon—Fri 10—11am & 6—9pm. Dorms **€16.95**

★ **Les Bonnets Rouges** 3 rue de la Thaumassière ☎ 02 48 65 79 92, ⓦ bonnetsrouges.bourges.fr. This family-run *chambre d'hôte* is a pocket of calm in a striking seventeenth-century house just off rue Bourbonnoux. Shabby-chic decor and eclectic furnishings make each room unique – the "Suite Romance" is particularly beautiful. **€76**

**Camping Robinson** 26 bd de l'Industrie ☎ 02 48 20 16 85. Decent-sized, three-star site located south of the hostel. Bus Beugnon, from Nation, stop "Val D'Auron", or a 10min walk from the *gare routière*. Closed mid-Nov to March. **€14.50**

★ **Oustal en Berry** 7 rue Félix-Chédin ☎ 02 48 70 26 64, ⓦ oustalenberry.fr. Two minutes from the station and set in a nineteenth-century merchant's house with pretty gardens, these four themed *chambres d'hôtes* are inspired by the lives of famous French women – the "Colette" is decked out in rich creams and gold; the Coco Chanel in elegant monochrome. The hosts are genuine and friendly, serving up delicious home-made cakes and jams for breakfast (included), around a communal table. **€90**

7

**Villa C** 20 av Henri-Laudier ☎02 18 15 04 00, ⓦhotelvillac.com. Close to the train station, this upmarket urban boutique hotel has just ten rooms; ask for the "Villa Terrasse", which has its own terrace. Breakfast €13. €95

## EATING AND DRINKING

Bourges's main centre for eating is along rue Bourbonnoux, which is crammed with restaurants, pubs and bars. Alternatively, pick up picnic goodies at the Halle St-Bonnet market (Tues–Fri 8am–12.30pm, 3.30–7pm, Sat 8am–7pm, Sun 8am–1pm).

**Au Rez de Chaussée** 8 rue Porte Jaune ☎02 48 65 99 60. Creative French cuisine and enthusiastic service help make this one of Bourges's most popular restaurants. Be sure to book ahead. Mains around €20. Tues & Thurs noon–2pm & 7–10pm, Wed noon–2pm, Fri & Sat noon–2pm & 7–11pm.

**Cak'T** Promenade des Remparts ☎02 48 24 94 60, ⓦcak-t.com. Tucked under the old ramparts just off rue Bourbonnoux, this refined tearoom serves home-made quiches and tarts at lunchtime and is a local favourite for afternoon tea. It's just off the main street, so look out for the sign. Tues–Sat noon–2pm & 3–6pm, Sun 3–6pm.

**La Crêperie des Remparts** 59 rue Bourbonnoux ☎02 48 24 55 44. Great-value, freshly made crêpes, galettes (from €6.40) and salads, best enjoyed in the sun-trap garden at the back of the restaurant. Tues–Sat noon–2pm & 7–10pm.

**Les Petits Plats du Bourbon** Hôtel de Bourbon Mercure Bourges, 60 av Jean-Jaurès ☎02 48 70 79 90, ⓦlespetitsplatsdubourbon.com. In the impressive setting of the choir of the seventeenth-century Abbaye de St-Ambroix, this contemporary bistro serves modern French market cuisine. For lunch try a cocotte (casserole) with an appetizer and dessert (€18); evening menus start at €27. Mon 7.15–9.30pm, Tues–Sat 11.45am–1.45pm & 7.15–9.45pm.

**Les 3 P'tits Cochons** 27 av Jean-Jaurès ☎02 48 65 64 96, ⓦrestaurant-3ptitscochons.fr. Head here for a lively local vibe and some great bistro-style and tapas cooking. Mains from around €13. DJs spin anything from electro to pop at weekends, special nights come with a door charge of usually no more than €4. Mon & Sat 5pm–2am, Wed–Fri 11am–2pm & 5pm–2am

# The Cher and Indre

Of all the Loire's many tributaries, the slow-moving **Cher** and **Indre** are closest to the heart of the region, watering a host of châteaux as they flow northwest from this little-visited region to the south. Twenty kilometres southeast of Tours, spanning the Cher, the **Château de Chenonceau** is perhaps the quintessential Loire château for its architecture, site, contents and atmosphere. Further upstream, **Montrichard** and **St-Aignan** make quieter diversions from the endless stream of castle tours. To the south is the **Château de Valençay**, with its exquisite Empire interiors. A short drive west of here, on the River Indre itself, is the lovely town of **Loches**, which possesses the most magnificent medieval citadelle in the region.

## Château de Chenonceau

Daily: April & May 9.30am–7pm; June & Sept 9.30am–7.30pm; July & Aug 9.30am–8pm; Oct 9.30am–6.30pm; Nov to mid-Feb 9.30am–5pm; mid-Feb to March 9.30am–5.30pm • Last entrance 1hr before close • Château, gardens and galleries €14, with iPod audioguide €18 • ☎08 20 20 90 90, ⓦchenonceau.com

The gentle River Cher flows so slowly and passively between the exquisite arches of the **Château de Chenonceau** that you're almost always assured of a perfect reflection. The château is not visible from the road, so you have to pay before even getting a peek at the residence. While the tree-lined path to the front door is dramatic, wind your way through the gardens for a more intimate approach; they were laid out under Diane de Poitiers, mistress of Henri II. During summer the place teems with people and it can become uncomfortably crowded, so try to visit first thing.

### Inside the château

Visits are unguided – a relief, for there's an endless array of arresting tapestries, paintings, ceilings, floors and furniture on show (although you could opt for the worthwhile iPod guided tour).

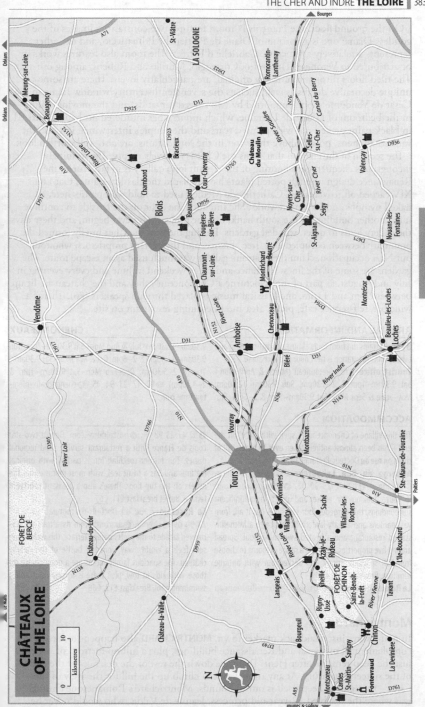

CHÂTEAUX
OF THE LOIRE

0       10
kilometres

N

On the **ground floor**, the François I$^{er}$ room features two contrasting images of the goddess Diana; one is a portrait of Diane de Poitiers by Primaticcio, and the other represents a relatively aristocratic Gabrielle d'Estrées. The room also features works by or attributed to Veronese, Tintoretto, Correggio, Murillo and Rubens, among others. The tiled floors throughout, many original, are particularly lovely. There are some unique decorative details as well, such as the seventeenth-century window frame in the César de Vendôme room, supported by two carved caryatids, and the moving ceiling in the bedroom of Louise de Lorraine, which mourns her murdered husband Henri III in black paint picked out with painted tears and the couple's intertwined initials. The vaulted **kitchens**, poised above the water in the foundations, are also well worth a look.

The section of the château that spans the Cher is relatively empty. The seemingly incongruous chequerboard flooring of the elegant **long gallery** is in fact true to the Renaissance design, though potted plants have replaced the classical statues that Louis XIV carried off to Versailles. Catherine de Médicis used to hold wild parties here, all naked nymphs and Italian fireworks. She intended the door on the far side to continue into another building on the south bank, but the project was never begun, and these days the gallery leads to quiet, wooded gardens. During the war, the Cher briefly formed the boundary between occupied and "free" France, and the current proprietors, who rode out Nazi occupation, claim the château's gallery was much used as an escape route. The gardens are some of the finest in France and every weekend in June and every evening in July and August, as part of the "Nocturne à Chenonceau", they and the château are lit up between 9pm and 11pm, and classical music is played through speakers (€6). There's a wine bar, self-service café, picnic area and fine-dining restaurant on site.

## ARRIVAL AND INFORMATION
CHENONCEAUX

**By train** Trains run from Tours almost hourly from 6am and take 30min. The station is next door to the château.

**Tourist office** 1 rue Bretonneau (March & April Mon–Sat 9.30am–1pm & 2–5.30pm, Sun 9.30am–12.30pm; May–June & Sept Mon–Sat 9.30am–1pm & 2–6pm, Sun 9.30am–12.30pm; July & Aug Mon–Sat 9.30am–7pm, Sun 9.30am–12.30pm & 2–6pm; Oct & Nov Mon–Sat 9.30am–1pm & 2–5.30pm; Dec–Feb Mon–Sat 9.30am–1pm & 2–4.30pm) ☎02 47 23 94 45, ⓦchenonceaux-blere-tourisme.com.

## ACCOMMODATION

The tiny village of Chenonceaux – spelt with an "x" on the end – has been almost entirely taken over by hotels, all of them on rue du Docteur-Bretonneau.

**Auberge du Bon Laboureur** 6 rue du Docteur-Bretonneau ☎02 47 23 90 02, ⓦbonlaboureur.com. If you're looking for peace and quiet in magnificent surroundings, this gorgeous four-star hotel has it all, from vast gardens and a leafy lantern-lit terrace to a Michelin-starred restaurant and a heated swimming pool. Spread around five properties, there are a range of rooms to choose from, all spacious, sunny and decked out with antique furniture. Breakfast €18. **€149**

**Le Relais Chenonceaux** 10 rue du Docteur-Bretonneau ☎02 47 23 98 11, ⓦhostelduroy.com. Decent two-star Logis de France with a restaurant serving solid regional dishes. This former coaching inn is packed with original features and has a rustic feel, with most rooms under the rafters on the top floor. There's also a pleasant courtyard terrace. Buffet breakfast €11. **€67**

**La Roseraie** 7 rue du Docteur-Bretonneau ☎02 47 23 90 09 ⓦchenonceaux.com. From its attractive, ivy-covered facade to the pretty garden terrace, this welcoming spot feels a world away from the bustle of the nearby château. The spacious family rooms are a good choice for those with kids in tow, plus there is a restaurant and a swimming pool. Breakfast €12. **€68**

# Montrichard

In many ways just a laidback market town, **MONTRICHARD** also happens to have a full complement of medieval and Renaissance buildings, plus a hilltop fortress, of which just the keep remains after Henri IV broke down the rest of the defences at the end of the sixteenth century. At any time, you can climb up the hill for the view of the Cher – though the keep itself is out of bounds. Montrichard's Romanesque church was where the disabled 12-year-old princess, Jeanne de Valois, who would never be able to have children, married her cousin the Duc d'Orléans. When he became King Louis XII, after the unlikely death of Charles VIII at Amboise, politics dictated that he marry Charles VIII's widow, Anne of Brittany. Poor Jeanne was divorced and sent off to govern Bourges, where she founded a new religious order and eventually took the veil herself, before dying in 1505.

### ARRIVAL AND INFORMATION

**By bus** There are four buses a day from Blois (line #6).

**Tourist office** Housed in the Maison Ave Maria, an ancient house with saints and beasts sculpted down its beams, on rue du Pont (April–June & Sept Mon–Sat 9.30am–12.30pm

MONTRICHARD

& 2–6pm, Sun 10am–1pm; July & Aug daily 10am–6pm; Oct–March Mon–Fri 10am–noon & 2–5pm); ☎02 54 32 05 10, ⓦducheralaloire.com

### ACCOMMODATION AND EATING

**Le Bellevue** 24 quai de la République ☎02 54 32 06 17, ⓦhotel-le-bellevue41.com. Located down by the river, *Le Bellevue* offers basic rooms – it's worth asking for one with a river view. There's a decent riverside restaurant serving traditional French cuisine (lunch menu from €16.50). Breakfast €9.50. €98

**Camping Couleurs du Monde** 1 rond-point de Montparnasse, Faverolles-sur-Cher ☎02 54 32 06 08, ⓦcamping-couleurs-du-monde.com. On the opposite bank of the Cher overlooking Montrichard, this four-star campsite with a swimming pool and a pizzeria is in a lovely rural location. There's an aquatic centre in the town. Take bus #6 from Montrichard or it's a twenty-minute walk. Closed Oct–Feb. €24.50

★ **L'Escale des Châteaux de la Loire** 12 rue de Pont,

Angé ☎02 54 32 58 21, ⓦescale-chateaux-loire.fr. A fun, eco-friendly take on the humble campsite, this unique space is unlike anywhere else in the region. Kids will love sleeping in a traditional yurt or tipi, but there are also romantic wooden cabins, treehouses and eco-pods (tiny wooden huts) available. There's a tranquil yet convivial vibe, and lots of play and recreational areas. Closed Oct–March. Breakfast €10. Treehouses (4 people) €160, cabins (4 people) €115, tipis and yurts €80, eco-pods €65

**La Villa** 34 rue de Sully ☎02 54 32 07 34. A busy spot right on the main sqaure, this typically French restaurant serves up a good range of *galettes*, crêpes, salads and burgers (from around €8). Upstairs, although quieter, has tables with a good view over the square. Tues–Sat noon–2.30pm & 7–10pm, Sun noon–2.30pm.

## Bourré

Three kilometres to the east of Montrichard, the hills around **BOURRÉ** are riddled with enormous, cave-like quarries, dug deep to get at the famous château-building stone that gets whiter as it weathers.

Some of the caves are now used to cultivate mushrooms, a peculiar process that you can witness at the **Cave Champignonnière** (40 rte des Roches; April–Sept daily guided visits at 10am, 11am, 2pm, 3pm, 4pm & 5pm; mid-Feb to March 11am, 3pm & 4pm; €12; ☎02 54 32 95 33, ⓦle-champignon.com). The tour also takes you to a "subterranean city" sculpted in recent years as a tourist attraction, and there's an excellent shop including rare varieties of mushrooms, mushroom soup, dried mushrooms, and so on.

You can also visit a troglodyte dwelling at **La Magnanerie** (4 chemin de la Croix-Bardin; guided visits only, with English information sheets available: Mon & Wed–Sun mid-Feb to mid-March 2.30pm; April to mid-July & Sept–Oct 11am, 2.30pm & 4pm; July & Aug 11.30am, 2.30am, 3.30pm, 4.30pm & 5.30pm;€8; ☎02 54 75 50 79, ⓦmagnanerie-troglo.fr), where the owner demonstrates how his ancestors lived, quarrying the soft stone using huge saws and producing silk in a chamber riddled with silkworm niches.

## St-Aignan

**ST-AIGNAN**, 15km southeast of Montrichard, is a small town comprising a cluster of houses below a huge Romanesque collegiate church and sixteenth-century private château. The lofty **Collégiale de St-Aignan** (daily 9am–7pm, Sun closed during services at 10.30am) features some fine capitals carved in the twelfth century, though many more are nineteenth-century recreations. The crypt is renowned for its remarkably preserved, brightly coloured twelfth- and thirteenth-century frescoes, some of which show the beginnings of naturalistic Gothic tendencies.

A flight of 144 steps climbs from the collégiale to the grand gravelled terrace of the **château**, enclosed on one side by the L-shape of the Renaissance logis, and on the other by the remnants of the eleventh-century fortress. Private ownership means it's closed to visitors, but you're free to stroll around – the far corner of the terrace leads through to a great view of the river, reached via a flight of steep steps.

One of the region's biggest tourist attractions is the excellent **ZooParc de Beauval** (daily: 9am–dusk; adult €31, child €25; ☎ 02 54 75 50 00, ⓦ zoobeauval.com), 2km to the south of town on the D675. The space given to the animals is ample and it's part of a Europe-wide programme for breeding threatened species in captivity.

## INFORMATION AND TOURS                                    ST-AIGNAN

**Tourist office** 60 rue Constant-Ragot (Jan–Feb & Oct–Dec Mon–Sat 10am–12.30pm & 2–5.30pm; March–May Mon–Sat 9.30am–12.30pm & 2–6pm; June–Sept Mon–Sat 9.30am–12.30pm & 2–6.30pm, Sun 10am–1pm (and also 2–5pm July & Aug); ☎ 02 54 75 22 85, ⓦ saintaignan-tourism.co.uk), just off the car-park-like place Président-Wilson, in the upper part of town.

**Boat tours** The tourist office has details of various boat trips on the Cher: Tasciaca (daily July & Aug, Sat & Sun in Sept; ☎ 06 89 12 55 77) leave from quai Jean-Jacques Delorme in St Aignan on hour-long guided cruises.

## ACCOMMODATION AND EATING

**Camping des Cochards** 1 rue du Camping, Seigy ☎ 02 54 75 15 59, ⓦ lescochards.com. Four-star campsite stretching along the riverbank near Seigy with ample camping space and cabins for rent. Amenities include grocery store, bar with a small restaurant, games and TV room, washing machines and dryers. Closed Oct–March. **€24.50**

**Le Grand Hôtel St-Aignan** 7 quai Jean-Jacques Delorme ☎ 02 54 75 18 04, ⓦ grand-hotel-saint-aignan. com. The modern furnishings, large windows and big comfy beds make these rooms excellent value, particularly the well-sized family rooms (€120). Choose from airy, riverside rooms or cosy attic hideaways with a view of the château. There's also a good restaurant with menus from €29.50. Breakfast €11. **€71**

★ **Les Jardins de Beauval** ☎ 02 54 75 60 00, ⓦ leshotelsdebeauval.com. This three-star hotel, located right next to the zoo, has a pool, restaurant and spa on site. Inspired by Thai and Indonesian architecture, large, comfortable rooms housed in pavilions are dotted around a landscaped lake, with wildfowl paddling around. The package deals, including zoo entry and breakfast, are good value. Closed mid-Nov to mid-March. **€115**

**Le Mange-Grenouille** 10 rue Paul-Boncour ☎ 02 54 71 74 91, ⓦ lemangegrenouille.fr. Hands down the best restaurant in town, this charming little spot is housed in a beautiful sixteenth-century building, with outside seating in a leafy courtyard. The signature dish might be the grenouilles (frogs), but there's plenty more to get excited about, including delicious home-made ice creams and sorbets. Lunch menus from €16. Tues–Fri noon–2pm & 7–9pm, Sat 7–9.30pm, Sun noon–2pm.

# Château de Valençay

20km southeast of St-Aignan on the main Blois–Châteauroux road • Daily: mid-March to April 10.30am–6pm; May & Sept 10am–6pm; June 9.30am–6.30pm; July & Aug 9.30am–7pm; Oct to mid-Nov 10.30am–5pm • Château €13.50 audioguide free • ☎ 02 54 00 10 66, ⓦ chateau-valencay.fr

An elegant marriage of classical and Renaissance styles, with its domed round tower and beautifully manicured gardens, the refined **Château de Valençay** paints a striking picture. Originally built to show off the wealth of a sixteenth-century financier, the lasting impression today is the legacy of its greatest owner, the Prince de Talleyrand.

One of the great political operators and survivors, Talleyrand owes most of his fame to his post as Napoleon's foreign minister. A bishop before the Revolution, with a reputation for having the most desirable mistresses, he proposed the nationalization of church property, renounced his bishopric, escaped to America during the Terror,

THE CHÂTEAU DE CHAMBORD UP CLOSE

backed Napoleon and continued to serve the state under the restored Bourbons. One of his tasks for the emperor was keeping Ferdinand VII of Spain entertained for six years here after the king had been forced to abdicate in favour of Napoleon's brother Joseph. The Treaty of Valençay, signed in the château in 1813, put an end to Ferdinand's forced guest status, giving him back his throne. The interior is consequently largely First Empire: elaborately embroidered chairs, Chinese vases, ornate inlays to all the tables, faux-Egyptian details, finicky clocks and chandeliers. A single discordant note is struck by the leg brace and shoe displayed in a glass cabinet along with Talleyrand's uniforms – the statesman's deformed foot was concealed in every painting of the man, including the one displayed in the portrait gallery of the graceful Neoclassical wing.

### Car museum

Daily: April–May & Sept–Oct 10.30am–12.30pm & 2–6pm; June 10am–12.30pm & 2–6.30pm; July & Aug 10am–12.30pm & 1.30–7pm • €5.50 • ⓦ musee-auto-valencay.fr

In Valençay village, about 100m from the château gates, the **car museum** houses an excellent collection of sixty-odd mostly pre-war cars, with the oldest dating from 1898. There are plenty of old posters and car parts to look at too, and some interesting temporary exhibitions.

## Loches

**LOCHES**, 42km southeast of Tours, is the obvious place to head for in the Indre valley. Its walled citadelle is by far the most impressive of the Loire valley fortresses, with its unbreached ramparts and the Renaissance houses below still partly enclosed by the outer wall of the medieval town. Tours is only an hour away by bus, but Loches makes for a quiet, relatively un-touristy base for exploring the Cher valley, or the lesser-known country to the south, up the Indre.

### The old town

The **old town**, ringed by the sturdy **citadelle** (daily Jan–March & Oct–Dec 9.30am–5pm; April–Sept 9am–7pm) is dominated by the Tour St-Antoine belfry, close to the handsome place du Marché that links rue St-Antoine with Grande Rue. Two fifteenth-century gates to the old town still stand: the **Porte des Cordeliers**, by the river at the end of Grande Rue, and the **Porte Picois** to the west, at the end of rue St-Antoine. Rue du Château, lined with Renaissance buildings, leads to the twelfth-century towers of **Porte Royale**, the main entrance to the citadelle.

### Collégiale de St-Ours

In front of the Musée Lansyer is the Romanesque church, the **Collégiale de St-Ours**, with its distinctive roofline – the nave bays are capped by two octagonal stone pyramids, sandwiched between more conventional spires. The porch has some entertainingly grotesque twelfth-century monster carvings, and the stoup, or basin for holy water, is a Gallo-Roman altar. The church's highlight is the shining white tomb of Agnès Sorel, the mistress of the Dauphin Charles VII, a beautiful recumbent figure tenderly watched over by angels. The alabaster is rather more pristine than it should be, as it had to be restored after anticlerical Revolutionary soldiers mistook her for a saint – an easy error to make.

### Logis Royal

Daily: April–Sept 9am–7pm; Oct–March 9.30am–5pm • €9 including the *donjon* • ⓣ 02 47 59 01 32, ⓦ citeroyaleloches.fr

The northern end of the citadelle is taken up by the **Logis Royal**, or Royal Lodgings, of Charles VII and his three successors. It has two distinct halves; the older section was built in the late fourteenth century as a pleasure palace for the Dauphin Charles and

Agnès Sorel. A copy of Charles's portrait by Fouquet can be seen in the antechamber to the Grande Salle, where in June 1429 he met Joan of Arc, who came here victorious from Orléans to give the defeatist Dauphin another pep talk about coronations.

From the Logis Royal, cobbled streets lined with handsome townhouses wind through to the far end of the elevated citadelle, to the *donjon*, the best preserved of its kind in Europe. You can climb up to the top of the massive keep, but the main interest lies in the dungeons and lesser towers. The Tour Ronde was built under Louis XI and served as a prison for his adviser, Cardinal Balue, who was kept locked up in a wooden cage in one of the upper rooms. Perhaps he was kept in the extraordinary graffiti chamber on the second floor, which is decorated with an enigmatic series of deeply carved, soldier-like figures estimated to date from the thirteenth century. From the courtyard, steps lead into the bowels of the Martelet, home to a more famous prisoner: Ludovico "il Moro" Sforza, duke of Milan, patron of Leonardo da Vinci and captive of Louis XII. In the four years he was imprisoned here, from 1500, he decorated his cave-like cell with ruddy wall paintings, still faintly visible.

### The Caravaggios of Philippe de Béthune

Next to the Église St-Antoine • Daily 10am–6.45pm • Free

Loches is home to one of the art world's many scandals: in 2006, art historians discovered **two paintings** – *La Cène à Emmaüs* and *L'Incrédulité de Saint Thomas* – in the loft of the Église St-Antoine which were believed to be the work of Caravaggio, brought from Rome by Philippe de Béthune, baron and minister of King Henry IV's court. After extensive testing, experts declared that yes, they were indeed the work of the old Master. However, local gossip has it that after Loches's mayor refused to let the pictures go to Paris to be displayed in the Louvre, preferring instead to keep them for the town, experts since have declared them to be fake.

## ARRIVAL AND INFORMATION    LOCHES

**By train and bus** Trains (50min) and buses (1hr) from Tours run hourly (less frequently on weekends) and arrive at the *gare SNCF* on the east side of the Indre.

**Tourist office** Housed in a modern wood-topped building on place de la Marne (March & April Mon–Sat 9.30am–12.30pm & 2–6pm; May & June Mon–Sat 9am–12.30pm & 1.30–6pm, Sun 10am–12.30pm & 2.30–5pm; July &

Aug Mon–Sat 9am–12.30pm & 1.30–7pm, Sun 10am–12.30pm & 2–6pm; Sept Mon–Sat 9am–12.30pm & 1.30–6.30pm, Sun 10am–12.30pm & 2–5pm; Oct Mon–Sat 9.30am–12.30pm & 2–5.30pm; Nov–Feb Mon–Sat 10am–12.30pm & 2.30–5pm; ☏ 02 47 91 82 82, ⓦ loches-valdeloire.com).

## ACCOMMODATION

**Camping La Citadelle** ☏ 02 47 59 05 91 ⓦ lacitadelle. com. Located right next to the abbey in Beaulieu-les-Loches, 1km across the river, the comfortable *La Citadelle* campsite is set between two branches of the Indre and has two swimming pools and also children's play areas. Closed mid-Oct to March. **€30**

★ **La Closerie Saint-Jacques** 37 rue Balzac ☏ 02 47 91 63 12, ⓦ lacloseriesaintjacques.com. Three dazzling designer rooms, named after the city *portes*. Truly jaw-dropping attention to detail with antiques, original artworks, timber-beamed ceilings and luxurious fabrics. Owned by a charming couple who also offer delicious evening meals (book ahead). Breakfast included. **€130**

**De France** 6 rue Picois ☏ 02 47 59 00 32, ⓦ hotel defrance-loches.com. Old-fashioned and characterful, with a beautiful ivy-covered courtyard, a decent restaurant and off-street parking. Housed in a former coaching inn, rooms are good value, albeit a little faded. Breakfast €9.90. **€58**

**Luccotel** 12 rue des Lézards ☏ 02 47 91 30 30, ⓦ luccotel.com. Around a 10min walk above the old town, but boasting a restaurant, covered pool, loungers, tennis court and a superb terrace with beautiful views. Rooms are comfortable and well-priced, and there are cheaper, motel-style abodes out back. Breakfast €10. **€64**

## EATING AND DRINKING

**Gerbe d'Or** 22 rue Balzac ☏ 02 47 91 67 63, ⓦ restaurant lagerbedor.fr. Organic, local and seasonal food with hearty

portions and accommodating service. There's a leafy terrace open in the summer months and special dishes for kids and vegetarians. *Menus* from €14.50. Tues noon–1.30pm, Wed–Sun noon–1.30pm & 7.30–9pm.

**La Loire en Tonneaux** 29 Grande Rue ☎07 81 86 55 00. Both a restaurant and *cave à vins*, this is a lively spot to sample regional wines, with knowledgeable, English-speaking owners who are happy to make recommendations. Order a platter of charcuterie, cheese or nibbles to accompany your drinks, or attend one of the regular tastings, held throughout the summer. Daily 10.30am–11pm.

**Le P'tit Restau** 6 Grande Rue ☎02 47 19 85 32, ⊛leptitrestau.fr. This charming little restaurant with a young team offers three starters, mains and desserts, which change weekly. Local, seasonal produce goes to make French dishes with international influences. Lunch menus from €15. Mon–Tues & Fri–Sun noon–2pm & 7.30–10pm.

# Blois and around

The château at **BLOIS**, the handsome former seat of the dukes of Orléans, is magnificent and its great facade rises above the modern town like an Italianate cliff. There are stretches of woodland within striking distance including the **Forêt de Blois** to the west on the north bank of the Loire, and the **Parc de Chambord** and **Forêt de Boulogne**, further upstream. To the south and east, the forested, watery, game-rich area known as the **Sologne** lies between the Loire and Cher, stretching beyond Orléans almost as far as Gien.

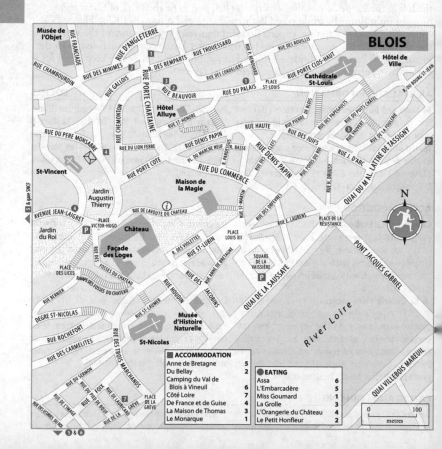

| ■ ACCOMMODATION | |
|---|---|
| Anne de Bretagne | 5 |
| Du Bellay | 2 |
| Camping du Val de Blois à Vineuil | 6 |
| Côté Loire | 7 |
| De France et de Guise | 4 |
| La Maison de Thomas | 3 |
| Le Monarque | 1 |

| ● EATING | |
|---|---|
| Assa | 6 |
| L'Embarcadère | 5 |
| Miss Goumard | 1 |
| La Grolle | 3 |
| L'Orangerie du Château | 4 |
| Le Petit Honfleur | 2 |

# The château

Daily: April–June & Sept–Oct 9am–6.30pm; July & Aug 9am–7pm; Nov–March 10am–5pm • €12, plus €3 for guided tour • **Guided tours in English** July & Aug daily 10.30am, 1.15pm & 3pm• **Son et lumière** April–May & Sept 10pm, June–Aug 10.30pm • €10.50 with audioguideor €19.50 including château entry • ☎ 02 54 90 33 33, ⓦ chateaudeblois.fr

The **Château de Blois** was home to six kings, and countless more aristocratic and noble visitors. The impression given is one of grandiloquent splendour, mixed with awe-inspiring spectacle, especially the superb spiral staircase that takes centre stage in the Renaissance **north wing**. The classical **west wing** was built in the 1630s by François Mansart for Gaston d'Orléans, brother of Louis XIII. To the south side, you go back in time 140-odd years to Louis XII's St-Calais chapel, which contrasts with the more exuberant brickwork of his flamboyant Gothic **east wing**.

Mansart's breathtaking staircase leads you round to the less interesting **François I**$^{er}$ **wing**; the garish decor here dates from Félix Duban's mid-nineteenth-century efforts to turn an empty barn of a château into a showcase for sixteenth-century decorative motifs. One of the largest rooms is given over to paintings of the notorious murder of the Duke of Guise and his brother, the Cardinal of Lorraine, by Henri III. As leaders of the radical Catholic League, the Guises were responsible for the summary execution of Huguenots at Amboise. The king had summoned the States-General to a meeting in the Grande Salle, only to find that an overwhelming majority supported the duke, along with the stringing up of Protestants, and aristocratic over royal power. Henri had the duke summoned to his bedroom in the palace, where he was ambushed and hacked to death, while the cardinal was murdered in prison the next day. Their deaths were avenged a year later when a monk assassinated the king himself.

The château was also home to Henri III's mother and manipulator, Catherine de Médicis, who died here a few days after the murders in 1589. The most famous of her rooms is the study, where, according to Alexandre Dumas' novel, *La Reine Margot*, she kept poison hidden in secret caches in the skirting boards and behind some of the 237 narrow carved wooden panels; they now contain small Renaissance *objets d'art*. In the nineteenth century, revolutionaries were tried in the Grande Salle for conspiring to assassinate Napoléon III, a year before the Paris Commune of 1870. You can return to the courtyard via the Salle des États, where the arches, pillars and fireplaces are another riot of colour. Across the courtyard to the ground floor of the François Ier wing, you'll find the **architecture rooms**, which display original stonework from the staircase and dormer windows.

Summer visitors can usually just turn up at the gate for the 45-minute **son et lumière** – it's one of the best in the region, rising above the usual mix of melodrama, light and musical effects by making the most of the château's fascinating history and lovely courtyard setting, and thrillingly recreates the murder of the Duke of Guise.

# The rest of the town

Just below the château on rue St-Laumer is the **Église St-Nicolas** (April–Nov 9am–6.30pm; Nov–March 9am–5pm), which once belonged to an abbey. The choir is a handsome example of the humble Benedictine treatment of the Romanesque style.

## Maison de la Magie

1 place du Château • April–Aug daily 10am–12.30pm & 2–6.30pm; Sept Mon–Fri 2–6.30pm, Sat & Sun 10am–12.30pm & 2–6.30pm • €10 or €19.50 with château entry • ☎ 02 54 90 33 33, ⓦ maisondelamagie.fr

The **Maison de la Magie** faces the château on the far side of the esplanade. With three floors of interactive illusions, magic tricks and live performances throughout day, it offers an excellent few hours' distraction. Highlights include learning how to perform card tricks and a section devoted to Houdini.

## Cathédrale St-Louis and around

Place St-Louis • Mon–Fri & Sun 8am–7pm; Sat 9am–6pm

Located in the east of town, the Gothic **Cathédrale St-Louis** leans against a weighty bell tower whose lowest storey dates from the twelfth century. The interior is unexceptional, but an interesting feature is the modern stained-glass windows, completed in 2003 by the Dutch artist Jan Dibbets. Leading off place St-Louis, rue du Palais connects with rue St-Honoré, where, at no. 8, you'll find the elaborate Hôtel Alluye; the private house of the royal treasurer Florimond Robertet, it is one of the few surviving relics of Blois' golden years under Louis XII.

## ARRIVAL AND DEPARTURE
BLOIS

**By train** The *gare SNCF* is on av Jean-Laigret – the main street leading east from the *gare SNCF* to place Victor-Hugo and the château.

Destinations Amboise (every 20min; 13min); Angers (at least 6 times daily; 1hr 22min); Beaugency (every 40min; 17min); Meung-sur-Loire (every 20min; 23min); Orléans (every 20min; 27min); Paris (at least every 2hr; 1hr 24min);

Saumur (at least 6 times daily; 1hr); Tours (at least hourly; 36min).

**By bus** The *gare routière* is directly in front of the *gare SNCF*, with buses leaving up to three times a day for Cheverny and Chambord.

Destinations Chambord (3 daily; 45min); Cour-Cheverny (7 daily; 20min); St-Aignan (2–3 daily; 1hr 10min).

## GETTING AROUND

**By bicycle/on foot** If you have time and the inclination, it's particularly pleasant to be able to visit the châteaux around Blois by bicycle or on foot. Ask at the tourist office (see below) for walking and cycling maps.

**By bus** Local public transport in the area is very poor, with even the main routes served by only a couple of commuter buses a day. Note, however, that the local bus company Rémi (ⓦremi-centrevaldeloire.fr) runs return coach trips to Chambord, Cheverny and Beauregard from April–June & Sept–Oct Wed, Sat & Sun and July & Aug daily with

departures from Blois' *gare SNCF* tickets are bought on the bus (€6 return) and will give you a discount on the entry price on presentation at the various châteaux.

**By taxi** Taxi Radio Blois ☎ 02 54 78 07 65 run excursions to the area's châteaux; expect to pay around €44 for a return trip to Cheverny including an hour's waiting time.

**Bike rental** Détours de Loire, 39 av Docteur Jean-Laigret (☎ 02 54 56 07 73, ⓦ detoursdeloire.com), and Les Vélos Verts, Gare de Blois (☎ 02 54 74 57 05, ⓦ lesvelosverts. com).

## INFORMATION

**Tourist office** 23 place du Château (April–Sept daily 9am–7pm; Oct–March Mon–Sat 10am–12.30pm & 2–5pm; ☎ 02 54 90 41 41, ⓦ bloischambord.com). The office

organizes hotel rooms for a small fee and has information on day coach tours of Chambord and Cheverny. It also sells combined tickets to various local châteaux.

## ACCOMMODATION

**Anne de Bretagne** 31 av Jean-Laigret ☎ 02 54 78 05 38, ⓦ hotelannedebretagne.com. A short walk from the train station, this charming, vine-covered hotel is a tranquil spot, with a lovely sunny terrace out front in the summer months. Inside, the dark wood floors, bold red walls and British-inspired pop art adorning the hallways make a great first impression, but the rooms themselves are a bit cramped and lacklustre. Buffet breakfast €9. **€70**

**Du Bellay** 12 rue des Minimes ☎ 02 54 78 23 62, ⓦ hoteldubellay.com. *Du Bellay* is looking a little frayed around the edges these days, but it's still the best budget option in the *centre ville*. Some rooms are better than others, but all are clean and functional, with natural daylight, and the staff are friendly and helpful. Rooms with shared bathrooms start from €30 and a continental breakfast is €6. **€50**

**Camping du Val de Blois à Vineuil** ☎ 02 54 79 93 57, ⓦ camping-loisir-blois.com. On the south bank of the river, 4km from the town centre, this well-serviced

three-star campsite has a swimming pool, mini-golf and playground, plus bikes and kayaks for rent. Closed Nov–March. **€22.70**

**Côté Loire** 2 place de la Grève ☎ 02 54 78 07 86, ⓦ coteloire.com. This charming hotel, with beautiful views over the river, makes a tranquil alternative to the central hotels. Each room has its own character, but the attic rooms are most unique, with sloping ceilings and dramatic wooden beams. The adjoining restaurant is open Tues to Sat for lunch and dinner. Breakfast €11. **€62**

**De France et de Guise** 3 rue Gallois ☎ 02 54 78 00 53, ⓦ hotel-france-guise.com. Built in the nineteenth century on the site of the old ramparts, this historic hotel provides a pleasant mix of old-world charm and modern amenities. Rooms on the lower floors can be noisy, but the owners are extremely friendly and the location is hard to beat. Ask for a room with a park view. Breakfast €8. **€65**

★ **La Maison de Thomas** 12 rue Beauvoir ☎ 09 81 84 44 59, ⓦ lamaisondethomas.fr. On a pedestrian street in the heart of town, this delightful B&B, run by a wonderfully hospitable couple, has stylishly decorated rooms with original timber beams, polished wood floors and quirky touches. The Renaissance suite is huge and excellent value, while rooms facing the road are sunny all day long. Breakfast included. **€101**

**Le Monarque** 61 rue Porte Chartraine ☎ 02 54 78 02 35, ⓦ hotel-lemonarque.com. Cheerful, well-located hotel with a popular on-site restaurant and lots of character. The impressive collection of Tintin posters and memorabilia livens up what would otherwise be very straightforward and functional rooms. Breakfast €9.50. **€69**

## EATING AND DRINKING

**Assa** 189 quai Ulysse-Besnard ☎ 02 54 78 09 01, ⓦ assarestaurant.com. The focus is on local, seasonal foods at this stylish Michelin-starred restaurant and the menus are tweaked daily, in accordance with its name – *Assa* means "morning" in Japanese. Menus start from €49 and feature modern French cuisine with a notable Asian influence. Wed & Fri–Sat 12.15–1.30pm & 7.30–9pm, Thurs 7.30–9pm, Sun 12.15–1.30pm.

**L'Embarcadère** 16 quai Ulysse-Besnard ☎ 02 54 78 31 41, ⓦ lembarcadere.fr. A little distance out of town but worth the effort, this locals' favourite serves fresh seafood, juicy grills and show-stopping desserts. Tuck into Normandy oysters, *moules de bouchot* or expertly cooked veal, with lunch *menus* from €15.90. Mon–Thurs & Sun noon–2pm & 7–9.30pm, Fri & Sat noon–2pm & 7–10pm.

**Miss Goumard** 20 rue du Palais ☎ 02 54 58 96 99. Cute and cosy vintage-style tearoom with a good but limited choice of healthy lunch dishes, organic where possible, and with vegetarian and vegan options. There's an excellent selection of sweet treats too; the carrot cake is a popular option. And the juices are delicious. Tues–Sat noon–6.30pm.

**La Grolle** 5 rue Vauvert ☎ 02 36 23 64 65, ⓦ augredevin-

lagrolle.com. Cheese is the star of the show at this Savoyard restaurant with chalet-style decor. Try the baked Camembert (€13.50) or a homemade burger topped with Reblochon (€15). They own a wine shop nearby (Au Gré de Vin; 28 av du Maréchal-Maunoury; ☎ 02 54 58 74 97), which organizes tasting evenings. Tues–Sat noon–2pm & 7–9pm.

**L'Orangerie du Château** 1 av Jean-Laigret ☎ 02 54 78 05 36, ⓦ orangerie-du-chateau.fr Housed in a striking fifteenth-century building at the foot of the château, this is the swankiest option in town. The Michelin-starred cuisine is as decadent as the surroundings, but expect the attitude and price points to match. *Menus* change seasonally and start from €41 (four courses). Tues–Sat noon–1.45pm & 7–9pm.

**Le Petit Honfleur** 18 rue Beauvoir ☎ 09 72 34 06 48. The atmospheric timber-framed interiors and pretty flower-lined terrace make this a romantic spot, especially in the evening. Try the Normandy-themed *menu* Petit Honfleur (€26), which includes a delicious *poulet vallée d'Auge*, regional cheeses and *teurgoule* (rice pudding) dessert. Tues–Sat noon–2pm & 7.30–9.30pm.

# Château de Chaumont

Daily: Feb–March 10am–6pm; April & Oct 10am–7pm; May–Aug 10am–8pm; Sept 10am–7.30pm; Nov–Jan 10am–5.30pm • €18 (May–Oct), €12 (Nov–March) • ☎ 02 54 20 99 22, ⓦ domaine-chaumont.fr

Catherine de Médicis forced Diane de Poitiers to hand over Chenonceau in return for the **Château de Chaumont**, 20km downstream from Blois. Diane got a bad deal, but this is still one of the lovelier châteaux.

The original fortress was destroyed by Louis XI in the mid-fifteenth century in revenge for the part its owner, Pierre d'Amboise, played in the "League of Public Weal", an alliance of powerful nobles against the ever-increasing power of the monarch. Pierre found his way back into the king's favour, and with his son, Charles I^er of Amboise, built much of the quintessentially medieval castle that stands today. The Renaissance design is more obvious in the courtyard, which today forms three sides of a square, the fourth side having been demolished in 1739 to improve the spectacular views over the river. Inside, the heavy nineteenth-century decor of the ground-floor rooms dates from the ownership of the Broglie family, but a few rooms on the first floor have been remodelled in Renaissance style. The large council chamber is particularly fine, with seventeenth-century majolica floor tiles and walls adorned with intricate sixteenth-century tapestries showing the gods of each of the seven planets known at the time.

## The grounds

Daily 10am–dusk • Free

The Broglie family also transformed the **landscaped park** into the fashionable English style and built the remarkable *belle époque* **stables**, with their porcelain troughs and elegant electric lamps for the benefit of the horses at a time before the château itself was wired – let alone the rest of the country. A corner of the château grounds hosts the annual **Festival des Jardins** (May–Oct), which shows off the extravagant efforts of contemporary garden designers.

### Boat trips

📞 06 88 76 57 14, 🌐 milliere-raboton.net • 1hr 30min to 10hr • €20–105

Throughout the year, you can secure the best view of the château from the deck of a traditional Loire boat, which leave from the quay immediately below the château. The regular dawn excursions are best for wildlife spotting, or you can organize longer trips and even camp out.

## Château de Cheverny

Daily: April–Sept 9.15am–6.30pm; Oct–March 10am–5pm • €11.50 • 📞 02 54 79 96 29, 🌐 chateau-cheverny.fr

Fifteen kilometres southeast of Blois, the **Château de Cheverny** is the quintessential seventeenth-century château. Built between 1604 and 1634, and little changed since, it presents an immaculate picture of symmetry, harmony and the aristocratic good life. This continuity may well be because descendants of the first owners still own, live in and go hunting from Cheverny today. Its stone, from Bourré on the River Cher, lightens with age, and the château gleams in its acres of rolling parkland. The interior decoration has only been added to, never destroyed, and the extravagant display of paintings, furniture, tapestries and armour against the gilded, sculpted and carved walls and ceilings is extremely impressive. The most precious objects are hard to pick out from the sumptuous whole, but some highlights are the painted wall panels in the dining room telling stories from Don Quixote; the vibrant, unfaded colours of the Gobelin tapestry in the arms room; and the three rare family portraits by François Ier's court painter, François Clouet.

Inspired by the Château de Cheverny, Hergé created Marlinspike Hall (Château de Moulinsart in French) as a country home for Captain Haddock in the *Adventures of Tintin* and the Hergé Foundation has a small but fascinating permanent **exhibition** at the château, which is worth a visit.

You can explore the elegant **grounds** on foot, or take a tour on a little train or by boat (April to mid-Nov; €16.50 including château entry). The **kennels** near the main entrance are worth a peek too: a hundred lithe hounds mill and loll about while they wait for the next stag; feeding time (11.30am; April to mid-Sept daily; mid-Sept to March Mon & Wed–Fri) is something to be seen. Cheverny's hunt culls around thirty deer a year, as set by the National Forestry Office.

## Château de Beauregard

March Mon–Fri 1.30–6.30pm, Sat & Sun 10.30am–6.30pm; April–June & Sept to mid-Oct daily 10.30am–6.30pm; July & Aug daily 10am–7pm; mid-Oct to mid-Nov daily 1.30–5pm • Guided tours in English (1hr) daily at noon • €12.50 • 📞 02 54 70 41 65, 🌐 beauregard-loire.com

A pleasant cycle ride from Blois, the little-visited **Château de Beauregard**, 7km south of Blois on the D956 to Contres, lies in the Forêt de Russy. It was – like Chambord – one of François Ier's hunting lodges, but its transformation in the sixteenth century was one of beautification rather than aggrandizement. It was added to in the seventeenth century and the result is sober and serene, at eas e in its manicured geometric park.

The highlight of the château is a richly decorated, long **portrait gallery**, whose floor of Delft tiling depicts an army on the march. The walls are entirely panelled with 327 portraits of kings, queens and great nobles, including European celebrities such as Francis Drake, Anne Boleyn and Charles V of Spain. All of France's kings are represented, from Philippe VI (1328–50), who precipitated the Hundred Years' War, to Louis XIII (1610–43), who occupied the throne when the gallery was created. Kings, nobles and executed wives alike are given equal billing – except for Louis XIII, whose portrait is exactly nine times the size of any other.

It's worth strolling down through the grounds to the sunken Jardin des Portraits, a Renaissance-influenced creation by contemporary landscaper Gilles Clément, who was responsible for Paris's futuristic Parc André-Citroën (see page 108).

## Château de Chambord

Daily: April–Oct 9am–6pm; Nov–March 9am–5pm • Guided tours in English (1hr): daily July–Sept at 11.15am; €5 • €13; parking €6 • T 02 54 50 40 00, W chambord.org

The **Château de Chambord**, François I^er's little "hunting lodge", is the largest of the Loire châteaux and one of the most extravagant commissions of its age. Its patron's principal objective – to outshine the Holy Roman Emperor Charles V – would, he claimed, leave him renowned as "one of the greatest builders in the universe". If you are going to visit – and it's one of the region's absolute highlights – try to arrive early and avoid weekends, when the crush of visitors can be overwhelming.

Before you even get close, the gargantuan scale of the place is awe-inspiring: there are more than 440 rooms and 85 staircases, and a petrified forest of 365 chimneys runs wild on the roof. In architectural terms, the mixture of styles is as outrageous as the size. The Italian architect Domenico da Cortona was chosen to design the château in 1519 in an effort to establish prestigious Italian Renaissance art forms in France, though the labour was supplied by French masons. The château's plan (attributed, fancifully, to da Vinci) is pure Renaissance: rational, symmetrical and totally designed to express a single idea – the central power of its owner. Four hallways run crossways through the central keep, at the heart of which the Great Staircase rises up in two unconnected spirals before opening out into the great lantern tower, which draws together the confusion on the roof like a great crown.

The cold, draughty size of the château made it unpopular as an actual residence – François I^er himself stayed there for just 42 days in total – and Chambord's role in history is slight. A number of rooms on the first floor were fitted out by Louis XIV and his son, the Comte de Chambord, and they feel like separate apartments within the unmanageable whole. You can explore them freely, along with the adjacent eighteenth-century apartments, where the château was made habitable by lowering ceilings, building small fireplaces within the larger ones, and cladding the walls with the fashionable wooden panelling known as boiseries.

The second floor houses a rambling **Museum of Hunting** where, among the endless guns and paintings that glorify hunting, are two superb seventeenth-century tapestry cycles: one depicts Diana, goddess of the hunt; another, based on cartoons by Lebrun, tells the story of Meleager, the heroic huntsman from Ovid's *Metamorphoses*.

The **Parc de Chambord** around the château is an enormous walled game reserve – the largest in Europe. Wild boar roam freely, though red deer are the beasts you're most likely to spot. You can explore on foot, or by bike or boat – both rentable from the jetty where the Cosson passes alongside the main facade of the château.

### ACCOMMODATION AND EATING — CHÂTEAU DE CHAMBORD

**Au Relais d'Artémis** 1 av de Chambord, Bracieux T 02 54 46 41 22, W restaurant-relais-artemis-41.fr. A popular choice with locals and visitors alike, serving classic French *terroir* cooking in its leafy garden. *Menus* from €20. Wed–Sun noon–2pm & 7–9pm.

**De la Bonn'heure** 9 rue René-Masson, Bracieux T 02 54 46 41 57, W hoteldelabonnheure.com. Set around floral gardens, this friendly hotel has sunny rooms with doors onto the terrace and a tranquil vibe. Wi-fi is in public areas and some rooms only. You can hire a bike here for €10 a day. Breakfast buffet €10. **€65**

★ **Max Vauché Chocolatier & Choco'Bar** 22 Les Jardins

du Moulin, Bracieux ☎ 02 54 46 07 96, ⓦ maxvauche-chocolatier.com. Master chocolatier Max Vauché runs this chocolate boutique, where it's possible to enjoy chocolate-making workshops or take an hour-long behind-the-scenes tour (€4.70; several times daily, with English tours at 11.30am & 2.30pm in July & Aug). The neighbouring *Choco'Bar* serves up an array of decadent hot chocolates, coffees and sweet treats. July–Aug Tues–Sat 10.30am–noon & 2–6.30pm, Sun 3–6.30pm; Sept–June Sat 10.30am–noon & 2–6.30pm, Sun 3–6.30pm.

★ **Le Relais de Chambord** Place St-Louis, opposite the château ☎ 02 54 81 01 01, ⓦ relaisdechambord.com. This stylish new boutique hotel and restaurant in a former coaching inn is a breath of fresh air to the area. Rooms and suites are white and minimalist, with black and white photos of the château decorating the walls. The hip restaurant, Le Grand St-Michel, serves Mediterranean-fusion dishes made with local, seasonal produce (main courses €23–33). Breakfast buffet €18. €180

## The Sologne

Stretching southeast of Blois, the **Sologne**, depending on the weather and the season, can be one of the most dismal areas in central France: damp, flat, featureless and foggy. At other times its forests, lakes, ponds and marshes have a quiet magic – in summer, for example, when the heather is in bloom and the ponds are full of water lilies, or in early autumn when you can collect mushrooms. Wild boar and deer roam here, not to mention the ducks, geese, quails and pheasants that far outnumber the small human population. It was this remote, mystical landscape that provided the setting for Alain Fournier's novel *Le Grand Meaulnes*; Fournier himself spent his childhood in La Chapelle d'Angillon, 34km north of Bourges, and the story's famous "fête étrange" took place in the Sologne.

**GETTING AROUND AND INFORMATION**        **THE SOLOGNE**

**By car/on foot** Two *grandes randonnées* lead through the Sologne, both variants of the main GR3 along the Loire. The northern GR3C runs through Chambord and east mostly along forest roads to Thoury and La Ferté-St-Cyr, where it rejoins the southern branch, the GR31, which takes a more attractive route through Bracieux and along footpaths through the southern part of the Forêt de Chambord. There are numerous other well-signposted walking paths.
**Tourist offices** There are tourist offices in most of Sologne's towns and villages (ⓦ sologne-tourisme.fr).

# Tours and around

Straddling a spit of land between the rivers Loire and Cher, the ancient cathedral city of **TOURS** is the chief town of the Loire valley. It has the usual feel of a mid-sized provincial city, with some discordant shifts between the strikingly grand and stripped-down modern. Its charms, however, include some good bars and restaurants, an interesting collection of museums – including an above-average Beaux-Arts museum – and many fine buildings, most notably the Cathédrale St-Gatien.

The city's two distinct old quarters lie on either side of rue Nationale, the busy shopping street that forms the town's main axis, while the main tourist area lies around picturesque place Plumereau, some 600m to the west. Tours is also the main transport link to the great châteaux of **Villandry**, **Langeais**, **Azay-le-Rideau** and **Amboise**.

## The cathedral quarter

The great west towers of the **Cathédrale St-Gatien**, standing on the square of the same name, are visible all over the city. Their surfaces crawl with decorated stone in the Flamboyant Gothic style, and even the Renaissance belfries that cap them share the same spirit of refined exuberance. Inside, the style moves back in time, ending with a relatively severe High Gothic east end – built in the thirteenth century – and its glorious stained-glass windows. A door in the north aisle leads to the recently reopened fourteenth-century **Cloître de la Psalette**.

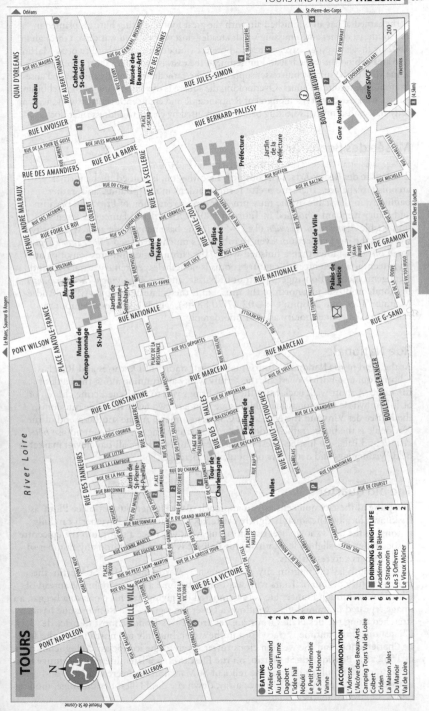

TOURS

● EATING

| | |
|---|---|
| L'Atelier Gourmand | 4 |
| Au Lapin qui Fume | 2 |
| Dagobert | 5 |
| L'idée hall | 7 |
| Nobuki | 8 |
| Le Petit Patrimoine | 3 |
| Le Saint Honoré | 1 |
| Vanne | 6 |

■ ACCOMMODATION

| | |
|---|---|
| L'Adresse | 2 |
| L'Alcove des Beaux-Arts | 3 |
| Camping Tours Val de Loire | 8 |
| Colbert | 1 |
| Criden | 6 |
| La Maison Jules | 5 |
| Du Manoir | 4 |
| Val de Loire | 7 |

■ DRINKING & NIGHTLIFE

| | |
|---|---|
| Académie de la Bière | 6 |
| Le Strapontin | 1 |
| Les 3 Orfèvres | 3 |
| Le Vieux Mûrier | 7 |

The cathedral has an unfinished air, with the great foot of a flying buttress planted in the southeast corner and a missing south arcade – lost when a road was driven through in 1802 by the same progressive, anticlerical prefect who destroyed the basilica of St-Martin. The area behind the cathedral and museum, to the east, is good for a short stroll. There's a fine view of the spidery buttresses supporting the cathedral's painfully thin-walled apse from place Grégoire de Tours. Overlooking the square is the oldest wing of the archbishop's palace, whose end wall is a mongrel of Romanesque and eighteenth-century work, with an early sixteenth-century projecting balcony once used by clerics to address their flock.

## Musée des Beaux-Arts

18 place François-Sicard • Daily except Tues 9am–12.45pm & 2–6pm • €6 • ☎ 02 47 05 68 73

The **Musée des Beaux-Arts**, just south of the cathedral, is housed in the former archbishop's palace. There are pretty formal gardens in the grounds, and, rather bafflingly, in the stable by the museum entrance, a recreation of Fritz, the Barnum and Bailey elephant who died in Tours in 1904. Other than Mantegna's intense, unmissable *Agony in the Garden* (1457–59) in the basement, there are few celebrity works in the large collection. Even Rembrandt's much-advertised *Flight into Egypt* is a small oil study rather than a finished work. The chronological progression of palatial seventeenth- and eighteenth-century rooms is nonetheless extremely attractive, and local gems include Boulanger's portrait of Balzac, and the engravings *The Five Senses* by Abraham Bosse. Just north of the museum is the Château de Tours (25 av André-Malraux; Tues–Sun 2–6pm; €4; ☎ 02 47 70 88 46), which hosts good temporary exhibitions of contemporary art and photography.

## Rue Nationale

At the head of **rue Nationale**, Tours' main street, statues of Descartes and Rabelais – both Touraine-born – overlook the scruffy walkways running along the bank of the Loire. A short walk back from the river brings you to the Benedictine church of St Julien, whose old monastic buildings are home to two fairly missable museums, the Musée des Vins and the Musée du Compagnonnage. At the southern end of rue Nationale is the huge, traffic-ridden place Jean-Jaurès, the site of the grandiose *hôtel de ville* and Palais de Justice. West of place Jean-Jaurès, a huge all-day **flower market** is held Wednesdays and Saturdays on boulevard Béranger.

## The old quarter

The pulse of the city quickens as you approach **place Plumereau** – or place Plum' as it's known locally. The square's tightly clustered, ancient houses have been carefully restored as the city's showpiece, transforming what was once a slum into the epicentre of social life. The slightly less touristy **rue Colbert** is where you'll find any number of excellent bars and restaurants.

To the south lay the pilgrim city once known as **Martinopolis** after St Martin, the fourth-century bishop of Tours who went on to become a key figure in the spread of Christianity through France. He is remembered for giving half his cloak to a beggar, an image repeated in stained-glass windows all over the region. The Romanesque basilica stretched along rue des Halles from rue des Trois-Pavés-Ronds almost to place de Châteauneuf: the outline is traced out in the street, but only the north tower, the **Tour de Charlemagne**, and the western clock tower survived the iconoclastic Huguenot riots of 1562. The **Basilique de St-Martin**, on rue Descartes, is a late nineteenth-century neo-Byzantine affair built to honour the relics of St Martin, rediscovered in 1860 and now housed in the crypt. A short distance away, down rue des Halles, lies the huge, modern **Halles**, or covered market.

# Prieuré de St-Cosme

April–May & Sept–Oct daily 10am–6pm; June–Aug daily 10am–7pm; Nov–March daily except Tues 10am–12.30pm 2–5pm • €6 • Take bus #3 from outside the Palais de Justice, on place Jean-Jaurès, to the "La Pléiade" stop • ☎ 02 47 37 32 70, ⓦ prieure-ronsard.fr

In May, when the roses are in full bloom, the **Prieuré de St-Cosme**, 3km west of the centre, is one of the most appealing sights in the area even if it is hemmed in by suburbs and barred off from the nearby Loire by a trunk road. Once an island priory, now a semi-ruin, it was here that Pierre de Ronsard, France's greatest Renaissance poet, lived as prior from 1565 until his death in 1585. Vestiges of many monastic buildings survive but the most affecting sight is the lovingly tended **garden of roses**, which has some two thousand rose bushes, and 250 varieties – including the tightly rounded pink rose called "Pierre de Ronsard".

## ARRIVAL AND DEPARTURE

## TOURS

**By air** The Aéroport Tours Val de Loire (☎ 02 47 49 37 00, ⓦ tours.aeroport.fr) is situated 6km northeast of Tours. Tram A serves the city centre. A taxi costs €15–30.

**By train** The *gare SNCF* is situated southeast of the cathedral district, facing the Centre des Congrès Vinci. Destinations Amboise (frequent; 20min); Azay-le-Rideau (8 daily; 30min); Blois (frequent; 40min); Chenonceaux (8 daily; 30min); Chinon (8 daily; 45min); Langeais (10 daily;

20min); Le Mans (8 daily; 1hr); Montrichard (11 daily; 40min); Orléans (frequent; 1hr 30min); Paris (hourly; 1hr 34min); Saumur (frequent; 45min).

**By bus** The *gare routière* is directly outside the train station. Destinations Amboise (8 daily; 50min); Azay-le-Rideau (3 daily; 50min); Chinon (3 daily; 1hr 10min); Loches (12 daily; 50min); Richelieu (3 daily; 1hr 50min); Villandry (July & Aug only; 2 daily; 30min).

## GETTING AROUND

**Bike rental** Détours de Loire, 35 rue Charles-Gille ☎ 02 47 61 22 23, ⓦ detoursdeloire.com. The Détours de Loire scheme allows you to drop off the bike at various locations along the river, for a small charge.

**Car rental** Avis, gare de Tours ☎ 02 47 20 53 27; Europcar, 194 av Maginot ☎ 02 47 85 85 85; Hertz, 57 rue Marcel-Tribut ☎ 02 47 75 50 00. All offer pick-up and drop-off at Tours airport or the *gare SNCF*.

## INFORMATION AND TOURS

**Tourist office** On the corner of rue Bernard-Palissy and busy bd Heurteloup (April–Sept Mon–Sat 8.30am–7pm, Sun 10am–12.30pm & 2.30–5pm; Oct–March Mon–Sat 9am–12.30pm & 1.30–6pm, Sun 10am–1pm; ☎ 02 47 70 37 37, ⓦ tours-tourism.co.uk), just across the square from the train and bus stations; it offers information on château tours.

**Château tours** Several companies offer château tours from Tours, including Acco Dispo (☎ 06 82 00 64 51, ⓦ accodispo-tours.com), Loire Valley Tours (☎ 02 47 79 40 20, ⓦ loire-valley-tours.com) and Touraine Évasion (☎ 06 07 39 13 31, ⓦ tourevasion.com). Expect to pay €25–39 for a half-day or €60 for a full-day tour per person, visiting up to five châteaux and excluding admission fees.

## ACCOMMODATION

★ **L'Adresse** 12 rue de la Rôtisserie ☎ 02 47 20 85 76, ⓦ hotel-ladresse.com. The neutral colour scheme, white-painted beams and parquet floors of *L'Adresse* are effortlessly chic, but the real highlights are the details – huge beds, plush duvets, sparkling new bathrooms and big windows. Despite the cool surroundings, there's a friendly and unpretentious family feel. Breakfast €10. **€85**

**L'Alcôve des Beaux-Arts** 40 rue de la Préfecture ☎ 02 47 05 05 00, ⓦ hoteldesartstours.com. Located 5min from the station, this friendly B&B is no-frills but good value. Rooms are a little cramped, but nonetheless light and cheerful, some with little balconies. **€77**

**Camping Tours Val de Loire** 61 rue de Rochepinard, St-Avertin ☎ 02 47 27 87 47, ⓦ onlycamp.fr. Next to the river on the opposite bank to the city (south), this four-star campsite has surprisingly few facilities, yet there's

plenty you could want nearby including swimming pools and children's play areas. The good news is that it's well equipped for cyclists, and bikes are available to rent in July and August. Take bus #3 or #19 to stop "L'Essart". **€21.50**

**Colbert** 78 rue Colbert ☎ 02 47 66 61 56, ⓦ tours-hotel-colbert.fr. If you want a hotel at the heart of the action, this is the place, with a huge selection of bars and restaurants right on the doorstep. The friendly hosts (and equally friendly dogs) and sunny garden terrace are an added bonus. Buffet breakfast €8.50. **€61**

**Criden** 65 bd Heurteloup ☎ 02 47 20 81 14, ⓦ criden-tours.com. Modish, Parisian-themed decor sets this place apart, with arty black-and-white photos and cosy lounge areas. Rooms are spotless and surprisingly quiet despite being a short stroll from the train station, plus there's a large sunny terrace where you can enjoy breakfast (€8.50).

**7**

**7**

## STAYING IN A CHÂTEAU

One of the great privileges of visiting the Loire is that there are a variety of châteaux that accommodate visitors. The standards range enormously: at the top end of the market, you are guaranteed deluxe accommodation, with room service, all mod cons, excellent food and all the amenities you would expect from a top-class hotel; at the other end, it's a bed and breakfast in someone's house, which can be pot luck. The following are the pick of the hotels in the Tours area:

**Château D'Artigny** Nr Montbazon (take D17 from there) ☎ 02 47 34 30 30, ⊛ grandesetapes.com/en/castle-hotel-artigny-loire. Stunning, beautifully restored château originally owned by the perfumier François Coty, and decorated in a Neoclassical style. The rooms are all large, lavishly appointed and comfortable, while the excellent restaurant has sweeping views across the Loire valley. You can take cookery classes and enjoy wine tastings, but if that all sounds too tiring, there's a pool, jacuzzi, spa and sauna to relax in. Breakfast buffet €24. €185

**Domaine de Beauvois** Nr Luynes ☎ 02 47 55 50 11, ⊛ younancollection.com. Much of the appeal of this beautiful sixteenth-century mansion comes from its peaceful seclusion, with long country walks and beautiful bike rides the order of the day. There are some lovely, quirky touches in the rooms, too, which have beamed ceilings and painted frescoes, and the restaurant offers excellent food. Buffet breakfast included. €169

**Domaine de la Tortinière** Nr Montbazon ☎ 02 47 34 35 00, ⊛ tortiniere.com. Delightful family-run boutique hotel, with friendly bilingual owners. Rooms range from the modestly comfortable to the spectacularly luxurious (such as the suites in the turrets, complete with circular bedrooms) and very good food is served in the dining room, overlooking an open-air swimming pool. Buffet breakfast €20. €189

Parking is available in the underground car park (€5). €73

★ **La Maison Jules** 45 rue Jules-Simon ☎ 06 83 84 71 22, ⊛ lamaisonjules.com. This gorgeous B&B in a nineteenth-century mansion near the cathedral has five elegant rooms; for a romantic stay book Grégoire, under the eaves. Breakfast is taken in the garden in summer, and, in winter, guests can choose a book from the library and snuggle up by the fireplace. €145

**Du Manoir** 2 rue Traversière ☎ 02 47 05 37 37, ⊛ hotel-du-manoir-tours.fr. Set in a peaceful location equidistant from the cathedral and train station, this tastefully restored, nineteenth-century townhouse has comfortable, homely rooms. Prices are negotiable and breakfast (€9.50) is served in the atmospheric stone-walled cellar downstairs. Limited private parking so book head. €75

★ **Val de Loire** 33 bd Heurteloup ☎ 02 47 05 37 86, ⊛ hotelvaldeloire.fr. This elegant townhouse has spotless modern rooms with a mix of carpets and wooden floors. Opt for a garden view. Buffet breakfast €9. €88

## EATING

**L'Atelier Gourmand** 37 rue Etienne-Marcel ☎ 02 47 38 59 87, ⊛ lateliergourmand.fr. A trendy, ultra-modern restaurant with superb fresh market cuisine not far from rue Colbert. Head here for lunch, when the *formule* is €21. Daily noon–2pm & 7.30–10.30pm.

**Au Lapin qui Fume** 90 rue Colbert ☎ 02 47 66 95 49, ⊛ aulapinquifume.fr. With its bright yellow furniture and adorable rabbit logo this place sticks out amid the myriad restaurants along rue Colbert. The terrine de *lapin* (rabbit) is the star turn, and there are plenty of other meat and fish dishes too, and the hearty portions will fill you up. Save room for the lavender-poached apricots with pistachio ice cream. Evening *menus* from €25. Tues–Sat 11.45am–2pm & 6.45–10pm; July & Aug open Mon.

★ **Dagobert** 31 rue du Grand-Marché ☎ 02 47 61 76 14. With its chequerboard floors, dark wood beams and shelves crammed with old books, this elegant bar-bistro appears lifted from another era. The menu livens things up, putting a modern twist on old classics, plus there's a large variety of regional wines from the on-site *cave*. The evening *menu* is €30 or else opt for a *planche apéro* (€15) with cheeses and charcuterie to accompany your wine. Mon & Thurs–Sun 6pm–2am.

**L'idée hall** 47 rue de la Victoire ☎ 09 81 16 92 29. Cheery local restaurant and wine bar a short walk north the covered market. The good-value menu (three courses €24) offers delicious traditional French dishes, such as *terrine de campagne* (country pâté), *steak frites* and *soupe de fraises* (strawberry smoothie dessert). Naturally, there's an impressive selection of local wines. Tues & Thurs–Sat noon–2pm & 7.15–9.45pm, Wed 7.15–9.45pm.

**Nobuki** 3 rue Buffon ☎ 02 47 05 79 79, ⊛ nobuki.fr. A welcome alternative to the usual French fare, this Japanese restaurant is sleek and modern, and the sushi is top-notch. *Menus* from €19.50. Mon–Thurs noon–2pm, Fri noon–2pm & 7–10pm.

**Le Petit Patrimoine** 58 rue Colbert ☏ 02 47 66 05 81, ⓦ lepetitpatrimoine.fr. Romantic little place serving rich, lovingly prepared Loire dishes and good Loire wines; it's always packed with locals, so make a reservation. The foie gras, served with *pain aux figues* is a particular speciality. *Menus* from €18.80. Tues–Sat noon–2pm & 7–10pm.

★ **Le Saint-Honoré** 7 place des Petites Boucheries ☏ 02 47 61 93 82, ⓦ lesainthonoretours.fr. With its wooden beams, stone-brick walls and underground wine cellar, this family-run restaurant is cosy and traditionally

French. Best of all, the hearty *terroir* cuisine is made with fruit and veg straight from the chef's own kitchen garden. Try the famous *pâté de Tours*. *Menus* from €29. Mon–Fri noon–3pm & 7–10pm.

**Vanne** 23 rue Georges-Courteline ☏ 09 65 10 88 81. A small but ambient place with modern interiors hidden behind a timber-fronted facade, *Vanne* has made a name for itself serving flavoursome Korean cuisine. The dishes are limited but expertly executed and evening *menus* start at €20. Mon–Tues & Thurs–Sat noon–2pm & 7–9pm.

## DRINKING AND NIGHTLIFE

**Académie de la Bière** 41 rue Lavoisier ☏ 02 47 05 31 74. Stocking over 170 different varieties of beer from across the globe, this is a lively, student-friendly pub, just around the corner from the cathedral. Happy hour is 8–10pm, with discounts on draught beer and soft drinks, plus there's a small dancefloor. Wed–Sat 8pm–5am.

**Le Strapontin** 23 rue de Châteauneuf ☏ 02 47 47 02 74. Bright red walls and neo-punk artwork give *Le Strapontin* a cool, youthful vibe, but the live jazz and sizeable wine and beer list draws a slightly more grown-up crowd. Daily 5pm–2am.

**Les 3 Orfèvres** 6 rue des Orfèvres ☏ 02 47 64 02 73,

ⓦ 3orfevres.com. A popular haunt for locals, backpackers and language students, just off place Plumereau, with live bands and DJs. The club doesn't really get going until after midnight, but certainly jumps when it does, playing a mix of rock and pop. Wed–Sat: live bands from 8–11pm, closes around 6am.

**Le Vieux Mûrier** 11 place Plumereau ☏ 02 47 61 04 77. The oldest bar in the area and in prime position on the square. Cosy, retro, scarlet and smoky-yellow interiors and an always-packed terrace, make this one of the most popular choices for solo or group outings. Tues–Sat 11–2am, Sun 2–9pm.

## DIRECTORY

**Health** Centre Hospitalier Tours, 2 bd Tonnellé; ☏ 02 47 47 47 47.

**Police** Commissariat Général, 70–72 rue Marceau ☏ 02 47 33 80 69.

# Amboise

Twenty kilometres upstream of Tours, **AMBOISE** is one of the highlights of the Loire region, with its beguiling mix of beauty, excellent gastronomy and genuine sense of history. The château dominates the town, but there are many other attractions, most famously Leonardo da Vinci's residence of **Clos-Lucé**. Amboise draws a busy tourist trade in high season, which may detract from the quieter pleasures of strolling around town, but does mean it's a lively destination.

## Château d'Amboise

Daily: April–June 9am–6.30pm; July & Aug 9am–7pm; Sept & Oct 9am–6pm; first two weeks Nov & March 9am–5.30pm; mid-Nov to Jan 9am–12.30pm & 2–4.45pm; Feb 9am–12.30pm & 1.30–5pm • €12.80 including Histopad, • ⓦ chateau-amboise.com

The remains of the château d'Amboise, once five times its present size, but much reduced by wars and lack of finance, still represent a highly impressive accomplishment. It was in the late fifteenth century, following his marriage to Anne of Brittany at Langeais, that Charles VIII decided to turn the old castle of his childhood days into an extravagant palace, adding the Flamboyant Gothic wing that overlooks the river, and the chapelle de St-Hubert, perched incongruously atop a buttress of the defensive walls. But not long after the work was completed, he managed to hit his head, fatally, on a doorframe. He left the kingdom to his cousin, Louis XII, who spent most of his time at Blois but built a new wing at Amboise (at right angles to the main body) to house his nearest male relative, the young François d'Angoulême, thereby keeping him within easy reach. When the young heir acceded to the throne as François I$^{er}$ he didn't forget his childhood home. He embellished it with classical stonework (visible on the east facade of the Louis XII wing), invited

Leonardo da Vinci to work in Amboise under his protection, and eventually died in the château's collegiate church.

Henri II continued to add to the château, but it was during the reign of his sickly son, François II, that it became notorious. The **Tumult of Amboise** was one of the first skirmishes in the Wars of Religion. Persecuted by the young king's powerful advisers, the Guise brothers, Huguenot conspirators set out for Amboise in 1560 to "rescue" their king and establish a more tolerant monarchy under their tutelage. But they were ambushed by royal troops in the woods outside the town, rounded up and summarily tried in the Salle des Conseils. Some were drowned in the Loire below the château, some were beheaded in the grounds, and others were hung from the château's balconies.

After such a colourful history, the interior of the château is comparatively restrained, though the various rooms still retain some sense of their historical grandeur. The last French king, Louis-Philippe, also stayed in the château, hence the abrupt switch from the solid Gothic furnishings of the ground floor to the 1830s post-First Empire style of the first-floor apartments. The most recently renovated parts of the château are the **underground passageways**, which have been both dungeons and larders in their time. The **Tour des Minimes**, the original fifteenth-century entrance, is the most architecturally exciting part of the castle, with its massive internal ramp, leading down to the pleasant gardens.

## Clos-Lucé

Daily: Jan 10am–6pm; Feb–June & Sept–Oct 9am–7pm; July & Aug 9am–8pm; Nov & Dec 9am–6pm; • €15.50, mid-Nov to Feb €13.50 • Last entry 1hr before close • ☏ 02 47 57 00 73, ⊛ vinci-closluce.com

Following his campaigns in Lombardy, François Ier decided that the best way to bring back the ideas of the Italian Renaissance was to import one of the finest exponents of the new arts. In 1516, **Leonardo da Vinci** ventured across the Alps in response to the royal invitation, carrying with him the *Mona Lisa* among other paintings. For three years before his death in 1519, he made his home at the **Clos-Lucé**, at the end of rue Victor-Hugo. Leonardo seems to have enjoyed a semi-retirement at Amboise, devoting himself to inventions of varying brilliance and impracticability, and enjoying conversations with his royal patron, but it seems that no work of any great stature was produced there. The house – an attractive brick mansion with Italianate details added by Charles VIII – is now a museum to Leonardo, dotted with models of his inventions – including wooden flying machines. A fresco of the *Annunciation of Mary*, thought to be either his work, or that of one of his disciples, has been restored in the Oratory. His workshop has recently been renovated and is now on show to the public for the first time.

### ARRIVAL AND INFORMATION
### AMBOISE

**By train** The *gare SNCF* is on the north bank of the river, at the end of rue Jules-Ferry, about 1km from the château. There are frequent connections to Tours (at least 4 hourly; 17min) and Blois (2 hourly; 20min).

**By bus** Rémi's line C runs between Tours and Amboise (11 daily Mon–Sat).

**Tourist office** Information on Amboise and the vineyards of the Touraine-Amboise *appellation*, is available at the riverfront tourist office on quai du Général-de-Gaulle (April–June & Sept–Oct Mon–Sat 9.30am–6pm, Sun 10am–1pm & 2–5pm; July & Aug Mon–Sat 9am–7pm, Sun 10am–6pm; Nov–March Mon–Sat 10am–12.30pm & 2–5pm; ☏ 02 47 57 09 28, ⊛ amboise-valdeloire.com).

### GETTING AROUND

**Bike rental** Cycles Richard, 2 rue Nazelles, near the station (☏ 02 47 57 01 79), or Locacycle, on 2bis rue Jean-Jacques-Rousseau (☏ 02 47 57 00 28).

**Canoe rental** Club de Canoë-Kayak, at the Base de l'Île d'Or (☏ 02 47 23 26 52, ⊛ loire-aventure.com), rents out canoes and also runs guided trips.

### ACCOMMODATION

**Au Charme Rabelaisien** 25 rue Rabelais ☏ 02 47 57 53 84, ⊛ au-charme-rabelaisien.com. Four stunning, individually designed rooms in a charming timber-fronted B&B, with vintage furniture, bathrobes, minibar and other boutique hotel mod cons. There's a pool and shady garden too. Breakfast €14. **€145**

**Belle-Vue** 12 quai Charles-Guinot ☎02 47 57 02 26, ⓦ hotel-bellevue-amboise.com. A long-established three-star *Logis de France*, located by the waterfront just below the château, and home to the swish *Lounge B* bar-restaurant. Recently refurbished, the rooms here are modern and comfortable with a striking colour palette and unique touches. Closed Jan to mid-March. Breakfast €13. **€89**

**Le Blason** 11 place Richelieu ☎02 47 23 22 41, ⓦ leblason.fr. A top budget option, with comfortable, well-furnished rooms in a quiet corner, just a few minutes' walk from the château. Rooms are cosy, with a splash of colour and exposed wood beams, while the bathrooms are modern and equipped with rain showers. Breakfast €8. **€66**

**Camping de l'Île d'Or** Île d'Or ☎02 47 57 23 37, ⓦ camping-amboise.com. Pleasant, leafy two-star campsite on a little island in the middle of the Loire, with a pool, tennis courts and football pitch nearby. Closed Oct–March. **€12.50**

**Le Choiseul** 36 quai Charles-Guinot ☎02 47 30 45 45, ⓦ grandesetapes.com/chateau-hotel-choiseul-amboise. Widely acknowledged to be the best hotel in Amboise, this luxurious place has grandly appointed and very comfortable rooms, an excellent restaurant and all the other touches you'd expect, including a pool, stunning views and a gourmet restaurant, *Le 36* (see below). Breakfast €24. **€143**

**Éthic Étapes** 1 rue Commire ☎02 47 30 60 90, ⓦ iledor-amboise.fr. A clean and comfy youth hostel located on the same island as the campsite (see above). Single and double rooms and dorms are available, and it's well equipped for cyclists. Breakfast included. **€25**

★ **Le Vieux Manoir** 13 rue Rabelais ☎02 47 30 41 27, ⓦ le-vieux-manoir.com. Run by an utterly charming American couple, this lovingly restored manor house is one of the best bed and breakfasts in the region. Original wood beams, sweet decor and beautiful gardens bursting with flowers add to the traditional feel, while the glass of Loire wine waiting on your arrival is a nice touch. **€160**

## EATING AND DRINKING

### EATING

**Restaurant Le 36** ☎02 47 30 45 45. With its opulent dining room overlooking the Loire and idyllic garden terrace, this is the top choice for gourmet cuisine in Amboise, located in the equally stunning *Le Choiseul* hotel (see above). You'll pay for the privilege but it's worth it, with extravagant dishes and some unconventional pairings. *Menus* €31–79. Daily noon–2pm & 7.30–9pm.

**Les Arpents** 5 rue d'Orange ☎02 36 20 92 44, ⓦ restaurant-lesarpents.fr. Superbly crafted and presented dishes made with local, seasonal produce are on the menu in this stylish restaurant. You could try fish of the day (€23) with béarnaise sauce or opt for the excellent-value lunch menu (€17). Leave room for the chocolate and blackcurrant cake. Tues–Sat noon–2pm & 7–9pm, Sun 2–2.30pm.

★ **La Fourchette** 9 rue Malebranche ☎06 11 78 16 98. This small bistro has fast earned itself a reputation for unique and tasty, home-cooked dishes, and it's excellent value, with mains starting from just €12. The friendly, intimate vibe is all part of the experience, but it means that booking ahead is essential. Mon 7–8.30pm, Tues &Thurs–Sat 12.15–1.30pm & 7–8.30pm.

**Galland Épicerie de Terroirs** 27 rue Nationale ☎02 47 23 14 79. This welcoming local delicacies shop stocks more than 1000 different products from small producers and specializes in Loire valley wines, local cheeses and charcuterie. You're welcome to stop by for a tasting in the wine section at the back of the shop. Call ahead if you're in a group. Daily 9.30am–7.30pm.

**La Pause du Temps** 80 rue Nationale ☎09 81 97 55 57, ⓦ lapausedutemps.fr. A simple café with a nice courtyard terrace. The small, regularly changing menu features the likes of pork with thyme and a quinoa burger, both at €16. It's well priced and therefore popular so come early. You can buy frozen yoghurt to take out. Wed–Sat 9am–9pm, Sun 9am–2pm.

### DRINKING

**Caveau des Vignerons d'Amboise** At the base of the château. If you're keen to taste some of the local wine, head to this welcoming place, which offers a wide variety to sip and buy. Daily 10am–7pm; closed Nov–March.

**Caves Duhard** 56 rue du Rocher des Violettes ☎02 47 57 20 77, ⓦ caves-duhard.fr. Tucked away deep in a sixteenth-century *cave*, three generations of enthusiastic specialists have dedicated themselves to the wines of the Loire valley. Drop by for a tasting. Daily 10am–6pm.

**Le Shaker** 3 quai François-Tissard, Île d'Or. With an award-winning mixologist and a terrace with wonderful views across to the château, this is the place to go for a late cocktail. Try a White Lady (gin, cointreau and egg white). Daily 6pm–3am.

# Château de Villandry

Gardens: Daily April–May & Sept 9am–7pm; July & Aug 9am–7.30pm; Oct 9am–6.30pm; end Oct to mid-Nov & mid– to end Feb 9am–5.30pm; mid-Nov to mid-Feb 9am–5pm. Château: closes 1hr before gardens, last entry 30min before closing • €11 (€8.50 Nov–

March) château and gardens, €7 (€4.50 Nov–March) gardens only • ☎ 02 47 50 02 09, ⓦ chateauvillandry.fr • Buses run daily in July & Aug from Tours' *gare routière*

Even if gardens aren't normally your thing, those at the Château de Villandry are unmissable. Thirteen kilometres west of Tours along the Cher, this recreated Renaissance **garden** is as much symbolic as ornamental or practical. At the topmost level is a large, formal water garden in the elevated classical spirit. Next down, beside the château itself, is the ornamental garden, which features geometrical arrangements of box hedges symbolizing different kinds of love: tender, passionate, fickle and tragic. But the highlight, spread out at the lowest level across 12,500 square metres, is the *potager*, or Renaissance kitchen garden. Carrots, cabbages and aubergines are arranged into intricate patterns, while rose bowers and miniature box hedges form a kind of frame. Even in winter, there is almost always something to see, as the entire area is replanted twice a year. At the far end of the garden, overlooked by the squat tower of the village church, beautiful vine-shaded paths run past the medieval herb garden and the maze.

The elegant château was erected in the 1530s by one of François I$^{er}$'s royal financiers, Jean le Breton, though the keep – from which there's a fine view of the gardens – dates back to a twelfth-century feudal castle. It's worth a visit if only for the magnificent views over the grounds, but pales in comparison to its gardens. Le Breton's Renaissance structure is arranged around three sides of a *cour d'honneur*, the fourth wing having been demolished in the eighteenth century.

## Château de Langeais

Daily: Feb & March 9.30am–5.30pm; April–June & Sept to mid-Nov 9.30am–6.30pm; July & Aug 9am–7pm; mid-Nov to Jan 10am–5pm • €9.80 • ☎ 02 47 96 72 60, ⓦ chateau-de-langeais.com

Twenty-three kilometres west of Tours, the small riverside town of **LANGEAIS** huddles in the shadow of its forbidding château, which was built to stop any incursions up the Loire by the Bretons. This threat ended with the marriage of Charles VIII and Duchess Anne of Brittany in 1491, which was celebrated in the castle, and a diptych of the couple portrays them looking less than joyous at their union – Anne had little choice in giving up her independence. The main appeal here is in the way that the interior has resisted modernization, to give a genuine sense of what life would have been like in the fifteenth century, including fascinating tapestries, some rare paintings and a number of *chaires* (seigneurial chairs). The banqueting hall has a large U-shaped table, piled high with imitation food, while in the huge marriage chamber is the gilded and bejewelled wedding coffer of Charles and Anne.

### ARRIVAL AND INFORMATION

**By train** The *gare SNCF* is 5min away on foot from the castle and has a regular service to Tours (10 daily; 20min) and Saumur (9 daily; 25min).

### ACCOMMODATION AND EATING

LANGEAIS

**L'Ange est Rêveur** 5 place Pierre-de-Brosse ☎ 02 47 96 55 97, ⓦ langeaisreveur.fr. Set in the shadow of the château de Langeais, this exquisite *chambre d'hôte* has five romantic rooms with spotless wood floors, vintage chandeliers and canopy beds. Breakfast included. €75

★ **Au Coin des Halles** 9 rue Gambetta ☎ 02 47 96 37 25, ⓦ aucoindeshalles.com. A surprisingly modern addition to this pleasantly old-fashioned town, with fragrant, appetizing creations served in a decidedly funky dining room space. There's a good-sized terrace at the back so you can eat alfresco in the summer. *Menus* from €17.50. Mon–Tues & Fri–Sun 12.15–2pm & 7.15–9pm.

**Errard Hosten** 2 rue Gambetta ☎ 02 47 96 82 12. On the small road leading to the château, this is a classic and welcoming place to stay. Rooms are spacious, with most offering a good view over the square, plus there's a decent restaurant, which serves a bistro *menu* for lunch and a gastronomic *menu du terroir* in the evening. *Menus* €19.50–61. Breakfast €13. Closed mid-Dec to Jan. €84

**La Maison de Rabelais** 2 place Pierre-de-Brosse ☎ 02 47 96 82 20. A delightful tearoom and chocolatier opposite the château, which serves snacks and salads, but specializes in ice-cream sundaes and decadent chocolate concoctions. Daily 8.30am–7pm June–Sept; closed Mon Oct–May.

## Azay-le-Rideau

**Château** Daily: April–June & Sept 9.30am–6pm; July & Aug 9.30am–11pm; Oct–March 10am–5.15pm • €10.50 • ⓦ azay-le-rideau.fr

Even without its striking château, the quiet village of **AZAY-LE-RIDEAU** would bask in its serene setting, complete with an old mill by the bridge and curious, doll-like Carolingian statues embedded in the facade of the church of St Symphorien. Perhaps unsurprisingly, it has become a magnet for tourists. On its little island in the Indre, the **château** is one of the loveliest in the Loire: perfect turreted early Renaissance, pure in style right down to the blood-red paint of its window frames. Visiting the interior, furnished in mostly period style, doesn't add much to the experience although the grand staircase is worth seeing, and it's fun to look out through the mullioned windows across the moat and park and imagine yourself the *seigneur*. In summer, the château is illuminated from 7–11pm.

### ARRIVAL AND INFORMATION                          AZAY-LE-RIDEAU

**By train** The *gare SNCF* is awkwardly situated a 15min walk west of the centre, along avenue Adélaïde-Riché. Trains from Tours (Mon–Fri 9 daily, Sat & Sun 5 daily; 30min) call at Azay-le-Rideau on their way to Chinon (Mon–Fri 10 daily, Sat & Sun 6 daily; 20min) roughly every 2hr.
**By bus** The bus stop is next to the tourist office on the main road.

**Tourist office** 4 rue du Château (May–June & Sept Mon–Sat 9.30am–1pm & 2–6pm, Sun 10am–1pm & 2–5pm; July & Aug Mon–Sat 9.30am–1pm & 2–7pm, Sun 10am–1pm & 2–6pm; Oct–March Mon–Sat 10am–12.30pm & 2–6pm; ☎ 02 47 45 44 40, ⓦ azay-chinon-valdeloire.com).
**Bike rental** Azay le Rideau Cycles, 13 rue Carnot (☎ 02 47 45 40 94, ⓦ azaylerideaucycles.com).

### ACCOMMODATION

★ **Biencourt** 7 rue de Balzac ☎ 02 47 45 20 75, ⓦ hotelbiencourt.fr. Built in the sixteenth century as a coaching inn, this charming small hotel was later the village school. The 17 rooms are simply but stylishly decorated, with all mod cons. The buffet breakfast (€11) features local farm produce and can be eaten on the flower filled patio on warm days. **€74**
**Camping du Sabot** 1 rue du Stade, signposted off the D84 to Saché ☎ 02 47 45 42 72, ⓦ onlycamp.fr. This large and well-organized campsite, upstream from the château, has a grocery store, with bread and pastries to order, plus washing machines, picnic tables, hot showers, and free wi-fi. Closed Nov–March. **€22.70**

**Le Grand Monarque** 3 place de la République ☎ 02 47 45 40 08, ⓦ legrandmonarque.com. As the name suggests, this option is indeed rather grand, and has a wide range of chic rooms, some with exposed beams and stone walls. There's a shady terrace to enjoy breakfast or a pre-supper drink if it's warm. Buffet breakfast €13. **€90**
**Troglododo** Rte des Granges ☎ 02 47 45 31 25, ⓦ troglododo.fr. The unusual rooms offered by M. et Mme Sarrazin are housed in troglodyte chambers hollowed out of the rock. Bright splashes of colour, stylish lighting and funky fabrics make this a unique spot, and it can get booked up a fair way in advance; don't even think about turning up in summer without a reservation. Breakfast €13. **€80**

### EATING AND DRINKING

**Côté Cour** 19 rue Balzac ☎ 02 47 45 30 36, ⓦ cotecour-azay.com. Arguably the best restaurant in town, serving a small menu of local seasonal dishes. The house speciality is a delicious dried pear salad. *Menus* from €18.50 to €32. Mon–Tues & Thurs–Sun noon–2pm & 7–8.30pm.
**Les Grottes** 23 rue de Pineau ☎ 02 47 86 22 96. While

decent, the food at this atmospheric cave restaurant is nothing remarkable, but it's popular for its unique setting, inside a quirky troglodyte dwelling. There's a breezy terrace out front for the claustrophobic. *Menus* from €20. Daily noon–2pm & 7–10pm; closed Thurs Oct–May.

## Château d'Ussé

Daily: mid-Feb to March & Sept–Oct 10am–6pm; April–Aug 10am–7pm; • €14 • ☎ 02 47 95 54 05, ⓦ chateaudusse.fr

Fourteen kilometres west of Azay-le-Rideau, as the Indre approaches its confluence with the Loire, is the Château d'Ussé in **RIGNY-USSÉ**. With its shimmering white towers and terraced gardens, this is the ultimate fairy-tale château – so much so that it's supposed to have inspired Charles Perrault's classic retelling of the Sleeping Beauty myth. The exterior resembles nothing so much as a Disney fantasy, while inside things are more restrained, apart from the rather kitsch Sleeping Beauty tableaux.

The château's gardens, designed by Le Nôtre, are pleasant to wander in, featuring a lovely Renaissance chapel, while the surrounding vineyards produce a sparkling Cuvée Prestige Brut, which is for sale in the grounds.

### ACCOMMODATION AND EATING — RIGNY-USSÉ

**Le Clos d'Ussé** Rigny-Ussé ⓣ 02 47 95 55 47, ⓦ leclosdusse.fr. This simple, but welcoming family-run hotel-restaurant is the only one in the tiny village of Rigny-Ussé, just a short stroll from the château. The contemporary rooms are cosy and comfortable, and there's a leafy terrace on which to enjoy breakfast (€9). **€80**

**Domaine de la Juranvillerie** 15 rue des Fougères ⓣ 02 47 95 57 85, ⓦ lajuranvillerie.com. Behind the château, in a tranquil, wooded fold of the valley, *Domaine de la Juranvillerie* is arguably the region's most unique *chambre d'hôte*, run by a charming older couple. The seventeenth-century farmhouses have been beautifully restored in traditional style, but with all mod cons, plus there's an "enchanted" forest, medieval garden and a natural swimming pool. For the full experience, prebook a place on the weekly medieval costumed dinner (€28). Breakfast is included. **€75**



# Chinon and around

**CHINON** lies on the north bank of the Vienne, 12km from its confluence with the Loire, and is surrounded by some of the best vineyards in the Loire valley. While the cobbled medieval streets and half-timbered townhouses give a marvellous sense of history, it's a quiet town, and the actual sights won't keep you occupied for any more than a day or two. However, the tree-lined promenades and hilltop château are undeniably pretty and the growing population of English expats bring an international flavour to the many cafés, restaurants and bars.

## The royal fortress

Daily: March–April & Sept–Oct 9.30am–6pm; May–Aug 9.30am–7pm; Nov–Feb 9.30am–5pm • €9 • ⓣ 02 47 93 13 45, ⓦ forteressechinon.fr • To get there, walk from town or take the free lift from the car park near the tourist office

Chinon's château, strictly speaking, is actually a fortress, rather than a typical Renaissance castle, perched high on a hill over the town, with a stunning view over the Vienne.

A fortress existed here from the Iron Age until the time of Louis XIV, the age of its most recent ruins. Henry Plantagenet added a new castle to the first medieval fortress on the site, built by his ancestor Foulques Nerra, and died here, crying vengeance on his son Richard, who had treacherously allied himself with the French king Philippe-Auguste. After a year's siege in 1204–5, Philippe-Auguste finally took the castle from the English King John, ending the Plantagenet rule over Touraine and Anjou.

Over two hundred years later, Chinon was one of the few places where the Dauphin Charles, later Charles VII, could safely stay while Henry V of England held Paris and the title to the French throne. When Joan of Arc arrived here in 1429, she was able to talk her way into meeting him. The story depicted in a tapestry on display on the site is that as Joan entered the great hall, the Dauphin remained hidden anonymously among the assembled nobles, as a test, but Joan picked him out straight away. Joan herself claimed that an angel had appeared before the court, bearing a crown. She begged him to allow her to rally his army against the English. To the horror of the courtiers, Charles said yes. The reality is rather more prosaic: records show that Joan attended a small meeting with the king, so already knew who he was.

The fortress has been sensitively and impressively restored. The **Logis Royal**, or royal quarters, includes the apartments of Charles VII and Mary of Anjou, and visitors can also explore the **middle castle**, the **Fort Coudray** and the **Fort Saint George**. There's also an excellent **Joan of Arc museum** on site, where you can see fragments of bone said to have been rescued from under the stake where she died.

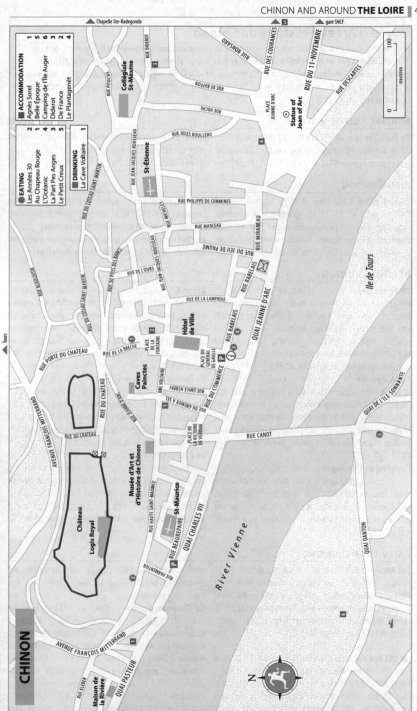

**CHINON**

**■ ACCOMMODATION**
| | |
|---|---|
| Agnès Sorel | 1 |
| Belle Époque | 5 |
| Camping de l'Île Auger | 6 |
| Diderot | 3 |
| De France | 2 |
| Le Plantagenêt | 4 |

**● EATING**
| | |
|---|---|
| Les Années 30 | 2 |
| Au Chapeau Rouge | 1 |
| L'Océanic | 4 |
| La Part Pes Anges | 3 |
| Le Petit Creux | 5 |

**■ DRINKING**
| | |
|---|---|
| La Cave Voltaire | 1 |

7

## Musée d'Art et d'Histoire de Chinon

44 rue Haute St-Maurice • March to mid-Sept daily except Tues 2.30–6.30pm; mid-Sept to mid-Nov Mon & Thurs–Sun 2–6pm • €3

The **Musée d'Art et d'Histoire de Chinon** has some diverting oddments of sculpture, pottery and paintings related to the town's history, as well as a fascinating recreation of a room in a sixteenth-century inn. The top floor is given over to temporary exhibitions of contemporary art.

### ARRIVAL AND DEPARTURE

CHINON

**By train** The *gare SNCF* lies to the east of the town, from where rue du Dr-P.-Labussière and rue du 11-novembre lead to place Jeanne-d'Arc, where there's a carving of Joan in mid-battle charge. Keep heading west and you'll soon reach the old quarter. Frequent trains to Tours depart daily (45min–1hr).

### INFORMATION

**Tourist office** 1 rue Rabelais (daily 10am–1.30pm & 2–7pm; ☎02 47 93 17 85, ⓦazay-chinon-valdeloire. com). The office can provide addresses of local vineyards where you can taste Chinon's famous red wine, and details of walking and biking trails in the nearby Forêt de Chinon.

**Canoe rental** Chinon Loisirs Activités Nature by the campsite (☎06 23 82 96 33, ⓦloisirs-nature.fr; April–Oct) rents out canoes and runs guided trips in summer.
**Market** An antiques and flea market takes place every third Sun of the month, while regular market day is Thurs.

### ACCOMMODATION

★ **Agnès Sorel** 4 quai Pasteur ☎02 47 93 04 37, ⓦhotel-agnes-sorel.com. A notch above most other two-star hotels, *Agnès Sorel* feels like home the moment you step through the door. Rooms are light, airy and spacious, with wooden floors, gleaming bathrooms and chic yet unpretentious decor. Opt for a room with a balcony overlooking the river. Breakfast €8.50. **€68**

**Belle Époque** 14 av Gambetta ☎02 47 93 00 86, ⓦhotelbelle-epoque.com. What it lacks in pizzazz, this homely guesthouse more than makes up for with warm, friendly service. Well located directly opposite the station, rooms are basic but cosy and clean, plus there's private parking and a lively café-restaurant downstairs. Breakfast €8.50. **€60**

**Camping de l'Île Auger** ☎02 47 93 08 35, ⓦcamping-chinon.com. Clean, well-serviced campsite with ample shady spots on the south bank of the Vienne. Bungalows and discounts for long stays are possible, plus swimming pool access and wi-fi for an extra fee. Closed Nov–March. **€15**

**Diderot** 7 rue Diderot ☎02 47 93 18 87, ⓦhoteldiderot. com. Housed in a beautifully restored fifteenth-century building, this solidly bourgeois hotel offers an old-fashioned welcome from the jam-making proprietor. The flower-filled garden and breakfast terrace is the main highlight, where you can indulge in an array of home-made jams and pastries (€10). **€70**

**De France** 47–49 place du Général-de-Gaulle ☎02 47 93 33 91, ⓦbestwestern.fr. There's nothing remarkable about this hotel, but it does have everything you'd expect from a Best Western – big comfy beds, TV & minibar and a great breakfast buffet. It's hard to beat the location, though – right over the main square. Breakfast €13. **€99**

**Le Plantagenêt** 12 place Jeanne-d'Arc ☎02 47 93 36 92, ⓦhotel-plantagenet.com. Homely and welcoming, this historic hotel has a range of traditional and modern rooms, plus a pretty summer garden and veranda. There are bikes available to rent, and a huge breakfast spread including home-made cakes and crêpes. Breakfast €11.50. **€72**

### EATING AND DRINKING

**Les Années 30** 78 rue Haute St-Maurice ☎02 47 93 37 18, ⓦlesannees30.com. With cosy, timeless decor and a flowery lantern-lit terrace right beneath the castle, this is a romantic spot for a dinner date. The menu is traditionally French, but with some adventurous dishes and Far Eastern-influenced flavours. *Menus* from €27. Mon & Thurs–Sun 12.15–1.30pm & 7.30–8.45pm.

★ **La Cave Voltaire** 13 rue Voltaire ☎02 47 93 37 68. A wine bar and shop offering a huge range of regional wines, along with a fully stocked bar and an array of appetizers. Host Patrice speaks excellent English and is incredibly knowledgeable and passionate about local and organic

wines, making wine-tasting fun for both connoisseurs and lay people. May–Oct daily 10.30am–11pm; days and times vary in winter.

**Au Chapeau Rouge** 49 place du Général-de-Gaulle ☎02 47 98 08 08, ⓦauchapeaurouge.fr. Run by a husband-and-wife team, this is a popular choice, with a limited but well-executed menu and an emphasis on regional cuisine. Grab a seat on the pretty, flower-lined terrace and order the "discovery" *menu* (€32). Tues–Sat noon–1pm & 7.30–8.30pm, Sun noon–1pm.

**L'Océanic** 13 rue Rabelais ☎02 47 93 44 55, ⓦloceanic-chinon.com. The place to go if you're in the mood for some

> **WINE TASTING IN CHINON**
>
> Though it's better with a good meal, if you want to try a glass of Chinon you could visit the **Caves Painctes** (📞 02 47 93 30 44, 🕸 chinon.com), off rue Voltaire, a deep cellar carved out of the rock where a local winegrowers' guild runs tastings. "Paincte" was supposedly the name of a wine cellar owned by the father of Rabelais, who was born at the manor farm of La Devinière, 6km southwest of town, where there's a good but rather dry museum on Rabelais' life. Tastings take place July & Aug Tues–Sun 11am, 3pm, 4.30pm & 6pm and cost around €3.

local fish, this popular haunt has everything from Tsarskaya oysters and *moules*, to crab gratin and monkfish. There's also an impressive cheese selection. Four-course *menu* €28.50. Tues–Sat noon–1.30pm & 7.30–9.30pm, Sun noon–1.30pm.

**La Part des Anges** 5 rue Rabelais 📞 02 47 93 99 93, 🕸 lapartdesanges-chinon.com. Justifiably popular family-run affair, with an open kitchen and unique,

beautifully presented cuisine. *Menus* from €23. Wed–Sun noon–2pm & 7.30–9pm.

**Le Petit Creux** 5 rue du Faubourg St-Jacques 📞 02 47 93 04 44. Good-value, bright and cheerful pizzeria just across the bridge from the main town. This is standard fare, but reliable, with pizzas (tomato or cream base) around €11.50 and salads around €9. Mon & Thurs–Sun 11.30am–2.30pm & 6.30–10.30pm.

## Tavant

Sixteen kilometres southeast of Chinon is the village of **TAVANT** which hides the great **St-Nicolas church** (June–Sept Tues–Sat 1.15–5.45pm; Oct–May ask at the mairie; crypt €3). The appeal lies in the twelfth-century Romanesque wall paintings in its crypt, which rank among the finest in Europe. Today, just fragments survive in the upper church, as well as a giant figure of Christ in Majesty on the half-dome of the apse. If the chapel isn't open when you arrive, ask for the guardian at the nearby *mairie* (25 rue Grande).

# Saumur and around

**SAUMUR** is a good-sized town notable for two things in particular: its excellent **sparkling wine** (some would say as good as champagne) and its wealth of aristocratic **military** associations, based on its status as home to the French Cavalry Academy. The *centre ville*, with its warren of cobblestone lanes and jumble of half-timbered buildings and grand white tufa townhouses, runs along the waterfront in the shadows of the majestic **château**.

The stretch of the Loire from Chinon to Angers, which passes through Saumur, is particularly lovely, with the added draw of the bizarre troglodyte dwellings carved out of the cliffs. The land on the south bank, under grapes and sunflowers, gradually rises away from the river, with long inactive windmills still standing, while across the water cows graze in wooded pastures.

## The château

April to mid-June & mid-Sept to Oct Tues–Sun 10am–1pm & 2–5.30pm; mid-June to mid-Sept daily 10am–6.30pm; closed Nov–March • €6; €7 in summer • 📞 02 41 40 24 40, 🕸 chateau-saumur.fr

Set high above town, Saumur's impressive **château** may seem oddly familiar, but then its famous depiction in *Les Très Riches Heures du Duc de Berry*, the most celebrated of all the medieval illuminated prayer books, is reproduced all over the region. It was largely built in the latter half of the fourteenth century by Louis Ier, Duc d'Anjou, who wanted to compete with his brothers Jean de Berry and Charles V. The threat of marauding bands of English soldiers made the masons work flat out – they weren't even allowed to stop for feast days.

## Notre-Dame de Nantilly and the church of St-Pierre

Down by the public gardens south of the château, Saumur's oldest church, **Notre-Dame de Nantilly** (daily 9am–6pm, closes 5pm in winter; ☎02 41 83 30 31), houses a large tapestry collection in its Romanesque nave, which is put on display in the summer. The original Gothic church of **St-Pierre**, in the old town, is closed for renovation works; once it re-opens it's worth taking a look at the Counter-Reformation façade, built as part of the church's efforts to overawe its persistently Protestant population.

## École Nationale d'Équitation

Av de l'École Nationale d'Équitation, St-Hilaire St-Florent • Closed Mon morning, Sat afternoon, all day Sun and holidays; mid-Feb to mid-April & mid-Oct to Nov tours at 10am, 11am, 2.30pm & 4pm; mid-April to mid-Sept tours every 30min from 10am–4pm • Guided tours from €8, galas €35 • ☎ 02 41 53 50 60, ⓦ ifce.fr/cadre-noir

Saumur's cavalry heritage is displayed in all its glory at the **École Nationale d'Équitation**, home to the much-acclaimed Cadre Noir riding team, where famed *écuyers* (riding masters) such as Philippe Karl and François Bacher honed their skills. For budding equestrians, touring the grounds offers a fascinating insight into the roots of French classical dressage, with the opportunity to peek into the stables and tack rooms, meet the horses and, if you're lucky, watch the young horses and riders in their daily training. Even the non-horsey will be impressed by the galas and public performances, with mesmerizing dressage displays set to music, including the crowd-pleasing "airs above the ground" (school movements in which the horses leap and rear).

## Musée des Blindés

1043 rte de Fontevraud • Daily: Jan–April & Oct–Dec Mon–Fri 10am–5pm, Sat & Sun 11am–6pm; May, June, Sept daily 10am–6pm; July & Aug daily 9.30am–6.30pm • Free guided tours throughout July & Aug • €8.50 • ☎ 02 41 83 69 95, ⓦ museedesblindes.fr

The history of the tank – traditionally considered as cavalry not infantry – is covered in the **Musée des Blindés**, to the southeast of Saumur's centre. Around 250 vehicles are on display in an exhibition room showing tanks from 1917 to the present day.

## St-Hilaire-St-Florent

Take bus #5 from rue Portail Louis

A large number of manufacturers of the famous Saumur sparkling wine cluster in the suburb of **St-Hilaire-St-Florent**, and are especially prominent along the riverside rue Ackerman and rue Léopold-Palustre. Particularly good cellars include Ackerman-Laurance, Bouvet-Ladubay, Langlois-Château, Gratien & Meyer, Louis de Grenelle and Veuve Amiot; choosing between them is a matter of personal taste, and possibly a question of opening hours, though most are open daily throughout the warmer months (generally 10am–6pm).

### ARRIVAL AND DEPARTURE SAUMUR

**By train** The *gare SNCF* is on Saumur's north bank: turn right onto av David-d'Angers and take bus #30 to the centre or cross the bridge to the island on foot.

Destinations Angers (frequent; 30min); Nantes (frequent; 60–90min); Tours (frequent; 40min).

**By bus** The *gare routière* is situated on the south bank, on place Balzac.

### GETTING AROUND

**By car** Much of Saumur's old town is pedestrianized but it's easy to get in and out by car. Free public car parks are located along the waterfront outside the tourist office, in place du Chardonnet and in place Marc-Leclerc on the Île d'Offard.

**Bike rental** There are several bike rental outlets in Saumur – ask for a list at the tourist office. Expect to pay €10 for a half-day and €15 for a full day.

## INFORMATION

**Tourist office** 8bis quai Carnot (mid-May to late Sept Mon–Sat 9.15am–7pm, Sun 10.30am–5.30pm; late Sept to mid-May Mon–Sat 9.15am–12.30pm & 2–6pm, Sun 10am–noon; ⓣ 02 41 40 20 60, ⓦ ot-saumur.fr). The old quarter, around St-Pierre and the castle, lies immediately behind the *hôtel de ville*, on the riverbank just east of the bridge.

**La Maison des Vins d'Anjou et de Saumur** 7 quai Carnot (May–Oct Mon 2–7pm, Tues–Sat 9.30am–1pm & 2–7pm, Sun 10.30am–1pm; Nov & Dec Fri & Sat 10.30am–12.30pm & 2.30–6pm; closed Jan–March; ⓣ 02 41 38 45 83, ⓦ vins-de-saumur.com). The Maison has addresses of wine growers and *caves* to visit.

## ACCOMMODATION

**Camping l'Île d'Offard** Rue de Verden, Île d'Offard ⓣ 02 41 40 30 00, ⓦ saumur-camping.com. Set in a quiet corner of the *Île d'Offard*, with waterfront tent and caravan pitches, ample picnic areas and a swimming pool. Closed Nov–Feb. Camping **€43**

★ **Château de Verrières** 53 rue d'Alsace ⓣ 02 41 38 05 15, ⓦ chateau-verrieres.com. One of the finest buildings in the town is given over to this exceptional B&B. The rooms are lavish, the atmosphere luxurious, there's a two-hectare garden to potter around, a swimming pool and a spacious terrace. Breakfast €24, free parking. **€215**

★ **Le Londres** 48 rue d'Orléans ⓣ 02 41 51 23 98, ⓦ lelondres.com This hotel is as charming as the couple who run it and every inch of it has been designed with care. Elements of the original nineteenth-century building remain, but it's the quirky decor that makes it truly unique. Each room is themed and named accordingly ("Rose Bonbon", "Blue Garden", "L'Anglais") plus there are fresh pastries delivered daily from a local patisserie, views of the château, and two self-contained apartments. Breakfast €12. Private parking €9. **€100**

**St-Pierre** 8 rue Haute-St-Pierre ⓣ 02 41 50 33 00, ⓦ saintpierresaumur.com. A luxurious boutique hotel hidden down a side street close to the busy place St-Pierre, at the foot of the château. Each room is individually decorated, with textured wallpapers, chandeliers and vintage furnishings, and the exterior is equally impressive – a refurbished seventeenth-century stone building with timber-fronting and castle-like turrets. Breakfast €15.50. **€130**

**Le Volney** 1 rue Volney ⓣ 02 41 51 25 41, ⓦ levolney.com This simple budget hotel has no frills, but it's still great value, with clean rooms, decent showers and comfy beds. The cheerful management and central location are also pluses. Some rooms have shared showers. Breakfast €8.50. **€45**

## EATING AND DRINKING

**L'Alchimiste** 6 rue de Lorraine ⓣ 02 41 67 65 18, ⓦ lalchimiste-saumur.fr. Innovative cuisine with an emphasis on local, seasonal foods is served up in this elegant restaurant, a short stroll from the Cadre Noir. Tuck into langoustine risotto, followed by local speciality *crémet d'Anjou* and a sweet digestif – the *whisky carambar* is delicious. *Menus* from €21. Tues–Sat noon–2.30pm & 7.30–10pm.

**Bistrot Les TonTons** 1 place St-Pierre ⓣ 02 41 59 59 40. The place to go to enjoy charcuterie and cheese plates

## TROGLODYTE DWELLINGS AROUND SAUMUR

For centuries, the soft tufa rock that lines the Loire has been riddled with underground caves and troglodyte dwellings carved into the cliff sides, making up one of the largest and most varied collections of troglodyte sites in Europe. Today, many of the caves serve a new purpose: as traditional wine *caves*, where wines are stored and aged; as atmospheric galleries filled with rock sculptures; as hotels or restaurants; or, perhaps most uniquely, as cellars for cultivating mushrooms. The closest caves to Saumur are in St-Hilaire-St-Florent, where the star attraction is the Pierre et Lumière (ⓦ pierre-et-lumiere.com), which exhibits miniature sculptures of some of the Loire's most iconic churches and châteaux. Other notable highlights include the spectacular lightshow at the cavern-like Perrières (ⓦ les-perrieres.com) in Doué-la-Fontaine and the wine caves around Montsoreau and Turquant.

### VISITING THE CAVES

There are dozens of sites around Saumur for visitors to explore, but a lack of guided tours means it's best to visit the caves independently by car or to hire a private guide. Many tours of the Abbaye de Fontevraud (see below) or nearby sights also include a stop at one of the mushroom or wine caves. There's normally no need to book ahead, but it's best to check the opening times at the tourist office (see above) as they can vary greatly and many are closed in the low season. Entrance is typically between €2–9.

(from €18) at any time, plus a delicious selection of grills and seasonal dishes. The portions are more than generous – the foie gras starter feeds at least two greedy people – and there's a superb wine list featuring local organic, biodynamic wines. Tues–Thurs 10am–10pm, Fri & Sat 10am–midnight.

**L'Escargot** 30 rue du Maréchal-Leclerc ☎02 41 51 20 88. Just outside the busy old town, this traditional restaurant is worth seeking out. Unsurprisingly, it's the *escargots* (snails) that take centre stage, cooked up in a variety of delicious sauces, while the rest of the menu is limited but expertly executed. *Menus* from €19. Mon & Thurs–Sun noon–1pm & 7.30–9.30pm, Sat 7.30–9.30pm.

**Le Gambetta** 12 rue Gambetta ☎02 41 67 66 66, ⓦrestaurantlegambetta.fr. Saumur's only Michelin-starred restaurant is a complete sensory experience, with show-stopping creations that taste as good as they look. For the full effect, put yourself at the mercy of chef Mickaël Pihours and opt for the *Curiosité* menu (€38–45). Tues & Thurs–Sat noon–2pm & 7.15–9.15pm, Sun noon–2pm.

**Le Grand Bleu** 6 rue du Marché ☎02 41 67 41 83. A romantic spot in the evening hours with the leafy terrace lit by chandeliers, *Le Grand Bleu* specializes in fish and seafood. Try the pan-fried eel or the flaming garlic and whisky *gambas. Menus* €16–34. Daily noon–2pm & 7–9pm.

**Le Pot de Lapin** 35 rue Rabelais ☎02 41 67 12 86. A relaxed vibe and exceedingly friendly staff make this contemporary bistro-restaurant a hotspot among both locals and out-of-towners. The varied menu is the real highlight, with a huge choice of starters and tapas. Mains from €14. Tues–Sat noon–2pm & 7–9pm.

# The Abbaye de Fontevraud

Daily: late Jan to Feb & early Nov to Dec 9.30am–6pm; April–Oct 9.30am–7pm • €11 • ☎02 41 51 73 52, ⓦfontevraud.fr • Bus #1 runs from Saumur, but times change frequently so ask at the tourist office (see below) for details

At the heart of the stunning Romanesque complex of the **Abbaye de Fontevraud**, 16km southeast of Saumur, are the tombs of the Plantagenet royal family, eerily lifelike works of funereal art that powerfully evoke the historical bonds between England and France. A religious community was established in around 1100 as both a nunnery and a monastery with an abbess in charge – an unconventional move, even if the post was filled solely by queens and princesses. The remaining buildings date from the twelfth century and are immense, built to house and separate not only the nuns and monks but also the sick, lepers and repentant prostitutes. There were originally five separate institutions, of which three still stand in graceful Romanesque solidity. In 1804 Napoleon decided to transform the building into a prison, which continued till 1963 and inspired writer Jean Genet, whose book *Miracle of the Rose* was partly based on the recollections of a prisoner incarcerated here. Part of the building is now a smart boutique hotel and restaurant (☎02 46 46 10 10, ⓦhotel-fontevraud.com).

The abbey church is an impressive space, not least for the four tombstone **effigies**: Henry II, his wife Eleanor of Aquitaine, who died here, their son Richard the Lionheart and daughter-in-law Isabelle of Angoulême, King John's queen. The strange domed roof, the great cream-coloured columns of the choir and the graceful capitals of the nave add to the effect. Elsewhere in the complex you can explore the magnificent cloisters, the chapterhouse, decorated with sixteenth-century murals, and the vast refectory. All the cooking for the religious community, which would have numbered several hundred, was done in the now restored Romanesque kitchen, an octagonal building as extraordinary from the outside (with its 21 spiky chimneys) as it is within.

## INFORMATION

**Tourist office** Place St-Michel (April–June Tues–Sat 9.30am–1pm & 2.30–6pm, Sun 10.30am–1pm; July–Sept Mon–Sat 9.30am–1pm & 2.30–6pm, Sun 10.30am–1pm & 2–5pm; ☎02 41 51 79 45, ⓦot-saumur.fr). The abbey is

## ABBAYE DE FONTEVRAUD

now the Centre Culturel de l'Ouest (CCO), the cultural centre for western France, and is used for a great many activities, from concerts to lectures, art exhibitions and theatre.

## ACCOMMODATION AND EATING

**Croix Blanche** 7 place des Plantagenêts ☎02 41 51 71 11, ⓦhotel-croixblanche.com. Located opposite the Abbaye, this historic seventeenth-century coaching inn with slate roofs and tufa walls has been bought bang up to date, and the themed rooms each have a creative twist. Some are due to be renovated in 2018/19. There's also an excellent on-site restaurant, brasserie and flower-filled terrace. Buffet breakfast €14. **€95**

# Angers and around

**ANGERS**, capital of the ancient county of Anjou, is a hugely likeable, vibrant town, which seems to happily straddle the ancient and modern worlds. For fans of heritage tourism, it has two stunning **tapestry** series, the fourteenth-century *Apocalypse* and the twentieth-century *Le Chant du Monde*, plus its own hilltop **château**. Along with its interesting cultural aspects, the city has a strong selection of shops, bars and restaurants as well as a thriving nightlife.

## The château and Apocalypse tapestry

Daily: May–Aug 9.30am–6.30pm; Sept–April 10am–5.30pm • €9 • ☏ 02 41 86 48 77, ⓦ chateau-angers.fr

The **Château d'Angers** is a formidable early medieval fortress, with its mighty kilometre-long curtain wall reinforced by seventeen circular towers. Inside are a few miscellaneous remains of the counts' royal lodgings and chapels, but the chief focus is the astonishing *Tapestry of the Apocalypse*. Woven between 1373 and 1382 for Louis I$^{er}$ of Anjou, it was originally 140m long, of which 100m now survives. Treated as a masterpiece from the start, the tapestry's reputation rests on its superb detail and stunning colours, preserved today by the very low light levels in the long viewing hall. If you plan to follow the apocalypse story right through, the English-language audioguide comes in handy, but a

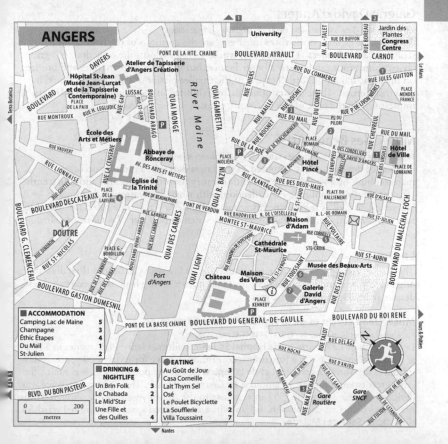

Bible would be even better. In brief: the Day of Judgement is signalled by the breaking of the seven seals – note the four horsemen – and the seven angels blowing their trumpets. As the battle of Armageddon rages, Satan appears first as a seven-headed red dragon, then as the seven-headed lion-like Beast. The holy forces break the seven vials of plagues, whereupon the Whore of Babylon appears mounted on the Beast. She is challenged by the Word of God, seen riding a galloping horse, who chases the hordes of Satan into the lake of fire, allowing the establishment of the heavenly Jerusalem. It's spellbinding, operatic stuff, and its sheer grandeur will appeal whatever your religious views.

## The cathedral

4 rue St-Christophe • Daily 8am–7pm

The most dramatic approach to the **Cathédrale St-Maurice** is via the quayside, passing through an arch of greenery, then scaling the long flight of steps to the mid-twelfth-century portal, which shows another version of the apocalypse. Built in the 1150s and 1160s, the cathedral exemplifies the Plantagenet style and is among the earliest examples in France of this influential architectural development. The interior is somewhat prosaic, but the fifteenth-century windows are impressive.

## Galerie David d'Angers

33bis rue Toussaint • Tues–Sun 10am–6pm • €4 • ☎ 02 41 05 38 90, ⓦ musees-angers.fr

Arguably the greatest stoneworks in Angers are the creations of the famous local sculptor **David d'Angers** (1788–1856), whose *Calvary* adorns the cathedral. His great civic commissions can be seen all over France, but the large-scale marbles and bronzes on the cathedral are almost all copies of the smaller plaster of Paris works created by the artist himself. These plaster originals are exhibited in the **Galerie David d'Angers**, set impressively in the nave of the thirteenth-century Église Toussaint.

## Musée des Beaux-Arts

14 rue du Musée • Tues–Sun 10am–6pm • €6 • ☎ 02 41 05 38 00, ⓦ musees.angers.fr

The **Musée des Beaux-Arts** is housed in the Logis Barrault, a proudly decorated mansion built by a wealthy late fifteenth-century mayor. Eighteenth- and nineteenth-century paintings dominate the collection, with works by Watteau, Chardin and Fragonard, as well as Ingres' operatic *Paolo et Francesca* – the same subject depicted by Rodin in *The Kiss* – and a small collection devoted to Boucher's *Les Génies des Arts*.

## La Doutre

The district facing the château across the Maine is known as **La Doutre** (literally, "the other side"), and still has a few mansions and houses dating from the medieval period, despite redevelopment over the years.

### Musée Jean Lurçat et de la Tapisserie Contemporaine

4 bd Arago • Tues–Sun 10am–6pm • €6 • ☎ 02 41 24 18 45, ⓦ musees.angers.fr

In the north of La Doutre is the **Hôpital St-Jean**, built by Henry Plantagenet in 1174 as a hospital for the poor, a function it continued to serve for nearly 700 years. Today it houses the **Musée Jean Lurçat et de la Tapisserie Contemporaine**, which contains the city's great twentieth-century tapestry, *Le Chant du Monde*. The tapestry sequence was designed by Jean Lurçat in 1957 in response to the Apocalypse tapestry, though he died nine years before its completion. It hangs in a vast vaulted space, the original ward for the sick, or **Salle des Malades**.

The first four tapestries deal with La Grande Menace, the threat of nuclear war: first the bomb itself; then Hiroshima Man, flayed and burnt with the broken symbols of belief dropping from him; then the collective massacre of the Great Charnel House; and the last dying rose falling with the post-Holocaust ash through black space – the End of Everything. From then on, the tapestries celebrate the joys of life: Man in Glory in Peace; Water and Fire; Champagne – "that blissful ejaculation", according to Lurçat; Conquest of Space; Poetry; and Sacred Ornaments. Subject matter and treatment are intense, and the setting helps: it's a huge echoey space, with rows of columns supporting soaring Angevin vaulting. The artist's own commentary is available in English.

There are more modern tapestries in the building adjoining the Salle des Malades, where the collection includes several of Lurçat's paintings, ceramics and tapestries, along with the highly tactile but more muted abstract tapestries of Thomas Gleb and Josep Grau Garriga.

## Abbaye de Ronceray and Église de la Trinité

On La Doutre's central square, place de la Laiterie, is the church of the ancient **Abbaye de Ronceray**, which is used to mount art exhibitions, and is worth visiting just to see the Romanesque galleries of the old abbey and admire their beautiful murals. When there's no exhibition, you can only visit by guided tour – enquire at the tourist office (see below). Inside the adjacent twelfth-century **Église de la Trinité**, an exquisite Renaissance wooden spiral staircase fails to mask a great piece of medieval bodging used to fit the wall of the church around part of the abbey that juts into it.

### ARRIVAL AND DEPARTURE ANGERS

**By train** The *gare SNCF* is just south of the centre, 1 esplanade de la Gare. Trams run regularly from outside into town.

Destinations Le Mans (frequent; 40min); Nantes (frequent; 40min); Paris (frequent; 1hr 40min); Saumur (frequent; 20–30min); Tours (frequent; 1hr–1hr 25min).

**By bus** The *gare routière* is near the train station on place Pierre-Semard.

Destinations Doué-la-Fontaine (5 daily; 50min); St-Georges-sur-Loire (3 daily; 45min).

### GETTING AROUND

**Bike rental** Espace 2 Roues, 45 rue Beaurepaire ☎02 41 87 69 46, ⓦespace-2-roues.fr. From €15/1 day, €30/3 days.

**Boat rental** Numerous companies rent out canoes and run guided kayak trips on the five rivers in the vicinity of Angers. Try: Canoë-Kayak Club d'Angers, 75 av du Lac de Maine (on the Maine and Lac de Maine) ☎02 41 72 07 04, ⓦckca.fr; or Club de Canoë-Kayak les Ponts de Cé, 30 rue Maximin-Gélineau, Les Ponts de Cé (on the Loire) ☎02 41 44 65 15, ⓦcanoekayakdespontsdece.fr.

**Car rental** At the *gare SNCF* are Avis (☎☎02 41 88 20 24), Europcar (☎☎02 41 87 87 10) and Hertz (☎☎02 41 88 15 16).

### INFORMATION

**Tourist office** Place Kennedy (May–Sept Mon–Sat 10am–7pm, Sun 10am–6pm; Oct–April Mon & Wed–Sat 10am–5.30pm, Tues 1.30–5.30pm, Sun 10am–1pm; ☎02 41 23 50 00, ⓦtourisme.destination-angerscom), facing the château; it sells a city pass (€15 for 24hr, €24 for 48hr, €33 for 72hr), which allows access to the tapestries as well as some of the city's museums and attractions. Free wi-fi is also available.

**Festivals and events** In summer, during the Festival Tempo Rives, there are free outdoor concerts performed on the Maine riverbanks, near Le Quai theatre, opposite the castle, with everything from electro and rock to disco and reggae. In Sept, the festival Les Accroche Coeurs hosts three days of theatre, live music and street performances.

**La Maison des Vins d'Anjou et de Saumur** Just across from the castle and a minute from the tourist office, La Maison des Vins (5bis place Kennedy; May–Sept Tues–Sat 10.30am–1pm & 3–7pm; Oct–April Tues–Sat 10.30am–1pm & 2.30–6.30pm), is staffed with helpful wine experts, who can arrange visits to local wine growers and *caves*.

### ACCOMMODATION

**Camping Lac de Maine** 49 av du Lac de Maine ☎02 41 81 97 37, ⓦcampingangers.com. Agreeably situated next to a lake, across from *Éthic Étapes*, complete with extensive sports facilities and heated pool. Mobile homes, caravan and tent pitches are available. Closed Nov–March. **€29.80**

**Champagne** 34 av Denis-Papin ☎ 02 41 25 78 78, ⓦ hoteldechampagne.com. Smart furnishings and cheerful decor make the rooms feel much bigger than they are, and the well-sized bathrooms look brand new. The biggest selling point though, is the location, right next to the main bus and train station, and within walking distance of the central attractions. Breakfast €10. **€90**

**Éthic Étapes** Lac de Maine 49, av du lac de Maine ☎ 02 41 22 32 10, ⓦ ethic-etapes-angers.fr. Clean, modern and well-furnished hostel, with rooms sleeping up to four and either private or shared bathrooms. An excellent spot for budget travellers or families, with a 200-acre park, 14-hole golf course and lake right on the doorstep, but you'll need to take the bus into town. **€52.30**

★ **Du Mail** 8 rue des Ursules ☎ 02 41 25 05 25, ⓦ hoteldumail.fr. With its bold red foyer, plush hall carpets and chandeliers, it's obvious that this super-stylish boutique hotel has just been renovated and the bathrooms are still gleaming. There's a leafy terrace to enjoy an *apéro* in the courtyard and a choice of uniquely decorated rooms, each with all mod cons. Parking €7. Breakfast €11. **€81**

**St-Julien** 9 place du Ralliement ☎ 02 41 88 41 62, ⓦ hotelsaintjulien.com. The exceedingly friendly, English-speaking owner and unbeatable location (right on the central place du Ralliement) are St-Julien's biggest selling points and it's great value for money. There's a range of rooms, all well-equipped and spotless, even if the decor is a little bland. Breakfast €9.50. **€77**

## EATING

**Au Goût du Jour** 14 rue de la Roë ☎ 02 41 23 73 19. Simple, well-executed French cuisine is the order of the day here, with beautiful presentation and chic surroundings. Best of all is the price – a three-course dinner *menu* will set you back just €25.50. Tues–Fri noon–1pm & 7.30–9pm, Sat 7.30–9pm.

**Casa Corneille** 8 rue Corneille ☎ 02 41 88 33 64. Tucked away down a side street off the main drag, *Casa Corneille* is small, but elegant and the menu follows suit, with limited choices, but excellent execution. Make a reservation to ensure you get a seat. *Menus* €28–36. Tues–Fri 12.15pm–1.30pm & 7.30–9.15pm, Sat 7.30–9.15pm.

★ **Lait Thym Sel** 65 rue Beaurepaire ☎ 02 41 72 08 64. A hip and popular new restaurant. And with good reason – the food here is excellent. The chef and his wife, who takes care of front of house, have worked in fair few Michelin-starred eating places. Here it's all about the seven-course tasting menu – a steal at €38. Tues–Sun 8–9pm.

**Osé** 19 rue Toussaint ☎ 02 41 31 45 63. Open just a few years, this unique café has already earned itself a legion of local fans and it's a lively lunch spot, with an emphasis on organic, seasonal dishes. Take time to browse the modern art, hand-crafted ceramics and array of herbal teas on sale in

the adjoining shop too. Mon–Wed 12.15–1.45pm, Thurs & Fri 12.15–1.45pm & 7.15–9pm, Sat 12.15–2pm.

**Le Poulet Bicyclette** 39 rue Jules-Guitton ☎ 02 41 34 83 45, ⓦ lepouletbicyclette.fr. Senegalese chef Abdoul brings the flavours of Africa to France at this tiny, yet atmospheric restaurant. Tuck into traditional dishes such as *saka-saka* (€13.50), *chicken yassa* (€11) or *tiakry* (€5) and wash it down with a glass of sweet *bissap* juice. Mon–Sat noon–3pm & 7–11pm.

**La Soufflerie** 8 place du Pilori ☎ 02 41 87 45 32. Popular café specializing in soufflés, both large and savoury (around €12.50) and small and sweet (around €11). Tues–Sat noon–2pm & 7–10pm.

**Villa Toussaint** 43 rue Toussaint ☎ 02 41 88 15 64, ⓦ lavillatoussaint.fr. Just across from the tourist office at the foot of the château, this is a smart choice for a sightseeing break, with a leafy terrace offering plenty of shade. Much of the food is Asian-themed and served tapas style (between €3–8), so you can pick a range of sushi, sashimi and nems to share, and add a few French-inspired dishes like chorizo and foie gras. Tues–Sat noon–2pm & 7.15–10.30pm.

## DRINKING AND NIGHTLIFE

**Un Brin Folk** 26 rue du Mail ☎ 02 44 85 58 04. Stripped-down hipster bar, with a varied playlist from old-skool country to new-skool breaks, this is the kind of place to sip wine on a sofa. There's an eclectic menu of *tartines* (around €10) with toppings from smoked duck to local organic cheese, plus a wide range of dessert specials. Wed–Sat noon–2.30pm & 7–10.30pm.

**Le Chabada** 56 bd du Doyenné ⓦ lechabada.com. Try this spot for less mainstream music; it hosts gigs most nights of the week.

**Le Mid'Star** 23 quai Félix-Faure ☎ 02 41 95 71 70. Angers' biggest and best-known clubbing venue, playing electro, pop and disco; €10, or €15 including a drink (women go free Thurs & Fri). Thurs–Sat midnight–late.

★ **Une Fille et des Quilles** 66 rue Baudrière ☎ 02 41 72 23 86. Angers' newest and most popular wine bar, thanks to its excellent wine list (400 labels, organic and mostly from the Loire) and friendly service. Low-key jazzy background music doesn't detract from chatting. Mon–Fri noon–3pm & 6.30pm–2am, Sat 6.30pm–2am.

## Château du Plessis-Bourré

March & Oct Tues–Sun 2–5pm; April–June & Sept Tues pm to Sun 10am–6pm; July–Aug daily 10am–6pm • €9.50 • ☎ 02 41 32 06 72, ⓦ plessis-bourre.com • Irigo bus #43 runs from Angers to Écuillé

Five years' work at the end of the fifteenth century produced the fortress of **Le Plessis-Bourré**, in the village of Écuillé, between the Sarthe and Mayenne rivers. Despite the vast, full moat, spanned by an arched bridge with a still-functioning drawbridge, it was built as a luxurious residence rather than a defensive castle. The treasurer of France at the time, Jean Bourré, received important visitors here, among them Louis XI and Charles VIII.

Given the powerful medieval exterior, the first three rooms on the ground floor come as a surprise; they are beautifully decorated and furnished in the Louis XVI, Louis XV and Régence styles, respectively, though things revert to type in the Gothic Salle du Parlement. The highlight of the tour comes in the Salle des Gardes, just above, where the original, deeply coffered ceiling stems from Bourré's fashionable interest in alchemy. Every inch is painted with allegorical scenes: sixteen panels depict alchemical symbols such as the phoenix, the pregnant siren and the donkey singing Mass, while eight cartoon-like paintings come with morals attached – look out for "Chicheface", the hungry wolf that only eats faithful women, whose victim is supposed to be Jean Bourré's wife.

## Château de Serrant

Mid-March to May & Sept to mid-Nov Wed–Sun 9.45am–5.15pm; June daily 9.45am–5.15pm; July & Aug daily 9.45am–5.15pm; • €8 • ☎ 02 41 39 13 01, ⓦ chateau-serrant.net • Anjoubus buses #10 and #22 run to St-Georges-sur-Loire from Angers bus station – the tourist office has timetables

At the Château de Serrant, 15km west of Angers beside the N23 near **ST-GEORGES-SUR-LOIRE**, the combination of dark-brown schist and creamy tufa give a rather pleasant cake-like effect to the exterior. The building was begun in the sixteenth century and added to up until the eighteenth century. In 1755 it belonged to an Irishman, Francis Walsh, to whom Louis XV had given the title Count of Serrant as a reward for Walsh's help against the old enemy, the English. The Walsh family married into the ancient La Trémoille clan, whose descendants – via a Belgian offshoot – still own the château. The massive rooms of the interior are packed with all the trappings of old wealth, with much of the decor dating from the late nineteenth and early twentieth centuries. Tours show off the grand Renaissance staircase, the sombre private chapel designed by Mansart, a bedroom prepared for Napoleon and the attractive vaulted kitchens.

# Nantes and around

Over the last fifteen years, the rejuvenated, go-ahead city of **NANTES** has transformed itself into a likeable metropolis that deserves to figure on any tourist itinerary. At the heart of this ambitious regeneration project stands a must-see attraction, the **Machines de l'Île** – home of the Grand Éléphant – but the city as a whole is also scrubbed, gleaming, and suffused with a remarkable energy. In 2013, Nantes became the first French city to be awarded European Green Capital.

As the capital of an independent Brittany, Nantes was a considerable medieval centre. Great wealth came later, however, with the growth of Atlantic trade; by the end of the eighteenth century, it was the principal port of France. An estimated 500,000 Africans were carried into **slavery** in the Americas in vessels based here, and even after abolition in 1817 the trade continued illegally. Subsequently the port declined, and heavy industry and wine production became more important. For more than fifty years now, since it was transferred to the Pays de la Loire in 1962, Nantes has no longer even been in Brittany.

Recent redevelopment schemes have shifted the focus of the city back towards the **Loire** itself. For visitors, nonetheless, once you've seen the machines, the main areas you're likely to spend time in are the older **medieval city**, concentrated around the cathedral, with the **Château des Ducs** prominent in its southeast corner, and the elegant **nineteenth-century town** to the west.

## Château des Ducs

**Castle** Daily July & Aug 8.30am–8pm; Sept–June 8.30am–7pm• Free **Musée d'Histoire Urbaine** July–Aug daily 10am–7pm, Sept–June Tues–Sun 10am–6pm • €8 inc. temporary exhibitions • ☎ 08 11 46 46 44, ⓦ chateaunantes.fr

Though no longer on the waterfront, the **Château des Ducs** still preserves the form in which it was built by two of the last rulers of independent Brittany, François II, and his daughter Duchess Anne, born here in 1477. The list of famous people who have been guests or prisoners, defenders or belligerents, of the castle includes Gilles de Rais (Bluebeard), publicly executed in 1440; Machiavelli, in 1498; John Knox as a galley-slave in 1547–49; and Bonnie Prince Charlie preparing for Culloden in 1745. In addition, the **Edict of Nantes** was signed here in 1598 by Henri IV, ending the Wars of Religion by granting a degree of toleration to the Protestants. It had far more crucial consequences when it was revoked, by Louis XIV, in 1685.

The stout **ramparts** of the château remain pretty much intact, and most of the encircling moat is filled with water, surrounded by well-tended lawns that make a popular spot for lunchtime picnics. Visitors can enter the courtyard, and also stroll atop the ramparts for fine views over the city, for no charge.

The incongruous potpourri of buildings that encircle the courtyard within include the fascinating **Musée d'Histoire Urbaine**, which was renovated in 2016. Highlights of the city's history museum include a fascinating scale model of the city in the thirteenth century, and a determined attempt to come to terms with Nantes' slave-trading past, with its display of pitiful trinkets used to buy slaves in Africa. You can learn more about this dark period of Nantes' history at the Mémorial de l'Abolition de l'Esclavage on Quai de la Fosse (mid-May to mid-Sept 9am–8pm; mid-Sept to mid-May 9am–6pm; free).

## Cathédrale de St-Pierre-et-St-Paul

Place St-Pierre • Daily 8.30am–7pm

The fifteenth-century **Cathédrale de St-Pierre-et-St-Paul** has had an unfortunate history. It was used as a barn during the Revolution, while in 1800 the Spaniards Tower, the arsenal of the château 200m south, exploded, shattering its stained glass. The building was then bombed during World War II, and damaged by fire in 1972. Restored and reopened, its soaring height and lightness are emphasized by its clean white stone. It contains the tomb of François II and his wife Margaret – with symbols of Power, Strength and Justice for him and Fidelity, Prudence and Temperance for her.

## Musée des Beaux-Arts

10 rue Clemenceau • Mon, Wed & Fri–Sun 11am–7pm, Thurs 11am–9pm • €8 • ☎ 02 51 17 45 00, ⓦ museedartsdenantes. nantesmetropole.fr

Nantes' **Musée des Beaux-Arts**, east of the cathedral, was partially closed in 2011 for a six-year renovation project to create 30 percent more exhibition space including a new building, the Cube, devoted to contemporary art. The galleries are now more accessible and much lighter. Highlights of its permanent collection, which has works from the thirteenth to twenty-first centuries, include Gentileschi's *Diana the Huntress*, Monet's *Nymphéas* and Kapoor's *Sister*. It also has good temporary exhibitions and a swish new restaurant.

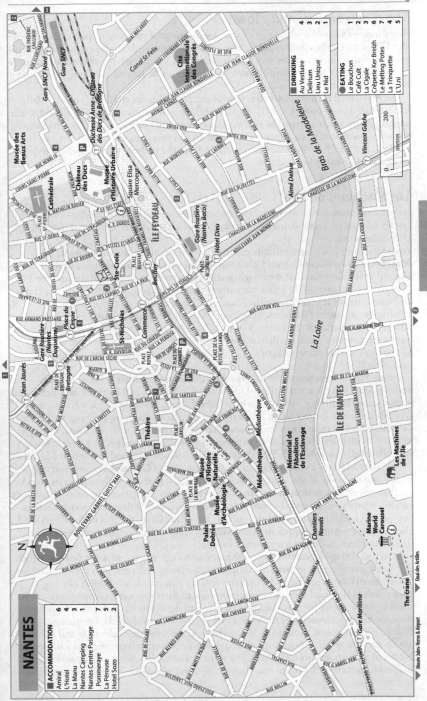

**NANTES**

**ACCOMMODATION**
| | |
|---|---|
| Amiral | 6 |
| L'Hôtel | 4 |
| La Manu | 3 |
| Nantes Camping | 1 |
| Nantes Centre Passage Pommeraye | 7 |
| La Pérouse | 5 |
| Hôtel Sozo | 2 |

**DRINKING**
| | |
|---|---|
| Au Vestiaire | 4 |
| Delirium | 3 |
| Lieu Unique | 2 |
| Le Nid | 1 |

**EATING**
| | |
|---|---|
| Le Bouchon | 1 |
| Café Cult | 2 |
| La Cigale | 3 |
| Crêperie Ker Breizh | 6 |
| Le Melting Potes | 7 |
| La Trinquette | 4 |
| L'Uni | 5 |

0 ——— 200 metres

7

## The nineteenth-century town

The financier Graslin took charge of the development of the western part of Nantes in the 1780s, when the city was at its richest. **Place Royale**, with its distinctive fountain, was laid out at the end of the eighteenth century, as was the nearby **place Graslin**, home to the elaborately styled **Grand Théâtre** and the not-to-be-missed *La Cigale* brasserie, which dates from 1895.

The **Muséum d'Histoire Naturelle**, west of the place Graslin at 12 rue Voltaire (daily except Tues 10am–6pm; €4; ☏02 40 41 55 00, ✆museum.nantes.fr), is a Victorian-era anachronism, where among the eccentric assortment of oddities you'll find rhinoceros toenails, a coelecanth, an Aepyornis egg and an Egyptian mummy. There's even a complete tanned human skin, taken in 1793 from the body of a soldier whose dying wish was to be made into a drum.

## Les Machines de l'Île

**7**

Parc des Chantiers, bd Léon-Bureau • Feb to mid-April & Nov–Dec Tues–Sun afternoon only; mid-April to June & Sept–Oct Tues–Sun; July–Sept daily; closed Jan • Elephant €8.50; carousel: €8.50 fairground mode or €6.90 discovery mode; gallery €8.50 • ☏ 08 10 12 12 25, ✆ lesmachines-nantes.fr

Inaugurated in 2007, and initially centring on the fabulous **Grand Éléphant**, the **Machines de l'Île** is a truly world-class attraction, which is continuing to develop and expand year after year. Part *hommage* to the sci-fi creations of Jules Verne and the blueprints of Leonardo da Vinci, part street-theatre extravaganza, this is the lynchpin of Nantes' urban regeneration. The "machines" in question are the astonishing contraptions created by designer/engineer François Delarozière and artist Pierre Orefice; the "island" is the Île de Nantes, a 3km-long, whale-shaped island in the Loire, ten minutes' walk southwest of the tourist office, that was once the centre of the city's shipbuilding industry. It's now quite a hip spot for eating, drinking and nightlife.

Twelve metres high and eight metres wide, the **Grand Éléphant** is phenomenally realistic, down to the articulation of its joints as it "walks", and its trunk as it flexes and sprays water. In 2018 it was fitted with a hybrid engine to make it more eco-friendly. Visitors can see it for free when it emerges for regular walks along the huge esplanade outside, which is arguably more impressive than paying for a ride. That said, riding a gigantic mechanical elephant is an experience in itself, and you get to wander through its hollow belly and climb the spiral stairs to the balconies around its canopied howdah.

The latest addition to the machines, the **Marine Worlds Carousel**, is a vast merry-go-round on the banks of the Loire. Unveiled in 2012, it consists of three separate tiers of oddball subaquatic devices. There are two options for visiting the carousel – "Discovery mode", where you can tour but not ride the carousel, and "Fairground mode", where you get to climb on board creatures such as the Giant Crab, the Bus of the Abyss, and the Reverse-Propelling Squid, each individually manoeuvrable. The next big project, The Heron Tree, is due for completion in 2021.

As well as riding the carousel or elephant, visitors can pay to enter the **Gallery**, which displays a changing assortment of completed machines, and peek into the vast hangars where the machines are kept and constructed. It's a worthwhile addition offering a closer look at the machines and demonstrations of their moveable components.

The opening times for the Machines de l'Île and departure times for the elephant vary enormously throughout the year, so it's a good idea to check before visiting. Rides can't be booked in advance; tickets are sold for same-day rides only and there are no combined ticket discounts, although family passes are available and a discount is offered for entrance to the gallery. If you need clarification, head to the tourist office (opposite the carousel; July & Aug daily 9am–6pm) where they'll explain everything in English.

RIDING THE GRAND ÉLÉPHANT AT LES MACHINES DE L'ÎLE, NANTES

**7**

## ARRIVAL AND DEPARTURE

**NANTES**

**By plane** Services to Nantes' airport (ⓦnantes.aeroport. fr), 12km southwest of the city and connected by regular buses, include flights from London Gatwick and Luton.

**By train** Nantes' *gare SNCF*, with regular TGVs to Paris, Lyon and Bordeaux, has two exits; for most facilities (tramway, buses, hotels) use Accès Nord. The station is getting a futuristic makeover by architect Rudy Ricciotti and is due to be completed late 2019.

Destinations Bordeaux (2 daily; 4hr 43min); Le Croisic (10 daily; 1hr 10min); Paris-Montparnasse (6 TGVs daily; 2hr 25min).

**By bus** Nantes has two main bus stations. The one just south of the centre on allée Baco, near place Ricordeau, is used by buses heading south and southwest, while the one where the cours des 50 Otages meets rue de l'Hôtel-de-Ville serves routes that stay north of the river.

## GETTING AROUND

**By public transport** Trams run along the old riverfront, past the *gare SNCF* and the two bus stations (ⓦtan.fr). Flat-fare tickets, at €1.70, are valid for one hour, or 24hr tickets are available for €5.60. Tickets must be bought before boarding.

**Bike rental** Nantes' share bike scheme is run by Bicloo (ⓦbicloo.nantesmetropole.fr), with more than 100 stations located all over the city. The first 15min are free.

## INFORMATION

**Tourist offices** Nantes has tourist offices at 9 rue des États, facing the château (July & Aug daily 9am–7pm; Sept–June Mon–Sat 10am–6pm, Sun 10am–5pm; ☎08 92 46 40 44, ⓦnantes-tourisme.com), and in the Parc des Chantiers alongside the Machines de l'Île (July & Aug daily 9am–6pm). Both sell the Pass Nantes (€25/24hr, €35/48hr, €45/72hr), which offers free entry to numerous attractions, plus tours, river cruises and unlimited public transport.

## ACCOMMODATION

**Amiral** 26bis rue Scribe ☎02 40 73 56 69, ⓦhotel-nantes.fr. Contemporary, eco-friendly hotel on a lively pedestrianized street just north of place Graslin, and well located for the city's nightlife. All the en-suite rooms have double-glazing, but some noise still creeps in. Cheaper rates at weekends. Breakfast €11. **€112**

**L'Hôtel** 6 rue Henri-IV ☎02 40 29 30 31, ⓦnanteshotel. com. The dark walls and soft lighting give this fashion-forward hotel an edge, but the rooms are still light and airy, with designer decor and views of the château. Just a few years old, everything in this hotel still looks brand new and the genial welcome is a plus. Breakfast €14. **€109**

**La Manu** 2 place de la Manufacture ☎02 40 29 29 20. Nantes' hostel, which has a cafeteria, is housed in a postmodern former tobacco factory a few hundred metres east of the *gare SNCF*, 5min from the centre on tramway #1. Beds in four- or six-bed dorms; rates include breakfast. If you're not a YHA or HI member, you'll need to purchase membership on arrival. Closed mid-Dec to early Jan. **€ 22.10**

**Nantes Camping** 21 bd du Petit-Port ☎02 40 74 47 94, ⓦnantes-camping.fr. Well-managed eco-friendly five-star campsite, with a pool, in a pleasant tree-shaded setting north of the city centre on tram route #2 (stop "Morrhonnière"). Minimum three-night stay in July & Aug. Open all year. **€25**

**Nantes Centre Passage Pommeraye** 2 rue Boileau ☎02 40 48 78 79, ⓦaccorhotels.com. Chic, extremely friendly boutique hotel with spacious, stylish rooms, beautiful bathrooms and hallways displaying striking artworks by local artists. With its central location, and good buffet breakfast (€11) it's extremely good value. At the time of writing, the hotel was being renovated after having been taken over by AccorHotels. **€65**

★ **La Pérouse** 3 allée Duquesne ☎02 40 89 75 00, ⓦhotel-laperouse.fr. Superb contemporary building ingeniously integrated with the older architecture that surrounds it. The interior is decorated with 1930s furniture, stucco walls and high-tech touches like flatscreen TVs. An original, comfortable and friendly place to stay, with excellent breakfasts (€16). **€99**

★ **Hotel Sozo** 16 rue Frédéric-Cailliaud ☎02 51 82 40 00, ⓦsozohotel.fr. A four-star boutique hotel set in a remarkable nineteenth-century chapel, this is a veritable masterpiece of design. The vaulted ceilings, white stone walls and stained-glass windows are divine, but you still have all mod cons, alongside concierge service, hot and cold buffet breakfast (€17) and private parking. **€141**

## EATING AND DRINKING

**Le Bouchon** 7 rue Bossuet ☎02 40 20 08 44, ⓦle-bouchon-nantes.com. From the charming, timber-fronted facade to the candlelit walled garden, this is a romantic spot for a dinner date, but there's a well-priced lunch menu too, with *formules* from €14. Tues–Fri noon–2pm & 7.45– 10pm, Sat 7.45–10.30pm.

**Café Cult** 2 rue des Carmes ☎02 40 47 18 49, ⓦcafe-cult.com. Friendly, good-value café in a beautiful old half-timbered house. Plat du jour €12.50 and cheap drinks later on, when it becomes a lively bar. Mon–Sat noon–2am.

★**La Cigale** 4 place Graslin ☎02 51 84 94 94, ⓦlacigale.com. Exquisite *belle époque* brasserie, with a history dating from 1895, and opulent surroundings adorned with colourful mosaics. There's fine cuisine served in the formal indoor dining room, or you can indulge in a decadent French-style afternoon tea ("Pause Gourmande", €9) and choose from an array of sweet treats. Daily 7.30am–12.30am.

**Crêperie Ker Breizh** 11 rue de la Héronnière ☎02 40 69 80 20. In keeping with its Breton origins, Nantes has a fair few crêperies and this is one of the best thanks to some interesting *galette* fillings: one of the "specials" is scallops in a coconut curry sauce (€8.30). Make sure you try the salted caramel for dessert. Tues–Sat noon–2pm & 7–9.30pm.

**Le Melting Potes** 26 bv de la Prairie au Duc ☎02 40 35 18 10, ⓦmeltingpotesnantes.com. Funky, youthful burger joint with a big range of well-priced burgers (from €9.50), including vegetarian and gluten-free options. There are regular theme nights too, including a salsa evening, live comedy and blind tastings. Mon–Fri noon–2pm & 7.30–10.30pm, Sat 7.30–10.30pm.

**La Trinquette** 3 quai de la Fosse ☎02 51 72 39 05. This laidback central bar, with friendly English-speaking owners, serves *tartines* (from €6.80) and *croque monsieurs* to go with its fine *apéritifs*, and gets especially lively on market day (Sat), when DJs play. Mon–Fri 8.30am–10pm, Sat 8am–10pm.

★**L'U.ni** 36 rue Fouré ☎02 40 73 53 05. With show-stopping contemporary cuisine served in sleek surroundings, *L'U.ni* is quickly climbing the ranks to become one of Nantes' most fashionable restaurants. For the full experience, opt for the six-course *menu dégustation* (€63). Wed–Sat noon–1.30pm & 7.30–9.30pm, Sun 7.30–9.30pm.

## DRINKING AND NIGHTLIFE

Nantes has a vibrant and varied nightlife, but it's at its best during university terms – in July and August most locals head to the beach. The majority of bars and clubs are around rue Jean-Jacques-Rousseau in the old town, but the *Hangar à Bananes* on the l'île de Nantes is also lively, and the pubs and music venues on rue du Maréchal-Joffre, north of the château, have a laidback, local vibe.

**Au Vestiaire** 2 place de la Petite Hollande ☎02 40 47 79 05. This popular local pub right opposite the Saturday market is an atmospheric spot to grab a beer (from €3), and it doubles up as a sports bar, screening both local and international football and rugby fixtures. Mon–Sat 4pm–2am.

**Delirium** 19 allée Baco ☎02 40 08 90 77, ⓦdelirium cafe.fr. The mind-boggling array of bottled and draught beers (around €3.50) will impress even the most hard-to-please beer-lover, and the entire bar is decorated with beer caps and bottles from around the globe. Do as the locals do and order a platter of *saucisson* to share. Mon 10.30am–12.30pm, Tues–Fri 10.30am–2am, Sat 3.30pm–2am, Sun 3.30pm–12.30am.

**Lieu Unique** Quai Ferdinand-Favre ☎02 51 82 15 00, ⓦlelieuunique.com. As unique as its name proclaims, this former LU biscuit factory now hosts concerts, theatre, dance, art exhibitions, a bookshop, a brasserie and a great bar. Mon 11am–8pm, Tues–Thurs 11am–midnight, Fri & Sat 11am–3am, Sun 3–8pm.

★**Le Nid** Tour Bretagne, place de Bretagne ☎02 40 35 36 49, ⓦlenidnantes.com. Located on the 32nd floor of Nantes' tallest building – the drab 144m skyscraper, Tour Bretagne – this is the city's highest bar, with unbeatable panoramic views from its open-air observation platform. *Le Nid* (The Nest) takes its name to the extreme, with a gigantic stork dominating the room and chairs that resemble cracked eggs designed by Jean Jullien – look out over the city and you might even spot splattered eggs painted on some of the rooftops. You'll have to pay €1 to ride the elevator to the top, but there's no obligation to buy a drink if you just want to enjoy the view. July & Aug Mon–Wed 2.15pm–midnight, Thurs 2.15pm–4am, Fri 2.15pm–2am, Sat 10am–2am, Sun 10am–midnight; see website for off-season hours.

# Guérande

About 80km west of Nantes (an hour or so's drive), the picturesque walled town of **GUÉRANDE** stands on the southwestern edge of the Grande-Brière marshes. Guérande derived its fortune from controlling the saltpans that form a chequerboard across the surrounding inlets. This "white country" is composed of bizarre-looking *oeillets*, each 70 to 80 square metres, in which sea water has been collected and evaporated since Roman times, leaving piles of white salt.

A tiny yet lively town, Guérande is still entirely enclosed by its stout fifteenth-century **ramparts**. A spacious promenade leads right the way around the outside, passing four fortified gateways and for half its length, the broad old moat remains filled with water. Within the walls, pedestrians throng the narrow, cobbled streets during high season, and it makes a great day out especially on Wednesdays and Saturdays, when a market is held by the central **church of St-Aubin**.

## INFORMATION

**Tourist office** 1 place du Marché-aux-Bois, just outside the Porte St-Michel (June & Sept Mon–Sat 10am–12.30pm & 2–6pm, Sun 10am–1pm & 3–5pm; July & Aug daily 9.30am–7pm; Oct–May Mon–Sat 10am–-12.30pm & 2–6pm; ☎ 02 40 24 96 71, ⓦ ot-guerande.fr).

## ACCOMMODATION AND EATING

**Goût'Thé** 30 rue de Saillé ☎ 02 4001 88 83, ⓦ goutthe. com. Charming tearoom with delicious cakes (from €3.20) and a *plat du jour*, like a goats' cheese salad, from €5.50. There's a good choice of teas but the spicy hot chocolate is a winner on colder days. April–Oct Tues–Sat 10am–7pm, Sun 3–7pm; Nov–March Tues-Sat 10am–7pm.

**Au Gré des Marées** 3 rue Vannetaise ☎ 02 40 53 79 35, ⓦ augredesmarees-fruitsdemer.fr. If you're looking to sample the local seafood, this is the place to go; it has a fresh daily menu featuring langoustines, clams, prawns, whelks, periwinkles and lobster, among others. Order oysters to share (€15 a dozen) or indulge in a varied seafood platter (from €26). Daily 10.30am–2pm & 6–9pm.

★ **La Guérandière** 5 rue Vannetaise ☎ 02 40 62 17 15, ⓦ guerandiere.com. Perfectly bridging the gap between stylish and homely, this beautifully restored manor house is a true home from home. Each of the four rooms is attractively decorated and adorned with choice knick-knacks and antique-style furnishings, plus there's a large leafy garden and a home-made breakfast. **€87**

★ **Roc-Maria** 1 rue des Halles ☎ 02 40 24 90 51, ⓦ hotel-creperie-rocmaria.com. Tucked down an alley just off the main street, this pretty fifteenth-century townhouse would be the town's best kept secret if only it weren't so popular. The rooms are bright and modern, with spotless bathrooms and stone-brick walls that keep it cool even in the midsummer heat. The friendly staff all speak English and the crêperie downstairs serves perfectly cooked *galettes* (around €6–12). Restaurant closed Mon (except July & Aug). Breakfast €7.30. **€74**

# La Baule

With its dramatic crescent of sand and endless Riviera-style oceanfront boulevard, lined with palm-tree-fronted hotels and residences, the upscale resort of **LA BAULE** firmly imagines itself in the south of France. Parisians flock here during the summer months and it can be fun if you feel like a break from the more subdued Atlantic-coast attractions – the beach is undeniably impressive and there's a suitably upmarket selection of shops and restaurants to choose from.

## ARRIVAL AND INFORMATION

**By train** La Baule's *gare SNCF*, served by TGVs from Paris, is on place Rhin-et-Danube, away from the seafront.

**Tourist office** 8 place de la Victoire, near the *gare SNCF* and the *gare routière* (April–June & Sept Mon–Sat 10am–12.30pm & 2–6pm, Sun 10am–1pm & 3–5pm; July & Aug daily 9.30am–7pm; Oct–March closed Sun pm; ☎ 02 40 24 34 44, ⓦ labaule-guerande.com).

## ACCOMMODATION AND EATING

**Le Billot** 17 av des Pétrels ☎ 02 40 60 00 00, ⓦ le-billot. fr. This funky restaurant is deserving of its recent surge in popularity and the attention to detail is instantly noticeable. The emphasis is on fresh, seasonal and often home-grown ingredients – the oysters are delicious (from €7.90) and even the humble tartare de boeuf (raw minced beef) gets a gourmet makeover (€15.90). Reservations advised. Tues-Sun 12.15–1.45pm & 7.15–9.45pm.

**Lutétia** 13 av Olivier-Guichard ☎ 02 40 60 25 81, ⓦ lutetia-labaule.com. Split across a striking Art Deco building and a grand Bauloise-style villa, this beautiful boutique hotel is strolling distance from the beach. Each room is uniquely decorated, with King-size beds, bright modern decor and all the mod cons, and there's also a luxurious spa and gourmet restaurant on site. Breakfast €13. **€130**

**Villa Cap d'Ail** 145 av du Maréchal de-Lattre-de-Tassigny ☎ 02 40 60 29 30, ⓦ villacapdail-labaule.com. This charming stone-brick villa has been stylishly renovated, but retains much of its original early twentieth-century charm. The 22 rooms each have a distinct theme, from understated chic to sumptuous red, and the vibrant dining room offers a cheery backdrop for breakfast (€11). **€93**

# Le Croisic

Some 10km west of La Baule, sheltering from the ocean around the corner of the headland, the small port of **LE CROISIC** makes an attractive and more peaceful alternative base to La Baule. These days it's basically a pleasure port, but there's still an active fishing industry with about sixteen boats going out daily (however, the fish market is closed to the public). The rocky coastline isn't ideal for swimming, but there are still a few patches of sand for sunbathing and it's a scenic choice for a coastal walk.

## ACCOMMODATION AND EATING                                    LE CROISIC

**Le Bot** 6 rue de la Marine ☎ 02 40 23 02 07, ⓦ creperie-le-bot.fr. Running since 1936, this well-established crêperie whips up a huge range of buckwheat *galettes* and crêpes right in front of you. The most decadent is *"La Duchesse Anne"*, heaped with caramelized apples, vanilla ice cream and hot caramel sauce (€8.80) – pair it with a pitcher of artisan cider (€6.90). Tues–Sat noon–2.30pm & 7–9.30pm, Sun noon–3pm & 7–9pm.

**Camping l'Océan** 15 rte de la Maison-Rouge ☎ 02 40 23 07 69, ⓦ camping-ocean.com. The fanciest of the array of campsites along the rocky sea coast known as the Grande Côte, with its own aquapark, restaurant, and mobile homes for rent along with traditional camping pitches. Seven nights' minimum stay in July & Aug. Closed Oct–March. €53

★ **Les Nids** 15 rue Pasteur ☎ 02 40 23 00 63, ⓦ hotellesnids.com. This supremely friendly two-star hotel is deserving of another star thanks to a complete renovation that has left no detail unchecked. Behind the gleaming white facade, everything is spotless, rooms are well-equipped, all with balcony or terrace, and each with a personal touch, plus there's a small indoor swimming pool, a lovely walled garden and kids' play area. Breakfast €9.60. €76

★ **L'Océan** Plage de Port-Lin ☎ 02 40 62 90 03, ⓦ restaurantlocean.com. A modern seafront fantasy perched on the rocks, with panoramic glass windows and balconies overlooking the ocean, it's easy to see where this hotel got its name. Everything in the rooms looks brand new, while the lavish on-site restaurant and bistro serve up an array of fresh fish and seafood. Breakfast €18. €185

**Le Saint Alys** 3 quai Hervé-Rielle ☎ 02 40 23 58 40. The warm welcome here makes you feel like you've been invited for dinner at a friend's, while the food itself is exquisite, beautifully presented and full of flavour. *Menus* from €32. Reservation required. Mon & Thurs–Sat 12.15–2pm & 7.15–9pm, Tues & Sun 12.15–2pm.

# Le Mans

**LE MANS**, the historic capital of the Maine region, is synonymous with its famous 24-hour car race, which takes place in June. During the rest of the year, it's a much quieter place; what it lacks in obvious beauty it makes up for in historical background, being the favourite home of the Plantagenet family, the counts of Anjou, Touraine and Maine. The old quarter, in the shadow of the magnificent cathedral, is unusually well preserved, while outside town you can visit the serene Cistercian abbey of Épau and, of course, the racetrack, a must-see pilgrimage for petrolheads.

## The old quarter

The complicated web of the **old quarter** sprawls over the hillside above the River Sarthe, to the north of the central place de la République. Its medieval streets – a hotchpotch of intricate Renaissance stonework, medieval half-timbering and sculpted pillars – and grand classical facades, are still encircled by the original third-century Gallo-Roman walls, supposedly the best preserved in Europe and running for several hundred metres. Steep, walled steps lead up from the river, and longer flights descend on the southern side of the enclosure, using old Gallo-Roman entrances. If it all looks familiar, that's because it's often used in films; both Leonardo di Caprio in *The Man in the Iron Mask* and Gérard Depardieu in *Cyrano de Bergerac* stomped up its cobbled streets.

## Le Carré Plantagenêt

2 rue Claude-Blondeau • Tues–Sun 10am–6pm • €5 • ☎ 02 43 47 46 45, ⓦ lemans-tourisme.com

This earnest **archeological museum** details the history of Le Mans, from prehistoric times to the fifteenth century. The highlights are an exquisite enamel portrait of Henry

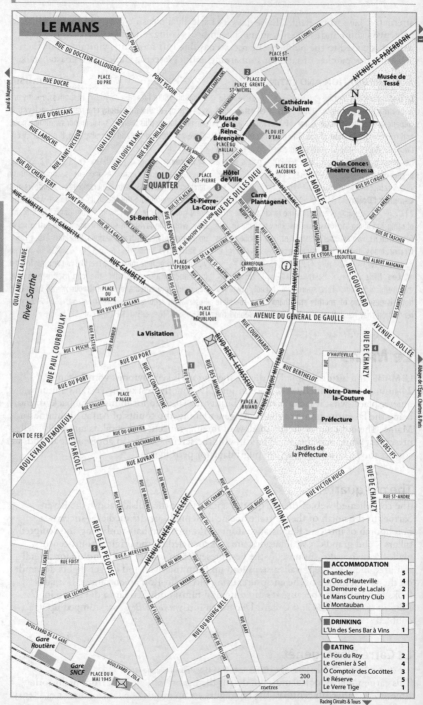

**LE MANS**

**ACCOMMODATION**
| Chantecler | 5 |
| Le Clos d'Hauteville | 4 |
| La Demeure de Laclais | 2 |
| Le Mans Country Club | 1 |
| Le Montauban | 3 |

**DRINKING**
| L'Un des Sens Bar à Vins | 1 |

**EATING**
| Le Fou du Roy | 2 |
| Le Grenier à Sel | 4 |
| Ó Comptoir des Cocottes | 3 |
| Le Réserve | 5 |
| Le Verre Tige | 1 |

Racing Circuits & Tours

II's father, Geoffroi Le Bel, a room of religious sculptures and six beautifully preserved and rather eerie slumbering statues.

## Cathédrale St-Julien

Place St-Michel • Daily Easter-Sept 9am–7pm, Oct–Easter 9am–5pm

The high ground of the old town has been sacred since ancient times, as testified by a strangely human, pink-tinted menhir now propped up against the southwest corner of the very impressive **Cathédrale St-Julien**, which crowns the hilltop. The nave of the cathedral was only just completed when Geoffroi Plantagenêt, the count of Maine and Anjou, married Matilda, daughter of Henry I of England, in 1129, thus founding the English dynastic line. Inside, for all the power and measured beauty of this Romanesque structure, it's impossible not to be drawn towards the vertiginous High Gothic choir, which is filled with coloured light filtering through the stained-glass windows.

## Musée de Tessé

2 av de Paderborn • Tues–Fri 10am–noon & 2–6pm, Sat & Sun 10am–12.30pm & 2–6pm • €5 • ☎ 02 43 47 38 51, ⊛ lemans-tourisme.com

Follow the 1850s road tunnel from the north side of the old quarter, past the monument to Wilbur Wright – who tested an early flying machine in Le Mans – to place du Hallai. From here, you can walk northeast alongside the park to the **Musée de Tessé**. It's a mixed bag of paintings, furnishings and sculptures, but the highlight is the basement collection of mummies, including two full-scale reconstructions of ancient Egyptian tombs, one of which is of Queen Nofretari, wife of Ramses II.

### ARRIVAL AND DEPARTURE — LE MANS

**By train** The *gare SNCF* is located at place du 8 mai 1945. Tramlines connect the train station to the *centre ville*, cathedral and the Musée de Tessé.
Destinations Angers (frequent 48min); Nantes (frequent 1hr 33min); Paris (frequent; 1hr 30min); Rennes (frequent; 1hr); Saumur (2 daily; 1hr 50min); Tours (frequent; 1hr 39min).

**By bus** The *gare routière* is located right next door to the *gare SNCF*, with frequent services to all towns in the region run by a variety of independent bus companies. A tram runs to place de la République, where the city bus terminal is located.

### INFORMATION

**Tourist office** Rue de l'Étoile (April–Sept Mon–Sat 9am–6pm; Oct–March 10am–6pm; ☎ 02 43 28 17 22, ⊛ lemans-tourisme.com). There is a second office in the old town at the Maison de Pillier Rouge, 41–43 Grande Rue (May–Sept Sun & public hols only 2.30–6pm).
**Festivals and events** On summer nights in July and Aug, the cathedral, the Gallo-Roman walls and various other sites around the old town and walls are illuminated in Le Mans' son et lumière show, "La Nuit des Chimères" (⊛ nuitdeschimeres.com). The displays are free and last two hours, starting at dusk.
**Bike rental** The city has a bike rental scheme with both traditional and electric bikes. There's also SETRAM bike rental at the north side of the train station (49 av du Général-de-Gaulle; Mon–Fri 8.30–7pm Sat 10am–noon & 2–7pm; €3/1 day; ☎ 02 43 24 76 76, ⊛ setram.fr).
**Markets** There's a daily market in the covered halls on place du Marché, plus a bric-a-brac market on Wed, Fri (when there's also food) and Sun mornings on place du Jet-d'Eau, below the cathedral in the new town.

### ACCOMMODATION

**Chantecler** 50 rue de la Pelouse ☎ 02 43 14 40 00, ⊛ hotelchantecler.fr. Quiet, professionally run hotel, offering spacious and well-fitted-out rooms and free parking. Good choice for the station as it's only a 5min walk away, or a 10min stroll to place de la République. Breakfast €12. **€102**
**Le Clos d'Hauteville** 2 rue d'Hauteville ☎ 02 43 23

26 80, ⊛ leclosdhauteville.com. A pocket of tranquillity within walking distance of the main attractions, this welcoming B&B offers excellent value for money. It's a cosy, family affair, with three well-sized, tastefully decorated rooms and a pretty garden, plus breakfast and private parking are included. **€85**
**La Demeure de Laclais** 4bis place du Cardinal-Grente

7

**7**

## LE MANS RACING

The first 24-hour car race at Le Mans was run as early as 1923, on the present 13.6km Sarthe circuit, with average speeds of 92kph (57mph) – these days, the drivers average around 330kph (205mph). The **Sarthe circuit**, on which the now world-renowned **24 Heures du Mans** car race takes place every year in mid-June, stretches south from the outskirts of the city, along ordinary roads. When the competition isn't on, the simplest way to get a taste of the action is just to take the main road south of the city towards Tours, a stretch of ordinary highway which follows the famous Mulsanne straight for 5.7km – a distance that saw race cars reach speeds of up to 375kph, until two chicanes were introduced in 1989. Alternatively, visit the **Musée des 24 heures du Mans** (9 place Luigi-Chinetti; Daily May–Sept 10am–7pm; Oct–April 10am–6pm; Oct–Dec daily except Tues 11am–5pm; €8.50; ☎02 43 72 72 24, ⊚lemans-musee24h.com) on the edge of the Bugatti circuit – the dedicated track section of the main Sarthe circuit, where the race starts and finishes. It parades some 150 vehicles dating as far back as 1873, ranging from the humble 2CV to classic Lotus and Porsche race cars. The focus of the museum is the characters who made the race famous. Vintage newsreel along with newspapers and mannequins in period costume keep this interesting even for non-car fans.

### TICKETS

During the race weekend, you'll need a ticket to get anywhere near the circuit. Buy them direct from the organizers at ⊚lemans.org, or via the tourist office; they cost €82 for the whole event, €32–39 for trial days (Wed & Thurs), and €50 for race day, which is always on a Sunday. You'll need a separate ticket (€55–105) to get access to the grandstands and be sure to book well in advance. Many enthusiasts' clubs and ticket agencies offer tour packages including accommodation – otherwise impossible to find at race times – and the crucial parking passes; try ⊚clubarnage.com or look through the adverts in a motor-sports magazine. True petrolheads can book themselves a place at one of the circuit-side campsites. Outside of race days, you can watch practice sessions, and there's the bikers' 24 Heures Moto in early April and the Le Mans Classic in July.

☎02 43 81 91 78, ⊚lademeuredelaclais.fr. The stylish, wood-floored rooms in this charming *chambre d'hôte* are made all the more appealing by the soothing colour schemes and cathedral views. There's also a small garden and breakfast is included, with home-made yoghurt and jams. **€115**

**Le Mans Country Club** Chemin de la Ragotterie, Yvré-l'Évêque ☎02 43 82 11 00, ⊚lemans-countryclub.com. This surprisingly affordable château is in the heart of the countryside, yet just a 10min drive from the centre of town. Thoroughly modernized and renovated inside, it still retains some character, with its original beams and sloping ceilings. Breakfast €16.50. **€119**

**Le Montauban** 17 rue Montauban ☎02 43 24 32 08, ⊚lemontauban.fr. Dove grey and white decor, and modern touches, make this one very stylish *chambre d'hôte* but the best part is the vaulted swimming pool and gym in the basement. Breakfast included. **€95**

### EATING AND DRINKING

**Le Fou du Roy** 2 Impasse Sainte-Catherine ☎02 43 28 45 03. One of the very few establishments open on Monday and Sunday nights in the old town, this atmospheric restaurant has tapestries on its walls and a small terrace for eating outside on fine days. Traditional French cuisine with decent grills. *Menus* from €21. Mon & Thurs–Sun noon–1.30pm & 7–10pm.

**Le Grenier à Sel** 26 place de l'Éperon ☎02 43 23 26 30, ⊚restaurant-le-grenier-a-sel.fr. Classic French fare served in smart surroundings, with evening *menus* from €45. Don't be put off by the simplistic menu – what it lacks in creative flair, it more than makes up for in quality and the garlic-stuffed *escargots* and braised veal are cooked to perfection. Mon–Tues & Thurs–Fri noon–1.30pm &

7.30–9.30pm, Wed noon–1.30pm, Sat 7.30–9.30pm.

**Ô Comptoir des Cocottes** 10 place St-Pierre ☎02 43 28 65 24, ⊚comptoirdescocottes.fr. Quirky restaurant that specializes in dishes cooked and presented in little casserole pots, such as cod with citrus fruits. Leave room for the Carambar rice pudding. *Menus* from €9.90 to €22.90. Tues–Sat 10am–3pm & 6–10.30pm, Sun 10am–5pm.

**La Réserve** 34 place de la République ☎02 43 52 82 82, ⊚restaurantlareserve.fr. The hippest restaurant on the huge place de la République serves exceptional meat and fish dishes (from €17) with a weekly changing menu, alongside an enviable wine list and a selection of unique cocktails. Reserve a table on the huge terrace or snuggle up in the dark interior with its stylish decor and ornate chairs.

Tues–Thurs noon–2.15pm & 7–10.15pm, Fri noon–2.15pm & 7–11pm, Sat noon–3pm & 7–11.15pm.

**Le Verre Tige** 48 Grand Rue ☎02 43 28 39 00. The atmospheric stone-brick cellar of *Le Verre Tige* has a bohemian feel and the menu is equally eclectic, specializing in *tartines* (around €14.50) – plates of bread, charcuterie, cheese and salads. Tues–Sat 9am–2pm & 5.30pm–midnight.

**L'Un des Sens Bar à Vins** 9 rue Dr Leroy-Rue ☎02 43 80 94 81, ⓦlundessens-lemans.fr. Stylish local haunt with an ever-changing menu of seasonal dishes and local wines, beautifully presented and served by enthusiastic waiters. Lunch deals start from €16 for a main, accompanied by a glass of wine. Mon–Fri 10am–3pm & 5–11pm, Sat noon–11pm.

## The Abbaye de L'Épau

Jan Thurs & Sun 11am–6pm; April–Sept daily 10am–7pm; Oct–Dec & Feb–March Mon & Wed–Sun 11am–6pm • €5.50 • ☎02 43 84 22 29, ⓦepau.sarthe.com • Take the tram to "Épau"

If car racing holds no romance, there's another outing from Le Mans of a much quieter nature – the Cistercian **Abbaye de l'Épau**, 4km out of town off the Chartres–Paris road. The abbey was founded in 1229 by Queen Berengaria, consort of Richard the Lionheart, and it stands in a rural setting on the outskirts of the Bois de Changé, largely unaltered since its fifteenth-century restoration. The visit includes the dormitory, with the remains of a fourteenth-century fresco, the scriptorium and the abbey church, home to the tomb of Queen Berengaria.

7

# Burgundy

**432** Auxerre and around

**438** The Yonne valley

**442** The Canal de Bourgogne

**446** The Morvan

**455** Nevers

**457** Dijon

**463** The Côte d'Or

**467** The Saône valley

BEAUNE'S MULTI-HUED HÔTEL-DIEU

# Burgundy

At the very heart of the country, Burgundy is one of France's most prosperous regions. Its peaceful way of life, celebrated wine, delicious food and numerous outdoor activities all combine to make this region the ideal place to discover and appreciate la vie française. Wine is, of course, the region's most obvious attraction, and devotees head straight for the great vineyards, whose produce has played the key role in the local economy since Louis XIV's doctor prescribed wine as a palliative for the royal dyspepsia. Wine tasting is particularly big business around Chablis, Mâcon and Beaune.

For centuries Burgundy's powerful **dukes** remained independent of the French crown, and during the Hundred Years' War they even sided with the English, selling them the captured Joan of Arc. By the fifteenth century their power extended over all of Franche-Comté, Alsace and Lorraine, Belgium, Holland, Picardy and Flanders, and their state was the best-organized and richest in Europe. Burgundy finally fell to the French kings when Duke Charles le Téméraire (the Bold) was killed besieging Nancy in 1477.

There's evidence everywhere of this former wealth and power, both secular and religious: the dukes' capital of **Dijon**, the great abbeys of **Vézelay** and **Fontenay**, the ruins of the monastery of **Cluny** (whose abbots' influence was second only to the pope's), and a large number of imposing châteaux. During the Middle Ages, Burgundy – along with Poitou and Provence – became one of the great church-building areas in France. Practically every village has its Romanesque church, especially in the country around **Cluny** and **Paray-le-Monial**, and where the Catholic Church built, so had the Romans before, with their legacy visible in the substantial Roman remains at **Autun**. There's more history on show at **Alésia**, the scene of Julius Caesar's epic victory over the Gauls in 52 BC.

Between bouts of gastronomic indulgence, you can engage in some moderate activity: for **walkers** there's a wide range of hikes, from gentle walks in the Côte d'Or to relatively demanding treks in the Parc Régional du Morvan.

## GETTING AROUND                                                                           BURGUNDY

**By bus and train** Burgundy has a pretty good transport network, with departmental buses filling in most of the gaps left by the SNCF, albeit with somewhat skeletal timetables (⟨w⟩viaobigo.fr). For the smaller towns and villages you usually need to reserve the day before you want to travel and it's not always possible to do a round trip on the same day.

**By bike** Many of the canal towpaths form part of a rapidly expanding network of cycle paths (⟨w⟩burgundy-by-bike.com).

# Auxerre and around

Most travellers to Burgundy arrive in **AUXERRE**, the chief population and industrial centre in the north of Burgundy – and with good reason. A very pretty and historic town of narrow lanes and lovely open squares, it looks its best from **Pont Paul-Bert** over the river **Yonne** and the riverside quays. From here you get a lovely view of moored houseboats and barges, with churches soaring dramatically and harmoniously above the surrounding rooftops.

To enjoy some local colour, and pick up some local produce, try the **market** in place de l'Arquebuse (Tues & Fri morning).

BASILICA OF STE-MARY LA MADELEINE, VÉZELAY

# Highlights

**❶ Cuisine** Gourmands, prepare to indulge – Burgundy has given us *boeuf bourguignon, escargots, gougères, jambon persillé*, Dijon mustard and many other delectable dishes; for some of the best food around, head to the *Côte Saint-Jacques* restaurant in Joigny. See page 435

**❷ Noyers-sur-Serein** Buried in beautiful countryside east of Auxerre, this stunningly unspoilt medieval town has the added bonus of an impressive museum. See page 441

**❸ Vézelay** One of France's earliest UNESCO sites, this small village with the gigantic Romanesque basilica of Mary Magdalene features among Burgundy's most historic locations. See page 448

**❹ Dijon** This affluent and cosmopolitan city still reflects the fabulous wealth of the powerful medieval dukes. The spectacular Neoclassical frontage of the Palais des Ducs and the newly renovated Musée des Beaux-Arts are must-see attractions. See page 457

**❺ The Côte d'Or** Home to Burgundy's most renowned vineyards, and now a UNESCO site, the towns and villages that line the road from Dijon to Beaune are full of possibilities for wine tasting. See page 463

**❻ Beaune's Hôtel-Dieu** Topped by a myriad of glazed, multicoloured tiles, the medieval hospice at Beaune also houses Rogier van der Weyden's *Last Judgement*. See page 465

HIGHLIGHTS ARE MARKED ON THE MAP ON PAGE 434

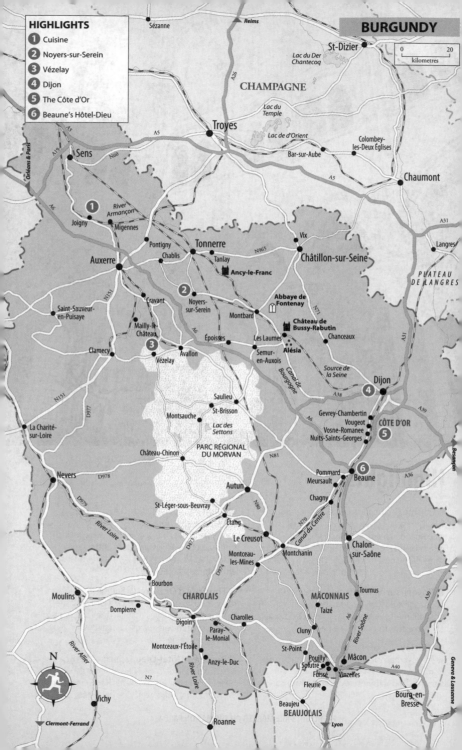

## THE FOOD OF BURGUNDY

The richness of Burgundy's **cuisine** is largely due to two factors: the region's wines and its possession of one of the world's finest breeds of beef cattle, the Charolais. **Wines** are often used in the preparation of sauces, especially *à la bourguignonne*. Essentially, this means that the dish is cooked in a red wine sauce to which baby onions, mushrooms and lardons (pieces of bacon) are added. The classic Burgundy dishes cooked in this manner are *bœuf bourguignon* and *coq au vin*. Another term that frequently appears on menus is *meurette*, which is also a red wine sauce but made without mushrooms and flambéed with a touch of marc brandy. It's used with eggs, fish and poultry as well as red meat.

**Snails** (*escargots*) are hard to avoid in Burgundy, and the local style of cooking involves stewing them for several hours in white wine with shallots, carrots and onions, then stuffing them with garlic and parsley butter and finishing them off in the oven. **Other specialities** include the parsley-flavoured ham (*jambon persillé*); calf's head (*tête de veau*, or *sansiot*); and a *pauchouse* of river fish (that is, poached in white wine with onions, butter, garlic and lardons).

Like other regions of France, Burgundy produces a variety of **cheeses**. The best known are the creamy white Chaource, the soft St-Florentin from the Yonne valley, the orange-skinned Époisses and the delicious goat's cheeses from the Morvan. And then there is **gougère**, a savoury pastry made with cheese, best eaten warm with a glass of Chablis.

# L'Abbaye St-Germain

Place St-Germain • **Abbey & museum** April–June & Sept–Oct Mon & Wed–Sun 10am–noon & 2–6pm; July & Aug daily 10am–12.30pm & 1.30–6pm; Nov–March Mon & Wed–Sun 10am–noon & 2–5pm • Free **Crypt** Guided tours only hourly 10am, 11am, 2pm, 3pm & 4pm (and 5pm in summer) • €7 • ☎ 03 86 18 02 90/8, ⊠ auxerre.fr

The most interesting of Auxerre's many churches is the airy, light abbey church of **St-Germain**, famous for its ten-ribbed vaults; it contains three of only five in existence worldwide. The monks' former dormitories, around a classical cloister, now house a historical and archeological **museum**, but the real highlight is the **crypt** where the tomb of St Germain, fourth bishop of Auxerre (378–448), was the epicentre of the bishops' burial catacombs. The tomb is empty – St Germain's remains were used for various reliquaries and what was left was desecrated by Huguenots in 1567. The crypt is one of the few surviving examples of Carolingian architecture, with its plain barrel vaults still resting on their thousand-year-old oak beams. Its wonderfully vivid and expressive ochre **frescoes** are the oldest in France, dating back to around 850 AD.

# Cathédrale St-Étienne

Place St-Étienne • Daily 9am–6pm **Crypt** & treasury April to mid-Oct Tues–Sat 10.15am–1pm & 2.15–5.30pm, Sun 3.15–5.30pm; mid-Oct to March Sat 10.15am–1pm & 2.15–5.30pm • €3 crypt, €2 treasury • ☎ 03 86 52 31 68

The **cathedral** was built between 1215 and 1560 but remains unfinished; the southernmost of the two west front towers has never been completed. Look out for the richly detailed sculpture of the porches and the glorious colours of the original thirteenth-century glass that still fills the windows of the choir, despite the savagery of the Wars of Religion and the Revolution. There has been a church on the site since about 400 AD, though nothing visible survives earlier than the eleventh-century **crypt**. Among its frescoes is a unique depiction of a warrior Christ mounted on a white charger, accompanied by four mounted angels. Upstairs, manuscripts, chalices and a number of interesting ivory ornaments are displayed in the **treasury**.

# St-Sauveur-en-Puisaye

An interesting side trip from Auxerre, about forty minutes away by car, is the village of **ST-SAUVEUR-EN-PUISAYE**, the birthplace, in 1873, of the French novelist Colette (1873–1954). The **Maison de Colette**, her childhood home, at 8–10 rue Colette (visits by guided tours

**8**

in French; April–June Wed–Sun 10am–1pm & 2–7pm; July & Aug daily 10am–1pm & 2–7pm; Sept & Oct Wed–Sun 10am–1pm & 2–6pm; Nov & Dec Sat & Sun 10am–1pm & 2–5pm; €11; ☎03 86 45 66 20, ⓦmaisondecolette.fr), opened to the public in 2016 following restoration. There's also an exhibition relating to her life, including a reconstruction of her apartment in Paris, personal items and original manuscripts in the local château (April–Oct Mon & Wed–Sun 10am–6pm; €7; ☎03 86 45 61 95, ⓦmusee-colette.com).

## ARRIVAL AND DEPARTURE
### AUXERRE AND AROUND

**By train** The *gare SNCF*, on rue Paul-Doumer, is across the river from the town; take bus #1 (every 20min; €1.20) which circles the centre until arriving at the *gare routière*.

Destinations Avallon (6 daily; 1hr); Clamecy (3 daily; 50min); Dijon (10–15 daily; 2hr; change at Laroche-Migennes); Joigny (35min–50min); Laroche-Migennes (every 30min–1hr; 30min); Montbard (5 daily; 1hr 30min);

Paris Bercy (16 daily; 1hr 50min); Sens (6 daily; 1hr).

**By bus** The *gare routière* is on the north side of town, on rue des Migraines.

Destinations Avallon (1–2 daily; 1hr 20min); Chablis (2–5 daily; 35min); Sens (2–5 daily; 40min); Tonnerre (2–5 daily; 1hr 10min). See ⓦviamobigo.fr.

## GETTING AROUND

**Bike rental** You can rent bikes from La Maison du Vélo (Place Achille-Ribain; €6/2hr; €20/day; ☎03 86 46 24 99, ⓦmaison-velo.jimdo.com).

**By bus** Electric shuttle buses (free) go around hilly Auxerre city centre every 15 min.

**Car rental** There are car hire firms all over town, including

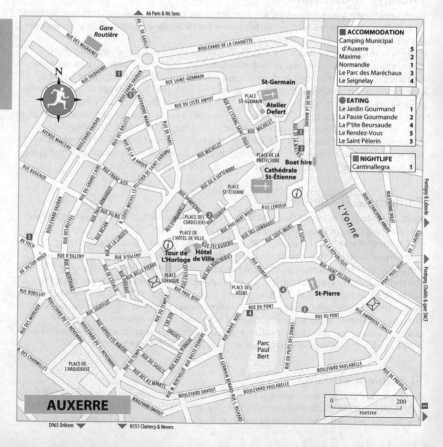

a few near the *gare SNCF*. Try @ rhinocarhire.com to get the best price.

**Taxis** Ask at the tourist office.

## INFORMATION

**Tourist office** The tourist office (April daily 9.30am–12.30pm & 2–6pm; May–June daily 9am–6pm; July & Aug daily 9am–7pm; Sept Mon–Sat 9.30am–6pm, Sun 9.30am–1.30pm & 2–5pm; Oct Mon–Sat 9am–noon & 1–5pm, Sun 9.30am–1.30pm & 2–5pm; Nov–March Tues–Sat 9am–noon & 1–5pm; ✆ 03 86 52 06 19, @ ot-auxerre.

fr) stands by the river at 2 quai de la République, with an annexe on place de l'Hôtel-de-Ville.

**Festivals** The Garçon la Note festival (@ garcon-la-note. com) sees free music concerts on café terraces around the city every night in July and Aug.

## ACCOMMODATION

**Camping Municipal d'Auxerre** 8 rte de Vaux ✆ 03 86 52 11 15. Located next to the riverside football ground, this is a pleasant and deliciously shady site on the south side of town. It takes pets and also has a handy little shop. Closed Oct to mid-April. **€15**

★ **Maxime** 2 quai de la Marine ✆ 03 86 52 14 19, @ hotel-lemaxime.com. Stylish and luxurious hotel on the banks of the Yonne. Rooms have been decorated in soft pastel shades. Some have wonderful river views but are not necessarily more expensive. The bar in the vaulted cellar is quite something. Breakfast €14. **€119**

**Normandie** 41 bd Vauban ✆ 03 86 52 57 80, @ hotel normandie.fr. Just outside the old town centre, this fairly swanky, creeper-covered hotel occupies a former nineteenth-century country house, with elegant old furniture throughout

and modern trimmings in the guest rooms. Facilities include a sauna, a gym and a billiards room. Buffet breakfast €9.80. **€94**

**Le Parc des Maréchaux** 6 av Foch ✆ 03 86 51 43 77, @ leparcdesmarechaux.com. An oasis of quiet just off one of the main roads radiating from the centre, this nineteenth-century mansion has a large garden with ancient trees to breakfast under. The decor is golden and brown, with each room named after a French marshal. A Victorian bar and a heated pool complete the picture. Breakfast €11. **€79**

**Le Seignelay** 2 rue du Pont ✆ 03 86 52 03 48, @ leseignelay.com. A traditional little hostelry with friendly staff, a good restaurant and private courtyard for summer dining. Bedrooms are cosy, but this is probably the best deal in town. Free garage parking for bikes and motorbikes. Breakfast €7.50. **€68**

## EATING AND DRINKING

Place de l'Hôtel-de-Ville is a good spot to head to for an aperitif, especially in summer, as there are several bars and cafés with sunny terraces.

★ **Le Jardin Gourmand** 56 bd Vauban ✆ 03 86 51 53 52, @ lejardingourmand.com. Sparkling glass, crisp linen and immaculate decor; this is truly fine dining. Although the menu changes regularly, you are guaranteed gastronomic dishes made from locally sourced ingredients. Lunch *menus* from €58, while the tasting menu will set you back €132. Reserve in advance. Wed–Sat noon–1.45pm & 7.30–9.15pm, Sun noon–1.45pm.

★ **La Pause Gourmande** 1 rue Fourier ✆ 03 86 33 98 87, @ lapausegourmande-89.com. Those with a sweet tooth shouldn't miss this cake shop and tearoom; chef David usually has around 35 different *pâtisseries* on offer. At lunchtime, there's a good selection of traditional French dishes, from around €18 for a main course. Restaurant: Tues–Sat noon–1.30pm; tearoom and shop: Tues & Thurs–Sat 9am–5.30pm, Wed 9am–1.30pm.

**La P'tite Beursaude** 55 rue Joubert ✆ 03 86 51 10 21,

@ laptitebersaude.fr. With exposed beams and waitresses wearing traditional Morvan dress, this restaurant has a rustic feel to it. Specializing in regional cuisine, it has *menus* from €19 (lunch) and €27 (dinner). The rib-eye steaks are particularly tasty. Reservations advised. Mon & Fri–Sun noon–1.45pm & 7.30–9pm, Wed–Thurs 7.30–9pm.

**Le Rendez-Vous** 37 rue du Pont ✆ 03 86 51 46 36, @ restaurant-lerendezvous.fr. Old-fashioned family cuisine in very untraditional surroundings; the paintings on the wall might make you think you've stumbled into Picasso's atelier. On warm evenings the restaurant spills out onto the terrace; three-course set *menu* at €36. May–Oct Mon–Thurs noon–2pm & 7.30–9.30pm, Fri until 10pm; Nov–April Mon–Thurs noon–2pm, Fri noon–2pm & 7.30–9.30pm.

★ **Le Saint-Pèlerin** 56 rue Saint-Pèlerin ✆ 03 86 52 77 05, @ restaurant-lesaintpelerin.fr. The centrepiece of this quiet, relaxed dining room is the wood fire on which the restaurant's speciality *grillades* are prepared. Good choice of meats and fish, with *menus* from €14.90–29.90. Tues–Sat noon–2pm & 7.15–10pm.

## ENTERTAINMENT

**Cantinallegra** 4 quai de la Marine ✆ 03 86 34 28 47, @ cantinallegra.com. This riverside restaurant and wine bar serving organic food and wine has weekly jazz concerts

off season. See website for details. Tues–Sat noon–1.30pm & 7–9pm but check website.

8

# The Yonne valley

Burgundy begins just south of Fontainebleau, near where the river **Yonne** joins the Seine, and follows the Yonne valley through the historic towns of **Sens** and **Joigny** before it reaches Auxerre. Scattered in a broad corridor to the east and west in the riverbanks of the Yonne's tributaries – the **Armançon**, **Serein**, **Cure** and **Cousin** – is a fascinating collection of abbeys, châteaux, towns, villages and other sites as ancient as the history of France. They all deserve a visit, for reasons ranging from architecture (**Pontigny**) and wine (**Chablis**) to sheer secluded beauty (**Noyers-sur-Serein**).

## Sens

The northernmost town in Burgundy, **SENS** is a relaxed place on the banks of the Yonne, but surprisingly lively at night when restaurants stay open well beyond the 9pm curfew encountered in many French provincial cities. Because of its **Monday market**, restaurants and museums stay open on Monday, too, unlike other cities in the Yonne; Tuesday tends to be Sens' rest day.

The town's name commemorates the Senones, the Gallic tribe who all but captured Rome in 390 BC; they were only thwarted by the Capitoline geese cackling and waking the garrison. Sens' heyday as a major ecclesiastical centre was in the twelfth and thirteenth centuries, when **Thomas Becket** spent four years in exile here under the protection of Louis IX of France. Sens is proud of this connection: from the stained glass in the cathedral to its local microbrewery with its Thomas Becket beer, there are numerous reminders of the "English saint".

### Cathedral of St-Étienne

Place de la République • **Cathedral** Mon–Sat 8am–6pm • **Musée de Sens** June–Sept daily except Tues 10am–noon & 2–6pm; Oct–May Mon, Thurs & Fri 2–6pm, Wed, Sat & Sun 10am–noon & 2–6pm, • €6 • ☎ 03 86 64 46 22, ⓦ musees-sens.fr

The town's ancient centre is dominated by the **Cathedral of St-Étienne**. Built between 1130 and 1180, this was the first of the great French Gothic cathedrals and, having been built without flying buttresses – these were added later for stability – its profile is relatively wide and squat. The architect who completed it, William of Sens, went on to rebuild the choir of Canterbury Cathedral in England. The story of Thomas Becket's murder is told in the twelfth-century windows in the north aisle of the choir. The **treasury** contains a number of rich tapestries and vestments – including those of Becket himself. In summer, an impressive son et lumière enlivens the facade each evening.

### Musée de Sens

Originally designed to accommodate the ecclesiastical courts next to the cathedral, the thirteenth-century **Palais Synodal** now houses part of the **Musée de Sens**, built over the old Roman Baths, which you can visit in the basement. The highlight is an extensive **art collection** including statues by Rodin and a lively crowd scene by Brueghel the Younger.

---

**ARRIVAL AND INFORMATION**                  **SENS**

**By train** The *gare SNCF* is on place François-Mitterrand beyond the Yonne. Change at Laroche-Migennes for Auxerre.
Destinations Dijon (15 daily; 2hr 30min); Joigny (18–21 daily; 20min); Laroche-Migennes (18–21 daily; 28min); Paris Bercy (15 daily; 1hr 14min); Tonnerre (8–10 daily; 1hr 10min).

**Tourist office** Place Jean-Jaurès (July & Aug Mon–Sat 9.30am–1pm & 2–6.30pm; Sept–June Mon–Sat 9.30am–12.30pm & 2–6pm (closed Tues Nov–April); Sun May–Oct 10.30am–1pm & 2–4.30pm.; ☎ 03 86 65 19 49, ⓦ tourisme-sens.com). You can download a free town tour "Sens Unique Tour" from the website.

## ACCOMMODATION

**Les 5 Sens** 33 rue du Général-de-Gaulle ☎06 10 12 57 65, ⍈lescinqsens.eu. A delightful little B&B in the centre of the town. The tastefully decorated rooms feature tiled or flagstone floors and the whole house is richly beamed. **€75**

★ **De Paris et de la Poste** 97 rue de la République ☎03 86 65 17 43, ⍈hotel-paris-poste.fr. The grandest

hotel in Sens, opposite the elaborate facade of the 1904 town hall, with large, comfortable rooms around a sizeable garden, each one individually decorated. The lively bar downstairs is worth popping into even if you're not a guest. Breakfast €15, parking €8. **€77**

## EATING AND DRINKING

The café terraces on place de la République are a great spot for a drink or light meal and are open quite late by French provincial standards.

**Au P'tit Creux** 3 rue de Brennus ☎03 86 64 99 29. This friendly, bustling crêperie on the doorstep of the cathedral has substantial *menus* from €22.50 and a great selection of salads. Mon & Thurs–Sun noon–2pm & 7–10pm.

**La Madeleine** À la pointe de l'Île, quai Boffrand ☎03 86 65 09 31, ⍈restaurant-lamadeleine.fr. Sens' best restaurant, under Patrick Gaultier, a gregarious personality even for a one-star Michelin chef. Classic setting, superb service and heavenly food (*menus* €49–120, but well worth the indulgence). Booking essential well in advance. Tues 8–9.15pm, Wed–Sat 12.30–1.15pm & 8–9.15pm.

# Joigny

As you travel south from Sens, the next place of any size on the Yonne is **JOIGNY**, a mini-Auxerre with the river dividing an old, hilly medieval quarter from the more modern, post-eighteenth-century town. The first fort was constructed here at the end of the tenth century, but much of the original settlement was destroyed by a fire in 1530. Joigny is worth an overnight visit and makes a pleasant rest stop, particularly on market days (Wed & Sat).

Buildings worthy of attention are the classical **Château des Gondi**, built by Cardinal Gondi in the sixteenth century, the church of **St-Thibault** (daily 9am–6pm), which is in late Gothic flamboyant style, and the remains of the twelfth-century ramparts on Chemin de la Guimbard.

On **rue Montant-au-Palais** – the street leading up to the sixteenth-century church of **St-Jean** (daily 9am–6pm), with its masterpiece of a ceiling – there are several remarkable half-timbered houses that somehow escaped the 1530 conflagration. They include the best known, **Maison du Pilori**, which combines Gothic and Renaissance styles, with some carvings strangely reminiscent of crocodile heads, and the **Maison Jesse** that has Christ's own family tree carved on its ridge. Down by the bridge, there is a wonderful Victorian closed market hall (1887).

**8**

## ARRIVAL AND INFORMATION

**By train** The *gare SNCF* is a long way south in the new town. It's a straight 20min walk up avenues de Gaulle and Gambetta to the bridge over the river and the old town. Destinations Dijon (12 daily; 2hr 20min); Paris Bercy (15 daily; 1hr 20min); Sens (15 daily; 20min).

**Tourist office** 4 quai Henri-Ragobert (July & Aug Mon 2–5pm, Tues–Fri 9.30am–noon & 2–6.30pm, Sat 9am–12.30pm & 2–6pm, Sun 10am–1pm; Sept –June Tues–Fri 9.30am–noon & 2–6pm, Sat 9am–12.30pm & 2.30–5.30pm; ☎03 86 62 11 05, ⍈joigny-tourisme.com).

## ACCOMMODATION AND EATING

★ **La Côte Saint-Jacques** 14 Faubourg de Paris ☎03 86 62 09 70, ⍈cotesaintjacques.com. A five-star marvel of a hotel with wonderful views over the Yonne and a two-star Michelin restaurant (*menus* €79–238) under chef Jean-Michel Lorain, (who offers half-day cookery classes from €125, once a month). Apartments and suites range from the secluded and romantic to penthouse extravaganzas; ask for a river-view room if you can. An award-winning spa, unbeatable service and a memorable breakfast feast (€29, and worth every euro) make this hotel really stand

out. Restaurant open Tues 7.30–10.00pm, Wed–Sun noon–2pm & 7.30–10.00pm. **€380**

**Paris-Nice** Rond-point de la Résistance ☎03 86 62 06 72, ⍈leparisnice.fr. The food is excellent and the portions generous; the menu is pretty comprehensive too, everything from pizzas to *pâté maison* and all very well presented; the shady tables in the garden are almost always filled by locals on summer lunch-times. They also have reasonably priced double rooms to rent for €58. Tues–Sat noon–2pm & 7.30–9pm, Sun noon–2pm.

## Pontigny

**PONTIGNY** lies 25km east of Joigny, and has a beautifully preserved twelfth-century Cistercian **abbey church** (daily 9am–7pm; free; ☎03 86 47 54 99, ⍟abbayedepontigny. com), standing on the edge of the village. There's no tower, no stained glass and no statuary to distract from its austere lines, though the sombre effect is somehow compensated for by the seventeenth-century choir that occupies much of the nave. There are classical music concerts here several times a year.

Three Englishmen played a major role in the abbey's early history, all of them archbishops of Canterbury. Thomas Becket took refuge from Henry II in the abbey in 1164, before moving to Sens in 1166; Stephen Langton similarly hid here during an argument over his eligibility for the primacy from 1207 to 1213; finally, Saint Edmund of Abingdon retired here in 1240, after unsuccessfully trying to stand up to Henry III. Saint Edmund's relics lie in a seventeenth-century tomb inside the abbey.

## Chablis and around

Some 16km south of Pontigny, the pretty red-roofed village of **CHABLIS** is home to the region's famous dry white wines. Lying in the valley of the **River Serein**, the town is surrounded by rows of vines, interspersed with yellow splashes of fields full of sunflowers. While wandering around the wealthy, modern village take a look at the side door of the **church of St-Martin**, which is decorated with ancient horseshoes belonging to sick horses left by visiting pilgrims – St-Martin being the protector of horsemen.

The wacky **Corkscrew and Vineyard Museum** (4 rue de l'Équerre; Mon–Fri 8am–noon & 2–5pm; Sat by appointment; €2; ☎03 86 42 43 76, ⍟chablis-geoffroy. com) at **Beine**, a ten minutes' drive west of Chablis, is great fun; spot the phallic and occasionally X-rated bottle-openers and corkscrews, and indulge in a little wine tasting.

### ARRIVAL AND INFORMATION

**By bus** Buses stop at place St-Martin in the middle of town. There are very few daily buses to Tonnerre (20min) and Auxerre (40min); they have to be reserved in advance (⍟tourisme-chablis.fr/data/pdf/bus).
**Tourist office** 1 rue du Maréchal-de-Lattre-de-Tassigny (daily 10am–12.30pm & 1.30–6pm; ☎03 86 42 80 80,

### CHABLIS AND AROUND

⍟tourisme-chablis.fr). They can provide lots of information about local vineyards and wine tasting.
**Taxis** Public transport runs at awkward times and you may have to book a taxi on ☎03 86 42 11 15. It costs around €35 to the nearest train station in Tonnerre.

### ACCOMMODATION

**Camping de Chablis** Just outside Chablis ☎03 86 42 44 39, ⍟ville-chablis.fr/camping-municipal. Beautiful site beside the River Serein, outside the village. It's small, and far and away the cheapest place to stay in the area, and so gets booked well in advance; call the tourist office outside the season to secure a place. Closed Oct–May. **€14.50**

★ **Hostellerie des Clos** 18 rue Jules-Rathier ☎03 86 42 10 63, ⍟hostellerie-des-clos.fr. Sumptuous hotel on the banks of the Serein; the building was previously the

hospice, recently converted and charmingly decorated. The light and airy dining room is the setting for a gastronomic restaurant, which features truffle-laden dishes, foie gras and oysters. *Menus* from €45. Breakfast is €14 and there's free parking. **€103**
**Du Vieux Moulin** 18 rue des Moulins ☎03 86 42 47 30, ⍟larochewines.com. A luxurious mix of traditional and contemporary architecture, with stylish rooms, excellent service and an outstanding restaurant. Breakfast €12. Free parking. **€145**

### EATING AND DRINKING

**Le Mâchon Vigneron** 14 rue Auxerroise ☎03 86 42 14 44, ⍟machonvigneron.fr. Priding itself on the freshness of its ingredients, this restaurant occupies a vigneron's eighth to twelfth-century cellars and specializes in sauces based on Chablis; have pork cheeks braised in Chablis with potato gratin. Lunch *menus* from €16 including a glass of wine. Closed Jan. Wed, Thurs & Swun 10am–2.30pm &

3–6.30pm, Fri & Sat until 10pm.
**Le Syracuse** 19 av du Maréchal-de-Lattre-de-Tassigny ☎03 86 42 19 45. Dine either in the garden, soaking up the sun, or in the thirteenth-century vaulted dining room, and choose a pizza (€10) or a *menu du jour* for €15.50. A perfect spot for lunch. Tues–Sat noon–2pm & 7–9pm, Sun noon–1.45pm.

### CHABLIS WINES

The combination of fossilized/limestone Jurassic soil, as well as a perfect vineyard climate with hard, wet winters and dry, sunny summers have made the village of Chablis one of the best-known names in dry white wines. Chablis (Ⓦ chablis-wines.com) follows the four Burgundy denominations in its own, particular way: the plots on a plateau are the cheapest, denominated as **Petit-Chablis**. The ones with a northern or eastern orientation (and thus limited sun exposure) are simply called **Chablis**. Those facing south or west are much more expensive and classified into 40 **premiers crus**. At the top of the pyramid are 103 hectares on the west side of the Serein facing south and comprising just seven **Grand Crus** that many believe produce the finest dry white wine in France: Blanchot, Bougros, Le Clos, Grenouilles, Preuses, Valmur and Vaudésirs. You can pick up a premier cru bottle in local cellars for €20 and a Grand Cru for less than €40.

### TASTINGS AND TOURS

For **tastings** try domain Jean-Marc Brocard in Préhy (☎ 03 86 41 49 00, Ⓦ brocard.fr); they use a unique biodynamic model of viniculture which they are happy to explain to you (in English). **Vititours** offer English-speaking tours that end in tastings (90min; €25; ☎ 06 11 47 82 98, Ⓦ chablis-vititours.fr). They can pick you up from any hotel within a 35km radius of Chablis, which includes Auxerre, for longer tours of 2.5hr (€75) or a full day (€150). The hotel *Du Vieux Moulin* (see below) also offers tastings of its own domain Laroche.

## Noyers-sur-Serein

Ⓦ noyers-et-tourisme.com

Around 23km southeast of Chablis – you'll need to drive or take a taxi (about €40 from Tonnerre or Montbard train stations) – you come to the beautiful little town of **NOYERS-SUR-SEREIN**. It's classed as one of Les Plus Beaux Villages de France (Ⓦ france-beautiful-villages.org). Half-timbered and arcaded houses ornamented with rustic carvings – particularly those on place de la Petite-Étape-aux-Vins and around place de l'Hôtel-de-Ville – are corralled inside a loop of the river and the town walls; you can pass a few pleasant hours wandering the path between the river and the irregular walls with their robust towers. The Serein here is as pretty as in Chablis, but Noyers, being remarkably free of commercialism, has more charm.

### Musée des Arts Naïfs et Populaires

25 rue de l'Église • June & Sept daily except Tues 11am–12.30pm & 2–6pm; July & Aug daily except Tues 10am–6.30pm; Oct–Dec & Feb–May Sat & Sun 2.30–6.30pm • €4 • ☎ 03 86 82 89 09

For a small-town museum, the **Musée d'Art Naïf** certainly punches above its weight. It comprises one of the best collections in the country of "art naïf" – that is, works by painters who had no formal training and were often manual workers lacking even basic schooling. One, Augustine Lesage, worked as a miner for sixty years before he started painting. Some star exhibits include Gérard Lattier's morbid comic-strip-style work, the excellent collages of Louis Quilici and the dreamy early twentieth-century paintings of Jacques Lagrange.

### ACCOMMODATION AND EATING

NOYERS-SUR-SEREIN

★ **Auberge du Pot d'Étain** 24 rue Bouchardat, L'Isle-sur-Serein ☎ 03 86 33 88 10, Ⓦ potdetain.com. An unassuming little auberge in the village of L'Isle-sur-Serein, 10km south of Noyers. The cuisine here (*menus* €29–50) is truly Burgundian, and the hefty sixty-page wine list has been acknowledged as among the top five in France. They also have nine comfortable rooms too. Breakfast €10, parking €3. **€65**

★ **Côté-Serein Chambres de la Tour Cachée** 9 rue de Venoise ☎ 06 42 07 43 64. A stunning medieval manor, with outdoor pool and charming gardens, on the banks of the Serein. Bedrooms are beautifully appointed, all have river views and the welcome is warm. Breakfast €12. **€89**

★ **Le Gratin Mondain** 10 Petite Rue ☎ 06 98 58 22 11, Ⓦ chambre-hote-bourgogne.fr. Gorgeous guest accommodation in a seventeenth-century half-timbered house with two elegant bedrooms and a separate duplex suite. Marguerite, the enthusiastic hostess, can make dinner

(€20) with 48hrs notice. Breakfast €10. €72
**Restaurant la Vieille Tour** 1 rue de la Porte-Peinte ☏ 03 86 82 87 36. This highly regarded restaurant serving traditional French cuisine and usually including a vegetarian option, has three-course *menus* from €27 and a good-value wine list. The dining room is small and reservations are a must. Mon–Wed, Sat & Sun noon–2pm & 7.15–9pm, Fri 7.15–9pm.

# The Canal de Bourgogne

East of Joigny, and conveniently close to the TGV stop of Laroche-Migennes, the **Canal de Bourgogne** branches off to the north of the River Yonne southeast towards Dijon. Along or close to the canal are several places of interest: the beautiful town of **Tonnerre**, the Renaissance châteaux of **Tanlay** and **Ancy-le-Franc**, the **Abbaye de Fontenay**, and the site of Julius Caesar's victory over the Gauls at **Alésia**. Just east of the canal, perched above the River Armançon, lies the picturesque town of **Semur-en-Auxois**. Further east the Canal encompasses the upper reaches of the River Seine: at **Châtillon-sur-Seine** is the famous Celtic Treasure of Vix.

## Tonnerre and around

On the Paris–Sens–Dijon TGV train route, **TONNERRE** is a great base for exploring this corner of the region, and far cheaper than Chablis, just 18km away. Although not as prosperous as its world-renowned neighbour, it is much prettier, since it was not bombed during the war – unlike Chablis – and it has several sights well worth a look. Another string to its bow is the local golden, fruity Chardonnay – a fairly recent *appellation contrôlée* in Burgundy, recognized in 2006.

Tonnerre is also an excellent starting point for **cycling** along the **Canal de Bourgogne**; from here to Dijon it's four or five days of easy cycling through some superb countryside. You don't even have to worry about luggage: Bag Transfer (☏03 86 41 43 22, ⌨bagtransfert.com) will pick up your bags and take it to your next stop for a fee.

### Hôtel-Dieu

Entrance through the tourist office, place Marguerite-de-Bourgogne • April–Sept Mon–Sat 9.30am–12.30pm & 1.30–6pm, Sun 10am–12.30pm & 2–6pm; Oct–March Mon, Tues & Thurs–Sat 9.30am–noon & 1.30–5.30pm • €10

The **Hôtel-Dieu**, a huge medieval hospice founded in 1293 by Marguerite de Bourgogne, has a grand 100m-long column-free hall that is used today for village functions and the occasional concert. Don't miss the eighteenth-century sundial that forms an elongated figure of eight. The first floor houses the town's museum, where interesting exhibits include a papal bull to Marguerite de Bourgogne and a wonderfully realistic sculpture of the *Entombment of Christ* by Klaus Sluter (1454).

---

#### CHEVALIER D'ÉON: THE CROSS-DRESSING DIPLOMAT

Tonnerre's quirkiest claim to fame is that it was the birthplace of the great eighteenth-century cross-dresser, **Chevalier d'Éon**. Born in the **Hôtel d'Uzès** in 1728, still the most magnificent structure in Tonnerre, d'Éon went about his important diplomatic missions for King Louis XV dressed in women's clothes. He fell out with the king, however, and, when he was in exile in London, wore a (male) dragoon's uniform – yet still bookmakers took bets on his sex. When Louis XVI ascended to the throne he allowed d'Éon to return to France – but exiled in Tonnerre – and also recognized his claim to be a woman and to dress as such. After the Revolution, Chevalier d'Éon slowly slid into debt, and died penniless in London in 1810. An autopsy determined that he was undoubtedly a man. A museum (Hôtel Chevalier d'Éon, 22 rue du Pont; April–Oct Sat & Sun 10am–6pm; guided tours at 10.30am, 3pm & 5pm; €10; ☏06 86 37 25 63) in Tonnerre features much of his correspondence as well as his lavish silk dresses and other personal effects.

## Fosse Dionne

Rue de la Fosse Dionne

Tonnerre's most unlikely attraction sits at the foot of the steep hill crowned by the church of St-Pierre. The **Fosse Dionne** is a fascinating blue-green "mystic" pool encircled by a washhouse that dates from 1758. A number of legends are attached to the spring (the name derives from Divona, Celtic goddess of water), including suggestions that it was a gateway to hell or the lair of a ferocious basilisk slain by bishop St-Jean de Réôme. Divers have penetrated 360m along a narrow underwater passageway and 61m in depth with no end in sight, but further exploration was banned in 1996, after several explorers died in these attempts. However, a new attempt was authorized in 2018.

## Château de Tanlay

8km southeast of Tonnerre • April–Nov daily except Tues 10am–12.30pm & 2.15–6pm • Guided tours 10am, 11.30am & hourly 2.15–5.15pm • €10, free entry to gardens • ☏ 03 86 75 70 61, ⓦ chateaudetanlay.fr

The romantic **Château de Tanlay** is a pleasant 8km cycle along the canal southeast from Tonnerre. This early sixteenth-century construction, very French in feel, is only slightly later in date than its near neighbour, but those extra few years were enough for the purer Italian influences visible in Ancy to have become Frenchified. Encircling the château are water-filled moats and standing guard over the entrance to the first grassy courtyard is the grand lodge, from where you enter the château across a stone drawbridge.

## Château d'Ancy-le-Franc

8

25km southeast of Tonnerre • April–June & Sept Tues–Sun 10.30am–12.30pm & 2–6pm; July & Aug Mon 1.30–6pm, Tues–Sun 10.30am–6pm; Oct to mid-Nov Tues–Sun 10.30am–12.30pm & 2–5pm • Guided tours 10.30am, 11.30am, 2pm, 3pm & 4pm, plus April–Sept 5pm • Château €10; château & park €13 • ☏ 03 86 75 14 63, ⓦ chateau-ancy.com • No public transport

The **Château d'Ancy-le-Franc** was built in the mid-sixteenth century for the brother-in-law of the notorious Diane de Poitiers, mistress of Henri II. More Italian than French, with its textbook classical countenance, it is the work of the Italian Sebastiano Serlio, one of the most important architectural theorists of the Renaissance, who was brought to France in 1540 by François Ier to work on his palace at Fontainebleau. The exterior is elegant but austere, but the inner courtyard is a refined embodiment of the principles of classical architecture. Some of the apartments are sumptuous, decorated by the Italian artists Primaticcio and Niccolò dell'Abbate, both of whom also worked at Fontainebleau. **Concerts** are occasionally held in the courtyard, the price of which includes a tour of the château.

## Musée du Pays Châtillonnais

14 rue de la Libération, Châtillon-sur-Seine • Mon & Wed–Sun 10am–5.30pm; closed Tues Sept–June • €7 • ☏ 03 80 91 24 67, ⓦ musee-vix.fr

For anyone interested in pre-Roman France, there is one compelling reason to visit **CHÂTILLON-SUR-SEINE**, around 30km east of Tonnerre: the so-called **Treasure of Vix**, discovered in 1953 6km northwest of Châtillon. The finds, from the sixth-century BC tomb of a Celtic princess buried in a four-wheeled chariot, include the famous **Vase of Vix**, which, weighing 208kg and at 1.64m high, is the largest bronze vase of Greek origin known from antiquity; it has a superbly modelled high-relief frieze round its rim, and Gorgons' heads for handles. The treasure is displayed in the **Musée du Pays Châtillonnais**, which also boasts an impressive collection of objects from Celtic, Gallo-Roman and medieval periods found in the Châtillonnais region.

## Montbard and around

One base worth knowing about if you're counting on **public transport** in the area is the rather unexciting hillside town of **MONTBARD**, on the main line between Dijon and Paris and where buses leave for both Châtillon and Semur.

### Abbaye de Fontenay

6km from Montbard • Daily: April–Oct 10am–6pm; mid-Nov to mid-April 10am–noon & 2–5pm • Guided visits hourly except 1pm • €10 or €12 guided • ☎ 03 80 92 15 00, ⓦ abbayedefontenay.com

The UNESCO World Heritage Site of **Abbaye de Fontenay** is the biggest draw in the area. Founded in 1118, it's the only Burgundian monastery to survive intact, despite conversion to a paper mill in the early nineteenth century. It was restored in the early 1900s to its original form, while the gardens were re-landscaped in 2008 in full harmony with its Romanesque structure. It is one of the world's most complete monastic complexes, including a caretaker's lodge, guesthouse and chapel, dormitory, hospital, prison, bakery, kennels and abbot's house, as well as a church, cloister, chapterhouse and even a forge.

On top of all this, the abbey's setting, at the head of a quiet stream-filled valley enclosed by woods of pine, fir, sycamore and beech, is superb. There's a bucolic calm about the place, particularly in the graceful cloister, and in these surroundings the spartan simplicity of Cistercian life seems appealing. Hardly a scrap of decoration softens the church and there's no direct lighting in the nave, just an otherworldly glow from the square-ended apse. A new hiking/biking trail (84km) links the abbey with the Basilique Ste-Marie-Madeleine in Vézelay (see page 448).

## Alésia and around

A few kilometres south of Montbard, on Mont Auxois, above the village of **ALISE-STE-REINE** is **Alésia**. It was here in 52 BC that the Gauls, united under the leadership of Vercingétorix, made their last stand against the military might of Rome. Julius Caesar himself commanded the Roman army, which surrounded the final Gallic stronghold and starved the Gauls out, bloodily defeating all attempts at escape. Vercingétorix surrendered to save his people, was imprisoned in Rome for six years until Caesar's formal triumph, and then strangled. The **battle** was a fundamental turning point in the fortunes of the region, as Gaul remained under Roman rule for four hundred years.

### Muséoparc d'Alésia

1 rte des Trois-Ormeaux, Alise-Ste-Reine • Daily: April–June, Sept & Oct 10am–6pm; July & Aug 10am–7pm; Nov, Feb & March 10am–5pm; closed Dec & Jan • €12 • ☎ 03 80 96 96 23, ⓦ alesia.com

The modern **Muséoparc d'Alésia**, inaugurated in 2012, brings the battle of Alésia to life with a visitor centre, a museum and a multimedia exhibition about Gallo-Roman life. You can also visit excavations, including the theatre and a Gallo-Roman house.

### Vercingétorix statue

On the hilltop opposite the Muséoparc d'Alésia, and visible from far and wide, is a great bronze **statue of Vercingétorix**. Erected by Napoléon III, whose influence popularized the rediscovery of France's pre-Roman roots, the statue represents Vercingétorix as a romantic Celt – half virginal Christ, half long-haired 1970s heartthrob. On the plinth is inscribed a quotation from Vercingétorix's address to the Gauls as imagined by Julius Caesar: "United and forming a single nation inspired by a single ideal, Gaul can defy the world." Napoléon III signs his dedication, "Emperor of the French", inspired by a vain desire to gain legitimacy by linking his own name to that of a "legendary" Celt.

### Château de Bussy-Rabutin

8km east of Alésia, on the D954 • Daily: mid-May to mid-Sept 9.15am–1pm & 2–6pm; mid-Sept to mid-May 9.15am–noon & 2–5pm • €8 • ☎ 03 80 96 00 03, ⓦ chateau-bussy-rabutin.fr

The handsome **Château de Bussy-Rabutin**, a French National monument, was built for Roger de Rabutin, a member of the Academy in the reign of Louis XIV and a notorious womanizer. The scurrilous tales of life at the royal court told in his book *Histoires Amoureuses des Gaules* earned him a spell in the Bastille, followed by years of exile in this château. There are some interesting portraits of great characters of the age, including its famous female beauties, each underlined by an acerbic little comment such as: "The most beautiful woman of her day, less renowned for her beauty than the uses she put it to".

## Semur-en-Auxois

Sitting on a rocky bluff, **SEMUR-EN-AUXOIS**, an extraordinarily beautiful small fortress town, is a place of cobbled lanes, medieval gateways and ancient gardens tumbling down to the River Armançon, 13km west of Alésia. All roads here lead to place Notre-Dame, a handsome square dominated by the large thirteenth-century **church of Notre-Dame**, characterized by its huge entrance porch and the narrowness of its nave. Inside, the windows of the second chapel on the left commemorate the dead of World War I – Semur was the general headquarters of the American 78th division, and the battlefields were not far away.

In front of the church are the four sturdy towers of Semur's once-powerful **castle**, all that remains after the body of the fortress was dismantled in 1602 because of its usefulness to enemies of the French crown. You can explore the winding streets around the castle – there's scarcely a lane in town without some building of note – and continue down to the delightful stretch of river between the Pont Pinard and the Pont Joly, from where there are beautiful views of the town.

## Époisses

Cheese connoisseurs might like to take a 12km hop west of Semur on the Avallon road to the village of **ÉPOISSES**, not only for its château (gardens year-round; €2; castle July & Aug daily except Tues 10am–noon & 3–6pm; €8; ⓦchateaudepoisses.com), but also for its distinctive, soft orange-skinned cheese of the same name, the manufacture of which involves it being washed in *marc de Bourgogne*. Try a little bite at the fromagerie Berthaut on the place du Champ de Foire: they make their own and would be delighted to instruct you in the art.

## The source of the Seine

The **source of the Seine** lies some 15km southeast of Alésia. No more than a trickle here, it rises in a tight little vale of beech woods. The spring is now covered by an artificial grotto complete with a languid nymph, Sequana, spirit of the Seine. In Celtic times it was a place of worship, as is clear from the numerous votive offerings discovered there, including a neat bronze of Sequana standing in a bird-shaped boat, now in the archeological museum in Dijon.

## ARRIVAL AND INFORMATION          CANAL DE BOURGOGNE

### TONNERRE

**By train** The *gare SNCF* is just a 10min walk from the centre of town.

Destinations Alésia/Les Laumes (15 daily; 35min); Dijon (15 daily; 1hr 5min); Laroche-Migennes (15 daily; 24min); Montbard (15 daily; 25min); Paris Bercy (15 daily; 2hr).

**By bus** Buses stop in front of the train station. See ⓦviamobigo.fr or ask for information at the tourist office.

Destinations Auxerre (4–6 daily; 1hr 10min); Chablis (4–6 daily; 20min); Noyers-sur-Serein (4 daily; 40min); Tanlay (4 daily; 15min).

**Tourist office** 12 rue Campenon (April–June & Sept Tues–Sat 10am–noon & 2–6pm; July & Aug daily 10am–6pm; Nov–March Mon, Tues & Thurs–Sat 10am–noon & 2–5pm; ⓣ03 86 55 14 48, ⓦtourisme-tonnerre.fr). They rent bikes (€4/hr; €20/day) and offer a free town trail leaflet.

### MONTBARD

**By train** The *gare SNCF* is at place Henri-Vincenot, south of town.

Destinations Auxerre (5 daily; 1hr 30min); Dijon (every 30min–1hr; 35min); Laroche-Migennes (9–10 daily;

50min); Les Laumes-Alésia (hourly; 8min); Tonnerre (15 daily; 25min).

**By bus** Buses stop by the *gare SNCF*.
Destinations Châtillon-sur-Seine (6–9 daily; 40min); Dijon (2–5 daily; 35min).

**ALÉSIA**
**By train** Trains go as far as the station of Les Laumes–Alésia, from where it's a 3km ascent to the site.
**By taxi** You can book or order taxis from Montbard station to Alésia (☎ 06 08 82 20 61 or ☎ 03 80 92 31 49).

## ACCOMMODATION

**TONNERRE**
**Du Centre** 63–64 rue de l'Hôpital ☎ 03 86 55 10 56, ⓦ hotel-tonnerre.com. Located opposite the *Hôtel-Dieu* in the centre of town, this is a relaxed, provincial hotel and its popular little restaurant, *Le P'tit Gourmet*, offers good value bistro-style cooking (*menus* from €13). Breakfast €7. **€55**

★ **Ferme de la Fosse Dionne** 11 rue de la Fosse Dionne ☎ 03 86 54 82 62, ⓦ ferme-fosse-dionne.fr. A sensitively restored former farm, with lovely rooms in bright colours and a beamed, covered balcony overlooking a small courtyard directly opposite the spring. The friendly owners also offer a three-course meal for €22 in the evening. Parking free, breakfast included. **€82**

**SEMUR-EN-AUXOIS**
**La Côte d'Or** 1 rue de la Liberté ☎ 03 80 97 24 54, ⓦ auxois.fr. This central former coaching inn has been attractively renovated, keeping many original features such as bare stone walls and beams. The tapas bar/wine bar/tearoom is a good place to relax by the fire in winter. Breakfast €12. **€95**

**Des Cymaises** 7 rue du Renaudot ☎ 03 80 97 21 44, ⓦ hotelcymaises.com. Traditional hotel in the medieval city proper, housed in a grand old mansion with a walled court-yard. Rooms – some with sloping roofs – are of high standard with a great many exposed beams. Breakfast €9. **€79**

★ **La Fontainotte** 4 rue de la Fontaignotte ☎ 03 80 96 61 26, ⓦ lafontaignotte.com. This smart guest house with an equally swish restaurant (main courses €18), in a seventeenth-century manor house, is the brainchild of French film producer Charles Gassot. The five bedrooms are stylishly decorated and spacious. There are three lounges, one of which has a pool table. Breakfast included. **€160**

## EATING AND DRINKING

**TONNERRE**
★ **Autour du Pressoir** Place Marguerite ☎ 03 86 54 81 05. A *bar à vin* in the lovely central town square offering large *assiettes* of local produce and an extensive wine list including Chablis, Tonnerrois and Aligoté. Eat and drink (plat du jour and a glass of wine for around €10), then buy the ingredients and wines from the shop inside. Mon–Sat 10am–7pm, Sun 10am–5pm.

**Le Saint-Père** 2 rue Georges-Pompidou ☎ 03 86 55 12 84, ⓦ le-saint-pere.com. The place to try Burgundy cuisine, this is family cooking at its best, served in splendid country mansion surroundings. Lunch *menus* start from €14.50 and evening *menus* from €25.50. Mon & Thurs–Sat noon–1.30pm & 7–8.30pm, Tues & Sun noon–1.30pm, open Sun eve July & Aug.

# The Morvan

The **Morvan** region (ⓦ morvan.com) lies in the middle of Burgundy between the valleys of the Loire and the Saône, stretching roughly from **Clamecy**, **Vézelay** and **Avallon** in the north to **Autun** in the south. It's a land of wooded hills and, with poor soil and pastures only good for a few cattle, villages and farms are few and far between. In the nineteenth century, supplying firewood and charcoal to Paris was the main business and large tracts of hillside are still covered in coniferous plantations. Wet nursing was also an important part of the economy, with local peasant women leaving their homes and families to feed the children of the French aristocracy and Parisian bourgeoisie, a practice that continued well into the twentieth century. Ideally, you'll have a car or bike to explore this area as public transport is limited.

The World War II occupation was felt profoundly in the Morvan, firstly because it was stripped of its machinery, equipment and forestry products; and secondly because it became a centre for the **Resistance**. As a result the locals suffered terribly from reprisals and forced labour programmes.

## CHÂTEAU LIVING

Burgundy – and in particular the area to the east and south of the Morvan – is one of the prime **château** regions in France. Many are still in the hands of old families like the **château de Vauban – Champignolles** in **Bazoches du Morvan** (ⓦ chateau-de-vauban.com), now a wedding and events venue, whose owner is related to Vauban, the great French fortification builder, or the **château de Chastellux** (Easter–Sept; visits at 11.15am, 2.30pm & 4.30pm; €10, free entry to gardens; ☎ 03 86 49 04 83, ⓦ chateau-de-chastellux.com), whose remoteness and association with a feudal aristocratic class places them several steps above a simple stately mansion.

As the upkeep of such massive structures becomes more and more expensive, many château owners rent their properties to large families or groups. Depending on numbers, costs can be as low as £300 per week, but take note: wi-fi may not penetrate the thick stone walls, and you will almost invariably need your own car; some places come with a cook and a maid, and occasionally the owners may still live on the premises (though you might never even bump into them). The range of experiences is broad, however, and you should be able to find something to suit your tastes – from **Château de Missery** near Saulieu (ⓦ chateaudemissery. com), who offer weekend cookery courses and wine tastings for about a dozen people, to **Château de Tailly** (ⓦ chateaudetailly.com), which is split into three buildings and can accommodate smaller parties of guests. Check ⓦ oliverstravels.com for a selection of options.

The creation of a **Parc Régional** in 1970 did something to promote the area as a place for outdoor activities, but it was the election of François Mitterrand, local politician and former mayor of **Château-Chinon**, as president of the Republic that rescued the Morvan from oblivion. In addition to lending it some of the glamour of his office, he took concrete steps to beef up the local economy. West of the Morvan, the landscape softens as it descends towards the River Loire and the fine medieval town of **Nevers**, on Burgundy's western border. These days, the area is very popular with mountain bikers thanks to the Grande Traversée du Morvan route (330 km).

8

# Avallon

Approaching **AVALLON** along the N6 from the north, you might not give the place a second look. The southern aspect is altogether more promising: a small, ancient town clustered high on a ridge above the wooded valley of the River Cousin, looking out over the hilly, sparsely populated country of the Morvan regional park. Once a staging post on the Roman Via Agrippa from Lyon to Boulogne, it's an attractive place of stone facades and sleepy cobbled streets, and well worth a visit.

Bisecting the town north to south, the narrow **Grande-Rue Aristide-Briand** leads past the arch of the fifteenth-century **Tour de l'Horloge** – the 49m spire of which dominates the town – to the pilgrim church of **St-Lazare**, on whose battered Romanesque facade you can still decipher graceful carvings of the zodiac signs; inside, in the southeastern chapel, there is a wonderful trompe l'oeil of the Virgin Mary.

Take a stroll down to the lime-shaded **Promenade de la Petite Porte**, where you can walk the perimeter of the outside walls, which afford precipitous views across the plunging valley of the Cousin.

## Musée de l' Avallonnais

5 rue du Collège • April–Sept Wed–Mon 2–6pm; Oct, Nov & Jan–March Sat & Sun 2–6pm • €3 • ☎ 03 86 34 03 19, ⓦ museeavallonnais.com

The archeological section of the **Musée de l'Avallonais** includes a second-century mosaic from a Gallo-Roman villa, while the highlight of the fine arts department is Alfred Boucher's sculpture of a very life-like Jason pinching the Golden Fleece.

## Musée du Costume

6 rue Belgrand • April–Nov daily 10.30am–12.30pm & 1.30–5.30pm • €5 • ☎ 03 86 34 19 95

The rather quaint **Musée du Costume**, housed in a seventeenth-century mansion just off Grande-Rue, features a collection of regional dresses among furniture and *objets d'art* of this period. They host a special exhibition every summer concentrating on historical fashions.

## ARRIVAL AND INFORMATION
AVALLON

**By train** The *gare SNCF* is to the northeast of town about a 15min walk from the centre.

Destinations Auxerre (1–2 daily; 1hr 10min); Montbard (1–2 daily; 1hr 50min).

**By bus** Trans-Yonne buses stop at place Vauban.

Destinations Auxerre (1–2 daily; 1hr 10min); Dijon (1–3 daily; 2hr–2hr 30min); Semur-en-Auxois (1–3 daily; 1hr); Vézelay (summer only 1–3 daily; 30min, check with tourist office for current timetable).

**By bike** The Grande Traversée du Morvan mountain biking route (330km) links Avallon with Autun via Saulieu.

**Tourist office** In a fifteenth-century house at 6 rue Bocquillot, between the clock tower and St-Lazare (April–June Mon–Sat 10am–1pm & 2–6pm; July & Aug Mon 2–6pm, Tues–Sat 10am–1pm & 2–6pm, Sun 10am–1pm; 10am–6.30pm; Sept–March Tues–Sat 9.30am—-12.30pm & 2–5.30pm; ☎03 86 34 14 19, ⓦavallon-morvan.com).

## ACCOMMODATION

**Camping Municipal de Sous-Roche** Rue Sous-Roche ☎03 86 34 10 39, ⓦcampingsousroche.com. Attractive, classy riverside site 2km south of town inside the Parc du Morvan and close to many hiking and mountain-biking trails. Features a small shop, café, BBQ and *pétanque* court. Closed mid-Oct to March. €15.40

**Les Capucins** 6 av Doumer ☎03 86 34 06 52, ⓦavallonlescapucins.com. Delightful mid-range *hôtel de charme* housed in a nineteenth-century mansion close to the train station, with pleasant en-suite rooms all boasting a/c. There's also a decent restaurant (three-course menu €18). Excellent value. Breakfast €9. €68

★**Château de Vault Lugny** 4km east of Avallon ☎03 86 34 07 86, ⓦlugny.fr. A gorgeous thirteenth- to sixteenth-century château, set in sweeping parkland,

housing a peaceful and luxurious five-star hotel. The spacious bedrooms are all decorated in period style, while there's an incredible indoor pool in the old cave, tennis court, and wine-tasting opportunities. The restaurant is open daily and serves delicious regional cuisine, with much of the produce grown on site in the *potager gastronomique*. Breakfast €26. Closed Oct to mid-March. Weekdays €327

**Le Moulin des Ruats** 23 rue des Isles Labaumes, 4km west of Avallon ☎03 86 34 97 00, ⓦmoulindesruats.com. If you have a car, try this eighteenth-century former flour mill on the scenic valley road to Vézelay. Some of the calm, elegant rooms have a view of the River Cousin, and the restaurant is renowned for its regional cuisine (*menus* from €35). Breakfast €14. Closed mid-Nov to mid-Feb. €93

## EATING AND DRINKING

**Dame Jeanne** 59 Grande Rue Aristide Briand ☎03 86 34 58 71, ⓦdamejeanne.fr. This refined tearoom and café in a seventeenth-century house, which has long opening hours, offers an excellent breakfast and does light dishes for around €11, served in its flowery courtyard. Its specialities are *gougères* with spices. Mon–Wed, Fri & Sat 8am–7pm.

**Relais des Gourmets** 47 rue de Paris ☎03 86 34 18 90, ⓦrelaisdesgourmets.com. Excellent little restaurant, bedecked with scarlet geraniums. In the peaceful inner courtyard, you can lounge beneath the ancient olive trees

and sample beef and snails. *Menus* from €22, and there's even a menu for vegetarians. Wed–Sun noon–2pm & 7–9pm.

★**Le Vaudésir** 84 rue de Lyon ☎03 86 34 14 60, ⓦrestaurant-levaudesir.com. Excellent restaurant with an all-female team. Chef Cécile uses the finest local ingredients to create beautifully presented traditional French dishes, such as duck tart with spicy foie gras sauce. Menus start at €20. Tues & Thurs–Sat noon–1.30pm & & 7–8.30pm, Wed & Sun noon–1.30pm.

## Vézelay

The tourist buses winding their way up the steep incline to **VÉZELAY** should not deter you from visiting this attractive hilltop hamlet, which is surrounded by ramparts and has some of the most picturesque, winding streets and crumbling buildings in Burgundy. While the main draw is undeniably the Basilique Ste-Marie-Madeleine (Basilica of St Mary Magdalene), Vézelay is also a popular destination for art-lovers, with its many small galleries and antique shops on rue St-Pierre, and an impressive art collection in the **Musée Zervos**. Vézelay is classed as one of Les Plus Beaux Villages de France (ⓦfrance-beautiful-villages.org).

## Basilique St-Marie-Madeleine
Top of rue St-Pierre • Daily sunrise–sunset (usually 8pm); guided visits Tues–Sat 9–11am & 2.30–5pm, Sun 9–10.30am & 2.30–5pm • Free, €4.50 for a guided visit • ☎ 03 86 33 39 50, ⓦ basiliquedevezelay.org

Pilgrims journey to Vézelay to venerate the relics of Mary Magdalene (1120), housed in one of the seminal buildings of the Romanesque period – the **Basilique Ste-Marie-Madeleine** – one of the first UNESCO-inscribed sites in France. On the church's west front, the colossal narthex was added to the nave in 1140 to accommodate the swelling numbers of pilgrims. Inside, your eye is drawn to the sculptures of the central doorway, on whose tympanum a Pentecostal Christ is shown swathed in exquisitely figured drapery. From Christ's outstretched hands, the message of the Gospel shoots out to the apostles in the form of beams of fire, while the frieze below depicts the converted and the pagans – among those featured are giants, pygmies (one mounting his horse with a ladder), a man with breasts and huge ears, and dog-headed heathens. The arcades and arches are edged with fretted mouldings, and the supporting pillars are crowned with finely cut capitals, depicting scenes from the Bible, classical mythology, allegories and morality stories. The orientation of the church is such that, during the summer solstice, the sun coming through the south windows creates a line of nine luminous spots bisecting the nave floor.

## Musée de l'Oeuvre Viollet-le-Duc
Place du Cloître • Easter–June & Sept Sat & Sun 2–6pm; July & Aug daily 2–6pm • €3 • ☎ 03 86 33 24 62

The **Musée de l'Oeuvre Viollet-le-Duc**, which takes up two rooms of the old monks' dormitory, houses the best sculptures from the St Mary Magdalene basilica as well as the mouldings created by Viollet-le-Duc during the basilica's restoration.

## Musée Zervos
Rue Saint-Étienne • Mid-March to June & Sept to mid-Nov Mon & Wed–Sun 10am–6pm; July & Aug daily 10am–6pm • €3 • ☎ 03 86 32 39 26, ⓦ musee-zervos.fr

Occupying the house where Romain Rolland, the Nobel prize for literature winner, lived and died in 1944, the **Musée Zervos** is well worth a visit. Exhibits include a number of interesting modernist works, including pieces by Picasso, Kandinsky, Miró, Calder and Giacometti.

8

### ARRIVAL AND INFORMATION VÉZELAY

**By train** Take the Avallon-bound train and stop at Sermizelles (10km away) where you can continue to Vézelay on the twice-daily shuttle bus or by prebooked taxi (Cyril Taxi, ☎ 03 86 33 19 06 or Annette Devry Taxis, ☎ 03 86 32 36 63).
**By car** Vézelay is 14km from Avallon on the D957 and 48km away from Auxerre on the N6 and then the N151. There are car parks at the bottom of the hill (€2–5).

**By bike** A new cycle route (84km) links Vézelay with the Abbaye de Fontenay.
**Tourist office** 12 rue St-Étienne (July & Aug Mon–Sat 10am–1pm & 2–6pm, Sun 10am–12.30pm & 2–5.30pm; Sept–June Tues–Sat 10am–1pm & 2–6pm; ☎ 03 86 33 23 69, ⓦ vezelaytourisme.com).

### ACCOMMODATION

★ **Les Glycines** Rue St-Pierre ☎ 03 86 32 35 30, ⓦ glycines-vezelay.com. This beautiful mid-eighteenth-century hotel looks oddly English, but inside it is charmingly French; check out the Zervos suite with its 250-year-old wallpaper. The appealing courtyard faces the main street, while inside there's a cosy, atmospheric restaurant (*menus* from €22.50). Breakfast €12. **€80**

**De la Poste et du Lion d'Or** Place du Champ de Foire ☎ 03 73 53 03 20, ⓦ hplv-vezelay.com. A grand and luxurious choice, which reopened in 2017 following a very successful renovation. The simply furnished rooms have imposing old wooden furniture and great views of either the old town or the sweeping valley behind. The gourmet restaurant has *menus* from €26. Breakfast €14. **€135**

### EATING AND DRINKING

Beer fans should try one of the award-winning organic brews from the Brasserie de Vézelay (ⓦ brasseriedevezelay. com).

★ **Le Bougainville** 28 rue St-Pierre ☎ 03 86 33 27 57. The finest regional cuisine served in a genteel dining room with *menus* from €27 including the house wine. The home-made terrine is a delicious combination of *Époisses* cheese, ham and artichoke. You must try the cheese board too: it groans enticingly with up to thirty excellent cheeses. Mid-Feb to mid-Nov Mon & Thurs–Sun noon–2pm & 7–9pm.

★ **À la Fortune du Pot** 6 place du Champ de Foire ☎ 03 86 33 32 56, ⓦ fortunedupot.com. This hugely popular restaurant serves wonderful home-cooked Burgundian specialities in comfortable, welcoming surroundings. Even the organic bread is baked daily on the premises. A must-try is the *boeuf bourguignon*, served with dauphinoise potatoes. Mon & Thurs–Sun noon–2pm & 7–10pm.

# Clamecy

ⓦ clamercynivernais-tourisme.fr

**CLAMECY**, 23km west of Vézelay on the banks of the River Yonne, has less to offer than its rustic neighbours, but is worth a day-trip. It was the centre of the Morvan's logging trade from the sixteenth century up until the completion of the Canal du Nivernais in 1834; woodcutting gangs working in the hills floated their logs down the river as far as Clamecy, where they were made up into great rafts for shipment on to Paris.

Winding your way up the narrow streets that lead to the well-preserved historic town centre, you'll pass a number of fifteenth- to eighteenth-century buildings, particularly on **rue de la Monnaie**, **rue de la Tour** and **rue Bourgeoise**. At the top of the hill is the church of **St Martin**, a veritable gem of flamboyant Gothic architecture, parts of which date back to the twelfth century.

## Romain Rolland Art and History Museum

Av de la République • May–Sept Mon & Wed–Sat 10am–noon & 2–6pm, Sun 2–6pm; Oct–April Wed–Sat 10am–noon & 2–6pm, Sun 2–6pm • €3 • ☎ 03 86 27 17 99

Clamecy's **Romain Rolland Art and History Museum** has a broad range of things to see, including three whole rooms of Gallo-Roman objects and a fine art collection that spans the last five centuries. The modernist posters designed by renowned poster artist Charles Loupot and the collection of paintings donated by President Mitterrand are especially worth seeking out.

# Saulieu

An old market town with a reputation for its gastronomy, **SAULIEU** suffered as a result of the depopulation of the Morvan. Every year the town waits hungrily for its **Gourmet festival** on the third weekend of May, Les Journées Gourmandes, featuring local Michelin-starred chefs, mountains of meat, rivers of wine and all manner of local produce. There's also a celebration of the local Charolais cows on the third weekend of August. Saulieu is a good springboard for the cycling, hiking and riding possibilities in the Parc du Morvan (see page 454), but unless you come during the festival it's not overly exciting as a base.

## Basilique St-Andoche

Easter–Nov Tues–Sat 9am–noon & 2–6.30pm, Sun 2–6.30pm; Nov–Easter Tues–Sat 9am–noon & 2–4.30pm • Free

The main sight of Saulieu old town is the twelfth-century **Basilique St-Andoche**, noted for its lovely Romanesque capitals of the school of Gislebertus, the master sculptor of Autun, as well as its impressive church organ.

## Musée François-Pompon

3 rue du Docteur-Roclore • April–Sept Mon 10am–12.30pm, Wed–Sat 10am–12.30pm & 2–6pm, Sun & public hols 10.30am–noon & 2.30–5pm; Oct–Dec & March Mon 10am–12.30pm, Wed–Sat 10am–12.30pm & 2–5.30pm, Sun & public hols 10.30am–noon & 2.30–5pm • €3 • ☎ 03 80 64 19 51

Next door to the basilica, the **Musée François-Pompon** is fun to visit, with good local folklore displays and a large collection of works by the local nineteenth-century animal

8

sculptor, François Pompon. One room is devoted to the gourmet past of the town, with a particular dedication to local three-Michelin-star chef **Bernard Loiseau** who committed suicide in 2003.

## ARRIVAL AND INFORMATION

**By bus** Buses stop in front of the *gare SNCF*. Book in advance (☎0800 21 32 33).
Destinations Montbard (4 daily; 1hr).
**Tourist office** 24 rue d'Argentine (April Tues–Sat 10am–1pm & 2–6pm; May & Sept Mon–Sat 10am–noon

& 2–6pm, Sun 10am–1pm & 2–6pm; June–Aug Mon–Sat 10am–noon & 2–7pm, Sun 10am–1pm & 2–5pm; Oct–March Tues–Sat 10am–noon & 2–5pm; ☎03 80 64 00 21, ⓦsaulieu-morvan.fr).

## ACCOMMODATION AND EATING

★ **Hostellerie de la Tour d'Auxois** 1 rue Sallier ☎03 80 64 36 19, ⓦtourdauxois.com. A lovely hotel right in the heart of the town, it has a large pool, a garden, and a great restaurant (closed Mon, Tues & Sat lunch) serving classic Burgundian *menus* from €27. Breakfast €13. **€99**

★ **Le Relais Bernard-Loiseau** 2 rue d'Argentine ☎03 80 90 53 53, ⓦbernard-loiseau.com. This five-star hotel-restaurant-spa was created by the famed chef Bernard

Loiseau (and made even more famous after his suicide in 2003 following a long bout of depression). It is an elegant, beyond-luxurious place of rich woods, stone arches and plush furnishings that exude wealth. *Menus* at the two-star Michelin restaurant (closed Tues & Wed), which has been continued by his widow, start at €75 for lunch and €150 for dinner. Free parking. Breakfast €30. **€165**

# Autun

With its Gothic spire rising against the backdrop of the Morvan hills, **AUTUN** is scarcely bigger than the circumference of its **walls**; most of the enclosure still consists of Roman fortifications that have been maintained through the centuries. The emperor Augustus founded the town in about 10 BC as part of a massive and, ultimately, highly successful campaign to pacify the brooding Celts of defeated Vercingétorix. The splendour of Augustodunum, as it was called, was designed to eclipse the memory of Bibracte, the neighbouring capital of the powerful tribe of the Aedui. Autun did indeed become one of the leading cities of Roman Gaul until it was sacked by the Arabs in 725 AD. Today, it is a picturesque provincial town, and an excellent base for exploring the surrounding countryside, particularly the Parc du Morvan.

## The Gallo-Roman remains

This town's past remains very tangible, and two of its four Roman gates survive: **Porte St-André**, spanning rue de la Croix-Blanche in the northeast, and **Porte d'Arroux** in the northwest. In a field just across the River Arroux stands a lofty section of wall known as the **Temple of Janus**, which was probably part of the sanctuary of an unknown deity. On the east side of town, on avenue du 2ème Dragon, you can see the remains of what was the largest **Roman theatre** in Gaul, which had a capacity of fifteen thousand – in itself a measure of Autun's importance at that time. A Roman festival, with re-enactments, takes place here on the first weekend of August. The most enigmatic of the Gallo-Roman remains in the region is the **Pierre de Couhard**, off Faubourg St-Pancrace to the southeast of the town. It's a 27m-tall stone pyramid situated on the site of one of the city's necropolises, thought to date from the first century, and most probably a cenotaph.

## Cathédrale St-Lazare

Place du Terreau • Daily 8am–7pm • €2

Autun's great twelfth-century **Cathédrale St-Lazare** was built nearly a thousand years after the Romans had departed, and its greatest claim to artistic fame lies in its sculptures, the work of Gislebertus, generally accepted as one of the most outstanding Romanesque sculptors.

The tympanum of the **Last Judgement** above the west door bears his signature – *Gislebertus hoc fecit* ("Gislebertus made this") – beneath the feet of Christ. To his left are the Virgin Mary, the saints and the apostles, with the saved rejoicing below them; to the right the Archangel Michael disputes souls with Satan, who tries to cheat by leaning on the scales, while the damned despair beneath. During the eighteenth century the local clergy decided the tympanum was an inferior work and plastered over it, saving it from almost certain destruction during the Revolution. The interior of the cathedral, whose pilasters and arcading were modelled on the Roman architecture of the city's gates, was also decorated by Gislebertus, who carved most of the capitals himself. Some of the finest are now exhibited in the old chapter library, up the stairs on the right of the choir, among them a beautiful *Flight into Egypt* and *The Death of Cain*. You can find out more about the sculptor and the town's heritage at the Espace Gislebertus (daily: July & Aug 10am–7pm; April–June & Sept–Oct 10am–1pm & 2–6pm; free), an interpretation centre opposite the cathedral.

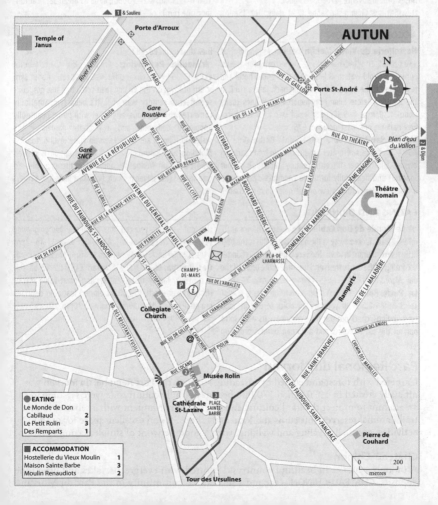

**AUTUN**

8

Temple of Janus
Porte d'Arroux
River Arroux
RUE DE PARIS
Porte St-André
RUE DE GAILLON
RUE DU FAUBOURG ST-ANDRÉ
Gare Routière
RUE CARION
RUE DE PARIS
RUE DE LA CROIX-BLANCHE
Gare SNCF
AVENUE DE LA RÉPUBLIQUE
RUE DE 23ÈME RMIA
GRAND RUE
BOULEVARD LAUREAU
BOULEVARD MAZAGRAN
R. MAZAGRAN
RUE DU THÉÂTRE ROMAIN
Plan d'eau du Vallon
RUE BERNARD RENAUT
RUE DES CITÉS
RUE DE LA CROIX VERTE
RUE DE LA GRILLE
RUE DE LA GRANDE-VERTU
RUE GUERIN
BOULEVARD FRÉDÉRIC LATOUCHE
PROMENADE DES MARBRES
AVENUE DU 2ÈME DRAGONS
Théâtre Romain
RUE DU FAUBOURG ST-ANDOCHE
AVENUE DU GÉNÉRAL DE GAULLE
RUE PERNETTE
RUE JEANNIN
Mairie
RUE DE PARPAS
RUE ST-CHRISTOPHE
CHAMPS-DE-MARS
RUE DE L'ARQUEBUSE
PLACE L'HARMASSE
RUE DES MARBRES
RUE DE LA MALADIÈRE
Ramparts
RUE DE L'ARBALÈTE
BD. DES RÉSISTANTS FUSILLÉS
RUE ST-SAUGE
RUE ST-ANTOINE
Collegiate Church
RUE ST-SAUGE R. L'ANCIENNE
RUE CHANGARNIER
RUE DU DR GILLOT
RUE PIOLIN
CHEMIN DES BAGOTS
CHEMIN DES MANILLES
RUE COCAND
Musée Rolin
RUE SAINT-BRANCHEZ
RUE DU FAUBOURG SAINT-PANCRACE
Cathédrale St-Lazare
PLACE SAINTE-BARBE
Pierre de Couhard
Tour des Ursulines

**EATING**
| | |
|---|---|
| Le Monde de Don Cabillaud | 2 |
| Le Petit Rolin | 3 |
| Des Remparts | 1 |

**ACCOMMODATION**
| | |
|---|---|
| Hostellerie du Vieux Moulin | 1 |
| Maison Sainte Barbe | 3 |
| Moulin Renaudiots | 2 |

0    200
metres

## Musée Rolin

3 rue des Bancs • Mon & Wed–Sun April–Sept 10am–1pm & 2–6pm; Oct–March 10am–noon & 2–5pm; • €6.50 • ☎ 03 85 52 09 76

Just outside the cathedral is the **Musée Rolin** which occupies a Renaissance hotel that was once home to Nicolas Rolin, Chancellor of Philippe le Bon. In addition to interesting Gallo-Roman (and even Greek) pieces, the star attractions are Gislebertus's representation of Eve as an unashamedly sensual nude, and Jean Hey's brilliantly coloured *Nativity*.

## ARRIVAL AND INFORMATION                                    AUTUN

**By train** The nearest train station is Le Creusot-Montceau TGV, about 30 mins' drive, which is served by regular shuttle buses.

Destinations Lyon (11 daily; 45min); Paris Gare de Lyon (7 daily; 1hr 20min) .

**By bus** The *gare routière* is very near the train station. Book buses 24hr in advance (☎ 0800 853 000).

Destinations Chalon-sur-Saône (2–4 daily; 1hr 15min);

Épinac (3–5 daily; 25min).

**Tourist office** The tourist office is at 13 rue du Général-Demetz on Champs-de-Mars (April–June Mon–Sat 10am–noon & 2pm, Sun 10am–2pm; July & Aug Mon–Sat 9.30am–12.30pm & 2–6pm, Sun 10am–2pm; Sept & Oct Mon–Sat 10am–noon & 2–6pm; Nov–March Tues–Sat 10am–12.30pm & 2–5.30pm; ☎ 03 85 86 80 38, ⦿ autun-tourisme.com).

## ACCOMMODATION

**Hostellerie du Vieux Moulin** Chemin Jeanne-Barrat ☎ 03 85 52 10 90, ⦿ hostellerie-duvieuxmoulin-autun. com. Lovely old watermill housing a mid-priced hotel and restaurant at the gates of the Morvan park. Take a stroll in the gardens before dining on regional specialities (daily noon–1.30pm & 7–9.30pm). Closed Dec to mid-March. Free parking, breakfast included. **€75**

**Maison Sainte-Barbe** 7 place Sainte-Barbe ☎ 03 85 86 24 77, ⦿ maisonsaintebarbe.com. Run by a charming owner, this former fifteenth-century rectory has four spacious and beautifully furnished *chambres d'hôtes*, and a lovely garden with a view of the neighbouring chapel.

Breakfast included. **€82**

★ **Moulin Renaudiots** Chemin du Vieux-Moulin ☎ 03 85 86 97 10, ⦿ moulinrenaudiots.com. About 3km south of town on the Chalon road you'll find this gorgeous seventeenth-century watermill. It's been sympathetically converted to a spacious, airy hotel with huge, beautifully appointed bedrooms and a peaceful garden – the welcoming hosts are quite keen on wine tasting, too. On Mondays and Saturdays a *table d'hôte* option is offered (€54), while on Wednesday and Fridays there's a splendid cold spread (€22). Free parking, breakfast included. **€140**

## EATING AND DRINKING

★ **Le Monde de Don Cabillaud** 4 rue des Bancs ☎ 07 60 94 21 10. Tucked away in the old quarter, this is the best little fish restaurant in town. The very limited menu changes according to the catch: fresh and fuss-free is the order of the day. *Menus* from €28. Tues–Sat noon–1.30pm & 7–9pm.

**Le Petit Rolin** 1 parvis du Chanoine Denis-Grivot ☎ 03 85 86 15 55. If you care for quick service in good surroundings, check out this little crêperie – its walls form part of the old ramparts and a Roman column props up

the roof – where you can dine on *cuisine bourguignonne* (€13–24) or crêpes (€6–11). April–Oct daily 11am–2pm & 7–10pm; Nov & Dec Wed–Sun 11am–2pm & 7–10pm.

**Des Remparts** 17 rue Mazagran ☎ 03 85 52 54 02. A convivial family restaurant serving great-value *menus* (from €15 at lunch, €22.50 for dinner) featuring delicious regional specialities. Wed 10am–2.30pm, Thurs–Mon 10am–2.30pm & 6–10pm.

# Parc Régional du Morvan

Carpeted with forest and etched by cascading streams, the **Parc Régional du Morvan** was officially created in 1970, when 170,000 hectares of hilly countryside were set aside in an attempt to protect the local cultural and physical environment with a series of nature trails, animal reserves, museums and local craft shops. It's an excellent place for **outdoor activities**, especially cycling and walking, with a good network of simple accommodation.

## Château-Chinon

Although it nestles in beautiful countryside dotted with evergreens, lakes and limestone deposits, **CHÂTEAU-CHINON** – the most substantial community in the Parc du Morvan

– is a place to drive through rather than stay overnight. It is of interest, however, for its President Mitterrand connections; he was mayor here from 1959 to 1981, and thanks largely to him, the village now boasts a major hosiery factory and military printing works, both of which have provided much-needed employment to an isolated and often forgotten region.

### Musée du Septennat

6 rue du Château • May–June & Sept Wed–Mon 10am–1pm & 2–6pm; July & Aug daily 10am–1pm & 2–7pm; Feb–April & Oct–Dec Wed–Mon 10am–noon & 2–6pm • €4 • ☎ 03 86 85 19 23

The **Musée du Septennat**, housed in the converted eighteenth-century convent of St Claire, displays the gifts Mitterrand received as head of state, including carpets from the Middle East, ivory from Togo, Japanese puppets, and a bizarre table decorated with butterfly wings.

## INFORMATION AND ACCOMMODATION

**Information centre** The park's main information centre, the Maison du Parc, is 13km from Saulieu in beautiful grounds about 1km outside St-Brisson on the D6 (April to mid-Nov Mon–Fri 9.30am–12.30pm & 2–5.30pm, Sat & Sun 10am–12.30pm & 2–5.30pm; July & Aug daily 10am–1pm & 2–6pm; mid-Nov to March Wed–Fri 9.30am–12.30pm & 2–5.30pm; ☎03 86 78 79 57, ⓦtourisme. parcdumorvan.org).

**Website** You can download cycling, walking and activities brochures from ⓦ tourisme.parcdumorvan.org.

## PARC RÉGIONAL DU MORVAN

**Accommodation** Every other village in the park seems to have its own campsite and the larger ones often have a couple of simple hotels as well. There are seven campsites and several small hotels around the large, wooded Lac des Settons, the main resort in the heart of the park, which has watersports facilities, café-restaurants and small beaches. The plain, modern village of Montsauche, 4km northwest of the lake, is a good base for provisions, including camping gas, and has a municipal campsite; Moux, a similar distance to the southeast, is another possible alternative.

## ACTIVITIES

**Cycling** There is a plethora of cycle routes in the Parc du Morvan, and tourist offices throughout the Morvan region sell large-scale maps. Mountain bikers should check out the Grande Traversée du Morvan (330km) route. Bikes are available from most camp-sites in the area: for a complete list ask at any tourist office, or check online.

**Hiking** For walkers, the most challenging trip is the three-to four-day hike along the GR13 footpath, crossing the park

from Vézelay to Mont Beuvray and taking in the major lakes, which are among the park's most developed attractions. There are also numerous less strenuous possibilities including the 4km walk from Saulieu to Lac Chamboux.

**Climbing** There is excellent rock climbing near Avallon and Dun les Places.

**Horseriding** Horseriding is a fairly popular way of seeing the park, and numerous *gîtes* offer pony trekking.

# Nevers

Some 60km west of the Parc du Morvan, **NEVERS**, on the confluence of the rivers Loire and Nièvre, is a strange place, where motorbikers and boy racers drawn to the Formula One racing ring at nearby **Magny-Cours** mingle in the streets with religious pilgrims come to pay their respects to **Bernadette of Lourdes**, gourmands attracted by the local **nougatine**, and shoppers out to buy fine hand-painted pottery. **Faïence**, as it's called, has been a hallmark of Nevers since the seventeenth century, and is painted in the deep colour known as *bleu de Nevers*; there's even a museum celebrating the renowned earthenware.

**Place Carnot** is the hub of the centre; nearby, just above the tourist office, you'll find the fifteenth-century **Palais Ducal** (mid-April to Sept Mon–Sat 9am–6.30pm, Sun 10am–1pm & 2–6pm; Oct to mid-April Mon–Sat 9am–12.30pm & 2–6pm; free), former home of the dukes of Nevers, which has octagonal turrets and a central tower adorned with elegantly carved hunting scenes.

That aside, Nevers' main attractions are its religious monuments. The stunning **Cathédrale de St-Cyr** (daily 9am–noon & 2–6pm), with its wonderful display of jutting gargoyles, reveals French architectural styles from the tenth to the sixteenth centuries and, with its modern stained-glass windows, brings things right up to the present. The cathedral even manages to have two apses, one Gothic, the other Romanesque.

On the far side of the commercial pedestrian precinct around rue Mitterrand is the even more interesting and aesthetically satisfying late eleventh-century **church of St-Étienne** (daily 9am–noon & 2–6pm).

## Espace Bernadette (old convent of St-Gildard)

34 rue St-Gildard • **Convent** Daily: April–Oct 8am–12.30pm & 3.30–7.30pm; Nov–March 8am–noon & 2–6pm • Free **Museum** Daily: April–Oct 8am–12.30pm & 3.30–7.30pm; Nov–March 8am–noon & 2–6pm • Free • ☎ 03 86 71 99 50, ⓦ sainte-bernadette-soubirous-nevers.com

Of spiritual rather than architectural appeal is the **Espace Bernadette**, in the old **convent of St-Gildard**, where Bernadette of Lourdes ended her days. A steady flow of pilgrims comes to visit her tiny, embalmed body, displayed in a glass-fronted **shrine**, in the convent chapel. A small but very engaging **museum** displays some of her belongings and correspondence.

## Musée de la Faïence et des Beaux-Arts

15 rue St-Genest • May–Sept Tues–Sun 10am–6.30pm, Oct–April Tues–Fri 1–5.30pm, Sat & Sun 2–6pm • €6 • ☎ 03 86 68 44 60, ⓦ musee-faïence.nevers.fr

A stunning museum, designed by architect Benoît Crépet, and housed in the restored Abbaye de Notre-Dame, has finally given a fitting home to many of the town's world-famous pieces. Don't miss the original *Vierge à la Pomme*, by Denis Lefebvre, or the deep cobalt-blue *Plat Vénus, l'Amour et Mercure*, both dating from the seventeenth century. There's also a large collection of sparkling enamelled glass. But it's the faïence that takes centre stage; it has been in production here for four centuries and has graced the tables of princes and peasants alike. There are engaging multimedia presentations showcasing the evolution of the craft; and if you're still keen to see more, drop in to see the artisans at work in Faïence Bleue, 22 rue du 14 Juillet, or Fayencerie d'Art de Nevers at 11 and 88b avenue Colbert.

## Musée Archéologique du Nivernais

Porte de Croux • June–Oct Thurs–Sun 2–6pm • €2 • ☎ 03 86 57 05 16

Housed in the Porte de Croux, a fourteenth-century crenellated tower forming part of the original ramparts of the city, this museum has been a long time coming. Bought by Denis de Vertpré in 1847, it was bequeathed to the town on condition that it was restored and used as a museum for the antiquities of the area. There are some fascinating local archeological remains, dating as far back as the Bronze Age, as well as numerous marbles of Greek and Roman origin and a huge and impressive Gallo-Roman mosaic.

### ARRIVAL AND INFORMATION　　　　　　　　　　　　　　NEVERS

**By train and bus** The train and bus stations are next to each other at the west of the town centre; from here, avenue de Gaulle leads east to place Carnot (15min).

Destinations (train) Clermont-Ferrand (5–7 daily; 1hr 45min); Le Creusot (5–7 daily; 1hr 30min); Dijon (5–7 daily; 2hr 20min); Lyon (3–4 daily; 3hr); Paris Bercy (6–9 daily; 2–3hr).

**Tourist office** Below the Palais Ducal (April–Sept Mon–Sat 9.30am–6.30pm, Sun 10am–1pm & 2–6pm; Oct–March Mon 2–6pm, Tues–Sat 10am–12.30pm & 2–6pm; ☎ 03 86 68 46 00, ⓦ nevers-tourisme.com).

**Racing and karting** You can go karting on the Magny-Cours circuit on certain dates (☎ 03 86 21 80 00, ⓦ circuitmagnycours.com). Check the website for details of races.

### ACCOMMODATION

Accommodation is at an absolute premium on rally days, so check your dates carefully or book well in advance.

**Beauséjour** 5bis rue St-Gildard ☎ 03 86 61 20 84, ⓦ hotel-beausejour-nevers.com. Close to the station and opposite the convent of St-Gildard, this hotel offers very reasonably priced rooms (the cheaper ones have shared facilities) and friendly service. It's fine for an overnight stay. Breakfast €8.30. **€49**

**Best Western Diane** 38 rue du Midi ☎ 03 86 57 28 10, Ⓦ bestwestern.com. Just a short walk from the station, this is an excellently situated hotel, with a tennis court, indoor pool and a golf course; the buffet breakfast is served in a vaulted room in the St Laurent tower. Closed parking available €10. Breakfast €14. **€96**

**Camping de Nevers** Rue de la Jonction ☎ 03 86 36 40

75, Ⓦ aquadis-loisirs.com. A lovely campsite, next to the river across the Pont de Loire, which offers a splendid view of the Palais Ducal and Cathédrale de St-Cyr. There's a bar, internet access, a *pétanque* court and badminton. Closed Nov–March. **€16.50**

**De Clèves** 8 rue St-Didier ☎ 03 86 61 15 87, Ⓦ hoteldecleves.fr. A quiet and comfortable hotel in the centre of town, always popular and packed to the gunwales on race days. It's run by welcoming and energetic owners, eager to help, but ask for any information you require on arrival, as reception is not always open. Breakfast €7.50; garage €6. **€75**

### EATING AND DRINKING

**La Botte de Nevers** Rue du Petit Château ☎ 03 86 61 16 93, Ⓦ labottedenevers.fr. Easily spotted due to the wonderful wrought-iron sign outside, this is a place of many *menus* – they start at €30, but it's worth paying more for the best Charolais steaks this side of the Morvan. Tues 7–9pm, Wed–Sat noon–1.30pm & 7–9pm, Sun noon–1.30pm.

**La Cour St-Étienne** 33 rue St-Étienne ☎ 03 86 36 74 57, Ⓦ restaurant-la-cour.com. Attractive restaurant with an elegant half-timbered dining room, which serves high-quality, traditional food, with *menus* starting at €28.90.

Mon 7–9.30pm, Tues–Sat noon–2pm & 7–9.30pm, Sun noon–2pm.

**Jean-Michel Couron** 21 rue St-Étienne ☎ 03 86 61 19 28, Ⓦ jm-couron.com. Located in a former chapel, Jean-Michel Couran's restaurant gives traditional dishes a touch of modern flair, offering gourmet French cuisine at reasonable prices. Try the exquisite langoustine tails with pressed peas and whipped coconut cream, if it's on. The desserts are mini works of art and the cheeses are wonderful too. *Menus* €37, €50.50 and €59. Wed–Sat noon–1.15pm & 7.45–9pm, Sun noon–1.15pm.

# Dijon

In Celtic times, **DIJON** held a strategic position on the tin merchants' route from Britain to the Adriatic. It became the capital of the dukes of Burgundy around 1000 AD, and in the fourteenth and fifteenth centuries, under the auspices of dukes Philippe le Hardi (the Bold – as a boy, he had fought the English at Poitiers), Jean sans Peur (the Fearless), Philippe le Bon (the Good – he sold Joan of Arc to the English), and Charles le Téméraire (also the Bold), Dijon flourished. The dukes used their tremendous wealth and power – especially their control of Flanders, the dominant manufacturing region of the age – to make this one of the greatest centres of art, learning and science in Europe. It lost its capital status on incorporation into the kingdom of France in 1477 but has remained one of the country's pre-eminent provincial cities. Today, it's an affluent university city: elegant, modern and dynamic, especially when the students are around. Locals are currently looking forward to the opening of the Cité Internationale de la Gastronomie et du Vin (Ⓦ citedelagastronomie-dijon.fr), a new centre celebrating Burgundy's food and wine, due to open in 2020.

Dijon is not enormous and the area you'll want to see is confined to the eminently walkable centre. Two recently built **tramlines** have transformed the place, with cars being forced out onto the outskirts; if you have driven to Dijon, you are advised to leave the car at your hotel and forget about it until you leave. **Rue de la Liberté** forms the spine of the city, running east from the wide, attractive **place Darcy** and the eighteenth-century triumphal arch of **Porte Guillaume** – once a city gate – past the **palace** of the dukes of Burgundy on the semicircular **place de la Libération**. From this lovely, classical square, rue Rameau continues directly east to place du Théâtre, from where rue Vaillant leads on to the **church of St Michel**. Most places of interest are within ten minutes' walk to the north or south of this main axis, which is lined with smart shops, mammoth department stores and graceful old houses.

8

## The Palais des Ducs

Place de la Libération • **Tour Philippe-le-Bon** Guided tours only April–Nov 11 daily; Dec–March 6 tours Sat & Sun, 3 tours Wed • €3

The focus of a visit to Dijon is inevitably the seat of its former rulers, the **Palais des Ducs**, which stands at the hub of the city. Facing the main courtyard is the relaxed **place de la Libération**, built by Jules Hardouin-Mansart, one of the architects of Versailles, towards the end of the seventeenth century. It's now something of a suntrap on a good day, and the decision to close it to traffic has stimulated a boom in café trade. The fourteenth-century Tour de Bar dominates the courtyard in front of the east wing, and now houses the **Musée des Beaux-Arts**, while the loftier, fifteenth-century **Tour Philippe-le-Bon** (316 steps) can be visited only on guided tours. The vista from the

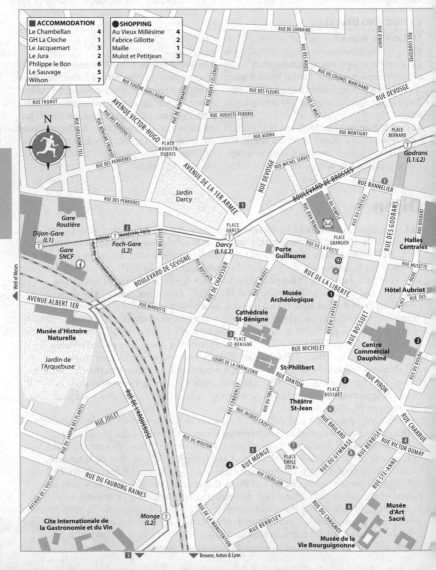

**■ ACCOMMODATION**
| Le Chambellan | 4 |
| GH La Cloche | 1 |
| Le Jacquemart | 3 |
| Le Jura | 2 |
| Philippe le Bon | 6 |
| Le Sauvage | 5 |
| Wilson | 7 |

**● SHOPPING**
| Au Vieux Millésime | 4 |
| Fabrice Gillotte | 2 |
| Maille | 1 |
| Mulot et Petitjean | 3 |

top is particularly worthwhile for the views of the glazed Burgundian tiles of the Hôtel de Vogüé and the cathedral; on a clear day the Jura Mountains loom on the horizon.

## Musée des Beaux-Arts

1 rue Rameau • Daily except Tues: June–Sept 10am–6.30pm; Oct–May 9.30am–6pm • Free, €4 for audioguide • ☎ 03 80 74 52 09,
Ⓦ beaux-arts.dijon.fr

The **Musée des Beaux-Arts** has an interesting collection of works from the Middle Ages to the twentieth century; among the highlights are the Flemish paintings, particularly the *Nativity* by the so-called Master of Flémalle, a shadowy figure who ranks with van Eyck as one of the first artists to break from the chilly stranglehold of International

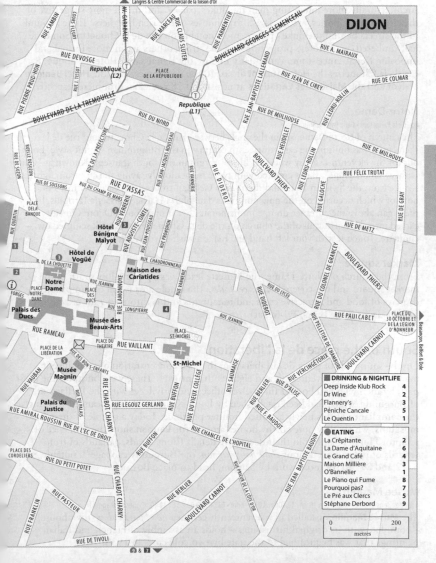

**DIJON**

Langres & Centre Commercial de la Toison d'Or

Besançon, Belfort & Dole

8

■ **DRINKING & NIGHTLIFE**

| Deep Inside Klub Rock | 4 |
| Dr Wine | 2 |
| Flannery's | 3 |
| Péniche Cancale | 5 |
| Le Quentin | 1 |

● **EATING**

| La Crêpitante | 2 |
| La Dame d'Aquitaine | 6 |
| Le Grand Café | 4 |
| Maison Millière | 3 |
| O'Bannelier | 1 |
| Le Piano qui Fume | 8 |
| Pourquoi pas? | 7 |
| Le Pré aux Clercs | 5 |
| Stéphane Derbord | 9 |

0                    200
        metres

Gothic, Burgundy's homespun phase of Gothic art. However, due to renovation, the fifty rooms usually showing works from the seventeenth to twenty-first century are closed; they are scheduled to reopen at the end of 2019.

Visiting the museum also provides the opportunity to see the surviving portions of the original ducal palace, including the vast **kitchen** and the magnificent **Salle des Gardes**. Displayed here are the lavish, almost decadent, **tombs** of Philippe le Hardi and Jean sans Peur and his wife, Marguerite de Bavière, with their startling, painted effigies of the dead, surrounded by gold-plated angels.

## Quartier Notre-Dame

Architecturally more interesting than the dukes' palace, and much more suggestive of the city's former glories, are the lavish townhouses of the rich burghers. These abound in the streets behind the duke's palace, most notably on **rue de la Chouette**. Some are half-timbered, with storeys projecting over the street, others are in more formal and imposing Renaissance stone. Particularly fine are the Renaissance **Hôtel de Vogüé**, 8 rue de la Chouette, the **Hôtel Aubriot** at no. 40 rue des Forges, plus the **Hôtel Bénigne Malyot** and the **Maison des Cariatides** at nos. 1 and 28 rue Chaudronnière respectively.

### Notre-Dame
Rue de la Préfecture • Daily 9am–6.30pm • Free

The church of **Notre-Dame**, set in the angle between rue de la Chouette and rue de la Préfecture, was built in the early thirteenth century in the Burgundian Gothic style. Look out for the eleventh-century wooden "black" Virgin in the south transept. Known as "Our Lady of Good Hope", she is credited with twice miraculously saving the city from fighting – once from the Swiss in 1513 and then when German troops left peacefully in 1944, both of which occurred on the now notorious date of 9/11. The **Tapisserie Terribilis**, below the organ above the entrance door, commemorates her protection of Dijon. Outside, carved into the north wall of the church on rue de la Chouette, is a small, sculpted owl – chouette. Touch it with your left hand and make a wish as you walk past.

### Market square

From the church of Notre-Dame, rue Musette leads west, passing just south of the **market square** and the covered *halles centrales*. The whole area is full of sumptuous displays of food and attractive cafés and restaurants and is thronged with crowds on market days (Tues, Thurs, Fri & Sat).

## South of the place de la Libération

On the south side of place de la Libération, there's a concentration of magnificent **mansions** from the seventeenth and eighteenth centuries. These were built, for the most part, by men who had bought themselves offices and privileges with the Parliament of Burgundy, which had been established by Louis XI in 1477 as a means of winning the compliance of this newly acquired frontier province. Today a couple of them hold **museums**, while a few noteworthy houses around **rue Vauban** show the influence of sculptor Hugues Sambin in their decorative details (lions' heads, garlands of fruit, tendrils of ivy and his famous *chou bourguignon*, or "Burgundy cabbage"), notably, nos. 3, 12 and 21. To see more work by Sambin, head to place Bossuet.

### Musée Magnin
4 rue des Bons-Enfants • Tues–Sun 10am–12.30pm & 1.30–6pm • €3.50 • ☎ 03 80 67 11 10, ⓦ musee-magnin.fr

The **Musée Magnin**, installed in a seventeenth-century *hôtel particulier* (townhouse) – complete with its original furnishings – holds an assembly of French and Italian paintings that was bequeathed to the state by two collectors in 1938.

## Musée d'Art Sacré

15 rue Ste-Anne • Mon & Wed–Sun 9.30am–12.30pm & 2–6pm • Free • ☎ 03 80 48 80 90

One of two museums housed in the Monastère de Bernardine, the **Musée d'Art Sacré** contains an important collection of church treasures. Highlights include a seventeenth-century statue of St Paul, the first in the world to be restored using an extraordinary technique that involves injecting the stone with resin and then solidifying the resulting compound using gamma rays. Formerly crumbling to dust, the statue is now completely firm.

## Musée de la Vie Bourguignonne

17 rue Ste-Anne • Mon & Wed–Sun 9.30am–12.30pm & 2–6pm • Free • ☎ 03 80 48 80 90

The **Musée de la Vie Bourguignonne**, which, like the Musée d'Art Sacré is in the Monastère de Bernardine, explores nineteenth-century Burgundian life, and features costumes, furniture and a number of fun reconstructions of rooms and shops.

# Jardin de l'Arquebuse and around

Below the train station the small, landscaped **Jardin de l'Arquebuse** provides an oasis of calm in the town, with joggers and *boules* players sharing the space with families enjoying a leisurely stroll. The **Natural History Museum** stands by its gate, while the city's **Botanical Garden** dominates its middle.

# The Well of Moses

Centre Hospitalier Spécialisé de la Chartreuse, av Albert-1er • Daily: April–Sept 9.30am–12.30pm & 2–6pm; Oct–March 9.30am–12.30pm & 2–4.30pm • €3.50 • Bus #3, stop Av Albert-1er

Around 1km west of Dijon train station lies the old **Carthusian Monastery of Champmol**, built by Philippe le Hardi, which was destroyed in the Revolution and is now a medical centre. However, many make the long journey on foot or by bus to visit one of Burgundy's masterpieces: the **Well of Moses**, a magnificent medieval sculpture by Claus Sluter in the grounds. Ask at the on-site tourist office about guided tours.

## ARRIVAL AND DEPARTURE | DIJON

**By train** The *gare SNCF* is at the end of the tramline B. A few minutes' walk outside the station on av Foch is the stop for tramline A.

Destinations Beaune (1–3 hourly; 25min); Besançon (1–3 hourly; 1hr); Bourg-en-Bresse (5 daily; 1hr 45min); Chalon-sur-Saône (1–3 hourly; 40min); Laroche-Migennes (10–12 daily; 1hr 30min); Lyon (hourly; 2hr); Mâcon (hourly; 1hr 10min); Nevers (5–7 daily; 2hr 20min); Nuits St-Georges (1–3 hourly; 20min); Paris Bercy (6 daily 3hr); Paris-Lyon (every 30min–1hr; 1hr 30min); Reims (every 30min–1hr; 3hr 20min); Tonnerre (10–12 daily; 1hr); Troyes (daily; 2hr 10min).

**By bus** The *gare routière* is next door to the train station.

Destinations Avallon (1–5 daily; 2hr–2hr 30min); Montbard (5 daily; 40min).

## GETTING AROUND

**By tram** The city has a great many tram stops, making cars unnecessary in the centre (☞ divia.fr; €1.40 single).

**Bike rental** Dijon is very bicycle-friendly; rent bicycles from ☞ divia.fr/page/diviavelodi, which has 400 stations around the city.

**Car rental** Many people rent a car from Dijon to explore the nearby vineyards. Car companies at the train station include Avis, Sixt and Enterprise.

## INFORMATION

**Tourist office** The central office is near place Notre-Dame at 11 rue des Forges (April–Sept Mon–Sat 9.30am–6.30pm, Sun & public hols 10am–6pm; Oct–March Mon–Sat 9.30am–1pm & 2–6pm, Sun & public hols 10am–4pm; ☎ 08 92 70 05 58, ☞ destinationdijon.com). There's a second office at the Centre Hospitalier Spécialisé de la Chartreuse, by the Well of Moses.

**Tours** You can book guided city tours that include the Well of Moses (€8), or longer minibus tours of local vineyards (from €62) at the tourist office.

8

**Passes** The tourist office sells the Dijon City Pass (from €25/24hr), which offers free entry to some sights, free public transport, free tastings and free guided tours.

## ACCOMMODATION

**Le Chambellan** 92 rue Vannerie ☎03 80 67 12 67, ⓦhotel-chambellan.com. A no-frills two-star hotel with comfortable, modernized rooms and sparkling bathrooms, clustered around a pretty seventeenth-century courtyard. Breakfast €7.50. Special deal with nearby parking, €7/day. **€55**

★ **GH La Cloche** 14 place Darcy ☎03 80 30 12 32, ⓦhotel-lacloche.com. Here, at the best hotel in Dijon, a grand luxury pile built in 1882, you get luxurious rooms and a gourmet restaurant (menus from €28.50). Famed past guests include Napoléon III, Rodin, Saint-Saëns, Maurice Chevalier and Grace Kelly, among others. There's a sauna and fitness centre, a beautiful *terrasse* and secure parking (€15). Breakfast €23. **€179**

★ **Le Jacquemart** 32 rue Verrerie ☎03 80 60 09 60, ⓦhotel-lejacquemart.fr. Run by the same charming management as *Le Chambellan* (see above), this elegant hotel has comfortable and quiet, high-ceilinged rooms. Breakfast €7.50, parking €6. **€67**

★ **Le Jura** 14 av Foch ☎03 80 41 61 12, ⓦoceania hotels.com. By far the best of the huddle of options in the av Foch opposite the *gare SNCF*, this mid-nineteenth-century hotel is a famous Dijon landmark. The spacious, comfortable rooms have been modernized and are surprisingly quiet. The much-photographed old lift with its clocks will charm you even as you enter the reception. Breakfast €15, nearby parking €15. **€144**

**Philippe le Bon** 18 rue Ste-Anne ☎03 80 30 73 52, ⓦhotelphilippelebon.com. Refined old building in an agreeable garden opposite the Musée de la Vie Bourguignonne. The most expensive rooms are lovely; full of character and beautifully restored; the others are plush but a little bland in comparison. Great restaurant in the garden below; you can buy its wines at reception. Breakfast €17. **€115**

**Le Sauvage** 64 rue Monge ☎03 80 41 31 21, ⓦhotel lesauvage.com. A delightful former coaching inn with large and elegant rooms overlooking a vine-draped courtyard. Despite being in the liveliest quarter of town, it's peaceful. Breakfast €8, parking €5. **€57**

★ **Wilson** 1 rue de Longvic ☎03 80 66 82 50, ⓦwilson-hotel.com. This is a good place to stay if you have a car; it's a ten-minute walk north to the centre. The seventeenth-century former coaching inn has bags of character and retains its original features. There's a delicious breakfast buffet made with local produce (€14) and the bar, with its open fire, is a nice spot to sip a Burgundy in winter. Parking €10. **€76**

## EATING

Dijon has a number of excellent restaurants, particularly around rue Monge, while pretty place Émile-Zola is packed with the open-air tables of reasonably priced brasseries.

**La Crêpitante** 31 rue Verrerie ☎03 45 08 17 25, ⓦlacrepitante.com. This new crêperie in an attractive old building is a breath of fresh air, marrying organic Burgundian produce and Breton dishes. Try the oeufs en meurette in a galette (€12.50) or a seasonal special. You must try the salted caramel for dessert. Tues–Sat 1.45am–1.45pm & 7–9.30pm.

★ **La Dame d'Aquitaine** 23 place Bossuet ☎03 80 30 45 65, ⓦladamedaquitaine.fr. Possibly the best restaurant in Dijon, according to the locals; it's set in the thirteenth-century crypt of the magnificent seventeenth-century *Perreney de Balleure* hôtel particulier. It has everything: ambience, friendly service, good food and *menus* starting at €29. Booking recommended. Mon–Wed 7–9pm, Thurs–Sat noon–2pm & 7–9pm.

**Le Grand Café** 5 rue du Château ☎03 80 30 97 26, ⓦbrasserie-legrandcafe.com. A Dijonnais institution, this is a very popular, grand bar/brasserie/wine bar/restaurant, depending on the time of day. You can have a plat du jour for €9.50, salads for €12 or just sip a coffee and relax. May–Oct Mon–Thurs 8am–midnight, Fri & Sat 8am–1am; Nov–April Mon–Thurs 8am–9pm, Fri & Sat 8am–11pm.

★ **Maison Millière** 10 rue de la Chouette ☎03 80 30 99 99, ⓦmaison-milliere.fr. Don't miss out on dining in this 1483 building – so photogenic that part of the film *Cyrano de Bergerac*, starring Gérard Depardieu, was filmed here. The back garden is almost as delightful as the €29 *menu bourguignon*, and in winter the historic upstairs dining room makes a cosy alternative. After you've sampled the local food, you can pop into the adjoining shop and stock up on ingredients. Booking is a must. Tues–Sun: restaurant noon–2pm (Tues–Thurs & Sun) & 7–9.30pm (Fri & Sat); shop 10am–7pm.

**O'Bannelier** 24 rue Bannelier ☎03 80 30 86 91, ⓦobannelier.wordpress.com. Nice, stylish little restaurant, run by a young couple, serving traditional Burgundian cuisine made with local produce. A three-course lunch is good value at €18 and main courses start at €14. To finish, the *café gourmand* (coffee with a selection of small desserts, €8) is usually a good choice. Mon, Tues & Thurs noon–1.30pm, Fri–Sun noon–1.30pm & 7–9.30pm.

**Le Piano qui Fume** 36 rue Berbisey ☎03 80 30 35 45, ⓦlepianoquifume.com. A restaurant that prides itself on the freshness and topicality of its *menus*, made with seasonal ingredients. Its motto is "Cuisine is an art and art is patience". Highly rated by the locals. *Menus* from €31, booking advised. Mon & Tues noon–1.45pm, Thurs–Sat noon–1.45pm & 7–9.45pm.

**Pourquoi pas?** 13 rue Monge ☎ 03 80 50 11 77. A Dijon stalwart, serving fresh, sophisticated French cuisine at very reasonable prices. There's a short, but good-value wine list, a good cheese board and the desserts are simply wonderful. *Menus* from €29 or try the four-course *menu surprise* (€48) where the chef chooses the dishes for you. Booking essential, two weeks in advance in season. Tues–Fri 7.15–9.15pm, Sat noon–1.30pm & 7.15–9.15pm.

**Le Pré aux Clercs** 13 place de la Libération ☎ 03 80 38 05 05, ⓦ lepreauxclercs.fr. This smart brasserie, part of three-Michelin-star chef Georges Blanc's empire, serves traditional French cuisine with the added bonus of an excellent wine list and views of the Ducal palace. *Menus* start at €26 and they also have some stylish rooms and suites to rent (from €110). Daily noon–2pm & 7–10pm.

★ **Stéphane Derbord** 10 place du Président-Wilson ☎ 03 80 67 74 64, ⓦ restaurantstephanederbord.fr. Next to Hôtel Wilson (see Accommodation), this is the place to go for a special meal. Creative Burgundian cuisine is on the menu at this Michelin-starred restaurant. Expect the likes of perch and frog cannelloni followed by pigeon breast rubbed with vanilla seeds. Lunch menu €30, evening menus from €55. Tues–Sat noon–1.45pm & 7.30–9.15pm.

## DRINKING AND NIGHTLIFE

Dijon is an important university city as well as one of France's main conference centres, with a nightlife to span the spectrum. Rue Berbisey is a good place to start a night out.

**Deep Inside Klub Rock** 16 rue Victor-Dumay ☎ 03 80 54 20 66. The place to go for a hot and sweaty night out if you like live rock music. The bar, with a good selectin of beers, is on the ground floor and the stage is in the cellar. Gigs take place several nights a week starting at 8.30/9pm. Mon–Sat 6pm–2am.

**Dr Wine** 5 rue Musette ☎ 03 80 53 35 16, ⓦ drwine. fr. Popular wine bar, restaurant and shop, in an old *hôtel particulier*, with more than 1,000 labels on the menu and around 25 by the glass (€4–12). Decent food to soak it up with too (three courses €19.90). Tues–Sat 10am–3pm & 6pm–2am.

**Flannery's** 4 place St-Bénigne ☎ 03 80 44 94 33, ⓦ flannerys.fr. A popular Irish bar (which one isn't?) with a particularly good selection of whiskeys. Big-screen sport and live gigs on Tuesdays attract many students. Guinness €6 a pint. Daily 4.30pm–2am.

★ **Péniche Cancale** Port du Canal ☎ 03 80 43 15 72, ⓦ penichecancale.com. At the small port west of the city centre, this barge is not only a restaurant and hip bar but hosts live world music gigs or DJs from Thurs to Sat (entry fee varies for events). April–Sept Tues & Wed 6pm–midnight, Thurs–Sat 6pm–2am; Oct–March Thurs–Sat 7pm–2am.

**Le Quentin** 6 rue Quentin ☎ 03 80 30 15 05. Cool café-bar with lounge music inside and a terrace outside that looks onto the market. Ideal for people-watching on market days or for an *apéro* on a sunny evening. Mon & Wed 5pm–1am, Tues & Fri 11am–2pm & 5pm–2am, Thurs 5pm–2am, Sat 11am–2am.

## SHOPPING

Dijon, with its range of gastronomic specialties, from spicy condiments to sticky, sweet pastries, is a particularly good place to buy foodie gifts. Listed here are the best shops in their own genre.

**Au Vieux Millésime** 82 rue Monge ☎ 03 80 41 28 79, ⓦ auvieuxmillesime.com. As capital of the Burgundy region, Dijon presides over some great winemaking country: sommelier Ludovic Flexas offers helpful advice on wines from the region and further afield; prices start at around €6. Tues–Fri 10am–12.30pm & 2–7pm, Sat 10am–7pm.

**Fabrice Gillotte** 21 rue du Bourg ☎ 03 80 30 38 88, ⓦ fabrice-gillotte.com. One of Dijon's numerous foodie specialities is chocolate, and Gillotte is the city's most famous *chocolaterie*. Absolutely irresistible. Mon 2–7pm, Tues–Fri 9.15am–noon & 2–7pm, Sat 9am–12.30pm & 2–7pm.

**Maille** 32 rue de la Liberté ☎ 03 80 30 41 02, ⓦ maille. com. Dijon is, of course, the high temple of mustard, with many producers, but Maille is the greatest of them all, with a history stretching back nearly 300 years and around 80 mustards currently on its lists. This store sells a wide range, from mild-tasting to cauterizing. Mon–Sat 10am–7pm.

**Mulot et Petitjean** 13 place Bossuet ☎ 03 80 30 07 10, ⓦ mulotpetitjean.fr. Visit the beautiful headquarters of this renowned producer of *pain d'épices*, a kind of gingerbread made with honey and spices and eaten with butter or jam. Mon 2–7pm, Tues–Sat 9am–noon & 2–7pm.

# The Côte d'Or

South of Dijon, the attractive countryside of the **Côte d'Or** is characterized by the steep scarp of the *côte*, wooded along the top and cut by sheer little valleys called *combes*, where local rock climbers hone their skills. Spring is a good time to visit this region;

8

you can avoid the crowds and the landscape is a dramatic symphony of browns – trees, earth and vines – punctuated by millions of bone-coloured vine stakes, standing like crosses in a vast war cemetery. The main administrative and shopping centre is the beautiful city of **Beaune**, south of which is the **Great Wine Route** which checks off the big names in Burgundy winemaking.

## The Great Wine Route

The place names that line the legendary **Great Wine Route** Nationale 74 – Gevrey-Chambertin, **Vougeot**, Vosne-Romanée, Nuits-St-Georges, **Pommard**, Volnay, **Meursault** – are music to the ears of wine buffs. These prosperous villages are full of wine cellars where you can get good advice on different vintages; you can taste and buy direct from the source at most of the **vineyards** by just turning up and asking.

### Château du Clos-de-Vougeot

Clos de Vougeot, some 20km south of Dijon between Gévrey-Chambertin and Nuits-St-Georges • Daily: April–Oct 9am–6.30pm (Sat until 5pm); Nov–March 10am–5pm • €7.50 • ☎ 03 80 62 86 09, ⓦ closdevougeot.fr

If you're interested in French wine culture, it's worth visiting the **Château du Clos-de-Vougeot** to see the winemaking process. Particularly impressive are the mammoth thirteenth-century winepresses installed by the Cistercian monks who owned these vineyards for nearly seven hundred years. The land now belongs to more than eighty different owners, each growing and marketing their own wine.

### Le Cassissium

On the outskirts on Nuits-St-Georges • April to mid-Nov daily 10am–1pm & 2–7pm; mid-Nov to March Tues–Sat 10.30am–1pm & 2–5.30pm; 90min guided tours • €9.50 • ☎ 03 80 62 49 70, ⓦ cassissium.fr

Fans of cassis (blackcurrant liqueur) should drop by **Le Cassissium**, where you can enjoy a comprehensive guided tour of the cassis factory and learn about the history of the

---

### THE WINES OF BURGUNDY

Burgundy farmers have been growing grapes since Roman times, and Burgundy's **wines** are some of the most renowned in the world. In recent years, though, Burgundy's vineyards, and those in other regions of France, have suffered due to competition from the southern hemisphere. However, because of stringent legal restrictions banning watering and other interference, French wines, more than others, remain a faithful reflection of the *terroir* where they are produced, and Burgundy experts remain confident that the climate and soil of their region will fight off any temporary economic challenges.

Burgundy's best wines come from a narrow strip of hillside called the **Côte d'Or** that runs southwest from Dijon to Santenay, and is divided into two regions, Côte de Nuits (the better reds) and Côte de Beaune (the better whites). The vineyards here (small parcels of land known as climats) became a UNESCO World Heritage Site in 2015. High-quality wine is certainly produced further south as well though, in the **Mâconnais** and on the **Côtes Chalonnaises**. Reds from the region are made almost exclusively from the Pinot Noir grape, while whites are largely from Chardonnay. Fans of bubbly should look out for the often highly regarded **sparkling** whites, which crop up across the region and won't set you back half as much as a bottle of Champagne.

The single most important factor determining the "character" of wines is the **soil**. In both the Côte d'Or and **Chablis** (see page 441), its character varies over very short distances, making for an enormous variety of taste. Chalky soil makes a wine drier and more acidic – while clay brings more fruitiness and body to it.

For an **apéritif** in Burgundy, you should try kir, named after the man who was both mayor and MP for Dijon for many years after World War II – two parts dry white wine, traditionally *aligoté*, and one part cassis. To round the evening off there are many **liqueurs** to choose from, but Burgundy is particularly famous for its marcs, of which the best are matured for years in oak casks.

blackcurrant. For some delicious artisanal cassis head up the hill along the D109 to the hamlet of Concoeur and the boutique of Ferme Fruirouge (2 pl de l'Église; Mon & Thurs–Sun 9am–noon & 2–7pm; ⓦfruirouge.fr).

### Château de Pommard

15 rue Marey-Monge, near Beaune • "Experiences" (see below) need to be pre-booked • ☎ 03 80 22 07 99, ⓦ chateaudepommard.com

Apart from being one of the great names in Burgundy, having been established in 1726 to furnish the tables of Louis XV, the **Château de Pommard** offers a variety of interesting "experiences" from educational tastings (€20) to learning about the climats (vineyard tour, €30) and joining in the grape harvest (€100). Since 2014 the business has been owned by American entrepreneur Michael Baum who is easing the château into the twenty-first century – they even hold a rock festival, Rootstock, in July (ⓦrootstockmusic.com).

### Olivier Leflaive

10 place du Monument, Puligny-Montrachet • Restaurant: Mon–Sat noon–1.30pm & 7–8.30pm • Tastings €20 for four wines; double rooms from €190 • ☎ 03 80 21 37 65, ⓦ olivier-leflaive.com

The Leflaive family has been making wine for more than 370 years, but **Olivier Leflaive**, the current family head (now retired), was the first in 2007 to combine the concept of a vineyard tour, wine tastings, a gourmet meal (*menu* €65) and four-star lodgings all in one location, including several premiers and grands crus.

### Château de Meursault

Meursault • Daily: May–Sept 10am–6.30pm; Oct–April 10am–noon & 2–6pm • Tastings from €21.50, must be pre-booked • ☎ 03 80 26 22 75, ⓦ chateau-meursault.com

The **Château de Meursault** in Meursault is one of the oldest estates in Burgundy, with extensive and beautiful grounds. It is the most prestigious producer of Burgundy Chardonnay, and is open to the public for tastings, during which you'll see their magnificent twelfth to sixteenth-century cellars.

## Beaune

**BEAUNE**, the principal town of the Côte d'Or, manages to maintain its attractively ancient air, despite a near-constant stream of wine aficionados using the place as their base. Narrow cobbled streets and sunny squares dotted with cafés make it a lovely, albeit expensive, spot to sample the region's wine. The Saturday-morning market is well worth a visit.

### Hôtel-Dieu (Hospices de Beaune)

Place de la Halle • Daily: April to mid-Nov 9am–6.30pm; mid-Nov to March 9–11.30am & 2–5.30pm; last admission 1hr before closing • €11.30 • ☎ 03 80 24 45 00, ⓦ hospices-de-beaune.com

Beaune's chief attraction is the fifteenth-century hospital, the **Hôtel-Dieu**, founded in 1443 by chancellor of Burgundy, Nicholas Rolin. As grateful ex-patients or their families donated vine plots to the hospital, the town prospered quickly to become the centre of the local wine trade. The cobbled courtyard is surrounded by a wooden gallery overhung by a massive roof patterned with diamonds of variegated tiles – green, burnt sienna, black and yellow – and similarly multicoloured steep-pitched dormers and turrets. Inside is a vast paved hall with a glorious arched timber roof, the Grande Salle des Malades, with the original enclosed wooden beds. Passing through two smaller, furnished wards, one with some stunning seventeenth-century frescoes, then the kitchen and the pharmacy, you reach a dark chamber housing the splendid fifteenth-century altarpiece of the *Last Judgement* by Rogier van der Weyden and the tapestry of St Éloi, which is comparable to the *Lady and the Unicorn* in the Musée National du Moyen Âge in Paris (see page 91).

8

## Marché aux Vins

7 rue de l'Hôtel-Dieu • Daily: April–Nov 10am–7pm; Dec–March 10am–noon & 2–7pm • €10 allows you to sample 4 wines, €15 for 6 wines • ☎ 03 80 25 08 20, ⓦ marcheauxvins.com

If you're keen to indulge in a **wine-tasting** session, head to the **Marché aux Vins**, where you can wander freely through the atmospheric Église des Cordeliers and its caves, sampling the wines. Note, however, that the operative word here is "sample".

## Musée du Vin de Bourgogne

Rue d'Enfer • 10am–1pm & 2–6pm; March, Oct & Nov Wed–Sun; April–Sept Mon & Wed–Sun; • €4.80 • ☎ 03 80 22 08 19

The former residence of the dukes of Burgundy now houses the **Musée du Vin de Bourgogne**, featuring, among other things, giant winepresses, a collection of traditional tools of the trade and a relief map of the vineyards that helps to make sense of it all.

## Fallot Moutarderie

31 rue du Faubourg-Bretonnière • Tours daily 10am–4.30pm • €10 • ☎ 03 80 22 10 10, ⓦ fallot.com

Surprisingly, French mustard – even Dijon – cannot be termed *appellation contrôlée* because most mustard seeds are imported from Canada nowadays. Only Fallot – established in 1840 – can claim to produce some brands with all ingredients (including seeds and verjuice) that are sourced locally with old-fashioned recipes. The **Fallot Moutarderie** offers a quirky and fun tour of the factory, finishing off with a hefty plate of mustard-related amuse-bouches at the end.

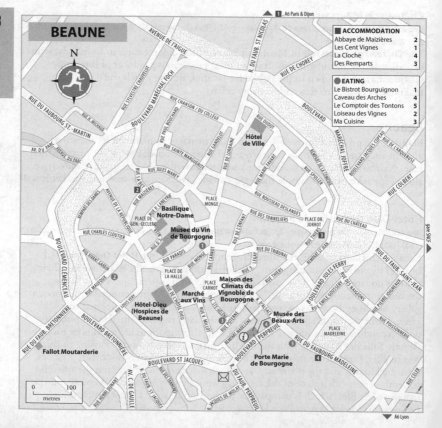

## ARRIVAL AND INFORMATION

**By train** The *gare SNCF* is east of the centre on av du 8-septembre, a 5min walk from the old walls. Local buses also stop here.

Destinations Chalon-sur-Saône (1–3 hourly; 45min); Dijon (1–3 hourly; 25min); Lyon (hourly; 1hr 10min); Mâcon (1–3 hourly; 50min).

**Tourist office** The well-managed tourist office, who organize a number of tours, is at 6 bd Perpreuil (April, May & Mon–Sat 9am–6.30pm, Sun 9.30am–6pm; June–Sept Mon–Sat 9am–7pm, Sun 9am–6pm; Nov–March Mon–Sat 9.30am–12.30pm & 1.30–6pm, Sun 10am–12.30pm

## BEAUNE

& 1.30–5pm; ☏ 03 80 26 21 30, ⓦ beaune-tourism.com). There is a smaller information point by the Hôtel-Dieu. Next to the main tourist office on bd Perpreuil is the Maison des Climats du Vignoble de Bourgogne (daily 9am–noon & 1.30–6pm; free), opened in 2017, which explains the Côte d'Or's unique wine-growing area following its UNESCO listing in 2015.

**Bike rental** Bourgogne Randonnées, 7 av 8-septembre near the train station (March–Oct Mon–Sat 9am–noon & 1.30–6pm, Sun 10am–noon & 2–6pm; €19/day; ☏ 03 80 22 06 03, ⓦ bourgogne-randonnees.fr).

## ACCOMMODATION

★ **Abbaye de Maizières** 19 rue Maizières ☏ 03 80 24 74 64, ⓦ hotelabbayedemaizieres.com. Located in a twelfth-century abbey, this hotel has beautifully decorated rooms with exposed stone walls, wall hangings and medieval-style tapestries. Air-conditioned and with a great restaurant (dinner only 7–9pm); the only minor quibble is the lack of a lift. Beware the steep stairs and watch your head as you come in. Breakfast €20. **€159.50**

**Les Cent Vignes** 10 rue Auguste-Dubois ☏ 03 80 22 03 91, ⓔ campinglescentvignes@mairie-beaune.fr. This popular and very pretty campsite with a tennis court and swimming pool is about 1km north of town, off rue du Faubourg-St-Nicolas (the N74 to Dijon), before the bridge over the *autoroute*. Booking is advisable. Closed Nov to mid-March. **€16.50**

**La Cloche** 40 rue du Faubourg-Madeleine ☏ 03 80 24 66 33, ⓦ hotel-lacloche-beaune.com. Located near the station, this hotel offers sympathetically decorated rooms that complement the elegant old building and the knowledgeable staff are happy to advise on the best wine tours. Breakfast €12, parking €5.50. **€74**

**Des Remparts** 48 rue Thiers ☏ 03 80 24 94 94, ⓦ hotel-remparts-beaune.com. Run by Élyane, a delightful former headmistress, this is a wonderful hotel, sensitively restored and full of old beams and ancient stone. You can still see the ramparts that give it its name from the windows of some of the more expensive rooms. They rent bikes too. Breakfast €13. **€132**

## EATING

★ **Le Bistrot Bourguignon** 8 rue Monge ☏ 03 80 22 23 24. This relaxed and friendly bistro and wine bar specializes in regional cuisine (main courses around €20) and prides itself on having been the first wine bar in Burgundy to serve wine by the glass – and it's not just any old vin de table: your host is particularly passionate about regional wines. Tues–Sat 12.15–2pm & 7.15–10pm.

**Caveau des Arches** 10 bd Perpreuil ☏ 03 80 22 10 37, ⓦ caveau-des-arches.com. Excellent dining in a gorgeously renovated cellar, and surprisingly affordable given the plush surroundings. The great-value *menu bourguignon* costs just €26. Booking recommended. Tues–Sat noon–1.30pm & 7–9.30pm.

**Le Comptoir des Tontons** 22 rue du Faubourg-Madeleine ☏ 03 80 24 19 64, ⓦ lecomptoirdestontons. com. Just outside the town walls, this down-to-earth restaurant serves a lot of organic produce, including wine.

Three-course *menu* €43. Booking recommended. Tues–Sat 7–10.30pm.

★ **Loiseau des Vignes** 31 rue Maufoux ☏ 03 80 24 12 06, ⓦ bernard-loiseau.com. A beautiful Michelin-star restaurant serving exquisitely presented food, which is part of the empire of the late three-Michelin-star chef Bernard Loiseau (see page 452). Don't expect hearty Burgundian cooking: these platters are works of art, accompanied by a superb wine list – more than seventy available by the glass. Lunch is available from a very reasonable €25 and dinner from €59. There's even a lush garden for summer dining. Tues–Sat noon–2pm & 7–10pm.

**Ma Cuisine** Passage Ste-Hélène ☏ 03 80 22 30 22. A simple yet stylish restaurant serving traditional French cuisine, with *menus* from €28 to €70 and a wine list with no fewer than 900 wines, dazzling even the Michelin inspectors. Mon, Tues, Thurs & Fri noon–1.45pm & 7–9.45pm.

# The Saône valley

The **Saône valley** south from **Chalon-sur-Saône** via **Tournus** all the way to **Mâcon** is prosperous and modern, nourished by tourism, industry (especially metalworking), and the wine trade. But turn your back on the river and head west and you immediately enter a different Burgundy, full of hilly pastures and woodland. This country is best known for its produce: the white wines of the **Mâconnais** are justly renowned, and the handsome white cattle that luxuriate in the green fields of the **Charolais** are an obvious sign that this is serious beef territory.

In the past, the region was famed for its religious institutions; almost every village clusters under the tower of a Romanesque church, spawned by the authority of the great abbey at **Cluny**. Many large and powerful abbeys were established in the eleventh and twelfth centuries under the aegis of Cluny.

## Chalon-sur-Saône

**CHALON** is a sizeable port and bustling town on a broad meander of the Saône. Its old riverside quarter has an easy charm, and the town itself makes a cheap and cheerful base for exploring the more expensive areas of the Côte d'Or.

The highlight of the **old town**, set just back from the river, is the lively **place St-Vincent**, where you can sit outside a café and admire the twin towers of the Romanesque cathedral, surrounded by medieval timber-framed houses. The Saône **quays**, meanwhile, provide some nice, though not always shaded, walking opportunities.

### Musée Niépce

28 quai des Messageries • Daily except Tues: July & Aug 10am–6pm; Sept–June 9.30am–11.45am & 2–5.45pm • Free • ☎ 03 85 48 41 98, Ⓦ museeniepce.com

Not far from the tourist office is the unusual **Musée Niépce**. Nicéphore Niépce, who was born in Chalon, is credited with inventing photography in 1816 – though he named it "heliography". The museum possesses a fascinating range of cameras, from the first machine ever to the Apollo moon mission's equipment, plus an interesting selection of photographs.

### ARRIVAL AND INFORMATION

**By train** *Gares SNCF* and *routière* are a 15min walk west of the centre, following av Jean-Jaurès and bd de la République.
Destinations (train) Dijon (1–3 hourly; 40min); Lyon (hourly; 1hr 20min); Mâcon (hourly; 30min).
Destinations (bus) Autun (2–4 daily; 1hr 15min); Cluny (5 daily; 1hr 20min); Le Creusot (2–5 daily; 1hr 20min); Mâcon (5 daily; 2hr).
**Tourist office** 4 place du Port Villiers, by the riverside (April–Oct daily 9.30am–12.30pm & 2–6pm; Nov–March Tues–Sat 9.30am–12.30pm & 2–5.30pm; ☎ 03 85 48 37 97, Ⓦ achalon.com).

### ACCOMMODATION

★ **À La Villa Boucicaut** 33bis av Boucicaut ☎ 03 85 90 80 45, Ⓦ la-villa-boucicaut.fr. Undoubtedly the nicest place to stay in Chalon, this peaceful hotel is a few minutes' walk from the stations. Run by a charming couple, who designed each of the beautifully furnished and decorated rooms themselves. They can also arrange wine tastings. Breakfast €11.50, parking €7. **€99**

**Camping du Pont de Bourgogne** Rue Julien-Leneveu, St-Marcel ☎ 03 85 48 26 86, Ⓦ camping-chalon.com. Cross the most northerly of Chalon's bridges and head east – the campsite is 1km out of town on the south bank of the Saône in St-Marcel. It offers cycles for hire, and a bar-restaurant. Closed Oct–March. **€17.50**

**Le St-Georges** 32 av Jean-Jaurès ☎ 03 85 90 80

---

**CHALON FESTIVALS**

You may be tempted to visit Chalon during the pre-Lent **carnival** (Feb or March), which features a parade of giant masks and a confetti battle, or for one of the most remarkable festivals in Burgundy, the three-day **Montgolfiades** which has a display and a race of dozens of multi-coloured hot-air balloons; it take place in the last weekend of May (Ⓦ montgolfiades71.com). As most of the sponsors are wine producers, the event is a great excuse to drink and be merry.

50, ⓦle-saintgeorges.fr. A lovely boutique hotel in a nineteenth-century building in the centre of Chalon. It has a huge Nuxe spa, sauna and hammam suite and its own, very good, restaurant owned by three-Michelin-star chef Georges Blanc. Breakfast €15, parking on site €7. **€122**

## EATING AND DRINKING

Rue de Strasbourg, on the so-called Île aux Restos, is lined with excellent places to eat, while the small river island of St-Laurent across the eponymous bridge is the nightlife centre, filled with good bars.

**Le Bistrot** 31 rue de Strasbourg ☎ 03 85 93 22 01. Tomato-red outside and chic to an almost Parisian degree inside, this restaurant is not difficult to spot. Chef Patrick Mézière offers serious quality for around €36, with lunch *menus* at €21. Much of the produce is grown by the man himself, on his potager outside the town. Some premiers crus on the wine list, which is highly commendable. Tues–

Sat noon–1.30pm & 7.30–9pm.

**Chez Jules** 11 rue de Strasbourg ☎ 03 85 48 08 34, ⓦrestaurant-chezjules.com. This husband and wife enterprise is a good choice for traditional favourites, with special focus on Burgundian cuisine. *Menus* €28.50–34. Mon–Wed noon–1.30pm & 7–9.30pm, Fri & Sat noon–1.30pm & 7–10.30pm.

**Le Majorelle** 13 place St-Vincent ☎ 03 85 94 04 16. You get good, solid *menus* with some great desserts in this unassuming brasserie, but also the fastest service in the laidback square of St-Vincent. Dishes €11–19. Daily 9am–9.15pm.

# Tournus

Graced by ancient, golden buildings, **TOURNUS** is a beautiful little town on the banks of the Saône, 28km south of Chalon. Its main attraction is the old abbey church of **St-Philibert**, one of the earliest and thus most influential Romanesque buildings in Burgundy. Its construction began around 900 AD but the present building dates back to the first half of the eleventh century. The facade, with its powerful towers and simple decoration of Lombard arcading, is somewhat reminiscent of a fortress.

## Hôtel-Dieu

April–Oct Wed–Sun 10am–1pm & 2–6pm • ☎ 03 85 51 23 50 • €5

To the south of town is the **Hôtel-Dieu**, a seventeenth-century charity hospital. You can still see the rows of solid, oak beds, in which patients lay until 1982, but the real highlight is the elaborate dispensary, complete with a host of faïence pots and hand-blown glass jars. The building also houses the **Musée Greuze**, which pays homage to one of Tournus' best-known citizens, the Enlightenment painter Jean-Baptiste Greuze.

## ACCOMMODATION                                                     TOURNUS

**Greuze** 5 place de l'Abbaye ☎ 03 85 51 77 77, ⓦhotelgreuze.fr. Four-star hotel that offers plush rooms with all luxuries as well as a spa which stocks wine-based beauty products. They also have an attached Michelin-

starred restaurant (1 rue Albert-Thibaudet; menus from €41; ⓦrestaurant-greuze.fr). The bedrooms are all lovely, but the most expensive offer a stunning view of the abbey. Breakfast buffet €14. Free parking. **€170**

# Mâcon

**MÂCON** is a lively, prosperous town built by the River Saône, 58km south of Chalon and 68km north of Lyon, with excellent transport connections between the two. A centre for the wine trade, with a surprisingly relaxed, holiday resort atmosphere in summer, thanks to its long café-lined **riverbank** and free outdoor concerts in late June, July and August; it also boasts the best **nightlife** between Dijon and Lyon. It is, however, a nightmare to drive around and parking is problematic, so it's not recommended as a base for a regional wine-tasting tour for anyone renting a car.

## Musée des Ursulines

5 rue des Ursulines • Tues–Sat 10am–noon & 2–6pm, Sun 2–6pm • €3 • ☎ 03 85 38 90 38

The **Musée des Ursulines** is based in a seventeenth-century convent with a chequered history, having served not only as a convent but also as a prison and then as a barracks.

8

**8**

## ALPHONSE LAMARTINE: THE GREAT ROMANTIC

Often compared to Lord Byron, **Alphonse Lamartine** (1790–1869) is one of the best known of the French Romantic poets. He was born and grew up in Milly (now called Milly-Lamartine), about 15km west of Mâcon, and published his first poetic work, *Méditations poétiques*, in 1820. After the 1830 Revolution in Paris, he became involved in politics and was elected to the Chambre des Députés in 1833.

Lamartine, having acquired a reputation as a powerful orator on the weighty questions of the day – like the abolition of slavery and capital punishment – had his finest hour as the leading figure in the provisional government of the Second Republic, which was proclaimed from the Hôtel de Ville in Paris on February 23, 1848. He withdrew from politics when reactionary forces let the army loose on the protesting workers of Paris and Marseille in June 1848. Retiring to St-Point, he continued to write and publish until his death in 1869.

The museum itself features Gallo-Roman artefacts, an exhibition dedicated to Mâcon's history, and a collection of sixteenth- to twentieth-century paintings. On the first floor is a section devoted to Lamartine, the nineteenth-century French Romantic poet (see box above), who was born in Mâcon in 1790 and whose name you will see everywhere.

### ARRIVAL AND INFORMATION

MÂCON

**By train** The *gare SNCF* lies on rue Bigonnet at the southern end of rue Victor-Hugo; TGV trains leave from Mâcon-Loché station 6km out of town. There is a shuttle between the two train stations (Line E) or it's a short taxi ride (€20).
Destinations Bourg-en-Bresse (6 daily; 30min); Chalon-sur-Saône (1–3 hourly; 30min); Dijon (1–3 hourly; 1hr–1hr 20min); Lyon (hourly; 1hr).

**By bus** The *gare routière* is next to the train station.
Destinations Charolles (2–3 daily; 1hr 10min); Cluny (2–3 daily; 30min); Paray-le-Monial (2–3 daily; 1hr 30min); Tournus (1 daily; 50min).

**Tourist office** 1 place St-Pierre (April to mid-June, Sept & Oct Mon–Sat 9.30am–12.30pm & 2–6pm (open Sun in June); mid-June to Aug daily 9am–7pm; Nov–April Tues–Sat 10am–noon & 2–5pm; ☎03 85 21 07 07, ⓦmacon-tourism.com). Among their many brochures and information on the local area they offer a free walking map of the city with all sights clearly marked.

**Cruises** Book at the tourist office for day-long (April–Oct; about €65 with lunch) or half-day cruises on the River Saône (€13).

### ACCOMMODATION

★ **Best Western Plus d'Europe et d'Angleterre** 92–109 quai Jean-Jaurès ☎03 85 38 27 94, ⓦhotel-europeangleterre-macon.com. A nineteenth-century pile that's been brought back to former glory (Colette and the Aga Khan were visitors), this stylish hotel has finely furnished, high-ceilinged rooms, some of which have river views. The downstairs wine bar has a good selection of Burgundy and Rhône wines and regularly hosts tastings. Breakfast €14. Parking €12. **€95**

**Camping Municipal** 1 rue des Grandes-Varennes ☎03 85 38 16 22. This large, local campsite, with excellent facilities including heated pool, bar and a good restaurant, is a better base for touring the Mâconnais with a car than the city itself. It's about 3km north of town off bd du Général-de-Gaulle, a continuation of the N6. Closed mid-Oct to mid-March. **€17**

**Du Nord Quai Jean-Jaurès** ☎03 85 38 08 68, ⓦhotel-dunord.com. Beautiful hotel on the banks of the Saône, offering well-appointed rooms; most have a wonderful view of the river, but check on booking. Breakfast €8. **€90**

### EATING AND DRINKING

**Les Arts** 219 quai Lamartine ☎03 85 32 08 49. The most popular of the many bars on quai Lamartine, with friendly service, large TV screen and cocktails at €7. Sun–Wed 7am–midnight, Thurs–Sat 7am–2am.

★ **Le Poisson d'Or** 266 allée du Parc ☎03 85 38 00 88, ⓦlepoissondor.com. The place to go if you're fed up with *boeuf bourguignon*, this lovely riverside restaurant with a

*terrasse* hanging over the Saône, is a fish-lovers' paradise. Father and son team Pascal and Jefferson Calloud are the talented chefs. If fish isn't your thing though, there's still plenty of choice, such as the buttery *grenouilles*. Menus €30–68. Mon & Thurs–Sat noon–1.30pm 7.30pm–9.15pm, Tues & Sun noon–1.30pm.

# The Mâconnais

The **Mâconnais** wine-producing country lies to the west of the Saône, a 20km-wide strip stretching from Tournus to just south of Mâcon. The region's best white wines, including all the grands crus and some of the best white grands crus, labelled **Pouilly-Fuissé**, come from the southern part of this strip, around the pretty villages of **Pouilly**, **Vinzelles** and **Fuissé**.

## Musée Départemental de Préhistoire

Solutré-Pouilly • Daily: April–Sept 10am–6pm; Oct–March 10am–5pm • €5 • ☎ 03 85 35 82 81, ⓦ rochedesolutre.com

Directly above the villages of Pouilly, Vinzelles and Fuissé rises the distinctive and precipitous 500m rock of **Solutré**, which served as an ambush site for hunters in prehistoric times – around 20,000 BC. The bones of 100,000 horses have been found in the soil beneath the rock, along with mammoth, bison and reindeer carcasses. The history and results of the excavations are displayed in a museum at the foot of the rock, the **Musée Départemental de Préhistoire**.

A steep path climbs to the top of the rock, where, on a clear day, you get a superb view as far as Mont Blanc and the Matterhorn. Look down on the huddled roofs of **Solutré-Pouilly** and you'll see that the slopes beneath you are covered with the vines of the Chardonnay grape, which makes the exquisite greenish Pouilly-Fuissé wine.

| ACCOMMODATION | THE MÂCONNAIS |
|---|---|

★ **La Source des Fées** Rte du May, Fuissé ☎ 03 85 35 67 02, ⓦ lasourcedesfees.com. A distinctive farmhouse *gîte*, whose name, "Fairy Spring", alludes to a nearby spring where fairies were supposed to have appeared. Convenient (only a 5min drive from the TGV station at Mâcon-Loché) and comfortable, with enormous rooms and suites plus three-course dinners (€30) that are renowned in the area. Rates include wine tasting, breakfast and parking. **€128**

**8**

# Cluny

Scattered among the houses of the attractive modern-day town, the **abbey of CLUNY** is the Saône Valley's major tourist destination. The monastery was founded in 910 AD in response to the corruption of the existing church, and it took only a couple of vigorous early abbots to transform the power of Cluny into a veritable empire. Second only to that of the pope, the abbot's power in the Christian world made even monarchs tremble. However, Cluny's spiritual influence gradually declined and the abbey became a royal gift in the twelfth century. Centuries later, in the wake of the Revolution, Hugues de Semur's vast and influential eleventh-century **church**, which had been the largest building in Christendom until the construction of St Peter's in Rome, was dismantled. The most exciting thing that has happened since has been the burial of Mme Danielle Mitterrand, the former French President's wife, in the town cemetery in 2011; her grave attracts many visitors.

## The abbey

Place de l'Abbaye • Abbey Daily: April–June & Sept 9.30am–6pm; July & Aug 9.30am–7pm; Oct–March 9.30am–5pm • €9.50, includes entry to Clos Vougeot (see page 464) • ☎ 03 85 59 15 93, ⓦ cluny-abbaye.fr **Haras de Cluny** Guided tours April–June, Sept & Oct Tues–Sat 3.30pm, Sun 11am & 3.30pm; July & Aug Tues–Sat 11am, 2.30pm & 4.30pm; • €7 • ☎ 03 85 59 85 19, ⓦ ifce.fr/haras-nationaux/nos-sites **Tour des Fromages** April Mon–Sat 9.30am–1pm & 2–6.30pm; May–Sept daily 9.30am–6.30pm; Oct daily 9.30am–12.30pm & 2.30–5pm; Nov–March Mon–Sat 9.30am–12.30pm & 2.30–5pm • €2.50

What you see of the former **abbey** today is an octagonal belfry and the huge south transept. Standing amid these fragments of a once huge construction gives a tangible and poignant insight into the Revolution's enormous powers of transformation. Access to the belfry is through the Grande École des Ingénieurs, one of France's elite higher-education institutions, and you can often see the students in their grey lab coats. At the back of the abbey is one of France's national stud farms, **Haras de Cluny**, which you can visit, but only on a guided tour. The **Musée d'Art et d'Archéologie**, in the fifteenth-century palace of the last freely elected abbot, helps to flesh out the ruins by renting tablet PCs which provide a representation of what the abbey looked like as you stand on particular spots; from the top of the **Tour des Fromages** (120 steps, entered via the tourist office) an amazing virtual reality screen projects the old buildings onto a live cam that shows the street below.

## ARRIVAL AND INFORMATION CLUNY

**By bus** Buses from both Mâcon (4–6 daily; 30min) and Chalon-sur-Saône (2–5 daily; 1hr 20min) stop on Porte-de-Paris, a 5min walk from the town centre.
**Tourist office** Beside the Tour des Fromages, 6 rue

Mercière (April Mon–Sat 9.30am–1pm & 2–6.30pm; May–Sept daily 9.30am–6.30pm; Oct daily 9.30am–12.30pm & 2.30–5pm; Nov–March Mon–Sat 9.30am–12.30pm & 2.30–5pm; ☎ 03 85 59 05 34, ⓦ cluny-tourisme.com).

## ACCOMMODATION

**De Bourgogne** Place de l'Abbaye ☎ 03 85 59 00 58, ⓦ hotel-cluny.com. Right in the centre of Cluny, built in the walls of the old abbey, this hotel has well-appointed rooms, which look either onto the abbey or the pretty breakfast garden. If you can, splash out for the suite Lamartine at €166. Parking €10, breakfast €11. Great restaurant, too. Closed Dec & Jan. **€99**
**Le Clos de l'Abbaye** 6 place du Marché ☎ 03 85 59 22 06, ⓦ closdelabbaye.fr. An excellent mid-range choice, run by a friendly couple. There are five stylishly decorated rooms in this eighteenth-century building, three of which have a view of the abbey. Breakfast included. **€70**
★ **Le Potin Gourmand** 4 place du Champ de Foire ☎ 03 85 59 02 06, ⓦ potingourmand.com. A lovely, rambling old building, with charming and individually decorated

rooms, set around a courtyard and garden. It also owns a beautiful rustic restaurant that combines local produce with exotic flavours: try the splendid tournedos of Charolais beef with celeriac purée and fresh red-onion pickle (closed lunch & dinner Mon, and Tues lunch; menus from €20). Closed mid-Jan to mid-Feb. Breakfast €13. **€140**
**Hostellerie d'Héloïse** 7 rte de Mâcon ☎ 03 85 59 05 65, ⓦ hostelleriedheloise.com. This recently converted mid-priced establishment, on the banks of the Grosne, used to be the old railway hotel. Light, contemporary and ideal for a stopover, its glory is the attached restaurant (see below), a delight after a long day of travel. Note that both reception and restaurant are closed on Wed, Thurs lunch and Sun eve. Free parking, breakfast €11. **€72**

## EATING AND DRINKING

**Café du Centre** 4 rue Municipale ☎ 03 85 59 10 65. Right in the centre of town, with a charming terrace, this lively, old-fashioned bistro offers simple, tasty dishes and a great selection of salads from €9.50. Tues–Sat 7am–10pm, Sun until 2pm.
**La Nation** 21 rue Lamartine ☎ 03 85 59 05 45. A modern, spacious brasserie with outdoor seating, outstanding service and great plats du jour from €10. The house pichet at €5.50 for 25cl is fantastic value. Daily 8am–10pm; food served noon–2pm & 7–9pm.

★ **La Table d'Héloïse** 7 rte de Mâcon ☎ 03 85 59 05 65, ⓦ hostelleriedheloise.com. A wonderful restaurant attached to the hotel of the same name, serving good, solid Burgundian cuisine followed by delectable desserts. The classic menu de terroir featuring snails under a pastry crust and a cut-with-a-fork tender pavé de Charolais is excellent value at €36. Note that the best tables are on the sun-filled terrasse overlooking the river. Menus from €28, reservations advised. Mon–Tues & Fri–Sat noon–1.45pm & 7.30–8.45pm, Thurs 7.30–8.45pm, Sun noon–1.45pm.

# The Charolais

The **Charolais** takes its name from the pretty little water-enclosed market town of **CHAROLLES**, with its 32 bridges, on the main N79 road. In turn, it gives its name to one of the world's most illustrious breeds of cattle: the white, curly-haired, stocky Charolais, bred for its lean meat. Throughout this region, scattered across the rich farmland, are dozens of small villages, all with Romanesque churches, the offspring of Cluny's vigorous youth.

## Paray-le-Monial

Some 14km west of Charolles, across countryside that becomes ever gentler and flatter as you approach the broad valley of the Loire, is **PARAY-LE-MONIAL**, whose major attraction is its **Basilique du Sacré-Coeur** (daily 9am–8pm). Not only is it an exquisite building in its own right, with a marvellously satisfying arrangement of apses and chapels stacking up in sturdy symmetry to a fine octagonal belfry, it's the best place to get an idea of what the abbey of Cluny looked like, as it was built shortly afterwards in devoted imitation of the mother church.

8

# Poitou-Charentes and the Atlantic coast

476 Poitiers and around

482 Parthenay

483 Niort

484 The Marais Poitevin

485 Les Sables-d'Olonne and around

487 The Île de Noirmoutier

488 La Rochelle and around

492 The Île de Ré

494 Rochefort and around

498 The Île d'Oléron

499 Royan

502 Saintes

504 Cognac

506 Angoulême and around

509 Bordeaux and around

516 The Bordeaux wine region

524 The Côte d'Argent

ÎLE DE RÉ LIGHTHOUSE AND MUSEUM

**9**

# Poitou-Charentes and the Atlantic coast

Newsstands selling *Sud-Ouest* remind you where you are: this is not the Mediterranean, certainly, but in summer the quality of the light, the warm air, the fields of sunflowers and the shuttered siesta-silence of the farmhouses give you the first exciting promises of the south. While foreign tourists flock to Paris or the Riviera when summer arrives, the discerning French head for the west coast. Straddling the regions of Poitou-Charentes, Aquitaine and Pays-de-la-Loire, it's an area of great variety, with Roman cities, rustling marshes, a beautiful wine region and miles of sandy coast, dotted with small islands and slumbering coastal villages.

The coastline is rich in **beaches**, which are especially lovely on the pine-covered, sandy **Côte d'Argent**, south of Bordeaux. The historic port **La Rochelle** is a pleasing mix of Renaissance mansions and ice-cream stalls, and the islands are delightful: **Noirmoutier**, small and idyllic; **Ré**, with long beaches, windswept plains and flashy Parisian guests; **Oléron**, unaffected and blue-collar; and romantic **Île d'Aix**, tiny and windswept. The islands are popular in July and August, but best in late spring or early autumn when the crowds slip away.

Inland, the cities make ideal weekend breaks: elegant **Bordeaux**, with unrivalled dining, nightlife and shopping; young and lively **Poitiers**; and cool, creative **Angoulême**, home to the comic strip. For walkers and cyclists there is the **Marais Poitevin**, a lace-like mass of intertwined canals, and for lovers of Romanesque piety, a long stretch of the church-lined **route to Santiago de Compostela**, the medieval pilgrim path to the shrine of St Jacques (also known as St James and Santiago) in Spain. The finest of the churches, among the best in all of France, are in the countryside around Saintes and Poitiers.

It is a region of seafood – fresh and cheap in markets, restaurants and oyster bars for miles inland. Around Bordeaux are some of the world's top **vineyards**, producing robust reds (claret) and sweet whites like Sauternes. Baked specialities include **macarons**, invented in Saint-Émilion, and *canelés* (sweet pastries made from custard-like batter, and flavoured with rum and vanilla) from Bordeaux.

| **GETTING AROUND** | **POITOU-CHARENTES** |
|---|---|

Bigger towns are well connected by trains, and most smaller towns and villages are accessible by regular but infrequent buses. Off the main routes, particularly in the wine region and on the islands, renting a car or bike is a good idea.

# Poitiers and around

**POITIERS**, sitting on a hilltop overlooking two rivers, is a charming country town whose long and sometimes influential history – as the seat of the dukes of Aquitaine, for instance – is discernible in the winding lines of the streets and the breadth of architectural fashions represented in its buildings. Its pedestrian precincts and wonderful central gardens make for comfortable sightseeing, while the large student population ensures a lively atmosphere in the restaurants and pavement cafés.

**Place du Maréchal-Leclerc** is the heart of the café and restaurant scene, and to the north **place Charles-de-Gaulle** is home to the Marché de Notre-Dame, the covered market (Tues–Sat 6am–8pm), and to outdoor markets held on Tuesday, Thursday, Friday and Saturdays mornings. Between is a rabbit warren of medieval streets.

# Highlights

❶ **Marais Poitevin** A labyrinth of canals, marshes, pastures and ruins, dubbed "green Venice". See page 484

❷ **Île de Ré** Misty beaches, glistening salt marshes, fishing boats, green-shuttered cottages and designer wellies. See page 492

❸ **Île d'Aix** A minuscule island in the Bay of Biscay, where Napoleon made his final stand. See page 496

❹ **Angoulême** Maybe the best-kept secret in France – beautiful, historic, lively, full of things to do, and hardly a tourist in sight. See page 506

❺ **Bordeaux** Known as "La Belle au bois dormant" (Sleeping Beauty), an elegant, serene city notwithstanding the bustling wine bars, cafés, shops and gourmet restaurants. See page 509

❻ **Wine country** Rolling vineyards, magnificent châteaux and the robust flavours of Margaux, Sauternes, St-Émilion, Pauillac, Cognac… the list goes on. See pages 516 and 524

❼ **Dune du Pyla** Europe's largest dune is a mighty mountain of golden sand and the views from the top span the entire Côte d'Argent. See page 527

**HIGHLIGHTS ARE MARKED ON THE MAP ON PAGE 478**

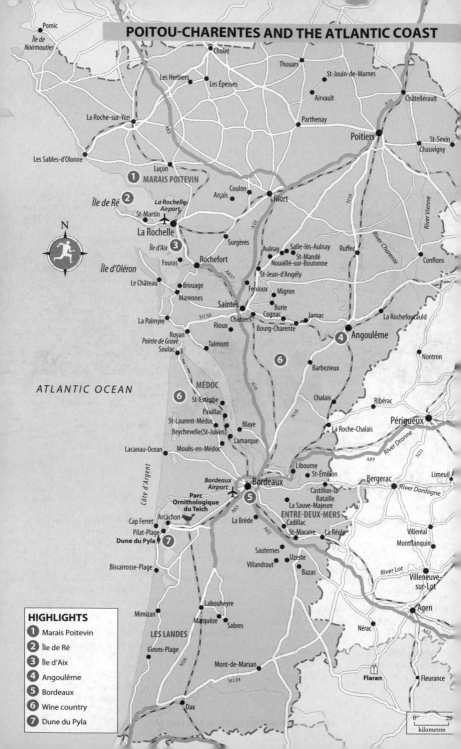

# The church of Notre-Dame-la-Grande

Rue Gambetta cuts north past the old **Palais de Justice** (Mon–Fri 10am–noon, 3–5pm; free), whose nineteenth-century facade hides an older core, including a magnificent Gothic knights' hall. The Palais peers down on one of the most famous churches in France, **Notre-Dame-la-Grande** (daily 9am–7pm), built in the twelfth century during the reign of Eleanor. The most exceptional thing about the church is the west front. The facade is not conventionally beautiful, squat and loaded as it is with detail to a degree that the modern eye could regard as fussy. And yet it's this detail which is enthralling, ranging from the domestic to the disturbingly anarchic. Such elaborate sculpted facades – and domes like pine cones on turret and belfry – are the hallmarks of the Poitou brand of Romanesque. Inside the church, the original Romanesque frescoes are gone, except in the apse vault above the choir, and the crypt. The columns and vaults were repainted by Joly-Leterme in 1851.

# Cathédrale St-Pierre

At the eastern edge of the old town stands the enormous, pale-faced **Cathédrale St-Pierre** (daily 9am–7pm, till 5pm in winter). Some of the stained glass dates from the twelfth century, notably the Crucifixion in the central window of the apse, which supposedly features Henry II and Eleanor. The grand eighteenth-century organ, the Orgue Clicquot, is the cathedral's most striking feature – often put to good and deafening use in summer concerts.

# Baptistère St-Jean

April to mid-June Tues–Sun 2–6pm; mid-June to Sept daily 10.30am–12.30pm & 2–6pm; Oct–March Tues–Sun 2–4pm • €3

In the middle of rue Jean-Jaurès is the patched-up fourth-century **Baptistère St-Jean**, reputedly the oldest Christian building in France. The "font" is an octagonal pool sunk into the floor. Water pipes uncovered in the bottom suggest the water couldn't have been more than 30–40cm deep, which casts doubt on the popular belief that early Christian baptism was by total immersion.

# Musée Sainte-Croix

3bis rue Jean-Jaurès; mid-June to mid-Sept Tues–Sun 10am–6pm; mid-Sept to mid-June Tues–Fri 10am–6pm, Sat & Sun 1–6pm • €4.50, free on Tues and 1st Sun of the month • ⓦ musees-poitiers.org

The town museum, the **Musée Sainte-Croix**, features an interesting Gallo-Roman section with some handsome glass, pottery and sculpture, notably a first-century white marble Minerva. From here, you can cross Pont-Neuf to take the **riverside path** – on the right once you're across the bridge – upstream to Pont St-Cyprien for a picturesque amble.

## ARRIVAL AND DEPARTURE                                      POITIERS

**By plane** Poitiers-Biard Airport (ⓣ05 49 30 04 40, ⓦ poitiers.aeroport.fr) is a short taxi ride (around €12) from the centre.

**By train** The gare SNCF is on boulevard du Grand-Cerf, part of the ring road encircling Poitiers.

Destinations Angoulême (9–20 daily; 45min–1hr 15min); Bordeaux (11–14 daily; 1hr 45min–2hr 30min); Futuroscope (6–17 daily; 10min); La Rochelle (17–23 daily;

1hr 20min–1hr 45min); Limoges (4–8 daily; 2hr); Niort (12–15 daily; 45min); Paris-Montparnasse (10–14 daily; 1hr 25min–2hr 5min); Tours (2–4 daily; from 1hr).

**By bus** The gare routière is on boulevard du Grand-Cerf, next to the gare SNCF.

Destinations Châteauroux (1–3 daily; 2hr 10min); Chauvigny (1–3 daily; 45min); Le Blanc (1–2 daily; 1hr 10min); Parthenay (4–9 daily; 55min); St-Savin (1–2 daily; 45min).

## INFORMATION AND GETTING AROUND

**Tourist office** The tourist office (Mon–Sat 9.30am–6pm; ⓣ05 49 41 21 24, ⓦ ot-poitiers.fr) is a 15min walk from the station, at 45 place Charles-de-Gaulle, and can supply

walkers and cyclists with maps and guides. The Maison du Tourisme, the tourist office for the Vienne region, is at 33 place Charles-de-Gaulle (mid-July to Aug daily 9am–9pm;

Sept to mid-July Mon–Fri 9am–7pm, Sat 10am–1pm & 2–7pm; ☏ 05 49 37 48 58, ⊛ tourisme-vienne.com).

**By bike** Hire bikes from Cyclamen (60 bd Pont-Achard; ☏ 05 49 8813 25; closed Sun & Mon).

**By car** Cars can be rented from National/Citer (97 bd du Grand-Cerf; ☏ 05 49 58 51 58) and Hertz (105 bd du Grand-Cerf; ☏ 05 49 37 48 48).

## ACCOMMODATION

**Auberge de Jeunesse** 1 allée Roger-Tagault ☏ 05 49 30 09 70, ⊛ hifrance.org. Clean, functional hostel that's beginning to look a bit dated. Take bus #3 from the station to "Trois Bourdons", from where it's a 15-minute walk. Well signposted, it's to the right off the N10 Angoulême road. Dorm €15.70

**Les Cours du Clain** 117 chemin de la Grotte-Calvin ☏ 06 10 16 09 55, ⊛ lescoursduclain-poitiers.com. Situated 3.5km southwest of the centre, this B&B in a striking early nineteenth-century château is surrounded by landscaped gardens, with a pool and five sizeable rooms. The hostess is warm and helpful, and the atmosphere tranquil. €100

**De l'Europe** 39 rue Carnot ☏ 05 49 88 12 00, ⊛ hotel-europe-poitiers.com. Good-value spacious rooms in a large hotel, once a coach house, in the centre of Poitiers.

Rooms are almost identical in design; only some are accessible by lift. If you're a light sleeper avoid rooms on the road side. Parking €7; breakfast €10.40. €75.20

**Le Grand Hôtel** 28 rue Carnot ☏ 05 49 60 90 60, ⊛ grandhotelpoitiers.fr. With a sunny terrace and secure parking, this is as private and convenient as you can get, right in the heart of the city. Rooms are warm but unflashy, with everything you'd expect from a Best Western, including a/c, and the buffet breakfast (€12.50) is generous. €116

**Du Plat d'Étain** 7 rue du Plat d'Étain ☏ 05 49 41 04 80, ⊛ poitiers-leplatdetain.com. A no-frills budget option, this classic French hotel offers basic but clean rooms. There's no a/c and it can get noisy, but it's walking distance from all the main sights, has private parking (limited so book ahead) and very competitive deals. €56.80

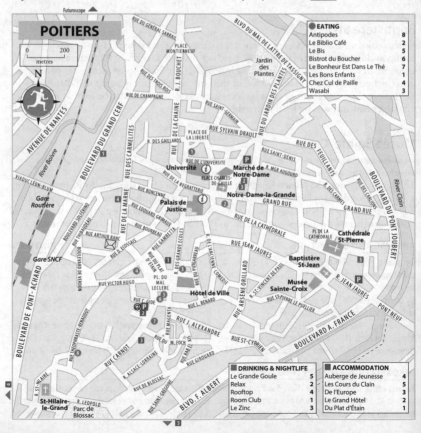

**POITIERS**

0    200
metres

N

Futuroscope ▲

| ● EATING | |
| --- | --- |
| Antipodes | 8 |
| Le Biblio Café | 2 |
| Le Bis | 5 |
| Bistrot du Boucher | 6 |
| Le Bonheur Est Dans Le Thé | 7 |
| Les Bons Enfants | 1 |
| Chez Cul de Paille | 4 |
| Wasabi | 3 |

| ■ DRINKING & NIGHTLIFE | | ■ ACCOMMODATION | |
| --- | --- | --- | --- |
| Le Grande Goule | 5 | Auberge de Jeunesse | 4 |
| Relax | 2 | Les Cours du Clain | 5 |
| Rooftop | 4 | De l'Europe | 3 |
| Room Club | 1 | Le Grand Hôtel | 2 |
| Le Zinc | 3 | Du Plat d'Étain | 1 |

## EATING AND DRINKING

Poitiers has the highest percentage of students of any city in France, which means lots of busy bars and cafés. You can ask about student and youth offers at the Centre Régional d'Information Jeunesse (CRIJ), 64 rue Gambetta (☎ 05 49 60 68 68).

### CAFÉS AND RESTAURANTS

★ **Antipodes** 65 rue Théophraste-Renaudot ☎ 05 49 42 02 93, ⍾restaurant-antipodes.fr. The name is a reference to the chef's tireless roving, which provides the inspiration behind the fusion menu at this delightful twelfth-century barrel-vaulted cellar restaurant – expect intriguing combinations like chocolate parfait with black olive oil. Ingredients are from its garden and local farms and there's live jazz on Thursdays. Formules from €11.50. Mon–Fri noon–2.30pm & 7–10pm, Sat 7–10pm.

**Le Biblio Café** 71bis rue de la Cathédrale ☎ 09 71 52 53 35, ⍾bibliocafe.fr. A peppy student café dispensing stimulants (coffee), depressants (beer) and performance enhancers (books) to the local youth. Mon & Sun 11am–9pm, Tues–Sat 11am–10pm.

**Le Bis** 4 rue Saint-Nicolas ☎ 05 49 50 77 91, Funky, fashionable surroundings with equally innovative cuisine make this bistro a hit with local gastronomes. Choose between dining alfresco out front or sitting beneath back-lit origami stag-heads indoors. *Menus* from €19.50. Tues–Thurs noon–2pm, 7–10pm, Fri & Sat noon–2pm & 7–11pm.

**Bistrot du Boucher** 31 rue Carnot ☎ 05 49 03 37 02, ⍾bistrotduboucher.fr. This chain restaurant serves up food that's fresh, hearty and tasty, at low prices, with a traditionally French atmosphere and a focus on quality, local meat. Daily *menus* €22.90–33.80. Daily noon–1.45pm & 7–9.45pm.

★ **Le Bonheur est dans le Thé** 7 rue Carnot ☎ 05 49 41 44 48 ⍾lebonheurestdanslethe.fr. Hidden down a (well-marked) alleyway off rue Carnot, this sprightly teahouse offers a peaceful escape from the bustle of the *centre ville*, with bright tables set around a flower-filled courtyard. There's a range of teas, as well as fresh juices and aperitifs, home-made cakes and pastries, and wholesome, organic brunch and lunch dishes, including vegetarian and vegan options. Mains from €10.90. Tues–Thurs noon–3pm, Fri & Sat noon–3pm & 7–11pm.

**Les Bons Enfants** 11bis rue Cloche-Perse ☎ 05 49 41 49 82. A very small, unpretentious restaurant, with a focus on local produce – especially Pineau, an aperitif from Charentes. Book in advance. Menus €11–29. Tues–Sat noon–1.15pm & 7–9.45pm.

**Chez Cul de Paille** 3 rue Théophraste-Renaudot ☎ 05 49 41 07 35. This cosy restaurant attracts a mixed clientele of both locals and students for its short but sweet menu that has poisson du jour for just €13, plus fantastic value set menus from €10. Events are often held here, too. Tues–Sat noon–2pm & 7pm–2am.

**Wasabi** 11 rue du Chaudron-d'Or ☎ 05 49 52 21 16, ⍾wasabi-poitiers.com. A popular sushi bar with fresh, inexpensive sushi, sashimi and grilled meat (set *menus* starting from €9) and outdoor seating. There's 10 percent discount on takeaways. Mon–Sat 11am–2.30pm & 6–11pm.

### BARS, CLUBS AND VENUES

**La Grand'Goule** 46 rue du Pigeon Blanc ⍾lagoule.fr. Where the freshers go – three storeys, three bars and three smoking rooms. Discounted entry with student card. Tues–Sat midnight–6am.

**Relax** 20 place Charles-de-Gaulle ☎ 05 49 41 13 64. Friendly bar popular with both students and 30-somethings, serving draft beer at €2.40 and cocktails at €6. Stop by for an aperitif or fresh fruit smoothie in the afternoon. Mon–Sat 3pm–2am.

**Rooftop** 6 rue de la Marne ☎ 05 49 47 99 76, ⍾rooftop-poitiers.com. A modern café sited atop the TAP theatre with bright furnishings and outdoor seating on a vast sunny terrace. There's food on offer, but it's best to grab a beer and enjoy the varied entertainment, from live music to DJs. Mon–Fri 11am–2pm & 6pm–1.30am, Sat 6pm–1.30am.

**Room Club** 37 bd du Grand-Cerf ⍾room-club.fr. Small club playing largely electro music, but also hosts popular event nights, such as hip hop and house parties. Cover from €7. Thurs–Sat midnight–7am.

**Le Zinc** 196 Grand'Rue ⍾lezincdepoitiers.fr. Don't let the grungy facade put you off – modelled on a Belgian brasserie, this place has a warm, rustic atmosphere, over 20 kinds of beer (many Belgian), plus regular live gigs. Mon–Sat 6pm–2am.

## DIRECTORY

**Police** 38 rue de la Marne (☎ 05 49 60 60 00).

**Taxis** Poitiers Taxi (☎ 06 95 83 13 62); Taxis Indépendants (☎ 05 49 01 10 01).

# Around Poitiers

North of Poitiers is the cinema theme park **Futuroscope**. There are also a number of safari parks; the best is monkey reserve **Vallée des Singes** ("Valley of the Apes"; daily March–Nov 10am–5pm; €20; ⍾la-vallee-des-singes.fr), thirty minutes' drive south,

9

near Romagne. More traditional attractions can be found east of Poitiers at **Chauvigny** and **St-Savin** – medieval towns with fine Romanesque churches. Both are accessible by bus, but you'll need an early start to see the two in one day.

### Futuroscope

8km north of Poitiers • May–Sept daily 10am–9.30pm; Oct–April weekends and school holidays; 10am–9pm • Adult day pass €45; children 5–16 €37; under-5s free; discounts available online • ☏ 05 49 49 59 06 • ⊛ futuroscope.com

The enormous cinematic theme park **Futuroscope** is France's second-biggest theme park after Disneyland Paris, drawing more than 46 million visitors since it opened in 1987. With ambitious virtual-reality rides, dazzling multimedia and audiovisual exhibitions, and mind-boggling robotic displays, it's a thrilling journey into the future for all ages and you'll need at least a full day to take it all in. Don't miss the award-winning 4-D cinema show *The Time Machine*; the new Fun Xperiences Arena, where participants can test their strength, agility and mind skills; and the spectacular live shows.

The park can be reached by train from Paris and Poitiers, or by bus from Poitier's *hôtel de ville* or *gare SNCF*, and English-language iPod commentary is available (free, but you'll need to leave ID). The hotels and restaurants on site are largely uninspiring and overpriced, so pack a picnic and make the most of the ample lawn space instead.

### Chauvigny

A bustling market town on the banks of the Vienne, **Chauvigny** is home to the imposing ruins of five **medieval castles** that stand atop a precipitous rock spur, and the intriguing Romanesque **church of St-Pierre**. Take rue du Château from the central place de la Poste and you'll pass the ruins of the Château Baronnial, which once belonged to the bishops of Poitiers and now hosts birds of prey shows, and the Château d'Harcourt, whose north tower houses exhibitions, before coming to the church, St-Pierre.

The choir capitals inside St-Pierre are gruesome and delightful, each depicting a vision of damnation. Monsters – bearded, winged, scaly, human-headed with burning manes – grab hapless humans – naked, struggling, puny – ripping their bowels out and crushing their heads. Counterbalancing these horrors are joyous depictions of the Nativity.

If you can, come on Saturday and visit the **market** held between the church of Notre-Dame and the river; it sells a selection of local food – oysters, prawns, crayfish, cheeses galore and pâtés in aspic.

### St-Savin

Scarcely more than a hamlet, **St-Savin** is worth visiting for the UNESCO-listed **abbey church** (daily 10am–noon & 2–6pm; €8; ⊛ abbaye-saint-savin.fr), which was built in the eleventh century. The vault is decorated with murals depicting scenes from Genesis and Exodus, including Noah with a three-decked ark and Pharaoh's horses on the shores of the Red Sea. On the first floor, in what were originally the monks' cells, is a very good multimedia **museum** of Romanesque art history, medieval monastic life and architecture.

# Parthenay

Directly west of Poitiers is the small town of **PARTHENAY**, once an important stop on the pilgrim routes to Compostela. Its faded medieval splendour is worth a glance if you're heading north to Brittany, or west to the sea.

From the train station, avenue de Gaulle leads straight to the central place du Drapeau, from where you can cut through the shopping district to the Gothic **Porte de l'Horloge**, the fortified gateway to the old citadelle on a steep-sided neck of land above a loop in the River Thouet.

Through the gateway, on rue de la Citadelle, the Romanesque **church of Sainte-Croix** faces the *mairie* across a small garden. The view over the western ramparts and the **gully** of St-Jacques, with its muddle of medieval houses and vegetable plots, is spectacular. Further along rue de la Citadelle is a handsome but badly damaged Romanesque door, all that remains of the castle chapel of **Notre-Dame-de-la-Couldre**. The castle itself is gone, but from its site you can look down on the twin-towered **gateway**, and the **Pont St-Jacques**, a thirteenth-century bridge through which nightly flocks of pilgrims poured into the town for shelter and security. To reach it, turn left under the Tour de l'Horloge and down the medieval lane known as **Vau St-Jacques**. The lane is very atmospheric, with crooked half-timber dwellings crowding up to the bridge.

There are three beautiful **Romanesque churches** within easy reach of Parthenay. One is a twenty-minute walk away at **Parthenay-le-Vieux**. The others are at **Airvault**, 20km northeast of Parthenay, and **St-Jouin-de-Marnes**, 9km northeast of Airvault; unfortunately, neither of these are accessible by public transport.

## ARRIVAL AND DEPARTURE PARTHENAY

**By bus** Unfortunatley the train station at Parthenay no longer operates, so if travelling by public transport bus is your only option. Buses arrive and depart from the former gare SNCF, just to the east of the town centre.
Destinations Nantes (2–3 daily; 2hr 20min); Poitiers (4–9 daily; 55min).

## INFORMATION

**Tourist office** 22 bd de la Meilleraye (Mon 9am–noon & 1.30–5.30pm, Tues–Sat 10am–1pm & 2–6pm; ☎ 05 49 94 03 77, ⓦ cc-parthenay-gatine.fr).

## ACCOMMODATION

**Le Bois Vert** 14 rue de Boisseau ☎ 05 49 64 78 43, ⓦ camping-boisvert.com. Four-star site that's part of the huge Base de Loisirs riverbank recreation area, about 3km west of Parthenay on the D949. April–Oct. **€26.50**

★ **Le Grand Logis** 7 rue Bélisaire-Ledain ☎ 05 49 70 22 00, legrandlogisparthenay.com. A bucolic medieval lodge, straight out of Arthurian legend, converted into a snug B&B sitting quietly in a leafy garden. Breakfast included. **€55**

**Saint Jacques** 13 Av du 114ème Régiment d'Infanterie ☎ 05 49 64 33 33, ⓦ hotel-parthenay.com. Though it's nothing to write home about, this unfussy hotel is a decent choice for an overnight stay, with simply furnished rooms and a handy central location (though ask for a room that's not facing the main road). Breakfast €9. **€59**

## EATING AND DRINKING

★ **Aut' Fouée** 33 rue de la Vau St-Jacques ☎ 05 49 64 77 93. With its bright facade, regal red shutters and climbing roses, Aut' Fouée looks right at home among the timber-fronted houses of the Saint-Jacques quarter. Step inside and you'll be transported back to medieval times, with bread baked in front of you, hearty pots of terrine and portions fit for a king. Set menu: €24.50, lunch formule €11.50. Fri & Sat noon–1.30pm, 7–8.45pm, Sun noon–1.30pm.

**La Citadelle** 9 place Georges-Picard ☎ 05 49 64 12 25. A busy local bistro serving excellent wine and food (mains start at €12) to hungry locals. La Citadelle's partner-restaurant, L'Enoteka, at 47 rue Jean-Jaurès, is more of the same for slightly lower prices. Mon noon–1.30pm, Tues–Thurs noon–1.30pm & 7–9.30pm, Fri noon–1.30pm & 7–10pm, Sat 7–10pm.

**Le Fin Gourmet** 28 rue Ganne ☎ 05 49 64 04 53, ⓦ lefingourmet.com. High-quality traditional cuisine in a quaint, stone-walled medieval house. Everything is made on site, even the bread. Menus from €28. Tues & Thurs–Sat noon–1.30pm & 7.30–9pm, Wed 7.30–9pm, Sun noon–1.30pm.

# Niort

The medieval town of **NIORT**, built on two small hills, sits some 50km southwest of Poitiers and makes a useful stopover if your goal is the Marais Poitevin (see page 484). The most interesting part of the town is the mainly pedestrian area around **rue Victor-Hugo** and **rue St-Jean**, which is full of stone-fronted or half-timbered medieval houses. The old **town hall** on rue St-Jean is a triangular building of the early sixteenth century with lantern, belfry and ornamental machicolations, perhaps capable of repelling drunken revellers but no match for catapult or sledgehammer. Along the

9

tree-lined river **Sèvre Niortaise** lie the ruins of a glove factory, the last vestige of Niort's once thriving leather industry. At the time of the Revolution, it kept more than thirty cavalry regiments in breeches. Today, Niort's bourgeois reputation is thanks to its new key industry: insurance. Accordingly, restaurants are usually packed at lunchtime, and well-heeled shoppers throng the pedestrianized streets, giving it an animated, affluent feel. Just downstream is the **market hall** and, beyond, vast and unmistakable on a slight rise, the keep of a **castle** begun by Henry II of England.

## ARRIVAL AND INFORMATION

NIORT

**By train** From the *gare SNCF* on place Pierre-Semard it's a 15min walk to the tourist office. Take rue de la Gare as far as rue du 14-juillet, then turn right into place de la Brèche. Destinations Paris Montparnasse (8 daily; 2–3hr); La Rochelle (17–23 daily; 35min); Poitiers (12–15 daily; 45min).
**By bus** Buses go from place de la Brèche, including 3–6 daily to Coulon (Mon–Sat 20min).

**Tourist office** 2 rue Brisson (daily 10am–6.30pm; ☎ 05 49 24 18 79, ⓦ niortmaraispoitevin.com). They have helpful maps of the town and plenty of information about walking itineraries around the Marais, and also sell large-scale maps of cycle routes (€1).
**Car rental** A number of car rental agencies line rue de la Gare by the station, including Avis at no. 89 (☎ 05 49 24 36 98).

## ACCOMMODATION

★ **Maison La Porte Rouge** 68 av de La Rochelle ☎ 05 49 28 41 62, ⓦ maisonlaporterouge.com. With its stylish decor and elegant lounge, this exquisite *chambre d'hôte* takes the best bits of a boutique hotel and adds the charm and intimacy of a B&B. Themed rooms range from crisp monochrome to preppy chic, plus there's a swimming pool, leafy garden and two self-contained studios. Breakfast included. Rooms and studios from €85
**Moka** 84 rue de la Gare ☎ 05 49 76 15 15, ⓦ mokahotel niort.com. Excellent value, right by the train station, with

free street parking overnight, a decent buffet breakfast (€9) and various deals available throughout the year. The smart rooms are painted in earthy colours, with splashes of colour in the furnishings. €65
**Particulier** La Chamoiserie, 10 rue de l'Espingole ☎ 05 49 78 07 07, ⓦ hotelparticulierniort.com. Boutique hotel close to the *donjon*, with sixteen beautiful modern rooms, complete with luxurious bedspreads and plush robes. There's also parking (book ahead; €9), a grand lounge area and a breakfast room overlooking the pretty garden. Breakfast €12. €98

## EATING AND DRINKING

**L'Adress** 1 rue des Iris ☎ 05 49 79 41 06, ⓦ restaurant-ladress.fr. With an idyllic location, this modern, glass-fronted restaurant makes a dazzling first impression. Thankfully, the menu is up to par too – fresh, colourful and innovative, with a big emphasis on presentation and dishes like roasted pigeon, smoked aubergine caviar or home-made sorbet topped with sparkling sugar. *Menus* from €20. Tues–Sat noon–2pm & 7.30–9pm.
**La Dolce Vita** 46 rue St-Jean ☎ 05 49 17 14 89, ⓦ ladolcevita-niort.fr. A family-run Italian restaurant, with rich, plentiful food and a warm atmosphere. There's a range of pasta dishes and pizzas (from €12.90), and food is available for takeaway too. Tues–Sat noon–2pm & 7–9.45pm.
**Le P'tit Rouquin** 92 rue de la Gare ☎ 05 49 24 05 34, ⓦ leptitrouquin.com. An authentic French bistro with red chequered curtains, rustic interiors and cosy stone-walled courtyard. The menu rotates with seasonal ingredients,

but look out for popular staples like the steak *tartare* with basil or creamy seafood risotto with walnut oil. There's also an organic wine list. *Menu* €27. Mon–Thurs noon–2pm & 7–10pm, Fri noon–2pm.
**Restaurant du Donjon** 7 rue Brisson ☎ 05 49 24 01 32, ⓦ restaurant-le-donjon.com. A monochrome facade, leather seats and black and white artwork set the scene at this central restaurant, located right opposite the tourist office. *Menus* start from €16.50 and include unadventurous classics like risotto, duck confit and profiteroles. Mon–Sat noon–2.30pm & 7–10.30pm.
★ **La Terrine** 48 rue Saint-Jean ☎ 05 49 26 79 48. An atmospheric lunch spot, transforming locally-sourced ingredients into delicious *salads*, omelettes and *tatins*. Opt for the *L'Ardoise Terre et Mer* (€19.50) – a platter of regional delicacies like foie gras, ratatouille and langoustines. Tues–Fri noon–2pm & 7–10pm, Sat 7–10pm.

# The Marais Poitevin

An endless maze of green pools and streams, wild irises, ruined churches, hidden marshes and golden orioles, the **Marais Poitevin** is a beautiful part of the world. Known as "La Venise Verte" (Green Venice), it was created when seventeenth-century Dutch engineers drained a wet marsh by constructing a network of *rigoles* – tiny canals banked with poplars. The marshes lie across three *départements*, so getting information on the whole area, which is the size of the Isle of Wight, is difficult. Tourist offices stock an invaluable free map and guide called *Marais Poitevin: Carte Découverte*. When walking or cycling stick to the marked paths, as shortcuts invariably end in wet socks.

## Coulon and around

You can access the eastern part of the marsh from pretty **COULON** (the "capital" of the Marais) 11km from Niort. Ten kilometres west is the quaint village of Arçais, dominated by a nineteenth-century château, and another place to hire canoes and punts, or find accommodation.

### INFORMATION AND GETTING AROUND

**Tourist office** Place de la Coutume (Mon–Sat 10am–1pm & 2–6pm, ☎08 20 00 00 79, ⓦ marais-poitevin.fr); the office has a free museum that explores the history of the area and can provide a list of local campsites and *chambres d'hôtes*.

**By bike and boat** You can hire bikes and boats from Le Marais Poitevin (6 rue de l'Église, Coulon; ☎05 49 35 14 14, ⓦ lemaraispoitevin.fr; bike hire €10 per day; guided boat tour €12.50 per person; boat hire without a guide €20).

### ACCOMMODATION

**Le Central** 4 rue d'Autremont ☎05 49 35 90 20, ⓦ hotel-lecentral-coulon.com. Breezy country-style rooms with wood floors, pretty fabrics and fresh flowers make this friendly hotel a top choice. There's a/c throughout, private parking and a restaurant. Breakfast €10. **€88**
**Au Marais** 46–48 quai Louis-Tardy ☎05 49 35 90 43. It's hard to beat the location of this blue-shuttered, riverside

hotel. With just 18 rooms, it has an intimate feel, though the bright rooms (some of which have river views) are more charming that the common areas. Breakfast €8.90. **€82**
**Le Paradis** 29 rue Sainte-Sabine, Le Vanneau ☎05 49 35 33 95, ⓦ gite-le-paradis.com. This rustic house sits deep into the marshes with five spacious rooms, a large garden and two rental cottages. Breakfast included. **€64**

### EATING AND DRINKING

★ **Central** 4 rue d'Autremont ☎05 49 35 90 20, ⓦ hotel-lecentral-coulon.com. A nostalgic country hotel restaurant with an elegant dining room and superb cooking,

using all local ingredients and perfect for leisurely weekend lunches. *Menus* from €21.50. Tues–Sat noon–1.30pm & 7.45–9pm, Sun noon-1.30pm.

# Les Sables-d'Olonne and around

**LES SABLES-D'OLONNE** is an unpretentious seaside resort, a far cry from the boutiques and designer wellies of Île de Ré (see page 492), though they share the same stretch of coast. The town was founded in 1218, became a harbour under Louis XI, and peaked in the seventeenth century as the cod-fishing capital of France. Today the town is famous for **watersports** – the Vendée Globe sailing race (ⓦ vendeeglobe.org) starts here; there's a big sailing school and opportunities for windsurfing, kayaking, waterskiing and surfing. It's also a friendly place, with safe beaches and plenty of holiday rentals, ideal for families.

Les Sables-d'Olonne's **Musée de l'Abbaye Sainte-Croix** on rue de Verdun (ⓦ lemasc. fr/masc; Tues–Fri 2–6pm; Sat & Sun 11am–1pm & 2–6pm; €5) houses a respectable modern art collection. Don't miss a stroll up from the seafront to the Île Penotte quarter, where the houses are decorated with colourful seashell mosaics (*coquillages*).

### INFORMATION

LES SABLES-D'OLONNE

**Tourist office** 1 promenade Joffre (April–June & Sept daily 10am–12.30pm & 2–6pm; July & Aug daily 9.30am–7pm; Oct–March Mon–Thurs & Sat 10am–12.30pm & 1.30–5.30pm, Fri 1.30–5.30pm; ☎02 51 96 85 85, ⓦ lessablesdolonne-tourisme.com).

**Parking** The town has a one-way system and you have to pay at meters even on Sundays. Alternatively, park in one of the residential streets at the eastern end of the beach, or in quieter La Chaume, and take the passenger ferry over.

9

### ACCOMMODATION

**Antoine** 60 rue Napoléon ⓣ 02 51 95 08 36, ⓦ antoinehotel.com. The flower-framed door and white shutters offer a cheery first impression at this basic, clean and homely spot just three minutes from the port. There's garage parking available (€9), but the narrow lanes are a struggle if you've got a big car. In July & August half-board is required. Breakfast €9. Open March to mid-Oct. €75

**Le Calme des Pins** 43 av Aristide-Briand ⓣ 02 51 21 03 18, ⓦ calmedespins.com. A three-star family-run hotel, 5min from the beach, with 45 rooms (many with a sea view) and a bold red, grey and white colour scheme that adds a dash of originality. There's also a generous, varied buffet breakfast (€9), private parking, a spa and sauna, plus a tranquil garden. €73

**Camping La Dune des Sables** Rte de l'Aubrai ⓣ 02 51 32 31 21, ⓦ chadotel.com. Small site that's friendly and convenient rather than luxurious, with laundry, restaurant, shop, pools, great beaches, kids' club and rental cabins with fridge and crockery. April–Sept. €37

**Les Embruns** 33 rue du Lieutenant Maurice-Anger ⓣ 02 51 95 25 99, ⓦ hotel-sables-d-olonne.com. Located in the attractive La Chaume quarter, just 400m from the beach, this place is friendly, clean and English-speaking, with individually decorated rooms in a country-chic style. Breakfast €8.70, parking €6. €78

### EATING AND DRINKING

There are good fish restaurants around the port, at quai Guiné, and opposite on quai des Boucanniers, reachable via shuttle ferry (July & Aug daily 7am–1am; Easter hols, June & Sept Mon–Thurs 7am–10pm, Fri– Sun 7am–midnight; Oct–May Mon–Thurs 7am–8pm, Fri & Sat 8am–10pm, Sun 8am–8pm; €1.10). The covered market, Halles Centrales (June–Sept daily 8am–1pm; closed Mon Oct–May) stocks fresh local fish, dairy, fruit, vegetables, herbs and bread.

**Le Cabestan** 17 quai Guiné ⓣ 02 51 95 07 50, ⓦ cabestan85.com. With its red, white and blue colour scheme, naval posters and menu hung on a gigantic buoy, the nautical theme is strong at this small quayside restaurant. Unsurprisingly, freshly caught fish and seafood feature heavily on the menu with specialities including langoustines and *moules*. *Menus* from €22. Tues & Sun noon–1.15pm, Wed–Sat noon–1.15pm & 7–9.15pm.

**Le Fatra** 21 quai George-V ⓣ 02 51 32 68 73, ⓦ le-fatra.com. An excellent little restaurant with a terrace, changing seasonal menus, views of the port, friendly service and a wine list that carefully complements the menu. Book ahead. Lunch *menu* €14, dinner *menu* €25. Thurs & Sun noon–2pm, Tues, Wed, Fri & Sat noon–2pm & 7.30–10pm.

## Puy du Fou

April–Sept & school holidays Daily from 9.30am. Closing times vary from 7pm to 10.30pm, depending on the evening show schedule • Adult €40, child €29, discounts online for advance booking • ⓣ 08 20 09 10 10, ⓦ puydufou.com

About 80km inland from Les Sables-d'Olonne is the "historical theme park", **Puy du Fou**, in **Les Épesses** village. Highlights include *Mousquetaire de Richelieu,* set in a 17th-century theatre and featuring sword fighting and flamenco, and *Vikings*, featuring wild animals and a Viking warship. The best show is the La *Cinéscénie* – a sound and light display with fireworks, staged after sunset (June to September).

### ARRIVAL AND INFORMATION — PUY DU FOU

**Public transport** A shuttle bus runs from Angers TGV station and Puy du Fou but must be booked in advance (3 daily; 1hr 30min; €28 return; check website for details.)

**Tourist office** The tourist office in Cholet (ⓣ 02 41 49 80 00, ⓦ ot-cholet.fr) can provide additional information about transport.

### ACCOMMODATION

**Château de la Flocellière** 85700 la Flocellière ⓣ 02 51 57 22 03, ⓦ chateaudelaflocelliere.com. This spectacular castle, 11km southeast of Puy du Fou overlooking miles of rolling farmland, was one of the first in a growing trend of B&Bs offering not a holiday but a social milieu where guests are greeted by a countess, and can dine with the gentry. More B&Bs like this can be found at ⓦ bienvenueauchateau.com. €160

**La Crémaillère** 2 rue de la Libération, Les Espesses ⓣ 02 51 57 30 01. An inexpensive village hotel, 3km from Puy du Fou, with eleven simple, comfortable rooms and a restaurant providing traditional meals. Breakfast €8.50. €60

**La Libaudière** Pouzauges ⓣ 02 51 57 52 68, ⓦ chambresdhotesvendee.com. Children will love sleeping in a yurt, treehouse or floating cabin on the lake at this country B&B, 21km southeast from Puy du Fou, and a 30min drive. The hosts are friendly and the breakfast is excellent. Yurt €75, treehouse €125, standard B&B €63

# The Île de Noirmoutier

9

The Impressionist painter, Renoir, loved **ÎLE DE NOIRMOUTIER**, an island of sandy inlets, pine forests and salt marshes. At 20km-long, and 60km north of Les Sables-d'Olonne, Noirmoutier enjoys a warm microclimate, responsible for its figs and early-flowering mimosa. Tourism is the island's main economy, but it also produces salt, fine spring potatoes, and an abundance of cod, oysters, eels and squid.

The little village of **Noirmoutier-en-l'Île**, the busiest of the island's six villages, has a twelfth-century **castle** once owned by the Black Prince (now containing a museum), a **church** with a Romanesque crypt, an **aquarium**, a good **market** (year-round Fri; April–Sept also Tues & Sun) on place de la République, and many of the island's restaurants, port-side bars and cafés.

Inland, the saltwater dykes are the only reminder that you're out to sea, while the pretty whitewashed and ochre-tiled houses in the villages are typical of the Vendée and southern Brittany. Spring weather is often stormy and the summer heat entices mosquitoes, so come prepared.

The most famous **beach**, Plage des Dames, with its painted bathing huts, is a ten-minute cycle east of Noirmoutier-en-l'Île. The beaches on the west and south coasts are the quietest in summertime. Near Fort Larron there is a bird reserve with avocets, egrets and redshanks, and in La Guérinière a butterfly park.

## GETTING THERE AND AROUND      ÎLE DE NOIRMOUTIER

The best way to reach the island is via the spectacular, 4.5km-long causeway, "Le Gois", which is covered twice a day with water. Otherwise, the D38 crosses via a permanant bridge and there are daily buses from Nantes (see page 420), taking 1hr 45min.

**By bike** Cycling is the ideal way to explore: there are paths around almost the entire perimeter, it's perfectly flat, and the traffic is regularly jammed. Of the dozens of bike rental outlets, Vel-hop, 55 av Joseph-Pineau (☎ 02 51 39 01 34, ⓦ cyclhop.fr; €11 per day) will deliver to your hotel.

**By bus** In July and Aug Noirmoutier-en-l'Île has a free "park and ride" shuttle bus service from the town down to a number of beaches (daily 9am–7pm).

## INFORMATION

**Tourist office** Rue du Général-Passaga, Noirmoutier-en-l'Île (April–June & Sept daily 9.30am–12.30pm & 2–6pm; July & Aug daily 9.30am–7pm; Oct–March Mon–Sat 9.30am–12.30pm & 2–5.30pm; ☎ 02 51 39 80 71, ⓦ ile-noirmoutier.com). Find information on all the island's activities, from fishing to windsurfing, lists of campsites, and basic maps of cycle routes.

## ACCOMMODATION

★ **La Chaize** 23 av de la Victoire ☎ 02 51 39 04 62, ⓦ hotel-noirmoutier.com. Effortlessly chic with its spotless wood floors and faux-fur throws, this luxe hotel is excellent value. There are superior rooms with jacuzzi baths and terraces, freestanding apartments in the garden, and great family rooms with a fun mezzanine sleeping area for the kids, plus private parking and a heated indoor pool. Breakfast €10. **€80**

**L'Île Ô Château** 11 rue des Douves ☎ 02 51 39 02 72, ⓦ ileochateau.com. Despite a prime location at the foot of the castle, this is a haven of tranquillity, with light, airy rooms, rattan floors and muted colours, each with a personal touch. The hosts, Marianne and Ange, are delightful and run the hotel like an oversized B&B, plus there's a central courtyard and pool to cool off during the summer months. Breakfast €12. **€90**

**Les Prateaux** 8 allée du Tambourin ☎ 02 51 39 12 52, ⓦ lesprateaux.com. Well-furnished, carpeted rooms with huge comfy beds and either balconies or terraces. This place can get busy and a bit impersonal during the high season, but it's ideally placed in the pine woods, right next to Plage des Dames. **€145**

## EATING AND DRINKING

**Le Grand Four** 1 rue de la Cure ☎ 02 51 39 61 97, ⓦ legrandfour.com. A genteel country-house restaurant with candy-coloured shutters and an ivy-covered facade, this charming spot has been serving fine local dishes to visitors since 1956. It's especially lovely in the summer when you can sit out front. *Menus* from €34. Tues, Wed, Fri & Sat 12.15–2pm & 7.15–9.30pm, Thurs 7.15–9.30pm, Sun 12.15–2pm.

**9**

★ **La Marine** 5 rue Marie-Lemonnier ☎ 02 51 39 23 09, ⓦ alexandrecouillon.com. Memorable Michelin-starred cooking from celebrated chef Alexandre Couillon, who presents a *menu* that changes depending on the catch of the day. Daily *menus* €88 (4 courses) to €238 (*dégustation* with wine). Mon & Thurs–Sat 12.15–1.30pm & 7.15–9pm, Sun 12.15–1.30pm.

**Le Roman Bleu** 1 rue Boucharde ☎ 02 51 39 03 88, ⓦ leromanbleu.com. A warm, family-run restaurant with enthusiastic service, good food, and well-matched wines.

Tuck into a risotto of prawns, mussels and cockles (€18.90), followed by chocolate *babou* cake, made to a family recipe (€9). Tues–Sat noon–2pm & 7–9.30pm, Sun noon–2.30pm.

**La Table d'Élise** Rue Marie-Lemonnie ☎ 02 28 10 68 35. The bistro version of *La Marine*, next door, overseen by the same chef, with simpler versions of the same food at a fraction of the price. Lunch *menu* €21.50, dinner *menu* €29. Thurs–Mon 12.15–2pm & 7.15–9pm; Sun lunch only.

# La Rochelle and around

Known as "La Ville Blanche" (the White City), **LA ROCHELLE** is a delicate concoction of pale limestone, warm light and sea air. The city was one of the most important ports in France during the Renaissance, and its rich past is visible in its grand arcades, turrets and timber-framed houses. Due to the foresight of mayor Michel Crépeau, the city's historic centre and waterfront were wrested from developers, and its streets freed of traffic in the 1970s. Controversial at the time, the policy has since been adopted across the country – even surpassing Crépeau's successful yellow bicycle plan.

Eleanor of Aquitaine gave La Rochelle a charter in 1199, releasing it from feudal obligations. This spurred rapid growth through salt and wine trade. The Wars of Religion devastated the town, which turned Protestant, and was ruthlessly besieged by Cardinal Richelieu in 1627. The English dispatched the Duke of Buckingham to their aid, but he was caught napping on the Île de Ré and suffered defeat. By the end of 1628 Richelieu had starved the city into submission. Out of the pre-siege population of 28,000, only 5000 survived. The walls were demolished and the city's privileges revoked. La Rochelle later became the principal port for trade with the French colonies in the Caribbean Antilles and Canada. Many of the settlers, especially in Canada, came from this part of France.

The area around La Rochelle is ideal for young families, with miles of safe, sandy **beaches**. Visiting in August is best avoided, unless you're camping, or book accommodation months in advance.

## The Vieux Port

The **Vieux Port**, where pleasure boats are moored, is the heart of the town. You can stroll very pleasantly for an hour or more along the seafront in either direction from the harbour: down to the **Port des Minimes**, a vast marina development 2km south of the centre, or west, along a promenade and strip of parkland, towards **Port Neuf**. Dominating the inner harbour, the heavy Gothic gateway of the **Porte de la Grosse Horloge** touches the entrance to the old town to the north, and to the south reaches towards the tree-lined pedestrianized cours des Dames, where sailors' wives used to await their husbands' return. Leading north from the Porte de la Grosse Horloge, rue du Palais runs towards the cathedral and museums on rue Thiers.

## The Towers

Daily: April–Sept 10am–1pm & 2.15–6.30pm, Oct–March 10am–1pm & 2.15–5.30pm• ⓦ tours-la-rochelle.fr • €6; €9 for all three towers

La Rochelle is home to three famous towers. **Tour St-Nicolas**, on the east side of the mouth of the harbour, is the most architecturally interesting, with two spiral staircases that intertwine but never meet. On the opposite bank is **Tour de la Chaîne**, which houses an exhibition on seventeenth-century emigration to French Canada. You can climb along the old city walls to the third tower, just behind Tour de la Chaîne, known as the **Tour de la Lanterne**, or Tour des Quatre-Sergents – after four sergeants imprisoned and executed for defying the Restoration monarchy in 1822. All three towers have fine views back to the port, and the entry ticket includes a trip on the **electric ferry** (*passeur*), which tirelessly crosses the water all day (€1).

## The rue du Palais and around

The area around La Rochelle's main shopping street, **rue du Palais**, is beautiful. Lining the street are eighteenth-century houses, some grey-stone, some half-timbered, with

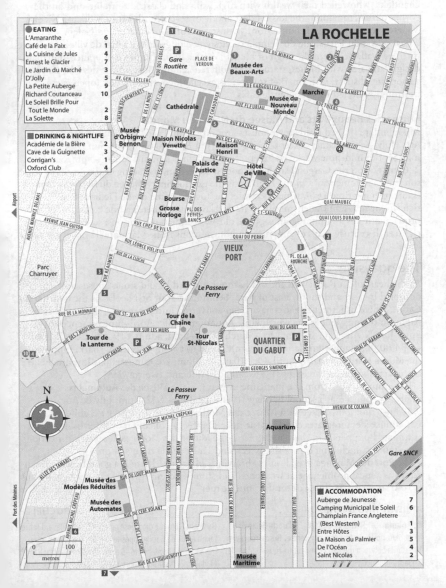

**EATING**
| | |
|---|---|
| L'Amaranthe | 6 |
| Café de la Paix | 1 |
| La Cuisine de Jules | 4 |
| Ernest le Glacier | 7 |
| Le Jardin du Marché | 3 |
| D'Jolly | 5 |
| La Petite Auberge | 9 |
| Richard Coutanceau | 10 |
| Le Soleil Brille Pour Tout le Monde | 2 |
| La Solette | 8 |

**DRINKING & NIGHTLIFE**
| | |
|---|---|
| Académie de la Bière | 2 |
| Cave de la Guignette | 3 |
| Corrigan's | 1 |
| Oxford Club | 4 |

**ACCOMMODATION**
| | |
|---|---|
| Auberge de Jeunesse | 7 |
| Camping Municipal Le Soleil | 6 |
| Champlain France Angleterre (Best Western) | 1 |
| Entre Hôtes | 3 |
| La Maison du Palmier | 5 |
| De l'Océan | 4 |
| Saint Nicolas | 2 |

**9**

distinctive Rochelais-style slates, overlapping like fish scales. The shops are a step back from the street beneath ground-floor arcades. Among the finest buildings are the **Hôtel de la Bourse** – actually the Chamber of Commerce – and the **Palais de Justice** with its colonnaded facade, both on the left-hand side. A few metres further on, in **rue des Augustins**, is **Maison Henri II**, built in 1555 and complete with loggia, gallery and slated turrets, where the regional tourist board has its offices. Place de Verdun itself is rather characterless, home to an uninspiring, humpbacked, eighteenth-century **cathedral** on the corner and the bike rental park.

West of rue du Palais you'll find the homes of eighteenth-century shipowners and chandlers, who veiled their wealth with high walls and classical restraint, and on the corner of **rue Fromentin**, the less modest abode of seventeenth-century doctor Nicolas Venette, who adorned his house front with statues of Hippocrates and Galen.

East of rue du Palais, rue du Temple carries you alongside the **hôtel de ville**'s attractive fortified wall. Begun in the reign of Henri IV, it's a beautiful piece of Franco-Italianate design, adorned with niches, statues and coffered ceilings. Just up rue des Merciers, a shopping district, is the **market square**; its excellent covered market (open every morning) is circled by simple little cafés.

### Musée des Beaux-Arts and Musée du Nouveau Monde

Museums are stashed inside townhouses around rue du Palais. The **Musée des Beaux-Arts** (July–Sept weekdays except Tues 10am–1pm & 1.45–6pm, Sat–Sun 2–6pm; mid-Sept to mid-June weekdays except Tues 9.30am–12.30pm & 1.45–5pm, Sat–Sun 2–6pm; €6) on rue Gargoulleau has a modest collection, including exotic works by local son Eugène Fromentin. On rue Fleuriau is the extraordinary **Musée du Nouveau Monde** (same opening times; €6), which occupies the former home of the Fleuriau family, rich shipowners and traders mixed up in the slave trade. There's a fine collection of prints, paintings and photographs of the old West Indian plantations; seventeenth- and eighteenth-century maps of America; and illustrations from Marmontel's novel *Les Incas*.

## The quayside

At the heart of La Rochelle is the old harbour, banked by old stone houses now occupied by bars and shops. East of here, behind the Tour St-Nicolas, is the **quartier du Gabut**, where fishermen's shacks have been converted into more bars, shops and cafés. Right on the quayside is the worthwhile **Aquarium** (daily: April–June & Sept 9am–8pm; July & Aug 9am–11pm; Oct–March 10am–8pm; adults €19, children €14; ☎05 46 34 00 00, ⓦaquarium-larochelle.com), home to twenty species of shark. Opposite is the **Musée Maritime** (daily: April–Oct 10am–6.30pm; €9; ⓦmuseemaritimelarochelle.fr), which showcases three ships – a weather station and two trawlers.

Ten minutes' walk from the maritime museum is the **Musée des Automates** (daily: 2–7pm; French school holidays 10am–12.30pm & 2–7pm; July & Aug 9.30am–7pm; joint ticket with Musée des Modèles Réduits, adults €12, children €8; ⓦmuseedesautomates.com) on rue de la Désirée, a collection of three hundred automated puppets. On the same street is the **Musée des Modèles Réduits**, with various scale models, including cars, a shipwreck and La Rochelle train station.

The **Port des Minimes** itself houses thousands of yachts. There is a good beach, which serves as a local promenade at weekends and summer evenings. You can get here by bus (#10 from place Verdun), or on the "**bus de mer**".

---

**ARRIVAL AND DEPARTURE**                                    **LA ROCHELLE**

**By plane** La Rochelle airport (ⓦlarochelle.aeroport.fr) is 6km northwest of the city centre. Buses run every 10–30min between the airport and centre (bus #1 Mon–Fri 5.45am–10pm, Sat 6.30am–19pm).

**By train** From the grandiose *gare SNCF* on boulevard Joffre, take avenue de Gaulle opposite to reach the town centre. Destinations Bordeaux (6–8 daily; 2hr 20min–3hr); Nantes (3 daily; 2hr 35min); Niort (17–23 daily; 35min); Paris-

Montparnasse (6–8 daily; 3hr–4hr); Poitiers (17–23 daily; 1hr 20min–1hr 45min); Rochefort (10–20 daily; 20min); Saintes (7–12 daily; 50min–1hr).

**By bus** The main bus station, or *gare routière*, is situated in place de Verdun, a 10min walk to the north of the old harbour.

**By ferry** Ferries serve the nearby island of St-Martin de Ré (ⓦ inter-iles.com; 3–14 weekly; 1hr; €15.50–22.50).

## GETTING AROUND

**By bike** There are two municipal bike stations, run by Yélo (ⓦ yelo.agglo-larochelle.fr): one in place de Verdun (all year), the other on quai Valin near the tourist office (May–Sept only). On handing over ID you get half an hour of free bike time; after this it's €1 per half hour for up to two hours, then €3 per half-hour afterwards.

**By boat** Yélo also operates the "Bus de Mer" boat, which runs from the old port to Minimes (Daily: June hourly from 9am–7pm except 1pm; July–Aug 8.30am–11.30pm; April–May & Sept 10am–7pm except 1pm; Oct–March weekends and school holidays only 10am–6pm except 1pm; €3).

**By car** Car rental is available from all major companies outside the station, such as Rent-A-Car, 29 av du Général-de-Gaulle (ⓣ 05 46 27 27 27).

## INFORMATION

**Tourist office** Quai Georges-Simenon (March & Oct Mon 10am–1pm & 2–6pm, Tues–Sat 10am–1pm & 2–6pm, Sun 10am–1pm; April–June & Sept Mon–Sat 9am–6pm, Sun 9am–5pm; July & Aug daily 9am–7pm; Nov–Feb Tues–Sat 10am–1pm & 2–5pm ; ⓣ 05 46 41 14 68, ⓦ larochelle-tourisme.com).

**Passes and tours** The tourist office sells the La Rochelle City Pass (1 day €28, 2 days €38, 3 days €48; ⓦ larochelle-citypass.com), covering all city transport and discount entry into attractions.

## ACCOMMODATION

Accommodation is expensive and scarce in summer, so booking is essential even for campers. There's no such thing as a budget hotel here, though an outstanding youth hostel goes some way to making amends. As an alternative to hotels, the tourist office has a list of self-catering apartments around Les Minimes.

**Auberge de Jeunesse** Av des Minimes ⓣ 05 46 44 43 11, ⓦ fuaj-aj-larochelle.fr. A convenient modern hostel overlooking the marina at Port des Minimes, with all facilities, including a bar, TV room, garden, laundry room, veranda and cafeteria. Bus #4 or follow the signs from the train station. Dorms €18, singles €39

**Camping Municipal Le Soleil** Av Michel-Crépeau ⓣ 05 46 44 42 53. In a good location near the hostel, and close to the beaches, this site is often crowded with raucous young holiday-makers. Take bus #4 from place de Verdun to Les Minimes. Open late June to late Sept. €15.90

★ **Champlain France Angleterre (Best Western)** 30 rue Rambaud ⓣ 05 46 41 23 99, ⓦ hotelchamplain.com. A splendid old mansion stuffed with polished mahogany and chandeliers, this is a three-star hotel that looks like it has two stars more; located five minutes from the port and surrounded by restaurants. Secure parking is an extra €8. €111

**Entre Hôtes** 8 rue Réaumur ⓣ 05 16 85 93 33, ⓦ entre-hotes.com. Effortlessly blending boutique hotel style with the ambiance of a *chambre d'hôte*, this elegant B&B has five plush rooms with garden views. Opt for the "Insolite" room, housed in the vaulted cellar with original stonework and its own terrace. €145

★ **La Maison du Palmier** 23 place du Maréchal-Foch ⓣ 05 46 50 31 96, ⓦ lamaisondupalmier.com. Tiny yet elegant B&B built around a central courtyard, with three spacious, individually decorated rooms. There's an excellent breakfast and helpful, friendly service. No private parking. €133

**De l'Océan** 36 cours des Dames ⓣ 05 46 41 31 97, ⓦ hotel-ocean-larochelle.com. Smack bang in the middle of the action, this affordable two-star hotel has small but comfortable a/c rooms, many with views of the port. One of the best bargains in town. €77

**Saint Nicolas** 13 rue Sardinerie et place de la Solette ⓣ 05 46 41 71 55, ⓦ hotel-saint-nicolas.com. A convenient, comfortable central hotel tucked away in a quiet courtyard, with a/c, private parking (€10), 24hr reception and a bar-lounge. €93

## EATING AND DRINKING

As long as you avoid the tourist traps on cours des Dames, eating well is easy in La Rochelle. Rue St-Jean-du-Pérot is the stomping ground of more discerning gastronomes, while cheaper, local haunts can be found around the market square.

**L'Amaranthe** 14 rue Bletterie ⓣ 05 17 83 07 21, ⓦ lamaranthe.net. Pretty surroundings dotted with fresh flowers and a rotating menu of home-made dishes sourced from organic, local produce. *Menus* from €16 (lunch) and €24 (dinner). Tues–Sat 12.15–1.45pm & 7.15–9.30pm.

**Café de la Paix** 54 rue Chaudrier ⓣ 05 46 41 39 79. A beautifully preserved *belle époque* café that dates back to 1895, adorned with antique chandeliers and gilded mirrors. The food is a bit overpriced, but it's a grand setting for an afternoon coffee break. Mon–Sat 7am–9pm.

**La Cuisine de Jules** 5 rue Thiers ⓣ 05 46 41 50 91, ⓦ www.lacuisinedejules.fr. *La Cuisine de Jules* is a cut

**9**

above other mid-range restaurants and thus popular with in-the-know locals. The bright, modern interior is complemented by well-portioned food and good service – try the pan-fried cuttlefish. *Menus* from €24.50. Tues–Sat noon–2pm & 7–10pm.

★ **Ernest le Glacier** 15–16 rue du Port/48 cours des Dames, Ⓦ ernest-le-glacier.com. The only place in La Rochelle to buy your ice cream, *Ernest* uses the best ingredients and boasts a myriad of imaginative flavours ranging from the decadent (*macaron*, lemon meringue, *canelés de Bordeaux*) to the downright bizarre (lime and basil, liquorice, rice pudding). Enjoy a simple cornet (€3.50) or go all-out with a 10-flavour tasting bowl (€12). Rue du Port: Tues, Fri & Sat noon–11pm, Wed, Thurs & Sun noon–7pm; cours des Dames: Mon & Sun 12.30–7pm; Wed–Sat 12.30–11pm.

**Le Jardin du Marché** 5bis rue Gargoulleau Ⓣ 05 46 41 06 42. A satisfying place for breakfast (from €4), with good tea and excellent hot chocolate, crêpes and pastries, or lunch (*tartines*, from €12.50). Enjoy people-watching on the terrace, or head to the quiet inner courtyard to eat beneath shady palm fronds. Mon–Sat 8am–6pm.

**D'Jolly** 16 rue Chaudrier Ⓣ 05 46 41 26 95. A well-stocked cache of pastries, cakes and chocolates, where raspberry tarts, rose *macarons* and artisan ice creams beckon in passers-by. Mon 10am–7.30pm, Tues–Sat 9am–7.30pm, Sun 9am–1pm & 3–7.30pm.

**La Petite Auberge** 25 rue St-Jean-du-Pérot Ⓣ 05 46 41 28 43, Ⓦ lapetiteauberge17.fr. A champion seafood restaurant with crab, scallops, monkfish, sardines, salmon and the like, and a wine list stretching to Spain. Three-course *menu* €31.50. Mon–Sat noon–2pm & 7–10.30pm, closed Mon and Wed lunchtime.

★ **Richard Coutanceau** Plage de la Concurrence Ⓣ 05 46 41 48 19, Ⓦ coutanceaularochelle.com. On the seafront west of the old harbour, with panoramic views over the beach and sea, this Michelin-starred restaurant is a veritable gallery of gastronomy. Reservations essential. *Menus* €70–140. Tues–Sat 12.15–1.30pm & 7.30–9.30pm.

★ **Le Soleil Brille Pour Tout le Monde** 13 rue des Cloutiers Ⓣ 05 46 41 11 42. Decked out with luminous yellow furniture and cutesy sun motifs, this family-run restaurant is as vibrant and cheery as its name suggests. The good vibes infuse the food too, with fresh market ingredients whipped into delicious *tartes*, varied salads and great vegetarian options (mains from €10). Tues–Sat 12.15–2pm, 7.30–10pm.

**La Solette** 11 rue de la Fourche. On a cobbled square off rue St-Nicolas, this friendly café serves a limited choice of fresh, tasty home-cooked meals (salmon *tartare*, steak and chips, burgers). Don't be put off by the slightly shabby frontage – locals aren't and the terrace seating is always packed in summer. Lunch *menus* from €13. Mon–Thurs & Sun noon–2pm & 7–10.30pm, Fri & Sat noon–2pm & 7pm–midnight.

### NIGHTLIFE AND ENTERTAINMENT

While nightlife along rue St-Nicolas is active all year round, the lively, late night student bars on the quai de Gabut, behind the tourist office, quieten in the holidays. The monthly magazine *Sortir 17* (Ⓦ sortir17.com) has listings for mainstream and classical music events, as well as theatre and film. In mid-July La Rochelle hosts a major festival of French-language music, Les Francofolies (Ⓦ francofolies. fr), which features French and international musicians, and draws some 100,000 visitors.

### BARS AND CLUBS

**Académie de la Bière** 10 cour du Temple, off rue des Templiers. A low-key beer bar containing ample *blondes*, *brunes* and *blanches*. Mon–Sat 10am–2am.

**Cave de la Guignette** 8 rue St-Nicolas Ⓦ la-guignette.

fr. With its peeling paint, low lighting and barrels for tables, this well-stocked wine cellar, formerly frequented by sailors, is atmospheric or dingy depending on your taste. Try the namesake *guignette*, a potent home-made aperitif. Mon–Sat 10.30am–1.30pm & 4.30–9pm, Sun 4.30–9pm.

**Corrigan's** 20 rue des Cloutiers Ⓦ corrigans.fr. Decisive proof that Irish bars don't always have to be ghastly fakes, this classic pub hosts regular live music, including traditional Irish sessions each Sunday, and pub quizzes. There's a convivial vibe, good Guinness on tap and a mix of locals and expats. Tues–Sat 6pm–2am, Sun 7pm–1am.

**Oxford Club** Promenade de la Concurrence Ⓦ oxford-club.fr. Two DJs, two dancefloors and a techno/house line-up, alongside 70s/80s nights and karaoke Sundays. Wed–Sun 11pm–5am.

# The Île de Ré

With misty beaches, green-shuttered cottages and lonely coves, **Île de Ré** is one of the loveliest places in western France. Out of season the economy rests on oysters and mussels, while in high season 400,000 visitors pass through, many of them rich Parisians, and the island is a little less tranquil. The Île de Ré is a rung higher on the French resort prestige ladder than Noirmoutier (see page 487), and three rungs above Oléron (see page 498), so designer boutiques, high-class restaurants and luxury hotels are the norm.

# St-Martin

The island's capital, **ST-MARTIN**, is the centre of tourist life. At its heart is the harbour, filled with a democratic mix of flat-bottomed oyster boats and gleaming yachts. Around the water are less democratic shops, bars and cafés. This is the main tourist drag, to be avoided at all cost on hot August afternoons. To the east of the harbour you can walk along the **fortifications** – redesigned by Vauban in the seventeenth century – to the citadelle. From 1860 to 1938, this was the departure point for *bagnards* – prisoners sentenced to hard labour in French Guiana and New Caledonia.

# The rest of the island

The bird reserve, **Maison du Fier et Réserve Naturelle**, in the village of **Les Portes-En-Ré** (daily except Sat morn: April–June & Sept–Oct 10am–12.30pm & 2.30–6pm; July & Aug 10am–12.30pm & 2.30–7pm; €5, ⓦile-de-re.lpo.fr/maison-du-fier), is a must for nature lovers. The **Écomusée du Marais Salant** (mid-March to mid-April & mid-Sept to Oct Tues–Sat 2.30–5pm; mid-April to mid-June 2.30–6pm; mid-June to mid-Sept 10am–12.30pm & 2–7pm; adults €5.50, children €2.70–4.90; ⓦmarais-salant.com) near the village of **Loix**, offers a glimpse into salt harvesting. A little further inland, through a maze of salt and oyster beds, is the pretty village of **Ars-En-Ré**, recognizable by its distinctive church steeple, painted black and white to help sailors navigate the coastline.

## ARRIVAL AND INFORMATION | ÎLE DE RÉ

**By bus** Regular buses run from place de Verdun in La Rochelle to St-Martin.

**By car** The toll bridge (mid-June to mid-Sept €16, mid-Sept to mid-June €8) is a short drive from La Rochelle.

**By boat** Inter-Îles in La Rochelle makes boat trips to St-Martin (1hr; €15.50–22.50).

**Tourist office** Each village on the island has its own tourist office, but the branch by St-Martin harbour (daily: Sept–

June 9.30am–6pm; July & Aug 9.30am–7pm ☎ 5 46 09 00 55, ⓦiledere.com) is the biggest and most comprehensive, with maps of the island's cycle routes.

**Bike rental** There are operators across the island like Cyclosurf (☎ 05 46 30 19 51, ⓦcyclo-surf.com) and Cycland (☎ 05 46 09 08 66, ⓦcycland.fr). A day's cycle hire for an adult is around €11 per day and for a child €8.

## ACCOMMODATION

A reliable and exhaustive source of the campsites on the island is ⓦcampings-ile-de-re.com.

**Camp du Soleil** Ars-en-Ré ☎ 05 46 29 40 62, ⓦcampdusoleil.com. A solid three-star campsite with grassy pitches, cabins and mobile homes of all varieties, TV room, games, playground and pool. Late March to Sept. **€28.10**

**Le Clocher** 14 place Carnot, Ars-en-Ré ☎ 05 46 29 41 20, ⓦhotel-le-clocher.com. With free parking, family rooms, and comparatively low prices, this is Ré's version of a budget hotel. It's still a cut above the average three-star hotel though, with wooden floors, white panelled walls and modern furnishings adding a stylish stamp. The relaxed bar is a bonus. **€114**

★ **La Galiote en Ré** 7 rue du 8-mai, La Flotte-en-Ré ☎ 05 46 09 50 95, ⓦhotellagaliote.com. Pale wood furnishings, patterned cushions and fresh flowers give this well-kept small hotel an effusive charm and the generous, English-speaking hosts are equally welcoming. It's within easy walking distance of the pretty village of La Flotte, with secure parking, and a delicious, home-made breakfast. **€149**

**L'Île Blanche** 9 chemin des Bardonnières, La Flotte ☎ 05 46 09 52 43, ⓦileblanche.com. Around 1.5km from the sea, this family-orientated site has outdoor and covered pools, tennis, volleyball, over 200 mobile homes and cottages, table tennis, football pitch and a restaurant. Most accommodation available for weekend or weekly reservations only. Easter–Sept **€835/week**

**Le Sénéchal** 6 rue Gambetta, Ars-en-Ré ☎ 05 46 29 40 42, ⓦhotel-le-senechal.com. A countrified boutique hotel dropped into a rustic seaside village, *Le Sénéchal* has chic decor, a bright courtyard, a small outdoor pool and a lounge with board games; the so-called "Beautiful" rooms boast their own fireplaces. Breakfast €14. Closed Jan. **€139**

**De Toiras** 1 quai Job-Foran, St-Martin ☎ 05 46 35 40 32, ⓦhotel-de-toiras.com. Those with money to burn can live like royalty at this opulent five-star haven – a splurge of unbridled Napoleonic decadence, with rooms and suites named after famous aristocrats, generals and presidents. Expect top-notch service, a gourmet restaurant, courtyard garden and stately decor, with a price tag to match. **€310**

**9**

## EATING AND DRINKING

★**Ben-Hur Char à Huîtres** Av Victor-Bouthillier, Saint-Martin-de-Ré ☎06 99 21 20 73. The epitome of island dining, with colourful tables outside by the Ben-Hur boat, from which the freshest seafood is served up. It would be remiss to come here and not try the oysters (from €8 for six), but other delights on the menu include prawns sautéed with peppers, and grilled sardines (€11.50). Often has live music during the summer: expect dancing to start later on in the evenings. Daily 11.30am–10.30pm.

**Le Bistrot du Marin** 10 quai Nicolas-Baudin, St-Martin ☎05 46 68 74 66. Fresh, well put-together meals in the heart of St-Martin, with a pleasant interior and seating on the quayside. Plat du jour €15, desserts from €6.90. There are no reservations so get there early. Fri–Tues 8am–2am, Wed 8am–3pm.

**L'Écailler** 3 quai de Sénac, La Flotte ☎05 46 09 56 40, ⓦlecailler-iledere.com. Amid the bustle of La Flotte's scenic harbour, this splendid fish restaurant is justifiably one of the island's top eateries. There's a huge variety of

fish and seafood à la carte (mains from €32). Bookings recommended. Mid-April to mid-Nov Wed–Sun 12.15–2pm & 7.30–10pm.

**La Martinière** 12 rue de Sully in St-Martin/9 quai de Sénac in La Flotte ⓦla-martiniere.fr. Satisfy your sweet tooth with one of the thirty-three ice-cream and 20 sorbet flavours at this old-fashioned ice-cream store, which dates back to 1970. Home-made and sourced from fresh, local ingredients, you'll find flavours like mojito, star anise, cinnamon, marshmallow and cappuccino, starting from €3. Easter–Sept daily: St-Martin 10.30am–1pm & 2.30–7.30pm; La Flotte 9am–9.30pm.

**L'Océan** 172 rue Saint-Martin, Bois Plage-en-Ré ☎05 46 09 23 07, ⓦre-hotel-ocean.com. This hotel restaurant is a lovely spot to tuck into fresh, local oysters (from €11), langoustine cannelloni and delicious home-made fish soup (€8) in tranquil surroundings. Closed mid-Nov to mid-Feb. Mon, Wed & Thurs 12.15–1.45pm, Tues & Fri–Sun 12.15–1.45pm & 7.15–9pm.

# Rochefort and around

Colbert, Louis XIV's navy minister, built **ROCHEFORT** in the seventeenth century to repel the English and watch over Protestant-leaning La Rochelle (see page 488). It remained an important naval base for centuries, with its shipyards, sail-makers, munition factories and a hospital. Built on a strict grid plan, the town is a monument to the tidiness of the military mind. **Place Colbert** is just as the seventeenth century left it, complete with lime trees and cobblestones brought from Canada as ships' ballast. The banks of the **Charente** river are beautiful, dominated by the eighteenth-century Royal Ropeworks and the stark, majestic Transporter Bridge, built in 1900.

## Musée d'Art et d'Histoire and Maison Pierre Loti

The explorers Pierre Loti – alias novelist Julien Viaud (1850–1923) – and the Lesson brothers haunt Rochefort's **Musée d'Art et d'Histoire** at 63 rue de Gaulle (Tues–Sun 10.30am–12.30pm & 2–6pm; €4), which houses exotic objects brought back from expeditions, and nautical artworks. The **Maison Pierre Loti** is still undergoing significant renovations, and so the museum now houses collections from his home and a 3D experience that allows you to take a guided tour of the building (reservations recommended; €8). The house itself is part of a row of modestly proportioned grey-stone houses, outwardly a model of petit bourgeois conformity, and inside an outrageous and fantastical series of rooms decorated to exotic themes, from medieval gothic to an Arabian room complete with minaret. You can see how the house suited Loti's private life: he threw extravagant fancy dress parties and, rather more scandalously, fathered more children with his Basque mistress, kept in a separate part of the house, than with his French wife.

## Corderie Royale, Hermione and Musée National de la Marine

**Corderie Royale** Daily: April–Sept 10am–7pm; Oct–March 10am–12.30pm & 2–6pm; adults €10, children €5; ⓦcorderie-royale.com **Hermione** Daily: Feb–March 10am–12.30pm & 2–6pm; April–June & Sept 10am–7pm; July & Aug 9am–7pm; adults €12, children €6; ⓦhermione.com
**Musée National de la Marine** April–Sept daily 10am–7pm; Oct–March Wed–Mon 1.30–6pm; adults €6.50; ⓦmusee-marine.fr

The **Corderie Royale**, or Royal Ropeworks, off rue Toufaire, is a rare example of seventeenth-century industrial architecture, substantially restored after damage in World War II. Between 1660 and the Revolution it furnished the entire French navy with rope. From here, you can stroll through gardens by the river and examine the rest of the admirably restored **Arsenal**. After a few minutes, you will come to Rochefort's latest pride and joy: a shipyard devoted to meticulously rebuilding the **Hermione**, the frigate aboard which La Fayette set sail from here in 1780 to assist the American bid for independence from the British. The completed ship set sail to America in summer 2015 to retrace her original voyage, but is back in port and open to visitors (though she does still take infrequent long voyages – check website for latest). A **combined ticket**, available at both museums and the tourist office, will get you into the Corderie Royale and the Hermione (€19). The **Musée National de la Marine** is a short walk from the Hermione and has a collection of sculptures and models of the Arsenal.

## ARRIVAL AND INFORMATION ROCHEFORT

**By train** The *gare SNCF* is located at the northern end of avenue du Président Thomas-Wilson, a 15min walk from the centre of town.

Destinations La Rochelle (10–20 daily; 20min); Saintes (7–12 daily; 35min).

**By bus** The bus station is in the centre at place de Verdun, where it crosses De Gaulle. Line G runs hourly from here to the *gare SNCF*.

Destinations Château d'Oléron (4–5 daily; 50min–1hr

10min); La Fumée-Île d'Aix (5–7 daily; 40min); Marennes (5–7 daily; 40min).

**Tourist office** The main tourist office is on avenue Sadi-Carnot (July & Aug daily 10am–6.30pm; April–June & Sept daily 10am–12.30pm & 2–6pm; Oct–March Mon–Sat 10am–12.30pm & 2–5.30pm; ☎05 46 99 08 60, ⓦrochefort-ocean.com).

**Bike rental** You can hire bikes from the outside the tourist office (from €12/day; make sure you have ID).

## ACCOMMODATION

**La Caravelle** 34 rue Jean-Jaurès ☎05 46 99 02 53, ⓦhotel-caravelle-rochefort.com. Simple but pleasant rooms, many of which are enlivened by splashes of colour. Breakfast €9.50. **€78**

**Municipal campsite** ☎05 46 82 67 70, ⓦville-rochefort.fr/decouvrir/camping-le-rayonnement. Utilitarian-looking campsite with kids' club, wi-fi, barbecues and mobile home access. It's a long haul if you've arrived at the *gare SNCF*: about half an hour's walk. March–Nov. **€13**

★ **Palmier sur Cour** 55 rue de la République ☎05 46

89 72 55, ⓦpalmiersurcour.com. A magnificent, broad-halled townhouse B&B in the centre, with a sunny garden and three bedrooms, adorned with paintings and antique books. Freshly baked cakes and biscuits are served for breakfast. Breakfast included. **€95**

**Roca Fortis** 14 rue de la République ☎05 46 99 26 32, ⓦhotel-rochefort.fr. Reasonably priced three-star central hotel opposite *Palmier sur Cour* with comfort-able modern rooms, a garden and a comprehensive breakfast (€10). **€85**

## EATING AND DRINKING

**Cap Nell** 1 quai Bellot ☎05 46 87 31 77, ⓦcapnell.com. Quayside dining, with a stylish modern interior, roomy outdoor terrace, and excellent seafood. Three-course *menus* from €22. Daily noon–2pm & 7.30–10pm (high season open all day).

**La Cave Passe à Table** 94bis Rue de la République ☎05 46 74 05 01, ⓦlacavepasseatable.com. The sister restaurant of its namesake in Saintes, this winery-cum-restaurant offers a wide range of wines by the glass. The three-course *menus* change daily (€17.50–18.50) but popular dishes include *magret de canard* (duck), filet mignon, and apricot tart. Tues–Thurs 9.30am–6pm, Fri & Sat 9.30am–10pm.

**Les Jardins du Lac** 3 chemin de Fontchaude, Trizay ☎05 46 82 03 56, ⓦles-jardins-du-lac-restaurant.fr. This chic country-hotel restaurant has views over a lake and

serves delicate gourmet meals. It's 11km southeast from Rochefort, so drive out on a Sunday for a long walk and leisurely lunch. *Menus* from €40. Tues–Sat 12.30–1.45pm & 7–8.45pm, Sun 12.30–1.45pm.

★ **Le Marydiane** 72 rue Jean-Jaurès ☎05 46 99 07 11, ⓦle-marydiane.com. Simple, seasonal ingredients get an original makeover at this homely restaurant, with dishes like squid ink risotto, succulent beef with mini crêpes and caramel nut panna cotta. There's a changing daily *menu* (€22). Mon & Wed noon–2pm, Tues & Thurs–Sat noon–2pm & 7.15–10pm.

★ **Pistache Chocolat** Place Colbert ☎05 46 87 11 96, ⓦpistache-chocolat.fr. It's not even a café – just a bakery and chocolatier, with a few tables on the street, but the sweets, cakes and bread (hand-kneaded because there's no room for a machine) are the best in town. Enjoy hot

**9**

chocolate, vanilla cupcakes, apple and cinnamon *macarons* or home-made peppermint ice cream. Tues–Sat 6.30am–7.30pm, Sun 6.30am–7pm.
**La Villette** 15 av Général-de-Gaulle ☎ 05 46 99 05 72.

Simple but tasty food is served up in this old-fashioned bistro and bar, popular with workers from the nearby market. With mains from €10, you'll have plenty of money left for shopping too. Mon–Sat noon–7pm.

## Fouras

The low-key seaside town of **FOURAS**, 30km south of La Rochelle, and accessible by bus #5 from La Rochelle (45min), is the main embarkation point for Île d'Aix (see below). The ferry dock, **Pointe de la Fumée**, is at the tip of a 3km long peninsula. The finger of land is hemmed in by fortresses, intended to protect the Charente against Norman attack, but later useful in repelling the Dutch and English.

### Fort Vauban and Île Madame

The seventeenth-century **Fort Vauban** (June to mid-Sept daily except Mon, 10am–noon & 3–6.30pm, Sept–May Sat & Sun 2.30–5.30pm; €4) now houses a small local history museum. From its esplanade there's a panorama of neighbouring forts and islands, including **Île Madame**, accessible at low tide from Port des Barques, via the Passe aux Boeufs causeway. The island also has a grim history as the internment site, and in most cases death site, of scores of priests from the region, victims of the anti-clerical terror unleashed in the 1790s.

### INFORMATION                                                           FOURAS

**Tourist office** Fouras's tourist office, which also serves the Île d'Aix, is situated on avenue du Bois Vert on the peninsula (July & Aug daily 9am–1pm & 2–6.30pm; April–June & Sept daily 9am–12.30pm & 2–6pm, Sun 10am–12.30pm & 2.30–6pm; Feb, March & Oct Mon–Sat 9.30am–12.30pm & 2–5.30pm; Nov–Jan Mon–Fri 9am–12.30pm & 2–5.30pm; ☎ 05 46 84 60 69, ⌨ rochefort-ocean.com).

### ACCOMMODATION

**Grand Hôtel des Bains** 15 rue du Général-Bruncher ☎ 05 46 84 03 44, ⌨ grandhotel-desbains.fr. Light, airy and tastefully decorated rooms make this former coaching inn a welcoming choice, plus there's a beautiful, flower-filled terrace to enjoy your breakfast (€11.90). The market and beach are both within a short stroll. **€89**

★ **La Roseraie** 2 rue Éric-Tabarly ☎ 05 46 84 64 89, ⌨ hotel-fouras.com. Cute as a button and neat as a pin, this adorable beach hotel is worth more than its two-star rating. The friendly owners, tree-lined garden and close proximity to the beach are added bonuses. Breakfast €8. **€60**

### EATING AND DRINKING

**L'Archipel** 2 av Philippe-Janet ☎ 05 46 83 30 37. Bright restaurant by the sea with ample windows and terrace seating to make the most of its position. Unsurprisingly, the emphasis is on seafood but – surprisingly – with a Caribbean twist, such as a Creole salad with crab samosas, prawns and pineapple (€15.60). Menus from €24.80. Mon–Wed 7–8.30pm, Thurs & Sun noon–2pm & 7–8.30pm,

Fri & Sat noon–2pm & 7–9pm.
**Ti Sable** Av Charles-de-Gaulle ☎ 05 46 84 61 10. With ample terrace seating and a view of the beachfront, this is Fouras's top restaurant for good reason. There's a varied menu with a focus on seafood and it's great value for money with menus from €20. Wed–Sun noon–2pm & 7–10pm.

## Île d'Aix

Lying in the Bay of Biscay like a forgotten croissant, **ÎLE D'AIX** (pronounced "eel dex"), just 2km long, has a population of only 200. It's a romantic place – frequented by abdicating emperors, wild birds and hollyhocks. It's also well-defended, with forts and ramparts. Over the course of history the island, particularly **Fort Liédot**, has often served as a prison, notably during the Crimean was and World War I. The best time to visit is in spring or autumn, avoiding the midsummer crowds; hire a bicycle, cycle round the perimeter of the island in an hour or two, paddle in the sea, and enjoy lunch at *Hôtel Napoléon*.

## Musée Napoléon

Napoleon lived on Île d'Aix for three days in July 1815, planning his escape to America, only to find himself on the way to St Helena and exile. Now his former home, the **Musée Napoléon** (April–Oct daily except Tues in Oct: 9.30am–12.30pm & 2–6pm; Nov–March daily except Tues: 9.30am–12.30pm & 2–5pm; €4.50; ⓦmusees-nationaux-napoleoniens.org), exhibits his clothing, art and arms. Napoleon's white dromedary camel, from whose back he conducted his Egyptian campaign, is lodged nearby at the **Musée Africain**, though it was closed at the time of research for extensive renovations; it should reopen in June 2020.

### ARRIVAL AND DEPARTURE — ÎLE D'AIX

**By ferry** Ferries connect Île d'Aix with Fouras (Pointe de la Fumée ⓣ 08 20 16 00 17, ⓦservice-maritime-iledaix.com) daily. Boats leave at least hourly in summer and a minimum of five times daily in winter; the journey takes approximately 30min. Buy tickets (adult return €9.80 in winter, €14.90 in summer) at the dock 30min before departure. In summer there are also ferries from La Rochelle and Oléron.

**Getting around** You can hire bikes from Cyclaix on rue Marengo (April to mid-Nov daily 9an–6pm; €12/day), or pick up a horse and carriage from place d'Austerlitz.

### ACCOMMODATION

**Napoléon** Rue Gourgaud ⓣ05 46 84 00 77, ⓦhotel-ile-aix.com. Sophisticated hotel with 18 modern rooms that have unfortunately become a little bland since being renovated, and views of the lighthouses and Fort Boyard. Just make sure you request a sea view. Breakfast €12. __€120__

**Résidence** Fort de la Rade ⓣ 01 58 21 55 50, ⓦpv-holidays.com. Spotless modern apartments and studios, with fully equipped kitchens, making this a popular choice for families and groups. There's an outdoor pool and it's just a few minutes' stroll from the port. Studio for two people per week: __€240__

### EATING AND DRINKING

**Les Paillots** ⓣ05 46 84 66 24. A simple seaside restaurant with a menu of fresh seafood, ship's galley decor and a terrace; a useful fallback if *Chez Joséphine* is full. Breakfast by reservation, *menus* from €21. Daily 9.30am–3.30pm & 7–10.30pm.

**Restaurant Chez Joséphine** Hôtel Napoléon ⓣ05 46 84 00 77, ⓦhotel-ile-aix.com/restaurant-josephine. With a pleasing modern menu of French classics and modish design, *Chez Joséphine* is an urban island wrapped in a rural island. *Menus* from €24. Daily noon–2.30pm & 7.30–9.30pm, closed Nov to early spring (date dependent on weather).

## Brouage and around

Eighteen kilometres southwest of Rochefort is **BROUAGE**, another seventeenth-century military base. The way into the town is through the **Porte Royale** in the north wall of the original fortifications. Locked inside, Brouage seems abandoned and somnolent; even the sea has retreated, and all that's left of the harbour is a series of pools (*claires*), where oysters are reared. Just south of Brouage, the oyster village of **Marennes** is the centre of production in a region that supplies over sixty percent of France's requirements.

### OYSTERS

Marennes' speciality is fattening *creuses* oysters, a species bred in France since the 1970s. It's a lucrative but precarious business, vulnerable to storm damage, temperature changes, salinity in the water, the ravages of starfish and umpteen other natural disasters.

Oysters begin life as minuscule larvae, which are "born" about three times a year. When a birth happens, the oystermen are alerted by a special radio service, and they all rush out to place their "collectors" – usually arrangements of roofing tiles – for the larvae to cling to. They mature there for eight or nine months, and are then scraped off and moved to *parcs* in the tidal waters of the sea. Finally, they're taken to *claires* – shallow rectangular pools where they are kept permanently covered by water that's less salty than sea water. Here they fatten up and acquire the greenish colour the market expects. With "improved" modern oysters, the whole cycle, which used to take five years, now takes about two.

**9**

Brouage forms a tight grid lined with low two-storey houses. On the second street to the right is a memorial to Samuel de Champlain, the local boy who founded the French colony of Québec in 1608. In the same century, Brouage witnessed the last pangs of a royal romance when Cardinal Mazarin, successor of Richelieu, locked up his niece, Marie Mancini, to keep her from her young sweetheart, Louis XIV. The politics of the time made the Infanta of Spain a more useful consort for the King of France. Louis gave in, while Marie pined on the battlements of Brouage. Returning from his marriage in St-Jean-de-Luz, Louis dodged his escort and stole away to see her. Finding her gone, he slept in her room and paced the battlements in her footsteps.

## INFORMATION

**Tourist office** Place Chasseloup-Laubat (April–June & Sept Tues–Sat 9.30am–12.30pm & 3–6pm; July & Aug daily 9.30am–1pm & 3–7pm; Oct–March Tues–Sat 10am–12.30pm & 3–5.30pm; ☎ 05 46 85 04 36, ⊚ www.tourisme-marennes.fr). Ask here about trips to the oyster beds (see page 497).

## ACCOMMODATION

**Le Brouage** 16 rue de Québec ☎ 05 46 85 03 06. This sweet hotel has simple, unfussy rooms in a green-shuttered building. The wood-beamed restaurant serves up oysters and other seafood specialities, with menus from €22. Open mid-March to Nov. **€59**

**Le Héron Cendré** 71 av du Général-de-Gaulle, La Tremblade ☎ 05 46 75 73 49, ⊚ hotelleheron.fr. Just a 30min drive to the centre of Île d'Oléron, this friendly hotel makes a money-saving alternative to the pricey island resorts, with quiet surroundings, bright rooms, private parking and beach-inspired decor. Breakfast €9. **€79**

# The Île d'Oléron

Joined to the mainland by a bridge just north of Marennes, the **ÎLE D'OLÉRON** is France's largest island after Corsica, a laid-back, unaffected fishing island and coastal resort.

Outside the tourist season, the island is a peaceful retreat: a patchwork of little villages, pine forests and gleaming muddy tributaries lined with fishing boats. Taken over by holiday-makers in July and August, it loses much of its tranquillity.

The main town in the south of the island, **Le Château**, is named after the **citadelle** that still stands, along with some seventeenth-century **fortifications**. The town thrives on its traditional oyster farming and boat building, and there's a lively **market** in place de la République every morning. The chief town and most picturesque of the island's settlements is **St-Pierre** in the north, whose market square has an unusual thirteenth-century monument, **La Lanterne des Morts**. The best beach is at **La Brée les Bains**, in the northeast. Activities abound, from cycling to **surfing**, and a great **aqua park** opens between June and September in Dolus d'Oléron in the centre of the island.

A pleasant place to spend an afternoon is **Pôle-Nature Marais aux Oiseaux** (daily: April–June & Sept 10am–1pm & 2–6pm; July & Aug 10am–7pm; €4.50; ⊚ marais-aux-oiseaux.fr), the bird park. Located a short distance off the D126 between St-Pierre and Dolus, right in the middle of the island, it's a breeding centre with many rare and endangered species.

## GETTING THERE AND AROUND                    ÎLE D'OLÉRON

Oléron can be reached by buses #6 and #7 from Rochefort (1hr), and in July and August minibuses connect the main towns on the island; ⊚ transports.nouvelle-aquitaine.fr for timetables.

## INFORMATION

**Tourist office** Place de la République in Le Château (April–June, Sept & Oct Mon–Sat 9.30am–12.30pm & 2.30–6.30pm; July & Aug Mon–Sat 9.30am–7pm, Sun 9.30am–1pm; Nov–Feb Mon–Fri 10am–12.30pm & 2.30–5.30pm; ☎ 05 46 85 65 23, ⊚ ot-chateau-oleron.fr). Bikes can be rented from Vélos 17 (☎ 05 46 47 14 05, ⊚ velos17loisirs.com), which has outlets in all the towns on the island. A day's cycle hire is around €13 for both adults and children.

## ACCOMMODATION

What Île d'Oléron does best is mid-range family-orientated beach hotels. Prices rise by 30–50 percent in high season and most hotels are closed Nov–March. For stays of a week or longer, tourist offices have lists of rental apartments.

**L'Albatros** 11 bd du Dr-Pineau, St-Trojan-les-Bains ☎ 05 46 76 00 08, ⓦ albatros-hotel-oleron.com. A little gem of a seaside hotel with a selection of cosy garden bungalows or sea-view rooms, and an excellent on-site restaurant. Breakfast €12.50. €115

**Face aux Flots** 24 rue du Moulin, La Cotinière ☎ 05 46 47 10 05, ⓦ hotel-faceauxflots-oleron.com. A family-run three-star hotel in a smart 1930s building, right by the beach. Rooms are small but sunny and modern, with balconies and many with an ocean view, plus there's a pool, bar and friendly service. The only downside is that there's no lift. Breakfast €11. €78

**Pertuis d'Antioche** Off the D273 ☎ 05 46 47 92 00 ⓦ camping-antiochedoleron.com. A mere 150m from the beach, with mobile home rental, swimming pool, paddling pool, jacuzzi and solarium, this is a pricey but luxurious option for campers looking for something a little better than the usual. April–Sept. €36

**De la Plage** 51 bd du Capitaine-Leclerc, La Cotinière ☎ 05 46 47 28 79, ⓦ oleronhotel.com. Quiet, simple family hotel in the suburbs of La Cotinière, with rooms and studio flats (with kitchenette). All rooms have a terrace or a balcony, and there's a heated pool (open April–Oct). The hotel is an easy 10min walk from the shops, restaurants and harbour. Breakfast €9.20. €89

**Le Square** Place des Anciens Combattants, St-Pierre ☎ 05 46 47 00 35, ⓦ le-square-hotel.fr. Decent value two-star hotel with pretty blue-and-white rooms that make the most of their limited space, plus a palm-lined private pool, free parking and a games room. It's just minutes away from the restaurants and shops of St-Pierre, so punt for a room at the back if you want peace and quiet. Breakfast €7. €79

## EATING AND DRINKING

**Au Gré du Vin** 1 place de la République, Le Château d'Oléron ☎ 05 46 85 02 73. Arguably some of the most beautiful plates of food on the island, complemented by excellent wines and superlative service. Thurs–Mon noon–2pm & 7–10pm.

★ **Les Jardins d'Aliénor** 11 rue du Maréchal-Foch, Le Château d'Oléron ☎ 05 46 76 48 30, ⓦ lesjardinsdalienor. com. A haute-rustic hotel and gourmet restaurant, where memorable gourmet cuisine is served in a gorgeous, walled garden. *Menus* start from €49, but mains such as tuna steak start at €25. Summer Tues–Sun, Winter Wed–Sun: noon–2pm & 7–10pm.

**Le Jour du Poisson** 3 rue de l'Ormeau, St-Denis ☎ 05 46 75 76 21. A small but celebrated restaurant specializing – unsurprisingly – in fish and as popular with the locals as it is with tourists. Mains start at €15. Thurs 7.30–9pm, Fri–Mon noon–1.30pm & 7.30–9pm.

★ **Le Saint-Pierre** 19 rue de la République, St-Pierre ☎ 05 46 47 14 39. A lovable cottage restaurant serving island staples like *moules-frites* (from €11), home-made burgers (from €12) and artisan ice creams with flavours like 'Cognac' and 'Coco Chanel'. Sept–June Tues–Sat noon–2pm & 7–10pm; July & Aug daily.

# Royan

Before World War II, **ROYAN** was a glorious seaside resort, drawing the cream of society with its luxury hotels and casinos. The town is still popular, but the glory days are gone – a victim of Allied bombing and 1950s town planning. But Royan still has its **beaches**, which are lovely, particularly out towards the northern suburb of Pontaillac.

In a weather-beaten square behind the waterfront is Gillet and Hébrard's uncompromising masterpiece, the **church of Notre-Dame** (1955–58). Tall concrete columns roar upwards, surging into a 65-metre bell tower, which looks rather like the prow of Noah's ark. The inside fulfils the promise of the outside with triangular columns and metres of stained glass. Royan's highlight is the area around **boulevard Garnier**, which leads southeast from Rond-Point-de-la-Poste along the beach. The area once housed Paris's good and great, including Émile Zola who lived at **Le Rêve**, 58 bd Garnier.

## Excursions from Royan

There are various **cruises** from Royan in season – ask at the tourist office – including one to the **Cordouan lighthouse**, built by the Black Prince. There's

**9**

also a 20min **ferry** (7 daily; one-way: pedestrians €3.30, bicycles €1.70, motorbikes €10.70, cars €23.70) that crosses to the headland on the other side of the Gironde, **Pointe de Grave**. From there, a bicycle trail and the GR8 walking trail head down the coast through the pines and dunes to the bay of Arcachon.

An ideal bicycle or picnic excursion just over an hour's ride from Royan is to **Talmont**, 16km up the Gironde on the GR360. Apart from a few ups and downs through the woods outside Royan, it's all level terrain. The low-lying village clusters around the beautiful twelfth-century **church of Ste-Radegonde**, perched on a cliff above the Gironde.

## ARRIVAL AND INFORMATION                                            ROYAN

**By train** The *gare SNCF* is on place de la Gare near cours de l'Europe.
**Destinations** Angoulême (4–7 daily; 1hr 30min); Saintes (3–13 daily; 30min).
**Tourist office** Bd de la Grandière (April to mid-June Mon–Sat 9am–12.30pm & 2–6pm, Sun 10am–12.30pm; mid-June to Aug daily: 9am–7pm; Sept–March Mon–Sat

9am–12.30pm & 2–5.30pm; ☏ 05 46 08 17 50, ⓦ royan-tourisme.com).
**Bike rental** Hire bikes for €12 per day from Cycles Horseau (107 cours de l'Europe; ☏ 05 46 39 96 43).
**Car rental** The major car rental firms are based near the station.

## ACCOMMODATION

Accommodation in Royan is overpriced and scarce in high season – you might be better off making it a day-trip from Saintes or Rochefort.
**Les Bleuets** 21 façade de Foncillon ☏ 05 46 38 51 79, ⓦ hotel-les-bleuets.com. A good-value, nautical-themed hotel opposite Foncillon beach, with views of the Gironde and the Atlantic. Rooms are clean and for an extra €30 you can get a sea view. Breakfast €8.50. **€80**
**Camping Clairefontaine** 16 rue du Colonel-Lachaud, on the outskirts of Royan ☏ 05 46 39 08 11, ⓦ campeole. co.uk. A four-star campsite with a range of cabins and chalets, 300m from the beach, with a swimming pool and faux beach in the grounds. May to mid-Oct. **€27**
**Family Golf Hotel** 28 bd Garnier ☏ 05 46 05 14 66,

ⓦ family-golf-hotel.com. Despite a slightly incongruous mix of chandeliers and rattan furnishings, rooms here are breezy and cheerful, many with balconies looking out over the ocean. The location is hard to beat, right on the beach. Breakfast €12. **€110**
**Miramar** 173 av de Pontaillac ☏ 05 46 39 03 64, ⓦ hotel-miramar-royan.fr. In prime beachside location, this well-run hotel has large, comfortable rooms decked out with chic nautical-inspired decor, a bar and a sea-view terrace. Breakfast €12. **€124**
**Rêve de Sable** 10 place du Maréchal-Foch ☏ 05 46 06 52 25, ⓦ revedesable.com. Inexpensive and comfortable, this small three-star hotel is a few minutes' walk from the beach, and right in the heart of town. **€103**

## EATING AND DRINKING

★ **L'Aquarelle** 71a rte de Montil ☏ 05 46 22 11 38, ⓦ laquarelle.net. Boasting a rural location, this Michelin-starred eatery is worth the 10min journey from Royan. Delightfully eccentric dishes marry unusual flavours like foie gras with coconut or duck with sweet ginger, and the post-dinner coffee comes with an array of hand-crafted sweets and chocolates. *Menus* will set you back as much as €120, but the €37 lunch *menu* is best for cash-strapped foodies. Tues 7–9.15pm, Wed–Sat noon–3.30pm & 7–9.15pm, Sun noon–3.15pm.
**Les Filets Bleus** 14 rue Notre-Dame ☏ 05 46 05 74 00. Behind its humble blue and white facade, this local favourite serves up classic, unfussy cuisine, with a mouthwatering range of fish and seafood. *Menus* from €19. Tues–Sat noon–2pm & 7–9pm.

**Le Petit Bouchon** 8 quai de l'Amiral-Meyer ☏ 05 46 22 08 82, ⓦ lepetitbouchon17.com. Smack bang on the seafront with a spacious terrace overlooking the colourful marina, *Le Petit Bouchon* should be an overpriced tourist trap, but instead it's atmospheric and well-priced, with *menus* from €24. Mid-Feb to June & Sept to mid-Nov Tues–Sat noon–2pm & 7–10pm, Sun noon–2pm; July & Aug daily noon–2pm & 7–10pm.
**La Table Notre-Dame** 11 rue des Bains ☏ 05 46 05 89 75. A great find, this relaxed restaurant decked out in greys and browns has a sophisticated feel. The short menu includes the likes of duck breast with Pineau des Charentes (€19), while the formules (from €15) are excellent value. Mon–Sat noon–1.15pm & 7–9.30pm.

**9**

# Saintes

**SAINTES** was once more important than its modest size suggests; it was the capital of the province of Saintonge and a little cog in the Roman machine. The city retains an atmosphere of grandeur and reminders of past greatness, including a marvellous amphitheatre and two Romanesque pilgrim churches.

## Abbaye aux Dames

Daily: Jan–March & Nov 2–6pm; April & May 10am–12.30pm & 2–7pm; June–Sept 10am–7pm; Oct & Dec 10am–12.30pm & 2–6pm • €8 • ⓦ abbayeauxdames.org

The abbey church, the **Abbaye aux Dames**, is as unique as Notre-Dame in Poitiers. A sculpted doorway conceals the plain, domed interior, but its most unusual feature is the eleventh-century tower, by turns square, octagonal and lantern-shaped. A visit to the abbey is now described as a "music adventure", with music accompanying – and adding to – your experience, the highlight of which is the rather wonderful Musical Carousel (Tues–Sun 10am–12.30pm & 2–7pm; €2.50). A classical music festival takes place in the abbey in mid-July.

## Arc de Germanicus and the Musée Archéologique

On the riverbank is the Roman **Arc de Germanicus**, a triumphal arch built in 19 AD and dedicated to Germanicus Caesar, as well as his uncle, the emperor Tiberius, and cousin Drusus. Germanicus died later that year, most likely poisoned by Tiberius – he was becoming too popular. In a stone building next door is the **Musée Archéologique** (April–Sept Tues–Sat 10am–12.30pm & 1.30–6pm, Sun 2–6pm; Oct–March Tues–Sat 1.30–5pm, Sun 2–5pm; €3), which provides a glimpse into Roman Saintes.

## Cathédrale de St-Pierre

A footbridge crosses from the Musée Archéologique to the covered market on the west bank of the river. Nearby is place du Marché and the **Cathédrale de St-Pierre**, a tubby Romanesque church with an imposing Neoclassical facade, where John Calvin preached from 1536 to 1564.

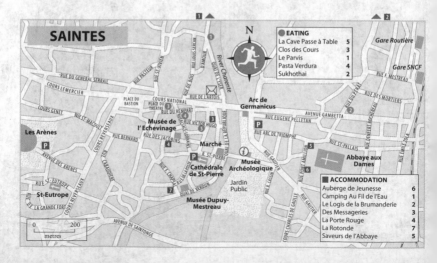

> **PINEAU DES CHARENTES**
> Roadside signs throughout the Charente advertise **Pineau des Charentes**, a sweet liqueur made by blending lightly fermented grape must and cognac. It's drunk chilled as an aperitif, or with oysters. **Pineau** is also used to make local specialities like *moules au Pineau* (mussels cooked with *Pineau*, tomatoes, garlic and parsley) and *lapin à la saintongeaise* (rabbit casseroled with *Pineau rosé*, shallots, garlic, tomatoes, thyme and bay leaves).

## Les Arènes

May–Sept daily 10am–7pm; Oct–April Tues–Sat 10am–12.30pm & 1.30–5pm, Sun 2–5.30pm • €4

Saintes' Roman heritage is best seen at **Les Arènes**, one of the finest amphitheatres in France. The remains are perhaps all the more extraordinary for their location: this monumental vestige from an ancient past, now a little grassy in parts, sits embedded in a valley almost completely surrounded by bland suburbia; a forgotten, sleeping relic dating from 40 AD, also the oldest surviving Roman ruins in France. To find it take the small footpath beginning by 54 cours Reverseaux. On the way back from the amphitheatre call in at the eleventh-century **church of St-Eutrope**, with its carved choir and atmospheric crypt; it houses the third-century tomb of Saintes' first bishop, Eutropius.

## Around Saintes

There are a number of marvellous Romanesque churches reachable by car from Saintes. In **Fenioux**, 29km to the north towards St-Jean-d'Angély, there's St-Europe with its mighty spire, while the church at **Rioux**, 12km south, has an intricate facade. Best of all is the twelfth-century pilgrim **church St-Pierre**, at **Aulnay**, 37km northeast of Saintes, with its facade depicting Christ in Majesty and St Peter, crucified upside down, with two lithe soldiers balancing on the arms of his cross to hammer nails into his feet.

Some 12km from Saintes, at Port d'Envaux, is the fantastic open-air gallery **Les Lapidiales** (ⓦlapidiales.org). Here, many of Europe's best sculptors have carved into the disused stone quarry, creating a magnificent permanent collection that grows yearly.

### ARRIVAL AND INFORMATION
### SAINTES

**By train** Saintes' *gare SNCF* is on avenue de la Marne at the east end of the main road, avenue Gambetta.

Destinations Angoulême (4–7 daily; 1hr 20min); Cognac (6 daily; 20min); Rochefort (7–12 daily; 35min); Royan (3–13 daily; 30min).

**By bus** The bus station is on Galerie du Bois-d'Amour, behind quai de l'Yser.

Destinations Cognac (up to 5 daily; 35min); Rochefort (1–2 daily; 1hr min); St-Pierre d'Oléron (2–3 daily; 2hr 10min).

**Tourist office** Place Bassompierre by the Arc Germanicus (May–June & Sept daily 9.30am–12.30pm & 1.30–6pm; July–Aug daily 9am–7pm; Oct–April Mon–Sat 10am–12.30pm & 1.30pm–5pm; ☎05 46 74 23 82, ⓦsaintes-tourisme.fr). The office offers bike hire, maps with self-guided walking tours and free wi-fi, and also organizes regular guided tours and boat trips on the Charente during the summer.

### ACCOMMODATION

**Auberge de Jeunesse** 7 place Geoffroy-Martel ☎05 46 92 14 92, ⓦfuaj-aj-saintes.org. In a superb location behind the Abbaye aux Dames, the facilities here are modern and breakfast is included, though rooms could do with a bit of an update. Reception: Mon–Fri 8am–noon & 5–10pm, Sat & Sun 8–10am & 6–10.30pm. Dorms €17.50, twins €47

**Camping Au Fil de l'Eau** 8 rue Courbiac ☎05 46 93 08 00, ⓦcamping-saintes-17.com. This campsite occupies expansive grounds by the River Charente, and has a laundrette, *pétanque* and table tennis, mini-golf, river

fishing and a restaurant. Mid-April to mid-Oct. €15

**Le Logis de la Brumanderie** 57 rte de la Brumanderie ☎06 89 35 25 60, ⓦlabrumanderie.com. Surrounded by vineyards, this family-run B&B 3km from Saintes is clean, comfortable and quiet, with English-speaking hosts, a separate entry for guests, and easy access to golf, tennis and riding. There's also a *gîte* that sleeps three people. €65

**Des Messageries** Rue des Messageries ☎05 46 93 64 99, ⓦhotel-des-messageries.com. A large, pleasant chain hotel with garage parking on a quiet central courtyard. Most rooms have a/c and all have TV and minibar, and there's a

**9**

well-stocked breakfast buffet (€9.50). €106

**La Porte Rouge** 15 rue des Jacobins ☎ 05 46 90 46 71, �ⓦ sites.google.com/site/moniquepotel/home. An authentic sixteenth-century building, converted by friendly Franco-New Yorkers into a book-lined, art-filled home with guest rooms. The views of the town are spectacular, the location central, and there's a small walled garden. Prices can rise up to €160. €85

**La Rotonde** 2 rue Monconseil ☎ 06 87 51 70 92, ⓦ chambres-hotes-saintes.com. A princely B&B which could give most luxury hotels a run for their money, with its open fires, fresh flowers, antique sideboards and the Charente flowing beneath the windows. Some rooms have kitchenettes. €102

**Saveurs de l'Abbaye** 1 place St-Pallais ☎ 05 46 94 17 91, ⓦ saveurs-abbaye.com. A sleek but inexpensive hotel opposite the Abbaye aux Dames, with parquet floors and light rooms (ask for one on the top floor). A decent restaurant (closed Sun & Mon) has set *menus* from €18. €72

### EATING AND DRINKING

**La Cave Passe à Table** 27 rue St-Michel ☎ 05 46 74 05 01, ⓦ lacavepasseatable.com. Half vintner's, half restaurant, pocket-sized *La Cave* sells 20 wines by the glass (from €3.50), and a three-course daily *menu* (€17) served at tables in the shop front. Tues–Thurs 10am–7pm, Fri & Sat 10am–10pm.

**Clos des Cours** 2 place du Théâtre ☎ 05 46 74 62 62, ⓦ closdescours.com. An upmarket central restaurant run by a passionate couple, whose world travels have added a unique edge to their fantastic French cooking. Lunch *menus* from €15.50, dinner from €30. Mon–Sat noon–2pm & 7–9pm, Sun 10am–2pm.

**Le Parvis** 12bis quai de l'Yser ☎ 05 46 97 78 12, ⓦ restaurant-le-parvis.fr. Located along the riverside a short stroll from the *centre ville*, this deservedly popular restaurant has a tranquil garden terrace and thoughtfully presented gourmet cuisine. They also run cooking classes. Evening *menus* at €30. Tues–Sat noon–1pm & 7.15–9pm.

**Pasta Verdura** 7 rue du Rempart ☎ 05 46 74 98 22. A funky modern lunch-bar with plenty of healthy lunch choices including organic salads, vegetarian options and artisan ice creams. Eat in or take away, with lunch *formules* at €11. Daily 11.30am–5pm.

**Sukhothai** 113 av Gambetta ☎ 05 46 91 88 08, ⓦ sukhothai.fr. Fresh, piquant Thai cooking served in cheery surroundings, with an option to take away. Three-course *menu* €28.50. Tues–Sat noon–2pm & 7–10pm.

# Cognac

Anyone who does not already know what **COGNAC** is about will quickly nose its quintessential air as they stroll about the medieval lanes of the town's riverside quarter. For here is the greatest concentration of *chais* (warehouses), where the high-quality brandy is matured, its fumes blackening the walls with tiny fungi. Cognac *is* cognac, from the tractor driver and pruning-knife wielder to the manufacturer of corks, bottles and cartons. Untouched by recession (almost 98 percent of production is exported), it is likely to thrive as long as the world has sorrows to drown – a sunny, prosperous, self-satisfied little place.

Cognac has a number of medieval stone and half-timbered buildings in the narrow streets of the old town, of which rue Saulnier and rue de l'Isle-d'Or make atmospheric backdrops for a stroll, while picturesque **Grande-Rue** winds through the heart of the old quarter to the *chais*, down by the river. The attractive *hôtel de ville* is set in pleasant gardens just to the east.

## Around Cognac

The gentle landscape around Cognac is good for walking and cycling. One worthwhile walk is the towpath or *chemin de halage* that follows the south bank of the Charente from Cognac upstream to Pont de la Trâche, then on to the idyllic village of **Bourg-Charente** (about 8km in all), with its castle and Romanesque church. Alternatively, follow the GR4 the other way to the hamlet of **Richemont**, 5km northwest of Cognac, where you can swim in the pools of the tiny River Antenne, below an ancient church on a steep bluff in the woods.

### Jarnac

One marvellous excursion is upstream to **Jarnac**, from where you can take boat trips on the Charente, arranged by the Jarnac tourist office (7 quai de l'Orangerie; April–June

## COGNAC IN COGNAC

No trip to Cognac is complete without investigating the drink behind the town. All the major houses open their doors, and bottles, to visitors, so you can pick the one that appeals to your interests: **Otard** (127 bd Denfert-Rochereau; ☎05 45 36 88 86, ⓦbaronotard.com; tours from €11) is historical – the birthplace of François Ier in 1494, and a prison for British prisoners after the Seven Years'War; vast **Rémy Martin** (20 rue de la Société Vinicole; ☎05 45 35 76 66, ⓦremymartin.com; from €20) ferries visitors round on a little train; **Camus** (ⓦcamus.fr) is still a family-run outfit; at **Hennessy** (ⓦhennessy.com) you can cross the river on a boat to visit the storehouses; **Meukow** (ⓦmeukowcognac.com) is run by a family of Franco-Russian entrepreneurs; and at **Martell** (ⓦmartell.com) you can visit the founder's home, and a replica of a traditional cognac barge. You will find more historical information at **Écomusée du Cognac** (☎05 46 94 91 16; April–Sept daily 10am–12.30pm & 2.30–6.30pm; adults €7) an 18km drive northwest of Cognac, which shows the evolution of the distillation process and includes tasting of cognacs and liqueurs. Follow the D731 to St-Jean-d'Angély for 13km as far as Burie, then turn right onto the D131, 4km from Migron.

& Sept Tues–Fri 9.30am–12.30pm & 1.30–5.30pm; July & Aug Mon 1.30–5.30, Tues–Fri 9.30am–12.30pm & 1.30–5.30pm, Sat 9.30am–12.30pm; Oct–March Tues–Fri 9am–12.30pm; ☎05 45 81 09 30, ⓦtourism-cognac.com). The town proudly boasts its connection with the late President Mitterrand, who was born and buried here. The **Musée François-Mitterrand**, 10 quai de l'Orangerie (mid-April to mid-Sept Wed–Fri 2–6pm, Sat & Sun 10am–12.30pm & 2–6pm; €4; ☎05 45 81 38 88), houses a permanent exhibition on Mitterrand's public works.

### ARRIVAL AND INFORMATION                                          COGNAC

**By train** To walk to the central place François-Ier from the *gare SNCF* on bd de Paris, go down rue Mousnier, right on rue Taransaud, past the PTT and up rue du 14-Juillet. The square is dominated by an equestrian statue of the king, and in fine weather the cafés here teem with locals.

**Tourist office** 16 rue du 14-Juillet (April–June & Sept Mon–Sat 9.30am–5.30pm; July & Aug Mon–Sat 9.30am–6.30pm, Sun 9.30am–1pm; Oct–March Mon–Sat 10am–5pm, closed Tues morning; ☎05 45 82 10 71, ⓦtourism-cognac.com), where you can book tours of the Cognac houses – same-day tours are often available in June–Aug, with English guides – as well as get information on river trips.

### ACCOMMODATION

**Camping de Cognac** Bd de Châtenay ☎05 45 32 13 32, ⓦcampingdecognac.com. Three-star campsite on the tree-lined banks of the river. Late April to mid-Sept. **€18**

**Le Cheval Blanc** 6 place Bayard ☎05 45 82 09 55, ⓦhotel-chevalblanc.fr. Clean, no-frills accommodation in the centre of town. Probably the best-value central option and there are cheaper weekend deals available. **€71**

**Gîtes de Brives** 23 rte des Romains ☎05 46 93 15 34, ⓦgitesdecognac.eu. Family rental cottages (for 2, 4–6 or 6–7) and sweet B&B rooms set in large grounds, 13km from town. There's also a big swimming pool, children's play area, *boules* court, volleyball, badminton, table tennis and gym. Rental €450–1300 per week. B&B per night **€75**

★ **Quai des Pontis** 16 rue des Pontis ☎05 45 32 47 40, ⓦquaidespontis.com. If you fell asleep reading *Wind In The Willows* and dreamt up a hotel, it might look like *Quai des Pontis*: a few acres of grassy land on a riverbank, with birds singing, a handful of luxuriously refitted gypsy caravans, and long-legged fishing huts (priciest but best). A golf cart delivers luggage to the "rooms", and breakfast (€10.30 per person) is left in a hamper at your door. There's also a disused factory, converted into traditional B&B accommodation near the road, plus a number of modern lodges (some with river views) that have kitchenettes. Caravans **€98**, cabins **€108**, B&B **€88**, lodges **€90**

**L'Yeuse** 65 rue de Bellevue ☎05 45 36 82 60, ⓦyeuse. fr. An old-fashioned château hotel located on the outskirts of town, with the heavy florals and furniture popular in the 1960s, a hilly garden and a comfortable bar. Guests have free use of the mini-spa (hamam, sauna, jacuzzi). **€139**

### EATING

Picnickers should visit the food market on place d'Armes (Tues–Sun 8am–1pm).

**Bistro de Claude** 55 rue Grande ☎05 45 82 60 32, ⓦbistro-de-claude.com. Tucked up a sleepy cobblestone lane in the old town, this is a Cognac institution, with fine food, knowledgeable staff, 25 types of cognac and a

**9**

smart, cosy interior. Dress is smart-casual, and the service is leisurely, so allow a couple of hours for dinner. Evening *menu* €36. Mon–Fri noon–1.30pm & 7.30–9.30pm.

**Torréfaction Marignan** 16 rue d'Angoulême ☎ 05 45 82 12 92. Suffused with the dark, warm smell of chocolate, coffee and apricots, this admirable coffee house stocks 300 kinds of tea and has previously been awarded the distinction of Best Coffee Roaster in France. Tues–Sat 8.30am–7pm.

**Le Chantilly** 146 av Victor-Hugo ☎ 05 45 32 43 07. Simple but tasty food is the order of the day at this friendly,

no-frills bistro, plus there's a quiet terrace out back. Don't be put off by its fast-food joint frontage – the food is quality and well-priced with *menus* from €12 and dishes like couscous and paella to take away. Daily noon–2pm.

**Le St-Jacques** 8 rue des Minotiers ☎ 05 45 82 25 78. Jolly worker's bistro with tables so close you can almost taste your neighbour's soup. Piquant, robust cooking and friendly service. Daily *menus* from €13 and the bar is open all day, with wi-fi available for customers. Mon–Sat 7am–3pm & 5–9pm.

# Angoulême and around

Perched on a plateau above a meander in the River Charente, hilly **ANGOULÊME** is the capital of its department. The town's splendid architectural muddle attests to a history of conquest and re-conquest stretching back to the sixth century, when the Franks took it from the Visigoths. An industrial powerhouse, Angoulême once manufactured paper for the whole of France, but only a few mills struggled into the twenty-first century. Today, it's better known for its comic strips, illustration and animation, and some 200,000 enthusiasts descend on Angoulême each January for the International Comics Festival.

## The old town

The **old town** is a natural hilltop fortress. On the southern edge stands the **cathedral**, whose west front offers a dense exposition on twelfth-century theology, culminating in a Risen Christ surrounded by angels. A lively frieze beneath the tympanum commemorates the recapture of Spanish Zaragoza from the Moors; a bishop transfixes a Moorish giant with his lance, while legendary military commander Roland (Charles the Great's nephew) kills the Moorish king.

Wandering the old town you'll see brightly coloured **comic strips** and murals painted on various town walls. The city is a world leader of *bandes dessinées*, or comic books, and the tourist office has a leaflet detailing the location of every wall mural.

## Cité Internationale de la Bande Dessinée

121 rue de Bordeaux • July & Aug Tues–Fri 10am–7pm, Sat & Sun 2–7pm; June–Sept Tues–Fri 10am–6pm, Sat & Sun 2–6pm • €7 for the museum, library and reading room; free for library only; free for under-18s; free for all first Sundays Oct–June • ⓦ citebd.org

The **Cité Internationale de la Bande Dessinée** owns an impressive collection of original drawings including favourites like Astérix, Peanuts and Tintin, and traces the 150-year development of the comic. The building includes a vast library, with many in English.

### ARRIVAL AND INFORMATION

ANGOULÊME

**By train** Angoulême can be reached by train from Cognac, Limoges and Poitiers. From the *gare SNCF*, avenue Gambetta leads uphill to the town centre (15min).
Destinations Bordeaux (16–22 daily; 1hr–1hr 30min); Poitiers (9–12 daily; 45min–1hr 15min); Royan (4–7 daily; 1hr 30min); Saintes (4–7 daily; 1hr 30min).
**By bus** Buses leave from either the train station or place

Bouillaud.
**Tourist office** 7bis rue du Chat (July & Aug Mon–Sat 9am–6.30pm, Sun 9.30am–1pm; Sept–June Mon & Wed–Fri 9am–12.30pm & 1.30–6pm, Tues 11am–12.30pm & 1.30–6pm, Sat 9.30am–12.30pm & 1.30–5.30pm; ☎ 05 45 95 16 84, ⓦ angouleme-tourisme.com), on place des Halles, opposite the large covered market (mornings).

### ACCOMMODATION

**Camping du Plan d'Eau** Impasse des Rouyères, St Yrieix ☎ 06 88 69 11 74, ⓦ camping-angouleme.fr.

Sparkling three-star site with cabins that can be reached by #3 bus to St Yrieix from the Hôtel de Ville. €13.70

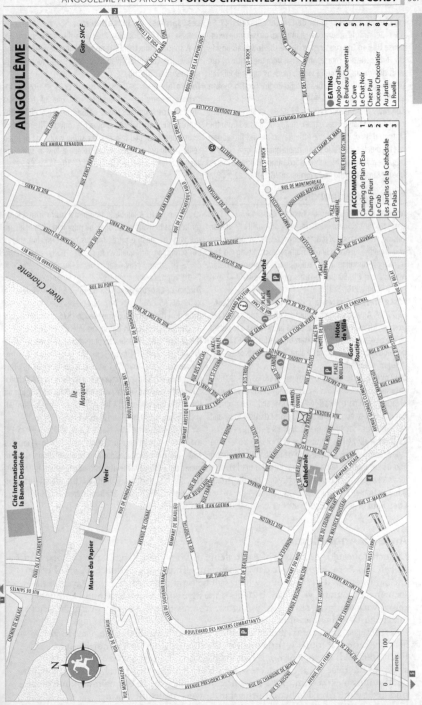

# ANGOULÊME

**Gare SNCF**

River Charente

Île Marquet

Weir

Cité Internationale de la Bande Dessinée

Musée du Papier

**● EATING**

| | |
|---|---|
| Angolo d'Italia | 2 |
| Le Bruleau Charentais | 6 |
| La Cave | 5 |
| Le Chat Noir | 3 |
| Chez Paul | 7 |
| Duceau Chocolatier | 8 |
| Au Jardin | 4 |
| La Ruelle | 1 |

**■ ACCOMMODATION**

| | |
|---|---|
| Camping du Plan d'Eau | 1 |
| Champ Fleuri | 2 |
| Le Crab | 5 |
| Les Jardins de la Cathédrale | 4 |
| Du Palais | 3 |

Marché

Hôtel de Ville

Gare Routière

Cathédrale

0 100 metres

N

9

★**Champ Fleuri** Chemin de l'Hirondelle ☎ 05 45 68 35 84, ⓦ champ-fleuri.com. Rambling, picturesque farmhouse B&B in the countryside above the town, alongside the Hirondelle golf course, only 3min from the centre by car, with five rooms, beautiful views, gardens and a pool. Tall people should avoid the beamed BD Room. English spoken and breakfast is included. €100

**Le Crab** 27 rue Kléber ☎ 05 45 93 02 93, ⓦ hotel-le-crab. com. Tucked down a backstreet, clearly signposted from the station, this *Logis* hotel is a little frayed around the edges, but it's quiet, secure and comfortable enough for a night or two. The owners are friendly and accommodating and there's free off-street parking and a restaurant. Breakfast €7. €68

**Les Jardins de la Cathédrale** 35 rue Waldeck-Rousseau ☎ 05 45 22 59 87, ⓦ lesjardinsdelacathedrale. fr. A spacious nineteenth-century family home slumbering below the cathedral, with two cosy guest rooms, both spotless, if a little frilly. €70

**Du Palais** 4 place Francis-Louvel ☎ 05 45 92 54 11, ⓦ hotel-angouleme.fr. Undoubtedly one of the most atmospheric hotels in town, housed in a graceful 18th-century building that was originally a convent. The romantic rooms boast original features like stone walls and beamed ceilings, though if possible ask to see a few as some are vastly better than others. Breakfast €7.50–11.50. €86

## EATING AND DRINKING

**Angolo d'Italia** 43 rue de Genève ☎ 05 45 90 51 74, ⓦ restaurant-angolo-italia.fr. Good-quality Italian cuisine, with a range of pastas and pizzas, reasonable prices and friendly service. Choose from alfresco dining on the terrace or snuggling in the atmospheric stone-brick cellar. Menus from €19.80. Tues–Thurs noon–2pm & 7–10pm (till 10.30pm Fri & Sat).

★**Le Bruleau Charentais** 10 rue de Beaulieu ☎ 05 45 69 72 17. An authentic chophouse with a roaring open fire from which molten camembert and juicy steaks are pulled by the pink-nosed chef. Grills start from as little as €11, with generous portions, chips and salad. Book ahead. Mon–Sat 7.30pm–midnight.

**La Cave** 13 rue Ludovic-Trarieux ☎ 06 08 86 83 93, ⓦ lacaveangouleme.com. A classy wine bar with a vast array of Tariquet, Mainart, Michel Juillot, cognac and champagne to drink in or take home, plus they organize château tours and tastings. Tues–Sat 10.30am–12.30pm & 3–8pm.

**Le Chat Noir** 24 rue de Genève ☎ 05 45 95 26 27. The faded facade of this popular café belies its humble charm and it's in prime position right opposite the market. Join locals for a post-shopping coffee or bite to eat on the terrace – menus from €13.40. Daily 9am–midnight.

**Chez Paul** 8 place Francis-Louvel ☎ 05 45 90 04 61, ⓦ chez-paul.fr. A laidback, traditional bistro with a large terrace, garden and a bar, open till midnight. Best of all are the very reasonable prices (*menus from* €18), but there's no scrimping on quality. April–Oct daily noon–2pm & 7–10.30pm; Nov–March Mon–Sat noon–2pm & 7–10.30pm.

**Duceau Chocolatier** 18 place de l'Hôtel-de-Ville ☎ 05 45 95 06 42, ⓦ chocolaterie-duceau.com. A truly delightful chocolate shop; founded in 1876, with more than 40 chocolates made in-house, an interior as delectable as the praline, and a celebrated pure chocolate ganache. Mon 2.30–7pm, Tues–Fri 9am–7pm, Sat 9am–1pm & 2–7pm.

**Au Jardin** 5 rue Ludovic-Trarieux ☎ 05 45 90 07 97. A relaxed, bright fuchsia restaurant is a particularly great choice for vegetarians and vegans, with lots of salads and the like on the menu (mains around €10). Mon–Fri noon–2.30pm all year round, plus June–Aug Mon & Tues 7–9pm.

★**La Ruelle** 6 rue Trois Notre-Dame ☎ 05 45 95 15 19, ⓦ laruelle-angouleme.fr. Reinvented French favourites with surprising combinations and an international flair are presented with panache at this modern, urban restaurant. For the full experience, opt for the six-course *menu dégustation* (€57). Tues–Fri noon–2pm & 7.30–9.30pm, Sat 7.30–9.30pm.

## Around Angoulême

**La Rochefoucauld**, 22km east of Angoulême, is home to a Renaissance **château** (Jan & Feb Sun 2pm; March–Dec daily except Tues 10am–7pm; adult €10, child €5) on the banks of the River Tardoire, which still belongs to the family that gave the town its name a thousand years ago. It stages a massive son et lumière (sound and light show) with a brigade-sized cast in August. It's now possible to stay overnight here: see ⓦ chateau-la-rochefoucauld.com.

Further east, the country becomes hillier and more wooded. One place to visit is the beautiful, if touristy, little town of **Confolens**, about 40km northeast of La Rochefoucauld. Its ancient houses are stacked up a hillside above a broad brown sweep of the river Vienne, here crossed by a long narrow medieval bridge. It's worth continuing an extra 6km to the romantic little village of **St-Germain-de-Confolens**, huddled by the riverside beneath the stark towers of a ruined castle.

# Bordeaux and around

9

The city of **BORDEAUX** cuts a fine figure, towering above the west bank of the River Garonne, a blend of Neoclassical grandeur and modern innovation. The Romans set up a lively trading centre here, and the city still functions as the transport hub for Aquitaine. First-rate museums, excellent shopping, fine restaurants and lively nightlife make Bordeaux an absorbing place to spend a long weekend. Don't miss the spectacular new Cité du Vin if you have even a cursory interest in the city's wine history.

The hills of **Entre-Deux-Mers** and the medieval town of **St-Émilion** are well worth visiting in their own right. The vast pine forests of **Les Landes**, stretching towards the Dune du Pyla (the largest sand dune in Europe) and the glistening, wild Atlantic beaches of the **Côte d'Argent**, are magical, but you'll need your own transport to holiday there.

## Vieux Bordeaux

At the heart of the old town centre is **place de la Bourse**. Behind and to the west is the **Grand Théâtre** (☎05 56 00 85 95, ⊛opera-bordeaux.com) on place de la Comédie. Built by the architect Victor Louis in 1780, on the site of a Roman temple, the lofty exterior is adorned with pillars, Muses and Graces. Inside are flamboyant trompe l'oeil paintings; to get in, attend an opera or ballet (seats in the gods from as little as €15), or ask at the tourist office about a guided tour.

Smart streets radiate out from here: the city's main shopping streets, **rue Ste-Catherine** and the **cours de l'Intendance** to the south and west, and the sandy, tree-lined **allées de Tourny** to the northwest. The narrow streets around **place du Parlement** and **place St-Pierre** – lined with ancient townhouses doubling up as bistros, boutiques and vintage shops – make for a pleasant stroll.

Crossing the river just south of the fifteenth-century Porte Cailhau is the impressive **Pont de Pierre** – "Stone Bridge". It was built on Napoleon's orders during the Spanish campaigns, with seventeen arches in honour of his victories. The views of the river and quays from here are stunning, especially at dusk.

## Place Gambetta and around

In the middle of **place Gambetta** is a valiant attempt at an English garden. It's a quiet place, showing no trace of its bloody history; the guillotine lopped off three hundred heads here during the Revolution. On one corner stands the **Porte Dijeaux**, an old city gate.

### Cathédrale St-André and Tour Pey-Berland

**Cathedral** daily: June & Sept Mon 3–7.30pm, Tues–Sat 10am–1pm & 3–7.30pm, Sun 9.30am–1pm & 3–7.30pm; Oct–May Mon 2–7pm, Tues, Thurs & Fri 10am–noon & 2–6pm, Wed & Sat 10am–noon & 2–7pm, Sun 9.30am–noon & 2–6pm **Tower** June–Sept daily 10am–1.15pm & 2–6pm; Oct–May Tues–Sun 10am–12.30pm & 2–5pm; adults €6

South of place Gambetta is the **Cathédrale St-André**, built between the eleventh and fifteenth centuries, with twin steeples over the north transept, and an adjacent bell tower, the fifteenth-century **Tour Pey-Berland**. The interior of the cathedral, begun in the twelfth century, is vast and impressive, even if there's not much of artistic interest apart from the choir, which provides one of the few complete examples of the late Gothic style known as Rayonnant, and some finely carved doors.

### Musée des Beaux-Arts and Musée des Arts Décoratifs

Bordeaux's best museums are scattered in the streets around the cathedral. Directly behind the classical hôtel de ville is the **Musée des Beaux-Arts** (⊛musba-bordeaux.fr; Wed–Mon 10am–6pm; €5). It has a small star-studded European art collection, featuring Titian and Rubens, and good temporary exhibitions. The **Musée des Arts Décoratifs** (⊛madd-bordeaux.fr; Tues–Sun 11am–6pm; €5), two blocks north on rue Bouffard, is

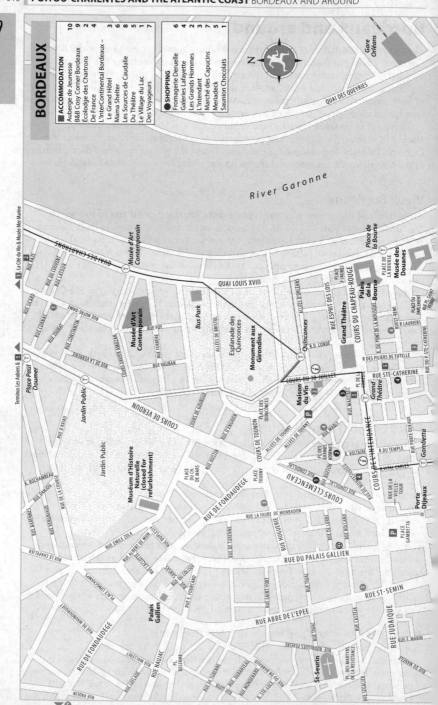

**BORDEAUX**

**◼ ACCOMMODATION**

| | |
|---|---|
| Auberge de Jeunesse | 10 |
| B&B Cosy Corner Bordeaux | 9 |
| Écolodge des Chartrons | 2 |
| De France | 4 |
| L'InterContinental Bordeaux – Le Grand Hôtel | 3 |
| Mama Shelter | 6 |
| Les Sources de Caudalie | 8 |
| Du Théâtre | 5 |
| Le Village du Lac | 1 |
| Des Voyageurs | 7 |

**● SHOPPING**

| | |
|---|---|
| Fromagerie Deruelle | 6 |
| Galeries Lafayette | 4 |
| Les Grands Hommes | 2 |
| L'Intendant | 3 |
| Marché des Capucins | 7 |
| Meriadeck | 5 |
| Saunion Chocolats | 1 |

River Garonne

Gare Orléans

QUAI DES QUERIES

QUAI LOUIS XVIII

Musée d'Art Contemporain

Place de la Bourse

Musée des Douanes

Bus Park

Esplanade des Quinconces

Monument aux Girondins

Palais de la Bourse

Grand Théâtre

COURS DU CHAPEAU-ROUGE

Maison du Vin

Cours du 30 Juillet

Grand Théâtre

COURS DE L'INTENDANCE

Porte Dijeaux

Place Paul Doumer

Jardin Public

Muséum d'Histoire Naturelle (closed for refurbishment)

COURS DE VERDUN

COURS CLEMENCEAU

Place Tourny

Place Gambetta

RUE DU PALAIS GALLIEN

Palais Gallien

RUE ABBE DE L'EPEE

St-Seurin

RUE ST-SEMIN

RUE JUDAIQUE

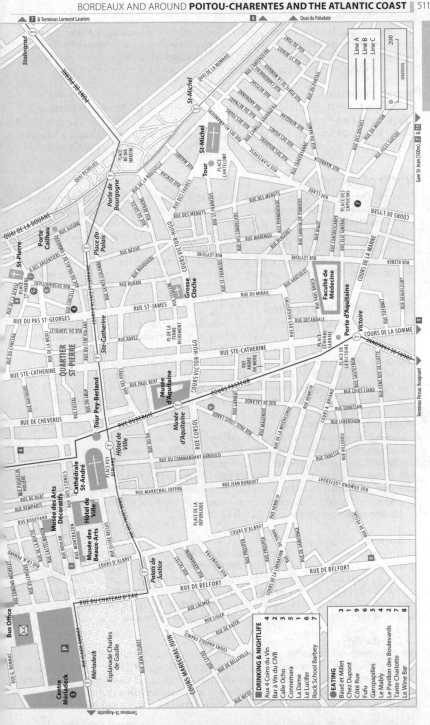

**DRINKING & NIGHTLIFE**

| | |
|---|---|
| Aux 4 Coins du Vin | 4 |
| Bar à Vin du CIVB | 2 |
| Calle Ocho | 3 |
| Connemara | 1 |
| La Dame | 5 |
| Le Lucifer | 6 |
| Rock School Barbey | 7 |

**EATING**

| | |
|---|---|
| Baud et Millet | 3 |
| Chez Dupont | 9 |
| Côté Rue | 6 |
| Fufu | 5 |
| Garopapilles | 4 |
| Le Mably | 1 |
| Le Pavillon des Boulevards | 7 |
| Tante Charlotte | 2 |
| Le Wine Bar | 8 |

9

housed in a handsome eighteenth-century house, where the beautifully restored period rooms evoke the grandeur of the Ancien Régime. As well as an impressive collection of eighteenth- and nineteenth-century furnishings and porcelain, the museum also hosts a series of temporary exhibitions devoted to Art Deco and contemporary design.

## Musée d'Aquitaine

To the southeast of the cathedral, on busy cours Pasteur, is the **Musée d'Aquitaine** (Tues–Sun 11am–6pm; €5), which traces the region's development since Roman times through artefacts and artworks. Highlights include the "Venus with Horn", a bas-relief discovered in the Dordogne in 1911, which is thought to be at least 20,000 years old.

# North of the centre

North of the Grand Théâtre, cours du 30-juillet leads into the bare, gravelly expanse of the **esplanade des Quinconces**. On the west side is the **Monument aux Girondins**, a glorious *fin-de-siècle* ensemble of statues and fountains built in honour of the local deputies to the 1789 Revolutionary Assembly. During World War II the occupying Nazis made plans to lower French morale by melting the monument down. Fortunately the local Resistance got there first and, under cover of darkness, dismantled the monument piece by piece, hiding it in a barn in the Médoc until after the war.

# Jardin Public and around

To the northwest of the city centre is the beautiful formal park, the **Jardin Public**, containing the city's botanical gardens as well as a small **natural history museum** (closed for refurbishment until 2019; contact tourist office for updates). Behind, to the west and north, lies a quiet, provincial quarter of two-storey stone houses that includes rue du Dr-Albert-Barraud, where you can see the **Palais Gallien**, a third-century arena - all that remains of Burdigala, Aquitaine's Roman capital; tours can be arranged with the tourist office (€3). Nearby, on place Delerme, is the unusual round **market hall**.

## Musée d'Art Contemporain

7 rue Ferrère • ⓦ capc-bordeaux.fr; Tues & Thurs–Sun 11am–6pm, Wed 11am–8pm • €7

To the east of the Jardin Public, close to the river, is the **Musée d'Art Contemporain** on rue Ferrère, occupying a converted nineteenth-century warehouse. The vast, arcaded hall is magnificent in its own right, and provides an ideal setting for the post-1960 sculpture and installations by artists like Richard Long and Sol LeWitt. The main space is used for temporary exhibitions. There's a superb collection of art books in the library and a café-restaurant on the roof (lunch only).

## Chartrons

Following the curve of the river north from the Musée d'Art Contemporain, you'll reach the down-at-heel but historic **Chartrons**, once the wine district. It's becoming increasingly cool, sprouting artists' studios, vintage shops and restaurants, as well as a Sunday Farmer's market on the quay. The **Musée du Vin et du Négoce** (ⓦ museeduvinbordeaux.com; daily 10am–6pm; adults €10), on rue Borie, depicts the history of the wine trade, with an inevitable focus on Bordeaux.

## La Cité du Vin

1 esplanade de Pontac • ☎ 05 56 16 20 20, ⓦ laciteduvin.com • Mon–Fri 10am–6pm, Sat & Sun 10am–7pm • €20

The city's most audacious piece of contemporary architecture is home to the fantastic Cité du Vin, strikingly set by the Garonne in the north of the city. Arguably the city's finest museum, the visit includes a digital guide through exhibits that take you from wine cultivation and production to the history of the wine trade and current trends.

Perhaps best of all, the tour ends with a glass of wine in the Belvedere, which offers spectacular panoramic views over the city.

## Musée Mer Marine

89 rue des Étrangers • ☎ 05 57 19 77 73, ⓦ mmmbordeaux.com • Mon & Wed–Fri 10am–6pm, Sat & Sun 10am–7pm • €9

Another striking addition to northern Bordeaux is the Musée Mer Marine, set by the water in the area that was – appropriately for this museum – the city's thriving port in the nineteenth century. At the time of research, the museum had not yet fully opened and was only hosting temporary exhibitions; its permanent collection is due to open in spring 2019 and aims to combine historic maritime artefacts with an opportunity to glimpse life under the water, while also examining the effect climate change has on the oceans.

## ARRIVAL AND DEPARTURE

BORDEAUX

**By plane** Bordeaux-Mérignac airport is 12km west of the city and connected by shuttle buses (ⓦ 30direct.com; roughly hourly; €7.20) to the city. Budget airlines from the UK include Flybe (Birmingham, Southampton) and easyJet (Liverpool, London).

**By train** Arriving by train, you'll find yourself at Gare St-Jean, 3km south of the city centre; bus #16 and tramline C run into town.

Destinations Angoulême (16–22 daily; 1hr–1hr 30min); Arcachon (15–25 daily; 50–55min); Bayonne (9 daily; 1hr 40min–2hr 10min); Bergerac (7–14 daily; 1hr 15–1hr 30min); Biarritz (9 daily; 2hr–2hr 45min); Brive (2–3 daily; 2hr 35min); Hendaye (6–9 daily; 2hr 30min); La Rochelle (6–8 daily; 2hr–2hr 20min); Lourdes (6–10 daily; 2hr 20min–3hr); Marseille (6 daily; 4hr); Mont de Marsan (5–6 daily; 1hr 30min); Nice (3–8 daily; 9–10hr); Paris-Montparnasse (1–2

hourly; 4hr); Périgueux (8–14 daily; 1hr–1hr 25min); Pointe de Grave (7–9 daily to Lesparre; 1hr 20min; then bus #713 to Pointe de Grave 1–5 daily Mon–Sat; 1hr); Poitiers (11–14 daily; 1hr 45min–2hr 30min); Saintes (6–9 daily; 1hr 40min); St-Émilion (7–14 daily; 40min); St-Jean-de-Luz (8–10 daily; 2hr–2hr 40min); Toulouse (10–16 daily; 2hr–2hr 40min).

**By bus** There's no central bus station, but bus stops congregate on the south side of the esplanade des Quinconces, on allées de Munich (where you'll also find the information centre – ☎ 05 56 43 68 43, ⓦ infotbc. com). Exceptions are the bus to Blaye, which leaves from "Buttinière" (take tramline A) and buses to Margaux and Pauillac, which leave from "place Ravezies" (tramline C).

Destinations Blaye (4–7 daily; 1hr 45min); Cap Ferret (6–12 daily; 1hr 30min); Lacanau (5 daily; 2hr 15min); Pauillac (3–7 daily; 45min–1hr 10min).

## GETTING AROUND

**By tram** Tram services (ⓦ infotbc.com) operate on the three lines regularly between 4.30am and midnight, and extend several kilometres into Bordeaux's suburbs. You can either purchase single tickets (€1.70) or packs of ten (€13.20) from machines at tram stops or newsagents (tabacs). You can also buy an unlimited-use pass, available for between one and seven days.

**Parking** There are numerous underground car parks in the centre, though it's cheaper to use the ones next to the tram stations on the east bank of the Garonne: buy a round-

trip park-and-ride ticket (€4.50) and hop on a tram to the centre. For more information see ⓦ infotbc.com.

**Bike rental** Liberty Cycles (☎ 05 56 92 77 18; closed Mon morning, Sat afternoon & Sun) at 104 cours d'Yser rents out bikes from €11 per day. Another option is Station Vélo Services at 36 Place de Stalingrad. Both shops do repairs.

**Car rental** Numerous rental firms are located in and around the train station, including Europcar ☎ 08 25 00 42 46; Hertz ☎ 08 25 00 24 00; and National/Citer ☎ 05 56 92 19 62. They all have outlets at the airport as well.

## INFORMATION

**Tourist office** Bordeaux's main tourist office, near the Grand Théâtre on 12 cours du 30-juillet (Mon–Sat 9am–6.30pm, Sun 9.30am–5pm; ☎ 05 56 00 66 00, ⓦ bordeaux-tourisme.com), can book accommodation, and city and

vineyard tours (see page 516). A Bordeaux City Pass (1 day €29, 2 days €39, 3 days €43) is also available, offering free museum entry, public transport, walking and bus tours, and various discounts.

## ACCOMMODATION

It's better to lodge in the centre than venture out to rue Charles-Domercq and cours de la Marne, which are rife with grimy one- and two-star hotels. Book well ahead if visiting during the Vinexpo trade fair (in odd-numbered years) or the Fête du Vin (in even-numbered years) in June.

**Auberge de Jeunesse** 22 cours Barbey ☎ 05 56 33 00 70, ⓦ auberge-jeunesse-bordeaux.com. A decent private hostel with a warm, relaxed vibe and a mix of modern dorms and doubles. Located just off cours de la Marne, it's a 10min walk from gare St-Jean. Kitchen and laundry

**9**

facilities are available, and breakfast is included. **€24.50**

**B&B Cosy Corner Bordeaux** 241 cours de la Somme ☎ 05 56 31 96 85, ⓦ chambre-hotes-bordeaux.com. Welcoming, English-speaking hosts, bright, cheery rooms and a hearty breakfast (included) make this a good choice, especially for families. It's about a 15min walk from the centre, but close to the bus and tram stations. Minimum three night stay in high season. **€80**

**Écolodge des Chartrons** 23 rue Raze, Chartrons ☎ 05 56 81 49 13, ⓦ ecolodgedeschartrons.com. Located on a quiet road in Chartrons, a 10min walk from the centre, *Écolodge* is a beautifully restored eco-friendly B&B, with a glass-roofed courtyard where splendid breakfasts are served. There are four rooms with books, slate bathrooms, antique paintings, private parking, and a discreet but helpful hostess. Breakfast included. **€147**

**De France** 7 rue Franklin ☎ 05 56 48 24 11, ⓦ hotel-france-bordeaux.fr. In a really handy, central location, this unfussy two-star hotel is a decent option for a short stay. Rooms are on the small side, but comfortable, bright and modern. Breakfast (€8) can be served in your room for no extra charge. **€94**

**L'InterContinental Bordeaux – Le Grand Hôtel** Place de la Comédie ☎ 05 57 30 44 44, ⓦ ghbordeaux.com. A great city hotel, right in the centre. It's timeless luxury all the way here, with brass-buttoned porters, concierge service, two bars (including a summer-only rooftop one), two Gordon Ramsay restaurants and valet parking, as well as an excellent breakfast, an opulent spa and pool, a jacuzzi on the roof, and rooms equipped with everything imaginable. **€306**

★ **Mama Shelter** 19 rue Poquelin-Molière ☎ 05 57 87 70 60, ⓦ mamashelter.com/bordeaux. Fashionably eclectic, with sleek decor, stunning spacious rooms and a show-stopping rooftop terrace, *Mama Shelter* is hands-down one of the city's coolest hotels. Rooms are bang up to date, including iMac computers with internet, radio and movies on demand, minibars, plump duvets and million-dollar views. Book online for cheapest rates. Breakfast €17; parking €19. **€119**

**Les Sources de Caudalie** Château Smith Haut Lafitte, Martillac ☎ 05 57 83 83 83, ⓦ sources-caudalie.com. Fifteen minutes' drive from Bordeaux, *Les Sources* is a five-star spa hotel, part of the Château Smith Haut Lafitte empire, that specializes in grape-based spa treatments. The setting is luxuriously faux-rustic, there's a Michelin-starred restaurant, tranquil grounds, and vineyards on every side, giving the air a vinous sweetness. **€319**

★ **Du Théâtre** 10 rue Maison-Daurade ☎ 05 56 79 05 26, ⓦ hotel-du-theatre.com. A personality-packed budget choice, carefully thought out to maximize space and add a personal touch. Bright wall stencils, a few choice kitsch furnishings and well-designed bathrooms mean even the tiny single rooms are perfectly comfortable, plus there's a 24-hr English-speaking reception and an unbeatable location, right in the heart of town. The only downside is the wi-fi, which is a bit temperamental in the top-floor rooms. Breakfast €8. **€96**

**Le Village du Lac** Bd Jacques Chaban-Delmas ☎ 05 57 87 70 60, ⓦ camping-bordeauxlac.com. A lovely lakeside campsite located 8km north of the centre near the tramline, with rental cottages (kitchenette, TV, a/c, bathroom, terrace), camping, camper vans, swimming pool, shops, laundrette and secure parking. **€33**

**Des Voyageurs** 3bis av Thiers ☎ 05 56 86 18 00, ⓦ hotel-voyageurs-bordeaux.com. This small, two-star hotel is a short, picturesque walk from the centre across the Pont de Pierre, and represents the best value for money in Bordeaux. It has helpful staff and clean, well-furnished rooms. Breakfast €8. **€75**

## EATING AND DRINKING

Bordeaux is packed with good restaurants to suit any budget and the streets around rue du Parlement St-Pierre and rue St-Rémi are full of places to eat, while upmarket options crowd around place du Parlement and towards Chartrons. The student population ensures a collection of young, lively bars, especially around place de la Victoire, and the city has a strong gay scene.

## RESTAURANTS

★ **Baud et Millet** 19 rue Huguerie ☎ 05 56 79 05 77, ⓦ http://baudetmillet.com. Running since 1986, this local institution takes guests on a journey through the cheeses of France, with a mind-boggling array of cheese-inspired dishes. Select a bottle of wine from the shelf and order langres profiteroles (€9) or splash out on unlimited access to the cheese cave (€32). Portions are generous and staff are keen to guide you. Mon–Sat 11am–11pm.

**Chez Dupont** 45 rue Notre-Dame ☎ 05 56 81 49 59, ⓦ chez-dupont.com. A romantic, old-fashioned restaurant in Chartrons, with wooden floors, vintage posters and waistcoated waiters. Food is fresh from the market, with mains (such as tuna sashimi risotto) from €18.90 and huge portions. Tues–Sat noon–2pm & 7.30–10.30pm.

**Côté Rue** 14 rue Paul-Louis-Lande ☎ 05 56 49 06 49, ⓦ cote-rue-bordeaux.fr. The epitome of contemporary Bordeaux, with a relaxed feel, creative cuisine and bright modern art on the walls – it's no surprise that locals flock here. Dishes might include the likes of scallops with pumpkin foam or crab-stuffed ravioli, all beautifully presented. Lunch menus from €30, dinner €56. Daily 11.30am–10.30pm.

**Fufu** 37 rue St-Rémi ☎ 05 56 52 10 29, ⓦ restuarantfufu.com. A well-loved Japanese noodle bar in the heart of town; eat at the long bar, watching the chefs fry your noodles, or take away a hot box of ramen (from €10.50) and perch on a bench next to the Garonne, a few minutes' walk away. Daily 11.30am–10.30pm.

★ **Garopapilles** 62 rue Abbé-de-l'Épée ☎ 09 72 45 55 36, ⓦ garopapilles.com. The open kitchen and attached *cave à vin* – lending its 200-strong wine list – help make eating here an experience more than just an indulgence. The cuisine brings out rustic local flavours through creative culinary techniques, with a mouthwatering three-course lunch *menu* at €35 and a five-course evening *menu* at €90. Regular wine tastings are also held on site. Book ahead. Tue–Fri 12.15–2pm, Thu–Fri 7.30-9pm.

**Le Mably** 12 rue Mably ☎ 05 56 44 30 10, ⓦle-mably. com. Decorous Art Nouveau interiors and daily *menus* (€18–35) that change with the seasons and employ fresh, local produce. Book a table on the sunny terrace in summer and dine beneath the imposing Notre-Dame church. Mon–Sat noon–2.30pm & 7.45–10.30pm.

**Le Pavillon des Boulevards** 120 rue Croix-de-Seguey ☎05 56 81 51 02 ⓦlepavillondesboulevards. fr. The elegant setting and exemplary service are to be expected at this Michelin-starred restaurant, but there's nothing traditional about the menu. Dishes are inventive, sometimes surprising and always delicious, with plenty of fish and seafood, and lunch *menus* from €35. Tues–Sat noon–1.30pm & 8–9.30pm.

★**Tante Charlotte** 7 rue des Bahutiers ☎ 09 82 60 13 12. This popular restaurant has a hip bourgeois feel to it, with silver chairs and cushions, black and white photos on the walls and candlelit tables. Stick with the theme and order the *menu à boudoir*, which includes succulent meat dishes, delicious home-made desserts and a huge range of aperitifs to choose from. Tues–Sat 7.45pm–2am.

★**Le Wine Bar** 19 rue des Bahutiers ☎05 40 25 15 74, ⓦlewinebar-bordeaux.com. A genial, thoroughly charming bar-restaurant near the river, run by two sisters and their husbands, with 60 types of wine (from 27 countries) sold by the glass and simple, delicious Italian snacks (cheese or ham and bread, salads, bruschetta, soup in winter). Their tiramisu is a local favourite. Wine served only when bought with food. Sun–Thurs 7pm–midnight, Fri & Sat noon–2pm & 7pm–midnight.

## BARS, CLUBS AND VENUES

★**Aux 4 Coins du Vin** 8 rue de la Devise ☎05 57 34 37 29, ⓦaux4coinsduvin.com. Where good grapes go when they die. There are 40 wines available, mostly red and mostly French, but a few whites and foreign wines, and you can taste by the glass, half-glass or quarter-glass. Pleasing tasting plates accompany the wine, big enough for two or three to share. Mon–Tues 6pm–midnight, Mon & Tues 6pm–midnight, Wed–Sat 6pm–1am.

**Bar à Vin du CIVB** 1 cours du 30-juillet ☎ 05 56 00 43 47, ⓦbaravin.bordeaux.com. Set on the ground floor of the Maison du Vin de Bordeaux, the CIVB (Bordeaux Wine Council) offers two parts edification to one part intoxication. A full range of Bordeaux wines (reds, dry and sweet whites, rosés, clarets and sparkling whites) are available. Mon–Sat 11am–10pm.

**Calle Ocho** 24 rue des Piliers-de-Tutelle ☎05 56 48 08 68, ⓦcalle-ocho.eu. Bordeaux's best-known salsa bar has an unrivalled party vibe and is packed out most nights till 2am. There's real Cuban rum and mojitos too. Mon–Sat 5pm–1.45am.

**Connemara** 18 cours d'Albret, ⓦconnemara-pub.com. As Irish as a pub as ever you'll find. The Guinness is cold and the football always pulls a good crowd. Happy hour 6–8pm daily, and weekly live music and open-mic nights. Mon 5pm–2am, Tues–Fri 11.30am–2am, Sat noon–2am, Sun 7pm–1am.

**La Dame** 1 quai Armand-Lalande ☎05 57 10 20 50. An old petrol barge moored in the north of the city provides one of Bordeaux's liveliest nightlife spots. Come for above-board or port-side cocktails, or head below deck to the popular nightclub. Tues & Wed 10am–3pm & 5pm–2am, Thurs & Fri 10am–3pm & 5pm–6am, Sat 10am–6am.

**Le Lucifer** 35 rue Pessac ☎05 56 99 09 02. A lively pub-style joint with a good mix of students and locals, *Le Lucifer* is a hit with beer-lovers thanks to its huge range of bottled and draught brews (mostly Belgian) and hosts regular live music nights. They don't accept cards, so be sure to bring cash. Mon–Sat 5.30pm–2am, Sun 9pm–2am.

**Rock School Barbey** 18 cours Barbey ☎05 56 33 66 00, ⓦrockschool-barbey.com. Bordeaux's premier venue for rock, which hosts well-known international bands. Daily 10am–1pm & 2pm–6am.

## SHOPPING

Bordeaux's so-called "Golden Triangle" – the area bordered by the cours de l'Intendance, allées de Tourny and cours Clemenceau – is lined with designer stores, jewellery boutiques and wine shops. Alternatively, head to the pedestrianized rue Sainte-Catherine, which has all the usual high street brands and outlets. A popular Sunday market is held along quai des Chartrons.

**Fromagerie Deruelle** 66 rue du Pas-St-Georges ⓦfromagerie-deruelle.com. Bordeaux isn't exactly short on superlative fromageries (cheese shops) but this small shop is one of the best, with an extensive range of 150 different cheeses, complemented by knowledgeable, friendly staff. In addition to fromage, you can also pick up other dairy products like yoghurts and eggs, plus charcuterie, wine and oils – not to mention some fabulous home-made (and cheese-based) desserts. Mon 3.30–7.30pm, Tues–Sat 10am–1.30pm & 3.30–7.30pm.

**Galeries Lafayette** 11–19 rue Sainte-Catherine ⓦgalerieslafayette.com. France's most famous department store has a huge range of women's clothing, including a number of top-name designers, plus a gigantic cosmetic and perfume floor, luxury foods and souvenirs. There's a men's store on rue de la Porte-Dijeaux, and the tourist office offers 10 percent discount coupons. Mon–Sat

**9**

9.30am–8pm, Sun 11am–7pm.

**Les Grands Hommes** 12 place des Grands-Hommes ⓦ lesgrandshommes.com. An elegant domed shopping mall at the epicentre of the "Golden Triangle", *Les Grands Hommes* has a small selection of upmarket jewellery, accessories and homeware boutiques, plus a Carrefour supermarket. Head to the ground floor, where the artisan food stalls are excellent quality, if slightly overpriced. Shops: Mon–Sat 10am–7.30pm Carrefour: Mon–Sat 9am–9pm.

**L'Intendant** 2 allées de Tourny ⊕ 05 56 48 01 29, ⓦ intendant.com. One of the city's best wine shops, with over 1200 Bordeaux wines straight from the châteaux. It's worth a peek just to marvel at the grand spiral stair-well, which towers with neatly stacked wines. Mon–Sat 10am–7.30pm.

**Marché des Capucins** Place des Capucins ⊕ 05 56 92 26 29. Bordeaux's main covered market hall is an epicurean journey through France, with fresh fruits, vegetables, meats, fish and seafood, breads and pastries from around the country. Stock up on edible souvenirs like Bordeaux speciality *canelés* or enjoy lunch at one of the many food stalls. Tues–Fri 6am–1pm, Sat & Sun 5.30am–2.30pm.

**Meriadeck** 57 rue du Château d'Eau ⊕ 05 56 93 00 15, ⓦ meriadeck.com. Bordeaux's biggest shopping centre, with three floors of shops and restaurants, including clothing stores like H&M, Zara and Mango, and a gigantic two-floor Auchan supermarket. Parking is free for the first 90 minutes. Mon–Sat 10am–8pm, Auchan: Mon–Sat 8.30am–9.30pm, Sun 8.30am–12.30pm.

**Saunion Chocolats** 56 cours Clemenceau ⊕ 05 56 48 05 75, ⓦ saunion.fr. Decadent chocolates and confectionary hand-crafted by one of Bordeaux's most renowned chocolatiers, with products starting at just a few euros, plus delicious artisan ice creams in summer. Mon–Sat 9.30am–7.15pm, Sun 10am–7pm.

## DIRECTORY

**Books and newspapers** Presse Gambetta, on place Gambetta, sells all the main English-language papers in addition to some regional guides and maps, while Bordeaux's largest bookstore, Mollat, 15 rue Vital-Carles (Mon–Sat 9.30am–7.30pm, 1st Sun of month 2–6pm), has a wide selection.

**Cinema** Watch original-language (*version originale* or *v.o.*) films at the wonderful arthouse cinema Utopia, 5 place Camille-Jullian (⊕ 05 56 52 00 03, ⓦ www.cinemas-utopia.org). For Hollywood blockbusters there's the seventeen-screen Megarama (⊕ 05 56 40 66 70, ⓦ megarama.fr) across the Pont de Pierre in the old gare d'Orléans. Check the free weekly *Bordeaux Plus* for listings.

**Consulate** UK, 353 bd du Président-Wilson ⊕ 05 57 22 21 10; USA, 89 quai des Chartons ⊕ 01 43 12 48 65.

**Health** Centre Hospitalier Pellegrin-Tripode, place Amélie-Raba-Léon (⊕ 05 56 79 56 79), to the west of central Bordeaux.

**Police** Commissariat Central, 23 rue François-de-Sourdis (⊕ 05 57 85 77 77 or ⊕ 17 in emergencies).

# The Bordeaux wine region

Touring the local **vineyards** and sampling a few home-grown wines is one of the great pleasures of Bordeaux. The wine regions lie in a great semicircle around the city, starting with the **Médoc** in the north, then skirting east through **St-Émilion**, before finishing south of the city among the vineyards of the **Sauternes**. In between, the less prestigious districts are also worth investigating, especially **Blaye**, to the north of Bordeaux, and **Entre-Deux-Mers**, to the east.

You will quickly see that there's more to the region than wine. Many of the Médoc's eighteenth-century châteaux are architectural treasures, while a vast fortress dominates the town of Blaye, and there's an older, ruined castle at Villandraut on the edge of the Sauternes. St-Émilion, loved by tourists, is the prettiest of the wine towns, and has the unexpected bonus of a cavernous underground church. For scenic views you can't beat the green, gentle hills of Entre-Deux-Mers and its ruined abbey, **La Sauve-Majeur**.

## GETTING AROUND                                                                    BORDEAUX WINE REGION

**By train** There are train lines from Bordeaux running north through the Médoc to Margaux and Pauillac, and south through the Garonne valley to St-Macaire and La Réole. St-Émilion lies on the Bordeaux–Sarlat line, but the station is a couple of kilometres from the town.

**By bus** There's a comprehensive regional bus network –

pick up timetables at the tourist office. Several different companies operate buses; the largest is Citram Aquitaine (ⓦ citram.fr).

**By bike** Cycling is an appealing mode of transport, and many of the towns are connected by well-marked tarmac cycle paths.

# The Médoc

The landscape of **THE MÉDOC**, a patch of land between the Atlantic coast forests and the Gironde, is monotonous: gravel plains, the brown water of the estuary, and gravelly soil. The D2 wine road, heading off the N15 from Bordeaux, passes through Margaux, St-Julien, Pauillac and St-Estèphe, where many of the famous châteaux reside.

## Château Margaux

20km north of Bordeaux • By appointment only Mon–Fri; closed Aug and during harvest • ☎ 05 57 88 83 83, ⓦ chateau-margaux.com • Free

One of the loveliest châteaux in the Médoc, **Margaux** is an eighteenth-century villa set in extensive, sculpture-dotted gardens close to the west bank of the Gironde. Its wine, a classified Premier Grand Cru, already world-famous in the 1940s and 1950s, went through a rough patch in the two succeeding decades but improved in the 1980s, after the estate was bought by a Greek family.

In the small village of **Margaux** itself, there's a **Maison du Vin** (7 place de la Trémoille; Mon–Fri 9am–6pm; ☎ 05 57 88 70 82, ⓦ maisonduvindemargaux.com), which can help find accommodation, and advise on visits to the *appellation*'s châteaux. A little further down the road, at number 2, is La Cave d'Ulysse (Mon–Fri 9am–7pm, Sat 10am–7pm; ⓦ caveulysse.com), which gives free tastings from a variety of Margaux châteaux.

## Fort Médoc and Lamarque

The ruins of **Fort Médoc** sit between Margaux and St-Julien, on the D2 road with views over the estuary. It was designed by prolific military architect Vauban in the seventeenth century, and the ruins make good scrambling. Southwards is the pretty village of **Lamarque**, which is full of flowers and has a distinctive, minaret-like church tower. The port, where you can take a ferry (4–9 daily; one-way passengers €2.70, cycles €1.80, cars €14.30) across the muddy Gironde to Blaye, is a couple of kilometres away.

## Pauillac

**PAUILLAC** is the largest and most attractive town in the Médoc, perched on the banks of the Gironde estuary and home to a cluster of waterfront cafés and restaurants. A strategic base for exploring the wine-growing region, it's close to some of Bordeaux's most important vineyards; no fewer than three of the top five Grands Crus hail from here.

### INFORMATION                                              PAUILLAC

**Maison du Tourisme et du Vin** On the waterfront (Mon–Sat 9.30am–12.30pm & 2–6.30pm, Sun 10.30am–12.30pm & 3–6pm; ☎ 05 56 59 03 08, ⓦ pauillac-medoc. com); they can provide a list of *gîtes* and arrange bike hire and châteaux visits.

### ACCOMMODATION                                            PAUILLAC

★ **Le Coeur des Vignes** 19 chemin du Marronnier, St-Lambert ☎ 06 26 90 36 40 ⓦ coeurdesvignes.com. Just under 4km south of Pauillac is this utterly delightful B&B. The four individually decorated rooms are modern and light-filled, while retaining a sense of the nineteenth-century house itself. There's a lovely garden, a terrace with a pool, and a lounge with a fireplace – plenty of places to relax after choosing a bottle of wine from their well-curated list. €110

**Les Phoenix** 21 rue Jean-Mermoz ☎ 05 56 59 62 48, ⓦ caruso33.net/les-phoenix-pauillac.html. This is a budget B&B with simple but spacious rooms and shared bathrooms, as well as friendly hosts, free parking and an excellent breakfast (included). €52

### EATING AND DRINKING

**Café Lavinal** P. Desquet, Bages ☎ 5 57 75 00 09. With its sunny terrace and English-speaking waiters, this bright, pleasant bistro is understandably popular with tourists, but the quality of food remains high – expect interesting takes on the usual bistro staples, such as confit lamb with bulgur wheat. Menus from €28. It's a 5min drive from Pauillac in the village of Bages. Mon–Sat noon–2pm & 7.30–9pm.

**Château Cordeillan** Rte des Châteaux, Bages ☎ 05

**9**

## THE WINES OF BORDEAUX

The Bordeaux wine region circles the city, enjoying near-perfect climatic conditions and soils ranging from limestone to sand and pebbles. It's the largest quality wine district in the world, producing around 500 million bottles a year – over half of France's quality wine output and ten percent, by value, of the world's wine trade.

The Gironde estuary, fed by the Garonne and the Dordogne rivers, determines the lie of the land. The **Médoc** lies northwest of Bordeaux, between the Atlantic coast and the River Gironde, where the vines, deeply rooted in poor, gravelly soil, produce good, full-bodied red wines. The region's **eight appellations** are Médoc, Haut Médoc, St-Estèphe, Pauillac, St-Julien, Moulis en Médoc, Listrac-Médoc and Margaux. Southwest of Bordeaux, the vast vineyards of **Graves** produce the best of the region's dry white wines, along with punchy reds, from some of the most prestigious communes in France, like Pessac, Talence, Martillac and Villenave d'Ornon. They spread down to Langon and envelop the areas of **Sauternes** and **Barsac**, where the sweet white dessert wines are considered among the best in the world.

East of the Gironde estuary and the Dordogne, the **Côtes de Blaye** produce some good-quality white table wines, mostly dry, and a smaller quantity of reds. The **Côtes de Bourg**, an area that spreads down to the renowned St-Émilion region, specializes in solid whites and reds. Here, there are a dozen producers who have earned the Premiers Grands Crus Classés classification, and their wines are full, rich reds that don't have to mature as long as the Médoc wines. Lesser-known neighbouring areas include the vineyards of **Pomerol**, **Lalande** and **Côtes de Francs**, all producing reds similar to St-Émilion but at more affordable prices.

Between the Garonne and the Dordogne is **Entre-Deux-Mers**, which yields large quantities of inexpensive, drinkable table whites, mainly from the Sauvignon grape. Stretching along the north bank of the Garonne, the vineyards of the **Côtes de Bordeaux** feature fruity reds and a smaller number of dry, sweet whites.

The **classification** of Bordeaux wines is a complex business. Apart from the usual *appellation d'origine protégée* (AOP) labelling, the wines of the Médoc châteaux are graded into five crus, or growths. These were established as early as 1855, based on the prices the wines had fetched over the last few hundred years. Four were voted the best or **Premier Grand Cru Classé**: Margaux, Lafitte, Latour and Haut-Brion. With the exception of Château Mouton-Rothschild, which moved up a class in 1973 to become the fifth Premier Grand Cru Classé, there have been no official changes, so divisions between the crus should not be taken too seriously.

### BUYING WINE AND VISITING CHÂTEAUX

If you're interested in **buying wine**, head for the châteaux, where you'll get the best price and the opportunity to sample and receive expert advice before purchasing. To **visit the châteaux**, ask at the Maison du Vin or tourist office in each wine-producing village.

---

56 59 24 24, ⓦcordeillanbages.com. A first-rate two-Michelin-starred gourmet restaurant in opulent surroundings. Prices are as high as you'd expect for such an experience (*menu* €89–155) but it's an undeniably lovely setting, and the restaurant is refreshingly modern and unstuffy. Dress smartly. April–Nov Wed–Sun 12.30–1.30pm & 7.30–9.30pm.

## The Médoc châteaux

Organize to visit the most famous of the **Médoc châteaux** – Château Lafite-Rothschild (4km northwest of Pauillac; ☏05 56 59 26 83, ⓦlafite.com), and Château Latour (3km south of Pauillac; ☏05 56 73 19 80, ⓦchateau-latour.com) – either directly or through the Maison du Vin.

## St-Estèphe

North of Pauillac is the wine commune of **ST-ESTÈPHE**, Médoc's largest *appellation*, consisting predominantly of Crus Bourgeois – a level below Cru Classé (see page 516) – vineyards belonging to the local *cave coopérative*, **Marquis de St-Estèphe**, on the D2 towards Pauillac (Mon–Fri 8.30am–12.15pm & 2–6pm; ☏05 56 73 35 30, ⓦmarquis-saint-estephe.fr). One of the *appellation*'s five Crus Classés is the distinctive **Château Cos** d'Estournel, with its flamboyant nineteenth-century pagoda; the *chais* (warehouses) can be visited by appointment (☎05 56 73 15 50, ⓦestournel.com; English spoken, reserve a week ahead). St-Estèphe is a slow-moving village dominated by the eighteenth-century **church of St-Étienne**, with its highly decorative interior. The small, homespun **Maison du Vin** (April–June & mid-Sept to early Nov Mon–Fri 10am–noon & 2–6pm, Sat 2–6pm; July to mid-Sept Mon–Sat 10am–7pm; early Nov to March 10am–noon & 2–5pm; ☎05 56 59 30 59, ⓦvins-saint-estephe.com) is hidden in the church square.

## ACCOMMODATION                                                   ST ESTÈPHE

**Château Les Ormes Pez** 29 rte des Ormes de Pez ☎05 56 73 24 00, ⓦlesormesdepez.com. A comfortable family hotel in a handsome château, with a pool (unheated) and large walled garden, surrounded by vineyards, just outside the village. Breakfast included. **€149**

**Château Pomys** Rte de Poumey ☎05 56 59 73 44, ⓦchateaupomys.com. Although it looks like an Italian villa, with its imposing facade and manicured garden, this is a wine château, a long walk from the village. There's a small restaurant and ten converted rooms – all comfortable, clean and pleasant, but with few amenities, which is reflected in the prices. Summer only. Breakfast €14. **€100**

# Blaye

According to legend, the great Frankish hero Roland was buried in Blaye, which was a port of the Gaul Santones in pre-Roman times. The town played a crucial role in the wars against the English, and the French Wars of Religion. The citadelle was built by the great military engineer Vauban, but has never seen action. Blaye has a long history of viniculture, as the area was originally planted by the Romans, and is also known for the messy-looking sweet confectionery, pralines, made here since the seventeenth century. Another speciality is caviar; legend has it that it was introduced to residents by noble Russians who fled to France during the Russian Revolution.

## INFORMATION                                                        BLAYE

**Tourist office** The office on rue des Minimes (daily: March–May & Oct 10am–12.30pm 2–5.30pm; June–Sept 10am–6.30pm; Nov–Feb 10am–12.30pm & 2–5pm; ☎05 57 42 12 09, ⓦtourisme-blaye.com) has details on wine tasting/tours and can book rooms.

## ACCOMMODATION

**Camping Municipal La Citadelle** Citadelle de Vauban ☎05 57 42 00 20. Situated in green, tree-lined grounds, inside the old citadelle, and 5min from the *centre ville* this is an old school campsite, with room for just 36 tents, electricity and bathrooms. **€10**

★ **Château Bavolier** St Christoly-de-Blaye ☎05 57 42 59 74, ⓦchateau-bavolier.com. It's hard not to lavish praise on Bavolier, 15min by car from Blaye: an enchanting scale-model palace, run as a two-room B&B by its English owners. It was built in the seventeenth century by a consul to the king and nestles in 5 acres of garden in the heart of wine country. Splendidly renovated, the interior is luxurious, the hostess attentive, and the setting magical. Closed during winter. Book the master suite for a regal experience. Breakfast €10. **€138**

**Domaine des Deux-Cèdres** 26 rte des Astéries ☎05 57 64 88 65, ⓦdomainedesdeuxcedres.com. Striking, colourful rooms, enhanced with homely knick-knacks, and delicious home-cooked cuisine available on request. There are four rooms available, along with a *gîte*, set amid the vineyards, and a swimming pool. Breakfast included. **€102**

★ **Villa Saint-Simon** 8 cours du Général-de-Gaulle ☎05 57 42 99 66, ⓦvillastsimon.com. A skilfully renovated nineteenth-century townhouse opposite Blaye port, with five tastefully decorated rooms named after local châteaux.

---

## WINES OF BLAYE

The green slopes north of the Garonne were planted long before the Médoc. Wine here is powerful, richly coloured, fruity, and cheaper than on the opposite riverbank. The **Côtes de Bourg** and **Côtes de Blaye** are quintessential pleasant, inexpensive reds. Visit the **Maison du Vin de Blaye** on cours Vauban (Mon–Sat 9am–12.30pm & 2–7pm) to stock up. You can get a good bottle for around €5.

**9**

English-speaking hosts Les and Clarissa – oenophile and artist, respectively – extend a warm welcome that goes far beyond the average B&B. Excellent value wine tours and tastings are offered exclusively to guests and tailored to both the seasoned connoisseur and the wine-loving amateur, plus there's a well-stocked wine shop. If you're on a tight budget, ask about the ground-floor room. **€98**

**Villa Saint-Simon Apartments** 9 rue St-Simon ☎06 62 76 22 72, ⓦapartmentsbordeaux.com. These one- to three-bedroom fully furnished apartments, run by the same team as *Villa Saint-Simon*, have impeccable style, with chic furnishings and beautiful wooden floors, offset by striking artwork. Ask about weekly discounts. **€135**

## EATING AND DRINKING

**★La Galerie** 9 rue St-Simon ☎05 57 68 50 65, ⓦlagalerieblaye.com. Stone-brick walls adorned with mesmerizing artworks from a changing roster of local and international artists make this an atmospheric spot for a relaxing meal, and produce is grown out back. Wine tastings are held in the underground cellar on request, while the restaurant has the self-proclaimed best wine list in town. Order a selection of tapas (€13.90) or tuck into the succulent barbecued duck breast (€19.80), but save space for the delectable puddings. Tues 8am–2pm, Thurs–Sun 8am–2pm.

**Le Gavroche** 14 rue Neuve ☎05 57 58 21 03. At the base of the *citadelle*, this cosy restaurant with bare stone walls and beamed ceilings is a great spot for enjoying traditional, meat-heavy dishes like duck parmentier and rabbit terrine. Mon, Thurs & Sun noon–12.30pm, Tues, Wed, Fri & Sat noon–8.30pm.

**Le Plaisance au Port** 4 place Marchal, Bourg-sur-Gironde ☎05 57 68 45 34. An urban-looking country restaurant 14km southeast of Blaye, with long, curved windows overlooking the estuary, and well-cooked dishes like monkfish with fresh pesto, or red snapper with peppers and olives. Mains €14–19. Daily 11.30am–midnight.

# St-Émilion

**ST-ÉMILION**, 35km east of Bordeaux, and a short train trip, is an essential visit. The old grey houses of this fortified medieval town straggle down the steep south-hanging slope of a low hill, with the green froth of the summer's vines crawling over its walls. Many of the growers still keep up the old tradition of planting roses at the ends of the rows, which in pre-pesticide days served as an early-warning system against infection, the idea being that the most common bug, oidium, went for the roses first, giving three days' notice of its intentions.

## The old town

The best way to see St Émilion is on a **guided tour**. Tours begin at the **grotte de l'Ermitage**, where it's said that St Émilion lived as a hermit in the eighth century, sleeping on a stone ledge. The tour continues in the half-ruined **Trinity Chapel**, which was converted into a cooperage (barrel-makers') during the Revolution. Striking frescoes are still visible. Across the yard is a passage beneath the **belfry** leading to the **catacombs**, where three chambers dug out of the soft limestone were used as an ossuary between the eighth and eleventh centuries.

Below is the church itself. Simple and huge, the entire structure – barrel vaulting, great square piers and all – was hacked out of the rock. The interior was once painted, but only faint traces survived the Revolution, when it was used as a gunpowder factory. Every June the wine council – *La Jurade* – assembles here in red robes to judge last year's wine and decide whether each *viticulteur*'s produce deserves the *appellation contrôlée* rating. Behind the tourist office is a grand view of the **moat** and old town **walls**. To the right is the twelfth-century **collegiate church**, with a handsome but mutilated doorway, and a fourteenth-century **cloister**, accessible through the tourist office (daily 9.30am–6.30pm; free).

## Local vineyards

Many local vineyards hold wine tastings: Château Fonplegade (☎05 57 74 43 11, ⓦfonplegade.com; appointment only) is friendly and close to the train station, while Château Canon (☎05 57 55 23 45, ⓦchateaucanon.com; appointment only), west of

**9**

town, has splendid architecture. **Maison du Vin**, next door to the tourist office (daily 10am–12.30pm & 2–6pm; ⓦvins-saint-emilion.com), can advise you on which vineyards to visit, and sells local wines at a fair price.

## ARRIVAL AND INFORMATION                                    ST-ÉMILION

**By train** The small, unmanned gare de Saint-Émilion is on the Sarlat–Bergerac–Libourne–Bordeaux rail route, and about 1.6km from the village (just turn right at the station and follow the road). The nearest mainline station is at Libourne (served by the TGV), a 40-minute walk from Saint-Émilion.

**Tourist office** Place des Créneaux by the belfry (daily 9.30am–12.30pm & 1.30–6pm; ☎ 05 57 55 28 28, ⓦsaint-emilion-tourisme.com), organizes town tours (10am–5.30pm, one or two a day in English; adult €13, under-10s free) and vineyard tours by bus, tourist train or bike (June–Sept; some in English; starting from €14). They also have bikes for rent (from €18 per day).

## ACCOMMODATION

**Camping Yelloh!** ☎ 05 57 24 75 80, ⓦcamping-saint-emilion.com. Two km northwest of St-Émilion, on the road to Montagne, this four-star campsite is well-maintained and has cottages and houseboats for rent, as well as a restaurant and takeaway, corner shop, swimming pools, boating lake, bike rental and a free shuttle bus to town. Late April to mid-Sept. **€40**

**Château Franc-Pourret** 1 La Gomerie ☎ 06 70 21 00 24, ⓦfranc-pourret.com. This family château, 15min by foot from St-Émilion, and set amid a sea of vines and rose bushes, has two homely guestrooms. The hostess is welcoming and English-speaking, the organic, home-made breakfast (included) is delicious, and wine tours can be organized (book in advance). **€119**

★ **La Gomerie** 5 La Gomerie ☎ 05 57 24 68 85, ⓦchambreshotessaintemilion.com. A rustic cottage hidden away in the vineyards, *La Gomerie* is a quiet retreat from the bustle of St-Émilion. Bare stone walls and dark wood furnishings give the rooms a distinctive character and it's excellent value for the price. Don't arrive after dark as the turn-off is easy to miss even in daylight; free parking. Breakfast included. **€74**

**Hostellerie de Plaisance** 5 place du Clocher ☎ 05 57 55 07 55, ⓦhostelleriedeplaisance.com. Those with trust funds to blow can do so with flair and extravagance here; in the heart of town, with five stars, first-class dining, spectacular views and sumptuous rooms. Breakfast €32. Open mid-Feb to mid-Dec. **€320**

## EATING AND DRINKING

St-Émilion has a handful of excellent, reasonably priced restaurants, and a lot of dross, so do some research before eating out, and make reservations.

**Chai Pascal** 37 rue Gaudet ☎ 05 57 24 52 45, ⓦchai-pascal.com. A welcoming family-run bistro and wine bar with a concise, quality menu of traditional dishes. Mains start from €12.50. Daily noon–11pm.

**Lard & Bouchon** 22 rue Gaudet ☎ 05 57 24 28 53, ⓦlardetbouchon.fr. Hidden away in an arched brick wine cellar, this is a cool spot to escape the blazing summer sun. Bistro-style *menus* start from €29 and there's an excellent choice of local wines by the glass or bottle. Tues–Sat noon–2pm & 7–9pm, daily in July & Aug.

★ **Macarons de St-Émilion** 9 rue Gaudet ☎ 05 57 24 72 33, ⓦmacarons-saint-emilion.fr. Beneath its unassuming red-and-white-striped awning, this tiny store is heaped with home-made *macarons* (€9 for 24), *canelés* and artisan treats. Owner Nadia Fermingier uses an original *canelé* recipe, invented by nuns in the 1620s, and locals rave that they're the best in France. June–Oct Mon–Sat 8am–7.30pm, Sun 9am–7.30pm; Nov–May Mon–Sat 8am–7pm, Sun 9am–7pm.

**Restaurant Le Tertre** 5 rue du Tertre-de-la-Tente ☎ 05 57 74 46 33, ⓦrestaurant-le-tertre.com. Stashed halfway up a dizzyingly steep cobblestone street, you won't want to drink too much if you're eating here. It's worth the climb, though – snag a prime view on one of the cosy outdoor platforms or head into the wood-beamed, stone-walled restaurant and gorge on the hearty three-course regional *menu* (€25). Book ahead. Feb & March Mon, Tues & Fri–Sun 12–1.15pm & 7–9.15pm; April–Nov Thurs–Tues 12–1.15pm & 7–9.15pm.

# Entre-Deux-Mers

**Entre-Deux-Mers** ("between two seas") lies between the tidal waters of the Dordogne and Garonne. It's the most attractive area in the wine region, with gentle hills and medieval villages. Its wines, including the Premières Côtes de Bordeaux, are mainly dry whites, produced by over forty *caves coopératives*. They're considered good, albeit not up to the level of Médocs or dry Graves produced to the south.

## La Sauve-Majeure

ⓦ abbaye-la-sauve-majeure.fr • June–Sept daily 10am–1.15pm, 2–6pm; Oct–May Tues–Sun 10.30am–1pm, 2–5.30pm • €7.50

Around 25km east of Bordeaux is the ruined eleventh-century abbey **La Sauve-Majeure**, an important stop for pilgrims en route to Santiago de Compostela in Spain. Thick woods once surrounded the abbey – in fact its name is from the Latin *silva major* (large forest). All that remains today are the Romanesque apse and apsidal chapels, and outstanding sculpted capitals in the chancel. The best illustrate stories from the Old and New Testaments; a pensive Daniel in the lions' den is particularly winning. There's a small **museum** at the entrance, with some keystones from the fallen roofs.

## St-Macaire and around

If you're heading south through Entre-Deux-Mers, Langon is the first town you come to, but it's best to postpone your rest stop until pretty **ST-MACAIRE**, across the Garonne. The village still has its original **gates** and **battlements** and there's a beautiful medieval church, the **Église-Prieuré**, with beautifully restored wall paintings.

La Réole, 18km east, is full of medieval buildings on narrow, hilly streets – pick up a map from the tourist office on place Richard-Coeur-de-Lion. You can take a look at France's oldest **town hall**, constructed in the twelfth century by Richard the Lionheart, and the well-preserved **Abbaye des Bénédictins**, which has a fantastic view over the River Garonne and the surrounding countryside.

### INFORMATION                                              ST MACAIRE AND AROUND

**Tourist office** 52 rue André-Bénac, La Réole (Tues–Sat 10am–    1pm & 2–6pm; ☎ 05 56 61 13 55, ⓦ entredeuxmers.com).

### ACCOMMODATION AND EATING

**L'Abricotier** 2 rue François-Bergoeing, St-Macaire ☎ 05 56 76 83 63, ⓦ restaurant-labricotier.com. A genial local hotel-restaurant with a shady terrace and tasty daily *menus* from €23. The three rooms upstairs have a simple homeliness, and with free parking and breakfast for €8, it's an excellent budget choice. Restaurant Wed–Sun noon–2pm & 7.30–9pm. **€70**

**Les Feuilles d'Acanthe** 6 rue Carnot, St-Macaire ☎ 05 56 62 33 75, ⓦ hotel-saint-macaire.fr. Easy to locate in the centre of town, this twelve-room hotel has an excellent restaurant with daily *menus* from €16.90. Rooms are sparsely furnished with uninspiring decor, incongruous against the attractive stone walls and wood beams, but there's a jacuzzi and some great views. Closed Dec–Jan. Breakfast €11. **€110**

## Sauternes and around

**SAUTERNES** is a slumbering village surrounded by vines and dominated by the **Maison du Sauternes** (Mon–Fri 9am–7pm, Sat & Sun 10am–7pm, shorter hours in winter; ☎ 05 56 76 69 83, ⓦ maisondusauternes.com) at one end of the village, and a pretty church at the other. The *maison* looks like a treasure-trove, with its rows of golden bottles with white labels, and it's a non-profit organization, offering tastings, expert advice and competitive prices.

### ACCOMMODATION                                                          SAUTERNES

★ **La Sauternaise** 22 rue Principale ☎ 06 78 00 64 18, ⓦ chambres-sauternes.com. Offering four individually designed, luxurious rooms with wellness facilities, this B&B is a step above the usual offerings and boasts a hard-to-beat location in the centre of the village. A gourmet breakfast is included, and

they offer a great selection of wines for purchase. **€120**
**Relais du Château d'Arche** ☎ 05 56 76 66 55, ⓦ chateau-arche.fr. A luxurious château-hotel and vineyard on the D125 just outside Sauternes (heading north) with nine rooms. Breakfast €10. **€150**

### EATING AND DRINKING

**Auberge Les Vignes** 23 rue Principale ☎ 05 56 76 60 06, ⓦ aubergelesvignes.fr. Understated elegance with a sunny terrace right on the main street, this is a good place for fish and oysters, as well as local specialities like

*cassolette d'escargots* (snail casserole). There's also a sizeable wine list and a lunch *menu* at €16. Tues–Sat noon–2pm & 7.30–9.30pm, Sun noon–2pm.
**Restaurant Saprien** 14 rue Principale ☎ 05 56 76 60

**9**

## SAUTERNES

The **Sauternes** region, which extends southeast from Bordeaux for 40km along the left bank of the Garonne, is an ancient winemaking area, first planted during the Roman occupation. The distinctive golden wine of the area is sweet, round, full-bodied and spicy, with a long aftertaste. It's not necessarily a dessert wine, either; try it with Roquefort cheese. Gravelly terraces with a limestone subsoil help create the delicious taste, but mostly it's due to a peculiar microclimate of morning autumn mists and afternoons of sun and heat which causes *Botrytis cinerea* fungus, or "noble rot", to flourish on the grapes, letting the sugar concentrate and introducing some intense flavours. When the grapes are picked they're not a pretty sight: carefully selected by hand, only the most shrivelled, rotting bunches are taken. The wines of Sauternes are some of the most sought-after in the world, with bottles of **Château d'Yquem**, in particular, fetching thousands of euros. Sadly, that particular château does not offer tastings, but you can wander around the buildings and grounds, two minutes' drive north of Sauternes.

87, ⓦrestaurant-le-saprien.fr. With its shady garden terrace right at the foot of the vineyards, this is a romantic place to escape the sun or dine beneath the stars. The cuisine is classic French, with a good mix of meat and fish dishes and lunch *menus* from €14. Tues–Sat noon–2pm & 7.30–9pm, Sun noon–2pm.

### Around Sauternes

Ten kilometres south of Sauternes is the little town of **Villandraut**, overlooked by a great mammoth of a ruined château (April–June Sat & Sun 10am–1pm & 3–6.30pm; July–Sept daily 10am–1pm & 3–6.30pm; Oct–April by appointment only; €5). It was built by Pope Clement V, who caused the Papal Schism (1378) by moving his papacy to Avignon. You can visit Clement's tomb in **Uzeste** en route to **Bazas**, 15km east. At the heart of Bazas is the wide, arcaded place de la Cathédrale, where the **St-Jean-Baptiste cathedral** is a harmonious blend of Romanesque, Gothic and classical styles.

### ACCOMMODATION                                    AROUND SAUTERNES

★**Le Sorbet** Sorbet, Bazas ☎06 32 31 74 64, ⓦausorbet.com. A delightful country cottage with friendly hosts, a pretty garden and eco credentials, this charming *chambre d'hôte* has two beautifully decorated, cosy rooms. Breakfast included. **€90**

# The Côte d'Argent

At over 200km, the **CÔTE D'ARGENT** is the longest, straightest, sandiest stretch of coast in Europe. Behind the endless beaches, which reach from the mouth of the Gironde all the way to Biarritz, are high sand dunes, and the largest forest in Western Europe, **Les Landes**. There's no coast road, only a cycle path, built at the end of World War II. It winds through more than 75km of pine-forested dunes from the upmarket holiday town of Cap Ferret, to Soulac in the north. The lack of conventional tourist sights means that outside July and August the coast does not get many visitors, and away from the main resorts it's possible to find deserted stretches of coastline, even in August.

## Arcachon

On Friday nights in the summer, Bordeaux's residents flee the city, making for **ARCACHON**, the oldest beach resort on the Côte d'Argent. In August the white beaches bustle, and blue and yellow cruise boats buzz around the wooden jetties.

Many of Arcachon's houses date from that brief period in the nineteenth century when the public's taste resembled that of a seven-year-old girl: extravagant, frilly bungalows sit in rose-filled gardens, inscribed with names like "Mirabelle" and "Claire de Lune" in curly italics. The town is made up of four little districts, named after the seasons. The seafront promenades and shopping streets of **ville d'été** (summer town) are full of ice-cream stalls and fishing nets. **Ville d'hiver** (winter town), south of the beach, is a place of broad, quiet streets and Second Empire mansions. To get there, follow the boulevard de la Plage west of Jetée Thiers until you reach the pedestrianized rue de Maréchal-de-Lattre-de-Tassigny; there a lift carries you up to the flower-filled, wooded **Parc Mauresque**, just below ville d'hiver. Residential **ville d'automne** (autumn town) stretches eastwards along boulevard de la Plage, a gentle 15min walk from ville d'été; the beaches are a little quieter here.

## Parc Ornithologique du Teich

Daily 10am–6pm/8pm (winter/summer) • €8.90 • ⓦ reserve-ornithologique-du-teich.com

At **Le Teich**, about 14km east of Arcachon, one of the most important expanses of wetlands remaining in France has been converted into a bird sanctuary, the **Parc Ornithologique du Teich**. There are no hotels in Le Teich, but there are campsites, and it's an easy day-trip from Arcachon by train.

## INFORMATION
## ARCACHON

**Tourist office** Théâtre Olympia, 21 av du Général-de-Gaulle (April–June & Sept Mon–Sat 9am–6pm, Sun 10am–1pm & 2–5pm; July & Aug daily 9am–7pm; Oct–March Mon–Fri 9am–1pm & 2–6pm, Sat 9am–1pm & 2–5pm; ☎ 05 57 52 97 97; ⓦ arcachon.com).

**Boat trips** In summer boats leave the jetties of Thiers and Eyrac on various cruises, including to the Île aux Oiseaux (1hr 45min; €16), and the Arcachon basin/Dune du Pyla (4hr; €30). There's also a regular boat service from here to Cap Ferret on the opposite peninsula (30min; €14 return). Discounted tickets for all excursions are available from the tourist office. Check ⓦ bassin-arcachon-info.com for timetables.

## ACCOMMODATION

**Le Camping Club** 5 allée de la Galaxie ☎ 05 56 83 24 15, ⓦ camping-arcachon.com. An excellent four-star campsite in town with a bar, restaurant, and shop (July & Aug only), playground, BBQs, volleyball and bike rental. Closed Nov–Dec. **€110**

**Le Dauphin** 7 av Gounod ☎ 05 56 83 02 89, ⓦ dauphin-arcachon.com. This unpretentious hotel in an attractive nineteenth-century building has simple but pleasant rooms, some of which have balconies. There's an outdoor swimming pool, and the beach is just a few streets away. **€140**

**La Plage** 10 av Nelly-Deganne ☎ 05 56 83 06 23, ⓦ hotelarcachon.com. The slick monochrome facade and identikit balconies of *La Plage* look somewhat incongruous against the fanciful Arcachonaise villas on the same block. Behind the urban frontage, however, the rooms are comfortable and there's private parking, a fitness room and a well-stocked breakfast buffet. Breakfast €13. **€140**

★ **Ville d'hiver** 20 av Victor-Hugo ☎ 05 56 66 10 36, ⓦ hotelvilledhiver.com. Impressively transformed from a nineteenth-century water plant, this unique hotel offers free-standing blocks of rooms, dotted around a charming garden. Warm wood furnishings, contemporary decor and balconies afford each room its own character and privacy, but best of all is the outdoor swimming pool, housed in the old purification tank. Breakfast €13. **€200**

## EATING AND DRINKING

★ **Le Cabane de l'Aiguillon** Bd Pierre-Loti ☎ 05 56 54 88 20, ⓦ lacabanedelaiguillon.com. The hut here sells oysters all year round, but come in fair weather to enjoy the produce outside, under the leafy pergola and by the water's edge. In addition to oysters, you can also enjoy clams, whelks and prawns, simply accompanied by bread, lemon and white wine. Hard to beat. Take-away daily 9am–7.30pm. Terrace dining in good weather only daily 11am–5pm.

**Le Cabestan** 6bis av du Général-de-Gaulle ☎ 05 56 83 18 62. A straight-shooting seafood restaurant with warm service and traditional surroundings, this is the place to tuck into Arcachon's famous oysters. Mains from €16. Wed–Sun noon–2pm & 7–9.15pm, July–Aug also Tues 7–9.15pm.

Closed Jan.

★ **Pâtisserie Alain Guignard** 11 av Notre-Dame-des-Passes. An Arcachon institution with a twenty-year pedigree. Indulge your sweet tooth with fruit crumble, *canelés*, layer cake, chocolate cake, biscuits, fruit tarts, coffee and éclairs. Daily 8.30am–7.30pm.

**La Table du Boucher** 16 rue du Maréchal-de-Lattre-de-Tassigny ☎ 05 56 54 06 28. Head to this welcoming local joint if you want a change from fish and seafood – the meat-heavy menu is cooked to perfection. The *andouillette* (€14.90) and veal with confit onions (€16.90) are both delicious, but you can't go wrong with steak and chips. Tues–Sun noon–2pm & 7.30–10.30pm; July & Aug daily.

**9**

# Cap Ferret

The tiny peninsula town of **CAP FERRET** crashed onto the tourist scene in the 1920s, when Jean Cocteau began holidaying here: "We row, we nap, we roll in the sand, we stroll around naked, in a landscape like Texas", he wrote in Letters from Piquey (1923). Polite society wanted to join in, and Cap Ferret quickly became a well-heeled holiday resort. Surrounded by the Landes of Gascony and the Pays de Buch, the peninsula is full of wooded enclaves, quiet coves and long sandy beaches, and if you're happy to go off the beaten track, it's possible to escape the crowds even in mid-summer.

## INFORMATION
CAP FERRET

**Tourist office** 12 av de l'Océan (April–Sept daily 10am–1pm & 3–6pm; ☎ 05 56 60 63 26, ⓦ lege-capferret.com), just down from the jetty. A P'tit train tour runs from outside the tourist office – €3.35 for the short circuit.

**Boats** Passenger ferries run all year round between Cap Ferret and nearby Arcachon (30min; €14 return; buy tickets at the jetty; ⓦ bassin-arcachon-info.com). Bikes can be

taken on board. Ferries also run to Dune du Pyla and Le Moulleau, and a number of boat cruises and tours are also available.

**Bike hire** Many hotels offer bike rental, or else Locabeach (between the jetty and the Tourist Office; ☎ 05 56 60 49 46) rents bikes (€13/day), electric bikes (€32/day) and scooters (from €50/day).

## ACCOMMODATION

**Camping Brémontier** Le Grand Crohot Océan ☎ 05 56 60 03 99, ⓦ campingbremontier.fr. 10km north of Cap Ferret in a protected pine forest with a shop and bread delivery, bike rental, a supervised beach and a sailing club. Open May–Sept. **€18.90**

**Chez Annie** 7 rue des Roitelets ☎ 05 56 60 66 25, ⓦ chezannie-capferret.com. Run by the affable Annie, who speaks very little English but is happy to mime, this is a home away from home, right down to the home-made crêpes and apricot jam at breakfast. The three well-furnished wood cabins are comfortable and spotless, the beach is a short walk away and there's a pretty garden to relax in. **€130**

★ **La Maison du Bassin** 5 rue des Pionniers ☎ 05 56 60 60 63, ⓦ lamaisondubassin.com. Oak floors, plush beds and chandeliers add a restrained elegance to the small but perfectly formed rooms at this hotel, which has the feel of a

bourgeois summer home. The attached restaurant, with its huge terrace hemmed in by vines, is also excellent (menus from €28) and the staff are attentive and knowledgeable about the area. Breakfast from €15. **€165**

★ **Des Pins** 23 rue des Fauvettes ☎ 05 56 60 60 11, ⓦ hoteldespins.eu. Des Pins feels like a genteel Edwardian boarding house, with fresh, pale rooms off a wood-panelled hall. There are sleeping cabins in the garden and a gypsy caravan. The only downside is bad soundproofing. Closed mid–Nov to Jan. Breakfast €12. **€80**

**Yamina Lodge** 169 av de Bordeaux ☎ 05 56 60 14 89, ⓦ yamina-lodge.com. Three rooms and a villa in purpose-built, wooden cabins nestled beneath towering pine trees, this is an idyllic spot to unwind. Country-style interiors with wicker furnishings and fine wood floors add to the Zen feel, plus there are roomy terraces, bikes for hire and a romantic jacuzzi. Breakfast €12. Closed winter. **€180**

## EATING AND DRINKING

**Pinasse Café** 2bis av de l'Océan ☎ 05 56 03 77 87, ⓦ pinasse-cafe.com. Right next to Cap Ferret's main jetty, where the Arcachon boat disembarks, *Pinasse* is a tourist honeypot, but against all odds it's also an excellent little restaurant, serving an array of fresh seafood (€4–63). Secure a table on the picturesque terrace and watch as the ships come in, with the waves lapping beneath you. Daily

9.30am–11pm.

**So Phare Away** 32 av Nord du Phare ☎ 06 70 93 59 79. A quality, varied menu with fresh, piquant seafood and fish dishes for around €25, but the big selling point is the surroundings. Bright interiors, quirky log furniture and a bamboo-covered terrace. Summer daily noon–2pm & 7.30–11pm; winter Sat & Sun noon–2pm & 7.30–11pm; closed mid-Jan to mid-Feb.

# Les Landes

South of Bordeaux is **LES LANDES**, the largest pine forest in Western Europe. Nearly 10,000 square kilometres long, it was declared a *parc naturel régional* in 1970. It's a beautiful place, but inhospitable and lonely, strong on outdoor pursuits but with few cultural attractions.

**Mont de Marsan** makes a good base for exploring the inland part of Les Landes. It's the administrative heart of the region, 100km south of Bordeaux, and served by regular

## THE DUNE DU PYLA

**The Dune du Pyla** (or Dune du Pilat) is the largest dune in Europe – a vast white lunar landscape of windswept sand, 100m high, 12km south of Arcachon. It's an arduous climb, so take the steps to the top if you're not up for the challenge, but the adventurous shouldn't miss the long, hair-raising slide down to the sea, over slopes as steep as an Olympic ski-jump. Bus #1 leaves from the *gare SNCF* in Arcachon every hour from July to September – two to seven a day in other months. If you're driving, note that the car park costs €4 for two hours. Three minutes away by car is *Hôtel La Co(o)rniche* (46 bd Louis-Gaume; ☎ 05 56 22 72 11, ⓦ lacoorniche-pyla.com; €590); the terrace, with views of the bay and dunes, is the ideal spot for cocktails or a plate of oysters (from €14).

trains. **Parc Jean-Rameau**, on the north bank of the river Douze, is the prettiest part of the town. If you're lucky enough to be in the area in mid-July, you can enjoy Les Fêtes Madeleine (ⓦfetesmadeleine.fr), a week of parades, sports, flamenco and bullfighting, when the town's Basque identity asserts itself.

### INFORMATION

**Tourist office** 1 place Charles-de-Gaulle, Mont-de-Marsan (Jan–March & Nov–Dec Mon–Fri 9am–12.30pm & 1.30–6pm, Sat 9am–1pm; April–June & Sept–Oct Mon–Sat 9.30am–6pm, Sun 10am–5pm; July & Aug Mon–Sat 9am–6.30pm, Sun 10am–5pm; ☎ 05 58 05 87 37, ⓦtourisme-montdemarsan.fr)
**Activities** The tourist office provides maps of local walking

### LES LANDES

and cycling routes and also organizes a guided tour of Mont-de-Marsan in English (July & Aug, from the office Mon–Sat 10.30am). Another outdoor activity on offer is canoeing on one of the three rivers whose confluence is at the town. For canoe hire try Canoë Loisir (☎ 05 58 45 62 21, ⓦ canoeloisir. fr) in nearby Roquefort.

### ACCOMMODATION

**Les Prés d'Eugénie** Eugénie-les-Bains ☎ 05 58 05 06 07, ⓦ michelguerard.com. An idyllic retreat marooned on its own estate, where you'll sleep in a renovated nineteenth-century colonial mansion, surrounded by manicured gardens and vineyards, dine on three-Michelin-starred cuisine, and be pampered in a luxurious spa – this kind of luxury comes at quite a price, of course. There are also a variety of deals, spa breaks and cooking classes available. €630
**Le Renaissance** 225 av de Villeneuve ☎ 05 58 51 51

51, ⓦ le-renaissance.com. Comfortable, spotless rooms in this mid-size country hotel 1km from the centre of Mont-de-Marsan, with a swimming pool, restaurant and lovely gardens. Breakfast €11.50. €99
**Le Richelieu** 3 rue Robert-Wlérick ☎ 05 58 06 10 20, ⓦ hotel-richelieu-montdemarsan.com. Reliable and friendly hotel, with a decent on-site restaurant, private parking and comfortable, well-equipped rooms right in the centre of town. Part of the *Citadel* chain, it's smart and functional rather than stylish, but good value. €72

### EATING AND DRINKING

**Le Bistrot de Marcel** 1 rue Pont du Commerce ☎ 05 58 75 09 71, ⓦ lebistrotdemarcel.fr. Traditional cuisine sourced from local ingredients and served in a prime location overlooking the Midouze river. Service is leisurely, so make a night of it and order the *menu du sud-ouest* (€30.90). Mon–Fri noon–2pm & 7.30–10.30pm, Sat

7.30–10.30pm.
**Brûlerie Montoise** 1 rue du 4-septembre ☎ 05 58 75 02 63. The coffee is roasted daily, the teas are plentiful and the cakes are fresh – what more do you need for a sightseeing break? Tues–Sat 9am–noon, 2–7pm.

# The Limousin, Dordogne and the Lot

**533** The Limousin

**542** The Dordogne

**567** The Lot

BEYNAC-ET-CAZENAC

# The Limousin, Dordogne and the Lot

The oval area bordered to the east by the uplands of the Massif Central and to the west by the Atlantic plains was the most contested between the English and the French during the Hundred Years' War, and has been most in demand among English visitors and second-home buyers in more recent times. Although it doesn't coincide exactly with either the modern French administrative boundaries or the old provinces of Périgord and Quercy, which constitute the core of the region, the land here has a physical and geographical homogeneity thanks to its great rivers: the Dordogne, the Lot and the Aveyron, all of which drain westwards from the Massif Central into the mighty Garonne.

From **Limoges** in the province of Limousin in the north to the Garonne valley in the south, the country is gently hilly, full of lush hidden valleys and miles of woodland, mainly oak. The northerly **Limousin** is slightly greener and wetter, the south more open and arid. But you can travel a long way without seeing a radical shift, except in the uplands of the **Plateau de Millevaches**, where the rivers plunge into gorges and the woods are beech, chestnut and conifer plantations. The other characteristic landscape is the *causses*, the dry scrubby limestone plateaux found between the Lot and Dordogne and the Lot and Aveyron. Where the rivers have cut their way through the limestone, the valleys are walled with overhanging cliffs, riddled with fissures, underground streams and caves. And in these caves – especially in the valley of the Vézère around **Les Eyzies** – is some of the most awe-inspiring **prehistoric art** to be found anywhere in the world.

The other great artistic legacy of the area is the Romanesque sculpture, most notably adorning the churches at **Souillac** and **Beaulieu-sur-Dordogne**, but all modelled on the supreme example of the cloister of St-Pierre in the quiet town of **Moissac**. Hilltops through the region are marked by splendid **fortresses** of purely military design, such as **Bonaguil**, **Najac**, **Biron**, **Beynac** and **Castelnaud**, which more than compensate for the dearth of luxurious châteaux.

The charm of the area undoubtedly lies in the landscapes and the dozens of harmonious small towns and villages. Some, like **Sarlat** and **Rocamadour**, are so well known that they are overrun with tourists in the height of summer. Others, like **Figeac**, **Villefranche-de-Rouergue**, **Gourdon**, **Montauban**, **Monflanquin** and the many *bastides* (fortified towns) that pepper the area between the Lot and Dordogne, have a quieter, more local charm, where the greatest pleasure lies in wandering the narrow streets of their old towns. Unsurprisingly, many villages in the region feature on the prestigious list of *Les Plus Beaux Villages de France* (ⓦ france-beautiful-villages.org)

The wartime Resistance was very active in these out-of-the-way regions, and the roadsides are dotted with memorials to those killed in ambushes or shot in reprisals. There is also one chilling monument to wartime atrocity: the ruined village of **Oradour-sur-Glane**, still as the Nazis left it after massacring the population and setting fire to the houses.

## GETTING AROUND

**THE LIMOUSIN, DORDOGNE AND THE LOT**

All of the region's main towns are linked by rail and/or bus services, while a fair number of smaller places have sporadic public transport links. To really make the most of the area, though, you'll need your own vehicle – car rental is available in all of the major towns.

JARDINS DE MARQUEYSSAC

# Highlights

**❶ Brantôme** This old abbey town, scenically set on an island in the middle of the Dronne, makes a great base for leisurely boat trips on the river. See page 543

**❷ Cuisine** Foie gras, truffles and *pommes sarladaises* – Dordogne is the place to sample French country cooking at its best. See page 543

**❸ Monpazier** The finest of numerous *bastides* (fortified towns) in the region, particularly resplendent in the late afternoon sun. See page 551

**❹ Sarlat-la-Canéda** Wander the narrow lanes of this archetypal medieval town, with its lovely *vieille ville* of honey-coloured stone; time

your visit to coincide with one of the excellent weekly produce markets. See page 552

**❺ Centre International d'Art Pariétal (Lascaux IV)** Don't miss the new state-of-the-art reconstruction of the prehistoric Lascaux cave. See page 558

**❻ Jardins de Marqueyssac** Extraordinary gardens, perched on a rocky promontory, with astounding views over the Dordogne and its picturesque villages. See page 562

**❼ Cité Internationale de la Tapisserie** Watch the weavers at work on a Tolkien tapestry at this new centre celebrating Aubusson's high-quality needlework. See page 538

**HIGHLIGHTS ARE MARKED ON THE MAP ON PAGE 532**

# The Limousin

The **Limousin** – the country around **Limoges** – is hilly, wooded, wet and not particularly fertile: ideal pasture for the famous Limousin cattle. This is herdsman's country, and it's the widespread use of the shepherd's cape known as a *limousine* that gave its name to the car. The modern Limousin region stretches south to the Dordogne valley to include **Brive and Turenne**. But while these places, together with Limoges itself, are not without interest, the star of the show is the countryside – especially in the east on the **Plateau de Millevaches**.

10

## Limoges

**LIMOGES** is a pleasant city, if not one that calls for a long stay. It's famed for its crafts – enamel in the Middle Ages and, since the eighteenth century, exceptionally **fine china** – and in 2017 was classed as a UNESCO Creative City. Around 1200 people are employed by twenty factories in the porcelain industry, which has an annual turnover of €120 million. On first glance, its centre is rather blighted by the ugly concrete buildings of **place de la République**, but delving into the quiet streets beyond, particularly **rue de la Boucherie** and around, reveals a more atmospheric and charming side to Limoges. Although the local council is doing what it can to brighten up public places with experimental ceramic arts.

### Cathédrale St-Étienne

Place St-Étienne • Daily: April–Oct 9am–6pm; Nov–March 9am–5pm • ⓦ cathedrale-limoges.fr

The **Cathédrale St-Étienne** was begun in 1273 and modelled on the cathedral of Amiens, though only the choir, completed in the early thirteenth century, is pure Gothic. The rest of the building was added piecemeal over the centuries, the western part of the nave not until 1876. The most striking external feature is the sixteenth-century facade of the north transept, built in full Flamboyant style with elongated arches, clusters of pinnacles and delicate tracery in window and gallery. At the west end of the nave, the tower, erected on a Romanesque base that had to be massively reinforced to bear the weight, has octagonal upper storeys, in common with most churches in the region. It once stood as a separate campanile and probably looked the better for it. Inside, the effects are much more pleasing. The sense of soaring height is accentuated by all the upward-reaching lines of the pillars, the net of vaulting ribs, the curling, flame-like lines, and, as you look down the nave, by the narrower and more pointed arches of the choir.

### Musée des Beaux-Arts de Limoges

1 place de l'Évêché • April–Sept daily except Tues 9.30am–noon & 2–6pm; Oct–March Mon & Wed–Sat 10am–noon & 2–5pm, Sun 2–5pm • €5 • ☎ 05 55 45 98 10, ⓦ museebal.fr

The best of the city's museums – with its showpiece collections of enamelware dating back to the twelfth century – is the **Musée des Beaux-Arts de Limoges** in the old bishop's palace next to the cathedral. The large, attractive exhibition space charts the progression from the simple Byzantine-influenced *champlevé* (copper filled with enamel) to seventeenth- and eighteenth-century work that uses a far greater range of colours and indulges in elaborate, virtuoso portraiture.

### The Botanical Garden

Daily sunrise to sunset • Free

Behind the cathedral, the **botanical garden** feels like a tucked away gem, descending gracefully towards the River Vienne and split into three different sections, including the historic garden, which, unsurprisingly, is the oldest of the three, with around fifteen hundred beautifully presented plants spread out in neat – but not too ordered – lines.

## The old quarter

Stretching roughly north from the River Vienne to the ugly, modern place de la République, the partly renovated **old quarter** is a charmingly jumbled mix of predominantly timbered buildings. It's the best part of the city for a stroll, with the most interesting area lying immediately south and east of the market. Here you'll find rue de la Boucherie, for a thousand years the domain of the butchers' guild, and arguably the most attractive of Limoges's streets. The dark, cluttered **chapel of St-Aurélien**, halfway along, belongs to the guild, while one of their former shophouses at no. 36 makes an interesting little museum, the **Maison de la Boucherie** (closed at the time of writing; free). At the top of the street, in place de la Motte, is the attractive **market hall** (Tues–Sat 7am–2pm, Sun 8am–1pm), at its best and liveliest during the week.

### St-Michel-des-Lions

Place St-Michel

The fourteenth- and fifteenth-century **church of St-Michel-des-Lions**, tucked away near the market hall, is named after the two badly weathered Celtic lions guarding the

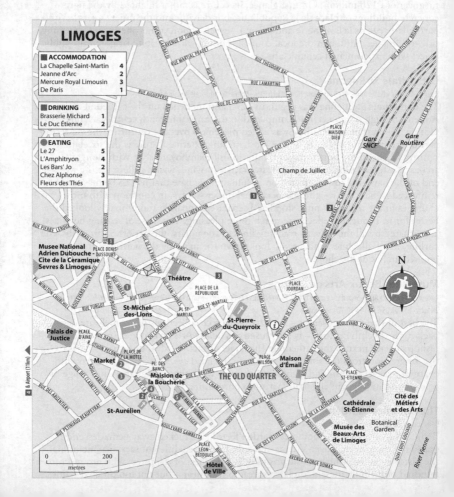

**LIMOGES**

**■ ACCOMMODATION**
| La Chapelle Saint-Martin | 4 |
| Jeanne d'Arc | 2 |
| Mercure Royal Limousin | 3 |
| De Paris | 1 |

**■ DRINKING**
| Brasserie Michard | 1 |
| Le Duc Étienne | 2 |

**● EATING**
| Le 27 | 5 |
| L'Amphitryon | 4 |
| Les Bars' Jo | 2 |
| Chez Alphonse | 3 |
| Fleurs des Thés | 1 |

south door and topped by one of the most elegant towers in the region. The inside is dark and atmospheric, with two beautiful, densely coloured fifteenth-century windows either side of the choir.

### St-Pierre-du-Queyroix

Rue St-Pierre

The **church of St-Pierre-du-Queyroix** sits under a typically Limousin belfry, and the interior, partly twelfth-century, has the same slightly pink granite glow as the cathedral. There's some fine stained glass here, including an eye-catching window at the end of the south aisle depicting the Dormition of the Virgin, and signed by the great enamel artist Jean Pénicault in 1510.

## Musée National Adrien-Dubouché – Cité de la Céramique Sèvres & Limoges

8bis place Winston-Churchill • Daily except Tues 10am–12.30pm & 2–5.45pm • €7, €8 combined ticket with Fondation Bernardaud • ⓦ musee-adriendubouche.fr

The best place to see Limoges's renowned **porcelain** is in **Musée National Adrien-Dubouché – Cité de la Céramique Sèvres & Limoges**, a short walk west of the old quarter. The strikingly renovated museum's interestingly presented collection includes samples of the local product and china displays from around the world, as well as various pieces from celebrity services ordered for the likes of Abraham Lincoln, Queen Elizabeth and sundry French royals. You can buy a combined ticket for a guided tour of Fondation Bernardaud (27 av Albert-Thomas; June-Sept Mon–Sat 9.45–11.15am & 1.30–4.15pm; ⓦbernardaud.fr), a porcelain maker dating from 1863.

### ARRIVAL AND INFORMATION

LIMOGES

**By plane** Limoges Bellegarde airport (ⓦ aeroportlimoges. com) is 11km northwest of the city. Taxis to the city centre cost around €24–33 (there is no public transport).

**By train** Limoges's magnificent Art Deco gare des Bénédictins lies slightly northeast of the centre on avenue de-Gaulle, from where it's a 5min walk to central place de la République.

Destinations Aubusson (daily; 1hr 55min); Bordeaux (10 daily; 2hr 30min); Brive-la-Gaillarde (17 daily; 1hr 10min); Eymoutiers-Vassivière (5–8 daily; 50min); Périgueux (14 daily; 1hr 20min); St-Léonard-de-Noblat (7 daily; 21min); Solignac-la-Vigen (5 daily; 10min).

**By bus** The *gare routière* is next to the train station; however, it's usually more convenient to use the bus stops on places Jourdan and Winston-Churchill. Note that buses to Solignac depart only from place Winston-Churchill.

Destinations Aubusson (2–3 daily; 1hr 50min); Oradour-sur-Glane (Mon–Sat 3 daily; 35min); St-Léonard-de-Noblat (3 daily; 40min); Solignac (Mon–Fri 2 daily; 40min).

**Tourist office** 12 bd de Fleurus (May–June & Sept Mon–Sat 10am–5.30pm, Sun 10am–1pm; July & Aug Mon–Sat 10am–7pm, Sun 10am–1pm; Oct–April Mon–Sat 10am–1pm & 2–5pm; ☎ 05 55 34 46 87, ⓦ limoges-tourisme.com).

### ACCOMMODATION

★ **La Chapelle Saint-Martin** Nieul, 10km northwest of Limoges ☎ 05 55 75 80 17, ⓦ chapellesaintmartin.com. Set within beautiful grounds that stretch down towards a lake, this luxurious hotel is just 15 minutes' drive from central Limoges but feels like a different world. Rooms are spacious and sumptuous, without being fussy, and there's an outdoor swimming pool, tennis courts and a Michelin-star restaurant. **€185**

**Jeanne d'Arc** 17 av de-Gaulle ☎ 05 55 77 67 77, ⓦ hotel jeannedarc.fr. A recent renovation has made this old hotel, close to the train station, an appealing option, though it can be a case of pot luck as some rooms feel more elegant and modern than others. **€60**

**Mercure Royal Limousin** Place de la République ☎ 05 55 34 65 30, ⓦ mercure.com. Sitting on the vast place de la République on the edge of the old quarter, the *Mercure* is an unattractive, concrete affair, though the rooms are comfortable and a decent size. More expensive rooms have balconies looking over the square. **€76**

★ **De Paris** 5 cours Vergniaud ☎ 05 55 77 56 96, ⓦ hoteldeparis-limoges.com. Next to the Champ de Juillet park, a charming nineteenth-century hotel where breakfast is served on Limoges china. The bedrooms might be a little old-fashioned but are not devoid of charm (most have marble fireplaces) and are generally airy and pleasant. **€55**

### EATING

Limoges has an abundance of good and not too expensive places to eat; however, if you're in town on a Sunday you'll find choices to be extremely limited. It's advisable to book on Saturday evenings when restaurants can quickly fill up.

**10**

**Le 27** 27 rue Haute-Vienne ☎ 05 55 32 27 27, 🌐 ka.le27.com. Conceived as a traditional brasserie – complete with oyster bar – but with modern sensibilities, this is one of the best places to eat in town, and is headed by Gilles Dudognon, one half of the team behind *La Chapelle Saint Martin* (see page 535). Expect lots of fresh fish and local meat, such as Limousin steak (€27), on the regularly changing menu. Mon–Sat noon–2pm & 7.45–10.30pm.

**L'Amphitryon** 26 rue de la Boucherie ☎ 05 55 33 36 39, 🌐 amphitryon-limoges.fr. This elegant restaurant serves subtle and sophisticated cuisine, with a good choice of seafood as well as beef, veal and other local specialities. The lunchtime *formule* is excellent value at just €23; evening *menus* start at €45. Tues–Sat noon–1.30pm & 7.45–9.30pm.

★ **Les Bars' Jo** Market hall, place de la Motte ☎ 05 55 32 32 79. For a good-value lunch and a lively atmosphere, head straight to the market hall to join the locals round the colourful communal tables here. Bright pictures of market life and animals adorn the walls, and the menu makes use of the best market produce, ranging from plates of cheese (€4.80) to seafood platters (€35), with excellent-value *menus* from €14.50. Mon–Sat 7am–3pm.

**Chez Alphonse** 5 place de la Motte ☎ 05 55 34 34 14, 🌐 chezalphonse.fr. A welcoming and very popular bistro, complete with red-check tablecloths and bustling waiters, which specializes in local, seasonal dishes, such as roast lamb or rabbit *chasseur* (mains from €16). Mon–Wed noon–2pm & 7.30–10.30pm, Thurs–Sat noon–2.30pm & 7.30–11pm.

**Fleurs des Thés** 12 rue des Filles Notre-Dame ☎ 05 55 33 48 06. Lovely little tearoom serving organic cakes, with vegetarian, vegan and gluten-free options; try the matcha muffin. On Tuesday and Thursday there's a vegetarian platter for lunch (€9.60). Tues & Thurs noon–6pm, Wed & Fri–Sat 2–6pm.

### DRINKING

★ **Brasserie Michard** 8 place Denis-Dussoubs ☎ 05 55 79 37 98, 🌐 bieres-michard.com. A friendly microbrewery bar serving its own very decent beers – the Ambrée is particularly nice (€2.80). Enjoy either inside the large but cosy interior, or on the terrace overlooking the square. Tues & Wed 4pm–midnight, Thurs until 1am, Fri &Sat until 1.30am.

**Le Duc Étienne** 19 rue de la Boucherie. A relaxed, wood-timbered bar in the old quarter, which gets very busy and spills out into place St-Aurélien on warm evenings. Mon–Wed 2pm–1am, Thurs–Sat 2pm–2am, Sun 6pm–1am.

## Around Limoges

The countryside **around Limoges** may not have quite the same appeal as that further south, but it's peppered with interesting small towns and villages that make great day-trips from the city.

### Solignac and around

A dozen kilometres south of Limoges in the lovely wooded valley of the Briance, the village of **SOLIGNAC** is notable for its Romanesque church and the nearby Château de Châlucet.

#### The abbey church of Solignac

Daily 9am–5.30pm

With the tiled roofs of its octagonal apse and neat little brood of radiating chapels, the **abbey church of Solignac** is utterly charming in its simplicity, striking a sturdy pose beside the main road through the village. The twelfth-century facade has little adornment, as the granite is too hard to permit intricate carving. Inside it's beautiful, with a flight of steps leading down into the nave with a dramatic view of the length of the church. There are no aisles, just a single space roofed with three big domes – an absolutely plain Latin cross in design.

#### Château de Châlucet

5km east of Solignac in St-Jean-de-Ligoure • Daily: April to June, Sept & Oct 10.30am–12.30pm & 1.30–6.30pm; July & August 10.30am–6.30pm • Guided tours €5 • No public transport • ☎ 05 55 00 96 55, 🌐 chalucet.com

The **Château de Châlucet** lies 5km up the valley of the Briance to the east of Solignac. At the highest point of the climb there is a dramatic view across the valley to the romantic, ruined keep of the castle, rising above the woods. Built in the twelfth century, the château was in English hands during the Hundred Years' War and, in the lawless aftermath, became the lair of a notorious local brigand, Perrot le Béarnais. It was dismantled in 1593 for harbouring Protestants and has been much restored recently.

| **ARRIVAL AND DEPARTURE** | **SOLIGNAC AND AROUND** |
|---|---|
| **By train** Solignac-Le Vigen station is 1km northeast of the village centre and is served by trains from Brive-la-Gaillarde (3–7 daily; 1hr 10min) and Limoges (2–4 daily; 10min). | **By bus** Bus #44 from Limoges (Mon–Fri daily; 40min) arrive at place Georges-Lemaigre-Dubreuil, just a few minutes' walk north of the abbey. |

## St-Léonard-de-Noblat

**ST-LÉONARD-DE-NOBLAT**, 20km east of Limoges, is an appealing little market town of narrow streets and medieval houses with jutting eaves and corbelled turrets. There's a very lovely eleventh- and twelfth-century church, with a six-storey tower, high dome and simple, barrel-vaulted interior – the whole in grey granite.

### HistoRail

18 rue de Beaufort • Mid-June to mid-Sept Mon–Fri 2–6pm • €6 • ⓦ historail.com

The little railway museum of **Historail** is completely charming; run entirely by volunteers, it boasts a fun collection of both full-sized and model trains through the ages. Outside, a specially erected model train set meanders through the flowers and around a small pond.

| **ARRIVAL AND ACCOMMODATION** | **ST-LÉONARD-DE-NOBLAT** |
|---|---|
| **By train** St-Léonard's train station is around a 20min walk southwest of the old town.<br>Destinations Eymoutiers-Vassivière (5–8 daily; 25min); Limoges (4–8 daily; 25min).<br>**By bus** SNCF bus #R9 from Limoges (from place Churchill, place Jourdan & the *gare routière*) stops at St-Léonard's train station and in the town centre. | Destinations Aubusson (1–3 daily; 1hr 10min); Limoges (2–4 daily; 35min).<br>**Relais St-Jacques** 6 bd Adrien-Pressemane ⓣ 05 55 56 00 25, ⓦ lerelaissaintjacques.com. This small hotel has nine rooms, decked out smartly in earthy tones. The good restaurant (*menus* from €23) serves Limousin beef and home-made foie gras. Restaurant daily noon–1.45pm & 7–9pm. **€65** |

## Oradour-sur-Glane

Some 25km northwest of Limoges, the village of **ORADOUR-SUR-GLANE** stands just as the soldiers of the SS left it on June 10, 1944, after killing 642 of the inhabitants in reprisal for attacks by French *maquisards*. On arriving, the SS took the men of the village into barns, where they opened fire with machine guns, deliberately aiming low to wound rather than kill, before setting the barns alight – only six men escaped, one of whom was shot dead shortly after. Meanwhile, the women and children were shepherded into the church, where a gas bomb was set off – when this failed, the soldiers let loose with machine guns and grenades, before, again, setting the church, and its inhabitants, and then the rest of the village, on fire. The entire village, which sits to the southeast of the modern village, has been preserved as a shrine.

### The Centre de la Mémoire

Daily: Feb & Nov to mid-Dec 9am–5pm; March to mid-May & mid-Sept to Oct 9am–6pm; mid-May to mid-Sept 9am–7pm; closed 16 Dec–Jan • Exhibition €7.80 • ⓦ www.oradour.org • Bus #12 from Limoges (Mon–Sat 3 daily; 35min)

It's well worth taking the time to visit the exhibition at the **Centre de la Mémoire**, which sets the historical context for the events of June 1944 and attempts to explain how – and why – such acts of brutality took place. Most of the displays are in French, but there's enough English translation and photographs to give a good sense of the content.

### The village

Daily: Feb & Nov to mid-Dec 9am–5pm; March to mid-May & mid-Sept to Oct 9am–6pm; mid-May to mid-Sept 9am–7pm • Free

Access to the **village** is only possible through the Centre de la Mémoire, though it's not necessary to visit the exhibition in order to do so. An underground passage leads

**10**

from beside the ticket desk into the village itself, where a sign admonishes *Souviens-toi* ("Remember"), and the main street leads past roofless houses gutted by fire. Telephone poles, iron bedsteads and gutters are fixed in tormented attitudes where the fire's heat left them; pre-war cars rust in the garages; cooking pots hang over empty grates; last year's grapes hang wizened on a vine whose trellis has long rotted away. To the north of the village a dolmen-like slab on a shallow plinth covers a crypt containing relics of the dead, and the awful list of names, while to the southeast, by the stream, stands the church where the women and children – five hundred of them – were burnt to death.

## Rochechouart

**ROCHECHOUART**, a lovely little walled town roughly 45km west of Limoges, is most famous for being the site, two million years ago, of one of the largest **meteorites** ever to hit earth, a monster 1.5km in diameter and weighing some 6 billion tonnes. The traces of this cosmic calamity still attract the curiosity of astronomers, though the only evidence that a lay person might notice is the unusual-looking breccia stone many of the region's older buildings are made of: the squashed, shattered, heat-transformed and reconstituted result of the collision.

### Musée Départemental d'Art Contemporain

Daily except Tues: March–Sept 10am–12.30pm & 1.30–6pm; Oct to mid-Dec 10am–12.30pm & 2–5pm • €4.60 • ⓦ www.musee-rochechouart.com

One building using the stone from the meteor impact is the handsome **château** that stands at the town's edge. It started life as a rough fortress before 1000 AD, was modernized in the thirteenth century (the sawn-off keep and entrance survive from this period) and embellished with Renaissance additions in the fifteenth. Until it was acquired as the *mairie* in 1832, it had belonged to the de Rochechouart family for eight hundred years. Today it houses the very well-regarded **Musée Départemental d'Art Contemporain**, which includes an important collection of works by the Dadaist Raoul Haussmann, who died in Limoges in 1971. In another room, decorated with its original sixteenth-century frescoes of the Labours of Hercules, the British artist Richard Long has created a special installation of white stones, while in the garden Giuseppe Penone's metal sculpture grapples with a tree.

### ARRIVAL AND INFORMATION                                    ROCHECHOUART

**By bus** Bus #21 between Limoges and Rochechouart (Mon–Sat 1–2 daily; 1hr 15min) stop on rue Maurice-Thorez, a short walk southeast of central place Octave-Marquet.

**Tourist office** 6 rue Victor-Hugo (April–June & Sept Mon–Sat 10am–noon & 2–5pm; July & Aug Mon–Sat 10am–12.30pm & 2.30–6pm; Oct–March Mon–Fri 10am–12.30pm & 2–5pm; ☎ 05 55 03 72 73, ⓦ tourisme-meteorite.com).

### ACCOMMODATION

**De France** Place Octave-Marquet ☎ 05 55 03 77 40, ⓦ hoteldefrance-rochechouart.fr. This lovely blue-shuttered building has simple, if rather unexciting, rooms above a decent restaurant that serves a menu of Limousin specialities (€24). Restaurant Mon–Sat noon–2pm & 7.30–8.45pm, Sun noon–2pm. **€55**

## Aubusson

A neat grey-stone town in the bottom of a ravine formed by the River Creuse, **AUBUSSON**, 85km east of Limoges, is mainly of interest as a centre for weaving **tapestries** – second only to the Gobelins workshops in Paris. In 2009, the town's tapestry production was recognized by UNESCO on its list of intangible cultural heritage, and as a result schools started teaching the craft for the first time in almost twenty years.

Two museums provide a good background. **La Cité Internationale de la Tapisserie**, rue des Arts (July & Aug Mon & Wed–Sun 10am–6pm, Tues 2–6pm; Sept–June Mon & Wed–Sun 9.30am–noon & 2–6pm; €8; ⓦ cite-tapisserie.fr), opened in 2016, charts the history of Aubusson tapestries over six centuries, up to the modern-day works of Jean

Lurçat (see page 414); the Cité's weavers are currently creating thirteen tapestries and a carpet based on the works of JRR Tolkien, which are due to be completed in 2021. The **Maison du Tapissier**, next to the tourist office at 63 rue Vieille (Mon–Sat 10am–noon & 2–5pm; €5), gives an overview of weaving techniques and local history, displayed in the sixteenth-century home of a master weaver.

| ARRIVAL AND INFORMATION | AUBUSSON |
|---|---|

**By train** Aubusson's train station is just under 1km (about 10min walk) northwest of the town centre; daily trains run to Limoges (1hr 45min).
**By bus** All buses, including bus #R9 to Limoges (1–3 daily; 1hr 50min) and St-Léonard-de-Noblat (1–3 daily; 1hr), stop at the small *gare routière*, on the south side of the river on

avenue des Lissiers, opposite the Musée de la Tapisserie.
**Tourist office** Rue Vieille (June & Sept Mon–Sat 10am–12.30pm & 2–6pm; July & Aug Mon–Sat 10am–1pm & 2–6pm, Sun 10am–noon & 2–5pm; Oct–May Mon–Sat 10am–noon & 2–5pm, closed Mon Nov–Feb; ☎05 55 66 32 12, ⓦaubusson-felletin-tourisme.com).

### ACCOMMODATION AND EATING

★ **À la Terrade** 6 rue Alfred-Assolant ☎05 55 67 72 22, ⓦlesmaisonsdupont.com. This bistro in four-star aparthotel Les Maisons du Pont is in a very pretty sixteenth-century building with a riverside terrace. The two-course lunch is good value at €16.50 and the wines are organic and biodynamic. Wed–Sun noon–2.30pm & 7–9.30pm.

**Le France** 6 rue des Déportés ☎05 55 66 10 22, ⓦaubussonlefrance.com. A charming hotel on the main road through the town centre, offering elegant rooms decorated in an unfussy mix of traditional and contemporary styles. There's also a good restaurant serving traditional French cuisine (*menus* from €29). **€89**

# The Plateau de Millevaches

**Millevaches** (ⓦpnr-millevaches.fr), the plateau of a thousand springs, is undulating upland country rising to 800–900m in altitude, on the northern edge of the Massif Central, with a wild and sparsely populated landscape and villages few and far between. Those that do exist appear small, grey and sturdy, inured to the buffeting of upland weather. It's a magnificent country of conifer plantations and natural woodland – of beech, birch and chestnut – interspersed with reed-fringed tarns, man-made lakes and pasture grazed by sheep and cows, much of it now designated a **natural regional park**. It's an area to walk or cycle in, or at least savour at a gentle pace, stopping in the attractive, country inns scattered across the plateau.

The small town of **Eymoutiers** has a primitive architectural beauty and an old-world charm; nearby, the **Lac de Vassivière** offers all sorts of sports activities and a beautiful setting for a contemporary art museum.

## Lac de Vassivière

The man-made **Lac de Vassivière**, with 45km of indented shoreline, provides some lovely spots for walking and cycling. In summer, it is a popular destination for watersports enthusiasts, with opportunities for sailing, windsurfing and water skiing, among other activities. The jumping-off point for the lake, **EYMOUTIERS**, 45km southeast of Limoges, is an upland town of tall, narrow stone houses crowding round a much-altered Romanesque **church**.

### Centre International d'Art et du Paysage

Île de Vassivière • July & Aug daily 11am–1pm & 27pm; Sept–June Tues–Fri 2–6pm, Sat & Sun 11am–1pm & 2–6pm • €4 • ☎05 55 69 27 27, ⓦciapiledevassiviere.com

An island in the Lac de Vassivière, accessible by causeway, provides a wonderful home for the **Centre International d'Art et du Paysage**, a contemporary art centre where many of the pieces lie scattered among the trees. There's also a hall hosting temporary exhibitions, and a number of works dotted among the trees. You can head over to the island without having to visit the art centre, which is well worth it for the lakeside views and tranquil pathways, and there are a number of spots that are perfect for paddling.

## ARRIVAL AND INFORMATION

**By train** Eymoutiers-Vassivière train station is just a few minutes' walk north of Eymoutiers centre. During the summer months, it's possible to travel by restored steam train between Limoges and Eymoutiers (€28 return; see ⓦ trainvapeur.com).

Destinations Limoges (5–8 daily; 50min); St-Léonard-de-Noblat (5–8 daily; 25min).

**Getting to the lake** Getting to Lac de Vassivière by public transport is only possible between July and Aug, when TER run "Passauvert" services from Limoges. The €7 fare includes the round-trip journey by train (depart 10.01am)

## LAC DE VASSIVIÈRE AND AROUND

to Eymoutiers, and then on by bus to the lake. It's also possible to pick up the Passauvert in Eymoutiers (€3; depart 11.03am). Buses make the return journey at 5.56pm, though you should check all times online (ⓦ lelacdevassiviere.com) for up-to-date details.

**Tourist office** Maison de Vassivière in Auphelle, on the western shore of the lake (April Mon–Fri 9.30am–12.30pm & 2–5pm, Sat 2–5pm; May, June & Sept daily 9.30am–12.30pm & 2–5.30pm; July & Aug daily 2.30–6.30pm; Nov–March Mon–Fri 9.30am–12.30pm & 2–5pm; ☎ 05 55 69 76 70, ⓦ lelacdevassiviere.com).

## ACCOMMODATION AND EATING

**La Caravelle** Port de Crozat ☎ 05 55 57 06 75, ⓦ la-caravelle-vassiviere.com. The rooms at this lakeside hotel have had a contemporary makeover and all benefit from their own private balcony or terrace with fabulous lake views. It has the best of the lakeside restaurants (open daily; *menus* from €25), serving traditional French cuisine. They also rent out pedalos (from €8 for 30min). **€75**

**Les Cerisiers** 14 rue Pierre-et-Marie-Curie, Eymoutiers ☎ 05 55 69 68 32, ⓦ lescerisiers87.com. A charming B&B run by two Brits, set in an old townhouse, a short walk from

the centre of Eymoutiers. There are just two simple but very pleasant bedrooms, plus a lovely garden and a dining room with a log-burning stove. Three-course dinners are available for €20. **€52**

**Les Terrasses du Lac** Vauveix ☎ 05 55 64 76 77, ⓦ campings-vassiviere.fr. The best of the three campsites by the lake, in a prime position right by the water. Some of the pitches boast beautiful views, and the campsite is particularly popular with families, though it's generally quiet and relaxed. Closed Nov to March. **€17**

# Brive-la-Gaillarde and around

**BRIVE-LA-GAILLARDE** is a major rail junction and the nearest thing to an industrial centre for miles around. Nevertheless, it has an attractive old town and makes an agreeable base for exploring the Corrèze *département* and its beautiful villages, as well as the upper reaches of the Vézère and Dordogne rivers. Numerous streets fan out from the central square, **place du Général-de-Gaulle**, which is home to a number of turreted and towered houses, some dating back to the thirteenth century.

## Church of St-Martin

Place du Général-de-Gaulle

At Brive's heart is the much-restored **church of St-Martin**, originally Romanesque in style, though only the transept, apse and a few comically carved capitals survive from that era. St Martin himself, a Spanish aristocrat, arrived in pagan Brive in 407 AD on the feast of Saturnus, smashed various idols and was promptly stoned to death by the outraged onlookers.

## Musée Labenche

26bis bd Jules-Ferry • Daily except Tues: May–Sept 10am–12.30pm & 1.30–6pm; Oct–April 2–6pm • €5 • ⓦ museelabenche.brive.fr

One of the town's most impressive buildings is the sixteenth-century Hôtel de Labenche, now the **Musée Labenche**. The museum traces the history of Brive with a number of different displays, including the town's archeological finds and a fine collection of seventeenth-century tapestries.

## Turenne

**TURENNE**, just 16km south of Brive, was capital of the viscountcy of Turenne, whose most illustrious *seigneur* was Henri de la Tour d'Auvergne – the "Grand Turenne", who was born in 1611 and rated by Napoleon as the finest tactician of modern times.

Mellow stone houses crowd in the lee of the sharp bluff on whose summit sprout two towers, all that remains of the castle.

### The château

April–June, Sept & Oct daily 10am–noon & 2–6pm; July & Aug daily 10am–7pm; Nov–March Sun 2–5pm • €3.40 • ☎ 05 55 85 90 66, ⓦ chateau-turenne.com

Though little remains of Turenne's **château**, it is possible to visit one of the towers, the Tour de César, and the beautiful gardens that surround it. They also have a room to rent on a B&B basis (€80). The real reason to climb up here, however, is for the fabulous views over the surrounding countryside. Two routes lead to the château – the steepest leads directly through the pretty village, or follow the road that curves around the hill, which will take you past the attractive church before coming to the château itself.

### Collonges-la-Rouge

With its red-sandstone houses, pepper-pot towers and pink-candled chestnut trees, **COLLONGES-LA-ROUGE**, 7km east of Turenne, is the epitome of rustic charm – but make sure you get here early in the day, or after 5pm, to avoid the crowds. Though small-scale, there's a certain grandeur about the place, befitting the status of the resident Turenne administrators. On the main square a twelfth-century **church** testifies to the imbecility of shedding blood over religious differences: in the sixteenth century, Protestant and Catholic conducted their services here simultaneously, side by side. Outside, the covered **market hall** still retains its old-fashioned baker's oven.

## ARRIVAL AND DEPARTURE                    BRIVE-LA-GAILLARDE AND AROUND

### BRIVE-LA-GAILLARDE
**By plane** Brive Dordogne Valley airport (☎ 05 55 22 40 00, ⓦ aeroport-brive-vallee-dordogne.com) is 13km south of town. There's no public transport but taxis meet flights and car rental is available onsite.

**By train** The *gare SNCF* is at the top of avenue Jean-Jaurès, a 5min walk south of the old town.
Destinations Bordeaux (9 daily; 3hr 37min); Cahors (8 daily; 1hr 10min); Figeac (7 daily; 1hr 30min); Gourdon (8 daily; 39min); Limoges (17 daily; 1hr); Montauban (6 daily; 2hr 15min); Périgueux (6 daily; 1hr 25min); Rocamadour-Padirac (7 daily; 40min); Solignac-le-Vigen (5 daily; 1hr 24min); Souillac (8 daily; 23min); Toulouse (7 daily; 3hr 11min)

**By bus** The *gare routère* is on place du 14 Juillet, but some buses depart from the *gare SNCF* instead; check schedules

online at ⓦ cftaco.fr.
Destinations Beaulieu-sur-Dordogne (Mon–Sat 2–3 daily; 1hr 5min–1hr 30min); Collonges la Rouge (Mon–Sat 2–7 daily; 45min); Montignac (Mon–Fri daily; 1hr 30min); Turenne (Mon–Fri daily; 25min).

### TURENNE
**By bus** Buses to and from Brive (Mon–Fri 2–3 daily; 25min) and Collonges-la-Rouge (Mon–Fri 1–2 daily; 8min) stop on the main road, close to the tourist office.

### COLLONGES-LA-ROUGE
**By bus** Buses from Brive (Mon–Sat 2–6 daily; 40min) and Turenne (Mon–Fri 2–3 daily; 11min) stop on the main road at the top of the village, near the permit holders' car park.

## INFORMATION

### BRIVE-LA-GAILLARDE
**Tourist office** Place du 14-Juillet (April–June & Sept Mon–Sat 9am–12.30pm & 1.30–6.30pm; July & Aug Mon–Sat 9am–7pm, Sun 11am–5pm; Oct–March Mon–Sat 9am–noon & 2–6pm; ☎ 05 55 24 08 80, ⓦ brive-tourisme.com).

### TURENNE
**Tourist office** On the main road, close to the road that leads up into the village (Easter–April & Sept Mon–Wed & Fri–Sun 10am–12.30pm & 2–6pm; May & June closed Wed & Sat am; July & Aug daily 10am–12.30pm & 2.30–6.30pm; ☎ 05 55 24 08 80).

## ACCOMMODATION

### BRIVE-LA-GAILLARDE
**Auberge de Jeunesse** 56 av du Maréchal-Bugeaud ☎ 05 55 24 34 00, ⓦ fuaj.org/Brive-la-Gaillarde. Housed

in a grand old mansion just a short walk from the centre, this is a fairly standard FUAJ hostel, with a kitchen for guests' use and dorms sleeping three or four people; the selling point, however, is the lovely garden. Open Feb–Sept. **€15.40**

**Le Collonges** 3 place Winston-Churchill ☎ 05 55 74 09 58, ⓦ hotel-collonges.com. A welcoming hotel, just across the ring road from the old town. Rooms are decorated in muted greys and browns, with striking modern furniture completing the look. The terrace is a good spot for a cold drink. **€72**

★ **Le Miel des Muses** 21 av Jean-Jaurès ☎ 05 55 23 79 65, ⓦ lemieldesmuses.fr. Brive's boutique hotel has nine stylish, spacious rooms; all are named after grapes – "Noah" has direct access to the roof terrace and pool. There's also a trendy, vintage-style brasserie, *Le Comptoir St-Sernin*, which serves platters and tapas (*menus* from €11). Restaurant daily noon–2pm & 7–11pm. **€89**

**La Truffe Noir** 22 bd Anatole-France ☎ 05 55 92 45 00, ⓦ la-truffe-noire.com. Brive's grandest hotel, though its position on the ring road around the old town leaves something to be desired. Despite the impressive lobby, the rooms are ordinary, though they're well equipped and air-conditioned. It has a good restaurant serving local cuisine (lunch menu €24). **€99**

### TURENNE

**La Maison des Chanoines** ☎ 05 55 85 93 43, ⓦ maison-des-chanoines.com. This lovely little hotel is housed in one of Turenne's most beautiful buildings, which dates back to the sixteenth century. The homely (if a little old-fashioned) rooms feature floral fabrics and dark-wood furniture – the best boast their own private terraces. Meals are served in the atmospheric dining room, or on the garden terrace during the summer months. Open April–Sept. **€85**

## EATING AND DRINKING

### BRIVE-LA-GAILLARDE

★ **Bistrot Chambon** 8 rue des Échevins ☎ 05 55 22 36 83, ⓦ bistrot-chambon.fr. Bustling, contemporary corner bistro serving elegant but unpretentious food. At lunch, the dish of the day, which ranges from a herby roast guinea fowl to sirloin steak with Dauphinois potatoes, costs just €13.50 – though be sure to leave room for the heavenly desserts. Dinner *menu* €31. Tues–Thurs noon–2pm & 7.15–9.30pm, Fri & Sat noon–2pm & 7.15–10.15pm.

**Café l'Arrosoir** 13 rue du Lieutenant-Colonel-Farro ☎ 05 55 23 41 78. A modern little corner café with ample seating outside, serving up *tartines gourmandes* such as cabécou cheese with *magret de canard* (€8.20), plus *croque monsieur* and larger *plats du jour* (€7.80). Mon–Sat 8am–7pm.

**Le Lamparo** 20 rue du Lieutenant-Colonel-Farro ☎ 05 55 24 27 59. The tables outside this fish shop are inevitably rammed with locals, but it's worth grabbing one if you can for a great dining experience. The short menu offers up the best of the produce for sale inside and includes a seafood platter (€25) or six oysters for just €9, and there's wine to wash it all down with. Tues–Sat 8am–12.30pm & 3–7pm.

# The Dordogne

To the French, the **Dordogne** is a river. To the British, it is a much looser term, covering a vast area roughly equivalent to what the French call Périgord, which starts south of Limoges and includes the Vézère and Dordogne valleys. The Dordogne is also a *département*, with fixed boundaries that pay no heed to either definition. The central part of the *département*, around Périgueux and the River Isle, is known as **Périgord Blanc**, after the light, white colour of its rock outcrops; the southeastern half around Sarlat as **Périgord Noir**, said to be darker in aspect because of the preponderance of oak woods. To confuse matters further, the tourist authorities have added another two colours to the Périgord patchwork: **Périgord Vert**, the far north of the *département*, so called because of the green of its woods and pastureland; and **Périgord Pourpre** in the southwest, purple because it includes the wine-growing area around Bergerac.

This southern region is also known for its **bastides** – fortified towns – built during the turbulent medieval period when there was almost constant conflict between the French and English. In the reaches of the **upper Dordogne**, the colour scheme breaks down, but the villages and scenery in this less travelled backwater still rival anything the rest of the region has to offer.

## Périgord Vert

The close green valleys of **Périgord Vert** are very rural, with plenty of space and few people, large tracts of wood and uncultivated land. Less well known than the Périgord

## THE FOOD AND WINE OF PÉRIGORD

The two great stars of Périgord cuisine are **foie gras** and **truffles** (*truffes*). Foie gras is best eaten either chilled in succulent, buttery slabs, or lightly fried and served with a fruit compote to provide contrasting sweetness and acidity. Truffle is often dished up in omelettes and the rich *périgourdin* sauces which accompany many local meat dishes, but to appreciate the delicate earthy flavour to the full, you really need to eat truffle on its own, with just a salad and some coarse country bread.

The other mainstay of Périgord cuisine is the grey Toulouse **goose**, whose fat is used in the cooking of everything, including the flavourful potato dish, *pommes sarladaises*. The goose fattens well: *gavé* or crammed with corn, it goes from six to ten kilos in weight in three weeks, with its liver alone weighing nearly a kilo. Some may find the process off-putting, but small local producers are very careful not to harm their birds, if for no other reason than that stress ruins the liver. Geese are also raised for their meat alone, which is cooked and preserved in its own thick yellow grease as *confits d'oie*, which you can either eat on its own or use in the preparation of other dishes, like cassoulet. **Duck** is used in the same way, both for foie gras and *confits*. *Magret de canard*, or duck-breast fillet, is one of the favourite ways of eating duck and appears on practically every restaurant menu.

Another goose delicacy is *cou d'oie farci* – goose neck stuffed with sausage meat, duck liver and truffles, while a favourite salad throughout the region is made with warm *gésiers* or goose gizzards. Other less challenging specialities include stuffed *cèpes*, or wild mushrooms; *ballottines*, fillets of poultry stuffed, rolled and poached; the little flat discs of goat's cheese known as *cabécou* or *rocamadour*; and for dessert there's *pastis*, a light apple tart topped with crinkled, wafer-thin pastry laced with armagnac.

The **wines** should not be scorned, either. There are both reds and whites from the vineyards of Bergerac, of which the sweet, white Monbazillac is the most famous. Pécharmant is the fanciest of the reds, but there are some very drinkable Côtes de Bergerac, much like the neighbouring Bordeaux and far cheaper. The **Cahors** region, which produces fine, dark, almost peppery reds, was awarded the prestigious 2016 Vignoble de l'Année by the well-regarded Bettane-Deseauve wine guide (**⊙**bettanedesseauve.com). This places the region's wines on a par with those from the better-known vineyards of St-Émilion and Châteauneuf-du-Pape.

**10**

Noir, its largely granite landscape bears a closer resemblance to the neighbouring Limousin than to the rest of the Périgord. It's partly for this reason that in 1998 the most northerly tip, together with the southwestern part of the Haute-Vienne, was designated as the **Parc Naturel Régional Périgord-Limousin** in an attempt to promote "green" tourism in this economically fragile and depopulated area.

It's undoubtedly in the countryside that the region's finest monuments lie. One of the loveliest stretches is the **valley of the Dronne**, from **Aubeterre** on the Charente border through **Brantôme** to the marvellous Renaissance château of **Puyguilhem** and the picture-postcard village of **St-Jean-de-Côle**, and on to the Limousin border, where the scenery becomes higher and less intimate.

### Brantôme

The picturesque old town of **BRANTÔME** sits on an island in the River Dronne, whose still, water-lilied surface mirrors the limes and weeping willows of the riverside gardens. The countryside that surrounds the town, along the **River Dronne**, remains largely undisturbed, though Brantôme itself is firmly on the tourist trail. This is one of the most tranquil and beautiful parts of the Dordogne, best savoured at a gentle pace, perhaps by bike, on a **boat trip**, or even by canoeing along the river.

### The abbey

Bd Charlemagne, north bank of the river • Caves & museum Feb, March & Oct–Dec daily except Tues 10am–noon & 2–5pm; April–May & Sept daily 10am–6pm; July & Aug daily 10am–7pm • €6

**10**

Brantôme's former **Benedictine abbey** has been the town's focus ever since it was founded, possibly by Charlemagne. Its most notorious abbot, Pierre de Bourdeilles, was the sixteenth-century author of scurrilous tales of life at the royal court.

The first monastery on the site is thought to have been troglodytic in origin, and the caves against which the later abbey was built were initially very important for worship, but over time were relegated to outhouses and storage. The **caves** here are arguably the most fascinating feature of the abbey; they're hugely atmospheric, not least the Last Judgement Cave, where the origins of the huge bas-relief remain an enigma, but is thought to date back to the fifteenth century. Admission also includes entry to the **Musée Fernand Desmoulin**, dedicated to the illustrator and painter best remembered for the 75 drawings he did between 1900 and 1902, apparently under the influence of three different spirits – the drawings, especially compared to Desmoulin's non-spirit work, are surprisingly modern, and some are undeniably eerie.

## ARRIVAL AND INFORMATION BRANTÔME

**By bus** Buses between Angoulême (1–3 daily; 1hr 5min) and Périgueux (1–3 daily; 35min) stop in front of the gendarmerie on avenue du Docteur-Devillard, just a couple of minutes' walk southeast of the town centre.

**Tourist office** Housed in the old Église Notre-Dame, directly across the river from the abbey church (March & Oct–Dec Mon & Wed–Sun 10am–noon & 2–5pm; April & May daily 10am–1pm & 2–6pm; June & Sept daily 10am–6pm; July & Aug daily 10am–6.30pm; ☎ 05 53 05 80 63, ⓦ perigord-dronne-belle.fr).

**Boat trips Brantôme** Croisières (Tour des Gardes, rue Pierre-de-Bourdeille; April & Oct 2–4pm; May 2–5pm; June & Sept 11am & 2–5pm; July & Aug 11am, noon & 2–6pm; €8 (April–Oct; ☎ 05 53 04 74 71, ⓦ brantomecroisieres. com) offers 50-minute boat trips up the Dronne in a 49-seater electric boat.

**Canoe rental Brantôme** Canoë, route de Thiviers (from €10/hour; reservations essential during July & Aug; ☎ 05 53 05 77 24, ⓦ brantomecanoe.com); also offers stand-up paddleboarding.

## ACCOMMODATION

**Au Nid des Thés** 13 rue Victor-Hugo ☎ 05 53 02 75 49, ⓦ au-nid-des-thes.fr. A small *chambre d'hôte* attached to a little tearoom, on a shop-filled pedestrianized street in the heart of Brantôme. The four rooms, all with sweet names – caramel, nougat, chocolat, praline – are large and airy, and in fine weather breakfast is served in the garden. **€90**

**Coligny** 8 place de Gaulle ☎ 05 53 05 71 42, ⓦ hotel-coligny.fr. A pleasant hotel facing the river, with eight contemporary rooms, decked out in soothing earth colours. The restaurant's riverside terrace is a great spot for a drink. **€63**

★ **Les Jardins de Brantôme** 33 rue de Mareuil ☎ 05 53 05 88 16, ⓦ lesjardinsdebrantome.com. With seven

elegant, individually decorated rooms staggered up a gentle hillside, just a short walk from the town centre, *Les Jardins de Brantôme* offers the kind of sophisticated, unstuffy accommodation that you don't often find in rural France. It's run by a friendly husband and wife team and there's a small, lovely pool that catches the afternoon sun. **€125**

**Le Peyrelevade** 1km east of Brantôme on the D78 Thiviers road ☎ 05 53 05 75 24, ⓦ camping-dordogne. net. A very pleasant campsite, set among lovely wooded grounds, with both a heated swimming pool and its own private riverside beach. Closed Oct–April. **€25**

## EATING AND DRINKING

**Le Bar du Marché** 16 rue Victor-Hugo ☎ 05 53 05 80 49. The colourful tables spilling out of the front of this café across the river from the abbey make it a popular choice on sunny days. The menu covers all the usual Perigordian specialities, such as *magret de canard* (€13), plus pizzas from €8. Daily 10am–10pm.

**La Récré Gourmande** Rue Jacquette-de-Montbron

☎ 05 53 45 77 04, ⓦ larecregourmande.fr. Arguably the best place to eat in town, serving hearty regional food either beneath the trees in the lovely garden or in the stylish beamed dining room. On the menu you'll find the likes of the *Périgourdine* (€19.50), a duck burger topped with foie gras, and copious salads (from €16.70). Daily 11am–2am.

## Bourdeilles

**BOURDEILLES**, 16km down the Dronne from Brantôme by a beautiful back road, is a sleepy backwater. Its shady riverbanks are perfect for picnics, with trees drooping into the water. The ancient village clusters round its château on a rocky spur above the river; at the other end of rue de l'Église, the lovely "Jardin Médiéval" (free), next to the church, offers beautiful views over the water-lily-strewn river and the château and houses that line it.

### The château

Feb, March, Nov & Dec Tues–Sun 10am–12.30pm & 2–5pm; April to June, Sept & Oct daily 10am–1pm & 2–6pm; July & Aug daily 10am–7.30pm • €8.10 • ⓦ 05 53 03 73 36

Bourdeilles' **château** consists of two buildings: one a thirteenth-century fortress, the other an elegant Renaissance residence begun by the lady of the house as a piece of unsuccessful favour-currying with Catherine de Médici – unsuccessful because Catherine never came to stay, and the château remained unfinished. Climb the octagonal keep for a good view over the town's clustered roofs and along the valley of the Dronne.

**10**

The château is now home to an exceptional collection of **furniture** and **religious statuary** bequeathed to the state by its former owners. Among the more notable pieces are some splendid Spanish dowry chests and a sixteenth-century Rhenish Entombment with life-sized statues, embodying the very image of the serious, self-satisfied medieval burgher. The *salon doré*, the room in which de Médici was supposed to sleep, has also been preserved.

### ARRIVAL AND ACCOMMODATION

### BOURDEILLES

**By car** There's no public transport to Bourdeilles; parking (free) is available at the top of the hill, near the church, and outside the *hôtel de ville*, across the river from the *Hostellerie Les Griffons*.

**Hostellerie Le Donjon** Place de la Halle ⓣ 05 53 04 07 50, ⓦ hostellerie-ledonjon.fr. This appealing B&B in a seventeenth-century townhouse on the main street offers views of the château from some of its rooms, all of which are arranged around a charming courtyard. *Table d'hôte* is available (€26) on reservation. **€80**

**Hostellerie Les Griffons** ⓣ 05 53 45 45 35, ⓦ griffons. fr. Bourdeilles' most upmarket option, set in a gorgeous sixteenth-century house beside the old bridge. Rooms are hugely atmospheric, with original features like wood beams and bare stone walls. The walled garden houses a small pool. Closed Nov–Easter. **€130**

## Aubeterre-sur-Dronne

Rather touristy, but very beautiful with its ancient galleried and turreted houses, **AUBETERRE-SUR-DRONNE** hangs on a steep hillside above the river some 30km downstream of Ribérac. South of Aubeterre, the country gradually changes. Farmland gives way to an extensive forest of oak and sweet chestnut, bracken and broom, interspersed with sour, marshy pasture, and is very sparsely populated. It's ideal cycling and picnicking country.

### Église Monolithe

Rue St-Jean • Daily: 9.30am–7pm • €5

Aubeterre's principal curiosity is the cavernous **Église Monolithe**, carved out of the soft rock of the cliff face in the twelfth century, with its rock-hewn tombs going back to the sixth. A (blocked-off) tunnel connects with the **château** on the bluff overhead.

### Church of St-Jacques

Following the road through the village and up the hill from central place Trarieux brings you to the extremely beautiful church of **St-Jacques**, with its eleventh-century facade sculpted and decorated in the richly carved Poitiers style. The interior is barely adorned, and all the more atmospheric in its simplicity.

### ARRIVAL AND INFORMATION

### AUBETERRE-SUR-DRONNE

**By bus** A daily bus runs to and from Angoulême (Mon–Sat 1–2 daily; 1hr 5min) from a bus stop near the tourist office.

**Tourist office** 8 place du Champ-de-Foire, beside the main car park (July & Aug daily 9.30am–1pm & 2–6.30pm; Sept–June Mon–Sat 9.30am–12.30pm & 2–6pm; ⓣ 05 45 98 57 18, ⓦ sudcharentetourisme.fr).

## ACCOMMODATION

**Aubeterre Plage Camping** Route de Ribérac ☎ 06 87 29 18 36, ⓦ camping-aubeterre.fr. This campsite has an enviable position by the river, at the foot of Aubeterre, with a sandy beach, pleasant pitches, and plenty of space for children to run around. **€20**

**Hostellerie du Périgord** Route de Ribérac, beside the bridge ☎ 05 45 98 50 46, ⓦ hostellerie-perigord.com. It's a steep walk up the hill to the centre of the village from here, but this is a lovely place to stay, with comfortable, modern rooms. There's an outdoor pool, spa and fitness room, and a smart restaurant serving local specialities (lunch *menu* €15.50). **€85**

**10**

## St-Jean-de-Côle

ST-JEAN-DE-CÔLE, 20km northeast of Brantôme, ranks as one of the loveliest villages in the Dordogne. Its ancient houses huddle together in typical medieval fashion around a wide sandy square dominated by the charmingly ill-proportioned eleventh-century **church of St-Jean-Baptiste** and the rugged-looking **Château de la Marthonie** (not open to the public). The château, which dates from the twelfth century, has acquired various additions in a pleasingly organic fashion.

### ARRIVAL AND INFORMATION                                    ST-JEAN-DE-CÔLE

**By car** There is no public transport to St-Jean-de-Côle. Parking is available on the main road or behind the *mairie*.

**Tourist office** 19 rue du château (April–June & Sept–Oct Tues–Fri 9.30am–12.30pm & 2–5.30pm, Sat 2–5.30pm; July–Sept daily 10am–1pm & 2–6.30pm; ☎ 05 53 62 14 15, ⓦ perigord-limousin-tourisme.com).

### EATING AND DRINKING

**Le Saint Jean** Rte de Nontron ☎ 09 70 35 57 20, ⓦ le-stjean.fr. A popular restaurant with a lovely terrace under canopies, on the main road through the village. The *formule* is excellent value at €19.50, and often includes duck, while the *menu du terroir* is a great way to try local specialities (€34). Mon–Thurs & Sun noon–2pm & 7–8pm, Fri & Sat noon–2.30pm & 7–9pm.

## Château de Puyguilhem

Villars, around 10km west of St-Jean-de-Côle • April & Sept daily 10am–12.30pm & 2–5.30pm; May–Aug daily 10am–12.30pm & 2–6.30pm; Oct–March Wed–Sun 10am–12.30pm & 2–5.30pm • €6 • ☎ 05 53 54 82 18, ⓦ chateau-puyguilhem.fr

The **Château de Puyguilhem** sits on the edge of a valley backed by oak woods, just outside the village of **VILLARS**. It was erected at the beginning of the sixteenth century on the site of an earlier military fortress. With its octagonal tower, broad spiral staircase, steep roofs, magnificent fireplaces and false dormer windows, it's a perfect example of French Renaissance architecture. From the gallery at the top of the stairs you get a close-up of the roof and window decoration, as well as a view down the valley, which once was filled by an ornamental lake.

## Grotte de Villars

North of Villars • Daily: April–June & Sept 10am–noon & 2–7pm; July & Aug 10am–7.30pm; Oct 2–6pm • €9.20 • ⓦ grotte-villars.com

The **Grotte de Villars**, north of the village of the same name, boasts a few prehistoric paintings – notably of horses, and a still unexplained scene of a man and a bison. The main reason for coming here, however, is to see the impressive array of stalactites and stalagmites.

## Château de Hautefort

40km east of Périgueux, bus #9 • March & early Nov Sat & Sun 2–6pm; April & May daily 10am–12.30pm & 2–6.30pm; June–Aug daily 9.30am–7pm; Sept daily 10am–6pm; Oct daily 2–6pm • €10 • ☎ 05 53 50 51 23, ⓦ chateau-hautefort.com

The **Château de Hautefort** enjoys a majestic position at the end of a wooded spur above its feudal village. A magnificent example of good living on a grand scale, the castle has an elegance that is out of step with the usual rough stone fortresses of Périgord. The approach is across a wide esplanade flanked by formal gardens, over a drawbridge, and into a stylish Renaissance courtyard, open to the south. In 1968 a fire gutted the castle, but it has since been meticulously restored using traditional techniques; it's all unmistakably new, but the quality of the craftsmanship is superb.

# Périgueux

**PÉRIGUEUX**, capital of the *département* of the Dordogne and a central base for exploring the countryside of Périgord Blanc, is a small, busy market town with an attractive medieval and Renaissance core of stone-flagged squares and narrow alleys harbouring richly ornamented merchants' houses. The main hub of the modern town is the tree-shaded **boulevard Montaigne**, which marks the western edge of the *vieille ville*.

Place de la Clautre sits at the heart of the renovated streets of the medieval town, the most attractive of which is the narrow **rue Limogeanne**, lined with Renaissance mansions, now turned into boutiques and delicatessens, intermingled with fast-food outlets. Roman Périgueux, known as **La Cité**, lies to the west of the town centre, towards the train station.

### Cathédrale St-Front

Place de la Clautre • Daily: April–June, Sept & Oct 8.30am–7pm; July & Aug 9am–7.30pm; Nov–March 8.30am–6pm

The square, pineapple-capped belfry of the domed and coned **Cathédrale St-Front** surges far above the roofs of the surrounding medieval houses. When it was rebuilt in 1173 following a fire, it was one of the most distinctive Byzantine churches in France, modelled on St Mark's in Venice and the Holy Apostles in Constantinople, and even today, seeing it rising above the city it suggests something a little more exotic than the town itself. The Byzantine influence is still evident in the interior in the Greek-cross plan – unusual in France – and in the massive clean curves of the domes and their supporting arches. The big Baroque altarpiece in the gloomy east bay, which is carved in walnut wood and depicts the Assumption of the Virgin, is worth a look, too.

### Musée d'Art et d'Archéologie du Périgord

22 cours Tourny • April–Sept Mon & Wed–Fri 10.30am–5.30pm, Sat & Sun 1–6pm; Oct–March Mon & Wed–Fri 10am–5pm, Sat & Sun 1–6pm • €5.50, combined ticket with Musée Vesunna €9 • ☎ 05 53 06 40 70, ⓦ perigueux-maap.fr

The **Musée d'Art et d'Archéologie du Périgord** is best known for its extensive and important prehistoric collection and some beautiful Gallo-Roman mosaics. Exhibits include copies of a 70,000-year-old skeleton, the oldest yet found in France, and a beautiful engraving of a bison's head.

### Musée Gallo-Romain Vesunna

La Cité • April–June & Sept Tues–Fri 9.30am–5.30pm, Sat & Sun 10am–12.30pm & 2.30–6pm; July & Aug daily 10am–7pm; Oct–March Tues–Fri 9.30am–12.30pm & 1.30–5pm, Sat & Sun 10am–12.30pm & 2.30–6pm • €6 • ☎ 05 53 35 40 12, ⓦ perigueux-vesunna.fr

The most prominent vestige of Roman Périgueux is the high brick **Tour de Vésone**, the last remains of a temple to the city's guardian goddess, which stands in a public garden just south of the train tracks. Beside the tower, the foundations of an exceptionally well-preserved Roman villa form the basis of the **Musée Gallo-Romain Vesunna**. This was no humble abode: the villa, complete with under-floor heating, thermal baths and colonnaded walkways around the central garden with its cooling pond and fountains, boasted at least sixty rooms. You can see the remains of first-century murals of river and marine life, the colours still amazingly vibrant, and here and there, graffiti of hunting scenes, gladiatorial combat and even an ostrich.

---

**ARRIVAL AND INFORMATION** | **PÉRIGUEUX**

**By plane** Périgueux's small airport (☎ 05 53 02 79 79), at Bassilac, 7km east of the city, is served by flights to and from Paris (Mon–Fri 2 daily; 1hr). There is no public transport; a taxi will cost around €20, and cars can be hired through Taxi Périgueux (☎ 05 53 09 09 09; book in advance).

**By train** The *gare SNCF* lies to the west of town at the end of rue des Mobiles-du-Coulmiers, the continuation of rue du

Président-Wilson.

Destinations Bordeaux (9–15 daily; 1hr 15min–1hr 30min); Brive-la-Gaillarde (5–9 daily; 55min–1hr 5min); Les Eyzies (4–8 daily; 30min); Limoges (8–12 daily; 1hr–1hr 25min).

**By bus** Regional buses run by CFTA Périgord (☎ 05 55 86 07 07, ⓦ cftaco.fr) leave from both the train station and the

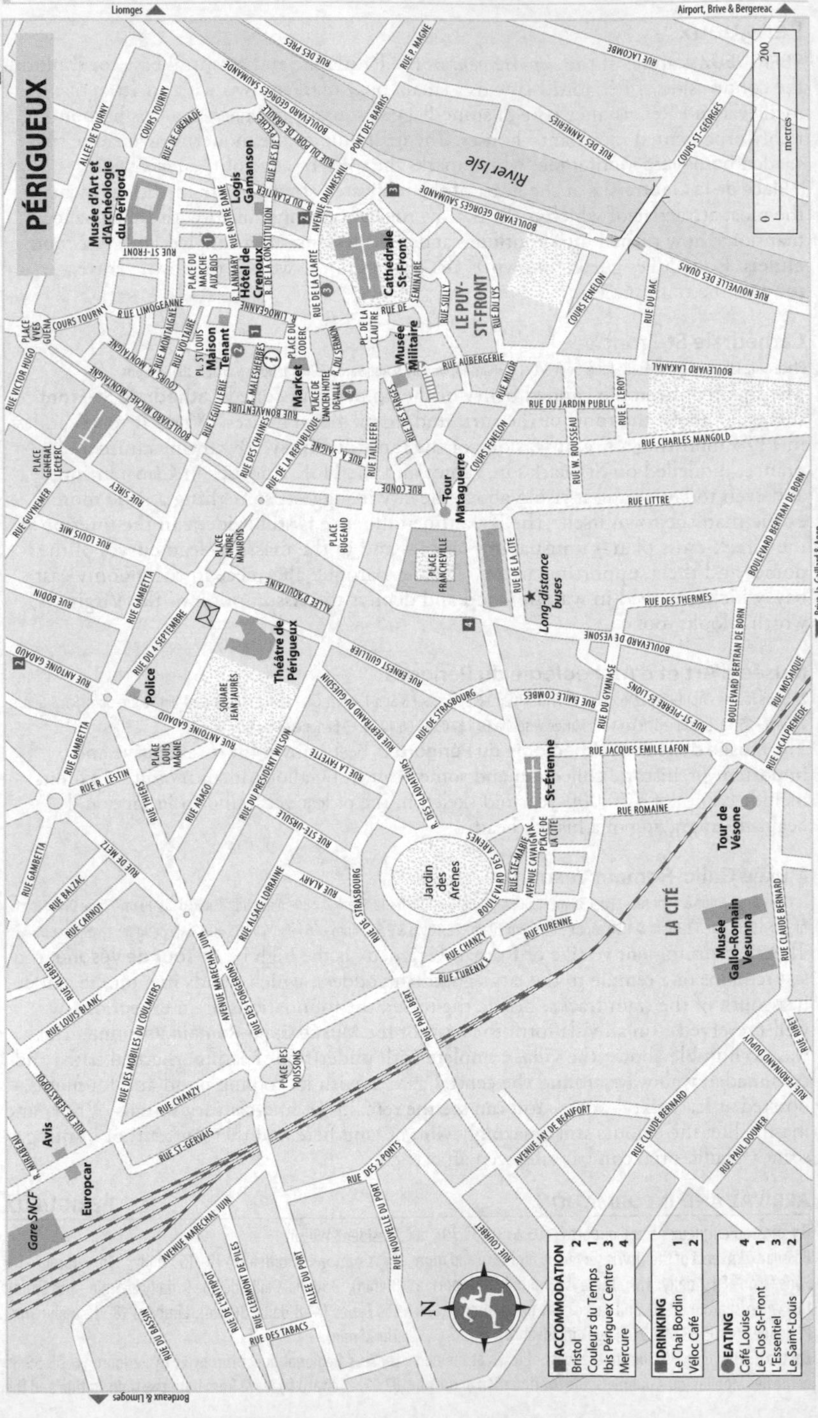

PÉRIGUEUX
Liomges
Airport, Brive & Bergereac
Brive-la-Gaillard & Agen
Bordeaux & Limoges
0
200
metres
River Isle
Musée d'Art et d'Archéologie du Périgord
Logis Gamanson
Hôtel de Crenoux
Maison Tenant
Market
Cathédrale St-Front
LE PUY-ST-FRONT
Musée Militaire
Tour Mataguerre
PLACE FRANCHEVILLE
Long-distance buses
Théâtre de Périgueux
SQUARE JEAN JAURÈS
Police
St-Étienne
Jardin des Arènes
Tour de Vésone
LA CITÉ
Musée Gallo-Romain Vesunna
Gare SNCF
Avis
Europcar
PLACE YVES GUÉNA
PLACE GÉNÉRAL LECLERC
PLACE ANDRÉ MAUROIS
PLACE BUGEAUD
PLACE LOUIS MAGNE
PLACE DES POISSONS
PLACE DU MARCHE AUX BOIS
PLACE DU CODERC
PL. ST LOUIS
PLACE DE L'ANCIEN HOTEL DE VILLE
PL. DE LA CLAUTRE
BOULEVARD GEORGES SAUMANDE
RUE DES PRES
RUE P. MAGNE
RUE LACOMBE
RUE DES TANNERIES
COURS ST-GEORGES
RUE NOUVELLE DES QUAIS
RUE DU BAC
COURS FENELON
BOULEVARD LAKANAL
RUE CHARLES MANGOLD
RUE LITTRE
BOULEVARD BERTRAN DE BORN
RUE DES THERMES
BOULEVARD DE VESONE
RUE EMILE COMBES
RUE ST-PIERRE ES LIONS
RUE JACQUES EMILE LAFON
RUE ROMAINE
RUE MOSAIQUE
RUE LACALPRENEDE
RUE CLAUDE BERNARD
RUE RIBEYT
RUE FERDINAND DUPUY
RUE PAUL DOUMER
AVENUE JAY DE BEAUFORT
RUE COURBET
RUE NOUVELLE DU PORT
RUE DES 2 PONTS
ALLEE DU PORT
RUE DES TABACS
RUE CLERMONT DE PILES
RUE DE L'ENTREPOT
RUE DU BASSIN
AVENUE MARECHAL JUIN
RUE ST-GERVAIS
RUE DE SEBASTOPOL
R. MIRABEAU
RUE CHANZY
RUE DES MOBILES DU COULMIERS
RUE LOUIS BLANC
RUE KLEBER
RUE CARNOT
RUE BALZAC
RUE GAMBETTA
RUE DE METZ
RUE THIERS
RUE R. LESTIN
RUE ARAGO
RUE ANTOINE GADAUD
RUE DU 4 SEPTEMBRE
RUE BODIN
RUE LOUIS MIE
RUE GUYNEMER
RUE SIREY
RUE VICTOR HUGO
COURS TOURNY
ALLEE DE TOURNY
RUE DE GRENADE
RUE ST-FRONT
RUE LIMOGEANNE
RUE MONTAIGNE
RUE VOLTAIRE
COURS M. MONTAIGNE
BOULEVARD MICHEL MONTAIGNE
RUE EGUILLERIE
R. MALESHERBES
RUE BONAVENTURE
RUE DES CHAINES
RUE DE LA RÉPUBLIQUE
RUE A. SAIGNE
RUE TAILLEFER
RUE CONDE
RUE DES FARGES
RUE DU SERMON
RUE DE LA CLARTÉ
R. DE LA CONSTITUTION
R. LANMARY
RUE NOTRE DAME
RUE DES DEUX PONTS
RUE DU PORT DE GRAULE
BOULEVARD GEORGES SAUMANDE
PONT DES BARRIS
AVENUE DAUMESNIL
R. DU PLANTIER
RUE DE SEMINAIRE
RUE SULLY
RUE DU LYS
RUE AUBERGERIE
RUE MILOR
RUE DU JARDIN PUBLIC
RUE E. LEROY
RUE W. ROUSSEAU
RUE DE LA CITE
ALLEE D'AQUITAINE
RUE ERNEST GUILLIER
RUE BERTRAND DU GUESCLIN
RUE DE STRASBOURG
RUE LA FAYETTE
RUE DU PRESIDENT WILSON
R. DES GLADIATEURS
RUE STE-URSULE
RUE ALARY
RUE ALSACE LORRAINE
RUE DES FORGERONS
AVENUE MARECHAL JUIN
RUE PAUL BERT
RUE TURENNE
RUE CHANZY
BOULEVARD DES ARENES
RUE STE-MARIE
AVENUE CAVAIGNAC
PLACE DE LA CITE
RUE DU GYMNASE
ACCOMMODATION
Bristol 2
Couleurs du Temps 1
Ibis Périgueux Centre 3
Mercure 4
DRINKING
Le Chai Bordin 1
Véloc Café 2
EATING
Café Louise 4
Le Clos St-Front 1
L'Essentiel 3
Le Saint-Louis 2
N

10

more central rue de la Cité, behind place Francheville. Destinations Angoulême (1–3 daily; 1hr 40min); Bergerac (3–6 daily; 1hr–1hr 30min); Brantôme (1–3 daily; 50min); Montignac (Mon–Fri 1–2 daily; 1hr); Sarlat (1–3 daily; 1hr 15min–1hr 45min).

**Tourist office** 9bis place du Coderc (June 15–30 & Sept 1–17 Mon–Sat 9am–12.30pm & 2–6pm, Sun 10am–1pm; July & Aug Mon–Sat 9am–7pm, Sun 10am–6pm; Sept 18 to June 14 Mon–Sat 9am–12.30pm & 2–6pm; ☎ 05 53 53 10 63, ⓦ tourisme-perigueux.fr).

## ACCOMMODATION

★ **Bristol** 37 rue Antoine-Gadaud ☎ 05 53 08 75 90, ⓦ bristolfrance.com. A 5min walk from the centre, this welcoming hotel remains a good choice, though a recent refurbishment means it's not quite the bargain it used to be. Rooms are large and bright, with a/c, and there's free parking. **€80**

★ **Couleurs du Temps** 20 bd Albert-Claveille ☎ 06 79 81 83 71, ⓦ couleursdutempsdordogne.blogspot.com. Overlooking the Parc de la Préfecture, this charming B&B in a characterful 1930s house has two TV-free rooms. Both are decorated in retro style and have sitting areas with tea and coffee. If you don't want breakfast, owner Luc knocks €5 off the room price. **€75**

**Ibis Périgueux Centre** 8 bd Georges-Saumande ☎ 05 53 53 64 68, ⓦ ibis.com. The only hotel in the city where all the rooms boast either a river or – even better – a cathedral view, which makes up for their otherwise bare functionality. The lobby is deceptively grand, but staff are helpful, and good discounts online often bring prices down to €59. **€86**

**Mercure** 7 place Francheville ☎ 05 53 06 65 00, ⓦ mercure.com. A good central location on the main square and contemporary decor with a theme based around the Lascaux cave drawings make this four-star hotel an attractive option. The downside is no onsite parking. Breakfast €16. **€86**

## EATING AND DRINKING

The best area to look for places to eat is the *vieille ville*, particularly around place St-Louis, place St-Silain and in the streets behind the tourist office.

**Café Louise** 10 place de l'Ancien-Hôtel-de-Ville ☎ 05 53 08 93 85. This intimate *maison gourmande* is very popular for its blend of Italian and French flavours. *Menus* start from €15 and might include dishes like ravioli of foie gras. The dining room has an understated, relaxed elegance, while in fine weather you can sit out on the lovely *place*. Wed–Sun noon–midnight.

**Le Chai Bordin** 8 rue de la Sagesse ☎ 09 81 89 40 65, ⓦ lechaibordin.com. This wine shop is the place to come to sample some of the region's excellent wines, with its great atmosphere and people spilling out into the little side street on warm evenings. Tues & Wed 10am–12.30pm & 3–9pm, Thurs & Fri 10am–12.30pm & 3–10pm, Sat 9.30am–3pm & 3.30–10pm.

★ **Le Clos St-Front** 5 rue de la Vertu ☎ 05 53 46 78 58, ⓦ leclossaintfront.com. High-quality *menus*, using local ingredients, served in a leafy, walled courtyard or elegant dining rooms. You can eat for less than €30, but the €46 *menu* will enable you to choose the best dishes on offer,

such as turbot braised in nettle-infused butter. Tues & Sun noon–1.30pm, Wed–Sat noon–1.30pm & 7–9pm.

**L'Essentiel** 8 rue de la Clarté ☎ 05 53 35 15 15, ⓦ restaurant-perigueux.com. An elegant but unfussy Michelin-starred restaurant, close to the cathedral. With *menus* starting from €29 at lunch and €47 at dinner, it's also surprisingly good value – expect choices like roast pigeon with Jerusalem artichokes and an offal *pastilla*. Tues–Sat noon–2pm & 7.30–10pm.

**Le Saint-Louis** 26bis rue Eguillerie ☎ 05 53 53 53 90. An unpretentious bar-brasserie on one of the city's loveliest squares. Sit out under the umbrellas on the cobblestones, or inside the surprisingly smart interior. *Menus* start from €20 in the evenings, including dishes such as scallops in a creamy pepper sauce. Mon–Sat 10am–11pm.

★ **Véloc Café** 7 av Daumesnil ☎ 06 33 48 22 89. This bike rental shop is also a cute retro café where you can enjoy a coffee, Bergerac wine, craft beer or light lunch made with seasonal, local produce (€9.50). The terrace overlooks the cathedral and is a great place to while away an hour or two in fine weather. Mon–Sat 7.30pm–8.30pm, Sun 7.30am–2pm; open until 11pm in summer.

# Périgord Pourpre

The **Périgord Pourpre** takes its name from the wine-growing region concentrated in the southwest corner of the Dordogne *département*, most famous for the sweet white wines produced around **Monbazillac**. The only town of any size is **Bergerac**, which makes a good base for exploring the vineyards and the uplands to the south. These are peppered with *bastides*, medieval fortified towns (see page 550), such as the beautifully preserved **Monpazier**, and here also you'll find the **Château de Biron**, which dominates the countryside for miles around.

## Bergerac

**BERGERAC**, "capital" of Périgord Pourpre, lies on the riverbank in the wide plain of the Dordogne. Once a flourishing port for the wine trade, it is still the main market centre for the surrounding maize, vine and tobacco farms. Devastated in the Wars of Religion, when most of its Protestant population fled overseas, Bergerac is now essentially a modern town with some interesting and attractive reminders of the past.

### The vieille ville

The compact **vieille ville** is an appealing area to wander through, with numerous late medieval houses and one or two beautiful squares. The splendid seventeenth-century Maison Peyrarède on rue de l'Ancien-Pont houses the informative **Musée du Tabac** (April & May Tues–Sat 10am–noon & 2–6pm, Sun 2.30–6.30pm; June–Sept daily 10am–1pm & 2–6pm; Oct–March Tues–Fri 10am–noon & 2–6pm, Sat 10am–noon; €4), which details the history of the plant, with collections of pipes and tools of the trade. Unsurprisingly, it rather skims over the negative side of tobacco use. Wine-lovers should make a beeline for the **Maison des Vins**, 1 rue des Récollets (Mon–Sat 10am–1pm & 2–7pm; free; ☎05 53 63 57 55, ⓦvins-bergeracduras.fr), which offers free tastings and beginners' courses (July & Aug; €5). It also sells a selection of local wines, many under €10, and provides information about visiting the surrounding vineyards.

### ARRIVAL AND INFORMATION

BERGERAC

**By air** The airport (☎05 53 22 25 25, ⓦbergerac.aeroport. fr) lies 5km southeast of Bergerac (€20–25 by taxi), and serves quite a few UK cities courtesy of BA, Flybe, Jet2 and Ryanair. A number of car rental companies are based

---

### BASTIDES

**Bastides**, from the Occitan word *bastida*, meaning a group of buildings, were the new towns of the thirteenth and fourteenth centuries. Although they are found all over southwest France, from the Dordogne to the foothills of the Pyrenees, there is a particularly high concentration in the area between the Dordogne and Lot rivers, which at that time formed the disputed "frontier" region between English-held Aquitaine and Capetian France.

That said, the earliest *bastides* were founded largely for economic and political reasons. They were a means of bringing new land into production – in an era of rapid population growth and technological innovation – and thus extending the power of the local lord. But as tensions between the French and English forces intensified in the late thirteenth century, so the motive became increasingly military. The *bastides* provided a handy way of securing the land along the frontier, and it was generally at this point that they were fortified.

As an incentive, anyone who was prepared to build, inhabit and defend the *bastide* was granted various benefits in a founding charter. All new residents were allocated a building plot, garden and cultivable land. The charter might also offer asylum to certain types of criminal or grant exemption from military service and would allow the election of consuls charged with day-to-day administration – a measure of self-government remarkable in feudal times. Taxes and judicial affairs, meanwhile, remained the preserve of the representative of the king or local lord under whose ultimate authority the *bastide* lay.

The other defining feature of a *bastide* is its layout. They are nearly always square or rectangular in shape and are divided by streets at right angles to each other, producing a chequerboard pattern. The focal point is the market square, often missing its covered *halle* nowadays, but generally still surrounded by arcades, while the church is relegated to one side.

The busiest *bastide* founders were Alphonse de Poitiers, on behalf of the French crown, after he became Count of Toulouse in 1249, and King Edward I of England (1272–1307), who wished to consolidate his hold on the northern borders of his Duchy of Aquitaine. The former chalked up a total of 57 *bastides*, including **Villeneuve-sur-Lot** (1251) and **Monflanquin** (1252), while Edward was responsible for **Beaumont** (1272) and **Monpazier** (1284), among others. While many *bastides* retain only vestiges of their original aspect, both Monpazier and Monflanquin have survived almost entirely intact.

at the airport, including Avis (☎ 05 53 61 24 83, ⓦ avis.fr) and Europcar (☎ 05 53 61 61 61, ⓦ europcar.fr). There's no public transport from the town.

**By train** The station is on avenue du 108ème Régiment-d'Infanterie, a 10min walk northeast of the old town, which is best reached by following boulevard Victor-Hugo to place de la République.

Destinations Bordeaux (9–15 daily; 50min–1hr); Sarlat (6–9 daily; 1hr 15min); Trémolat (6–9 daily; 25–40min).

**By bus** Bus #3 to Périgueux (Mon–Fri 3–5 daily; 1hr 15min) arrives and departs from the gare SNCF.

**Tourist office** 97 rue Neuve-d'Argenson (April–June, Sept & Oct Mon–Sat 9.30am–1pm & 2–7pm; July & Aug Mon–Sat 9.30am–7pm; Nov–March Mon–Wed, Fri & Sat 9.30am–1pm & 2–6.30pm, Thurs 10am–1pm & 2–6.30pm; ☎ 05 53 57 03 11, ⓦ pays-bergerac-tourisme.com). A second office opens in summer behind the Maison des Vins in the Cloître des Récollets (July & Aug daily 10.30am–1pm & 2–6.30pm).

**Bicycle rental** Apolo Cycles, 15 impasse des Grenouillets (€15/day; ☎ 06 20 64 59 25, ⓦ apolo-cycles.com).

## ACCOMMODATION

**De Bordeaux** 38 place Gambetta ☎ 05 53 57 12 83, ⓦ hotel-bordeaux-bergerac.com. Bergerac's smartest town-centre hotel, though some of the rooms could do with a little updating, just a short walk north of the old town. A bonus is the outdoor swimming pool set in the attractive garden. **€90**

**Château les Merles** 3 Chemin des Merles, Mouleydier ☎ 05 53 63 13 42, ⓦ lesmerles.com. Stylish contemporary hotel in a gorgeous château 15km east of Bergerac. The restaurant serves delicious modern Perigordian cuisine, and there's a picturesque pool and a golf course. **€160**

**Le Colombier de Cyrano et Roxanne** 17 rue du Grand-Moulin ☎ 05 53 57 96 70, ⓦ lecolombierdecyrano.fr. This two-bedroom chambre d'hôte is set on a particularly lovely place, which is crammed full of old timbered buildings. There are just two sweet, boho rooms, one of which benefits from its own hammock-strung terrace. **€79**

**La Pelouse** 8 rue Jean-Jacques-Rousseau ☎ 05 53 57 06 67, ⓦ entreprisefrery.com/camping-la-pelouse. This shady campsite is on the south bank of the river, a pleasant 15min walk from the old town. The basic facilities include a laundry and a bakery. **€11.10**

## EATING AND DRINKING

**La Blanche Hermine** 16 place Louis-de-la-Bardonnie ☎ 05 53 57 63 42, ⓦ facebook.com/CreperieLaBlanche Hermine. A cheerful crêperie opposite the covered market dishing up an imaginative range of buckwheat crêpes as well as copious salads – all at very reasonable prices (from €5.40). Tues–Sat noon–10.30pm.

★ **La Cocotte des Halles** 14 place du Marché-Couvert ☎ 05 53 24 10 00. A real locals' place attached to the covered market that looks like it hasn't changed for years – spotty brown tablecloths, orange wooden chairs and

tiled floor – but boasting excellent, unpretentious food. The menus, starting from €16, are great value and include dishes like swordfish with lime alongside more usual offerings like confit de canard. Mon–Sat 9am–3pm.

**La Table du Marché Couvert** 21 place du Marché-Couvert ☎ 05 53 22 49 46, ⓦ table-du-marche.com. This smart, modern bistro offers some of the more interesting dishes in town, such as hake with a tomato marmalade, on its daily menus (from €26 at lunchtime, €39 at dinner). Tues–Sat noon–1.45pm & 7.15–9.30pm.

## Monpazier and around

**MONPAZIER**, founded in 1284 by King Edward I of England (who was also Duke of Aquitaine), is one of the most complete of the surviving bastides. Picturesque and placid though it is today, the village has a hard and bitter history, being twice – in 1594 and 1637 – the centre of peasant rebellions provoked by the misery following the Wars of Religion. Both uprisings were brutally suppressed: the 1637 peasants' leader was broken on the wheel in the square.

Monpazier follows the typical bastide layout (see box opposite), with a grid of streets built around a gem of a central square. Deep, shady arcades pass under all the houses, which are separated from each other by a small gap to reduce fire risk; at the corners the buttresses are cut away to allow the passage of laden pack animals. You can find out more about these fortified towns in **Le Bastideum** (8 rue Galmot; Tues–Sun 10.30am–1pm & 2.30–6pm; €4.80; ⓦ bastideum.fr).

### Château de Biron

8km southwest of Monpazier • Feb & March Tues–Sun 10am–12.30pm & 2–5pm; April–June, Sept & Oct daily 10am–1pm & 2–6pm; July & Aug daily 10am–7.30pm; Nov & Dec 10am–12.30pm & 2–5pm • €8.50 • ☎ 03 53 63 13 39

**10**

The vast **Château de Biron** was begun in the eleventh century and added to piecemeal afterwards. It's worth paying for an audioguide (€2.50) if you're after a bit more background information (descriptions in the château itself are in French only), but you can wander at your own will around the rooms and the grassy courtyard, where there is a restored Renaissance chapel and guardhouse with tremendous views over the roofs of the feudal village below.

## ARRIVAL AND INFORMATION                                        MONPAZIER AND AROUND

**By car** There is no public transport to Monpazier; parking (free) is available on Foirail Nord, directly outside the north gate to the *bastide*.
**Tourist office** Place des Cornières (Feb–May & Oct–Dec Mon–Fri 9am–12.30pm & 2–5.30pm; June & Sept daily 10am–12.30pm & 2.30–6pm; July & Aug daily 10am–12.30pm & 2–7pm; ☎ 05 53 22 68 59, ⓦ pays-bergerac-tourisme.com).

## ACCOMMODATION

**Chez Edèll** 2 rue Notre-Dame ☎ 05 53 63 26 71, ⓦ chezedell.com. Lovely little B&B by the south gate of the bastide, with three pristine, stylish rooms and an apartment for two people. Breakfast is taken on the small outdoor terrace in summer. €65

★ **Edward 1ᵉʳ** 5 rue St-Pierre ☎ 05 53 22 44 00, ⓦ hoteledward1er.com. A gorgeous, stately hotel a few minutes' walk from the main square, with friendly and helpful Dutch owners. The rooms have a rustic chic, with lots of white furniture and luxurious fabrics, and are very comfortable. An extension has seen the hotel grow in size, but it still retains its intimate feel, and guests now have the choice of a couple of peaceful lounge areas. The owners also run two excellent restaurants (see below). €155

**Moulin de David** 4km south of Monpazier, off the road to Villeréal ☎ 05 53 22 65 25, ⓦ moulindedavid.com. A very pleasant and well-equipped four-star campsite, in a peaceful and shady setting by a brook; there's a choice of three swimming pools, one of which has slides. You can also rent bikes here. €30

## EATING AND DRINKING

**Bistrot 2** Foirail Nord ☎ 05 53 22 60 64, ⓦ bistrot2.fr. If *Éléonore* (see below) is full, try this lovely bistro, run by the same people; it's a more informal place, a few streets to the north, with *menus* from €15.75 featuring lots of Perigord ingredients, including (in season) the delicious local white asparagus. Closed Nov to mid-March. Daily noon–10pm.

★ **Restaurant Éléonore** 5 rue St-Pierre ☎ 05 53 22 44 00, ⓦ restauranteleonore.com. The elegant restaurant at the Edward 1ᵉʳ hotel (see above) is the best and most atmospheric place to eat in town, with an elegant dark-blue dining room. On warm evenings, tables are set up outside, with swallows swooping overhead. The menu changes daily and reflects local, seasonal produce, with a choice of three to five courses (from €31.50). Reservations required. May–Sept Thurs noon–2pm, Mid-March to June & Sept to mid-Nov daily 7.30–9pm.

# Périgord Noir

**Périgord Noir** encompasses the central part of the valley of the Dordogne, and the valley of the Vézère. This is the distinctive Dordogne country: deep-cut valleys between limestone cliffs, with fields of maize in the alluvial bottoms and dense oak woods on the heights, interspersed with patches of not very fertile farmland. Plantations of walnut trees (cultivated for their oil), flocks of low-slung grey geese (their livers enlarged for foie gras) and prehistoric-looking stone huts called *bories* are all hallmarks of Périgord Noir.

The well-preserved medieval architecture of **Sarlat**, the wealth of **prehistory** and the staggering cave paintings of the **Vézère valley**, and the stunning beauty of the château-studded **Dordogne** have all contributed to making this one of the most heavily touristed inland areas of France. If possible, it's worth coming out of season, but if you can't, seek accommodation away from the main centres, and always drive along the back roads – the smaller the better – even when there is a more direct route available.

## Sarlat-la-Canéda

**SARLAT-LA-CANÉDA**, the "capital" of Périgord Noir, lies in a hollow between hills 10km or so back from the Dordogne river and is undoubtedly the big tourist draw of the region.

You hardly notice the modern town, as it's the mainly fifteenth- and sixteenth-century houses of the *vieille ville* in mellow, honey-coloured stone that draw the attention.

The **vieille ville** is an excellent example of medieval organic urban growth. It was also the first town to benefit from culture minister André Malraux's law of 1962, which created the concept of a *secteur sauvegardé* (protected area), and boasts no fewer than 73 protected buildings and monuments. The old centre is violated only by the straight swath of the rue de la République which cuts through its middle. The west side, devoid of any standout sights, remains relatively quiet (and all the more atmospheric), whereas the east side, where most people wander, is full of sun-facing bars and restaurants.

**10**

### Cathédrale St-Sacerdos and around

#### Place du Peyrou

Sarlat's cathedral is rather large and unexciting, and mostly dates from its seventeenth-century renovation. Adjoining the cathedral is the more impressive facade of the seventeenth-century **Palais Episcopal**, while opposite stands the town's finest house, the **Maison de La Boétie** (not open to the public) where the poet and humanist Étienne de La Boétie was born in 1530. It has gabled tiers of windows and a characteristic steep roof stacked with heavy limestone tiles (*lauzes*).

For a better sense of the medieval town, wander through the cool, shady lanes and courtyards – **cour des Fontaines** and **cour des Chanoines** – around the back of the

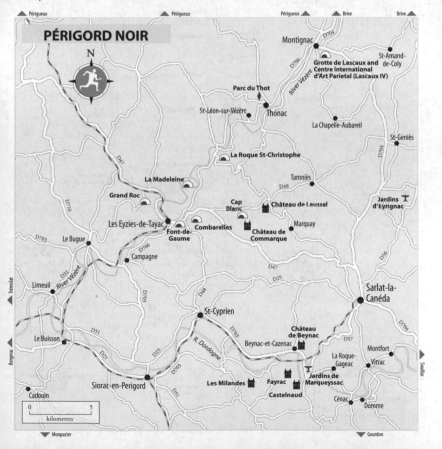

cathedral. On a slope directly behind the cathedral stands the curious twelfth-century coned tower, the **Lanterne des Morts**, whose exact function has escaped historians, though the most popular theory is that it was built to commemorate St Bernard, who performed various miracles when he visited the town in 1147.

### Belvédère de Sarlat (Ascenseur Panoramique)

Église Ste-Marie • April–Dec variable between 9am & 9pm; check with tourist office (see below) for current hours • April–Oct €5, Nov & Dec €4 • Tickets on site are by credit card only, or can be purchased from the tourist office • ☎ 05 53 31 45 42

**10**

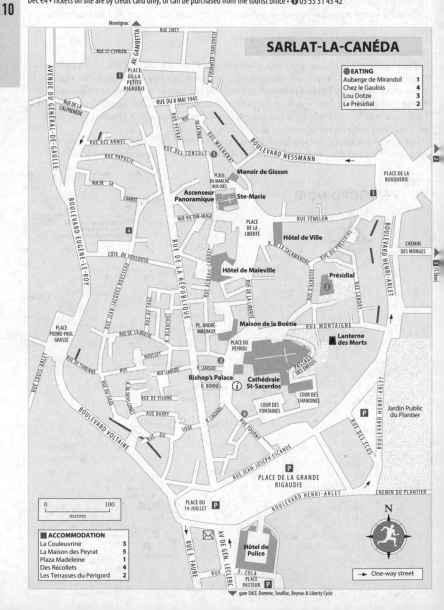

> **SARLAT MARKET**
>
> In a region famous for its **markets**, Sarlat's twice-weekly (Wed & Sat) offering is particularly notable for its size and the range of produce on offer. Of the two, the Saturday market is the largest, spreading down from northerly avenue Gambetta to place du 14-juillet. The stalls that crowd the main drag are a rather uninspired selection of clothes, shoes and mass-produced crafts; veer off towards place de la Liberté, however, and you'll find stalls selling everything from seasonal fruit and veg (not to mention truffles) to foie gras, walnut wine and nougat. It's an irresistible Sarlat experience but get there early as most stalls start packing up around 12.30pm.

**10**

Arguably the best view of Sarlat is from the top of the **Belvédère de Sarlat** (look out for signs for the *ascenseur panoramique*), a glass-sided lift designed by architect Jean Nouvel and built into the tower of the church of Ste-Marie (now the covered market). The visit lasts twelve minutes and takes you up 35m to the very top of the tower (which was conveniently never roofed) and affords fabulous 360° views over the town's attractive rooftops – a guide is on hand to point out the landmarks.

## ARRIVAL AND INFORMATION                                    SARLAT-LA-CANÉDA

**By train** The *gare SNCF* is just under 2km south of the old town, about a 20min walk.
**Destinations** Bergerac (7–8 daily; 1–1hr 25min); Bordeaux (7–8 daily; 2hr 30min–2hr 50min); Trémolat (7–8 daily; 40min).
**By bus** Buses depart from place Pasteur, just south of place du 14-juillet; see ⓦ transperigord.fr for details.
**Destinations** Montignac (Mon–Fri 1–2 daily; 30min); Périgueux (1–2 daily; 1hr 45min); Souillac (2–3 daily; 1hr).

**Tourist office** 3 rue Tourny (April–June & Sept Mon–Sat 9am–6pm, Sun 10am–1pm & 2–5pm; July & Aug Mon–Sat 9am–7.30pm, Sun 10am–1pm & 2–6pm; Oct Mon–Sat 9am–12.30pm & 2–5pm, Sun 10am–1pm; Nov–March Mon–Sat 10am–noon & 2–5pm; ☎ 05 53 31 45 45, ⓦ sarlat-tourisme.com).
**Bike rental** Liberty Cycle, on the D704 towards Souillac, just east of the *gare SNCF* (☎ 07 81 24 78 79, ⓦ liberty-cycle.com), rents bikes from €22 a day.

## ACCOMMODATION

**La Couleuvrine** 1 place de la Bouquerie ☎ 05 53 59 27 80, ⓦ la-couleuvrine.com. One of the nicest and most reasonable places to stay in Sarlat, occupying a tower in the former ramparts on the northeast side of the *vieille ville*. Most of the rooms are quite small, though cosily furnished with solid dark furniture and pretty fabrics. The restaurant has a dinner menu for €30. **€75**

★ **La Maison des Peyrat** La Plane Basse, 1.3km east of the centre ☎ 05 53 59 00 32, ⓦ maisondespeyrat.com. On a hill overlooking the town and countryside, this quaint hotel, in a building that dates back to the fourteenth century, has ten contemporary rooms which retain original features. There's also a very nice pool and breakfast is served on the patio in summer. Closed mid-Nov to March. Rooms **€69**

**Plaza Madeleine** 1 place de la Petite-Rigaudie ☎ 05 53 59 10 41, ⓦ hoteldelamadeleine-sarlat.com. A recent renovation has given the *Plaza Madeleine* a smart, almost Parisian feel, with lots of dark colours and statement lights. There's a heated outdoor pool and a spa, and an intimate bar with a great terrace for people-watching. **€165**

**Des Récollets** 4 rue Jean-Jacques-Rousseau ☎ 05 53 31 36 00, ⓦ hotel-recollets-sarlat.com. A good-value place, with functional rooms set in an old cloister around a little courtyard, on an atmospheric side street on the quieter western side of the old town. **€59**

**Les Terrasses du Périgord** About 2.5km north of Sarlat near Proissans village ☎ 05 53 59 02 25, ⓦ terrasses-du-perigord.com. A really lovely campsite, with spacious pitches beneath the trees, and panoramic views of the surrounding countryside. There's a covered pool and an outdoor pool. Closed Oct–March. **€26.40**

## EATING

**Auberge de Mirandol** 7 rue des Consuls ☎ 05 53 29 53 89, ⓦ restaurant-auberge-mirandol-sarlat.fr. An attractive and popular restaurant serving reasonably priced local delicacies in a fifteenth-century house, complete with its own *cave*. *Menus* from €17.90. Mid-Feb to Nov daily noon–2pm & 7–9pm; closed Mon out of season.

★ **Chez le Gaulois** 1 rue Tourny ☎ 05 53 59 50 64. A delightful little place specializing in cheese and charcuterie, with tables in the cosy interior or outside on the cobbled street. There's a good choice of both hot (*fondue*) and cold dishes (most around €13). April–June & Sept–Feb Tues–Sat noon–2pm & 7–9pm; July & Aug daily noon–2pm & 7–10pm.

**Lou Dotze** place du Peyrou ☎ 05 53 59 20 08,

Ⓦfacebook.com/loudotze. This friendly little crêperie doesn't look like much on first glance, but the *galettes* (from €7.80) are delicious, the service never anything less than charming, and the position – right opposite the cathedral – is hard to beat. Daily: late April to June, Sept & Dec 9am–4pm & 6pm–midnight; July & Aug 9am–midnight.

**Le Présidial** 6 rue Landry ☎05 53 28 92 47, Ⓦlepresidial.fr. A beautiful setting, in a lovely seventeenth-century mansion, with tables out in the walled garden in summer. Expect the usual local dishes like *confit de canard*, plus more interesting options like trio of cod, sea bream and skate with lemongrass (lunch *menu* €19.50, dinner *menu* from €29.50). Mon & Thurs 7–9pm, Tues, Wed, Fri & Sat noon–1.30pm & 7–9pm.

## The Vézère valley

The **valley of the River Vézère** between **Limeuil** and **St-Amand-de-Coly** justifiably styles itself as the **prehistory** capital of the world. The high, rocky outcrops overlooking acres of thick forest are riddled with caves which have provided shelter for humans for tens of thousands of years. It was here that the first skeletons of **Cro-Magnon people** – the first Homo sapiens, tall and muscular with a large skull – were unearthed in 1868 by labourers building the Périgueux–Agen train line. Since then, an incomparable wealth of archeological and artistic evidence of late Stone Age people has been revealed, most famously in the breathtakingly sophisticated **cave paintings** of **Lascaux** and **Font de Gaume**.

Away from the throngs of visitors at the caves, there is much to appreciate in the peace and quiet of the Vézère valley. It's best enjoyed from a **canoe**, where you'll often find yourself alone in a bend of the river, rather than part of a vast armada, as tends to be the case on the Dordogne.

### Limeuil

Built into the steep slope at the confluence of the Dordogne and Vézère rivers, the beautiful village of **LIMEUIL** is a picturesque place to while away a couple of hours. From the riverbank – an ideal picnic spot, with a pebbly beach that's the perfect spot for a dip in the water – the narrow, cobbled rue du Port leads steeply uphill, winding in between medieval houses and through the old gateways. At the top, the best views out over the village and surrounding countryside have been monopolized by the **Parc Panoramique** (April & Oct Mon–Fri & Sun 10am–6pm; May, June & Sept Mon–Fri & Sun 10am–6pm, Sat 2–6pm; July & Aug daily 10am–8pm; €8; Ⓦjardins-panoramiques-limeuil.com), a wilderness of trees, shrubs and crumbling stone walls.

### Trémolat and around

Set back from the river, the picturesque village of **TRÉMOLAT** is worth a stop for its two superlative dining opportunities, both of which are part of the luxurious *Le Vieux Logis* hotel (see page 561). Most people pass through the village on their way to the **Cingle de Trémolat**, a short drive west on the D31, where a viewpoint allows you to see the river as it meanders through the countryside. The best view, however, is just above this – to reach it, take the turning just after the car park for the Cingle (if coming from Trémolat), towards "Belvédère et Calvaire du Rocamadour", and pull over when you reach the tower. On clear days, the river takes on a mirror-like consistency, and you can see Trémolat's stately church rising up from the green fields that surround.

### Les Eyzies-de-Tayac

The main base for visiting many of the region's prehistoric painted caves is **LES EYZIES-DE-TAYAC**, a one-street village lined with gift shops and foie gras outlets. There are more prehistoric caves around Les Eyzies than you could possibly hope to visit in one day and they are all UNESCO World Heritage Sites. The compulsory tours are tiring, so it's best to just do a couple rather than attempt them all. In town, it's worth visiting the excellent **Musée National de Préhistoire** (1 rue du Musée; June & Sept daily except

**A PREHISTORY MYSTERY**

Most of the **caves** around Les Eyzies were not used as permanent homes, and there are various theories as to the purpose of such inaccessible spots. Most agree that they were sanctuaries and, if not actually places of worship, at least had religious significance. One suggestion is that making images of animals that were commonly hunted – like reindeer and bison – or feared – like bears and mammoths – was a kind of sympathetic magic intended to help men either catch or evade these animals. Another is that they were part of a fertility cult: sexual images of women with pendulous breasts and protuberant behinds are common. Others argue that these cave paintings served educational purposes, making parallels with Australian aborigines who used similar images to teach their young vital survival information as well as the history and mythological origins of their people. But much remains unexplained – the abstract signs that appear in so many caves, for example, and the arrows that clearly cannot be arrows, since Stone Age arrowheads looked different from these representations.

**10**

Tues 9.30am–6pm; July & Aug daily 9.30am–6.30pm; Oct–May daily except Tues 9.30am–12.30pm & 2–5.30pm; €6; ⓦmusee-prehistoire-eyzies.fr), which contains many important prehistoric artefacts found in the various caves in the region. Look out for the oil lamp from Lascaux and the exhibits from La Madeleine, to the north of Les Eyzies, including a superb bas-relief of a bison licking its flank.

### Grotte de Font-de-Gaume

1.5km from Les Eyzies on the D47 to Sarlat • Daily except Sat: mid-May to mid-Sept 9.30am–5.30pm; mid-Sept to mid-May 9.30am–12.30pm & 2–5.30pm • €10; just seventy-eight tickets are available each day, only twenty-six are available to book in advance • ☎ 05 53 06 86 00, ⓦ site-les-eyzies.fr

Since its discovery in 1901, dozens of polychrome paintings have been found in the **Grotte de Font-de-Gaume**. The **cave** was first settled by Stone Age people during the last Ice Age – about 25,000 BC – when the Dordogne was the domain of roaming bison, reindeer and mammoths. The entrance is no more than a fissure concealed by rocks and trees above a small lush valley, leading to a narrow twisting passage. The first painting you see is a frieze of bison, reddish-brown in colour, massive, full of movement and very far from the primitive representations you might expect. Further on comes the most miraculous image of all, a **frieze** of five bison discovered in 1966 during cleaning operations. The colour, remarkably sharp and vivid, is preserved by a protective layer of calcite. Shading under the belly and down the thighs is used to give three-dimensionality with a sophistication that seems utterly modern. Another panel consists of superimposed drawings, a fairly common phenomenon in cave painting, sometimes the result of work by successive generations, but here an obviously deliberate technique. A reindeer in the foreground shares legs with a large bison behind to indicate perspective.

Stocks of **artists' materials** have also been found here: kilos of prepared pigments; palettes – stones stained with ground-up earth pigments; and wooden painting sticks. Painting was clearly a specialized, perhaps professional, business, reproduced in dozens of caves located in the central Pyrenees and northern Spain.

### Grotte des Combarelles

2km from Les Eyzies on the D47 towards Sarlat • Daily except Sat: mid-May to mid-Sept 9.30am–5.30pm; mid-Sept to mid-May 9.30am–12.30pm & 2–5.30pm • €10; just forty-two tickets are available each day and can be purchased from the Font-de-Gaume ticket office, only seven are available for advance booking • ☎ 05 53 06 86 00, ⓦ site-les-eyzies.fr

The **Grotte des Combarelles** was discovered in 1910. The innermost part of the cave is covered with **engravings** from the Magdalenian period (about 12,000 years ago). Drawn over a period of two thousand years, many are superimposed one upon another, and include horses, reindeer, mammoths and stylized human figures – among the finest are the heads of a horse and a lioness.

**10**

## Abri du Cap Blanc

7km east of Les Eyzies • Daily except Sat: mid-May to mid-Sept 10am–6pm; mid-Sept to mid-May 10am–12.30pm & 2–5.30pm • €8; two-hundred tickets are available each day, only thirty-five are available for advance booking • ☎ 05 53 06 86 00, ⓦ site-les-eyzies.fr

Not a cave but a natural rock shelter, the **Abri du Cap Blanc** lies on a steep wooded hillside. The shelter contains a **sculpted frieze** of horses and bison dating from the Middle Magdalenian period, about 14,000 years ago. Of only ten surviving prehistoric sculptures in France, this is undoubtedly the best. The design is deliberate, with the sculptures polished and set off against a pockmarked background. But what makes this place extraordinary is not just the large scale, but the high relief of some of the sculptures. This was only possible in places where light reached in, which in turn brought the danger of destruction by exposure to the air. Cro-Magnon people actually lived in this shelter, and a female skeleton some two thousand years younger than the frieze was found here.

## Grotte du Grand Roc

2km north of Les Eyzies, off the D47 • Feb & March Tues–Sun 10am–12.30pm & 2–5pm; April–June, Sept & Oct daily 10am–1pm & 2–6pm; July & Aug daily 10am–7.30pm; Nov & Dec Tues–Sun 10am–12.30pm & 2–5pm • €8.20 • ☎ 05 53 06 92 70

As well as prehistoric cave paintings, you can see some truly spectacular **stalactites** and **stalagmites** in the area around Les Eyzies. Some of the best examples can be found in the **Grotte du Grand Roc**, whose entrance is high up in the cliffs that line much of the Vézère valley. There's a great view from the mouth of the cave and, inside, along some 80m of tunnel, a fantastic array of rock formations.

## La Roque St-Christophe

9km northeast of Les Eyzies along the D706 to Montignac • Daily: Jan 10am–5pm; Feb, March & Oct to mid-Nov 10am–6pm; April–June & Sept 10am–6.30pm; July & Aug 10am–8pm; mid-Nov to Dec 10am–5.30pm • €8.75 • ☎ 05 53 50 70 45, ⓦ roque-st-christophe.com

The enormous prehistoric dwelling site of **La Roque St-Christophe** is made up of about a hundred **rock shelters** on five levels, hollowed out of the limestone cliffs. The whole complex is nearly 1km long and about 80m above ground level, where the River Vézère once flowed. The earliest traces of occupation go back over 50,000 years. There are frequent guided visits in summer, or you can just take an English-language leaflet and wander at your own pace.

## Montignac

The small, attractive town of **MONTIGNAC** is the main base for visiting the **Lascaux cave**. It's a more appealing place than Les Eyzies, with several wooden-balconied houses leaning appealingly over the river, a good **market** (Wed & Sat) and a lively annual **arts festival** (last week of July; ⓦ festivaldemontignac.fr), featuring international folk groups.

## Grotte de Lascaux and Centre International de l'Art Pariétal (Lascaux IV)

1.2km southeast of Montignac (15min walk) • 1hr guided tours (see website for times of tours in English): Jan–March & Nov–Dec 10am–6pm; April–June & Sept 9am–7.30pm; July & Aug 8am–9.30pm; Oct 9.30am–7pm; last admission 2hr before closing • €17, €21 with Parc du Thot • ☎ 05 53 50 99 10, ⓦ lascaux.fr

The **Grotte de Lascaux**, 2km south of Montignac on the D704, was discovered in 1940 by four boys who stumbled across a deep cavern decorated with marvellously preserved **paintings** of animals. Executed by Cro-Magnon people 17,000 years ago, the paintings are among the finest examples of prehistoric art in existence. There are five or six identifiable styles, and subjects include bison, mammoths and horses, plus the biggest known prehistoric drawing, of a 5.5m bull with an astonishingly expressive head and face. In 1948, the cave was opened to the public, and over the next fifteen years more than a million tourists came to see it. Sadly, because of deterioration caused by the heat and breath of visitors, the cave had to be closed in 1963; then visitors had to be content with the replica known as **Lascaux II**, 200m from the original site, until 2016.

This has now been replaced with a new visitor centre, the **Centre International de l'Art Pariétal (Lascaux IV)**, at a safe distance from the original. The ambitious new building has been designed to blend into the surrounding landscape and is half buried in the hill on which it is built; there are great views from the roof. The replica has been designed to create the feeling of being inside the original cave, and other areas, including a 3D cinema and temporary exhibitions, allow visitors to better understand the historical and cultural context. There's also a nice café here serving traditional French and regional dishes.

For an enhanced appreciation of the cave itself, especially if you have children, it's worth visiting the museum at **Parc du Thot** first (see below).

### Parc du Thot

Le Thot, near Thonac, around 7km down the Vézère from Lascaux IV • Daily: Feb & March 10am–5.30pm; April–June, Sept & Oct 10am–6pm; July & Aug 10am–7.30pm; Nov & Dec 10am–5pm • €9.50, €21 with Lascaux IV • ☎ 05 53 50 70 44, ⓦ lascaux.fr

**Parc du Thot** is a combined animal park and museum with a very interesting video showing the construction of the replica cave, along with mock-ups of prehistoric scenes and live examples of some of the animals featured in the paintings. Here you'll see European bison, wolves, long-horned cattle and Przewalski's horses, rare and beautiful animals from Mongolia believed to resemble the prehistoric wild horse – notice the erect mane.

### St-Amand-de-Coly

Nine kilometres east of Montignac, the village of **ST-AMAND-DE-COLY** boasts a superbly beautiful fortified Romanesque church, a magical venue for concerts in the summer. Despite its bristling military architecture, the twelfth-century church manages to combine great delicacy and spirituality, with its purity of line and simple decoration most evocative in the low sun of late afternoon or early evening. Its defences left nothing to chance: the walls are 4m thick, a ditch runs all the way round, and a passage once skirted the eaves, with numerous positions for archers to rain down arrows, and blind stairways to mislead attackers.

---

**ARRIVAL AND INFORMATION**                                  **THE VÉZÈRE VALLEY**

#### LIMEUIL

**By car** There is no public transport to Limeuil. Parking is available at both ends of the village (for a fee).

**Canoe rental** Canoës Rivières Loisirs, place du Port (May to mid-Sept daily 9am–5pm; ☎ 05 53 63 38 73, ⓦ canoes-rivieres-loisirs.fr).

#### TRÉMOLAT

**By train** Trémolat's small train station is 1km south of town.

Destinations Bergerac (5 daily; 25min); Bordeaux (5 daily; 2hr 20min); Sarlat (6 daily; 40min).

#### LES EYZIES-DE-TAYAC

**By train** The train station is about 0.5km northwest of town, on the Périgueux–Agen train line (Périgueux 6 daily; 30min).

**Tourist office** On the main street (Jan–March, Nov & Dec Mon–Fri 10–12.30pm & 2–5pm; April & Oct Mon–Sat 9.30am–12.30pm & 2–6pm; May, June & Sept Mon–Sat 9.30am–12.30pm & 2–6pm, Sun 9.30am–12.30pm; July

& Aug daily 9am–6.30pm; ☎ 05 53 06 97 05, ⓦ lascaux-dordogne.com).

**Canoe rental** Canoës Vallée Vézère (April–Sept; ☎ 05 53 05 10 11, ⓦ canoesvalleevezere.com), by the river near *Les Glycines*.

#### MONTIGNAC

**By bus** Buses stop at place Tourny, just off rue du 4-septembre, south of the river.

Destinations Brive-la-Gaillarde (Mon–Fri daily; 1hr); Périgueux (1–3 daily; 1–1hr 55min); Sarlat (Mon–Sat 1–2 daily; 25min).

**Tourist office** Place Bertrand-de-Born (Jan–March, Nov & Dec Mon–Fri 10am–12.30pm & 2–5pm; April & Oct Mon–Sat 9.30am–12.30pm & 2–6pm; May, June & Sept Mon–Sat 9.30am–12.30pm & 2–6pm, Sun 9.30am–12.30pm; July & Aug daily 9am–6.30pm; ☎ 05 53 51 82 60, ⓦ lascaux-dordogne.com).

**Canoe rental** Les 7 Rives on the north side of the river, near place d'Armes (daily 9.30am–6.30pm; ☎ 05 53 50 19 26).

**ACCOMMODATION AND EATING**

## LIMEUIL

**Au Bon Accueil** At the top of the hill ☎ 05 53 63 30 97, ⊛ au-bon-accueil-limeuil.com. Celebrated restaurant up at the top of the hill, with a small terrace. *Menus* start from €20 and include *tourin* – a garlic soup that's a speciality of the region – and rabbit casserole in mustard sauce. They also run a four-room *chambre d'hôte* just down the hill; rooms are simple but pleasant enough. April–Oct daily noon–2pm & 7–9pm. **€80**

**Le Chai** On the main road, by the river ☎ 05 53 63 39 36. This sweet restaurant has a lovely spot close to the river, with tables outside in the fragrant walled garden. The menu boasts a number of Perigordian specialities – try one of the *assiettes* for a good sampling of local produce (€27.50) – as well as pizzas (from €9.50). Mon, Tues & Thurs–Sun noon–2pm & 7–9pm, daily in July & Aug.

## TRÉMOLAT AND AROUND

★ **Bistrot de la Place** On the main road in Trémolat, just opposite the turning to Le Vieux Logis ☎ 05 53 22 80 06, ⊛ vieux-logis.com. The cheaper and more relaxed restaurant of *Le Vieux Logis* (see below), the *Bistrot de la Place* serves unpretentious but sophisticated food in the centre of the village itself – you'll struggle to find food as good as this at such low prices anywhere else in the region. The emphasis is on seasonal ingredients, such as local asparagus in spring and duck with cherries in summer. Three-course lunch *formule* €19. Mid-April to mid-Oct daily noon–1.30pm & 7.30–9pm; mid-Oct to mid-April Wed–Sun noon–1.30pm & 7.30–9pm.

★ **Le Vieux Logis Trémolat** ☎ 05 53 22 80 06, ⊛ vieux-logis.com. A peaceful and intimate *Relais et Châteaux* property set among beautiful gardens. Rooms are luxurious and unfussy, but the real reason to come here is for its two eating options, one of which is the *Bistrot de la Place* (reviewed above). The swankier of the two is the on-site Michelin-starred gourmet restaurant, which serves sublime food using local ingredients (*menus* from €55). Restaurant mid-April to mid-Oct daily noon–1.30pm & 7–9pm; mid-Oct to mid-April Wed–Sun noon–1.30pm & 7–9pm. **€180**

## LES EYZIES-DE-TAYAC

Les Eyzies hotels are pricey and may require half-board in high season, while most are closed in winter. When it comes to eating, you're best off dining in one of the hotel restaurants. **Des Falaises** Av de la Préhistoire ☎ 05 53 06 97 35. At the quieter end of the main drag, this is the cheapest option

in town. Rooms are fairly plain, but enlivened with colourful bed covers, and all are en suite. **€40**

**Les Glycines** Av de Laugerie ☎ 05 53 06 97 07, ⊛ les-glycines-dordogne.com. Elegant hotel and spa near the tiny railway station, offering very pretty, romantic rooms and three wooden "lodges", elevated among the trees. The hotel's *potager* provides much of the produce used in the fine dining restaurant (*menus* from €65), and the more casual bistro (menus from €31). Closed Nov–March. Restaurant daily 7–9pm, bistro daily noon–2pm. **€165**

★ **Le Moulin de la Beune** Rue du Moulin ☎ 05 53 06 94 33, ⊛ moulindelabeune.com. In a glorious setting, right by the River Beune, this ivy-covered hotel offers calm, spacious rooms. The restaurant is one of the best in town, with a lovely garden terrace at the back (*menus* from €23). Closed Dec to mid-April. Restaurant Mon–Sat 7–9.30pm. **€85**

## MONTIGNAC

Montignac hotels, as everywhere around here, get booked up quickly in summer. All of the hotels have restaurants – the one at *Hostellerie de la Roseraie* is particularly good.

**Aux Berges de Vézère** Place Tourny ☎ 05 53 50 56 31, ⊛ restaurant-montignac.fr. This chic restaurant with a lovely riverside terrace has a surprisingly good-value lunch menu Monday to Friday with a plat du jour for €10.90 and pizzas from €8.70. Otherwise, you'll find traditional regional dishes made with organic local produce. July & Aug daily noon–2pm & 7–9pm, closed Sun eve and Mon Sept–June.

★ **De Bouilhac** Av du Professeur-Faurel ☎ 05 53 51 21 46, ⊛ hoteldebouilhac-montignac.fr. This renovated seventeenth-century château offers the most stylish accommodation and smartest dining option in the town centre. The restaurant, in a vaulted stone room with a grand fireplace, serves traditional regional cuisine; main courses from €16 at lunchtime and an evening menu for €39. **€125**

**Le Moulin du Bleufond** Av Aristide-Briand ☎ 05 53 51 83 95, ⊛ bleufond.com. On the riverbank 500m downstream from the centre of Montignac, this is a well-tended and very popular three-star campsite, with a great pool. Closed mid-Oct to March. **€27.50**

**De la Roseraie** Place d'Armes ☎ 05 53 50 53 92, ⊛ laroseraie-hotel.com. This ivy- and wisteria-clad hotel, in a nice location near the river on a quiet square, has pretty, period rooms, plus a pool and flower-filled garden, and a great restaurant (*menus* from €31). Restaurant Mon–Wed & Fri–Sun 7.15–9pm. Closed Nov–March. **€90**

**10**

## The middle Dordogne valley

The most familiar images of the River Dordogne are those from around **Beynac** and **La Roque-Gageac**, where the scenery is at its most spectacular, with clifftop châteaux facing each other across the valley. The most imposing of these date from the Hundred

Years' War, when the river marked the frontier between French-held land to the north and English territory to the south. Further upstream, the hilltop *bastide* village of **Domme** offers stunning views, but is as crowded as Sarlat in summer.

Just south of the river, the **Abbaye de Cadouin** lies tucked out of harm's way in a fold of the landscape, hiding a lovely Gothic cloister. The train line from Bergerac to Sarlat runs along the river for this stretch, offering some wonderful views but unfortunately not stopping anywhere very useful; to appreciate the villages in this area, you need your own transport or, better still, a canoe.

**10**

## Abbaye de Cadouin

6km south of Le Buisson • **Cloister** Feb, March, Nov & Dec Tues–Sun 10am–12.30pm & 2–5pm; April–June, Sept & Oct Sun–Fri 10am–1pm & 2–6pm; July & Aug daily 10am–7.30pm • €7 • ⓦ abbaye-de-cadouin.com

For eight hundred years, until 1935, the twelfth-century Cistercian **Abbaye de Cadouin** drew flocks of pilgrims to wonder at a piece of cloth first mentioned by Simon de Montfort in 1214 and thought to be part of Christ's shroud. In 1935 the two bands of embroidery at either end were shown to contain an Arabic text from around the eleventh century. Since then the main attraction has been the finely sculpted but badly damaged capitals of the Flamboyant Gothic **cloister**. Beside it stands a Romanesque **church** with a stark, bold front and wooden belfry roofed with chestnut shingles (chestnut trees abound around here – their timber was used in furniture-making and their nuts ground for flour during frequent famines). Inside the church, the nave is slightly out of alignment; this is thought to be deliberate and perhaps a vestige of pagan attachments, as the three windows are aligned so that at the winter and summer solstices the sun shines through all three in a single shaft.

## Jardins de Marqueyssac

Daily: Feb, March & Oct to mid-Nov 10am–6pm; April–June & Sept 10am–7pm; July & Aug 9am–8pm, candlelit evenings Thurs 7pm–midnight; mid-Nov to Jan 2–5pm; • €9.80; candlelit evenings €15 • ☎ 05 53 31 36 36, ⓦ marqueyssac.com

The gorgeous **Jardins de Marqueyssac**, sitting on top of a wooded promontory that rises above a wide meander in the Dordogne, are one of the most magical sights in the region. At times, the gardens feel like a Tim Burton fantasy – quirky, maze-like topiary is the first thing that greets you upon entering – while at others it's like being in the heart of a forest, with only the rustle of birds in the trees above disturbing the peace. Though the gardens were originally laid out in the seventeenth century, what you see today is the result of extensive restoration work from the late 1990s.

Three paths lead through the grounds to the **Belvedere**, which juts out from the cliff with stupendous views over the river towards La Roque-Gageac and, in the opposite direction, Castelnaud. The gardens are even more magical during the special candlelit evenings on Thursdays in July and August when you can explore to the accompaniment of a live jazz band.

## Château de Castelnaud

Daily: Feb, March & Oct to mid-Nov 10am–6pm; April–June & Sept 10am–7pm; July & Aug 9am–8pm; mid-Nov to Jan 2–5pm • €10.80 • ☎ 05 53 31 30 00, ⓦ castelnaud.com

The partially ruined **Château de Castelnaud** is a true rival to Beynac (see below) in terms of impregnability – although it was successfully captured by the bellicose Simon de Montfort as early as 1214. The English held it for much of the Hundred Years' War, and it wasn't until the Revolution that it was finally abandoned. Fairly heavily restored in recent years, it now houses a highly informative **museum of medieval warfare**. Its core is an extensive collection of original weaponry, including all sorts of bizarre contraptions, and a fine assortment of armour. Costumed events and demonstrations take place throughout the year.

Beynac-et-Cazenac

Clearly visible on an impregnable cliff on the north bank of the river, the eye-catching village and castle of **BEYNAC-ET-CAZENAC** was built in the days when the river was the only route open to traders and invaders. By road, it's 3km to the **château** (daily 10am–6.30pm; €8; ☎05 53 29 50 40, ⍟chateau-beynac.com) but a steep lane leads up through the village and takes only fifteen minutes by foot. It's protected on the landward side by a double wall; elsewhere the sheer drop of almost 200m does the job. The flat terrace at the base of the keep, which was added by the English, conceals the remains of the houses where the beleaguered villagers lived. Richard the Lionheart held the place for a time, until a gangrenous wound received while besieging the castle of Châlus, north of Périgueux, ended his term of blood-letting.

La Roque-Gageac

The village of **LA ROQUE-GAGEAC** is almost too perfect, its ochre-coloured houses sheltering under dramatically overhanging cliffs. It inevitably pulls in the tourist buses, and since the main road separates the village from the river, the noise and fumes of the traffic can become rather oppressive in summer. The best way to escape is to slip away through the lanes and alleyways that wind up through the terraced houses.

Domme

High on a cliff on the river's south bank, **DOMME** is an exceptionally well-preserved *bastide*. Its attractions, in addition to its position, include three original thirteenth-century **gateways** and a section of the old **walls**. From the northern edge of the village, marked by a drop so precipitous that fortifications were deemed unnecessary, you look out over a wide sweep of river country. Beneath the village is a warren of **caves** (daily: Feb to mid-Nov & Christmas hols; contact the tourist office for times & tickets; €8.50) in which the townspeople took refuge in times of danger. Unfortunately, the rock formations can't compare with the area's other caves; the only good point is the exit onto the cliff face with a panoramic lift up to the top.

## ARRIVAL AND INFORMATION
## THE MIDDLE DORDOGNE VALLEY

There is no public transport to any of these villages. Parking at each is readily available, for a fee.

### DOMME
**Tourist office** Place de la Halle (daily: March & Oct to mid-Nov 10am–12.30pm & 1.30–5pm; April 9.30am–6.30pm; May, June & Sept 9.30am–6.30pm; July & Aug 9.30am–7pm; ☎05 53 31 71 00, ⍟perigordnoir-valleedordogne.com).

## ACCOMMODATION AND EATING

### ABBAYE DE CADOUIN
**De l'Abbaye** Place de l'Abbaye ☎05 53 63 40 93. A small restaurant opposite the abbey, serving hearty, reasonably priced meals (*menus* from €14.50), all starting with a complementary helping of the delicious house *tourin* (garlic soup). Tues–Sat noon–1.30pm & 7–9pm, Sun noon–1.30pm.

★ **Auberge de Jeunesse** ☎05 53 73 28 78, ⍟fuaj.org. This excellent FUAJ hostel is situated in part of the abbey itself, with dorms in the monks' old sleeping quarters, and some great double rooms. Closed Dec & Jan. Dorms €24, doubles €50.20

**Les Songes de l'Abbaye** 11 place de l'Abbaye ☎05 53 63 94 18, ⍟songesdelabbaye.com. A stylish B&B with four comfortable, contemporary rooms: one has twin beds,

one a four-poster. The owners are organic farmers and have an *épicerie* on the building's ground floor. €80

### BEYNAC-ET-CAZENAC
**Du Château** On the D703 ☎05 53 29 19 20, ⍟hotel-chateau-dordogne.com. The best of Beynac's hotels, with fresh, bright rooms, a small pool and a good restaurant (*menus* from €17.50) with a terrace overlooking the river; though it's on the busy main road, rooms are double-glazed and some have a/c. €87

**Le Capeyrou** Off the D703 ☎05 53 29 54 95, ⍟camping lecapeyrou.com. In an enviable position along the river, with the château making a rather magnificent backdrop, this leafy campsite is, unsurprisingly, a popular spot, with its own sandy beach and a large swimming pool. Closed Oct–April. €28.40

10

**10**

#### LA ROQUE-GAGEAC

★ **La Belle Étoile** On the D703 ☎ 05 53 29 51 44, ⓦ hotel-belle-etoile-dordogne.fr. A really lovely small hotel in a prime position across the road from the river. Rooms are spacious and cool; it's worth splashing out an extra €20 for a river view. The restaurant serves good traditional cuisine and has a lovely river-view terrace (*menus* from €29). Closed Nov–March. Restaurant Tues & Thurs–Sun 12.30–1.30pm & 7.30–9pm; Wed 7.30–9pm. **€68**

#### DOMME

★ **La Borie Blanche** Via the D46E3, 5.6km east of Domme ☎ 05 53 28 11 24. Delicious authentic regional cuisine is on offer at this restaurant in a quaint old farmhouse in the countryside just outside Domme. *Menus* range from €17 to €20 and include the likes of grilled beef from the chef/farmer's own cattle with roast potatoes. There's a shady terrace for summer dining. Booking required. Easter to Nov daily noon–2pm & 7–9pm.

**L'Esplanade** 2 rue Pontcarral ☎ 05 53 28 31 41, ⓦ esplanade-perigord.com. The most luxurious place to stay in Domme, right on the cliff edge, with panoramic views from some of the rooms, which are sumptuously decorated. There's also a gourmet restaurant (menus from €35). Closed Nov–March. **€99**

# The upper Dordogne valley

East of Sarlat and Domme, you leave the crowds of Périgord Noir behind, but the Dordogne valley retains all of its beauty and interest. **Martel** and **Carennac** are wonderfully preserved medieval villages, and there are exceptional examples of Romanesque sculpture in the churches at **Souillac** and **Beaulieu**. Travel is difficult without a car, but Souillac is reachable by train and has bus routes to Sarlat and Martel. Cyclists can follow the *voie verte*, a 23km-long cycle route from Sarlat to Souillac along a decommissioned train track.

## Souillac

The first place of any size east of Sarlat is **SOUILLAC**, at the confluence of the Borrèze and Dordogne rivers and on a major road junction. Virginia Woolf stayed here in 1937 and was pleased to meet "no tourists … England seems like a chocolate box bursting with trippers afterward"; things have changed little today, and the town has an understated charm, once you head into the winding streets west of the main road through the centre.

### Church of Ste-Marie
Rue Morlet

Roofed with massive domes like the cathedrals of Périgueux and Cahors, the spacious interior of the twelfth-century **church of Ste-Marie** creates just the atmosphere for cool reflection on a summer's day. On the inside of the west door are some of the most wonderful Romanesque sculptures, including a seething mass of beasts devouring each other. The greatest piece of craftsmanship, though, is a **bas-relief of Isaiah**, fluid and supple, thought to be by one of the artists who worked at Moissac.

### Musée de l'Automate
Rue Morlet • April–June & Sept–Oct Tues–Sun 2–6pm; July & Aug daily 10am–12.30pm & 2–6.30pm • €7 • ☎ 05 65 37 07 07, ⓦ musee-automate.fr

The **Musée de l'Automate** contains an impressive collection of nineteenth- and twentieth-century mechanical dolls and animals, which dance, sing and perform magical tricks; look out for the irresistible laughing man.

---

**ARRIVAL AND INFORMATION**                                               **SOUILLAC**

**By train** The train station is just over 1km northwest of the town centre.

Destinations Brive-la-Gaillarde (8 daily; 23min); Cahors (8 daily; 40min); Gourdon (8 daily; 15min); Montauban (6 daily; 1hr 23min); Toulouse (6 daily; 2hr).

**By bus** Buses arrive and depart from both the train station and the more central avenue de Sarlat.

Destinations Martel (1–2 daily; 30min); Sarlat (1–2 daily; 40min).

**Tourist office** Boulevard Louis-Jean-Malvy (Jan–March, Nov & Dec Tues–Fri 10am–noon & 2–5pm; April–June,

Sept & Oct Mon–Sat 10am–12.30pm & 2–6pm; July & Aug Mon–Sat 9.30am–1pm & 2–6.30pm, Sun 10am–1pm; ☎ 05 65 33 22 00, ⊛ vallee-dordogne.com).

**Canoe rental** Copeyre Canoë, Les Ondines, just south of central Souillac (from €16; ☎ 05 65 32 72 61, ⊛ copeyre. com). Also rents out SUPs and mountain bikes.

**10**

## ACCOMMODATION AND EATING

**Le Beffroi** 6 place St-Martin ☎ 05 65 37 80 33. Situated on a pretty square, in the shadow of the church of St-Martin, this friendly restaurant is a great choice for simple but tasty meals, especially under the lovely, wisteria-shaded terrace. The local trout is particularly recommended (€16). Mon noon–2pm, Tues–Sat noon–2pm & 7–9pm.

★ **Château de la Treyne** 7km southeast of Souillac, towards Lacave ☎ 05 65 27 60 60, ⊛ chateaudelatreyne. com. Arguably the best place to stay in the region, *Château de la Treyne* is the epitome of luxury – owners (and staff) who instantly make you feel like old friends, sumptuous but unfussy rooms, and the most enviable of positions, overhanging the Dordogne itself. In fine weather, you

can enjoy the restaurant's Michelin-starred cuisine on the candlelit riverside terrace as the sun sets in the distance, an unashamedly romantic experience. €300

**Les Ondines** La Borgne, 1km south of the old town ☎ 05 65 37 86 44, ⊛ camping-lesondines.com. A large riverside campsite that's very family-oriented, with a heated pool, children's playground and a bouncy castle. Closed Oct–April. €24

**Le Pavillon St-Martin** 5 place St-Martin ☎ 05 65 32 63 45, ⊛ hotel-saint-martin-souillac.com. Directly opposite the brooding church of St-Martin, this attractive, sixteenth-century shuttered building has eleven beautifully renovated rooms, full of character. €58

# Martel

About 15km east of Souillac and set back even further from the river, **MARTEL** is a minor medieval masterpiece, built in a pale, almost white stone, offset by warm reddish-brown roofs. A Turenne-administered town (see page 540), its heyday came during the thirteenth and fourteenth centuries, when the viscounts established a court of appeal here.

## Place des Consuls

The main square, **place des Consuls**, is mostly taken up by the eighteenth-century **market hall** (market Sat & Wed), but on every side there are reminders of the town's illustrious past, most notably in the superb Gothic **Hôtel de la Raymondie**. Begun in 1280, it served as the Turenne law courts, though it doubled as the town's refuge, hence the distinctive corner turrets. Facing it is the **Tour des Pénitents**, one of the medieval towers that gave the town its epithet, *la ville aux sept tours* ("the town with seven towers"). The Young King Henry, son of Henry II, died in the striking **Maison Fabri**, in the southeast corner of the square. One block south, rue Droite leads east to the town's main **church**, St-Maur, which was built in a fiercely defensive, mostly Gothic style, and has a finely carved Romanesque tympanum depicting the Last Judgement above the west door.

## Tourist train

About 200m south of town, near the Relais Ste-Anne • April–Sept • €10.50 return • ☎ 05 65 37 35 81, ⊛ trainduhautquercy.info

One way to soak up the scenery is on the **steam and diesel tourist trains** (*trains à vapeur*) that run on a restored line between Martel and St-Denis. The trains, which depart from an old station, afford wonderful views as they climb the steep cliffs overlooking the river valley. It's worth choosing a seat on the right-hand side of the train (facing in the direction of travel), for the best views.

## ARRIVAL AND INFORMATION                     MARTEL

**By bus** Buses from Brive (weekly; 1hr) and Souillac (Mon–Sat 1–2 daily; 30min) stop on the main road, just a short walk from the town square.

**Tourist office** Cour de la Raymondie (April–June, Sept &

Oct Mon–Sat 9am–noon & 2–6pm; July & Aug daily 9am–7pm; Nov–March Mon–Fri 9am–noon & 2–5pm; ☎ 05 65 33 22 00, ⊛ martel.fr).

## ACCOMMODATION AND EATING

**Auberge des 7 Tours** ☎ 05 65 37 30 16, ⊛ auberge7 tours.com. The position of this small hotel, just a short

walk north of the town centre, affords lovely views of the surrounding countryside from its terrace. Rooms are plain

**10**

but bright, and there's a decent restaurant on site (*menus* from €14). Restaurant Tues–Fri noon–2pm & 7–9pm, Sat 7–9pm, Sun noon–2pm. **€70**

**Camping les Falaises** Gluges, 5km south from Martel ☎ 05 65 37 37 78, ⓦ camping-lesfalaises.com. In a lovely position by the Dordogne, this pleasant campsite offers lots of shady pitches and canoeing and kayaking opportunities right on the doorstep. There's a supervised river beach at Gluges in summer. Closed Sept to mid-June. **€14.40**

**Plein Sud** Place des Consuls. A charming little place opposite the covered market, with tables out on the square, serving decent pizzas (from €8) and more interesting mains

like tuna steak (€15.50). April–Sept Tues–Sat noon–3pm & 7–9.30pm, Sun noon–3pm.

★ **Relais Ste-Anne** Rue du Pourtanel ☎ 05 65 36 40 56, ⓦ relais-sainte-anne.com. The nicest place to stay is this ivy-covered former girls' boarding school, surrounded by attractive gardens with a small heated pool and a fine restaurant (*menus* from €30). The rooms are furnished in a tasteful mix of contemporary and modern styles, some with their own terrace. Closed Dec–March. Restaurant Mon & Wed–Sat 7.30–8.30pm (also Tues in July & Aug), Sun 12.30–1.30pm & 7.30–8.30pm. **€95**

## Carennac

**CARENNAC** is without doubt one of the most beautiful villages along the Dordogne river. Elevated just above the south bank, 13km or so east of Martel, it's best known for its typical Quercy architecture, its Romanesque priory, where the French writer Fénelon spent the best years of his life, and for its greengages.

### Church and cloisters

**Cloisters** April–June, Sept & Oct Mon–Sat 10am–noon & 2–5.30pm; July & Aug daily 9.30am–12.30pm & 2–6.30pm • €3

Carennac's major feature, as so often in these parts, is the Romanesque tympanum – in the Moissac style – above the west door of its church, the **Église St-Pierre**. Christ sits in majesty with the Book of Judgement in his left hand, with the apostles and adoring angels below him. Next to the church, don't miss the old **cloisters and chapterhouse**, which contain an exceptionally expressive life-size *Entombment of Christ*.

### ARRIVAL AND INFORMATION                                          CARENNAC

**By car** There is no public transport to Carennac. There are a number of free car parks just off the main road above the village.

**Tourist office** Cour du Prieuré (April–June, Sept & Oct

Mon–Sat 10am–12.30pm & 2–6pm, Sun 2–6pm; July & Aug daily 9.30am–1pm & 2–7pm; ☎ 05 65 33 22 00, ⓦ vallee-dordogne.com).

### ACCOMMODATION AND EATING

**La Farga** ☎ 05 65 33 18 97, ⓦ lafarga.wordpress.com. This welcoming *chambre d'hôte* on the main street has five appealingly simple, tastefully decorated rooms and one apartment, some overlooking the garden with its heated pool and children's play area. Meals using local organic ingredients are available for both lunch and dinner (€15 and €20 respectively) in the communal dining room. **€65**

**Hostellerie Fénelon** ☎ 05 65 10 96 46, ⓦ hotel-

fenelon.com. This is the village's only hotel, with comfortable, pleasant – if not hugely modern – rooms, the nicer ones overlooking the river. It also has a pool and a good restaurant specializing in traditional regional cuisine (*menus* from €19). Closed mid-Nov to mid-March. Restaurant May–Sept daily noon–2pm & 7–9pm; Oct–April Sat & Sun noon–2pm & 7–9pm. **€59**

## Beaulieu-sur-Dordogne

In a picturesque spot on the banks of the Dordogne, **BEAULIEU-SUR-DORDOGNE** boasts an appealing and atmospheric old town that is particularly pleasant to explore in late afternoon when the pale-stone buildings glow in the setting sun. Beaulieu is especially known for being home to one of the great masterpieces of Romanesque sculpture, on the porch of the **church of St-Pierre**. This doorway is unusually deep-set, with a tympanum presided over by an oriental-looking Christ with one arm extended to welcome the chosen. All around him is a complicated pattern of angels and apostles, executed in characteristic "dancing" style, similar to that at Carennac. The dead raise the lids of their coffins hopefully, while underneath a frieze depicts monsters crunching heads. Take the opportunity also to wander north along rue de la Chapelle past some handsome sculpted facades and down to the river.

## ARRIVAL AND INFORMATION

**BEAULIEU-SUR-DORDOGNE**

**By bus** Buses run to and from Brive (Mon–Sat 1–3 daily; 1hr), alighting and departing from place du Champs-du-Mars, just west of place Marbot.
**Tourist office** Place Marbot (April–June & Sept Mon–Sat 9.30am–12.30pm & 2.30–6pm, Sun 9.30am–12.30pm;

July & Aug Mon–Sat 9.30am–1pm & 2.30–7pm, Sun 9.30am–1pm; Oct Mon–Sat 9.30am–12.30pm & 2.30–6pm; Nov–March Mon–Sat 10am–12.30pm & 2.30–5pm; ☎ 05 65 33 22 00, ⓦ vallee-dordogne.com).

## ACCOMMODATION AND EATING

**Camping des Îles** Bd Rodolphe-de-Turenne ☎ 05 55 91 02 65, ⓦ campingdesiles.com. As its name suggests, this large campsite is set on its own island in the Dordogne, just a short walk from the old town. It's a great choice for families, with a swimming pool and adventure playground on site, plus archery and canoe rental. Closed mid-Sept to mid-April. **€27.50**
**Côté Dordogne** 20 bd Rodolphe-de-Turenne ☎ 05 55 91 29 29. The best time to come to this restaurant is in summer so that you can sit on the terrace next to the river. But the food is great year round, with a good-value lunch

*formule* at €13.50. Expect traditional French dishes such as *pâté en croûte* with walnut liqueur to start, and duck confit for main. Daily 12.15–2pm & 7.15–9pm.
**Les Flots Bleus** 17 place du Champ-de-Mars ☎ 05 55 91 06 21, ⓦ hotel-flotsbleus.com. Boasting an enviable position right by the river, *Les Flots Bleus* has just seven bright and very pleasant rooms – it's worth paying an extra €10 for a view. The riverside terrace is a popular spot for a drink throughout the day, and the restaurant has a great reputation (*menus* from €21.50), serving local specialities. Closed mid-Nov to Feb. **€74**

**10**

# The Lot

While the old provinces of **Haut Quercy** and **Quercy** – the land between the Dordogne and the Lot rivers and between the Lot and the Garonne, Aveyron and Tarn – largely correspond to the modern-day Lot *département*, it makes sense, for convenience's sake, to group them together with the gorges of the River **Aveyron** and Villefranche-de-Rouergue on the edge of the province of Rouergue.

The area is hotter, drier, less well known and, with few exceptions, less crowded than the Dordogne, though no less interesting. The cave paintings at **Pech-Merle** are on a par with those at Les Eyzies, while **Najac** has a ruined castle (and fabulous views) to rival those of the Dordogne. The towns of **Figeac** and **Villefranche-de-Rouergue** are without equal, as is the village of **St-Antonin-Noble-Val**, and stretches of country such as that below **Gourdon**, around **Les Arques** where Ossip Zadkine had his studio, and the **Célé valley**.

## Rocamadour and around

Halfway up a cliff in the deep and abrupt canyon of the Alzou stream, the spectacular setting of **ROCAMADOUR** is hard to beat. Since medieval times the town has been inundated by pilgrims drawn by the supposed miraculous ability of Rocamadour's Black Madonna. Nowadays, pilgrims are outnumbered by more secular-minded visitors, who fill the lanes lined with shops peddling incongruous souvenirs, but who come here mainly to wonder at the sheer audacity of the town's location, built almost vertically into its rocky backdrop.

### Brief history

Legend has it that the history of Rocamadour began with the arrival of **Zacchaeus**, a tax-collector in Jericho at the time of Christ. According to one legend he was advised by the Virgin Mary to come to France, where he lived out his years as a hermit. When in 1166 a perfectly preserved body was found in a grave high up on the rock, it was declared to be Zacchaeus, or **St Amadour**. The place soon became a major pilgrimage site and a staging post on the road to Santiago de Compostela in Spain. St Bernard, numerous kings of England and France and thousands of others crawled up the chapel steps on their knees to pay their respects and seek cures for their illnesses. Young King Henry, son of Henry II of England, was the first to plunder the shrine, but he was easily outclassed by the Huguenots, who tried in vain to burn the saint's corpse and finally resigned themselves simply to hacking it to bits. A reconstruction was produced in the nineteenth century, in an attempt to revive the flagging pilgrimage.

## Chapelle Notre-Dame

Rocamadour is easy enough to find your way around. There's just one street, rue de la Couronnerie, strung out between two medieval gateways. Above it, the steep hillside supports no fewer than seven churches. There's a lift dug into the rock face (€2.60 single, €4.20 return), but it's far better to climb the 233 steps of the Via Sancta, up which the devout drag themselves on their knees, to the little **Chapelle Notre-Dame** where the miracle-working twelfth-century Black Madonna resides. The tiny, crudely carved walnut statue glows in the mysterious half-light, but the rest of the chapel is unremarkable. From the rock above the entrance door hangs a rusty sword, supposedly Roland's legendary blade, Durandal.

## The ramparts

Daily 8am–7pm • €2

Just east of the Chapelle Notre-Dame you can either hop in a lift (€4.20 return) or take a winding, shady path, *Le Calvaire*, past the Stations of the Cross, to the top of the hill, where you can walk around the ancient **ramparts** and enjoy vertiginous views across the valley.

## Gouffre de Padirac

20km east of Rocamadour • Daily 90min guided tours: April–June 9.30am–6.30pm; July 9am–8.30pm; Aug 8am–9.30pm; Sept & Oct 9.30am–5.30pm • €13.50 • ☎ 05 65 33 64 56, ⌨ gouffre-de-padirac.com

An enormous limestone sinkhole, about 100m deep and more than 100m wide, the **Gouffre de Padirac** gives access to an underground river network containing some spectacular rock formations and magical lakes, and is very, very popular. Visits are partly on foot, partly by boat, and in wet weather you'll need a waterproof jacket. It's advisable to book online in advance in the height of summer, which will allow you to jump the invariably long queue, and to check opening hours as they can change from day to day.

### ARRIVAL AND INFORMATION — ROCAMADOUR AND AROUND

**By car** Getting to Rocamadour without your own transport is awkward. The best place to park is in L'Hospitalet, on the hilltop above Rocamadour (which has the best view of the town).

**By train** Rocamadour-Padirac *gare SNCF* on the Brive–Capdenac line is 3km from Rocamadour; it's a fairly straightforward walk along the main road (D673), or you can call a taxi (☎ 06 86 18 71 55).

Destinations Brive-la-Gaillarde (7 daily; 40min); Figeac (6 daily; 36min); Turenne (2 daily; 25min).

**Tourist office** There are two tourist offices (☎ 05 65 33 22 00, ⌨ vallee-dordogne.com): the main one in L'Hospitalet (April–June, Sept & Oct daily 10am–12.30pm & 2–5pm; July & Aug daily 9.30am–7pm), and a second next to the *hôtel de ville*, on rue de la Couronnerie (April–June, Sept & Oct daily 10am–12.30pm & 2–5pm; July & Aug daily 9.30am–7pm; Nov–March daily 10am–noon & 2–5pm).

### ACCOMMODATION

Rocamadour's hotels close for the winter, and you need to book early in summer.

**Beau Site** Rue de la Couronnerie ☎ 05 65 33 63 08, ⌨ bestwestern-beausite.com. Rocamadour's most luxurious hotel, in the heart of the village, offers surprisingly unexciting rooms in a beautiful old building; more modern rooms are on offer in the annex. The sunny, tucked-away terrace is a real bonus, and guests can use the pool at its sister hotel *Bellaroc*, located 1km away. Closed mid-Nov to Easter. €105

**Belvédère** L'Hospitalet ☎ 05 65 33 63 25, ⌨ hotel-le-belvedere.fr. Though you're not in the medieval city here, you can benefit from some of the most fabulous views of it from a number of the bedrooms and the restaurant at this modern hotel. Like *Beau Site*, guests can also use the pool at

the nearby *Bellaroc* hotel. Closed mid-Nov to Easter. **€73**
**Le Troubadour** Belveyre, on the D763, 1km north of L'Hospitalet ☎05 65 33 70 27, ⊛hotel-troubadour. com. It's worth staying outside of the medieval city at the charming *Troubadour*, set among expansive grounds. With just ten rooms in the eighteenth-century farmhouse, it has a homely feel, and there's a swimming pool and a restaurant (eves only; *menu* €33) on site. **€90**

### EATING AND DRINKING

**Les Jardins de la Louve** Far end of rue de la Couronnerie ☎05 65 33 62 93. At the quieter end of the main street, this pleasant restaurant is one of the more appealing in town, with both a shady terrace and a lovely garden. The *plat du jour* is good value at €12.50, and lighter dishes are also on offer. Closed mid-Nov to Easter. Daily noon–2pm & 7–9pm.

**Le Jehan de Valon** Rue de la Couronnerie ☎05 65 33 63 08, ⊛bestwestern-beausite.com. The *Beau Site*'s gourmet restaurant provides fabulous views over the valley from its terrace, and serves up seasonal, local dishes like Quercy lamb with a white bean casserole. Closed Nov to mid-Feb. *Menus* from €27. Daily 12.15–2pm & 7.15–9pm.

## Gourdon

**GOURDON** lies between Sarlat and Cahors, conveniently served by the Brive–Toulouse train line, and makes a quiet, agreeable base for visiting some of the major places in this part of the Dordogne and Lot. It's 17km south of the River Dordogne and pretty much at the eastern limit of the luxuriant woods and valleys of Périgord, which give way quite suddenly, at the line of the N20, to the arid limestone landscape of the **Causse de Gramat**.

It is a striking town, its medieval centre of yellow-stone houses attached like a swarm of bees to a prominent hilltop, neatly ringed by modern boulevards containing all the commerce. The main street through the old town, with a fortified **gateway** at one end, is rue du Majou. It's lined all the way up with splendid stone houses, some, like the **Maison du Sénéchal** at no. 17, dating back to the fourteenth century and extended during the sixteenth. At the top you emerge into a lovely, intimate square in front of the massive but not particularly interesting fourteenth-century **church of St-Pierre**. From the square, steps climb to the top of the hill, where the castle once stood and from where there is a superb view stretching for miles.

### ARRIVAL AND INFORMATION
GOURDON

**By train** The station is roughly 1km northeast of the centre; from the station, walk south on avenue de la Gare, then turn right onto avenue Gambetta to reach the boulevard encircling the old town. Destinations Brive-la-Gaillarde (8 daily; 40min); Cahors (8 daily; 26min); Montauban (6 daily; 1hr 10min); Souillac (8 daily; 15min); Toulouse (6 daily; (1hr 45min).

**Tourist office** 20 bd des Martyrs (March–June, Sept & Oct Mon–Sat 9.30am–noon & 2–6pm; July & Aug Mon–Sat 9.30am–7pm, Sun 9.30am–12.30pm; Nov–Feb Mon–Sat 10am–noon & 2–5pm; ☎05 65 27 52 50, ⊛tourisme-gourdon.com).

### ACCOMMODATION AND EATING

**Hostellerie de la Bouriane** Place du Foirail ☎05 65 41 16 37, ⊛hotellabouriane.fr. A smart, traditional hotel, with comfortable rooms, though some are a little on the dark side. The restaurant is especially popular for Sunday lunch, with *menus* from €32. Restaurant May to mid-Oct Tues–Sat 7.30–8.45pm, Sun 12.15–1.30pm & 7.30–8.45pm; mid-Oct to April closed Sun eve. Closed mid-Jan to mid-March. **€82**
★ **La Métairie des Songes** Flagel, 4km south east of Gourdon ☎05 65 32 19 33, ⊛lametairie-gourdon.com.

This gorgeous B&B in an eighteenth-century farmhouse set in 3.5km of parkland is noted for its good food. The four elegant rooms are named after Impressionist painters and furnished with antiques. Don't miss the four-course dinner (€34). **€65**
★ **Le Pot Occitan** 39 bd Mainiol ☎05 65 41 11 81. A charming, relaxed restaurant, decorated with bright cushions and books on Americana, serving up simple, hearty dishes like the *formule du boucher* – sirloin steak, chips, salad and a generous slice of Cantal – for around €17. Daily 11.30am–3pm & 7–10pm.

## Les Arques

The exquisite hamlet of **LES ARQUES**, 27km southwest of Gourdon, is set among quiet, remote, small-scale farming country, emptied of people by the slaughter of the two world wars and by migration to the towns in search of jobs. The village itself is attractive, but notable mainly as the home of the Russian Cubist/Expressionist sculptor **Ossip Zadkine**, who bought an old house by the church here in 1934, and for its excellent restaurant (see below).

## Musée Zadkine

Tues–Sun: April–Oct 10.30am–12.30pm & 2.30–6.30pm; Oct–Dec & Feb–March 2–6pm • €3 • ☎ 05 65 22 83 37

Even if you've no real interest in the sculptor's work, Les Arques' **Musée Zadkine** is a fascinating stop, with a compelling collection of his statues. It's the ones in the basement that really steal the show, with *Orphée* taking pride of place; awe-inspiring in its size, this wood-carved sculpture appears to change as you view it from different sides, and the attention to detail is quite astounding.

## The church

Les Arques' small twelfth-century **church** is beautiful in its unadorned simplicity. Above the door, Zadkine's huge crucifixion works perfectly against the bare stone walls and the simple stained-glass windows, while in the tiny crypt, his *Pieta* has been created in such a way that the shading on the figures makes them appear almost two dimensional.

### EATING                                                                                LES ARQUES

★ **La Récréation** On the main road, as you enter the village ☎ 05 65 22 88 08, ⓦ la-recreation-restaurant.com. Set in the old village school, this wonderful restaurant serves up copious, delicious meals beneath the chestnut trees of the old school yard and in one of the converted classrooms (*menus* from €26). On a summer night, with the swifts flying overhead, it's idyllic. Reservations highly recommended. March–Oct Mon, Tues & Fri–Sun noon–1.30pm & 7.30–9.15pm.

# Cahors

**CAHORS**, on the River Lot, was the capital of the old province of Quercy. In its time, it has been a Gallic settlement; a Roman town; a briefly held Moorish possession; a town under English rule; a bastion of Catholicism in the Wars of Religion, sacked in consequence by Henri IV; a university town for 400 years; and birthplace of the politician Léon Gambetta (1838–82), after whom so many French streets and squares are named. Modern Cahors is a sunny southern backwater, with two interesting sights in its **cathedral** and the remarkable **Pont Valentré**. The city sits on a peninsula formed by a tight loop in the River Lot and is small and easily walkable.

While you're in the Cahors area, don't miss out on the local **wine**, heady and black but dry to the taste and not at all plummy like the Gironde wines from Blaye and Bourg, which use the same Malbec grape.

## Cathedral

Place Jean-Jacques-Chapou • 9am–noon & 2–7pm • St Gausbert's chapel closed to the public, though it is occasionally included on city tours – ask at the tourist office

Dominating the centre is the **Cathedral**, which, consecrated in 1119, is the oldest and simplest in plan of the Périgord-style churches. The exterior is not exciting: a heavy square tower dominates the plain west front, whose best feature is the north portal, where a Christ in Majesty dominates the tympanum, surrounded by angels and apostles, while cherubim fly out of the clouds to relieve him of his halo. Side panels show scenes from the life of St Stephen. The outer ring over the portal shows a line of naked figures being stabbed and hacked with axes.

Inside, the cathedral is much like Périgueux's St-Front, with a nave lacking aisles and transepts, roofed with two big domes; in the first are fourteenth-century frescoes of the stoning of St Stephen, while over the west door are faded but beautiful Creation scenes from the same era. To the right of the choir a door opens into a delicate **cloister** in the Flamboyant style, still retaining some intricate, though damaged, carving. On the northwest corner pillar the Virgin is portrayed as a graceful girl with broad brow and ringlets to her waist. In the cloister's northeast corner, **St Gausbert's chapel** holds the Holy Coif, a cloth said to have covered Christ's head in the tomb, which according to legend was brought back from the Holy Land in the twelfth century by Bishop Géraud de Cardaillac.

**10**

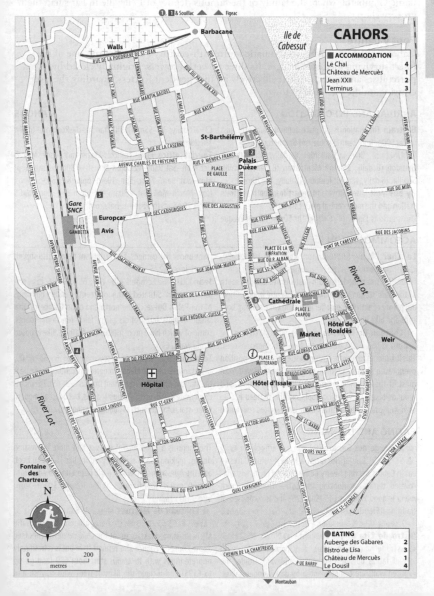

**10**

## The old town

The area around the cathedral is filled by a warren of narrow lanes, most of them now handsomely restored. Many of the houses, turreted and built of thin, flat brick, date from the fourteenth and fifteenth centuries. As you wander, look out for the many little "secret gardens" scattered around the town.

Immediately south of the cathedral, the lime-bordered **place Jean-Jacques-Chapou** commemorates a local trade unionist and Resistance leader, killed in a German ambush on July 17, 1944. Next to it is the covered **market** and a building still bearing the name Gambetta, where the family of the famous deputy of Belleville in Paris had their grocery shop.

## Pont Valentré

Cahors is best known for its dramatic fourteenth-century **Pont Valentré**, one of the finest surviving medieval bridges. Its three powerful towers, originally closed by portcullises and gates, made it effectively an independent fortress, guarding the river crossing on the west side of town.

## ARRIVAL AND INFORMATION CAHORS

**By train** The station is on place Jouinot-Gambetta, just under 500m from central boulevard Gambetta.

Destinations Brive-la-Gaillarde (8 daily; 1hr 10min); Gourdon (8 daily; 25min); Montauban (8 daily; 45min); Souillac (8 daily; 42min); Toulouse (8 daily; 1hr 20min).

**By bus** Most buses arrive and depart from both the train station and the more central place Lafayette.

Destinations Figeac (4–6 daily; 1hr 50min); Puy-l'Évêque (3–10 daily; 35–55min); Villefranche-de-Rouergue (daily; 1hr 25min).

**Tourist office** Place François-Mitterrand (April, May & Oct Mon–Sat 9am–12.30pm & 1.30–6.30pm; June–Sept Mon–Sat 9am–7pm, Sun 10am–6pm & 1.30–5.30pm; Nov–March Mon–Sat 9.30am–12.30pm & 2–6pm; ☎05 65 53 20 65, ⓦ tourisme-cahors.com).

## ACCOMMODATION

**Le Chai** 52 av André-Breton ☎05 36 04 00 80, ⓦ hifrance.org/auberge-de-jeunesse/cahors-le-chai. html. This smart modern youth hostel is situated just south of the train station, overlooking the Valentré bridge. There are plenty of activities on offer including wine tasting, boat trips and bike hire. €22.40

★ **Château de Mercuès** Mercuès, 8km northwest of Cahors ☎05 65 20 00 01, ⓦ chateaudemercues.com. This luxurious thirteenth-century castle has a prime position overlooking the Lot, with views of the river enjoyed from most of the charming rooms. The beautifully landscaped grounds boast a swimming pool, and the château has its own vineyard nearby, with an impressive vaulted cellar built

right under the gardens. The restaurant here is also superb (see below). €275

**Jean XXII** 2 rue Edmond-Albe ☎05 65 35 07 66, ⓦ hotel-jeanxxii.com. Situated in the fourteenth-century buildings of the Palais Duèze, at the north end of bd Gambetta, this small, friendly hotel offers plain, fairly functional rooms, some of which have more interesting features, like exposed stone walls. €75

**Terminus** 5 av Charles-de-Freycinet ☎05 65 53 32 00, ⓦ balandre.com. An elegant nineteenth-century house near the station, with a fine restaurant (*menus* €23–65). The rooms don't quite match up to the public areas, but boast all modern three-star comforts such as double-glazing and a/c. €75

## EATING AND DRINKING

★ **Auberge des Gabares** 24 place Champollion ☎05 65 53 91 47. One of the nicest and best-value places to eat in Cahors, serving hearty home cooking on its wisteria-covered terrace overlooking the Lot – the daily lunch *menu* is good value at €15 (Sun €26) and is composed of traditional French cuisine. Tues & Thurs–Sat noon–2pm & 7–9.30pm, Wed & Sun noon–2pm.

**Bistro de Lisa** 67 bd Gambetta ☎05 65 35 22 35, ⓦ bistrodelisa.com. A smart, very popular bistro, with lots of tables outside beside the boulevard. Inside, the exposed walls are complemented by dark wooden tables.

The menu is a good mix of classics and more interesting dishes, making use of regional produce like Limousin beef, and the *frites* alone are worth a trip here. Lunch *menus* from €14.90, *plat du jour* from €8.90. Mon–Sat 7.30am–1am, Sun 9am–1am.

★ **Château de Mercuès** Mercuès, 8km northwest of Cahors ☎05 65 20 00 01, ⓦ chateaudemercues.com. The Michelin-starred restaurant at the *Château de Mercuès* (see above) oozes elegance and refined style but is refreshingly unpretentious with it. *Menus* start from €89 (and go up to €195) and include the likes of trout with crayfish and mushrooms, with a hibiscus and nettle sauce. Be sure to keep room for the impressive cheese selection. Tues–Sat 7.15–9.30pm, Sun noon–1.30pm.

**Le Dousil** 124 rue Nationale ☎ 05 65 53 19 67. A small, cosy wine bar that's a great place to sample local wines, alongside plates of cheese and meat (from €8.90), or more substantial dishes like cassoulet (from €16.40). Mon, Tues & Sun 6.30–10.30pm, Wed–Sat 11am–2pm & 6.30pm–10.30pm.

## St-Cirq-Lapopie

The pale stone houses of **ST-CIRQ-LAPOPIE**, staggered down the steep hillside above the south bank of the Lot, appear almost fairy-tale-like as you approach from the east. The village was saved from ruin when poet André Breton came to live here in the early twentieth century, and though it's now an irresistible draw for the tour buses, with its cobbled lanes, half-timbered houses and flower-strewn balconies, it's still well worth a visit, especially early or late in the day, when the buildings glow in the sunlight. From behind the tourist office (see below), a steep path leads up to the top of the cliff, once the site of the town's château, for commanding views over the river valley.

10

### ARRIVAL AND INFORMATION                              ST-CIRQ-LAPOPIE

**By bus** The only way to get to St-Cirq-Lapopie by public transport is by bus from Cahors to Tour-de-Faure (3–5 daily; 40–50min), from where it's a steep 2km walk up the hill.

**Tourist office** Place du Sombral (daily: April, May & Oct 10am–1pm & 2–6pm; June & Sept 10am–6pm; July & Aug 10am–7pm; Nov–March 9.30am–12.30pm & 2–5pm; ☎ 05 65 31 31 31, ⊚ saint-cirqlapopie.co.uk).

### ACCOMMODATION AND EATING

**Auberge du Sombral** Place du Sombral ☎ 05 65 31 26 08, ⊚ lesombral.com. This attractive auberge on the village's main square offers charming, if somewhat plain, rooms with modern bathrooms, above a popular restaurant (*menus* from €19.80). Closed mid-Nov to March. Restaurant Sun–Thurs noon–2pm, Fri & Sat noon–2pm & 7–9pm. €60

**Camping de la Plage** ☎ 05 65 30 29 51, ⊚ camping plage.com. Down by the river, this well-run campsite has lovely pitches among the trees, and various activities on offer, including swimming, canoeing and horseriding. Closed Nov to March. €24

**Le Cantou** Below the church ☎ 05 65 35 59 03. With its cosy, stone-walled interior, this appealing restaurant is excellent value, with *menus* starting at €19 and surprisingly international dishes ranging from sesame duck *brochettes* to "Tex Mex"-style chicken. Mid-March to mid-Nov daily noon–2pm & 7–9pm.

**L'Oustal** Rue de la Pélissaria ☎ 05 65 31 20 17. A cute place tucked away just south of the church, with a handful of tables on an outside terrace, offering dishes such as trout *persillade* and rice (*menus* from €19). Easter to mid-Nov daily except Thurs noon–2pm & 7–9pm.

**Le Saint Cirq** Tour de Faure, opposite the village ☎ 05 65 30 30 30, ⊚ hotel-lesaintcirq.com. Though not in St-Cirq itself, there's no doubt that *Le Saint Cirq* boasts the best position, with fabulous views across to the village. Rooms are decked out in muted colours with tiled floors and rustic-chic furnishings, and the pool enables you to soak up more of those great panoramas. €118

## Downstream from Cahors

West of Cahors the vine-cloaked banks of the Lot are dotted with ancient villages. Of these, dramatic **Puy-l'Évêque** is served by SNCF buses that thread along the valley from Cahors to Monsempron-Libos, on the Agen–Périgueux train line. You'll need your own transport, however, to reach the splendid **Château de Bonaguil**, in the hills northwest of here, worth the effort for its elaborate fortifications and spectacular position. From here the Lot valley starts to get ugly and industrial; strike due west instead to **Monflanquin**, a *bastide* that is well worth a visit for its hilltop location and almost perfect arcaded central square.

### Puy-l'Évêque

**PUY-L'ÉVÊQUE** is probably the prettiest village in the entire valley, with many grand houses built in honey-coloured stone and overlooked by both a **church** and the **castle** of the bishops of Cahors. The best view is from the bridge across the Lot.

## ARRIVAL AND INFORMATION PUY-L'ÉVÊQUE

**By bus** Buses from Cahors (4–10 daily; 40min) depart from and arrive at place du Rampeau, on the main road at the top of the village, and place des Platanes, just east of *Hôtel Henry*.

**Tourist office** 12 Grand'Rue (April–June & Sept–Oct Mon–Fri 9.30am–12.30pm & 2–5pm, Sat 9.30am–12.30pm; July & Aug Mon–Fri 9.30am–6.30pm, Sat 9.30am–1pm & 3–6.30pm; Nov–March Mon–Fri 9.30am–12.30pm & 2–5pm, Sat 9.30am–12.30pm; ☎05 65 21 37 63, ⓦtourisme-lot-vignoble.com).

## ACCOMMODATION AND EATING

**Bellevue** Place de la Truffière ☎05 65 36 06 60, ⓦhotelbellevue-puyleveque.com. Perched on the cliff edge, this modern hotel has stylish rooms – some with a four-poster bed – and a good restaurant with panoramic views over the village and river (*menus* from €19.50). Restaurant Tues–Sun noon–1.30pm; Tues & Thus–Sat 7.30–9pm. **€76**

**Le Pigeonnier** Promenade du Héron ☎05 65 21 37 77. Situated directly across the river from the village, this simple crêperie boasts lovely views from its grassy terrace and serves *galettes* from €7 and large salads from €8.20. May–Sept Tues–Fri & Sun noon–2pm & 7–9.30pm, Sat 7–9.30pm; Oct–April Fri & Sun noon–2pm & 7–9.30pm, Sat 7–9.30pm.

## Château de Bonaguil

16km northwest of Puy-l'Évêque • March–June, Sept & Oct daily 10am–5.30pm; July & Aug daily 10am–7pm; Nov–Feb during school holidays only daily 2–5pm • €9.50 • ☎05 53 41 90 71, ⓦchateau-bonaguil.com

The imposing **Château de Bonaguil** is spectacularly perched on a wooded spur. Dating largely from the fifteenth and sixteenth centuries, with a double ring of walls, five huge towers and a narrow boat-shaped keep designed to resist artillery, Bonaguil was the last of a dying breed, completed just when military architects were abandoning such elaborate fortifications. As it attracts around two thousand visitors a day during summer, it's advisable to get here early.

## Monflanquin

The pretty village of **MONFLANQUIN**, founded by Alphonse de Poitiers in 1256, is one of the region's perfectly preserved *bastides*, not too touristy and impressively positioned on the top of a hill that rises sharply from the surrounding country. It conforms to the regular pattern of right-angled streets leading from a central square to the four town gates. The square – **place des Arcades** – with its distinctly Gothic houses, derives a special charm from being tree-shaded on a slope.

### Musée des Bastides

Place des Arcades • April–June & Sept–Oct Mon–Sat 9.30am–12.30pm; July & Aug daily 9.30am–1pm • €4 • ☎05 53 36 40 19, ⓦmonflanquin-museedesbastides.com

The surprisingly high-tech little **Musée des Bastides**, above the tourist office, details the life and history of *bastides*. Most of the information is in English, and the various models bring the *bastides* to life; children in particular will enjoy the more hands-on aspects of the exhibition.

## ARRIVAL AND INFORMATION MONFLANQUIN

**By car** Parking is available at the top of the *bastide*, and halfway up the hill.

**Tourist office** Place des Arcades (April–June & Sept Mon & Wed–Sat 9.30am–12.30pm & 2–5pm, Tues 9.30am–12.30pm; July & Aug daily 9.30am–1pm & 2–6pm; Oct–March Wed, Fri & Sat 9.30am–12.30pm & 2–5pm, Thurs 9.30am–12.30pm; ☎05 53 36 40 19, ⓦcoeurdesbastides.com).

## ACCOMMODATION AND EATING

⭐ **La Bastide** Place des Arcades ☎05 53 36 77 05. This friendly little crêperie, decked out with old signs and potted plants, has tables outside on the shady terrace – grab one facing down the hill for views over the countryside. The *formule* is good value at €12, and *galettes* start from €6.50.

Tues, Wed, Fri & Sat noon–11pm, Thurs 11am–11pm, Sun noon–3pm.

**Les Bourdeaux** 3km south of Monflanquin ☎05 53 49 16 57, ⓦlesbourdeaux.com. Just a short drive from Monflanquin, this gorgeous old blue-shuttered farmhouse has been turned into a welcoming *chambre d'hôte* by its Dutch owners. The pick of the three rooms is Champagne, with its own terrace; the swimming pool has beautiful views of the countryside, and there's an outdoor kitchen and dining space for guests' use. €95

# Figeac

**FIGEAC**, on the River Célé, 71km east of Cahors, is a beautiful town with an unspoilt medieval centre not too encumbered by tourism. Like many other provincial towns hereabouts, it owes its beginnings to the foundation of an abbey in the early days of Christianity in France, one that quickly became wealthy because of its position on the pilgrim routes to both Rocamadour and Compostela. In the Middle Ages it became a centre of tanning, which partly accounts for why many houses' top floors have *solelhos*, or open-sided wooden galleries used for drying skins and other produce. It was the Wars of Religion that pushed it into eclipse, for Figeac sided with the nearby Protestant stronghold of Montauban and suffered the same punishing reprisals by the victorious royalists in 1662. The **church of St-Sauveur**, near the river, maintains its lovely Gothic chapterhouse decorated with heavily gilded but dramatically realistic seventeenth-century carved wood panels illustrating the life of Christ.

## Hôtel de la Monnaie and around

In the old town centre, the **Hôtel de la Monnaie** surveys place Vival. It's a splendid building dating back to the thirteenth century, when the city's mint was located in this district. In the streets radiating off to the north of the square there's a delightful range of houses of the medieval and classical periods, both stone and half-timbered, adorned with carvings and colonnettes and interesting ironwork. At the end of these streets are the two adjacent squares of **place Carnot** and **place Champollion**, both of great charm. The former is the site of the old *halles*, under whose awning cafés now spread their tables.

## Musée Champollion

Place Champollion • April–June, Sept & Oct Tues–Sun 10.30am–12.30pm & 2–6pm; July & Aug daily 10.30am–6.30pm; Nov–March Tues–Sun 2–5.30pm • €5 • ☎ 05 65 50 31 08, ⓦ musee-champollion.fr

Jean-François Champollion, who cracked Egyptian hieroglyphics by deciphering the triple text of the Rosetta Stone, was born at 4 impasse Champollion, just off place Champollion. The house now forms part of the excellent **Musée Champollion**, dedicated to the history of writing, from the very earliest cuneiform signs some 50,000 years ago. The most interesting exhibits relate to Champollion's life and work, including original manuscripts tracing his and others' progress towards cracking the hieroglyphs. Beside the museum, a larger-than-life reproduction of the Rosetta Stone forms the floor of the tiny **place des Écritures**, above which is a little garden planted with tufts of papyrus.

## ARRIVAL AND INFORMATION                                                          FIGEAC

**By train** The *gare SNCF* is a 5min walk to the south of the old town, across the river at the end of rue de la Gare and avenue des Poilus.

**Destinations** Brive-la-Gaillarde (6 daily; 1hr 40min); Cordes-Vindrac (6 daily; 1hr 46min); Najac (6 daily; 50min); Rocamadour-Padirac (6 daily; 35min); Toulouse (6 daily; 3hr); Turenne (4 daily; 1hr); Villefranche-de-Rouergue 6 daily; 35min).

**By bus** Buses arrive at and depart from the train station.

Destinations Cahors (4–6 daily; 1hr 40min); Gourdon (weekly; 1hr 40min); Rocamadour (weekly; 50min); Souillac (weekly; 1hr 15min); Villefranche-de-Rouergue (4–6 daily; 40min).

**Tourist office** Hôtel de la Monnaie, place Vival (April–June & Sept–Oct Mon–Sat 9am–12.30pm & 2–6pm (also Sun 10am–1pm June & Sept); July & Aug Mon–Sat 9am–6.30pm, Sun 10am–6.30pm; Nov–March Mon–Fri 10am–12.30pm & 2–6pm, Sat 10am–12.30pm & 2–5pm; ☎ 05 65 34 06 25, ⓦ tourisme-figeac.com).

## ACCOMMODATION

**Des Bains** 1 rue du Griffoul ☎ 05 65 34 10 89, ⓦ hotel desbains.fr. Just across the river from the old town, with lovely views from its restaurant terrace, in a building that used to house the town swimming baths. Rooms are light

10

and airy, if a little spartan. €56

**Champollion** 3 place Champollion ☎ 05 65 34 04 37. Small hotel on this bustling square, with smart rooms above a popular café-bar. Two have views over the square. €64

**La Domaine du Surgié** 2km east of Figeac ☎ 05 61 64 88 54, ⚲ domainedusurgie.com. This well-equipped riverside campsite has two pools (including water slides)

and is a great choice for families. Bikes and canoes for rent. Closed mid-Sept to mid-May. €26

**Le Quatorze** 14 place de l'Estang ☎ 05 65 14 08 92, ⚲ le-quatorze.fr. This lovely shuttered old building houses fourteen appealing bedrooms, the best of which have views over the old town. The courtyard garden is an extra bonus. €79

## 10

## EATING

**La Dînée du Viguier** 4 rue Boutaric ☎ 05 65 50 08 08, ⚲ ladineeduviguier.fr. This mid-range restaurant is in the atmospheric surrounds of the former guard room of the town's twelfth-century castle (now a four-star hotel). You can have a two-course lunch for €23.50 but splash out for the five-course chef's menu (€49), featuring creative versions of traditional French dishes using local produce. Tues–Fri noon–2pm & 7–9pm, Sat 7–9pm, Sun noon–2pm.

★ **La Mémé du Quercy** 1 place Vival ☎ 09 83 55 06 07. A very popular little place serving up tasty dishes (from €12)

made with the produce of twenty-three local artisans and farmers, whose goodies can be bought in the on-site shop. Delicious desserts and good wine too. Mon & Wed–Sun 9am–7pm.

**Pizzeria del Portel** 9 rue Orthabadial ☎ 05 65 34 53 60, ⚲ restaurant-delportel.net. A convivial pizzeria serving an extensive menu of pizzas, seasonal salad platters, *moules* and the like, with the benefit of outside seating (mains from €9). Tues–Sun noon–2pm & 7–10pm.

# Grotte de Pech-Merle

Cabrerets, 30km east of Cahors • Late March to June & Sept to mid-Nov daily 9.30am–noon & 1.30–5pm; July & Aug 9.15am–5pm • €13; visitors are limited to seven hundred per day – it's advisable to book ahead in July and Aug either by phone or online, three or four days ahead • ☎ 05 65 31 27 05, ⚲ pechmerle.com

Discovered in 1922, the **Grotte de Pech-Merle** is less accessible than the caves at Les Eyzies, well hidden on the scrubby hillsides above Cabrerets, which lies 15km from Marcilhac and 4km from Conduché. The cave itself is far more beautiful than those at Padirac or Les Eyzies, with galleries full of the most spectacular stalactites and stalagmites – structures tiered like wedding cakes, hanging like curtains, or shaped like discs or pearls.

The first **drawings** you come to are in the "Chapelle des Mammouths", executed on a white calcite panel that looks as if it's been specially prepared for the purpose. There are horses, bison – charging head down with tiny rumps and arched tails – and tusked, whiskery mammoths. Next comes a vast chamber where the glorious horse panel is visible on a lower level; it's remarkable how the artist used the relief of the rock to do the work, producing an utterly convincing mammoth in just two black lines. The ceiling is covered with finger marks, preserved in the soft clay. You pass the skeleton of a cave hyena that has been lying there for 20,000 years – wild animals used these caves for shelter and sometimes, unable to find their way out, starved to death. And finally, the most spine-tingling experience at Pech-Merle: the footprints of an adolescent preserved in a muddy pool.

The admission price includes an excellent film and **museum**, where prehistory is illustrated by colourful and intelligible charts, a selection of objects (rather than the usual ten thousand flints), skulls, and beautiful slides displayed in wall panels.

# The valley of the Aveyron

Thirty-odd kilometres south of Figeac, **Villefranche-de-Rouergue** lies on a bend in the River Aveyron, clustered around its perfectly preserved, arcaded market square. From here the Aveyron flows south through increasingly deep, thickly wooded valleys, past the hilltop village of **Najac**, and then turns abruptly west as it enters the **Gorges de l'Aveyron**. The most impressive stretch of this gorge begins just east of **St-Antonin-de-Noble-Val**, an ancient village caught between soaring limestone cliffs; from here, it's an easy trip to the dramatically sited village of **Cordes-sur-Ciel**, though it sits upon the Cérou, rather than the Aveyron.

## Villefranche-de-Rouergue

No medieval junketing, barely a craft shop in sight, VILLEFRANCHE-DE-ROUERGUE must be as close as you can get to what a French provincial town used to be like. It's a small place, lying on a bend in the Aveyron, 35km south of Figeac and 61km east of Cahors across the **Causse de Limogne**. Built as a *bastide* by Alphonse de Poitiers in 1252 as part of the royal policy of extending control over the recalcitrant lands of the south, the town became rich on copper from the surrounding mines and its privilege of minting coins. From the fifteenth to the eighteenth centuries, its wealthy residents built the magnificent houses that grace the cobbled streets to this day.

**10**

### Place Notre-Dame

Villefranche is home to one of the loveliest *bastide* squares in the region, **place Notre-Dame**. It's built on a slope and you enter at the corners underneath the buildings. All the houses are arcaded at ground-floor level, providing for a **market** (Thurs) where local merchants and farmers spread out their weekly produce – the quintessential Villefranche experience. The houses are unusually tall and some are very elaborately decorated, notably the so-called **Maison du Président Raynal** on the lower side at the top of rue de la République.

The square's east side is dominated by the **church of Notre-Dame** with its colossal porch and bell tower, nearly 60m high. The interior has some fine late fifteenth-century stained glass, carved choir stalls and misericords. On the boulevard that forms the northern limit of the old town, the seventeenth-century **Chapelle des Pénitents-Noirs** (bd de Haute Guyenne; April, May & Oct Tues–Sat 2–5pm; June & Sept daily 2–6pm; July & Aug daily 10.30am–1pm & 2–6pm; €4).

### Chartreuse St-Sauveur

1km out of town on the Gaillac road • April & May Tues–Sat 2–5pm; June daily 2–6pm; July & Aug daily 10.30am–6pm; Sept daily 10.30am–noon & 2–6pm; Oct Thurs–Sat 2–7pm • €5

The **Chartreuse St-Sauveur** was completed in the space of ten years from 1450, giving it a singular architectural harmony, and has a very beautiful cloister and choir stalls by the same master as Notre-Dame in Villefranche (which, by contrast, took nearly three hundred years to complete).

### ARRIVAL AND INFORMATION

### VILLEFRANCHE-DE-ROUERGUE

**By train** The *gare SNCF* lies a couple of minutes' walk south across the Aveyron from the old town and is served by regular trains to Figeac (6 daily; 35min) and Najac (6 daily; 15min).

**By bus** Buses pull in at the train station; those from Figeac also stop on the more central place de la Liberté.

Destinations Figeac (1–4 daily; 35min); Najac (Mon–Fri 1–3 daily; 45min).

**Tourist office** Promenade du Guiraudet (May, June & Sept Mon–Sat 9am–noon & 2–6pm; July & Aug Mon–Fri 9am–12.30pm & 2–7pm, Sat 9am–noon & 2–6pm, Sun 10am–12.30pm; Oct–April Mon–Fri 9am–noon & 2–5pm, Sat 9am–noon; ☏ 05 65 45 13 18, ⊕ tourisme-villefranche-najac.com).

### ACCOMMODATION

**Camping du Rouergue** 1.5km south of Villefranche on the D47 to Monteil ☏ 05 65 45 16 24, ⊕ campingdu rouergue.com. Attractive tree-shaded pitches, separated by hedges, plus a small swimming pool and children's playground. Closed Oct to mid-April. **€16**

★ **Les Fleurines** 17 bd Haute-Guyenne ☏ 05 65 45 86 90, ⊕ lesfleurines.com. Old and new come together at this striking hotel – the boulevard-facing entrance is all sleek lines and contemporary, while the opposite side, adjacent to the Chapelle des Pénitents-Noirs, boasts the original, beautifully restored brickwork of the old hospital that was originally housed here. The modern rooms are decorated in calming whites and greys, and there's also a number of apartments available. **€89**

**Les Terrasses de la Maison Pago** 29 rue Montlauzeur ☏ 05 65 81 59 26, ⊕ maisonpago.fr. An old canning factory has been stylishly converted into *chambres d'hôtes*, in a great position in the old town. There are three individually decorated rooms, and the real bonus are the two terraces, one of which affords views over the orange-tiled roofs of the town. **€86**

## EATING AND DRINKING

**L'Assiette Gourmande** Place André-Lescure ☎ 05 65 45 25 95. One of the best places to eat in town, *L'Assiette* specializes in local cuisine (*menus* from €15), such as a delicious salad of foie gras and smoked duck breast. Mon, Fri–Sat noon–1.30pm & 7.30–9pm, Tues, Thurs & Sun noon–1.30pm.

**Côté Saveurs** 5 rue Belle-Isle ☎ 05 65 65 83 64, ☞ cote-saveurs.fr. Elegant, inventive food is served at this modern gastronomic restaurant, with the menu changing seasonally. *Menus* start at a very good value €23, and the beautifully presented food might include the likes of veal carpaccio or hake with risotto. Tues–Sat noon–1.30pm & 7.30–8.30pm.

## Najac

**NAJAC** occupies an extraordinary site on a conical hill isolated in a wide bend in the deep valley of the Aveyron, 25km south of Villefranche-de-Rouergue. Its magnificent **castle**, which graces many a travel poster, sits right on the peak of the hill, while the half-timbered and stone-tiled village houses tail out in a single street along the narrow back of the spur that joins the hill to the valley side.

### Najac château

Daily: April–June & Sept–Oct 10.30am–1pm & 3–5.30pm; July & Aug 10.30am–7pm • €5.50 • ☞ 05 65 29 71 65

Najac's **château** is a model of medieval defensive architecture and was endlessly fought over because of its impregnable position in a region once rich in silver and copper mines. In one of the chambers of the keep are sculpted portraits of St Louis, king of France, his brother Alphonse de Poitiers and Jeanne, the daughter of the count of Toulouse, whose marriage to Alphonse was arranged in 1229 to end the Cathar wars by bringing the domains of Count Raymond and his allies under royal control. It was Alphonse who "modernized" the castle and made the place we see today – a model in one of the turrets shows his fortifications as they were in the castle's prime in 1253. The main reason to visit, however, is the magnificent all-round view from the top of the keep, a full 200m above the river.

### Church of St-Jean

April–Sept daily 10am–noon & 2–6pm; Oct Sun 10am–noon & 2–6pm • Free

In the centre of what was the medieval village, at the foot of the castle, stands the sturdy **church of St-Jean**, which the villagers of Najac were forced by the Inquisition to build at their own expense in 1258 as a punishment for their conversion to Catharism. In addition to a collection of reliquaries and an extraordinary iron cage for holding candles, the church has one architectural oddity: its windows are solid panels of stone from which the lights have been cut out in trefoil form.

## ARRIVAL AND INFORMATION                                                           NAJAC

**By train** The train station is on the other side of the river from the village, 2km by road.
Destinations Figeac (6 daily; 51min); Villefranche-de-Rouergue (6 daily; 15min).
**By bus** The daily bus from Villefranche-de-Rouergue (Mon–Fri 1–3 daily; 35min) arrives at and departs from

place du Faubourg.
**Tourist office** 25 place du Faubourg (May, June & Sept Mon–Sat 9.30am–12.30pm & 2–6pm, Sun 9.30am–12.30pm; July & Aug daily 9.30am–6.30pm; Oct–April Tues–Sat 10am–12.30pm & 2–5pm; ☎ 05 65 29 72 05, ☞ tourisme-villefranche-najac.com).

## ACCOMMODATION AND EATING

**L'Oustal del Barry** 2 place Sol-del-Barry ☎ 05 65 29 74 32, ☞ oustaldelbarry.com. This very comfortable hotel has simple but warmly decorated rooms, with solid wood furnishings; the best room has a balcony with wonderful panoramic views of the château and countryside. Its restaurant is renowned for its subtle and inventive cuisine

(*menus* from €21). Restaurant mid-March to Oct daily 12.30–1.45pm & 7.15–8.45pm; Nov & Dec Mon–Tues & Thurs–Sun 12.30–1.45pm. Closed Nov–March. **€65**
**Tartines & Campagne** 31 rue du Bourguet ☎ 05 65 29 57 47. A sweet little café on the way to the château, with a streetside terrace that enjoys views over the countryside, serving light dishes like *croque monsieur* (€8) and salads (from €8.50). April–Oct Mon–Wed 10.30am–5.30pm, Fri–Sun 10.30am–10.30pm.

## St-Antonin-Noble-Val

One of the finest and most substantial towns in the valley is **ST-ANTONIN-NOBLE-VAL**, 30km southwest of Najac. It sits on the bank of the Aveyron beneath the beetling cliffs of the Roc d'Anglars and has endured all the vicissitudes of the old towns of the southwest: it went Cathar, then Protestant, and each time was walloped by the alien power of the kings from the north. Yet, in spite of all this, it recovered its prosperity, manufacturing cloth and leather goods, and was endowed by its wealthy merchants with a marvellous heritage of medieval houses in all the streets leading out from the lovely **place de la Halle**. It's on this square that you'll find the town's finest building, the **Maison des Consuls**, whose origins go back to 1125.

### ARRIVAL AND INFORMATION　　　　　　　　　　　　　ST-ANTONIN-NOBLE-VAL

**By bus** Buses to and from Montauban (1–2 daily; 1hr) stop on avenue Paul-Benet, to the north of the old town.
**Tourist office** Place de la Mairie (March & Oct Mon 2–5.30pm, Tues–Sat 10am–12.30pm & 2–5.30pm, Sun 10am–1pm; April Mon–Sat 9.30am–12.30pm & 2–6pm, Sun 9.30am–1pm; May–June & Sept Mon–Sat 9.30am–12.30pm & 2–6pm, Sun 9.30am–1pm & 2–5pm; July & Aug daily 9am–1pm & 2–7pm; Nov–Feb Mon & Sat 2–5pm, Tues–Fri 10am–12.30pm & 2–5pm; ☎ 05 63 30 63 47, ⓦ tourisme-saint-antonin-noble-val.com).

### ACCOMMODATION AND EATING

**Café de la Halle** 9 place de la Halle ☎ 05 63 30 61 74, ⓦ café-bar-saintantonin.fr. This sweet, simple café on the market square is the nicest spot in St Antonin to sit with a drink, with ample seating on the cobblestones under the shade of a tree. Daily 7.30am–midnight.
**La Résidence** 37 rue Droite ☎ 05 63 67 37 56, ⓦ laresidence-france.com. Smart and welcoming, and arguably the best *chambre d'hôte* in St-Antonin. Rooms are large and airy, pick of which is La Tulipe, which has its own roof terrace. **€115**
**La Table d'Antoine** 5 place Payrols ☎ 05 63 26 02 07. This attractive tearoom serves breakfast, lunch and dinner, with the plat du jour at €8. Regulars come here for the cakes, such as bergamot cheesecake (€5). Mon & Wed 9am–5.30pm, Thurs–Sun 9am–9.30pm.

## Cordes-sur-Ciel

**CORDES-SUR-CIEL**, perched on a conical hill 25km southeast of St-Antonin, is one of the region's must-see sights. Founded in 1222 by Raymond VII, Count of Toulouse, it was a **Cathar** stronghold, and the ground beneath the town is riddled with tunnels for storage and refuge in time of trouble. As one of the southwest's oldest and best-preserved *bastides*, complete with thirteenth- and fourteenth-century houses climbing steep cobbled lanes, Cordes is inevitably a major tourist attraction: medieval banners flutter in the streets and artisans practise their crafts, giving it, at times, the feel of an open-air museum. When the mist rolls into the valley below, it's not hard to see why the town was given the suffix "sur-Ciel" – or, "in the sky".

The main pleasure of visiting Cordes is in wandering the streets up to the top of the hill, from where you can enjoy – on clear days – fabulous views over the surrounding countryside. There are a handful of museums, including the **Musée Charles-Portal**, 1 rue Saint-Michel (April–May & Sept to mid-Nov Fri–Sun 2.30–6pm; June–Aug Mon & Wed–Sun 2.30–6.30pm; €3; ⓦ museecharlesportal.fr), which recounts the history of the town, and the **Musée d'Art Moderne et Contemporain** (mid-March to mid-Nov daily except Tues 10am–12.30pm & 2–6pm; €4; ☎ 05 63 56 14 79, ⓦ mamc. cordessurciel.fr), which is set in the beautiful fourteenth-century Maison du Grand Fauconnier and features works by the figurative painter Yves Brayer, who lived here from 1940.

## ARRIVAL AND INFORMATION

**By train** The nearest station is at Cordes-Vindrac, 5km west of town; it takes about an hour to walk to Cordes itself, or you can request a pick-up by shuttle bus (☎ 05 63 56 14 80). Destinations Figeac (4–6 daily; 1hr 20min); Najac (4–6 daily; 45min); Toulouse (4–6 daily; 1hr 5min); Villefranche (4–6 daily; 45min).

**By bus** Bus #707 from Albi stops at "La Bouteillerie" at the foot of the town near Porte de l'Horloge (3–5 daily; 40min).

**Tourist information** Maison Gaugiran, 38–42 rue Raimond-VII (April–June, Sept & Oct Mon 2–6pm; Tues–Sat 10.30am–12.30pm & 2–6pm, Sun 10.30am–12.30pm & 2–5pm; July & Aug Mon–Sat 9.30am–1pm & 2–6.30pm, Sun 10am–1pm & 2–6pm; Nov–March Mon–Sat 10.30am–12.30pm & 2–4pm, Sun 2–5pm; ☎ 05 63 56 00 52, ⊛ cordessurciel.fr).

## ACCOMMODATION AND EATING

**L'Escuelle des Chevaliers** 87 Grande Rue Raimond-VII ☎ 09 66 86 14 40, ⊛ lescuelledeschevaliers.fr. This medieval restaurant, complete with costumed waiters and original dishes such as pork with ginger accompanied by pea puree (*menu* €20), is a cut above your usual theme restaurants. As a result, it gets booked up, so you'll need to reserve in advance. They also do B&B (year round). Restaurant April–Oct Mon–Sat noon–2pm & 7–9pm, Sun noon–2pm. **€72**

**Hostellerie du Vieux Cordes** 21 rue St-Michel ☎ 05 63 53 79 20, ⊛ hotelcordes.fr. A sweet – if a little old-fashioned – hotel in town, with the nicest of the rooms boasting features like exposed stone walls and views over the countryside. The atmospheric restaurant offers *menus* from €16.50. Restaurant Tues–Sun noon–2pm & 7–9pm. **€68**

★ **Le Secret du Chat** 16 Le Planol ☎ 06 95 48 18 10, ⊛ chambres-cordes-tarn-charme-lesecretduchat.com. Arguably the most atmospheric place to stay in Cordes is this charming B&B, tastefully decorated with interesting antique finds. Dinner is available for guests throughout the year, with advance notice. **€120**

# Montauban

The prosperous, provincial city of **MONTAUBAN** is capital of the largely agricultural *département* of Tarn-et-Garonne. It lies on the banks of the River Tarn, 53km from Toulouse, close to its junction with the Aveyron and their joint confluence with the Garonne. With an attractive old centre, interesting shops, some great places to eat, and a laidback feel, it makes a particularly pleasant base for a few days. The greatest delight is simply to wander the streets of the compact city centre, with their lovely pink-brick houses.

The city's **history** goes back to 1144, when the count of Toulouse decided to found a *bastide* here as a bulwark against English and French royal power. In fact, it's generally regarded as the first *bastide*, and that plan is still clearly evident in the old city centre.

Montauban has enjoyed periods of great prosperity, as one can guess from the proliferation of fine townhouses. The first followed the suppression of the Cathar heresy and the final submission of the counts of Toulouse in 1229, and was greatly enhanced by the building of the Pont-Vieux in 1335, which made it the best crossing-point on the Tarn in these parts. The Hundred Years' War did its share of damage, as did Montauban's opting for the Protestant cause in the Wars of Religion, but by the time of the Revolution it had become once more one of the richest cities in the southwest, particularly successful in the manufacture of cloth.

## Place Nationale

Montauban's finest feature is **place Nationale**, the *bastide*'s central square, which was rebuilt after a fire in the seventeenth century and is surrounded on all sides by exquisite double-vaulted arcades with the octagonal belfry of St-Jacques showing above the western rooftops.

## Church of St-Jacques

Rue de la République

First built in the thirteenth century on the pilgrim route to Compostela, the **church of St-Jacques** is a much more atmospheric prospect than the cathedral (see page 582).

Inside, the church is dark and in need of repair, but its varying murals are testament to the fact that it was added to up until the eighteenth century.

## Musée Ingres

19 rue de l'Hôtel-de-Ville • The museum is closed for renovation until the end of 2019 • ☎ 05 63 22 12 91, ⓦ museeingres.montauban.com

The former bishop's residence is now the **Musée Ingres**, based on a collection of drawings and paintings that artist Jean-Auguste-Dominique Ingres, a native of Montauban, left to the city on his death. The museum also contains a substantial collection of sculptures by another native, Émile-Antoine Bourdelle. While the museum is undergoing renovation, some of its collection will be on show at the **Chapelle de l'Ancien Collège** (1 rue du Collège; April–June & Oct daily 10am–noon & 2–6pm; July–Sept daily 10am–6pm; Nov–March Mon–Sat 10am–noon & 2–6pm, Sun 2–6pm; free).

## Cathédrale Notre-Dame

Place Notre-Dame

The **Cathédrale Notre-Dame** is a cold fish: an austere and unsympathetic building erected just before 1700 as part of the triumphalist campaign to reassert the glories of the Catholic faith after the cruel defeat and repression of the Protestants. Apart from being a rare example of a French cathedral built in the classical style, its most interesting features are the statues of the four evangelists that triumphantly adorn the facade. Those on show now are recent copies, but the weather-beaten originals can be seen just inside.

### ARRIVAL AND INFORMATION
MONTAUBAN

**By train** The *gare SNCF* is southeast of the old town, across the river on avenue Roger-Salengro.
Destinations Bordeaux (9 daily; 2hr); Brive-la-Gaillarde (7 daily; 3hr 11min); Cahors (8 daily; 42min); Gourdon (7–9 daily; 1hr 10min); Moissac (4–6 daily; 20min); Souillac (7–9 daily; 1hr 30min); Toulouse (16 daily; 30min).

**Tourist office** 4 rue du Collège (May, June, Sept & Oct Mon–Sat 9.30am–12.30pm & 2–6.30pm; July & Aug Mon–Sat 9.30am–6.30pm, Sun 10am–12.30pm; Nov to April Mon–Sat Mon–Sat 9.30am–12.30pm & 1.30–6pm; ☎ 05 63 63 60 60, ⓦ montauban-tourisme.com).

### ACCOMMODATION

**Abbaye des Capucins** 6–8 quai de Verdun ☎ 05 63 22 00 00, ⓦ hotel-montauban-restaurant-spa-reunion. com. The most atmospheric place to stay in town is this luxury hotel in a former abbey, which dates back to the seventeenth century. Despite lots of original features, the overall feel is surprisingly modern; it also benefits from an outdoor pool. **€108**

**Du Commerce** 9 place Roosevelt ☎ 05 63 66 31 32, ⓦ hotel-commerce-montauban.com. This is next to the cathedral, and has small, simply furnished rooms; the buffet breakfast (€9) is good value. **€60**

**Mercure** 12 rue Notre-Dame ☎ 05 63 63 17 23, ⓦ mercure.com. Chain hotel in an eighteenth-century building opposite the cathedral offering large rooms and four-star services, as well as a reasonably priced restaurant. **€81**

### EATING

★ **Crumble Tea** 25 rue de la République ☎ 05 63 20 39 43. A delightful little teashop crammed with tea miscellanea (much of it for sale), in a small courtyard off rue de la République. There's an excellent array of home-made cakes (from €3.50), plus a good-value lunch *menu* (€11.50). Mon–Sat 10am–6pm.

★ **Le Ventadour** 2 quai Villebourbon ☎ 05 63 63 34 58, ⓦ le-ventadour.com. In the atmospheric surrounds of a seventeenth-century former coaching inn next to the river, this "gastro-bistrot" serves good traditional French cuisine for a ridiculously reasonable price (three-course *menu* €15.90). Mon–Fri noon–2pm.

# Moissac

**MOISSAC**, 30km northwest of Montauban, is remarkable only for its beautiful Romanesque abbey church. The town suffered terrible damage during the flood of

March 1930, when the Tarn, swollen by a sudden thaw in the Massif Central, burst its banks, destroying 617 houses and killing 120 people. The modern town is rather bland, in great contrast to the outstanding church and its cloister, which has made Moissac a household name in the history of art.

## Abbey church of St-Pierre

Place Durand-de-Bredon • Daily: April–June & Oct 10am–noon & 2–6pm; July–Sept 10am–7pm; Nov–March 2–5pm • €6.50

The cloister and porch of the **abbey church of St-Pierre** is a supreme masterpiece of Romanesque sculpture. Indeed, the fact that it has survived numerous wars, including siege and sack by Simon de Montfort senior in 1212 during the crusade against the Cathars, is something of a miracle. During the Revolution it was used as a gunpowder factory and billet for soldiers, who damaged many of the sculptures. In the 1830s it only escaped demolition to make way for the Bordeaux–Toulouse train line by a whisker.

Legend has it that Clovis the Frank first founded a monastery here, though it seems more probable that its origins belong in the seventh century, which saw the foundation of so many monasteries throughout Aquitaine. The first Romanesque church on the site was consecrated in 1063 and enlarged in the following century. The famous south **porch**, with its magnificent tympanum and curious wavy door jambs and pillars, dates from this second phase of building, and its influence can be seen in the decoration of porches on countless churches across the south of France. It depicts Christ in Majesty, surrounded by the evangelists and the elders of the Apocalypse as described by St John in the Book of Revelation. There's more fine carving in the capitals inside the porch, and the interior of the church, which was remodelled in the fifteenth century, is interesting too, especially for some of the wood and stone statuary it contains.

## The abbey cloister

The **cloister** adjoining the abbey is at its most peaceful first thing in the morning. It surrounds a garden shaded by a majestic cedar, and its pantile roof is supported by 76 alternating single and double marble columns. Each column supports a single inverted wedge-shaped block of stone, on which are carved with extraordinary delicacy all manner of animals and plant motifs, as well as scenes from Bible stories and the lives of the saints.

### ARRIVAL AND INFORMATION                                    MOISSAC

**By train** The train station is just over 500m southwest of the abbey church.
Destinations Montauban (4–6 daily; 20min); Toulouse (5–7 daily; 1hr 5min).
**Tourist office** 1 bd de Brienne (April–June & Oct Mon–Sat

9am–noon & 2–6pm, Sun 10am–1pm & 3–6pm; July & Aug daily 9am–7pm; Sept daily 9am–6pm; Nov–March Mon 2–5pm, Tues–Sat 10am–noon & 2–5pm; ☎05 32 09 69 36, ⑩ tourisme-moissac-terresdesconfluences.fr).

### ACCOMMODATION AND EATING

★ **Moulin de Moissac** ☎05 63 32 88 88, ⑩ www. lemoulindemoissac.com. Occupying a large, not particularly attractive former mill on the river, Moissac's top hotel has lovely, atmospheric rooms, many with bare stone walls and river views, and an excellent spa on site. The restaurant has a wonderful riverside terrace, with *menus* from €20. Restaurant Mon–Fri & Sun noon–2pm & 7.30–9.30pm, Sat 7.30–9.30pm. **€120**

★ **Le Pigeonnier** 4 rue Poumel ☎09 51 38 79 92. On the eastern outskirts of town, this old pigeonnier is now a quirky restaurant with a lovely outdoor terrace. There's no menu; diners eat, at a communal table, whatever the chef prepares. There's usually a good selection of vegetarian dishes, and live music on Saturday evenings. Booking is advised. *Menus* from €15. Tues–Fri 11.30am–2.30pm, Sat 6.30–10.30pm.

# The Pyrenees

**586** The Pays Basque

**600** The Central Pyrenees

**615** The Eastern Pyrenees

THE CIRQUE DE GAVARNIE, "NATURE'S COLOSSEUM"

# The Pyrenees

Basque-speaking, wet and green in the west; craggy, snowy, Gascon-influenced in the middle; dry, Mediterranean and Catalan-speaking in the east – the Pyrenees are physically beautiful, culturally varied and less developed than the Alps. The whole range is marvellous walkers' country, especially the central region around the Parc National des Pyrénées, with its 3000-metre-high peaks, streams, forests and wildlife. If you're a committed hiker, it's possible to traverse these mountains, usually from the Atlantic to the Mediterranean, along the GR10.

**11**

As for the more conventional tourist attractions, the **Côte Basque** – peppered with fun-loving towns like **Bayonne** and **Biarritz** – is lovely, sandy but very popular, and suffers from seaside sprawl and a surfeit of caravan-colonized campsites. The foothill towns are on the whole rather dull, although **Pau** merits at least a day, while monstrously kitsch **Lourdes** has to be seen whether you're a devout pilgrim or not. **Roussillon** in the east, focused on busy **Perpignan**, has beaches every bit as popular as those of the Côte Basque, some nestled into the compact coves of its southern rocky coast, while its interior consists of craggy terrain split by spectacular canyons and sprouting a crop of fine Romanesque abbeys and churches – **St-Michel-de-Cuixà**, **St-Martin-du-Canigou** and **Serrabona** being the most dramatic – and a landscape bathed in Mediterranean light. Finally, the sun-drenched foothills just to the northwest harbour the famous **Cathar castles**, legacies of the once-independent and ever-rebellious inhabitants of southwestern Languedoc.

# The Pays Basque

The three **Basque provinces** – Labourd (Lapurdi), Basse Navarre (Behe Nafarroa) and Soule (Zuberoa) – share with their Spanish neighbours a common language – Euskera – and a strong sense of identity. The language is widely spoken, and Basques refer to their country as Euskal-herri (or, across the border in Spain, Euskadi). You'll see bilingual French/Euskera toponym signage and posters throughout the region (sometimes only in Euskera), so in this section we have given the Euskera for all locations in brackets after the French.

Apart from the language and the traditional broad beret, the most obvious manifestations of Basque national identity are the ubiquitous *trinquets* (enclosed) or *frontons* (open) concrete courts in which the national game of **pelota** is played. Pairs of players wallop a hard leather-covered ball, either with their bare hands or a long basketwork extension of the hand called a *chistera* (in the variation known as *cesta punta*), against a high wall blocking one end of the court. It's extraordinarily dangerous – the ball travels at speeds of up to 200kph – and knockouts or worse are not uncommon.

## The Côte Basque

Barely 30km long from the Spanish frontier to the mouth of the Adour, the **Basque coast** is made up of scattered rocky outcrops and beautiful sandy beaches. Most surfers head for Biarritz, Hendaye (near the border) or Anglet (just north of Biarritz) which all offer surf hire and schooling. Reasonably priced accommodation is not difficult to find – except from mid-July and throughout August, when space should be reserved at least six weeks in advance.

# Highlights

❶ **Surfing the Côte Basque** Catch a wave at Biarritz, Europe's top destination for both boogie-boarders and classic surfers. See page 592

❷ **Cauterets** Several lake-spangled valleys above this agreeable spa offer superb trekking, whether modest day-loops or more ambitious multi-day traverses. See page 611

❸ **The Cirque de Gavarnie** A vast alpine amphitheatre with wind-blown cascades and traces of glacier. See page 613

❹ **Niaux cave** The upper Ariège valley hosts a cluster of prehistoric caves painted by Cro-Magnon humans over 10,000 years ago; Niaux

contains the best preserved and most vivid of these images. See page 617

❺ **Cathar castles** The imposing castles of the upper Aude and Corbières region testify to southwestern Languedoc's era of independence. See page 622

❻ **Musée d'Art Moderne, Céret** An astonishing collection of paintings from the prime movers of the early twentieth-century avant-garde. See page 632

❼ **Petit Train Jaune** Rumble up the dramatic Têt valley of Roussillon in an open-car, narrow-gauge train. See page 635

**HIGHLIGHTS ARE MARKED ON THE MAP ON PAGE 588**

## Biarritz

Up until the 1950s, **BIARRITZ** (Miarritze) was the Monte-Carlo of the Atlantic coast, transformed by Napoléon III during the mid-nineteenth century into a playground for monarchs, aristos and glitterati. With the 1960s rise of the Côte d'Azur, however, the place went into seemingly terminal decline, despite having been discovered by the first surfers in 1957. But from the early 1990s, Biarritz was rediscovered by Parisian yuppies, a new generation of the international surfing fraternity and a slightly alternative family clientele, who together have put the place back on the map.

The focus of Biarritz is the **Casino Municipal**, just behind the Grande Plage, now restored to its 1930s grandeur, while inland the town forms a surprisingly amorphous, workaday sprawl, where you'll find fancy shops and restaurants on main drags and cosier eateries light up the otherwise tenebrous side streets after sundown.

The **halles**, divided into a seafood wing and a produce, cheese and ham division, is friendly and photogenic, the streets around it lined with places to eat and drink. To the west, **place de l'Atalaye**, high above the port and named for a nearby whalers' lookout tower, is fringed by elegant mansions; just below, characterful if touristy **rue du Port-Vieux** leads down to its namesake beach.

### Musée Asiatica

1 rue Guy-Petit • Daily 2–6.30pm; July & Aug plus school holidays Mon–Fri 10.30am–6pm, Sat & Sun 2–6pm • €11 • ☎ 05 59 22 78 78, Ⓦ museeasiatica.com

Exhibiting the private collection of Chinese, Indian and Tibetan art specialist Michel Postel, the atmospherically presented **Musée Asiatica** holds eastern riches, including medieval jades, textiles and religious icons.

### Musée Historique de Biarritz

Rue Broquedis • Sept–June Tues–Sat 10am–12.30pm & 2–6.30pm; July & Aug Tues–Sat 10.30am–1pm & 2.30–6.30pm • €4 • ☎ 05 59 24 86 28, Ⓦ musee-historique-biarritz.fr

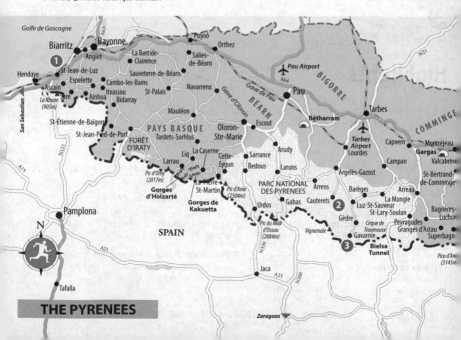

THE PYRENEES

Sited in a former Anglican church, the volunteer-run **Musée Historique de Biarritz** holds a smallish collection of photos, clothing and other artefacts that trace the town's fortunes from its beginnings as a medieval whaling station to its *belle époque* heyday.

### Musée de la Mer

Plateau de l'Atalaye • Nov–March daily 9.30am–7pm, April–June & Sept–Oct daily 9.30am–8pm, July & Aug daily 9.30am–midnight • €14.90 • ☏ 05 59 22 75 40, ⓦ aquariumbiarritz.com

The **Musée de la Mer** is one of Europe's great aquarium collections, based on the life found throughout the course of the Gulf Stream from the Caribbean to the Bay of Biscay and beyond. The many tanks offer spectacular sub-aquatic views of deep sea, mangrove and coral habitats where you'll come face to face with hammerhead sharks, rays, turtles and seals as well as pretty, multicoloured coral fish and the less pretty but decidedly more interesting moray eels.

## ARRIVAL AND DEPARTURE BIARRITZ

**By plane** Biarritz airport sits 4km inland from the town centre, just off the D810. Bus #14 from the airport heads into Biarritz. Flights are mostly domestic although a few no-frills routes exist to and from Ireland and England.

**By train** The *gare SNCF* is 4km southeast of the centre at the end of avenue Foch/avenue Kennedy in the *quartier* known as La Négresse (take bus A1 to or from square d'Ixelles).

Destinations Bordeaux (hourly; 2hr 15min); Hendaye (hourly; 35min); Irún (1 to 3 daily; 45min).

**By bus** There are no long-distance bus routes serving Biarritz but buses for local destinations Anglet (bus #10) and Bayonne (buses A1 & A2) can be picked up from avenues Edouard-VII and Louis-Barthou respectively, beside the tourist office.

**Public transport** There are two free shuttle buses (*navettes*): one makes a city centre circuit and another goes to the plage de la Côte des Basques – both can be boarded at av de Londres.

## INFORMATION

**Tourist office** Situated just inland from Grande Plage on Square d'Ixelles (Oct–March Mon–Fri 9am–6pm, Sat 10am–noon & 2–5pm, Sun10am–3pm; April–July & mid

Sept–end Sept Mon–Fri 9am–6pm, Sat–Sun 10am–5pm; Aug–mid Sept daily 9am–7pm; ☏ 05 59 22 37 10, ⓦ biarritz.fr).

11

**HIGHLIGHTS**

1 Surfing the Côte Basque
2 Cauterets
3 The Cirque de Gavarnie
4 Niaux cave
5 Cathar castles
6 Musée d'Art Moderne, Céret
7 Petit Train Jaune

**Bicycle and scooter rental** Solibo at 24 rue Peyroloubilh (☎ 05 59 24 94 47, ⓦ sobilo-scooters.com) offers bicycles for €20 a day.

**Surf rental and surf lessons** There are numerous surf schools in Biarritz all offering the same thing for the same price. Expect to pay €18 a day to hire a surfboard or bodyboard plus €12 for a wetsuit. If it's your first time, note that 90min group lessons cost €40–45 each. Kids can also learn (from aged seven and up provided they can swim) for

€35 a lesson. To surf on Plage de la Côte des Basques (see page 592) head down to the shorefront and pick from any of the surf-hire tents that are just past the restaurants on bd du Prince-de-Galles. To book ahead try La Vague Basque, bd du Prince-de-Galles (☎ 06 62 76 17 32, ⓦ vaguebasque.fr). To surf on Grande Plage (see page 592) go to Plums surf school on rue Gardères (☎ 05 59 24 10 79, ⓦ touradour. com/shops/plums).

## ACCOMMODATION

**Alcyon** 8 rue de la Maison-Suisse ☎ 05 59 22 64 60, ⓦ hotel-alcyon-biarritz.com. A modern four-star establishment in a listed nineteenth-century building a short stroll from Grande Plage. The moderately spacious rooms are impeccably clean and come with bathrooms and balconies. Unfortunately, the hotel offers no parking but staff can point you to possible parking spots. **€95**

**Biarritz Camping** 28 rte d'Harcet ☎ 05 59 23 0012, ⓦ biarritz-camping.fr. 1km behind plage de la Milady and 3km south of town, this reasonably basic campsite is the nearest to Biarritz, with a small pool, play park and shop; 10min walk to the beach. Also indoor accommo-dation (bungalow huts and static homes) available for four to six people. Early April to Sept. Camping **€34**, bungalow huts (weekly) **€675**

**La Maison du Lierre** 3 av du Jardin-Public ☎ 05 59 24 06 00, ⓦ hotel-maisondulierre-biarritz.com. Central

hotel with well-proportioned, wood-floored rooms some of which have balconies. It's bright and clean inside and has a delightful private garden out back. **€90**

**Hotel Palym** 7 rue du Port-Vieux ☎ 05 59 24 16 56, ⓦ hotel-palym-biarritz.fr. With a variety of old-fashioned rooms and a ground floor bar-restaurant, this is a solid budget option, though owing to nearby bars isn't great for those looking for an early night. **€65**

**Surf Hostel Biarritz** 27 av de Migron ☎ 07 65 66 22 22, ⓦ surfhostelbiarritz.com. The hippest hostel on the west coast, with bikes, boards and a hearty breakfast all included in the price. Its Achilles heel is that it's a bit out of the way; however hostel shuttle buses run to and from the surf as well as the train station and airport. Open March–Oct; booking essential. **€40**

## BASQUE COUNTRY CUISINE

Although **Basque cooking** shares many of the dishes of the southwest and the central Pyrenees – in particular **garbure**, a thick potato, carrot, bean, cabbage and turnip soup enlivened with pieces of pork, ham or duck – it does have distinctive recipes. One of the best known is the Basque omelette, *pipérade*, made with tomatoes, peppers and often Bayonne ham, and actually more like scrambled eggs. Another delicacy is sweet red peppers, or *piquillos*, stuffed whole with *morue* (salt cod). *Poulet basquaise* is also common, especially as takeaway food: pieces of chicken browned in pork fat and casseroled in a sauce of tomato, ground Espelette chillis, onions and a little white wine. In season there's a chance of *salmi de palombe*, an onion-and-wine-based stew of wild doves netted or shot as they migrate north over the Pyrenees.

With the Atlantic adjacent, **seafood** is also a speciality. The Basques inevitably have their version of fish soup, called *ttoro*. Another great delicacy is elvers or *piballes*, caught as they come up the Atlantic rivers. Squid are common, served here as *txiperons*, either in their own ink, stuffed and baked or stewed with onion, tomato, peppers and garlic. All the locally caught fish – tuna (*thon*), sea bass (*bor*), sardines (*sardines*) and anchovies (*anchois*) – are regular favourites, too.

**Cheeses** mainly comprise the delicious ewe's-milk *tommes* and *gasna* from the high pastures of the Pyrenees. Puddings include the *Gâteau Basque*, an almond-custard pie often garnished with preserved black cherries from Itxassou. As for **alcohol**, the only Basque AOC wine is the very drinkable Irouléguy – as red, white or rosé – while the local digestif liqueur is the potent green or yellow Izzara.

Spanish influences run deep here and in many of the bars you'll find a tantalizing choice of *pintxos* – the Basque equivalent of tapas – comprising bite-sized snacks, often skewered, that offer an efficient way to sample a wider selection of regional produce.

**11**

## EATING

★**Bar Jean** 5 rue des Halles ☎05 59 24 80 38, ⓦbarjean-biarritz.fr. Not to be confused with *Café Jean* on the same street, this semi-subterranean tapas bar serves creative bites and seafood meals to a lively clientele into the wee small hours. Noisy, yet intimate, and with a lengthy list of fine Riojas, this is the perfect place to pass an evening. Tapas around €3.50, paella €20. Daily 9am–3pm & 6.30pm–1.30am; Oct–May closed Tues & Wed; closed Jan.

**Le Clos Basque** 12 rue Louis-Barthou ☎05 59 24 24 96. Upmarket, modern(ish) and consistently lauded French restaurant serving a host of favourites like steak frites, veal and lobster. All good value at €27 for three courses. Tues–Sun noon–2pm & 7.45–9.30pm

**Le Comptoir du Foie Gras** 1 rue du Centre ☎05 59 22 57 42. As the name would suggest this convivial tapas bar stakes its reputation on its foie gras. The place is as much about the drinking as the eating with cocktails starting at €8 and sharing platters hovering around the €10 mark. Mon–Thurs 8am–11pm, Fri–Sat 9am–2am, Sun 11am–4pm.

**Miremont Pâtissier** Place Clemenceau ☎05 59 24 01 38, ⓦmiremont-biarritz.fr. Established in 1872, *Miremont* still sets the standard in patisserie arts. The cakes (ranging from €2.50–7.50) that greet you as you enter this opulent boutique-cum-tearoom-cum-restaurant are devastatingly pretty, such as their Béret Rouge, a white chocolate mousse covered with raspberry paste. The café-restaurant through the back has nice sea views if you can take your eyes off your cake. Daily 9am–8pm.

**Le Surfing** Plage de la Côte des Basques, 9 bd Prince-de-Galles ☎05 59 24 78 72, ⓦlesurfing.fr. A sea-view shrine to the sport positioned near the water's edge, this place is festooned with antique surfboards and serves tasty fish and chips for €13 and a wide selection of unusually creative vegetarian dishes like polenta fried in butter and sage for €9. Wed–Sun 9am–2.30pm & 7.30–10.30pm.

**La Table d'Aranda** 87 av de la Marne ☎05 59 22 16 04, ⓦtabledaranda.fr. Basque slow food restaurant a 10min walk from the centre. First appearances are deceptive, with the tacky flashing neon sign and dated exterior, but all is forgiven when the top-quality food arrives – usually starting with an amuse-bouche. Hearty yet refined country cuisine is offered, such as delicious white truffles broken over locally sourced veal with a port reduction (€23). *Menus* start at €16 for two plates. Daily noon–1.45pm & 7.45–9.45pm; Sept–June closed Sun & Mon.

## Bayonne

**BAYONNE** (Baïona) stands back some 5km from the Atlantic, a position that until recently protected it from any real touristic exploitation. The city is effectively the

11

## BIARRITZ BEACHES

Of Biarritz's six beaches, three are **surfable**, although in summer months and especially at weekends there's not always a lot of space in the water. Parking is near impossible at any time of the year, let alone summer, so consider taking the free *navette* service (see page 589).

**Grande Plage** is the legendary beach on which to show off your board and suntan; it's sited on the north edge of the old town by the famous casino. With its golden sand, beautiful views and famous backdrop, people descend here in their droves in order to see and be seen. Consequently restrictions on the number of bathers and surfers come into force at busier times. **Plage Miramar**, extending northeast of Grande Plage, offers more space but deadly currents so there's no surfing here. **Plage Marbella** and **Plage de la Côte des Basques**, south of the rocky outcrop, have two clear kilometres of sand and surf although the latter loses its sandy beach at high tide leaving perilous rocks to circumnavigate on the way back to land. A number of surf schools and board-hire companies can be found at the north end near the old town.

**Plage du Port-Vieux**, a petite little cove beach in the old town that has gentle waves, and **Plage Milady**, on the southern edge of town, are ideal for non-surfing beachgoers and families. The latter has better parking provisions and a playground although the waves can still be pretty choppy.

economic and political capital of the Pays Basque and to the lay person, at least, its Basque flavour predominates, with tall half-timbered dwellings and woodwork painted in the traditional green and red.

Sitting astride the confluence of the River Adour and the much smaller Nive, Bayonne is a small-scale, easily manageable city, at the hub of all major road and rail routes from the north and east. Although there are no great sights, it's a pleasure to walk the narrow streets of the old town, which is still wrapped in the fortifications of **Sébastien le Preste de Vauban**, Louis XIV's military engineer. West of the Nive in Grand Bayonne, the town's fourteenth-century **castle** dominates. The oldest part, the Château-Vieux, is a genuine example of no-nonsense late medieval fortification. Just west lies the little **Jardin Botanique**, built on a bastion of the Vauban fortifications. Around the corner on magnolia-shaded place Pasteur is the **Cathédrale Ste-Marie**, with its twin towers and steeple rising with airy grace above the town, best viewed from within its own cloister.

The smartest, most commercial streets in town extend northeast from the cathedral: rue Thiers leading to the *hôtel de ville*, and rue de la Monnaie, leading into rue Port-Neuf, with its chocolate *confiseries* and restaurants. South and west of the cathedral, along rue des Faures and rue d'Espagne, there's exemplary half-timbering and a bohemian, artsy-craftsy feel, where antique shops and rare-book dealers alternate with the odd bar or restaurant.

East of the cathedral, the Nive's riverside quays are the city's most picturesque focus, with their sixteenth-century arcaded houses across the Nive on the Petit Bayonne side.

### Musée Basque

37 quai des Corsaires • April–June & Sept Tues–Sun 10am–6.30pm; July & Aug Fri–Wed 10am–6.30pm, Thurs 10am–8.30pm; Oct–March Tues–Sun 10.30am–6pm • €7.50, free for under 26s and for all on first Sun of each month plus Thurs after 6.30pm in July and Aug • ☎ 05 59 59 08 98, ⓦ musee-basque.com

Exhibits in the **Musée Basque** illustrate traditional Basque life using a collection of farm implements – solid-wheeled oxcarts, field rollers and the like, as well as *makhilak* (innocent-looking carved, wooden walking sticks with a concealed steel spear tip at one end, used by pilgrims and shepherds for self-protection). The seafaring gallery features a superb rudder handle carved as a sea monster, a wood-hulled fishing boat, and a model of Bayonne's naval shipyards dating to 1805.

### ARRIVAL AND DEPARTURE                                                    BAYONNE

**By plane** Biarritz airport is 6km southwest of Bayonne. From the airport, either buses #14 or C (C is quicker) will take you into town.

**By train** The *gare SNCF* is just off place de la République on the north bank of the Adour.

Destinations Bordeaux (hourly; 2hr); Hendaye (every 10–30min; 35min); St-Jean-de-Luz (every 10–30min; 20min); Pau (6–11 daily; 1hr 20min).

**By bus** The *gare routière* for destinations in Béarn, Basse Navarre and Soule is next to the train station. For Biarritz take either #A1 or #A2 (every 10–20min Mon–Sat and every 50min on Sun).

## INFORMATION

**Tourist office** 25 place des Basques (July & Aug Mon–Sat 9am–7pm, Sun 10am–1pm; Sept–June Mon–Fri 9am–6.30pm, Sat 10am–6pm; ⓣ 08 20 42 64 64, ⓦ bayonne-tourisme.com). Free bike hire is available here, provided you bring ID and a credit card as a security deposit.

## ACCOMMODATION

**Des Arceaux** 26 rue Port-Neuf ⓣ 05 59 59 15 53. Comfortable hotel with pastel-hued rooms furnished with an agreeable mishmash of antique and faux-antique furniture. The ubiquitous bolster pillows might leave you with a sore neck in the morning, though. **€60**

**Côte Basque** 2 rue Maubec ⓣ 05 59 55 10 21, ⓦ hotel-cotebasque.fr. Tastefully modernized hotel in a central if slightly noisy location just across from the station. Family suites are available for an extra €21. **€62**

## EATING, DRINKING AND ENTERTAINMENT

The most popular areas for eating and drinking are along the right bank of the Nive or along quai Jauréguiberry on the Grand Bayonne side.

**Auberge du Cheval Blanc** 68 rue Bourgneuf, Petit Bayonne ⓣ 05 59 59 01 33, ⓦ cheval-blanc-bayonne.com. Housed in a pretty eighteenth-century timber house on a side street, this unassuming restaurant, specializing in seafood, has recently reclaimed Bayonne's only Michelin star. While the menu lacks some of the complexity of typical fine dining, the flavour combinations are inventive and successful like their pumpkin cream with chicken stock, shrimps and bacon. Weekday *menus* €25, weekend from €45. Daily noon–1.30pm & 7.45–9.30pm; closed Sat noon, Sun eve, Mon & first week of July.

**Le Chistera** 42 rue Port-Neuf, Grand Bayonne ⓣ 05 59 59 25 93, ⓦ lechistera.com. The best option out of a row of three similar restaurants under the arcades here, offering fish soup, Basque chicken and *pipérade*. The €16.80 three-course menu culminating with home-made desserts is good value. Tues–Sun noon–2.30pm & Thurs–Sun 7.30–9.30pm.

**Chocolat Cazenave** 19 Arceaux Port-Neuf, Grand Bayonne ⓣ 05 59 59 03 16, ⓦ chocolats-bayonne-cazenave.fr. The local chocolate tradition is duly honoured with a handful of chocolatiers on, or around, this street. This, the most famous one, serves frothy chocolate beverages in flowery porcelain teacups at tables under the arcade or in its Art Nouveau interior. Tues–Sat 9.15am–noon & 2–7pm.

**La Karafe** 25 quai Jaureguiberry ⓣ 05 59 25 69 26, ⓦ lakarafe.fr. If you've acquired a taste for *pintxos* (tapas) then this cheap and lively wine bar is the place to go. For around €3 a *pintxo* you can sample local sheep cheese, chorizo and *magret de canard* or for €6.50 try the mini skewered burgers. Glasses of wine range from €2.50 up to €9 for a glass of Champagne Rosé. Sun–Thurs 5.30pm–2am, Fri & Sat noon–2.30pm & 5.30pm–2am.

**Xafla** 27 quai Amiral-Dubourdieu ⓣ 05 59 56 79 22, ⓦ restaurant-a-table-bayonne.fr. Historic little waterfront snackery offering locally sourced, often organic and mostly vegan titbits like the crunchy mushroom croquettes (€6.50) as well as regional beer and wine. Tues noon–2.30pm, Wed–Sat noon–10pm, Sun noon–4pm.

# St-Jean-de-Luz

With its fine sandy bay – the most protected of the Basque beaches – and magnificent old quarter speckled with half-timbered mansions, **ST-JEAN-DE-LUZ** (Donibane Lohitzun) remains the most attractive resort on the Basque coast, despite being fairly overrun by holidaying families in peak season. As the only natural harbour between Arcachon and Spain, it has long been a major port, with whaling and cod-fishing the traditional occupations of its fleets. Even now, St-Jean remains one of France's busiest fisheries, and the principal one for landing anchovy and tuna.

## Maison Louis XIV

6 place Louis-XIV • Guided visits only (35min): June & Sept 11am, 3pm, 4pm, 5pm; July & Aug Wed–Mon 10.30am–12.30pm & 2.30–6.30pm; also open during some public holidays • €6.50 • ⓣ 05 59 26 27 58, ⓦ www.maison-louis-xiv.fr

The wealth and vigour of St-Jean's seafaring and mercantile past is evident in surviving seventeenth- and eighteenth-century townhouses. One of the finest, adjacent to the *hôtel de ville* on plane-tree-studded place Louis-XIV, is the turreted **Maison Louis XIV**, built for the Lohobiague family in 1635, but renamed after the young King Louis stayed here for a month in 1660 during the preparations for his marriage to Maria Teresa, Infanta of Castile.

## The church of St-Jean-Baptiste

Rue Gambetta • Mon–Fri 8.30am–noon & 2–6.30pm, Sat 8.30am–noon & 2–7.30pm, Sun 8am–noon & 3–7.30pm • Free • ☎ 05 59 26 08 81

King Louis' wedding took place in the **church of St-Jean-Baptiste** on pedestrianized rue Gambetta, the main shopping-and-tourism street today. The door through which they left the church – right of the existing entrance – has been sealed up ever since. Even without this curiosity, the church deserves a look inside: the largest French Basque church, it has a barn-like nave roofed in wood and lined on three sides with tiers of dark oak galleries accessed by wrought-iron stairways. The galleries, a distinctive feature of Basque churches, were reserved for the men, while the women sat at ground level. Equally Basque is the elaborate gilded retable of tiered angels, saints and prophets behind the altar. Hanging from the ceiling is an *ex voto* model of the Empress Eugénie's paddle steamer, the *Eagle*, which narrowly escaped being wrecked outside St-Jean in 1867.

## ARRIVAL AND INFORMATION

ST-JEAN-DE-LUZ

**By train** St-Jean's *gare SNCF* is on av de Verdun on the southern edge of the town centre, 500m from the beach. Destinations Bayonne (every 10–30min; 20min); Biarritz (every 10–30min; 12min); Hendaye (every 10–30min; 10min).

**By bus** Buses arrive at the *halte routière* diagonally opposite the trains.

Destinations Bayonne (10 daily; 55min); Biarritz (12 daily; 25min); Hendaye (10 daily; 25min).

**Tourist office** 20 bd Victor-Hugo (April–June & Sept Mon–Sat 9am–12.30pm & 2–7pm, Sun 10am–1pm; July & Aug Mon–Sat 9am–7.30pm, Sun 10am–1pm & 3–7pm; Oct–March Mon–Sat 9am–12.30pm & 1.30–6.30pm, Sun 10am–1pm; ☎ 05 59 26 03 16, ⦿ www.saint-jean-de-luz.com).

## ACCOMMODATION

★ **Les Goélands** 4–6 av d'Etcheverry ☎ 05 59 26 10 05, ⦿ hotel-lesgoelands.com. Consists of two *belle époque* villas 300m from the beach and old town, with jazzy interiors and en-suites plus some rooms with balconies and sea views. If you've got kids and a large budget opt for the "Family connecting rooms" (from €149–166). There's also a restaurant and well-tended gardens to relax in. Free parking. Easter–Oct. **€119**

**Kapa Gorry** 9 rue Paul-Gelos ☎ 05 59 26 04 93, ⦿ hotel-kapa-gorry.com. A good budget option near the northern edge of the beach and 500m from the centre. The rooms are clean if a little unhomely. Downstairs there is a reading room, dining room and terrace where a simple breakfast can be taken (€6.50). **€82**

**La Marisa** 16 rue Sopite ☎ 05 59 26 95 46, ⦿ hotel-lamarisa.com. A stone's throw or two from the beach within the old town, this hotel oozes charm and eccentricity, with its wood panelling and antique furniture complementing the seafaring artwork. There is a well-stocked reading/common room and rear garden to relax in. Closed mid-Dec to mid-Feb. **€110**

## EATING AND DRINKING

**Le Brouillarta** 48 Promenade Jacques-Thibaud ☎ 05 59 51 29 51, ⦿ restaurant-lebrouillarta.com. For a sea view try this fishy restaurant across the road from the middle section of the beach. The food here is rustic yet refined, using high-quality, fresh ingredients and a dose of creative flair. Three-course *menus* range from €25 (weekday lunch *menu*) to €41 (all other times). Mon & Thurs–Sun 12.30–2pm & 7.30–10pm.

**Le Kaiku** 17 rue de la République ☎ 05 59 26 13 20, ⦿ kaiku.fr. Basque/French cuisine romantically served in a lovely medieval old stone and timber building yards from the beach. Seafood features heavily on the menu while

meat enthusiasts should opt for roasted Kintoa (a Basque breed of pig) served with gaspacho and powdered black olives. Vegetarians are usually accommodated for with mainstays like aubergine and mushroom risotto. Prices range from the four-course €38 lunch to the €76 five-course discovery menu commencing with fancy amuse-bouches. Daily 12.30–2pm & 7.30–10pm.

★ **Zoko Moko** 6 rue Mazarin ☎ 05 59 08 01 23, ⦿ zoko-moko.com. Blazing a trail in fine cuisine, *Zoko Moko* has become a reason to visit this town. Expect vibrant, colourful platters based around crustaceans, fish or meat and wash it all down with the regional Irouleguy Dom Brana (€38).

*Menus* here start at €26 for a quick three-course lunch up to the tasting *menu* for €77, which includes amuse-bouches plus four courses and glasses of wine designed to accompany each plate. July–Sept daily 12.30–2pm & 7.30–10pm; Oct–June Mon & Thurs–Sun same hours.

# Inland Labourd and Basse Navarre

Without your own transport, the simplest forays into the soft, seductive landscapes of the Basque hinterland – **Labourd** (Lapurdi) and **Basse Navarre** (Behe Nafarroa) – are along the St-Jean-de-Luz–Sare bus route past **La Rhune**, **Ascain** and **Sare**, or the Bayonne–St-Jean-Pied-de-Port train line through the **Vallée de Nive**. Both give a representative sample of the area.

## GETTING AROUND                                    INLAND LABOURD AND BASSE NAVARRE

**By bus** Four to five buses a day (weekend service March–Oct only), run by Le Basque Bondissant (ⓦbasque-bondissant.com), ply the route from St-Jean-de-Luz, stopping also at Ascain, Col de St-Ignace and Sare.
**Destinations** (by bus) Ainhoa (from Cambo-les-Bains) (2 daily; 25min); Cambo-les-Bains (from Bayonne) (2–8 daily; 30min); Espelette (from Cambo-les–Bains) (3 daily; 10min); La Bastide-Clairence (from Bayonne) (2 daily; 35min); Sare (from St-Jean-de-Luz via Ascain) (5 daily; 30min).
**Destinations** (by train) Cambo-les-Bains (from Bayonne) (4 daily; 23min); St-Jean-Pied-de-Port (from Bayonne) (4 daily; 1hr 18min).

11

## La Rhune

The 905-metre cone of **La Rhune** (Larrun), straddling the frontier with Spain, is the westernmost skyward thrust of the Pyrenees before they decline into the Atlantic. As *the* landmark of Labourd, in spite of its unsightly multipurpose antennae, it's a predictably popular vantage point, offering fine vistas way up the Basque coast and east along the Pyrenees.

A rack-and-pinion **tourist train** (mid-Feb to June & Sept–Oct every 35min 9.30am–11.30am & 2–4pm; July & Aug every 35min 8.30am–5.30pm; €19; ☎05 59 54 20 26, ⓦrhune.com) runs up to the top of the cone from **Col de St-Ignace**, on the road to Sare. The railway line's steep gradient up (constructed between 1912 and 1924), ensures that the antediluvian carriages trundle at a leisurely 9km/hr; the ascent takes 35 minutes, but you should allow over two hours for the round trip. A bus service to Col de St-Ignace is available from the St-Jean-de-Luz bus station.

## Ascain

Like so many Labourdan villages, **Ascain** (Azkaine), just southeast of St-Jean-de-Luz, is postcard-perfect to the point of tweeness, with its galleried church, *fronton* and polychrome, half-timbered houses. It's the ideal base for exploring La Rhune although most visitors only stop briefly on their way to Sare and beyond.

## INFORMATION                                                              ASCAIN

**Tourist office** Across the road from the church (May–June Mon–Sat 9am–12.30pm & Mon–Fri 2–5.30pm; July & Aug Mon–Fri 9am–12.30pm & 2–6.30pm, Sat 9.30am–12.30pm & 2–6pm, Sun 10am–1pm; mid-Sept to mid-April Mon–Fri 9am–12.30pm & 2–5.30pm; ☎05 59 54 00 84).

## ACCOMMODATION AND EATING

**De La Rhune** Next to the church ☎05 59 54 00 04, ⓦhoteldelarhune.com. This former village post office on place du Fronton was regularly visited in the early nineteenth century by writer Pierre Loti who, inspired by the window view of La Rhune, wrote the novel *Ramuntcho* in room 21. The bedrooms are comfortable but lack the charm and character that you might expect from a building of this vintage. The restaurant delivers two courses for €15 of simple home-made Basque cuisine served in the pleasant garden out at the back. **€98**
**Xoko Ona** Place Pierre-Loti ☎05 24 33 71 18. Vibrant tapas bar and restaurant with a quick fire, no nonsense three course €20 menu featuring duck confit, fries and salad or grilled prawns with rice among the options. Sun & Tues–Thues 9am–8pm, Fri–Sat 9am–12.30pm.

**11**

## Sare

Seven kilometres southeast from Ascain, **Sare** is a perfectly proportioned knoll-top village, with traditional half-timbered houses and a typically Basque church, with its three tiers of balconies. It's centred around the place du Fonton, with its pelota court at one end and restaurants at the other.

### INFORMATION SARE

**Tourist office** Place du Fronton (April to June & Sept Mon–Fri 9am–12.30pm & 2–5.30pm plus Sat 9.30am–12.30pm; July & Aug Mon–Sat 9am–12.30pm & 2–6.30pm, Sun 10am–1pm; Oct–March Mon–Fri 9am–12.30pm & 2–5.30pm; ☎ 05 59 54 20 14, ⓦ sare.fr). Look for postings on the wall inside the tourist information office for upcoming pelota matches that take place in the court opposite. Games are scheduled on Mondays at 8.30pm in summer but are at irregular times throughout the rest of the year.

### ACCOMMODATION AND EATING

**Arraya** On the village square ☎ 05 59 54 20 46, ⓦ arraya.com. A former hospice on the Santiago de Compostela pilgrimage route dating back to the sixteenth century, *Arraya* is now a charming and unpretentious hotel as well as the village's most accomplished restaurant. Rooms are sumptuously presented with embroidered fabrics and antique furnishings, befitting of the ceiling's oak beams. The ground-floor restaurant makes a decent stab at haute cuisine, delivering pretty Basquaise platters of trout and lamb with *menus* from €19 that culminate with a slice of top-notch *gâteau basque*. Restaurant open 12.30–2pm & 7.30–10pm, closed Sun eve, Mon & Tues lunch (except July to mid-Sept). Hotel open April–Oct. Rooms **€104**

**Camping La Petite Rhune** Follow the D406 for 1km south of Sare (campsite is signposted left) ☎ 05 59 54 23 97, ⓦ lapetiterhune.com. A nicely shaded three-star site with playground, tennis and the all-important pool. Also offers *gîtes* and chalets all year round. Mid-June to mid-Sept. Camping **€24**, chalets (four person, minimum stay 3 nights) **€100**

**VVF** 200m north of the church ☎ 04 73 43 06 41, ⓦ vvfvillages.fr. A good, centrally located budget option if you're travelling in a group or en famille (a kids' club is included). The lodging offers four beds spread across two uncharming rooms plus a mini kitchen and balcony. Easter to mid-Oct. Minimum stay 3 nights. **€42**

## Ainhoa

A mere 8km east from Sare on the GR10 brings you to **Ainhoa**, a gem of a village. It consists of little more than a single street lined with substantial, mainly seventeenth-century houses, whose lintel plaques offer mini-genealogies as well as foundation dates. Take a look at the bulky towered **church** with its gilded Baroque altarpiece of prophets and apostles in niches, framed by Corinthian columns.

### INFORMATION AINHOA

**Tourist office** On the side street opposite the church (March–May & Sept–Oct Mon–Fri 9am–noon & 2–5pm plus Sat 10am–12.30pm in Sept; July & Aug Mon–Fri 9am– 1pm & 2–6.30pm, Sat 10am–12.30pm; Nov–Feb Mon–Fri 9am–noon & 2–5pm; ☎ 05 59 29 93 99, ⓦ ainhoa.fr).

### ACCOMMODATION AND EATING

**Auberge Alzate** On the main street ☎ 05 59 29 77 15. The village's most economical eatery (although still a bit pricey) with its €16 *menu* featuring Basque favourites, veal and duck. The cheapest lunch option is *omelette au fromage de brebis* (sheep's cheese) for €8 enhanced by home-made *frites* Mon, Wed–Sun 9am–9pm; July–Aug daily 9am–10pm; closed Dec to mid-Feb.

**Chambre d'hôte Ohantzea** Rue Principale ☎ 05 59 29 57 17, ⓦ ohantzea.com. The cheapest accommodation in town by a long shot, this lovely old building (one of only two blue painted buildings in town) is perfectly pleasant, offering three spacious rooms with queen-sized beds, as well as an inviting back garden to unwind in. Breakfast included. April–Oct. **€80**

**Ithurria** On the north edge of the village ☎ 05 59 19 92 11, ⓦ ithurria.com. The most luxurious option in the village, this seventeenth-century villa (originally built to house Santiago de Compostela pilgrims) ameliorated with a pool, sauna, and exotic garden, has well-equipped doubles and family apartments. The gourmet restaurant beneath holds a Michelin star for its perfect regional cuisine. The *menus* offer the best value, ranging from €45–90, and include roasted lamb embellished with sautéed girolles and rocket pesto with regional cakes or cheese for afters. Noon–2pm & 7.30–9pm, closed Wed & Thurs lunch (except July & Aug). Hotel open April–Oct. **€145**

## Espelette

Six kilometres northeast of Ainhoa, **Espelette** is a somewhat busy village of wide-eaved houses, with a church notable for its heavy square tower, painted ceiling and keyhole-shaped, inscribed-slab gravestones (the oldest are by the church, under the lime trees). The village's principal source of renown is its dark-red **chilli peppers** – much used in Basque cuisine, and hung to dry in summer on many house fronts.

### INFORMATION                                    ESPELETTE

**Tourist office** In the seventeenth-century château (Nov–March Mon–Fri 9am–12.30pm & 2–5pm; April–May Mon–Fri 9am–12.30pm & 2–6pm; June, Sept & Oct Mon–Fri 9am–12.30pm & 2–6pm, Sat 9am–1pm; July & Aug 9am–12.30pm & 2–6.30pm, Sat 9.30am–12.30pm & 2–6pm, Sun 9am–1pm; ☎05 59 93 95 02, ⓦespelette.fr).

### ACCOMMODATION AND EATING

**Aintzina** 440 Karrika Nagusia. ☎05 59 93 91 62. Delicious, no-nonsense Basque home cooking; prepared with a mighty pinch of the local ground peppers. Aim for the house speciality of slow cooked veal in sweet and local peppers and wine, part of the €25 three-course menu. Fri–Tues noon–2pm Mon–Tues & Fri–Sat 7–9pm

**Euzkadi** 285 Karrika Nagusia ☎05 59 93 91 88, ⓦhotel-restaurant-euzkadi.com. Traditional hotel, with a facade proudly emblazoned with the local *piment* crop, offering stylish, spacious rooms with bathrooms. The quieter rooms face the pool to the rear while the downstairs restaurant offers quality *pipérade* and *elzekaria* (bean and cabbage soup) within *menus* of €20–31. Vegetarian meals provided on demand. Restaurant open 12.30–2pm & 7.30–8.45pm; closed Mon & Tues low season. **€87**

★ **Maison Éliza Bidea** Xerrendako karrika ☎05 59 93 96 51. Peacefully tucked away by a leafy riverbank and housed in a beautiful eighteenth-century building, this hotel is a bohemian embodiment of the proprietor's creativity. Minimalists beware – there are knick-knacks everywhere. Guests are permitted to prepare their own meals in the kitchen, and the house restaurant (open to demand) will provide three-course Basque-style meals for €18. **€68**

## Cambo-les-Bains

Six kilometres east of Espelette is **Cambo-les-Bains** (Kanbo), an established spa resort with a favourable microclimate that made it ideal for the treatment of tuberculosis in the nineteenth century. Its other historical attribute is that it was the birthplace of the **gâteau basque** (see page 591), now ubiquitous throughout the region. The "new" town, with its ornate houses and hotels, radiates out from the baths over the heights above the River Nive, while the old quarter of Bas Cambo lies beside the river and *gare SNCF*.

### Villa Arnaga

1.5km northwest of town on the Bayonne road • Daily: April–May & Oct 9.30am–12.30pm & 2–6pm; June & Sept 9.30am–6pm; July–Aug 10am–7pm • €8.30 • ☎05 59 29 83 92, ⓦarnaga.com

The main sight around Cambo-les-Bains is the **Villa Arnaga**, built for Edmond Rostand, author of *Cyrano de Bergerac*, who came here to cure his pleurisy in 1903. This larger-than-life Basque house, painted in deep-red trim, overlooks an almost surreal formal garden with discs and rectangles of water and segments of grass punctuated by blobs, cubes and cones of topiary box, with a distant view of green hills. Inside it's very kitsch, with a minstrels' gallery, fake pilasters, allegorical frescoes, numerous portraits and various memorabilia.

### INFORMATION                              CAMBO-LES-BAINS

**Tourist office** 3 av de la Mairie (Mon–Sat 10am–1pm & 2–6.30pm; Sun 9am–1pm ☎05 59 29 70 25, ⓦcambolesbains.com).

### ACCOMMODATION AND EATING

**Hostellerie du Parc** Av de la Mairie ☎05 59 93 54 54, ⓦhotel-parc-cambo.com. Homely, clean and central hotel with comfortable en-suite rooms equipped with TV and fridge. Out the back there is a lovely secluded garden with Black Rock chickens dust-bathing in the shade. Closed first two weeks of Jan. **€78**

★ **Tarterie Au Déjeuner sur l'Herbe** 17 place Duhalde, just off rue du Centre ☎05 59 42 67 17. A transfixingly beautiful window display of artisan pies, tarts and cakes lures you into this adorable café-restaurant. *Tourtes* (with a pastry top) at €8.50 and *tartes* (without) for €7.50 come with a wealth of different fillings from courgette & goat's cheese to salmon and scallops. For a sweet tooth, the choice appears limitless, but the rhubarb meringue pie is the one not to miss. Sun–Fri noon–7pm.

## La Bastide-Clairence

Nineteen kilometres northeast of Cambo lies arguably the most perfectly preserved village in the Basque region, **La Bastide-Clairence** (Bastida), which dates back to the fourteenth century. Resting on the northeastern perimeter with Béarn, historically this predominantly Bascaise village has seen tolerant cohabitation of the two cultures – a progressive inclination that was put to good use in the sixteenth century by Spanish and Portuguese Jews who settled here after fleeing the Spanish inquisition. There is still a fascinating Jewish graveyard next to the Christian one by the fourteenth-century church. The main focus of the village however is its symmetrical arcaded square, with its bar/restaurants and an old forge open to the public gaze.

### INFORMATION  LA BASTIDE-CLAIRENCE

**Tourist office** In the arcaded square (July & Aug 10am–1pm & 3–7pm, plus June & Sept Sat 10am–noon; Sept–June Mon–Fri 9.30am–12.30pm & 2–6pm, closes at noon on Wed; ☎05 59 29 65 05, ⊛labastideclairence-pays-basque.com).

### ACCOMMODATION & EATING

**Bar Restaurant Les Arceaux** Place des Arceaux ☎05 59 29 66 70. One of two restaurant options in the heart of the village, this friendly place, which doubles as the village newsagent, has changing €10 and €12 *menus* of regional cuisine. Dine inside, or under shade in the lovely *place*. Tues–Sun 7.30am–9pm; closed Jan.

**Maison Marchand** Rue Notre-Dame ☎05 59 29 18 27, ⊛maison.marchand.pagesperso-orange.fr. In a lovely old half-timbered house, this family B&B offers four characterful en-suite rooms and a well-tended garden, complete with resident cats. Breakfasts come with delicious warm bread, croissants, local cheese and jam. A hospitality tray in the rooms is also provided. On Mondays and Thursdays the proprietors cook a veritable feast for guests (€25pp including unlimited wine) using the finest regional produce. Closed Nov–March. **€65**

## St-Jean-Pied-de-Port

About 33km southeast of Cambo, the old capital of Basse Navarre, **ST-JEAN-PIED-DE-PORT** (Donibane Garazi), lies in a circle of hills at the foot of the Bentarte pass into Spain. Part of France since the 1659 Treaty of the Pyrenees, it was an important stop on the **Santiago de Compostela pilgrimage** in the Middle Ages.

The old town consists of a single cobbled street, **rue de la Citadelle**, which runs downhill from the fifteenth-century **Porte St-Jacques** – the gate by which pilgrims entered the town, St Jacques being French for Santiago – to the **Porte Notre-Dame**, commanding the bridge over the Nive, with its constantly photographed view of balconied houses overlooking the stream.

### ARRIVAL AND INFORMATION  ST-JEAN-PIED-DE-PORT

**By train** The *gare SNCF* is at the end of av Renaud, a 10min walk north of the centre.
Destinations Bayonne (3–5 daily; 1hr 20min); Cambo-les-Bains (3–5 daily; 45min).

**Tourist office** 14 place Charles-de-Gaulle (July & Aug Mon–Sat 9am–7pm, Sun 10am–1pm & 2–5pm; Sept–June Mon–Sat 9am–noon & 2–6pm; ☎05 59 37 03 57, ⊛pyrenees-basques.com).

### ACCOMMODATION

*Chambres d'hôtes*, as well as cheaper dormitory lodgings for pilgrims and hikers, are numerous: try along rue de la Citadelle.

**Chambre d'hôte Errecaldia** 5 chemin St-Jacques ☎05 59 49 17 02, ⊛errecaldia.com. Quietly situated beneath the grounds of the seventeenth-century citadelle, yet central enough to dip in and out of town. The spacious rooms within come with a cracking view over the modern town and beyond. **€75**

**Gîte d'étape Ultreia** 8 rue de la Citadelle ☎06 80

88 46 22, ⓦultreia64.fr. Friendly hostel predominantly frequented by pilgrims or walkers and thus has a 10pm curfew. The cheapest dorm has seven beds, or if you book ahead you can have a private room. Breakfast is €5. Bunks €22, private room €56

**Des Remparts** 16 place Floquet ☎05 59 37 13 79,

ⓦhoteldesremparts.fr. The best budget choice among the hotels, this relatively quiet place (when the windows are shut) is located just before you cross the Nive coming into town on the Bayonne road. Try to get a room overlooking the inner courtyard. €67

### EATING AND DRINKING

**Cave des États de Navarre** Rue d'Espagne ☎05 59 49 10 48. This watering hole on the southern side of the Nive is an excellent place to sample local produce. Local ciders and wines sold by the glass (from €4) wash down the tasty Basquaise tapas accompaniments (from €4.50). Mon & Wed–Sun 9.30am–8pm.

**Paxkal Oillarburu** 8 rue de l'Église ☎05 59 37 06 44. Offering three-course *menus* from €15, and excellent, well-proportioned rustic dishes that include *garbure* and Iraty trout in garlic butter. You may need to evoke the patience of

St Jacques to dine in this very popular restaurant at busier times. Book ahead in summer. Mon & Wed–Sun 12.30–2.30pm & 7.30–8.45pm; open Tues July & Aug only.

**Restaurant Les Pyrénées** Place Charles-de-Gaulle ☎05 59 37 01 01, ⓦhotel-les-pyrenees.com. The town's gourmet option delivers exquisite, delicate plates using decadent ingredients. Beyond the reach of most budgets, the *menus* at this Michelin-starred restaurant range from €42 up to an eye-watering €115. Daily 12.15–1.45pm & 7.45–9pm; closed mid-Nov to end Nov & Jan.

## Haute Soule

East of the Nive valley, you enter largely uninhabited country, the old Basque county known as the **Haute Soule**, threaded only by the GR10 and a couple of minor roads. The border between Basse Navarre and Soule skims the western edge of the **Forêt d'Iraty**, one of Europe's largest surviving beech woods, a popular summer retreat and winter cross-country skiing area. There are no shops or proper hotels until you reach **Larrau**, the only real village hereabouts, though the scattered hamlet of Ste-Engrâce in the east of the district has accommodation, as do Licq and Tardets-Sorholus, foothill settlements some way down the valley.

Haute Soule is a land of open skies, where griffon vultures turn on the thermals high above countless flocks of sheep (their occasional corpses providing sustenance). It's not a great distance between the Nive valley and Béarn, but the slowness of the roads and the grandeur of the scenery seem to magnify it.

### The Forêt d'Iraty

To drive to the **Forêt d'Iraty** (Irati), follow the D301 east out of the Nive valley from the junction on the D428, where the forest is signposted. The road is steep, narrow and full of tight hairpins and ambling livestock but as you climb up the steep spurs and around the heads of labyrinthine gullies, ever more spectacular views open out over the valley of the Nive, St-Jean and the hills beyond. Solar-powered sheep ranches abound, with cheese on sale. Beech copses fill the gullies, shadowing the lighter grass whose green is so intense it seems almost theatrical – an effect produced by a backdrop of purplish rock outcrops.

### Larrau

The first thing you notice coming into **LARRAU** (Larraiñe) from the west is how different the architecture is from the villages in Labourd and Basse Navarre. In contrast to the usual painted, half-timbered facades and tiled roofs, the houses here are grey and stuccoed, with Béarnais-style, steep-pitched slate roofs to shed heavy snow. Despite its size, it's nonetheless very quiet – almost dead out of season.

#### Gorges d'Holzarté

The **Gorges d'Holzarté**, 4km southeast of Larrau, is one of several local gorges, cutting deep into northern slopes of the ridge that forms the frontier with Spain. A short track leads from *Auberge Logibar* (3km east of Larrau) across a lively, chilly stream to a car park,

11

---

**OSSAU-IRATY CHEESE**

Native to the Basque country and Béarn, this AOC ewe's **cheese**, with its delightfully nutty flavour, is developed in the summer-grazing huts extending along the Basque coast up to the Col d'Aubisque in the Pyrenees national park. Look out for **Route du Fromage** signs (w ossau-iraty.fr) while travelling about the Basque hinterland and buy direct from the shepherds themselves. The true artisan cheese often has small holes and should not stick to the palate.

---

from where a steep path – a variant of the GR10 – climbs through beech woods in about 45 minutes to the junction of the Holzarte gorge with the **Gorges d'Olhadubi**. Slung across the mouth of the latter is a spectacular Himalayan-style **suspension bridge**, the *passerelle*, which bounces and swings alarmingly as you walk out over the 180-metre drop.

### Gorges de Kakuetta

15km east of Larrau on the D113 · Mid-March to mid-Nov 8am–nightfall · €6 · ☎ 05 59 28 60 83, w sainte-engrace.com

The **Gorges de Kakuetta** is truly dramatic and, outside peak season, not crowded at all; allow about two hours to visit. It pays to be well shod – the metal catwalk or narrow path, by turns, are slippery in places and provided with safety cables where needed. The walls of the gorge rise up to 300m high and are scarcely more than 5m apart in spots, so little sunlight penetrates except at midday from May to July. The air hangs heavy with mist produced by dozens of seeps and tiny waterfalls, nurturing tenacious ferns, moss and other vegetation that thrives in the hothouse atmosphere. Within an hour, the path brings you to a small cave beyond which only technical climbers need apply; just before it a twenty-metre waterfall (which you can walk behind) gushes out of a hole in the rock.

### ACCOMMODATION AND EATING                                         LARRAU

**Auberge Logibar** 3km east of Larrau on the D26 ☎ 05 59 28 61 14, w auberge-logibar.com. Perfectly positioned for lay-walker hikes to the Gorges d'Holzarté, just over 1km to the south, this welcoming *gîte* has simple private rooms and dorms. The bar-restaurant downstairs has *menus* from €12 with lamb, trout, *cèpes* and other locally sourced ingredients, served until 3pm. They also provide takeaway sandwiches and snacks throughout the day. Closed Dec–Feb. Dorms €15, doubles €35

**Camping Ibarra** Just off the D113, 13km east of Larrau ☎ 05 59 28 73 59, w ibarra-chantina.com. Attractive riverside campsite just 3km from the Gorges de Kakuetta. Easter to mid-Oct. €10.90

**Hôtel-Restaurant Etchémaïté** Just off the D26 on the east side of the village ☎ 05 59 28 61 45, w hotel-etchemaite.fr. Nicely renovated old hotel with bright spacious rooms, some with balconies and views over the town and mountains. The excellent restaurant offers decent value, three-course *menus* (ranging between €20 and €36) that include grilled sardines and braised lamb. Food available 12.30–2.30pm & 7.30–9pm. Closed Jan to mid-Feb. €74

# The Central Pyrenees

The **Central Pyrenees**, immediately east of the Pays Basque, hosts the range's highest mountain peaks, the most spectacular section by the border being protected within the **Parc National des Pyrénées**. Highlights – apart from the lakes, torrents, forests and 3000-metre peaks around **Cauterets** – are the cirques of **Lescun**, **Gavarnie** and **Troumouse**, each with its distinctive character. And for less *sportif* interests, there's many a flower-starred mountain meadow accessible by car, especially near **Barèges**, in which to picnic. The only real urban centres are **Pau**, a probable entry point to the area, the dull city of **Tarbes**, and pilgrimage target, **Lourdes**.

## Pau

From humble beginnings as a crossing on the Gave de Pau (*gave* is "mountain river" in Gascon dialect), **PAU** became the capital of the ancient viscountcy of

Béarn in 1464, and of the French part of the kingdom of Navarre in 1512. In 1567 its sovereign, Henri d'Albret, married the sister of French King François I$^{er}$, Marguerite d'Angoulême, who transformed the town into a centre of the arts and nonconformist thinking.

The least-expected thing about Pau is its **English connection**: seduced by its climate and persuaded (mistakenly) of its curative powers by Scottish doctor Alexander Taylor, the English flocked to Pau throughout the nineteenth century, bringing along their cultural idiosyncrasies – fox-hunting, horse racing, polo, croquet, cricket, golf (the first eighteen-hole course in continental Europe in 1860, and the first to admit women), tea salons and parks. When the railway arrived here in 1866, the French came, too: writers like Victor Hugo, Stendhal and Lamartine, as well as socialites. The first French rugby club opened here in 1902, after which the sport spread throughout the southwest.

Pau has few must-see sights or museums, so you can enjoy its relaxed elegance without any sense of guilt. The parts to wander in are the streets behind the **boulevard des Pyrénées**, especially the western end, which stretches along the escarpment above the Gave de Pau, from the castle to the Palais Beaumont, now a convention centre, in the English-style **Parc Beaumont**. On a clear day, the view from the boulevard encompasses a broad sweep of the highest Pyrenean peaks, with the distinctive Pic du Midi d'Ossau slap in front of you. In the narrow streets between the castle and ravine-bed chemin du Hédas are numerous cafés, restaurants, bars and boutiques, with the main Saturday **market** in the *halles* just northeast on place de la République.

## The Château Musée National

Rue du Château • Daily guided tours: mid-June to mid-Sept 9.30am–5.45pm; mid-Sept to mid-June 9.30–11.45am & 2–5pm • €7; free first Sun of month, children free; exterior unenclosed gardens free • ☎ 05 59 82 38 00, ⓦ musee-chateau-pau.fr

The **château** is very much a landmark building, though not much remains of its original fabric beyond the southeastern brick keep built in 1370. Louis-Philippe renovated it in the nineteenth century after two hundred years of dereliction, and Napoléon III and Eugénie titivated it further with stellar vaulting, chandeliers and

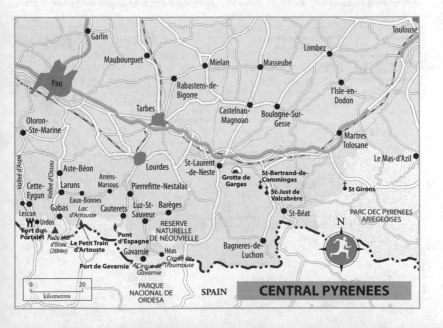

coffered ceilings. The **Musée National** inside is visitable by a French-only, one-hour guided tour, the only way to see the vivid eighteenth-century tapestries with their wonderfully observed scenes of rural life, or Henri IV memorabilia like the giant turtle shell that purportedly served as his cradle.

## Musée Bernadotte

6 rue Tran • Tues–Sun 10am–noon & 2–6pm • €3; children free • ☎ 05 59 27 48 42

A short distance northeast of the château, the mildly interesting **Musée Bernadotte** is the birthplace of the man who, having served as one of Napoleon's commanders, went on to become Charles XIV of Sweden. As well as fine pieces of traditional Béarnais furniture, the house contains some valuable works of art collected over his lifetime.

## Musée des Beaux-Arts

10 rue Mathieu-Lalanne • Daily except Tues 10am–noon & 2–6pm • €5; children free • ☎ 05 59 27 33 02

Pau's second worthwhile museum, the **Musée des Beaux-Arts**, has an eclectic collection of little-known works from European schools spanning the fourteenth to twentieth centuries; the only really world-class items are Rubens' *The Last Judgement* and Degas' *The Cotton Exchange*, a slice of finely observed *belle époque* New Orleans life.

---

### ARRIVAL AND INFORMATION                                          PAU

**By plane** Pau airport is 6 miles northwest of Pau. The airport currently serves only domestic and a handful of southern European routes. The #20 bus runs from the airport to the *gare SNCF* hourly from 7.22am–7.10pm, while another runs from the *gare SNCF* to the airport hourly from 6.40am–7.10pm. The fare is €1.

**By train** The *gare SNCF* (trains and *SNCF* buses) is just south of the old centre, by the riverside. A free funicular links the train station to the bd des Pyrénées, opposite place Royale.
Destinations Bordeaux (5 daily; 2hr 15min); Oloron Ste-

Marie (for the Vallée d'Aspe change here) (9 daily, fewer at weekends; 35min); Paris (4 direct daily; 5hr 39min); Tarbes (approx. hourly; approx. 40min).

**By bus** CITRAM buses leave from the *gare SNCF*.
Destinations Laruns and the Vallée d'Ossau (3 daily, 4 at weekends; 1hr).

**By car** Parking is predictably nightmarish; there are a few free spaces to the west of the centre around place de Verdun or to the east beyond Park Beaumont, otherwise shell out for kerbside meters or use the giant underground car park at

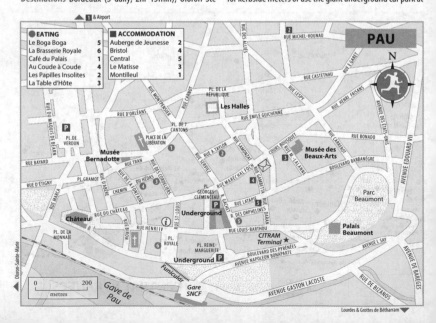

| EATING | | ACCOMMODATION | |
|---|---|---|---|
| Le Boga Boga | 5 | Auberge de Jeunesse | 2 |
| La Brasserie Royale | 6 | Bristol | 4 |
| Café du Palais | 1 | Central | 5 |
| Au Coude à Coude | 4 | Le Matisse | 3 |
| Les Papilles Insolites | 2 | Montilleul | 1 |
| La Table d'Hôte | 3 | | |

PAU

## THE PARC NATIONAL DES PYRÉNÉES

The **Parc National des Pyrénées** was created in 1967 to protect at least part of the high Pyrenees from modern touristic development – ski resorts, paved roads, mountaintop restaurants, car parks and other inappropriate amenities. It extends for more than 100km along the Spanish border from Pic de Laraille (2147m), south of Lescun, in the west, to beyond Pic de la Munia (3133m), almost to the Aragnouet–Bielsa tunnel. Varying in altitude between 1070m and 3298m at the Pic de Vignemale, south of Cauterets, the park includes the spectacular Gavarnie and Troumouse cirques, as well as 220 lakes, more than a dozen valleys and about 400km of marked walking routes.

By the **banning of hunting** and all dogs and vehicles (except local herders), the park has also provided sanctuary for many rare, endangered species of birds and mammals. These include chamois, marmots, stoats, genets, griffon vultures, golden eagles, eagle owls and capercaillies, to say nothing of the rich and varied flora. The most celebrated animal – extinct as of 2004 – is the Pyrenean **brown bear**, whose pre-1940 numbers ran to as many as two hundred; the thirty-plus current specimens are descended from re-introduced (in 2006 and 2018) Slovenian brown bears. Although largely herbivorous, bears will take livestock opportunistically, and most mountain shepherds are their remorseless enemies. To appease the shepherds, local authorities pay prompt and generous compensation for any losses, but the restocking programme remains highly controversial, with pro- and anti-bear graffiti prominent on the road approaches to the park, and troublesome animals being shot illegally by aggrieved farmers or herders on a regular basis.

The **GR10** runs through the entire park on its 700-kilometre journey from coast to coast, starting at Banyuls-sur-Mer on the Mediterranean and ending at Hendaye-Plage on the Atlantic.

place Georges-Clemenceau.

**Tourist office** Place Royale (July & Aug Mon–Sat 9am–6.30pm, Sun 9.30am–1pm & 2–5pm; Sept–June Mon–Sat 9am–6pm, Sun 9.30am–1pm; ☏ 05 59 27 27 08, ⓦ pau-pyrenees.com).

## ACCOMMODATION

**Auberge de Jeunesse** 30 rue Michel-Hounau ☏ 05 59 11 05 05, ⓦ habitat-jeunes-pau-asso.fr. It's not pretty to look at but this small youth hostel has a friendly, convivial atmosphere and is within easy reach of the town centre. Dorms are not too crowded, having either two beds or four beds per room, and all bedding is included in the rate. The facilities available include kitchen, computer room and laundry, plus breakfast for just €3. Advance booking is advisable as there are only ten beds in the hostel. **€19.80**

**Bristol** 3 rue Gambetta ☏ 05 59 27 72 98, ⓦ hotelbristol-pau.com. Right in the heart of the city, this long-standing boutique hotel is surprisingly well proportioned for its location. Large rooms and en-suites, as well as a bar and a sunny terrace to take breakfast (€12), make for a comfortable stay. Free parking. **€109**

**Central** 15 rue Léon-Daran ☏ 05 59 27 72 75, ⓦ hotel centralpau.com. Offers 28 personalized rooms – some more tasteful than others – with comfy beds, en-suites and, most importantly, soundproofing. The hotel can garage your car for €5.50 per day. Breakfast €8. **€66**

**Le Matisse** 17 rue Mathieu-Lalanne ☏ 05 59 92 16 35, ⓦ le-matisse-fr.book.direct/en-gb. Friendly and relatively quiet budget hotel opposite the Musée des Beaux-Arts. The rooms are nothing to get excited about; small with plain furnishings but have a toilet, shower, TV and tea-making facilities. **€55**

**Montilleul** 47 av Jean-Mermoz ☏ 05 59 32 93 53, ⓦ montilleul-fr.book.direct. A nice cheap option although a good 30min walk north of the centre, this small, family-run hotel is simple and clean. The excellent continental breakfasts have a selection of tasty jams worthy of the €8.50 price tag. The #5 bus passes by on its way to and from town and the *gare SNCF*; for those with their own transport, the hotel offers free parking. **€40**

## EATING

★ **Le Boga Boga** 19 rue des Orphelines ☏ 05 59 83 71 44, ⓦ lebogaboga.fr. One of three favoured bars on this narrow side street serving drinks and tapas late into the night. Allow €15–20 for tapas depending on how much alcohol you need to soak up. The Spanish wine menu starts at €18 a bottle or try the harder stuff, like a caffeine-laced Mojito Bull for €8.50. Tues–Sun 6pm–2am.

**La Brasserie Royale** 5 place Royale ☏ 05 59 27 72 12, ⓦ brasserie-royale.com. Popular, upscale brasserie with *carte* and three-course *menus* from €19 up – even the cheapest nets you a solid marinated pork with house *pipérade* main. There's been an establishment here since

1843, and the current interior with swirling fans and original art (larger parties can book the back room) vies for allure with tables on the *place* in fine weather. Noon–2.15pm & 7.30–10.30pm; closed Sun.

**Café du Palais** 7 rue St-Jacques ☎05 59 27 74 08, ⓦcafedupalaispau.com. Pavement café/brasserie just off the picturesque place de la Libération offering breakfasts from €7 and attractive hot plates and salads. Two-course *menus* with coffee are €14 and there are also a couple of vegetarian options on the carte. Mon–Sat 8am–8pm.

**Au Coude à Coude** 3 rue du Hédas ☎05 59 83 32 62. Cute pavement café with a strong focus on home-made food right down to the house bread. The three course menu for €25 will fill you up on things like quiches, aubergine bakes and *galettes*. Tues–Sat 10am–10pm, Sun 10am–6pm.

★ **Les Papilles Insolites** 5 rue Alexandre-Taylor ☎05 59 71 43 79, ⓦlespapillesinsolites.blogspot.co.uk. An exciting option for wine-lovers, this part-vintners, part-restaurant provides an intimate setting where you dine at dimly lit tables surrounded by the *cave*'s stock. If you like a wine, take home a case. The *menu* offers fancy meat-focused dishes supported by seasonal veg; three courses for €21. Wed–Sat 3–11pm; closed Sun–Tues.

**La Table d'Hôte** 1 rue du Hédas ☎05 59 27 56 06. Elegant bare-brick restaurant in a former warehouse, one of the first to colonize this trendy area. There's a heavy emphasis on red meat and seafood on the carte although they also have a three-course vegetarian menu for €19. Noon–1.30pm & 7.30–9.30pm.

# Salies-de-Béarn

Fifteen kilometres northwest from Pau is **SALIES-DE-BÉARN**, a typical Béarnais village of winding lanes and flower-decked houses with brightly painted woodwork. The River Saleys, hardly more than a stream here, runs through the middle of it, separating the old village from the nineteenth-century quarter that sprang up to exploit the powerful saline spring for which it has long been famous. You can try the curative waters at the wonderful **thermal baths** at cours du Jardin-Public (10am–noon & 2–7pm; closes at 6pm at weekends; 1hr entry includes use of the jacuzzi for €10; ☎05 59 38 10 11, ⓦthermes-de-salies.com), "curative" pools – one salty, one not – in an old but modernized thermal establishment.

### ARRIVAL AND INFORMATION                                        SALIES-DE-BÉARN

**By bus** One bus route serves Salies-de-Béarn, originating at the train station in Orthez (on the Pau–Bordeaux train line) (3 daily; 25min).

**Tourist office** Rue des Bains (mid April–June Mon–Sat 9.30am–noon & 2–6pm; July–Oct Mon–Sat 9.30am–12.30 & 2–6.30pm, Sun 9am–1pm; Nov–mid April Mon, Thurs & Sat 10am–noon & 2.30–5pm, Tues, Wed & Fri 2.30–5pm ; ☎05 59 38 00 33, ⓦtourisme-bearn-gaves.com).

### ACCOMMODATION AND EATING

**La Demeure Saint-Martin** 42 rue Saint-Martin ☎05 62 82 47 29, ⓦlademeuresaintmartin.com. A quasi sacro-bohemian retreat, this twelfth-century presbytery bears the hallmarks of its age as well as of its eccentric owner. Adorned with quirky personal effects, this building feels loved. Rooms are equipped with a basin and shower while the toilet is in the hall. Breakfast is served in your room: home-made cake, bread and jams for €10. **€90**

**La Terrasse** 2 rue Loume ☎05 59 38 09 83. With its large terrace – hence the name – enviably positioned overlooking the Saleys river, its unsurprising that this restaurant-bar is so popular. The menu holds no great surprises; just hearty Béarnais home cooking and quaffably good wine. Three courses start at €17. Noon–2pm & 7–10pm; Oct–June closed Thurs & Sun eves & all Mon; July–Sept closed Mon.

# Sauveterre-de-Béarn

Heading south from Salies-de-Béarn, the D933 winds over hilly farming country to **SAUVETERRE-DE-BÉARN**, a pretty country town beautifully set on a bluff high above the Gave d'Oloron, just before it mingles with the Saison. From the terrace by the thirteenth-century **church of St-André** – over-restored but still retaining a fine west-portal relief of Christ in Glory – you look down over the river and the remains of fortified, half-ruined **Pont de la Légende**, while at the west end of the compact *cité médiévale* stand the ruins of a Gaston Fébus **château**. A pedestrian-only lane leads down to the bridge and river, full of bathers on hot days despite its murky greenness.

## ARRIVAL

**SAUVETERRE-DE-BÉARN**

**By bus** One bus from Orthez (on the Pau–Bordeaux train line) stops by the main place Royale (3 daily Mon–Fri, 1 on Sat; 35min).

## ACCOMMODATION

**La Maison de Navarre** 1 chemin de Navarre ☎ 06 98 53 30 21. On the western edge of town, this guest house and restaurant has pleasant rooms and an attractive formal garden round the back with a swimming pool and a terrace to dine al fresco. The kitchen draws produce and inspiration from local and neighbouring regions with dishes like foie gras with *piment béarnais*. Three course menus start at €18. Restaurant noon–2pm except Thurs and Sat, Fri–Sat 7.30–9.30pm. **€91**

# Navarrenx

From Sauveterre-de-Béarn, the D936 bears southeast along the flat valley bottom 20km away on the Pau–Mauléon bus route to **NAVARRENX**, a sleepy, old-fashioned market town built as a *bastide* in 1316 and still surrounded by its medieval walls. Having crossed the medieval bridge over the Gave d'Oloron – claimed here as the salmon-fishing capital of France – you enter from the west by the fortified Porte St-Antoine.

## ACCOMMODATION

**NAVARRENX**

**Hôtel Le Commerce** Place des Casernes ☎ 05 59 66 50 16, ⊚ logishotels.com. The lovingly preserved exterior of this hotel with its grey-blue shutters and mansard roof contrasts with its modern, sometimes futuristic interior. It's a comfortable and friendly hotel offering substantial breakfasts for €8pp, and you can also take the half-board option for €125 (for two) and sample the terraced restaurant's vibrant cuisine. Closed Jan. **€78**

# Lourdes

**LOURDES**, 37km southeast of Pau, has one principle function. Over seven million Catholic pilgrims arrive here yearly, and the town is totally dedicated to looking after and, on occasion, exploiting them. Lourdes was hardly more than a village before 1858, when Bernadette Soubirous, 14-year-old daughter of a poor local miller, had the first of eighteen visions of the Virgin Mary in the Grotte de Massabielle by the Gave de Pau. Since then, Lourdes has become the most visited attraction in this part of France, many pilgrims hoping for a miraculous cure for conventionally intractable ailments.

Myriad shops are devoted to the sale of unbelievable religious kitsch: Bernadette and/or the Virgin in every shape and size, adorning barometers, thermometers, plastic tree trunks, empty bottles that you can fill with holy water, bellows, candles and illuminated plastic grottoes. Clustered around the miraculous grotto are the churches of the Domaine de la Grotte, an annexe to the town proper that sprang up in the century following Bernadette's visions. The first to be built was an underground crypt in 1866, followed by the flamboyant double **Basilique du Rosaire et de l'Immaculée Conception** (1871–83), and then in 1958 by the massive subterranean **Basilique St-Pie-X**, which can apparently fit 20,000 people at a time. The **Grotte de Massabielle** itself is the focus of pilgrimage – a moisture-blackened overhang by the riverside with a marble statue on high of the Virgin, where pilgrims queue to circumambulate, stroking the grotto wall with their left hand. To one side are taps for filling souvenir containers with the holy spring water; to the other are the *brûloirs* or rows of braziers where enormous votive candles burn, prolonging the prayers of supplicants.

## The château

**Musée Pyrénéen** 25 rue du Fort Daily: April–May 9am–noon & 1.30–6.30pm, no lunch break June–Sept; Oct–March daily 9am–noon & 2–6pm, 5pm on Fri · €7 · ☎ 05 62 42 37 37, ⊚ lourdes-visite.com

Lourdes' only secular attraction is its spectacular **château**, poised on a rocky bluff east of the Gave de Pau, and guarding the approaches to the valleys and passes of the central

Pyrenees. Inside is the surprisingly excellent **Musée Pyrénéen**. Its collections include Pyrenean fauna, all sorts of fascinating pastoral and farming gear, and an interesting section on the history of Pyrenean mountaineering.

### Grottes de Bétharram

St-Pé-de-Bigorre, 8 miles west of Lourdes just off the D937 • Guided visits only late March to June & Sept–Oct daily 9am–noon & 1.30–5.30pm; July–Aug 9am–6pm; mid-Feb to late March Mon–Thurs tours at 2.30pm & 4pm, Fri 2.30pm only; tours last 1hr 20min • Adult €14.50, child €9 • ☎ 05 62 41 80 04, ⓦ betharram.com

One worthwhile excursion from Lourdes, particularly for families, is to this large system of caves. Part of the eighty-minute tour around its spectacular stalactites and stalagmites takes place in a barge on an underground lake; the remaining kilometre is by miniature railway.

### ARRIVAL AND INFORMATION                                              LOURDES

**By plane** The Tarbes-Lourdes airport is currently served by no-frills flights from Britain. Take the "Maligne Gave" #2 bus into town (€2).

**By train** Lourdes' *gare SNCF* is on the northeast edge of the town centre, at 33 av de la Gare.
Destinations Bayonne (6 daily; 1hr 40min); Pau (20 daily; 30min); Tarbes (21 daily; 15min).

**By bus** The *gare routière* is in central place Capdevieille.

Destinations Cauterets (6 daily; 55min); Gavarnie (1 daily; 1hr 40min); Tarbes (9–14 daily; 30min).

**Tourist office** Place Peyramale (Nov–March Mon–Sat 9am–noon & 2–5.30pm; April to June Mon–Sat 9am–12.30pm & 1.30–6.30pm, Sun 10am–12.30pm; July & Aug Mon–Sat 9am–7pm, Sun 10am–6pm; Oct Mon–Sat 9am–12.30pm & 1.30–6pm; ☎ 05 62 42 77 40, ⓦ lourdes-infotourisme.com).

### ACCOMMODATION

Lourdes has more hotels than any city in France outside Paris and consequently competition is intense.

**Au Berceau de Bernadette** 44 bd de la Grotte ☎ 05 62 42 76 58, ⓦ berceau-bernadette-lourdes.com. Pray at your convenience at this *petite résidence* with its own DIY chapel. Religious imagery is present throughout the building without being too overbearing while the rooms offer space, comfort and hot beverages in your room – a

rarity in France – plus breakfast is included. Closed Nov–March. **€60**

**Méditerranée** 23 av du Paradis ☎ 05 62 94 72 15, ⓦ lourdeshotelmed.com. Overlooking the river, this modern hotel rises above the town's tatty norm. The rooms are bright and well equipped if a little on the pokey side. Continental breakfast buffet is an additional €13. **€65**

### EATING AND DRINKING

**Brasserie Le Van Gogh** 16 place Marcadal ☎ 05 62 93 90 86. Stylish café, restaurant and bar that pays homage to the great painter with replicas adorning the walls and tankers of beer brewing on the ceiling. It's a popular haunt for thirty-somethings at weekends with punters spilling out onto the large pavement seating area outside. If you fancy a bite, there's crowd-pleasing faves like chicken and rice for €10. Sun–Thurs 8am–1am, Fri & Sat 8am–2am, closes at 5pm on Wed. Food served until 9pm

**O Piment Rouge** 37 rue de la Grotte ☎ 05 62 41 47 87, ⓦ restaurant-piment-rouge.com. The default strategy when looking for a restaurant in Lourdes should always be

to stay off the main tourist drag. Not so with this gem of a restaurant that serves simple but not simplistic Basque/French platters in a cosy timbered building. Three-course *menus* range from €19 to €29 and might include foie gras, lamb and profiteroles. Thur–Tues noon–1.45pm & 7–9.30pm, closed Tues & Wed between Nov & March.

**Le Palacio** 28 place du Champ-Commun ☎ 05 62 94 00 59, ⓦ restaurant-lourdes-palacio.fr. Just out of reach of the touristic concourse trappings, *Le Palacio* offers solid French cuisine served on the sunny *place*. You can dine on a budget here with their *plat du jour* for €8.50 or pizzas starting at €7. Daily noon–1.30pm & 7–9.30pm.

## The Vallée d'Aspe

The **Vallée d'Aspe** presents the central Pyrenees at their most undeveloped, primarily because inappropriate topography and unreliable snow conditions have precluded ski-resort construction.

## GETTING AROUND AND INFORMATION

**By train** The train from Pau serves the grey town of Oloron-Ste-Marie (8 daily; 40min), which sits 45km west of Lourdes. From there, the bus that goes deeper into the valley is sometimes coordinated to depart from the train station eight minutes later.

**By bus** Five buses daily journey up the valley, through the Tunnel du Somport into Spanish territory. Destinations on the way include Bedous (33min), Pont-de-Lescun (a 5km walk from Lescun village) (40min), Cette Eygun (42min), Etsaut (48min), and Urdos (55min).

## Lescun

Some 35km south of Pau, southwest of the N134 and valley floor, the ancient stone-and-stucco houses of **LESCUN** huddle on the northeast slopes of a huge and magnificent green **cirque**. The floor of the cirque and the lower slopes, dimpled with vales and hollows, have been gently shaped by generations of farming, while to the west the town is overlooked by the great grey molars of Le Billare, Trois Rois and Ansabère, beyond which rises the storm-lashed bulk of the **Pic d'Anie** (2504m).

## ARRIVAL AND INFORMATION

The bus from Oloron-Ste-Marie stops in the valley floor below Lescun; then it's a three-mile hike up the hill to the village. Alternatively, you can hop off a couple of stops early and take a taxi from Bedous. Taxis can be taken from the garage on the southern end of town. Ideally, phone or email ahead to book: ☎ 05 59 34 70 06 or ✉ gerard.lepretre@wanadoo.fr.

## ACCOMMODATION

**Camping Le Lauzart** Turn left onto the D340 just before Lescun village and continue for one mile ☎ 05 59 34 78 80, ⓦ camping-gite-lescun-pyrenees.com. This lush green campsite has a stupendous position with unimpeded views of the peaks. The site owners sell basic provisions and might even cook breakfast or dinner for you bearing in mind there's no restaurant in the village. May–Sept. €12.60

**Chambres d'Hôtes Pic d'Anie** Place Centrale ☎ 05 59 34 71 54, ⓦ hebergement-picdanie.fr. A characterful old building full of plants and ancient wooden furniture that give insight into the house's past. The bedrooms are on the small side but are at least en suite and there's also a reading room, handy for the frequent rain showers. Breakfast €8. April to mid-Sept. €50

**Gîte Pic d'Anie** Opposite the Chambres d'Hôtes Pic d'Anie. Run by the same establishment as the *Chambres d'Hôtes Pic d'Anie*, the simple and clean interior here lacks the charm of its neighbouring accommodation but at least has cooking facilities in this restaurant-less town. Supplies can be bought from the shop across the road. Breakfast €8. €16

## Cette-Eygun

A couple of kilometres beyond the turn-off for Lescun is **CETTE-EYGUN**, a pretty little village with a few good walking opportunities, but the main reasons to come here are to dine and sleep it off at the beautiful *Château d'Arance* (see below) with its bird's-eye view of the valley.

## ACCOMMODATION AND EATING

★ **Le Château d'Arance** ☎ 05 59 34 75 50, ⓦ chateau darance.com. Converted and modernized twelfth-century stone manor house with spectacular, unhampered views. Internally, the hotel in places lacks the charm promised by its well-restored exterior, but the bedrooms come with all the conveniences you would expect for the price and are thus comfortable. On summer evenings the château's vaulted restaurant spills out onto the dramatically set terrace (leisurely breakfasts – €9 – are also enjoyed here), where you can sample the food you see being produced across the valley. Catch of the day (fresh trout or salmon) is usually on the set menu, as is the Basque cheese platter, all washed down with a nice €15 bottle of Béarnais wine. *Menus* start at €20. Restaurant open noon–2pm & 7.30–9pm; closed Mon Nov–Feb. Reservation essential if not a guest. €70

## Urdos

Some 10km south of Cette-Eygun, **URDOS** is the last village on the French side of the frontier, and has one of the best hotel-restaurants (see below) in the valley. From here, you (and the odd bus) can continue through the free tunnel under the **Col de Somport** and on to Canfranc in Spain, the terminus for trains from Jaca, though in fine weather the far more scenic road over the pass is not too strenuous a drive.

Further upstream – about two miles north of Urdos – at one of the narrowest, rockiest, steepest points of the Aspe squats the menacing nineteenth-century **Fort du Portalet** (guided tours only: mid-April to June & Sept–Oct Wed 2.30pm & Sun 10am; July & Aug 10am & 2.30pm, Sun just 10am; €10; reservation only via ☎05 59 34 57 57 or online at ⓦtourisme-aspe.com/fort-du-portalet.html). Built to defend against Spanish incursions, the garrison housed over four hundred men and could withstand a week's siege in total autonomy. In the 1940s it served as a prison for Socialist premier Léon Blum under Pétain's Vichy government, and then for Pétain himself after the liberation of France. Today the fort is undergoing major restoration work and visits are temporarily limited.

### ACCOMMODATION AND EATING                                                                                       URDOS

★ **Des Voyageurs** Rte du Col du Somport ☎ 05 59 34 88 05, ⓦhotel-voyageurs-valleeaspe.com. Good old-fashioned hotel that has made a name for itself – at least locally – for its fine restaurant. The €15.50 set *menu* kicks off with a robust and filling *garbure* followed by a more delicate main course of trout, stuffed with ceps. Restaurant 12.15–2pm & 7.30–9pm; closed Mon & Sun eve. Breakfast is €6.50. The hotel is closed mid-Oct to Nov. Doubles **€52**

## Vallée d'Ossau

A destination for hikers, cyclists and snow-sports enthusiasts rather than casual day-trippers, the route up the **Ossau valley** rises fast towards the gnarled eminence of the Pic du Midi and the Cirque d'Anéou on the Spanish border. Outside winter the landscape is lush and green, with high pastures grazed by the sheep whose milk provides the distinctive Ossau-Iraty cheese (see page 600), a Béarn/Basque delicacy not to be missed. Near the Col, look out for marmots (a type of rodent), that never stray far from their burrows. The villages on the way are little reason to stick around – except for unremarkable Laruns, in order to stock up on supplies, and the two spa resorts of Eaux-Chaudes and Eaux-Bonnes, which retain charm even if they have seen more prosperous times.

### GETTING AROUND AND INFORMATION                                                              VALLÉE D'OSSAU

**By bus** From Pau, four buses daily call at Laruns (1hr 5min) before turning east towards Eaux-Bonnes (1hr 15min) and Gourette (1hr 30min). For destinations south to the border change at Laruns for one of two coordinated buses that stop at Eaux-Chaudes (10min) and Gabas (25min).
**Tourist office** Place de la Mairie, in Laruns village (Sept to mid-July daily 9am–noon & Mon–Sat 2–6pm; mid-July to Aug Mon–Sat 9am–7.30pm & Sun 9am–6pm; ☎05 59 05 31 41).
**Maison du Parc** Next to the tourist office (mid-June to mid-Sept Mon–Fri 9am–noon & 2–5.30pm; closed Sat & Sun and every second Fri; ☎05 59 05 41 59).

## Eaux-Chaudes

The D934 road from Laruns towards the Spanish border winds steeply into the upper reaches of the Gave d'Ossau valley, passing through **EAUX-CHAUDES** spa village: an attractive ghost town of a place, somewhat run-down but unspoilt by development and an ideal base for climbers and walkers. The perfect place to rest weary bones is the **Thermes des Eaux-Chaudes**, next to the river (May–Oct Mon–Sat 9am–noon & 3.30–6.30pm; ☎05 59 05 31 41, ⓦeauxchaudes.fr). It's in a lovely vintage building, and offers the usual spa facilities and treatments, from jet showers (€10) to massages (€45). Further en route, the **Pic du Midi d'Ossau** comes into view, with its craggy, mitten-shaped summit (2884m) – it's a classic Pyrenean landmark.

### ACCOMMODATION AND EATING                                                               EAUX-CHAUDES

**Auberge La Caverne** Southern edge of the village ☎ 05 59 05 34 40, ⓦaubergelacaverne.com. Run by a hard-working couple who offer both dorms and en-suite doubles in a jolly, old building. Reasonably priced *table d'hôte* meals

11

## LE PETIT TRAIN D'ARTOUSTE

**Le Petit Train d'Artouste** (late May to early Sept 9am–5pm hourly (every 30min in July & Aug); €17 one-way; €25 return; ☎ 05 59 05 36 99, ⓦ altiservice.com) chugs along a spectacular miniature railway line that runs ten vertiginous kilometres southeast through the mountains from **Lac de Fabrèges**, 13km south of Eaux-Chaudes, to **Lac d'Artouste**. Built in the 1920s to service a hydroelectric project and later converted for tourist purposes, this is a beautiful trip, lasting about four hours there and back, including the initial *télécabine* ride from the base of **Pic de la Sagette** (2031m). Tickets can be purchased from the tourist office in the resort at Lac de Fabrèges and the *télécabine* leaves from next door.

are also available starting from €8 for a crêpe, €12 for dishes like Basque chicken; or, if you're just passing through, stop for a drink on the flowery terrace. Service any time of the day. Open May–Oct & mid-Dec to mid-Feb. Dorms half-board €50, rooms half-board €110

★ **Chambre d'hôte Baudot** Place Henri-IV ☎ 05 59 05 34 51, ⓦ chambre-hote-baudot.com. Impeccably restored old hotel next to the spa offering understated charm and good value. The three-storey nineteenth-century building has large en-suite rooms and breakfasts by a log fire when the air gets a bit nippy. June–Sept. Rates include breakfast. €65

## Eaux-Bonnes

The only way of reaching the Gave de Pau by road without going back towards Pau is along the minor D918 east over the Col d'Aubisque, via Eaux-Bonnes and **Gourette**, 12km east of Laruns and the favourite **ski centre** of folk from Pau. The base development is ugly but the skiing, on 28 north-facing runs from a top point of 2400m, is more than respectable. You can of course stay here, but the once thriving spa village of **EAUX-BONNES**, 8km below Gourette, is more elegant and pleasant. Save for the unattractive tourist info hut, the village remains undeveloped and thus retains a certain charm especially out of high season when you practically have the town to yourself.

### INFORMATION EAUX-BONNES

**Tourist office** In the central *place* (Mon–Fri 9.30am–noon & 2–5.30pm; July & Aug Mon–Sat 9.30am–5.30pm; ☎ 05 59 05 12 17, ⓦ gourette.com).

### ACCOMMODATION AND EATING

**Hôtel des Eaux-Bonnes** 19 rue Louis-Barthou ☎ 05 59 50 33 06. This old-fashioned hotel offers spacious rooms spread round a central indoor courtyard overlooking a quirky fish pond containing trout. Needless to say, trout appears on the hotel's restaurant menu along with other regional mainstays. The three-course *menu* costs €19.50. €55

## Arrens-Marsous

The Col d'Aubisque (1709m), a grassy saddle with a souvenir stall/café on top, usually sees the Tour de France whizz through, making the pass irresistible to any French cyclist worth their salt. Once over the next mound – the lower Col de Soulor (1475m) – the route descends, 18km in all, to attractive **ARRENS-MARSOUS**, at the head of the Val d'Azun.

### INFORMATION ARRENS-MARSOUS

**Tourist office** Housed in the Maison du Val d'Azun in the village centre (mid-June to mid-Sept only Mon–Sat 9am– noon & 2–6pm, Sun 9am–12.30pm; ☎ 05 62 97 49 49, ⓦ valdazun.com).

### ACCOMMODATION

**Chambre d'hôte La Condorinette** 3 rue de la Gourgoutière, Marsous ☎ 05 62 92 06 39, ⓦ chambres hotes.pyrenees-65.com. Friendly B&B offering colourful double rooms plus a two-bed family suite. The wood-burning stove in the lounge/dining room makes for a pleasant backdrop to the substantial breakfasts provided and on warmer days you can eat outside in the orchard garden. Evening meals are also provided for €26 and offer simple but delicious home cooking with a strong but not exclusive emphasis on Béarnaise cuisine. May–Oct. Doubles €68, family suite €125

# The Gave de Pau

From its namesake city, the **Gave de Pau** forges southeast towards the mountains, bending sharply south at Lourdes and soon fraying into several tributaries: the **Gave d'Azun**, the **Gave de Cauterets**, the **Gave de Gavarnie** and the **Gave de Bastan**, dropping from the Col du Tourmalet. **Cauterets**, 30km due south of Lourdes, and **Gavarnie**, 37km southeast of Argelès, are busy, established resorts on the edge of the national park, but the countryside they adjoin is so spectacular that you forgive their deficiencies. If you want a smaller, more manageable base, then either **Barèges**, up a side valley from the spa resort of **Luz-St-Sauveur**, or Luz itself, are better bets. But pick your season well – or even the time of day – and you can enjoy the most popular sites in relative solitude. At Gavarnie few people stay the night, so it's quiet early or late, and the **Cirque de Troumouse**, which is just as impressive (though much harder to get to without a car), has far fewer visitors.

## Cauterets

**CAUTERETS** is a pleasant if unexciting little town that owes its fame and rather elegant Neoclassical architecture (especially on boulevard Latapie-Flurin) to its spa, and more recently to its role as one of the main Pyrenean ski and mountaineering centres. The town is small and easy to get around; most of it is still squeezed between the steep wooded heights that close the mouth of the Gave de Cauterets valley.

**11**

### ARRIVAL AND INFORMATION
CAUTERETS

**By bus** Buses arrive at the lovely old *gare* on av de la Gare on the north edge of the centre from Lourdes (6 daily & one extra on Fri; 55min).

**Tourist office** Place du Maréchal-Foch (July & Aug Mon–Sat 9am–noon & 2–7pm, Sun 9am–noon & 2–6pm; Sept–

June Mon–Sat 9am–noon & 2–5pm; ☎05 62 92 50 50, ⓦcauterets.com).

**Maison du Parc** Av de la Gare, on the northern edge of the centre (Mon–Fri 9.30am–noon & 3–6.30pm; ☎05 62 92 52 56). A good source of walking maps and hiking route advice.

### ACCOMMODATION

**Camping La Prairie** Rte de Pierrefitte (D920) ☎05 62 92 07 04, ⓦcampinglaprairie.over-blog.com. A 5min walk north of the town centre – and one of a number of campsites on this side of town – *La Prairie* is predominantly a canvas site with a few basic facilities and consequently is the cheapest of the bunch. Mid-May to mid-Oct. **€13**

**Le Lion d'Or** 12 rue Richelieu ☎05 62 92 52 87, ⓦhotel-cauterets.fr. One of the town's more charming options, this hotel has been in the same family for a century yet is

tastefully decorated with a combination of antiques and quaint furnishings and sits around the corner from a nice open-air thermal pool. **€84**

**Le Pas de l'Ours** 21 rue de la Raillère ☎05 62 92 58 07, ⓦlepasdelours.com. Clean and warm hotel and *gîte d'étape* with so much pine cladding, it's almost a sauna. The double rooms offer reasonably good value but if you're alone or on a budget, the six-bed dorms are the town's best option. Dorm **€22**, doubles (B&B) **€84**

### EATING

**La Crêperie du Gave** Galerie Aladin, rue de Belfort ☎05 62 45 09 96. Located on the west side of the river, this small, economical restaurant serves *galettes* with a drink from €5.50 to €9.90 or three-course *menus* including wine/cider for €13. Noon–2pm & 7–9pm, closed Sun eve & Mon. During school holidays: daily noon–2pm, 4.30–5.30pm & 7–9pm.

**Les Halles de Cauterets** Av du Général-Leclerc. For tantalizing takeaway food, visit this indoor market with its rotisseries selling hot meals by the kilo. Stuff your picnic hamper with roast lamb or vegetable gratin or if you're off on a hike, get delicious sandwiches made up for you. The *fromagerie* attached to the Halles sells wonderful aged *brebis*. Daily 9am–noon & 2–6pm.

## Luz-St-Sauveur

The only road approach to the cirques Gavarnie and Troumouse is through **LUZ-ST-SAUVEUR**, astride the GR10. Like Cauterets, this was a nineteenth-century spa, patronized by Napoléon III and Eugénie, and elegant Neoclassical facades in the left-bank St-Sauveur quarter date from then.

The **St-André church** (approximately daily mid-May to end Sept 3–6pm; free) on place de la Comporte at the top of Luz's medieval, right-bank quarter is the town's principal sight. Built in the late eleventh century, it was fortified in the fourteenth by the Knights of St John with a crenelated outer wall and two stout towers. The north entrance sports a handsome portal surmounted by a Christ in Majesty carved in fine-grained local stone.

## ARRIVAL AND INFORMATION                                    LUZ-ST-SAUVEUR

**By bus** The service between Lourdes and Barèges stops outside the tourist office on place du 8-mai. There is one direct bus from Lourdes that runs on school days and 4 to 5 indirect buses daily that involve a co-ordinated change at

Pierrefitte Nestallas, a few kilometres north of Luz.
**Tourist office** On the edge of the central place du 8-mai (Mon–Sat 9am–noon & 2–6.30pm, Sun 9am–noon; ☏ 05 62 92 30 30, ⓦ luz.org).

## ACCOMMODATION

★ **Le Montaigu** Rte de Vizos ☏ 05 62 92 81 71, ⓦ hotel montaigu.com. This modern three-star hotel sits in a semi-rural position beneath the ruined tenth-century château Ste-Marie (a 5min uphill saunter). The rooms have large balconies with cracking south-westerly views to the high Pyrenees. Breakfast included. Doubles **€102**, half-board **€142**

**Les Templiers** 6 place de la Comporte ☏ 05 62 92 81 52, ⓦ hotel-luz.com. With en-suite rooms looking onto a beautiful eleventh-century church, this rustic gem, clad in Virginia creeper and climbing rose, is centrally located in a peaceful square. The hotel also runs an organic crêperie downstairs and provides a tasty €7.50 breakfast. **€79**

## EATING

★ **Chez Christine** 3 rue Dossun-Prolongée ☏ 05 62 92 86 81. Although this is predominantly a pizzeria, the quality of the own-made pasta and desserts plus locally sourced meat dishes make this a superb all-rounder. Vegetarians

will find a lot to choose from here including cheesy fondues for €18 (min two persons) and pizzas starting at €8. Mon, Tues & Thurs–Sat 7–9.30pm.

## Gavarnie

Once poor and depopulated, **Gavarnie** village found the attractions of mass tourism – much of it excursions from Lourdes – too seductive to resist, and it's now filled with souvenir shops and snack bars.

## ARRIVAL AND INFORMATION                                            GAVARNIE

**By car** If you drive in, a parking fee (May to Oct 8am–5pm; €5) is charged; otherwise there is ample free parking around the shops and hotels.
**By bus** Buses leave the *gare routière* in Lourdes at 8.58am, stop at Luz-St-Sauveur at 9.53am and head on to Gavarnie's tourist office. The bus back to Lourdes departs at 5.30pm. The journey takes 1hr 40min.

**Tourist office** By the car park (Mon–Sat 9am–noon & 2–6pm; plus Sun during July & Aug & during the ski season 9am–noon & 2–6pm; ☏ 05 62 92 49 10, ⓦ gavarnie.com).
**Maison du Parc** On the main drag past the car park (Mon–Thurs 8.30am–noon & 1.30–6pm & Fri 8.30am–noon; ☏ 05 62 92 42 48).

## ACCOMMODATION

**La Bergerie** Chemin du Cirque ☏ 05 62 92 48 41, ⓦ camping-gavarnie-labergerie.com. Surely one of the most stunningly located Pyrenean campsites, with views compensating for basic facilities. The site has a laundry room and a small bar serving wine and *pression* beer. June–Sept. **€11.70**
★ **Compostelle** Rue de l'Église ☏ 05 62 92 49 43, ⓦ compostellehotel.com. Thanks to its elevated position next to the beautiful old church, this pretty hotel has the best views in town onto the cirque. Inside, the decor may not be that of a deluxe hotel but it's all clean and functional. Breakfast €7.50. Closed Oct to mid-Jan. Doubles **€53**, half-board **€56pp**
**Gîte Auberge Le Gypaète** Below the main car park

behind the tourist office ☏ 05 62 92 40 61, ⓦ legypaete. pagesperso-orange.fr. Nice little stone cottage with a wall humorously covered in climbing footholds. Inside there's a large dining area and, incredibly, 45 beds jammed in, literally to the rafters. Most guests opt for the hearty half-board option and wash it down with a €5 half-litre of house wine. There's free internet here and picnics on request for €9. Dorms **€15**, half-board **€36**
**Vignemale** Across the river at the end of the village ☏ 05 62 92 40 00, ⓦ hotel-vignemale.com. For three-star luxury, this hotel, astride the *gave*, offers spacious rooms and balconies with unimpeded views to the cirque. Closed mid-Oct to mid-May. **€150**

## THE CIRQUE DE GAVARNIE

Victor Hugo called it "Nature's Colosseum" – a magnificent, natural amphitheatre scoured out by glaciers. Over 1500m high, the Gavarnie cirque consists of three sheer bands of rock streaked by seepage and waterfalls, separated by sloping ledges covered with snow and glacier remnants. On the east, it's dominated by the jagged **Astazou** and **Marboré** peaks, both over 3000m. In the middle, a cornice sweeps round to the **Brèche de Roland**, a curious vertical slash, 100m deep and about 60m wide, said to have been hewn from the ridge by Roland's sword, Durandal. In winter, there's good beginner-to-intermediate **skiing** at the nearby 24-run resort of **Gavarnie-Gèdre**, with great views of the cirque from the top point of 2400m.

From Gavarnie village an unmade road follows the river towards the cirque, gradually narrowing as the gradient and the drama increases. It's a moderately easy hour's walk in each direction but if you prefer, hire a horse from the edge of town for €25. The broad track ends at the *Hôtel du Cirque et de la Cascade*, once a famous meeting place for mountaineers and now a popular snack bar in summer.

To get to the foot of the cirque walls, you face a steeper, final half-hour on a dwindling, increasingly slippery path which ends in a spray-bath at the base of the **Grande Cascade**, fed by Lago Helado on the Spanish side, and at 423m the highest waterfall in Europe. This plummets and fans out in three stages down the rock faces – a fine sight in sunny weather, with rainbows in the wind-teased plumes. For a bit of serenity the best time to see the cirque is at dusk when, even in summer, you could have it all to yourself.

### EATING AND INFORMATION

★ **Les Cascades** Next to the Maison du Parc ☎ 05 62 92 40 17. A gastronomic highlight of the town, this restaurant presents fresh regional platters with low food-mile ingredients. All with the added benefit of tables overlooking the cirque. *Menus* range from €16–35. May–Oct Mon–Sat noon–1.30pm & 7–8.30pm.

## The Cirque de Troumouse

Much bigger than Gavarnie and, in bad weather, rather intimidating, the **Cirque de Troumouse** forms a 10km wall of curved rock shorn by glacial action. A mere 22km by road from Gavarnie village, it would be inconceivable to visit one cirque and not the other. Just north of Gavarnie the D922 forks to the right leading up a wild valley whose only habitations are the handful of farmsteads and a pilgrimage chapel, with its ancient polychrome statuette of the Virgin and Child, that make up the scattered hamlet of **HÉAS** – among the loneliest outposts in France before the road in was constructed.

### GETTING THERE                                          CIRQUE DE TROUMOUSE

**By car** After 8km up the D922 from Gavarnie, vehicles need to pay a toll (€5) although only when the booth is open: May–Oct 9am–5pm, depending on the weather.

### ACCOMMODATION AND EATING

**Auberge de la Munia** Héas ☎ 05 62 92 48 39, ⓦ aubergedelamunia.com. With a handful of plain rooms and an attractive garden this is the most appealing place to stay in this remote valley. Many stop off at the auberge's restaurant when returning from the cirque and the proportions are in keeping with hiker appetites. Expect hearty stews with meat, veg and beans and delightfully calorific puddings like blueberry *clafoutis*. Three-course *menus* are €20. Food available 7.30–8.30pm; closed when there is no B&B. **€66**, half-board **€50pp**

## Barèges

The only major village in the Cirque de Bastan is **BARÈGES**, primarily a skiing, mountaineering and paragliding centre, and the most congenial, low-key resort around the Gave de Pau.

### ARRIVAL AND INFORMATION                                BARÈGES

**By bus** Buses stop on rue du Dr-Ducos one block from the tourist office. There is one direct service from Lourdes that runs on school days and 4 to 5 indirect buses daily that involve a coordinated change at Pierrefitte Nestallas, a

> ### SKIING AND HIKING AROUND BARÈGES
>
> With its links to the adjacent, equal-sized *domaine* of **La Mongie** over 10km east on the far side of the Col du Tourmalet, Barèges offers access to the largest **skiing** area in the French Pyrenees, including downhill pistes totalling 125km (1850–2400m) and 31km of cross-country trails through the Lienz plateau forest (1350–1700m). Beginners' runs finishing in Barèges village are much too low (1250m) to retain snow, so all skiers usually have to start from the Tournaboup or Tourmalet zones. High-speed, state-of-the-art chair lifts are the rule at Barèges, and runs have been regraded to make the resort more competitive, but La Mongie over the hill, despite its hideous purpose-built development, offers even higher, longer pistes. For more information consult ⓦ grand-tourmalet.com.
>
> The **GR10** passes through Barèges on its way southeast into the lake-filled **Néouvielle Massif**, part of France's oldest (1935) natural reserve, and a great **hiking** area. The best trailhead for **day-hikes** lies 3km east of Barèges on the D918 at **Pont de la Gaubie** (you'll see a small car park and an abandoned snack bar), from where the classic seven-hour day-loop takes in the Vallée des Aygues Cluses plus the lakes and peak of Madamète, followed by a descent via Lac Nère and Lac dets Coubous back to Gaubie.

**11**

few kilometres north of Luz-St-Sauveur. From Lourdes (5 indirect Mon–Sat & 4 Sun; 1hr 5min).

**Tourist office** Place Urbain-Cazaux (July & Aug Mon–Sat 9am–12.30pm & 2–6.30pm, Sun 10am–noon & 4–6pm; Sept–June closes 5pm; ☎ 05 62 92 16 00, ⓦ grand-tourmalet.com). Can supply ski-lift passes.

### ACCOMMODATION

**La Montagne Fleurie** 21 rue Ramon ☎ 05 62 92 68 50, ⓦ montagnefleurie.fr. The best value out of the handful of hotels lining the main road, this eighteenth-century building has been restored with dignity and thought. Breakfast is a little on the pricey side at €9.50, however evening meals are traditional, varied and inexpensive at €17. **€82.50**

# The Comminges

Stretching from Luchon almost to Toulouse, the **Comminges** is an ancient feudal county encompassing the upper Garonne river valley. It also hosts one of the finest buildings in the Pyrenees, a magnificent cathedral built over three distinct periods in **St-Bertrand-de-Comminges**.

## St-Bertrand-de-Comminges

The grey fortress-like **cathedral** (April & Oct Mon–Sat 10am–noon & 2–6pm, Sun 2–6pm; May–Sept Mon–Sat 9am–7pm, Sun 2–5pm; Nov–Feb Mon–Sat 10am–noon & 2–6pm, Sun 2–5pm; admission to cloister and choir €5) of **ST-BERTRAND-DE-COMMINGES** commands the plain from its knoll-top position, the austere white-veined facade and heavily buttressed nave totally subduing the clutch of fifteenth- and sixteenth-century houses huddled at its feet. To the right of the west door a Romanesque twelfth-century cloister with carved capitals looks out across a lush valley to the foothills, haunt of Resistance fighters during World War II. In the aisleless interior, the church's great attraction is the central choir, built by Toulousain craftsmen and installed 1523–35. The 66 elaborately carved stalls, each one the work of a different craftsman, are a feast of virtuosity, mingling piety, irony and satire. During the summer (mid-July to mid-Aug), the cathedral and St-Just in Valcabrère, both with marvellous acoustics, host the musical Festival du Comminges (ⓦ festival-du-comminges.com).

## St-Just de Valcabrère

April–Sept 10am–7pm; Oct noon–6pm; Nov–March Sat & Sun only 2–6pm • €3 • ☎ 05 61 95 44 44

One mile east of St-Bertrand, there's an exquisite Romanesque church – the **St-Just de Valcabrère** – whose square tower rises above a cypress-studded cemetery. The north portal is girded by four elegant full-length sculptures and overtopped by a relief of Christ in Glory borne heavenward by angels. Both interior and exterior are full of recycled masonry from the Roman **Lugdunum Convenarum**, whose remains are visible at the crossroads just beyond the village.

### The Grottes de Gargas

About 6km from St-Bertrand in the direction of St-Laurent are the **Grottes de Gargas** (guided tours daily every 30min: July & Aug 10am–6pm; rest of year 10.30am– 5.30pm Tues–Sun, but reservations usually necessary; €10.50; ☎ 05 62 98 81 50, Ⓦ grottesdegargas.fr), renowned for their 231 prehistoric painted hand-prints outlined in black, red, yellow or white. The prints seem to be deformed – perhaps the result of leprosy, frostbite or ritual mutilation, though no one really knows why.

---

**INFORMATION**                                          **ST-BERTRAND-DE-COMMINGES**

**Tourist office** In the nineteenth-century Olivétain chapel and monastery on the cathedral square (May–Sept Mon– Sat 9am–7pm, Sun 2–5pm; otherwise Mon–Sat 10am–

noon & 2–5pm; ☎ 05 61 95 44 44). The office doubles as a festival box office.

---

**ACCOMMODATION AND EATING**

**Chez Simone** Rue du Musée ☎ 05 61 94 91 05. Specializing in wood-pigeon stew, this friendly family-run restaurant serves hearty regional food with little concession for vegetarians. There's a lovely terrace outside and the beam-ceilinged interior has nice views and a fireplace. Three-course *menus* begin at €20. Daily noon–2pm plus mid-July to mid-Sept 7–9pm; closed Jan and when there's snow.

**Du Comminges** Place du Bout du Pont ☎ 05 61 88 31 43, Ⓦ hotelducomminges.fr. This beautiful old building, part obscured by climbing plants, looks onto the cathedral. First impressions are good: there's a charming original oak front door and inside the exposed beams and heavy wood furniture add to the hotel's vintage atmosphere. The cheapest rooms have a shower but no toilet. The buffet breakfast costs €8. May to mid-Oct. **€65**

# The Eastern Pyrenees

The dominant climatic influence of the **Eastern Pyrenees**, excluding the misty Couserans region, is the Mediterranean; the climate is warmer, the days sunnier, the landscape more arid than elsewhere in the Pyrenees. Dry-weather plants like cistus, broom and thyme make their appearance, and the foothills are planted with vines. The proximity of Spain is evident, with much of the territory definitively incorporated into France in 1659 previously belonging to historical Catalonia. Like the rest of the Pyrenees, the countryside is spectacular, and densely networked with hiking trails. Historical sights, except the painted caves of the **Ariège** and the Cathar castles and medieval towns of the **upper Aude**, are concentrated towards the coast in French Catalonia and along the Tech and Tet valleys.

## Val d'Ariège

Whether you're coming from the western Pyrenees or heading south from the major transport hub of Toulouse, the **Val d'Ariège** marks the start of the transition to the Mediterranean zone. The river, extending from high peaks along the Andorran border around the spa of Ax-les-Thermes down to agricultural plains north of **Foix**, forms the main axis of the eponymous *département*. In between lie a wealth of **caves**, most notably near Tarascon and Le-Mas-d'Azil. Transport is no problem as long as you stick to the valley.

### Foix

France's smallest *départemental* capital, **FOIX**, lies 82km south of Toulouse on the Toulouse–Barcelona train line. It's an agreeable country town of narrow alleys and sixteenth- to seventeenth-century half-timbered houses, with an old quarter squeezed between the rivers Ariège and Arget.

Built one millennia ago on top of an existing seventh-century fortification, Foix's **château** (Feb–April & Oct–Dec & Jan weekends 10.30am–noon & 2–5.30pm; early May Mon–Fri 10.30am–noon & 2–5.30pm, Sat & Sun 10am–6pm; mid-May to June & early Sept 10am–6pm; July & Aug 10am–6.30pm; €6.70; ☎05 61 05 10 10) with its three distinctive hilltop towers, has seen its fair share of controversy: its counts sided against the Albigensians during their eleventh-century Cathar genocide and after the Revolution it became a home to political prisoners. Today it houses the small Musée de l'Ariège.

## ARRIVAL AND INFORMATION                                        FOIX

**By train** The *gares SNCF* and *routière* are together on av de la Gare, off the N20 on the right (east) bank of the Ariège. Destinations Ax-les-Thermes (13 daily, 8 on Sun, 45min); Latour-de-Carol (7 daily, 3 on Sun; 1hr 40min); Tarascon-sur-Ariège (10 daily, 8 on Sun; 15min); Toulouse (14 daily, 12 on Sun; 1hr 10min).

**Tourist office** 29 rue Théophile-Delcasse (July & Aug 9.30am–7pm, Sun 9.30am–12.30pm & 2–6pm; Sept–mid-June Mon–Sat 9.30am–noon & 2–6pm, mid-June–end-June Mon–Sat 9.30am–noon & 2–6pm,

Sun 9.30am–12.30pm & 2–6pm. ☎05 61 65 12 12, ⓦtourisme-foix-varilhes.fr).

**Boat trips** 6km north of Foix on the D1, boat trips set off for a 1.5km trip along Europe's longest underground river, the Rivière Souterraine de Labouiche. The trips (April–June & Sept 10–11am & 2–4.30pm; July–Aug 9.30am–5pm; Oct to mid-Nov Tues–Fri 2–4pm, Sat & Sun 10–11am & 2–4.30pm; €11.40; ☎05 61 65 04 11, ⓦlabouiche.com) take in the usual stalagtites and stalacmites and a beautiful waterfall.

## ACCOMMODATION

**Auberge Le Léo** 16 rue Noël-Peyrevidal ☎05 61 65 09 04, ⓦleodefoix.com. More an activity centre (rafting and the like) than a hostel but ideal if you're on a budget. The rooms are basic and pokey but come with bathrooms attached and free parking outside. Economical weekday lunches (noon–2pm) are available downstairs with

traditional *menus* costing €14. **€27pp**

**Lons** 6 place Duthil ☎05 34 09 28 00, ⓦhotel-lons-foix. com. This hotel is the quietest and most comfortable option in town, with a respected restaurant attached (*menus* from €13.90). Restaurant open daily noon–2pm & 7.30–9pm. Closed late Dec to early Jan. **€89**

## EATING

The prime area for eating is around rue de la Faurie in the town centre.

★ **Le Jeu de l'Oie** 17 rue de la Faurie ☎05 61 02 69 39. Does classic French country-bistro cuisine – cassoulet, duck dishes, terrines, offal, good desserts, Leffe draught beer

– at low prices (three-course *menus* with a glass of wine €17.50), which guarantees a lunch-time crush. Vegetarians can partake of the menu too with *tarte tatin* of vegetables followed by pesto tagliatelle. Tues–Sat noon–2.30pm & 7–10.30pm.

# Niaux

Some 21km south of Foix, the rather ordinary village of **Niaux** has found itself at the centre of the French Magdalenian era (approx 15,000 BC–7000 BC). Its surrounding hills of scrub-topped limestone conceal great cave systems (see box opposite) – rock carved by water over millennia, home to prehistoric hominids and the archeological treasures they left behind.

## ACCOMMODATION AND EATING                                    NIAUX

**La Petite Auberge de Niaux** Turn right as you enter Niaux village from the north ☎05 61 05 79 79, ⓦaubergedeniaux.com. Although predominantly a fine restaurant, the owners offer a two-bedroomed *gîte* with lounge, kitchenette and balconies overlooking the river. There's usually a 2-night minimum stay. The restaurant is nicely tucked away in an old stone building with alfresco dining an option in the garden. A wide variety of *menus*

are available with alluring names such as "Temptation", "Montagne" and "Terre d'Ariège" and a vegetarian *menu*, a rare occurrence, even makes an appearance. All high-end, regional cooking in idyllic surroundings. *Menus* range from €14.75–48. Restaurant open Tues–Sat noon–2pm & Tues–Sun 7.30–9pm. Usually closed mid-Nov to mid-Feb. **€75**

## PREHISTORIC PYRENEES

The following are a selection of the best prehistoric sights in the Pyrenees:

**Grotte de Niaux** 22km south of Foix (45min guided visits: Jan weekends, Feb & March Tues–Sun 3 daily 11am–4.15pm; April–June 5 daily 11am–4.15pm (1.30pm in English); July & Aug 10 daily between 9.45am–5.30pm (9.45am & 12.15pm in English); Sept–June 7 daily 10.15am–4.30pm (10.15am & 1pm in English); Oct 5 daily between 11am–4.15pm (1.30pm in English); Nov & Dec Wed–Sun 3 daily 11am–4.15pm; €12; advance reservations mandatory ☎ 05 61 05 10 10, ✉ info@grands-sites-ariege.fr). A huge cave complex under an enormous rock over-hang 2km north of the hamlet of Niaux. There are 4km of galleries in all, with paintings of the Magdalenian period scattered throughout, although tours see just a fraction of the complex. No colour is used to render the subjects – horses, ibex, stags and bison – just a dark outline and shading to give body to the drawings, executed with a "crayon" made of bison fat and manganese oxide.

**Grotte de la Vache** Alliat, 2km across the valley west from Niaux (90min guided tours: April–June & Sept Tues–Sat 10.30pm; July & Aug daily 11am, 2, 3, 4 & 5pm; otherwise by arrangement; €7; ☎ 05 61 05 10 10, ✇ grotte-de-la-vache.org). A relatively rare example of an inhabited cave where you can observe hearths, embossed bones, tools and other remnants in situ that date back 14,000 years.

**Grotte de Bédeilhac** Above Bédeilhac village; take the D618 from Tarascon towards Saurat; after 5km, the cave entrance yawns in the Soudour ridge (75min guided tours: April–June, Sept & school holidays Tues–Sun 2pm & 4pm; July & Aug daily 11am–5pm, Oct Wed–Fri 2pm & Sat–Sun 4pm, Nov–March Sat–Sun 10am; €9; ☎ 05 61 05 10 10, ✇ grotte-de-bedeilhac. org). Inside are examples of every known technique of Paleolithic art; while not as immediately powerful as at Niaux, its diversity – including modelled stalagmites and mud reliefs of beasts – compensates.

**Parc de la Préhistoire** 2km west of Tarascon on the D23 (April–June & Sept–Oct Mon–Fri 10am–6pm & weekends 10am–7pm, closed Mon in Sept & Oct; July & Aug daily 10am–8pm, last entry 5.30pm; €11.50; ☎ 05 61 05 10 10). This museum presents a circuit of discovery that shows the life and art of people from the Magdalenian period who lived in this area 14,000 years ago. Outdoor exhibits here feature engaging workshop demonstrations on archeology, prehistoric hunting, fire-making and art techniques, as well as a recreated encampment.

# The Pays de Sault

The **Pays de Sault** – a magnificent upland bounded by the rivers Ariège and Aude, and the D117 road from Foix to Quillan – marks the start of "Cathar country" (see page 622). The region's main town, **Lavelanet**, is a nondescript place on the banks of the River Touyre, 28km from Foix and 35km from Quillan, that offers little beyond bus connections – including north to **Mirepoix** covered on opposite, though it's not strictly in the *pays*.

## Roquefixade

ROQUEFIXADE sits roughly 19km east of Foix en route to Lavelanet; the ruined eleventh-century castle (free, unenclosed) towering above the village sets the scene for further Cathar exploration of the region.

### ACCOMMODATION ROQUEFIXADE

**Auberge des Troubadours** Just northeast of the village and well signposted ☎ 05 34 14 04 48, ✇ gite-etape-roquefixade.com. Dorm beds and family rooms in a beautiful old house in idyllic countryside. Ideally located for gentle hikes, although the *gîte* is also frequented by trekkers completing the final leg of the "Sentier Cathare", a 12-day route from the Mediterranean coast. The *gîte* does breakfasts for €7 and packed lunches for €10. All year. **€19pp**

## Montségur

The tiny village of **MONTSÉGUR**, a small distance south of Lavelanet, straggles in long terraces at the foot of its castle-rock, a modified version of a *bastide* (the original settlement was up by the castle). The castle itself (daily: Feb, Nov & Dec 11am–4pm; March & Oct 10am–5pm; April–June & Sept 10am–6pm; July–Aug 9am–7pm; Dec 10am–4pm, closed Jan; €5.50 (€6.50 in July & Aug); ✇ montsegur.fr) is not strictly

Cathar but actually a remnant of a fortification built on Cathar ruins to protect France from southern raiders. A garrison remained there until the Treaty of the Pyrenees in the seventeenth century. All that remains today are the stout, now truncated curtain walls and keep. The space within is terribly cramped, and you can easily imagine the sufferings of the six hundred or so persecuted Cathars.

## ACCOMMODATION

**Gîte Le Barry** Comus village ☎ 04 68 20 33 69, ⓦ gites-comus.com. Comus village has two good *gîtes d'étape*, *Barry du Haut* in the old rectory and *Barry d'en Bas* in the old town hall. You can also camp outside. All meals are provided:

breakfast is €7, a hot meal €20 and picnic provisions €10. Here you're just 2.5km shy of the D613 road between Ax-les-Thermes and Quillan, with two daily buses (not weekends) to the latter. Camping €10, dorms €23

## INFORMATION

**Tourist office** In the village *place* (July–Sept 10am–1pm

& 2–6pm; ☎ 05 61 01 06 94, ⓦ montsegur.fr).

## MONTSÉGUR

## ACCOMMODATION AND EATING

★ **Les Deux Petits Pois** 8km east of Montségur in Fougax-et-Barrineuf ☎ 05 61 01 46 90, ⓦ lesdeuxpetits pois.com. English/Canadian-run *chambre d'hôte* opposite the post office which has three lovely en-suite rooms, and offers a copious breakfast and vegetarian dinner on request for €25. **€80**

**La Patate Qui Fume** 118 rue du Village ☎ 05 61 02 65 07, ⓦ patatequifume.com. Turn right as soon as you enter

Montségur village from the south and you'll find this nice little restaurant offering alfresco dining. *Menus* ranging from €16 to €29 offer three home-made courses, with a vegetarian platter making an unexpected appearance next to the usual suspects of *magret de canard* and trout. For something slightly unusual, try the duck burger. Reservations in the evening only. April–Oct Mon–Sun noon–2pm & 7.30–8.30pm.

## Mirepoix

If you're heading north from Lavelanet towards Carcassonne, it's definitely worth stopping in at **MIREPOIX**, a late thirteenth-century *bastide* built around one of the finest surviving arcaded market squares – **Les Couverts** – in the country. The square is bordered by houses dating from the thirteenth to the fifteenth centuries, and a harmonizing modern *halle* on one side, but its highlight is the medieval **Maison des Consuls** (council house), whose rafter-ends are carved with dozens of unique portrayals of animals and monsters, and caricatures of medieval social groups and professions, as well as ethnic groups from across the world. Just south of Les Couverts is the early

---

### THE FALL OF MONTSÉGUR

Between 1204 and 1232, Montségur's castle was reconstructed by Guilhabert de Castres as a strongpoint for the **Cathars** (see page 622). By 1232 it – and the village at the base of the *pog* or rock pinnacle – had become the effective seat of the beleaguered Cathar Church, under the protection of a garrison commanded by Pierre-Roger de Mirepoix, with a population of some five hundred, clergy as well as ordinary believers fleeing Inquisition persecution.

Provoked by de Mirepoix's raid on Avignonet in May 1242, in which the eleven chief Inquisitors were hacked to pieces, the forces of the Catholic Church and the king of France laid siege to the castle in May 1243. By March 1244, Pierre-Roger, despairing of relief, agreed to terms. At the end of a fortnight's truce, the 225 Cathar civilians who still refused to recant their beliefs were burnt on a communal pyre on March 16.

Four men who had escaped Montségur unseen on the night of March 15 recovered the Cathar "treasure", hidden in a cave for safekeeping since late 1243, and vanished. Two of them later reappeared in Lombardy, where these funds were used to support the refugee Cathar community there for another 150 years. More recent New Age-type speculations, especially in German writings, identify this "treasure" as the Holy Grail, and the Cathars themselves as the Knights of the Round Table.

---

**A GORGE-OUS WALK**

From either Montségur or Fougax-et-Barrineuf, you can take an impressive half-day walk through the **Gorges de la Frau**, emerging at Comus hamlet in the heart of the Pays de Sault. The route from Montségur initially follows the "Sentier Cathare" until linking up with the **GR107** in the valley of the Hers river, which has carved out the gorge. Alternatively, starting from Fougax, just follow the minor D5 south along the Hers for 16km until the tarmac dwindles to a rough, steep track as you enter the gorges proper, where thousand-metre-high cliffs admit sunlight only at midday. The defile ends some 3.5km before Comus, where the track broadens and the grade slackens.

---

Gothic cathedral of **St-Maurice** which is claimed to have the largest undivided nave in France, supported only by airy rib vaulting.

### ARRIVAL AND INFORMATION | MIREPOIX

**By bus** Buses stop on cours du Colonel-Petit-Pied, one block north of the central place.
Destinations Lavelanet (1–7 daily; 25min); Toulouse (1–3 daily; 1hr 50min).

**Tourist office** Place du Maréchal-Leclerc, the main square (July & Aug Mon–Sat 9.15am–6.30pm, Sun 10am–6pm; Sept–June Mon–Sat 9.15am–12.15pm & 2–6pm, Sun 2–6pm; ☎05 61 68 83 76, ⓦtourisme-mirepoix.com).

### ACCOMMODATION AND EATING

**Camping Les Nysades** 2km east on the Limoux road (D626) ☎05 61 60 28 63, ⓦcamping-mirepoix-ariege. com. A small campsite that welcomes tents and caravans but with few facilities. Easter–Sept. **€16**

**Chambre d'hôte La Ferme de Boyer** 3km west of Mirepoix on the D119, the turning is on the left just past Besset village ☎05 61 68 93 41, ⓦfermeboyer.iowners. net. In a lovely eighteenth-century farmstead set back from the main road, this B&B offers a relaxing environment with its large garden and pool. Families can opt for the self-contained two-bedroomed cottage and either use the good kitchen facilities or let the hosts provide dinner for around €30. Doubles **€80**, cottage **€150**

**Maison des Consuls** 6 place du Maréchal-Leclerc ☎05 61 68 81 81, ⓦmaisondesconsuls.com. Extravagantly furnished hotel tucked into the medieval square and with a small patio out the back, to relax away from the masses. The more expensive rooms have private terraces overlooking the *place*. Breakfasts from €6.50–€16. **€90**

★**Les Remparts** 6 cours Louis-Pons-Tande ☎05 61 68 12 15, ⓦhotelremparts.com. The best-value accommodation in town, if you're looking for a mid-range hotel. The building may be old but the bedroom decor is sympathetically modern and comfortable. The hotel's restaurant targets gourmands with its typically small but pretty portions on big plates. That said, the ingredients are very fresh, seasonal and mostly local. Menus €25–64. Restaurant open Fri–Sun noon–1.45pm & Mon–Sat 7.15–9.30pm. **€75**

## Camon

Near enough to Mirepoix, 13km to the southeast, to make a pleasant day excursion, this walled medieval village is home to a twelfth to fourteenth-century **fortified Benedictine abbey** at the summit (now a *chambre d'hôte*).

### ACCOMMODATION AND EATING

★**L'Abbaye-Château de Camon** ☎05 61 60 31 23, ⓦchateaudecamon.com. A truly special retreat for those with deep pockets. There's a large pool, a part of the original cloister, eighteenth-century canvases in the lounge, a frescoed chapel, plus all the echoing galleries and spiral staircases you could want; the gourmet restaurant does dinner for all comers (€48 *table d'hôte*; Thurs–Tues 7.30–9pm). **€140**

## Vallée de l'Aude

South of Carcassonne, the D118 and the (mostly disused) rail line both forge steadily up the twisting **Vallée de l'Aude** between scrubby hills and vineyards, past **L'Abbaye de St-Hilaire** and its carved sarcophagus, river-straddling **Limoux** and sleepy **Alet-les-Bains**, before reaching **Quillan** where the topography changes. The route squeezes through

11

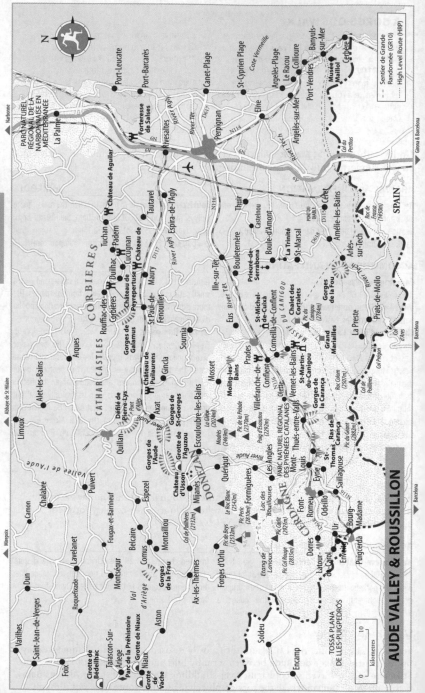

**AUDE VALLEY & ROUSSILLON**

Sentier de Grande
Randonnée (GR10)

High Level Route (HRP)

— N —

PARC NATUREL
REGIONAL DE LA
NARBONNAISE EN
MEDITERRANÉE

Narbonne

La Palme

Port-Leucate

Port-Barcarès

Canet-Plage

St-Cyprien Plage

Côte Vermeille

Argelès-Plage

Le Racou

Collioure

Banyuls-
sur-Mer

Port-Vendres

Musée
Maillol

Cerbère

Rivesaltes

6N

6V

Perpignan

N114

Elne

Argelès-sur-Mer

Girona & Barcelona

Forteresse
de Salses

River Agly

River Têt

D617

N9

6V

6N

Col du
Perthus

SPAIN

Château de Aguilar

Tautavel

N116

Thuir

Castelnou

Boule-d'Amont

La Trinité
St-Marsal

Amélie-les-Bains

Roc de
Frausa
(1450m)

PONT DU
DIABLE

D115

Céret

Arles-
sur-Tech

River Tech

Barcelona

CORBIÈRES

Tuchan

Padern

Cucugnan

Château de

Rouffiac-des-
Corbières

Château de
Peyrepertuse

Duilhac

Maury

River Agly

Espira-de-l'Agly

Ille-sur-Têt

Bouleternère

Prieuré-de-
Serrabona

Boule-d'Amont

Col
d'Ares

Prats-de-Mollo

La Preste

Gorges
de la Fou

Chalet des
Cortalets

Pic du
Canigou
(2784m)

MASSIF DU CANIGOU

Grand
Marlailles

Col de
Pradelles

Col Pregon

Gorges de
Galamus

St-Paul-de-
Fenouillet

Soulnia

Ginda

Château de
Puilaurens

Eus

River Têt

St-Michel-
de-Cuixà

Cornella-de-Conflent

Prades

Villefranche-de-
Conflent

Vernet-les-Bains

St-Martin-
du-Canigou

Roc Colom
(2507m)

CATHAR CASTLES

Défilé de
Pierre-Lys

Pont
d'Alies

Gorges de
St-Georges

Grotte de
l'Aguzou

Escouloubre-les-Bains

Mosset

Molitg-les-
Bains

Confent

Olette

N116

Gorges de
la Caranca

St-
Thomas

Ras de
Carança

Pic du Géant
(2882m)

Abbaye de St Hilaire

Alet-les-Bains

Arques

Limoux

Chalabre

Puivert

Quillan

River Aude

Axat

Gorges
de l'Aude

Axat

Madres
(2469m)

La Calm
(2024m)

Pic de la Pelade
(2370m)

Puig d'Escoutou
(2299m)

Les Angles

Mont-
Louis

Thuès-entre-Valls

Eyne

DONEZAN

Vallée de l'Aude

Milhepoix

Camon

Chalabre

Roquefixade

Lavelanet

Montségur

Fougax-et-Barrineuf

Belcaire

Comus

Espezel

Montaillou

Gorges
de la Frau

Col de Pailhères
(2132m)

Mijanès

Château
d'Usson

Quérigut

Le Roc Blanc
(2542m)

Pic Péric
(2810m)

Lac des
Bouillouses

Formiguères

Etang de
Lanoux

Pic Carlit
(2921m)

Pic Col Rouge
(2835m)

PARC NATUREL REGIONAL
DES PYRÉNÉES CATALANES

Font-
Romeu

Odeillo

Bourg-
Madame

CERDAGNE

Ur

Enveitg

Latour-
de-Carol

Dorres

Puigcerdà

TOSSA PLANA
DE LLES-PUIGPEDROS

Val
d'Ariège

Varilhes

Saint-Jean-de-Verges

Foix

Tarascon-Sur-
Ariège

Grotte de
Bédeilhac

Parc de la Préhistoire

Grotte de Niaux

Grotte
de
Vache

Niaux

Aston

Ax-les-Thermes

Forges d'Orlu

Soldeu

Encamp

Dun

Roquefixade

Pic de Pailhères
(2532m)

Pic Carlit
(2921m)

Saillagouse

Pic du Géant

0        10
kilometres

awesome gorges either side of **Axat** before emerging near the river's headwaters on the Capcir plateau, east of the Carlit massif. It's a magnificent drive or slightly hair-raising cycle-ride up to isolated **Quérigut**, then easier going on to **Formiguères**.

## GETTING AROUND · VALLÉE DE L'AUDE

Transport is heavily subsidized in Languedoc and regional train and bus journeys cost just €1.

**By train** A train line runs south from Carcassonne.

Destinations Alet-Les-Bains (2–4 daily Mon–Sat; 45min); Limoux (4–6 daily Mon–Sat; 30min); Quillan (2–4 daily Mon–Sat; 1hr 10min).

**By bus** The bus follows the same route as the train line from Carcassonne, covering the timetable gaps and part routes.

Destinations Alet-Les-Bains (3 daily; 40min); Limoux (3 daily; 30min); Quillan (3 daily; 1hr 10min).

## Limoux and around

Some 24km south of Carcassonne, **LIMOUX** life revolves around pretty **place de la République** in the heart of the old town, with its Friday market, brasseries and cafés, and the nineteenth-century **promenade du Tivoli**, in effect a bypass road on the west. Previously known for its wool and leather-tanning trades, Limoux's recent claim to fame is the excellent regional sparkling wine, Blanquette de Limoux, a cheaper alternative to champagne.

### Abbaye de St-Hilaire

16km south of Carcassonne · Daily: April–June & Sept–Oct 10am–6pm; July & Aug 10am–7pm; Nov–March 10am–5pm · €5.50 · ☎ 04 68 69 62 76, Ⓦ saint-hilaire-aude.fr

Blanquette de Limoux sparkling wine was supposedly invented in 1531 at the **Abbaye de St-Hilaire**, which dominates the centre of the eponymous village (11km northeast by minor road). The Gothic cloister (always open) doubles as the village square, but the main attraction is the so-called **sarcophagus** in the south chapel of the thirteenth-century cathedral. This is one of the masterpieces of the mysterious **Maître de Cabestany**, an itinerant sculptor whose work – found across the eastern Pyrenees on both sides of the border – is distinguished by the elongated fingers, pleated clothing and cat-like, almond-eyed faces of the human figures. Here, the arrest of evangelizing **St Sernin** (Saturnin) – patron of Toulouse – his martyrdom through dragging by a bull and his burial by female disciples, is portrayed on three intricately carved side panels of what's actually a twelfth-century marble reliquary too small to contain a corpse.

## ARRIVAL AND INFORMATION · LIMOUX

**By train** The train station is to the east of the town on av de la Gare.

Destinations Carcassonne (4–8 daily; 30min); Quillan (4–8 daily; 35min).

**By car** Free parking is on the riverbanks by the picturesque old bridge.

**Tourist office** 7 av du Pont de France, inconveniently positioned north of the centre (July & Aug daily 9am–12.30pm & 2–7pm; Sept–June Mon–Fri 10am–12.30pm & 2–5pm, Sat 10am–12.30pm & 1.30–4pm; ☎ 04 68 31 11 82, Ⓦ limoux.fr).

## ACCOMMODATION AND EATING

Hotel accommodation is not in plentiful supply in Limoux and what there is does not inspire. Best go for a nearby B&B. **Chambre d'hôte Le Hothouse** 25 chemin Tour de la Badoque ☎ 04 68 31 66 83, Ⓦ chambredhote-lehothouselimoux.blogspot.co.uk. A charming little B&B just outside town with characterful rooms, hammocks next to the pool, and in lush surroundings. **€80**

**La Goutine** 10 rue de la Goutine ☎ 04 68 74 34 07. A healthy option, this organic and vegetarian restaurant is something of a rarity in France. Expect delicious quinoa dishes, as well as tofu sausage and bean stew. Three courses for a very reasonable €21. Tues–Sat noon–2.30pm, plus Fri & Sat 7–10pm.

## Alet-les-Bains

South of Limoux, an essential halt is the small thermal resort of **ALET-LES-BAINS**; the spa on the outskirts is incidental to the unspoilt half-timbered houses and arcaded *place* inside the fortifications. The **Abbaye Ste-Marie d'Alet** (July & Aug daily 10am–12.30pm & 2.30–7pm; Sept–June Mon–Thurs 2–6pm, Fri–Sun 10am–noon & 2–6pm; €5; ☎04 68 69 93 56, ⊛info.aletlesbains.free.fr) on av Nicolas-Pavillon – attached to the tourist office (which has the keys) – is a sandstone Romanesque abbey that was sacked by the Huguenots in the sixteenth century. Today there remains only the church and chapterhouse overlooking what's left of a gallery of the cloisters and the northern gateway of the monastery.

## ACCOMMODATION AND EATING
ALET-LES-BAINS

★ **Hostellerie de l'Évêché** 2 rue Nicolas-Pavillon, by the abbey ☎04 68 69 90 25, ⊛hotel-eveche.com. Occupying the old bishop's palace, this beautiful hotel and restaurant, astride the river, and within its own parkland, is a wonderful stopover. Dinner is served either in the atmospheric stone-walled annex or outside under the huge copper beech trees. The gourmet *menus* range from €31 for three courses to €52 for five from which you can sample an excellent cassoulet. Children can play outside in the secure gardens in between courses. Service noon–2pm & 7.30–9pm. April–Oct. **€78**

## Quillan

**Quillan**, 28km upstream from Limoux, is a useful staging post en route south into the mountains or east to the Cathar castles (see below). The only monument is the ruined castle, burnt by the Huguenots in 1575 and partly dismantled in the eighteenth century.

## ARRIVAL AND INFORMATION
QUILLAN

**By bus and train** The *gare SNCF* and *gare routière* sit together on the main bypass road.
**Tourist office** Square A. Tricoire, opposite the train station

(July & Aug daily 9.30am–7pm; Sept–June Mon–Sat 9.30am–noon & 2.30–6pm; ☎04 68 20 07 78, ⊛quillan. fr).

## ACCOMMODATION

**Camping Sapinette** 21 rue René-Delpech ☎04 68 20 13 52, ⊛camping-quillan.fr. A nice municipal site surrounded by pine trees on a hill, with moderately good leisure facilities including a pool and playground. April–Oct. **€19.60**
**Chambre d'hôte Nidelice** 28 bd Jean-Bourrel ☎09 63 40 15 10, ⊛nidelice.com. Located in a relatively peaceful boulevard, this friendly B&B is tastefully decorated with rustic rooms and stripped pine floors. The town's many bars and restaurants are just outside. **€59**

**Hôtel-Restaurant Cartier** 31 bd Charles-de-Gaulle ☎04 68 20 05 14, ⊛hotelcartier.com. Notable for its Art Deco facade, this hotel may not be a beacon of modernity, but it has comfortable and spacious rooms (including family suites for €94) and a great restaurant, where you can sample cuttlefish in a creamy saffron sauce within the €22 three-course menu – or for €5 extra, upgrade to a huge cassoulet. Vegetarians are also well catered for here. Late March to mid-Dec. **€70**

## The Cathar castles

Romantic and ruined, the medieval fortresses that pepper the hills between Quillan and Perpignan have become known as the **Cathar castles**, though actually many were built either before or after the Cathar era. Roussillon, Languedoc and the eastern Ariège were the twelfth-century sect's power base. Their name derives from the Greek word for "pure" – *katharon* – as they abhorred the materialism and worldly power of the established Church, and they were initially pacifist, denying the validity of feudal vows or allegiances. While the Cathars probably never accounted for more than ten percent of the population, they included many members of the nobility and mercantile classes, which alarmed the ruling powers.

Once disputational persuasion by the ecclesiastical hierarchy proved fruitless, Pope Innocent III anathemized the Cathars as heretics in 1208 and persuaded the French king to mount the first of many "Albigensian" crusades, named after Albi, a Cathar

THE CATHAR CASTLE OF PEYREPERTUSE

stronghold. Predatory northern nobles, led for a decade by the notoriously cruel Simon de Montfort, descended on the area with their forces, besieging and sacking towns, massacring Cathar and Catholic civilians alike, laying waste or seizing the lands of local counts. The effect of this brutality was to unite both the Cathars and their Catholic neighbours in southern solidarity against the barbarous north. Though military defeat became inevitable with the capitulation of Toulouse in 1229 and the fall of Montségur in 1244, it took the informers and torturers of the Holy Inquisition another 180 years to root out Catharism completely.

## Puilaurens

10km east of Axat • Feb & March Sat & Sun 10am–5pm; April & Oct to mid-Nov daily 10am–5pm; May daily 10am–6pm; June & Sept daily 10am–7pm; July & Aug daily 9am–8pm • €7 • ☎ 04 68 20 65 26

The westernmost Cathar castle, **Puilaurens**, perches atop a hill at 700m, its fine crenelated walls sprouting organically from the rock outcrops. It sheltered many Cathars up to 1256, when Chabert de Barbera, the region's *de facto* ruler, was captured and forced to hand over this citadelle and Quéribus (see below) further east to secure his release. The castle remained strategically important – being close to the Spanish border – until 1659, when France annexed Roussillon and the frontier was pushed south. Highlights of a visit are the **west donjon** and **southeast postern gate**, where you're allowed briefly on the curtain wall for views, and the **Tour de la Dame Blanche**, with its rib-vaulted ceiling.

## Quéribus

Overlooks village of Cucugnan, halfway between Quillan and the sea • Daily: Feb 10am–5.30pm; March 10am–6pm; April–June & Sept 9.30am–7pm; July & Aug 9am–8pm; Oct 10am–6.30pm; Nov to first week of Jan 10am–5pm • €7 • ☎ 04 68 45 03 69

The history of **Quéribus** is similar to that of Puilaurens, and it too held out until 1255 or 1256; not reduced by siege, its role as a Cathar sanctuary ended with the capture of the luckless Chabert, though the garrison escaped to Spain. Spectacularly situated above the Grau de Maury pass 6km north of the Quillan–Perpignan road, the castle balances on a storm-battered rock pinnacle above sheer cliffs – access is forbidden in bad weather. Because of the cramped topography, the space within the walls is stepped in terraces, linked by a single stairway and dominated by the polygonal keep. The high point, in all senses, is the so-called **Salle du Pilier**, whose vaulted ceiling is supported by a graceful pillar sprouting a canopy of intersecting ribs. A spiral staircase leads to the roof terrace and fantastic views (best outside summer) in every direction, including Canigou, the Mediterranean and northwest to the next Cathar castle, Peyrepertuse.

## Peyrepertuse

Just west of Quéribus • Daily: Dec & Jan 10am–4.30pm; Feb & Nov 10am–5pm; March & Oct 10am–6pm; April–June & Sept 9am–7pm; July & Aug 9am–8pm • €7 • ☎ 04 68 45 69 40, ⓦ peyrepertuse.com.

If you only have time for one of the Cathar castles, make it the **Château de Peyrepertuse**, not only for the unbeatable site and stunning views, but also because it's unusually well preserved. The castle was obtained by treaty with the Kingdom of Aragón in 1258, and most of the existing fortifications were built afterwards, staying in use until 1789. The 3.5-km access road starts in Duilhac village or, alternatively, you can walk up from Rouffiac des Corbières village to the north via the GR36 – a tough, hot climb of over an hour. Either way the effort is rewarded, for Peyrepertuse is among the most awe-inspiring castles anywhere, draped the length of a jagged rock-spine with sheer drops at most points. Access is banned during fierce summer thunderstorms, when (as at Quéribus) the ridge makes an ideal lightning target.

Tickets are sold by the southerly car park, but you then walk fifteen minutes through thickets of box to the entrance on the north side. The bulkiest fortifications enclose the lower, eastern end of the ridge, with a **keep** and **barbican** controlling the main gate. Things get increasingly airy as you progress west along the ridge past and through various cisterns, chapels and bastions, culminating in a **stairway** of over a hundred steps carved into the living rock, which leads to a keep, tower and the **chapel of San Jordi** at the summit.

## Aguilar

Just east of Tuchan • Daily: mid-April to mid-June 10.30am–5.30pm; mid-June to mid-Sept 9am–7pm; mid-Sept to Oct 11am–5pm; closed Nov to mid-April • €4 • ☎ 04 68 45 51 00

Overlooking the Côtes de Roussillon-Villages wine *domaine* is the isolated, thirteenth-century **Château d'Aguilar**; perched at the end of a steep, one-lane drive, its hexagonal curtain wall shelters a keep, with the châtelain's lodge on the top floor.

### VISITING THE CASTLES

**By train** The Train du Pays Cathare et du Fenouillèdes (☎ 04 68 20 04 00, ⓦ tpcf.fr) runs from Rivesaltes or Espira de Agly, just north of Perpignan, to Axat, stopping at the main towns along the Cathar way. The service (sometimes only St-Paul-de-Fenouillet to Axat) runs April, May & Oct Sun &

Wed; June Tues, Wed & Sun; July Sun–Fri; Aug Tues–Sun; Sept Tues, Wed, Fri & Sun (adult fare €13–21 depending on distance).

**Passeport des Sites du Pays Cathare** If you're planning on visiting several of the Cathar-related and other medieval

**11**

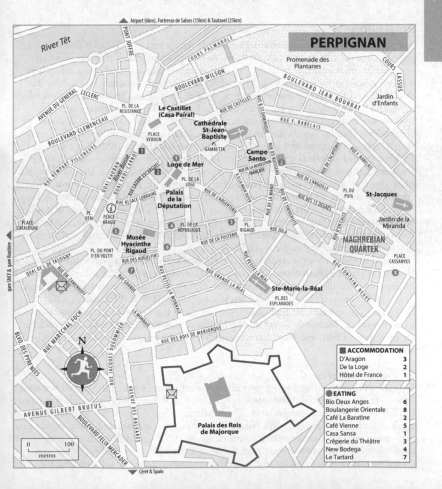

sites in the Aude, consider purchasing the Le Passeport des Sites du Pays Cathare, available for €4 at any of the nineteen participating monuments in the *département*. The card (valid per calendar year) gives €1 off adult admission, and a free child admission, for the ramparts of Carcassonne, Lastours, Saissac, Caunes-Minervois, St-Hilaire, Lagrasse, Fontfroide, Puilaurens, Usson, Peyrepertuse, Quéribus, Aguilar and other sites. For more information see ⓦ payscathare.org.

## Cucugnan

**Cucugnan**, fifty kilometres east of Quillan, halfway to the coast, is a popular base for visiting Quéribus (and Peyrepertuse) and there's ample accommodation in *chambres d'hôtes* and hotels.

### ACCOMMODATION CUCUGNAN

**Auberge de Cucugnan** 2 place de la Fontaine ☎ 04 68 45 40 84. The smallish, modern rooms (with en-suite) here contrast with the building's stone facade and charming restaurant. The food is, on the whole, of a high standard but not particularly original. *Menus* from €20; closed Thurs. **€65**

★ **Auberge du Vigneron** 2 rue Achille-Mir ☎ 04 68 45 03 00, ⓦ auberge-vigneron.com. Comfortable, timeless hotel above an excellent restaurant with a terrace overlooking the hills. The half-board option is excellent value; many of the restaurant ingredients come from the hotel's own garden. Restaurant closed Mon. **€90**; half-board **€83pp**

# Roussillon

The area comprising the eastern fringe of the Pyrenees and the lowlands down to the Mediterranean is known as **Roussillon**, or **French Catalonia**. Catalan power first emerged in the tenth century under the independent counts of Barcelona, who then became kings of Aragón as well in 1163. The Catalan zenith was reached during the thirteenth and fourteenth centuries, when the Franco–Catalan frontier traced the Corbières hills north of Perpignan. But Jaume I of Aragón and Valencia made the mistake of dividing his kingdom between his two sons at his death in 1276, thus ensuring continuous see-saw battles and annexations that ended only with the Treaty of the Pyrenees, negotiated by Louis XIV and the Spanish king in 1659.

Although there's no real separatist impetus among French Catalans today, their sense of identity remains strong: the language is very much alive (not least in bilingual place signage), and their red-and-yellow flag is ubiquitous. The **Pic du Canigou**, which completely dominates Roussillon despite its modest (2784m) elevation, shines as a powerful beacon of Catalan nationalism, attracting hordes of Catalans from across the border to celebrate St John's Eve (June 23–24). At the feet of the Canigou, the little town of **Prades**, place of exile from Franco's Spain of cellist Pablo (Pau) Casals, served as a focus of Catalan resistance until 1975.

Most of the region's attractions are easily reached by public transport from Roussillon's capital, **Perpignan**. The coast and foothills between it and the Spanish frontier are beautiful, especially at **Collioure**, though predictably crowded and in most places overdeveloped. You'll find the finest spots in the **Tech** and **Têt valleys** which slice southwest towards the high peaks, among them the Romanesque monasteries of **Serrabona**, **St-Michel-de-Cuixà** and **St-Martin-du-Canigou**, the world-class modern art museum at **Céret**, and **Mont Canigou** itself, lapped by foothill orchards of peaches and cherries.

## Perpignan and around

This far south, climate and geography alone would ensure a palpable Spanish influence. Moreover, a good part of **PERPIGNAN**'s population is of Spanish origin – refugees from the Civil War and their descendants. The southern influence is further augmented by a substantial contingent of North Africans, including both Arabs and white French settlers repatriated after Algerian independence in 1962. Given its relatively grubby appearance, few will want to stay here for more than a day or two; if you have your own transport, you may prefer to base yourself somewhere in the surrounding area.

## Casa Païral

Place de Verdun • 10.30am–6.30pm; closed bank holidays • €2 • ☎ 04 68 35 42 05

The best place to begin explorations of Perpignan is at **Le Castillet**, built as a gateway in the fourteenth century and now home to the **Casa Païral**, an interesting museum of Roussillon's Catalan rural culture and the anti-French rebellions of 1661–74, when the tower held captured Catalan insurgents.

## Place de la Loge

A short distance from place de Verdun down rue Louis-Blanc lies **place de la Loge**, focus of the pedestrianized heart of the old town, with a voluptuous Venus statue by Aristide Maillol (see page 631) in the centre. Dominating the cafés and brasseries of the narrow square is Perpignan's most interesting building, the Gothic **Loge de Mer** (1397). Designed to hold the city's stock exchange and maritime court, it features gargoyles, lancet windows and lacy balustrades up top. Adjacent stand the sixteenth-century **hôtel de ville**, with its magnificent wrought-iron gates and with another Maillol (*La Méditerranée*) in the courtyard, and the fifteenth-century **Palais de la Députation**, once the parliament of Roussillon.

## Cathédrale St-Jean-Baptiste

Place Gambetta • Mon–Sat 8am–6pm (closes 7pm June–Sept), Sun 2–6pm • Free • Campo Santo Oct–April Tues–Sun 11am–5pm; closed May–Sept

From place de la Loge, rue St-Jean leads northeast to the fourteenth-century **Cathédrale St-Jean** on place Gambetta, its external walls built of alternating bands of river stones and brick. The dimly lit interior is most interesting for its elaborate Catalan altarpieces and for the fourteenth-century, Rhenish polychrome Crucifixion known as the *Dévôt Christ*; it's in the fifth side chapel along the north wall, and was probably brought from the Low Countries by a travelling merchant. Out of the side door, a few steps on the left, you'll find the entrance to the **Campo Santo**, a vast enclosure that's one of France's oldest cemeteries, occasionally used for summer concerts.

## The Maghrebian and Romany quarters

South of the cathedral, rue de la Révolution-Française and rue de l'Anguille lead into the teeming, dilapidated **Maghrebian and Romany quarter**, where women congregate on the secluded inner lanes but are seldom seen on the busier thoroughfares. Here you'll find North African shops and cafés, especially on rue Llucia, and a daily market on place Cassanyes. Uphill and north from this stands the elegant church of **St-Jacques** (Tues–5pm 11am–5pm; free), which was built in two phases in the fourteenth and eighteenth centuries; it abuts **La Miranda gardens**, atop a section of the old city walls.

## Palais des Rois de Majorque

Rue des Archers • Daily: June–Sept 10am–6pm; Oct–May 9am–5pm • €4 • ☎ 04 68 34 96 26

A twenty-minute walk southwest through place des Esplanades brings you to the main entrance of the **Palais des Rois de Majorque**, which crowns the hill that dominates

**11**

---

### CATALAN CUISINE

Characterized by the wide variety of ingredients that grow throughout the different climates between the mountains and the sea, Catalonia's distinctive food depends on its use of contrasting (sweet, savoury and sour) flavours within the five fundamental **sauces** of Catalan cuisine. The most important of these is **sofregit**, a tomato-based sauce with caramelized onion that's used ubiquitously. The most popular traditional dishes include *ollada* (pork stew), *bullinada* (similar to paella but with potatoes instead of rice) and regional favourite, *boles de picolat* (meatballs). Catalans have a sweet tooth too and produce a variety of custardy desserts like *pa d'ous* (flan) and *crema catalane* as well as the wonderful sweet wines of Banyuls and Rivesaltes.

the southern part of the old town. Although Vauban's walls surround it now, and it's suffered generally from on-going military use until 1946, the two-storey palace and its partly arcaded courtyard date originally from the late thirteenth century. There are frequent worthwhile temporary exhibits in the former king's apartments.

## Musée Hyacinthe Rigaud

16 rue de l'Ange, near place Arago • June–Sept 10.30am–7pm; Oct–May Tues–Sun 11am–5.30pm • €8 • ☎ 04 68 35 43 40

The collection at the **Musée Hyacinthe Rigaud** is devoted largely to Catalan painters, most notably Minorcan-born **Pierre Daura** (1896–1976), a Republican and godson of Pablo Casals long exiled in the US: his sympathies are evident in two symbolic canvases of the post-Civil-War Republican refugee camps at nearby Argelès. One room has a few Maillol sketches and statues, and three portraits by Picasso.

## Forteresse de Salses

Guided tours: April–Sept 10am–6.30pm; Oct–March 10am–12.45pm & 2–5.15pm • €8 • ⓦ salses.monuments-nationaux.fr • Trains to Salses depart from Perpignan every 30min (13min)

An interesting stop 15km north of Perpignan is the **Forteresse de Salses**, in the town of Salses-le-Château. This late fifteenth-century Spanish-built fort, on the north end of town, was one of the first to be designed with a ground-hugging profile to protect it from artillery fire. It housed around one thousand troops and was entirely self-sufficient with wells, irrigation systems and even a bakery within the walls. Tours are in French but afterwards you will be able to explore some parts on your own.

## Tautavel

**Tautavel**, 25km northwest of Perpignan off the St-Paul-de-Fenouillet road, might not have much to see, but is interesting anthropologically. In 1971 the remains of the oldest known European hominid – dated to around 450,000 years old – were discovered in the nearby Caune d'Arago cave, and a reconstruction of the skull and other cave finds are displayed in the village's **Musée de la Préhistoire** (Sept–mid-July 10am–12.30pm & 2–6pm; mid-July–Aug 10am–7pm; €8; ☎04 68 29 04 76, ⓦ450000ans.com).

## ARRIVAL AND INFORMATION | PERPIGNAN

**By plane** From the airport at Rivesaltes, 6km north (no-frills flights from UK), there are shuttle buses every 30min into town (€1), which call at bd St-Assiscle to link up with the *gare routière* and *gare SNCF*.

**By train** The train station is at the end of av du Général-de-Gaulle to the west of the city centre; it is connected to the bus station by way of a tunnel under the tracks. All regional train journeys cost €1.

Destinations Barcelona (3 daily; 2hr 30min); Collioure (8–12 daily; 25min); Narbonne (approx every 30min; 30–45min); Villefranche (8 daily; 55min).

**By bus** The bus station is on bd Saint-Assiscle, to the west of the city centre. All regional bus journeys cost €1.

Destinations Banyuls-sur-Mer (4 daily except Sun; 45min); Céret (15 daily; 40min); Collioure (3 daily; 45min); Latour-de-Carol (2–3 daily; 2hr); Prades (approx every 30min; 55min); via the Tech valley to Prats-de-Molló (2–3 daily; 1hr 40min); Quillan (2 daily; 2hr); Tet valley to Mont-Louis (3–4 daily; 2hr 15min).

**Tourist office** Place de la Loge (June to Sept Mon–Sat 9am–7pm, Sun 10am–5pm; rest of year Mon–Sat 9am–6pm, Sun 11am–1pm; ☎ 04 68 66 30 30, ⓦ perpignantourisme.com).

## ACCOMMODATION

**D'Aragon** 17 av Gilbert-Brutus ☎04 68 54 04 46, ⓦ aragon-hotel.com. A bit out of the way, but handy for the Palais des Rois de Majorque, *Aragon* is a two-star with simple, unfussy rooms and parking nearby. **€66**

**De la Loge** 1 Fabriques d'en Nabot ☎04 68 34 41 02, ⓦ hoteldelaloge.fr. Smack in the centre of town, this is a tastefully renovated medieval mansion with a central courtyard, on a quiet alley. Try to get a room facing the courtyard if you want a peaceful sleep. **€70**

★ **Hôtel de France** 28 quai Sadi-Carnot ☎04 68 84 80 35, ⓦ hoteldefrance-perpignan.fr. Central and simple, this old hotel is a good option for couples or groups on a budget. Rooms have delightful views onto the river Basse and, if you crane your neck out on the balcony, the Castillet too. Double rooms **€62**, Quad rooms **€110**

**EATING**

For a city of Perpignan's size, restaurants, bars and clubs are quite thin on the ground. However, there's the Trobades festival celebrating the medieval heritage of the region (in late September) and other events like the October-long Jazzèbre festival. But Perpignan's best-known spectacle is La Procession de la Sanch, the Good Friday procession of red-hooded penitents that goes from the church of St-Jacques to the cathedral between 3pm and 5pm. Nightlife is largely confined to wine/tapas bars in the narrow alleyways of the old centre while young clubbers journey to the modern coastal resort of Canet Plage at weekends.

**Bio Deux Anges** 39 rue des Augustins ☎ 04 68 08 78 32, ⓦ biodeuxanges.com. Organic, vegetarian restaurant with nutritionally balanced *menus* from €17 based around whole grains such as quinoa and Camargue rice. Tues–Sat 9am–7pm.

★ **Boulangerie Orientale** 4 place Cassanyes ☎ 04 68 67 09 58. Savour the scent of a true boulangerie as you enter this gourmet tribute to France's colonial past. Serves a selection of French and North African breads plus irresistibly sticky pastries for little more than €1. Daily 8am–5pm.

**Café La Baratine** Place de la Révolution-Française ☎ 04 68 62 83 27. A delightful bistro-café on the edge of the St-Jacques quarter with shaded tables next to an old marble well. Tues–Sat noon–2pm & 7–9.30pm.

**Café Vienne** 3 place Arago ☎ 04 68 34 80 00. Specializing in seafood, this large nonstop pavement restaurant churns out three courses for €14 rising to €25 in the evening. The €25 "Oyster Seller's Tray", with all manner of tasty crustaceans is the highlight. Fri–Sat 10am–midnight; Sun–Thurs noon–11pm.

**Casa Sansa** 2 rue Fabriques-Couvertes ☎ 04 68 50 48 01. In a smart side street, this place, with its bullfight posters and old photos on the wall, serves traditional regional dishes such as *suquet-bouillabaisse*, a Catalan take on the famous Marseillais fish broth. *Menus* start at around €20. Tues–Sat noon–2pm & 7–11pm.

**Crêperie du Théâtre** 12 rue du Théâtre ☎ 04 68 34 29 06. ⓦ creperie-du-theatre.fr. Inexpensive option and well set up for customers with special diets including vegan and gluten free. The cheapest *menu* at €12.50 includes a choice of *galettes*, a salad and a drink while for €17 you get an extra salad and dessert. Mon–Sat noon–9.30pm

**New Bodega** 3bis rue Voltaire ☎ 04 68 35 21 87, ⓦ lanew-bodega.e-monsite.com. A tapas restaurant rather than bar, with severely limited seating – booking is advisable at weekends. It's straightforward classic tapas: *patatas bravas*, *gambas planxa* *calamari* and the like, with prices mostly hovering around the €6 mark, and all joyfully prepared behind the large glass screen next to the tables. Tues–Sat noon–11pm.

★ **Le Tartard** 6 rue Sainte-Magdeleine ☎ 09 54 38 53 58. A restaurant for more adventurous carnivores, this is the place to try tartare. Every dish is vibrant, with accompaniments chosen as much for their colour as their contrasting tastes: try the tuna and ham tartare served with Spanish *pan con tomate* and sweet garlic confit. *Menus* from €14. Tues–Sat noon–3pm & 7–11pm.

## Castlenou

Twenty kilometres southwest of Perpignan, beyond the winemaking town of Thuir, is **CASTELNOU**, one of the best-preserved villages in the Pyrenees. Surrounded by rolling hills of sun-baked scrub and oak, there's little sign of modernization for miles around, save for the road to the village. Through the pedestrianized fourteenth-century portal, the village rambles up towards the pentagon-shaped **Château de Castelnou** (Oct–April Sat–Wed 11am–5pm; May–Sept daily 10am–7pm; €5.50; ☎ 04 68 53 22 91, ⓦ castelnou.com) – a worthwhile ascent for the views alone. First inhabited in 990 AD, the château served as the military and administrative capital to the Viscount of Vallespir until 1321. Despite its elevated position, it was besieged several times, notably by the kings of Majorca and Aragón in 1285 and 1295. There's a car park at the base of the village or up the hill behind the castle.

**ACCOMMODATION AND EATING** CASTELNOU

★ **Chambre d'hôte/Crêperie La Figuera** 3 Carrer de la fond d'Avall ☎ 04 68 53 18 42, ⓦ la-figuera.com. In a truly idyllic spot at the base of the village with a gorgeous terrace cloaked with plants and flowers, and tables beneath rambling fig trees. The restaurant produces simple Catalan dishes and *galettes* from €8 or you can just stop by for a quick drink (Easter–Sept noon–2pm & 7–9pm; nonstop service at busier times). €75

# The Côte Vermeille

The **Côte Vermeille**, where the Pyrenees meet the sea, is the last patch of French shoreline before Spain, its seaside villages once so remote that the Fauvist painters of the early 1900s hid out here. Mass tourism may have ended any sense of exclusivity but outside of high season there is solitude and peace among the wide empty beaches; interspersed between modern resorts like **Port-Barcarès** (north east of Perpignan), **Canet Plage** and **Argelès-sur-Mer**. The coastline remains sandy and straight almost until the border before being pushed east by the up-surging Pyrenean chain, where the prettier cove towns of **Collioure** and **Banyuls** are found.

## Collioure

Some thirty kilometres southeast of Perpignan, **COLLIOURE** is achingly picturesque. Palm trees line the curving main beach of **Port d'Avall**, while slopes of vines and olives rise to ridges crowned with ruined forts and watchtowers. Its setting and monuments inspired Henri Matisse and André Derain to embark in 1905 on their explosive Fauvist colour experiments.

Collioure is dominated by its twelfth-century **Château-Royal** (daily: 9am–5pm; July & Aug 10am–7pm; €4; ☎04 68 82 06 43), founded by the Templars and subject to later alterations by the kings of Mallorca and Aragón, and again after the Treaty of the Pyrenees gave Collioure to France. The mediocre permanent "collection" inside scarcely merits the entrance fee; attend instead a concert in the courtyard.

The second landmark in the town is the **Église Notre-Dame-des-Anges** (daily: 9am–noon & 2–6pm; free; ☎04 68 82 06 43), which features in every postcard and tourist brochure of the region. With its belfry dating back to the middle ages, this building served as a beacon for the port until the late seventeenth century when the rest of the church was adjoined. Behind it two small **beaches** are divided by a causeway leading to the **chapel of St-Vincent**, built on a former islet, while west from here a concrete path follows the rocky shore to the bay of **Le Racou**.

Just north of the château lies the **old harbour**, still home to a handful of brightly painted lateen-rigged fishing boats – now more likely used as pleasure craft – all that remains of Collioure's traditional fleet. Beyond this, the stone houses and sloping lanes of the old **Mouré** quarter are the main focus of interest.

### INFORMATION                                                    COLLIOURE

**Tourist office** Place du 18-juin (April–June & Sept 9am–noon & 2–6pm; July & Aug Mon–Sat 9am–7pm & Sun 10am–5pm; Oct–March Mon–Sat 9am–noon & 2–5pm; ☎04 68 82 15 47, ⌨collioure.com).

### ACCOMMODATION

★ **L'Arapède** Rte de Port-Vendres ☎04 68 98 09 59, ⌨arapede.com. This spacious, modern hotel fifteen minutes' walk away from the centre of the town has ample parking (drivers should note that Collioure can be a parking nightmare) and a beautiful clifftop garden patio with pool. There's also a mini beach five minutes away. Closed mid-Nov to late-March. **€105**

**La Girelle** Plage d'Ouille ☎04 68 81 25 56, ⌨campingla girelle.unblog.fr. Enviably positioned next to a nice little sandy beach, this mostly tent-only site, ten minutes' walk from Collioure, offers a decent range of services including a grocer, fridge lockers and a snack-bar restaurant that hosts regular paella evenings. A handful of basic chalets can be rented by the week for €595 if you book well in advance. April–Sept. **€32**

**Hostellerie des Templiers** 12 av Camille-Pelletan ☎04 68 98 31 10, ⌨hotel-templiers.com. The most central place to stay, this atmospheric hotel celebrates Collioure's art heritage (Picasso frequented the bar downstairs) with paintings screening the bar and corridor walls. The hotel itself rambles into an annex that backs on to an occasionally noisy nightclub. Closed mid-Nov to Jan. **€95**

### EATING

**Le Cinquième Péché** 18 rue de la Fraternité ☎04 68 98 09 76, ⌨le-cinquieme-peche.com. Collioure's most innovative restaurant, and perhaps the only place in France creating Japanese-French fusion. Expect colourful platters combining the uncommon bedfellows of fruit and fish to the delight of any adventurous palate. Two-course *menus* cost €19. Tues–Sat 12.15–1.45pm & 7.30–9pm.

**Paco** 18 rue Rière ☎04 68 82 90 91. There are a few tapas options in town but this is easily the best. Open year-round, there's a convivial atmosphere that spills onto the narrow lane as locals and tourists effortlessly mingle with one another over generous platters of calamari, razor clams and cured hams. Tapas are from €3.50 upwards. 11am–3pm & 5.30pm–12.30am; closed Tues.

## Banyuls-sur-Mer

South towards **BANYULS-SUR-MER**, 10km from Collioure, both the main highway and minor D914 wind through attractive vineyards, with the Albères hills rising steeply on the right. Make sure you sample the dark, full-bodied Banyuls dessert **wine**, an *appellation* that applies only to the vineyards of the Côte Vermeille. The town itself, facing a broad sweep of pebble beach, is pleasant but lacks the overt charm of Collioure.

On the seafront avenue du Fontaulé, the **Biodiversarium** (10am–12.30pm & 2–6.30pm; €9.50; ☎04 68 88 73 39, ⓦbiodiversarium.fr) aquarium, run by Sorbonne university's marine biology department, has tanks containing a comprehensive collection of the region's submarine life; this is protected in a nearby *réserve marine*, France's best, which can be explored with local **scuba outfitters**.

Four kilometres southwest of town in the Vallée de Roume, signposted from the top of avenue de Gaulle, is the **Musée Maillol** (May–Sept 10am–noon & 3–6pm; Oct–April 10am–noon & 2–5pm; €5;☎04 68 88 57 11), which is devoted to the works of sculptor **Aristide Maillol** (1861–1944), who was born near Banyuls. He is buried under his statue *La Pensée* in Banyuls.

11

### INFORMATION BANYULS-SUR-MER

**Tourist office** Diagonally opposite the *mairie* on the seafront (July & Aug 9am–7pm; Sept–June Mon–Sat 9am–noon & 2–6pm; ☎04 68 88 31 58, ⓦbanyuls-sur-mer.com).

### ACCOMMODATION & EATING

**Les Elmes** At the eponymous sandy cove 1.5km north of town ☎04 58 88 03 12, ⓦhotel-des-elmes.com. Slap bang on the beachfront, this hotel has excellent facilities including a hot tub, sauna, terrace and an in-house restaurant (*La Littorine*) downstairs. The rooms are comfortable and well equipped but aim for the sea-view ones instead of the road outlook if you can afford extra. If you dine here, it may be a bit pricey, but you're in for a treat; €27 buys you the two perfectly balanced, elegant-looking dishes from the gourmet *menu*. **€88**

**Le Fanal** Av Pierre-Fabre ☎04 68 98 65 88, ⓦpascal-borrell.com. Classic French cuisine from a Michelin-starred chef served alfresco on tables overlooking the marina. The service can be a little slow but it's well worth the wait. The two course €24 menu might include a very fresh catch of the day and a mouth-watering chocolate millefeuille. Daily noon–2pm & 7–10pm

**Les Pieds dans l'Eau** Rue des Elmes ☎06 27 34 81 66, ⓦlocations-vacances-banyuls.ch. A self-catering apartment complex ideal for couples and families. Right on the sandy beach and just far enough away from the main road, it's an extremely relaxing spot. In high season there is a minimum stay period of one week. **€500** per week

## Vallée de Tech

The D115 winds its way through the beautiful **Vallée de Tech** starting at the border town, Le Boulou, then westwards through pretty little **Céret**, capital of the Vallespir region. Further upstream, the road passes through the dilapidated spa town, Amélie-les-Bains, and scruffy Arles-sur-Tech, whose only attraction is the sumptuous **Abbaye de Ste-Marie**. Just past Arles, the narrow Gorges de la Fou is well worth an outing, before you continue west to the captivating medieval walled town of **Prats-de-Mollo**, which is guarded by a menacing Vauban fortification.

### GETTING AROUND VALLÉE DE TECH

**By bus** Destinations to and from Perpignan along the Tech valley include Amélie-les-Bains (10 daily; 55min); Arles-sur-Tech (10 daily; 1hr); Céret (15 daily; 40min); and Prats-de-Mollo (2–3 daily; 1hr 40min).

## Céret

**Céret** is a delightful place, with a wonderfully shady old town overhung by huge plane trees; the central streets are narrow and winding, opening onto small squares like **plaça de Nou Reigs** ("Nine Spouts" in Catalan), named after its central fountain; on avenue d'Espagne, two remnants of the medieval walls, the **Porte de France** and **Porte d'Espagne**, are visible. The town's main sight, however, is the remarkable **Musée d'Art Moderne** (July to mid-Sept 10am–7pm; mid-Sept to June Tues–Sun 10am–5pm; €8; ☎04 68 87 27 76, ⊛musee-ceret.com) at 8 bd du Maréchal-Joffre. Between about 1910 and 1935, Céret's charms – coupled with the residence here of the Catalan artist and sculptor Manolo – drew a number of avant-garde artists to the town, including Matisse and Picasso, who personally dedicated a number of pictures to the museum. The holdings are too extensive to mount everything at once, but there are works on show by Chagall, Miró, Pignon, Picasso and Dufy, among others.

## INFORMATION CÉRET

**Tourist office** 5 rue Saint-Ferréol (July–Aug Mon–Sat 9am–7pm, Sun 9am–1pm; Sept–Oct & May–June Mon–Fri 9am–12.30pm & 2–6pm, Sat 9am–12.30pm & 2–5pm; Nov–April Mon–Fri 9am–12.30pm & 2–5pm, Sat 9am–1pm; ☎04 68 87 00 53, ⊛vallespir-tourisme.fr).

## ACCOMMODATION & EATING

**Restaurant La Fontaine** Plaça de Nou Reigs ☎04 68 09 27 46. Few could resist dining in this beautiful, traffic-free marbled square shaded by vast plane trees. If you have a family, this is the perfect place for a relaxing meal while the kids dip hands in and out of the marbled fountain. The *plat du jour* costs €10. Mon–Tues & Thurs–Fri 10am–3pm & 6–10pm, Sat & Sun 9am–11pm.

★ **Vidal** 4 place Soutine ☎04 68 87 00 85, ⊛hotelceret. com. A tastefully converted eighteenth-century episcopal palace within the old town walls, *Vidal* is now a charming and unpretentious hotel that has a decent restaurant, *Del Bisbe*, attached. Its first-floor terraced restaurant, shaded by vines, serves tasty, if not ground-breaking, regional dishes including lamb roasted with pistachios. The three-course *menu* costs €29. Noon–2pm & 7.30–9.30pm; closed Tues & Wed. Hotel and restaurant closed Nov. **€55**

## Abbaye de Ste-Marie

Arles-sur-Tech • July & Aug 9am–7pm; Sept–June Mon–Sat 9am–noon & 2–6pm; also Sun April–Oct 2–5pm • €4 • ☎04 68 83 90 66

The Romanesque **Abbaye de Ste-Marie**, in Arles-sur-Tech, 14km from Céret, has Carolingian origins, thought to account for the back-to-front alignment of the altar at the west end and entrance at the east. Entry is via the pleasant thirteenth-century cloister. The unique and compelling feature of the massive church interior is a band of still vividly coloured twelfth-century **frescoes** high up in the apse of the eastern anti-chapel dedicated to St-Michel and which, appropriately, feature the archangel.

## Gorges de la Fou

Ten miles west of Céret mid-March–June & Sept daily 10am–5.30pm; July–Aug daily 9.30am–6.30pm; Oct–mid-Nov 10am–4pm • €10 • ☎04 68 39 16 21

The world's narrowest canyon, the **Gorges de la Fou**, spans a spectacular 2km cut through the southeastern flank of Pic du Canigou; at some parts the walls are only one metre apart. Aided by a metal catwalk, the ascent through the gorge is not overly arduous.

## Prats-de-Mollo

Beyond the Gorges de la Fou, the D115 climbs steadily, between valley sides thick with walnut, oak and sweet chestnut, 19km to **PRATS-DE-MOLLO**, the end of the bus line. Prats is the last French town before the **Spanish frontier**, 13km beyond at Col d'Arès, but it has none of the usual malaise of border towns and is the most attractive place in the valley since Céret. Hub of the newer quarter is **El Firal**, the huge square used for markets since 1308 (it takes place on Fridays); the walled and gated **ville haute** just south makes for a wonderful wander, with its steep cobbled streets and a weathered church that has marvellous ironwork on the door. The old town's walls were rebuilt in the seventeenth century after the suppression of a local revolt against onerous taxation imposed by Louis XIV on his new, post-Treaty Pyrenees holdings.

Vauban's fortress, the **Fort Lagarde** (guided visits: April–June & Sept–Oct Tues–Sun 2–6pm; July & Aug daily 10.30am–1pm, 3.30pm & 5–6.30pm; €5; ☎04 68 39 70 83;

enquire about guided tours at the tourist office) sits on the heights above the town. It was built in 1677 as much to intimidate the local population as to keep the Spanish out.

## INFORMATION

### PRATS-DE-MOLLO

**Tourist office** Place le Fioral (April–Oct 9am–6pm; Nov–March Mon–Fri 10am–5pm; ☎04 68 39 70 83, ⓦpratsdemollolapreste.com).

## ACCOMMODATION AND EATING

**Le Bellevue** Rue El Firal ☎04 68 39 72 48, ⓦhotel-le-bellevue.fr. Overlooking the *place*/Friday market, just outside the town wall, this appealing hotel offers private parking and rooms with balconies for a little extra. Its restaurant has seasonal *menus* from €20. Closed Dec to mid-Feb. **€57**

**Hostellerie Le Relais** 3 place Josep de la Trinxeria ☎04 68 39 71 30, ⓦhotelrestaurantlerelais.com. Cheerful pastel-hued rooms and a south-facing garden restaurant serving an exciting range to suit all budgets including paella and Catalan meatballs, with two-course *menus* starting from €14. **€70**

**Village Liberté** Rte du Col d'Arès, 100m south of the old town ☎04 68 39 72 78, ⓦvvf-villages.com. A small family holiday village with petite studios, two-room apartments and leisure facilities including a nice pool. Advance booking essential. Easter–Oct. **€80**

# Saint-Marsal and around

The only direct route between the **valleys of the Tech and the Têt**, best covered by car or cycle, is the D618 from Amélie-les-Bains to Bouleternère. It's 44 slow kilometres of mountain road, twisting through hillside meadows and magnificent oak forests, past isolated *masies* (Catalan farmsteads). Halfway there is the tiny village of **Saint-Marsal**, which offers the first amenities en route and is well worth the stop.

## Prieuré de Serrabona

Daily except major holidays 10am–6pm • €4 • ☎04 68 84 09 30

On the D84 just past Boule d'Amont, you'll come across one of the finest examples – arguably *the* finest – of Roussillon Romanesque. The interior of the **Prieuré de Serrabona** (consecrated 1151) is starkly plain, making the beautifully carved column capitals of its rib-vaulted tribune even more striking: lions, centaurs, griffins and human figures with Asiatic faces and hairstyles – motifs brought back from the Crusades – executed in pink marble from Villefranche-de-Conflent, by students of the Maître d'Cabestany, if not himself.

# The Têt valley

The upper **Têt valley**, known as the **Pays de Conflent**, is utterly dominated by the **Pic du Canigou**. The valley bottoms are lush with fields and orchards, but the vast and uncompromising mountain presides over all. As you continue upstream, the valley steepens and buckles as magnificent gorges carve in from the surrounding mountains and scalding water bleeds from the valley's northern flank. Ancient shepherd villages, basking in Mediterranean glow, peer down on the road below. Crisscrossing the Têt, the vintage **Train Jaune** (see page 635) groans its way towards the Cerdagne plateau.

## Prades (Prada) and around

The chief valley town is **Prades**, easily accessible by train and bus on the Perpignan–Villefranche–Latour-de-Carol route, and one obvious starting point for all excursions in the Canigou region. Although there are no great sights beyond the **church of St-Pierre** (free entry) in central place de la République, the town enjoys a status disproportionate to its size. This is largely thanks to Catalan cellist Pablo (Pau) Casals, who was a fierce opponent of the Franco regime in Spain, and consequently settled here as an exile. In 1950 he instituted the internationally renowned **chamber music**

**festival** (⊕prades-festival-casals.com), held annually from late July to mid-August, the usual venue being the abbey of St-Michel-de-Cuixà (see below).

The thriving Tuesday morning market is not to be missed, with its produce strongly influenced by Catalan and North African culture; you'll find paella, churros and fresh Moroccan spices, traded to the sounds of accordion buskers and congregations of elderly men chatting in French-Catalan dialect.

### Abbaye St-Michel-de-Cuxà

May–Sept daily 9.30–11.50am & 2–6pm; Oct–April Mon–Sat 9.30–11.50am & 2–5pm • €6 • ☎ 04 68 96 15 35, ⓘ abbaye-cuxa.com

Three kilometres south of Prades stands one of the loveliest abbeys in France, the eleventh-century **St-Michel-de-Cuxà**. Although mutilated after the Revolution it is still beautiful, with its crenelated tower silhouetted against the wooded – sometimes snowy – slopes of Canigou. You enter via the labyrinthine, vaulted crypt, with its round central chamber, before proceeding to the church with its strange Visigothic-style "keyhole" arches. But the glory of the place is the **cloister** and its twelfth-century column capitals.

## ARRIVAL AND INFORMATION

PRADES AND AROUND

**By bus** The bus depot is on av du Général-de-Gaulle on the east side of town.

Destinations Latour-de-Carol (2–3 daily; 1hr); Perpignan (approx. every half-hour; 55min).

**By train** The *gare* is two blocks south of the bus depot on bd de la Gare.

Destinations Perpignan (8 daily; 45min); Villefranche (8 daily; 10min).

**Tourist office** 10 place de la République (April, May & Oct Mon–Fri 9am–noon Sat 9am–1pm; June & Sept Mon–Sat 9am–noon & 2–6pm, Sun 9am–1pm; July & Aug Mon–Sat 9am–1pm, 2–6.30pm, Sun 9am–1pm; Nov to March Mon–Fri 9am–noon & 2–5pm, Sat 9.30am–12.30pm. ☎ 04 68 05 41 02, ⊕prades-tourisme.fr).

## ACCOMMODATION

★ **Castell Rose** Chemin de la Litera ☎ 04 68 96 07 57, ⊕castellrose-prades.com. Sumptuous *chambre d'hôte* in a converted manor house with a pool and tennis court. Although just a short walk from the centre of Prades, it's a very peaceful and secluded spot, thanks to the extensive grounds and the glorious views south to the Massif du Canigou. This outlook is also enjoyed from the homely bedrooms, particularly the ones with private balconies. **€110**

**Chambre d'hôte Maison Prades** 51 av du Général-de-Gaulle ☎ 04 68 05 74 27, ⊕maisonprades.com. With its big bright rooms looking up to the Pic du Canigou and down to the sunny garden, this *chambre d'hôte* looks after its guests well. Breakfasts (included) are copious, delicious and healthy. **€75**

**Le Grand Hôtel** Molitg-les-Bains, 6km north of Prades ☎ 04 68 05 00 50, ⊕grandhotelmolitg.com. If money is no object and you have transport, then this old and charmingly dishevelled spa hotel, beautifully set in a secluded valley next to a river, is a fine choice. Bathe in the hotel's thermal waters, or more appealingly, the gentle flowing river below. The hotel's gourmet restaurant has high standards and fairly high prices; a two-course meal costs €32. **€120**

**L'Oasis** Molitg-les-Bains, 6km north of Prades ☎ 04 68 05 00 92, ⊕l-oasis-molitg-les-bains.fr. More down-to-earth than *Le Grand Hôtel* across the road, this budget option offers exceptional value with its basic, but clean rooms. **€68**

## EATING

A number of appealing pavement café-restaurants ring the central *place* and while they offer a pleasant place to stop for a kir or two the food tends to be of poor quality.

★ **Restaurant Le Galie** 3 av du Général-de-Gaulle ☎ 04 68 05 53 76, ⊕restaurantlegalie.com. With its bold, flavourful and typically colourful Catalan-inspired dishes, you'll forgive this small restaurant's rather sombre atmosphere. For a light lunch, try the exquisite home-made smoked beef tenderloin with cep mustard sauce, leaving room for their home-made *éclair Paris*. *Menus* start at €24 for two courses. Noon–2pm & 7–9.30pm; closed Mon & Tues eve plus all Wed.

## Eus

The village of **Eus**, a five-minute drive northeast of Prades, claims to be the sunniest in France; it's certainly one of the prettiest. Built among massive granite boulders that litter these elevated slopes, narrow cobbled lanes wind up to the ruined château and imposing eighteenth-century church of St Vincent. A number of easy hikes begin from the entrance to the village through the olive groves and gnarled green oak forests.

| DRINKING | EUS |
|---|---|

**Des Goûts et des Couleurs** Place de la République ☎ 06 09 53 32 47. No visit to Eus would be complete without visiting this convivial pavement bar occupying its own little *place*. Opening hours approximately mid-March to mid-Nov daily 11am–7pm.

## Villefranche-de-Conflent

Some six kilometres up the Têt from Prades, the medieval garrison town of **Villefranche-de-Conflent** is dwarfed by sheer limestone escarpments, and is undoubtedly one of the most beautiful in France. Founded in 1092 by the counts of Cerdagne to block incursions from rivals in Roussillon, then remodelled by Vauban in the seventeenth century after annexation by France, its streets and fortifications have remained untouched by subsequent events. Worth a visit is St-Jacques church, with its primitively carved thirteenth-century baptismal font just inside the door; you can also walk the walls for €4.50 when the tourist office is open.

11

### Château-Fort Libéria

Daily: 10am–6pm; May & June 10am–7pm; July–Aug 9am–8pm • €11 or €7 if you fancy walking up • ⑩ fort-liberia.com

In 1681, Vauban constructed the **Château-Fort Libéria** on the heights above Villefranche-de-Conflent to protect it from "aerial" bombardment. Getting there involves taking the jeep, which leaves from near the town's main gate; you can return to Villefranche by descending a subterranean stairway of a thousand steps, emerging at the end of rue St-Pierre.

### St-Martin-du-Canigou

A 30min walk (no car access) above the hamlet of Casteil, itself eight kilometres south of Villefranche in the Vallée de Cady. French guided tours: Tues–Sun 10am, 11am, 2pm, 3pm, 4pm; plus June–Sept Mon–Sat hourly between 10am & 5pm; Sun/hols 10am, 12.30pm, 2pm, 3pm 4pm & 5pm; closed Jan • €6 • ⑩ stmartinducanigou.org

The stunning abbey of **St-Martin-du-Canigou**, founded in 1001, resurrected from ruins between 1902 and 1982, and now inhabited by a working religious community, occupies a narrow promontory of rock surrounded by chestnut and oak woods, while above it rises the precipitous slopes of the Pic du Canigou. Below, the ground drops vertically into the ravine of the Cady stream rushing down from the Col de Jou. What you see is a beautiful little garden and cloister overlooking the ravine, a low-ceiling, atmospheric chapel beneath the church, and the main church itself.

| INFORMATION | VILLEFRANCHE-DE-CONFLENT |
|---|---|

**Tourist office** 33 rue St-Jacques (Feb, Oct & Nov 10.30am–noon & 2–4pm; March–May 10.30am–5pm; June & Sept 9.30am–5pm; July & Aug 9.30am–8pm; Dec 2–4pm; closed Jan; ☎ 04 68 96 22 96, ⑩ villefranchedeconflent-tourisme.fr).

---

### PETIT TRAIN JAUNE

One of the most spectacular train rides in the world, the **Petit Train Jaune** runs between Villefranche-de-Conflent and La Tour-de-Carol (with onward links towards Toulouse or Barcelona) in the upper Cerdagne, and is a wonder of early twentieth-century engineering. Built to link up the villages of the high Pyrenees with Perpignan, the antique narrow-gauge carriages now mostly carry tourists, cyclists and skiers. The most spectacular section of the route is in the upper Têt between Olette and Mont-Louis, where you'll trundle over gorges and massive viaducts. The summertime frequency of the trains makes it practical to hop off and on, allowing you to explore the areas around smaller, isolated stations, many of them *haltes facultatives* (ask to be set down). Outside summer, the timetable is somewhat unreliable, as the ageing train system needs regular maintenance.

## ACCOMMODATION

**Camping Les Cerisiers** Chemin de la Peña, Vernet-les-Bains (6km south of Villefranche) ☎04 68 05 60 38, ⓦ camping-lescerisiers.com. Unlike other campsites in the area, this pleasant little site is peacefully tucked away from any kind of main road. It's also well located for attempts to summit the Pic du Canigou. There are a few facilities here: sauna, hot tub, free wi-fi and little shop, while Vernet covers all other needs. Mid-March to mid-Oct. €20

**Chambre d'hôte de l'Ancienne** 31 rue St-Jacques ☎04 68 05 76 78, ⓦ ancienneposedelacite.com. Tastefully restored historic building within the walls of Villefranche offering three large en-suite rooms, a welcome tray and access to the house sauna. €85

## EATING

★ **Boulangerie Pâtisserie Miras** 13 rue Saint-Jacques ☎04 68 05 85 90, ⓦ boulangerie.miras.free.fr. Run by a genuine artisan *boulanger*, this is the ideal place to sample the *bunyete*, a Catalan speciality akin to a pancake-doughnut-cross (€2.50). This attractive little shop proudly bakes its breads and pastries in a 1930s cast iron, wood-fired oven. Oct–Feb Tues–Sat 7am–12.30pm & 3–7pm, Sun 7am–12.30pm & 2–5pm; March–Sept daily 7am–7pm.

**La Senyera** 81 rue Saint-Jean ☎04 68 96 17 65, ⓦ lasenyera.fr. This beautiful and atmospheric restaurant has the best reputation in town and is where the locals choose to dine. All the dishes display a refreshingly sophisticated flair for a touristic hub like Villefranche, although there are a few gimmicks such as slates acting as plates. Budget around €25–35 for a generous meal. Noon–2pm & 7.30–9pm; Nov–March closed Wed & all eves except Sat; April–Oct closed Wed & Tues–Thurs eve; closed mid-Oct to mid-Nov & first week of July.

## The upper Têt

Ten or so kilometres west of Villefranche, the mountains close in, dwarfing the valley and road below. As you turn right just past the village of **Olette** the road leads to the picture-perfect shepherd's village of **Evol**, overlooked by the old fortress of the So Viscounts. Further up the Têt, most of the settlements are high on the mountainside, connected by ancient footpaths and dry-stone terraces, the most breathtaking of which is **Canaveilles**; from the main road it's three kilometres of vertiginous single-track hairpins to reach this characterful old village. If you cross the main N166 road from the foot of Canaveilles and follow the well-trodden path to the river, you'll see a stone basin with scalding thermal water pouring in from the mountainside with a makeshift sluice gate in the river for temperature adjustment. Some 3km further on the south side of the valley, the wild, wooded **Gorges de la Carança** (Thuès-Entre-Valls is the nearest village) cuts south through the mountains towards Spain.

One trip worth making, particularly after a heavy day's trekking, is to **Les Bains de St-Thomas** (daily 10am–7.30pm; July, Aug, winter holidays and Feb 10am–8.40pm; closed for two weeks in the middle of June; €7; ☎04 68 97 03 13, ⓦ bains-saint-thomas.fr). Signposted from Fontpedrouse, 11km west of Olette, there are three open-air thermal pools here set at a pleasant 36–38°C, and located in a beautiful, mountainous pine forest.

## ACCOMMODATION AND EATING                         UPPER TÊT VALLEY

There is a real dearth of accommodation options in this well-touristed area, except for holiday homes that usually rent by the week. Crucially there are no restaurants here either; the nearest are either back in Villefranche or up in Mont-Louis.

**La Fontaine** In the centre of Olette ☎04 68 97 03 67. An excellent, English-run *chambre d'hôte* with five very tasteful rooms including a family suite. Breakfast is provided here but for all other meals in this town there is only a café across the road selling sandwiches. Closed Jan. €65

## The Cerdagne

Twenty kilometres up from Olette, the Mediterranean climate slips away as the gradient flattens onto the wide, grassy **Cerdagne** plateau, whose once-powerful counts controlled lands from Barcelona to Roussillon. It's a region that's never been sure whether it is Spanish or French. After the French annexation of Roussillon, it was partitioned, with Spain retaining – as it still does – the enclave of Lliva. The Petit Train

Jaune (see page 635) snakes laboriously across the entire plateau, though stations aren't always convenient for the settlements they nominally serve.

## Mont-Louis

Easterly gateway to the region, the little garrison town of **Mont-Louis**, built by Vauban in 1679–82, is France's highest fortified town. The top citadelle is still a training school for paratroops and marines. Today the town is an attractive halfway station between the Mediterranean and Andorra, and has a few shops, bars and restaurants.

**ACCOMMODATION AND EATING**        **MONT-LOUIS**

**La Volute** 1 place d'Armes ☎ 06 21 58 01 80, ⓦ lavolute. wix.com/lavolute. Gîte set in the seventeenth-century former governor's mansion, with a garden atop a section of the ramparts overlooking the moat and mountains beyond. Sleeps 4 to 15 people. Minimum stay of one week outside of low season. **€1350** per week

**Le Dagobert** 8 bd Vauban ☎ 04 68 04 14 32, ⓦ miel-

lerucherdelours.fr. Situated in the Fort's old hospital this restaurant provides an atmospheric setting with its high, granite vaulted walls and ceiling. On offer you'll find bistro favourites plus a few regional specialities like *boles de picolat*, a Catalan meatball stew. Three-course *menus* cost €18. Wed–Sun 12.30–2.30pm & 7–9pm.

## Les Lacs des Bouillouses

The Têt ultimately has its source in the Carlit massif, which looms above the lovely **Lacs des Bouillouses**. This huge park in the high Pyrenees is strikingly beautiful; the sky is a different, purer kind of blue and the river and lake waters are clear and fresh. There are moderately difficult, circular hikes around the lakes that feed into the main reservoir as well as idyllic picnic beaches along the banks of the gentle river. Wild swimming in the summer months is a more than appealing prospect. To get here, turn north from Mont-Louis and from there it's well signposted.

**11**

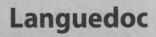

# Languedoc

**640** Eastern Languedoc

**656** Southern Languedoc

**669** Western Languedoc

CARCASSONNE IN THE SNOW

# Languedoc

In many ways, Languedoc is more an idea than a geographical entity. The modern *région* covers only a fraction of the lands where Occitan or the *langue d'oc* – the language of *oc*, the southern Gallo-Latin word for *oui* – once dominated, which stretched south from Bordeaux and Lyon into Spain and northwest Italy. The heartland today is the Bas Languedoc – the coastal plain and dry, stony vine-growing hills between Carcassonne and Nîmes. It's here that the Occitan movement has its power base, demanding recognition of its linguistic and cultural distinctiveness.

Languedoc's long-contested history has left it with a tremendous variety of sights for the visitor. **Nîmes** has extensive Roman remains, while the medieval town of **Carcassonne** is a must-see, a gateway to the romantic Cathar castles to the south. There's also splendid ecclesiastical architecture in **Albi** and **St-Guilhem-le-Désert**. **Montpellier**'s university ensures it has a buzz that outstrips the city's modest size, while **Toulouse**, the cultural capital of medieval and modern Languedoc, though officially outside the administrative *région*, is a high point of any itinerary.

The many other attractions include great swathes of **beach** where – away from the major resorts – you can still find a kilometre or two to yourself, along with wonderful dramatic landscapes and river gorges, from the **Cévennes** foothills in the east to the **Montagne Noire** and **Corbières** hills in the west.

**12**

# Eastern Languedoc

Heading south from Paris via Lyon and the Rhône valley, you can go one of two ways: east to Provence and the Côte d'Azur – which is what most people do – or west to **Nîmes**, Montpellier and the comparatively untouched Languedoc coast. Nîmes makes a good introduction to the area; it's a beautifully modernized town, blending crisp architecture and wide, leafy boulevards with impressive Roman monuments, including the spectacular **Pont du Gard** nearby. **Montpellier** is also worth a day or two, not so much for historical attractions as for a heady vibrancy and easy access to the ancient villages, churches and fine scenery of the upper **Hérault valley**, which forms the heartland of the Languedoc. It's a lovely rural region that has resolutely resisted the power of Northern France since the Middle Ages.

## Nîmes

On the border between Provence and Languedoc, **NÎMES** is inescapably linked to two things – denim and Rome. The latter's influence resulted in some of the most extensive **Roman remains** in Europe, while the former (*de Nîmes*), was manufactured for the first time in this city's textile mills and exported to the southern USA in the nineteenth century to clothe slaves. The city is well worth a visit, in part for the ruins and the narrow lanes of the compact old city, but also to experience its energy and direction, having enlisted the services of a galaxy of architects and designers – including Norman Foster, Jean Nouvel and Philippe Starck – in a bid to wrest southern supremacy from neighbouring Montpellier.

### Les Arènes

L'Amphithéâtre, place des Arènes • Daily: March & Oct 9am–6pm; April, May & Sept 9am–6.30pm; June 9am–7pm; July & Aug 9am–8pm; Nov–Feb 9.30am–5pm (closed during events) • €10 • ☎ 04 66 21 82 56, ⓦ arenes-nimes.com

WATER-JOUSTING, SÈTE

# Highlights

❶ **The bulls of Languedoc** Whether in a bullfight at Les Arènes or eaten as a succulent *boeuf à la gardienne*, the *taureaux* of the plains of Languedoc are famous. See page 645

❷ **Pont du Gard** This graceful aqueduct is an emblem of southern France and a tribute to Roman determination. See page 647

❸ **St-Guilhem-le-Désert** The ancient Carolingian monastery and the tiny hamlet at its feet present a quintessential Occitan panorama. See page 652

❹ **Water-jousting** A Setois tradition, in which teams of rowers charge at each other in gondolas. See page 655

❺ **Carcassonne** The Middle Ages come alive in this walled fortress town. See page 664

❻ **The Canal du Midi** Cycling, walking or drifting along this lovely canal is the most atmospheric way of savouring France's southwest. See page 666

❼ **Les Abattoirs, Toulouse** This former slaughterhouse contains an important collection of modern and contemporary art. See page 672

❽ **Toulouse-Lautrec museum, Albi** The most comprehensive collection of Toulouse-Lautrec's work is in the former Bishop's Palace of his home town. See page 678

**HIGHLIGHTS ARE MARKED ON THE MAP ON PAGE 642**

The focal point of the city is a first-century Roman arena, known as **Les Arènes**, at the junction of boulevards de la Libération and Victor-Hugo. One of the best-preserved Roman amphitheatres in the world, its arcaded two-storey facade conceals massive interior vaulting, riddled with corridors and supporting raked tiers of seats with a capacity of more than twenty thousand spectators, whose staple fare was the blood and guts of gladiatorial combat. When Rome's sway was broken by the barbarian invasions, the arena became a fortress and eventually a slum, home to an incredible two thousand people when it was cleared in the early 1800s. Today it has recovered something of its former role, with passionate summer crowds still turning out for some blood-letting – Nîmes has the most active bullfighting scene outside Spain.

## The hôtel de ville and around

Just to the north of the Roman arena lies the warren of narrow streets that makes up Nîmes' compact old town. Among the mostly seventeenth- and eighteenth-century mansions you'll find the **hôtel de ville**, set between rue Dorée and rue des Greffes, the interior of which has been redesigned by the architect Jean-Michel Wilmotte to combine high-tech design with classical stone. Look out for the stuffed crocodiles suspended from chains above the stairwells – a gift from wealthy eighteenth-century burghers.

A few minutes from the *hôtel de ville*, at the eastern end of rue des Greffes, is the **Muséum d'Histoire Naturelle** (Tues–Sun 10am–6pm; free). Housed in a seventeenth-

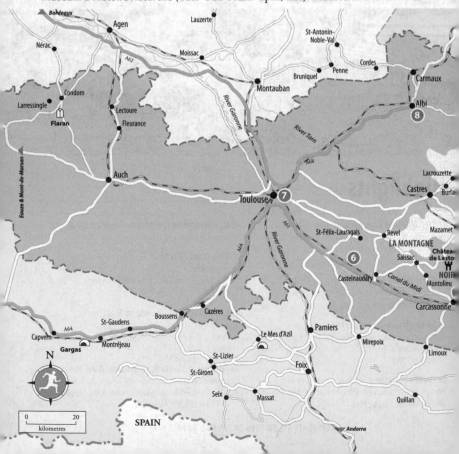

century Jesuit chapel at 13 bd de l'Admiral-Courbet, the museums are full of Roman bits and bobs, assorted curios, and stuffed animals.

## Musée du Vieux Nîmes

Plaçe aux Herbes • Tues–Sun 10am–6pm • €5 • ☎ 04 66 76 73 70, 🖰 nimes-tourisme.com

The resident Protestants were responsible for many of the splendid seventeenth- and eighteenth-century *hôtels* built in the streets around the cathedral – rues de l'Aspic, Chapitre, Dorée and Grand'Rue, among others. At the end of Grand'Rue, the former bishop's palace is now the **Musée du Vieux Nîmes**, which has displays of Renaissance furnishings and decor and documents relating to local history.

## Cathédrale Notre-Dame-et-St-Castor

Rue Saint-Castor • free • ☎ 04 66 67 27 72, 🖰 nimes.catholique.fr

The **Cathédrale Notre-Dame-et-St-Castor** sports a handsome sculpted frieze on the west front, illustrating the story of Adam and Eve, and a pediment inspired by the Maison Carrée. It's practically the only existing medieval building in town, as most were destroyed in the turmoil that followed the Michelade, the St Michael's Day massacre of Catholic clergy and notables by Protestants in 1567. Despite brutal repression in the wake of the Camisard insurrection of 1702, Nîmes was, and remains, a dogged Protestant stronghold. Apart from that, the cathedral is of little interest, having been

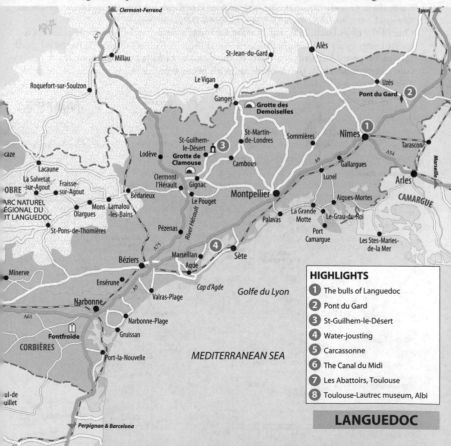

**HIGHLIGHTS**

1. The bulls of Languedoc
2. Pont du Gard
3. St-Guilhem-le-Désert
4. Water-jousting
5. Carcassonne
6. The Canal du Midi
7. Les Abattoirs, Toulouse
8. Toulouse-Lautrec museum, Albi

**LANGUEDOC**

seriously mutilated in the Wars of Religion and significantly altered in the nineteenth century. The author Alphonse Daudet was born in its shadow, as was Jean Nicot – a doctor, no less – who introduced tobacco into France from Portugal in 1560 and gave his name to the world's most widely consumed drug.

Meandering west from the cathedral are the narrow lanes of the medieval city, at the heart of which is the delightful **place aux Herbes**, where there are two or three cafés and bars and a fine twelfth-century house on the corner of rue de la Madeleine.

## Porte d'Auguste

Rue Nationale

North of the cathedral stands Nîmes' surviving Roman gate, **Porte d'Auguste** at the end of rue Nationale, the former Roman main street. Already a prosperous city on the Via Domitia, the main Roman road from Italy to Spain, Nîmes did especially well under Augustus. He gave the city its walls, remnants of which surface here and there, and its gates, as the inscription on the Porte records. He is also responsible for the chained crocodile, which figures on Nîmes' coat of arms. The image was copied from an Augustan coin struck to commemorate Augustus's defeat of Antony and Cleopatra after he settled veterans of that campaign on the surrounding land.

## Maison Carrée

Place de la Maison-Carrée • Daily: March 10am–6pm; April, May & Sept 10am–6.30pm; June 10am–7pm; July & Aug 9.30am–8pm; Oct 10am–1pm & 2–6pm; Nov–Feb 10am–1pm & 2–4.30pm • €6 • ☎ 04 66 21 82 56, ⓦ maisoncarree.eu

One of the city's landmarks, the **Maison Carrée** is a neat, jewel-like temple celebrated for its integrity and harmonic proportions. Built in 5 AD, it's dedicated to the adopted sons of Emperor Augustus – all part of the business of inflating the imperial personality cult. No surprise, then, that Napoleon, with his love of flummery, took it as the model

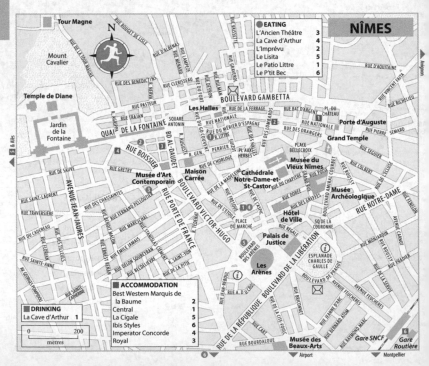

**NÎMES**

● EATING
| | |
|---|---|
| L'Ancien Théâtre | 3 |
| La Cave d'Arthur | 4 |
| L'Imprévu | 2 |
| Le Lisita | 5 |
| Le Patio Littre | 1 |
| Le P'tit Bec | 6 |

■ ACCOMMODATION
| | |
|---|---|
| Best Western Marquis de la Baume | 2 |
| Central | 1 |
| La Cigale | 5 |
| Ibis Styles | 6 |
| Imperator Concorde | 4 |
| Royal | 3 |

■ DRINKING
| | |
|---|---|
| La Cave d'Arthur | 1 |

## BULLFIGHTING

Nîmes' great passion is **bullfighting**, and its *férias* are attended by both aficionados and fighters at the highest level. The wildest and most famous is the **Féria de Pentecôte**, which lasts five days over the Whitsun weekend. A couple of million people crowd into the town (hotel rooms need to be booked a year in advance), and seemingly every city native opens a bodega at the bottom of the garden for dispensing booze. There are *corridas*, which end with the killing of the bull, *courses* where *cocards* are snatched from the bull's head, and semi-amateur *courses libres* when a small posse of bulls is run through the streets. Two other *férias* take place: one at carnival time in February; the other, the Féria des Vendanges, in the third week of September at grape harvest time. Events have been marked over the years by small but vocal protests and in 2006 several organizers of the local *tauromachie* world were injured by letter bombs. The **tourist office** can supply full details and advise about accommodation if you want to visit at *féria* time.

for the Madeleine church in Paris. The temple stands in its own small square opposite rue Auguste, where the Roman forum used to be, with pieces of Roman masonry scattered around.

## Musée d'Art Contemporain

Carré d'Art, Place de la Maison-Carrée • Tues–Sun 10am–6pm • €5, free 1st Sun of each month (see website for temporary exhibits) • ☏ 04 66 76 35 70, ⓦ carreartmusee.com

On the west side of place de la Maison-Carrée stands a gleaming example of the architectural boldness characteristic of the city, the **Carré d'Art**, by British architect Norman Foster. In spite of its size, this box of glass, aluminium and concrete sits modestly among the ancient roofs of Nîmes, its slender portico echoing that of the Roman temple opposite. Light pours in through the walls and roof, giving it a grace and weightlessness that makes it not in the least incongruous.

Inside, the excellent **Musée d'Art Contemporain** contains an impressive collection of French and Western European art from the last four decades, focusing on French art since the 1960s, works relating to Mediterranean identity, and German and British artists. The roof-terrace café overlooks the Maison Carrée.

## Jardin de la Fontaine and around

Perhaps the most refreshing thing you can do in Nîmes is head west of the centre to the **Jardin de la Fontaine**, France's first public garden, created in 1750. Behind the formal entrance, where fountains, nymphs and formal trees enclose the **Temple de Diane**, steps climb the steep wooded slope, adorned with grottoes and nooks and artful streams, to the **Tour Magne** (daily: March & Oct 9.30am–1pm & 2–6pm; April & May 9.30am–6.30pm; June 9am–7pm; July & Aug 9am–8pm; Sept 9.30am–1pm & 2–6.30pm Nov–Feb 9.30am–1pm & 2–4.30pm; €3.50). The 32m tower, left over from Augustus's city walls, gives terrific views over the surrounding country – as far, it is claimed, as the Pic du Canigou on the edge of the Pyrenees. At the foot of the slope flows the gloriously green and shady **Canal de la Fontaine**, built to supplement the rather unsteady supply of water from the *fontaine*, the Nemausus spring, whose presence in a dry, limestone landscape gave Nîmes its existence.

## Musée des Beaux-Arts

Rue de la Cité-Foulc • Tues–Sun 10am–6pm • Free (temporary exhibitions €5) • ☏ 04 66 76 71 82, ⓦ nimes.fr

The **Musée des Beaux-Arts**, in rue de la Cité-Foulc, prides itself on a huge Gallo-Roman mosaic showing the Marriage of Admetus. Originally housed in the tiny Maison Carrée, its collection now includes 3600 works from the fifteenth to the nineteenth centuries, including paintings by Rubens, Subleyras, and Delaroche.

## OCCITAN IDENTITY

A good part of the political character of Languedoc derives from resentment of domination by remote and alien Paris, aggravated by the area's traditional poverty. In recent times this has been focused on Parisian determination to drag the province into the modern world, with massive tourist development on the coast and the drastic transformation of the cheap wine industry. It is also mixed up with a collective folk memory of the thirteenth-century massacre of the Cathars and the subsequent obliteration of the brilliant langue d'Oc troubadour tradition, as well as the brutal repression of the Protestant Huguenots around 1700 and support of the revolutions of 1789 and 1848. The resulting antipathy towards central authority has made an essentially rural and conservative population vote traditionally for the Left – except during the first decade of this century, which saw wide support for Le Pen's resurgent Front National. Although a sense of **Occitan** identity and culture remains strong in the region, it has very little currency as a spoken or literary language, despite the popularity of university-level language courses and the foundation of Occitan-speaking elementary schools.

## South of town

Out on the southern edge of town, you'll find examples of the revolutionary civic architecture for which Nîmes was once famed. Jean Nouvel's pseudo-Mississippi-steamboat housing project, named **Nemausus** after the deity of the local spring that gave Nîmes its name, squats off the Arles road behind the *gare SNCF*, and the magnificent sports stadium, the **Stades des Costières**, by Vittorio Gregotti, looms close to the *autoroute* along the continuation of avenue Jean-Jaurès.

### ARRIVAL AND INFORMATION
NÎMES

**By plane** The Camargue airport (☎04 66 70 49 49, ⊛aeroport-nimes.fr), shared by Nîmes and Arles, lies 15km southeast of the city. A shuttle service links it to the town centre (2–4 daily, timed with flights; "Gambetta" or "Imperator" stop; €6.80). By taxi, the trip will cost at least €25 (€35 at night).

**By train** The *gare SNCF* is 10min walk southeast of the city centre at the end of av Feuchères.

Destinations Arles (every 20–30min; 30–40min); Avignon (every 20–30min; 30min); Béziers (every 20–30min; 1hr 15min); Carcassonne (every 20–30min; 2hr 5min–3hr 10min); Clermont-Ferrand (every 20–30min; 5–6hr); Marseille (every 20–30min; 40min–1hr 15min); Montpellier (every 20–30min; 30min); Narbonne (every 20–30min; 1hr 45min); Paris (every 20–30min; 3hr–9hr

30min); Perpignan (hourly; 2hr 45min); Sète (every 20–30min; 48min).

**By bus** The *gare routière* is just behind the train station. Destinations Aigues-Mortes (hourly; 55min); Ganges (2–3 daily; 1hr 30min); La Grande-Motte (2–9 daily; 1hr 30min); Le Grau-du-Roi (hourly; 1hr 15min); Le Vigan (3–5 daily; 1hr 50min); Pont du Gard (8 daily; 45min); Sommières (8 daily; 45min); Uzès (30min–1hr).

**Tourist office** 6 bd des Arènes (Mon–Sat 9am–7.pm,Sun 10am–6pm); plus an offshoot office on Pavilion Esplanade Charles-de-Gaulle (Mon–Sat 9.30am–5.30pm, Sun 10am–5pm). Both ☎04 66 58 38 00, ⊛nimes-tourisme.com.

**Passes** If you're planning on making the rounds of museums and monuments, pick up the Pass Nîmes Romaine from the first monument you visit (€13).

### ACCOMMODATION

★ **Best Western Marquis de la Baume** 21 rue Nationale ☎04 66 76 28 42, ⊛bestwestern.com. Atmospheric chain hotel nestled on a side street in a seventeenth-century townhouse. The modern furnishings throughout don't detract from the building's impeccably restored ceiling vaults, painted joists and sandstone stairs. **€100**

**Central** 2 place du Château ☎04 66 67 27 75, ⊛hotel-central.org. Just behind the temple and the Porte d'Auguste, with English-speaking management, this small, cosy hotel features simple but comfortable rooms –

although the top floor gets hot in summer. Secure parking available. **€80**

**La Cigale** 257 chemin de l'Auberge de Jeunesse, 2km northwest of the centre ☎04 66 68 03 20, ⊛fuaj.org. Set in airy, park-like surroundings this youth hostel's olive tree-laden terrace provides quiet respite from the bustle of the old city, 2km to the southeast. Take bus #2 direction "Alès/ Villeverte" from the *gare SNCF* to stop "Stade" – the last bus goes at 8pm. July & Aug membership required; Sept–June no curfew. Camping **€9.50**, dorms **€21.90**, doubles **€49**

**Ibis Styles Nîmes** Gare Centre 19 allée Boissy-d'Anglas ☎ 04 66 05 54 30, ⌨ ibis.com. At this dazzlingly modern edifice with matching interior, the staff are friendly and helpful, the breakfast a generous spread and the location, just behind the *gare SNCF*, makes it an attractive option if you're travelling by rail. **€75**

**Impérator Concorde** Quai de la Fontaine ☎ 04 66 21 90 30, ⌨ hotel-imperator.com. The city's finest choice, and a favourite of Ernest Hemingway's, located by the Jardin de la Fontaine. Luxuriously appointed rooms, excellent service and private parking. Prices are severely hiked during *férias*. **€185**

★ **Royal** 3 bd Alphonse-Daudet ☎ 04 66 58 28 27, ⌨ royalhotel-nimes.com. The *Royal* has a cool Spanish-style decor that draws in passing *toreros*. The rooms are individually decorated with an Iberian flavour, and the place exudes a certain chic. It's also home to the *Bodeguita* tapas bar, which spills enticingly out over the place d'Assas. **€92**

## EATING

The best places to hang out for coffee and drinks are the numerous little squares scattered through the old town: place de la Maison-Carrée, place du Marché and place aux Herbes.

**L'Ancien Théâtre** 4 rue Racine ☎ 04 66 21 30 75. Just a 5min stroll west from the Maison Carrée, with solid local cuisine, and home-made breads and pastries. *Menus* from €18. Tues–Fri noon–1.45pm & 7–9pm, Sat 6–9pm.

★ **L'Imprévu** 6 place d'Assas ☎ 04 66 38 99 59. A chic and surprisingly inexpensive little restaurant serving seasonal, classical dishes with a modern twist. It features an interior terrace decorated with local art. *Menus* from €22. Noon–2pm & 7.30–10pm, closed Tues & Sat afternoon and all Wed.

★ **Le Lisita** 2 bd des Arènes ☎ 04 66 67 29 15, ⌨ lelisita.com. Hands-down, the city's best *gastronomic* restaurant, run by two former staff of Michel Roux's famous London restaurant *Le Gavroche*. It also enjoys an unbeatable location overlooking Les Arènes. *Menus* start at a very reasonable €29. Daily noon–10pm.

**Le Patio Littre** 10 rue Littre ☎ 04 66 67 22 50, ⌨ restaurant-patio-littre-nimes.com. Modern but unstuffy restaurant centred on French cuisine with occasional Asian and vegetarian entries on to the carte like their delicate quinoa risotto with multicolour veg. Further tables are found out back on the enclosed leafy patio. *Menus* from €19. Wed–Sun noon–2pm & 7–10pm.

**Le P'tit Bec** 87 bis rue de la République ☎ 04 66 38 05 83, ⌨ restaurant-lepetitbec.fr The best mid-range place for typical Gardoise cuisine. The dining room is pleasant and airy and there's further seating in the enclosed patio outsite. *Menus* range between €18 and €48. Tues–Fri 11.30am–1.15pm & 6.30–9.45pm

## DRINKING

**La Cave d'Arthur** 35 rue Fresque ☎ 06 17 26 42 26. Cosy beer cavern in the heart of old Nîmes purveying an enviable selection of bottled brews from around the world. Tues–Sat 5pm–2am.

# North of Nîmes

Some 20km to the northeast of Nîmes is the **Pont du Gard**, the greatest surviving stretch of a 50km-long Roman aqueduct and a popular tourist destination, while 17km beyond, near the start of the aqueduct, the picturesque hilltop town of **Uzès** has a number of good places to stay.

## The Pont du Gard

Built in the middle of the first century AD to supply fresh water to the city, and with just a 17m difference in altitude between start and finish, the **Roman aqueduct** north of Nîmes was quite an achievement, running as it does over hill and dale, through a tunnel, along the top of a wall, into trenches and over rivers; the **Pont du Gard** carries it over the River Gardon. Today the bridge is a UNESCO World Heritage Site and something of a tourist trap, but is nonetheless a supreme piece of engineering and a brilliant combination of function and aesthetics; it made the impressionable Rousseau wish he'd been born Roman.

Three tiers of **arches** span the river, with the covered water conduit on the top rendered with a special plaster waterproofed with a paint apparently based on fig juice. A visit here used to be a must for French journeymen masons on their traditional tour of the country, and many of them have left their names and home towns carved on the stonework. Markings made by the original builders are still visible on individual stones in the arches.

**12**

### Site Pont du Gard

**Museum** 400 rte du Pont-du-Gard, Vers-Pont-du-Gard • Opens daily 9am; Dec–Feb closes 5pm; March & Oct closes 6pm; April–June & Sept closes 7pm; July–Aug closes 8pm • €8.50 • English-language audioguides and tours available; book tours 2 weeks in advance • ☎ 04 66 37 50 99, ⓦ pontdugard.fr

The Pont du Gard features an extensive multimedia complex, the **Site Pont du Gard**, which includes a state-of-the-art **museum**, botanical **gardens** and a range of regular children's activities. With the swimmable waters of the Gardon and ample picnic possibilities available, you could easily spend a day here.

## Uzès

**UZÈS** is a lovely old town perched on a hill above the River Alzon. Half a dozen medieval towers – the most fetching is the windowed Pisa-like **Tour Fénestrelle**, tacked onto the much later cathedral – rise above its tiled roofs and narrow lanes of Renaissance and Neoclassical houses. The latter were the residences of the seventeenth- and eighteenth-century local bourgeoisie, who had grown rich, like their fellow Protestants in Nîmes, on textiles. From the mansion of Le Portalet, with its view out over the valley, walk past the Renaissance church of **St-Étienne** and into the medieval place aux Herbes, where there's a Saturday morning market, and up the arcaded rue de la République. The Gide family used to live off the square, and the young André spent summer vacations there with his granny.

### Le Duché castle

Place Duché • Daily guided tours (60min) Sept–June 10am–noon & 2–6pm, July–Aug 10am–12.30pm & 2–6.30pm • €18; tower only €13 • ☎ 04 66 22 18 96, ⓦ duche-uzes.fr

**Le Duché castle**, still inhabited by the same family a thousand years on, is dominated by its original keep, the **Tour Bermonde**. Guided tours take in exhibits of local history and vintage cars. Opposite, the courtyard of the eighteenth-century **hôtel de ville** holds summer concerts.

### ARRIVAL AND INFORMATION                                    UZÈS

**By bus** Uzès is served by daily buses from Nîmes (50min).

**Tourist office** Place Albert-1ᵉʳ (June–Sept Mon–Fri 10am–6/7pm, Sat & Sun 10am–1pm & 2–5pm; Oct–May Mon–Fri 10am–12.30pm & 2–6pm, Sat & Sun 10am–1pm; ☎ 04 66 22 68 88, ⓦ uzes.fr ).

### ACCOMMODATION

**Hostellerie Provençale** 1-3 rue de la Grande Bourgade ☎ 04 66 22 11 06, ⓦ hostellerieprovencale.com. Set in two old village houses south of the church of St-Étienne, this hotel features a/c, en-suite rooms. Breakfast can be taken on the terrace and is included in the room rate. **€105**

**La Maison d'Uzès** 18 rue du Docteur-Blanchard ☎ 04 66 20 07 00, ⓦ lamaisonduzes.fr. Spa hotel set in a gorgeously renovated listed mansion dating from the seventeenth century and just a stone's throw from the Duché. The nine rooms have spectacular views over the rooftops of Uzès. **€239**

★ **La Taverne** 4 rue Xavier-Sigalon ☎ 04 66 22 13 10, ⓦ lataverne-uzes.com. This small, welcoming hotel with good amenities is just behind the tourist office. Rooms are basic but clean and well kept, and there is a beautiful, shady terrace for enjoying breakfast or an afternoon break. **€75**

# Montpellier

A thousand years of trade and intellectual activity have made **MONTPELLIER** a teeming, energetic city. Benjamin of Tudela, the tireless twelfth-century Jewish traveller, reported its streets crowded with traders from every corner of Egypt, Greece, Gaul, Spain, Genoa and Pisa. After the king of Mallorca sold it to France in 1349 it became an important university town in the 1500s, counting the radical satirist François Rabelais among its alumni. Periodic setbacks, including almost total destruction for its Protestantism in 1622, and depression in the wine trade in the early years of the twentieth century, have done little to dent its progress. Today it vies with Toulouse for the title of the most dynamic city in the south, a quality you'll appreciate as you explore the atmospheric pedestrianized streets of the **old town**. The reputation of its university especially, founded in the thirteenth century and most famous for its medical school, is a long-standing one: more than sixty thousand students still set the intellectual and cultural tone of the city, the average age of whose residents is said to be just 25. In many senses the best time to visit is during the academic year (Oct–May), when the city teems with students. The nearest **beaches** for a dip are at Palavas (tram direction "Odysseum" to Port Marianne, then bus #28), but the best are slightly to the west of the town.

Montpellier is renowned for its **cultural life**, and hosts a number of annual **festivals**, notably Montpellier Danse (late June to mid-July), and for music, Le Festival de Radio-France et de Montpellier (July).

## Place de la Comédie

At the hub of the city's life, joining the old part to its newer additions, is **place de la Comédie**, or "L'Oeuf" ("the egg"). This colossal oblong square, paved with cream-coloured marble, has a fountain at its centre and cafés either side. One end is closed by the **Opéra**, an ornate nineteenth-century theatre; the other opens onto the **Esplanade**, a beautiful tree-lined promenade that snakes its way to the **Corum concert hall**, which is dug into the hillside and topped off in pink granite, with splendid views from the roof.

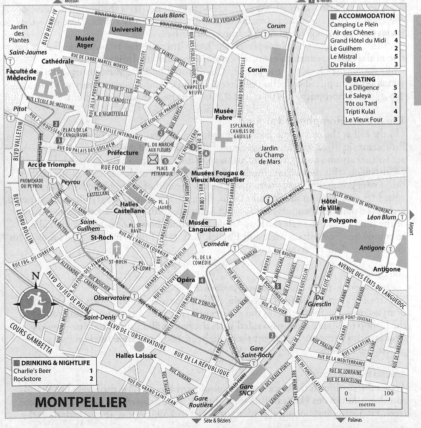

12

### Musée Fabre

39 bd Bonne Nouvelle • Tues–Sun 10am–6pm • €8 (€10 for temp exhibitions) • ☎ 04 67 14 83 00, ⓦ museefabre.montpellier3m.fr

South of the Corum is the **Musée Fabre**, the city's most trumpeted museum and one of the largest in the Languedoc. Its huge collection features seventeenth- to nineteenth-century European painting, including works by Delacroix, Zurbaran, Raphael, Jan van Steen and Veronese, as well as ceramics and contemporary art.

### The old town

From the northwest side of L'Oeuf, **rue de la Loge** and **rue Foch**, built in the 1880s during Montpellier's own Haussmann-izing spree, slice through the heart of the old city. Either side of them, a maze of narrow lanes slopes away to the encircling modern boulevards. Few buildings survive from before the 1622 siege, but the city's busy bourgeoisie quickly made up for the loss, proclaiming their financial power through austere seventeenth- and eighteenth-century mansions. Known as "Lou Clapas" (rubble), the area is rapidly being restored and gentrified. It's a pleasure to wander through, and to come upon secretive little squares like the places St-Roch, St-Ravy and de la Canourgue.

#### Place Jean-Jaurès and around

**Place Jean-Jaurès** is a focal point in the city's student life: on fine early evenings you get the impression that half the population is sitting here and in the adjacent place du Marché-aux-Fleurs. Through the Gothic doorway of no. 10 is the so-called palace of the kings of Aragon, named after the city's thirteenth-century rulers. Close by is the **Halles Castellane**, a graceful, iron-framed market hall.

A short walk from place Jean-Jaurès, the lively little rue des Trésoriers-de-France has one of the best seventeenth-century houses in the city, the **Hôtel Lunaret**, at no. 5, while round the block at 7 rue Jacques-Coeur you'll find the **Musée Languedocien**, which houses a mixed collection of Greek, Egyptian and other antiquities (Mon–Sat 2.30/3pm–5.30/6pm; €7; ☎04 67 52 93 03, ⓦmusee-languedocien.com).

### The Arc de Triomphe and around

On the hill at the end of rue Foch, from which the royal artillery bombarded the Protestants in 1622, the formal gardens of the **Promenade du Peyrou** look out across the city and away to the Pic St-Loup, which dominates the hinterland behind Montpellier, with the distant smudge of the Cévennes visible beyond. At the farther side a swagged and pillared water tower marks the end of an eighteenth-century aqueduct modelled on the Pont du Gard. Beneath the grand sweep of its double-tiered arches is a daily fruit and veg market and a huge Saturday **flea market**. At the city end of the promenade, the vainglorious **Arc de Triomphe** shows Louis XIV as Hercules, stomping on the Austrian eagle and English lion, forcefully reminding the locals of his victory over their Protestant "heresy".

#### The cathédrale

1 rue Saint-Pierre • Free • ☎ 04 67 66 04 12, ⓦ cathedrale-montpellier.fr

Montpellier's long-suffering **cathédrale**, with its massive porch, sports a patchwork of styles from the fourteenth to the nineteenth centuries. Inside is a memorial to the bishop of Montpellier, who sided with the half-million destitute vine-growers who came to demonstrate against their plight in 1907 and were fired on by government troops.

#### Around the cathédrale

Across the road from the cathédrale, on boulevard Henri-IV is the lovely but slightly run-down **Jardin des Plantes** (Tues–Sun: July & Sept noon–8pm; Oct–May 2–6pm; free), France's oldest botanical garden, founded in 1593. Above the cathedral, in the university's prestigious medical school on rue de l'École-de-Médecine, is the **Musée Atger** which has a distinguished academic collection of French and Italian drawings (Mon, Wed & Fri 1.30–5.45pm; closed school summer hols; free).

## ARRIVAL AND INFORMATION

## MONTPELLIER

**By plane** Montpellier-Méditerranée Airport (w montpellier. aeroport.fr), is 8km southeast of town beside the Étang de Mauguio; from here a *navette* (timed for flights; 15min; €1.60) runs to the bus stop on rue de Crète (by the Léon Blum tram stop); a taxi will cost at least €25–30, depending on the time of day and traffic conditions.

**By train** The *gare SNCF* is at the opposite end of rue Maguelone from the central place de la Comédie.

Destinations Arles (hourly; 1hr 20min); Avignon (every 20–30min; 1hr 15min–2hr); Béziers (every 20–30min; 40min); Carcassonne (every 20–30min; 1hr 15min); Lyon (every 20–30min; 1hr 40min–3hr 30min); Marseille (every 20–30min; 2hr 20min); Mende (every 20–30min; 3hr 40min–4hr 30min); Narbonne (every 20–30min; 45min–1hr 15min); Paris (every 20–30min; 3hr 15min–6hr); Perpignan (hourly; 2hr 15min); Sète (every 20–30min; 15–20min); Toulouse (every 20–30min; 2hr 15min–2hr 55min).

**By bus** The *gare routière* (t 04 67 92 01 43) is next to the train station.

Destinations Aigues-Mortes (2–4 daily; 1hr); Bédarieux (3–4 daily; 1hr 35min); Gignac (for St-Guilhem: 6–8 daily; 40min); La Grande-Motte (8–12 daily, hourly in summer; 1hr 5min); Grau-du-Roi (4–8 daily; 1hr 10min); Lodève (4 daily; 1hr 15min); Millau (2–8 daily; 2hr 20min); Palavas (local service); Rodez (1–3 daily; 3hr 55min); St-Pons-de-Thomières (1–3 daily; 2hr 55min); Le Vigan (3–5 daily; 1hr 40min).

**By car** Much of the city centre is pedestrianized, but you can park on the streets outside the centre and there are many well-signed municipal garages.

**Tourist office** At the east end of place de la Comédie, opposite the Polygone shopping centre (Mon–Sat 9.30am–7.30pm & Sun 10am–5pm; t 04 67 60 60 60, w montpellier-france.com). The tourist office sells the one-, two- and three-day City Card (from €13.50), which covers public transport and gives free admission to many sites as well as other discounts.

## GETTING AROUND

**By bus and tram** TAM (w tam-voyages.com) city buses and trams run between the stations and outer districts as far as Palavas (€1.40; day ticket €4.30).

**By bike** There are more than 150km of bike paths running

throughout the city and to the sea. You can rent bikes at Montpellier's municipal Vélomagg (€0.50/30min; w tam-way.com) stations around town.

## ACCOMMODATION

**Camping Le Plein Air des Chênes** t 04 67 02 02 53, w sandaya.fr. Situated 5km from Montpellier town centre (take bus #22 or 36), this 4-star campsite has plenty of amenities, including an airy restaurant, heated pool and tennis courts. It enjoys a particularly peaceful setting surrounded by ancient oak woods. April to mid-Oct. **€38**

★ **Grand Hôtel du Midi** 22 bd Victor-Hugo t 04 67 92 69 61, w grandhoteldumidimontpellier.com. This sumptuous old pile has undergone an extensive re-fit; all the rooms are individually decorated and the buffet breakfast is generous. You step from the door straight onto the humming place de la Comédie, right in the heart of the town. **€133**

**Le Guilhem** 18 rue Jean-Jacques-Rousseau t 04 67 52 90 90, w leguilhem.com. Beautifully restored

sixteenth-century townhouse, with cheerful rooms mostly overlooking quiet gardens, and a sunny breakfast terrace. Part of the Best Western chain. **€100**

**Le Mistral** 25 rue Boussairolles t 04 67 58 45 25, w hotel-le-mistral.com. An unassuming but comfortable little hotel in a Neoclassical building, just five minutes from the central station and a short walk from the place de la Comédie. It's the city's best economy option. Also offers garage parking (€5 extra). **€80**

**Du Palais** 3 rue du Palais des Guilhem t 04 67 60 47 38, w hoteldupalais-montpellier.fr. Tastefully renovated eighteenth-century mansion on the west side of the old town, blending modern and antique touches. An excellent mid-range option. **€90**

## EATING

★ **La Diligence** 2 place Pétrarque t 04 67 66 12 21, w la-diligence.com. Atmospheric vaulted medieval setting for innovative dishes with Asian influences. This deservedly popular restaurant is home to some of the finest cuisine in the city – fusion at the highest level. *Menus* €52–90 (€31 at lunch). Tues–Fri noon–2pm & 7.30–10pm, Sat & Mon

7.30–10pm.

**Le Saleya** 4 place du Marché-aux-Fleurs t 04 67 60 53 92. A long-standing Montpellier institution. In fine weather, join the locals at the outdoor tables to feast on a daily selection of market-fresh fish and regional food (*menus* from €15.90). Mon–Sat noon–2pm & 7–10.30pm.

**12**

**Tôt ou Tard** 7 place de la Chapelle Neuve ☎ 04 67 66 08 09. Situated in a classic French, plane tree shaded square with tables spilling out from all the restaurants that surround. You can eat a full meal here or drop in for an aperitif and share a few tapas at around €6 a piece. Mon–Tues 5pm–12.30am, Wed–Sun 10–12.30am.

**Tripti Kulai** 20 rue Jacques-Coeur ☎ 04 67 66 30 51, ⓦ triptikulai.com. Quirky, friendly vegetarian/vegan restaurant. Dishes, including a good choice of salads, have an oriental flair, and the lassis and home-made chai are superb. Weekday *menus* from €12. Mon–Sat noon–2.30pm & 6–9.30pm.

**Le Vieux Four** 59 rue de l'Aiguillerie ☎ 04 67 60 55 95. Carnivores will love this cosy, candlelit place specializing in *grillades au feu de bois* – meats roasted on an open spit. If you fancy something lighter, they also do a vegetarian platter and butter-roasted cod in Sichuan pepper. *Menus from* €19.50. Tues–Fri noon–2pm, Wed–Sun 7.30–10pm.

## DRINKING AND NIGHTLIFE

In addition to its clubs, bars and live music, Montpellier has a very lively theatre scene, as well as a tradition of engaging *cafés littéraires* on a variety of themes. For what's on at the various venues, look for posters around town or check the free weekly listings magazine, *Olé*, (ⓦ ole-mag.com).

**Charlie's Beer** 22 rue Aristide-Ollivier ☎ 04 67 58 89 86, ⓦ lepetitzinc.wix.com/charlies-beer. There are more than sixty beers on tap at this venerable, grungy old Montpellier institution. Live music at weekends. Daily 6pm–1am.

**Rockstore** 20 rue de Verdun ☎ 04 67 06 80 00, ⓦ rockstore.fr. Montpellier's rock 'n' roll heart, featuring a regular slate of bands and djs from Europe, North America and beyond. The bar, *Le Café Rock*, has a sophisticated, confident ambience. Daily 7.30pm–5am.

# St-Guilhem-le-Désert and around

The small town of **Gignac** lies amid vineyards 30km west of Montpellier. It is here that the main road (and buses) turn off for the glorious abbey and village of **ST-GUILHEM-LE-DÉSERT**, which lies in a side ravine, 6km further north up the Hérault beyond the famed medieval Pont du Diable. A ruined castle spikes the ridge above, and the ancient tiled houses of the village ramble down the banks of the rushing Verdus, which is everywhere channelled into carefully tended gardens.

## Abbaye de Gellone

Place de la Liberté • Daily 8am–12.10pm & 2.30–6.20pm • Free • ☎ 04 67 57 58 83, ⓦ saintguilhem-valleeherault.fr/l-abbaye-de-gellone

The grand focus of St-Guilhem-le-Désert is the tenth- to twelfth-century **Abbaye de Gellone**, founded at the beginning of the ninth century by St Guilhem, comrade-in-arms of Charlemagne. The church is a beautiful and atmospheric building, though architecturally impoverished by the dismantling and sale of its cloister – now in New York – in the nineteenth century. It stands on place de la Liberté, surrounded by honey-coloured houses and arcades with traces of Romanesque and Renaissance domestic styles in some of the windows. The interior of the church is plain and somewhat severe compared to the warm colours of the exterior, best seen from rue Cor-de-Nostra-Dama/Font-du-Portal, where you get the classic view of the perfect apse.

## Grotte de Clamouse

Rte de Saint-Guilhem-le-Désert • Guided tours: Nov, Feb & March Mon–Fri 2.30pm, Sat & Sun 11am, 2.30 & 4pm; April, May & Oct hourly 10.30am–4.30pm; June & Sept hourly 10.30am–5.30pm; July & Aug regular tours between 10.30am–6pm • €10.80; €6.70 3 to 11 year-olds; €8 12 to 18 year-olds • ☎ 04 67 57 71 05, ⓦ clamouse.com

Cave enthusiasts will enjoy the **Grotte de Clamouse**, an extensive and beautiful stalactite cave that is entered along a subterranean river before it opens up into three expansive grottoes. It is on the road between Gignac and St-Guilhem-le-Désert.

## Grotte des Demoiselles

St-Bauzille-de-Putois • Guided tours: Jan Mon–Sat 11am, 1, 2.30 & 4 & 6pm; Feb daily 11am, 1, 2.30 & 4pm; March daily 11am, 2.30, 4pm, Sun 1pm also; April & May daily 10.30 & 11.30am, 1, 2, 3, 4, 5 & 6.30pm; June Mon–Fri 10.30 & 11.30am, 1, 2, 3, 4, 5 & 6.30pm, Sat & Sun 10.30 & 11.30am, 1, 2.30, 3.30, 4.30, 5.30 & 7pm; July & Aug regular tours 10am–7.30pm; Sept daily 10.30 & 11.30am, 1.30, 2.30, 3.30, 4.30, 5.30 & 7pm; Oct daily 11am, 1, 2.30 & 4.30pm, Sun also 11.30am & 3.30pm; Nov Mon–Sat 2, 2.30, 4 & 5.30pm, Sun 11am, 1, 2.30

& 4pm; Dec Mon–Sat 2, 2.30, 4 & 5.30pm, Sun 11am, 1, 2.30 & 4pm • €11.50, range of reduced rates for children according to their age • ☎ 04 67 73 70 02, ⓦ demoiselles.com

North of St-Guilhem, after passing through dramatic river gorges almost as far as Ganges, you reach the **Grotte des Demoiselles**, the most spectacular of the region's many caves: a set of vast cathedral-like caverns hung with stalactites descending with millennial slowness to meet the limpid waters of eerily still pools. Located deep inside the mountain, it's reached by an hourly funicular.

### ACCOMMODATION                        ST-GUILHEM-LE-DÉSERT AND AROUND

**Domaine de Pélican** 34150 Gignac ☎ 04 67 57 68 92, ⓦ domainedepelican.fr. The closest campsite to St-Guilhem is on this wine *domaine* and *ferme/auberge* near Aniane on the road back down to Gignac. The restaurant serves up such delights as lamb cutlets with a crust of fresh spring garlic. Closed Dec–April. B&B **€90**, camping **€16.50**

**Le Guilhaume d'Orange** 2 av Guillaume d'Orange ☎ 04 67 57 24 53, ⓦ guilhaumedorange.com. Set near the top of the old village, this welcoming hotel features ten unique and spacious rooms, tastefully appointed, if not long on amenities. Half- and full-board available. **€75**

## Lodève

Around 25km northwest of Gignac, at the point where the swift A75 *autoroute* brings heavy traffic down from Clermont-Ferrand, sits **LODÈVE**, a town at the confluence of the Lergues and Soulondres rivers. In addition to being a pleasant, old-fashioned place at which to pause on your way up to Le Caylar or La Couvertoirade, it also has an **art museum** that puts on world-class temporary exhibitions. The **cathedral** – a stop on the pilgrim route to Santiago de Compostela – is also worth a look, as is the unusual World War I **Monument aux Morts**, in the adjacent park, by local sculptor Paul Dardé. This unsettling *mise en scène* of civilians mourning a soldier who has fallen on the field is a departure from the usual stiff commemorations of the "Morts pour la France". More of his work is displayed at the **Musée de Lodève** at place Georges-Auric (Nov–March Mon–Fri 10am–1pm & 2–6pm, Sat 10am–1pm; April–May Mon–Sat 10am–1pm & 2–6pm; June–Sept daily 10am–1pm & 2–6pm; Oct Tues–Sun 10am–1pm & 2–6pm; €6–10 depending on exhibitions; ☎ 04 67 88 86 10) and the **Halle Dardé** (daily 9am–7pm; free; ☎ 04 67 88 86 44) off the place du Marché. There's a big market on Saturdays, and local farmers bring in their produce three times a week in summer.

### ARRIVAL AND INFORMATION                                            LODÈVE

**By bus** The *gare routière* (☎ 04 67 88 86 44) is next to the tourist office.
Destinations Millau (4 daily; 55min); Montpellier (4 daily; 1hr–1hr 15min); connections to other destinations via Clermont l'Hérault (6 daily; 25min).

**Tourist office** 7 place de la République (May, June & Sept Mon–Sat 10am–1pm & 2–6pm; July & Aug Mon–Sat 10am–-1pm & 2–6pm, Sun 10am–12.30pm & 3.30–6pm; Oct–April Mon–Fri 9.30am–12.30pm & 2–6pm, Sat 10am–1pm; ☎ 04 67 88 86 44, ⓦ tourisme-lodevois-larzac.com).

### ACCOMMODATION

**Du Nord** 18 bd de la Liberté ☎ 04 67 44 10 08, ⓦ hoteldu nord-lodeve.fr. This friendly, family-run establishment offers large a/c rooms, each with TV, private bath and balcony, and larger rooms for families and groups. **€65**

## The Languedoc coast

There is a beguiling, bucolic air about the **Languedoc coast**: its breezy, golden strands are often cut off from the sea by marshy, reed-fringed *étangs* (lagoons) and for this reason it doesn't suffer the frenzied holiday crowds of its neighbours. However, the area does have a lot going for it, enjoying long hours of sunshine, 200km of sporadically populated sand and an abundance of wildlife; you'll likely spot a few baby-pink flamingos. A few holiday resorts have sprung up, sometimes engulfing once quiet fishing towns, but there's more than enough unexploited territory to make this coast a good getaway, and many of the old towns have managed to sustain their character and traditions.

## The coast east of Montpellier

The oldest of the new resorts, on the fringes of the Camargue, **La Grande-Motte** is a 1960s vintage beachside Antigone – a "futuristic" planned community which has aged as gracefully as the bean bag and eight-track tape. In summer, its seaside and streets are crowded with semi-naked bodies; in winter, it's a depressing, wind-battered place with few permanent residents.

### Le Grau-du-Roi

A little way east of La Grande-Motte are **Port-Camargue**, with a sprawling, modern marina, and **LE GRAU-DU-ROI**, which manages to retain something of its character as a working fishing port. Tourist traffic still has to give way every afternoon at 4.30pm when the swing bridge opens and lets in the trawlers to unload the day's catch onto the quayside, from where it's whisked off to auction – *la criée* – now conducted largely by electronic means rather than shouting.

### Aigues-Mortes

The town of **AIGUES-MORTES** ("dead waters") was built as a fortress port by Louis IX in the thirteenth century for his departure on the Seventh Crusade. Its massive walls and towers remain virtually intact. Outside the ramparts, amid drab modern development, flat saltpans lend a certain otherworldly appeal, but inside all is geared to tourism. If you visit (daily 10am–5.30; May–Aug 10am–7pm; €8; ☎04 66 53 61 55, ⓦaigues-mortes-monument.fr), consider a climb up the **Tour de Constance** on the northwest corner of the town walls, where Camisard women were imprisoned (one such, Marie Durand, was incarcerated here for 38 years); or take a walk along the wall, where you can gaze out over the weird mist-shrouded flats of the Camargue.

| ACCOMMODATION | THE COAST EAST OF MONTPELLIER |
|---|---|

**Les Arcades** 23 bd Gambetta, Aigues-Mortes ☎04 66 53 81 13, ⓦhotel-aigues-mortes-piscine.com. This fine hotel is set within a renovated, listed sixteenth-century home tucked within the walls of Aigues-Mortes. There are nine individually appointed, en-suite and a/c rooms and outside, an appealing terrace and swimming pool. **€100**

**Azur Bord de Mer** Place Justin, La Grande Motte ☎04 67 56 56 00, ⓦhotelazur.net. Set dramatically on the extremity of the quay, this is the most appealing among the town's dozen or so near-identical hotels; aim for the garden room that has direct access to its own private patio. **€169**

**Camping Le Garden** Av de la Petite Motte, La Grande Motte ☎04 67 56 50 09, ⓦlegarden.fr. A good campsite with excellent facilities a couple of minutes' walk from the beach (two-night minimum stay in high season). Closed mid Oct–Feb. **€47**

## Sète

Some 28km southwest of Montpellier, twenty minutes away by train, **SÈTE** has been an important port for three hundred years. The upper part of the town straddles the slopes of the Mont St-Clair, which overlooks the vast Bassin de Thau, a breeding ground of mussels and oysters, while the lower part is intersected by waterways lined with tall terraces and seafood restaurants. Sète's crowded and vibrant pedestrian streets are scattered with café tables, and the town has a lively workaday bustle in addition to its tourist activity. Things are at their height during the summer *joutes nautiques* (see page 655).

A short climb up from the harbour is the **cimetière marin**, the sailors' cemetery, where poet Paul Valéry is buried. Near the cemetery are the small **Musée Paul Valéry**, 148 rue Denoyer (April–Oct daily 9.30am–7pm; Nov–March Tues–Sun 10am–6pm; €9.70; ☎04 99 04 76 16, ⓦmuseepaulvalery-sete.fr), and the **Espace Brassens**, 67 bd Camille-Blanc (June–Sept daily 10am–6pm; Oct–May Tues–Sun 10am–noon & 2–6pm; €5.80; ☎04 99 04 76 26, ⓦespace-brassens.fr), which is dedicated to the locally born singer-songwriter Georges Brassens; the latter will be of little interest to non-fans. More intriguing is the found art collection at the **Musée International des Arts Modestes** at 23 quai du Maréchal-de-Lattre-de-Tassigny (April–Sept daily 9.30am–7pm; Oct–March Tues–Sun noon–2pm & 2–6pm; €5.60; ☎04 99 04 76 44, ⊛miam.org).

## ARRIVAL AND INFORMATION                                                    SÈTE

**By train** The *gare SNCF*, on the main Nîmes-Toulouse line, lies 1km north of the tourist office on place André-Cambon.

**By bus** Regular buses to Montpellier (5–16 daily; 1hr 5min) arrive at the *gare routière*, on quai de la République, on the eastern edge of the town centre.

**By ferry** Ferries for Morocco (1–2 weekly) and Mallorca (1–3 weekly) depart from the *gare maritime* at 4 quai d'Alger (☎04 67 46 15 22, ⊛sete.port.fr).

**Tourist office** 60 Grand'rue Mario-Roustan (April–June & Sept Mon–Sat 9.30am–6, Sun 10am–5pm; July & Aug daily 9.30am–7pm; Oct–March Mon–Sat 9.30am–5.30pm, Sun 10am–1pm; ☎04 67 04 71 71, ⊛tourisme-sete.com). They have a good array of English-language information, and sell the "City Pass" that gives discounted entry to all three of the town's museums.

## ACCOMMODATION AND EATING

**Grand Hôtel** 17 quai du Maréchal-de-Lattre-de-Tassigny ☎04 67 74 71 77, ⊛legrandhotelsete.com. This artily renovated hotel, dating from 1882, combines *belle époque* splendour with modern touches. Rooms are luxurious and service is impeccable. **€130**

★ **L'Orque Bleue** 10 quai Aspirant-Herber ☎04 67 74 72 13, ⊛hotel-orquebleue-sete.com. A charmingly sophisticated little hotel overlooking the main canal and fishing port. Request a canalside room (more expensive at €130) with their French windows opening onto shallow balconies offering an ideal vantage spot for water-jousting.

All rooms have en-suite bathrooms. **€95**

**La Palangrotte** Rampe Paul-Valéry ☎04 67 74 80 35. This local standby is famous for its mussels and bouillabaisse, solid wine list and vegan menu. Meals from €13. Tues & Wed–Sat noon–2pm & 7–9.30pm, Sun noon–2pm.

**Villa Salis** 7 rue du Général-Revest ☎04 67 53 46 68, ⊛fuaj.org. HI hostel high up on the hill above town with splendid views of the harbour. It's set in a perfect wooded glade, and features a kitchen, basic shop and cycle hire. Closed Oct to March. **€21**

## Marseillan
⊛marseillan.com

Lying at the southern end of the Bassin de Thau, around 45km southwest of Montpellier, the picturesque fishing village of **MARSEILLAN** is as laden with history as any of its more famous neighbours. Founded by the Phoenicians, it was eventually cut off from the sea by the basin. Not many people come here nowadays, preferring the more vivacious charms of its seafront namesake, Marseillan-Plage. But a visit here rewards you with a delightful, seventeenth century market filled with stalls every Tuesday, as well as an attractive old port and a maze of cobbled streets.

But it's a drink that really put Marseillan on the modern-day map: it's home to the first, and arguably finest, of vermouths, Noilly Prat (pronounced "nwarlly pra"). The town is therefore the spiritual birthplace of the dry martini, so favoured by 007 – although the locals scorn any form of embellishment and knock it back just as it is. You can visit the famous distillery at 1 rue Noilly (May–Sept daily 10–noon & 2.30–7pm; March, April & Oct–Dec daily 10am–noon & 2.30–5.30pm; Jan & Feb open by booking only; guided tours range from €5.50–€35; ☎04 67 77 20 15, ⊛noillyprat.com).

---

## JOUTES NAUTIQUES

**Water-jousting** is a venerable Languedoc tradition that pits boat-borne jousting teams against each other in an effort to unseat their opponents. Two sleek boats, each manned by eight oarsmen and bearing a lance-carrying jouster, charge at each other on a near head-on course. As the boats approach, the jousters attempt to strike their adversary from his mount. There are about a dozen *sociétés de joutes* in Sète itself, and you can see them in action all through the summer.

**12**

## Agde and around

Midway between Sète and Béziers, at the western tip of the Bassin de Thau, the old town of **AGDE** is the most interesting of the coastal towns. Originally Phoenician, and maintained by the Romans, it thrived for centuries on trade with the Levant. Outrun as a seaport by Sète, it later degenerated into a sleepy fishing harbour.

Today, it's a major tourist centre with a good deal of charm, notably in the narrow back lanes between rue de l'Amour and the riverside, where fishing boats tie up. There are few sights apart from the impressively fortified **cathedral**, though the **waterfront** is attractive, and by the bridge you can watch the Canal du Midi slip modestly into the River Hérault on the very last leg of its journey from Toulouse to the Bassin de Thau and Sète.

### Cap d'Agde

**CAP D'AGDE** lies to the south of Mont St-Loup, 7km from Agde. The largest (and by far the most successful) of the newer resorts, it sprawls out from the volcanic mound of St-Loup in an excess of pseudo-traditional buildings that offer every type of facility and entertainment – all of which are expensive. It is perhaps best known for its colossal **Village Naturiste**, one of the largest in France, with the best of the beaches, space for 20,000 visitors, and its own restaurants, banks, post offices and shops. Access is possible if you're not actually staying there (visitors to 8pm only; ⓦen.capdagde.com/discover/naturism). If you have time to fill, head for the **Musée de l'Éphèbe**, Mas de la Clape (June–Sept daily 10am–6.30pm; Oct–May Mon–Fri 10am–5.30pm, Sat & Sun 10.30am–5pm; €6; ☏04 67 94 69 60, ⓦmuseecapdagde.com), which displays antiquities discovered locally, including many unique and rare pieces drawn from the sea around here.

**12**

### ARRIVAL AND INFORMATION                                                 AGDE AND AROUND

**By train** The *gare SNCF* is at the end of av Victor-Hugo. Destinations Avignon (12 daily; 1hr 40min–2hr 19min); Narbonne (16 daily; 30min); Nîmes (16 daily; 1hr 10min); Perpignan (12 daily; 1hr 10min); Toulouse (8 daily; 1hr 45min–2hr 15min).

**By bus** Hourly buses run between Agde and Cap d'Agde, stopping at the *gare SNCF*, the bridge and La Promenade.

**Tourist office** Rond-point du Bon Accueil, the roundabout at the entrance to Cap d'Agde, travelling from the *cité* (July–Sept

Mon–Sat 9am–7pm, Sun 10am–1pm & 2.30–6.30pm; Oct–March Mon–Sat 9am–noon & 2–6pm; April–June daily 9am–12.30pm & 2–6pm; ☏04 67 01 04 04, ⓦcapdagde.com).

**Boat tours** Boat trips of the Canal du Midi and the coast are organized by Le Millésime (from €7; ☏04 67 01 71 93, ⓦagde-croisiere-peche.com), Trans Cap (from €11; ☏06 08 47 22 32, ⓦtranscapcroisieres.com) and boat hire by Agde Croisières (€44 per hour; ☏04 46 78 14 60, ⓦagde-croisiere-location.com

### ACCOMMODATION

**La Voile d'Or** Place du Globe, Cap d'Agde ☏04 67 01 04 11, ⓦlavoiledor.com. This modern resort-style place may lack atmosphere but offers spacious rooms with balconies. It

has two pools and is a stroll away from the seaside. Closed mid-Nov to Feb. **€135**

### EATING

**Le Jardin de Beaumont** Rte de Florensac ☏04 67 21 19 23, ⓦbeaumont-holidays.com. A wine *domaine* 3km north of Agde, where you can dine on salads and local specialities, and enjoy excellent wines indoors or out. *Menus* €16–25. July & Aug daily noon–2pm & 7–10pm, opens 10am on Sun; Sept–June Mon–Sat noon–2pm, Sun 10am–2pm.

**La Table de Stéphane** 2 rue du Moulin-à-Huile ☏04 67 26 45 22, ⓦlatabledestephane.com. This famous local restaurant, set about 2km east of Agde's old town, features elaborate creations such as quail ballotine with foie gras, rhubarb and summer truffle. *Menus* from €32. Tues–Fri noon–2pm & 7–9.30pm, Sat 7–9.30pm, Sun noon–2pm.

# Southern Languedoc

**Southern Languedoc** presents an exciting and varied landscape, its coastal flats stretching south from the mouth of the Aude towards Perpignan, interrupted by occasional low, rocky hills. Just inland sits **Béziers**, its imposing cathedral set high above the languid River Orb, girded in the north by the amazingly preserved Renaissance town of **Pézenas** and in the south by the pre-Roman settlement of the **Ensérune**. It's also a gateway to the spectacular uplands of the **Monts de l'Espinouse** and the **Parc Naturel Régional du Haut Languedoc**, a haven for ramblers. Just south of Béziers, the ancient Roman capital of **Narbonne** guards the mouth of the Aude. Following the course of this river, which is shadowed by the historic **Canal du Midi**, you arrive at the quintessential medieval *citadelle*, the famous fortress town of **Carcassonne**. Once a shelter for renegade **Cathar** heretics, this is also a fine departure point for the Cathar castles – a string of romantic ruins.

# Béziers

Though no longer the rich city of its nineteenth-century heyday, **BÉZIERS** has admirable panache. The town is the capital of the Languedoc **wine** country and a focus for the **Occitan** movement, as well as being the birthplace of Resistance hero **Jean Moulin**. The town is also home to two great Languedocian adopted traditions: English **rugby** and the Spanish **corrida**, both of which are followed with a passion. The best time to visit is during the mid-August **féria**, a raucous four-day party that can be enjoyed even if bullfighting isn't to your taste.

### Cathédrale St-Nazaire

Plan des Albigeois • ☏ 04 67 28 22 89

The finest view of the old town is from the west, as you come in from the direction of Carcassonne: crossing the willow-lined River Orb by the Pont-Neuf, you can look upstream at the sturdy arches of the **Pont-Vieux**, above which rises a steep-banked hill crowned by the **Cathédrale St-Nazaire** which, with its crenellated towers, resembles a castle more than a church. The best approach to the cathedral is up the medieval lanes at the end of Pont-Vieux, rue Canterelles and passage Canterellettes. Its architecture is mainly Gothic, the original building having burned down in 1209 during the sacking of Béziers, when Armand Amaury's crusaders massacred some seven thousand people at the church of the Madeleine for refusing to hand over about twenty Cathars. "Kill them all", the pious abbot is said to have ordered, "God will recognize his own!"

From the top of the cathedral **tower**, there's a superb view out across the vine-dominated surrounding landscape. Keep an eye on small children, however, lest they slip through the potentially perilous gaps in the wall. Next door, you can wander through the ancient **cloister** and out into the shady **bishop's garden** overlooking the river.

### Musée des Beaux-Arts

Place de la Révolution • Sept–June Tues–Sat & 1st Sun of month noon–5pm: July & Aug daily 10am–6pm • €3; ticket includes entrance to Hôtel Fayet • ☏ 04 67 49 04 66, ⓦ ville-beziers.fr

Steps away from the cathedral, **place de la Révolution** is home to the **Musée des Beaux-Arts** which, apart from an interesting collection of Greek Cycladic vases, won't keep you long.

### Musée du Biterrois

Caserne Saint-Jacques Rampe du 96ᵉᵐᵉ Régiment d'Infanterie • Oct–March Tues–Sat & 1st Sun of month; April–Sept Sat & 1st Sun of month: 10am–noon & 2–6pm • €3 • ☏ 04 67 36 81 61, ⓦ ville-beziers.fr

The **Musée du Biterrois** holds an important collection ranging from locally produced pottery to funerary monuments and artefacts dredged from ancient shipwrecks, but the highlight is the "treasure of Béziers" – a rich cache of silver platters found in a nearby field.

12

## ARRIVAL AND INFORMATION

**By train** From the *gare SNCF* on bd Verdun, the best way into town is through the landscaped gardens of the Plateau des Poètes opposite the station entrance and up the allées Paul-Riquet.

Destinations Agde (18 daily; 10min); Arles (10–14 daily; 2hr 10min); Avignon (4–10 daily; 2hr); Bédarieux (4–8 daily; 40min); Carcassonne (22 daily; 45min–1hr 45min); Clermont-Ferrand (3 daily; 6–7hr); Marseille (8 daily; 3hr 10min); Millau (4–6 daily; 2hr); Montpellier (26 daily; 45min); Narbonne (18 daily; 14min); Nîmes (20 daily; 1hr 15min); Paris (30 daily; 4hr 30min–12hr); Perpignan (18 daily; 40min–1hr); Sète (23 daily; 25min).

**By bus** The *gare routière* (☎04 67 28 36 41, ⓦbeziers-transports.com) is on place de Gaulle, at the northern end of the *allées*.

Destinations Agde (2 daily; 4–6 daily in summer; 25min); Bédarieux (generally up to 2 daily; 1hr); Castres (2 daily; 2hr 50min); Mazamet (2 daily; 2hr); Pézenas (4–11 daily; 32min); La Salvetat (generally up to 2 daily; 2hr 10min); St-Pons-de-Thomières (4 daily; 1hr 20min).

**Tourist office** 3 place Gabriel-Péri (daily 9am–6/7pm; ☎04 99 41 36 36, ⓦbeziers-in-mediterranee.com).

**Bike rental** If you fancy pottering along the Canal du Midi, note that bikes are available for rent; enquire at the tourist office.

## ACCOMMODATION

**Les Berges du Canal** 2120 rte de Narbonne ☎04 67 39 36 09, ⓦlesbergesducanal.com. The nearest campsite to Béziers is outside Villeneuve-lès-Béziers, about 4km southeast of the town centre. Closed mid Oct–mid March. **€27**

**Impérator** 28 allées Paul-Riquet ☎04 67 49 02 25, ⓦhotel-imperator.fr. A notch above the rest but still an excellent deal, this hotel is set in a gracious renovated mansion. There's an elegant bar reserved exclusively for guests and a peaceful inner courtyard for summer dining. **€75**

**Des Poètes** 80 allées Paul-Riquet ☎04 67 76 38 66, ⓦhoteldespoetes.net. Set at the southern end of the *allées* overlooking a garden, this basic but pleasant hotel offers doubles, twins and family rooms. Double **€60**, Family **€90**

## EATING

★ **Dolce Vita chez Jpetto** 23 bd de Verdun ☎04 67 93 33 10, ⓦdolcevitajpetto.fr. Across the road from the station this restaurant is worth missing your train for. The wood-fired pizzas are as good as any in Naples and, as a bonus, you get to watch the pizzaiolo spinning and throwing the dough around in the open kitchen. *Pizzas* from €9.50. Tues–Sun noon–2pm & 7–10.30pm.

★ **Le Patio** 21 rue Française ☎04 67 49 09 45, ⓦrestaurant-patio.fr. A lovely spot, tucked away in the side streets; everything is home-made and delicious especially when eaten outside in the charming courtyard under the shade of a huge old olive tree. Well patronized by locals. *Menus* €17.50–29. Daily except Sun lunch: noon–2pm & 7.30–9.30pm.

# Pézenas

**PÉZENAS** lies 18km east of Béziers. Market centre of the coastal plain, it looks across to rice fields and shallow lagoons, hazy in the heat and dotted with pink flamingos. The town was catapulted to glory when it became the seat of the parliament of Languedoc and the residence of its governors in 1465, and reached its zenith in the late seventeenth century when the prince Armand de Bourbon made it a "second Versailles". The legacy of this illustrious past can be seen in the town's exquisite array of fourteenth- to seventeenth-century mansions. Pézenas also plays up its association with **Molière**, who visited several times with his troupe in the mid-seventeenth century, when he enjoyed the patronage of Prince Armand, and put on plays at the **Hôtel d'Alfonce** on rue Conti.

## Musée Vulliod St-Germain

3 rue Albert-Paul-Alliés • Oct–mid Nov & mid Feb–May Tues–Sun 10am–noon & 2–5.30pm; June–Sept Tues–Sun 10am–noon & 2–7pm • €3 • ☎04 67 98 90 59, ⓦpezenas-tourisme.fr

Although Molière features in the eclectic **Musée Vulliod St-Germain**, housed in a sixteenth-century palace tucked away in the north end of the old town, it's the grand salon, with its Aubusson tapestries and seventeenth- and eighteenth-century furniture, that steals the show.

## The town mansions

The tourist office, at the main entrance to the old town, distributes a guide to all the town's eminent houses, taking in the former **Jewish ghetto** on rue des Litanies and rue Juiverie, but you can just as easily follow the explanatory plaques posted all over the centre, starting at the east end of rue François-Outrin where it leaves the town's main square, place du 14-juillet.

### ARRIVAL AND INFORMATION                                                     PÉZENAS

**By bus** The *gare routière* is at the south east end of the square on the riverbank, with frequent buses to Montpellier, Béziers and Agde.

**Tourist office** Place des États du Languedoc (July & Aug Mon, Tues, Thurs & Sat 9am–7pm, Wed & Fri 9am–10pm,

Sun 10am–7pm; Sept–June Mon–Sat 9am–noon & 2–6pm, Sun 10am–noon & 2–5pm; ☎ 04 67 98 36 40, ⓦ pezenas-tourisme.fr).

**Market** There's a huge market each Sat on cours Jean-Jaurès, along the river.

### ACCOMMODATION

**Molière** 40 place du 14-juillet ☎ 04 67 98 14 00, ⓦ hotel-le-moliere.com. Charming nineteenth-century hotel on the edge of the old town, with en-suite rooms and a lovely old salon. **€92**

**Le Saint-Germain** 6 av Paul-Vidal ☎ 04 67 09 75 75, ⓦ hotel-saint-germain-pezenas.com. Functional, but with a small pool and private parking, and en-suite rooms decorated in cool, muted colours. **€80**

### EATING

Anyone with a sweet tooth should sample two local delicacies: flavoured sugar-drops called *berlingots*, and *petits pâtés* – bobbin-shaped pastries related to mince pies, reputedly introduced by the Indian cook of Clive of India, who stayed in Pézenas in 1770.

★ **L'Entre Pots** 8 av Louis-Montagne ☎ 04 67 90 00 00, ⓦ restaurantentrepots.com. A place for a treat, this Michelin-starred restaurant is the best in Pézenas. Sumptuous, beautifully presented cuisine that's reasonably priced and professionally served. *Menus* start at around

€27. Reservations advised. Noon–2pm & 7.30–10pm: July & Aug closed Mon; rest of the year closed Sun & Mon.

**Les Palmiers** 50 rue Mercière ☎ 04 67 09 42 56, ⓦ lespalmiers.restaurant. A beautiful and welcoming establishment serving inventive Mediterranean-style food. This is not haute cuisine, but the menu features a variety of excellently prepared dishes. *Menus* from €22. Mon–Sat noon–2pm & 7–9.30pm, Sun noon–2pm.

**12**

# Narbonne and around

On the Toulouse–Nice main train line, 25km west of Béziers, is **NARBONNE**, once the capital of Rome's first colony in Gaul, Gallia Narbonensis, and a thriving port in classical times and the Middle Ages. Plague, war with the English, and the silting up of its harbour finished it off in the fourteenth century. Today, it's a pleasant provincial city with a small but well-kept old town, dominated by the great truncated choir of its cathedral and bisected by a grassy esplanade on the banks of the Canal de la Robine.

## Horreum Romain

7 rue Rouget-de-Lisle · June–Sept daily 10am–6pm; Oct–May Wed–Mon 10am–noon & 2–5pm · €4 · ☎ 04 68 90 30 65, ⓦ mairie-narbonne.fr

One of the few Roman remnants in Narbonne is the **Horreum**, at the north end of rue Rouget-de-Lisle, an unusual underground grain store divided into a series of small chambers leading off a rectangular passageway.

## Cathédrale St-Just-et-St-Pasteur

Rue Armand-Gauthier · **Salle du Trésor** July–Sept daily (except Tues morn) 10–11.45am & 2–5.45pm; Oct–June daily 2–5pm · €6 · ☎ 04 68 32 09 82, ⓦ narbonne-tourisme.com

At the opposite end of Rouget de Lisle from the Horreum, close to the attractive tree-lined banks of the **Canal de la Robine**, is Narbonne's other principal attraction, the enormous Gothic **Cathédrale St-Just-et-St-Pasteur**. With the Palais des Archevêques and its 40m-high keep, it forms a massive pile of masonry that dominates the restored lanes of the old town. In spite of its size, this is actually only the choir of a much more ambitious church, whose construction was halted to avoid wrecking the city walls. The immensely tall interior has some beautiful fourteenth-century stained glass in the chapels on the northeast side of the apse and imposing Aubusson tapestries – one of the most valuable of these is kept in the **Salle du Trésor**, along with a small collection of ecclesiastical treasures.

## Museum of Art and Archeology Museum

Place de l'Hôtel-de-Ville · Daily: June–Sept 10am–6pm; Oct–May 10am–noon & 2–5pm · €4 · ☎ 04 68 90 31 34, ⓦ narbonne-tourisme.com

The **place de l'Hôtel-de-Ville**, next to the cathedral, is dominated by the great towers of St-Martial, the Madeleine and Bishop Aycelin's keep. From there the passage de l'Ancre leads through to the **Palais des Archevêques** (Archbishops' Palace), which houses a fairly ordinary **Museum of Art** and a good **Archeology Museum**, whose interesting Roman remains include a massive 3.5m wood and lead ship's rudder, and a huge mosaic.

## Abbaye de Fontfroide

Fontfroide, 15km southwest of Narbonne · Guided tours daily lasting 1hr 30min: April–June & Sept 11am, 2pm & 3pm; July & Aug 11am, noon, 3pm, 4pm & 5pm; Oct–March 11am & 3pm · €11.50 · ☎ 04 68 45 11 08, ⓦ fontfroide.com

A good side trip from Narbonne – just 15km southwest, but impossible without transport of your own – is the lovely **Abbaye de Fontfroide**, which enjoys a beautiful location tucked into a fold in the dry cypress-clad hillsides. The extant buildings go back to the twelfth century, with some elegant seventeenth-century additions in the entrance and courtyards, and were in use from their foundation until 1900, first by Benedictines, then Cistercians. It was one of the Cistercian monks, Pierre de Castelnau, whose murder as papal legate sparked the notorious Albigensian Crusade against the Cathars in 1208.

Visits to the restored abbey are only possible on a **guided tour**. Star features include the cloister, with its marble pillars and giant wisteria creepers, the church itself, some fine ironwork and a rose garden. The stained glass in the windows of the lay brothers' dormitory consists of fragments from churches in north and eastern France damaged in World War I.

| ARRIVAL AND INFORMATION | NARBONNE AND AROUND |
|---|---|

**By train** Narbonne is on the main train lines to Perpignan, Toulouse and Nîmes; the *gare SNCF* is at 1 bd Frédéric-Mistral on the northwest side of town.

**By bus** Buses to Gruissan (3–6 daily; 45min) and Narbonne-Plage (2–8 daily; 45min) stop at the *gare routière*, next to the train station.

**Tourist office** 31 rue Jean-Jaurès, next to the cathedral (April to mid-Sept daily 9am–7pm; mid-Sept to March Mon–Sat 10am–12.30pm & 1.30–6pm; ☎ 04 68 65 15 60, ⓦ narbonne-tourisme.fr).

## ACCOMMODATION

**Les Mimosas** Chaussée de Mandirac ☎ 04 68 49 03 72, ⓦ camping-les-mimosas.fr. The nearest campsite is 6km south of Narbonne on the Étang de Bages (there is no public transport). Open April to mid Oct. **€40**

**MJC Centre International de Séjour** Place Salengro ☎ 04 68 32 01 00, ⓦ cis-narbonne.com. The best budget accommodation in town is this modern, friendly and completely accessible youth hostel. Half board **€30.75**

★ **Villa Ambrosia** 3 allée Ambrosia ☎ 06 32 63 10 72, ⓦ villa-ambrosia.fr. Beautifully decorated *chambres d'hôtes* five minutes from the town centre. Breakfast is generous and an air of peace pervades the whole establishment. **€120**

**Will's Hotel** 23 av Pierre-Sémard ☎ 04 68 90 44 50, ⓦ willshotel-narbonne.com. A homely backpackers' favourite near the station, set in a 150-year-old house. Spacious rooms feature a/c and en-suite showers. The management is very welcoming and English is spoken. **€55**

## EATING

**L'Estagnol** 5 cours Mirabeau ☏04 68 65 09 27, ⓦlestagnol.fr. Across the canal from the old town, this local favourite attracts the crowds with its simple, good-value food. *Menus* €13–32. Mon–Sat noon–3pm & 7.30–11.30pm.

★ **La Table Saint Crescent** 68 av du Général-Leclerc ☏04 68 41 37 37. Everything at this Michelin-star-gazing restaurant is presented with exquisite precision, from roasted saddle of lamb with a fresh baby vegetable sauce and honey vinaigrette to the perfectly cooked lobster. *Menus* €35–95; reservations are recommended. Daily: noon–1.30pm & 8–9.30pm.

## Parc Naturel Régional du Haut Languedoc

Embracing Mont Caroux in the east and the Montagne Noire in the west, the **Parc Naturel Régional du Haut Languedoc** is the southernmost extension of the Massif Central. The west, above Castres and Mazamet, is Atlantic in feel and climate, with deciduous forests and lush valleys, while the east is dry, craggy and calcareous. Except in high summer you can have it almost to yourself. Buses serve the Orb valley – where you'll find the small, unremarkable town of Bédarieux – and cross the centre of the park to **La Salvetat** and **Lacâune**, but you really need transport of your own to make the most of it.

### Olargues

Near the eastern edge of the park sits the medieval village of **OLARGUES**, scrambling up the south bank of the Jaur above its thirteenth-century single-span bridge. The steep twisting streets, presumably almost unchanged since the bridge was built, lead up to a thousand-year-old belfry crowning the top of the hill. With the river and gardens below, the ancient and earth-brown farms on the infant slopes of Mont Caroux beyond, and swifts swirling round the tower in summer, you get a powerful sense of age and history.

### St-Pons-de-Thomières

**ST-PONS-DE-THOMIÈRES**, 18km west of Olargues, is on the Béziers–Castres and Béziers–La Salvetat bus routes, as well as the Bédarieux–Mazamet route. This is the "capital" of the park, with the **Maison du Parc** housed around the corner from the local **tourist office** at 1 place du Forail. Sights include the **cathedral** (July & Aug 8am–6pm; Sept–June Wed 9am–2pm, Thurs–Tues 9am–6pm) – a strange mix of Romanesque and classical – and a small and reasonably interesting **Musée de Préhistoire Régionale**, which is next to the Maison du Parc (Tues–Sun 10am–noon & 3–6pm; April–June closed Mon, Tues & Wed; €3.50; ☏04 67 97 39 34).

### The park's uplands

The uplands of the park are wild and little travelled, dominated by the towering peak of **Mont Caroux** and stretching west along the ridge of the **Monts de l'Espinouse**. This is prime hiking territory, where thick forest of stunted oak alternates with broad mountain meadows, opening up on impressive vistas. Civilization appears again to the west in the upper Agout valley, where **Fraïsse-sur-Agout** and **La Salvetat** have become thriving bases for outdoor recreation, and to the north, at the medieval spa town of **Lacaune**. There's no transport crossing the uplands, but the D180 takes you from Le Poujol-sur-Orb, 2km west of Lamalou-les-Bains, to Mont Caroux and L'Espinouse.

#### Into the Agout valley

The D180 is the most spectacular way to climb into the park. Soon after leaving the main highway, you'll pass the **Forêt des Écrivains-Combattants**, named after the French writers who died in World War I. Just above the hamlet of Rosis, the road levels out in a small mountain valley, whose slopes are brilliant yellow with broom in June. Continuing north, the D180 climbs another 12km above deep ravines, offering spectacular views to the summit of **L'Espinouse**. The Col de l'Ourtigas is a good place to stretch your legs and take in the grandeur. Here the landscape changes from Mediterranean cragginess to marshy moor-like meadow and big conifer plantations, and the road begins to descend west into the valley of the River Agout. It runs through tiny Salvergues, with its plain workers' cottages and a striking fortress-church; Cambon, where the natural woods begin; and postcard-pretty **Fraïsse-sur-Agout**.

### La Salvetat-sur-Agout

**LA SALVETAT-SUR-AGOUT** is an attractive mountain town 10km west of Fraïsse between the artificial lakes of La Raviège and Laouzas. Built on a hill above the river, with car-wide streets and houses clad in huge slate tiles, it's usually half asleep except at holiday time, when it becomes a busy outdoor activities centre.

### Lacaune and around

**LACAUNE** makes a pleasant stop if you're crossing the park. Set 45km east of Castres, surrounded by rounded wooded heights, it's very much a mountain town. It was one of the centres of Protestant Camisard resistance at the end of the seventeenth century, when its inaccessibility was ideal for clandestine worship. The air is fresh, and the town, though somewhat grey in appearance because of the slates and drab stucco common throughout the region, is cheerful enough.

From Lacaune to Castres the most agreeable route is along the wooded **Gijou valley**, following the now defunct train track, past minuscule Gijounet and **Lacaze**, where a nearly derelict **château** strikes a picturesque pose in a bend of the river.

**12**

## ARRIVAL AND INFORMATION PARC NATUREL RÉGIONAL DU HAUT LANGUEDOC

### BÉDARIEUX
**By train and bus** The *gare SNCF*, in place Pierre-Seymard on the southwest edge of the old town, meets trains from Béziers (every hour & a half daily; 35–45min), and buses from Béziers (Mon–Sat 3 daily; 1hr 30min), Montpellier (1–4 daily; 1hr 25min) and St-Pons via Olargues (1–4 daily; 40min–1hr 10min).
**Tourist office** 1 rue de la République (Mon–Fri 9am–noon & 2–6pm, Sat 9am–noon; ☎ 04 67 95 08 79, ⓦ bedarieux.fr).

### OLARGUES
**Tourist office** Av de la Gare (Mon–Sat 10am–1pm & 3–7pm, Sun 10am–1pm; ☎ 04 67 23 02 21 ⓦ olargues.org).

### ST-PONS-DE-THOMIÈRES
**By bus** There are buses to St-Pons from Castres (Mon–Sat 1–4 daily; 1hr–1hr 30min) and La Salvetat (Mon–Sat 2 daily; 40min).

**Tourist office** Place du Foirail (April–June & Sept Tues–Sat 9.30am–12.30pm & 2–6pm; July & Aug daily 10am–1pm & 3–7pm; Oct–March Fri–Sun 9.30am–12.30pm ☎ 04 67 97 06 65, ⓦ minervoix-caroux.com).

### LA SALVETAT-SUR-AGOUT
**Tourist office** Place des Archers (July & Aug Mon–Fri 9am–12.30pm & 2–7pm, Sat 10am–12.30pm & 3–7pm, Sun 10am–12.30pm; ☎ 04 11 95 08 07, ⓦ salvetat-tourisme.fr).

### LACAUNE
**By bus** Buses from Castres stop at Lacaune (Mon–Sat 1–4 daily; 50min).
**Tourist office** Place du Général-de-Gaulle (July & Aug Mon–Fri 9.30am–12.30pm & 2–7pm, Sat & Sun 10am–12.30, Sat 3–7pm; Sept to Easter Tues–Sat 10am–noon & 2–5pm; Easter to June Mon–Sat 10am–noon & 2–6pm; ☎ 05 32 11 09 45, ⓦ lacaune.com). You can rent bikes here.

## ACCOMMODATION AND EATING

### BÉDARIEUX
**La Forge** 22 av de l'Abbé-Tarroux ☎ 04 67 95 13 13. An excellent restaurant with a cosy, vaulted dining room, delightful outdoor seating and *menus* ranging from €17 to €37. Tues & Thurs–Sat noon–2pm & 7–9.30pm, Mon

7–9.30pm, Wed & Sun noon–2pm. Closed part Nov & part Jan.
**De l'Orb** Parc Phoros, Rte de Saint-Pons ☎ 04 67 23 35 90, ⓦ hotel-orb.com. This is the town's only hotel: a decent, if basic, place. Located on the south end of town

along av Jean-Jaurès, about 500m south of the Pont Vieux. All rooms are en suite. **€51**

## OLARGUES

**Camping Orlargues** North of Olargues ☎04 67 97 71 50, ⓦcampingolargues.wix.com/lebaous. This beautiful, riverside campsite is just a 5min walk north of town. Closed Sept–April. **€18.50**

★ **Les Quatr' Farceurs** Rue de la Comporte ☎04 67 97 81 33, ⓦolargues.co.uk. This friendly, English-owned B&B is widely recognized as one of the area's best accommodation options. The rooms are comfortable, if basic, and the abundant home-cooked meals (€25) are accompanied by free-flowing wine. **€65**

## ST-PONS-DE-THOMIÈRES

★ **Les Cerisiers du Jaur** Rte de Bédarieux ☎04 67 95 30 33, ⓦcerisierdujaur.com. The well-equipped campsite is on the main road east to Bédarieux. **€19**

## LA SALVETAT-SUR-AGOUT

**La Plage** Lac de la Raviège ☎04 67 97 69 87, ⓦhotel-la-salvetat-sur-agout.fr. Inexpensive rooms and generous portions of home-cooked local food (menus from €14) are on offer at this small lakeside hotel 1km from the town centre. **€62**

## LACAUNE

**Calas** 4 place de la Vierge ☎05 63 37 03 28, ⓦpageloisirs.com/calas. This small hotel's main draw is not the pool or the comfortable and well-equipped rooms, but its highly praised, fourth-generation bistro, where house specialities include pigeon and pigs' feet with truffles. *Menus* €16–38. Restaurant Easter–Oct daily noon–1.30pm & 7.30–9pm; Oct–Easter Sun–Thurs noon–1.30pm & 7.30–9pm, Fri & Sat noon–1.30pm. **€40**

**Domaine Le Clot** Les Vidals ☎05 63 37 03 59, ⓦdomaineleclot.com. This small but beautifully sited campsite on the Murat road also boasts a restaurant. Closed Nov–March. **€15.70**

# Carcassonne

**12**

Right on the main Toulouse–Montpellier train link, **CARCASSONNE** couldn't be easier to reach. For anyone travelling through this region it is a must – one of the most dramatic, if also most-visited, towns in the whole of Languedoc. Carcassonne owes its division into two separate "towns" to the wars against the Cathars. Following Simon de Montfort's capture of the town in 1209, its people tried in 1240 to restore their traditional ruling family, the Trencavels. In reprisal, King Louis IX expelled them from the **Cité**, only permitting their return on the condition that they built on the low ground by the River Aude – what would become the **ville basse**.

A major summertime event worth catching is the **Festival de Carcassonne** from late June to mid-August, featuring world-class dance, theatre and music. The high point is the mammoth fireworks display on Bastille Day (July 14).

## Cité

To reach the Cité from the *ville basse*, take bus #2 from outside the station, or a *navette* from Square Gambetta. Alternatively, walk it in less than 30min, crossing the Pont-Vieux and climbing rue Barbacane, past the church of St-Gimer to the sturdy bastion of the Porte d'Aude (this is effectively the back entrance – the main gate is Porte Narbonnaise, on the east side)

The attractions of the well-preserved and lively *ville basse* notwithstanding, everybody comes to Carcassonne to see the **Cité**, the double-walled and turreted fortress that crowns the hill above the River Aude. From a distance it's the epitome of the fairy-tale medieval town. Viollet-le-Duc rescued it from ruin in 1844, and his "too-perfect" restoration has been furiously debated ever since. It is, as you would expect, a real tourist trap. Yet, in spite of the chintzy cafés, craft shops and the crowds, you'd have to be a very stiff-necked purist not to be moved at all.

### Château Comtal

1 rue Viollet-le-Duc • Daily: April–Sept 10am–6.30pm; Oct–March 9.30am–5pm; guided tours only, several in English • €9• ☎04 68 11 70 70, ⓦcarcassonne.monuments-nationaux.fr

There is no charge for admission to the streets or the grassy *lices* – "lists" – between the walls, though cars are banned from 10am to 6pm. However, to see the inner fortress of the **Château Comtal** and walk the walls, you'll have to join a **guided tour**. These assume some knowledge of French history, and point out the various phases in the construction of the fortifications, from Roman and Visigothic to Romanesque and the post-Cathar adaptations of the French kings.

### St-Nazaire

Place St-Nazaire • Mon–Fri 8.45am–12.45pm & 1.45–5/6pm, Sat & Sun 8.45–10.30am & 2–5/6pm • Free • ☎ 04 68 10 24 30 • ⓦ carcassonne.org

Don't miss the beautiful **church of St-Nazaire**, towards the southern corner of the Cité at the end of rue St-Louis. It's a serene combination of nave with carved capitals in the Romanesque style and a Gothic choir and transepts, along with some of the loveliest stained glass in Languedoc. In the south transept is a tombstone believed to belong to Simon de Montfort. You can also climb the **tower** for spectacular views over the Cité.

## ARRIVAL AND DEPARTURE
## CARCASSONNE

**By plane** Carcassonne airport lies just west of the city (☎ 04 68 71 96 46, ⓦ aeroport-carcassonne.com). A *navette* (€6; departs 45 mins before each departing flight; 15min) leaves from outside the terminal and stops at the *gare SNCF*, square Gambetta and the Cité; a taxi to the centre will cost €10–17.

**By train** The *gare SNCF* is in the *ville basse* on the north bank of the Canal du Midi at the northern limits of the old town.

Destinations Arles (4–8 daily; 2hr 40min–3hr 30min);

Béziers (22 daily; 45min–1hr 45min); Bordeaux (18–22 daily; 3hr 20min–4hr 30min); Limoux (16 daily; 25min); Marseille (12–18 daily; 3hr 20min–5hr 30min); Montpellier (18 daily; 1hr 30min–4hr); Narbonne (22 daily; 35min); Nîmes (26 daily; 2hr 5min–3hr 10min); Quillan (6 daily; 1hr 15min); Toulouse (22 daily; 45min–1hr).

**By bus** The *gare routière* (ⓦ carcassonne-agglo.fr) is a series of bus stops, with no actual building, located on bd de Varsovie on the northwest side of town, south of the canal.

12

CARCASSONNE: VILLE BASSE

Gare SNCF
PROMENADE DU CANAL
Canal du Midi
Jardin Chénier
BOULEVARD OMER SARRAUT
Toulouse
AV. DU PRES ROOSEVELT
AVENUE PIERRE SEMARD
BOULEVARD DE VARSOVIE
Regional Bus Stops
PONT MARENGO
R. PROSPER MONTAGNE
ROUTE MINERVOISE
RUE FOURTEL
RUE HUGUES BERNARD
RUE MAURICE SARRAUT
RUE L. ROLLIN
RUE ANTOINE MARTY
N
RUE DE LA LIBERTÉ
RUE JEAN BRINGER
RUE GEORGES CLEMENCEAU
RUE D'ALSACE
RUE DU PALAIS
RUE D'ALSACE
RUE DU 4 SEPTEMBRE
RUE ARMAGNAC
RUE DU 4 SEPTEMBRE
BOULEVARD JEAN-JAURÈS
RUE DE STRASBOURG
RUE DE LORRAINE

● EATING
L'Écurie 2
Robert Rodriguez 1

RUE JULES SAUZEDE
RUE DU DOCTEUR ALBERT TOMEY
RUE DE LA RÉPUBLIQUE
RUE MAZAGRAN
RUE VICTOR HUGO
RUE DE L'AIGLE D'OR
RUE BARBÈS
RUE FÉDOU
RUE COSTE REBOULH
RUE PIERRE GERMAIN
PLACE CARNOT
PL DE L DE TASSIGNY
RUE DE VERDUN
RUE JEAN BRINGER
RUE DE VERDUN
RUE DES ÉTUDES
RUE LITTRÉ
Maison des Mémoires
PLACE EGGENFELDEN
Centre National d'Études Cathares
ⓘ
Musée des Beaux-Arts
SQUARE GAMBETTA
SQUARE GAMBETTA
BOULEVARD CAMILLE PELLETAN
BOULEVARD PAUL SABATIER
RUE AIMÉ RAMOND
RUE JULES SAUZEDE
RUE CHARTRAN
RUE COURTEILHAC
RUE AIMÉ RAMOND
AVENUE MULLOT-PONT NEUF
RUE VOLTAIRE
Cathédrale
RUE VOLTAIRE
RUE DU PONT VIEUX
River
BOULEVARD BARBÈS
Porte des Jacobins
BOULEVARD CDT ROUMENS
RUE DES TROIS COURONNES
Chapel
RUE PONT VIEUX
RUE DE LA DIGUE
QUAI BELLEVUE
Aude
0 200 metres
R. CAPELET
PLACE DU GL DE GAULLE
RUE MARCEAU
RUE DE LA CRECHE BLEUE
RUE BASSE
RUE LARAIGNON
Limoux
La Cité

**12**

## THE CANAL DU MIDI

The **Canal du Midi** runs for 240km from the River Garonne at Toulouse via Carcassonne to the Mediterranean at Agde. It was the brainchild of **Pierre-Paul Riquet**, a minor noble and tax collector, who succeeded in convincing Louis XIV (and more importantly, his first minister, Colbert) of the merits of linking the Atlantic and the Mediterranean via the Garonne.

The work, begun in 1667, took fourteen years to complete, using tens of thousands of workers. The crux of the problem from the engineering point of view was how to feed the canal with water when its high point at Naurouze, west of Carcassonne, was 190m above sea level and 58m above the Garonne at Toulouse. Riquet responded by building a system of reservoirs in the Montagne Noire, channelling run-off from the heights down to Naurouze. He spent the whole of his fortune on the canal and, sadly, died just six months before its inauguration in 1681.

The canal was a success and sparked a wave of prosperity along its course, with traffic increasing steadily until 1857, when the Sète–Bordeaux railway was opened, reducing trade on the canal to all but nothing. Today, the canal remains a marvel of engineering and beauty, incorporating no fewer than 99 locks (*écluses*) and 130 bridges, almost all of which date back to the first era of construction. The canal has, since its construction, been known for the lovely plane trees that line riverbank. Sadly, a wilt infection was discovered in 2006 and since then the trees have been systematically cut down. They will be replaced, however the view will not be the same for many years to come. You can follow the canal by road, and many sections have foot or bicycle paths, but the best way to see it is, of course, by boat. Outfits in all the major ports rent houseboats and barges, and there are many cruise options to choose from as well. Other sources of information include ⓦcanalmidi.com and ⓦfrench-waterways.com, plus the tourist offices in Carcassonne and Toulouse.

**Boat rental and cruises** Le Boat (☏1 800 734 5491, ⓦleboat.com or Locaboat (☏03 86 91 72 72, ⓦlocaboat.com), both have a number of branches in Languedoc and the Midi.

**Information** Voies Navigables de France, 2 Port St-Étienne in Toulouse (☏05 61 36 24 24, ⓦsudouest.vnf. fr); they also have English-speaking offices at the major canal ports.

## INFORMATION

**Tourist office** 28 rue de Verdun (April–June, Sept Mon–Sat 9am–6pm, Sun 10am–1pm; July & Aug 9am–7pm; Oct Mon–Sat 9am–6pm; Nov–March Mon–Sat 9.30am–12.30pm & 1.30–5.30pm; ☏04 68 10 24 30, ⓦtourisme-carcassonne.fr). There's also an annexe (April–June & Sept daily 9am–6pm; Oct daily 9.30am–5.30pm; Nov–March Tues–Sun 9.30am–1pm & 1.30–5.30pm) just inside Porte Narbonnaise, the main gate to the Cité.

**Discount pass** If you are planning on visiting other medieval sites near Carcassonne (including the Cathar castles), you could buy the Passeport aux Sites du Pays Cathare (€4), which gives you a discounted admission price to many castles and monuments.

## ACCOMMODATION

**Auberge de Jeunesse** Rue Trencavel ☏04 68 25 23 16, ⓦfuaj.org; map p.667. This modern, clean hostel, in the heart of the Cité, offers the cheapest accommodation in town and tends to get booked up well in advance. **€23.50**

**Campsite la Cité** Rte St-Hilaire ☏04 68 10 01 00, ⓦcampingcitecarcassonne.com; map p.667. Tucked away amid parkland to the south of town, the local campsite can be reached by local bus (line #8) or on foot (about 20min) from the Cité. Closed mid-Oct to March. Minimum stay of one week in July & Aug. **€33**

★ **De la Cité** Place Auguste-Pierre-Pont ☏04 68 71 98 71, ⓦhoteldelacite.com; map p.667. Carcassonne's luxury option, with prices to match, with rooms and suites in an opulent medieval manor house, a heated swimming pool and stunning views from the battlemented walls. **€375**

**Le Donjon** 2 rue du Comte-Roger ☏04 68 11 23 00, ⓦhotel-donjon.fr; map p.667. A shade less luxurious than the Cité and a good deal less expensive, this hotel offers four-star amenities in a medieval building near the castle. The rooms are spacious and airy. **€119**

**Espace Cité** 132 rue Trivalle ☏04 68 25 24 24, ⓦhotel espacecite.fr; map p.667. Just outside the main gate of the Cité, and offering Carcassonne's best value for money – excellent location, en-suite rooms, mod cons and efficient service at reasonable prices. All-you-can-eat breakfast buffet is €9. **€82**

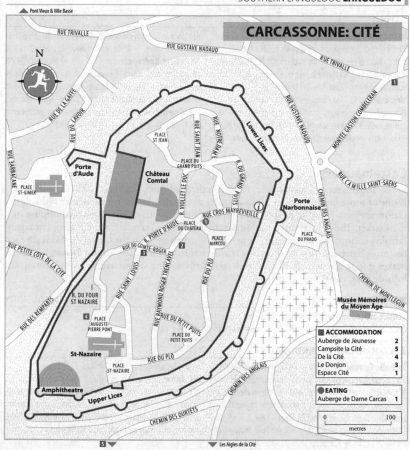

CARCASSONNE: CITÉ

**ACCOMMODATION**

| | |
|---|---|
| Auberge de Jeunesse | 2 |
| Campsite la Cité | 5 |
| De la Cité | 4 |
| Le Donjon | 3 |
| Espace Cité | 1 |

**EATING**

| | |
|---|---|
| Auberge de Dame Carcas | 1 |

## CASSOULET

The magnificent **cassoulet** is a dish with age-old origins. It was apparently first concocted when the town was besieged by Edward, the Black Prince, during the Hundred Years war and was deemed so sustaining that the townspeople not only survived, but put the English to rout. According to tradition it would be assembled in a deep earthenware bowl, the **cassole**, from which the dish takes its name, and taken to the village bread oven, where it would slowly transform to an unctuous, aromatic masterpiece. Little has changed through the ensuing centuries: the bread ovens have gone, and a few cosmopolitan ingredients have found their way into the mix, but essentially the dish is the same, and so is the method. Although Castelnaudry is universally accepted as the home of the original recipe, both Toulouse and Carcassonne have their own varieties. It's essentially just a form of the beans and bones stew that's found all over southern Europe; in this case the beans should be the local Tarbais, grown around Pamiers, Pau and Tarbes. Castelnaudry purists insist on duck or goose confit, Toulouse sausage and a little pork. In Toulouse they include mutton, and, crucially, a breadcrumb crust. Carcassonne eschews the confit and frequently adds a partridge or similar game bird. The locals have long been arguing over their various interpretations, but the salient fact remains, this is one of the great peasant dishes of France.

## EATING

**Auberge de Dame Carcas** 3 place du Château ☎ 04 68 71 23 23, ⓦdamecarcas.com; map p.667. A traditional bistro offering cassoulet with duck confit (€18) and other regional dishes. Daily: July & Aug noon–2pm & 7–10pm; Sept–June noon–2pm & 7–9.30pm.

★ **L'Écurie** 43 bd Barbès ☎ 04 68 72 04 04, ⓦrestaurant-lecurie.fr; map p.665. Sophisticated local cuisine including some splendid fish dishes; try the Nordic salad with smoked salmon and marinated tuna. They also do a very good casssoulet. *Menus* €16–30. Mon–Sat noon–1.30pm & 7–9.30pm, Sun noon–1.30pm.

★ **Robert Rodriguez** 39 rue Coste-Reboulh ☎ 04 68 47 37 80; map p.665. Carcassonne's most flamboyantly experimental restaurant combines local, fresh ingredients in inventive permutations. What's on offer changes according to season and the chef's inclinations, with *menus* at €45–80. Tues–Sat noon–1.30pm & 8–9.30pm.

# Castelnaudary

Some 36km west of Carcassonne, on the main road from Toulouse, **CASTELNAUDARY** is one of those innumerable French country towns that boasts no particular sights but is nonetheless a pleasure to spend a couple of hours in, having a coffee or shopping in the market. Today it serves as an important commercial centre for the rolling Lauragais farming country hereabouts, as it once was for the traffic on the Canal du Midi. In fact, the most flattering view of the town is still that from the canal's **Grand Bassin**, which makes it look remarkably like a Greek island town, with its ancient houses climbing the hillside from the water's edge.

## INFORMATION                                                          CASTELNAUDARY

**12**

**Tourist office** Place de la République (Mon–Sat 9.30am– noon & 2–6pm; ☎ 04 68 23 05 73, ⓦcastelnaudary- tourisme.com).

## ACCOMMODATION AND EATING

**La Belle Époque** 55 rue du Général-Dejean ☎ 04 68 23 39 72, ⓦlabelle-epoque-castelnaudary.com. This is one of the best places to try Castelnaudary's signature dish, the cassoulet. Otherwise there is a selection of regional meat and fish options. *Menus* from €23. April–June & Sept–Nov Thurs–Mon noon–2pm & 7–9.30pm; July & Aug daily noon–2pm & 7–9.30pm; Nov–March Mon & Thurs noon–2pm, Fri–Sun noon–2pm & 7–9.30pm.

**Du Canal** 88 av Arnaut-Vidal ☎ 04 68 94 05 05, ⓦhotelducanal.com. A comfortable and beautifully located canalside hotel with large rooms. There is secure parking, a splendid terrace, and guests have use of a fridge and freezer. Family rooms are also available. **€75**

# The Montagne Noire

There are two good routes from Carcassonne north into the **Montagne Noire**, which forms the western extremity of the Parc Naturel Régional du Haut Languedoc: Carcassonne–Revel and Carcassonne–Mazamet by the valley of the Orbiel. Neither is served by public transport, but both offer superlative scenery.

## Montolieu

**MONTOLIEU**, semi-fortified and built on the edge of a ravine, has set itself the target of becoming France's **secondhand book capital**, with its shops overflowing with dog-eared and antiquarian tomes. Drop in to the Librairie Booth, by the bridge over the ravine, for English-language titles.

## Saissac

**SAISSAC**, 8km beyond Montolieu, is an upland village surrounded by conifers and beechwood, interspersed with patches of rough pasture, with gardens terraced down its steep slopes. Remains of towers and fortifications poke out among the ancient houses, and on a spur below the village stand the romantic ruins of its castle and the church of St-Michel.

## St-Papoul Abbey

5 place Monseigneur-de-Langle April–June, Sept & Oct daily 10am–noon & 2–6pm; July & Aug daily 10am–7pm; Nov, Dec & Feb & March Sat & hols 10am–noon & 2–5pm, Sun 2–5pm • €5 • ☎ 04 68 94 97 75, ⊕ abbaye-saint-papoul.fr

Some 14km west of Saissac on the D103 (or just a few kilometres southwest of the *Bout du Monde* campsite), the ancient village of **ST-PAPOUL**, with its walls and Benedictine **abbey**, makes for a gentle side trip. The abbey is best known for the sculpted corbels on the exterior of the nave, executed by the "Master of Cabestany". These can be viewed free at any time, although the interior of the church and its pretty fourteenth-century cloister are also worth a peek.

## Revel

The "main" D629 road winds down through the forest past the Bassin de St-Férréol, which was constructed by Riquet to supply water to the Canal du Midi, and on to **REVEL**. Revel is a *bastide* dating from 1342, featuring an attractive arcaded central square with a superb wooden-pillared medieval *halle* in the middle. Now a prosperous market town (Saturday is market day), it makes an agreeably provincial stopover.

## Châteaux de Lastours

16km north of Carcassonne • Nov–March occasional openings: check website; April–June & Sept daily 10am–6pm; July & Aug daily 9am–8pm; Oct daily 10am–5pm • €7 • ☎ 04 68 77 56 02, ⊕ chateauxdelastours.fr

The most memorable site in the **Montagne Noire** is the **Châteaux de Lastours**, the most northerly of the Cathar castles. There are, in fact, four castles here – their ruined keeps jutting superbly from a sharp ridge of scrub and cypress that plunges to rivers on both sides. The two oldest, Cabaret (mid-eleventh century) and Surdespine (1153), fell into de Montfort's hands in 1211, after their lords had given shelter to the Cathars. The other two, Tour Régine and Quertinheux, were added after 1240, when the site became royal property, and a garrison was maintained here as late as the Revolution. A path winds up from the roadside, bright in early summer with iris, cistus, broom and numerous other plants.

**12**

### ACCOMMODATION AND EATING

### THE MONTAGNE NOIRE

**Auberge du Midi** 34 bd Gambetta, Revel ☎ 05 61 83 50 50, ⊕ hotelrestaurantdumidi.com. A hotel and restaurant in a refined old nineteenth-century mansion, with basic amenities but very friendly and welcoming owners. It also has the town's best restaurant, where you can dine on *terroir* cuisine inside or on a shaded terrace. *Menus* €22–48. Restaurant daily noon–2pm & 7–10pm. **€65**

**Domaine du Lampy-Neuf** 4km north of Saissac on the D4 ☎ 04 68 24 46 07, ⊕ domainelampy-neuf.com. This lakeside estate, set among the rich woods of the Montagne Noire, features its own arboretum. It offers beautiful, comfortable rooms, as well as excellent regional meals (€25) for guests. An ideal base for exploring the region. **€70**

# Western Languedoc

**Toulouse**, with its sunny, cosmopolitan charms, is not only the main town in **Western Languedoc** but also a very accessible kick-off point for anywhere in the southwest of France. Of the places nearby, **Albi**, with its highly original cathedral and comprehensive collection of Toulouse-Lautrec paintings, is the number-one priority. West of Toulouse the land opens up into the broad plains of the **Gers**, a sleepy and rather dull expanse of wheat fields and rolling hills. Those in search of a solitary, little-visited France will enjoy its uncrowded monuments, especially any lover of rich terrines and a mellow, warming Armagnac.

## Toulouse

**TOULOUSE** is one of the most vibrant provincial cities in France. Long an **aviation** centre – St-Exupéry and Mermoz flew out from here on their pioneering airmail flights over Africa and the Atlantic in the 1920s – Toulouse is now home to Aérospatiale, the driving force behind Concorde, Airbus and the Ariane space rocket. Moreover, the city's 120,000 students make it third only to Paris and Lyon as a **university** centre.

This is not the first flush of pre-eminence for Toulouse. From the tenth to the thirteenth centuries the counts of Toulouse controlled much of southern France. They maintained a resplendent court, renowned especially for its troubadours, the poets of courtly love whose work influenced Petrarch, Dante and Chaucer and thus the whole course of European poetry. The arrival of the hungry northern French nobles of the Albigensian Crusade put an end to that; in 1271 Toulouse became crown property.

The beautiful old city – **La Ville Rose** – lies within a rough hexagon clamped round a bend in the wide, brown River Garonne and contained within a ring of nineteenth-century boulevards, including Strasbourg, Carnot and Jules-Guesde. The Canal du Midi, which here joins the Garonne on its way from the Mediterranean to the Atlantic, forms a further ring around this core. There are three very good museums and some real architectural treasures in the churches of **St-Sernin** and **Les Jacobins** and in the magnificent Renaissance townhouses – *hôtels particuliers* – of the merchants who grew rich on the woad-dye trade. It's all very compact and easily walkable.

On Sunday mornings the whole of place St-Sernin turns into a marvellous, teeming **flea market**, and there are **book markets** on Thursday mornings in place Arnaud-Bernard, and all day Saturday in place St-Étienne.

## Place du Capitole

**Place du Capitole** is the centre of the city's social life. Its smart cafés throng with people at lunchtime and in the early evening, when the dying sun flushes the pink facade of the big town hall opposite. This is the scene of a mammoth Wednesday **market** for food, clothes and junk, and a smaller organic food market on Tuesday and Saturday mornings. From place du Capitole, a labyrinth of narrow medieval streets radiates out to the town's other squares, such as place Wilson, the more intimate place St-Georges, the delightful triangular place de la Trinité and place St-Étienne, in front of the cathedral.

## The Capitole

Place du Capitole • Mon–Fri 8.30am–7pm, Sun 10am–7pm • Free • ☏ 05 61 22 34 12, ⊛ toulouse-tourisme.com

Occupying the whole of the eastern side of the eponymous square, the **Capitole** has been the seat of Toulouse's city government since the twelfth century. In medieval times it housed the *capitouls*, who made up the oligarchic and independent city council from which its name derives. Today, these medieval origins are disguised by an elaborate pink-and-white classical facade (1750) of columns and pilasters, from which the flags of Languedoc, the Republic and the European Union are proudly flown. If there are no official functions taking place, you can peek inside the Salle des Illustres and a couple of other rooms covered in flowery, late nineteenth-century murals and some more subdued Impressionist works by Henri Martin.

## The hôtels particuliers

Many of the old *capitouls* built their **hôtels** in the dense web of now mainly pedestrianized streets around the Capitole. The material they used was almost exclusively the flat Toulousain brick, whose rosy colour gives the city its "Ville Rose" nickname. It is an attractive material, lending a small-scale, detailed finish to otherwise plain facades, and setting off admirably any wood- or stonework. Although many of the *hôtels* survive, they are rarely open to the public, so you have to do a lot of nonchalant sauntering into courtyards to get a look at them. The best known, open to visitors thanks to its very handsome Bemberg collection of paintings, is the **Hôtel d'Assézat**, at the river end of rue de Metz. Other fine houses exist just to the south: on rue Pharaon, in place des Carmes, on rue du Languedoc and on rue Dalbade, where the Hôtel Clary (also known as de Pierre) at no. 25 is unusual for being built of stone.

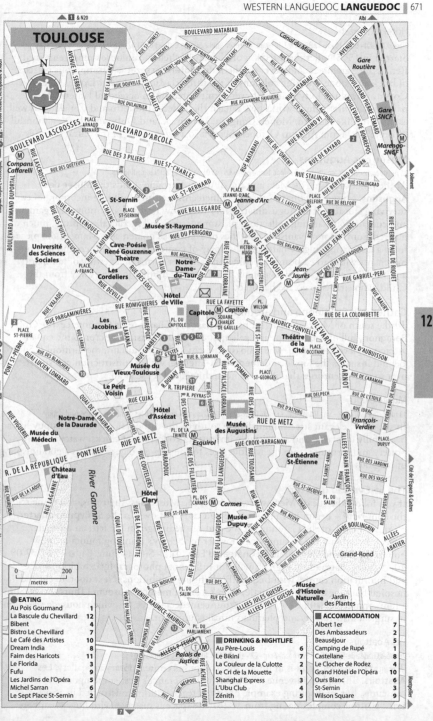

**TOULOUSE**

12

1 & N20

**EATING**

| | |
|---|---|
| Au Pois Gourmand | 1 |
| La Bascule du Chevillard | 12 |
| Bibent | 4 |
| Bistro Le Chevillard | 7 |
| Le Café des Artistes | 10 |
| Dream India | 8 |
| Faim des Haricots | 11 |
| Le Florida | 3 |
| Fufu | 9 |
| Les Jardins de l'Opéra | 5 |
| Michel Sarran | 6 |
| Le Sept Place St-Sernin | 2 |

**DRINKING & NIGHTLIFE**

| | |
|---|---|
| Au Père-Louis | 6 |
| Le Bikini | 7 |
| La Couleur de la Culotte | 2 |
| Le Cri de la Mouette | 1 |
| Shanghaï Express | 3 |
| L'Ubu Club | 4 |
| Zénith | 5 |

**ACCOMMODATION**

| | |
|---|---|
| Albert 1er | 7 |
| Des Ambassadeurs | 2 |
| Beauséjour | 5 |
| Camping de Rupé | 1 |
| Castellane | 8 |
| Le Clocher de Rodez | 4 |
| Grand Hôtel de l'Opéra | 10 |
| Ours Blanc | 6 |
| St-Sernin | 3 |
| Wilson Square | 9 |

## Hôtel d'Assézat

Place d'Assézat • Daily 10am–12.30pm & 1.30–6pm, Wed open until 8.30pm • €10 • ☎ 05 61 12 06 89, ⓦ fondation-bemberg.fr

Started in 1555 under the direction of Nicolas Bachelier, Toulouse's most renowned Renaissance architect, and never finished, the **Hôtel d'Assézat** is a sumptuous palace of brick and stone, sporting columns of the three classical orders of Doric, Ionic and Corinthian, plus a lofty staircase tower surmounted by an octagonal lantern. The paintings within include works by Cranach the Elder, Tintoretto and Canaletto as well as moderns like Pissarro, Monet, Gauguin, Vlaminck, and Dufy, and there's a roomful of Bonnards. From April to October there's also a *salon de thé* in the entrance gallery.

## Musée des Augustins

21 rue de Metz • Wed 10am–9pm, Thurs–Mon 10am–6pm • €6 • ☎ 05 61 22 21 82, ⓦ augustins.org

At the junction of rue de Metz and rue d'Alsace-Lorraine stands the **Musée des Augustins**. Outwardly unattractive, the nineteenth-century building incorporates two surviving cloisters of an Augustinian priory (one now restored as a monastery garden) and contains outstanding collections of Romanesque and medieval sculpture, much of it saved from the now-vanished churches of Toulouse's golden age. Many of the pieces form a fascinating, highly naturalistic display of contemporary manners and fashions: merchants with forked beards touching one another's arms in a gesture of familiarity, and the Virgin represented as a pretty, bored young mother looking away from the Child, who strains to escape her hold.

## Cathédrale St-Étienne and around

**12**

To the south of Musée des Augustins, just past the Chambre de Commerce, **rue Croix-Baragnon**, full of smart shops and galleries, opens at its eastern end onto the equally attractive **place St-Étienne**, which boasts the city's oldest fountain, the Griffoul (1546). Behind it stands the lopsided **Cathédrale St-Étienne**, whose construction was spread over so many centuries that it makes no architectural sense at all.

## Musée Dupuy

13 rue de la Pléau • Tues–Sun 10am–6pm • €5 • ☎ 05 61 22 95 40, ⓦ musees-midi-pyrenees.fr/musees/musee-paul-dupuy

In the quiet, elegant streets immediately south of the cathedral, the **Musée Dupuy** has a beautifully displayed and surprisingly interesting collection of clocks, watches, clothes, pottery and furniture from the Middle Ages to the present day, as well as a good display of religious art.

## The St-Cyprien quarter

If you follow the rue de Metz westward from the Musée des Augustins, you come to the **Pont-Neuf** – begun in 1544 – where you can cross over to the **St-Cyprien quarter** on the left bank of the Garonne. At the end of the bridge on the left, an old water tower, erected in 1822 to supply clean water to the city's drinking fountains, now houses the **Galerie Municipale du Château d'Eau** (Tues–Sun 1–7pm; €4; ☎ 05 61 77 09 40, ⓦ galeriechateaudeau.org), a small but influential photography exhibition space and information centre, with frequently changing exhibitions. Next door, in the old hospital buildings at 2 rue Viguerie, there's a small **medical museum** (Thurs, Fri & Sun 11am–5pm; free; ☎ 05 61 77 84 25, ⓦ museemedecine.free.fr), which houses a selection of surgical instruments and pharmaceutical equipment.

## Les Abattoirs

76 allées Charles-de-Fitte • Wed–Sun noon–6pm • €7 • ☎ 05 34 51 10 60, ⓦ lesabattoirs.org

The star of the left bank is undoubtedly Toulouse's contemporary art gallery, **Les Abattoirs**. This splendid venue is not only one of France's best contemporary art museums, but an inspiring example of urban regeneration, constructed in a vast brick abattoir complex dating from 1828. The space is massive, with huge chambers perfectly suited to displaying even the largest canvases. The collection comprises over two thousand works (painting, sculpture, mixed- and multimedia) by artists from 44 countries; the most striking piece is undoubtedly Picasso's massive 14m by 20m theatre backdrop, *La dépouille du Minotaure en costume d'Arlequin*, painted in 1936 for Romain Rolland's *Le 14 juillet*, and which towers over the lower gallery.

## Church of Les Jacobins

69 rue Pargaminières • Tues–Sun 9am–7pm • Free, cloisters €5 • ☎ 05 61 22 23 82, ⊕ jacobins.toulouse.fr

A short distance west of place du Capitole, on rue Lakanal, is the church of **Les Jacobins**. Constructed in 1230 by the Order of Preachers (Dominicans), which St Dominic had founded here in 1216 to preach against Cathar heretics, the church is a huge fortress-like rectangle of unadorned brick, buttressed – like Albi cathedral – by plain brick piles, quite unlike what you'd normally associate with Gothic architecture. The interior is a single space divided by a central row of ultra-slim pillars from whose minimal capitals spring an elegant splay of vaulting ribs – 22 from the last in line – like palm fronds. Beneath the altar lie the bones of the philosopher St Thomas Aquinas. On the north side, you step out into the calming hush of a **cloister** with a formal array of box trees and cypress in the middle, and its adjacent art **exhibition hall**.

## St-Sernin

Place St-Sernin • **Basilique** Oct–May Mon–Sat 8.30am–6pm, Sun 8.30am–7.30pm; June–Sept Mon–Sat 8.30am–7pm, Sun 8.30am–7.30pm • Free • **Ambulatory & crypt** June–Sept Mon–Sat 10am–6pm, Sun 11.30–6pm; Oct–May Mon–Sat 10am–noon & 2–5.50pm, Sun 2–5.30pm; €2.50 • ☎ 05 61 11 02 22, ⊕ basilique-saint-sernin.fr

From the north side of place du Capitole, **rue du Taur** leads past the belfry wall of **Notre-Dame-du-Taur**, whose diamond-pointed arches and decorative motifs are the acme of Toulousain bricklaying skills, to place St-Sernin. Here you're confronted with the largest Romanesque church in France, the UNESCO-listed **basilica of St-Sernin**, begun in 1080 to accommodate the passing hordes of Santiago pilgrims, and one of the loveliest examples of its genre. Its most striking external features are the octagonal brick belfry with rounded and pointed arches, diamond lozenges, colonnettes and mouldings picked out in stone, and the apse with nine radiating chapels. Entering from the south, you pass under the Porte Miégeville, whose twelfth-century carvings launched the influential Toulouse school of sculpture. Inside, the great high nave rests on brick piers, flanked by double aisles of diminishing height, surmounted by a gallery running right around the building. The fee for the **ambulatory** is worth it for the exceptional eleventh-century marble reliefs on the end wall of the choir and for the extraordinary wealth of reliquaries in the spacious **crypt**.

## Musée St-Raymond

1ter place St-Sernin • Tues–Sun 10am–6pm • €5 • ☎ 05 61 22 31 44, ⊕ saintraymond.toulouse.fr

Right outside the basilica of St-Sernin is the city's archeological museum, **Musée St-Raymond**, housed in what remains of the block built for poor students of the medieval university. It contains a large collection of objects ranging from prehistoric to Roman, as well as an excavated necropolis in the basement.

## Cité de l'Espace

Av Jean-Gonord, beside exit 17 of the A612 *périphérique* on the road to Castres • Feb–Aug daily 10am–5/7pm • €21, children €15.50, under-5s free • ☎ 05 67 22 23 24, ⊕ cite-espace.com • Bus #19 from place Marengo (school hols only)

At the **Cité de l'Espace**, out in the suburbs to the east, the theme is space and space exploration, including satellite communications, space probes and, best of all, the opportunity to walk inside a mock-up of the Mir space station – fascinating, but chilling. Many of the exhibits are interactive and you could easily spend a half-day here, especially if you're with children.

12

## Aeroscopia

6 rue Roger-Béteille • Daily 9.30am–6pm (7pm during school holidays); last entrance 1hr before closing • €12.50–24, under-6s free • Guided tours, normally in French • ☎ 05 34 39 42 00, ⓦ musee-aeroscopia.fr

Toulouse's major new aerospace museum – **Aeroscopia** – is located right next to the airport, Blagnac, and celebrates the city's close links with air travel, past, present and future. There are all sorts of sleek flying machines on display, from huge commercial Airbuses and leisure-led light aircraft to supersonic military planes, drones and aerofoils. Along with exhibits such as model airplanes and fascinating behind-the-scenes information of how these remarkable machines are made and then handled in mid-air, you can take a tour around the giant factory, including a couple of themed ones – the first focusing on the first unsung pioneers of the industry and another concentrating on military aviation.

### ARRIVAL AND DEPARTURE
### TOULOUSE

**By plane** Aéroport Toulouse–Blagnac (☎ 08 25 38 00 00, ⓦ toulouse.aeroport.fr) is 5km northwest of the town centre. An airport shuttle (every 20min 5.45–12.10am, returning 5.05am–9.40pm; tickets can be bought from driver for €8) sets you down at the bus station, with stops on allées Jean-Jaurès and place Jeanne-d'Arc. The new tramline is an alternative to the *navette*: tram T2 (€6.10) goes every 9 to 15min from the airport to Palais de Justice

**By train** The *gare SNCF*, better known as *gare Matabiau*, is at 80 bd Pierre-Sémard (☎ 08 92 35 35 35). To reach the city centre takes just 5min by métro to Capitole, or 20min on foot (turn left out of the station, cross the canal and head straight down allées Jean-Jaurès).

Destinations Albi (17 daily; 1hr); Auch (18–20 daily; 1hr

15min–2hr 30min); Ax-les-Thermes (6 daily; 1hr 55min); Bayonne (18–22 daily; 2hr 25min–3hr 45min); Bordeaux (18–22 daily; 2hr 30min); Castres (11 daily; 1hr 5min); Foix (13 daily; 47min–1hr 15min); La-Tour-de-Carol (6 daily; 2hr 30min); Lourdes (8–16 daily; 1hr 40min); Lyon (14–18 daily; 4–6hr); Marseille (22 daily; 3hr 30min–6hr); Mazamet (11 daily; 1hr 30min–1hr 55min); Paris (13 daily; 5hr 20min–6hr 45min); Pau (6–10 daily; 2hr–2hr 30min); Tarascon-sur-Ariège (13 daily; 1hr 20min); Tarbes (6–13 daily; 1hr 45min).

**By bus** The *gare routière* (☎ 05 61 61 67 67) is next to the train station, on bd Pierre-Sémard.

Destinations Albi (12–16 weekly; 2hr 40min); Carcassonne (1 daily; 2hr 20min); Castres (8–12 weekly; 1hr 40min–2hr).

### GETTING AROUND

**Transport passes** Tisseo-Connex (☎ 05 61 41 70 70, ⓦ tisseo.fr) tickets (€2) cover one hour's transport by métro and city buses within the city centre.

**Taxi** Capitole ☎ 05 34 25 02 50.

**Bike rental** The municipal bike system, VélôToulouse (subscribe for €10/week; ⓦ velo.toulouse.fr), rents bikes for free for up to 30min then €1.20/day or €5/week there-after from over 200 automated stations.

### INFORMATION

**Tourist office** Square Charles-de-Gaulle (June–Sept Mon–Sat 9am–7pm, Sun 10am–6pm; Oct–May Mon–Sat 9.30am–6pm, Sun 10am–6pm; ☎ 08 92 18 01 80, ⓦ toulouse-tourisme.com). The Capitole métro stop is right outside.

**Discount pass** The Pass Tourisme card (€18, €28 & €35 for 1, 2 & 3 days respectively) offers free public transport and entry to the city's museums and monuments plus discounts at a range of other attractions.

### ACCOMMODATION

**Albert 1ᵉʳ** 8 rue Rivals ☎ 05 61 21 17 91, ⓦ hotel-albert1.com. This small, comfortable and good-value hotel is set in a quiet side street just off the Capitole and close to the central market in place de Victor-Hugo. Check for special weekend deals. **€79**

**Des Ambassadeurs** 68 rue de Bayard ☎ 05 61 62 65 84. Very friendly little hotel with a perfect location, just down the road from *gare* Matabiau and a ten-minute walk from the Capitole – a surprisingly good deal given the price. **€74**

**Beauséjour** 4 rue Caffarelli ☎ 05 61 62 77 59, ⓦ hotelbeausejourtoulouse.com. Basic, but dirt cheap,

and with a great copper-balconied facade and sound-proofed rooms. Best of the hotels in the slightly dodgy but engagingly gritty neighbourhood around place de Belfort. **€55**

**Camping Le Rupé** Chemin du Pont du Rupé ☎ 05 61 70 07 35, ⓦ camping-toulouse.com. Toulouse's nearest campsite. Take bus #59, to the "Rupé" stop. **€21**

**Castellane** 17 rue Castellane ☎ 05 61 62 18 82, ⓦ castellanehotel.com. A cheerful hotel with a wide selection of room sizes and types – most are bright and quiet. One of the few wheelchair-accessible hotels in this price range. **€74**

**Le Clocher de Rodez** 14 place Jeanne-d'Arc ☎ 05 61 62 42 92, ⊛ hotel-clocher-toulouse.com. Right in the heart of the city, a stone's throw from lovely St-Sernin and the Capitole, this hotel is also very handily placed for the *gare*. Staff are extremely helpful and, unusually, the hotel offers secure parking. Despite its size, it exudes a very personal hospitality. €100

★ **Grand Hôtel de l'Opéra** 1 place du Capitole ☎ 05 61 21 82 66, ⊛ grand-hotel-opera.com. Originally a seventeenth-century convent, the *grande dame* of Toulouse's hotels presides over the place du Capitole. The rich decor, peppered with antiques and artwork, underlines the atmosphere of sophistication, and there's also a fitness centre. Substantial online discounts. €200

**Ours Blanc** 25 place Victor-Hugo ☎ 05 61 21 62 40, ⊛ hotel-oursblanc.com. Right by the covered market and steps from the Capitole, this welcoming hotel is one of the city's better bargains. Decorated in cool whites, it has a refined air about it. €79

**St-Sernin** 2 rue St-Bernard ☎ 05 61 21 73 08, ⊛ hotel stsernin.com. Nicely renovated old hotel in one of the best districts of the old town, around the basilica – close to all the action, but far enough away to provide peace in the evening. €95.

**Wilson Square** 12 rue d'Austerlitz ☎ 05 61 21 67 57, ⊛ hotel-wilson.com. Good value, well-kept place at the top end of rue d'Austerlitz with a good selection of bars and restaurants on your doorstep. €89

## EATING

Place Arnaud-Bernard, a popular arty hangout, is a great place to lounge in a café, while place du Capitole is the early evening meeting place. Place St-Georges remains popular, though its clientele is no longer convincingly bohemian, and place Wilson also has its enthusiasts. For lunch, a great informal option is the row of five or six small restaurants jammed in on the mezzanine floor above the gorgeous food market in place Victor-Hugo, off boulevard de Strasbourg. They are all closed on Monday, and cost as little as €12 for market-fresh *menus*. The food and atmosphere are perfect.

### CAFÉS

**Bibent** 5 place du Capitole ☎ 05 34 30 18 37, ⊛ maison constant.com/bibent. Located on the south side of the square, this is Toulouse's most distinguished café, with exuberant plasterwork, marble tables and cascading chandeliers. Daily 7am–11pm.

**Le Café des Artistes** 13 place de la Daurade ☎ 05 61 12 06 00. Lively café overlooking the Garonne. A perfect spot to watch the sun set on warm summer evenings, as floodlights pick out the brick buildings along the *quais*. Mon–Sat 11am–1/2am, Sun noon–10pm.

**Le Florida** 12 place du Capitole ☎ 05 61 23 94 61, ⊛ leflorida-capitole.fr. Relaxed café with a retro air. One of the most pleasant places to hang out on the central square. Daily 6am–1am.

### RESTAURANTS

**Au Pois Gourmand** 3 rue Émile-Heybrard ☎ 05 34 36 42 00, ⊛ pois-gourmand.fr. Great location in a riverside nineteenth-century house with a beautiful patio. The quality French cuisine does not come cheap, but is of a high standard, and the *carte* presents a pleasant departure from purely regional dishes. *Menus* from €45 to €79. Take bus #66 or #14 from métro St-Cyprien-République. Mon–Fri noon–1.30pm & Mon–Sat 7.30–9.30pm.

**La Bascule du Chevillard** 14 av Maurice-Hauriou ☎ 05 61 55 24 30. A Toulouse institution. Its chrome interior is pure Art Deco and the food well prepared and presented. The menu includes regional dishes like cassoulet, *foie de canard* and oysters from the Bay of Arcachon. Meals €25 and up. Mon–Sat noon–2pm & 8–11pm.

**Bistro Le Chevillard** 4 bv du Maréchal-Leclerc ☎ 05 61 21 32 02, ⊛ chezcarmen.fr. Family-run for two generations, this is one of the last of the traditional slaughterhouse-side meat emporia. Unsurprisingly, the menu offers a bowel busting array of the finest cuts with rich sauce accompaniments. *Menus* from €17. Mon–Fri noon–2pm & Mon–Sat 8–11pm.

**Dream India** 7 rue des Gestes ☎ 09 81 81 29 87. A sight for sore eyes for curry lovers, this back street restaurant serves all the usual Anglo-Indian favourites like chicken tikka masala for €10.50. Daily 11.30am–2pm & 6.30–11pm.

**Faim des Haricots** 3 rue du Puits Vert ☎ 05 61 22 49 25, ⊛ lafaimdesharicots.fr. Toulouse's best vegetarian option, particularly noted for its delicious tartes and all-you-can-eat buffets, it also has generous *formules* starting at €15.40. Daily noon–2.30pm & 7–10.30pm.

★ **Fufu** 32 rue Sainte-Ursule ☎ 05 62 17 74 46, ⊛ restaurantfufu.com. A cosy little Japanese noodle and ramen bar, tucked away in the backstreets offering top-quality fast food including vegetarian options like *yasai yakisoba* for €10.50. Sun–Thurs 11.30am–10.30pm, Fri & Sat 11.30am–11pm

**Les Jardins de l'Opéra** 1 place du Capitole ☎ 05 61 23 07 76, ⊛ lesjardinsdelopera.com. The *Grand Hôtel*'s restaurant is Toulouse's best and most luxurious. If you fancy a splurge you will pay for it – a basic *menu* starts at €32, and dinner can run to over €100 – but the food is outstanding. Tues–Sat noon–2pm & 8–10pm.

★ **Michel Sarran** 21 bd Armand-Duportal ☎ 05 61 12 32 32, ⊛ michel-sarran.com. Justifiably renowned *restaurant gastronomique*, holding two Michelin stars. It's a 15min walk from the place du Capitole (follow rue des Lois and rue des Salenques to the end, and turn left). Imaginative dishes with a strong Mediterranean streak are

**12**

served with style and warmth. *Menus* range from €60 to €145. Sept–July Mon, Tues, Thurs & Fri noon–1.45pm & 8–9.45pm, Wed 8–9.45pm.

★ **Le Sept Place St-Sernin** 7 place St-Sernin ☎ 05 62 30 05 30, ⓦ restaurant-sept.fr. A small house behind the basilica conceals a lively and cheerful restaurant serving inventive and original cuisine with a constantly changing *carte*, followed by dazzling desserts. If you like a tingle to your palate, try the *moelleux au piment d'espelette*. *Menus* from €32 at lunch time and from €78 in the eves. Mon–Fri noon–2pm & 8–9.45pm, Sat 8–9.45pm.

## DRINKING AND NIGHTLIFE

### BARS

★ **Au Père-Louis** 45 rue des Tourneurs ☎ 05 61 21 33 45, ⓦ au-pere-louis.fr. Granddaddy of the Toulouse drinking scene and a local institution, this historic bar first opened its doors in 1889 and has hardly changed since. There's a huge choice of wines, beers and cocktails, but try the house speciality, *quinquina* (a strong, aromatic aperitif with a quinine base), and pair it with some of the excellent ham. Daily 10am–3.30pm & 6–11pm.

**La Couleur de la Culotte** 14 place St-Pierre ☎ 05 34 44 97 01, ⓦ lacouleurdelaculotte.com. Great little café during the day, bar/club at night, right in the heart of the city and a favourite hangout for students. Mon–Fri 9am–2am, Sat 10am–3am, Sun 10am–2am.

### CLUBS

**Le Cri de la Mouette** 78 allée de Barcelone ☎ 05 62 30 05 28, ⓦ lecridelamouette.com. Popular club on a converted canal boat, featuring reggae, rock, funk and soul. Daily 11pm–5am.

**Shanghaï Express** 12 rue de la Pomme ☎ 05 61 23 37 80. One of the city's most established gay and lesbian clubs, which attracts a mixed crowd including transvestites and transsexuals. Wed–Sun 12.30–7am.

**L'Ubu Club** 16 rue St-Rome ☎ 05 31 61 56 13, ⓦ allforyou.fr. Long-standing pillar of the city's dance scene, which remains as popular as ever. Wed–Sun 11.30pm–7am.

### LIVE MUSIC

**Le Bikini** rue Théodore-Monod, Parc Technologique du Canal ☎ 05 62 24 09 50, ⓦ lebikini.com. On the city's southern outskirts, this is *the* hangout for Toulouse rockers, and a prime venue for live gigs. Thurs–Sun 8pm–2am.

**Zénith** 11 av Raymond-Badiou ☎ 05 62 74 49 49. The city's biggest concert venue (with 9000 seats), specializing in rock. The tourist office has details of all live gigs.

### THEATRE

**Cave-Poésie René-Gouzenne** 71 rue du Taur ☎ 05 61 23 62 00, ⓦ cave-poesie.com. Home to decidedly bohemian literary workshops, concerts and gatherings. Hours vary.

**Théâtre de la Cité** 1 rue Pierre-Baudis ☎ 05 34 45 05 05, ⓦ tnt-cite.com. Live theatre featuring a varied programme of top-notch French and foreign productions.

**Odyssud** 4 av du Parc, Blagnac ☎ 05 61 71 75 15, ⓦ odyssud.com. Major venue featuring both theatre and opera. Take bus #66.

## DIRECTORY

**Consulates** Canada, 10 rue Jules-de-Resseguier (☎ 05 61 52 19 06, ✉ toulouse@international.gc.ca); USA, 25 allées Jean-Jaurès (☎ 05 34 41 16 19, ⓦ fr.usaembassy.gov). Closest British Consulate is in Bordeaux, at 353 bd Wilson (☎ 05 57 22 21 10; ⓦ gov.uk/government/world/france; there is an Honorary Consulate in Toulouse (☎ 05 61 30 37 91).

**Health** For medical emergencies contact SAMU (☎ 115). The network of university hospitals has facilities all over the city. For non-emergencies check their website for the appropriate centre (ⓦ chu-toulouse.fr). For a pharmacy out of hours, try Pharmacie de Nuit, 70–76 allées Jean-Jaurès, entry on rue Arnaud-Vidal (daily 8pm–8am; ☎ 05 61 62 38 05).

# Albi

**ALBI**, 77km and an hour's train ride northeast of Toulouse, is a small town with two unique sights: a museum containing the most comprehensive collection of **Toulouse-Lautrec**'s work (Albi was his birthplace); and a remarkable **Gothic cathedral**. Its other claim to fame comes from its association with Catharism; though not itself an important centre, it gave its name – Albigensian – to both the heresy and the crusade to suppress it.

## Cathédrale Ste-Cécile

Place Ste-Cécile • Mon–Sat 9.30am–6pm, Sun 9.30–10.15am & 1.30–5.30pm • Choir €5; treasury €2; choir & treasury €6 • ☎ 05 63 38 47 40, ⓦ paroisse-albi-sud.fr

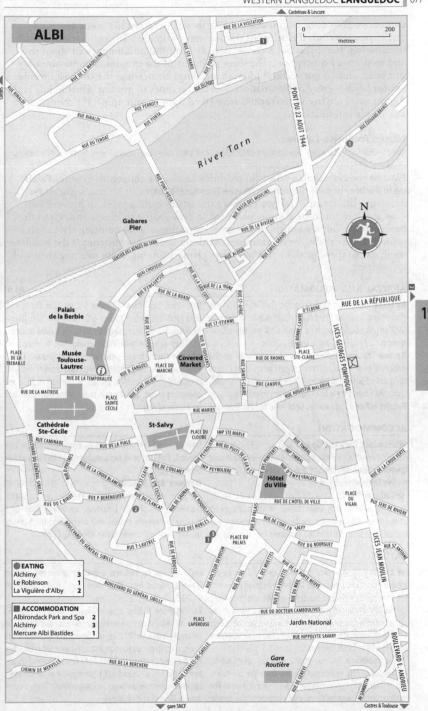

Castelnau & Lescure

## ALBI

0 ——————— 200
metres

RUE DE LA VISITATION

RUE STE MARIE

RUE PORTA

RUE DE LA MADELEINE

RUE DU PORT

PONT DU 22 AOÛT 1944

Cordes

RUE RINALDI

RUE PERROTY

RUE RINALDI

RUE PORTA

RUE EDOUARD BRANLY

RUE DU TENDAT

River Tarn

Gabares
Pier

RUE BASSE DES MOULINS

RUE DE LA RIVIÈRE

SENTIER DES BERGES DU TARN

RUE ALHON

RUE ÉMILE GRAND

N

QUAI CHOISEUL

RUE D'ENGUEYSSE

RUE DE LA CROIX DE LA VIGNE

RUE DE LA BUADE

RUE DE LA RÉPUBLIQUE

D'ELBENE

RUE ST-AFRIC

RUE ST-ÉTIENNE

RUE BONNE-CAMBE

12

Palais
de la Berbie

RUE DE LA SOUQUE

RUE D. FOUSSANTS

PLACE
STE-CLAIRE

Musée
Toulouse-
Lautrec

ⓘ

RUE D. FARGUES

PLACE DU
MARCHÉ

Covered
Market

RUE DE RHONEL

RUE SAINT-CLAIRE

LICES GEORGES POMPIDOU

PLACE
DE LA
TREBAILLE

RUE DE LA TEMPORALITÉ

RUE SAINT JULIEN

RUE CANDEIL

RUE DE LA MAITRISE

PLACE
SAINTE
CÉCILE

RUE AUGUSTIN MALROUX

Cathédrale
Ste-Cécile

RUE CAMINADE

RUE DE LA PIALE

St-Salvy

RUE MARIES

PLACE DU
CLOÎTRE

IMP STE MARIE

RUE TIMBAL

IMP TIMBAL

RUE DE LA CROIX VERTE

BOULEVARD DU GÉNÉRAL SIBILLE

RUE D. PRÊTRES

RUE DE LA CROIX BLANCHE

RUE DE L'OULMET

RUE PEYROLIÈRE

RUE DU PUITS DE LA GRÂCE

RUE DES PÉNITENTS

RUE D'EMPEYRALOTS

BOULEVARD DU C. BIROT

RUE P BERENGUIER

RUE DU PLANCAT

RUE ST CLAIR

RUE Pte CÉCILE

IMP PEYROLIÈRE

RUE DE SAHNAL

RUE ROQUELAURE

Hôtel
du Ville

PLACE
DU
VIGAN

RUE SERE DE RIVIÈRE

BOULEVARD DU GÉNÉRAL SIBILLE

RUE T-LAUTREC

RUE DES NOBLES

RUE DE VERDOUSE

③

PLACE DU
PALAIS

RUE DU PALAIS

RUE DE L'HÔTEL DE VILLE

RUE DE L'ORT EN SALVY

RUE DU BOURGUET

LICES JEAN MOULIN

RUE ST ANTOINE

② 

RUE DOCTEUR DEVOISIN

RUE DU SEL

R. DES MUETTES

RUE DE LA PORTE-NEUVE

RUE DE LA VIOLETTE

RUE DU MAIL

RUE DU DOCTEUR CAMBOULIVES

BOULEVARD DU GÉNÉRAL SIBILLE

PLACE
LAPEROUSE

Jardin National

RUE HIPPOLYTE SAVARY

BOULEVARD E. ANDRIEU

CHEMIN DE MERVILLE

RUE DE LA BERCHERE

AVENUE CHARLES-DE-GAULLE

RUE DE GRAVE

Gare
Routière

Castres & Toulouse

gare SNCF

Rd GAMBETTA

### ● EATING
| | |
|---|---|
| Alchimy | 3 |
| Le Robinson | 1 |
| La Viguière d'Alby | 2 |

### ■ ACCOMMODATION
| | |
|---|---|
| Albirondack Park and Spa | 2 |
| Alchimy | 3 |
| Mercure Albi Bastides | 1 |

**Cathédrale Ste-Cécile**, begun about 1280, dwarfs the town like some vast bulk carrier run aground, the belfry its massive superstructure. The comparison sounds unflattering, but this is not a conventionally beautiful building; it's all about size and boldness of conception. The sheer plainness of the exterior is impressive on this scale, and it's not without interest: arcading, buttressing, the contrast of stone against brick – every differentiation of detail becomes significant. During July and August there are free **organ recitals** here (Wed 5pm & Sun 4pm); the tourist office can supply information.

## Musée Toulouse-Lautrec

Place Ste-Cécile • Oct–March Wed–Mon 10am–noon & 2–5.30pm; April & May daily 10am–noon & 2–6pm; June–Sept daily 9am–6pm • €9 • ☎ 05 63 49 48 70, ⓦ musee-toulouse-lautrec.net

Next to the cathedral, a powerful red-brick castle, the thirteenth-century **Palais de la Berbie**, houses the superb **Musée Toulouse-Lautrec**. It contains paintings, drawings, lithographs and posters from the artist's earliest work to his very last – an absolute must for anyone interested in *belle époque* seediness and, given the predominant Impressionism of the time, the rather offbeat painting style of its subject. But perhaps the most impressive thing about this museum is the building itself, its parapets, gardens and walkways giving stunning views over the river and its bridges.

### ARRIVAL AND INFORMATION                                              ALBI

**By train** Trains from Cordes-Vindrac (3–4 daily; 1hr–1hr 30min) and Toulouse (16 daily; 1–2hr) pull in to the *gare SNCF* on place Stalingrad; it's a 10min walk north into town along avs du Maréchal-Joffre and de-Gaulle.

**By bus** The *gare routière*, on place Jean-Jaurès on the southeast edge of the old town, meets buses from Castres (6–8 daily; 50min) and Cordes (Mon–Sat 1–4 daily; 35min). Some SNCF buses leave from here, others from the *gare*.

**Tourist office** 42 rue Mariès (mid-June to Sept Mon–Sat 9am–7pm, Sun 10am–12.30pm & 2.30–5pm; Oct to mid-June Mon–Sat 9am–12.30pm & 2–6/6.30pm, Sun 10am–12.30pm & 2–6.30pm; ☎ 05 63 36 36 00, ⓦ albi-tourisme. fr). They sell the "Albi Pass", giving free or discounted admission to the town's sights and some restaurants (€12).

**Festivals** The town hosts three good annual festivals, dedicated to jazz in May, theatre at the end of June and beginning of July, and classical music at the end of July and beginning of August.

### ACCOMMODATION

**Albirondack Park and Spa** 31 allée de la Piscine ☎ 05 63 60 37 06, ⓦ albirondack.fr. Set in a wooded glade near town, this beautiful campsite also has cabins and Airstream trailers. Open all year. €30

★ **Alchimy** 10–12 place du Palais ☎ 05 63 76 18 18, ⓦ alchimyalbi.fr. Airy, understated luxury in the heart of the town. All the rooms are beautifully appointed and feature spacious bathrooms equipped to the highest standards and the staff cannot do enough to ensure your comfort. This chic hotel has a renowned restaurant too (see below). €129

**Mercure Albi Bastides** 41 rue Porta ☎ 05 63 47 66 66, ⓦ mercure.com/fr/hotel-1211-hotel-mercure-albi-bastides/index.shtml. Luxurious accommodation in a massive eighteenth-century mill overlooking the banks of the Tarn, and with views of the cathedral. €120

### EATING

★ **Alchimy** 10–12 place du Palais ☎ 05 63 54 14 69, ⓦ alchimyalbi.fr. A beautiful, light-filled dining room sets the tone for this elegant brasserie serving exquisite food; try the butter-roasted cod or the lamb with creamy morel sauce. A three-course dinner for two will set you back over €100 with wine: it's pricey, but worth the splurge. *Menus* from €16.90 at lunch. Daily noon–2pm & 7.30–11pm.

★ **Le Robinson** 142 rue Édouard-Branly ☎ 05 63 46 15 69. Set in the woods just upriver from the old town, this restaurant's environs alone make it worth a visit. The outdoor terrace and location, well away from the centre, make it ideal for children, especially when the weather is good. *Menus* from €28. Wed–Sun noon–2.30pm & 7–9.30pm. Closed Nov–March.

**La Viguière d'Alby** 7 rue Toulouse-Lautrec ☎ 05 63 54 76 44, ⓦ restaurant-viguiere-alby-tarn81.fr. An Albigeois *terroir* institution, serving hearty local dishes in quiet, unpretentious surroundings. The wine list is excellent and the food never disappoints. For a hearty regional classic, aim for the house cassoulet (€19) or if you're an adventurous carnivore, consider the tripe and saffron stew. Daily noon–3pm & Mon–Sat 7–9.30pm.

# Castres

In spite of its industrial activities, **CASTRES**, 40km south of Albi and 55km east of Toulouse, has kept a lot of its charm in the streets on the right bank of the Agout and, in particular, the riverside quarter where the old tanners' and weavers' houses overhang the water. The centre is a bustling, businesslike sort of place, with a big morning **market** on Saturdays on place Jean-Jaurès.

## Musée Goya

Hôtel de ville • July & Aug daily 10am–6pm; Sept & April–June Tues–Sun 9am–noon & 2–6pm; Oct–March Tues–Sun 9am–noon & 2–5pm • €5 • ☎ 05 63 71 59 30, ⓦ ville-castres.fr

Next to the rather unremarkable old cathedral, the former bishop's palace holds the *hôtel de ville* and Castres' **Musée Goya**, home to the biggest collection of Spanish paintings in France outside the Louvre. Goya is represented by some lighter political paintings and a large collection of engravings, while other famous Iberian artists on show include Murillo and Velázquez.

## Musée Jean-Jaurès

2 place Pélisson • July & Aug daily 10am–noon & 2–6pm; May, June & Sept Tues–Sun 10am–noon & 2–6pm; Oct–March Tues–Sat 10am–noon & 2–5pm • €3 • ☎ 05 63 62 41 83, ⓦ ville-castres.fr

Getting to the **Musée Jean-Jaurès**, dedicated to the city's famous native son, takes you through the streets of the old town, past the splendid seventeenth-century **Hôtel Nayrac**, on rue Frédéric-Thomas. The slightly hagiographic museum pays tribute to one of France's boldest and best political writers, thinkers and activists of modern times.

**12**

## ARRIVAL AND INFORMATION
CASTRES

**By train** The *gare SNCF* lies 1km southwest of the town centre on av Albert-1er. Trains and SNCF buses arrive from Toulouse (11 daily; 1hr 5min).

**By bus** The *gare routière* is beside the train station on av Albert-1er, with bus services to Albi (6–8 daily; 50min); Lacaune (Mon–Sat 1–4 daily 50min); Revel (Mon–Sat 1–6, 45min); St-Pons (Mon–Sat 1–4 daily; 1hr–1hr 30min); Toulouse (8–12 weekly; 1hr 40min–2hr).

**Tourist office** 2 place de la République (Sept–June Mon–Sat 9.30am–12.30pm & 2–6pm, Sun on bank hols & June 2.30–4.30pm; July & Aug Mon–Sat 9.30am–6.30pm,Sun 10.30am–noon & 2.30–5pm; ☎ 05 63 62 63 62, ⓦ tourisme-castres.fr). You can buy the Passe Tourisme (€6.50) here; it gives reductions on museums, shops and restaurants.

## ACCOMMODATION

**Camping de Gourjade** Rte de Roquecourbe ☎ 05 63 59 33 51, ⓦ campingdegourjade.net. The municipal campsite is in a riverside park 2km northeast of town on the road to Roquecourbe; it's accessible by river-taxi (return €6). Closed Oct–March. **€16.50**

**Grand Hôtel de Castres** 11 rue de la Libération ☎ 05 63 37 82 20, ⓦ grandhoteldecastres.com. This is in the centre of old Castres, and has splendid views over the river, and contemporary decor. **€92**

★ **Renaissance** 17 rue Victor-Hugo ☎ 05 63 59 30 42, ⓦ hotel-renaissance.fr. This cosy three-star hotel in the heart of old Castres has a variety of rooms, including junior suites. Expect wooden floors and comfortable furnishings. **€84**

**Rivière** 10 quai Tourcaudière ☎ 05 63 59 04 53, ⓦ hotelriviere.pagesperso-orange.fr. A basic, welcoming and good-value option with tidy if nondescript rooms, the best of which have views over the Agout. **€58**

## EATING AND DRINKING

**La Mandragore** 1 rue Malpas ☎ 05 63 59 51 27. This local favourite is praised both for its *gastronomique* cuisine, its *terroir* standbys, and its wine selection. Dine inside or on the terrace. *Menus* €16–32. Tues–Sat noon–2pm & 7–9pm.

**Le Médiéval** 44 rue Milhau-Ducommun ☎ 05 63 51 13 78. A homely little restaurant with a great atmosphere, friendly staff and a riverside location. Four-course *menu* €39. Reservation recommended in eves. Tues–Sun noon–2pm & 7–9pm.

## ARMAGNAC

**Armagnac** is a mellow, golden brandy distilled in the district extending into the Landes and Lot and Garonne *départements*, divided into three distinct areas: Haut-Armagnac (around Auch), Ténarèze (Condom) and Bas-Armagnac (Eauze), in ascending order of output and quality. Growers of the grape like to compare brandy with whisky, equating malts with the individualistic, earthy Armagnac distilled by small producers, and blended whiskies with the more consistent, standardized output of the large-scale houses. Armagnac grapes are grown on sandy soils and, importantly, the wine is distilled only once, giving the spirit a lower alcohol content but more flavour. Aged in local black oak, Armagnac matures quickly, so young Armagnacs are relatively smoother than corresponding Cognacs.

Distilled originally for medicinal reasons, Armagnac has many claims heaped upon it. Perhaps the most optimistic are those of the priest of Eauze de St-Mont, who held that the eau de vie cured **gout** and hepatitis. More reasonably, he also wrote that it "stimulates the spirit if taken in moderation, recalls the past, gives many joys, above all else, conserves youth. If one retains it in the mouth, it unties the tongue and gives courage to the timid."

Many of the producers welcome visitors and offer tastings, whether you go to one of the bigger *chais* (storehouse) of Condom or Eauze, or follow a faded sign at the bottom of a farm track. For more **information**, contact the Bureau National Interprofessionnel de l'Armagnac (ⓦ armagnac.fr).

## The Gers

West of Toulouse is the *département* of **Gers**, which lies at the heart of the historic region of Gascony. In the long struggle for supremacy between the English and the French in the Middle Ages it had the misfortune to form the frontier zone between the English base at Bordeaux and the French at Toulouse. The attractive if unspectacular rolling agricultural land is dotted with ancient, honey-stoned farms. Settlement is sparse and – with the exception of **Auch**, the capital – major monuments are largely lacking, which keeps it well off the beaten tourist trails.

The region is perhaps best known for its stout-hearted mercenary warriors – of whom Alexandre Dumas' d'Artagnan and Edmond Rostand's Cyrano de Bergerac are the supreme literary exemplars – its rich cuisine (Gers is the biggest producer of **foie gras** in the country), and its **Armagnac**.

### Auch

The sleepy provincial capital of the Gers, **AUCH** is most easily accessible by rail from Toulouse, 78km to the east. The **old town**, which is the only part worth exploring, stands on a bluff overlooking the tree-lined River Gers, with the **cathedral** towering dramatically over the town.

#### Cathédrale Ste-Marie

Rue Arnaud-de-Moles • Daily: July–Aug 9.30am–7pm; Sept–June 9.30am–12.30pm & 2–6pm; closed during services • €2 • ☎ 05 62 05 04 64, ⓦ auch-tourisme.com

The **Cathédrale Ste-Marie** alone makes a trip to Auch worthwhile. Although not finished until the latter part of the seventeenth century, it is built in broadly late Gothic style, with a classical facade. Of particular interest are the choir stalls and the stained glass; both were begun in the early 1500s, though the windows are clearly of Renaissance inspiration, while the choir remains Gothic. The eighteen windows, unusual in being a complete set, parallel the scenes and personages depicted in the stalls. They are the work of a Gascon painter, Arnaud de Moles, and are equally rich in detail.

#### The old town

Immediately south of the cathedral, in the tree-filled place Salinis, is the 40m-high **Tour d'Armagnac**, which served as an ecclesiastical court and prison in the fourteenth century. Descending from here to the river is a **monumental stairway** of 234 steps, with a statue of d'Artagnan gracing one of the terraces. From place de la République, in front of the cathedral's main west door, rue d'Espagne connects with rue de la Convention and what is left of the narrow medieval stairways known as the **pousterles**, which give access to the lower town. On the north side of place de la République, the tourist office inhabits a splendid, half-timbered fifteenth-century house on the corner with rue Dessoles, a pedestrianized street that has an array of fine buildings.

### Musée des Jacobins

4 place Louis-Blanc • Feb, March, Nov & Dec Mon–Fri 2–5pm, Sat & Sun 10am–noon & 2–5pm; April Oct daily 10am–noon & 2–6pm • €4 • ☎ 05 62 05 74 79, ⓦ musee-jacobins.auch.fr

Just down the steps to the east of rue Dessoles, on place Louis-Blanc, the former convent, now the **Musée des Jacobins**, houses one of the best collections of pre-Columbian and later South American art in France. Also of interest is its small collection of traditional Gascon furniture, religious artefacts and Gallo-Roman remains.

## ARRIVAL AND INFORMATION                                                    AUCH

**By train** The *gare SNCF* is on av Pierre-Mendès across the river from the cathedral, a 10min walk east.

**By bus** The *gare routière* is next to the train station.
Destinations Bordeaux (1 daily; 3hr 40min); Condom (1–2 daily; 40min); Lectoure (4–8 daily; 40min); Montauban (generally up to 3 daily; 2hr); Tarbes (3–4 daily; 2hr);
Toulouse (1–4 daily; 1hr 30min).

**Tourist office** 3 place de la République (May, June & Sept Mon–Sat 9.15am–6pm, Sun & hols 10am–12.30pm; July & Aug Mon–Sat 9.30am–-6.30pm, Sun 10am–12.15pm & 3–5.30pm; Oct–April Mon–Sat 9.15am–6pm ☎ 05 62 05 22 89, ⓦ auch-tourisme.com).

## ACCOMMODATION

**Château Les Charmettes** 21 rte de Duran ☎ 05 62 62 10 10, ⓦ chateaulescharmettes.com. The best hotel in the area, in a country estate 2km northwest of the town centre. Amenities include a pool, jacuzzi, tennis courts, and a stunning garden setting. An ideal base for exploring the region. **€160**
**De France** 2 place de la Libération ☎ 05 62 61 71 71, ⓦ hoteldefrance-auch.com. Right by the *mairie* and only
a few minutes' walk west of the cathedral, this beautiful old hotel has a variety of rooms, all en suite, and it's worth paying a little more for a larger one. The restaurant is good, too (see below). **€83**
**Robinson** Rte de Tarbes ☎ 05 62 05 02 83, ⓦ hotel robinson.net. A fairly basic but clean budget option in a lovely setting. **€55**

## EATING

**De France** 2 place de la Libération ☎ 05 62 61 71 71, ⓦ hoteldefrance-auch.com. This well-regarded hotel restaurant tilts towards the *gastronomique*. There is also a separate brasserie serving less complex and less expensive dishes. Weekday lunch *menus* from €25, although à la carte will set you back considerably more. Tues–Fri noon–2pm
& 7–9.30pm, Sat 7–9.30pm, Sun noon–2pm.
**La Table d'Oste** 7 rue Lamartine ☎ 05 62 05 55 62, ⓦ latabledoste.com. Good Gascon and Languedocian cuisine, including foie gras, duck and cassoulet. *Menus* €26–29. Mon 7–9.30pm, Tues–Sat noon–1.30pm & 7–9.30pm.

**12**

# The Massif Central

**684** Auvergne

**706** The southwest

**711** Les Causses

**716** The Cévennes and Ardèche

LE PUY-EN-VELAY

# 13 The Massif Central

Thickly forested and sliced by numerous rivers and lakes, the once volcanic uplands of the Massif Central are geologically the oldest part of France and culturally one of the most firmly rooted in the past. Industry and tourism have made few inroads here, and the people remain rural and somewhat taciturn, with an enduring sense of regional identity.

The Massif Central takes up a huge portion of the centre of France, but only a handful of towns have gained a foothold in its rugged terrain: **Le Puy**, spiked with theatrical pinnacles of lava, is the most compelling, with its steep streets and majestic cathedral; the spa town of **Vichy** has an antiquated elegance and charm; formerly industrial **Clermont-Ferrand**, the biggest town in the Massif, has a certain cachet in the black volcanic stone of its historic centre and its stunning physical setting beneath the **Puy de Dôme**, a 1464m-high volcanic plug. There is pleasure, too, in the unpretentious provinciality of **Aurillac**, in the untouched medieval architecture of smaller places like **Murat**, **Besse**, **Salers**, **Orcival**, **Sauveterre-de-Rouergue** and **La Couvertoirade**, and in the hugely influential abbey of **Conques**. But, above all, this is a region where you come to see the landscapes rather than towns, churches or museums.

Many of France's greatest rivers rise in the Massif Central: the **Dordogne** in the Monts-Dore; the **Loire** on the slopes of the Gerbier de Jonc in the east; and two tributaries of the Garonne, the **Lot** and the **Tarn**, in the Cévennes. It is these last two rivers that create the distinctive character of the southern parts of the Massif Central, dividing and defining the special landscapes of the *causses*, or limestone plateaux, with their stupendous gorges. This is territory tailor-made for walkers or lovers of the **outdoors**.

## Auvergne

The heart of the Massif Central is the **Auvergne**, a wild and unexpected scene of extinct volcanoes (*puys*), stretching from the grassy domes and craters of the **Monts-Dômes** to the eroded skylines of the **Monts-Dore**, and the deep ravines of the **Cantal mountains** to the forest of darkly wooded pinnacles surrounding Le Puy. It's one of the poorest regions in France and has long remained outside the main national lines of communication: much of it is higher than 1000m and many roads fall victim to snowfall in winter.

If travelling by public transport, you'll have to pass through **Clermont-Ferrand**, the Auvergne capital and a city of dramatic historical associations – it was the site of Pope Urban II's speech, which launched the First Crusade in 1096. The small towns in the spectacular **Parc Naturel Régional des Volcans d'Auvergne** are home to numerous treasures, including the Basilique Notre-Dame in **Orcival**, the lively market town of **Murat** and the surprising grandeur of **Salers**; at **St-Nectaire** you can see a beautiful small church displaying the distinct Auvergnat version of Romanesque; and even **St-Flour** and **Aurillac** have an agreeable provincial insularity.

### Clermont-Ferrand and around

The most dramatic approach to **CLERMONT-FERRAND** is from the Aubusson road or along the scenic rail line from Le Mont-Dore, both of which cross the chain of the Monts-Dômes just north of the Puy de Dôme. Descending through the leafy western suburbs, you get marvellous views of the black towers of the **cathedral**, which sits atop the volcanic stump that forms the hub of the old town.

THE MILLAU VIADUCT

# Highlights

❶ **Puy de Dôme** Some 400m above Clermont-Ferrand, this long-extinct volcano offers staggering vistas of the Massif Central. See page 690

❷ **Le Puy-en-Velay** Built on volcanic rocks, this ancient town offers intriguing reminders of how similar the Byzantine and Romanesque styles once were. See page 701

❸ **Conques** Modern pilgrims trek to this monastery town, once an important way station on the route to Santiago de Compostela. See page 709

❹ **The Millau viaduct** Designed by Sir Norman Foster, the viaduct is a miracle of modern engineering. See page 713

❺ **Canoeing** The river gorge of the Tarn provides excellent opportunities for kayaking and canoeing. See page 713

❻ **Gorges de l'Ardèche** From the natural bridge at Pont d'Arc, the rushing Ardèche has carved out a dramatic descent through wooded and cave-riddled cliffs. See page 721

**HIGHLIGHTS ARE MARKED ON THE MAP ON PAGE 686**

**13**

---

### PARC DES VOLCANS D'AUVERGNE

The **Parc Naturel Régional des Volcans d'Auvergne** consists of three groups of extinct volcanoes – the **Monts-Dômes** (see page 687), the **Monts-Dore** (see page 694) and the **Monts du Cantal** (see page 697) – linked by the high plateaux of Artense and the Cézallier. It's a vast, sparsely populated place, and the mountains have few crags or individual rock faces. The steep upper slopes, grassy and treeless, are known as *montagnes à vaches* (mountains for cows), traditionally providing pasture for the cows that produce **St-Nectaire** cheese. You can still see the (now mainly ruined) primitive stone huts, or *burons*, of their herdsmen, scattered along the slopes.

**Maison du Parc** Château de Montlosier, 20km southwest of Clermont-Ferrand ☎04 73 65 64 26, ⓦwww.parcdesvolcans.fr. The park headquarters oversees various subsidiary *maisons du parc*, each devoted to different themes or activities: fauna and flora, the lives of the herdsmen, peat bogs and so on.

April & May daily except Tues 10am–12.30pm & 1.30–5.30pm; June–Sept daily 10am–12.30pm & 1.30–6.30pm; Oct and school holidays daily except Tues 10am–12.30pm & 1.30–5.30pm; winter holidays Sat & Sun 9.30am–12.30pm & 1.30–6.30pm.

---

Although its location is magnificent, almost encircled by the wooded and grassy volcanoes of the **Monts-Dômes**, in the twentieth century the town was a typical smokestack industrial centre, the home base of Michelin tyres. Today, however, focusing on the service industries and with two universities, Clermont-Ferrand is very different. Many of the old factories have been demolished, avenues have been widened for tramways, and derelict blocks have become shopping malls. As a result, the old centre has a surprisingly hip and youthful feel, with cafés on the central **place de Jaude** – well placed for the morning sun – often full of students taking advantage of the free wi-fi offered around the square; come evening, nearby pavement bars fill up as the city's boutiques and galleries shut up shop for the day.

For one week in February, during the **International Short Film Festival** (ⓦclermont-filmfest.com), Clermont-Ferrand becomes as renowned in the film world as Cannes.

### Brief history

Clermont-Ferrand's roots, both as a spa and a communications and trading centre, go back to Roman times. It was just outside the town, on the plateau of Gergovia to the south, that the Gauls, under **Vercingétorix**, won their only victory against Julius Caesar's invading Romans. In the Middle Ages, the rival towns of Clermont and Montferrand were ruled respectively by a bishop and the count of Auvergne. Louis XIII united them in 1630, but it was not until the rapid **industrial expansion** of the late nineteenth century that the two really became indistinguishable.

### Cathédrale Notre-Dame de l'Assomption

**Cathedral** Mon–Sat 7.45am–noon & 2–6pm, Sun and holidays 9am–noon & 3–8pm • Free • ⓦcathedrale-catholique-clermont.fr

As you enter the appealing medieval quarter, clustered in a characteristic muddle around the cathedral, Clermont's status as a *ville noire* becomes immediately apparent. The colour is not due to pollution, but to the black volcanic rock used to construct many of its buildings. The dark and sombre **Cathédrale Notre-Dame de l'Assomption**, standing at the centre and highest point of the old town, is the most striking example of this practice. Begun in the mid-thirteenth century, it was not finished until the nineteenth, under the direction of Viollet-le-Duc, who was the architect of the west front and those typically Gothic spires. The gloomy **interior** is startlingly illuminated by the brilliantly coloured rose windows in the transept and the stained-glass windows in the choir, most of which date back to the fourteenth century. Remnants of medieval frescoes survive, too: a particularly beautiful Virgin and Child adorns the right wall of the Chapelle Ste-Madeleine and an animated battle scene between the Crusaders and Muslims unfolds on the central wall of the Chapelle St-Georges. Unfortunately it's no longer possible

13

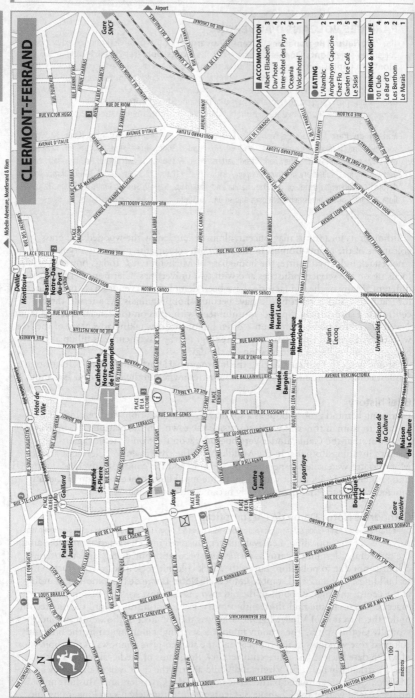

CLERMONT-FERRAND

| ACCOMMODATION | |
|---|---|
| Albert Elisabeth | 3 |
| Dav'hotel | 4 |
| Inter-hôtel des Puys | 2 |
| Oceania | 5 |
| Volcanhotel | 1 |

| ● EATING | |
|---|---|
| L'Alambic | 2 |
| Amphitryon Capucine | 1 |
| Chez Flo | 3 |
| Garden Ice Café | 5 |
| Le Sisisi | 4 |

| ■ DRINKING & NIGHTLIFE | |
|---|---|
| 101 Club | 4 |
| Le Bar d'O | 3 |
| Les Berthom | 2 |
| Le Marais | 1 |

to climb the **Tour de la Bayette**, but it's worth checking if this has changed as the views across the city towards the Puy de Dôme are particularly impressive on a fine day.

## Basilique Notre-Dame-du-Port
Rue du Port • Daily 10am–6pm • Free • ⓦ notredamedeclermont.fr

Northeast of the cathedral, down the elegant old rue du Port, stands Clermont's other great church, the Romanesque **Basilique Notre-Dame-du-Port** – a century older than the cathedral and in almost total contrast, built from softer arkose (a type of sandstone) in pure Auvergnat Romanesque style. Check out the Madonna and Child in the tympanum of the south door in the strangely stylized local form. Both figures are stiff and upright, the Child more like a dwarf than an infant. It was near here (in all probability in Place Delille) that Pope Urban II called for the **First Crusade** in 1095, preaching to a vast crowd who received his speech with shouts of *Dios lo volt* (Occitan for "God wills it"), which became the battle cry of the crusaders.

## L'Aventure Michelin
32 rue du Clos-Four • April–June daily 10am–6pm; July & Aug daily 10am–7pm; Sept–March Tues–Sun 10am–6pm • €9.50 • ☎ 04 73 98 60 60, ⓦ laventure.michelin.com

It feels somewhat incongruous that this French provincial capital is the world headquarters of a colossal global brand. Yet **L'Aventure Michelin**, in the old Michelin factory, is an enjoyable place to learn about one of the most innovative industries in France – and one that is still going strong. The company, which invented not only the radial tyre but also the folding map, originated in 1829 thanks partly to the ingenuity of Charles Mackintosh, the Scotsman of waterproof raincoat fame, whose niece married Édouard Daubrée, a Clermont sugar manufacturer, and brought with her ideas about making rubber goods that she had learnt from her uncle. In 1889, the company became Michelin and Co, named after new owner Édouard Michelin, just in time to catch the development of the automobile and the World War I aircraft industry. L'Aventure Michelin runs through the rest of the story: how the company rode the wave of the car boom; how it started producing maps in 1900 to inform customers where to find petrol; and how they started adding **restaurants** nearby and rating them with stars. Finally, of course, there is Michelin Man himself: the only marketing mascot that has survived unchanged for more than a century.

---

### THE FOOD OF THE AUVERGNE AND MASSIF CENTRAL

Don't expect anything overly refined from the cuisine of the Auvergne and Massif Central: it started as solid peasant food, as befits a traditionally poor and rugged region. The best-known dish is **potée auvergnate**, a kind of cabbage soup, with added potatoes, pork or bacon, beans and turnips – easy to make and very nourishing. Another popular cabbage dish is **chou farci**: cabbage stuffed with pork and beef and cooked with bacon.

Two potato dishes are very common – **la truffade** and **l'aligot**. For *truffade*, the potatoes are sliced and fried in lard, then fresh Cantal cheese is added; for an *aligot*, the potatoes are puréed and mixed with cheese. Less palatable for the squeamish is **tripoux**, usually a stuffing of either sheep's feet or calf's innards, cooked in a casing of stomach lining. **Fricandeau**, a kind of pork pâté, is also wrapped in sheep's stomach.

**Clafoutis** is a popular fruit tart in which the fruit is baked with a batter of flour and egg simply poured over it. The classic fruit ingredient is black cherries, though pears, blackcurrants or apples can also be used.

The Auvergne and the Ardèche in the east produce some wines, though these are not of any great renown. **Cheese**, however, is a different story. In addition to the great cow's milk cheeses – St-Nectaire (see page 695), Laguiole, Cantal, Fourme d'Ambert and Bleu d'Auvergne – this region also produces the prince of all cheeses, **Roquefort**, made from sheep's milk at the edge of the Causse du Larzac near Millau.

**13**

## Musée Bargoin and Muséum Henri Lecoq

**Musée Bargoin** 45 rue Ballainvilliers • Tues–Sat 10am–noon & 1–5pm, Sun 2–7pm • €5, €10 for the "Pass découverte" which allows entry to all metropolitan museums • ☎ 04 43 76 25 50 • **Muséum Henri Lecoq** 15 rue Bardoux • May–Sept Tues–Sat 10am–noon & 2–6pm, Sun 2–6pm; Oct–April Tues–Sat 10am–noon & 2–5pm, Sun 2–5pm • €5 or €10 for the "Pass découverte" which allows entry to all metropolitan museums • ☎ 04 43 76 25 60

Elegant **Rue Ballainvilliers**, with its shuttered-window eighteenth-century facades, leads to the **Musée Bargoin**. Archeological finds on display here include some fascinating domestic items: Roman shoes, baskets, pieces of dried fruit, glass and pottery, as well as a remarkable burial find from nearby Martres-de-Veyre, dating back to the second century AD. There is also a diverse collection of tapestries and textiles. Directly behind is the **Muséum Henri Lecoq**, which is billed as "the only general natural history museum" in the region. Although there are lots of stairs, the museum is well suited to children, with a treasure-hunt-style game hidden around the exhibitions. The stuffed animal exhibit provides a decent insight into local wildlife, but the public garden full of beautiful trees is what makes a visit here truly worthwhile.

## Montferrand

**Montferrand**, standing some 2.5km northeast of the centre, is today little more than a suburb of Clermont, with a couple of interesting museums including the excellent **Musée d'Art Roger-Quilliot**. Built on a grid, its principal streets, rue de la Rodade and rue Jules-Guesde (named after the founder of the French Communist Party – Montferrand was home to many of the Michelin factory workers), are still lined with fine townhouses once owned by medieval merchants and magistrates. Only the highly successful Montferrand **rugby team** keeps the old town's name alive.

### Musée d'Art Roger-Quilliot (MARQ)

Place Louis-Deteix • Tues–Fri 10am–6pm, Sat & Sun 10am–noon & 1–6pm • €5 or €10 for the "Pass découverte" which allows entry to all metropolitan museums • ☎ 04 43 76 25 25 • Tram #A from place de Jaude

Housed in a daringly renovated eighteenth-century Ursuline convent, the **Musée d'Art Roger-Quilliot** holds a broad collection of more than two thousand works of art dating from medieval times right up to the present day. Notable pieces include a stunning enamelled reliquary of Thomas Becket and a space dedicated to mathematician Blaise Pascal.

## Vulcania

Rte de Mazayes, St-Ours-les-Roches • mid-April to June daily 10am–6pm; July & Aug daily 10am–6/6.30pm; late March & Sept to early Nov Wed–Sun 10am–6pm• €24.50–28 depending on season; English audioguide €3.50 • ☎ 04 73 19 70 00, ⓦ vulcania.com • A *navette* leaves the *gare SNCF*, stopping by place de Jaude on its way (June to August; mid-April to May & Sept to early Nov with reservation 48hr in advance ☎ 04 73 26 97 75)

Set in a beautiful site in the middle of the *puys* 17km west of Clermont-Ferrand, the interactive **Vulcania** science park is a big hit with families and kids who want to learn about the formation and lifetime of volcanoes. Rides, geysers, electric trains and films all serve to present the subject of geology in an engaging and entertaining way.

## Riom

Just 15km north of Clermont-Ferrand, **RIOM** is a sedate and provincial town that makes a worthwhile lunch stop if you're on the way up to Vichy. It's an aloof, old-world kind of place, still Auvergne's judicial capital, and its Renaissance architecture, fashioned out of the local black volcanic stone, is undeniably striking. There's an interesting museum on the region's folk traditions, the **Musée Régional d'Auvergne**, at 10bis Rue Delille (May, June & Sept to mid-Nov Tues–Sun 2–5.30pm; July & Aug 2.30–6pm; free).

## Puy de Dôme

15km west of Clermont-Ferrand • **Path** Accessible from the car park of the Col de Ceyssat (Ceyssat mountain pass), situated along the D941 (signposted from place de Jaude) • May, June, Sept & Oct Sat, Sun & public holidays 12.30–5pm; July & Aug daily 10am–5pm

· **Rack railway** Jan–March & mid-Oct to Dec 10am–5pm; April to mid-July & mid-Aug to mid-Oct 9am–7pm; mid-July to mid-Aug 9am–8.40pm · €13 return · ⓦ panoramiquedesdomes.fr · A *navette* runs to the entrance from the *gare SNCF* via place de Jaude (6 daily early April to early Nov; €3 return; ☎ 04 73 44 68 68) · ⓦ puydedome.com

Visiting Clermont-Ferrand without climbing the **Puy de Dôme** (1465m), the closest and highest peak of the Monts-Dômes, in the **Parc Naturel Régional des Volcans d'Auvergne** (see page 687), would be like visiting Athens without seeing the Acropolis. And if you choose your moment – early in the morning or late in the evening – you can easily avoid the worst of the crowds. You can climb to the top of the puy ("peak") in about an hour (2.3km) or take a rack railway, the **Panoramique des Dômes**, which brings you to the top in thirteen minutes.

The result of a volcanic explosion about 10,000 years ago, the Puy is a steep 400m from base to summit. Although the weather station buildings and enormous television mast are pretty ugly close up, the sense of airy elevation and the staggering views (as far as the Cantal mountains and even to Mont Blanc when conditions are favourable) more than compensate. The on-site café-bar *Épicure* is a great spot to watch paragliders jumping off from the summit, and you'll also get a bird's-eye view of the other volcanic summits to the north and south, largely forested and including the perfect, 100m-deep grassy crater of the **Puy de Pariou**.

Just below the summit are the scant remains of a substantial **Roman temple**, dedicated to the god Mercury, some of the finds from which are displayed in Clermont-Ferrand's Musée Bargoin.

## ARRIVAL AND INFORMATION
### CLERMONT-FERRAND AND AROUND

**By plane** The city airport (☎ 04 73 62 71 00, ⓦ clermont-aeroport.com) at Aulnat, 7km east, serves mainly domestic flights. A local bus (#20; €1.50 one-way) connects with the town centre via the tram station at Musée d'Art Roger-Quilliot. Destinations Nice (weekly; 1hr); Paris (daily; 55min).

**By train** The *gare SNCF* is on av de l'Union Soviétique, a 10min bus journey from place de Jaude, at the western edge of the cathedral hill. There are buses to the centre (€1.50). A taxi costs around €10.
Destinations Aurillac (6 daily; 2hr 25min); Lyon (5–8 daily; 2hr 30min); Le Puy (2–3 daily; 2hr 10min); Murat (4–6 daily; 1hr 40min); Nevers (6–9 daily; 1hr 30min); Nîmes (2–4 daily; 4hr 10min–5hr 15min); Paris-Bercy (7–8 daily;

3hr 30min); Riom (roughly every 30min; 10min); St-Flour (1 daily; 1hr 50min); Toulouse (1–4 daily; 5hr 50min); Vichy (17–29 daily; 30min).

**By bus** The intercity *gare routière* is at place Gambetta-Les Salins (☎ 04 73 93 13 61; ⓦ gare-routiere-clermont-fd. com), though some buses stop by the *gare SNCF*.
Destinations Le Mont-Dore (3 daily; 1hr 20min); Mende (3 daily; 2hr 55min); St-Étienne (3–5 daily; 1hr 45min–3hr 15min); St Flour (3 daily; 1hr 15min–2hr 40min).

**Tourist office** Place de la Victoire (July & Aug Mon–Fri 9am–7pm, Sat & Sun 10am–7pm; Sept–June Mon–Fri 9am–6pm, Sat & Sun 10am–1pm & 2–6pm; ☎ 04 73 98 65 00, ⓦ clermontferrandtourism.com).

## GETTING AROUND

Everywhere in Clermont-Ferrand is accessible by bus, *navette* or tram. There's a city transport information kiosk, Boutique T2C, at 24 bd Charles-de-Gaulle (☎ 04 73 28 70 00, ⓦ t2c.fr).

**By bike** With 60km of routes in special lanes along the tramline, the city is a joy for cyclists, although not always

flat. Bicycles are available at extremely low prices (€3/day) and for long-term rental from one of the city's thirty-plus "C. vélo" automated rental stations. The office is on av de l'Union Soviétique (Mon–Fri 9am–1pm, & 2–5.30pm, Sat 9.15am–12.15pm & 1–5pm, ⓦ www.c-velo.fr).

## ACCOMMODATION

### CLERMONT-FERRAND
**Albert Elisabeth** 37 av Albert-Elisabeth ☎ 04 73 92 47 41, ⓦ hotel-albertelisabeth.com. Well-run family hotel that's handy for the station. With smart, monochrome rooms and a/c, it offers special weekend rates and breakfast for €8.50. €89

**Dav'hotel** 10 rue des Minimes ☎ 04 73 93 31 49,

ⓦ davhotel.fr. Tucked away in a small street behind the place de Jaude with modern, artsy decor. Rooms adjoining *Le Cosmic* bar tend to be noisy, so specify a quiet room unless you want to hang out till closing time (which is not such a hardship). Breakfast €7.50. €80

★ **Inter-hôtel des Puys** 16 place Delille ☎ 04 73 91 92 06, ⓦ hoteldespuys.com. A modern, three-star offering

**13**

spacious rooms, some with balconies. Its first-rate gourmet restaurant and breakfast room has splendid views of the town and the Puy de Dôme, and there's an indoor garage. Breakfast €16. €90

**Océania** 82 bd François-Mitterrand ☎04 73 29 59 59, ⓦoceaniahotels.com. A central four-star with gym, hammam and jacuzzi, plus a covered garage (€15/night). Rooms offer nice views and there's a good restaurant with a large breakfast buffet €15. €126

**Volcanhôtel** 6 rue Sainte-Rose ☎04 73 19 66 66, ⓦvolcanhotel.fr. Well-located near rue de l'Ange, with

rather plain, no-frills rooms. Avoid the "budget" rooms which are verging on pokey and not worth the money. Breakfast €8.50. €86

**RIOM**

**Le Pacifique** 52 av de Paris ☎04 73 38 15 65, ⓦhotel-lepacifique-riom.com. Good-sized, airy rooms with colourful decor, in a small hotel near the A71. Promotions include a package that includes tickets to Vulcania. Free private parking. Closed mid-Dec to mid-Jan. Breakfast €9. €76

## EATING

The best restaurants in Clermont-Ferrand are around the conspicuously modern covered food market, in place St-Pierre just off rue des Gras.

### CLERMONT-FERRAND

**L'Alambic** 6 rue Ste-Claire ☎04 73 36 17 45, ⓦalambic. restaurant.online.fr. A *terroir* restaurant with a high-end feel, excellent food and service, and mid-range prices. Try the *truffade* or the cassoulet with Puy lentils for €19. Mon & Wed 7–10pm, Tues & Thurs–Sat noon–2pm & 7–10.15pm.

**Amphitryon Capucine** 50 rue Fontgiève ☎04 73 31 38 39, ⓦamphitryoncapucine.com. Great service, quality products and good-value *menus*, especially the *menu Esquisse* at €35. Tues–Sat noon–1.45pm & 7.30–9.30pm.

**Chez Flo** 18 rue du Cheval-Blanc ☎04 73 31 11 52, ⓦchezflo.fr. Difficult to find but worth it: a low-ceilinged, cosy brasserie with smiling service and excellent-value local cuisine. Basic *menu* €15.90, but go, if you can, for the three-course gourmet *menu* at €26. Tues noon–2pm, Wed–Sat noon–2pm & 7.15–10pm.

**Garden Ice Café** 48 place de Jaude ☎04 73 93 40 97, ⓦgardenicecafe.com. Good service, great burgers and friendly banter in this sports-bar-brasserie facing place de Jaude. Dishes from €9.50 and *menus from* €19.80. Mon–Sat 7am–1am, Sun 9am–midnight.

**Le Sisisi** 14 rue Massillon ☎04 73 14 04 28, ⓦlesisisi. com. Cool, contemporary bistro with stripped wooden floors that's popular with night owls due to its late hours. Mains, such as roast pork with hazelnut pesto, start from €17.50. Booking recommended. Tues–Fri noon–3pm & 6.30pm–2am, Sat 6.30pm–2am.

### RIOM

**Le Flamboyant** 21bis rue de l'Horloge ☎04 73 63 07 97, ⓦrestaurant-le-flamboyant.com. This sophisticated restaurant tucked down a pedestrianized street is arguably one of Riom's best, with a sleek, modern (yet unpretentious) feel. The seasonal menus are great value at €35 and include the likes of quail stuffed with foie gras, and local cheeses. Mon, Wed & Sun noon–1.30pm, Tues & Thurs–Sat noon–1.30pm & 7.30–9.45pm.

## DRINKING AND NIGHTLIFE

**101 Club** 3 rue du Coche ⓦoneooneclub.com. Known for its eclectic programme that runs the full gamut from electronica and deep house to funk and pop, as well as regular international DJs. Thus–Sun midnight–5.30am.

**Le Bar d'O** 5 place de la Victoire ☎04 73 91 43 14. This appealing wine bar has a somewhat retro feel (though that's potentially more by accident than design) but is a popular and pleasant choice for a glass or two of wine, especially in summer when you can sit out on the square. Mon & Tues 8am–10pm, Wed–Fri 8am–midnight, Sat 8am–12.30am.

**Les Berthom** 6 place de l'Étoile ☎04 73 31 01 65, ⓦlesberthom.com. A good range of Belgian and French beer at a decent price (as ever with the *Berthom* chain), plus a pleasant setting just off place de Jaude. Mon–Wed 5pm–1am, Thurs & Fri 5pm–2am, Sat 4pm–2am, Sun 4pm–midnight.

**Le Marais** 49 rue Fontgiève ☎04 73 40 06 56, ⓦlemaraisbar.com. Clermont's main gay and lesbian venue has theme nights during the week – from karaoke to drag shows – and disco *soirées* on Fri and Sat. Thurs–Sun 8pm–2am.

## Vichy

**VICHY**, 50km north of Clermont-Ferrand, is famous for two things: its World War II puppet government under Marshal Pétain (see Contexts), and its curative sulphurous **springs**, which attract thousands of ageing and ailing visitors, or *curistes*, every year. The town is almost entirely devoted to catering for its largely elderly, genteel population, which swells several-fold in summer, though attempts are being made to rejuvenate Vichy's image by appealing to a younger, fitness-conscious generation. Still, with Clermont-Ferrand's nightlife so close, young people don't flock here, except in July and August when the rather good riverside **beaches** on the banks of the Allier become a big draw.

There's a real *fin-de-siècle* atmosphere about Vichy, and the best reason to come is to see its fine *belle époque*, Art Nouveau and Art Deco **architecture**, of which a prime example is the **Hôtel de ville** near place Charles-de-Gaulle. The tourist office offers afternoon **tours** (in French) showcasing different periods and also a brochure with suggested walking tours. If you are strolling on your own, you'll find more striking examples in **rue de Russie**, **rue de Belgique** and **rue Alquié**, and around the old town between the church of **St Blaise**, the river and the town's main spring, the **Sources des Célestines**. There are also four parks on the right bank of the Allier, providing pleasant, wooded river walks. The most famous is the **Parc de Napoléon III**, an English garden created for Napoléon III.

## Parc des Sources

**Hall des Sources** Mid-Feb to Dec Mon–Sat 7am–5.30pm • Free

Vichy revolves around the **Parc des Sources**, a stately tree-shaded park that takes up most of the centre. At its north end stands the **Hall des Sources**, an enormous iron-framed greenhouse in which people sit and chat or read newspapers, while the various waters emerge from a large tiled stand in the middle, beside the just-visible remains of the Roman foundation. The *curistes* line up to get their prescribed cupful from the Sources des Célestines, which is the only spring whose water is bottled and widely drunk. The fountains become progressively more sulphurous and foul, with the Source de l'Hôpital, which has its own circular building at the far end of the park, being almost unbelievably nasty. Each of the springs is prescribed for a different ailment and the tradition is that, apart from the Célestines, they must all be drunk on the spot in order to work – a dubious but effective way of drawing in the crowds.

## Thermes Les Dômes Vichy

132 bd des États-Unis • daily 8am–noon & 2–7pm; call to check availability • ☎ 04 70 97 39 59, ⓦ vichy-thermes-domes-hotel.fr

Directly behind the Hall des Sources, on the leafy **Esplanade Napoléon III**, is the Byzantine-style former Grand Établissement Thermal bathhouse, now the **Thermes Les Dômes Vichy**, decorated with Moorish arches, gold-and-blue domes and ceramic panels of voluptuous mermaids. All that remains of the original building is the grand entrance hall, with its fountain and two beautiful murals, *La Bain* and *La Source*, from 1903. Nowadays, Thermes Les Dômes Vichy offers thermal hydrotherapy treatments and health retreats with medical experts in a contemporary facility.

## Church of St-Blaise

Not far from the Parc de Napoléon III on the right bank, the old town boasts the eccentric **church of St-Blaise** at 3 rue Sainte-Cécile. This is actually two churches in one, with a stunning 1931 Art Deco Notre-Dame-des-Malades attached to the original seventeenth-century church. Inside there's an Auvergne Black Virgin which stands surrounded by plaques offered by grateful worshippers who were cured by the sulphurous waters.

| **ARRIVAL AND INFORMATION** | **VICHY** |
|---|---|

**By train** The *gare SNCF* is a 10min walk from the centre, at the end of rue de Paris.

Destinations Clermont-Ferrand (17–29 daily; 30min); Paris-Bercy (7 daily; 2hr 50min).

**By bus** Buses, including services from Ambert (3 daily; 2hr 10min), pull in to the *gare routière* on the corner of rue Doumier and rue Jardet, by the central place Charles-de-Gaulle. There's public transport information on ☎ 04 70 30 17 30.

**Tourist office** 19 rue du Parc (April–June & Sept Mon–Sat 9.30am–noon & 1.30–6.30pm, Sun 3–6pm; July & Aug Mon–Sat 9.30am–7pm, Sun 10am–noon & 2.30–7pm; Oct–March Mon–Sat 9.30am–noon & 1.30–6pm; ☎ 08 25 77 10 10, ⓦ vichy-tourisme.com).

**13**

## ACCOMMODATION

**De Grignan** 7 place Sévigné ☎ 04 70 32 08 11, ⓦ hoteldegrignan.fr. Surprisingly contemporary rooms in this central hotel, some of which have handy kitchenettes. There's also a spa, complete with a hammam and sauna. Good discounts available online. €95.60

★ **Midland** 4 rue de l'Intendance ☎ 04 70 97 48 48, ⓦ hotel-midland.com. The most pleasant of several good-value lodgings in the city, this quiet, grand neo-Baroque

hotel also houses the excellent restaurant *Le Derby's*. Breakfast €10; check the full or half-board options. Closed mid-Nov to mid-April. **€79**

**Du Rhône** 8 rue de Paris ☎ 04 70 98 63 45, ⓦ vichy-hoteldurhone.net. Though the rooms aren't going to win any awards for their design, they are good value and cheerful, and in a good central position. €58

## EATING AND DRINKING

There are several brasseries and cafés in the area around the junction of rue Clemenceau and rue de Paris.

**Maison Decoret** 15 rue du Parc ☎ 04 70 97 65 06, ⓦ maisondecoret.com. A must-try restaurant, with eclectic dishes drawing on flavours from places as diverse as Oaxaca and Marseille. Lunch €45, *menus* €75–125. Mon & Thurs–Sun 12.15–1.30pm & 8–9.15pm; closed last two weeks of Aug and first week of Sept.

**Le Montreize** 22 place d'Allier ☎ 04 70 59 99 44. Everyone's favourite Vichy restaurant, offering traditional

dishes – and best known for the Auvergnat burger (€14), made with local beef, bacon and cheese sauces. *Menus* from €20. Mon–Sat noon–1.30pm & 7–9pm, Sun noon–1.30pm.

**La Table d'Antoine** 8 rue Burnol ☎ 04 70 98 99 71, ⓦ latabledantoine.com. A good, affordable option for haute cuisine, under chef Antoine Suillat. *Menus* from €26.90. Tues–Sat 12.15–1pm & 7.30–8.45pm (8.30pm in winter), Sun 12.15–1pm.

## SHOPPING

★ **Galerie de l'Opéra** 6 rue du Casino ☎ 04 70 31 90 27. One of the delights of a visit to Vichy is hunting for *objets d'art*; this is the best shop, with the highly knowledgeable

Alain Cannet de Valdère at your service. Wed–Sun noon–6pm, Mon & Tues by appointment only.

# The Monts-Dore

The **Monts-Dore**, part of the Parc Naturel Régional des Volcans d'Auvergne (see page 687), lie about 50km southwest of Clermont. Volcanic in origin – the main period of activity was around five million years ago – they are much more rugged and more obviously mountainous than their gentler, younger neighbours, the Monts-Dômes. Their centre is the precipitous, plunging valley of the River Dordogne, which rises on the slopes of the **Puy de Sancy**, at 1885m the highest point in the Massif Central, just above the little town of **Le Mont-Dore**.

## Le Mont-Dore

Squeezed out along the narrow wooded valley of the infant Dordogne, grey-slated **LE MONT-DORE** is the gateway to the region. An altogether wholesome and civilized sort of place, it's a long-established spa resort, with Roman remains testifying to just how old it is. Its popularity goes back to the eighteenth century, when roads replaced the old mule paths and made access possible, but reached its apogee with the opening of the railway around 1900.

### Établissement Thermal

Mon–Sat early April to early Nov • From €45 • ☎ 04 73 65 05 10, ⓦ chainethermale.fr

The **Établissement Thermal** – the baths, which give Le Mont-Dore its *raison d'être* – are in the middle of town and certainly worth visiting. Early every morning, the *curistes* stream into the neo-Byzantine halls – an extravaganza of tiles, striped columns and ornate ironwork – hoping for a remedy in this self-proclaimed "world centre for treatment of asthma".

### Puy de Sancy

**Cable car** May–June, Sept & Oct daily 9am–noon 1.30–5pm; July & Aug daily 9am–6pm • €10.20 return

For walkers the principal attraction of Le Mont-Dore is the nearby **Puy de Sancy** (1885m), which the Grande Randonnée (GR) 4 hiking trail passes. Accessible by **cable car** since 1936, it's the highest mountain in the Massif Central and one of the most visited sights in the region. Formerly known as the "Mountain of the Cross" thanks to the crucifix on the summit, its jagged skyline blocks the head of the Dordogne valley, 3km away.

## Orcival

Some 27km southwest of Clermont and about 20km north of Le Mont-Dore, lush pastures and green hills punctuated by the abrupt eruptions of the *puys* enclose the small village of **ORCIVAL**. A pretty place founded by the monks of La Chaise-Dieu (see page 704) in the twelfth century, it makes a suitable base for hiking in the region.

### Notre-Dame d'Orcival

Daily: Easter–Nov 8am–noon & 2–7.30pm; Nov–Easter 8am–6pm • Free

Orcival is dominated by the stunning twelfth-century church of **Notre-Dame d'Orcival**, built from dark-grey volcanic stone and fanned with tiny chapels. One of five major Lower Auvergne Romanesque churches, it counted no fewer than 24 priests in the mid-1200s, and the ironwork on the north door, with its curious forged human head motif, dates from that era. Inside, attention focuses on the choir, neatly and harmoniously contained by the semicircle of pillars defining the ambulatory. Mounted on a stone column in the centre is the celebrated **Virgin of Orcival**, a gilded and enamelled twelfth-century statue; she has been the object of a popular cult since the Middle Ages and is still carried through the streets on Ascension Day.

## St-Nectaire and around

**ST-NECTAIRE** lies 26km southeast of Orcival, midway between Le Mont-Dore and Issoire. It comprises the old village of **St-Nectaire-le-Haut**, overlooked by the magnificent Romanesque **church of St-Nectaire** and the tiny spa of **St-Nectaire-le-Bas**, whose main street is lined with grand but fading *belle époque* hotels. The two sections are separated by a **salt marsh**, one of the biggest in France and an area of protected plant life. Among the town's other curiosities are caverns, the **Grottes de Cornadore** (daily 10am–noon & 2–6/7pm; €6.90; ☎04 73 88 57 97, ✺grottes-du-cornadore. com), former underground Roman baths dug into 340-million-year-old granite, plus an exhibition on the cheese-making process and the chance to visit a ripening cellar at the **Maison du Fromage** (daily: 10am–noon & 2–7pm; €5.90; ☎04 73 88 57 96, ✺maison-du-fromage.com).

For walks out of St-Nectaire, take the D150 past the church through the old village towards the **Puy de Mazeyres** (919m), and turn up a path to the right for the final climb to the summit (1hr). From here you get a superb aerial view of the surrounding countryside, which is notable for its menhirs and other prehistoric megaliths; the

---

### ST-NECTAIRE CHEESE

The cheese of **St-Nectaire** has been growing in reputation ever since Louis XIV had it regularly served at his table, and only cheeses made from herds grazing in a limited area to the south of the Monts-Dore are entitled to the *appellation d'origine contrôlée*, the governmental agricultural quality control. The cheese is made in two stages: first, a white creamy cheese or *tomme* is produced. This is then matured for two to three months in a cellar; the resulting mould on the skin produces the characteristic smell, taste and yellowy-grey colour. There are, in fact, two kinds of St-Nectaire cheese: **fermier** and **laitier**. The *fermier* (farmhouse) is the strongest and tastiest, and some of it is still made entirely on local farms, using just the milk from one herd of cows. Increasingly, however, farmers make the *tomme* using the milk of lots of different herds and then sell it on to wholesalers to produce the *laitier* (dairy) cheese, which is more of an industrial product, with an automated refining stage.

**13**

tourist office has information on how to find them. Alternatively, follow the D966 along the Couze de Chambon valley to **Saillant**, where the stream cascades down a high lava rock face in the middle of the village.

## Basilica of St-Nectaire

Daily: April–Oct 9am–7pm; Nov–March 10am–5pm • Free

Like the church in Orcival and Notre-Dame-du-Port in Clermont, the **Basilica of St-Nectaire** is one of the most striking examples of the Auvergne's Romanesque architecture. The carved capitals around the apse retain the tantalizing hues of the paint that once covered the whole interior, while the church's treasures include a magnificent gilded bust of St Baudime (the third-century missionary of the Auvergne, parish founder and purported brother of Saint Nectarius), a polychrome *Virgin in Majesty* and two enamelled plaques, all dating from the twelfth century.

## Besse

Fifteen or so kilometres south of St-Nectaire, and 11km south of the sleepy little village of Murol, **BESSE** is one of the prettiest and oldest villages in the region. Its fascinating winding streets of lava-built houses – some fifteenth-century – sit atop the valley of the Couze de Pavin, with one of the original fortified town **gates** still in place at the upper end of the village.

Besse became wealthy due to its role as the principal market for the farms on the eastern slopes of the Monts-Dore, and its cooperative is still one of the main producers of St-Nectaire cheese (see page 695). The annual **festivals** of the Montée and Dévalade, marking the ascent of the herds to the high pastures in July and their descent in autumn, are still celebrated by the procession of the Black Virgin of Vassivière from the **church of St-André** in Besse to the chapel of **La Vassivière**, west of **Lac Pavin**, and her journey back again in autumn (July 2 and the first Sun after Sept 21).

## Lac Pavin and around

**Lac Pavin** lies 5km west of Besse, on the way to the purpose-built downhill ski resort of **Super-Besse** (both are connected to Besse by an hourly *navette*). It's a perfect volcanic lake, filling the now wooded crater. The D978 passes the lake and the nearby **Puy de Montchal**, whose summit (1407m) gives you a fine view over several other lakes and the rolling plateau south towards Égliseneuve-d'Entraigues, 13km away by road.

---

### ARRIVAL AND INFORMATION                                    THE MONTS-DORE

**LE MONT-DORE**

**By train** The *gare SNCF* is at av Guyot-Dessaigne at the entrance to the town; a 10min walk down av des Belges gets you to the centre.

**By bus** The *gare routière* is next to the *gare SNCF*. Buses from Clermont-Ferrand and Vichy are operated by Faure (☎ 04 73 39 97 15) and Cars André (☎ 04 71 78 00 49) and cost €2. In winter, there is an hourly bus service from Besse to Super-Besse (€1.60) and a free continuous shuttle service between ski stations (ⓦ sancy.com).

Destinations Clermont-Ferrand (4–5 daily; 1hr 35min); Sancy (July & Aug 4–5 daily; 15min).

**Tourist office** 25 av de la Libération (Jan, March & Dec 9am–noon & 2–6pm; Feb daily 9am–6.30pm; Apri, May & Sept–Oct Mon–Sat 9am–noon & 2–6pm, Sun 10am–noon & 2–7.30pm; July & Aug Mon–Sat 9am–6.30pm, Sun 9am–12.30pm & 2–6pm; Nov Mon–Sat 9am–noon & 2–5pm; ☎ 04 73 65 20 21, ⓦ sancy.com). The helpful staff will advise you about walking, cycling and skiing possibilities, as well as offer excursions to otherwise inaccessible places in the area.

---

### ACCOMMODATION AND EATING

**LE MONT-DORE**

**Grand Hôtel** 2 rue Meynadier ☎ 04 73 65 02 64, ⓦ hotel-mont-dore.com. A stately nineteenth-century mansion with charming owners, who will organize tours,

family activities and just about everything else for you. Good off-season offers. Breakfast €8.50. **€77**

**Helvétia** 5 rue de la Saigne ☎ 04 73 65 26 73, ⓦ helvetia-montdore.com. Homely, welcoming hotel by the river, offering good half- and full-board rates. Breakfast €6.80. Closed mid-Oct to mid-Dec. **€52**

### ORCIVAL
**Camping de la Haute-Sioule** St-Bonnet-Près-Orcival ☎ 04 73 65 83 32, ⓦ camping-auvergne.info. Some 5km north of the village on a hillside with wonderful views of the surrounding mountains, this is a delightful base for the summer season. Closed Oct–April. **€16.60**

### ST-NECTAIRE
**Les Bains Romains** ☎ 04 73 88 57 00, ⓦ hotel-bains-romains.com. Near the town centre, this top-notch Mercure hotel, converted from an old baths, offers a spa with treatments, elegant sitting areas, chic bedrooms and plush

swimming pool. The restaurant is also very good (*mains* from €20). Breakfast €15.60. Good discounts available online. **€83**
**De la Paix** ☎ 04 73 88 49 07, ⓦ hotel-delapaix.net. This hotel, at the base of the GR30 footpath below the church, offers airy, comfortable rooms and a reasonably priced restaurant (local *menus* from €15). Breakfast €8.50. **€55**

### MUROL
**Le Grillon** Lac Chambon ☎ 04 73 88 60 66, ⓦ hotel-grillon.com. This cute lakeside hotel has bright, somewhat old-fashioned rooms, of which some have balconies. The restaurant serves local specialities, on the terrace if desired; the half-board offers are excellent, and there are big discounts for multi-night stays. Closed mid-Nov to Feb. Breakfast €10. **€60**

## The Monts du Cantal

The **Monts du Cantal**, also known as the Cantal Massif, forms the most southerly extension of the Parc des Volcans (see page 687). Still nearly 80km in diameter and once 3000m high, it is one of the world's largest volcanoes (albeit extinct), shaped like a wheel without a rim. The hub of the Monts du Cantal is formed by the three great conical peaks that survived the erosion of the original single cone: **Plomb du Cantal** (1855m), **Puy Mary** (1787m) and **Puy de Peyre-Arse** (1686m).

From this centre a series of deep-cut wooded valleys radiates out like spokes. The most notable are the **valley of Mandailles** and the **valleys of the Cère and Alagnon** in the southwest, where the road and rail line run, and in the north the **valleys of Falgoux and the Rhue**. Between the valleys, especially on the north side, are huge expanses of gently sloping grassland, including the **Plateau du Limon**. This grassland has for centuries been the mainstay of life in the Cantal, as summer pasture for the cows whose milk makes the firm yellow **Cantal cheese** which is pressed in the form of great crusty drums. But this tradition has long been in serious decline; as elsewhere, many of the herds are now beef cattle and tourism is on the increase, based in particular around walking, horseriding and skiing.

### Aurillac
**AURILLAC**, the lively provincial capital of the Cantal, lies on the west side of the mountains, 98km east of Brive and 160km from Clermont-Ferrand. Though it has good mainline train connections and has a population of around 30,000, it remains one of the most out-of-the-way French provincial capitals. The annual **international street theatre festival** (ⓦ aurillac.net), held in the last week in August, attracts over 400 performance companies from all over Europe and fills the town with rather more exotic characters than are normally to be seen in these parts.

---

### ROUTE DES CRÊTES
The sinuous and spectacular **Route des Crêtes** (mountain ridge road) between Aurillac and Tournemire (30km) gives you the best view of the Cantal mountain range, and reaches a pass at the Col de Bruel (1308m). Good stops include Croix de Cheules, for a commanding view over the valleys below, and the village of St-Jean-de-Dône, which has a Templar chapel. From Tournemire, return to Aurillac via St-Cernin or continue to Salers. The *Chalet du Puy Mary* restaurant (ⓦ lepuymary.com), at Pas de Peyrol on the junction of the D680 and the D17, has a staggering westerly view, perfect for watching the sunset over the mountains. These roads close in the winter; check in Aurillac before you set off.

**13**

The most interesting area of Aurillac is the kernel of old streets, now largely pedestrianized and full of good shops, just northeast of the central **place du Square**. **Rue Duclaux** leads through to the attractive **place de l'Hôtel-de-Ville**, where big markets are held (Wed & Sat) in the shadow of the handsome orange-and-grey **Hôtel de Ville**, built in Neoclassical style in 1803. Beyond it, the continuation of **rue des Forgerons** leads to the beautiful little **place St-Géraud**, with a Romanesque house that was probably part of the original abbey guesthouse, and the externally rather unprepossessing **church of St-Géraud**, which nonetheless has a beautifully ribbed late Gothic ceiling.

### Muséum des Volcans

Rue du Château Saint-Étienne • Mid-June to Aug Tues–Fri 10am–noon & 2–6pm; Sept to mid-June Tues–Fri 2–6pm • €5 • ☏ 04 71 48 07 00

On a steep bluff overlooking the east end of town towers the eleventh-century keep of the Château St-Étienne. The keep holds the town's most worthwhile museum, the **Muséum des Volcans**, which has a good section on the relationship between humankind and volcanoes and a splendid view over the mountains to the east.

### ARRIVAL AND INFORMATION

AURILLAC

**By train** The *gare SNCF* is on place Sémard, a 10min walk from the central place du Square along av de la République and rue de la Gare.

Destinations Clermont-Ferrand (6 daily; 2hr 25min); Toulouse (4 daily; 3hr 50min).

**By bus** The *gare routière* is next to the *gare SNCF*. Bus timetables to local destinations are online at ⓦ stabus.fr.

**Tourist office** 7 rue des Carmes (Jan–March & Nov–Dec Mon–Sat 9.30am–noon & 1.30–5.30pm; April–June Mon–Sat 9am–noon & 1.30–6pm; July & Aug Mon–Sat 9am–12.30pm & 1.30–7pm, Sun 10am–3pm; Sept Mon–Sat 9am–noon & 1.30–6.30pm; ☏ 04 71 48 46 58, ⓦ www. iaurillac.com).

### ACCOMMODATION

★ **Des Carmes** 20 rue des Carmes ☏ 04 71 48 01 69, ⓦ hoteldescarmes.fr. A real find in a great, central position. Rooms are sophisticated and contemporary in style with a monochrome palette, and there's a great restaurant downstairs. **€98**

**Grand Hôtel de Bordeaux** 2 av de la République ☏ 04 71 48 01 84, ⓦ hotel-de-bordeaux.fr. An Aurillacoise institution for 150 years, set in a nineteenth-century mansion. Now part of Best Western, they offer three-star accommodation with modern, airy bedrooms and attentive service. Breakfast €12. **€92**

**La Thomasse** 26 rue du Docteur-Louis-Mallet ☏ 04 71 48 26 47, ⓦ hotel-la-thomasse.com. This appealing ivy-

clad hotel is just ten-minutes' drive from the centre of town in a suburban location – but don't let that put you off. Once inside, it feels more like a country retreat, with cosy, light-filled rooms, a bar and an outdoor pool. **€89**

**Rocher du Cerf** Laveissière, 40km southwest of Aurillac ☏ 04 71 49 50 14, ⓦ lerocherducerf.com. A pretty spa chalet with all its rooms offering memorable views of the Monts du Cantal. Half-board packages for two are very competitive. Breakfast €7.50. **€65**

**Du Square** 15 place du Square ☏ 04 71 48 24 72, ⓦ hotel-le-square.com. Smart, comfortable hotel near the centre of town, some rooms with balconies. A restaurant is attached (menus from €14.90). Breakfast €8. **€59**

### EATING AND DRINKING

★ **L'Arsène sur Cour** 18 rue Arsène-Vermenouze ☏ 04 71 48 48 97, ⓦ aurillac-restaurant.com. This cosy restaurant serves up a small but decent menu with an emphasis on beef (*côte de boeuf* €45) and hearty salads. Save room for the delectable desserts. Book ahead in summer to get a table on the terrace. Tues–Fri noon–2pm

& 7–9pm, Sat noon–2pm & 7–10pm.

**Kerry Pub** 6 rue du Consulat ☏ 04 71 48 64 91. Lively Irish pub that shows sports and serves Irish and local beer. It's the best bet for a drink midweek when everywhere else has closed. Tues–Sat 11am–2pm.

## Salers

**SALERS** lies 42km north of Aurillac, at the foot of the northwest slopes of the Cantal and within sight of the Puy Violent. Scarcely altered in size or aspect since its sixteenth-century heyday, it remains an extraordinarily homogeneous example of the architecture of that time. If things appear rather grand for a place so small, it's because the town became the administrative centre for the highlands of the Auvergne in 1564, and home

**13**

of its magistrates. Exploiting this history is really all it has left, but Salers still makes a very worthwhile visit.

If you arrive by the Puy Mary road, you'll enter town near the **church**, which is worth a look for the super-naturalistic statuary of the *Entombment of Christ* (1496). From here, the cobbled **rue du Beffroi** leads uphill, under the massive clock tower, and into the central **place Tyssandier-d'Escous**. This is a glorious little square, surrounded by fifteenth-century mansions with pepper-pot turrets, mullioned windows and carved lintels, among them the **Maison des Templiers**, which houses the small **Musée de Salers**. Before you leave town, head out to the **Promenade de Barrouze** for the view out across the surrounding green hills and the Puy Violent.

### Musée de Salers

Rue des Templiers • April–June, Sept & Oct Mon–Thurs & Sun 10am–12.30pm & 2–5.30pm, Sat 2–5.30pm; July & Aug Mon–Thurs & Sun 10am–12.30pm & 2–6.30pm, Sat 2–6.30pm • €5 • ☎ 04 71 40 75 97

Though the **Musée de Salers** itself is rather dull, with exhibitions on the Salers cattle breed, traditional costumes and the local cheese-making industry, it's worth having a look at the vaulted ceiling of the entrance passageway, with its carved lions and heads of saints, such as that of St John the Baptist framed by wild flowing hair.

**Tourist office** Place Tyssandier-d'Escous (daily 9.30am– 7pm; ☎ 04 71 40 58 08, ⓦ salers-tourisme.fr).

### ACCOMMODATION AND EATING

**Le Gerfaut** Rte du Puy-Mary ☎ 04 71 40 75 75, ⓦ salers-hotel-gerfaut.com. Luxurious yet affordable, with stunning views and a small swimming pool, this is probably the nicest option in Salers. The restaurant offers meals to residents, with half-board options. Closed mid-Nov to Easter. **€88**

**Des Remparts** Promenade de Barrouze ☎ 04 71 40 70 33, ⓦ salers-hotel-remparts.com. Large, modern, comfortable rooms, in an attractive building in the centre of the village. Its excellent restaurant specializes in Auvergnat cuisine (*menus* from €21). Breakfast €11. **€108**

## Murat

**MURAT**, on the eastern edge of the Cantal, is the closest town to the high peaks and a busy little place, its cafés and shops uncharacteristically bustling for this region. It is also the easiest to access, lying on the N122 road and main train line, about 40km southwest of Salers. Rather than any particular sight, it's the ensemble of grey stone houses, nestled against the backdrop of the steep basalt cliffs of the **Rocher Bonnevie**, that attracts – especially as you approach from the east along the D680. Many of the houses date from the fifteenth and sixteenth centuries and are packed in together on the town's medieval lanes, which meander around castle ruins and are overlooked by a huge white statue of the Virgin Mary. Facing the town, perched on the distinctive mound of the **Rocher Bredons**, by the village of **Albepierre**, there's the lovely Romanesque **Église de Bredons** (July & Aug Tues–Sun 2–5pm; Sept–June arrange a viewing at the *mairie* of Albepierre or call ☎ 04 71 20 02 80) which contains some wonderful eighteenth-century altarpieces.

### Maison de la Faune

Place de l'Hôtel-de-ville • Ask at the *mairie* for opening hours • €4.80 • ☎ 04 71 20 00 52, ⓦ murat.fr

One of Murat's finest sixteenth-century buildings opens to the public in summer as the **Maison de la Faune** (the House of Fauna), with an impressive exhibition on the wildlife of the Parc des Volcans. Displays contain stuffed animals such as mountain goats and weasels, birds including swallows and goldfinches, and numerous cabinets of butterflies and other insects.

**By train** The *gare SNCF* is on the main road, av du Dr Louis-Mallet.

**Tourist office** Place de l'Hôtel-de-ville (Mon–Fri 8.30am–noon & 1.30–5pm, Sat 9am–noon; ☎ 04 71 20 09 47, ⓦ murat.fr).

**13**

## ACCOMMODATION AND EATING

**Les Messageries** 18 av du Dr-Mallet ☎04 71 20 04 04, ⓦhotel-les-messageries.com. Comfortable hotel with family rooms, a gym, a skating rink in winter and a restaurant serving hearty meals (€29.90), including home-made *terrines* and fruit tarts. In high season (Feb & Aug), half-board is compulsory and a two-night stay the minimum, otherwise breakfast is €10. **€77**

**Les Stalapos** rue du Stade ☎04 71 20 01 83, ⓦmurat. fr. A cheerful, shady municipal campsite below the *gare SNCF*, with free wi-fi throughout and lots of good facilities. Closed Oct–April. **€9.40**

## St-Flour

Seat of a fourteenth-century bishopric, **ST-FLOUR** stands dramatically on a cliff-girt basalt promontory above the River Ander, 92km west of Le Puy and 92km south of Clermont-Ferrand. Prosperous in the Middle Ages because of its strategic position on the main road from northern France to Languedoc and the proximity of the grasslands of the Cantal, whose herds provided the raw materials for its tanning and leather industries, it fell into somnolent decline in modern times, only partially reversed in the last thirty-odd years.

The wedge of old streets that occupies the point of the promontory surrounding the cathedral has considerable charm and is the main attraction. The best time to come is on a Saturday morning when the old town fills up with **market stalls** selling sausages, cheese and other local produce. If you're in a car, you can park it in the chestnut-shaded square, **Les Promenades**. The narrow streets of the old town lead off from Les Promenades and converge on the **place d'Armes**, with its **cathedral**, some attractive old arcaded buildings housing a couple of cafés, and the town's two **museums**.

### Cathédrale St-Pierre

Place d'Armes • Jan–June & Sept–Dec daily 9am–6pm; July & Aug daily 8.30am–7pm • Free

The fourteenth-century **Cathédrale St-Pierre** backs onto the edge of the cliff, with a terrace giving good views out over the countryside. The Gothic grey volcanic exterior is fairly run of the mill, but inside you will see a fine vaulted ceiling and a number of works of art including some frescoes and most notably a carved, painted woodcarving of a Black Christ with a strikingly serene expression, dating from the thirteenth century.

### Musée Alfred Douët

17 place d'Armes • April–June & Oct Wed–Sat 2–6pm; July–Sept daily 10.30am–6.30pm; Nov–March Thurs & Fri 2–5pm; • €4 • ☎04 71 60 44 99, ⓦmusee-douet.com

At the north end of the place d'Armes, in a fine fourteenth-century building, the **Musée Alfred Douët** houses a private collection of French, Italian and Flemish artworks as well as tapestries, weapons and antique furniture. The view from the cliffs behind the museum gives a sense of St-Flour's impregnable position.

### Musée de la Haute-Auvergne

1 place d'Armes • April–June & Oct Wed–Sat 2–6pm; July–Sept daily 10.30am–6.30pm; Nov–March Thurs & Fri 2–5pm • €6.50 • ☎04 71 60 22 32

At the south end of the place d'Armes, the current *hôtel de ville*, formerly the episcopal palace (1610), acts as the interesting **Musée de la Haute-Auvergne**, whose collections include some beautifully carved Auvergnat furniture. The former bishop's private chapel houses some twelfth-century treasures, and also on display are a range of exquisitely made traditional musical instruments, such as the *cabrette*, a kind of accordion peculiar to the Auvergne.

## ARRIVAL AND INFORMATION

ST-FLOUR

**By train** The *gare SNCF* is on av Charles-de-Gaulle in the lower town. A few trains from Clermont-Ferrand and Aurillac stop here, but most journeys involve changing at Neussargues onto a SNCF bus, which can drop you off on the

Promenades in the old town, saving you the walk up.

**Tourist office** 17bis place d'Armes (April & mid-Sept to Oct Mon–Sat 9am–noon & 2–6pm; May Mon–Sat 9am–noon & 2–6pm, Sun 10am–12.30pm & 2.30–5pm; June & early Sept Mon–Sat 9am–12.30pm & 2–6.30pm, Sun 10am– 12.30pm & 2.30–5.30pm; July & Aug Mon–Sat 9am–7pm, Sun 10am–12.30pm & 2.30–6pm; Nov–March Mon–Fri 9am–noon & 2–6pm, Sat 9.30am–12.30pm; ☎ 04 71 60 22 50, ⓦ saint-flour.com).

## ACCOMMODATION AND EATING

**Grand Hôtel de l'Europe** 12–13 Cours Spy-des-Ternes ☎ 04 71 60 03 64, ⓦ saint-flour-europe.com. Well-sited hotel just outside the historic centre in front of the main free municipal car park. All rooms have great views, satellite TV and safes. The restaurant has a panoramic view and serves good local dishes. Breakfast €10.90. €64

**La Maison des Planchettes** 7 rue des Planchettes ☎ 04 71 60 10 08, ⓦ hotelrestaurantlesplanchettes.fr. Old-style hotel in a magnificent building, which offers full board in simple yet comfortable rooms at low prices. The good Auvergnat restaurant attached has *menus* from €13. Breakfast included with the half-board option, otherwise €8. €73

# Le Puy-en-Velay

Right in the middle of the Massif Central, **LE PUY-EN-VELAY**, often shortened to Le Puy, is one of the most remarkable towns in the whole of France, with a landscape and architecture that are totally theatrical. Slung between the higher mountains to east and west, the countryside erupts in a chaos of volcanic acne: everywhere is a confusion of abrupt conical hills, scarred with dark outcrops of rock and topknotted with woods. Even in the centre of the town, these volcanic thrusts burst through. Le Puy is also somewhat inaccessible: the three main roads out all cross passes that are more than 1000m high, which causes problems in winter.

In the past, Le Puy enjoyed influence and prosperity because of its ecclesiastical institutions, which were supported in part by the production of the town's famous green lentils (*lentilles vertes*). Recently, however, Le Puy has fallen somewhat on hard times, and its traditional industries – tanning and lace – have essentially gone bust. However, in the maze of steep cobbled streets and steps that terrace the **Rocher Corneille**, lacemakers still do a fine trade, with their doilies and shawls hanging enticingly outside souvenir shops. Le Puy was – and still is, to a lesser extent – also a centre for pilgrims embarking on the 1600km trek to **Santiago de Compostela** (history has it that Le Puy's Bishop Godescalk was the first pilgrim to make the journey, in the tenth century). The specific starting point is **place du Plot**, scene of a lively Saturday market, and **rue St-Jacques**.

If you happen to be in town in the third week of September you are in luck: the five-day **King of the Birds** festival engulfs the old town in a colourful feast of Renaissance costumes (ⓦ roideloiseau.com). The event celebrates the traditional bird-hunting competition introduced to Le Puy by Charles V in 1524, where the winner would be proclaimed "king" for a year. The modern-day festival celebrated its thirtieth edition in 2015 and brings in some six thousand costumed revellers each year.

## Notre-Dame-de-France

**Climb** Daily: mid-March to April 9am–6pm; May, June & Sept 9am–7pm; July & Aug 9am–7.30pm; Oct to mid-Nov & Feb to mid-March 10am–5pm • €4 • ☎ 04 71 04 11 33

It would be hard to lose your bearings in Le Puy – wherever you go there's no losing sight of the **Notre-Dame-de-France**, the colossal, brick-red statue of the Virgin and Child that towers above the town on the **Rocher Corneille**, 755m above sea level and 130m above the lower town. The Virgin was cast in 1860 from 213 guns captured at Sebastopol and painted red to match the tiled roofs below. Renovated in 2012, visitors can climb up to the statue's base and, irreverent though it may seem, even up inside it. From here you get stunning views of the city, the church of St-Michel atop its needle-pointed pinnacle a few hundred metres northwest, and the surrounding volcanic countryside.

**13**

## Cathédrale Notre-Dame-du-Puy

Daily: mid-July to mid-Aug 6.30am–10pm; mid-Aug to mid-July 6.30am–7pm • Free • ☎ 04 71 05 98 74, ⓦ cathedraledupuy.org

The main focus in the **old town** is the Byzantine-looking **Cathédrale Notre-Dame-du-Puy**, begun in the eleventh century and decorated with multicoloured layers of stone and mosaic patterns and roofed with a line of six domes. It's best approached up the steep, cobbled rue des Tables, where you get the full theatrical force of its five-storey west front towering above you. In the rather exotic eastern gloom of the interior, a black-faced Virgin in spreading lace and golden robes stands on the main altar, the copy of a revered original destroyed during the Revolution; another copy is still paraded through the town every August 15. Don't miss the so-called **Fever Stone**, whose origins may have been as a prehistoric dolmen and which was reputed to have the power of curing fevers. Other treasures are displayed at the back of the church in the sacristy, beyond which is the entrance to the exceptionally beautiful eleventh- and twelfth-century **cloister**, with its carved capitals and one of the oldest wrought-iron gates in France. Its chapterhouse has a Byzantine-inspired fresco of the Crucifixion painted around 1200. The surrounding ecclesiastical buildings and the **place du For**, on the south side of the cathedral, all date from the same period and form a remarkable ensemble.

## Hôtel Dieu

2 rue Becdelièvre • mid-April to early Nov Tues–Sun 1.30–6.30pm • Free • ☎ 04 71 07 00 00, ⓦ hoteldieu.info

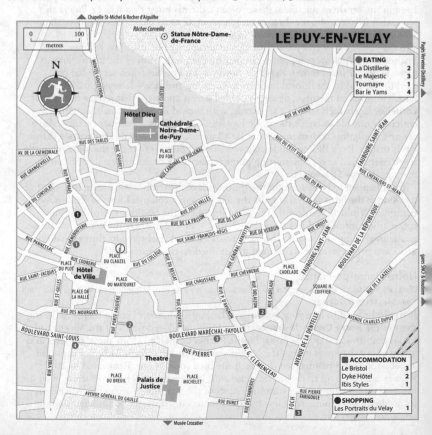

Next to the cathedral, housed in the old hospital of Le Puy, which was still operating until the 1980s, is the **Hôtel Dieu**, a modern museum of regional history that uses extensive audiovisual aids. Ask to be shown the reconstructed ancient pharmacy in the basement, the best room in the museum, which is not always open because it needs constant surveillance.

## Chapelle St-Michel d'Aiguilhe

Daily: Feb to mid-March 2–5pm; mid-March to April & Oct to mid-Nov 9.30am–5.30pm; May to early July & Sept 9am–6.30pm; mid-July to Aug 9am–7pm; Christmas hols 2–5pm • €3.50 • ☎ 04 71 09 50 03, ⓦ rochersaintmichel.fr

It's a fifteen-minute, signposted walk from the cathedral to the **Chapelle- St-Michel**, perched atop the 82m-high needle-pointed lava pinnacle of the **Rocher d'Aiguilhe**. The Romanesque church, built on Bishop Godescalk's return from his pilgrimage to Santiago de Compostela and consecrated in 962, is a beauty in its own right, and its improbable situation atop this striking column of rock is quite extraordinary – it's a long haul up 265 steps to the entrance. In 1275, the building's bell tower fell down and was not reconstructed until the nineteenth century, when the plaster in the chapel was removed and the beautiful original frescoes uncovered. In the **sanctuary**, there is a display of sacred artefacts that had been hidden in the altar and were only discovered in 1955; among these items is a wooden crucifix, thought to have been brought from Spain by a pilgrim.

## ARRIVAL AND INFORMATION
### LE PUY-EN-VELAY

**By train** The *gare SNCF* is on place du Maréchal-Leclerc, around a 15min walk from the central place du Clauzel. Destinations Clermont-Ferrand (2–3 daily; 2hr 10min); Lyon (5–8 daily; 2hr 15min); St-Étienne (6–8 daily; 1hr 30min).

**By bus** The *gare routière* faces the *gare SNCF* on place du Maréchal-Leclerc. There is one direct bus daily to Clermont-Ferrand (2hr 45min), but most involve changing on to a

SNCF train at St-Georges-d'Aurac or Issoire.

**Tourist office** 2 place du Clauzel (Easter–June & Sept Mon–Fri 8.30am–noon & 1.30–6pm, Sat 9am–12.30pm & 2–5.30pm, Sun 10am–12.30pm & 2–5pm; July & Aug Mon–Sat 8.30am–7pm, Sun 10am–12.30pm & 2–5pm; Oct–Easter Mon–Sat 8.30am–noon & 1.30–5.45pm, Sun 10am–noon; ☎ 04 71 09 38 41, ⓦ ot-lepuyenvelay.fr).

## ACCOMMODATION

**Le Bristol** 9 av Foch ☎ 04 71 09 13 38, ⓦ hotelbristol-lepuy.com. A former pilgrims' hostel in one of the area's oldest buildings. The restaurant, *La Table de Félix*, offers regional dishes from €9.60. Good half-board options. Breakfast €10; garage parking €5. **€72**

**Dyke Hôtel** 37 bd du Maréchal-Fayolle ☎ 04 71 09 05 30, ⓦ dykehotel.fr. This basic two-star is five minutes' walk from the train station and ten minutes from the town's historic area, and so is always popular – make sure to book

ahead. Cars can park in the private garage for €6; motorbikes and bicycles are free. Breakfast €6.50. **€51**

**Ibis Styles** 47 bd du Maréchal-Fayolle ☎ 04 71 09 32 36, ⓦ ibis.com. A convenient location (especially for drivers) and great-value family suites. The attached restaurant, *Taverne de Maître Kanter*, serves beautifully presented food in a lively venue, with *menus* from €28. The wi-fi's reliable, too. Garage €6. Breakfast included. **€111**

## EATING AND DRINKING

**La Distillerie** 11 rue porte Aiguière ☎ 04 71 04 91 12, ⓦ brasserie-la-distillerie.fr. Le Puy's most atmospheric pub/brasserie; bold brass and wood furnishing in a spot tucked away from the main street in a shaded terrace. It offers an impressive selection of regional speciality beers and liqueurs, including local favourite *verveine*, a sweet herbal concoction. Mon–Fri 9am–1pm, Sat 9am–1.30pm.

★ **Le Majestic** 8 bd du Maréchal-Fayolle ☎ 04 71 09 06 30. With a classy ambiance and good location, this brasserie serves high-end versions of regional food at a decent price.

*Menus* including salads for €17.50 and a small *terrasse* at the back. Mon–Sat 8am–1am, Sun 10am–8pm.

**Tournayre** 12 rue Chènebouterie ☎ 04 71 09 58 94, ⓦ restaurant-tournayre.com. A local favourite, located in a seventeenth-century building with a vaulted ceiling, specializing in regional food (*menus* €30–58). Wed–Sat noon–2pm. & 7.30–9pm, Sun noon–2pm.

**Bar le Yams** 1 place Laines ☎ 04 61 09 72 36. A lively brasserie for an evening drink and the best place to try the local green lentil beer, which is available in many of Le Puy's bars and clubs. Daily 7pm–1am.

**13**

## SHOPPING

★ **Les Portraits du Velay** 10 rue Raphaël ☎04 71 06 00 94, ⓦlacebook.net. Shopping in Le Puy means buying traditional lace and embroidery goods; this shop, opened by lacemaker Didier in 1998, offers the best selection. Daily 9.30am–12.30pm & 2.30–6.30pm.

# North of Le Puy

**North of Le Puy**, the D906 crosses a vast and terminally depopulated area of pine-clad uplands – now the **Parc Naturel Régional Livradois-Forez** – and continues all the way to Vichy, via the historic town of **La Chaise-Dieu** and the old industrial centre of **Ambert**.

## La Chaise-Dieu

The little town of **LA CHAISE-DIEU** is renowned for the **Abbey church of St-Robert** whose square towers dominate the town. In July and August, an old diesel **panoramic train** runs between here and Ambert (from €16 return; ☎04 73 82 43 88, ⓦagrivap.fr), a leisurely and hugely enjoyable way to see the region.

### Abbey church of St-Robert

**Abbey church** March–May & Oct Mon–Sat 9am–noon & 2–6pm, Sun 2–6pm; June to mid Aug & Sept Mon–Sat 9am–noon & 2–6.30pm, Sun 2–6.30pm; Nov–Feb Mon–Sat 9am–noon & 2–5pm, Sun 2–5pm; closed second fortnight in Aug • €4 • ☎04 71 00 06 06, ⓦabbaye-chaise-dieu.com

Founded in 1044 and restored in the fourteenth century at the expense of Pope Clement VI, who had served as a monk here, the **Abbey church of St-Robert** was destroyed by the Huguenots in 1562, burnt down in 1692, and remained unfinished when the Revolution brought a wave of anticlericalism; it was only really completed in the twentieth century. Its interior contains the tomb of Clement VI, some magnificent Flemish tapestries of Old and New Testament scenes hanging in the choir – which also boasts some fine Gothic stalls – and a celebrated fresco of the **Danse Macabre**, depicting Death plucking at the coarse plump bodies of 23 living figures, representing the different classes of society. "It is yourself", says the fifteenth-century text below.

The remarkable **Salle de l'Écho**, part of the Abbey complex, was once used for hearing confession from the sick and dying. The acoustics are such that two people can turn their backs on each other, stand in opposite corners and still have a perfectly audible conversation just by whispering. Unfortunately, it was closed for reconstruction at the time of research; check website for up-to-date information.

## Ambert

Some 25km north of La Chaise-Dieu, the little town of **AMBERT** was, from the fourteenth to eighteenth centuries, the centre of papermaking in France. It especially supplied the printers of Lyon, a connection that brought the region into contact with new ideas, in particular the revolutionary teachings of the Reformed Church. In the still-operating **Richard de Bas paper mill**, just east of town, the **Musée Historique du Papier** (daily: July & Aug 9.30am–7pm; Jan–June & Sept–Dec 9.30am–12.30pm & 2–6pm; €7.90; ☎04 73 82 03 11, ⓦricharddebas.com) features exhibits on everything from papyrus to handmade medieval samples.

### INFORMATION

**NORTH OF LE PUY**

**Tourist office** Place de la Mairie, La Chaise-Dieu (April Tues–Sat 10am–noon & 2–5.30pm; May, June & Sept Tues–Sun 10am–12.30pm & 2–5.30pm; July & Aug daily 10am–12.30pm & 2–6.30pm; Jan–March & Oct–Dec Tues–Sat 10am–noon & 2–5pm; ☎04 71 00 01 16).

KAYAKING IN THE GORGES DE L'ARDÈCHE

**13**

### ACCOMMODATION AND EATING

**De l'Écho** Place de l'Écho, La Chaise-Dieu ☎ 04 71 00 00 45, ⓦ echo-et-abbaye.com. This sweet hotel offers a handful of pleasant rooms, of which the so-called "character rooms" are the most impressive – the Lafayette suite includes a vaulted room that dates back to the seventeenth century. The cosy restaurant serves menus from €24.50 with an emphasis on local produce. Breakfast €9. **€69**

# The southwest

In the southwestern corner of the Massif Central, the landscapes start to change and the altitude begins to drop. The wild, desolate moorland of the **Aubrac** is cut and contained by the savage gorges of **the Lot and Truyère rivers**, in the confluence of which lies the unspoiled village of **Entraygues** ("between the waters" in Occitan). To the south, the arid plateaux form a sort of intermediate step to the lower hills and coastal plains of Languedoc.

The town of **Rodez**, the capital of the old province of the **Rouergue** – renamed Aveyron after the Revolution – also has much more of a Mediterranean feel, with its pink sandstone cathedral offering a stark contrast to the dark volcanic structures of the Auvergne. The town is certainly worth a visit, though its attractions need not keep you for more than a day. The two great architectural draws of the southwest are **Conques**, with its medieval village and magnificent abbey, which owes its existence to the Santiago pilgrim route (now the GR65), and the perfect little *bastide* of **Sauveterre-de-Rouergue**.

## The Aubrac

**The Aubrac** lies to the south of St-Flour, east of the valley of the River Truyère and north of the valley of the Lot. It's a region of bleak, windswept uplands with long views and huge skies, dotted with glacial lakes and granite villages hunkered down from the weather. The highest points are between 1200m and 1400m, and there are more cows up here than people; you see them grazing the boggy, peaty pastures, divided by dry-stone walls and turf-brown streams. There are few trees, save for a scattering of willow and ash and the occasional stand of hardy beeches on the tops, and only the abandoned shepherds' huts testify to more populous times. It's an area that's invisible in bad weather, but which, in good conditions, has a raw beauty, little disturbed by tourism or modernization.

### Aubrac and around

The marathon **GR65** from Le Puy to Santiago de Compostela in Spain crosses the Aubrac mountains from northeast to southwest en route to Conques. The tiny village of **AUBRAC**, which gave its name to the region, owes its existence to this Santiago pilgrim route; around 1120, a way station was opened here for the express purpose of providing shelter for the pilgrims on these inhospitable heights. Little remains today, beyond the windy **Tour des Anglais**.

The waymarked **Tour d'Aubrac** footpath does a complete circuit of the area in around ten days, starting from the town of **AUMONT-AUBRAC**, 40km from Aubrac, which is a much better option for accommodation.

### St-Urcize

In the wildest and most starkly beautiful part of the Aubrac region, the close-huddled village of **ST-URCIZE**, 13km north of Aubrac, hangs off the side of the valley of the River Hère; it has a lovely Romanesque church at its centre, a poignant **World War I memorial**, and a statue of the Virgin Mary up on a platform that looks over the surrounding countryside. The village is ghostly out of season; most of the unspoiled granite houses are owned by people who live elsewhere.

**13**

### LAGUIOLE: KNIVES AND CHEESE

Laguiole **knives**, which draw hordes of French to the town's many shops, are characterized by a long, pointed blade and a bone handle that fits the palm; the genuine article should bear the effigy of a bee stamped on the clasp that holds the blade open. The industry started here in the nineteenth century, then moved to industrial Thiers, outside Clermont-Ferrand, before returning in 1987. At this point, the **Société Laguiole** (the only outlet for the genuine article) opened a Philippe Starck-designed factory on the St-Urcize road, with a giant knife projecting from the roof of the windowless all-aluminium building. They have a shop on the main through-road, on the corner of the central marketplace (ⓦ www.forge-de-laguiole.com).

Laguiole's **cheesemaking** tradition (ⓦ aubrac-laguiole.com) dates back to the twelfth century; unpasteurized cow's milk is formed into massive cylindrical cheeses, and aged up to eighteen months. To sample or buy, try the factory outlet on the north edge of town.

## Laguiole

Seventeen kilometres west of St-Urcize, **LAGUIOLE** passes for a substantial town in these parts; if you don't have a car your only chance of getting in or out of town is on the morning bus to Rodez. Derived from the Occitan word for "little church", it's a name that now stands for knives and cheese.

### ACCOMMODATION AND EATING

#### AUBRAC AND AROUND

**Chez Camillou** 10 route du Languedoc, Aumont Aubrac ☏ 04 66 42 80 22, ⓦ camillou.com. Finding a great, comfortable three-star hotel in the proverbial middle of nowhere is priceless; finding its excellent hotel restaurant *Cyril Attrazic* (Wed–Sun) is little short of a miracle. Closed mid-Nov to mid-March. Breakfast €11.90. €̄101

**De la Dômerie** Aubrac ☏ 05 65 44 28 42, ⓦ hoteldomerie. com. Friendly hotel, in the same family for generations, with each room decorated and furnished in a different style. Try the Aubrac steak in the restaurant (menus from €24.50). Breakfast €12. Closed mid-Nov to end Jan. €̄72

**Relais de Peyre** 9 av du Languedoc, Aumont Aubrac ☏ 04 66 42 86 14, ⓦ lerelaisdepeyre.com. Less grand than the *Chez Camillou* nearby, but no less comfortable, this hotel also has a good-value restaurant serving burgers and pizzas from €12.80. Breakfast €8. Closed Jan. €̄57

#### ST-URCIZE

**Remise** Le Bourg ☏ 04 71 23 20 02, ⓦ aubrac-chez remise.com. A hidden gem out in the wilderness; a classy

### THE AUBRAC MOUNTAINS

hotel with modern, whitewashed rooms and a restaurant with *tartes au cantal* and local cheeses; *menus* from €209. Closed Dec–March. Breakfast €9. €̄70

#### LAGUIOLE

**L'Aubrac** 17 allée Amicale ☏ 05 65 44 32 13, ⓦ hotel-aubrac.fr. A café, hotel and restaurant in the centre of Laguiole, offering a wide range of rooms from singles to six-person family suites. Breakfast includes a local baker's delicacy, *fouace*. €̄70

**La Ba** 4 rue Bardière ☏ 05 65 51 68 30, ⓦ la-ba.fr. The tiny *La Ba*, a cross between a café-restaurant, fancy wine bar and hotel, also offers ski lessons in winter. Rooms are on the small side, but are cosy and well appointed. Breakfast €10. €̄59

**Gilles Moreau** 2 allée Amicale ☏ 05 65 44 31 11, ⓦ gilles-moreau.fr. Pleasant hotel, with a heated swimming pool and spa treatments. On site is a good restaurant with *menus* from €28. Parking €10, breakfast €13. Closed Jan to mid-Feb. €̄69

## Rodez

A particularly beautiful and out-of-the-way stretch of country lies on the southwest of the Massif Central, bordered roughly by the valley of the **River Lot** in the north and the **Viaur** in the south, which denotes the edge of the Aveyron *département*. The upland areas are open and wide, with views east to the mountains of the Cévennes and south to the Monts de Lacaune and the Monts de l'Espinouse. The only place of any size, accessible on the main train and bus routes, is Aveyron's capital, **RODEZ**, an active and prosperous town with a charming, renovated centre and a fine **cathedral**.

**13**

## The old town

Built on high ground above the River Aveyron, the **old town**, dominated by the massive red sandstone **Cathedral of Notre-Dame**, is visible for kilometres around. All approaches lead to the **place d'Armes**. From the back of the cathedral to the north and the south, a network of well-restored medieval streets connects place de-Gaulle, place de la Préfecture and the attractive place du Bourg, with its fine sixteenth-century houses. In place Foch, just south of the cathedral, the Baroque chapel of the old **lycée** is worth a look for its amazing painted ceiling, while in **place Raynaldy**, the modern **hôtel de ville** and the **médiathèque** quite successfully graft modern styles onto old buildings.

### Cathedral of Notre-Dame

Place d'Armes • Daily 8am–6.30pm • Free

The **Cathedral of Notre-Dame**, with its fortress-like west front, sits next to the seventeenth-century bishop's palace on the place d'Armes – both buildings were incorporated into the town's defences. The Gothic cathedral, its plain facade relieved only by an elaborately flowery rose window, was begun in 1277 and took three hundred years to complete. Towering over the square is the cathedral's 87m-high **belfry**, rebuilt after the original burned down and nowadays intricately decorated with fabulous pinnacles, balustrades and statuary. The impressively spacious interior, architecturally as plain as the facade, is adorned with a magnificently extravagant seventeenth-century walnut organ loft and fifteenth-century choir stalls.

### Musée Fenaille

14 place Eugène-Raynaldy • April– June & Tues–Sat 11am–7pm, Sun 2–7pm; July & Aug Mon 2–7pm & Tues–Sat 10am–7pm; Oct–March Tues–Fri 10am–noon & 2–6pm, Sat 11am–6pm, Sun 2–6pm • €11 • ☎ 05 65 73 84 30, ⓦ musee-fenaille.com

The **Musée Fenaille** is the main museum in Rodez, holding an impressive permanent collection of historical artefacts found in Aveyron, and hosting temporary exhibitions each summer that showcase the work of local artists. The big attraction is the top floor, which is devoted to carved **menhirs** dating back more than three thousand years; don't miss the anthropomorphic Neolithic statue-menhir of the Dame de Saint-Sernin.

### Musée Denys-Puech

Place Georges-Clemenceau • July & Aug Tues–Sun 2–7pm, Sept–June Wed–Sun 2–6pm • Free • ☎ 05 65 77 89 60, ⓦ musee-denys-puech.rodezagglo.fr

Behind place Raynaldy is the **Musée Denys-Puech**, which has a permanent collection celebrating the work of Denys Puech (1854–1942), one of the most important post-Rodin French sculptors. Other permanent displays feature works from local artists, such as the orientalist painter Maurice Bompard and the engraver Eugène Viala, and the museum presents three special exhibitions of contemporary art per year.

---

### ARRIVAL AND INFORMATION                                                   RODEZ

**By plane** Rodez airport (ⓦ aeroport-rodez.fr) is 7km north of town. There is no shuttle to Rodez; a taxi costs €15–20 (20–40min).

Destinations Paris (1–2 daily; 1hr 15).

**By train** The *gare SNCF* is on av Joffre, on the northern edge of town.

Destinations Toulouse (7–11 daily; 2hr 20min).

**By bus** The *gare routière* (☎ 05 65 68 11 13) is on av Victor-Hugo.

Destinations Entrayges (up to 4 daily; 1hr 10min); Laguiole (1–3 daily; 1hr 30min); Millau (7–10 daily; 1hr 25min).

**Tourist office** 10–12 place de la Cité (July & Aug Mon–Sat 9.30am–7pm, Sun 10am–1pm & 2–5pm; Sept–June Mon–Sat 9.30am–12.30pm & 2–6pm; ☎ 05 65 75 76 77, ⓦ tourisme.grand-rodez.com).

## ACCOMMODATION

**Du Clocher** 4 rue Séguy ☎ 05 65 68 10 16, ⊚ hotel-clocher.com. Hotel with a nice yellow and ochre colour scheme and stylish rooms with large plasma screens. Great half-board option. Breakfast €9. **€50**

**Mercure Rodez Cathédrale** 1 av Victor-Hugo ☎ 05 65 68 55 19, ⊚ accorhotels.com. With a beautiful 1930s Art Deco facade, this four-star hotel provides stylish accommodation by the cathedral. The arty character

continues next door in the *Maurice Bompard* bar, which features Venetian frescoes by the eponymous painter. Some free parking places. Breakfast €12.90. **€95**

**La Tour Maje** 1 bd Gally ☎ 05 65 68 34 68, ⊚ hotel tourmaje.fr. A comfortable three-star in a modern building with plenty of amenities, rather incongruously tacked onto a medieval tower. Breakfast €13. **€95**

## EATING AND DRINKING

**Les Arômes** 5 rue Ste-Catherine ☎ 05 65 87 24 41, ⊚ lesaromes-restaurant.fr. Though it doesn't look much from outside, this little restaurant serves up some surprisingly sophisticated food. *Menus* start at €21 and might include snails cooked in duck fat, or roast lamb with thyme. Wed–Sat noon–2pm & 7–9.30pm, Sun noon–2pm.

**Bistro Les Colonnes** 6 place d'Armes ☎ 05 65 68 00 33. This is a great place to view the cathedral (especially from the patio and at night), with long hours and large portions to boot. The good-value *menus* start at €12.50 and cocktails at €5. Sun–Wed 8am–1am, Thurs–Sat 8am–2am.

**L'Harmonie** 12 rue de la Madeleine ☎ 05 65 68 63 62,

⊚ restaurant-harmonie.fr. Opposite the Église Saint-Amans, this small but smart restaurant is one of Rodez's best, though is just open for lunch. The short but sweet menu might include the likes of a warm goat's cheese salad with honey and country ham, or a risotto with pesto, and *menus* start at just €13.50. Mon–Sat noon–2pm.

**Le Kiosque** Av Victor-Hugo ☎ 05 65 68 56 21, ⊚ lekiosque-rodez.fr. With a brilliant location in the middle of Rodez's Jardin du Foirail, this restaurant focuses on seafood and fish (six oysters €10; sixteen shrimp €9) but also offers a variety of local *menus* such as the Aveyronnais for €22.50. Tues–Sat noon–1.45pm & 7.15–9.50pm.

# Sauveterre-de-Rouergue

Forty kilometres southwest of Rodez, **SAUVETERRE-DE-ROUERGUE** makes the most rewarding side trip in this part of Aveyron if you have your own vehicle. It is a perfect, otherworldly *bastide*, founded in 1281, with a large, wide central square, part cobbled, part gravelled, and surrounded by stone and half-timbered houses built over arcaded ground floors. Narrow streets lead off to the outer road, and are lined with stone-built houses the colour of rusty iron. On summer evenings, *pétanque* players come out to roll their *boules* beneath chestnut and plane trees, while swallows and swifts swoop and dive overhead.

## ACCOMMODATION AND EATING                                     SAUVETERRE-DE-ROUERGUE

**La Grappe d'Or** Bd Lapérouse Tour de Ville ☎ 05 65 72 00 62, ⊚ hotel-restaurant-rodez.fr. A charming hotel whose restaurant offers an excellent *formule* at €14.50, with dishes like *gésiers chauds* and *tripoux* as well as pizza, and, for dessert, cheese, ice cream and *fouace* (a sweet cake). Breakfast €7. Hotel closed Nov–March; restaurant open all year. **€40**

**Le Sénéchal** At the entrance to the village ☎ 05 65 71 29 00, ⊚ hotel-senechal.fr. Four-star business hotel, yet with a Mediterranean-style terracotta colour scheme, featuring an indoor pool and an excellent, Michelin-starred restaurant with traditional and tasting *menus* at €33–125. Breakfast €17. Closed Jan to mid-March. **€135**

# Conques

**CONQUES**, 37km north of Rodez, is one of the great villages of southwest France. It occupies a spectacular position on the flanks of the steep, densely wooded gorge of the little **River Dourdou**, a tributary of the Lot. It was its **abbey** that brought Conques into existence, after a hermit called Dadon settled here around 800 AD and founded a community of Benedictine monks, one of whom is said to have pilfered the relics of the martyred girl, Sainte-Foy, from the monastery at Agen. Known for her ability to cure blindness and liberate captives, Sainte-Foy's presence brought the pilgrims flocking, earning the abbey a prime place on the pilgrimage route to Santiago de Compostela.

**13**

The **village** is very small, largely depopulated and mainly contained within medieval **walls**, parts of which still survive, along with three of its **gates**. The houses date mainly from the late Middle Ages, and the whole ensemble of cobbled lanes and stairways is a pleasure to stroll through. There are two main streets, the old **rue Haute**, or "upper street", which was the route for the pilgrims coming from Estaing and Le Puy and passing onto Figeac and Cahors through the **Porte de la Vinzelle**; and the lane, now **rue Charlemagne**, which leads steeply downhill through the **Porte de Barry** to the river and the ancient **Pont Romain**, with the little **chapel of St-Roch** off to the left, from where you get a fine view of the village and church.

In summer, Conques hosts a prestigious **classical music festival**, most of the concerts taking place at the abbey church.

## Abbey Church of Sainte-Foy

**Church** Daily 7.30am–10pm • Free • **Treasury** Daily: April–Sept 9.30am–12.30pm & 2–6.30pm; Oct–March 10am–noon & 2–6pm • €6.50 including Musée Fau

At the village's centre, dominating the landscape, stands the Romanesque **Abbey Church of Sainte-Foy**, begun in the eleventh century, whose giant pointed towers are echoed in those of the medieval houses clustered tightly around it. Its plain, fortress-like facade rises on a small cobbled square beside the tourist office and pilgrims' fountain, the slightly shiny silver-grey schist prettily offset by the greenery and flowers of the terraced gardens.

In startling contrast to this plainness, is the elaborately sculpted *Last Judgement* in the twelfth-century **tympanum** above the door, which admonishes all who see it to eschew vice and espouse virtue. Christ sits in judgement in the centre, with the chosen on his right hand, among them Dadon the hermit and the emperor Charlemagne. Meanwhile, his left hand directs the damned to Hell, which is (as usual) much more graphically and interestingly portrayed, with all its gory tortures, than the bliss of Paradise depicted in the bottom left panel.

The **treasury** was a crucial destination for pilgrims on the Santiago de Compestela route; the main goal was to see Sainte-Foy's relics displayed in the choir, encircled by a lovely wrought-iron screen. A piece of skull in the reliquary has been authenticated and the church was added to the list of UNESCO World Heritage Sites in 1998. There is some fine carving on the capitals, especially in the triforium arches; to see them, climb to the **organ loft**, which gives you a superb perspective on the whole interior.

On summer evenings, around 9.30pm, the abbey church hosts organ and piano concerts called the **Nocturne des Tribunes** (May–Sept daily; tickets from the tourist office, €6; no children under 12) – a stunning way to experience the beauty of the place.

---

### ARRIVAL, INFORMATION AND TOURS

### CONQUES

**By car** You need a car to reach Conques. There's a car park 450m outside the village centre as you arrive from the D901 (€4).

**Tourist office** Le Bourg (daily: April–Sept 9.30am– 12.30pm & 2–6.30pm; Oct–March 10am–noon & 2–6pm; ☎ 05 65 72 85 00, ⊛ tourisme-conques.fr). Guided tours leave from here (1 or 2 daily; 45min; €4.50).

---

### ACCOMMODATION AND EATING

**Auberge St-Jacques** Rue Gonzague-Florens ☎ 05 65 72 86 36, ⊛ aubergestjacques.fr. Located near the abbey church, this old-fashioned but well-maintained hotel is good value and also has a popular restaurant, with *menus* from €21. Breakfast €9. **€60**

**Camping Beau Rivage** Le Moulin Neuf, on the bank of the Dourdou, 400m below Conques ☎ 05 65 69 82 23, ⊛ campingconques.com. A simple, efficient campsite with a pretty good restaurant and a few cottages available for rent as well (€48). Breakfast €7. Closed Oct–March. **€35**

**Moulin de Cambelong** Le Moulin, just off the D901 ☎ 05 65 72 84 77, ⊛ moulindecambelong.com. A four-star hotel where the rooms have spacious wooden balconies with great views of the river. Its one-star Michelin restaurant, under chef Hervé Busset, specializes in duck dishes (*menus* from €40). Breakfast €18. **€150**

★ **Sainte Foy** Opposite the abbey church ☎ 05 65 69 84 03, ⓦ hotelsaintefoy.com. Pleasant, if rather dated, rooms, some with a view, and a good restaurant serving food on the beautifully shaded patio. Wi-fi access only around reception area. Breakfast €13.50, garage €15. **€105**

**De la Terrasse** Vieillevie, 6km east of Conques ☎ 04 71 49 94 00, ⓦ hotel-terrasse.com. A good hotel with an even better restaurant (*menus* €28–40), a pretty sun terrace and a small pool. Canoe rental is also available. Breakfast €10. Closed mid-Nov to March. **€68**

## The upper Lot valley

The most beautiful stretch of the **Lot Valley** is the 21.5km between the bridge of Coursavy, below **Grand-Vabre** (just north of Conques), and **Entraygues**: deep, narrow and wild, with the river running full and strong, as yet unaffected by the dams higher up, with scattered farms and houses high on the hillsides among long-abandoned terracing. The shady, tree-tunnelled road is level and not heavily used, making it ideal for cycling.

## Entraygues and around

Lying right where the Lot meets the equally beautiful River Truyère, **ENTRAYGUES**, with its riverside streets and attractive grey houses, has an airy, open feel. The brown towers of a thirteenth-century **château** overlook the meeting of the waters, and a magnificent four-arched **bridge** of the same date crosses the Truyère a little way upstream, alongside the ancient tanners' houses.

### Château de Calmont d'Olt

Espalion, 10km south of Entraygues • April & Sept–Nov Mon–Wed & Fri–Sun 2–6pm; May & June Mon–Wed & Fri–Sun 10am–6pm; July & Aug daily 10am–7pm • €9 in summer, otherwise €5.50 • ☎ 05 65 44 15 89 ⓦ chateaucalmont.org

The **Château de Calmont d'Olt** is a considerably restored, atmospheric old fortress dating from the eleventh century, on the very peak of an abrupt bluff, 535m high and a stiff 1km climb above the town of **ESPALION** on the south bank – its views of the town and the country beyond are unbeatable. Regular children's activities include demonstrations of medieval siege engines and artillery.

**INFORMATION**                                    **ENTRAYGUES AND AROUND**

**Tourist office** Place de la République (April–June & Sept Mon–Sat 10am–12.15pm & 2–6pm; July & Aug Mon–Sat 9.30am–12.30pm & 2–7pm, Sun & holidays 10am–12.30pm; Oct–March Mon 2–6pm, Tues–Fri 10am–12.15pm & 2–6pm, Sat to 5pm); ☎ 05 65 44 56 10, ⓦ tourisme-entraygues.com). Here you'll get information about walking, mountain biking, fishing and canoeing in the area.

**ACCOMMODATION AND EATING**

**Du Centre** 1 place de la République ☎ 05 65 44 51 19, ⓦ hotelducentre-12.com. One of those wonderful, friendly hotels that you find in rural France, offering everything with a smile: spotless rooms, a shady terrace overlooking the central square right in the middle of town, a bar and a restaurant offering family cooking with *menus* €13–18.50. Breakfast €7. **€45**

**Lion d'Or** 6 Tour de Ville ☎ 05 65 44 50 01, ⓦ hotel-lion-or.com. First-rate hotel with a covered swimming pool, jacuzzi, sauna and even mini-golf and tennis, plus a garden, assorted family-friendly amenities and attached restaurant (*menu du terroir* €21, other *menus* available). The decor is a mix of cosy furniture and upbeat artwork. A studio apartment is also available for weekly rentals (€320). Breakfast €8.50. Closed mid-Nov to March. **€58**

# Les Causses

The **Parc Naturel Régional des Grands Causses** merges naturally with the **Causses and Cévennes** UNESCO Heritage Site and it is only human administrators who have artificially separated one from the other. The park, most of which lies in the *département* of **Lozére**, is sculpted by the canyon of **Gorges du Tarn**,

**13**

where the deep limestone cliffs are a barrier to even mobile signals. Moulded over millennia, this is a spectacular country of narrow valleys, granite gorges and small villages built precariously on slopes such as the **Cirque of Navacelles**. The gateway to it all is the appealing town of **Millau**; further south the village of **Roquefort-Sur-Soulzon** is home to the famed cheese, while the Cistercian **Abbaye de≈Silvanès** and the Templar village of **La Couvertoirade** provide history in spades.

# Millau

The lively town of **MILLAU** occupies a beautiful site in a bend of the River Tarn at its junction with the Dourbie. It's enclosed on all sides by impressive white cliffs, formed where the rivers have worn away the edges of the *causses*, especially on the north side, where the spectacular table-top hill of the **Puech d'Andan** stands sentinel over the town. Millau owes its original prosperity to its position on the ford where the Roman road from Languedoc to the north crossed the Tarn, marked today by the truncated remains of a medieval **bridge** surmounted by a watermill, which juts out into the river beside the modern bridge. Speaking of bridges, nowadays the most famous thing about Millau is, oddly, the construction that allows visitors to bypass it: a spectacular **viaduct** (see box opposite) that lies just to the west of town, near Creissels.

From the Middle Ages until modern times, thanks to its proximity to the sheep pastures of the *causses*, the town was a major manufacturer of **leather**, especially gloves. Although outclassed by cheaper producers in the mass market, Millau still leads in the production of top-of-the-range goods.

The town's clean and well-preserved old streets have a summery, southern charm. Whether you arrive from the north or south, you'll find yourself sooner or later in **place du Mandarous**, the main square, where avenue de la République, the road to Rodez, begins. South of here, the **old town** is built a little way back from the river to avoid floods and is contained within an almost circular ring of shady boulevards.

## Place Foch

The rue Droite cuts through the centre, linking three squares: place Emma-Calvé, place des Halles and place Foch. The prettiest by far is **place Foch**, with its café shaded by two big plane trees and its houses supported on stone pillars; some date back to the twelfth century. In one corner is the **church of Notre-Dame**, which is worth a look for its octagonal, Toulouse-style belfry, originally Romanesque.

### Musée de Millau

Place Foch • July & Aug Tues–Sun 10am–12.30pm & 2–6pm; Sept–June Mon–Sat 10am–12.30pm & 2–6pm • €5 • ☎ 05 65 59 01 08, ⓦ museedemillau.fr

The very interesting **Musée de Millau**, housed in the Hôtel de Pégayrolles, a stately eighteenth-century mansion, has thirty exhibition rooms focusing on the bizarre combination of archeology and gloves. Here you can see the magnificent red pottery of the Graufesenque works, as well as the complete skeleton of a 180-million-year-old plesiosaurus.

## Place Emma-Calvé and around

**Place Emma-Calvé** and the adjoining **place du Beffroi** have been subject to some questionable attempts at reconciling old stonework with contemporary urban design. The **clock tower** by the post office on place du Beffroi is worth a climb for the great all-round view, if open. Take a look also in the streets off the square – rue du Voultre, rue de la Peyrollerie and their tributaries – for a sense of the old working-class and bourgeois districts.

### THE VIADUC DE MILLAU: AN UNSURPASSABLE BYPASS

Although it looks like little more than the A75/E11 *autoroute* on the map, the €400 million **Viaduc de Millau** (ⓦ leviaducdemillau.com), which opened to traffic in 2004, is still the tallest bridge in the world. Designed by British architect Norman Foster and French engineer Michel Virlogeux, it was originally conceived to alleviate congestion for one of the main France–Spain holiday travel routes. The toll bridge costs from €6.92 to cross (depending on vehicle type and time of day) – instead, consider taking the D992 to pass underneath it, an experience that moves from breathtaking to completely surreal at sunrise or sunset.

## La Graufesenque

Av Louis-Balsan, 2km southeast of the centre just upstream on the south bank of the Tarn • April–June, Sept & Oct Wed–Sun 10am–12.30pm & 2–6pm; July & Aug Tues–Sun 10am–12.30pm & 2.30–6pm • €4.40 • ☎ 05 65 60 11 37, ⓦ graufesenque.com

Clear evidence of the town's importance in Roman times (when it was called Condatomagus) can be seen in the **La Graufesenque** Gallo-Roman site, whose renowned bright red terracotta wares (*terra sigillata*) were distributed throughout the Roman world. This is the archeological site only; the finds can be seen in the Musée de Millau.

### ARRIVAL AND INFORMATION
### MILLAU

**By train** The *gare SNCF* is on rue de Belfort; it's a walk of around 10min down rue Alfred-Merle to the main square, place du Mandarous.
Destinations Clermont-Ferrand (1 daily; 4hr 35min).
**By train** The *gare routière* is outside the train station.
Destinations Millau (7–10 daily; 1hr 25min).

**Tourist office** Place du Beffroi (April–June & Sept Mon–Sat 9am–12.30pm & 2–6pm, Sun 10am–4pm; July & Aug daily 9.30am–7pm; Oct–March Mon–Sat 9.30am–12.30pm & 2–5.30pm; ☎ 05 65 60 02 42, ⓦ millau-viaduc-tourisme.fr).

### ACCOMMODATION

**De la Capelle** 7 place de la Fraternité ☎ 05 65 60 14 72, ⓦ hotel-millau-capelle.com. Cheerful, modern hotel with fine views of the Puech d'Andan, this is a good-value option, especially for families; double rooms can sleep up to four people. Breakfast €7. **€65**
★ **Château de Creissels** Place du Prieur, Creissels ☎ 05 65 60 16 59, ⓦ chateau-de-creissels.com. Set just under 3km southwest of central Millau, this graceful hotel in a twelfth-century château offers luxurious but unpretentious rooms, decorated in either "contemporary" or "château" style, and most boasting a balcony or terrace. The real selling point of its position are the views afforded on the Viaduc de Millau – best enjoyed from the outdoor pool. There's also a gym, a library and a celebrated restaurant.

Breakfast €12. **€129**
**Des Causses** 2 rue Mathieu-Prévot ☎ 05 65 60 03 19, ⓦ hotel-des-causses.com. Set in an attractive building, this two-star hotel with colourful furnishings and stylish decor is known in the area for its restaurant (Mon–Sat 6–9pm; mains from €19), which serves up interesting local and international dishes such as a Finnish meat stew or saucisse d'Aveyron with aligot. Breakfast €12.80. **€89**
**Les Érables** Rte de Millau-Plage ☎ 05 65 59 15 13, ⓦ campingleserables.fr. A shaded, three-star campsite, not overly crowded and near a leisure centre. Free wi-fi at reception. Closed Oct–March, reception closed noon–3.30pm April–June & Sept. **€17**

### EATING AND DRINKING

**Estanco** 20 bd Richard ☎ 05 65 60 01 64, ⓦ estanco. fr. Not one restaurant but two – a more casual pizzeria downstairs, and fabulous seafood upstairs, with an atmospheric terrace that's perfect in summer. It's a bit off the beaten track but well worth seeking out. Mixed grilled fish for €16.50. Tues–Sat 10am–3pm & 7.30–11pm.

**La Mangeoire** 10 bd de la Capelle ☎ 05 65 60 13 16, ⓦ restaurantmillau.com. *Maître restaurateur*-accredited restaurant, which has been in the same family for five decades, serving grilled fish, oysters, meat and game dishes, with *menus* from a *formule du jour* at €17, €25 or €29. Tues–Sun noon–2pm & 7–10pm.

## The Gorges du Tarn

Millau is the gateway to the spectacular **Gorges du Tarn**, which cuts through the limestone plateaux of the Causse de Sauveterre and the Causse Méjean in a

**13**

precipitous trench 400–500m deep and 1000–1500m wide. Its sides, cloaked with woods of feathery pine and spiked with pinnacles of eroded rock, are often sheer and always very steep, creating within them a microclimate in sharp distinction to the inhospitable plateaux above. The permanent population is tiny, though there's plenty of evidence of more populous times in the abandoned houses and once-cultivated terraces.

The most attractive section of the gorge runs northeast for 53km from the pretty village of **Le Rozier**, 21km northeast of Millau, to **Ispagnac**. A narrow and very twisty road follows the left bank of the river from Le Rozier, but it's not the best way to see the scenery. For drivers, the best views are from the road to St-Rome-de-Dolan above Les Vignes, and from the roads out of La Malène and the attractive **Ste-Énimie**. But it is far nicer to **walk**, or hire a **boat**. There are two beautiful **caves** about 25km up the Jonte river from Le Rozier.

## Aven Armand

Daily: late March to early July & late Aug to early Nov 10am–noon & 1.30–5pm; second half of July & Aug 10am–6pm • Guided visits only; €12.50 • ☎ 04 66 45 61 31, ⓦ aven-armand.com

**Aven Armand**, a cave on the edge of the Causse Méjean, is fitted with a funicular that takes you more than 100m underground. Its great attraction is the hundreds of stalagmite columns, including the world's tallest stalagmite towering 30m above the cave floor.

## The Grotte de Dargilan

Daily: April–June & Sept 10.30am–5pm; July & Aug 10.15am–6.30pm; Oct 2–4pm • Guided tours only; €11.50 • ☎ 04 66 45 60 20, ⓦ grotte-dargilan.com

The **Grotte de Dargilan**, on the south side of the river on the edge of the Causse Noir, and known as the "pink cave" from the colour of its iron oxide deposits, is one of France's most beautiful stalactite caverns. Grey manganese salts mix with white stalactites and ochre ferrous hues to give delicate "drapery" effects – a contrast to the sheer vastness of some of the structures in the lower caverns.

---

**GETTING AROUND**                          **THE GORGES DU TARN**

**By boat** Better than driving around the Gorges du Tarn is to walk, or follow the river's course by boat or canoe; for rental, try Le Soulio (May–Sept; ☎ 04 66 48 81 56, ⓦ le-soulio.com).

---

**ACCOMMODATION AND EATING**

**Auberge de la Cascade** St-Énimie ☎ 04 66 48 52 82, ⓦ aubergecascade.com. Hotel with panoramic views, a good bar and restaurant (*menus* €19.90, €25.80, €31 and €43) with options including local trout. The full-board option is only marginally more expensive than half-board. One of the few options in the area offering disabled access. Closed mid-Oct to Easter. **€66**

**Auberge du Moulin** St-Énimie ☎ 04 66 48 53 08, ⓦ aubergedumoulin48.com. A three-star converted stone mill (the owner is the grandson of the original miller), where all rooms have views of either the village below or the Tarn and lush garden. Good restaurant with *gigot d'agneau* (leg of lamb) and a range of *menus* from €14.90–39. Breakfast €9, picnic lunch €9. Closed Nov–Easter. **€79**

**Grand Hôtel des Voyageurs** Le Rozier ☎ 05 65 62 60 09, ⓦ hotelrestaurant-gorgesdutarn.com. You can get excellent value at this friendly and unpretentious hotel; if you are travelling alone, half-board from €49, including breakfast, works out the more economical option. Closed Nov–Easter. Breakfast €8.30. **€57**

**Le Vallon** Ispagnac ☎ 04 66 44 21 24, ⓦ hotel-ispagnac.com. A small hotel with an excellent *terroir* restaurant (from €16) and veranda, offering family-size rooms and good-value half-board from €56 per person. They also own a small campsite, 200m from the hotel (☎ 04 66 44 21 24, ⓦ camping-cerisiers.com; €15.60). Breakfast €8.50. Closed Nov–March. **€56**

## South of Millau

On the edge of the Parc Régional des Grands Causses, the village of **Roquefort-sur-Soulzon** – which has little to it apart from cheese-making, with almost every building

**13**

devoted to the process – and the medieval **Abbey of Sylvanès** are relatively isolated spots, best visited on a return trip from Millau, if you are prepared to drive through some of the most rural and bucolic parts of France.

The main *autoroute* heads southeast and traverses the barren and windswept **Causse du Larzac**. Two photo opportunities lie not far off the highway: the quaint village of **La Couvertoirade** and the great panoramic vision of the **Cirque de Navacelles**.

## Sylvanès Abbey

Sylvanès • Jan to mid-March & Nov to mid-Dec Mon–Fri 9.30am–12.30pm & 2–6pm; mid-March to June, Sept & Oct daily 9.30am–12.30pm & 2–6pm; July & Aug daily 9.30am–1pm & 2–7pm • €3 • ☎ 05 65 98 20 20, ⓦ sylvanes.com

Deep in the isolation of the *causses*, 26km south of Roquefort, squats the twelfth-century Cistercian **Abbaye de Sylvanès**, founded in 1137 and the first Cistercian house in the region. Having largely survived the depredations of war and revolution, the abbey serves today as a centre for sacred music and dance from the world over. Although you'll have to manage your own transport, it's worth visiting not only for the evocative setting, but also for the excellently preserved thirteenth-century church and the surviving monastic buildings, including a refectory and scriptorium dating back to the 1100s.

## La Couvertoirade

**LA COUVERTOIRADE**, 45km south of Millau, is billed as a perfect "Templar" village, although in fact its present remains post-date the dissolution of that Order in the late thirteenth century. It's still a striking site, completely enclosed by its towers and walls and almost untouched by renovation. Its forty remaining inhabitants live by tourism, and you have to pay to walk around the **ramparts** (daily: March & Oct to mid-Nov 10am–noon & 2–5pm; April to June & Sept 10am–noon & 2–6pm; July & Aug 10am–7pm; €3; English audioguide €6.50; ☎ 05 65 58 55 59, ⓦ lacouvertoirade.com). Just outside the walls on the south side is a *lavogne*, a paved water hole of a kind seen all over the *causse* for watering the flocks whose milk is used for Roquefort cheese.

## Cirque de Navacelles

Some 5km south of La Couvertoirade, you can turn off at **Le Caylar** to drive another 20km south on the stunning road to **St-Maurice-Navacelles**, a small and sleepy hamlet centring on a fine World War I memorial by Paul Dardé. From here, head north to the **Cirque de Navacelles**, 10km away on the D25 past the beautiful ruined seventeenth-century sheep farm of La Prunarède. The cirque is a widening in the 150m-deep trench of the Vis gorge, formed by a now dry loop in the river that has left a neat pyramid of rock sticking up in the middle like a wheel hub. An ancient and scarcely inhabited hamlet survives in the bottom – a bizarre phenomenon in an extraordinary location, and you get a bird's-eye view of it from the edge of the cliff above.

# The Margeride

The wild, rolling and sparsely populated wooded hills of the **Margeride**, east of Aubrac and Aveyron, are best visited in conjunction with the Causses, although strictly speaking they are not part of that region. Using your own transport, take the D4, a slow but spectacular route east (92km) to Le Puy, crossing the forested heights of **Mont Mouchet**, at 1465m the highest point of the Margeride. A side turning, the D48 (signposted), takes you to the national **Resistance monument**. It is located by the woodman's hut that served as HQ to the local Resistance commander in June 1944. Here, Resistance fighters battled to delay German reinforcements moving north to strengthen defences against the D-Day landings in Normandy.

**13**

The Margeride also has two wildlife parks – **Wolves Of Gévaudan**, in Hameau de Ste-Lucie (April–June, Sept & Oct daily 10am–5.30pm; July & Aug daily 9.45am–7pm; Nov–March varying days 10am–5pm; €9; ☎04 66 32 09 22, ⓦloupsdugevaudan.com) and, 40km northeast, the **European Bison Reserve** at Ste-Eulalie-en-Margeride (daily 10am–5pm; €16; ☎04 66 31 40 40, ⓦbisoneurope.com). **St-Alban-sur-Limagnole**, a quiet village conveniently situated between the two, is a good spot for lunch or an overnight stay.

## ACCOMMODATION AND EATING                                    THE MARGERIDE

★ **Relais St-Roch** rue du Carreirou, St-Alban-sur-Limagnole ☎04 66 31 55 48, ⓦrelais-saint-roch.fr. Housed in a nineteenth-century mansion built in pink arkose stone, this three-star hotel, its rooms decorated with traditional wallpapers and fabrics, can best be admired from the pool. There's also a lovely terrace and a decent restaurant, *La Petite Maison*. Closed Oct to mid-April. Breakfast €18. **€155**

# The Cévennes and Ardèche

The **Cévennes** mountains and **River Ardèche** form the southeastern defences of the Massif Central, overlooking the Rhône valley to the east and the Mediterranean littoral to the south. The bare landscapes found in the western edge of the mountain range are clearly those of the central Massif, but around Mont Aigoual and its radiating valleys, and the tributary valleys of the Ardèche, the feel is distinctly Mediterranean: deep, dry, and clothed in forests of sweet chestnut, oak and pine.

Remote and inaccessible country until well into the twentieth century, the region has bred rugged and independent inhabitants. For centuries it was the most resolute stronghold of Protestantism in France, and it was in these valleys that the persecuted Protestants put up their fiercest resistance to the tyranny of Louis XIV and Louis XV. In World War II, it was heavily committed to the Resistance, while after 1968, it became the domain of hippies – some of whom remain.

## Parc National des Cévennes and around

The **Parc National des Cévennes** was created in 1970 to protect and preserve the life, landscape, flora, fauna and architectural heritage of the Cévennes. North to south, it stretches from **Mende** on the Lot to **Le Vigan** and includes both **Mont Lozère** and **Mont Aigoual**. Access, to the periphery at least, is surprisingly easy, thanks to the Paris–Clermont–Alès–Nîmes train line and the Montpellier–Mende link. In July and August, it's wise to book ahead for **accommodation**; otherwise you could find yourself sleeping outdoors; the **main information office** for the park is at Florac (see page 718).

---

### THE STEVENSON TRAIL

In 1878, the author Robert Louis Stevenson took a walking trail through Haute-Loire, Ardèche, Lozère and the Cévennes with Modestine, a donkey he bought in Le Monastier-sur-Gazeille near Le Puy and sold at journey's end in the former Protestant stronghold of St-Jean-du-Gard. The journey is described in *Travels with a Donkey* (see Contexts), a book that has captured the imagination of so many with its line "I travel for travel's sake; the great affair is to move." Today you can follow the **Chemin de Stevenson** in a variety of ways: walking it, while a car transports your luggage (La Malle Postale; ☎04 71 04 21 79, ⓦlamallepostale.com); on a packaged hike (Cévennes Évasion Voyage Nature; ☎04 66 45 18 31, ⓦcevennes-evasion.com); or even by hiring a donkey (Chik'Anes; ☎04 63 89 00 98, ⓦchikanes.com). For more information and a full list of operators, check ⓦchemin-stevenson.org.

## Mende

Capital of the Lozère *département*, **MENDE** lies well down in the deep valley of the Lot at the northern tip of the Parc des Cévennes, and 40km north of Florac, with train and bus links to the Paris–Nîmes and Clermont–Millau lines. It's an attractive southern town that spirals its way out from the impressive **cathedral**; it's pleasant to take a quiet wander in the old town's minuscule squares and narrow medieval streets, with their bulging houses. Mende is also a useful stop-off point for last-minute supplies before you head off to the mountains.

In **rue Notre-Dame**, which separated the Christian from Jewish quarters in medieval times, the thirteenth-century house at no. 17 was once a synagogue. If you carry on down to the river, you'll see a thirteenth-century stone bridge, the **Pont Notre-Dame**, with its worn cobbles.

### The cathedral

Place Urbain-V • Daily 9am–7pm • Free

Standing against the haze of the mountain background, Mende's main landmark, the **cathedral**, owes its construction to Pope Urban V, who was born locally. Although work began in 1369, progress was hampered by war and natural disasters and the building wasn't completed until the end of the nineteenth century. Inside is a handsome choir and, suspended from the clerestory, eight great Aubusson tapestries, depicting the life of the Virgin. She's also present in one of the side chapels of the choir in the form of a statue made from olive wood, thought to have been brought back from the Middle East during the crusades.

### ARRIVAL AND INFORMATION | MENDE

**By train** The *gare SNCF* is on av de la Gare across the river, 600m north of the centre.

Destinations Nîmes (2 daily; 3hr 10min).

**By bus** Buses, most of which are local, leave from the *gare SNCF*.

Destinations Clermont-Ferrand (3 daily; 2hr 55min); Le Puy (Mon–Sat 1 daily; 1hr 40min); Rodez (up to 1 daily; 2hr 30min); St-Flour (2 daily; 2hr).

**Tourist office** Place du Foirail (June & Sept Mon & Wed–Sat 9am–noon & 2–6pm; July & Aug Mon 9am–7pm, Sun 10am–5pm; Oct–May Mon & Wed–Fri 9am–noon & 2–6pm, Tues 10am–noon & 2–6pm, Sat 9am–noon; ☎ 04 66 94 00 23, ⓦot-mende.fr).

### ACCOMMODATION AND EATING

**De France** 9 bd Lucien-Arnault ☎ 04 66 65 00 04, ⓦhoteldefrance-mende.com. Central, comfortable hotel with private parking – essential in Mende. The large, white rooms have good facilities, and there's a refined restaurant offering French cuisine on *menus* from €31–56. Breakfast €12. Closed Christmas to mid-Jan. €98

**Pont-Roupt** 2 av du 11-novembre ☎ 04 66 65 01 43, ⓦhotel-pont-roupt.fr. A five-minute walk from the centre and facing the river, this classy hotel offers an indoor pool, terrace, spa and good restaurant; dishes include *truite au lard* and *salade au Roquefort*. *Menus* from €30. Buffet breakfast €12.50. €120

## Mont Lozère and around

**Mont Lozère** is a windswept and desolate barrier of granite and yellow grassland, rising to 1699m at the summit of **Finiels**. It is still grazed by herds of cows, but in nothing like the numbers of bygone years when half the cattle in Languedoc came up here for their summer feed. Snowbound in winter and wild and dangerous in bad weather, it has claimed many a victim among lost travellers. In some of the squat granite hamlets on the northern slopes, like **Servies**, **Auriac** and **Les Sagnes**, you can still hear the bells, known as *clochers de tourmente*, that tolled in the wind to give travellers some sense of direction when the cloud was low.

If you're travelling by car from Mende, the way to the summit is via the village of **Le Bleymard**, about 30km to the east on the bank of the infant River Lot. From Le Bleymard, the D20 winds 7km up through the conifers to join the GR7 hiking trail, which has taken a more direct route from Le Bleymard. This is the route that

**13**

Stevenson took, waymarked as the "Tracé Historique de Stevenson" (see page 716). Road and footpath run together as far as the **Col de Finiels**, where the GR7 strikes off on its own to the southeast. The source of the River Tarn is about 3km east of the Col, the summit of Lozère 2km to the west. From the Col, the road and Stevenson's route drop down in tandem, through the lonely hamlet of Finiels to the village of **Le Pont-de-Montvert**.

## Le Pont-de-Montvert

At the pretty but touristy village of **LE PONT-DE-MONTVERT**, a seventeenth-century **bridge** crosses the Tarn by a stone tower that once served as a tollhouse. In this building in 1702, the Abbé du Chayla, a priest appointed by the Crown to reconvert the rebellious Protestants enraged by the revocation of the Edict of Nantes, set up a torture chamber to coerce the recalcitrant. Incensed by his brutality, a group of rebels led by one Esprit Séguier attacked and killed him on July 23. Reprisals were extreme; nearly twelve thousand were executed, thus precipitating the Camisards' guerrilla war against the state. At the edge of the village, there's a museum on the life and character of the region, the **Maison du Mont Lozère** (July & Aug daily 10.30am–12.30pm & 2.30–6pm; €2.50; ☎04 66 45 80 73, ⓦlozere.fr).

## Florac

Situated 39km south of Mende, **FLORAC** lies in the bottom of the trench-like valley of the Tarnon, just short of its junction with the Tarn. Behind the village rises the steep wall that marks the edge of the Causse Méjean. When you get here, you will have already passed the frontier between the northern and Mediterranean landscapes; the dividing line seems to be the **Col de Montmirat** at the western end of Mont Lozère. Once you begin the descent, the scrub and steep gullies and the tiny abandoned hamlets, with their houses oriented towards the sun, speak clearly of the south.

The village, with some two thousand inhabitants, is strung out along the left bank of the Tarnon and the main street, **avenue Jean-Monestier**. There's little to see, though the close lanes of the village up towards the valley side have their charms, especially the shaded **place du Souvenir**. In summer it is worth visiting the Sunday **market**, when you'll find the tiny streets packed with merchants and local produce.

## INFORMATION
FLORAC

**Centre d'Information du Parc National des Cévennes** 6bis place du Palais (May & June Mon–Fri 9am–noon & 2–7pm, Sat & Sun 10am–1pm & 3–6pm; July & Aug Mon–Fri 9am–1pm & 2–7pm, Sat & Sun 10am–1pm & 4–7pm; Sept & Oct Mon–Fri 9am–noon & 2–6pm, Sat & Sun 10am–1pm & 3–6pm; Nov & Dec Mon–Wed & Fri 9am–noon & 1.30–5.30pm, Thurs 1.30–5.30pm; ☎04 66 49 53 00, ⓦcevennes-parcnational.fr). A wide stock of brochures about the region, from its flora, fauna and traditions to local activities and routes for walkers, cyclists, canoeists and horse riders. It also supplies a list of *gîtes d'étape* in the park and can provide information for anyone

following Stevenson's route (see page 716), including where to hire a donkey.

**Tourist office** 33 av Jean-Monestier (April–Oct daily 9.30am–noon & 2–6pm; Nov–March Mon & Wed–Fri 9.30am–noon & 2–5.30pm; ☎04 66 45 01 14, ⓦvacances-cevennes.com). The office provides details on guided treks around the national park, plus medical information.

**Mountain bike rental** Cévennes Évasion, 1 place Boyer (☎04 66 45 18 31, ⓦcevennes-evasion.com; €20/day). They also offer a Stevenson trail route and week-long deals with bike rental and hotel stays.

## ACCOMMODATION AND EATING

**Les Gorges du Tarn** 48 rue du Pêcher ☎04 66 45 00 63, ⓦhotel-gorgesdutarn.com. An airy and sunny hotel that also offers rather plain self-catering apartments for weekly stays in addition to its simply-furnished rooms. Its *L'Adonis* restaurant (daily 7–8.30pm) is worth visiting even if you don't stay; it offers a *formule midi* for €23 and a variety of

*menus* from €29. Breakfast €11. Closed Nov–Easter. **€69**

**Grand Hôtel du Parc** 47 av Jean-Monestier ☎04 66 45 03 05. A solid three-star with a pool, a large, pleasant garden and an excellent restaurant with *menus* from €25–42. Buffet breakfast €9. Closed Nov–Easter. **€60**

## Mont Aigoual

You can travel up the beautiful valley of the Tarnon to the **Col de Perjuret**, where a right turn will take you on to the **Causse Méjean** and to the strange rock formations of **Nîmes-le-Vieux** and a left turn along a rising ridge a further 15km to the 1565m summit of **Mont Aigoual** (GR6, GR7, GR66). From this vantage point, it is said that you can see a third of France, from the Alps to the Pyrenees, with the Mediterranean coast from Marseille to Sète at your feet. The summit is a relatively large plateau with the ground dropping away steeply into the valley of the River Hérault on the south side; the view and the exposure to the elements is dramatic. At the top is an **observatory** which has been in use for more than a century. A small but interesting **exhibition** (May–Sept daily 10am–noon & 1–6pm; free) shows modern weather-forecasting techniques alongside displays of old barometers and weather vanes.

The **descent** to Le Vigan by the valley of the Hérault is superb; a magnificent twisty road follows the deepening ravine through dense beech and chestnut woods and over bridges, to come out at the bottom in rather Italianate scenery, with tall, close-built villages and vineyards beside the stream.

### ACCOMMODATION AND EATING                                   MONT AIGOUAL

**Les Bruyères** Valleraugue ☎ 04 67 82 20 06, 🌐 hotel-valleraugue.com. In a leafy riverside setting in the charming village of Valleraugue, this hotel once served as a stopping point for stagecoaches, and retains a slightly old-fashioned feel. Rooms are large and airy, and there's a pool, riverside bar, unfussy restaurant and games room, plus parking (€7/day). Breakfast €9. Closed Oct–April. **€59**

**Le Touring** L'Éperou ☎ 04 67 82 60 04, 🌐 hotel-restaurant-touring.com. A real family hotel, just below the summit, with rooms that have the rustic feel of a log cabin. Breakfast €8.50, half-board €53pp, midweek *menus* from €16; this is a good place to try the delicious local *charcuterie* or *saucisse aligot* (sausage with cheesy mashed potato). Free private parking. Closed April & Dec. **€62**

## Le Vigan

Some 64km from Montpellier and 29km from St-Guilhem-le-Desert, **LE VIGAN** makes a good starting point for exploring the southern part of the Cévennes. It's a leafy, cool and thoroughly agreeable place, at its liveliest during the **Fête d'Isis** at the beginning of August and the colossal **fair** that takes over the Parc des Châtaigniers for a couple of days in September.

The prettiest part of the town is around the central **place du Quai**, shaded by lime trees and bordered by cafés and brasseries. From here it's just a two-minute walk south, down rue Pierre-Gorlier, to the gracefully arched **Pont Vieux**. Beside it stands the **Musée Cévenol**.

### Musée Cévenol

1 rue des Calquières • April–June, Sept & Oct Wed–Sun 10am–noon & 2–6pm; July & Aug Tues–Sun 10am–1pm & 3–6.30pm • €5 • ☎ 04 67 81 06 86, 🌐 museecevenol-levigan.jimdo.com

The **Musée Cévenol** offers a well-presented look at traditional rural occupations in the area, including woodcutting, butchery, shepherding and wolf-hunting. There's also a room devoted to the area's best-known twentieth-century writer, André Chamson, whose novels are steeped in the traditions and countryside of the Cévennes. Interestingly, Coco Chanel also features: she had local family connections and it seems found inspiration for her designs in the *cévenol* silks. Housed in an old tannery, the building itself holds plenty to interest visitors.

### INFORMATION                                                LE VIGAN

**Tourist office** Place du Marché (July & Aug Mon–Sat 9am–12.30pm & 2–6.30pm, Sun and public holidays 9.30am–12.30pm; Easter–June, Sept & Oct Mon–Fri 9am–12.30pm & 2–6pm, Sat 9am–12.30pm & 2–6pm; Nov–Easter Mon 2–5.30pm Tues–Fri 9am–12.30pm & 2–5.30pm, Sat 9am–12.30pm; ☎ 04 67 81 01 72, 🌐 tourismecevennesnavacelles.com).

**13**

## ACCOMMODATION AND EATING

**Auberge Cocagne** Avèze, 3km south of Le Vigan ☎04 67 81 02 70, ⓦauberge-cocagne-cevennes.com. Unfortunately the shuttered, early seventeenth-century building is contrasted against rather uninspiring rooms, but this remains a charming place to stay, with friendly hosts. Restaurant *menus* from €20. Private parking. Breakfast €8.50. Closed mid-Dec to mid-Feb. **€72**

**Mas de la Prairie** Av du Sergeant-Triaire ☎04 67 81 80 80, ⓦmasdelaprairie.fr. Comfortable hillside hotel with many amenities including a swimming pool, solarium and restaurant with *menus* for €20 and €30. Rooms are a bit of a mixed bag so ask to see a few if possible. Closed mid-Nov to April. Breakfast €12. **€60**

**Le Val de l'Arre** Rte du Pont de la Croix, 2km upriver from Le Vigan ☎04 67 81 02 77, ⓦvaldelarre.com. A shaded riverside campsite near Le Vigan, on the opposite bank. Facilities include wi-fi (not free), a snack bar, shops that offer local produce and a pool. Closed Oct–March. **€25.50**

## St-Jean-du-Gard and around

Some 58 winding kilometres northeast of Le Vigan, **ST-JEAN-DU-GARD** was the centre of Protestant resistance during the Camisard war in 1702–04. It straggles along the bank of the River Gardon, crossed by a graceful, arched eighteenth-century bridge, and a number of picturesque old houses that still survive along the main street, **Grande-Rue**.

### Musée du Désert

Mas Soubeyran, near Mialet • Daily: March–June & Sept–Nov 9.30am–noon & 2–6pm; July & Aug 9.30am–6.30pm • €6 • ☎04 66 85 02 72, ⓦmuseedudesert.com

Signposts at St-Jean direct you to the museum at Mas Soubeyran, a minuscule hamlet of beautiful rough-stone houses in a gully above the village of Mialet, about 8km away. The **Musée du Désert** is in the house that once belonged to Rolland, one of the Camisards' self-taught but most successful military leaders, and it remains much the same as it would have looked in 1704, the year he died. It catalogues the appalling sufferings and sheer dogged heroism of the **Protestant Huguenots** in defence of their freedom of conscience; and the "desert" they had to traverse between the Revocation of the Edict of Nantes in 1685 and the promulgation of the Edict of Tolerance in 1787, which restored their original rights (full emancipation came with the Declaration of the Rights of Man in the first heady months of the Revolution in 1789). Unsurprisingly, the brutality the Protestants faced led to armed rebellion, inspired by the prophesying of the lay preachers who had replaced the banished priests, calling for a holy war. The rebels were hopelessly outnumbered, however, and the revolt was ruthlessly put down in 1704. **Memorabilia** on display includes documents, private letters and lists of those who died for their beliefs, including five thousand who died as galley slaves (*galériens pour la foi*) and the women who were immured in the Tour de Constance prison in Aigues-Mortes.

### La Bambouseraie

552 rue de Montsauve • daily: late Feb to mid-March, Oct & Nov 9.30am–6pm; mid-March to mid-July & mid-Aug to Sept 9.30am–7pm; mid-July to mid-Aug 9.30am–8pm; last entry 30min before closing time; €11.20; ☎04 66 61 70 47, ⓦbambouseraie.com

Thirteen kilometres southeast of St-Jean towards Anduze, Générargues is noteworthy for **La Bambouseraie**, an extraordinary and appealing garden consisting of a huge number of bamboos of all shapes and sizes (as well as other plants); the project was started in 1855 by local entrepreneur Eugène Mazel. An easy way to get here is to take the **steam train** from St-Jean-du-Gard; it takes just ten minutes.

## INFORMATION                                                                    ST-JEAN-DU-GARD AND AROUND

**Tourist office** Maison Rouge, Musée des Vallées Cévenoles (daily: April–June, Sept & Oct 10.30am–1pm & 2–5.30pm; July & Aug 10am–6pm; ☎04 66 85 32 11, ⓦcevennes-tourisme.fr). They can advise you about the steam train between St-Jean and Anduze (April–Oct at least 3 daily; check website for details; €16 return; ☎04 66 60 59 00, ⓦtrainavapeur.com).

**ACCOMMODATION AND EATING**

**L'Oronge** Place de la Révolution ☎ 04 66 86 05 52, ⓦ hoteloronge.com. Housed in a seventeenth-century stone building where Stevenson stayed in 1879, this is a popular choice for its sense of history, and the rooms are pleasant enough, with exposed stonework. Cute restaurant with great *menus* from €17.50. Breakfast €8.50, €2 supplement for charcuterie. **€66**

# Northern Ardèche

North of the Cévennes, the Ardèche river starts carving the gorge towards the southeast within sloping forests of pine, spruce and, lower down, **chestnut** trees. This is a land of beautiful villages, some – such as **Vogüé**, **Jaujac** or **Antraigues-sur-Volane** – etched onto the volcanic basalt slopes. Chestnut cream, chestnut biscuits and a very drinkable 21 percent proof chestnut liqueur are all available to taste in **Aubenas**, the main administrative centre, but the town lacks good hotels, so it is best visited on a day-trip.

If you want to stay in the northern Ardèche, nearby **Vals-les-Bains** and **Neyrac-les-Bains** are better options. Apart from the thermal spas that dominate the area, this is where you will also find the regional **Bourganel Brewery** (ⓦ bieres-bourganel.fr) with – surprise – its chestnut-flavoured beer.

## Aubenas

Some 91km southeast of Le Puy, **AUBENAS** sits high on a hill overlooking the middle valley of the River Ardèche. The central knot of streets with their cobbles and bridges, occupying the highest point of town around **place de l'Hôtel-de-ville**, have great charm, particularly towards place de la Grenette and place 14-juillet. Place de l'Hôtel-de-ville is dominated by the eleventh-century **château**, from which the local *seigneurs* ruled the area right up until the Revolution. At the time of research, the graceful château was undergoing significant restoration; once works have finished it should again be possible to take a guided tour – contact the tourist office for more information. There's a magnificent view of the Ardèche snaking up the valley from under an arch beside the castle. Other sights include the heavily restored thirteenth-century **St-Laurent church**, which has the curious seventeenth-century hexagonal **Dôme Benoît chapel**.

**INFORMATION** **NORTHERN ARDÈCHE**

**Tourist office** place de l'Airette, Aubenas (July & Aug Mon–Sat 9am–7pm, Sun 9am–1pm; Sept–June Mon–Sat 9am–noon & 2–6pm; ☎ 04 75 89 02 03, ⓦ aubenas-vals.com). One of the best tourist offices for maps and information on everything (even parking) in the whole of the Ardèche.

**ACCOMMODATION AND EATING**

★ **Le Carré des Maîtres** 6 av P.-Ribeyre, Vals-les-Bains ☎ 04 75 94 00 89,. A great wine bar with themed evenings and a good selection of local wines, plus a terrace overlooking a stream. The daily set *menu* is always guaranteed to be top quality (€23). April to mid-Nov Tues 7–9pm, Wed–Sun 11am–1.30pm & 7–9pm.

★ **Château Clément** Vals-les-Bains ☎ 04 75 88 33 53, ⓦ chateauclement.com. A family-friendly Third Republic château with carved walnut wood-panelling and a huge double revolution staircase leading to rooms ranging from the super-modern to the highly traditional. Rates include breakfast and views over the valley of Vals-les-Bains, and there are amenities aplenty, including a pool, spa – and the most glorious grounds. **€200**

**Du Levant** Neyrac-les-Bains ☎ 04 75 36 41 07, ⓦ hotel-levant.com. An old coach house in the same family for six generations, also site of the famous restaurant by Claude Brioude (*menus* €22–58). The hotel offers half- or full-board. Breakfast €9. **€96**

# The Gorges de l'Ardèche

The **Gorges de l'Ardèche** begins at the **Pont d'Arc**, a very beautiful 54m-high stone arch that the river has cut for itself through the limestone, just downstream from **Vallon**,

**13**

itself 39km south of Aubenas. The gorge continues for about 35km to **St-Martin-d'Ardèche** in the valley of the Rhône.

The gorge winds back and forth, much of the time dropping 300m straight down to the almost dead-flat scrubby Plateau des Gras. It's beautiful, but a tourist trap; the road following the rim, with spectacular viewpoints at regular intervals, is jammed with traffic in **summer**, when you should book accommodation well in advance. The river, down at the bottom, which is where you really want to be to appreciate the grandeur of the canyon, is likewise packed with canoes in high season.

## Aven Marzal

Signposted from the main Ardèche gorge road • **Caves** Daily: April to early July & Sept to mid-Oct 11.30am–4.30pm; July & Aug 10.30am–5.30pm; obligatory guided visits approximately every hour in July and Aug, falling to 4 per day in other months • €9.50, joint ticket with zoo €15.50 • **Zoo** Daily: mid-Feb to mid-March 2–4.30pm; mid-March to early July & Sept to mid-Oct 10.30am–5.30pm; July & Aug 9.30am–7pm • €8.50 • ☎ 04 75 04 12 45, ⓦ aven-marzal.com

The Ardèche plateau is riddled with caves. **Aven Marzal**, a stalactite cavern north of the main gorge road, has a prehistoric **zoo**, filled with reconstructions of dinosaurs and various friends. Note that the frequency of visits to the cave depends on the number of people who are present on any one day.

## Aven Orgnac

Signposted from Orgnac L'Aven • 90min tours daily: Feb & March 10.30am–noon & 2–4.45pm; April–June & Sept 10am–noon & 2–5.30pm; July & Aug 9.30am–7pm; Oct to mid-Nov 9.30am–noon & 2–4.30pm; Christmas hols 2.15–4.30pm • €13.50; additional €2.50 for Cité de la Préhistoire • ☎ 04 75 38 65 10, ⓦ orgnac.com

Best of the area's caves, to the south of the gorge, is the **Aven Orgnac**, one of France's most important and colourful stalactite formations. In addition to the normal tours, you can also opt for two "*visites spéléologiques*", which are hard-core caving tours that last either three or eight hours; reserve two weeks ahead. There's also a very good prehistory museum, the **Cité de la Préhistoire**.

## La Caverne du Pont d'Arc Museum

Free shuttle from Vallon Pont d'Arc • hours vary but generally at least 9.30am–5.30pm daily; see website for details • €15 • ☎ 04 75 94 39 40, ⓦ cavernedupontdarc.fr

The most important cave in the Ardèche, France, and arguably in the world, is the **Chauvet cave**, which features in Werner Herzog's award-winning 2010 documentary *The Cave of Forgotten Dreams*; it can be spotted from the car park at the Pont d'Arc. The discovery in 1994 of this immense natural prehistoric sanctuary amazed archeologists: it contained no fewer than 425 individual animal paintings of exceptional quality and technique, dating back 36,000 years. Remarkably, the whole cave system was painstakingly replicated and opened as **La Caverne du Pont d'Arc Museum** in 2015. An hour-long tour takes visitors along a raised walkway, past 27 panels that display hundreds of engravings and drawings of 15 species of animals. The final panel, the staggering 12m-long Lion Panel, shows 92 animals, which – thanks to intricate shading techniques from the artists – seem to come to life in the darkness.

### ARRIVAL AND INFORMATION                    THE GORGES DE L'ARDÈCHE

**By bus** The Vallon bus station is by the tourist office. In July & Aug there is a daily shuttle from Vallon to Pont d'Arc (daily 9.30am–6.45pm every 30–50min; last return from Pont d'Arc 7.30pm). See ⓦ lesept.fr for up-to-date timetables for the region.
Destinations Aubenas (Mon–Sat 2–4 daily; 1hr 45min);

Avignon (1 daily; 1hr 30min).
**Tourist office** 1 place de l'Ancienne Gare, Vallon (April, May & Oct Mon–Fri 9am–noon & 2–5pm, Sat 9am–noon & 2–4pm; June–Sept Mon–Sat 9am–7pm, Sun 9am–-5pm; Nov–March Mon–Fri 9am–noon & 2–5pm, Sat 9am–noon; ☎ 04 28 91 24 10, ⓦ pontdarc-ardeche.fr).

### ACCOMMODATION

Finding accommodation in the area can be a problem during the high season. This is really a place to get back to nature, so camping is the best option.

★ **Le Belvédère** Rte des Gorges de l´Ardèche ☎ 04 75 88 00 02, ⓦ hotel-ardeche-belvedere.com. Close to the Pont d'Arc, this is the hotel to stay in if you want to be in the middle of the action. There's a wonderful terrace with a pool, fantastic views from the restaurant, and activities on the river can be arranged. It offers unbeatable-value off-season packages, which include full board, hiking and kayaking. Breakfast €11. **€95**

**Camping L'Ardéchois** La Roche ☎ 04 75 88 06 63, ⓦ ardechois-camping.com. Palatial and award-winning five-star campsite with the option of private bathrooms. There are two swimming pools, restaurants, takeaways, entertainment and sports activities; especially focused on families and children. Closed Oct–March. **€60**

**Le Manoir du Raveyron** 140 rue Henri-Barbusse, Vallon ☎ 04 75 88 03 59, ⓦ manoir-du-raveyron.com. The best hotel near Vallon, 300m from the centre of the village, this is a converted sixteenth-century manor house – with a jacuzzi – and scenic backdrop and a good restaurant (daily 7–8.30pm; *menu* €30). Breakfast included. Closed Nov to mid-March. **€95**

13

# The Alps and Franche-Comté

**729** Grenoble

**735** The Chartreuse massif

**737** The Hautes-Alpes

**743** Chambéry and around

**749** The Isère valley and the Vanoise

**750** Annecy

**755** Mont Blanc

**762** Lake Geneva

**765** Besançon

**769** Lons-le-Saunier and around

**774** Belfort

ALPINE PERFECTION

# The Alps and Franche-Comté

**14**

The wild and rugged landscape of the Alps, formed by the collision of continental tectonic plates over tens of millions of years, and the eroding actions of multiple glaciers and fast-flowing rivers, contains some of Europe's most stunning mountain landscapes. King of all it surveys, and Europe's highest peak, is Mont Blanc, which sits pretty over the Chamonix valley below, itself the region's premier sporting playground. On offer are some of the most thrilling outdoor activities on the continent, from world-class skiing and mountain climbing, to superb road cycling and the most gentle of valley walks. While resorts like Chamonix absorb the lion's share of adrenaline-seeking visitors to the Alps, there are excellent alternatives, notably the Queyras and Écrins national parks.

Yet you'll also find plenty of charming villages and towns to explore, notably **Grenoble**, the economic capital of the Alps, which possesses a vibrant nightlife and lively cultural scene. **Chambéry**, too, offers stimulating cultural attractions alongside some wonderful Italianate architecture, while easy-going **Annecy** is a town whose picture-postcard lakeside setting is sure to delight. Close by, the genteel spa resort of **Aix-les-Bains** presents further possibilities for lake-bound fun, as does **Lake Geneva**, whose pristine shoreline is punctuated by well turned-out towns and villages like **Évian** and **Yvoire**. Further south, **Briançon**, one of the highest towns in Europe, offers Vauban's formidable fortress as a reminder of the tumultuous past of this region on France's eastern frontier.

The region of **Franche-Comté**, which lies to the northwest of Lake Geneva, was once ruled by the Grand Dukes of Burgundy, and annexed by France in the late seventeenth century. The four *départements* of Franche-Comté – the Territoire de Belfort, the Haute-Saône, the Doubs and the Jura are generally far more rural and less touristy than those in Rhone-Alpes. The region's capital, **Besançon**, is an attractive town built around imposing fortifications, developed by the French military engineer Vauban (see page 739) during the late 1600s.

Lying in the rich agricultural valley to the south of Besançon, the quiet town of **Lons-le-Saunier** provides a gateway to the Jura Mountains to the east. Composed of gentle, forested slopes in the west, of more sheer crags in the east and of high-forested plateaux in between, these mountains have long been popular for cross-country skiing, but the varied terrain also provides plenty of good trails for hikers. Note that the official *département* of Jura in the south of Franche-Comté does not contain the whole of the mountain range commonly known as the Jura; these mountains also stretch northward into the Doubs *département* as well as into Switzerland. A particular highlight in these mountains is the **Région des Lacs**, which possesses beautiful lakes, pine forests and small farming communities as well as ski resorts. At the northern tip of the region is the historic town of **Belfort**, a rewarding destination in itself, and one that makes a handy base for exploring the area.

## INFORMATION          THE ALPS AND FRANCHE-COMTÉ

**Getting around** Travelling around the Alps and Franche-Comté is relatively easy, with frequent trains between the major towns and resorts, while during the skiing season of December to April and the summer months of July and August, more bus services become available. The more remote areas of the Alps and Jura are difficult to reach without a car, but anyway are best explored on foot or by bicycle. Drivers should remember that some high passes in the east of the region, including the Col du Galibier and the Col de l'Iseran, can remain closed well into June. This can force you to make long detours into Italy via expensive Alpine tunnels.

**Useful websites** ⓦ auvergnerhonealpes-tourisme.com and ⓦ savoie-mont-blanc.com provide excellent introductions to the region. For the Franche-Comté area, check out ⓦ franche-comte.org.

ANNECY

# Highlights

**❶ Skiing and snowboarding** Test your skills from December to April in any number of world-class resorts, like Chamonix, Méribel and Val d'Isère. See pages 736, 759 and 752

**❷ Parc Naturel Régional du Queyras** Walk or drive through the empty mountain landscapes of the Queyras to St-Véran, one of the highest villages in Europe. See page 742

**❸ Annecy** Take a leisurely cruise on Annecy's beautiful lake and wander through the narrow lanes of its historic old town. See page 750

**❹ Aiguille du Midi** Brave one of the world's highest cable-car ascents for a spectacular view of Mont Blanc, the highest peak in Europe. See page 759

**❺ Lake Geneva** Enjoy the sedate pleasures of Évian and Yvoire on the French side of this huge and scenic lake, or hop on one of the frequent ferries to Switzerland. See page 762

**❻ Besançon** Explore the imposing Citadelle, the intriguing museums and the inviting cafés of the capital of Franche-Comté. See page 765

**❼ Jura Mountains** Far less visited than the Alps, this sublimely forested landscape is perfect for an abundance of outdoor pursuits, in particular cross-country skiing, hiking and mountain biking. See page 771

**HIGHLIGHTS ARE MARKED ON THE MAP ON PAGE 728**

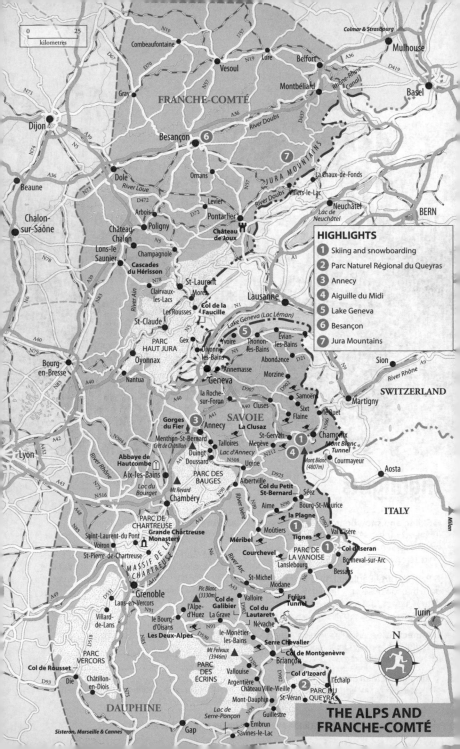

THE ALPS AND
FRANCHE-COMTÉ

**HIGHLIGHTS**

1 Skiing and snowboarding
2 Parc Naturel Régional du Queyras
3 Annecy
4 Aiguille du Midi
5 Lake Geneva
6 Besançon
7 Jura Mountains

SWITZERLAND

ITALY

FRANCHE-COMTÉ

JURA MOUNTAINS

SAVOIE

DAUPHINÉ

PARC
HAUT JURA

PARC DES
BAUGES

PARC DE
CHARTREUSE

MASSIF DE LA
CHARTREUSE

PARC
VERCORS

PARC
DES
ÉCRINS

PARC DE
LA VANOISE

PARC DU
QUEYRAS

0          25
kilometres

N

**Accommodation** Many of the hotels outside the main towns – and in particular the ski resorts – are often seasonal (closed in late spring and late autumn) and invariably over-priced, though booking ahead will often get you the best deals. There are plentiful campsites as well as hostels and *refuges* (huts), the former mostly open year-round, the latter generally open between mid-June and September.

# Grenoble

Set serenely at the confluence of the Drac and Isère rivers, **GRENOBLE**, the self-styled "capital of the Alps", is, at just 213m above sea level, France's lowest city, watched over by the snowcapped peaks of the Belledonne, Vercors and Chartreuse massifs. It's a vibrant and cosmopolitan place, home to more than 60,000 students and a lively cultural scene, while at its centre is a quirky maze of streets, where modern and medieval buildings are packed close together. Its restaurants and cafés, meanwhile, provide relaxing spots in which to sit and admire the grandeur of this fantastic mountain setting.

Settled by the Celtic Allobroges tribe, who called their settlement Cularo, it was renamed Gratianopolis by the Romans in the fourth century and became the seat of a bishop. The city was annexed by France in the fourteenth century, and it was here, far from Paris, that a local uprising in 1788 (known as the Journée des Tuiles) initiated the French Revolution. Grenoble is the final stop on the Route Napoléon; the French emperor arrived here on March 7, 1815, declaring "Before Grenoble, I was an adventurer. In Grenoble, I was a prince." The prosperity of the city was originally founded on glove-making, but in the nineteenth century its economy diversified to include industries as varied as mining and hydroelectric power, while more recently it has forged a reputation as a centre for scientific research in the electronic and nuclear industries.

## The téléphérique

Quai Stéphane-Jay • Times are complex but it's roughly May–Sept daily 9.15am–11.45pm (July & Aug till 12.15am, Mon from 11am; April & Oct Tues–Sun 9.30am–11.45pm; Nov–Feb Tues–Sun 11am–6.30pm, Fri & Sat till 11.45pm; closed three weeks in Jan • €8.20 return • ☎ 04 76 44 33 65, ⓦ bastille-grenoble.fr

---

### HIKING AND CLIMBING IN THE ALPS AND FRANCHE-COMTÉ

There are seven national or regional parks in the area covered by this chapter: Vanoise, Chartreuse, Bauges, Écrins, Queyras, Vercors and Haut Jura. All of these contain gentle day-walks and more demanding treks – not least classic long-distance paths like the Tour du Mont Blanc – which require one or two weeks' walking. Most of these routes are clearly marked and dotted with *refuge* huts; the routes are also described in high detail by the Topo-guides guidebooks (see page 49). Nonetheless, even the most experienced walkers or skiers treat these mountains and their unpredictable weather conditions with due respect. Even low-level walks in the Alps during summer often require a good level of fitness and specialist equipment, such as crampons or ice axes. You should take account of the weather conditions (which can vary considerably between the valleys and peaks), of the potentially debilitating effects of high altitude, and of the serious danger of avalanches.

The Alps were the first great centre for European rock climbers in the nineteenth century and still offer countless routes that can be enjoyed by both novices and world-class climbers. Hugely popular too are *via ferrata* courses, in which wires and ladders are bolted onto the rock so that even inexperienced climbers (wearing harnesses and ropes) can make ascents which would otherwise be impossible for them. There are *via ferrata* courses being developed across the whole region, but at present two of the largest centres for this popular sport are at Serre Chevalier and in the Parc National des Écrins.

The **Bureau Info Montagne** office in Grenoble and the **Office de Haute Montagne** in Chamonix can provide information on the best guides and the most up-to-date information on all the GR paths and the best *via ferrata* courses, while local tourist offices often produce detailed maps of walks in their own areas.

The best way to start your tour of the city is to take the **téléphérique** to **Fort de la Bastille** on the steep slopes above the northern bank of the Isère. One of the world's first urban cable cars, built in 1934, it's a hair-raising ride as you're whisked swiftly into the air in a transparent glass ball towards the Bastille 263m above. The journey is not for those of a claustrophobic disposition, though one alternative is to climb the steep footpath from the St-Laurent church on the northern bank of the Isère. For the more adventurous, there's a *via ferrata* along the walls leading up to the Bastille, comprising two fairly difficult stages, each around forty-five minutes long. If you fancy having a go, contact the Maison de la Montagne (see page 733).

## Fort de la Bastille

The **Bastille's** main draw is its spectacular **views**. At your feet, the Isère flows under old bridges which join the St-Laurent quarter (a home for Italian immigrants in the late 1800s) on the northern bank of the river to the nucleus of the medieval town. Even this far south, if you look northeast on a clear day you can see the distant white peaks of Mont Blanc further up the deep valley of the Isère. To the east, snowfields gleam in the high gullies of the Belledonne massif (2978m). To the southeast is the peak of Le Taillefer (2807m), while further to the south you can make out the mountain pass which the

| ■ ACCOMMODATION | | | ● EATING | | | | ■ DRINKING | |
|---|---|---|---|---|---|---|---|---|
| Auberge de Jeunesse | 7 | Le Grand Hôtel | L'Auberge Napoléon | 5 | La Gratin Dauphinois | 4 | La Boîte à Sardines | 2 |
| Brit Hôtel Suisse et | | Grenoble | 3 | Café de la Table Ronde | 1 | Jardin du Thé | 8 | Le Café des Arts | 1 |
| Bordeaux | 2 | Institut | 1 | Chardon Bleu | 7 | Le Rousseau | 6 | | |
| Camping Le Bois | | Okko | 5 | La Ferme à Dédé | 2 | | | | |
| de Cornage | 6 | Park Hotel | | La Gazzetta | 3 | | | | |
| De l'Europe | 4 | Grenoble | 8 | | | | | | |

## FOOD AND DRINK IN THE ALPS AND FRANCHE-COMTÉ

Most characteristic of Alpine cuisine is the liberal amount of cheese made from the local cow, ewe and goat milk. The *fromageries* of Franche-Comté and the Northern Alps are full of cheeses like Roblochon, Tome des Bauges, Emmental, Chèvre, Comté and Beaufort. These are found not just in the famous fondue, but also *raclette* and *tartiflette* (both cheese-based dishes served with ham and potatoes). Other cheeses worth seeking out include the smooth blue-veined Bleu de Gex, produced exclusively in the Pays de Gex region, and creamy Saint-Marcellin, from the Grenoble area.

Many restaurants feature **fish** (notably salmon and trout) from the Alpine lakes and use locally grown herbs, like thyme, basil and rosemary. These herbs are particularly in evidence in the Southern Alps around Briançon, where they are often used to flavour the *saucisson* (cured sausage), which you'll find in many a morning shopping market.

The region produces many light and fruity varieties of **wine**, of which the most popular is the dark red Mondeuse, with its faint taste of raspberries. By contrast, the expensive *vin jaune* from the Jura is a potent, golden wine, made from Sauvignon grapes with a fermentation process similar to that of sherry – it remains in the cask for 6–10 years before being bottled. *Vin jaune* is a favourite accompaniment for the local cheeses of Franche-Comté, and is used in speciality dishes such as *poulet au vin jaune* (chicken in a creamy sauce flavoured by the wine). It's also worth sampling some regional **liqueurs**. The most famous of these is undoubtedly **Chartreuse**, the drink produced by Carthusian monks since the sixteenth century, which contains 130 different herbs and is known as the "elixir of life", while Chambéry is famous for its high-quality **vermouth**, including the unique Chambéryzette, flavoured with strawberries.

14

famous Route Napoléon crosses on its way northwards from the Mediterranean. This was the road towards Paris that Napoleon took after his escape from Elba in March 1815. Finally, to the west you can admire Moucherotte (1901m), one of the highest peaks of the Vercors massif, and the mountain which most seems to dominate the city beneath.

### Musée des Troupes de Montagne

Tues–Sun 11am–6pm, closed Jan • €3, including audioguide • ☏ 04 76 00 92 25, ⊚ museedestroupesdemontagne.fr

Although the well-preserved nineteenth-century fortifications were never tested in battle, part of the Fort de la Bastille now houses the **Musée des Troupes de Montagne**, dedicated to the history of the French mountain troops. The first alpine units were formed in 1888, since which time they've been engaged in many major combat situations, not least both World Wars, while more recent missions have included Bosnia and Afghanistan. The equipment and uniform on display testify to the exacting terrain and conditions the Chasseurs Alpins, or "Les diables bleus" (The Blue Devils), are often required to operate in.

## Musée Dauphinois

30 rue Maurice-Gignoux • Daily except Tues: June–Aug 10am–7pm; Sept–May 10am–6pm • Free • ☏ 04 57 58 89 01, ⊚ musee-dauphinois.fr

Up a steep cobbled path opposite the St-Laurent footbridge, the **Musée Dauphinois** is located in a former convent, and is devoted to the history, arts and crafts of the Dauphiné province. In the basement, there's a Baroque chapel with grey and gold wall paintings depicting episodes from the New Testament and scenes from the life of St-François-de-Sales, the convent's founder. In the museum proper, there's plenty of information on the lives of the rugged and self-sufficient Dauphinois mountain people, but perhaps the most memorable exhibit details the evolution of skiing in the area over the last four thousand years, right through to the modern winter sports that came to Grenoble when it hosted the 1968 Winter Olympics.

## Musée Archéologique Grenoble Saint-Laurent

Place St-Laurent • Daily except Tues 10am–6pm • Free • ☏ 04 76 44 78 68, ⊚ musee-archeologique-grenoble.fr

Housed within the former **Église St-Laurent** is the superbly renovated **Musée Archéologique**, whose spectacular hoard of grave goods was unearthed from some 1500 graves. Evidence points to pagan and Christian worship dating back as far as the fourth century, with earthenware, jewellery and coins among the many precious items recovered. Its centrepiece, though, is an eighth-century crypt and a medieval cloister.

## The old town

The narrow streets of the **old town** on the southern bank of the Isère, particularly around places Grenette, Vaucanson, Verdun and Notre-Dame, make up the liveliest and most colourful quarter of the city. Here, too, there is plenty of cultural interest, not least one of France's most renowned art collections.

### Musée de Grenoble

5 place de Lavalette • Daily except Tues 10am–6.30pm • €8, free first Sun of the month • ☎ 04 76 63 44 44, ⓦ museedegrenoble.fr

A vast modern complex down by the riverbank, the **Musée de Grenoble** is home to one of the country's most prestigious art collections. The classical wing has a fine spread of masterpieces spanning the thirteenth to nineteenth centuries. Pieces by Rubens, Veronese, and Canaletto take centre stage in the first few rooms, followed by nineteenth-century luminaries Gauguin, Renoir, and local hero, Henri Fantin-Latour. Once you've absorbed those, there is still a further two dozen or so rooms of twentieth-century and modern art to negotiate, including works by Chagall, Matisse, Picasso and Warhol, to name but a few. If you can summon the energy, take a peek at the basement collection of Egyptian antiquities.

### Musée de l'Ancien Évêché

2 rue Très-Cloîtres • Mon, Tues, Thurs & Fri 9am–6pm, Wed 1–6pm, Sat & Sun 11am–6pm • Free • ☎ 04 76 03 15 25, ⓦ ancien-eveche-isere.fr

Housed in the old bishop's palace, the **Musée de l'Ancien Évêché** offers a brisk tour through Grenoble's history from the Stone Age onwards. The remains of the Roman town walls and a fifth-century **baptistry** are on show in the basement, while upstairs you will find the oldest human skull found in the Alps, dating back 11,000 years, Iron Age jewellery and many Roman artefacts, including a colourful mosaic floor panel depicting a pair of parrots. The absence of any English captioning does, however, make this a frustrating visit.

### Musée de la Résistance et de la Déportation de l'Isère

14 rue Hébert • Mon, Wed, Thurs, Fri 9am–6pm, Tues 1.30–6pm, Sat & Sun 10am–6pm • Free • ☎ 04 76 42 38 53, ⓦ resistance-en-isere.fr

As sobering as it is insightful, the excellent **Musée de la Résistance et de la Déportation de l'Isère** relates the history of the Nazi occupation of the Dauphiné, from where some 2600 people were deported, including a thousand Jews. Alongside the wealth of poignant and personal wartime memorabilia, the role of the Resistance fighters is given due prominence, Isère being one of the major centres of the Resistance movement in France during World War II. The combination of guerrilla warfare activities, intelligence, and clandestine publications such as *Les Allobroges* (established in 1942) were all, ultimately, key to ensuring Allied success.

---

**ARRIVAL AND DEPARTURE**                                   **GRENOBLE**

**By plane** Grenoble-Isère airport (☎ 04 76 65 48 48, ⓦ grenoble-airport.com) is 45km to the northwest of the city. Buses run hourly from the airport to the *gare routière* in Grenoble (45min; €14.50), and in winter, there are also frequent buses between the airport and the ski resorts of Les Deux-Alpes and L'Alpe d'Huez (1hr 30min; €40).

**By train** The *gare SNCF* is at the western end of avenue Félix-Viallet, just ten minutes' walk from the centre.

Destinations Annecy (11 daily; 1hr 45min); Briançon, changing at Gap (5 daily; 4hr 20min); Chambéry (frequent; 45min–1hr); Lyon (every 30min; 1hr 25min); Paris-Lyon (8 daily; 3hr).

**By bus** The *gare routière* is next to the *gare SNCF*.

Destinations Le Bourg-d'Oisans (6 daily; 1hr); Briançon (2 daily; 2hr 40min); Chambéry (hourly; 2hr); Col du Lautaret (2 daily; 1hr 50min); La Grave (2 daily; 1hr 30min); St-Pierre-de-Chartreuse (6 daily; 1hr 10min).

## INFORMATION

**Tourist office** In the ugly concrete building at 14 rue de la République (July–Sept Mon–Sat 10am–7pm, Sun 9am–noon; Oct–June Mon 1–6pm, Tues–Fri 10am–6pm, Sat 10am–1pm & 2–6pm; ☏ 04 76 42 41 41, ⊛ grenoble-tourisme.com).

**Maison de la Montagne** The "House of the Mountains", in the same building as the tourist office (Mon–Fri 9.30am–12.30pm & 1–6pm, Sat 10am–1pm & 2–5pm; ☏ 04 76 44 67 03, ⊛ grenoble-montagne.com), is the place to go for info on mountain activities in the region, including walking

suggestions, detailed information on *refuges* (including taking bookings), weather conditions and guides. Maps are also sold here.

**Grenoble Passes** If you're in town for more than a day or two, it might be worth considering buying a Grenoble Pass (⊛ grenoblepass.com) from the tourist office, which you can get for one (€19), two (€28), or three (€48) days: among its benefits are free public transport, a guided tour of the Old Town and a return trip on the *téléphérique*.

## GETTING AROUND

With the exception of the hilly north bank of the Isère, Grenoble is compact and flat enough to negotiate by foot. That said, there's a useful bus and tram system in place should you start to flag.

**Public transport** This comprises five tramlines – the most useful of which are lines A and B which pass outside the train station and go through the city centre – in addition to a host of bus lines. You can pick up the handy tram and bus map at the public transport office (TAG), which is located at 49 avenue Alsace-Lorraine (Mon–Fri 7.15am–6.30pm, Sat 9.30am–6pm).

**Tickets** A single ticket costs €1.60, but better value is the one-day *Visitag* (€5.40). If you're staying longer, consider

the three-day *Visitag* (€12) or a *carnet* of ten (€14.50). Tickets for buses can be bought from the driver (€2.10), but tickets for trams must be bought at machines outside tram stations or at the TAG office.

**Bike rental** Metrovélo in the underpass of the *gare SNCF*, place de la Gare; €3 per day, including helmet and lock; ☏ 08 20 22 38 38, ⊛ metrovelo.fr. There's also an excellent little fold-out map (Le plan du cycliste urbain) available.

**Taxi** Grenoblois 14 rue de la République ☏ 04 76 54 42 54, ⊛ taxi-grenoble38.fr. Provides a 24hr radio taxi service.

**Car hire** All the following have outlets at or opposite the *gare SNCF*: Avis ☏ 04 56 40 61 35; Europcar ☏ 08 25 88 70 90; Hertz ☏ 04 76 86 55 80.

## ACCOMMODATION

**Auberge de Jeunesse** 10 av du Grésivaudan ☏ 04 76 09 33 52, ⊛ fuaj.org. This modern hostel has comprehensive facilities including common room, laundry, cycle storage, restaurant and self-catering kitchen, which is useful as there's a supermarket close by. It's 5km south of the city centre in a large park in Échirolles; bus #1 to the "Quinzaine" stop or tram A to "La Rampe". Breakfast included. From **€20**

**Brit Hôtel Suisse et Bordeaux** 6 place de la Gare ☏ 04 76 47 55 87, ⊛ grenoble-center-brithotel.fr. Opposite the railway station, this grand nineteenth-century building – take a look up at the fabulous tiled facade – has been neatly refashioned with sparkling all cream and white rooms (including triples and quads) enhanced with the odd splash of colour. Note that the entrance is on avenue Félix-Viallet. Breakfast €8. **€55**

**Camping Le Bois de Cornage** 110 chemin du Camping, Vizille ☏ 04 76 68 12 39, ⊛ campingvizille.com. Around 15km from the city centre, this three-star campsite has a swimming pool, playground, restaurant and pizzeria on site. Take bus #3000 from the *gare routière* in Grenoble and get off at stop "Place du Château" in Vizille. Open April–Oct. Chalets are available by the week and sleep six people. Camping **€18**, chalet **€485** per week

**De l'Europe** 22 place Grenette ☏ 04 76 46 16 94, ⊛ hoteleurope.fr. With its stuccoed facade and elegant, wrought-iron balconies, Grenoble's oldest hotel promises much,

but the rooms themselves – a mix of standard and superior – are on the simple side. Still, they're well turned out and the location overlooking a central square is arguably the best in the city. Breakfast €9.50. Weekend rates are cheaper. **€69**

**Le Grand Hôtel Grenoble** 5 rue de la République ☏ 04 76 51 22 59, ⊛ grand-hotel-grenoble.com. The city's most luxurious hotel, whose triple-glazed rooms are surprisingly modest in size, though boast sumptuous beds with the crispest of linen, grey silk curtains, and glass-fronted cupboards – the dazzling bathrooms, meanwhile, are tiled brilliant-white and feature walk-in showers. Expect the likes of salmon and foie gras for breakfast (€15). **€140**

**Institut** 10 rue Barbillon ☏ 04 76 46 36 44, ⊛ institut-hotel.fr. Two blocks in from the train station, this friendly two-star *Logis* hotel provides small and functional but neatly presented, a/c rooms, and on the whole represents pretty good value for money. Triples and quads available too. Breakfast €8.90. **€55**

★ **Okko** 23 rue Hoche ☏ 04 85 19 00 10, ⊛ okkohotels.com. The central concept at *Okko* is the Club Lounge, a kitchen-cum-lounge where guests are free to kick back and avail themselves of snacks and drinks (one glass of wine, the remainder non-alcoholic) all day long, then around 6pm, a delicious buffet spread (cheese, meats etc) appears. With all this going on, it's easy to forget that you've got a room to go to; modestly sized, but snappily designed, the neat little

**14**

extras like bottles of water and a Nespresso machine round things off brilliantly. Breakfast is included. **€95**

**Park Hotel Grenoble** 10 place Paul-Mistral ☎ 04 76 85 81 23, ⓦ park-hotel-grenoble.fr. Within comfortable walking distance of the centre, the *Park* is a sparkling addition to the city's hotel scene, its plush, heavily glassed rooms furnished in various hues of red and grey offset with black trim. Impeccably serviced too. Trams A and C stop close by. Breakfast €19. **€129**

## EATING, DRINKING AND NIGHTLIFE

### CAFÉS AND RESTAURANTS

**L'Auberge Napoléon** 7 rue Montorge ☎ 04 76 87 53 64, ⓦ auberge-napoleon.fr. The city's most upmarket, if not most well-regarded, restaurant, offering fine evening-only cuisine such as Limousin veal tenderloin with hot foie gras, and hot poached oysters with black radish. The heavily glassed and mirrored decor might be a bit much for some, but it's all part of the package. Starters €14, mains €28. Closed first two weeks Aug. Mon–Sat 7.30–9.30pm.

**Café de La Table Ronde** 7 place St-André ☎ 04 76 44 51 41, ⓦ restaurant-tableronde-grenoble.com. Allegedly France's second-oldest café, founded in 1739, this has always been a hotspot for writers, artists and tourists. The mirrored interior is an atmospheric place to linger over a coffee, but when the sun comes out, the terrace is as enjoyable a place as any to quaff a beer or two. Alternatively, try a cup of Green Chaud (Chartreuse with hot chocolate). Daily noon–2.30pm & 7–11pm. Closed Sun in winter.

**Chardon Bleu** 23 av Alsace-Lorraine ☎ 04 76 12 05 93, ⓦ auchardonbleu.com. Big, bold and bright café-cum-patisserie that doles out a whole lot more besides irresistible-looking home-made pastries and coffee, namely quiches, lasagne, and a tasty little *pâté en croûte*, as well as breakfasts (€7.50) and a *plat du jour* (€9.95). Park yourself down on a stool at one of the simple plastic tables or take your grub with you. Mon–Sat 6.45am–7.45pm.

★ **La Ferme à Dédé** 24 rue Barnave ☎ 04 76 54 00 33, ⓦ restaurantlafermeadede.com. You could be forgiven for thinking you were halfway up a mountain in this fun, almost Lyonnais bouchon-style restaurant, with its red-and-white-checked tablecloths and randomly scattered alpine junk. Big menu featuring hearty sausage casseroles, gooey Savoyard fondues, and local favourites, *raclette* and *tartiflette*. Packed to the gills most nights. Starters €10, mains €14. Daily noon–2.30pm & 7–11.30pm.

**La Gazzetta** 30 av Félix-Viallet ☎ 04 76 50 22 22, ⓦ gazzetta.fr. A cut above your average Italian, *La Gazzetta* offers sublimely crafted dishes like mushroom and foie gras ravioli, and pappardelle with crayfish and asparagus tips. The risotto dishes are also worth a shot, or you could just settle for a pizza. The black and orange colour scheme, big bay windows and mezzanine-level seating lend the place a with-it, lounge-like vibe. Pizza €9, pasta €13. Mon–Fri noon–2pm & 7–10pm, Sat 7–10.30pm.

**Le Gratin Dauphinois** 52 av Félix-Viallet ☎ 04 56 17 75 47, ⓦ jaimelegratindauphinois.com. As the name suggests, gratins dishes (€17) is what it's all about at this perky little establishment, for example gratin ravioles with crayfish, or gratin ravioles with blue Vercor cheese, accompanied by a fresh seasonal salad. *Menus* from €12–27. Mon–Fri 11am–2pm & 7–10pm.

★ **Jardin du Thé** 2 rue Millet ☎ 04 76 27 09 45. Straddling two sides of a pleasantly shaded pedestrianized street, the glass-fronted "Tea Garden" is a delightful spot to rest up and sample one (or more) of some three hundred varieties of tea, piled high in bright red tins, alongside a home-made scone or cookie. Note: you won't find any coffee here. Mon–Sat 9.30am–8pm.

**Le Rousseau** 3 rue Jean-Jacques-Rousseau ☎ 04 76 62 04 18. Diminutive place tucked away down a little side street off place Ste-Claire, featuring white, rough-hewn walls, cool blue spotlights, and perfectly set tables. Expect dishes like salmon and cream *ravioles*, and seared foie gras with apples. *Menus* from €27. Starters €12, mains €16. Tues–Sat noon–2pm & 7–10.30pm.

### BARS

**La Boîte à Sardines** 1 place Claveyson ☎ 04 76 44 27 84. Cool name, cool place – which just about sums up the "Box of Sardines", a quirky, easy-going watering hole where you can sup on a crisp draught Belgian beer (€3.50–6) or a mojito while contemplating the rather peculiar decor. Mon 5pm–1am, Tues–Sat noon–1am.

**Le Café des Arts** 36 rue St-Laurent ☎ 04 76 54 65 31, ⓦ lecafedesarts38.fr. Entertainment-wise, there's little reason to visit the north bank, but this place is the exception. From Thursdays through to Saturdays, there's a humdinger of a live music programme, from African blues and Balkan jazz to classical and chanson – on these nights you can enjoy a very reasonably priced concert with dinner (Thurs €15, Fri & Sat €20). Wed 5–11pm, Thurs–Sat 7pm–midnight.

## DIRECTORY

**Bookshops** BD Fugue, rue Jean-François-Hache (Mon 10am–7pm, Tues–Sat 9.30am–7pm; ☎ 04 38 37 18 36), is the place to go for French-language comic books, and it also has a super little Tintin-themed café. Librairie des Alpes, 1 rue Casimir-Périer (Tues–Sat 10am–noon & 3–7pm; ☎ 04 76 51 57 98) has an excellent collection of new and secondhand coffee-table books on the Alps.

**Festivals** Grenoble's premier annual event is Cabaret Frappé (ⓦ cabaret-frappe.com), a week-long celebration of contemporary jazz, soul, world and experimental music held at venues around town in late July. In keeping with the musical vibe, the superb Détours de Babel (ⓦ detoursdebabel.fr), from mid-March through to early April, proposes a different theme each year, for example,

Music and Politics, or Music and Identity.

**Health** Centre Hospitalier Universitaire (CHU) ☎ 04 76 76 50 25; ambulance Alp'Azur (a private ambulance company) ☎ 04 76 21 11 11.

**Pharmacy** There are several large pharmacies in the centre which have long opening hours. Pharmacie Victor-Hugo, 2 bd Agutte-Sembat (daily 8am–8pm) ☎ 04 76 46 04 15.

**Police** 36 bd du Maréchal-Leclerc ☎ 04 76 60 40 40.

# The Chartreuse massif

ⓦ chartreuse-tourisme.com

Nestling a short way north of Grenoble, the **Chartreuse massif** is a place of spectacular landscapes, including sharp limestone peaks, mountain pastures and large areas of pine forest. Designated in 1995 as the **Parc Naturel Régional de la Chartreuse** the landscape provides wonderful opportunities for all manner of recreational pursuits. The **Maison de la Montagne** office in Grenoble (see page 733) can offer advice on many of these activities, and also publishes descriptions of the various hiking routes in the area.

## The Grande Chartreuse Monastery and Musée de la Grande Chartreuse

**Musée de la Grande Chartreuse** • April, May, Sept to early Nov daily except Thurs 2–6pm; June–Aug daily except Thurs 10am–6.30pm, Sun 2–6.30pm • €8.50, including audioguide • ☎ 04 76 88 60 45, ⓦ musee-grande-chartreuse.fr

The massif's main local landmark is the **Grande Chartreuse Monastery**, situated up the narrow Gorges des Guiers Morts, southeast of St-Laurent-du-Pont, and some 35km from Grenoble. Carthusian monks and nuns seek a life of contemplation following the example of their founder, the eleventh-century monk St Bruno, a life which involves long periods of solitude, silence, work and prayer. Members of the order live in cells and meet only for Mass and a weekly communal meal, eaten in silence. Since 1605, however, the Carthusians have also become famous as the producers of various **Chartreuses**, powerfully alcoholic herbal elixirs ranging from the better-known green and yellow variants to a number of gentler fruit and nut liqueurs. The monastery is not open to the public, but near the village of **St-Pierre-de-Chartreuse**, 5km back on the Grenoble road, you can visit the **Musée de la Grande Chartreuse**, formerly La Correrie monastery, which illustrates the life of the Carthusian Order.

## Voiron

**Caves de la Chartreuse** 10 bd Edgar-Kofler • March–Oct daily 10am–12.30pm & 2–6.30pm; Nov–Feb Mon–Fri 10am–12.30pm & 2–6pm • free, but guided tours in English (June–Aug daily at noon) cost €15 • ☎ 04 76 05 81 77, ⓦ chartreuse.fr

For those interested in the local liqueurs, a visit to **VOIRON**, 30km west of the park and on the train line from Grenoble to Lyon, is most definitely in order. Here, you'll find the **Caves de la Chartreuse**, where the "elixir of life" has been bottled since 1737. These days, the herbs (some 130 of them) are picked, crushed and mixed in great secrecy at the monastery by just two monks, before being transferred to the distillery here in Voiron. It is the monks, too, who decide when the liqueur is ripe for bottling, which is typically several years into the maturation process. Following an informative 3-D film on the history of the monastery and the secret manuscript with the recipe of the original liqueur (which dates from 1605), you are taken through the world's largest liqueur cellars – built in 1860 and some 160 metres long – before the real highlight of the tour; a tasting of one of the beverages themselves.

## Le Bourg-d'Oisans

Connecting Grenoble to Briançon, the **N91** twists through the precipitous valley of the Romanche and over the **Col du Lautaret** (2058m), which is kept open all year round and crossed at least a couple of times a day (and more often during the skiing season) by the Grenoble–Briançon bus. The first major settlement on the route, **LE BOURG-D'OISANS** (known as "Le Bourg"), 20km southeast of Grenoble, is of no great interest in itself, but it sits in a beautiful position in the valley and is a good base for summer sports. It's particularly popular with cyclists.

14

### INFORMATION                                          LE BOURG D'OISANS

**Tourist office** On quai Girard, by the river in the middle of town (July & Aug daily 9am–7pm; Sept–June Mon–Sat 9am–noon & 2–6pm; ☎ 04 76 80 03 25, ⓦ bourgdoisans.com); you can pick up lots of excellent information on hiking routes here. **Maison du Parc National des Écrins** 120 rue Gambetta (July & Aug daily 10am–noon & 3–6pm; Sept–June Mon–

Fri 9–11am & 1.30–4pm; ☎ 04 76 80 00 51, ⓦ ecrins-parcnational.fr); they can also advise on hiking possibilities within the park boundary.
**Bicycle rental** Road and mountain bikes from Au Cadre Rouge, 20 rue du Général-de-Gaulle (☎ 04 76 80 13 81), for €27 per day; they also do repairs.

## La Grave

Continuing on the N91 towards La Grave past the modern ski resort of **Les Deux-Alpes**, you'll pass two waterfalls issuing from the north side of the valley: early summer run-off enhances the 300m plume of the **Cascade de la Pisse**, while, 6km further on is the near-vertical fall of churning whitewater called the **Saut de la Pucelle** ("the virgin's leap") – a breathtaking sight.

**LA GRAVE**, 18km on from the Barrage du Lac du Chambon, lies at the foot of the Col du Lautaret, facing the majestic glaciers of the north side of **La Meije** (3984m). While it lies at the heart of a large and testing ski area, La Grave, with its small collection of stone buildings, could not be a more different environment than Les Deux-Alpes. In addition to the skiing opportunities, it's also a good base for walkers and climbers; the **GR54** passes to the northwest of the village, and there are also two equipped *via ferrata* courses nearby (an easier one at Arsine and a tougher course at the Mines du Grand Clot).

---

### SKIING IN THE ALPS

With their long and varied runs, extensive lift networks, and superb après-ski, the French Alps offer some of the best skiing not just in Europe, but in the world. Skiing first became a recreational sport here in the early 1900s but the industry really began to boom in the Alps during the 1960s with the construction of dozens of high-altitude, purpose-built resorts that ensured good lasting snow cover. Some of these resorts have their detractors: the modern architects often created sprawling concrete settlements that had little in common with the traditional farming villages lower in the valleys, and in so doing they earned France a lasting reputation for "ski factories". Nonetheless, few can knock the efficiency of these resorts. They have an abundance of hotels, equipment outlets and ski schools, while at many you can simply clip your skis on at the hotel door and be skiing on some of the most challenging pistes on earth within minutes.

Although downhill is the most common form of the sport at all the resorts, **cross-country** or **nordic skiing** has become increasingly popular on gentler slopes (particularly around Morzine and in the Parc Naturel Régional du Queyras), while there are also several famous routes for **ski touring** (a form of cross-country skiing with uphill sections and across much longer distances), not least the **Haute Route** between Chamonix and Zermatt (Switzerland) and the **Grande Traversée des Alpes**, which leads south from Thonon-les-Bains on Lake Geneva through several national parks. There are also plenty of opportunities for **snowboarding** with many resorts having developed snow parks expressly for snowboarders.

The ski **season** runs from December to late April, with high season over Christmas and New Year, February half-term and (to a lesser extent) Easter.

If you don't want to walk, then an easier way of appreciating the stunning vistas is provided by the *télécabine* (mid-June to early Sept & late Dec to early May; €23 return), which rises sharply from the centre of the village to the 3200m summit of **Le Rateau**, just west of La Meije. The 35-minute ride is value for money considering that the view of the barely accessible interior of the Écrins is normally seen only by the most intrepid mountaineers. The lift also provides access to acres of off-piste skiing, and the freezing conditions of the mountain's northerly face make it ideal for ice climbing.

From La Grave it's only 11km to the top of the **Col du Lautaret**, a pass which is generally kept clear for traffic during the winter months, despite its high altitude (2057m). Around the col is a huge expanse of meadow long known to botanists for its glorious variety of Alpine flowers, which are seen at their best in mid-July.

**14**

### INFORMATION AND ACCOMMODATION                                   LA GRAVE

**Bureau des Guides** Place du Téléphérique (mid-Dec to mid-May & mid-June to mid-Sept; ☎04 76 79 90 21, ⓦguidelagrave.com). Provides guides for the different hiking paths in the area, as well as guides for activities such as caving, canyoning and mountain biking.

**Hôtel Castillan** ☎04 76 70 90 04, ⓦle-castillan.com. A large, welcoming hotel plumb in the centre of the village that's inevitably popular with skiers and cyclists; rooms are on the simple side, but they're cheap and there's also a pool and sauna. Triples and quads available too. Breakfast €9. **€48**

# The Hautes-Alpes

The **Hautes-Alpes** make up the area of high mountains to the southeast of Grenoble and south of the Massif de la Vanoise. To the east lies the Italian border and to the south, the Alpes de Provence. The region is sliced in two by the Durance valley, with the **Parc National des Écrins** lying on the western side of the divide and the **Parc Naturel Régional du Queyras** on the eastern. At the head of the Durance valley, where the Guisane and Durance rivers converge, is the ancient fortified city of **Briançon** which makes an excellent base for exploring the surrounding region.

## Briançon

Located 100km east of Grenoble along the N91, **Briançon** is the capital of the Écrins and one of Europe's highest towns at 1350m above sea level. The town is essentially split between the steep, narrow streets of the **ville haute** (also known as the Cité Vauban), which sits high above the urban spread of the modern and charmless lower town (**ville basse**), itself of little interest save for the **Télécabine de Prorel** (Dec–April & July–Aug; €14.50 return), which shoots up from avenue René-Froger, linking Briançon with the Serre-Chevalier ski resort. It also provides a head start to mountain walkers.

### Ville haute
English-language tours take place throughout the year on Tuesdays at 4pm (€7.50)

The **ville haute** looms on the cusp of a rocky outcrop high above the Durance and Guisane valleys. Fortified originally by the Romans to guard the road from Milan to Vienne, it's encircled by lofty ramparts and sheer walls constructed by the French architect and soldier Sébastien Le Preste de Vauban in the seventeenth century.

The highest point of the fortifications is the **citadelle**, which looks over the strategic intersection of five valleys and guards the start of the climb to the desolate and windswept **Col de Montgenèvre**, one of the oldest and most important passes into Italy. There are four **gates**: portes Dauphine and Pignerol lie to the north, porte d'Embrun to the southwest and porte de la Durance to the east. If you come by car the best option is to park at the **Champ de Mars** at the top of the hill and enter the town through the porte Pignerol. From here the narrow main street, Grande Rue – known as the *grande gargouille* because of the "gurgling" stream running down the middle – tips steeply downhill, bordered by mostly eighteenth-century houses. Almost halfway down and to the right is the sturdy **collegiate church**, designed under the supervision of Vauban, again with an eye to defence. Beyond it, there's a fantastic **view** from the walls, especially on a clear starry night, when the snows on the surrounding barrier of mountains give off a silvery glow. Continuing further down Grande Rue, and turning left, you'll find the blocky **Cordeliers church**, Briançon's sole surviving medieval building; it's only occasionally open to visitors, but there are some colourful, well-preserved fifteenth-century murals inside.

**14**

## ARRIVAL AND INFORMATION

BRIANÇON

**By train** The *gare SNCF* is on av de la République in the *ville basse*; local buses #1 and #3 (€1.50) link the station and the Champ de Mars in the *ville haute*.

Destinations (train) Embrun (6 daily; 45min); Gap (6 daily; 1hr 25min); Marseille (3 daily; 4hr 30min).

Destinations (bus) Col du Lautaret (2 daily; 50min); Gap (8 daily; 1hr 45min); La Grave (2 daily; 1hr 10min); St-Véran via Guillestre (1–2 daily; 1hr 40min); Vallouise via Argentière (1 daily; 2hr).

**Tourist office** In the *ville haute* at 1 place du Temple, close to the porte Pignerol gateway (July & Aug daily 9am–noon & 2–7pm; Sept–June Mon–Fri 9am–noon & 2–6pm; ☏ 04

92 21 08 50, ⊚ serre-chevalier.com).

**Bureau des Guides** In the *ville basse* at 24 rue Centrale (July & Aug Mon–Fri 10am–noon & 3–7pm, Sat 3–7pm, Sun 10am–1pm; Sept–June daily 5–7pm; ☏ 04 92 20 15 73, ⊚ guides-briancon.com), this is the place to head to for information about outdoor activities in the mountains.

**Maison du Parc National des Écrins** Place du Médecin-Général-Blanchard in the *ville haute* (July & Aug daily 10am–noon & 3–7pm; Sept–June Mon–Fri 2–5pm; ☏ 04 92 21 42 15, ⊚ ecrins-parcnational.fr), provides maps for those venturing into the nearby Écrins massif.

## ACCOMMODATION

There's a half-decent choice of hotels in town, although most are located down in the dull *ville basse*, with just a couple of options in the old town.

**Camping des Cinq Vallées** St-Blaise ☏ 04 92 21 06 27, ⊚ camping5vallees.com. Located 2km south of the town, this welcoming campsite has all the facilities you'd expect of a three-star site, including heated outdoor pool, shop, laundry, playground and pizzeria. June to mid-Sept. **€21**

**De la Chaussée** 4 rue Centrale ☏ 04 92 21 10 37, ⊚ hotel-de-la-chaussee.com. Super *ville basse* option offering a slice of Alpine chic amid the modern, grey surrounds; pine-panelled walls and ceilings, chunky wooden furnishings, sliding wooden doors and sweet little bathrooms with cute sinks and wood-framed mirrors. Breakfast €11. **€95**

**Parc** Avenue du 159E Ria ☏ 04 92 20 37 47, ⊚ soleil vacances.com. Briançon's largest hotel occupies most of

the lower town's small central park, and while the rooms are nothing out of the ordinary, they're generously proportioned and do have splendid views of the surrounding mountains. Breakfast €10. **€75**

**Des Remparts** 14 av Vauban ☏ 04 92 21 08 73, ⊚ hotel desremparts.eu. The location, just inside the porte Pignerol, is fabulous, but the eight rooms, some of which have a shower and some just a sink, are extremely basic at best – which is why it's as cheap as chips. The bar is the reception. Breakfast €6. **€35**

**Vauban** 13 av du Général-de-Gaulle ☏ 04 92 21 12 11, ⊚ hotel-vauban-briancon.com. Close to both the station and ski lift, this is a decent lower town option, with carpeted, pine-clad rooms (including triples) – most with balcony – that offer fair value for money. Smart little billiard/bar lounge and a decent breakfast spread (€10) to set you on your way. **€78**

## EATING AND DRINKING

When it comes to eating and drinking, make tracks for the *ville haute*, which is chock-a-block with cafés and restaurants, but choose carefully as some of these can be rather hit and miss.

**Au Plaisir Ambré** 26 Grande Rue ☏ 04 92 52 63 46, ⊚ auplaisirambre.com. Refined cooking in a handsome restaurant offering several short *menus* (from €26) featuring some deliciously meaty dishes such as veal sweetbreads in garlic crumbs and hazelnut juice, and pigeon with mash and roasted pears. Fri–Tues noon–2pm & 7–9.30pm.

**Le Panier Alpin** 50 Grande Rue ☏ 04 86 99 57 13. For something light, this gorgeous, and very arty, *épicerie-cum-*

tearoom is just the ticket. An *assiette dégustation*, consisting of a selection of local cheeses, cured meats and salad, will set you back around €12, or just rest up with a *grand crème* or sticky chocolate fondue (€5). The adjoining shop sells a mouthwatering variety of local foodstuffs. July & Aug & Dec–April daily 10.30am–11pm, rest of year Tues–Sat 10.30am–7pm, Sun 2.30–6.30pm.

**Le Rustique** 36 rue du Pont d'Asfeld ☏ 04 92 21 00 10, ⊚ restolerustique.fr. For a taste of the delicious local trout, head to this cheerfully decorated restaurant just off the main drag; have it fried, grilled or baked, and accompanied by almond and cream, red berries, or calvados. Otherwise, expect juicy lamb and beef dishes prepared various ways. *Menus* from €31. Starters €11, mains €17. Tues–Sun noon–2pm & 7–10pm.

**Les Templiers** 20 rue du Temple ☎ 04 92 20 29 04. Ostensibly a pizzeria, this nicely vaulted restaurant right next to the tourist office also serves up regional staples like *raclettes*, fondues and *tourtons*, fried, ravioli-like parcels, popular in the mountain areas. *Menus* from €20. Starters €8, mains €16. Tues–Sun noon–2.30pm & 6–10pm.

## The Parc National des Écrins and Vallouise

The Écrins national park is worth a trip for the sheer variety of sports that it offers in a much less crowded setting than Mont Blanc. The best base for exploring the area is the village of **Vallouise**, 19km southwest of Briançon on the D902. From Vallouise, there are several excellent shorter walks that take you into the heart of the Écrins or you can follow the GR54, which makes a circuit of the park and passes through the village.

Vallouise itself centres around the Romanesque **church of St-Étienne**, which has a gorgeous, partly frescoed porch. The buildings lining the two or three streets fanning out from here are typical of the region; striking, three-storey farmhouses consisting of a vaulted ground floor (for livestock), a first-floor living quarter, and an upper floor which would have served as a granary.

### ARRIVAL AND INFORMATION

VALLOUISE

Reaching Vallouise by public transport is difficult: your best bet is to take a train from Briançon to L'Argentière-la-Bessée, from where you could either hitch or hang around for one of the very infrequent buses to Vallouise.

**Tourist office** Place de l'Église (Tues–Sat 9am–12.30pm & 2–5.30pm; ☎ 04 92 23 36 12, ⍟ paysdesecrins.com).

**Bureau des Guides** Hut in the main car park (☎ 04 92 23 32 29, ⍟ guides-ecrins.com).

**Maison du Parc des Écrins** Located on the road that turns left before you enter Vallouise, and has all the information you need on the park, including local hikes (mid-June to mid-Sept daily 10am–noon & 2–6pm; mid-Sept to mid-June Tues–Fri 10am–noon & 1–5pm; ☎ 04 92 23 58 08, ⍟ ecrins-parcnational.fr).

### ACCOMMODATION AND EATING

**Les Vallois** Rière Pont ☎ 04 92 23 33 10, ⍟ lesvallois.com. Pleasant chalet-style accommodation down by the river offering pine-heavy rooms, some of which feature a balcony overlooking the hotel garden, and swimming pool. The combined bar-restaurant is worth a stop if you're feeling peckish and offers a good-value *plat du jour* for €9.90 and *menus* from €15. Breakfast €9. **€89**

## Briançon to the Queyras

The direct road from Briançon to Queyras (the D902) is a beautiful route that ascends steeply to the 2360m **Col d'Izoard** before descending into the **Casse Déserte**, a wild, desolate region with an abundance of scree running down from the peaks above. If the Col d'Izoard is closed (or if you don't fancy driving on the high, winding mountain roads), you can reach the Queyras from the north or the south on the N94.

### VAUBAN AND HIS FORTRESSES

The citadelle in Briançon is just one example (albeit a spectacular one) of the many fortifications built on France's eastern borders by **Sébastien Le Preste de Vauban** (1633–1707), a Marshal and engineer in the army of Louis XIV. In all, Vauban built 33 fortresses and strengthened countless others in order to defend the new lands won by **Louis**, the so-called **"Sun King"**, during the wars of the seventeenth century. Vauban was highly innovative in the design of his fortresses, which were often built in the shape of a star so that the various defensive bastions could defend each other with covering fire. The other spectacular fortifications planned and constructed by him in the Alps and Franche-Comté are the citadelles at Besançon and Mont-Dauphin. Twelve of Vauban's fortresses, dotted around France, are now included on UNESCO's World Heritage List.

14

## Mont-Dauphin

**Guided tours Jan–May Tues–Sun 10am & 2.30pm; June & Sept daily 10am & 3.30pm; July & Aug daily 10am, 2.30pm & 3.30pm; Oct–Dec Wed, Sat & Sun 3.30pm • €6 • ☎ 04 92 45 42 40, Ⓦ montdauphin-vauban.fr • Regular trains from Briançon stop at the *gare SNCF* in Mont-Dauphin, though the station is situated down on the main road, from where it's a long uphill slog to reach the fortress.**

From Briançon, the River Durance meanders through a wide valley following the N94 until, some 30km later, the brooding grey fortress of **MONT-DAUPHIN** hoves into view. Spread across the wide Plateau des Milles Vents ("a thousand winds"), and with commanding views towards the Durance and the Guil, Mont-Dauphin was constructed in 1692, and so named after the eldest son of King Louis XIV, upon whose orders Vauban was requested to build it. Sizing up its gargantuan walls, it's not difficult to see why this was considered the ideal spot from which to repel the Duke of Savoie's advancing troops. Crossing the moat, you enter the village via the thick-set porte de Briançon, from where the main road spears down to the porte d'Embrun. The grid-like streets fanning out from here, lined with houses built from the local pink Guillestre marble, are well inhabited today (around 170 people), with the odd café in situ to cater to passing tourists.

## Embrun

From Mont-Dauphin, the River Durance continues alongside the N94 for 17km to **EMBRUN**, an attractive little town of narrow streets on a rocky bluff above the Durance and an excellent base if you want to spend a longer time exploring the Parc du Queyras. Embrun has been a fortress town for centuries. Emperor Hadrian made it the capital and main religious centre for this region, and from the third century to the Revolution it was the seat of an archbishopric.

### Cathédrale Notre-Dame and Tour Brune

**Guided tours in English of the cathedral and treasury mid-June to mid-Sept Thurs at 10am • €4.50, must be booked at the tourist office (see opposite) Tour Brune: mid-June to mid-Sept Tues–Sat 10am–12.30pm & 3–6.30pm, Sun 9am–noon**

Embrun's chief sight is its twelfth-century **Cathédrale Notre-Dame**, the largest in the French Alps, which has inspired numerous imitations throughout the region. The elaborate main porch, guarded by stone lions, and the fifteenth-century rose window, are especially impressive. The interior, meanwhile, is striking for its wide Gothic arches and rib-vaulted ceiling, which is composed of alternate bands of black and white bricks. Just behind the cathedral is the formidable-looking **Tour Brune** (Brown Tower), which was built in the thirteenth-century as a watchtower, though today it hosts exhibitions run by the Écrins National Park.

### Lac de Serre-Ponçon

Embrun nestles at the northeastern corner of the **Lac de Serre-Ponçon**, a wide expanse of water created by the damming of the Durance in the late 1950s (completed in 1961), thus making it one of the largest man-made lakes in Europe. The lake is a great spot to indulge in water-bound activities such as canoeing, waterskiing and windsurfing; the best place to organize such activities is **Savines-Le-Lac**, 10km southwest of Embrun on the southern shore. This is also the place from where most of the lake cruises depart.

## ARRIVAL AND INFORMATION — EMBRUN

**By train and bus** The *gare SNCF* and *gare routière* are a five-minute walk east of town on place de la Gare. There are daily trains and buses from Embrun to Briançon, as well as to Mont-Dauphin–Guillestre.

**Tourist office** Inside the former chapel of the Cordeliers on place du Général-Dosse (July & Aug Mon–Sat 9am–7pm, Sun 10am–12.30pm & 4–7pm; Sept–June Mon–Sat 9am–noon & 2–6pm; ☎ 04 92 43 72 72, Ⓦ serreponcon-tourisme.com), which is itself notable for the beautiful medieval frescoes which adorn the walls and ceilings. Staff can provide information on nearby walking routes, as well as on the wide range of other locally available outdoor activities including rafting, sailing and climbing, and watersports on nearby Lac de Serre-Ponçon.

## ACCOMMODATION AND EATING

**Camping La Vieille Ferme** ☎ 04 92 43 04 08, ⓦ camping embrun.com. Located at the southern end of town, this is the most comfortable and most conveniently sited campsite in the area. There's an on-site restaurant, and they also organize lots of river activities. They've also got pyramid tents for hire, sleeping up to five, plus two- and three-bed apartments sleeping up to six also available. May–Sept. Camping €33, pyramid tents €525 apartments €735 per week.

**De la Mairie** Place Eugène-Barthelon ☎ 04 92 43 20 65, ⓦ hoteldelamairie.com. Occupies a sunny location on the town's main square. There are two categories of room available; the rather boring, pine-walled "Montagnarde" rooms, and the considerably more appealing (and not much more expensive) "Gustavienne" rooms, complete with cool saloon doors that separate bedroom and bathroom. Breakfast €10. €67

**L'Ogow** 72 rue de la Liberté ☎ 04 92 43 58 84. A smiling Tintin cut-out welcomes you to this accommodating restaurant, which relies on regional specialities like *tourtons* and *ravioles*. If the weather's warm, head for the sunny terrace out back. Starters €10, mains €12. Daily noon–2.30pm & 7–10pm.

★ **Le Pigeonnier** 2 rue Victor-Maurel ☎ 04 92 43 89 63, ⓦ pigeonnier.net. This gorgeous seventeenth-century house, set within lush, Mediterranean-style gardens, offers three stunning rooms, each furnished with parquet flooring, marble fireplace, floor-to-ceiling customs, and a chaise longue. The bathrooms, meanwhile, are enormous and magnificent, fitted with double sinks and stand-alone baths. Factor in a host of other delightful little touches, and the expense seems worth it. April–Oct. €130

# Gap

Sitting some 10km west from Savines-Le-Lac via the N94 is the departmental capital, **GAP**, a small, pleasant town on the Route Napoléon, whose origins reach back to Roman times. Gap prospered in the Middle Ages, partly thanks to its position on the pilgrim route to Santiago de Compostela, but suffered badly in the sixteenth-century Wars of Religion, and was burnt to the ground by the invading forces of the Duke of Savoy in 1692. Today the pedestrianized streets of the walled old town are lined with elegant, mainly eighteenth-century buildings and social life revolves around the café-filled place Jean-Marcellin. The house where Bonaparte spent a night in March 1815 is just off the square at 19 rue de France (look for the mural on the facade). Gap's massive Romanesque-style **cathedral** on place St-Arnoux, was completed in 1904, and incorporates elements from older churches, including marble altars and carved wooden angels.

## Musée Départemental

6 av du Maréchal-Foch • July & Aug daily 10am–noon & 2–6pm; Sept–June Mon & Wed–Fri 2–5pm, Sat & Sun 2–6pm • Free • ☎ 04 92 51 01 58

Located beyond the walled town, the **Musée Départemental** houses an intermittently stimulating collection of local Iron Age and Roman archeological finds, folk crafts and paintings. The most interesting exhibits are the exquisitely carved *coffre*, wooden trunks from the Queyras region which would have been used either as safes or were purely for ornamental purposes; look out, too, for the miniature versions of these. Down in the basement, a mummified infant's foot takes centre stage.

### Domaine de Charance and Pic de Charance

A few kilometres north of the town centre (and accessible via free shuttle buses in July and August) are the lovely gardens of the **Domaine de Charance** (free), which, at around 1000m, offer fantastic views over the surrounding countryside and Gap's famous apple and pear orchards. The grand eighteenth-century château is closed to visitors, but the beautiful terraced gardens, featuring numerous apple trees and 500 species of roses, are worth the trip alone. Behind the château is a wilder "English" garden, woodland and photogenic lake. Reasonably fit walkers can follow the trail from here to the **Pic de Charance** (1852m), which should take around three hours.

## ARRIVAL AND INFORMATION
GAP

**By train** The *gare SNCF* is just east of the centre on av des Alpes.

Destinations Briançon (6 daily; 1hr 15min).

**Tourist office** In the heart of the old town at 1 place Jean-

14

Marcellin (July & Aug Mon–Sat 9am–7pm; Sun 9am–1pm; Sept–June Mon–Fri 9am–12.30pm & 1.30–6pm, Sat 9am–4pm; ☎ 04 92 52 56 56, ⓦ gap-tallard-vallees.fr), staff here can provide information on nearby mountain-biking routes and the airborne activities, such as paragliding, parachuting and hot-air ballooning, for which the surrounding region is especially well known. They've also got free bike rental.

## ACCOMMODATION

**La Cloche** 2 place Alsace-Lorraine ☎ 04 92 51 02 52. Eight rather austere rooms above an old town café offer rooms with and without shower and next to nothing by way of furnishings. Still, you get a TV, and there are some decent views of the square from the shuttered windows. Breakfast €6. **€35–50**

**Station Gap-Bayard** ☎ 04 92 50 16 83, ⓦ gap-bayard. com. You'll need your own transport to get here, as it's 7km north of town on RN85, but the best thing about staying in one of these clean and bright rooms – including eight-bed dorms – are the fantastic views over a stunning golf course

(green fee €55). Half-board dorms **€41**, half-board doubles **€60**

★ **Les Trois Chardons Bleus** 26 av du Commandant-Dumont ☎ 06 52 67 09 41, ⓦ 3chardonsbleus.fr. The "Three Blue Thistles" is a delightful, family-run guesthouse ten-minutes' walk north-east of the centre, with three sweet rooms (Attic, Zen and Larch Flower) packed with simple homely charms; wall pictures, potted plants, little fluffy towels and so on. A bit tricky to find as it's set back from the road and behind a gate. **€79**

## EATING

**Le Bouchon** 4 La Placette ☎ 04 92 46 02 43, ⓦ lebouchon-gap.fr. Very friendly and consistently good restaurant whose cracking *plat du midi* (€15) and *plat du soir* (€25) are likely to feature dishes such as *confit* mackerel fillets with eggplant caviar, while the homemade ice cream is a great way to finish off. Tues–Sat noon–1.30pm & 8–10pm.

**Le Lavandin** 1 La Placette ☎ 04 92 51 15 46, ⓦ lelavandin.fr. Sweet little rustically decorated restaurant renowned for its marvellous savoury pies (leek and salmon, pear and Roquefort; €9), served with a soup of the day and a green salad; the desserts (€5) are terrific too, such as crème

brûlée with lavender, and a wonderfully gooey chocolate fondant. Mon, Tues & Thurs–Sat noon–2pm & 7–9pm.

**La Menthe Poivrée** 20 rue du Centre ☎ 09 52 77 55 73. Hidden away just off place Grenette, "The Peppermint" is Gap's standout restaurant, though it's not nearly as expensive as its smart, shallow-vaulted interior might suggest – and what's more, with just half a dozen tables, there's ample room to relax. And the food's not half-bad either, with exemplary dishes like lobster ravioli, and duck leg with spiced sweet cinnamon and polenta. *Menus* from €17. Tues–Sun noon–2pm & 7.30–10pm.

# Parc Régional du Queyras

ⓦ queyras.com

Spreading southeast of Briançon to the Italian border, the **Parc Régional du Queyras** is much more Mediterranean in appearance than the mountains to the north, with only shallow soils and low scrub covering the mountainsides. The open land along the park's rolling roads makes it particularly enjoyable to spend a few hours driving up to **St-Véran**, an Alpine village near the Italian border. There are some good walking opportunities: the **GR58** or **Tour du Queyras** path runs through St-Véran on its circuit of the park, and the **GR5** passes Ceillac and Arvieux on its way from Briançon towards Embrun.

## Guillestre

The road into the Queyras park follows the River Guil from Mont-Dauphin. The first stop is **GUILLESTRE**, a pretty mountain village that only really comes to life in summer. Its houses, in typical Queyras style, have open granaries on the upper floors and its sixteenth-century church has an intriguing porch (reminiscent of the cathedral at Embrun) with squatting lions carved from limestone.

## INFORMATION AND ACCOMMODATION                                    GUILLESTRE

**Tourist office** Place Salva (July & Aug daily 9.30am–7pm; Sept–June Mon–Sat 9.30am–12.30pm & 2.30–6pm; ☎ 04 92 24 77 61, ⓦ queyras-montagne.com) can advise on all aspects of visiting the Queyras.

**Le Catinat Fleuri** 100 chemin d'Eygliers ☎ 04 92 45 07

62, ⓦ catinat-fleuri.com. A 5min walk uphill from the tourist office, the rooms here, like the building itself, are rather plain, but the complex does boast two superb pools (one indoor, one outdoor), tennis court, verdant gardens and spots for camping between June and October (€13). Breakfast €8. **€69**

### Château Queyras and around

Late June to mid-Sept Mon–Fri 10.15am–6.45pm, Sat & Sun 1–6.45pm • €10 • ☎ 04 92 21 98 58, ⌨ fortqueyras.fr

Continuing along the D947 from Guillestre, you'll come to the fortress of **Château Queyras** which bars the way so completely that there's scarcely room for the road to squeeze around its base. There was probably a fortification of some kind here in the fourteenth century, though it wasn't until Vauban got his hands on it in the early eighteenth century that it took on its present shape – decommissioned at the end of World War II, it's now privately owned. Just beyond the fort is **Château-Ville-Vieille**, a small village with a few old houses and a church still intact. A right turn here takes you towards St-Véran, but if you stay on the road parallel to the River Guil, you will pass through the villages of Aiguilles, Abriès and L'Échalp (all with *gîtes d'étape*), to the **Belvédère du Viso**, close to the Italian border and the **Monte Viso**, at 3841m the highest peak in the area.

### St-Véran

Seven kilometres south of Château-Ville-Vieille lies **ST-VÉRAN**, which at 2042m is one of the highest villages in Europe. Its houses are part stone part timber, and the seventeenth-century **Église de St-Véran** stands prettily on the higher of the two streets, with its white tower silhouetted against the bare crags on the other side of the valley. The **GR58** passes south of the village; waymarked and easy to follow, the path eventually turns right down to the river, before continuing up the opposite bank through woods of pine and larch till the chapel of Notre-Dame-de-Clausis. There, above the line of trees, it crosses to the right bank of the stream and ends in the **Col de Chamoussière** (2884m), about three and a half hours from St-Véran. The ridge to the right of the col marks the frontier with Italy.

#### INFORMATION AND ACCOMMODATION                                    ST-VÉRAN

**Tourist office** Halfway down the main high street (Mon–Sat 9am–12.30pm & 2–5.30pm; also open Sun in high season; ☎ 04 92 45 82 21, ⌨ saintveran.com). In July and August, Petit Mathieu buses (☎ 04 92 46 71 56) link the village with the *gare SNCF* in Guillestre, although it's best to contact the tourist office for the most up-to-date times.

**Les Chalets du Villard** ☎ 04 92 45 82 08, ⌨ leschaletsduvillard.fr. One of the most tranquil places to stay in the village, offering spacious studio apartments with kitchen facilities and private terraces, as well as a spa, tennis court and on-site restaurant. Mid-Dec to April & June to mid-Sept. Two people sharing **€130**

# Chambéry and around

Nestling in a valley to the north of the Chartreuse Massif, the town of **CHAMBÉRY** commands the entrance to the mountain passes which lead towards Italy, and has thus held an important strategic position for the various armies and merchants who have crossed the Alps over the centuries. The town grew up around the château built by Count Thomas of Savoie in 1232, and became the Savoyard capital, enjoying a golden age in the fourteenth and fifteenth centuries. Although superseded as capital by Turin in 1562, it remained an important commercial and cultural centre, and the philosopher Rousseau spent some of his happiest years in the town during the 1730s. Only incorporated into France in 1860, modern Chambéry is a bustling provincial town with a wealth of grand Italianate architecture and a strong sense of its regional identity.

## Fontaine des Éléphants and rue de Boigne

Halfway down the broad, leafy boulevard de la Colonne is Chambéry's most famous monument, the extravagant and somewhat off-scale **Fontaine des Éléphants**. The fountain was erected in 1838 in homage to Général Comte de Boigne (1751–1830), a local boy who amassed a fortune working as a mercenary in India and subsequently used much of his vast wealth to fund major urban developments in his home town. Appropriately enough, de Boigne has a street named after him, hence **rue de Boigne**,

**14**

which, with its elegant colonnades, is immediately reminiscent of Turin. At its bottom end, rue de Boigne opens up on to the café-lined **place St-Léger**, which hosts a **flea market** on the second Saturday of every month. Heading east along place St-Léger you'll come to the fine old **rue de la Croix-d'Or**, the hub of aristocratic Chambéry in the seventeenth century and now home to numerous restaurants.

## Musée Savoisien and Cathédrale St-François

**Musée Savoisien** Square de Lannoy-de-Bissy • Mon & Wed–Sun 10am–noon & 2–6pm • €3 • ☎ 04 79 33 44 48, Ⓦ musee-savoisien.fr

A few paces from the Fontaine des Éléphants, the **Musée Savoisien** chronicles the history of Savoie from the Bronze Age onwards, though it is currently closed pending extensive renovations. When it does reopen (2020 at the earliest), expect a diverse mix of Iron Age pottery, Roman bronzes, and paintings. Its centrepiece, however, is the Cruet Mural, a remarkably well-preserved set of thirteenth-century wall paintings depicting battle scenes and life at the royal court. The building itself is a former Franciscan monastery, hence the lovely little cloister. Right next to the museum stands the town's main ecclesiastical sight, the **Cathédrale St-François**; dating from the 1400s, it has an interior decorated in elaborate nineteenth-century trompe l'oeil, supposedly one of the largest in Europe. Note, too, upon entering, the fine early sixteenth-century carved wood portal.

## Château des Ducs de Savoie

May, June & Sept Tues–Sun 2.30pm; July & Aug daily 10.30am, 2.30pm, 3.30pm & 4.30pm; Oct–April Tues–Sun 2.30pm • €6 • ☎ 04 79 70 15 94

A massive and imposing structure, the **Château des Ducs de Savoie** originally dates from the twelfth century, though nothing remains from this time. What you see today, including the Gatehouse, towers and Chamber of Accounts, dates mostly from the fourteenth and fifteenth centuries, which is when it also became the main home of the Dukes of Savoy. The Baroque Holy Chapel, or **Sainte-Chapelle**, in the internal

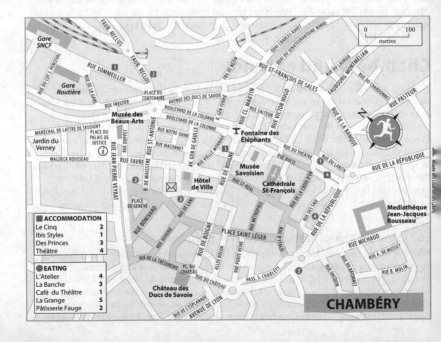

CHAMBÉRY

courtyard, was once the repository of the Turin Shroud; the shroud was damaged in a fire in 1532 and was transferred to the Duke's new court in Turin in 1578. Today, the château is occupied by the *préfecture*, and the interior is only accessible on a guided tour, which begins from the adjacent place du Château.

## Musée des Beaux-Arts

Place du Palais de Justice • Mon & Wed–Sun 10am–noon & 2–6pm • Free, €3 for exhibitions • ☎ 04 79 33 75 03

The small but beautifully presented **Musée des Beaux-Arts** is devoted largely to works by lesser-known Italian artists from the Renaissance; the pride of the collection is the fifteenth-century *Portrait of a Young Man*, attributed to Paolo Uccello. The remainder of the collection is given over to French painters from the late nineteenth and early twentieth centuries, with the emphasis, not surprisingly, on bucolic lake and mountain scenes, such as *Vue du Lac du Bourget* by Ginain.

## Musée des Charmettes

Chemin des Charmettes • April–Nov daily except Tues 10.30am–6pm; Dec–March Sat & Sun 10am–4.30pm • Free • ☎ 04 79 33 39 44

Two kilometres south of town on the rustic chemin des Charmettes is Rousseau's Chambéry address, **Les Charmettes**. This country cottage is now home to the **Musée des Charmettes**, a museum focused on Rousseau's writing and domestic life. The house is beautifully furnished in the style of the day, while the walls of the downstairs dining and music rooms manifest Italian-style trompe l'oeil paintings, though these were completed after Rousseau's time. Adjacent to the house, the lovely formal gardens – with abundant herbs and fruits – are laid out just as Rousseau would have remembered them. He only lived here a short while (1736–42), with his companion Madame de Warens, but claimed to have "savoured a century of life and a complete and pure happiness" in this isolated and tranquil location. Look out for open-air events taking place here on summer evenings.

### ARRIVAL AND INFORMATION

CHAMBÉRY

**By train** The *gare SNCF* is on rue Sommeiller, 500m north of the old town.

Destinations Aix-les-Bains (frequent; 15min); Annecy (hourly; 55min); Bourg-St-Maurice (every 1–2hr; 2hr); Geneva (5 daily; 1hr 30min); Grenoble (frequent; 45min–1hr); Lyon (hourly; 1hr 25min); Paris-Lyon (7 daily; 2hr 50min).

**Tourist office** 5 place du Palais de Justice (July & Aug Mon–Sat 9am–6.30pm, Sun 10am–1pm; Sept–June Mon–Sat 9am–12.30pm & 2–6pm; ☎ 04 79 33 42 47, ⓦ chambery-tourisme.com).

**Bicycle rental** Le Vélostation (ⓦ velostation-chambery. fr) is an excellent bike hire scheme located at the *gare SNCF* (€4.50 for half a day, €6 for full day).

**Market** Chambéry's main food market, selling everything from regional cheeses to live poultry, sets up on place du Palais de Justice on Saturday mornings.

### ACCOMMODATION

★ **Le Cinq** 22 du Faubourg-Reclus ☎ 04 79 33 51 18, ⓦ hotel-chambery.com. The location, on a fairly busy crossroads, won't win any awards, but this sparkling boutique hotel gets it right on pretty much every other level. The cool, navy-blue and charcoal-grey rooms come with some playful touches like bunched lampshades, there's a stunning basement pool, and the buffet breakfast (though not cheap) is terrific. Breakfast €15. **€110**

**Ibis Styles** 154 rue Sommeiller ☎ 04 79 62 37 26, ⓦ accorhotels.com. A few paces along from the train station, this *Styles* hotel is possessed of no little colour and sparkle; rooms are warm, welcoming and modern and are either road or rail facing. There's a lovely lounge bar to kick back in too. Breakfast €10. **€55**

**Des Princes** 4 rue de Boigne ☎ 04 79 33 45 36, ⓦ hotel desprinces.com. The sense of colonial grandeur is unmistakable in the Indian-themed decor of this refined hotel. The rooms are a real mix of styles and tastes, from the heavily wood- and timber-furnished, Alpine-style rooms, to those with sharper, more contemporary design features, such as frosted-glass doors that separate the bedroom and bathroom. Breakfast €11.50. **€89**

**Théâtre** 9 rue Denfert-Rochereau ☎ 04 79 85 76 79, ⓦ theatrehotelchambery.com. It's not exactly run through with character, and the rooms are a little on the small side, but the price and location do compensate somewhat – that said, it can get noisy in these parts. The more expensive rooms have balconies overlooking the place du Théâtre. Breakfast €9. **€68**

## EATING AND DRINKING

★ **L'Atelier** 59 rue de la République ☎04 79 70 62 39, ⓦatelier-chambery.com. Former post house that's now a trendy bistro comprising two vividly coloured rooms and an easy-going wine bar. Sophisticated and contemporary dishes like cappuccino of cauliflower soup, and saddle of rabbit roasted with mustard and foie gras; alternatively, pop along for tapas night on a Tuesday. *Menus* €17 to €36. Tues–Sat noon–2pm & 7.30–10pm.

**La Banche** 10 place de l'Hôtel-de-Ville ☎04 79 85 36 10, ⓦla-banche.fr. Chambéry's oldest restaurant has been here in some form or other since the sixteenth century, and it remains a welcoming little place, with old-fashioned velvet chairs and small wooden tables with paper tablecloths set around a large meat-cutter, and vintage ads on the walls; the short menu consists of typical brasserie dishes, like fillet of cod in *sauce vierge*, and poached pear crumble in gingerbread ice cream. *Plat du jour* €12. Starters €8, mains €15. Tues–Sat noon–2pm & 7.30–10pm.

**Café du Théâtre** 14 rue Denfert-Rochereau ☎04 79 25 56 10. This traditional café-brasserie with outdoor seating, attached to the venerable theatre, is a popular place for locals to enjoy afternoon coffees and evening aperitifs. They also serve light meals, like crêpes and *croque monsieur*. *Plats du jour* from €9. Daily 7am–1.30am.

**La Grange** 33 place Monge ☎04 79 85 60 31, ⓦrestaurantlagrange.com. One of a clutch of restaurants in this little quarter, a homely, thick-wood panelled restaurant offering a variety of Savoyard specialities like *raclette* and *croziflette* (similar to *tartiflette*, but instead uses Savoyard pasta made from buckwheat), though you'll find most diners chomping their way through one of the deliciously sticky fondues. *Menus* from €23. Starters €10, mains €15. Mon–Sat noon–2pm & 7–10.30pm.

**Pâtisserie Fauge** 6 place de Genève ☎04 79 33 36 77. Savoury bites, sandwiches, and *galettes*, as well as an eye-popping selection of artfully presented cakes and chocolates, are just some of the tasters available at this perky patisserie which has been at it since 1908. Mon 10am–7pm, Tues–Sat 8am–7pm, Sun 8am–12.30pm.

# Aix-les-Bains

Thirteen kilometres north of Chambéry is **AIX-LES-BAINS**, one of France's premier spa resorts. The town's waters have been famous for their healing qualities since Roman times but most of the elegant buildings here date from Aix's *belle époque* heyday of the late 1800s, when members of European high society dropped by to relax and take the waters; Queen Victoria was a frequent visitor. These days, Aix-les-Bains is a sedate and genteel place, with thousands of French pensioners descending on the town throughout the year for state-funded thermal treatments. The spa centre, **Les Thermes Nationaux d'Aix-les-Bains,** was formerly housed in the impressive (though now sadly redundant, save for the tourist office) Art Deco building on place Maurice-Mollard, but these days you'll find it at **Thermes Chevalley** (daily 10am–7.30pm, Fri till 9.30pm; ☎04 79 35 68 66, ⓦvalvital. fr; weekdays €19, weekends €21), a five-minute walk uphill behind here on route du Revard. There are also some parks to amble through and plenty of cafés where you can sit back with a *pastis* and watch the world go slowly by. Aix is also the best base for enjoying the sights and outdoor activities at the nearby **Lac du Bourget** (see page 748).

## Arc de Campanus and the Musée Lapidaire

The activities and sights of the town are focused around place Maurice-Mollard, where the most eye-catching landmark is **Arc de Campanus**, a Roman arch erected in the first century BC as a funerary monument. The large Roman baths that once stood near here are said to have incorporated over 24 kinds of marble; of the surviving ruins in the square (some of which back on to the *mairie*), the most intact is the Temple de Diane, a rectangular monument which now houses the **Musée Lapidaire** where there's a small collection of Gallo-Roman ceramics and statues – there are no set opening times or entry price, so check first with the tourist office if you wish to visit.

## Musée Faure

10 bd des Côtes • Wed–Sun: April–Oct 10am–12.30pm & 1.30–6.30pm; Nov–March 10am–12.30pm & 1.30–5pm • €5 • ☎04 79 61 06 57

Heading west from place Maurice-Mollard, up rue Divat, you'll come to an elegant roadside villa which now houses the marvellous **Musée Faure**. Named after the

**14**

> ## WATERSPORTS ON LAC DU BOURGET
>
> Whatever your favourite watersport, the Lac du Bourget is likely to have a club and good facilities available. Here are a few options:
>
> **Sailing** Club Nautique Voile d'Aix-les-Bains on boulevard Barrier at the Grand Port (☎04 79 34 10 74, ⓦcnva.com; yachts (with and without a skipper; €180–250/half day), dinghy's (€25/hr), as well as sailboards €18, stand-up paddles €12 and kayaks €13).
>
> **Waterskiing and wakeboarding** Ski Club Nautique, at Baie de Mémard to the north of the Grand Port (☎06 46 65 31 81, ⓦaixnride.fr; €40 for waterskiing and wakeboarding lessons, plus stand-up paddles for rent €12/hr).
>
> **Kayaking and stand-up paddling** Entente Nautique Aviron d'Aix-les-Bains, 22 av Daniel-Rops (☎04 79 88 12 07, ⓦavironaix.fr; €12/hr).
>
> **Boat trips** From the Grand Port, Bateaux du Lac du Bourget (☎04 79 63 45 00, ⓦcompagnie desbateauxdulac.fr) run daily sightseeing cruises on the lake between April and October (1hr, €13.50; 1hr 30min, €16.50), as well as more expensive lunch, dinner and evening cruises.

eponymous pharmacologist, the gallery holds a relatively small but superb collection of nineteenth-century Impressionist art, featuring works by Sisley, Sargent, Pissarro and Cézanne, whose grey-skied *Vue de Bonnières* was one of the painter's first attempts at a landscape. There are some lovely Degas pastels too, in particular *Danseuses Mauves* (Ballerinas in Mauve). Degas' versatility is evident from one or two of his sculptures up on the second floor, which is otherwise dominated by Rodin pieces.

### Lac du Bourget and Abbaye d'Hautecombe

It's 2km from the town centre to the Grand Port on the Lac du Bourget, but if that's too long a walk, note that bus #2 departs every 30min from outside the tourist office in Aix-les-Bains, passing the *gare SNCF* on the way. Also, between April and October, the ubiquitous *petit train* (€7) trundles down to the lake hourly between 2pm & 6pm, departing from the *hôtel de ville*

Connected to the River Rhône by the Canal de Savières, the **Lac du Bourget** is France's biggest natural lake, at 18km long and 3.5km wide, and a place of great beauty, a protected wildlife reserve and home to the now scarce European beaver. "Nowhere could one find such perfect concord between water, mountains, earth and sky", enthused the nineteenth-century French writer Balzac, and it's clear what attracted him and so many other poets and artists to this place. The lake's "Côte Sauvage" rises precipitously above the sparkling blue water on its western bank, which is dominated at its southern end by the looming presence of the **Dent du Chat** (1390m).

There are daily boat trips (30min) to the picturesque **Abbaye d'Hautecombe** (audioguide tours in English and other languages; Mon & Wed–Sun 10–11.15am & 2–5pm; €3.50; ☎04 79 54 58 80, ⓦchemin-neuf.fr) on the western side of the lake. Founded some time around 1140 by Amadeus of Clermont, the abbey functioned as a Cistercian community until the French Revolution, after which time it fell into ruin. Revived in 1824, a Benedictine congregation took over after World War I, but these monks left in 1992 and it's now administered by the Catholic Chemin Neuf community. The abbey is the final resting place of many members of the Savoie royals, the first of whom to be buried here was Humbert (Umberto III) in 1189; the last king and queen of Italy, Umberto II de Savoie (died 1983) and his wife Marie-José (died 2001) are also buried here. The Abbaye lies close to the village of St-Pierre de Curtille, and is also accessible to cars via the D18 road.

### ARRIVAL AND INFORMATION AIX-LES-BAINS

**By train** The *gare SNCF* in Aix-les-Bains is on the southern side of the town centre on bd du Président-Wilson, from where it's a brief stroll up av Charles-de-Gaulle to the central place Maurice-Mollard.
Destinations Annecy (frequent; 40min); Chambéry (frequent; 15min).

**Tourist office** Inside the enormous former spa building on place Maurice-Mollard (July & Aug Mon–Sat 9am–12.30pm & 2–6.30pm, Sun 10am–noon & 2–6pm; Oct–May Mon–Sat 9am–noon & 2–6pm; ☎04 79 88 68 00, ⓦaixlesbains-rivieradesalpes.com).

## ACCOMMODATION

**Aix-les-Bains Hostel** Promenade du Sierroz ☎ 04 79 88 32 88, ⓦ auberge-aix-les-bains.com. In a fabulous location just a stone's throw from the lake, this well-equipped hostel (including laundry, self-service kitchen and restaurant) offers three-, four-, five- and six-bedded dorms, as well as doubles. Breakfast included. Mid-Feb to mid-Nov. Dorms **€24.50**, doubles **€30**

**Camping du Sierroz** Bd Robert-Barrier ☎ 04 79 61 89 89, ⓦ camping-sierroz.com. Some 400m along from the hostel, this is the largest and best kept of the several lakeshore campsites. Facilities include shop and restaurant, *pétanque* and ping-pong, and plenty of play areas for kids. May–Oct. **€23.60**

**Le Carré d'Aix** 94 rue du Casino ☎ 04 70 35 57 58, ⓦ lecarredaix.com. Elegant, privately run hotel with nineteen idiosyncratic rooms spread over four floors leading off a fine, wrought-iron spiral staircase. The walls and fabrics are coloured in gorgeous shades of chocolate brown and charcoal grey, though it's the quirky furnishings and assorted accoutrements garnered from the owner's travels that steal the show; for example in one room you might find an old leather trunk, and in another an old-fashioned telephone. Breakfast €8. **€60**

★ **Savoy** 21 av Charles-de-Gaulle ☎ 04 79 35 13 33, ⓦ hotel-savoy-aixlesbains.com. It's not nearly as grand as it sounds, and it's a little frayed around the edges, but this welcoming hotel, in a renovated nineteenth-century building, provides high-ceilinged, parquet-floored rooms, all with shower facilities – the family rooms are incredibly spacious. Breakfast €8. **€59**

## EATING AND DRINKING

**L'Arbre à Palabres** 12 place du Revard ☎ 04 79 88 39 37, ⓦ restaurant-arbre-palabres.fr. About 50m down from place Maurice-Mollard, there's not much that this tidy café/pizzeria doesn't do; burgers, salads, *moules*, and the full range of Savoyard specialities. It's also a good spot for an early morning pick-me-up, with decent coffee and a substantial breakfast going for €6. *Plat du jour* €9.90. Starters €9, mains €13. Tues & Sun 8.30am–7pm, Wed–Sat 8.30am–11.30pm.

★ **Chez Fanny** 102 rue de Genève ☎ 04 79 35 07 67. Sitting pretty on a little cobbled square, this neat, mirror-lined café is the perfect place to rest up over lunch; savoury tarts, salads, hot sandwiches, burgers and desserts, or a *plat du jour* for €7.90. Mon–Sat 7.30am–7pm, Sun 8am–noon.

**La Rotonde** Square Jean-Moulin ☎ 04 79 35 00 60, ⓦ rotonde-aixlesbains.com. Perched on the edge of the park, the smart and spacious *Rotonde* packs them in for its extensive *menus*, including some excellent wok-prepared dishes, tartare and carpaccio plates, and more offbeat choices like clafoutis with chorizo, and tiramisu with parmesan. If you just fancy a drink, take a seat inside the lounge bar. *Menus* from €18.50. Starters €8, mains €16. Daily noon–2pm & 7–10.30pm.

# The Isère valley and the Vanoise

The **Massif de la Vanoise**, a rugged set of mountains east of Chambéry, rises to heights of over 3500m, and offers challenging routes for skiers, particularly along the steep slopes of the **Isère valley**. The glacier-capped southeast quadrant of the Vanoise forms the **Parc National de la Vanoise**, where hikers will find some of the most spectacular GR trails in France. The easiest road access to the Massif is from Chambéry or Grenoble, although driving the winding and precipitous old highways from Annecy or Chamonix is an adventure in itself.

The A43 from Chambéry cuts between the Massif des Bauges to the north and the Vanoise to the south, following the path of the lower Isère River as it flows down from Albertville. Following the river by road from here involves a 180km journey south,

## WALKING IN THE PARC NATIONAL DE LA VANOISE

The **Parc National de la Vanoise** (ⓦ vanoise-parcnational.fr) occupies the eastern end of the Vanoise Massif. It's extremely popular, with over 500km of marked paths, including the **GR5**, **GR55** and **GTA** (Grande Traversée des Alpes), and numerous *refuges* along the trails. For in-depth information on the various routes, head for the tourist offices in Val d'Isère, Bourg-St-Maurice and Méribel.

To cross the park, you can take the **GR55** from the Lac de Tignes and over the **Col de la Vanoise**. You can then connect with the **GR5**, which brings you out at the southern end of the park in the town of Modane. There are countless shorter but equally beautiful walks in the park. Settlements in the Arc Valley, like Bessans, are decent bases to start exploring the park, but even the ski resorts of Tignes, Val d'Isère and Méribel are good starting points.

north and south again back to its source high in the mountains near the **Col de l'Iseran** (2770m), close to the Italian frontier. From Albertville, the N90 climbs southeast along the bends of the Isère River for 50km to Moûtiers, the turn-off for the massive **Les Trois Vallées** ski region. At Moûtiers, the river course swings northeast and following it will lead you to **Bourg-St-Maurice**, the town at the midpoint of the upper Isère valley. At Séez, a couple of kilometres further east, the road comes to an important junction: the N90 continues to climb steeply towards the **Col du Petit St-Bernard** (2188m), while the D902 heads south towards **Val d'Isère**.

## The Col de l'Iseran

From the ski resort of Val d'Isère, the **D902** veers south from the river and climbs towards the **Col de l'Iseran** (2770m), the highest pass with a paved road in the Alps. Despite the dangers of weather and the arduous climb, the pass has been used for centuries, mainly because it is by far the quickest route between the remote upper valleys of the Isère and Arc. From October to June, the pass is blocked by snow, but in summer, it's a must-see sight for tourists with cars, who have the option of moving on to the much less touristy villages of the **Arc valley** that lie beyond the pass. If the weather is good and you are reasonably fit, you should consider walking from here along a steep path to the **Pointe des Lessières** (3041m), which offers beautiful views of the Vanoise Massif, as well as the fearsome Italian side of Mont Blanc.

# Annecy

Lying 50km to the south of Lake Geneva, **ANNECY**, set on a sparkling turquoise lake, the Lac d'Annecy, is one of the most beautiful and popular resort towns of the French Alps. It enjoyed a brief moment of political and religious importance in the early sixteenth century, when Geneva embraced the Reformation and the Catholic bishop, François de Sales, decamped here with a train of ecclesiastics and a prosperous, cultivated elite.

These days, the delights of the town lie not just in its historical monuments, like the imposing château on the hill or the stronghold of the Palais de l'Île closer to the lake, but also in the stunning scenery. Annecy's old town is a bewitching warren of passages and arcaded houses that date from the sixteenth century and are divided by peaceful little branches of the **Canal du Thiou**. Many of the houses here are ringed by canalside railings overflowing with geraniums and petunias in summer; added to the cool shade offered by the arcades, these flowers make the town's pedestrianized streets a delight to wander around on a sunny day. At the height of summer, however, you can barely move for the crowds, so you'd do well to take to the streets as early as you can in the morning.

## The Château

**Musée and observatoire** Place du Château • June–Sept daily 10.30am–6pm; Oct–May daily except Tues 10am–noon & 2–5pm • €5.50, combined ticket for this and the Palais de l'Île costs €7.20 • ☎ 04 50 33 87 30, 🌐 musees.agglo-annecy.fr

From rue de l'Île on the Canal du Thiou's south bank, the narrow rampe du Château leads up to the **Château**, the former home of Genevois counts and the dukes of Nemours, a junior branch of the house of Savoy. There has been a castle on this site since the eleventh century, but the Nemours found the old fortress a little too rough for their taste and added more refined living quarters in the sixteenth century. These now house the collections of the **Musée du Château** and **Observatoire Régional des Lacs Alpins**. In the latter, there are some intriguing exhibits about the geology and marine life of the local lakes, while the former contains folk art and handicrafts from across the region. The main attractions, however, are the castle itself and the views it provides of the lake below. Concerts are regularly held in the ballroom during summer.

## Rue Ste-Claire and the cathedral

At the base of the château is **rue Ste-Claire**, the main street of the old town, with arcaded shops and houses, as well as plentiful cafés and restaurants. Running parallel to rue Ste-Claire, on the other side of the canal, is rue Jean-Jacques-Rousseau which passes the city's **cathedral**, where Rousseau once sang as a chorister. It was in Annecy that Rousseau met Madame de Warens and eventually converted to Catholicism. One of the highlights of the cathedral is its mid-nineteenth-century organ, which is put to good use in July and August when the wonderful Organ Festival is staged here. Moreover, one-hour organ concerts are held here every Wednesday in July and August at 6.30pm.

**14**

## Palais de l'Île

**Centre d'Interprétation de l'Architecture** • June–Sept daily 10.30am–6pm; Oct–May daily except Tues 10am–noon & 2–5pm • €3.80, combined ticket for this and the Château costs €7.20 • ☎ 04 56 49 40 37, ⓦ musees.agglo-annecy.fr

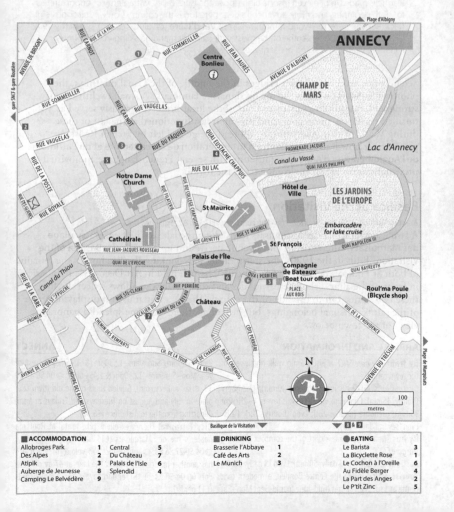

| ■ ACCOMMODATION | | | ■ DRINKING | | ● EATING | |
|---|---|---|---|---|---|---|
| Allobroges Park | 1 | Central | 5 | Brasserie l'Abbaye | 1 | Le Barista | 3 |
| Des Alpes | 2 | Du Château | 7 | Café des Arts | 2 | La Bicyclette Rose | 1 |
| Atipik | 3 | Palais de l'Isle | 6 | Le Munich | 3 | Le Cochon à l'Oreille | 6 |
| Auberge de Jeunesse | 8 | Splendid | 4 | | | Au Fidèle Berger | 4 |
| Camping Le Belvédère | 9 | | | | | La Part des Anges | 2 |
| | | | | | | Le P'tit Zinc | 5 |

**14**

---

### SKIING IN THE SAVOIE

Unquestionably, the Savoie region offers some of the world's greatest skiing. To begin with, there's **Les Trois Vallées** (Ⓦles3vallees.com), one of the world's largest linked skiing areas (some 600km), with endless off-piste possibilities. Its four component resorts are glitzy **Courchevel** (Ⓦcourchevel.com), which also has by far the finest restaurants of any French ski resort; the under-rated and family-oriented **Les Menuires** (Ⓦlesmenuires.com); **Val Thorens** (Ⓦvalthorens.com), the highest resort in Europe and much favoured by younger crowds and the snowboarding set; and **Méribel** (Ⓦmeribel.net), traditionally dominated by British tourists, and which therefore perhaps explains its status as the party capital of the Three Valleys. Despite the British imports, though, the small wooden chalets which climb the eastern side of the valley do manage to give the resort a traditional Savoyard feel. Less well known is the **Paradiski** ski area, on the slopes above Bourg-St-Maurice, which comprises the resorts of **Les Arcs** (Ⓦlesarcs.com) and **La Plagne** (Ⓦla-plagne.com), linked together by a giant double-decker *téléphérique* that swings over the Ponthurin valley. The former is accessible from the town via a funicular railway, and offers excellent snow and terrain for all levels, while La Plagne is made up of eleven resorts high above the Isère valley, with plenty of opportunities for both beginners and more advanced skiers; here too is the country's only public bobsleigh track. Beyond here, the world-famous resort of **Val d'Isère** (Ⓦvaldisere.com), site of the 1992 Olympic downhill, offers some of the most varied and demanding skiing in the country, including year-round skiing on its glacier.

---

Serenely pitched between two bridges in the middle of the Canal du Thiou, the photogenic **Palais de l'Île** is the town's signature landmark. A small twelfth-century stronghold, beautifully constructed out of the local stone, it variously served as a fortified residence, mint, court and prison; it last functioned as the last of these during World War II, and you can still read the graffiti left by French Resistance prisoners. It now houses the **Centre d'Interprétation de l'Architecture et du Patrimoine de l'Agglomération d'Annecy**, a museum with several French-language audiovisual presentations on urban environments in the region.

## Basilica of the Visitation

20 av de la Visitation • Daily 7am–noon & 2–7pm • **Museum** Daily 9am–noon & 2–5pm • Free

A stroll south on rue des Marquisats leads along the lake to the free, grassy **plage des Marquisats**. Alternatively, take avenue de Trésum up towards the **Basilica of the Visitation**. Built in the 1920s, the stern, rather ugly-looking Basilica houses the remains of both St François de Sales and St Jane de Chantal, held in Art Deco-style reliquaries in front of the altar – elsewhere, mosaics and stained-glass windows reflect the lives of these two saints. Off to the side of the church, there's a tiny museum displaying some of the saints' personal belongings, but best of all, there are some splendid panoramic views of the town below.

### ARRIVAL AND INFORMATION
ANNECY

**By train** The *gare SNCF* is just a 5min walk northwest of the town centre.

Destinations Aix-les-Bains (frequent; 40min); Chambéry (hourly; 45min); Chamonix via St-Gervais (every 1–2hr; 2hr 35min); Grenoble (hourly; 2hr); Lyon (hourly; 2hr); Paris-Lyon (several daily; 4hr).

**By bus** The *gare routière* is part of the complex involving the *gare SNCF*.

Destinations Geneva (6 daily; 50min); Lyon (5 daily; 2hr).

**Tourist office** Inside the Centre Bonlieu, a modern civic centre at 1 rue Jean-Jaurès (mid-June to mid-Sept Mon–Sat 9am–6.30pm, Sun 9am–12.30pm & 1.45–6pm; rest of year Mon–Sat 9am–12.30pm & 1.45–6pm; ☎04 50 45 00 33, Ⓦlac-annecy.com). Guided tours of the old town take place in July and August on Tuesdays and Fridays at 4pm, departing from the tourist office (€6.50).

**Bicycle rental** There's excellent bike rental at Roul' ma poule, 4 rue des Marquisats (€15 half-day, €20 per day; ☎04 50 27 86 83, Ⓦannecy-location-velo.com) which also has another branch just around the lake at 47 av du Petit Port (☎04 50 23 31 15) renting kayaks and paddleboards (€11 per hr).

## ACCOMMODATION

**Allobroges Park** 11 rue Sommeiller ☎04 50 45 03 11, ⓦallobroges.com. A solid and comfortable (if slightly overpriced) three-star set back from the road in its own little courtyard. The warm, thickly carpeted rooms (of which there are four categories) enjoy lots of light thanks to high windows, and there's a snazzy lobby bar where you can kick back with a nightcap before hitting the sack. Breakfast €10. **€109**

**Des Alpes** 12 rue de la Poste ☎04 50 45 04 56, ⓦhotel annecy.com. A warm welcome awaits at this diminutive hotel just a stone's throw from the *gare SNCF*. Chalet-style rooms with pine-laced walls and just about every other bit of furniture culled from some sort of timber. Triples and quads available. Breakfast €8.50. **€81**

★ **Atipik** 19 rue Vaugelas ☎04 50 52 84 33, ⓦatipik hotel.fr. A super-value option midway between the stations and the old town. The individually themed rooms – some of which have balconies overlooking a canal – are by no means large, but they are elegantly furnished, mostly in natural woods. Charmingly staffed too. Breakfast €9.50. **€80**

**Auberge de Jeunesse** 4 rte du Semnoz ☎04 50 45 33 19, ⓦfuaj.org/annecy. Serene, forest-fringed location over-looking the lake 2km away from the town centre, with four- and five-bed dorms plus good facilities including laundry, games room and bar, bike rental and kitchens; for €10, you can have a two-course dinner. Take bus #6 to stop "Hôtel de Police", from where it's a five-minute walk. Open all year. Dorms **€22.50**

**Camping Le Belvédère** 8 rte du Semnoz ☎04 50 45 48 30, ⓦannecy-camping-municipal.fr. A two-minute walk up from the hostel, this tidy municipal campsite is a great spot for families, with several play areas and mini-golf to keep kids entertained – and an on-site bar for adults. There are also a dozen or so lovely wooden chalets sleeping up to seven. March–Oct. **€17.50**; chalet per night **€96** per week **€510**

**Central** 6 rue Royale ☎04 50 45 05 37, ⓦhotel centralannecy.fr. While the exterior of this one-star hotel promises little, inside you will find a cheerily run affair offering fourteen occasionally garish, but never dull, rooms, some of which have shared toilet and shower facilities. Rooms either look out over a quiet courtyard or down on to one of the town's canals. Breakfast €8. **€70**

**Du Château** 16 rampe du Château ☎04 50 45 27 66, ⓦannecy-hotel.com. Situated a few paces down from the château, sixteen cottage-like rooms inform this handsome nineteenth-century stone building high above the terracotta tiled-roofs of the old town; chunky wooden bedsteads, wicker chairs and pretty, home-made textiles are all standard features. Breakfast €9. **€70**

**Palais de l'Isle** 13 rue Perrière ☎04 50 45 86 87, ⓦpalaisannecy.com. In a pitch-perfect setting right by the canal in the heart of the old town, the *Palais* is a labyrinth of narrow corridors concealing crisp, designer-furnished rooms painted in either yellow or sky blue, some of which overlook the canal, others the street. Breakfast €12. **€130**

**Splendid** 4 quai Eustache-Chappuis ☎04 50 45 20 00, ⓦhotel-annecy-lac.fr. In an enviable spot overlooking the grassy expanse of the Champ de Mars, the *Splendid* is one of the more expensive options in town, but its polished, burgundy-and-black-coloured rooms, and big, tiled bathrooms with oversized mirrors are pretty much what you'd expect for the price. Tea- and coffee-making facilities are a welcome touch too. Breakfast €14. **€123**

## EATING AND DRINKING

The town's restaurants are, on the whole, pretty commendable, though the string of establishments by the canal along quai Perrière are apt to serving unimaginative fodder for the tourist masses. Elsewhere, there are few more enjoyable things to do on a warm summer's evening in Annecy than to park yourself down by one of the canalside cafés and soak up the local architecture. Away from here, rue Ste-Claire offers some promising possibilities for a late-night drink or two.

### CAFÉS AND RESTAURANTS

★ **Le Barista** 2 passage Gruffaz ☎09 84 29 61 44, ⓦbarista-cafe.fr. There are very few places to get decent coffee in Annecy, but this is definitely one of them. Secreted away inside an arcaded passage overlooking a canal, and with all but three tables outside and two inside, *Le Barista* serves up delicious, lovingly crafted espressos, ristrettos and flat whites, though nothing beats one of their cold brews on a hot day. Tues–Fri 9.30am–6.30pm, Sat 9am–7pm.

---

### BEACH LIFE

If you (or, as is more likely, the kids) have had enough of traipsing around town, then you might consider retreating to one of Annecy's two excellent, albeit grassy, **beaches**. One is located over on the northeast corner, near the *Imperial Hotel*, while the other – which is shallower and therefore much better suited to families – is on the western shore just south of the port. Both are open roughly mid-June to mid-September, have shower and toilet facilities, and are fully supervised.

**14**

## LAC D'ANNECY CRUISES

A **lake cruise** is the most relaxing way to travel between Annecy and the other settlements around the lake. Compagnie des Bateaux, 2 place aux Bois (☎04 50 51 08 40, ☳annecy-croisieres.com), run several boats daily from the quai Napoléon-III (which is where you buy tickets), including a one-hour trip (€14.60), and a two-hour jolly (€18.80) which briefly stops off at various points around the lake. They also run 2–3hr cruises which include lunch or dinner (as well as dancing in the evening) on the MS *Libellule*; prices start at €57 for a lunch cruise and €60 for a dinner cruise.

**La Bicyclette Rose** 29 rue Sommeiller ☎04 50 05 16 51. The Pink Bicycle packs 'em in for its super tasty breakfasts (pancakes, smoked salmon, scrambled eggs and bacon), gut-busting brunches and *tartines* (€8.50); the sunny interior, complete with communal tables and box shelves rammed with all manner of curios, looks fab. Tues–Fri 7.30am–6pm, Sat 8am–6pm, Sun 8am–3pm.

**Le Cochon à l'Oreille** Quai Perrière ☎04 50 45 92 51, ☳cochon-annecy.com. Slightly weird-looking place – unless you're into porcelain pigs, of which there are hundreds – which might explain the preponderance of pork on the menu. Kids will love it, as might the parents, as there are excellent baby-changing facilities here. Starters €8, mains €15. Daily noon–2pm & 7–10pm; closed Mon mid-Nov to mid-April.

**Au Fidèle Berger** 2 rue Royale ☎04 50 45 00 32, ☳aufideleberger.fr. "The Faithful Shepherd" is a genteel, ever-busy *salon de thé* that makes for a nice spot to relax with a coffee or pot of Darjeeling, though while you're here it'd be remiss not to sample one of their deliciously creamy pastries. Breakfasts and light dishes, such as salads, are also on the menu. Tues–Fri 9.15am–7pm, Sat 9am–7.15pm.

**La Part des Anges** 23 rue Sommeiller ☎04 50 60 07 14, ☳restaurant-lapartdesanges.com. Slick restaurant and wine bar sited well away from the tourist track and catering to a more discerning crowd. On a constantly rotating menu, you might find the likes of salmon carpaccio with mint oil, and fillet of trout with almonds and risotto *crémeux*. The restaurant itself looks impressive, heavily mirrored walls bearing down on black-cloth-covered tables and velvet cushioned seating. *Menus* from €24. Starters €12, mains €21. Closed first three weeks August. Tues–Sat noon–2pm & 7–10pm; wine bar opens at 6pm.

**Le P'tit Zinc** 11 rue du Pont-Morens ☎04 50 51 12 93. This popular little bistro is one of the few canalside places to retain any semblance of charm, and is a great place to indulge in the local Savoyard favourites, particularly a superb *tartiflette* and some excellent fondues. Starters €8, mains €18. Daily 11.30am–2.30pm & 6.30–10.30pm.

### BARS

**Brasserie l'Abbaye** 4 rue du Pâquier ☎04 50 45 12 88, ☳abbaye-annecy.com. This lively brick-lined bar/brasserie also has a large outdoor terrace where you can kick back with one of their Belgian brews, though they're not cheap at around €5 a pop. Light munchies available too, like pizza and *moules marinières*. Daily 8am–1am.

**Café des Arts** 4 passage de l'Isle ☎04 50 51 56 40. Despite its position right in the heart of the tourist zone, squeezed onto the tip of the Palais de l'Île, this mellow café-bar remains a true local's favourite. Chill out on the sunny cobbled terrace with an espresso, or cool off inside the brick-lined bar with a pint, particularly on Wednesdays when there's live music. Daily 10am–midnight.

**Le Munich** 1 quai Perrière ☎04 50 45 02 11, ☳lemunich.com. Vaguely reminiscent of a Bavarian beer hall, *Le Munich* is where the serious drinking takes place; around a dozen or so draught beers, mostly German (Krombacher, Munchen) and Belgian (including Trappist beers); and to soak it all up, get your chops around one of their monster-sized burgers, like the no-nonsense Fat Bastard. Closed Jan. Daily 8am–2am.

## Around Annecy

While the tourist crowds that flock to Annecy in the summer high season may only be bearable for a day or two, there are plenty of places around the lake to escape to and run wild. As well as **boat tours**, **cycling** is an especially enjoyable means of appreciating the beauty of the Lac d'Annecy. Cycling the 40km road circuit of the lake is a very popular Sunday morning activity among sporty Annéciens; a traffic-free cycle route follows the west shore down to Faverges. The surrounding hills offer walking and mountain-biking excursions to suit all levels of ability and fitness. Experienced walkers should enjoy the relatively undemanding ascent of **La Tournette** (2351m) on the eastern side of the lake, while gentler walks and cycle routes are plentiful in the forested **Semnoz mountains** on the lake's west side. This is also a great spot for tandem paragliding.

### Château de Menthon

April–June & Sept–Oct Fri–Sun & hols 2–6pm; July & Aug daily noon–7pm • €8.50 • ☎ 04 50 60 12 05, ⓦ chateau-de-menthon.com

Close to the village of **Menthon-St-Bernard** on the eastern shore of the lake is the grand, turreted **Château de Menthon**. The fortress has been inhabited since the twelfth century and was the birthplace of St Bernard, the patron saint of mountaineers – indeed, the castle remains in the hands of the de Menthon family. In the nineteenth century, however, it was extensively renovated in the romantic Gothic revival style and now possesses an impressive library containing some 12,000 books. On weekends, costumed actors relate the château's history.

### The Gorges du Fier

Daily: mid-March to mid-June & mid-Sept to mid-Oct 9.30am–6.15pm; mid-June to mid-Sept 9.30am–7.15pm • €5.70 • ☎ 04 50 46 23 07, ⓦ gorgesdufier.com

Some 10km west of Annecy, the River Fier has cut a narrow crevice through the limestone rock at the **Gorges du Fier**, which is signposted off the D14 at Lovagny. It's an awe-inspiring landscape of often bizarre geology, with eroded cliff faces, narrow rock fissures and curiously sculpted boulders, all formed by the rushing waters of the river below. Once you are inside the 300m-long gorge, you traverse a high-level walkway pinned to the gorge side. The crevice is so narrow that when it rains heavily the water can rise by around 25m in just a few hours. There's a shop, café and free car park on site.

# Mont Blanc

Fifty kilometres to the east of Annecy on the Swiss and Italian borders looms **Mont Blanc** (4807m), Western Europe's highest peak. First climbed in 1786 by Jacques Balmat and Michel-Gabriel Paccard, two intrepid gentlemen from Chamonix, the mountain and its surrounding valleys are now the biggest tourist draw to the Alps.

The closest airport is in Geneva, but if you're coming from France then Annecy is the easiest city from which to approach the mountain, and, of the two road routes, the one east via Megève is the more picturesque. The two main approach roads to Mont Blanc come together at Le Fayet, a village just outside St-Gervais-les-Bains, where the **Tramway du Mont Blanc** begins its 75-minute haul to the **Nid d'Aigle** (2375m), a vantage point on the northwest slope (€37.50 return; ⓦ compagniedumontblanc.fr/chamonix.com). Experienced mountaineers can press on from here along the famous Goûter ridge to the summit of Mont Blanc itself.

If you are heading into Italy from Chamonix, the most direct road is the N205, which takes you south out of Chamonix, then through the 11.6km **Mont Blanc Tunnel** (one-way €44.40, return €55.40), and brings you out on the road to Aosta and Milan.

## Chamonix-Mont-Blanc

The bustling, cosmopolitan town of **CHAMONIX** (known officially as Chamonix-Mont-Blanc) is the primary French base for outdoor activities on or around Mont Blanc. "Cham" throngs with visitors throughout the year, and although it may have long since had its village identity submerged in a sprawl of tourist development, flashy restaurants and boutiques, the stunning backdrop of glaring snowfields, eerie blue glaciers and ridges of sharp peaks that surround Mont Blanc are ample compensation.

Naturally, the mountains provide the main sights and activities, but on days when the bad weather sets in, there are a few things to do in town. Otherwise, it's a case of just chilling out in one of the town's many convivial restaurants or bars.

**14**

**14**

## Musée Alpin and Espace Tairraz

**Musée Alpin** 89 av Michel-Croz • Daily except Tues: mid-Dec to mid-June 10am–noon & 2–6pm; July & Aug 10am–1pm & 2–6pm; closed Nov to mid-Dec • €5.90 • ☎ 04 50 55 29 46, ⓦ chamonix.com **Espace Tairraz** Esplanade St-Michel • Daily: July & Aug 10am–6pm; Sept–June 2–6pm • €5.90 • ☎ 04 50 55 53 93

Housed inside the early twentieth-century Chamonix Palace, the occasionally illuminating **Musée Alpin** is full of exhibits which detail the life of the valley since the first tourists began to arrive in the eighteenth century, though more interesting are the extensive displays on the history of winter sports in the region and the various cabinets stuffed with mountaineering equipment.

The **Espace Tairraz** exhibition centre is home to the **Musée des Cristaux**, a beautiful collection of minerals hewn from the mountains hereabouts, foremost among which are the stunning, smoky-coloured quartz crystal and the vivid red fluorite crystal. The centre also hosts temporary photography exhibitions of the mountains.

### ARRIVAL AND DEPARTURE · CHAMONIX-MONT-BLANC

**By train and bus** The *gare SNCF* and *gare routière* are on rue des Allobroges, a short walk to the south of place du Triangle-de-l'Amitié. Le Mulet is a free, year-round shuttle bus (daily 7am–8.15pm; every 10–15min) which does a loop of the town starting at Chamonix Sud bus station and passing Aiguille du Midi and the gare SNCF.

Destinations (train) Annecy via St Gervais (8 daily; 2hr 20min).
Destinations (bus) Geneva (2 daily; 2hr); other resorts in the Chamonix-Mont-Blanc area: Argentière (frequent; 20 min); Les Houches (frequent; 15min); Servoz (frequent; 20min).

### INFORMATION

**Tourist office** 85 place du Triangle-de-l'Amitié (daily: mid-April to mid-June & mid-Sept to mid-Dec 9am–12.30pm & 2–6pm; mid-June to mid-Sept 9am–7pm; mid-Dec to mid-April 8.30am–7pm; ☎ 04 50 53 00 24, ⓦ chamonix. com); while you're here, pick up a copy of the bi-monthly *Chamonix argentière magazine*, which has details of all the town and region's events and activities. ⓦ chamonix.net is also an excellent source of information on the town.

**CHAMONIX**

| ■ ACCOMMODATION | |
|---|---|
| Auberge de Jeunesse | 9 |
| Camping La Mer de Glace | 5 |
| Le Chamonix | 2 |
| Le Faucigny | 1 |
| Hameau Albert-1er | 8 |
| Le Morgane | 7 |
| Pointe-Isabelle | 6 |
| Richemond | 4 |
| Vert Hôtel | 3 |

| ● EATING | |
|---|---|
| Albert-1er | 6 |
| L'Atelier Café | 5 |
| L'Atmosphère | 4 |
| Le Bartavel | 2 |
| Le Cap Horn | 3 |
| L'Impossible | 7 |
| Panier des 4 Saisons | 1 |

| ■ DRINKING | |
|---|---|
| Bar du Moulin | 1 |
| Bighorn Bistro and Bakery Bar | 2 |
| Les Caves | 1 |
| Élévation 1904 | 4 |
| Moo Bar | 3 |

**Compagnie des Guides** Inside the Maison de la Montagne at 190 place de l'Église (daily 8.30am–noon & 2.30–7.30pm; ☎04 50 53 00 88, ⓦchamonix-guides.com); established in 1821, this excellent organization can provide guides for just about every mountain activity going, from off-piste skiing, snowshoeing and heli-skiing in the winter, to hiking, mountaineering and rock climbing in the summer; they offer a superb summer programme for kids too (ⓦcham-aventure.com). The same building houses the Office de Haute Montagne (Mon–Sat 9am–noon & 3–6pm, also Sun in July & Aug; ☎04 50 53 22 08, ⓦchamoniarde.

com), where you can get details and suggestions for all the local hiking routes, advice on *refuges*, as well as up-to-the-minute information on weather conditions.

**Bicycle rental** Any number of places in town offer bike rental, though one particularly good outfit is Zéro G, 90 av Ravanel-le-Rouge (daily 9am–12.30pm & 3.30–7pm; ☎04 50 53 01 01, ⓦzerogchamonix.com).

**Leisure centre** The Richard Bozon Sports Centre, at 214 av de la Plage (☎04 50 53 23 70) has ice-skating, swimming, tennis and squash, a climbing wall, sauna and hamam.

## ACCOMMODATION

There's plenty of accommodation to go around in Chamonix, but given the volume of tourist traffic in and around town, you'd do well to book in advance, whatever the time of year. The tourist office also offers a reservation service (☎04 50 53 23 33, ⓦbooking.chamonix.com), which can find you a room at even the busiest times. High season in Chamonix is December to March and mid-June to mid-September, while a number of establishments close in May and October; note that hotel prices can vary wildly according to the time of year, but regardless, you'll often find the best rates online. If you're staying in a Chamonix hotel or at the hostel, then you should receive a free *Carte d'Hôte* on arrival; this guest card entitles you to free transport on the resort's public buses and on the SNCF train line between Servoz and Vallorcine.

**Auberge de Jeunesse** 127 montée Jacques-Balmat, Les-Pèlerins-en-Haut ☎04 50 53 14 52, ⓦauberge-chamonix.com. This large hostel, 2.5km out of the town centre, has two- four- and six-bed rooms, and although there's no communal kitchen, they do offer cheap, three-course meals in the evening (€13). Bus #2 to the "Auberge de Jeunesse" stop, just below the hostel. Mid-May to Sept & Dec–April. Breakfast included. Dorms **€26**

**Camping La Mer de Glace** 200 chemin de la Bagna, Les Praz ☎04 50 53 44 03, ⓦchamonix-camping.com. This beautifully secluded site, 2km northeast of Chamonix, offers decent facilities including laundry, kids' play area, shop and bar. May–Sept. **€25**

**Le Chamonix** 11 rue de l'Hôtel-de-Ville ☎04 50 53 11 07, ⓦhotel-le-chamonix.com. Long-standing climbers and hikers hotel that's creaking at the seams a bit, but still perfectly acceptable (if overpriced), with a varied selection of pine-furnished doubles, triples and quads (some with bunks), some of which have views up to Mont Blanc. Breakfast €11. **€98**

**Le Faucigny** 118 place de l'Église ☎04 50 53 01 17, ⓦhotelfaucigny-chamonix.com. A gem of a hotel within a few paces of the main square, *Le Faucigny* has 28 crisply decorated rooms furnished in white-tinted pine and smart greys, with those on the second floor positioned under the mansard roof. At 4pm each day, you can pop down to the library-like lounge and help yourself

to some complimentary tea, coffee and cake along with a newspaper, and you can also enjoy the spa, with its jacuzzi and sauna; there's free bike rental too. Breakfast €12. **€150**

★ **Hameau Albert-1ᵉʳ** 38 route du Bouchet ☎04 50 53 05 09, ⓦhameaualbert.fr. Run by the same family since 1903, this fantastic hotel is actually a beautifully arranged complex set within gorgeous gardens complete with a little brook and laden with fruit trees and herb beds. The accommodation itself comprises Alpine-style cabins, furnished in either rustic style, with roaring fireplaces, or in more modern fashion with white-washed wood, and super-cool contemporary rooms in the main building; wherever you stay, the views up to Mont Blanc are stunning. A gorgeous, combined indoor/outdoor pool, and spa, rounds things off beautifully. Breakfast €25. **€235**

**Le Morgane** 145 av de l'Aiguille-du-Midi ☎04 50 53 57 15, ⓦmorgane-hotel-chamonix.com. Sophisticated, and very expensive, hotel, with minimalist rooms conceived in wood and stone and coloured in muted browns and beiges. There's also a gorgeous basement pool, sauna and hamam, while the top-floor terrace offers superb views of Mont Blanc. Free bike rental. Breakfast €15. **€190**

**Pointe-Isabelle** 165 av Michel-Croz ☎04 50 53 12 87, ⓦpointeisabelle.com. Just two-minutes' walk from the *gare SNCF*, this sparky hotel is far more appealing than its unprepossessing exterior suggests; soothing rooms are decorated in fetching deep purple and charcoal grey colours, with superbly designed wet rooms, and balconies from which to enjoy the marvellous mountain views. Closed mid-Oct to early Dec. Breakfast €13.50. **€98**

**Richemond** 228 rue du Docteur-Paccard ☎04 50 53 08 85, ⓦrichemond.fr. An imposing early twentieth-century structure set back from the busy main street, the *Richemond* has been managed by the same family for three generations, hence its rather old-fashioned, but still very charming, manner. The rooms are a mix of old and new, though all are gradually being renovated; ask for a balcony room with views across to Mont Blanc. Closed mid-April to mid-June, and mid-Sept to mid-Dec. Breakfast €10.50. **€105**

**Vert Hôtel** 964 rte des Gaillands ☎04 50 53 13 58,

**14**

verthotel.com. Around 1km west of the town centre, close to the Lac du Gaillands, the "Green Hotel" is a welcoming, family-friendly place, offering a lovely mix of rooms, the mountain view and balcony rooms being slightly pricier. Lots of people also come here to enjoy the atmospheric lounge bar-cum-restaurant, which does fabulous cocktails and delicious food. Bus #1 stops just outside. Breakfast €9. **€70**

## EATING AND DRINKING

Given Chamonix's year-round popularity, it's no surprise that the town is rammed with places to eat and drink, and the quality is, on the whole, pretty high – though prices can be too. Chamonix's geographical location is reflected in its Swiss and Italian culinary influences, but there's certainly no shortage of high-end French cuisine if you're prepared to spend a little extra. For live music head for the pubs and clubs of rue des Moulins or Chamonix Sud.

### CAFÉS AND RESTAURANTS

★ **Albert-1er** 38 rte du Bouchet 04 50 53 05 09, hameaualbert.fr. Chamonix's only two-starred Michelin restaurant is headed by chef Pierre Maillet, who produces some wonderfully conceived dishes like veal sweetbread with walnut crust, green apple and mountain lovage, and roasted lobster with home-made black pudding and lobster claw polenta, with many of the ingredients plucked from the kitchen garden; the wine, too, is more than a match for the food. The decor is formal, but contemporary, and though it might be a little too stiff for some, there's no denying that you'll be in for an evening to remember. *Menus* from €49. Closed mid-Oct to early Dec. Mon & Fri–Sun 12.30–2pm & 7.15–9.30pm, Tues & Thurs 7.15–9.30pm.

**L'Atelier Café** Quai d'Arve 04 50 53 32 36. Cafés are ten a penny in Chamonix, but this easy-going and colourful establishment serves up great coffee and pasties, alongside light lunches (bagels, *croques*), breakfasts and brunches. In winter, retreat to the cosy interior, with its thick-set stone walls and little wooden stools and tables. Daily 8.30am–10pm.

**L'Atmosphère** 123 place Balmat 04 50 55 97 97, restaurant-atmosphere.com. The main appeal of this good-looking restaurant is its covered balconied terrace perched just a metre or so above the rushing waters of the Arve River – and there's a tremendous wine cellar to boot. As far as the food goes, take your pick from beautifully conceived seasonal dishes like pan-fried duck foie gras with morello cherries, and saddle of hare with chanterelle mushrooms and pan-fried pumpkins – the hot stone grill dishes are worth a punt, too. Starters €12, mains €21. Daily noon–2pm & 7–11pm.

**Le Bartavel** 26 cour du Bartavel 04 50 53 97 19. With its sprawling terrace edging out towards place Balmat, this is a solid bet if you don't want to break the bank. Pizza (€10) and pasta (€12) form the mainstay of a long menu, which also features soups, salads, crêpes and *grillades*. Daily 9am–11.30pm.

**Le Cap Horn** 74 rue des Moulins 04 50 21 80 80, caphorn-chamonix.com. The entrance to this most contemporary of restaurants is through a fine timber-framed porch, a theme continued inside with three floors of wood and slate and a slightly peculiar mix of Alpine and nautical decor. It's an intriguing menu that very much fuses far eastern and French cuisine, for example Asian braised pork cheek with truffles, fried onions and bao bread. Starters €10, mains €18. Daily noon–3pm & 7–10.30pm.

**L'Impossible** 9 chemin du Cry 04 50 53 20 36, restaurant-impossible.com. Well worth the 10min walk from the town centre for its cosy farmhouse interior and thrilling Italian-inspired dishes like steamed cuttlefish with eggplant sauce, black rice and ginger, and gorgonzola, walnut and spinach ravioli with peach and mascarpone sauce. Starters €14, mains €25. Daily 6.30–10.30pm. Closed Nov & Tues in May–June & Sept–Oct.

---

## CHAMONIX EVENTS

Inevitably, many of the town's biggest annual events revolve around the mountains; the **World Climbing Championships** in mid-July sees some of the world's finest alpinists roll into town to tackle a series of speed and technical climbs on an enormous artificial wall, while, in mid-August, the four-day **Fête des Guides de Chamonix (Mountain Guides Festival)** celebrates the work of the local guides, with live music, folklore events, climbing demonstrations, and a grand procession to bless the ropes and ice axes. During the last week of August, it's the **Ultra-Trail du Mont Blanc** (ultratrailmontblanc.com), which starts and ends in Chamonix but also crosses Swiss and Italian territory; at 166km-long, this single stage ultra-marathon is one of the world's toughest endurance tests, though the best athletes manage to complete it in a remarkable twenty hours or so. The town's main music event is the **Cosmo Jazz Festival** (cosmojazzfestival.com) at the end of July, which attracts some of the world's most accomplished jazz musicians to venues around town as well as some terrific mountain locations.

**14**

## SKIING IN CHAMONIX

Despite its fame, Chamonix is not the most user-friendly of ski resorts and access to the slopes relies on shuttle buses, trains or a car. For advanced skiers, however, it's probably one of the best places in the Alps since it offers an impressive range of challenging runs and off-piste itineraries. It's not so much a single resort as a chain of unconnected ski areas set along both sides of the Chamonix valley and dominated by Mont Blanc. The **Brévent** and **Flégère** areas on the southern slopes both have a good variety of pistes and provide some fine views of the Mont Blanc massif across the valley, while **Argentière–Les Grands Montets** is a colder, north-facing area that is well-suited to advanced skiers. The famous **Vallée Blanche** can be accessed by cable car from the Aiguille du Midi; skiing here involves a 20km descent which passes many crevasses and is not patrolled, so a guide is strongly recommended. Closer to Chamonix itself, the **Les Planards** and **Le Savoy** areas require artificial snow and snow cannons to stay open, but they are good spots for beginners to hone their technique. There are plenty of **ski schools** in Chamonix, which provide lessons for skiers and snowboarders, as well as guides. The ESF office (☎04 50 53 22 57, Ⓦesfchamonix.com) is situated in the Maison de la Montagne; the guides here hold special lessons on the famous runs of the Vallée Blanche.

**Panier des 4 Saisons** 262 rue du Docteur-Paccard ☎04 50 53 98 77, Ⓦrestaurant-panierdes4saisons.com. Ignore the rather uninviting location up a grubby side alley, this lovely restaurant rustles up some of the finest food in town; casserole of Burgundian *escargots* in parsley and garlic butter, and roasted veal T-bone with rosemary jus and polenta, and for veggies, there's a scrummy goat-cheese ravioli in leek fondue. Starters €12, mains €24. Mon–Sat noon–2pm & 7.30–10.30pm.

### BARS AND CLUBS

**Bar du Moulin** 80 rue des Moulins ☎06 07 24 88 18. Below *Le Cap Horn* restaurant, this terrific little cellar bar is arguably the best après-ski hangout in town; an evening here usually starts quite sedately, but don't be fooled – the pace picks up quickly as the night wears on and it becomes quite the party place, often with an appearance by a stellar name DJ. Wed–Sun 4pm–2am.

**Bighorn Bistro and Bakery Bar** 77 place Edmond-Desailloud ☎04 57 44 62 84, Ⓦblghornbistro.com. Easy-going, American-run bistro-cum-bar, hence the impressive line-up of imported artisan beers from the likes of the Brooklyn Brewery and the Boulevard Brewing Company; soak it all up with a handcrafted sandwich, fat burger or one of the gut-busting dishes from the brunch menu. Mon–Wed 4–11pm, Thurs–Sun 11am–11pm.

**Les Caves** 74 rue des Moulins ☎04 50 21 80 80. Kick back with a cocktail or a glass of red wine, and a plate of tapas, in the sophisticated basement wine-bar-cum-jazz club of *Le Cap Horn*. There's music most nights, which invariably starts with a low-key jazz or blues session before a DJ or band takes over later in the evening. Daily 6pm–2am.

**Élévation 1904** 259 av Michel-Croz ☎04 50 53 00 52. Whether it's an early morning cappuccino or a pint at sundown, you'll find all the cool dudes – or so they like to think – hanging out on the alfresco terrace of this buzzing little bar opposite the train station. Daily 7.30am–1.30am.

**Moo Bar** 239 av Michel-Croz ☎04 50 55 33 42, Ⓦmoobarcuisine.com. Equal part restaurant, equal part bar, this good-time place offers both a lunch and evening menu (burgers, surprisingly enough; pulled pork, beef and truffle; €14.50) and a terrific selection of drinks, namely cocktails, wine and ice-cold beers – there's even a self-service beer station; regular live music too. Daily 9am–1am.

# Excursions in the Chamonix Valley

Alongside the walking and skiing opportunities around Chamonix, there are several exhilarating excursions using the various ski lifts and mountain railways; it may be worth getting a **multipass** that covers all the lifts in the area (€65 for 24 hours, €77.50/88 for two/three consecutive days). These can be purchased online, at the tourist office, or at the foot of each cable-car ascent.

## Aiguille du Midi téléphérique

May to mid-June & Sept 8am–5pm; mid-June to Aug 6.30am–6pm; Oct 8.30am–4pm; Jan–April 8.30am–4.30pm • €61.50 return • ☎04 50 53 22 75, Ⓦmontblancnaturalresort.com

Easily the most famous excursion in the area is the **téléphérique** to the **Aiguille du Midi** (3842m), one of the longest cable-car ascents in the world, rising 3000m above the valley

**14**

floor in two extremely steep stages – anyone even remotely suffering from vertigo should forget about this particular excursion. Although the trip is absurdly expensive, penny-pinching by buying a ticket only as far as the Plan du Midi (2310m) is a waste of money: go all the way or not at all. If you do go up, make the effort to be on your way before 9am, as the summits tend to cloud over towards midday, and huge crowds may force you to wait for hours if you try later. Take warm clothes – even on a summer's day it'll be below zero at the top – and sunblock is also advisable to protect against the glare off the snow.

The Aiguille is an exposed granite pinnacle on which a restaurant and the *téléphérique* dock are precariously balanced. Here, too, is an extraordinary new skywalk called **Step into the Void**, an all-glass box suspended some 1000 metres above empty space – an astonishing feat of engineering, this really is not for the faint-hearted. Even if you're not willing to brave the skywalk (it's included in the price of the cable car) the views up here are incredible. At your feet is the snowy plateau of the **Col du Midi**, with the glaciers of the Vallée Blanche and Géant sloping down the mountainside. From the Aiguille, the Three Monts climbing route takes mountaineers up the steep snowfield and exposed ridge to the summit of Mont Blanc with its final cap of ice. On the horizon lies rank upon rank of snow- and ice-capped monsters receding into the distance. Perhaps most impressive of all is the view from east to south, in which the Aiguille Verte, Triollet and the Jorasses, with the Matterhorn and Monte Rosa, form a cirque of needle-sharp peaks and sheer crags.

## Montenvers rack railway

Daily: May–June & Sept–Oct 8.30am–5pm; July & Aug 8am–6.30pm; Nov–April 10am–4.30pm; closed Oct • €32.50 return • ☎ 04 50 53 22 75, ⓦ montblancnaturalresort.com

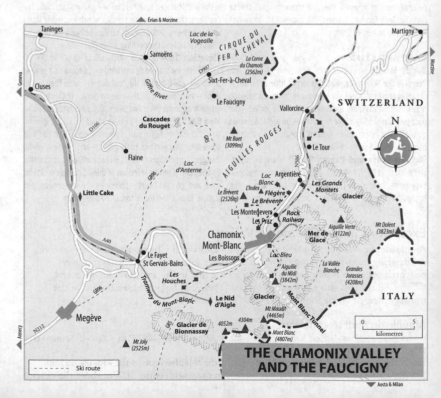

THE CHAMONIX VALLEY AND THE FAUCIGNY

## CLIMBING MONT BLANC AND THE TOUR DU MONT BLANC

Climbing Mont Blanc is not a task that should be undertaken lightly, as testified by the number of lives claimed by the mountain each year. It is a semi-technical climb and fast-changing weather conditions mean that a guide is essential. There are several different routes, the most popular of which is the Goûter ridge route (three days), which ascends from the Nid d'Aigle at the top of the Tramway du Mont Blanc. The best season for climbing the mountain is mid-June to September (when the majority of *refuges* are also open), but even in this period, it should only be attempted by fit, acclimatized and well-prepared mountaineers.

The classic way for walkers to admire Mont Blanc without putting themselves through the dangers of an ascent is to undertake the **Tour du Mont Blanc**, a 250km circuit of the mountain across French, Swiss and Italian terrain. The trail normally takes eight to twelve days, during which you can either camp or stay at the *refuges* (€20–25) en route. Many of the *refuges* provide food and other supplies, but it's worth checking the latest details with the **Office de Haute Montagne** in Chamonix, which can also provide maps of the route. Even in early July, many of the passes can still be covered in snow, so walkers should carry crampons and heavy-duty waterproofs. Several tour companies in Chamonix can provide guides for the walk, though the venerable Compagnie des Guides (see page 757) is your best bet.

**14**

If you haven't tired of superb panoramic views, you can make for the **Montenvers rack railway**, a train service which has been running up from Chamonix to the Mer de Glace (1913m) on the flanks of Mont Blanc since 1908; indeed the advent of the Montenvers rack railway effectively signalled the beginning of Alpine tourism in the region. Taking around twenty minutes, the little red train chugs its way up to the "Sea of Ice", which, at 7km long and nearly 2000m at its widest point, is by far the largest glacier in the Alps. At the top you have the option of walking for twenty minutes or taking a short cable-car ride (an additional €6) down into an **ice cave** freshly carved out of the Mer de Glace every summer – this is usually open between mid-June and September. Another excellent possibility is to make the relatively easy hike from Montenvers to the Plan du Midi (2hr) and take the cable car back down to Chamonix from there.

### Hiking and climbing

There are countless excellent **shorter walks** around Chamonix, including many on the northern side of the valley amid the lower but nonetheless impressive peaks of the **Aiguilles Rouges**. One easy, picturesque trail takes you from the village of Les Praz (just to the northeast of Chamonix itself) to **Lac Blanc**. Take the *téléphérique* from Les Praz to Flégère and then the gondola to L'Index (a combined ticket is €29). The walk to the lake and back from L'Index takes around 2hr 30min and requires good walking boots.

### The Faucigny and the Cirque du Fer-à-Cheval

To the north of Chamonix is the **Faucigny**, a region of wide glacial valleys, gentle forested slopes and peaceful little villages that seem a world away from the party atmosphere of the resorts further south. **Samoëns**, lying 15km away from Chamonix, is one such village; despite its relatively low altitude, it has become popular with **skiers** thanks to a short transfer time from Geneva and its proximity to the Grand Massif ski area (particularly the purpose-built resort of **Flaine**) via the Express du Grand Massif, a *télécabine* to the south of the village.

If you head east from Samoëns along the D907, you follow the valley as it narrows into the Gorges des Tines before opening out again at another delightful little village, **SIXT-FER-À-CHEVAL**. This pretty village lies on the confluence of two branches of the river Giffre: the Giffre-Haut, which comes down from Salvagny, and the Giffre-Bas, which flows all the way from the **Cirque du Fer-à-Cheval**. The cirque is a horseshoe-shaped ridge famed for the rugged beauty of its cliffs and waterfalls, and it is this which makes the journey away from Chamonix truly memorable.

The cirque begins about 6km from Sixt and you can reach it easily via the footpath on the left bank of the Giffre-Bas. It is a vast semicircle of limestone walls, up to 700m in height and 4–5km long, from which spring countless waterfalls, particularly in the summer months. The left-hand end of the cirque is dominated by a huge spike of rock known as La Corne du Chamois (The Goat's Horn). At its foot the valley of the Giffre bends sharply north to its source in the glaciers above the Fond de la Combe. The bowl of the cirque is thickly wooded except for a circular meadow in the middle where the road ends.

**14**

# Lake Geneva

The crescent-shaped expanse of **Lake Geneva** (known as Lac Léman in France) is some 73km long, 14km wide and an impressive 310m deep; it has always been a natural border with Switzerland to the north. Even in summer, the lake is subject to violent storms, yet the experience of sailing across its waters on a calm day is delightful, and should not be missed. On the French side of the lake, the spa resort of **Évian-les-Bains** (of bottled water fame) and the picturesque village of **Yvoire** are the main sites of interest. **Thonon-les-Bains**, a larger town situated between these two landmarks, is the starting point of the renowned touring route, the **Route des Grandes Alpes**, and a gateway to the beautiful Chablais region to the south of the lake. North of the lake, close to the Swiss border, is the peaceful spa town of **Divonne-les-Bains**, and the green pastures of the Pays de Gex region, renowned for its blue cheese and scenic hiking and cycling routes.

## Évian-les-Bains

The most well-known French spa resort on Lake Geneva, **ÉVIAN** maintains a clinical orderliness that wouldn't be out of place on the opposite side of the water. The spa aside, there are a certainly a couple of attractions that merit an afternoon's sightseeing, although simply taking a stroll along the waterfront, or a leisurely trip on the lake is good enough reason to spend some time here.

### The Évian Spa and waterfront

**Les Thermes Évian Spa** Place de la Libération • Mon–Fri 9am–8pm, Sat 9am–6pm • €30 for day access to pools, sauna and fitness facilities, €20 for pools and sauna only • ☎ 04 50 75 02 30, ⓦ lesthermesevian.com

**Thermes Évian Spa** offers all manner of treatments, but most people come here just to wallow in the warming, Évian-sourced thermal waters; the entrance fee includes access to the various pools, sauna, jacuzzi, hamam and fitness centre. Just beyond the spa, and elegantly laid out with squares of immaculately mown grass, perfectly clipped hedges and colourful flowerbeds, the **waterfront** strip is the town's focal point. Its main promenade is fronted by a quartet of fine *belle époque* buildings, not least the grand, glazed brick and stone **Palais Lumière**, built as a pump-room in 1902 and adorned with gorgeous stained-glass windows and Art Nouveau frescoes – today it's a cultural centre, hosting regular exhibitions. Next door is the **town hall**, the former summer residence of celebrated photographer Antoine Lumière, while a little further along is the prepossessing **theatre** building which has been functioning as such since 1885. Completing this showy line-up of buildings, and which no self-respecting spa resort would be without, is the **casino** (1912), topped by a "Neo-Byzantine" dome and elegant scalloped arcade.

### Pré-Curieux water gardens

May–Sept 3 boats daily: 10am, 1.45pm, 3.30pm • €12.60 for boat trip and tour of gardens • ☎ 04 50 83 30 62, ⓦ evian-tourisme.com

Situated by the lake on the town's western outskirts and accessible only by a boat that leaves from the centre of Évian are the **Pré-Curieux** water gardens. Set around a colonial-style house, where you can views some displays, these picturesque lakeside gardens are divided into various water-based ecosystems (including ponds, marshes and a waterfall), each of which exhibits different forms of plant and animal life. Tickets for the gardens are available at the small kiosk in front of the casino and boats leave from the nearby quay.

## The funicular

Rue du Port • May–Sept daily 10am–12.30pm & 1.15–7.10pm • Free • ☎ 04 50 26 35 35.

One thing not to miss is the town **funicular**, which departs from its gorgeous little Art Nouveau station behind the Palais Lumière and rattles its way uphill to the suburb of Neuvecelle, some 750m distant. Opened in 1907 to transport guests from the Cachat spring up to the *Évian Royal Hotel*, the line then closed in the 1960s, remaining dormant for the best part of three decades before being extended (there are now six stops) and reopened in 2002. The best way to experience it is to ride to the top, grab a drink at the hut, and then walk back down, the path more or less following the line of the funicular. Bikes can be transported on the trailer, also free of charge.

## L'Espace Évian and Source Cachat

19 rue Nationale • April–Sept Tues–Sun 10am–noon & 2–6.30pm • Free • ☎ 04 50 84 80 29

Having lain redundant for years, the Évian company's former offices – itself a fine bit of Art Nouveau architecture dating from 1903 – have been spruced up and now house an exhibition on the town's most famous product. As informative as the interactive exhibitions are, the emphasis here is very much on trying to promote as many of the company's products as possible. Up the hill, on avenue des Sources, you can admire the **Source Cachat**, discovered in 1789 by count Jean-Charles de Lazier. Make sure you do as the locals do and take a bottle along, though there is often a bit of a scrum around the fountain from whence the nicely chilled water spouts. The water itself is now bottled at an industrial estate in Amphion, 3km along the lakeside; tours of the site, which includes a visit to the Évian exhibition and a tour around the production line, are now possible, but must be booked in advance (☎ 04 50 84 80 18, ⓦ evianexperience.com).

## ARRIVAL AND INFORMATION
ÉVIAN-LES-BAINS

**By train** The *gare SNCF* lies on the hill a 10min walk to the southwest of the town centre on av de la Gare.
Destinations Annecy via Annemasse (several daily; 2hr); Geneva via Annemasse (several daily; 1hr); Thonon-les-Bains (every 2hr; 10min).

**By bus** The *gare routière*, from which you can catch buses to Thonon-les-Bains and Yvoire, is next to the tourist office on quai Baron-de-Blonay.

**By ferry** The Compagnie Générale de Navigation (☎ 84 81 18 48, ⓦ cgn.ch) operate a dozen or so ferries per day across the lake to Lausanne in Switzerland (€19 single, €32.80 return); departures are from the Port on avenue Jean-Léger and the ride takes thirty-five minutes.

**Tourist office** Place d'Allinges (May, June & Sept Mon–Fri 9am–noon & 2–6.30pm, Sat 9am–noon & 2–6pm, Sun 10am–noon & 3–6pm; July & Aug Mon–Fri 9.30am–6.30pm, Sat & Sun 10am–6pm; Oct–April Mon–Fri 9am–noon & 2–6pm, Sat till 5pm; ☎ 04 50 75 04 26, ⓦ evian-tourisme.com).

## ACCOMMODATION

**Évian Express** 32 av de la Gare ☎ 04 50 75 15 07, ⓦ hotel-evianexpress.net. Appropriately named joint positioned directly opposite the *gare SNCF*, this welcoming, warmly run place is the antithesis of your average station hotel; bright, boldly coloured and spotless rooms sleeping two- to four-people, some of which have fantastic lake views – and it's the cheapest option in town. Reception open 8am–noon & 2–9pm. Breakfast €8.50. **€75**

**De France** 59 rue Nationale ☎ 04 50 75 00 36, ⓦ hotel-france-evian.fr. Distinguished eighteenth-century building overlooking one of the town's biggest squares, concealing a mix of fairly ordinary rooms and a bunch of larger, more polished rooms, which aren't actually that much more expensive; triples and quads available too Breakfast €9. **€85**

**Littoral** 9 av de Narvik ☎ 04 50 75 64 00, ⓦ hotel-littoral-evian.com. Rooms at this personable little hotel are neatly fashioned either in thick pine wood or a slightly more contemporary style, but the best thing going for this place is its super position near the water, which ensures that many of the rooms have head-on lake views. Breakfast €11.50. **€95**

14

**14**

## EATING AND DRINKING

**Instant Gourmand** 10 rue de l'Église ☎ 04 50 04 74 98. Fabulous backstreet restaurant with barely half a dozen tables, inside and out, but with an intriguing little menu featuring the likes of scallop ceviche, pan-fried skate with tandoori yoghurt sauce, and clafoutis *cerise* and balsamic vinegar. Starters €11, mains €20. Tues–Sat noon–1.30pm & 7–9.30pm.

**La Pizza** 4 place Charles-de-Gaulle ☎ 04 50 75 05 36, ⓦ lapizzaevian.com. The name is hardly inspiring, and there's little to suggest that there's anything particularly special about this place, but the pizzas – many made with crème fraîche – are absolutely cracking, and go for around €8. They also have a selection of interesting three-course *menus* from €15, on top of which you also get a glass of house sangria. Mon & Wed–Sun noon–2pm & 7–11pm.

# Yvoire

Occupying a picture-postcard setting 25km to the west of Évian is the absurdly pretty medieval village of **YVOIRE**, where narrow cobbled lanes lined with artisan shops and chunky stone-built houses slope down to the water's edge, and every street corner seemingly abounds with colourful flowers. Although the village heaves with day-trippers – notably Japanese – in the summer months, you can still find some peace and quiet. Today the most visible reminder of Yvoire's medieval past is the old **castle** along with the two stone gateways, both dating from the fourteenth century.

## Labyrinthe-Jardin des Cinq Sens

Rue du Lac • Daily: mid-April to early-Oct 10am–6.30pm • €12 • ☎ 04 50 72 88 80, ⓦ jardin5sens.net

Yvoire's one main attraction is the **Labyrinthe-Jardin des Cinq Sens**, formerly the kitchen gardens of the now privately-owned castle. This wonderful display of immaculate formal gardens – incorporating some 1500 varieties – is designed to stimulate each of the five senses: fruit bushes appeal to your taste buds; the foliage in the Jardin des Textures encourages you to touch; geraniums provide vivid colours; lilies and honeysuckle produce attractive perfumes, while the central aviary is filled with birdsong.

## ARRIVAL AND INFORMATION

In the absence of a train or bus station most people make their way here by car, hence the preponderance of car parks located just outside the medieval core.

**Boat trips** From Port de Plaisance ferries (☎ 84 81 18 48, ⓦ cgn.ch) make the short trip to Nyon (12 daily; €32.80 return) on the opposite side of the lake, with less regular ferries to Lausanne (3 daily; €57.30) and Geneva (4 daily;

€45.50).

**Tourist office** Place de la Mairie (Nov–March Mon–Fri 9.30am–12.30pm & 1.30–5pm, Sat 11am–3pm; April–June & Sept–Oct Mon–Sat 9.30am–12.30pm & 1.30–5pm, Sun noon–4pm; July & Aug daily 9.30am–6.30pm; ☎ 04 50 72 80 21, ⓦ yvoiretourism.com).

## ACCOMMODATION AND EATING

**Le Jules Verne** ☎ 04 50 72 80 08, ⓦ hoteljulesverne. com. Most of the rooms in this upmarket hotel, superbly located down by the port, face lakewards, while those down on the ground floor have the added bonus of their own terraced garden. In a nod to the eponymous explorer, the breakfast room is decked out with colourful hot-air balloons. March–Oct. Breakfast €18. **€160**

**La Traboule** Grande Rue ☎ 04 50 72 83 73, ⓦ la-

---

## THE ROUTE DES GRANDES ALPES

Winding its way over mountain passes and secluded valleys all the way from Thonon-les-Bains to Menton on the Mediterranean coast is the most renowned tourist route of the French Alps, the 684km **Route des Grandes Alpes**. The route crosses six Alpine passes over 2000m, three of which – the Col de la Cayolle, the Col d'Izoard and the Col de Vars – were only paved in 1934. The complete route opened in 1937 and has been a popular touring route for drivers, walkers and cyclists ever since. It can be covered in a couple of days by car, but only by rushing through the stunning mountain landscapes and intriguing settlements (including Morzine, Valloire, Briançon and Barcelonnette) that line the route.

traboule.fr. While it can't boast a grand lakeside setting like most of Yvoire's restaurants, this is a beautiful-looking place with little potted flowers adorning immaculately laid tables. Inevitably lake fish (in particular perch fillet) take pride of place, but there are also some superb cheese-based dishes on the menu. Starters €12, mains €18. Wed–Sun 11.45–2.30pm & 6.45–9.30pm.

**Le Vieux Logis** Grande Rue ☎04 50 72 80 24, ⓦ levieuxlogis.com. Tucked away in the heart of the medieval village, this sweet little family-run hotel and restaurant offers plenty of charm, even though the furnishings are nothing particularly special. Mid-Feb to Nov. Breakfast €10. €̶8̶7̶

# Besançon

The capital of Franche-Comté, **BESANÇON**, is an attractive town of handsome stone buildings that sits between the northern edge of the Jura Mountains and a loop of the wide River Doubs. It is this natural defensive position that has defined the town's history. Besançon was briefly a Gallic fortress before Caesar smashed the Gauls' resistance in 58 BC. Strong outer walls were developed during the Middle Ages and the indefatigable military engineer Vauban added the still-extant citadelle in the seventeenth century in order to guard the natural breach in the river, and a large French army presence remained in the area until well into the twentieth century.

For the most part, visitors are unlikely to stray far from the old town, which is squeezed into a tight loop of the Doubs. Its pedestrianized streets and narrow walkways conceal a wealth of good museums and cosy cafés. From the main tourist office on the far side of the river, the **rue de la République** leads across the pont de la République and into the heart of the old town, to the central **place du 8-septembre** and the sixteenth-century **hôtel de ville**. The principal street, **Grande Rue**, cuts across place du 8-septembre along the line of an old Roman road. At its northwestern end is another bridge, the modern **Pont Battant**, a replacement for the original Roman bridge into the city, which (in a testament to Roman engineering) survived until 1953. Just before the bridge is the liveliest part of town, filled with inviting cafés and bars.

## Musée des Beaux-Arts et d'Archéologie

Place de la Révolution • Daily except Tues 9.30am–noon & 2–6pm • €5 • ☎ 03 81 87 80 49, ⓦ mbaa.besancon.fr

In the main square just off the northern end of Grande Rue, the **Musée des Beaux-Arts et d'Archéologie** exhibits a fabulous hoard of Egyptian antiquities, notably a beautiful wood-stuccoed and painted sarcophagus, in addition to some fine Roman mosaics and bronzes. The fine art collection, meanwhile, spans the late fifteenth- to early twentieth centuries, with key works by Rembrandt, Renoir and Matisse. The museum is reopening in 2019 after undergoing a major refurbishment.

## Musée du Temps

96 Grande Rue • Tues–Sat 9.15am–noon & 2–6pm; Sun 10am–6pm • €5, €2.50 Sat, free Sun • ☎ 03 81 87 81 50, ⓦ mdt.besancon.fr

Horologists will delight in the comprehensive display of clocks at the **Musée du Temps**, housed inside the sixteenth-century **Palais Granvelle**. Packed with interactive exhibits on the important local clock-making industry, which reached its zenith here in the nineteenth century, there are all manner of fabulous timepieces to admire, from exquisitely produced watches and table clocks to grandfather clocks and navigational instruments. The museum's star exhibit, however, is Foucault's Pendulum, a thirteen-metre-high apparatus conceived by the eponymous physicist as a means of demonstrating how the earth rotated.

## Maison Victor Hugo

140 Grande Rue • Daily except Tues 10.30am–6pm, Nov–March till 5.30pm • €2.50 • ☎ 03 81 87 85 35

A plaque at no.140 Grande Rue indicates that this house was the birthplace of Victor Hugo, in 1802 – however, he only lived here for six weeks, and never returned to the city.

The house celebrates the author's life and works, with first editions, signed letters and pamphlets – though there is very little by way of personal effects. Much is also made of his tireless campaigns fighting for the rights of the poor and disadvantaged – indeed he gave many speeches to the French National Assembly on the subject – which, in turn, fuelled many of his most well-known works, not least *Les Misérables*, which took seventeen years to complete. Look out, too, for a miniature bronze bust of Hugo by Rodin; apparently, Hugo was so irritated by Rodin's presence that the sculptor had to work largely from sketches.

## Castan Square and Porte Noire

Across the way from Maison Victor Hugo stands the idyllic **Castan Square**, which takes its name from the archeologist who, in 1870, discovered the remains of what was most probably a Roman theatre – fronted by eight Corinthian columns of varying height, it's now a delightful English-style garden. Just beyond here is the **Porte Noire** ("Black

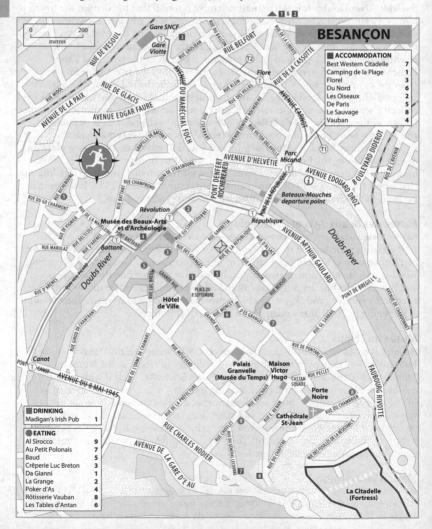

**BESANÇON**

| ■ ACCOMMODATION | |
|---|---|
| Best Western Citadelle | 7 |
| Camping de la Plage | 1 |
| Florel | 3 |
| Du Nord | 6 |
| Les Oiseaux | 2 |
| De Paris | 5 |
| Le Sauvage | 8 |
| Vauban | 4 |

| ■ DRINKING | |
|---|---|
| Madigan's Irish Pub | 1 |

| ● EATING | |
|---|---|
| Al Sirocco | 9 |
| Au Petit Polonais | 7 |
| Baud | 5 |
| Crêperie Luc Breton | 3 |
| Da Gianni | 1 |
| La Grange | 2 |
| Poker d'As | 4 |
| Rôtisserie Vauban | 8 |
| Les Tables d'Antan | 6 |

Gate"), something of a misnomer for this almost whiter than white triumphal arch built in the second century AD in honour of Emperor Marcus Aurelius. Given its age, the ornamentation is remarkable, particularly on the inside of the arch and the recesses on the other side.

## Cathédrale St-Jean and Horloge Astronomique

**Horloge Astronomique** Hourly guided visits in French; April–Sept daily except Tues 9.50–12.30pm & 1.50–5.30pm; Oct–Dec & Feb–March daily except Tues & Wed same hours • €3.50 • ☎ 03 81 81 12 76, ⓦ horloge-astronomique-besancon.fr

Through the porte Noire is the eighteenth-century **Cathédrale St-Jean** (closed Tues), whose spare but imposing interior manifests high Romanesque arches leading upwards to a magnificent rib-vaulted ceiling. The principal interest here, though, is the **Horloge Astronomique**, a remarkable astronomical clock built between 1858 and 1860 which contains some 30,000 parts and indicates over a hundred terrestrial and celestial positions.

## The citadelle

99 rue des Fusillés de la Résistance • Daily: April–June & Sept–Oct 9am–6pm; July & Aug 9am–7pm; Nov–March 10am–5pm; Jan closed first two weeks • €10.80, includes entrance to all museums; €2 for audioguide • ☎ 03 81 87 83 33, ⓦ citadelle.com

A steep fifteen-minute climb from the cathedral (or bus #17 if you don't fancy that), Vauban's vast and spectacular **citadelle** lords it over the old town below. There's much to see and do here, and you could quite easily spend several hours exploring the walls, turrets and ditches (that Vauban left as traps for any potential assailants), not to mention several museums and a **zoo**, which has been cleverly incorporated into the fortification trenches.

Inevitably, the **Musée de la Résistance et de la Déportation** is a rather sobering affair, though it does a superb job detailing the activities of the wartime resistance movement, both locally and throughout France. The **Musée Comtois**, meanwhile, has some lovely displays pertaining to the lives and traditions of the local populace, with collections of pottery, furniture and puppets, and a magnificent assemblage of seventeenth- and eighteenth-century cast-iron firebacks. Squarely one for the kids, the **Musée d'Histoire Naturelle** contains an aquarium, insectarium and noctarium.

## ARRIVAL AND INFORMATION                                         BESANÇON

**By train** The *gare de Besançon-Viotte* is at the end of av Maréchal-Foch, a 10min walk north of the old town, while the *gare de Besançon Franche-Comté* TGV station (part of the high-speed LGV Rhin-Rhône line) is some 10km north of town; trains connect the two stations roughly every 60–90min.
Destinations Belfort (hourly; 1hr 15min); Bourg-en-Bresse (6 daily; 1hr 50min); Dijon (hourly; 1hr); Lons-le-Saunier (hourly; 1hr 10min); Paris-Lyon (6 daily; 2hr 30min).

**By bus** There is an extensive bus network, with several major stops, including one at the *gare de Besançon-Viotte*, as well as two tramlines (tram #2 passes by the *gare de Besançon-Viotte*); tickets for buses and trams – which can be bought at machines by the stops – cost €1.40 for a single journey, or there's a day pass for €4.30.

**Tourist office** The tourist office is on the northern bank by

the pont de la République at 2 place de la Première Armée Française (July & Aug daily 10am–6pm; Sept–June Mon–Sat 10am–12.30pm & 1.30–6pm, Sun 10am–1pm; ☎ 03 81 80 92 55, ⓦ besancon-tourisme.com).

**Bicycle rental** Bikes can be hired from some thirty Velocité stations dotted around town (€1 subscription then €1/hr or €4/day; ⓦ velocite.besancon.fr).

**River boats** On the other side of the pont de la République from the tourist office, two cruise boat companies (Bateau le Vauban; ⓦ bateau-besancon.fr and Vedettes de Besançon; ⓦ vedettesdebesancon.com) offer 75-minute trips along the Doubs, following its course around the outer limits of the town centre; both operate between April and October with between two and five trips daily depending upon the month (€12).

## ACCOMMODATION

**Best Western Citadelle** 13 rue du Général-Lecourbe ☎ 03 81 81 33 92, ⓦ bestwerncitadelle.com. Set in a quieter corner of the old town, this friendly hotel has seen a welcome renovation, with two categories of room (standard

and deluxe) available in two buildings, though all are boldly coloured and come with extras like coffee machines. There's a choice of a standard breakfast (€13) or an "Express" breakfast (€7), the latter served from 5am onwards in the

**14**

fantastic vaulted basement. €86

**Camping de la Plage** 12 rte de Belfort, Chalezeule ☎ 03 81 88 04 26, ⓦ campingdebesancon.com. Located 5km out of town, this campsite has a restaurant, pool and plenty of opportunities for various sporting activities. They've also got bungalows sleeping four. Mid-March to Oct. €19; bungalows €50

**Florel** 6 rue de la Viotte ☎ 03 81 80 41 08, ⓦ hotel-florel.fr. Easily the most appealing of the three hotels opposite the *gare de Besançon-Viotte*, *Florel* offers bright, modern rooms, each fashioned in a different colour, while the more expensive deluxe rooms also have a private terrace. Breakfast €11. €89

**Du Nord** 8 rue Moncey ☎ 03 81 81 34 56, ⓦ hotel-du-nord-besancon.com. Central hotel with comfortable, high-ceilinged rooms painted in strong oranges and reds, and furnished to a decent standard, though the street-facing ones can be a little noisy. Breakfast €9. €75

**Les Oiseaux** 48 rue des Cras ☎ 03 81 40 32 00, ⓦ habitatjeuneslesoiseaux.fr. A 15min walk from the *gare de Besançon-Viotte* along rue de Belfort, but difficult to find; head for the tourist office, where you can catch the #5 bus and get off at the "Les Oiseaux" stop, which is next to the hostel. Singles and doubles only, and although there's no communal kitchen, there is a restaurant and breakfast is included in the price. Singles €35; doubles €50

**De Paris** 33 rue des Granges ☎ 03 81 81 36 56, ⓦ besanconhoteldeparis.com. The high, brown plastic chairs lining the reception corridor are a bit weird, but that aside, this former coaching inn has infinite class; tastefully decorated rooms with big plump beds, thick curtains and soft carpets, and super-shiny bathrooms. Breakfast €13. €92

★ **Le Sauvage** 6 rue du Chapitre ☎ 03 81 82 00 21, ⓦ hotel-lesauvage.com. Set amid a pretty, deliciously fragrant garden, *Le Sauvage* is the most restful spot in town; gorgeous, parquet-floored rooms decorated in muted browns are the order of the day. Breakfast, meanwhile, can be taken outside on the raised terrace, with fabulous views of the town and surrounding woods; there's a fabulously cosy bar too. Breakfast €15. €98

★ **Vauban** Quai Vauban ☎ 03 81 82 02 08, ⓦ hotel-vauban. fr. A fantastic riverside setting marks this discreet little hotel out as one of the city's most enticing possibilities. Occupying one of the narrow arcaded houses along this strip, the rooms are necessarily modest in size, but they are smartly fashioned and possess all the necessary mod cons. Breakfast €11. €84

## EATING AND DRINKING

### CAFÉS AND RESTAURANTS

**Al Sirocco** 1 rue Chifflet ☎ 03 81 82 24 05. This always-buzzing pizzeria looks great with its glazed, wood-framed windows that open up onto the street, and its earthy wooden furniture. Pizzas are prepared in a large brick-fired oven before being delivered steaming hot to your table; deliciously fresh pasta dishes, ice creams and sorbets too. Pizza and pasta €12. Tues–Sat noon–2pm & 7–10pm.

**Au Petit Polonais** 81 rue des Granges ☎ 03 81 81 23 67. Founded in 1870, this veteran of the Besançon restaurant scene provides a small but tasty range of standard brasserie-type fare, such as hamburger and fries, and quiche and salad. Starters €9. mains €14. Tues–Sun noon–2pm & 7–10pm.

**Baud** 4 Grande Rue ☎ 03 81 81 20 12, ⓦ baudbesancon. com. Nearly a century old, this glittering chocolatier-cum-café provides an irresistible array of cakes, pastries and chocolates to nibble on, as well as *plats chauds* (€13.50) and salads (€8.50), plus lots of teas and coffees. Tues–Sat 8am–7.30pm, Sun 8am–1pm.

**Crêperie Luc Breton** 7 rue Luc-Breton ☎ 03 81 81 13 45. This stylish central crêperie provides *galettes* galore, such as chopped steak with mushrooms and crème fraîche, as well as a stack of sweet and savoury crêpes, some of quite mouth-watering proportions, like caramelized apples, raisins and cinnamon with calvados (€5–10). Mon–Sat noon–2pm & 7–11pm.

**Da Gianni** 9 rue Richebourg ☎ 03 81 81 42 96. There are some superb Italian restaurants in town, but this place really takes some beating. Sparky, enthusiastically staffed place serving scrummy antipasti, like calamari carpaccio, steaming bowls of pasta (€12), thin crust pizzas (€11), and genuinely excellent Italian ice cream. Reservations advised. Mon–Sat noon–2pm & 7–10pm.

**La Grange** 17 av Cusenier ☎ 03 81 50 82 97, ⓦ lagrange-restaurant.fr. Welcoming Alpine-styled restaurant where mountain food is very much the order of the day. The menu, in the form of a newspaper, features lots of fondue dishes, the most appealing of which is the fondue *bourguignonne*, whereby delicious hunks of beef are dipped into sizzling oil – follow that, perhaps, with a fondue *au toblerone* – it's all great fun. Daily 8am–10.30pm, Fri & Sat till 11.30pm.

★ **Poker d'As** 14 square Saint-Amour ☎ 03 81 81 42 49. Don't be deceived by the austere, wood-clad frontage, this wonderfully old-fashioned establishment is a delight. Sit down at chunky, beautifully engraved wooden tables, admire the copper pots and bells strung along the walls, and tuck into the likes of loin of rabbit with zucchini and roasted tomato coulis. Starters €12, mains €18. Tues–Sat noon–1.30pm & 7.30–9.30pm.

**Rôtisserie Vauban** 30B rue Rivotte ☎ 03 81 50 88 88, ⓦ rotisserie-vauban.fr. Secreted away down a small side street just below the citadelle, this buzzy little restaurant is a cracking find. The menu comprises some half a dozen roasted/grilled meat dishes – for example a quarter or half chicken, caramelized pork ribs, and suckling pig – all as tasty as they are filling. €13–17. Takeaway too. Tues–Sat noon–2pm & 7–9.30pm, Sun noon–2pm.

**Les Tables d'Antan** 18 rue Bersot ☎03 81 83 04 42, ⓌIestablesdantan.fr. Manifesting exposed brick and timber bound walls and flagstone flooring, this diminutive establishment is known for its *gratin* and salted crumble dishes, for example *gratin au mont d'or* (zucchini with salted beef and white wine) or crumble *sarladais* (*sarladaises* potatoes and duck confit with *griottines* and thyme) washed down with one of the local beers. Scrummy. Mains €17.

Wed–Sat noon–2pm & 7–10pm, Mon & Tues 7–10pm.

**BARS**

**Madigan's Irish Pub** 17 place du 8-septembre ☎03 81 81 17 44, Ⓦmadigans-irishpub.com. Lively, good-time party place where you can sup on a range of French and international beers (€5 for 50cl) – including an impressive selection of American craft beers – or choose from one of the brews of the moment. Mon–Wed 10am–1am, Thurs–Sat 10am–2am, Sun 2pm–2am.

**14**

# Lons-le-Saunier and around

The origins of the sleepy little spa town of **LONS-LE-SAUNIER** date back to Roman times, although most of the town was destroyed by a fire in the early seventeenth century, and much of the old town you see today dates mainly from the 1700s. Lons was once a major, and very prosperous, centre for winemaking and salt production, and the legacy of this era can still be seen in the grand townhouses and public buildings. These days it's a rather quiet place, but there's a handful of sights worth spending a lazy afternoon looking over. A good day to visit is Thursday, as that's when people from all over roll into town for the enormous **market**.

## Place de la Liberté and Musée Rouget de Lisle

24 rue du Commerce • July & Aug: Mon–Fri 10am–noon & 2–6pm, Sat & Sun 2–5pm • €1 • ☎03 84 47 29 16

The ideal place to start your tour of the town is the sunny **place de la Liberté**, where the theatre clock at the eastern end chimes a familiar half-dozen notes from *La Marseillaise* to honour Lons' most famous citizen, Rouget de Lisle; he composed the anthem during his time as a campaigner in the French revolutionary army during the early 1790s.

Running north from place de la Liberté is the attractive colonnaded thoroughfare of **rue du Commerce**, where you'll find some of Lons' oldest buildings. No. 24 is the house where de Lisle was born, in 1760, and now accommodates the **Musée Rouget de Lisle**; as well as lots of personal effects, it's also of interest for its fine eighteenth-century interior and furnishings.

## Musée des Beaux-Arts and La Maison de la Vache qui Rit

**Musée des Beaux-Arts** Place Philibert-de-Chalon • Tues–Fri 2–5pm, Sat & Sun 2–6pm • €2 • ☎03 84 47 64 30 **La Maison de la Vache qui Rit** 25 rue Richebourg • May–June & Sept–Oct daily except Mon 10am–1pm & 2–6pm; July & Aug daily 10am–7pm; Nov–April daily except Mon 2–6pm • €7.50 • ☎03 84 47 54 10, Ⓦlamaisondelavachequirit.com

At the northern end of rue du Commerce at place Philibert-de-Chalon stands the **Musée des Beaux-Arts**, which houses an intermittently interesting collection of nineteenth-century sculptures, including those of the local artist Jean-Joseph Perraud. Eminently more exciting, and something that'll be of great interest to spreadable cheese enthusiasts, is the **La Maison de la Vache qui Rit**, a multimedia museum dedicated to the locally produced Laughing Cow cheese. Returning south along rue Richebourg to avenue Jean-Moulin, you'll come to a statue of de Lisle himself. It was created by Frédéric Bartholdi, the man who designed New York's Statue of Liberty.

## Spa Lédonia

4 rue de Pavigny • Mon–Fri 10am–7pm, Sat 9am–7pm, Sun 9am–1pm • Spa treatments from €20 • ☎03 84 24 38 18, Ⓦvalvital.fr

**14**

A left turn at the Lisle statue leads to the peaceful, tree-lined **Parc Édouard-Guenon**, where you'll find the delightfully ornate *fin-de-siècle* **Spa Lédonia**, or mineral baths. The baths are now run by **Thermes Valvital**, and have a sauna, Turkish bath and jacuzzi.

## ARRIVAL AND INFORMATION                                       LONS-LE-SAUNIER

**By train** The *gare SNCF* is on bd Gambetta, a ten-minute walk south of place de la Liberté; head straight down av Aristide-Briand (opposite the station entrance) to reach the centre.
Destinations Belfort (7 daily; 2hr 40min); Besançon (hourly; 1hr 10min); Lyon Part Dieu (6 daily; 1hr 25min);

Paris-Lyon via Bourg-en-Bresse (6 daily; 3hr).
**Tourist office** In the theatre building on place du 11-novembre (July & Aug Mon–Sat 10am–6pm, Sun 9am–1pm; Sept–June Mon–Fri 9am–12.30pm & 2–5.30pm, Sat 10am–noon & 2–4pm; ☎03 84 24 65 01, ⓦlonslesaunier.fr).

## ACCOMMODATION

**Gambetta** 4 bd Gambetta ☎03 84 24 41 18, ⓦhotel-gambetta-lons.com. A friendly, family-run place opposite the *gare SNCF*, whose rooms are infinitely more appealing than the dull exterior would suggest; modern, colourful and with a/c, they're also well insulated from the passing traffic, of which there is quite a lot. Breakfast €8.50. **€58**
**Du Parc** 9 av Jean-Moulin ☎03 84 86 10 20, ⓦhotel-parc.fr. The most central option, overlooking the main square, and although what furnishings there are are a bit plastic, the rooms are well-kept. There's also a popular

restaurant downstairs, as well as parking for cars and bikes. Breakfast €8. **€74**
**Parenthèse** 186 chemin du Pin ☎03 47 55 44, ⓦhotel-jura.com. If you've got wheels, and a bit more cash to spare, then this lovely, isolated hotel, some 2km north of Lons in the pretty little village of Chille, is perfect. Super-smart rooms, each one named after, and displaying a piece of work by, a well-known artist. Excellent spa facility including a gorgeous pool. Breakfast €15. **€90**

## EATING AND DRINKING

★ **La Comédie** 65 place de la Comédie ☎03 84 24 20 66, ⓦrestaurant-la-comedie.fr. Understatedly smart-looking restaurant with Venetian-style ball masks adorning the burgundy/grey walls, nicely spaced out tables, and a delightful wood-decked terrace out the back. The menu is far from exhaustive, and it is on the expensive side, but dishes like bresse chicken with comté polenta and *griottines* (morello cherries), and veal tenderloin tartar with seaweed butter will more than satisfy. Starters €18, mains €22. Tues–Sat noon–2pm & 7.30–9.30pm.
**Pelen** 1 rue Saint-Désiré ☎03 84 24 31 39, ⓦpelen.fr. For truly indulgent pastries and chocolates, don't miss this place just off place de la Liberté, which has been doling out

delicious cakes, crêpes and bowls of ice cream since 1899. The ground-floor chocolate shop, meanwhile, is sure to fulfil all your sweet-toothed fantasies. Mon–Fri 9am–12.15pm & 2.30–7pm, Sat till 7.15pm, Sun till 12.30pm.
**La Table de Perraud** 11 place Perraud ☎03 84 86 49 68, ⓦrestaurant-latabledeperraud.com. Bare brick walls, a fine timber ceiling and beautifully laid tables make for a warm and welcoming setting at this upscale restaurant that's not dissimilar to (though a little cheaper than) *La Comédie*; a refreshingly unfussy *menu* featuring the likes of charolais beef tartar with fries, and profiteroles with hot chocolate. Starters €10, mains €18. Tues–Sat 11.45am–1.30pm & 7.30–9.30pm.

# The Région des Lacs

If you drive east for 20km along the N78 road from Lons, you'll enter the **Région des Lacs**, an area of woods, pastures and lakes strung out along the valley of the River Ain. During the journey, the road begins its ascent to the peaks and gorges that define the border with Switzerland. With each bend in the climbing road, the views down to the tiny villages become all the more impressive. Some of the lakes charge parking fees during the day, but after 6pm, when the crowds and swimming supervisors have gone home, they are deserted and serenely peaceful – the perfect place for an evening picnic at sunset.

## Clairvaux-les-Lacs

The Région des Lacs' main town is **CLAIRVAUX-LES-LACS**. It's here that the River Ain flows into the northern tip of the serpentine **Lac de Vouglans**, which is dammed 25km downstream. The **Grand Lac**, just south of town, is the focus of summer resort activity, with a beach area and watersports facilities. It's calm and scenic, in spite of all the camping activity going on around it.

## INFORMATION AND ACCOMMODATION                                           CLAIRVAUX-LES-LACS

**Office du Tourisme du Pays des Lacs** 36 Grande-Rue (April–June & Sept Mon–Sat 9am–noon & 2–6pm; July & Aug Mon–Sat 9.30am–6.30pm, Sun 9am–1pm; Oct–March Mon–Wed & Fri 10am–noon & 4–6pm; ☎ 03 84 25 27 47, ⓦ juralacs.com), is the place to find information about the region and outdoor activities such as boat and bike rental and the 46 hiking routes in the area.

**La Chaumière du Lac** 21 rue du Savior, Grand Lac ☎ 03 84 25 81 52, ⓦ la-chaumiere-du-lac.fr. Good-value lakeside hotel with ten comfortable rooms (including two family rooms), some with a balcony offering lake views. The hotel also has a restaurant serving local fish and cheese (*menus* €19–32). **€60**

## Lac de Chalain and around

Some 16km north of Clairvaux, near the village of **DOUCIER** and surrounded by hills, **Lac de Chalain** is a much more impressive setting. It's also a very popular spot for **camping**, hence the prices can be high.

One reason this area is so popular with campers is its proximity to the **Cascades du Hérisson** (ⓦ cascades-du-herisson.fr), the septet of waterfalls that has become one of the Jura's best-known natural spectacles. If you are **driving**, you can reach the main car park for the Cascades by passing through Val-Dessous, a village just to the southeast of Doucier, and then heading for the Parking de l'Éventail. A well-signposted path takes you from the car park to the highest of the falls, which descend a breathtaking 255m over just 7km. A gentle walk of around ten minutes from the car park leads to the prettiest of the falls, the **Éventail**. If you continue upstream, you'll arrive at the **Grand Saut** fall, where the water plummets down a sheer drop of some sixty metres. If you follow the pathway behind the waterfall, you can ascend a steep trail as it leads past several smaller springs as well as a drinks kiosk; from here another path leads south to the village of Bonlieu. Finally, the path ends at the uppermost fall, which is known as **Saut Girard**, close to the village of **ILAY**. In all, the walk should take around three hours for reasonably fit walkers.

## Les Rousses

A couple of kilometres before the frontier with Switzerland is the ski resort of **LES ROUSSES**, an outstanding area for cross-country skiing. Les Rousses is also very handy for hikers looking to explore the **Parc Naturel Régional du Haut-Jura** (ⓦ parc-haut-jura. fr), the regional park which runs south from Champagnole across the southern Jura Mountains. There are several **GR** footpaths which can be accessed from Les Rousses. **GR9** passes through here as it moves along the crest of the ridge towards the Col de la Faucille; the **GR559**, a 95-km long route which takes you on a tour of the lakes of

---

### SKIING AND BIKING IN THE JURA

The high plateaux of the Jura Mountains (ⓦ jura-tourism.com) guarantee good snow cover in winter, but they also lack the steep gradients of the Alpine peaks further to the south; it is this high but level terrain which has made the Jura into France's most popular destination for **cross-country skiing**, or *ski de fond*. The goal of any superfit *fondeur* is the 175km **Grande Traversée du Jura** (GTJ), which crosses the high plateau from Villers-le-Lac to Giron, a town in the south of the Parc Naturel Régional du Haut-Jura.

The same gentle topography and established infrastructure that enable cross-country skiing have made this region an ideal high-summer venue for **mountain biking**, with hundreds of waymarked cross-country skiing pistes used out of season as trails for adventurous mountain bikers. The 360km **GTJ–VTT**, which starts near Montbéliard (just to the south of Belfort), has become the greatest long-distance biking challenge in the area. Many people cycle on the road; there aren't many cars, so if you can handle the hills, then go for it.

Franche-Comté, begins here and ends in Lons-le-Saunier; even the much longer **GR5** passes within a few kilometres of the resort.

## INFORMATION

**Tourist office** 495 rue Pasteur (July & Aug, plus mid-Dec to mid-March daily 9am–noon & 2–6pm; mid-March to June, plus Sept to mid-Dec Mon–Sat 9am–noon & 2–6pm; ☎03 84 60 04 31, ⓦlesrousses.com) can provide information on the local skiing conditions. The ESF is also based in the tourist office (☎03 84 60 01 61, ⓦedf-lesrousses.com); their ski instructors organize lessons focusing specifically on cross-country skiing techniques.

## ACCOMMODATION

**Auberge de Jeunesse** 3.5km outside Les Rousses in Le Bief-de-la-Chaille ☎03 84 60 02 80, ⓦfuaj.org. Decent hostel located in an old farmhouse by a stream. Late Dec to March & mid-May to mid-Sept. Breakfast included. **€18.50**
**La Ferme du Père François** 214 rue Pasteur ☎03 84 60 34 62, ⓦperefrancois.fr. The warm, family-run *"Farm of Father François"* hotel offers smart, beautifully lit rooms featuring lots of solid pine furnishings and inviting red-and-white checked bedspreads and curtains. There's a very good restaurant here too. Breakfast €12. **€115**
**La Redoute** 357 route Blanche ☎03 84 60 00 40, ⓦhotel-des-rousses.com. Accomplished *Logis* hotel just around the corner from *La Ferme* in the centre of the village with 25 unspectacular but comfortable rooms, including triples and quads, plus a commendable restaurant. Breakfast €10. **€72**

# Château-Chalon

Some 10km to the north of Lons on the N83 road towards Besançon, the route known locally as the **Route des Vins du Jura**, you come to a turn-off on the D120 for **Voiteur**. This is an unremarkable provincial town, but just beyond it is one of the prettiest villages in Franche-Comté. **CHÂTEAU-CHALON** is a delight to wander around, with a beautiful church, the twelfth-century **Église Saint-Pierre**, and a medieval keep, which is all that remains of the grand Benedictine Abbey which once stood here. As well as having a stunning position on top of a high rocky outcrop, the village is also noted for the unique variety of *vin jaune*, and there are several vineyards operating around the town. A good choice if you want to sample a range of local and regional wines is the vineyard of Jean Berthet-Bondet on the rue de la Tour (contact the vineyard to organize a tour; Mon–Sat 10am–noon & 2–6.30pm; ☎03 84 44 60 48, ⓦberthet-bondet.net), which offers tasting sessions, though do call in advance.

# Poligny

Lying at the southern end of the Culée de Vaux valley, the attractive little town of **POLIGNY** is the cheese capital of Franche-Comté, and you'll find several superb *fromageries* on place des Déportés, the lovely, café-fringed main square. There's another cheese shop on rue Notre-Dame, opposite the **Église Notre-Dame**, which is just one example of several fine medieval churches scattered along the valley. Standing in an overgrown grass square, and featuring a marvellous steeple, this one dates from the eleventh century.

## Maison du Comté

Av de la Résistance • Guided tours April–June & Sept–Oct Tues–Sun 2pm, 3.15pm & 4.30pm; July & Aug daily 10am, 11.30am & hourly 2.15–5.15pm • €5 • ☎03 84 87 78 40, ⓦmaison-du-comte.com

Cheese aficionados won't want to miss the **Maison du Comté**, an old *fromagerie* that's now the headquarters of the Comité Interprofessionel du Gruyère du Comté, France's favourite cheese. The guided tour begins with a twenty-minute film (with English subtitles), followed by various displays, animated models and, best of all, a tasting session.

## INFORMATION AND ACCOMMODATION

**Tourist office** 20 place des Déportés (Mon–Sat 10am–12.30pm & 1.30–6pm; July & Aug also Sun 9.30am–12.30pm; ☎03 84 37 24 21, ⓦpoligny-tourisme.com); pick up one of their handy little self-guided leaflets outlining the town's surprisingly numerous historical sites.

**De la Vallée Heureuse** Rte de Genève ☎ 03 84 37 12 13, ⓦ hotelvalleeheureuse.com. Located around 800m east of town in a lovely old converted mill, and while it's not cheap, the eleven rooms are beautifully designed (some with balcony), and the hotel possesses excellent facilities, namely indoor and outdoor pools, sauna, jacuzzi and restaurant. Breakfast €14. **€110**

## Arbois

Serious wine-lovers should head for **ARBOIS**, 10km to the north of Poligny. Wine emporia line the central place de la Liberté, all of which entreat you to sample the unusual local reds, whites and rosés in the shop windows. Of these local wines, the sweet *vin de paille* is the rarest; the name derives from its grapes, which are dried on beds of straw during the production process, thus giving the wine a strong aftertaste.

### Musée de la Vigne et du Vin

March–June, Sept & Oct daily except Tues 10am–noon & 2–6pm; July & Aug daily 10am–noon & 2–6pm; Nov–Feb daily except Tues 2–6pm • €3.50 • ☎ 03 84 66 40 45, ⓦ arbois.fr

A few kilometres south of town on the D469 is the Château Pécauld, where you'll find the **Musée de la Vigne et du Vin**, which details the development and production of wine in the Jura. The surrounding vineyards illustrate the work of the local wine growers, while the cellars and galleries trace the changing methods of wine production over the years. The château also has wine-tasting sessions, which must be booked in advance (☎ 03 84 66 40 53).

### Maison de Louis Pasteur

83 rue de Courcelles • daily: Feb–April & Oct 2–6pm; May–Sept 9.30am–12.30pm & 2–6pm; guided tours hourly (May–Sept only) • €6.80 • ☎ 03 84 66 11 72, ⓦ terredelouispasteur.fr

At the far end of rue de Courcelles, just by the bridge, stands the **Maison de Louis Pasteur**, a former tannery and childhood home of the eponymous scientist, who, in 1885, discovered the rabies vaccine – indeed, a local nine-year-old boy by the name of Joseph Meister became the first, fortunate, recipient of the vaccine that same year. Born in nearby Dole, but schooled in Arbois, Pasteur regularly returned to the house in adulthood, eventually re-settling here following the death of his father in 1865. On view are many of his personal effects, as well as his laboratory, bedroom and lounge, complete with billiard table.

---

**ARRIVAL AND INFORMATION**                **ARBOIS**

**By train** The *gare SNCF* is a 20min walk northwest of town on av de la Gare; head straight down av Pasteur, then rue de Courcelles to reach the centre.

**Tourist office** 17 rue de l'Hôtel-de-Ville (mid-June to mid-Sept Mon–Sat 9am–12.30pm & 1.30–6.30pm, Sun 10am– 12.30pm & 3–5.30pm; mid-Sept to mid-June Mon–Sat 10am–12.30pm & 2–5.30pm; ☎ 03 84 66 55 50, ⓦ arbois. com); staff can provide details of vineyards in the area that offer tasting sessions of local wine.

---

**ACCOMMODATION AND EATING**

**La Balance Mets et Vins** 47 rue de Courcelles ☎ 03 84 37 45 00, ⓦ labalance.fr. Great-looking restaurant located on the main road close to Maison de Louis Pasteur, with copper-tinted walls and brick pillars running its length. The food, such as *savagnin* risotto with scallops and crispy asparagus, is terrific, while the chef here prepares many of his dishes with the local drink, for example, rooster with morels and *vin de paille*. Menus €20–65. Starters €16, mains €21. Tues–Sat noon–2pm & 7–9pm.

**Camping Les Vignes** 5 rue de la Piscine ☎ 06 14 26 09 85. Large, well-maintained municipal site 1km east of the centre, with grocery store, snack bar, swimming pool and play areas. Mid-March to Oct. **€20.50**

**Maison Jeunet** 9 rue de l'Hôtel-de-Ville ☎ 03 84 66 05 67, ⓦ maison-jeunet.com. Fantastically classy – but very expensive – boutique hotel offering twelve rooms of unbridled luxury; lush green carpets, beautifully patterned armchairs and fancy artwork inform the bedrooms, while bright white designer basins and walk-in showers are the most striking aspects of the gloriously shiny bathrooms. Breakfast €23. **€142**

**Les Messageries** 2 rue de Courcelles ☎ 03 84 66 15 45, ⓦ hotel-arbois.com. Located in an old stone townhouse full of character, the thoroughly modern rooms are spartanly furnished but clean and bright, with large flatscreen TVs and bedside reading lamps. There are also four "economy" rooms without shower (€47). Breakfast €12. **€79**

14

# Belfort

Nestled in the gap between two mountain ranges – the Vosges to the north and the Jura to the south – lies **BELFORT**, a town assured of a place in French hearts for its history as an insurmountable stronghold on this obvious route for invaders. The town is remembered particularly for its long resistance to a siege during the 1870 Franco–Prussian War; it was this resistance that spared it the humiliating fate of being annexed into the German empire, a fate suffered by much of neighbouring Alsace-Lorraine. The commanding officer at the time was one Colonel Denfert-Rochereau (known popularly as the "Lion of Belfort"), who earned himself the honour of numerous street names throughout the country, as well as that of a Parisian square and métro station.

Finding your way around Belfort is easy enough. The town is sliced in two by the River Savoureuse: the **new town** to the west is the commercial hub, while the quieter, and far prettier, **old town** lies across to the east, beneath the impressive edifice of the red **citadelle**.

## Citadelle

**Musée d'Histoire** April–June & Sept daily except Tues 10am–12.30pm & 2–6pm; July & Aug daily 10am–12.30pm & 2–6pm; Oct–March daily except Tues 2–6pm • €7 • ☏ 03 84 90 40 70

The **citadelle** was built by Vauban on the site of a medieval keep, of which only a single tower to the north of the castle remains. It's a stiff climb to the top, but there are excellent views of Belfort's old town and of the surrounding countryside once you do make it. Vauban was also responsible for a new set of fortifications surrounding Belfort, and from the castle you can see how these moulded the old town into a pentagonal shape. The street plan is still largely unchanged. The citadelle now houses the **Musée d'Histoire**, which displays exhibits on the town's military history, as well as many Bronze and Iron Age artefacts.

On your way up to the castle, look out for an 11m-high red sandstone **lion** carved out of the rock face. It was designed by Frédéric Bartholdi, of Statue of Liberty fame, as a monument to commemorate the 1870 siege, and was completed in 1880.

## Musée des Beaux-Arts and Donation Maurice Jardot

**Musée des Beaux-Arts** Daily except Tues: April–May 10am–noon & 2–6pm; June–Sept 10am–6pm; Oct–March 10am–noon & 2–5pm • €2 • ☏ 03 84 22 16 73 **Donation Maurice Jardot** 8 rue de Mulhouse Same times as Musée d'Histoire • €2 • ☏ 03 84 54 25 51

Art-lovers should head to the **Musée des Beaux-Arts**, located in Tour 41 in the lower part of the fortifications, where paintings by the likes of Dürer and Doré and sculptures by Rodin and Carrière are on display; it was, though, closed at the time of writing and slated to reopen in 2020.

Also worth a visit is the **Donation Maurice Jardot** (also known as the Musée d'Art Moderne) on the northern edge of the new town. It was founded at the behest of Maurice Jardot, an associate of Daniel-Henry Kahnweiler, one of the most noted art dealers of the twentieth century; when Jardot died in 1997, he left 150 works of art to the town, including some by Chagall, Braque and Picasso.

---

### ARRIVAL AND INFORMATION
BELFORT

**By train** The *gare SNCF* and departure point for local buses is at the end of Faubourg-de-France, the main shopping street in the new town.

Destinations Besançon (frequent; 1hr 15min); Montbéliard (frequent; 15min); Mulhouse (hourly; 35min); Paris-Est (4 daily; 4hr).

**Tourist office** 2 rue Clemenceau (Mon–Fri 9am–12.30pm & 2–6pm, Sat till 5pm; ☏ 03 84 55 90 90, ⊕ belfort-tourisme.com). To reach the tourist office from the *gare SNCF*, walk for ten minutes down Faubourg-de-France as far as the river, then turn left and walk along quai Charles-Vallet until you reach rue Clemenceau. They've got free internet access, and, usefully, toilets too.

## EUROCKÉENNES

First staged in 1989, today **Eurockéennes** (ⓦeurockeennes.fr) is one of France's biggest and most diverse annual rock festivals, attracting top international artists (Queens of the Stone Age, Nine Inch Nails) as well as plenty of up-and-coming French acts. The four-day festival takes place over the first weekend in July in a lovely setting on the shores of the Lac du Malsaucy, 6km northeast of Belfort, and the vibe is suitably relaxed and friendly, despite crowds in excess of 100,000. Tickets are reasonably priced (day passes €49, three-day pass €122, four-day pass €154), and there's a free campsite nearby with 12,000 spaces for those who want the full rock festival experience.

**14**

### ACCOMMODATION

**Camping L'Étang des Forges** Rue du Général-Béthouart ☎03 84 22 54 92, ⓦcamping-belfort.com. The best local campsite, a few kilometres north of the old town next to Lake Forges; here you'll find decent amenities, including a grocery store, swimming pool, volleyball court, snack bar and restaurant; they've also got bikes for hire. April–Oct. **€18**

**Grand Hôtel du Tonneau d'Or** 1 rue du Général-Reiset ☎03 84 58 57 56, ⓦtonneaudor.fr. The lobby of this hotel, housed in an impressive building dating from 1902, is quite something; a monumental Neoclassical staircase with stained-glass windows either side. The rooms, meanwhile, are spacious and modern, with mostly grey tones. Breakfast €13. **€97**

**Habitat Jeunes Belfort** 6 rue de Madrid ☎03 84 21 39 16, ⓦhabitatjeunes90.org. Located 1km west of the railway line, this housing association also offers a small number of hostel rooms plus a communal kitchen and restaurant. Open year-round. Breakfast €2.20. Dorms **€20**

**Saint-Christophe** Place d'Armes ☎03 84 55 88 88, ⓦhotelsaintchristophe.com. In an historic building at the heart of the old town, the *Saint-Christophe* has neat, colourfully painted rooms, sleeping one- to four-, though some are a little on the boxy side. Ask for a room with a view over the square. Breakfast €9. **€74**

### EATING AND DRINKING

**Aux 2 Coqs** 6 place de l'Étuve ☎03 84 22 33 05. Secreted away in a narrow back alley, next to a soothing fountain, the "Two Roosters" is by far the most sophisticated outfit in town; here you can sample some fabulously creative dishes like monkfish and pike mousse, and fried escalope of foie gras with spice mango compote. Starters €12, mains €19.

Mon & Wed–Sun 11.45am–2.30pm & 6.45–10pm; Tues 6.45–10pm.

**Bar Le Central** 2 place Corbis ☎03 84 21 28 56. The most enjoyable place in town to sit down with a coffee or linger with a beer and watch the world go by on this busy, new town main square. Mon–Sat 7am–1am.

# The Rhône valley

**778** Lyon

**797** Beaujolais

**798** Vienne

**801** St-Étienne

**802** South to Valence

**804** Valence

**806** Montélimar

BEAUJOLAIS VINEYARD

# The Rhône valley

The Rhône valley stretches down from the compelling city of Lyon, the second-biggest city in France, to just north of Orange, in Provence. The north–south route of ancient armies, medieval traders and modern rail and road, the valley has experienced some industrialization, but this has done little to affect the verdant, vine-dotted beauty of the countryside. Following the River Rhône is of limited appeal, with the exception of the scenic stretch of vineyards and fruit orchards between the Roman city of Vienne and the distinctly southern city of Valence. The nougat capital of Montélimar, further south still, also wears its charms well. But the big magnet is, of course, the gastronomic paradise of Lyon, with its unrivalled concentration of world-class restaurants.

**15**

## GETTING AROUND

Getting up and down the Rhône Valley couldn't be simpler, with plentiful trains – both regional and TGV – plying the route between Lyon and Montélimar. Travelling by car will, inevitably, allow you to dictate things at your own pace, though having your own wheels is pretty much imperative if you wish to explore the Beaujolais region, as bus services here are virtually non-existent.

# Lyon

Viewed from the Autoroute du Soleil, the first impression of **LYON** is of a major confluence of rivers and roads, around which only petrochemical industries thrive. In fact, from the sixteenth century right up until the postwar dominance of metalworks and chemicals, silk was the city's main industry, generating the wealth that left behind a multitude of Renaissance buildings. But what has stamped its character most on Lyon is the commerce and banking that grew up with its industrial expansion. Today, with its eco-friendly tram system, high-tech industrial parks home to international companies, Lyon is a modern city *par excellence*; moreover, with a Eurostar link to London, Lyon is more accessible than ever.

Most French people find themselves here for business rather than for recreation: it's a get-up-and-go place, with an almost Swiss sense of cleanliness, order and efficiency. But as a manageable slice of urban France, Lyon certainly has its charms. Foremost among these is **gastronomy**; there are more restaurants per Gothic and Renaissance square metre of the old town than anywhere else on earth, and the city could form a football team with its superstars of the international chef circuit.

Lyon offers superb cultural attractions, too, from a raft of fine churches, notably the mighty Basilica Notre-Dame up on Fourvière, to half a dozen exceptional museums, chief among them the stunning new **Musée des Confluences**, the constantly absorbing **Gallo-Roman museum**, and the wonderful **Gadagne museum**, with its marvellous puppetry displays. Urban explorers, meanwhile, will enjoy staking out Lyon's distinctive older quarters and its winding, secret *traboules*. As if that weren't enough, Lyon's nightlife, cinema and theatre, its antique markets, music and other cultural festivities might tempt you to stay just that little bit longer.

Lyon is organized into nine arrondissements. Of most interest to visitors is the **Presqu'île** (1$^{er}$ and 2$^e$ arrondissements), the tongue of land between the rivers Saône and Rhône, and **Vieux Lyon** (5$^e$) on the west bank of the Saône, where the Romans built

# Highlights

**❶ Musée des Confluences** The gleaming centrepiece of the revamped Confluence district, Lyon's architectural marvel houses a remarkable collection of natural, historical and scientific artefacts. See page 781

**❷ Lyon's restaurants** Food is king here, with award-winning chefs and Michelin stars galore, though for an alternative take on Lyonnais cuisine, make a beeline for one of the city's famous bouchons. See page 792

**❸ Beaujolais** Take a trip around this verdant countryside dotted with pretty hilltop villages and lush vineyards yielding some of the country's most distinctive wines, such as Cru Beaujolais. See page 797

**❹ Musée Gallo-Romain** Vienne is run through with Roman remains, though this vast plot, across the river in St-Romain-en-Gal, offers the most intriguing insight into the daily life and domestic architecture of Roman France. See page 800

**❺ Montélimar nougat** Without doubt, the best place to gorge on the moreish bonbon made of sweet honey and crunchy nuts. See page 806

HIGHLIGHTS ARE MARKED ON THE MAP ON PAGE 780

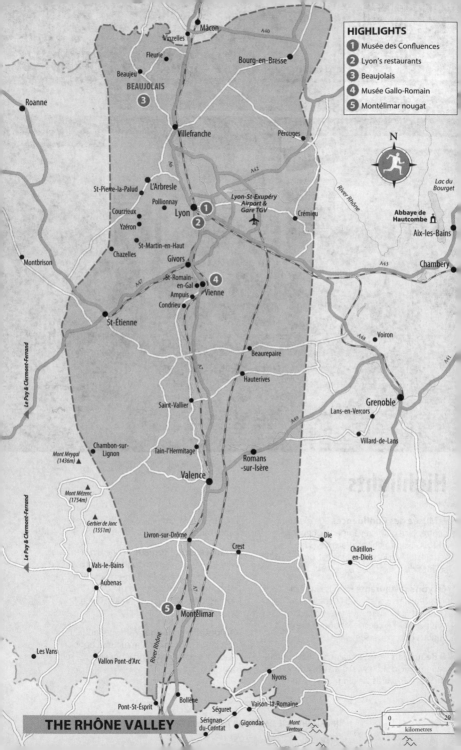

## HIGHLIGHTS

1. Musée des Confluences
2. Lyon's restaurants
3. Beaujolais
4. Musée Gallo-Romain
5. Montélimar nougat

N

THE RHÔNE VALLEY

Mâcon
Vinzelles
Fleurie
Beaujeu
**BEAUJOLAIS**
3
Bourg-en-Bresse
Roanne
Villefranche
Pérouges
St-Pierre-la-Palud
L'Arbresle
Pollionnay
Lyon-St-Exupéry
Airport &
Gare TGV
Courzieux
Lyon
1
2
Crémieu
Yzéron
Chazelles
St-Martin-en-Haut
Givors
Montbrison
St-Romain-en-Gal
4
Vienne
Ampuis
Condrieu
St-Étienne
Voiron
Beaurepaire
Hauterives
Saint-Vallier
Grenoble
Lans-en-Vercors
Chambon-sur-Lignon
Villard-de-Lans
Mont Meygal (1436m)
Tain-l'Hermitage
Romans-sur-Isère
Mont Mézenc (1754m)
Valence
Gerbier de Jonc (1551m)
Livron-sur-Drôme
Crest
Die
Châtillon-en-Diois
Vals-le-Bains
Aubenas
5
Montélimar
Les Vans
Vallon Pont-d'Arc
River Rhône
Nyons
Pont-St-Ésprit
Bollène
Séguret
Vaison-la-Romaine
Sérignan-du-Comtat
Gigondas
Mont Ventoux

Lac du Bourget
Abbaye de Hautcombe
Aix-les-Bains
Chambery

Le Puy & Clermont-Ferrand

kilometres
0          20

their capital of Gaul, Lugdunum. To the north of the Presqu'île is the old silk-weavers' district of **La Croix-Rousse** (4$^e$). Other well-touristed areas include modern Lyon on the east bank of the Rhône (3$^e$), at the heart of which is the bustling commercial area around Part-Dieu, and, north of here, **Parc de la Tête d'Or**, the city's main green space.

## The Presqu'île

The Presqu'île, or peninsula, is most visitors' first port of call. Its dominant feature is **place Bellecour**, whose pink gravelly acres were first laid out in 1617, and which offer fabulous views up to the looming bulk of Notre-Dame de Fourvière. The southern portion of the peninsula starts around Perrache station, beyond which lies the Confluence district, whose regeneration continues apace.

Running south from place Bellecour is **rue Auguste-Comte** which is full of antique shops selling heavily framed eighteenth-century art works; **rue Victor-Hugo**, a pedestrian precinct full of chic shops, continues north of place Bellecour on rue de la République, all the way up to the back of the *hôtel de ville*.

To the north of place Bellecour at the top of quai St-Antoine is the **quartier Mercière**, the old commercial centre of the town, with sixteenth- and seventeenth-century houses lining rue Mercière, and the **church of St-Nizier**, whose bells used to announce the nightly closing of the city's gates. In the silk-weavers' uprising of 1831, workers fleeing the soldiers took refuge in the church, only to be massacred. Today, traces of this working-class life are almost gone, edged out by bars, restaurants and designer shops, the latter along rue du Président Édouard-Herriot and the long pedestrian rue de la République in particular.

15

### Musée des Confluences

86 quai Perrache • Tues, Wed & Fri 11am–7pm, Thurs 11am –10pm, Sat & Sun 10am–7pm • €9 • ☎ 04 28 38 12 12, Ⓦ museedesconfluences.fr

Occupying the thinnest wedge of land at the confluence of the Saône and Rhône rivers, the sparkling new **Musée des Confluences** is an extraordinary glass-and-steel structure that could have been plucked from the set of a *Star Wars* film. Its permanent exhibition is arranged thematically into four sections, the first of which, "Eternity", gets to grips with life and death; the most notable, and spooky, exhibit is a Peruvian mummy, in the seated position with arms and legs clasped to its chest. In Egyptian society, animals were mummified too (being considered incarnations of gods), as evidenced by the crocodiles, rams, eagles and suchlike on display in the "Species" exhibition, which also contains a stunning collection of butterflies and bugs. "Societies", meanwhile, ponders upon man's ability to create – look out for the superb Berliet motor car from 1908 and Cockcroft and Walton's particle accelerator – while, finally, "Origins" traces the various theories of evolution; the (literally) unmissable highlight here is a skeleton of the Camarasaurus, which roamed North America in the late Jurassic period.

### Musée Historique des Tissus and Musée des Arts Décoratifs

34 rue de la Charité • Tues–Sun 10am–6pm • €10 • ☎ 04 78 38 42 00, Ⓦ mtmad.fr

The fine **Musée Historique des Tissus**, housed in the eighteenth-century former town palace of the Duke of Villeroy, doesn't quite live up to its claim to cover the history of decorative cloth through the ages, but it does have brilliant collections from certain periods. Particularly outstanding are the exhibits from Egypt and Persia, notably a remarkably well-preserved baby's bonnet, and a quite gorgeous Persian silk kaftan gilded with silver metal-wrapped threads. The main hall is given over to oversized carpets from Ottoman Turkey and the once all-powerful Iranian Safavid dynasty, while upstairs, Chinese tapestries and Japanese kimonos are the most prominent items on show.

15

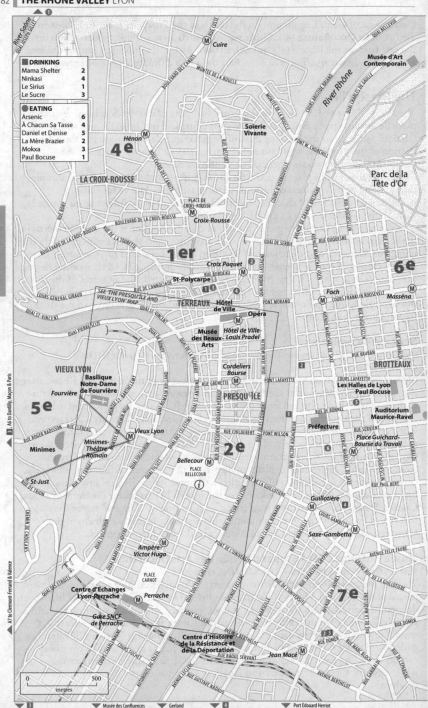

■ DRINKING
Mama Shelter 2
Ninkasi 4
Le Sirius 1
Le Sucre 3

● EATING
Arsenic 6
À Chacun Sa Tasse 4
Daniel et Denise 5
La Mère Brazier 2
Mokxa 3
Paul Bocuse 1

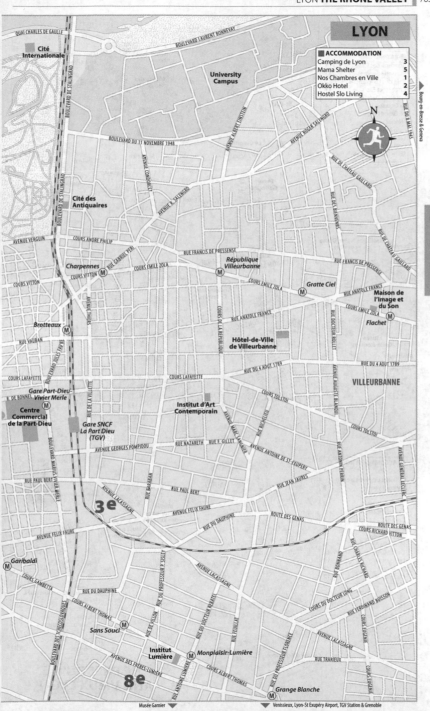

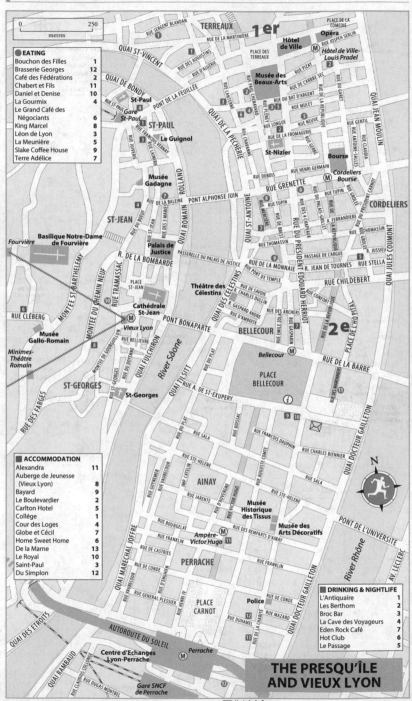

THE PRESQU'ÎLE
AND VIEUX LYON

**● EATING**

| | |
|---|---|
| Bouchon des Filles | 1 |
| Brasserie Georges | 12 |
| Café des Fédérations | 2 |
| Chabert et Fils | 11 |
| Daniel et Denise | 10 |
| La Gourmix | 4 |
| Le Grand Café des | |
| Négociants | 6 |
| King Marcel | 8 |
| Léon de Lyon | 3 |
| La Meunière | 5 |
| Slake Coffee House | 9 |
| Terre Adélice | 7 |

**■ ACCOMMODATION**

| | |
|---|---|
| Alexandra | 11 |
| Auberge de Jeunesse | |
| (Vieux Lyon) | 8 |
| Bayard | 9 |
| Le Boulevardier | 2 |
| Carlton Hotel | 5 |
| Collège | 1 |
| Cour des Loges | 4 |
| Globe et Cécil | 7 |
| Home Sweet Home | 6 |
| De la Marne | 13 |
| Le Royal | 10 |
| Saint-Paul | 3 |
| Du Simplon | 12 |

**■ DRINKING & NIGHTLIFE**

| | |
|---|---|
| L'Antiquaire | 1 |
| Les Berthom | 2 |
| Broc Bar | 3 |
| La Cave des Voyageurs | 4 |
| Eden Rock Café | 6 |
| Hot Club | 7 |
| Le Passage | 5 |

## LYON'S MURALS

Lyon's fascination with **mural art** can be traced back to the late 1970s, when a group of students thought it a good idea to introduce some colour to the city's grimescape, while simultaneously bringing art to the masses. The Musée Garnier murals aside, the easiest ones to track down are the Mur des Canuts in Croix-Rousse, a brilliant, illusory piece depicting everyday life of the district's inhabitants, including, of course, the old silk-weavers; La Fresque des Lyonnais on the corner of rue de la Martinière and Quai St-Vincent, which honours Lyon's most famous citizens, such as the Lumière brothers, Garnier and Bocuse; and La bibliothèque (The City Library), just down the road on the corner of rue de la Platière and Quai de la Pecherie. Check out Ⓦcite-creation.com for more information.

The stuff produced in Lyon itself reflects the luxurious nature of the silk trade: seventeenth- to nineteenth-century hangings and chair covers, including hangings from Marie-Antoinette's bedroom at Versailles, from Empress Josephine's room at Fontainebleau and from the palaces of Catherine the Great of Russia. There are also some lovely twentieth-century pieces – including Sonia Delaunay's *Tissus Simultanés* – and couture creations from Worth and Mariano Fortuny to Paco Rabanne and Christian Lacroix.

The adjoining **Musée des Arts Décoratifs** is something of an anti-climax after the textile museum, with its rather dour displays of faïence, porcelain, furniture and eighteenth-century rooms removed from old houses in the Presqu'île. There is, though, a collection of superb modern silverware by noted architects, including Richard Meier and Zaha Hadid.

### Place des Terreaux

Flanked by cafés and bars, elongated **place des Terreaux** has as its focal point a monumental nineteenth-century **fountain**. Originally intended for residence in Bordeaux, it was designed by Bartholdi, of Statue of Liberty fame, although the rows of watery jets that sprout up unexpectedly across the rest of the square are a modern addition. The square's eastern end is dominated by the even more monumental *hôtel de ville*, its facade crawling with ostentatious statuary. Just off place des Terreaux, behind the *hôtel de ville* is Lyon's **opera house**, radically redesigned in 1993 by Jean Nouvel. Its original Neoclassical elevations are now topped by a huge glass Swiss roll of a roof, and the interior's now entirely black with silver stairways climbing into the darkness.

### Musée des Beaux-Arts

20 place des Terreaux • Mon, Wed, Thurs, Sat & Sun 10am–6pm, Fri 10.30am–6pm • €8; audioguide included • ☎ 04 72 10 17 40, Ⓦ mba-lyon.fr

Housed in a former Benedictine abbey, the collections of the **Musée des Beaux-Arts** are second in France only to those in the Louvre. The museum is organized roughly by genre, with nineteenth- and twentieth-century sculpture in the ex-chapel on the ground floor. The first floor houses a particularly interesting collection of Egyptian artefacts including coffins, amulets and stone tablets, in addition to a selection of medieval French, Dutch, German and Italian woodcarving and antiquities, coins and *objets d'art*. Upstairs, twentieth-century painting is represented by Picasso (*Woman Seated on the Beach*) and Matisse, and there are also works by Braque, a brace of Bonnards and a gory Francis Bacon. The nineteenth century is covered by the Impressionists and their forerunners, Corot and Courbet; there are works by the Lyonnais artists Antoine Berjon and Fleury Richard, and from there you can work your way back through Rubens, Zurbarán, El Greco, Tintoretto and more. Here too is Rembrandt's *The Stoning of St Steven*, his earliest known work completed in 1625 at the age of just nineteen. For some respite from traipsing the many halls, make for the lovely garden, where there are sculptures by the likes of Rodin and Bourdelle.

15

## La Croix-Rousse

**La Croix-Rousse** is the old silk-weavers' district and spreads up the steep slopes of the hill above the northern end of the Presqu'île. Although increasingly gentrified, it's still predominantly a working-class area, but barely a couple of dozen people operate the modern high-speed computerized looms that are kept in business by the restoration and maintenance of France's palaces and châteaux.

Along with Vieux Lyon, it was in this district that the **traboules** flourished. Officially the *traboules* are public thoroughfares during daylight hours, but you may find some closed for security reasons. The long climb up the part-pedestrianized **Montée de la Grande Côte**, however, still gives an idea of what the *quartier* was like in the sixteenth century, when the *traboules* were first built. One of the original *traboules*, **Passage Thiaffait** on rue Réné-Leynaud, has been refurbished to provide premises for young couturiers.

### Soierie Vivante

21 rue Richan • Tues 1.30–6pm, Wed–Sat 9am–noon & 1.30–6pm; guided tours 2pm & 4pm • €7 • ☎ 04 78 27 17 13, ⓦ soierie-vivante. asso.fr • Ⓜ Croix-Rousse

One of the few remaining silk-worker's ateliers in Lyon is the former trimming workshop of one Madame Létourneau, now run by **Soierie Vivante** (Living Silk Association). A tour of the workshop includes a demonstration of the three beautiful Jacquard looms dating from 1870, the only ones of this type still functioning in Lyon. If you can't make it along for a demonstration, you can still have a nose around, and there's also a giftshop selling some lovely silk wares.

## Vieux Lyon

Reached by one of the three *passerelles* (footbridges) crossing the Saône from Terreaux and the Presqu'île, **Vieux Lyon** is made up of the three villages of St-Jean, St-Georges and St-Paul at the base of the hill overlooking the Presqu'île. South of place St-Paul, the cobbled streets of Vieux Lyon, pressed close together beneath the hill of **Fourvière**, form a backdrop of Renaissance and medieval facades, bright night-time illumination and a swelling chorus of well-dressed Lyonnais in search of supper or a midday splurge.

### Musée Gadagne

1 place du Petit-Collège • Wed–Sun 10.30am–6.30pm • €6 each or €8 for both museums, including audioguide • ☎ 04 78 42 03 61, ⓦ gadagne.musees.lyon.fr

---

### THE SILK STRIKE OF 1831

Though the introduction of the Jacquard loom of 1804 made it possible for one person to produce 25cm of silk in a day instead of taking four people four days, **silk workers**, or *canuts* – whether masters or apprentices, and especially women and child workers – were badly paid whatever their output. As the price paid for a length of silk fell by over fifty percent, attempts to regulate the price were ignored by the dealers, even though hundreds of skilled workers were languishing in debtors' jails.

On November 21, 1831, the *canuts* called an all-out **strike**. As they processed down the Montée de la Grande Côte with their black flags and the slogan "Live working or die fighting", they were shot at and three people died. After a rapid retreat uphill they built barricades, assisted by half the National Guard, who refused to fire cannon at their "comrades of Croix-Rousse". Following three days of battle, and with the bourgeoisie running scared, the *canuts'* employers called upon outside aid, and 30,000 extra troops arrived to quash the rebellion. Some 600 people were killed or wounded, and in the end the silk industrialists were free to pay whatever pitiful fee they chose, but the uprising was one of the first instances of organized labour taking to the streets during the most revolutionary fifty years of French history.

Housed in a splendid fifteenth-century Renaissance mansion, the **Musée Gadagne** comprises two very fine museums. Two floors are given over to the **Musée d'Histoire de Lyon**, which offers a comprehensive chronological overview of the city's development, from antiquity to the modern day.

Better still is the **Musée des Marionnettes du Monde**, showcasing the many different forms of puppetry from both France and around the world, including Venetian glove puppets, Javanese rod puppets, and Chinese shadow puppets. In France, puppet theatres first appeared in the sixteenth-century, developing strong regional identities, as here in Lyon, around the turn of the nineteenth century, particularly with the advent of shadow and paper theatres. Pride of place in the collection goes to the nineteenth-century Lyonnais creations, Guignol and Madelon – the French equivalents of Punch and Judy, who also make an appearance.

## Cathédrale St-Jean

Place St-Jean • Mon–Fri 8.15am–7.45pm, Sat & Sun & holidays 8am–7pm • Free

Standing on the square of the same name is the twelfth- to fifteenth-century **Cathédrale St-Jean**, whose imposing facade lacks most of its statuary as a result of various wars and revolutions. The interior is conspicuously bland, save for some lovely thirteenth-century stained glass above the altar and in the rose windows of the transepts, and a sixteenth-century astronomical clock in the northern transept; its mechanism is cloaked by a beautiful Renaissance casing and is capable of computing moveable feast days (such as Easter) until the year 2019; a new one is planned for 2020, which will apparently work until 2084. On the strike of noon, 2pm, 3pm and 4pm the figures of the Annunciation go through an automated set piece, heralded by the lone bugler at the top of the clock. Note, though, that extensive restoration work – on both the exterior and interior – is likely to last until 2020, though it does remain open.

To the rear of the cathedral, an archeological garden contains the scant remains of two of Lyon's earliest churches, Ste-Croix and St-Étienne, the latter with a very pronounced arch still standing.

## Musée Gallo-Romain and Roman Theatres

17 rue Cléberg • **Musée Gallo-Romain** Tues–Sun 10am–6pm • €6 (Thurs free) • ☎ 04 72 38 49 30, ⓦ musees-gallo-romains.com
**Theatres** Mid-April to mid-Sept 7am–9pm; mid-Sept to mid-April 7am–7pm • Free • Funicular Fourvière/Minimes

Well worth the short trek up to Fourvière, the underground **Musée Gallo-Romain** showcases exhibits from prehistoric times to 7 AD, the sheer number and splendour of which serve to underline Roman Lyon's importance. Among the many highlights is a fragment of the so-called "Claudian Table", a fine bronze engraving of a speech by the Lyon-born Emperor Claudius, discovered in 1528 by a Lyonnais cloth-maker. Elsewhere, look out for a superb Bronze Age processional chariot, and some remarkably well-preserved mosaics – "In the Circus", for example, recalls the city's standing as one of Roman Gaul's most popular centres of entertainment.

Alongside the museum, dug into the hillside, stand the substantial remains of two ruined **theatres** – the larger of which was built by Augustus in 15 BC and extended in the second century by Hadrian to seat 10,000 spectators. Nowadays, they are the focal point for the **Nuits de Fourvière** music and film festival each summer.

## Basilique Notre-Dame de Fourvière

Place de Fourvière • Daily 7am–7pm • Rooftop tours 2.30pm & 4pm: April, May, Oct Wed & Sun; June–Sept daily (plus 11am Mon–Sat);
Nov 2.30pm & 3.30pm; 1hr 15min • Rooftop tours €7 • ☎ 04 78 25 13 01, ⓦ fourviere.org • Funicular Fourvière

A hulking, incredibly ornate wedding cake of a church, the **Basilique Notre-Dame de Fourvière** was built, like the Sacré-Coeur in Paris, in the aftermath of the 1871 Commune to emphasize the defeat of the godless socialists. And like the Sacré-Coeur, its hilltop position has become a defining element in the city's skyline. Overblown it may be, but the interior is utterly dazzling, from the marble statues and stained glass to the

> ## TOP TRABOULES
>
> All around Lyon lurk *traboules*, alleyways and tunnelled passages originally built to provide shelter from the weather for the silk-weavers as they moved their delicate pieces of work from one part of the manufacturing process to another. The streets running down from boulevard de la Croix-Rousse, as well as many in Vieux Lyon, are intersected by these *traboules*. Usually hidden by plain doors, they are impossible to distinguish from normal entryways, proving an indispensable escape network for pre-war gangsters and wartime Resistance fighters. Look out for subtle signs on the walls indicating the presence of a *traboule*.
>
> **Vieux Lyon** Find the aptly named *longue traboule*, a dark winding passage connecting 27 rue du Boeuf with 54 rue St-Jean.
>
> **Vieux Lyon** A *traboule* lies behind the door of 28 rue St-Jean, leading to the serene courtyard of a fifteenth-century palace.
>
> **La Croix-Rousse** Go up rue Réné-Leynaud, passing St-Polycarpe on your right, then take rue Pouteau via a *passage*. Turn right into rue des Tables Claudiennes, and enter no. 55 emerging opposite 29 rue Imbert-Colomes. Climb the stairs into 14bis, cross three courtyards and climb the steps, where you finally arrive at place Colbert.

gold and turquoise mosaic wall panels, depicting events such as Joan of Arc in Orléans and The Battle of Lepanto. Take a look, too, down in the crypt, where there's some beautifully executed stonework, plus an ornate turquoise mosaic ceiling in the apse.

It's well worth partaking in the Basilica **tour**, which includes a look behind the scenes, a march to the top of the observation tower and, best of all, a vertigo-inducing rooftop walk – if you can't stomach that, you can take in the magnificent citywide views from the esplanade. From here, the **montée St-Barthélémy** footpath winds back downhill to Vieux Lyon through the hanging gardens.

## Modern Lyon

On the skyline from Fourvière, you can't miss the gleaming pencil-like skyscraper that belongs to Lyon's home-grown Crédit Lyonnais bank. This is the centrepiece of **Part-Dieu**, a business-culture-commerce hub which includes one of the biggest public libraries outside Paris, a mammoth concert hall and a busy shopping centre. While it's not the most aesthetically pleasing area, you don't have to go far to enjoy some culture.

### Halles de Lyon Paul Bocuse

102 cours Lafayette • Market Tues–Sat 7am–7pm (restaurants till 10.30pm), Sun 7am–1pm (restaurants till 4.30pm) • ☎ 04 78 62 39 33, ⓦ halles-de-lyon-paulbocuse.com • Trolleybus #3, stop "Les Halles Paul Bocuse"

Named in honour of Lyon's most celebrated chef, who died in 2018, the **Halles indoor market** has been a temple of food since 1859 (albeit one relocated here in 1971), with goodies ranging from oysters and truffles to spiced sausages and cheeses, as well as chocolate, confectionery, wine and much more. This is not your average market though, and whether you're buying, eating or drinking (there are some fantastic bars and restaurants here too), it's not cheap.

### Institut Lumière

25 rue du Premier-Film • Tues–Sun 10am–6.30pm • €7 • ☎ 04 78 78 18 95, ⓦ institut-lumiere.org • Ⓜ Monplaisir-Lumière

Film buffs won't want to miss the enlightening **Institut Lumière**, housed within the grandiose Art Nouveau villa that was, for a period, the home of Antoine Lumière, father of Auguste and Louis, two of the earliest pioneers of film. The emphasis here is very much on the earliest forms of photographic techniques, which subsequently paved the way for film. Prize exhibits include early magic lanterns, the first cinematograph (1885), and the first ever autochromes, or colour plates, one of which is a picture of Antoine's third daughter relaxing in the Winter Garden. Don't miss the stunning collection of photos by celebrated Lumière photographer, Gabriel Veyre – the quality is so good that it's hard to believe they were taken in the 1930s. Meanwhile, in the basement projection room, you can view some entertaining cinematic clips including the first film, *Les Sorties des Usines Lumière*, showing workers leaving the Lumière factory. In the theatre across the way, several different films are shown nightly.

### Centre d'Histoire de la Résistance et de la Déportation

14 av Berthelot • Wed–Sun 10am–6pm • €6 • ☎ 04 78 72 23 11, ⓦ chrd.lyon.fr • ⓜ Perrache/Jean-Macé

Housed within the former military medical school used by the Gestapo during World War II, the **Centre d'Histoire de la Résistance et de la Déportation** makes for a sobering but worthwhile visit. In addition to a library of books, videos, memoirs and other documents recording experiences of resistance, occupation and deportation to the camps, there's an exhibition space housed over the very cellars and cells in which Klaus Barbie, the Gestapo boss of Lyon, tortured and murdered his victims. After living in Bolivia for years under a false identity, Barbie was extradited to France in 1987, aged 74, and tried in Lyon for crimes against humanity, for which he was sentenced to life imprisonment; the centrepiece of the exhibition is a moving and unsettling 45-minute video of the trial in which some of his victims recount their terrible ordeal – it's in French but ask to have it subtitled.

**15**

### Musée Garnier

4 rue des Serpollières • Tues–Sat 2–6pm • €8 • ☎ 04 78 75 16 75, ⓦ museeurbaintonygarnier.com • Tram #4, stop "États-Unis Musée Tony Garnier"

One of France's most influential urban planners, Lyon-born Tony Garnier (1869–1948), was responsible for many of the city's key architectural sites, though his presence looms particularly large in the rather anonymous 8ᵉ arrondissement. The **Musée Garnier** is not a museum in the conventional sense, rather it's an open-air exhibition of murals painted on the ends of apartment blocks, each one depicting a period of the city's history, such as the factory workers at the old blast furnaces, or some of Garnier's many architectural contributions, like Stade Gerland, the hospital, or the abattoir (now the Halle Tony Garnier). Garnier actually designed and lived in the squat building opposite the museum, and, fittingly, there's a mural of the great man close by.

---

**ARRIVAL AND DEPARTURE**                                                                  **LYON**

#### BY PLANE

**Lyon-Saint Exupéry International Airport** (☎ 08 26 80 08 26, ⓦ lyonaeroports.com) is 25km to the southeast of the city, just off the Grenoble *autoroute*. Taxi aside (€50–60), the only way of reaching the city centre is the Rhône Express tram (every 15–30min 4.25am–midnight; €16.10; ⓦ rhoneexpress.fr), which terminates at Part-Dieu train station. Note that there are no services from the airport's TGV station into Lyon. There are also regular buses from the airport to Grenoble, Chambéry and Annecy.

#### BY TRAIN

Central Lyon has two train stations: Gare de Perrache on the Presqu'île is used mainly for ordinary trains rather than TGVs; and Part-Dieu (TGV) is in the 3ᵉ arrondissement to the east of the Presqu'île. Some TGV trains from Paris give

the option of getting off at either station. Part-Dieu is the station for all Eurostar trains.

**Destinations** (from La Part-Dieu or Perrache) Avignon (10 daily; 2hr 20min–2hr 40min); Avignon TGV (hourly; 1hr 10min); Bourg-en-Bresse (10 daily; 55min–1hr 30min); Clermont-Ferrand (8 daily; 2hr 20min–2hr 40min); Dijon (hourly; 2hr); Grenoble (every 30min; 1hr 15min–1hr 50min); Lille-Europe (8 daily; 3hr 10min); Marseille (frequent; 1hr 40min–3hr 45min); Montélimar (10 daily; 1hr 35min); Orange (9 daily; 2hr 5min); Paris (every 30min; 2hr); Paris CDG Airport (9 daily; 2hr 10min); Meximieux (for Pérouges) (every 30–60min; 30min); St-Étienne (frequent; 50min); Valence (frequent; 1hr 10min); Valence TGV (frequent; 35min); Vienne (frequent; 20–35min); Villefranche (frequent; 25–40min).

---

**INFORMATION**

**Tourist office** The main tourist office stands on the southeast corner of place Bellecour (daily 9am–6pm;

☎ 04 72 77 69 69, ⓦ lyon-france.com). There's also an information desk in Terminal 2 of the airport.

**Guided tours** Numerous guided tours (2hr; €12–15, free with Lyon City Card, see box below) are offered by the tourist office; for example, the silk tour explores the former silk-workers district of Croix-Rousse, another tour delves into the complex web of Lyon's famous *traboules*, and there's a gastronomic tour, complete with tasting. Lyon Bike Tour run guided city tours by electric bike (from €30; ⓦ lyonbiketour. com), meeting by the Palais de Justice on quai Romain-Rolland – all except the shortest tour (1hr 30min) include a culinary pit stop.

## GETTING AROUND

Lyon is an eminently walkable city, but you may wish to make use of the excellent public transport system if hopping between the Presqu'île, Vieux Lyon and modern Lyon.

**Public transport** This comprises four métro lines, four tramlines, as well as trolleybuses, buses and two funiculars (*ficelle*). The métro runs 5am–12.15am, with the most important bus lines running until 10 or 11pm. You can pick up the handy métro, tram and bus map at any of the city transport (TCL) offices around the city.

**Tickets** A single ticket costs €1.90, but better value is the one-day *Ticket Liberté* (€5.80), or a *carnet* of ten (€16.90). A single ride on the funicular costs €2.80. Tickets, which can be bought at machines outside métro and tram stations or at any of the TCL offices, are valid for one hour after they have been validated on board.

**Car rental** All the main car hire companies have offices at the airport and at Perrache and Part-Dieu train stations.

Note that car rental outlets at the airport are situated on the opposite side to the main terminals, and accessed via a shuttle bus.

**Bike rental** Vélo'v (ⓦ velov.grandlyon.com) is a pick-up and drop-off bike hire scheme with stations all over the city. After subscribing (€4 for one day), the first thirty minutes are free, after which it's a per-minute billing system up to a maximum of €35.

**Boat trips** Les Bateaux Lyonnais (Naviginter), 13bis quai Rambaud, 2e ☎ 04 78 42 96 81, ⓦ lesbateauxlyonnais.com. Leaving from quai des Célestins, boats run up the Saône to Île Barbe or down to the confluence with the Rhône (March & Nov–Dec Fri–Sun; April–Oct daily); €14). The same company offers lunch and dinner cruises from €50.

**Taxis** Taxi Radio Lyon (☎ 04 72 10 86 86, ⓦ taxilyon.com); expect to pay a €2 starting fee then around €0.76 per km; note, though, that there is a minimum fare of €7.

## ACCOMMODATION

Lyon has an abundance of accommodation, with a liberal sprinkling of terrific hotels, including an increasing number of *chambres d'hôtes*, throughout the city, though the greatest concentration is in the Presqu'île and Vieux Lyon. In many places breakfast is not included in the rate, and quite often works out to be a hefty add-on. The following are marked on the map on page 784, unless otherwise stated.

### HOTELS

**Alexandra** 49 rue Victor-Hugo, 2e ☎ 04 78 37 75 79, ⓦ hotel-alexandra-lyon.fr; Ⓜ Ampère Victor-Hugo; map p.784. Entered via a brick passageway, just off a lively pedestrian zone, this decent hotel possesses thirty or so almost identically furnished rooms: warm bedrooms and designer bathrooms coloured in cool greys and blacks with splashes of red. The seven rooms to the rear – one of which is a family room with a mezzanine – have direct access to a sunny wood-decked terrace. Breakfast €16. **€89**

**Bayard** 23 place Bellecour, 2e ☎ 04 78 37 39 64, ⓦ hotel

bayard.fr; Ⓜ Bellecour; map p.784. Sister hotel to the Alexandra the similarly accomplished (but cheaper) *Bayard* occupies an enviable spot across from the enormous main square. Differently styled rooms are available, though the square-facing ones are the most appealing, featuring high ceilings, parquet flooring and period furnishings. Breakfast €14. **€79**

**Le Boulevardier** 5 rue de la Fromagerie, 1er ☎ 04 78 28 48 22, ⓦ leboulevardier.fr; Ⓜ Cordeliers; map p.784. The fourteen rooms squeezed into this centuries-old building are small and possess little natural light, though this is amply compensated for by the bright decor, cooling, exposed stone walls and the occasional vintage piece; the bathrooms, too, are immaculate. Note, though, that the stairs are steep and there's no lift, while the downstairs bar (which functions as the reception) can get noisy. Breakfast €7. **€79**

**Carlton Hotel** 4 rue Jussieu, 2e ☎ 04 78 42 56 51, ⓦ sofitel.accorhotels.com; Ⓜ Cordeliers; map p.784.

15

---

## LYON CITY CARD

The great-value **Lyon City Card** (€25, €35, €45 or €55 for one, two, three or four days; ⓦ lyoncitycard.com) grants unlimited access to the métro, bus, tramway and funicular, over twenty museums (including the Roman ruins in St-Romain-en-Gal; see page 800), guided city tours (including the Fourvière Basilica tour) and river cruise trips. The card is available from the tourist office and the major TCL offices.

The resolutely stylish Carlton retains most of its original – mostly Art Deco – features, notably stained-glass windows, glass-beaded chandeliers and, best of all, a splendid wrought-iron lift. The rooms themselves are no less sumptuous, with throws, carpets and floral wallpaper decorated in vivid shades of red, offset in black and white; a splendid Turkish hamam rounds things off nicely. Breakfast €25. **€200**

**Collège** 5 place St-Paul, 5ᵉ ☎04 72 10 05 05, ⌨college-hotel.com; Ⓜ Vieux-Lyon; map p.784. There's much that'll make you smile about this wonderful school-themed hotel, from the library-like reception to the breakfast room furnished like a classroom. The concept is continued in the completely all-white rooms – categorized from undergraduate (cheapest) to postgraduate (most expensive) – with lockers for cupboards and recycled school desks for tables. Better still, each floor has a vintage refrigerator stocked with drinks which guests are free to avail themselves of. Breakfast €17. **€139**

**Cour des Loges** 2–8 rue du Boeuf, 5ᵉ ☎04 72 77 44 44, ⌨courdesloges.com; Ⓜ Vieux-Lyon; map p.784. Lyon's most luxurious residence is set in a seventeenth-century former Jesuit college, at the centre of which is a stunning glazed atrium. The sixty or so rooms are predominantly fashioned in decadent Renaissance style, roughly half of which have mezzanine-level flooring and wet-room-style open spaces with attractive metal-framed showers. A spa with pool, sauna and Turkish bath complete the hotel's impressive set-up. Breakfast €27. **€225**

**Globe et Cécil** 21 rue Gasparin, 2ᵉ ☎04 78 42 58 95, ⌨globeetcecilhotel.com; Ⓜ Bellecour; map p.784. No one room is the same in this welcoming, family-run hotel near place Bellecour, which is some feat given that there are more than sixty of them. Each one is appointed with the sort of careful touch and individuality that you might find in your own home, so expect to find vibrant colours, wrought-iron or carved wooden bedsteads, oak bureaus, marble fireplaces and the like. Breakfast €12. **€155**

**Home Sweet Home** 6 rue Cléberg, 5ᵉ ☎04 72 32 15 66, ⌨home-sweet-home-lyon.com; Ⓜ Vieux Lyon/Minimes; map p.784. Sweet and quirky guesthouse just 100m down the road from the Musée Gallo-Romain, with three pretty rooms bursting with colour and providing super views across town, though bathroom facilities are shared. The friendly owner provides a substantial breakfast which you can enjoy on the little terrace. Note that the sign on the wall says Villa Romaine – just buzz in. **€72**

★ **Mama Shelter** 13 rue Domer, 7ᵉ ☎04 78 02 58 00, ⌨mamashelter.com; Ⓜ Jean Mace; map p.782. This cool upbeat place – part of the hipster chain of hotels – is terrific. The Starck designed rooms (four sizes from Small Mama to XL Mama) come complete with microwave, cartoon masks and an iMac TV screen with free on-demand movies – mind you, you'll probably spend most of your time down in the

rocking restaurant/bar. The breakfast (€17) will keep you going well into the afternoon. **€79**

**De la Marne** 78 rue de la Charité, 2ᵉ ☎04 78 37 07 46, ⌨hoteldelamarne.fr; Ⓜ Perrache; map p.784. Despite the rather grubby exterior, this friendly, well-managed hotel is actually not a bad place to bed down for the night, and it's one of the cheapest lodgings going in the Presqu'île. Twenty-three perky rooms available though you'd do well to plump for one in the courtyard annexe, which is not only quieter but also possesses a family room. Breakfast €7. Triples and quads available too. **€75**

★ **Nos Chambres en Ville** 12 rue René-Leynaud, 2ᵉ ☎04 78 27 22 30, ⌨chambres-a-lyon.com; Ⓜ Croix Paquet; map p.782. Secreted away up in Croix-Rousse, this former silk-weaver's residence has been converted into a warm and welcoming guesthouse. The three cleverly conceived rooms (two with shower, one with bath) manifest the original grey stone walls and exposed beams, but there are also touches of contemporary chic. Similarly, the communal lounge area – which guests are invited to use – has been sensitively renovated. Tricky to find as there's no sign outside, but you'll be given a code to punch in when you reserve. Closed Aug. **€90**

★ **Okko Hotel** 14bis quai du Général-Sarrail, 6ᵉ ☎04 28 00 02 50, ⌨okkohotels.com; Ⓜ Foch; map p.782. The focal point of this wonderfully original hotel is Le Club, a kitchen-cum-lounge area where guests are free to help themselves to unlimited (non-alcoholic) drinks and snacks throughout the day, in addition to a glass of wine and aperitifs (cheeses, meats etc) around 6pm; the rooms, though modestly sized, are both functional and easy on the eye, with nice touches, too, like Nespresso machines and bottles of water located in neat little compartments above the desk. Riverside rooms are worth paying the small extra for. **€129**

**Le Royal** 20 place Bellecour, 2ᵉ ☎04 78 37 57 31, ⌨lyonhotel-leroyal.com; Ⓜ Bellecour; map p.784. A landmark building since its inception as Lyon's first hotel in 1893, *Le Royal* remains a cut above most places in town. Rooms are impeccably styled in one of two colour schemes – red or blue – and are upholstered throughout with Toile de Jouy fabrics. The service is first-class, and nothing is too much trouble for the obliging staff – though at these rates, that is to be expected. Breakfast €27. **€155**

**Saint-Paul** 6 rue de la Lainerie, 5ᵉ ☎04 78 28 13 29, ⌨hotelsaintpaul.eu; Ⓜ Vieux Lyon; map p.784. Occupying a superb old town location, in one of the city's oldest buildings (possibly late fourteenth-century), this age-old hotel is well worth a punt. The more functional rooms to the rear face inwards onto a darkened courtyard, so receive little light, while those at the front are larger, brighter and have retained the original beamed ceilings. For late risers, continental breakfast (€12) is served until 11am. **€79**

**15**

**15**

**Du Simplon** 11 rue Duhamel, 2ᵉ ☎04 78 37 41 00, ⓦhotel-simplon-lyon.com; ⓜPerrache; map p.784. The unprepossessing exterior actually conceals a homely, and very popular, little hotel, run by a friendly lady with a penchant for cherries, as evidenced by the many cherry-adorned *objets* in the lounge and breakfast room. The rooms, meanwhile, are cosily decorated in different colours, and although a touch boxy and with smallish bathrooms, are meticulously clean. **€89**

## HOSTELS AND CAMPSITE

**Auberge de Jeunesse (Vieux Lyon)** 41–45 montée du Chemin-Neuf, 5ᵉ ☎04 78 15 05 50, ⓦfuaj.org; ⓜVieux-Lyon/Minimes; map p.784. Modern hostel set in a steep part of the old town with fantastic views over Lyon. Dorms sleep four to seven people, plus ensuite doubles, and there's a kitchen for use, as well as a laundry. Avoid the climb from Vieux Lyon métro station and take the funicular to Minimes, from where it's a five-minute walk back down the hill. Breakfast included. Dorms **€18**, doubles **€50**

**Camping de Lyon** Dardilly ☎04 78 35 64 55, ⓦcamping-lyon.com; map p.782. North along the A6 from Lyon or by bus #89 (stop "Camping International") from the gare de Vaise. Alternatively, take #3 from *Hôtel-de-ville*. Pleasant, green site with plenty of pitches, as well as a gypsy caravan sleeping four, wood/canvas tents sleeping four or five, and mobile homes sleeping two to six. Facilities include a heated outdoor pool, bar, restaurant (July & Aug only), shop and laundry. Open year-round. Camping **€22.50**, gypsy caravan **€95** wood/canvas tent **€62**, mobile home **€74**

★ **Hostel Slo Living** 5 rue Bonnefoi, 7ᵉ ☎04 78 59 06 90, ⓦslo-hostel.com; ⓜSaxe-Gambetta; map p.782. There are currently few better hostels in France than *Slo*, an easy-going place whose attractively designed, all-white rooms (four-, six- and eight-bedded dorms and private doubles) are located either side of a lovely wood-decked patio where you can play a game of *boules* or just kick back with a beer. Buffet breakfast €5. Dorms **€25**, doubles **€75**

## EATING AND DRINKING

Few cities anywhere in Europe, let alone France, can rival Lyon for the quality of its food, and there are currently fifteen restaurants here with one or more Michelin stars. However, while these temples of gastronomy continue to raise standards, the humble bouchon remains as popular as ever, and really is an experience not to be missed – note that some of the more upscale restaurants are closed on Saturdays and Sundays, with others closing on Mondays. While decent coffee remains hard to source, Lyon's café culture is slowly improving, and it's now possible to find some terrific spots to sip an espresso (or tea), particularly up in the Croix-Rousse district. Otherwise, you can join the masses on place des Terreaux and the streets of Vieux Lyon.

## CAFÉS

**À Chacun Sa Tasse** 2 rue du Griffon, 1ᵉʳ ☎04 72 87 06 45; ⓜCroix-Paquet; map p.782. Secreted away on the edge of the Croix-Rousse district, this mellow, vaguely Art Deco-styled teahouse is the place to sup on one (or more) of the one hundred or so brews on offer; take a seat at one of the glass-topped tables downstairs, or, better still, slump back into one of the squishy leather chairs upstairs. Mon–

Fri 8am–7pm, Sat 9am–7pm.

**Mokxa** 3 rue de l'Abbé-Rozier, 1ᵉʳ ☎04 27 01 48 71; ⓦCroix-Paquet; map p.782. Cheerful little café on a sunny little square in Croix-Rousse that has gained a loyal following, particularly among the laptop crowd. Very reasonably priced flat whites, cappuccinos, chai lattes and similar served by knowledgeable staff, though service can be slow. Tues–Fri 8am–-7pm, Sat 9am–7pm, Sun 2–9pm (closed last Sun in the month).

**Slake Coffee House** 9 rue de l'Ancienne-Préfecture, 2ᵉ ☎04 78 38 24 38, ⓦslake-coffee.com; ⓜCordeliers; map p.784. Sleek brick and wood-lined establishment offering a decent selection of coffees brewed various ways (chemex, French Press, V60, etc), best enjoyed with a muffin or slice of cheesecake. Mon–Fri 8am–7pm, Sat 10am–7pm, Sun 11am–7pm.

★ **Terre Adélice** 1 place de la Baleine, 5ᵉ ☎04 78 03 51 84; ⓦVieux-Lyon; map p.784. Sparkling ice-cream parlour on a pretty old town square, though it's the sorbets that the locals really come here for. Choose, if you can, from over one hundred flavours, from the sublime (Armagnac brandy and prune) to the ridiculous (cucumber, liquorice).

---

## THE BOUCHON

No visit to Lyon is complete without a visit to a **bouchon**, the traditional Lyonnais eating establishment. Its provenance most likely comes from the time when inns serving wine would attach small bundles of straw to their signs, indicating that horses could be cared for (*bouchonnés*) while the coachmen went inside to have a drink. The food may not be to everyone's taste – *andouillette* (hot cooked tripe sausage) and *pieds de veau* (calves' feet) are typical staples – but the dishes are usually beautifully cooked and they're wonderfully convivial places. While many bouchons claim to be authentic, only 22 are certified, the best of which are found in the Presqu'île.

One scoop €2.80, two scoops €4.70. May–Sept daily 1pm–midnight, March, April & Oct Mon–Thurs 1–6.30pm, Fri–Sun 1–11.30pm, Nov–Feb Fri–Sun 1–6.30pm.

## RESTAURANTS

**Arsenic** 132 rue Pierre-Corneille, 7ᵉ ☎09 62 39 85 55, ⓦarsenicrestaurant.com; ⓜPlace Guichard; map p.782. Unfortunate name, but there's nothing unfortunate about the food, or indeed the concept, whereby young chefs from around the world are brought in to learn their trade alongside the restaurant's senior chefs. Dishes like tuna, broccoli and hibiscus, and scorpionfish, celery and shiitake (dishes comprise just three words, or ingredients) are unlikely to disappoint. Three courses €32, four courses €40. Mon–Fri noon–2pm & 7.30–9.30pm.

**Bouchon des Filles** 20 rue du Sergent-Blandan, 2ᵉ ☎04 78 30 40 44; ⓜHôtel-de-Ville-Louis Pradel; map p.784. As the name suggests, this is an all-female-run establishment, and a fine one it is too, which you'd expect from two ladies who served their apprenticeships at the *Café des Fédérations* (see below); the restaurant's signature dish is indisputably the *croustille de boudin aux pommes* (black pudding with apple and herbs wrapped in pastry), one of the choices on the fixed-price four-course *menu*, which, at €27, is great value. Daily 7pm–10pm, plus Fri–Sun noon–2pm.

**Brasserie Georges** 30 cours de Verdun, 2ᵉ ☎04 72 56 54 54, ⓦbrasseriegeorges.com; ⓜPerrache; map p.784. Row upon row of crisply laid tables with red leather seating, and friezes poised above the heavily mirrored walls, make for quite a setting in this cavernous Art Deco brasserie founded in 1836. *Choucroutes* (sauerkraut served with sausages and other meats) are the house speciality, though there are plenty of Lyonnais dishes on the menu. Terrific home-brewed craft beers too. Starters €10, mains €18. Mon–Thurs 11.30am–11pm, Fri & Sat till 12.15am.

★ **Café des Fédérations** 8–10 rue du Major-Martin, 1ᵉʳ ☎04 78 28 26 00, ⓦrestaurant-cafedesfederations-lyon.com; ⓜHôtel-de-Ville; map p.784. One of Lyon's most enduring and celebrated bouchons, serving the earthiest of Lyonnais specialities such as marinated tripe and black pudding, and veal brains fried in butter Provençal. Cheerful green-and-white-checked tables are complemented by rough wooden floorboards and jovial pictures on the walls. A good time is guaranteed. Three-course lunch €20.50, dinner €29. Mon–Sat noon–2pm & 7–10pm.

**Chabert et Fils** 11 rue des Marronniers, 2ᵉ ☎04 78 37 01 94, ⓦchabertrestaurant.fr; ⓜBellecour; map p.784. Noisy, chaotic and a great deal of fun, this age-old bouchon is the pick of the many restaurants packed along this street. It offers much more than just the usual bouchon staples, for example, stew of veal with spring vegetables, and duck with morello cherries – unusually, the menu is also available in English. Starters €10, mains €15. Mon–Thurs & Sun noon–2pm & 7–11pm, Fri & Sat till 11.30pm.

★ **Daniel et Denise** 156 rue de Créqui, 3ᵉ ☎04 78 60 66 53, ⓦdanieletdenise.fr; ⓜPlace Guichard; map p.782; and 36 rue Tramassac, 5ᵉ ☎04 78 60 66 53; ⓜVieux-Lyon; map p.784. If you've only got time to try one bouchon, make it this one. Run by charismatic *meilleur ouvrier de France*, Joseph Viola, this little corner restaurant will charm your socks off from the moment you step inside the old-fashioned interior, with its red-and-white-check-clothed tables, tiled flooring, and copper pots. On the menu are deliciously tasty dishes like sirloin of Angus beef with black pepper and cognac, and crème brûlée with bourbon vanilla – though do not leave without trying a slice of Viola's *pâté en croûte*, a sensational crusty foie gras and sweetbread pâté. Two-course lunch menu €21, three-course dinner menu €33. Closed Aug. Mon–Fri noon–2pm & 7–10pm.

**La Gourmix** 7 place Antonin-Poncet, 1ᵉʳ ☎04 78 38 09 36, ⓦgourmix.fr; ⓜHôtel-de-Ville; map p.784. The concept is as simple as it is brilliant: three mini'wichs (mini baguettes) – and you can choose from over 100, including foie gras and *jambon cru* – with a side of crisps or salad and a drink, all for just €10; beer and wine is also served though that is extra. Mon–Fri 11.30am–3pm & 6.30–10pm, Sat 11.30am–10.30pm.

**Le Grand Café des Négociants** 1 place Francisque-Régaud, 2ᵉ ☎04 78 42 50 05, ⓦlesnegociants.com; ⓜCordeliers; map p.784. Despite its unenviable position on a busy junction, this venerable old place – dating from 1864 – is always rammed, be it the sumptuously gilded brasserie, serving both regional and traditional dishes (and continental and American-style breakfasts), or the bustling outdoor terrace – the ideal spot for coffee or beer. *Menus* €35. Starters €13, mains €22. Daily 7am–1am; restaurant noon–midnight.

**King Marcel** 31 rue Mercière, 1ᵉʳ ☎04 78 42 28 50, ⓦkingmarcel.fr; ⓜCordeliers; map p.784. Choose from one of six juicy burgers (made from Charolais beef), throw in some thick-cut fries and a green salad, then take a seat at one of the dinky tables (spread over two floors) and wait for it to be brought to you. Takeaway too. Burgers from €8.50. Mon–Wed 11am–10pm, Thurs–Sun til 11pm.

**Léon de Lyon** 1 rue Pléney, 1ᵉʳ ☎04 72 10 11 12, ⓦbistrotsdecuisiniers.com; ⓜHôtel-de-Ville; map p.784. The distinctive orange and green stained-glass frontage conceals a distinguished brasserie serving original culinary creations as well as traditional Lyonnais recipes. There's plenty of seating inside, but in warmer weather the pavement terrace is a more convivial spot to dine. Starters €14, mains €21. Closed first three weeks Aug. Daily noon–2.30pm & 7–11.30pm.

★ **La Mère Brazier** 12 rue Royale, 1ᵉʳ ☎04 78 23 17 20, ⓦlamerebrazier.com; ⓜCroix-Paquet; map p.782.

**15**

**15**

## THE MÈRES LYONNAISES

Lyon's standing as one of the world's finest gastronomic destinations is in no small part down to the **Mères Lyonnaises**, or "Mothers of Lyon". Originally house cooks for the middle and upper classes, many of these women ultimately became surplus to requirements, so instead opened up their own businesses, serving food that combined grande bourgeoisie cuisine with more humble fare of the kind you might find in a bouchon, hence dishes such as pullet hen with black truffles, and pike *quenelle* casserole. Leading the way were women like Mère Fillioux and Mère Eugénie Brazier, the latter establishing her eponymous restaurant on rue Royale, which is also where Paul Bocuse completed his apprenticeship.

Established in 1921 by Mme Brazier, one of the original Mères Lyonnaises and the first woman to attain three Michelin stars, this magnificent restaurant is now headed up by superstar chef Mathieu Viannay, who currently has two stars. This is about as good, and as expensive, as it gets in Lyon, with a menu as brilliant as it is bold, for example poached quail eggs with Corsican honey and sorrel, and roasted veal sweetbreads with crispy rice soufflé and smoked eel juice. Starters €45, mains €70. Closed Aug. Mon–Fri noon–2pm & 7.30–11pm.

**La Meunière** 11 rue Neuve, 1ᵉʳ ☎04 78 28 62 91, ⓦlameuniere.fr; ⓜHôtel-de-Ville; map p.784. Dyed-in-the-wool bouchon whose happily carewown demeanour is manifest in age-old furnishings and faded wall prints. Seating is arranged around a central "guest" table laden with various cuts of meat, cheeses and pâtés, while the menu features the likes of veal kidneys with port wine and a mustard sauce. Good fun and good value. Starters €9.50, mains €18. Tues–Sat noon–2pm & 7.30–9.30pm.

**Paul Bocuse** 40 rue de la Plage, Collonges-au-Mont-d'Or ☎04 72 42 90 90, ⓦbocuse.fr; map p.782. Some 6km north of the city, on the west bank of the Saône, you can't miss the oversized signage proclaiming Lyon's most famous restaurant, named after its late celebrity chef. High-end French gastronomy is the bill of fare, with luxurious dishes such as scallop of foie gras pan-cooked with raspberries, and braised veal sweetbreads with Ivoire sauce, though you will, inevitably, be paying through the nose. Starters €45, mains €70. *Menus* from a wallet-busting €175. Daily noon–2pm & 8–10pm.

## NIGHTLIFE AND ENTERTAINMENT

Lyon packs a pretty mean punch when it comes to nightlife and entertainment, with a wide range of bars and clubs, alongside some great live music, opera and theatre. The best places to wander if you are looking for a bar are rue Mercière, the area around place des Terreaux and the Opéra and the streets of Vieux Lyon, though the riverboat bars along the banks of the Rhône are popular too.

Lyon's cinematic history is also extremely rich, thanks largely to the pioneering work of the Lumière brothers (see page 788). For avant-garde, classic and obscure films, usually in their original language, check the listings for the cinemas CNP Terreaux, Bellecour, Fourmi Lafayette, Opéra and Ambiance.

### BARS AND CLUBS

**L'Antiquaire** 20 rue Hippolyte-Flandrin, 1ᵉʳ ☎06 34 21 54 65; ⓜHôtel-de-Ville ; map p.784. A novel presence in Lyon, this gorgeous, candlelit bar will satisfy even the most demanding cocktail connoisseur, with a terrific range of drinks (€8–10), though it'd be remiss not to try the house special, a luscious Bacardi Fizz. You won't have the privilege, but regulars have their own liquor lockers. Mon–Wed & Sun 6.30pm–1am, Thurs–Sun till 3am.

**Les Berthom** 24 rue Pizay, 1ᵉʳ ☎09 62 25 14 34, ⓦlesberthom.fr; ⓜHôtel-de-Ville; map p.784. An industrial aesthetic prevails at this good-time bar, with its exposed brick walls and ceilings, stripped wooden flooring and chunky wooden stools and tables. The beer, meanwhile, is mostly of the Belgian variety (including Trappist and fruit varieties) – and there are some organic ones too – but at around €6 a pop it's not cheap. Mon–Fri & Sun 5pm–1am, Sat 4pm–2am.

**Broc Bar** 20 rue Lanterne, 1ᵉʳ ☎04 78 30 82 61; ⓜHôtel-de-Ville; map p.784. There's nothing obviously exciting about this street-corner café-cum bar, with its battered-looking red and yellow tables and chairs, but the terrace is invariably packed with punters idly chatting over a daytime coffee or an evening beer. Mon 7am–11pm, Tues–Sat 7am–1am, Sun 10am–9pm.

**La Cave des Voyageurs** 7 place St-Paul, 5ᵉ ☎04 78 28 92 28, ⓦlacavedesvoyageurs.fr; ⓜVieux-Lyon; map p.784. Earthy, two-floored brick-lined wine bar serving hundreds of varieties of wine from all over France that you can taste and take away; better still, enjoy a glass with a plate of charcuterie. Tues–Sat 5pm–1am.

**Eden Rock Café** 68 rue Mercière, 1ᵉʳ ☎04 78 38 28 18, ⓦedenrockcafe.com; ⓜCordeliers; map p.784. One of the city's better live music venues, staging straight down-the-line rock music, with the same band typically playing on consecutive nights from Thursday through to Saturday. Sun–Wed 4.30pm–1am, Thurs–Sat 4.30pm–3am.

**Hot Club** 26 rue Lanterne, 1ᵉʳ ☎04 78 39 54 74, ⓦhotclubjazzlyon.com; ⓜHôtel-de-Ville; map p.784. Hidden away down a seedy side street, the discreet entrance conceals a fine vaulted cellar playing host to a high class programme of jazz, swing, blues and funk, and has been doing so since 1948. Tickets €10. Closed July & Aug. Wed–Sat 9pm–1am.

★**Mama Shelter** 13 rue Domer, 7ᵉ ☎04 78 02 58 00, ⓦmamashelter.com; ⓜJean Mace; map p.782. In the uber-hip hotel of the same name, this is party central and consequently rammed most nights of the week; table football, ping-pong and inflatable rubber rings running the length of the ceiling all contribute to the good-time vibe, while DJs crank up the atmosphere from Thursday to Saturday. Daily 6pm–1.30am.

**Ninkasi** 267 rue Marcel-Mérieux, 7ᵉ ☎04 72 76 89 00, ⓦninkasi.fr; ⓜGerland; map p.782. *Ninkasi* is actually a collective of some half a dozen bars scattered across the city, though this, the original bar down in the Gerland district, remains the most prominent. A high-spirited crowd is drawn here nightly to down a few refreshing house brews and soak up some cracking music, be it live bands or world-renowned DJs. Mon–Wed 10am–1am, Thurs 10am–2am, Fri & Sat 10am–4am, Sun 10am–midnight.

**Le Passage** 8 rue du Plâtre, 1ᵉʳ ☎04 78 28 11 16, ⓦle-passage.com; ⓜHôtel-de-Ville; map p.784. Intimate, utterly seductive wine bar set against a gothic backdrop of leather seating, candle-topped tables, and soft red lights. A glass of wine can be anything from €5 to €15, although in such luxurious surroundings you might just be tempted to splash out on champagne. Tues & Wed 7am–1am, Thurs–Sat 7pm–3am.

**Le Sirius** Opposite 4 quai Augagneur, 3ᵉ ☎04 78 71 78 71, ⓦlesirius.com; ⓜLa Guillotière; map p.782. Laidback boat bar on the River Rhône with an impressive roster of DJs, a diverse programme of live music, including world, rock and soul, and jazz jam sessions on Tuesdays. Friendly staff and late opening too. Daily 2pm–3am.

★**Le Sucre** 50 quai Rambaud, 2ᵉ ⓦle-sucre.eu; map p.782. Disused sugar factory on the banks of the Rhône that has been brilliantly converted into a vibrant cultural hub, the focal point of which is a rooftop bar playing host to an array of events, including techno club nights. Fri 6.30pm–1am, Sat 4pm–5am, Sun 4–11pm.

## THEATRE, MUSIC AND FILM

**Institut Lumière** 25 rue du Premier-Film, 8ᵉ ☎04 78 78 18 95, ⓦinstitut-lumiere.org; ⓜMontplaisir-Lumière. Housed in the former "Hangar" on the site of the old Lumière factories, this superbly renovated theatre offers a terrifically varied programme of film, both domestic and foreign. Tickets €9.

**Opéra de Lyon** 1 Place de la Comédie, 1ᵉʳ ☎04 69 85 54 54, ⓦopera-lyon.com; ⓜHôtel-de-Ville. One of the best opera houses in France, it's also home to the well-regarded Lyon Opera Ballet company. Cheap tickets are sold just before performances begin. Box office Tues–Sat noon–7pm.

**Théâtre des Célestins** 4 rue Charles-Dullin, 2ᵉ ☎04 72 77 40 00, ⓦtheatredescelestins.com; ⓜBellecour. Beautiful, gilded residence on a lovely little square staging less radical stuff than most places but offering a highly competent programme of works nonetheless. Box office Tues–Sat 12.15–6.45pm.

**Théâtre National Populaire** 8 place Lazare-Goujon ☎04 78 03 30 00, ⓦtnp-villeurbanne.com; ⓜGratte-Ciel. Located a short way east of the city centre in Villeurbanne, the TNP stands as Lyon's most prominent theatre, staging the biggest, blowsiest productions. Box office Tues–Fri 2–7pm, Sat 2–7pm.

## DIRECTORY

**Health** SAMU – emergency medical attention ☎15; Police ☎17; SOS Médecins ☎04 78 83 51 51. Hospitals: Croix-Rousse, 93 Grand rue de la Croix Rousse ☎04 72 07 10 46; Hôpital Édouard-Herriot, 5 place d'Arsonval, 3ᵉ ☎04 72 11 76 45. For house calls contact the medical referral centres (☎04 72 33 00 33).
**Police** The main commissariat is at 47 rue de la Charité, 2ᵉ ☎04 78 42 26 56.

# Pérouges

Thirty-four kilometres northeast of Lyon, on the N84, is **PÉROUGES**, a lovely village of cobbled alleyways and ancient houses. Its charm has not gone unnoticed by the French film industry either – historical dramas such as *The Three Musketeers* were filmed within its fortifications – nor by some of the residents, who have fought long and hard for preservation orders on its most interesting buildings. The result is an immaculate work of conservation. Local traditional life is also thriving in the hands of a hundred or so workers who still weave locally grown hemp.

The simple and beautiful church of **Marie-Madeleine**, close to the medieval gate that serves as the entry point to Pérouges, is worth an exploration. Built around 1440, its style is primarily early Gothic with Romanesque features. The central square, the

**place de la Halle**, and Pérouges' main street, the **rue du Prince**, have some of the best-preserved French medieval remains. The **lime tree** on place de la Halle is a symbol of liberty, and was planted in 1792.

### ARRIVAL AND INFORMATION

PÉROUGES

**By train** From Lyon, you will arrive at the train station in Meximieux from where it's a 10min walk to Pérouges.
Destinations Lyon (every 30–60min; 30min).
**Tourist office** Just outside the fortifications on Route de la

Cité (May–Aug daily 10am–1pm & 1.30–5pm; April, Sept & Oct Mon–Fri 10am–noon & 2–5pm, Sat & Sun 2–5pm; Nov–March Mon–Fri 10.30am–noon & 2–4.30pm; ☎ 09 67 12 70 84, ⓦ perouges.org).

### ACCOMMODATION AND EATING

**Auberge du Coq** Rue des Rondes ☎ 04 74 61 05 47. Those with a modest wallet should head for this pretty, stone-walled restaurant, where good-value *menus* are available from €18.50; snail casserole and *coq au vin, cuisses de grenouille* (frogs' legs), or roast chicken with mushrooms are standards. Do sample the local speciality, the deliciously sugary *galette pérougienne*. Wed–Sat noon–2pm & 7–10.30pm, Sun noon–2pm.

**Hostellerie de Pérouges** Place du Tilleul ☎ 04 74 61 00 88, ⓦ hostelleriedeperouges.com. This hotel, lodging within a cluster of gorgeous medieval houses scattered around the square, has a range of rooms from three- to four-stars, though all are prepared to an exceptionally high standard – four-poster beds and period furnishings are typical features. Breakfast €17. **€136**

# Beaujolais

Around 30km northeast of Lyon, the countryside becomes increasingly hilly as you approach the **Beaujolais** region, where the light, fruity red wines hail from. Fashionable to drink when it is young, Beaujolais is made from the Gamay grape, which thrives on the area's granite soil. Of the three Beaujolais appellations, the best are the *crus*, which come from the northern part of the region between St-Amour and Brouilly. If you have your own transport, you can follow the *cru* trail that leads up the D68 to St-Amour, before wending your way along the D31. Beaujolais Villages produces the most highly regarded *nouveau*, which comes from the middle of the region, while plain Beaujolais are produced in the vineyards southwest of Villefranche-sur-Saône.

## Oingt

There are any number of delightful Beaujolais villages you could head for, but if time is a limiting factor, then head to **Oingt**, around 15km southwest of Villefranche (see below). Oingt is typical of the villages in this "Golden Stones" region, so called because of the distinctive ochre-yellow colour of its buildings. The narrow, sun-dappled streets of this splendidly fortified village lead up to the evocative **church of St Matthews**, and, across the way, the chunky, circular observation tower, from where there are superlative views of the surrounding vineyards. Arts and crafts also play a big part in village life here, and you'll find workshops liberally scattered throughout the streets.

## Villefranche

Thirty-five kilometres north of Lyon, **Villefranche** is both an excellent base for an exploration of the Beaujolais region and a worthwhile destination in itself. Rue Nationale is the long, gently dipping main axis of town, where you'll find smart shops, cafés and patisseries, and the striking **church of Notre-Dame**, which has a fine tower with a soaring spire and ferocious-looking gargoyles. Secreted away behind many of the handsome two- and three-storey buildings lining rue Nationale are some beautifully restored Renaissance courtyards, like the **Italian House**, at no. 407, which features a superb wooden gallery with a spiral staircase leading to a watchtower –

some of these courtyards you can enter freely, but for others you should contact the tourist office (see below), who can arrange guided tours. If you're planning on visiting the Beaujolais region and want to gather a picnic, try the superb **covered market** on boulevard Jean-Jaurès.

### ARRIVAL AND INFORMATION — VILLEFRANCHE

**By train** The train station is on place de la Gare, from where it's an easy 5min walk down rue de la Gare to the main street, rue Nationale.

**Destinations** Lyon (frequent; 25–40min).

**Tourist office** Just off rue Nationale, at 96 rue de la Sous-Préfecture (May–Sept Mon–Fri 9am–6pm, Sat 9am–12.30pm & 1.30–6pm; Oct–April Mon–Fri 10am–5pm, Sat 10am–12.30pm & 1.30–5pm; ☎04 74 07 27 40, ⓦvillefranche-beaujolais.fr); the friendly staff are more than willing to assist with any aspect of visiting the Beaujolais wine region.

### ACCOMMODATION, EATING AND DRINKING

**Bar 91** 91 rue Stalingrad ☎04 74 03 14 10. If you can't make it to the Beaujolais region, then a stop at this vibrant, modern wine bar near the station will be some compensation. A slick wood and brick aesthetic with mismatched tables and chairs, floor-to-ceiling windows through which to soak up the sun, tasting sessions, live music and kiddie-friendly facilities make this a super little place. You can also pick up a *plat du jour* for €9. Mon 11.30am–2.30pm, Tue–Fri 11.30am–10.30pm, Sat 9am–1pm & 4–11pm.

**Plaisance** 96 av de la Libération ☎04 74 65 33 52, ⓦhotel-plaisance.com. Accomplished Best Western hotel at the southern end of town (fronting the large car park), offering decently sized, smartly furnished rooms in assorted fetching colours (plum, lime green, turquoise), some with bath, some with shower. **€89**

# Vienne

As you head south from Lyon on the A7, a twenty-kilometre stretch of oil refineries and factories, steel and chemical works may well tempt you to make a beeline for the lavender fields of Provence further south. However, a short detour off the *autoroute* leads to **VIENNE**, which, along with **St-Romain-en-Gal**, just across the river, once prospered as Rome's major wine port and entrepôt on the Rhône. Many Roman monuments survive to attest to this past glory, while several important churches recall Vienne's medieval heyday: it was a bishop's seat from the fifth century and the home town of twelfth-century Pope Calixtus II. The town has undoubtedly maintained its character and sense of purpose, and the compact old quarter makes for enjoyable wandering. Moreover, the **Saturday market** is one of the largest in the country, and you'll find all the main squares and streets choc-a-bloc with merchants selling everything from cheese, fruit and veg to textiles and pottery.

## The Roman monuments

Roman monuments are scattered liberally around the streets of Vienne, including the magnificently restored **Temple d'Auguste et de Livie**, a perfect, scaled-down version of Nîmes' Maison Carrée, on place du Palais, and the remains of the **Jardin Archéologique de Cybèle**, off place de Miremont, which were discovered in 1938 on the site of a former hospital. Off to one side are the substantial remains of two magnificent archways, which would have formed the entrances to the old Roman Forum. The city symbol, however, is the **Pyramid**, a neat 25-metre-high obelisk located on boulevard Fernand Point, outside the famous restaurant of the same name; it's the only surviving relic from the city's Roman circus.

### Théâtre Antique

Rue du Cirque • April–Aug daily 9.30am–1pm & 2–6pm; Sept & Oct Tues–Sun 9.30am–1pm & 2–6pm; Nov–March Tues–Fri 9.30am–12.30pm & 2–5pm, Sat & Sun 1.30–5.30pm • €3 or €6 combined ticket (see box opposite) • ☎04 74 85 39 23

Best of all the Roman monuments in Vienne is the magnificent **Théâtre Antique**, sited at the base of Mont Pipet to the north of town. Built around 40 AD, in its heyday it could seat up to 13,000 spectators, making it one of the largest such venues in Roman antiquity. After falling into a state of disrepair, a lengthy period of restoration concluded in 1938. While it's a bit of a slog to get up here, it's definitely worth the effort for the view of the town and river from the very top seats. Better still, the theatre is a quite superb venue for the many concerts held in Vienne throughout the summer, not least during the Jazz Festival.

## Musée Archéologique Église St-Pierre

Place St-Pierre • April–Oct Tues–Sun 9.30am–1pm & 2–6pm; Nov–March Tues–Fri 9.30am–12.30pm & 2–5pm, Sat & Sun 1.30–5.30pm
• €3 or €6 combined ticket • ☎ 04 74 85 20 35

The **Musée Archéologique Église St-Pierre** stands on the site of one of France's first cathedrals, the origins of which date from the fifth century. The building has suffered much reconstruction and abuse since, including a stint as a factory in the nineteenth century, though the monumental portico of the former church is still striking. Today, the cool, haunting interior retains the atmosphere of an architectural salvage yard, housing substantial but broken chunks of Roman columns, capitals and cornices, though there are some splendid fresco fragments and mosaics to admire.

## Cathédrale St-Maurice

Place St-Paul • Daily 9am–6pm • Free

Completely out of proportion with its surrounds, the monumental **Cathédrale St-Maurice** was pieced together between the eleventh and sixteenth centuries – hence the somewhat unwieldy facade, a combination of Romanesque and Gothic, which appears as if its upper half has been dumped on top of a completely alien building. The interior, with its 90m-long vaulted nave, is impressive though, spare and elegant, with some modern stained-glass windows, traces of fifteenth-century frescoes, and seventeenth-century tapestries, one representing St Maurice.

## Église and Cloître de St-André-le-Bas

Place du Jeu-de-Paume • April–Oct Tues–Sun 9.30am–1pm & 2–6pm; Nov–March Tues–Fri 9.30am–12.30pm & 2–5pm, Sat & Sun 1.30–5.30pm • €3 or €6 combined ticket • ☎ 04 74 78 71 06

The **Église** and **Cloître de St-André-le-Bas** on place du Jeu de Paume, a few streets north of the cathedral, date from the ninth and twelfth centuries. The back tower of the church, on rue de la Table Ronde, is a remarkable monument, studded with tiny carved stone faces, while the cloister is entered via a small garden a few paces across from the church; beyond the room where temporary exhibits are held, this beautiful little Romanesque affair manifests slender, chalky columns and walls decorated with local tombstones, some dating from the fifth century.

**15**

---

### VIENNE MUSEUM PASS AND AUDIOGUIDE

The Théâtre Antique, Église and Cloître de St-André-le-Bas, Musée des Beaux-Arts et d'Archéologie, Musée de la Draperie (currently closed) and Musée Archéologique St-Pierre can be visited on a **single ticket** (€6), which can be picked up at any of the sites and is valid for 48 hours; a pass for all these museums plus the Musée Gallo-Romain costs €8. Audioguides (€5), available from the tourist office, will give you more information on the city's glorious past at each of the main temples and ruins.

## Musée Gallo-Romain

St-Romain-en-Gal • Tues–Sun 10am–6pm • €6 or €8 combined ticket, free first Sun each month; audioguide included • ☎ 04 74 53 74 01, Ⓦ musee-site.rhone.fr.

Across the Rhône from Vienne, several hectares of Roman ruins constitute the site of **ST-ROMAIN-EN-GAL**, also the name of the modern town surrounding it. Before exploring the excavations, you enter the vast glass and steel building holding the **Musée Gallo-Romain**, which is dominated by some superb mosaics, though those on display are just a fraction of the 250 or so that were discovered along the riverbank; the most outstanding example is the olive-green-coloured Punishment of Lycurgus, which is placed in a separate room on the upper floor.

The site itself – discovered as recently as 1967 – attests to a significant community dating from the first century BC to the third AD, and comprises domestic houses, a craftsmen's district including the significant remains of a fulling mill, a commercial area with market halls and warehouses, and, most impressive of all, the wrestlers' baths, complete with marble toilets that display some remarkable frescoes.

**15**

### ARRIVAL AND INFORMATION                                    VIENNE

**By train** The train station is at the top of cours Brillier, which runs down to the riverfront.
Destinations Lyon (frequent; 20–35min); Valence (frequent; 45min).
**Tourist office** In a large pavilion at the bottom of cours Brillier (March–June & Sep–Oct daily 9am–noon & 1.30– 6pm; July & Aug Mon–Sat 9am–7pm, Sun 9am–noon & 1.30–6pm; Nov–Feb Mon–Sat 9am–noon & 1.30–6pm; ☎ 04 74 53 70 10, Ⓦ vienne-tourisme.com).
**Bike hire** Available from the tourist office; €3 for half a day, €5 per day.

### ACCOMMODATION

**Grand Hôtel de la Poste** 47 cours Romestang ☎ 04 74 85 02 04, Ⓦ hoteldelaposte38.com. The building is beginning to show its age, and the rooms are a little frayed around the edges, but it's clean, fairly priced, and the location, overlooking a pretty, tree-lined *cours*, is perfect. Triples, quads and family rooms also available. Closed last two weeks in August. Breakfast €9. **€69**

**La Pyramide** 14 bd Fernand-Point ☎ 04 74 53 01 96, Ⓦ lapyramide.com. Part of the prestigious Relais & Châteaux group, this gorgeous – but very expensive – establishment offers nineteen immaculately turned out rooms, in addition to a few apartments, finished in either maple or light grey wood panelling; the detail is wonderful, right down to the inlaid crystals in the light switches. Ask for a room overlooking the lush gardens. Breakfast €25. **€240**

### EATING

**Le Cloître** 2 rue des Cloîtres ☎ 04 74 31 93 57, Ⓦ le-cloitre.net. Nicely tucked in next to the Cathédrale St-Maurice, this unassuming but polished little restaurant serves some interesting variations on classic dishes such as duck foie gras with fig chutney and gingerbread, and iced soufflé with Chartreuse and dark chocolate sauce. *Menus* €17–37. Starters €11.50, mains €14. Mon–Fri noon–2pm & 7.30–9.30pm.

**L'Estancot** 4 rue de la Table Ronde ☎ 04 74 85 12 09. Sweet, family-run establishment next to the Église St-André-le-Bas, whose tightly packed ranks of tables make for an intimate venue; *criques* are the speciality here, delicious savoury potato pancakes served various ways (escalope of foie gras with port, Charolais beef with spinach), though they're not especially cheap (€26). *Menus* from €24. Tues–Sat noon–1.30pm & 7.30–9.30pm.

★ **La Pyramide** 14 bd Fernand-Point ☎ 04 74 53 01 96, Ⓦ lapyramide.com. *La Pyramide* was one of France's premier restaurants in the 1930s, when its then-owner, Fernand Point, garnered three Michelin stars. Today, under

### VIENNE JAZZ FESTIVAL

Vienne takes great pride in hosting Jazz à Vienne (Ⓦ jazzavienne.com), arguably the country's finest **international jazz festival**. Taking place from the end of June for two weeks, not only does it attract some very big names (Gregory Porter, Gilberto Gil, Angélique Kidjo), but most concerts are held in the fabulous surrounds of the Théâtre Antique. That said, you'll find events also occurring in restaurants and bars all over town – it's a great time to be here.

the stewardship of Patrick Henriroux and with two stars to its name, this magnificent establishment remains one of the hottest addresses around, and if you're willing to stump up, you can feast on the likes of red mullet with beef's heart in a tomato sauce and pistil saffron, and a warm Grand Marnier soufflé. The more informal, yet very classy, PH3 bistro won't make such a dent in the wallet, with a two-course lunchtime *formule* express for €23. In summer, meals are served out on the sublime garden terrace, with its neatly clipped hedges and colourful flowerbeds. *Menus* from €64. Starters €45, mains €65. Closed Feb. Thurs–Mon noon–2pm & 7.30–9.30pm. PH3 Daily same times.

# St-Étienne

**ST-ÉTIENNE**, 51km southwest of Lyon, was until recently a bland town. Almost entirely industrial, it is a major armaments manufacturer, enclosed for kilometres around by mineworkings, warehouses and factory chimneys. Like many other industrial centres, it fell on hard times, and the demolition gangs have moved in to raze its archaic industrial past. Only in the last decades has equilibrium been restored thanks to a concerted programme to revitalize the town, which includes a number of excellent museums. St-Étienne has also become an important design centre, as evidenced by the excellent **Biennale Internationale du Design de Saint-Étienne** in March/April of odd-numbered years.

## Musée d'Art Moderne et Contemporain

La Terrasse Wed–Mon 10am–6pm • €6, free every first Sun of the month • ☎ 04 77 79 52 52, ⓦ mam-st-etienne.fr

A justified detour for anyone with an interest in twentieth-century art, the **Musée d'Art Moderne et Contemporain** stands at the terminus of tram T2 from St-Étienne's central station. It is quite an unexpected treasure house of contemporary work, both pre- and post-World War II, with a good modern American section in which Andy Warhol and Frank Stella figure prominently, along with work by Rodin, Matisse, Léger and Ernst. There are many rooms filled entirely with French art, imaginatively laid out to exciting effect.

## Musée d'Art et d'Industrie

2 place Louis-Comte • Wed–Mon 10am–6pm • €6 • ☎ 04 77 49 73 00, ⓦ musee-art-industrie.saint-etienne.fr

The fine **Musée d'Art et d'Industrie** gives a real flavour of St-Étienne's strong industrial heritage, with space given over to three of the city's most prominent industries, namely bicycles, weaponry and textiles. The first of these documents the city's affinity with two wheels, from the manufacture of the first French bicycle here in 1886 through to the industry's development in a sporting context, not least of course the Tour de France; there are over 350 *vélocipèdes* on display. The exhibition on weaponry documents the gunsmithing industry in St-Étienne, alongside an impressive assemblage of arms and armour, while Textiles concentrates on the development of the revolutionary Jacquard loom alongside an exquisite collection of ribbons and silks.

## ARRIVAL AND INFORMATION

ST-ÉTIENNE

**By train** The main *gare* is at Châteaucreux in the business quarter, 10min away from the centre by tram. However there are four more stations in St-Étienne depending on the direction of the destinations. Take care to check which one you are leaving from/arriving at.

Destinations Lyon (3–4 hourly; 50min–1hr); Paris (10 daily; 2hr 45min–3hr 30min); Le Puy-en-Velay (1 hourly; 1hr 30min).

**Tourist office** 16 av de la Libération (Tues–Sat 10am–12.30pm & 2–6.30pm; mid-July to mid-Aug Tues–Fri 10am–6.30pm, Sat 10am–12.30pm & 2–6.30pm; ☎ 04 77 49 39 00, ⓦ saint-etiennetourisme.com); the office is around ten minutes' walk from Châteaucreux station along avenue Denfert-Rochereau.

**Bicycle rental** There are around twenty-five 24/7 rental points around town (pre-registration only; ☎ 09 69 32 42 00, ⓦ velivert.fr).

15

## ACCOMMODATION AND EATING

**Café Basque** 15 rue des Martyrs de Vingre ☏ 04 77 95 10 14. Atmospheric brick and stone-walled restaurant with smartly laid tables, though there is some pavement seating too; the food, chalked up on a board, is unpretentious and beautifully cooked, for example *ballotine* of veal, and filet mignon skewers. Starters €11, mains €16. Tues–Sat noon–2pm & 7.30–9.30pm.

**Inter-Hôtel Le Cheval Noir** 11 rue François-Gillet ☏ 04 77 33 41 72, ⓦ hotel-chevalnoir.fr. "The Black Horse"

hotel is a perfectly acceptable two-star establishment offering strikingly painted rooms (including a number of multi-bedded rooms) some of which have bath, some with shower. Breakfast €9. **€75**

**Terminus du Forez** 31 av Denfert-Rochereau ☏ 04 77 32 48 47, ⓦ hotel-terminusforez.com. Central, funky three-star *Logis* hotel with two different, if slightly bizarre, decors: Egyptian or Neoclassical. Free parking, good restaurant and, amazingly, breakfast available 24/7 for €9. **€77**

# South to Valence

15

Between Vienne and Valence are some of the oldest, most celebrated **vineyards** in France: the renowned Condrieu–Côte Rôtie, Hermitage and Crozes-Hermitage *appellations*. If you've got any spare luggage space, it's well worth stopping to pick up a bottle from the local co-op; even their *vin ordinaire* is superlative and unbelievably cheap, considering its quality. As you head south of Vienne, on the west bank, the first region is the **Côte Rôtie**, characterized by incredibly steep terraces which produce powerful, ruby-red wines cultivated from the Syrah grape, though occasionally mixed with Viognier. The welcoming Corps de Loups winery in Tupin et Semons offers excellent tours and tasting (daily 9am–noon & 2–6.30pm; ☏ 09 53 87 84 64, ⓦ corpsdeloup.com).

A little further south is the tiny area producing one of the most exquisite and oldest French white wines, Condrieu, and close by is one of the most exclusive – Château-Grillet – an *appellation* covering just this single château (☏ 04 74 59 51 56, ⓦ chateau-grillet.com).

Between **St-Vallier** and **Tain l'Hermitage**, the Rhône becomes more scenic, with the Alps looming into view soon after Tain. In spring you're more likely to be conscious of orchards everywhere rather than vines. Cherries, pears, apples, peaches and apricots, as well as bilberries and strawberries, are cultivated in abundance and sold at roadside stalls.

## Tain-l'Hermitage

**TAIN-L'HERMITAGE**, accessible from both the N7 and the A7, is unpretentious and uneventful, but if you have a weakness for wine or chocolate, you'll love this place. If your visit happens to fall on the last weekend in February you can try out wines from 78 vineyards in the Foire aux Vins des Côtes du Rhône Septentrionales, and on the third weekend of September, the different wine-producing villages celebrate their cellars in the **Fête des Vendanges**. But at any time of the year you can go bottle-hunting along the N86 for some 30km north of Tain along the right bank, following the *dégustation* signs and then crossing back over between Serrières and Chanas. Tain also boasts the oldest suspension bridge over the Rhône, on the opposite side of which is pretty **Tournon-Sur-Rhône**, which marks the border with the Ardeche region.

### Cave de Tain

22 rte de Larnage • **Tours** May–Sept daily 10.30am & 3.30pm; Oct–April Sat & Sun 10.30am & 3.30pm • €5.50 **Shop** July & Aug Mon–Sat 9am–7pm, Sun 10am–12.30pm & 2–6pm; rest of year Mon–Sat 9am–12.30pm & 2–6.30pm, Sun 10am–12.30pm & 2–6pm • ☏ 04 75 08 91 86, ⓦ cavedetain.com

There are cellars all over town where you can taste and buy wine but, for ease and expertise, head to the **Cave de Tain**, where they have all the wines of the distinguished Hermitage and Crozes-Hermitage *appellations* you'll ever need, and at ridiculously low prices too. If you don't make it for one of the **tours** – which includes sampling four wines – then pop into the shop, which has excellent English notes throughout, as well as a tasting area where you're welcome to sample any of the wines on display. From the *gare SNCF*, walk down avenue du Dr-Durand before turning left along rue du Noir and then rue Louis-Pinard – it's signposted from there.

## Valrhona Cité du Chocolat

12 av du Président-Roosevelt • Mon–Sat 9am–7pm, Sun 10am–6.30pm • €10.50 • ☎ 04 75 09 27 27, ⓦ valrhona.com and ⓦ citeduchocolat.com

As you go along the main RN7, beyond the junction with the RN95, the irresistible waft of cocoa signals the famous **Chocolaterie Valrhona**. Founded in 1922, Valrhona has become one of the world's leading chocolate manufacturers, and now exports to more than seventy countries worldwide; there's even a school for pastry chefs here. A chocoholics dream, the smell and taste sensation that is the **Cité du Chocolat** discovery centre takes visitors through each stage of the production process via a series of cleverly designed interactive activities, though naturally the best part is the tasting itself, of which there is plenty. Once done, pop into the shop, which offers further, limitless tasting possibilities, though it's inconceivable that you'll leave empty-handed.

### ARRIVAL AND INFORMATION

**By train** The train station is on av du Dr-Durand, from where it's a five-minute walk down to the main road, av Jean-Jaurès.
Destinations Lyon (hourly; 1hr 10min); Valence (hourly; 10min); Vienne (hourly; 40min).

### TAIN L'HERMITAGE

**Tourist office** Cross av Jean-Jaurès and it's next to the church at place du 8-mai-45 (daily 10am–noon & 2–6pm; ☎ 04 75 08 06 81, ⓦ ardeche-hermitage.com); they have an extensive list of vineyards.

### ACCOMMODATION AND EATING

**Les 2 Côteaux** 18 rue Joseph-Péala ☎ 04 75 08 33 01, ⓦ hotel-les-2-coteaux-26.com. Superbly located down by the suspension bridge, the cheerful "Two Hillsides" offers eighteen cool, sunlit rooms, though there's little by way of decor; it's well worth paying the €10 extra for one of the river-facing rooms. Breakfast €12. **€73**

**Le Pavillon de L'Ermitage** 69 av Jean-Jaurès ☎ 04 75 08 65 00, ⓦ pavillon-ermitage.com. The exterior and lobby are unlikely to elicit much enthusiasm, and it's a little overpriced, but the differently coloured rooms are decently sized, and come with extras like tea- and coffee making facilities; the main appeal, however, is the tidy outdoor pool. Breakfast €12. **€90**

**Le Quai** 17 rue Joseph-Péala ☎ 04 75 07 05 90. Opposite *Les 2 Côteaux*, hence with similarly lovely views of the Rhône from its breezy terrace, this upmarket but unstuffy restaurant serves delicious, inventive cuisine like pike dumplings with mushrooms and Nantua sauce; as you might expect here, the wine list is exceptional. Starters €15, mains €20. Daily noon–2.30pm & 7–10.30pm.

# Hauterives

**Palais Idéal** 8 rue du Palais • Daily: Jan & Dec 9.30am–4.30pm; Feb, March, Oct & Nov 9.30am–5.30pm; April–June & Sept 9am–6.30pm; July & Aug 9.30am–7pm • €7.50 • ☎ 04 75 68 81 19, ⓦ facteurcheval.com

**HAUTERIVES**, 25km northeast of Tain, is a small unspoilt village, save for one remarkable creation – the manic, surreal **Palais Idéal** built by a local postman by the name of Ferdinand Cheval (1836–1924). The house is truly bizarre, a bubbling frenzy reminiscent of the *modernista* architecture of Spain, with features that recall Thai or Indian temples. The eccentric building – conceived, apparently, when Cheval stumbled across an odd-looking stone on one of his daily rounds – took thirty-three years to carve; he also designed his equally bizarre tombstone nearby. Various Surrealists have paid homage to the building and psychoanalysts have given it much thought, but ultimately it defies all classification.

# Romans-sur-Isère

**Musée International de la Chaussure** 2 rue Ste-Marthe • Tues–Sat 10am–5pm, Sun 2.30–6pm • €5 • ☎ 04 75 05 51 81, ⓦ ville-romans.fr

Like Hauterives, **ROMANS-SUR-ISÈRE**, 27km further south and 15km east of the Rhône at Tain, is dominated by one thing; its shoemaking industry, which was to the fore here in the nineteenth century. Housed in the former Convent of the Visitation, the vast **Musée International de la Chaussure** traces the history of shoemaking and tanning throughout the ages, accompanied by a staggering 16,000 items of footwear from around the world. Your toes will curl in horror at the extent to which women have been immobilized by their footwear from ancient times to the present on every continent, while at the same time you can't help but admire the craziness of some of the creations. Among the highlights of the collection are some mummified feet from ancient Egypt, and a pair of boots as worn by Napoleon. If inspired to replenish your own shoe stock, drop in to the Charles Jourdan factory shop at 1 bd Voltaire or the large shopping outlet, Marques Avenue, along avenue Gambetta. You'll find, in any case, the pleasant old town is, inevitably, peppered with shoe shops.

| ARRIVAL AND INFORMATION | ROMANS-SUR-ISÈRE |
|---|---|
| **Train station** The train station (which is named Romans-Bourg de Péage, after its sister town across the river) is a 5min walk north of central place Charles-de-Gaulle on place Carnot. | **Tourist office** 62 bd Gambetta (Mon–Sat 9am–12.30pm & 1.30–6pm, also May–Sept Sun 9.30am–12.30pm; ☎ 04 75 02 28 72, ⊛ valence-romans-tourisme.com). |

### ACCOMMODATION

**L'Orée du Parc** 6 av Gambetta ☎ 04 75 70 26 12, ⊛ hotel-oreeparc.com. Housed in a 1920s mansion a short walk from town, this is about as restful an option as you could wish for; ten silky smooth rooms, some of which overlook a leafy garden complete with pool and terrace; bike rental too. Breakfast €13. **€94**

# Valence

At an indefinable point along the Rhône, there's an invisible sensual border, and by the time you reach **VALENCE**, you know you've crossed it. The quality of light is different and the temperature higher, bringing with it the scent of eucalyptus and pine, and the colours and contours suddenly seem worlds apart from the cold lands of Lyon and the north.

Valence is the obvious place to celebrate your arrival in the **Midi** (as the French call the south), a spruce town made up of tidy boulevards, large public areas and fresh-looking facades as well as a very pleasant old quarter. Although Valence is not particularly big on sights, the superb Musée de Valence does give the town a key cultural focus; gastronomy, meanwhile, has always been important here, and there are also many convivial bars in which to while away a few hours in the sun.

## Musée de Valence

4 place des Ormeaux • Tues 2–6pm, Wed–Sun 10am–6pm • €5 • ☎ 04 75 79 20 80, ⊛ museedevalence.fr

Occupying the greater part of the former Episcopal Palace, the **Musée de Valence** offers a comprehensive and beautifully presented collection of art and archeology from the Drôme and Rhône valley regions. The lower floors contain a voluminous collection of art work, though it's singularly notable for the work of one Hubert Robert, whose ten years in Rome depicting its antiquities – manifest here in a superb series of red chalk sketches – earned him the sobriquet, "Robert of the Ruins".

The archeological exhibition upstairs is rich in local finds, such as a notched cave bone from the Thaïs cave in Drôme, and fossilized remains from Montrebut, though these pale in comparison to two marvellous (albeit partially effaced) mosaics, discovered by renowned archeologist Michel Vignard in 1967 in a villa near Saint-Paul-Les-Romans: *Orpheus Charming the Animals* and *The Labours of Hercules*, the latter one of only eight such mosaics known to exist.

# Cathédrale St-Apollinaire

The focus of Vieux Valence, the **Cathédrale St-Apollinaire**, was consecrated in 1095 by Pope Urban II (who proclaimed the First Crusade), and was largely reconstructed in the seventeenth century. More work was carried out later, including the horribly mismatched nineteenth-century tower, but the interior still preserves its original Romanesque grace – especially the columns around the ambulatory.

# The côtes

Between the cathedral and **Église de St-Jean** at the northern end of Grande-Rue, which has preserved its Romanesque tower and porch capitals, are some of the oldest and narrowest streets of Vieux Valence. They are known as **côtes**: côte St-Estève just northwest of the cathedral; côte St-Martin off rue du Petit-Paradis; and côte Sylvante off rue du Petit-Paradis' continuation, rue Ambroise-Paré. Diverse characters who would have walked these steep and crooked streets include Rabelais, a student at the university founded here in 1452 and suppressed during the Revolution, and the teenage Napoleon Bonaparte, who began his military training as a cadet at the artillery school.

**15**

# Maison des Têtes and the Maison Dupré-Latour

Though Valence lacks the cohesion of the medieval towns and villages further south, it does have several vestiges of the sixteenth-century city, most notably the Renaissance **Maison des Têtes** at 57 Grande-Rue. Try to have a look at the ceiling in the passageway here (office hours only), where sculpted roses transform into the cherub-like heads after which the palace is named. Also worth a look is the **Maison Dupré-Latour**, on rue Pérollerie, which has a superbly sculptured porch and spiral staircase.

## ARRIVAL AND INFORMATION — VALENCE

**Train and bus stations** The *gare SNCF* and *gare routière* are just a 5min walk from the old town on rue Denis-Papin. Note that the TGV station (where Eurostar trains also stop) is 10km northeast of Valence, along the *autoroute* to Romans, though regional trains do stop here too. Regular shuttles (€1.20) and trains connect the *gare TGV* with the *gare SNCF*. Destinations (train) Gap Grenoble (frequent; 1hr–1hr 40min); Lyon (frequent; 1hr 10min); Montélimar (frequent; 30min); Tain-l'Hermitage (frequent; 10min); Vienne (frequent; 50min).

**Tourist office** 11 bd Bancel, the main thoroughfare (Mon–Sat 9am–12.30pm & 1.30–6pm, also May–Sept Sun 9.30am–12.30pm; ☎ 04 75 44 90 40, ⓦ valence-romans-tourisme.com).

## ACCOMMODATION

**De France** 16 bd du Général-de-Gaulle ☎ 04 75 43 00 87, ⓦ hotel-valence.com. Super-smart establishment on the main boulevard with fully soundproofed rooms decorated in tasteful palettes such as lime green and mauve, while the sumptuous beds certainly invite a good night's sleep. Little touches like proper coffee machines round things off nicely. In warmer weather, breakfast (€8 or €16) can be taken on the summery terrace. **€90**

**De Lyon** 23 av Pierre-Sémard ☎ 04 75 41 44 66, ⓦ hoteldelyon.com. A stock two-star bang opposite the train station, offering averagely sized rooms, decorated mostly in white to offset the brightly coloured bedspreads. There are also rooms for families and rooms with wheelchair-accessible bathrooms. Breakfast €8. **€66**

**Les Négociants** 27 av Pierre-Sémard ☎ 04 75 44 01 86, ⓦ hotelvalence.com. Cheaper and infinitely more appealing than *De Lyon* next door, this chic little hotel features softly lit, a/c rooms with minimalist, chocolate-brown-coloured furnishings and shuttered windows to help insulate from passing traffic. Breakfast €8.50. **€54**

## EATING AND DRINKING

**Chez Grand-Mère** 3 place de la Pierre ☎ 04 75 62 09 98. Set on a pretty, tree-shaded square, this homely, timber-framed restaurant – complete with retro junk – lets diners make up their own three-course *formule* from anything chalked up on the board for just €19.80. Local dishes feature highly, such as the baked tomato and basil *ravioles*. Starters €8, mains €15. Tues–Sat noon–2pm & 7–10pm.

**Daily Pic** 3 place Championnet ☎ 04 75 25 08 08. The bright and breezy concept of Anne-Sophie Pic (see page 806), this is a somewhat more affordable alternative, whereby you select your dishes from the chill cabinet (for example poached cod with orange vinaigrette for a main, and coffee and raspberry tiramisu for dessert) and take them to your table, paying when you've finished; dishes between €4–7, or choose the *menu du jour* for €14.90. Tues–Sat 9.30am–7.30pm, Sun & Mon 10am–6pm.

★ **L'Épicerie** 18 place Saint-Jean ☎ 04 75 42 74 46, ⓦ restaurant-valence-lepicerie.com. The pick of the town centre restaurants, comprising three contrasting but equally gorgeous dining areas. The long-time resident chef, Pierre Sève, is just as likely to take and deliver your order, which could include the likes of *grillotteés* salad with bacon and ravioli Dauphiné, chicken liver cake with tomato coulis, or iced nougat. *Menus* from €24. Starters €12, mains €22. Closed mid-July to mid-Aug. Mon–Fri noon–2pm & 7–10pm.

**Pic** 285 av Victor-Hugo ☎ 04 75 44 15 32, ⓦ anne-sophie-pic.com. Overseen by three Michelin-starred chef Anne-Sophie Pic (granddaughter of the restaurant's founder), this is not an experience you (or your wallet) will forget in a hurry. Technically brilliant, sumptuous food, such as roasted blue lobster smoked with red fruits and lavender, and white *mille feuille* with Tahitian vanilla cream, jasmine jelly and pepper emulsion. *Menus* €120–340. Tues–Sat noon–2pm & 7.30–9.30pm, Sun noon–2pm.

# 15 Montélimar

If you didn't know it before, you'll soon realize what makes the attractive town of **MONTÉLIMAR**, 40km south of Valence, tick: nougat. Shops and signs everywhere proclaim the glory of the stuff, which has been made here for centuries. The *vieille ville* is made up of narrow lanes that radiate out from the main street, **rue Pierre-Julien**, which runs from the one remaining medieval **gateway** on the nineteenth-century ring of boulevards at place St-Martin, south past the **church of Sainte-Croix**, and on to place Marx-Dormoy.

## Musée de la Miniature

19 rue Pierre-Julien • July & Aug daily 9.30am–noon & 2–6pm; Sept–Dec & mid-Feb to June Wed–Sun 2–6pm • €3 • ☎ 04 75 53 79 24

Located opposite the post office, the small but utterly charming **Musée de la Miniature** is the one attraction to visit if you're short of time. Viewed through microscopes, many of these delightful 1/12 scale miniatures are highly amusing, such as the violin-playing grasshopper, and a pair of mosquitoes playing chess; look out, too, for an exquisite model of Noah's Ark, made entirely from paper.

## Château des Adhémar

Plateau de Narbonne • July & Aug daily 10am–6pm; Sept–June daily 10am–12.30pm & 2–6pm • €6 • ☎ 04 75 00 62 30

High above the old town is the impressive **Château des Adhémar**, which originally belonged to the family after whom the town ("Mount of the Adhémars") was named. The castle is mostly fourteenth-century, but also boasts a fine eleventh-century chapel with some patchy frescoes, and twelfth-century living quarters, which are now used exclusively for contemporary art exhibitions. It's a stiff little walk up here, but there are lovely views from the ramparts.

## Fabrique et Musée d'Arnaud Soubeyran

Zone Commerciale Sud (RN7) • Mon–Sat 9am–7pm, Sun 10am–noon & 2.30–6.30pm • Free • ☎ 04 75 51 01 35, ⓦ nougatsoubeyran. com • Bus line 1 from outside the train station towards Soleil Levant; stop "A. Pontaimery"

If the sheer number of places offering nougat still hasn't sated your appetite, then pay a visit to the **Fabrique et Musée d'Arnaud Soubeyran**, where they've been churning out the stuff since 1837; now, they concoct eighty tonnes of the stuff each year – the essential ingredients being lavender honey and almonds from Provence, vanilla and pistachios. There's also a fun museum outlining the history of nougat, while the shop sells many flavours, including delicious orange and lavender, as well as a stack of other sweet tempters.

## ARRIVAL AND INFORMATION

**MONTÉLIMAR**

**By train** The *gare SNCF* is on the western side of town, from where it's a 5min walk through the gardens to the main boulevard.

**Tourist office** A 10min walk from the station on Montée Saint-Martin (Allées Provençales) (Mon–Sat 9.30am–12.30pm & 2–6pm, July & Aug 9.30am–6.30pm; ☎ 04 75 01 00 20, ⓦ montelimar-tourisme.com).

## ACCOMMODATION AND EATING

**La Petite France** 34 impasse Raymond-Daujat ☎ 04 75 46 07 94. Tucked away down a side street, this intimate little spot is a firm favourite among locals; some cracking *menus* from €22, which might feature the likes of foie gras with spiced apple chutney and ginger or roasted guinea fowl in fig sauce. Tues–Sat noon–1.30pm & 7–9pm.

**Sphinx** 19 bd Marre-Desmarais ☎ 04 75 01 86 64, ⓦ sphinx-hotel.fr. Initially, this place doesn't hold out much promise, but enter the courtyard and you'll discover a quite lovely seventeenth-century townhouse accommodating classically furnished, predominantly red, rooms with the snazziest of bathrooms and a host of neat little touches. The husband and wife owners couldn't be more helpful. Breakfast €9. **€85**

**15**

# Provence

**810** West Provence

**851** Central Provence

**858** Northeast Provence

FUN TIMES IN THE GORGES DU VERDON

# Provence

Arguably the most irresistible region of France, Provence ranges from the snowcapped mountains of the southern Alps to the delta plains of the Camargue, and boasts Europe's greatest canyon, the Gorges du Verdon. Fortified towns guard its ancient borders; villages perch defensively on hilltops; and great cities like Arles, Aix and Avignon are full of cultural glories. The sensual inducements of Provence include sunshine, food and wine, and the heady scent of Mediterranean vegetation. Small wonder it has for so long attracted the rich and famous, the artistic and reclusive, and throngs of summer visitors.

The Mediterranean shoreline of Provence is covered separately in Chapter 17. Away from the coastal resorts, **inland Provence** remains remarkably unscathed. Evidence of its many inhabitants – Greeks, Romans, raiding Saracens, schismatic popes, and an endless succession of competing counts and princes – remains everywhere apparent. Provence only became fully integrated into France in the nineteenth century and, though just a tiny minority speak the **Provençal** language, the accent is distinctive even to a foreign ear. In the east, the rhythms of speech become clearly Italian.

The main difficulty in visiting Provence lies in choosing where to go. In the west, along the **Rhône valley**, are the Roman cities of **Orange**, **Vaison-la-Romaine**, and **Arles**, and the papal city of **Avignon**, with its fantastic summer festival. **Aix-en-Provence**, the mini-Paris of the region, was home to Cézanne, for whom the **Mont Ste-Victoire** was an enduring subject, while Van Gogh is forever linked with **St-Rémy** and Arles. The **Gorges du Verdon**, the **Parc National du Mercantour** along the Italian border, **Mont Ventoux** northeast of Carpentras, and the flamingo-filled lagoons of the **Camargue** offer stunning and widely disparate landscapes.

**16**

---

**GETTING AROUND**                                                         **PROVENCE**

Much the fastest way to get to and around Provence is on the high-speed TGV trains, which stop at Orange, Avignon and Aix en route to Marseille or Nice. Note, however, that TGV stations tend to be a long way outside the towns they serve, and distinct from the *gares SNCF* used by local trains. A couple of lines that originate in Nice make great sightseeing routes into the mountains – the Train des Merveilles up to Tende (see page 862), and the narrow-gauge Chemins de Fer de Provence to Digne-les-Bains (see page 857). To explore the mountains and rural areas, however, there's no substitute for a car.

# West Provence

The richest area of Provence, the Côte d'Azur apart, is the **west**. Most of the large-scale production of fruit, vegetables and wine is based here, in the low-lying plains beside the Rhône and the Durance rivers. The only heights are the rocky outbreaks of the Dentelles and the Alpilles, and the narrow east–west ridges of Mont Ventoux, the Luberon and Mont Ste-Victoire. The two dominant cities of inland Provence, **Avignon** and **Aix**, both have rich histories and stage lively festivals; Arles, Orange and Vaison-la-Romaine hold impressive Roman remains. Around the Rhône delta, the **Camargue** is a unique self-contained enclave.

## Orange

Thanks to its spectacular **Roman theatre**, the small town of **ORANGE**, west of the Rhône and 20km north of Avignon, is famous out of all proportion to its size. Founded

# Highlights

**❶ Avignon** The former city of the popes complements its monuments and museums by staging a dynamic annual theatre festival. See page 819

**❷ Medieval hilltop villages** Les Baux and Gordes are the most famous, but many others are equally picturesque, and much less frequented. See pages 831 and 846

**❸ Arles** With its impressive Roman remains, delightful ancient core, and intimate association with Van Gogh, Arles is an under-appreciated jewel. See page 832

**❹ La Camargue** The marshland of the Rhône delta is home to white horses, flamingos and unearthly landscapes. See page 839

**❺ Aix-en-Provence** This beautiful city is a wonderful place for café idling, and hosts the region's most vibrant markets. See page 847

**❻ Les Gorges du Verdon** The largest canyon in Europe, with stunning views and a full range of hikes. See page 854

**❼ Haute-Provence** The Parc National du Mercantour and the Vallée des Merveilles are Alpine glories off the beaten path. See page 857

**HIGHLIGHTS ARE MARKED ON THE MAP ON PAGE 812**

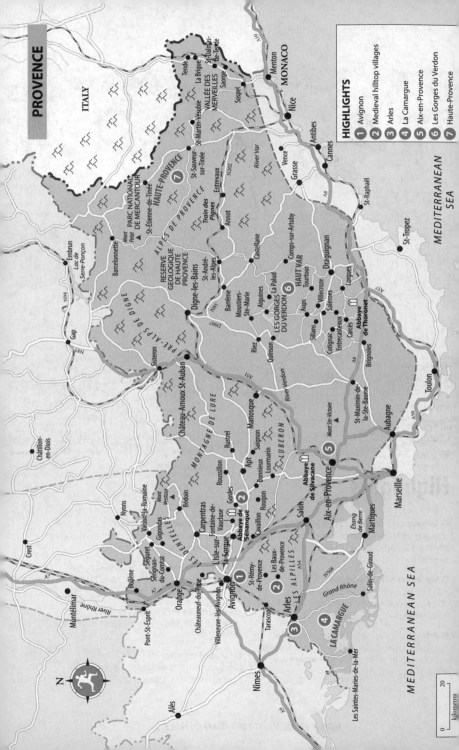

# PROVENCE

ITALY

MONACO

MEDITERRANEAN SEA

MEDITERRANEAN SEA

N

**HIGHLIGHTS**

1 Avignon
2 Medieval hilltop villages
3 Arles
4 La Camargue
5 Aix-en-Provence
6 Les Gorges du Verdon
7 Haute-Provence

**HAUTE-PROVENCE**

PARC NATIONAL DE MERCANTOUR

VALLÉE DES MERVEILLES

RÉSERVE GÉOLOGIQUE DE HAUTE PROVENCE

ALPES DE PROVENCE

PRÉ-ALPES DE DIGNE

Train des Pignes

LES GORGES DU VERDON

HAUT VAR

MONTAGNE DE LURE

MONTAGNE DE LURE

LUBERON

LES DENTELLES

LES ALPILLES

LA CAMARGUE

Menton
Nice
Antibes
Cannes
St-Raphaël
St-Tropez
Toulon
Marseille
Martigues
Aubagne
Draguignan
Lorgues
Brignoles
Abbaye de Thoronet
St-Maximin-de-la-Ste-Baume
Mont Ste-Victoire
Aix-en-Provence
Salon
Grasse
Vence
St-Sauveur-sur-Tinée
St-Martin-Vésubie
La Brigue
Tende
St-Dalmas-de-Tende
Saorge
Sospel
Entrevaux
Annot
Castellane
Comps-sur-Artuby
Tourtour
Villecroze
Salernes
Sillans
Cotignac
Entrecasteaux
Carcès
St-André-les-Alpes
Moustiers-Ste-Marie
Aiguines
La Palud
Alps
Barrême
Riez
Quinson
River Verdon
Digne-les-Bains
St-Etienne-de-Tinée
Barcelonnette
Mont Pelat
Embrun
Lac de Serre-Ponçon
Gap
Sisteron
Château-Arnoux St-Auban
Manosque
Rustrel
Roussillon
Apt
Saignon
Bonnieux
Lourmarin
Abbaye de Silvacane
Rougon
Cavaillon
Gordes
Abbaye de Sénanque
Fontaine-de-Vaucluse
L'Isle-sur-la-Sorgue
Carpentras
Bédoin
Mont Ventoux
Vaison-la-Romaine
Gigondas
Séguret
Sérignan-du-Comtat
Orange
Châteauneuf-du-Pape
Villeneuve-lès-Avignon
Avignon
St-Rémy-de-Provence
Les Baux-de-Provence
Tarascon
Arles
Nîmes
Alès
Les Saintes-Maries-de-la-Mer
Salin-de-Giraud
Grand Rhône
Étang de Berre
Martigues
Crest
Nyons
Bollène
Pont-St-Esprit
Montélimar
Châtillon-en-Diois
River Rhône

0 — 20
kilometres

## PROVENÇAL FOOD AND DRINK

The appetizing cuisine of Provence bursts with Mediterranean influences. **Olives** are a defining ingredient, whether in sauces and salads, tarts and pizzas; mixed with capers in tapenade; or simply accompanying the traditional Provençal aperitif of *pastis*. Another Provençal classic, **garlic**, is used in *pistou*, a paste of olive oil, garlic and basil, and *aïoli*, the name for both a garlic mayonnaise and the dish in which it's served with salt cod.

Vegetables – tomatoes, capsicum, aubergines, courgettes and onions – are often made into **ratatouille**, while **courgette flowers**, stuffed with *pistou* or tomato sauce (*fleurs de courgettes farcies*), are an exquisite delicacy.

Sheep, taken up to the mountains in summer, provide the staple **meat**; you'll find the finest, *agneau de Sisteron*, roasted with Provençal herbs as *gigot d'agneau aux herbes*. **Fish** too is prominent on traditional menus, with freshwater trout, salt cod, anchovies, sea bream, monkfish, sea bass and whiting all ubiquitous, along with wonderful seafood such as clams, periwinkles, sea urchins and oysters.

**Sweets** include almond *calissons* from Aix and candied fruit from Apt, while the **fruit** – melons, white peaches, apricots, figs, cherries and Muscat grapes – is unbeatable. **Cheeses**, such as Banon, wrapped in chestnut leaves and marinated in brandy, and the aromatic Picadon, from the foothills of the Alps, are invariably made from goat's or ewe's milk.

The best **wines** come from around the Dentelles, notably Gigondas, and from Châteauneuf-du-Pape. To the east are the light, drinkable, but not particularly special wines of the Côtes du Ventoux and the Côtes du Luberon *appellations*. With the exception of the Côteaux des Baux around Les Baux, and the Côtes de Provence in the Var, the best wines of southern Provence come from along the coast.

**16**

as Aurisio in 35 BC, it became associated with both fruit and colour in the eighth century, when Charlemagne made it the seat of the counts of Orange, a title that passed to the Dutch crown in the sixteenth century.

The Roman theatre is the one must-see attraction. Otherwise, with its medieval street plan, fountained squares, ancient porticoes and courtyards, and Thursday-morning market, Orange is attractive to stroll around, and makes a quiet base for exploring the region.

## Théâtre Antique

Daily: March & Oct 9.30am–5.30pm; April, May & Sept 9am–6pm; June–Aug 9am–7pm, closing early on event days; Nov–Feb 9.30am–4.30pm • €9.50 including Musée d'Art et d'Histoire; €8.50 for last hour of each day • ☎ 04 90 50 17 60, ⌨ theatre-antique.com

The enormous wall of the **Théâtre Antique** dominates Orange's medieval centre. Said to be the world's best-preserved Roman theatre, it's the only one with its stage wall still standing. Later a fort, slum and prison before its reconstruction in the nineteenth century, the Théâtre now hosts musical performances in summer and is also open as an archeological site.

Spreading a colossal 36m high by 103m wide, its outer face resembles a monstrous prison wall, despite the ground-level archways leading into the backstage areas. The **stage**, originally sheltered by a mighty awning, could accommodate throngs of performers, while the acoustics allowed a full audience to hear every word.

Though missing most of its original decoration – which you can see reproduced using the new virtual-reality headsets – the inner side of the wall above the stage is extremely impressive. Below columned niches, empty of their statues, a larger-than-life representation of Augustus looks down centre stage. Seating was allocated strictly by rank; an inscription "EQ Gradus III" (third row for knights) remains visible near the orchestra pit.

The best **viewpoint** over the entire theatre, on St-Eutrope hill, can be accessed free of charge from both east and west. As you look down towards the stage, the ruins at your feet are those of the short-lived seventeenth-century castle of the princes of Orange. Louis XIV had it destroyed in 1673, and the principality of Orange was officially annexed to France forty years later.

## Musée d'Art et d'Histoire

Rue Madeleine-Roch • Daily: March & Oct 9.45am–12.30pm & 1.30–5.30pm; April, May & Sept 9.15am–6pm; June–Aug 9.15am–7pm; Nov–Feb 9.45am–12.30pm & 1.30–4.30pm • €5.50, or €9.50 with Théâtre • ☎ 04 90 50 17 60, ⊛ theatre-antique.com

The **Musée d'Art et d'Histoire**, across from the Théâtre, covers local history from the Romans onwards, and also hosts temporary exhibitions. Artefacts taken from the Théâtre complex include the largest known Roman land-survey maps, carved on marble, along with a couple of sphinxes and a mosaic floor.

## ARRIVAL AND INFORMATION                                    ORANGE

**By train** The *gare SNCF* is on av Frédéric-Mistral, 800m east of the centre.
Destinations Avignon (20 daily; 20min); Paris (2 daily; 3hr 30min).

**By bus** The *gare routière* is on bd Édouard-Daladier, 250m east of the theatre.
Destinations Avignon (21 daily; 50min); Carpentras (3 daily; 40–45min); Châteauneuf-du-Pape (3 daily; 25min);

Vaison-la-Romaine (10 daily; 1hr).

**By car** Parking is very limited in the city centre; for short stays, park along cours Aristide-Briand, or overnight in the underground car park east of the theatre near the bus station.

**Tourist office** 5 cours Aristide-Briand (July & Aug Mon–Sat 9am–6pm, Sun 9am–12.30pm; Sept–June Mon–Sat 9am–12.30pm & 2–6pm; ☎ 04 90 34 70 88, ⊛ otorange.fr).

## ACCOMMODATION

**Arène** 8 place de Langes ☎ 04 90 11 40 40, ⊛ hotel-arene.fr. Very presentable hotel, spreading through five buildings on a quiet, pedestrianized – if not especially attractive – square, with spacious rooms, two pools and a Provençal restaurant. **€130**

**Glacier** 46 cours Aristide-Briand ☎ 04 90 34 02 01, ⊛ le-glacier.com. Comfortable, cosy Provençal-style rooms in yellows and blues with pretty quilts and floral curtains. All en-suite and a/c, they vary widely in size and amenities;

the smallest are tiny. Good breakfasts in the pavement café downstairs. Nov–Feb closed Fri–Sun. **€95**

**L'Herbier** 8 place aux Herbes ☎ 04 90 34 09 23, ⊛ lherbierdorange.com. A good budget option, set in a seventeenth-century house overlooking a pretty square near the Théâtre Antique. Rooms are simple and clean, and include some good-value family options; all have at least showers. **€68**

**St-Florent** 4 rue du Mazeau ☎ 04 90 34 18 53, ⊛ hotel-

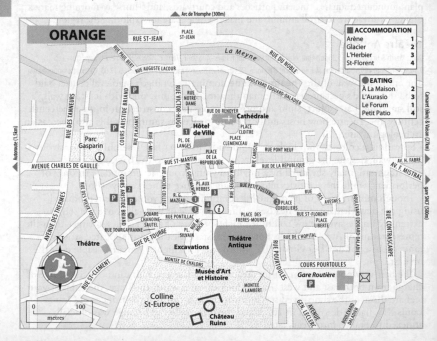

orange-saintflorent.com. Central, inexpensive hotel, with appealingly kitsch decor and a wide range of rooms; some have four-poster beds, all are en-suite, and there are some cheaper singles. **€61**

### EATING AND DRINKING

**À La Maison** 4 place des Cordeliers ☎04 90 60 98 83. Friendly café-restaurant that spills out onto a little square facing the Théâtre, with tables circling a fountain. There's a daily *plat du jour* for €10.50 and a three-course lunch *formule* for €16; the €27.50 dinner *menu* includes a delicious *velouté* of *petits pois*, followed by cod *aïoli*. Tues–Sat noon–1.30pm & 7.30–9.30pm, Sun 10am–4pm.

**L'Aurasio** 9 rue du Mazeau ☎04 32 81 13 19, ⓦlarausio. eatbu.com. This delightful little family-run restaurant, with outdoor seating facing the Théâtre, has quickly established itself at the forefront of the local dining scene. The lunch *formule* costs €19.50, the one dinner menu is €29.50, featuring French meat and fish classics prepared and presented with modern flair. Thurs–Sun noon–1.15pm & 7–9pm.

**Le Forum** 3 rue du Mazeau ☎04 90 34 01 09, ⓦrestaurant-leforum-orange.fr. Small, intimate restaurant near the Théâtre. The changing €29 *menu* revolves around seasonal ingredients; in January, truffles feature heavily, while in May, it's asparagus. Reserve ahead. Daily except Tues noon–1.30pm & 7–10pm.

**Petit Patio** 58 cours Aristide-Briand ☎04 90 29 69 27. Provençal restaurant, in a pleasant garden courtyard not far west of the Théâtre. At lunchtime, €19 buys two courses plus wine and coffee; dinner *menus* cost €29 or €39, and abound in zestful local produce. Mon, Tues, Fri & Sat noon–1.15pm & 7.30–9.30pm, Wed & Thurs noon–1.15pm.

**16**

# Châteauneuf-du-Pape

The large village of **CHÂTEAUNEUF-DU-PAPE**, between Avignon and Orange, takes its name from the summer palace of the Avignon popes. Its rich ruby-red **wine** ranks among the most renowned in France. Commercial activity centres on the main road that loops around Châteauneuf's small central hill. Walk up from the busy little **place du Portail**, and you're swiftly in a tangle of sleepy, verdant alleyways. A couple of intact castle walls still crown the top of the hill, but they simply define a hollow shell, freely accessible at all times.

## Musée du Vin Brotte

Rd Pierre-de-Luxembourg • Daily: mid-April to May & mid-Sept to mid-Oct 9am–1pm & 2–7pm; June to mid-Sept 9am–7pm; mid-Oct to mid-April 9am–noon & 2–6pm • Free • ☎04 90 83 59 44, ⓦwww.brotte.com

The best place to learn about local wines is the **Musée du Vin Brotte**, southwest of the centre. As well as providing a good historical overview of the wine industry, covering regional geology, it illustrates traditional tools and techniques, offers free tasting, and sells the Brotte family's own wine.

## INFORMATION

**Tourist office** 3 rue de la République (June–Sept Mon–Sat 9.30am–6pm; Oct–May Mon, Tues & Thurs–Sat 9.30am–12.30pm & 2–6pm; ☎ 04 90 83 71 08, ⓦ ccpro. fr/tourisme).

## ACCOMMODATION AND EATING

**Garbure** 3 rue Joseph-Ducos ☎ 04 90 83 75 08, ⓦ la-garbure.com. Cosy, very central village hotel, with eight cheerful rooms and a decent restaurant, with dinner *menus* from €30 and terrace seating across the street. Garage parking for €10. Restaurant closed Sun in low season, hotel closed 2 weeks in Nov. **€90**

**Le Verger des Papes** 4 montée du Château ☎ 04 90 83 50 40, ⓦ vergerdespapes.com. This utterly delightful

### CHÂTEAUNEUF-DU-PAPE

restaurant, well away from the traffic near the château at the top of the hill, serves traditional food on a peaceful panoramic terrace with *menus* at €22 for lunch, €33 for dinner. July & Aug Mon–Sat noon–2pm & 7.30–9.30pm, Sun noon–2pm; March–June & Sept to late Dec Tues, Wed & Sun noon–2pm, Thurs–Sat noon–2pm & 7.30–9.30pm.

# Vaison-la-Romaine

The charming old town of **VAISON-LA-ROMAINE**, 27km northeast of Orange, is divided into two distinct halves, connected by a single-arched Roman bridge across the River Ouvèze. Throughout its history, Vaison's centre has shifted from one side to the other. Now known as the **Haute Ville**, and topped by a ruined twelfth-century castle, the steep, forbidding hill south of the river was the site of the original Celtic settlement. The **Romans**, however, built their homes on the flatter land north of the river. That's now the modern town centre, so the medieval *haute ville* remains a self-contained and largely unspoiled village.

## Roman ruins

Av du Général-de-Gaulle • Daily: 2nd half of Feb, Nov & Dec 10am–noon & 2–5pm; March & Oct 10am–noon & 2–5.30pm; April & May 9.30am–6pm; June–Sept 9.30am–6.30pm; closed early Jan to mid-Feb • €9 with cathedral cloisters • ☎ 04 90 36 50 48

Vaison's two excavated **Roman residential districts** lie either side of the main road through the town centre. While you can peek through the railings for free, you'll get a much better sense if you pay for admission, which also enables you to visit the excellent museum.

### Vestiges de Puymin

Vaison's eastern cluster of Roman remains, the **Vestiges de Puymin**, stretches up a gentle hillside. The ground plans of several mansions and houses are discernible in the foreground, while higher up the **museum** holds ornamental items unearthed from the ruins. Everyday artefacts include mirrors of silvered bronze, lead water pipes, weights and measures, taps shaped as griffins' feet and dolphin doorknobs, and there are some impressive statues and stelae. A tunnel through the hillside leads to an ancient **theatre**, which seats seven thousand people during the July **dance festival** (ⓦ vaison-danses.com).

### Vestiges de la Villasse

Vaison's smaller, western Roman ruins, the **Vestiges de la Villasse**, reveal a clear picture of the layout of a comfortable, well-serviced Roman town. As well as a row of arcaded shops, they include patrician houses (some with mosaics still intact), a basilica and the baths.

## Haute Ville

From the south side of the **Pont Romain**, the sturdy ancient bridge across the River Ouvèze, a cobbled lane climbs upwards towards place du Poids and the fourteenth-century gateway to the medieval **haute ville**. More steep zigzags take you past the Gothic gate and overhanging portcullis and into the heart of this sedate, largely uncommercialized *quartier*. All the squares hold pretty fountains and flowers, and right at the top, from the twelfth- to sixteenth-century **castle**, you'll have a great view of Mont Ventoux. Every Tuesday in summer, Vaison's **market** spreads up into the *haute ville*.

### ARRIVAL AND INFORMATION

### VAISON-LA-ROMAINE

**By bus** The *gare routière* is on av des Choralies, east of the centre.

Destinations Avignon (3 daily; 1hr 25min); Orange (10 daily; 1hr).

**Tourist office** Place du Chanoine-Sautel, between the two Roman sites (April–May & Sept Mon–Sat 9.30am–noon

& 2–5.45pm, Sun 9.30am–noon; June Mon–Fri 9.30am–1pm & 2–5.45pm, Sat 9.30am–noon & 2–5.45pm, Sun 9.30am–noon; July & Aug Mon–Fri 9.30am–6.45pm, Sat & Sun 9.30am–12.30pm & 2–6.45pm; Oct–March Mon–Sat 9.30am–noon & 2–5.45pm; ☎ 04 90 36 02 11, ⓦ vaison-ventoux-tourisme.com).

### ACCOMMODATION

★ **Le Beffroi** 2 rue de l'Évêché ☎ 04 90 36 04 71, ⓦ le-beffroi.com. Beautiful, luxurious rooms in a sixteenth-century residence in a lovely *haute ville* setting, with a pool, and a great restaurant enjoying views over the valley. Hotel closed late Jan to late March, and mid-Nov to early Dec; restaurant closed Tues, and Nov–Easter. **€120**

**Burrhus** 1 place Montfort ☎ 04 90 36 00 11, ⓦ burrhus. com. Modern, freshly styled bedrooms in the heart of town, with tiled floors and very comfortable beds. The cheapest rooms are very small, and the square gets noisy at weekends, but the sunny breakfast balcony is a real plus, and they offer free garage parking. **€69**

★ **L'Évêché** 14 rue de l'Évêché ☎ 06 03 03 21 42, ⓦ eveche.free.fr. Lovely B&B in the *haute ville*, with five comfortable modern rooms and a homely atmosphere. Enjoy coffee and croissants on the little terrace at the back. **€89**

**La Fête en Provence** Place du Vieux-Marché ☎ 04 90 36 36 43, ⓦ hotellafete-provence.com. Gorgeous, comfortable, contemporary rooms, studios and duplex apartments, surrounding a pool and flower-decked patio, in the *haute ville*. There's also a romantic restaurant (closed Wed). **€80**

### EATING AND DRINKING

**L'Auberge de la Bartavelle** 12 place Sus-Auze ☎ 04 90 36 02 16, ⓦ restaurant-bartavelle.fr. A lively place, serving decent and affordable specialities from southwest France – rabbit ravioli, *confit de canard* and the like – on *menus* costing from €16.50 for lunch, €23 at dinner. Tues–Thurs & Sat 12.15–1.30pm & 7.15–9.30pm, Fri 7.15–9.30pm, Sun 12.15–1.30p; closed Jan.

**La Lyriste** 45 cours Taulignan ☎ 04 90 36 04 67. Of several restaurants along this quiet boulevard, the *Lyriste* stands out for its changing, high-quality *menus*, based around themes like cheese, exotic fruits or scallops. The

*plat du jour* costs €11.50, and there's a simple but great value €23.50 *menu découverte* in the evening. Tues, Thurs & Fri noon–1.30pm & 7.15–9.30pm, Wed & Sun noon–1.30pm, Sat 7.15–9.30pm.

**O' Natur'Elles** 36 place Montfort ☎ 04 90 65 81 67. Organic bistro on the main square, specializing in succulent savoury platters of local delicacies like *pissaladière*. At €15–20, they're not particularly cheap, but they're ideal for vegetarians. Meat and fish mains also available, for around €20. Mon & Wed–Sun noon–1.30pm & 7.30–9.30pm, Tues noon–1.30pm.

## Mont Ventoux

**MONT VENTOUX**, whose outline repeatedly appears upon the horizon from the Rhône and Durance valleys, rises some 20km east of Vaison. White with snow, black with storm-cloud shadow or reflecting myriad shades of blue, the barren pebbles of the uppermost 300m are like a weathervane for all of western Provence. Winds can accelerate to 250km per hour around the meteorological, TV and military masts and dishes on the summit, but if you can stand still for a moment the view in all directions is unbelievable.

Long renowned as among the most fearsome challenges on the Tour de France, the climb up Mont Ventoux is attempted by hundreds of **cyclists** each day in summer. Most start at one of two small towns low on its western flanks – **Malaucène**, on the D938 10km southeast of Vaison, or livelier **Bédoin,** another dozen kilometres southeast. The D974 loops between the two via the summit of Mont Ventoux, a total haul of 42km; the anticlockwise circuit from Bédoin offers a marginally gentler

16

gradient. Coming this way, you reach a stone cairn 1km short of the very top, well above the tree line, that commemorates British cyclist **Tom Simpson**, who died here in 1967 from heart failure on one of the hottest days ever recorded in the Tour de France. According to race folklore his last words were "Put me back on the bloody bike."

## Dentelles de Montmirail

Running northeast to southwest between Vaison and Carpentras, the jagged hilly backdrop of the **DENTELLES DE MONTMIRAIL** is best appreciated from the contrasting landscape of level fields, orchards and vineyards lying to their south and west. The range is named after lace (*dentelles*) – the limestone protrusions were thought to resemble the contorted pins on a lacemaking board – though the alternative connection with teeth (*dents*) is equally appropriate.

The area is best known for its wines. On the western and southern slopes lie the wine-producing villages of **Gigondas**, **Séguret**, **Beaumes-de-Venise**, **Sablet**, **Vacqueyras** and, across the River Ouvèze, **Rasteau**. Each carries the distinction of having its own individual *appellation contrôlée* within the Côtes du Rhône or Côtes du Rhône Villages areas: in other words, their wines are exceptional.

### Séguret

The star Dentelles village is **SÉGURET**, whose name means "safe place" in Provençal. This alluring spot, 9km southwest of Vaison-la-Romaine, blends into the side of a rocky cliff; a ruined castle soars high above. Amid its steep cobbled streets, vine-covered houses and medieval structures, look out for an old stone laundry and a belfry with a one-handed clock.

### Gigondas

**GIGONDAS**, 14km southwest of Séguret, is a worthwhile stop, its main draw being its exquisite **red wine**, which is strong, with an aftertaste of spice and nuts. Sampling the varieties could not be easier; the **Syndicat des Vins** runs a *caveau des vignerons* (daily 10am–noon & 2–6pm) in place de la Mairie where you can taste and ask advice about the produce from forty different *domaines*.

| INFORMATION | DENTELLES DE MONTMIRAIL |
|---|---|

**GIGONDAS**
**Tourist office** Rue du Portail (April–June, Sept & Oct Mon–Sat 9.30am–12.30pm & 2.30–6pm; July & Aug Mon– Sat 9.30am–12.30pm & 2.30–6.30pm, Sun 9.30am–1pm; Nov–March Mon–Sat 10am–noon & 2–5pm; ☎ 04 90 65 85 46, ⊕ www.gigondas-dm.fr).

## ACCOMMODATION AND EATING

**SÉGURET**
★ **Bastide Bleue** Rte de Sablet ☎ 04 90 46 83 43, ⊕ bastidebleue.com. This delightful rural villa, at the foot of the hill below Séguret, offers simple but attractive en-suite rooms, plus a pool. Its rustic dining room, closed Tues & Wed in low season, serves good *menus* from €29 in the evening. **€81.50**

**GIGONDAS**
★ **Les Florets** Rte des Dentelles ☎ 04 90 65 85 01, ⊕ hotel-lesflorets.com. Charming hotel, 2km north of Gigondas towards Séguret, with elegant and very comfortable rooms and an excellent restaurant (closed Wed) that serves *menus* from €25 lunch, €28 dinner. Closed Jan to mid-March. **€120**

**Gîte d'Étape des Dentelles** Le village ☎ 04 90 65 80 85, ⊕ gite-dentelles.com. This simple, inexpensive *gîte*, at the entrance to the village, offers two large shared dorms, ten very plain double rooms, and one triple, none of them en suite. Closed Jan & Feb. Dorms **€18**, doubles **€40**

**L'Oustalet** Place du Village ☎ 04 90 65 85 30, ⊕ restaurant-oustalet.fr. Thanks to a dynamic chef, this modern restaurant, with seating indoors and out on a pleasant shaded terrace, offers the best dining in the village centre. Full dinner *menus* start at €38. They also offer three contemporary styled rooms, from €160 per night. Tues–Sat noon–2pm & 7–9pm; also Sun noon–2pm in summer.

16

# Carpentras

The faded provincial town of **CARPENTRAS** dates back to 5 BC, when it was the capital of a Celtic tribe. The Greeks who founded Marseille came to Carpentras to buy honey, wheat, goats and skins, and the Romans had a base here. For a brief period in the fourteenth century, it became the papal headquarters and gave protection to Jews expelled from France.

In Carpentras today, immaculately restored squares and fountains alternate with decayed streets of seventeenth- and eighteenth-century houses, some forming arcades over the pavement.

## Synagogue de Carpentras and around

Place de la Juiverie • Mon–Thurs 10am–noon & 3–5pm, Fri 10am–noon & 3–4pm; closed Jewish holidays • Free • ☎ 04 90 63 39 97, ⓦ synagoguedecarpentras.fr

A seventeenth-century construction on fourteenth-century foundations, the **Synagogue de Carpentras** is the oldest surviving place of Jewish worship in France. The **porte de la Juiverie**, on the southern side of the fifteenth-century **Cathédrale St-Siffrein** nearby, is so named because Jews used to pass through it to enter the cathedral in chains. Inside, they would be unshackled as converted Christians.

## ARRIVAL AND INFORMATION                                    CARPENTRAS

**By train** Carpentras' *gare SNCF* is 400m southwest of the centre.
Destinations Avignon (half-hourly; 40min); Vaison-la-Romaine (6 daily; 1hr).
**By bus** Buses arrive either at the *gare routière* on place Terradou (from Avignon, Vaison, and other points north and west), or on av Victor-Hugo (from Marseille, Aix and Cavaillon).
Destinations Avignon (frequent; 35–45min); Cavaillon

(2–5 daily; 45min); Gigondas (1–3 daily; 30min); L'Isle-sur-la-Sorgue (5 daily; 20min); Marseille (3 daily; 1hr 15min–2hr 5min); Orange (3 daily; 40–45min); Vaison (4 daily; 45min).
**Tourist office** 374 av Jean-Jaurès (July & Aug Mon–Sat 9am–1pm & 2–7pm, Sun 9.30am–1pm; Sept–June Mon & Wed–Sat 9.30am–12.30pm & 2–6pm, Tues 9.30am–12.30pm & 3–6pm; ☎ 04 90 63 00 78, ⓦ ventouxprovence.fr).

16

## ACCOMMODATION

**Comtadin** 65 bd Albin-Durand ☎ 04 90 67 75 00, ⓦ le-comtadin.com. Nicely restored traditional hotel, on the peripheral boulevard a short walk from the town centre. Light, double-glazed rooms and a sunny breakfast patio. **€110**
**Fiacre** 153 rue Vigne ☎ 04 90 63 03 15, ⓦ hotel-du-fiacre.com. Grand eighteenth-century townhouse, with a central courtyard and nicely decorated rooms, two with

terraces and two with balconies. The friendly owners can help plan walking and cycling tours. **€80**
**Lou Comtadou** Rte St-Didier, 881 av Pierre-de-Coubertin ☎ 04 90 67 03 16, ⓦ campingloucomtadou.com. Very pleasant, well-equipped three-star campsite, in shaded rural surroundings 1km south of the centre. Closed Oct to mid-March. **€25**

## EATING AND DRINKING

**Chez Serge** 90 rue Cottier ☎ 04 90 63 21 24, ⓦ chez-serge.com. Welcoming bistro in an old mansion, serving changing daily *plats* in the courtyard beneath the shade of a huge tree. The great-value lunch *menu* is €19, dinner *menus* start at €32, with a major emphasis on truffles in season; there's also a wide selection of €12 pizzas. Daily: June–Sept noon–2pm & 7.30–10pm, Oct–May noon–1.30pm

& 7.30–9.30pm.
**Pâtisserie Jouvaud** 40 rue de l'Évêché ☎ 04 90 63 15 38, ⓦ patisserie-jouvaud.com. This cosy tearoom and patisserie, which also has three tables on the pedestrian street outside, makes a fabulous stop-off for tea and cakes. Daily 9am–7.30pm.

# Avignon

Capital of the Catholic Church during the early Middle Ages and for centuries a major artistic centre, **AVIGNON** remains an unmissable destination. During the **Festival d'Avignon** in July, it becomes *the* place to be in Provence.

Low medieval **walls** still encircle Avignon's old centre, as it nestles up against a ninety-degree bend in the Rhône river. Their gates and towers restored, the ramparts

**POPES AND ANTIPOPES – THE INTRIGUING HISTORY OF AVIGNON**

The first **pope** to come to Avignon, **Clement V**, was invited by the astute King Philippe le Bel in 1309, ostensibly to protect him from impending anarchy in Rome. In reality, Philip saw a chance to extend his power by keeping the pope in Provence, during what came to be known as the Church's "Babylonian captivity". Clement's successor, **Jean XXII**, who had previously been bishop of Avignon, re-installed himself happily in the episcopal palace. The next Supreme Pontiff, **Benedict XII**, acceded in 1334; accepting the impossibility of returning to Rome, he replaced the bishop's palace with an austere fortress, now known as the **Vieux Palais**.

Though Gregory XI finally moved the Holy See back to Rome in 1378, that didn't mark the end of the papacy here. After Gregory's death in Rome, dissident local cardinals elected their own pope in Avignon, provoking the Western Schism, a ruthless struggle for control of the Church's wealth. That lasted until **Benedict XIII** – now officially deemed to have been an **antipope** – fled into self-exile near Valencia in 1409. It was Benedict who built Avignon's walls in 1403, when under siege by French forces loyal to Rome. Avignon itself remained papal property until the Revolution.

As home to one of Europe's richest courts, fourteenth-century Avignon attracted princes, dignitaries, poets and raiders, who arrived to beg from, rob, extort and entertain the popes. According to Petrarch, the overcrowded, plague-ridden papal entourage was "a sewer where all the filth of the universe has gathered".

**16**

dramatically mark the historic core off from the formless sprawl of the modern city beyond. Despite their menacing crenellations, however, they were never a formidable defence. The major monuments occupy a compact quarter up against the river, just beyond the principal **place de l'Horloge**, at the northern end of rue de la République, the chief axis of the old town.

Avignon can be dauntingly crowded, and stiflingly hot, in summer. But it's worth persevering, not simply for the colossal **Palais des Papes**, home to the medieval popes, and its fine crop of museums and ancient churches, but also the sheer life and energy that throbs through its lanes and alleyways.

## Palais des Papes

Daily: March 9am–6.30pm; April–June & Sept–Oct 9am–7pm; July 9am–8pm; Aug 9am–8.30pm; Nov–Feb 9.30am–5.45pm; last ticket 1hr before closing • €12, or €14.50 with Pont St-Bénézet • ☎ 04 32 74 32 74, ⓦ palais-des-papes.com

Avignon's vast **Palais des Papes** soars above the cobbled place du Palais at the north end of the walled city, overlooking the curving Rhône. Although the palace was built primarily as a fortress, and equipped with massive stone vaults and battlements, the two pointed towers that hover above its gate are incongruously graceful. Inside, so little remains of its original decoration and furnishings that the denuded interior leaves hardly a whiff of the corruption and decadence of fat, feuding cardinals and their mistresses; the thronging purveyors of jewels, velvet and furs; the musicians, chefs and painters competing for patronage; and the riotous banquets and corridor schemings. Simply look at the virtual-reality "Histopad" tablet that's loaned to each visitor, however, and the palace springs to colourful life.

### Vieux Palais

Visits to the Palais des Papes begin in the original **Vieux Palais**, constructed from 1335 onwards, under Benedict XII. The first building you enter, the **Pope's Tower**, is accessed via the vaulted **Treasury**, where the Church's deeds and finances were handled. Four large holes in the floor of the smaller downstairs room, now covered by glass, held the papal gold and jewels. The same cunning storage device was used in the **Chambre du Camérier** or Chamberlain's Quarters, off the Jesus Hall upstairs. In the adjoining **Papal Vestiary**, the Pope had a small library and would dress before receiving sovereigns and ambassadors in the **Consistoire** of the Vieux Palais, on the other side of the Jesus Hall.

On the floor above, the **kitchen** offers powerful testimony to the scale of papal gluttony. Major feasts were held in the **Grand Tinel**, or dining room, where only the pope was allowed to wield a knife. During the conclave that elected each new pope, the cardinals were locked into this room, adjourning to conspire in chambers to the south and west.

### Palais Neuf

Despite its name, the **Palais Neuf** is only a few years newer than the Vieux Palais – it was erected by the next Pope, Clement VI. The transition from the old to the new palace is now imperceptible, but brings you immediately to the twin highlights of any visit. Clement's **bedroom**, adorned with wonderful entwined oak- and vine-leaf motifs, and his study, the **Chambre du Cerf**, filled with superb hunting and fishing scenes, provide the tour's first dash of real-life colour, as opposed to the virtual reality of the Histopads. Austerity resumes in the cathedral-like proportions of the **Grande Chapelle**, or **Chapelle Clémentine**, beyond, and in the **Grande Audience**, its twin in terms of volume on the floor below.

The circuit also includes a walk along the roof terraces, which offer such tremendous views that it's worth heading up a little higher to the rooftop café even when the signs insist that it's closed.

### Petit Palais

Daily except Tues 10am–1pm & 2–6pm • Free • ☏ 04 90 86 44 58, ⓦ petit-palais.org

Immediately north of the Palais de Papes, the **Petit Palais** contains a first-rate collection of thirteenth- to fifteenth-century painting and sculpture, mostly by masters from northern Italian cities. Visitors can watch as the masters wrestle with and finally conquer the representation of perspective – a revolution from medieval art, where the size of figures depended on their importance rather than position within the picture.

**16**

### Pont St-Bénézet

Daily: March 9am–6.30pm; April–June & Sept–Oct 9am–7pm; July 9am–8pm; Aug 9am–8.30pm; Nov–Feb 9.30am–5.45pm; last ticket 1hr before closing • €5, or €14.50 with Palais des Papes • ☏ 04 32 74 32 74, ⓦ palais-des-papes.com

Now merely jutting halfway out towards the Île de la Barthelasse, the twelfth-century **Pont St-Bénézet** originally reached all the way to Villeneuve, and was the only bridge to cross the Rhône between Lyon and the Mediterranean. A picturesque ruin since a flood in 1668, with just four of its 22 arches surviving, this is the bridge immortalized in *Sur le pont d'Avignon*. While that song has existed for five centuries, its modern words and tune come from nineteenth-century French operettas. It's generally agreed that the lyrics should really say "*Sous le pont*" (under the bridge) rather than "*Sur le pont*" (on the bridge), and that it refers to goings-on on the Île de la Barthelasse either of the general populace, who would dance on the island on feast days, or of the thief and trickster clientele of a tavern there, dancing with glee at the arrival of more potential victims.

The narrow bridge itself is open for visits. Displays beneath its landward end explain the history of both bridge and song. After that, you're free to walk to the end and back, and dance upon it too for that matter.

### Rocher des Doms

Commanding lovely views from its hilltop position north of the Palais des Papes, the peaceful **Rocher des Doms** park is Avignon's best spot for a picnic. The steep climb up is rewarded with relaxing lawns, fountains and ducks, as well as a little café.

### Place de l'Horloge

Frenetically busy year-round, Avignon's café-lined **place de l'Horloge** holds the imposing **hôtel de ville** and **clock tower**, as well as the **Opéra**. Around the square,

▲ 1 (500m)

N

**ÎLE DE LA BARTHELASSE**

Swimming Pool

Boat to Île de la Barthelasse

Pont St-Bénézet

BOULEVARD DE LA LIGNE

Porte du Rocher

Porte du Rhône

Musée du Petit Palais

Rocher des Doms

Cathédrale Notre-Dame-des-Doms

Cinema Utopia

CHEMIN DE L'ÎLE PIOT

BOULEVARD DU RHÔNE

RUE REMPART DU RHÔNE

RUE FERRUCE

RUE LIMASSET

RUE DES GROTTES

RUE GRANDE FUSTERIE

RUE CHIRON

RUE DE LA BALANCE

PLACE DU PALAIS

CHEMIN DE BAGATELLE

PONT DALADIER

Porte de l'Oulle

PLACE CRILLON

R. BARONCELLI

RUE LIMAS

RUE ST-ÉTIENNE

RUE LIMAS

RUE PETITE FUSTERIE

RUE RACINE

Conservatoire de Musique

RUE MOLIÈRE

RUE CORNEILLE

RUE J. VILAR

RUE DE MONS

Palais des Papes

RUE PEYROLLERIE

RUE BANASTERIE

CHEMIN DE L'ÎLE PIOT

River Rhône

Cruises Mireio

RUE DE LA PLAISANCE

RUE DU MAIL

Opéra

PLACE DE L'HORLOGE

Maison Jean Vilar

PASSAGE DE L'ORATOIRE

St-Agricol

Hôtel de Ville

St-Pierre

PLACE CARNOT

ALLÉE DE L'OULLE

BOULEVARD DE L'OULLE

RUE JOSEPH-VERNET

RUE SAINT-THOMAS D'AQUIN

RUE ST-ANDRÉ

RUE FÉLIX GRAS

RUE ST-AGRICOL

RUE DES MARCHANDS

Palais du Roure

PLACE DU CHANGE

RUE DU VIEUX-

RUE VIEUX SEXTIER

RUE VIALA

RUE DU ROURE

PLACE DE LA PRINCIPALE

RUE BANCASSE

RUE GALANTE

RUE PTE. CALADE

RUE VICTOR HUGO

Musée Vouland

Musée Calvet

RUE BASILE

RUE DE LA BOULQUERIE

RUE DES FOURBISSEURS

RUE FIGUIERE

RUE DU COLLÈGE DE LA CROIX

St-Didier

RUE DE LA RÉPUBLIQUE

Porte St-Dominique

RUE D'ANNANELLE

Musée Requien

RUE HORACE VERNET

RUE BOISSERIN

RUE THÉODORE AUBANEL

PLACE ST-DIDIER

RUE DU ROI RENE

RUE LANTERNE

RUE SAINT-ANDRÉ

Mediathèque Ceccano

RUE DES 3 FALCONS

RUE LABOUREUR

BOULEVARD ST-DOMINIQUE

RUE VELOUTERIE

RUE ST-CHARLES

Musée Lapidaire

RUE F. MISTRAL

Musée Angladon

RUE DES ÉTUDES

RUE JOSEPH-VERNET

RUE DE PORTAIL-BOQUIER

RUE VIOLETTE

RUE DES LICES

Collection Lambert

BOULEVARD RASPAIL

BOULEVARD RASPAIL

Agricole Perdiguier

RUE AGRICOL PERDIGUIER

PLACE DES CORPS SAINTS

RUE ST-MICHEL

RUE DE L'OBSERVANCE

COURS JEAN-JAURÈS

TCRA Office

RUE DE LA BOURSE

AVENUE L. DE TASSIGNY

RUE ST-CHARLES

Anc. Couvent des Célestins

Porte St-Roch

RUE DU REMPART SAINT-ROCH

Porte St-Charles

Porte de la République

RUE PAUL-MÉRINDOL

BOULEVARD ST-ROCH

COURS PRES KENNEDY

BOULEVARD ST-ROCH

AVENUE EISENHOWER

AVENUE DE BLANCHISSAGE

AVENUE MONCLAR-NORD

PLACE DE LA RÉPUBLIQUE

Gare Routière

**AVIGNON**

Gare SNCF

▼ Gare TGV (4km)

Villeneuve-lès-Avignon (1.5km) ▲    Free Parking (1km) ▲    Nîmes (44km) ▲

16

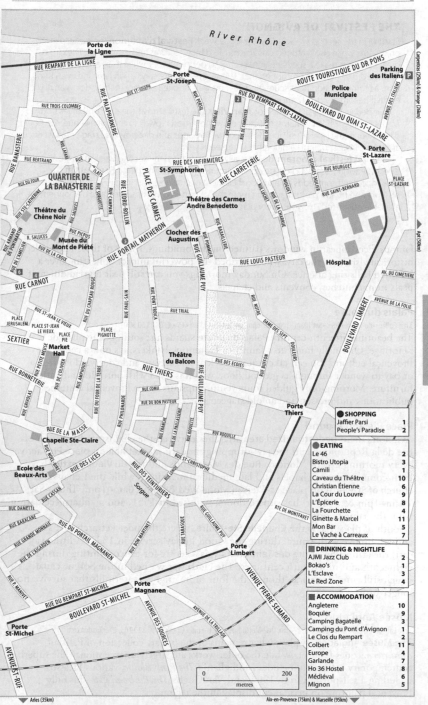

River Rhône

Porte de
la Ligne

RUE REMPART DE LA LIGNE

ROUTE TOURISTIQUE DU DR PONS

Porte
St-Joseph

Parking
des Italiens

RUE ST-JOSEPH

RUE DU REMPART SAINT-LAZARE

Police
Municipale

RUE PERCIL

RUE TROIS COLOMBES

RUE SVIRIN

BOULEVARD DU QUAI ST-LAZARE

RUE CREMADE

RUE D'AMOUYER

RUE DE LA TOUR

Porte
St-Lazare

RUE BANASTERIE

RUE BERTRAND

RUE LANTIN

RUE 3 PILATS

RUE DES INFIRMIÈRES

St-Symphorien

RUE CARRETERIE

RUE GEORGES TAULIER

RUE BOURGUET

PLACE
ST-LAZARE

QUARTIER DE
LA BANASTERIE

RUE DU FOUR

RUE STE-CATHERINE

RUE SALUCES

RUE SORGUETTE

PLACE DES CARMES

RUE LEROU-ROLLIN

RUE CAMPANE

Théâtre des Carmes
Andre Benedetto

RUE LICHEL

RUE DE LA CHARRUE

RUE DE LA CHARME

RUE SAINT-BERNARD

Théâtre du
Chêne Noir

R. SALUCES

RUE PICPUS

Musée du
Mont de Piété

RUE ARMAND
DE PONTMARTIN

RUE DE L'IMELIER

RUE DE LA CROIX

RUE PORTAIL MATHERON

Clocher des
Augustins

RUE BARAILLÈRE

RUE POMMIER

RUE GUILLAUME PUY

RUE LOUIS PASTEUR

Hôpital

AV. DU CIMETIÈRE

RUE CARNOT

RUE ST-JEAN LE VIEUX

RUE DU CHAPEAU ROUGE

RUE PAUL SAIN

RUE PONT TROUCA

RUE TRIAL

RUE NOTRE
DAME DES SEPT

DOULEURS

AVENUE DE LA FOLIE

BOULEVARD LIMBERT

PLACE
JÉRUSALEM

PLACE ST-JEAN
LE VIEUX

PLACE
PIE

PLACE
PIGNOTTE

SEXTIER

Market
Hall

RUE PETITE MEUSE

RUE DE L'OLIVIER

RUE AMPHOUX

Théâtre
du Balcon

RUE DES ÉCOLES

RUE BUFFON

RUE BONNETERIE

RUE GRIVOLAS

RUE THIERS

RUE GUILLAUME PUY

Porte
Thiers

RUE DU FOUR DE LA TERRE

RUE COMU

RUE PHILONARDE

RUE DU BON PASTEUR

Chapelle Ste-Claire

RUE DE LA MASSE

RUE NOTRE DAME

RUE FRANCHE

RUE DE LA BALLISSERIE

RUE BOUQUERIE

RUE ROQUILLE

Ecole des
Beaux-Arts

RUE DES LICES

RUE BATEAU

RUE LIGNE

RUE ST-CHRISTOPHE

RUE CASSAN

RUE DES TEINTURIERS

Sorgue

RUE DAMETTE

RUE GUILLAUME PUY

RTE DE MONTFAVET

RUE BARACANE

RUE GRANDE MONNAIE

RUE DU PORTAIL MAGNANEN

RUE BON MARTINET

RUE TARASQUE

Porte
Limbert

RUE DE LAIGARDEN

RUE B MANTVEL

Porte
Magnanen

AVENUE PIERRE SEMARD

Porte
St-Michel

RUE DU REMPART ST-MICHEL

BOULEVARD ST-MICHEL

AVENUE DES SOURCES

AVENUE DE LA TRILLADE

AVENUES T-RUF

0        200
metres

Arles (35km)

Aix-en-Provence (75km) & Marseille (95km)

Carpentras (25km) & Orange (26km)

Apt (50km)

16

**SHOPPING**
Jaffier Parsi          1
People's Paradise      2

**EATING**
Le 46                  2
Bistro Utopia          3
Camili                 1
Caveau du Théâtre     10
Christian Étienne      6
La Cour du Louvre      9
L'Épicerie             8
La Fourchette          4
Ginette & Marcel      11
Mon Bar                5
Le Vache à Carreaux    7

**DRINKING & NIGHTLIFE**
AJMI Jazz Club         2
Bokao's                1
L'Esclave              3
Le Red Zone            4

**ACCOMMODATION**
Angleterre            10
Boquier                9
Camping Bagatelle      3
Camping du Pont d'Avignon  1
Le Clos du Rempart     2
Colbert               11
Europe                 4
Garlande               7
Ho 36 Hostel           8
Médiéval               6
Mignon                 5

---

**THE FESTIVAL OF AVIGNON**

Starting in the second week in July, the three-week **Festival d'Avignon** focuses especially on theatre, while also featuring classical music, dance, lectures and exhibitions. The city's great buildings make a spectacular backdrop to performances, while its streets throng with bright-eyed performers promoting their shows. Everywhere stays open late, and everything from accommodation to obscure fringe events gets booked up very quickly; doing anything normal becomes virtually impossible.

Founded in 1947 by actor-director **Jean Vilar**, the festival hosts theatre companies from across Europe. While big-name directors draw the largest crowds to the main venue, the Cour d'Honneur in the Palais des Papes, lesser-known troupes and directors also stage new works, and the festival spotlights a different culture each year.

The main **festival programme** is usually available from the second week in May on ⓦ festival-avignon.com; tickets go on sale around mid-June. The fringe **Festival Off** (ⓦ avignonleoff.com) adds an additional element of craziness and magic, with innovative, obscure and bizarre performances in more than a hundred venues. The Carte d'Abonnement, available online for €16, gives thirty percent off all fringe shows.

---

famous faces appear in windows painted on the buildings. Many of these figures depict historical visitors to the city, who described the powerful impact of hearing over a hundred bells ring at once. On Sunday mornings you can still hear myriad different peals from churches, convents and chapels.

**16**

## Palais du Roure

3 rue Collège-du-Roure • Tues–Sat 10am–1pm & 2–6pm, guided tour 11am • €5 • ☎ 04 13 60 50 01

The beautiful fifteenth-century **Palais du Roure** stands just south of the place de l'Horloge. Originally home to a family of Florentine bankers, it's now a centre for Provençal culture. You can take a quick peek at its gateway and courtyard for free, or pay to wander through its ground floor, which is filled with portraits and antique furniture. Morning-only guided tours venture upstairs to see Provençal costumes, publications and presses, and an old stagecoach.

## Place Pie and around

Avignon's main **pedestrianized area** stretches between the chainstore blandness of rue de la République and the jaw-dropping modern **market hall** on **place Pie**, active every morning except Monday. **Rue des Marchands** and **rue du Vieux-Sextier** have their complement of chapels and late medieval mansions, while the Renaissance **church of St-Pierre** on place St-Pierre (Mon–Wed & Sun 10am–1pm; Thurs–Sat 10am–1pm & 2–6pm) has superb doors, sculpted in 1551, and an altarpiece dating from the same period.

South of place Pie is the **Chapelle Ste-Claire**, where the poet Petrarch first saw and fell in love with Laura, during the Good Friday service in 1327. A little way east, the atmospheric **rue des Teinturiers** was a centre for calico printing during the eighteenth and nineteenth centuries. The cloth was washed in the Sorgue canal, which still runs alongside, though the four of its mighty watermills that survive no longer turn.

## Musée Angladon

5 rue Labourer • April–Sept Tues–Sun 1–6pm; Oct–March Tues–Sat 1–6pm • €8 • ☎ 04 90 82 29 03, ⓦ angladon.com

The **Musée Angladon** displays what remains of the private collection of Parisian *couturier* Jacques Doucet. While the older works are largely unexceptional, the superb contemporary collection includes Modigliani's *The Pink Blouse*, various Picassos, including a self-portrait from 1904, and Van Gogh's *The Railroad Cars*, his only Provençal painting on permanent display in the region.

## Musée Calvet

65 rue Joseph-Vernet • Daily except Tues 10am–1pm & 2–6pm • Free • ☎ 04 90 86 33 84, ⓦ musee-calvet.org

The excellent, airy **Musée Calvet** is housed in a lovely eighteenth-century palace. Highlights include Antonio Forbera's extraordinary *Le Chevalet du Peintre*, a trompe l'oeil painting from 1686 depicting the artist's easel, complete with sketches and palette; a wonderful gallery of languorous nineteenth-century marble sculptures; and works by Soutine, Manet and Joseph Vernet, as well as Jacques-Louis David's subtle, moving *Death of Joseph Barra*. Look out for the easily missed Flemish room behind the ticket desk. There are also some much more ancient artefacts, like enigmatic stelae from the fourth-century BC, carved with half-discernible faces, and assorted Egyptian treasures.

## Musée Lapidaire

27 rue de la République • Daily except Mon 10am–1pm & 2–6pm • Free • ☎ 04 90 85 75 38, ⓦ musee-lapidaire.org

Housed in a former Baroque chapel, the **Musée Lapidaire** is home to larger pieces from the archeological collection of its sister museum, the Musée Calvet. Besides Egyptian statues and Etruscan urns, it abounds in Roman and Gallo-Roman sarcophagi, and early renditions of the mythical Tarasque, a dragon-like creature said to have terrorized nearby Tarascon.

## Collection Lambert

5 rue Violette • July & Aug daily 11am–7pm; Sept–June Tues–Sun 11am–6pm • €10 • ☎ 04 90 16 56 20, ⓦ collectionlambert.fr

Avignon's major contemporary art gallery, the thoughtfully curated **Collection Lambert**, is principally devoted to the lovingly amassed artworks that were donated to the city by collector Yvon Lambert in 2011. Each year, though, its superb spaces also house a large-scale temporary exhibition devoted to a specific contemporary artist, as well as showing off previous such shows. The permanent display includes pieces created by Jean-Michel Basquiat for Lambert's Paris gallery in 1988, as well as works by Cy Twombly, Anselm Kiefer and Roni Horn.

**16**

### ARRIVAL AND DEPARTURE

AVIGNON

**By train (gare SNCF)** Avignon's *gare SNCF* is just outside the walls south of the old city.

Destinations (*gare SNCF*) Arles (hourly; 20min); Carpentras (half-hourly; 40min); Cavaillon (9–14 daily; 35min); Lyon (12 daily; 2hr 30min); Marseille (14 daily; 1hr 5min–1hr 55min); Orange (20 daily; 20min); Tarascon (12 daily; 12min); Valence (12 daily; 1hr 10min).

**By train (gare TGV)** Avignon's TGV station, 2km south of the city and served by high-speed trains en route between Paris and the Riviera, is linked by regular trains with the *gare SNCF* (5min; €1.80), as well as frequent buses into town (daily, 2–4 hourly; €3; ⓦ tcra.fr). A taxi into town (call ☎ 04 90 82 20 20) can cost €15 or more.

Destinations (*gare TGV*) Aix-en-Provence TGV (22 daily; 20min); Lille-Europe (5 daily; 4hr 30min); London St Pancras (1–5 weekly; 6hr); Lyon (14 daily; 1hr); Marseille (every 30min; 35min); Paris (17 daily; 2hr 40min); Paris CDG Airport (5 daily; 3hr 10min); Valence TGV (9 daily; 30–40min).

**By bus** Avignon's *gare routière* is alongside the *gare SNCF*, just outside the walls south of the old city. For timetables, visit ⓦ sudest-mobilites.fr and ⓦ lieutaud.fr.

Destinations Aix-en-Provence (3–7 daily; 1hr 15min); Arles (6 daily; 1hr); Carpentras (frequent; 35–45min); Cavaillon (7 daily; 35min); Digne (3–5 daily; 3hr 30min); Fontaine-de-Vaucluse (8 daily; 1hr); L'Isle-sur-la-Sorgue (10 daily; 40min); Orange (21 daily; 50min); St-Rémy (8 daily; 40min); Vaison (3 daily; 1hr 25min).

**By plane** Avignon-Caumont airport, 8km southeast of the centre (☎ 04 90 81 51 51, ⓦ avignon.aeroport.fr), is connected with Birmingham and Southampton on Flybe (ⓦ flybe.com), and linked to the town centre and *gare TGV* by bus #22 (€1.40).

**By car** Driving into Avignon involves negotiating a nightmare of junctions and one-way roads. The easiest parking options for day-trippers are two free, guarded car parks, connected with the town centre by free shuttle buses: Île Piot (daily 24hr), on the Île de la Barthelasse between Avignon and Villeneuve, and Parking des Italiens (Mon–Sat 7.30am–8.30pm), beside the river northeast of the old town. The oversubscribed parking spaces inside the walls are expensive; check whether your hotel offers free or discounted parking.

### GETTING AROUND

**By bus** The main TCRA local bus stops are on cours du Président-Kennedy and outside porte de l'Oulle facing the river (tickets €1.40 each; book of 10 tickets €12.50; one-day pass €3.50; ⓦ tcra.fr).

**By ferry** Free river ferries cross from east of Pont St-Bénézet to the Île de la Barthelasse, site of the city's campsites (March & Oct Wed 2–5.15pm, Sat & Sun 10–11.45am & 2–5.15pm; April–June & Sept daily 10am–12.15pm & 2–6.15pm; July & Aug daily 11am–8.45pm).

**By bike** Provence Bike, immediately east of the *gare SNCF* at 7 av St-Ruf (☎04 90 27 92 61, ⓦprovence-bike.com), rents bicycles, scooters and motorbikes.

**By taxi** There's a taxi rank on place Pie (☎04 90 82 20 20).

## INFORMATION AND TOURS

**Tourist office** 41 cours Jean-Jaurès, at the southern end of the city (April–June & Aug–Oct Mon–Sat 9am–6pm, Sun 10am–5pm; July daily 9am–7pm; Nov–March Mon–Fri 9am–6pm, Sat 9am–5pm, Sun 10am–noon; ☎04 32 74 32 74, ⓦot-avignon.fr).

**Boat trips** In summer, from a base just south of place Crillon, Cruises Mireio (☎04 90 85 62 25, ⓦmireio.net) offer 45-minute river trips on the Rhône (April–Sept, see website for schedule; €12), as well as dinner cruises upstream towards Châteauneuf-du-Pape and downstream to Arles (€42.50–92, meal included).

## ACCOMMODATION

In general, Avignon's hotels and B&Bs are very reasonably priced. Bear in mind, though, that during July's festival, many establishments charge significantly higher rates than those shown below.

### HOTELS AND B&BS

**Angleterre** 29 bd Raspail ☎04 90 86 34 31, ⓦhotel dangleterre.fr. Located in a quiet neighbourhood in the southwest corner of the old city, well away from night-time noise, this is a traditional hotel with plain, low-priced rooms, many of them very small but equipped with reasonable bathrooms. **€90**

★ **Boquier** 6 rue du Portail-Boquier ☎04 90 82 34 43, ⓦhotel-boquier.com. Extremely welcoming little hotel near the tourist office, with funkily decorated, widely differing, and consistently inexpensive en-suite rooms, some very small, some sleeping three or four. **€69**

★ **Le Clos du Rempart** 35 rue Crémade ☎04 90 86 39 14, ⓦclosdurempart.com. Delightful B&B in a pretty nineteenth-century house in the northeast corner of the city with two large, luxurious and very peaceful en-suite rooms; there's a wonderful wisteria-covered breakfast terrace and a hammock to doze in on sunny afternoons. **€175**

**Colbert** 7 rue Agricol-Perdiguier ☎04 90 86 20 20, ⓦavignon-hotel-colbert.com. At the south end of town and handy for local trains and buses, this hotel has warmly and imaginatively decorated rooms, mostly large and all a/c, plus a pleasant central courtyard complete with fountain. The helpful owners are always ready with suggestions. Closed Nov–March. **€74**

**Europe** 12 place Crillon ☎04 90 14 76 76, ⓦheurope. com. Very comfortable upscale hotel, in a sixteenth-century townhouse. Unpretentiously classy, it's set back in a shaded courtyard, with bright, modern, soundproofed rooms, home-made breakfasts and an excellent restaurant. **€225**

★ **Garlande** 20 rue Galante ☎04 90 80 08 85, ⓦhoteldegarlande.com. Stylish little family-run hotel, in a pedestrian street near the Palais des Papes. Each of the eleven generally spacious rooms has its own colour scheme and Provençal touches, as well as a decent bathroom with bath or shower. Closed Feb. **€98**

**Médiéval** 15 rue de la Petite Saunerie ☎04 90 86 11 06, ⓦhotelmedieval.com. Very central hotel in a fine seventeenth-century townhouse, with very reasonable rates (even during the festival) and a lovely garden courtyard, but rather plain, dated rooms of widely varying sizes. **€88**

**Mignon** 12 rue Joseph-Vernet ☎09 70 35 37 67, ⓦhotel-mignon.com. The decor may be a little fussy for some tastes, but this small hotel is amazing value for money considering its spotless little rooms and fantastic location on a chic street. **€69**

### HOSTELS AND CAMPSITES

**Camping Bagatelle** 25 allée Antoine-Pinay, Île de la Barthelasse ☎04 90 86 30 39, ⓦcampingbagatelle. com. This three-star campsite, dominated by camping-cars, is the closest to Avignon city centre, visible as you cross the Daladier bridge; bus #20 from the post office, or 15min walk from place de l'Horloge. It's nothing special, but there's a laundry, shop and café, as well as basic hostel facilities, with beds in four- or six-person dorms, plus private rooms sleeping from two to four, with and without en-suite bathrooms; all hostel rates include breakfast. Open all year. Dorms **€22.17**, rooms **€59**, camping **€26.50**

**Camping du Pont d'Avignon** 10 chemin de la Barthelasse, Île de la Barthelasse ☎04 90 80 63 50, ⓦaquadis-loisirs.com. Well-shaded four-star site, with a lovely pool, on the island directly facing Pont St-Bénézet across the river, a fair walk from the centre but accessible on bus route #20. Closed late Nov to Feb. **€25.60**

**Ho 36 Hostel** 17 rue de la République ☎04 32 40 50 60, ⓦho36hostels.com. Stylish independent hostel, in a prime central location, that's a major favourite among young international visitors. Rooms are clean and fresh, with a/c; some are dorms sleeping 4–8 in individually curtained beds, others are en-suite private doubles. Kitchen facilities are minimal, but the on-site café serves tapas plus €5 continental breakfasts. Dorms **€22**, doubles **€75**

16

## EATING AND DRINKING

### RESTAURANTS

**Le 46** 46 rue de la Balance ☎04 90 85 24 83, ⊛le46 avignon.com. This smart modern bistro, with a street-front terrace near the Palais des Papes, serves superb regional dishes using fresh market produce. At lunchtime, you can get a €14–16 *plat du jour*, often fresh fish, or a large salad; dinner is *à la carte*, with starters at around €9.50 and typical mains €16–20. Mon–Fri noon–2.30pm & 7–10.30pm, Sat & Sun noon–2.30pm.

**Caveau du Théâtre** 16 rue des Trois-Faucons ☎04 90 82 60 91, ⊛caveaudutheatre.com. Friendly bistro, with pretty painted walls, jolly red tables on the street, and occasional live jazz, serving delicious dishes like braised ox cheek (€19) or huge mixed salads (€16). Lunch *menu* €15, three-course dinner *menu* €29. Mon–Fri noon–2.30pm & 7pm–midnight, Sat 7pm–midnight; closed second half of Aug.

★ **Christian Étienne** 10 rue de Mons ☎04 84 88 51 27, ⊛christian-etienne.fr. Avignon's best-known gourmet restaurant, in a twelfth-century mansion, with a terrace overlooking the place du Palais. Mouthwatering Provençal delights include a whole *menu* devoted to tomatoes, or perhaps lobster with ginger, asparagus and sesame seeds followed by orange and carrot macaroons with almond sorbet. Dinner *menus* range from €75 to the €130 *menu confiance*, in which the chef brings whatever takes his fancy, but you can sample the restaurant's pleasures on a three-course, no-choice €35 lunch *menu*. Mon, Tues & Fri–Sun noon–1.30pm & 7–9.15pm, open daily in July.

**La Cour du Louvre** 23 rue St-Agricol ☎09 70 35 15 86, ⊛restaurantlacourdulouvre.fr. Hidden peacefully away from the old-town bustle in a delightful interior courtyard at the end of a *cour*, with a romantic atmosphere and good Mediterranean cooking. Although there's a €14.50 lunchtime *plat du jour*, set *menus* start at €35. Mon–Sat noon–2.15pm & 7–10pm.

**L'Épicerie** 10 place St-Pierre ☎04 90 82 74 22. Gloriously traditional Provençal restaurant, with an old-fashioned dining room and check-clothed tables set out on a tiny cobbled square that's almost impossible to find. The €16 lunch *formule* is great value, while a mixed deli plate of savoury specialities costs €21.50, and conventional plates like duck or beef approach €30. Daily noon–2.30pm & 7–10pm; closed Tues & Wed in low season, plus all Jan & Feb.

**La Fourchette** 17 rue Racine ☎04 90 85 20 93, ⊛la-fourchette.net. Bright, busy yet refined restaurant, open weekdays only and serving up classic and sophisticated fish and meat dishes – try the tasty scallops in port and beetroot sauce – with a €15 *plat du jour* and a €38 dinner *menu*. Mon–Fri 12.15–1.45pm & 7.15–9.45pm; closed first 3 weeks in Aug.

**Ginette & Marcel** 27 place des Corps-Saints ☎04 90 85 58 70. The most attractive of several restaurants on this lively, youthful little square. If you sit outside, be sure to have a peek at the interior – it's a fun evocation of a 1950s French grocery, filled with funky bric-a-brac. Salads and €7 *tartines* are the speciality, and you can get a substantial meal for around €10, or even a bowl of cornflakes for €2. Mon–Sat 10.30am–11pm.

### CAFÉS

**Camili** 155 rue de la Carreterie ☎04 90 27 38 50, ⊛camili-booksandtea.com. This cosy tearoom sells organic and fairtrade tea, coffee and juices, as well as home-made cakes, pastries and snacks; has a garden patio; and doubles as a book exchange, with a truly enormous stock of English books. It also offers English and French classes and knitting evenings. Tues–Sat noon–7pm.

### BARS

**Bistro Utopia** La Manutention, 4 rue de l'Escalier Ste-Anne ☎04 90 82 65 36. A hotbed of intellectual ferment, this ultra-cool warehouse-like bar stands at the entrance to the Utopia arts/cinema complex. Mon–Fri noon–midnight, Sat & Sun 2pm–midnight.

**Mon Bar** 17 rue du Portail-Mathéron ☎06 61 13 29 39. Pleasantly old-fashioned café, 400m east of the place du Palais and steeped in the lore of Avignon, with a laidback atmosphere. Coffee costs just €1 until 10am, and they serve a €12 lunch *menu*. Daily 7am–2am.

**La Vache à Carreaux** 14 rue de la Peyrolerie ☎04 90 80 09 05, ⊛vache-carreaux.fr. This intimate, homely wine bar styles itself a "restaurant de fromage et vins". Cheese is indeed prominent on the food menu, which features €12.50 baked half-camemberts alongside large salads from €9.50. Daily noon–3pm & 7pm–1am.

**16**

## NIGHTLIFE AND ENTERTAINMENT

Though Avignon saves its energy for the festival, the city is busy with nightlife and cultural events year round, and plenty of classical concerts are performed in churches, usually for free.

### LIVE MUSIC AND CLUBS

**AJMI Jazz Club** La Manutention, 4 rue de l'Escalier Ste-Anne ☎04 90 86 08 61, ⊛jazzalajmi.com. This popular club, in a busy arts complex behind the Palais des Papes, hosts a year-round programme of major acts along with some adventurous new jazz and improvised music; check the website for the latest schedule. Hours vary.

**Bokao's** 9bis bd du quai St-Lazare ☎04 90 82 47 95, ⊛bokaos.fr. Mainstream, youth-oriented club, in a converted barn with outdoor space, across from the river just outside the walls, playing an eclectic mix of music. Thurs–Sat midnight–6am.

**L'Esclave** 12 rue du Limas ☎04 90 85 14 91. Avignon's best known gay and lesbian bar, with regular DJs, drag shows and karaoke nights at ground level, and more secluded areas upstairs. Mon–Sat 11.45pm–7am, Sun 11pm–7am.

**Le Red Zone** 25 rue Carnot ☎04 65 81 74 13. Sweaty, very crimson club where DJs play anything from salsa to electro according to the night. Tues–Sat midnight–7am.

### THEATRE AND CINEMA

**Cinéma Utopia** La Manutention, 4 rue de l'Escalier Ste-Anne ☎04 90 82 65 36, ⓦwww.cinemas-utopia. org. Part of a hip converted warehouse complex that also includes *Bistro Utopia* and the *AJMI Jazz Club*, this wildly popular venue shows a busy repertory programme of films from all over the world, many in *version originale* (undubbed).

**Opéra** Place de l'Horloge ☎04 90 14 26 00, ⓦopera grandavignon.fr. Avignon's most prestigious venue for classical opera and ballet, with a season running from October to June.

**Théâtre du Balcon** 38 rue Guillaume-Puy ☎04 90 85 00 80, ⓦtheatredubalcon.org. Venue staging everything from African music and twentieth-century classics to contemporary theatre.

**Théâtre des Carmes André Benedetto** 6 place des Carmes ☎04 90 82 20 47, ⓦtheatredescarmes.com. Set up by, and now named after, one of the founders of Festival Off, this theatre specializes in avant-garde performances.

**Théâtre du Chêne Noir** 8bis rue Ste-Catherine ☎04 90 86 74 87, ⓦchenenoir.fr. Programmes at this eclectic theatre range from mime or musicals to Molière.

### SHOPPING

**Jaffier Parsi** 42 rue des Fourbisseurs ☎04 90 86 08 55. Everything you might need to equip your Provençal kitchen, from discounted Le Creuset cookware to colourful ceramic casseroles. Mon 2–7pm, Tues–Sat 9am–7pm.

**People's Paradise** 7 rue des Trois-Faucons ☎04 90 86 43 74, ⓦpeoplesparadise.fr. This warehouse-like clothing, style, graphic design and general accessories store is a beacon on Avignon's fashion scene. Mon–Sat 10am–7pm.

### DIRECTORY

**Emergencies** Doctor/ambulance ☎15; Hospital, Centre Hospitalier H. Duffaut, 305 rue Raoul-Follereau (☎04 32 75 33 33, ⓦch-avignon.fr).

**Markets** Flea market: place des Carmes (Sun morning). Flowers: place des Carmes (Sat morning). Food: in the covered halls on place Pie (Tues–Fri 6am–1.30pm; Sat & Sun 6am–2pm).

**Police Municipale** 13 quai St-Lazare ☎08 00 00 84 00 or ☎04 90 85 13 13.

# Villeneuve-lès-Avignon

Pretty and prosperous, though little more than a village at its core, **VILLENEUVE-LÈS-AVIGNON** (also spelled Villeneuve-lez-Avignon) climbs a rocky escarpment above the west bank of the Rhône, looking down across the river upon its older and larger neighbour from behind far more convincing fortifications. Despite ongoing rivalry, Villeneuve has effectively been a suburb of Avignon for most of its history, as well as holding palatial residences constructed by the cardinals and a great monastery founded by Pope Innocent VI.

Officially belonging to Languedoc rather than Provence, Villeneuve might be better known were it further from Avignon, whose monuments it almost matches in scale. It is, however, a very different – and really rather sleepy – kind of place, where daily activity centres around the lovely little place Jean-Jaurès. As such, it retains a timelessness that bustling Avignon inevitably lacks. Whatever time of year you visit it's certainly worth a day spent exploring.

**Market** days in Villeneuve's place Charles-David are Thursday, for food, and Saturday for bric-a-brac.

## Fort St-André

**Fort St-André** Daily: June–Sept 10am–6pm; Oct–May 10am–1pm & 2–5pm • €6, €9 with La Chartreuse • ☎04 90 25 45 35, ⓦfort-saint-andre.fr **Abbey** Tues–Sun: March 10am–1pm & 2–5pm; April 10am–1pm & 2–6pm; May–Sept 10am–6pm; Oct 10am–5pm; closed Nov–Feb • €7 • ☎04 90 25 55 95, ⓦabbayesaintandre.fr

Originally, Villeneuve-lès-Avignon was enclosed within the walls of the enormous **Fort St-André**, on a rise to the east. Then, in 1770, the course of the Rhône shifted 1km south, and the fort lost its strategic importance. Now a hollow shell, it can be reached by climbing either from place Jean-Jaurès, or up the steeper rue Pente Rapide, a cobbled street that leads from the north side of place Charles-David.

Once you pass through the fort's vast white walls, via a bulbous, double-towered gateway, you're on what used to be the town's narrow main street. Buying a ticket for the fort itself allows you to continue up the street, passing tumbledown ruins, and then walk along the parapets, where a cliff-face terrace offers tremendous views across the river. You can also pay separately to visit its former **abbey**, which has gardens of olive trees, ruined chapels, lily ponds and dovecotes.

## La Chartreuse du Val de Bénédiction

58 rue de la République • Daily: April–Sept 9.30am–6.30pm; Oct–March 10am–5pm; closed 1st half of Jan • €8, €9 with Fort St-André • ☎ 04 90 15 24 24, ⓦ chartreuse.org

One of France's largest Carthusian monasteries, **La Chartreuse du Val de Bénédiction**, spreads below the Fort St-André. Founded by the sixth Avignon pope, Innocent VI, it was sold after the Revolution. Today its buildings are totally unembellished, and except for the Giovanetti frescoes in the chapel, all its artworks have been dispersed. Visitors can wander around unguided, through the three cloisters, the church, chapels, cells and communal spaces, though there's little to see. It's one of the best venues of the Festival of Avignon (see page 824).

## Musée Pierre-de-Luxembourg

3 rue de la République • May–Oct Tues–Sun 10am–12.30pm & 2–6pm; Nov–April Tues & Thurs–Sun 2–5pm, Wed 10am–noon & 2–5pm • €3.80 • ☎ 04 90 27 49 66

The **Musée Pierre-de-Luxembourg**, just off the central place Jean-Jaurès, holds treasures from the fourteenth-century **Église Collégiale Notre-Dame** nearby, including a rare fourteenth-century smiling Madonna and Child carved from a single tusk of ivory. Paintings taken from the Chartreuse include the stunning *Coronation of the Virgin*, painted in 1453 by Enguerrand Quarton.

## Tour Philippe-le-Bel

Feb, March, Oct & Nov Tues & Thurs–Sun 2–5pm, Wed 10am–noon & 2–5pm; April–Sept Tues–Sun 10am–12.30pm & 2–6pm; closed Dec–Jan • €2.50 • ☎ 04 32 70 08 57

The stout **Tour Philippe-le-Bel**, south of the centre beside the main road from Avignon, was built to guard the western end of Avignon's Pont St-Bénézet. The tricky climb to the top is rewarded with an overview of Villeneuve and Avignon.

### ARRIVAL AND INFORMATION
### VILLENEUVE-LÈS-AVIGNON

**By bus** The #11 bus (every 30min) takes 10min to ply between Villeneuve's place Charles-David and Avignon's cours du Président-Kennedy.

**Tourist office** Place Charles-David (Jan–April & Nov Mon–Fri 9–12.30pm & 2–5pm, Sat 9am–12.30pm; May, June & Sept Mon–Sat 9am–12.30pm & 2–6pm; July & Aug daily 9am–6pm; closed Dec; ☎ 04 90 03 70 60, ⓦ ot-villeneuvelezavignon.fr).

### ACCOMMODATION

★ **L'Atelier** 5 rue de la Foire ☎ 04 90 25 01 84, ⓦ hoteldelatelier.com. Very tasteful rooms in a charming sixteenth-century house with a central stone staircase bathed in light, plus huge open fireplaces and a delightful courtyard garden with terraces. **€83**

**Camping Municipal de la Laune** Chemin St-Honoré ☎ 04 90 25 76 06, ⓦ camping-villeneuvelezavignon. com. Spacious, well-shaded three-star site off the D980, north of town near the municipal swimming pool, on local bus route #5. Closed mid-Oct to March. **€26**

**Jardins de la Livrée** 4bis rue du Camp de Bataille ☎ 04 86 81 00 21, ⓦ www.la-livree.fr. Five clean, comfortable B&B rooms in an old house in the centre of the village, with a swimming pool; rates include parking and breakfast. The appealing Mediterranean restaurant downstairs (closed Mon) serves a €29 dinner *menu*. The one drawback is the noise of passing trains. **€105**

**Prieuré** 7 place du Chapitre ☎ 04 90 15 90 15, ⓦ leprieure. com. Luxurious former priory, set in peaceful flower-filled gardens. Its opulent rooms abound in tapestries, finely carved

16

doors, oak ceilings and baronial trappings, while the top-quality dining room serves Provençal cuisine with a gourmet twist, with lunch *menus* from €36 and dinner at €80 and €110. Closed Jan to mid-Feb & Nov. €233

**YMCA hostel** 7bis chemin de la Justice ☎04 90 25 46 20, ⓦymca-avignon.fr. Beautifully situated hostel,

overlooking the river by Pont du Royaume (the extension of Pont Daladier). Balconied rooms holding from one to four single beds, with and without en-suite facilities, plus an open-air swimming pool. Stop "Pont d'Avignon" on buses from Avignon to Villeneuve. Shared-bath double €38, en-suite €55

### EATING AND DRINKING

★ **Les Jardins d'Été de la Chartreuse** Cloître St-Jean, La Chartreuse ☎04 90 15 24 23, ⓦchartreuse.org. A truly memorable experience; in summer only, you can thread your way through the labyrinthine old monastery (you don't have to pay for admission) to find this open-air restaurant in a secluded courtyard. Some tables have lovely sunset views. Friendly service and *menus* of substantial Provençal cuisine from €19, plus early-evening drinks and snacks. Late May to early Sept daily 11.30am–10pm.

**Naturabsolu** 10 place St-Marc ☎09 50 76 05 57, ⓦnaturabsolu.fr. Predominantly vegan and organic restaurant on the main square, with indoor and outdoor seating, which serves a daily €12.50 raw plate as well as large salads and a €15 *plat du jour*, along with fresh smoothies and juices. Daily specials can include fish or chicken, however. Mon, Tues & Thurs–Sat noon–3pm & 6–9.30pm.

## St-Rémy-de-Provence

The dreamy, little-changed community of **ST-RÉMY-DE-PROVENCE**, where Van Gogh painted some of his most lyrical works, nestles against the northern base of the Alpilles, 30km from either Arles or Avignon. St-Rémy is a beautiful spot, centring on a charmingly low-key old town, the **vieille ville**, an enchanting tangle of narrow lanes and ancient alleyways interspersed with peaceful little squares. Despite the presence of boutiques, restaurants, and a couple of cafés, the core remains surprisingly sleepy; instead virtually all the town's commercial life takes place on the four busy boulevards that ring the entire ensemble.

Several exceptional sites and attractions lie within walking distance to the south: Van Gogh's hospital of **St-Paul-de-Mausole**, a **Roman arch**, and the ruins of ancient **Glanum**. St-Rémy is also famous as the birthplace of sixteenth-century astrologer **Nostradamus**.

### St-Paul-de-Mausole

Av Vincent-van-Gogh • Daily: April–Sept 9.30am–6.45pm; Oct–March 10.15am–5.15pm; last admission 30min before closing • €5 • ☎04 90 92 77 00, ⓦsaintpauldemausole.fr

The former monastery of **St-Paul-de-Mausole**, where **Vincent van Gogh** was a voluntary psychiatric patient between May 1889 and May 1890, stands just under 2km south of St-Rémy's old town. Visiting is a profoundly moving experience. Amazingly enough, it's still a psychiatric hospital, and although tourists are kept well clear of the active area, you get a real sense of its ongoing work. Displays in the church and cloisters contrast Van Gogh's diagnosis and treatment with modern-day practices, and you can see a mock-up of his former room and walk in the glorious gardens, planted with lavender and poppies. Vincent was allowed to wander around the town and Alpilles, so long as he stayed within an hour's walk of the hospital.

### Glanum

Rte des Baux-de-Provence, 1600m south of central St-Rémy • April–Sept daily 9.30am–6pm; Oct–March Tues–Sun 10am–5pm • €8, car parking €3 • ☎04 90 92 23 79, ⓦsite-glanum.fr

The impressive ancient settlement of **GLANUM** was dug from alluvial deposits at the foot of the Alpilles. Gallo-Greeks, probably from Massalia (Marseille), built a city here between the second and first centuries BC. Then the Gallo-Romans constructed another town, which lasted until the third century AD; a Roman triumphal arch and mausoleum, known as **Les Antiques**, still stand beside the main road nearby and are freely accessible around the clock.

16

A footpath drops from the site entrance to run through the ruins of Glanum itself, which can be hard to decipher. Greek levels can be most readily distinguished from the Roman by the building materials: the earlier civilization used massive hewn rocks, as opposed to the smaller, more accurately shaped stones preferred by the Romans.

At the site's southern end, where it narrows into a ravine, a Greek edifice stands around the **spring** that made this location so desirable. Steps lead down to a pool, with a slab above for the libations of those too sick to descend. The Gallo-Romans directed the water through canals to heat houses and, of course, to the **baths** that lie near the site entrance.

## ARRIVAL AND INFORMATION

ST-RÉMY-DE-PROVENCE

**By bus** The main bus stop is in place de la République, on the eastern edge of the old town.

Destinations Arles (8 daily; 50min); Avignon (8 daily; 40min); Les Baux (4 daily; 15min).

**Tourist office** Place Jean-Jaurès, just south of the old town

(mid-April to June & Sept to mid-Oct Mon–Sat 9.15am–12.30pm & 2–6.30pm, Sun 10am–12.30pm; July & Aug Mon–Sat 9.15am–6.30pm, Sun 10am–5pm; mid-Oct to mid-April Mon–Sat 9.15am–12.30pm & 2–5.30pm; ☎ 04 90 92 05 22, ⓦ saintremy-de-provence.com).

## ACCOMMODATION

**Gounod** 18 place de la République ☎ 04 90 92 06 14, ⓦ hotel-gounod.com. Comfortable central hotel, where the ornately decorated rooms in the main villa combine antique furnishings with bright modern linens; there's also a modern garden annex, centred around a swimming pool. Rates include breakfast. Closed Feb & March. **€110**

**Mas de Nicolas** Av Plaisance-du-Touch ☎ 04 90 92 27 05, ⓦ www.camping-masdenicolas.com. Spacious, well-shaded four-star municipal site with its own pool, 800m from the centre on a turning off the rte de Mollèges. Closed mid-Oct to mid-March. **€29.60**

**Pegomas** 3 av Jean-Moulin ☎ 04 90 92 01 21, ⓦ camping pegomas.fr. The nearest site to the town centre, this three-star option, 1km east towards Cavaillon, has a pool, a bar and a small shop. Closed late Oct to mid-March. **€28.50**

★**Le Soleil** 35 av Pasteur ☎ 04 90 92 00 63, ⓦ hotelsoleil.com. Very welcoming hotel, set back from the main road 350m south of the centre towards Glanum, with a pool and private parking. Pleasant, spacious rooms; three self-contained apartments; and a bar but no restaurant. **€127**, apartments **€175**

★ **Sous les Figuiers** 3 av Taillandier ☎ 04 32 60 15 40, ⓦ hotelsouslesfiguiers.com. Gorgeous place just north of the old town, run by a creative team of photographer and painter. Of the fourteen well-appointed rooms, the finest eleven cost extra, and have their own private garden terraces; there are no TVs, but there's a swimming pool and an on-site artist's studio (art classes available). Closed mid-Jan to mid-March. **€129**

## EATING AND DRINKING

**L'Aile ou la Cuisse** 5 rue de la Commune ☎ 04 32 62 00 25, ⓦ restaurantlaileoulacuisse.com. Very romantic, upscale restaurant in the old town. The changing €30 dinner *menu* features succulent fish and meat specials, but doesn't include their signature whole roasted (small) cockerel, which costs €24.90 à la carte. They also have a deli selling posh picnic items and delectable jams and olive oils. Daily noon–2.30pm & 7–10pm; closed Sun eve & Tues mid-Nov to March.

**La Cassolette** 53 rue Carnot ☎ 04 90 92 40 50. Inexpensive little restaurant in the old town, serving great-value French cuisine. The prize seats are out on the pavement of this tiny street; inside things are a bit more

formal. A simple €14 *menu* is served for both lunch and dinner; the €20 evening *menu* includes fish soup followed by *taureau*, while the €26 option is a definite step up, featuring a *grand aïoli*. No credit cards. Daily noon–1.30pm & 7.30–9.30pm.

**L'Estagnol** 7 bd Marceau ☎ 04 90 92 05 95, ⓦ restaurant-lestagnol.com. Peaceful, elegant restaurant, with exposed-stone walls, near the northwest corner of the peripheral boulevard. Summer delights on the largely Provençal €30 *menu* include cold courgette soup and the strawberry "soup" for dessert. Tues–Sun noon–2pm & 7.15–9.30pm; closed Sun eve in winter.

16

# Les Baux-de-Provence

The unreal fortified village of **LES BAUX-DE-PROVENCE** perches atop the Alpilles ridge, 15km northeast of Arles. The ruins of its eleventh-century **castle** merge almost imperceptibly into the plateau, whose rock is both foundation and part of the structure. The village itself, straggling over the hilltop just below, is a too-good-to-be-true collection of sixteenth- and seventeenth-century churches, chapels and mansions. To avoid crowds of summer day-trippers, it's best to turn up late in the day.

## The château

Daily: March & Oct 9.30am–6.30pm; April–June & Sept 9am–7pm; July & Aug 9am–8pm; Nov–Feb 10am–5pm; last entry 1hr before closing • April–Sept €10.50, Oct–March €8.50 • ☎ 04 90 49 20 02, ⓦ chateau-baux-provence.com

The only entrance to the enormous **château** at Les Baux is via turnstiles at the end of the main village street. These lead first to open ground below the walls, which is scattered with replica siege engines and catapults, and then to footpaths over and through buildings that include the ruins of the feudal castle demolished on Richelieu's orders, the partially restored **Chapelle Castrale** and the **Tour Sarrasine**. The higher you climb, the more spectacular the views become.

## The Carrières de Lumières

D27 • Daily: March & Oct–Dec 10am–6pm; April–Jun & Sept 9.30am–7pm; July & Aug 9.30am–7.30pm; last entry 1hr before closing • €12.50 • ☎ 04 90 54 47 37, ⓦ carrieres-lumieres.com

It's said that Dante took his inspiration for the nine circles of the *Inferno* from the **Val d'Enfer** (Valley of Hell), immediately north of Les Baux. Jean Cocteau used its contorted rocks and bauxite quarries as a location for his 1959 film, *Le Testament d'Orphée*. Those quarries have now been turned into an audiovisual experience called the **Carrières de Lumières**. Projection is continuous, so you don't have to wait to go in. Images are projected over the floor, ceilings and walls of the vast rectangular caverns, accompanied by music that resonates strangely in the captured space. The precise content changes each year, but makes little difference; the experience is mind-blowing.

| INFORMATION | LES BAUX-DE-PROVENCE |
|---|---|

**Tourist office** Maison du Roy, rue Porte-Mage (daily: April–Sept Mon–Fri 9am–6pm, Sat & Sun 10am–5.30pm; Oct–March Mon–Fri 9.30am–5pm, Sat & Sun 10am–5.30pm; ☎ 04 90 54 34 39, ⓦ lesbauxdeprovence.com).

### ACCOMMODATION AND EATING

**Hostellerie de la Reine Jeanne** ☎ 04 90 54 32 06, ⓦ la-reinejeanne.com. The village's one moderately priced hotel, near the tourist office. Very friendly staff, six simple rooms with views of the *citadelle*, a daily €16 *plat du jour*, and good *menus* starting at €35. Closed mid-Jan to mid-Feb. **€59**

★ **Oustau de Baumanière** ☎ 04 90 54 33 07, ⓦ oustau debaumaniere.com. Luxurious and spectacularly situated complex, stretching from below the castle rock up to the former quarries. Accommodation is offered in villas and buildings old and new, varying from opulently traditional to more contemporary, and there are three pools, two restaurants and a spa. *Menus* in the main restaurant start at €100 for lunch, €175 for dinner. Closed Nov–Feb, except Christmas. **€315**

**Le Prince Noir** Rue de l'Orme ☎ 04 90 54 39 57, ⓦ leprincenoir.com. An eccentric B&B in the home of an artist, in the uppermost house in the village. Choose between the one comfortable bedroom or the two luxurious suites; two-night minimum stay. Room **€108**, suite **€155**

**Les Variétés** 29 rue du Trencat ☎ 04 90 54 55 88. The most affordable restaurant in the village, open in the daytime only, has a lovely interior courtyard and sells good salads and pasta dishes for around €10. Daily 11.30am–5pm; closed Oct–Feb.

# Arles

With its sun-kissed golden stone, small-town feel and splendid setting on the east bank of the Rhône, **ARLES** ranks high among southern France's loveliest cities. It's also one of the oldest, with the extraordinary Roman amphitheatre at its heart, **Les Arènes**, simply the most famous of several magnificent monuments. Originally a Celtic settlement, Arles later became the Roman capital of Gaul, Britain and Spain. For centuries, the port of Arles prospered from trade up the Rhône, especially when enemies blockaded its eternal rival, Marseille. Decline set in with the arrival of the railways, however, and

the town where **Van Gogh** spent a lonely and miserable period in the late nineteenth century had itself become inward-looking and depressed.

Thankfully, however, Arles today is pleasantly laidback – at its liveliest on Saturdays, when Camargue farmers come in for the weekly **market** – and a delightful place simply to stroll around. Its compact central core, tucked into a ninety-degree curve in the river, is small enough to cross on foot in a few minutes. While ancient ruins are scattered everywhere, the heart of the Roman city, the **place du Forum**, remains the hub of popular life. Medieval Arles, on the other hand, centred on what's now the place de la République, the pedestrianized site of both the **Cathédrale St-Trophime** and the *hôtel de ville*. The one area where the city's former **walls** have survived lies to the east, in a quiet and attractive little corner. Sadly, the **riverfront**, once teeming with bars and bistros, was heavily damaged during World War II.

## Roman Arles

Arles is still recognizable as the **Roman** city thrust to greatness when Julius Caesar built an entire fleet here within a month. After using the ships to win control of Rome, he

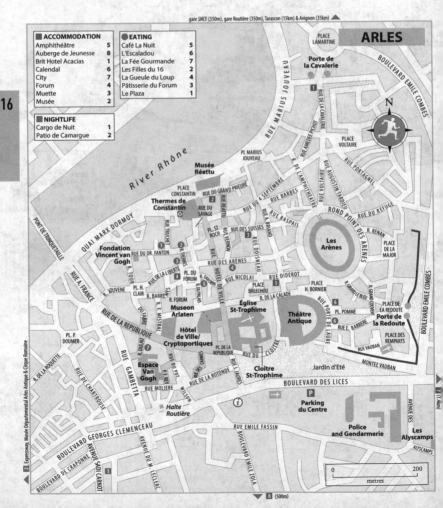

| ACCOMMODATION | |
|---|---|
| Amphithéâtre | 5 |
| Auberge de Jeunesse | 8 |
| Brit Hotel Acacias | 1 |
| Calendal | 6 |
| City | 7 |
| Forum | 4 |
| Muette | 3 |
| Musée | 2 |

| EATING | |
|---|---|
| Café La Nuit | 5 |
| L'Escaladou | 6 |
| La Fée Gourmande | 7 |
| Les Filles du 16 | 2 |
| La Gueule du Loup | 4 |
| Pâtisserie du Forum | 3 |
| Le Plaza | 1 |

| NIGHTLIFE | |
|---|---|
| Cargo de Nuit | 1 |
| Patio de Camargue | 2 |

---

**THE RENCONTRES INTERNATIONALES DE LA PHOTOGRAPHIE**

Europe's most prestigious annual **photography festival**, the **Rencontres d'Arles** (Ⓦ rencontres-arles.com), takes over more than a dozen venues throughout the city between July and late September. Visitors can either pay from €6 for admission to a single exhibition, or buy passes – €35 for one day, €42 for the whole festival – from ticket offices in the place de la République and elsewhere.

---

devastated Marseille for supporting his enemy Pompey, and Arles became a major port. The Mediterranean was closer to the city then, and the wheat fields of the Camargue became known as the "granary of Rome". Arles' relative isolation after the empire crumbled allowed its heritage to be preserved.

## Les Arènes

Daily: March, April & Oct 9am–6pm; May–June & Sept 9am–7pm; July & Aug 9am–8pm; Nov–Feb 10am–5pm • €9 with Théâtre Antique • ☎ 08 91 70 03 70, Ⓦ arenes-arles.com

Constructed at the end of the first century AD, the dramatic amphitheatre known as **Les Arènes** was the largest Roman building in Gaul. Looming above the city, it measures 136m long by 107m wide; its two tiers of sixty arches each (the lower Doric, the upper Corinthian) were originally topped by a third, and thirty thousand spectators would cram beneath its canvas roof to watch gladiator battles. During the Middle Ages, it became a fortress, sheltering over two hundred dwellings and three churches; now it's once more used for entertainment. While it's impressive from the outside, it's only worth paying for admission when a performance – a bullfight, perhaps, or a concert – is taking place.

## Théâtre Antique

Entrance on rue du Cloître • Daily: March, April & Oct 9am–6pm; May–Sept 9am–7pm; Nov–Feb 10am–5pm • €9 with Les Arènes • ☎ 04 90 18 41 20

Only one pair of columns in Arles' **Théâtre Antique** is still standing, all the statuary has been removed, and the sides of the stage are littered with broken chunks of stone. Quarried to build churches after the Romans left, it later became part of the city's fortifications. There's little to see on an ordinary day, but it's an atmospheric venue for performances and festivals.

## Cryptoportiques

Accessed via the *hôtel de ville*, place de la République • Daily: March, April & Oct 9am–6pm; May–Sept 9am–7pm; Nov–Feb 10am–5pm • €4.50

Arles' most unusual – and spookiest – Roman remains, the **Cryptoportiques**, are reached via stairs that descend from inside the *hôtel de ville*. No one knows quite what these huge, dark and dank underground galleries were; they may have simply propped up one side of the town's level open forum, which stood above. Empty now, they're gloriously atmospheric for a fifteen-minute subterranean stroll.

## Thermes de Constantin

Rue du Grand-Prieuré • Daily: March, April & Oct 9am–6pm; May–Sept 9am–7pm; Nov–Feb 10am–5pm • €4 • ☎ 04 90 49 36 74

All that now remains of the imperial palace that once extended along the Rhône waterfront are the ruins of the **Thermes de Constantin**, Provence's largest Roman baths. You can see the heating system beneath a thick floor and the divisions between the different areas, but there's nothing to help you imagine the original. The most striking feature, the elegant high wall of an apse that sheltered one of the baths, in alternating stripes of orange brick and grey masonry, is best viewed from outside.

## Les Alyscamps

Av des Alyscamps • Daily: March, April & Oct 9am–6pm; May–Sept 9am–7pm; Nov–Feb 10am–5pm • €4.50 • ☎ 04 90 49 36 74

---

### BULLFIGHTS IN THE ARENA

**Bullfighting** comes in two styles in Arles and the Camargue. In the **courses camarguaises**, held at *fêtes* from late spring to early autumn (the most prestigious is Arles' Cocarde d'Or, on the first Monday in July), *razeteurs* run at the bulls hoping to pluck ribbons and cockades tied to their horns, cutting them free with barbed gloves. The drama and grace lie in the style with which the men leap over the barrier away from the bull, and the competition for prize money. In this gentler bullfight, people are rarely injured and the bulls are not killed.

More popular, however, are the brutal Spanish-style **corridas**, consisting of a strict ritual leading up to the all-but-inevitable death of the bull. After its entry into the ring, the bull is subjected to the *bandilleros* who stick decorated barbs in its back; the *picadors*, who lance it from horseback; and finally, the *torero*, who endeavours to lead the bull through a graceful series of movements before killing it with a single sword stroke to the heart. In one *corrida* six bulls are killed by three *toreros*, for whom injuries (sometimes fatal) are not uncommon.

Outsiders may disapprove, but *tauromachie* (as it's known hereabouts) has a long history in the region, and offers the opportunity to experience Arles' Roman arena in use. Les Arènes stages bullfighting events between Easter and September, including non-fatal *courses camarguaises* at 5.30pm each Wednesday & Friday from early July until late August, and Spanish-style *corridas* in late April, early July and September. **Tickets** cost from €12 for the *courses camarguaises* up to €99 for a prime spot at a *corrida* (ⓦarenes-arles.com).

---

Arles' Roman necropolis, **Les Alyscamps**, lies a few minutes' walk south of boulevard des Lices. Originally much larger, it was regarded as Europe's most hallowed Christian burial ground long after the Roman era had ended; until the twelfth century, mourners far upstream would launch sumptuous coffins to float down the Rhône, for collection at Arles. Only one alleyway now survives, while the finest of its sarcophagi and statues are long gone. Nonetheless, ancient tombs still line the shaded walk, as painted by Van Gogh, and the tranquil stroll ends at the wonderfully simple Romanesque church of **St-Honorat**.

### Musée Départemental Arles Antique

Av 1ère Division France Libre • Daily except Tues 10am–6pm • €8, free first Sun of each month • ☎ 04 13 31 51 03, ⓦ www.arles-antique. cg13.fr • 15min walk southwest of place du Forum; served by free shuttle buses from *gare SNCF*, every 30min 7.10am–7.10pm

The superb **Musée Départemental Arles Antique**, the best place to get an overall sense of Roman Arles, stands southwest of the centre. Open-plan, flooded with light and immensely spacious, it starts with regional prehistory, then leads through the Roman era. The story of Arles is traced from Julius Caesar's legionnaire base up to the height of its importance as a fifth-century trading centre.

Excellent models show the changing layout of the city and the sheer size of its monuments, while topics explored include medicine, industry and agriculture, and the use of water power. A new extension proudly displays a miraculously preserved flat-bottomed boat that was discovered in the Rhône in 2004, and is thought to have been used to transport massive blocks of stone. Overhead walkways enable visitors to admire fabulous mosaics, while sculptures on the sarcophagi salvaged from Les Alyscamps (see above) depict everything from music and lovers to gladiators and Christian miracles.

The museum is positioned on the axis of the second-century **Cirque Romain**, an enormous chariot racetrack that stretched back 450m and seated twenty thousand spectators. Little is now discernible on the ground, however.

### Église St-Trophime

Place de la République • **Cathedral** Mid-April to June Mon–Sat 8am–noon & 2–6pm, Sun 9am–1pm & 3–7pm; July–Sept Mon–Sat 8am–noon & 2–6pm, Sun 9am–1pm & 3–7pm; Oct to mid-April daily 8am–noon & 2–6pm • Free **Cloisters** Daily: April & Oct 9am–noon & 2–6pm; May–Sept 9am–7pm; Nov–March 10am–noon & 2–5pm • €5.50

Arles' **Église St-Trophime** is simply one inconspicuous facade among many on place de la République. Superb twelfth-century Provençal stone carving around its doorway depicts the Last Judgement, trumpeted by angels playing with the enthusiasm of jazz musicians. Inside, the high nave is decorated with d'Aubusson tapestries, while there's more Romanesque and Gothic stone carving in the beautiful **cloisters**, reached by a separate entrance to the right.

## Musée Réattu

10 rue du Grand-Prieuré • Tues–Sun: March–Oct 10am–6pm; Nov–Feb 10am–5pm • July & Aug €9, Sept–June €8; €12 with Fondation Vincent van Gogh • ☎ 04 90 49 37 58, ⓦ museereattu.arles.fr

The must-see **Musée Réattu**, in a fifteenth-century priory beside the river, centres on 57 ink and crayon sketches by Pablo Picasso, made between December 1970 and February 1971. Among the split faces, clowns and hilarious mythical Tarasque, there's a beautifully simple portrait of Picasso's mother, painted in 1923. Other twentieth-century pieces include *Odalisque*, Zadkine's polychromed sculpture of a woman playing a violin, and Mario Prassinos' black-and-white studies of the Alpilles.

### ARRIVAL AND INFORMATION
ARLES

**By train** Arles' *gare SNCF* is on av Pauline-Talabot, a few blocks north of Les Arènes.
Destinations Avignon (17 daily; 20min); Avignon TGV (8 daily; 50min); Lyon (7–9 daily; 2hr 30min); Marseille (hourly; 50min–1hr); Nîmes (8 daily; 30min); Tarascon (12 daily; 10min).
**By bus** Most buses arrive at the unstaffed *gare routière* on av Pauline-Talabot, but local services stop on bd Georges-Clemenceau, east of rue Gambetta.
Destinations Aix (9 daily; 1hr 20min); Avignon (6 daily; 1hr); Avignon TGV (11 daily; 50min); Les Baux (5 daily; 40min); Nîmes (11 daily; 1hr 5min); Les Saintes-Maries-de-la-Mer (9 daily; 50min); St-Rémy (8 daily; 50min); Tarascon

(10 daily; 20min).
**By car** Drivers are better off parking on the periphery, such as in the "Centre" car park on bd des Lices, than venturing into the central maze of narrow one-way streets.
**Tourist office** Bd des Lices (Easter–Sept Mon–Sat 9am–6.45pm, Sun 10am–1pm; Oct Mon–Sat 9am–5.45pm, Sun 10am–1pm; Nov–Easter Mon–Sat 9am–4.45pm, Sun 10am–1pm; ☎ 04 90 18 41 20, ⓦ arlestourisme.com). The €16 *Pass Avantage* and the more restricted €12 *Pass Liberté* offer admission to various permutations of sites.
**Bike rental** 1 Véloc, 12 rue de la Cavalerie (☎ 04 86 32 27 05, ⓦ 1veloc.fr).

**16**

## VAN GOGH IN ARLES

On February 21, 1888, **Vincent van Gogh** arrived in Arles from Paris, to be greeted by snow and a bitter Mistral wind. Within a year, he painted such canvases as *The Sunflowers*, *Van Gogh's Chair*, *The Red Vines* and *The Sower*. He always lived near the station, staying first at the Hôtel Carrel, 30 rue de la Cavalerie, then the Café de la Gare, and finally the so-called "Yellow House", at 2 place Lamartine.

Van Gogh found few kindred souls in Arles, but managed to persuade **Paul Gauguin** to join him in October. Their relationship soured when the November weather forced them to spend more time indoors. Precisely what transpired on December 23, 1888 may never be known. According to Gauguin, Van Gogh, feeling threatened by his friend's possible departure, attacked first Gauguin and then himself. He cut off the lower part of his **left ear**, wrapped it in newspaper, and handed it to a prostitute. Gauguin duly left Arles, and although Vincent's wound soon healed, his mental health swiftly deteriorated. In response to a petition from thirty of his neighbours, he was packed off to the **Hôtel-Dieu** hospital, from where he moved on to St-Rémy (see page 830).

None of Van Gogh's paintings remains in Arles, and the Yellow House was destroyed by World War II bombing. Vestiges of the city that he knew survive, however. Behind the Réattu museum, lanterns line the river wall where he'd wander, wearing candles on his hat, watching the night-time light: *The Starry Night* shows the Rhône at Arles, while the distinctive Pont Langlois drawbridge is still there on the southern edge of town. The Hôtel-Dieu hospital itself, on rue du Président-Wilson, is now the **Espace Van Gogh**, housing a bookshop and a *salon de thé*.

The **Fondation Vincent van Gogh** runs a gallery at 33 rue du Dr-Fanton (daily 11am–6pm, closed Mon Oct–April; €9, or €12 with Musée Réattu; ☎ 04 90 93 08 08, ⓦ fondation-vincentvangogh-arles.org). It owns no works by Van Gogh, however; instead, changing exhibitions by contemporary artists explore themes associated with the celebrated artist.

## ACCOMMODATION

★ **Amphithéâtre** 5–7 rue Diderot ⓣ04 90 96 10 30, ⓦhotelamphitheatre.fr. Very central hotel, with inviting and charmingly decorated public spaces, and spacious a/c rooms that abound in warm colours, tiles and wrought-iron work, and have large well-equipped bathrooms. The four-person rooms and suites are also good value. €89

**Auberge de Jeunesse** 20 av du Maréchal-Foch ⓣ04 90 96 18 25, ⓦfuaj.org. Old-style hostel, 500m south of the centre – from the *gare SNCF*, take bus #3 to stop "Clemenceau" or bus #2 to stop "Fournier" – with rock-hard beds in large dorms, and spartan facilities. Bike hire available. Reception 7–10am & 5–11pm (midnight in summer). Rates include breakfast, only served until 9am. Closed Nov–Feb. Dorms €20.50

**Brit Hotel Acacias** 2 rue de la Cavalerie ⓣ04 90 96 37 88, ⓦhotel-acacias.com. Modern, simple but cheerfully decorated – and soundproofed – rooms in a friendly hotel, not far from the train station, with free parking nearby. Closed late Oct to March. €93

**Calendal** 5 rue Porte-de-Laure ⓣ04 90 96 11 89, ⓦlecalendal.com. Welcoming hotel, overlooking the Théâtre Antique and glowing at sunset, with bright a/c rooms facing a pleasant shaded garden; rates include access to the indoor spa. €139

**City** 67 rte de Crau ⓣ04 90 93 08 86, ⓦcamping-city.com. The closest campsite to town, 1.5km southeast on the Crau bus route, this three-star is not particularly attractive, but it offers a certain amount of shade, plus a restaurant and a pool. Closed Oct–March. €20

**Forum** 10 place du Forum ⓣ04 90 93 48 95, ⓦhotelduforum.com. Run by the same family for almost a century, this venerable hotel, in Arles' most appealing little square, offers plain but sizeable and tasteful rooms, plus a tiny pool and a bar that's barely changed since Picasso hung out here sixty years ago. €100

★ **Muette** 15 rue des Suisses ⓣ04 90 96 15 39, ⓦhotel-muette.com. Charming old stone hotel, close to Les Arènes, where the pleasant, tranquil rooms are decked out in beiges and creams, with rough-hewn terracotta-tiled floors and lots of Van Gogh touches, down to the (artificial) sunflowers on the tables. Larger suites sleep up to five. Nice buffet breakfast (€10), and friendly management. Closed Jan & Feb. €87

**Musée** 11 rue du Grand-Prieuré ⓣ04 90 93 88 88, ⓦhoteldumusee.com. Small, good-value, family-run place, set in a seventeenth-century mansion in a quiet spot opposite Musée Réattu, with a pretty, flower-filled terrace, and its own art gallery. Two-night minimum stay in summer. Closed Jan & first 2 weeks of March & Dec. €80

16

## EATING AND DRINKING

### RESTAURANTS

**L'Escaladou** 23 rue Porte-de-Laure ⓣ04 90 96 70 43, ⓦlescaladou-restaurant-arles.com. Behind its old-fashioned facade, near the upper side of the Théâtre Antique, this local favourite holds three substantial and usually very busy dining rooms. It can be noisy and not exactly romantic, but the service is friendly, and seafood lovers are in for a real treat, in the shape of the sumptuous and magnificently garlicky €28 Arlesian bouillabaisse. The one set *menu* costs €26 for three courses. Mon, Wed & Fri–Sun noon–2pm & 7–9.30pm.

**La Fée Gourmande** 39 rue Dulau ⓣ04 90 18 26 57. This friendly, slightly kitsch little restaurant has established such a reputation for its high-class home-style cooking that reservations are essential. Changing daily specials like the house speciality, melt-in-your-mouth slow-cooked lamb, cost around €25. Wed–Fri 11.30am–3pm, Sat 11.30am–3pm & 7–9pm, Sun 7–9pm.

**Les Filles du 16** 16 rue du Dr-Fanton ⓣ04 90 93 77 36, ⓦle16restaurant.com. Friendly little traditional bistro, just off the place du Forum and run, as the name suggests, by the daughters of the original owner. The lunch *formule* costs just €16, while for dinner you can get a three-course *menu* for €28, or simply order a *plat*, such as the succulent seasonal *tellines* (clams), or the €17 *gardiane de taureau*. Mon–Fri noon–1.45pm & 7–9.30pm.

★ **La Gueule du Loup** 39 rue des Arènes ⓣ04 90 96 96 69, ⓦrestaurant-lagueuleduloup.fr. Cosy stone-walled restaurant, squeezed into a venerable townhouse, with the open kitchen plus four tables downstairs, and the main dining room upstairs. Elaborate and delicate Provençal dishes include a courgette-blossom mousse and turbot on a bed of puréed aubergine. *Menus* from €18 lunch, €33 dinner; reservations recommended. Mon 7.30–9.30pm, Tues–Sat noon–1.45pm & 7.30–9.30pm.

**Le Plaza** 28 rue du Dr-Fanton ⓣ04 90 96 33 15. Smart but very friendly place, also known as *La Paillote*, where good *menus* full of Provençal starters and main courses such as *estouffade de taureau* (bull) range €24–34.50; the €26 seafood option includes a classic *aïoli*. Reserve for outdoor seating. Mon, Tues & Thurs–Sun noon–1.30pm & 7–9.30pm, Wed 7–9.30pm.

### CAFÉS

**Café La Nuit** 11 place du Forum ⓣ04 90 96 44 56. Immortalized in Van Gogh's *Café Terrace at Night* – though it's not the same café depicted in *The Night Café*, which was near the station – this long-established café remains *the* place to enjoy Arles' pretty central square. Have a drink on the terrace and you'll find yourself in quite a few holiday snaps; don't eat here though, the food is very poor. Daily 9am–midnight.

**Pâtisserie du Forum** 4 rue de la Liberté ☎ 04 90 96 03 72. *Salon de thé* with a whole patisserie full of goodies to go with the Earl Grey, plus ice cream and hot chocolate. Tues–Sat 7am–7.30pm, Sun 7am–12.30pm.

## NIGHTLIFE

### LIVE MUSIC

**Cargo de Nuit** 7 av Sadi-Carnot ☎ 04 90 49 55 99, ⓦ cargodenuit.com. This lively venue puts on an excellent and eclectic line-up of live jazz, electronic and world music concerts, and also comedy. It's only open when an event is scheduled, when the bar section also serves tapas. Schedule varies, but especially likely to be open Fri & Sat; bar opens 8pm, concerts start 9.30pm.

**Patio de Camargue** 49 chemin Barriol ☎ 04 90 49 51 76, ⓦ chico.fr. Arles was the original base for the world-conquering *Gipsy Kings* group. Founder-member Chico now runs this riverfront restaurant-cum-music venue, roughly 1km southwest of the centre, which puts on regular dinner concerts; they're typically on Saturday nights, and cost upwards of €50; check website for current schedules.

# The Camargue

Spreading across the Rhône delta, and defined by the Petit Rhône to the west, the Grand Rhône to the east, and the Mediterranean to the south, the drained, ditched and protected land known as the **CAMARGUE** is utterly distinct from the rest of Provence. With land, lagoon and sea sharing the same horizontal plain, its shimmering horizons appear infinite.

The whole of the Camargue is a Parc Naturel Régional, which sets out to balance tourism, agriculture, industry and hunting against the indigenous ecosystems. When the Romans arrived, the northern part of the Camargue was a forest; they felled the trees to build ships, then grew wheat. These days, especially since the northern marshes were drained and re-irrigated after World War II, the main crop is **rice**.

The Camargue is split into two separate sections by the large **Étang du Vaccarès**, a lagoon that's out of bounds to visitors. Most people focus their attention on the western Camargue, home to the sizeable town of **Saintes-Maries-de-la-Mer**, and also commercial attractions such as wildlife parks and activity operators. It is possible, however, to take a quick look at both the western and eastern halves of the Camargue within a single day.

## The western Camargue

The **western** side of the Camargue is busy all summer with tourists, who flock down its main artery, the D570, towards **Saintes-Maries-de-la-Mer**. Take the time to explore the marshes and dunes en route, or follow the waterfront nature trails.

16

---

## BULLS, BIRDS AND BEAVERS: CAMARGUAIS WILDLIFE

The Camargue is a treasure trove of bird and animal species, both wild and domestic. Its most famous denizens are its **bulls** and **white horses**, both of which roam in semi-liberty. Born dark brown or black, the Camargue horse turns white in around its fourth year.

An estimated 2500 of the region's **gardians** or herdsmen – ten percent of them women – remain active. A hardy bunch, they play a major role in preserving Camarguais traditions. Their traditional homes, or *cabanes*, are thatched, windowless one-storey structures, with bulls' horns over the door to ward off evil spirits. Throughout the summer, the *gardians* are kept busy, with spectacles involving bulls and horses in every village arena; winter is a good deal harder.

Camargue **wildlife** ranges from wild boars, beavers and badgers, tree frogs, water snakes and pond turtles, to marsh and seabirds and birds of prey. The best season for **birdwatching** lasts from April to June. Of the region's fifty thousand or so **flamingos**, ten thousand remain in winter (Oct–March), when the rest migrate to Africa.

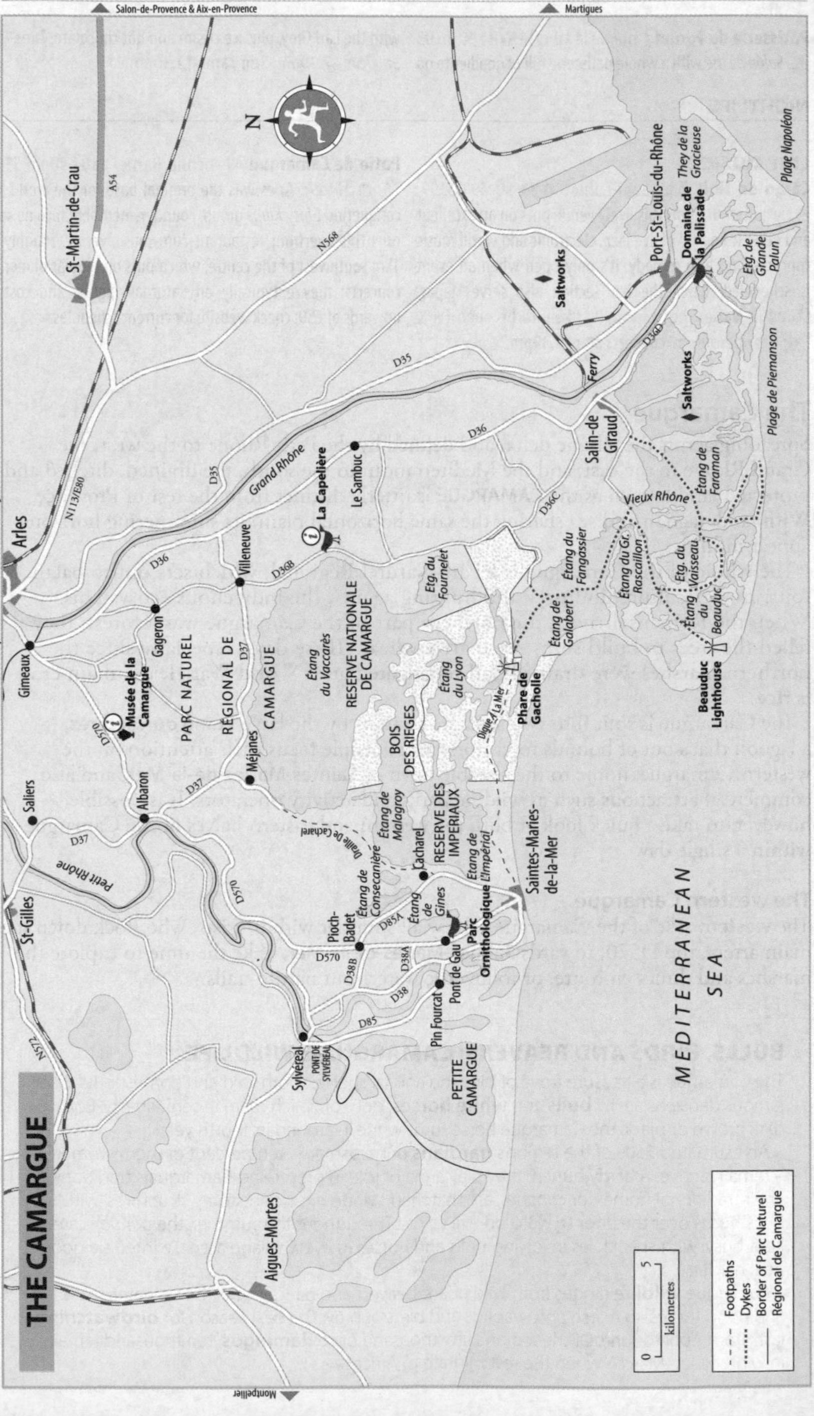
THE CAMARGUE
16
Salon-de-Provence & Aix-en-Provence
Martigues
Tarascon & Avignon
Nîmes & Montpellier
Montpellier
St-Martin-de-Crau
A54
N568
N113/E80
Arles
Gimeaux
Gageron
Villeneuve
La Capelière
Le Sambuc
Grand Rhône
D35
D36
D36B
D36C
D36D
D37
D570
Musée de la Camargue
PARC NATUREL RÉGIONAL DE CAMARGUE
RESERVE NATIONALE DE CAMARGUE
Etang du Vaccarès
Etg. du Fournelet
Etang du Lyon
BOIS DES RIEGES
RESERVE DES IMPERIAUX
Etang de Malagroy
Etang de Consecanière
Etang de l'Impérial
Etang de Gines
Draille De Cacharel
Digue à La Mer
Phare de Gacholle
Etang de Galabert
Étang du Fangassier
Étang du Gr. Rascaillon
Etg. du Vaisseau
Etang du Beauduc
Beauduc Lighthouse
Vieux Rhône
Étang de Faraman
Salin-de Giraud
Ferry
Saltworks
Saltworks
Port-St-Louis-du-Rhône
Domaine de la Palissade
They de la Gracieuse
Plage Napoléon
Etg. de Grande Palun
Plage de Piemanson
MEDITERRANEAN SEA
Saintes-Maries-de-la-Mer
Parc Ornithologique
Pont de Gau
Cacharel
Pioch-Badet
Pin Fourcat
D38
D38A
D38B
D85
D85A
Méjanes
Albaron
Saliers
Petit Rhône
St-Gilles
N572
Sylvéreal
PONT DE SYLVÉREAL
PETITE CAMARGUE
Aigues-Mortes
N
0
5
kilometres
Footpaths
Dykes
Border of Parc Naturel Régional de Camargue

## Musée de la Camargue

D570, 10km southwest of Arles • Daily: April–Sept 9am–12.30pm & 1–6pm; Oct–March 10am–12.30pm & 1–5pm; closed Sat & Sun in Jan • €5 • ☎ 04 90 97 10 82, ☜ parc-camargue.fr

Adjoining the main Camargue **information centre**, the **Musée de la Camargue** documents the history, traditions and livelihoods of the Camarguais people, with particular emphasis on rice, wine and bulls. Its excellent displays are not very accessible if you don't read French, though.

## Parc Ornithologique du Pont de Gau

Pont de Gau, 4km north of Saintes-Maries • Daily: April–Sept 9am–7pm; Oct–March 10am–6pm • €7.50 • ☎ 04 90 97 82 62, ☜ parcornithologique.com

The **Parc Ornithologique du Pont de Gau** makes a great stop before you reach Saintes-Maries. Paths lead around and over three separate lagoons in a thirty-acre marsh, making birdwatching easy. Flamingos are abundant, while some less easily spotted species, such as owls and vultures, are kept in aviaries.

## Saintes-Maries-de-la-Mer

Although most Camargue visitors head straight to **SAINTES-MARIES-DE-LA-MER**, 37km southwest of Arles, this attractive but commercialized seaside village has much more in common with France's other Mediterranean beach resorts than with the wild and empty land that surrounds it.

Saintes-Maries is most famous for its annual **gypsy festival** on May 24–25, when Romanies celebrate **Sarah**, their patron saint. She was the Egyptian servant of the two "Maries" in the town's name: **Mary Jacobé**, the aunt of Jesus, and **Mary Salomé**, mother of two of the Apostles, who were said to have landed here in a boat without sails and oars after being driven out of Palestine.

A line of **beaches**, sculpted into little crescents by stone breakwaters and busy with bathers and windsurfers in summer, stretches away west from Saintes-Maries' central core of white-painted, orange-tiled houses, while the pleasure **port** to the east offers boat trips to the lagoons and fishing expeditions. The town **market** takes place on place des Gitans every Monday and Friday.

**16**

## Église des Saintes-Maries

Place Jean-XXIII • **Rooftop** Daily: July & Aug Mon–Sat 10am–sunset, Sun 1pm–sunset; March–June & Sept to mid-Nov Mon–Sat 10am–noon & 2–5pm, Sun 2–5pm • €2.50 • ☎ 04 90 97 80 25, ☜ sanctuaire-des-saintesmaries.fr

---

### HIKING THE DIGUE À LA MER

Constructed in the nineteenth century to stop the incursions of seawater that precluded agriculture in the southern Camargue, the low-lying sea dyke known as the **Digue à la Mer** stretches across the mouth of the Rhône. Hiking the rough, narrow track along the top is a wonderful wilderness experience, with open water to either side, flamingos and other birds flying overhead, and the wind roaring in your ears.

While the dyke itself is roughly 12km long, connecting trails at either end make it possible to walk the whole way between Saintes-Maries-de-la-Mer and Salin-de-Giraud. The entire 31km route takes around six hours, with no facilities en route, so most visitors content themselves with an out-and-back round-trip from one end or the other. The Phare de Gacholle lighthouse in the middle, open as an information centre on summer weekends, makes an obvious turn-around point (July & Aug Sat & Sun 11am–5pm).

If you're coming from Saintes-Maries-de-la-Mer, simply head 1km east of town, staying close to the sea; the trail starts from the Plage de l'Est, where drivers pay a €4.50 admission fee. Coming from Salin-de-Giraud, you can park beside the Étang de Fangassier at trailheads either 7km west or 13km northwest of town.

The spiders-web tangle of streets and alleyways at the heart of old Saintes-Maries opens out into spacious squares around the grey-gold Romanesque **Church of Saintes-Maries**. Fortified in the fourteenth century in response to frequent attacks by pirates, the church has beautifully pure lines and fabulous acoustics. Its high, barrel-vaulted interior provided shelter for all the villagers; it even holds its own freshwater well.

At the far end, steps lead down to the low **crypt**, where the tinselled, sequined and dark-skinned statue of Sarah is surrounded by candles. Access to certain areas is restricted, following the theft of precious relics in 2009.

Although you can't climb to the top of the tower, you can pay to scramble onto and over the church **roof**, for great views over the town.

## The eastern Camargue

Cut through by the final canalized stretch of the Grand Rhône, the little-visited **eastern** side of the Camargue is less agricultural and more industrial, but has its own share of wildlife reserves and tranquil refuges, as well as the quiet little village of **Salin-de-Giraud**.

**Salt** evaporation was first undertaken here by the Romans, and the Camargue now holds one of the biggest saltworks in the world. Saltpans and pyramids add an extra-terrestrial feel to the landscape.

### La Capelière

D36B, 23km south of Arles and 19km northwest of Salin-de-Giraud • April–Sept daily 9am–1pm & 2–6pm; Oct–March daily except Tues 9am–1pm & 2–5pm • €3 • ☎ 04 90 97 00 97, 🖥 snpn.com/reservedecamargue

**La Capelière**, the information centre for the eastern Camargue, holds faded displays on Camargue wildlife and how to see it. Outside, a short but excellent 1.5km initiation trail circles a small lagoon, and there are superb **birdwatching** opportunities from camouflaged hides equipped with telescopes.

| ARRIVAL AND INFORMATION | THE CAMARGUE |
|---|---|

### SAINTES-MARIES-DE-LA-MER

**By bus** Buses from Arles (9 daily; 50min) arrive at the north end of place Mireille, 400m short of the sea.

**Tourist office** 5 av Van-Gogh, on the seafront (daily: April–June & Sept 9am–7pm; July & Aug 9am–8pm; Oct 9am–6pm; Nov–March 9am–5pm; ☎ 04 90 97 82 55, 🖥 saintesmaries.com).

### TOURS AND ACTIVITIES

**River trips** The paddle steamer *Le Tiki III* offers 90min trips from the mouth of the Petit Rhône, 2.5km west of Saintes-Maries-de-la-Mer (mid-March to Oct 1–5 daily; €12; ☎ 04 90 97 81 68, 🖥 tiki3.fr), and so does the Camargue from Saintes-Maries itself (mid-March to mid-Oct 1–4 daily; €12; ☎ 06 17 95 81 96, 🖥 bateau-camargue.com).

**Horseriding** Around thirty Camargue farms offer horseriding, costing from around €20/hr up to €100/day. Recommended options include Chez Élise (☎ 06 24 28 30 82, 🖥 elise-camargue.fr); you can find full lists at 🖥 saintesmaries.com and 🖥 promenades-a-cheval.com.

**Cycling** Bikes can be rented in Saintes-Maries-de-la-Mer from Le Vélociste on place Mireille (☎ 04 90 97 83 26, 🖥 www.levelociste.fr), and in Salin-de-Giraud from Mas St Bertrand (☎ 04 42 48 80 69, 🖥 mas-saint-bertrand.com).

**Canoeing and kayaking** Canoes and kayaks are available from Kayak Vert in Sylvéréal, 17km northwest of Saintes-Maries-de-la-Mer (☎ 04 66 73 57 17, 🖥 kayakvert-camargue.fr) and cost from €10 for 1hr.

**Jeep safaris** Camargue Safari (☎ 04 90 93 60 31, 🖥 safari-4x4-gallon.camargue.fr) offer jeep safaris, starting from Arles or Saintes-Maries, for €36 for 3hr and upwards.

### ACCOMMODATION

**Bleu Marine** 15 av du Dr-Cambon, Saintes-Maries-de-la-Mer ☎ 04 90 97 77 00, 🖥 hotel-bleu-marine.com. Friendly, peaceful retreat at the western end of town, with simple but immaculate rooms, a nice pool and easy parking. €83

**Cacharel** Rte de Cacharel, 4km north of Saintes-Maries ☎ 04 90 97 95 44, 🖥 hotel-cacharel.com. Sixteen luxurious rooms in one of the Camargue's oldest farms, with open fires to warm you in winter, a pool to cool off in summer, and horseriding available year-round, but no restaurant. €151

**Camping Sunêlia Le Clos du Rhône** Rte d'Aigues-Mortes ☎ 04 90 97 85 99, 🖥 camping-leclos.fr. Busy four-star site at the mouth of the Petit Rhône, 800m west of Saintes-Maries along an easy seaside path, and offering a pool, laundry and shop, but not all that much shade. Closed mid-Nov to March. **€29.70**

**Hostellerie du Pont de Gau** Rte d'Arles, Pont de Gau, 4km north of Saintes-Maries ☎ 04 90 49 96 99, ⓦ pontdegau.com. Simple but pleasant motel-like rooms alongside a really excellent restaurant, near the Parc Ornithologique. Closed Jan to mid-Feb. **€90**

★ **Mangio Fango** Rte d'Arles, Saintes-Maries-de-la-Mer ☎ 04 90 97 80 56, ⓦ hotelmangiofango.com. Tranquil farmhouse, overlooking the Étang des Launes 600m north of central Saintes-Maries, with a Mediterranean twist. Stylish, comfortable rooms (get one at the back, with a balcony, if possible), pricey restaurant, spa and steam

room, and a pool surrounded by lush green foliage. From mid-Nov to Dec, the place is open weekends only. **€165**

**Mas de Pioch** Pioch-Badet, 10km north of Saintes-Maries ☎ 04 90 97 50 06, ⓦ manadecavallini.com. Great-value B&B in a converted nineteenth-century hunting inn just off the main road; large rooms, capable of sleeping up to 6 guests, plus a pool. Book well in advance. **€55**

**Méditerranée** 4 av F-Mistral, Saintes-Maries-de-la-Mer ☎ 04 90 97 82 09, ⓦ hotel-mediterranee.org. Decked out in jolly flowers, this simple budget hotel has pretty Provençal-style rooms and stands in the heart of the town on the main restaurant street, seconds from the sea. The cheapest rooms share toilets, and there are some well-priced 4-person options. **€58**

### EATING AND DRINKING

Of a summer evening, Saintes-Maries is very lively indeed, with flamenco or gypsy-jazz guitarists and buskers everywhere. Camarguais specialities include *tellines*, tiny, shiny shellfish served with garlic mayonnaise; *gardiane de taureau*, bull's meat cooked in wine, vegetables and Provençal herbs; and *poutargue des Saintes-Maries*, a mullet roe dish.

**Casa Romana** 6 rue Joseph-Roumanille, Saintes-Maries-de-la-Mer ☎ 04 90 97 83 33. Friendly Provençal restaurant, with outdoor seating near the church. At lunchtime, two daily €15 *plats du jour* such as mussels or

*taureau*, also feature on a €20.50 *menu*; the evening *menu* is €29. Tues 5.30–10pm, Wed–Sun noon–2pm & 7–10pm; closed Jan.

**Les Embruns** 11 av de la Plage ☎ 04 90 97 92 40. Welcoming brasserie on the seafront road, just 100m from the old town bustle, with a street terrace and a bright, modern dining room. Seafood specials include a daily catch for under €20, stuffed squid, and fresh oysters or mussels, and there's a simple but good-value €19.50 *menu*. Daily noon–2pm & 7–10pm; closed Mon in low season.

**16**

# The River Sorgue

As you head east from Avignon to the Luberon, try to find time to pause at two delightful spots on the River Sorgue: the pretty market town of **L'Isle-sur-la-Sorgue**, and **Fontaine-de-Vaucluse**, which guards the source of the river a little further east.

## L'Isle-sur-la-Sorgue

**L'ISLE-SUR-LA-SORGUE**, 30km east of Avignon, straddles five branches of the River Sorgue, with little canals and waterways running through and around the centre. These waters were once filled with otters and beavers, eels, trout and crayfish, and turned the power wheels of a medieval cloth industry. Tanneries, dyeing works, and subsequently silk and paper manufacturing, all ensured considerable prosperity for the "island".

Nowadays, the blackened waterwheels turn for show only, and the mills and tanneries stand empty. In summer, though, L'Isle is a cheerful place, particularly on Sundays, when people arrive for its well-known **antiques market**, which centres on the Village des Antiquaires on avenue de l'Égalité and spills out onto the boulevards.

While claims to be the Venice of Provence may stretch a point, L'Isle-sur-la-Sorgue is a pleasant place to spend an afternoon. The central **place de l'Église** and **place de la Liberté** offer reminders of past prosperity, most obviously in the Baroque seventeenth-century **church** (Tues–Sat: July & Aug 10am–noon & 3–6pm, Sun 3–6pm; Sept–June 10am–noon & 3–5pm).

## Fontaine-de-Vaucluse

The source of the River Sorgue is a mysterious tapering fissure, 7km east of L'Isle-sur-la-Sorgue at the foot of towering 230m cliffs. Among the most powerful natural springs in the world, and compellingly beautiful into the bargain, it's a hugely popular tourist attraction. All access is via a gentle 500m footpath from the ancient riverside village of

**FONTAINE-DE-VAUCLUSE.** Both the village and the full length of the path are heavily (albeit reasonably tastefully) commercialized, but it's still a gorgeous spot, with the glorious green river cascading beneath thickly wooded slopes.

## INFORMATION                                                    THE RIVER SORGUE

### L'ISLE-SUR-LA-SORGUE

**Tourist office** Place de la Liberté (Mon–Sat 9am–12.30pm & 2.30–6pm, Sun 9am–12.30pm; ☎ 04 90 38 04 78, ⓦ oti-delasorgue.fr).

### FONTAINE-DE-VAUCLUSE

**Tourist office** In the village centre (April–Sept Mon–Sat 10am–5pm, Sun 9.30am–1pm; Oct–March Mon–Fri 9–12.30pm & 1.30–5pm; ☎ 04 90 20 32 22, ⓦ oti-delasorgue.fr).

## ACCOMMODATION AND EATING

### L'ISLE-SUR-LA-SORGUE

**Bistrot de l'Industrie** 2 quai de la Charité ☎ 09 70 35 81 75, ⓦ bistrot-de-lindustrie.com. This traditional old bistro serves three-course weekday lunches for €17.70, with evening main dishes at around €18 and pizzas also available, to be enjoyed at secluded riverside tables. Mon & Thurs–Sun noon–2.30pm & 7–9.30pm, Tues noon–2.30pm.

★ **La Prévôté** 4 rue J.J.-Rousseau ☎ 04 90 38 57 29, ⓦ la-prevote.fr. Charming hotel, arrayed around a quiet courtyard behind the church in the old town. The five rooms, at varying prices, are decked out in beautiful terracotta tiles, wooden beams and Provençal quilts; a small, superb restaurant (closed Mon lunch, Wed lunch & all Tues), serves top-quality *menus* from €24 for lunch, €46 for dinner. **€160**

### FONTAINE-DE-VAUCLUSE

★ **Auberge La Figuière** ☎ 04 90 20 37 41, ⓦ lafiguiere-provence.fr. Simple but attractive B&B rooms in the heart of the village, with terracotta tiles, tasteful Provençal furnishings and walk-in showers. With tables spread across a flowery courtyard, the restaurant (closed Mon) serves a great-value €25 *menu*. Closed Oct to mid-Feb. **€72**

**Restaurant Philip** Chemin de la Fontaine ☎ 04 90 20 31 81. Gorgeous riverside spot, en route to the spring. At the very least, it's worth enjoying a quick drink on the bar section of its long, peaceful terrace, but the food is good too, with full *menus* starting at €30. Daily: Easter to mid-June & Sept noon–5pm; mid-June to Aug noon–9pm.

**L'Hôtel du Poète** ☎ 04 90 20 34 05, ⓦ hoteldupoete. com. Despite its uninspiring exterior, this former watermill, just outside the village below the main D25 on the river's north bank, offers luxurious accommodation, with large, comfortable rooms and a pool, but no restaurant. Closed mid-Nov to Feb. **€98**

## The Luberon

East of Avignon and north of Aix, the beautiful wine-growing, lavender-carpeted valley of the **Luberon** has long been a favoured escape for well-heeled Parisian, Dutch and British visitors, not to mention artists. The Luberon's northern face is damper and more alpine in character than the Mediterranean-scented southern slopes, and gets extremely cold in winter. It's almost all wooded, except for the summer sheep pastures at the top, and there's just one main route across, the Combe de Lourmarin. One sizeable town, likeable **Apt**, and countless small **villages** cling stubbornly to the Luberon foothills. With their impossibly narrow cobbled streets, tumbledown houses strewn with flowers, and sun-baked *places*, they make wonderful days out and even better places to stay.

### Apt

The only town base for exploring the Luberon, bustling little **APT** has one of the oldest cathedrals in Provence. It's especially worth visiting on a Saturday for the lively **market** when, as well as every imaginable Provençal edible, there are barrel organs, jazz musicians and stand-up comics on show.

### Bonnieux

It's very easy to get lost among the narrow, twisting lanes of **BONNIEUX**, which is built on several interlocking levels, 12km southwest of Apt. If all else fails, head to the top

16

> ### PARC NATUREL RÉGIONAL DU LUBERON
>
> Aiming to conserve the natural fauna and flora, and limit development, the **Parc Naturel Régional du Luberon** covers much of the Luberon. It's administered by the **Maison du Parc**, which runs an information centre at 60 place Jean-Jaurès in Apt (Mon–Fri 8.30am–noon & 1.30–6pm; April–Aug also Sat 8.30am–noon; ☎004 90 04 42 00, ⓦparcduluberon.fr). Under the rubric **Le Luberon à Vélo** (ⓦleluberonavelo.com), assorted hotels, campsites and cycle hire and repair shops jointly promote cycle tourism throughout the region.

of the hill and dinky twelfth-century *église haute*, to enjoy marvellous views across the valley. **Market day** is Friday.

## Ménerbes

Surrounded by sweeping countryside and perched on a hill 23km southwest of Apt, the village of **MÉNERBES** boasts a fine collection of medieval and Renaissance-era houses and a dominant sixteenth-century citadelle. **Market day** is Thursday.

### Maison de la Truffe et des Vins

Place de l'Horloge • Daily: April–Oct 10am–12.30pm & 2.30–6.30pm • ☎ 04 90 72 38 37, ⓦ vin-truffe-luberon.com

If you're feeling overwhelmed by the multitude of local road signs directing you to wine-tasting caves or châteaux, head to the elegant **Maison de la Truffe et des Vins**, which sells wines from all three of Luberon's *appellations* at wholesale prices. They also offer wine and truffle-tasting, have a good open-air restaurant, and double as the local tourist office.

## Gordes and around

**GORDES**, 20km west of Apt or 12km north of Ménerbes, is an incredibly picturesque Provençal village much favoured by Parisian media personalities, film directors, artists and the like. A cluster of magnificent, honey-coloured buildings clinging to a sheer rock face, it's a spectacular sight. **Market day** is Tuesday.

At the top of the village, a church and houses surround a mighty twelfth- to sixteenth-century **château**, which houses the paintings of the contemporary Flemish artist **Pol Mara**, who lived locally (daily 10am–noon & 2–6pm; €4).

### Village des Bories

3.5km east of Gordes, off the D2 • Daily 9am–sunset • €6 • ☎ 04 90 72 03 48, ⓦ levillagedesbories.com

A collection of peculiar dry-stone dwellings on the hillside east of Gordes is known as the **Village des Bories**. Although such buildings were first constructed in the Bronze Age, most of these constructions – sheep-pens, wine vats, bread-ovens and the like – date from the eighteenth century, and remained occupied until little more than a hundred years ago.

### Abbaye de Sénanque

D177, 4km north of Gordes • Self-guided visits Mon–Sat 9.30–11am; 1hr guided tours, in French, to a very intricate schedule; see website for full details, and reserve online, at least 48hr in advance • €7.50 • ☎ 04 90 72 02 05, ⓦ senanque.fr

Set amid much-photographed lavender fields in a deep cleft in the hills, the substantial and austere twelfth-century Cistercian **Abbaye de Sénanque** is still active as a monastery. You can visit its church, cloisters and all its main rooms, while a shop sells the monks' produce, including liqueur, honey and lavender essence.

### Abbaye de Silvacane

D561A, 29km south of Apt • April & May Tues–Sun 10am–1pm & 2–5.30pm, June–Sept daily 10am–6pm, Oct–March Tues–Sun 10am–1pm & 2–5pm • €7.50 • ☎ 04 42 50 41 69, ⓦ abbaye-silvacane.com

Drivers en route between Aix and Apt pass close to the Cistercian **Abbaye de Silvacane**, just south of the Durance. Constructed like Sénanque in the twelfth century, the abbey

16

is now, after a long history of abandonment and evictions, a monastic institution once again. Isolated from the surrounding villages on the bank of the Durance, its architecture has hardly changed in seven hundred years; you can visit the stark, pale-stoned splendour of the church, its cloisters and surrounding buildings.

## Roussillon

The houses in the village of **ROUSSILLON**, 10km east of Gordes, radiate all the different shades of the seventeen ochre tints that were once quarried here. As colourful as an artist's palette, the town attracts a multitude of painters, potters and sculptors, whose works are on show and for sale throughout the town. Its main square is crammed with shops and restaurants, and **market day** is Thursday.

### Sentiers des Ocres

Daily mid-Feb to Dec; hours change monthly, up to 9am–7.30pm in July & Aug • €2.50 • ⓦ roussillon-provence.com

A short signposted stroll from the village centre brings you to Roussillon's abandoned ochre quarries, now a stunning natural park full of brilliantly coloured and oddly shaped rocks and pinnacles. Two trails, known as the **Sentiers des Ocres**, loop through this extraordinary landscape – the shorter takes around 20 minutes – repeatedly emerging from gentle, shady woodlands into patches of stark, exposed multi-hued ochre.

### Conservatoire des Ocres

D104 • daily: Feb & March 10am–5pm; April–June, Sept & Oct daily 10am–6pm; July & Aug daily 10am–7pm; Nov & Dec 2–5pm; Jan by reservation only • €7, includes optional guided tour • ⓣ 04 90 05 66 69, ⓦ okhra.com

The **Conservatoire des Ocres**, 1.5km southeast of Roussillon on the D104, tells the full story of the Luberon's ochre industry. As well as demonstrating washing, draining, settling and drying procedures, it hosts fascinating exhibitions.

## ARRIVAL AND INFORMATION                                        THE LUBERON

### APT
**By bus** Buses from Aix (2 daily; 1hr 45min) and Avignon (7 daily; 1hr 20min) stop at the *gare routière* on av de la Libération, east of the centre, but also drop passengers in the central place de la Bouquerie.
**Tourist office** 788 av Victor-Hugo (July & Aug Mon–Sat 9.30am–12.30pm & 2–6.30pm; Sept–June Mon–Sat 9.30am–12.30pm & 2–6pm; ⓣ 04 90 74 03 18, ⓦ luberon-apt.fr).
**Bike hire** Luberon Bike Shop, 669 av Victor-Hugo (ⓣ 06 48 72 16 13, ⓦ luberonbikeshop.com).

### GORDES
**Tourist office** In the château (Mon–Sat 9am–12.30pm & 2–6pm, Sun 10am–12.30pm & 2–6.30pm; ⓣ 04 90 72 02 75, ⓦ gordes-village.com).

### ROUSSILLON
**Tourist office** Place de la Poste (July & Aug Mon–Sat 9.30am–12.30pm & 2–6.30pm, Sun 9.30am–12.30pm; Sept–June Mon–Sat 9.30am–12.30pm & 2–6pm; ⓣ 04 90 05 60 25, ⓦ otroussillon.pagesperso-orange.fr).

## ACCOMMODATION

### APT
**Camping Les Cèdres** 63 impasse de la Fantaisie ⓣ 04 90 74 14 61, ⓦ camping-les-cedres.eu. Pleasant, shady and very inexpensive little campsite, within easy walking distance of the centre across the bridge from place St-Pierre. Closed mid-Nov to mid-Feb. €12
**Le Couvent** 36 rue Louis-Rousset ⓣ 04 90 04 55 36, ⓦ loucouvent.com. This pretty former convent, now run as a guesthouse, is Apt's most attractive option, with five stylish, simple, spacious rooms and a pool. Rates include breakfast. €99

**Le Palais** 24bis place Gabriel-Péri ⓣ 04 90 04 89 32, ⓦ hotel-restaurant-apt.fr. Simple but very charming and friendly hotel in the heart of town, overlooking the central square and somehow squeezing ten rooms into its slender frame. Breakfast costs €6 extra. €58

### BONNIEUX
★ **Le Clos du Buis** Rue Victor-Hugo ⓣ 04 90 75 88 48, ⓦ leclosdubuis.com. Very pleasant little hotel in a former boulangerie near the centre of the village, with ten a/c rooms, a pool, private parking and views of Mont Ventoux.

16

The breakfast buffet costs €12. €126

★ **Mas del Sol** Chemin des Foulans ☎ 04 90 75 94 80, ⓦ chambres-dhotes-bonnieux-luberon.com. Immaculate B&B, 2.5km northwest of the village centre towards Goult, run by a friendly couple and offering five modern rooms with a pool and tremendous views. Two-night minimum stay. €160

### GORDES

**Bastide de Gordes** Le Village ☎ 04 90 72 12 12, ⓦ bastide-de-gordes.com. Luxurious hotel, built into the ramparts of the old village. Some rooms have vaulted ceilings, there's a lavish spa as well as an outdoor pool, and the terrace boasts stunning views. €430

### ROUSSILLON

**Le Clos de la Glycine** Place de la Poste ☎ 04 90 05 60 13, ⓦ luberon-hotel.fr. Swanky hotel-restaurant in the heart of the hill village, where several of the sumptuous rooms enjoy fabulous views over the valley, and the excellent restaurant *David* serves *menus* from €38. €135

**La Maison des Ocres** 457 av Dame-Sirmonde, rte de Gordes ☎ 04 90 05 60 50, ⓦ lamaisondesocres-hotel.com. Charming, ochre-coloured hotel, where the nicest of the eighteen rooms, which sleep up to four, have private terraces, and there's a very relaxing garden. €123

## EATING

### APT

★ **L'Intramuros** 120–124 rue de la République ☎ 04 90 06 18 87. Inventive bistro-style food served in eccentric, cluttered surroundings, with *plats* like beef cheeks cooked and served in sealed jars for €18.50, pizzas for €13–15, and mixed *antipasti* platters from €12.50. Mon–Sat noon–1.30pm & 7–9pm; closed Mon Sept–April.

**Le Platane** 25 rue Jules-Ferry ☎ 04 90 04 74 36. Very pleasant Provençal restaurant, in an old-town back-alley with a raised roof terrace. Lunch starts at €14, dinner at €22, and there are plenty of options for vegetarians. Tues–Sat noon–2pm & 7–9pm.

### BONNIEUX

**Le Fournil** 5 place Carnot ☎ 04 90 75 83 62, ⓦ www.lefournil-bonnieux.com. Lovely Provençal dishes laced with olive oil and garlic, Luberon and Ventoux wines and a pretty terrace fringing a fountain-dominated *place*; two-course lunch for €25, dinner from €49.80. Tues & Sat 7.30–9pm, Wed–Fri & Sun noon–2pm & 7.30–9pm.

### GORDES

**L'Artégal** Place du Château ☎ 04 90 72 02 54. Romantic village restaurant, serving fabulous food on a terrace facing the château. For lunch you can get a huge salad for €17 or three courses for €28; full dinner *menus* start at €39. Mon & Thurs–Sun 12.15–2pm & 7.15–9.15pm, Tues 12.15–2pm.

### ROUSSILLON

**La Treille** 4 rue du Four ☎ 04 90 05 64 47. Pretty little restaurant in the heart of the old village, festooned with a climbing vine (*treille*), and offering a lovely shaded patio. Salads from €13, a three-course lunch for €19.50, and Provençal favourites classics à la carte in the evening, typically at €20–30. Mon, Tues, Thurs, Fri & Sun noon–3pm & 7–10pm, Sat noon–3pm.

**16**

# Aix-en-Provence

Were it not for the great metropolis of Marseille, just 30km south, **AIX-EN-PROVENCE** would be the dominant city of central Provence. Historically, culturally and socially, the two cities are moons apart, and for visitors the tendency is to love one and hate the other. Aix is more immediately attractive, a stately and in parts pretty place that's traditionally seen as conservative. The proudest moment in its history was its fifteenth-century heyday as an independent fiefdom under the beloved King René of Anjou, while in the nineteenth century it was home to close friends Paul Cézanne and Émile Zola. Today, the youth of Aix dress immaculately; hundreds of foreign students, particularly Americans, come to study here; and there's a certain snobbishness, almost of Parisian proportions.

The tangle of medieval lanes at the city's heart, known as **Vieil Aix**, is a great monument in its entirety, an enchanting ensemble that's far more compelling than any individual building or museum it contains. With so many streets alive with people; so many tempting restaurants, cafés and shops; a fountained square to rest in every few minutes; and a backdrop of architectural treats from the sixteenth and seventeenth centuries, it's easy to while away days enjoying its pleasures. On Saturdays, and to a lesser extent Tuesdays and Thursdays, the centre is taken up with some of the finest **markets** in Provence.

## Cathédrale St-Sauveur

Place des Martyrs-de-la-Résistance • Daily 8am–7.30pm • ⓦ cathedrale-aix.net

The **Cathédrale St-Sauveur**, at the north end of Vieil Aix, is a conglomerate of fifteenth-to sixteenth-century buildings. The finest of its many medieval art treasures is a dazzling triptych by Nicolas Froment, *Le Buisson Ardent*, which has become a Provençal icon. Commissioned by King René in 1475, the painting has been restored to a jewel-like intensity; the burning bush of the title is not the one seen by Moses, but an allegory of the virginity of Mary.

## Musée des Tapisseries

28 place des Martyrs-de-la-Résistance • Daily except Tues: mid-April to mid-Oct 10am–12.30 & 1.30–6pm, mid-Oct to mid-April 10am–12.30 & 1.30–5pm • €3.50 • ☎ 04 42 23 09 91

AIX-EN-PROVENCE

**16**

**■ ACCOMMODATION**

| Auberge de Jeunesse du Jas de Bouffan | 9 |
| Augustins | 3 |
| Camping Arc-en-Ciel | 5 |
| Camping Chantecler | 6 |
| Cardinal | 4 |
| Cézanne | 8 |
| Globe | 2 |
| Le Pigonnet | 10 |
| Le Prieuré | 1 |
| St-Christophe | 7 |

**● EATING**

| Le Bistrot des Philosophes | 1 |
| Crep Sautière | 7 |
| Le Formal | 8 |
| Mitch | 5 |
| Poivre d'Âne | 2 |
| La Table des Saisons | 3 |
| La Tomate Verte | 6 |
| Le Zinc d'Hugo | 4 |

**■ NIGHTLIFE**

| Le Scat | 1 |

**● SHOPPING**

| La Taverne de Platon | 1 |

**FESTIVAL D'AIX-EN-PROVENCE**

The undoubted highlight of Aix's busy annual calendar is the **Festival d'Aix-en-Provence**, dedicated to opera and classical music and held during the first three weeks of July. Tickets for major events cost anything from €20 to as much as €240, and go on sale in February, either online (ⓦfestival-aix.com), from the box office on place de l'Archevêché (☎0820 922 923), or at FNAC stores.

The former bishop's palace, the **Ancien Archevêché**, just south of the cathedral, houses the enjoyable **Musée des Tapisseries**. Highlights among its seventeenth- and eighteenth-century tapestries include nine scenes from *Don Quixote*, woven in the 1730s. In one, he's being divested of his armour by maidens who can't conceal their smiles.

## Musée Granet

Place St-Jean-de-Malte • Tues–Sun: early July to mid-Oct 10am–7pm; mid-Oct to early July noon–6pm • early July to mid-Oct €8.50, mid-Oct to early July €5.50 • ☎ 04 42 52 88 32, ⓦ www.museegranet-aixenprovence.fr

Aix's largest museum, the extensively modernized **Musée Granet**, is in the **quartier Mazarin**, a peaceful seventeenth-century residential district south of cours Mirabeau. Each summer it plays host to a high-class temporary exhibition, while its permanent collection covers art and archeology.

**Paul Cézanne**, who studied in this building when it was an art school, is represented by minor canvases such as *Bathsheba*, *The Bathers* and *Portrait of Zola*, assorted student pieces, and even one of his paint-encrusted palettes. There's also a small Rembrandt self-portrait; a similarly small Picasso from 1937, *Femme au Ballon*; several Giacomettis and a couple of Morandis; and a whole room of depictions of ruins by François Granet (1775–1849), whose collection originally formed the nucleus of the museum. Ancient finds from the pre-Roman Oppidum d'Entremont are displayed downstairs.

## Atelier Cézanne

9 av Paul-Cézanne • April & May daily 10am–12.30pm & 2–6pm; June–Sept daily 10am–6pm; Oct, Nov & March daily 10am–12.30 & 2–5pm; daily English tour 5pm (April–Sept) or 4pm (Oct–March) • €6.50 • ☎ 04 42 21 06 53, ⓦ atelier-cezanne.com • Bus #5 from Rotonde V-Hugo

While Paul Cézanne used many studios in and around Aix, he finally had a house built for the purpose in 1902, overlooking the city 750m north of the cathedral. It was here that he painted the *Grandes Baigneuses*, the *Jardinier Vallier* and some of his greatest still lifes. The **Atelier Cézanne** remains exactly as it was at the time of his death in 1906: coat, hat, wineglass and easel, the objects he liked to paint, his pipe, a few letters and drawings … everything save the pictures he was working on.

## Jas de Bouffan

Rte de Galice, 4km west of central Aix • closed for renovations at time of research; check website for the latest opening hours and prices • ☎ 04 42 16 11 61, ⓦ cezanne-en-provence.com • Bus #8

In 1859, when Paul Cézanne was 20 years old, his father bought an elegant Provençal manor known as the **Jas de Bouffan**, which remained in the family for forty years. Rather reluctantly, Cézanne senior gave his son free rein to paint the walls of the drawing room, but all traces have now been removed. Paul Cézanne frequently depicted the grounds, however, including the rambling gardens and duck-filled pond. In principle, it's open for guided tours, but having become somewhat shabby it was recently closed for renovations. It should have reopened by the time you read this; check online.

## Oppidum d'Entremont

3km north of central Aix • April & May Mon & Wed–Fri 9am–noon & 2–6pm, plus first Sat & Sun of month, 9am–noon & 2–6pm; June–Aug daily except Tues 9am–noon & 2–6pm; Sept daily except Tues 9am–noon & 2–5pm; Oct–March Mon & Wed–Fri 9am–noon & 2–5pm, plus first Sat & Sun of month, 9am–noon & 2–5pm • Free • ⓦ www.entremont.culture.gouv.fr • Bus #20 from cours Sextius

The **Oppidum d'Entremont** is the site of a Gallic settlement built more than two hundred years before the Romans established Aix. You'll find the remains of a fortified

16

enclosure, as well as excavations of the residential and commercial quarters of the town. Statues and trinkets unearthed here are displayed in Aix's Musée Granet.

## ARRIVAL AND INFORMATION

AIX-EN-PROVENCE

**By train** As well as a *gare SNCF*, just south of the centre on rue Gustave-Desplaces, Aix is served by a TGV station, 16km southwest, from which regular minibuses (every 30min: daily 4am–11.30pm; €5; ☎ 08 10 00 13 26) run to the *gare routière* in town.

Destinations from gare SNCF Marseille (every 20–30min; 40–50min).

Destinations from TGV Avignon TGV (22 daily; 20min); Marseille (frequent; 15min); Paris (8 daily; 3hr); Paris CDG Airport (4 daily; 3hr 30min).

**By bus** The *gare routière* is on av de l'Europe, on the south side of the old town.

Destinations Apt (2 daily; 1hr 45min); Arles (9 daily; 1hr 20min); Avignon (3–7 daily; 1hr 15min); Carpentras (3–4

daily; 1hr 30min); Cavaillon (4 daily; 1hr 20min); Marseille (very frequent; 30–50min); Sisteron (2 daily; 2hr).

**By car** Driving into Aix can be confusing: the ring of boulevards encircling the old town essentially form one giant roundabout, circulating anticlockwise; hotels are signposted off in yellow. Parking in the old town is nightmarish; the ring is probably the best bet for on-street parking, while good underground car parks are dotted along the circuit.

**Tourist office** 300 av Guiseppe-Verdi, in a shopping mall just west of cours Mirabeau (April–Sept Mon–Sat 8.30am–7pm, Sun 10am–1pm & 2–6pm; Oct–March Mon–Sat 8.30am–7pm, Sun 10am–1pm & 2–6pm; ☎ 04 42 16 11 61, ⊛ aixenprovencetourism.com).

## ACCOMMODATION

In high season, it's essential to reserve a hotel room at least a couple of months in advance. The tourist office offers bookings on ⊛ aixenprovencetourism.com.

### HOTELS

**Augustins** 3 rue de la Masse ☎ 04 42 27 28 59, ⊛ hotel-augustins.com. Classy central hotel, housed in a fourteenth-century monastery on the southern edge of the old core; the rooms are dependably comfortable, though they don't quite live up to the promise of the public areas, and the breakfast is skimpy for the €12 price. **€109**

**Cardinal** 24 rue Cardinale ☎ 04 42 38 32 30, ⊛ hotel-cardinal-aix.com. Welcoming, rather old-fashioned establishment in a quiet though very central neighbourhood, with 29 sizeable, great-value, antique-furnished a/c rooms, including six very fancy suites in an annexe just up the street. **€80**

**Cézanne** 40 av Victor-Hugo ☎ 04 42 91 11 11, ⊛ hotel aix.com. Smart modern boutique hotel, close to the *gare SNCF*, offering opulent bedrooms styled in honour of local poster boy Cézanne. The huge buffet breakfast is €19.50 extra, but at least there's free (if cramped) parking. **€162**

**Globe** 74 cours Sextius ☎ 04 42 26 03 58, ⊛ hoteldu globe.com. There's a slight chain-like feel to this large hotel, a 10min walk from the centre, but the standard rooms are adequate, and there are also some much cheaper "student" singles – not en suite – and family rooms. Modern breakfast room and rooftop terrace. Closed mid-Dec to mid-Jan. **€104**

**Le Pigonnet** 5 av du Pigonnet ☎ 04 42 59 02 90, ⊛ hotel pigonnet.com. Five-star luxury in the beautiful setting of an eighteenth-century *bastide* surrounded by lush gardens, 10min on foot southwest from the *quartier* Mazarin and boasting a pool, spa and fancy restaurant. **€261**

**Le Prieuré** 458 rte de Sisteron ☎ 04 42 21 05 23, ⊛ aix-en-provence-hotel-le-prieure.fr. Old-fashioned hotel in a former priory 2km north of the centre, which overlooks but doesn't have access to a magnificent seventeenth-century landscaped park. The 23 rooms haven't been updated in a while, but have a vintage charm. **€85.50**

**St-Christophe** 2 av Victor-Hugo ☎ 04 42 26 01 24, ⊛ hotel-saintchristophe.com. Comfortable 1930s-style hotel above a popular brasserie, close to the station and cours Mirabeau; some of its plush Art Deco rooms have private terraces, while the cheapest have showers not baths. **€110**

### HOSTEL AND CAMPSITES

**Auberge de Jeunesse du Jas de Bouffan** 3 av Marcel-Pagnol ☎ 04 42 20 15 99, ⊛ auberge-jeunesse-aix.fr. Rather institutional-looking hostel, 2km west of the centre, with small dorm rooms, a restaurant, baggage deposit, tennis and volleyball courts, as well as parking. Catch bus #2 to stop "V. Vasarély". Closed mid-Dec to mid-Jan. **€23.75**

**Camping Arc-en-Ciel** 50 av Malacrida, Pont des Trois-Sautets ☎ 04 42 26 14 28, ⊛ campingarcenciel. com. Located 2km southeast of town on bus #3, near the *Chantecler* site (see below), this small, clean fifty-pitch site has very good facilities, including a pool, plus shopping close at hand. Closed Oct–March. **€21.20**

**Camping Chantecler** 41 av du Val St-André, rte de Nice ☎ 04 42 26 12 98, ⊛ campingchantecler.com. Spacious campsite, set in a big park 2km southeast of the centre on bus #3, surrounding a Provençal country house and featuring a large pool and a restaurant that's open for all meals. Open all year. **€24.30**

## EATING

**Le Bistrot des Philosophes** 20 place des Cardeurs ☎ 04 42 21 64 35, ⓦ lebistrotdesphilosophes.com. One of the classier offerings on tourist-oriented place des Cardeurs, with hearty *plats* and a spacious outdoor terrace. Mixed platters of smoked salmon and foie gras, or main dishes like grilled tuna with *confit* aubergine, cost €23 and up. Daily noon–2.30pm & 7–10.30pm.

**Crep Sautière** 18 rue Bédarrides ☎ 04 42 27 91 60. Delicious, fresh crêpes at €6–10, to take away or enjoy while squashed into the cosy, vaulted and often packed restaurant. Tues–Sat noon–2pm & 7.30–11pm.

**Le Formal** 32 rue Espariat ☎ 04 42 27 08 31, ⓦ www.restaurant-leformal.com. You could easily miss this inconspicuous central restaurant, housed in a medieval cellar (it's entirely indoors) stocked with superlative wines. Don't let the name put you off; "Le Formal" is just the surname of the chef. Beautifully presented contemporary cuisine is served on *menus* priced at €46 and €52, though you can get a two-course lunch, including a mini-bouillabaisse, for €28. Tues–Fri noon–1.30pm & 7.15–9.30pm, Sat 7.15–9.30pm.

**Mitch** 26 rue des Tanneurs ☎ 04 42 26 63 08. Chic, intimate contemporary restaurant in the old town, open for dinner only and serving changing *menus* at €39 and €49 that depend on the freshest market ingredients and feature dishes like stuffed squid with a *rouille* foam. Indoor and outdoor seating. Mon–Sat 7.30–10pm.

★ **Le Poivre d'Âne** 40 place des Cardeurs ☎ 04 42 21 32 66, ⓦ www.restaurantlepoivredane.com. Small, dinner-only restaurant on the fringes of the popular place des Cardeurs, with seating inside and out. Book ahead to enjoy great-value, wide-ranging set *menus* of creative local cuisine, from €39 to €49. Daily 7.30–10pm; closed Wed in winter.

**La Table des Saisons** 6 rue Lieutaud ☎ 04 42 22 97 07, ⓦ latabledessaisons.com. If you're looking for a substantial snack rather than a full meal, this friendly deli/tearoom makes an ideal stop-off. The daily selection of savoury tarts, with vegetarian as well as fish or meat toppings, or large mixed salads cost from €14; there's a €15.50 *plat du jour*, including a coffee; and they also offer soup in winter. July & Aug Mon & Thurs–Sun noon–10pm, Tues noon–3pm; Sept–June Mon, Tues & Sun noon–2pm, Thurs–Sat noon–2pm & 7–10pm.

**La Tomate Verte** 15 rue des Tanneurs ☎ 04 42 60 04 58, ⓦ latomateverte.com. This pared-down (and very green) modern bistro serves imaginative and beautifully presented southern-French cuisine, such as a poached medley of fresh fish, and has some tables out on the street. Three-course *menus* from €29 for lunch, €36 for dinner. Tues–Sun 10.30am–10.30pm.

**Le Zinc d'Hugo** 22 rue Lieutaud ☎ 04 42 27 69 69, ⓦ zinc-hugo.com. Snug wine bar with inventive cuisine. On weekdays there's an €13.50 lunchtime *plat du jour*; €29.50 gets you a delicious *assiette comptoir* of charcuterie, cheeses and salad; there's also a €35 set *menu*; and typical mains like stuffed sea bass cost €20–26. Tues–Sat noon–2.30pm & 7–10.30pm.

**16**

## NIGHTLIFE

**Le Scat** 11 rue de la Verrerie ☎ 04 42 23 00 23, ⓦ facebook.com/ScatClub. Eclectic, cave-like late-night club, nominally jazz but putting on live music of all genres. Tues–Sat 11.30pm–6am; live music Wed–Fri.

## SHOPPING

**La Taverne de Platon** 25 rue des Tanneurs ☎ 06 33 05 88 21, ⓦ latavernedeplaton.com. Part antiques store, part art gallery, and part junk shop, this oddball emporium revamps and defaces old advertisements, wine labels and found objects into idiosyncratic artworks, under the slogan "beauty is in the eye of the beholder", and also sells everything from bowler hats to Goth jewellery. Tues–Sat 10.30am–8pm.

# Central Provence

In **central Provence**, it's the landscapes rather than the towns that dominate. The gentle hills and tranquil villages of the **Haut-Var** make for happy exploration by car or bike, before the foothills of the Alps close in around the citadelle town of **Sisteron** and **Dignes-les-Bains** further east.

The most exceptional geographical feature is the **Gorges du Verdon** – Europe's answer to the Grand Canyon. So long as you have your own transport, good bases for exploring the majestic peaks, cliffs and lakes of this spectacular area include the small market town of **Aups**, south of the Gorges, and to the northeast, **Castellane**, a centre for sports and activities.

## Aups

The neat and very pleasant village of **AUPS**, 90km northeast of Aix, makes an ideal stopover for drivers touring the Haut-Var or the Grand Canyon du Verdon. While holding all the facilities visitors might need, it remains a vibrant, lived-in community, still earning its living from agriculture, and at its best on Wednesdays and Saturdays, when **market** stalls fill its central squares and the surrounding streets.

Aups centres on three ill-defined and inter-connected **squares**: place Frédéric-Mistral, the smaller place Duchâtel slightly uphill to the left, and the tree-lined gardens of place Martin-Bidouré to the right. Beyond these, the tangle of old streets, and the sixteenth-century clock tower with its campanile, make it an enjoyable place to explore.

### INFORMATION                                                    AUPS

**Tourist office** Place Frédéric-Mistral (May to mid-July & mid-Aug to Sept Mon–Sat 9am–12.30pm & 2–5.30pm; mid-July to mid-Aug Mon–Sat 9am–12.30pm & 2.30– 6.30pm, Sun 9am–12.30pm; Oct–April Mon, Tues, Thurs & Fri 9am–12.30pm & 2–5.30pm, Wed & Sat 9am–12.30pm; ☏04 94 84 00 69, ⓦaups-tourisme.com).

### ACCOMMODATION AND EATING

★ **Auberge de la Tour** Rue Aloisi ☏04 94 70 00 30, ⓦaubergedelatour-aups.com. Appealing and great-value hotel, where the tasteful, airy, well-equipped rooms sleep up to four, and surround a sunny, peaceful, plant-filled courtyard restaurant that serves good *menus* ranging from €22 up to €39 for the gourmet all-truffle option. Closed Oct–March, restaurant also closed Tues Sept–June. **€60**

**Camping L'Oasis du Verdon** Rte de Tourtour ☏04 94 70 00 93, ⓦcampinglespres.com. This well-shaded three-star site, to the right off allée Charles-Boyer just 300m southeast of the town centre, has a bar, snack bar and heated pool. Closed mid-Oct to March. **€24**

**Grand Hôtel** Place Duchâtel ☏04 94 70 10 82, ⓦgrand-

hotel-aups.com. Traditional village hotel, just off the main square, with six plain but adequate en-suite rooms; some sleep up to four. The popular and hugely efficient garden restaurant in front serves excellent *menus* at €17–29.50, and there's a nice bar plus off-street parking. **€59**

**St-Marc** Rue Aloisi ☏04 94 70 06 08, ⓦhotel-restaurant-lesaintmarc83.com. Rickety, earthy, but very characterful old rooms (sleeping up to five people; not all en-suite) in a former olive-oil mill above a good restaurant, where a delicious octopus stew costs €18, and there's a €25 dinner *menu*; they also make pizzas over a wood fire. Closed Tues & Wed Sept–June, plus second half Nov. **€65**

## Haut-Var villages

The **villages** of the Haut-Var are among the prettiest in all Provence. Bask in their tranquillity and beauty, wander the maze-like lanes and admire the glorious, verdant landscape. The main historical sight is the serene **Abbaye du Thoronet**.

### Villecroze

It would be easy to drive straight through charming **VILLECROZE**, 8km southeast of Aups, without realizing its lovely, peaceful old quarter was even there. The inconspicuous walled medieval village, immediately south of the main D557, is a joy to stroll around, with its lovely vaulted stone arcades.

Villecroze sits beneath a water-burrowed cliff, on its northern side. The **gardens** around the base are delightfully un-Gallic and informal, and intriguing **grottoes** in its flanks are open to visitors in summer (April & May Wed–Sun 2–5pm; June Wed–Sun 10am–1pm & 2–5pm; July & Aug daily 10am–noon & 4–6pm; Sept Wed–Sun 10am–noon & 2–5pm; Oct Wed–Sun 1–4pm; €4; ☏04 94 67 50 00).

### Salernes

Compared with Villecroze, **SALERNES**, 5km west, is quite a metropolis, with a thriving tile-making industry and enough near-level irrigated land for productive agriculture. Twenty or so studios and shops, large and small, sell a huge range of **pottery** and **tiles**, while on Sunday and Wednesday a **market** takes place beneath the ubiquitous plane trees on the *cours*.

## Sillans-la-Cascade

Tiny **SILLANS-LA-CASCADE**, 9km southwest of Aups, is a sleepy village that has clung on to a brief stretch of ancient ramparts. Down below, on the Bresque River, a stunning **waterfall**, reached by a twenty-minute walk along a delightful and clearly signed path from the main road, gushes into a turquoise pool where swimming is sadly prohibited.

## Cotignac

**COTIGNAC**, 15km southwest of Aups, is the Haut-Var village *par excellence*, with a shaded main square for *pétanque* and passages and stairways bursting with begonias, jasmine and geraniums leading through a cluster of medieval houses. More gardens sprawl at the foot of the bubbly rock cliff that forms the back wall of the village, which is threaded with troglodyte walkways.

## Abbaye du Thoronet

Off the D79, 16km southeast of Cotignac • April–Sept daily 10am–6.30pm; Oct–March Mon–Sat 10am–1pm & 2–5pm, Sun 10am–noon & 2–5pm • €8 • ☎ 04 94 60 43 96, ⓦ le-thoronet.fr

The last of the three great Cistercian monasteries of Provence, the **Abbaye du Thoronet** remains even less scarred by time than Silvacane and Sénanque. During the Revolution, it was kept intact as a remarkable monument of history and art; it's now used occasionally for concerts. It was first restored in the 1850s, while a more recent campaign has brought it to clear-cut perfection. The interior spaces, delineated by walls of pale rose-coloured stone, are inspiring.

**16**

### INFORMATION                                     HAUT-VAR VILLAGES

**SALERNES**
**Tourist office** Place Gabriel-Péri (July & Aug Mon–Sat 9.15am–12.15pm & 1.45–7pm, Sun 9.30am–12.30pm; Sept–June Tues–Thurs & Sat 9.15am–12.15pm & 1.45–6pm, Fri 2–6pm; ☎ 04 94 70 69 02, ⓦ ville-salernes.fr).

**COTIGNAC**
**Tourist office** Pont de la Cassole (April–June & Sept Tues–Fri 9am–12.30pm & 2–6pm, Sat 9am–12.30pm & 2–4pm; July & Aug Mon–Sat 9am–12.30pm & 2–7pm, Sun 9am–1pm; Oct–March Tues, Wed & Fri 9am–12.30pm & 2–6pm, Thurs 2–6pm, Sat 9am–12.30pm; ☎ 04 94 04 61 87, ⓦ ot-cotignac.provenceverte.fr).

### ACCOMMODATION AND EATING

**VILLECROZE**
★ **La Bohème** Villecroze ☎ 04 94 70 80 04. Delightful, very floral café and tearooms, just inside the walls of the medieval enclave, with tables out on the alley, an enticing suntrap. Breakfast (€6) is served, along with cooked brunches (€10), afternoon tea, smoothies and cakes. Daily 9am–1pm & 4–8pm; closed Mon in low season.
**Le Colombier** Rte de Draguignan ☎ 04 94 70 63 23, ⓦ lecolombier-var.com. Charming hotel-restaurant, south of the village along the D557, with six sizeable and tastefully decorated rooms with terraces, and a peaceful garden. *Menus* in the restaurant (closed Sun eve & Mon) start at €29. Closed mid-Nov to mid-Dec. **€125**

**SALERNES**
**L'Odyssée** 5 rue des 4-Coins ☎ 04 94 68 02 32, ⓦ l-odyssee-de-salernes.com. Friendly, high-class restaurant with seating on the main square, serving changing daily

*menus* that focus on local, and especially organic, produce; *plats* like beef tartare or risotto typically cost €16–21. Concerts and theatre performances in winter. Daily except Thurs noon–1.30pm & 7.30–9.30pm.

**SILLANS-LA-CASCADE**
**Les Pins** 1 Grande Rue ☎ 04 94 04 63 26, ⓦ www. restaurant-lespins.com. The five simple en-suite rooms here are well priced but very ordinary; the patio restaurant (closed Sun eve, Tues eve, and all Mon Oct–March), is considerably better, with lunch at €20 and dinner *menus* from €28. **€70**

**COTIGNAC**
**Restaurant du Cours** 18 cours Gambetta ☎ 04 94 04 78 50, ⓦ restaurant-hotelducours.fr. Sun-kissed pavement restaurant – not to be confused with the *Brasserie du Cours* – at the heart of the village's social life, decked out with

bright yellow tablecloths and serving top-quality *menus* at €14 for lunch, €22–32 in the evening. July & Aug daily noon–2pm & 7–10pm; closed Tues eve & Wed in low season, plus late Dec to early March.

★ **Le Temps de Pose** Place de la Mairie ☎ 04 94 77 04 69 17. This quaint, flower-bedecked café on a quiet square makes an ideal spot for breakfast, a light lunch or a reviving cup of tea. Tasty, fresh sandwiches and quiches cost around €8, a large salad or daily *plat* more like €10. July & Aug daily 8.30am–10pm; Sept–June Tues–Sun 8.30am–7pm.

## The Gorges du Verdon

The breathtaking beauty and majesty of the **Gorges du Verdon**, also known as the Grand Canyon du Verdon, almost match its American counterpart, albeit on a much smaller scale. Peppered with spectacular viewpoints, plunging crevices up to 700m deep, and glorious azure-blue lakes, the area is absolutely irresistible; try not to leave Provence without spending at least a day here. The river falls from Rougon at the top of the gorge, disappearing into tunnels, decelerating for shallow, languid moments and finally exiting in full, steady flow at the **Pont du Galetas** at the western end of the canyon. Alongside is the huge artificial **Lac de Sainte-Croix**, which is great for swimming when the water levels are high; otherwise the beach becomes a bit sludgy.

With so many hairpin bends and twisting, narrow roads, it takes a full, rather exhausting day to **drive** right round the Gorges. Many visitors choose instead to trace either its north or south rim. The entire circuit being 130km long, this is **cycling** country only for the preternaturally fit.

Local outfitters and guides offer **activities** including climbing, rafting, canoeing, canyoning, cycling and horseriding.

### Moustiers-Ste-Marie

The loveliest village on the fringes of the gorge, **MOUSTIERS-STE-MARIE** occupies a magnificent site near its western end. Set high on a hillside, just out of sight of both canyon and lake, it straddles a plummeting stream that cascades between two golden cliffs. A star slung between them on a chain, originally suspended by a returning Crusader, completes the perfect picture.

Moustiers gets crowded in summer, when visitors throng its winding lanes and pretty bridges, and fill its stores and galleries. To escape, puff your way up to the aptly named chapel of **Notre-Dame de Beauvoir**, high above the village proper.

### The north rim

The spectacular and tortuous D952 runs more or less parallel to the **north rim** of the gorge for 45km east from Moustiers to Castellane. For the best close-up views, head south near the village of **La Palud-sur-Verdon** halfway along, and follow the **Route des Crêtes**.

#### La Palud-Sur-Verdon

Peace, tranquillity and incredible scenery reign supreme in the principal pit stop along the northern rim, **LA PALUD-SUR-VERDON**, 20km southeast of Moustiers. Even if you're just passing through, take the time to wander around the narrow, rambling streets and enjoy a meal or drink at a traditional restaurant or café.

#### The Route des Crêtes

To admire the very best of the Gorges du Verdon, detour off the D952 onto the dramatic **Route des Crêtes**, which loops away both from the centre of La Palud, and from another intersection a short distance east. There's nothing to stop you driving straight off into the canyon on its highest stretches, and at some points you look down a sheer 800m drop to the sliver of water below. As the mid-section of the Route des Crêtes is one-way (westbound only), to see it all you have to start from the more scenic eastern end. The road closes each winter from November 15 to March 15.

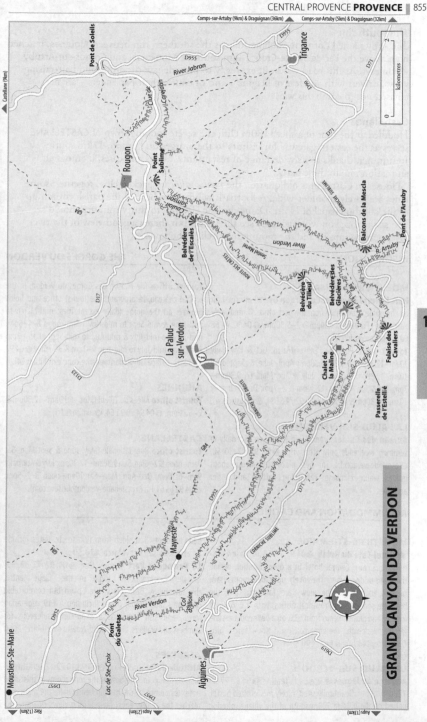

Comps-sur-Artuby (9km) & Draguignan (36km)
Comps-sur-Artuby (5km) & Draguignan (32km)

Castellane (9km)

D955

Pont de Soleils

Trigance

D955

River Jabron

D90

D71

Clue de Carejuan

Rougon

Point Sublime

D23

CORNICHE SUBLIME

Balcons de la Mescla

Couloun Samson

D84

Pont de l'Artuby

Belvédère de l'Escalès

River Verdon

R. Artuby

Sentier Martel

ROUTE DES CRÊTES

Belvédères des Glacières

Belvédère du Tilleul

D17

La Palud-sur-Verdon

D23

Chalet de la Maline

Falaise des Cavaliers

D952

D71

Passerelle de l'Estellié

CORNICHE RIVE DROITE

D952

D71

Mayreste

D952

Moustiers-Ste-Marie

D957

Lac de Ste-Croix

River Verdon

Col d'Illoire

Pont du Galetas

D71

CORNICHE SUBLIME

D19

Aiguines

D957

D957

Riez (12km)

Aups (27km)

Aups (13km)

N

**GRAND CANYON DU VERDON**

16

0 2 kilometres

## The south rim

The aptly named **Corniche Sublime** follows the southern rim between **Aiguines**, perched high above the **Lac de Sainte-Croix** 14km south of Moustiers, and **Comps-sur-Artuby**, 40km east. As this road was built expressly to provide jaw-dropping and hair-raising views, drivers with any fear of heights – and of course their passengers – are best advised not to come this way.

## Castellane

Huddled at the foot of a sheer 180m cliff, the severe-looking town of **CASTELLANE** serves as the eastern gateway for visitors to the Gorges du Verdon, 17km southwest. In summer, thanks to its wide range of restaurants, hotels and cafés, it enjoys an animation rare in these parts.

Houses in Castellane's old quarter, the *vieille ville*, are packed close together; some lanes are barely shoulder-wide. A footpath winds from behind the parish church up to the clifftop chapel of Notre-Dame du Roc. Twenty to thirty minutes should see you at the top; you won't actually see the gorge, but there's a good view of the river disappearing into it, and the mountains circling the town.

### INFORMATION — THE GORGES DU VERDON

#### MOUSTIERS-STE-MARIE

**Parc Naturel Régional du Verdon** Overall information on the gorge is available from the park office, Domaine de Valx (Mon–Fri 9am–12.30pm & 2–5.30pm; ☎ 04 92 74 68 00, ⓦ parcduverdon.fr).

**Tourist office** Place de l'Église (March, Oct & Nov daily 10am–12.30pm & 2.30–5.30pm; April–June & Sept daily 10am–12.30pm & 2–6pm; July & Aug Mon–Fri 9.30am–7pm, Sat & Sun 9.30am–12.30pm & 2–7pm; Dec–Feb daily 10am–12.30pm & 2–5pm; ☎ 04 92 74 67 84, ⓦ moustiers.fr).

#### LA PALUD-SUR-VERDON

**Bureau des Guides** Grande Rue (hours erratic; daily in summer, weekends only otherwise; ☎ 04 92 77 30 50, ⓦ escalade-verdon.fr). The best place to find out about guided walks, climbing, canyoning, rafting and other activities.

**Tourist office** The Maison des Gorges du Verdon, in the central château, incorporates the tourist office and holds displays on the gorge (daily except Tues: mid-March to mid-June & mid-Sept to mid-Nov 10am–noon & 4–6pm; mid-June to mid-July & mid-Aug to mid-Sept 10am–1pm & 4–7pm; mid-July to mid-Aug 9–1pm & 3–7pm; ☎ 04 92 77 32 02, ⓦ lapalud-verdontourisme.com; exhibition €4).

#### AIGUINES

**Tourist office** Allées du Tilleul (Mon–Fri 9am–12.30pm & 2–5.30pm; ☎ 04 94 70 21 64, ⓦ aiguines.fr).

#### CASTELLANE

**Tourist office** Rue Nationale (May, June & Sept Mon–Sat 9am–noon & 2–6pm, Sun 9.30am–12.30pm; July & Aug daily 9am–6.30pm; Oct–April Mon–Sat 10am–noon & 2–5pm; ☎ 04 92 83 61 14, ⓦ castellane-verdontourisme.com).

### ACCOMMODATION AND EATING

#### MOUSTIERS-STE-MARIE

★ **Hôtel-Café du Relais** ☎ 04 92 74 66 10, ⓦ lerelais-moustiers.com. Central hotel in a great location beside the main bridge, where the lovely upgraded rooms have modern bathrooms. The views are fantastic, and the brasserie serves good Provençal dishes, with a €16 lunch *formule* and dinner *menus* from €35, on a *belle époque*-style terrace overlooking the stream. Closed Nov–March, plus Tues except in July & Aug. **€90**

#### LA PALUD-SUR-VERDON

**Auberge de Jeunesse** Rte de la Maline ☎ 04 92 77 38 72, ⓦ fuaj.org. Beautifully sited, nicely modernized hostel, poised on the hillside 500m south of the village, offering beds in rooms that sleep from two to six. Rates include breakfast. Closed Oct–March. **€20.50**

**Le Perroquet Vert** Grande Rue ☎ 04 92 77 33 39, ⓦ leperroquetvert.com. Right in the village centre, this townhouse B&B offers three plain but comfortable bedrooms plus simple meals including a €19 vegetarian *menu*, and also serves as a shop-cum-rendezvous for climbers and walkers. Closed mid-Nov to mid-March. **€60**

#### AIGUINES

**Altitude 823** Grande Rue ☎ 04 98 10 22 17, ⓦ altitude 823-verdon.com. The best of the nine rooms in this small hotel-restaurant, at the hairpin bend where the main road reaches the centre, enjoy far-reaching views down to the lake. Breakfast is included. Closed Nov to mid-March. €117

**Le Galetas** Quartier Vernis ☎ 04 94 70 20 48, ⓦ camping legaletas.wix.com. Aiguines' large and rather plain municipal campsite is a long way down from the village, almost within diving distance of the lake. No reservations. Closed mid-Oct to March. €16

**Le Vieux Château** Place de la Fontaine ☎ 04 94 70 22 95, ⓦ hotelvieuxchateau.fr. Appealing *Logis de France* hotel, housed in an eighteenth-century coaching inn in the heart of the village, with bright, albeit simple rooms and

a nice terrace bar and restaurant that serves a €28 *menu terroir* and a decent €14 *plat du jour*, such as *aïoli* or trout. Closed Nov–March. €85

### CASTELLANE

★ **Commerce** Place Marcel-Sauvaire ☎ 04 92 83 61 00, ⓦ hotel-du-commerce-verdon.com. Comfortable and very central, Castellane's finest hotel has modernized rooms that sleep up to four, plus a restaurant (closed Mon) that serves wonderful food, both indoors and beside the small pool. Rates include buffet breakfast. Closed Nov–Easter. €115

# Alpes de Haute-Provence

North of Castellane, the **Route Napoléon** passes through the barren scrubby rocklands of the **Alpes de Haute-Provence**. The road was built in the 1930s to commemorate the great leader's journey north through Haute-Provence on return from exile on Elba in 1815, in the most audacious and vain recapture of power in French history. Using mule paths still deep with winter snow, Napoleon and his seven hundred soldiers forged ahead towards **Digne-les-Bains** and **Sisteron** on their way to Grenoble – a total of 350km – in just six days. One hundred days later, he lost the battle of Waterloo, and was subsequently dispatched to the island of St Helena for permanent exile.

## Digne-les-Bains

By far the largest community in the Provençal Alps, the faded spa town of **DIGNE-LES-BAINS**, is best seen as a convenient base for trips into the mountains, rather than a destination in its own right, though it does feature one interesting **museum**.

### Musée Alexandra David-Néel

27 av du Maréchal-Juin, 1.2km southwest of the centre • Guided tours, by advance reservation only. Tues–Sun 10.30am & 2pm, with an extra 3.30pm tour only when both earlier tours are full • Free • ☎ 04 92 31 32 38, ⓦ alexandra-david-neel.com

The **Musée Alexandra David-Néel** is dedicated to the memory of an extraordinary, tenacious explorer who spent more than fourteen years travelling the length and breadth of Tibet. David-Néel lived out the remainder of her life in this house, eventually dying in 1969, aged almost 101. It's stuffed with photographs tracing her journeys, as well as Tibetan ornaments, masks and paintings.

## Sisteron

**SISTERON**, 25km northwest of Digne on the Route Napoléon, was once the most important mountain gateway to Provence. The site has been fortified since time immemorial; even now, half-destroyed by the Anglo-American bombardment of 1944, its magnificent **citadelle** (daily: April & Oct 9am–6pm, May 9am–6.30pm, June & Sept 9am–7pm, July & Aug 9am–7.30pm; 1st half of Nov 10am–5pm €6.60; ⓦ www.citadelledesisteron.fr) stands as a fearsome sentinel over the city and the solitary bridge across the River Durance. The views from the ramparts, built in 1370, are breathtaking,

**16**

---

### CHEMINS DE FER DE PROVENCE

Also known as the **Train des Pignes**, in honour of the pine cones originally used as fuel, the narrow-gauge **Chemins de Fer de Provence** connects Dignes-les-Bains with Nice, with stops including Annot and St-André-les-Alpes. It's a stupendous ride, with four trains daily taking around 3hr 20min to cover the full route, for a one-way fare of €24.10. The scenery includes glittering rivers, lush dark-green forests, dramatic cliff faces and plunging gorges. For full details, see ⓦ trainprovence.com.

while a small **historical museum** lies just inside. Further up is the vertiginous late medieval chapel, **Notre-Dame-du-Château**, which has been restored to its Gothic glory.

## ARRIVAL AND INFORMATION

### ALPES DE HAUTE-PROVENCE

### DIGNE-LES-BAINS

**By train** The gare Chemin de Fer de la Provence (see page 857), with trains to and from Nice (4 daily; 3hr 20min), is on av Pierre-Sémard, on the west bank of the river.

**By bus** The *gare routière* is on rond-point-du-11-novembre-1918. Destinations Avignon (3–5 daily; 3hr 30min); Barcelonnette (2 daily; 1hr 30min); Sisteron (9 daily; 1hr 15min).

**Tourist office** place du Tampinet (April–June & Sept Mon–Sat 9am–noon & 2–6pm, Sun 9.30am–noon & 2.30–6pm;

July & Aug Mon–Sat 8.30am–12.30pm & 1.30–6.30pm, Sun 9.30am–noon & 2.30–4.30pm; Nov–March Mon–Fri 9am–noon & 2–5pm, Sat 9am–1pm; ☎04 92 36 62 62, ⓦot-dignelesbains.fr).

### SISTERON

**Tourist office** Place de la République (July & Aug Mon–Sat 9am–7pm, Sun 10am–5pm; Sept–June Mon–Sat 9am–noon & 2–5pm; ☎04 92 61 36 50, ⓦsisteron-buech.fr).

## ACCOMMODATION AND EATING

### DIGNE-LES-BAINS

**Central** 26 bd Gassendi ☎04 92 31 31 91. Spacious, comfortable budget hotel, on a bustling street in the heart of town near the tourist office. The cheapest of its simple antique-furnished rooms lack en-suite facilities. Closed Jan. **€55**

★ **Le Chaudron** 40 rue de l'Hubac ☎04 92 31 24 87. This excellent old-town restaurant, run by a very friendly husband-and-wife team, offers pavement seating in summer, and a cosy upstairs dining room in winter. The €29 dinner *menu* focuses on substantial baked dishes from their wood-fired oven, and at lunchtime there's a good €12.80 *plat du jour*. Mon, Tues & Fri–Sun noon–1.30pm & 7.30–9.15pm.

**Villa Gaia** 24 rte de Nice ☎04 92 31 21 60, ⓦhotel-villagaia-digne.com. Stately, peaceful eighteenth-century

country house, 3km southwest of the centre and offering ten very comfortable guest rooms of varying sizes, along with spa facilities. There's no public restaurant, but guests can have dinner for €28. Closed Nov to mid-April. **€92**

### SISTERON

**Grand Hôtel du Cours** Allée de Verdun ☎04 92 61 04 51, ⓦhotel-lecours.com. This old-fashioned, family-run hotel, just a few steps from the cathedral, is the perfect place to appreciate the genteel charms of Sisteron, and has a good restaurant. Closed Jan & Feb. **€81**

**Tivoli** 21 place René-Cassin ☎06 51 36 17 75. Decent two-star hotel just off place de la République. Cheerful and good value, with revamped decor, parking and a terrace with views towards the citadelle. **€59**

# Northeast Provence

Depending on the season, the **northeastern corner of Provence** can be two different worlds. In winter, the sheep and shepherds find warmer pastures, leaving the snowy heights to horned mouflons, chamois and the perfectly camouflaged ermine. The villages where shepherds came to summer markets are battened down for the long cold haul, while modern conglomerations of Swiss-style chalet houses, sports shops and nightclubs come to life around the ski lifts. The seasonal dichotomy is especially evident in towns like **Colmars-les-Alpes** and **Barcelonnette**.

The **Alpes-Maritimes** make up much of northeastern Provence, encompassing most of the magnificent **Parc National du Mercantour**, which runs south of Barcelonnette to the Italian border villages of Tende, Breil-sur-Roya and Sospel.

## Colmars-les-Alpes

Even when spookily empty out of season, the charming village of **COLMARS-LES-ALPES** makes an ideal journey's break on the western periphery of the Parc National du Mercantour. Tucked away in the Haut-Verdon valley, behind imposing, honey-coloured walls and large seventeenth-century *portes*, it comes to life in winter as a base for skiiers, as well as during its summer medieval fair (second Sun in Aug).

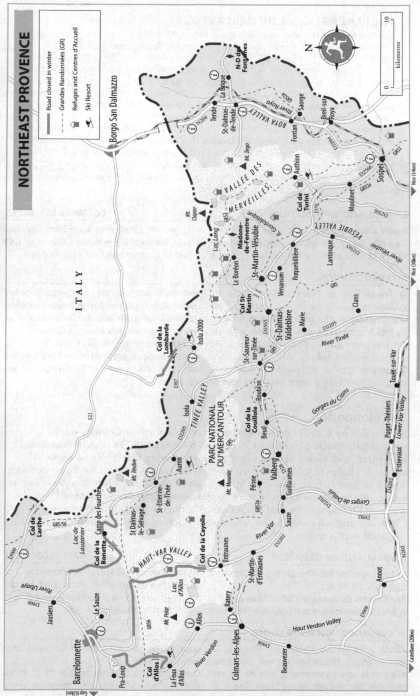

## NORTHEAST PROVENCE

| | |
|---|---|
| ━━━ | Road closed in winter |
| ---- | Grandes Randonnées (GR) |
| 🏠 | Refuges and Centres d'Accueil |
| 🎿 | Ski Resort |

N

0 ───── 10
kilometres

**ITALY**

Borgo San Dalmazzo

N-D des Fontaines

La Brigue
Tende
St-Dalmas-de-Tende
Saorge
River Roya
Breil-sur-Roya

**ROYA VALLEY**
Fontan
D2204
N204
GR52

Mt. Bego
Luthion
Sospel
Nice (34km)
D2566
GR52a

**VALLÉE DES MERVEILLES**
Mt. Clapier
Lac Long
Col de Turini
Moulinet
D70
D2566

Madone-de-Fenestre
R. Gordolasque
St-Martin-Vésubie
Le Boréon
Roquebillière
Venanson
Lantosque
River Vésubie
**VÉSUBIE VALLEY**
D2565
Nice (30km)
GR5

Col de la Lombarde
Isola 2000
Col St-Martin
St-Dalmas-Valdeblore
Marie
Clans
D2565
D2205

St-Sauveur-sur-Tinée
River Tinée
Touët-sur-Var

**TINÉE VALLEY**
Isola
D2205

Roubion
Col de la Couillole
Beuil
Gorges du Cians
Lower Var Valley
D28

**PARC NATIONAL DU MERCANTOUR**
Mt. Ténibre
Auron
St-Etienne-de-Tinée
Mt. Mounier
Péone
Valberg
Guillaumes
Sauze
River Var
GR52a
D902
Puget-Théniers
Entrevaux
D4202
Gorges de Daluis
D2202

Col de Larche
Lac de Lauzanier
Camp des Fourches
St-Dalmas-le-Selvage
GR5/56

Col de la Bonette
**HAUT-VAR VALLEY**
(Col de la Cayolle)
Entraunes
St-Martin-d'Entraunes
N202
D902

River Ubaye
Jausiers
Le Sauze
D900
Gap (62km)

Barcelonnette
Castellane (20km)

Pra-Loup
Col d'Allos
La Foux d'Allos
Mt. Pelat
Allos
Lac d'Allos
GR56
Ratery
Colmars-les-Alpes
River Verdon
Haut Verdon Valley
Beauvezer
Annot
D908
D908

16

**16**

---

## THE PARC NATIONAL DU MERCANTOUR

The **Parc National du Mercantour** is a long, narrow band of mountains, near the Italian border, that runs for 75km from south of Barcelonnette to Sospel, 16km north of the Mediterranean. A haven for wildlife, it holds colonies of chamois, mouflon, ibex and marmots, breeding pairs of golden eagles and other rare birds of prey, great spotted woodpeckers and hoopoes, blackcocks and ptarmigan. Grey wolves, which disappeared in the 1930s, started to venture back from neighbouring Italy during the 1990s, and there's now thought to be a small but stable wolf population. The flora too is special, with unique species of lilies, orchids and Alpine plants, including the rare multi-flowering saxifrage.

Numerous paths cross the park, including the GR5 and GR52, with *refuge* huts providing basic food and bedding for hikers. The **Maisons du Parc** in Barcelonnette, St-Étienne-de-Tinée and St-Martin-Vésubie can provide maps and accommodation details as well as advice on footpaths and weather conditions; see also ⓦ mercantour.eu. Camping, lighting fires, picking flowers, playing radios or disturbing the delicate environment is strictly outlawed.

---

### ARRIVAL AND INFORMATION                    COLMARS-LES-ALPES

**Tourist office** Outside the walls, facing the porte des Glacis (May & June Mon–Sat 9am–noon & 2–6pm, Sun 9.30am–12.30pm; July & Aug Mon–Sat 9am–12.30pm & 2–6.30pm, Sun 9.30am–noon & 2–5.30pm; Sept–April Mon–Sat 9am–noon & 2–6pm, Sun 9.30am–noon; ☎ 04 92 83 41 92, ⓦ colmarslesalpes-verdontourisme.com).

### ACCOMMODATION

**Le France** Place de France ☎ 04 92 83 42 93, ⓦ hotellefrance-colmarslesalpes.com. Colmars' one hotel, an old-fashioned but very appealing place just across the D908 from the walled town, has a garden restaurant that serves pizza in summer, and a splendid old bar. Closed early Jan to mid-Feb. **€68**

**Gassendi** Rue St-Joseph ☎ 09 64 48 07 04, ✉ gassendi@gmail.com. Year-round *gîte d'étape*, housed in a hideously pebble-dashed monstrosity that's actually a twelfth-century Templar hospice. The six dorms have ten beds each, and there's a couple of private double rooms. Rates include breakfast; an evening meal costs €16 extra. Dorms **€24**, doubles **€64**

**Les Pommiers** Quartier du Tallier ☎ 04 92 83 41 56. Attractive, simple campsite, amid the orchards of a working farm, 10min walk southwest of the village. Closed late Sept to April. **€15**

---

# Barcelonnette

Surrounded by majestic snowcapped peaks, 44km north of Colmars via the terrifying mountain pass of the Col d'Allos, **BARCELONNETTE** is an immaculate little place, with sunny squares where old men wearing berets play *pétanque*. All the houses have tall gables and deep eaves, and a more ideal spot for doing nothing would be hard to find. It owes its Spanish-sounding name, "Little Barcelona", to its foundation in the thirteenth century by Raimond Béranger IV, count of Provence, whose family came from the Catalan city. Although snow falls here around Christmas and stays until Easter, and there are several ski resorts nearby, summer is the main tourist season.

### ARRIVAL AND INFORMATION                    BARCELONNETTE

**By bus** Connections with Digne (2 daily; 1hr 30min) and Gap (4 daily; 1hr 30min).

**Parc National du Mercantour information centre** 10 av de la Libération (mid-June to mid-Sept daily 10am–noon & 2.30–6.30pm; ☎ 04 92 81 21 31, ⓦ mercantour.eu).

**Tourist office** Off place Frédéric-Mistral (July & Aug daily 9am–7pm; Sept–June Mon–Sat 9am–noon & 2–6pm; ☎ 04 92 81 04 71, ⓦ barcelonnette.com).

### ACCOMMODATION AND EATING

**Azteca** 3 rue François-Arnaud ☎ 04 92 81 46 36, ⓦ azteca-hotel.fr. Pleasant hotel, in a nineteenth-century villa built by an emigrant returned from Mexico, steps away from the centre and enjoying superb views of the mountains. Avoid the over-priced "Mexican" rooms, below the breakfast terrace. **€78**

**Cheval Blanc** 12 rue Grenette ☎ 04 92 81 00 19, ⓦ chevalblancbarcelonnette.com. Inexpensive central hotel, consisting of a rambling labyrinth of widely varying rooms above an attractive bar and restaurant (closed Sun, and open evenings only in winter) where *menus* start at €25. Closed Nov. €75

**Le Poivre d'Âne** 49 rue Manuel ☎ 04 92 81 48 67, ⓦ le-poivre-ane-barcelonnette.fr. This welcoming restaurant,

known for its hearty portions of mountain favourites, is much larger than it looks; beyond its main-street terrace there's a cosy covered courtyard at the back. As well as a €16 lunch *menu* and €27 dinner *menu*, they offer all-you-can-eat *churrasco* grilled meats for €32 and cheese-and-potato *tartiflette* for €23. Mon–Sat noon–2pm & 7–9.30pm.

# The Alpes-Maritimes

With their economy driven mostly by tourism, the towns of the **Alpes-Maritimes** make great bases for exploring the Parc du Mercantour. From Barcelonnette it's a wonderful journey across the Cime de la Bonette pass, which at an altitude of more than 2800m is claimed to be the highest "inter-valley" road in Europe. The road – the D64 – is only open for three months of the year, from the end of June until September. The air is cold even in summer and the green and silent spaces of the approach to the summit, circled by barren peaks, are magical.

## St-Étienne-de-Tinée

South of la Bonette, the D64 switchbacks down into the Tinée valley. Its highest town, **ST-ÉTIENNE-DE-TINÉE**, springs awake for sheep fairs, held twice every summer, and the Fête de la Transhumance at the end of June. At the west end of town, a cable car then chair lift climb to the summit of **La Pinatelle**, linking the village to the ski resort of **Auron**.

## St-Martin-Vésubie

In lovely little **ST-MARTIN-VÉSUBIE**, 60km southeast of St-Étienne-de-Tinée in the Vésubie valley, a cobbled, narrow street with a channelled stream runs through the old quarter beneath the overhanging roofs and balconies of Gothic houses.

The annual highlight at the **Alpha wolf reserve** in Le Boréon, a small, scenic mountain retreat 8km north, comes in spring, when visitors can see newborn wolf cubs (July & Aug daily 10am–6pm, last admission 4.30pm; April–June, Sept–Oct & school hols daily 10am–5pm, last admission 3.30pm; €14; ☎ 04 93 02 33 69, ⓦ alpha-loup.com).

**16**

---

**INFORMATION**                        **THE ALPES-MARITIMES**

**ST-ÉTIENNE-DE-TINÉE**
**Tourist office** 1 rue des Communes-de-France, at the northern end of the village, doubles as information centre for the Parc du Mercantour (daily: 10.30am–1pm & 3–7pm; ☎ 04 93 02 41 96, ⓦ auron.com, ⓦ mercantour.eu).

**ST-MARTIN-VÉSUBIE**
**Tourist office** Place du Général-de-Gaulle (July & Aug daily 8.30am–12.30pm & 2–7.30pm; Sept–June Mon–Sat 9am–noon & 2–6pm, Sun 9am–noon; ☎ 04 93 03 21 28, ⓦ saintmartinvesubie.fr).

---

**ACCOMMODATION AND EATING**

**ST-ÉTIENNE-DE-TINÉE**
**Camping du Plan d'Eau** ☎ 04 93 02 41 57, ⓦ camping duplandeau.com. Small, summer-only municipal site, in a nice verdant location at the edge of the village, beside a little lake. Closed Oct–May. €15

**Le Régalivou** 8 bd d'Auron ☎ 04 93 02 49 00, ⓦ leregalivou.free.fr. Lively hotel-restaurant, perched above the village centre, which has a large terrace, and stays open year-round. Fourteen en-suite rooms and a hearty restaurant, serving pizzas and grilled meats. €75

**ST-MARTIN-VÉSUBIE**
**Châtaigneraie** Allée de Verdun ☎ 04 93 03 21 22, ⓦ raiberti.com. Imposing, summer-only hotel, set in lovely gardens near the village centre. Comfortable en-suite rooms that sleep up to five – many have balconies – plus a pool and a good restaurant. Closed Oct–May. €70

★ **La Pierre Bleue** 163 bd Raoul-Audibert ☎ 04 93 03 37 86, ⓦ silvana.giordanengo.free.fr/LaPierreBleue. Delightful, secluded B&B, set in lush gardens and offering five lovely en-suite rooms; the friendly hosts also cook superb dinners for €32, using fresh local ingredients. Closed Oct–May. €106

## The Roya valley

The thickly forested **Roya valley** runs from Col de Tende on the French–Italian border down to Breil-sur-Roya. The roads that follow the river are narrow and steep, so driving is usually slow. In the **upper** valley, the highlight is the **Vallée des Merveilles**, a jumble of lakes and tumbled rocks on the western flank of Mont Bego. Down in the **lower** valley, don't miss the sleepy Italianate town of **Sospel**.

### Tende

**TENDE**, the highest town on the Roya, guards the access to the Col de Tende, which connects Provence with Piedmont but is now bypassed by a road tunnel. As recently as 1947, it still belonged to Italy. While not especially attractive, it's a busy little place that has plenty of cheap accommodation, along with places to eat, bars and shops.

#### Musée des Merveilles

Av du 16-septembre-1947 • daily except Tues: mid-June to mid-Sept 10am–6pm, mid-Sept to mid-June 10am–5pm; closed 2 weeks in Nov • Free • ☎ 04 93 04 32 50, ⓦ www.museedesmerveilles.com

Tende's beautifully designed **Musée des Merveilles** details the geology, archeology and traditions of the Vallée des Merveilles. Alongside dioramas depicting the daily lives of Copper Age and Bronze Age peoples, reproductions of the rock designs are displayed, with attempts to decipher the beliefs and myths that inspired them. Whether or not you go to the valley itself, the museum provides an invaluable insight into an intriguing subject, though you'll need reasonable French to understand the exhibits.

### Saorge

Reached by a side road that climbs steeply east from the main road at **Fontan**, 12km south of Tende, **SAORGE** is a gorgeous mountainside village of twisting, tunnelling little alleyways and tottering tower-like houses. Follow the main lane all the way to the far end to reach an exquisite seventeenth-century **Baroque monastery**, designated a national monument (Feb–April & Oct daily except Tues 10am–12.30pm & 2–5pm; May–Sept daily 10am–12.30pm & 2–6pm; €6; ☎04 93 04 55 55, ⓦmonastere-saorge.fr).

### Sospel

The best place to take a relaxed break in the lower Roya valley is **SOSPEL**, a dreamy Italian-looking town that spans the gentle River Bévéra 36km south of St-Dalmas-de-Tende. Its main street, avenue Jean-Médecin, follows the Bévéra on its southern bank; halfway down, the thirteenth-century **Vieux Pont** spans the river. Much of the town centre is made up of dark, narrow lanes, but **place St-Michel** at its heart, and dominated by the Cathédrale St-Michel, holds some wonderful peaches-and-cream Baroque facades and arcaded houses.

---

### EXPLORING THE VALLÉE DES MERVEILLES

The first recorded visitor to stumble on the **Vallée des Merveilles**, a fifteenth-century traveller who had lost his way, described it as "an infernal place with figures of the devil and thousands of demons scratched on the rocks". That's a pretty accurate description, except that some of the carvings depict animals, tools, people working and mysterious symbols – and they date back to the second millennium BC.

The valley is best approached from **St-Dalmas-de-Tende**, 4km south of Tende. The easiest route is the 10km hike (6–8hr there and back) that starts at the *Refuge Les Mesches*, 8km west on the D91. The engravings are beyond the *Refuge des Merveilles*. Note that certain areas are out of bounds unless accompanied by an official guide – and remember that blue skies and sun can quickly turn into violent hailstorms and lightning, so go prepared, properly shod and clothed, and take your own food and water. For details of **guided walks**, contact Tende's tourist office (see page 863).

## ARRIVAL AND INFORMATION                    THE ROYA VALLEY

### TENDE

**By train** The Train des Merveilles, designed for sightseers and offering English commentary in summer, leaves Nice daily at 9.23am, and reaches Tende at 11.24am (€16 each way, or €16 day pass July–Sept only ). Regular ordinary trains run along the same line.

**Tourist office** 103 av du 16-septembre-1947 (daily 9am–noon & 2–6pm; ☎04 83 93 98 82, ⓦtendemerveilles.com).

### SOSPEL

**By train** The *gare SNCF* is southeast of town on av A-Borriglione.

Destinations Fontan (1–3 daily; 40min); Nice (4 daily; 50min); St-Dalmas-de-Tende (3 daily; 45min); Tende (3 daily; 55min).

**Tourist office** 1 place St-Pierre (Mon 10am–12.30pm & 1.30–6pm, Tues–Fri 9.30am–6pm, Sat 9.30am–4.45pm; ☎04 93 04 15 80, ⓦsospel-tourisme.com).

## ACCOMMODATION AND EATING

### TENDE

**La Margueria** 19 av du 16-septembre-1947 ☎04 93 04 60 53. Popular pizzeria, with beams strung with dried herbs and garlic, stuffed foxes on the walls, and a good range of other Italian specialities. Daily noon–2pm & 7.30–9.30pm; closed Tues Oct–June.

**Miramonti** 5 rue Antoine-Vassalo ☎04 93 04 61 82, ⓦlemiramonti.fr. Inexpensive and very central hotel-restaurant that's handy for the station. The cheapest of its six clean, plain rooms lack en-suite facilities. Closed mid-Nov to mid-Dec; restaurant closed Wed. €43

### SAORGE

**Petite Épicerie** 68 rue Revelli ☎09 67 38 10 83, ⓦlapetiteepiceriesaorge.blogspot.co.uk. This little deli on the main alleyway through the village doubles as a great-value bistro, serving mixed vegetable or charcuterie platters for around €12, and an excellent €13.50 *plat du jour*, at a couple of outdoor tables. April–June & Sept–Dec

daily except Tues 8am–2pm & 5–8pm; July & Aug daily 8am–9pm.

### SOSPEL

**Hôtel des Étrangers** 7 bd de Verdun ☎04 93 04 00 09, ⓦsospel.net. Slightly faded but still very acceptable hotel, just across the town's eastern bridge, with a covered pool; its riverfront restaurant, *Bel Aqua* (closed Tues & Wed lunch), serves *menus* from €32. Closed Nov to mid-March. €75

**Mas Fleuri** Quartier La Vasta ☎04 93 04 14 94, ⓦcamping-mas-fleuri.com. The closest to central Sospel of the four local campsites, 2km upstream (northwest) along the D2566, this two-star site has a pool. Closed Nov–March. €20.60

**Souta Loggia** 5 place St-Nicolas ☎04 93 87 93 75. Cool café/bar, stretching beneath and beyond the arcades of a fine old square just north of the river. Hip soundtrack, plus a *menu* of €13–15 salads and changing *plats* including steaks and pasta specials. Daily 8am–10pm.

**16**

# The Côte d'Azur

**866** Marseille

**881** Cassis

**882** La Ciotat

**883** Bandol and around

**884** Hyères and around

**889** The Corniche des Maures

**891** The Massif des Maures

**893** St-Tropez and around

**898** Ste-Maxime

**899** Fréjus and around

**902** Cannes and around

**909** Antibes and around

**912** Above the Baie des Anges

**916** Nice

**925** The Corniches

**928** Monaco

**932** Menton

LE VIEUX PORT, MARSEILLE

# 17 The Côte d'Azur

The Côte d'Azur polarizes opinion like few places in France. To some it remains the most glamorous of all Mediterranean playgrounds; to others, it's an overdeveloped victim of its own hype. Yet at its best – in the gaps between the urban sprawl, on the islands, in the remarkable beauty of the hills, the impossibly blue water after which the coast is named and in the special light that drew so many artists to paint here – it captivates still.

The ancient city of **Marseille** possesses its own earthy magnetism, while right on its doorstep there's swimming and sailing in the pristine waters of the **Calanques national park**. To the east the family resorts of **La Ciotat** and **St Raphaël**, sedate **Hyères** and Roman **Fréjus** hold their own in the face of huge media hype, while true Mediterranean magic is to be found in the scented vegetation, silver beaches, secluded islands and medieval perched villages like **Grimaud** and **La Garde-Freinet**. You can escape to the wonderful unspoilt landscapes of the **Îles d'Hyères**, with some of the best flora and fauna in Provence, then contrast the beachcomber charm of **La Croix-Valmer** with the flashy ebullience of its overhyped neighbour, **St-Tropez** – unmissable if only for a day-trip, though you need to be prepared to contend with huge crowds in summer.

Once an inhospitable shore with few natural harbours, the seventy-odd kilometres of the Riviera between **Cannes** and **Menton** blossomed in the nineteenth century as foreign aristocrats began to winter in the region's mild climate. In the interwar years the toffs were gradually supplanted by new elites – film stars, artists and writers – and the season switched to summer. Nowadays, the **Riviera** is an uninterrupted sprawl of hotels, serried apartment blocks and secluded villas, with liner-sized yachts bobbing at anchor. Attractions remain, however, notably in the legacies of the artists who stayed here: Bonnard, Picasso, Léger, Matisse, Renoir and Chagall. **Nice** has real substance as a major city, while **Monaco** intrigues visitors with its tax-haven opulence and comic-opera independence.

The months to avoid are July and August, when room prices soar, overflowing campsites become health hazards and locals get short-tempered, and November, when many museums, hotels and restaurants close.

---

**GETTING AROUND**             **THE CÔTE D'AZUR**

**By bus** Regular buses run along much of the coast, but heavy traffic makes it extremely slow in high season.

**By train** Frequent trains link the major cities along the coast. Note that the main rail line turns inland between Toulon and Fréjus.

**By bike** Though you can cycle, distances between destinations are large, and you probably won't get very far unless you're Tour de France material.

**By car** Driving around the Côte d'Azur is the most convenient option, though summer traffic along the coast and in the cities can be infernal.

---

# Marseille

France's greatest port, **MARSEILLE** has (thankfully) shaken off much of its old reputation for sleaze and danger to attract a wider range of visitors. What they discover is an earthy, vibrant city, where the attractions of a metropolis meet those of the coast, its hitherto down-at-heel appearance scrubbed up since its stint as European Capital of Culture 2013. The march of progress is not relentless: occasionally last year's prestige civic project still becomes this year's broken, bottle-strewn fountain. But that's Marseille. If you don't like your cities gritty, it may not be for you. See beyond the intermittent squalor, though, and chances are you will warm to this cosmopolitan, creative place.

ÎLE DE PORQUEROLLES

# Highlights

**① Vieux Port, Marseille** The old trading port, with its restaurants, beautiful sunsets and nightlife, attracts the most colourful characters in southern France. See page 869

**② Les Calanques** The limestone cliffs between Marseille and Cassis make for excellent hikes leading to isolated coves in which to go swimming. See page 881

**③ Îles de Porquerolles and St-Honorat** These well-preserved islands offer a glimpse of what much of the coast must have looked like a

hundred years ago. See pages 885 and 904

**④ Massif des Maures** This undeveloped range of hazy coastal hills is a world apart from the glitz and glamour of the Côte. See page 891

**⑤ Fondation Maeght** Modern art, architecture and landscape fuse to create a stunning visual experience. See page 914

**⑥ Nice** The Riviera's capital of street life is laidback, surprisingly cultured and easy to enjoy, whatever your budget. See page 916

HIGHLIGHTS ARE MARKED ON THE MAP ON PAGE 868

**17**

### Brief history

Founded by the Greeks some two and a half millennia ago, the most renowned and populated metropolitan area in France after Paris and Lyon has both prospered and been ransacked over the centuries. It has lost its privileges to French kings and foreign armies, recovered its fortunes, suffered plagues, religious bigotry, republican and royalist terror and had its own Commune and Bastille-storming. It was the march of Marseillais revolutionaries to Paris in 1792 that gave the *Hymn of the Army of the Rhine* its name of *La Marseillaise*, later to become the national anthem. Occupied by the Germans during World War II, it became a notably cosmopolitan place in the postwar years, when returning *pieds noirs* (European settlers from Algeria) were joined by large communities of Maghreb origin and by migrants from the Comoros archipelago, a former French colony in the Indian Ocean.

## The Vieux Port and around

The cafés around the **Vieux Port**, where glistening fish are sold on the quay straight off the boats, are wonderful spots to observe the city's street life. Particularly good in the afternoon is the north (Le Panier) side, where the terraces are sunnier and the views better. A **ferry** (every 10 min; daily 7.30am–8.30pm; €0.50) shuttles across the port from the *hôtel de ville* on the north side to the quai Rive-Neuve opposite. Immediately to the north of the Vieux Port beyond the Fort St-Jean, the **Esplanade du J4** is the focus of the city's new cultural quarter.

### Fort St-Nicolas

Two **fortresses** guard the harbour entrance. The construction of **St-Nicolas**, on the south side of the port, represented the city's final defeat as a separate entity: Louis XIV ordered the new fort to keep an eye on the city after he had sent in an army, suppressed the city's council, fined it, arrested all opposition and set ludicrously low limits on Marseille's subsequent expenditure and borrowing.

### Abbaye St-Victor

3 rue de l'Abbaye • Daily 9am–7pm • Crypt €2 • ☎ 04 96 11 22 60, ⓦ saintvictor.net • Bus #81 from Vieux Port

A short way inland from the Fort St-Nicolas, above the Bassin de Carénage, is Marseille's oldest church, the **Abbaye St-Victor**. Originally part of a monastery

---

#### FOOD AND WINE OF THE CÔTE D'AZUR

As part of Provence, the **Côte d'Azur** shares its culinary fundamentals of olive oil, garlic and herbs, gorgeous vegetables and fruits, goat's cheeses and, of course, the predominance of fish. The fish soups – Marseille's **bouillabaisse**, and **bourride**, accompanied by a garlic and chilli-flavoured mayonnaise known as *rouille* – are served all along the coast, as are **fish** covered with Provençal herbs and grilled over an open flame. **Seafood** – from spider crabs to clams, sea urchins to crayfish, crabs, lobster, mussels and oysters – are piled onto huge *plateaux de fruits de mer*, which may not reflect this coast's harvest but do demonstrate the luxury associated with it.

The **Italian influence** is strong, from ravioli stuffed with spinach to thin-crust pizzas and every sort of pasta as a vehicle for anchovies, olives, garlic and tomatoes. Nice has its own specialities, such as *socca*, a chickpea flour pancake, *pissaladière*, a pizza-like tart with anchovies and black olives, *salade niçoise* and *pan bagnat*, both of which combine egg, olives, salad, tuna and olive oil, and mesclun, a salad of bitter leaves: consequently, Nice is about as good a spot to enjoy cheap street food as you'll find. *Petits farcis* – stuffed aubergines, peppers or tomatoes – are a standard feature on Côte d'Azur *menus*.

The best of the Côte **wines** come from Bandol: Cassis too has its own *appellation*, and around Nice the Bellet wines are worth discovering. Fancy cocktails are a Côte speciality, but *pastis* is the preferred tipple.

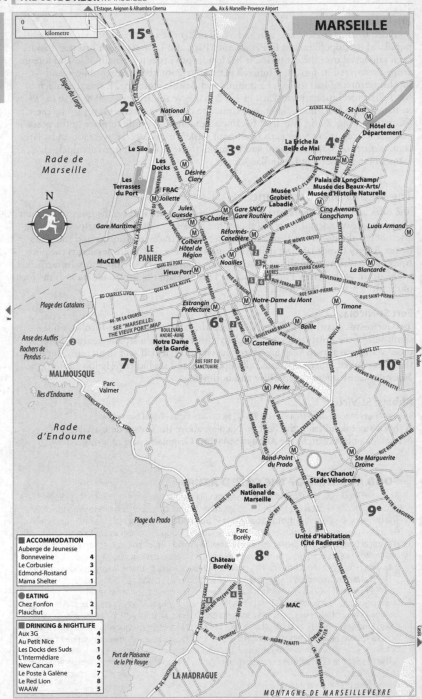

**MARSEILLE**

L'Estaque, Avignon & Alhambra Cinema

Aix & Marseille-Provence Airport

0 ——— 1
kilometre

15e

2e

National

Le Silo

Les Docks

Désirée
Clary

Les
Terrasses
du Port

FRAC

Joliette

Jules
Guesde

St-Charles

Gare Maritime

MuCEM

LE
PANIER

Colbert
Hôtel de
Région

QUAI DU PORT

Vieux Port

Noailles

BD CHARLES LIVON

QUAI DE RIVE NEUVE

Plage des Catalans

AV. DE LA COURSE

Estrangin
Préfecture

SEE "MARSEILLE:
THE VIEUX PORT" MAP

Anse des Auffes

Rochers de
Pendus

MALMOUSQUE

Îles d'Endoume

Parc
Valmer

Rade
d'Endoume

Rade de
Marseille

N

3e

La Friche la
Belle de Mai

Chartreux

Musée
Grobet-
Labadié

Palais de Longchamp/
Musée des Beaux-Arts/
Musée d'Histoire Naturelle

Cinq Avenues
Longchamp

Luois Armand

Réformés-
Canebière

Gare SNCF/
Gare Routière

La Blancarde

Notre-Dame du Mont

Timone

6e

Notre Dame
de la Garde

Baille

Castellane

Périer

Rond-Point
du Prado

Ballet
National de
Marseille

Parc Chanot/
Stade Vélodrome

Ste Marguerite
Drôme

Plage du Prado

Parc
Borély

Unité d'Habitation
(Cité Radieuse)

9e

Château
Borély

8e

MAC

Port de Plaisance
de la Pte Rouge

LA MADRAGUE

MONTAGNE DE MARSEILLEVEYRE

St-Just

Hôtel du
Département

4e

Gare SNCF/
Gare Routière

10e

Toulon

7e

Montredon

**ACCOMMODATION**

| | |
|---|---|
| Auberge de Jeunesse Bonneveine | 4 |
| Le Corbusier | 3 |
| Edmond-Rostand | 2 |
| Mama Shelter | 1 |

**EATING**

| | |
|---|---|
| Chez Fonfon | 2 |
| Plauchut | 1 |

**DRINKING & NIGHTLIFE**

| | |
|---|---|
| Aux 3G | 4 |
| Au Petit Nice | 3 |
| Les Docks des Suds | 1 |
| L'Intermédiaire | 6 |
| New Cancan | 2 |
| Le Poste à Galène | 7 |
| Le Red Lion | 8 |
| WAAW | 5 |

## MARSEILLE ORIENTATION

Marseille is divided into fifteen **arrondissements** spiralling out from the city's focal point, the **Vieux Port**. Due north lies the old town, Le Panier, site of the original Greek settlement of Massalia, and beyond that the regenerated area of Euroméditerranée, centred on the Esplanade du J4. The wide boulevard leading from the head of the Vieux Port, **La Canebière**, is the central east–west axis of the town, with the main shopping streets to the south. The main north–south axis is **rue d'Aix**, becoming cours Belsunce then rue de Rome, avenue du Prado and finally boulevard Michelet. The bohemian quarter around place Jean-Jaurès and cours Julien lies east of rue de Rome. From the headland west of the Vieux Port, the corniche heads south past the city's most favoured residential districts towards the beaches and nightlife of the **Plage du Prado**.

founded in the fifth century on the burial site of various martyrs, the church was built, enlarged and fortified – a vital requirement given its position outside the city walls – over a period of two hundred years from the middle of the tenth century. It looks and feels like a fortress, though the interior has an austere power and the **crypt** is a fascinating, crumbling warren containing several sarcophagi, including one with the remains of St Maurice.

### Musée des Civilisations d'Europe et de la Méditerranée (MuCEM)

7 promenade Robert-Laffont/Esplanade du J4 • Daily except Tues: May–June & Sept–Oct 11am–7pm; July & Aug 10am–8pm; Nov–April 11am–6pm; • €9.50. English audioguide €3.50 • ⓦ mucem.org • Bus #60 from Vieux Port

**Fort St-Jean**, on the north side of the harbour, dates from the Middle Ages, when Marseille was an independent republic; immaculately restored, it now forms one half of the **Musée des Civilisations d'Europe et de la Méditerranée (MuCEM)**, an ethnographic museum of national status that was the showpiece of Marseille 2013. The other half of the museum – including its main exhibition space – is on the Esplanade du J4 in a striking modernist box by Algerian-born architect Rudy Ricciotti. The two halves are linked by a roof-level footbridge.

### Musée Regards de Provence

Allée Regards de Provence • Tues–Sun 10am–6pm; last admission at 5.30pm • Documentary film €4, two temporary exhibitions €6.50; *billet couplé* to see everything €8.50 • ⓦ museeregardsdeprovence.com • ⓂJoliette

Occupying the fine 1948-built *station sanitaire* (sanitary station; built for the purposes of infection control in the port), the **Musée Regards de Provence** displays works from the Fondation Regards de Provence's 850-strong collection of art from and about the region, including works by Ziem, Dufy and Monticelli. While the artists are generally not from the front rank of international fame, standards are high and the museum building itself is a delight.

### The cathedral and Les Docks

At the landward end of J4 is the massive late nineteenth-century **Cathédrale de la Nouvelle Major** (daily except Tues: summer 10am–7pm; winter 10am–6pm), architecturally a blend of neo-Romanesque and neo-Byzantine, with a distinctive pattern of alternating bands of stone. To the north is **Les Docks**, a grandiose, nineteenth-century warehouse now converted into offices, shops and restaurants. Opposite Les Docks on the waterside is **Les Terrasses du Port**, a slick shopping mall.

## Notre-Dame-de-la-Garde

Rue Fort-du-Sanctuaire • Daily: April–Sept 7am–7.15pm; Oct–March 7am–6.15pm • Free • **Museum** Tues–Sun: April-Sept 10am–6pm; Oct–March 10am–5pm • €5 • ☎ 04 91 13 40 80, ⓦ notredamedelagarde.com • Bus #60 or tourist train from Vieux Port

**17**

The best view of the Vieux Port is from the **Palais du Pharo**, on the headland beyond Fort St-Nicolas, or, for a wider angle, from **Notre-Dame-de-la-Garde**, the city's Second-Empire landmark atop the La Garde hill, the highest point of the city. It is crowned by a monumental gold Virgin that gleams to ships far out at sea. Inside, model ships hang from the rafters while ex votos depict the shipwrecks, house fires and car crashes from which the Virgin has supposedly rescued grateful believers. Many of the most visually striking models are now displayed in the little **museum** beneath the basilica.

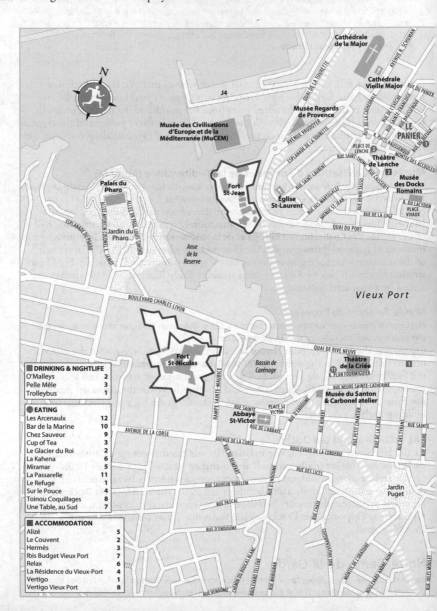

**DRINKING & NIGHTLIFE**

| | |
|---|---|
| O'Malleys | 2 |
| Pelle Mêle | 3 |
| Trolleybus | 1 |

**EATING**

| | |
|---|---|
| Les Arcenaulx | 12 |
| Bar de la Marine | 10 |
| Chez Sauveur | 9 |
| Cup of Tea | 3 |
| Le Glacier du Roi | 2 |
| La Kahena | 6 |
| Miramar | 5 |
| La Passarelle | 11 |
| Le Refuge | 1 |
| Sur le Pouce | 4 |
| Toinou Coquillages | 8 |
| Une Table, au Sud | 7 |

**ACCOMMODATION**

| | |
|---|---|
| Alizé | 5 |
| Le Couvent | 2 |
| Hermès | 3 |
| Ibis Budget Vieux Port | 7 |
| Relax | 6 |
| La Résidence du Vieux-Port | 4 |
| Vertigo | 1 |
| Vertigo Vieux Port | 8 |

# Le Panier

To the north of the Vieux Port is the oldest part of Marseille, **Le Panier**, where, up until the last war, tiny streets, steep steps and houses of every era formed a *vieille ville* typical of the Côte. In 1943, however, with Marseille under German occupation, the quarter became an unofficial ghetto for **Untermenschen** of every sort, including Resistance fighters, Communists and Jews. The Nazis gave the twenty thousand inhabitants one day's notice to leave; many were deported to the camps. Dynamite was laid, and

**MARSEILLE: THE VIEUX PORT**

**17**

everything from the waterside to rue Caisserie was blown sky-high, except for three old buildings that appealed to the fascist aesthetic: the seventeenth-century **hôtel de ville**, on the quay; the **Hôtel de Cabre**, on the corner of rue Bonneterie and Grande-Rue; and the **Maison Diamantée**, on rue de la Prison.

At the junction of rue de la Prison and rue Caisserie, the steps of montée des Accoules lead up to **place de Lenche**, site of the Greek *agora* and a good café stop. What's left of old Le Panier is above here, though many of the tenements have been demolished.

## Hospice de la Vieille Charité

2 rue de la Charité • **Musée d'Archéologie Méditerranéenne** Tues–Sun: mid-May to mid-Sept 9.30am–6.30pm; mid-Sept to mid-May 10am–6pm • €6 • ☎ 04 91 14 58 97, ⓦ musee-archeologie-mediterraneenne.marseille.fr **Musée d'Arts Africains, Océaniens et Amérindiens** Tues–Sun: mid-May to mid-Sept 9.30am–6.30pm; mid-Sept to mid-May 10am–6pm • €6 • ☎ 04 91 14 58 38, ⓦ maaoa. marseille.fr • Ⓜ Joliette

At the top of rue du Réfuge stands the restored **Hospice de la Vieille Charité**, a seventeenth-century workhouse with a gorgeous Baroque chapel surrounded by columned arcades; only the tiny grilled exterior windows recall its original use. It's now a cultural centre, a venue for temporary exhibitions and contains two museums: the **Musée d'Archéologie Méditerranéenne**, that has some very beautiful pottery and glass and an Egyptian collection with a mummified crocodile; and the **Musée d'Arts Africains, Océaniens et Amérindiens**, with beautiful objects from as far afield as Mali and Vanuatu, and a room devoted to Mexico.

# La Canebière and around

**La Canebière**, the occasionally tatty boulevard that runs for about 1km down to the port, is the city's hub, though it's more a place to move through than to linger in. It takes its name from the hemp (*canabé*) that once grew here and was used for the town's rope-making trade. La Canebière neatly divides the moneyed southern *quartiers* and the ramshackle **quartier Belsunce** to the north – a mainly Arab area of old, narrow streets.

## Mémorial de la Marseillaise

23–25 rue Thubaneau • Tues & Fri at 10.30am & 3pm • €6 (tickets from Musée d'Histoire de Marseille; valid for both) • ☎ 04 91 91 91 97, ⓦ musee-histoire-marseille-voie-historique.fr • Tram #2 or #3, stop "Belsunce Alcazar"

The main reason for visiting the *quartier* Belsunce is to visit the **Mémorial de la Marseillaise**, which presents the story of France's national anthem with some panache in the old real tennis court in which it was first performed in Marseille. You can listen to various versions of Rouget de Lisle's 1792 anthem – which was actually composed in Strasbourg – and discover more about the Marseille volunteers and their epic march on Paris.

## Centre Bourse

2 rue Henri-Barbusse • ⓦ bourse.klepierre.fr • Tram #2 or #3, stop "Belsunce Alcazar"

Immediately west of cours Belsunce, the ugly but useful **Centre Bourse** shopping complex provides a stark contrast to this tatty but historic area. Behind it is the **Jardin des Vestiges**, where the ancient port extended, curving northwards from the present quai des Belges. Excavations have revealed a stretch of the Greek port and bits of the **city wall** with the bases of three square towers and a gateway, dated to the second or third century BC.

### Musée d'Histoire de Marseille

Centre Bourse • Tues–Sun 10am–6pm, till 7pm mid-May to mid-Sept • €6 • ☎ 04 91 55 36 63, ⓦ musee-histoire-de-marseille.marseille.fr

Within the Centre Bourse, the **Musée d'Histoire de Marseille** presents finds from excavations of the Jardin des Vestiges, including a third-century wreck of a Roman trading vessel. There are also models of the city and of its vanished nineteenth-century transporter bridge, which dominated the entrance to the Vieux Port until it was blown up by the retreating Germans in 1944.

## The Palais Longchamp and around

22 bd Longchamp • **Musée des Beaux-Arts** • Tues–Sun: mid-May to mid-Sept 9.30am–6.30pm; mid-Sept to mid-May 10am–6pm • €6 • ☎ 04 91 14 59 30, ⓦ musee-des-beaux-arts.marseille.fr **Musée d'Histoire Naturelle** Tues–Sun: July to mid-Sept 9.30am–6.30pm; mid-Sept to July 10am–6pm • €6 • ☎ 04 91 14 59 50, ⓦ museum-marseille.org • ⓜ Longchamp–Cinq-Avenues or tram #2 same stop

The **Palais Longchamp**, 2km east of the port at the end of boulevard Longchamp, forms the grandiose conclusion of an aqueduct that once brought water from the Durance to the city. The palace's north wing houses the **Musée des Beaux-Arts** with a fair selection of old masters, including paintings by Rubens, Tiepolo and Jordaens, plus works by the nineteenth-century painters Corot and Courbet. Well represented too are Provençal painters of the nineteenth century, including Félix Ziem. The southeastern wing is occupied by the **Musée d'Histoire Naturelle**, where the oldest parts of the collection of stuffed animals and fossils date back to the eighteenth century.

### Musée Grobet-Labadié

140 bd Longchamp • Closed for renovation • ⓦ musee-grobet-labadie.marseille.fr • ⓜ Longchamp–Cinq-Avenues or tram #2 same stop

Opposite the Palais Longchamp, the **Musée Grobet-Labadié** is an elegant late nineteenth-century townhouse filled with exquisite *objets d'art*, representing the tastes of a typical family from Marseille's affluent merchant class at its zenith. It was closed for renovation at the time of writing.

### La Friche la Belle de Mai

41 rue Jobin • Mon–Sat 8.30am–midnight, Sun 8–10pm • Free access during opening hours • Tour Panorama Wed–Fri 2–7pm, Sat & Sun 1–7pm • Price depends on exhibition • ⓦ lafriche.org • ⓜ St-Charles or tram #2 direction "Longchamp"

**La Friche la Belle de Mai** is an arts centre equally focused on the production and consumption of culture, housed in a former tobacco factory near the gare St-Charles. There are artists' studios and a television studio as well as all kinds of performance – from circus to dance, music and theatre – and art exhibitions; many events are free of charge. The **Tour Panorama** exhibition venue has a vast roof terrace that offers views over the city and is the venue for DJ nights and live music sets in summer (usually Fri & Sat 7–11pm; free). There's also a puppet theatre, Théâtre Massalia, and a skate park here.

## South of La Canebière

The prime shopping district of Marseille is encompassed by three streets running **south from La Canebière**: rue Paradis, rue St-Ferréol and **rue de Rome**. The most elegant boutiques and galleries cluster in the area around the **Musée Cantini**.

### Musée Cantini

19 rue Grignan • mid-May to mid-Sept Tues–Sun 9.30am–6.30pm; mid-Sept to mid-May Tues–Sun 10am–6pm • €6; free first Sun of month • ☎ 04 91 54 77 75, ⓦ musee-cantini.marseille.fr • ⓜ Estrangin Préfecture

Fauvists and Surrealists are well represented at the **Musée Cantini**, a good little museum of modern art, along with works by Matisse, Léger, Picasso, Ernst, Le Corbusier, Miró and Giacometti.

### Cours Julien

ⓜ Notre-Dame-du-Mont–Cours-Julien

A few blocks east of rue de Rome is one of the most pleasant places to idle in the city, **cours Julien**, with its pools, fountains, pavement cafés and boutiques, buried under graffiti and populated by Marseille's bohemian crowd and diverse immigrant

**17**

community. Streets full of bars and music shops lead east to **place Jean-Jaurès**, locally known as "la Plaine", where the market is a treat, particularly on Saturdays.

## The corniche and around

For the corniche, take bus #83 from the Vieux Port; the quickest way to the beaches is by bus #19 from Ⓜ Rd-Pt-du-Prado

The most popular stretch of sand close to the city centre is the **plage des Catalans**, a few blocks south of the Palais du Pharo. This marks the beginning of Marseille's **corniche**, avenue J.-F.-Kennedy, which follows the cliffs past the dramatic statue and arch of the **Monument aux Morts des Orients**.

South of the monument, steps lead down to a picturesque inlet, **Anse des Auffes**, where there are small fishing boats beached on the rocks and narrow stairways leading nowhere. The corniche then turns inland, bypassing the **Malmousque peninsula**, whose coastal path gives access to tiny bays and rocky beaches – perfect for swimming when the mistral wind is not blowing. The corniche ends at the **Parc Balnéaire du Prado**, the city's main sand beach.

## Parc Borély

**Park** Daily 7am–9pm • Free • **Botanical garden** Tues–Sun: April–Oct 10am–noon & 1–6pm; Nov–March 10am–noon & 1–5pm • €3
**Château Borély** 134 av Clot Bey • Tues–Sun: mid-May to mid-Sept 9.30am–6.30pm; mid-Sept to mid-May 10am–6pm • €6 • Ⓦ musee-borely.marseille.fr • Bus #19 or #83, stop "Parc Borély"

A short way up **avenue du Prado** from the beach, avenue du Park-Borély leads into the city's best green space, the **Parc Borély**, which has a boating lake, rose gardens, palm trees and a botanical garden.

The eighteenth-century **Château Borély** itself is a museum of decorative arts, housing collections hitherto scattered in various locations across the city, including fashion and eighteenth- and nineteenth-century ceramics from the Marseille area.

## MAC

69 av de Haïfa • Tues–Sun: mid-May to mid-Sept 9.30am–6.30pm; mid-Sept to mid-May 10am–6pm • €9 • Ⓦ mac.marseille.fr • Bus #23 or bus #45 from Ⓜ Rd-Pt-du-Prado, stop "Haïfa Marie-Louise"

Between Montredon and **boulevard Michelet**, the main road out of the city, is the contemporary art museum, **MAC**. The permanent collection includes works from the 1960s to the present day by Buren, Christo, Klein, Niki de Saint Phalle, Tinguely and Warhol, as well as Marseillais artists César and Ben.

### Unité d'Habitation (Cité Radieuse)

280 bd Michelet • Open access 9am–6pm • Guided tours in French Tues–Sat 2pm & 4pm; during school hols also in French and English Sat at 10am. €10; book via tourist office • Ⓦ marseille-citeradieuse.org • Bus #21 from Ⓜ Rd-Pt-du-Prado to "Le Corbusier"

Set back just west of boulevard Michelet stands a building that broke the mould, Le Corbusier's seventeen-storey block of flats, the **Unité d'Habitation**, designed in 1946 and completed in 1952. It's also known as the Cité Radieuse, and many architects the world over have tried to imitate it. Up close, its status as a revolutionary example is apparent: at ground level the building is decorated with Le Corbusier's famous human figure, the Modulor; on the third floor there is a hotel and restaurant. Take the lift to the top to view the iconic rooftop recreation area; it's here that Le Corbusier's ocean liner inspiration is most obvious.

## The Château d'If

Île d'If • April–Sept daily 10am–6pm; Oct–March Tues–Sun 10am–5pm • €6 • Ⓦ chateau-if.fr • Boats depart quai de la Fraternité on the Vieux Port in Marseille every 30min–1hr (weather permitting)

The **Château d'If**, on the tiny island of If, is best known as the penal setting for Alexandre Dumas' *The Count of Monte Cristo*. Having made his watery escape after fourteen years of incarceration as the innocent victim of treachery, the hero of the piece, Edmond Dantès, describes the island thus: "Blacker than the sea, blacker than the sky, rose like a phantom the giant of granite, whose projecting crags seemed like arms extended to seize their prey". In reality, most prisoners went insane or died before leaving. The sixteenth-century castle and its cells are horribly well preserved, and the views back towards Marseille are fantastic. Note that **ferries** may not run when the mistral blows because it's too difficult to land.

## ARRIVAL AND DEPARTURE                                                   MARSEILLE

**By plane** The city's airport, the Aéroport Marseille-Provence (☎0820 811 414, ⓦmarseille-airport.com), is 20km northwest of the city, linked to the *gare SNCF* by bus (every 15min 4.10am–11.30pm; 25min; €8.30; ⓦnavettemarseilleaeroport.com).

Destinations Bristol (3 weekly; 1hr 55min); Edinburgh (2 weekly; 2hr 30min); London Gatwick (up to 3 flights daily; 1hr 50min); London Heathrow (3 daily; 1hr 55min); London Stansted (1–2 daily; 2hr 5min); Manchester (2 weekly; 2hr 10min); Montréal (7 weekly; 8hr 15min); Paris CDG (up to 6 daily; 1hr 30min).

**By train** The *gare SNCF* St-Charles (☎36 35) is on the northern edge of the 1er arrondissement on square Narvik. From the station, a monumental staircase leads down to bd d'Athènes and on to La Canebière, Marseille's main street.

Destinations Aix-en-Provence (26–29 daily; 45min); Aix-en-Provence TGV (approx. 2 hourly; 11–12min); Arles (every 20min–1hr; 48min–1hr 13min); Avignon Centre (approx hourly; 1hr 15min–1hr 56min); Avignon TGV (3–4 hourly; 27–50min); Cannes (hourly; 2hr 10min); Cassis (every 30min–1hr; 18min); La Ciotat (every 30min–1hr; 25min); Les Arcs for Draguignon (hourly; 1hr 25min); Lyon Part-Dieu (every 30min–1hr; 1hr 40min–3hr 30min); Nice (every 30min–2hr; 2hr 40min); Paris Gare de Lyon (every 30min–1hr; 3hr 20min); St Raphaël (every 30min–2hr; 1hr 340min); Sisteron (4–7 daily; 2hr 10min).

**By bus** The *gare routière* is integrated with the gare St-Charles on rue Honnorat (☎0891 024 025, ⓦlepilote.com). Destinations Aix-en-Provence via *autoroute* (every 5min at peak times; 30–50min); Cassis (12 daily; 45–50min).

**By ferry** La Méridionale, 4 quai d'Arenc (☎0970 83 30 30, ⓦlameridionale.fr), runs ferries to Corsica. CORSICA linea, 23 place de la Joliette (☎0825 88 80 88, ⓦcorsicalinea.com), runs services to Algeria, Tunisia, Sardinia and Corsica.

## GETTING AROUND

### BY PUBLIC TRANSPORT
**Bus, tram and métro** Marseille has an efficient public transport network (ⓦrtm.fr). The métro and trams run from 5am until just after midnight; buses run from 5 or 6am until 9pm, after which night-bus services take over until around 12.45am.

**Information** You can get a plan of the transport system from most métro stations' *points d'accueil* (daily 6.50am–7.40pm) or at the RTM office at the Centre Bourse (6 rue des Fabres; Mon–Fri 8.30am–6pm).

**Tickets and passes** Flat-fee single tickets for buses, trams and the métro can be used for journeys combining all three as long as they take less than 1hr and involve no more than one métro ride. You can buy individual tickets (€1.70) from bus drivers, and from métro ticket offices or machines on métro stations and tram stops. Two-journey *Cartes 2 voyages* (€3.40) and ten-journey *Cartes 10 voyages* (€14) can be bought from métro stations, RTM kiosks and shops displaying the RTM sign. Consider also the good-value one-day *Pass XL 24h* (€5.20) and three-day *Pass XL 72h* (€10.80), available from the same outlets. Tickets must be tapped on the card reader at métro gates or on board.

**Ferry** RTM runs a ferry between the Vieux Port and Pointe Rouge in the south of the city for easier access to the beaches and *calanques* (late April to Sept daily 8am–7pm; hourly; €5).

### BY BIKE
Blue bicycles belonging to Le Vélo scheme (ⓦlevelo-mpm.fr) can be rented from 130 rental points in the city using a bank card (€1 for seven-day membership, after which first 30min is free, €1 for each additional 30min). Electric bikes can be rented from ITINbikes, 22 rue de la Loge (Tues–Sat 9am–5.30pm; ☎04 91 63 17 25) and mountain bikes from Tandem, 16 av du Parc-Borély (daily 9am–6pm; ☎04 91 22 64 80).

### BY TAXI
Taxi Radio Marseille ☎04 91 02 20 20; Taxi Marseillais ☎04 91 92 92 92.

## INFORMATION

**Tourist office** 11 La Canebière, just up from the Vieux Port (Mon–Sun 9am–6pm; ☎0826 500 500, ⓦmarseille-tourisme.com).

**Marseille City Pass** If you intend visiting several of

17

Marseille's museums it's worth considering the Marseille City Pass, which for €26 (one day) €33 (two days) or €41 (three days) includes free admission to museums, city guided tours, entry to the Château d'If and free travel on métros and buses.

## ACCOMMODATION

### HOTELS

**Alizé** 35 quai des Belges, 1er ⓣ 04 91 33 66 97, ⓦ alize-hotel.com; ⓜ Vieux Port; map p.872. Comfortable, attractive three-star hotel on the Vieux Port. Public areas are a little gloomy but rooms are modern, soundproofed and a/c; the more expensive ones look out onto the Vieux Port. €109

**Le Corbusier** Unité d'Habitation, 280 bd Michelet, 8e ⓣ 04 28 31 39 22, ⓦ hotellecorbusier.com; bus #21 from ⓜ Rd-Pt-du-Prado to "Le Corbusier"; map p.870. Landmark hotel on the third floor of this renowned architect's iconic high-rise, with fabulous views and a variety of room styles, from simple studios and a large wheelchair-accessible room to elegant mini suites with access to a large eighth-floor balcony. €99

**Le Couvent** 6 rue Vieille, 2e ⓣ 06 12 31 48 79, ⓦ fonderievieille.com; ⓜ Joliette; map p.872. A real find, tucked away in the warren of streets that lead from the Vieux Port to Le Panier, with just nine smart, modern suites in a seventeenth-century convent. The suites boast both living areas and kitchens, and lots of original features from the original building. Two-night minimum stay. €130

**Edmond-Rostand** 31 rue Dragon, 6e ⓣ 04 91 37 74 95, ⓦ hoteledmondrostand.com; ⓜ Estrangin Préfecture; map p.870. Smart, friendly three-star in the antiques district, a short walk from the Vieux Port. Comfortable, smallish a/c rooms with contemporary furnishings, en-suite bath and free wi-fi. €150

**Hermès** 2 rue Bonneterie, 2e ⓣ 04 96 11 63 63, ⓦ hotelmarseille.com; ⓜ Vieux Port; map p.872. Two-star just off the Vieux Port, with plain but comfortable rooms with free wi-fi and flatscreen TV. Some have terraces, and there's a roof terrace with fabulous views over the Vieux Port. €85

**Ibis Budget Vieux Port** 46 rue Sainte, 1er ⓣ 0892 680 582, ⓦ ibis.com; ⓜ Vieux Port; map p.872. This budget chain hotel is worth a stay for its location alone, close to the Vieux Port. Situated in a historic building, though the rooms are quite bare-bones and can feel more youth-hostel chic than hotel – that said, it's incredibly popular, so book ahead. €67

★ **Mama Shelter** 64 rue de la Loubière, 6e ⓣ 04 84 35 20 00, ⓦ mamashelter.com; ⓜ Baille or Notre-Dame-du-Mont; map p.870. Marseille sister of the hip Paris original, combining stylish design and boutique hotel comforts – including iMacs for TV, free wi-fi and free on-demand movies – with budget prices. There's a restaurant, bar, a reserved strip of beach and parking. €80

**Relax** 4 rue Corneille, 1er ⓣ 04 91 33 15 87, ⓦ hotelrelax.fr; ⓜ Vieux Port; map p.872. Homely and very friendly budget hotel, right next to the Opéra and near all the action. Public areas are a little overstuffed in style; rooms are simpler, a/c and soundproofed. Prices are keen for the central location. €65

**La Résidence du Vieux-Port** 18 quai du Port, 2e ⓣ 04 91 91 91 22, ⓦ hotel-residence-marseille.com; ⓜ Vieux Port; map p.872. Sunny rooms decorated with primary-coloured artworks in a prime location overlooking the port; some rooms have balconies overlooking the water. The restaurant is equally bright and cheerful, with a much-coveted terrace. €180

### HOSTELS

**Auberge de Jeunesse Bonneveine** Impasse Bonfils, av J.-Vidal, 8e ⓣ 04 91 17 63 30, ⓦ ajmarseille.org; ⓜ Rd-Pt-du-Prado, then bus #44 (direction "Floralia Rimet", stop "Place Bonnefon") or night bus #583 from Centre Bourse; map p.870. Attractive modern hostel just 200m from the plage du Prado. Facilities include wi-fi, restaurant and bar. Rates include breakfast. Open 24hr. Closed mid-Dec to mid-Jan. Dorms €24.70, doubles €27.90

★ **Vertigo** 42 rue des Petites-Maries, 1er ⓣ 04 91 91 07 11; ⓜ St-Charles ⓦ hotelvertigo.fr; map p.872. Funky backpacker hotel and hostel near the train and bus stations, with simple, stylish rooms and two-sixteen-bed mixed dorms, youthful staff, 24hr reception and a bar in the lobby. En-suite double rooms fill up fast, so book those in advance. Dorms from €20, doubles €70

★ **Vertigo Vieux Port** 38 rue du Fort-Notre-Dame, 7e ⓣ 04 91 54 42 95, ⓦ hotelvertigo.fr; ⓜ Estrangin Préfecture; map p.872. This sister hostel to *Vertigo* has a similarly cool atmosphere, with accommodation in simple twin rooms or four- to eight-bed mixed or all-female dorms, all en suite. Rates include breakfast and wi-fi. Dorms €24, twins €64

## EATING

Good restaurant hunting grounds include cours Julien and around (international options), the Vieux Port (touristy and fishy), the Corniche and plage du Prado (glitzy and pricey). Rue Sainte is good for smart, fashionable dining close to the Vieux Port.

## CAFÉS AND BARS

**Bar de la Marine** 15 quai Rive-Neuve, 1er ☎ 04 91 54 95 42; ⓜ Vieux Port; map p.872. A favourite bar for Vieux Port lounging, doubly famous as the inspiration for Pagnol's Marseille trilogy and as a location from the film *Love, Actually*. It's open from breakfast: at lunchtime you might tuck into a €12 *plat du jour*; in the evening pizzas (from €12.50) anchor down the mojitos and wine. Sun–Wed 7am–2am, Thurs–Sat 7am–3pm.

**Cup of Tea** 1 rue Caisserie, 2e ☎ 04 91 90 84 02; ⓜ Vieux Port; map p.872. A gorgeous Le Panier bookshop and *salon de thé* strategically located midway up the climb from the Vieux Port to the Vieille Charité. Huge selection of speciality teas, including green tea or rooibos from €3.50; coffee from €1.80. Mon–Sat 8.30am–7pm.

**Le Glacier du Roi** 4 place de Lenche, 2e ☎ 04 91 91 01 16; ⓜ Joliette; map p.872. Arguably the best ice cream in the city, with a wonderful array of flavours to eat in or take away (two scoops €4), such as fig and caramel, plus a number of decadent desserts. Wed–Mon 8.30am–7pm.

★ **Plauchut** 168 La Canebière, 1er ☎ 04 91 48 06 67, ⓦ plauchut.com; ⓜ Réformés-Canebière; map p.870. Beautiful old *pâtissier-chocolatier-glacier* and *salon de thé*, established in 1820, selling delicious home-made ice cream (from €2.50), croissants, *calissons* and *macarons*, plus *pogne* (a type of brioche), sandwiches (from €4) and traditional *navettes* – a hard orange-scented biscuit sold by weight. Tues–Sun 8am–8pm.

## RESTAURANTS

★ **Les Arcenaulx** 25 cours d'Estienne-d'Orves, 1er ☎ 04 91 59 80 30, ⓦ les-arcenaulx.com; ⓜ Vieux Port; map p.872. This classy place has an atmospheric and intellectual vibe, as it's also a bookshop; there's a €26 lunch *menu* and a six-course *menu découverte* for €65; otherwise, expect to pay around €21 for the likes of *tartare de boeuf* with *frites* and salad. Mon–Sat noon–2pm & 7.30–10.30pm; July & Aug also closed Mon.

**Chez Fonfon** 140 Vallon des Auffes, 7e ☎ 04 91 52 14 38, ⓦ chez-fonfon.com; bus #83; map p.870. There's no debate about the quality of the bouillabaisse (€53) here, for this chic restaurant overlooking a small fishing harbour is one of an elite band guarding the true recipe of the dish. Daily noon–2pm & 7–10pm.

**Chez Sauveur** 10 rue d'Aubagne, 1er ☎ 04 91 54 33 96, ⓦ chezsauveur.fr; ⓜ Noailles; map p.872. Established in 1943, this modest Sicilian restaurant close to the marché des Capucins is renowned locally for its excellent wood-fired pizzas (from €9), including a few made with *brousse*, a type of goat's cheese. Tues–Sat 11.30am–10.30pm.

**La Kahena** 2 rue de la République, 2e ☎ 04 91 90 61 93, ⓦ lakahena.fr; ⓜ Vieux Port; map p.872. Great Tunisian restaurant just off the Vieux Port, with a bright interior, elaborate patterned tiles, couscous from €10 and lamb *brochettes* for €16. There are delectable displays of sticky pastries, and a few North African bottles on the wine list. Daily noon–2pm & 7–10pm.

**Miramar** 12 quai du Port, 2e ☎ 04 91 91 10 40, ⓦ lemiramar.fr; ⓜ Vieux Port; map p.872. Everyone who's ever been to – or lived in – Marseille will have an opinion on where to go for the best *bouillabaisse*, and this classic gastronomic restaurant in the Vieux Port is undoubtedly one of the main contenders. Though the menu covers a whole range of exquisite seafood (and meat) options, you'd be foolish not to try the *bouillabaisse* (€69). You can even learn to cook it here (contact tourist office for details). Tues–Sun noon–2.30pm & 7–10.30pm.

★ **La Passarelle** 52 rue Plan Fourmiguier, 7e ☎ 04 91 33 03 27; ⓜ Vieux Port or bus #82 or #83; map p.872. Relaxed and informal restaurant tucked behind La Criée theatre, with a short, daily-changing seasonal menu featuring the likes of seared tuna with sweet pepper hummus. Main courses around €22. The garden terrace is one of the prettiest (and most peaceful) in the city. Daily 11am–2pm & 6–11.30pm; garden terrace open April–Oct.

★ **Le Refuge** 22 rue du Refuge, 2e ☎ 09 81 06 46 48, ⓦ lerefugedupanier.com; ⓜ Joliette; map p.872. Tucked away in Le Panier, this little restaurant is loved by both locals and tourists alike. Priding themselves on unpretentious gourmet food, the seasonal menu might include dishes such as octopus salad or sea bream with almond and dried fruit rice, plus delectable desserts, and in fine weather you can sit out on the lovely terrace. *Menus* from €16. Sun & Mon noon–3pm, Thurs–Fri noon–3pm & 7.30–10.30pm.

★ **Sur le Pouce** 2 rue des Convalescents, 1er ☎ 04 91 56 13 28; ⓜ St-Charles; map p.872. Lively and inexpensive Tunisian restaurant in the *quartier* Belsunce, with a huge range of couscous from €5.50–10, plus grills, Merguez sausages and *brochettes* from around €6. One of the city's best budget options. Daily noon–3.30pm & 6–11.30pm.

**Toinou Coquillages** 3 cours Saint-Louis, 1er ☎ 04 91 33 14 94, ⓦ toinou.com; ⓜ Noailles; map p.872. Popular with locals and visitors alike for the choice of more than forty types of shellfish, served in the restaurant and sold fresh from the counter at the front. *Plateaux* from €14.70; they also do fish and chips. Daily 11.30am–10pm.

**Une Table, au Sud** 2 quai du Port, 2e ☎ 04 91 90 63 53, ⓦ unetableausud.com; ⓜ Vieux Port; map p.872. Stylish, Michelin-starred gastronomic restaurant overlooking the Vieux Port. Chef Ludovic Turac's contemporary take on Provençal cooking includes dishes such as roast veal sweetbread with potato *churros*, and sole with hazelnut butter. The three-course daily lunch *menu* costs €36, otherwise *menus* start at €58. Tues–Sat noon–2pm & 7.30–10pm, Sun noon–2pm.

**17**

## DRINKING

**Au Petit Nice** 28 place Jean-Jaurès, 1er ☎04 91 48 43 04; Ⓜ Notre-Dame-du-Mont; map p.870. A Marseille institution in the most bohemian quarter of the city. The terrace is the place to head for on Saturday during the market, and there's a great selection of reasonably priced beers (from €2 *pression*, €3 in bottles). Mon–Thurs 11am–2am, Fri & Sat 8am–2am.

**O'Malley's** 9 quai Rive-Neuve, 1er; ☎04 91 33 65 50; Ⓜ Vieux Port; map p.872. Celtic trappings plus live music daily at 9pm and daily happy hour (5–9pm), when pints start at €5. Mon–Tues & Sun 3pm–1.15am, Wed & Thurs 3pm–2.15am, Fri & Sat 3pm–3.15am.

**Le Red Lion** 231–233 av Pierre-Mendès-France, 8e ☎04 91 25 17 17, Ⓦ pub-redlion.com; bus #19; map p.870. Large British-style pub close to the beach with a big selection of beers including Kronenbourg, Grimbergen and Guinness; draught beer from €5. The interior is dark and warren-like; as soon as the sun shines everyone crowds onto the narrow terrace at the front. Mon–Thurs & Sun 4pm–2am, Fri & Sat 4pm–4am.

## NIGHTLIFE AND ENTERTAINMENT

Of the various free local arts newspapers *Ventilo* and *Sortir* are the most useful; pick them up from tourist offices, museums and cultural centres, or FNAC in the Centre Bourse: this bookstore – and the tourist office's ticket bureau – are the best places for tickets and information.

### LIVE MUSIC AND CLUBS

**Les Docks des Suds** 12 rue Urbain V, 2e ☎04 91 99 00 00, Ⓦ docks-des-suds.org; tram #2, stop "Arenc le Silo"; map p.870. Vast warehouse that hosts Marseille's annual Fiesta des Suds world-music festival (Oct) and is a regular live venue for hip-hop, electro and world music. Closed Aug. Hours vary.

**L'Intermédiaire** 63 place Jean-Jaurès, 6e ☎06 87 87 88 21; Ⓜ Notre-Dame-du-Mont; map p.870. Loud, hip club and bar with regular live bands and DJs and a highly eclectic music policy. Thurs–Sat 6pm–2am.

**Pelle Mêle** 8 place aux Huiles, 1er ☎04 91 54 85 26; Ⓜ Vieux Port; map p.872. Intimate and lively jazz club and piano bar just off the Vieux Port, with frequent live sets. A big range of whiskies from €9. Mon–Sat 5.30pm–2am; live music Wed–Sat 7.30–11.30pm.

**Le Poste à Galène** 103 rue Ferrari, 5e ☎04 91 47 57 99, Ⓦ leposteagalene.com; Ⓜ Notre-Dame-du-Mont; map p.870. Intimate and popular bar and live venue with regular live pop, folk, jazz, rock and electro, plus 1980s and 1990s DJ nights (Sat from 11pm; €7) and a bar. Concerts start at 9pm.

**Trolleybus** 24 quai Rive-Neuve, 7e ☎04 91 54 30 45, Ⓦ letrolley.com; bus #83; map p.872. Atmospheric bar, club and live venue in a series of vaulted, themed seventeenth-century catacombs that once housed an arsenal; DJ nights have an emphasis on electro. Spirits are priced by the bottle. Thurs–Sat midnight–6am.

**WAAW** 17 rue Pastoret, 6e ☎04 91 42 16 33, Ⓦ waaw. fr; Ⓜ Notre-Dame-du-Mont; map p.870. This is *the* place to come in Marseille, whether you're a tourist, a local, or even *en famille*. Part cultural centre, part restaurant, part cocktail bar, part dancehall – one thing's for sure – it does all of it brilliantly. Tues–Sat 6pm–midnight; restaurant from 7pm.

### LGBT CLUBS

**Aux 3G** 3 rue St-Pierre, 5e ☎04 91 48 76 36, Ⓦ aux3g. com; Ⓜ Notre-Dame-du-Mont; map p.870. Marseille's only lesbian bar, close to La Plaine market and regularly packed for its weekend karaoke and DJ nights, when they spin anything from dance music to eighties hits. Gay men are also welcome. Admission €5. Thurs 7.30pm–midnight, Fri 8pm–midnight, Sat 8pm–2am.

**New Cancan** 3 rue Sénac, 1er ☎04 91 48 59 76, Ⓦ newcancan.com; Ⓜ Noailles; map p.870. It's pretty cheesy, but the *New Cancan* is nevertheless Marseille's only gay disco and something of a local institution. Free entry Thurs & Sun; otherwise door charge with *conso* (free drink). Wed–Sun midnight–7am.

### THEATRES AND CONCERT HALLS

**Ballet National de Marseille** 20 bd Gabès, 8e ☎04 91 32 72 72, Ⓦ ballet-de-marseille.com; Ⓜ Rond-Point du Prado. The home venue of the famous dance company, founded in 1972 by Roland Petit. Now under the direction of Emio Greco and Pieter C. Scholten, the company also performs at the Opéra, Le Silo and at La Criée theatre, as well as touring.

**Espace Julien** 39 cours Julien, 6e ☎04 91 24 34 10, Ⓦ espace-julien.com; Ⓜ Notre-Dame-du-Mont. Vibrant, municipally run arts centre staging everything from live comedy to jazz, electro and rock bands. There's a large main auditorium and a second, more intimate venue, the *Café Julien*.

**La Friche la Belle de Mai** 41 rue Jobin, 3e ☎04 95 04 95 95, Ⓦ lafriche.org; Ⓜ St-Charles or tram #2 direction "Longchamp". Interdisciplinary arts complex occupying a former industrial site in the north of the city, hosting theatre, dance, live music, circus, puppetry and art exhibitions. Live DJ nights on the roof in summer.

**Opéra** 2 rue Molière, 1er ☎04 91 55 11 10, Ⓦ opera. marseille.fr; Ⓜ Vieux Port. High opera and symphony concerts by the Orchestre Philharmonique de Marseille in a magnificent setting, part Neoclassical, part Art Deco. Cheapest opera tickets are for the amphitheatre at the very top of the auditorium; fifty of these are held back until just before a performance.

**Le Silo** 35 quai du Lazaret, 2e ☎04 91 90 00 00, Ⓦ silo-marseille.fr; tram #2, stop "Arenc le Silo". This 1920s-built former dockside grain silo has been converted into a 2000-seat multi-purpose concert venue and hosts everything from ballet to rock, swing and jazz-funk.

**Théâtre National la Criée** 30 quai Rive-Neuve, 7ᵉ ☎04 91 54 70 54, ⊚theatre-lacriee.com; bus #83. Marseille's most prestigious stage for drama, home base of the Théâtre National de Marseille and occasional venue for ballet.

### CINEMAS
**Château de la Buzine** 56 traverse de la Buzine, 11ᵉ

☎04 91 45 27 60, ⊚labuzine.com; bus #50 from Castellane to La Valentine, then bus #51. It's a long trek from the centre, but the villa that Pagnol dreamed of turning into a *cinemathèque* is now exactly that – and a fantastic place to see his classic films. Matinées and evening screenings; tickets €7.70.

**Le Gyptis** 136 rue Loubon, 3ᵉ ☎04 95 04 95 95, ⊚lafriche.org; ⊕St-Charles. Arthouse cinema in Belle de Mai, with a separate children's programme and occasionally showing undubbed (*v.o.*) English-language films. Performance times vary; tickets €6.

### DIRECTORY
**Consulates** UK, 10 place de la Joliette, 2ᵉ (☎01 44 51 31 00); USA, place Varian-Fry, 6e (☎01 43 12 48 85).
**Health** Ambulance ☎15; doctor ☎3624; 24hr casualty department at Hôpital de la Conception, 147 bd Baille, 5ᵉ (☎04 91 38 00 00); medical emergencies for travellers at SOS Voyageurs, Gare St-Charles, 3ᵉ (☎04 91 62 12 80);

for an out-of-hours pharmacy (*pharmacie de garde*) see ⊚pharmaciesdegardemarseille.wordpress.com.
**Laundry** 102 rue Sainte (daily 7am–9pm).
**Police** Commissariat Central, 2 rue Antoine-Becker, 2ᵉ (24hr; ☎04 91 39 80 00).

# Cassis

Many people rate chic little **CASSIS**, 23km east of Marseille, as the best resort this side of St-Tropez; hemmed in by cliffs, its development has been necessarily modest, making it a pleasant stop-over or day-trip from Marseille. Be sure to try the local Cassis white wines.

The spectacular clifftop **route des Crêtes** links Cassis with La Ciotat; regular belvederes allow you to stop and take the perfect shot of distant headlands receding into the sunset – vertigo permitting. The route is closed during high winds.

## The calanques

Boat trips from around €16–23 • Forest fire information ☎08 11 20 13 13, ⊚calanques-parcnational.fr • If walking, call the information line before setting out as from June to September access is controlled according to a colour-coded alert level: orange means free access, red means access 6–11am only and black means the massifs are closed altogether

Portside posing and sunbathing aside, don't miss a boat trip to the **calanques** – pristine fjord-like inlets that cut deep into the limestone cliffs between Cassis and Marseille, declared a national park in 2012. Several companies operate from the port; be prepared for rough seas. If you're feeling energetic, follow the well-marked GR98 footpath from Port-Miou on the western side of the town. It's a four-hour round trip on foot to the *calanque*, **En Vau**, where you can reach the shore. The water is deep blue and swimming between the cliffs is pure heaven. The fire risk is high; smoking and fires are prohibited and you're advised not to attempt the walk in high winds. There are no refreshment stops, so take water.

### ARRIVAL AND INFORMATION                                                              CASSIS

**By bus** Buses from Castellane in Marseille (12 daily; 35–45min) arrive at *rond-point de la Gendarmerie* from where it's a short walk to the port and beach.
**By train** The *gare SNCF* is 3.5km from town, connected by bus (7.15am–8.25pm every 35min–1hr; 18min).
Destinations Bandol (every 30min–1hr; 18min); La Ciotat (every 30min–1hr; 6min); Marseille (every 30min–1hr;

18min); St-Cyr/Les Lecques (every 30min–1hr; 11min).
**Tourist office** Quai des Moulins (Feb–April Mon–Sat 9.30am–12.30pm & 2–6pm, Sun 10am–12.30pm; May & June Mon–Sat 9am–6.30pm, Sun 9.30am–12.30pm & 3–6pm; July & Aug Mon–Sat 9am–7pm, Sun 9.30am–12.30pm & 3–6pm; Oct Mon–Sat 9.30am–12.30pm; Nov–Jan Mon–Sat 9.30am–12.30pm & 2–5pm, Sun 10am––

**17**

12.30pm; ☏ 08 92 39 01 03, ⓦ ot-cassis.com).

**Activities** You can rent kayaks or boats in Cassis, sometimes

including a skipper, and there are a couple of diving outfits; the tourist office has details.

## ACCOMMODATION

**Le Cassiden** 7 av Victor-Hugo ☏ 04 42 01 39 58, ⓦ hotel-le-cassiden.fr. Just back from the port, this appealing hotel has ten small but bright, modern rooms with simple decor and en-suite shower; all are double-glazed and a/c. Good value for the standard. **€88**

**Cassis Hostel** 4 av du Picouveau ☏ 09 54 37 99 82, ⓦ cassishostel.com. Pleasant budget option in a suburban setting a short walk from the port, with accommodation in double rooms or four- and six-bed dorms. Facilities include a pool, free wi-fi and a kitchen. Breakfast included. Dorms **€30**, doubles **€85**

**Les Cigales** Inland just off the D559 on the edge of the village ☏ 04 42 01 07 34, ⓦ campingcassis.com. Cassis's most central campsite is a two-star affair, a 15min walk

from the port, with free wi-fi and 250 pitches. Closed early Nov to late March. **€23.60**

**Le Jardin d'Émile** 23 av de l'Amiral-Ganteaume ☏ 04 42 01 80 55, ⓦ lejardinemile.fr. This sunny guesthouse has an enviable location overlooking Bestouan Beach. The six rooms, largely painted in bright colours, are a delight – full of character and comfort – and some even boast sea views. Breakfast (€13) is served on the sea-view terrace. **€115**

**Les Roches Blanches** 9 av des Calanques ☏ 04 42 01 09 30, ⓦ roches-blanches-cassis.com. Cassis's best hotel is in an idyllic setting amid pines on the Presqu'île, west of the port. Rooms have modern decor, bathrooms and a/c and many have either a balcony or terrace. There's a pool, plus direct access to the sea. Parking €15. **€240**

## EATING AND DRINKING

**Le Chaudron** 4 rue Adolphe-Thiers ☏ 04 42 01 74 18. Esteemed, old family-run bistro in the streets behind the port, with modern decor; expect traditional dishes with a twist, such as duck breast with honey and lavender (€18.50). *Menus* from €23. Mon & Wed–Fri 7pm–1am, Sat & Sun noon–3pm & 7pm–1am.

**Le Clos des Arômes** 10 rue Abbé-P.-Mouton ☏ 04 42 01 71 84, ⓦ leclosdesaromes.fr. Classic Provençal cooking in a simple, rustic dining room or in a pretty garden, with wood-fired pizza from €10 and dishes such as *daube à l'ancienne*, penne with calamari ragout or grilled fish. *Menus* from €30. Daily noon–2.30pm & 7.30–10pm.

# La Ciotat

Cranes still loom over the little port of **LA CIOTAT**, where vast oil tankers were once built. Today, the unpretentious town relies on tourism and yachting and is less a place for sightseeing than relaxing, with a lively waterfront and good, sandy beaches on the eastern side of the port. The streets of the old town, apart from **rue des Poilus**, are uneventful, though the increasing numbers of boutiques and *agents immobiliers* reflect the change from shipyard to pleasure port.

## The Eden Cinema

25 bd Clemenceau • Screening times vary • Tickets €7.50 • ⓦ edencinemalaciotat.com

In 1895, **Auguste and Louis Lumière** filmed the first moving pictures in La Ciotat – the town's main claim to fame. The world's oldest movie house, the **Eden Cinema**, still stands today: it was carefully restored to coincide with Marseille's stint as European Capital of Culture in 2013 and is once again a functioning cinema, with a varied programme that includes documentaries and film classics.

## Parc du Mugel

Daily: April–Sept 8am–8pm; Oct–March 9am–6pm • Free • Bus #30 from port, stop "Mugel"

Take a walk through the **Parc du Mugel**, with its strange cluster of rock formations on the promontory beyond the shipyards. A path leads up through overgrown vegetation to a narrow terrace overlooking the sea. Two stops before the park on bus #30 (Figuerolles) you can reach the **Anse de Figuerolles** *calanque* down the avenue of the same name, and its neighbour, the **Gameau**.

## ARRIVAL AND INFORMATION

**By train** The *gare SNCF* is 5km from the town, connected to the Vieux Port by buses #10 and #40 (every 30–40min; 20min).

Destinations Bandol (every 30min–1hr; 11min); Cassis (every 30min–1hr; 6min); Marseille (every 20min–1hr; 25min); St Cyr-Les Lecques (every 30min–1hr; 4min).

**Tourist office** Bd Anatole-France (June–Sept Mon–Sat 9am–8pm, Sun 10am–1pm; Oct–May Mon–Sat 9am–noon & 2–6pm; ☎ 04 42 08 61 32, ⌨ en.laciotat.info).

**Boat trips** For a blissful afternoon offshore, take Navette Île Verte, which makes the crossing to the islet of Île Verte (daily: April–June & Sept hourly 10am–5pm; July & Aug hourly 9am–6.45pm; Oct enquire at Vieux Port or call; €13 return; ☎ 06 63 59 16 35, ⌨ laciotat-ileverte.com). Catamaran Le Citharista runs trips to the *calanques*, using its namesake catamaran, a glass-bottomed boat or (in July & Aug) a semi-rigid open boat – this last giving the chance to take a dip (late March to end Oct except during bad weather; up to 9 daily in high season; €18–32; ☎ 06 09 35 25 68; ⌨ visite-calanques.fr).

## ACCOMMODATION

**Corniche du Liouquet** Corniche du Liouquet, rte des Lecques ☎ 04 42 83 28 82, ⌨ hotel-corniche-ciotat.com. Stunningly situated by the sea to the east of town, this small three-star hotel has just twelve contemporary rooms with a/c and Ligne Roset furnishings. Most rooms also have a terrace. Breakfast €14. **€113**

**Miramar** 3 bd Beaurivage, La Ciotat-Plage ☎ 04 42 83 33 79, ⌨ hotelmiramarlaciotat.fr. Spacious and comfortable – though not stylish – family-run hotel in the beach suburb of La Ciotat-Plage, right on the palm-fringed seafront, with a/c en-suite rooms, some with balconies, plus free wi-fi. There's also a restaurant. **€81**

**La Rotonde** 44 bd de la République ☎ 04 42 08 67 50, ⌨ hotel-larotonde-ciotat.fr. Good-value, non-smoking two-star 200m from the port. All rooms have private bath, and flatscreen TV; cheaper rooms lack a/c, and around half the rooms have balconies. **€104**

**Du Soleil** 751 av Émile-Bodin ☎ 04 42 71 55 32, ⌨ camping-dusoleil.com. The most central of La Ciotat's campsites, around 1.5km from the beach and harbour, is this place, a small two-star site with on-site restaurant and takeaway. Closed Oct–March. Camping **€28**, mobile homes **€70**, bungalows **€80**

## EATING AND DRINKING

**Roche Belle** Corniche du Liouquet ☎ 04 42 71 47 60, ⌨ roche-belle.fr. In an idyllic setting near the sea between La Ciotat and Les Lecques, with a shady terrace and dishes such as squid on polenta with pine nuts. There's a three-course *menu* at €36.50 and they serve Bandol wines. Lunch *formule* €22; à la carte mains from around €27. Tues–Sat noon–1.30pm & 7.30–9.30pm; July & Aug also open Sun.

**De la Vigne à l'Olivier** 44 quai François-Mitterrand ☎ 04 86 33 27 02. Classy Italian restaurant/café and wine bar at the far side of the port, with charcuterie and cheese platters from €16, fresh pasta from €15 and wines by the glass from €5. Daily 6pm–midnight.

# Bandol and around

Across La Ciotat bay are the fine sand and shingle beaches of **Les Lecques**, an offshoot of the inland town of **St-Cyr-sur-Mer**, to which it is fused by modern suburbs. From the Port de la Madrague at the eastern end of Les Lecques' bay a signposted 10km **coastal path** runs through a stretch of secluded beaches and unspoilt *calanques* to the unpretentious resort of **BANDOL**. Inland, *dégustation* signs announce the *appellation* Bandol, whose **vineyards** produce some of the best wines on the Côte. The reds are highly reputed; the pale rosé is sublime on a warm summer's evening. To taste or buy, visit the **Oenothèque des Vins de Bandol**, place Lucien-Artaud, opposite the casino on the seafront (Mon–Sat 10am–1pm & 3–7pm, Sun 10am–1pm; ☎ 04 94 29 45 03, ⌨ maisondesvins-bandol.com).

## ARRIVAL AND INFORMATION
BANDOL AND AROUND

**By train** Bandol station is uphill from the port; infrequent free shuttle buses link it with Embarcadère, close to the tourist office. It's generally easiest to reach Bandol via St-Cyr/Les Lecques station in St-Cyr-sur-Mer, 2km inland, from which regular trains run to Bandol.

Destinations from St Cyr-Les Lecques La Ciotat (every 30min–1hr 30min; 4min).

Destinations from Bandol La Ciotat (every 30min–1hr 30min; 11min); Marseille (every 30min–1hr; 45min).

**Tourist office** On Bandol's quayside at allée Alfred-Vivien (June–Sept daily 9am–7pm; Oct–May daily 10am–6pm; ☎ 04 94 29 41 35, ⌨ bandoltourisme.fr).

**17**

## ACCOMMODATION

**Golf Hotel** Plage de Renécros, Bandol ☎04 94 29 45 83 ⓦgolfhotel.fr. Pleasant two-star on this pretty sandy cove just a short walk from Bandol. Some of the rooms have terraces overlooking the beach. Secure parking. Breakfast €11. **€108**

**Le Key Largo** 19 corniche Bonaparte, Bandol ☎04 94 29 46 93, ⓦhotel-key-largo.com. Simple, bright rooms right by the sea near the port. Some have balconies and sea views. Breakfast (€10) can be served in your room for no extra charge. **€92**

# Hyères and around

HYÈRES is the oldest resort on the Côte, listing Queen Victoria and Tolstoy among its early admirers. Set back from the coast, it lost out when the focus of tourism switched from winter convalescence to the beach. Today it exports cut flowers and exotic plants – the most important being the date palm, which graces every street – and it's a garrison town. Walled, medieval **old Hyères** perches on the slopes of Casteou hill, 5km from the sea; below it lies the **modern town**, with its elegant villas in fanciful pseudo-Moorish styles; avenue Gambetta is its main north–south axis. At the coast, the **Presqu'Île de Giens** is leashed to the mainland by an isthmus, known as **La Capte**, and a parallel sand bar enclosing salt flats.

## The lower vieille ville

From place Clemenceau, a medieval gatehouse – the **Porte Massillon** – opens into the *vieille ville* on rue Massillon, which is lined with tempting shops selling fruit and vegetables, chocolate, soaps, olive oil and wine. It ends at **place Massillon**, a perfect Provençal square with terraced cafés overlooking the twelfth-century **Tour des Templiers** (July & Aug Tues–Sat 10am–7pm; Sept–June Tues–Sat 10am–5pm; free), the remnant of a Knights Templar fort elegantly converted into exhibition space for contemporary art.

## The upper vieille ville

Behind the Tour des Templiers, rue Ste-Catherine leads uphill to place St-Paul, from which you have a panoramic view over the Golfe de Giens. Wide steps fan out from the Renaissance door of the former collegiate **church of St-Paul** (July & Aug Tues–Sat 10am–1pm & 4–7pm; Sept–June Tues–Sat 10am–1pm & 2–5pm; free), whose distinctive belfry is pure Romanesque, as is the choir, though the simplicity of the design is masked by the collection of votive offerings hung inside. To the right of St-Paul, a Renaissance house bridges rue St-Paul, its turret supported by a pillar rising beside the steps. Through this arch you can head up rue Ste-Claire to **Parc Ste-Claire** (daily 8am–5.30/6/7pm; free), the exotic gardens around **Castel Ste-Claire**, once home to the American writer Edith Wharton. Cobbled paths continue up the hill towards the **Parc St-Bernard** (daily 8am–5/6.30/7/7.30pm; free), which is full of almost every Mediterranean flower known.

### Villa Noailles and around

Montée de Noailles • Sat–Thurs 2–7pm, Fri 3–9pm • Free • ☎04 98 08 01 98, ⓦvillanoailles-hyeres.com

The **Villa Noailles**, a Cubist mansion enclosed within part of the old citadel walls, was designed by Mallet-Stevens in the 1920s and housed all the luminaries of Dada and Surrealism. It now hosts contemporary art and design exhibitions. Still further up the hill are the immaculate remains of the eleventh-century **castle**, whose keep and towers give stunning views out to the Îles d'Hyères and east to the Massif des Maures.

## The Hyères coast

If you're keen on the ancient history of this coast, the **Site Archéologique d'Olbia** (June –Aug Mon–Fri 9.30am–noon & 2.30–6pm, Sat & Sun 2.30–6pm; April–

May, Sept & Oct Mon & Wed–Fri 9.30am–noon & 2–5.30pm, Sat & Sun 2–5.30pm; Nov–March groups only, by appointment; €2.80; ☎04 94 65 51 49) in Almanarre is worth a visit for its Greek, Roman and medieval remains, including those of the abbey of Saint-Pierre de l'Almanarre. Along the eastern shore of the isthmus linking Hyères to the **Presqu'île de Giens** there are plenty of sandy **beaches**. Alternatively, take the **route du Sel** (closed to motorised traffic 9pm–5am, and mid-Oct to April) along the western shore for a glimpse of the flamingos on the adjoining saltpans and of the kitesurfers at the southern end of the windy plage de l'Almanarre.

## The Îles d'Hyères

The wild, scented greenery and fine sand beaches of the **Îles d'Hyères** are a reminder of what much of the mainland was like half a century ago. You can **stay** on all three main islands, though accommodation is scarce, coveted and expensive. Visitors should observe signs forbidding smoking (away from the ports), flower-picking and littering. The fire risk in summer is extreme: at times large sections of the islands are closed off and visitors must stick to marked paths.

A haven from tempests in ancient times, then the peaceful home of monks and farmers, the **Îles d'Hyères** became, from the Middle Ages, the target of piracy and coastal attacks. The three main islands, **Porquerolles**, **Port-Cros** and **Levant**, are covered in half-destroyed, rebuilt or abandoned forts, dating from the sixteenth century to the twentieth, when the German gun positions on Port-Cros and Levant were put out of action by the Americans. There's also still a military presence on Porquerolles and indeed ninety percent of Île du Levant is a missile testing range; the tiny bit of this island spared by the military is the **nudist colony** of Heliopolis, set up in the 1930s.

The islands' fragile environment is protected by the Parc National de Port-Cros and the Conservatoire Botanique de Porquerolles.

### Île de Porquerolles

The most easily accessible island is **Île de Porquerolles**, whose village, also called **PORQUEROLLES**, has a few hotels and restaurants, plenty of cafés, a supermarket and fruit stall and interminable games of *boules*. It dates from a nineteenth-century military settlement, and still focuses around the central **place d'Armes**. In summer it teems with day-trippers, but there is some activity all year round. This is the only cultivated island, with a few olive groves and three Côtes de Provence *domaines*, which you can visit.

Porquerolles is big enough to find yourself alone amid its stunning landscapes. The **lighthouse**, south of the village, and the *calanques* to its east make good destinations for an hour's walk, though the southern shoreline is mostly cliffs, with scary paths meandering close to the edge through exuberant maquis scrub.

#### Maison du Parc

Daily: early July to mid-Sept 9.30am–12.30pm & 2.30–6.30pm; April to early July & mid-Sept to late Oct 9.30am–12.30pm & 2–6pm; mid to late March & late Oct to mid-Nov 9.30am–12.30pm & 1.30–5.50pm • Free • ☎04 94 58 07 24

Just off the path to the lighthouse at the southern end of the village is the **Maison du Parc**, which has a garden of palms from around the world and information on the national park's activities. It also organizes guided walks on themes including the island's flora and fauna.

#### The beaches

The most fabled (and distant) of the beaches is the **plage Notre-Dame**, 3km northeast of the village just before the *terrain militaire* on the northeastern tip. The nearest to the village is the sandy **plage de la Courtade**, which you pass on the way to Notre-Dame. Facilities are minimal – there are earth toilets and places to park bikes at

**17**

Courtade. The smaller **plage d'Argent** west of the village has a good **restaurant**, while at the island's mistral-blasted western tip idyllic beaches bracket an isthmus that leads to the pink-painted, seventeenth-century **Fort du Grand Langoustier** (unfortunately closed to the public).

## Île de Port-Cros

The dense vegetation and hills of **Île de Port-Cros** make exploration tougher than Porquerolles, though it's less than half the size – take water with you. Aside from ruined forts and the buildings around the port, the only significant intervention is the extensive network of paths; you're not supposed to stray from these and it would be difficult to do so given the thickness of the undergrowth. The entire island is a protected zone, and has the richest fauna and flora of all the islands. Kestrels, eagles and sparrowhawks nest here; there are shrubs that flower and bear fruit at the same time. One kilometre from the port (and a 45min walk) is a beach, the **plage de la Palud**, with an underwater trail for snorkellers; it takes longer to reach Mont Vinaigre, the island's highest point, via the **Vallon de la Solitude** – a three-hour round trip. From here there are views over the island's south coast and the islet of Gabinière. Except for those close to the beaches, the island's 30km of paths are liable to close at times of high fire risk.

| ARRIVAL AND DEPARTURE | HYÈRES AND AROUND |
|---|---|

### HYÈRES

**By plane** Toulon-Hyères airport (☎08 25 01 83 87, ⓦ toulon-hyeres.aeroport.fr) lies between Hyères and Hyères-Plage, 3km from the centre, to which it's connected by an infrequent bus service (#63; hourly; 20min).
Destinations London City (3 weekly in summer; 2hr); Paris Orly (up to 8 daily; 1hr 25min); Southampton (weekly in summer; 1hr 50min).

**By train** The *gare SNCF* is on place de l'Europe, with frequent buses (#29 or #67) to the town centre, 1.5km north, and up to six daily runs to Toulon (23min).

**By bus** Buses arrive and depart from place du Maréchal-Joffre, two blocks south of the entrance to the old town (☎04 94 03 87 03, ⓦ reseaumistral.com).
Destinations Le Lavandou (up to 15 daily; 35min); St-Tropez (up to 15 daily; 1hr 35min); Toulon (up to 14 daily; 1hr); Tour Fondue (for Porquerolles: every 15–30min; 36min).

### ÎLES D'HYÈRES

**From Bandol** Quai d'Honneur. Three weekly excursions to Porquerolles in summer; the trip includes 6hr on the island (☎04 94 32 51 41, ⓦ atlantide1.com).

**From La Tour Fondue** Presqu'île de Giens. The closest port to Porquerolles; all year round to Porquerolles (☎04 94 58 21 81, ⓦ tlv-tvm.com).

**From Le Lavandou** *Gare maritime* (☎04 94 71 01 02, ⓦ vedettesilesdor.fr). The closest port to Port-Cros and Levant, with services to both from mid-April to early Oct and summer services to Porquerolles (1–4 daily mid-Feb to June & Sept to early Nov; 6–8 daily July & Aug). The same line runs infrequent seasonal services from Cavalaire and La Croix-Valmer to Port-Cros and Porquerolles.

**From La Londe** Port Miramar. Services to Porquerolles and Port-Cros (April–Oct; ☎04 94 48 01 00, ⓦ bateliers delacotedazur.com), plus St-Tropez (June–Sept). The same line runs services to Porquerolles from Toulon (June–Aug).

**From Port d'Hyères** Hyères-Plage. Services to Port-Cros and Levant all year (☎04 94 58 21 81, ⓦ tlv-tvm.com).

**From St-Raphaël** Quai Nomy, Vieux Port. Excursions to Porquerolles (July & Aug weekly ☎04 94 95 17 46, ⓦ bateauxsaintraphael.com).

**From Toulon** Quai Cronstadt. Summer trips to Porquerolles (May–Sept ☎04 94 46 24 65, ⓦ lesbateliersdelarade.com).

## INFORMATION

### HYÈRES

**Tourist office** Near the *gare routière* at Rotonde du Park Hôtel, 16 av de Belgique (July & Aug Mon–Sat 9am–6pm, Sun 9am–1pm; April–June & Sept Mon–Fri 9am–6pm, Sat 9am–4pm; Oct–Mar Mon–Fri 9am–5pm, Sat 9am–4pm; ☎04 94 01 84 50, ⓦ hyeres-tourisme.com).

**Bike rental** Amotos, 10 rue Jean-d'Agrève, near port St-Pierre (Tues–Sat 9am–noon & 2.30–6.30pm; ☎04 94 38 79 45, ⓦ amotos.fr).

### ÎLE DE PORQUEROLLES

**Tourist office** There's a booth by the harbour in

**17**

Porquerolles (July & Aug Mon–Sat 9am–6pm, Sun 9am–1pm; April–June & Sept Mon–Fri 9am–6pm, Sat 9am–4pm; Oct–Mar Mon–Fri 9am–5pm, Sat 9am–4pm; ☎ 04 94 58 33 76, ✆ hyeres-tourisme.com), where you can get island maps for €3.

**Bike rental** There are several outlets in Porquerolles including Le Cycle Porquerollais, rue de la Ferme (daily 8.45am–5,30pm; ☎ 04 94 58 30 32), and L'Indien, place d'Armes (☎ 04 94 58 30 39, ✆ lindien.fr).

## ACCOMMODATION

### HYÈRES

**Le Calypso** 36 av de la Méditerranée ☎ 04 94 58 02 09, ✆ hotelcalypso.fr. Basic and friendly hotel close to Port St-Pierre, handy for the beach and for trips to the islands. The eleven simple rooms have double glazing and flatscreen TVs; some also have a terrace or small garden. Closed Dec to mid-Feb. Breakfast €7. **€56**

**Camping Bernard** Rue des Saraniers 5 ☎ 04 94 66 30 54. Two-star campsite just 50m from the sea in Le Ceinturon, with 100 pitches and plenty of shade; facilities include a free wi-fi point and children's games. Closed Oct–Easter. **€22.90**

**Camping Clair de Lune** 27 av du Clair-de-Lune ☎ 04 94 58 20 19, ✆ campingclairdelune.com. Four-star campsite and caravan park on the Presqu'île de Giens, with free wi-fi. They also have bungalows and mobile homes. Closed mid-Nov to early Feb. Camping **€40**; mini bungalow **€469** per week, mobile homes from **€775** per week

**Du Soleil** 24 rue du Rempart ☎ 04 94 65 16 26, ✆ hotel-du-soleil.fr. Twenty assorted en-suite rooms in a renovated house at the top of the *vieille ville*, close to parc St-Bernard and the Villa Noailles. Decor is simple, and the location peaceful. **€110**

### ÎLE DE PORQUEROLLES

**L'Arche de Porquerolles** place d'Armes ☎ 04 94 58 33 71, ✆ larchedeporquerolles.fr. Eleven unflashy, modern rooms with a/c above a restaurant in the village with en-suite showers, wooden floors and flatscreen TVs. Some rooms also have terraces and sea views. Closed mid-Nov to March. **€170**

**Les Medes** 2 rue de la Douane ☎ 04 94 12 41 24, ✆ hotel-les-medes.fr. Quite smart, modern three-star hotel close to place d'Armes with a/c and a garden with an artificial waterfall. Accommodation varies from bright rooms to suites and a duplex apartment with kitchenettes and living rooms. Closed early Nov to late Dec. **€195**

### ÎLE DE PORT-CROS

**Le Manoir** ☎ 04 94 05 90 52, ✆ hotel-lemanoirportcros. com. The island's principal hotel, in a leafy garden beneath tall eucalyptus and with a pool. Doubles with bath or shower; half-board only. Its *restaurant gastronomique* overlooks the water and serves a *prix-fixe* menu for €57. Closed Oct–April. €270

**Provençale** ☎ 04 94 05 90 43, ✆ hostellerie-provencale. com. Airy en-suite, a/c rooms above a restaurant, with terrace or balcony. More luxurious rooms have sea views and access to a swimming pool. Closed Nov to mid-April. **€175**

## EATING AND DRINKING

### HYÈRES

★ **Le Jardin de Saradam** 35 av de Belgique ☎ 04 94 65 97 53, ✆ lejardindesaradam.com. Reliable North African restaurant close to the *gare routière* with a pretty garden and filling couscous and tagines on offer from around €14. Book ahead. Tues 7–9.30pm, Wed–Sat noon–2pm & 7–9.30pm, Sun noon–2pm.

**Pradeau Plage** 1420 av des Arbanais ☎ 04 94 58 29 06, ✆ pradeauplage.com. In an enviable waterside position looking towards the Île de Porquerolles, just steps from the beach, this relaxed restaurant serves up – unsurprisingly – a seafood-heavy menu. Expect the likes of seafood brochettes (prawns, scallops and tuna; €25) and fritto misto (€14.50). Closed Nov–March. Daily noon–3pm & 7–10pm.

**Le Tison d'Or** 1 rue du Maréchal-Gallieni ☎ 04 94 00 95 53. This small restaurant serves up a short set *menu* (€35) of surprisingly modern takes on traditional ingredients, such as a foie gras crème brûlée or lobster poached in a Thai-style sauce. Tues–Sat noon–1.30pm. & 7–9pm.

### ÎLE DE PORQUEROLLES

**L'Olivier** Le Mas du Langoustier ☎ 04 94 58 30 09, ✆ langoustier.com. If you want gourmet cuisine you'll need to make the trek to the idyllic and Michelin-starred restaurant of the *Mas du Langoustier* hotel in the west of the island, which has *menus* starting from €95 and dishes such as lobster tail with pomelo butter on the *carte*. Late April to early Oct Wed–Sun 12.30–2pm & 7–9.30pm; daily July & Aug.

**La Plage d'Argent** Plage d'Argent ☎ 04 94 58 32 48, ✆ plage-dargent.com. *Gault Millau*-listed place right on the beach, serving salads from around €20 and seafood from around €21, plus snacks for eating on the sand if you prefer something more casual. Mid-April to Sept daily 9am–6pm; open until 10/11pm Tues, Thurs & Sat in July & Aug.

# The Corniche des Maures

**17**

The Côte really gets going with the resorts of the **Corniche des Maures**, where multimillion-dollar residences lurk in the hills, luxurious yachts bob in the bays, and seafront prices become alarming.

The Corniche itself is spectacular, with beaches that shine silver (from the mica crystals in the sand), tall dark pines, oaks and eucalyptus to shade them, glittering rocks of purple, green and reddish hue and chestnut-forested hills keeping winds away. No wonder the French president's official retreat, the Fort de Brégançon, is here (guided tours July & Sept only, bookable only through Bormes-les-Mimosas tourist office; €10).

## Bormes-les-Mimosas

Seventeen kilometres east of Hyères, chic **BORMES-LES-MIMOSAS** is medieval in flavour, with a ruined but restored **castle** at the summit of its hill, protected by spiralling lines of pantiled houses backing onto immaculately restored flights of steps. The mimosas here, and all along the Côte d'Azur, are no more indigenous than Porsches: the tree was introduced from Mexico in the 1860s, but the town still has some of the most luscious climbing flowers of any Côte town, and in summer, the displays of bougainvillea and oleander are impressive.

### ARRIVAL AND INFORMATION
BORMES-LES-MIMOSAS

**By bus** Hyères–St-Tropez buses stop at Pin some distance below the medieval village, from where there's a free shuttle bus daily outside high season; in July and Aug it may be easier to continue the short distance to Le Lavandou (up to 8 daily buses; 25min) and change there.

**Tourist office** 1 place Gambetta (April–May & mid to late Sept Mon–Fri 8.30am–noon & 1.30–5pm, Sat 9am–noon; June & Sept Mon–Sat 9am–12.30pm & 2–6pm, Sun 9am–1pm; July & Aug daily 9.30am–12.30pm & 2.30–6.30pm; Oct–March Mon–Sat 9am–12.30pm & 2–5.30pm; ☎04 94 01 38 38, ⓦbormeslesmimosas.com).

### ACCOMMODATION

**Bellevue** 14 place Gambetta ☎04 94 71 15 15, ⓦbellevuebormes.com. Attractive hotel/restaurant at the entrance to the medieval village with a/c, country-style en-suite rooms with wi-fi, flatscreen TV and safe. The best rooms are those with a sea view, but they are more than double the price of the cheapest double room. Full- and half-board available. Closed mid-Nov to late Jan. **€49**

**Clau Mar Jo** 895 chemin de Bénat ☎04 94 71 53 39, ⓦcamping-clau-mar-jo.fr. Four-star mobile-home park just below the main road between the village and Le Lavandou, with good facilities including a swimming pool, children's play area and a gym. Closed early Nov to March. From **€889**/week for four in high season.

**Hostellerie du Cigalou** Place Gambetta ☎04 94 41 51 27, ⓦhostellerieducigalou.com. Classy three-star hotel opposite the *Bellevue*, and a member of the *Châteaux & Hôtels Collection*. It has a mimosa-shaded swimming pool and twenty tastefully decorated, themed a/c rooms with bath, safe and flatscreen TV. **€189**

### EATING AND DRINKING

★**Le Jardin** 1 ruelle du Moulin ☎04 94 71 14 86. In summer, you can sit out on arguably the nicest terrace in town, under oleander trees, while in the winter meals are served in the cosy dining room. The short menu makes use of seasonal local produce – expect the likes of an asparagus salad with *jambon cru* (€15) in spring, for example. Mains from €22. Feb & Oct Thurs–Sun noon–1.30pm & 7–9.30pm; March–June Wed–Sun noon–1.30pm & 7–9.30pm; July–Sept Tues–Sat 7–10pm, Sun noon–1.30pm & 7–10pm.

**Pâtes...et Pâtes** 1 rue Pierre-Toesca ☎04 94 64 85 75. At the foot of the medieval village, this restaurant serves good pasta from around €10, with a big choice of sauces; fancier dishes include the smoked salmon with cream for €15.70. July & Aug Mon & Wed–Sun 7–10.30pm; Sept, Oct & Feb–June Mon–Wed noon–2pm & 7–10.30pm, Sat & Sun 7–10.30pm.

**La Tonnelle de Gil Renard** 23 place Gambetta ☎04 94 71 34 84, ⓦrestaurant-la-tonnelle.com. Rather chic, *Gault Millau*-listed restaurant at the entrance to the old village, with dishes such as tuna with spelt risotto, and duck with celery gratin. *Menus* from €33, otherwise *plats* around €24. Wed–Sun noon–1.30pm & 7–9.30pm.

**17**

# Le Lavandou and around

**LE LAVANDOU**, a few kilometres east of Bormes, is a pleasantly unpretentious seaside town known for its good beaches. Its name derives from *lavoir* or "washhouse" rather than "lavender". From the central promenade of quai Gabriel-Péri the sea is all but invisible thanks to the pleasure boats moored at the three harbours; demand from restaurateurs also keeps a few fishing boats in business. There's a sandy beach in town, but the fabled silver sands are to the east at **Aiguebelle**, **Le Rossignol**, **Cavalière**, **Pramousquier** and across the municipal boundary in **Le Canadel** and **Le Rayol**. It's hardly open countryside, but this is one of the most unspoilt sections of the Côte, with a well-made cycle track parallel to the coast road. You can follow the sinuous D27 up to the Col du Canadel for breathtaking views and beautiful cork-oak woodland, and, in Le Rayol, visit a superb garden, the **Domaine du Rayol** (daily: July & Aug 9.30am–7.30pm; April–June, Sept & Oct 9.30am–6.30pm; Nov–March 9.30am–5.30pm; €11; ☏04 98 04 44 00, ⓦdomaineeurayol.org), which has plants from differing parts of the world that share the Mediterranean climate.

## ARRIVAL AND INFORMATION
LE LAVANDOU AND AROUND

**By bus** Buses from Bormes and Hyères stop at the *gare routière* on av de Provence.
Destinations La Croix-Valmer (up to 8 daily; 35min); Rayol Canadel (up to 8 daily; 15min); St-Tropez (up to 15 daily; 55min).
**Tourist office** Opposite the port at quai Gabriel-Péri (late June to mid-Sept Mon–Sat 9am–12.30pm & 2–7pm, Sun 9.30am–12.30pm & 3.30–6.30pm; mid-season Mon–Sat 9am–12.30pm & 2.30–6pm; low season Mon–Fri 9am–noon & 2.30–5.30pm, Sat 9am–noon; ☏04 94 00 40 50, ⓦot-lelavandou.com).

## ACCOMMODATION AND EATING

**L'Oustaou** 20 av du Général-de-Gaulle ☏04 94 71 12 18, ⓦlavandou-hotel-oustaou.com. Le Lavandou's best budget option – a clean, family-run place in the town centre, just minutes from the beach and port. It's well known and gets busy, so it might be worth booking ahead. The cheapest rooms are a little on the small size – it's worth paying a little more for a bigger one if you can. **€56**

**La Plage** 14 rue des Trois-Dauphins ☏04 94 05 80 74, ⓦlhoteldelaplage.com. Unpretentious three-star hotel right on the pretty sandy cove of Aiguebelle, with uncluttered modern decor, a restaurant (tapas from €8.50, mains from €17) and a broad terrace with bar. Rooms have en-suite bath and a/c, and many have sea views and balconies. **€102**

# La Croix-Valmer

Beyond Le Rayol the corniche climbs through 3km of open countryside, scarred almost every year by fires. As abruptly as this wilderness commences, it ends with the sprawling family resort of **Cavalaire-sur-Mer**. From here another exceptional stretch of coastline, dressed only in its natural covering of rock and woodlands, is visible across the Baie de Cavalaire. This is the **Domaine de Cap Lardier**, a wonderful coastal conservation area around the southern tip of the St-Tropez peninsula, easily accessible from **LA CROIX-VALMER**. The resort's rather characterless centre is 2.5km from the sea; vineyards between the two produce a very decent Côte de Provence.

## ARRIVAL AND INFORMATION
LA CROIX-VALMER

**By bus** Buses stop at plage du Débarquement and at the Croix de Constantin in the village. From mid-June to mid-Sept free shuttle buses connect the village centre with plage de Gigaro (every 45min) and plage du Débarquement (every 30min). Destinations Hyères (up to 15 daily; 1hr 15min); Le Lavandou (up to 15 daily; 35min); St-Tropez (up to 15 daily; 20min).
**Tourist office** 287 rue Louis-Martin, just up from the junction of the D559 and D93 (July & Aug daily 9.30am–12.30pm & 3.30–7pm; April–June & Sept Mon–Sat 9.15am–noon & 2–6pm, Sun 9.15am–noon; Oct–March Mon–Fri 9.15am–noon & 2–6pm, Sat 9.15am–noon; ☏04 94 55 12 12, ⓦlacroixvalmertourisme.com).

## ACCOMMODATION

**La Bienvenue** Rue Louis-Martin ☏04 94 17 08 08, ⓦhotel-la-bienvenue.com. Family-run, three-star hotel close to the tourist office, with light, neutral decor and pleasant, unfussy rooms. Breakfast is served in the garden, and there's private parking (free). Breakfast €12.50. Closed Dec–Feb. **€150**

**Le Château de Valmer** Bd de Gigaro ☎ 04 94 55 15 15, ⓦ chateauvalmer.com. Luxurious old Relais & Châteaux mansion in an idyllic setting between pines, palms and vines just back from the plage de Gigaro, with double and three- and four-bed family rooms, cottages on the estate and a few treehouses. Spa and leisure facilities include two pools, sauna, hamam and gym. Closed Oct–April. **€460**

**Sélection** 310 bd de la Mer ☎ 04 94 55 10 30, ⓦ selectioncamping.com. Four-star campsite, 400m from the sea and with excellent facilities including a heated pool, bar, restaurant, takeaway, shop and plenty of activities. Closed mid-Oct to mid-March. **€50**

### EATING AND DRINKING

**Les Moulins de Paillas** Plage de Gigaro ☎ 04 94 79 71 11, ⓦ lesmoulinsdepaillas.com. The big-selling point of this hotel restaurant is undoubtedly its wonderful terrace that looks out over the sea – you could easily lose hours eating lunch here. The largely Italian menu ranges from pizzas (from €14) to linguini with clams (€23) and grilled sea bream with fennel (€28). Mid-May to Sept daily 12.30–2pm & 7.30–9.30pm.

# The Massif des Maures

Between Hyères and Fréjus the coast's bewitching hinterland is the wooded, hilly **Massif des Maures**. The highest point of these hills stops short of 800m, but the quick succession of ridges, the sudden drops and views, and the curling, looping roads, are pervasively mountainous. In spring, the sombre forest is enlivened by millions of wild flowers and the roads are busy with cyclists; in winter, this is the haunt of hunters. Amid the brush crawl the last of the endangered Hermann's tortoises, once found along the entire northern Mediterranean coast.

## Collobrières and around

At the heart of the Massif is the ancient village of **COLLOBRIÈRES**, reputed to have been the first place in France to learn from the Spanish that a certain tree plugged into bottles allows a wine industry to grow. From the Middle Ages until supplanted by the sweet chestnut, cork production was the major business here.

### Confiserie Azuréenne

Bd Koenig • Daily: summer 9.30am–12.30pm & 1.30–7.30pm; winter 9.30am–12.30pm & 2–6pm • ☎ 04 94 48 07 20, ⓦ confiserieazureenne.com

Collobrières' church, *mairie* and houses don't seem to have changed much for a century, but the **Confiserie Azuréenne** exudes efficiency and modernity in the manufacture of all things chestnut: ice cream, jam, nougat, purée and *marrons glacés*. There's an exhibition that explains the production process and a small terrace on which to enjoy the delicious ice cream.

### La Chartreuse de la Verne

Off the D14 • Daily: June–Aug daily except during high fire risk 11am–6pm; Sept–May 11am–5pm • €6 • ☎ 04 94 43 48 28 or ☎ 04 94 48 08 00 for fire-risk information, ⓦ diocese-frejus-toulon.com/Monastère-Notre-Dame-de-Clémence • If you arrive by car, you have to park at the visitor car park, several hundred metres back from the monastery

Hidden in the forest, 12km from Collobrières towards Grimaud, is a huge and now largely restored twelfth-century monastery, **La Chartreuse de la Verne**, abandoned at the time of the Revolution. These days it looks a little too pristine, though there's no denying the wonder of its setting.

## Grimaud

**GRIMAUD**, 25km east of Collobrières along the twisting D14 and more easily reached from St-Tropez or La Croix-Valmer, is a film set of a **village perché**. The cone of houses enclosing the eleventh-century church and culminating in the ruins of a medieval castle appears as a single, perfectly unified entity, though the effect of timelessness is undermined by the glass lift that whisks visitors up into the village from the main road – handy, when it's in working order. The most vaunted street is the arcaded **rue des Templiers**, which leads up to the Romanesque **Église de St-Michel** and a house of the Knights Templar, while the view from the **castle** ruins (free) is superb. Back on the main road through the village is a small folk museum, the **Musée des Arts et Traditions Populaires** (May–June & Sept Mon–Sat 2.30–6pm; July & Aug Tues–Sat 2.30–6pm; Oct–April Mon–Sat 2–5.30pm; free; ☎04 94 43 39 29).

## Port Grimaud

The entrance is well signed off the N98

Grimaud's celebrated coastal extension, **PORT GRIMAUD**, stands at the head of the Golfe de St-Tropez, just north of La Foux. Created in the 1960s with waterways for roads and with yachts everywhere, it's exquisitely tasteful, though surrounded by car parks rather than lavender fields and with a mild air of artificiality. The inhabitants include a certain Joan Collins. You don't have to pay to visit, but you can't explore properly without renting a boat or joining a boat tour; prices vary significantly by boat and time of year – your best bet is to head down to the harbour and check out the numerous operators.

## La Garde-Freinet

The peaceful village of **LA GARDE-FREINET**, set in forested hills 10km northwest of Grimaud, was founded in the late twelfth century by people from the nearby villages of Saint-Clément and Miremer. The original fortified settlement sat further up the hillside, and the foundations of the **fortress** are still visible above the village beside the ruins of a fifteenth-century castle (take the path from La Planette car park at the northwestern end of the village; 1hr 30min). The medieval charm, easy walks to stunning panoramas and twice-weekly **market** (Wed and Sun) make it an alluring spot, and many expats have bought property here. Happily, though, attempts to "do a St-Tropez" by making it trendy and expensive seem – thus far – doomed to failure.

### ARRIVAL AND INFORMATION

### THE MASSIF DES MAURES

#### COLLOBRIÈRES

**By bus** Collobrières is served by infrequent buses from Hyères (1–2 daily; 50min) and Toulon (up to 3 daily; 1hr 50min).
**Tourist office** Bd Charles-Caminat (Tues–Sat 9am–12.30pm & 2–5.30pm; ☎04 94 48 08 00, ⓦcollobrieres-tourisme.com). They can supply details of walks in the surrounding hills.

#### GRIMAUD

**By bus** Buses link St-Tropez to Grimaud (1–2 daily; 30min) and Port Grimaud (up to 7 daily; 5min). There are also connections from Grimaud village to La Garde-Freinet (4–5 daily; 15min).
**Tourist office** On the RD558 next to the lift up to the old village (April–June & Sept Mon–Sat 9am–1pm & 2–6pm; July & Aug daily 9am–1pm & 2.30–7pm; Oct–March 9am–12.30pm & 2–5.30pm; ☎04 94 55 43 83, ⓦgrimaud-provence.com).

#### LA GARDE-FREINET

**By bus** Buses from Grimaud (4–5 daily; 15min) and St-Tropez (1–2 daily; 45min) arrive at parking du Stade on the main road at the entrance to the village.
**Tourist office** Chapelle St-Jean (April–June & Sept Mon–Fri 9am–12.30pm & 2–5.30pm, Sat 9.30am–12.30pm; July & Aug Mon–Sat 9.30am–1pm & 2.30–6.30pm, Sun 9.30am–12.30pm; Oct–March Mon–Fri 9.30am–12.30pm & 2–5pm; ☎04 94 56 04 93, ⓦla-garde-freinet-tourisme. fr). They can provide details for the entire Maures region, including suggested walks and hikes (in English), such as the spectacular 21km GR9 route des Crêtes.
**Conservatoire du Patrimoine** Next door to the tourist office in the Chapelle St-Jean (April–Oct Mon–Sat 9am–1pm & 2–5pm; Nov–March Mon–Fri 9am–1pm & 2–5pm; ⓦconservatoiredufreinet.org). They organize guided walks on local topics and have exhibits on local history.

#### GETTING AROUND

**On foot** Much of the Massif is inaccessible even to walkers. However, the GR9 footpath follows the highest and most northerly ridge from Pignans on the N97 past Notre-Dame-des-Anges, La Sauvette, La Garde-Freinet and down to the head of the Golfe de St-Tropez.

**By bike** For cyclists, the D14 that runs for 42km through the middle, parallel to the coast, from Pierrefeu-du-Var, north of Hyères, to Cogolin near St-Tropez, is manageable and stunning, climbing from 150m to 411m above sea level.

## ACCOMMODATION

### COLLOBRIÈRES

**Des Maures** 19 bd Lazare-Carnot ☎04 94 48 07 10, ⓦhoteldesmaures.fr. Simple but spacious and very good-value rooms above a restaurant and bar in the centre of the village, facing the river at the back. Competitive half-board available. €65

★ **Notre-Dame** 15 av de la Libération ☎04 94 48 07 13, ⓦhotel-notre-dame.eu. Surprisingly chic for the deeply rural location, this boutique-style hotel has ten individually decorated rooms with huge bathrooms, a lovely patio restaurant by the river and a pool. There's limited parking – reserve in advance. €98

### GRIMAUD

**Camping Charlemagne** Le Pont de Bois, rte de Collobrières ☎04 94 43 22 90, ⓦcamping-charlemagne.com. Four-star campsite on the road to Collobrières.

Facilities include a restaurant, pizzeria, barbecue, bakery and games room, and there's wi-fi too. €31

### LA GARDE-FREINET

**Camping de Bérard** 5km along the RD558 to Grimaud ☎04 94 43 21 23, ⓦcampingberard.com. Three-star campsite with a swimming pool, free wi-fi, a shop, restaurant and bar, plus musical evenings and plenty of games facilities. Closed Nov–Feb. €17.20

**Le Mouron Rouge** 1115 rte du Lac, 1km north of La Garde-Freinet ☎04 94 43 66 33, ⓦlemouronrouge.com. Lovely *chambre d'hôte* in a rustic setting, with well-equipped apartments and studios (both sleeping 2–4) and a double room with private terrace. There's a *boules* pitch and a large pool. Weekly lets only in high season. Double €875/week, apartments €1625/week, studios €1425/week

## EATING AND DRINKING

### COLLOBRIÈRES

★ **La Petite Fontaine** 6 place de la République ☎04 94 48 00 12. Congenial, affordable *Gault Millau*-listed restaurant, serving hearty, rustic food – *daube de boeuf*, home-made terrines, *tarte aux pommes* with chestnut purée – on €26 and €33 *menus* as well as reasonably priced à la carte. Tues–Sat noon–1.30pm & 7–9pm, Sun noon–1.30pm.

**Cave des Vignerons de Collobrières** Near Hôtel Notre-Dame at the western entrance to the village ☎04 94 48 07 26. A good place to buy the local Côtes de Provence wines. Mon–Sat 9.30am–12.30pm & 2–5.30pm.

### GRIMAUD

**Le Pâtissier du Château** 19 place des Aliziers ☎04 94 43 21 16, ⓦpatisserieduchateau.com. Bakery and tearoom selling wonderful cakes and fresh, nutty breads,

plus breakfasts (€10), omelettes (from €5) and a €13 set lunch. Daily except Wed 7am–7pm.

### LA GARDE-FREINET

**Le Carnotzet** 7 place du Marché ☎04 94 43 62 73. Lively bar, art gallery and restaurant with a terrace on the village's most exquisite square. *Plats du jour* from €13, *menu* €25; live jazz Thurs evenings in July & Aug. Mon & Thurs–Sun noon–2.30/3pm & 7–10/10.30pm, Tues 7–10/10.30pm.

**La Faucado** 33 bd de l'Esplanade ☎04 94 79 67 37, ⓦlafaucado.fr. *Restaurant gastronomique* with mains around €35; it's rather overpriced, but serves beautiful dishes, such as veal kidneys in Madeira or roast monkfish with basil, from local produce in a pretty garden setting. Mon, Tues & Thurs–Sat 7.30–10pm, Wed & Sun noon–1.30pm & 7.30–10pm.

# St-Tropez and around

As the summer playground of Europe's youthful rich, **ST-TROPEZ** is among the most overhyped – and in July and August overcrowded – spots in the Mediterranean. It remains undeniably glamorous, its vast yachts and infamous champagne "spray" parties creating an air of hedonistic excess in high summer. Alas, partaking of its designer charms can seriously dent your budget at any time of the year.

## Brief history

The **origins** of St-Tropez are unremarkable: a fishing village that grew up around a port founded by Marseille's Greeks, destroyed by Saracens in 739 and finally fortified

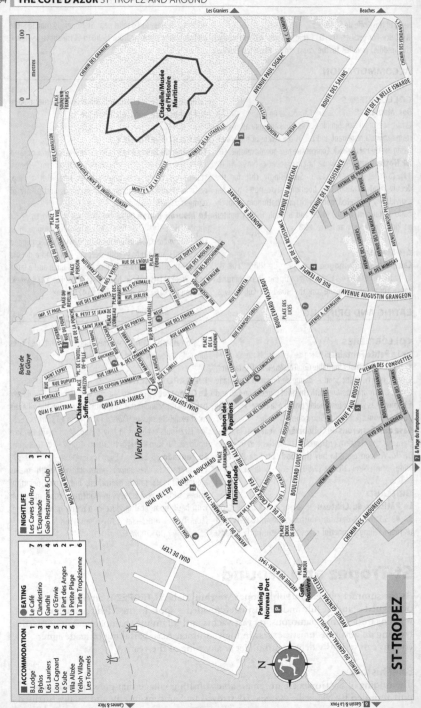

ST-TROPEZ

| ACCOMMODATION | |
|---|---|
| B.Lodge | 1 |
| Byblos | 3 |
| Les Lauriers | 3 |
| Lou Cagnard | 4 |
| Le Sube | 2 |
| Villa Alizée | 6 |
| Yelloh Village | 5 |
| Les Tournels | 7 |

| ● EATING | |
|---|---|
| Le Café | 7 |
| Clandestino | 3 |
| Gandhi | 4 |
| Le G'Envie | 5 |
| La Part des Anges | 2 |
| La Petite Plage | 1 |
| La Tarte Tropézienne | 6 |

| ■ NIGHTLIFE | |
|---|---|
| Les Caves du Roy | 3 |
| L'Esquinade | 1 |
| Gaio Restaurant & Club | 2 |

in the late Middle Ages. Its sole distinction was its inaccessibility: stuck on a small peninsula that never warranted proper roads, reached only by boat till the end of the nineteenth century.

Soon after, bad weather forced the painter **Paul Signac** to moor in St-Tropez. He promptly decided to build a house there, to which he invited his friends. Matisse was one of the first to accept, with Bonnard, Marquet, Dufy, Dérain, Vlaminck, Seurat and Van Dongen following suit, and by World War I St-Tropez was an established **bohemian** hangout. The 1930s saw a new influx, of writers as much as painters: Cocteau, Colette and Anaïs Nin, whose journal records "girls riding bare-breasted in the back of open cars". In 1956, Roger Vadim filmed Brigitte Bardot here in **Et Dieu … Créa la Femme**; the cult of Tropezian sun, sex and celebrities promptly took off and the place has been groaning under the weight of visitors ever since.

## The Vieux Port and around

The **Vieux Port**, rebuilt after its destruction in World War II, defines the French word *frimer*, which means to stroll ostentatiously in places like St-Tropez. You'll either love it or hate it. The other pole of St-Tropez's life, south of the Vieux Port, is **place des Lices**, where you can sit on benches in the shade of the plane trees and watch, or join, the *boules* games.

### Musée de l'Annonciade

Place Georges-Grammont • mid-July to Sept daily 10am–6pm; Oct & Dec to mid-July Tues–Sun 10am–6pm • €6 • ☎ 04 94 17 84 10

The marvellous **Musée de l'Annonciade** occupies a deconsecrated sixteenth-century chapel on place Georges-Grammont, right on the Vieux Port. It features works by Signac, Matisse and most of the other artists who worked here: you'll see grey, grim, northern views of Paris, Boulogne and Westminster, and then local, brilliantly sunlit scenes by the same brushes – the museum is unrivalled outside Paris for its collection of French art between 1890 and 1940.

### Château Suffren and around

Up from the port, at the end of quai Jean-Jaurès, you enter place de l'Hôtel-de-Ville, where you'll find the **Château Suffren**, built in 980 by Count Guillaume 1er of Provence, and the very pretty *mairie*. A street to the left leads down to the rocky **baie de la Glaye**, while straight ahead rue de la Ponche passes through an ancient gateway to place du Revelin above the exceptionally pretty **fishing port** and its tiny beach.

## The Citadelle

1 montée de la Citadelle • Daily: April–Sept 10am–6.30pm; Oct–March 10am–5.30pm • €3 • ☎ 04 94 97 59 43

If you turn inland from the sea and walk upwards, you finally reach the open space around the sixteenth-century **Citadelle**, which offers glorious views of the gulf and town that haven't changed much since they were painted by St-Tropez's bohemian newcomers a century ago. It houses the well-presented **Musée de l'Histoire Maritime**, which charts St-Tropez's long and often surprising association with the sea – from its historic role as a centre for coastal trade and participation in the "maritime caravan" between ports of the Ottoman Empire to the torpedo factory built here by the British on the eve of World War I.

## The St-Tropez beaches

Transport from St-Tropez is provided by a minibus service in summer from place des Lices to Salins (5 daily; 15min); or bus #7705 to Ramatuelle (at least 6 daily; 9min); by car, you'll have to pay high parking charges at all the beaches – the approach roads are designed to make it impossible to park for free on the verge

**17**

The beach within easiest walking distance of St-Tropez is **Les Graniers**, below the Citadelle just beyond the port des Pêcheurs along rue Cavaillon. From there, a path follows the coast around the **baie des Canebiers**, with its small beach, to Cap St-Pierre, Cap St-Tropez, the very crowded **Les Salins** beach and right round to Tahiti-Plage, about 11km away.

Tahiti-Plage is the start of the almost straight, 5km north–south **Pampelonne** beach, the world initiator of the topless bathing cult. The water is shallow for 50m or so, and the beach is exposed to the wind, and sometimes scourged by dried sea vegetation and garbage. **Bars** and restaurants line the beach, all with patios and sofas, serving cocktails, gluttonous ice creams and full-blown meals. **Le Club 55** on boulevard Patch (☏04 94 55 55 55, ⓦclub55.fr) is the original and most famous, while **Nikki Beach**, route de l'Épi (☏04 94 79 82 04, ⓦnikkibeach.com), is the celebrity hangout.

## Gassin

In delightful contrast to the overcrowded coast, the interior of the **St-Tropez peninsula** remains undeveloped, thanks to government intervention, complex ownerships and the value of some local wines. The best view of this richly green countryside is from the hilltop village of **GASSIN**, just 8km from St-Tropez. Gassin is the shape and size of a ship perched on a summit; once an eighth-century Muslim stronghold, it's an excellent place for a big dinner, taken outside by the village wall where you can sit and enjoy a spectacular panorama east over the peninsula.

### ARRIVAL AND DEPARTURE                    ST-TROPEZ AND AROUND

**By bus** Buses drop you at the *gare routière* on av du Général-de-Gaulle.

Destinations Hyères (up to 15 daily; 1hr 40min); Le Lavandou (up to 15 daily; 55min); St-Raphaël (up to 15 daily; 1hr 25min).

**By car** Beware of driving to St-Tropez in summer – traffic jams start in earnest at Ste-Maxime, where the D25 from the *autoroute* joins the coast road; it can take 2hr to crawl the remaining 16km into St-Tropez. There is (paid) parking

in the vast Parking du Nouveau Port at the entrance to the village.

**By ferry** The quickest way to reach St-Tropez in summer – except by helicopter – is the ferry from Ste-Maxime on the opposite side of the gulf (mid-Feb to early Jan, every 15min in high season; 15min; €7.50 single, €13.50 return). In summer there are also ferries from Port Grimaud, Les Issambres and Cogolin's marina (☏04 94 49 29 39, ⓦbateauxverts.com).

### INFORMATION

**Tourist office** Quai Jean-Jaurès (April–June, Sept & early Oct daily 9.30am–12.30pm & 2–7pm; July & Aug daily 9.30am–1.30pm & 3–7.pm; Oct (after les Voiles) to March Mon–Sat 9.30am–12.30pm & 2–7pm; ☏04 94 97 45 21,

ⓦsainttropeztourisme.com).

**Bike rental** Bikes and motorbikes can be rented at Rolling Bikes, 50 av du G.-Leclerc (☏04 94 97 09 39, ⓦrolling-bikes.com).

### ACCOMMODATION

You'll be lucky to find a room in high season. The tourist office can help (€15), but – transport permitting – you might be better off staying elsewhere.

**B. Lodge** 12 rue de l'Aïoli ☏04 94 97 06 57, ⓦhotel-b-lodge.com. Overlooking the citadelle, this attractive boutique-style hotel is in a quieter setting than places in the centre and has stylish decor and its own bar. There is a/c, free wi-fi and pets are welcome, but parking is a headache. **€220**

**Byblos** Av Paul-Signac ☏04 94 56 68 00, ⓦbyblos.com. A member of the *Leading Hotels of the World* group, the Byblos is a perennial favourite if money really is no object and you need to be with the in-crowd; expect suitably

sumptuous rooms and a very cool evening bar scene. Closed Nov–April. Breakfast €40. **€855**

**Les Lauriers** 5 rue du Temple ☏04 94 97 04 88, ⓦhotelleslauriers.net. Just behind place des Lices, this friendly, relaxed three-star has eighteen a/c rooms and a garden. Rooms are individually decorated, with deep colours and vibrant wallpaper. Breakfast €12. **€190**

**Lou Cagnard** 18 av Paul-Roussel ☏04 94 97 04 24, ⓦhotel-lou-cagnard.com. Pretty, affordable option with Provençal-style rooms – fourteen of them with a/c – in a relatively tranquil location with a garden and secure private parking. Seven-night minimum stay June–Sept and during les Voiles. **€85**

**Le Sube** 23 quai de Suffren ☎ 04 94 97 30 04, ⊕ hotel subesainttropez.com. One of St-Tropez's oldest-established hotels, though rooms are bright and comfortable (and all have a/c). Some rooms offer fantastic views over the port. It's right in the thick of the action, and there's a classy bar. Closed Nov–March. €180

**Villa Alizée** 14 chemin Ste-Bonaventure ☎ 06 08 62 65 29, ⊕ villaalizee.com. Relaxed *chambre d'hôte* with four individually decorated rooms, situated just under 3km west

of St-Tropez, off the coast road. There's an pool in the lovely gardens, and it's possible to rent the entire villa. Breakfast included. €180

**Yelloh Village Les Tournels** Rte des Tournels, 3km from Ramatuelle ☎ 04 94 55 90 90, ⊕ tournels.com. Five-star campsite with an extensive, heated outdoor pool with water slides, plus an indoor pool and spa. It's more geared to chalet lets than tents, but they do welcome campers too. Closed Nov–March. €72

## EATING AND DRINKING

### ST-TROPEZ

St-Tropez restaurants are notoriously expensive, with style over substance almost an art form. Avoid the Vieux Port if you're on a tight budget; better value is to be found in the streets behind it, particularly up towards the church and Citadelle.

**Le Café** Place des Lices ☎ 04 94 97 44 69, ⊕ lecafe.fr. Old-school, landmark brasserie with a terrace facing onto place des Lices. Pasta from €14, meat dishes, including brasserie classics such as beef *tartare* from around €18; fish mains from €26. Daily 8am–2am.

**Clandestino** 24 rue du Portail-Neuf ☎ 09 83 66 78 28. A rare treat in central St-Tropez – an appealing restaurant serving reasonably priced food. The Italian menu won't win any awards for originality but the food is decent and prices start at €16 for mains. Mon, Wed–Fri & Sun 7–11.30pm, Tues & Sat noon–3pm & 7–11.30pm.

**Gandhi** 3 quai de l'Épi ☎ 04 94 97 71 71, ⊕ gandhisai. com. Near the parking du Nouveau Port, this small, busy Indian restaurant has earned a good reputation for its familiar line-up of tandooris, vindaloos and biryanis. Lunch *formule* €19.50, main dishes from around €14. Daily except Wed noon–1.45pm & 7–10pm; closed Dec & Jan.

**Le G'Envie** 67 rue du Portail-Neuf ☎ 04 94 79 85 09. A petite restaurant that's well worth seeking out for its unpretentious gourmet food. The seasonal menu may include delicious dishes such as prawn risotto or tuna tartare (*menu* €39); the lunch formule at €21 is excellent value. Expect to queue. Tues–Sun noon–midnight.

**La Part des Anges** 7 rue de l'Église ☎ 04 94 96 19

50. Very pleasant little restaurant serving decent food at modest prices in a pretty, atmospheric lane just down from St-Tropez's church, with pasta from €16 and grilled meat or fish from around €20. There are also specials on the blackboard. Daily except Wed noon–2.30pm & 7–11pm; closed Nov–March.

**La Petite Plage** 9 quai Jean-Jaurès ☎ 04 94 17 01 23, ⊕ lapetiteplage-saint-tropez.com. Upmarket seafood restaurant and cocktail bar on the Vieux Port that has a very chic beach boho vibe going on, with sand scattered on the floor. It's not cheap, of course – though there's a handful of mains for under €30 – but it's hard to beat the location and standards are very high. Daily 9am–3am.

★ **La Tarte Tropézienne** place des Lices ☎ 04 94 97 94 25, ⊕ latartetropezienne.fr. Patisserie claiming to have invented the moreish eponymous sponge and custard cake (€5.50 for an enormous individual tart), though you no longer have to come to St-Tropez to sample it – the company is now a chain. Good, too, for takeaway lunch food such as croque-monsieur (€3). Daily 6.30am–8.30pm.

### GASSIN

★ **Bello Visto** 9 place des Barrys ☎ 04 94 56 17 30, ⊕ bellovisto.eu. Good Provençal specialities on a €28 *menu*, with dishes like sea bass braised in white wine or veal with *lardo di colonnata* and anchovy *jus*. They have rooms, also. March–May & Oct Wed noon–2.30pm, Fri–Tues noon–2.30pm & 7–9.30pm; June–Sept daily noon–2.30pm & 7–9.30pm.

## NIGHTLIFE

In season St-Tropez stays up late. The *boules* games on place des Lices continue until well after dusk and the portside spectacle doesn't falter until the early hours. In addition to the places listed below, La Petite Plage (see above) is another fabulous (if expensive, of course) evening spot.

**Les Caves du Roy** Byblos, 27 av du Maréchal-Foch ☎ 04 94 56 68 00, ⊕ lescavesduroy.com. Still the place to see and be seen, the *Caves du Roy* lets you rub shoulders with rap stars and supermodels – if your face and clothes pass muster on the door. Music is a mix of current dance hits and oldies from the 1970s and 1980s. Late April to July & Sept

to early Oct Fri & Sat, July & Aug daily.

**L'Esquinade** 2 rue du Four ☎ 04 94 56 26 31. Gay-friendly club spinning house, disco and electro music. Unlike most of St-Tropez's clubs it's open year-round. Daily midnight–7am.

**Gaïo Restaurant & Club** 4 rue du 11-novembre ☎ 04 94 97 89 98, ⊕ gaio.club. The veteran nightclub Papagayo has been transformed into this super-glamorous restaurant and nightclub which is beloved by celebrities. Come for the dancing rather than the food (which is Japanese-Peruvian fusion). Daily 8pm–6am.

# 17 Ste-Maxime

Facing St-Tropez across its gulf, **STE-MAXIME** is the perfect Côte stereotype: palmed corniche and enormous pleasure-boat harbour, beaches crowded with bronzed windsurfers and water-skiers, and an Art Deco casino presiding over the seafront. It sprawls a little too much, merging with its northern neighbours to create a continuous suburban strip up to Fréjus. But if hardly as colourful as St-Tropez, it's less pretentious and the beaches are cleaner; though if your **budget** denies you the pleasures of watersports, you might find Ste-Maxime a little lacking in diversions. You can, at least, eat at reasonable cost, since there are plenty of crêperies, *glaciers* and snack places along the central avenue Charles-de-Gaulle. There's also an **Aqualand** water park with all manner of ingenious water slides just off the D25 Le Muy road north of town, though this isn't cheap, either (late June to end Aug daily 10am–6/7pm; €28, children €20.50; ⓦ aqualand.fr).

## The Ste-Maxime beaches

For the spenders, the east-facing **plage de la Nartelle**, 5km east from the centre towards Les Issambres, is the strip of sand to head for. Here, at **Barco Beach** (Feb–Nov; ☎ 04 94 96 46 49, ⓦ barcobeach.com) and its five neighbours, you'll pay for shaded, cushioned comfort, grilled fish or meat and elaborate cocktails; as dusk falls some of the beach concessions also offer live music. A kilometre or so further on, **plage Les Éléphants** recalls the town's link to Jean de Brunhoff – creator of Babar the elephant – who had a holiday home in Ste-Maxime.

## The markets

Ste-Maxime's *vieille ville* has several good **markets**: a covered flower and food market on rue Fernand-Bessy (July & Aug Mon–Sat 8am–1pm & 4.30–8pm, Sun 8am–1pm; Sept–June Tues–Sun 8am–1pm); a daily fish market on the port (8am–noon); a Thursday morning food market on place du Marché; a weekly flea market on promenade Simon-Lorière (Wed 8am–6pm) and arts and crafts in the pedestrian streets (mid-June to mid-Sept daily 4–11pm).

## Musée du Phonographe et de la Musique Mécanique

Parc St-Donat, rte du Muy • Wed–Sun: May–Sept 10am–noon & 4–6pm; Oct by arrangement • €4 • ☎ 04 94 96 50 52

High up in the Massif des Maures on the road to Le Muy, some 10km north of Ste-Maxime, is the marvellous **Musée du Phonographe et de la Musique Mécanique**, the result of one woman's amazing forty-year obsession with collecting audio equipment. She has amassed a wide selection of automata, musical boxes and pianolas, plus one of Thomas Edison's "talking machines" dating from 1878.

### ARRIVAL AND INFORMATION                                          STE-MAXIME

**By bus** Buses from St-Tropez (up to 15 daily; 35min) and St-Raphaël (up to 15 daily; 50min) stop outside the tourist office.

**By ferry** If you're heading for St-Tropez from Ste-Maxime, an alternative to the bus is to go by boat (see page 896).

**Tourist office** 1 promenade Simon-Lorière (daily: April–

June & Sept 9am–12.30pm & 2–6.30pm; July & Aug daily 9am–7pm; Oct–March 9am–noon & 2–6pm; ☎ 08 26 20 83 83, ⓦ sainte-maxime.com).

**Bike rental** Rent Bike Location, 15 rue Magali (☎ 04 94 43 98 07, ⓦ rentbike-location.com).

### ACCOMMODATION

**Castellamar** 8 av G.-Pompidou ☎ 04 94 96 19 97, ⓦ hotelcastellamar.wordpress.com. The best of the

cheaper hotels, on the west side of the river, but still close to the town centre and the sea, with a bar, lounge and tree-

shaded terrace. Closed mid-Oct to mid-March. €77
**Les Cigalons** 34 av du Croiseur Léger-le-Malin ☎ 04 94 96 05 51, ⓦ campingcigalon.com. Two-star seaside campsite east of town, just 50m from the beach, with wi-fi, children's games and *boules*. It also rents out holiday bungalows. Closed mid-Oct to late March. Camping €31, bungalows from €600/week
**Matisse** 11 bd Frédéric-Mistral ☎ 04 94 96 18 33, ⓦ hotel-matisse.com. Stylish and central three-star hotel with Matisse-themed decor and a pool. There are various

categories and styles of room but all have a/c and either bath or shower. Open all year round. €140
**Villa des Anges** Off the D559, 3km southwest of Ste-Maxime ☎ 04 94 96 29 10, ⓦ hotelvilladesanges.fr. Just a short walk from the beach, this relaxed small hotel is a bit overpriced given the rooms – which are bright if a bit twee – but the outdoor pool, the sea views from the terrace, and the short walk to the beach more than make up for it. Breakfast €14. Closed Dec–March. €159

### EATING

**La Crevette** 30 rue Gambetta ☎ 04 94 96 03 88, ⓦ lacrevette.eu. Just a few streets back from the port, this unpretentious bistro has a pleasant terrace and a great value lunch *formule* (€15.50). Expect a mix of traditional and international dishes – such as couscous with lamb and *merguez* (spicy sausage). Mon–Fri 7am–1am, Sat & Sun 9am–1am.

**La Belle Aurore** 5 bd Jean-Moulin ☎ 04 94 96 02 45, ⓦ belleaurore.com. Elegant *restaurant gastronomique* with a stunning setting on the water's edge with views across to St-Tropez. There's a €48 five-course *menu*; otherwise it's around €30 for a main course. Closed Oct–April. Tues & Thurs–Sun noon–2pm & 7.30–9.30pm.

# Fréjus and around

**FRÉJUS** – along with its neighbour **ST-RAPHAËL**, 3km east – dates back to the Romans. It was established as a naval base under Julius Caesar and Augustus, and its ancient port – known as Forum Julii – consisted of 2km of quays connected by a walled canal to the sea (which was considerably closer then). After the battle of Actium in 31 BC, the ships of Antony and Cleopatra's defeated fleet were brought here. Little remains of the Roman walls that circled the city, and the once-important port silted up and was filled in after the Revolution. Today you can see a scattering of **Roman remains**, along with the medieval **Cité Épiscopale**, or cathedral complex, which takes up two sides of **place Formigé**, the marketplace and heart of both contemporary and medieval Fréjus.

The area between Fréjus and the sea is now the suburb of **Fréjus-Plage**, with a vast 1980s marina, **Port-Fréjus**. Both Fréjus and Fréjus-Plage merge with St-Raphaël, which in turn merges with **Boulouris** to the east.

## The Roman remains

A tour of the Roman remains gives you a good idea of the extent of Forum Julii, but they are scattered throughout and beyond the town centre and take a full day to get around. Turning right out of the *gare SNCF* and then right down boulevard Séverin-Decuers brings you to the **Butte St-Antoine**, against whose east wall the waters of the port would have lapped, and which once was capped by a fort. It was one of the port's defences, and one of the ruined **towers** may have been a lighthouse. A path around the southern wall follows the quayside (some stretches are visible) to the medieval **Lanterne d'Auguste**, which was built on the Roman foundations of a structure marking the entrance of the canal into the ancient harbour. If you retrace your steps back to the centre, you'll come to rue des Moulins, and the arcades of the **Porte d'Orée**, positioned on the former harbour's edge alongside what was probably a bath complex.

## The amphitheatre

Rue Henri-Vadon • April–Sept Tues–Sun 9.30am–12.30pm & 2–6pm; Oct–March Tues–Sat 9.30am–noon & 2–4.30pm • €2 • ⓦ frejus.fr

**17**

Taking a left turn from the station, passing the Roman **porte des Gaules** and heading along rue Henri-Vadon, brings you to the **amphitheatre**, which has a capacity of around ten thousand. Fit to host concerts again after a refurbishment in 2012, its upper tiers have been reconstructed, but the vaulted galleries on the ground floor are largely original.

### The Roman theatre and around

Av du Théâtre Romain • April–Sept Tues–Sun 9.30am–12.30pm & 2–6pm; Oct–March Tues–Sat 9.30am–noon & 2–4.30pm • Free • ⓦ frejus.fr

The **Roman theatre** is north of the old town. Its original seats have long gone, though it's still used for shows in summer. To the northeast, in the parc de la Villa Aurélienne at the far end of avenue du XVème-Corps-d'Armée, you can see six arches of the 40km **aqueduct**, which was once as high as the ramparts.

## The cathedral complex

48 rue du Cardinal-Fleury • **Cloisters** June–Sept daily 10am–12.30pm & 1.45–6.30pm; Oct–May Tues–Sun 10am–1pm & 2–5pm • €6; info sheets in English available • ☎ 04 94 52 14 01, ⓦ cloitre-frejus.fr • **Musée Archéologique** April–Sept Tues–Sun 9.30am–12.30pm & 2–6pm; Oct–March Tues–Sat 9.30am–noon & 2–4.30pm • €2 • ⓦ frejus.fr

The oldest part of the **cathedral complex** is the **baptistry**, built in the fourth or fifth century and so contemporary with the decline of the city's Roman founders. Its two doorways are of different heights, signifying the enlarged spiritual stature of the baptized. Bits of the early Gothic **cathedral** may belong to a tenth-century church, but its best features, apart from the bright diamond-shaped tiles on the spire, are Renaissance: the choir stalls, a wooden crucifix on the left of the entrance and the intricately carved doors with scenes of a Saracen massacre, only opened for the guided tours. The most engaging component of the whole ensemble, however, are the **cloisters**. In a small garden of scented bushes around a well, slender twelfth-century marble columns support a fourteenth-century ceiling painted with apocalyptic creatures. The treasures of the **Musée Archéologique**, on the upper storey of the cloisters, include a complete Roman mosaic of a leopard and a copy of a double-headed bust of Hermes.

## St-Raphaël

Fréjus' neighbour **ST-RAPHAËL** became fashionable at the turn of the twentieth century, but lost many of its *belle époque* mansions and hotels to World War II bombardment. All the same, you may prefer to stay here rather than in Fréjus for its livelier, family-friendly atmosphere and easy access to the **beaches**, which stretch west of the port into Fréjus-Plage and east of the Jardin Bonaparte to the modern **Marina Santa Lucia**, which offers opportunities for every kind of watersport. When you're tired of sea and sand, you can lose whatever money you have left at the **Casino Barrière** (ⓦ casinosbarriere. com) on Square de Gand overlooking the Vieux Port.

---

**OUTDOOR FUN AROUND FRÉJUS**

Around Fréjus, rugged terrain for cyclists is found in the forested hills of the **Massif de l'Estérel** to the northeast of town; there are more than 100km of signposted trails in and around Fréjus. Tourist offices in Fréjus and St-Raphaël sell maps and **guides** to the Estérel for €8.50–11.70. There are also cycle trails at the **Base Nature François-Léotard** (daily: July & Aug 7.30am–midnight; Sept–June 7.30am–11pm; free; ☎ 04 94 51 91 10), a large public park just west of Port-Fréjus on the coast, as well as a beach, a public swimming pool and sports pitches. Opposite the Base Nature is Fréjus' water park, **Aqualand**, with all manner of water slides and pools (ⓦ aqualand.fr).

## The vieille ville

The **vieille ville**, beyond place Carnot on the inland side of the railway line, is no longer the town's commercial focus but a good place to stroll and browse. The fortified Romanesque church of **San Raféu** on rue des Templiers, has fragments of the Roman aqueduct that brought water from Fréjus in its courtyard, along with a local **history and underwater archeology museum** (March–June & Sept Tues 9am–12.30pm, Wed–Sat 9am–12.30pm & 2–5pm; July–Sept Tues–Sat 10am–6pm; Nov–Feb Tues 2–5pm, Wed–Fri 10am–12.30pm & 2–5pm, Sat 10–12.30pm; free; ⓦ musee-saintraphael. com). You can climb to the top of the fortified tower to view the town and sea.

# Notre-Dame-de-Jérusalem

Rte de Cannes • April–Sept Tues–Sun 9.30am–12.30pm & 2–6pm; Oct–March Tues–Sat 9.30am–noon & 2–4.30pm • €3, or €6 with Fréjus' Pass • ⓦ frejus.fr

Just off the RN7 at La Tour de Mare, 5.6km from the centre of Fréjus, is the last of Jean Cocteau's artistic landmarks, the chapel of **Notre-Dame-de-Jérusalem**. Conceived as the church for a failed artistic community, the octagonal building was not completed until after Cocteau's death in 1963, and the interior was completed to Cocteau's plans by Édouard Dermit. The Last Supper scene inside includes a self-portrait of Cocteau.

## ARRIVAL AND DEPARTURE                                  FRÉJUS AND AROUND

### FRÉJUS

**By train** Trains to St-Raphaël are much more frequent than those to Fréjus, so it's often easiest to alight there and take the #1, #2, #4 or #14 Agglobus, which run with varying frequency between the two towns (15–35min). There are also trains between St-Raphaël and Fréjus *gare SNCF*, which is on the south side of the *vieille ville* (14–17 daily; 3min).

**By bus** The *gare routière* is on the north side of the town centre at rue Gustave-Bret close to the tourist office (☎ 04 94 53 78 46).

### ST-RAPHAËL

**By train** St-Raphaël's *gare SNCF*, on the Marseille–Ventimiglia line, is on rue Waldeck-Rousseau in the centre of town.

Destinations Cannes (every 20min–1hr; 26–38min); Fréjus (14–17 daily; 3min); Nice (every 10min–1hr; 50min–1hr 15min).

**By bus** The *gare routière* is at Square du Docteur-Régis, across the rail line behind the train station.

Destinations Fréjus (frequent; 15–35min); Ste-Maxime (up to 15 daily; 50min); St-Tropez (up to 13 daily; 1hr 25min–1hr 45min).

## INFORMATION

### FRÉJUS

**Tourist office** Le Florus II, 249 rue Jean-Jaurès (June & Sept Mon–Sat 9.30am–12.30pm & 2.30–6pm; July & Aug daily 9.30am–7pm; Oct–May Mon–Sat 9.30am–noon & 2–6pm; ☎ 04 94 51 83 83, ⓦ frejus.fr).

**Passes** If you're planning to visit most of Fréjus's sights, it may be worth getting the seven-day Fréjus' Pass (€6), which gives access to the amphitheatre, Roman theatre, Notre-Dame-de-Jérusalem and the Musée Archéologique.

**Bike rental** Booking Bikes, 43 rue Grisolle (☎ 04 83 12 52 64, ⓦ booking-bikes.com).

**Market days** Wed and Sat.

### ST-RAPHAËL

**Tourist office** Quai Albert-1er (July & Aug daily 9am–7pm; Sept–June Mon–Sat 9am–12.30pm & 2–6.30pm; ☎ 04 94 19 52 52, ⓦ saint-raphael.com).

**Boat trips** Les Bateaux de Saint-Raphaël offer boat trips to St-Tropez and the *calanques* of the Estérel coast from quai Nomy on the south side of the Vieux Port (ticket office April & May Mon–Sat 9am–noon & 2–6pm, Sun 2–6pm; June & Sept daily 9am–noon & 2–6pm; July & Aug Mon–Thurs & Sat 9am–7pm, Fri 9am–7pm & 9–10.30pm, Sun 9–11.45am & 1.30–7pm; Oct Mon 2–5pm, Tues–Sat 9am–noon & 2–5pm; ☎ 04 94 95 17 46, ⓦ bateauxsaintraphael.com).

## ACCOMMODATION

### FRÉJUS

**Les Acacias** 370 rue Henri-Giraud, 2.5km from the old town, close to the pagoda Hong Hien ☎ 04 94 53 21 22, ⓦ campingacacias.fr. Leafy, moderate-sized three-

star campsite with 81 pitches, children's play facilities, a swimming pool, spa and gym. Closed Nov–March. **€41**
**Aréna** 139–145 rue du Général-de-Gaulle ☎ 04 94 17 09 40, ⓦ hotel-frejus-arena.com. Comfortable four-star hotel in

**17**

three buildings grouped around a pool and luxuriant garden, close to the *gare SNCF*. Rooms have flatscreen TV and a/c. There's also a good restaurant. Closed late Oct to Nov. **€124**

**Auberge de Jeunesse Fréjus/Saint-Raphaël** 627 chemin du Counillier ☎04 94 53 18 75, ⓦfuaj.org. Fréjus' hostel is set amid ten hectares of umbrella pines 2km northeast of the centre. It's close to the pagoda Hong Hien and served by the infrequent bus #10 from Fréjus or St-Raphaël *gare routière*. Reception 8.30am–noon & 5.30–9/10pm. Breakfast included. **€19.28**

**Le Flore** 35 rue Grisolle ☎04 94 51 38 35. The nicest budget option in the old town is this pretty, wisteria-clad two-star. It won't win any awards for decor but rooms have free wi-fi a/c and flatscreen TV, and there are two triples and one four-bed room. Breakfast €7.50. **€65**

**ST-RAPHAËL**

**Agay Soleil** 1152 bd de la Plage, Agay ☎04 94 82 00 79, ⓦagay-soleil.com. Three-star campsite on the horseshoe-shaped bay of Agay, east of St-Raphaël on the breathtaking corniche de l'Estérel, with mobile homes and chalets to rent as well as pitches. Closed Nov to late March. **€34**

**Excelsior** Promenade René-Coty ☎04 94 95 02 42, ⓦexcelsior-hotel.com. The handsome old *Excelsior* is one of the rare seafront survivors from St-Raphaël's pre-war heyday, with 32 tastefully decorated a/c rooms plus a restaurant and English-style pub. More expensive rooms have sea views. **€204**

**Nouvel Hôtel** 66 av Henri-Vadon ☎04 94 95 23 30, ⓦnouvelhotel.net. Pleasant two-star hotel between the *gare SNCF* and the beach; all the rooms are different, and they have singles and triples as well as doubles. There's also a restaurant, so half-board is possible. Breakfast €7. **€85**

**Du Soleil** 47 bd du Domaine du Soleil ☎04 94 83 10 00, ⓦhotel-dusoleil.com. Charming non-smoking hotel occupying a very pretty old villa east of the town centre. All twelve rooms have flatscreen TV, bath or shower and most have a balcony or terrace. There's also a handful of studios in a separate building, with kitchenettes, making them perfect for families. Bus #8 to Les Plaines. Breakfast €9. **€96**

## EATING, DRINKING AND ENTERTAINMENT

**FRÉJUS**

**Cadet Rousselle** 25 place Agricola ☎04 94 53 36 92. Perennially popular crêperie with a wide choice of sweet crêpes and savoury *galettes* (from €4.50). They also serve main-course-sized salads from €6.50. Tues, Wed & Fri–Sun (daily July & Aug) noon–1.30pm & 6.30–8.30pm, Thurs 6.30–8.30pm.

**Le Jardin de l'Aréna** 145 rue du Général-de-Gaulle ☎04 94 17 09 40, ⓦhotel-frejus-arena.com. You can dine on the leafy terrace at the *Aréna* hotel's *restaurant gastronomique*, and enjoy dishes like lobster parmentier or veal with thyme jus. Lunchtime *formule* €20; *menus* €24–40. Tues–Sat noon–2.30pm & 7–9.30pm, Sun noon–2.30pm.

**Le Provençal** 44 place Dou-Maiet ☎04 94 40 59 15. This cosy restaurant with a small terrace serves up some of the best, and least pretentious, food in town. The seasonal menu changes regularly, but might include a cold petits pois soup with feta, crab cakes, and blueberry pancakes with crème fraîche. *Menus* from €22. Mon noon–1.30pm, Thurs 7–9.30pm, Fri–Sun noon–1.30pm & 7–9.30pm.

**ST-RAPHAËL**

**Le Bishop** 84 rue Jean-Aicard ☎04 94 95 04 63. Popular restaurant dishing up Provençal staples at reasonable prices, a couple of blocks back from the beach. Stuffed rabbit €16, *aïoli* €22; *menus* from €23. July & Aug Mon–Sat noon–2pm & 7–10pm; Sept–June Tues–Sat noon–2pm & 7–10pm, Sun noon–2pm.

**Blue Bar** 133 rue Jules-Barbier ☎04 94 95 15 87. There's a big range of Belgian beers from €5.50 at this unpretentious, pubby place on the seafront. Cocktails cost around €10 and they serve fancy ice creams (€7.50) and *plats du jour* (*formule* €14.90). Daily 7am–2am.

**La Brasserie** 6 av de Valescure ☎04 94 95 25 00, ⓦlabrasserietg.fr. Traditional Provençal dishes are cooked to a high standard at this smart modern restaurant on the edge of the *vieille ville*. Lunchtime *plat du jour* €14, *formule* €18, evening *menu* €30. Mon–Sat noon–2.30pm & 7–10.30pm.

**Elly's** 54 rue de la Liberté ☎04 94 83 63 39, ⓦelly-s.com. Elegant restaurant serving the likes of black tiger prawn risotto, and beef cheek ravioli with ginger and lemongrass, with fancy Bordeaux and Burgundies alongside Provençal wines. Mains from €24. Tues–Sat noon–3pm & 7–9.30pm; closed first week of June.

**La Réserve** Promenade René-Coty ☎06 27 13 88 99, ⓦla-reserve.fr. Swish seafront disco, improbably situated beneath a road junction, that attracts some big-name international DJs. Entry with *conso* €15, spirits priced by the bottle, beers €9. Summer nightly 11.30pm–7am; winter Fri & Sat only.

# Cannes and around

With its immaculate seafront hotels and exclusive beach concessions, glamorous yachts and designer boutiques, **CANNES** is in many ways the definitive Riviera resort, a place where appearances count, especially during the **film festival** in May, when the orgy of self-promotion reaches its annual peak. The ugly seafront Palais des Festivals is the heart of the film festival but also hosts conferences, tournaments and trade shows. Despite its glittery image Cannes works surprisingly well as a big seaside resort, with plenty of free, sandy public beaches. You'll find the non-paying **beaches** to the west of Le Suquet towards the suburb of **La Bocca** along the **plages du Midi**, though there's also a tiny public section of beach on **Plage de la Croisette**, just east of the Palais des Festivals.

Just offshore, the peaceful **Îles de Lérins** – **Ste-Marguerite** and **St-Honorat** – offer a sublime, easily accessible contrast to the frenetic town, while further out are the towns of **Vallauris**, with its interesting Picasso connections, and **Grasse**, famed for its perfume.

## Promenade de la Croisette

**Promenade de la Croisette** is certainly the sight to see, with its palace hotels – the *Martinez* and *Carlton* – on one side and their private beaches on the other. It's possible to find your way down to the beach without paying, but not easy (you can of course walk along it below the rows of sun beds). The hotel beaches are where you're most likely to spot a star during the film festival – or at least the paparazzi crowding around them.

## Le Suquet

The old town, known as **Le Suquet** after the hill on which it stands, provides a great panorama of the curve of Cannes' bay. On its summit stand the remains of the fortified priory lived in by Cannes' eleventh-century monks, and the beautiful twelfth-century **Chapelle Ste-Anne**.

### Musée de la Castre

6 rue de la Castre • April–June & Sept Tues–Sun 10am–1pm & 2–6pm; late night Wed until 9pm in June & Sept; July & Aug daily 10am–7pm, Wed until 9pm; Oct–March Tues–Sun 10am–1pm & 2–5pm • €6 • ☎ 04 89 82 26 26

The **Musée de la Castre**, in the remains of Cannes' eleventh-century priory, holds an extraordinary collection of musical instruments from all over the world, along with pictures and prints of old Cannes and an ethnology and archeology section.

## Îles de Lérins

The **Îles de Lérins** would be lovely anywhere, but at just fifteen minutes' ferry ride from frantic Cannes, they're not far short of paradise – though that very proximity means neither is exactly a desert island in peak season. Of the two, **Ste-Marguerite** is busier than its neighbour, **St-Honorat**, whose abbey is often used for spiritual retreats.

### Île Ste-Marguerite

**Île Ste-Marguerite** is beautiful, and large enough for visitors to find seclusion by following the trails that lead away from the congested port, through the Aleppo pines and woods of evergreen oak that are so thick they cast a sepulchral gloom. The western end is the most accessible, but the lagoon here is brackish, so the best places to swim are along the rocky southern shore, reached most easily along the **allée des Eucalyptus**. The channel between Ste-Marguerite and St-Honorat is, however, a popular anchorage for yachts, so you're unlikely to find solitude.

### Fort Ste-Marguerite

April & May daily 10.30am–1.15pm & 2.15–5.45pm; June–Sept daily 10am–5.45pm; Oct–March Tues–Sun 10.30am–1.15pm & 2.15–4.45pm • €6.50, includes museum • ☎ 04 89 82 26 26

Dominating the island is the **Fort Ste-Marguerite**, a Richelieu commission that failed to prevent the Spanish occupying both of the islands between 1635 and 1637. Later,

**17**

Vauban rounded it off, presumably for Louis XIV's *gloire* – since the strategic value of enlarging a fort facing the mainland without upgrading the one facing the sea is pretty minimal. There are cells to see, including the one in which Dumas' **Man in the Iron Mask** is supposed to have been held, and the **Musée de la Mer**, containing mostly Roman local finds but also remnants of a tenth-century Arab ship.

### Île St-Honorat

Owned by monks almost continuously since its namesake and patron founded a monastery here in 410 AD, **Île St-Honorat**, the smaller southern island, was home to a famous bishops' seminary, where St Patrick trained before setting out for Ireland. There are a couple of places to eat but no bars, hotels or cars: just vines, lavender, herbs and olive trees mingled with wild poppies and daisies, and pine and eucalyptus

| ◼ ACCOMMODATION | |
|---|---|
| Alizé | 5 |
| Canberra | 2 |
| Chanteclair | 7 |
| InterContinental Carlton | 6 |
| Provence | 3 |
| Simone | 1 |
| La Villa Tosca | 4 |

| ● EATING | |
|---|---|
| Aux Bons Enfants | 3 |
| Barbarella | 6 |
| Chez Vincent & Nicolas | 4 |
| Da Bouttau Auberge Provençale | 5 |
| Noisette | 1 |
| La Palme d'Or | 2 |

| ◼ DRINKING & NIGHTLIFE | |
|---|---|
| Backstage | 2 |
| Le Baôli | 4 |
| Club 7 | 3 |
| Pint House | 1 |

trees shading the paths beside the white rock shore. The present **abbey** buildings (ⓦabbayedelerins.com) date mostly from the nineteenth century, though some vestiges of the medieval and earlier constructions remain in the austere church and the cloisters. You can visit the eleventh-century fortified monastery on the water's edge and the abbey church, see the chapels dotted around the island, and purchase the abbey's sought-after wines and liqueurs.

## Vallauris

Pottery and Picasso are the attractions of **VALLAURIS**, an otherwise unremarkable town in the hills above Golfe-Juan, 6km northeast of Cannes. It was here that Picasso first began to use clay, thereby reviving the town's traditional craft. Today the main street, **avenue Georges-**

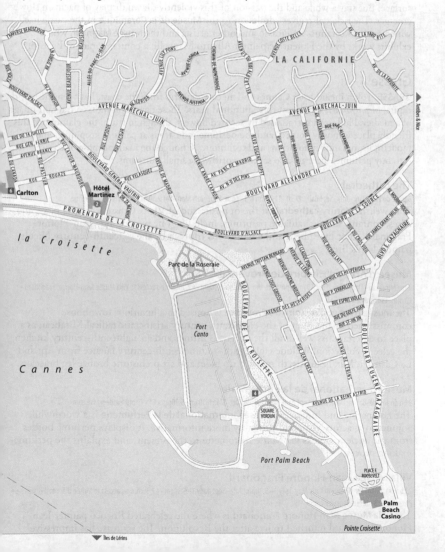

**17**

Clemenceau, sells nothing but pottery, much of it garish bowls or figurines that could feature in souvenir shops anywhere. The bronze statue of **Man with a Sheep**, the artist's gift to the town, stands in the main square, place Paul-Isnard, beside the church and castle.

## The Musée National Pablo Picasso

Place de la Libération du 24-août-1944 • July & Aug daily 10am–12.45pm & 2.15–6.15pm; Sept–June daily except Tues 10am–12.15pm & 2–5pm • €6, includes Musée de la Céramique/Musée Magnelli • ☎ 04 93 64 71 83, ⓦ musee-picasso-vallauris.fr

In 1952, Picasso was asked to decorate the deconsecrated early medieval **chapel** in the castle courtyard; his subject was war and peace. The space, now the **Musée National Pablo Picasso**, is tiny, with the architectural simplicity of an air-raid shelter, and at first it's easy to be unimpressed by the painted panels covering the vault – as many critics still are – since the work looks mucky and slapdash, with paint-runs on the plywood panel surface. But stay a while and the passion of this violently drawn display of pacifism slowly emerges. The ticket also gives admission to the **Musée de la Céramique** in the castle itself, which exhibits ceramics by Picasso and other artists and the **Musée Magnelli**, which exhibits works by the Florentine painter Alberto Magnelli, a contemporary of Picasso.

# Grasse

**GRASSE**, 16km inland from Cannes and an easy day-trip from the coast, has been the world capital of *parfumiers* for almost three hundred years. These days it promotes a fragrant image of a medieval hill town surrounded by scented flowers, though in truth, the glamour of this friendly place is mostly bottled, and the **perfume** industry is at pains to keep quiet about modern, unromantic innovations and techniques. Though the main purpose of coming here is to buy perfume, there are also several worthwhile small **museums**.

## The cathedral

8 place du Petit-Puy • July–Sept daily 09.30–11.30am & 3–6pm; Sept–July Mon–Sat 9.30–11.30am & 3–5pm • Free

The twelfth-century **cathedral**, at the opposite end of Vieux Grasse from the place aux Aires, contains various valuable paintings, including one by local boy Jean-Honoré Fragonard, three by Rubens and a wondrous triptych by the sixteenth-century Niçois painter Louis Bréa.

## Musée d'Art et d'Histoire de Provence

2 rue Mirabeau • Daily: May–Sept 10am–7pm; Oct–April 10am–5.30pm • €2, including access to Villa Musée Jean-Honoré Fragonard • ⓦ museesdegrasse.com

The **Musée d'Art et d'Histoire de Provence** is housed in a luxurious townhouse commissioned by the sister of the eighteenth-century aristocratic radical Mirabeau as a place to entertain. As well as all the gorgeous fittings and an eighteenth-century kitchen, the eclectic collections include eighteenth- to nineteenth-century faïence from Apt and Le Castellet, Mirabeau's death mask, a tin bidet and six prehistoric bronze leg bracelets.

## Musée International de la Parfumerie

2 bd du Jeu-de-Ballon; Daily: May–Sept daily 10am–7pm; Oct–March 10am–5.30pm • €4 • ⓦ museesdegrasse.com

The fascinating and interactive **Musée International de la Parfumerie** is a worthwhile adjunct to a factory visit, and probably more informative. It displays perfume bottles from the ancient Greeks via Marie Antoinette to the present, and explains the perfume-making process.

## Villa Musée Jean-Honoré Fragonard

23 bd Fragonard • mid-April to early May daily 1–5.30pm; July–Sept daily 1–6.30pm • €2, including access to Musée d'Art et d'Histoire de Provence • ⓦ museesdegrasse.com

The **Villa Musée Jean-Honoré Fragonard** is where the celebrated Rococo painter Jean-Honoré Fragonard returned to live after the Revolution. The staircase has impressive

**17**

## SNIFFING AROUND THE PERFUME FACTORIES

There are thirty or so **parfumeries** in and around Grasse, most of them making not perfume but essences-plus-formulas, sold to Dior, Lancôme, Estée Lauder and the like, who make up their own brand-name perfumes.

The ingredients that the "nose" – as the creator of the perfume's formula is known – has to play with include resins, roots, moss, beans, bark, civet (a secretion from the cat-like civet), ambergris (whale vomit), bits of beaver and musk from Tibetan goats. You can visit three local **showrooms** for free, which include overpoweringly fragrant shops and guided tours, in English, of the traditional perfume factory set-up (the actual working industrial complexes are strictly out of bounds).

**Fragonard** 3 rue Jean-Ossola ⓦfragonard.com. Daily 10am–6.30pm.
**Galimard** 73 rte de Cannes ⓦgalimard.com. Daily: April–June & Sept 9am–6pm; July & Aug 9am–

6.30pm; Oct–March 9am–noon & 2–6pm.
**Molinard** 60 bd Victor-Hugo ⓦmolinard.com. July & Aug daily 9.30am–7pm; Sept–June Mon–Sat 9.30am–6.30pm, Sun 10am–6pm.

wall paintings by his son Alexandre-Évariste, while the salon is graced by copies of **Love's Progress in the Heart of a Young Girl**, which Jean-Honoré painted for Madame du Barry.

## ARRIVAL AND DEPARTURE
**CANNES AND AROUND**

### CANNES
**By train** The *gare SNCF* is on rue Jean-Jaurès, five blocks north of the Palais des Festivals on the seafront.
Destinations Antibes (up to 5 hourly; 12min), Grasse (1–2 hourly; 30min); Nice (up to 5 hourly; 24–34min); St-Raphaël (every 20min–1hr; 26–38min).
**By bus** There are two *gares routières*: one on place B.-Cornut-Gentille between the *mairie* and Le Suquet, serving coastal destinations; and the other, next to the *gare SNCF*, for local buses – however some services for destinations inland, including Grasse, depart from bd d'Alsace on the north side of the Voie Rapide. Palm Bus (☎08 25 82 55 99, ⓦpalmbus.fr; €1.50) runs numerous day and night buses, serving all of Cannes and the surrounding area.
Destinations Antibes (every 10–20min; 30min); Grasse (every 25–30min; 50–55min); Nice (every 10–20min; 1hr 20min-2hr); Vallauris (1–3 hourly; 25min).

### ÎLES DE LÉRINS
Boats for both islands leave from Cannes' quai des Îles at the seaward end of the quai Max-Laubeuf.
**To St-Honorat** Compagnie Planaria (Jan & Feb 4 daily; March & Oct–Nov 7 daily; April–June & Sept 9 daily; July & Aug 10 daily; the last boat back to Cannes leaves 4.30pm from Oct–March. 5.30pm in April–June & Sept, and

6.30pm in July & Aug; €16.50; ☎04 92 98 71 38, ⓦcannes-ilesdelerins.com).
**To Ste-Marguerite** Three companies – Horizon (☎04 92 98 71 36, ⓦhorizon-lerins.com), Riviera Lines (☎04 92 98 71 31, ⓦriviera-lines.com) and Trans Côte d'Azur (☎04 92 00 42 30, ⓦtrans-cote-azur.com) – run to Ste-Marguerite (up to 18 daily 7.30am–4.30pm; €15).

### VALLAURIS
**By bus** Regular buses from Cannes (#18 from bd d'Alsace north of the *gare SNCF*) and from Golfe-Juan SNCF arrive at the rear of the château.
Destinations Antibes (every 10–20min; 35min); Cannes (1–3 hourly; 25min).

### GRASSE
**By bus** Grasse's *gare routière* is just north of the old town at place de la Buanderie.
Destinations Cannes (every 25–30min; 50–55min); Nice (every 25–50min; 1hr 20min).
**By train** Trains from Cannes (1–2 hourly; 25min) arrive at Grasse's *gare SNCF*, south of the *vieille ville*; it's a stiff walk uphill, so take the Funix shuttle bus (Mon–Sat every 15min; €1.50) to reach the centre of town.

## INFORMATION

### CANNES
**Tourist offices** There are three tourist offices in Cannes (all ☎04 92 99 84 22, ⓦcannes-destination.com): Palais des Festivals, 1 bd de la Croisette (daily: March–June, Sept & Oct

9am–7pm; July & Aug 9am–8pm; Nov–Feb 10am–6pm); 1 rue Pierre-Sémard in Cannes-La Bocca (Tues–Sat: April–Oct 9am–12.30pm & 2.30–6pm; Nov–March 9am–12.30pm & 1.30–5pm); and at the *gare SNCF* (Mon–Sat 9am–1pm & 2–6pm).

**17**

**Bike rental** Bikes can be rented from Élite Rent a Bike, 19 av du Maréchal-Juin (☎04 93 94 30 34, ⓦelite-rentabike. com), or Holiday Bikes, also at 19 av du Maréchal-Juin (☎04 97 06 30 63, ⓦloca-bike.fr).

**VALLAURIS**

**Tourist office** 4 av Georges-Clemenceau (Mon–Sat 9am–noon & 2–5pm; ☎04 93 63 18 38, ⓦvallauris-golfe-juan.

fr). There is a car park nearby, just off the D135.

**GRASSE**

**Tourist office** at the *gare routière*, place de la Buanderie (July–Sept Mon–Sat 9am–7pm, Sun 10am–1pm & 2–5pm; May–June & Oct Mon–Sat 9am–6pm, Sun 10am–6pm; Nov–April Mon–Sat 9am–1pm & 2–5pm; ☎04 93 36 66 66, ⓦpaysdegrassetourisme.fr).

## ACCOMMODATION

### CANNES

**Alizé** 29 rue du Bivouac Napoléon ☎04 97 06 64 64, ⓦhotel-alize-cannes.fr. A central hotel with large, bright and soundproofed rooms with a/c and cable TV – great value in the lower end of this price range. **€109**

★ **Canberra** 120 rue d'Antibes ☎04 97 06 95 00, ⓦhotel-cannes-canberra.com. Classy, understated and intimate four-star hotel with elegant, 1950s-inspired decor and large rooms with a/c and flatscreen TV. There's a heated pool in the garden plus a sauna, gym, restaurant and cocktail bar. **€288**

**Chanteclair** 12 rue Forville ☎04 93 39 68 88, ⓦhotelchanteclair.com. About as cheap as you'll get in the centre of Cannes, right next to the old town, and with a private courtyard where you can eat breakfast (€8). Rooms are small but all have shower; most also have WC. **€75**

**InterContinental Carlton** 58 La Croisette ☎04 93 06 40 06, ⓦ-carlton-cannes.com. Legendary landmark *belle époque* seafront palace hotel that featured in Hitchcock's *To Catch a Thief*. Rooms are a/c and decorated in a tasteful but conservative style, with pay-per-view movies, wi-fi and marble bathroom. **€577**

**Provence** 9 rue Molière ☎04 93 38 44 35, ⓦhotel-de-

provence.com. Charmingly decorated and well-appointed three-star hotel just off rue d'Antibes, with pale colours, a/c, a bar and a luxuriant garden. Some rooms have balconies and the suite has a large terrace. **€161**

**Simone** 16 rue Hélène-Vagliano ☎04 93 99 51 00, ⓦhotelsimone.com. Conveniently located on a side street close to the station, this is a great find, with bright, contemporary rooms, which makes up for them being on the cosy side. Check the website for good deals. **€120**

**La Villa Tosca** 11 rue Hoche ☎04 93 38 34 40, ⓦvilla-tosca.com. Smart three-star hotel in a graceful balconied building just a few blocks from the sea. Well-equipped, a/c rooms have flatscreen TV; some also have balconies. There is a cheaper two-star sister hotel – the *PLM* – a few doors down. Rates in summer can drop to €80 with advance booking. **€130**

### GRASSE

**Hôtel du Patti** 1 place du Patti ☎04 93 36 01 00, ⓦhotelpatti.com. Just below the bus station and on the edge of the old town, this pleasant two-star hotel has an airy modern lobby and 73 a/c rooms with bath or shower. Breakfast €12. **€99**

## EATING AND DRINKING

### CANNES

Cannes has restaurants catering for every budget, with rue Meynadier, Le Suquet and quai St-Pierre being the best places to look. You can buy your own food in the Forville market two blocks behind the *mairie* (Tues–Sun 7am–1pm).

**Aux Bons Enfants** 80 rue Meynadier ⓦaux-bons-enfants-cannes.com. Small and friendly, though less rustic than it used to be, this family-run stalwart – established in 1920 – serves very reliable Provençal cuisine with *menus* from €24 and dishes such as octopus *daube* Marseille-style or grilled *andouillette*. Cash only. Jan–Nov Tues–Sat noon–2pm & 7–10pm; open Mon during school hols.

**Barbarella** 16 rue Saint-Dizier, Le Suquet ☎04 93 38 87 38. Stylish, fun and gay-friendly restaurant and cabaret, with themed evenings and bistro fare with a Provençal accent in dishes such as duck breast with honey sauce or

salmon *tartare*. *Plat du jour* €13. Mon–Sat 7pm–late.

**Chez Vincent & Nicolas** 92 rue Meynadier ☎04 93 68 35 39, ⓦchezvincentetnicolas.fr. Slightly quirky and original choice, with a lovely setting in a square just off the main street. The scallops wrapped in bacon are worth a try. Meat or fish mains start at around €19. Daily 7–11.30pm.

**Da Bouttau Auberge Provençale** 10 rue Saint-Antoine, Le Suquet ☎04 92 99 27 17, ⓦdabouttau.com. Established in 1860, this stylish restaurant is the oldest in Cannes. It serves Niçois specialities and creative dishes such as lentil pasta with artichokes, and goat's cheese *pastille* with confit onions. *Menu* €35; two-course lunch *formule* €24. Daily noon–2pm & 7.15–11pm.

**Noisette** 4 rue Tony-Allard ☎04 93 39 70 35. This cosy, bright place serves up some of the best Italian food in town, in unpretentious surroundings. Expect squid-ink pasta, an incredibly fresh *caprese* salad, and a perfect tiramisu. Mains from €18. Tues–Sat noon–2 & 7–9pm.

**La Palme d'Or** Hôtel Martinez, 73 bd de la Croisette ☎ 04 92 98 74 14. The place to go and celebrate if you've just won a film festival prize; it has held two Michelin stars for a quarter of a century. Lunch *menu* €70; evening *menus* start at €205. Tues–Sat 12.30–1.30pm & 8–10pm.

### ÎLES DE LÉRINS

Taking a picnic to the islands is a good idea, particularly out of season, though there are reasonably priced snack stalls, two restaurants on Ste-Marguerite (April–Oct) and one on St-Honorat near the landing stage (daily for lunch; closed mid-Nov to mid-Dec).

### GRASSE

**Au Comptoir** 9 rue Dominique-Conte ☎ 04 93 36 90 25. Lively little *bar à vins* on the fringe of the *vieille ville*, with a chalked-up selection of tapas and sharing platters (around €12) to soak up the wines. Tues–Sat 11am–11pm.

**La Bastide Saint-Antoine** 48 rue Henri-Dunant ☎ 04 93 70 94 94, ⓦ jacques-chibois.com. The best place to eat in Grasse is the Michelin-starred restaurant at this elegant small hotel, which serves *cuisine gourmande* with a Provençal twist in dishes such as bream in a *bouillabaisse* sauce with cardamom carrots. Lunch *menus* €66; otherwise *menus* from €185. Daily noon–2.30pm & 8–10.30pm; closed early Nov to early Dec.

**Fougassettes Venturini** 1 rue Marcel-Journet ☎ 04 93 36 20 47. *Confiserie* where you can buy the eponymous *fougassettes* – a sweet flatbread flavoured with orange blossom (€1.80). It also sells candied fruits, candied rose petals and Marseille-style *navettes* (€3 for 100g). Tues–Sat 9am–12.30pm & 3–6.30pm.

## NIGHTLIFE

### CANNES

There are tons of trendy, exclusive bars and clubs, especially in the grid of streets known as the Carré d'Or, bounded by rue Macé, rue V.-Cousin, rue Dr G.-Monod and rue des Frères Pradignacs.

**Backstage** 17 rue Gérard-Monod ☎ 06 73 50 42 03. The biggest and flashiest of the trendy lounge/bar/clubs in the tight little knot of streets between rue d'Antibes and la Croisette, with dramatic black decor, varying free themed nights and a terrace at the front. Daily 6pm–2.30am.

**Le Baôli** Port Pierre-Canto ☎ 04 93 43 03 43, ⓦ baolicannes.com. If you want to rub shoulders with celebrities and big-name international DJs, head to this exclusive exotic (and expensive) outdoor disco-restaurant with palms lit up at night – dress the part. March & April Sat & Sun; May–Oct daily: restaurant (€70–80) from 8pm, club midnight–dawn.

**Club 7** 7 rue Rouguière ☎ 06 09 55 22 79. Gay disco and cabaret club just off rue Félix-Faure, with regular events all year round including drag shows and live music. Free entry. Daily 12.15am–7am.

**Pint House** 19 rue des Frères Pradignacs ☎ 04 93 38 90 10, ⓦ pinthouse.fr. Irish-style pub with live rugby on TV; the beers are mostly French or Belgian (*pression* from €3.80, bottles from €5.50). A bit of a relief from the trying-too-hard excess of much Cannes nightlife. Daily 6pm–5am.

# Antibes and around

Graham Greene, who lived in **ANTIBES** for more than twenty years, considered it the only place on this stretch of coast to have preserved its soul. And although Antibes and its twin, **Juan-les-Pins**, have not escaped the overdevelopment that blights the region, they have avoided its worst excesses. Antibes itself is a pleasing old town, extremely animated, with one of the finest **markets** on the coast and the best **Picasso collection** in its ancient seafront castle; and the southern end of the **Cap d'Antibes** still has its woods of pine, in which some of the most exclusive mansions on the Riviera hide. North of Antibes is lovely **Biot**, with its fascinating Fernand Léger connections.

## Musée Picasso

Place Mariejol · Mid-June to mid-Sept Tues–Sun 10am–6pm; mid-Sept to mid-June Tues–Sun 10am–1pm & 2–6pm · €8, or €10 pass with other Antibes museums · ☎ 04 92 90 54 28, ⓦ antibes-juanlespins.com

Lording it over the Antibes ramparts and the sea, the sixteenth-century **Château Grimaldi** is a beautifully cool, light space, with a terrace garden filled with sculptures by Germaine Richier, Miró and others – some on long-term loan. In 1946 Picasso was offered the dusty building as a studio. Several prolific months followed before he

**17**

moved to Vallauris (see page 908), leaving his Antibes output to what is now the **Musée Picasso**. Although he donated other works later on, the bulk of the collection belongs to this one period: there are nudes, fauns and still lifes plus sculpture and ceramics made at the Madoura workshop in Vallauris. Temporary exhibitions focus on particular aspects of the collection, which also includes anguished canvases by Nicolas de Staël, who stayed in Antibes for a few months from 1954 to 1955.

## Cathédrale d'Antibes

Rue du Saint-Esprit

Alongside the castle is the **Cathédrale d'Antibes**, built on the site of an ancient temple. The choir and apse survive from the Romanesque building that served the city in the Middle Ages while the nave and stunning ochre facade are Baroque. Inside, in the south transept, is a sumptuous medieval altarpiece surrounded by immaculate panels of tiny detailed scenes.

## Cap d'Antibes

**Plage de la Salis**, the longest Antibes beach, runs along the eastern neck of **Cap d'Antibes**, with no big hotels squatting its sands – amazingly rare on the Riviera. To the south, at the top of chemin du Calvaire, there are superb views from the **Chapelle de la Garoupe** (Fri 2.30–5pm; free; ꤮garoupe.free.fr), which contains Russian spoils from the Crimean War and hundreds of **ex votos**. To the west, on boulevard du Cap between chemins du Tamisier and G.-Raymond, you can wander around the **Jardin Thuret** (Mon–Fri: summer 8am–6pm; winter 8.30am–5.30pm; free), botanical gardens belonging to a national research institute. Back on the east shore, further south, lies a second public beach, **plage de la Garoupe**. From here a coastal footpath circles the cape to join the chemin des Douaniers.

### Around the Southern Cap

At the southern end of the Cap d'Antibes, on avenue L.D.-Beaumont, stands the grandiose **Villa Eilenroc** (Wed & first & third Sat of month 2–5pm; €2), designed by Charles Garnier, architect of the casino at Monte-Carlo, and surrounded by lush gardens. There are more sandy coves and little harbours along the western shore, where you'll also find the **Espace Mer et Littoral**, at the end of avenue J.-F.-Kennedy in a former Napoleonic coastal battery; it presents changing exhibitions on the marine and coastal environments (mid-June to mid-Sept Tues–Sat 10am–6.30pm; free). Much of the southern tip of the **cap** is a warren of private roads, including the area around the fabled **Hôtel du Cap Eden Roc** and the so-called "bay of millionaires".

## Juan-les-Pins

**JUAN-LES-PINS**, less than 2km from the centre of Antibes, had its heyday in the interwar years, when the summer season on the Riviera first took off and the resort was the haunt of film stars like Charlie Chaplin, Maurice Chevalier and Lilian Harvey, the

---

**ANTIBES MARKET**

One block from the sea, the morning **covered market** (June–Aug daily 6am–1pm; Sept–May closed Mon) overflows with Provençal goodies and cut **flowers**, the traditional and still-flourishing Antibes business. In the afternoons a **craft market** (mid-June to Sept Tues–Sun 3pm–midnight; Oct to mid-June Fri–Sun only) takes over, and when the stalls pack up, café tables take their place.

polyglot London-born musical star who lingered here until 1968, long after her fame had faded. Juan-les-Pins isn't as glamorous as it once was either, though it still has a casino and a certain cachet, and the beaches are sand.

# Biot

The *village perché* of **BIOT**, 8km north of Antibes, is where Fernand Léger lived for a few years at the end of his life. The village itself – famous for its hand-blown bubble glass – is beautiful, full of craft shops and ateliers selling everything from glassware to fine art and handbags.

## Musée National Fernand Léger

316 chemin du Val-de-Pôme • Daily except Tues: May–Oct 10am–6pm; Nov–April 10am–5pm • €5.50 (€7.50 during temporary exhibitions) • ☎ 04 93 53 87 28, Ⓦ musee-fernandleger.fr • Bus #10 from Antibes or Biot *gare SNCF* (every 30–45min; 25min from Antibes/5min from Biot), stop "F. Léger"

A stunning collection of the artist's intensely life-affirming works, created between 1905 and 1955, is on show at the **Musée National Fernand Léger**, in a building that is itself an expression of his art, custom-built to accommodate the vibrant mosaics that adorn its exterior walls. The museum is just east of the village on the chemin du Val-de-Pôme.

## ARRIVAL, INFORMATION AND GETTING AROUND — ANTIBES AND AROUND

**By train** Antibes' *gare SNCF* lies north of the old town at the top of av Robert-Soleau. Turn right out of the station and a 3min walk along av R.-Soleau will bring you to place de-Gaulle at the entrance to the *vieille ville*.
Destinations Cannes (up to 5 hourly; 10–13min); Nice (up to 5 hourly; 17–21min).
**By bus** The *gare routière* is east of the train station on place Guynemer, with frequent buses between the two. Local Envibus services link Antibes to its neighbours: bus #2 goes to Cap d'Antibes, bus #1 to Juan-les-Pins and #10 to Biot. Destinations Biot (every 15–4min; 30min); Cap d'Antibes (every 30–45min; 12min); Juan-les-Pins (every 10–15min; 19min).

**Tourist office** 42 av R.-Soleau (April–June & Sept Mon–Sat 9.30am–12.30pm & 2–6pm, Sun 9am–1pm; July & Aug daily 9am–7pm; Oct–March Mon–Sat 9am–12.30pm & 1.30–5pm, Sun 9am–1pm (closed Sun in Jan & Nov); ☎ 04 22 10 60 10, Ⓦ antibesjuanlespins.com). There's an annexe in Juan-les-Pins (6 chemin des Sables; 04 22 10 60 01; same hours).
**Bike rental** Holiday Bikes, 93 bd Wilson in Juan-les-Pins (☎ 04 93 61 51 51, Ⓦ loca-bike.fr).
**Bookshop** Antibes Books, 13 rue Georges-Clemenceau (Mon & Sun 11am–6pm, Tues–Sat 10am–7pm (summer daily 10am–7pm); ☎ 04 93 61 96 47, Ⓦ antibesbooks.com) is a well-stocked and very friendly English bookshop.

## ACCOMMODATION

### ANTIBES

**Backpackers House** 22 rue des Casemates, Antibes ☎ 04 97 04 75 46, Ⓦ frenchrivierahostel.com. Popular hostel right in the thick of things in Antibes, with smart, comfortable dorms sleeping five to eight. Facilities include a tour desk and a communal kitchen and lounge. **€35**
★ **La Jabotte** 13 av Max-Maurey, Antibes ☎ 04 93 61 45 89, Ⓦ jabotte.com. Just a short walk from the plage de la Salis, this friendly place has beautifully decorated rooms

in vibrant, cheerful colours – book in advance. The cheapest double has a shower, but shared WC facilities. Downstairs rooms all have private terraces, while the two upstairs rooms are the only ones with TVs. **€174**
**Logis de la Brague** 1221 rte de Nice ☎ 04 93 33 54 72, Ⓦ camping-logisbrague.com. As with all campsites near Antibes, this three-star site is north of the city in the *quartier* of La Brague (bus #10 or one train stop to "Gare de Biot"); this one is closest to the station. Closed Oct–April. **€28**

**17**

**La Marjolaine** 15 av du Docteur-Fabre, Juan-les-Pins ☎ 04 93 61 06 60; ⓦ lamarjolainefrance.com. Sixteen traditionally styled rooms in a lovely a/c villa with a leafy terrace and a handy location between Juan-les-Pins train station and the beach. Closed Nov–Feb. **€105**

**Le Mas Djoliba** 29 av de Provence, Antibes ☎ 04 93 34 02 48, ⓦ hotel-djoliba.com. Pleasant – if a little old-fashioned – hotel with a pool, *boules* and a fabulous garden; it's a great hideaway from the bustle of town and not too far from the beach. Closed Nov to mid-March. **€145**

**Pré Catelan** 27 av des Palmiers ☎ 04 93 61 05 11, ⓦ precatelan.fr. Peaceful and very comfortable hotel, in attractive gardens on the corner of av des Lauriers, near the sea and the station, with spacious rooms, some sleeping four, and a heated swimming pool. **€215**

**Le Relais du Postillon** 8 rue Championnet, Antibes ☎ 04 93 34 20 77, ⓦ relaisdupostillon.com. Located in Antibes old town, this charming two-star above a low-key bar feels like an old inn, with its individually styled a/c rooms and lots of exposed stonework. **€85**

**BIOT**

**Les Arcades** 14–16 place des Arcades ☎ 04 93 65 01 04, ⓦ hotel-restaurant-les-arcades.com. Book well in advance to stay in this appealing old hotel/restaurant in the medieval centre of the village, full of old-fashioned charm and with huge rooms and an excellent restaurant, which doubles as an art gallery (*menu* €35). Very good value for this neck of the woods. **€60**

## EATING, DRINKING AND ENTERTAINMENT

Antibes' old town is rich in eating and drinking options; Juan-les-Pins isn't quite so well endowed, but does have several discos and cocktail bars. In Biot, the best place to eat is in the *Les Arcades* hotel restaurant.

**De Bacon** 664, bd de Bacon, Cap d'Antibes ☎ 04 93 61 50 02, ⓦ restaurantdebacon.com. With excellent fish and a sea view, this locally renowned restaurant offers a €55 set lunch; otherwise, *menus* from €85 except during high season – mains otherwise start at an eyewatering €70. March–Oct Tues 7.30–10pm, Wed–Sun noon–2pm & 7.30–10pm.

**Brûlot** 3 rue Frédéric-Isnard, Antibes ☎ 04 93 34 17 76, ⓦ brulot.fr. A stalwart of the restaurant scene in Antibes' old town, dishing up classic regional dishes like *socca, salade niçoise* and tripe. Lunch *formule* €14.90, *menus* €24–45. Mon–Sat 4–11pm.

**Le Pam–Pam** 137 bd Wilson, Juan-les-Pins ☎ 04 93 61 11 05, ⓦ pampam.fr. Perennially popular cocktail bar with

a Polynesian-meets-Brazilian ambience and frequent live music and dance spectacles. Fruit and gewgaw-bedecked cocktails from €12. Daily 3pm–4.30am.

**La Passagère Hôtel Belles Rives**, 33 bd Édouard-Baudoin, Juan-les-Pins ☎ 04 93 61 02 79, ⓦ bellesrives. com. Modern Mediterranean delights using regional produce served in lovely, restored Art Deco surroundings with wonderful views over the bay. *Menus* (from €105) might include tuna with yuzu cream or crab open ravioli. March–May & Oct–Dec Wed–Sun 12.30–2pm & 7.30–9.30pm; June–Sept daily 7.30–10pm.

**Les Vieux Murs** 25 promenade Amiral-de-Grasse, Antibes ☎ 04 93 34 06 73, ⓦ lesvieuxmurs.com. *Restaurant gastronomique* serving classy food such as green asparagus tart with diced confit veal or swordfish with lobster broth, in a perfect setting on the castle ramparts. *Menu* €36, otherwise main courses from €30. Daily noon–10pm.

# Above the Baie des Anges

Between Antibes and Nice, the **Baie des Anges** laps at a long stretch of undistinguished twentieth-century resorts. The old towns, such as **Cagnes**, lie inland. Cagnes is associated with Renoir – as is **St-Paul-de-Vence**, which houses the wonderful modern art collection of the Fondation Maeght. **Vence** has a small chapel decorated by Matisse, and is a relaxing place to stay.

## Cagnes

**CAGNES** is a confusing agglomeration, consisting of the seaside district of **Cros-de-Cagnes**, the immaculate medieval village of **Haut-de-Cagnes** overlooking the town from the northwest, and **Cagnes-sur-Mer**, the traffic-choked town centre wedged between the two.

### Les Collettes – the Musée Renoir

Chemin des Collettes • Daily except Tues: April & May 10am–noon & 2–6pm; June–Sept 10am–1pm & 2–6pm; Oct–March 10am–noon & 2–5pm • €6 • ⓦ cagnes-tourisme.com • Free shuttle bus #45 from Cagnes-sur-Mer bus station (July & Aug only); it's about 10min on foot

**17**

**Les Collettes**, the house that Renoir had built in 1908 and where he spent the last twelve years of his life, is now a **museum**, encompassing the house and olive and rare orange groves surrounding it. One of the two studios in the house – north-facing to catch the late afternoon light – is arranged as if Renoir had just popped out. Renoir's work is represented by several sculptures, some beautiful watercolours and ten paintings from his Cagnes period. Visitors can also see the family kitchen and hall on the ground floor.

## Château Grimaldi

Place du Château, Haut-de-Cagnes • Daily: April–June & Sept 10am–noon & 2–6pm; July & Aug 10am–1pm & 2–6pm; Oct–March 10am–noon & 2–5pm • €4 • ☏ 04 92 02 47 35 • Free shuttle bus #44 from bus station; by foot, it's a steep ascent from av Renoir along rue du Général-Bérenger and montée de la Bourgade

Arty **Haut-de-Cagnes** lives up to everything dreamed of in a Riviera *village perché*. The ancient village backs up to a crenellated feudal **château** which has a stunning Renaissance interior, housing museums of local history, olive cultivation, the **donation Solidor** – a diverse collection of paintings of the famous cabaret artist Suzy Solidor – plus an **olive museum** and exhibition space for **contemporary art**.

### ARRIVAL AND INFORMATION

**CAGNES**

**By train** The *gare SNCF* Cagnes-sur-Mer (one stop from the *gare SNCF* Cros-de-Cagnes) is southwest of the centre alongside the *autoroute*; turn right on the northern side of the *autoroute* along av de la Gare to head into town. The sixth turning on your right, rue des Palmiers, leads to the tourist office.
Destinations Antibes (up to 4 hourly; 6–13min); Cannes (2–3 hourly; 18–24min); Nice (up to 4 hourly; 16min).

**By bus** Buses #42, #56 and #200 all make the short run from the *gare SNCF* to the *gare routière* on square Bourdet. Destinations Cannes (every 15–20min; 57min); Nice (every 15–20min; 36min).
**Tourist office** 6 bd du Maréchal-Juin (July & Aug Mon–Sat 9am–1pm & 2–6pm; Sept–June Mon–Fri 9am–noon & 2–6pm, Sat 9am–noon; ☏ 04 93 20 61 64, ⓦ cagnes-tourisme.com).

### ACCOMMODATION

**Aéva** 22 bd de la Plage ☏ 04 93 73 39 52, ⓦ hotel-aeva.fr. Red seafront hotel in Cros-de-Cagnes offering appealing (if not hugely exciting) en suites with sound-proofing, satellite TV and safes. There's a classy restaurant facing the sea, and a separate aparthotel, too. **€130**

**Le Val Fleuri** 139 Vallon des Vaux ☏ 04 93 31 21 74, ⓦ campingvalfleuri.fr. Three-star campsite approximately 4km from the sea (bus #41) with a heated pool, snack bar and children's play area. They also rent out studio flats and mobile homes. Closed Oct–March. **€27**

### EATING, DRINKING AND ENTERTAINMENT

**Fleur de Sel** 85 montée de la Bourgade ☏ 04 92 20 33 33, ⓦ restaurant-fleurdesel.com. This elegant restaurant serves dishes such as lobster with black truffle oil or scallops with carrot tagliatelle, lemon juice, caviar and yuzu; *menus* from €36. April–Sept daily except Wed 7–9.30pm; Oct–March Fri–Tues 7–9.30pm.

**Josy-Jo** 2 rue du Planastel ☏ 04 93 20 68 76, ⓦ restaurant-josyjo.com. Charming restaurant in the space that served as Soutine's workshop in the interwar years, with an oleander-shaded terrace and refined Provençal dishes. *Formule* €29, otherwise around €27–48 for main courses à la carte. Mon & Tues 7.30–10pm, Wed–Sat noon–2pm & 7.30–10pm.

## St-Paul-de-Vence

The fortified village of **ST-PAUL-DE-VENCE** is home to one of the best artistic treats in the region: the remarkable **Fondation Maeght**, created in the 1950s by Aimé and Marguerite Maeght, art collectors and dealers who knew all the great artists who worked in Provence.

### Fondation Maeght

623 chemin des Gardettes • Daily: July–Sept 10am–7pm; Oct–June 10am–6pm • €16 • ☏ 04 93 32 81 63, ⓦ www.fondation-maeght.com

Through the gates of the **Fondation Maeght** is a sublime fusion of art, modern architecture and landscape. Alberto Giacometti's *Cat* stalks along the edge of the grass;

Miró's *Egg* smiles above a pond; it's hard not to be bewitched by the Calder mobile swinging over watery tiles, by Léger's *Flowers, Birds and a Bench* on a sunlit rough stone wall, or by the clanking tubular fountain by Pol Bury. The building itself is superb: multi-levelled, flooded with daylight and housing a fabulous collection of works by Bonnard, Braque, Miró, Chagall and Léger, among others. Not everything is exhibited at any one time, apart from what is permanently featured in the garden.

### The vieux village

St-Paul-de-Vence's other famous sights are in the busy but beautiful **vieux village**. The hotel-restaurant **La Colombe d'Or** at the entrance to the village is celebrated for the art on its walls, donated in lieu of payment for meals by the then-impoverished Braque, Picasso, Matisse and Bonnard in the lean years following World War I – though it doesn't exactly encourage casual visitors. You could instead make the pilgrimage to the simple grave of **Marc Chagall** on the right-hand side of the little **cemetery** (open during daylight hours) at the southern end of the village, running the gauntlet of the boutiques and galleries on rue Grande to get there.

| ARRIVAL AND INFORMATION | ST-PAUL-DE-VENCE |
|---|---|
| **By bus** The Nice–Vence bus #400 has two stops in St-Paul: alighting at the Fondation Maeght stop, the first on the way up from Nice, the Fondation is a left turn up the hill from the roundabout; from the village centre, head uphill along the steep street opposite the entrance to the village itself. | Destinations Nice (every 30min–1hr; 1hr); Vence (every 30min–1hr; 7min).<br>Tourist office 2 rue Grande (daily: June–Sept 10am–7pm; Oct–May 10am–6pm; ☎04 93 32 86 95, ⓦsaint-pauldevence.com). |

| ACCOMMODATION AND EATING | |
|---|---|
| **La Colombe d'Or** Place du Général-de-Gaulle ☎04 93 32 80 02, ⓦla-colombe-dor.com. Famous for its stellar collection of modern art, the *Colombe d'Or* has thirteen elegant rooms and twelve apartments, plus a *restaurant* | *gastronomique*, valet parking, a heated outdoor pool, sauna and gardens – not to mention a idyllic terrace. Closed Nov–Christmas. **€360** |

# Vence

Long one of the less pretentious of Côte d'Azur towns, **VENCE** is slowly succumbing to a chi-chi makeover. Blessed with ancient houses, gateways, fountains, chapels and a **cathedral** containing Roman funeral inscriptions and a Chagall mosaic, in the 1920s it became a haven for painters and writers: André Gide, Raoul Dufy, D.H. Lawrence (who died here in 1930 while being treated for tuberculosis contracted in England) and Marc Chagall were all long-term visitors, along with **Matisse** whose work is the reason most people come.

### Chapelle du Rosaire

466 av Henri-Matisse • April–Oct Tues, Thurs & Fri 10am–noon & 2–6pm, Wed & Sat 2–6pm; early Nov & mid-Dec to March Tues, Thurs & Fri 10am–noon & 2–5pm, Wed & Sat 2–5pm • €7 • ☎04 93 58 03 26, ⓦchapellematisse.com

Towards the end of World War II, Matisse moved to Vence to escape Allied bombing of the coast, and his legacy is the exciting **Chapelle du Rosaire**, off the road to St-Jeannet, which leaves the town from carrefour Jean-Moulin at the top of avenue des Poilus. The chapel was his last work – consciously so – and not, as some have tried to explain, a religious conversion. "My only religion is the love of the work to be created, the love of creation, and great sincerity", he said in 1952 when the five-year project was completed.

The drawings on the chapel walls – black outline figures on white tiles – were executed by Matisse with a paintbrush fixed to a 2m-long bamboo stick specifically to remove his own stylistic signature from the lines. He succeeded in this to the extent that many people are disappointed, not finding the "Matisse" they expect. Yet it is a

**17**

total work – every part of the chapel is Matisse's design – and one that the artist was content with.

## ARRIVAL AND INFORMATION
VENCE

**By bus** Vence's *gare routière* is at place du Maréchal-Juin, a short walk from the tourist office.
Destinations Nice (every 30min–1hr; 55min–1hr 15min);

St-Paul-de-Vence (every 30min–1hr; 7min).
**Tourist office** Place du Grand-Jardin (Mon–Sat 9am–8pm; ☎ 04 93 58 06 38, ⓦ vence-tourisme.fr).

## ACCOMMODATION

**Le 2 Bed & Bistrot** 2 rue des Portiques ☎ 04 93 24 42 58, ⓦ le2avence.fr. Four stylish a/c rooms – including a junior suite and a loft with private roof terrace that gives stunning views over the surrounding hills – in a *chambre d'hôte* in the heart of Vieux Vence, above a bistro. **€108**
**Domaine de la Bergerie** 1330 chemin de la Sine ☎ 04 93 58 09 36, ⓦ camping-domainedelabergerie. com. Three-star campsite 3km west of town off the road to Tourettes-sur-Loup, with a pool and *pétanque* pitch. They

also rent small chalet-like pods (€42). Closed mid-Oct to late March. **€28**
**Villa Roseraie** Av Henri-Giraud ☎ 04 93 58 02 20, ⓦ www.villaroseraie.com. Three-star comforts in a villa that dates from 1929, with a palm-fringed pool, a garden, private parking and a bar. The rooms are decorated in Provençal style and some have private patio or terrace. Two-night minimum in high season. **€111**

## EATING

★ **Auberge des Seigneurs** 1 rue du Dr-Binet ☎ 04 93 58 04 24, ⓦ auberge-seigneurs.fr. Lovely, very friendly old inn, set into the walls of Vieux Vence. The restaurant, which spreads onto a panoramic terrace just outside the walls, serves a fine array of Provençal specialities on *menus* costing from €24 at lunch, €35 at dinner. Tues–Sat noon–1.30pm & 7–9pm. **€90**

**La Farigoule** 15 av Henri-Isnard ☎ 04 93 58 01 27, ⓦ lafarigoule-vence.fr. This very pretty restaurant – with a wood-beamed interior and a courtyard garden – is a good bet for a special meal, with *menus* at €32 and €70 and Côtes de Provence wines. Wed–Sun noon–1pm & 7.30–9.30pm; closed late Nov to Christmas.

# Nice

The capital of the Riviera and fifth-largest city in France, **NICE** lives off a glittering reputation. Far too large to be considered simply a beach resort, it has all the advantages and disadvantages of a major city: superb culture, shopping, eating and drinking, but also crime, graffiti and horrendous traffic, all set against a backdrop of blue skies, sparkling sea and sub-tropical greenery kept lush by sprinklers.

Popularized by English aristocrats in the eighteenth century, Nice reached its zenith in the *belle époque* of the late nineteenth century, and has retained its historical styles almost intact: the medieval rabbit warren of **Vieux Nice**, the Italianate facades of **modern Nice** and the rich exuberance of **fin-de-siècle residences** dating from when the city was Europe's most fashionable winter retreat. It has mementos from its time as a Roman regional capital, and earlier still, when the Greeks founded the city. The **museums** are a treat for art-lovers, and though its politics are conservative Nice doesn't

## NICE ORIENTATION

Shadowed by mountains that curve down to the Mediterranean east of its port, Nice divides fairly clearly between old and new. **Vieux Nice**, the old town, groups about the hill of **Le Château**, its limits signalled by **boulevard Jean-Jaurès**, built along the course of the River Paillon. Along the seafront, the celebrated **promenade des Anglais** runs a cool 5km until forced to curve inland by the sea-projecting runways of the airport. The central square, **place Masséna**, is at the bottom of the modern city's main street, **avenue Jean-Médecin**, to the north is the exclusive hillside suburb of **Cimiez**, while the port lies on the eastern side of **Le Château**.

**17**

**NICE MUSEUMS**

Access to Nice's museums is via a €10 ticket that is valid for 24 hours and allows entry to all of the municipal museums and galleries. If you're planning more than you can sensibly cram into one day, however, it's worth considering the €20 **Ticket 7 Jours**, which gives unlimited access to all within a seven-day period. Note, however, that the Musée National Marc Chagall and Musée des Arts Asiatiques are not municipal museums and are not covered by the ticket. The **French Riviera Pass** (€26/24hr, €38/48hr, €56/72hr; ⓦ frenchrivierapass.com) gives access to all, and to numerous other museums and attractions along the Riviera.

feel stuffy; it has a highly visible LGBT community and spirited nightlife; and despite its historic centre it feels as though it continues to update itself – seen best, perhaps, in its ultra-modern tramway and smartened up public spaces. Conservative it may be, but Nice does not rest on its laurels.

## Parc de la Colline du Château

Daily: April–Sept 8.30am–8pm; Oct–March 8.30am–6pm • Take the lift by the Tour Bellanda at the eastern end of quai des États-Unis (Daily: June–Aug 9am–8pm, April, May & Sept 9am–7pm; Oct–March 10am–6pm; free), climb montée du Château from the old town or take the tourist train from place Masséna (10am–5/6/7pm; €10)

For initial orientation, fantastic sea and city views and the scent of Mediterranean vegetation, head for the **Parc de la Colline du Château**. It's where Nice began, as the ancient Greek city of Nikaïa, hence the mosaics and stone vases in mock-Grecian style. Despite the name, there's no château, just wonderful views over the scrambled rooftops and gleaming mosaic tiles of Vieux Nice and along the sweep of the promenade des Anglais.

## Vieux Nice

**Vieux Nice** has been much gentrified in recent years, but the restaurants, boutiques and little art galleries still coexist with humbler shops, there's washing strung between the tenements, and away from the showpiece squares a certain shabbiness lingers. Tourism now dominates Vieux Nice: throbbing with life day and night in August, much of it seems deserted in November. It is best explored on foot.

The central square is **place Rossetti**, where the soft-coloured Baroque **Cathédrale de Ste-Réparate** (Mon–Fri 9am–noon & 2–6pm, Sat 9am–noon & 2–7.30pm, Sun 9am–1pm & 3–6pm; ⓦ cathedrale-nice.fr) just manages to be visible in the concatenation of eight narrow streets. There are cafés to relax in, and a fabulous ice-cream parlour, *Fenocchio*, with an extraordinary choice of flavours.

### Cours Saleya

The old town's real magnet is **cours Saleya** and the adjacent place Pierre-Gautier and place Charles-Félix. These wide-open, sunlit spaces – fringed with grandiloquent municipal buildings and Italianate chapels – are the site of the city's main **market**. Café and restaurant tables fill the *cours* on summer nights, and presiding over it all is the Baroque **Chapelle de la Miséricorde** with its elliptical nave and exceptionally rich ornamentation. The **market** on the Cours is a treat, with gorgeous, colourful displays of fruit, vegetables, cheeses and sausages, plus cut flowers and potted roses, mimosa and other scented plants. On Monday the stalls sell bric-a-brac and second-hand clothes.

### Palais Lascaris

15 rue Droite • Daily except Tues: mid-June to mid-Oct 10am–6pm; mid-Oct to mid-June 11am–6pm • €10 • ☎ 04 93 62 72 40

Grandest survivor of Vieux Nice's Baroque town mansions is the **Palais Lascaris**, a seventeenth-century palace built by the Duke of Savoy's Field-Marshal, Jean-Paul

17

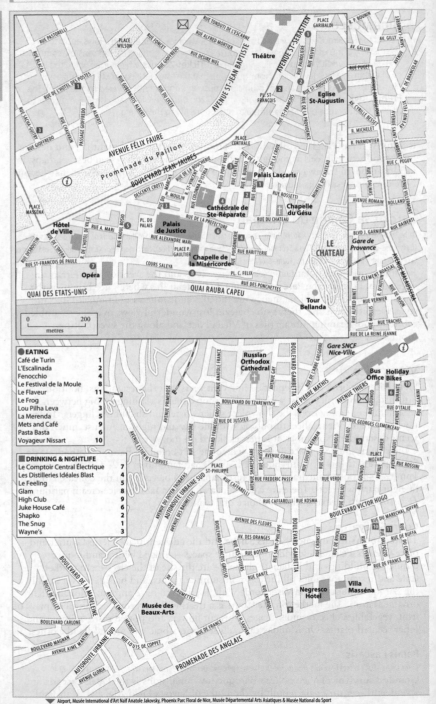

**EATING**

| | |
|---|---|
| Café de Turin | 1 |
| L'Escalinada | 2 |
| Fenocchio | 4 |
| Le Festival de la Moule | 8 |
| Le Flaveur | 11 |
| Le Frog | 7 |
| Lou Pilha Leva | 3 |
| La Merenda | 5 |
| Mets and Café | 9 |
| Pasta Basta | 6 |
| Voyageur Nissart | 10 |

**DRINKING & NIGHTLIFE**

| | |
|---|---|
| Le Comptoir Central Électrique | 7 |
| Les Distilleries Idéales Blast | 4 |
| Le Feeling | 5 |
| Glam | 8 |
| High Club | 9 |
| Juke House Café | 6 |
| Shapko | 2 |
| The Snug | 1 |
| Wayne's | 3 |

▼ Airport, Musée International d'Art Naïf Anatole Jakovsky, Phoenix Parc Floral de Nice, Musée Départemental Arts Asiatiques & Musée National du Sport

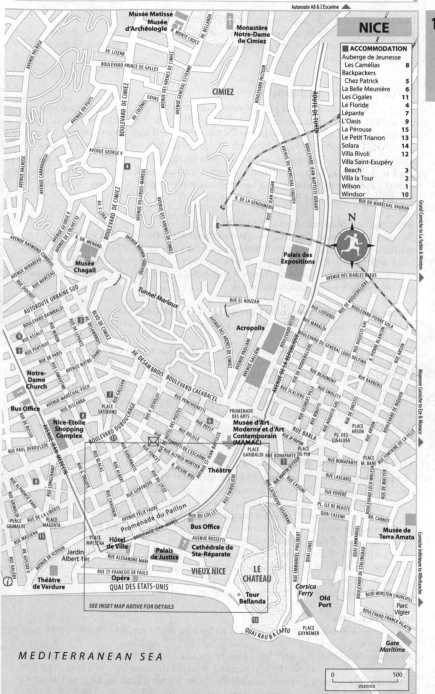

Autoroute A8 & L'Escarène

## NICE

### ACCOMMODATION

| | |
|---|---|
| Auberge de Jeunesse Les Camélias | 8 |
| Backpackers Chez Patrick | 5 |
| La Belle Meunière | 6 |
| Les Cigales | 11 |
| Le Floride | 4 |
| Lépante | 7 |
| L'Oasis | 9 |
| La Pérouse | 15 |
| Le Petit Trianon | 13 |
| Solara | 14 |
| Villa Rivoli | 12 |
| Villa Saint-Exupéry Beach | 3 |
| Villa la Tour | 2 |
| Wilson | 1 |
| Windsor | 10 |

MEDITERRANEAN SEA

0    500
metres

**17**

Lascaris, whose family arms, engraved on the ceiling of the entrance hall, bear the motto "Not even lightning strikes us". It's all very sumptuous, with frescoes, tapestries and chandeliers, along with a five-hundred-strong collection of historic musical instruments.

## Place Masséna and around

Stately, largely pedestrianized **place Masséna** is the city's hub. Built in 1835 across the path of the River Paillon and renovated in 2007, it is graced by seven white resin human figures by Spanish artist Jaume Plensa, suspended high above the ground and illuminated by night. Steps on the south of the square lead to Vieux Nice; the new town lies to the north. Immediately to the west lie the **Jardins Albert-1$^{er}$**, where the Théâtre de Verdure occasionally hosts concerts, including the annual jazz festival; to the east, the **Promenade du Paillon** – a twelve-hectare urban park – follows the course of the river, dividing Vieux Nice from the modern city.

### Avenue Jean-Médecin to rue Masséna

Running north from place Masséna, **avenue Jean-Médecin** is the city's nondescript main shopping street. **Designer** boutiques sit west of place Masséna on rue du Paradis and rue Alphonse-Karr. Both these streets intersect with the pedestrianized **rue Masséna** and the end of **rue de France** – true holiday territory, all ice-cream parlours and big brasseries, and always crammed.

### Musée d'Art Moderne et d'Art Contemporain (MAMAC)

Place Yves-Klein • Tues–Sun: mid-June to mid-Oct 10am–6pm; mid-Oct to mid-June 11am–6pm • €10 • ☎ 04 97 13 42 01, ⓦ mamac-nice.org

The covered course of the Paillon northeast of place Masséna is the site of the city's prestige projects from the 1990s to date. Most appealing of these is the marble **Musée d'Art Moderne et d'Art Contemporain**, or MAMAC, which has rotating exhibitions of avant-garde French and American movements from the 1960s to the present. New Realism (smashing, burning, squashing and wrapping the detritus or mundane objects of everyday life) and Pop Art feature strongly with works by Warhol, Klein, Lichtenstein, César, Arman and Christo.

## The promenade des Anglais

The point where the Paillon flows into the sea marks the beginning of the **promenade des Anglais**, created by nineteenth-century English residents for their afternoon strolls. Today, along with lots of traffic, it boasts some of the most fanciful turn-of-the-twentieth-century architecture on the Côte d'Azur. At nos. 13–15, the Palais de la Méditerranée is once again a luxurious **casino**, though the splendid Art Deco facade is all that remains of the 1930s original.

On 14 July 2016 the promenade was the scene of a terrorist attack in which a truck was driven into the large crowd of people that had gathered to watch the Bastille Day fireworks; 86 people were killed, and over 450 injured. There is currently a temporary memorial in the garden of the Musée Masséna.

### Musée Masséna

65 rue de France/35 promenade des Anglais • Daily except Tues: mid-June to mid-Oct 10am–6pm; mid-Oct to mid-June 11am–6pm • €10 • ☎ 04 93 91 19 10

The **Musée Masséna**, the city's local history museum, charts Nice's development from Napoleonic times up to the 1930s. Housed in a villa that was built at the turn of the twentieth century as a private residence for Prince Victor d'Essling, Duc de Rivoli, it's worth a look to see the sumptuous interior of an aristocratic house from Nice's heyday.

**17**

## NICE BEACHES

The **beach** below the promenade des Anglais is all pebbles and mostly public, with showers provided. It's not particularly clean and you need to watch out for broken glass. There are fifteen private beaches, clustering at the more scenic, eastern end of the bay close to Vieux Nice. If you don't mind rocks, you might want to try the string of coves beyond the port that starts with the **plage de la Réserve**, opposite Parc Vigier (bus #38).

### Musée des Beaux-Arts

33 av des Baumettes • Tues–Sun 10am–6pm • €10 • ☎ 04 92 15 28 28, ⓦ www.musee-beaux-arts-nice.org • Bus #3, #9 #10, #22, stop "Rosa Bonheur"

If you head 1km or so down the promenade from the astonishingly opulent *Negresco Hotel* and head a couple of blocks inland you will come to the **Musée des Beaux-Arts**, where the chief attraction is the collection of 28 works by Raoul Dufy, who is intimately connected with the visual image of Nice.

### Musée International d'Art Naïf Anatole Jakovsky

Château Sainte-Hélène, av de Fabron • Daily except Tues: mid-June to mid-Oct 10am–6pm; mid-Oct to mid-June 11am–6pm • €10 • ☎ 04 93 71 78 33 • Bus #8, #9, #10, #23, #52, stop "Fabron Musée d'Art Naïf"

Continuing southwest along the promenade des Anglais beyond the Musée des Beaux-Arts and towards the airport, you'll come to the **Musée International d'Art Naïf Anatole Jakovsky**, home to a surprisingly good collection of amateur art from around the world.

### Phoenix Parc Floral de Nice and the Musée Départemental des Arts Asiatiques

405 promenade des Anglais • **Park** Daily: April–Sept 9.30am–7.30pm; Oct–March 9.30am–6pm • €5 • ☎ 04 92 29 77 01, ⓦ parc-phoenix.org • **Musée Départemental des Arts Asiatiques** Daily except Tues: July & Aug 10am–6pm; Sept–June 10am–5pm • Free • ☎ 04 92 29 37 00, ⓦ www.arts-asiatiques.com • Bus #9, #10 or #23 from Nice

Right out by the airport, the **Phoenix Parc Floral de Nice** is a cross between a botanical garden, aviary and tacky theme park. The best reason to head out here, however, is to see the **Musée Départemental des Arts Asiatiques**, located in a beautiful building designed by Japanese architect Kenzo Tange, on the edge of the park (but not part of it). It houses a collection of ethnographic artefacts, including silk goods and pottery, as well as traditional and contemporary art.

## Russian Orthodox Cathedral

Av Nicolas-II • Daily: April–Oct 9am–noon & 2–6pm; Nov–May 9.30am–noon & 2–5.30pm • Free • Bus #71, stop "Tzarewitch"

The most exotic of western Nice's flamboyant flights of architectural fancy is the **Russian Orthodox Cathedral**, at the end of avenue Nicolas-II, which runs off boulevard Tsaréwitch. Note that men should not be bare chested, and women should have both head and shoulders covered (scarves can be borrowed near the entrance).

## Cimiez

Bus #15, #17 #20 or #24, stop "Arènes/Musée Matisse"

Packed with vast *belle époque* piles, many of them former hotels, the northern suburb of **Cimiez** has always been posh. The heights of Cimiez were the social centre of the local elite some 1700 years ago, when the town was capital of the Roman province of Alpes-Maritimae. Part of a small amphitheatre still stands, and excavations of the **Roman baths** have revealed enough detail to distinguish the sumptuous and elaborate facilities for the top tax official and his cronies, the plainer public baths and a separate complex for women. All the finds, plus an illustration of the town's history up to the Middle Ages, are displayed in the **Musée d'Archéologie**, 160 av des Arènes de Cimiez (daily

**17**

except Tues: mid-June to mid-Oct 11am–6pm; mid-Oct to mid-June 10am–6pm; €10; ☎04 93 81 59 57).

## Musée Matisse

164 av des Arènes de Cimiez • Daily except Tues: mid-June to mid-Oct 11am–6pm; mid-Oct to mid-June 10am–6pm • €10 • ☎04 93 81 08 08, ⓦ musee-matisse-nice.org

The seventeenth-century villa lying between the Roman excavations and the arena is the **Musée Matisse**. Matisse spent his winters in Nice from 1916 onwards, and then from 1921 to 1938 rented an apartment overlooking place Charles-Félix. It was here that he painted his most sensual, colour-flooded canvases of odalisques posed against exotic draperies. As well as the Mediterranean light, Matisse loved the cosmopolitan aspect of Nice and the presence of fellow artists Renoir, Bonnard and Picasso in neighbouring towns. He died in Cimiez in November 1954, aged 85.

## Jardin du Monastère de Cimiez and around

Place Jean-Paul-II • **Church** Daily except Wed 9am–6pm • Free • **Gardens** Daily 9am–6pm • Free

The Roman remains and the Musée Matisse back onto an old olive grove, at the eastern end of which are the sixteenth-century buildings and exquisite gardens of the **Jardin du Monastère Notre-Dame de Cimiez**. The oratory has brilliant murals illustrating alchemy, while the church houses three masterpieces of medieval painting by Louis and Antoine Bréa. On the north side of the monastery is the **Cemetery** of Cimiez (daily: May–Aug 8am–6.45pm; March, April, Sept & Oct 8am–5.45pm; Nov–Feb 8am–4.45pm); the simple tomb of **Matisse** is signposted on the left-hand side.

## Musée Chagall

Av du Docteur-Ménard • Daily except Tues: May–Oct 10am–6pm; Nov–April 10am–5pm • €8, €10 during temporary exhibitions; free first Sun of month • ☎04 93 53 87 20, ⓦ musee-chagall.fr • Bus #15, stop "Musée Chagall"

At the foot of Cimiez hill, just off boulevard Cimiez, **Chagall's Biblical Message** is housed in a **museum** built specially for the work and opened by the artist in 1972. The rooms are light, white and cool, with windows allowing you to see the greenery of the garden beyond the indescribable shades between pink and red of the five *Song of Songs* canvases. The seventeen paintings of the Biblical Message are all based on the Old Testament and complemented with etchings and engravings.

## ARRIVAL AND DEPARTURE
NICE

**By plane** Aéroport Nice-Côte d'Azur (☎0820 423 333, ⓦ nice.aeroport.fr), which has flights from several regional British airports, New York, Montréal and Paris, is at the western end of the promenade des Anglais. Two fast buses connect with the city: #99 goes to the *gare SNCF* on av Thiers (every 30min between 7.53am and 8.53pm); #98 goes to the *Promenade des Arts* (up to 4 hourly between 5.40am and 11.45pm). For either the fare is €6. Taxis are plentiful and cost about €32 into town. At the time of writing, the second tram line was due to partly open at the end of 2018, which will eventually (hopefully in summer 2019) continue on to the city centre, providing an easy, quick route into the city. For up-to-date information see ⓦ lignesdazur.com.

**By train** Nice's *gare SNCF* (☎36 35) is on av Thiers on the northern edge of the city centre.

Destinations Antibes (up to 5 hourly; 17–21min); Cannes (up to 5 hourly; 24–34min); Marseille (every 30min–2hr; 2hr 35min–2hr 57min); Menton (up to 4 hourly; 30–46min); Monaco (up to 4 hourly; 18–24min); St-Raphaël (every 10min–1hr; 50min–1hr 15min); Sospel (7–11 daily; 48–1hr); Villefranche (up to 4 hourly; 7min).

**By bus** Buses generally pull in along av de Verdun near place Masséna; Menton and Monaco buses arrive at the port.

Destinations Cannes (up to 4 hourly; 1hr 32min); Menton (every 4 hourly; 1hr 10min–1hr 30min); Monaco (up to 4 hourly; 37min); St-Paul-de-Vence (every 30min–1hr; 1hr); Vence (every 30min–1hr; 1hr 10min).

**By ferry** Ferries to Corsica are run by Corsica Ferries, quai du Commerce (☎0825 095 095, ⓦ corsica-ferries.fr).

## GETTING AROUND

**By bus and tram** Buses and trams in Nice and surrounding towns are provided by Lignes d'Azur, whose main office is at 1 rue d'Italie (Mon–Fri 7.30am–7pm, Sat 8.30am–3pm; ☎08 1006 1006, ⓦ lignesdazur.com). A single tramline

## THE CHEMINS DE FER DE PROVENCE

The **Chemins de Fer de Provence** runs one of France's most scenic and fun railway routes, from the Gare de Provence on rue Alfred-Binet (at least 4 daily; 3hr 15min; ⊛ trainprovence. com). The line runs up the Var valley into the hinterland of Nice to Digne-les-Bains, and climbs through spectacular scenery as it goes. There are steam train excursions on Sundays from May to October.

loops in a "V" shape from the northern suburbs through the city centre to the northeastern suburbs; a second east–west line serving the airport is scheduled to start opening at the end of 2018, with full operation (to the city centre) by summer 2019. Buses are frequent until early evening (roughly 8.30–9.40pm), after which five Noctrambus night buses serve most areas from the promenade des Arts next to MAMAC until 1.10am; the tram continues until 1.35am to Henri Sappia and until 1.50am to Hôpital Pasteur. You can buy a single ticket (€1.50) or a day pass (€5) on the bus; ten-journey multipasses (€10) and seven-day passes (€15) are available from *tabacs*, kiosks, newsagents and from Lignes d'Azur offices, where you can also pick up a free route map. You can also buy tickets from machines at tram stops using coins or credit cards.

**By taxi** Central Taxi Riviera (☎ 04 93 13 78 78, ⊛ taxis-nice. fr); Taxis Niçois Indépendents (☎ 04 93 88 25 82).
**By bike** Nice has an on-street bicycle rental scheme, Vélo Bleu (☎ 04 93 72 06 06; ⊛ www.velobleu.org), with 175 rental stations scattered throughout the city, and extending into Cagnes-sur-Mer and St Laurent du Var. You have to sign up online or call toll-free from the bike station (€1.50/day, €5/week), after which the first 30min is free; it costs €1 for the next 30min and €2/hr thereafter. Payment is by credit card. If you want to rent a mountain bike, electric bike, scooter or motorbike, try Holiday Bikes, 34 av Auber (☎ 04 93 16 01 62, ⊛ loca-bike.fr).
**Car rental** Major commercial agencies are based at the airport and *gare SNCF*. You can rent an electric car using the Autobleue rental scheme (⊛ auto-bleue.org; registration fee €24, rates from €0.15/minute).

## INFORMATION

**Tourist office** In front of the *gare SNCF* on av Thiers (June–Sept daily 9am–7pm; Oct–May Mon–Sat 9am–6pm, Sun 10am–5pm; ☎ 04 92 14 46 14, ⊛ en.nicetourisme.com).

There is another branch at 5 promenade des Anglais (June–Sept daily 9am–7pm; Oct–April Mon–Sat 9am–6pm; May Mon–Sat 9am–6pm, Sun 10am–5pm).

## ACCOMMODATION

Sleeping on the beach is illegal and for campsites you'll need to head west to Cagnes-sur-Mer (see page 914).

### HOTELS

**Les Cigales** 16 rue Dalpozzo ☎ 04 97 03 10 70, ⊛ hotel-lescigales.com. Clean, a/c and smart three-star hotel 150m from the promenade des Anglais, with soundproofed en-suite rooms with satellite TV and safe, plus a sun terrace for guests. Good value for the price and location. **€216**
★ **Le Floride** 52 bd de Cimiez ☎ 04 93 53 11 02, ⊛ hotel-floride.fr. Clean, friendly, good-value two-star hotel in Cimiez, with some spacious en-suite doubles and a few cheap singles with WC and shower. Rooms at the front have a/c – those at the shadier back make do with fans. Private parking. Closed mid-Feb to mid-March. **€74**
**Lépante** 6 rue Lépante ☎ 04 93 62 20 55, ⊛ hotellepante. com. Two-star hotel in a central *belle époque* building, with a/c and a first-floor sunny terrace where breakfast is served in fine weather. The elegant, country-style rooms have soundproofing, private bath and free wi-fi. **€101**
★ **L'Oasis** 23 rue Gounod ☎ 04 93 88 12 29, ⊛ hotel niceoasis.com. Tucked off the street in a palm-shaded garden setting, this three-star former Russian guesthouse – Lenin and Chekhov are former guests – has nice, upgraded

a/c rooms, secure private parking (€15/night) and a terrace where you can take breakfast in fine weather. Breakfast €12. **€104**
**La Pérouse** 11 quai Rauba-Capeu ☎ 04 93 62 34 63, ⊛ hotel-la-perouse.com. The best-situated hotel in central Nice, at the foot of Le Château, and with a rooftop pool and fabulous views over the promenade des Anglais and Baie des Anges. Rooms have marble bathrooms and individually controlled a/c. **€247**
**Le Petit Trianon** 11 rue du Paradis ☎ 04 93 87 50 46, ⊛ lepetittrianon.fr. Sweet, if a little old-fashioned, these a/c and soundproofed rooms have a great location in an old apartment block in the pedestrian zone close to the beach. **€110**
**Solara** 7 rue de France ☎ 04 93 88 09 96, ⊛ hotelsolara. com. Simple but attractive and bright a/c rooms on the fourth and fifth floors of a building in the pedestrian shopping area close to the beach, accessed by a tiny lift. Rooms on the fifth floor have balconies. Good value and central. **€90**
**Villa Rivoli** 10 rue Rivoli ☎ 04 93 88 80 25, ⊛ villa-rivoli. com. Sweet hotel in a *belle époque* building a short walk from the promenade des Anglais and beach, with pleasant a/c en-suite rooms with pretty, traditional decor. Some rooms have small balconies; there's free wi-fi. **€109**

17

**Villa la Tour** 4 rue de la Tour ⓣ04 93 80 08 15, ⓦvilla-la-tour.com. Tucked down a side street in Vieux Nice, with charming, themed a/c en-suite rooms with satellite TV and safe, including a few with balconies or views over the city. Room styles (and rates) vary quite widely. There's also a bar/restaurant. €86

**Wilson** 39 rue de l'Hôtel des Postes ⓣ04 93 85 47 79, ⓦhotel-wilson-nice.com. A stylish and gay-friendly budget guesthouse on the third floor in a great location, with individually themed rooms, the cheapest of which have washbasin only. Free wi-fi, but no lift. €50

**Windsor** 11 rue Dalpozzo ⓣ04 93 88 59 35, ⓦwww.hotelwindsorrnice.com. Smart boutique-style and gay-friendly "art hotel" with individually styled rooms, some with frescoes, and many of them quite striking. There's also a spa with sauna and steam bath, and a small pool in a partially shaded garden, overgrown with bamboo. €137

### HOSTELS

**Auberge de Jeunesse Les Camélias** 3 rue Spitalieri ⓣ09 72 35 70 82, ⓦhifrance.org. Very central HI hostel in a fine old villa with a pretty garden tucked behind the Nice Étoile shopping centre, with accommodation in three- to seven-bed dorms, wi-fi, bar, laundry and kitchen facilities. Closed mid-Dec to early Jan. €29.90

**Backpackers Chez Patrick** First floor (the hostel downstairs is nothing to do with them), 32 rue Pertinax ⓣ04 93 80 30 72, ⓦchezpatrick.com. Clean, a/c hostel close to the station. There are no breakfast facilities but there's a fridge, microwave, washing machine, a safe, and no curfew. Accommodation is in four- to six-bed dorms or doubles. Dorms €30, doubles €76

**La Belle Meunière** 21 av Durante ⓣ04 93 88 66 15, ⓦbellemeuniere.com. Efficient, clean and friendly back-packer place in a lovely old bourgeois house, with accommodation in double, twin, triple or four-bed rooms, or dorms that sleep up to five. There's a laundry service, private parking and a terrace at the front; it feels a bit dated in places but it remains a solid, central choice. Dorms €35, doubles €86

★ **Villa Saint-Exupéry Beach** 6 rue Sacha-Guitry ⓣ04 93 16 13 45, ⓦvillahostels.com. Well-equipped, a/c hostel close to place Masséna and Vieux Nice with bar, 24hr gym, movie lounge, secure lockers and free wi-fi. Accommodation is in doubles, twins or private three- or four-bed rooms, or in dorms (sleeping 3–14); there are some women-only dorms. Dorms €42.95, twins €130

## EATING

**Café de Turin** 5 place Garibaldi ⓣ04 93 62 29 52, ⓦcafedeturin.fr. A local institution, the *Café de Turin* dominates one corner of place Garibaldi. The emphasis is on raw seafood, with *panachés* of *fruits de mer* from €37, plus a few shellfish-based cooked options. They don't take reservations, so be prepared to queue. Daily 8am–10pm.

**L'Escalinada** 22 rue Pairolière ⓣ04 93 62 11 71, ⓦescalinada.fr. Good Niçois specialities at this old restaurant at the foot of a stepped side street in Vieux Nice, such as stockfish (a dried fish dish; €26) and courgette fritters (€8); *menu* €26. Service is efficient, but occasionally a bit gruff. Daily 11.30am–3.30pm & 6.30–11.30pm.

★ **Fenocchio** 2 place Rossetti ⓣ04 93 80 72 52, ⓦfenocchio.fr. A firm Vieux Nice favourite, this excellent *glacier* serves a vast range of ice creams, with flavours like salted caramel and violet alongside more familiar offerings. On warm nights, skip the restaurant desserts and head here instead. One scoop €2.50, two €4. They have two other shops, on rue de la Poissonnerie and boulevard Jean-Jaurès (the latter open till 1am). Daily 9am–midnight.

**Le Festival de la Moule** 20 cours Saleya ⓣ04 93 62 02 12. If you like mussels, come to this unpretentious all-you-can-eat *moules-frites* place on cours Saleya. There are various sauces to choose from, and a pot is €14.90 with free refills; they also serve omelettes, salads and fish. Daily except Wed 11am–10pm.

**Le Flaveur** 25 rue Gubernatis ⓣ04 93 62 53 95, ⓦrestaurant-flaveur.com. Stylish restaurant with creative dishes, such as tandoori monkfish with black rice cream or suckling lamb with fennel, that make this a local favourite. *Menus* €89–150. Tues–Fri noon–1.45pm & 7.30–10pm, Sat 7.30–10pm.

★ **Le Frog** 3 rue Milton-Robbins ⓣ04 93 85 85 65, ⓦrestaurantgroupesnice.fr. Quirky, trendy little restaurant close to the opera serving up variations on classic French cooking, including frogs' legs and snails. The *tourte aux blettes* – sweet Swiss chard tart – is seriously good. Formules from €13. Daily: noon–2.30pm & 7–11.30pm.

**Lou Pilha Leva** 10 rue Collet ⓣ04 93 13 99 08. *Socca* fresh from the pan is much the best thing to eat at this rock-bottom street-food place: *socca* costs €2.80, *pissaladière* €3.20, *pan bagnat* (a tuna, olive and salad sandwich) €4.50. You can take away or eat at the benches outside. Daily 11am–10pm.

★ **La Merenda** 4 rue Raoul-Bosio, no phone; ⓦlamerenda.net. Chef Dominique le Stanc quit the Michelin-starred *Chantecler* to cook classic Niçois dishes at this tiny, legendary place in Vieux Nice. *Plats du jour* including *tripes à la niçoise* from €15; stockfish at €23. Cash only. Reserve in advance (in person only). Mon–Fri noon–1.15pm & 7–9pm.

**Mets and Café** 28 rue Assalit ⓣ04 93 80 30 85. Busy budget brasserie close to many of the backpacker hostels, serving up traditional French food and with a €13 lunchtime *formule*. Mon–Sat 11.30am–3pm.

**Pasta Basta** 18 rue de la Préfecture ⓣ04 93 80 03 57. No-frills pasta place with seven types of fresh and two dried pasta varieties and a choice of eighteen sauces. Pasta from €4.60, sauce from €5, and rough wine by the *pichet* from €4.50. Try the *merda de can* (buckwheat gnocchi). Mon–Fri noon–2pm & 7–11pm, Sat noon–11pm, Sun noon–11pm.

★ **Voyageur Nissart** 19 rue d'Alsace-Lorraine ☎ 04 93 82 19 60, ⓦ voyageurnissart.com. Excellent food like

*maman* used to make, in a setting that couldn't be more typically French – chequered tablecloths and all. *Menus* start at €15.90; one focuses on Niçois specialities like *daube* and *petits farcis*. Tues–Fri & Sun noon–2.30pm & 7–10.30pm, Sat 7–10.30pm.

## NIGHTLIFE AND ENTERTAINMENT

Vieux Nice is the centre of Nice's pub and club scene, much of it anglophone in character. As for nightclubs, bouncers judging how much you're going to spend, or exclusive membership lists, are the rule. There are two big casinos – the Casino Barrière Le Ruhl-Nice (1 promenade des Anglais; ☎ 04 97 03 12 22) and the Palais de la Méditerranée (15 promenade des Anglais; ☎ 04 92 14 68 00). Nice's LGBT scene is active, and for LGBT visitors the city has a relaxed feel. The annual Pink Parade takes place in early summer. The Mardi Gras Carnival opens the year's events in February (ⓦ nicecarnaval.com), with the second week of July taken up by the Nice Jazz Festival (ⓦ nicejazzfestival.fr).

### BARS

★ **Le Comptoir Central Électrique** 10 rue Bonaparte ☎ 04 93 14 09 62. Stylishly distressed café/bar in the hip "petit Marais" district, with 1950s furniture, a few tables facing the street, a long list of wines by the glass (€5.50), and cocktails from €9. There's also food. Mon–Sat 8.30am–12.30am, Sun 5pm–12.30am.

★ **Les Distilleries Idéales Blast** 24 rue de la Préfecture ☎ 04 93 62 10 66. Probably the prettiest bar in Vieux Nice, with high vaulted ceilings and a florid, *fin de siècle* steampunk look including wall paintings by a local artist. Charcuterie and cheese platters (€7) help soak up the €9 cocktails. Eight draught beers including two types of Grimbergen; happy hour pints are just €5.10. Daily 9am–12.30am.

**Juke House Café** 8 rue Defly ☎ 04 93 80 02 22. Tiny, American-style cocktail and tapas bar that draws a young crowd. Happy hour is 6–8pm, when cocktails cost €5–6 and draught beers start at €2.50. The food menu is a mix of tapas, burgers and salads, and as the name suggests, there's a jukebox. Tues–Sat 5pm–midnight.

**The Snug** 22 rue Droite ☎ 09 63 08 02 12. Smaller and more low-key than most of Nice's Irish bars, with a friendly,

pubby atmosphere, live music, open-mic night (Mon) and Guinness and Kilkenny to drink (pints €6.50); they also serve food (from €7), including a Sunday roast. Mon–Thurs 4pm–12.30am, Fri 4pm–2am, Sat noon–2am, Sun noon–12.30am.

**Wayne's** 15 rue de la Préfecture, ☎ 04 93 13 46 99, ⓦ waynes.fr. This big, boisterous bar is one of the lynchpins of the Vieux Nice nightlife scene, very popular with anglophone expats and with sport on big-screen TVs plus live rock bands every night. Daily 10am–2am.

### CLUBS AND LIVE MUSIC

**Le Feeling** 14 rue Pertiax ☎ 06 18 44 43 45, ⓦ discotheque-lefeeling.com. Popular club with a relaxed feel, with frequent theme evenings, plus a restaurant that does karaoke. Entrance €10–20. Often open midweek – check website for details. Fri & Sat 8.30pm–5am.

**Glam** 6 rue Eugène-Emmanuel ☎ 04 93 87 29 67, ⓦ leglam.org. Nice's liveliest lesbian and gay club, with guest DJs, a dance and pop-oriented music policy and theme nights ranging from bears to pop. Entry varies but typically €10–15 with a free drink. Fri–Sun 11.50pm–5am.

**High Club** 45 promenade des Anglais ☎ 06 16 95 75 87, ⓦ highclub.fr. Large seafront disco that attracts big-name international DJs and live PAs. There's also an eighties-themed club, *Studio 47*, aimed at the over-25s, plus a LGBT-friendly club, *Sk'High*. Ooccasional free nights, but entrance usually €10. Fri & Sat 11.45pm–6am.

★ **Shapko** 5 rue Rossetti ☎ 09 54 94 69 31, ⓦ shapkobar.fr. Intimate and friendly Vieux Nice music bar on two levels, with a relaxed crowd and eclectic live music, from slap bass jazz to funk and soul; Sunday night is dedicated to Brazilian samba and bossa nova. Live music daily, usually from around 9pm. Daily 6–11.30pm.

## DIRECTORY

**Consulate** Canada, 10 rue Lamartine (☎ 04 93 92 93 22).
**Health** SAMU ☎ 15; Riviera Emergency Medical Services (English-speaking doctors; ☎ 04 93 92 55 55); Hôpital Pasteur, 30 voie Romaine (☎ 04 92 03 77 77).

**Pharmacy** 66 av Jean-Médecin (Mon–Sat 24hr, Sun 7pm–midnight; ☎ 04 93 62 54 44).
**Police** 1 av du Maréchal-Foch (☎ 04 92 17 22 22).

# The Corniches

Three **corniche roads** run east from Nice to the independent principality of Monaco and to Menton, the last town of the French Riviera. Each provides a superb means of

**17**

seeing the most mountainous stretch of the Côte d'Azur. Napoleon built the **Grande Corniche** on the route of the Romans' Via Julia Augusta, and the **Moyenne Corniche** dates from the first quarter of the twentieth century, when aristocratic tourism on the Riviera was already causing congestion on the lower, coastal road, the **Corniche Inférieure**. The upper two are the classic location for car commercials, and for movie car crashes. Real deaths occur too – most notoriously Princess Grace of Monaco – a bitter irony, since the corniches had been the backdrop to one of her greatest film successes, *To Catch a Thief*.

## The Corniche Inférieure

Although buses take all three corniche roads, the train runs only along the lower, **Corniche Inférieure**, and if you don't have your own transport this is the easiest route to take. The attractions include the pretty resorts of **Villefranche-sur-Mer** and **Beaulieu-sur-Mer** and two remarkable villas that hark back to the Riviera's aristocratic heyday.

### Villefranche-sur-Mer

**VILLEFRANCHE-SUR-MER** is on the far side of Mont Alban from Nice. The cruise liners attracted by its beautiful bay can somewhat spoil the ambience, but as long as your visit doesn't coincide with the sudden rush of a shore excursion, the **old town**, with its fishing boats, sixteenth-century citadelle and the covered medieval **rue Obscure** running beneath the houses, is a charming place to while away an afternoon.

#### Chapelle de St-Pierre

Wed–Sun: mid-March to mid-Sept 9.30am–noon & 3–7pm; mid-Sept to mid-March 9.30am–12.30pm & 2–6pm • €3

Villefranche's tiny harbour is overlooked by the medieval **Chapelle de St-Pierre**, decorated by Jean Cocteau in 1957 in shades he described as "ghosts of colours". The drawings portray scenes from the life of St Peter and homages to the women of Villefranche and the gypsies.

#### Villa Éphrussi

Saint-Jean-Cap-Ferrat • Feb–June & Sept–Oct daily 10am–6pm; July & Aug daily 10am–7pm; Nov–Jan Mon–Fri 2–6pm, Sat & Sun 10am–6pm • €14 • ☎ 04 93 01 33 09, ⓦ villa-ephrussi.com

On the main road along the neck of the **Cap Ferrat peninsula**, between Villefranche and Beaulieu, stands the **Villa Éphrussi**, surrounded by elaborate gardens. Built in 1912 for a Rothschild heiress, it overflows with decorative art, paintings, sculpture and artefacts ranging from the fourteenth to the nineteenth centuries, and from European to Far Eastern origins.

#### Villa Kérylos

Impasse Gustave-Eiffel, Beaulieu-sur-Mer • Daily: May–Aug 10am–7pm; Sept–April 10am–5pm • €11.50 • ☎ 04 93 01 01 44, ⓦ villakerylos.fr • The villa is a 5min walk from Beaulieu train station

The main reason to visit attractive, *belle époque* **BEAULIEU-SUR-MER** is the **Villa Kérylos**, a near-perfect reproduction of an ancient Greek villa that's on the seafront, just east of the casino. Théodore Reinach, the archeologist who had it built in 1900, lived here for twenty years, in the manner of an Athenian citizen, taking baths with his male friends and assigning separate suites to women.

## The Moyenne Corniche

Of the three corniche roads east of Nice, the **Moyenne Corniche** is the most photogenic, a real cliff-hanging, car-chase highway. Eleven kilometres from Nice, the medieval village of **ÈZE** winds round its conical rock just below the corniche. No other *village perché* is more infested with pseudo-artisans and others catering to rich tourists, and it requires a major mental feat to recall that the tiny vaulted passages and stairways were designed with defence in mind. At the summit, a cactus garden, the **Jardin Exotique** (daily: July–Sept 9am–7.30pm; Oct–June 9am–4.30/6.30pm; €6; ⓦjardinexotique-eze. fr) covers the site of the former castle.

## The Grande Corniche

At every other turn on the **Grande Corniche**, you're invited to park your car and enjoy a *belvédère*. At certain points, such as **Col d'Èze**, you can turn off upwards for even higher views; bus #82 from Villefranche goes here.

### Trophée d'Auguste

Av Albert-1er, La Turbie • Tues–Sun: mid-May to mid-Sept 9.30am–1pm & 2.30–6.30pm; mid-Sept to mid-May 10am–1.30pm & 2.30–5pm • €6 • ☎ 04 93 41 20 84, ⓦ trophee-auguste.fr• Infrequent buses (#116; 35min) from Nice to La Turbie

Eighteen stunning kilometres from Nice, you reach the village of **LA TURBIE** and its **Trophée d'Auguste**, a huge monument raised in 6 BC to celebrate the subjugation of the tribes of Gaul. Originally a statue of Augustus Caesar stood on the 45m-high plinth, which was pillaged, ransacked for building materials and blown up over the centuries. Painstakingly restored in the 1930s, it now stands statueless, 35m high; viewed from a distance, it still looks imperious.

### Roquebrune

As the Grande Corniche descends towards Cap Martin, it passes the eleventh-century castle of **ROQUEBRUNE**, its village nestling round the base of the rock. The **castle** (June–Sept 10am–1pm & 2.30–7pm; Feb–May daily 10am–12.30pm & 2–6pm; Nov–Jan daily except Fri 10am–12.30pm & 2–5pm; €5) has been kitted out enthusiastically in medieval fashion, while the tiny vaulted passages and stairways of the village are almost too good to be true. One thing that hasn't been restored is the vast millennial **olive tree** that lies just to the east of the village on the chemin de Menton.

### Cap Martin

Southeast of Roquebrune old town is the peninsula of **Cap Martin**, with a **coastal path** giving access to a wonderful shoreline of white rocks, secluded beaches and wind-bent pines. The path is named after **Le Corbusier**, who spent several summers in Roquebrune. He drowned off Cap Martin in 1965 and his grave – designed by himself – is in the **cemetery** (square J near the flagpole), high above the old village. You can also visit his **cabanon** (beach house) and the architect Eileen Gray's stunning 1920s modernist **Villa E-1027** on a guided tour (advance bookings only on ☎06 48 72 90 53 or ⓦcapmoderne.com; €18).

---

## ACCOMMODATION AND EATING

### THE CORNICHE INFÉRIEURE

**La Belle Étoile** 1 rue du Baron-de-Brès, Villefranche-sur-Mer ☎ 04 97 08 0941. The bright white dining room of this tucked-away restaurant creates a bit of an island feel, but the small menu is very much a modern take on traditional French food. Mains from €31. Mon & Wed–Fri 7–9.30pm, Sat noon–1.30pm & 7–9.30pm.

**La Darse** 32 av du Général-de-Gaulle, Villefranche-sur-Mer ☎ 04 93 01 72 54, ⓦ hoteldeladarse.com. Two-star hotel in a charming spot overlooking the nineteenth-century naval harbour, with fourteen a/c rooms, some with sea-facing balconies and some sleeping up to three.

Breakfast €10. Closed mid-Nov to mid-Feb. **€88**

**Le Havre Bleu** 29 bd du Maréchal-Joffre, Beaulieu-sur-Mer ☎04 93 01 01 40, ⓦlehavrebleu.com. Appealing two-star hotel in a lovely blue-shuttered building that feels more tranquil than you'd expect from the location. Rooms are simply furnished and enlivened with bright fabrics, and the best have a private terrace. **€89**

### THE GRANDE CORNICHE

**Café de la Fontaine** 4 av du Général-de-Gaulle, La Turbie ☎04 93 28 52 79. Excellent bistro on the main road through La Turbie, run by the same team as the two-

**17**

Michelin-starred *Hostellerie Jérôme* in the old village and with a chalked-up selection of classic dishes like saddle of rabbit *à la niçoise* or lamb with shallots; main courses from €15. Daily noon–3pm & 7–11pm.

**Les Deux Frères** 1 place des Deux-Frères, Roquebrune ☎ 06 80 86 22 41, ⓦ lesdeuxfreres.com. The best-located hotel in Roquebrune village, worth booking in advance to try to get a sea-view room; there are just eight a/c rooms, varying widely in style and price. The hotel also has a good restaurant with €32 and €53 *menus*. Restaurant Wed–Sun noon–1.30pm & 7.30–9.30pm. €120

# Monaco

Viewed from a distance, there's no mistaking the cluster of towers that is **MONACO**. Postwar redevelopment rescued the tiny principality from economic decline but elbowed aside much of its previous prettiness – not for nothing was **Prince Rainier**, who died in 2005, known as the Prince Bâtisseur ("Prince Builder"). This tiny state, no bigger than London's Hyde Park, retains its comic opera independence: it has been in the hands of the autocratic Grimaldi family since the thirteenth century, and in theory would become part of France were the royal line to die out. Along with its wealth, Monaco latterly acquired a reputation for wheeler-dealer **sleaze**. On his accession in 2005, the US-educated Prince Albert II set about trying to get the principality off an OECD list of uncooperative tax havens, declaring he no longer wished Monaco to be known – in the words of Somerset Maugham – as "a sunny place for shady people".

The oldest part of the principality is **Monaco-Ville**, around the palace on the rocky promontory, with the **Fontvieille** marina in its western shadow. **La Condamine** is the old port on the other side of the promontory; the ugly bathing resort of **Larvotto** extends to the eastern border; and **Monte-Carlo** is in the middle.

One time not to visit is during the Formula 1 **Monaco Grand Prix** in May – no viewpoint is accessible without a ticket and prices soar to ridiculous levels.

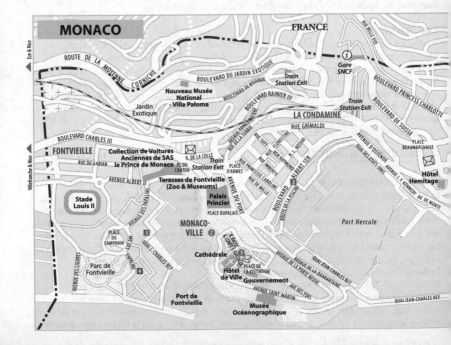

# Monte-Carlo

**MONTE-CARLO** is where the real money is flung about, and its famous **casino** demands to be seen. Adjoining it is the gaudy **opera house**, and around the place du Casino – which has recently seen the completion of a major renovation – are

**17**

> **PHONING MONACO**
> Monaco's international code is 00377 and numbers have eight digits (omit 0 when dialling from outside the principality).

more casinos, palace-hotels and *grands cafés*. Though the hotel around it is being part-demolished and rebuilt, the American Bar of the **Hôtel de Paris** is *the* place for the elite to meet, while the turn-of-the-twentieth-century **Hermitage** has a beautiful Gustave Eiffel iron-and-glass dome.

### Casino de Monte-Carlo

Place du Casino • Daily 9am–noon for tours; gaming starts from 2pm • Morning tour €17; casino entry after 2pm €17; additional €10 for the Salons Privés • ☎ +377 98 06 21 21, ⓦ casinomontecarlo.com• Bus #1or #6

Entrance to **Casino de Monte-Carlo** is restricted to over-18s and you will need ID; dress code is rigid, with shorts and T-shirts frowned upon, and jackets are recommended after 8pm. Photography is prohibited and bags and large coats are checked at the door. The first halls are the **Salle Renaissance** – an anteroom– and the **Salle Europe** where serried ranks of slot machines stand below ceilings of *fin-de-siècle* extravagance, while the more subdued **Salle des Amériques** is devoted to table games – roulette, blackjack and craps. Of the **Salons Privés**, the giddily opulent **Salle Médecin** and the **Salles Touzet** are also devoted to table games; as their name suggests, the **Salons Super Privés** are more intimate, and you won't see them on morning tours.

### Villa Sauber

17 av Princesse-Grace • Daily 10am–6pm • €6, including Villa Paloma • ☎ +377 98 98 91 26 • ⓦ nmnm.mc • Bus #5 or #6

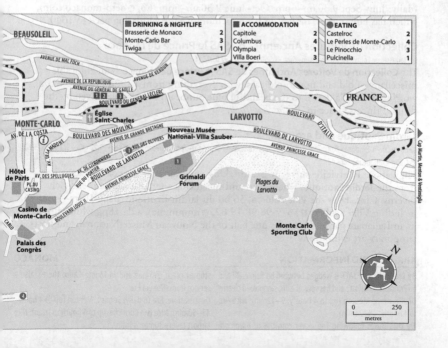

| ■ DRINKING & NIGHTLIFE | | ■ ACCOMMODATION | | ● EATING | |
|---|---|---|---|---|---|
| Brasserie de Monaco | 2 | Capitole | 2 | Castelroc | 2 |
| Monte-Carlo Bar | 3 | Columbus | 4 | Le Perles de Monte-Carlo | 4 |
| Twiga | 1 | Olympia | 1 | Le Pinocchio | 3 |
| | | Villa Boeri | 3 | Pulcinella | 1 |

**17**

The **Villa Sauber** is one of the few surviving *belle époque* villas in the principality, set amid concrete apartment blocks. It comprises one half of the **Nouveau Musée National**, and presents interesting temporary art exhibitions, often on Monaco-related themes.

## Monaco-Ville

The old town of **MONACO-VILLE** (bus #1 or #2) has been spared the developers' worst. On place du Palais you can watch the **changing of the guard** at 11.55am, then take a self-guided tour around the Lilliputian **Palais Princier** (April to mid-Oct daily 10am–6/7pm; €8; ☎+377 93 25 18 31, ⦿palais.mc) – the voice on the audioguide is that of Prince Albert himself. Afterwards, see the tombs of Prince Rainier and Princess Grace in the nineteenth-century **cathedral** (daily 8.30am–6/7pm; free).

### Musée Océanographique

Av Saint-Martin • Daily: April–June & Sept 10am–7pm; July & Aug 9.30am–8pm; Oct–March 10am–6pm • €11–16, depending on season • ☎+377 93 15 36 00, ⦿oceano.org

One of Monaco's best sights is the aquarium in the basement of the imposing **Musée Océanographique**, where the fishy beings outdo the weirdest Kandinsky or Hieronymus Bosch creations. A serious scientific institution as well as a visitor attraction, the museum celebrated its centenary in 2010.

## Fontvieille

**FONTVIEILLE**, below the rock of Monaco-Ville, has a number of interesting museums: the **Musée Naval** (daily 10am–6pm; €4), crammed full with 250 model ships; the **zoological gardens** (March–May 10am–noon & 2–6pm; June–Sept 9am–noon & 2–7pm; Oct–Feb 10am–noon & 2–5pm; €5), with exotic birds, hippopotamuses and lemurs; and the museum of stamps and coins, the **Musée des Timbres et des Monnaies** (daily: July–Sept 9.30am–6pm; Oct–June 9.30am–5pm; €3; ⦿oetp-monaco.com), which has rare stamps, money and commemorative medals dating back to 1640.

### Collection de Voitures Anciennes de SAS le Prince de Monaco

Les Terrasses de Fontvieille • Daily 10am–6pm • €6.50 • ☎+377 92 05 28 56

The **Collection de Voitures Anciennes de SAS le Prince de Monaco** is an enjoyable miscellany of old and not-so-old cars, with everything from a 1928 Hispano-Suiza worthy of Cruella de Vil to the beautiful blue Sunbeam convertible driven by the future Princess Grace in *To Catch a Thief*.

### Jardin Exotique and around

62 bd du Jardin-Exotique • Daily: Feb–April & Oct 9am–6pm, May–Sept 9am–7pm; Nov–Jan 9am–5pm • €7.20 • ☎+377 93 15 29 80, ⦿jardin-exotique.mc • Bus #2

High above Fontvieille there are breathtaking panoramas of the coast as far as Italy from the **Jardin Exotique**, where cacti and succulents alternate with mineral-rich caverns. Close by is the **Villa Paloma**, 56 bd du Jardin-Exotique (daily 10am–6pm; €6, including Villa Sauber; ☎+377 98 98 19 62, ⦿nmnm.mc), a dazzling white villa set in an Italianate garden. It forms one half of the Nouveau Musée National, and hosts temporary art exhibitions.

---

**ARRIVAL AND INFORMATION**                                          **MONACO**

**By train** The *gare SNCF* is wedged between bd Rainier-III and bd Princesse-Charlotte and has several exits, signposted clearly. Destinations Menton (up to 4 hourly; 9–12min); Nice (up to 4 hourly; 18–24min).

**By bus** Buses following the lower corniche or *autoroute* stop at place d'Armes and in Monte-Carlo; there's also a service from Nice via Èze

Destinations Èze (6 daily; 30min); Menton (up to 4 hourly; 45–50min); Nice (via Corniche, up to 4 hourly; 51min); Nice airport (every 30min; 45min).

**Tourist office** 2a bd des Moulins (Mon–Sat 9am–7pm, Sun 11am–1pm; ☏ +377 92 16 61 66, ⊛ visitmonaco.com), with a branch at the *gare SNCF* (Mon–Fri 9am–5.15pm, Sat 10am–5.15pm).

## GETTING AROUND

**By bus** Municipal buses ply the length of the principality from around 7am to just after 9pm (€2 single; one-day pass €5.50; ⊛ cam.mc); after 9pm a single night bus route runs (Mon–Fri until 12.20am; Sat & Sun until 4am).

**By ferry** A ferry (8am–8pm; €1.50) shuttles across the harbour every 20min.

**Lifts** Clean and convenient lifts – marked on the tourist office's map – link the lower and higher streets and can save you a lot of breathless hill climbing.

## ACCOMMODATION

The best area for reasonably priced hotels is Beausoleil, a short walk uphill into France from Monte-Carlo. Monaco has no campsite, and caravans are illegal. Camper vans have to be parked at the Parking des Écoles, in Fontvieille, and even then not overnight.

**Capitole** 19 bd du Général-Leclerc, Beausoleil ☏ +377 04 93 28 65 65, ⊛ hotel-capitole.fr. This three-star hotel is one of Beausoleil's nicest, just 300m from the Casino, with plain but pleasant rooms with a/c, sound-proofing, safe and flatscreen TV. There's a pleasant breakfast room on the ground floor. €199‾

**Colombus** 23 av des Papalins, Fontvieille ☏ +377 04 92 05 90 00, ⊛ columbusmonaco.com. This place overlooks the sea in Fontvieille, and offers boutique hotel comforts in cool shades and natural materials for a fraction of the price of the palace hotels. Rooms are soundproofed, with a/c, and there's a pool and a bar. €289‾

**Olympia** 17bis bd du Général-Leclerc, Beausoleil ☏ +377 04 93 78 12 70, ⊛ olympiahotel.fr. More traditional than its near neighbour *Capitole*, this comfortable three-star hotel in Beausoleil is a good mid-range option. €130‾

**Villa Boeri** 29 bd du Général-Leclerc, Beausoleil ☏ +377 04 93 78 38 10, ⊛ hotelboeri.com. Cheerful and welcoming two-star in Beausoleil with a nice terrace at the front. The a/c rooms are soundproofed, with satellite TV and bath or shower and WC. €120‾

## EATING AND DRINKING

**Castelroc** Place du Palais ☏ +377 93 30 36 68, ⊛ castelrocmonaco.com. Opposite the Palais Princier with a terrace overlooking Fontvieille, this smart restaurant isn't cheap, but it's a good place to sample traditional Monégasque dishes like *barbajuans* – samosa-like triangles stuffed with Swiss chard and cheese (€13.50). *Menus* from €48. Mon & Sun 9am–5pm, Tues–Sat 9am–10pm.

★ **Les Perles de Monte-Carlo** 47 quai Jean-Charles-Rey ☏ +377 97 77 84 31, ⊛ perlesdemontecarlo. com. That this place started life as an oyster farm (which it remains today) alone makes it stand out from the other offerings in Monaco – add to that its position on the tip of a quay in Fontvieille, looking out at the city and its rocky coastline, and the fact that the seating is all outside, and you know you've found somewhere particularly special. Unsurprisingly, oysters are top billing (€25 for twelve with a glass of wine). Reserve ahead. Mon–Sat 8am–5pm, Thurs & Fri 8am–5pm & 8–11pm.

**Le Pinocchio** 30 rue du Comte-Félix-Gastaldi ☏ +377 93 30 96 20, ⊛ lepinocchiomonaco.com. A reliable, good-value Italian in a narrow street in Monaco-Ville dishing up hearty portions from a long menu of antipasti and pasta, including the likes of *saltimbocca* or veal *milanese* from €20 and pasta from €16. Daily noon–2.30pm & 7–10.30pm.

**Pulcinella** 17 rue du Portier ☏ +377 93 30 73 61, ⊛ pulcinella.mc. Traditional Italian restaurant between the Casino and Larvotto beach. The view – of a motorway flyover – isn't the best, but the food is relatively good value for the location. *Spaghetti vongole* €19, risotto with yellow peppers, burrata and prawns €19; more elaborate dishes include fillet of beef (€37). Lunch *formule* €19. Daily noon–2pm & 7.30–11pm.

## DRINKING AND NIGHTLIFE

**Brasserie de Monaco** 36 rte de la Piscine ☏ +377 97 98 51 20, ⊛ brasseriedemonaco.com. Situated on the port and with Monaco's only beer brewed on the premises – including wheat beers and amber ale – this smart place has DJs nightly from 6pm and a burgers-to-salads food menu (mains from €14, pizzas from €10). Pints €7. Daily noon–2am.

**Monte-Carlo Bar** 1 av Prince-Pierre ☏ +377 92 05 73 80, ⊛ montecarlo-bar.com. If you want to drink somewhere that's about as low-key and unpretentious as it gets, this is your place. It's a pretty typical French café, from the lino floor to the red chairs and awning outside; beers start at €14.30, and mains from €11.30. Daily 8am–4pm.

**Twiga** 10 av Princesse-Grace ☏ +377 99 99 25 50, ⊛ twigasumosan.com. This is where to go if you're in Monaco to see and be seen – much loved by the jet-setting crowd (and suitably, can be accessed by boat). There's a stylish contemporary restaurant, a lounge and shisha bar by the water, and an incredibly sleek club that gets going after 1am. Dress to impress. Daily 7pm–3am.

# 17 Menton

Of all the Côte d'Azur resorts, **MENTON**, ringed by mountains, is the warmest and most Italianate, being right on the border. In 1861 a British doctor, James Henry Bennet, published a treatise on the benefits of Menton's mild climate to tuberculosis patients, and soon thousands of well-heeled sufferers were flocking here in the vain hope of a cure. Menton's biggest event of the year is the **Fête du Citron** in February, when the lemon-flavoured bacchanalia includes processions of floats decorated entirely with the fruit.

## Musée Jean Cocteau Collection Séverin Wunderman

2 quai de Monléon • Daily except Tues 10am–6pm • €10 • ☎ 04 89 81 52 50, ⓦ museecocteaumenton.fr

The **promenade du Soleil** runs along the pebbly beachfront of the Baie du Soleil, stretching from the quai Napoléon-III past the casino towards Roquebrune. The most diverting building is the striking new structure opened in 2011 to house the **Musée Jean Cocteau Collection Séverin Wunderman**, which exhibits all facets of the polymath artist's work from before World War I to the 1950s; it also mounts temporary exhibitions. You can also visit the seventeenth-century bastion by the quai Napoléon-III nearby, restored according to Cocteau's plans between 1958 and 1963. It contains ceramics and pictures of his Mentonnais lovers in the *Inamorati* series.

## Église St-Michel and around

**Church** Parvis de la Basilique St-Michel • Mon–Fri 10am–noon & 3–5pm • **Chapel** By arrangement with the tourist office only

As the *quai* bends around the western end of the Baie de Garavan from the Cocteau museum, a long flight of pebbled steps leads up into the **vieille ville** to the **Parvis de la Basilique**, an attractive Italianate square hosting concerts in summer and giving a good view out over the bay. The frontage of the **Église St-Michel** proclaims its Baroque supremacy in perfect pink-and-yellow proportions; climbing a few steps further will reward you with the beautiful facade of the **chapel of the Pénitents-Blancs** in apricot and white.

## The château cemetery

Daily 7am–5pm • Free

Menton's crumbling **cemetery**, at the top of the old town on the site of the town's château, is hauntingly sad – many of the young tuberculosis sufferers who ended their days in Menton are buried here – but also bewitchingly beautiful, with views along the coast into Italy.

## Palais Carnolès

3 av de la Madone • Closed at the time of research for renovation • Bus #7

An impressive collection of paintings from the Middle Ages to the twentieth century are displayed in the slightly crumbly **Palais Carnolès**, the old summer residence of the princes of Monaco; it was closed at the time of research but should reopen during the lifetime of this guide. Of the early works, the *Madonna and Child with St Francis* by Louis Bréa is exceptional. The most recent works include canvases by Graham Sutherland, who spent some of his final years in Menton.

---

**ARRIVAL AND INFORMATION** | **MENTON**

**By train** Menton's *gare SNCF* is at the end of av de la Gare, off av de Verdun/ Boyer, a broad double boulevard that bisects the modern part of town.

Destinations Monaco (up to 4 hourly; 9–12min); Nice (up to 4 hourly; 30–46min).

**By bus** The *gare routière* is north of the *gare SNFC* on av de

Sospel, which is the northern continuation of av de Verdun. Destinations Monaco (up to 4 hourly; 30–46min); Nice (up to 4 hourly; 1hr 10min–1hr 30min); Nice airport (hourly; 1hr 15min).

**Tourist office** 8 av Boyer (July & Aug daily 9am–7pm; Sept–June Mon–Sat 9am–12.30pm & 2–6pm, Sun 2–6pm; ☎04 92 10 50 00, ⓦ menton.fr).

## ACCOMMODATION

★ **Lemon** 10 rue Albert-1er ☎04 93 28 63 63, ⓦ hotel-lemon.com. Appealing budget hotel a couple of minutes' walk from the train station, run by a friendly young couple. Simple but modern en-suite rooms, some with balconies, and a pretty garden. A good choice at the price. **€69**

**Napoléon** 29 porte de France, Baie de Garavan ☎04 93

35 89 50, ⓦ napoleon-menton.com. One of the smartest choices in town, this modern, friendly hotel is right on the seafront between the old town and Italian border, with understated contemporary decor, a pool, gym and stylish, jungly garden on site. **€226**

## EATING AND DRINKING

**Côté Sud** 15 quai Bonaparte ☎06 31 11 48 70, ⓦ cotesud menton.com. One of the more promising budget options facing the port, with stylish modern decor, a vast selection of pizzas from €7.50, pasta and main course salads around €10; meat or fish mains from around €20. Mon–Sat 7pm–midnight, Sun noon–3pm & 7–midnight.

**Fleur de Sel** 48 rue Jules-Guesde ☎03 66 96 06 15. Bright, modern crêperie set a couple of roads back from the sea, with a good range of sweet and savoury options (such as the Savoyard with ham, *jambon cru*, raclette and potato).

The lunchtime *formule* is great value at €14.50. Mon & Tues noon–2pm, Wed–Sat noon–2pm & 7–10pm.

**Mirazur** 30 av Aristide-Briand ☎04 92 41 86 86, ⓦ mirazur.fr. Rising culinary star Mauro Colagreco has bagged two Michelin stars for this swish 1930s-style dining room by the Italian border; it's one of the Riviera's hottest culinary tickets. *Menus* €110–210. Mid-July to Aug Tues 7.15–10.15pm, Wed–Sun 12.15–2.15pm & 7.15–10.15pm; mid-Feb to mid-July & Sept–Oct Wed–Sun 12.15–2.15pm & 7.15–10.15pm.

# Corsica

940 Bastia and around

946 Cap Corse

949 The Nebbio (U Nebbiu)

952 The Balagne (A Balagna)

958 The Réserve Naturelle de
Scandola

960 Porto (Portu) and around

966 Ajaccio (Aiacciu)

972 Le Golfe de Valinco

975 Sartène (Sartè) and
around

977 Bonifacio (Bonifaziu) and
around

982 Porto-Vecchio and around

985 Aléria

986 Corte (Corti) and around

989 Central Corsica

SAILING IN GIROLATA BAY, CORSICA

# Corsica

More than six million people visit Corsica each year, drawn by the mild climate and some of the most diverse landscapes in all Europe. Nowhere in the Mediterranean has beaches finer than the island's perfect half-moon bays of white sand and transparent water, or seascapes more dramatic than the red porphyry Calanches of the west coast. Even though the annual visitor influx now exceeds the island's population nearly twenty times over, tourism hasn't spoilt the place: there are a few resorts, but overdevelopment is rare and high-rise blocks are confined to the main towns.

**Bastia**, capital of the north, was the principal Genoese stronghold, and its fifteenth-century citadelle has survived almost intact. It's first and foremost a Corsican city, and commerce rather than tourism is its main concern. Also relatively undisturbed, the northern Cap Corse harbours inviting sandy coves and fishing villages such as **Macinaggio** and **Centuri-Port**. Within a short distance of Bastia, the fertile region of the Nebbio contains a scattering of churches built by Pisan stoneworkers, the prime example being the Cathédrale de Santa Maria Assunta at the appealingly chic little port of **St-Florent**.

To the west of here, **L'Île-Rousse** and **Calvi**, the latter graced with an impressive citadelle and fabulous sandy beach, are major targets for holiday-makers. The spectacular **Scandola nature reserve** to the southwest of Calvi is most easily visited by boat from the tiny resort of **Porto**, from where walkers can also strike out into the wild **Gorges de Spelunca**. **Corte**, at the heart of Corsica, is the best base for exploring the mountains and gorges of the interior which form part of the **Parc Naturel Régional** that runs almost the entire length of the island.

Sandy beaches and rocky headlands punctuate the west coast all the way down to **Ajaccio**, Napoleon's birthplace and the island's capital, where pavement cafés and palm-lined boulevards teem with tourists in summer. Slightly fewer make it to nearby **Filitosa**, greatest of the many prehistoric sites scattered across the south. **Propriano**, the area's principal resort, lies close to stern **Sartène**, former seat of the wild feudal lords who once ruled this region and still the quintessential Corsican town.

More megalithic sites lie south of Sartène on the way to **Bonifacio**, a comb of ancient buildings perched atop furrowed white cliffs at the southern tip of the island. Equally popular, **Porto-Vecchio** provides a springboard for excursions to the amazing beaches of the south. The eastern plain has less to boast of, but the Roman site at **Aléria** is worth a visit for its excellent museum.

## Brief history

Set on the western Mediterranean trade routes, Corsica has always been of strategic and commercial appeal. Greeks, Carthaginians and Romans came in successive waves, driving native Corsicans into the interior. The Romans were ousted by Vandals, and for the following thirteen centuries the island was attacked, abandoned, settled and sold as a nation state, with generations of islanders fighting against foreign government. In 1768 France bought Corsica from Genoa, but nearly two and half centuries of French rule have had a limited effect and the island's Baroque churches, Genoese fortresses, fervent Catholic rituals and a Tuscan-influenced indigenous language and cuisine show a more profound affinity with Italy.

Corsica's uneasy relationship with the mainland has worsened in recent decades. Economic neglect and the French government's reluctance to encourage Corsican language and culture spawned a nationalist movement in the early 1970s, whose

# Highlights

**❶ Plage de Saleccia** Soft white shell sand, turquoise water and barely a building in sight. See page 952

**❷ Calvi** Corsica's hallmark resort, framed by snow peaks and a spectacular blue gulf. See page 954

**❸ The GR20** Gruelling 170km footpath, which takes in spectacular mountain scenery – but is only for the fit. See page 958

**❹ Girolata** The last fishing village on the island still inaccessible by road, set against a backdrop of red cliffs and dense maquis. See page 959

**❺ Les Calanches de Piana** A mass of terracotta-red porphyry, eroded into dogs' heads, witches and devils. See page 963

**❻ Filitosa menhirs** Among the western Mediterranean's greatest archeological treasures, unique for their carved faces. See page 976

**❼ Boat trips from Bonifacio** Catch a *navette* from the harbour visited by Odysseus for imposing views of the famous chalk cliffs and *haute ville*. See page 982

**❽ Corte** A nationalist stronghold, with loads of eighteenth-century charm and a rugged mountain setting. See page 986

**HIGHLIGHTS ARE MARKED ON THE MAP ON PAGE 938**

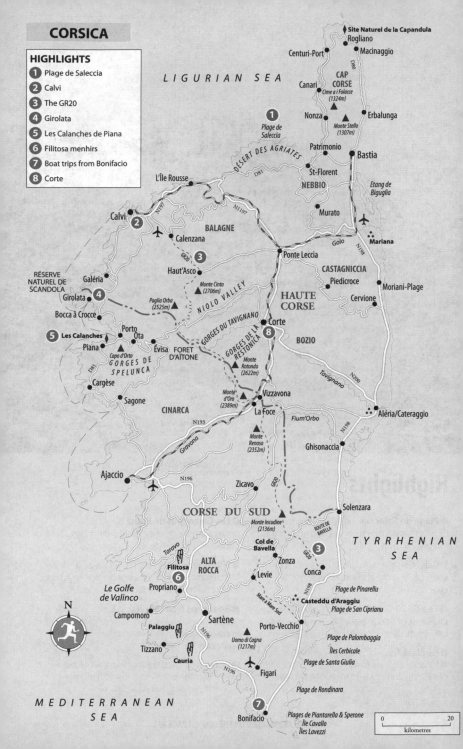

clandestine armed wing – the FLNC (Fronte di Liberazione Nazionale di a Corsica) – and its various offshoots were until recently engaged in a bloody conflict with the state.

Relations between the island's hardline nationalists and Paris may be perennially fraught, but there's little support among ordinary islanders for total independence. Bankrolled by Paris and Brussels, Corsica is the most heavily subsidized region of France. Moreover, Corsicans are exempt from social security contributions and the island as a whole enjoys preferential tax status.

Opinion, however, remains divided on the best way forward for the island. While centre-right parties push for an all-out promotion of tourism as a socio-economic cure-all, local nationalist groups resist large-scale development, claiming it will irrevocably damage the pristine environment visitors come to enjoy. Meanwhile, bombings of second homes – a feature of island life since the 1980s – has given way to a marked increase in assassinations and counter killings, most of them linked to organized crime and corruption rather than feuds between nationalist factions, as in the past. Corsica has the highest per capita murder rate of any European region – a statistic attributed by locals to the failure of the French government to address ingrained social and economic problems, but which has roots deep in the island's cultural DNA.

**18**

The extent to which violence is nowadays a symptom of mob influence rather than part of the liberation struggle was dramatically underlined in June 2014, when the FLNC announced a definitive end to its armed conflict with the French state. The announcement came in the wake of a particularly bloody period for the island, during which several prominent figures, including politicians, lawyers and civil servants, were gunned down.

Mainland politics often seems to bear little reflection of those in Corsica; this was particularly illustrated in the 2017 elections when Macron's landslide victory didn't involve his party gaining a single seat on the island. Instead, its three new MPs were from the Pè a Corsica (For Corsica) alliance, with aims for greater autonomy for the island – though this seems unlikely to happen under Macron. Whether or not this will cause renewed friction in the region remains to be seen.

## THE FOOD AND DRINK OF CORSICA

It's the herbs – thyme, marjoram, basil, fennel and rosemary – of the maquis (the dense, scented scrub covering lowland Corsica) that lend the island's cuisine its distinctive aromas.

You'll find the best **charcuterie** in the hills of the interior, where pork is smoked and cured in the cold cellars of village houses – it's particularly delicious in Castagniccia, where wild pigs feed on the chestnuts which were once the staple diet of the locals. Here you can also taste chestnut fritters (*fritelli a gaju frescu*) and chestnut porridge (*pulenta*) sprinkled with sugar or eau de vie. **Brocciu**, a soft mozzarella-like cheese made with ewe's milk, is found everywhere on the island, forming the basis for many dishes, including omelettes and cannelloni. *Fromage corse* is also very good – a hard **cheese** made in the sheep- and goat-rearing central regions, where *cabrettu à l'istrettu* (kid stew) is a speciality.

**Game** – mainly stews of hare and wild boar but also roast woodcock, partridge and wood pigeon – features throughout the island's mountain and forested regions. Here blackbirds (*merles*) are made into a fragrant pâté, and eel and trout are fished from the unpolluted rivers. **Sea fish** like red mullet (*rouget*), bream (*loup de mer*) and a great variety of shellfish is eaten along the coast – the best crayfish (*langouste*) comes from around the Golfe de St-Florent, whereas oysters (*huîtres*) and mussels (*moules*) are a speciality of the eastern plain.

Corsica produces some excellent, and still little-known, **wines**, mostly from indigenous vine stocks that yield distinctive, herb-tinged aromas. Names to look out for include: Domaine Torraccia (Porto-Vecchio); Domaine Fiumicicoli (Sartène); Domaine Saparale (Sartène); Domaine Gentille (Patrimonio); Domaine Leccia (Patrimonio); and Venturi-Pieretti (Cap Corse). In addition to the usual whites, reds and rosés, the last of these makes the sweet muscat for which Cap Corse was renowned in previous centuries. Another popular aperitif is the drink known as Cap Corse, a fortified wine flavoured with quinine and herbs. Note that **tap water** is particularly good quality in Corsica, coming from the fresh mountain streams.

Corsica's troubled underbelly, however, is largely invisible to visitors. Political graffiti and bullet-scarred signposts, which used to be ubiquitous, are fast becoming a thing of the past, while the drive-by shootings and mafia assassinations which dominate the local press tend to occur well away from the resorts.

## GETTING THERE

### BY FERRY
Four companies run services between the mainland and Corsica: Corsica Ferries (ⓦ corsica-ferries.fr; from Nice and Toulon), Corsica Linea (ⓦ corsicalinea.com; from Marseille), La Méridionale (ⓦ lameridionale.fr; from Marseille) and Moby (ⓦ mobylines.com; from Nice). Journeys take between five and twelve hours on either regular ferries or much faster giant hydrofoils ("NGV", or *navire à grande vitesse*). Corsica Ferries, Corsica Linea and Moby also run services to various Italian ports (including to Sardinia).
**Fares** Fares fluctuate according to the season, with the lowest between October and May; during July and August ticket prices sometimes more than treble. A one-way crossing for a foot passenger costs anything from €30.50 to €75 per person, plus €60 to €250 per vehicle, depending on the date of the journey.
**Tickets** Ferry tickets for all companies can be booked via

their websites. Note that reservations are essential for journeys in July and August.

### BY AIR
Direct flights to Corsica depart from several major French cities, including Paris, Marseille, Lyon and Nice. The largest operators are Air France (ⓦ airfrance.co.uk) and Air Corsica (ⓦ aircorsica.com), who fly to Bastia, Ajaccio, Calvi and Figari year-round. In addition, easyJet (ⓦ easyjet.com) fly daily from Paris to Bastia and Ajaccio, Ryanair (ⓦ ryanair. com) fly daily to Figari from Paris, Transavia (ⓦ transavia. com) fly from Nantes to Ajaccio three times weekly and XL Airways (ⓦ xlairways.com) fly to Figari during the summer season from Paris CDG.
**Fares** Return fares start at around €100 low season with easyJet, and peak at around €440 for weekend departures with Air France in July and August.

## GETTING AROUND

### BY CAR
With public transport woefully inadequate, the most convenient way of getting around Corsica is by rental car. All the big firms have offices at airports and towns across the island, allowing you to collect and return vehicles in different places. Even if your budget won't stretch to a week, it's worth renting for a couple of days to explore remote beaches and the back roads of the interior.

### BY BUS
Bus services have massively reduced across the island in recent years, with several lines stopping altogether. Expect a couple of daily services to major destinations out of Bastia and Ajaccio, and along the east coast to Porto-Vecchio and Bonifacio; elsewhere in the island, services tend to peter out in the winter months or are even more infrequent. Getting accurate timetable information for bus services can also be difficult – the best way to check information is at a tourist office or, better still, online at ⓦ corsicabus.org.
**Fares and timetables** Prices are reasonable: tickets for

the 2hr trip between Bastia and Calvi cost €16. Rundowns of journey times and frequencies appear in the relevant accounts throughout this chapter.

### BY TRAIN
Corsica's diminutive train, the recently revamped *Micheline* or *Trinighellu* (little train; ⓦ cf-corse.fr), travels through the mountains from Ajaccio to Bastia via Corte, with a branch line running northwest to Calvi. Thanks to new trains over the last few years, journeys are now more comfortable (and smoother) than ever – though unfortunately no quicker.
**Fares and timetables** A single journey between Bastia and Ajaccio costs €25 (note that bus services along this route were suspended indefinitely in the summer of 2015 due to competition from the railway). If you are planning on travelling a fair bit by train, you might consider the seven-day Carte Zoom (€50). Again, timetable information and fares appear on ⓦ corsicabus.org, though they no longer seem to be regularly updated.

# Bastia and around

The dominant tone of Corsica's most successful commercial town, **BASTIA**, is one of charismatic dereliction, as the city's industrial zone is spread onto the lowlands to the south, leaving the centre of town with plenty of aged charm. The old quarter, known as the Terra Vecchia, comprises a tightly packed network of haphazard streets, flamboyant Baroque churches and lofty tenements, their crumbling golden-grey walls set against a backdrop of maquis-covered hills.

The city dates from Roman times, when a base was set up at Biguglia to the south, beside a freshwater lagoon. Little remains of the former colony, but the site merits a day-trip for the well-preserved pair of Pisan churches at Mariana, rising from the southern fringes of Poretta airport. Bastia began to thrive under the Genoese, when wine was exported to the Italian mainland from Porto Cardo, forerunner of Bastia's Vieux Port, or Terra Vecchia. Despite the fact that in 1811 Napoleon appointed Ajaccio capital of the island, initiating a rivalry between the two towns which exists to this day, Bastia soon established a stronger trading position with mainland France. The Nouveau Port, created in 1862 to cope with the increasing traffic with France and Italy, became the mainstay of the local economy, exporting chiefly agricultural products from Cap Corse, Balagne and the eastern plain.

The centre of Bastia is not especially large, and all its sights can easily be seen in a day without the use of a car. The spacious **place St-Nicolas** is the obvious place to get your bearings: open towards the sea and lined with shady trees and cafés, it's the main focus of town life. Running parallel to it on the landward side are boulevard Paoli and rue César-Campinchi, the two main shopping streets, but all Bastia's historic sights lie within **Terra Vecchia**, the old quarter immediately south of place St-Nicolas, and **Terra Nova**, the area surrounding the citadelle. Tucked away below the imposing, honey-coloured bastion is the much-photographed **Vieux Port**, with its boat-choked marina encircled by crumbling eighteenth-century tenement buildings.

## Terra Vecchia

From place St-Nicolas the main route into Terra Vecchia is **rue Napoléon**, a narrow street with some ancient offbeat shops and a pair of sumptuously decorated chapels on its east side. The first of these, the **Oratoire de St-Roch**, is a Genoese Baroque extravagance built in 1604, with walls of finely carved wooden panelling and a magnificent gilt organ.

### Oratoire de L'Immaculée Conception

The **Oratoire de L'Immaculée Conception** was built in 1609 as the showplace of the Genoese in Corsica, who used it for state occasions. The austere white-marble facade belies a flamboyant interior of gilt and velvet, whose centrepiece (behind the High Altar) is a copy of Bartolomé Esteban Murillo's celebrated depiction of the Immaculate Conception (the original hangs in Madrid's El Prado museum). During the British rule of the island in 1795, the chapel was used as the seat of the regional parliament.

### Place du Marché

The **place de l'Hôtel-de-Ville**, to the rear of the Oratoire de L'Immaculée Conception, is commonly known as **place du Marché** after the lively farmers' market that takes place here each morning, from around 7am until 2pm. Dominating the south end of the square is the **church of St-Jean-Baptiste**, an immense ochre edifice that dominates the Vieux Port. Its twin campaniles are iconic of the city, but the interior – a Rococo overkill of multicoloured marble – is less impressive.

### Vieux Port

The oldest and most photogenic part of Bastia is the **Vieux Port** – a secretive zone of dark alleys, vaulted passageways and seven-storey houses packed around the base of the church of St-Jean-Baptiste. Site of the original Roman settlement of Porto Cardo, the harbour later bustled with Genoese traders, but since the building of the ferry terminal and commercial docks to the north it has become a backwater.

18

▲ 1 & Cap Corse

## BASTIA

0        100
metres

AVENUE EMILE SARI

RUE DU COMM LUCE DE CASABIANCA

RUE CHANOINE LESCHI

North Ferry
Terminal

Préfecture

BOULEVARD GÉNÉRAL GRAZIANI

RUE CÉSAR CAMPINCHI

Objectif
Nature

RUE CHANOINE LESCHI

RUE DU NOUVEAU PORT

Nouveau
Port

Airport
Bus Stop

SQ
ST-VICTOR

Jetée St-Nicolas

& St-Florent

Gare
SNCF

ROND-
POINT
LECLERC

AV. MAL SÉBASTIANI

Gare
Routière

South Ferry
Terminal

3  Buses to Aléria,
Porto-Vecchio,
Bonifacio

RUE G PÉRI

AV. F. PIETRI

i

Buses
to Calvi

4

1

RUE CONVENTIONNEL
SALICETI

PLACE
SAINT-
NICOLAS

VOIE RAPIDE
PROMENADE DES QUAIS

BOULEVARD GEN DE GAULLE

RUE CÉSAR CAMPINCHI

BOULEVARD PAOLI

5

RUE MIOT

CHEMIN DE L'HÔPITAL MILITAIRE

RUE NAPOLÉON

1

Oratoire de
St-Roch

QUAI DES MARTYRS DE LA LIBERATION

Théâtre

BOULEVARD GÉNÉRAL GIRAUD

RUE FAVALELLI

RUE CÉSAR CAMPINCHI

Oratoire de
l'Immaculée
Conception

RUE COMMANDANT-MÈGRE

TERRA
VECCHIA

RUE DES TERRASSES

3

PLACE DE
L'HÔTEL DE VILLE

2

St-Jean-
Baptiste

BOULEVARD PAOLI

6

RUE GEN CARBUCCIA

5

Vieux
Port

VOIE RAPIDE

St-
Charles

RUE DU COLLE

QUAI DU SUD

Palais
de Justice

BOULEVARD AUGUSTE GAUDIN

Jardin
Romieu

Tunnel

Jetée
du Dragon

Oratoire de Monserato

Porte Louis-XVI

CHEMIN DES FILLIPINES

Palais des
Gouverneurs
(Bastia Museum)

PLACE DU
DONJON

7

TERRA
NOVA

4

PLACE
GUASCO

Jardin
Romieu

Oratoire
Ste-Croix

Ste-Marie

PLACE
D'ARMES

Citadelle

N

VOIE RAPIDE

▼ 2 , La Marana, Étang de Biguglia, Poretta Airport, Corte, Porto-Vecchio, Bonifacio & Ajaccio

### ● SHOPPING
| | |
|---|---|
| Chez Mireille | 2 |
| Mattei | 1 |

### ■ ACCOMMODATION
| | |
|---|---|
| Best Western | 2 |
| Central | 5 |
| Napoléon | 4 |
| Les Orangers | 1 |
| Du Palais | 6 |
| Les Voyageurs | 3 |

### ● EATING
| | |
|---|---|
| A Casarella | 7 |
| A Tana | 3 |
| Chez Huguette | 5 |
| Glacier Raugi | 1 |
| Palais des Glaces | 2 |
| Le Petit Vincent | 6 |
| La Table du Marché | 4 |

### ■ DRINKING & NIGHTLIFE
| | |
|---|---|
| L'Empire Bar | 1 |
| La Madrague Club | 2 |

## Terra Nova

The military and administrative core of old Bastia, **Terra Nova** (or the citadelle) is focused on **place du Donjon**, which gets its name from the squat round tower that formed the nucleus of Bastia's fortifications: it was used by the Genoese to incarcerate Corsican patriots, among them the nationalist rebel Sampiero Corso in 1657, who was held in the dungeon for four years.

### Palais des Gouverneurs

**Musée de Bastia** May–June & Sept Tues–Sun 10am–6.30pm; July & Aug daily 10am–6.30pm; Oct–April Tues–Sat 9am–noon & 2–5pm • €5 • ☎ 04 95 31 09 12, ⓦ musee-bastia.com

Facing the place du Donjon is the impressive fourteenth-century **Palais des Gouverneurs**, a building with a distinctly Moorish feel originally built for the Genoese governor and bishop. It became a prison after the French transferred the capital to Ajaccio, and was then destroyed during a British attack of 1794 (in which an ambitious young captain named Horatio Nelson played a decisive part). The subsequent rebuilding was not the last, as parts of it were mistakenly blown up by American B-52s in the bungled attack of 1943 which devastated the city centre on the day after the island's liberation. Today, the Palais hosts the state-of-the-art **Musée de Bastia**, which charts the city's evolution as a trade and artistic centre. Its collection includes part of Cardinal Fesch's famous hoard of Renaissance art (see page 969).

### Église Ste-Marie and Oratoire Sainte-Croix

If you cross the place du Donjon and follow rue Notre-Dame you come out at the **Église Ste-Marie**. Built in 1458 and overhauled in the seventeenth century, the church was the cathedral of Bastia until 1801, when the bishopric was transferred to Ajaccio. Inside, its principal treasure is a small silver statue of the Virgin (housed in a glass case on the right wall as you face the altar), which is carried through Terra Nova and Terra Vecchia on August 15, the Festival of the Assumption. Immediately behind Ste-Maire in rue de l'Évêché stands the **Oratoire Sainte-Croix**, a sixteenth-century chapel decorated in Louis XV style, with lashings of rich blue paint and gilt scrollwork. It houses another holy item, the *Christ des Miracles*, a blackened oak crucifix much venerated by Bastia's fishermen.

## L'Oratoire de Monserato

One of Bastia's most extraordinary monuments, the **Oratoire de Monserato**, lies a pleasant two-kilometre uphill walk from the town centre. The building itself looks unremarkable from the outside, but its interior houses the much-revered **Scala Santa**, a replica of the Holy Steps of the Basilica of Saint John of Lateran in Rome. Penitents who ascend it on their knees as far as its high altar may be cleansed, or so it is believed, of all sins, without the intercession of a priest.

### ARRIVAL AND DEPARTURE | BASTIA

#### BY FERRY

**Nouveau Port** All ferries arrive and depart from the Nouveau Port, just a five-minute walk from place St-Nicolas and the centre of town. Toilet facilities are inside the South Terminal, where there's a left luggage counter (*consigne*). Taxis queue outside at disembarkations times.

**Ferry offices** Corsica Ferries, av Pascal Lota, ☎ 04 95 32 95 95, ⓦ corsicaferries.com; Corsica Linea, Nouveau Port ☎ 08 25 88 80 88, ⓦ corsicalinea.com; Moby, 1 rue du Commandant Luce-de-Casabianca ☎ 04 95 34 84 94,

ⓦ mobylines.com; La Méridionale, Port de Commerce ☎ 09 70 83 20 20, ⓦ lameridionale.fr.

#### BY PLANE

Bastia's Poretta airport (☎ 04 95 54 54 54, ⓦ bastia. aeroport.fr) is 16km south of town, just off the route nationale (N193). Shuttle buses to and from the centre coincide with flights; the stop at the airport (marked by a single post with a small timetable on it) is easy to miss – it stands immediately outside the terminal concourse, 20m

**18**

from the exit. Tickets cost €9. You can be dropped at the north side of place du Maréchal-Leclerc, across the square from the train station. This is also the departure points for travellers heading in the other direction (ie, out to the airport). Taxis charge a hefty €48/66 (Mon–Fri day/Sun & evenings after 7pm) for the 20–30min trip.

### BY BUS

Bastia doesn't have a proper bus station, which can cause confusion, with services arriving and departing from different locations around the north side of the main square. Roughly speaking, services to smaller, rural destinations – including Cap Corse and St-Florent – operate out of the *gare routière*, at the north end of place St-Nicolas behind the

*hôtel de ville*. Buses for Bonifacio, Porto-Vecchio and services to the east coast can be picked up outside the Rapides Bleus office, at the roadside opposite the main post office on av du Maréchal-Sébastiani. Services for Calvi via L'Île Rousse depart from outside the train station. Departure points are marked on our map, but should be checked in advance at the tourist office. Note that bus services from Bastia have greatly reduced over recent years, a pattern that is likely to continue.

Destinations Aléria/Cateraggio (2–3 daily; 1hr 20min); Calvi (1–2 daily; 2hr); Erbalunga (daily; 30–50mins); L'Île Rousse (1–2 daily; 1hr 30min); Porto-Vecchio (2 daily; 2hr 50min); St-Florent (2–3 daily; 45min).

### INFORMATION

**Tourist office** At the north end of place St-Nicolas (June to mid-Sept daily 8am–8pm; mid-Sept to May Mon–Fri 8.30am–6pm, Sat 9am–6pm; ☎04 95 54 20 40, ⊛bastia-tourisme.com), but don't expect advice about other parts of the island; the staff are basically there to hand out glossy

leaflets, bus timetables and free fold-out maps, nothing more. **Health Centre** Centre Hospitalier de Bastia, Furiani ☎04 95 59 11 11.

**Left luggage** The Nouveau Port terminal has a small *consigne*.

### GETTING AROUND

**Taxis** There are ranks outside the *gare routière*, train station and Nouveau Port. Otherwise call direct: Bleus Bastiais (☎04 95 32 70 70); VTC 2B (☎06 22 33 27 60).
**Bike rental** Bike-Rental-Corsica.com hires out a variety of bikes (from e-bikes to mountain bikes, plus motorbikes and scooters) and can deliver them straight to your hotel or even

the airport (☎04 95 44 49 67, ⊛bike-rental-corsica.com).
**Car rental** Avis 1bis rue José-Luccioni, ☎04 95 31 95 64, airport ☎04 95 54 55 46; Europcar, 3 rue du Chanoine-Leschi ☎04 95 31 59 29, airport ☎04 95 30 09 50; Hertz, Immeuble Novelty, av Pierre-Giudicelli ☎04 95 31 14 24, airport ☎04 95 30 05 00.

### ACCOMMODATION

**Best Western** Av Jean-Zuccarelli ☎04 95 55 05 10, ⊛corsica-hotels.fr. Hardly the most characterful option, but the location (on the hill above town) is attractive, and rooms are bright an spacious, if a tad overpriced. Central a/c. **€170**
★ **Central** 3 rue Miot ☎04 95 31 71 12, ⊛centralhotel. fr. Eighteen pleasantly furnished rooms (plus a handful of larger studios), with textured walls and sparkling bathrooms, just off the southwest corner of place St-Nicolas. By far the most pleasant and best-value place to stay in the centre. Advance reservation essential. **€120**
**Napoléon** 43/45 bd Paoli ☎04 95 31 60 30, ⊛hotel-napoleon-bastia.fr. Smart – if a little basic – two-star in a central location. The rooms have small fridges and effective a/c. Welcoming management by Bastia standards. Copious breakfasts included. **€95**
**Les Orangers** Miomo, 5km north of town ☎04 95 33

24 09, ⊛camping-lesorangers.com. The most convenient campsite if you're relying on public transport; frequent buses leave from the top of place St-Nicolas opposite the tourist office. Set among eucalyptus, its just a short walk to the beach and has a small pool. Closed Nov–March. **€28**
**Du Palais** 2 bd Paoli ☎04 95 31 06 94, ⊛hotel-palais-bastia-centre.com. Pleasant hotel in a central location, offering bright, contemporary rooms of varying sizes. Ask for a room at the back if you are a light sleeper. The quadruple rooms are good value for families. **€70**
**Les Voyageurs** 9 av du Maréchal-Sébastiani ☎04 95 34 90 80, ⊛hotel-lesvoyageurs-bastia.com. Smart three-star near the train station, with friendly staff and rooms decorated with striking, bright photography and other artwork. The larger, more expensive ones have baths instead of showers. No views to speak of, but fine for a night or two. Secure parking (€7) and central a/c. **€115**

### EATING, DRINKING & NIGHTLIFE

Lined with smart café-restaurants, place St-Nicolas is the place to be during the day, particularly between noon and 3pm, when the rest of town is deserted. Along boulevard Paoli and rue César-Campinchi, chi-chi *salons de thé* offer

elaborate patisseries, local chestnut flan and doughnuts (*beignets*). The Casanis factory is on the outskirts in Lupino, so *pastis* is indisputably the town's tipple – order a "Casa" and you'll fit in well. A couple of cheesy discos, and unwelcoming bars, offer some nightlife, but you'll have to search hard for a crowded venue outside weekends in summer. The best source of information about all events is the daily local paper *Corse-Matin* (ⓦ corsematin.com).

## CAFÉS AND RESTAURANTS

★ **A Casarella** 6 rue Ste-Croix ☎ 04 95 32 02 32. Innovative Corsican-French cuisine served on a terrace on the edge of the citadelle. The chef's specialities are traditional dishes of the Balagne, such as *casgiate* (nuggets of fresh cheese baked in fragrant chestnut leaves) or the rarely prepared *storzapretti* – balls of brocciu, spinach and herbs in tomato sauce. Mains from around €20. April–Nov daily noon–2.30pm & 6.30pm–midnight; closed Dec–March.

**A Tana** 22 rue Posta Vecchia ☎ 04 95 38 71 18. Just west of the quai des Martyrs, this unpretentious Italian restaurant serves up excellent and reasonably priced dishes in a convivial atmosphere. Pizzas from €14.50, pasta from €16. Mon–Sat noon–2.30pm & 7.30–10.30pm.

**Chez Huguette** Rue de la Marine, Vieux Port ☎ 04 95 31 37 60, ⓦ chezhuguette.fr. A cut above the competition on the Vieux Port, this place should be your first choice if you want to splash out on seafood to remember. The location on the quayside, facing St-Jean-Baptiste, is perfect, and the cooking sublime, from the Étang de Diane oysters to their impeccably fresh catch of day and – if you're really not counting your euros – their exquisite Cap Corse lobster, which could set you back as much as €200 for a large one (for two). Otherwise, mains start around a more reasonable €22. Reservation recommended. Daily 11.30am–2.25pm & 6.30–10.30pm.

**Glacier Raugi** 2bis rue du Chanoine-Colombani ☎ 04 95 31 22 31. Corsica's greatest ice-cream maker, from an illustrious line of local *glaciers*. They also serve pizzas, but skip the savoury food for the desserts (from €4) or simply get a cone to take away and enjoy by the sea. Mon–Sat 9.30am–midnight, Sun 9am–1pm & 4pm–midnight.

★ **Palais des Glaces** Place St-Nicolas ☎ 04 95 31 05 01, ⓦ lepalaisdesglaces.com. One of the few dependable lunch spots on the main square, frequented as much by Bastiais as visitors. Mains start at €14.50 and include wok-fried prawns or grilled swordfish, served under swish awnings beneath the plane trees. Daily 6am–midnight.

**Le Petit Vincent** Rue du Dragon ☎ 04 20 00 14 67. In an elevated position in the Terra Nova, with a glorious terrace overlooking the sea, this little restaurant is a delight. Expect a mix of Provençal and Asian flavours on the menu, such as *pissaladière*, or beef fillet in satay sauce. Mains from €19. Mon 6.30–11pm, Tues–Sat noon–2.30pm & 6.30–11pm.

**La Table du Marché** Place du Marché ☎ 04 95 31 64 25. Offering far better value than most places on the nearby Vieux Port, this smart terrace restaurant serves a tempting €32 *menu régional* featuring local crayfish, east-coast oysters and *filets de St-Pierre*. The à la carte menu is dominated by fancier gastro seafood, and is much more expensive. Mon–Sat noon–2pm & 7–10pm, plus Sun in July & Aug.

## BARS AND CLUBS

**L'Empire-Bar** 21 rue Napoléon ☎ 04 20 04 53 37. Classy but unpretentious bar in a good location, which is especially popular on weekend evenings. Decent wines on offer, but even better cocktails. Tues–Sat noon–2pm & 7–10.30pm, Sun noon–2pm.

**La Madrague Club** Lucciani, 10km south of Bastia on the airport road ☎ 04 95 30 02 50. This is currently the only *boîte* (club) of note in the city. It attracts a fairly young crowd, and you'll need a car to get there. Entry is €15 including a drink. Fri & Sat 10pm–late.

## SHOPPING

**Chez Mireille** 5 rue des Terrasses ☎ 04 95 32 41 05. A Bastiais institution for decades, this small family-run deli sells a selection of wonderful Castagniccian specialities, such as traditional *canistrelli* biscuits baked with lemon and white wine, and perfect *fiadone*. Tues–Sat 9am–1pm & 3–7.30pm.

**Mattei** Bd du Général-de-Gaulle ☎ 04 95 32 44 68. The wonderful Art Deco facade of this established wine merchants hints at the institution that it is. In addition to wine, they sell liqueurs from all over the island, including the famous local quinine-based aperitif, Cap Corse, which they bottle themselves. Daily 10am–8pm.

# South of Bastia

Fed by the rivers Bevinco and Golo, the **ÉTANG DE BIGUGLIA**, to the south of the city, is the largest lagoon in Corsica, and one of its best sites for rare migrant birds. The Roman town of **MARIANA**, on the southern shore of the *étang*, can be approached by taking the turning for Poretta airport, 16km along the N193, or the more scenic coastal route through **LA MARANA**. Mariana was founded in 93 BC as a military colony, but today's houses, baths and basilica are too ruined to be of great interest. It's only the square baptistry, with its remarkable mosaic floor decorated with dancing dolphins and fish looped around bearded figures representing the four rivers of paradise, that warrants a detour.

**18**

Adjacent to Mariana stands the **church of Santa Maria Assunta**, known as **La Canonica**. Built in 1119 close to the old capital of Biguglia, it's the finest of around three hundred churches built by the Pisans in their effort to evangelize the island. Modelled on a Roman basilica, the perfectly proportioned edifice is decorated outside with Corinthian capitals plundered from the main Mariana site and with plates of Cap Corse marble. Another ancient church, **San Parteo**, built in the eleventh and twelfth centuries, stands 300m further south.

**18**

# Cap Corse

Until Napoléon III had a coach road built around **Cap Corse** in the nineteenth century, the promontory was effectively cut off from the rest of the island, and relied on Italian maritime traffic for its income – hence its distinctive Tuscan dialect. Many Capicursini later left to seek their fortunes in the colonies of the Caribbean, which explains the distinctly ostentatious mansions, or *palazzi*, built by the successful émigrés (nicknamed "les Américains") on their return. For all the changes brought by the modern world, Cap Corse still feels like a separate country, with wild flowers in profusion, vineyards and quiet, traditional fishing villages.

Forty kilometres long and only fifteen across, the peninsula is divided by a spine of mountains called the Serra, which peaks at **Cima di e Folicce**, 1324m above sea level. The coast on the east side of this divide is characterized by tiny ports, or *marines*, tucked into gently sloping river-mouths, alongside coves which become sandier as you go further north. The villages of the western coast are sited on rugged cliffs, high above the rough sea and tiny rocky inlets that can be glimpsed from the corniche road.

## GETTING AROUND — CAP CORSE

**By bus** The villages of Macinaggio and Pietracorbara are connected to Bastia's *gare routière* by bus. During the summer, there are usually three departures a day (in both directions; Mon–Sat), but from September to June this drops to just one a day (Mon–Fri only), departing Macinaggio at 6.30am and Pietracorbara 15 minutes later, then returning north in the evening from Bastia at 6pm. More frequent services run between Erbalunga and Bastia (Mon–Sat; 20min). It's advisable to check all timings before departure via the Bastia tourist office (see page 944) or online at ⓦ corsicabus.org.

## Erbalunga

Built along a rocky promontory 10km north of Bastia, the small port of **ERBALUNGA** is the highlight of the east coast, with its aged, pale buildings stacked like crooked boxes behind a small harbour and ruined Genoese watchtower. A little colony of French artists lived here in the 1920s, and the village has drawn a steady stream of admirers ever since. Come summer it's transformed into something of a cultural enclave, with concerts and art events adding a spark to local nightlife. The town is most famous, however, for its Good Friday procession, known as the **Cerca** (Search), which evolved

---

### CAP CORSE DRIVING TIPS

If you're driving on Cap Corse, bear in mind that **petrol stations** are few and far between, so fill up whenever you can: there are pumps in Bastia, Rogliano and Erbalunga (but check on the ground as things can change quickly). It's also worth noting that by heading in a **clockwise direction**, you'll be on the safer inside lane of the road all the way around (local driving styles are especially perilous along the windy west coast, where there's little room for error if you're forced to suddenly *serrer à droite*). That said, photographers may want to proceed in the opposite direction (starting at Bastia) to benefit from the early-morning and late-evening light.

from an ancient fertility rite. Hooded penitents, recruited from the ranks of a local religious brotherhood, form a spiral known as a *Granitola*, or snail, which unwinds as the candlelit procession moves into the village square.

## ACCOMMODATION                                      ERBALUNGA

★ **Castel Brando** On the main square ☎ 04 95 30 10 30, ⊛ castelbrando.com. Shaded by a curtain of mature date palms, this elegant, stone-floored *palazzu* is like a *belle époque* backdrop to a classic Visconti movie. The elegant

rooms have unfussy period furnishings, with the welcome addition of air conditioning, a lovely pool, spa and ample parking. Closed mid-Nov to mid-March. **€200**

## EATING AND DRINKING

**A Piazzetta** In the tiny square behind the harbour ☎ 04 95 33 28 69. The village's budget option, serving quality pizzas, veal in Cap Corse liqueur, excellent *moules-frites* and possibly Corsica's best sorbets. *Menus* from €20; count on €25–30 à la carte. Cash only. March–Dec daily noon–2pm & 7–10pm.

★ **Le Pirate** On the harbourside ☎ 04 95 33 24 20,

⊛ restaurantlepirate.com. Don't be fooled by their rudimentary website – well-heeled Bastiais flock year round to this restaurant on the waterfront for its famous *haute gastronomie*. Local seafood and meat delicacies dominate their set *menus* (€42/75/195 for lunch/dinner). Daily noon–3pm & 7–11pm.

# Macinaggio

A port since Roman times, well-sheltered **MACINAGGIO**, 20km north of Erbalunga, was developed by the Genoese in 1620 for the export of olive oil and wine to the Italian peninsula. The Corsican independence leader, Pascal Paoli, landed here in 1790 after his exile in England, whereupon he kissed the ground and uttered the words "*O ma patrie, je t'ai quitté esclave, je te retrouve libre*" ("Oh my country, I left you as a slave, I rediscover you a free man"). There's not much of a historic patina to the place nowadays, but with its packed **marina** and line of colourful seafront awnings, Macinaggio has a certain appeal, made all the stronger by its proximity to some of the wildest landscape on the Corsican coast.

Another reason to linger is to sample the superb **Clos Nicrosi** wines, grown in the terraces above the village, which you can taste at the *domaine*'s little shop on the north side of the Rogliano road, opposite the *U Ricordu* hotel.

## Site Naturel de la Capandula

North of the town lie some beautiful stretches of sand and clear sea – an area demarcated as the **Site Naturel de la Capandula**. A marked footpath, known as **Le Sentier des Douaniers** (see page 948) because it used to be patrolled by customs officials, threads its way across the hills and coves of the reserve, giving access to an area that cannot be reached by road. The **Baie de Tamarone**, 2km along this path, is a good place for diving and snorkelling. Just behind the beach, the *piste* forks: follow the left-hand track for twenty minutes and you'll come to a stunning arc of turquoise sea known as the **rade de Santa Maria**, site of the isolated Romanesque **Chapelle Santa-Maria**. The bay's other principal landmark is the huge **Tour Chiapelle**, a ruined three-storeyed watchtower dramatically cleft in half and entirely surrounded by water.

## INFORMATION                                      MACINAGGIO

**Tourist office** Located in the port (July & Aug Mon–Sat 9am–noon & 2–7pm, Sun 9am–noon; Sept Mon–Sat 9am–noon & 2–6pm, Sun 9am–noon; Oct–May Mon–Fri 9am–noon & 2–6pm; ☎ 04 95 35 40 34, ⊛ macinaggiorogliano-capcorse.fr).

**Boat trips** The San Paulu launch runs a twice-daily shuttle

service for walkers between Macinaggio and Centuri-Port (May–Dec; by reservation only; €17), as well as half-day excursions to outlying beauty spots (€28). Timetables are published online at ⊛ sanpaulu.com, and on leaflets at the tourist office. You can also phone the company direct on ☎ 06 14 78 14 16.

18

**18**

## LE SENTIER DES DOUANIERS

The roadless northern tip of Cap Corse is among the few stretches of coastline on the island crossed by a waymarked path, **Le Sentier des Douaniers**. Following the yellow splashes of paint, it's possible to trace it all the way from Macinaggio to Centuri-Port (or vice versa) in seven to eight hours, taking in the picturesque Santa Maria and Agnello towers en route.

The **tourist office** in Macinaggio will furnish you with a free **map** and route description. Being mostly flat, the route presents no great physical challenges, although you should be aware of the force of the sun along this stretch of coast. In July and August, set off at dawn and aim to rest up in the shade (of which there's precious little) between 11.30am and 4pm. **Water** can also be a problem as there are no springs.

### ACCOMMODATION

**U Libecciu** Rte de la Plage ☎04 95 35 43 22, ⓦu-libecciu.com. The best option in Macinaggio is this welcoming, modern three-star, located down the lane leading from the marina to the plage de Tamarone. Smallish rooms without balconies, or larger ones with terraces. There's also a pleasant swimming pool and a basic bar. Closed mid-Nov to mid-March. **€104**

**U Stazzu** 1km north of the harbour, signposted off the Rogliano road ☎04 95 35 43 76, ⓦcamping-u-stazzu.jimdo.com. Basic site on the edge of the village. The ground slopes and is rock hard, but it's cheap, there's ample shade and easy access to the nearby beach; the site's little café serves particularly good breakfasts and pizzas. There's also a number of bungalows that sleep up to four people, available by the week. Closed Oct to mid-March. Camping **€20**, bungalows **€560/week**

### EATING AND DRINKING

**Le Vela d'Oro** Down a narrow alleyway running off the little square, opposite the port ☎04 95 35 42 46. Capcorsin seafood specialities – such as local crayfish in home-made spaghetti – served in a cosy dining room decorated with old nautical maps. *Menus* from €19–25. Mid-March to Dec daily noon–2.30pm & 7.30–10pm; closed Wed out of season.

## Centuri-Port

When Dr Johnson's biographer, James Boswell, arrived here from England in 1765, the former Roman settlement of **CENTURI-PORT** was a tiny fishing village, recommended to him for its peaceful detachment from the dangerous turmoil of the rest of Corsica. Not much has changed since Boswell's time: Centuri-Port exudes tranquillity despite a serious influx of summer residents, many of them artists who come to paint the fishing boats in the slightly prettified harbour, where the grey-stone wall is highlighted by the green serpentine roofs of the encircling cottages, restaurants and bars. The only drawback is the beach, which is disappointingly muddy and not ideal for sunbathing.

### ACCOMMODATION AND EATING                                   CENTURI-PORT

**L'Auberge du Pêcheur** Rue du Port ☎04 95 35 60 14. Basic, but appealing hotel in the old-school Mediterranean mode: no TVs or a/c, but idyllic views out of its shuttered, front-side rooms over the harbour (ask for No. 4). Everything's impeccably clean, the beds are comfy and the staff genuinely welcoming. Great little seafood restaurant on the ground floor, ten steps from the water. Closed Nov–Easter. **€85**

**De la Jetée** At entrance to the port ☎09 70 35 61 51, ⓦhotel-de-la-jetee-centuri.fr. The *Jetée* has 14 spacious, airy rooms, most with balconies overlooking the harbour. Furnishings are bland but adequate, and there's a busy, good-value terrace restaurant tacked on the back. Half-board is also available. Closed Oct–March. **€70**

**Vieux Moulin** At the entrance to the village ☎04 95 35 60 15, ⓦle-vieux-moulin.net. Centuri's most stylish option: a converted *maison d'Américain* with a wonderful terrace and attractively furnished en-suite rooms. There's also a restaurant with a lovely terrace overlooking the sea. Closed Nov–Feb. **€100**

## Nonza

Set high on a black rocky pinnacle that plunges vertically into the sea, the village of **NONZA**, 18km south of Centuri, is one of the highlights of the Cap Corse shoreline.

It was formerly the main stronghold of the da Gentile family, and the remains of their **fortress** are still standing on the overhanging cliff. Reached by a flight of six hundred steps, Nonza's long grey **beach** is discoloured as a result of pollution from the now disused asbestos mine up the coast. This may not inspire confidence, but the locals insist it's safe (they take their own kids there in summer), and from the bottom you get the best view of the tower, which looks as if it's about to topple into the sea.

### ACCOMMODATION AND EATING

NONZA

**Casa Lisa** At the bottom of the village ☎04 95 37 83 52, ⓦcasalisa.free.fr. Lovely rooms with exposed beams, original tiled floors and shuttered windows looking across the gulf to the Désert des Agriates. Breakfast €7. Cards not accepted. Closed Nov–March. **€75**

**Casa Maria** Chemin de la Tour ☎04 95 37 80 95, ⓦcasamaria-corse.com. Four pleasantly furnished rooms (and one pricier family suite), housed in a restored schist building above the square. Breakfast is served on a delightful outdoor terrace with lovely views. There's also an apartment that sleeps up to six people and can be hired by the week. Cards not accepted. Closed Nov–March. Doubles **€105,** apartment **€700/week**

★ **La Sassa** Near the Tour Génoise ☎04 95 38 55 26, ⓦlasassa.com. One of the loveliest café-restaurants on the island, La Sassa occupies a plum location on a craggy spur below the tour, with a to-die-for view over the beach from its teak deck. A chilled young crew serve succulent charcoal-grilled meat, pasta and salads at restrained prices, as well as artisanal ice creams and craft beers and ciders, to a soundtrack of Corsican lounge grooves – particularly atmospheric at sunset time when the surrounding rocks are floodlit. *Menus* from €24–34. Late April to Sept daily 11am–11pm.

**18**

# The Nebbio (U Nebbiu)

Taking its name from the thick mists that sweep over the region in winter, the **Nebbio** has for centuries been one of the most fertile parts of the island, producing honey, chestnuts and some of the island's finest wine. An amphitheatre of rippled chalk hills, vineyards and cultivated valleys surrounds the area's main town, **St-Florent**, half an hour's drive west over the mountain from Bastia at the base of Cap Corse. Aside from EU subsidies, the major money earner here is viticulture: the village of **Patrimonio** is the wine-growing hub, with *caves* offering *dégustations* lined up along its main street.

St-Florent is the obvious base for day-trips to the beautifully preserved Pisan church of Santa Maria Assunta, just outside the town, and the **Désert des Agriates**, a wilderness of parched maquis-covered hills across the bay whose rugged coastline harbours one of Corsica's least accessible, but most picturesque, beaches.

### GETTING AROUND

THE NEBBIO

**By bus** The principal public transport serving the Nebbio is the twice-daily bus from Bastia to St-Florent, operated by Transports Santini (☎04 95 37 02 98). Timings can be checked at ⓦcorsicabus.org, or at the tourist office in St-Florent.

## St-Florent

Viewed from across the bay, **ST-FLORENT** (San Fiurenzu) appears as a bright line against the black tidal wave of the Tenda hills, the pale stone houses seeming to rise straight out of the sea, overlooked by a squat circular citadelle. It's a relaxed town, with a decent beach and a good number of restaurants, but the key to its success is the **marina**, which is jammed with expensive boats throughout the summer. Neither the tourists, however, nor indeed St-Florent's proximity to Bastia, entirely eclipse the air of isolation conferred on the town by its brooding backdrop of mountains and scrubby desert.

In Roman times, a settlement called Cersunam – referred to as Nebbium by chroniclers from the ninth century onwards – existed a kilometre east of the present village. The ancient port was eclipsed by the harbour that developed around the new Genoese citadelle in the fifteenth century, which prospered as one of Genoa's strongholds, and it was from here that Pascal Paoli (see page 968) set off for London in 1796, never to return.

## Place des Portes and the citadelle

**Place des Portes**, the centre of village life, has café tables facing the sea in the shade of plane trees, and in the evening fills with strollers and *pétanque* players. The fifteenth-century circular **citadelle** can be reached on foot from place Doria at the seafront in the old quarter. Destroyed by Nelson's bombardment in 1794, it was renovated in the 1990s and affords superb views from its terrace.

**18**

## Church of Santa Maria Assunta

June–Oct Mon–Fri 9.30am–noon & 3–6.30pm; off season, key obtainable through tourist office • €2

Just a kilometre to the east of the town down a small lane running off place des Portes, on the original site of Cersanum, you come to the **church of Santa Maria Assunta** – the so-called "cathedral of the Nebbio" – a fine example of Pisan Romanesque architecture. Built in warm yellow limestone, the building has gracefully symmetrical blind arcades decorating its western facade, and at the entrance twisting serpents and wild animals adorning the pilasters on each side of the door. In the nave, immediately to the right of the entrance stands a glass case containing the mummified figure of St Flor, a Roman soldier martyred in the third century.

### ARRIVAL AND DEPARTURE                                    ST-FLORENT

**By bus** Transports Santini buses (☎04 95 37 02 98) run from Bastia's *gare routière* to St-Florent up to three times daily (Mon–Sat), pulling into the village car park behind the marina. This is also the departure point for return buses to Bastia, which depart four times daily from June to September, and up to three times daily (Mon–Sat) the rest of the year.

**Tickets** You can purchase tickets on the bus or book in advance from Transports Santini's travel agency on St-Florent's main street, rue du Centre, just below the post office.

### INFORMATION

**Tourist office** Next to the post office at the top of the village (Mon–Fri 9am–noon & 2–6pm, Sat 9am–noon; ☎04 95 37 06 04, ⊛corsica-saintflorent.com), 100m north of place des Portes.

**Shops and services** The large Spar, next to the bridge in the marina, is the best-stocked supermarket in the area, and is even open on Sundays. Every other facility you could possibly want for a beach, camping or watersports holiday is available at the cavernous Corse Plaisance, a little further south down the road.

### ACCOMMODATION

**Camping Kalliste** Rte de la Plage ☎04 95 37 03 08, ⊛camping-saintflorent.fr. Closest to town and most congenial. Facilities include five outdoor pools (though all relatively small), a kids' playground, a restaurant and a bar. In addition to pitches, mobile homes and safari tent-style lodges are also available. Closed Oct–May. Camping **€47,** lodge **€151**

**L'Europe** Place des Portes ☎04 95 35 32 91, ⊛hotel-europe2.com. Appealing old building in the village centre next to the square, with original flagstone floors and modern comforts. Rooms are on the small side for the price, but all are en suite and well aired, and some overlook the

---

## TRIPS TO THE DESERT

Excursion boats run out of St-Florent marina to the superb beaches – Lotu and Saleccia – across the bay in the Désert des Agriates. The *Popeye* (☎04 95 37 19 07 or ☎06 62 16 23 76; ⊛lepopeye.com) and *Corse Croisières* (☎06 10 38 27 65) leave at regular intervals throughout the day from 9am, the last service returning around 4pm (or later in July & Aug); tickets cost €16 for the return trip to Lotu, or €25 for the round trip to Saleccia in a powerful inflatable.

From Lotu, an all-terrain 4WD runs via a rough track inland to Saleccia. The firm Saleccia Off Road (☎06 64 00 38 92, ⊛saleccia-off-road.com) offers packages that could include the outward and return trips by boat; from €25.

marina. €118

**Maxime** Chemin de la Cathédrale, just off place des Portes ☏04 95 37 05 30, ⓦhotel-maxime-saint-florent. fr. Bright, modern hotel in the centre. Rooms to the rear of the building have French windows and little balconies overhanging a small water channel. Closed Dec–Feb. €92

**Santa Maria** Lieu-dit Cisternino ☏04 95 37 04 44. On the Bastia road, just outside of the town centre, this is an elegant three star. All rooms have a/c and are decorated in soothing, muted colours; the best have balconies with views of either St-Florent or the sea. €168

**Tettola** On the Bastia road, 2km northeast of town ☏04 95 37 08 53, ⓦhoteltettola.com. The big selling point of this unpretentious hotel is its swimming pool that overlooks the sea. The a/c rooms are bright and comfortable, and half have balconies with sea views. €115

### EATING

**L'Europe** Place des Portes ☏04 95 35 32 91, ⓦhotel-europe2.com. Local meat, seafood and pasta specialities are the mainstays of this rather fancy but good-value bistro on the waterfront (part of the hotel of the same name), where you can dine on tables overlooking the port. The *menu corse (€29)* is recommended and includes *soupe de poissons* and a squid and cuttlefish risotto. Easter–Oct daily noon–2.30pm & 7–11pm; Nov–Easter closed Mon, Tues & Sun eve.

**La Gaffe** St-Florent marina ☏04 95 37 00 12, ⓦrestaurant-saint-florent.com. One of the town's top seafood restaurants, where you can order pasta with spider crab or sea bass carpaccio, with mains €29–33, or a *menu* at €55. Daily except Wed noon–2.30pm & 7–10pm.

**La Rascasse** St-Florent marina ☏04 95 37 06 09, ⓦlarascasse.corsica. Renowned for its imaginative spins on local seafood: lobster cannelloni, mussel and chestnut fritters, and rockfish sautéed in cured ham. Mains from €45; *menus* at €58–70. Mid-March to Oct daily except Mon (July & Aug daily) noon–2pm & 7–10.30pm.

## Patrimonio (Patrimoniu)

As you leave St-Florent by the Bastia road, the next village you come to, after 6km, is **PATRIMONIO**, centre of the first Corsican wine region to gain *appellation contrôlée* status. Apart from the renowned local muscat, which can be sampled in the village or at one of the *caves* along the route from St-Florent, Patrimonio's chief asset is the sixteenth-century **church of St-Martin**, occupying its own little hillock and visible for kilometres around. The colour of burnt sienna, it stands out vividly against the rich green vineyards and chalk hills. In a garden 200m south of the church stands a limestone **statue-menhir** known as U Nativu, a late megalithic piece dating from 900–800 BC. A carved T-shape on its front represents a breastbone, and two eyebrows and a chin can also be made out.

The U Nativu menhir takes pride of place next to the stage at Patrimonio's annual open-air guitar festival (ⓦfestival-guitare-patrimonio.com), held in the last week of July next to the church, when performers and music aficionados from all over Europe converge on the village.

## The Désert des Agriates

Extending westwards from the Golfe de St-Florent to the mouth of the Ostriconi River, the **Désert des Agriates** is a vast area of uninhabited land, dotted with clumps of cacti and scrub-covered hills. It may appear inhospitable now, but during the time of the Genoese this rocky moonscape was, as its name implies, a veritable breadbasket (*agriates* means "cultivated fields"). In fact, so much wheat was grown here that the Italian overlords levied a special tax on grain to prevent any build-up of funds that might have financed an insurrection. Fires and soil erosion eventually took their toll, however, and by the 1970s the area had become a total wilderness.

Numerous crackpot schemes to redevelop the Désert have been mooted over the years – from atomic weapon test zones to concrete Club-Med-style resorts – but during the past few decades the government has gradually bought up the land from its various owners (among them the Rothschild family) and designated it as a protected nature reserve.

## The beaches

A couple of rough *pistes* wind into the desert, but without some kind of 4WD vehicle the only feasible way to explore the area and its rugged coastline, which includes two of the island's most beautiful **beaches**, is on foot. From St-Florent, a pathway winds northwest to **Plage de l'Ostriconi**, just off the main Calvi highway (T30), in three easy stages. The first takes around 5hr 30min, and leads past the famous **Martello tower** and much-photographed **plage du Lotu** to **plage de Saleccia**, a huge sweep of soft white sand and turquoise sea that was used as a location for the invasion sequences in the film *The Longest Day.*

From plage de Saleccia, it takes around three hours to reach the second night halt, **plage de Ghignu**, where a simple *gîte d'étape* provides basic facilities. The last stretch to l'Ostriconi can be covered in under six hours. Note that the only water sources along the route are at Saleccia and Ghignu, so take plenty with you.

### GETTING THERE

Excursion boats leave at regular intervals throughout the day from the jetty in St-Florent marina, ferrying passengers across the gulf to and from plages du Lotu and Saleccia. See page 950 for more details.

### ACCOMMODATION

**Paillers du Ghignu** Plage de Ghignu ☏ 04 95 57 10 10, ✉ ghignu@haute-corse.fr. This superbly remote *gîte d'étape* offers the most far-flung accommodation in coastal Corsica. Housed in a converted shepherd's hut close to the shoreline, its only facilities are basic bunks (no mattresses), hot showers and toilets – you'll need to bring a sleeping bag, food and drink. Reservations essential. Closed mid-Oct to April. €12

**U Paradisu** Plage de Saleccia ☏ 04 95 37 82 51, ⊛ camping-uparadisu.com. Well set-up campsite with pitches for tents in shady scrub behind the dunes, plus a scattering a delightful dry-stone cottages with bunks that can be rented nightly by coast walkers (outside of high season only; no linen provided) and more luxurious cabins. Cash only. Closed Oct–April. Camping €14, bunks €18

# The Balagne (A Balagna)

The **Balagne**, the region stretching west from the Ostriconi valley as far as the redcliffed wilderness of Scandola, has been renowned since Roman times as "Le Pays de l'Huile et Froment" (Land of Oil and Wheat). Backed by a wall of imposing, pale grey mountains, the characteristic outcrops of orange granite punctuating its spectacular coastline shelter a string of idyllic beaches, many of them sporting ritzy marinas and holiday complexes. These, along with the region's two honeypot towns, **L'Île Rousse** and **Calvi**, get swamped in summer, but the scenery more than compensates. In any case, Calvi, with its cream-coloured citadelle, breathtaking white-sand bay and mountainous backdrop, should not be missed.

## L'Île Rousse

Developed by Pascal Paoli in the 1760s as a "gallows to hang Calvi", the port of **L'ÎLE ROUSSE** (Isula Rossa) simply doesn't convince as a Corsican town, its palm trees, smart shops, neat flower gardens and colossal pink seafront hotel creating an atmosphere that has more in common with the French Riviera. Pascal Paoli had great plans for his new town on the Haute-Balagne coast, which was laid out from scratch in 1758 as a port to export the olive oil produced in the region. A large part of it was built on a grid system, quite at odds with the higgledy-piggledy nature of most Corsican villages and towns. Thanks to the busy trading of wine and oil, it soon began to prosper and, two and a half centuries later, still thrives as a successful port. These days, however, the main traffic consists of holiday-makers, lured here by brochure shots of the nearby beaches. This is officially the hottest corner of the island, and the town is deluged by sun-worshippers in July and August. It's undoubtedly an attractive place, but given the proximity of Calvi, and so much unspoilt countryside on its doorstep, you may prefer to stop here for little more than lunch or a coffee on the square.

### Place Paoli

All roads in L'Île Rousse lead to **place Paoli**, a shady square that's open to the sea and has as its focal point a fountain surmounted by a bust of "U Babbu di u Patria" ("Father of the Nation"), one of many local tributes to Pascal Paoli. There's a Frenchified covered **market** at the entrance to the square, which is home to a daily fresh produce market, and a popular artisan-cum-antiques sale on Saturday mornings; on the west side rises the imposing facade of the **church of the Immaculate Conception.**



### Île de la Pietra

To reach the **Île de la Pietra**, the islet that gives the town its name, continue north from the top of the promenade, passing the station on your left. Once over the causeway, you can walk through the crumbling mass of red granite as far as the lighthouse at the far end, from where the view of the town is spectacular, especially at sundown, when you get the full effect of the red glow of the rocks.

### The town beach

Immediately in front of the promenade, the **town beach** is a crowded Côte d'Azur-style strand, blocked by ranks of sun loungers and parasols belonging to the row of lookalike café-restaurants behind it. Two much more enticing beaches, **Bodri** and **Ghjunchitu**, lie a couple of kilometres around the headland to the west; you can get there on the two daily train services between L'Île Rousse and Calvi (alight at "Botri").

## ARRIVAL AND DEPARTURE — L'ÎLE ROUSSE

**By train** The train station (T 04 95 60 00 50) is on route du Port, 500m south of where the ferries arrive. Two services daily run to Bastia, and to Calvi via the beaches and villages en route.

**By bus** The Bastia–Calvi bus, operated twice daily by Les Beaux Voyages (T 04 95 65 11 35, W beauxvoyagesencorse.com), stops just south of place Paoli in the town's main thoroughfare, av Piccioni. Tickets can be purchased from the driver.

**By ferry** Passenger ferries from Nice, Marseille and Toulon, and the Italian port of Savona, dock at the quayside on the northwest side of the centre, a 10min walk from the town centre.

## INFORMATION

**Tourist office** Av de Calizi (April, May & Oct Mon–Sat 10am–noon & 2–6pm; July & Aug Mon–Sat 10am–1pm & 3–6pm; Nov–March Mon–Fri 9am–noon & 2–6pm; T 04 95 60 04 35, W balagne-corsica.com).

## ACCOMMODATION

**Le Bodri** 3km west off the main Calvi rd T 04 95 60 10 86, W campinglebodri.com. Just 200m from the beach, and set among extensive grounds of eucalyptus and pine trees, this very pleasant campsite does get rammed in summer, though it's pleasantly quiet outside the *grandes vacances*. It's possible to reach it by train – alight at "Botri". Closed Oct–April. €24

**Cala di L'Oru** Bd Pierre-Pasquini T 04 95 60 14 75, W hotel-caladiloru.com. Relaxed three-star hotel, swathed in greenery, on the outskirts of town. The rooms are functional without being bland, and a good-sized pool is a welcome bonus. Generous discounts low- and mid-season. Closed Nov–March. €120

**Le Grillon** 10 av Paul-Doumer T 04 95 60 00 49, W hotel-grillon.net. The best cheap hotel in town, just 1km from the centre on the St-Florent/Bastia road. Nothing special, but quiet and immaculate. Half board available. Closed Nov–Feb. €75

**Les Oliviers** 1km east of town, on rte de Bastia T 04 95 60 19 92, W camping-oliviers.com. Well-shaded site on the eastern outskirts, sandwiched between the highway and cliffs. Closed Oct to early April. €20.50

**Santa Maria** Rte du Port T 04 95 63 05 05, W hotelsantamaria.com. Next to the ferry port and affiliated to the Best Western chain, this is one of the larger and better-value three-star places. Their a/c rooms have small balconies or patios opening onto a garden and pool, and there's exclusive access to a tiny pebble beach. €180

**18**

**Splendid** Av du Comte-Valéry ☎ 04 95 60 00 24, ⓦ lesplendid-hotel.com. Well-maintained, 1930s-style building with a small curvi-form pool and some sea views from upper floors. Rooms are in need of a refresh, but the price isn't bad given the central location. Closed mid-Nov to April. €̲1̲1̲7̲

### EATING AND DRINKING

Though there's an abundance of mediocre eating places in the narrow alleys of the old town, a few restaurants do stand out, some offering stylish gourmet *menus* and others serving superb fresh seafood. The best cafés are found under the plane trees lining the southern side of place Paoli.

**L'Escale** Rue Notre-Dame ☎ 04 95 60 10 53. Giant fresh mussels, prawns and crayfish from the east coast *étangs* are the thing here, served in various *menus* (from €25) on a spacious terrace looking across the tramway line to the bay. Brisk, courteous service, copious portions and for once the house white (by the glass or *pichet*) is palatable. Daily noon–2.30pm & 7–11pm.

**Le Morgan** Av Piccioni ☎ 06 72 38 90 68. Unpretentious modern restaurant serving up an interesting an varied menu that covers everything from XXL burgers (€17.90) and chicken risotto (€14.50) to tuna tartare (€21) and grilled prawns (€24), all beautifully presented. Mon–Sat 9am–11pm.

**U Pasquale Paoli** 2 place Paoli ☎ 04 95 46 67 70. Gastronomic renditions of Corsican standards are the forte of this excellent restaurant: the octopus in olive oil and lemon confit is hard to top, and there are plenty of wonderful vegetarian options. Count on à la carte mains around €21–39. Mon–Wed & Fri–Sun noon–2pm & 7.30–10pm, Thurs 7.30–10pm.

# Calvi

Seen from the water, **CALVI** is a beautiful spectacle, with its three immense bastions topped by a crest of ochre buildings, sharply defined against a hazy backdrop of mountains. Located twenty kilometres west along the coast from L'Île Rousse, the town began as a fishing port on the site of the present-day *ville basse* below the citadelle, and remained just a cluster of houses and fishing shacks until the Pisans conquered the island in the tenth century. Not until the arrival of the Genoese, however, did the town become a stronghold when, in 1268, Giovaninello de Loreto, a Corsican nobleman, built a huge citadelle on the windswept rock overlooking the port and named it Calvi. A fleet commanded by Nelson launched a brutal two-month attack on the town in 1794; he left saying he hoped never to see the place again, and very nearly didn't see anywhere else again, having sustained the wound that cost him his sight in one eye.

The French concentrated on developing Ajaccio and Bastia during the nineteenth century, and Calvi became primarily a military base. A hangout for European glitterati in the 1950s, the town these days has the ambience of a slightly kitsch Côte d'Azur resort, whose glamorous marina, souvenir shops and fussy boutiques jar with the down-to-earth villages of its rural hinterland. It's also an important base for the French Foreign Legion's parachute regiment, the 2ème REP, and immaculately uniformed legionnaires are a common sight around the bars lining avenue de la République.

Social life in Calvi focuses on the restaurants and cafés of the **quai Landry**, a spacious seafront walkway linking the marina and the port. This is the best place to get the feel of the town, but the majority of Calvi's sights are found within the walls of the **citadelle**.

## The citadelle

"Civitas Calvis Semper Fidelis" – always faithful – reads the inscription of the town's motto, carved over the ancient gateway into the fortress. The best way of seeing the citadelle is to follow the ramparts connecting the three immense bastions, the views from which extend out to sea and inland to Monte Cinto. Within the walls the houses are tightly packed along tortuous stairways and narrow passages that converge on the place d'Armes. Dominating the square is the **Cathédrale St-Jean-Baptiste**, set at the highest point of the promontory. This chunky ochre edifice was founded in the thirteenth century, but was partly destroyed during the Turkish siege of 1553 and then suffered extensive damage twelve years later, when the powder magazine in the governor's palace exploded. It was rebuilt in the form of a Greek cross. The church's great treasure is the **Christ des Miracles**, which is housed in the chapel on the right of the choir; this crucifix was brandished at marauding Turks during the 1553 siege, an act which reputedly saved the day.

## La Maison Colomb

To the north of place d'Armes in rue de Fil stands **La Maison Colomb**, the shell of a building which Calvi believes – as the plaque on the wall states – was Christopher Columbus's birthplace, though the claim rests on pretty tenuous, circumstantial evidence. The house itself was destroyed by Nelson's troops during the siege of 1794, but as recompense a statue was erected in 1992, the five-hundredth anniversary of Columbus's "discovery" of America; the date of this historic landfall, October 12, is now a public holiday in Calvi.

## The beach

Calvi's **beach** sweeps round the bay from the end of quai Landry, but most of the first kilometre or so is owned by bars which rent out sun loungers for a hefty price. To avoid these, follow the track behind the sand, which will bring you to the start of a more secluded stretch. The sea might not be as sparklingly clear as at many other Corsican beaches, but it's warm, shallow and free of rocks.

### ARRIVAL AND DEPARTURE CALVI

**By plane** Ste-Catherine airport, served by domestic and international flights, lies 7km south of Calvi (☎ 04 95 65 88 88, ⌨ www.calvi.aeroport.fr); the only public transport into town is by taxi, which shouldn't cost more than €25 weekdays (or €30 on weekends).

**By train** The train station (Gare CFC ☎ 04 95 65 00 61), on av de la République close to the marina, is the terminus for regular long-distance trains to Bastia and Ajaccio, as well as villages and resorts along the route of the seasonal tramway. For timetable and fare info, go to ⌨ corsicabus.org) Destinations Ajaccio (2 daily; 4hr 10min); Bastia (2 daily; 3hr); Corte (2 daily; 2hr 24min); L'Île Rousse (2 daily; 30min).

**By bus** Buses to and from Bastia and towns along the north coast (Les Beaux Voyages ☎ 04 95 65 11 35, ⌨ beauxvoyagesencorse.com; daily) stop outside the train station on place de la Porteuse d'Eau, whereas those from Porto, run by SAIB (mid-May to June & mid-Sept to end Sept Mon–Sat; July to mid-Sept daily; ☎ 04 95 22 41 99) work from the roadside behind the marina.

Destinations Bastia (1–2daily; 2hr); L'Île Rousse (2 daily; 30min); Porto (1 daily; 2hr 30min).

**By boat** Ferries no longer run to/from Calvi; it's best to travel via L'Île Rousse instead.

### INFORMATION

**Tourist office** Chemin de la plage (March & Nov Mon–Fri 9am–noon & 2–6pm; April & Oct Mon–Sat 9am–noon & 2–6pm; May, June & Sept Mon–Sat Mon–Sat 9am–noon & 2–6pm, Sun 9.30am–12.30pm; July & Aug Mon–Sat 9am–7pm, Sun 9am–1pm; ☎ 04 95 65 16 67, ⌨ balagne-corsica.com).

**Bicycle rental** Garage d'Angeli, 4 quartier-neuf (☎ 04 95 65 02 13, ⌨ garagedangeli.com), from €14 per day. Take along your credit card or passport, which they'll need to secure the deposit.

### ACCOMMODATION

Accommodation is easy to find in Calvi except during the jazz festival (third week of June).

**Camping Bella Vista** Rte de Pietramaggiore, 1km southeast of the centre (700m inland from the beach) ☎ 04 95 65 11 76, ⌨ www.camping-bellavista.com. The best option for backpackers as it's much closer to the centre of town than the competition – though you pay a couple of euros per night extra for the privilege. Plenty of shade, nice soft ground and clean toilet blocks, plus an on-site pizzeria. Closed mid-Oct to March. €30

**La Caravelle** Marco Plage, 1km south of centre ☎ 04 95 65 95 50, ⌨ hotel-la-caravelle.com. An impeccably clean, modern hotel virtually on the beach, with ground-floor rooms set around a garden; those on the first floor are more luxurious. Buffet breakfasts are served on a sunny patio, and there's a nice bar-restaurant. Good value in this bracket considering the location, quality of the property and service. €192

**Casa Vecchia** Rte de Santore ☎ 04 95 65 09 33, ⌨ hotel-casa-vecchia.com. Pleasant apartments, all with a balcony or terrace, in a leafy garden, south of town, and 300m from the beach. Friendly management. Closed Oct–March. €150

18

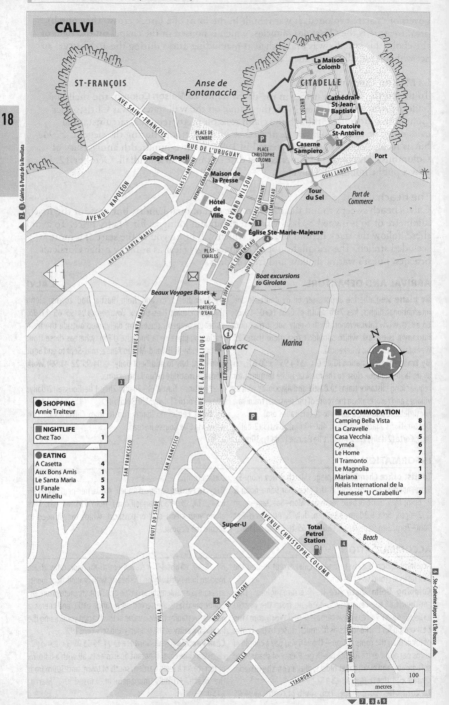

CALVI

18

ST-FRANÇOIS

Anse de Fontanaccia

La Maison Colomb

CITADELLE

Cathédrale St-Jean-Baptiste

Oratoire St-Antoine

Caserne Sampiero

Port

PLACE DE L'OMBRE

PLACE CHRISTOPHE COLOMB

Garage d'Angeli

RUE DE L'URUGUAY

Maison de la Presse

Hôtel de Ville

Église Ste-Marie-Majeure

Tour du Sel

Port de Commerce

QUAI LANDRY

AVENUE NAPOLÉON

AVENUE SANTA MARIA

PL ST-CHARLES

AVENUE SANTA MARIA

RUE JOFFRE

RUE CLEMENCEAU

QUAI LANDRY

Boat excursions to Girolata

Beaux Voyages Buses

LA PORTEUSE D'EAU

Gare CFC

Marina

N

AVENUE DE LA RÉPUBLIQUE

LE PILICHETU

SAN FRANCESCO

SAN FRANCESCO

ROUTE DU STADE

Super-U

AVENUE CHRISTOPHE COLOMB

Total Petrol Station

Beach

ROUTE DE SANTORE

VILLA

VILLA

VILLA

ROUTE DE LA PIETRA-MAGGIORE

STAGNONE

**● SHOPPING**
Annie Traiteur — 1

**■ NIGHTLIFE**
Chez Tao — 1

**● EATING**
A Casetta — 4
Aux Bons Amis — 1
Le Santa Maria — 5
U Fanale — 3
U Minellu — 2

**■ ACCOMMODATION**
Camping Bella Vista — 8
La Caravelle — 4
Casa Vecchia — 5
Cyrnéa — 6
Le Home — 7
Il Tramonto — 2
Le Magnolia — 1
Mariana — 3
Relais International de la Jeunesse "U Carabellu" — 9

0        100
metres

7, 8 & 9

★ **Cyrnea** Rte de Bastia ☎ 04 95 65 03 35, ⊛ hotel-cyrnea.fr. Large budget hotel, a twenty-minute walk south of town, and 300m from the beach. Good-sized rooms for the price, all with bathrooms and balconies (ask for one with "vue sur les montagnes" to the rear), and there's even a pleasant outdoor pool. Outstanding value for money, especially in high season. Closed Nov to mid-April. €98

★ **Le Home** Rte de Pietramaggiore ☎ 04 95 65 02 04, ⊛ residence-lehome.com. Comfortable, a/c chalet studios and apartments set in beautiful gardens a five-minute walk from the beach and old town. Impeccably clean, they're equipped with hobs, coffee makers, toasters and microwaves for basic self-catering, and have balconies. Friendly management. Weekly rentals only. €847/week.

**Il Tramonto** Rte de Porto ☎ 04 95 65 04 17, ⊛ hotelil tramonto.com. Excellent little hotel, with clean, comfortable and light rooms on the far north side of town. Definitely worth splashing out on one with "vue sur la mer", which have little terraces and a superb panorama over Punta de la Revellata. €110

**Le Magnolia** Rue d'Alsace-Lorraine ☎ 04 95 65 19 16, ⊛ hotel-le-magnolia.com. Nineteenth-century townhouse with belle époque decor and the atmosphere of an elegantly old-fashioned pension, set behind high walls in the heart of the historic quarter. The eponymous magnolia tree shades a lovely terrace restaurant where breakfast is served in the mornings. Welcoming management. €135

★ **Mariana** Av Santa Maria ☎ 04 95 65 31 38. It's a bit of a steep uphill walk to this pleasant hotel, but this location does mean that many of the rooms have wonderful views over the town, the sea and the surrounding countryside. All rooms benefit from balconies, but they vary a lot in decoration – from rather old-fashioned and a little frilly to smart and modern. There's a fabulous rooftop pool with a bar, plus a sauna and hammam. €163

**Relais International de la Jeunesse "U Carabellu"** 4km from the centre of town on rte Pietramaggiore ☎ 04 95 65 14 16, ⊛ clajsud.fr. Follow the N197 for 2km, turn right at the sign for Pietramaggiore, and the hostel – two little houses with spacious, clean dormitories, family and double rooms, looking out over the gulf – is in the village another 2km further up the lane. Book in advance. Closed Nov–March. Beds €20/33 (B&B/half-board)

## EATING AND DRINKING

### RESTAURANTS

★ **A Casetta** 16 rue Clemenceau ☎ 04 95 65 32 15. This fabulous deli has just a handful of tables on a lovely harbour-view from which you can enjoy sharing plates (from €14) of Corsican specialities – from cheese to saucisse to terrines – all beautifully presented. Mon–Sat 11am–5pm.

**Aux Bons Amis** 11 rue Clemenceau ☎ 04 95 65 05 01. Cosy restaurant decorated with fishing paraphernalia serving up surprisingly sophisticated dishes. The focus is – unsurprisingly – on fish, with menus from €24 including dishes like carpaccio of red tuna. Tues, Thurs & Fri noon–2pm, Sat & Sun noon–2pm & 7–11pm.

**Le Santa Maria** Next to the Église Ste-Marie-Majeure, rue Clemenceau ☎ 04 95 64 04 19. A popular four-course tourist menu (€20) and paella (€25) are the main offerings here, served in an atmospheric little square in front of the church, with pichets of house wine or, if you can stretch to it, the wonderful Clos Culombu. April–Oct daily 9am–3pm & 5pm–midnight.

★ **U Fanale** Rte de Porto, just outside the centre of town on the way to Punta de la Revellata ☎ 04 95 65 18 82. Worth the walk out here for their delicious, beautifully presented Corsican specialities – mussels or lamb simmered in ewe's cheese and white wine, a fine soupe corse, and melt-in-the-mouth fiadone (traditional flan). Menus €24–40 plus a full à la carte choice (count on €35–50), and pizzas from €18. You can dine outside in the garden or inside their salle panoramique, with views across the bay to Punta de la Revellata. March–Dec daily noon–2.30pm & 7–11pm; closed Tues lunchtime.

**U Minellu** Off bd Wilson, nr Ste-Marie-Majeure ☎ 04 95 65 05 52, ⊛ u-minellu.fr. Wholesome Corsican specialities served in a narrow stepped alley, or on a shady terrace with pretty mosaic tables. Their menu features courgette fritters, fish en papillote and a cheese platter – good value at €21.50. March–Oct Mon, Tues & Thurs–Sat noon–1.30pm & 7–10pm, Wed 7–10pm, Sun 7–10pm.

### BAR

**Chez Tao** Rue St-Antoine, in the citadelle ☎ 04 95 65 00 73, ⊛ cheztao.com. Legendary bar-nightclub, opened in 1935 in the wake of the Bolshevik Revolution by a Muslim White Russian, and long the haunt of the Riviera's glitterati. Now turned into a pricey piano bar from 11.30pm–2am, after which DJs take over. Daily 10.30pm–6am.

## SHOPPING

**Annie Traiteur** 5 rue Clemenceau ☎ 04 95 65 49 67. Recommended for local specialities and other authentic souvenirs, including a huge range of wines, olive oil, honey, charcuterie, liqueurs and canistrelli biscuits. They also prepare fresh bastelles (pasties) with spinach and local brocciu. Daily 7am–8pm, open till 11.30pm in July & Aug.

# The Réserve Naturelle de Scandola

The extraordinary **Réserve Naturelle de Scandola** takes up the promontory dividing the Balagne from the Golfe de Porto. Composed of striking red porphyry granite, its sheer cliffs and gnarled claw-like outcrops were formed by Monte Cinto's volcanic eruptions 250 million years ago, and subsequent erosion has fashioned shadowy caves, grottoes and gashes in the rock. Scandola's colours are as remarkable as the shapes, the hues varying from the charcoal grey of granite to incandescent rusty purple.

The headland and its surrounding water were declared a nature reserve in 1975 and now support significant colonies of seabirds, dolphins and seals, as well as 450 types of seaweed and some remarkable fish such as the grouper, a species more commonly found in the Caribbean. In addition, nests belonging to the rare Audouin's gull are visible on the cliffs, and you might see the odd fish eagle (*Balbuzard pêcheur*) – there used to be only a handful of nesting pairs at one time, but careful conservation has increased their numbers considerably over the past two decades.

## GETTING THERE                                          RÉSERVE NATURELLE DE SCANDOLA

**By boat** Scandola is off-limits to hikers and can be viewed only by boat (Colombo Lines ☎ 04 95 62 32 10, ⓦ colombo-line.com), which means taking one of the daily excursions from Calvi or Porto. These leave morning and afternoon from Calvi, and from Porto at various intervals throughout the daytime and early evening (April–Oct), the first two stopping for two hours at Girolata (see page 959) and returning in the late afternoon. It's a fascinating journey and well worth the steep fare, although it's a good idea to take a picnic if you're on a tight budget, as the restaurants in Girolata are very pricey.

---

### THE GR20

Winding some 170km from Calenzana (12km from Calvi) to Conca (22km from Porto-Vecchio), the **GR20** is Corsica's most demanding long-distance footpath. Only one-third of the 18,000 to 20,000 hikers who start it each season complete all sixteen stages, which can be covered in ten to twelve days if you're in good physical shape – if you're not, don't even think about attempting this route. Marked with red-and-white splashes of paint, it comprises a series of harsh ascents and descents, sections of which exceed 2000m and become more of a scramble than a walk, with stanchions, cables and ladders driven into the rock as essential aids. The going is made tougher by the necessity of carrying a sleeping bag, all-weather kit and two or three days' food with you. That said, the rewards more than compensate. The GR20 takes in the most spectacular mountain terrain in Corsica and along the way you can spot the elusive mouflon (mountain sheep), glimpse lammergeier (a rare vulture) wheeling around the crags, and swim in ice-cold torrents and waterfalls.

The first thing you need to do before setting off is get hold of the Parc Régional's indispensable **Topo-guide**, published by the Fédération Française de la Randonnée Pédestre, which gives a detailed description of the route, along with relevant sections of IGN contour maps, lists of *refuges* and other essential information. Most good bookshops in Corsica stock them, or call at the park office in Ajaccio (see page 970).

The route can be undertaken in either **direction**, but most hikers start in the north at Calenzana, tackling the most demanding *étapes* early on. The hardship is alleviated by extraordinary mountainscapes as you round the Cinto massif, skirt the Asco, Niolo, Tavignano and Restonica valleys, and scale the sides of Monte d'Oro and Rotondo. At Vizzavona on the main Bastia–Corte–Ajaccio road, roughly the halfway mark, you can call it a day and catch a bus or train back to the coast, or press on south across two more ranges to the needle peaks of Bavella.

**Accommodation** along the route is provided by **refuges**, where, for around €11–20, you can take a hot shower, use an equipped kitchen and bunk down on mattresses. Usually converted *bergeries*, these places are staffed by wardens during the peak period (June–Sept). Advance reservations can be made online via the national park (PNRC) website, ⓦ parc-corse.org, for an advance payment of €5 per bed; any un-booked places are allocated on a first-come-first-served basis, so be prepared to bivouac if you arrive late. Another reason to be on the trail soon after

## Girolata

Connected by a mere mule track to the rest of the island (1hr 30min on foot from the nearest road), the tiny fishing haven of **GIROLATA**, immediately east of Scandola, has a dreamlike quality that's highlighted by the vivid red of the surrounding rocks. A short stretch of stony beach and a few houses are dominated by a stately watchtower, built by the Genoese in the seventeenth century in the form of a small castle on a bluff overlooking the cove. For most of the year, this is one of the most idyllic spots on the island, with only the odd yacht and party of hikers to threaten the settlement's tranquillity. From June to September, though, daily boat trips from Porto and Calvi ensure the village is swamped during the middle of the day, so if you want to make the most of the scenery and peace and quiet, walk here and stay a night in one of the *gîtes*.

The head of the Girolata trail is at **Bocca â Crocce** (Col de la Croix), on the Calvi–Porto road, from where a clear path plunges downhill through dense maquis and forest to a flotsam-covered cove known as **Cala di Tuara** (30min). The more rewarding of the two tracks that wind onwards to Girolata is the gentler one running left around the headland, but if you feel like stretching your legs, follow the second, more direct route uphill to a pass.

18

### ACCOMMODATION                                                                           GIROLATA

**La Cabane du Berger** On the beach ☎04 95 20 16 98. Basic *gîte d'étape* offering a choice of accommodation in dorms or small wood cabins in the garden behind (these accommodate two people); you can also put your tent up here. Meals are served in their quirky wood-carved bar, but the food isn't up to much. Closed Nov–April; no cards. Dorms €45 (half-board obligatory)

**Le Cormoran Voyageur** Among the houses at the

---

dawn is that it allows you to break the back of the *étape* before 2pm, when clouds tend to bubble over the mountains and obscure the views.

The **weather** in the high mountains is notoriously fickle. A sunny morning doesn't necessarily mean a sunny day, and during July and August violent storms can envelop the route without warning. It's therefore essential to take good wet-weather gear with you, as well as a hat, sunblock and shades. In addition, make sure you set off on each stage with adequate **food** and **water**. At the height of the season, most *refuges* sell basic supplies (*alimentation* or *ravitaillement*), but you shouldn't rely on this service; ask hikers coming from the opposite direction where their last supply stop was and plan accordingly (basic provisions are always available at the main passes of Col de Vergio, Col de Vizzavona, Col de Bavella and Col de Verde). The *refuge* wardens (*gardiens*) will be able to advise you on how much water to carry at each stage.

Finally, a word of **warning**: each year, injured hikers have to be air-lifted to safety off remote sections of the GR20, normally because they strayed from the marked route and got lost. Occasionally, fatal accidents also occur for the same reason, so always keep the paint splashes in sight, especially if the weather closes in – don't rely purely on the many cairns that punctuate the route, as these sometimes mark more hazardous paths to high peaks.

### GETTING TO THE TRAILHEAD

Getting to **Calenzana** from Calvi, trailhead for the GR20, is no easy feat given the sporadic nature of public transport. It's straightforward enough during July and August, when two daily buses leave from the Porteuse d'Eau roundabout in Calvi (2.30pm & 7.30pm; €10); but for the rest of the year, this service only operates once daily on Mondays, Tuesdays, Thursdays and Fridays (3.30pm). Timetables may be consulted at ⓦcorsicabus.org, or via the bus company, Beaux Voyages (☎04 95 65 11 35, ⓦbeauxvoyagesencorse.com).

If you find yourself heading off to the GR20 on a day when the bus isn't running, you can jump in an expensive cab (around €40 from Calvi airport or Lumio, the nearest train station to Calenzana), or, if you're part of a group, hire a car for the day, drive your fellow walkers to Calenzana and catch a cab yourself back up the hill after dropping the car off. Be warned, if you're tempted to cover the stretch on foot, that the road makes a seriously unpleasant, and in places downright dangerous, walk – especially at night (when, inevitably, the taxi fare rises to around €60).

**18**

north end of the cove ☎04 95 20 15 55. Eighteen dorm spaces and a small restaurant overlooking the boat jetty.

Open July & Aug only; no cards. Dorms €48 (half-board obligatory)

## EATING

Unless you're staying at one of the *gîtes*, you'll be better off paying a little extra to eat at one of the two restaurants just up the steps. For a quick bite before heading back up the path, look no further than the little Bastella shop down on the beach, which sells tasty Corsican pasties (*bastelles*), filled with spinach, onions and brocciu.

**A Bastella** On the beach ☎06 19 28 36 13. Located at the far end of the beach, this little snack hut serves freshly made sandwiches and delicious Corsican pasties (*bastelles*) made with local brocciu, spinach and tomatoes, and also rustles up inexpensive wood-baked pizzas (from €12.50). May–Sept daily 11am–6pm.

★ **Le Bel Ombra** ☎04 95 20 15 67, ⓦbel-ombra. com. The pricier of the village's two places to eat, with a terrace overlooking the bay where you can tuck into fresh local seafood specialities, including fresh Scandola lobster. *Menus* from €17. No cards. Daily 11.30am–2.30pm & 7.30–9.30pm.

**Le Bon Espoir** Next door to Le Bel Ombra ☎07 69 16 02 10, ⓦrestaurant-girolata.com. Same view, similar seafood menu (*menu* €24) – the main difference is that the fish comes straight off the *patron*'s own boat. April–Sept daily 11.30am–2.15pm & 7.30–9.30pm.

# Porto (Portu) and around

The overwhelming proximity of the mountains, combined with the pervasive eucalyptus and spicy scent of the maquis, give **PORTO**, 30km south of Calvi, a uniquely intense atmosphere that makes it one of the most interesting places to stay on the west coast. Except for a watchtower erected here by the Genoese in the second half of the sixteenth century, the site was only built upon with the onset of tourism since the 1950s; today the village is still so small that it can become claustrophobic in July and August, when overcrowding is no joke. Off season, the place becomes eerily deserted, so you'd do well to choose your times carefully; the best months are May, June and September.

The crowds and traffic jams tend to be most oppressive passing the famous **Calanches**, a huge mass of weirdly eroded pink rock just southwest of Porto, but you can easily sidestep the tourist deluge in picturesque **Piana**, which overlooks the gulf from its southern shore, or by heading inland from Porto through the **Gorges de Spelunca**. Forming a ravine running from the sea to the watershed of the island, this spectacular gorge gives access to the equally grandiose **Forêt d'Aïtone**, site of Corsica's most ancient Laricio pine trees and a deservedly popular hiking area. Throughout the forest, the river and its tributaries are punctuated by strings of *piscines naturelles* (natural swimming pools) – a refreshing alternative to the beaches hereabouts. If you're travelling between Porto and Ajaccio, a worthwhile place to break the journey is the clifftop village of **Cargèse** where the two main attractions are the Greek church and spectacular beach.

## Vaïta and the marina

Eucalyptus-bordered **route de la Marine** links the two parts of the resort. The village proper, known as **Vaïta**, comprises a strip of supermarkets, shops and hotels 1km from the sea, but the main focus of activity is the small **marina**, located at the avenue's end.

Overlooking the entrance to the harbour is the much-photographed **Genoese Tower** (April–Oct daily 9am–5.30pm; €2.50), a square chimney-shaped structure that was cracked by an explosion in the seventeenth century, when it was used as an arsenal. An awe-inspiring view of the crashing sea and maquis-shrouded mountains makes it worth the short climb.

**18**

---

**BOAT TRIPS FROM PORTO**

A number of firms run **boat excursions** out of Porto harbour between April and October. Most follow comparable itineraries around the Gulf, combining a tour of the **Réserve Naturelle de Scandola** headland with a stop at **Girolata**, and cruises around the Calanches de Piana. The main difference between them is the kind of vessels they use, which vary from converted fishing boats to superfast inflatables. Tickets should be booked in advance direct from the operators (not from the tourist office), who have stalls around the marina, and prices can vary slightly according to demand and time of year. Reduced tariffs for **children** apply to all of the following.

**Compagnie Nave Va** Hôtel Cyrnée, just behind the tourist office ☎04 95 26 15 16, ⓦnaveva. com. The largest firm, with 11 boats running tours around the island, including one that accommodates up to 150 people. Scandola and Girolata daily departures 9.30am and 2.30pm, €38; Calanches de Piana four daily; €25.

**Corse Adrénaline** north side of the marina ☎06 23 06 44 93, ⓦcorseadrenaline.fr. Former fisherman, François-Xavier, and partner Coralie run this scarlet-coloured, 12-seater speedboat, with 600 horsepower of out-board oomph to whisk you between the sites. Contrary to appearances, it's actually the most stable of the smaller boats in Porto – thus more comfortable if the sea's choppy; €30–60, depending on the trip.

**Pass Partout** Anthony Boutique ☎06 85 12 29 15, ⓦlepasspartout.com. This firm specializes in small semi-rigid boats carrying only twelve passengers – a disincentive if there's a big swell, but it allows entry to narrow defiles and caves in the Calanches. Tariffs €26–60, depending on extent and duration of trip.

**Porto Linea** Hôtel Monte Rossu, just off the square ☎04 95 22 28 63, ⓦportolinea.com. The smaller of this outfit's two boats, the *Mare Nostrum II*, carries only twelve people. Scandola and Girolata €45–48; Calanches de Piana cruises €29–55.

**Via Mare** Hotel du Golfe at the foot of the tower ☎06 07 28 72 72, ⓦviamare-promenades. com. This outfit runs the biggest boat in the gulf, with frequent trips (at least three daily) to Scandola (€38) and the Calanches (€26), or longer tours combining both (€47).

---

## The beach

The **beach** consists of a pebbly cove south beyond the shoulder of the massive rock supporting the tower. To reach it from the marina, follow the little road that skirts the rock, cross the wooden bridge which spans the River Porto on your left, then walk through the car park under the trees. Although it's rather rocky and exposed, and the sea very deep, the great crags overshadowing the shore give the place a vivid, wild atmosphere.

### ARRIVAL AND INFORMATION

**By bus** Buses from Calvi, via Galéria, and from Ajaccio, via Cargèse, pull into the junction at the end of route de la Marine, opposite the Banco supermarket, en route to the marina. Timetables are posted at the stops themselves, and at the tourist office.

**Tourist office** Porto's tourist office is down in the marina (May, June & Sept daily 9am–noon & 2–6pm; July & Aug daily 9am–7pm; Oct–April Mon–Fri 9am–noon & 2–5pm; ☎04 95 26 10 55, ⓦporto-tourisme.com), and is of use primarily as a source of Topo-guides and brochures for hikes in the area.

**Diving and sea kayaking** The clear waters of the gulf offer superlative diving. Working out of the marina next to the footbridge, the Centre de Plongée du Golfe (☎06 87 23 60 29, ⓦplongeeporto.com) runs courses for beginners and will take out more experienced divers with their own equipment; you can also fill your gas bottles here and go snorkelling (€20). In addition, the Centre de Plongée du Golfe have unsinkable canoes for rent – ideal for paddling into the hidden coves around Porto.

### ACCOMMODATION

Competition between hotels is more cut-throat in Porto than in any other resort on the island. During slack periods towards the beginning and end of the season, most places engage in a full-on price war, pasting up cheaper tariffs than their neighbours – all of which is great for punters. In late July and August, however, the normal high rates prevail.

**Le Belvédère** Porto marina ☎04 95 26 12 01, ⓦhotelrestaurant-lebelvedere-porto.com. This three-star is the smartest of the hotels overlooking the marina, with great views of Capo d'Orto from its comfortable rooms and terraces. Reasonable rates given the location. **€93**

**Brise de Mer** On the left of rte de la Marine as you approach the tower from the village, opposite the telephone booths ☎04 95 26 10 28, ⊛brise-de-mer. com. A large, somewhat old-fashioned place with very friendly service and a congenial terrace restaurant. Worth spending an extra €4–5 for a room at the back as these have the best views. Closed mid-Oct to March. **€88**

**Camping Les Oliviers** At the east end of the village, next to the bend in the main road ☎04 95 26 14 49, ⊛camping-oliviers-porto.com. Top-notch four-star site, boasting a huge, multilayered pool and a fitness centre. Closed early Nov to March. **€35.60**

**Camping Sol e Vista** At the main road junction near the supermarkets ☎04 95 26 15 71, ⊛camping-sole-e-vista.fr. A superb location on shady terraces ascending a steep hillside with a small café at the top. Great views of Capo d'Orto cliffs opposite, and immaculate toilet blocks, plus it boasts a large curvi-form pool overlooking the bay.

They also have some pleasant bungalows on site. Closed Dec–March. Camping **€36**, bungalows **€920/week**

**Le Colombo** At the top of the village opposite the turning for Ota ☎04 95 26 10 14, ⊛hotel-colombo-porto.com. An informal, sixteen-room hotel overlooking the valley. The rooms are functional but clean and airy, and there's a well-shaded garden for breakfast. Closed mid-Oct to March. **€100**

★ **Corsica** Rte de la Marine ☎ 04 95 26 10 89, ⊛hotel-corsica-porto.com. Only 5 mins' uphill walk from the marina, this recently re-vamped two-star offers great value for money, with spacious, well furnished rooms (most have private terraces) and a lovely pool. The location is quiet, and offers fine views of the towering Capo d'Orto crags behind. Closed Nov–March. **€93**

**Le Golfe** At the base of the rock in the marina ☎04 95 26 12 31, ⊛hotel-le-golfe-porto.com. Small, cosy and unpretentious; rooms are decorated in muted colours and all benefit balconies with sea views; larger rooms have nice sitting areas. The brasserie downstairs is a bonus. Closed Nov–April. **€58**

### EATING AND DRINKING

The overall standard of restaurants in Porto is poor, with overpriced food and indifferent service the norm, particularly during high season. There are, however, a couple of noteworthy exceptions:

**A Stretta** In the marina ☎04 95 27 12 49. Appealing modern restaurant with just a few tables and an owner who likes to get to know his customers. Expect lots of exquisite fresh fish on offer, included in the tapas-style starters (€12.50); mains from €26.50 – the *menu* is excellent value at €39.50. Daily noon–2pm & 7–8.15pm.

**Le Moulin** Pont de Porto ☎04 95 26 12 09. A charming riverside restaurant just outside of town, with an appealing terrace with river views, and a decent *menu* (€24) of local specialities. Try the veal stew if it's on offer. March–Nov daily 11.30am–2pm & 6.30–10pm.

# The Calanches

The UNESCO-protected site of the **Calanches**, 5km southwest of Porto, takes its name from *calanca*, the Corsican word for creek or inlet, but the outstanding characteristics here are the vivid orange and pink rock masses and pinnacles which crumble into the dark-blue sea. Liable to unusual patterns of erosion, these tormented rock formations and porphyry needles, some of which soar 300m above the waves, have long been associated with different animals and figures, of which the most famous is the Tête de Chien (Dog's Head) at the north end of the stretch of cliffs. Other figures and creatures conjured up include a Moor's head, a monocled bishop, a bear and a tortoise.

One way to see the fantastic cliffs of the Calanches is by boat from Porto. Alternatively, you could drive along the corniche road that weaves through the granite archways on its way to Piana. Eight kilometres along the road from Porto, the *Roches Bleues* café is a convenient landmark for walkers.

## Piana

Picturesque **PIANA** occupies a prime location overlooking the Calanches, but for some reason does not suffer the deluge of tourists that Porto endures. Retaining a sleepy feel, the village comprises a cluster of pink houses ranged around an eighteenth-century church and square, from the edge of which the panoramic views over the Golfe de Porto are sublime.

★ **Les Roches Rouges** Rte de Porto ☎04 95 27 81 81, ⊚lesrochesrouges.com. Having lain empty for two decades, this elegant old *grand hôtel* rising from the eucalyptus canopy on the outskirts was restored with most of its original fittings and furniture intact, and possesses loads of *fin-de-siècle* style. The rooms are huge and light, with large shuttered windows, but make sure you get one facing the water. Non-residents are welcome to drop in for a sundowner on the magnificent terrace, or for a meal in the fresco-covered restaurant, whose *menus gastronomiques* (€39–49), dominated by local seafood delicacies, are as sophisticated as the ambience. Count on €65–90 for three courses à la carte. Closed Nov–March. **€130**

**18**

# The Gorges de Spelunca

Spanning the 2km between the villages of **Ota** and **Évisa**, a few kilometres inland from Porto, the **Gorges de Spelunca** are a formidable sight, with bare orange granite walls, 1km deep in places, plunging into the foaming green torrent created by the confluence of the rivers Porto, Tavulella, Onca, Campi and Aïtone. The sunlight, ricocheting across the rock walls, creates a sinister effect that's heightened by the dark jagged needles of the encircling peaks. The most dramatic part of the gorge can be seen from the road, which hugs the edge for much of its length.

## Évisa

**ÉVISA**'s bright orange roofs emerge against a lush background of chestnut forests about 10km from Ota, on the eastern edge of the gorge, and the village makes the best base for hiking in the area. Situated 830m above sea level, it caters well for hikers and makes a pleasant stop for a taste of mountain life – the air is invariably crisp and clear, and the food particularly good.

---

### CALANCHES WALKS

The rock formations visible from the road are not a patch on what you can see from the waymarked **trails** winding through the Calanches, which vary from easy ambles to strenuous stepped ascents. An excellent leaflet highlighting the pick of the routes is available free from tourist offices. Whichever one you choose, leave early in the morning or late in the afternoon to avoid the heat in summer, and take plenty of water.

• **Walk one** The most popular walk is to the Château Fort (1hr), which begins at a sharp hairpin in the D81, 700m north of the *Café Les Roches Bleues* (look for the car park and signboard at the roadside). Passing the famous Tête de Chien, it snakes along a ridge lined by dramatic porphyry forms to a huge square chunk of granite resembling a ruined castle. Just before reaching it there's an open platform from where the views of the gulf and Paglia Orba, Corsica's third-highest mountain, are superb – one of the best sunset spots on the island – but bring a torch to help find the path back.

• **Walk two** For a more challenging extension to Walk one, begin instead at the *Café Les Roches Bleues*. On the opposite side of the road, two paths strike up the hill: follow the one on your left (nearest the stream, as you face away from the café), which zigzags steeply up the rocks, over a pass and down the other side to rejoin the D81 in around 1hr 15min. About 150m west of the spot where you meet the road is the trailhead for the Château Fort walk, with more superb views.

• **Walk three** A small oratory niche in the cliff by the roadside, 500m south of *Café Les Roches Bleues*, contains a Madonna statue, Santa Maria, from where the wonderful *sentier muletier* (1hr) climbs into the rocks above. Before the road was blasted through the Calanches in 1850, this old paved path, an extraordinary feat of workmanship supported in places by dry-stone banks and walls, formed the main artery between the villages of Piana and Ota. After a very steep start, the route contours through the rocks and pine woods above the restored mill at Pont de Gavallaghiu, emerging after one hour back on the D81, roughly 1.5km south of the starting point. Return by the same path.

## ACCOMMODATION

**Camping Acciola** 3km out of Évisa ☎04 95 26 23 01, ⓦacciola.com. A small site, in the depths of nowhere, with a café-bar and great panorama over the mountains. Take the D84 for 2km, and turn right at the T-junction towards Cristinacce; *Acciola* lies another 400m on your left. **€18.40**

**Scopa Rossa** On the east edge of the village ☎04 95 26 20 22, ⓦhotelscoparossa.com. In a lovely location elevated above the village, this unfussy hotel has simple, if unexciting, rooms and a restaurant serving Corsican specialities. Half board is available. **€66**

## EATING

**A Tràmula** In the middle of the village ☎04 95 23 08 94. Traditional local cuisine – quality charcuterie, veal's tongue in *vin de myrthe*, chestnut crêpes and other delights – with ingredients sourced in or from the farms in the immediate area. Ask for a table on the tiny balcony overlooking the valley. You can also buy local produce here. Mains €12–25; *menu* at €26. April–Sept daily noon–3pm & 6–10.30pm; Oct–March, eves only.

# Cargèse (Carghjese)

Sitting high above a deep-blue bay on a cliff scattered with olive trees, **CARGÈSE**, 20km southwest of Porto, exudes a lazy charm that attracts hundreds of well-heeled summer residents to its pretty white houses and hotels. The full-time locals, half of whom are descendants of Greek refugees who fled the Turkish occupation of the Peloponnese in the seventeenth century, seem to accept with nonchalance this inundation – and the proximity of a large Club Med complex – but the best times to visit are May and late September, when Cargèse is all but empty.

## The Roman Catholic and Greek churches

Two churches stand on separate hummocks at the heart of the village, a reminder of the old antagonism between the two cultures (resentful Corsican patriots ransacked the Greeks' original settlement in 1715 because of the newcomers' refusal to take up arms against their Genoese benefactors). The **Roman Catholic church**, built for the minority Corsican families in 1828, is one of the latest examples of Baroque in Corsica, with a trompe l'ocil ceiling. The **Greek church**, however, is the more interesting of the two: a large granite Neo-Gothic edifice built in 1852 to replace a building that had become too small for its congregation. Inside, the outstanding feature is an unusual iconostasis, a gift from a monastery in Rome, decorated with uncannily modern-looking portraits. Behind it hang icons brought over from Greece with the original settlers – the graceful Virgin and Child, to the right-hand side of the altar, is thought to date as far back as the twelfth century.

## Plage de Pero

The best beach in the area, **plage de Pero**, is 2km north of the village – head up to the junction with the Piana road and take the left fork down to the sea.

### ARRIVAL AND INFORMATION | CARGÈSE

**By bus** Autocars Roger Ceccaldi buses (☎04 95 21 38 06, ⓦautocars-ceccaldi-ajaccio.fr) pass through Cargèse en route to and from Ajaccio and Porto, stopping outside the tiny main square in the centre of the village. The service runs twice times daily in July and August and daily (Mon–Sat) from September to June.

**Tourist office** The village's tourist office stands on rue du Dr-Dragacci (July–Sept daily 9am–1pm & 2.30–7pm; Oct– June Mon–Fri 9am–1pm & 2.30–5.30pm; ☎04 95 26 41 31, ⓦcargese.net).

**Boat trips** Launch trips to the Calanches and Scandola run daily out of Cargèse in season, costing €30/55 respectively (☎04 95 28 02 66, ⓦnaveva.com). Tickets may be purchased on departure or, to secure a place in high season, in advance from the tourist office.

### ACCOMMODATION

**Camping Torraccia** 4km north of Cargèse on the main road ☎04 95 26 42 39, ⓦcamping-torraccia.com. Well shaded under olive groves, its best pitches are at the top of the hill, looking inland towards Capo Vitullo (1331m); they also have simple wood bungalows that can be rented on a daily basis out of season, or by the week from late June to

**18**

August. Camping **€17.60**, bungalows **€950/week**

**Le Continental** Top of the village, near the turning for plage de Pero ☎ 04 95 26 42 24, ⓦ continentalhotel. free.fr. Cosy, mostly sea-facing rooms (not all en suite) overlooking the main road just past place St-Jean. Clean, efficient, and good value. **€80**

**Cyrnos** Rue de la République ☎ 04 95 26 49 47, ⓦ hotel-cyrnos.torraccia.com. Simple hotel on the main street offering smallish and plain but clean rooms with mountain or sea views; the glass-partitioned balconies of the *vue sur la mer* rooms look out over the church to the bay. **€40**

★ **Les Lentisques** Plage de Pero ☎ 04 95 26 42 34, ⓦ leslentisques.com. Head down the lane dropping downhill from the junction at the top of the village to reach this congenial, family-run three-star. Nestled in the dunes behind the area's nicest beach, it has a large, breezy breakfast hall and simple rooms (fully en suite and sea-facing), though some could do with an update, and there's also a fair-sized pool. **€164**

**Punta e Mare** Up the lane past the Spar supermarket ☎ 06 89 72 41 81, ⓦ locations-cargese.com. Secluded, unpretentious hotel tucked away on the quiet outskirts of the village. There's ample parking, and the rooms, though on the small side, are bright, well kept and have little loggias. **€105**

**St-Jean** Overlooking the crossroads ☎ 04 95 26 46 68, ⓦ lesaintjean.com. Smart rooms, some with sea views, balconies. Duplex family rooms are particularly spacious. There's a smart restaurant, but it's the lovely terrace with its sea views that really steals the show. **€70**

## EATING AND DRINKING

A fair number of restaurants are scattered about the village, as well as the standard crop of basic pizzerias, but the most tempting place to eat is down in the harbour.

**U Rasaghiu** In the marina ☎ 04 95 26 48 60. Consists of two adjacent outlets: the first does *spécialités corses* and seafood dishes (including lobster in garlic sauce), at reasonable prices (*menu* €24); the second offers huge pizzas to eat in or takeaway (€12–17). They also lay on live polyphony music two or three evenings each week in season; it gets very popular (and lively). Feb–Nov daily noon–2.30 & 6–midnight.

# Ajaccio (Aiacciu)

Edward Lear claimed that on a wet day it would be hard to find so dull a place as **AJACCIO**, a harsh judgement with an element of justice. The town has none of Bastia's sense of purpose and can seem to lack a definitive identity of its own, but it is a relaxed and good-looking place, with an exceptionally mild climate, and a wealth of smart cafés, restaurants and shops.

Although it's an attractive idea that Ajax, hero of the Trojan War, once stopped here, the name of Ajaccio actually derives from the Roman *Adjaccium* (place of rest), a winter stop-off point for shepherds descending from the mountains to stock up on goods and sell their produce. This first settlement was destroyed by the Saracens in the tenth century, and modern Ajaccio grew up around the citadelle founded in 1492. **Napoleon** gave the town international fame, but though the self-designated *Cité Impériale* is littered with statues and street names related to the Bonaparte family, you'll find that the Napoleonic cult has a less dedicated following here than you might imagine: the emperor is still considered by many Ajacciens as a self-serving Frenchman rather than as a Corsican.

Since the early 1980s, Ajaccio has gained an unwelcome reputation for nationalist violence. The most infamous terrorist atrocity of recent decades was the murder, in February 1998, of the French government's most senior official on the island, Claude Érignac, who was gunned down as he left the opera. However, separatist violence rarely (if ever) affects tourists here, and for visitors Ajaccio remains memorable for the things that have long made it attractive – its battered old town, relaxing cafés and the encompassing view of its glorious bay.

The core of the **old town** – a cluster of ancient streets spreading north and south of **place Foch**, which opens out to the seafront by the port and the marina – holds the most interest. Nearby, to the west, **place de Gaulle** forms the modern centre and is the source of the main thoroughfare, **cours Napoléon**, which extends parallel to the sea almost 2km to the northeast. West of place de Gaulle stretches the modern part of town fronted by the **beach**, overlooked at its eastern end by the citadelle.

## Place Foch

Once the site of the town's medieval gate, **place Foch** lies at the heart of old Ajaccio. A delightfully shady square sloping down to the sea, it gets its local name – place des Palmiers – from the row of palms bordering the central strip. Dominating the top end, a fountain of four marble lions provides a mount for the inevitable statue of Napoleon. A humbler effigy occupies a niche high on the nearest wall – a figurine of Ajaccio's patron saint, **La Madonnuccia**, dating from 1656, a year in which Ajaccio's

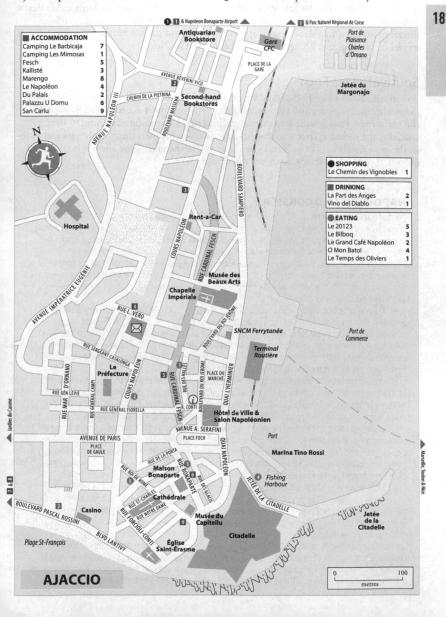

**ACCOMMODATION**

| | |
|---|---|
| Camping Le Barbicaja | 7 |
| Camping Les Mimosas | 1 |
| Fesch | 5 |
| Kallisté | 3 |
| Marengo | 8 |
| Le Napoléon | 4 |
| Du Palais | 2 |
| Palazzu U Domu | 6 |
| San Carlu | 9 |

**SHOPPING**

| | |
|---|---|
| Le Chemin des Vignobles | 1 |

**DRINKING**

| | |
|---|---|
| La Part des Anges | 2 |
| Vino del Diablo | 1 |

**EATING**

| | |
|---|---|
| Le 20123 | 5 |
| Le Bilboq | 3 |
| Le Grand Café Napoléon | 2 |
| O Mon Bato! | 4 |
| Le Temps des Oliviers | 1 |

**AJACCIO**

local council, fearful of infection from plague-struck Genoa, placed the town under the guardianship of the Madonna in a ceremony conducted on this spot.

## Salon Napoléonien

Mid-June to mid-Sept Mon 2–5.45pm Tues–Sun 9–11.45am & 2–5.45pm; mid-Sept to mid-June Mon–Fri 9–11.45am & 2–4.45pm • €2.30 • ⓦ ajaccio.fr

At the northern end of place Foch stands the **hôtel de ville** of 1826. Its first floor is given over to the **Salon Napoléonien**, which contains a replica of the ex-emperor's death mask, along with a solemn array of Bonaparte family portraits and busts. A smaller medal room has a fragment from Napoleon's coffin and part of his dressing case, plus a model of the ship that brought his body back from St Helena.

## South of place Foch

The south side of place Foch, standing on the former dividing line between the poor district around the port and the bourgeoisie's territory, gives access to **rue Bonaparte**, the main route through the latter quarter. Built on the promontory rising to the citadelle, the secluded streets in this part of town – with their dusty buildings and hole-in-the-wall restaurants lit by flashes of sea or sky at the end of the alleys – retain more of a sense of the old Ajaccio than anywhere else.

---

### NAPOLEON AND CORSICA

**Napoleon Bonaparte** was born in Ajaccio in 1769, a year after the French took over the island from the Genoese. They made a thorough job of it, crushing the Corsican leader Paoli's troops at Ponte Nuovo and driving him into exile. Napoleon's father Carlo, a close associate of Paoli, fled the scene of the battle with his pregnant wife in order to escape the victorious French army. But Carlo's subsequent behaviour was quite different from that of his former leader – he came to terms with the French, becoming a representative of the newly styled Corsican nobility in the National Assembly, and using his contacts with the French governor to get a free education for his children.

At the age of 9, Napoleon was awarded a scholarship to the **Brienne military academy**, an institution specially founded to teach the sons of the French nobility the responsibilities of their status, and the young son of a Corsican Italian-speaking household used his time well, leaving Brienne to enter the exclusive **École Militaire** in Paris. At the age of 16 he was commissioned into the artillery. When he was 20 the Revolution broke out in Paris and the scene was set for a remarkable career.

Always an ambitious opportunist, Napoleon obtained leave from his regiment, returned to Ajaccio, joined the local Jacobin club and – with his eye on a colonelship in the Corsican militia – promoted enthusiastically the interests of the Revolution. However, things did not quite work out as he had planned, for **Pascal Paoli** had also returned to Corsica.

Carlo Bonaparte had died some years before, and Napoleon was head of a family that had formerly given Paoli strong support. Having spent the last twenty years in London, Paoli was pro-English and had developed a profound distaste for revolutionary excesses. Napoleon's French allegiance and his Jacobin views antagonized the older man, and his military conduct didn't enhance his standing at all. Elected second-in-command of the volunteer militia, Napoleon was involved in an unsuccessful attempt to wrest control of the citadelle from royalist sympathizers. He thus took much of the blame when, in reprisal for the killing of one of the militiamen, several people were gunned down in Ajaccio, an incident which engendered eight days of civil war. In June 1793, Napoleon and his family were chased back to the mainland by the Paolists.

Napoleon promptly renounced any special allegiance he had ever felt for Corsica. He Gallicized the spelling of his name, preferring Napoléon to his baptismal Napoleone. And, although he was later to speak with nostalgia about the scents of the Corsican countryside, he put the city of his birth fourth on the list of places he would like to be buried.

## Maison Bonaparte

Rue Saint-Charles • April–Sept Tues–Sun 10am–12.30pm & 1.15–5.30pm, Oct–March Tues–Sun 10.30am–12.30pm & 1.15–4.30pm • €7 • ☎ 094 95 21 43 89, ⓦ musee-maisonbonaparte.fr

Napoleon was born in what's now the colossal **Maison Bonaparte**, on rue Saint-Charles, off the west side of rue Bonaparte. The house passed to Napoleon's father in the 1760s and here he lived, with his wife and family, until his death. But in May 1793, the Bonapartes were driven from the house by Paoli's partisans, who stripped the place down to the floorboards. Requisitioned by the English in 1794, Maison Bonaparte became an arsenal and a lodging house for English officers until Napoleon's mother Letizia herself funded its restoration. Owned by the state since 1923, the house now bears few traces of the Bonaparte family's existence. One of the few original pieces of furniture left in the house is the wooden sedan chair in the hallway – the pregnant Letizia was carried back from church in it when her contractions started. The upper floors house an endless display of portraits, miniatures, weapons, letters and documents.

**18**

## The cathedral

Mon–Fri 10am–6pm; no tourist visits on Sat or Sun

Napoleon was baptized in 1771 in the **cathedral**, on rue Forcioli-Conti. Modelled on St Peter's in Rome, it was built in 1587–93 on a much smaller scale than intended, owing to lack of funds – an apology for its diminutive size is inscribed in a plaque inside, on the wall to the left as you enter. Inside, to the right of the door, stands the font where he was dipped at the age of 23 months. Before you go, take a look in the chapel to the left of the altar, which houses a gloomy Delacroix painting of the Virgin.

# North of place Foch

The dark narrow streets backing onto the port to the north of place Foch are Ajaccio's traditional trading ground. Each weekday and Saturday morning (and on Sundays during the summer), the square directly behind the *hôtel de ville* hosts a small **fresh produce market** where you can browse and buy top-quality fresh produce from around the island, including myrtle liqueur, wild-boar sauces, ewe's cheese from the Niolo valley and a spread of fresh vegetables, fruit and flowers.

## Palais Fesch: Musée des Beaux Arts

50–52 rue Cardinal Fesch • Daily: May–Oct 9.15am–6pm; Nov–April 9am–5pm, Thurs, Fri & Sat noon–5pm • €8 • ⓦ musee-fesch.com

Behind here, the principal road leading north off the place Foch is rue **Cardinal-Fesch**, a delightful meandering street lined with boutiques, cafés and restaurants. Halfway along, set back from the road behind iron gates, stands Ajaccio's – indeed Corsica's – finest art gallery, the resplendent **Palais Fesch: Musée des Beaux-Arts**. Cardinal Joseph Fesch was Napoleon's step-uncle and bishop of Lyon, and he used his lucrative position to invest in large numbers of paintings, many of them looted by the French armies in Holland, Italy and Germany. His bequest to the town includes seventeenth-century French and Spanish masters, but it's the Italian paintings that are the chief attraction: Titian, Bellini, Veronese, Botticelli and Michelangelo are all represented in state-of-the-art air-conditioned galleries.

## Chapelle Impériale

50–52 rue du Cardinal-Fesch • April–June & Sept Mon 1–5.15pm, Tues–Sun 9.15am–12.15pm & 2.15–5.15pm; July & Aug Mon 1.30–6pm, Tues–Thurs 9–6.30pm, Fri 9am–6.30pm & 9pm–midnight, Sat & Sun 10.30am–6pm; Oct–March Tues–Sat 9.15am–12.15pm & 2.15–5.15pm • €1.50

The **Chapelle Impériale** stands across the courtyard from the Musée des Beaux-Arts. With its gloomy monochrome interior the chapel itself is unremarkable, and its interest lies in the crypt, where various members of the Bonaparte family are buried. It was the cardinal's dying wish that all the Bonaparte family be brought together under one roof, so the chapel was built in 1857 and the bodies – all except Napoleon's – subsequently ferried in.

## Les Îles Sanguinaires

Municipal buses (line #5) run roughly twice hourly to Punta della Parata from cours Napoléon and place de Gaulle, passing a string of small beaches en route

The largest of the islets, Mezzo Mare (or Grande Sanguinaire), is topped by a lighthouse where Alphonse Daudet spent ten days in December 1862. Tufts of gorse, a square watchtower (la Tour de Castellucciu) and crashing surf give the place a dramatic air. Without the luxury of your own vessel, the only way to get a close look at them is to join the daily boat excursion from Porticcio and Ajaccio run by Nave Va (see below). You can, however, enjoy the iconic view of the islands from **Punta della Parata**, the narrow, rocky headland facing them from the mainland. A ten-minute clamber from the car park at the road's end takes you up to the **Tour de la Parata**, a 12m-tall watchtower built of dark grey granite in 1608. One of the last of its kind erected by the Genoese to guard the coast against Barbary pirates, it sports the rusting remains of Corsica's first aerial telegraph, installed in the latter half of the eighteenth century.

### ARRIVAL AND DEPARTURE                                              AJACCIO

#### BY PLANE
Served by domestic and international flights, Ajaccio's Napoléon Bonaparte (formerly Campo dell'Oro) Airport (☎04 95 23 56 56, ⚙www.2a.cci.fr/Aeroport-Napoleon-Bonaparte-Ajaccio.html) is 8km south of town around the bay. Shuttle buses, or *navettes* (hourly 6am–10.45pm; ☎04 95 23 29 41) provide an inexpensive link with the centre, stopping at the train sation – tickets cost €5 one-way, and the journey takes around 20min. This is also the best place to pick up buses from the centre to the airport. Taxis charge around €20–25 for the trip, and slightly more on Sundays, holidays and after 7pm.

#### BY BOAT
Ferries dock at the gare Maritime on quai L'Herminier (☎04 95 51 21 80). Facilities are limited to a toilet and waiting area, where Corsica Ferries has a booking counter; La Méridionale has an office nearby. There's no left luggage here at present.
**Ferry offices** Corsica Ferries, counter inside the gare Maritime (☎04 95 50 78 82, ⚙corsicaferries.com); La Méridionale, on the quayside a 5min walk north of the terminal building along bd Sampiero (☎04 91 99 45 09, ⚙lameridionale.fr).

#### INFORMATION
**Tourist office** 3 boulevard du Roi-Jérôme (April–June & Sept Mon–Sat 8am–7pm, Sun 9am–1pm; July & Aug Mon–Sat 8am–8.30pm, Sun 9am–1pm & 4–7pm; Oct–March Mon–Fri 8.30am–12.30pm & 2–6pm, Sat 8.30am–12.30pm & 2–5pm; ☎04 95 51 53 03, ⚙ajaccio-tourisme.com). They hand out large free glossy maps and post transport timetables for checking departure times.
**National Park Office** Anyone planning a long-distance

Destinations Marseille (up to 4 weekly; 12hr overnight); Nice (up to 6 weekly; 5hr 25min); Toulon (up to 3 daily; 5hr 55min).

#### BY BUS
Long-distance buses work from the lay-by outside the gare Maritime. All of the various companies have booking and information counters inside the departures hall (to the right of the building as you enter).
Destinations Bonifacio (1–2 daily; 3hr 15min); Cargèse (1 daily; 1hr 15min); Évisa (1 daily; 2hr 5min); Porto (1 daily; 1hr 55min); Porto-Vecchio (1–2 daily; 3hr 10min); Propriano (1–2 daily; 1hr 35min); Sartène (1–2 daily; 1hr 45min).

#### BY TRAIN
The train station lies almost a kilometre north along bd Sampiero (☎04 95 23 11 03, ⚙ter-sncf.com), a continuation of the quai l'Herminier.
Destinations Bastia (4 daily; 3hr 30min); Calvi (2 daily; 4hr); Corte (4 daily; 1hr 30min); L'Île Rousse (2 daily; 3hr 35min).

hike should head for the office of the national parks association, the Parc Naturel Régional de Corse, 19 av Georges-Pompidou, 4km northwest of the centre (Mon–Fri 8am–noon & 2–6pm; ☎04 95 51 79 00, ⚙pnr.corsica), where you can buy Topo-guides, maps, guidebooks and leaflets.
**Hospital** Centre Hospitalier, 27 av Impératrice-Eugénie ☎04 95 29 90 90; for an ambulance, call ☎15.

## GETTING AROUND

**Car rental** Rent-a-Car, 52 cours Napoléon (☎04 95 51 34 45) and the airport (☎04 95 23 56 36); and Avis, 1 rue Colonna d'Istria (☎04 95 23 92 55) and the airport (☎04 95 23 56 90).

**Bus** The most useful of the Municipal bus routes crisscrossing the city is line #5, which runs a few times hourly from place de Gaulle to Parata for the Îles Sanguinaires.

**Boat trips** Nave Va (☎04 95 51 31 31, ⊛naveva.com) operate popular gulf cruises from Ajaccio's Marina Tino Rossi, departing at 2.40pm. Tickets cost €27. The same firm also runs longer day-trips north as far as Scandola, and south around the coast to Bonifacio.

## ACCOMMODATION

18

Ajaccio suffers from a dearth of inexpensive accommodation, but there are a fair number of mid- and upscale places. Whatever your budget, it's essential to book ahead, especially for weekends between late May and September, when beds are virtually impossible to come by at short notice.

**Camping Le Barbicaja** 4.5km west along the rte des Sanguinaires ☎04 95 52 01 17, ⊛camping-barbicaja. com. Close to the beach and easier to reach by bus (#5 from place de Gaulle) than *Les Mimosas*, but more crowded, and altogether grottier. Closed Nov–March. **€17**

**Camping Les Mimosas** 3km northwest of town ☎04 95 20 99 85, ⊛camping-lesmimosas.com. A shady and well-organized site with clean toilet blocks, friendly management and fair rates – though a long trudge if you're loaded with luggage. Closed Nov–April. **€16**

**Fesch** 7 rue du Cardinal-Fesch ☎04 95 51 62 62, ⊛hotel-fesch.com. Surprisingly smart three-star hotel in a superb, central location. All the rooms have double glazing (a bonus in this part of town) and the more expensive ones benefit from private terraces. **€115**

★ **Kallisté** 51 cours Napoléon ☎04 95 51 34 45, ⊛hotel-kalliste-ajaccio.com. Efficient hotel in an eighteenth-century tenement, with plenty of parking space. Soundproofed rooms for up to four people, all with cable TVs and bathrooms. The staff speak English. **€79**

★ **Marengo** 12 bd Mme-Mère ☎04 95 21 43 66, ⊛hotel-marengo.com. A 10min walk west of the centre, up a quiet side street off bd Mme-Mère. Slightly boxed in by tower blocks, but it's a secluded, quiet and pleasant small hotel (with only 18 rooms) away from the city bustle,

though rates feel a bit too steep in high season. Closed mid-Nov to mid-March. **€119**

**Le Napoléon** 4 rue Lorenzo-Vero ☎04 95 51 54 00, ⊛hotel-napoleon-ajaccio.fr. Dependable upper-mid-scale hotel slap in the centre of town, on a side road off cours Napoléon, in a revamped Second Empire building. Comfortable, very welcoming and good value for the location, though peak season tariffs are high. **€130**

**Du Palais** 5 av Bévérini-Vico ☎04 95 22 73 68, ⊛hoteldupalaisajaccio.com. Well-run mid-scale place, a 10min walk north of the centre, within easy reach of the train station. The rooms are on the small side, but they're impeccably clean. Ask for one at the rear of the building if you want peace and quiet. **€85**

**Palazzu U Domu** 17 rue Bonaparte ☎04 95 50 00 20, ⊛palazzu-domu.com. The only place resembling a boutique hotel in Ajaccio, housed in a former mansion of the Pozzo di Borgo clan. Using natural materials such as teak and slate, it manages to fuse Imperial elegance with contemporary designer chic. The effect of all the dark wood and stone is a touch sombre and some of the rooms are on the gloomy side, but this is as cool as accommodation in the Imperial City gets, and it's right in the middle of the old quarter (all the other luxury hotels are well out of town). **€298**

**San Carlu** 8 bd Danielle-Casanova ☎04 95 21 13 84, ⊛hotel-sancarlu.com. Sited opposite the citadelle and close to the beach, this three-star hotel is the poshest option on the waterfront, with sunny, well-furnished rooms, all fully a/c, and a special suite for disabled guests in the basement – but no parking. Closed Dec. **€109**

## EATING, DRINKING AND ENTERTAINMENT

At mealtimes, the alleyways and little squares of Ajaccio's old town become one large, interconnecting restaurant terrace lit by rows of candles. All too often, however, the breezy locations and views of the gulf mask indifferent cooking and inflated prices. With the majority of visitors spending merely a night or two here in transit, only those places catering for a local clientele attempt to provide real value for money. Bars and cafés jostle for pavement space along cours Napoléon, generally lined with people checking out the promenaders, and on place de Gaulle, where old-fashioned cafés and *salons de thé* offer a still more sedate scene. If you fancy a view of the bay, try one of the flashy cocktail bars that line the seafront on bd Lantivy, which,

along with the casino, a few cinemas and a handful of overpriced clubs, comprise the sum total of Ajaccio's lacklustre nightlife.

### RESTAURANTS

**Le 20123** 2 rue du Roi-de-Rome ☎04 95 21 50 05, ⊛20123.fr. Decked out like a small hill village, complete with fountain and parked Vespa, the decor here's a lot more frivolous than the food: serious Corsican gastronomy features on a single €37 *menu*. Top-notch cooking, and organic AOC wine. No cards. Noon–2.30pm & 7–11.30pm. Closed Mon, except in July & Aug.

**Le Bilboq (Chez Jean-Jean)** 2 rue des Glacis, just off

**18**

place Foch ☎04 95 51 35 40. The eponymous patron (a former fisherman and boxer) of this legendary seafood joint is Ajaccio's undisputed "lobster king" – and there's only one thing on the menu: local *langouste*, served grilled with spaghetti. Dine alfresco on a narrow alley terrace, or inside, regaled by the music of Tino Rossi (which, unlike the lobster, is definitely an acquired taste). Dessert, should you have room, is a delicious chestnut tart. Count on €60–80 per head for three courses, plus wine. Daily 6.30–10.30pm.

**Le Grand Café Napoléon** 10 cours Napoléon ☎04 95 21 42 54. With its studiously Second Empire decor, this is Ajaccio's most genteel meeting place. Drop by for a pastry at the chi-chi *salon de thé*, or dine in Napoléon III splendour in the restaurant. *Menus* from €24; or around €60–70 for three courses, plus wine. Mon–Sat 7am–11pm.

★ **O Mon Bato!** Vieux Port Tino Rossi ☎07 69 76 05 15. This seafood restaurant onboard a boat could be really gimmicky but manages to pull it off with aplomb, creating the perfect place to sip chilled rosé and watch the (other) boats bob in the harbour. The short carte is resolutely anchored in the sea, with dishes such as *soupe de poisson* to start (€15) and grilled red mullet for mains (€24). Wed–Sun noon–2.30pm & 7pm–2am.

**Le Temps des Oliviers** 1 rue des Halles ☎04 95 28 36 72. Run by a pair of young sisters, this upbeat backstreet bistro occupies a secluded spot on a traffic-free alley behind the tourist office. It serves quality Italian dishes: the pizzas (cooked on a state-of-the-art Morello oven; €11–22) are sublime, and so are the risotto and *grillades*. DJs play most Thursday evenings. Get there early for a table outside on the terrace. Sun–Thurs 7.30–11pm, Fri & Sat 7.30pm–12.30am.

**BARS**

**La Part des Anges** Diamant II, bd Lantivy ☎04 95 21 29 34. Lively wine bar below the place de Gaulle, near the Casino, popular with a bourgeois 18–30 crowd. Live jazz and DJs on Fri & Sat during the summer. At lunchtime it doubles as a gastro-bar, serving inventive light bites (around €25 per head). Daily 7am–2am.

**Vino del Diablo** Port de l'Amirauté ☎04 95 22 70 10. This cool, modern tapas bar is a good place ot head throughout the evening – though it's worth booking if you want to eat. Later in the evenings DJs take to the decks. Mon–Sat 6pm–2am.

**SHOPPING**

**Le Chemin des Vignobles** 16 av Noël-Francini ☎04 95 51 46 61. Stocks the broadest selection of Corsican wines of any shop on the island. Tues–Sat 10am–noon & 2.30–7.30pm.

# Le Golfe de Valinco

From Ajaccio, the vista of whitewashed villas and sandy beaches lining the opposite side of the gulf may tempt you out of town when you first arrive. On closer inspection, however, **Porticcio** turns out to be a faceless string of leisure settlements for Ajaccio's smart set, complete with tennis courts, malls and flotillas of jet-skis. Better to skip this stretch and press on south along the T40 highway which, after scaling the **Col de Celaccia**, winds down to the stunning **Golfe de Valinco**. A vast blue inlet bounded by rolling, scrub-covered hills, the gulf presents the first dramatic scenery along the coastal highway. It also marks the start of militant and Mafia-ridden south Corsica, more closely associated with vendetta, banditry and separatism than any other part of the island. Many of the mountain villages glimpsed from the roads hereabouts are riven with age-old divisions, exacerbated in recent years by the spread of organized crime and nationalist violence. But the island's seamier side is rarely discernible to the hundreds of thousands of visitors who pass through each summer, most of whom stay around the small port of **Propriano**, at the eastern end of the gulf. In addition to offering most of the area's tourist amenities, this busy resort town lies within easy reach of the menhirs at **Filitosa**, one of the western Mediterranean's most important prehistoric sites.

**GETTING AROUND**            **THE GOLFE DE VALINCO**

The Golfe de Valinco region is reasonably well served by public transport, with buses running two to three times per day between Ajaccio and Bonifacio, via Propriano and Sartène. Note, however, that outside July and August there are no services along this route on Sundays.

# Propriano (Pruprià)

Tucked into the narrowest part of the Golfe de Valinco, the small port of **PROPRIANO**, 57km southeast of Ajaccio, centres on a fine natural harbour that was exploited by the ancient Greeks, Carthaginians and Romans, but became a prime target for Saracen pirate raids in the sixteenth century, when it was largely destroyed. Redeveloped in the 1900s, it now boasts a thriving marina, and handles ferries to Marseille and Sardinia.

### The beaches

During the summer, tourists come here in droves for the area's **beaches**. The nearest of these, **plage du Lido**, lies 1km west, just beyond the Port de Commerce, but it's nowhere near as pretty as the coves strung along the northern shore of the gulf around **Olmeto plage**. You can reach Olmeto on the three daily buses from Propriano to Porto.

**18**

## ARRIVAL AND INFORMATION

**By boat** Ferries from the mainland and Sardinia dock in the Port de Commerce, a 10min walk from rue du Général-de-Gaulle, the town's main street. La Méridionale operate all services from here; they are represented in Propriano by Voyages Sorba, 15 quai l'Herminier (☎ 04 95 76 04 36, ⓦ sorba-voyages.com).

**By bus** Buses go from the roadside next to the church on rue de la Miséricorde/Montée de l'Église, above the village

centre.

Destinations Ajaccio (2–3 daily; 1hr 45min); Porto-Vecchio (2–3 daily; 1hr 45min); Sartène (2–3 daily; 20min).

**Tourist office** Quai St-Érasme (June & Sept Mon–Sat 9am–1pm & 3–7pm; July & Aug daily 8am–8pm; Oct–May Mon–Fri 9am–1pm & 3–6pm; ☎ 04 95 76 01 49, ⓦ lacorsedesorigines.com).

## ACCOMMODATION

**Arcu di Sole** Rte de Baracci ☎ 04 95 76 05 10, ⓦ hotel-arcudisole.com. A large modern pink building with green shutters, just off the main Ajaccio road, 3km northeast of town (turn inland by the Total petrol station). The ground-floor rooms have little balconies; those to the rear are pleasantly shaded. No views to speak of, but there's a garden pool, gourmet restaurant, tennis courts and mini-golf for the kids. Closed mid-Oct to March. **€108**

**Beach Hôtel** 38 av Napoléon ☎ 04 95 76 17 74, ⓦ beachhotel-propriano.com. Spacious and comfortable en-suite rooms in a four-storey block overlooking the Port de Commerce and plage du Phare. Note that wi-fi is only available in the sea-facing rooms and reception. **€96**

**Bellevue** Av Napoléon ☎ 04 95 76 01 86, ⓦ hotel-bellevue-propriano.com. The cheapest central hotel, half-way down av Napoléon and bang opposite the marina; the rooms are cheerfully decorated – some have balconies with a view of the gulf. The bar is lively and popular with locals. Rates in August and September include breakfast. **€95**

**Camping Colomba** 3km northeast along rte de Baracci ☎ 04 95 76 06 42, ⓦ campingcolomba.com. Take the right-hand turning off the main road by the Total petrol

station to reach this medium-sized, peaceful four-star with good facilities (including a gourmet restaurant and a pool) and plenty of shade – the best of the sites are within walking distance of town. Closed Oct–March. **€20.50**

**U Fracintu Gîte Hôtel** 7km northeast of Propriano at Burgo ☎ 04 95 76 15 05, ⓦ gite-hotel-valinco.fr. One of the largest hikers' hostels in Corsica, with room for 65 people in two- and three-bed rooms, plus a gîte with four-bed dorms. Lovely views across the valley from its terrace, and right next to the Mare a Mare Sud trailhead. Advance booking essential. Dorm rates include half-board, doubles include breakfast. Closed Nov–April. Dorms **€51**, doubles **€66**

**Le Lido** 42 av Napoléon ☎ 04 95 76 06 37, ⓦ le-lido.com. This low-rise hotel on the outskirts of Propiano, which dates from the 1930s, is head and shoulders above the competition – not least in its unsurpassed beachside location. The eleven rooms are ranged around a cool courtyard – seven have terraces jutting on the sand behind – and there's also a very sophisticated gourmet restaurant. Closed Oct–May. **€160**

## EATING AND DRINKING

Propriano has more than its fair share of duff restaurants – most of them lining the marina. The swish terraced establishments on the waterfront along av Napoléon can be relied upon for fresh croissants at breakfast and maybe a pizza, but few live up to their location when it comes to serious cooking. For that, you'll have to stick to the places

reviewed below, or the rather expensive restaurant in Le Lido (menus €85–225).

★ **Chez Charlot** Viggianello, 4.4km east up the D19 ☎ 04 95 76 00 06. Down-to-earth village cuisine – Corsican soup, veal bruschettas, stuffed courgettes, roast pork, tripe, rabbit stew and pan-fried snapper – offered on a superb-

**18**

value €20 *menu*. You can eat indoors or out on the fabulous narrow terrace next to the church which surveys the entire gulf. Reservation essential in high season. Daily noon–1.30pm & 7.30–10pm.

**Le Croco d'Île** 7 quai L'Herminier ☎04 95 73 27 85. Dependable pizzeria on the quayside next to where the ferries dock. A bit out of the way, but the wood-fired pizzas are juicy and they do a range of sensibly priced grilled meats (from €16.50), as well as seafood. Live music most evenings in summer. *Menu* €17.50. Daily noon–2.30pm & 7–11pm.

**No Stress Café – Bischof** 24 av Napoléon ☎04 95 51 27 78. This place occupies a prime spot, with great views over the harbour from its rear terraces. Charcoal-grilled local meat specialities are their forté, but they also do a mean prawn risotto and proper pizzas for those on tighter budgets. *Menus* from €22. Daily 8am–10pm

★ **Tempi Fa** 7 rue Napoléon ☎04 95 76 06 52, ⓦ tempi-fa.com. Done out in rustic Corsican style, with

exposed stone walls and sides of ham dangling from the rafters, *Tempi Fa* functions as a local produce boutique by day and a lively tapas bar in the evenings, where you can order plates of top-notch charcuterie, local cheese, Alta Rocca olives and Rizzanese wines, while perched on stools around old barrels on the terrace or inside a cosy dining hall with antique tiled floors and wooden ceilings. Charcuterie plates from €19.90; *menus* €24.90–34.90. March–Dec daily noon–2.30pm & 7.30–11pm.

**Terra Cotta** 31 av Napoléon ☎04 95 74 23 80. One of the swankiest restaurants in town, with tables in a cool, Moroccan-style bistro, or out on a seafront terrace. The cooking is uncompromisingly sophisticated, using only the freshest local seafood, and the service smiling. *Formules* at lunchtime from €26; evening *menu* €56; reservations recommended in the evenings. Closed mid-Oct to May. Mon–Sat noon–2pm & 7.30–10pm.

# Filitosa

April–Oct 9am–sunset, out of season by arrangement only • €7 • ☎ 04 95 74 00 91, ⓦ filitosa.fr

Set deep in the countryside of the fertile Vallée du Taravo, the extraordinary **Station Préhistorique de Filitosa**, 17km north of Propriano, comprises a wonderful array of statue-menhirs and prehistoric structures encapsulating some eight thousand years of history. There's no public transport to the site; vehicles should be parked in the small car park five minutes' walk from the entrance in the village.

Filitosa was settled by Neolithic farming people who lived here in rock shelters until the arrival of navigators from the east in about 3500 BC. These invaders were the creators of the menhirs, the earliest of which were possibly phallic symbols worshipped by an ancient fertility cult. When the seafaring people known as the Torréens (after the towers they built on Corsica) conquered Filitosa around 1300 BC, they destroyed most of the menhirs, incorporating the broken stones into the area of dry-stone walling surrounding the site's two *torri*, or towers, examples of which can be found all over the south of Corsica. The site remained undiscovered until a farmer stumbled across the ruins on his land in the late 1940s.

## The Filitosas

**Filitosa V** looms up on the right shortly after the main entrance to the site. The largest statue-menhir on the island, it's an imposing spectacle, with clearly defined facial features and a sword and dagger outlined on the body. Beyond a sharp left turn lies the *oppidum* or central monument, its entrance marked by the **eastern platform**, thought to have been a lookout post. The cave-like structure sculpted out of the rock is the only evidence of Neolithic occupation and is generally agreed to have been a burial mound. Straight ahead, the Torréen **central monument** comprises a scattered group of menhirs on a circular walled mound, surmounted by a dome and entered by a corridor of stone slabs and lintels. Nobody is sure of its exact function.

Nearby **Filitosa XIII** and **Filitosa IX**, implacable lumps of granite with long noses and round chins, are the most impressive of the menhirs. Filitosa XIII is typical of the figures made just before the Torréen invasion, with its vertical dagger carved in relief – **Filitosa VII** also has a clearly sculpted sword and shield. **Filitosa VI**, from the same period, is remarkable for its facial detail. On the eastern side of the central monument stand some vestigial Torréen houses, where fragments of ceramics dating from 5500 BC were discovered; they represent the most ancient finds on the site, and some of them are displayed in the museum.

### The western monument

The **western monument**, a two-roomed structure built underneath another walled mound, is thought to have been some form of Torréen religious building. A flight of steps leads to the foot of this mound, where a footbridge opens onto a meadow that's dominated by five statue-menhirs arranged in a semicircle beneath a thousand-year-old olive tree. A bank separates them from the quarry from which the megalithic sculptors hewed the stone for the menhirs – a granite block is marked ready for cutting.

### The museum

The **museum** is a downbeat affair, but the artefacts themselves are fascinating. The major item here is the formidable **Scalsa Murta**, a huge menhir dating from around 1400 BC and discovered at Olmeto. Like other statue-menhirs of this period, this one has two indents in the back of its head, which are thought to indicate that these figures would have been adorned with headdresses. Other notable exhibits are **Filitosa XII**, which has a hand and a foot carved into the stone, and **Trappa II**, a strikingly archaic face.

# Sartène (Sartè) and around

Prosper Mérimée famously dubbed **SARTÈNE** *"la plus corse des villes corses"* ("the most Corsican of Corsican towns"), but the nineteenth-century German chronicler Gregorovius put a less complimentary spin on it when he described it as a "town peopled by demons". Sartène hasn't shaken off its hostile image, despite being a smart, better-groomed place than many small Corsican towns. The main square, place Porta, doesn't offer many diversions once you've explored the enclosed *vieille ville*, and the only time of year Sartène teems with tourists is at Easter for **U Catenacciu**, a Good Friday procession that packs the main square with onlookers.

Close to Sartène are some of the island's best-known **prehistoric sites**, most notably Filitosa, the megaliths of **Cauria** and the **Alignement de Palaggiu** – Corsica's largest array of prehistoric standing stones – monuments from which are displayed in the town's excellent museum.

## Place Porta and Santa Anna

**Place Porta** – its official name, place de la Libération, has never caught on – forms Sartène's nucleus. Once the arena for bloody vendettas, it's now a well-kept square opening onto a wide terrace. Flanking the north side is the **church of Ste-Marie**, built in the 1760s but completely restored to a smooth granitic appearance. Inside the church, the most notable feature is the weighty wooden cross and chair carried through the town by hooded penitents during the Easter **Catenacciu** procession.

A flight of steps to the left of the **hôtel de ville**, formerly the governor's palace, leads past the post office to a ruined **lookout tower** (*échauguette*), which is all that remains of the town's twelfth-century ramparts. This apart, the best of the *vieille ville* is to be found behind the *hôtel de ville* in the **Santa Anna** district, a labyrinth of constricted passageways and ancient fortress-like houses. Featuring few windows and often linked to their neighbours by balconies, these houses are entered by first-floor doors which would have been approached by ladders – dilapidated staircases have replaced these necessary measures against unwelcome intruders.

## Musée Départemental de Préhistoire Corse et d'Archéologie

Bd Jacques-Nicolai • June–Sept daily 10am–6pm; Oct–May Mon–Fri 10am–5pm • €4 • ⑳ prehistoire-corse.org

A noteworthy attraction in Sartène is the swish **Musée Départemental de Préhistoire Corse et d'Archéologie**. Exhibits comprise mostly Neolithic and Torréen pottery fragments, in addition to some bracelets and glass beads from the Iron Age, and painted ceramics from the thirteenth to sixteenth centuries.

## ARRIVAL AND INFORMATION                                           SARTÈNE

**By bus** Arriving in Sartène by bus, you'll be dropped either at the top of av Gabriel-Péri or at the end of cours Général-de-Gaulle. Destinations: Ajaccio (1–3 daily; 1hr 45min); Propriano

(1–3 daily; 10min).
**Tourist office** Cours Soeur-Amélie (summer only Mon–Fri 9am–noon & 2.30–6pm; ☎ 04 95 77 15 40, ⓦ lacorsedesorigines.com).

## ACCOMMODATION

**Camping Olva** 6km north of Sartène, off the D69 ☎ 04 95 77 11 58. Shady three-star site, with lots of hiking trails into the forest on its doorstep. There's a lovely pool, sports field, tennis court and even a gym, and a variety of static accommodation on offer as well. Closed Oct–April. Camping **€21.30**, Lodge **€450/week**
**Domaine de Croccano** 3km down the D148 ☎ 04 95 77 11 37, ⓦ corsenature.com. This gorgeous eighteenth-century farmhouse B&B, hidden in a fold of the Rizzanese valley, has breathtaking views over the Sartenais from its vine-covered terraces. There's just three rooms: one double,

a room that sleeps four, and another that sleeps five; all have private bathrooms. Rates drop by up to €30/night for weekly stays. Closed Dec & Jan. **€120**
**San Damianu** Just across the bridge from the vieille ville, beneath the convent of the same name ☎ 04 95 70 55 41, ⓦ sandamianu.fr. A four-star hotel occupying a plum spot with spectacular views over the town and valley. Rooms are airy and bright, if a little bland, but it offers all the comforts and amenities you'd expect for a hotel in this class, including a lovely pool and teak sun terrace. **€185**

## EATING

In addition to the restaurants listed below, cafés cluster around place Porta, and are great places for crowd-watching.
**Le Jardin de l'Échauguette** Next to the Échauguette in the vieille ville ☎ 06 20 40 71 49. Delightful garden restaurant on a shade-dappled terrace, tucked away on the edge of the medieval ramparts (get here early for a table with the best valley views). The food's refined *gastro corse* at friendly prices: grouper *croustillant* with almonds in red wine sauce; chicken liver with fresh mint; Sartenaise veal stew on a bed of creamy polenta. *Menus* from €24. April–Sept daily noon–3pm & 6.30–11pm.
**Restaurant du Cours ("Chez Jean")** 20 cours Soeur-Amélie ☎ 04 95 77 19 07. Wholesome, honest *cuisine*

*sartenaise* (pork stews, stuffed courgettes and local liver sausage grilled over an open fire), as well as inexpensive pizzas, served in a stone-walled inn. In winter they cook in the open hearth. House *menus* €16–24.50. Daily noon–3pm & 6.30–11pm.
**U Sirenu** Rte de Bonifacio ☎ 04 95 77 21 85, ⓦ usirenu. fr. The interior of this restaurant feels very rustic and cosy (there's even a fireplace for the winter), but the main reason to come here is to dine on the wonderful terrace, which has expansive views of the surrounding hills. The *menu* features local specialities, including wild boar, plus charcuterie and cheese plates (mains €14–20). Meals finish with a glass of house liquor. Daily 11.30am–2pm & 7–9.30pm.

# The megalithic sites

Sparsely populated today, the rolling hills of the southwestern corner of Corsica are rich in prehistoric sites. The megaliths of **Cauria**, standing in ghostly isolation 10km southwest from Sartène, comprise the Dolmen de Fontanaccia, the best-preserved monument of its kind on Corsica, while the nearby alignments of **Stantari** and **Renaggiu** have an impressive congregation of statue-menhirs.

More than 250 menhirs can be seen northwest of Cauria at **Palaggiu**, another rewardingly remote site. Equally wild is the coast hereabouts, with deep clefts and coves providing some excellent spots for diving and secluded swimming.

As you snake your way through the maquis, the **Dolmen de Fontanaccia** eventually comes into view on the horizon, crowning the crest of a low hill amid a sea of vegetation. A blue sign at the parking space indicates the track to the dolmen, a fifteen-minute walk away.

Known to the locals as the **Stazzona del Diavolu** (Devil's Forge), a name that does justice to its enigmatic power, the Dolmen de Fontanaccia is in fact a burial chamber from around 2000 BC. This period was marked by a change in burial customs – whereas bodies had previously been buried in stone coffins in the ground, they were now placed above, in a mound of earth enclosed in a stone chamber. What you see today is a great stone table, comprising six huge granite blocks nearly 2m high, topped by a stone slab that remained after the earth eroded away.

The twenty "standing men" of the **Alignement de Stantari**, 200m to the east of the dolmen, date from the same period. All are featureless, except two which have roughly sculpted eyes and noses, with diagonal swords on their fronts and sockets in their heads where horns would probably have been attached.

Across a couple of fields to the south is the **Alignement de Renaggiu**, a gathering of forty menhirs standing in rows amid a small shadowy copse, set against the enormous granite outcrop of Punta di Cauria. Some of the menhirs have fallen, but all face north to south, a fact that seems to rule out any connection with a sun-related cult.

### GETTING THERE · THE MEGALITHIC SITES

**By car** To reach the Cauria megalithic site, you need to turn off the T40 about 3km west of Sartène, at the Col de l'Albitrina (291m), taking the D48 towards Tizzano. Four kilometres along this road a left turning brings you onto a winding road through maquis. Keep going until you see the Dolmen de Fontanaccia, about 2km later.

## Palaggiu

The **Alignement de Palaggiu** holds the largest concentration of menhirs in Corsica. Stretching in straight lines across the countryside like a battleground of soldiers, the 258 menhirs include three statue-menhirs with carved weapons and facial features – they are amid the first line you come to. Dating from around 1800 BC, the statues give few clues as to their function, but it's a reasonable supposition that proximity to the sea was important – the famous Corsican archeologist Roger Grosjean's theory is that the statues were some sort of magical deterrent to invaders.

### GETTING THERE · PALAGGIU

**By car** To reach the Palaggiu by road (there are no buses covering this route), regain the D48 from Sartène and head southwards past the Domaine la Mosconi vineyard (on your right, 3km after the Cauria turn-off), 1500m beyond which a green metal gate on the right side of the road marks the turning. From here a badly rutted dirt track leads another 1200m to the stones, lost in the maquis, with vineyards spread over the hills in the half-distance.

# Bonifacio (Bonifaziu) and around

**BONIFACIO** enjoys a superbly isolated location at Corsica's southernmost point, a narrow peninsula of dazzling white limestone creating a town site unlike any other. The much-photographed **haute ville**, a maze of narrow streets flanked by tall Genoese tenements, rises seamlessly out of sheer cliffs that have been hollowed and striated by the wind and waves, while on the landward side the deep cleft between the peninsula and the mainland forms a perfect natural harbour. A haven for boats for centuries, this inlet is nowadays a chic marina that attracts yachts from around the Med. Its geography has long enabled Bonifacio to maintain a certain temperamental detachment from the rest of Corsica, and the town today remains distinctly more Italian than French in atmosphere. It retains Renaissance features found only here, and its inhabitants have their own dialect based on Ligurian, a legacy of the days when this was practically an independent Genoese colony.

Such a place has its inevitable drawbacks: exorbitant prices, overwhelming crowds in July and August and a commercial cynicism that's atypical of Corsica as a whole. However, the old town forms one of the most arresting spectacles in the Mediterranean, and warrants at least a day-trip. If you plan to come in peak season, try to get here early in the day before the bus parties arrive at around 10am.

18

## BONIFACIO

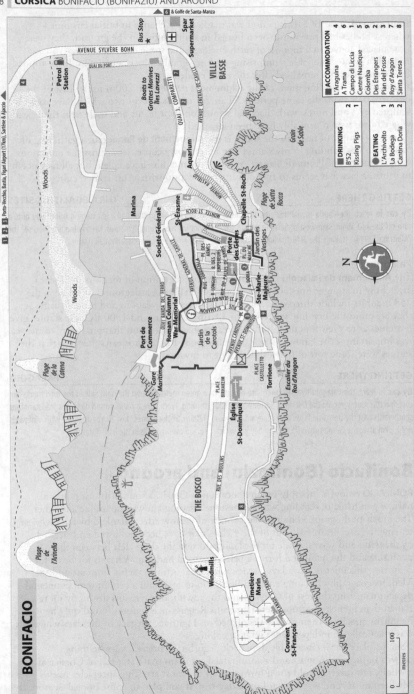

6 & Golfe de Santa-Manza

T1. T2. T3 ▶ Porto-Vecchio, Bastia, Figari Airport (17km), Sartène & Ajaccio ▲

Bus Stop

Spar Supermarket

AVENUE SYLVÈRE BOHN

QUAI DU PORT

Petrol Station

Boats to Grottes Marines Îles Lavezzi

QUAI J. COMPARETTI

AVENUE GÉNÉRAL-DE-GAULLE

VILLE BASSE

Aquarium

Grain de Sable

Woods

Woods

Woods

Marina

St-Érasme

MONTÉE ST-ROCH

Chapelle St-Roch

Plage de Sutta Rocca

Société Générale

Porte des Gênes

Jardin des Vestiges

RUE DES 2 EMPEREURS

PL DES 2 EMPEREURS

PL DU MARCHÉ

RUE LONGUE

RUE DOMENICA

RUE DORIA

Ste-Marie-Majeure

N

Port de Commerce

Roman Column/ War Memorial

QUAI BANDA DEL FERRO

AVENUE GÉNÉRAL-DE-GAULLE

RUE DU PALAIS-DE-GARDE

RUE ST-JEAN-BAPTISTE

RUE J. SCARBON

Jardin de la Carotola

Plage de la Catena

Gare Maritime

AVENUE CAROTOLA

AVENUE ST-DOMINIQUE

RUE DE BONAPARTE

PLACE CASTELLETTO

Torrione

Escalier du Roi d'Aragon

PLACE BIR-HAKEIM

Église St-Dominique

RUE DES MOULINS

THE BOSCO

Plage de l'Arinella

Windmills

Cimetière Marin

RUE ST-FRANÇOIS

Couvent St-François

Sardinia ▼

0 — 100
metres

### ACCOMMODATION
| | |
|---|---|
| L'Araguina | 4 |
| A Trama | 6 |
| Campo di Liccia | 1 |
| Centre Nautique | 5 |
| Colomba | 9 |
| Des Etrangers | 2 |
| Plan del Fosse | 3 |
| Roy d'Aragon | 7 |
| Santa Teresa | 8 |

### DRINKING
| | |
|---|---|
| B'52 | 2 |
| Kissing Pigs | 1 |

### EATING
| | |
|---|---|
| L'Archivolto | 1 |
| La Bodega | 3 |
| Cantina Doria | 2 |

## Montée Rastello

At the end of the café-lined **quai Comparetti**, just before the **port commercial** where ferries leave for Sardinia, a flight of steps – **Montée Rastello** – lead uphill to the **haute ville**. The climb is rewarded by a magnificent view of the white limestone cliffs tapering to Capu Persutau, and the huge lump of fallen rock face called the Grain de Sable. The tiny **Chapelle St-Roch**, at the head of the steps, was built on the spot where the last plague victim died in 1528; another, narrower stone staircase twists down to the tiny beach of **Sutta Rocca**.

## Bastion de l'Étendard

April–Sept daily 9.30–5.30pm; Oct–May 10am–4.30pm • €2.50

Montée St-Roch takes you up the final approach to the citadelle walls, entered via the great **Porte de Gênes**, once the only gateway to the *haute ville*. It opens on to the place des Armes, where you can visit the **Bastion de l'Étendard**, sole remnant of the fortifications destroyed during a siege in 1554. While exploring the narrow streets, look out for flamboyant marble escutcheons above the doorways and double-arched windows separated by curiously stunted columns. Many of the older houses did not originally have doors; the inhabitants used to climb up a ladder which they would pull up behind them to prevent a surprise attack.

## Ste-Marie-Majeure

Cutting across rue du Palais de Garde brings you to the church of **Ste-Marie-Majeure**, originally Romanesque but restored in the eighteenth century, though the richly sculpted belfry dates from the fourteenth century. The facade is hidden by a loggia where the Genoese municipal officers used to dispense justice in the days of the republic. The church's treasure, a fragment of the True Cross, was saved from a shipwreck in the Straits of Bonifacio; for centuries after, the citizens would take the relic to the edge of the cliff and pray for calm seas whenever storms raged. It is kept under lock and key in the sacristy, along with an ivory cask containing relics of St Boniface.

## Torrione and the Escalier du Roi d'Aragon

Escalier du Roi d'Aragon April–Oct daily 10am–4.30pm • €2.50

Rue Doria leads towards the Bosco; at the end of this road a left down rue des Pachas will bring you to the **Torrione**, a 35-metre-high lookout post built in 1195 on the site of Count Bonifacio's castle. Descending the cliff from here are the **Escalier du Roi d'Aragon**'s 187 steps, which were said to have been built in one night by the Aragonese in an attempt to gain the town in 1420, but in fact they had already been in existence for some time and were used by the people to fetch water from a well.

## The Bosco

To the west of the Torrione lies the **Bosco**, a quarter named after the wood that used to cover the far end of the peninsula in the tenth century. In those days a community of hermits dwelt here, but nowadays the limestone plateau is open and desolate. The entrance to the Bosco is marked by the **Église St-Dominique**, a rare example of Corsican Gothic architecture – it was built in 1270, most probably by the Templars, and later handed over to the Dominicans.

Beyond the church, rue des Moulins leads on to the ruins of three **windmills** dating from 1283, two of them decrepit, the third restored. Behind them stands a memorial to the 750 people who died when a troopship named *Sémillante* ran aground here in

**18**

1855, on its way to the Crimea: one of the many disasters wreaked by the notoriously windy straits.

The tip of the Bosco plateau is occupied by the **Cimetière Marin**, its white crosses standing out sharply against the deep blue of the sea. Open until sundown, the cemetery is a fascinating place to explore, with its flamboyant mausoleums displaying a jumble of architectural ornamentations. Next to the cemetery stands the **Couvent St-François**, allegedly founded after St Francis sought shelter in a nearby cave – the story goes that the convent was the town's apology to the holy man, over whom a local maid had nearly poured a bucket of slops. Immediately to the south, the **Esplanade St-François** commands fine views across the bay to Sardinia.

## ARRIVAL AND DEPARTURE                                BONIFACIO

**By car** Most of the town's car parks lie to the left of the marina as you arrive. The municipal ones charge around €2.80 per half-day; launch operators also have their own lots further down the lane towards Pertusato, where you can park for free if you buy a ticket for one of their boat trips.
**By bus** Buses drop passengers in the marina, next to the tourist office. For services to Ajaccio, you'll need to change buses at Scupetu.
Destinations Ajaccio (2–3 daily; 3hr 30min); Porto-Vecchio

(2–4 daily; 30–40min), Scupetu (2–3 daily; 20min).
**By plane** Figari airport, 17km north of Bonifacio (☎ 04 95 71 10 10, ⊛ www.2a.cci.fr), handles flights from mainland France and a few charters from the UK. A seasonal *navette* runs two to four times daily from the airport to Porto-Vecchio, from where you can pick up a connecting bus to Bonifacio. The only other option. (aside from car hire) is to take a taxi into town – around €45.

## INFORMATION

**Tourist office** The tourist office in the *haute ville*, at the bottom of rue F.-Scamaroni (April–June & Sept daily 9am–6pm; July & Aug daily 9am–8pm; Oct & Nov Mon–Fri 9am–5pm; Nov–March Mon–Fri 9am–4pm; ☎ 04 95 73 11 88, ⊛ bonifacio.fr) has audioguides for hire in English and French (€5 for 1hr 30min tour).
**Care hire** Cars may be rented from Avis, at Figari airport (☎ 04 95 71 00 01); Europcar, Port de Plaisance (☎ 04 95 73

10 99), Hertz, at Figari airport (☎ 04 95 71 04 16).
**Banks** Bonifacio doesn't have an abundance of banks. There are two central ATMs: at Société Générale, 38 rue St-Érasme, and La Banque Postale, rue St-Dominique, but note that they frequently run out of bills, so get to them early in the day if you need cash. Avoid the rip-off *bureaux de change* dotted around town.

## ACCOMMODATION

Finding a place to stay can be a chore, as the hotels are quickly booked up in high season; for a room near the centre, reserve well in advance, and brace yourself for a lot of noise at night if you nab a room on the quayside – Bonifacio becomes a proper party town when the Italians descend in August. Better still, save yourself the trouble, and a considerable amount of money, by finding a room somewhere else and travelling here for the day; tariffs in this town are the highest on the island. The same applies to the large campsites dotted along the road to Porto-Vecchio, which can get very crowded.
**L'Araguina** Av Sylvère-Bohn ☎ 04 95 73 02 96, ⊛ campingaraguina.fr. The closest campsite to town, but unwelcoming, cramped in season, and with inadequate washing and toilet facilities. Avoid unless desperate – though it's undoubtedly the most convenient option if you're backpacking. Closed mid-Oct to March. **€22**
**A Trama** 1.5km from Bonifacio along the rte de Santa Manza ☎ 04 95 73 17 17, ⊛ a-trama.com. Discreet hotel hidden behind a screen of maquis, palms, pines and dry-stone chalk walls. The chalet rooms, all with private

terraces, are grouped around a garden and pool; some could do with modernizing, but the lovely outside space is ample compensation, especially if you're travelling with kids, and there's a classy restaurant (*Le Clos Vatel*). Expensive in high summer, but more affordable off season. **€212**
**Campo di Liccia** 3km north towards Porto-Vecchio ☎ 04 95 73 03 09, ⊛ campingdiliccia.com. Well shaded and large, so you're guaranteed a place. There's a pleasant pool (plus a kids' pool), a playground and an outdoor gym; wi-fi is only available in the reception and bar. Closed Oct–March. **€21.60**
**Centre Nautique** On the marina ☎ 04 95 73 02 11, ⊛ centre-nautique.com. Very chic (with prices to match) but relaxed hotel on the waterfront, fitted out with mellow wood and nautical charts. No rooms here – just suites and apartments, all stylishly furnished and most benefitting from sea views, though their breakfasts are a rip-off (€12) – you get much better value at the quayside cafés. **€350**
**Colomba** Rue Simon-Varsi ☎ 04 95 73 73 44, ⊛ hotel-bonifacio-corse.fr. The only hotel worthy of note in the thick of the old quarter occupies a smartly renovated

medieval tenement on one of the *haute ville's* prettiest streets. It offers twelve classically furnished, en-suite rooms, some with shuttered widows opening to magnificent sea views. Parking available. Closed Nov–March. €167

**Des Étrangers** 4 av Sylvère-Bohn ☎ 04 95 73 01 09, ⓦ hoteldesetrangers.fr. Simple rooms (the costlier ones have TV and a/c, but it costs just €5 more for a room with both) facing the main road, just up the main Porto-Vecchio road from the port. Nothing special, but good value for Bonifacio, especially in July & Aug. Closed Nov–March. €60

**Pian del Fosse** 4km out of town on the rte de Santa Manza ☎ 04 95 73 16 34, ⓦ camping-piandelfosse.com. Big three-star campsite that's very peaceful and quiet in June & September (during the summer holidays they hold live concerts so expect it to be a little noisier), and well placed for the beaches. There's a children's playground, plus table tennis available. Closed mid-Oct to March. €22.10

**Roy d'Aragon** 13 quai J.-Comparetti ☎ 04 95 73 03 99, ⓦ royaragon.com. A very pleasant, modern Best Western in a prime location on the quayside. Rooms are bright and comfortable, though a little on the small side; the best have views of the port and a private terrace. There's a café right by the water, and parking just a short walk away. Closed Nov–March. €145

**Santa Teresa** Quartier St-François ☎ 04 95 73 11 32, ⓦ hotel-santateresa.com. Large, modern and efficient three-star on the clifftop overlooking the Cimetière Marin, note-worthy for its stupendous views across the straits to Sardinia. Not all of the very smart rooms are sea-facing, though, so ask for "*vue sur la mer avec balcon*" when you book. Closed Nov–March. €160

## EATING, DRINKING AND NIGHTLIFE

Eating possibilities in Bonifacio might seem unlimited, but it's best to avoid the chintzy restaurants in the marina, few of which merit their exorbitant prices. For a snack, try the boulangerie-pâtisserie *Faby Noël*, 4 rue St-Jean-Baptiste, in the *haute ville*, a tiny local bakery serving Bonifacien treats such as *pain des morts* (sweet buns with walnuts and raisins) and *migliacis* (buns made with fresh ewe's cheese), in addition to the usual range of spinach and *brocciu bastelles*, baked here in the traditional way – on stone. For a scrumptious, budget Bonifacien breakfast you can buy a *pain des morts* warm out of the oven at the *Pâtisserie Sorba* (3 rue St-Érasme; follow the smell of baking bread to the bottom of the Montée Rastello steps) and take it to *Bar du Quai* a couple of doors down.

### RESTAURANTS

**L'Archivolto** Rue de l'Archivolto ☎ 04 95 73 17 58. With its candlelit, antique- and junk-filled interior, this would be the most commendable place to eat in the *haute ville* were the cooking a little less patchy and the prices fairer. But it still gets packed out – reservations are recommended – and the couple that own it are charming. Lunch *menus* around €25; evening à la carte only, around €40–50 for three courses. Easter–June & Sept–Oct Mon–Sat noon–3pm & 6–11pm; July & Aug daily noon–3pm & 6–11pm.

**La Bodega** Place Bonaparte ☎ 06 73 75 94 70. This small restaurant seats less than twenty people and is all the

better for it – it's cosy and charming, and serves up great Corsican food. Try the *aubergines à la Bonifacienne* (€13) or the *Mita-Mita* plate of charcuterie, cheese and *pain de morts* (€13.50). Excellent value all round. Daily noon–10pm.

★ **Cantina Doria** 27 rue Doria ☎ 04 95 73 50 49. Down-to-earth Corsican specialities at down-to-earth prices. Their popular three-course €21 *menu* – which includes the house speciality, aubergines *à la bonifacienne* – offers unbeatable value for the *haute ville*, though you'll soon bump up your bill if you succumb to the temptations of the excellent wine selection. June to mid-Sept daily noon–2.30pm & 7–11pm; March–May & mid-Sept to Oct closed Sat.

### BARS

**B'52** Quai Comparetti ☎ 06 32 82 18 69, ⓦ b52bonifacio. com. Hippest of the waterfront lounge bars, hosting DJs on weekends and throughout peak season. There's a pleasant outdoor deck. Mid-June to mid-Sept daily 8pm–2am.

**Kissing Pigs** Quai Banda del Ferro ☎ 04 95 73 56 09. Curiously themed wine bar boasting the world's largest collection of kissing pig photos and other snout-related ephemera. They serve all the island's top wines (by the glass and carafe, as well as bottle), accompanied by fragrant *charcuterie maison* (try the pungent two-year-old *figatellu*), *grillades*, flans and salads. *Menus* €19.50 and €20.50. Daily except Wed 11.30am–3.30pm & 6.30–11pm.

# Around Bonifacio

There are impressive views of the citadelle from the **cliffs** at the head of the Montée Rastello (reached via the pathway running left from the top of the steps), but they're not a patch on the spectacular panorama from the sea. Throughout the day, a flotilla of excursion **boats** (see page 982) ferries visitors out to the best vantage points, taking in a string of caves and other landmarks only accessible by water en route, including the **Îles Lavezzi**, the scattering of small islets where the troop ship *Sémillante* was

**18**

---

## BOAT TRIPS FROM BONIFACIO

From the moment you arrive in Bonifacio, you'll be pestered by touts from the many boat companies running excursions out of the harbour. There are more than a dozen of these, but they all offer more or less the same routes, at the same prices.

Lasting between thirty and forty-five minutes, the shorter trips take you out along the cliffs to the *grottes marines* (sea caves) and *calanches* (inlets) below the old town; tickets cost €19–27 depending on the demand and how well you can haggle.

Longer excursions out to the **Îles Lavezzi**, part of the archipelago to the east of the straits of Bonifacio, cost around €35–45. Most companies offer a shuttle (*navette*) service, allowing you to spend as much time as you like on the islands before returning. Boats go out past the Grain de Sable and Phare du Pertusato and then moor at the main island of **Lavezzi**, beside the **cimetière Achiarino**. Buried in two walled cemeteries are the victims of the *Sémillante* shipwreck of 1855, in which 773 crew members and soldiers bound for the Crimean War were drowned after their vessel was blown onto the rocks.

Classified as a nature reserve since 1982, the islets are home to several rare species of **wild flower**, and offer fabulous **snorkelling** and some exquisite shell-sand **beaches**. A network of footpaths runs between them, well waymarked, as you're not permitted to wander off into the fragile vegetation.

---

shipwrecked in 1855 and now designated as a nature reserve. The whole experience of bobbing around to an amplified running commentary is about as touristy as Bonifacio gets, but it's well worth enduring just to round the mouth of the harbour and see the *vieille ville*, perched atop the famous chalk cliffs. The Lavezzi islets themselves are surrounded by wonderfully clear sea water, offering Corsica's best snorkelling. On your way back, you skirt the famous **Île Cavallo**, or "millionaire's island", where the likes of Princess Caroline of Monaco and other French and Italian glitterati have luxury hideaways.

### The beaches

The **beaches** within walking distance of Bonifacio are generally smaller and less appealing than most in southern Corsica. For a dazzling splash of turquoise, you'll have to follow the narrow, twisting lane east of town in the direction of Pertusatu lighthouse, turning left when you see signs for **Piantarella**, Corsica's kitesurfing hotspot. A twenty-minute walk south around the shore from there takes you past the remains of a superbly situated Roman villa to a pair of divine little coves, Grand Sperone and Petit Sperone – both shallow and perfect for kids.

Another superb beach in the area is **Rondinara**, a perfect shell-shaped cove of turquoise water enclosed by dunes and a pair of twin headlands. Located 10km north (east of N198), it's sufficiently off the beaten track to remain relatively peaceful (outside school holidays). Facilities are minimal, limited to a smart wooden beach restaurant, paying car park and campsite (see below). Shade is at a premium, so come armed with a parasol.

**ACCOMMODATION**                                                                         **THE BEACHES**

**Camping Rondinara** Rodinara beach ☎ 04 95 70 43 15, ⓦ rondinara.fr. Facilities at Rodinara beach are minimal but include this well set-up campsite, which boasts its own | pool, bar, pizzeria and grocery store, and is only a ten minute walk from the sand. Closed Oct to mid-May. **€24.80**

# Porto-Vecchio and around

Set on a hillock overlooking a beautiful deep blue bay, **PORTO-VECCHIO**, 25km north of Bonifacio, was rated by James Boswell as one of "the most distinguished harbours in Europe". It was founded in 1539 as a second Genoese stronghold on the east coast, Bastia being well established in the north. The site was perfect: close to the unexploited and fertile plain, it benefited from secure high land and a sheltered harbour, although the mosquito population spread malaria and wiped out the first Ligurian settlers within months. Things began to take off mainly thanks to the cork industry, which still thrived well into the twentieth century. Today most revenue comes from tourists, the vast majority of them well-heeled Italians who flock here for the fine outlying **beaches**. To the northwest, the little town of **Zonza** makes a good base for exploring the dramatic forest that surrounds one of Corsica's most awesome road trips, the **route de Bavella**.

18

Around the centre of town there's not much to see, apart from the well-preserved **fortress** and the small grid of **ancient streets** backing onto the main place de la République. East of the square you can't miss the **Porte Génoise**, which frames a delightful expanse of sea and saltpans and through which you'll find the quickest route down to the modern marina, which is lined with cafés and restaurants.

## ARRIVAL AND INFORMATION
PORTO-VECCHIO

**By plane** Figari airport (☎ 04 95 71 10 10, ⓦ www.2a.cci.fr), 28km southwest, is served by weekly charter flights to various destinations in northern Europe, and by domestic departures to several cities on the French mainland. A seasonal *navette* runs two to four times daily from the marina; tickets cost €4 single. Timetable information appears online at ⓦ corsicabus. org, or on the tourist office website. Taxis charge around €50, depending on the time of day.

**By bus** Porto-Vecchio doesn't have a bus station; instead, the various companies who come here stop and depart outside their agents' offices on the edge of the *haute ville*. Destinations Ajaccio (2–4 daily; 3hr 30min); Bastia (2 daily; 2hr 45min–3hr); Bonifacio (1–4 daily; 30–40min); Propriano (2–4 daily; 1hr 40min); Sartène (2–4 daily; 1hr 35min).

**Tourist office** Porto-Vecchio's efficient tourist office (Mon–Sat 9am–12.30pm & 2–6.30pm; ☎ 04 95 70 09 58, ⓦ ot-portovecchio.com) is on rue du Maréchal-Leclerc.

## ACCOMMODATION

As most visitors staying in this region during the summer come for fly-drive villa holidays, hotel accommodation is thin on the ground, especially at the bottom end.

**Goéland** Port de Plaisance ☎ 04 95 70 14 15, ⓦ hotel goeland.com. Charming hotel, set on a little man-made beach looking across the gulf, with large rooms, some of which have teak terraces overlooking the water. Rates include breakfast; and food served on the waterfront lawn is wonderful. **€260**

**Holzer** 12 rue Jean-Jaurès ☎ 04 95 70 05 93, ⓦ hotel-holzer.com. Labyrinthine place with rather cramped, unexciting rooms, but immaculately clean and very central. **€149**

**Matonara** Just north of the centre at the Quatre-Chemins intersection ☎ 04 95 70 37 05, ⓦ camping-matonara.fr. Lying within easy reach of the Hyper U supermarket, this is the most easily accessible site in the area. Pitches are shaded by cork trees. Bring plenty of mozzie repellent. Closed Nov–April. **€19**

**Mistral** Rue Jean-Nicoli ☎ 04 95 70 08 53, ⓦ lemistral. eu. Comfortable mid-range three-star, slightly removed from the noisy centre of town. There's a lovely flower-filled, shady terrace outside. Fully a/c. **€110**

**Panorama** 12 rue Jean-Nicoli ☎ 04 95 70 07 96. Basic pension-style place just above the old town, with parking spaces and various types of rooms (nos. 8 and 9 on the top floor are the cosiest, though without toilets). Not all that well maintained, but usually the cheapest in town. **€100**

★ **San Giovanni** 2km south of Porto-Vecchio on the D659 towards Arca ☎ 04 95 70 22 25, ⓦ hotel-san-giovanni.com. Thirty comfortable, bright and airy rooms set in landscaped gardens, with a heated pool, jacuzzi, sauna, tennis court, ping pong table and children's games area. It's well run, peaceful and great value. **€185**

## EATING AND DRINKING

**A Furana** Rue Borgo ☎ 04 95 70 58 03, ⓦ restaurant-afurana.fr. Fragrant local cuisine served in a vaulted Genoese dining hall, or on a romantic terrace boasting panoramic gulf views. *Menus* from €27. Daily noon–2pm & 7–10.30pm.

★ **La Table de Nathalie** 4 rue Jean-Jaurès ☎ 04 95 71 65 25. Ask any local where to dine at in town and they'll invariably direct you to this cosy bistro. Run by an enthusiastic and welcoming husband and wife team, it serves dishes prepared from only the freshest local ingredients. Try the slow-roast lamb, *porcelet* with caramelized foie gras or succulent home-made burgers. Most dishes €18–30 (*plat du jour* €16.50) – great value given the quality of cuisine. Reservation recommended.

18

Mon 7–10pm, Tues–Sat noon–1pm & 7–10pm; also Mon lunch & Sun in high season.

**U Giramondu** 3 rue Pasteur ☎ 04 95 28 98 07. In a great location just outside the citadelle, this little, modern restaurant serves up tapas, separated on the menu by country – for example spring risotto (Italy), crispy chicken (America) and beef tartare (France) – ranging from €6 to €16. The terrace is a bonus in warm months. Daily 4pm–2am.

**U Sputinu** Place de l'Église ☎ 04 95 72 28 33. The pièce de résistance of this Corsican speciality place on the little square opposite the church is their copious *grande assiette* – a selection of quality charcuterie, cheese, spinach pasties (*bastelles aux épinards*) and savoury fritters (*migliacciu*) – served on rustic wooden plates. Dining outside during the summer months here is a delight. March–Oct Mon–Sat noon–3pm & 6–midnight.

## Golfe de Porto-Vecchio

Much of the coast of the **Golfe de Porto-Vecchio** and its environs is characterized by ugly development and hectares of swampland, yet some of the clearest, bluest sea and whitest beaches on Corsica are also here. The most frequented of these, Palombaggia and Santa Giulia, can be reached by **bus** from the town in summer, timetables for which are posted in the tourist office and online at ⓦcorsicabus.org; at other times you'll need your own transport. You'll also have to travel independently to reach the **Casteddu d'Araggiu**, one of the island's best-preserved Bronze Age sites, which stands on a ledge overlooking the gulf to the north of town.

### The beaches

A golden semicircle of sand edged by short twisted umbrella pines and red rocks, the **plage de Palombaggia** is south Corsica's trademark beach, and indisputably one of the most beautiful bays in Europe. Come here outside the school holidays and you'll find it hard to resist the striking colours and serene, clear water. But in summer the crowds can be simply overwhelming. One possible compromise is to press on south to two other smaller, less famous beaches just beyond Palombaggia – **Cala di la Folaca** and the **plage d'Acciaju** – where the sand is just as white and the water equally translucent. Narrow access lanes and *pistes* drop down to them from the main road at regular intervals, but the best way to enjoy this exquisite string of coves is by walking along them.

A few kilometres further south along the same road takes you over the Bocca di l'Oru to the plage de **Santa Giulia**, a spectacular white-sand beach and turquoise bay. The presence of several sprawling holiday villages and facilities for windsurfing and other watersports ensures large crowds from early in the season, but the colours alone warrant a detour. Shallow and crystal-clear, the water is especially good for little ones.

North of Porto-Vecchio, the first beach worth a visit is **San Ciprianu**, a half-moon bay of white sand, reached by turning right off the D468 at the VITO petrol station and following the road down to the sea. If you instead carry on for another 8km, you'll come to the even more picturesque beach at **Pinarellu**, an uncrowded, long sweep of soft white sand with a Genoese watchtower and, like the less inspiring beaches immediately north of here, benefiting from the spectacular backdrop of the Massif de l'Ospédale.

### Casteddu d'Arragiu

The coast between Porto-Vecchio and Solenzara is strewn with **prehistoric monuments**. The most impressive of these, **Casteddu d'Araggiu**, lies 12km north along the D759. From the site's car park (signposted off the main road), it's a twenty-minute stiff uphill climb through maquis and scrubby woodland to the ruins. Built in 2000 BC, the *casteddu* consists of a complex of chambers built into a massive circular wall of pink granite from the top of which the views over the coastal belt are superb.

## The route de Bavella

Starting from just north of the resort of **Solenzara** on the east coast, and winding 40km through the mountains to the picture-postcard-pretty mountain village of **ZONZA**, the

---

**THE DOMAINE DE TORRACCIA**

A short way inland from Pinarellu, the hamlet of Lecci, on the main Porto-Vecchio–Bastia highway, marks the turning for one of Corsica's finest vineyards, the **Domaine de Toraccia** (Ⓦ domaine-de-torraccia.com). Produced with traditional vine stock and labour-intensive organic cultivation methods, its flagship cuvée is the Oriu, a dense, smoky *vin de garde* that's the ideal accompaniment to local mountain charcuterie and ewe's cheese. Made from hundred-percent Vermentino, Torraccia's white, by contrast, is bone dry and tinged with herbs – perfect with seafood.

You can sample the *domaine's* full list – along with their equally delicious olives and olive oil – at the **vineyard** itself (Mon–Sat: summer 8am–8pm; winter 8am–noon & 2–6pm; free), where there's an engaging exhibition of old Corsican photographs to peruse. With the exception of the Oriu, they're all available *en vrac* (straight out of the *cuves* in demi-jars) at less than half the bottle price.

---

**18**

D268 – known locally as the **route de Bavella** – is perhaps the most dramatic road in all Corsica. The road penetrates a dense expanse of old pine and chestnut trees as it rises steadily to the **Col de Bavella** (1218m), where a towering statue of **Notre-Dame-des-Neiges** marks the windswept pass itself. An amazing panorama of peaks and forests spreads out from the col: to the northwest the serrated granite ridge of the Cirque de Gio Agostino is dwarfed by the pink pinnacles of the Aiguilles de Bavella; behind soars Monte Incudine.

### Bavella

Just below the Col de Bavella the seasonal hamlet of **BAVELLA** comprises a handful of congenial cafés, corrugated-iron-roofed chalets and hikers' hostels from where you can follow a series of waymarked **trails** to nearby viewpoints. Deservedly the most popular of these is the two-hour walk to the **Trou de la Bombe**, a circular opening that pierces the Paliri crest of peaks. From the car park behind the *Auberge du Col* follow the red-and-white waymarks of GR20 for 800m, then head right when you see orange splashes.

# Aléria

Built on the estuary at the mouth of the River Tavignano on the island's east coast, 40km southeast of Corte along the N200, **ALÉRIA** was first settled in 564 BC by a colony of Greek Phocaeans as a trading port for copper and lead, as well as wheat, olives and grapes. After an interlude of Carthaginian rule, the Romans arrived in 259 BC, built a naval base and re-established its importance in the Mediterranean. Aléria remained the east coast's principal port right up until the eighteenth century. Little is left of the historic town except Roman ruins and a thirteenth-century Genoese fortress, which stands high against a background of chequered fields and green vineyards. To the south, a strip of modern buildings straddling the main road makes up the modern town, known as **Cateraggio**, but it's the village set on the hilltop just west of here that's the principal focus for visitors.

### The Site

**Musée Jérôme Carcopino** Mid-May to Sept daily 8am–noon & 2–7pm; Oct to mid-May Mon–Sat 8am–noon & 2–5pm • €2 • Ⓦ aleria.fr

Before looking around the ruins of the ancient city, set aside an hour for the **Musée Jérôme Carcopino**, housed in the Fort Matra. It holds remarkable finds from the **Roman site**, including Hellenic and Punic coins, rings, belt links, elaborate oil lamps decorated with Christian symbols, Attic plates and a second-century marble bust of Jupiter Ammon. Etruscan bronzes fill another room, with jewellery and armour from the fourth to the second century BC.

A dusty track leads from here to the Roman site itself (closes 90min before museum; same ticket), where most of the excavation was done as recently as the 1950s. Most of the site still lies beneath ground and is undergoing continuous digging, but the balneum (bathhouse), the base of Augustus's triumphal arch, the foundations of the forum and traces of shops have already been unearthed.

### GETTING THERE                                                         ALÉRIA

**By bus** Aléria/Cateraggio can be reached on any of the daily buses running between Bastia and the south of the island via the east coast (summer 1 daily Mon–Sat; winter 1–3 weekly winter).

### EATING

**Aux Coquillages de Diana** 1.2km north of Aléria: look for a sign on the right (east) side of the road pointing the way down a surfaced lane ☏ 06 76 10 00 03, ⊚ restaurant-coquillagesdediana-aleria.com. This famous seafood restaurant, resting on stilts above the water, is the place to sample the local Nustale oysters, hauled fresh each day from the nearby Étang de Diane lagoon. It serves a great-value €32 seafood platter, featuring clams, mussels and a terrine made from dried mullet's eggs called *poutargue* – the kind of food one imagines the Romans must have feasted on when they farmed the *étang* two millennia ago. Daily: May–Sept noon–2.30pm & 7.30–10pm; Oct–Dec & Feb–April noon–2.30pm.

# Corte (Corti) and around

Stacked up the side of a wedge-shaped crag against a spectacular backdrop of granite mountains, **CORTE** epitomizes *l'âme corse*, or "Corsican soul" – a small town marooned amid a grandiose landscape, where a spirit of dogged patriotism is never far from the surface. Corte has been the home of Corsican nationalism since the first National Constitution was drawn up here in 1731, and was also where **Pascal Paoli**, "U Babbu di u Patria" ("Father of the Nation"), formed the island's first democratic government later in the eighteenth century. Self-consciously insular and grimly proud, it can seem an inhospitable place at times, although the presence of the island's only university lightens the atmosphere noticeably during termtime, when the bars and cafés lining its long main street fill with students. For the outsider, Corte's charm is concentrated in the tranquil *haute ville*, where the forbidding **citadelle** – site of a modern **museum** – presides over a warren of narrow, cobbled streets.

## Haute ville

The old **haute ville**, immediately above Corte's main street, cours Paoli, centres on **place Gaffori**, which is dominated by a statue of General Gian-Pietru Gaffori pointing vigorously towards the church. On its base a bas-relief depicts the siege of the Gaffori house by the Genoese, who attacked in 1750 when the general was out of town and his wife Faustina was left holding the fort. Their residence still stands, right behind, and you can clearly make out the bullet marks made by the besiegers.

For the best view of the citadelle, follow the signs uphill to the viewing platform, the **Belvédère**, which faces the medieval tower, suspended high above the town on its pinnacle of rock and dwarfed by the immense crags behind. The platform also gives a wonderful view of the converging rivers and encircling forest – a summer bar adds to the attraction.

Just above place Gaffori, left of the gateway to the citadelle, stands the **Palais National**, a great, solid block of a mansion that's the sole example of Genoese civic architecture in Corte. Having served as the seat of Paoli's government for a while, it became the Università di Corsica in 1765, offering free education to all (Napoleon's father studied here). The university closed in 1769 when the French took over the island after the Treaty of Versailles, not to be resurrected until 1981. Today, several modern buildings have been added, among them the Paoli Tech Engineering School, which has a focus on sustainable construction and renewable energy, among other things.

## The Museu di a Corsica and citadelle

April to mid-June & mid-Sept to Oct daily except Mon 10am–6pm; mid-June to mid-Sept daily 10am–8pm; Nov–March Tues–Sat 10am–5pm • €5.30 • ⓦ www.musee-corse.com

The monumental gateway just behind the Palais National leads from place Poilu into Corte's Genoese citadelle, whose lower courtyard is dominated by the modern buildings of **Museu di a Corsica**, a state-of-the-art museum housing the collection of ethnographer Révérend Père Louis Doazan, a Catholic priest who spent 27 years amassing a vast array of objects relating to the island's traditional transhumant and peasant past: principally old farm implements, craft tools and peasant dress.

The museum's entrance ticket also admits you to Corte's principal landmark, the **citadelle**. The only such fortress in the interior of the island, the Genoese structure served as a base for the Foreign Legion from 1962 until 1984, but now houses a pretty feeble exhibition of nineteenth-century photographs. It's reached by a huge staircase of Restonica marble, which leads to the medieval tower known as the **Nid d'Aigle** (Eagle's Nest). The fortress, of which the tower is the only original part, was built in 1420, and the barracks were added during the mid-nineteenth century. These were later

18

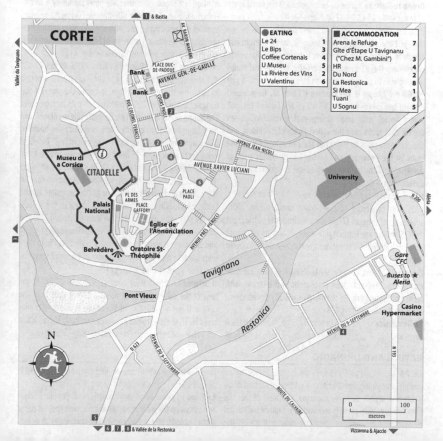

CORTE

| EATING | | ACCOMMODATION | |
|---|---|---|---|
| Le 24 | 1 | Arena le Refuge | 7 |
| Le Bips | 3 | Gîte d'Étape U Tavignanu | |
| Coffee Cortenais | 4 | ("Chez M. Gambini") | 3 |
| U Museu | 5 | HR | 4 |
| La Rivière des Vins | 2 | Du Nord | 2 |
| U Valentinu | 6 | La Restonica | 8 |
| | | Si Mea | 1 |
| | | Tuani | 6 |
| | | U Sognu | 5 |

18

converted into a prison, in use as recently as World War II, when the Italian occupiers incarcerated Corsican Resistance fighters in tiny cells. Adjacent to the cells is a former **watchtower** which at the time of Paoli's government was inhabited by the hangman.

## ARRIVAL AND DEPARTURE CORTE

**By bus** Unfortunately, bus services from Corte have over recent years been completely scaled back, making it near-impossible to get to and from the town by bus. There is still a service to Aléria (July & Aug daily Mon–Sat; 10am; 1hr), but it must be reserved in advance (by 9pm the day before; ☎ 04 95 46 22 89).

**By train** The *gare CFC* (☎ 04 95 46 00 97) is at the foot of the hill near the university.

Destinations Ajaccio (3–5 daily; 2hr); Bastia (3–5 daily; 1hr 45min); Calvi (2 daily; 2hr 30min); L'Île Rousse (2 daily; 2hr).

**By car** For those who are driving, the best place to park is at the top of av Jean-Nicoli, the road which leads into town from Ajaccio.

## INFORMATION

**Tourist office** Just inside the main gates of the citadelle, near the museum (mid-April to June & Sept Mon–Fri 9am–noon & 2–6pm; July Mon–Fri 9am–6pm, Sat 9am–2pm; Aug Mon–Fri 9am–6pm, Sat & Sun 9am–2pm; Oct to mid-April Mon–Fri 9am–noon & 2–6pm; ☎ 04 95 46 26 70, ⓦ corte-tourisme.com). In the same building is the information office of the Parc Régional (same hours and phone number).

## ACCOMMODATION

**Arena le Refuge** Vallée de la Restonica, 3km southwest of town ☎ 04 95 46 09 13, ⓦ hotel-arena-lerefuge.com. Pleasant, family run hotel in a lovely rural location by the river, just a short distance from town. Rooms are bright and simply furnished, with terraces or balconies that open onto the garden. There's a restaurant on-site, but the real bonus is being able to swim in the river. Closed Oct–March. **€120**

★ **Gîte d'Étape U Tavignanu ("Chez M. Gambini")** Behind the citadelle ☎ 04 95 46 16 85. Run-of-the-mill hikers' hostel with small dorms and a relaxing garden terrace that looks over the valley. Peaceful, secluded, and the cheapest place to stay after the campsites. Follow the signs for the Tavignano trail (marked with orange spots of paint) around the back of the citadelle. Breakfast included. Easter to mid-Oct. **€20**

**HR** 12 av du 9-septembre ☎ 04 95 45 11 11, ⓦ hotel-hr.com. This converted concrete-block gendarmerie, 200m southwest of the *gare CFC*, looks grim from the outside, but its 125 rooms are comfortable enough and its rates rock bottom; bathroom-less options are the best deal. No credit cards. **€55**

**Du Nord** 22 cours Paoli ☎ 09 74 56 48 39, ⓦ hoteldunord-corte.com. Pleasant, clean place right in the centre, with plenty of Second Empire charm. Its variously priced rooms are large for the tariffs. **€123**

**La Restonica** Vallée de la Restonica, 2km southwest from town ☎ 04 95 45 25 25, ⓦ hotelrestonica.com. Sumptuous comfort in a wood-lined riverside hotel set up by a former French-national footballer, Dominique Colonna. Hunting trophies, old paintings, salon with open fireplace and leather-upholstered furniture create an old-fashioned atmosphere, and there's a large pool and garden terrace. **€120**

★ **Si Mea** 3 av du Pont de l'Orta ☎ 04 95 65 08 23, ⓦ hotelsimea-corte.fr. In a quiet, off-track, elevated location on the eastern fringe of Corte, this small hotel occupies a renovated 1930s building set in its own grounds. The boutique-style rooms have been artfully decorated, and have large beds with quality linen, and balconies boasting panoramic views of the town and mountains. Excellent value for the price. 10–15 mins' walk from the centre. **€95**

**Tuani** Vallée de la Restonica, 7km southeast ☎ 04 95 46 11 65. Too far up the valley without your own car, but the wildest and most atmospheric of the campsites around Corte, overlooking a rushing stream, deep in the woods. Ideally placed for an early start on Monte Rotondo. There's a lovely, breezy restaurant that serves up decent pizza, pasta and charcuterie platters, often using ingredients from their own garden, plus a kids' playground and a small shop on-site. Mid-April to mid-Sept. **€21**

**U Sognu** Rte de la Restonica ☎ 04 95 46 09 07. At the foot of the valley, this campsite is a 15min walk from the centre. It has a good view of the citadelle, plenty of poplar trees for shade, and toilets in a converted barn. There's also a small bar and restaurant (in summer). May–Sept. **€18**

## EATING AND DRINKING

**Le 24** 24 cours Paoli ☎ 04 95 46 02 90. Served by an enthusiastic young crew against a backdrop of vaulted stone walls and stylish designer furniture, the food in this hip Corsican speciality place is innovative yet full of traditional flavours. Try the sublime chocolate mousse if it's on the menu. Mains (such as prawn linguine) are around €21. March to mid-Feb daily noon–2pm & 7–10pm.

**Le Bips** 14 cours Paoli ☎ 04 95 46 04 48. Popular budget restaurant on the main drag, serving fragrant, copious pasta dishes, salads, steaks and some local specialities at down-to-earth rates. Hidden away in an eighteenth-century cellar, it's tricky to find: you have to cut down a back alley of the main street to a rear door. And expect to wait for a table unless you arrive early. Expect to pay around €25 per person a la carte. Later on in the evening its focus is very much on drinking. Daily 11.30am–2.30pm & 7pm–midnight.

**Coffee Cortenais** 3 cours Paoli. An American restaurant probably isn't what you expect – or even want – in the middle of Corsica, but this relaxed restaurant is one of the best bets in town for a relatively cheap (not to mention decent) meal. Burgers are (unsurprisingly) the star attraction here, starting at a very reasonable €11.50. Mon–Sat 11.30am–11pm.

**U Museu** Rampe Ribanelle in the haute ville at the foot of the citadelle, 30m down rue Colonel-Feracci ⓣ 04 95 61 08 36, ⓦ restaurant-umuseu.com. Congenial and well-situated place on a terrace at the foot of the citadelle walls. Try the €22 *menu corse*, featuring lasagne in wild boar sauce, trout, and *tripettes*. Great value for money, and the house wines are local AOC. June–Sept daily noon–2.30pm & 7–10.30pm; Oct–May closed Sun.

**La Rivière des Vins** 5 rampe Ste-Croix ⓣ 04 95 46 37 04. On a leafy square in the old quarter, this little Corsican speciality resto-cum-wine bar does a roaring trade largely thanks to its "plateau gourmand", which loads a mint-and-brocciu *omelette*, generous helping of charcuterie, traditional grilled liver sausages (*figatteli*), pan-fried potatoes and all the trimmings on to a single, filling platter. Also on the menu are a range of succulent wood-grilled steaks and bruschettas. *Mains* €14–28. Closed Dec–Feb. Daily noon–3pm & 6–11pm; closed lunchtimes on weekends.

**U Valentinu** 1 place Paoli ⓣ 04 95 61 19 65. This great little Italian restaurant on the main street serves Corte's best pizzas, baked to perfection in a wood oven. The dining hall is spacious, staff are friendly, portions copious and prices reasonable. Go for one of their Corsican speciality options, featuring mountain charcuterie and ewe's cheese. Mains €9–20. Daily noon–2.30pm & 7–10.30pm.

18

# Central Corsica

**Central Corsica** is a nonstop parade of stupendous scenery, and the best way to immerse yourself in it is to get onto the region's ever-expanding network of trails and forest tracks. The ridge of granite mountains forming the spine of the island is closely followed by the epic **GR20** footpath (see page 958), which can be picked up from various villages and is scattered with *refuge* huts, most of them offering no facilities except shelter. For the less active there are also plenty of roads penetrating deep into the **forests** of Vizzavona, La Restonica and Rospa Sorba, crossing lofty passes that provide exceptional views across the island. The most popular attractions in the centre, though, are the magnificent **gorges** of **La Restonica** and **Tavignano**, both within easy reach of Corte.

## Gorges du Tavignano

A deep cleft of ruddy granite beginning 5km to the west of Corte, the **Gorges du Tavignano** offers one of central Corsica's great walks, marked in yellow paint flashes alongside the broad cascading River Tavignano. You can pick up the trail from opposite the Chapelle Sainte-Croix in Corte's *haute ville* and follow it as far as the Lac de Nino, 30km west of the town, where it joins the GR20.

### ACCOMMODATION — CENTRAL CORSICA

**A Sega** ⓣ 04 95 51 79 00. Situated at 1192m amid glorious pine forest, this ranks among Corsica's best-run *refuges* and serves as a welcome stop off on the long trek up the valley to Lac de Nino. It takes around 3.5–4hr to reach on foot (there's no access road), and offers dorm beds, bivouac, filling breakfasts and evening meals and can supply packed lunches (€12). Dorm beds have to be booked through the PNRC website (ⓦ parc-corse.org); meals in advance by phone. Bivouac €7, dorms €14, half-board in bivouac €44, half-board in dorm €55

## Gorges de la Restonica

The glacier-moulded rocks and deep pools of the **Gorges de la Restonica** make the D936 running southwest from Corte the busiest mountain road in Corsica – if you come in high summer, expect to encounter traffic jams all the way up to the car park at the **Bergeries de Grotelle**, 15km from Corte. **Minibuses** run from Chjarasgiolu, about 4km from Corte, to the Bergeries, costing €13 (4 daily; Aug only; ☎04 95 46 02 12); taxis charge around €40. The gorges begin after 6km, just beyond where the route penetrates the **Forêt de la Restonica**, a glorious forest of chestnut, Laricio pine and the tough maritime pine endemic to Corte. Not surprisingly, it's a popular place to walk, picnic and bathe in the many pools fed by the cascading torrent of the River Restonica, easily reached by scrambling down the rocky banks.

From the *bergeries*, a well-worn path winds along the valley floor to a pair of beautiful glacial lakes. The first and larger, **Lac de Melo**, is reached after an easy hour's hike through the rocks. One particularly steep part of the path has been fitted with security chains, but the scramble around the side of the passage is perfectly straightforward, and much quicker. Once past Lac de Melo, press on for another forty minutes along the steeper marked trail over a moraine to the second lake, **Lac de Capitello**, the more spectacular of the pair. Hemmed in by vertical cliffs, the deep turquoise-blue pool affords fine views of the Rotondo massif on the far side of the valley, and in clear weather you can spend an hour or two exploring the surrounding crags.

MENHIR AT FILITOSA, CORSICA

# Contexts

993     History

1012     Art

1022     Architecture

1028     Cinema

1035     Books

1038     French

1047     Glossary of architectural terms

# History

Ever since Julius Caesar observed that "Gaul" was divided into quite distinct parts, and then conquered and unified the country, France has been perceived as both a nation and a collection of fiercely individualistic *pays*, or localities. The two Frances have often come into conflict. Few countries' governments have centralized as energetically, or have imposed such radical change from above. Equally, few peoples have been so determined to hold on to their local traditions. Charles de Gaulle famously complained that it was impossible to govern a country with 246 different kinds of cheeses. Yet each of those cheese-making regions, as de Gaulle was well aware, was proud to belong to the kind of impossibly, quarrelsomely traditional nation that could have so many cheeses.

The themes of nationalism and localism, of central control and popular resistance, of radicalism and conservatism, continue to define France today. What follows is necessarily a brief account of major events in the country's past.

## Caves to Celts

Traces of human existence are rare in France until about 50,000 BC. Thereafter, beginning with the stone tools of the Neanderthal "Mousterian civilization", they become ever more numerous, with an especially heavy concentration of sites in the Périgord region of the Dordogne, where, near the village of Les Eyzies, remains were discovered in 1868 of a late Stone Age people, subsequently dubbed "Cro-Magnon". Flourishing from around 25,000 BC, these cave-dwelling hunters seem to have developed quite a sophisticated culture, the evidence of which is preserved in the beautiful paintings and engravings on the walls of the region's caves.

By 10,000 BC, human communities had spread out widely across the whole of France, and by about 7000 BC, **farming and pastoral communities** had begun to develop. By 4500 BC, the first **dolmens** (megalithic stone tombs) showed up in Brittany, while dugout canoes dating back to the same epoch have been unearthed in Paris. It seems that a thriving trade followed the rivers, while the land between was heavily forested.

By 1800 BC, the **Bronze Age** had arrived in the east and southeast of the country, and trade links had begun with Spain, central Europe, southern Britain and around the Mediterranean – **Greek colonists** founded Massalia (Marseille) in around 600 BC.

The first Celts made an appearance in around 500 BC. Whether these were the same people known to the Romans as "long-haired" Gauls isn't certain. Either way, the inhabitants of France were far from shaggy-haired barbarians. The Gauls, as they became known, invented the barrel and soap, and were skilful manufacturers and

| 1,800,000 BC | 400,000 BC | 28,000–30,000 BC | 18,000–15,000 BC |
|---|---|---|---|
| Appearance of first stone tools in France | Traces of fire left at Terra Amata, Nice | Chauvet cave in Archèche is painted; Neanderthals disappear | Lascaux cave art, Dordogne: artistic peak of the Upper Paleolithic |

prolific traders – as was proved by the "chariot tomb" of **Vix**, where the burial goods included rich gold jewellery, a metal-wheeled cart and elaborate Greek vases.

## Roman Gaul

By 100 BC the **Gauls** had established large **hilltop towns with merchant communities**. The area equivalent to modern **Provence** became a Roman colony in 118 BC and, in 58 BC, when **Julius Caesar** arrived to complete the Roman conquest of Gaul, there were perhaps fifteen million people living in the area now occupied by modern France. **Tribal rivalries** made the Romans' job of conquering the north fairly easy, and when the Gauls finally united under **Vercingétorix** in 52 BC, it only made their defeat at the battle of **Alésia** more final.

This **Roman victory** was one of the major turning points in the history of France, fixing the frontier between Gaul and the Germanic peoples at the Rhine, thus saving Gaul from disintegrating because of internal dissension and making it a Roman province. During the five centuries of peace that followed, the Gauls farmed, manufactured and traded, became urbanized and educated – and learnt Latin. The emperor Augustus founded numerous cities – including Autun, Limoges and Bayeux – built roads and settled Roman colonists on the land. Vespasian secured the frontiers beyond the Rhine, thus ensuring a couple of hundred years of peace and economic expansion.

Serious **disruptions** of the Pax Romana only began in the third century AD. Oppressive aristocratic rule and an economic crisis turned the destitute peasantry into gangs of marauding brigands – precursors of the medieval *jacquerie* (see page 996). But most devastating of all, there began a series of incursions across the Rhine frontier by various restless **Germanic tribes**, the first of which, the Alemanni, pushed down as far as Spain, ravaging farmland and destroying towns.

In the fourth century the reforms of the emperor **Diocletian** secured some decades of respite from both internal and external pressures. Towns were rebuilt and fortified, foreshadowing feudalism and the independent power of the nobles. By the fifth century, however, the Germanic invaders were back: **Alans**, **Vandals** and **Suevi**, with **Franks** and **Burgundians** in their wake. While the Roman administration assimilated them as far as possible, granting them land in return for military duties, they gradually achieved independence from the empire.

## The Franks and Charlemagne

By 500 AD, the **Franks**, who gave their name to modern France, had become the dominant invading power. Their most celebrated king, **Clovis**, consolidated his hold on northern France and drove the Visigoths out of the southwest into Spain. In 507 he made the until then insignificant little trading town of Paris his capital and became a Christian, which inevitably hastened the **Christianization** of Frankish society.

Under the succeeding **Merovingian** dynasty the kingdom began to disintegrate until, in 732, **Charles Martel** reunited the kingdom and saved western Christendom from the northward expansion of Islam by defeating the Spanish Moors at the **battle of Poitiers**.

| 7000 BC | 3600 BC | 1800 BC | 600 BC |
|---------|---------|---------|--------|
| Neolithic farming begins | The first megaliths appear in Brittany | Start of the Bronze Age; walled citadelles built | Greek colonists found Massalia (Marseille) |

In 754 Charles's son, Pépin, had himself crowned king by the pope, thus inaugurating the **Carolingian dynasty** and establishing for the first time the principle of the divine right of kings. His son was **Charlemagne**, who extended Frankish control over the whole of what had been Roman Gaul, and far beyond. On Christmas Day in 800, he was crowned emperor of the **Holy Roman Empire**, though the kingdom again fell apart following his death in squabbles over who was to inherit various parts of his empire. At the Treaty of Verdun in 843, his grandsons agreed on a division of territory that corresponded roughly with the extent of modern France and Germany.

Charlemagne's administrative system had involved the royal appointment of counts and bishops to govern the various provinces of the empire. Under the destabilizing attacks of Norsemen/Vikings (who evolved into the Normans) during the ninth century, Carolingian kings were obliged to delegate more power and autonomy to these **provincial governors**, whose lands, like **Aquitaine** and **Burgundy**, already had separate regional identities as a result of earlier invasions. Gradually the power of these governors overshadowed that of the king, with his lands confined solely to the Île de France. When the last Carolingian died in 987, it was only natural that they should elect one of their own number to take his place. This was **Hugues Capet**, founder of a dynasty that lasted until 1328.

## The rise of the French kings

The years 1000 to 1500 saw the gradual extension and consolidation of the power of the **French kings**, accompanied by the growth of a centralized administrative system and bureaucracy. Foreign policy was chiefly concerned with restricting papal interference in French affairs and checking the English kings' continuing involvement in French territory. Conditions for the overwhelming majority of the population, meanwhile, remained remarkably unchanged.

Surrounded by vassals much stronger than themselves, **Hugues Capet** and his successors remained weak throughout the eleventh century, though they made the most of their feudal rights. At the beginning of the twelfth century, having successfully tamed his own vassals in the Île de France, Louis VI had a stroke of luck. **Eleanor**, daughter of the powerful duke of Aquitaine, was left in his care on her father's death, so he promptly married her off to his son, the future Louis VII. The marriage ended in divorce, however, and in 1152 Eleanor married Henry of Normandy, shortly to become **Henry II** of England. Thus the **English** crown gained control of a huge chunk of French territory, stretching from the Channel to the Pyrenees. Though their fortunes fluctuated over the ensuing three hundred years, the English rulers remained a perpetual thorn in the side of the French kings, with a dangerous potential for alliance with any rebellious French vassals.

**Philippe Auguste** (1179–1223) made considerable headway in undermining English rule by exploiting the bitter relations between Henry II and his three sons, one of whom was **Richard the Lionheart**. By the end of his reign Philippe had recovered all of Normandy and the English possessions north of the Loire.

For the first time, the royal lands were greater than those of any other French lord. The foundations of a systematic administration and civil service had been established

| 450 BC | 58–52 BC | 406 AD | 732 AD |
|---|---|---|---|
| Arrival of the Gauls | Julius Caesar conquers Gaul | Frank and Germanic tribes settle | Northward advance of the Moors halted at Battle of Poitiers |

in **Paris**, and Philippe had firmly and quietly marked his independence from the papacy by refusing to take any interest in the **crusade** against the heretic Cathars of Languedoc. When Languedoc and Poitou came under royal control in the reign of his son Louis VIII, France was by far the greatest power in western Europe.

## The Hundred Years' War

In 1328 the Capetian monarchy had its first succession crisis, which led directly to the ruinous **Hundred Years' War** with the English. Charles IV, last of the line, had only daughters as heirs, and when it was decided that France could not be ruled by a queen, the English king, **Edward III** claimed the throne of France for himself – on the grounds that his mother was Charles's sister.

The French chose **Philippe, Count of Valois**, instead, and Edward acquiesced for a time. But when Philippe began whittling away at his possessions in Aquitaine, Edward renewed his claim and embarked on war. With its population of about twelve million, France was the far richer and more powerful country, but its army was no match for the superior organization and tactics of the English. Edward won an outright victory at **Crécy** in 1346 and seized the port of Calais as a permanent bridgehead. Ten years later, his son, the Black Prince, actually took the French king, Jean le Bon, prisoner at the **battle of Poitiers**.

Although by 1375 French military fortunes had improved to the point where the English had been forced back to Calais and the Gascon coast, the strains of war and administrative abuses, as well as the madness of Charles VI, caused other kinds of damage. In 1358 there were **insurrections** among the Picardy peasantry (the *jacquerie*) and among the townspeople of Paris under the leadership of Étienne Marcel. Both were brutally repressed, as were subsequent risings in Paris in 1382 and 1412.

When it became clear that the king was mad, two rival camps began to vie for power: the **Burgundians**, led by the king's cousin and Duke of Burgundy, Jean sans Peur, and the **Armagnacs**, who gathered round the Duke of Orléans, Charles's brother. The situation escalated when Jean sans Peur had Orléans assassinated, and when fighting broke out between the two factions, they both called on the English for help. In 1415 Henry V of England inflicted another crushing defeat on the French army at **Agincourt**. The Burgundians seized Paris, took the royal family prisoner and recognized Henry as heir to the French throne. When Charles VI died in 1422, the English and their Burgundian allies assumed control of much of France, leaving the young French heir, the Dauphin Charles, barely clinging on to a rump state around the Loire valley.

The French state might well have been finally exterminated had it not been for the arrival at court, in 1429, of **Joan of Arc**, a 17-year-old peasant girl who promised divine support for an aggressive military campaign. The English were driven back from their siege of Orléans, the Dauphin crowned as Charles VII at Reims in July 1429, Paris was retaken in 1436 and the English finally driven from France altogether (except for a toehold at Calais) in 1453. Joan's own end was less triumphant: she fell into the hands of the Burgundians and was burnt at the stake for heresy in 1431 (see page 370).

From the 1450s, court life was centred on pleasure-seeking in the Loire valley. Even for the peasantry life grew less hard. The threats of war and plague steadily receded, and from 1450 the harvests did not fail for seventy unbroken years. The population

| 800 AD | 987 AD | 1152 | 1163 |
|---|---|---|---|
| Charlemagne crowned Holy Roman Emperor | Capetian Dynasty founded by Hugues Capet | England's Henry II marries Eleanor of Aquitaine | Cornerstone laid of Notre-Dame de Paris, France's pre-eminent Gothic cathedral |

began to grow again, and a kind of peasant aristocracy took shape in the form of the smallholder *fermiers*. In the towns, meanwhile, the *aisés*, or well-to-do merchants and artisans, began to form the basis of what would become the bourgeoisie.

By the end of the fifteenth century, Dauphiné, Burgundy, Franche-Comté and Provence were under royal control, and an effective standing army had been created. The taxation system had been overhauled, and France had emerged from the Middle Ages a rich, powerful state, firmly under the centralized authority of an absolute monarch.

## The Wars of Religion

After half a century of self-confident but inconclusive pursuit of military glory in Italy, brought to an end by the **Treaty of Cateau-Cambrésis** in 1559, France was plunged into another period of devastating internal conflict. The **Protestant** ideas of Luther and Calvin had gained widespread adherence among all classes of society, despite sporadic brutal attempts by François I and Henri II to stamp them out.

**Catherine de Médicis**, acting as regent for her son, later Henri III, implemented a more tolerant policy, provoking violent reaction from the ultra-Catholic faction led by the **Guise** family. Their massacre of a Protestant congregation coming out of church in March 1562 began a civil **War of Religion** that, interspersed with ineffective truces and accords, lasted for the next thirty years.

Well organized and well led by the Prince de Condé and Admiral de Coligny, the **Huguenots** – French Protestants – kept their end up very successfully, until Condé was killed at the battle of Jarnac in 1569. Three years later came one of the blackest events in the memory of French Protestants, even today: the **massacre of St Bartholomew's Day**. Coligny and three thousand Protestants who had gathered in Paris for the wedding of Marguerite, the king's sister, to the Protestant Henri of Navarre were slaughtered at the instigation of the Guises, and the bloodbath was repeated across France, especially in the south and west where the Protestants were strongest.

In 1584 Henri III's son died, leaving his brother-in-law, **Henri of Navarre**, heir to the throne, to the fury of the Guises and their Catholic league, who seized Paris and drove out the king. In retaliation, Henri III murdered the Duc de Guise, and found himself forced into alliance with Henri of Navarre, whom the pope had excommunicated. In 1589 Henri III was himself assassinated, leaving Henri of Navarre to become Henri IV of France. It took another four years of fighting and the abjuration of his faith for the new king to be recognized. "Paris is worth a Mass," he is reputed to have said.

Once on the throne, Henri IV set about reconstructing and reconciling the nation. By the **Edict of Nantes** of 1598, the Huguenots were accorded freedom of conscience, freedom of worship in certain places, the right to attend the same schools and hold the same offices as Catholics, their own courts and the possession of a number of fortresses as a guarantee against renewed attack, the most important being La Rochelle and Montpellier.

## Kings and cardinals

In the seventeenth century, France was largely ruled by just two kings, **Louis XIII** (1610–43) and **Louis XIV** (1643–1715). In the *grand siècle*, as the French call it, or "Great

| 1328 | 1346 | 1348–1352 | 1415 |
| --- | --- | --- | --- |
| Start of the Hundred Years' War with the English | Edward III is victorious at Battle of Crécy | The Black Death ravages France | King Henry V of England inflicts crushing defeat at Battle of Agincourt |

Century", the state grew ever stronger, ever more centralized, and ever more embodied in the person of the king. France also expanded significantly, with frontiers secured in the Pyrenees, on the Rhine and in the north; conflict with the neighbouring Habsburg kings of Spain and Austria, however, helped exhaust the state's resources.

Louis XIII had the good fortune to be served by the extraordinarily capable minister **Cardinal Richelieu**, who began his services by crushing a revolt led by Louis XIII's brother Gaston, Duke of Orléans. He then confronted Protestantism. Believing that the Protestants' retention of separate fortresses within the kingdom was a threat to security, and the absolute power of the king, he attacked and took La Rochelle in 1627. Although he was unable to extirpate their religion altogether, Protestants were never again to present a military threat.

Richelieu also actively promoted economic self-sufficiency – **mercantilism** – by encouraging the growth of the luxury craft industries. France was to excel in textile production right up to the Revolution. On the foreign front, he built up the navy and granted privileges to companies involved in establishing **colonies** in North America, Africa and the West Indies. He adroitly kept France out of actual military engagement, meanwhile, by funding the Swedish king and general, Gustavus Adolphus, to make war against the Habsburgs in Germany. When in 1635 the French were finally obliged to commit their own troops, they made significant gains against the Spanish in the Netherlands, Alsace and Lorraine, and won Roussillon for France.

### The Sun King

Richelieu died just a few months before Louis XIII in 1642. As Louis XIV was still an infant, his mother, Anne of Austria, acted as regent, served by Richelieu's protégé, **Cardinal Mazarin**, who was hated as much as his predecessor was by the traditional aristocracy and the *parlements* (the supreme courts of law), who were anxious that their privileges, including the collection of taxes, would be curtailed. Spurred by these grievances, which were exacerbated by the ruinous cost of the Spanish wars, various groups in French society combined in a series of revolts, known as the **Frondes**. The first Fronde, in 1648, was led by the *parlement* of Paris, which resented royal oversight of tax collection. It was quickly followed by an aristocratic Fronde, supported by various peasant risings round the country. All were suppressed easily enough.

In 1659 Mazarin successfully brought the Spanish wars to an end. Two years later **Louis XIV** came of age, declaring that he would rule without a first minister. He embarked on a long struggle to modernize the administration. The war ministers, Le Tellier and his son Louvois, provided Louis with a well-equipped and well-trained professional army that could muster some 400,000 men by 1670. But the principal reforms were carried out by **Colbert**, who tackled corruption, set up a free-trade area in northern and central France, established the French East India Company, and built up the navy with a view to challenging the commercial supremacy of the Dutch.

Alongside his promotion of wise governance, Louis XIV certainly liked to gild his own throne, earning himself the title Le Roi Soleil, the **"Sun King"**. His grandiosity was expressed in two ruinously expensive forms: his extravagant new royal palace at Versailles and incessant military campaigns. His war against the Dutch, in 1672, ultimately resulted in the acquisition of Franche-Comté and a swathe of Flanders, including the city of Lille. In 1681 he simply grabbed Strasbourg, and got away with it.

| 1431 | 1562 | 1572 | 1598 |
|---|---|---|---|
| Jeanne d'Arc burned at the stake | Guise family massacres Protestants to start 30-year War of Religion | St Bartholomew's Day Massacre, Paris | Edict of Nantes grants Huguenots freedom of worship |

In 1685, under the influence of his very Catholic mistress, Madame de Maintenon, the king removed all privileges from the **Huguenots** by revoking the Edict of Nantes. The result was devastating. Many of France's most skilled artisans, its wealthiest merchants and its most experienced soldiers were Protestants, and they fled the country in huge numbers – over 200,000 by some estimates. Protestant countries promptly combined under the auspices of the League of Augsburg to fight the French. Another long and exhausting war followed, ending, most unfavourably for Louis XIV, in the **Peace of Rijswik** (1697).

No sooner was this concluded than Louis became embroiled in the question of who was to succeed the moribund Charles II of Spain as ruler of the Habsburg domains in Europe. William of Orange, now king of England as well as ruler of the Dutch United Provinces, organized a Grand Alliance against Louis. The so-called **War of the Spanish Succession** broke out and dragged on until 1713, leaving France totally impoverished. The Sun King, finally, was eclipsed. He died in 1715, after ruling for 72 years over a country that had grown to dominate Europe, and had become unprecedentedly prosperous, largely because of colonial trade. Louis XIV's power and control, however, had masked growing tensions between central government and traditional vested interests.

### Louis XV and the parlements

Louis XIV had outlived both his son and grandson. His successor, **Louis XV**, was only 5 when his great-grandfather died. During the **Regency**, the traditional aristocracy and the *parlements* scrambled to recover a lot of their lost power and prestige. An experiment with government by aristocratic councils failed, however, and attempts to absorb the immense national debt by selling shares in an overseas trading company ended in a huge collapse. When the prudent and reasonable **Cardinal Fleury** came to prominence upon the regent's death in 1726, the nation's lot began to improve (though the disparity in wealth between the countryside and the towns continued to increase). The Atlantic seaboard towns grew rich on slavery and trade with the American and Caribbean colonies, though in the middle of the century France lost out to England in the **War of Austrian Succession** and the **Seven Years War** – both in effect contests for control of America and India. The need to finance the wars led to the introduction of a new tax, the Twentieth, which was to be levied on everyone. The *parlement*, which had successfully opposed earlier taxation and fought the Crown over its religious policies, dug its heels in again, leading to renewed conflict over Louis' pro-Jesuit religious policy.

The division between the *parlements* and the king and his ministers only sharpened during the reign of **Louis XVI**, which began in 1774. Strangely enough, the one radical attempt to introduce an effective and equitable tax system led directly to the Revolution. Calonne, finance minister in 1786, tried to get his proposed tax approved by an **Assembly of Notables**, a device that had not been employed for more than a hundred years. His purpose was to bypass the *parlement*, which could be relied on to oppose any radical proposal. The attempt backfired, with the *parlement* demanding a meeting of the **Estates-General**, representing the nobles, the clergy and the bourgeoisie – this being the only body competent to discuss such matters. As law and order began to break down, the king gave in and agreed to summon the Estates-General on May 17, 1789.

| 1661 | 1664 | 1685 | 1759 |
|------|------|------|------|
| Louis XIV, the "Sun King", comes of age; start of Absolute Monarchy | First performance of Molière's *Tartuffe* | Louis revokes the Edict of Nantes, forcing mass exodus of Huguenot soldiers, artisans and merchants | Voltaire publishes his magnum opus, *Candide* |

## Revolution and empire

Against a background of deepening economic crisis and general misery, the Estates-General proved unusually radical. On June 17, 1789, the Third Estate – the representatives of the bourgeoisie – seized the initiative and declared itself the National Assembly, joined by some of the lower clergy and liberal nobility. Louis XVI appeared to accept the situation, and on July 9 the National Constituent Assembly declared itself. However, the king then called in troops, unleashing the anger of the people of Paris, the **sans-culottes** (literally, "without trousers").

On July 14 the *sans-culottes* stormed the fortress of the **Bastille**, symbol of the oppressive nature of the king's **"ancien régime"**. Throughout the country, peasants attacked landowners' châteaux, destroying records of debt and other symbols of oppression. On the night of August 4, the Assembly abolished the feudal rights and privileges of the nobility – a momentous shift of gear in the Revolutionary process. Later that month they adopted the **Declaration of the Rights of Man**. In December church lands were nationalized.

Bourgeois elements in the Assembly tried to bring about a compromise with the nobility, with a view to establishing a constitutional monarchy, but these overtures were rebuffed. Émigré aristocrats were already working to bring about foreign invasion to overthrow the Revolution. In June 1791 the king was arrested trying to escape from Paris. The Assembly, following an initiative of the wealthier bourgeois **Girondin** faction, decided to go to war to protect the Revolution.

On August 10, 1792, the *sans-culottes* set up a **Revolutionary Commune** in Paris and imprisoned the king, marking a radical turn in the Revolution. A new National Convention was elected and met on the day the ill-prepared Revolutionary armies finally halted the Prussian invasion at Valmy. A major rift swiftly developed between the **Jacobins** and *sans-culottes* and the more moderate **Girondins** over the abolition of the monarchy. The radicals carried the day, and, in January 1793, Louis XVI was executed. By June, the Girondins had been ousted.

**Counter-Revolutionary forces** were gathering in the provinces and abroad. A Committee of Public Safety was set up as chief organ of the government. Left-wing popular pressure brought laws on general conscription and price controls and a deliberate policy of secularization, and **Robespierre** was pressed onto the Committee as the best hope of containing the pressure from the streets, marking the beginning of the **Terror**.

As well as ordering the death of the hated queen, **Marie Antoinette**, Robespierre felt strong enough to guillotine his opponents on both Right and Left. But the effect of so many rolling heads was to cool people's faith in the Revolution; by mid-1794, Robespierre himself was arrested and executed, and his fall marked the end of radicalism. More conservative forces gained control of the government, deregulating the economy, limiting suffrage and establishing a five-man executive Directory, in 1795.

### Napoleon

In 1799, **General Napoleon Bonaparte**, who had made a name for himself as commander of the Revolutionary armies in Italy and Egypt, returned to France and took power in a coup d'état. He became First Consul, with power to choose officials and initiate legislation. He redesigned the tax system, created the Bank of France, replaced the power of local institutions by a corps of *préfets* answerable to himself, and

| **1762** | **1789** | **1793** |
|---|---|---|
| Rousseau's *Du contrat social* revolutionizes political thought | French Revolution ends the monarchy | Marie Antoinette is guillotined on the place de la Concorde, nine months after her husband, Louis XVI |

made judges into state functionaries – in short, laid the foundations of the modern French administrative system.

Although alarmingly revolutionary in the eyes of the rest of Europe, Napoleon was no Jacobin. He restored unsold property to émigré aristocrats, reintroduced slavery in the colonies, and recognized the Church once more. The authoritarian, militaristic nature of his regime, meanwhile, became more and more apparent. In 1804 he crowned himself **emperor** in the presence of the pope.

The tide began to turn in 1808. Spain, which was then under the rule of Napoleon's brother, rose in revolt, aided by the British, and in 1812, Napoleon threw himself into the disastrous **Russian campaign**. He reached Moscow, but the long retreat in terrible winter conditions annihilated his veteran Grande Armée. The nation was now weary of the burden of unceasing war and in 1814 Napoleon was forced to abdicate by a coalition of European powers. They installed **Louis XVIII**, brother of the decapitated Louis XVI, as monarch. In a last effort to recapture power, Napoleon escaped from exile in Elba and reorganized his armies, only to meet final defeat at **Waterloo** on June 18, 1815. Louis XVIII was restored to power.

## Restorations and revolutions

In the **White Terror**, which followed Napoleon's downfall, aristocrats attempted to expunge out all trace of the Revolution and restore the *ancien régime*. Louis XVIII resisted these moves, however, at least until the Duc de Berry was assassinated in an attempt to wipe out the Bourbon family. In response to reactionary outrage, the king was forced to dismiss his moderate royalist minister, Decazes. Censorship became more rigid and education was once more subjected to the authority of the Church. Then, in 1824, Louis was succeeded by the thoroughly reactionary **Charles X**, who pushed through a law indemnifying émigré aristocrats for property lost during the Revolution.

When the liberal opposition won a majority in the elections of 1830, the king dissolved the Chamber and restricted the already narrow suffrage. Barricades went up in the streets of Paris. Charles X abdicated and parliament was persuaded to accept **Louis-Philippe**, Duc d'Orléans, as king. On the face of it, divine right had been superseded by popular sovereignty as the basis of political legitimacy. The **1814 Charter**, which upheld Revolutionary and Napoleonic reforms, was reaffirmed, censorship abolished, the tricolour restored as the national flag, and suffrage widened.

However, the **Citizen King**, as he was called, had somewhat more absolutist notions about being a monarch. He began the colonization of Algeria and resisted attempts to enfranchise even the middle ranks of the bourgeoisie. A growing economic crisis brought bankruptcies, unemployment and food shortages, helping to radicalize the growing urban working class, whose hopes of a more just future received a theoretical basis in the **socialist writings** and activities of Blanqui, Fourier, Louis Blanc and Proudhon, among others.

### 1848 and the Second Republic

In February 1848 workers and students took to the streets, and when the army fired on a demonstration and killed forty people, civil war appeared imminent. The Citizen King fled to England, a provisional government was set up and a **republic** proclaimed.

| **1795** | **1804** | **1815** |
|---|---|---|
| Rouget de Lisle's *La Marseillaise* adopted as French national anthem | Napoleon crowned emperor | Napoleon defeated at Waterloo; the monarchy is re-established |

The government quickly extended the vote to all adult males – an unprecedented move for its time. But by the time elections were held in April, a new tax designed to ameliorate the financial crisis had antagonized the countryside, and a massive conservative majority was re-elected. Three days of bloody street fighting at the barricades followed, when General Cavaignac, who had distinguished himself in the suppression of Algerian resistance, turned the artillery on the workers. More than 1500 were killed and 12,000 arrested and exiled.

A reasonably democratic constitution was drawn up and elections called to choose a president. To everyone's surprise, Louis-Napoléon, nephew of the emperor, romped home. In spite of his liberal reputation, he restricted the vote again, censored the press and pandered to the Catholic Church. In 1852, following a coup and further street fighting, he had himself proclaimed **Emperor Napoléon III**.

## Empire and Commune

Napoléon III's authoritarian regime oversaw rapid growth in industrial and economic power. When he came to power, over half the country subsisted on the land (a figure down from three-quarters at the Revolution), two-thirds of road traffic took the form of a mule, and France itself remained a semi-continent made up as much of wilderness – forests, mountains, moorlands and grassy wastes – as land under cultivation. The peasant population was overwhelmingly enmired in debt, poverty and hunger: in 1865, life expectancy for those who made it to 5 years old was 51 years.

Industrialization, however, was now under way, and the explosive expansion of the railways began to lift the provinces out of their previous isolation. By 1888, 22,000 miles of track had been laid. Disaster, however, was approaching in the shape of the **Franco–Prussian** war. Involved in a conflict with Bismarck and the rising power of Germany, Napoléon III declared war. The French army was quickly defeated and the emperor himself taken prisoner in 1870. The result at home was a universal demand for the proclamation of a **third republic**. The German armistice agreement insisted on the election of a national assembly to negotiate a proper peace treaty. France lost Alsace and Lorraine and was obliged to pay hefty war reparations.

Outraged by the monarchist majority re-elected to the new Assembly and by the attempt of its chief minister, Thiers, to disarm the National Guard, the people of Paris created their own municipal government known as **the Commune**. However, it had barely existed two months before it was savagely crushed. On May 21, the **"semaine sanglante"** began in which government troops fought with the Communards street by street, massacring around 25,000, the last of them lined up against the wall of Père Lachaise cemetery and shot. It was a brutal episode that left a permanent scar on the country's political and psychological landscape.

## The Third Republic

In the wake of the Commune, competing political factions fought it out for control. Legitimists supported the return of a Bourbon to the throne, while Orléanists supported the heir of Louis-Philippe. Republicans, of course, would have none of either. Thanks in part to the intransigence of the Comte de Chambord, the Bourbon claimant who refused to accept a constitutional role, the Third Republic was declared. The Crown Jewels were sold off in 1885, and France never again seriously considered having a monarch.

| 1848 | 1832 | 1851 | 1852 |
|------|------|------|------|
| Founding of the Second Republic | Chopin performs his debut concert in Paris | Louis Napoléon stages coup d'état | Baron Haussmann hired to rebuild the French capital |

## The War years

In the years preceding **World War I**, the country enjoyed a period of renewed prosperity. Yet the conflicts in the political fabric of French society remained unresolved. With the outbreak of war in 1914, France found itself swiftly overrun by Germany and its allies, and defended by its old enemy, Britain. The cost of the war was even greater for France than for the other participants because it was fought largely on French soil. Over a quarter of the eight million men called up were either killed or injured; industrial production fell to sixty percent of the pre-war level. This – along with memories of the Franco–Prussian war of 1870 – was the reason that the French were more aggressive than either the British or the Americans in seeking war reparations from the Germans.

In the postwar struggle for recovery the interests of the urban working class were again passed over, save for Clemenceau's eight-hour-day legislation in 1919. As the **Depression** deepened in the 1930s, Nazi power across the Rhine became ever more menacing. In 1936, the left-wing **Front Populaire** won the elections with a handsome majority, ushering in **Léon Blum**, France's first Socialist and first Jewish prime minister. He pushed through progressive reforms, but his government quickly fell – and the Left would remain out of power until 1981. France meanwhile, had more pressing concerns, as it was drawn into war by the German invasion of Poland, in September 1939.

## World War II

For eight months, France waited out what it called a *drôle de guerre*, or "funny kind of war". Then, in May 1940, Germany attacked – with terrifying speed. In just six weeks, France was overrun as the government fled south, along with up to ten million refugees, or roughly a quarter of the population. **Maréchal Pétain**, a conservative veteran of World War I, emerged from retirement to sign an armistice with Hitler and head the collaborationist **Vichy government**, which ostensibly governed the southern part of the country, while the Germans occupied the strategic north and the Atlantic coast. Pétain's prime minister, Laval, believed it was his duty to adapt France to the new authoritarian age heralded by the Nazi conquest of Europe.

There has been endless controversy over who collaborated, how much and how far it was necessary. One thing at least is clear: Nazi occupation provided a good opportunity for out-and-out French fascists to track down Communists, Jews, Resistance fighters, freemasons – all those who they considered "alien" bodies in French society. While some Communists were involved in the **Resistance** right from the start, Hitler's attack on the Soviet Union in 1941 brought them into the movement on a large scale. Resistance numbers were further increased by young men taking to the hills to escape conscription as labour in Nazi industry. General de Gaulle's radio appeal from London on June 18, 1940, resulted in the Conseil National de la Résistance, unifying the different Resistance groups in May 1943.

Although British and American governments found him irksome, **de Gaulle** was able to impose himself as the unchallenged spokesman of the Free French. Even the Communists accepted his leadership. Representatives of his provisional government moved quickly into liberated areas of France behind the Allied advance after D-Day, thereby saving the country from localized outbreaks of civil war – and saving France, in de Gaulle's view, from the threat of Communist uprising.

| 1857 | 1870–1871 | 1888 | 1889 |
|---|---|---|---|
| Charles Baudelaire publishes *Les fleurs du mal* | Franco–Prussian War and Siege of Paris lead to the bloodbath of the Commune | After a fight with Gauguin in Arles, painter Vincent Van Gogh cuts off his own ear | Eiffel Tower is built |

## PARIS UNDER SIEGE

On September 1, 1870, when news of Napoléon III's surrender to Kaiser Wilhelm at the Battle of Sedan reached Paris, it was, ironically, greeted with **jubilation** rather than dismay. George Sand declared the fall of the Second Empire "a third awakening", while crowds poured on to the streets to sing the Marseillaise, confident that with the end of the bellicose regime the Prussian invaders would pack up and turn for home. What none of the merrymakers realized, however, was that the Prussian armies were on the brink of encircling their city and intent on crushing it.

The siege was regarded as a bit of a joke at the start. Secure behind a ten-metre-tall wall reinforced by 93 bastions, earthworks and landmines, Parisians had stockpiled grain, while huge herds of sheep and oxen grazed in the Bois de Boulogne – a scene as bucolic as it was ominous.

Within a month, however, the joke had turned sour. The authorities had grossly under-provisioned. Fresh meat and bread quickly ran out. The bourgeoisie were forced to slaughter their carriage horses and pets (and even – famously – the contents of the municipal zoo, including its much loved elephants). The working classes, meanwhile, resorted to mice and sewer rats, growing hungrier and more restless with each passing day.

Entirely cut off from the rest of the country for over three months, the city's only means of communication with the war cabinet in Tours were hastily constructed **hot-air balloons**. Some of these red-striped behemoths were blown out to sea and never seen again. Others pitched up in Prussia. One even landed on the snow-covered mountains of Norway. But the majority, having survived fusillades from the enemy lines, made haphazard landings in rural France, where their pilots, precious mail sacks and carrier pigeons were spirited away by local patriots.

As the chill of the worst winter in living memory began to bite, however, indiscriminate bombardment from Herr Krupp's massive guns stationed on the outskirts sapped what little will remained. By early January, the world's most glittering and sophisticated city – home to Zola, Hugo, Renoir and Degas, which only two years previously had hosted the Great Exhibition – had been brought to its knees.

Bismarck's plan had always been to choke the capital from outside, and in the end, dissent from inside Paris rather than the shells raining upon it brought about the end of the siege. After months of relentless cold and starvation, the Red Clubs and 350,000-strong National Guard – their ranks swollen by members of an angry, politicized underclass consigned by Haussmann's rebuilding of Paris to slum quarters on the city's fringes – lost patience with the ineffectual leadership of General Trochu and threatened **rebellion**. To avert a bloodbath, Trochu secretly dispatched a message to Bismarck requesting an armistice.

The Prussian terms were harsh, and intended to humiliate. After a triumphant ceremony at the Palace of Versailles where the **surrender** was formally accepted, 30,000 Uhlans staged a victory march down the Champs-Élysées. This ordeal, coupled with crippling reparations, contributed in no small part to the punitive conditions later imposed on Germany in the Treaty of Versailles – one of the principal causes of World War II.

### The aftermath of war

France emerged from the war demoralized, bankrupt and bomb-wrecked. Almost half its people were peasants, still living off the land, and its industry was in ruins. Under a new constitution, in which **French women** were granted the vote for the first time, elections resulted in a large and squabbling left-wing majority. De Gaulle

| 1903 | 1907 | 1900–1904 | 1913 |
|---|---|---|---|
| The first ever Tour de France is staged | The game of *pétanque* is invented in La Ciotat on the Côte d'Azur | Pablo Picasso resides at the Bateau Lavoir in Paris: his Blue Period | Marcel Proust completes the first volume of *À la recherche du temps perdu* (*Remembrance of Things Past*) |

resigned in disgust. The new **Fourth Republic** was weak and fractious, but thanks in part to American aid in the form of the Marshall Plan, France achieved enormous industrial **modernization and expansion** in the 1950s. The country opted to remain in the US fold, but at the same time aggressively and independently pursued **nuclear technology**, finally detonating its own atom bomb in early 1960. France also took the lead in promoting closer **European integration**, a process culminating in 1957 with the creation of the European Economic Community.

## Colonial wars

On the surrender of Japan to the Allies in 1945, **Vietnam**, the northern half of the French Indochina colony, came under the control of Ho Chi Minh and his Communist organization, Vietminh. An eight-year armed struggle ended with French defeat at Dien Bien Phu and partition of the country at the Geneva Conference in 1954 – at which point the Americans took over in the south, with well-known consequences.

In the same year the **Algerian war of liberation** began. The French government was legally, economically and, it felt, morally committed to maintaining its rule over Algeria. Legally, the country was a *département*, an integral part of France, and the million-odd settlers, or **pieds noirs**, were officially French. And there was oil in the south. By 1958, half a million troops, most of them conscripts, had been committed to a bloody and brutal war that cost some 700,000 lives.

By 1958, it began to seem as if the government would take a more liberal line towards Algeria. In response, hard-line Rightists among the settlers and in the army staged a putsch and threatened to declare war on France. General de Gaulle let it be known that in its hour of need and with certain conditions – that is, stronger powers for the president – the country might call upon his help. Thus, on June 1, 1958, the National Assembly voted him full powers for six months and the Fourth Republic came to an end.

## De Gaulle and his successors

As prime minister, then newly powerful president of the **Fifth Republic**, de Gaulle wheeled and dealed with the *pieds noirs* and Algerian rebels. Meanwhile the war

---

### THE DREYFUS AFFAIR

From 1894, the **Dreyfus Affair** dramatically widened the split between Right and Left. Captain Dreyfus was a Jewish army officer convicted of spying for the Germans and shipped off to the penal colony of Devil's Island. It soon became clear that he had been framed – by the army itself – yet they refused to reconsider his case. The affair immediately became an issue between the anti-Semitic, Catholic Right and the Republican Left, with Radical statesman Clemenceau, Socialist leader Jean Jaurès and novelist Émile Zola coming out in favour of Dreyfus. Charles Maurras, founder of the fascist Action Française – precursor of Europe's Blackshirts – took the part of the army.

Dreyfus was officially rehabilitated in 1904, but in the wake of the affair the more radical element in the Republican movement began to dominate the administration, bringing the army under closer civilian control and dissolving most of the religious orders. In 1905 the Third Republic affirmed its anti-clerical roots by introducing a law on the separation of church and state.

---

| 1914–1918 | 1919 | 1926 | 1929 |
|---|---|---|---|
| World War I causes massive casualties in northeastern France | Treaty of Versailles restores territories lost in the Franco–Prussian War | Coco Chanel launches her "little black dress" in American *Vogue* | The start of the Great Depression; Jean-Paul Sartre meets Simone de Beauvoir at the École Normale in Paris |

continued, and violence in France – including a secret massacre of two hundred demonstrating French Algerians in Paris in 1961 – escalated. Eventually, in 1962, a referendum gave an overwhelming "yes" to **Algerian independence**, and *pieds noirs* refugees flooded into France. At the same time, a French labour shortage led to massive recruitment campaigns for workers in North Africa, Portugal, Spain, Italy and Greece. When the immigrants arrived in France, however, they found themselves under-paid, ill-housed and discriminated against both socially and officially.

De Gaulle's leadership was haughty and autocratic in style, and his quirky strutting on the world stage irritated France's partners. He blocked British entry to the European Economic Community, cultivated the friendship of the Germans, rebuked the US for its imperialist policies in Vietnam, withdrew from NATO, refused to sign a nuclear test ban treaty and called for a "free Québec".

Still, the sudden boiling over of **May 1968** took everyone by surprise. Beginning with student protests at the University of Nanterre, outside Paris, the movement of revolt rapidly spread to the Sorbonne and out into factories and offices. On the night of May 10, barricades went up in the streets of the Quartier Latin in Paris, and the CRS (riot police) responded by wading in. A **general strike** followed, and within a week more than a million people were out, marching under vaguely radical slogans. De Gaulle appealed to the nation to elect him as the only effective barrier against left-wing dictatorship, and dissolved parliament. The "silent majority", frightened and shocked by *les événements* – "the events", as they were nervously called – voted massively in his favour. When the smoke cleared, little had changed.

### Pompidou and Giscard

Having petulantly staked his presidency on the outcome of yet another referendum (on a couple of constitutional amendments) and lost, de Gaulle once more took himself off to his country estate and retirement. He was succeeded as president in 1969 by his business-oriented former prime minister **Georges Pompidou** and then, in 1974, by **Valéry Giscard d'Estaing**, who announced that his aim was to make France "an advanced liberal society". But, aside from reducing the voting age to 18 and liberalizing divorce laws, little progress was made. Giscard fell foul of various scandals and fell out with his ambitious prime minister, **Jacques Chirac**, who set out to challenge the leadership with his own RPR Gaullist party.

The Left seemed well placed to win the coming 1978 elections, until the fragile union between the Socialists and Communists cracked, the latter fearing their roles as the coalition's junior partners. The result was another right-wing victory, with Giscard able to form a new government, grudgingly supported by the RPR. Law and order and immigrant controls were the dominant features of Giscard's second term.

## The Mitterrand and Chirac era

When **François Mitterrand** won the presidential elections over Giscard in 1981, inaugurating the first Socialist government for decades, expectations were sky high. By 1984, however, the flight of capital, inflation and budget deficits had forced a complete turnaround, and the 1986 parliamentary election saw the Right, under Jacques Chirac, winning a clear majority in parliament. Thus began a period marked by what the

| 1934 | 1935 | 1939–1945 | 1948 |
|---|---|---|---|
| Gypsy guitarist Django Rheinhardt and violin virtuoso Stéphane Grappelli form the Hot Club de France Quintette | Edith Piaf's breakthrough performance at *Le Gerny* nightclub | World War II; Paris and northern France occupied by Nazis; the south is ruled by the puppet Vichy regime | Citroën unveils the iconic 2CV motor car |

French call **cohabitation**, in which the head of state (the president) and head of government (the prime minister) belong to opposite sides of the political divide.

As prime minister, Chirac embarked on a policy of privatization and monetary control, but the greatest change of the era was instituted by Mitterrand. In 1992, the president staked his reputation on the **Maastricht referendum** on creating closer political union in Europe. The vote was carried by a narrow margin in favour. On the whole, poorer rural areas voted "No" while rich urbanites and political parties voted "Yes". Only the extreme end of the political spectrum, the Communists and the Front National, remained determinedly anti-Europe.

In the 1990s, emerging scandals over cover-ups, corruption and the dubious war records of senior politicians tainted both the major parties, and Mitterrand tottered on to the end of his presidential term, looking less and less like the nation's favourite uncle. Several mayors ended up in jail, but it seemed as if the Paris establishment was above the law. By the time Mitterrand finally stepped down, he had been the French head of state for fourteen years, during a period when crime rose and increasing numbers of people found themselves excluded from society by racism, poverty and homelessness. Support for extreme Right policies propelled Jean-Marie Le Pen's Front National from a minority faction to a serious electoral force.

### Chirac's first presidency

Elected as president in 1995 and winning a second mandate in 2002, Chirac showed himself every bit as astute a politician as Mitterrand, and no less prone to scandal and controversy. An early sign of the rocky road ahead came when his prime minister, Alain Juppé, introduced **austerity measures**, designed to prepare France for European monetary union. Reforms to pensions and healthcare spending provoked a series of damaging strikes in 1995 and 1996, and led to growing popular disenchantment with the idea of closer European integration.

The **Front National** played up their image of standing up for the small man against the corrupt political establishment, and at municipal elections in June 1995 gained control of three towns, including the major port of Toulon. The **Algerian bomb attacks** which rocked Paris in the mid-1990s – designed to punish France for supporting Algeria's anti-Islamist military government – further played into the hands of the far Right and diminished public confidence in the government as guardian of law and order.

Feeling increasingly beleaguered and unable to deliver on the economy, Chirac called a snap parliamentary election in May 1997. His gamble failed spectacularly, and he was forced into a weak **cohabitation** with a Socialist parliament headed by **Lionel Jospin**, who promptly introduced the 35-hour working week, a 50:50 gender quota for representatives of political parties and, in 1999, the **Pacs** or Pacte Civil de Solidarité, a contract giving cohabiting couples, particularly gay couples, almost the same rights as married people.

### Skeletons in the mayoral cupboard

The most persistent **corruption scandals** focused on the finances of the Paris town hall, dating back to the 1980s. In 1995 it was revealed that Alain Juppé had rented a luxury flat in Paris for his son at below-market rates, and in 1998 the conservative Paris mayor **Jean Tibéri** was implicated in a scam involving subsidized real estate and fake

| 1954–1962 | 1959 | 1961 | 1968 |
|---|---|---|---|
| Algerian War of Independence | François Truffaut's *Les quatre-cents coups* (*The 400 Blows*) epitomizes French Nouvelle Vague (New Wave) cinema | Johnny Hallyday's cover of *Let's Twist Again* tops every chart in Europe | Student revolts and national strike cripple the country |

town-hall jobs – with real salaries – for party activists and relatives. Prosecutors edged ever closer to Chirac himself. In 2001 the president was accused of using some three million francs in cash from illegal sources to pay for luxury holidays, and in 2003 it was revealed that in eight years in office as mayor of Paris he and his wife had run up grocery bills of 2.2 million euros – over half of which had been reimbursed in cash. When investigating magistrates tried to question Chirac he claimed presidential immunity, a position that was upheld by France's highest court. But finally, in late 2011, the old fox was run to ground, charged with creating fictional jobs for political cronies and friends in need. The jury found him guilty and Chirac, by then 79 years old, was given a two-year suspended prison sentence for embezzling public funds, abuse of trust and illegal conflict of interest. Due to his age and status as former head of state, he was not required to go to prison.

### The election earthquake

In the run-up to the **presidential elections of 2002**, everyone in France assumed that the race was between Chirac and Jospin. Both far Left and far Right were damagingly split – and Front National leader, **Jean-Marie Le Pen**, had lost much support for punching a woman Socialist candidate in 1998. Lionel Jospin's hopes had been bolstered by the election of Socialist **Bertrand Delanoë** as Mayor of Paris in March 2001 but in the run-up to the elections the economy began to falter, unemployment was once more on the rise and fears over crime were widespread. Chirac talked up issues of immigration and law and order and when the results of the first round came through, Jospin had been beaten into third place by Le Pen – leaving Chirac and Le Pen to stand against each other in the final run-off in May.

The result was widely referred to as an "earthquake", shaking voters out of their disillusioned apathy. On May 1, 800,000 people packed the boulevards of Paris to protest against Le Pen and Socialists called on their supporters to vote for Chirac. He duly swept the board and, in the **ensuing parliamentary elections**, his new right-wing party, the **Union for a Presidential Majority**, swept convincingly to power. In an attempt to address widespread concerns about lack of representation and government accountability, one of Chirac's first measures was a **devolution** bill, giving more power to 26 regional assemblies and ending centuries of central government steadily accruing power to itself.

### Iraq, Muslims and climate change

In March 2003, a reinvigorated Chirac declared that he would wield France's Security Council veto if the US tried to table a resolution that contained an ultimatum leading to war in Iraq. Both the nationalist Right and anti-imperialists on the Left lapped it up in an orgy of anti-Americanism, and even some international observers applauded France's principled defence of international law, or perhaps of European power. Others saw Chirac's actions as cynical political posturing.

Either way, the result was an almighty spat that seriously damaged the cherished Franco–American relationship. One thing France's tough stance wasn't based on was any particularly pro-Arab or pro-Islamic bias, despite the presence of 5 million or more **Muslims** in France – the largest community in Europe. During 2003, Chirac presided over a government setting expulsion targets for illegal immigrants and enacting a

| 1981 | 1995 | 1998 | 2002 |
|------|------|------|------|
| Mitterrand becomes President of the Republic | Chirac voted President | Zidane's dream team beat Brazil 3-0 in the FIFA World Cup, then win the UEFA Euros two years later | The Euro replaces French Franc |

hugely controversial bill – though it was backed by almost two-thirds of the population and passed in parliament by 494 votes to 36 – banning "ostensibly religious" signs, notably Islamic headscarves, from schools and hospitals. Proposing the measure in December 2003, Chirac avowed that "secularity is one of the republic's great achievements … We must not allow it to be weakened."

In 2003 **climate change** also bludgeoned its way onto the headlines, due to Parisian temperatures in August regularly topping 40ºC (104ºF) – more than ten degrees above the average maximum for that time of year. Fifteen thousand people died. No one seemed willing to take responsibility for doing anything about it.

## Reforms, resistance and riots

Faced with an ageing population, unemployment flatlining at around ten percent and a budget deficit persistently exceeding the eurozone's three-percent ceiling, the newly confident Right decided it would reform the public sector once and for all. First to go under the knife would be the state's generous pensions and unemployment benefits, then worker-friendly hiring and firing rights, and finally the world-leading health service. Most of France saw the programme less as prudent milk-rationing and more as the sending of their sacred cows to slaughter. By mid-May 2003, two million workers were out on strike; and on May 26 half a million protested in the streets of Paris. And this was only in defence of pensions.

In the regional elections of March 2004, the electoral map turned a furious pink. Then, in the referendum of May 2005, 55 percent of French voters rejected the proposed new EU constitution when all the major political parties had urged them to vote "Yes". French voters, it seemed, did not want to join the new, economically liberal, globalized world.

Neither did disaffected French youths. In October 2005, two teenagers in a run-down suburb outside Paris were electrocuted while hiding from police they believed were chasing them. Local anger led speedily to three weeks of nightly, nationwide riots and confrontations. Youths torched cars, buses, schools and even police and power stations – anything connected with the hated state. Almost 9000 vehicles and property worth €200 million went up in smoke, and almost 2900 people were arrested. The ambitious Interior Minister, Nicolas Sarkozy, demanded the neighbourhoods be cleaned with power hoses. Young people who actually lived in the "hot" suburbs saw the main cause as anger at **racism** and social and economic exclusion. Many of the worst-affected areas were home to communities of largely African or North African origin, where youth unemployment ran as high as fifty percent – double the already high average among young people.

Even as the *banlieue* burned, Prime Minister Dominique de Villepin attempted to tackle the problem of youth unemployment and economic stagnation by giving small companies the right to dismiss new employees without having to give cause. This looked suspiciously like neoliberal or "Anglo-Saxon" capitalism. So, in October 2005, a million workers across the country marched against the new labour law. When, in early 2006, the laws were to be extended to all companies employing workers under the age of 26, the young responded with fury. In March, students in Paris **occupied the Sorbonne**, in conscious imitation of May 1968. And just as in 1968, people protested across France in their millions – only this time in the hope not that France would

| 2003 | 2005 | 2007 | 2011 |
| --- | --- | --- | --- |
| Severe heat wave leaves 15,000 dead | Urban riots by immigrant communities across the country | Nicolas Sarkozy wins presidential election | The Muslim veil, or hejab, is banned in French schools |

radically change, but that everything would stay the same. On April 10, Dominique de Villepin withdrew the law.

## Sarko

In the wake of the employment rights debacle, Nicolas Sarkozy, by now known popularly (and not affectionately) as "Sarko", was confirmed as the UMP's candidate for the 2007 presidential election. By a narrow margin, he defeated his centrist Socialist rival, **Ségolène Royal**. He had promised ongoing, radical reform, but major surprises followed his victory. First, he appointed a notably conciliatory cabinet. Next, his wife left him, and he took up with the model, singer and Euro-jetsetter Carla Bruni, marrying her in February 2008. Suddenly, the media spotlight was on his presidency, and it was asking more questions about the lifts in his shoes than his economic policies.

Then came the global financial crisis of 2008–09. Suddenly, the "Anglo-Saxon" form of market-led, laissez-faire capitalism seemed exactly what French socialists had always said it was: a debt-fuelled castle built on sand. In response, Sarkozy performed an astonishing political about-turn, pledging to wield the power of the state to ensure stability. Strong-state *dirigisme* was back. National reform, again, would have to wait. France never teetered on the edge of banking meltdown like its Atlantic rivals, but it was hit by recession nonetheless. In 2009, unemployment in France began racing towards the ten percent figure.

The usual **corruption scandals**, meanwhile, started to circle over Sarkozy's beleaguered administration. In 2009, his former political associate Dominique de Villepin was tried for his alleged role in the Clearstream affair, a supposed smear campaign in which a fake list of dodgy bank accounts, containing Sarkozy's name, was passed to an investigating judge. Rumours surfaced of kickbacks from French arms sales to Pakistan, allegedly used to fund Édouard Balladur's (Prime Minister 1993–1995) election campaign in the mid-1990s. Sarkozy was later accused of becoming a "French Berlusconi", by putting pressure on his powerful media friends to ensure a compliant press. Then members of his party were accused of accepting illegal donations from the L'Oréal heir and France's wealthiest woman, Liliane Bettencourt. In July 2010, Sarkozy himself was forced into making an unprecedented TV address to deny ever receiving money stuffed into an envelope – none of which did much to bolster the popularity of a leader widely perceived, with his jet-set lifestyle and glamorous marriage, as having lost touch with the Man in the Street.

As France's public debt spiralled and industrial output plummeted through 2011, the "President of the Rich" was increasingly seen as failing to deliver on his electoral pledges, while standing by as the mega-wealthy benefited from tax breaks and legal loopholes.

### "Mr Normal"

It was to distinguish himself from his adversary's high-rolling lifestyle that Socialist Party candidate, **François Hollande**, declared himself "Mr Normal" in the run-up to the 2012 elections. A moderate social-democrat from the central French province of Corrèze, Hollande had served as First Secretary of his party, but had long remained in the shadow of his wife, former presidential candidate, Ségolène Royal. The marriage, however,

| 2012 | 2015 |
|---|---|
| François Hollande defeats Sarkozy in closely fought presidential election | Series of Islamist terrorist shootings occur throughout France, including an attack at the Parisian headquarters of satirical magazine *Charlie Hebdo*, which kills 12 staff members, and then, later in the year, co-ordinated attacks in the capital killing 130 |

collapsed shortly after Royal's bid for the presidency in 2007, when it emerged that Hollande was involved with a *Paris Match* political journalist, Valérie Trierweiler.

In spite of the interest in his private life, Hollande went on to emerge victorious from the 2012 battle with Sarkozy for the French presidency – an acrimonious campaign in which the far Right National Front candidate, Marine Le Pen, shocked many by polling nearly 18 percent of the vote.

When the Socialist Party won an outright majority in the parliamentary elections soon after, Hollande's new administration had the mandate it needed to push through the keystones of its manifesto: a 75 percent tax on earnings over €1 million, and rapid expansion of the state sector as a means of stimulating growth. It didn't take long for public cynicism in his leadership to emerge as the economy remained stubbornly stagnant and his popularity rating sunk to a record low for a French president. Even his flagship tax on millionaires was quietly removed from the statute book after tantrums from rich people like actor Gérard Depardieu, who took up residency in Russia as a protest.

### 2015 terrorist attacks and a political revolution

2015 was a particularly traumatic year for France, following a number of devastating terrorist incidents in the capital. In January, the Paris office of the satirical magazine *Charlie Hebdo* was attacked leaving 12 people (including eight staff members) dead, though this wasn't the first time the publication had been targeted by extremists; on this occasion a branch of Al Qaeda claimed responsibility. Then, in November a series of coordinated attacks across the capital left 130 dead, 90 of whom lost their lives at the Bataclan theatre whilst attending a concert – these the deadliest attacks in western Europe since the Madrid train bombings in 2004.

On the political front, seismic changes were afoot. In the 2017 presidential elections, former Minister of Economy, **Emmanuel Macron** – who had founded the centrist/liberal leaning La République En Marche! party just a year earlier and was just 39 – triumphed handsomely in a second round run off against Marine Le Pen's National Front who, remarkably (though troublingly for many), managed to increase their vote share (from 2012) to 21 percent in the first round. Even though the by now deeply unpopular Hollande had decided not to seek re-election, the Socialists were nowhere to be seen. Whilst Macron's arrival has undoubtedly been a breath of fresh air, the honeymoon is now well and truly over, as France's youngest president since Napoleon continues to power on with his controversial programme of domestic reform – not least in the shake-up of the state railway operator SNCF. Whilst there was some brief respite in the form of the national football team's glorious World Cup victory in Moscow in July 2018 (the second in its history), further trouble lay ahead as the year drew to a close with the so-called *gilets jaunes* (Yellow Vests), a grassroots citizen's protest movement that was initially borne out of Macron's decision to raise taxes on fuel; this soon escalated into a wider anti-government movement, the result of which was some of the worst civil disorder France had witnessed for years.

In April 2019, the whole world watched on as a fire ravaged through Notre-Dame cathedral. The stone structure was thankfully saved but the entire roof collapsed. Financial pledges from within France and all around the world came pouring in immediately, creating a controversy within the country and abroad in these times of austerity.

| **2017** | **2018** | **2019** |
|---|---|---|
| Emmanuel Macron is elected French president | France win the World Cup for a second time, beating Croatia 4–2 in the final. The anti-government movement "gilets jaunes" causes ongoing civil disorder | Fire ravages Notre-Dame |

# Art

Since the Middle Ages, France has held – with occasional gaps – a leading position in the history of European painting, with Paris, above all, attracting artists from the whole continent. The story of French painting is one of richness and complexity, partly due to this influx of foreign painters and partly due to the capital's stability as an artistic centre.

## Beginnings

In the late Middle Ages, the itinerant life of the nobles led them to prefer small and transportable works of art; splendidly **illuminated manuscripts** were much praised and the best painters, usually trained in Paris, continued to work on a small scale until the fifteenth century. Many illuminators were also panel painters, and foremost among them was **Jean Fouquet** (c.1420–81). Born in Tours in the Loire valley, he became court painter to Charles VIII, drawing from both Flemish and Italian sources and utilizing the new fluid oil technique that had been perfected in Flanders.

Two other fifteenth-century French artists could be said to represent distinctive northern and southern strands. **Enguerrand Quarton** (c.1410–c.1466) was the most famous Provençal painter of the time. His *Coronation of the Virgin*, which hangs at Villeneuve-lès-Avignon, ranks as one of the first city/landscapes in the history of French painting: Avignon itself is faithfully depicted and the Mont Ste-Victoire, later to be made famous by Cézanne, is recognizable in the distance. The Master of Moulins, active in the 1480s and 1490s, was noticeably more northern in temperament, painting both religious altarpieces and portraits commissioned by members of the royal family or the fast-increasing bourgeoisie.

## Mannerism and Italian influence

At the end of the fifteenth and the beginning of the sixteenth centuries, the French invasion of Italy brought both artists and patrons into closer contact with the Italian Renaissance.

The most famous of the artists who were lured to France was **Leonardo da Vinci** who spent the last three years of his life (1516–19) at the court of François Ier. From the Loire valley, which until then had been his favourite residence, the French king moved nearer to Paris, where he had several palaces decorated. Italian artists were once again called upon, and two of them, **Rosso** and **Primaticcio**, who arrived in France in 1530 and 1532, respectively, were to shape the artistic scene in France for the rest of the sixteenth century.

Both artists introduced to France the latest Italian style, **Mannerism**, with its emphasis on the fantastic, the luxurious and the large-scale decorative. It was first put to the test in the revamping of the palace at Fontainebleau, and most French artists worked at the château at some point in their career, or were influenced by its homogeneous style, leading to what was subsequently called the **School of Fontainebleau**.

**Antoine Caron** (c.1520–1600), who often worked for Catherine de Médicis, the widow of Henri II, contrived complicated allegorical paintings in which elongated figures are arranged within wide, theatre-like scenery packed with ancient monuments and Roman statues. Even the Wars of Religion, raging in the 1550s and 1560s, failed to rouse French artists' sense of drama, and representations of the many massacres then going on were detached and fussy in tone.

Portraiture tended to be more inventive, and very French in its general sobriety. The portraits of **Jean Clouet** (c.1485–1541) and his son **François** (c.1510–72), both official painters to François Ier, combined sensitivity in the rendering of the sitter's features with a keen sense of abstract design in the arrangement of the figure, conveying with great clarity social status and giving clues to the sitter's profession.

## The seventeenth century

In the **seventeenth century**, Italy continued to be a source of inspiration for French artists, most of whom were drawn to Rome, at that time the most exciting artistic centre in Europe, dominated by Italian painters such as Michelangelo Merisi da Caravaggio and Annibale Carracci.

Some French painters like **Moïse Valentin** (c.1594–1632) worked in Rome and were directly influenced by Caravaggio; others, such as the great painter from Lorraine, **Georges de la Tour** (1593–1652), benefited from his innovations at one remove, gaining inspiration from the Utrecht Caravaggisti who were active at the time in Holland. La Tour produced deeply felt religious paintings in which figures appear to be carved out of the surrounding gloom by the magical light of a candle. Sadly, his output was very small – just some forty or so works in all.

Humble subjects and attention to naturalistic detail were also important aspects of the work of the **Le Nain brothers**, especially **Louis** (1593–1648), who depicted with great sympathy, but never with sentimentality, the condition of the peasantry. He chose moments of inactivity or repose within the lives of the peasants, and his paintings achieve timelessness and monumentality by their very stillness. The other Italian artist of influence, the Bolognese **Annibale Carracci** (d. 1609), impressed French painters not only with his skill as a decorator but, more tellingly, with his ordered, balanced landscapes, which were to prove of prime importance for the development of the classical landscape in general, and in particular for those painted by **Claude Lorrain** (1604/5–82). Born in Lorraine, Claude studied and travelled in Italy, which would provide him with subjects of study for the rest of his life. His landscapes are airy compositions in which religious or mythological figures are lost within an idealized, Arcadian nature, bathed in tranquil light.

Landscapes, harsher and even more ordered, but also recalling the Arcadian mood of antiquity, were painted by the other French painter who elected to make Rome his home, **Nicolas Poussin** (1594–1665). Like Claude, Poussin selected his themes from the rich sources of Greek, Roman and Christian myths and stories; unlike Claude, however, his figures are not subdued by nature but rather dominate it, in the tradition of the masters of the High Renaissance, such as Raphael and Titian, whom he greatly admired. Poussin only briefly returned to Paris, called by the king, Louis XIII, to undertake some large decorative works quite unsuited to his style or character.

Many other artists visited Italy, but most returned to France, the luckiest to be employed at the court to boost the royal images of Louis XIII and XIV and their respective ministers, Richelieu and Colbert. **Simon Vouet** (1590–1649), **Charles Le Brun** (1619–90) and **Pierre Mignard** (1612–95) all performed that task with skill, often using ancient history and mythology to suggest flattering comparisons with the reigning monarch.

The official aspect of their works was paralleled by the creation of the new **Academy of Painting and Sculpture** in 1648, an institution that dominated the arts in France for the next few hundred years, if only by the way artists reacted against it. **Philippe de Champaigne** (1602–74), a painter of Flemish origin, alone stands out at the time as remotely different, removed from the intrigues and pleasures of the court and instead strongly influenced by the teaching and moral code of Jansenism, a purist and severe form of the Catholic faith. But it was the more courtly, fun-loving portraits and paintings by such artists as Mignard that were to influence most of the art of the following century.

## The early eighteenth century

The semi-official art encouraged by the foundation of the Academy became more frivolous and light-hearted in the **eighteenth century**. The court at Versailles lost its attractions, and many patrons now were to be found among the hedonistic bourgeoisie and aristocracy living in Paris. History painting, as opposed to genre scenes or portraiture, retained its position of prestige, but at the same time many artists tried their hands at landscape, genre, history or decorative works, often merging aspects of one genre with another. **Salons**, at which painters exhibited their works, were held with increasing frequency and bred a new phenomenon in the art world – the art critic.

Possibly the most complex personality of the eighteenth century was **Jean-Antoine Watteau** (1684–1721). Primarily a superb draughtsman, Watteau's use of soft and yet rich, light colours reveals how much he was struck by the great seventeenth-century Flemish painter Rubens. His subtle depictions of dreamy couples, often seen strolling in delicate, mythical landscapes, are known as "*fêtes galantes*". They convey a mood of melancholy and poignancy largely lacking in the works of followers such as Nicolas Lancret and J.B. Pater.

The work of **François Boucher** (1703–70) was probably more representative of the eighteenth century: the pleasure-seeking court of Louis XV found the lightness of morals and colours in his paintings immensely congenial. Boucher's virtuosity is seen at its best in his paintings of women, always rosy, young and fantasy-erotic. **Jean-Honoré Fragonard** (1732–1806) continued this exploration of licentious themes but with an exuberance, a richness of colour and a vitality (*The Swing*) that was a feast for the eyes and raised the subject to a glorification of love. Far more restrained were the paintings of **Jean-Baptiste-Siméon Chardin** (1699–1779), who specialized in homely genre scenes and still lifes, painted with a simplicity that belied his complex use of colours, shapes and space to promote a mood of stillness and tranquillity. **Jean-Baptiste Greuze** (1725–1805) chose stories that anticipated reaction against the laxity of the times; the moral, at times sentimental, character of his paintings was all-pervasive, reinforced by a stage-like composition well suited to cautionary tales.

## Neoclassicism

This new seriousness became more severe with the rise of **Neoclassicism**, a movement for which purity and simplicity were essential components of the systematic depiction of edifying stories from the classical authors. Roman history and legends were the most popular subjects. Many of the paintings of **Jacques-Louis David** (1748–1825) are reflections of republican ideals and of contemporary history, from the *Death of Marat* to events from the life of Napoleon, who was his patron. For the emperor and his family, David painted some of his most successful portraits – *Madame Récamier* is not only an exquisite example of David's controlled use of shapes and space and his debt to antique Rome, but can also be seen as a paradigm of Neoclassicism.

Two painters, **Jean-Antoine Gros** (1771–1835) and **Baron Gérard** (1770–1837), followed David closely in style and in themes (portraits, Napoleonic history and legend), but often with a touch of softness and heroic poetry that pointed the way to Romanticism.

**Jean-Auguste-Dominique Ingres** (1780–1867) was a pupil of David; he also studied in Rome before coming back to Paris to develop the purity of line that was the essential and characteristic element of his art. His effective use of it to build up forms and bind compositions can be admired in conjunction with his recurrent theme of female nudes bathing, or in his magnificent and stately portraits that depict the nuances of social status.

## Romanticism

Completely opposed to the stress on drawing advocated by Ingres, two artists created, through their emphasis on colour, form and composition, pictures that look forward to the later part of the nineteenth century and the Impressionists. **Théodore Géricault** (1791–1824), whose short life was dominated by the heroic vision of the Napoleonic era, explored dramatic themes of human suffering in such paintings as *The Raft of the Medusa*, while his close contemporary, **Eugène Delacroix** (1798–1863), epitomized the **Romantic movement** – its search for emotions and its love of nature, power and change.

Delacroix was deeply aware of tradition, and his art was influenced, visually and conceptually, by the great masters of the Renaissance and the seventeenth and eighteenth centuries. In many ways he may be regarded as the last great religious and decorative French painter, but through his technical virtuosity, freedom of brushwork and richness of colours, he can also be seen as the essential forerunner of the Impressionists.

Other painters working in the Romantic tradition were still haunted by the Napoleonic legends, as well as by North Africa (Algeria) and the Middle East, which had become better known to artists and patrons alike during the Napoleonic wars. These were the subjects of paintings by **Horace Vernet** (1789–1863), **Théodore Chassériau** (1819–56) and the enormously popular but now little-regarded giant of old-fashioned classicism, **Jean-Louis-Ernest Meissonier** (1815–91).

Among their contemporaries was **Honoré Daumier** (1808–79): very much an isolated figure, influenced by the boldness of approach of caricaturists, he was content to depict everyday subjects such as a laundress or a third-class rail car – caustic commentaries on professions and politics that work as brilliant observations of the times.

## Landscape painting and realism

The first part of the **nineteenth century** saw nature, unadorned by artistic conventions, become a subject for study. Running parallel to this was the realization that painting could be the visual externalization of the artist's own emotions and feelings. **Jean-Baptiste-Camille Corot** (1796–1875) started to paint landscapes that were influenced as much by the unpretentious and realistic country scenes of seventeenth-century Holland as by the balanced compositions of Claude. His loving and attentive studies of nature were much admired by later artists, including Monet.

At the same time, a whole group of painters developed similar attitudes to landscape and nature, helped greatly by the practical improvement of being able to buy oil paint in tubes rather than as unmixed pigments. Known as the **Barbizon School** after the village on the outskirts of Paris around which they painted, they soon discovered the joy and excitement of *plein-air* (open-air) painting. **Théodore Rousseau** (1812–67) was their nominal leader, his paintings of forest undergrowth and forest clearings displaying an intimacy that came from the immediacy of the image. **Charles-François Daubigny** (1817–78), like Rousseau, often infused a sense of drama into his landscapes.

**Jean-François Millet** (1814–75) is perhaps the best-known associate of the Barbizon group, though he was more interested in the human figure than simple nature. Landscapes, however, were essential settings for his figures; indeed, his most famous pictures are those exploring the place of people in nature and their struggle to survive. *The Sower*, for instance, reflected a typical Millet theme, suggesting the heroic working life of the peasant. As is so often the case for painters touching on new themes or on ideas that are uncomfortable to the rich and powerful, Millet enjoyed little success during his lifetime, and his art was only widely appreciated after his death.

The moralistic and romantic undertone in Millet's work was something that **Gustave Courbet** (1819–77) strove to avoid. After an initial resounding success in the Salon exhibition of 1849, he endured constant criticism from the academic world and patrons alike, his scenes of ordinary life regarded as unsavoury and wilfully ugly. Breaking with the Salon tradition, Courbet put on a private exhibition of some forty of his works. Inscribed on the door in large letters was one word: "**Realism**".

# Impressionism

Like Courbet, **Edouard Manet** (1832–83) was strongly influenced by Spanish painters. Unlike Courbet, however, he never saw himself as a rebel or avant-garde painter – yet his technique and his themes were both new and shocking. Manet used bold contrasts of light and very dark colours, giving his paintings a forcefulness that critics often took for a lack of sophistication. And his detractors saw much to decry in his reworking of an old subject originally treated by the sixteenth-century Venetian painter, Giorgione, *Le Déjeuner sur l'Herbe*. Manet's version was shocking because he placed naked and dressed figures together, and because the men were dressed in the costume of the day, implying a pleasure party too specifically contemporary to be "respectable".

Manet's most successful pictures are reflections of ordinary life in bars and public places, where respectability was certainly lacking. To Manet, painting was to be enjoyed for its own sake and not as a tool for moral instruction – in itself an outlook that marked a definite break with the past. From the 1870s, Manet began to adopt the new techniques of painting out of doors, and his work became lighter and freer. He began to be seen as a much-admired member of a burgeoning group of mould-breaking young painters, alongside **Claude Monet** (1840–1926). Born in Le Havre, Monet came into contact with **Eugène Boudin** (1824–98), whose colourful beach scenes anticipated the way the Impressionists approached colour. Monet discovered that, for him, light and the way in which it builds up forms and creates an infinity of colours was the element that governed all representations. Under the impact of Manet's bright hues and his unconventional attitude ("art for art's sake"), Monet soon began using pure colours side by side, blended together to create areas of brightness and shade.

In 1874, a group of thirty artists exhibited together for the first time. Among them were some of the best-known names of this period of French art: Degas, Monet, Renoir, Pissarro. One of Monet's paintings was entitled *Impression: Sun Rising*, a title that was singled out by the critics to ridicule the colourful, loose and unacademic style of these young artists. Overnight they became, derisively, the "**Impressionists**".

**Camille Pissarro** (1830–1903) was slightly older than most of them and seems to have played the part of an encouraging father figure, always keenly aware of any new development or new talent. Not a great innovator himself, Pissarro was a very gifted artist whose use of Impressionist technique was supplemented by a lyrical feeling for nature and its seasonal changes. But it was really with **Monet** that Impressionist theory ran its full course: he painted and repainted the same motif under different light conditions, at different times of the day, and in different seasons, producing whole series of paintings such as *Grain Stacks*, *Poplars* and, much later, his *Water Lilies*.

**Auguste Renoir** (1841–1919), who started life as a painter of porcelain, was swept up by Monet's ideas for a while, but soon felt the need to look again at the old masters and to emphasize the importance of drawing. Renoir regarded the representation of the female nude as the most taxing and rewarding subject that an artist could tackle. Like Boucher in the eighteenth century, Renoir's nudes are luscious, but rarely, if ever, erotic – although in his later paintings they can become cloyingly, almost overpoweringly, sweet. Better were his portraits of women fully clothed, both for their obvious and innate sympathy and for their keen sense of design.

**Edgar Degas** (1834–1917) was yet another artist who, although he exhibited with the Impressionists, did not follow their precepts very closely. The son of a rich banker, he was trained in the tradition of Ingres: design and drawing were an integral part of his art, and, whereas Monet was fascinated mainly by light, Degas wanted to express movement in all its forms. His pictures are vivid expressions of the body in action, usually straining under fairly exacting circumstances – dancers and circus artistes were among his favourite subjects – as well as more mundane depictions of laundresses and other working women.

Like so many artists of the day, Degas had his imagination fired by the discovery of **Japanese prints**, which could for the first time be seen in quantity. These provided him with new ideas of composition, not least in their asymmetry of design and the use of large areas of unbroken colour. **Photography**, too, had an impact, if only because it finally liberated artists from the task of producing accurate, exacting descriptions of the world.

Degas' extraordinary gift as a draughtsman was matched only by that of the Provençal aristocrat **Henri de Toulouse-Lautrec** (1864–1901). Toulouse-Lautrec, who had broken both his legs as a child, was unusually small, a physical deformity that made him particularly sensitive to free and vivacious movements. A great admirer of Degas, he chose similar themes: people in cafés and theatres, working women and variety dancers all figured large in his work. But, unlike Degas, Toulouse-Lautrec looked beyond the body, and his work is scattered with social comment, sometimes sardonic and bitter. In his portrayal of Paris prostitutes, there is sympathy and kindness; to study them better he lived in a brothel, revealing in his paintings the weariness and sometimes gentleness of these women.

## Post-Impressionism

Though a rather vague term, as it's difficult to date exactly when the backlash against Impressionism took place, **Post-Impressionism** represents in many ways a return to more formal concepts of painting – in composition, in attitudes to subject and in drawing.

**Paul Cézanne** (1839–1906), for one, associated only very briefly with the Impressionists and spent most of his working life in relative isolation, obsessed with rendering, as objectively as possible, the essence of form. He saw objects as basic shapes – cylinders, cones, and so on – and tried to give his painting a unity of texture that would force the spectator to view it not so much as a representation of the world but rather as an entity in its own right, as an object as real and dense as the objects surrounding it. It was this striving for pictorial unity that led him to cover the entire surface of the picture with small, equal brush strokes which made no distinction between the textures of a tree, a house or the sky.

The detached, unemotional way in which Cézanne painted was not unlike that of the seventeenth-century artist Poussin, and he found a contemporary parallel in the work of **Georges Seurat** (1859–91). Seurat was fascinated by current theories of light and colour, and he attempted to apply them in a systematic way, creating different shades and tones by placing tiny spots of pure colour side by side, which the eye could in turn fuse together to see the colours mixed out of their various components. This **pointillist** technique also had the effect of giving monumentality to everyday scenes of contemporary life.

While Cézanne, Seurat and, for that matter, the Impressionists sought to represent the outside world objectively, several other artists – the **Symbolists** – were seeking a different kind of truth, through the subjective experience of fantasy and dreams. **Gustave Moreau** (1840–98) represented, in complex paintings, the intricate worlds of the romantic fairy tale, his visions expressed in a wealth of naturalistic details. The style of **Puvis de Chavannes** (1824–98) was more restrained and more obviously concerned with design and the decorative. And a third artist, **Odilon Redon** (1840–1916), produced some weird and visionary graphic work that especially intrigued Symbolist writers; his less numerous works in colour belong to the later part of his life.

The subjectivity of the Symbolists was of great importance to the art of **Paul Gauguin** (1848–1903). He started life as a stockbroker who collected Impressionist paintings, a Sunday artist who gave up his job in 1883 to dedicate himself to painting.

During his stay in Pont-Aven in Brittany, Gauguin worked with a number of artists who called themselves the **Nabis**, among them **Paul Sérusier** and **Émile Bernard**. He began exploring ways of expressing concepts and emotions by means of large areas of colour and powerful forms, and developed a unique style that was heavily indebted to his knowledge of Japanese prints and of the tapestries and stained glass of medieval art. His search for the primitive expression of primitive emotions took him eventually to the Pacific, where, in Tahiti, he found some of his most inspiring subjects.

A similar derivation from Symbolist art and a wish to exteriorize emotions and ideas by means of strong colours, lines and shapes underlies the work of **Vincent Van Gogh** (1853–90), a Dutch painter who came to live in France. Like Gauguin, with whom he had an admiring but stormy friendship, Van Gogh started painting relatively late in life, lightening his palette in Paris under the influence of the Impressionists, and then heading south to Arles where, struck by the harshness of the Mediterranean light, he turned out such frantic expressionistic pieces as *The Reaper* and *Wheatfield with Crows*. In all his later pictures the paint is thickly laid on in increasingly abstract patterns that follow the shapes and tortuous paths of his deep inner melancholy.

**Édouard Vuillard** (1868–1940) and **Pierre Bonnard** (1867–1947) explored the Nabi artists' interest in Japanese art and in the decorative surface of painting. They produced intimate images in which figures and objects blend together in complicated patterns. In the works of Bonnard, in particular, the glowing design of the canvas itself becomes as important as what it's trying to represent.

## Fauvism, Cubism, Surrealism

The **twentieth century** kicked off to a colourful start with the **Fauvist** exhibition of 1905, an appropriately anarchic beginning to a century which, in France above all, was to see radical changes in attitudes towards painting. The painters who took part in the exhibition included, most influentially, **Henri Matisse** (1869–1954), **André Derain** (1880–1954), **Georges Rouault** (1871–1958) and **Albert Marquet** (1875–1947), and they were quickly nicknamed the Fauves (Wild Beasts) for their use of bright, wild colours that often bore no relation whatsoever to the reality of the object depicted. Skies were just as likely to be green as blue since, for the Fauves, colour was a way of composing, of structuring a picture, and not necessarily a reflection of real life. Raoul Dufy (1877–1953) used Fauvist colours in combination with theories of abstraction to paint an effervescent industrial age.

Fauvism was just the beginning: the first decades of the twentieth century were a time of intense excitement and artistic activity in Paris, and painters and sculptors from all over Europe flocked to the capital to take part in the liberation from conventional art that individuals and groups were gradually instigating. This loose, cosmopolitan grouping of artists gradually became known as the **École de Paris**, though it was never a "school" as such. **Pablo Picasso** (1881–1973) was one of the first to arrive in Paris – from Spain, in 1900. He soon started work on his first Blue Period paintings, which describe the sad and squalid life of itinerant actors in tones of blue. Later, while Matisse was experimenting with colours and their decorative potential, Picasso came under the sway of Cézanne and his organization of forms into geometrical shapes. He also learned from so-called "primitive", and especially African, sculpture, and out of these studies came a painting that heralded a definite new direction, not only for Picasso's own style but for the whole of modern art – *Les Demoiselles d'Avignon*. Executed in 1907, this painting combined Cézanne's analysis of forms with the visual impact of African masks.

It was from this semi-abstract picture that Picasso went on to develop the theory of **Cubism**, inspiring artists such as **Georges Braque** (1882–1963) and **Juan Gris** (1887–1927), another Spaniard, and formulating a whole new movement. The Cubists' aim was to depict objects not so much as they saw them but rather as they knew them to be: a bottle and a guitar were shown from the front, from the side and from the back as if the eye could take in all at once every facet and plane of the object. Braque and Picasso first analysed forms into these facets (analytical Cubism), then gradually reduced them to series of colours and shapes (synthetic Cubism), among which a few recognizable symbols such as letters, fragments of newspaper and numbers appeared. The complexity of different planes overlapping one another made the deciphering of Cubist paintings sometimes difficult, and the very last phase of Cubism tended increasingly towards abstraction.

Spin-offs of Cubism were many: such movements as **Orphism**, headed by **Robert Delaunay** (1885–1941) and **Francis Picabia** (1879–1953), who experimented not with objects but with the colours of the spectrum. **Fernand Léger** (1881–1955), one of the main exponents of the so-called School of Paris, exploited his fascination with Cubism's smoothness and the power of the colour spectrum to create geometric and monumental compositions of technical imagery that were indebted to both Cézanne and Cubism.

The war, meanwhile, had affected many artists: in Switzerland, **Dada** was born out of the scorn artists felt for the petty bourgeois and nationalistic values that had led to the bloodshed. It was best exemplified in the work of the Frenchman **Marcel Duchamp** (1887–1968), who selected everyday objects ("ready-mades") and elevated them, without modification, to the rank of works of art simply by putting them on display – his most notorious piece was a urinal which he called *Fontaine* and exhibited in New York in 1917. His conviction that art could be made out of anything would be hugely influential.

Dada was a literary as well as an artistic movement, and through one of its main poets, André Breton, it led to the inception of **Surrealism**. It was the unconscious and its dark unchartered territories that interested the Surrealists: they derived much of their imagery from Freud and even experimented in words and images with free-association techniques. Strangely enough, most of the "French" Surrealists were foreigners, primarily the German **Max Ernst** (1891–1976) and the Spaniard **Salvador Dalí** (1904–89), though Frenchman **Yves Tanguy** (1900–55) also achieved international recognition. Mournful landscapes of weird, often terrifying images evoked the landscape of nightmares in often very precise details and with an anguish that went on to influence artists for years to come. **Picasso**, for instance, shocked by the massacre at the Spanish town of Guernica in 1936, drew greatly from Surrealism to produce the disquieting figures of his painting of the same name.

## Towards Nouveau Réalisme

At the outbreak of **World War II** many artists emigrated to the US, where the economic climate was more favourable. France was no longer the artistic melting pot of Europe, though Paris itself remained full of vibrant new work. Sculptors like the Romanian **Brancusi** (1876–1957) and the Swiss **Giacometti** (1886–1966) lived most of their lives in the city. Reacting against the rigours of Cubism, many French artists of the 1940s and 1950s opened themselves instead to the language and methods of American Abstract Expressionism that was emanating from a vibrant New York. French painters such as **Pierre Soulages** (b.1919) and **Jean Dubuffet** (1901–85) pursued **Tachisme**, also known as **l'Art informel**. Dubuffet was heavily influenced by **Art Brut** – that is, works created by children, prisoners or the mentally ill. He produced thickly textured, often childlike paintings, pioneering the depreciation of traditional artistic materials and methods, fashioning junk, tar, sand and glass into the shape of human beings. His work (which provoked much outrage) influenced the French-born American, **Arman** (1928–2005), and **César** (1921–98), both of whom made use of scrap metals – their output ranging from presentations of household debris to towers of crushed and compressed cars.

These artists, among others, began to constitute what would be seen as the last coherent French art movement of the century: **Nouveau Réalisme**. A phenomenon largely of the late 1950s and 1960s, this movement rejected traditional materials and artistic genres, and concentrated instead on the distortion of the objects and signs of contemporary culture. It is often compared to Pop Art. Nouveau Réaliste sculpture is best represented by the works of the Swiss **Jean Tinguely** (1925–91), whose work was concerned mainly with movement and the machine, satirizing technological civilization. His most famous work, executed in collaboration with **Niki de Saint Phalle** (1926–2002), is the exuberant fountain outside the Pompidou Centre, featuring fantastical birds and beasts shooting water in all directions.

A founder member of Nouveau Réalisme, though resisting all classification, was **Yves Klein** (1928–1962) who laid the foundations for several currents in contemporary art. He is seen as a precursor of minimalism thanks to his exhibition "Le Vide" in 1958, in which he redefined the void and the immaterial as having a pure energy. He was fascinated by the colour blue, which he considered to possess a spiritual quality. He even patented his own colour, International Klein Blue, employing it in a series of "body prints" in which he covered female models with paint, thus prefiguring performance art.

## Conceptual and contemporary

The chief legacy of Surrealism in 1960s France was the way in which avant-garde artists regularly banded together – and often quickly disbanded – around ideological or conceptual manifestos. These groups were not art schools as such, more conscious experiments in defining and limiting what art could be, in the search for political or theoretical meaning – in search, some would say, of coherence. One of the first such self-constituted groups of the 1960s, **GRAV** (Groupe de recherche d'art visuel) played with abstraction in the form of mirrors, visual tricks and **kinetic art** – which had a strong heritage in France from Duchamp and Alexander Calder. Among the leading figures were **François Morellet** (1926–2016), who focused on geometric works, and the Argentine-born **Julio Le Parc** (b.1928). GRAV's goal, as its 1963 *Manifesto* declared, was to demystify art by tricking the spectator into relaxing in front of the artwork.

Perhaps the most significant group launched itself in January 1967, when Daniel Buren, Olivier Mosset, Michel Parmentier and Niele Toroni removed their own works from the walls of the Salon de la Jeune Peinture, in protest against the reactionary nature of painting itself – and, paradoxically, to reaffirm the relevance of painting as an art form existing in itself, without interpretation. It was an early taste of the politics of 1968. The works of **BMPT** – the name was taken from the four men's surnames – focused on abstract colour, often in regular patterns. The best-known of the four, **Daniel Buren** (b.1938), caused a furore in 1985–86 with his installation in the courtyard of the Palais Royal that consisted of numerous black-and-white, vertically striped columns of differing heights. Now, however, this one-time *enfant terrible* has become one of France's most respected living artists.

Following BMPT's lead, the geometrically abstract **Supports-Surfaces** group emerged in Nice in 1969, founded by **Daniel Dezeuze** (b.1942), **Jean-Pierre Pincemin** (1944–2005) and **Claude Viallat** (b.1936), among others. The group stressed the importance of the painting as object – as paint applied to a surface.

The 1977 opening of the Musée National d'Art Moderne, in Paris's Pompidou Centre, was a sign of the increased state support that French contemporary art was beginning to attract – a support that would be hugely boosted in the early 1980s by the active buying policy of the Socialist government. The landmark Pompidou exhibition of 1979, *Tendances de l'art en France*, showed artists in three groupings. The first was broadly abstract, the second, figurative. It was the third, however, which would look most prophetic of future directions; it focused on **conceptual artists**, many of them working with unconventional materials. This third group included the BMPT iconoclasts, along with three artists who would become landmark figures in French contemporary art: **Christian Boltanski** (b.1944) and **Annette Messager** (b.1943) – who were then husband and wife – and **Bertrand Lavier** (b.1949). All three work with found objects: Boltanski's often harrowing work has even employed personal property lost in public places, while Messager has drawn on toys and needlework to create unsettling works, often challenging perceptions of women. Lavier, meanwhile, is best known for playing with art and reality – principally by applying paint to industrial objects.

A quintessentially French reaction to minimalist and conceptual art emerged in 1981 with **Figuration Libre**, a movement which absorbed comic-strip art and graffitti in an explosion of punk creativity. Among the key figures were **Jean-Charles Blais** (b.1956), **Robert Combas** (b.1957), **François Boisrond** (b.1959) and **Hervé di Rosa** (b.1959). Despite such breakout movements, the juggernaut of conceptual art has continued to roll on through the last two decades. Large-scale installation has become important, particularly in the works of **Jean-Marc Bustamante** (b.1952) and **Jean-Luc Vilmouth** (1952–2015), who have been known to co-opt buildings, resulting in a blurring of the aesthetic and the functional. Artists crossing and re-crossing generic boundaries is another ongoing theme. Bustamante, for example, whose principal medium is photography, collaborated for four years with the sculptor Bernard Bazile (b.1952) under the name **Bazile Bustamante**.

A new generation of artists is using non-traditional media, including video, photography, electronic media and found objects. Recent work could hardly be more diverse, but a common thread seems to be the use of films and installations which explore the relationships between reality and fiction, between interiority and the exterior world – ideas which resonate in the films, puppet shows and "public interventions" of **Pierre Huyghe** (b.1962). Huyghe is often associated with – and has worked with – the Algerian-born **Philippe Parreno** (b.1964), who in 2006 co-directed (with Douglas Gordon) a feature film which followed the footballer Zinédine Zidane for ninety minutes of relentless close-up. Two other associated artists are **Dominique Gonzalez-Foerster** (b.1965), who works with films, photographs, installations and even métro stations and shop windows to create worlds where fantasy and reality seem to overlap, and **Claude Closky** (b.1963), whose "books" and videos restructure everyday flotsam and jetsam. Closky has declared, "My work bears on all that daily life has made banal, on things that are never called into question." Similarly eclectic in his choice of media is **Fabrice Hybert** (b.1961), who has created the world's largest-ever bar of soap (at 22 tons) and a working television studio. His playful, interactive work taps into what he describes as the "enormous reservoir of the possible". **Sophie Calle** (b.1953) blends texts and photographs; among her most publicized works have been her intimate documentations of the lives of both strangers and – after she asked her mother to hire a private detective for the purpose – Calle herself.

In such a multimedia milieu, some critics have claimed that painting is moribund in France. Bucking this trend is the celebrated Lyonnais painter **Marc Desgrandchamps** (b.1960). He may work with traditional oils, but Desgrandchamps is hardly a traditionalist. His figures often appear partially transparent, or are presented as fragments, thus overlaying the perception of reality with doubt and disquiet.

# Architecture

France's architectural legacy reflects the power and personality of church and the state, the "great men" vying to outdo their peers with lavish statements in stone. Many of France's architectural trends were born in Italy – Romanesque, Renaissance and Baroque – but they were refined and developed in uniquely French ways. Rococo grew from Baroque, Neoclassicism came from the Renaissance, and Art Nouveau was a brilliant, confused jumble of Baroque features combined with the newly developed cast-iron industry. France's last great architectural flowerings can be seen in the work of the early twentieth-century modernists, Auguste Perret and Le Corbusier, but the contemporary scene is potentially as exciting, with Jean Nouvel and Christian de Portzamparc as its pre-eminent stars.

## The Romans

The **Romans**, who had colonized the south of France by around 120 BC, were fine town planners, linking complexes of buildings with straight roads punctuated by decorative fountains, arches and colonnades. They built essentially in the Greek style, and their large, functional buildings were concerned more with strength and solidity than aesthetics. A number of substantial Roman building works survive: in **Nîmes** you can see the Maison Carrée, the best-preserved Roman temple still standing, and the Temple of Diana, one of just four vaulted Roman temples in Europe. Gateways remain at **Autun**, **Orange**, **Saintes** and **Reims**, and largely intact amphitheatres can be seen at Nîmes and **Arles**. The **Pont du Gard** aqueduct outside Nîmes is still a magnificent and ageless monument of civil engineering, built to carry the town's fresh water over the gorge, and Orange has its massive theatre, with Europe's only intact Roman facade. There are excavated archeological sites at **Glanum** near **St-Rémy**, **Vienne**, **Vaison-la-Romaine** and **Lyon**.

## Romanesque

Charlemagne's ninth-century **Carolingian dynasty** attempted to revive the symbols of civilized authority by recourse to Roman models. Of this era, very few buildings remain, though the motifs of arch and vault and the plan of semicircular apse and basilican nave and aisles would be hugely influential.

The style later dubbed "**Romanesque**" (*Roman* in French, as opposed to *Romain* which, confusingly, means Roman/classical) only really developed from the eleventh century onwards. Classical Roman architecture was not so much a direct model as a distant inspiration, filtered partly through the Carolingian heritage and partly through Byzantine models – as imported by returning crusaders and arriving artisans from Italy. The new style was also shaped by the particular needs of monastic communities, which began to burgeon in the period, and the requirements of pilgrims, who began to tour shrines in ever-greater numbers.

The key characteristics of Romanesque are thick walls with small windows, round arches on Roman-style piers and columns, and a proliferation of stone sculpture and wall paintings – these last often being the first victims of wear-and-tear and iconoclasm. Romanesque is as diverse as the various regions of France. In the south, the classical inheritance of Provence is strong, with stone barrel vaults, aisleless naves and domes. **St-Trophime** at Arles (1150) has a porch directly derived from Roman models and, with the church at St-Gilles nearby, exhibits a delight in carved ornament peculiar to the south at this time. The presence of the wealthy and powerful Cluniac order, in Burgundy, made this region a veritable powerhouse of architectural experiment, while the south was the readiest route for the introduction of new cultural developments. The pointed arch and vault are probably owed to Spanish Muslim sources, and appear first in churches such as **Notre-Dame** at Avignon, Notre-Dame-la-Grande at Poitiers, the cathedral at **Autun** and **Ste-Madeleine** at Vézelay (1089–1206).

In Normandy, the nave with aisles is more usual, capped by twin western towers. The emphasis in general is on mass and size, and geometrical design is favoured over figurative sculpture. The **Abbaye aux Hommes** at Caen (1066–77) is typical – and also contains many of the elements later identified as "Gothic", notably ribbed vaults and spires.

## Gothic

The reasons behind the development of the **Gothic style** (twelfth to sixteenth centuries) lie in the pursuit of the sublime; to achieve great height without apparent great weight would seem to imitate religious ambition. Its development in the north is partly due to the availability of good building stone and soft stone for carving, but perhaps more to the growth of royal aspiration and power based in the Île de France, which, allied with the papacy, stimulated the building of the great **cathedrals** of Paris, Bourges, Chartres, Laon, Le Mans, Reims and Amiens in the twelfth and thirteenth centuries.

The Gothic phase is said to have begun with the building of the choir of the **abbey of St-Denis** near Paris in 1140. In France, the style reigned supreme until the end of the fifteenth century. Architecturally, it encompasses the development of spacious windows of coloured glass and the flying buttress, a rib of external stone that resists the outward push of the vaulting. But, above all, French Gothic is characterized by verticality.

In the south, as at Albi and Angers, the great churches are generally broader and simpler in plan and external appearance, with aisles often almost as high as the nave. Many secular buildings survive – some of the most notable in their present form being the work of Viollet-le-Duc, the pre-eminent nineteenth-century restorer – and even whole towns, for example **Carcassonne** and **Aigues Mortes**; **Avignon** has the bridge and the papal palace.

Even castles began to lend themselves to the disappearing walls of the Gothic style, as windows steadily increased in size in response to more settled times. Fine Gothic stone carving was applied to doors and windows, and roofscapes came alive with balustrades, sculpted gables and exquisite leadwork finials and ridges. Some of the most elaborate châteaux, as at **Châteaudun** and **Saumur**, in the Loire valley, were veritable palaces. Yet they still incorporated the old defensive feudal tower in their design, perhaps in the form of an elaborately sculpted open staircase. In the Dordogne region, a series of colonial settlements, the **bastides**, or fortified towns, are a refreshing antidote to triumphal French bombast.

## Renaissance

French military adventures in Italy in the early sixteenth century hastened the arrival of a new style borrowing heavily from the Italian **Renaissance**. The persistence of Gothic traditions, however, and the necessity of steep roofs and tall chimneys in the more northerly climate, gave the newly luxurious castles, or châteaux, a distinctively French emphasis on the vertical line, with an elaboration of detail on the facade at the expense of the clear modelling of form.

Gradually, these French forms were supplanted by a purely classical style – a development embodied by the **Louvre** palace, which was worked over by all the grand names of French architecture from Lescot in the early sixteenth century, via François Mansart and Claude Perrault in the seventeenth, to the later years of the nineteenth century.

At Blois and **Maisons-Lafitte** (1640), Mansart began to experiment with a new suavity and elegance, attitudes that appear again in the eighteenth century in the townhouses of the Rococo period. On the other hand, **Claude Perrault** (1613–88), who designed the great colonnaded east front of the Louvre, gives an austere face to the official architecture of despotism, magnificent but far too imperial to be much enjoyed by common mortals. The high-pitched roofs, which had been almost universal until then, are replaced here by the classical balustrade and pediment, the style grand but cold and supremely secular. Art and architecture were at the time organized by boards and academies, including the Académie Royale d'Architecture, and style and employment were strictly controlled by royal direction. With such a limitation of ideas at the source of patronage, it's hardly surprising that there was a certain dullness to the era.

## Baroque

In a similar way to the preceding century, the churches of the **seventeenth and eighteenth centuries** have a coldness quite different from the German, Flemish and Italian **Baroque**. When the Renaissance style first appeared in the early sixteenth century, there was no great need for new church building, the country being so well endowed from the Gothic centuries. **St-Étienne-du-Mont** (1517–1620) and **St-Eustache** (1532–89), both in Paris, show how old forms persisted with only an overlay of the new style.

It was with the Jesuits in the seventeenth century that the Church embraced the new style in order to combat the forces of rational disbelief. In Paris the churches of the **Sorbonne** (1653) and **Val-de-Grâce** (1645) exemplify this, as do a good number of other grandiose churches in the **Baroque** style, from **Les Invalides** at the end of the seventeenth century to the **Panthéon** of the late eighteenth century. Here is the Church triumphant, rather than the state, but no more beguiling.

The architect of Les Invalides was **Jules-Hardouin Mansart**, a product of the Académie Royale d'Architecture, which harked back to the ancient, classical tradition. Mansart also greatly extended the palace of **Versailles** and so created the CinemaScope view of France with that seemingly endless horizon of royalty. As an antidote to this pomposity, the **Petit Trianon** at Versailles is as refreshing now as it was to Louis XV, who had it built in 1762 as a place of escape for his mistress. This is even more true of that other pearl formed of the grit of boredom in the enclosed world of Versailles – **La Petite Ferme**, where Marie Antoinette played at being a milkmaid, which epitomizes the Arcadian and "picturesque" fantasy of the painters Boucher and Fragonard.

The lightness and charm that was undermining official grandeur with Arcadian fancies and **Rococo** decoration was, however, snuffed out by the Revolution. There's no real Revolutionary architecture: the necessity of order and authority soon asserted itself and an autocracy every bit as absolute returned with Napoleon, drawing on the old grand manner but with a stronger trace of the stern old Roman.

In Paris it was not the democratic Doric but the imperial Corinthian order that re-emerged triumphant in the church of the **Madeleine** (1806) and, with the **Arc de Triomphe** like some colossal paperweight, reimposed the authority of academic architecture in contrast to the fancy-dress structures of contemporary Regency England.

## The nineteenth century

The restoration of legitimate monarchy after the **fall of Napoleon** stimulated a revival of interest in older Gothic and early Renaissance styles, which offered a symbol of dynastic reassurance not only to the state but also to the newly rich. So in the private and commercial architecture of the nineteenth century these earlier styles predominate – in mine-owners' villas and bankers' headquarters.

From 1853, the overgrown and insanitary medieval capital was ruthlessly transformed into an urban utopia. In half a century, half of Paris was rebuilt. Napoléon III's authoritarian government provided the force – land was compulsorily purchased and boulevards bulldozed through old quarters – while banks and private speculators provided the cash. The poor, meanwhile, provided the labour – and were shipped out to the suburban badlands in their tens of thousands to make way for richer tenants. The presiding genius was Napoléon III's architect-in-chief, **Baron Haussmann** (1809–91). In his brave new city, every apartment building was seven storeys high. Every facade was built in golden limestone, often quarried from under the city itself, with unobtrusive Neoclassical details sculpted around the windows. Every second and fifth floor had its wrought-iron balcony and every lead roof sloped back from the street front at precisely 45 degrees.

Competing with Haussmann's totalitarian sobriety was a voluptuous, exuberant **neo-Baroque** strain, exemplified by Charles Garnier's Opéra in Paris (1861–74), and a third, engineering-led approach, embodied in the official **School of Roads and Bridges**. The teachings of Viollet-le-Duc, the great restorer who reinterpreted Gothic style as pure structure, led to the development of new techniques out of which "modern" architectural style was born. Iron was the first significant new material, often used in imitation of Gothic forms and destined to be developed as an individual architectural style in America. In the enormously controversial **Eiffel Tower** (1889), France set up a potent symbol of things to come.

## Le Corbusier to Art Deco

The sinuous, organic **Art Nouveau** style, which was at the height of fashion around the turn of the nineteenth and twentieth centuries, quickly found its winding way onto the facades of many Parisian buildings, including the department stores Printemps and La Samaritaine. The most famous expression of the style, however, is the entrances to the Paris métro, whose twisting metal railings and antennae-like orange lamps were deeply controversial when **Hector Guimard** first designed them in the 1900s. Few of the early entrances now remain, however (**Place des Abbesses** is one), partly because conservatives fought back under **Charles Garnier**, architect of the Opéra Garnier. He demanded classical marble and bronze porticoes for every station; his line was followed, on a less grandiose scale, wherever the métro steps surfaced by a major monument, thereby putting Guimard out of a job.

Even as Art Nouveau sought lithe and living forms, brutal **Modernism** powered ahead. Towards the end of the nineteenth century, France pioneered the use of reinforced concrete, most notably in buildings by **Auguste Perret**, such as his 1903 apartment house at 25 rue Franklin in Paris. Perret and other **modernists** designed gigantic skyscraper avenues and suburban rings, which now look like totalitarian horror-movie sets.

The more acceptable face of modernism, in the 1920s and 30s, was the simple geometry of the modern or International Style, which was allied to the glamorous **Art Deco look**; you're most likely to come across it in the capital, either on apartment block facades or in mega-projects such as the Palais de Tokyo.

The greatest proponent of this style was **Le Corbusier.** His stature may now appear diminished by the ascendancy of a blander style in concrete boxing, as well as by the significant technical and social failures of his buildings – not to mention his total disregard for historic streets and monuments – but he remains France's most influential modern architect. Surprisingly few of his works were ever built, but the **Cité Radieuse** in Marseille and plenty of lesser examples in Paris bear witness to the ideas of the man largely responsible for changing the face and form of buildings throughout the world.

# Contemporary

The miserable 1950s and 1960s buildings found all over the country are probably best skipped over. From the 1970s onwards, however, France again established itself as one of the most exciting patrons of international **contemporary architecture**. The **Pompidou Centre**, by **Renzo Piano** and **Richard Rogers**, derided, adored and visited by millions, maximizes space by putting the service elements usually concealed in walls and floors on the outside. It is one of the great contemporary buildings in western Europe – for its originality, popularity and practicality.

In the 1980s, under President Mitterrand's grandiose *grands projets*, it was decided that the axis from the Louvre to the Arc de Triomphe was to be extended westwards towards the **Grande Arche de la Défense**, symbol of the new La Défense business district. Designed by Von Spreckelsen, it isn't really an arch but a huge hollow cube. At the other end of the axis stands Ieoh Ming Pei's glass **pyramid** in the Cour Napoléon, the main entrance to the Louvre. Hugely controversial at first, it's now widely accepted and admired.

As part of the wider reorganization of the Louvre, the **Ministry of Finance** decamped to a new building in **Bercy** designed by Paul Chemetov and nicknamed the "steamboat" because of its titanic length and its anchoring in the Seine. Formerly full of wine warehouses, Bercy is now extensively redeveloped. Also in the Parc de Bercy stands Frank Gehry's (architect of Bilbao's Guggenheim Museum) free-form, exuberant **American Centre**. Another mega-project from broadly the same era is the **Parc de la Villette** complex, which was built on the site of an old abattoir. It houses the Cité des Sciences, Bernard Tschumi's 21 "*folies*" of urban life and the **Cité de la Musique** concert hall (also now known as Philharmonie 2) and conservatoire complex, designed by acclaimed architect Christian de Portzamparc to be like a symphony, its various sections creating a harmonious ensemble.

Perhaps the least successful of Mitterrand's grand projects was the **Bibliothèque Nationale**. Designed by Dominique Perrault, it's made up of four L-shaped tower blocks, resembling four open books, set around an inaccessible sunken garden. The most outstanding, by contrast, is arguably the **Institut du Monde Arabe**. Designed by **Jean Nouvel**, France's most eminent contemporary architect, it ingeniously marries high-tech architecture and motifs from traditional Arabic culture. Jean Nouvel's airy, green-themed buildings continue to multiply in Paris, from the Fondation Cartier, with its glass wall, to the curving, light-filled **Quai Branly** museum, which is surrounded by a lush garden designed by Gilles Clément, who landscaped the Parc André-Citroën.

Paris continues to find space for new architecture. The futuristically twisting double-ribbon of the **Passerelle Simone de Beauvoir** now bridges the Seine opposite Perrault's Bibliothèque. Upstream, the University Paris 7 is now installed in the massive **Grands Moulins de Paris** and **Halle aux Farines**, and a new school of architecture – appropriately enough – resides in the handsomely arched, late nineteenth-century **SUDAC** building. Christian de Portzamparc's blade-like **Tour Granite** is now one of the most distinctive silhouettes in the La Défense skyline, a vigorous foil to the incised cylinders of the twin Société Générale towers. Jakob Macfarlane's **Cité de la Mode et du Design** has a lime-green glass tube apparently pouring through it, while Frank Gehry's **Fondation Louis Vuitton** in the Bois de Boulogne looks less like the advertised "cloud of glass" than a glazed armadillo which has burst out of its own skin.

In **Marseille** there's Will Alsop's mammoth seat of regional government, while the first cathedral to be built in France since the nineteenth century, the **Cathédrale d'Évry**, masterminded by Swiss Mario Botta and finished in 1995, is a huge cylindrical red-brick tower which, besides being a place of worship, houses an art centre, concert hall and cinema screen. The new **European Parliament** building in **Strasbourg**, designed by the Architecture Studio group, was finished in 1997. A huge, boomerang-shaped structure with a glass dome and metal tower, it sits across the river from the eccentric, high-tech Richard Rogers-designed **European Court of Human Rights**.

Museums across the country continue to attract innovative architects. In **Nîmes,** Norman Foster's **Carré d'Art** modern art museum (1993) is characterized by its simple transparent design, while his **Musée de Préhistoire des Gorges du Verdon** (2001) in **Provence** uses local materials – part of the museum is folded into the landscape and blends on one side into an existing stone wall, while the entrance hall resembles the very caves the museum celebrates. Meanwhile, in Lyon, deconstructivist Wolf D. Prix's mesmerising glass-and-steel **Musée des Confluences** looks like something out of *Star Trek*, its setting at the confluence of the Rhône and Saône adding further drama.

The country's ever-advancing **transport network** has fuelled some of the most state-of-the-art design and engineering in Europe, as in **Roissy**, around the Charles-de-Gaulle airport, and at **Euralille**, the large complex around Lille's TGV/Eurostar station, masterminded by Dutch architect Rem Koolhaas. Most dramatic of all is the **Millau Viaduct**, a bridge so huge in scale and ambition that its impact could almost be described as geographical. Designed by engineer Michel Virlogeux and Norman Foster's firm, and opened in December 2004, its sleekness belies its size: the largest of its soaring white pylons is actually taller than the Eiffel Tower.

Even as they push towards a high-tech future, the French are particularly good at preserving the past – too good, some would say. A passion for restoring *"le patrimoine"* results in many fine old buildings being practically rebuilt – the dominant restoration theory in France is to restore to perfection rather than halt decay. More often than not, restoration is carried out by the **Maisons du Compagnonnage**, the old craft guilds, which have maintained traditional building skills, handing them down from master to apprentice (and only recently opened to women), while also taking on new industrial skills.

## Futures

In 2009 the government invited ten leading architectural firms to submit proposals for **Le Grand Pari** – the Greater, Greener Paris of the future. The architects envisioned new *"Grands Axes"*, avenues as radical as any bulldozed by Haussmann – but in this case linking city and *banlieue*. President Sarkozy favoured high-speed rail links down the Seine towards the port of Le Havre; Richard Rogers called for a green network covering the train lines leading out of the northern stations; Christian de Portzamparc wanted a high-speed elevated train running circles around the ring road. The radical left-wing architect Roland Castro mildly proposed that perhaps the suburbs might have their share of government offices and cultural institutions.

Meanwhile, real works progress apace in **Paris**, and beyond. From 2010 to 2016, the capital's old, murky underground mall of **Les Halles** was transformed by architect David Mangin into the light-filled spaces you can enjoy today, under a giant undulated roof (*canopée*). Also in 2010, the Louvre began work on its annex of glossy pavilions, sited in the northern town of Lens (it is a modest partner to the equally new Abu Dhabi annex, designed by – who else – Jean Nouvel), while the Pompidou Centre has opened its own curvaceously geometric satellite in **Metz**, designed by Shigeru Ban and Jean de Gastines to echo the shape of a Chinese hat. Back in Paris, the most intense developments are taking place in the Défense business district.. Here, the planned **Tour Phare** eco-scraper has been cancelled and is instead set to be replaced by the **Two Sisters**, two towers 200 and 100-metres high respectively, and linked by a skybridge part way up. Paris city council's decision to drop the legal ban on skyscrapers is likely to mean even grander projects in the near future, which may result in the capital losing its radical uniformity.

# Cinema

The first (satisfied) cinema audience in the world was French. Screened to patrons of the Grand Café, on Paris's boulevard des Capucines, in December 1895, Louis Lumière's single-reelers may have been jerky documentaries, but they were light years ahead of anything that had come before. Soon after, Georges Méliès' magical-fantastical features were proving a big hit with theatre audiences, and the twin cinematic poles of Realism and Surrealism had been established. France took to cinema with characteristic enthusiasm and seriousness. Ciné-clubs were formed all over the country, journals were published, critics made films and film-makers became critics. The avant-garde wing of French cinema acquired the moniker of French Impressionism, a genre characterized by directors such as Louis Delluc, Jean Epstein and Abel Gance, who used experimental, highly visual techniques to express altered states of consciousness. It was only a short step from here to the all-out Surrealism of the artist-polymath Jean Cocteau, and the Spanish director Luis Buñuel.

Towards the end of the 1920s, histrionic adaptations of novels, epic historical dramas and broad comedies attracted mass audiences, but the silent heyday ended abruptly with the advent of sound in 1929. Most silent stars faded into obscurity, but a number of directors successfully made the transition, notably Jean Renoir, the son of the painter, René Clair, Julien Duvivier, Jean Grémillon and Abel Gance. Among the newcomers were Jean Vigo, who died young in 1934, and Marcel Carné, who worked with the powerful scripts of the poet Jacques Prévert. The film-makers of the 1930s developed a bold new style, dubbed **Poetic Realism** for its pessimism, powerful visual aesthetic – high-contrast, often nocturnal – and devotion to "realistic", usually working-class, settings.

In 1936 the collector Henri Langlois set up the **Cinémathèque Française**, dedicated to the preservation and screening of old and art films – an indication of the speed with which the "*septième art*" had found its niche within the pantheon of French culture. Langlois played an important role in saving thousands of films from destruction during the war, but the occupation had surprisingly little effect on the industry. Renoir and Clair sought temporary sanctuary in Hollywood, and domestic production dipped, but hundreds of films continued to be made in Vichy France at a time when audiences sought the solace and comfort of the cinema in record numbers.

Postwar and pre-television, the late 1940s and early 1950s was another boom time for French cinema. Poetic Realism morphed into **film noir**, whose emphasis on darkness and corruption gave birth in turn to the thriller, a genre exemplified by the films of Henri-Georges Clouzot and Jean-Pierre Melville. During this period the mainstream cinema industry became highly organized and technically slick, and older directors such as Clair, Renoir and Jacques Becker made superbly controlled masterpieces spanning genres as diverse as thrillers, comedies and costume dramas.

The first shot of the coming revolution – a warning shot only – was fired by the acerbic young critic François Truffaut, writing in the legendary film magazine, **Les Cahiers du Cinéma**, in the mid-1950s. In opposition to what he and fellow critics dubbed *la tradition de qualité*, Truffaut envisaged a new kind of cinema based on the independent vision of a writer-director, an *auteur* (author), who would make films in a purer and more responsive manner. Directors such as Melville and Louis Malle – who made his first film with the diver Jacques Cousteau – were beginning to make moves in this direction, but Truffaut's vision was only fully realized towards the end of the decade, when the **Nouvelle Vague** ("New Wave") came rolling in. Claude Chabrol's *Les cousins*, Truffaut's own *Les quatre-cents coups*, Eric Rohmer's *Le Signe du lion*, Alain Resnais' *Hiroshima, mon amour* and Jean-Luc Godard's *À bout de souffle* were all released in 1959. The trademark freedom of these *auteur*-directors' films – loosely scripted, highly individualistic and typically shot on location – ushered in the modern era.

The 1960s was the heyday of the *auteur*. Truffaut established his pre-eminent status by creating an extraordinary oeuvre encompassing science fiction, thriller, autobiography and film noir, all his films characteristically elegant and excitingly shot. But the "new wave" hadn't carried all before it: René Clément, Henri-Georges Clouzot and even Jean Renoir were still working throughout the decade; Jean-Pierre Melville continued shooting his characteristically noir **films policiers** (crime-thrillers); and the Catholic director Robert Bresson carried on making films on his favourite theme of salvation. And Jacques Tati, the maverick genius behind the legendary comic character Mr. Hulot, made two of his greatest and most radical quasi-silent films, *Playtime* and *Trafic*, at either end of the 1960s.

The 1970s is probably the least impressive decade in terms of output, but a shot in the arm was delivered in the 1980s by the **Cinéma du Look**, a genre epitomized in the films of Jean-Jacques Beineix, Luc Besson and Léos Carax. Stylish, image-conscious and postmodern, films such as *Diva* and *Betty Blue* owed much to the look of American pulp cinema and contemporary advertising. Meanwhile, throughout the 1980s and into the 1990s, high-gloss costume dramas – historical or adaptations of novels – were the focus of much attention. Often called **Heritage Cinema**, the best films of this genre are the superbly crafted creations of Claude Berri, though Jean-Pierre Rappeneau's *Cyrano de Bergerac* is probably the internationally recognized standard-bearer. At the other end of the scale lies **cinéma beur**: naturalistic, socially responsible and low-budget films made by French-born film-makers of North African origin – *les beurs* in French slang. The newest trends in contemporary art cinema follow a related path of social realism. In recent years, a number of younger directors, notably Mathieu Kassovitz, have made films set in the deprived suburbs (*la banlieue*), creating a number of sub-genres that have been acclaimed variously as **New Realism**, **cinéma de banlieue** and **le jeune cinéma** ("young cinema").

Today, France remains the second-largest exporter of films in the world. The industry's continued health is largely due to the intransigence of the French state, which continues to protect and promote domestic cinema as part of its policy of **l'exception culturelle** – despite the complaints of the free-marketeers who would have the French market "liberalized". Half of the costs of making a feature film in France are paid for by state subsidies, levied on television stations, box-office receipts and video sales. Currently, American-made films capture around fifty percent of the French market, while home-grown productions make up around forty percent. But the future looks promising: recent years have seen the number of films made in France rise to almost two hundred a year, most of them domestically funded. A case in point is the 2011 world-wide hit *The Artist*, which won five Academy Awards, notably for Best Picture.

Note that the **films reviewed below** are only intended to point out a few landmarks of French cinema; we can't review every Godard film nor cover every significant director. As such, they can all be considered as highly recommended. Alternative English titles are given for those films renamed for the main foreign release.

## CINEMA PRE-1945

★ **L'Atalante** *Jean Vigo, 1934.* Aboard a barge, a newly married couple struggle to reconcile themselves to their new situation. Eventually, the wife, Juliette, tries to flee, but is brought back by the unconventional deck-hand, Père Jules, superbly portrayed by the great Michel Simon. This sensual and naturalistic portrait of a relationship was made just before Vigo died, and is his only feature film.

**La belle équipe/They Were Five** *Julien Duvivier, 1936.* A group of unemployed workers wins the lottery and sets up a cooperative restaurant. The version with an upbeat conclusion was a huge hit with contemporary audiences; Duvivier himself preferred his darker ending. Jean Gabin stars as the defeated hero, as in Duvivier's other greats, *La Bandéra* (1935) and the cult classic, *Pépé-le-Moko* (1937).

**Un chien andalou/An Andalusian Dog** *Luis Buñuel, 1929.* Made in collaboration with Salvador Dalí, this short opens with a woman's eye being cut into with a razor blade. While it doesn't get any less weird or shocking for the rest of its twenty-minute length, it's surprisingly watchable – when it came out, it was a big hit at Paris's Studio des Ursulines cinema. Buñuel further developed his Surrealist techniques in the feature-length talkie *L'âge d'or* (1930).

★ **Les enfants du paradis** *Marcel Carné, 1945.* Probably the greatest of the collaborations between Carné and the poet-scriptwriter, Jacques Prévert, this film is set in the low-life world of the popular theatre of 1840s Paris. Beautiful and worldly actress Garance (the great Arletty) is loved by arch-criminal Lacenaire, ambitious actor Lemaître, and brilliant, troubled mime Baptiste – unforgettably played by the top mime of the 1940s, Jean-Louis Barrault. The outstanding character portrayals and romantic, humane ethos are reminiscent of a great nineteenth-century novel.

**Le jour se lève/Daybreak** *Marcel Carné, 1939.* This brooding classic from the Poetic Realist stable has Jean Gabin, the greatest star of the era, playing another of his iconic working-class hero roles. After shooting his rival, the villainous old music-hall star Valentin, François (Gabin) is holed up in his guesthouse bedroom. In the course of the night, he recalls the events that led up to the murder. Also stars the great female idol of the 1930s, Arletty, and a superb script by the poet Jacques Prévert. Carné's *Hôtel du Nord* (1938) and *Quai des brumes* (1938) are in a similar vein.

**Le million** *René Clair, 1931.* In 1930 Clair had made the first great French talkie, *Sous les toits de Paris*, but it wasn't until *Le million* that the true musical film was born. A hunt for a lost winning lottery ticket provides plenty of opportunity for madcap comedy, suspense and romance.

★ **La règle du jeu/The Rules of the Game** *Jean Renoir, 1939.* Now hailed as the foremost masterpiece of the pre-war era, this was a complete commercial failure when it was released. The Marquis de la Chesnaye invites his wife, mistress and a pilot friend to spend a weekend hunting and partying in the countryside. Matching the four are a group of four servants with similarly interweaved love lives. Renoir himself plays Octave, who moves between the two groups. A complex, almost farcical plot based around misunderstanding and accusations of infidelity moves inexorably towards disaster.

## POSTWAR CINEMA

**Ascenseur pour l'échafaud/Elevator to the Gallows/Frantic** *Louis Malle, 1957.* This thriller is Louis Malle's remarkable debut. Two lovers (Jeanne Moreau and Maurice Ronet) murder the woman's husband but get trapped by a series of unlucky coincidences. Beautifully shot – especially when Jeanne Moreau wanders through the streets of Paris, accompanied by Miles Davis' superb original score – and as breathtaking as any Hitchcock film.

**La belle et la bête/Beauty and the Beast** *Jean Cocteau, 1946.* Cocteau's theatrical rendition of the "Beauty and the Beast" tale teeters on the edge of the surreal, but the pace is as compelling as any thriller. *Orphée* (1950) is more widely considered to be the director's masterpiece, a surreal retelling of the Orpheus tale in a setting strongly redolent of wartime France.

**Casque d'or/Golden Marie** *Jacques Becker, 1952.* Becker's first great film depicts the ultimately tragic romance between a gangster and a beautiful, golden-haired prostitute, portrayed with legendary seductiveness by Simone Signoret. Underneath the love story lurks the moral corruption of a brilliantly re-created turn-of-the-century Paris. Becker went on to make the seminal crime thriller, *Touchez pas au grisbi/Honour Among Thieves* (1953).

★ **Un condamné à mort s'est échappé/A Man Escaped** *Robert Bresson, 1956.* A prisoner, Fontaine (François Leterrier), calmly plans his escape from prison, working with a painstaking slowness that is brilliantly matched by the intensely absorbed camerawork. Working with real locations and amateur actors, Bresson echoed the work of the Italian Neo-realists, and foreshadowed the work of the Nouvelle Vague directors. Sometimes entitled *Le vent souffle où il veut*.

**Et ... Dieu créa la femme/And God Created Woman** *Roger Vadim, 1956.* This film should be called "And Roger Vadim created Brigitte Bardot", as its chief interest is not its harmless plot – love and adultery in St-Tropez – but its scantily clad main actress, who spends most of the time sunbathing and dancing in front of fascinated males. Deemed "obscene" by the moralizing authorities of the time, it helped liberate the way the body was represented in film.

**Les jeux interdits** *René Clément, 1952.* A small Parisian girl loses her parents and her dog in a Stuka attack on a column of refugees, and is rescued and befriended by a peasant boy. Together, they seek solace from the war by building an animal cemetery in an abandoned barn. This moving meditation on childhood and death extracted two remarkable performances from the child actors.

**Le salaire de la peur/The Wages of Fear** *Henri-Georges Clouzot, 1953.* This is the tensest, most suspense-driven of all the films made by the "French Hitchcock", focusing on four men driving an explosive-laden lorry hundreds of miles to a burning, third-world oil field. Tight and shatteringly sustained right up to the magnificent finale.

★ **Les vacances de Monsieur Hulot/Mr Hulot's Holiday** *Jacques Tati, 1951.* The slapstick comic mime Jacques Tati created his most memorable character in Hulot, the unwitting creator of chaos and nonchalant hero of this gut-wrenchingly funny film. So full of brilliantly conceived and impeccably timed sight gags that you hardly notice the innovative absence of much dialogue or plot. Groundbreaking cinema, and superlative entertainment. The later *Mon oncle* (1958) has an edgier feel, adopting a distinctly critical attitude to modern life.

## THE NOUVELLE VAGUE

**À bout de souffle/Breathless** *Jean-Luc Godard, 1959.* This is the film that came nearest to defining the Nouvelle Vague: insolent charm, cool music and sexy actors. Jean-Paul Belmondo is a petty criminal, Michel, while Jean Seberg plays Patricia, his American girlfriend. The film's revolutionary style, with its jerky, unconventional narrative, abrupt cuts and rough camerawork, proved one of the most influential of the twentieth century.

**Les cousins/The Cousins** *Claude Chabrol, 1959.* The Balzac-inspired plot centres around Charles (Gérard Blain), an earnest provincial student, who comes to live in Neuilly with his glamorous cousin Paul (Jean-Claude Brialy). A near-caricature of the Nouvelle Vague – idle students in the Quartier Latin, extravagant parties, convertible cars and exciting music.

**Hiroshima, mon amour** *Alain Resnais, 1959.* On her last days of shooting a film in Hiroshima, a French actress (Emmanuelle Riva) falls in love with a Japanese architect (Eiji Okada). Gradually, she reveals the story of her affair with a German soldier during the occupation, and her subsequent disgrace. Based on an original script by Marguerite Duras, Resnais' first film masterfully weaves together past and present in a haunting story of love and memory.

★ **Ma nuit chez Maude/My Night at Maud's** *Eric Rohmer, 1969.* Rohmer's career-long obsessions with sexuality, conversation, existential choices and the love triangle are given free rein in this moody, lingering portrait of a flirtation. Jean-Louis Trintignant plays a handsome egotist who, during the course of one long night, is drawn into a strange and inconclusive relationship with his friend's friend, the hypnotically attractive Maude (Françoise Fabian).

★ **Les quatre-cents coups/The 400 Blows** *François Truffaut, 1959.* A young *cinéphile* and critic turned filmmaker, François Truffaut triumphed at the 1959 Cannes film festival with this semi-autobiographical film, showing a Parisian adolescent (Jean-Pierre Léaud) trying to escape his lonely, loveless existence, and slowly drifting towards juvenile delinquency. Léaud's poignant performance, and Truffaut's sensitive, sympathetic observation, make this one of the most loveable films of the Nouvelle Vague.

## COMEDY AND SATIRE

**Belle de jour** *Luis Buñuel, 1966.* Catherine Deneuve plays Séverine, who lives out her sexual fantasies and obsessions in a brothel. At first sight, this is a far cry from Buñuel's pre-war collaborations with Dalí, though the film moves away from the initial acerbic comedy towards Surrealism.

**Bienvenue chez les Ch'tis** *Danny Boon, 2008.* The highest-grossing French film of all time, written and starring Danny Boon, has been largely ignored by the Anglophone world – largely because its humour is all-but un-translatable. It follows the fate of a postal manager sent from his cushy job in the south of France to one in the rainy north near Dunkirk, where the culture – and particularly impenetrable dialect, or ch-ti, of the locals – fuels many a pun and hilarious misunderstanding. The film had French audiences rolling in the aisles for months, and though the English subtitles inevitably fall short, it's worth persevering with for an insight into Gallic attitudes to regional differences.

★ **La cage aux folles/Birds of a Feather** *Édouard Molinaro, 1978.* Renato runs a cabaret nightclub at which his boyfriend, Albin, is the headlining drag act. When Renato's son, Laurent, decides to get married, the couple are drawn into an escalating farce as they try to present themselves as a conventional mother-and-son couple to Laurent's conservative in-laws. A supremely camp international hit.

**Le fabuleux destin d'Amélie Poulain/Amélie** *Jean-Pierre Jeunet, 2001.* This sentimental, feel-good portrait of a youthful ingenue wandering around a romanticized Montmartre was a worldwide hit. Amélie (Audrey Tautou) is on a mission to help the world find happiness; her own is harder to fix up.

★ **La grande vadrouille/Don't Look Now … We're Being Shot At!** *Gérard Oury, 1966.* For forty years, until the release of *Bienvenue chez les Ch'tis,* "The Big Jaunt" was France's biggest ever hit movie. Set in wartime Paris, it centres on three Allied soldiers parachuting down on a hapless conductor and decorator, played by stars Bourvil and Louis de Funès. In their desperation to be rid of the parachutists, the pair end up leading them to the free zone.

**Intouchables/The Untouchables** *Olivier Nakache 2011.* Based on the book *You Changed My Life* by Abdel Sellou, *Intouchables* has proved the feel-good blockbuster of the past few years, and one of the most successful French movies ever, shifting 19 million tickets in its first 16 weeks. It follows the story of Driss, a young, unemployed Senegalese man from the Parisian *banlieue,* who inadvertently finds himself taken on as the carer of a millionaire tetraplegic, Philippe. As the unlikely bond between the two grows, both lives are transformed, with predictable consequences – and what must be the cheesiest ending in the history of French cinema.

**Playtime** *Jacques Tati, 1967.* Tati once more plays Hulot, cinema's most radical slapstick creation. From a simple premise – he is showing a group of tourists round a futuristic Paris – he creates an intimately observed and perfectly controlled farce. Just as the city has somehow been transformed into a refined and faceless world of glass and steel, Tati's comedy has become infinitely subtle and reflective.

**Les visiteurs/The Visitors** *Jean-Marie Poiré, 1993.* A medieval knight and his squire are transported to present-day France, where they discover their castle has been turned into a country hotel by their descendants. The earthily comic encounters between time-travellers and modern middle-classes make for an extremely funny comedy of manners. French audiences so loved being sent up that this became the third most successful film in French history.

**Zazie dans le métro/Zazie** *Louis Malle, 1960.* In one of his few comedies, Malle successfully rendered novelist Raymond Queneau's verbal experiments by using cartoon-like visual devices. Ten-year-old Catherine Demongeot is perfect as the delightfully rude little girl driving everybody mad; and the film offers some great shots of Paris, climaxing in a spectacular scene at the top of the Eiffel Tower.

## DRAMAS/THRILLERS/FILMS POLICIERS

**L'armée des ombres/The Army in the Shadows** *Jean-Pierre Melville, 1969.* A small group of Resistance fighters, played by Yves Montand, Simone Signoret and Jean-Pierre Meurisse, are betrayed, questioned and then released. The tight, minimalist style creates a suffocating tension which culminates in an unforgettable conclusion.

★ **Le boucher/The Butcher** *Claude Chabrol, 1969.* A young schoolteacher in a tiny southwest village lives in an apartment above her school. Her loneliness is eased by a surprising fledgling romance with the local butcher – a kindly yet sinister figure – until a sequence of schoolgirl murders sows doubt in her mind. This would be gripping as a portrayal of village life even without the underlying tension and lurking violence.

★ **Caché/Hidden** *Michael Haneke, 2005.* The smooth bourgeois life of literary TV presenter Georges (Daniel Auteuil) and his wife Anne (Juliette Binoche) is disrupted when they receive a chillingly innocuous videotape of their own home under surveillance. In what has been widely read as a metaphor for France's attitude to its own colonial past, Georges is forced to confront a childhood friend, Majid (Maurice Bénichou), and his own troubled conscience.

**Coup de torchon/Clean Slate** *Bertrand Tavernier, 1981.* The setting is colonial West Africa, 1938. Ineffective, humiliated police chief Cordier (Philippe Noiret) decides to take murderous revenge on his wife, her lover, his mistress's husband and the locals he views as uniformly corrupt. As much an extremely black comedy as a true thriller.

★ **Irréversible** *Gaspar Noé, 2002.* One of the more disturbing films ever made: not just for the nightmarish rape and murder scenes but for the evisceration of the most terrifying elements of the male sexual psyche. A giddy, swooping camera traces the events of one night backwards in time from a brutal murder to a post-coital couple (Vincent Cassel and Monica Bellucci) getting ready for a party.

**Monsieur Hire** *Patrice Leconte, 1989.* A slow-moving, unsettlingly erotic psychological thriller. Michel Blanc plays the spookily impassive Monsieur Hire, a voyeur who witnesses his neighbour's boyfriend commit a murder, and becomes the prime suspect.

**Ne le dis à personne/Tell No one** *Guillaume Canet, 2006.* Disturbing psycho-thriller in which a doctor who is slowly rebuilding his life after the murder of his wife, eight years earlier, is suddenly implicated in two fresh murders. To complicate matters further, he is sent evidence that his wife is still alive. As much *Mulholland Drive* as *Frantic*, and more exciting than either.

★ **Pierrot-le-fou** *Jean-Luc Godard, 1965.* Godard's fascination with American pulp fiction is most brilliantly exploited in this highly charged and deeply sophisticated thriller. Accidentally caught up in a murderous gangland killing, Ferdinand (Jean-Paul Belmondo) flees with his babysitter (Godard's then-wife, Anna Karina) to the apparent safety of a Mediterranean island. The bizarre and tragic denouement is one of the great scenes of French cinema.

**Des dieux et des hommes/Of Gods and Men** *Xavier Beauvois, 2010.* When seven Trappist monks were kidnapped from the monastery of Tibhirine in Algeria and assassinated in 1996, the outcry in France was universal. Until their abduction, the monks had for decades lived in harmony with the Muslim population around them. This multi-award-winning drama recounts the story of their murder and its aftermath, focusing on the Trappists' relationship with their captors and with the Algerian government, as external events conspire to transform a peaceful situation into a violent tragedy.

## FILMS D'AMOUR

★ **L'ami de mon amie/Boyfriends and Girlfriends** *Eric Rohmer, 1987.* Two glossy young women in a flashy new town outside Paris – Cergy-Pontoise – become friends. While Blanche is away, Léa falls in love with Blanche's boyfriend Alexandre; when Blanche comes back, she in turn falls in love with Léa's boyfriend, Fabien. Behind the light comedy and seemingly inconsequential dialogue lurks a profound film about love and free will.

**Baisers volés/Stolen Kisses** *François Truffaut, 1968.* The third of Truffaut's five-part semi-autobiographical sequence, which began with *Les quatre-cents coups*, is probably the simplest and most delightful. Returning from military service, idealistic young Antoine Doinel (Jean-Pierre Léaud) mooches about Paris while working variously as a hotel worker, private detective and TV repairman. Through various amorous and bizarre adventures he slowly finds his way back towards the girl he loved and left behind. **La belle noiseuse** *Jacques Rivette, 1991.* "The beautiful troublemaker" originally stretched to four hours, though the more commonly screened "Divertimento" cut is half that length. A washed-out painter (the splendidly stuttering Michel Piccoli) lives in the deep south with his wife (Jane Birkin). An admiring younger painter offers his beautiful girlfriend (Emmanuelle Béart) as a nude model. Her fraught sittings become the catalyst for all the latent tensions in the two relationships to quietly explode.

**Un coeur en hiver/A Heart in Winter/A Heart of Stone** *Claude Sautet, 1992.* In this thoughtful, fresh ménage à trois scenario, violinist Camille (Emmanuelle Béart) is paired first with Maxime (André Dussolier), a violin-shop owner, and then with loner Stéphane (Daniel Auteuil), the chief craftsman. As the title "A Heart in Winter" suggests, this is a moody but ultimately sentimental film about love, and the fear of love.

**Le dernier métro/The Last Metro** *François Truffaut, 1980.* This huge commercial success stars Catherine Deneuve and Gérard Depardieu as two actors who fall in love while rehearsing a play during the German occupation. Wartime Paris is evoked through lavish photography and a growing feeling of imprisonment inside the confined space of the theatre. It swept the Césars that year, for Best Film,

Director, Actor and Actress.

**Le mari de la coiffeuse/The Hairdresser's Husband** *Patrice Leconte, 1990.* Leconte's film about a man who grows up obsessed with hairdressers, and ends up marrying one, epitomizes the best in French romantic film-making. A quirky, subtle and engagingly twisted portrait of an obsessive relationship.

**Les parapluies de Cherbourg/The Umbrellas of Cherbourg** *Jacques Demy, 1964.* Demy's most successful film also gave Catherine Deneuve one of her first great roles. It is an extraordinarily stylized musical, shot in bright, artificial-looking colours, and entirely sung rather than spoken. Demy twists disturbingly the traditional cheerfulness of the musical genre to give a dark, bitter ending to this story of love and abandonment, set during the Algerian war.

★ **Trois couleurs: rouge/Three Colours: Red** *Krzysztof Kieslowski, 1994.* The final part of Polish-born director's Kieslowski's "tricolore" trilogy is perhaps the most satisfying, though to get the most out of the powerful denouement, in which all the strands are pulled together through a series of chances and accidents, you really need to have watched *Bleu* and *Blanc* as well. A young model, Valentine (Irène Jacob), runs over a dog and traces its owner, a reclusive retired judge (Jean-Louis Trintignant) who assuages his loneliness by tapping his neighbours' phone calls. The film's "colour" is expressed through presiding red-brown tones and the theme of *fraternité*, the third principle of the French Republic.

## HERITAGE CINEMA

★ **Cyrano de Bergerac** *Jean-Paul Rappeneau, 1990.* It's hard to know what's finest about this extravagantly romantic film: Rostand's original story, set in seventeenth-century France, or Gérard Depardieu's landmark performance as the big-nosed swashbuckler-poet, Cyrano, who hopelessly loves the brilliant and beautiful Roxanne. The film's panache is matched by the verse dialogue – brilliantly rendered into English subtitles by Anthony Burgess. Hilarious, exciting and sublimely weepy.

★ **Jean de Florette** *Claude Berri, 1986.* This masterful adaptation of Marcel Pagnol's novel created the rose-tinted genre, *cinéma du patrimoine.* In the gorgeous setting of inland, pre-war Provence, Gérard Depardieu plays a deformed urban refugee struggling to create a rural utopia. He is opposed by the shrewd peasant Papet (Yves Montand) and a simpleton, Ugolin (Daniel Auteuil), who dreams of giant fields of carnations. The excellent sequel, *Manon des Sources* (1987), launched the stellar career of the improbably pouting Emmanuelle Béart.

**Au revoir les enfants/Goodbye, Children** *Louis Malle, 1987.* Malle's autobiographical tale is one of the finest film portraits of the war, and of school life in general. It is minutely observed, and desperately moving without being unduly sentimental. Three Jewish boys are hidden among the pupils at a Catholic boys' boarding school. Eventually, the Gestapo discover the ruse.

**La vie en rose** *Olivier Dahan 2007.* The star of this internationally acclaimed biopic, Marion Cotillard, won an Oscar for her compelling portrayal of the Parisian chanteuse, Edith Piaf – the first French woman to be honoured with an Academy Award for Best Actress – as well as BAFTAs and Golden Globes. The gongs were well deserved. Adopting a fractured narrative approach, the film flits with sustained intensity between the "Little Sparrow's" early life in Paris to the events leading up to and surrounding her death, framed by a stirring rendition of Piaf's iconic song, "Je ne regrette rien" – a much more deft and memorable ending than it sounds.

## CINÉMA DU LOOK

★ **37°2 le matin/Betty Blue** *Jean-Jacques Beineix, 1986.* Pouty Béatrice Dalle puts on a compellingly erotic performance as Betty, a free-thinking girl who lives in a beach house with struggling writer Zorg. The film opens in romantic mood with a sustained and passionate sex scene but rapidly spirals towards its disturbing ending. The film's intense and sometimes weird stylishness, along with its memorable score, made it an international hit.

**Les amants du Pont-Neuf** *Léos Carax, 1991.* Homeless painter Michèle (Juliette Binoche) is losing her sight. One day, on Paris's Pont-Neuf, she meets an indigent, fire-eating acrobat (Denis Lavant), and they tumble together into a consuming love, madly played out against the background of their life on the streets. An intense and beautiful film.

★ **Delicatessen** *Jean-Pierre Jeunet/Marc Caro,* 1991. Set in a crumbling apartment block in a dystopian fantasy city – Occupation Paris meets comic book – a grotesque local butcher murders his assistants and sells them as human meat, until his daughter falls in love with the latest butcher boy and the subterranean vegetarian terrorists find out. Hilarious and bizarre in equal measure, with superb cameos from the neighbours.

**Subway** *Luc Besson,* 1985. The favoured urban-nocturnal setting of the *cinéma du look* is given its coolest expression in *Subway*. A hock-headed Christophe Lambert is hunted by police and criminals alike for a cache of documents he shouldn't have. He hides out in the Paris métro where he manages to form a rock band – before being found by Isabelle Adjani. Film noir meets MTV.

## NEW REALISM: BEUR, BANLIEUE AND JEUNE

**Comme une image/Look at Me** *Agnès Jaoui, 2004.* Agnès Jaoui manages to be both sensitive and hard-hitting in this exploration of the dysfunctional relationship between a self-conscious, under-confident daughter (Marilou Berry) and her monstrously egotistical, literary lion of a father – a role played superbly by Jean-Pierre Bacri, who co-wrote the script with Jaoui.

**Girlhood** *Céline Sciamma, 2014.* With its almost exclusively black cast and focus on female characters, *Girlhood* offers a long overdue and fresh take on the coming-of-age-in-the-*banlieue* genre.

**La Haine/Hate** *Mathieu Kassovitz, 1995.* The flagship film of the *cinéma de banlieue*, films of the tough suburbs, centres on three friends: Hubert, of black African origin; Saïd, a *beur* (from North Africa); and Vinz, who is white and has Jewish roots – and a gun. They spend a troubled night wandering Paris before heading back to the *banlieue* and a violent homecoming. Brilliantly treads the line between gritty realism and street cool – the fact that it's shot in black-and-white helps, as does the soundtrack from French rapper MC Solaar, among others.

**Hexagone** *Malik Chibane, 1991.* Shooting in just 24 days, and using amateur actors, Chibane somehow pulled off exactly what he planned: to raise the profile of the new generation of *beurs*. The story is a simple enough rite-of-passage tale focused on five young friends who get in trouble, but the recurring motif of the sacrifice of Abraham gives it a thoughtful twist. The street-slang peppered script and cinematography – strong on handheld shots of the inner-city landscape – are superb.

★ **Un prophète** *Jacques Audiard, 2009.* A prison movie that becomes a gangland thriller, this film is lifted beyond the confines of either genre by its bitter political message and by its magnificent anti-hero, the *naïf*-but-turned-ruthless young Arab man played brilliantly by Tahir Rahim.

★ **La ville est tranquille/The Town Is Quiet** *Robert Guédiguian, 2000.* Notwithstanding its title, this harrowing film describes the dysfunctional society of a far-from-quiet city – Marseille – focusing on the hardships of Michèle (Ariane Ascaride), a 40-year-old woman working in a fish factory while fighting to save her heroin-addict daughter. After a series of light, happy tales, Robert Guédiguian magnificently turns here to a more realistic and political tone.

# Books

The most highly recommended books in this selection are marked by a ★ symbol.

## TRAVEL

**Marc Augé** *In the Metro*. A philosophically minded anthropologist descends deep into métro culture and his own memories of life in Paris. Brief and brilliant.

**Walter Benjamin** *The Arcades Project*. An all-encompassing portrait of Paris from 1830 to 1870, in which the *passages* are used as a lens through which to view Parisian society. Never completed, Benjamin's magnum opus is a kaleidoscopic assemblage of essays, notes and quotations, gathered under such headings as "Baudelaire", "Prostitution", "Mirrors" and "Idleness".

**Adam Gopnik** *Paris to the Moon*. Intimate and acutely observed essays from the Paris correspondent of *The New Yorker* on society, politics, family life and shopping.

**Julien Green** *Paris*. A collection of very personal sketches and impressions of the city, by an American who has lived all his life in Paris, writes in French, and is considered one of the great French writers of the century. Bilingual text.

**Richard Holmes** *Footsteps*. A marvellous mix of objective history and personal account, such as the tale of the author's own excitement at the events of May 1968 in Paris, which led him to investigate and reconstruct the experiences of the British in Paris during the 1789 Revolution.

**Michael de Larrabeiti** *French Leave*. In the summer of 1949, aged just 15, Michael de Larrabeiti set off on his own by bicycle to Paris from the UK. This book provides a wonderfully evocative testimony to his love of France as he looks back over fifty years of working and travelling throughout the country.

**Robert Louis Stevenson** *Travels with a Donkey*. Mile-by-mile account of Stevenson's twelve-day trek in the Haute Loire and Cévennes uplands with the donkey Modestine. His first book, *Inland Voyage*, took him round the waterways of the north.

## HISTORY

### GENERAL

**Eric Hazan** *The Invention of Paris*. Weighty but utterly compelling "psychogeographical" account of the city, picking over its history *quartier* by *quartier* in a thousand aperçus and anecdotes.

**★ Alistair Horne** *Seven Ages of Paris*. Highly readable narrative by the great British historian and journalist, tracing the capital's history from the twelfth century to the death of de Gaulle in 1969. Its brilliance lies in Horne's love of the quirky, and often seedy, side of life, where fashion, celebrity, street culture and a host of incidental characters combine to create a rich tableau that tells you a lot more than comparable academic histories.

**Andrew Hussey** *The French Intifada*. The "long war between France and its Arabs" made a timely appearance just after the *Charlie Hebdo* shootings and is indispensable reading for an understanding of the background to the simmering tensions between France and its Arab population.

**Colin Jones** *The Cambridge Illustrated History of France*. A political and social history of France from prehistoric times to the mid-1990s, concentrating on issues of regionalism, gender, race and class. Good illustrations and a friendly, non-academic writing style.

**Colin Jones** *Paris: Biography of a City*. Jones focuses tightly on the actual life and growth of the city, from the Neolithic past to the future. Five hundred pages flow by

easily, punctuated by thoughtful but accessible "boxes" on characters, streets and buildings whose lives were especially bound up with Paris's, from the Roman *arènes* to Zazie's métro. The best single book on the city's history.

**Ross King** *The Judgement of Paris*. High-octane account of the artistic culture wars of the 1860s and 1870s, focusing on the fascinating parallel lives of the well-established painter Meissonier and the radical upstart Manet.

**★ Graham Robb** *The Discovery of France*. Captivating, brilliant study of France which makes a superb antidote to the usual narratives of kings and state affairs. With affection and insight, and in fine prose, Robb describes a France of vast wastes inhabited by "faceless millions" speaking mutually unintelligible dialects, and reveals how this France was gradually discovered and, inevitably, "civilized".

**Graham Robb** *Parisians: An Adventure History of Paris*. Robb's equally compelling meanderings through the history of the nation's capital approaches the familiar from some beguilingly oblique angles, casting characters as diverse as Napoleon, Baudelaire, Haussmann, Hitler and Proust across a range of uniquely Parisian settings. The result reads like a sparkling modern novel, filled with revelations and fine storytelling.

**Robert Tombs & Isabelle Tombs** *That Sweet Enemy: The British and the French from the Sun King to the Present*. A fascinating, original and mammoth study of a strangely intimate relationship. The authors are a French woman and her English husband, and they engage in lively debate between themselves. Covers society, culture and personalities, as well as politics.

## THE MIDDLE AGES AND RENAISSANCE

**Natalie Zemon Davis** *The Return of Martin Guerre*. A vivid account of peasant life in the sixteenth century and a perplexing and titillating hoax in the Pyrenean village of Artigat.

★ **J.H. Huizinga** *The Waning of the Middle Ages*. Primarily a study of the culture of the Burgundian and French courts – but a masterpiece that goes far beyond this, building up meticulous detail to re-create the whole life and mentality of the fourteenth and fifteenth centuries.

**R.J. Knecht** *The French Renaissance Court*. The definitive work by a genuine authority. Not exactly a racy read, but successfully mixes high politics with sharp detail on life at court, backed up by plentiful illustrations.

**Marina Warner** *Joan of Arc*. Brilliantly places France's patron saint and national heroine within historical, spiritual and intellectual traditions.

## EIGHTEENTH AND NINETEENTH CENTURIES

**Vincent Cronin** *Napoleon*. An enthusiastic and engagingly written biography of France's emperor.

**Christopher Hibbert** *The French Revolution*. Well-paced and entertaining narrative treatment by a master historian.

**Alistair Horne** *The Fall of Paris*. A very readable and humane account of the extraordinary period of the Prussian siege of Paris in 1870 and the ensuing struggles of the Commune.

**Ross King** *The Judgement of Paris: The Revolutionary Decade That Gave the World Impressionism*. Lively account of the stormy early years when the Impressionists were refused entry to official exhibitions.

## SOCIETY AND POLITICS

**Julian Barnes** *Something to Declare*. This journalistically highbrow collection of 18 essays on French culture – films, music, the Tour de France, and, of course, Flaubert – wears its French-style intellectualism on its sleeve, but succeeds in getting under the skin anyway.

**Mary Blume** *A French Affair: The Paris Beat 1965–1998*. Incisive and witty observations on contemporary French life by the *International Herald Tribune* reporter who was stationed there for three decades.

★ **Jonathan Fenby** *On the Brink*. While the country isn't perhaps quite as endangered as the title suggests, this provocative book takes a long, hard look at the problems facing contemporary France, from unemployment to corruption in its self-serving, self-selecting ruling class.

★ **Mark Girouard** *Life in the French Country House*. Girouard meticulously re-creates the social and domestic

★ **Lucy Moore** *Liberty: The Lives and Times of Six Women in Revolutionary France*. This original book follows the lives of six influential – and very different women – through the Revolution, taking in everything from sexual scandal to revolutionary radicalism.

**Ruth Scurr** *Fatal Purity: Robespierre and the French Revolution*. This myth-busting biography of the "remarkably odd" figure of the man they called The Incorruptible, and who went on to orchestrate the notorious Terror, ends up being one of the best books on the Revolution in general.

## TWENTIETH CENTURY

**Marc Bloch** *Strange Defeat*. Moving personal study of the reasons for France's defeat and subsequent caving-in to fascism. Found among the papers of this Sorbonne historian after his death at the hands of the Gestapo in 1942.

**Carmen Callil** *Bad Faith: A Forgotten History of Family and Fatherland*. This quietly angry biography of the loathsome Louis Darquier, the Vichy state's Commissioner for Jewish Affairs, reveals the banality of viciousness in wartime France.

★ **Geoff Dyer** *The Missing of the Somme*. Structured round the author's visits to the war graves of northern France, this is a highly moving meditation on the trauma of World War I and the way its memory has been perpetuated.

**Jonathan Fenby** *The General: Charles de Gaulle and the France he Saved*. This monumental but utterly readable biography does not always get under the famously private president's skin, but does show how de Gaulle not only shaped but embodied the ideals and ambitions of the postwar nation – or a certain, proudly, idealistically reactionary segment of it, at least.

**Ian Ousby** *Occupation: The Ordeal of France 1940–1944*. Revisionist 1997 account which shows how relatively late resistance was, how widespread collaboration was, and why.

life that went on within the walls of French châteaux, starting with the great halls of early castles and ending with the commercial marriage venues of the twentieth century.

**Tim Moore** *French Revolutions: Cycling the Tour de France*. A whimsical bicycle journey along the route of the Tour by a genuinely hilarious writer. Lots of witty asides on Tour history and French culture.

**Jim Ring** *Riviera: The Rise and Rise of the Cote d'Azur*. A fascinating portrait of France's most anomalous region, taking in its discovery by aristocratic pleasure-seekers in the nineteenth century, the golden years of the 1920s when it was the playground of artists, film stars and millionaires, and the inevitable fall from grace.

**Charles Timoney** *Pardon My French: Unleash Your Inner Gaul*. Incisive and often very droll dissection of contemporary culture through the words and phrases that the French use all the time. Looks and maybe sounds like a gift book, but it's rather brilliant.

**Gillian Tindall** *Célestine: Voices from a French Village*. Intrigued by some nineteenth-century love letters left behind in the house she has bought in Chassignolles, Berry, Tindall researches the history of the village back to the 1840s. A brilliant, warm-hearted piece of social history.

**Lucy Wadham** *The Secret Life of France*. Funny and perceptive insider-eye view of the French, written by an expat who married one of them. Particularly good on women and female culture, and generally more intelligent than most in this genre.

**Theodore Zeldin** *The French*. A wise and original book that attempts to describe a country through the prism of the author's intensely personal conversations with a fascinating range of French people. Chapter titles include "How to be chic" and "How to appreciate a grandmother".

## ART, ARCHITECTURE AND POETRY

**Philip Ball** *Universe of Stone: Chartres Cathedral and the Triumph of the Medieval Mind*. Ball gets hopelessly sidetracked into potted histories of all kinds of aspects of medieval life, but at the core of this book is a fascinating letter of love to an extraordinary building.

**André Chastel** *French Art*. Authoritative, three-volume study by one of France's leading art historians. Discusses individual works of art in some detail – from architecture to tapestry, as well as painting – in an attempt to locate the Frenchness of French art. With glossy photographs and serious-minded but readable text.

★ **David Cairns** *Berlioz: The Making of an Artist 1803–1832*. The multiple-award-winning first volume of Cairns' two-part biography is more than just a life of the passionate French composer, it's an extraordinary evocation of post-Napoleonic France and its burgeoning Romantic culture.

★ **John Richardson** *The Life of Picasso*. No twentieth-century artist has ever been subjected to as much scrutiny as Picasso receives in Richardson's brilliantly illustrated biography, of which there are currently three volumes.

**Stephen Romer** (editor) *20th-Century French Poems*. A collection of around 150 French poems spanning the whole of the century. Although there's no French text, many of the translations are works of art in themselves, consummately rendered by the likes of Samuel Beckett, T.S. Eliot and Paul Auster.

**Rolf Toman** (editor) *Romanesque: Architecture, Sculpture, Painting*. Huge, sumptuously illustrated volume of essays on every aspect of the genre across Europe, with one chapter specifically devoted to France.

## GUIDES

**Glynn Christian** *Edible France*. A guide to food rather than restaurants: regional produce, local specialities, markets and best shops for buying goodies to bring back home. Dated, but still reliable for the provinces, if not Paris.

**Cicerone** *Walking Guides*. Neat, durable guides with detailed route descriptions. Dozens of titles including *Tour of Mont Blanc; Mountain Adventures Chamonix; Tour of the Oisans (GR54); French Alps (GR5); Corsica (GR20); Tour of the Queyras; The Pyrenean Trail (GR10); Walks and Climbs in the Pyrenees; Walking in the Alps*. Cycling guides include *The Way of Saint James (GR65)* and *Cycling the Canal du Midi*.

**Philippe Dubois** *Where to Watch Birds in France*. Maps, advice on when to go, habitat information, species' lists – everything you need.

**David Hampshire** *Living and Working in France*. An invaluable guide for anyone considering residence or work in France; packed with ideas and advice on job hunting, bureaucracy, tax, health and so on.

**Richard Holmes** *Fatal Avenue: A Traveller's History of the Battlefields of France and Flanders 1346–1945*. Excellent combination of guidebook and storytelling from a renowned military historian.

# French

French can be a deceptively familiar language because of the number of words and structures it shares with English. Despite this, it's far from easy, though the bare essentials are not difficult to master and can make all the difference. Even just saying "Bonjour Madame/Monsieur" and then gesticulating will often get you a smile and helpful service. People working in tourist offices, hotels and so on almost always speak English and tend to use it when you're struggling to speak French.

## Pronunciation

One easy rule to remember is that **consonants** at the ends of words are usually silent: the most obvious example is Paris, pronounced "Paree", while the phrase *pas plus tard* (not later) sounds something like "pa-plu-tarr". The exception is when the following word begins with a vowel, in which case you generally run the two together: *pas après* (not after) becomes "pazaprey". Otherwise, consonants are much the same as in English, except that: *ch* is always "sh", *c* is "s", *h* is silent, *th* is the same as "t", and *r* is growled (or rolled). And to complicate things a little, *ll* after *i* usually sounds like the "y" in yes – though there are exceptions, including common words like *ville* (city), and *mille* (thousand). And *w* is "v", except when it's in a borrowed English word, like *le whisky* or *un weekend*.

Vowels are the hardest sounds to get exactly right, but they rarely differ enough from English to make comprehension a problem. The most obvious differences are that *au* sounds like the "o" in "over"; *aujourd'hui* (today) is thus pronounced "oh-jor-dwi". Another one to listen out for is *oi*, which sounds like "wa"; *toi* (to you) thus sounds like "twa". Lastly, adding "m" or "n" to a vowel, as in *en* or *un*, adds a nasal sound, as if you said just the vowel with a cold.

### PHRASEBOOKS AND COURSES

**Rough Guide French Phrasebook** Mini dictionary-style phrasebook with both English–French and French–English sections, along with cultural tips, a menu reader and downloadable scenarios read by native speakers.

**Breakthrough French** One of the best teach-yourself courses, with three levels to choose from. Each comes with a book and CD-ROM.

**The Complete Merde! The Real French You Were Never Taught at School** More than just a collection of swearwords, this book is a passkey into everyday French, and a window into French culture.

**Oxford Essential French Dictionary** Very up-to-date French–English and English–French dictionary, with help on pronunciation and verbs, and links to free online products.

**Michel Thomas** A fast-paced and effective audio course that promises "No books. No writing. No memorizing", with an emphasis on spoken French, rather than conjugating verbs and sentence construction. ⓦ michelthomas.com.

## Basic words and phrases

French nouns are divided into masculine and feminine. This causes difficulties with adjectives, whose endings have to change to suit the nouns they qualify – you can talk about *un château blanc* (a white castle), for example, but *une tour blanche* (a white tower). If you're not sure, stick to the simpler masculine form – as used in this glossary.

### ESSENTIALS

| | |
|---|---|
| **hello (morning or afternoon)** bonjour | **thank you** merci |
| **hello (evening)** bonsoir | **please** s'il vous plaît |
| **good night** bonne nuit | **sorry** pardon/Je m'excuse |
| **goodbye** au revoir | **excuse me** pardon |

| | |
|---|---|
| **yes** oui | **a little** un peu |
| **no** non | **a lot** beaucoup |
| **OK/agreed** d'accord | **inexpensive** pas cher/bon marché |
| **help!** au secours! | **expensive** cher |
| **here** ici | **good** bon |
| **there** là | **bad** mauvais |
| **this one** ceci | **hot** chaud |
| **that one** celà | **cold** froid |
| **open** ouvert | **with** avec |
| **closed** fermé | **without** sans |
| **big** grand | **entrance** entrée |
| **small** petit | **exit** sortie |
| **more** plus | **man** un homme |
| **less** moins | **woman** une femme (pronounced "fam") |

## NUMBERS

| | |
|---|---|
| **1** un | **21** vingt-et-un |
| **2** deux | **22** vingt-deux |
| **3** trois | **30** trente |
| **4** quatre | **40** quarante |
| **5** cinq | **50** cinquante |
| **6** six | **60** soixante |
| **7** sept | **70** soixante-dix |
| **8** huit | **75** soixante-quinze |
| **9** neuf | **80** quatre-vingts |
| **10** dix | **90** quatre-vingt-dix |
| **11** onze | **95** quatre-vingt-quinze |
| **12** douze | **100** cent |
| **13** treize | **101** cent-et-un |
| **14** quatorze | **200** deux cents |
| **15** quinze | **300** trois cents |
| **16** seize | **500** cinq cents |
| **17** dix-sept | **1000** mille |
| **18** dix-huit | **2000** deux mille |
| **19** dix-neuf | **5000** cinq mille |
| **20** vingt | **1,000,000** un million |

## TIME

| | |
|---|---|
| **today** aujourd'hui | **now** maintenant |
| **yesterday** hier | **later** plus tard |
| **tomorrow** demain | **at one o'clock** à une heure |
| **in the morning** le matin | **at three o'clock** à trois heures |
| **in the afternoon** l'après-midi | **at ten thirty** à dix heures et demie |
| **in the evening** le soir | **at midday** à midi |

## DAYS AND DATES

| | |
|---|---|
| **January** janvier | **September** septembre |
| **February** février | **October** octobre |
| **March** mars | **November** novembre |
| **April** avril | **December** décembre |
| **May** mai | **Sunday** dimanche |
| **June** juin | **Monday** lundi |
| **July** juillet | **Tuesday** mardi |
| **August** août | **Wednesday** mercredi |

| | |
|---|---|
| **Thursday** jeudi | **March 2** le deux mars |
| **Friday** vendredi | **July 14** le quatorze juillet |
| **Saturday** samedi | **November 23** le vingt-trois novembre |
| **August 1** le premier août | **2019** deux mille dix-neuf |

## TALKING TO PEOPLE

When addressing people a simple *bonjour* is not enough; you should always use *Monsieur* for a man, *Madame* for a woman, *Mademoiselle* for a young woman or girl. This has its uses when you've forgotten someone's name or want to attract someone's attention. "Bonjour" can be used well into the afternoon, and people may start saying "bonsoir" surprisingly early in the evening, or as a way of saying goodbye.

**Do you speak English?** Parlez-vous anglais?

**How do you say it in French?** Comment ça se dit en français?

**What's your name?** Comment vous appelez-vous?

**My name is ...** Je m'appelle ...

**I'm ...** Je suis ...

**... English** ... anglais[e]

**... Irish** ... irlandais[e]

**... Scottish** ... écossais[e]

**... Welsh** ... gallois[e]

**... American** ... américain[e]

**... Australian** ...australien[ne]

**... Canadian** ... canadien[ne]

**... a New Zealander** ... néo-zélandais[e]

**... South African** ... sud-africain[e]

**I understand** Je comprends

**I don't understand** Je ne comprends pas

**Could you speak more slowly?** S'il vous plaît, parlez moins vite

**How are you?** Comment allez-vous?/ Ça va?

**Fine, thanks** Très bien, merci

**I don't know** Je ne sais pas

**Let's go** Allons-y

**See you tomorrow** À demain

**See you soon** À bientôt

**Leave me alone (aggressive)** Laissez-moi tranquille

**Please help me** Aidez-moi, s'il vous plaît

## FINDING THE WAY

**bus** autobus/bus/car

**bus station** gare routière

**bus stop** arrêt

**car** voiture

**train/taxi/ferry** train/taxi/bac or ferry

**boat** bâteau

**plane** avion

**shuttle** navette

**train station** gare (SNCF)

**platform** quai

**What time does it leave?** Il part à quelle heure?

**What time does it arrive?** Il arrive à quelle heure?

**a ticket to ...** un billet pour ...

**single ticket** aller simple

**return ticket** aller retour

**validate/stamp your ticket** compostez votre billet

**valid for** valable pour

**ticket office** vente de billets

**how many kilometres?** combien de kilomètres?

**how many hours?** combien d'heures?

**hitchhiking** autostop

**on foot** à pied

**Where are you going?** Vous allez où?

**I'm going to ...** Je vais à ...

**I want to get off at ...** Je voudrais descendre à ...

**the road to ...** la route pour ...

**near** près/pas loin

**far** loin

**left** à gauche

**right** à droite

**straight on** tout droit

**on the other side of** à l'autre côté de

**on the corner of** à l'angle de

**next to** à côté de

**behind** derrière

**in front of** devant

**before** avant

**after** après

**under** sous

**to cross** traverser

**bridge** pont

**town centre** centre ville

**all through roads (road sign)** toutes directions

**other destinations (road sign)** autres directions

**upper town** ville haute/haute ville

**lower town** ville basse/basse ville

**old town** vieille ville

### SIGN LANGUAGE

**Défense de ...** It is forbidden to ...

**Fermé** closed

**Ouvert** open

**Rez-de-chaussée (RC)** ground floor

**Sortie** exit

## QUESTIONS AND REQUESTS

The simplest way of asking a question is to start with *s'il vous plaît* (please), then name the thing you want in an interrogative tone of voice. For example:

**Where is there a bakery?** S'il vous plaît, où est la boulangerie?

**Which way is it to the Eiffel Tower?** S'il vous plaît, la route pour la Tour Eiffel?

**Can we have a room for two?** S'il vous plaît, une chambre pour deux?

**Can I have a kilo of oranges?** S'il vous plaît, un kilo d'oranges?

## QUESTION WORDS

**where?** où?
**how?** comment?
**how many/how much?** combien?
**when?** quand?

**why?** pourquoi?
**at what time?** à quelle heure?
**what is/which is?** quel est?

## ACCOMMODATION

**a room for one/two persons** une chambre pour une/ deux personne(s)
**a double bed** un grand lit/ un lit matrimonial
**a room with two single beds/twin** une chambre à deux lits
**a room with a shower** une chambre avec douche
**a room with a bath** une chambre avec salle de bain
**for one/two/three nights** pour une/deux/trois nuits
**Can I see it?** Je peux la voir?
**a room on the courtyard** une chambre sur la cour
**a room over the street** une chambre sur la rue
**first floor** premier étage
**second floor** deuxième étage
**with a view** avec vue
**key** clé
**to iron** repasser
**do laundry** faire la lessive
**sheets** draps

**blankets** couvertures
**quiet** calme
**noisy** bruyant
**hot water** eau chaude
**cold water** eau froide
**Is breakfast included?** Est-ce que le petit-déjeuner est compris?
**I would like breakfast** Je voudrais prendre le petit-déjeuner
**I don't want breakfast** Je ne veux pas le petit-déjeuner
**bed and breakfast** chambres d'hôtes
**Can we camp here?** On peut camper ici?
**campsite** camping/terrain de camping
**tent** tente
**tent space** emplacement
**hostel** foyer
**youth hostel** auberge de jeunesse

## DRIVING

**service station** garage
**service** service
**to park the car** garer la voiture
**car park** un parking
**no parking** défense de stationner/ stationnement interdit
**petrol/gas station** station d'essence
**fuel** essence
**unleaded** sans plomb
**leaded** super
**diesel** gazole

**oil** huile
**air line** ligne à air
**put air in the tyres** gonfler les pneus
**battery** batterie
**the battery is dead** la batterie est morte
**plug (for appliance)** prise
**to break down** tomber en panne
**petrol can** bidon
**insurance** assurance
**green card** carte verte
**traffic lights** feux rouges

## HEALTH MATTERS

**doctor** médecin
**I don't feel well** Je ne me sens pas bien
**medicines** médicaments
**prescription** ordonnance
**I feel sick** Je suis malade
**I have a headache** J'ai mal à la tête

**stomach ache** mal à l'estomac
**period** règles
**pain** douleur
**it hurts** ça fait mal
**chemist/pharmacist** pharmacie
**hospital** hôpital

condom préservatif

morning-after pill/emergency contraceptive pilule du lendemain

I'm allergic to … Je suis allergique à …

## OTHER NEEDS

bakery boulangerie

food shop alimentation

delicatessen charcuterie, traiteur

cake shop pâtisserie

cheese shop fromagerie

supermarket supermarché

to eat manger

to drink boire

tasting, eg wine dégustation, tasting

camping gas camping gaz

tobacconist tabac

stamps timbres

bank banque

money argent

toilets toilettes

police police

telephone téléphone

cinema cinéma

theatre théâtre

to reserve/book réserver

## RESTAURANT PHRASES

I'd like to reserve a table for two people, at eight thirty Je voudrais réserver une table pour deux personnes à vingt heures trente

I'm having the €30 set menu Je prendrai le menu à trente euros

Waiter! (never "garçon") Monsieur/Madame!/ s'il vous plaît!

the bill/check please l'addition, s'il vous plaît

# Food and dishes

## BASIC TERMS

l'addition bill/check

beurre butter

bio or biologique organic

bouteille bottle

carafe d'eau jug of water

la carte the menu

chauffé heated

couteau knife

cru raw

cuillère spoon

cuit cooked

emballé wrapped

à emporter takeaway

entrée starter

formule lunchtime set menu

fourchette fork

fumé smoked

gazeuse fizzy

lait milk

le menu set menu

moutarde mustard

oeuf egg

offert free

pain bread

pimenté spicy

plat main course

poivre pepper

salé salted/savoury

sel salt

sucre sugar

sucré sweet

table table

verre glass

vinaigre vinegar

## SNACKS

un sandwich/ une baguette a sandwich

...jambon beurre with ham and butter

...au fromage with cheese, no butter

...mixte with ham and cheese

...au pâté (de campagne) with pâté (country-style)

croque monsieur grilled cheese and ham sandwich

panini toasted Italian sandwich

tartine buttered bread or open sandwich, often with jam

oeufs eggs au plat fried à la coque boiled durs hard-boiled

brouillés scrambled

omelette omelette

...nature plain

...aux fines herbes with herbs

...au fromage with cheese

salade de tomates tomato salad

salade verte green salad

## PASTA (PÂTES), PANCAKES (CRÊPES), TARTES AND COUSCOUS

**nouilles** noodles
**pâtes fraîches** fresh pasta
**crêpe au sucre/ aux oeufs** pancake with sugar/ eggs
**galette** buckwheat pancake
**pissaladière** tart of fried onions with anchovies and black olives
**tarte flambée** thin pizza-like pastry topped with onion, cream and bacon
**couscous** steamed semolina grains, usually served with meat or veg, chickpea stew and chilli sauce
**couscous royal** couscous with spicy merguez sausage, chicken and beef or lamb kebabs

## SOUPS (SOUPES)

**bisque** shellfish soup
**bouillabaisse** soup with five fish
**bouillon** broth or stock
**bourride** thick fish soup
**consommé** clear soup
**garbure** potato, cabbage and meat soup
**pistou** parmesan, basil and garlic paste added to soup
**potage** thick vegetable soup
**potée auvergnate** cabbage and meat soup
**rouille** red pepper, garlic and saffron mayonnaise served with fish soup
**soupe à l'oignon** onion soup with a rich cheese topping
**velouté** thick soup, usually fish or poultry

## STARTERS (HORS D'OEUVRES)

**assiette de charcuterie** plate of cold meats
**assiette composée** mixed salad plate, usually cold meat and veg
**crudités** dressed raw vegetables
**hors d'oeuvres** combination of the above often with smoked or marinated fish

## FISH (POISSON), SEAFOOD (FRUITS DE MER) AND SHELLFISH (CRUSTACÉS OR COQUILLAGES)

**anchois** anchovies
**anguilles** eels
**barbue** brill
**baudroie** monkfish or anglerfish
**bigorneau** periwinkle
**brème** bream
**cabillaud** cod
**calmar** squid
**carrelet** plaice
**claire** type of oyster
**colin** hake
**congre** conger eel
**coques** cockles

**coquilles St-Jacques** scallops
**crabe** crab
**crevettes grises** shrimp
**crevettes roses** prawns
**daurade** sea bream
**éperlan** smelt or whitebait
**escargots** snails
**flétan** halibut
**friture** assorted fried fish, often like whitebait
**gambas** king prawns
**hareng** herring
**homard** lobster
**huîtres** oysters
**langouste** spiny lobster
**langoustines** saltwater crayfish (scampi)
**limande** lemon sole
**lotte de mer** monkfish
**loup de mer** sea bass
**maquereau** mackerel
**merlan** whiting
**moules (marinières)** mussels (with shallots in white wine sauce)
**oursin** sea urchin
**palourdes** clams
**poissons de roche** fish from shoreline rocks
**praires** small clams
**raie** skate
**rouget** red mullet
**saumon** salmon
**sole** sole
**thon** tuna
**truite** trout
**turbot** turbot
**violet** sea squirt

## FISH DISHES AND TERMS

**aïoli** garlic mayonnaise
**anchoïade** anchovy paste or sauce
**arête** fish bone
**assiette de pêcheur** assorted fish
**beignet** fritter
**darne** fillet or steak
**la douzaine** a dozen
**frit** fried
**friture** deep-fried small fish
**fumé** smoked
**fumet** fish stock
**gigot de mer** large fish baked whole
**grillé** grilled
**hollandaise** butter and vinegar sauce
**à la meunière** in a butter, lemon and parsley sauce
**mousse/mousseline** mousse
**pané** breaded
**poutargue** mullet roe paste

quenelles light dumplings

## MEAT (VIANDE) AND POULTRY (VOLAILLE)

**agneau (de pré-salé)** lamb (grazed on salt marshes)
**andouille** cold pork and tripe sausage
**andouillette** hot, cooked tripe sausage
**bavette** flank-like steak
**boeuf** beef
**boudin blanc** sausage of white meats
**boudin noir** black pudding
**caille** quail
**canard** duck
**caneton** duckling
**contrefilet** sirloin roast
**coquelet** cockerel
**la cuisson?** how would sir/ madam like his/her steak done?
**dinde/dindon** turkey
**entrecôte** rib steak
**faux filet** sirloin steak
**foie** liver
**foie gras** (duck/goose) liver
**gibier** game
**gigot (d'agneau)** leg (of lamb)
**grenouille (cuisses de)** frogs'(legs)
**langue** tongue
**lapin/lapereau** rabbit/young rabbit
**lard/lardons** bacon/diced bacon
**lièvre** hare
**merguez** spicy, red sausage
**mouton** mutton
**museau de veau** calf's muzzle
**oie** goose
**onglet** tasty, flank-like steak
**os** bone
**poitrine** breast
**porc** pork
**poulet** chicken
**poussin** baby chicken
**rillettes** pork mashed with lard and liver
**ris** sweetbreads
**rognons** kidneys
**rognons blancs** testicles
**sanglier** wild boar
**steak** steak
**tête de veau** calf's head (in jelly)
**tournedos** thick slices of fillet
**tripes** tripe
**tripoux** mutton tripe
**veau** veal
**venaison** venison

## MEAT AND POULTRY DISHES AND TERMS

**aïado** roast shoulder of lamb stuffed with garlic and
  other ingredients

**aile** wing
**blanquette, daube,** types of stew **estouffade,
  hochepôt, navarin, ragoût**
**blanquette de veau** veal in cream and mushroom
  sauce
**boeuf bourguignon** beef stew with Burgundy, onions
  and mushrooms
**brochette** kebab
**carré** best end of neck, chop or cutlet
**cassoulet** casserole of beans, sausages and duck/
  goose
**choucroute** sauerkraut with peppercorns, sausages,
  pork and ham
**civet** game stew
**confit** meat preserve
**coq au vin** chicken slow-cooked with wine, onions and
  mushrooms
**côte** chop, cutlet or rib
**cuisse** thigh or leg
**en croûte** in pastry
**épaule** shoulder
**farci** stuffed
**au feu de bois** cooked over wood fire
**au four** baked
**garni** with vegetables
**gésier** gizzard
**grillade** grilled meat
**grillé** grilled
**hâchis** chopped meat or mince hamburger
**magret de canard** duck breast
**marmite** casserole
**médaillon** round piece
**mijoté** stewed
**pavé** thick slice
**pieds et paques** mutton or pork tripe and trotters
**poêlé** pan-fried
**poulet de Bresse** chicken from Bresse
**râble** saddle
**rôti** roast
**sauté** lightly fried in butter
**steak au poivre (vert/rouge)** steak in a black
  peppercorn sauce (green/red peppercorn)
**steak tartare** raw chopped beef, topped with a raw
  egg yolk
**tagine** North African casserole
**viennoise** fried in egg and bread crumbs

## TERMS FOR STEAKS

**bleu** almost raw
**saignant** rare
**à point** medium rare
**bien cuit** well done
**très bien cuit** ruined

## GARNISHES AND SAUCES

**américaine** sauce of white wine, cognac and tomato

**auvergnate** with cabbage, sausage and bacon

**béarnaise** sauce of egg yolks, white wine, shallots and vinegar

**beurre blanc** sauce of white wine and shallots, with butter

**bonne femme** with mushroom, bacon, potato and onions

**bordelaise** in a red wine, shallot and bone-marrow sauce

**boulangère** baked with potatoes and onions

**bourgeoise** with carrots, onions, bacon, celery and braised lettuce

**chasseur** sauce of white wine, mushrooms and shallots

**châtelaine** with artichoke hearts and chestnut purée

**diable** strong mustard seasoning

**façon** in the style of …

**forestière** with bacon and mushroom

**fricassée** rich, creamy sauce

**mornay** cheese sauce

**pays d'auge** cream and cider

**périgourdine** sauce with foie gras and possibly truffles

**piquante** with gherkins or capers, vinegar and shallots

**provençale** sauce of tomatoes, garlic, olive oil and herbs

**savoyarde** with gruyère cheese

## VEGETABLES (LÉGUMES), GRAINS (FÉCULENTS), HERBS (HERBES) AND SPICES (ÉPICES)

**ail** garlic

**anis** aniseed

**artichaut** artichoke

**asperge** asparagus

**avocat** avocado

**basilic** basil

**betterave** beetroot

**blette/bette** Swiss chard

**cannelle** cinnamon

**capre** caper

**cardon** cardoon

**carotte** carrot

**céleri** celery

**champignons, cèpes,** mushrooms **ceps, girolles, chanterelles, pleurotes**

**chou (rouge)** (red) cabbage

**choufleur** cauliflower

**concombre** cucumber

**cornichon** gherkin

**échalotes** shallots

**endive** chicory

**épinards** spinach

**estragon** tarragon

**fenouil** fennel

**fèves** broad beans

**flageolets** flageolet beans

**gingembre** ginger

**haricots** beans

**...verts** green beans

**...rouges** kidney beans

**laurier** bay leaf

**lentilles** lentils

**maïs** maize (corn)

**menthe** mint

**moutarde** mustard

**oignon** onion

**panais** parsnip

**persil** parsley

**petits pois** peas

**piment rouge/vert** red/green chilli pepper

**pois chiche** chickpeas

**pois mange-tout** mange-tout

**pignons** pine nuts

**poireau** leek

**poivron (vert, rouge)** sweet pepper (green, red)

**pommes de terre** potatoes

**primeurs** spring vegetables

**radis** radish

**riz** rice

**safran** saffron

**sarrasin** buckwheat

**thym** thyme

**tomate** tomato

**truffes** truffles

## VEGETABLE DISHES AND TERMS

**à l'anglaise** boiled

**beignet** fritter

**duxelles** fried mushrooms and shallots with cream

**farci** stuffed

**feuille** leaf

**fines herbes** mixture of tarragon, parsley and chives

**gratiné** browned with cheese or butter

**à la grecque** cooked in oil and lemon

**jardinière** with mixed diced vegetables

**mousseline** mashed potato with cream and eggs

**à la parisienne** sautéed potatoes, with white wine and shallot sauce

**parmentier** with potatoes

**petits farcis** stuffed tomatoes, aubergines, courgettes and peppers

**râpée** grated or shredded

**à la vapeur** steamed

**en verdure** garnished with green vegetables

## FRUIT (FRUIT) AND NUTS (NOIX)

**abricot** apricot

amande almond
ananas pineapple
banane banana
brugnon, nectarine nectarine
cacahouète peanut
cassis blackcurrant
cerise cherry
citron lemon
citron vert lime
datte date
figue fig
fraise (des bois) strawberry (wild)
framboise raspberry
fruit de la passion passion fruit
grenade pomegranate
groseille redcurrant
mangue mango
marron chestnut (also châtaigne)
melon melon
mirabelle small yellow plum
myrtille bilberry
noisette hazelnut
noix walnuts; nuts
noix de cajou cashew nut
orange orange
pamplemousse grapefruit
pastèque watermelon
pêche peach
pistache pistachio
poire pear
pomme apple
prune plum
pruneau prune
raisin grape
reine-claude greengage

**FRUIT DISHES AND TERMS**
agrumes citrus fruits
beignet fritter
compôte stewed fruit

coulis sauce of puréed fruit
crème de marrons chestnut purée
flambé set aflame in alcohol
frappé iced

**DESSERTS (DESSERTS), PASTRIES (GÂTEAUX/VIENNOISERIES) AND CHEESES (FROMAGES)**
brebis sheep's milk cheese
bombe moulded ice-cream dessert
brioche sweet breakfast roll
charlotte custard and fruit in a lining of almond biscuits or sponge
chèvre goat's cheese
clafoutis almond and cherry desert
crème Chantilly vanilla-flavoured and sweetened whipped cream
crème fraîche sour cream
crème pâtissière thick, eggy pastry-filling
crêpe suzette thin pancake with orange juice and liqueur
fromage blanc cream cheese
gaufre waffle
glace ice cream
Île flottante/oeufs à la neige whipped egg-white floating on custard
macaron macaroon
madeleine small sponge cake
marrons Mont Blanc chestnut purée and cream on a rum-soaked sponge cake
palmier caramelized puff pastry
parfait frozen mousse, sometimes ice cream
petit-suisse a smooth mixture of cream and curds
petits fours bite-sized cakes/ pastries
plâteau de fromages cheeseboard
poires belle hélène pears and ice cream in chocolate sauce
tarte tatin upside-down apple tart
yaourt/yogourt yoghurt

# Glossary of architectural terms

These are either terms you'll come across throughout this book, or while travelling around.

**abbaye** abbey

**ambulatory** passage round the outer edge of the choir of a church

**apse** semicircular termination at the east end of a church

**Baroque** mainly seventeenth-century style of art and architecture, distinguished by ornate classicism

**basse ville/ville basse** lower town

**bastide** walled town

**capital** carved top of a column

**Carolingian** dynasty (and art, sculpture etc) named -after Charlemagne; mid-eighth to early tenth centuries

**château** mansion, country house, castle

**château fort** castle

**chevet** east end of a church

**choir** the eastern part of a church between the altar and nave, used by the choir and clergy

**classical** architectural style incorporating Greek and Roman elements: pillars, domes, colonnades, etc, at its height in France in the seventeenth century and revived, as Neoclassical, in the nineteenth century

**clerestory** upper storey of a church, incorporating the windows

**cloître** cloister

**donjon** castle keep

**église** church

**flamboyant** florid, late (c.1450–1540) form of Gothic

**Gallo-Roman** from the Roman era in France

**Gothic** late medieval architectural style characterized by pointed arches, verticality and light

**haute ville/ville haute** upper town

**hôtel (particulier)** mansion or townhouse

**Merovingian** dynasty ruling France and parts of Germany (and associated art etc) from sixth to mid-eighth centuries

**narthex** entrance hall of church

**nave** main body of a church

**porte** gateway

**Renaissance** classically influenced art/architectural style imported from Italy to France in the early sixteenth century

**retable** altarpiece

**Roman** Romanesque (easily confused with Romain, which means Roman)

**Romanesque** early medieval architecture distinguished by squat, rounded forms and naive sculpture, called Norman in Britain

**stucco** plaster used to embellish ceilings etc

**tour** tower

**transepts** transverse arms of a church

**tympanum** sculpted panel above a church door

**voussoir** wedge-shaped stones used in an arch or vault

# Small print and index

**1049** Small print

**1051** Index

**1061** Map symbols

## A ROUGH GUIDE TO ROUGH GUIDES

Published in 1982, the first Rough Guide – to Greece – was a student scheme that became a publishing phenomenon. Mark Ellingham, a recent graduate in English from Bristol University, had been travelling in Greece the previous summer and couldn't find the right guidebook. With a small group of friends he wrote his own guide, combining a contemporary, journalistic style with a thoroughly practical approach to travellers' needs.

The immediate success of the book spawned a series that rapidly covered dozens of destinations. And, in addition to impecunious backpackers, Rough Guides soon acquired a much broader readership that relished the guides' wit and inquisitiveness as much as their enthusiastic, critical approach and value-for-money ethos. These days, Rough Guides include recommendations from budget to luxury and cover more than 120 destinations around the globe, from Amsterdam to Zanzibar, all regularly updated by our team of roaming writers.

Browse all our latest guides, read inspirational features and book your trip at **roughguides.com**.

## Rough Guide credits

**Editor:** Carine Tracanelli
**Cartography:** Carte
**Managing editor:** Rachel Lawrence
**Picture editor(s):** Michelle Bhatia

**Cover photo research:** Michelle Bhatia
**Senior DTP coordinator:** Dan May
**Head of DTP and Pre-Press:** Rebeka Davies

## Publishing information

Fifteenth edition 2019

### Distribution

*UK, Ireland and Europe*
Apa Publications (UK) Ltd; sales@roughguides.com
*United States and Canada*
Ingram Publisher Services; ips@ingramcontent.com
*Australia and New Zealand*
Woodslane; info@woodslane.com.au
*Southeast Asia*
Apa Publications (SN) Pte; sales@roughguides.com
*Worldwide*
Apa Publications (UK) Ltd; sales@roughguides.com
**Special Sales, Content Licensing and CoPublishing**
Rough Guides can be purchased in bulk quantities
at discounted prices. We can create special editions,
personalised jackets and corporate imprints tailored to
your needs. sales@roughguides.com.

roughguides.com
Printed in China by CTPS
All rights reserved
© 2019 Apa Digital (CH) AG
License edition © Apa Publications Ltd UK

## Help us update

We've gone to a lot of effort to ensure that this edition of
**The Rough Guide to France** is accurate and up-to-date.
However, things change – places get "discovered", opening
hours are notoriously fickle, restaurants and rooms raise
prices or lower standards. If you feel we've got it wrong
or left something out, we'd like to know, and if you can
remember the address, the price, the hours, the phone
number, so much the better.

Please send your comments with the subject line
**"Rough Guide France Update"** to mail@uk.roughguides.
com. We'll credit all contributions and send a copy of the
next edition (or any other Rough Guide if you prefer) for
the very best emails.

## Acknowledgements

**Samantha Cook** Thanks to Carine Tracanelli and above all to Greg Ward.

## Photo credits

(Key: T-top; M-middle; B-bottom; L-left; R-right)

## ABOUT THE AUTHORS

**Samantha Cook** is a London-based writer and editor who has been nipping across the channel to Paris on a regular basis since the age of seven, and was responsible for the Paris chapter for this edition of the France guide. Among other titles, she has written Rough Guides to Paris; London; Vintage London; Kent Sussex & Surrey; Budget Accommodation in Britain; New Orleans; and Chick Flicks.

**Emma Gibbs** is a freelance writer and editor whose love affair with France developed after (or in spite of) countless holidays there as a child. She has also contributed to the Rough Guides to Europe on a Budget, Southeast Asia on a Budget and Laos.

**Norm Longley** has spent most of his working life in Europe – he is also the author of the Rough Guides to Romania, Slovenia and Budapest – but more recently has turned his hand to home shores, contributing to the Scotland, Wales and Ireland guides. Currently writing a guidebook to Somerset, he lives in the county and can occasionally be seen erecting marquees on The Rec in Bath.

**Keith Munro** has been a freelance writer since 2010 after a stretch working in London's music industry as a record label manager. A keen traveller, he spent a year in the French Pyrenees before returning to his childhood home of Edinburgh, and has since contributed to the Rough Guides to France, Scotland, Edinburgh and other travel-related publications.

**Victoria Trott** is an award-winning travel writer who specializes in France. She is the author of the latest edition of the Rough Guide to Languedoc & Roussillon and co-author of the current Rough Guide to Belgium & Luxembourg.

**Greg Ward** has been writing about France – and many other destinations – for Rough Guides since the early days.

# Index

## A

Abbaye d'Hautecombe 748
abers, the 332
Abri du Cap Blanc 558
accommodation 39
Agde 656
Agincourt, battle of 175, 996
Agout valley 662
Aguilar 624
Aigues-Mortes 654
Aiguille du Midi 759
Aiguilles Rouges 761
Ainhoa 596
airlines 32
Aix-en-Provence 15, 847
Aix-les-Bains 746
Ajaccio 966
Albert 189
Albi 676
Alençon 302
Aléria 444, 985
Alésia, battle of 994
Alet-les-Bains 620
Algerian war of independence 1005
Alpes de Haute-Provence 857
Alpes-Maritimes, the 861
Alps and Franche-Comté, the 726
Alsace-Lorraine 224
Ambert 704
Amboise 401
Amiens 192
Amiens cathedral 23
Amnéville 253
Andlau 236
Angers 413
Angoulême 506
Annecy 23, 750
Antibes 909
Apt 844
Arbois 773
Arcachon 524
architecture 1022
Ardèche 716
Ardennes, the 219
Arles 832
Armagnac 680
Arras 186
Arrens-Marsous 610
Arromanches 289
Art 1012
Art Deco 1025

Art Nouveau 1025
Ascain 595
ATMs 55
Aubenas 721
Aubeterre-sur-Dronne 545
Aubrac, the 706
Aubusson 538
Auch 680
Auguste, Phillipe 995
Aulnay 503
Aumont-Aubrac 706
Aups 852
Aurillac 697
Autoroute des Anglais 167
Autun 452
Auvergne 684
Auxerre 432
Avallon 447
Aven Armand (cave) 714
Aven Marzal 722
Aven Orgnac 722
Aveyron, the Valley of 576
Avignon 819
Avranches 294
Azay-le-Rideau 405
Azincourt 175

## B

Bagnoles-de-l'Orne 303
Baie des Anges 912
Baie des Trépassés 340
Balagne, the 952
Bandol 883
banks 55
Banyuls-sur-Mer 631
Barcelonnette 860
Barèges 613
Barfleur 293
Barneville-Carteret 293
Baroque architecture 1024
Barr 235
Basse Navarre 595
Bastia 940
bastides 25, 550
Bastille Day 20
Bastille, storming of 1000
Bavella 985
Bayeux 284
Bayeux Tapestry 17, 284, 287
Bayonne 591
Bazas 524
Beaugency 373

Beaujolais 797
Beaulieu-sur-Dordogne 566
Beaulieu-sur-mer 926
Beaumont-Hamel 190
Beaune 465
Beauport, Abbaye de 325
Beauvais 195
bed and breakfast 40
beer 43
Belfort 774
Belle-Île 356
Bénodet 345
Bergerac 550
Bergheim 236
Bernstein 236
Besançon 765
Besse 696
Beuvron-en-Auge 299
Beynac-et-Cazenac 563
Béziers 657
Biarritz 588
Biot 911
Blaye 519
Blois 390
Blum, Léon 1003
Bocage, the 304
Bonifacio 977
Bonnieux 844
Books 1035
Bordeaux 23, 509
Bordeaux wine region 516
Bormes-les-Mimosas 889
bouchons 20, 792
boules 48
Boulogne-sur-Mer 169
Bourdeilles 544
Bourg-Charente 504
Bourges 379
Bourré 385
Brantôme 543
Braque, Georges 266, 1018
Brest 336
Breton language 311
Briançon 737
Briare 377
Brignogan-Plages 333
Brittany 308
Brive-la-Gaillarde 540
Brouage 497
budgeting 51
bullfighting 48, 645, 836
Burgundy 432
buses to France 31
buses within France 36

# C

Cadouin, Abbaye de 562
Caen 281
Caesar, Julius 994
Cagnes 912
Cahors 570
Cairn du Barnenez 329
Calais 165
Calanches, the 963
calanques 881
Calanques, the 18
Calvi 954
Camaret 338
Camargue, the 839
Cambo-les-Bains 597
Cambrai 183
Camembert 300
Camon 619
camping 41
canal and river trips 37
Canal de Bourgogne 442
Canal du Midi 25, 666
Canaveilles 636
Cancale 320
Cannes 902
canoeing 50
Cap Corse 946
Cap d'Agde 656
Cap d'Antibes 910
Capet, Hugues 64, 995
Cap Ferret 526
Cap Martin 927
Carcassonne 20, 664
Carennac 566
Cargèse 965
Carhaix 348
Carnac 20, 352
Carpentras 819
car rental 38
Carrouges 303
Cascades du Hérisson 771
Cassel 163
Cassis 881
Cassoulet 667
Casteddu d'Arragiu 984
Castellane 856
Castelnaudary 668
Castlenou 629
Castres 679
Cathar castles 23, 621
Causses, Les 711
Cauterets 611
cave art, prehistoric 20, 557
cave painting 558, 576
caves, Troglodyte (Loire valley) 411
caving 50
cellphones 56
Centuri-Port 948

Cerdagne, the 636
Céret 631
Cette-Eygun 608
Cévennes, Parc National des 716
Cévennes, the 716
Cézanne, Paul 849, 1017
Chablis 440
Chagall, Marc 922
Chalon-sur-Saône 468
Chambéry 743
chambres d'hôtes 40
Chamonix-Mont-Blanc 755
champagne 207, 211
Champagne, region of 204
Channel Tunnel 30
Chantilly 148
Charlemagne 995
Charles de Gaulle 217, 1003
Charles X 1001
Charleville-Mézières 219
Charolais, the 472
Chartres 152
Chartreuse 735
Chartreuse massif 735
Château-Chalon 772
Château-Chinon 454
Château d'Amboise 401
Château d'Ancy-le-Franc 443
Château de Beauregard 394
Château de Biron 551
Château de Bonaguil 574
Château de Bussy-Rabutin 444
Château de Castelnaud 562
Château de Châlucet 536
Château de Chambord 395
Château de Chaumont 393
Château de Chenonceau 382
Château de Cheverny 394
Château de Hautefort 546
Château de la Ferté-St-Aubin 374
Château de Langeais 404
Château de Malbrouck 253
Château de Menthon 755
Château de Meung 372
Château de Pierrefonds 201
Château de Puyguilhem 546
Château de Serrant 417
Château de Tanlay 443
Château de Valençay 386
Château de Villandry 403
Château du Plessis-Bourré 417
Château d'Ussé 405
Château Hohlandsbourg 236
Château Kintzheim 236
Châteauneuf-du-Pape 815
Château Queyras 743
Château Burgundy (staying in) 447
Châteaux de Lastours 668

châteaux (Loire) 17
châteaux Loire, staying in 400
Châtillon-sur-Seine 443
Chaumont 217
Chauvet cave 722
Chauvigny 482
cheese 42, 300, 600, 695, 707
Chemins de Fer de Provence 857, 923
Cherbourg 291
Cher, the 382
children, travelling with 51
Chinon 406
Chirac, Jacques 1006
Cinema 1028
Circuit du Souvenir, the 190
Cirque de Gavarnie 613
Cirque de Navacelles 715
Cirque de Troumouse 613
Cirque du Fer-à-Cheval 761
Clairière de l'Armistice 201
Clairvaux-les-Lacs 770
Clamecy 450
Clécy 301
Clermont-Ferrand 684
climate 12, 52
climbing 49
climbing, Alps and Franche-Comté 729
climbing, Mont Blanc 761
Clos-Lucé 402
Cluny 471
Cocteau, Jean 932
Cognac 504
Col de l'Iseran 750
Col de St-Ignace 595
Col d'Izoard 739
Col du Lautaret 737
Col du Midi 760
Collioure 630
Collobrières 891
Collonges-la-Rouge 541
Colmar 238
Colmars-les-Alpes 858
Colombey-les-Deux-Églises 217
Comminges, the 614
Commune, the 1871 1002
Compiègne 199
Concarneau 346
conceptual art 1020
Confolens 508
Conques 709
contemporary architecture 1026
contemporary art 1020
Corbusier, Le 1025
Cordes-sur-Ciel 580
Corniche des Maures 889
Corniches, the (Côte d'Azur) 925
Corsica 936
Corte 986

costs 51
Côte Basque, the 586
Côte d'Albâtre, the 266
Côte d'Argent 524
Côte d'Azur, the 866
Côte de Goëlo 325
Côte de Granit Rose 327
Côte d'Émeraude 324
Côte d'Opale 173
Côte d'Or 463
Cotentin Peninsula 293
Côte Sauvage 356
Côte Vermeille, the 629
Cotignac 853
Coucy-le-Château-Auffrique 198
Coulon 485
Courchevel 752
Coutances 293
Crécy, battle of 174, 996
Credit and debit cards 55
Crèvecoeur-en-Auge 299
crime 52
cross-country skiing 736, 771
Crozon 337
Crozon peninsula, the 337
cubism 1018
Cucugnan 624
currency 55
cycling 15, 38, 47, 49
cycling, Loire 368

**D**

Dada 1019
Dalí, Salvador 1019
Dambach-la-Ville 236
da Vinci, Leonardo 402, 1012
D-Day beaches, the 288
Deauville 280
Degas, Edgar 1016
de Gaulle, Charles 217, 1003
Delacroix, Eugène 1015
Dentelles de Montmirail 818
d'Éon, Chevalier 442
Désert des Agriates 951
Devil's Wood 191
Dieppe 263
Digne-les-Bains 857
Digue à la Mer 841
Dijon 457
Dinan 321
Dinard 324
disabilities, travellers with 57
discount cards 52
Disneyland Paris 149
diving 50
Domfront 303
Domme 563
Dordogne, the 542

Douai 182
Douarnenez 340
Douaumont 256
Doucier 771
Dreyfus Affair, the 1005
drink 43
driving in France 36
driving to France 30
Dronne valley 543
drugs 53
Dune du Pyla 527
Dunkerque 158

**E**

Eaux-Bonnes 610
Eaux-Chaudes 609
Écomusée d'Alsace 242
Écrins, Parc National des 739
Eleanor of Aquitaine 995
electricity 53
embassies and consulates 53
Embrun 740
emergency numbers 53
Entraygues 711
Entre-Deux-Mers 522
entry requirements 53
Éperlecques 164
Épernay 15, 210
Époisses 445
Erbalunga 946
Ernst, Max 1019
Erquy 325
Espalion 711
Espelette 597
Essoyes 218
Étang de Biguglia 945
Étaples 173
Étretat 266
Eurockéennes 775
Eurotunnel 30
Eus 634
Évian-les-Bains 762
Évisa 964
Evol 636
Eymoutiers 539
Èze 926

**F**

Falaise 300
Faucigny, the 761
fauvism 1018
Fécamp 266
Fenioux 503
ferries from the UK 31
ferries within France 36
festivals 46

Figeac 575
Filitosa 974
film 1028
Finistère 330
Fleury 256
flights 29
flights within France 36
Florac 718
Foix 615
Fondation Maeght 914
Fontainebleau Château 151
Fontaine-de-Vaucluse 843
Fontenay, Abbaye de 15, 444
Fontevraud, Abbaye de 412
Fontfroide, Abbaye de 660
food 41
food and drink (by region)
    Burgundy 435
    Catalan 627
    in Alsace 224
    in Brittany 313
    in Champagne 216
    in Corsica 939
    in French Flanders 161
    in Périgord 543
    in Provence 813
    in the Alps and Franche-Comté 731
    in the Basque country 591
    in the Loire valley 371
    Massif Central 689
    Normandy 263
    on the Côte d'Azur 869
Forêt de Compiègne 201
Forêt d'Écouves 303
Forêt d'Iraty 599
Fort Médoc 517
Fouras 496
Fraïsse-sur-Agout 662
Franco–Prussian War, the 1002
Franks, the 994
Fréjus 899
French language 1038
Frondes, the 998
Futuroscope 482

**G**

Gap 741
Gassin 896
Gauguin, Paul 1017
Gaul, Roman 994
Gavarnie 612
Gave de Pau 611
Gavrinis 361
Germigny-des-Prés 375
Gers, the 680
Gertwiller 235
Gien 376
Gigondas 818

Girolata 959
Giscard d'Estaing, Valéry 1006
gîtes 40
Giverny 277
Glanum 830
Golfe de Porto-Vecchio 984
Golfe de Valinco 972
Golfe du Morbihan 358
Gordes 845
Gorges de Kakuetta 600
Gorges de la Fou 632
Gorges de la Frau 619
Gorges de l'Ardèche 23, 721
Gorges de la Restonica 989
Gorges de Spelunca 964
Gorges d'Holzarté 599
Gorges du Fier 755
Gorges du Tarn 713
Gorges du Tavignano 989
Gorges du Verdon, the 854
Gothic architecture 1023
Gouffre de Padirac 568
Gourdon 569
Gourette 610
GR5 749, 772
GR9 771
GR10 614
GR12 221
GR20 25, 958
GR54 736
GR55 749
GR58 743
GR65 706
GR107 619
GR559 771
Grande Corniche, the 927
Grande Traversée du Jura 771
Granville 294
Grasse 906
Grenoble 729
Grimaud 891
Grotte de Bédeilhac 617
Grotte de Clamouse 652
Grotte de Font-de-Gaume 557
Grotte de Lascaux 558
Grotte de la Vache 617
Grotte de Niaux 617
Grotte de Pech-Merle 576
Grotte des Combarelles 557
Grotte des Demoiselles 652
Grotte de Villars 546
Grotte du Grand Roc 558
Grottes de Bétharram 606
Grottes de Gargas 615
Guérande 423
Guillestre 742

H

Hang-gliding 50
Haussmann, Baron 65, 1025
Hauterives 803
Hautes-Alpes, the 737
Haute Soule 599
Haut-Jura, Parc Naturel Régional
   du 771
Haut Koenigsbourg 236
Haut Languedoc, Parc Naturel
   Régional du 662
Haut-Var villages 852
health 53
Héas 613
Henry II, King 995
Hesdin 174
hiking 49
hiking, Alps and Franche-Comté
   729
History 993
Hoëdic 357
Hollande, François 1010
Honfleur 278
horseriding 50
hospitals 54
hostels 40
hotels 39
Houat 357
Huelgoat 349
Hugo, Victor 86, 765
Huguenots 997, 999
Hunawihr 236
Hundred Years' War, the 996
Hyères 884

I

Ilay 771
Île Cavallo 982
Île d'Aix 496
Île de Batz 332
Île de Bréhat 326
Île de Noirmoutier 487
Île de Porquerolles 885
Île de Port-Cros 886
Île de Ré 492
Île de Sein 341
Île d'Oléron 498
Île d'Ouessant 333
Îles d'Hyères, the 885
Îles Glénan 345
Îles Lavezzi 981
Impressionism 1016
Indre, the 382
insurance 54
Inter-Celtic Festival 351
internet 54
Isère valley 749

Issenheim altarpiece, Colmar 25
Itterswiller 236

J

Jardin du Luxembourg, Paris 25
Jarnac 504
Joan of Arc 270, 273, 370, 996
Joigny 439
Josselin 349
joutes nautiques 655
Juan-les-Pins 910
Jumièges, abbaye de 277

K

Kaysersburg 237
Klein, Yves 1020

L

La Bastide-Clairence 598
La Baule 424
L'Aber-Wrac'h 333
Labourd 595
La Brée les Bains 498
La Bussière 377
Lacaune 663
Lac de Chalain 771
Lac de Serre-Ponçon 740
Lac de Vassivière 539
Lac du Bourget 748
La Chaise-Dieu 704
La Ciotat 882
La Coupole 164
La Couvertoirade 715
Lac Pavin 696
La Croix-Valmer 890
La Garde-Freinet 892
La Grande Boucle 12
La Grande-Motte 654
La Grave 736
Laguiole 707
Lake Geneva 762
La Marana 945
Lamarque 517
Lamartine, Alphonse 470
Lampaul 334
Langres 218
language 1038
Languedoc 640
Lannion 329
Laon 196
La Palud-Sur-Verdon 854
La Plagne 752
La Réole 523
La Rhune 595

La Rochefoucauld 508
La Rochelle 488
La Roque-Gageac 563
La Roque St-Christophe 558
Larrau 599
La Salvetat-sur-Agout 663
La Sauve-Majeure 523
La Targette 188
La Turbie 927
laundry 54
Le Bleymard 717
Le Bourg 326
Le Bourg-d'Oisans 736
Le Cateau-Cambrésis 184
Le Château (Île d'Oléron) 498
Le Conquet 333
Le Corbusier 1025
Le Croisic 424
Le Crotoy 175
Léger, Fernand 1019
Le Grau-du-Roi 654
Le Havre 268
Le Lac de Guerlédan 349
Le Lavandou 890
Le Mans 425
Le Mont-Dore 694
Le Palais 356
L'Épau, Abbaye de 429
Le Perche 303
Le Pont-de-Montvert 718
Le Puy-en-Velay 701
Les Andelys 276
Les Arcs 752
Les Arques 569
Les Baux-de-Provence 831
Lescun 608
Le Sentier des Douaniers 948
Les Épesses 486
Les Eyzies-de-Tayac 556
Les Gorges du Verdon 17
Les Lacs des Bouillouses 637
Les Landes 526
Les Menuires 752
Les Rousses 771
Les Sables-d'Olonne 485
Leszczynski, Stanislas 247
Le Touquet 172
Le Vigan 719
Lewarde 183
LGBT+ 55
L'Île Rousse 952
Lille 176
Limeuil 556
Limoges 533
Limousin, Dordogne and the
    Lot, the 530
Limousin, the 533
Limoux 620
Lisieux 298
L'Isle-sur-la-Sorgue 843

Livarot 299
Loches 388
Lochnagar 190
Locmariaquer 354
Locronan 339
Lodève 653
Loire châteaux 373
Loire, the 364
Longueval 191
Lons-le-Saunier 769
Lorient 351
Lot, the 567
Louis XIII 997
Louis XIV 997, 998
Louis XV 999
Louis XVI 999
Louis XVIII 1001
Lourdes 605
Louvre, the 17
Luberon, Parc Naturel Régional
    du 845
Luberon, the 844
Lumière brothers (Auguste and
    Louis) 788
Luz-St-Sauveur 611
Lyon 778

# M

Macinaggio 947
Mâcon 469
Mâconnais, the 471
Macron, Emmanuel 1011
magazines 45
mail 55
Malo-les-Bains 161
Manet, Edouard 1016
Mannerism 1012
maps 55
    Aix-en-Provence 848
    Ajaccio 967
    Albi 677
    Alsace and Lorraine 226
    Amiens 193
    Angers 413
    Angoulême 507
    Annecy 751
    Arles 834
    Around Paris 148
    Aude Valley and Roussillon 620
    Autun 453
    Auxerre 436
    Avignon 822
    Bastia 942
    Bayeux 286
    Beaubourg and Les Halles 79
    Beaune 466
    Besançon 766
    Biarritz 590

Blois 390
Bonifacio 978
Bordeaux 510
Boulogne-Sur-Mer 170
Bourges 380
Brittany 310
Burgundy 434
Caen 282
Cahors 571
Calais 166
Calvi 956
Cannes 904
Carcassonne: Cité 667
Carcassonne: Ville Basse 665
Central Pyrenees 601
Chambéry 744
Chamonix 756
Champagne and the Ardennes 206
Châteaux of the Loire 383
Cherbourg 291
Chinon 407
Clermont-Ferrand 688
Colmar 239
Concarneau 347
Corsica 938
Corte 987
Dieppe 264
Dijon 458
Dinan 321
France 6
Golfe de Morbihan 358
Grand Canyon du Verdon 855
Grenoble 730
Itineraries 27
Languedoc 642
La Rochelle 489
Le Havre 269
Le Mans 426
Le Puy-en-Velay 702
Lille 177
Limoges 534
Lyon 782
Main French Rail Routes 34
Marais, Île St-Louis and Bastille 82
Marseille 870
Marseille: The Vieux Port 872
Metro 120
Metz 250
Monaco 928
Montmartre and the Neuvième 112
Montpellier 649
Nancy 246
Nantes 419
Nice 918
Nîmes 644
Normandy 262
Northeast Provence 859
Orange 814
Orléans 369
Paris 66

Pau 602
Périgord Noir 553
Périgueux 548
Perpignan 625
Poitiers 480
Poitou-Charentes and the Atlantic coast 478
Provence 812
Quartier Latin 92
Quimper 342
Reims 208
Rennes 312
Rouen 271
Saintes 502
Sarlat-la-Canéda 554
St-Germain 96
St-Malo: Intra-Muros 317
Strasbourg 229
St-Tropez 894
The Alps and Franche-Comté 728
The Camargue 840
The Chamonix Valley and the Faucigny 760
The Champs-Élysées and around 70
The Côte d'Azur 868
The D-Day Beaches 288
The Limousin, Dordogne and the Lot 532
The Loire 366
The Massif Central 686
The North 160
The Presqu'île and Vieux Lyon 784
The Pyrenees 588
The Rhône valley 780
Toulouse 671
Tours 397
Trocadéro, Eiffel Tower and the Septième 102
Vannes 360
Marais Poitevin 484
Marennes 497
Margaux 517
Margeride, the 715
Mariana 945
Marie Antoinette 1000
Marquenterre, Parc Ornithologique du 175
Marseillan 655
Marseille 866
Martel 565
Martel, Charles 994
Massif Central, the 684
Massif des Maures 891
Matisse, Henri 184, 915, 922, 1018
May 1968 revolt 1006
media 45
Médoc, the 517
megalithic sites, Brittany 353
megalithic sites, Corsica 976
Mende 717

Ménerbes 845
Menthon-St-Bernard 755
Menton 932
Mercantour, Parc National du 860
Méribel 752
Metz 249
Meung-sur-Loire 372
Millau 712
Millet, Jean-François 1015
Millevaches 539
Mirepoix 618
Mittelbergheim 235
Mitterrand, François 1006
mobile phones 56
Moissac 582
Monaco 928
Monet, Claude 277, 1016
money 55
Monflanquin 574
Monpazier 551
Montagne Noire 668
Mont Aigoual 719
Montauban 581
Montbard 444
Mont Blanc 755, 761
Mont Blanc Tunnel (to Italy) 755
Mont-Dauphin 740
Mont de Marsan 526
Monte-Carlo 929
Montélimar 806
Montenvers rack railway 760
Montignac 558
Mont-Louis 637
Mont Lozère 717
Montolieu 668
Montpellier 648
Montreuil-sur-Mer 174
Montrichard 384
Monts-Dore 694
Monts du Cantal, the 697
Montségur 617
Mont St-Michel 18, 296
Mont Ventoux 817
Morgat 338
Morlaix 330
Mortagne-au-Perche 303
Morvan 446
Morvan, Parc Régional du 454
motorbikes 38
Moustiers-Ste-Marie 854
Moyenne Corniche, the 926
Mulhouse 242
Munster 241
Murat 699
Mûr-de-Bretagne 349

N
Najac 578
Nancy 245
Nantes 417
Nantes–Brest canal 348
Napoleon and Corsica 968
Napoleon Bonaparte 969, 1000
Napoléon III 1002
Narbonne 659
Navarrenx 605
Nebbio, the 949
Neoclassicism (art) 1014
Nevers 455
newspapers 45
Niaux 616
Nice 916
Nîmes 640
Niort 483
Niou 334
Noirmoutier-en-l'Île 487
Nonza 948
Normandy 260
north, The 158
Notre-Dame de Lorette 189
Nouveau Réalisme 1019
Nouvelle Vague cinema 1029
Noyers-sur-Serein 441
Noyon 201

O
Obernai 235
Occitan language 646
Oingt 797
Olargues 662
Olette 636
opening hours 55
Oradour-sur-Glane 537
Orange 810
Orbec 299
Orcival 695
Orléans 364
Ossau valley 609
Ouistreham 288
outdoor activities 49
oysters 497

P
Paimpol 325
Palaggiu 977
Paradiski 752
paragliding 50
Paray-le-Monial 472
Parc de la Préhistoire 617
Parc National de la Vanoise 749
Parc National des Cévennes 716

Parc National des Écrins 739
Parc National des Pyrénées 603
Parc National du Mercantour 860
Parc Naturel Régional des Volcans d'Auvergne 687
Parc Naturel Régional du Haut-Jura 771
Parc Naturel Régional du Haut Languedoc 662
Parc Naturel Régional du Luberon 845
Parc Ornithologique du Pont de Gau 841
Parc Ornithologique du Marquenterre 175
Parc Régional du Morvan 454
Parc Régional du Queyras 742
Paris 62
  accommodation 122
  airports 116
  Arc de Triomphe 70
  arrival 116
  Atelier Brancusi 80
  banks 146
  bars 136
  Bassin de la Villette 114
  Bastille 87
  Beaubourg 78
  Beaux Quartiers 109
  Belleville 116
  Bercy 88
  Berges de Seine 98
  Bibliothèque Nationale 78
  Bibliothèque Nationale de France 109
  boat trips 121
  Bois de Boulogne 110
  Bois de Vincennes 89
  buses 118
  bus stations 117
  Butte Montmartre 111
  Canal St-Martin 114
  catacombs 107
  Cathédrale de Notre-Dame 68
  Centre Pompidou 79
  Champs-Élysées 71
  Château de Vincennes 89
  cinemas 141
  Cinémathèque 88
  Cité de l'Architecture et du Patrimoine 101
  Cité des Sciences et de l'Industrie 115
  classical music 140
  clubs 139
  concert halls 140
  concert venues 138
  Conciergerie 68
  consulates 146
  Crypte Archéologique 69

cycling 121
dance 142
Défense, La 110
drinking 136
driving 117
eating 126
Église de la Madeleine 77
Eiffel Tower 100
embassies 146
festivals 143
film 141
flea markets 146
Fondation Louis Vuitton 110
Goutte d'Or 113
Grand Palais 72
history 62
Hôtel de Sully 87
Île de la Cité 65
Institut du Monde Arabe 90
Jardin Atlantique 107
Jardin d'Acclimatation 110
Jardin des Plantes 94
Jardin des Tuileries 73
Jardin du Luxembourg 100
Jeu de Paume 73
Jewish quarter 86
La Villette 114
Le 104 115
left luggage 147
Les Frigos 109
Les Halles 81
LGBT 142
listings 122
lost property 147
Louvre 74
Maison de Victor Hugo 86
Marais 81
markets 145
Mémorial de la Shoah 87
Mémorial des Martyrs de la Déportation 69
Ménilmontant 116
métro 118
Montmartre 111
Montmartre cemetery 113
Montparnasse 106
Montparnasse cemetery 107
Mosquée de Paris 94
Moulin Rouge 113
Musée Bourdelle 107
Musée Carnavalet 84
Musée d'Art et d'Histoire du Judaïsme 86
Musée d'Art Moderne de la Ville de Paris 101
Musée de la Mode 104
Musée de l'Armée 105
Musée de l'Homme 101
Musée de l'Orangerie 73
Musée de Montmartre 111

Musée des Archives Nationales 84
Musée des Arts Décoratifs 76
Musée des Beaux-Arts de la Ville de Paris 73
Musée des Egouts de Paris 105
Musée d'Orsay 95
Musée du Louvre 74
Musée du Quai Branly 104
Musée Jacquemart-André 72
Musée Marmottan 109
Musée National d'Art Moderne 80
Musée National des Arts Asiatiques-Guimet 104
Musée National du Moyen Age 91
Musée National Eugène Delacroix 99
Musée Picasso 84
Musée Rodin 106
Musée Yves Saint Laurent 104
music 138
nightlife 136
Observatoire de Paris 108
opera 141
Opéra-Bastille 88
Opéra District 77
Opéra-Garnier 77
Palais de Justice 68
Palais de la Découverte 72
Palais de Tokyo 104
Palais-Royal 78
Panthéon 91
Parc André-Citroën 108
Parc de Bercy 88
Parc de la Villette 114
Parc des Buttes-Chaumont 116
Parc Georges-Brassens 108
Parc Zoologique de Paris 89
passages 89
Père-Lachaise cemetery 116
Petit Palais 73
pharmacies 147
Philharmonie de Paris 115
Pigalle 113
Place de la Concorde 73
Place des Vosges 86
Place Vendôme 78
police 147
Pont-Neuf 68
Promenade Plantée 89
Quartier Latin 90
RER 118
Rue Mouffetard 94
Sacré-Coeur 112
Sainte-Chapelle 68
scooters 121
Seine, River 88
Sewers Museum 105
shopping 144
Sorbonne 91
St-Étienne-du-Mont 94

St-Germain 95
St-Germain-des-Prés 99
St-Ouen flea market 113
St-Séverin 90
St-Sulpice 100
taxis 121
theatre 141
tourist offices 122
Tour Montparnasse 106
train stations 117
transport 118
Trocadéro 101
Paris riots, 2005 1009
Parthenay 482
Patrimonio 951
Pau 600
Pauillac 517
Pays Basque, the 586
Pays d'Auge, the 298
Pays de Sault, the 617
Pegasus Bridge 289
pelota 48
perfume (Grasse) 907
Périgord Noir 552
Périgord Pourpre 549
Périgord Vert 542
Périgueux 547
Péronne 191
Pérouges 796
Perpignan 625
pétanque 10
Petit Train d'Artouste 610
Petit Train Jaune 635
pets, travelling with 31
Peyrepertuse 622
Pézenas 658
Philippe, Count of Valois 996
phones 56
phrasebooks 1038
Piana 963
Picardy 192
Picasso, Pablo 84, 906, 909, 1018
Pineau des Charentes 503
Pissarro, Camille 1016
Plateau de Langres 216
Plouescat 332
Plougrescant 327
Ploumanac'h 328
Pointe des Lessières 750
Pointe du Raz 341
Poitiers 476
Poitiers, battle of 994
Poitou-Charentes and the
    Atlantic coast 476
Poligny 772
Pompidou, Georges 1006
Pont-Audemer 298
Pont-Aven 348
Pont d'Ouilly 302
Pont du Gard 647

Pontigny 440
popes, Avignon 820
Porquerolles 885
Port-Clos 326
Port Grimaud 892
Porto 960
Porto-Vecchio 982
post 55
Post-Impressionism 1017
post offices 55
Poussin, Nicolas 1013
Prades 633
Prats-de-Mollo 632
Presqu'île de Quiberon 355
Propriano 973
Provence 810
public holidays 56
Puilaurens 622
puppetry 220
Puy de Dôme 690
Puy de Sancy 694
Puy du Fou 486
Puy-l'Évêque 573
Pyrénées, Parc National des 603
Pyrenees, the 586

## Q

Quéribus 622
Queyras, Parc Régional du 742
Quiberon 355
Quillan 621
Quimper 341
Quinéville 290

## R

racism 53
radio 45
rail passes 31, 36
realism (in art) 1015
Redon 349
refuge huts 41
Région des Lacs 770
Reims 204
Renaissance architecture 1023
Rennes 311
Renoir, Auguste 218, 912, 1016
Réserve Naturelle de Scandola
    958
Resistance, the 1003
Revel 669
Revin 221
Rhône valley, the 778
Richard the Lionheart 995
Richelieu, Cardinal 998
Richemont 504
Rigny-Ussé 405

Rimbaud, Arthur 220
Riom 690
Rioux 503
Riquewihr 237
Rocamadour 567
Rochechouart 538
Rochefort 494
Rodez 707
Roman architecture 1022
Romanesque architecture 1022
Romans-sur-Isère 803
Romanticism (art) 1014
Roquebrune 927
Roquefixade 617
Roscoff 330
Roubaix 182
Rouen 270
Rousseau, Théodore 1015
Roussillon 624
Roussillon (village) 846
route de Bavella 984
Route des Crêtes (Alsace) 242
Route des Crêtes (Massif Central)
    697
Route des Crêtes (Provence) 854
Route des Grandes Alpes 764
Route des Vins 235
Route Napoléon 857
Royan 499
Roya valley 862
rugby 48

## S

sailing 50
Saillant 696
Saintes 502
Saintes-Maries-de-la-Mer 841
Saint-Marsal 633
Saissac 668
Salernes 852
Salers 698
Salies-de-Béarn 604
Salin-de-Giraud 842
Samoëns 761
Sancerre 378
Saône valley, the 467
Saorge 862
Sare 596
Sarkozy, Nicolas 1010
Sarlat-la-Canéda 552
Sartène 975
Saulieu 450
Saumur 409
Sauternes 523
Sauveterre-de-Béarn 604
Sauveterre-de-Rouergue 709
Savines-Le-Lac 740

Scandola, Réserve Naturelle de 958
scooters 38
Second Republic, the 1001
Séguret 818
Seine, source of the 445
Sélestat 241
self-catering 40
Semnoz mountains 754
Semoy valley 221
Semur-en-Auxois 445
Sénanque, Abbaye de 845
Sens 438
Sentiers des Ocres 846
Sète 654
shopping 50
Siege of Paris 1870-1871 1004
Sillans-la-Cascade 853
Silvacane, Abbaye de 845
Sisteron 857
Site Naturel de la Capandula 947
Sixt-Fer-à-Cheval 761
skiing 49
   Alps 736
   Chamonix 759
   cross-country 736, 771
   Jura 771
   Savoie 752
smoking 56
snowboarding 49
Soissons 198
Solignac 536
Sologne, the 396
Somme battlefields 186
Somme, battle of the 189
Somme estuary 175
Sospel 862
Souillac 564
sports 47
St-Aignan 385
St-Amand-de-Coly 560
St-Antonin-Noble-Val 580
St-Benoît-sur-Loire 375
St-Bertrand-de-Comminges 614
St-Cirq-Lapopie 573
St-Denis 147
Ste-Marie-du-Mont 290
Ste-Maxime 898
St-Émilion 520
St-Estèphe 518
St-Étienne 801
St-Étienne-de-Tinée 861
Stevenson Trail 716
St-Florent 949
St-Flour 700
St-Gelven 349
St-Germain-de-Confolens 508
St-Guilhem-le-Désert 652
St-Hilaire, Abbaye de 620
St-Jean-de-Côle 546

St-Jean-de-Luz 593
St-Jean-du-Gard 720
St-Jean-Pied-de-Port 598
St-Just de Valcabrère 614
St-Léonard-de-Noblat 537
St-Lô 303
St-Macaire 523
St-Malo 316
St-Martin-d'Ardèche 722
St-Martin-Vésubie 861
St-Maurice-Navacelles 715
St-Mihiel 256
St-Nectaire 695
St-Omer 164
St-Ouen flea market, Paris 18
St-Papoul Abbey 669
St-Paul-de-Mausole 830
St-Paul-de-Vence 914
St-Pierre 498
St-Pons-de-Thomières 662
St-Raphaël 900
Strasbourg 228
St-Rémy-de-Provence 830
St-Romain-en-Gal 800
St-Sauveur-en-Puisaye 435
St-Savin 482
St-Tropez 893
studying in France 58
St-Urcize 706
St-Vaast-la-Hougue 293
St-Valéry-en-Caux 266
St-Valéry-Sur-Somme 175
St-Véran 743
Suisse Normande, the 301
Sully-sur-Loire 375
surfing 50
surrealism 1019
swimming 50
Sylvanès, Abbaye de 715
Symbolists, the 1017

T

Tain-l'Hermitage 802
Talmont 500
Tautavel 628
Tavant 409
teaching English 58
Tech Valley 631
television 45
temperature 52
Tende 862
terrorist attacks, 2015 1011
Têt valley 633
theft 52
Thiepval 190
Third Republic, the 1002
Thoronet, Abbaye du 853
Thury-Harcourt 301

time difference 57
tipping 57
Tonnerre 442
Toulouse 669
Toulouse-Lautrec, Henri 676, 1017
Tour de France 12, 47
Tour du Mont Blanc 761
tourist information offices 57
Tournus 469
tour operators 32
Tours 396
trains from the UK 30
trains in France 33
travel agents 32
Trégastel-Plage 328
Tréguier 327
Trémolat 556
Trouville 280
Troyes 213
Turenne 540

U

Urdos 608
Utah Beach 290
Uzès 648
Uzeste 524

V

Vaison-la-Romaine 816
Vaïta 960
Val d'Ariège 615
Val d'Isère 752
Valence 804
Vallauris 905
Vallée d'Aspe 606
Vallée de l'Aude 619
Vallée des Merveilles 862
Vallée de Tech 631
Vallée d'Ossau 609
Vallon 721
Vallouise 739
Val Thorens 752
van Gogh, Vincent 830, 837, 1018
Vannes 358
Vanoise, Parc National de la 749
Varengeville 266
Vauban fortresses 739
Vaux-le-Vicomte 150
vegetarian food 43
vegetarians 127
Vence 915
Vercingétorix 994
Verdon, Gorges du 17, 854
Verdun 254
Verdun, Battle of 255

Verdun cemeteries 257
Verdun memorials 255
Verne, Jules 193
Versailles 153
Vézelay 448
Vézère valley, the 556
Viaduc de Millau 713
Vichy 692
Vichy government, the 1003
Vienne 798
Village des Bories 845
Villandraut 524
Villars 546
Villecroze 852
Villedieu-les-Poêles 304
Villefranche 797
Villefranche-de-Conflent 635
Villefranche-de-Rouergue 577
Villefranche-sur-Mer 926
Villeneuve-lès-Avignon 828
Villers-Bretonneux 191
Vimoutiers 299
Vimy Ridge 188
Vitré 315
Vix, chariot tomb 994

Vix treasure 443
Voie Sacrée, La ("Sacred Way")
  256
Voiron 735
Volcans d'Auvergne, Parc Naturel
  Régional des 687

# W

walking 49
War of the Spanish Succession
  999
Wars of Religion, the 997
Waterloo, battle of 1001
watersports 50
Watteau, Jean-Antoine 1014
weather 12, 52
wildlife, Camarguais 839
William the Conqueror 300
Wimereux 171
windsurfing 50
wine 43
  Alsace 234
  Bordeaux 518

Burgundy 464
Chablis 441
Châteauneuf-du-Pape 815
Loire 371
Sancerre 378
Sauternes 524
Wissant 169
women travellers 58
working in France 58
World War I 18, 184, 186, 255,
  1003
World War II 18, 162, 1003

# Y

Yonne valley 438
Yvoire 764

# Z

Zonza 984

# Map symbols

The symbols below are used on maps throughout the book

| | | | | | | | |
|---|---|---|---|---|---|---|---|
| —— | International border | ✈ | Airport | ⚲ | Swimming pool | ⁙ | Ruin |
| —— | State/province boundary | Ⓜ | Métro station | ♈ | Gardens/fountain | ♜ | Fort/castle |
| --- | Chapter boundary | Ⓡ | RER station | ⊙ | Statue/memorial | ✲ | Viewpoint |
| ▪▪▪▪ | Motorway | Ⓣ | Tram stop | ♦ | Place of interest | ⚝ | Waterfall |
| ——— | Road | P | Parking | ⊠ | Gate | ⛰ | Mountain range |
| ▪▪▪▪ | Pedestrian road | ★ | Bus stop | ⚝ | Lighthouse | ▲ | Mountain peak |
| ▥▥▥ | Steps | ⛴ | Boat/ferry | ✗ | Battlefield | ⛰ | Refugio (mountain lodge) |
| —— | Tram route | 🛢 | Fuel station | ⛪ | Abbey | ⬭ | Stadium |
| ——— | Railway | ✉ | Post office | ♟ | Monastery | ▬ | Building |
| ——— | TGV line | ⓘ | Tourist office | ♟ | Museum | → | Church |
| ⋯⋯ | Funicular | @ | Internet access | ♜ | Tower | ☐ | Market |
| ---- | Cable car/téléphérique | ✚ | Hospital | ⁙ | Spring/spa | ⬚ | Park |
| - - | Ferry route | ⛷ | Skiing | ♜ | Château | ☐ | Beach |
| - - - | Footpath | ☸ | Nature reserve | ⌂ | Cave | ⊞ | Cemetery |
| —— | Wall | 🐾 | Zoo | | | | |

## Listings key

- ■ Accommodation
- ● Eating
- ■ Drinking/nightlife
- ● Shopping

# YOUR TAILOR-MADE TRIP
## STARTS HERE

**Tailor-made trips and unique adventures crafted by local experts**

Rough Guides has been inspiring travellers with lively and thought-provoking guidebooks for more than 35 years. Now we're linking you up with selected local experts to craft your dream trip. They will put together your perfect itinerary and book it at local rates.

**Don't follow the crowd – find your own path.**

## HOW ROUGHGUIDES.COM/TRIPS WORKS

**STEP 1**

Pick your dream destination, tell us what you want and submit an enquiry.

**STEP 2**

Fill in a short form to tell your local expert about your dream trip and preferences.

**STEP 3**

Our local expert will craft your tailor-made itinerary. You'll be able to tweak and refine it until you're completely satisfied.

**STEP 4**

Book online with ease, pack your bags and enjoy the trip! Our local expert will be on hand 24/7 while you're on the road.

# BENEFITS OF PLANNING AND BOOKING AT
## ROUGHGUIDES.COM/TRIPS

### PLAN YOUR ADVENTURE WITH LOCAL EXPERTS

Rough Guides' English-speaking local experts are hand-picked, based on their experience in the travel industry and their impeccable standards of customer service.

### SAVE TIME AND GET ACCESS TO LOCAL KNOWLEDGE

When a local expert plans your trip, you save time and money when you book, even during high season. You won't be charged for using a credit card either.

### MAKE TRAVEL A BREEZE: BOOK WITH PIECE OF MIND

Enjoy stress-free travel when you use Rough Guides' secure online booking platform. All bookings come witha money-back guarantee.

# WHAT DO OTHER TRAVELLERS THINK ABOUT ROUGH GUIDES TRIPS?

**Trip to Spain**

This Spain tour company did a fantastic job to make our dream trip perfect. We gave them our travel budget, told them where we would like to go, and they did all of the planning. Our drivers and tour guides were always on time and very knowledgable. The hotel accommodations were better than we would have found on our own. Only one time did we end up in a location that we had not intended to be in. We called the 24 hour phone number, and they immediately fixed the situation.

**Don A, USA**    ★★★★★

**Trip to Morocco**

Our trip was fantastic! Transportation, accommodations, guides - all were well chosen! The hotels were well situated, well appointed and had helpful, friendly staff. All of the guides we had were very knowledgeable, patient, and flexible with our varied interests in the different sites. We particularly enjoyed the side trip to Tangier! Well done! The itinerary you arranged for us allowed maximum coverage of the country with time in each city for seeing the important places.

**Sharon, USA**    ★★★★★

# PLAN AND BOOK YOUR TRIP AT
## ROUGHGUIDES.COM/TRIPS